To _____

From _____

On _____

Place me like a seal over your heart,
  like a seal on your arm;
 for love is as strong as death,
 its jealousy unyielding as the grave.
 It burns like a blazing fire,
  like a mighty flame.

Song of Songs 8:6

Our Wedding Date _____

Our Commitment Verse _____

Special Memories _____

Marriage

DEVOTIONAL BIBLE

Marriage

DEVOTIONAL BIBLE

NEW INTERNATIONAL VERSION

ZondervanPublishingHouse

Grand Rapids, MI 49530, USA

The Marriage Devotional Bible, New International Version®
© 2000 by The Zondervan Corporation
All rights reserved

Requests for information should be addressed to
The Zondervan Corporation
Grand Rapids, Michigan, 49530

Library of Congress Catalog Card Number 00-130183

Published by Zondervan Publishing House
Grand Rapids, Michigan, 49530, U.S.A.
http://www.zondervan.com

Printed in the United States of America
All rights reserved

00 01 02 03 04 05 8 7 6 5 4 3 2 1

You will be pleased to know that a portion of the purchase price
of your new NIV Bible has been provided to International Bible
Society to help spread the gospel of Jesus Christ around the world!

Contents

How to Use
the NIV MARRIAGE DEVOTIONAL BIBLE

Combining the marital counsel of acclaimed Christian marriage authors, Dave and Claudia Arp, Robert and Rosemary Barnes, and Les and Leslie Parrott, the *NIV Marriage Devotional Bible* offers these enriching features:

Daily Devotions: "Couple Minutes"
260 daily devotions tied to a Scripture passage help you as a married couple understand God's design for your marriage and give practical insights into achieving his ideal.

Weekend Devotions:
"Quiet Times With Each Other"
52 weekend devotions encourage you to take a step back, evaluate your union and enjoy God's presence together.

Book Introductions
An overview of each book in the Bible gives application points that will help you pick up the messages and themes in Scripture that will strengthen your marriage.

Quizzes: "Just Between You and Me"
55 marriage quizzes help reveal each of your needs, allowing you to discuss issues before they begin to hinder intimacy with God and each other.

Profiles: "Couples in the Bible"
Nearly 30 profiles show both good and bad examples of married couples from the Bible. This feature offers readers points of discussion and application to improve your relationship with God and you spouse.

Indexes:
The subject index will help you find certain topics from the devotions, such as communication, prayer, intimacy and finances.

The indexes for "Couples in the Bible" and "Just Between You and Me" will show you where to find each location of the profiles and quizzes.

The Word of God
Far more important than any of the tools we've provided is the text itself, the Word of God. The Bible is a supernaturally powerful book. The life-giving truth it offers is startlingly simple, yet deeply profound. It takes only a moment to receive its grace but a lifetime to fathom its meaning. God's Word is always current and always dynamic, no matter how fast or how much the world changes. It is full of the energy of youth and the wisdom of the ages.

It is our prayer that this Bible will help you incorporate the truth and wisdom of God's Word into your relationship, infusing your marriage with God's love and inviting Christ's presence into every season of your lives together.

If you have questions or remarks about this Bible, please write and tell us.

The Bible Editors
Zondervan Publishing House
5300 Patterson Avenue SE
Grand Rapids, MI 49530
www.zondervan.com

About the Authors

Dave and Claudia Arp are the founders and directors of Marriage Alive International, a marriage and family enrichment ministry. They have spent 20+ years putting together resources that help strengthen the family. They target the military and business communities, along with the church community. They've authored several books, including *The Second Half of Marriage* and *10 Great Dates*.

Bob and Rosemary Barnes run a residential treatment center for juvenile delinquent boys and girls. They also have a ministry for single moms. Bob is the executive director of Sheridan Family Ministries, and he writes a weekly newspaper column on the family. He and Rosemary give about 300 seminars per year. They've authored several books, including *Great Sexpectations*, *We Need to Talk*, and *Rock-Solid Marriage*.

Les and Leslie Parrott are co-directors of the Center for Relationship Development at Seattle Pacific University. It's a ground-breaking program dedicated to teaching the basics of good relationships. Their goal is to "solve problems before they begin." They've authored several books, including *Becoming Soul Mates*, *Saving Your Marriage Before It Starts*, and *Questions Couples Ask*.

Preface

THE NEW INTERNATIONAL VERSION is a completely new translation of the Holy Bible made by over a hundred scholars working directly from the best available Hebrew, Aramaic and Greek texts. It had its beginning in 1965 when, after several years of exploratory study by committees from the Christian Reformed Church and the National Association of Evangelicals, a group of scholars met at Palos Heights, Illinois, and concurred in the need for a new translation of the Bible in contemporary English. This group, though not made up of official church representatives, was transdenominational. Its conclusion was endorsed by a large number of leaders from many denominations who met in Chicago in 1966.

Responsibility for the new version was delegated by the Palos Heights group to a self-governing body of fifteen, the Committee on Bible Translation, composed for the most part of biblical scholars from colleges, universities and seminaries. In 1967 the New York Bible Society (now the International Bible Society) generously undertook the financial sponsorship of the project—a sponsorship that made it possible to enlist the help of many distinguished scholars. The fact that participants from the United States, Great Britain, Canada, Australia and New Zealand worked together gave the project its international scope. That they were from many denominations—including Anglican, Assemblies of God, Baptist, Brethren, Christian Reformed, Church of Christ, Evangelical Free, Lutheran, Mennonite, Methodist, Nazarene, Presbyterian, Wesleyan and other churches—helped to safeguard the translation from sectarian bias.

How it was made helps to give the New International Version its distinctiveness. The translation of each book was assigned to a team of scholars. Next, one of the Intermediate Editorial Committees revised the initial translation, with constant reference to the Hebrew, Aramaic or Greek. Their work then went to one of the General Editorial Committees, which checked it in detail and made another thorough revision. This revision in turn was carefully reviewed by the Committee on Bible Translation, which made further changes and then released the final version for publication. In this way the entire Bible underwent three revisions, during each of which the translation was examined for its faithfulness to the original languages and for its English style.

All this involved many thousands of hours of research and discussion regarding the meaning of the texts and the precise way of putting them into English. It may well be that no other translation has been made by a more thorough process of review and revision from committee to committee than this one.

From the beginning of the project, the Committee on Bible Translation held to certain goals for the New International Version: that it would be an accurate translation and one that would have clarity and literary quality and so prove suitable for public and private reading, teaching, preaching, memorizing and liturgical use. The Committee also sought to preserve some measure of continuity with the long tradition of translating the Scriptures into English.

In working toward these goals, the translators were united in their commitment to the authority and infallibility of the Bible as God's Word in written form. They believe that it contains the divine answer to the deepest needs of humanity, that it sheds unique light on our path in a dark world, and that it sets forth the way to our eternal well-being.

The first concern of the translators has been the accuracy of the translation and its fidelity to the thought of the biblical writers. They have weighed the significance of the lexical and grammatical details of the Hebrew, Aramaic and Greek texts. At the same time, they have striven for more than a word-for-word translation. Because thought patterns and syntax differ from language to language, faithful communication of the meaning of the writers of the Bible demands frequent modifications in sentence structure and constant regard for the contextual meanings of words.

A sensitive feeling for style does not always accompany scholarship. Accordingly the Committee on Bible Translation submitted the developing version to a number of stylistic consultants. Two of them read every book of both Old and New Testaments twice—once before and once after the last major revision—and made invaluable suggestions. Samples of the translation were tested for clarity and ease of reading by various kinds of people—young and old, highly educated and less well educated, ministers and laymen.

Concern for clear and natural English—that the New International Version should be idiomatic but not idiosyncratic, contemporary but not dated—motivated the translators and consultants. At the same time, they tried to reflect the differing styles of the biblical writers. In view of the international use of English, the translators sought to avoid obvious Americanisms on the one hand and obvious Anglicisms on the other. A British edition reflects the comparatively few differences of significant idiom and of spelling.

As for the traditional pronouns "thou," "thee" and "thine" in reference to the Deity, the translators judged that to use these archaisms (along with the old verb forms such as "doest," "wouldest" and "hadst") would violate accuracy in translation. Neither Hebrew, Aramaic nor Greek uses special pronouns for the persons of the Godhead. A present-day translation is not enhanced by forms that in the time of the King James Version were used in everyday speech, whether referring to God or man.

For the Old Testament the standard Hebrew text, the Masoretic Text as published in the latest editions of *Biblia Hebraica,* was used throughout. The Dead Sea Scrolls contain material bearing on an earlier stage of the Hebrew text. They were consulted, as were the Samaritan Pentateuch and the ancient scribal traditions relating to textual changes. Sometimes a variant Hebrew reading in the margin of the Masoretic Text was followed instead of the text itself. Such instances, being variants within the Masoretic tradition, are not specified by footnotes. In rare cases, words in the consonantal text were divided differently from the way they appear in the Masoretic Text. Footnotes indicate this. The translators also consulted the more important early versions—the Septuagint; Aquila, Symmachus and Theodotion; the Vulgate; the Syriac Peshitta; the Targums; and for the Psalms the *Juxta Hebraica* of Jerome. Readings from these versions were occasionally followed where the Masoretic Text seemed doubtful and where accepted principles of textual criticism showed that one or more of these textual witnesses appeared to provide the correct reading. Such instances are footnoted. Sometimes vowel letters and vowel signs did not, in the judgment of the translators, represent the correct vowels for the original consonantal text. Accordingly some words were read with a different set of vowels. These instances are usually not indicated by footnotes.

The Greek text used in translating the New Testament was an eclectic one. No other piece of ancient literature has such an abundance of manuscript witnesses as does the New Testament. Where existing manuscripts differ, the translators made their choice of readings according to accepted principles of New Testament textual criticism. Footnotes call attention to places where there was uncertainty about what the original text was. The best current printed texts of the Greek New Testament were used.

There is a sense in which the work of translation is never wholly finished. This applies to all great literature and uniquely so to the Bible. In 1973 the New Testament in the New International Version was published. Since then, suggestions for corrections and revisions have been received from various sources. The Committee on Bible Translation carefully considered the suggestions and adopted a number of them. These were incorporated in the first printing of the entire Bible in 1978. Additional revisions were made by the Committee on Bible Translation in 1983 and appear in printings after that date.

As in other ancient documents, the precise meaning of the biblical texts is sometimes uncertain. This is more often the case with the Hebrew and Aramaic texts than with the Greek text. Although archaeological and linguistic discoveries in this century aid in understanding difficult passages, some uncertainties remain. The more significant of these have been called to the reader's attention in the footnotes.

In regard to the divine name YHWH, commonly referred to as the *Tetragrammaton,* the translators adopted the device used in most English versions of rendering that name as "Lord" in capital letters to distinguish it from *Adonai,* another Hebrew word rendered "Lord," for which small letters are used. Wherever the two names stand together in the Old Testament as a compound name of God, they are rendered "Sovereign Lord."

Because for most readers today the phrases "the Lord of hosts" and "God of hosts" have little meaning, this version renders them "the Lord Almighty" and "God Almighty." These renderings convey the sense of the Hebrew, namely, "he who is sovereign over all the 'hosts' (powers) in heaven and on earth, especially over the 'hosts' (armies) of Israel." For readers unacquainted with Hebrew this does not make clear the distinction between *Sabaoth* ("hosts" or "Almighty") and *Shaddai* (which can also be translated

"Almighty"), but the latter occurs infrequently and is always footnoted. When *Adonai* and *YHWH Sabaoth* occur together, they are rendered "the Lord, the LORD Almighty."

As for other proper nouns, the familiar spellings of the King James Version are generally retained. Names traditionally spelled with "ch," except where it is final, are usually spelled in this translation with "k" or "c," since the biblical languages do not have the sound that "ch" frequently indicates in English— for example, in *chant*. For well-known names such as Zechariah, however, the traditional spelling has been retained. Variation in the spelling of names in the original languages has usually not been indicated. Where a person or place has two or more different names in the Hebrew, Aramaic or Greek texts, the more familiar one has generally been used, with footnotes where needed.

To achieve clarity the translators sometimes supplied words not in the original texts but required by the context. If there was uncertainty about such material, it is enclosed in brackets. Also for the sake of clarity or style, nouns, including some proper nouns, are sometimes substituted for pronouns, and vice versa. And though the Hebrew writers often shifted back and forth between first, second and third personal pronouns without change of antecedent, this translation often makes them uniform, in accordance with English style and without the use of footnotes.

Poetical passages are printed as poetry, that is, with indentation of lines and with separate stanzas. These are generally designed to reflect the structure of Hebrew poetry. This poetry is normally characterized by parallelism in balanced lines. Most of the poetry in the Bible is in the Old Testament, and scholars differ regarding the scansion of Hebrew lines. The translators determined the stanza divisions for the most part by analysis of the subject matter. The stanzas therefore serve as poetic paragraphs.

As an aid to the reader, italicized sectional headings are inserted in most of the books. They are not to be regarded as part of the NIV text, are not for oral reading, and are not intended to dictate the interpretation of the sections they head.

The footnotes in this version are of several kinds, most of which need no explanation. Those giving alternative translations begin with "Or" and generally introduce the alternative with the last word preceding it in the text, except when it is a single-word alternative; in poetry quoted in a footnote a slant mark indicates a line division. Footnotes introduced by "Or" do not have uniform significance. In some cases two possible translations were considered to have about equal validity. In other cases, though the translators were convinced that the translation in the text was correct, they judged that another interpretation was possible and of sufficient importance to be represented in a footnote.

In the New Testament, footnotes that refer to uncertainty regarding the original text are introduced by "Some manuscripts" or similar expressions. In the Old Testament, evidence for the reading chosen is given first and evidence for the alternative is added after a semicolon (for example: Septuagint; Hebrew *father*). In such notes the term "Hebrew" refers to the Masoretic Text.

It should be noted that minerals, flora and fauna, architectural details, articles of clothing and jewelry, musical instruments and other articles cannot always be identified with precision. Also measures of capacity in the biblical period are particularly uncertain (see the table of weights and measures following the text).

Like all translations of the Bible, made as they are by imperfect man, this one undoubtedly falls short of its goals. Yet we are grateful to God for the extent to which he has enabled us to realize these goals and for the strength he has given us and our colleagues to complete our task. We offer this version of the Bible to him in whose name and for whose glory it has been made. We pray that it will lead many into a better understanding of the Holy Scriptures and a fuller knowledge of Jesus Christ the incarnate Word, of whom the Scriptures so faithfully testify.

The Committee on Bible Translation

June 1978
(Revised Aug 1983)

Names of the translators and editors may be secured from the International Bible Society translation sponsors of the New International Version, 1820 Jet Stream Drive, Colorado Springs, Colorado 08921-3696 U.S.A.

Old
TESTAMENT

Genesis

The question
of when and how the world began has intrigued us
since, well, since the beginning. The book of Genesis is
about many beginnings—the beginning of the universe, the
beginning of humankind, the beginning of sin, and the
beginning of God's promises and his plan for salvation. It's a
book about why we began, and where God wants to take
us. It's about relationships—between God and his creation,
between God and humankind and between one person and
another. The book of Genesis recounts how God designed a
covenant with his chosen people and how he pledged his
love and faithfulness to them.

Marriage is a picture of that covenant. As you read,
notice how God used ordinary husbands and wives—Adam
and Eve, Abraham and Sarah, Isaac and Rebekah, Jacob and
Rachel—to fulfill his plan of salvation for all generations.

The Beginning

1 In the beginning God created the heavens and the earth. ²Now the earth was*a* formless and empty, darkness was over the surface of the deep, and the Spirit of God was hovering over the waters.

³And God said, "Let there be light," and there was light. ⁴God saw that the light was good, and he separated the light from the darkness. ⁵God called the light "day," and the darkness he called "night." And there was evening, and there was morning—the first day.

⁶And God said, "Let there be an expanse between the waters to separate water from water." ⁷So God made the expanse and separated the water under the expanse from the water above it. And it was so. ⁸God called the expanse "sky." And there was evening, and there was morning—the second day.

⁹And God said, "Let the water under the sky be gathered to one place, and let dry ground appear." And it was so. ¹⁰God called the dry ground "land," and the gathered waters he called

a2 Or possibly became

"seas." And God saw that it was good. ¹¹Then God said, "Let the land produce vegetation: seed-bearing plants and trees on the land that bear fruit with seed in it, according to their various kinds." And it was so. ¹²The land produced vegetation: plants bearing seed according to their kinds and trees bearing fruit with seed in it according to their kinds. And God saw that it was good. ¹³And there was evening, and there was morning—the third day.

¹⁴And God said, "Let there be lights in the expanse of the sky to separate the day from the night, and let them serve as signs to mark seasons and days and years, ¹⁵and let them be lights in the expanse of the sky to give light on the earth." And it was so. ¹⁶God made two great lights—the greater light to govern the day and the lesser light to govern the night. He also made the stars. ¹⁷God set them in the expanse of the sky to give light on the earth, ¹⁸to govern the day and the night, and to separate light from darkness. And God saw that it was good. ¹⁹And there was evening, and there was morning—the fourth day.

²⁰And God said, "Let the water teem with living creatures, and let birds fly above the earth across the expanse of the sky." ²¹So God created the great creatures of the sea and every living and moving thing with which the water teems, according to their kinds, and every winged bird according to its kind. And God saw that it was good. ²²God blessed them and said, "Be fruitful and increase in number and fill the water in the seas, and let the birds increase on the earth." ²³And there was evening, and there was morning—the fifth day.

²⁴And God said, "Let the land produce living creatures according to their kinds: livestock, creatures that move along the ground, and wild animals, each according to its kind." And it was so. ²⁵God made the wild animals according to their kinds, the livestock according to their kinds, and all the creatures that move along the ground according to their kinds. And God saw that it was good.

²⁶Then God said, "Let us make man in our image, in our likeness, and let them rule over the fish of the sea and the birds of the air, over the livestock, over all the earth,ᵃ and over all the creatures that move along the ground."

²⁷So God created man in his own
      image,

ᵃ26 Hebrew; Syriac *all the wild animals*

In the Beginning, God Created Marriage

Monday

GENESIS 1:1–31 The first sentence of Chaim Potok's novel, *In the Beginning*, reads " . . . all beginnings are hard." In the book the main character, David, describes how, one evening when he was nine years old, he burst into tears because a passage of a Bible commentary had proven too difficult for him to understand. David's mentor welcomed him warmly into his apartment and spoke in a gentle voice: "Be patient, David, beginnings are hard; you cannot swallow all the world at one time."

Have you ever felt like David? It's only natural when beginning something new— marriage included—to want instant maturity. But seasoned maturity takes time, and growing pains are inevitable. Looking back on your own beginnings as a couple, do you see ways God has helped you grow, not only in spite of, but even as a result of, difficult times?

As you reflect on the beginning of your own marriage, consider the fact that God made both of you in his image. This gift of being made in our heavenly Father's image is to be affirmed and celebrated (see verse 27). And your wedding anniversary is an ideal time for doing just that.

—*Les & Leslie*

Go to page 4 for your next devotional reading.

in the image of God he created
him;
male and female he created them.

²⁸God blessed them and said to them, "Be fruitful and increase in number; fill the earth and subdue it. Rule over the fish of the sea and the birds of the air and over every living creature that moves on the ground."
²⁹Then God said, "I give you every seed-bearing plant on the face of the whole earth and every tree that has fruit with seed in it. They will be yours for food. ³⁰And to all the beasts of the earth and all the birds of the air and all the creatures that move on the ground—everything that has the breath of life in it—I give every green plant for food." And it was so.

³¹God saw all that he had made, and it was very good. And there was evening, and there was morning—the sixth day.

2 Thus the heavens and the earth were completed in all their vast array.

²By the seventh day God had finished the work he had been doing; so on the seventh day he rested[a] from all his work. ³And God blessed the seventh day and made it holy, because on it he rested from all the work of creating that he had done.

Adam and Eve

⁴This is the account of the heavens and the earth when they were created.

When the LORD God made the earth and the heavens— ⁵and no shrub of the field had yet appeared on the earth[b] and no plant of the field had yet sprung up, for the LORD God had not sent rain on the earth[b] and there was no man to work the ground, ⁶but streams[c] came up from the earth and watered the whole surface of the ground— ⁷the LORD God formed the man[d] from the dust of the ground and breathed into his nostrils the breath of life, and the man became a living being.

⁸Now the LORD God had planted a garden in the east, in Eden; and there he put

Adam and Eve

GENESIS 2:4-25 Adam and Eve were, quite literally, made for each other. Their world was a garden and God was their friend. This passage shows God walking with them in the cool of the day. Their joyful innocence knew no bounds. But despite living in paradise, the first marriage was not problem-free. When Adam and Eve chose to believe the serpent and doubt God, they who had been innocent became guilty. They lost their paradise. Nevertheless, God remained faithful in the midst of their choices, blessing their union with his continued presence—and with the first children.

the man he had formed. ⁹And the LORD God made all kinds of trees grow out of the ground—trees that were pleasing to the eye and good for food. In the middle of the garden were the tree of life and the tree of the knowledge of good and evil.

¹⁰A river watering the garden flowed from Eden; from there it was separated into four headwaters. ¹¹The name of the first is the Pishon; it winds through the entire land of Havilah, where there is gold. ¹²(The gold of that land is good; aromatic resin[e] and onyx are also there.) ¹³The name of the second river is the Gihon; it winds through the entire land of Cush.[f] ¹⁴The name of the third river is the Tigris; it runs along the east side of Asshur. And the fourth river is the Euphrates.

¹⁵The LORD God took the man and put him in the Garden of Eden to work it and take care of it. ¹⁶And the LORD God commanded the man, "You are free to eat from any tree in the garden; ¹⁷but you must not eat from the tree of the knowledge of good and evil, for when you eat of it you will surely die."

¹⁸The LORD God said, "It is not good

---

*a*2 Or *ceased;* also in verse 3   *b*5 Or *land;* also in verse 6   *c*6 Or *mist*   *d*7 The Hebrew for *man (adam)* sounds like and may be related to the Hebrew for *ground (adamah);* it is also the name *Adam* (see Gen. 2:20).   *e*12 Or *good; pearls*
*f*13 Possibly southeast Mesopotamia

for the man to be alone. I will make a helper suitable for him."

[19]Now the LORD God had formed out of the ground all the beasts of the field and all the birds of the air. He brought them to the man to see what he would name them; and whatever the man called each living creature, that was its name. [20]So the man gave names to all the livestock, the birds of the air and all the beasts of the field.

But for Adam[a] no suitable helper was found. [21]So the LORD God caused the man to fall into a deep sleep; and while he was sleeping, he took one of the man's ribs[b] and closed up the place with flesh. [22]Then the LORD God made a woman from the rib[c] he had taken out of the man, and he brought her to the man.

[23]The man said,

"This is now bone of my bones

and flesh of my flesh;
she shall be called 'woman,'[d]
for she was taken out of man."

[24]For this reason a man will leave his father and mother and be united to his wife, and they will become one flesh. [25]The man and his wife were both naked, and they felt no shame.

The Fall of Man

3 Now the serpent was more crafty than any of the wild animals the LORD God had made. He said to the woman, "Did God really say, 'You must not eat from any tree in the garden'?"

[2]The woman said to the serpent, "We may eat fruit from the trees in the garden,

[a]20 Or *the man*　　*[b]21* Or *took part of the man's side*　　*[c]22* Or *part*　　*[d]23* The Hebrew for *woman* sounds like the Hebrew for *man*.

Marriage Takes Three

Tuesday

GENESIS 2:24　In the beginning, God created a lifelong relationship between a man and a woman, and he called it "marriage." Intended as the closest and most satisfying of all human relationships, the marriage bond remains strong when we follow the three principles found in this passage: leaving, cleaving and becoming one.

Leaving our families was the easy part for us. When we got married Dave's family lived in Naples, Italy. Actually he "left" several years before when he enrolled at Georgia Tech. Initially, it was easy for me (Claudia) to leave my family. After all, we would be living in Atlanta which was only a two-hour drive from my parents. Plus all I wanted was to be with Dave! Even pulling off a wedding between Christmas and New Years was simple.

But after the wedding, we were unprepared for the struggles we encountered. Family wasn't all we needed to leave, and it wasn't a one-time event. Over the years for us, leaving has involved realigning our priorities from what "I want for me" to what "we want for us"; this has included staying in the relationship through the hard times,

being faithful to each other and putting our relationship before other things like our jobs, hobbies and other interests.

The second challenge we faced in our marriage was to learn how to cleave to each other and to become soul mates. It's not easy to be vulnerable to another person—to open up and share intimate thoughts and feelings, and to be willing to give and receive emotional support—but it's the only way to become best friends.

Becoming one involves being skilled lovers. God created the sexual relationship, and it is with God's approval that, in the framework of marriage, we act on our passion for each other. In marriage we experience a unique sexual oneness.

Think about your marriage today. What might you still need to leave? Consider steps you might take to build a closer friendship, and think of ways you can add a little passion to your love life. Remember, in the beginning God created marriage. And it can be very, very good!

—*Dave & Claudia*

Go to page 8 for your next devotional reading.

³but God did say, 'You must not eat fruit from the tree that is in the middle of the garden, and you must not touch it, or you will die.' "

⁴"You will not surely die," the serpent said to the woman. ⁵"For God knows that when you eat of it your eyes will be opened, and you will be like God, knowing good and evil."

⁶When the woman saw that the fruit of the tree was good for food and pleasing to the eye, and also desirable for gaining wisdom, she took some and ate it. She also gave some to her husband, who was with her, and he ate it. ⁷Then the eyes of both of them were opened, and they realized they were naked; so they sewed fig leaves together and made coverings for themselves.

⁸Then the man and his wife heard the sound of the LORD God as he was walking in the garden in the cool of the day, and they hid from the LORD God among the trees of the garden. ⁹But the LORD God called to the man, "Where are you?"

¹⁰He answered, "I heard you in the garden, and I was afraid because I was naked; so I hid."

¹¹And he said, "Who told you that you were naked? Have you eaten from the tree that I commanded you not to eat from?"

¹²The man said, "The woman you put here with me—she gave me some fruit from the tree, and I ate it."

¹³Then the LORD God said to the woman, "What is this you have done?"

The woman said, "The serpent deceived me, and I ate."

¹⁴So the LORD God said to the serpent, "Because you have done this,

"Cursed are you above all the
    livestock
    and all the wild animals!
You will crawl on your belly
    and you will eat dust
    all the days of your life.
¹⁵And I will put enmity
    between you and the woman,
    and between your offspring^a and
    hers;
he will crush^b your head,
    and you will strike his heel."

¹⁶To the woman he said,

Marriage Takes Three

Genesis 2:24 gives three principles basic to a growing, loving marriage: leaving, cleaving and becoming one. To see how you are doing in following these principles in your marriage, check true or false for the following statements:

True False When I married my spouse, I moved my allegiance from my parents to my spouse.

True False I continue to make my spouse my top priority.

True False I take regular priority checkups and willingly reprioritize my commitments and time constraints.

True False My mate is my best friend.

True False I look for things that pull us together.

True False I try to avoid things that push us apart.

True False I would describe our love life as passionate.

True False I look for ways to add romance to our relationship.

"I will greatly increase your pains in
    childbearing;
with pain you will give birth to
    children.
Your desire will be for your husband,
    and he will rule over you."

¹⁷To Adam he said, "Because you listened to your wife and ate from the tree about which I commanded you, 'You must not eat of it,'

"Cursed is the ground because of
    you;
    through painful toil you will eat of
    it
    all the days of your life.
¹⁸It will produce thorns and thistles for
    you,
    and you will eat the plants of the
    field.
¹⁹By the sweat of your brow

^{a}15 Or *seed* ^{b}15 Or *strike*

you will eat your food
until you return to the ground,
    since from it you were taken;
for dust you are
    and to dust you will return."

²⁰Adam*ᵃ* named his wife Eve,*ᵇ* because she would become the mother of all the living. ²¹The LORD God made garments of skin for Adam and his wife and clothed them. ²²And the LORD God said, "The man has now become like one of us, knowing good and evil. He must not be allowed to reach out his hand and take also from the tree of life and eat, and live forever." ²³So the LORD God banished him from the Garden of Eden to work the ground from which he had been taken. ²⁴After he drove the man out, he placed on the east side*ᶜ* of the Garden of Eden cherubim and a flaming sword flashing back and forth to guard the way to the tree of life.

Cain and Abel

4 Adam*ᵈ* lay with his wife Eve, and she became pregnant and gave birth to Cain.*ᵈ* She said, "With the help of the LORD I have brought forth*ᵉ* a man." ²Later she gave birth to his brother Abel.

Now Abel kept flocks, and Cain worked the soil. ³In the course of time Cain brought some of the fruits of the soil as an offering to the LORD. ⁴But Abel brought fat portions from some of the firstborn of his flock. The LORD looked with favor on Abel and his offering, ⁵but on Cain and his offering he did not look with favor. So Cain was very angry, and his face was downcast.

⁶Then the LORD said to Cain, "Why are you angry? Why is your face downcast? ⁷If you do what is right, will you not be accepted? But if you do not do what is right, sin is crouching at your door; it desires to have you, but you must master it."

⁸Now Cain said to his brother Abel, "Let's go out to the field."*ᶠ* And while they were in the field, Cain attacked his brother Abel and killed him.

⁹Then the LORD said to Cain, "Where is your brother Abel?"

"I don't know," he replied. "Am I my brother's keeper?"

¹⁰The LORD said, "What have you done? Listen! Your brother's blood cries out to me from the ground. ¹¹Now you are under a curse and driven from the ground, which opened its mouth to receive your brother's blood from your hand. ¹²When you work the ground, it will no longer yield its crops for you. You will be a restless wanderer on the earth."

¹³Cain said to the LORD, "My punishment is more than I can bear. ¹⁴Today you are driving me from the land, and I will be hidden from your presence; I will be a restless wanderer on the earth, and whoever finds me will kill me."

¹⁵But the LORD said to him, "Not so*ᵍ*; if anyone kills Cain, he will suffer vengeance seven times over." Then the LORD put a mark on Cain so that no one who found him would kill him. ¹⁶So Cain went out from the LORD's presence and lived in the land of Nod,*ʰ* east of Eden.

¹⁷Cain lay with his wife, and she became pregnant and gave birth to Enoch. Cain was then building a city, and he named it after his son Enoch. ¹⁸To Enoch was born Irad, and Irad was the father of Mehujael, and Mehujael was the father of Methushael, and Methushael was the father of Lamech.

¹⁹Lamech married two women, one named Adah and the other Zillah. ²⁰Adah gave birth to Jabal; he was the father of those who live in tents and raise livestock. ²¹His brother's name was Jubal; he was the father of all who play the harp and flute. ²²Zillah also had a son, Tubal-Cain, who forged all kinds of tools out of*ⁱ* bronze and iron. Tubal-Cain's sister was Naamah.

²³Lamech said to his wives,

"Adah and Zillah, listen to me;
    wives of Lamech, hear my words.
I have killed*ʲ* a man for wounding
    me,
    a young man for injuring me.
²⁴If Cain is avenged seven times,
    then Lamech seventy-seven times."

ᵃ20,1 Or *The man*   *ᵇ20 Eve* probably means *living.*   *ᶜ24* Or *placed in front*   *ᵈ1 Cain* sounds like the Hebrew for *brought forth* or *acquired.*   *ᵉ1* Or *have acquired*   *ᶠ8* Samaritan Pentateuch, Septuagint, Vulgate and Syriac; Masoretic Text does not have *"Let's go out to the field."*   *ᵍ15* Septuagint, Vulgate and Syriac; Hebrew *Very well*   *ʰ16 Nod* means *wandering* (see verses 12 and 14).   *ⁱ22* Or *who instructed all who work in*   *ʲ23* Or *I will kill*

²⁵Adam lay with his wife again, and she gave birth to a son and named him Seth,ᵃ saying, "God has granted me another child in place of Abel, since Cain killed him." ²⁶Seth also had a son, and he named him Enosh.

At that time men began to call onᵇ the name of the LORD.

From Adam to Noah

5 This is the written account of Adam's line.

When God created man, he made him in the likeness of God. ²He created them male and female and blessed them. And when they were created, he called them "man.ᶜ"

³When Adam had lived 130 years, he had a son in his own likeness, in his own image; and he named him Seth. ⁴After Seth was born, Adam lived 800 years and had other sons and daughters. ⁵Altogether, Adam lived 930 years, and then he died.

⁶When Seth had lived 105 years, he became the fatherᵈ of Enosh. ⁷And after he became the father of Enosh, Seth lived 807 years and had other sons and daughters. ⁸Altogether, Seth lived 912 years, and then he died.

⁹When Enosh had lived 90 years, he became the father of Kenan. ¹⁰And after he became the father of Kenan, Enosh lived 815 years and had other sons and daughters. ¹¹Altogether, Enosh lived 905 years, and then he died.

¹²When Kenan had lived 70 years, he became the father of Mahalalel. ¹³And after he became the father of Mahalalel, Kenan lived 840 years and had other sons and daughters. ¹⁴Altogether, Kenan lived 910 years, and then he died.

¹⁵When Mahalalel had lived 65 years, he became the father of Jared. ¹⁶And after he became the father of Jared, Mahalalel lived 830 years and had other sons and daughters. ¹⁷Altogether, Mahalalel lived 895 years, and then he died.

¹⁸When Jared had lived 162 years, he became the father of Enoch. ¹⁹And after he became the father of Enoch, Jared lived 800 years and had other sons and daughters. ²⁰Altogether, Jared lived 962 years, and then he died.

²¹When Enoch had lived 65 years, he became the father of Methuselah. ²²And after he became the father of Methuselah, Enoch walked with God 300 years and had other sons and daughters. ²³Altogether, Enoch lived 365 years. ²⁴Enoch walked with God; then he was no more, because God took him away.

²⁵When Methuselah had lived 187 years, he became the father of Lamech. ²⁶And after he became the father of Lamech, Methuselah lived 782 years and had other sons and daughters. ²⁷Altogether, Methuselah lived 969 years, and then he died.

²⁸When Lamech had lived 182 years, he had a son. ²⁹He named him Noahᵉ and said, "He will comfort us in the labor and painful toil of our hands caused by the ground the LORD has cursed." ³⁰After Noah was born, Lamech lived 595 years and had other sons and daughters. ³¹Altogether, Lamech lived 777 years, and then he died.

³²After Noah was 500 years old, he became the father of Shem, Ham and Japheth.

The Flood

6 When men began to increase in number on the earth and daughters were born to them, ²the sons of God saw that the daughters of men were beautiful, and they married any of them they chose. ³Then the LORD said, "My Spirit will not contend withᶠ man forever, for he is mortalᵍ; his days will be a hundred and twenty years."

⁴The Nephilim were on the earth in those days—and also afterward—when the sons of God went to the daughters of men and had children by them. They were the heroes of old, men of renown.

⁵The LORD saw how great man's wickedness on the earth had become, and that every inclination of the thoughts of his heart was only evil all the time. ⁶The LORD was grieved that he had made man on the earth, and his heart was filled with pain. ⁷So the LORD said, "I will wipe mankind, whom I have created, from the face of the

---

ᵃ25 *Seth* probably means *granted.*   ᵇ26 Or *to proclaim*   ᶜ2 Hebrew *adam*   ᵈ6 *Father* may mean *ancestor;* also in verses 7-26.   ᵉ29 *Noah* sounds like the Hebrew for *comfort.*   ᶠ3 Or *My spirit will not remain in*   ᵍ3 Or *corrupt* earth—men and animals, and creatures that move along the ground, and birds of the air—for I am grieved that I have made them." [8]But Noah found favor in the eyes of the LORD.

[9]This is the account of Noah.

Noah was a righteous man, blameless among the people of his time, and he walked with God. [10]Noah had three sons: Shem, Ham and Japheth.

[11]Now the earth was corrupt in God's sight and was full of violence. [12]God saw how corrupt the earth had become, for all the people on earth had corrupted their ways. [13]So God said to Noah, "I am going to put an end to all people, for the earth is filled with violence because of them. I am surely going to destroy both them and the earth. [14]So make yourself an ark of cypress[a] wood; make rooms in it and coat it with pitch inside and out. [15]This is how you are to build it: The ark is to be 450 feet long, 75 feet wide and 45 feet high.[b] [16]Make a roof for it and finish[c] the ark to within 18 inches[d] of the top. Put a door in the side of the ark and make lower, middle and upper decks. [17]I am going to bring floodwaters on the earth to destroy all life under the heavens, every creature that has the breath of life in it. Everything on earth will perish. [18]But I will establish my covenant with you, and you will enter the ark—you and your sons and your wife and your sons' wives with you. [19]You are to bring into the ark two of all living creatures, male and female, to keep them alive with you. [20]Two of every kind of bird, of every kind of animal and of every kind of creature that moves along the ground will come to you to be kept alive. [21]You are to take every kind of food that is to be eaten and store it away as food for you and for them."

[22]Noah did everything just as God commanded him.

7 The LORD then said to Noah, "Go into the ark, you and your whole family, because I have found you righteous in this generation. [2]Take with you seven[e] of every kind of clean animal, a male and

[a]14 The meaning of the Hebrew for this word is uncertain.   [b]15 Hebrew *300 cubits long, 50 cubits wide and 30 cubits high* (about 140 meters long, 23 meters wide and 13.5 meters high)   [c]16 Or *Make an opening for light by finishing*   [d]16 Hebrew *a cubit* (about 0.5 meter)   [e]2 Or *seven pairs*; also in verse 3

Committed to the Right Goal

Wednesday

GENESIS 6   Diane had been married for a decade, and it had become a hard journey because her husband Bill was building his career and was hardly ever home. Bill's long hours at the office and weekly travel caused her to feel alienated and lonely. To add to Diane's discouragement, her friends had been urging her to abandon her difficult marriage. The world around her was saying, "It's ridiculous to stay committed to something that doesn't make you happy." The whole concept of commitment was confusing to Diane. She wondered why she found it so difficult to commit. Then she considered Noah and his level of commitment.

Noah made a commitment to God to build an ark. Noah hadn't committed to build the ark only until the job became difficult ... his commitment wasn't even to an ark. His commitment was to God. Noah had a whole

culture of distractions to deal with. To the pagan world around him, building an ark seemed incredibly foolish. And spending a lifetime working on it seemed even more foolish.

Building a marriage in today's world can often seem as difficult as Noah's project. How does one stay with that commitment when the going gets tough?

Diane had to refocus her commitment to God, the One who created the plan, rather than to the project at hand. Instead of complaining, she focused her energy on making the times Bill was home as meaningful as she could. Daily she asked God to bring Bill's heart home. Her commitment to God kept her focused during this long, often lonely "building project."

—Bob & Rosemary

Go to page 12 for your next devotional reading.

its mate, and two of every kind of unclean animal, a male and its mate, ³and also seven of every kind of bird, male and female, to keep their various kinds alive throughout the earth. ⁴Seven days from now I will send rain on the earth for forty days and forty nights, and I will wipe from the face of the earth every living creature I have made."

⁵And Noah did all that the LORD commanded him.

⁶Noah was six hundred years old when the floodwaters came on the earth. ⁷And Noah and his sons and his wife and his sons' wives entered the ark to escape the waters of the flood. ⁸Pairs of clean and unclean animals, of birds and of all creatures that move along the ground, ⁹male and female, came to Noah and entered the ark, as God had commanded Noah. ¹⁰And after the seven days the floodwaters came on the earth.

¹¹In the six hundredth year of Noah's life, on the seventeenth day of the second month—on that day all the springs of the great deep burst forth, and the floodgates of the heavens were opened. ¹²And rain fell on the earth forty days and forty nights.

¹³On that very day Noah and his sons, Shem, Ham and Japheth, together with his wife and the wives of his three sons, entered the ark. ¹⁴They had with them every wild animal according to its kind, all livestock according to their kinds, every creature that moves along the ground according to its kind and every bird according to its kind, everything with wings. ¹⁵Pairs of all creatures that have the breath of life in them came to Noah and entered the ark. ¹⁶The animals going in were male and female of every living thing, as God had commanded Noah. Then the LORD shut him in.

¹⁷For forty days the flood kept coming on the earth, and as the waters increased they lifted the ark high above the earth. ¹⁸The waters rose and increased greatly on the earth, and the ark floated on the surface of the water. ¹⁹They rose greatly on the earth, and all the high mountains under the entire heavens were covered. ²⁰The waters rose and covered the mountains to a depth of more than twenty feet.ᵃ, ᵇ ²¹Every living thing that moved on the earth perished—birds, livestock,

wild animals, all the creatures that swarm over the earth, and all mankind. ²²Everything on dry land that had the breath of life in its nostrils died. ²³Every living thing on the face of the earth was wiped out; men and animals and the creatures that move along the ground and the birds of the air were wiped from the earth. Only Noah was left, and those with him in the ark.

²⁴The waters flooded the earth for a hundred and fifty days.

8 But God remembered Noah and all the wild animals and the livestock that were with him in the ark, and he sent a wind over the earth, and the waters receded. ²Now the springs of the deep and the floodgates of the heavens had been closed, and the rain had stopped falling from the sky. ³The water receded steadily from the earth. At the end of the hundred and fifty days the water had gone down, ⁴and on the seventeenth day of the seventh month the ark came to rest on the mountains of Ararat. ⁵The waters continued to recede until the tenth month, and on the first day of the tenth month the tops of the mountains became visible.

⁶After forty days Noah opened the window he had made in the ark ⁷and sent out a raven, and it kept flying back and forth until the water had dried up from the earth. ⁸Then he sent out a dove to see if the water had receded from the surface of the ground. ⁹But the dove could find no place to set its feet because there was water over all the surface of the earth; so it returned to Noah in the ark. He reached out his hand and took the dove and brought it back to himself in the ark. ¹⁰He waited seven more days and again sent out the dove from the ark. ¹¹When the dove returned to him in the evening, there in its beak was a freshly plucked olive leaf! Then Noah knew that the water had receded from the earth. ¹²He waited seven more days and sent the dove out again, but this time it did not return to him.

¹³By the first day of the first month of Noah's six hundred and first year, the water had dried up from the earth. Noah

---

ᵃ20 Hebrew *fifteen cubits* (about 6.9 meters)
ᵇ20 Or *rose more than twenty feet, and the mountains were covered*

then removed the covering from the ark and saw that the surface of the ground was dry. [14]By the twenty-seventh day of the second month the earth was completely dry.

[15]Then God said to Noah, [16]"Come out of the ark, you and your wife and your sons and their wives. [17]Bring out every kind of living creature that is with you—the birds, the animals, and all the creatures that move along the ground—so they can multiply on the earth and be fruitful and increase in number upon it."

[18]So Noah came out, together with his sons and his wife and his sons' wives. [19]All the animals and all the creatures that move along the ground and all the birds—everything that moves on the earth—came out of the ark, one kind after another.

[20]Then Noah built an altar to the LORD and, taking some of all the clean animals and clean birds, he sacrificed burnt offerings on it. [21]The LORD smelled the pleasing aroma and said in his heart: "Never again will I curse the ground because of man, even though[a] every inclination of his heart is evil from childhood. And never again will I destroy all living creatures, as I have done.

[22]"As long as the earth endures,
seedtime and harvest,
cold and heat,
summer and winter,
day and night
will never cease."

God's Covenant With Noah

9 Then God blessed Noah and his sons, saying to them, "Be fruitful and increase in number and fill the earth. [2]The fear and dread of you will fall upon all the beasts of the earth and all the birds of the air, upon every creature that moves along the ground, and upon all the fish of the sea; they are given into your hands. [3]Everything that lives and moves will be food for you. Just as I gave you the green plants, I now give you everything.

[4]"But you must not eat meat that has its lifeblood still in it. [5]And for your lifeblood I will surely demand an accounting. I will demand an accounting from every animal. And from each man, too, I will demand an accounting for the life of his fellow man.

[6]"Whoever sheds the blood of man,
by man shall his blood be shed;
for in the image of God
has God made man.

[7]As for you, be fruitful and increase in number; multiply on the earth and increase upon it."

[8]Then God said to Noah and to his sons with him: [9]"I now establish my covenant with you and with your descendants after you [10]and with every living creature that was with you—the birds, the livestock and all the wild animals, all those that came out of the ark with you—every living creature on earth. [11]I establish my covenant with you: Never again will all life be cut off by the waters of a flood; never again will there be a flood to destroy the earth."

[12]And God said, "This is the sign of the covenant I am making between me and you and every living creature with you, a covenant for all generations to come: [13]I have set my rainbow in the clouds, and it will be the sign of the covenant between me and the earth. [14]Whenever I bring clouds over the earth and the rainbow appears in the clouds, [15]I will remember my covenant between me and you and all living creatures of every kind. Never again will the waters become a flood to destroy all life. [16]Whenever the rainbow appears in the clouds, I will see it and remember the everlasting covenant between God and all living creatures of every kind on the earth."

[17]So God said to Noah, "This is the sign of the covenant I have established between me and all life on the earth."

The Sons of Noah

[18]The sons of Noah who came out of the ark were Shem, Ham and Japheth. (Ham was the father of Canaan.) [19]These were the three sons of Noah, and from them came the people who were scattered over the earth.

[20]Noah, a man of the soil, proceeded[b] to plant a vineyard. [21]When he drank some of its wine, he became drunk and lay uncovered inside his tent. [22]Ham, the father of Canaan, saw his father's nakedness and told his two brothers outside.

---

[a]21 Or man, for   [b]20 Or soil, was the first

23But Shem and Japheth took a garment and laid it across their shoulders; then they walked in backward and covered their father's nakedness. Their faces were turned the other way so that they would not see their father's nakedness.

24When Noah awoke from his wine and found out what his youngest son had done to him, 25he said,

"Cursed be Canaan!
    The lowest of slaves
    will he be to his brothers."

26He also said,

"Blessed be the LORD, the God of
        Shem!
    May Canaan be the slave of
        Shem.a
27May God extend the territory of
        Japhethb;
    may Japheth live in the tents of
        Shem,
    and may Canaan be hisc slave."

28After the flood Noah lived 350 years. 29Altogether, Noah lived 950 years, and then he died.

The Table of Nations

10 This is the account of Shem, Ham and Japheth, Noah's sons, who themselves had sons after the flood.

The Japhethites

2The sonsd of Japheth:
    Gomer, Magog, Madai, Javan, Tubal, Meshech and Tiras.
3The sons of Gomer:
    Ashkenaz, Riphath and Togarmah.
4The sons of Javan:
    Elishah, Tarshish, the Kittim and the Rodanim.e 5(From these the maritime peoples spread out into their territories by their clans within their nations, each with its own language.)

The Hamites

6The sons of Ham:
    Cush, Mizraim,f Put and Canaan.
7The sons of Cush:
    Seba, Havilah, Sabtah, Raamah and Sabteca.

The sons of Raamah:
    Sheba and Dedan.

8Cush was the fatherg of Nimrod, who grew to be a mighty warrior on the earth. 9He was a mighty hunter before the LORD; that is why it is said, "Like Nimrod, a mighty hunter before the LORD." 10The first centers of his kingdom were Babylon, Erech, Akkad and Calneh, inh Shinar.i 11From that land he went to Assyria, where he built Nineveh, Rehoboth Ir,j Calah 12and Resen, which is between Nineveh and Calah; that is the great city.

13Mizraim was the father of
    the Ludites, Anamites, Lehabites, Naphtuhites, 14Pathrusites, Casluhites (from whom the Philistines came) and Caphtorites.
15Canaan was the father of
    Sidon his firstborn,k and of the Hittites, 16Jebusites, Amorites, Girgashites, 17Hivites, Arkites, Sinites, 18Arvadites, Zemarites and Hamathites.

Later the Canaanite clans scattered 19and the borders of Canaan reached from Sidon toward Gerar as far as Gaza, and then toward Sodom, Gomorrah, Admah and Zeboiim, as far as Lasha.

20These are the sons of Ham by their clans and languages, in their territories and nations.

The Semites

21Sons were also born to Shem, whose older brother wasl Japheth; Shem was the ancestor of all the sons of Eber.

22The sons of Shem:
    Elam, Asshur, Arphaxad, Lud and Aram.
23The sons of Aram:

---

a26 Or be his slave   b27 Japheth sounds like the Hebrew for extend.   c27 Or their   d2 Sons may mean descendants or successors or nations; also in verses 3, 4, 6, 7, 20-23, 29 and 31. e4 Some manuscripts of the Masoretic Text and Samaritan Pentateuch (see also Septuagint and 1 Chron. 1:7); most manuscripts of the Masoretic Text Dodanim   f6 That is, Egypt; also in verse 13   g8 Father may mean ancestor or predecessor or founder; also in verses 13, 15, 24 and 26.   h10 Or Erech and Akkad—all of them in i10 That is, Babylonia   j11 Or Nineveh with its city squares   k15 Or of the Sidonians, the foremost l21 Or Shem, the older brother of

Uz, Hul, Gether and Meshech.[a] 24Arphaxad was the father of[b] Shelah,
and Shelah the father of Eber. 25Two sons were born to Eber:
One was named Peleg,[c] because in his time the earth was divided; his brother was named Joktan. 26Joktan was the father of
Almodad, Sheleph, Hazarmaveth, Jerah, 27Hadoram, Uzal, Diklah, 28Obal, Abimael, Sheba, 29Ophir, Havilah and Jobab. All these were sons of Joktan.

30The region where they lived stretched from Mesha toward Sephar, in the eastern hill country.

31These are the sons of Shem by their clans and languages, in their territories and nations.

32These are the clans of Noah's sons, according to their lines of descent, within their nations. From these the nations spread out over the earth after the flood.

The Tower of Babel

11 Now the whole world had one language and a common speech. 2As men moved eastward,[d] they found a plain in Shinar[e] and settled there.
3They said to each other, "Come, let's make bricks and bake them thoroughly." They used brick instead of stone, and tar for mortar. 4Then they said, "Come, let us build ourselves a city, with a tower that reaches to the heavens, so that we may make a name for ourselves and not be scattered over the face of the whole earth."

5But the LORD came down to see the city and the tower that the men were building. 6The LORD said, "If as one people speaking the same language they have begun to do this, then nothing they plan to do will be impossible for them. 7Come, let us go down and confuse their language so they will not understand each other."

8So the LORD scattered them from there over all the earth, and they stopped building the city. 9That is why it was called Babel[f]—because there the LORD confused the language of the whole world. From there the LORD scattered them over the face of the whole earth.

From Shem to Abram

10This is the account of Shem.

Two years after the flood, when Shem

a23 See Septuagint and 1 Chron. 1:17; Hebrew Mash   b24 Hebrew; Septuagint father of Cainan, and Cainan was the father of   c25 Peleg means division.   d2 Or from the east; or in the east   e2 That is, Babylonia   f9 That is, Babylon; Babel sounds like the Hebrew for confused.

Communication Problems

Thursday

GENESIS 11   "It's not logical!" one says. The other responds, "What does logic have to do with it?" Both say, "If only you could understand me!"

Spouses misunderstand each other daily. In radio terms it's like one is talking on an AM channel and the other on an FM channel. Communication problems are nothing new—people at the tower of Babel had to deal with them, and so do spouses today.

Certainly the world would be a simpler place if everyone spoke the same language, and marriage would be easier if spouses always understood each other. But if you spoke the same "language" and always agreed with each other, your marriage could become very boring. Also, it could be tempting to take all the credit—instead of giving it to God. But not to worry; we all know that marriage doesn't work that way.

As we seek to understand each other, we have the opportunity to trust God in a tangible way that honors him. Instead of being consumed with "building our own edifice," we need to seek to understand our spouse. In so doing, we can build a loving, transparent relationship that demonstrates to others the reality of God's grace and goodness.

—Dave & Claudia

Go to page 14 for your next devotional reading.

was 100 years old, he became the father[a] of Arphaxad. ¹¹And after he became the father of Arphaxad, Shem lived 500 years and had other sons and daughters.

¹²When Arphaxad had lived 35 years, he became the father of Shelah. ¹³And after he became the father of Shelah, Arphaxad lived 403 years and had other sons and daughters.[b]

¹⁴When Shelah had lived 30 years, he became the father of Eber. ¹⁵And after he became the father of Eber, Shelah lived 403 years and had other sons and daughters.

¹⁶When Eber had lived 34 years, he became the father of Peleg. ¹⁷And after he became the father of Peleg, Eber lived 430 years and had other sons and daughters.

¹⁸When Peleg had lived 30 years, he became the father of Reu. ¹⁹And after he became the father of Reu, Peleg lived 209 years and had other sons and daughters.

²⁰When Reu had lived 32 years, he became the father of Serug. ²¹And after he became the father of Serug, Reu lived 207 years and had other sons and daughters.

²²When Serug had lived 30 years, he became the father of Nahor. ²³And after he became the father of Nahor, Serug lived 200 years and had other sons and daughters.

²⁴When Nahor had lived 29 years, he became the father of Terah. ²⁵And after he became the father of Terah, Nahor lived 119 years and had other sons and daughters.

²⁶After Terah had lived 70 years, he became the father of Abram, Nahor and Haran.

²⁷This is the account of Terah.

Terah became the father of Abram, Nahor and Haran. And Haran became the father of Lot. ²⁸While his father Terah was still alive, Haran died in Ur of the Chaldeans, in the land of his birth. ²⁹Abram and Nahor both married. The name of Abram's wife was Sarai, and the name of Nahor's wife was Milcah; she was the daughter of Haran, the father of both Milcah and Iscah. ³⁰Now Sarai was barren; she had no children.

³¹Terah took his son Abram, his grandson Lot son of Haran, and his daughter-in-law Sarai, the wife of his son Abram, and together they set out from Ur of the Chaldeans to go to Canaan. But when they came to Haran, they settled there.

³²Terah lived 205 years, and he died in Haran.

The Call of Abram

12 The LORD had said to Abram, "Leave your country, your people and your father's household and go to the land I will show you.

² "I will make you into a great nation
  and I will bless you;
I will make your name great,
  and you will be a blessing.
³ I will bless those who bless you,
  and whoever curses you I will
    curse;
and all peoples on earth
  will be blessed through you."

⁴So Abram left, as the LORD had told him; and Lot went with him. Abram was seventy-five years old when he set out from Haran. ⁵He took his wife Sarai, his nephew Lot, all the possessions they had accumulated and the people they had acquired in Haran, and they set out for the land of Canaan, and they arrived there.

⁶Abram traveled through the land as far as the site of the great tree of Moreh at Shechem. At that time the Canaanites were in the land. ⁷The LORD appeared to Abram and said, "To your offspring[c] I will give this land." So he built an altar there to the LORD, who had appeared to him.

⁸From there he went on toward the hills east of Bethel and pitched his tent, with Bethel on the west and Ai on the east. There he built an altar to the LORD and called on the name of the LORD. ⁹Then Abram set out and continued toward the Negev.

Abram in Egypt

¹⁰Now there was a famine in the land,

---

a10 Father may mean *ancestor;* also in verses 11-25.   *b12,13* Hebrew; Septuagint (see also Luke 3:35, and note at Gen. 10:24) *35 years, he became the father of Cainan. ¹³And after he became the father of Cainan, Arphaxad lived 430 years and had other sons and daughters, and then he died. When Cainan had lived 130 years, he became the father of Shelah. And after he became the father of Shelah, Cainan lived 330 years and had other sons and daughters*   *c7* Or *seed* and Abram went down to Egypt to live there for a while because the famine was severe. [11]As he was about to enter Egypt, he said to his wife Sarai, "I know what a beautiful woman you are. [12]When the Egyptians see you, they will say, 'This is his wife.' Then they will kill me but will let you live. [13]Say you are my sister, so that I will be treated well for your sake and my life will be spared because of you."

[14]When Abram came to Egypt, the Egyptians saw that she was a very beautiful woman. [15]And when Pharaoh's officials saw her, they praised her to Pharaoh, and she was taken into his palace. [16]He treated Abram well for her sake, and Abram acquired sheep and cattle, male and female donkeys, menservants and maidservants, and camels.

[17]But the LORD inflicted serious diseases on Pharaoh and his household because of Abram's wife Sarai. [18]So Pharaoh summoned Abram. "What have you done to me?" he said. "Why didn't you tell me she was your wife? [19]Why did you say, 'She is my sister,' so that I took her to be my wife? Now then, here is your wife. Take her and go!" [20]Then Pharaoh gave orders about Abram to his men, and they sent him on his way, with his wife and everything he had.

Abram and Lot Separate

13 So Abram went up from Egypt to the Negev, with his wife and everything he had, and Lot went with him. [2]Abram had become very wealthy in livestock and in silver and gold.

[3]From the Negev he went from place to place until he came to Bethel, to the place between Bethel and Ai where his tent had been earlier [4]and where he had first built an altar. There Abram called on the name of the LORD.

[5]Now Lot, who was moving about with Abram, also had flocks and herds and tents. [6]But the land could not support them while they stayed together, for their possessions were so great that they were not able to stay together. [7]And quarreling arose between Abram's herdsmen and the

Who Will You Serve?

Friday

GENESIS 13 The marriage relationship consists of a series of choices. The most significant choice is who you will serve with your marriage. Most married couples make this choice without thinking about it. Like Lot, they look around and see where many wonderful things abound, and then they pursue that direction. "Bigger" and "more" become the goals of their marriage.

In the early years of our marriage, this was a great conflict. I (Bob) felt the strong pull to focus all my energies on purchasing a home in the right neighborhood. Rosemary, on the other hand, believed that God would supply all our needs if we focused on him. It was a struggle in our marriage, until I realized that my preoccupation with the pursuit of things was futile. God had a better plan.

When Lot chose to move his life closer to the riches of the world, Abraham chose to serve only God. Abraham's total focus was pleasing to God. He knew that he could not serve both the things of the world, as well as God. Abraham knew that a choice had to be made.

The marriage team must make that same decision. Two masters cannot be served. The difficult decision must be made whether to serve God or serve things. The temptations dangling in front of each partner on the pages of catalogs and in advertisements can become very distracting. The decision of who or what our marriages will serve must be a daily choice and commitment.

There's nothing wrong with acquiring things. Abraham was a far wealthier person than Lot. Lot's mistake was that he focused too closely on the world . . . and failed. Abraham stayed focused on God . . . and prospered. The question to ask is, "What does our marriage serve? Does it serve God or does it serve the things of the world?"

—Bob & Rosemary

Go to page 29 for your next devotional reading.

herdsmen of Lot. The Canaanites and Perizzites were also living in the land at that time. [8]So Abram said to Lot, "Let's not have any quarreling between you and me, or between your herdsmen and mine, for we are brothers. [9]Is not the whole land before you? Let's part company. If you go to the left, I'll go to the right; if you go to the right, I'll go to the left."

[10]Lot looked up and saw that the whole plain of the Jordan was well watered, like the garden of the LORD, like the land of Egypt, toward Zoar. (This was before the LORD destroyed Sodom and Gomorrah.) [11]So Lot chose for himself the whole plain of the Jordan and set out toward the east. The two men parted company: [12]Abram lived in the land of Canaan, while Lot lived among the cities of the plain and pitched his tents near Sodom. [13]Now the men of Sodom were wicked and were sinning greatly against the LORD.

[14]The LORD said to Abram after Lot had parted from him, "Lift up your eyes from where you are and look north and south, east and west. [15]All the land that you see I will give to you and your offspring[a] forever. [16]I will make your offspring like the dust of the earth, so that if anyone could count the dust, then your offspring could be counted. [17]Go, walk through the length and breadth of the land, for I am giving it to you."

[18]So Abram moved his tents and went to live near the great trees of Mamre at Hebron, where he built an altar to the LORD.

Abram Rescues Lot

14 At this time Amraphel king of Shinar,[b] Arioch king of Ellasar, Kedorlaomer king of Elam and Tidal king of Goiim [2]went to war against Bera king of Sodom, Birsha king of Gomorrah, Shinab king of Admah, Shemeber king of Zeboiim, and the king of Bela (that is, Zoar). [3]All these latter kings joined forces in the Valley of Siddim (the Salt Sea[c]). [4]For twelve years they had been subject to Kedorlaomer, but in the thirteenth year they rebelled.

[5]In the fourteenth year, Kedorlaomer and the kings allied with him went out and defeated the Rephaites in Ashteroth Karnaim, the Zuzites in Ham, the Emites in Shaveh Kiriathaim [6]and the Horites in the hill country of Seir, as far as El Paran near the desert. [7]Then they turned back and went to En Mishpat (that is, Kadesh), and they conquered the whole territory of the Amalekites, as well as the Amorites who were living in Hazazon Tamar.

[8]Then the king of Sodom, the king of Gomorrah, the king of Admah, the king of Zeboiim and the king of Bela (that is, Zoar) marched out and drew up their battle lines in the Valley of Siddim [9]against Kedorlaomer king of Elam, Tidal king of Goiim, Amraphel king of Shinar and Arioch king of Ellasar—four kings against five. [10]Now the Valley of Siddim was full of tar pits, and when the kings of Sodom and Gomorrah fled, some of the men fell into them and the rest fled to the hills. [11]The four kings seized all the goods of Sodom and Gomorrah and all their food; then they went away. [12]They also carried off Abram's nephew Lot and his possessions, since he was living in Sodom.

[13]One who had escaped came and reported this to Abram the Hebrew. Now Abram was living near the great trees of Mamre the Amorite, a brother[d] of Eshcol and Aner, all of whom were allied with Abram. [14]When Abram heard that his relative had been taken captive, he called out the 318 trained men born in his household and went in pursuit as far as Dan. [15]During the night Abram divided his men to attack them and he routed them, pursuing them as far as Hobah, north of Damascus. [16]He recovered all the goods and brought back his relative Lot and his possessions, together with the women and the other people.

[17]After Abram returned from defeating Kedorlaomer and the kings allied with him, the king of Sodom came out to meet him in the Valley of Shaveh (that is, the King's Valley).

[18]Then Melchizedek king of Salem[e] brought out bread and wine. He was priest of God Most High, [19]and he blessed Abram, saying,

[a]15 Or seed; also in verse 16   [b]1 That is, Babylonia; also in verse 9   [c]3 That is, the Dead Sea   [d]13 Or a relative; or an ally   [e]18 That is, Jerusalem

"Blessed be Abram by God Most
   High,
   Creator*a* of heaven and earth.
20And blessed be*b* God Most High,
   who delivered your enemies into
   your hand."

Then Abram gave him a tenth of everything.
   21The king of Sodom said to Abram,
"Give me the people and keep the goods
for yourself."
   22But Abram said to the king of Sodom, "I have raised my hand to the LORD,
God Most High, Creator of heaven and
earth, and have taken an oath 23that I will
accept nothing belonging to you, not
even a thread or the thong of a sandal, so
that you will never be able to say, 'I made
Abram rich.' 24I will accept nothing but
what my men have eaten and the share
that belongs to the men who went with
me—to Aner, Eshcol and Mamre. Let them
have their share."

God's Covenant With Abram

15 After this, the word of the LORD
came to Abram in a vision:

"Do not be afraid, Abram.
   I am your shield,*c*
   your very great reward.*d* "

2But Abram said, "O Sovereign LORD,
what can you give me since I remain
childless and the one who will inherit*e*
my estate is Eliezer of Damascus?" 3And
Abram said, "You have given me no children; so a servant in my household will
be my heir."
   4Then the word of the LORD came to
him: "This man will not be your heir, but
a son coming from your own body will be
your heir." 5He took him outside and said,
"Look up at the heavens and count the
stars—if indeed you can count them." Then
he said to him, "So shall your offspring be."
   6Abram believed the LORD, and he
credited it to him as righteousness.
   7He also said to him, "I am the LORD,
who brought you out of Ur of the Chaldeans to give you this land to take possession of it."
   8But Abram said, "O Sovereign LORD,
how can I know that I will gain possession of it?"

9So the LORD said to him, "Bring me a
heifer, a goat and a ram, each three years
old, along with a dove and a young pigeon."
   10Abram brought all these to him, cut
them in two and arranged the halves opposite each other; the birds, however, he
did not cut in half. 11Then birds of prey
came down on the carcasses, but Abram
drove them away.
   12As the sun was setting, Abram fell
into a deep sleep, and a thick and dreadful darkness came over him. 13Then the
LORD said to him, "Know for certain that
your descendants will be strangers in a
country not their own, and they will be
enslaved and mistreated four hundred
years. 14But I will punish the nation they
serve as slaves, and afterward they will
come out with great possessions. 15You,
however, will go to your fathers in peace
and be buried at a good old age. 16In the
fourth generation your descendants will
come back here, for the sin of the Amorites has not yet reached its full measure."
   17When the sun had set and darkness
had fallen, a smoking firepot with a blazing torch appeared and passed between
the pieces. 18On that day the LORD made
a covenant with Abram and said, "To
your descendants I give this land, from
the river*f* of Egypt to the great river, the
Euphrates— 19the land of the Kenites,
Kenizzites, Kadmonites, 20Hittites, Perizzites, Rephaites, 21Amorites, Canaanites,
Girgashites and Jebusites."

Hagar and Ishmael

16 Now Sarai, Abram's wife, had borne
him no children. But she had an
Egyptian maidservant named Hagar; 2so
she said to Abram, "The LORD has kept
me from having children. Go, sleep with
my maidservant; perhaps I can build a
family through her."
   Abram agreed to what Sarai said. 3So
after Abram had been living in Canaan
ten years, Sarai his wife took her Egyptian
maidservant Hagar and gave her to her
husband to be his wife. 4He slept with
Hagar, and she conceived.

*a19 Or Possessor; also in verse 22   b20 Or And
praise be to   c1 Or sovereign   d1 Or shield; /
your reward will be very great   e2 The meaning of
the Hebrew for this phrase is uncertain.
f18 Or Wadi*

When she knew she was pregnant, she began to despise her mistress. ⁵Then Sarai said to Abram, "You are responsible for the wrong I am suffering. I put my servant in your arms, and now that she knows she is pregnant, she despises me. May the LORD judge between you and me."

⁶"Your servant is in your hands," Abram said. "Do with her whatever you think best." Then Sarai mistreated Hagar; so she fled from her.

⁷The angel of the LORD found Hagar near a spring in the desert; it was the spring that is beside the road to Shur. ⁸And he said, "Hagar, servant of Sarai, where have you come from, and where are you going?"

"I'm running away from my mistress Sarai," she answered.

⁹Then the angel of the LORD told her, "Go back to your mistress and submit to her." ¹⁰The angel added, "I will so increase your descendants that they will be too numerous to count."

¹¹The angel of the LORD also said to her:

"You are now with child
    and you will have a son.
You shall name him Ishmael,ᵃ
    for the LORD has heard of your
        misery.
¹²He will be a wild donkey of a man;
    his hand will be against everyone
    and everyone's hand against him,
and he will live in hostility
    towardᵇ all his brothers."

¹³She gave this name to the LORD who spoke to her: "You are the God who sees me," for she said, "I have now seenᶜ the One who sees me." ¹⁴That is why the well was called Beer Lahai Roiᵈ; it is still there, between Kadesh and Bered.

¹⁵So Hagar bore Abram a son, and Abram gave the name Ishmael to the son she had borne. ¹⁶Abram was eighty-six years old when Hagar bore him Ishmael.

The Covenant of Circumcision

17 When Abram was ninety-nine years old, the LORD appeared to him and said, "I am God Almightyᵉ; walk before me and be blameless. ²I will confirm my covenant between me and you and will greatly increase your numbers."

³Abram fell facedown, and God said to him, ⁴"As for me, this is my covenant with you: You will be the father of many nations. ⁵No longer will you be called Abramᶠ; your name will be Abraham,ᵍ for I have made you a father of many nations. ⁶I will make you very fruitful; I will make nations of you, and kings will come from you. ⁷I will establish my covenant as an everlasting covenant between me and you and your descendants after you for the generations to come, to be your God and the God of your descendants after you. ⁸The whole land of Canaan, where you are now an alien, I will give as an everlasting possession to you and your descendants after you; and I will be their God."

⁹Then God said to Abraham, "As for you, you must keep my covenant, you and your descendants after you for the generations to come. ¹⁰This is my covenant with you and your descendants after you, the covenant you are to keep: Every male among you shall be circumcised. ¹¹You are to undergo circumcision, and it will be the sign of the covenant between me and you. ¹²For the generations to come every male among you who is eight days old must be circumcised, including those born in your household or bought with money from a foreigner—those who are not your offspring. ¹³Whether born in your household or bought with your money, they must be circumcised. My covenant in your flesh is to be an everlasting covenant. ¹⁴Any uncircumcised male, who has not been circumcised in the flesh, will be cut off from his people; he has broken my covenant."

¹⁵God also said to Abraham, "As for Sarai your wife, you are no longer to call her Sarai; her name will be Sarah. ¹⁶I will bless her and will surely give you a son by her. I will bless her so that she will be the mother of nations; kings of peoples will come from her."

¹⁷Abraham fell facedown; he laughed and said to himself, "Will a son be born to a man a hundred years old? Will Sarah bear a child at the age of ninety?" ¹⁸And

---

ᵃ11 *Ishmael* means *God hears.*   ᵇ12 Or *live to the east / of*   ᶜ13 Or *seen the back of*   ᵈ14 *Beer Lahai Roi* means *well of the Living One who sees me.*   ᵉ1 Hebrew *El-Shaddai*   ᶠ5 *Abram* means *exalted father.*   ᵍ5 *Abraham* means *father of many.*

Abraham said to God, "If only Ishmael might live under your blessing!"

[19]Then God said, "Yes, but your wife Sarah will bear you a son, and you will call him Isaac.[a] I will establish my covenant with him as an everlasting covenant for his descendants after him. [20]And as for Ishmael, I have heard you: I will surely bless him; I will make him fruitful and will greatly increase his numbers. He will be the father of twelve rulers, and I will make him into a great nation. [21]But my covenant I will establish with Isaac, whom Sarah will bear to you by this time next year." [22]When he had finished speaking with Abraham, God went up from him.

[23]On that very day Abraham took his son Ishmael and all those born in his household or bought with his money, every male in his household, and circumcised them, as God told him. [24]Abraham was ninety-nine years old when he was circumcised, [25]and his son Ishmael was thirteen; [26]Abraham and his son Ishmael were both circumcised on that same day. [27]And every male in Abraham's household, including those born in his household or bought from a foreigner, was circumcised with him.

The Three Visitors

18 The LORD appeared to Abraham near the great trees of Mamre while he was sitting at the entrance to his tent in the heat of the day. [2]Abraham looked up and saw three men standing nearby. When he saw them, he hurried from the entrance of his tent to meet them and bowed low to the ground.

[3]He said, "If I have found favor in your eyes, my lord,[b] do not pass your servant by. [4]Let a little water be brought, and then you may all wash your feet and rest under this tree. [5]Let me get you something to eat, so you can be refreshed and then go on your way—now that you have come to your servant."

"Very well," they answered, "do as you say."

[6]So Abraham hurried into the tent to Sarah. "Quick," he said, "get three seahs[c] of fine flour and knead it and bake some bread."

[7]Then he ran to the herd and selected a choice, tender calf and gave it to a servant, who hurried to prepare it. [8]He then brought some curds and milk and the calf that had been prepared, and set these before them. While they ate, he stood near them under a tree.

[9]"Where is your wife Sarah?" they asked him.

"There, in the tent," he said.

[10]Then the LORD[d] said, "I will surely return to you about this time next year, and Sarah your wife will have a son."

Now Sarah was listening at the entrance to the tent, which was behind him. [11]Abraham and Sarah were already old and well advanced in years, and Sarah was past the age of childbearing. [12]So Sarah laughed to herself as she thought, "After I am worn out and my master[e] is old, will I now have this pleasure?"

[13]Then the LORD said to Abraham, "Why did Sarah laugh and say, 'Will I really have a child, now that I am old?' [14]Is anything too hard for the LORD? I will return to you at the appointed time next year and Sarah will have a son."

[15]Sarah was afraid, so she lied and said, "I did not laugh."

But he said, "Yes, you did laugh."

Abraham Pleads for Sodom

[16]When the men got up to leave, they looked down toward Sodom, and Abraham walked along with them to see them on their way. [17]Then the LORD said, "Shall I hide from Abraham what I am about to do? [18]Abraham will surely become a great and powerful nation, and all nations on earth will be blessed through him. [19]For I have chosen him, so that he will direct his children and his household after him to keep the way of the LORD by doing what is right and just, so that the LORD will bring about for Abraham what he has promised him."

[20]Then the LORD said, "The outcry against Sodom and Gomorrah is so great and their sin so grievous [21]that I will go down and see if what they have done is as bad as the outcry that has reached me. If not, I will know."

[22]The men turned away and went to-

---

[a]19 *Isaac* means *he laughs.*   [b]3 Or O *Lord*
[c]6 That is, probably about 20 quarts (about 22 liters)   [d]10 Hebrew *Then he*   [e]12 Or *husband*

ward Sodom, but Abraham remained standing before the LORD.*a* 23Then Abraham approached him and said: "Will you sweep away the righteous with the wicked? 24What if there are fifty righteous people in the city? Will you really sweep it away and not spare*b* the place for the sake of the fifty righteous people in it? 25Far be it from you to do such a thing—to kill the righteous with the wicked, treating the righteous and the wicked alike. Far be it from you! Will not the Judge*c* of all the earth do right?"

26The LORD said, "If I find fifty righteous people in the city of Sodom, I will spare the whole place for their sake."

27Then Abraham spoke up again: "Now that I have been so bold as to speak to the Lord, though I am nothing but dust and ashes, 28what if the number of the righteous is five less than fifty? Will you destroy the whole city because of five people?"

"If I find forty-five there," he said, "I will not destroy it."

29Once again he spoke to him, "What if only forty are found there?"

He said, "For the sake of forty, I will not do it."

30Then he said, "May the Lord not be angry, but let me speak. What if only thirty can be found there?"

He answered, "I will not do it if I find thirty there."

31Abraham said, "Now that I have been so bold as to speak to the Lord, what if only twenty can be found there?"

He said, "For the sake of twenty, I will not destroy it."

32Then he said, "May the Lord not be angry, but let me speak just once more. What if only ten can be found there?"

He answered, "For the sake of ten, I will not destroy it."

33When the LORD had finished speaking with Abraham, he left, and Abraham returned home.

Sodom and Gomorrah Destroyed

19 The two angels arrived at Sodom in the evening, and Lot was sitting in the gateway of the city. When he saw them, he got up to meet them and bowed down with his face to the ground. 2"My lords," he said, "please turn aside to your servant's house. You can wash your feet and spend the night and then go on your way early in the morning."

"No," they answered, "we will spend the night in the square."

3But he insisted so strongly that they did go with him and entered his house. He prepared a meal for them, baking bread without yeast, and they ate. 4Before they had gone to bed, all the men from every part of the city of Sodom—both young and old—surrounded the house. 5They called to Lot, "Where are the men who came to you tonight? Bring them out to us so that we can have sex with them."

6Lot went outside to meet them and shut the door behind him 7and said, "No, my friends. Don't do this wicked thing. 8Look, I have two daughters who have never slept with a man. Let me bring them out to you, and you can do what you like with them. But don't do anything to these men, for they have come under the protection of my roof."

9"Get out of our way," they replied. And they said, "This fellow came here as an alien, and now he wants to play the judge! We'll treat you worse than them." They kept bringing pressure on Lot and moved forward to break down the door.

10But the men inside reached out and pulled Lot back into the house and shut the door. 11Then they struck the men who were at the door of the house, young and old, with blindness so that they could not find the door.

12The two men said to Lot, "Do you have anyone else here—sons-in-law, sons or daughters, or anyone else in the city who belongs to you? Get them out of here, 13because we are going to destroy this place. The outcry to the LORD against its people is so great that he has sent us to destroy it."

14So Lot went out and spoke to his sons-in-law, who were pledged to marry*d* his daughters. He said, "Hurry and get out of this place, because the LORD is about to destroy the city!" But his sons-in-law thought he was joking.

15With the coming of dawn, the angels urged Lot, saying, "Hurry! Take your wife

a22 Masoretic Text; an ancient Hebrew scribal tradition *but the LORD remained standing before Abraham*   *b24* Or *forgive;* also in verse 26   *c25* Or *Ruler*   *d14* Or *were married to* and your two daughters who are here, or you will be swept away when the city is punished."

¹⁶When he hesitated, the men grasped his hand and the hands of his wife and of his two daughters and led them safely out of the city, for the LORD was merciful to them. ¹⁷As soon as they had brought them out, one of them said, "Flee for your lives! Don't look back, and don't stop anywhere in the plain! Flee to the mountains or you will be swept away!"

¹⁸But Lot said to them, "No, my lords,ᵃ please! ¹⁹Yourᵇ servant has found favor in yourᵇ eyes, and youᵇ have shown great kindness to me in sparing my life. But I can't flee to the mountains; this disaster will overtake me, and I'll die. ²⁰Look, here is a town near enough to run to, and it is small. Let me flee to it—it is very small, isn't it? Then my life will be spared."

²¹He said to him, "Very well, I will grant this request too; I will not overthrow the town you speak of. ²²But flee there quickly, because I cannot do anything until you reach it." (That is why the town was called Zoar.ᶜ)

²³By the time Lot reached Zoar, the sun had risen over the land. ²⁴Then the LORD rained down burning sulfur on Sodom and Gomorrah—from the LORD out of the heavens. ²⁵Thus he overthrew those cities and the entire plain, including all those living in the cities—and also the vegetation in the land. ²⁶But Lot's wife looked back, and she became a pillar of salt.

²⁷Early the next morning Abraham got up and returned to the place where he had stood before the LORD. ²⁸He looked down toward Sodom and Gomorrah, toward all the land of the plain, and he saw dense smoke rising from the land, like smoke from a furnace.

²⁹So when God destroyed the cities of the plain, he remembered Abraham, and he brought Lot out of the catastrophe that overthrew the cities where Lot had lived.

Lot and His Daughters

³⁰Lot and his two daughters left Zoar and settled in the mountains, for he was afraid to stay in Zoar. He and his two daughters lived in a cave. ³¹One day the older daughter said to the younger, "Our father is old, and there is no man around here to lie with us, as is the custom all over the earth. ³²Let's get our father to drink wine and then lie with him and preserve our family line through our father."

³³That night they got their father to drink wine, and the older daughter went in and lay with him. He was not aware of it when she lay down or when she got up.

³⁴The next day the older daughter said to the younger, "Last night I lay with my father. Let's get him to drink wine again tonight, and you go in and lie with him so we can preserve our family line through our father." ³⁵So they got their father to drink wine that night also, and the younger daughter went and lay with him. Again he was not aware of it when she lay down or when she got up.

³⁶So both of Lot's daughters became pregnant by their father. ³⁷The older daughter had a son, and she named him Moab;ᵈ he is the father of the Moabites of today. ³⁸The younger daughter also had a son, and she named him Ben-Ammi;ᵉ he is the father of the Ammonites of today.

Abraham and Abimelech

20 Now Abraham moved on from there into the region of the Negev and lived between Kadesh and Shur. For a while he stayed in Gerar, ²and there Abraham said of his wife Sarah, "She is my sister." Then Abimelech king of Gerar sent for Sarah and took her.

³But God came to Abimelech in a dream one night and said to him, "You are as good as dead because of the woman you have taken; she is a married woman."

⁴Now Abimelech had not gone near her, so he said, "Lord, will you destroy an innocent nation? ⁵Did he not say to me, 'She is my sister,' and didn't she also say, 'He is my brother'? I have done this with a clear conscience and clean hands."

⁶Then God said to him in the dream, "Yes, I know you did this with a clear conscience, and so I have kept you from sinning against me. That is why I did not

---

ᵃ18 Or No, Lord; or No, my lord   ᵇ19 The Hebrew is singular.   ᶜ22 Zoar means small.
ᵈ37 Moab sounds like the Hebrew for from father.
ᵉ38 Ben-Ammi means son of my people.

let you touch her. ⁷Now return the man's wife, for he is a prophet, and he will pray for you and you will live. But if you do not return her, you may be sure that you and all yours will die."

⁸Early the next morning Abimelech summoned all his officials, and when he told them all that had happened, they were very much afraid. ⁹Then Abimelech called Abraham in and said, "What have you done to us? How have I wronged you that you have brought such great guilt upon me and my kingdom? You have done things to me that should not be done." ¹⁰And Abimelech asked Abraham, "What was your reason for doing this?"

¹¹Abraham replied, "I said to myself, 'There is surely no fear of God in this place, and they will kill me because of my wife.' ¹²Besides, she really is my sister, the daughter of my father though not of my mother; and she became my wife. ¹³And when God had me wander from my father's household, I said to her, 'This is how you can show your love to me: Everywhere we go, say of me, "He is my brother." ' "

¹⁴Then Abimelech brought sheep and cattle and male and female slaves and gave them to Abraham, and he returned Sarah his wife to him. ¹⁵And Abimelech said, "My land is before you; live wherever you like."

¹⁶To Sarah he said, "I am giving your brother a thousand shekels*ᵃ* of silver. This is to cover the offense against you before all who are with you; you are completely vindicated."

¹⁷Then Abraham prayed to God, and God healed Abimelech, his wife and his slave girls so they could have children again, ¹⁸for the LORD had closed up every womb in Abimelech's household because of Abraham's wife Sarah.

The Birth of Isaac

21 Now the LORD was gracious to Sarah as he had said, and the LORD did for Sarah what he had promised. ²Sarah became pregnant and bore a son to Abraham in his old age, at the very time God had promised. ³Abraham gave the name Isaac*ᵇ* to the son Sarah bore him. ⁴When his son Isaac was eight days old, Abraham circumcised him, as God com-

Lot and His Wife

GENESIS 19:1-29   Lot was well connected; he was the nephew of the famous and powerful Abraham. He was rich—and getting richer with

COUPLES IN THE BIBLE

his large spread in the well-watered plains of the Jordan River. In Sodom he was well known as a city father. Lot could have been content and grateful for his good fortune. But he and his wife were enamored with the prosperous people of Sodom and longed for their acceptance. In spite of their mixed beliefs, God gave Lot and his wife an opportunity to flee Sodom before he destroyed it. But somewhere on a hillside, not far from town, Lot's wife turned for a last look at sin-city, the place she both loved and hated. At once, she became a pillar of salt. As for Lot, he lost everything except his life.

manded him. ⁵Abraham was a hundred years old when his son Isaac was born to him.

⁶Sarah said, "God has brought me laughter, and everyone who hears about this will laugh with me." ⁷And she added, "Who would have said to Abraham that Sarah would nurse children? Yet I have borne him a son in his old age."

Hagar and Ishmael Sent Away

⁸The child grew and was weaned, and on the day Isaac was weaned Abraham held a great feast. ⁹But Sarah saw that the son whom Hagar the Egyptian had borne to Abraham was mocking, ¹⁰and she said to Abraham, "Get rid of that slave woman and her son, for that slave woman's son will never share in the inheritance with my son Isaac."

¹¹The matter distressed Abraham greatly because it concerned his son. ¹²But God said to him, "Do not be so distressed about the boy and your maidservant. Listen to whatever Sarah tells you, because it is through Isaac that your offspring*ᶜ* will be reckoned. ¹³I will make the son of the

ᵃ16 That is, about 25 pounds (about 11.5 kilograms)   ᵇ3 Isaac means he laughs.
ᶜ12 Or seed

maidservant into a nation also, because he is your offspring."

¹⁴Early the next morning Abraham took some food and a skin of water and gave them to Hagar. He set them on her shoulders and then sent her off with the boy. She went on her way and wandered in the desert of Beersheba.

¹⁵When the water in the skin was gone, she put the boy under one of the bushes. ¹⁶Then she went off and sat down nearby, about a bowshot away, for she thought, "I cannot watch the boy die." And as she sat there nearby, she*a* began to sob.

¹⁷God heard the boy crying, and the angel of God called to Hagar from heaven and said to her, "What is the matter, Hagar? Do not be afraid; God has heard the boy crying as he lies there. ¹⁸Lift the boy up and take him by the hand, for I will make him into a great nation."

¹⁹Then God opened her eyes and she saw a well of water. So she went and filled the skin with water and gave the boy a drink.

²⁰God was with the boy as he grew up. He lived in the desert and became an archer. ²¹While he was living in the Desert of Paran, his mother got a wife for him from Egypt.

The Treaty at Beersheba

²²At that time Abimelech and Phicol the commander of his forces said to Abraham, "God is with you in everything you do. ²³Now swear to me here before God that you will not deal falsely with me or my children or my descendants. Show to me and the country where you are living as an alien the same kindness I have shown to you."

²⁴Abraham said, "I swear it."

²⁵Then Abraham complained to Abimelech about a well of water that Abimelech's servants had seized. ²⁶But Abimelech said, "I don't know who has done this. You did not tell me, and I heard about it only today."

²⁷So Abraham brought sheep and cattle and gave them to Abimelech, and the two men made a treaty. ²⁸Abraham set apart seven ewe lambs from the flock, ²⁹and Abimelech asked Abraham, "What is the meaning of these seven ewe lambs you have set apart by themselves?"

³⁰He replied, "Accept these seven lambs from my hand as a witness that I dug this well."

³¹So that place was called Beersheba,*b* because the two men swore an oath there.

³²After the treaty had been made at Beersheba, Abimelech and Phicol the commander of his forces returned to the land of the Philistines. ³³Abraham planted a tamarisk tree in Beersheba, and there he called upon the name of the LORD, the Eternal God. ³⁴And Abraham stayed in the land of the Philistines for a long time.

Abraham Tested

22 Some time later God tested Abraham. He said to him, "Abraham!"

"Here I am," he replied.

²Then God said, "Take your son, your only son, Isaac, whom you love, and go to the region of Moriah. Sacrifice him there as a burnt offering on one of the mountains I will tell you about."

³Early the next morning Abraham got up and saddled his donkey. He took with him two of his servants and his son Isaac. When he had cut enough wood for the burnt offering, he set out for the place God had told him about. ⁴On the third day Abraham looked up and saw the place in the distance. ⁵He said to his servants, "Stay here with the donkey while I and the boy go over there. We will worship and then we will come back to you."

⁶Abraham took the wood for the burnt offering and placed it on his son Isaac, and he himself carried the fire and the knife. As the two of them went on together, ⁷Isaac spoke up and said to his father Abraham, "Father?"

"Yes, my son?" Abraham replied.

"The fire and wood are here," Isaac said, "but where is the lamb for the burnt offering?"

⁸Abraham answered, "God himself will provide the lamb for the burnt offering, my son." And the two of them went on together.

⁹When they reached the place God had told him about, Abraham built an altar there and arranged the wood on it. He bound his son Isaac and laid him on the altar, on top of the wood. ¹⁰Then he

a16 Hebrew; Septuagint *the child*   *b31 Beersheba* can mean *well of seven* or *well of the oath.*

reached out his hand and took the knife to slay his son. [11]But the angel of the LORD called out to him from heaven, "Abraham! Abraham!"

"Here I am," he replied.

[12]"Do not lay a hand on the boy," he said. "Do not do anything to him. Now I know that you fear God, because you have not withheld from me your son, your only son."

[13]Abraham looked up and there in a thicket he saw a ram[a] caught by its horns. He went over and took the ram and sacrificed it as a burnt offering instead of his son. [14]So Abraham called that place The LORD Will Provide. And to this day it is said, "On the mountain of the LORD it will be provided."

[15]The angel of the LORD called to Abraham from heaven a second time [16]and said, "I swear by myself, declares the LORD, that because you have done this and have not withheld your son, your only son, [17]I will surely bless you and make your descendants as numerous as the stars in the sky and as the sand on the seashore. Your descendants will take possession of the cities of their enemies, [18]and through your offspring[b] all nations on earth will be blessed, because you have obeyed me."

[19]Then Abraham returned to his servants, and they set off together for Beersheba. And Abraham stayed in Beersheba.

Nahor's Sons

[20]Some time later Abraham was told, "Milcah is also a mother; she has borne sons to your brother Nahor: [21]Uz the firstborn, Buz his brother, Kemuel (the father of Aram), [22]Kesed, Hazo, Pildash, Jidlaph and Bethuel." [23]Bethuel became the father of Rebekah. Milcah bore these eight sons to Abraham's brother Nahor. [24]His concubine, whose name was Reumah, also had sons: Tebah, Gaham, Tahash and Maacah.

The Death of Sarah

23 Sarah lived to be a hundred and twenty-seven years old. [2]She died at Kiriath Arba (that is, Hebron) in the land of Canaan, and Abraham went to mourn for Sarah and to weep over her. [3]Then Abraham rose from beside his dead wife and spoke to the Hittites.[c] He said, [4]"I am an alien and a stranger among you. Sell me some property for a burial site here so I can bury my dead."

[5]The Hittites replied to Abraham, [6]"Sir, listen to us. You are a mighty prince among us. Bury your dead in the choicest of our tombs. None of us will refuse you his tomb for burying your dead."

[7]Then Abraham rose and bowed down before the people of the land, the Hittites. [8]He said to them, "If you are willing to let me bury my dead, then listen to me and intercede with Ephron son of Zohar on my behalf [9]so he will sell me the cave of Machpelah, which belongs to him and is at the end of his field. Ask him to sell it to me for the full price as a burial site among you."

[10]Ephron the Hittite was sitting among his people and he replied to Abraham in the hearing of all the Hittites who had come to the gate of his city. [11]"No, my lord," he said. "Listen to me; I give[d] you the field, and I give[d] you the cave that is in it. I give[d] it to you in the presence of my people. Bury your dead."

[12]Again Abraham bowed down before the people of the land [13]and he said to Ephron in their hearing, "Listen to me, if you will. I will pay the price of the field. Accept it from me so I can bury my dead there."

[14]Ephron answered Abraham, [15]"Listen to me, my lord; the land is worth four hundred shekels[e] of silver, but what is that between me and you? Bury your dead."

[16]Abraham agreed to Ephron's terms and weighed out for him the price he had named in the hearing of the Hittites: four hundred shekels of silver, according to the weight current among the merchants.

[17]So Ephron's field in Machpelah near Mamre—both the field and the cave in it, and all the trees within the borders of the field—was deeded [18]to Abraham as his property in the presence of all the Hittites who had come to the gate of the city.

---

[a]13 Many manuscripts of the Masoretic Text, Samaritan Pentateuch, Septuagint and Syriac; most manuscripts of the Masoretic Text *a ram behind* ⌐him⌐   [b]18 Or *seed*   [c]3 Or *the sons of Heth*; also in verses 5, 7, 10, 16, 18 and 20   [d]11 Or *sell*   [e]15 That is, about 10 pounds (about 4.5 kilograms)

¹⁹Afterward Abraham buried his wife Sarah in the cave in the field of Machpelah near Mamre (which is at Hebron) in the land of Canaan. ²⁰So the field and the cave in it were deeded to Abraham by the Hittites as a burial site.

Isaac and Rebekah

24 Abraham was now old and well advanced in years, and the LORD had blessed him in every way. ²He said to the chief[a] servant in his household, the one in charge of all that he had, "Put your hand under my thigh. ³I want you to swear by the LORD, the God of heaven and the God of earth, that you will not get a wife for my son from the daughters of the Canaanites, among whom I am living, ⁴but will go to my country and my own relatives and get a wife for my son Isaac."

⁵The servant asked him, "What if the woman is unwilling to come back with me to this land? Shall I then take your son back to the country you came from?"

⁶"Make sure that you do not take my son back there," Abraham said. ⁷"The LORD, the God of heaven, who brought me out of my father's household and my native land and who spoke to me and promised me on oath, saying, 'To your offspring[b] I will give this land'—he will send his angel before you so that you can get a wife for my son from there. ⁸If the woman is unwilling to come back with you, then you will be released from this oath of mine. Only do not take my son back there." ⁹So the servant put his hand under the thigh of his master Abraham and swore an oath to him concerning this matter.

¹⁰Then the servant took ten of his master's camels and left, taking with him all kinds of good things from his master. He set out for Aram Naharaim[c] and made his way to the town of Nahor. ¹¹He had the camels kneel down near the well outside the town; it was toward evening, the time the women go out to draw water.

¹²Then he prayed, "O LORD, God of my master Abraham, give me success today, and show kindness to my master Abraham. ¹³See, I am standing beside this spring, and the daughters of the townspeople are coming out to draw water. ¹⁴May it be that when I say to a girl, 'Please let down your jar that I may have a drink,' and she says, 'Drink, and I'll water your camels too'—let her be the one you have chosen for your servant Isaac. By this I will know that you have shown kindness to my master."

¹⁵Before he had finished praying, Rebekah came out with her jar on her shoulder. She was the daughter of Bethuel son of Milcah, who was the wife of Abraham's brother Nahor. ¹⁶The girl was very beautiful, a virgin; no man had ever lain with her. She went down to the spring, filled her jar and came up again.

¹⁷The servant hurried to meet her and said, "Please give me a little water from your jar."

¹⁸"Drink, my lord," she said, and quickly lowered the jar to her hands and gave him a drink.

¹⁹After she had given him a drink, she said, "I'll draw water for your camels too, until they have finished drinking." ²⁰So she quickly emptied her jar into the trough, ran back to the well to draw more water, and drew enough for all his camels. ²¹Without saying a word, the man watched her closely to learn whether or not the LORD had made his journey successful.

²²When the camels had finished drinking, the man took out a gold nose ring weighing a beka[d] and two gold bracelets weighing ten shekels.[e] ²³Then he asked, "Whose daughter are you? Please tell me, is there room in your father's house for us to spend the night?"

²⁴She answered him, "I am the daughter of Bethuel, the son that Milcah bore to Nahor." ²⁵And she added, "We have plenty of straw and fodder, as well as room for you to spend the night."

²⁶Then the man bowed down and worshiped the LORD, ²⁷saying, "Praise be to the LORD, the God of my master Abraham, who has not abandoned his kindness and faithfulness to my master. As for me, the LORD has led me on the journey to the house of my master's relatives."

²⁸The girl ran and told her mother's household about these things. ²⁹Now Rebekah had a brother named Laban, and

---

a2 Or *oldest*   *b7* Or *seed*   *c10* That is, Northwest Mesopotamia   *d22* That is, about 1/5 ounce (about 5.5 grams)   *e22* That is, about 4 ounces (about 110 grams) he hurried out to the man at the spring. [30]As soon as he had seen the nose ring, and the bracelets on his sister's arms, and had heard Rebekah tell what the man said to her, he went out to the man and found him standing by the camels near the spring. [31]"Come, you who are blessed by the LORD," he said. "Why are you standing out here? I have prepared the house and a place for the camels."

[32]So the man went to the house, and the camels were unloaded. Straw and fodder were brought for the camels, and water for him and his men to wash their feet. [33]Then food was set before him, but he said, "I will not eat until I have told you what I have to say."

"Then tell us," ˻Laban˼ said.

[34]So he said, "I am Abraham's servant. [35]The LORD has blessed my master abundantly, and he has become wealthy. He has given him sheep and cattle, silver and gold, menservants and maidservants, and camels and donkeys. [36]My master's wife Sarah has borne him a son in her[a] old age, and he has given him everything he owns. [37]And my master made me swear an oath, and said, 'You must not get a wife for my son from the daughters of the Canaanites, in whose land I live, [38]but go to my father's family and to my own clan, and get a wife for my son.'

[39]"Then I asked my master, 'What if the woman will not come back with me?'

[40]"He replied, 'The LORD, before whom I have walked, will send his angel with you and make your journey a success, so that you can get a wife for my son from my own clan and from my father's family. [41]Then, when you go to my clan, you will be released from my oath even if they refuse to give her to you—you will be released from my oath.'

[42]"When I came to the spring today, I said, 'O LORD, God of my master Abraham, if you will, please grant success to the journey on which I have come. [43]See, I am standing beside this spring; if a maiden comes out to draw water and I say to her, "Please let me drink a little water from your jar," [44]and if she says to me, "Drink, and I'll draw water for your camels too," let her be the one the LORD has chosen for my master's son.'

[45]"Before I finished praying in my heart, Rebekah came out, with her jar on her shoulder. She went down to the spring and drew water, and I said to her, 'Please give me a drink.'

[46]"She quickly lowered her jar from her shoulder and said, 'Drink, and I'll water your camels too.' So I drank, and she watered the camels also.

[47]"I asked her, 'Whose daughter are you?'

"She said, 'The daughter of Bethuel son of Nahor, whom Milcah bore to him.'

"Then I put the ring in her nose and the bracelets on her arms, [48]and I bowed down and worshiped the LORD. I praised the LORD, the God of my master Abraham, who had led me on the right road to get the granddaughter of my master's brother for his son. [49]Now if you will show kindness and faithfulness to my master, tell me; and if not, tell me, so I may know which way to turn."

[50]Laban and Bethuel answered, "This is from the LORD; we can say nothing to you one way or the other. [51]Here is Rebekah; take her and go, and let her become the wife of your master's son, as the LORD has directed."

[52]When Abraham's servant heard what they said, he bowed down to the ground before the LORD. [53]Then the servant brought out gold and silver jewelry and articles of clothing and gave them to Rebekah; he also gave costly gifts to her brother and to her mother. [54]Then he and the men who were with him ate and drank and spent the night there.

When they got up the next morning, he said, "Send me on my way to my master."

[55]But her brother and her mother replied, "Let the girl remain with us ten days or so; then you[b] may go."

[56]But he said to them, "Do not detain me, now that the LORD has granted success to my journey. Send me on my way so I may go to my master."

[57]Then they said, "Let's call the girl and ask her about it." [58]So they called Rebekah and asked her, "Will you go with this man?"

"I will go," she said.

[59]So they sent their sister Rebekah on

a36 Or *his*　　*b55* Or *she*

Isaac and Rebekah

GENESIS 25:19–34; 27:1–40
Sibling favoritism did untold damage to the storybook love affair of Isaac and Rebekah. In addition to the enormous wealth handed down to this couple from Abraham, God blessed them with the birth of twins. Esau was rough, physically strong and liked to hunt—his father's favorite. And Jacob was quiet and contemplative—his mother's favorite. When Esau, the outdoorsman, was about to receive his father's blessing and inheritance, Rebekah connived a scheme so that Jacob would receive his father's blessing instead. Her scheme worked and Isaac was fooled. But after the pattern of deception was established and recognized in the tents of Isaac, bitterness corroded every relationship in the family. Because of deception, Isaac and Rebekah's storybook marriage soured.

her way, along with her nurse and Abraham's servant and his men. ⁶⁰And they blessed Rebekah and said to her,

> "Our sister, may you increase
> to thousands upon thousands;
> may your offspring possess
> the gates of their enemies."

⁶¹Then Rebekah and her maids got ready and mounted their camels and went back with the man. So the servant took Rebekah and left.

⁶²Now Isaac had come from Beer Lahai Roi, for he was living in the Negev. ⁶³He went out to the field one evening to meditate,^a and as he looked up, he saw camels approaching. ⁶⁴Rebekah also looked up and saw Isaac. She got down from her camel ⁶⁵and asked the servant, "Who is that man in the field coming to meet us?"

"He is my master," the servant answered. So she took her veil and covered herself.

⁶⁶Then the servant told Isaac all he had done. ⁶⁷Isaac brought her into the tent of his mother Sarah, and he married Rebekah. So she became his wife, and he loved her; and Isaac was comforted after his mother's death.

The Death of Abraham

25 Abraham took^b another wife, whose name was Keturah. ²She bore him Zimran, Jokshan, Medan, Midian, Ishbak and Shuah. ³Jokshan was the father of Sheba and Dedan; the descendants of Dedan were the Asshurites, the Letushites and the Leummites. ⁴The sons of Midian were Ephah, Epher, Hanoch, Abida and Eldaah. All these were descendants of Keturah.

⁵Abraham left everything he owned to Isaac. ⁶But while he was still living, he gave gifts to the sons of his concubines and sent them away from his son Isaac to the land of the east.

⁷Altogether, Abraham lived a hundred and seventy-five years. ⁸Then Abraham breathed his last and died at a good old age, an old man and full of years; and he was gathered to his people. ⁹His sons Isaac and Ishmael buried him in the cave of Machpelah near Mamre, in the field of Ephron son of Zohar the Hittite, ¹⁰the field Abraham had bought from the Hittites.^c There Abraham was buried with his wife Sarah. ¹¹After Abraham's death, God blessed his son Isaac, who then lived near Beer Lahai Roi.

Ishmael's Sons

¹²This is the account of Abraham's son Ishmael, whom Sarah's maidservant, Hagar the Egyptian, bore to Abraham.

¹³These are the names of the sons of Ishmael, listed in the order of their birth: Nebaioth the firstborn of Ishmael, Kedar, Adbeel, Mibsam, ¹⁴Mishma, Dumah, Massa, ¹⁵Hadad, Tema, Jetur, Naphish and Kedemah. ¹⁶These were the sons of Ishmael, and these are the names of the twelve tribal rulers according to their settlements and camps. ¹⁷Altogether, Ishmael lived a hundred and thirty-seven years. He breathed his last and died, and he was gathered to his people. ¹⁸His descendants settled in the area from Havilah to Shur, near the border of Egypt, as you go toward Asshur. And they lived in hostility toward^d all their brothers.

---

^a63 The meaning of the Hebrew for this word is uncertain.   ^b1 Or *had taken*   ^c10 Or *the sons of Heth*   ^d18 Or *lived to the east of*

Jacob and Esau

[19]This is the account of Abraham's son Isaac.

Abraham became the father of Isaac, [20]and Isaac was forty years old when he married Rebekah daughter of Bethuel the Aramean from Paddan Aram[a] and sister of Laban the Aramean.

[21]Isaac prayed to the LORD on behalf of his wife, because she was barren. The LORD answered his prayer, and his wife Rebekah became pregnant. [22]The babies jostled each other within her, and she said, "Why is this happening to me?" So she went to inquire of the LORD.

[23]The LORD said to her,

"Two nations are in your womb,
    and two peoples from within you
        will be separated;
one people will be stronger than the
        other,
    and the older will serve the
        younger."

[24]When the time came for her to give birth, there were twin boys in her womb. [25]The first to come out was red, and his whole body was like a hairy garment; so they named him Esau.[b] [26]After this, his brother came out, with his hand grasping Esau's heel; so he was named Jacob.[c] Isaac was sixty years old when Rebekah gave birth to them.

[27]The boys grew up, and Esau became a skillful hunter, a man of the open country, while Jacob was a quiet man, staying among the tents. [28]Isaac, who had a taste for wild game, loved Esau, but Rebekah loved Jacob.

[29]Once when Jacob was cooking some stew, Esau came in from the open country, famished. [30]He said to Jacob, "Quick, let me have some of that red stew! I'm famished!" (That is why he was also called Edom.[d])

[31]Jacob replied, "First sell me your birthright."

[32]"Look, I am about to die," Esau said. "What good is the birthright to me?"

[33]But Jacob said, "Swear to me first." So he swore an oath to him, selling his birthright to Jacob.

[34]Then Jacob gave Esau some bread and some lentil stew. He ate and drank, and then got up and left.

So Esau despised his birthright.

Isaac and Abimelech

26 Now there was a famine in the land—besides the earlier famine of Abraham's time—and Isaac went to Abimelech king of the Philistines in Gerar. [2]The LORD appeared to Isaac and said, "Do not go down to Egypt; live in the land where I tell you to live. [3]Stay in this land for a while, and I will be with you and will bless you. For to you and your descendants I will give all these lands and will confirm the oath I swore to your father Abraham. [4]I will make your descendants as numerous as the stars in the sky and will give them all these lands, and through your offspring[e] all nations on earth will be blessed, [5]because Abraham obeyed me and kept my requirements, my commands, my decrees and my laws." [6]So Isaac stayed in Gerar.

[7]When the men of that place asked him about his wife, he said, "She is my sister," because he was afraid to say, "She is my wife." He thought, "The men of this place might kill me on account of Rebekah, because she is beautiful."

[8]When Isaac had been there a long time, Abimelech king of the Philistines looked down from a window and saw Isaac caressing his wife Rebekah. [9]So Abimelech summoned Isaac and said, "She is really your wife! Why did you say, 'She is my sister'?"

Isaac answered him, "Because I thought I might lose my life on account of her."

[10]Then Abimelech said, "What is this you have done to us? One of the men might well have slept with your wife, and you would have brought guilt upon us."

[11]So Abimelech gave orders to all the people: "Anyone who molests this man or his wife shall surely be put to death."

[12]Isaac planted crops in that land and the same year reaped a hundredfold, because the LORD blessed him. [13]The man became rich, and his wealth continued to grow until he became very wealthy. [14]He had so many flocks and herds and servants that the Philistines envied him. [15]So

---

[a]20 That is, Northwest Mesopotamia   [b]25 Esau may mean hairy; he was also called Edom, which means red.   [c]26 Jacob means he grasps the heel (figuratively, he deceives).   [d]30 Edom means red.   [e]4 Or seed

all the wells that his father's servants had dug in the time of his father Abraham, the Philistines stopped up, filling them with earth.

¹⁶Then Abimelech said to Isaac, "Move away from us; you have become too powerful for us."

¹⁷So Isaac moved away from there and encamped in the Valley of Gerar and settled there. ¹⁸Isaac reopened the wells that had been dug in the time of his father Abraham, which the Philistines had stopped up after Abraham died, and he gave them the same names his father had given them.

¹⁹Isaac's servants dug in the valley and discovered a well of fresh water there. ²⁰But the herdsmen of Gerar quarreled with Isaac's herdsmen and said, "The water is ours!" So he named the well Esek,ᵃ because they disputed with him. ²¹Then they dug another well, but they quarreled over that one also; so he named it Sitnah.ᵇ ²²He moved on from there and dug another well, and no one quarreled over it. He named it Rehoboth,ᶜ saying, "Now the LORD has given us room and we will flourish in the land."

²³From there he went up to Beersheba. ²⁴That night the LORD appeared to him and said, "I am the LORD, the God of your father Abraham. Do not be afraid, for I am with you; I will bless you and will increase the number of your descendants for the sake of my servant Abraham."

²⁵Isaac built an altar there and called on the name of the LORD. There he pitched his tent, and there his servants dug a well.

²⁶Meanwhile, Abimelech had come to him from Gerar, with Ahuzzath his personal adviser and Phicol the commander of his forces. ²⁷Isaac asked them, "Why have you come to me, since you were hostile to me and sent me away?"

²⁸They answered, "We saw clearly that the LORD was with you; so we said, 'There ought to be a sworn agreement between us'—between us and you. Let us make a treaty with you ²⁹that you will do us no harm, just as we did not molest you but always treated you well and sent you away in peace. And now you are blessed by the LORD."

³⁰Isaac then made a feast for them, and they ate and drank. ³¹Early the next morning the men swore an oath to each other. Then Isaac sent them on their way, and they left him in peace.

³²That day Isaac's servants came and told him about the well they had dug. They said, "We've found water!" ³³He called it Shibah,ᵈ and to this day the name of the town has been Beersheba.ᵉ

³⁴When Esau was forty years old, he married Judith daughter of Beeri the Hittite, and also Basemath daughter of Elon the Hittite. ³⁵They were a source of grief to Isaac and Rebekah.

Jacob Gets Isaac's Blessing

27 When Isaac was old and his eyes were so weak that he could no longer see, he called for Esau his older son and said to him, "My son."

"Here I am," he answered.

²Isaac said, "I am now an old man and don't know the day of my death. ³Now then, get your weapons—your quiver and bow—and go out to the open country to hunt some wild game for me. ⁴Prepare me the kind of tasty food I like and bring it to me to eat, so that I may give you my blessing before I die."

⁵Now Rebekah was listening as Isaac spoke to his son Esau. When Esau left for the open country to hunt game and bring it back, ⁶Rebekah said to her son Jacob, "Look, I overheard your father say to your brother Esau, ⁷'Bring me some game and prepare me some tasty food to eat, so that I may give you my blessing in the presence of the LORD before I die.' ⁸Now, my son, listen carefully and do what I tell you: ⁹Go out to the flock and bring me two choice young goats, so I can prepare some tasty food for your father, just the way he likes it. ¹⁰Then take it to your father to eat, so that he may give you his blessing before he dies."

¹¹Jacob said to Rebekah his mother, "But my brother Esau is a hairy man, and I'm a man with smooth skin. ¹²What if my father touches me? I would appear to be tricking him and would bring down a curse on myself rather than a blessing."

¹³His mother said to him, "My son, let

ᵃ20 *Esek* means *dispute.*   ᵇ21 *Sitnah* means *opposition.*   ᶜ22 *Rehoboth* means *room.*
ᵈ33 *Shibah* can mean *oath* or *seven.*
ᵉ33 *Beersheba* can mean *well of the oath* or *well of seven.*

the curse fall on me. Just do what I say; go and get them for me."

¹⁴So he went and got them and brought them to his mother, and she prepared some tasty food, just the way his father liked it. ¹⁵Then Rebekah took the best clothes of Esau her older son, which she had in the house, and put them on her younger son Jacob. ¹⁶She also covered his hands and the smooth part of his neck with the goatskins. ¹⁷Then she handed to her son Jacob the tasty food and the bread she had made.

¹⁸He went to his father and said, "My father."

"Yes, my son," he answered. "Who is it?"

¹⁹Jacob said to his father, "I am Esau your firstborn. I have done as you told me. Please sit up and eat some of my game so that you may give me your blessing."

²⁰Isaac asked his son, "How did you find it so quickly, my son?"

"The LORD your God gave me success," he replied.

²¹Then Isaac said to Jacob, "Come near so I can touch you, my son, to know whether you really are my son Esau or not."

²²Jacob went close to his father Isaac, who touched him and said, "The voice is the voice of Jacob, but the hands are the hands of Esau." ²³He did not recognize him, for his hands were hairy like those of his brother Esau; so he blessed him. ²⁴"Are you really my son Esau?" he asked.

"I am," he replied.

²⁵Then he said, "My son, bring me some of your game to eat, so that I may give you my blessing."

Jacob brought it to him and he ate; and he brought some wine and he drank. ²⁶Then his father Isaac said to him, "Come here, my son, and kiss me."

²⁷So he went to him and kissed him. When Isaac caught the smell of his clothes, he blessed him and said,

"Ah, the smell of my son
    is like the smell of a field
    that the LORD has blessed.
²⁸May God give you of heaven's dew
    and of earth's richness—

Mixed Blessing

GENESIS 27   "But Dad said I could!" How many times did I hear that line? Our children were experts at knowing which parent to approach with different requests. If it involved risk-taking—like rock climbing in the rain—they went to Dave. If it involved something like flexibility with curfew, schoolwork or social schedule, they would ask me. Face it, children are great at playing their parents against each other. Jacob and Esau were no exception.

Rebekah and Isaac were divided. Isaac loved Esau, and Rebekah loved Jacob (see Genesis 25:28). Rebekah was willing to risk deception to make sure that her favorite son received his father's blessing. What does this story say to twenty-first century marriages?

First, don't let your children sabotage your relationship. While you may naturally be drawn to the son or daughter who is more like you or shares your interests, work at achieving fair treatment in your roles as a parent.

Second, let your marriage model the kind of openness, other-centeredness and self-sacrificing love you desire in your children. Every single day, through your marriage relationship, you are mentoring your children and teaching them, by your actions, what a good relationship is all about.

—*Dave & Claudia*

Weekend Warm-up   *What message are you sending your children and loved ones through your marriage relationship?*   Go to page 37 for your next devotional reading.

an abundance of grain and new
wine.
²⁹May nations serve you
and peoples bow down to you.
Be lord over your brothers,
and may the sons of your mother
bow down to you.
May those who curse you be cursed
and those who bless you be
blessed."

³⁰After Isaac finished blessing him and Jacob had scarcely left his father's presence, his brother Esau came in from hunting. ³¹He too prepared some tasty food and brought it to his father. Then he said to him, "My father, sit up and eat some of my game, so that you may give me your blessing."

³²His father Isaac asked him, "Who are you?"

"I am your son," he answered, "your firstborn, Esau."

³³Isaac trembled violently and said, "Who was it, then, that hunted game and brought it to me? I ate it just before you came and I blessed him—and indeed he will be blessed!"

³⁴When Esau heard his father's words, he burst out with a loud and bitter cry and said to his father, "Bless me—me too, my father!"

³⁵But he said, "Your brother came deceitfully and took your blessing."

³⁶Esau said, "Isn't he rightly named Jacobᵃ? He has deceived me these two times: He took my birthright, and now he's taken my blessing!" Then he asked, "Haven't you reserved any blessing for me?"

³⁷Isaac answered Esau, "I have made him lord over you and have made all his relatives his servants, and I have sustained him with grain and new wine. So what can I possibly do for you, my son?"

³⁸Esau said to his father, "Do you have only one blessing, my father? Bless me too, my father!" Then Esau wept aloud.

³⁹His father Isaac answered him,

"Your dwelling will be
away from the earth's richness,
away from the dew of heaven
above.
⁴⁰You will live by the sword
and you will serve your brother.
But when you grow restless,

you will throw his yoke
from off your neck."

Jacob Flees to Laban

⁴¹Esau held a grudge against Jacob because of the blessing his father had given him. He said to himself, "The days of mourning for my father are near; then I will kill my brother Jacob."

⁴²When Rebekah was told what her older son Esau had said, she sent for her younger son Jacob and said to him, "Your brother Esau is consoling himself with the thought of killing you. ⁴³Now then, my son, do what I say: Flee at once to my brother Laban in Haran. ⁴⁴Stay with him for a while until your brother's fury subsides. ⁴⁵When your brother is no longer angry with you and forgets what you did to him, I'll send word for you to come back from there. Why should I lose both of you in one day?"

⁴⁶Then Rebekah said to Isaac, "I'm disgusted with living because of these Hittite women. If Jacob takes a wife from among the women of this land, from Hittite women like these, my life will not be worth living."

28 So Isaac called for Jacob and blessedᵇ him and commanded him: "Do not marry a Canaanite woman. ²Go at once to Paddan Aram,ᶜ to the house of your mother's father Bethuel. Take a wife for yourself there, from among the daughters of Laban, your mother's brother. ³May God Almightyᵈ bless you and make you fruitful and increase your numbers until you become a community of peoples. ⁴May he give you and your descendants the blessing given to Abraham, so that you may take possession of the land where you now live as an alien, the land God gave to Abraham." ⁵Then Isaac sent Jacob on his way, and he went to Paddan Aram, to Laban son of Bethuel the Aramean, the brother of Rebekah, who was the mother of Jacob and Esau.

⁶Now Esau learned that Isaac had blessed Jacob and had sent him to Paddan Aram to take a wife from there, and

ᵃ36 Jacob means he grasps the heel (figuratively, he deceives).   ᵇ1 Or greeted   ᶜ2 That is, Northwest Mesopotamia; also in verses 5, 6 and 7   ᵈ3 Hebrew El-Shaddai that when he blessed him he commanded him, "Do not marry a Canaanite woman," [7]and that Jacob had obeyed his father and mother and had gone to Paddan Aram. [8]Esau then realized how displeasing the Canaanite women were to his father Isaac; [9]so he went to Ishmael and married Mahalath, the sister of Nebaioth and daughter of Ishmael son of Abraham, in addition to the wives he already had.

Jacob's Dream at Bethel

[10]Jacob left Beersheba and set out for Haran. [11]When he reached a certain place, he stopped for the night because the sun had set. Taking one of the stones there, he put it under his head and lay down to sleep. [12]He had a dream in which he saw a stairway[a] resting on the earth, with its top reaching to heaven, and the angels of God were ascending and descending on it. [13]There above it[b] stood the LORD, and he said: "I am the LORD, the God of your father Abraham and the God of Isaac. I will give you and your descendants the land on which you are lying. [14]Your descendants will be like the dust of the earth, and you will spread out to the west and to the east, to the north and to the south. All peoples on earth will be blessed through you and your offspring. [15]I am with you and will watch over you wherever you go, and I will bring you back to this land. I will not leave you until I have done what I have promised you."

[16]When Jacob awoke from his sleep, he thought, "Surely the LORD is in this place, and I was not aware of it." [17]He was afraid and said, "How awesome is this place! This is none other than the house of God; this is the gate of heaven."

[18]Early the next morning Jacob took the stone he had placed under his head and set it up as a pillar and poured oil on top of it. [19]He called that place Bethel,[c] though the city used to be called Luz.

[20]Then Jacob made a vow, saying, "If God will be with me and will watch over me on this journey I am taking and will give me food to eat and clothes to wear [21]so that I return safely to my father's house, then the LORD[d] will be my God [22]and[e] this stone that I have set up as a pillar will be God's house, and of all that you give me I will give you a tenth."

Jacob Arrives in Paddan Aram

29 Then Jacob continued on his journey and came to the land of the eastern peoples. [2]There he saw a well in the field, with three flocks of sheep lying near it because the flocks were watered from that well. The stone over the mouth of the well was large. [3]When all the flocks were gathered there, the shepherds would roll the stone away from the well's mouth and water the sheep. Then they would return the stone to its place over the mouth of the well.

[4]Jacob asked the shepherds, "My brothers, where are you from?"

"We're from Haran," they replied.

[5]He said to them, "Do you know Laban, Nahor's grandson?"

"Yes, we know him," they answered.

[6]Then Jacob asked them, "Is he well?"

"Yes, he is," they said, "and here comes his daughter Rachel with the sheep."

[7]"Look," he said, "the sun is still high; it is not time for the flocks to be gathered. Water the sheep and take them back to pasture."

[8]"We can't," they replied, "until all the flocks are gathered and the stone has been rolled away from the mouth of the well. Then we will water the sheep."

[9]While he was still talking with them, Rachel came with her father's sheep, for she was a shepherdess. [10]When Jacob saw Rachel daughter of Laban, his mother's brother, and Laban's sheep, he went over and rolled the stone away from the mouth of the well and watered his uncle's sheep. [11]Then Jacob kissed Rachel and began to weep aloud. [12]He had told Rachel that he was a relative of her father and a son of Rebekah. So she ran and told her father.

[13]As soon as Laban heard the news about Jacob, his sister's son, he hurried to meet him. He embraced him and kissed him and brought him to his home, and there Jacob told him all these things. [14]Then Laban said to him, "You are my own flesh and blood."

---

[a]12 Or ladder   [b]13 Or There beside him
[c]19 Bethel means house of God.   [d]20,21 Or Since God . . . father's house, the LORD   [e]21,22 Or house, and the LORD will be my God, [22]then

Jacob Marries Leah and Rachel

After Jacob had stayed with him for a whole month, [15]Laban said to him, "Just because you are a relative of mine, should you work for me for nothing? Tell me what your wages should be."

[16]Now Laban had two daughters; the name of the older was Leah, and the name of the younger was Rachel. [17]Leah had weak[a] eyes, but Rachel was lovely in form, and beautiful. [18]Jacob was in love with Rachel and said, "I'll work for you seven years in return for your younger daughter Rachel."

[19]Laban said, "It's better that I give her to you than to some other man. Stay here with me." [20]So Jacob served seven years to get Rachel, but they seemed like only a few days to him because of his love for her.

[21]Then Jacob said to Laban, "Give me my wife. My time is completed, and I want to lie with her."

[22]So Laban brought together all the people of the place and gave a feast. [23]But when evening came, he took his daughter Leah and gave her to Jacob, and Jacob lay with her. [24]And Laban gave his servant girl Zilpah to his daughter as her maidservant.

[25]When morning came, there was Leah! So Jacob said to Laban, "What is this you have done to me? I served you for Rachel, didn't I? Why have you deceived me?"

[26]Laban replied, "It is not our custom here to give the younger daughter in marriage before the older one. [27]Finish this daughter's bridal week; then we will give you the younger one also, in return for another seven years of work."

[28]And Jacob did so. He finished the week with Leah, and then Laban gave him his daughter Rachel to be his wife. [29]Laban gave his servant girl Bilhah to his daughter Rachel as her maidservant. [30]Jacob lay with Rachel also, and he loved Rachel more than Leah. And he worked for Laban another seven years.

Jacob's Children

[31]When the LORD saw that Leah was not loved, he opened her womb, but Rachel was barren. [32]Leah became pregnant and gave birth to a son. She named him Reuben,[b] for she said, "It is because the LORD has seen my misery. Surely my husband will love me now."

[33]She conceived again, and when she gave birth to a son she said, "Because the LORD heard that I am not loved, he gave me this one too." So she named him Simeon.[c]

[34]Again she conceived, and when she gave birth to a son she said, "Now at last my husband will become attached to me, because I have borne him three sons." So he was named Levi.[d]

[35]She conceived again, and when she gave birth to a son she said, "This time I will praise the LORD." So she named him Judah.[e] Then she stopped having children.

30 When Rachel saw that she was not bearing Jacob any children, she became jealous of her sister. So she said to Jacob, "Give me children, or I'll die!"

[2]Jacob became angry with her and said, "Am I in the place of God, who has kept you from having children?"

[3]Then she said, "Here is Bilhah, my maidservant. Sleep with her so that she can bear children for me and that through her I too can build a family."

[4]So she gave him her servant Bilhah as a wife. Jacob slept with her, [5]and she became pregnant and bore him a son. [6]Then Rachel said, "God has vindicated me; he has listened to my plea and given me a son." Because of this she named him Dan.[f]

[7]Rachel's servant Bilhah conceived again and bore Jacob a second son. [8]Then Rachel said, "I have had a great struggle with my sister, and I have won." So she named him Naphtali.[g]

[9]When Leah saw that she had stopped having children, she took her maidservant Zilpah and gave her to Jacob as a wife. [10]Leah's servant Zilpah bore Jacob a son. [11]Then Leah said, "What good fortune!"[h] So she named him Gad.[i]

---

[a]17 Or delicate   [b]32 Reuben sounds like the Hebrew for he has seen my misery; the name means see, a son.   [c]33 Simeon probably means one who hears.   [d]34 Levi sounds like and may be derived from the Hebrew for attached.   [e]35 Judah sounds like and may be derived from the Hebrew for praise.   [f]6 Dan here means he has vindicated.   [g]8 Naphtali means my struggle.   [h]11 Or "A troop is coming!"   [i]11 Gad can mean good fortune or a troop.

¹²Leah's servant Zilpah bore Jacob a second son. ¹³Then Leah said, "How happy I am! The women will call me happy." So she named him Asher.ᵃ

¹⁴During wheat harvest, Reuben went out into the fields and found some mandrake plants, which he brought to his mother Leah. Rachel said to Leah, "Please give me some of your son's mandrakes."

¹⁵But she said to her, "Wasn't it enough that you took away my husband? Will you take my son's mandrakes too?"

"Very well," Rachel said, "he can sleep with you tonight in return for your son's mandrakes."

¹⁶So when Jacob came in from the fields that evening, Leah went out to meet him. "You must sleep with me," she said. "I have hired you with my son's mandrakes." So he slept with her that night.

¹⁷God listened to Leah, and she became pregnant and bore Jacob a fifth son. ¹⁸Then Leah said, "God has rewarded me for giving my maidservant to my husband." So she named him Issachar.ᵇ

¹⁹Leah conceived again and bore Jacob a sixth son. ²⁰Then Leah said, "God has presented me with a precious gift. This time my husband will treat me with honor, because I have borne him six sons." So she named him Zebulun.ᶜ

²¹Some time later she gave birth to a daughter and named her Dinah.

²²Then God remembered Rachel; he listened to her and opened her womb. ²³She became pregnant and gave birth to a son and said, "God has taken away my disgrace." ²⁴She named him Joseph,ᵈ and said, "May the LORD add to me another son."

Jacob's Flocks Increase

²⁵After Rachel gave birth to Joseph, Jacob said to Laban, "Send me on my way so I can go back to my own homeland. ²⁶Give me my wives and children, for whom I have served you, and I will be on my way. You know how much work I've done for you."

²⁷But Laban said to him, "If I have found favor in your eyes, please stay. I have learned by divination thatᵉ the LORD has blessed me because of you." ²⁸He added, "Name your wages, and I will pay them."

Jacob, Leah and Rachel

GENESIS 29:1—30:24 If you want to know why it is unwise to have more than one husband or wife, consider the example of Jacob, Leah and Rachel. Ironically, Jacob, who tricked his brother out of his birthright, was himself tricked by Laban, the father of Leah and Rachel. After working seven years for Rachel, he discovered the morning after his wedding that he had married Leah, not Rachel! After working seven more years, Jacob was then given Rachel. Imagine working fourteen years just for the right to marry the one you love! But then think about being married to two spouses at the same time. Jealousy was definitely a barrier to marital satisfaction. Leah, knowing that Jacob loved Rachel, tried to win him through bearing children. Rachel, jealous of her sister, gave her servant to Jacob. This made their marriage more dysfunctional. Later, God remembered Rachel and she conceived a son. Imagine the problems this blended family faced.

While laws today forbid having more than one spouse, we can still learn lessons from this marriage. Perhaps you're in a second marriage and you are jealous of the first spouse, or maybe you feel like your spouse is married to his or her job, or the children are more loved than you are. While we don't condone being married to two wives, we do respect Jacob for his commitment to work so hard for the one he loved.

²⁹Jacob said to him, "You know how I have worked for you and how your livestock has fared under my care. ³⁰The little you had before I came has increased greatly, and the LORD has blessed you wherever I have been. But now, when may I do something for my own household?"

³¹"What shall I give you?" he asked.

"Don't give me anything," Jacob replied. "But if you will do this one thing

---

ᵃ13 *Asher* means *happy.*   ᵇ18 *Issachar* sounds like the Hebrew for *reward.*   ᶜ20 *Zebulun* probably means *honor.*   ᵈ24 *Joseph* means *may he add.*   ᵉ27 Or possibly *have become rich and* for me, I will go on tending your flocks and watching over them: ³²Let me go through all your flocks today and remove from them every speckled or spotted sheep, every dark-colored lamb and every spotted or speckled goat. They will be my wages. ³³And my honesty will testify for me in the future, whenever you check on the wages you have paid me. Any goat in my possession that is not speckled or spotted, or any lamb that is not dark-colored, will be considered stolen."

³⁴"Agreed," said Laban. "Let it be as you have said." ³⁵That same day he removed all the male goats that were streaked or spotted, and all the speckled or spotted female goats (all that had white on them) and all the dark-colored lambs, and he placed them in the care of his sons. ³⁶Then he put a three-day journey between himself and Jacob, while Jacob continued to tend the rest of Laban's flocks.

³⁷Jacob, however, took fresh-cut branches from poplar, almond and plane trees and made white stripes on them by peeling the bark and exposing the white inner wood of the branches. ³⁸Then he placed the peeled branches in all the watering troughs, so that they would be directly in front of the flocks when they came to drink. When the flocks were in heat and came to drink, ³⁹they mated in front of the branches. And they bore young that were streaked or speckled or spotted. ⁴⁰Jacob set apart the young of the flock by themselves, but made the rest face the streaked and dark-colored animals that belonged to Laban. Thus he made separate flocks for himself and did not put them with Laban's animals. ⁴¹Whenever the stronger females were in heat, Jacob would place the branches in the troughs in front of the animals so they would mate near the branches, ⁴²but if the animals were weak, he would not place them there. So the weak animals went to Laban and the strong ones to Jacob. ⁴³In this way the man grew exceedingly prosperous and came to own large flocks, and maidservants and menservants, and camels and donkeys.

Jacob Flees From Laban

31 Jacob heard that Laban's sons were saying, "Jacob has taken everything our father owned and has gained all this wealth from what belonged to our father." ²And Jacob noticed that Laban's attitude toward him was not what it had been.

³Then the LORD said to Jacob, "Go back to the land of your fathers and to your relatives, and I will be with you."

⁴So Jacob sent word to Rachel and Leah to come out to the fields where his flocks were. ⁵He said to them, "I see that your father's attitude toward me is not what it was before, but the God of my father has been with me. ⁶You know that I've worked for your father with all my strength, ⁷yet your father has cheated me by changing my wages ten times. However, God has not allowed him to harm me. ⁸If he said, 'The speckled ones will be your wages,' then all the flocks gave birth to speckled young; and if he said, 'The streaked ones will be your wages,' then all the flocks bore streaked young. ⁹So God has taken away your father's livestock and has given them to me.

¹⁰"In breeding season I once had a dream in which I looked up and saw that the male goats mating with the flock were streaked, speckled or spotted. ¹¹The angel of God said to me in the dream, 'Jacob.' I answered, 'Here I am.' ¹²And he said, 'Look up and see that all the male goats mating with the flock are streaked, speckled or spotted, for I have seen all that Laban has been doing to you. ¹³I am the God of Bethel, where you anointed a pillar and where you made a vow to me. Now leave this land at once and go back to your native land.' "

¹⁴Then Rachel and Leah replied, "Do we still have any share in the inheritance of our father's estate? ¹⁵Does he not regard us as foreigners? Not only has he sold us, but he has used up what was paid for us. ¹⁶Surely all the wealth that God took away from our father belongs to us and our children. So do whatever God has told you."

¹⁷Then Jacob put his children and his wives on camels, ¹⁸and he drove all his livestock ahead of him, along with all the goods he had accumulated in Paddan Aram,ᵃ to go to his father Isaac in the land of Canaan.

¹⁹When Laban had gone to shear his

ᵃ18 That is, Northwest Mesopotamia

sheep, Rachel stole her father's household gods. ²⁰Moreover, Jacob deceived Laban the Aramean by not telling him he was running away. ²¹So he fled with all he had, and crossing the River,ᵃ he headed for the hill country of Gilead.

Laban Pursues Jacob

²²On the third day Laban was told that Jacob had fled. ²³Taking his relatives with him, he pursued Jacob for seven days and caught up with him in the hill country of Gilead. ²⁴Then God came to Laban the Aramean in a dream at night and said to him, "Be careful not to say anything to Jacob, either good or bad."

²⁵Jacob had pitched his tent in the hill country of Gilead when Laban overtook him, and Laban and his relatives camped there too. ²⁶Then Laban said to Jacob, "What have you done? You've deceived me, and you've carried off my daughters like captives in war. ²⁷Why did you run off secretly and deceive me? Why didn't you tell me, so I could send you away with joy and singing to the music of tambourines and harps? ²⁸You didn't even let me kiss my grandchildren and my daughters good-by. You have done a foolish thing. ²⁹I have the power to harm you; but last night the God of your father said to me, 'Be careful not to say anything to Jacob, either good or bad.' ³⁰Now you have gone off because you longed to return to your father's house. But why did you steal my gods?"

³¹Jacob answered Laban, "I was afraid, because I thought you would take your daughters away from me by force. ³²But if you find anyone who has your gods, he shall not live. In the presence of our relatives, see for yourself whether there is anything of yours here with me; and if so, take it." Now Jacob did not know that Rachel had stolen the gods.

³³So Laban went into Jacob's tent and into Leah's tent and into the tent of the two maidservants, but he found nothing. After he came out of Leah's tent, he entered Rachel's tent. ³⁴Now Rachel had taken the household gods and put them inside her camel's saddle and was sitting on them. Laban searched through everything in the tent but found nothing.

³⁵Rachel said to her father, "Don't be angry, my lord, that I cannot stand up in your presence; I'm having my period." So he searched but could not find the household gods.

³⁶Jacob was angry and took Laban to task. "What is my crime?" he asked Laban. "What sin have I committed that you hunt me down? ³⁷Now that you have searched through all my goods, what have you found that belongs to your household? Put it here in front of your relatives and mine, and let them judge between the two of us.

³⁸"I have been with you for twenty years now. Your sheep and goats have not miscarried, nor have I eaten rams from your flocks. ³⁹I did not bring you animals torn by wild beasts; I bore the loss myself. And you demanded payment from me for whatever was stolen by day or night. ⁴⁰This was my situation: The heat consumed me in the daytime and the cold at night, and sleep fled from my eyes. ⁴¹It was like this for the twenty years I was in your household. I worked for you fourteen years for your two daughters and six years for your flocks, and you changed my wages ten times. ⁴²If the God of my father, the God of Abraham and the Fear of Isaac, had not been with me, you would surely have sent me away empty-handed. But God has seen my hardship and the toil of my hands, and last night he rebuked you."

⁴³Laban answered Jacob, "The women are my daughters, the children are my children, and the flocks are my flocks. All you see is mine. Yet what can I do today about these daughters of mine, or about the children they have borne? ⁴⁴Come now, let's make a covenant, you and I, and let it serve as a witness between us."

⁴⁵So Jacob took a stone and set it up as a pillar. ⁴⁶He said to his relatives, "Gather some stones." So they took stones and piled them in a heap, and they ate there by the heap. ⁴⁷Laban called it Jegar Sahadutha,ᵇ and Jacob called it Galeed.ᶜ

⁴⁸Laban said, "This heap is a witness between you and me today." That is why it was called Galeed. ⁴⁹It was also called Mizpah,ᵈ because he said, "May the LORD keep watch between you and me

---

ᵃ21 That is, the Euphrates   ᵇ47 The Aramaic *Jegar Sahadutha* means *witness heap.*
ᶜ47 The Hebrew *Galeed* means *witness heap.*
ᵈ49 *Mizpah* means *watchtower.*

when we are away from each other. ⁵⁰If you mistreat my daughters or if you take any wives besides my daughters, even though no one is with us, remember that God is a witness between you and me."

⁵¹Laban also said to Jacob, "Here is this heap, and here is this pillar I have set up between you and me. ⁵²This heap is a witness, and this pillar is a witness, that I will not go past this heap to your side to harm you and that you will not go past this heap and pillar to my side to harm me. ⁵³May the God of Abraham and the God of Nahor, the God of their father, judge between us."

So Jacob took an oath in the name of the Fear of his father Isaac. ⁵⁴He offered a sacrifice there in the hill country and invited his relatives to a meal. After they had eaten, they spent the night there.

⁵⁵Early the next morning Laban kissed his grandchildren and his daughters and blessed them. Then he left and returned home.

Jacob Prepares to Meet Esau

32 Jacob also went on his way, and the angels of God met him. ²When Jacob saw them, he said, "This is the camp of God!" So he named that place Mahanaim.ᵃ

³Jacob sent messengers ahead of him to his brother Esau in the land of Seir, the country of Edom. ⁴He instructed them: "This is what you are to say to my master Esau: 'Your servant Jacob says, I have been staying with Laban and have remained there till now. ⁵I have cattle and donkeys, sheep and goats, menservants and maidservants. Now I am sending this message to my lord, that I may find favor in your eyes.' "

⁶When the messengers returned to Jacob, they said, "We went to your brother Esau, and now he is coming to meet you, and four hundred men are with him."

⁷In great fear and distress Jacob divided the people who were with him into two groups,ᵇ and the flocks and herds and camels as well. ⁸He thought, "If Esau comes and attacks one group,ᶜ the groupᶜ that is left may escape."

⁹Then Jacob prayed, "O God of my father Abraham, God of my father Isaac,

O LORD, who said to me, 'Go back to your country and your relatives, and I will make you prosper,' ¹⁰I am unworthy of all the kindness and faithfulness you have shown your servant. I had only my staff when I crossed this Jordan, but now I have become two groups. ¹¹Save me, I pray, from the hand of my brother Esau, for I am afraid he will come and attack me, and also the mothers with their children. ¹²But you have said, 'I will surely make you prosper and will make your descendants like the sand of the sea, which cannot be counted.' "

¹³He spent the night there, and from what he had with him he selected a gift for his brother Esau: ¹⁴two hundred female goats and twenty male goats, two hundred ewes and twenty rams, ¹⁵thirty female camels with their young, forty cows and ten bulls, and twenty female donkeys and ten male donkeys. ¹⁶He put them in the care of his servants, each herd by itself, and said to his servants, "Go ahead of me, and keep some space between the herds."

¹⁷He instructed the one in the lead: "When my brother Esau meets you and asks, 'To whom do you belong, and where are you going, and who owns all these animals in front of you?' ¹⁸then you are to say, 'They belong to your servant Jacob. They are a gift sent to my lord Esau, and he is coming behind us.' "

¹⁹He also instructed the second, the third and all the others who followed the herds: "You are to say the same thing to Esau when you meet him. ²⁰And be sure to say, 'Your servant Jacob is coming behind us.' " For he thought, "I will pacify him with these gifts I am sending on ahead; later, when I see him, perhaps he will receive me." ²¹So Jacob's gifts went on ahead of him, but he himself spent the night in the camp.

Jacob Wrestles With God

²²That night Jacob got up and took his two wives, his two maidservants and his eleven sons and crossed the ford of the Jabbok. ²³After he had sent them across the stream, he sent over all his posses-

---

ᵃ2 *Mahanaim* means *two camps.*   ᵇ7 Or *camps;* also in verse 10   ᶜ8 Or *camp* sions. ²⁴So Jacob was left alone, and a man wrestled with him till daybreak. ²⁵When the man saw that he could not overpower him, he touched the socket of Jacob's hip so that his hip was wrenched as he wrestled with the man. ²⁶Then the man said, "Let me go, for it is daybreak."

But Jacob replied, "I will not let you go unless you bless me."

²⁷The man asked him, "What is your name?"

"Jacob," he answered.

²⁸Then the man said, "Your name will no longer be Jacob, but Israel,ᵃ because you have struggled with God and with men and have overcome."

²⁹Jacob said, "Please tell me your name."

But he replied, "Why do you ask my name?" Then he blessed him there.

³⁰So Jacob called the place Peniel,ᵇ saying, "It is because I saw God face to face, and yet my life was spared."

³¹The sun rose above him as he passed Peniel,ᶜ and he was limping because of his hip. ³²Therefore to this day the Israelites do not eat the tendon attached to the socket of the hip, because the socket of Jacob's hip was touched near the tendon.

Jacob Meets Esau

33 Jacob looked up and there was Esau, coming with his four hundred men; so he divided the children among Leah, Rachel and the two maidservants. ²He put the maidservants and their children in front, Leah and her children next, and Rachel and Joseph in the rear. ³He himself went on ahead and bowed down to the ground seven times as he approached his brother.

⁴But Esau ran to meet Jacob and embraced him; he threw his arms around his neck and kissed him. And they wept. ⁵Then Esau looked up and saw the women and children. "Who are these with you?" he asked.

Jacob answered, "They are the children God has graciously given your servant."

⁶Then the maidservants and their children approached and bowed down. ⁷Next, Leah and her children came and bowed down. Last of all came Joseph and Rachel, and they too bowed down.

⁸Esau asked, "What do you mean by all these droves I met?"

ᵃ28 *Israel* means *he struggles with God.*
ᵇ30 *Peniel* means *face of God.*   ᶜ31 Hebrew *Penuel*, a variant of *Peniel*

Letting Go of a Grudge

Monday

GENESIS 33:1-4 Back in the 1870s a manufacturer of typewriters received complaints about the typewriter keys sticking together if the user went too fast. Engineers for the company decided that the best way to keep the keys from jamming was to slow the operator down. So they developed a less efficient keyboard with letters like "O" and "I" (two of the most frequently used letters in the alphabet) positioned for the relatively weaker ring and pinky fingers. Depressing these keys simply took more time. The problem was solved—no more jammed keys.

Since the time of that solution, however, typing technology and word processing have advanced significantly. Today's electric typewriters and word processors can go much faster than any human can type. The

problem is that we don't want to change the keyboard—even though it would help us type faster. The same reluctance to change—even to make life easier—applies to our relationships. Let's face it. We can hold onto a grudge for so long that we forget what it was about. Our marriage falls into the proverbial rut, and we simply ride it out—unless we change.

As you read about the reconciliation between Jacob and Esau, think about your capacity to let go of a grudge and make a change for the better. What do you think accounted for their change of heart, and what can their example teach you about change in your own marriage?

—*Les & Leslie*

Go to page 44 for your next devotional reading.

"To find favor in your eyes, my lord," he said.

9But Esau said, "I already have plenty, my brother. Keep what you have for yourself."

10"No, please!" said Jacob. "If I have found favor in your eyes, accept this gift from me. For to see your face is like seeing the face of God, now that you have received me favorably. 11Please accept the present that was brought to you, for God has been gracious to me and I have all I need." And because Jacob insisted, Esau accepted it.

12Then Esau said, "Let us be on our way; I'll accompany you."

13But Jacob said to him, "My lord knows that the children are tender and that I must care for the ewes and cows that are nursing their young. If they are driven hard just one day, all the animals will die. 14So let my lord go on ahead of his servant, while I move along slowly at the pace of the droves before me and that of the children, until I come to my lord in Seir."

15Esau said, "Then let me leave some of my men with you."

"But why do that?" Jacob asked. "Just let me find favor in the eyes of my lord."

16So that day Esau started on his way back to Seir. 17Jacob, however, went to Succoth, where he built a place for himself and made shelters for his livestock. That is why the place is called Succoth.a

18After Jacob came from Paddan Aram,b he arrived safely at thec city of Shechem in Canaan and camped within sight of the city. 19For a hundred pieces of silver,d he bought from the sons of Hamor, the father of Shechem, the plot of ground where he pitched his tent. 20There he set up an altar and called it El Elohe Israel.e

Dinah and the Shechemites

34 Now Dinah, the daughter Leah had borne to Jacob, went out to visit the women of the land. 2When Shechem son of Hamor the Hivite, the ruler of that area, saw her, he took her and violated her. 3His heart was drawn to Dinah daughter of Jacob, and he loved the girl and spoke tenderly to her. 4And Shechem

said to his father Hamor, "Get me this girl as my wife."

5When Jacob heard that his daughter Dinah had been defiled, his sons were in the fields with his livestock; so he kept quiet about it until they came home.

6Then Shechem's father Hamor went out to talk with Jacob. 7Now Jacob's sons had come in from the fields as soon as they heard what had happened. They were filled with grief and fury, because Shechem had done a disgraceful thing inf Israel by lying with Jacob's daughter—a thing that should not be done.

8But Hamor said to them, "My son Shechem has his heart set on your daughter. Please give her to him as his wife. 9Intermarry with us; give us your daughters and take our daughters for yourselves. 10You can settle among us; the land is open to you. Live in it, tradeg in it, and acquire property in it."

11Then Shechem said to Dinah's father and brothers, "Let me find favor in your eyes, and I will give you whatever you ask. 12Make the price for the bride and the gift I am to bring as great as you like, and I'll pay whatever you ask me. Only give me the girl as my wife."

13Because their sister Dinah had been defiled, Jacob's sons replied deceitfully as they spoke to Shechem and his father Hamor. 14They said to them, "We can't do such a thing; we can't give our sister to a man who is not circumcised. That would be a disgrace to us. 15We will give our consent to you on one condition only: that you become like us by circumcising all your males. 16Then we will give you our daughters and take your daughters for ourselves. We'll settle among you and become one people with you. 17But if you will not agree to be circumcised, we'll take our sisterh and go."

18Their proposal seemed good to Hamor and his son Shechem. 19The young man, who was the most honored of all his father's household, lost no time in doing what they said, because he was delighted

---

a17 Succoth means shelters.   b18 That is, Northwest Mesopotamia   c18 Or arrived at Shalem, a   d19 Hebrew hundred kesitahs; a kesitah was a unit of money of unknown weight and value.   e20 El Elohe Israel can mean God, the God of Israel or mighty is the God of Israel. f7 Or against   g10 Or move about freely; also in verse 21   h17 Hebrew daughter with Jacob's daughter. ²⁰So Hamor and his son Shechem went to the gate of their city to speak to their fellow townsmen. ²¹"These men are friendly toward us," they said. "Let them live in our land and trade in it; the land has plenty of room for them. We can marry their daughters and they can marry ours. ²²But the men will consent to live with us as one people only on the condition that our males be circumcised, as they themselves are. ²³Won't their livestock, their property and all their other animals become ours? So let us give our consent to them, and they will settle among us."

²⁴All the men who went out of the city gate agreed with Hamor and his son Shechem, and every male in the city was circumcised.

²⁵Three days later, while all of them were still in pain, two of Jacob's sons, Simeon and Levi, Dinah's brothers, took their swords and attacked the unsuspecting city, killing every male. ²⁶They put Hamor and his son Shechem to the sword and took Dinah from Shechem's house and left. ²⁷The sons of Jacob came upon the dead bodies and looted the city where[a] their sister had been defiled. ²⁸They seized their flocks and herds and donkeys and everything else of theirs in the city and out in the fields. ²⁹They carried off all their wealth and all their women and children, taking as plunder everything in the houses.

³⁰Then Jacob said to Simeon and Levi, "You have brought trouble on me by making me a stench to the Canaanites and Perizzites, the people living in this land. We are few in number, and if they join forces against me and attack me, I and my household will be destroyed."

³¹But they replied, "Should he have treated our sister like a prostitute?"

Jacob Returns to Bethel

35 Then God said to Jacob, "Go up to Bethel and settle there, and build an altar there to God, who appeared to you when you were fleeing from your brother Esau."

²So Jacob said to his household and to all who were with him, "Get rid of the foreign gods you have with you, and purify yourselves and change your clothes.

³Then come, let us go up to Bethel, where I will build an altar to God, who answered me in the day of my distress and who has been with me wherever I have gone." ⁴So they gave Jacob all the foreign gods they had and the rings in their ears, and Jacob buried them under the oak at Shechem. ⁵Then they set out, and the terror of God fell upon the towns all around them so that no one pursued them.

⁶Jacob and all the people with him came to Luz (that is, Bethel) in the land of Canaan. ⁷There he built an altar, and he called the place El Bethel,[b] because it was there that God revealed himself to him when he was fleeing from his brother.

⁸Now Deborah, Rebekah's nurse, died and was buried under the oak below Bethel. So it was named Allon Bacuth.[c]

⁹After Jacob returned from Paddan Aram,[d] God appeared to him again and blessed him. ¹⁰God said to him, "Your name is Jacob,[e] but you will no longer be called Jacob; your name will be Israel.[f]" So he named him Israel.

¹¹And God said to him, "I am God Almighty[g]; be fruitful and increase in number. A nation and a community of nations will come from you, and kings will come from your body. ¹²The land I gave to Abraham and Isaac I also give to you, and I will give this land to your descendants after you." ¹³Then God went up from him at the place where he had talked with him.

¹⁴Jacob set up a stone pillar at the place where God had talked with him, and he poured out a drink offering on it; he also poured oil on it. ¹⁵Jacob called the place where God had talked with him Bethel.[h]

The Deaths of Rachel and Isaac

¹⁶Then they moved on from Bethel. While they were still some distance from Ephrath, Rachel began to give birth and had great difficulty. ¹⁷And as she was having great difficulty in childbirth, the midwife said to her, "Don't be afraid, for you

---

[a]27 Or *because*   [b]7 *El Bethel* means *God of Bethel*.   [c]8 *Allon Bacuth* means *oak of weeping*.   [d]9 That is, Northwest Mesopotamia; also in verse 26   [e]10 *Jacob* means *he grasps the heel* (figuratively, *he deceives*).   [f]10 *Israel* means *he struggles with God*.   [g]11 Hebrew *El-Shaddai*   [h]15 *Bethel* means *house of God*.

have another son." 18As she breathed her last—for she was dying—she named her son Ben-Oni.*a* But his father named him Benjamin.*b*

19So Rachel died and was buried on the way to Ephrath (that is, Bethlehem). 20Over her tomb Jacob set up a pillar, and to this day that pillar marks Rachel's tomb.

21Israel moved on again and pitched his tent beyond Migdal Eder. 22While Israel was living in that region, Reuben went in and slept with his father's concubine Bilhah, and Israel heard of it.

Jacob had twelve sons:
23The sons of Leah:
  Reuben the firstborn of Jacob,
  Simeon, Levi, Judah, Issachar
  and Zebulun.
24The sons of Rachel:
  Joseph and Benjamin.
25The sons of Rachel's maidservant
  Bilhah:
  Dan and Naphtali.
26The sons of Leah's maidservant Zilpah:
  Gad and Asher.
These were the sons of Jacob, who were born to him in Paddan Aram.

27Jacob came home to his father Isaac in Mamre, near Kiriath Arba (that is, Hebron), where Abraham and Isaac had stayed. 28Isaac lived a hundred and eighty years. 29Then he breathed his last and died and was gathered to his people, old and full of years. And his sons Esau and Jacob buried him.

Esau's Descendants

36 This is the account of Esau (that is, Edom).

2Esau took his wives from the women of Canaan: Adah daughter of Elon the Hittite, and Oholibamah daughter of Anah and granddaughter of Zibeon the Hivite— 3also Basemath daughter of Ishmael and sister of Nebaioth.

4Adah bore Eliphaz to Esau, Basemath bore Reuel, 5and Oholibamah bore Jeush, Jalam and Korah. These were the sons of Esau, who were born to him in Canaan.

6Esau took his wives and sons and daughters and all the members of his household, as well as his livestock and all his other animals and all the goods he had acquired in Canaan, and moved to a land some distance from his brother Jacob. 7Their possessions were too great for them to remain together; the land where they were staying could not support them both because of their livestock. 8So Esau (that is, Edom) settled in the hill country of Seir.

9This is the account of Esau the father of the Edomites in the hill country of Seir.

10These are the names of Esau's sons:
  Eliphaz, the son of Esau's wife
  Adah, and Reuel, the son of
  Esau's wife Basemath.
11The sons of Eliphaz:
  Teman, Omar, Zepho, Gatam
  and Kenaz.
12Esau's son Eliphaz also had a
  concubine named Timna, who
  bore him Amalek. These were
  grandsons of Esau's wife Adah.
13The sons of Reuel:
  Nahath, Zerah, Shammah and
  Mizzah. These were grandsons
  of Esau's wife Basemath.
14The sons of Esau's wife Oholibamah daughter of Anah and granddaughter of Zibeon, whom she
  bore to Esau:
  Jeush, Jalam and Korah.

15These were the chiefs among Esau's descendants:
  The sons of Eliphaz the firstborn of
  Esau:
  Chiefs Teman, Omar, Zepho,
  Kenaz, 16Korah,*c* Gatam and
  Amalek. These were the chiefs
  descended from Eliphaz in
  Edom; they were grandsons of
  Adah.
17The sons of Esau's son Reuel:
  Chiefs Nahath, Zerah, Shammah
  and Mizzah. These were the
  chiefs descended from Reuel in

---

a18 Ben-Oni means *son of my trouble.*
b18 Benjamin means *son of my right hand.*
c16 Masoretic Text; Samaritan Pentateuch (see also Gen. 36:11 and 1 Chron. 1:36) does not have *Korah.*

Edom; they were grandsons of Esau's wife Basemath.

[18]The sons of Esau's wife Oholibamah:

Chiefs Jeush, Jalam and Korah.

These were the chiefs descended from Esau's wife Oholibamah daughter of Anah.

[19]These were the sons of Esau (that is, Edom), and these were their chiefs.

[20]These were the sons of Seir the Horite, who were living in the region:

Lotan, Shobal, Zibeon, Anah, [21]Dishon, Ezer and Dishan.

These sons of Seir in Edom were Horite chiefs.

[22]The sons of Lotan:

Hori and Homam.[a] Timna was Lotan's sister.

[23]The sons of Shobal:

Alvan, Manahath, Ebal, Shepho and Onam.

[24]The sons of Zibeon:

Aiah and Anah. This is the Anah who discovered the hot springs[b] in the desert while he was grazing the donkeys of his father Zibeon.

[25]The children of Anah:

Dishon and Oholibamah daughter of Anah.

[26]The sons of Dishon[c]:

Hemdan, Eshban, Ithran and Keran.

[27]The sons of Ezer:

Bilhan, Zaavan and Akan.

[28]The sons of Dishan:

Uz and Aran.

[29]These were the Horite chiefs:

Lotan, Shobal, Zibeon, Anah, [30]Dishon, Ezer and Dishan.

These were the Horite chiefs, according to their divisions, in the land of Seir.

The Rulers of Edom

[31]These were the kings who reigned in Edom before any Israelite king reigned[d]:

[32]Bela son of Beor became king of Edom. His city was named Dinhabah.

[33]When Bela died, Jobab son of Zerah from Bozrah succeeded him as king.

[34]When Jobab died, Husham from the land of the Temanites succeeded him as king.

[35]When Husham died, Hadad son of Bedad, who defeated Midian in the country of Moab, succeeded him as king. His city was named Avith.

[36]When Hadad died, Samlah from Masrekah succeeded him as king.

[37]When Samlah died, Shaul from Rehoboth on the river[e] succeeded him as king.

[38]When Shaul died, Baal-Hanan son of Acbor succeeded him as king.

[39]When Baal-Hanan son of Acbor died, Hadad[f] succeeded him as king. His city was named Pau, and his wife's name was Mehetabel daughter of Matred, the daughter of Me-Zahab.

[40]These were the chiefs descended from Esau, by name, according to their clans and regions:

Timna, Alvah, Jetheth, [41]Oholibamah, Elah, Pinon, [42]Kenaz, Teman, Mibzar, [43]Magdiel and Iram. These were the chiefs of Edom, according to their settlements in the land they occupied.

This was Esau the father of the Edomites.

Joseph's Dreams

37 Jacob lived in the land where his father had stayed, the land of Canaan.

[2]This is the account of Jacob.

Joseph, a young man of seventeen, was tending the flocks with his brothers, the sons of Bilhah and the sons of Zilpah, his father's wives, and he brought their father a bad report about them.

[3]Now Israel loved Joseph more than any of his other sons, because he had

---

[a]22 Hebrew *Hemam*, a variant of *Homam* (see 1 Chron. 1:39)   [b]24 Vulgate; Syriac *discovered water*; the meaning of the Hebrew for this word is uncertain.   [c]26 Hebrew *Dishan*, a variant of *Dishon*   [d]31 Or *before an Israelite king reigned over them*   [e]37 Possibly the Euphrates   [f]39 Many manuscripts of the Masoretic Text, Samaritan Pentateuch and Syriac (see also 1 Chron. 1:50); most manuscripts of the Masoretic Text *Hadar*

been born to him in his old age; and he made a richly ornamented[a] robe for him. ⁴When his brothers saw that their father loved him more than any of them, they hated him and could not speak a kind word to him.

⁵Joseph had a dream, and when he told it to his brothers, they hated him all the more. ⁶He said to them, "Listen to this dream I had: ⁷We were binding sheaves of grain out in the field when suddenly my sheaf rose and stood upright, while your sheaves gathered around mine and bowed down to it."

⁸His brothers said to him, "Do you intend to reign over us? Will you actually rule us?" And they hated him all the more because of his dream and what he had said.

⁹Then he had another dream, and he told it to his brothers. "Listen," he said, "I had another dream, and this time the sun and moon and eleven stars were bowing down to me."

¹⁰When he told his father as well as his brothers, his father rebuked him and said, "What is this dream you had? Will your mother and I and your brothers actually come and bow down to the ground before you?" ¹¹His brothers were jealous of him, but his father kept the matter in mind.

Joseph Sold by His Brothers

¹²Now his brothers had gone to graze their father's flocks near Shechem, ¹³and Israel said to Joseph, "As you know, your brothers are grazing the flocks near Shechem. Come, I am going to send you to them."

"Very well," he replied.

¹⁴So he said to him, "Go and see if all is well with your brothers and with the flocks, and bring word back to me." Then he sent him off from the Valley of Hebron.

When Joseph arrived at Shechem, ¹⁵a man found him wandering around in the fields and asked him, "What are you looking for?"

¹⁶He replied, "I'm looking for my brothers. Can you tell me where they are grazing their flocks?"

¹⁷"They have moved on from here," the man answered. "I heard them say, 'Let's go to Dothan.'"

So Joseph went after his brothers and found them near Dothan. ¹⁸But they saw him in the distance, and before he reached them, they plotted to kill him.

¹⁹"Here comes that dreamer!" they said to each other. ²⁰"Come now, let's kill him and throw him into one of these cisterns and say that a ferocious animal devoured him. Then we'll see what comes of his dreams."

²¹When Reuben heard this, he tried to rescue him from their hands. "Let's not take his life," he said. ²²"Don't shed any blood. Throw him into this cistern here in the desert, but don't lay a hand on him." Reuben said this to rescue him from them and take him back to his father.

²³So when Joseph came to his brothers, they stripped him of his robe—the richly ornamented robe he was wearing— ²⁴and they took him and threw him into the cistern. Now the cistern was empty; there was no water in it.

²⁵As they sat down to eat their meal, they looked up and saw a caravan of Ishmaelites coming from Gilead. Their camels were loaded with spices, balm and myrrh, and they were on their way to take them down to Egypt.

²⁶Judah said to his brothers, "What will we gain if we kill our brother and cover up his blood? ²⁷Come, let's sell him to the Ishmaelites and not lay our hands on him; after all, he is our brother, our own flesh and blood." His brothers agreed.

²⁸So when the Midianite merchants came by, his brothers pulled Joseph up out of the cistern and sold him for twenty shekels[b] of silver to the Ishmaelites, who took him to Egypt.

²⁹When Reuben returned to the cistern and saw that Joseph was not there, he tore his clothes. ³⁰He went back to his brothers and said, "The boy isn't there! Where can I turn now?"

³¹Then they got Joseph's robe, slaughtered a goat and dipped the robe in the blood. ³²They took the ornamented robe back to their father and said, "We found

---

a3 The meaning of the Hebrew for *richly ornamented* is uncertain; also in verses 23 and 32.
b28 That is, about 8 ounces (about 0.2 kilogram)

this. Examine it to see whether it is your son's robe."

[33]He recognized it and said, "It is my son's robe! Some ferocious animal has devoured him. Joseph has surely been torn to pieces."

[34]Then Jacob tore his clothes, put on sackcloth and mourned for his son many days. [35]All his sons and daughters came to comfort him, but he refused to be comforted. "No," he said, "in mourning will I go down to the grave[a] to my son." So his father wept for him.

[36]Meanwhile, the Midianites[b] sold Joseph in Egypt to Potiphar, one of Pharaoh's officials, the captain of the guard.

Judah and Tamar

38 At that time, Judah left his brothers and went down to stay with a man of Adullam named Hirah. [2]There Judah met the daughter of a Canaanite man named Shua. He married her and lay with her; [3]she became pregnant and gave birth to a son, who was named Er. [4]She conceived again and gave birth to a son and named him Onan. [5]She gave birth to still another son and named him Shelah. It was at Kezib that she gave birth to him.

[6]Judah got a wife for Er, his firstborn, and her name was Tamar. [7]But Er, Judah's firstborn, was wicked in the LORD's sight; so the LORD put him to death.

[8]Then Judah said to Onan, "Lie with your brother's wife and fulfill your duty to her as a brother-in-law to produce offspring for your brother." [9]But Onan knew that the offspring would not be his; so whenever he lay with his brother's wife, he spilled his semen on the ground to keep from producing offspring for his brother. [10]What he did was wicked in the LORD's sight; so he put him to death also.

[11]Judah then said to his daughter-in-law Tamar, "Live as a widow in your father's house until my son Shelah grows up." For he thought, "He may die too, just like his brothers." So Tamar went to live in her father's house.

[12]After a long time Judah's wife, the daughter of Shua, died. When Judah had recovered from his grief, he went up to Timnah, to the men who were shearing his sheep, and his friend Hirah the Adullamite went with him.

[13]When Tamar was told, "Your father-in-law is on his way to Timnah to shear his sheep," [14]she took off her widow's clothes, covered herself with a veil to disguise herself, and then sat down at the entrance to Enaim, which is on the road to Timnah. For she saw that, though Shelah had now grown up, she had not been given to him as his wife.

[15]When Judah saw her, he thought she was a prostitute, for she had covered her face. [16]Not realizing that she was his daughter-in-law, he went over to her by the roadside and said, "Come now, let me sleep with you."

"And what will you give me to sleep with you?" she asked.

[17]"I'll send you a young goat from my flock," he said.

"Will you give me something as a pledge until you send it?" she asked.

[18]He said, "What pledge should I give you?"

"Your seal and its cord, and the staff in your hand," she answered. So he gave them to her and slept with her, and she became pregnant by him. [19]After she left, she took off her veil and put on her widow's clothes again.

[20]Meanwhile Judah sent the young goat by his friend the Adullamite in order to get his pledge back from the woman, but he did not find her. [21]He asked the men who lived there, "Where is the shrine prostitute who was beside the road at Enaim?"

"There hasn't been any shrine prostitute here," they said.

[22]So he went back to Judah and said, "I didn't find her. Besides, the men who lived there said, 'There hasn't been any shrine prostitute here.' "

[23]Then Judah said, "Let her keep what she has, or we will become a laughingstock. After all, I did send her this young goat, but you didn't find her."

[24]About three months later Judah was told, "Your daughter-in-law Tamar is

---

[a]35 Hebrew *Sheol*   [b]36 Samaritan Pentateuch, Septuagint, Vulgate and Syriac (see also verse 28); Masoretic Text *Medanites*

guilty of prostitution, and as a result she is now pregnant."

Judah said, "Bring her out and have her burned to death!"

²⁵As she was being brought out, she sent a message to her father-in-law. "I am pregnant by the man who owns these," she said. And she added, "See if you recognize whose seal and cord and staff these are."

²⁶Judah recognized them and said, "She is more righteous than I, since I wouldn't give her to my son Shelah." And he did not sleep with her again.

²⁷When the time came for her to give birth, there were twin boys in her womb. ²⁸As she was giving birth, one of them put out his hand; so the midwife took a scarlet thread and tied it on his wrist and said, "This one came out first." ²⁹But when he drew back his hand, his brother came out, and she said, "So this is how you have broken out!" And he was named Perez.ᵃ ³⁰Then his brother, who had the scarlet thread on his wrist, came out and he was given the name Zerah.ᵇ

Joseph and Potiphar's Wife

39 Now Joseph had been taken down to Egypt. Potiphar, an Egyptian who was one of Pharaoh's officials, the captain of the guard, bought him from the Ishmaelites who had taken him there.

²The LORD was with Joseph and he prospered, and he lived in the house of his Egyptian master. ³When his master saw that the LORD was with him and that the LORD gave him success in everything he did, ⁴Joseph found favor in his eyes and became his attendant. Potiphar put him in charge of his household, and he entrusted to his care everything he owned. ⁵From the time he put him in charge of his household and of all that he owned, the LORD blessed the household of the Egyptian because of Joseph. The blessing of the LORD was on everything Potiphar had, both in the house and in the field. ⁶So he left in Joseph's care everything he had; with Joseph in charge, he

ᵃ29 Perez means breaking out.   ᵇ30 Zerah can mean scarlet or brightness.

God's Desires for Your Life

Tuesday

GENESIS 39:7 When Rosemary and I were both in graduate school, our finances were extremely limited. In fact, money was practically nonexistent. We knew God wanted us to be in school, but we sometimes wondered at what cost? Was he aware that we still needed to eat?! There are times in every marriage when we wonder if God is aware of our needs.

Joseph faced the question of needs. When his boss's wife said, "Come to bed with me," his sexual needs were probably in conflict with his commitment and loyalty to his boss.

Think about Joseph's situation. He was sold into slavery when he was seventeen. Purchased by an Egyptian master, he worked as a slave for over a decade. He must have wondered if this was it for his life. Would he ever get married? As a slave from seventeen on into his late twenties, would his physical needs ever be met? Then the boss's wife tempts him.

Joseph had to decide what he would do. Would he feed the desires of his body or would he stay committed to pleasing God? He knew he couldn't do both in this situation. The desires of his body would meet short-term needs. On the other hand, if Joseph trusted God and stayed pure, he would find far greater happiness.

While we were financially strapped in graduate school, many of our friends were already busy making money. As we watched them purchase many of the comforts we could not afford, we were tempted to quit this path God had put us on. We knew God wanted us where we were, but the pull to meet these short-term needs was great. Today as we look back, we see how God has used not only our education but also that time of trusting to mold us for his use.

Does it boil down to short-term needs versus God's desires for your life?

—**Bob & Rosemary**

Go to page 48 for your next devotional reading.

did not concern himself with anything except the food he ate.

Now Joseph was well-built and handsome, [7]and after a while his master's wife took notice of Joseph and said, "Come to bed with me!"

[8]But he refused. "With me in charge," he told her, "my master does not concern himself with anything in the house; everything he owns he has entrusted to my care. [9]No one is greater in this house than I am. My master has withheld nothing from me except you, because you are his wife. How then could I do such a wicked thing and sin against God?" [10]And though she spoke to Joseph day after day, he refused to go to bed with her or even be with her.

[11]One day he went into the house to attend to his duties, and none of the household servants was inside. [12]She caught him by his cloak and said, "Come to bed with me!" But he left his cloak in her hand and ran out of the house.

[13]When she saw that he had left his cloak in her hand and had run out of the house, [14]she called her household servants. "Look," she said to them, "this Hebrew has been brought to us to make sport of us! He came in here to sleep with me, but I screamed. [15]When he heard me scream for help, he left his cloak beside me and ran out of the house."

[16]She kept his cloak beside her until his master came home. [17]Then she told him this story: "That Hebrew slave you brought us came to me to make sport of me. [18]But as soon as I screamed for help, he left his cloak beside me and ran out of the house."

[19]When his master heard the story his wife told him, saying, "This is how your slave treated me," he burned with anger. [20]Joseph's master took him and put him in prison, the place where the king's prisoners were confined.

But while Joseph was there in the prison, [21]the LORD was with him; he showed him kindness and granted him favor in the eyes of the prison warden. [22]So the warden put Joseph in charge of all those held in the prison, and he was made responsible for all that was done there. [23]The warden paid no attention to anything under Joseph's care, because the

God's Desires for Your Life

Take a moment to answer each of these questions on your own. Then compare your answers to your spouse's.

Yes No I think it's difficult for me to tell the difference between need and want.

Yes No I can think of some unmet needs/wants in my life right now.

Yes No I would be embarrassed if any of these desires in my life would be known by the people around me.

Yes No One of my basic desires of life is to love my neighbor as myself — starting with my spouse.

Yes No Do I trust God to meet my needs?

LORD was with Joseph and gave him success in whatever he did.

The Cupbearer and the Baker

40 Some time later, the cupbearer and the baker of the king of Egypt offended their master, the king of Egypt. [2]Pharaoh was angry with his two officials, the chief cupbearer and the chief baker, [3]and put them in custody in the house of the captain of the guard, in the same prison where Joseph was confined. [4]The captain of the guard assigned them to Joseph, and he attended them.

After they had been in custody for some time, [5]each of the two men—the cupbearer and the baker of the king of Egypt, who were being held in prison—had a dream the same night, and each dream had a meaning of its own.

[6]When Joseph came to them the next morning, he saw that they were dejected. [7]So he asked Pharaoh's officials who were in custody with him in his master's house, "Why are your faces so sad today?"

[8]"We both had dreams," they answered, "but there is no one to interpret them."

Then Joseph said to them, "Do not interpretations belong to God? Tell me your dreams."

[9]So the chief cupbearer told Joseph his

dream. He said to him, "In my dream I saw a vine in front of me, ¹⁰and on the vine were three branches. As soon as it budded, it blossomed, and its clusters ripened into grapes. ¹¹Pharaoh's cup was in my hand, and I took the grapes, squeezed them into Pharaoh's cup and put the cup in his hand."

¹²"This is what it means," Joseph said to him. "The three branches are three days. ¹³Within three days Pharaoh will lift up your head and restore you to your position, and you will put Pharaoh's cup in his hand, just as you used to do when you were his cupbearer. ¹⁴But when all goes well with you, remember me and show me kindness; mention me to Pharaoh and get me out of this prison. ¹⁵For I was forcibly carried off from the land of the Hebrews, and even here I have done nothing to deserve being put in a dungeon."

¹⁶When the chief baker saw that Joseph had given a favorable interpretation, he said to Joseph, "I too had a dream: On my head were three baskets of bread.ᵃ ¹⁷In the top basket were all kinds of baked goods for Pharaoh, but the birds were eating them out of the basket on my head."

¹⁸"This is what it means," Joseph said. "The three baskets are three days. ¹⁹Within three days Pharaoh will lift off your head and hang you on a tree.ᵇ And the birds will eat away your flesh."

²⁰Now the third day was Pharaoh's birthday, and he gave a feast for all his officials. He lifted up the heads of the chief cupbearer and the chief baker in the presence of his officials: ²¹He restored the chief cupbearer to his position, so that he once again put the cup into Pharaoh's hand, ²²but he hangedᶜ the chief baker, just as Joseph had said to them in his interpretation.

²³The chief cupbearer, however, did not remember Joseph; he forgot him.

Pharaoh's Dreams

41 When two full years had passed, Pharaoh had a dream: He was standing by the Nile, ²when out of the river there came up seven cows, sleek and fat, and they grazed among the reeds. ³After them, seven other cows, ugly and gaunt, came up out of the Nile and stood beside those on the riverbank. ⁴And the cows that were ugly and gaunt ate up the seven sleek, fat cows. Then Pharaoh woke up.

⁵He fell asleep again and had a second dream: Seven heads of grain, healthy and good, were growing on a single stalk. ⁶After them, seven other heads of grain sprouted—thin and scorched by the east wind. ⁷The thin heads of grain swallowed up the seven healthy, full heads. Then Pharaoh woke up; it had been a dream.

⁸In the morning his mind was troubled, so he sent for all the magicians and wise men of Egypt. Pharaoh told them his dreams, but no one could interpret them for him.

⁹Then the chief cupbearer said to Pharaoh, "Today I am reminded of my shortcomings. ¹⁰Pharaoh was once angry with his servants, and he imprisoned me and the chief baker in the house of the captain of the guard. ¹¹Each of us had a dream the same night, and each dream had a meaning of its own. ¹²Now a young Hebrew was there with us, a servant of the captain of the guard. We told him our dreams, and he interpreted them for us, giving each man the interpretation of his dream. ¹³And things turned out exactly as he interpreted them to us: I was restored to my position, and the other man was hanged.ᶜ"

¹⁴So Pharaoh sent for Joseph, and he was quickly brought from the dungeon. When he had shaved and changed his clothes, he came before Pharaoh.

¹⁵Pharaoh said to Joseph, "I had a dream, and no one can interpret it. But I have heard it said of you that when you hear a dream you can interpret it."

¹⁶"I cannot do it," Joseph replied to Pharaoh, "but God will give Pharaoh the answer he desires."

¹⁷Then Pharaoh said to Joseph, "In my dream I was standing on the bank of the Nile, ¹⁸when out of the river there came up seven cows, fat and sleek, and they grazed among the reeds. ¹⁹After them, seven other cows came up—scrawny and very ugly and lean. I had never seen such ugly cows in all the land of Egypt. ²⁰The lean, ugly cows ate up the seven fat cows

ᵃ16 Or three wicker baskets   ᵇ19 Or and impale you on a pole   ᶜ22,13 Or impaled that came up first. 21But even after they ate them, no one could tell that they had done so; they looked just as ugly as before. Then I woke up.

22"In my dreams I also saw seven heads of grain, full and good, growing on a single stalk. 23After them, seven other heads sprouted—withered and thin and scorched by the east wind. 24The thin heads of grain swallowed up the seven good heads. I told this to the magicians, but none could explain it to me."

25Then Joseph said to Pharaoh, "The dreams of Pharaoh are one and the same. God has revealed to Pharaoh what he is about to do. 26The seven good cows are seven years, and the seven good heads of grain are seven years; it is one and the same dream. 27The seven lean, ugly cows that came up afterward are seven years, and so are the seven worthless heads of grain scorched by the east wind: They are seven years of famine.

28"It is just as I said to Pharaoh: God has shown Pharaoh what he is about to do. 29Seven years of great abundance are coming throughout the land of Egypt, 30but seven years of famine will follow them. Then all the abundance in Egypt will be forgotten, and the famine will ravage the land. 31The abundance in the land will not be remembered, because the famine that follows it will be so severe. 32The reason the dream was given to Pharaoh in two forms is that the matter has been firmly decided by God, and God will do it soon.

33"And now let Pharaoh look for a discerning and wise man and put him in charge of the land of Egypt. 34Let Pharaoh appoint commissioners over the land to take a fifth of the harvest of Egypt during the seven years of abundance. 35They should collect all the food of these good years that are coming and store up the grain under the authority of Pharaoh, to be kept in the cities for food. 36This food should be held in reserve for the country, to be used during the seven years of famine that will come upon Egypt, so that the country may not be ruined by the famine."

37The plan seemed good to Pharaoh and to all his officials. 38So Pharaoh asked them, "Can we find anyone like this man, one in whom is the spirit of God*a*?"

39Then Pharaoh said to Joseph, "Since God has made all this known to you, there is no one so discerning and wise as you. 40You shall be in charge of my palace, and all my people are to submit to your orders. Only with respect to the throne will I be greater than you."

Joseph in Charge of Egypt

41So Pharaoh said to Joseph, "I hereby put you in charge of the whole land of Egypt." 42Then Pharaoh took his signet ring from his finger and put it on Joseph's finger. He dressed him in robes of fine linen and put a gold chain around his neck. 43He had him ride in a chariot as his second-in-command,*b* and men shouted before him, "Make way*c*!" Thus he put him in charge of the whole land of Egypt.

44Then Pharaoh said to Joseph, "I am Pharaoh, but without your word no one will lift hand or foot in all Egypt." 45Pharaoh gave Joseph the name Zaphenath-Paneah and gave him Asenath daughter of Potiphera, priest of On,*d* to be his wife. And Joseph went throughout the land of Egypt.

46Joseph was thirty years old when he entered the service of Pharaoh king of Egypt. And Joseph went out from Pharaoh's presence and traveled throughout Egypt. 47During the seven years of abundance the land produced plentifully. 48Joseph collected all the food produced in those seven years of abundance in Egypt and stored it in the cities. In each city he put the food grown in the fields surrounding it. 49Joseph stored up huge quantities of grain, like the sand of the sea; it was so much that he stopped keeping records because it was beyond measure.

50Before the years of famine came, two sons were born to Joseph by Asenath daughter of Potiphera, priest of On. 51Joseph named his firstborn Manasseh*e* and said, "It is because God has made me forget all my trouble and all my father's household." 52The second son he named

a38 Or *of the gods*   *b43* Or *in the chariot of his second-in-command*; or *in his second chariot*
c43 Or *Bow down*   *d45* That is, Heliopolis; also in verse 50   *e51* *Manasseh* sounds like and may be derived from the Hebrew for *forget*.

Ephraim[a] and said, "It is because God has made me fruitful in the land of my suffering."

53The seven years of abundance in Egypt came to an end, 54and the seven years of famine began, just as Joseph had said. There was famine in all the other lands, but in the whole land of Egypt there was food. 55When all Egypt began to feel the famine, the people cried to Pharaoh for food. Then Pharaoh told all the Egyptians, "Go to Joseph and do what he tells you."

56When the famine had spread over the whole country, Joseph opened the storehouses and sold grain to the Egyptians, for the famine was severe throughout Egypt. 57And all the countries came to Egypt to buy grain from Joseph, because the famine was severe in all the world.

Joseph's Brothers Go to Egypt

42 When Jacob learned that there was grain in Egypt, he said to his sons, "Why do you just keep looking at each other?" 2He continued, "I have heard that there is grain in Egypt. Go down there and buy some for us, so that we may live and not die."

3Then ten of Joseph's brothers went down to buy grain from Egypt. 4But Jacob did not send Benjamin, Joseph's brother, with the others, because he was afraid that harm might come to him. 5So Israel's sons were among those who went to buy grain, for the famine was in the land of Canaan also.

6Now Joseph was the governor of the land, the one who sold grain to all its people. So when Joseph's brothers arrived, they bowed down to him with their faces to the ground. 7As soon as Joseph saw his brothers, he recognized them, but he pretended to be a stranger and spoke harshly to them. "Where do you come from?" he asked.

"From the land of Canaan," they replied, "to buy food."

8Although Joseph recognized his brothers, they did not recognize him. 9Then he remembered his dreams about them and said to them, "You are spies! You have come to see where our land is unprotected."

10"No, my lord," they answered. "Your

a52 Ephraim sounds like the Hebrew for twice fruitful.

Forgiveness Is a Choice

GENESIS 42 "Love means never having to say you're sorry" was a line in the popular 1960s movie Love Story. The wisdom of that phrase is debatable. But what's not debatable is that love means always having to forgive, even when your spouse fails to say "sorry."

The marriage relationship requires major doses of forgiveness. Whether it's forgiving differences in temperament or violations of trust, forgiveness is the bridge to getting over all those valleys.

You may ask, But what if my spouse hasn't asked for forgiveness yet? Can I forgive him before he asks? That's where we learn a great lesson from Joseph.

When Joseph's brothers came to Egypt—the same brothers who had sold him into slavery—Joseph has a chance to seek vengeance. Joseph's brothers don't recognize him and ask to buy food from him. But obviously Joseph has already decided to forgive them, even though they haven't yet asked. Without vengeance guiding his response to their need, he graciously gives them the food. Joseph forgave before they even asked! He chose to forgive them. As a basic principle of relationships, God requires that we forgive those who have wronged us, whether they ask or not.

Each of us has the freedom and responsibility to choose to forgive those who have offended us. The intimacy of marriage includes many moments of hurt. Love does mean having to say we are sorry, but more importantly, love means choosing to forgive, even before you are asked.

—*Bob & Rosemary*

Go to page 58 for your next devotional reading.

servants have come to buy food. ¹¹We are all the sons of one man. Your servants are honest men, not spies."

¹²"No!" he said to them. "You have come to see where our land is unprotected."

¹³But they replied, "Your servants were twelve brothers, the sons of one man, who lives in the land of Canaan. The youngest is now with our father, and one is no more."

¹⁴Joseph said to them, "It is just as I told you: You are spies! ¹⁵And this is how you will be tested: As surely as Pharaoh lives, you will not leave this place unless your youngest brother comes here. ¹⁶Send one of your number to get your brother; the rest of you will be kept in prison, so that your words may be tested to see if you are telling the truth. If you are not, then as surely as Pharaoh lives, you are spies!" ¹⁷And he put them all in custody for three days.

¹⁸On the third day, Joseph said to them, "Do this and you will live, for I fear God: ¹⁹If you are honest men, let one of your brothers stay here in prison, while the rest of you go and take grain back for your starving households. ²⁰But you must bring your youngest brother to me, so that your words may be verified and that you may not die." This they proceeded to do.

²¹They said to one another, "Surely we are being punished because of our brother. We saw how distressed he was when he pleaded with us for his life, but we would not listen; that's why this distress has come upon us."

²²Reuben replied, "Didn't I tell you not to sin against the boy? But you wouldn't listen! Now we must give an accounting for his blood." ²³They did not realize that Joseph could understand them, since he was using an interpreter.

²⁴He turned away from them and began to weep, but then turned back and spoke to them again. He had Simeon taken from them and bound before their eyes.

²⁵Joseph gave orders to fill their bags with grain, to put each man's silver back in his sack, and to give them provisions for their journey. After this was done for them, ²⁶they loaded their grain on their donkeys and left.

JUST BETWEEN you & me

Forgiveness Is a Choice

Take a moment to answer each of these questions on your own. Then compare your answers to your spouse's.

Yes   No   When I think about where our energies are going, I believe our marriage is focusing on the right priorities.

Yes   No   I think we have carefully spent time choosing the priorities we want to focus on.

Yes   No   Our family calendar reflects where our priorities are.

Yes   No   I sometimes feel trapped in the pursuit of the wrong priorities.

²⁷At the place where they stopped for the night one of them opened his sack to get feed for his donkey, and he saw his silver in the mouth of his sack. ²⁸"My silver has been returned," he said to his brothers. "Here it is in my sack."

Their hearts sank and they turned to each other trembling and said, "What is this that God has done to us?"

²⁹When they came to their father Jacob in the land of Canaan, they told him all that had happened to them. They said, ³⁰"The man who is lord over the land spoke harshly to us and treated us as though we were spying on the land. ³¹But we said to him, 'We are honest men; we are not spies. ³²We were twelve brothers, sons of one father. One is no more, and the youngest is now with our father in Canaan.'

³³"Then the man who is lord over the land said to us, 'This is how I will know whether you are honest men: Leave one of your brothers here with me, and take food for your starving households and go. ³⁴But bring your youngest brother to me so I will know that you are not spies but honest men. Then I will give your brother back to you, and you can trade^a in the land.'"

³⁵As they were emptying their sacks,

ª34 Or *move about freely*

there in each man's sack was his pouch of silver! When they and their father saw the money pouches, they were frightened. 36Their father Jacob said to them, "You have deprived me of my children. Joseph is no more and Simeon is no more, and now you want to take Benjamin. Everything is against me!"

37Then Reuben said to his father, "You may put both of my sons to death if I do not bring him back to you. Entrust him to my care, and I will bring him back."

38But Jacob said, "My son will not go down there with you; his brother is dead and he is the only one left. If harm comes to him on the journey you are taking, you will bring my gray head down to the grave[a] in sorrow."

The Second Journey to Egypt

43 Now the famine was still severe in the land. 2So when they had eaten all the grain they had brought from Egypt, their father said to them, "Go back and buy us a little more food."

3But Judah said to him, "The man warned us solemnly, 'You will not see my face again unless your brother is with you.' 4If you will send our brother along with us, we will go down and buy food for you. 5But if you will not send him, we will not go down, because the man said to us, 'You will not see my face again unless your brother is with you.' "

6Israel asked, "Why did you bring this trouble on me by telling the man you had another brother?"

7They replied, "The man questioned us closely about ourselves and our family. 'Is your father still living?' he asked us. 'Do you have another brother?' We simply answered his questions. How were we to know he would say, 'Bring your brother down here'?"

8Then Judah said to Israel his father, "Send the boy along with me and we will go at once, so that we and you and our children may live and not die. 9I myself will guarantee his safety; you can hold me personally responsible for him. If I do not bring him back to you and set him here before you, I will bear the blame before you all my life. 10As it is, if we had not delayed, we could have gone and returned twice."

11Then their father Israel said to them, "If it must be, then do this: Put some of the best products of the land in your bags and take them down to the man as a gift— a little balm and a little honey, some spices and myrrh, some pistachio nuts and almonds. 12Take double the amount of silver with you, for you must return the silver that was put back into the mouths of your sacks. Perhaps it was a mistake. 13Take your brother also and go back to the man at once. 14And may God Almighty[b] grant you mercy before the man so that he will let your other brother and Benjamin come back with you. As for me, if I am bereaved, I am bereaved."

15So the men took the gifts and double the amount of silver, and Benjamin also. They hurried down to Egypt and presented themselves to Joseph. 16When Joseph saw Benjamin with them, he said to the steward of his house, "Take these men to my house, slaughter an animal and prepare dinner; they are to eat with me at noon."

17The man did as Joseph told him and took the men to Joseph's house. 18Now the men were frightened when they were taken to his house. They thought, "We were brought here because of the silver that was put back into our sacks the first time. He wants to attack us and overpower us and seize us as slaves and take our donkeys."

19So they went up to Joseph's steward and spoke to him at the entrance to the house. 20"Please, sir," they said, "we came down here the first time to buy food. 21But at the place where we stopped for the night we opened our sacks and each of us found his silver—the exact weight— in the mouth of his sack. So we have brought it back with us. 22We have also brought additional silver with us to buy food. We don't know who put our silver in our sacks."

23"It's all right," he said. "Don't be afraid. Your God, the God of your father, has given you treasure in your sacks; I received your silver." Then he brought Simeon out to them.

24The steward took the men into Joseph's house, gave them water to wash their feet and provided fodder for their

a38 Hebrew *Sheol*   b14 Hebrew *El-Shaddai*

donkeys. 25They prepared their gifts for Joseph's arrival at noon, because they had heard that they were to eat there.

26When Joseph came home, they presented to him the gifts they had brought into the house, and they bowed down before him to the ground. 27He asked them how they were, and then he said, "How is your aged father you told me about? Is he still living?" 28They replied, "Your servant our father is still alive and well." And they bowed low to pay him honor.

29As he looked about and saw his brother Benjamin, his own mother's son, he asked, "Is this your youngest brother, the one you told me about?" And he said, "God be gracious to you, my son." 30Deeply moved at the sight of his brother, Joseph hurried out and looked for a place to weep. He went into his private room and wept there.

31After he had washed his face, he came out and and, controlling himself, said, "Serve the food."

32They served him by himself, the brothers by themselves, and the Egyptians who ate with him by themselves, because Egyptians could not eat with Hebrews, for that is detestable to Egyptians. 33The men had been seated before him in the order of their ages, from the firstborn to the youngest; and they looked at each other in astonishment. 34When portions were served to them from Joseph's table, Benjamin's portion was five times as much as anyone else's. So they feasted and drank freely with him.

A Silver Cup in a Sack

44 Now Joseph gave these instructions to the steward of his house: "Fill the men's sacks with as much food as they can carry, and put each man's silver in the mouth of his sack. 2Then put my cup, the silver one, in the mouth of the youngest one's sack, along with the silver for his grain." And he did as Joseph said.

3As morning dawned, the men were sent on their way with their donkeys. 4They had not gone far from the city when Joseph said to his steward, "Go after those men at once, and when you catch up with them, say to them, 'Why have you repaid good with evil? 5Isn't this

the cup my master drinks from and also uses for divination? This is a wicked thing you have done.' "

6When he caught up with them, he repeated these words to them. 7But they said to him, "Why does my lord say such things? Far be it from your servants to do anything like that! 8We even brought back to you from the land of Canaan the silver we found inside the mouths of our sacks. So why would we steal silver or gold from your master's house? 9If any of your servants is found to have it, he will die; and the rest of us will become my lord's slaves."

10"Very well, then," he said, "let it be as you say. Whoever is found to have it will become my slave; the rest of you will be free from blame."

11Each of them quickly lowered his sack to the ground and opened it. 12Then the steward proceeded to search, beginning with the oldest and ending with the youngest. And the cup was found in Benjamin's sack. 13At this, they tore their clothes. Then they all loaded their donkeys and returned to the city.

14Joseph was still in the house when Judah and his brothers came in, and they threw themselves to the ground before him. 15Joseph said to them, "What is this you have done? Don't you know that a man like me can find things out by divination?"

16"What can we say to my lord?" Judah replied. "What can we say? How can we prove our innocence? God has uncovered your servants' guilt. We are now my lord's slaves—we ourselves and the one who was found to have the cup."

17But Joseph said, "Far be it from me to do such a thing! Only the man who was found to have the cup will become my slave. The rest of you, go back to your father in peace."

18Then Judah went up to him and said: "Please, my lord, let your servant speak a word to my lord. Do not be angry with your servant, though you are equal to Pharaoh himself. 19My lord asked his servants, 'Do you have a father or a brother?' 20And we answered, 'We have an aged father, and there is a young son born to him in his old age. His brother is dead, and he is the only one of his mother's sons left, and his father loves him.'

21"Then you said to your servants, 'Bring him down to me so I can see him for myself.' 22And we said to my lord, 'The boy cannot leave his father; if he leaves him, his father will die.' 23But you told your servants, 'Unless your youngest brother comes down with you, you will not see my face again.' 24When we went back to your servant my father, we told him what my lord had said.

25"Then our father said, 'Go back and buy a little more food.' 26But we said, 'We cannot go down. Only if our youngest brother is with us will we go. We cannot see the man's face unless our youngest brother is with us.'

27"Your servant my father said to us, 'You know that my wife bore me two sons. 28One of them went away from me, and I said, "He has surely been torn to pieces." And I have not seen him since. 29If you take this one from me too and harm comes to him, you will bring my gray head down to the grave[a] in misery.'

30"So now, if the boy is not with us when I go back to your servant my father and if my father, whose life is closely bound up with the boy's life, 31sees that the boy isn't there, he will die. Your servants will bring the gray head of our father down to the grave in sorrow. 32Your servant guaranteed the boy's safety to my father. I said, 'If I do not bring him back to you, I will bear the blame before you, my father, all my life!'

33"Now then, please let your servant remain here as my lord's slave in place of the boy, and let the boy return with his brothers. 34How can I go back to my father if the boy is not with me? No! Do not let me see the misery that would come upon my father."

Joseph Makes Himself Known

45 Then Joseph could no longer control himself before all his attendants, and he cried out, "Have everyone leave my presence!" So there was no one with Joseph when he made himself known to his brothers. 2And he wept so loudly that the Egyptians heard him, and Pharaoh's household heard about it.

3Joseph said to his brothers, "I am Joseph! Is my father still living?" But his brothers were not able to answer him, because they were terrified at his presence.

4Then Joseph said to his brothers, "Come close to me." When they had done so, he said, "I am your brother Joseph, the one you sold into Egypt! 5And now, do not be distressed and do not be angry with yourselves for selling me here, because it was to save lives that God sent me ahead of you. 6For two years now there has been famine in the land, and for the next five years there will not be plowing and reaping. 7But God sent me ahead of you to preserve for you a remnant on earth and to save your lives by a great deliverance.[b]

8"So then, it was not you who sent me here, but God. He made me father to Pharaoh, lord of his entire household and ruler of all Egypt. 9Now hurry back to my father and say to him, 'This is what your son Joseph says: God has made me lord of all Egypt. Come down to me; don't delay. 10You shall live in the region of Goshen and be near me—you, your children and grandchildren, your flocks and herds, and all you have. 11I will provide for you there, because five years of famine are still to come. Otherwise you and your household and all who belong to you will become destitute.'

12"You can see for yourselves, and so can my brother Benjamin, that it is really I who am speaking to you. 13Tell my father about all the honor accorded me in Egypt and about everything you have seen. And bring my father down here quickly."

14Then he threw his arms around his brother Benjamin and wept, and Benjamin embraced him, weeping. 15And he kissed all his brothers and wept over them. Afterward his brothers talked with him.

16When the news reached Pharaoh's palace that Joseph's brothers had come, Pharaoh and all his officials were pleased. 17Pharaoh said to Joseph, "Tell your brothers, 'Do this: Load your animals and return to the land of Canaan, 18and bring your father and your families back to me. I will give you the best of the land of Egypt and you can enjoy the fat of the land.'

---

*a*29 Hebrew *Sheol*; also in verse 31   *b*7 Or *save you as a great band of survivors*

¹⁹"You are also directed to tell them, 'Do this: Take some carts from Egypt for your children and your wives, and get your father and come. ²⁰Never mind about your belongings, because the best of all Egypt will be yours.' "

²¹So the sons of Israel did this. Joseph gave them carts, as Pharaoh had commanded, and he also gave them provisions for their journey. ²²To each of them he gave new clothing, but to Benjamin he gave three hundred shekels*a* of silver and five sets of clothes. ²³And this is what he sent to his father: ten donkeys loaded with the best things of Egypt, and ten female donkeys loaded with grain and bread and other provisions for his journey. ²⁴Then he sent his brothers away, and as they were leaving he said to them, "Don't quarrel on the way!"

²⁵So they went up out of Egypt and came to their father Jacob in the land of Canaan. ²⁶They told him, "Joseph is still alive! In fact, he is ruler of all Egypt." Jacob was stunned; he did not believe them. ²⁷But when they told him everything Joseph had said to them, and when he saw the carts Joseph had sent to carry him back, the spirit of their father Jacob revived. ²⁸And Israel said, "I'm convinced! My son Joseph is still alive. I will go and see him before I die."

Jacob Goes to Egypt

46 So Israel set out with all that was his, and when he reached Beersheba, he offered sacrifices to the God of his father Isaac.

²And God spoke to Israel in a vision at night and said, "Jacob! Jacob!"

"Here I am," he replied.

³"I am God, the God of your father," he said. "Do not be afraid to go down to Egypt, for I will make you into a great nation there. ⁴I will go down to Egypt with you, and I will surely bring you back again. And Joseph's own hand will close your eyes."

⁵Then Jacob left Beersheba, and Israel's sons took their father Jacob and their children and their wives in the carts that Pharaoh had sent to transport him. ⁶They also took with them their livestock and the possessions they had acquired in Canaan, and Jacob and all his offspring went to

Egypt. ⁷He took with him to Egypt his sons and grandsons and his daughters and granddaughters—all his offspring.

⁸These are the names of the sons of Israel (Jacob and his descendants) who went to Egypt:

Reuben the firstborn of Jacob.
⁹The sons of Reuben:
    Hanoch, Pallu, Hezron and Carmi.
¹⁰The sons of Simeon:
    Jemuel, Jamin, Ohad, Jakin, Zohar and Shaul the son of a Canaanite woman.
¹¹The sons of Levi:
    Gershon, Kohath and Merari.
¹²The sons of Judah:
    Er, Onan, Shelah, Perez and Zerah (but Er and Onan had died in the land of Canaan).
    The sons of Perez:
    Hezron and Hamul.
¹³The sons of Issachar:
    Tola, Puah,*b* Jashub*c* and Shimron.
¹⁴The sons of Zebulun:
    Sered, Elon and Jahleel.
¹⁵These were the sons Leah bore to Jacob in Paddan Aram,*d* besides his daughter Dinah. These sons and daughters of his were thirty-three in all.

¹⁶The sons of Gad:
    Zephon,*e* Haggi, Shuni, Ezbon, Eri, Arodi and Areli.
¹⁷The sons of Asher:
    Imnah, Ishvah, Ishvi and Beriah.
    Their sister was Serah.
    The sons of Beriah:
    Heber and Malkiel.
¹⁸These were the children born to Jacob by Zilpah, whom Laban had given to his daughter Leah—sixteen in all.

¹⁹The sons of Jacob's wife Rachel:
    Joseph and Benjamin. ²⁰In Egypt, Manasseh and Ephraim were born to Joseph by Asenath

---

a22 That is, about 7 1/2 pounds (about 3.5 kilograms)   *b13* Samaritan Pentateuch and Syriac (see also 1 Chron. 7:1); Masoretic Text *Puvah*   *c13* Samaritan Pentateuch and some Septuagint manuscripts (see also Num. 26:24 and 1 Chron. 7:1); Masoretic Text *Iob*   *d15* That is, Northwest Mesopotamia   *e16* Samaritan Pentateuch and Septuagint (see also Num. 26:15); Masoretic Text *Ziphion* daughter of Potiphera, priest of On.[a]

[21]The sons of Benjamin:
Bela, Beker, Ashbel, Gera, Naaman, Ehi, Rosh, Muppim, Huppim and Ard.

[22]These were the sons of Rachel who were born to Jacob—fourteen in all.

[23]The son of Dan:
Hushim.

[24]The sons of Naphtali:
Jahziel, Guni, Jezer and Shillem.

[25]These were the sons born to Jacob by Bilhah, whom Laban had given to his daughter Rachel—seven in all.

[26]All those who went to Egypt with Jacob—those who were his direct descendants, not counting his sons' wives—numbered sixty-six persons. [27]With the two sons[b] who had been born to Joseph in Egypt, the members of Jacob's family, which went to Egypt, were seventy[c] in all.

[28]Now Jacob sent Judah ahead of him to Joseph to get directions to Goshen. When they arrived in the region of Goshen, [29]Joseph had his chariot made ready and went to Goshen to meet his father Israel. As soon as Joseph appeared before him, he threw his arms around his father[d] and wept for a long time.

[30]Israel said to Joseph, "Now I am ready to die, since I have seen for myself that you are still alive."

[31]Then Joseph said to his brothers and to his father's household, "I will go up and speak to Pharaoh and will say to him, 'My brothers and my father's household, who were living in the land of Canaan, have come to me. [32]The men are shepherds; they tend livestock, and they have brought along their flocks and herds and everything they own.' [33]When Pharaoh calls you in and asks, 'What is your occupation?' [34]you should answer, 'Your servants have tended livestock from our boyhood on, just as our fathers did.' Then you will be allowed to settle in the region of Goshen, for all shepherds are detestable to the Egyptians."

47 Joseph went and told Pharaoh, "My father and brothers, with their flocks and herds and everything they own, have come from the land of Canaan

and are now in Goshen." [2]He chose five of his brothers and presented them before Pharaoh.

[3]Pharaoh asked the brothers, "What is your occupation?"

"Your servants are shepherds," they replied to Pharaoh, "just as our fathers were." [4]They also said to him, "We have come to live here awhile, because the famine is severe in Canaan and your servants' flocks have no pasture. So now, please let your servants settle in Goshen."

[5]Pharaoh said to Joseph, "Your father and your brothers have come to you, [6]and the land of Egypt is before you; settle your father and your brothers in the best part of the land. Let them live in Goshen. And if you know of any among them with special ability, put them in charge of my own livestock."

[7]Then Joseph brought his father Jacob in and presented him before Pharaoh. After Jacob blessed[e] Pharaoh, [8]Pharaoh asked him, "How old are you?"

[9]And Jacob said to Pharaoh, "The years of my pilgrimage are a hundred and thirty. My years have been few and difficult, and they do not equal the years of the pilgrimage of my fathers." [10]Then Jacob blessed[f] Pharaoh and went out from his presence.

[11]So Joseph settled his father and his brothers in Egypt and gave them property in the best part of the land, the district of Rameses, as Pharaoh directed. [12]Joseph also provided his father and his brothers and all his father's household with food, according to the number of their children.

Joseph and the Famine

[13]There was no food, however, in the whole region because the famine was severe; both Egypt and Canaan wasted away because of the famine. [14]Joseph collected all the money that was to be found in Egypt and Canaan in payment for the grain they were buying, and he brought it to Pharaoh's palace. [15]When the money of the people of Egypt and Canaan was gone, all Egypt came to Joseph and said,

---

[a]20 That is, Heliopolis　[b]27 Hebrew; Septuagint *the nine children*　[c]27 Hebrew (see also Exodus 1:5 and footnote); Septuagint (see also Acts 7:14) *seventy-five*　[d]29 Hebrew *around him*　[e]7 Or *greeted*　[f]10 Or *said farewell to*

"Give us food. Why should we die before your eyes? Our money is used up."

16 "Then bring your livestock," said Joseph. "I will sell you food in exchange for your livestock, since your money is gone." 17So they brought their livestock to Joseph, and he gave them food in exchange for their horses, their sheep and goats, their cattle and donkeys. And he brought them through that year with food in exchange for all their livestock.

18When that year was over, they came to him the following year and said, "We cannot hide from our lord the fact that since our money is gone and our livestock belongs to you, there is nothing left for our lord except our bodies and our land. 19Why should we perish before your eyes—we and our land as well? Buy us and our land in exchange for food, and we with our land will be in bondage to Pharaoh. Give us seed so that we may live and not die, and that the land may not become desolate."

20So Joseph bought all the land in Egypt for Pharaoh. The Egyptians, one and all, sold their fields, because the famine was too severe for them. The land became Pharaoh's, 21and Joseph reduced the people to servitude,*a* from one end of Egypt to the other. 22However, he did not buy the land of the priests, because they received a regular allotment from Pharaoh and had food enough from the allotment Pharaoh gave them. That is why they did not sell their land.

23Joseph said to the people, "Now that I have bought you and your land today for Pharaoh, here is seed for you so you can plant the ground. 24But when the crop comes in, give a fifth of it to Pharaoh. The other four-fifths you may keep as seed for the fields and as food for yourselves and your households and your children."

25 "You have saved our lives," they said. "May we find favor in the eyes of our lord; we will be in bondage to Pharaoh."

26So Joseph established it as a law concerning land in Egypt—still in force today—that a fifth of the produce belongs to Pharaoh. It was only the land of the priests that did not become Pharaoh's.

27Now the Israelites settled in Egypt in the region of Goshen. They acquired property there and were fruitful and increased greatly in number.

28Jacob lived in Egypt seventeen years, and the years of his life were a hundred and forty-seven. 29When the time drew near for Israel to die, he called for his son Joseph and said to him, "If I have found favor in your eyes, put your hand under my thigh and promise that you will show me kindness and faithfulness. Do not bury me in Egypt, 30but when I rest with my fathers, carry me out of Egypt and bury me where they are buried."

"I will do as you say," he said.

31 "Swear to me," he said. Then Joseph swore to him, and Israel worshiped as he leaned on the top of his staff.*b*

Manasseh and Ephraim

48 Some time later Joseph was told, "Your father is ill." So he took his two sons Manasseh and Ephraim along with him. 2When Jacob was told, "Your son Joseph has come to you," Israel rallied his strength and sat up on the bed.

3Jacob said to Joseph, "God Almighty*c* appeared to me at Luz in the land of Canaan, and there he blessed me 4and said to me, 'I am going to make you fruitful and will increase your numbers. I will make you a community of peoples, and I will give this land as an everlasting possession to your descendants after you.'

5 "Now then, your two sons born to you in Egypt before I came to you here will be reckoned as mine; Ephraim and Manasseh will be mine, just as Reuben and Simeon are mine. 6Any children born to you after them will be yours; in the territory they inherit they will be reckoned under the names of their brothers. 7As I was returning from Paddan,*d* to my sorrow Rachel died in the land of Canaan while we were still on the way, a little distance from Ephrath. So I buried her there beside the road to Ephrath" (that is, Bethlehem).

8When Israel saw the sons of Joseph, he asked, "Who are these?"

9 "They are the sons God has given me here," Joseph said to his father.

a21 Samaritan Pentateuch and Septuagint (see also Vulgate); Masoretic Text *and he moved the people into the cities*   *b31* Or *Israel bowed down at the head of his bed*   *c3* Hebrew *El-Shaddai*   *d7* That is, Northwest Mesopotamia

Then Israel said, "Bring them to me so I may bless them."

[10]Now Israel's eyes were failing because of old age, and he could hardly see. So Joseph brought his sons close to him, and his father kissed them and embraced them.

[11]Israel said to Joseph, "I never expected to see your face again, and now God has allowed me to see your children too."

[12]Then Joseph removed them from Israel's knees and bowed down with his face to the ground. [13]And Joseph took both of them, Ephraim on his right toward Israel's left hand and Manasseh on his left toward Israel's right hand, and brought them close to him. [14]But Israel reached out his right hand and put it on Ephraim's head, though he was the younger, and crossing his arms, he put his left hand on Manasseh's head, even though Manasseh was the firstborn.

[15]Then he blessed Joseph and said,

"May the God before whom my
    fathers
  Abraham and Isaac walked,
the God who has been my shepherd
  all my life to this day,
[16]the Angel who has delivered me from
    all harm
  —may he bless these boys.
May they be called by my name
  and the names of my fathers
    Abraham and Isaac,
and may they increase greatly
  upon the earth."

[17]When Joseph saw his father placing his right hand on Ephraim's head he was displeased; so he took hold of his father's hand to move it from Ephraim's head to Manasseh's head. [18]Joseph said to him, "No, my father, this one is the firstborn; put your right hand on his head."

[19]But his father refused and said, "I know, my son, I know. He too will become a people, and he too will become great. Nevertheless, his younger brother will be greater than he, and his descendants will become a group of nations." [20]He blessed them that day and said,

"In your[a] name will Israel
  pronounce this blessing:
'May God make you like Ephraim
  and Manasseh.' "

So he put Ephraim ahead of Manasseh.

[21]Then Israel said to Joseph, "I am about to die, but God will be with you[b] and take you[b] back to the land of your[b] fathers. [22]And to you, as one who is over your brothers, I give the ridge of land[c] I took from the Amorites with my sword and my bow."

Jacob Blesses His Sons

49 Then Jacob called for his sons and said: "Gather around so I can tell you what will happen to you in days to come.

[2]"Assemble and listen, sons of Jacob;
  listen to your father Israel.

[3]"Reuben, you are my firstborn,
  my might, the first sign of my
    strength,
  excelling in honor, excelling in
    power.
[4]Turbulent as the waters, you will no
    longer excel,
  for you went up onto your father's
    bed,
  onto my couch and defiled it.

[5]"Simeon and Levi are brothers—
  their swords[d] are weapons of
    violence.
[6]Let me not enter their council,
  let me not join their assembly,
  for they have killed men in their
    anger
  and hamstrung oxen as they
    pleased.
[7]Cursed be their anger, so fierce,
  and their fury, so cruel!
  I will scatter them in Jacob
  and disperse them in Israel.

[8]"Judah,[e] your brothers will praise
    you;
  your hand will be on the neck of
    your enemies;
  your father's sons will bow down
    to you.
[9]You are a lion's cub, O Judah;
  you return from the prey, my son.

---

[a]20 The Hebrew is singular.   [b]21 The Hebrew is plural.   [c]22 Or *And to you I give one portion more than to your brothers—the portion* [d]5 The meaning of the Hebrew for this word is uncertain.   [e]8 *Judah* sounds like and may be derived from the Hebrew for *praise.*

Like a lion he crouches and lies
    down,
  like a lioness—who dares to rouse
    him?
[10]The scepter will not depart from
    Judah,
  nor the ruler's staff from between
    his feet,
until he comes to whom it belongs[a]
  and the obedience of the nations is
    his.
[11]He will tether his donkey to a vine,
  his colt to the choicest branch;
he will wash his garments in wine,
  his robes in the blood of grapes.
[12]His eyes will be darker than wine,
  his teeth whiter than milk.[b]

[13]"Zebulun will live by the seashore
  and become a haven for ships;
his border will extend toward
    Sidon.

[14]"Issachar is a rawboned[c] donkey
  lying down between two
    saddlebags.[d]
[15]When he sees how good is his resting
    place
  and how pleasant is his land,
he will bend his shoulder to the
    burden
  and submit to forced labor.

[16]"Dan[e] will provide justice for his
    people
  as one of the tribes of Israel.
[17]Dan will be a serpent by the roadside,
  a viper along the path,
that bites the horse's heels
  so that its rider tumbles backward.

[18]"I look for your deliverance, O LORD.

[19]"Gad[f] will be attacked by a band of
    raiders,
  but he will attack them at their
    heels.

[20]"Asher's food will be rich;
  he will provide delicacies fit for a
    king.

[21]"Naphtali is a doe set free
  that bears beautiful fawns.[g]

[22]"Joseph is a fruitful vine,
  a fruitful vine near a spring,
  whose branches climb over a
    wall.[h]
[23]With bitterness archers attacked him;

they shot at him with hostility.
[24]But his bow remained steady,
  his strong arms stayed[i] limber,
because of the hand of the Mighty
    One of Jacob,
  because of the Shepherd, the Rock
    of Israel,
[25]because of your father's God, who
    helps you,
  because of the Almighty,[j] who
    blesses you
with blessings of the heavens above,
  blessings of the deep that lies
    below,
  blessings of the breast and womb.
[26]Your father's blessings are greater
  than the blessings of the ancient
    mountains,
  than[k] the bounty of the age-old
    hills.
Let all these rest on the head of
    Joseph,
  on the brow of the prince among[l]
    his brothers.

[27]"Benjamin is a ravenous wolf;
  in the morning he devours the
    prey,
in the evening he divides the
    plunder."

[28]All these are the twelve tribes of Israel, and this is what their father said to them when he blessed them, giving each the blessing appropriate to him.

The Death of Jacob

[29]Then he gave them these instructions: "I am about to be gathered to my people. Bury me with my fathers in the cave in the field of Ephron the Hittite, [30]the cave in the field of Machpelah, near Mamre in Canaan, which Abraham bought as a burial place from Ephron the Hittite, along with the field. [31]There Abraham and his wife Sarah were buried, there

a10 Or until Shiloh comes; or until he comes to whom
tribute belongs   b12 Or will be dull from wine, /
his teeth white from milk   c14 Or strong
d14 Or campfires   e16 Dan here means he
provides justice.   f19 Gad can mean attack and
band of raiders.   g21 Or free; / he utters beautif
words   h22 Or Joseph is a wild colt, / a wild colt
near a spring, / a wild donkey on a terraced hill
i23,24 Or archers will attack . . . will shoot . . . will
remain . . . will stay   j25 Hebrew Shaddai
k26 Or of my progenitors, / as great as   l26 Or
the one separated from

Isaac and his wife Rebekah were buried, and there I buried Leah. [32]The field and the cave in it were bought from the Hittites.[a]"

[33]When Jacob had finished giving instructions to his sons, he drew his feet up into the bed, breathed his last and was gathered to his people.

50 Joseph threw himself upon his father and wept over him and kissed him. [2]Then Joseph directed the physicians in his service to embalm his father Israel. So the physicians embalmed him, [3]taking a full forty days, for that was the time required for embalming. And the Egyptians mourned for him seventy days.

[4]When the days of mourning had passed, Joseph said to Pharaoh's court, "If I have found favor in your eyes, speak to Pharaoh for me. Tell him, [5]'My father made me swear an oath and said, "I am about to die; bury me in the tomb I dug for myself in the land of Canaan." Now let

me go up and bury my father; then I will return.' "

[6]Pharaoh said, "Go up and bury your father, as he made you swear to do."

[7]So Joseph went up to bury his father. All Pharaoh's officials accompanied him— the dignitaries of his court and all the dignitaries of Egypt— [8]besides all the members of Joseph's household and his brothers and those belonging to his father's household. Only their children and their flocks and herds were left in Goshen. [9]Chariots and horsemen[b] also went up with him. It was a very large company.

[10]When they reached the threshing floor of Atad, near the Jordan, they lamented loudly and bitterly; and there Joseph observed a seven-day period of mourning for his father. [11]When the Canaanites who lived there saw the mourning at the threshing floor of Atad, they said, "The Egyptians are holding a sol-

[a]32 Or *the sons of Heth*   [b]9 Or *charioteers*

Trusting God in a Foreign Land

Thursday

GENESIS 50 Who or what do you put your trust in? Some put their trust in things. Others put their trust in people. But things will be gone in a flash. And people will inevitably disappoint us. If our happiness comes from things and people, we are vulnerable to misery.

Family members, on the other hand, are certainly significant in our lives. In fact, family should be a priority in our lives. Yet even a marriage can't be the ultimate place to look for security and happiness. That's too much pressure to put on a marriage. Happiness and security must come from something that can never leave or forsake a person.

When our first baby arrived, she turned our home into a foreign land. We were exhausted and didn't have hardly any time alone together. Intimacy seemed non- ... his was a time that we learned ... d's Word in a more intense way ... efore, believing that he would ... of happiness.

... similar lesson we learn from

Joseph. He grew up in a wealthy family where his doting father met his needs. Then one day to his shock he lost it all. Joseph's jealous brothers sold him into slavery. In one moment Joseph lost his things and his family.

During that long journey to Egypt, Joseph had to decide who or what he trusted. In good circumstances and in bad, where did he place his trust? Perhaps if it weren't for the difficult circumstances in that foreign land, Joseph would have never learned that he must focus on trusting God and God alone. Even though life came crashing down, Joseph knew he could trust God (see verse 20).

When life tries to harm you, God will use it for good to accomplish what he wants in your life and that "in all things God works for the good of those who love him" (Romans 8:28, page 1227). When you are in circumstances that seem to place you in that "foreign land," remember to place your trust in God alone.   —**Bob & Rosemary**

Go to page 63 for your next devotional reading.

emn ceremony of mourning." That is why that place near the Jordan is called Abel Mizraim.[a]

¹²So Jacob's sons did as he had commanded them: ¹³They carried him to the land of Canaan and buried him in the cave in the field of Machpelah, near Mamre, which Abraham had bought as a burial place from Ephron the Hittite, along with the field. ¹⁴After burying his father, Joseph returned to Egypt, together with his brothers and all the others who had gone with him to bury his father.

Joseph Reassures His Brothers

¹⁵When Joseph's brothers saw that their father was dead, they said, "What if Joseph holds a grudge against us and pays us back for all the wrongs we did to him?" ¹⁶So they sent word to Joseph, saying, "Your father left these instructions before he died: ¹⁷'This is what you are to say to Joseph: I ask you to forgive your brothers the sins and the wrongs they committed in treating you so badly.' Now please forgive the sins of the servants of the God of your father." When their message came to him, Joseph wept.

¹⁸His brothers then came and threw themselves down before him. "We are your slaves," they said.

¹⁹But Joseph said to them, "Don't be afraid. Am I in the place of God? ²⁰You intended to harm me, but God intended it for good to accomplish what is now being done, the saving of many lives. ²¹So then, don't be afraid. I will provide for you and your children." And he reassured them and spoke kindly to them.

The Death of Joseph

²²Joseph stayed in Egypt, along with all his father's family. He lived a hundred and ten years ²³and saw the third generation of Ephraim's children. Also the children of Makir son of Manasseh were placed at birth on Joseph's knees.[b]

²⁴Then Joseph said to his brothers, "I am about to die. But God will surely come to your aid and take you up out of this land to the land he promised on oath to Abraham, Isaac and Jacob." ²⁵And Joseph made the sons of Israel swear an oath and said, "God will surely come to your aid, and then you must carry my bones up from this place."

²⁶So Joseph died at the age of a hundred and ten. And after they embalmed him, he was placed in a coffin in Egypt.

a 11 Abel Mizraim means *mourning of the Egyptians.*
b 23 That is, were counted as his

Exodus

Moses tried to convince Pharaoh to release the millions of Israelites being held captive in his country. But Pharaoh thought he'd be a fool if he agreed. Why would he knowingly give up the cheap labor these slaves provided for his booming economy? Unfortunately for the Egyptians, letting the Israelites go wasn't just Moses' idea. It was also God's idea.

The book of Exodus is about discovering what it means to hear and to obey your heavenly Father. Listening to God may have something to do with moving by faith out of familiar surroundings into strange new territory, as it did with Moses and his people; or it may mean being faithful right where you are. In either case, the stories in Exodus ought to make one lesson clear: When it comes time to make a decision, a person can either obey God or plan on running into a lot of trouble.

The Israelites Oppressed

1 These are the names of the sons of Israel who went to Egypt with Jacob, each with his family: ²Reuben, Simeon, Levi and Judah; ³Issachar, Zebulun and Benjamin; ⁴Dan and Naphtali; Gad and Asher. ⁵The descendants of Jacob numbered seventy[a] in all; Joseph was already in Egypt.

⁶Now Joseph and all his brothers and all that generation died, ⁷but the Israelites were fruitful and multiplied greatly and became exceedingly numerous, so that the land was filled with them.

⁸Then a new king, who did not know about Joseph, came to power in Egypt. ⁹"Look," he said to his people, "the Israelites have become much too numerous for us. ¹⁰Come, we must deal shrewdly with them or they will become even more numerous and, if war breaks out, will join our enemies, fight against us and leave the country."

¹¹So they put slave masters over them to oppress them with forced labor, and

[a]5 Masoretic Text (see also Gen. 46:27); Dead Sea Scrolls and Septuagint (see also Acts 7:14 and note at Gen. 46:27) *seventy-five*

they built Pithom and Rameses as store cities for Pharaoh. [12]But the more they were oppressed, the more they multiplied and spread; so the Egyptians came to dread the Israelites [13]and worked them ruthlessly. [14]They made their lives bitter with hard labor in brick and mortar and with all kinds of work in the fields; in all their hard labor the Egyptians used them ruthlessly.

[15]The king of Egypt said to the Hebrew midwives, whose names were Shiphrah and Puah, [16]"When you help the Hebrew women in childbirth and observe them on the delivery stool, if it is a boy, kill him; but if it is a girl, let her live." [17]The midwives, however, feared God and did not do what the king of Egypt had told them to do; they let the boys live. [18]Then the king of Egypt summoned the midwives and asked them, "Why have you done this? Why have you let the boys live?"

[19]The midwives answered Pharaoh, "Hebrew women are not like Egyptian women; they are vigorous and give birth before the midwives arrive."

[20]So God was kind to the midwives and the people increased and became even more numerous. [21]And because the midwives feared God, he gave them families of their own.

[22]Then Pharaoh gave this order to all his people: "Every boy that is born[a] you must throw into the Nile, but let every girl live."

The Birth of Moses

2 Now a man of the house of Levi married a Levite woman, [2]and she became pregnant and gave birth to a son. When she saw that he was a fine child, she hid him for three months. [3]But when she could hide him no longer, she got a papyrus basket for him and coated it with tar and pitch. Then she placed the child in it and put it among the reeds along the bank of the Nile. [4]His sister stood at a distance to see what would happen to him.

[5]Then Pharaoh's daughter went down to the Nile to bathe, and her attendants were walking along the river bank. She saw the basket among the reeds and sent her slave girl to get it. [6]She opened it and saw the baby. He was crying, and she felt

sorry for him. "This is one of the Hebrew babies," she said.

[7]Then his sister asked Pharaoh's daughter, "Shall I go and get one of the Hebrew women to nurse the baby for you?"

[8]"Yes, go," she answered. And the girl went and got the baby's mother. [9]Pharaoh's daughter said to her, "Take this baby and nurse him for me, and I will pay you." So the woman took the baby and nursed him. [10]When the child grew older, she took him to Pharaoh's daughter and he became her son. She named him Moses,[b] saying, "I drew him out of the water."

Moses Flees to Midian

[11]One day, after Moses had grown up, he went out to where his own people were and watched them at their hard labor. He saw an Egyptian beating a Hebrew, one of his own people. [12]Glancing this way and that and seeing no one, he killed the Egyptian and hid him in the sand. [13]The next day he went out and saw two Hebrews fighting. He asked the one in the wrong, "Why are you hitting your fellow Hebrew?"

[14]The man said, "Who made you ruler and judge over us? Are you thinking of killing me as you killed the Egyptian?" Then Moses was afraid and thought, "What I did must have become known."

[15]When Pharaoh heard of this, he tried to kill Moses, but Moses fled from Pharaoh and went to live in Midian, where he sat down by a well. [16]Now a priest of Midian had seven daughters, and they came to draw water and fill the troughs to water their father's flock. [17]Some shepherds came along and drove them away, but Moses got up and came to their rescue and watered their flock.

[18]When the girls returned to Reuel their father, he asked them, "Why have you returned so early today?"

[19]They answered, "An Egyptian rescued us from the shepherds. He even drew water for us and watered the flock."

[20]"And where is he?" he asked his

a 22 Masoretic Text; Samaritan Pentateuch, Septuagint and Targums *born to the Hebrews*
b 10 Moses sounds like the Hebrew for *draw out.*

Amram and Jochebed

EXODUS 2:1–10 Becoming parents puts pressure on any marriage, but consider the pressure faced by Amram and Jochebed, the parents of Moses. Living in bondage and in a state of absolute helplessness and despair, Amram and Jochebed chose to trust in God's faithfulness to his covenant. How would you feel if you were having a baby and knew if he were a boy, he would be killed? Would you pray for a girl? What kind of pressure would this put on your marriage? Imagine the fear and anxiety Amram and Jochebed must have felt when the midwife told them they had a little boy baby. While we know little about the relationship between Amram and Jochebed, we can imagine the importance of loving and supporting each other during this trying time. Realizing the only chance of saving Moses was giving him away, Jochebed put their three-month old son in a basket and floated him down the Nile and prayed for God's protection.

Just as having a child stresses a marriage, losing a child is an even greater stress. But imagine their joy when Pharaoh's daughter unknowingly returned Moses to his family to be nursed and cared for. In their up-and-down family life, we would guess that their love for God and for each other helped them through the hard times. We can all admire their bravery and creativity that resulted in the protection of Moses who later played such an important role in Hebrew history.

daughters. "Why did you leave him? Invite him to have something to eat."

²¹Moses agreed to stay with the man, who gave his daughter Zipporah to Moses in marriage. ²²Zipporah gave birth to a son, and Moses named him Gershom,^{a} saying, "I have become an alien in a foreign land."

²³During that long period, the king of Egypt died. The Israelites groaned in their slavery and cried out, and their cry for help because of their slavery went up to God. ²⁴God heard their groaning and he remembered his covenant with Abraham, with Isaac and with Jacob. ²⁵So God looked on the Israelites and was concerned about them.

Moses and the Burning Bush

3 Now Moses was tending the flock of Jethro his father-in-law, the priest of Midian, and he led the flock to the far side of the desert and came to Horeb, the mountain of God. ²There the angel of the LORD appeared to him in flames of fire from within a bush. Moses saw that though the bush was on fire it did not burn up. ³So Moses thought, "I will go over and see this strange sight—why the bush does not burn up."

⁴When the LORD saw that he had gone over to look, God called to him from within the bush, "Moses! Moses!"

And Moses said, "Here I am."

⁵"Do not come any closer," God said. "Take off your sandals, for the place where you are standing is holy ground." ⁶Then he said, "I am the God of your father, the God of Abraham, the God of Isaac and the God of Jacob." At this, Moses hid his face, because he was afraid to look at God.

⁷The LORD said, "I have indeed seen the misery of my people in Egypt. I have heard them crying out because of their slave drivers, and I am concerned about their suffering. ⁸So I have come down to rescue them from the hand of the Egyptians and to bring them up out of that land into a good and spacious land, a land flowing with milk and honey—the home of the Canaanites, Hittites, Amorites, Perizzites, Hivites and Jebusites. ⁹And now the cry of the Israelites has reached me, and I have seen the way the Egyptians are oppressing them. ¹⁰So now, go. I am sending you to Pharaoh to bring my people the Israelites out of Egypt."

¹¹But Moses said to God, "Who am I, that I should go to Pharaoh and bring the Israelites out of Egypt?"

¹²And God said, "I will be with you. And this will be the sign to you that it is I who have sent you: When you have brought the people out of Egypt, you^b will worship God on this mountain."

¹³Moses said to God, "Suppose I go to

---

^{a}22 *Gershom* sounds like the Hebrew for *an alien there.* ^{b}12 The Hebrew is plural.

the Israelites and say to them, 'The God of your fathers has sent me to you,' and they ask me, 'What is his name?' Then what shall I tell them?"

¹⁴God said to Moses, "I AM WHO I AM.ᵃ This is what you are to say to the Israelites: 'I AM has sent me to you.' "

¹⁵God also said to Moses, "Say to the Israelites, 'The LORD,ᵇ the God of your fathers—the God of Abraham, the God of Isaac and the God of Jacob—has sent me to you.' This is my name forever, the name by which I am to be remembered from generation to generation.

¹⁶"Go, assemble the elders of Israel and say to them, 'The LORD, the God of your fathers—the God of Abraham, Isaac and Jacob—appeared to me and said: I have watched over you and have seen what has been done to you in Egypt. ¹⁷And I have promised to bring you up out of your misery in Egypt into the land of the Canaanites, Hittites, Amorites, Perizzites, Hivites and Jebusites—a land flowing with milk and honey.'

¹⁸"The elders of Israel will listen to you. Then you and the elders are to go to the king of Egypt and say to him, 'The LORD, the God of the Hebrews, has met with us. Let us take a three-day journey into the desert to offer sacrifices to the LORD our God.' ¹⁹But I know that the king of Egypt will not let you go unless a mighty hand compels him. ²⁰So I will stretch out my hand and strike the Egyptians with all the wonders that I will perform among them. After that, he will let you go.

²¹"And I will make the Egyptians favorably disposed toward this people, so that when you leave you will not go empty-handed. ²²Every woman is to ask her neighbor and any woman living in her house for articles of silver and gold and for clothing, which you will put on your sons and daughters. And so you will plunder the Egyptians."

ᵃ14 Or I WILL BE WHAT I WILL BE   ᵇ15 The Hebrew for LORD sounds like and may be derived from the Hebrew for I AM in verse 14.

Silence From Heaven

Friday

EXODUS 2:25 *Lord, are you listening? Do you see what I'm going through?* Haven't we all felt that at times? Especially when we feel like we have nowhere to turn. There are painful times in our marriages when we don't feel we can share the problems with anyone.

For example, there was a time when Bob was completely disinterested in our sexual relationship because he was greatly discouraged in his ministry. As a young wife, I didn't understand how this could affect him so much. Even though I was in such pain, I felt that this was too personal to share. I spent time praying, and it seemed like heaven was silent. For a long time there just didn't seem to be any improvement in our intimacy.

The children of Israel felt that same feeling that heaven was silent. They ". . . groaned in their slavery and cried out, and their cry for help because of their slavery went up to God" (verse 23). They must have

felt that, even though they were God's people, he had forgotten them or stopped listening. Yet we know that nothing could be further from the truth. God not only remembered them but also heard their groaning and looked on them with concern. Even though the Israelites didn't know it or see immediate evidence of it, God's great plan to deal with their desperate situation was already in motion. He was already answering their prayers through the preparation of their "deliverer" Moses.

What a great lesson for us when we are in difficult situations in our marriages—when we wonder if God is really hearing our prayers and seeing our needs. Just like his children in Egypt, God knows when you cry out to him. He sees, and he is concerned about you. He might already be in the process of answering your prayers.

—*Bob & Rosemary*

Go to page 66 for your next devotional reading.

Moses and Zipporah

EXODUS 2:21—4:18 Moses and Zipporah's marriage was cross-cultural. Moses met his wife in the foreign land of Midian where he fled after killing an Egyptian. Moses probably never intended to return to Egypt, but God had other plans. One day, as Moses was tending his father-in-law's flock, an angel appeared to him in a burning bush. Dramatically, God called Moses to return to Egypt and to lead his people out of bondage. Moses returned to Egypt with his wife and sons.

Cross-cultural marriages are more complicated, especially when the couple lives in a third culture. Though he grew up in Egypt, Moses identified with the Hebrew culture. Zipporah grew up in Midian. Even with God's help, we can imagine that they faced many challenges. Perhaps you have a cross-cultural marriage or maybe you and your spouse are from different backgrounds. Acknowledging these differences can enhance your relationship.

Not only was their marriage cross-cultural, but it was also, at times, long distance. When Moses was fighting the Amalekites, Zipporah, and their two sons returned to her father Jethro in Midian. We also know that Zipporah, with their sons and her father, visited Moses in the desert and that Moses willingly received advice from his father-in-law—something many are unwilling to do! When we look at marriages today, and all the complications with life in the twenty-first century, we can know God understands and is willing to meet all our special needs just as he did years ago for Moses and Zipporah.

Signs for Moses

4 Moses answered, "What if they do not believe me or listen to me and say, 'The LORD did not appear to you'?"

²Then the LORD said to him, "What is that in your hand?"

"A staff," he replied.

³The LORD said, "Throw it on the ground."

Moses threw it on the ground and it became a snake, and he ran from it. ⁴Then the LORD said to him, "Reach out your hand and take it by the tail." So Moses reached out and took hold of the snake and it turned back into a staff in his hand. ⁵"This," said the LORD, "is so that they may believe that the LORD, the God of their fathers—the God of Abraham, the God of Isaac and the God of Jacob—has appeared to you."

⁶Then the LORD said, "Put your hand inside your cloak." So Moses put his hand into his cloak, and when he took it out, it was leprous,ᵃ like snow.

⁷"Now put it back into your cloak," he said. So Moses put his hand back into his cloak, and when he took it out, it was restored, like the rest of his flesh.

⁸Then the LORD said, "If they do not believe you or pay attention to the first miraculous sign, they may believe the second. ⁹But if they do not believe these two signs or listen to you, take some water from the Nile and pour it on the dry ground. The water you take from the river will become blood on the ground."

¹⁰Moses said to the LORD, "O Lord, I have never been eloquent, neither in the past nor since you have spoken to your servant. I am slow of speech and tongue."

¹¹The LORD said to him, "Who gave man his mouth? Who makes him deaf or mute? Who gives him sight or makes him blind? Is it not I, the LORD? ¹²Now go; I will help you speak and will teach you what to say."

¹³But Moses said, "O Lord, please send someone else to do it."

¹⁴Then the LORD's anger burned against Moses and he said, "What about your brother, Aaron the Levite? I know he can speak well. He is already on his way to meet you, and his heart will be glad when he sees you. ¹⁵You shall speak to him and put words in his mouth; I will help both of you speak and will teach you what to do. ¹⁶He will speak to the people for you, and it will be as if he were your mouth and as if you were God to him. ¹⁷But take this staff in your hand so you can perform miraculous signs with it."

ᵃ6 The Hebrew word was used for various diseases affecting the skin—not necessarily leprosy.

Moses Returns to Egypt

18Then Moses went back to Jethro his father-in-law and said to him, "Let me go back to my own people in Egypt to see if any of them are still alive."

Jethro said, "Go, and I wish you well."

19Now the LORD had said to Moses in Midian, "Go back to Egypt, for all the men who wanted to kill you are dead." 20So Moses took his wife and sons, put them on a donkey and started back to Egypt. And he took the staff of God in his hand.

21The LORD said to Moses, "When you return to Egypt, see that you perform before Pharaoh all the wonders I have given you the power to do. But I will harden his heart so that he will not let the people go. 22Then say to Pharaoh, 'This is what the LORD says: Israel is my firstborn son, 23and I told you, "Let my son go, so he may worship me." But you refused to let him go; so I will kill your firstborn son.' "

24At a lodging place on the way, the LORD met ⌊Moses⌋ᵃ and was about to kill him. 25But Zipporah took a flint knife, cut off her son's foreskin and touched ⌊Moses'⌋ feet with it.ᵇ "Surely you are a bridegroom of blood to me," she said. 26So the LORD let him alone. (At that time she said "bridegroom of blood," referring to circumcision.)

27The LORD said to Aaron, "Go into the desert to meet Moses." So he met Moses at the mountain of God and kissed him. 28Then Moses told Aaron everything the LORD had sent him to say, and also about all the miraculous signs he had commanded him to perform.

29Moses and Aaron brought together all the elders of the Israelites, 30and Aaron told them everything the LORD had said to Moses. He also performed the signs before the people, 31and they believed. And when they heard that the LORD was concerned about them and had seen their misery, they bowed down and worshiped.

Bricks Without Straw

5 Afterward Moses and Aaron went to Pharaoh and said, "This is what the LORD, the God of Israel, says: 'Let my people go, so that they may hold a festival to me in the desert.' "

2Pharaoh said, "Who is the LORD, that I should obey him and let Israel go? I do not know the LORD and I will not let Israel go."

3Then they said, "The God of the Hebrews has met with us. Now let us take a three-day journey into the desert to offer sacrifices to the LORD our God, or he may strike us with plagues or with the sword."

4But the king of Egypt said, "Moses and Aaron, why are you taking the people away from their labor? Get back to your work!" 5Then Pharaoh said, "Look, the people of the land are now numerous, and you are stopping them from working."

6That same day Pharaoh gave this order to the slave drivers and foremen in charge of the people: 7"You are no longer to supply the people with straw for making bricks; let them go and gather their own straw. 8But require them to make the same number of bricks as before; don't reduce the quota. They are lazy; that is why they are crying out, 'Let us go and sacrifice to our God.' 9Make the work harder for the men so that they keep working and pay no attention to lies."

10Then the slave drivers and the foremen went out and said to the people, "This is what Pharaoh says: 'I will not give you any more straw. 11Go and get your own straw wherever you can find it, but your work will not be reduced at all.' " 12So the people scattered all over Egypt to gather stubble to use for straw. 13The slave drivers kept pressing them, saying, "Complete the work required of you for each day, just as when you had straw." 14The Israelite foremen appointed by Pharaoh's slave drivers were beaten and were asked, "Why didn't you meet your quota of bricks yesterday or today, as before?"

15Then the Israelite foremen went and appealed to Pharaoh: "Why have you treated your servants this way? 16Your servants are given no straw, yet we are told, 'Make bricks!' Your servants are being beaten, but the fault is with your own people."

17Pharaoh said, "Lazy, that's what you are—lazy! That is why you keep saying, 'Let us go and sacrifice to the LORD.' 18Now get to work. You will not be given

ᵃ24 Or ⌊Moses' son⌋; Hebrew him   ᵇ25 Or and drew near ⌊Moses'⌋ feet any straw, yet you must produce your full quota of bricks."

[19]The Israelite foremen realized they were in trouble when they were told, "You are not to reduce the number of bricks required of you for each day." [20]When they left Pharaoh, they found Moses and Aaron waiting to meet them, [21]and they said, "May the LORD look upon you and judge you! You have made us a stench to Pharaoh and his officials and have put a sword in their hand to kill us."

God Promises Deliverance

[22]Moses returned to the LORD and said, "O Lord, why have you brought trouble upon this people? Is this why you sent me? [23]Ever since I went to Pharaoh to speak in your name, he has brought trouble upon this people, and you have not rescued your people at all."

6 Then the LORD said to Moses, "Now you will see what I will do to Pharaoh: Because of my mighty hand he will let them go; because of my mighty hand he will drive them out of his country."

[2]God also said to Moses, "I am the LORD. [3]I appeared to Abraham, to Isaac and to Jacob as God Almighty,[a] but by my name the LORD[b] I did not make myself known to them.[c] [4]I also established my covenant with them to give them the land of Canaan, where they lived as aliens. [5]Moreover, I have heard the groan-

[a]3 Hebrew *El-Shaddai*   [b]3 See note at Exodus 3:15.   [c]3 Or *Almighty, and by my name the LORD did I not let myself be known to them?*

Bricks and Straw

EXODUS 5 Working conditions in Pharaoh's brick factory were already horrendous. Then he mandated that the Israelite brick makers gather their own straw. With the same required quota of bricks, getting enough straw became a huge problem. But they couldn't just decide not to use straw because the bricks wouldn't hold together; straw gives bricks texture and strength.

Taking this analogy and applying it to your relationship, ask yourself what is "the straw" in your marriage—what provides its texture and strength? The problems or obstacles you must overcome can actually be positive if you face them together.

When we consider our own marriage, we realize that we have grown closer and fortified our relationship more during the hard times than the easy times. During the seventies and early eighties we served as missionaries in Germany and Austria with Campus Crusade for Christ.

Our first year in Europe was the hardest year of our marriage. Moving to Germany with only six weeks notice with a baby, four- and six-year-old was traumatic. Then add no home for three months, no phone for eight months and no English-speaking friends. I was homesick. But Dave wasn't. He didn't understand how lonely I was. During those first few months we struggled in our relationship, but ultimately those struggles brought us closer together. We recommitted ourselves to each other, and our marriage became stronger.

What problems are you facing in your marriage? If you can look at them as "straws" rather than as problems, then together you can overcome them and strengthen your relationship. Remember that the Israelites were not alone in their problems. You may not have Moses and Aaron to represent you, but you do have God Almighty, who wants to empower your marriage and make it a model for others to follow.   —**Dave & Claudia**

Weekend Warm-up   *How do you handle problems as a couple?*

Go to page 77 for your next devotional reading.

ing of the Israelites, whom the Egyptians are enslaving, and I have remembered my covenant.

⁶"Therefore, say to the Israelites: 'I am the LORD, and I will bring you out from under the yoke of the Egyptians. I will free you from being slaves to them, and I will redeem you with an outstretched arm and with mighty acts of judgment. ⁷I will take you as my own people, and I will be your God. Then you will know that I am the LORD your God, who brought you out from under the yoke of the Egyptians. ⁸And I will bring you to the land I swore with uplifted hand to give to Abraham, to Isaac and to Jacob. I will give it to you as a possession. I am the LORD.' "

⁹Moses reported this to the Israelites, but they did not listen to him because of their discouragement and cruel bondage. ¹⁰Then the LORD said to Moses, ¹¹"Go, tell Pharaoh king of Egypt to let the Israelites go out of his country."

¹²But Moses said to the LORD, "If the Israelites will not listen to me, why would Pharaoh listen to me, since I speak with faltering lips*a*?"

Family Record of Moses and Aaron

¹³Now the LORD spoke to Moses and Aaron about the Israelites and Pharaoh king of Egypt, and he commanded them to bring the Israelites out of Egypt.

¹⁴These were the heads of their families*b*:

The sons of Reuben the firstborn son of Israel were Hanoch and Pallu, Hezron and Carmi. These were the clans of Reuben.

¹⁵The sons of Simeon were Jemuel, Jamin, Ohad, Jakin, Zohar and Shaul the son of a Canaanite woman. These were the clans of Simeon.

¹⁶These were the names of the sons of Levi according to their records: Gershon, Kohath and Merari. Levi lived 137 years.

¹⁷The sons of Gershon, by clans, were Libni and Shimei.

¹⁸The sons of Kohath were Amram, Izhar, Hebron and Uzziel. Kohath lived 133 years.

¹⁹The sons of Merari were Mahli and Mushi.

These were the clans of Levi according to their records.

²⁰Amram married his father's sister Jochebed, who bore him Aaron and Moses. Amram lived 137 years.

²¹The sons of Izhar were Korah, Nepheg and Zicri.

²²The sons of Uzziel were Mishael, Elzaphan and Sithri.

²³Aaron married Elisheba, daughter of Amminadab and sister of Nahshon, and she bore him Nadab and Abihu, Eleazar and Ithamar.

²⁴The sons of Korah were Assir, Elkanah and Abiasaph. These were the Korahite clans.

²⁵Eleazar son of Aaron married one of the daughters of Putiel, and she bore him Phinehas.

These were the heads of the Levite families, clan by clan.

²⁶It was this same Aaron and Moses to whom the LORD said, "Bring the Israelites out of Egypt by their divisions." ²⁷They were the ones who spoke to Pharaoh king of Egypt about bringing the Israelites out of Egypt. It was the same Moses and Aaron.

Aaron to Speak for Moses

²⁸Now when the LORD spoke to Moses in Egypt, ²⁹he said to him, "I am the LORD. Tell Pharaoh king of Egypt everything I tell you."

³⁰But Moses said to the LORD, "Since I speak with faltering lips, why would Pharaoh listen to me?"

7 Then the LORD said to Moses, "See, I have made you like God to Pharaoh, and your brother Aaron will be your prophet. ²You are to say everything I command you, and your brother Aaron is to tell Pharaoh to let the Israelites go out of his country. ³But I will harden Pharaoh's heart, and though I multiply my miraculous signs and wonders in Egypt, ⁴he will not listen to you. Then I will lay my hand on Egypt and with mighty acts of judgment I will bring out my divisions, my people the Israelites. ⁵And the Egyptians will know that I am the LORD when I

---

*a*12 Hebrew *I am uncircumcised of lips*; also in verse 30   *b*14 The Hebrew for *families* here and in verse 25 refers to units larger than clans.

stretch out my hand against Egypt and bring the Israelites out of it."

⁶Moses and Aaron did just as the LORD commanded them. ⁷Moses was eighty years old and Aaron eighty-three when they spoke to Pharaoh.

Aaron's Staff Becomes a Snake

⁸The LORD said to Moses and Aaron, ⁹"When Pharaoh says to you, 'Perform a miracle,' then say to Aaron, 'Take your staff and throw it down before Pharaoh,' and it will become a snake."

¹⁰So Moses and Aaron went to Pharaoh and did just as the LORD commanded. Aaron threw his staff down in front of Pharaoh and his officials, and it became a snake. ¹¹Pharaoh then summoned wise men and sorcerers, and the Egyptian magicians also did the same things by their secret arts: ¹²Each one threw down his staff and it became a snake. But Aaron's staff swallowed up their staffs. ¹³Yet Pharaoh's heart became hard and he would not listen to them, just as the LORD had said.

The Plague of Blood

¹⁴Then the LORD said to Moses, "Pharaoh's heart is unyielding; he refuses to let the people go. ¹⁵Go to Pharaoh in the morning as he goes out to the water. Wait on the bank of the Nile to meet him, and take in your hand the staff that was changed into a snake. ¹⁶Then say to him, 'The LORD, the God of the Hebrews, has sent me to say to you: Let my people go, so that they may worship me in the desert. But until now you have not listened. ¹⁷This is what the LORD says: By this you will know that I am the LORD: With the staff that is in my hand I will strike the water of the Nile, and it will be changed into blood. ¹⁸The fish in the Nile will die, and the river will stink; the Egyptians will not be able to drink its water.' "

¹⁹The LORD said to Moses, "Tell Aaron, 'Take your staff and stretch out your hand over the waters of Egypt—over the streams and canals, over the ponds and all the reservoirs'—and they will turn to blood. Blood will be everywhere in Egypt, even in the wooden buckets and stone jars."

²⁰Moses and Aaron did just as the LORD had commanded. He raised his staff in the presence of Pharaoh and his officials and struck the water of the Nile, and all the water was changed into blood. ²¹The fish in the Nile died, and the river smelled so bad that the Egyptians could not drink its water. Blood was everywhere in Egypt.

²²But the Egyptian magicians did the same things by their secret arts, and Pharaoh's heart became hard; he would not listen to Moses and Aaron, just as the LORD had said. ²³Instead, he turned and went into his palace, and did not take even this to heart. ²⁴And all the Egyptians dug along the Nile to get drinking water, because they could not drink the water of the river.

The Plague of Frogs

²⁵Seven days passed after the LORD struck the Nile. ¹Then the LORD said to Moses, "Go to Pharaoh and say to him, 'This is what the LORD says: Let my people go, so that they may worship me. ²If you refuse to let them go, I will plague your whole country with frogs. ³The Nile will teem with frogs. They will come up into your palace and your bedroom and onto your bed, into the houses of your officials and on your people, and into your ovens and kneading troughs. ⁴The frogs will go up on you and your people and all your officials.' "

⁵Then the LORD said to Moses, "Tell Aaron, 'Stretch out your hand with your staff over the streams and canals and ponds, and make frogs come up on the land of Egypt.' "

⁶So Aaron stretched out his hand over the waters of Egypt, and the frogs came up and covered the land. ⁷But the magicians did the same things by their secret arts; they also made frogs come up on the land of Egypt.

⁸Pharaoh summoned Moses and Aaron and said, "Pray to the LORD to take the frogs away from me and my people, and I will let your people go to offer sacrifices to the LORD."

⁹Moses said to Pharaoh, "I leave to you the honor of setting the time for me to pray for you and your officials and your people that you and your houses may be rid of the frogs, except for those that remain in the Nile."

¹⁰"Tomorrow," Pharaoh said.

Moses replied, "It will be as you say, so that you may know there is no one like the LORD our God. [11]The frogs will leave you and your houses, your officials and your people; they will remain only in the Nile."

[12]After Moses and Aaron left Pharaoh, Moses cried out to the LORD about the frogs he had brought on Pharaoh. [13]And the LORD did what Moses asked. The frogs died in the houses, in the courtyards and in the fields. [14]They were piled into heaps, and the land reeked of them. [15]But when Pharaoh saw that there was relief, he hardened his heart and would not listen to Moses and Aaron, just as the LORD had said.

The Plague of Gnats

[16]Then the LORD said to Moses, "Tell Aaron, 'Stretch out your staff and strike the dust of the ground,' and throughout the land of Egypt the dust will become gnats." [17]They did this, and when Aaron stretched out his hand with the staff and struck the dust of the ground, gnats came upon men and animals. All the dust throughout the land of Egypt became gnats. [18]But when the magicians tried to produce gnats by their secret arts, they could not. And the gnats were on men and animals.

[19]The magicians said to Pharaoh, "This is the finger of God." But Pharaoh's heart was hard and he would not listen, just as the LORD had said.

The Plague of Flies

[20]Then the LORD said to Moses, "Get up early in the morning and confront Pharaoh as he goes to the water and say to him, 'This is what the LORD says: Let my people go, so that they may worship me. [21]If you do not let my people go, I will send swarms of flies on you and your officials, on your people and into your houses. The houses of the Egyptians will be full of flies, and even the ground where they are.

[22]" 'But on that day I will deal differently with the land of Goshen, where my people live; no swarms of flies will be there, so that you will know that I, the LORD, am in this land. [23]I will make a distinction[a] between my people and

your people. This miraculous sign will occur tomorrow.' "

[24]And the LORD did this. Dense swarms of flies poured into Pharaoh's palace and into the houses of his officials, and throughout Egypt the land was ruined by the flies.

[25]Then Pharaoh summoned Moses and Aaron and said, "Go, sacrifice to your God here in the land."

[26]But Moses said, "That would not be right. The sacrifices we offer the LORD our God would be detestable to the Egyptians. And if we offer sacrifices that are detestable in their eyes, will they not stone us? [27]We must take a three-day journey into the desert to offer sacrifices to the LORD our God, as he commands us."

[28]Pharaoh said, "I will let you go to offer sacrifices to the LORD your God in the desert, but you must not go very far. Now pray for me."

[29]Moses answered, "As soon as I leave you, I will pray to the LORD, and tomorrow the flies will leave Pharaoh and his officials and his people. Only be sure that Pharaoh does not act deceitfully again by not letting the people go to offer sacrifices to the LORD."

[30]Then Moses left Pharaoh and prayed to the LORD, [31]and the LORD did what Moses asked: The flies left Pharaoh and his officials and his people; not a fly remained. [32]But this time also Pharaoh hardened his heart and would not let the people go.

The Plague on Livestock

9 Then the LORD said to Moses, "Go to Pharaoh and say to him, 'This is what the LORD, the God of the Hebrews, says: "Let my people go, so that they may worship me." [2]If you refuse to let them go and continue to hold them back, [3]the hand of the LORD will bring a terrible plague on your livestock in the field—on your horses and donkeys and camels and on your cattle and sheep and goats. [4]But the LORD will make a distinction between the livestock of Israel and that of Egypt, so that no animal belonging to the Israelites will die.' "

[5]The LORD set a time and said, "To-

[a]23 Septuagint and Vulgate; Hebrew will put a deliverance

morrow the LORD will do this in the land."
[6]And the next day the LORD did it: All the
livestock of the Egyptians died, but not
one animal belonging to the Israelites
died. [7]Pharaoh sent men to investigate
and found that not even one of the animals of the Israelites had died. Yet his
heart was unyielding and he would not
let the people go.

The Plague of Boils

[8]Then the LORD said to Moses and Aaron, "Take handfuls of soot from a furnace
and have Moses toss it into the air in the
presence of Pharaoh. [9]It will become fine
dust over the whole land of Egypt, and
festering boils will break out on men and
animals throughout the land."

[10]So they took soot from a furnace and
stood before Pharaoh. Moses tossed it
into the air, and festering boils broke out
on men and animals. [11]The magicians
could not stand before Moses because of
the boils that were on them and on all the
Egyptians. [12]But the LORD hardened Pharaoh's heart and he would not listen to
Moses and Aaron, just as the LORD had
said to Moses.

The Plague of Hail

[13]Then the LORD said to Moses, "Get
up early in the morning, confront Pharaoh and say to him, 'This is what the
LORD, the God of the Hebrews, says: Let
my people go, so that they may worship
me, [14]or this time I will send the full force
of my plagues against you and against
your officials and your people, so you
may know that there is no one like me in
all the earth. [15]For by now I could have
stretched out my hand and struck you and
your people with a plague that would
have wiped you off the earth. [16]But I have
raised you up[a] for this very purpose, that
I might show you my power and that my
name might be proclaimed in all the
earth. [17]You still set yourself against my
people and will not let them go. [18]There-
fore, at this time tomorrow I will send the
worst hailstorm that has ever fallen on
Egypt, from the day it was founded till
now. [19]Give an order now to bring your
livestock and everything you have in the
field to a place of shelter, because the hail
will fall on every man and animal that has

not been brought in and is still out in the
field, and they will die.' "

[20]Those officials of Pharaoh who
feared the word of the LORD hurried to
bring their slaves and their livestock inside. [21]But those who ignored the word of
the LORD left their slaves and livestock in
the field.

[22]Then the LORD said to Moses,
"Stretch out your hand toward the sky so
that hail will fall all over Egypt—on men
and animals and on everything growing
in the fields of Egypt." [23]When Moses
stretched out his staff toward the sky, the
LORD sent thunder and hail, and lightning
flashed down to the ground. So the LORD
rained hail on the land of Egypt; [24]hail fell
and lightning flashed back and forth. It
was the worst storm in all the land of
Egypt since it had become a nation.
[25]Throughout Egypt hail struck everything in the fields—both men and animals; it beat down everything growing in
the fields and stripped every tree. [26]The
only place it did not hail was the land of
Goshen, where the Israelites were.

[27]Then Pharaoh summoned Moses
and Aaron. "This time I have sinned," he
said to them. "The LORD is in the right,
and I and my people are in the wrong.
[28]Pray to the LORD, for we have had
enough thunder and hail. I will let you
go; you don't have to stay any longer."

[29]Moses replied, "When I have gone
out of the city, I will spread out my hands
in prayer to the LORD. The thunder will
stop and there will be no more hail, so
you may know that the earth is the
LORD's. [30]But I know that you and your
officials still do not fear the LORD God."

[31](The flax and barley were destroyed,
since the barley had headed and the flax
was in bloom. [32]The wheat and spelt,
however, were not destroyed, because
they ripen later.)

[33]Then Moses left Pharaoh and went
out of the city. He spread out his hands
toward the LORD; the thunder and hail
stopped, and the rain no longer poured
down on the land. [34]When Pharaoh saw
that the rain and hail and thunder had
stopped, he sinned again: He and his officials hardened their hearts. [35]So Pharaoh's heart was hard and he would not let

[a]16 Or *have spared you*

the Israelites go, just as the LORD had said through Moses.

The Plague of Locusts

10 Then the LORD said to Moses, "Go to Pharaoh, for I have hardened his heart and the hearts of his officials so that I may perform these miraculous signs of mine among them ²that you may tell your children and grandchildren how I dealt harshly with the Egyptians and how I performed my signs among them, and that you may know that I am the LORD."

³So Moses and Aaron went to Pharaoh and said to him, "This is what the LORD, the God of the Hebrews, says: 'How long will you refuse to humble yourself before me? Let my people go, so that they may worship me. ⁴If you refuse to let them go, I will bring locusts into your country tomorrow. ⁵They will cover the face of the ground so that it cannot be seen. They will devour what little you have left after the hail, including every tree that is growing in your fields. ⁶They will fill your houses and those of all your officials and all the Egyptians—something neither your fathers nor your forefathers have ever seen from the day they settled in this land till now.'" Then Moses turned and left Pharaoh.

⁷Pharaoh's officials said to him, "How long will this man be a snare to us? Let the people go, so that they may worship the LORD their God. Do you not yet realize that Egypt is ruined?"

⁸Then Moses and Aaron were brought back to Pharaoh. "Go, worship the LORD your God," he said. "But just who will be going?"

⁹Moses answered, "We will go with our young and old, with our sons and daughters, and with our flocks and herds, because we are to celebrate a festival to the LORD."

¹⁰Pharaoh said, "The LORD be with you—if I let you go, along with your women and children! Clearly you are bent on evil.ᵃ ¹¹No! Have only the men go; and worship the LORD, since that's what you have been asking for." Then Moses and Aaron were driven out of Pharaoh's presence.

¹²And the LORD said to Moses, "Stretch out your hand over Egypt so that locusts will swarm over the land and devour everything growing in the fields, everything left by the hail."

¹³So Moses stretched out his staff over Egypt, and the LORD made an east wind blow across the land all that day and all that night. By morning the wind had brought the locusts; ¹⁴they invaded all Egypt and settled down in every area of the country in great numbers. Never before had there been such a plague of locusts, nor will there ever be again. ¹⁵They covered all the ground until it was black. They devoured all that was left after the hail—everything growing in the fields and the fruit on the trees. Nothing green remained on tree or plant in all the land of Egypt.

¹⁶Pharaoh quickly summoned Moses and Aaron and said, "I have sinned against the LORD your God and against you. ¹⁷Now forgive my sin once more and pray to the LORD your God to take this deadly plague away from me."

¹⁸Moses then left Pharaoh and prayed to the LORD. ¹⁹And the LORD changed the wind to a very strong west wind, which caught up the locusts and carried them into the Red Sea.ᵇ Not a locust was left anywhere in Egypt. ²⁰But the LORD hardened Pharaoh's heart, and he would not let the Israelites go.

The Plague of Darkness

²¹Then the LORD said to Moses, "Stretch out your hand toward the sky so that darkness will spread over Egypt—darkness that can be felt." ²²So Moses stretched out his hand toward the sky, and total darkness covered all Egypt for three days. ²³No one could see anyone else or leave his place for three days. Yet all the Israelites had light in the places where they lived.

²⁴Then Pharaoh summoned Moses and said, "Go, worship the LORD. Even your women and children may go with you; only leave your flocks and herds behind."

²⁵But Moses said, "You must allow us to have sacrifices and burnt offerings to

ᵃ10 Or *Be careful, trouble is in store for you!*
ᵇ19 Hebrew *Yam Suph*; that is, Sea of Reeds

present to the LORD our God. ²⁶Our livestock too must go with us; not a hoof is to be left behind. We have to use some of them in worshiping the LORD our God, and until we get there we will not know what we are to use to worship the LORD."

²⁷But the LORD hardened Pharaoh's heart, and he was not willing to let them go. ²⁸Pharaoh said to Moses, "Get out of my sight! Make sure you do not appear before me again! The day you see my face you will die."

²⁹"Just as you say," Moses replied, "I will never appear before you again."

The Plague on the Firstborn

11 Now the LORD had said to Moses, "I will bring one more plague on Pharaoh and on Egypt. After that, he will let you go from here, and when he does, he will drive you out completely. ²Tell the people that men and women alike are to ask their neighbors for articles of silver and gold." ³(The LORD made the Egyptians favorably disposed toward the people, and Moses himself was highly regarded in Egypt by Pharaoh's officials and by the people.)

⁴So Moses said, "This is what the LORD says: 'About midnight I will go throughout Egypt. ⁵Every firstborn son in Egypt will die, from the firstborn son of Pharaoh, who sits on the throne, to the firstborn son of the slave girl, who is at her hand mill, and all the firstborn of the cattle as well. ⁶There will be loud wailing throughout Egypt—worse than there has ever been or ever will be again. ⁷But among the Israelites not a dog will bark at any man or animal.' Then you will know that the LORD makes a distinction between Egypt and Israel. ⁸All these officials of yours will come to me, bowing down before me and saying, 'Go, you and all the people who follow you!' After that I will leave." Then Moses, hot with anger, left Pharaoh.

⁹The LORD had said to Moses, "Pharaoh will refuse to listen to you—so that my wonders may be multiplied in Egypt." ¹⁰Moses and Aaron performed all these wonders before Pharaoh, but the LORD hardened Pharaoh's heart, and he would not let the Israelites go out of his country.

The Passover

12 The LORD said to Moses and Aaron in Egypt, ²"This month is to be for you the first month, the first month of your year. ³Tell the whole community of Israel that on the tenth day of this month each man is to take a lamb*a* for his family, one for each household. ⁴If any household is too small for a whole lamb, they must share one with their nearest neighbor, having taken into account the number of people there are. You are to determine the amount of lamb needed in accordance with what each person will eat. ⁵The animals you choose must be year-old males without defect, and you may take them from the sheep or the goats. ⁶Take care of them until the fourteenth day of the month, when all the people of the community of Israel must slaughter them at twilight. ⁷Then they are to take some of the blood and put it on the sides and tops of the doorframes of the houses where they eat the lambs. ⁸That same night they are to eat the meat roasted over the fire, along with bitter herbs, and bread made without yeast. ⁹Do not eat the meat raw or cooked in water, but roast it over the fire—head, legs and inner parts. ¹⁰Do not leave any of it till morning; if some is left till morning, you must burn it. ¹¹This is how you are to eat it: with your cloak tucked into your belt, your sandals on your feet and your staff in your hand. Eat it in haste; it is the LORD's Passover.

¹²"On that same night I will pass through Egypt and strike down every firstborn—both men and animals—and I will bring judgment on all the gods of Egypt. I am the LORD. ¹³The blood will be a sign for you on the houses where you are; and when I see the blood, I will pass over you. No destructive plague will touch you when I strike Egypt.

¹⁴"This is a day you are to commemorate; for the generations to come you shall celebrate it as a festival to the LORD—a lasting ordinance. ¹⁵For seven days you are to eat bread made without yeast. On the first day remove the yeast from your houses, for whoever eats anything with yeast in it from the first day through the

---

a3 The Hebrew word can mean *lamb* or *kid*; also in verse 4.

seventh must be cut off from Israel. ¹⁶On the first day hold a sacred assembly, and another one on the seventh day. Do no work at all on these days, except to prepare food for everyone to eat—that is all you may do.

¹⁷"Celebrate the Feast of Unleavened Bread, because it was on this very day that I brought your divisions out of Egypt. Celebrate this day as a lasting ordinance for the generations to come. ¹⁸In the first month you are to eat bread made without yeast, from the evening of the fourteenth day until the evening of the twenty-first day. ¹⁹For seven days no yeast is to be found in your houses. And whoever eats anything with yeast in it must be cut off from the community of Israel, whether he is an alien or native-born. ²⁰Eat nothing made with yeast. Wherever you live, you must eat unleavened bread."

²¹Then Moses summoned all the elders of Israel and said to them, "Go at once and select the animals for your families and slaughter the Passover lamb. ²²Take a bunch of hyssop, dip it into the blood in the basin and put some of the blood on the top and on both sides of the doorframe. Not one of you shall go out the door of his house until morning. ²³When the LORD goes through the land to strike down the Egyptians, he will see the blood on the top and sides of the doorframe and will pass over that doorway, and he will not permit the destroyer to enter your houses and strike you down.

²⁴"Obey these instructions as a lasting ordinance for you and your descendants. ²⁵When you enter the land that the LORD will give you as he promised, observe this ceremony. ²⁶And when your children ask you, 'What does this ceremony mean to you?' ²⁷then tell them, 'It is the Passover sacrifice to the LORD, who passed over the houses of the Israelites in Egypt and spared our homes when he struck down the Egyptians.'" Then the people bowed down and worshiped. ²⁸The Israelites did just what the LORD commanded Moses and Aaron.

²⁹At midnight the LORD struck down all the firstborn in Egypt, from the firstborn of Pharaoh, who sat on the throne, to the firstborn of the prisoner, who was in the dungeon, and the firstborn of all the livestock as well. ³⁰Pharaoh and all his offi-cials and all the Egyptians got up during the night, and there was loud wailing in Egypt, for there was not a house without someone dead.

The Exodus

³¹During the night Pharaoh summoned Moses and Aaron and said, "Up! Leave my people, you and the Israelites! Go, worship the LORD as you have requested. ³²Take your flocks and herds, as you have said, and go. And also bless me."

³³The Egyptians urged the people to hurry and leave the country. "For otherwise," they said, "we will all die!" ³⁴So the people took their dough before the yeast was added, and carried it on their shoulders in kneading troughs wrapped in clothing. ³⁵The Israelites did as Moses instructed and asked the Egyptians for articles of silver and gold and for clothing. ³⁶The LORD had made the Egyptians favorably disposed toward the people, and they gave them what they asked for; so they plundered the Egyptians.

³⁷The Israelites journeyed from Rameses to Succoth. There were about six hundred thousand men on foot, besides women and children. ³⁸Many other people went up with them, as well as large droves of livestock, both flocks and herds. ³⁹With the dough they had brought from Egypt, they baked cakes of unleavened bread. The dough was without yeast because they had been driven out of Egypt and did not have time to prepare food for themselves.

⁴⁰Now the length of time the Israelite people lived in Egypt[a] was 430 years. ⁴¹At the end of the 430 years, to the very day, all the LORD's divisions left Egypt. ⁴²Because the LORD kept vigil that night to bring them out of Egypt, on this night all the Israelites are to keep vigil to honor the LORD for the generations to come.

Passover Restrictions

⁴³The LORD said to Moses and Aaron, "These are the regulations for the Passover:

"No foreigner is to eat of it. ⁴⁴Any slave you have bought may eat of it after you have circumcised him, ⁴⁵but a temporary

---

[a]40 Masoretic Text; Samaritan Pentateuch and Septuagint *Egypt and Canaan*

resident and a hired worker may not eat of it. ⁴⁶"It must be eaten inside one house; take none of the meat outside the house. Do not break any of the bones. ⁴⁷The whole community of Israel must celebrate it.

⁴⁸"An alien living among you who wants to celebrate the LORD's Passover must have all the males in his household circumcised; then he may take part like one born in the land. No uncircumcised male may eat of it. ⁴⁹The same law applies to the native-born and to the alien living among you."

⁵⁰All the Israelites did just what the LORD had commanded Moses and Aaron. ⁵¹And on that very day the LORD brought the Israelites out of Egypt by their divisions.

Consecration of the Firstborn

13 The LORD said to Moses, ²"Consecrate to me every firstborn male. The first offspring of every womb among the Israelites belongs to me, whether man or animal."

³Then Moses said to the people, "Commemorate this day, the day you came out of Egypt, out of the land of slavery, because the LORD brought you out of it with a mighty hand. Eat nothing containing yeast. ⁴Today, in the month of Abib, you are leaving. ⁵When the LORD brings you into the land of the Canaanites, Hittites, Amorites, Hivites and Jebusites—the land he swore to your forefathers to give you, a land flowing with milk and honey—you are to observe this ceremony in this month: ⁶For seven days eat bread made without yeast and on the seventh day hold a festival to the LORD. ⁷Eat unleavened bread during those seven days; nothing with yeast in it is to be seen among you, nor shall any yeast be seen anywhere within your borders. ⁸On that day tell your son, 'I do this because of what the LORD did for me when I came out of Egypt.' ⁹This observance will be for you like a sign on your hand and a reminder on your forehead that the law of the LORD is to be on your lips. For the LORD brought you out of Egypt with his mighty hand. ¹⁰You must keep this ordinance at the appointed time year after year.

¹¹"After the LORD brings you into the land of the Canaanites and gives it to you, as he promised on oath to you and your forefathers, ¹²you are to give over to the LORD the first offspring of every womb. All the firstborn males of your livestock belong to the LORD. ¹³Redeem with a lamb every firstborn donkey, but if you do not redeem it, break its neck. Redeem every firstborn among your sons.

¹⁴"In days to come, when your son asks you, 'What does this mean?' say to him, 'With a mighty hand the LORD brought us out of Egypt, out of the land of slavery. ¹⁵When Pharaoh stubbornly refused to let us go, the LORD killed every firstborn in Egypt, both man and animal. This is why I sacrifice to the LORD the first male offspring of every womb and redeem each of my firstborn sons.' ¹⁶And it will be like a sign on your hand and a symbol on your forehead that the LORD brought us out of Egypt with his mighty hand."

Crossing the Sea

¹⁷When Pharaoh let the people go, God did not lead them on the road through the Philistine country, though that was shorter. For God said, "If they face war, they might change their minds and return to Egypt." ¹⁸So God led the people around by the desert road toward the Red Sea.ᵃ The Israelites went up out of Egypt armed for battle.

¹⁹Moses took the bones of Joseph with him because Joseph had made the sons of Israel swear an oath. He had said, "God will surely come to your aid, and then you must carry my bones up with you from this place."ᵇ

²⁰After leaving Succoth they camped at Etham on the edge of the desert. ²¹By day the LORD went ahead of them in a pillar of cloud to guide them on their way and by night in a pillar of fire to give them light, so that they could travel by day or night. ²²Neither the pillar of cloud by day nor the pillar of fire by night left its place in front of the people.

ᵃ18 Hebrew *Yam Suph*; that is, Sea of Reeds
ᵇ19 See Gen. 50:25.

14 Then the LORD said to Moses, 2"Tell the Israelites to turn back and encamp near Pi Hahiroth, between Migdol and the sea. They are to encamp by the sea, directly opposite Baal Zephon. 3Pharaoh will think, 'The Israelites are wandering around the land in confusion, hemmed in by the desert.' 4And I will harden Pharaoh's heart, and he will pursue them. But I will gain glory for myself through Pharaoh and all his army, and the Egyptians will know that I am the LORD." So the Israelites did this.

5When the king of Egypt was told that the people had fled, Pharaoh and his officials changed their minds about them and said, "What have we done? We have let the Israelites go and have lost their services!" 6So he had his chariot made ready and took his army with him. 7He took six hundred of the best chariots, along with all the other chariots of Egypt, with officers over all of them. 8The LORD hardened the heart of Pharaoh king of Egypt, so that he pursued the Israelites, who were marching out boldly. 9The Egyptians—all Pharaoh's horses and chariots, horsemen*a* and troops—pursued the Israelites and overtook them as they camped by the sea near Pi Hahiroth, opposite Baal Zephon.

10As Pharaoh approached, the Israelites looked up, and there were the Egyptians, marching after them. They were terrified and cried out to the LORD. 11They said to Moses, "Was it because there were no graves in Egypt that you brought us to the desert to die? What have you done to us by bringing us out of Egypt? 12Didn't we say to you in Egypt, 'Leave us alone; let us serve the Egyptians'? It would have been better for us to serve the Egyptians than to die in the desert!"

13Moses answered the people, "Do not be afraid. Stand firm and you will see the deliverance the LORD will bring you today. The Egyptians you see today you will never see again. 14The LORD will fight for you; you need only to be still."

15Then the LORD said to Moses, "Why are you crying out to me? Tell the Israelites to move on. 16Raise your staff and stretch out your hand over the sea to divide the water so that the Israelites can go through the sea on dry ground. 17I will harden the hearts of the Egyptians so that they will go in after them. And I will gain glory through Pharaoh and all his army, through his chariots and his horsemen. 18The Egyptians will know that I am the LORD when I gain glory through Pharaoh, his chariots and his horsemen."

19Then the angel of God, who had been traveling in front of Israel's army, withdrew and went behind them. The pillar of cloud also moved from in front and stood behind them, 20coming between the armies of Egypt and Israel. Throughout the night the cloud brought darkness to the one side and light to the other side; so neither went near the other all night long.

21Then Moses stretched out his hand over the sea, and all that night the LORD drove the sea back with a strong east wind and turned it into dry land. The waters were divided, 22and the Israelites went through the sea on dry ground, with a wall of water on their right and on their left.

23The Egyptians pursued them, and all Pharaoh's horses and chariots and horsemen followed them into the sea. 24During the last watch of the night the LORD looked down from the pillar of fire and cloud at the Egyptian army and threw it into confusion. 25He made the wheels of their chariots come off*b* so that they had difficulty driving. And the Egyptians said, "Let's get away from the Israelites! The LORD is fighting for them against Egypt."

26Then the LORD said to Moses, "Stretch out your hand over the sea so that the waters may flow back over the Egyptians and their chariots and horsemen." 27Moses stretched out his hand over the sea, and at daybreak the sea went back to its place. The Egyptians were fleeing toward*c* it, and the LORD swept them into the sea. 28The water flowed back and covered the chariots and horsemen—the entire army of Pharaoh that had followed the Israelites into the sea. Not one of them survived.

29But the Israelites went through the sea on dry ground, with a wall of water on their right and on their left. 30That day the LORD saved Israel from the hands of the

a9 Or charioteers; also in verses 17, 18, 23, 26 and 28 *b25 Or He jammed the wheels of their chariots* (see Samaritan Pentateuch, Septuagint and Syriac) *c27 Or from*

Egyptians, and Israel saw the Egyptians lying dead on the shore. ³¹And when the Israelites saw the great power the LORD displayed against the Egyptians, the people feared the LORD and put their trust in him and in Moses his servant.

The Song of Moses and Miriam

15 Then Moses and the Israelites sang this song to the LORD:

"I will sing to the LORD,
  for he is highly exalted.
The horse and its rider
  he has hurled into the sea.
²The LORD is my strength and my
    song;
  he has become my salvation.
He is my God, and I will praise him,
  my father's God, and I will exalt
    him.
³The LORD is a warrior;
  the LORD is his name.
⁴Pharaoh's chariots and his army
  he has hurled into the sea.
The best of Pharaoh's officers
  are drowned in the Red Sea.ᵃ
⁵The deep waters have covered them;
  they sank to the depths like a
    stone.

⁶"Your right hand, O LORD,
  was majestic in power.
Your right hand, O LORD,
  shattered the enemy.
⁷In the greatness of your majesty
  you threw down those who
    opposed you.
You unleashed your burning anger;
  it consumed them like stubble.
⁸By the blast of your nostrils
  the waters piled up.
The surging waters stood firm like a
    wall;
  the deep waters congealed in the
    heart of the sea.

⁹"The enemy boasted,
  'I will pursue, I will overtake them.
I will divide the spoils;
  I will gorge myself on them.
I will draw my sword
  and my hand will destroy them.'
¹⁰But you blew with your breath,
  and the sea covered them.
They sank like lead
  in the mighty waters.

¹¹"Who among the gods is like you,
  O LORD?
Who is like you—
  majestic in holiness,
  awesome in glory,
  working wonders?
¹²You stretched out your right hand
  and the earth swallowed them.

¹³"In your unfailing love you will lead
  the people you have redeemed.
In your strength you will guide them
  to your holy dwelling.
¹⁴The nations will hear and tremble;
  anguish will grip the people of
    Philistia.
¹⁵The chiefs of Edom will be terrified,
  the leaders of Moab will be seized
    with trembling,
the peopleᵇ of Canaan will melt
    away;
¹⁶ terror and dread will fall upon
    them.
By the power of your arm
  they will be as still as a stone—
until your people pass by, O LORD,
  until the people you boughtᶜ pass
    by.
¹⁷You will bring them in and plant
    them
  on the mountain of your
    inheritance—
the place, O LORD, you made for your
    dwelling,
  the sanctuary, O Lord, your hands
    established.
¹⁸The LORD will reign
  for ever and ever."

¹⁹When Pharaoh's horses, chariots and horsemenᵈ went into the sea, the LORD brought the waters of the sea back over them, but the Israelites walked through the sea on dry ground. ²⁰Then Miriam the prophetess, Aaron's sister, took a tambourine in her hand, and all the women followed her, with tambourines and dancing. ²¹Miriam sang to them:

"Sing to the LORD,
  for he is highly exalted.

ᵃ4 Hebrew Yam Suph; that is, Sea of Reeds; also in verse 22   ᵇ15 Or rulers   ᶜ16 Or created
ᵈ19 Or charioteers

The horse and its rider
　　he has hurled into the sea."

The Waters of Marah and Elim

22Then Moses led Israel from the Red Sea and they went into the Desert of Shur. For three days they traveled in the desert without finding water. 23When they came to Marah, they could not drink its water because it was bitter. (That is why the place is called Marah.ᵃ) 24So the people grumbled against Moses, saying, "What are we to drink?"

25Then Moses cried out to the LORD, and the LORD showed him a piece of wood. He threw it into the water, and the water became sweet.

There the LORD made a decree and a law for them, and there he tested them. 26He said, "If you listen carefully to the voice of the LORD your God and do what is right in his eyes, if you pay attention to his commands and keep all his decrees, I will not bring on you any of the diseases I brought on the Egyptians, for I am the LORD, who heals you."

27Then they came to Elim, where there were twelve springs and seventy palm trees, and they camped there near the water.

Manna and Quail

16 The whole Israelite community set out from Elim and came to the Desert of Sin, which is between Elim and Sinai, on the fifteenth day of the second month after they had come out of Egypt. 2In the desert the whole community grumbled against Moses and Aaron. 3The Israelites said to them, "If only we had died by the LORD's hand in Egypt! There we sat around pots of meat and ate all the food we wanted, but you have brought us out into this desert to starve this entire assembly to death."

4Then the LORD said to Moses, "I will rain down bread from heaven for you. The people are to go out each day and gather enough for that day. In this way I will test them and see whether they will follow my instructions. 5On the sixth day they are to prepare what they bring in, and that is to be twice as much as they gather on the other days."

6So Moses and Aaron said to all the Israelites, "In the evening you will know that it was the LORD who brought you out of Egypt, 7and in the morning you will see the glory of the LORD, because he has

ᵃ23 Marah means bitter.

The Good Ol' Days

Monday

EXODUS 16　The Israelites experienced God's goodness in miraculous ways—the Passover, the crossing of the Red Sea, and his provision of water in the desert. But in Exodus 16, the people grumble again, wishing for the "good ol' days" back in Egypt. So what did God do? He still sent manna in the morning but also meat in the evening. However, the Israelites' lack of trust and gratitude blocked their ability to appreciate how much God really loved and provided for them.

Before becoming too critical of the Israelites, stop and consider your own attitude in a difficult situation. Thinking back on those first few months when we moved to Germany, I (Claudia) couldn't stop thinking about the "good ol' days" in Knoxville. And to add to Dave's frustrations, I blamed him.

He was the one who was so excited about being here, not me. In the first few weeks I missed the joy of seeing God provide for us in very specific ways. For instance, Jim and Imogene, another missionary couple, loaned us their apartment while they were out of town. And one evening Frank and Judy (soon-to-be friends), sensing how needy we were, cancelled their plans and invited us and our boys over for dinner. And then there was Carl, the Volkswagen dealer we met while looking for a car; he loaned us his personal vehicle so we could look for a permanent place to live!

Why not take a few minutes and consider the miracles in your own life? Then remember to be grateful each day for your spouse and for God's provisions.　—*Dave & Claudia*

Go to page 81 for your next devotional reading.

heard your grumbling against him. Who are we, that you should grumble against us?" 8Moses also said, "You will know that it was the LORD when he gives you meat to eat in the evening and all the bread you want in the morning, because he has heard your grumbling against him. Who are we? You are not grumbling against us, but against the LORD."

9Then Moses told Aaron, "Say to the entire Israelite community, 'Come before the LORD, for he has heard your grumbling.' "

10While Aaron was speaking to the whole Israelite community, they looked toward the desert, and there was the glory of the LORD appearing in the cloud.

11The LORD said to Moses, 12"I have heard the grumbling of the Israelites. Tell them, 'At twilight you will eat meat, and in the morning you will be filled with bread. Then you will know that I am the LORD your God.' "

13That evening quail came and covered the camp, and in the morning there was a layer of dew around the camp. 14When the dew was gone, thin flakes like frost on the ground appeared on the desert floor. 15When the Israelites saw it, they said to each other, "What is it?" For they did not know what it was.

Moses said to them, "It is the bread the LORD has given you to eat. 16This is what the LORD has commanded: 'Each one is to gather as much as he needs. Take an omera for each person you have in your tent.' "

17The Israelites did as they were told; some gathered much, some little. 18And when they measured it by the omer, he who gathered much did not have too much, and he who gathered little did not have too little. Each one gathered as much as he needed.

19Then Moses said to them, "No one is to keep any of it until morning."

20However, some of them paid no attention to Moses; they kept part of it until morning, but it was full of maggots and began to smell. So Moses was angry with them.

21Each morning everyone gathered as much as he needed, and when the sun grew hot, it melted away. 22On the sixth day, they gathered twice as much—two omersb for each person—and the leaders

of the community came and reported this to Moses. 23He said to them, "This is what the LORD commanded: 'Tomorrow is to be a day of rest, a holy Sabbath to the LORD. So bake what you want to bake and boil what you want to boil. Save whatever is left and keep it until morning.' "

24So they saved it until morning, as Moses commanded, and it did not stink or get maggots in it. 25"Eat it today," Moses said, "because today is a Sabbath to the LORD. You will not find any of it on the ground today. 26Six days you are to gather it, but on the seventh day, the Sabbath, there will not be any."

27Nevertheless, some of the people went out on the seventh day to gather it, but they found none. 28Then the LORD said to Moses, "How long will youc refuse to keep my commands and my instructions? 29Bear in mind that the LORD has given you the Sabbath; that is why on the sixth day he gives you bread for two days. Everyone is to stay where he is on the seventh day; no one is to go out." 30So the people rested on the seventh day.

31The people of Israel called the bread manna.d It was white like coriander seed and tasted like wafers made with honey. 32Moses said, "This is what the LORD has commanded: 'Take an omer of manna and keep it for the generations to come, so they can see the bread I gave you to eat in the desert when I brought you out of Egypt.' "

33So Moses said to Aaron, "Take a jar and put an omer of manna in it. Then place it before the LORD to be kept for the generations to come."

34As the LORD commanded Moses, Aaron put the manna in front of the Testimony, that it might be kept. 35The Israelites ate manna forty years, until they came to a land that was settled; they ate manna until they reached the border of Canaan.

36(An omer is one tenth of an ephah.)

Water From the Rock

17 The whole Israelite community set out from the Desert of Sin, traveling from place to place as the LORD com-

---

a16 That is, probably about 2 quarts (about 2 liters); also in verses 18, 32, 33 and 36
b22 That is, probably about 4 quarts (about 4.5 liters)   c28 The Hebrew is plural.
d31 Manna means What is it? (see verse 15).

manded. They camped at Rephidim, but there was no water for the people to drink. ²So they quarreled with Moses and said, "Give us water to drink."

Moses replied, "Why do you quarrel with me? Why do you put the LORD to the test?"

³But the people were thirsty for water there, and they grumbled against Moses. They said, "Why did you bring us up out of Egypt to make us and our children and livestock die of thirst?"

⁴Then Moses cried out to the LORD, "What am I to do with these people? They are almost ready to stone me."

⁵The LORD answered Moses, "Walk on ahead of the people. Take with you some of the elders of Israel and take in your hand the staff with which you struck the Nile, and go. ⁶I will stand there before you by the rock at Horeb. Strike the rock, and water will come out of it for the people to drink." So Moses did this in the sight of the elders of Israel. ⁷And he called the place Massah*a* and Meribah*b* because the Israelites quarreled and because they tested the LORD saying, "Is the LORD among us or not?"

The Amalekites Defeated

⁸The Amalekites came and attacked the Israelites at Rephidim. ⁹Moses said to Joshua, "Choose some of our men and go out to fight the Amalekites. Tomorrow I will stand on top of the hill with the staff of God in my hands."

¹⁰So Joshua fought the Amalekites as Moses had ordered, and Moses, Aaron and Hur went to the top of the hill. ¹¹As long as Moses held up his hands, the Israelites were winning, but whenever he lowered his hands, the Amalekites were winning. ¹²When Moses' hands grew tired, they took a stone and put it under him and he sat on it. Aaron and Hur held his hands up—one on one side, one on the other—so that his hands remained steady till sunset. ¹³So Joshua overcame the Amalekite army with the sword.

¹⁴Then the LORD said to Moses, "Write this on a scroll as something to be remembered and make sure that Joshua hears it, because I will completely blot out the memory of Amalek from under heaven."

¹⁵Moses built an altar and called it The LORD is my Banner. ¹⁶He said, "For hands were lifted up to the throne of the LORD. The*c* LORD will be at war against the Amalekites from generation to generation."

Jethro Visits Moses

18 Now Jethro, the priest of Midian and father-in-law of Moses, heard of everything God had done for Moses and for his people Israel, and how the LORD had brought Israel out of Egypt.

²After Moses had sent away his wife Zipporah, his father-in-law Jethro received her ³and her two sons. One son was named Gershom,*d* for Moses said, "I have become an alien in a foreign land"; ⁴and the other was named Eliezer,*e* for he said, "My father's God was my helper; he saved me from the sword of Pharaoh."

⁵Jethro, Moses' father-in-law, together with Moses' sons and wife, came to him in the desert, where he was camped near the mountain of God. ⁶Jethro had sent word to him, "I, your father-in-law Jethro, am coming to you with your wife and her two sons."

⁷So Moses went out to meet his father-in-law and bowed down and kissed him. They greeted each other and then went into the tent. ⁸Moses told his father-in-law about everything the LORD had done to Pharaoh and the Egyptians for Israel's sake and about all the hardships they had met along the way and how the LORD had saved them.

⁹Jethro was delighted to hear about all the good things the LORD had done for Israel in rescuing them from the hand of the Egyptians. ¹⁰He said, "Praise be to the LORD, who rescued you from the hand of the Egyptians and of Pharaoh, and who rescued the people from the hand of the Egyptians. ¹¹Now I know that the LORD is greater than all other gods, for he did this to those who had treated Israel arrogantly." ¹²Then Jethro, Moses' father-in-law,

a7 Massah means *testing.*   *b7 Meribah* means *quarreling.*   *c16* Or *"Because a hand was against the throne of the LORD, the*   *d3 Gershom* sounds like the Hebrew for *an alien there.*   *e4 Eliezer* means *my God is helper.*

brought a burnt offering and other sacrifices to God, and Aaron came with all the elders of Israel to eat bread with Moses' father-in-law in the presence of God.

¹³The next day Moses took his seat to serve as judge for the people, and they stood around him from morning till evening. ¹⁴When his father-in-law saw all that Moses was doing for the people, he said, "What is this you are doing for the people? Why do you alone sit as judge, while all these people stand around you from morning till evening?"

¹⁵Moses answered him, "Because the people come to me to seek God's will. ¹⁶Whenever they have a dispute, it is brought to me, and I decide between the parties and inform them of God's decrees and laws."

¹⁷Moses' father-in-law replied, "What you are doing is not good. ¹⁸You and these people who come to you will only wear yourselves out. The work is too heavy for you; you cannot handle it alone. ¹⁹Listen now to me and I will give you some advice, and may God be with you. You must be the people's representative before God and bring their disputes to him. ²⁰Teach them the decrees and laws, and show them the way to live and the duties they are to perform. ²¹But select capable men from all the people—men who fear God, trustworthy men who hate dishonest gain—and appoint them as officials over thousands, hundreds, fifties and tens. ²²Have them serve as judges for the people at all times, but have them bring every difficult case to you; the simple cases they can decide themselves. That will make your load lighter, because they will share it with you. ²³If you do this and God so commands, you will be able to stand the strain, and all these people will go home satisfied."

²⁴Moses listened to his father-in-law and did everything he said. ²⁵He chose capable men from all Israel and made them leaders of the people, officials over thousands, hundreds, fifties and tens. ²⁶They served as judges for the people at all times. The difficult cases they brought to Moses, but the simple ones they decided themselves.

²⁷Then Moses sent his father-in-law on his way, and Jethro returned to his own country.

At Mount Sinai

19 In the third month after the Israelites left Egypt—on the very day—they came to the Desert of Sinai. ²After they set out from Rephidim, they entered the Desert of Sinai, and Israel camped there in the desert in front of the mountain.

³Then Moses went up to God, and the LORD called to him from the mountain and said, "This is what you are to say to the house of Jacob and what you are to tell the people of Israel: ⁴'You yourselves have seen what I did to Egypt, and how I carried you on eagles' wings and brought you to myself. ⁵Now if you obey me fully and keep my covenant, then out of all nations you will be my treasured possession. Although the whole earth is mine, ⁶youᵃ will be for me a kingdom of priests and a holy nation.' These are the words you are to speak to the Israelites."

⁷So Moses went back and summoned the elders of the people and set before them all the words the LORD had commanded him to speak. ⁸The people all responded together, "We will do everything the LORD has said." So Moses brought their answer back to the LORD.

⁹The LORD said to Moses, "I am going to come to you in a dense cloud, so that the people will hear me speaking with you and will always put their trust in you." Then Moses told the LORD what the people had said.

¹⁰And the LORD said to Moses, "Go to the people and consecrate them today and tomorrow. Have them wash their clothes ¹¹and be ready by the third day, because on that day the LORD will come down on Mount Sinai in the sight of all the people. ¹²Put limits for the people around the mountain and tell them, 'Be careful that you do not go up the mountain or touch the foot of it. Whoever touches the mountain shall surely be put to death. ¹³He shall surely be stoned or shot with arrows; not a hand is to be laid on him. Whether man or animal, he shall not be permitted to live.' Only when the ram's horn sounds a long blast may they go up to the mountain."

¹⁴After Moses had gone down the mountain to the people, he consecrated

---

ᵃ5,6 Or possession, for the whole earth is mine. 6You

them, and they washed their clothes. 15Then he said to the people, "Prepare yourselves for the third day. Abstain from sexual relations."

16On the morning of the third day there was thunder and lightning, with a thick cloud over the mountain, and a very loud trumpet blast. Everyone in the camp trembled. 17Then Moses led the people out of the camp to meet with God, and they stood at the foot of the mountain. 18Mount Sinai was covered with smoke, because the LORD descended on it in fire. The smoke billowed up from it like smoke from a furnace, the whole mountain*a* trembled violently, 19and the sound of the trumpet grew louder and louder. Then Moses spoke and the voice of God answered him.*b*

20The LORD descended to the top of Mount Sinai and called Moses to the top of the mountain. So Moses went up 21and the LORD said to him, "Go down and warn the people so they do not force their way through to see the LORD and many of them perish. 22Even the priests, who approach the LORD, must consecrate themselves, or the LORD will break out against them."

23Moses said to the LORD, "The people cannot come up Mount Sinai, because you yourself warned us, 'Put limits around the mountain and set it apart as holy.'"

24The LORD replied, "Go down and bring Aaron up with you. But the priests and the people must not force their way through to come up to the LORD, or he will break out against them."

25So Moses went down to the people and told them.

The Ten Commandments

20 And God spoke all these words:

2"I am the LORD your God, who brought you out of Egypt, out of the land of slavery.

3"You shall have no other gods before*c* me.

4"You shall not make for yourself an idol in the form of anything in heaven above or on the earth beneath or in the waters below. 5You shall not bow down to them or worship them; for I, the LORD your God, am a jealous God, punishing the children for the sin

a18 Most Hebrew manuscripts; a few Hebrew manuscripts and Septuagint *all the people*
b19 Or *and God answered him with thunder*
c3 Or *besides*

The Laws of Life and Love

Tuesday

EXODUS 20   Although God gave the Ten Commandments to his people more than 3,000 years ago, they are still relevant today. Almost 1,500 years after God gave the laws, Jesus upheld them, calling them the "commandments" and listing five of them for the rich young ruler (see Matthew 19:16–19). And in the Sermon on the Mount, Jesus showed that his coming had not canceled the commandments.

Jesus actually placed these laws on a higher level by demanding that the spirit as well as the legal aspects of the law be kept (see Matthew 5:17–28). And that's an important message for married couples. How many times have you tagged your spouse off base for not following the rules—any rules? But consider this fact: God never intended for the Ten Commandments to be a set of regulations by which anyone would earn salvation. At the heart of the covenant relationship lay an act of divine grace. God even prefaced the Ten Commandments with a reminder of his deliverance of his people from Egypt (see Exodus 20:2).

This is a great reminder for couples. We need to offer the same kind of grace to one another—before we make accusations, point our fingers and demand justice. Laws always need to be balanced with love.

—*Les & Leslie*

Go to page 86 for your next devotional reading.

of the fathers to the third and fourth generation of those who hate me, ⁶but showing love to a thousand ⌊generations⌋ of those who love me and keep my commandments.

⁷"You shall not misuse the name of the LORD your God, for the LORD will not hold anyone guiltless who misuses his name.

⁸"Remember the Sabbath day by keeping it holy. ⁹Six days you shall labor and do all your work, ¹⁰but the seventh day is a Sabbath to the LORD your God. On it you shall not do any work, neither you, nor your son or daughter, nor your manservant or maidservant, nor your animals, nor the alien within your gates. ¹¹For in six days the LORD made the heavens and the earth, the sea, and all that is in them, but he rested on the seventh day. Therefore the LORD blessed the Sabbath day and made it holy.

¹²"Honor your father and your mother, so that you may live long in the land the LORD your God is giving you.

¹³"You shall not murder.

¹⁴"You shall not commit adultery.

¹⁵"You shall not steal.

¹⁶"You shall not give false testimony against your neighbor.

¹⁷"You shall not covet your neighbor's house. You shall not covet your neighbor's wife, or his manservant or maidservant, his ox or donkey, or anything that belongs to your neighbor."

¹⁸When the people saw the thunder and lightning and heard the trumpet and saw the mountain in smoke, they trembled with fear. They stayed at a distance ¹⁹and said to Moses, "Speak to us yourself and we will listen. But do not have God speak to us or we will die."

²⁰Moses said to the people, "Do not be afraid. God has come to test you, so that the fear of God will be with you to keep you from sinning."

²¹The people remained at a distance, while Moses approached the thick darkness where God was.

Idols and Altars

²²Then the LORD said to Moses, "Tell the Israelites this: 'You have seen for yourselves that I have spoken to you from heaven: ²³Do not make any gods to be alongside me; do not make for yourselves gods of silver or gods of gold.

²⁴" 'Make an altar of earth for me and sacrifice on it your burnt offerings and fellowship offerings,ᵃ your sheep and goats and your cattle. Wherever I cause my name to be honored, I will come to you and bless you. ²⁵If you make an altar of stones for me, do not build it with dressed stones, for you will defile it if you use a tool on it. ²⁶And do not go up to my altar on steps, lest your nakedness be exposed on it.'

21 "These are the laws you are to set before them:

Hebrew Servants

²"If you buy a Hebrew servant, he is to serve you for six years. But in the seventh year, he shall go free, without paying anything. ³If he comes alone, he is to go free alone; but if he has a wife when he comes, she is to go with him. ⁴If his master gives him a wife and she bears him sons or daughters, the woman and her children shall belong to her master, and only the man shall go free.

⁵"But if the servant declares, 'I love my master and my wife and children and do not want to go free,' ⁶then his master must take him before the judges.ᵇ He shall take him to the door or the doorpost and pierce his ear with an awl. Then he will be his servant for life.

⁷"If a man sells his daughter as a servant, she is not to go free as menservants do. ⁸If she does not please the master who has selected her for himself,ᶜ he must let her be redeemed. He has no right to sell her to foreigners, because he has broken faith with her. ⁹If he selects her for his

ᵃ24 Traditionally *peace offerings*   ᵇ6 Or *before God*   ᶜ8 Or *master so that he does not choose her* son, he must grant her the rights of a daughter. [10]If he marries another woman, he must not deprive the first one of her food, clothing and marital rights. [11]If he does not provide her with these three things, she is to go free, without any payment of money.

Personal Injuries

[12]"Anyone who strikes a man and kills him shall surely be put to death. [13]However, if he does not do it intentionally, but God lets it happen, he is to flee to a place I will designate. [14]But if a man schemes and kills another man deliberately, take him away from my altar and put him to death.

[15]"Anyone who attacks[a] his father or his mother must be put to death.

[16]"Anyone who kidnaps another and either sells him or still has him when he is caught must be put to death.

[17]"Anyone who curses his father or mother must be put to death.

[18]"If men quarrel and one hits the other with a stone or with his fist[b] and he does not die but is confined to bed, [19]the one who struck the blow will not be held responsible if the other gets up and walks around outside with his staff; however, he must pay the injured man for the loss of his time and see that he is completely healed.

[20]"If a man beats his male or female slave with a rod and the slave dies as a direct result, he must be punished, [21]but he is not to be punished if the slave gets up after a day or two, since the slave is his property.

[22]"If men who are fighting hit a pregnant woman and she gives birth prematurely[c] but there is no serious injury, the offender must be fined whatever the woman's husband demands and the court allows. [23]But if there is serious injury, you are to take life for life, [24]eye for eye, tooth for tooth, hand for hand, foot for foot, [25]burn for burn, wound for wound, bruise for bruise.

[26]"If a man hits a manservant or maidservant in the eye and destroys it, he must let the servant go free to compensate for the eye. [27]And if he knocks out the tooth of a manservant or maidservant, he must let the servant go free to compensate for the tooth.

[28]"If a bull gores a man or a woman to death, the bull must be stoned to death, and its meat must not be eaten. But the owner of the bull will not be held responsible. [29]If, however, the bull has had the habit of goring and the owner has been warned but has not kept it penned up and it kills a man or woman, the bull must be stoned and the owner also must be put to death. [30]However, if payment is demanded of him, he may redeem his life by paying whatever is demanded. [31]This law also applies if the bull gores a son or daughter. [32]If the bull gores a male or female slave, the owner must pay thirty shekels[d] of silver to the master of the slave, and the bull must be stoned.

[33]"If a man uncovers a pit or digs one and fails to cover it and an ox or a donkey falls into it, [34]the owner of the pit must pay for the loss; he must pay its owner, and the dead animal will be his.

[35]"If a man's bull injures the bull of another and it dies, they are to sell the live one and divide both the money and the dead animal equally. [36]However, if it was known that the bull had the habit of goring, yet the owner did not keep it penned up, the owner must pay, animal for animal, and the dead animal will be his.

Protection of Property

22 "If a man steals an ox or a sheep and slaughters it or sells it, he must pay back five head of cattle for the ox and four sheep for the sheep.

[2]"If a thief is caught breaking in and is struck so that he dies, the defender is not guilty of bloodshed; [3]but if it happens[e] after sunrise, he is guilty of bloodshed.

"A thief must certainly make restitution, but if he has nothing, he must be sold to pay for his theft.

[4]"If the stolen animal is found alive in his possession—whether ox or donkey or sheep—he must pay back double.

[5]"If a man grazes his livestock in a field or vineyard and lets them stray and they graze in another man's field, he must

---

[a]15 Or *kills*   [b]18 Or *with a tool*   [c]22 Or *she has a miscarriage*   [d]32 That is, about 12 ounces (about 0.3 kilogram)   [e]3 Or *if he strikes him*

make restitution from the best of his own field or vineyard.

⁶"If a fire breaks out and spreads into thornbushes so that it burns shocks of grain or standing grain or the whole field, the one who started the fire must make restitution.

⁷"If a man gives his neighbor silver or goods for safekeeping and they are stolen from the neighbor's house, the thief, if he is caught, must pay back double. ⁸But if the thief is not found, the owner of the house must appear before the judges*ᵃ* to determine whether he has laid his hands on the other man's property. ⁹In all cases of illegal possession of an ox, a donkey, a sheep, a garment, or any other lost property about which somebody says, 'This is mine,' both parties are to bring their cases before the judges. The one whom the judges declare*ᵇ* guilty must pay back double to his neighbor.

¹⁰"If a man gives a donkey, an ox, a sheep or any other animal to his neighbor for safekeeping and it dies or is injured or is taken away while no one is looking, ¹¹the issue between them will be settled by the taking of an oath before the LORD that the neighbor did not lay hands on the other person's property. The owner is to accept this, and no restitution is required. ¹²But if the animal was stolen from the neighbor, he must make restitution to the owner. ¹³If it was torn to pieces by a wild animal, he shall bring in the remains as evidence and he will not be required to pay for the torn animal.

¹⁴"If a man borrows an animal from his neighbor and it is injured or dies while the owner is not present, he must make restitution. ¹⁵But if the owner is with the animal, the borrower will not have to pay. If the animal was hired, the money paid for the hire covers the loss.

Social Responsibility

¹⁶"If a man seduces a virgin who is not pledged to be married and sleeps with her, he must pay the bride-price, and she shall be his wife. ¹⁷If her father absolutely refuses to give her to him, he must still pay the bride-price for virgins.

¹⁸"Do not allow a sorceress to live.

¹⁹"Anyone who has sexual relations with an animal must be put to death.

²⁰"Whoever sacrifices to any god other than the LORD must be destroyed.*ᶜ*

²¹"Do not mistreat an alien or oppress him, for you were aliens in Egypt.

²²"Do not take advantage of a widow or an orphan. ²³If you do and they cry out to me, I will certainly hear their cry. ²⁴My anger will be aroused, and I will kill you with the sword; your wives will become widows and your children fatherless.

²⁵"If you lend money to one of my people among you who is needy, do not be like a moneylender; charge him no interest.*ᵈ* ²⁶If you take your neighbor's cloak as a pledge, return it to him by sunset, ²⁷because his cloak is the only covering he has for his body. What else will he sleep in? When he cries out to me, I will hear, for I am compassionate.

²⁸"Do not blaspheme God*ᵉ* or curse the ruler of your people.

²⁹"Do not hold back offerings from your granaries or your vats.*ᶠ*

"You must give me the firstborn of your sons. ³⁰Do the same with your cattle and your sheep. Let them stay with their mothers for seven days, but give them to me on the eighth day.

³¹"You are to be my holy people. So do not eat the meat of an animal torn by wild beasts; throw it to the dogs.

Laws of Justice and Mercy

23 "Do not spread false reports. Do not help a wicked man by being a malicious witness.

²"Do not follow the crowd in doing wrong. When you give testimony in a lawsuit, do not pervert justice by siding with the crowd, ³and do not show favoritism to a poor man in his lawsuit.

⁴"If you come across your enemy's ox or donkey wandering off, be sure to take it back to him. ⁵If you see the donkey of someone who hates you fallen down under its load, do not leave it there; be sure you help him with it.

⁶"Do not deny justice to your poor people in their lawsuits. ⁷Have nothing to

---

ᵃ8 Or *before God*; also in verse 9   *ᵇ9* Or *whom God declares*   *ᶜ20* The Hebrew term refers to the irrevocable giving over of things or persons to the LORD, often by totally destroying them.   *ᵈ25* Or *excessive interest*   *ᵉ28* Or *Do not revile the judges*   *ᶠ29* The meaning of the Hebrew for this phrase is uncertain.

do with a false charge and do not put an innocent or honest person to death, for I will not acquit the guilty.

[8]"Do not accept a bribe, for a bribe blinds those who see and twists the words of the righteous.

[9]"Do not oppress an alien; you yourselves know how it feels to be aliens, because you were aliens in Egypt.

Sabbath Laws

[10]"For six years you are to sow your fields and harvest the crops, [11]but during the seventh year let the land lie unplowed and unused. Then the poor among your people may get food from it, and the wild animals may eat what they leave. Do the same with your vineyard and your olive grove.

[12]"Six days do your work, but on the seventh day do not work, so that your ox and your donkey may rest and the slave born in your household, and the alien as well, may be refreshed.

[13]"Be careful to do everything I have said to you. Do not invoke the names of other gods; do not let them be heard on your lips.

The Three Annual Festivals

[14]"Three times a year you are to celebrate a festival to me.

[15]"Celebrate the Feast of Unleavened Bread; for seven days eat bread made without yeast, as I commanded you. Do this at the appointed time in the month of Abib, for in that month you came out of Egypt.

"No one is to appear before me empty-handed.

[16]"Celebrate the Feast of Harvest with the firstfruits of the crops you sow in your field.

"Celebrate the Feast of Ingathering at the end of the year, when you gather in your crops from the field.

[17]"Three times a year all the men are to appear before the Sovereign LORD.

[18]"Do not offer the blood of a sacrifice to me along with anything containing yeast.

"The fat of my festival offerings must not be kept until morning.

[19]"Bring the best of the firstfruits of your soil to the house of the LORD your God.

"Do not cook a young goat in its mother's milk.

God's Angel to Prepare the Way

[20]"See, I am sending an angel ahead of you to guard you along the way and to bring you to the place I have prepared. [21]Pay attention to him and listen to what he says. Do not rebel against him; he will not forgive your rebellion, since my Name is in him. [22]If you listen carefully to what he says and do all that I say, I will be an enemy to your enemies and will oppose those who oppose you. [23]My angel will go ahead of you and bring you into the land of the Amorites, Hittites, Perizzites, Canaanites, Hivites and Jebusites, and I will wipe them out. [24]Do not bow down before their gods or worship them or follow their practices. You must demolish them and break their sacred stones to pieces. [25]Worship the LORD your God, and his blessing will be on your food and water. I will take away sickness from among you, [26]and none will miscarry or be barren in your land. I will give you a full life span.

[27]"I will send my terror ahead of you and throw into confusion every nation you encounter. I will make all your enemies turn their backs and run. [28]I will send the hornet ahead of you to drive the Hivites, Canaanites and Hittites out of your way. [29]But I will not drive them out in a single year, because the land would become desolate and the wild animals too numerous for you. [30]Little by little I will drive them out before you, until you have increased enough to take possession of the land.

[31]"I will establish your borders from the Red Sea[a] to the Sea of the Philistines,[b] and from the desert to the River.[c] I will hand over to you the people who live in the land and you will drive them out before you. [32]Do not make a covenant with them or with their gods. [33]Do not let them live in your land, or they will cause you to sin against me, be-

a31 Hebrew Yam Suph; that is, Sea of Reeds
b31 That is, the Mediterranean c31 That is, the Euphrates

cause the worship of their gods will certainly be a snare to you."

The Covenant Confirmed

24 Then he said to Moses, "Come up to the LORD, you and Aaron, Nadab and Abihu, and seventy of the elders of Israel. You are to worship at a distance, ²but Moses alone is to approach the LORD; the others must not come near. And the people may not come up with him."

³When Moses went and told the people all the LORD's words and laws, they responded with one voice, "Everything the LORD has said we will do." ⁴Moses then wrote down everything the LORD had said.

He got up early the next morning and built an altar at the foot of the mountain and set up twelve stone pillars representing the twelve tribes of Israel. ⁵Then he sent young Israelite men, and they offered burnt offerings and sacrificed young bulls as fellowship offerings[a] to the LORD. ⁶Moses took half of the blood and put it in bowls, and the other half he sprinkled on the altar. ⁷Then he took the Book of the Covenant and read it to the people. They responded, "We will do everything the LORD has said; we will obey." ⁸Moses then took the blood, sprinkled it on the people and said, "This is the blood of the covenant that the LORD has made with you in accordance with all these words."

⁹Moses and Aaron, Nadab and Abihu, and the seventy elders of Israel went up ¹⁰and saw the God of Israel. Under his feet was something like a pavement made of sapphire,[b] clear as the sky itself. ¹¹But God did not raise his hand against these leaders of the Israelites; they saw God, and they ate and drank.

¹²The LORD said to Moses, "Come up to me on the mountain and stay here, and I will give you the tablets of stone, with the law and commands I have written for their instruction."

¹³Then Moses set out with Joshua his aide, and Moses went up on the mountain of God. ¹⁴He said to the elders, "Wait here for us until we come back to you. Aaron and Hur are with you, and anyone involved in a dispute can go to them."

¹⁵When Moses went up on the mountain, the cloud covered it, ¹⁶and the glory of the LORD settled on Mount Sinai. For six days the cloud covered the mountain, and on the seventh day the LORD called to

---

a5 Traditionally *peace offerings*   *b10* Or *lapis lazuli*

Intermission

Wednesday

EXODUS 23:12 Do you feel guilty when you relax? It's easy to be a "workaholic." When each day's to-do list extends into the next and the next, and the weekends are consumed with yard work, laundry and other household chores competing for attention, it's too easy to let Sunday become the weekly catch-up day. Then by Monday you're still tired and are in no way ready for the weekly cycle to begin again.

When we take time to rest, we will be renewed and invigorated for the coming week. Think for a moment of what activities might constitute "Sabbath refreshment." Consider the reviving power of worshiping together, taking a nap, going for a leisurely walk, reading a good book or leaving the television off. Or what about starting Sunday traditions? After our children left home, we missed the family rhythm—for instance, we didn't have to eat dinner at a certain time each evening—and realized we needed to initiate some structure. So we started the tradition of having cinnamon rolls for Sunday breakfast. Little rituals can add stability to a marriage relationship.

Resting from work on the Sabbath gives us time to reflect on God's blessings and on our marriage. Are you looking for time to invest in your spouse? You will find that your Sabbath intermission will energize your relationship both with God and with your spouse.

—Dave & Claudia

Go to page 94 for your next devotional reading.

Moses from within the cloud. [17]To the Israelites the glory of the LORD looked like a consuming fire on top of the mountain. [18]Then Moses entered the cloud as he went on up the mountain. And he stayed on the mountain forty days and forty nights.

Offerings for the Tabernacle

25 The LORD said to Moses, [2]"Tell the Israelites to bring me an offering. You are to receive the offering for me from each man whose heart prompts him to give. [3]These are the offerings you are to receive from them: gold, silver and bronze; [4]blue, purple and scarlet yarn and fine linen; goat hair; [5]ram skins dyed red and hides of sea cows[a]; acacia wood; [6]olive oil for the light; spices for the anointing oil and for the fragrant incense; [7]and onyx stones and other gems to be mounted on the ephod and breastpiece.

[8]"Then have them make a sanctuary for me, and I will dwell among them. [9]Make this tabernacle and all its furnishings exactly like the pattern I will show you.

The Ark

[10]"Have them make a chest of acacia wood—two and a half cubits long, a cubit and a half wide, and a cubit and a half high.[b] [11]Overlay it with pure gold, both inside and out, and make a gold molding around it. [12]Cast four gold rings for it and fasten them to its four feet, with two rings on one side and two rings on the other. [13]Then make poles of acacia wood and overlay them with gold. [14]Insert the poles into the rings on the sides of the chest to carry it. [15]The poles are to remain in the rings of this ark; they are not to be removed. [16]Then put in the ark the Testimony, which I will give you.

[17]"Make an atonement cover[c] of pure gold—two and a half cubits long and a cubit and a half wide.[d] [18]And make two cherubim out of hammered gold at the ends of the cover. [19]Make one cherub on one end and the second cherub on the other; make the cherubim of one piece with the cover, at the two ends. [20]The cherubim are to have their wings spread upward, overshadowing the cover with

them. The cherubim are to face each other, looking toward the cover. [21]Place the cover on top of the ark and put in the ark the Testimony, which I will give you. [22]There, above the cover between the two cherubim that are over the ark of the Testimony, I will meet with you and give you all my commands for the Israelites.

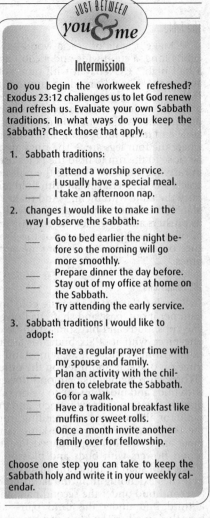

Intermission

Do you begin the workweek refreshed? Exodus 23:12 challenges us to let God renew and refresh us. Evaluate your own Sabbath traditions. In what ways do you keep the Sabbath? Check those that apply.

1. Sabbath traditions:
   ___ I attend a worship service.
   ___ I usually have a special meal.
   ___ I take an afternoon nap.

2. Changes I would like to make in the way I observe the Sabbath:
   ___ Go to bed earlier the night before so the morning will go more smoothly.
   ___ Prepare dinner the day before.
   ___ Stay out of my office at home on the Sabbath.
   ___ Try attending the early service.

3. Sabbath traditions I would like to adopt:
   ___ Have a regular prayer time with my spouse and family.
   ___ Plan an activity with the children to celebrate the Sabbath.
   ___ Go for a walk.
   ___ Have a traditional breakfast like muffins or sweet rolls.
   ___ Once a month invite another family over for fellowship.

Choose one step you can take to keep the Sabbath holy and write it in your weekly calendar.

---

[a]5 That is, dugongs   [b]10 That is, about 3 3/4 feet (about 1.1 meters) long and 2 1/4 feet (about 0.7 meter) wide and high   [c]17 Traditionally *a mercy seat*   [d]17 That is, about 3 3/4 feet (about 1.1 meters) long and 2 1/4 feet (about 0.7 meter) wide

The Table

23"Make a table of acacia wood—two cubits long, a cubit wide and a cubit and a half high.[a] 24Overlay it with pure gold and make a gold molding around it. 25Also make around it a rim a handbreadth[b] wide and put a gold molding on the rim. 26Make four gold rings for the table and fasten them to the four corners, where the four legs are. 27The rings are to be close to the rim to hold the poles used in carrying the table. 28Make the poles of acacia wood, overlay them with gold and carry the table with them. 29And make its plates and dishes of pure gold, as well as its pitchers and bowls for the pouring out of offerings. 30Put the bread of the Presence on this table to be before me at all times.

The Lampstand

31"Make a lampstand of pure gold and hammer it out, base and shaft; its flower-like cups, buds and blossoms shall be of one piece with it. 32Six branches are to extend from the sides of the lampstand—three on one side and three on the other. 33Three cups shaped like almond flowers with buds and blossoms are to be on one branch, three on the next branch, and the same for all six branches extending from the lampstand. 34And on the lampstand there are to be four cups shaped like almond flowers with buds and blossoms. 35One bud shall be under the first pair of branches extending from the lampstand, a second bud under the second pair, and a third bud under the third pair—six branches in all. 36The buds and branches shall all be of one piece with the lampstand, hammered out of pure gold.

37"Then make its seven lamps and set them up on it so that they light the space in front of it. 38Its wick trimmers and trays are to be of pure gold. 39A talent[c] of pure gold is to be used for the lampstand and all these accessories. 40See that you make them according to the pattern shown you on the mountain.

The Tabernacle

26 "Make the tabernacle with ten curtains of finely twisted linen and blue, purple and scarlet yarn, with cherubim worked into them by a skilled crafts-man. 2All the curtains are to be the same size—twenty-eight cubits long and four cubits wide.[d] 3Join five of the curtains together, and do the same with the other five. 4Make loops of blue material along the edge of the end curtain in one set, and do the same with the end curtain in the other set. 5Make fifty loops on one curtain and fifty loops on the end curtain of the other set, with the loops opposite each other. 6Then make fifty gold clasps and use them to fasten the curtains together so that the tabernacle is a unit.

7"Make curtains of goat hair for the tent over the tabernacle—eleven altogether. 8All eleven curtains are to be the same size—thirty cubits long and four cubits wide.[e] 9Join five of the curtains together into one set and the other six into another set. Fold the sixth curtain double at the front of the tent. 10Make fifty loops along the edge of the end curtain in one set and also along the edge of the end curtain in the other set. 11Then make fifty bronze clasps and put them in the loops to fasten the tent together as a unit. 12As for the additional length of the tent curtains, the half curtain that is left over is to hang down at the rear of the tabernacle. 13The tent curtains will be a cubit[f] longer on both sides; what is left will hang over the sides of the tabernacle so as to cover it. 14Make for the tent a covering of ram skins dyed red, and over that a covering of hides of sea cows.[g]

15"Make upright frames of acacia wood for the tabernacle. 16Each frame is to be ten cubits long and a cubit and a half wide,[h] 17with two projections set parallel to each other. Make all the frames of the tabernacle in this way. 18Make twenty frames for the south side of the tabernacle 19and make forty silver bases to go under them—two bases for each frame, one under each projection. 20For

a23 That is, about 3 feet (about 0.9 meter) long and 1 1/2 feet (about 0.5 meter) wide and 2 1/4 feet (about 0.7 meter) high   b25 That is, about 3 inches (about 8 centimeters)   c39 That is, about 75 pounds (about 34 kilograms)
d2 That is, about 42 feet (about 12.5 meters) long and 6 feet (about 1.8 meters) wide   e8 That is, about 45 feet (about 13.5 meters) long and 6 feet (about 1.8 meters) wide   f13 That is, about 1 1/2 feet (about 0.5 meter)   g14 That is, dugongs   h16 That is, about 15 feet (about 4.5 meters) long and 2 1/4 feet (about 0.7 meter) wide

the other side, the north side of the tabernacle, make twenty frames [21]and forty silver bases—two under each frame. [22]Make six frames for the far end, that is, the west end of the tabernacle, [23]and make two frames for the corners at the far end. [24]At these two corners they must be double from the bottom all the way to the top, and fitted into a single ring; both shall be like that. [25]So there will be eight frames and sixteen silver bases—two under each frame.

[26]"Also make crossbars of acacia wood: five for the frames on one side of the tabernacle, [27]five for those on the other side, and five for the frames on the west, at the far end of the tabernacle. [28]The center crossbar is to extend from end to end at the middle of the frames. [29]Overlay the frames with gold and make gold rings to hold the crossbars. Also overlay the crossbars with gold.

[30]"Set up the tabernacle according to the plan shown you on the mountain.

[31]"Make a curtain of blue, purple and scarlet yarn and finely twisted linen, with cherubim worked into it by a skilled craftsman. [32]Hang it with gold hooks on four posts of acacia wood overlaid with gold and standing on four silver bases. [33]Hang the curtain from the clasps and place the ark of the Testimony behind the curtain. The curtain will separate the Holy Place from the Most Holy Place. [34]Put the atonement cover on the ark of the Testimony in the Most Holy Place. [35]Place the table outside the curtain on the north side of the tabernacle and put the lampstand opposite it on the south side.

[36]"For the entrance to the tent make a curtain of blue, purple and scarlet yarn and finely twisted linen—the work of an embroiderer. [37]Make gold hooks for this curtain and five posts of acacia wood overlaid with gold. And cast five bronze bases for them.

The Altar of Burnt Offering

27 "Build an altar of acacia wood, three cubits[a] high; it is to be square, five cubits long and five cubits wide.[b] [2]Make a horn at each of the four corners, so that the horns and the altar are of one piece, and overlay the altar with bronze. [3]Make all its utensils of bronze—

its pots to remove the ashes, and its shovels, sprinkling bowls, meat forks and firepans. [4]Make a grating for it, a bronze network, and make a bronze ring at each of the four corners of the network. [5]Put it under the ledge of the altar so that it is halfway up the altar. [6]Make poles of acacia wood for the altar and overlay them with bronze. [7]The poles are to be inserted into the rings so they will be on two sides of the altar when it is carried. [8]Make the altar hollow, out of boards. It is to be made just as you were shown on the mountain.

The Courtyard

[9]"Make a courtyard for the tabernacle. The south side shall be a hundred cubits[c] long and is to have curtains of finely twisted linen, [10]with twenty posts and twenty bronze bases and with silver hooks and bands on the posts. [11]The north side shall also be a hundred cubits long and is to have curtains, with twenty posts and twenty bronze bases and with silver hooks and bands on the posts.

[12]"The west end of the courtyard shall be fifty cubits[d] wide and have curtains, with ten posts and ten bases. [13]On the east end, toward the sunrise, the courtyard shall also be fifty cubits wide. [14]Curtains fifteen cubits[e] long are to be on one side of the entrance, with three posts and three bases, [15]and curtains fifteen cubits long are to be on the other side, with three posts and three bases.

[16]"For the entrance to the courtyard, provide a curtain twenty cubits[f] long, of blue, purple and scarlet yarn and finely twisted linen—the work of an embroiderer—with four posts and four bases. [17]All the posts around the courtyard are to have silver bands and hooks, and bronze bases. [18]The courtyard shall be a hundred cubits long and fifty cubits wide,[g] with curtains of finely twisted linen five cubits[h] high,

---

[a]1 That is, about 4 1/2 feet (about 1.3 meters)
[b]1 That is, about 7 1/2 feet (about 2.3 meters) long and wide   [c]9 That is, about 150 feet (about 46 meters); also in verse 11   [d]12 That is, about 75 feet (about 23 meters); also in verse 13   [e]14 That is, about 22 1/2 feet (about 6.9 meters); also in verse 15   [f]16 That is, about 30 feet (about 9 meters)   [g]18 That is, about 150 feet (about 46 meters) long and 75 feet (about 23 meters) wide   [h]18 That is, about 7 1/2 feet (about 2.3 meters)

and with bronze bases. ¹⁹All the other articles used in the service of the tabernacle, whatever their function, including all the tent pegs for it and those for the courtyard, are to be of bronze.

Oil for the Lampstand

²⁰"Command the Israelites to bring you clear oil of pressed olives for the light so that the lamps may be kept burning. ²¹In the Tent of Meeting, outside the curtain that is in front of the Testimony, Aaron and his sons are to keep the lamps burning before the LORD from evening till morning. This is to be a lasting ordinance among the Israelites for the generations to come.

The Priestly Garments

28 "Have Aaron your brother brought to you from among the Israelites, along with his sons Nadab and Abihu, Eleazar and Ithamar, so they may serve me as priests. ²Make sacred garments for your brother Aaron, to give him dignity and honor. ³Tell all the skilled men to whom I have given wisdom in such matters that they are to make garments for Aaron, for his consecration, so he may serve me as priest. ⁴These are the garments they are to make: a breastpiece, an ephod, a robe, a woven tunic, a turban and a sash. They are to make these sacred garments for your brother Aaron and his sons, so they may serve me as priests. ⁵Have them use gold, and blue, purple and scarlet yarn, and fine linen.

The Ephod

⁶"Make the ephod of gold, and of blue, purple and scarlet yarn, and of finely twisted linen—the work of a skilled craftsman. ⁷It is to have two shoulder pieces attached to two of its corners, so it can be fastened. ⁸Its skillfully woven waistband is to be like it—of one piece with the ephod and made with gold, and with blue, purple and scarlet yarn, and with finely twisted linen.

⁹"Take two onyx stones and engrave on them the names of the sons of Israel ¹⁰in the order of their birth—six names on one stone and the remaining six on the other. ¹¹Engrave the names of the sons of Israel on the two stones the way a gem cutter engraves a seal. Then mount the stones in gold filigree settings ¹²and fasten them on the shoulder pieces of the ephod as memorial stones for the sons of Israel. Aaron is to bear the names on his shoulders as a memorial before the LORD. ¹³Make gold filigree settings ¹⁴and two braided chains of pure gold, like a rope, and attach the chains to the settings.

The Breastpiece

¹⁵"Fashion a breastpiece for making decisions—the work of a skilled craftsman. Make it like the ephod: of gold, and of blue, purple and scarlet yarn, and of finely twisted linen. ¹⁶It is to be square—a span*a* long and a span wide—and folded double. ¹⁷Then mount four rows of precious stones on it. In the first row there shall be a ruby, a topaz and a beryl; ¹⁸in the second row a turquoise, a sapphire*b* and an emerald; ¹⁹in the third row a jacinth, an agate and an amethyst; ²⁰in the fourth row a chrysolite, an onyx and a jasper.*c* Mount them in gold filigree settings. ²¹There are to be twelve stones, one for each of the names of the sons of Israel, each engraved like a seal with the name of one of the twelve tribes.

²²"For the breastpiece make braided chains of pure gold, like a rope. ²³Make two gold rings for it and fasten them to two corners of the breastpiece. ²⁴Fasten the two gold chains to the rings at the corners of the breastpiece, ²⁵and the other ends of the chains to the two settings, attaching them to the shoulder pieces of the ephod at the front. ²⁶Make two gold rings and attach them to the other two corners of the breastpiece on the inside edge next to the ephod. ²⁷Make two more gold rings and attach them to the bottom of the shoulder pieces on the front of the ephod, close to the seam just above the waistband of the ephod. ²⁸The rings of the breastpiece are to be tied to the rings of the ephod with blue cord, connecting it to the waistband, so that the breastpiece will not swing out from the ephod.

---

*a*16 That is, about 9 inches (about 22 centimeters)
*b*18 Or *lapis lazuli*   *c*20 The precise identification of some of these precious stones is uncertain.

29"Whenever Aaron enters the Holy Place, he will bear the names of the sons of Israel over his heart on the breastpiece of decision as a continuing memorial before the LORD. 30Also put the Urim and the Thummim in the breastpiece, so they may be over Aaron's heart whenever he enters the presence of the LORD. Thus Aaron will always bear the means of making decisions for the Israelites over his heart before the LORD.

Other Priestly Garments

31"Make the robe of the ephod entirely of blue cloth, 32with an opening for the head in its center. There shall be a woven edge like a collar*a* around this opening, so that it will not tear. 33Make pomegranates of blue, purple and scarlet yarn around the hem of the robe, with gold bells between them. 34The gold bells and the pomegranates are to alternate around the hem of the robe. 35Aaron must wear it when he ministers. The sound of the bells will be heard when he enters the Holy Place before the LORD and when he comes out, so that he will not die.

36"Make a plate of pure gold and engrave on it as on a seal: HOLY TO THE LORD. 37Fasten a blue cord to it to attach it to the turban; it is to be on the front of the turban. 38It will be on Aaron's forehead, and he will bear the guilt involved in the sacred gifts the Israelites consecrate, whatever their gifts may be. It will be on Aaron's forehead continually so that they will be acceptable to the LORD.

39"Weave the tunic of fine linen and make the turban of fine linen. The sash is to be the work of an embroiderer. 40Make tunics, sashes and headbands for Aaron's sons, to give them dignity and honor. 41After you put these clothes on your brother Aaron and his sons, anoint and ordain them. Consecrate them so they may serve me as priests.

42"Make linen undergarments as a covering for the body, reaching from the waist to the thigh. 43Aaron and his sons must wear them whenever they enter the Tent of Meeting or approach the altar to minister in the Holy Place, so that they will not incur guilt and die.

"This is to be a lasting ordinance for Aaron and his descendants.

Consecration of the Priests

29 "This is what you are to do to consecrate them, so they may serve me as priests: Take a young bull and two rams without defect. 2And from fine wheat flour, without yeast, make bread, and cakes mixed with oil, and wafers spread with oil. 3Put them in a basket and present them in it—along with the bull and the two rams. 4Then bring Aaron and his sons to the entrance to the Tent of Meeting and wash them with water. 5Take the garments and dress Aaron with the tunic, the robe of the ephod, the ephod itself and the breastpiece. Fasten the ephod on him by its skillfully woven waistband. 6Put the turban on his head and attach the sacred diadem to the turban. 7Take the anointing oil and anoint him by pouring it on his head. 8Bring his sons and dress them in tunics 9and put headbands on them. Then tie sashes on Aaron and his sons.*b* The priesthood is theirs by a lasting ordinance. In this way you shall ordain Aaron and his sons.

10"Bring the bull to the front of the Tent of Meeting, and Aaron and his sons shall lay their hands on its head. 11Slaughter it in the LORD's presence at the entrance to the Tent of Meeting. 12Take some of the bull's blood and put it on the horns of the altar with your finger, and pour out the rest of it at the base of the altar. 13Then take all the fat around the inner parts, the covering of the liver, and both kidneys with the fat on them, and burn them on the altar. 14But burn the bull's flesh and its hide and its offal outside the camp. It is a sin offering.

15"Take one of the rams, and Aaron and his sons shall lay their hands on its head. 16Slaughter it and take the blood and sprinkle it against the altar on all sides. 17Cut the ram into pieces and wash the inner parts and the legs, putting them with the head and the other pieces. 18Then burn the entire ram on the altar. It is a burnt offering to the LORD, a pleasing aroma, an offering made to the LORD by fire.

19"Take the other ram, and Aaron and his sons shall lay their hands on its head. 20Slaughter it, take some of its blood and

*a*32 The meaning of the Hebrew for this word is uncertain.   *b*9 Hebrew; Septuagint *on them* put it on the lobes of the right ears of Aaron and his sons, on the thumbs of their right hands, and on the big toes of their right feet. Then sprinkle blood against the altar on all sides. ²¹And take some of the blood on the altar and some of the anointing oil and sprinkle it on Aaron and his garments and on his sons and their garments. Then he and his sons and their garments will be consecrated.

²²"Take from this ram the fat, the fat tail, the fat around the inner parts, the covering of the liver, both kidneys with the fat on them, and the right thigh. (This is the ram for the ordination.) ²³From the basket of bread made without yeast, which is before the LORD, take a loaf, and a cake made with oil, and a wafer. ²⁴Put all these in the hands of Aaron and his sons and wave them before the LORD as a wave offering. ²⁵Then take them from their hands and burn them on the altar along with the burnt offering for a pleasing aroma to the LORD, an offering made to the LORD by fire. ²⁶After you take the breast of the ram for Aaron's ordination, wave it before the LORD as a wave offering, and it will be your share.

²⁷"Consecrate those parts of the ordination ram that belong to Aaron and his sons: the breast that was waved and the thigh that was presented. ²⁸This is always to be the regular share from the Israelites for Aaron and his sons. It is the contribution the Israelites are to make to the LORD from their fellowship offerings.ᵃ

²⁹"Aaron's sacred garments will belong to his descendants so that they can be anointed and ordained in them. ³⁰The son who succeeds him as priest and comes to the Tent of Meeting to minister in the Holy Place is to wear them seven days.

³¹"Take the ram for the ordination and cook the meat in a sacred place. ³²At the entrance to the Tent of Meeting, Aaron and his sons are to eat the meat of the ram and the bread that is in the basket. ³³They are to eat these offerings by which atonement was made for their ordination and consecration. But no one else may eat them, because they are sacred. ³⁴And if any of the meat of the ordination ram or any bread is left over till morning, burn it up. It must not be eaten, because it is sacred.

³⁵"Do for Aaron and his sons everything I have commanded you, taking seven days to ordain them. ³⁶Sacrifice a bull each day as a sin offering to make atonement. Purify the altar by making atonement for it, and anoint it to consecrate it. ³⁷For seven days make atonement for the altar and consecrate it. Then the altar will be most holy, and whatever touches it will be holy.

³⁸"This is what you are to offer on the altar regularly each day: two lambs a year old. ³⁹Offer one in the morning and the other at twilight. ⁴⁰With the first lamb offer a tenth of an ephahᵇ of fine flour mixed with a quarter of a hinᶜ of oil from pressed olives, and a quarter of a hin of wine as a drink offering. ⁴¹Sacrifice the other lamb at twilight with the same grain offering and its drink offering as in the morning—a pleasing aroma, an offering made to the LORD by fire.

⁴²"For the generations to come this burnt offering is to be made regularly at the entrance to the Tent of Meeting before the LORD. There I will meet you and speak to you; ⁴³there also I will meet with the Israelites, and the place will be consecrated by my glory.

⁴⁴"So I will consecrate the Tent of Meeting and the altar and will consecrate Aaron and his sons to serve me as priests. ⁴⁵Then I will dwell among the Israelites and be their God. ⁴⁶They will know that I am the LORD their God, who brought them out of Egypt so that I might dwell among them. I am the LORD their God.

The Altar of Incense

30 "Make an altar of acacia wood for burning incense. ²It is to be square, a cubit long and a cubit wide, and two cubits highᵈ—its horns of one piece with it. ³Overlay the top and all the sides and the horns with pure gold, and make a gold molding around it. ⁴Make two gold rings for the altar below the molding—two on opposite sides—to hold the poles used to carry it. ⁵Make the poles of acacia wood and overlay them with gold. ⁶Put the altar in front of the curtain that is before the

---

ᵃ28 Traditionally *peace offerings*   ᵇ40 That is, probably about 2 quarts (about 2 liters)
ᶜ40 That is, probably about 1 quart (about 1 liter)
ᵈ2 That is, about 1 1/2 feet (about 0.5 meter) long and wide and about 3 feet (about 0.9 meter) high

ark of the Testimony—before the atonement cover that is over the Testimony—where I will meet with you.

7"Aaron must burn fragrant incense on the altar every morning when he tends the lamps. 8He must burn incense again when he lights the lamps at twilight so incense will burn regularly before the LORD for the generations to come. 9Do not offer on this altar any other incense or any burnt offering or grain offering, and do not pour a drink offering on it. 10Once a year Aaron shall make atonement on its horns. This annual atonement must be made with the blood of the atoning sin offering for the generations to come. It is most holy to the LORD."

Atonement Money

11Then the LORD said to Moses, 12"When you take a census of the Israelites to count them, each one must pay the LORD a ransom for his life at the time he is counted. Then no plague will come on them when you number them. 13Each one who crosses over to those already counted is to give a half shekel,[a] according to the sanctuary shekel, which weighs twenty gerahs. This half shekel is an offering to the LORD. 14All who cross over, those twenty years old or more, are to give an offering to the LORD. 15The rich are not to give more than a half shekel and the poor are not to give less when you make the offering to the LORD to atone for your lives. 16Receive the atonement money from the Israelites and use it for the service of the Tent of Meeting. It will be a memorial for the Israelites before the LORD, making atonement for your lives."

Basin for Washing

17Then the LORD said to Moses, 18"Make a bronze basin, with its bronze stand, for washing. Place it between the Tent of Meeting and the altar, and put water in it. 19Aaron and his sons are to wash their hands and feet with water from it. 20Whenever they enter the Tent of Meeting, they shall wash with water so that they will not die. Also, when they approach the altar to minister by presenting an offering made to the LORD by fire, 21they shall wash their hands and feet so that they will not die. This is to be a last-

ing ordinance for Aaron and his descendants for the generations to come."

Anointing Oil

22Then the LORD said to Moses, 23"Take the following fine spices: 500 shekels[b] of liquid myrrh, half as much (that is, 250 shekels) of fragrant cinnamon, 250 shekels of fragrant cane, 24500 shekels of cassia—all according to the sanctuary shekel—and a hin[c] of olive oil. 25Make these into a sacred anointing oil, a fragrant blend, the work of a perfumer. It will be the sacred anointing oil. 26Then use it to anoint the Tent of Meeting, the ark of the Testimony, 27the table and all its articles, the lampstand and its accessories, the altar of incense, 28the altar of burnt offering and all its utensils, and the basin with its stand. 29You shall consecrate them so they will be most holy, and whatever touches them will be holy.

30"Anoint Aaron and his sons and consecrate them so they may serve me as priests. 31Say to the Israelites, 'This is to be my sacred anointing oil for the generations to come. 32Do not pour it on men's bodies and do not make any oil with the same formula. It is sacred, and you are to consider it sacred. 33Whoever makes perfume like it and whoever puts it on anyone other than a priest must be cut off from his people.' "

Incense

34Then the LORD said to Moses, "Take fragrant spices—gum resin, onycha and galbanum—and pure frankincense, all in equal amounts, 35and make a fragrant blend of incense, the work of a perfumer. It is to be salted and pure and sacred. 36Grind some of it to powder and place it in front of the Testimony in the Tent of Meeting, where I will meet with you. It shall be most holy to you. 37Do not make any incense with this formula for yourselves; consider it holy to the LORD. 38Whoever makes any like it to enjoy its fragrance must be cut off from his people."

a13 That is, about 1/5 ounce (about 6 grams); also in verse 15   b23 That is, about 12 1/2 pounds (about 6 kilograms)   c24 That is, probably about 4 quarts (about 4 liters)

Bezalel and Oholiab

31 Then the LORD said to Moses, [2]"See, I have chosen Bezalel son of Uri, the son of Hur, of the tribe of Judah, [3]and I have filled him with the Spirit of God, with skill, ability and knowledge in all kinds of crafts— [4]to make artistic designs for work in gold, silver and bronze, [5]to cut and set stones, to work in wood, and to engage in all kinds of craftsmanship. [6]Moreover, I have appointed Oholiab son of Ahisamach, of the tribe of Dan, to help him. Also I have given skill to all the craftsmen to make everything I have commanded you: [7]the Tent of Meeting, the ark of the Testimony with the atonement cover on it, and all the other furnishings of the tent— [8]the table and its articles, the pure gold lampstand and all its accessories, the altar of incense, [9]the altar of burnt offering and all its utensils, the basin with its stand— [10]and also the woven garments, both the sacred garments for Aaron the priest and the garments for his sons when they serve as priests, [11]and the anointing oil and fragrant incense for the Holy Place. They are to make them just as I commanded you."

The Sabbath

[12]Then the LORD said to Moses, [13]"Say to the Israelites, 'You must observe my Sabbaths. This will be a sign between me and you for the generations to come, so you may know that I am the LORD, who makes you holy.[a]

[14]" 'Observe the Sabbath, because it is holy to you. Anyone who desecrates it must be put to death; whoever does any work on that day must be cut off from his people. [15]For six days, work is to be done, but the seventh day is a Sabbath of rest, holy to the LORD. Whoever does any work on the Sabbath day must be put to death. [16]The Israelites are to observe the Sabbath, celebrating it for the generations to come as a lasting covenant. [17]It will be a sign between me and the Israelites forever, for in six days the LORD made the heavens and the earth, and on the seventh day he abstained from work and rested.' "

[18]When the LORD finished speaking to Moses on Mount Sinai, he gave him the two tablets of the Testimony, the tablets of stone inscribed by the finger of God.

The Golden Calf

32 When the people saw that Moses was so long in coming down from the mountain, they gathered around Aar-

---

[a]13 Or *who sanctifies you;* or *who sets you apart as holy.*

A Greenhouse for Couples

Thursday

EXODUS 31:12–18   Research has shown that couples who attend church, even *once* a month, increase their chances of staying married. Studies have also shown that churchgoers feel better about their marriages than those who don't worship together. Attending church provides couples with a shared sense of values and purpose in life. It also provides couples with a caring community of support.

To cultivate spiritual intimacy in your marriage without including the church is like trying to drive a car without a steering wheel. Billy Graham says that "church-goers are like coals in a fire. When they cling together, they keep the flame aglow; when they separate, they die out." The church is more than a group of people who come together. It is a group of people who are called together by the gospel of Christ's love and forgiveness. As Paul puts it, the church is called into the fellowship of God's Son (see 1 Corinthians 1:9).

From the beginning of our marriage, observing the Sabbath has been a systematic time of rest and renewal for our relationship. Dedicating a day of the week to attend church and worship with the body of Christ stabilizes our marriage and liberates us from the hectic pace that fills our other days.

—Les & Leslie

Go to page 102 for your next devotional reading.

on and said, "Come, make us gods[a] who will go before us. As for this fellow Moses who brought us up out of Egypt, we don't know what has happened to him."

[2]Aaron answered them, "Take off the gold earrings that your wives, your sons and your daughters are wearing, and bring them to me." [3]So all the people took off their earrings and brought them to Aaron. [4]He took what they handed him and made it into an idol cast in the shape of a calf, fashioning it with a tool. Then they said, "These are your gods,[b] O Israel, who brought you up out of Egypt."

[5]When Aaron saw this, he built an altar in front of the calf and announced, "Tomorrow there will be a festival to the LORD." [6]So the next day the people rose early and sacrificed burnt offerings and presented fellowship offerings.[c] Afterward they sat down to eat and drink and got up to indulge in revelry.

[7]Then the LORD said to Moses, "Go down, because your people, whom you brought up out of Egypt, have become corrupt. [8]They have been quick to turn away from what I commanded them and have made themselves an idol cast in the shape of a calf. They have bowed down to it and sacrificed to it and have said, 'These are your gods, O Israel, who brought you up out of Egypt.'

[9]"I have seen these people," the LORD said to Moses, "and they are a stiff-necked people. [10]Now leave me alone so that my anger may burn against them and that I may destroy them. Then I will make you into a great nation."

[11]But Moses sought the favor of the LORD his God. "O LORD," he said, "why should your anger burn against your people, whom you brought out of Egypt with great power and a mighty hand? [12]Why should the Egyptians say, 'It was with evil intent that he brought them out, to kill them in the mountains and to wipe them off the face of the earth'? Turn from your fierce anger; relent and do not bring disaster on your people. [13]Remember your servants Abraham, Isaac and Israel, to whom you swore by your own self: 'I will make your descendants as numerous as the stars in the sky and I will give your descendants all this land I promised them, and it will be their inheritance forever.' " [14]Then the LORD relented and did not bring on his people the disaster he had threatened.

[15]Moses turned and went down the mountain with the two tablets of the Testimony in his hands. They were inscribed on both sides, front and back. [16]The tablets were the work of God; the writing was the writing of God, engraved on the tablets.

[17]When Joshua heard the noise of the people shouting, he said to Moses, "There is the sound of war in the camp."

[18]Moses replied:

"It is not the sound of victory,
    it is not the sound of defeat;
    it is the sound of singing that I
      hear."

[19]When Moses approached the camp and saw the calf and the dancing, his anger burned and he threw the tablets out of his hands, breaking them to pieces at the foot of the mountain. [20]And he took the calf they had made and burned it in the fire; then he ground it to powder, scattered it on the water and made the Israelites drink it.

[21]He said to Aaron, "What did these people do to you, that you led them into such great sin?"

[22]"Do not be angry, my lord," Aaron answered. "You know how prone these people are to evil. [23]They said to me, 'Make us gods who will go before us. As for this fellow Moses who brought us up out of Egypt, we don't know what has happened to him.' [24]So I told them, 'Whoever has any gold jewelry, take it off.' Then they gave me the gold, and I threw it into the fire, and out came this calf!"

[25]Moses saw that the people were running wild and that Aaron had let them get out of control and so become a laughing-stock to their enemies. [26]So he stood at the entrance to the camp and said, "Whoever is for the LORD, come to me." And all the Levites rallied to him.

[a]1 Or *a god*; also in verses 23 and 31   [b]4 Or *This is your god*; also in verse 8   [c]6 Traditionally *peace offerings*

²⁷Then he said to them, "This is what the LORD, the God of Israel, says: 'Each man strap a sword to his side. Go back and forth through the camp from one end to the other, each killing his brother and friend and neighbor.'" ²⁸The Levites did as Moses commanded, and that day about three thousand of the people died. ²⁹Then Moses said, "You have been set apart to the LORD today, for you were against your own sons and brothers, and he has blessed you this day."

³⁰The next day Moses said to the people, "You have committed a great sin. But now I will go up to the LORD; perhaps I can make atonement for your sin."

³¹So Moses went back to the LORD and said, "Oh, what a great sin these people have committed! They have made themselves gods of gold. ³²But now, please forgive their sin—but if not, then blot me out of the book you have written."

³³The LORD replied to Moses, "Whoever has sinned against me I will blot out of my book. ³⁴Now go, lead the people to the place I spoke of, and my angel will go before you. However, when the time comes for me to punish, I will punish them for their sin."

³⁵And the LORD struck the people with a plague because of what they did with the calf Aaron had made.

33 Then the LORD said to Moses, "Leave this place, you and the people you brought up out of Egypt, and go up to the land I promised on oath to Abraham, Isaac and Jacob, saying, 'I will give it to your descendants.' ²I will send an angel before you and drive out the Canaanites, Amorites, Hittites, Perizzites, Hivites and Jebusites. ³Go up to the land flowing with milk and honey. But I will not go with you, because you are a stiff-necked people and I might destroy you on the way."

⁴When the people heard these distressing words, they began to mourn and no one put on any ornaments. ⁵For the LORD had said to Moses, "Tell the Israelites, 'You are a stiff-necked people. If I were to go with you even for a moment, I might destroy you. Now take off your ornaments and I will decide what to do with you.'" ⁶So the Israelites stripped off their ornaments at Mount Horeb.

The Tent of Meeting

⁷Now Moses used to take a tent and pitch it outside the camp some distance away, calling it the "tent of meeting." Anyone inquiring of the LORD would go to the tent of meeting outside the camp. ⁸And whenever Moses went out to the tent, all the people rose and stood at the entrances to their tents, watching Moses until he entered the tent. ⁹As Moses went into the tent, the pillar of cloud would come down and stay at the entrance, while the LORD spoke with Moses. ¹⁰Whenever the people saw the pillar of cloud standing at the entrance to the tent, they all stood and worshiped, each at the entrance to his tent. ¹¹The LORD would speak to Moses face to face, as a man speaks with his friend. Then Moses would return to the camp, but his young aide Joshua son of Nun did not leave the tent.

Moses and the Glory of the LORD

¹²Moses said to the LORD, "You have been telling me, 'Lead these people,' but you have not let me know whom you will send with me. You have said, 'I know you by name and you have found favor with me.' ¹³If you are pleased with me, teach me your ways so I may know you and continue to find favor with you. Remember that this nation is your people."

¹⁴The LORD replied, "My Presence will go with you, and I will give you rest."

¹⁵Then Moses said to him, "If your Presence does not go with us, do not send us up from here. ¹⁶How will anyone know that you are pleased with me and with your people unless you go with us? What else will distinguish me and your people from all the other people on the face of the earth?"

¹⁷And the LORD said to Moses, "I will do the very thing you have asked, because I am pleased with you and I know you by name."

¹⁸Then Moses said, "Now show me your glory."

¹⁹And the LORD said, "I will cause all my goodness to pass in front of you, and I will proclaim my name, the LORD, in your presence. I will have mercy on whom I will have mercy, and I will have compassion on whom I will have compassion. ²⁰But," he said, "you cannot see

my face, for no one may see me and live."

²¹Then the LORD said, "There is a place near me where you may stand on a rock. ²²When my glory passes by, I will put you in a cleft in the rock and cover you with my hand until I have passed by. ²³Then I will remove my hand and you will see my back; but my face must not be seen."

The New Stone Tablets

34 The LORD said to Moses, "Chisel out two stone tablets like the first ones, and I will write on them the words that were on the first tablets, which you broke. ²Be ready in the morning, and then come up on Mount Sinai. Present yourself to me there on top of the mountain. ³No one is to come with you or be seen anywhere on the mountain; not even the flocks and herds may graze in front of the mountain."

⁴So Moses chiseled out two stone tablets like the first ones and went up Mount Sinai early in the morning, as the LORD had commanded him; and he carried the two stone tablets in his hands. ⁵Then the LORD came down in the cloud and stood there with him and proclaimed his name, the LORD. ⁶And he passed in front of Moses, proclaiming, "The LORD, the LORD, the compassionate and gracious God, slow to anger, abounding in love and faithfulness, ⁷maintaining love to thousands, and forgiving wickedness, rebellion and sin. Yet he does not leave the guilty unpunished; he punishes the children and their children for the sin of the fathers to the third and fourth generation."

⁸Moses bowed to the ground at once and worshiped. ⁹"O Lord, if I have found favor in your eyes," he said, "then let the Lord go with us. Although this is a stiffnecked people, forgive our wickedness and our sin, and take us as your inheritance."

¹⁰Then the LORD said: "I am making a covenant with you. Before all your people I will do wonders never before done in any nation in all the world. The people you live among will see how awesome is the work that I, the LORD, will do for you. ¹¹Obey what I command you today. I will drive out before you the Amorites, Canaanites, Hittites, Perizzites, Hivites and Jebusites. ¹²Be careful not to make a treaty

with those who live in the land where you are going, or they will be a snare among you. ¹³Break down their altars, smash their sacred stones and cut down their Asherah poles.ᵃ ¹⁴Do not worship any other god, for the LORD, whose name is Jealous, is a jealous God.

¹⁵"Be careful not to make a treaty with those who live in the land; for when they prostitute themselves to their gods and sacrifice to them, they will invite you and you will eat their sacrifices. ¹⁶And when you choose some of their daughters as wives for your sons and those daughters prostitute themselves to their gods, they will lead your sons to do the same.

¹⁷"Do not make cast idols.

¹⁸"Celebrate the Feast of Unleavened Bread. For seven days eat bread made without yeast, as I commanded you. Do this at the appointed time in the month of Abib, for in that month you came out of Egypt.

¹⁹"The first offspring of every womb belongs to me, including all the firstborn males of your livestock, whether from herd or flock. ²⁰Redeem the firstborn donkey with a lamb, but if you do not redeem it, break its neck. Redeem all your firstborn sons.

"No one is to appear before me empty-handed.

²¹"Six days you shall labor, but on the seventh day you shall rest; even during the plowing season and harvest you must rest.

²²"Celebrate the Feast of Weeks with the firstfruits of the wheat harvest, and the Feast of Ingathering at the turn of the year.ᵇ ²³Three times a year all your men are to appear before the Sovereign LORD, the God of Israel. ²⁴I will drive out nations before you and enlarge your territory, and no one will covet your land when you go up three times each year to appear before the LORD your God.

²⁵"Do not offer the blood of a sacrifice to me along with anything containing yeast, and do not let any of the sacrifice from the Passover Feast remain until morning.

²⁶"Bring the best of the firstfruits of

ᵃ13 That is, symbols of the goddess Asherah
ᵇ22 That is, in the fall

your soil to the house of the LORD your
God.

"Do not cook a young goat in its
mother's milk."

27Then the LORD said to Moses, "Write
down these words, for in accordance with
these words I have made a covenant with
you and with Israel." 28Moses was there
with the LORD forty days and forty nights
without eating bread or drinking water.
And he wrote on the tablets the words of
the covenant—the Ten Commandments.

The Radiant Face of Moses

29When Moses came down from
Mount Sinai with the two tablets of the
Testimony in his hands, he was not aware
that his face was radiant because he had
spoken with the LORD. 30When Aaron and
all the Israelites saw Moses, his face was
radiant, and they were afraid to come
near him. 31But Moses called to them; so
Aaron and all the leaders of the community came back to him, and he spoke to
them. 32Afterward all the Israelites came
near him, and he gave them all the commands the LORD had given him on Mount
Sinai.

33When Moses finished speaking to
them, he put a veil over his face. 34But
whenever he entered the LORD's presence
to speak with him, he removed the veil
until he came out. And when he came out
and told the Israelites what he had been
commanded, 35they saw that his face was
radiant. Then Moses would put the veil
back over his face until he went in to
speak with the LORD.

Sabbath Regulations

35 Moses assembled the whole Israelite community and said to them,
"These are the things the LORD has commanded you to do: 2For six days, work is
to be done, but the seventh day shall be
your holy day, a Sabbath of rest to the
LORD. Whoever does any work on it must
be put to death. 3Do not light a fire in any
of your dwellings on the Sabbath day."

Materials for the Tabernacle

4Moses said to the whole Israelite community, "This is what the LORD has commanded: 5From what you have, take an
offering for the LORD. Everyone who is

willing is to bring to the LORD an offering
of gold, silver and bronze; 6blue, purple
and scarlet yarn and fine linen; goat hair;
7ram skins dyed red and hides of sea
cows*a*; acacia wood; 8olive oil for the
light; spices for the anointing oil and for
the fragrant incense; 9and onyx stones
and other gems to be mounted on the
ephod and breastpiece.

10"All who are skilled among you are
to come and make everything the LORD
has commanded: 11the tabernacle with its
tent and its covering, clasps, frames, crossbars, posts and bases; 12the ark with its
poles and the atonement cover and the
curtain that shields it; 13the table with its
poles and all its articles and the bread of
the Presence; 14the lampstand that is for
light with its accessories, lamps and oil
for the light; 15the altar of incense with its
poles, the anointing oil and the fragrant
incense; the curtain for the doorway at the
entrance to the tabernacle; 16the altar of
burnt offering with its bronze grating, its
poles and all its utensils; the bronze basin
with its stand; 17the curtains of the courtyard with its posts and bases, and the curtain for the entrance to the courtyard;
18the tent pegs for the tabernacle and for
the courtyard, and their ropes; 19the woven garments worn for ministering in the
sanctuary—both the sacred garments for
Aaron the priest and the garments for his
sons when they serve as priests."

20Then the whole Israelite community
withdrew from Moses' presence, 21and everyone who was willing and whose heart
moved him came and brought an offering
to the LORD for the work on the Tent of
Meeting, for all its service, and for the
sacred garments. 22All who were willing,
men and women alike, came and brought
gold jewelry of all kinds: brooches, earrings, rings and ornaments. They all presented their gold as a wave offering to the
LORD. 23Everyone who had blue, purple
or scarlet yarn or fine linen, or goat hair,
ram skins dyed red or hides of sea cows
brought them. 24Those presenting an offering of silver or bronze brought it as an
offering to the LORD, and everyone who
had acacia wood for any part of the work
brought it. 25Every skilled woman spun
with her hands and brought what she had

*a*7 That is, dugongs; also in verse 23

spun—blue, purple or scarlet yarn or fine linen. ²⁶And all the women who were willing and had the skill spun the goat hair. ²⁷The leaders brought onyx stones and other gems to be mounted on the ephod and breastpiece. ²⁸They also brought spices and olive oil for the light and for the anointing oil and for the fragrant incense. ²⁹All the Israelite men and women who were willing brought to the LORD freewill offerings for all the work the LORD through Moses had commanded them to do.

Bezalel and Oholiab

³⁰Then Moses said to the Israelites, "See, the LORD has chosen Bezalel son of Uri, the son of Hur, of the tribe of Judah, ³¹and he has filled him with the Spirit of God, with skill, ability and knowledge in all kinds of crafts— ³²to make artistic designs for work in gold, silver and bronze, ³³to cut and set stones, to work in wood and to engage in all kinds of artistic craftsmanship. ³⁴And he has given both him and Oholiab son of Ahisamach, of the tribe of Dan, the ability to teach others. ³⁵He has filled them with skill to do all kinds of work as craftsmen, designers, embroiderers in blue, purple and scarlet yarn and fine linen, and weavers—all of them master craftsmen and designers.

36 ¹So Bezalel, Oholiab and every skilled person to whom the LORD has given skill and ability to know how to carry out all the work of constructing the sanctuary are to do the work just as the LORD has commanded."

²Then Moses summoned Bezalel and Oholiab and every skilled person to whom the LORD had given ability and who was willing to come and do the work. ³They received from Moses all the offerings the Israelites had brought to carry out the work of constructing the sanctuary. And the people continued to bring freewill offerings morning after morning. ⁴So all the skilled craftsmen who were doing all the work on the sanctuary left their work ⁵and said to Moses, "The people are bringing more than enough for doing the work the LORD commanded to be done."

⁶Then Moses gave an order and they sent this word throughout the camp: "No man or woman is to make anything else as an offering for the sanctuary." And so the people were restrained from bringing more, ⁷because what they already had was more than enough to do all the work.

The Tabernacle

⁸All the skilled men among the workmen made the tabernacle with ten curtains of finely twisted linen and blue, purple and scarlet yarn, with cherubim worked into them by a skilled craftsman. ⁹All the curtains were the same size— twenty-eight cubits long and four cubits wide.ᵃ ¹⁰They joined five of the curtains together and did the same with the other five. ¹¹Then they made loops of blue material along the edge of the end curtain in one set, and the same was done with the end curtain in the other set. ¹²They also made fifty loops on one curtain and fifty loops on the end curtain of the other set, with the loops opposite each other. ¹³Then they made fifty gold clasps and used them to fasten the two sets of curtains together so that the tabernacle was a unit.

¹⁴They made curtains of goat hair for the tent over the tabernacle—eleven altogether. ¹⁵All eleven curtains were the same size—thirty cubits long and four cubits wide.ᵇ ¹⁶They joined five of the curtains into one set and the other six into another set. ¹⁷Then they made fifty loops along the edge of the end curtain in one set and also along the edge of the end curtain in the other set. ¹⁸They made fifty bronze clasps to fasten the tent together as a unit. ¹⁹Then they made for the tent a covering of ram skins dyed red, and over that a covering of hides of sea cows.ᶜ

²⁰They made upright frames of acacia wood for the tabernacle. ²¹Each frame was ten cubits long and a cubit and a half wide,ᵈ ²²with two projections set parallel to each other. They made all the frames of the tabernacle in this way. ²³They made twenty frames for the south side of the tabernacle ²⁴and made forty silver bases

ᵃ9 That is, about 42 feet (about 12.5 meters) long and 6 feet (about 1.8 meters) wide   ᵇ15 That is, about 45 feet (about 13.5 meters) long and 6 feet (about 1.8 meters) wide   ᶜ19 That is, dugongs   ᵈ21 That is, about 15 feet (about 4.5 meters) long and 2 1/4 feet (about 0.7 meter) wide to go under them—two bases for each frame, one under each projection. 25For the other side, the north side of the tabernacle, they made twenty frames 26and forty silver bases—two under each frame. 27They made six frames for the far end, that is, the west end of the tabernacle, 28and two frames were made for the corners of the tabernacle at the far end. 29At these two corners the frames were double from the bottom all the way to the top and fitted into a single ring; both were made alike. 30So there were eight frames and sixteen silver bases—two under each frame.

31They also made crossbars of acacia wood: five for the frames on one side of the tabernacle, 32five for those on the other side, and five for the frames on the west, at the far end of the tabernacle. 33They made the center crossbar so that it extended from end to end at the middle of the frames. 34They overlaid the frames with gold and made gold rings to hold the crossbars. They also overlaid the crossbars with gold.

35They made the curtain of blue, purple and scarlet yarn and finely twisted linen, with cherubim worked into it by a skilled craftsman. 36They made four posts of acacia wood for it and overlaid them with gold. They made gold hooks for them and cast their four silver bases. 37For the entrance to the tent they made a curtain of blue, purple and scarlet yarn and finely twisted linen—the work of an embroiderer; 38and they made five posts with hooks for them. They overlaid the tops of the posts and their bands with gold and made their five bases of bronze.

The Ark

37 Bezalel made the ark of acacia wood—two and a half cubits long, a cubit and a half wide, and a cubit and a half high.[a] 2He overlaid it with pure gold, both inside and out, and made a gold molding around it. 3He cast four gold rings for it and fastened them to its four feet, with two rings on one side and two rings on the other. 4Then he made poles of acacia wood and overlaid them with gold. 5And he inserted the poles into the rings on the sides of the ark to carry it. 6He made the atonement cover of pure

gold—two and a half cubits long and a cubit and a half wide.[b] 7Then he made two cherubim out of hammered gold at the ends of the cover. 8He made one cherub on one end and the second cherub on the other; at the two ends he made them of one piece with the cover. 9The cherubim had their wings spread upward, overshadowing the cover with them. The cherubim faced each other, looking toward the cover.

The Table

10They[c] made the table of acacia wood—two cubits long, a cubit wide, and a cubit and a half high.[d] 11Then they overlaid it with pure gold and made a gold molding around it. 12They also made around it a rim a handbreadth[e] wide and put a gold molding on the rim. 13They cast four gold rings for the table and fastened them to the four corners, where the four legs were. 14The rings were put close to the rim to hold the poles used in carrying the table. 15The poles for carrying the table were made of acacia wood and were overlaid with gold. 16And they made from pure gold the articles for the table—its plates and dishes and bowls and its pitchers for the pouring out of drink offerings.

The Lampstand

17They made the lampstand of pure gold and hammered it out, base and shaft; its flowerlike cups, buds and blossoms were of one piece with it. 18Six branches extended from the sides of the lampstand—three on one side and three on the other. 19Three cups shaped like almond flowers with buds and blossoms were on one branch, three on the next branch and the same for all six branches extending from the lampstand. 20And on the lampstand were four cups shaped like almond flowers with buds and blossoms. 21One bud was under the first pair of

a1 That is, about 3 3/4 feet (about 1.1 meters) long and 2 1/4 feet (about 0.7 meter) wide and high b6 That is, about 3 3/4 feet (about 1.1 meters) long and 2 1/4 feet (about 0.7 meter) wide c10 Or *He*; also in verses 11-29 d10 That is, about 3 feet (about 0.9 meter) long, 1 1/2 feet (about 0.5 meter) wide, and 2 1/4 feet (about 0.7 meter) high e12 That is, about 3 inches (about 8 centimeters) branches extending from the lampstand, a second bud under the second pair, and a third bud under the third pair—six branches in all. ²²The buds and the branches were all of one piece with the lampstand, hammered out of pure gold. ²³They made its seven lamps, as well as its wick trimmers and trays, of pure gold. ²⁴They made the lampstand and all its accessories from one talent^a of pure gold.

The Altar of Incense

²⁵They made the altar of incense out of acacia wood. It was square, a cubit long and a cubit wide, and two cubits high^b—its horns of one piece with it. ²⁶They overlaid the top and all the sides and the horns with pure gold, and made a gold molding around it. ²⁷They made two gold rings below the molding—two on opposite sides—to hold the poles used to carry it. ²⁸They made the poles of acacia wood and overlaid them with gold.

²⁹They also made the sacred anointing oil and the pure, fragrant incense—the work of a perfumer.

The Altar of Burnt Offering

38 They^c built the altar of burnt offering of acacia wood, three cubits^d high; it was square, five cubits long and five cubits wide.^e ²They made a horn at each of the four corners, so that the horns and the altar were of one piece, and they overlaid the altar with bronze. ³They made all its utensils of bronze—its pots, shovels, sprinkling bowls, meat forks and firepans. ⁴They made a grating for the altar, a bronze network, to be under its ledge, halfway up the altar. ⁵They cast bronze rings to hold the poles for the four corners of the bronze grating. ⁶They made the poles of acacia wood and overlaid them with bronze. ⁷They inserted the poles into the rings so they would be on the sides of the altar for carrying it. They made it hollow, out of boards.

Basin for Washing

⁸They made the bronze basin and its bronze stand from the mirrors of the women who served at the entrance to the Tent of Meeting.

The Courtyard

⁹Next they made the courtyard. The south side was a hundred cubits^f long and had curtains of finely twisted linen, ¹⁰with twenty posts and twenty bronze bases, and with silver hooks and bands on the posts. ¹¹The north side was also a hundred cubits long and had twenty posts and twenty bronze bases, with silver hooks and bands on the posts.

¹²The west end was fifty cubits^g wide and had curtains, with ten posts and ten bases, with silver hooks and bands on the posts. ¹³The east end, toward the sunrise, was also fifty cubits wide. ¹⁴Curtains fifteen cubits^h long were on one side of the entrance, with three posts and three bases, ¹⁵and curtains fifteen cubits long were on the other side of the entrance to the courtyard, with three posts and three bases. ¹⁶All the curtains around the courtyard were of finely twisted linen. ¹⁷The bases for the posts were bronze. The hooks and bands on the posts were silver, and their tops were overlaid with silver; so all the posts of the courtyard had silver bands.

¹⁸The curtain for the entrance to the courtyard was of blue, purple and scarlet yarn and finely twisted linen—the work of an embroiderer. It was twenty cubitsⁱ long and, like the curtains of the courtyard, five cubits^j high, ¹⁹with four posts and four bronze bases. Their hooks and bands were silver, and their tops were overlaid with silver. ²⁰All the tent pegs of the tabernacle and of the surrounding courtyard were bronze.

The Materials Used

²¹These are the amounts of the materials used for the tabernacle, the tabernacle of the Testimony, which were recorded at Moses' command by the Levites under the direction of Ithamar son of Aaron, the

^a24 That is, about 75 pounds (about 34 kilograms)   ^b25 That is, about 1 1/2 feet (about 0.5 meter) long and wide, and about 3 feet (about 0.9 meter) high   ^c1 Or He; also in verses 2-9   ^d1 That is, about 4 1/2 feet (about 1.3 meters)   ^e1 That is, about 7 1/2 feet (about 2.3 meters) long and wide   ^f9 That is, about 150 feet (about 46 meters)   ^g12 That is, about 75 feet (about 23 meters)   ^h14 That is, about 22 1/2 feet (about 6.9 meters)   ⁱ18 That is, about 30 feet (about 9 meters)   ^j18 That is, about 7 1/2 feet (about 2.3 meters)

priest. ²²(Bezalel son of Uri, the son of Hur, of the tribe of Judah, made everything the LORD commanded Moses; ²³with him was Oholiab son of Ahisamach, of the tribe of Dan—a craftsman and designer, and an embroiderer in blue, purple and scarlet yarn and fine linen.) ²⁴The total amount of the gold from the wave offering used for all the work on the sanctuary was 29 talents and 730 shekels,ᵃ according to the sanctuary shekel.

²⁵The silver obtained from those of the community who were counted in the census was 100 talents and 1,775 shekels,ᵇ according to the sanctuary shekel— ²⁶one beka per person, that is, half a shekel,ᶜ according to the sanctuary shekel, from everyone who had crossed over to those counted, twenty years old or more, a total of 603,550 men. ²⁷The 100 talentsᵈ of silver were used to cast the bases for the sanctuary and for the curtain—100 bases from the 100 talents, one talent for each base. ²⁸They used the 1,775 shekelsᵉ to make the hooks for the posts, to overlay the tops of the posts, and to make their bands.

²⁹The bronze from the wave offering was 70 talents and 2,400 shekels.ᶠ ³⁰They used it to make the bases for the entrance to the Tent of Meeting, the bronze altar with its bronze grating and all its utensils, ³¹the bases for the surrounding courtyard and those for its entrance and all the tent pegs for the tabernacle and those for the surrounding courtyard.

The Priestly Garments

39 From the blue, purple and scarlet yarn they made woven garments for ministering in the sanctuary. They also made sacred garments for Aaron, as the LORD commanded Moses.

ᵃ24 The weight of the gold was a little over one ton (about 1 metric ton).   ᵇ25 The weight of the silver was a little over 3 3/4 tons (about 3.4 metric tons).   ᶜ26 That is, about 1/5 ounce (about 5.5 grams)   ᵈ27 That is, about 3 3/4 tons (about 3.4 metric tons)   ᵉ28 That is, about 45 pounds (about 20 kilograms) ᶠ29 The weight of the bronze was about 2 1/2 tons (about 2.4 metric tons).

Bringing Our Children Before God

Friday

EXODUS 39:8, 14 Aaron was the spiritual leader of Israel. He was the link between the people and God as he officiated in the tabernacle. He was the one that God designated to teach and pray for the children of Israel. In Exodus 39, Aaron's beautifully ornamented ephod and priestly garments are described in detail. These were the garments he was to wear as he went about his priestly duties. In verse 14, we learn that part of the elaborate decorations on his chest were engraved stones representing each of the twelve tribes of Israel, the children of God. It was as if he were keeping the tribes before God as he went about his duties.

What a picture for us as married couples, as the spiritual leaders of our homes, to be bringing our children and future generations before the Lord. Throughout Scripture, we are challenged as a couple to maintain the responsibility of teaching the next genera-

tion and future generations about God and his precepts. The greatest impact we can have in this training process is to bring them before God in prayer.

When our daughter Torrey entered high school and our son Robey began middle school, I (Rosemary) felt an urgency to pray daily and regularly fast. As their mother, I saw this as my ministry and personal responsibility during this critical time in their lives.

We need to ask God for their protection and care. We need to ask him for wisdom in training and teaching them about him. We need to ask God to draw them to him and help them to grow in their knowledge and understanding of him. Just as Aaron kept the names of God's children before him, so we should keep the names of our loved ones before God.

—Bob & Rosemary

Go to page 133 for your next devotional reading.

The Ephod

[2]They[a] made the ephod of gold, and of blue, purple and scarlet yarn, and of finely twisted linen. [3]They hammered out thin sheets of gold and cut strands to be worked into the blue, purple and scarlet yarn and fine linen—the work of a skilled craftsman. [4]They made shoulder pieces for the ephod, which were attached to two of its corners, so it could be fastened. [5]Its skillfully woven waistband was like it—of one piece with the ephod and made with gold, and with blue, purple and scarlet yarn, and with finely twisted linen, as the LORD commanded Moses.

[6]They mounted the onyx stones in gold filigree settings and engraved them like a seal with the names of the sons of Israel. [7]Then they fastened them on the shoulder pieces of the ephod as memorial stones for the sons of Israel, as the LORD commanded Moses.

The Breastpiece

[8]They fashioned the breastpiece—the work of a skilled craftsman. They made it like the ephod: of gold, and of blue, purple and scarlet yarn, and of finely twisted linen. [9]It was square—a span[b] long and a span wide—and folded double. [10]Then they mounted four rows of precious stones on it. In the first row there was a ruby, a topaz and a beryl; [11]in the second row a turquoise, a sapphire[c] and an emerald; [12]in the third row a jacinth, an agate and an amethyst; [13]in the fourth row a chrysolite, an onyx and a jasper.[d] They were mounted in gold filigree settings. [14]There were twelve stones, one for each of the names of the sons of Israel, each engraved like a seal with the name of one of the twelve tribes.

[15]For the breastpiece they made braided chains of pure gold, like a rope. [16]They made two gold filigree settings and two gold rings, and fastened the rings to two of the corners of the breastpiece. [17]They fastened the two gold chains to the rings at the corners of the breastpiece, [18]and the other ends of the chains to the two settings, attaching them to the shoulder pieces of the ephod at the front. [19]They made two gold rings and attached them to the other two corners of the breastpiece

Bringing Our Children Before God

Take a moment to answer each of these questions on your own. Then compare your answers to your spouse's.

Yes No Praying for my children and teaching them about God is more important than dropping them off for sporting events.

Yes No Do I pray for each child every day?

Yes No I take the time to pray for the future spouse of each of my children.

Yes No Almost every day I spend time reading the Bible with my children.

Yes No Do I know that God has a plan for each of my children?

on the inside edge next to the ephod. [20]Then they made two more gold rings and attached them to the bottom of the shoulder pieces on the front of the ephod, close to the seam just above the waistband of the ephod. [21]They tied the rings of the breastpiece to the rings of the ephod with blue cord, connecting it to the waistband so that the breastpiece would not swing out from the ephod—as the LORD commanded Moses.

Other Priestly Garments

[22]They made the robe of the ephod entirely of blue cloth—the work of a weaver—[23]with an opening in the center of the robe like the opening of a collar,[e] and a band around this opening, so that it would not tear. [24]They made pomegranates of blue, purple and scarlet yarn and finely twisted linen around the hem of the robe. [25]And they made bells of pure gold and attached them around the hem

[a]2 Or He; also in verses 7, 8 and 22   [b]9 That is, about 9 inches (about 22 centimeters)   [c]11 Or lapis lazuli   [d]13 The precise identification of some of these precious stones is uncertain.   [e]23 The meaning of the Hebrew for this word is uncertain.

between the pomegranates. 26The bells and pomegranates alternated around the hem of the robe to be worn for ministering, as the LORD commanded Moses.

27For Aaron and his sons, they made tunics of fine linen—the work of a weaver— 28and the turban of fine linen, the linen headbands and the undergarments of finely twisted linen. 29The sash was of finely twisted linen and blue, purple and scarlet yarn—the work of an embroiderer— as the LORD commanded Moses.

30They made the plate, the sacred diadem, out of pure gold and engraved on it, like an inscription on a seal: HOLY TO THE LORD. 31Then they fastened a blue cord to it to attach it to the turban, as the LORD commanded Moses.

Moses Inspects the Tabernacle

32So all the work on the tabernacle, the Tent of Meeting, was completed. The Israelites did everything just as the LORD commanded Moses. 33Then they brought the tabernacle to Moses: the tent and all its furnishings, its clasps, frames, crossbars, posts and bases; 34the covering of ram skins dyed red, the covering of hides of sea cows*a* and the shielding curtain; 35the ark of the Testimony with its poles and the atonement cover; 36the table with all its articles and the bread of the Presence; 37the pure gold lampstand with its row of lamps and all its accessories, and the oil for the light; 38the gold altar, the anointing oil, the fragrant incense, and the curtain for the entrance to the tent; 39the bronze altar with its bronze grating, its poles and all its utensils; the basin with its stand; 40the curtains of the courtyard with its posts and bases, and the curtain for the entrance to the courtyard; the ropes and tent pegs for the courtyard; all the furnishings for the tabernacle, the Tent of Meeting; 41and the woven garments worn for ministering in the sanctuary, both the sacred garments for Aaron the priest and the garments for his sons when serving as priests.

42The Israelites had done all the work just as the LORD had commanded Moses. 43Moses inspected the work and saw that they had done it just as the LORD had commanded. So Moses blessed them.

Setting Up the Tabernacle

40 Then the LORD said to Moses: 2"Set up the tabernacle, the Tent of Meeting, on the first day of the first month. 3Place the ark of the Testimony in it and shield the ark with the curtain. 4Bring in the table and set out what belongs on it. Then bring in the lampstand and set up its lamps. 5Place the gold altar of incense in front of the ark of the Testimony and put the curtain at the entrance to the tabernacle.

6"Place the altar of burnt offering in front of the entrance to the tabernacle, the Tent of Meeting; 7place the basin between the Tent of Meeting and the altar and put water in it. 8Set up the courtyard around it and put the curtain at the entrance to the courtyard.

9"Take the anointing oil and anoint the tabernacle and everything in it; consecrate it and all its furnishings, and it will be holy. 10Then anoint the altar of burnt offering and all its utensils; consecrate the altar, and it will be most holy. 11Anoint the basin and its stand and consecrate them.

12"Bring Aaron and his sons to the entrance to the Tent of Meeting and wash them with water. 13Then dress Aaron in the sacred garments, anoint him and consecrate him so he may serve me as priest. 14Bring his sons and dress them in tunics. 15Anoint them just as you anointed their father, so they may serve me as priests. Their anointing will be to a priesthood that will continue for all generations to come." 16Moses did everything just as the LORD commanded him.

17So the tabernacle was set up on the first day of the first month in the second year. 18When Moses set up the tabernacle, he put the bases in place, erected the frames, inserted the crossbars and set up the posts. 19Then he spread the tent over the tabernacle and put the covering over the tent, as the LORD commanded him.

20He took the Testimony and placed it in the ark, attached the poles to the ark and put the atonement cover over it. 21Then he brought the ark into the tabernacle and hung the shielding curtain and

a 34 That is, dugongs

shielded the ark of the Testimony, as the LORD commanded him.

²²Moses placed the table in the Tent of Meeting on the north side of the tabernacle outside the curtain ²³and set out the bread on it before the LORD, as the LORD commanded him.

²⁴He placed the lampstand in the Tent of Meeting opposite the table on the south side of the tabernacle ²⁵and set up the lamps before the LORD, as the LORD commanded him.

²⁶Moses placed the gold altar in the Tent of Meeting in front of the curtain ²⁷and burned fragrant incense on it, as the LORD commanded him. ²⁸Then he put up the curtain at the entrance to the tabernacle.

²⁹He set the altar of burnt offering near the entrance to the tabernacle, the Tent of Meeting, and offered on it burnt offerings and grain offerings, as the LORD commanded him.

³⁰He placed the basin between the Tent of Meeting and the altar and put water in it for washing, ³¹and Moses and Aaron and his sons used it to wash their hands and feet. ³²They washed whenever they entered the Tent of Meeting or approached the altar, as the LORD commanded Moses.

³³Then Moses set up the courtyard around the tabernacle and altar and put up the curtain at the entrance to the courtyard. And so Moses finished the work.

The Glory of the LORD

³⁴Then the cloud covered the Tent of Meeting, and the glory of the LORD filled the tabernacle. ³⁵Moses could not enter the Tent of Meeting because the cloud had settled upon it, and the glory of the LORD filled the tabernacle.

³⁶In all the travels of the Israelites, whenever the cloud lifted from above the tabernacle, they would set out; ³⁷but if the cloud did not lift, they did not set out—until the day it lifted. ³⁸So the cloud of the LORD was over the tabernacle by day, and fire was in the cloud by night, in the sight of all the house of Israel during all their travels.

Leviticus

*We don't know
very much about how* the Israelites worshiped God
during their captivity in Egypt, but it's safe to say that after
living in a foreign land for generations, they had probably
slipped into some bad spiritual habits. The book of Leviticus
describes how God, through Moses, got these people back
on track in their relationship with him. And, although some
of the particulars listed here may seem strange, the
message of this book ought to be clear. God takes our relationship with him very seriously. He's not pleased when we
saunter through church every couple of weeks and casually
tip our hats to him. He's the Sovereign Lord of the universe,
and he deserves our disciplined worship.

Moving out of Egypt was no excuse for the Israelites to
get more sloppy with their spiritual discipline. For the
Israelites, there was no postponement of regular religious
rituals. As you read this book, think about how you and your
spouse are doing in this important area.

The Burnt Offering

1 The LORD called to Moses and spoke to him from the Tent of Meeting. He said, ²"Speak to the Israelites and say to them: 'When any of you brings an offering to the LORD, bring as your offering an animal from either the herd or the flock.

³" 'If the offering is a burnt offering from the herd, he is to offer a male without defect. He must present it at the entrance to the Tent of Meeting so that it*ᵃ* will be acceptable to the LORD. ⁴He is to lay his hand on the head of the burnt offering, and it will be accepted on his behalf to make atonement for him. ⁵He is to slaughter the young bull before the LORD, and then Aaron's sons the priests shall bring the blood and sprinkle it against the altar on all sides at the entrance to the Tent of Meeting. ⁶He is to skin the burnt offering and cut it into pieces. ⁷The sons of Aaron the priest are to put fire on the altar and arrange wood

ᵃ3 Or he

on the fire. [8]Then Aaron's sons the priests shall arrange the pieces, including the head and the fat, on the burning wood that is on the altar. [9]He is to wash the inner parts and the legs with water, and the priest is to burn all of it on the altar. It is a burnt offering, an offering made by fire, an aroma pleasing to the LORD.

[10]" 'If the offering is a burnt offering from the flock, from either the sheep or the goats, he is to offer a male without defect. [11]He is to slaughter it at the north side of the altar before the LORD, and Aaron's sons the priests shall sprinkle its blood against the altar on all sides. [12]He is to cut it into pieces, and the priest shall arrange them, including the head and the fat, on the burning wood that is on the altar. [13]He is to wash the inner parts and the legs with water, and the priest is to bring all of it and burn it on the altar. It is a burnt offering, an offering made by fire, an aroma pleasing to the LORD.

[14]" 'If the offering to the LORD is a burnt offering of birds, he is to offer a dove or a young pigeon. [15]The priest shall bring it to the altar, wring off the head and burn it on the altar; its blood shall be drained out on the side of the altar. [16]He is to remove the crop with its contents[a] and throw it to the east side of the altar, where the ashes are. [17]He shall tear it open by the wings, not severing it completely, and then the priest shall burn it on the wood that is on the fire on the altar. It is a burnt offering, an offering made by fire, an aroma pleasing to the LORD.

The Grain Offering

2 " 'When someone brings a grain offering to the LORD, his offering is to be of fine flour. He is to pour oil on it, put incense on it [2]and take it to Aaron's sons the priests. The priest shall take a handful of the fine flour and oil, together with all the incense, and burn this as a memorial portion on the altar, an offering made by fire, an aroma pleasing to the LORD. [3]The rest of the grain offering belongs to Aaron and his sons; it is a most holy part of the offerings made to the LORD by fire.

[4]" 'If you bring a grain offering baked in an oven, it is to consist of fine flour: cakes made without yeast and mixed with oil, or[b] wafers made without yeast and spread with oil. [5]If your grain offering is prepared on a griddle, it is to be made of fine flour mixed with oil, and without yeast. [6]Crumble it and pour oil on it; it is a grain offering. [7]If your grain offering is cooked in a pan, it is to be made of fine flour and oil. [8]Bring the grain offering made of these things to the LORD; present it to the priest, who shall take it to the altar. [9]He shall take out the memorial portion from the grain offering and burn it on the altar as an offering made by fire, an aroma pleasing to the LORD. [10]The rest of the grain offering belongs to Aaron and his sons; it is a most holy part of the offerings made to the LORD by fire.

[11]" 'Every grain offering you bring to the LORD must be made without yeast, for you are not to burn any yeast or honey in an offering made to the LORD by fire. [12]You may bring them to the LORD as an offering of the firstfruits, but they are not to be offered on the altar as a pleasing aroma. [13]Season all your grain offerings with salt. Do not leave the salt of the covenant of your God out of your grain offerings; add salt to all your offerings.

[14]" 'If you bring a grain offering of firstfruits to the LORD, offer crushed heads of new grain roasted in the fire. [15]Put oil and incense on it; it is a grain offering. [16]The priest shall burn the memorial portion of the crushed grain and the oil, together with all the incense, as an offering made to the LORD by fire.

The Fellowship Offering

3 " 'If someone's offering is a fellowship offering,[c] and he offers an animal from the herd, whether male or female, he is to present before the LORD an animal without defect. [2]He is to lay his hand on the head of his offering and slaughter it at the entrance to the Tent of Meeting. Then Aaron's sons the priests shall sprinkle the blood against the altar on all sides. [3]From the fellowship offering he is to bring a sacrifice made to the LORD by fire: all the fat that covers the inner parts or is connected to them, [4]both kid-

[a]16 Or *crop and the feathers*; the meaning of the Hebrew for this word is uncertain.   [b]4 Or *and*
[c]1 Traditionally *peace offering*; also in verses 3, 6 and 9

neys with the fat on them near the loins, and the covering of the liver, which he will remove with the kidneys. ⁵Then Aaron's sons are to burn it on the altar on top of the burnt offering that is on the burning wood, as an offering made by fire, an aroma pleasing to the LORD.

⁶" 'If he offers an animal from the flock as a fellowship offering to the LORD, he is to offer a male or female without defect. ⁷If he offers a lamb, he is to present it before the LORD. ⁸He is to lay his hand on the head of his offering and slaughter it in front of the Tent of Meeting. Then Aaron's sons shall sprinkle its blood against the altar on all sides. ⁹From the fellowship offering he is to bring a sacrifice made to the LORD by fire: its fat, the entire fat tail cut off close to the backbone, all the fat that covers the inner parts or is connected to them, ¹⁰both kidneys with the fat on them near the loins, and the covering of the liver, which he will remove with the kidneys. ¹¹The priest shall burn them on the altar as food, an offering made to the LORD by fire.

¹²" 'If his offering is a goat, he is to present it before the LORD. ¹³He is to lay his hand on its head and slaughter it in front of the Tent of Meeting. Then Aaron's sons shall sprinkle its blood against the altar on all sides. ¹⁴From what he offers he is to make this offering to the LORD by fire: all the fat that covers the inner parts or is connected to them, ¹⁵both kidneys with the fat on them near the loins, and the covering of the liver, which he will remove with the kidneys. ¹⁶The priest shall burn them on the altar as food, an offering made by fire, a pleasing aroma. All the fat is the LORD's.

¹⁷" 'This is a lasting ordinance for the generations to come, wherever you live: You must not eat any fat or any blood.' "

The Sin Offering

4 The LORD said to Moses, ²"Say to the Israelites: 'When anyone sins unintentionally and does what is forbidden in any of the LORD's commands—

³" 'If the anointed priest sins, bringing guilt on the people, he must bring to the LORD a young bull without defect as a sin offering for the sin he has committed. ⁴He is to present the bull at the entrance to the Tent of Meeting before the LORD. He is to lay his hand on its head and slaughter it before the LORD. ⁵Then the anointed priest shall take some of the bull's blood and carry it into the Tent of Meeting. ⁶He is to dip his finger into the blood and sprinkle some of it seven times before the LORD, in front of the curtain of the sanctuary. ⁷The priest shall then put some of the blood on the horns of the altar of fragrant incense that is before the LORD in the Tent of Meeting. The rest of the bull's blood he shall pour out at the base of the altar of burnt offering at the entrance to the Tent of Meeting. ⁸He shall remove all the fat from the bull of the sin offering—the fat that covers the inner parts or is connected to them, ⁹both kidneys with the fat on them near the loins, and the covering of the liver, which he will remove with the kidneys— ¹⁰just as the fat is removed from the ox*ᵃ* sacrificed as a fellowship offering.*ᵇ* Then the priest shall burn them on the altar of burnt offering. ¹¹But the hide of the bull and all its flesh, as well as the head and legs, the inner parts and offal— ¹²that is, all the rest of the bull—he must take outside the camp to a place ceremonially clean, where the ashes are thrown, and burn it in a wood fire on the ash heap.

¹³" 'If the whole Israelite community sins unintentionally and does what is forbidden in any of the LORD's commands, even though the community is unaware of the matter, they are guilty. ¹⁴When they become aware of the sin they committed, the assembly must bring a young bull as a sin offering and present it before the Tent of Meeting. ¹⁵The elders of the community are to lay their hands on the bull's head before the LORD, and the bull shall be slaughtered before the LORD. ¹⁶Then the anointed priest is to take some of the bull's blood into the Tent of Meeting. ¹⁷He shall dip his finger into the blood and sprinkle it before the LORD seven times in front of the curtain. ¹⁸He is to put some of the blood on the horns of the altar that is before the LORD in the Tent of Meeting. The rest of the blood he shall pour out at the base of the altar of burnt

---

ᵃ10 The Hebrew word can include both male and female.   *ᵇ10* Traditionally *peace offering*; also in verses 26, 31 and 35 offering at the entrance to the Tent of Meeting. ¹⁹He shall remove all the fat from it and burn it on the altar, ²⁰and do with this bull just as he did with the bull for the sin offering. In this way the priest will make atonement for them, and they will be forgiven. ²¹Then he shall take the bull outside the camp and burn it as he burned the first bull. This is the sin offering for the community.

²²" 'When a leader sins unintentionally and does what is forbidden in any of the commands of the LORD his God, he is guilty. ²³When he is made aware of the sin he committed, he must bring as his offering a male goat without defect. ²⁴He is to lay his hand on the goat's head and slaughter it at the place where the burnt offering is slaughtered before the LORD. It is a sin offering. ²⁵Then the priest shall take some of the blood of the sin offering with his finger and put it on the horns of the altar of burnt offering and pour out the rest of the blood at the base of the altar. ²⁶He shall burn all the fat on the altar as he burned the fat of the fellowship offering. In this way the priest will make atonement for the man's sin, and he will be forgiven.

²⁷" 'If a member of the community sins unintentionally and does what is forbidden in any of the LORD's commands, he is guilty. ²⁸When he is made aware of the sin he committed, he must bring as his offering for the sin he committed a female goat without defect. ²⁹He is to lay his hand on the head of the sin offering and slaughter it at the place of the burnt offering. ³⁰Then the priest is to take some of the blood with his finger and put it on the horns of the altar of burnt offering and pour out the rest of the blood at the base of the altar. ³¹He shall remove all the fat, just as the fat is removed from the fellowship offering, and the priest shall burn it on the altar as an aroma pleasing to the LORD. In this way the priest will make atonement for him, and he will be forgiven.

³²" 'If he brings a lamb as his sin offering, he is to bring a female without defect. ³³He is to lay his hand on its head and slaughter it for a sin offering at the place where the burnt offering is slaughtered. ³⁴Then the priest shall take some of the blood of the sin offering with his finger and put it on the horns of the altar of burnt offering and pour out the rest of the blood at the base of the altar. ³⁵He shall remove all the fat, just as the fat is removed from the lamb of the fellowship offering, and the priest shall burn it on the altar on top of the offerings made to the LORD by fire. In this way the priest will make atonement for him for the sin he has committed, and he will be forgiven.

5 " 'If a person sins because he does not speak up when he hears a public charge to testify regarding something he has seen or learned about, he will be held responsible.

²" 'Or if a person touches anything ceremonially unclean—whether the carcasses of unclean wild animals or of unclean livestock or of unclean creatures that move along the ground—even though he is unaware of it, he has become unclean and is guilty.

³" 'Or if he touches human uncleanness—anything that would make him unclean—even though he is unaware of it, when he learns of it he will be guilty.

⁴" 'Or if a person thoughtlessly takes an oath to do anything, whether good or evil—in any matter one might carelessly swear about—even though he is unaware of it, in any case when he learns of it he will be guilty.

⁵" 'When anyone is guilty in any of these ways, he must confess in what way he has sinned ⁶and, as a penalty for the sin he has committed, he must bring to the LORD a female lamb or goat from the flock as a sin offering; and the priest shall make atonement for him for his sin.

⁷" 'If he cannot afford a lamb, he is to bring two doves or two young pigeons to the LORD as a penalty for his sin—one for a sin offering and the other for a burnt offering. ⁸He is to bring them to the priest, who shall first offer the one for the sin offering. He is to wring its head from its neck, not severing it completely, ⁹and is to sprinkle some of the blood of the sin offering against the side of the altar; the rest of the blood must be drained out at the base of the altar. It is a sin offering. ¹⁰The priest shall then offer the other as a burnt offering in the prescribed way and make atonement for him for the sin he

has committed, and he will be forgiven.

11 " 'If, however, he cannot afford two doves or two young pigeons, he is to bring as an offering for his sin a tenth of an ephah[a] of fine flour for a sin offering. He must not put oil or incense on it, because it is a sin offering. 12He is to bring it to the priest, who shall take a handful of it as a memorial portion and burn it on the altar on top of the offerings made to the LORD by fire. It is a sin offering. 13In this way the priest will make atonement for him for any of these sins he has committed, and he will be forgiven. The rest of the offering will belong to the priest, as in the case of the grain offering.' "

The Guilt Offering

14The LORD said to Moses: 15"When a person commits a violation and sins unintentionally in regard to any of the LORD's holy things, he is to bring to the LORD as a penalty a ram from the flock, one without defect and of the proper value in silver, according to the sanctuary shekel.[b] It is a guilt offering. 16He must make restitution for what he has failed to do in regard to the holy things, add a fifth of the value to that and give it all to the priest, who will make atonement for him with the ram as a guilt offering, and he will be forgiven.

17"If a person sins and does what is forbidden in any of the LORD's commands, even though he does not know it, he is guilty and will be held responsible. 18He is to bring to the priest as a guilt offering a ram from the flock, one without defect and of the proper value. In this way the priest will make atonement for him for the wrong he has committed unintentionally, and he will be forgiven. 19It is a guilt offering; he has been guilty of[c] wrongdoing against the LORD."

6 The LORD said to Moses: 2"If anyone sins and is unfaithful to the LORD by deceiving his neighbor about something entrusted to him or left in his care or stolen, or if he cheats him, 3or if he finds lost property and lies about it, or if he swears falsely, or if he commits any such sin that people may do— 4when he thus sins and becomes guilty, he must return what he has stolen or taken by extortion, or what was entrusted to him, or the lost property

he found, 5or whatever it was he swore falsely about. He must make restitution in full, add a fifth of the value to it and give it all to the owner on the day he presents his guilt offering. 6And as a penalty he must bring to the priest, that is, to the LORD, his guilt offering, a ram from the flock, one without defect and of the proper value. 7In this way the priest will make atonement for him before the LORD, and he will be forgiven for any of these things he did that made him guilty."

The Burnt Offering

8The LORD said to Moses: 9"Give Aaron and his sons this command: 'These are the regulations for the burnt offering: The burnt offering is to remain on the altar hearth throughout the night, till morning, and the fire must be kept burning on the altar. 10The priest shall then put on his linen clothes, with linen undergarments next to his body, and shall remove the ashes of the burnt offering that the fire has consumed on the altar and place them beside the altar. 11Then he is to take off these clothes and put on others, and carry the ashes outside the camp to a place that is ceremonially clean. 12The fire on the altar must be kept burning; it must not go out. Every morning the priest is to add firewood and arrange the burnt offering on the fire and burn the fat of the fellowship offerings[d] on it. 13The fire must be kept burning on the altar continuously; it must not go out.

The Grain Offering

14" 'These are the regulations for the grain offering: Aaron's sons are to bring it before the LORD, in front of the altar. 15The priest is to take a handful of fine flour and oil, together with all the incense on the grain offering, and burn the memorial portion on the altar as an aroma pleasing to the LORD. 16Aaron and his sons shall eat the rest of it, but it is to be eaten without yeast in a holy place; they are to eat it in the courtyard of the Tent of Meeting. 17It must not be baked with yeast; I have given it as their share of the

a11 That is, probably about 2 quarts (about 2 liters)   b15 That is, about 2/5 ounce (about 11.5 grams)   c19 Or has made full expiation for his   d12 Traditionally peace offerings

offerings made to me by fire. Like the sin offering and the guilt offering, it is most holy. [18]Any male descendant of Aaron may eat it. It is his regular share of the offerings made to the LORD by fire for the generations to come. Whatever touches them will become holy.[a] "

[19]The LORD also said to Moses, [20]"This is the offering Aaron and his sons are to bring to the LORD on the day he[b] is anointed: a tenth of an ephah[c] of fine flour as a regular grain offering, half of it in the morning and half in the evening. [21]Prepare it with oil on a griddle; bring it well-mixed and present the grain offering broken[d] in pieces as an aroma pleasing to the LORD. [22]The son who is to succeed him as anointed priest shall prepare it. It is the LORD's regular share and is to be burned completely. [23]Every grain offering of a priest shall be burned completely; it must not be eaten."

The Sin Offering

[24]The LORD said to Moses, [25]"Say to Aaron and his sons: 'These are the regulations for the sin offering: The sin offering is to be slaughtered before the LORD in the place the burnt offering is slaughtered; it is most holy. [26]The priest who offers it shall eat it; it is to be eaten in a holy place, in the courtyard of the Tent of Meeting. [27]Whatever touches any of the flesh will become holy, and if any of the blood is spattered on a garment, you must wash it in a holy place. [28]The clay pot the meat is cooked in must be broken; but if it is cooked in a bronze pot, the pot is to be scoured and rinsed with water. [29]Any male in a priest's family may eat it; it is most holy. [30]But any sin offering whose blood is brought into the Tent of Meeting to make atonement in the Holy Place must not be eaten; it must be burned.

The Guilt Offering

7 " 'These are the regulations for the guilt offering, which is most holy: [2]The guilt offering is to be slaughtered in the place where the burnt offering is slaughtered, and its blood is to be sprinkled against the altar on all sides. [3]All its fat shall be offered: the fat tail and the fat that covers the inner parts, [4]both kidneys with the fat on them near the loins, and

the covering of the liver, which is to be removed with the kidneys. [5]The priest shall burn them on the altar as an offering made to the LORD by fire. It is a guilt offering. [6]Any male in a priest's family may eat it, but it must be eaten in a holy place; it is most holy.

[7]" 'The same law applies to both the sin offering and the guilt offering: They belong to the priest who makes atonement with them. [8]The priest who offers a burnt offering for anyone may keep its hide for himself. [9]Every grain offering baked in an oven or cooked in a pan or on a griddle belongs to the priest who offers it, [10]and every grain offering, whether mixed with oil or dry, belongs equally to all the sons of Aaron.

The Fellowship Offering

[11]" 'These are the regulations for the fellowship offering[e] a person may present to the LORD:

[12]" 'If he offers it as an expression of thankfulness, then along with this thank offering he is to offer cakes of bread made without yeast and mixed with oil, wafers made without yeast and spread with oil, and cakes of fine flour well-kneaded and mixed with oil. [13]Along with his fellowship offering of thanksgiving he is to present an offering with cakes of bread made with yeast. [14]He is to bring one of each kind as an offering, a contribution to the LORD; it belongs to the priest who sprinkles the blood of the fellowship offerings. [15]The meat of his fellowship offering of thanksgiving must be eaten on the day it is offered; he must leave none of it till morning.

[16]" 'If, however, his offering is the result of a vow or is a freewill offering, the sacrifice shall be eaten on the day he offers it, but anything left over may be eaten on the next day. [17]Any meat of the sacrifice left over till the third day must be burned up. [18]If any meat of the fellowship offering is eaten on the third day, it will not be accepted. It will not be credited to the one who offered it, for it is impure;

[a]18 Or Whoever touches them must be holy; similarly in verse 27   [b]20 Or each   [c]20 That is, probably about 2 quarts (about 2 liters)   [d]21 The meaning of the Hebrew for this word is uncertain.   [e]11 Traditionally peace offering; also in verses 13-37

the person who eats any of it will be held responsible.

[19]" 'Meat that touches anything ceremonially unclean must not be eaten; it must be burned up. As for other meat, anyone ceremonially clean may eat it. [20]But if anyone who is unclean eats any meat of the fellowship offering belonging to the LORD, that person must be cut off from his people. [21]If anyone touches something unclean—whether human uncleanness or an unclean animal or any unclean, detestable thing—and then eats any of the meat of the fellowship offering belonging to the LORD, that person must be cut off from his people.' "

Eating Fat and Blood Forbidden

[22]The LORD said to Moses, [23]"Say to the Israelites: 'Do not eat any of the fat of cattle, sheep or goats. [24]The fat of an animal found dead or torn by wild animals may be used for any other purpose, but you must not eat it. [25]Anyone who eats the fat of an animal from which an offering by fire may be[a] made to the LORD must be cut off from his people. [26]And wherever you live, you must not eat the blood of any bird or animal. [27]If anyone eats blood, that person must be cut off from his people.' "

The Priests' Share

[28]The LORD said to Moses, [29]"Say to the Israelites: 'Anyone who brings a fellowship offering to the LORD is to bring part of it as his sacrifice to the LORD. [30]With his own hands he is to bring the offering made to the LORD by fire; he is to bring the fat, together with the breast, and wave the breast before the LORD as a wave offering. [31]The priest shall burn the fat on the altar, but the breast belongs to Aaron and his sons. [32]You are to give the right thigh of your fellowship offerings to the priest as a contribution. [33]The son of Aaron who offers the blood and the fat of the fellowship offering shall have the right thigh as his share. [34]From the fellowship offerings of the Israelites, I have taken the breast that is waved and the thigh that is presented and have given them to Aaron the priest and his sons as their regular share from the Israelites.' "

[35]This is the portion of the offerings made to the LORD by fire that were allotted to Aaron and his sons on the day they were presented to serve the LORD as priests. [36]On the day they were anointed, the LORD commanded that the Israelites give this to them as their regular share for the generations to come.

[37]These, then, are the regulations for the burnt offering, the grain offering, the sin offering, the guilt offering, the ordination offering and the fellowship offering, [38]which the LORD gave Moses on Mount Sinai on the day he commanded the Israelites to bring their offerings to the LORD, in the Desert of Sinai.

The Ordination of Aaron and His Sons

8 The LORD said to Moses, [2]"Bring Aaron and his sons, their garments, the anointing oil, the bull for the sin offering, the two rams and the basket containing bread made without yeast, [3]and gather the entire assembly at the entrance to the Tent of Meeting." [4]Moses did as the LORD commanded him, and the assembly gathered at the entrance to the Tent of Meeting.

[5]Moses said to the assembly, "This is what the LORD has commanded to be done." [6]Then Moses brought Aaron and his sons forward and washed them with water. [7]He put the tunic on Aaron, tied the sash around him, clothed him with the robe and put the ephod on him. He also tied the ephod to him by its skillfully woven waistband; so it was fastened on him. [8]He placed the breastpiece on him and put the Urim and Thummim in the breastpiece. [9]Then he placed the turban on Aaron's head and set the gold plate, the sacred diadem, on the front of it, as the LORD commanded Moses.

[10]Then Moses took the anointing oil and anointed the tabernacle and everything in it, and so consecrated them. [11]He sprinkled some of the oil on the altar seven times, anointing the altar and all its utensils and the basin with its stand, to consecrate them. [12]He poured some of the anointing oil on Aaron's head and anointed him to consecrate him. [13]Then he brought Aaron's sons forward, put tunics on them, tied sashes around them

[a]25 Or fire is

and put headbands on them, as the LORD commanded Moses.

[14]He then presented the bull for the sin offering, and Aaron and his sons laid their hands on its head. [15]Moses slaughtered the bull and took some of the blood, and with his finger he put it on all the horns of the altar to purify the altar. He poured out the rest of the blood at the base of the altar. So he consecrated it to make atonement for it. [16]Moses also took all the fat around the inner parts, the covering of the liver, and both kidneys and their fat, and burned it on the altar. [17]But the bull with its hide and its flesh and its offal he burned up outside the camp, as the LORD commanded Moses.

[18]He then presented the ram for the burnt offering, and Aaron and his sons laid their hands on its head. [19]Then Moses slaughtered the ram and sprinkled the blood against the altar on all sides. [20]He cut the ram into pieces and burned the head, the pieces and the fat. [21]He washed the inner parts and the legs with water and burned the whole ram on the altar as a burnt offering, a pleasing aroma, an offering made to the LORD by fire, as the LORD commanded Moses.

[22]He then presented the other ram, the ram for the ordination, and Aaron and his sons laid their hands on its head. [23]Moses slaughtered the ram and took some of its blood and put it on the lobe of Aaron's right ear, on the thumb of his right hand and on the big toe of his right foot. [24]Moses also brought Aaron's sons forward and put some of the blood on the lobes of their right ears, on the thumbs of their right hands and on the big toes of their right feet. Then he sprinkled blood against the altar on all sides. [25]He took the fat, the fat tail, all the fat around the inner parts, the covering of the liver, both kidneys and their fat and the right thigh. [26]Then from the basket of bread made without yeast, which was before the LORD, he took a cake of bread, and one made with oil, and a wafer; he put these on the fat portions and on the right thigh. [27]He put all these in the hands of Aaron and his sons and waved them before the LORD as a wave offering. [28]Then Moses took them from their hands and burned them on the altar on top of the burnt offering as an ordination offering, a pleasing aro-ma, an offering made to the LORD by fire. [29]He also took the breast—Moses' share of the ordination ram—and waved it before the LORD as a wave offering, as the LORD commanded Moses.

[30]Then Moses took some of the anointing oil and some of the blood from the altar and sprinkled them on Aaron and his garments and on his sons and their garments. So he consecrated Aaron and his garments and his sons and their garments.

[31]Moses then said to Aaron and his sons, "Cook the meat at the entrance to the Tent of Meeting and eat it there with the bread from the basket of ordination offerings, as I commanded, saying,[a] 'Aaron and his sons are to eat it.' [32]Then burn up the rest of the meat and the bread. [33]Do not leave the entrance to the Tent of Meeting for seven days, until the days of your ordination are completed, for your ordination will last seven days. [34]What has been done today was commanded by the LORD to make atonement for you. [35]You must stay at the entrance to the Tent of Meeting day and night for seven days and do what the LORD requires, so you will not die; for that is what I have been commanded." [36]So Aaron and his sons did everything the LORD commanded through Moses.

The Priests Begin Their Ministry

9 On the eighth day Moses summoned Aaron and his sons and the elders of Israel. [2]He said to Aaron, "Take a bull calf for your sin offering and a ram for your burnt offering, both without defect, and present them before the LORD. [3]Then say to the Israelites: 'Take a male goat for a sin offering, a calf and a lamb—both a year old and without defect—for a burnt offering, [4]and an ox[b] and a ram for a fellowship offering[c] to sacrifice before the LORD, together with a grain offering mixed with oil. For today the LORD will appear to you.' "

[5]They took the things Moses commanded to the front of the Tent of Meeting, and the entire assembly came near

---

[a]31 Or I was commanded: [b]4 The Hebrew word can include both male and female; also in verses 18 and 19.   [c]4 Traditionally peace offering; also in verses 18 and 22

and stood before the LORD. ⁶Then Moses said, "This is what the LORD has commanded you to do, so that the glory of the LORD may appear to you."

⁷Moses said to Aaron, "Come to the altar and sacrifice your sin offering and your burnt offering and make atonement for yourself and the people; sacrifice the offering that is for the people and make atonement for them, as the LORD has commanded."

⁸So Aaron came to the altar and slaughtered the calf as a sin offering for himself. ⁹His sons brought the blood to him, and he dipped his finger into the blood and put it on the horns of the altar; the rest of the blood he poured out at the base of the altar. ¹⁰On the altar he burned the fat, the kidneys and the covering of the liver from the sin offering, as the LORD commanded Moses; ¹¹the flesh and the hide he burned up outside the camp.

¹²Then he slaughtered the burnt offering. His sons handed him the blood, and he sprinkled it against the altar on all sides. ¹³They handed him the burnt offering piece by piece, including the head, and he burned them on the altar. ¹⁴He washed the inner parts and the legs and burned them on top of the burnt offering on the altar.

¹⁵Aaron then brought the offering that was for the people. He took the goat for the people's sin offering and slaughtered it and offered it for a sin offering as he did with the first one.

¹⁶He brought the burnt offering and offered it in the prescribed way. ¹⁷He also brought the grain offering, took a handful of it and burned it on the altar in addition to the morning's burnt offering.

¹⁸He slaughtered the ox and the ram as the fellowship offering for the people. His sons handed him the blood, and he sprinkled it against the altar on all sides. ¹⁹But the fat portions of the ox and the ram—the fat tail, the layer of fat, the kidneys and the covering of the liver— ²⁰these they laid on the breasts, and then Aaron burned the fat on the altar. ²¹Aaron waved the breasts and the right thigh before the LORD as a wave offering, as Moses commanded.

²²Then Aaron lifted his hands toward the people and blessed them. And having sacrificed the sin offering, the burnt offer-

ing and the fellowship offering, he stepped down.

²³Moses and Aaron then went into the Tent of Meeting. When they came out, they blessed the people; and the glory of the LORD appeared to all the people. ²⁴Fire came out from the presence of the LORD and consumed the burnt offering and the fat portions on the altar. And when all the people saw it, they shouted for joy and fell facedown.

The Death of Nadab and Abihu

10 Aaron's sons Nadab and Abihu took their censers, put fire in them and added incense; and they offered unauthorized fire before the LORD, contrary to his command. ²So fire came out from the presence of the LORD and consumed them, and they died before the LORD. ³Moses then said to Aaron, "This is what the LORD spoke of when he said:

" 'Among those who approach me
    I will show myself holy;
in the sight of all the people
    I will be honored.' "

Aaron remained silent.

⁴Moses summoned Mishael and Elzaphan, sons of Aaron's uncle Uzziel, and said to them, "Come here; carry your cousins outside the camp, away from the front of the sanctuary." ⁵So they came and carried them, still in their tunics, outside the camp, as Moses ordered.

⁶Then Moses said to Aaron and his sons Eleazar and Ithamar, "Do not let your hair become unkempt,ᵃ and do not tear your clothes, or you will die and the LORD will be angry with the whole community. But your relatives, all the house of Israel, may mourn for those the LORD has destroyed by fire. ⁷Do not leave the entrance to the Tent of Meeting or you will die, because the LORD's anointing oil is on you." So they did as Moses said.

⁸Then the LORD said to Aaron, ⁹"You and your sons are not to drink wine or other fermented drink whenever you go into the Tent of Meeting, or you will die. This is a lasting ordinance for the generations to come. ¹⁰You must distinguish between the holy and the common, between the unclean and the clean, ¹¹and

---

ᵃ6 Or *Do not uncover your heads*

you must teach the Israelites all the decrees the LORD has given them through Moses."

¹²Moses said to Aaron and his remaining sons, Eleazar and Ithamar, "Take the grain offering left over from the offerings made to the LORD by fire and eat it prepared without yeast beside the altar, for it is most holy. ¹³Eat it in a holy place, because it is your share and your sons' share of the offerings made to the LORD by fire; for so I have been commanded. ¹⁴But you and your sons and your daughters may eat the breast that was waved and the thigh that was presented. Eat them in a ceremonially clean place; they have been given to you and your children as your share of the Israelites' fellowship offerings.ᵃ ¹⁵The thigh that was presented and the breast that was waved must be brought with the fat portions of the offerings made by fire, to be waved before the LORD as a wave offering. This will be the regular share for you and your children, as the LORD has commanded."

¹⁶When Moses inquired about the goat of the sin offering and found that it had been burned up, he was angry with Eleazar and Ithamar, Aaron's remaining sons, and asked, ¹⁷"Why didn't you eat the sin offering in the sanctuary area? It is most holy; it was given to you to take away the guilt of the community by making atonement for them before the LORD. ¹⁸Since its blood was not taken into the Holy Place, you should have eaten the goat in the sanctuary area, as I commanded."

¹⁹Aaron replied to Moses, "Today they sacrificed their sin offering and their burnt offering before the LORD, but such things as this have happened to me. Would the LORD have been pleased if I had eaten the sin offering today?" ²⁰When Moses heard this, he was satisfied.

Clean and Unclean Food

11 The LORD said to Moses and Aaron, ²"Say to the Israelites: 'Of all the animals that live on land, these are the ones you may eat: ³You may eat any animal that has a split hoof completely divided and that chews the cud.

⁴"'There are some that only chew the cud or only have a split hoof, but you must not eat them. The camel, though it chews the cud, does not have a split hoof; it is ceremonially unclean for you. ⁵The coney,ᵇ though it chews the cud, does not have a split hoof; it is unclean for you. ⁶The rabbit, though it chews the cud, does not have a split hoof; it is unclean for you. ⁷And the pig, though it has a split hoof completely divided, does not chew the cud; it is unclean for you. ⁸You must not eat their meat or touch their carcasses; they are unclean for you.

⁹"'Of all the creatures living in the water of the seas and the streams, you may eat any that have fins and scales. ¹⁰But all creatures in the seas or streams that do not have fins and scales—whether among all the swarming things or among all the other living creatures in the water—you are to detest. ¹¹And since you are to detest them, you must not eat their meat and you must detest their carcasses. ¹²Anything living in the water that does not have fins and scales is to be detestable to you.

¹³"'These are the birds you are to detest and not eat because they are detestable: the eagle, the vulture, the black vulture, ¹⁴the red kite, any kind of black kite, ¹⁵any kind of raven, ¹⁶the horned owl, the screech owl, the gull, any kind of hawk, ¹⁷the little owl, the cormorant, the great owl, ¹⁸the white owl, the desert owl, the osprey, ¹⁹the stork, any kind of heron, the hoopoe and the bat.ᶜ

²⁰"'All flying insects that walk on all fours are to be detestable to you. ²¹There are, however, some winged creatures that walk on all fours that you may eat: those that have jointed legs for hopping on the ground. ²²Of these you may eat any kind of locust, katydid, cricket or grasshopper. ²³But all other winged creatures that have four legs you are to detest.

²⁴"'You will make yourselves unclean by these; whoever touches their carcasses will be unclean till evening. ²⁵Whoever picks up one of their carcasses must wash his clothes, and he will be unclean till evening.

²⁶"'Every animal that has a split hoof not completely divided or that does not chew the cud is unclean for you; whoever

---

ᵃ14 Traditionally *peace offerings*   ᵇ5 That is, the hyrax or rock badger   ᶜ19 The precise identification of some of the birds, insects and animals in this chapter is uncertain.

touches ⌊the carcass of⌋ any of them will be unclean. ²⁷Of all the animals that walk on all fours, those that walk on their paws are unclean for you; whoever touches their carcasses will be unclean till evening. ²⁸Anyone who picks up their carcasses must wash his clothes, and he will be unclean till evening. They are unclean for you.

²⁹" 'Of the animals that move about on the ground, these are unclean for you: the weasel, the rat, any kind of great lizard, ³⁰the gecko, the monitor lizard, the wall lizard, the skink and the chameleon. ³¹Of all those that move along the ground, these are unclean for you. Whoever touches them when they are dead will be unclean till evening. ³²When one of them dies and falls on something, that article, whatever its use, will be unclean, whether it is made of wood, cloth, hide or sackcloth. Put it in water; it will be unclean till evening, and then it will be clean. ³³If one of them falls into a clay pot, everything in it will be unclean, and you must break the pot. ³⁴Any food that could be eaten but has water on it from such a pot is unclean, and any liquid that could be drunk from it is unclean. ³⁵Anything that one of their carcasses falls on becomes unclean; an oven or cooking pot must be broken up. They are unclean, and you are to regard them as unclean. ³⁶A spring, however, or a cistern for collecting water remains clean, but anyone who touches one of these carcasses is unclean. ³⁷If a carcass falls on any seeds that are to be planted, they remain clean. ³⁸But if water has been put on the seed and a carcass falls on it, it is unclean for you.

³⁹" 'If an animal that you are allowed to eat dies, anyone who touches the carcass will be unclean till evening. ⁴⁰Anyone who eats some of the carcass must wash his clothes, and he will be unclean till evening. Anyone who picks up the carcass must wash his clothes, and he will be unclean till evening.

⁴¹" 'Every creature that moves about on the ground is detestable; it is not to be eaten. ⁴²You are not to eat any creature that moves about on the ground, whether it moves on its belly or walks on all fours or on many feet; it is detestable. ⁴³Do not defile yourselves by any of these creatures. Do not make yourselves unclean by

means of them or be made unclean by them. ⁴⁴I am the LORD your God; consecrate yourselves and be holy, because I am holy. Do not make yourselves unclean by any creature that moves about on the ground. ⁴⁵I am the LORD who brought you up out of Egypt to be your God; therefore be holy, because I am holy.

⁴⁶" 'These are the regulations concerning animals, birds, every living thing that moves in the water and every creature that moves about on the ground. ⁴⁷You must distinguish between the unclean and the clean, between living creatures that may be eaten and those that may not be eaten.' "

Purification After Childbirth

12 The LORD said to Moses, ²"Say to the Israelites: 'A woman who becomes pregnant and gives birth to a son will be ceremonially unclean for seven days, just as she is unclean during her monthly period. ³On the eighth day the boy is to be circumcised. ⁴Then the woman must wait thirty-three days to be purified from her bleeding. She must not touch anything sacred or go to the sanctuary until the days of her purification are over. ⁵If she gives birth to a daughter, for two weeks the woman will be unclean, as during her period. Then she must wait sixty-six days to be purified from her bleeding.

⁶" 'When the days of her purification for a son or daughter are over, she is to bring to the priest at the entrance to the Tent of Meeting a year-old lamb for a burnt offering and a young pigeon or a dove for a sin offering. ⁷He shall offer them before the LORD to make atonement for her, and then she will be ceremonially clean from her flow of blood.

" 'These are the regulations for the woman who gives birth to a boy or a girl. ⁸If she cannot afford a lamb, she is to bring two doves or two young pigeons, one for a burnt offering and the other for a sin offering. In this way the priest will make atonement for her, and she will be clean.' "

Regulations About Infectious Skin Diseases

13 The LORD said to Moses and Aaron, ²"When anyone has a swelling or a rash or a bright spot on his skin that may become an infectious skin disease,[a] he must be brought to Aaron the priest or to one of his sons[b] who is a priest. [3]The priest is to examine the sore on his skin, and if the hair in the sore has turned white and the sore appears to be more than skin deep,[c] it is an infectious skin disease. When the priest examines him, he shall pronounce him ceremonially unclean. [4]If the spot on his skin is white but does not appear to be more than skin deep and the hair in it has not turned white, the priest is to put the infected person in isolation for seven days. [5]On the seventh day the priest is to examine him, and if he sees that the sore is unchanged and has not spread in the skin, he is to keep him in isolation another seven days. [6]On the seventh day the priest is to examine him again, and if the sore has faded and has not spread in the skin, the priest shall pronounce him clean; it is only a rash. The man must wash his clothes, and he will be clean. [7]But if the rash does spread in his skin after he has shown himself to the priest to be pronounced clean, he must appear before the priest again. [8]The priest is to examine him, and if the rash has spread in the skin, he shall pronounce him unclean; it is an infectious disease.

[9]"When anyone has an infectious skin disease, he must be brought to the priest. [10]The priest is to examine him, and if there is a white swelling in the skin that has turned the hair white and if there is raw flesh in the swelling, [11]it is a chronic skin disease and the priest shall pronounce him unclean. He is not to put him in isolation, because he is already unclean.

[12]"If the disease breaks out all over his skin and, so far as the priest can see, it covers all the skin of the infected person from head to foot, [13]the priest is to examine him, and if the disease has covered his whole body, he shall pronounce that person clean. Since it has all turned white, he is clean. [14]But whenever raw flesh appears on him, he will be unclean. [15]When the priest sees the raw flesh, he shall pronounce him unclean. The raw flesh is unclean; he has an infectious disease. [16]Should the raw flesh change and turn white, he must go to the priest. [17]The priest is to examine him, and if the sores have turned white, the priest shall pronounce the infected person clean; then he will be clean.

[18]"When someone has a boil on his skin and it heals, [19]and in the place where the boil was, a white swelling or reddish-white spot appears, he must present himself to the priest. [20]The priest is to examine it, and if it appears to be more than skin deep and the hair in it has turned white, the priest shall pronounce him unclean. It is an infectious skin disease that has broken out where the boil was. [21]But if, when the priest examines it, there is no white hair in it and it is not more than skin deep and has faded, then the priest is to put him in isolation for seven days. [22]If it is spreading in the skin, the priest shall pronounce him unclean; it is infectious. [23]But if the spot is unchanged and has not spread, it is only a scar from the boil, and the priest shall pronounce him clean.

[24]"When someone has a burn on his skin and a reddish-white or white spot appears in the raw flesh of the burn, [25]the priest is to examine the spot, and if the hair in it has turned white, and it appears to be more than skin deep, it is an infectious disease that has broken out in the burn. The priest shall pronounce him unclean; it is an infectious skin disease. [26]But if the priest examines it and there is no white hair in the spot and if it is not more than skin deep and has faded, then the priest is to put him in isolation for seven days. [27]On the seventh day the priest is to examine him, and if it is spreading in the skin, the priest shall pronounce him unclean; it is an infectious skin disease. [28]If, however, the spot is unchanged and has not spread in the skin but has faded, it is a swelling from the burn, and the priest shall pronounce him clean; it is only a scar from the burn.

[29]"If a man or woman has a sore on the head or on the chin, [30]the priest is to examine the sore, and if it appears to be more than skin deep and the hair in it is yellow and thin, the priest shall pronounce that person unclean; it is an itch,

[a]2 Traditionally *leprosy*; the Hebrew word was used for various diseases affecting the skin—not necessarily leprosy; also elsewhere in this chapter.   [b]2 Or *descendants*   [c]3 Or *be lower than the rest of the skin*; also elsewhere in this chapter

an infectious disease of the head or chin. [31]But if, when the priest examines this kind of sore, it does not seem to be more than skin deep and there is no black hair in it, then the priest is to put the infected person in isolation for seven days. [32]On the seventh day the priest is to examine the sore, and if the itch has not spread and there is no yellow hair in it and it does not appear to be more than skin deep, [33]he must be shaved except for the diseased area, and the priest is to keep him in isolation another seven days. [34]On the seventh day the priest is to examine the itch, and if it has not spread in the skin and appears to be no more than skin deep, the priest shall pronounce him clean. He must wash his clothes, and he will be clean. [35]But if the itch does spread in the skin after he is pronounced clean, [36]the priest is to examine him, and if the itch has spread in the skin, the priest does not need to look for yellow hair; the person is unclean. [37]If, however, in his judgment it is unchanged and black hair has grown in it, the itch is healed. He is clean, and the priest shall pronounce him clean.

[38]"When a man or woman has white spots on the skin, [39]the priest is to examine them, and if the spots are dull white, it is a harmless rash that has broken out on the skin; that person is clean.

[40]"When a man has lost his hair and is bald, he is clean. [41]If he has lost his hair from the front of his scalp and has a bald forehead, he is clean. [42]But if he has a reddish-white sore on his bald head or forehead, it is an infectious disease breaking out on his head or forehead. [43]The priest is to examine him, and if the swollen sore on his head or forehead is reddish-white like an infectious skin disease, [44]the man is diseased and is unclean. The priest shall pronounce him unclean because of the sore on his head.

[45]"The person with such an infectious disease must wear torn clothes, let his hair be unkempt,[a] cover the lower part of his face and cry out, 'Unclean! Unclean!' [46]As long as he has the infection he remains unclean. He must live alone; he must live outside the camp.

Regulations About Mildew

[47]"If any clothing is contaminated with mildew—any woolen or linen clothing, [48]any woven or knitted material of linen or wool, any leather or anything made of leather— [49]and if the contamination in the clothing, or leather, or woven or knitted material, or any leather article, is greenish or reddish, it is a spreading mildew and must be shown to the priest. [50]The priest is to examine the mildew and isolate the affected article for seven days. [51]On the seventh day he is to examine it, and if the mildew has spread in the clothing, or the woven or knitted material, or the leather, whatever its use, it is a destructive mildew; the article is unclean. [52]He must burn up the clothing, or the woven or knitted material of wool or linen, or any leather article that has the contamination in it, because the mildew is destructive; the article must be burned up.

[53]"But if, when the priest examines it, the mildew has not spread in the clothing, or the woven or knitted material, or the leather article, [54]he shall order that the contaminated article be washed. Then he is to isolate it for another seven days. [55]After the affected article has been washed, the priest is to examine it, and if the mildew has not changed its appearance, even though it has not spread, it is unclean. Burn it with fire, whether the mildew has affected one side or the other. [56]If, when the priest examines it, the mildew has faded after the article has been washed, he is to tear the contaminated part out of the clothing, or the leather, or the woven or knitted material. [57]But if it reappears in the clothing, or in the woven or knitted material, or in the leather article, it is spreading, and whatever has the mildew must be burned with fire. [58]The clothing, or the woven or knitted material, or any leather article that has been washed and is rid of the mildew, must be washed again, and it will be clean."

[59]These are the regulations concerning contamination by mildew in woolen or linen clothing, woven or knitted material, or any leather article, for pronouncing them clean or unclean.

---

[a]45 Or *clothes, uncover his head*

Cleansing From Infectious Skin Diseases

14 The LORD said to Moses, ² "These are the regulations for the diseased person at the time of his ceremonial cleansing, when he is brought to the priest: ³The priest is to go outside the camp and examine him. If the person has been healed of his infectious skin disease,ᵃ ⁴the priest shall order that two live clean birds and some cedar wood, scarlet yarn and hyssop be brought for the one to be cleansed. ⁵Then the priest shall order that one of the birds be killed over fresh water in a clay pot. ⁶He is then to take the live bird and dip it, together with the cedar wood, the scarlet yarn and the hyssop, into the blood of the bird that was killed over the fresh water. ⁷Seven times he shall sprinkle the one to be cleansed of the infectious disease and pronounce him clean. Then he is to release the live bird in the open fields.

⁸ "The person to be cleansed must wash his clothes, shave off all his hair and bathe with water; then he will be ceremonially clean. After this he may come into the camp, but he must stay outside his tent for seven days. ⁹On the seventh day he must shave off all his hair; he must shave his head, his beard, his eyebrows and the rest of his hair. He must wash his clothes and bathe himself with water, and he will be clean.

¹⁰ "On the eighth day he must bring two male lambs and one ewe lamb a year old, each without defect, along with three-tenths of an ephahᵇ of fine flour mixed with oil for a grain offering, and one logᶜ of oil. ¹¹The priest who pronounces him clean shall present both the one to be cleansed and his offerings before the LORD at the entrance to the Tent of Meeting.

¹² "Then the priest is to take one of the male lambs and offer it as a guilt offering, along with the log of oil; he shall wave them before the LORD as a wave offering. ¹³He is to slaughter the lamb in the holy place where the sin offering and the burnt offering are slaughtered. Like the sin offering, the guilt offering belongs to the priest; it is most holy. ¹⁴The priest is to take some of the blood of the guilt offering and put it on the lobe of the right ear of the one to be cleansed, on the thumb

of his right hand and on the big toe of his right foot. ¹⁵The priest shall then take some of the log of oil, pour it in the palm of his own left hand, ¹⁶dip his right forefinger into the oil in his palm, and with his finger sprinkle some of it before the LORD seven times. ¹⁷The priest is to put some of the oil remaining in his palm on the lobe of the right ear of the one to be cleansed, on the thumb of his right hand and on the big toe of his right foot, on top of the blood of the guilt offering. ¹⁸The rest of the oil in his palm the priest shall put on the head of the one to be cleansed and make atonement for him before the LORD.

¹⁹ "Then the priest is to sacrifice the sin offering and make atonement for the one to be cleansed from his uncleanness. After that, the priest shall slaughter the burnt offering ²⁰and offer it on the altar, together with the grain offering, and make atonement for him, and he will be clean.

²¹ "If, however, he is poor and cannot afford these, he must take one male lamb as a guilt offering to be waved to make atonement for him, together with a tenth of an ephahᵈ of fine flour mixed with oil for a grain offering, a log of oil, ²²and two doves or two young pigeons, which he can afford, one for a sin offering and the other for a burnt offering.

²³ "On the eighth day he must bring them for his cleansing to the priest at the entrance to the Tent of Meeting, before the LORD. ²⁴The priest is to take the lamb for the guilt offering, together with the log of oil, and wave them before the LORD as a wave offering. ²⁵He shall slaughter the lamb for the guilt offering and take some of its blood and put it on the lobe of the right ear of the one to be cleansed, on the thumb of his right hand and on the big toe of his right foot. ²⁶The priest is to pour some of the oil into the palm of his own left hand, ²⁷and with his right forefinger sprinkle some of the oil from his palm seven times before the LORD. ²⁸Some of the oil in his palm he is to put on the

ᵃ3 Traditionally *leprosy*; the Hebrew word was used for various diseases affecting the skin—not necessarily leprosy; also elsewhere in this chapter. ᵇ10 That is, probably about 6 quarts (about 6.5 liters)   ᶜ10 That is, probably about 2/3 pint (about 0.3 liter); also in verses 12, 15, 21 and 24 ᵈ21 That is, probably about 2 quarts (about 2 liters) same places he put the blood of the guilt offering—on the lobe of the right ear of the one to be cleansed, on the thumb of his right hand and on the big toe of his right foot. ²⁹The rest of the oil in his palm the priest shall put on the head of the one to be cleansed, to make atonement for him before the LORD. ³⁰Then he shall sacrifice the doves or the young pigeons, which the person can afford, ³¹one[a] as a sin offering and the other as a burnt offering, together with the grain offering. In this way the priest will make atonement before the LORD on behalf of the one to be cleansed."

³²These are the regulations for anyone who has an infectious skin disease and who cannot afford the regular offerings for his cleansing.

Cleansing From Mildew

³³The LORD said to Moses and Aaron, ³⁴"When you enter the land of Canaan, which I am giving you as your possession, and I put a spreading mildew in a house in that land, ³⁵the owner of the house must go and tell the priest, 'I have seen something that looks like mildew in my house.' ³⁶The priest is to order the house to be emptied before he goes in to examine the mildew, so that nothing in the house will be pronounced unclean. After this the priest is to go in and inspect the house. ³⁷He is to examine the mildew on the walls, and if it has greenish or reddish depressions that appear to be deeper than the surface of the wall, ³⁸the priest shall go out the doorway of the house and close it up for seven days. ³⁹On the seventh day the priest shall return to inspect the house. If the mildew has spread on the walls, ⁴⁰he is to order that the contaminated stones be torn out and thrown into an unclean place outside the town. ⁴¹He must have all the inside walls of the house scraped and the material that is scraped off dumped into an unclean place outside the town. ⁴²Then they are to take other stones to replace these and take new clay and plaster the house.

⁴³"If the mildew reappears in the house after the stones have been torn out and the house scraped and plastered, ⁴⁴the priest is to go and examine it and, if the mildew has spread in the house, it is a destructive mildew; the house is unclean. ⁴⁵It must be torn down—its stones, timbers and all the plaster—and taken out of the town to an unclean place.

⁴⁶"Anyone who goes into the house while it is closed up will be unclean till evening. ⁴⁷Anyone who sleeps or eats in the house must wash his clothes.

⁴⁸"But if the priest comes to examine it and the mildew has not spread after the house has been plastered, he shall pronounce the house clean, because the mildew is gone. ⁴⁹To purify the house he is to take two birds and some cedar wood, scarlet yarn and hyssop. ⁵⁰He shall kill one of the birds over fresh water in a clay pot. ⁵¹Then he is to take the cedar wood, the hyssop, the scarlet yarn and the live bird, dip them into the blood of the dead bird and the fresh water, and sprinkle the house seven times. ⁵²He shall purify the house with the bird's blood, the fresh water, the live bird, the cedar wood, the hyssop and the scarlet yarn. ⁵³Then he is to release the live bird in the open fields outside the town. In this way he will make atonement for the house, and it will be clean."

⁵⁴These are the regulations for any infectious skin disease, for an itch, ⁵⁵for mildew in clothing or in a house, ⁵⁶and for a swelling, a rash or a bright spot, ⁵⁷to determine when something is clean or unclean.

These are the regulations for infectious skin diseases and mildew.

Discharges Causing Uncleanness

15 The LORD said to Moses and Aaron, ²"Speak to the Israelites and say to them: 'When any man has a bodily discharge, the discharge is unclean. ³Whether it continues flowing from his body or is blocked, it will make him unclean. This is how his discharge will bring about uncleanness:

⁴" 'Any bed the man with a discharge lies on will be unclean, and anything he sits on will be unclean. ⁵Anyone who touches his bed must wash his clothes and bathe with water, and he will be unclean till evening. ⁶Whoever sits on anything that the man with a discharge sat on

---

[a] 31 Septuagint and Syriac; Hebrew 31such as the person can afford, one

must wash his clothes and bathe with water, and he will be unclean till evening.

7 " 'Whoever touches the man who has a discharge must wash his clothes and bathe with water, and he will be unclean till evening.

8 " 'If the man with the discharge spits on someone who is clean, that person must wash his clothes and bathe with water, and he will be unclean till evening.

9 " 'Everything the man sits on when riding will be unclean, 10and whoever touches any of the things that were under him will be unclean till evening; whoever picks up those things must wash his clothes and bathe with water, and he will be unclean till evening.

11 " 'Anyone the man with a discharge touches without rinsing his hands with water must wash his clothes and bathe with water, and he will be unclean till evening.

12 " 'A clay pot that the man touches must be broken, and any wooden article is to be rinsed with water.

13 " 'When a man is cleansed from his discharge, he is to count off seven days for his ceremonial cleansing; he must wash his clothes and bathe himself with fresh water, and he will be clean. 14On the eighth day he must take two doves or two young pigeons and come before the LORD to the entrance to the Tent of Meeting and give them to the priest. 15The priest is to sacrifice them, the one for a sin offering and the other for a burnt offering. In this way he will make atonement before the LORD for the man because of his discharge.

16 " 'When a man has an emission of semen, he must bathe his whole body with water, and he will be unclean till evening. 17Any clothing or leather that has semen on it must be washed with water, and it will be unclean till evening. 18When a man lies with a woman and there is an emission of semen, both must bathe with water, and they will be unclean till evening.

19 " 'When a woman has her regular flow of blood, the impurity of her monthly period will last seven days, and anyone who touches her will be unclean till evening.

20 " 'Anything she lies on during her period will be unclean, and anything she sits on will be unclean. 21Whoever touches her bed must wash his clothes and bathe with water, and he will be unclean till evening. 22Whoever touches anything she sits on must wash his clothes and bathe with water, and he will be unclean till evening. 23Whether it is the bed or anything she was sitting on, when anyone touches it, he will be unclean till evening.

24 " 'If a man lies with her and her monthly flow touches him, he will be unclean for seven days; any bed he lies on will be unclean.

25 " 'When a woman has a discharge of blood for many days at a time other than her monthly period or has a discharge that continues beyond her period, she will be unclean as long as she has the discharge, just as in the days of her period. 26Any bed she lies on while her discharge continues will be unclean, as is her bed during her monthly period, and anything she sits on will be unclean, as during her period. 27Whoever touches them will be unclean; he must wash his clothes and bathe with water, and he will be unclean till evening.

28 " 'When she is cleansed from her discharge, she must count off seven days, and after that she will be ceremonially clean. 29On the eighth day she must take two doves or two young pigeons and bring them to the priest at the entrance to the Tent of Meeting. 30The priest is to sacrifice one for a sin offering and the other for a burnt offering. In this way he will make atonement for her before the LORD for the uncleanness of her discharge.

31 " 'You must keep the Israelites separate from things that make them unclean, so they will not die in their uncleanness for defiling my dwelling place,a which is among them.' "

32These are the regulations for a man with a discharge, for anyone made unclean by an emission of semen, 33for a woman in her monthly period, for a man or a woman with a discharge, and for a man who lies with a woman who is ceremonially unclean.

---

a31 Or my tabernacle

The Day of Atonement

16 The LORD spoke to Moses after the death of the two sons of Aaron who died when they approached the LORD. ²The LORD said to Moses: "Tell your brother Aaron not to come whenever he chooses into the Most Holy Place behind the curtain in front of the atonement cover on the ark, or else he will die, because I appear in the cloud over the atonement cover.

³"This is how Aaron is to enter the sanctuary area: with a young bull for a sin offering and a ram for a burnt offering. ⁴He is to put on the sacred linen tunic, with linen undergarments next to his body; he is to tie the linen sash around him and put on the linen turban. These are sacred garments; so he must bathe himself with water before he puts them on. ⁵From the Israelite community he is to take two male goats for a sin offering and a ram for a burnt offering.

⁶"Aaron is to offer the bull for his own sin offering to make atonement for himself and his household. ⁷Then he is to take the two goats and present them before the LORD at the entrance to the Tent of Meeting. ⁸He is to cast lots for the two goats—one lot for the LORD and the other for the scapegoat.ᵃ ⁹Aaron shall bring the goat whose lot falls to the LORD and sacrifice it for a sin offering. ¹⁰But the goat chosen by lot as the scapegoat shall be presented alive before the LORD to be used for making atonement by sending it into the desert as a scapegoat.

¹¹"Aaron shall bring the bull for his own sin offering to make atonement for himself and his household, and he is to slaughter the bull for his own sin offering. ¹²He is to take a censer full of burning coals from the altar before the LORD and two handfuls of finely ground fragrant incense and take them behind the curtain. ¹³He is to put the incense on the fire before the LORD, and the smoke of the incense will conceal the atonement cover above the Testimony, so that he will not die. ¹⁴He is to take some of the bull's blood and with his finger sprinkle it on the front of the atonement cover; then he shall sprinkle some of it with his finger seven times before the atonement cover.

¹⁵"He shall then slaughter the goat for the sin offering for the people and take its blood behind the curtain and do with it as he did with the bull's blood: He shall sprinkle it on the atonement cover and in front of it. ¹⁶In this way he will make atonement for the Most Holy Place because of the uncleanness and rebellion of the Israelites, whatever their sins have been. He is to do the same for the Tent of Meeting, which is among them in the midst of their uncleanness. ¹⁷No one is to be in the Tent of Meeting from the time Aaron goes in to make atonement in the Most Holy Place until he comes out, having made atonement for himself, his household and the whole community of Israel.

¹⁸"Then he shall come out to the altar that is before the LORD and make atonement for it. He shall take some of the bull's blood and some of the goat's blood and put it on all the horns of the altar. ¹⁹He shall sprinkle some of the blood on it with his finger seven times to cleanse it and to consecrate it from the uncleanness of the Israelites.

²⁰"When Aaron has finished making atonement for the Most Holy Place, the Tent of Meeting and the altar, he shall bring forward the live goat. ²¹He is to lay both hands on the head of the live goat and confess over it all the wickedness and rebellion of the Israelites—all their sins—and put them on the goat's head. He shall send the goat away into the desert in the care of a man appointed for the task. ²²The goat will carry on itself all their sins to a solitary place; and the man shall release it in the desert.

²³"Then Aaron is to go into the Tent of Meeting and take off the linen garments he put on before he entered the Most Holy Place, and he is to leave them there. ²⁴He shall bathe himself with water in a holy place and put on his regular garments. Then he shall come out and sacrifice the burnt offering for himself and the burnt offering for the people, to make atonement for himself and for the people. ²⁵He shall also burn the fat of the sin offering on the altar.

²⁶"The man who releases the goat as a scapegoat must wash his clothes and

ᵃ8 That is, the goat of removal; Hebrew *azazel*; also in verses 10 and 26 bathe himself with water; afterward he may come into the camp. [27]The bull and the goat for the sin offerings, whose blood was brought into the Most Holy Place to make atonement, must be taken outside the camp; their hides, flesh and offal are to be burned up. [28]The man who burns them must wash his clothes and bathe himself with water; afterward he may come into the camp.

[29]"This is to be a lasting ordinance for you: On the tenth day of the seventh month you must deny yourselves[a] and not do any work—whether native-born or an alien living among you— [30]because on this day atonement will be made for you, to cleanse you. Then, before the LORD, you will be clean from all your sins. [31]It is a sabbath of rest, and you must deny yourselves; it is a lasting ordinance. [32]The priest who is anointed and ordained to succeed his father as high priest is to make atonement. He is to put on the sacred linen garments [33]and make atonement for the Most Holy Place, for the Tent of Meeting and the altar, and for the priests and all the people of the community.

[34]"This is to be a lasting ordinance for you: Atonement is to be made once a year for all the sins of the Israelites."

And it was done, as the LORD commanded Moses.

Eating Blood Forbidden

17 The LORD said to Moses, [2]"Speak to Aaron and his sons and to all the Israelites and say to them: 'This is what the LORD has commanded: [3]Any Israelite who sacrifices an ox,[b] a lamb or a goat in the camp or outside of it [4]instead of bringing it to the entrance to the Tent of Meeting to present it as an offering to the LORD in front of the tabernacle of the LORD—that man shall be considered guilty of bloodshed; he has shed blood and must be cut off from his people. [5]This is so the Israelites will bring to the LORD the sacrifices they are now making in the open fields. They must bring them to the priest, that is, to the LORD, at the entrance to the Tent of Meeting and sacrifice them as fellowship offerings.[c] [6]The priest is to sprinkle the blood against the altar of the LORD at the entrance to the Tent of Meeting and burn the fat as an

aroma pleasing to the LORD. [7]They must no longer offer any of their sacrifices to the goat idols[d] to whom they prostitute themselves. This is to be a lasting ordinance for them and for the generations to come.'

[8]"Say to them: 'Any Israelite or any alien living among them who offers a burnt offering or sacrifice [9]and does not bring it to the entrance to the Tent of Meeting to sacrifice it to the LORD—that man must be cut off from his people.

[10]"'Any Israelite or any alien living among them who eats any blood—I will set my face against that person who eats blood and will cut him off from his people. [11]For the life of a creature is in the blood, and I have given it to you to make atonement for yourselves on the altar; it is the blood that makes atonement for one's life. [12]Therefore I say to the Israelites, "None of you may eat blood, nor may an alien living among you eat blood."

[13]"'Any Israelite or any alien living among you who hunts any animal or bird that may be eaten must drain out the blood and cover it with earth, [14]because the life of every creature is its blood. That is why I have said to the Israelites, "You must not eat the blood of any creature, because the life of every creature is its blood; anyone who eats it must be cut off."

[15]"'Anyone, whether native-born or alien, who eats anything found dead or torn by wild animals must wash his clothes and bathe with water, and he will be ceremonially unclean till evening; then he will be clean. [16]But if he does not wash his clothes and bathe himself, he will be held responsible.' "

Unlawful Sexual Relations

18 The LORD said to Moses, [2]"Speak to the Israelites and say to them: 'I am the LORD your God. [3]You must not do as they do in Egypt, where you used to live, and you must not do as they do in the land of Canaan, where I am bringing you. Do not follow their practices. [4]You must obey my laws and be careful to follow my decrees. I am the LORD your God. [5]Keep

---

[a]29 Or *must fast*; also in verse 31   [b]3 The Hebrew word can include both male and female.   [c]5 Traditionally *peace offerings*   [d]7 Or *demons*

my decrees and laws, for the man who obeys them will live by them. I am the LORD.

6" 'No one is to approach any close relative to have sexual relations. I am the LORD.

7" 'Do not dishonor your father by having sexual relations with your mother. She is your mother; do not have relations with her.

8" 'Do not have sexual relations with your father's wife; that would dishonor your father.

9" 'Do not have sexual relations with your sister, either your father's daughter or your mother's daughter, whether she was born in the same home or elsewhere.

10" 'Do not have sexual relations with your son's daughter or your daughter's daughter; that would dishonor you.

11" 'Do not have sexual relations with the daughter of your father's wife, born to your father; she is your sister.

12" 'Do not have sexual relations with your father's sister; she is your father's close relative.

13" 'Do not have sexual relations with your mother's sister, because she is your mother's close relative.

14" 'Do not dishonor your father's brother by approaching his wife to have sexual relations; she is your aunt.

15" 'Do not have sexual relations with your daughter-in-law. She is your son's wife; do not have relations with her.

16" 'Do not have sexual relations with your brother's wife; that would dishonor your brother.

17" 'Do not have sexual relations with both a woman and her daughter. Do not have sexual relations with either her son's daughter or her daughter's daughter; they are her close relatives. That is wickedness.

18" 'Do not take your wife's sister as a rival wife and have sexual relations with her while your wife is living.

19" 'Do not approach a woman to have sexual relations during the uncleanness of her monthly period.

20" 'Do not have sexual relations with your neighbor's wife and defile yourself with her.

21" 'Do not give any of your children to be sacrificed[a] to Molech, for you must not profane the name of your God. I am the LORD.

22" 'Do not lie with a man as one lies with a woman; that is detestable.

23" 'Do not have sexual relations with an animal and defile yourself with it. A woman must not present herself to an animal to have sexual relations with it; that is a perversion.

24" 'Do not defile yourselves in any of these ways, because this is how the nations that I am going to drive out before you became defiled. 25Even the land was defiled; so I punished it for its sin, and the land vomited out its inhabitants. 26But you must keep my decrees and my laws. The native-born and the aliens living among you must not do any of these detestable things, 27for all these things were done by the people who lived in the land before you, and the land became defiled. 28And if you defile the land, it will vomit you out as it vomited out the nations that were before you.

29" 'Everyone who does any of these detestable things—such persons must be cut off from their people. 30Keep my requirements and do not follow any of the detestable customs that were practiced before you came and do not defile yourselves with them. I am the LORD your God.' "

Various Laws

19 The LORD said to Moses, 2"Speak to the entire assembly of Israel and say to them: 'Be holy because I, the LORD your God, am holy.

3" 'Each of you must respect his mother and father, and you must observe my Sabbaths. I am the LORD your God.

4" 'Do not turn to idols or make gods of cast metal for yourselves. I am the LORD your God.

5" 'When you sacrifice a fellowship offering[b] to the LORD, sacrifice it in such a way that it will be accepted on your behalf. 6It shall be eaten on the day you sacrifice it or on the next day; anything left over until the third day must be burned up. 7If any of it is eaten on the third day, it is impure and will not be accepted. 8Whoever eats it will be held responsible because he has desecrated

a21 Or to be passed through ⌜the fire⌝
b5 Traditionally peace offering

what is holy to the LORD; that person must be cut off from his people.

9 " 'When you reap the harvest of your land, do not reap to the very edges of your field or gather the gleanings of your harvest. 10Do not go over your vineyard a second time or pick up the grapes that have fallen. Leave them for the poor and the alien. I am the LORD your God.

11 " 'Do not steal.

" 'Do not lie.

" 'Do not deceive one another.

12 " 'Do not swear falsely by my name and so profane the name of your God. I am the LORD.

13 " 'Do not defraud your neighbor or rob him.

" 'Do not hold back the wages of a hired man overnight.

14 " 'Do not curse the deaf or put a stumbling block in front of the blind, but fear your God. I am the LORD.

15 " 'Do not pervert justice; do not show partiality to the poor or favoritism to the great, but judge your neighbor fairly.

16 " 'Do not go about spreading slander among your people.

" 'Do not do anything that endangers your neighbor's life. I am the LORD.

17 " 'Do not hate your brother in your heart. Rebuke your neighbor frankly so you will not share in his guilt.

18 " 'Do not seek revenge or bear a grudge against one of your people, but love your neighbor as yourself. I am the LORD.

19 " 'Keep my decrees.

" 'Do not mate different kinds of animals.

" 'Do not plant your field with two kinds of seed.

" 'Do not wear clothing woven of two kinds of material.

20 " 'If a man sleeps with a woman who is a slave girl promised to another man but who has not been ransomed or given her freedom, there must be due punishment. Yet they are not to be put to death, because she had not been freed. 21The man, however, must bring a ram to the entrance to the Tent of Meeting for a guilt offering to the LORD. 22With the ram of the guilt offering the priest is to make atonement for him before the LORD for

the sin he has committed, and his sin will be forgiven.

23 " 'When you enter the land and plant any kind of fruit tree, regard its fruit as forbidden.a For three years you are to consider it forbiddena; it must not be eaten. 24In the fourth year all its fruit will be holy, an offering of praise to the LORD. 25But in the fifth year you may eat its fruit. In this way your harvest will be increased. I am the LORD your God.

26 " 'Do not eat any meat with the blood still in it.

" 'Do not practice divination or sorcery.

27 " 'Do not cut the hair at the sides of your head or clip off the edges of your beard.

28 " 'Do not cut your bodies for the dead or put tattoo marks on yourselves. I am the LORD.

29 " 'Do not degrade your daughter by making her a prostitute, or the land will turn to prostitution and be filled with wickedness.

30 " 'Observe my Sabbaths and have reverence for my sanctuary. I am the LORD.

31 " 'Do not turn to mediums or seek out spiritists, for you will be defiled by them. I am the LORD your God.

32 " 'Rise in the presence of the aged, show respect for the elderly and revere your God. I am the LORD.

33 " 'When an alien lives with you in your land, do not mistreat him. 34The alien living with you must be treated as one of your native-born. Love him as yourself, for you were aliens in Egypt. I am the LORD your God.

35 " 'Do not use dishonest standards when measuring length, weight or quantity. 36Use honest scales and honest weights, an honest ephahb and an honest hin.c I am the LORD your God, who brought you out of Egypt.

37 " 'Keep all my decrees and all my laws and follow them. I am the LORD.' "

Punishments for Sin

20 The LORD said to Moses, 2"Say to the Israelites: 'Any Israelite or any

---

a23 Hebrew uncircumcised   b36 An ephah was a dry measure.   c36 A hin was a liquid measure.

alien living in Israel who gives[a] any of his children to Molech must be put to death. The people of the community are to stone him. [3]I will set my face against that man and I will cut him off from his people; for by giving his children to Molech, he has defiled my sanctuary and profaned my holy name. [4]If the people of the community close their eyes when that man gives one of his children to Molech and they fail to put him to death, [5]I will set my face against that man and his family and will cut off from their people both him and all who follow him in prostituting themselves to Molech.

[6]" 'I will set my face against the person who turns to mediums and spiritists to prostitute himself by following them, and I will cut him off from his people.

[7]" 'Consecrate yourselves and be holy, because I am the LORD your God. [8]Keep my decrees and follow them. I am the LORD, who makes you holy.[b]

[9]" 'If anyone curses his father or mother, he must be put to death. He has cursed his father or his mother, and his blood will be on his own head.

[10]" 'If a man commits adultery with another man's wife—with the wife of his neighbor—both the adulterer and the adulteress must be put to death.

[11]" 'If a man sleeps with his father's wife, he has dishonored his father. Both the man and the woman must be put to death; their blood will be on their own heads.

[12]" 'If a man sleeps with his daughter-in-law, both of them must be put to death. What they have done is a perversion; their blood will be on their own heads.

[13]" 'If a man lies with a man as one lies with a woman, both of them have done what is detestable. They must be put to death; their blood will be on their own heads.

[14]" 'If a man marries both a woman and her mother, it is wicked. Both he and they must be burned in the fire, so that no wickedness will be among you.

[15]" 'If a man has sexual relations with an animal, he must be put to death, and you must kill the animal.

[16]" 'If a woman approaches an animal to have sexual relations with it, kill both the woman and the animal. They must be

put to death; their blood will be on their own heads.

[17]" 'If a man marries his sister, the daughter of either his father or his mother, and they have sexual relations, it is a disgrace. They must be cut off before the eyes of their people. He has dishonored his sister and will be held responsible.

[18]" 'If a man lies with a woman during her monthly period and has sexual relations with her, he has exposed the source of her flow, and she has also uncovered it. Both of them must be cut off from their people.

[19]" 'Do not have sexual relations with the sister of either your mother or your father, for that would dishonor a close relative; both of you would be held responsible.

[20]" 'If a man sleeps with his aunt, he has dishonored his uncle. They will be held responsible; they will die childless.

[21]" 'If a man marries his brother's wife, it is an act of impurity; he has dishonored his brother. They will be childless.

[22]" 'Keep all my decrees and laws and follow them, so that the land where I am bringing you to live may not vomit you out. [23]You must not live according to the customs of the nations I am going to drive out before you. Because they did all these things, I abhorred them. [24]But I said to you, "You will possess their land; I will give it to you as an inheritance, a land flowing with milk and honey." I am the LORD your God, who has set you apart from the nations.

[25]" 'You must therefore make a distinction between clean and unclean animals and between unclean and clean birds. Do not defile yourselves by any animal or bird or anything that moves along the ground—those which I have set apart as unclean for you. [26]You are to be holy to me[c] because I, the LORD, am holy, and I have set you apart from the nations to be my own.

[27]" 'A man or woman who is a medium or spiritist among you must be put to death. You are to stone them; their blood will be on their own heads.' "

---

[a]2 Or *sacrifices*; also in verses 3 and 4   [b]8 Or *who sanctifies you*; or *who sets you apart as holy*   [c]26 Or *be my holy ones*

Rules for Priests

21 The LORD said to Moses, "Speak to the priests, the sons of Aaron, and say to them: 'A priest must not make himself ceremonially unclean for any of his people who die, ²except for a close relative, such as his mother or father, his son or daughter, his brother, ³or an unmarried sister who is dependent on him since she has no husband—for her he may make himself unclean. ⁴He must not make himself unclean for people related to him by marriage,ᵃ and so defile himself.

⁵" 'Priests must not shave their heads or shave off the edges of their beards or cut their bodies. ⁶They must be holy to their God and must not profane the name of their God. Because they present the offerings made to the LORD by fire, the food of their God, they are to be holy.

⁷" 'They must not marry women defiled by prostitution or divorced from their husbands, because priests are holy to their God. ⁸Regard them as holy, because they offer up the food of your God. Consider them holy, because I the LORD am holy—I who make you holy.ᵇ

⁹" 'If a priest's daughter defiles herself by becoming a prostitute, she disgraces her father; she must be burned in the fire.

¹⁰" 'The high priest, the one among his brothers who has had the anointing oil poured on his head and who has been ordained to wear the priestly garments, must not let his hair become unkemptᶜ or tear his clothes. ¹¹He must not enter a place where there is a dead body. He must not make himself unclean, even for his father or mother, ¹²nor leave the sanctuary of his God or desecrate it, because he has been dedicated by the anointing oil of his God. I am the LORD.

¹³" 'The woman he marries must be a virgin. ¹⁴He must not marry a widow, a divorced woman, or a woman defiled by prostitution, but only a virgin from his own people, ¹⁵so he will not defile his offspring among his people. I am the LORD, who makes him holy.ᵈ' "

¹⁶The LORD said to Moses, ¹⁷"Say to Aaron: 'For the generations to come none of your descendants who has a defect may come near to offer the food of his God. ¹⁸No man who has any defect may come near: no man who is blind or lame, disfig-ured or deformed; ¹⁹no man with a crippled foot or hand, ²⁰or who is hunchbacked or dwarfed, or who has any eye defect, or who has festering or running sores or damaged testicles. ²¹No descendant of Aaron the priest who has any defect is to come near to present the offerings made to the LORD by fire. He has a defect; he must not come near to offer the food of his God. ²²He may eat the most holy food of his God, as well as the holy food; ²³yet because of his defect, he must not go near the curtain or approach the altar, and so desecrate my sanctuary. I am the LORD, who makes them holy.ᵉ' "

²⁴So Moses told this to Aaron and his sons and to all the Israelites.

22 The LORD said to Moses, ²"Tell Aaron and his sons to treat with respect the sacred offerings the Israelites consecrate to me, so they will not profane my holy name. I am the LORD.

³"Say to them: 'For the generations to come, if any of your descendants is ceremonially unclean and yet comes near the sacred offerings that the Israelites consecrate to the LORD, that person must be cut off from my presence. I am the LORD.

⁴" 'If a descendant of Aaron has an infectious skin diseaseᶠ or a bodily discharge, he may not eat the sacred offerings until he is cleansed. He will also be unclean if he touches something defiled by a corpse or by anyone who has an emission of semen, ⁵or if he touches any crawling thing that makes him unclean, or any person who makes him unclean, whatever the uncleanness may be. ⁶The one who touches any such thing will be unclean till evening. He must not eat any of the sacred offerings unless he has bathed himself with water. ⁷When the sun goes down, he will be clean, and after that he may eat the sacred offerings, for they are his food. ⁸He must not eat anything found dead or torn by wild animals, and so become unclean through it. I am the LORD.

⁹" 'The priests are to keep my require-

ᵃ4 Or *unclean as a leader among his people*
ᵇ8 Or *who sanctify you;* or *who set you apart as holy*
ᶜ10 Or *not uncover his head*   ᵈ15 Or *who sanctifies him;* or *who sets him apart as holy*
ᵉ23 Or *who sanctifies them;* or *who sets them apart as holy*   ᶠ4 Traditionally *leprosy;* the Hebrew word was used for various diseases affecting the skin—not necessarily leprosy.

ments so that they do not become guilty and die for treating them with contempt. I am the LORD, who makes them holy.[a]

10" 'No one outside a priest's family may eat the sacred offering, nor may the guest of a priest or his hired worker eat it. 11But if a priest buys a slave with money, or if a slave is born in his household, that slave may eat his food. 12If a priest's daughter marries anyone other than a priest, she may not eat any of the sacred contributions. 13But if a priest's daughter becomes a widow or is divorced, yet has no children, and she returns to live in her father's house as in her youth, she may eat of her father's food. No unauthorized person, however, may eat any of it.

14" 'If anyone eats a sacred offering by mistake, he must make restitution to the priest for the offering and add a fifth of the value to it. 15The priests must not desecrate the sacred offerings the Israelites present to the LORD 16by allowing them to eat the sacred offerings and so bring upon them guilt requiring payment. I am the LORD, who makes them holy.' "

Unacceptable Sacrifices

17The LORD said to Moses, 18"Speak to Aaron and his sons and to all the Israelites and say to them: 'If any of you—either an Israelite or an alien living in Israel—presents a gift for a burnt offering to the LORD, either to fulfill a vow or as a freewill offering, 19you must present a male without defect from the cattle, sheep or goats in order that it may be accepted on your behalf. 20Do not bring anything with a defect, because it will not be accepted on your behalf. 21When anyone brings from the herd or flock a fellowship offering[b] to the LORD to fulfill a special vow or as a freewill offering, it must be without defect or blemish to be acceptable. 22Do not offer to the LORD the blind, the injured or the maimed, or anything with warts or festering or running sores. Do not place any of these on the altar as an offering made to the LORD by fire. 23You may, however, present as a freewill offering an ox[c] or a sheep that is deformed or stunted, but it will not be accepted in fulfillment of a vow. 24You must not offer to the LORD an animal whose testicles are bruised, crushed, torn or cut. You must

not do this in your own land, 25and you must not accept such animals from the hand of a foreigner and offer them as the food of your God. They will not be accepted on your behalf, because they are deformed and have defects.' "

26The LORD said to Moses, 27"When a calf, a lamb or a goat is born, it is to remain with its mother for seven days. From the eighth day on, it will be acceptable as an offering made to the LORD by fire. 28Do not slaughter a cow or a sheep and its young on the same day.

29"When you sacrifice a thank offering to the LORD, sacrifice it in such a way that it will be accepted on your behalf. 30It must be eaten that same day; leave none of it till morning. I am the LORD.

31"Keep my commands and follow them. I am the LORD. 32Do not profane my holy name. I must be acknowledged as holy by the Israelites. I am the LORD, who makes[d] you holy[e] 33and who brought you out of Egypt to be your God. I am the LORD."

23 The LORD said to Moses, 2"Speak to the Israelites and say to them: 'These are my appointed feasts, the appointed feasts of the LORD, which you are to proclaim as sacred assemblies.

The Sabbath

3" 'There are six days when you may work, but the seventh day is a Sabbath of rest, a day of sacred assembly. You are not to do any work; wherever you live, it is a Sabbath to the LORD.

The Passover and Unleavened Bread

4" 'These are the LORD's appointed feasts, the sacred assemblies you are to proclaim at their appointed times: 5The LORD's Passover begins at twilight on the fourteenth day of the first month. 6On the fifteenth day of that month the LORD's Feast of Unleavened Bread begins; for seven days you must eat bread made without yeast. 7On the first day hold a sacred as-

---

[a]9 Or who sanctifies them; or who sets them apart as holy; also in verse 16   [b]21 Traditionally peace offering   [c]23 The Hebrew word can include both male and female.   [d]32 Or made
[e]32 Or who sanctifies you; or who sets you apart as holy

sembly and do no regular work. [8]For seven days present an offering made to the LORD by fire. And on the seventh day hold a sacred assembly and do no regular work.' "

Firstfruits

[9]The LORD said to Moses, [10]"Speak to the Israelites and say to them: 'When you enter the land I am going to give you and you reap its harvest, bring to the priest a sheaf of the first grain you harvest. [11]He is to wave the sheaf before the LORD so it will be accepted on your behalf; the priest is to wave it on the day after the Sabbath. [12]On the day you wave the sheaf, you must sacrifice as a burnt offering to the LORD a lamb a year old without defect, [13]together with its grain offering of two-tenths of an ephah[a] of fine flour mixed with oil—an offering made to the LORD by fire, a pleasing aroma—and its drink offering of a quarter of a hin[b] of wine. [14]You must not eat any bread, or roasted or new grain, until the very day you bring this offering to your God. This is to be a lasting ordinance for the generations to come, wherever you live.

Feast of Weeks

[15]" 'From the day after the Sabbath, the day you brought the sheaf of the wave offering, count off seven full weeks. [16]Count off fifty days up to the day after the seventh Sabbath, and then present an offering of new grain to the LORD. [17]From wherever you live, bring two loaves made of two-tenths of an ephah of fine flour, baked with yeast, as a wave offering of firstfruits to the LORD. [18]Present with this bread seven male lambs, each a year old and without defect, one young bull and two rams. They will be a burnt offering to the LORD, together with their grain offerings and drink offerings—an offering made by fire, an aroma pleasing to the LORD. [19]Then sacrifice one male goat for a sin offering and two lambs, each a year old, for a fellowship offering.[c] [20]The priest is to wave the two lambs before the LORD as a wave offering, together with the bread of the firstfruits. They are a sacred offering to the LORD for the priest. [21]On that same day you are to proclaim a sacred assembly and do no regular work.

This is to be a lasting ordinance for the generations to come, wherever you live.

[22]" 'When you reap the harvest of your land, do not reap to the very edges of your field or gather the gleanings of your harvest. Leave them for the poor and the alien. I am the LORD your God.' "

Feast of Trumpets

[23]The LORD said to Moses, [24]"Say to the Israelites: 'On the first day of the seventh month you are to have a day of rest, a sacred assembly commemorated with trumpet blasts. [25]Do no regular work, but present an offering made to the LORD by fire.' "

Day of Atonement

[26]The LORD said to Moses, [27]"The tenth day of this seventh month is the Day of Atonement. Hold a sacred assembly and deny yourselves,[d] and present an offering made to the LORD by fire. [28]Do no work on that day, because it is the Day of Atonement, when atonement is made for you before the LORD your God. [29]Anyone who does not deny himself on that day must be cut off from his people. [30]I will destroy from among his people anyone who does any work on that day. [31]You shall do no work at all. This is to be a lasting ordinance for the generations to come, wherever you live. [32]It is a sabbath of rest for you, and you must deny yourselves. From the evening of the ninth day of the month until the following evening you are to observe your sabbath."

Feast of Tabernacles

[33]The LORD said to Moses, [34]"Say to the Israelites: 'On the fifteenth day of the seventh month the LORD's Feast of Tabernacles begins, and it lasts for seven days. [35]The first day is a sacred assembly; do no regular work. [36]For seven days present offerings made to the LORD by fire, and on the eighth day hold a sacred assembly and present an offering made to the LORD by fire. It is the closing assembly; do no regular work.

[a]13 That is, probably about 4 quarts (about 4.5 liters); also in verse 17   [b]13 That is, probably about 1 quart (about 1 liter)   [c]19 Traditionally *peace offering*   [d]27 Or *and fast*; also in verses 29 and 32

37("'These are the LORD's appointed feasts, which you are to proclaim as sacred assemblies for bringing offerings made to the LORD by fire—the burnt offerings and grain offerings, sacrifices and drink offerings required for each day. 38These offerings are in addition to those for the LORD's Sabbaths and*a* in addition to your gifts and whatever you have vowed and all the freewill offerings you give to the LORD.)

39" 'So beginning with the fifteenth day of the seventh month, after you have gathered the crops of the land, celebrate the festival to the LORD for seven days; the first day is a day of rest, and the eighth day also is a day of rest. 40On the first day you are to take choice fruit from the trees, and palm fronds, leafy branches and poplars, and rejoice before the LORD your God for seven days. 41Celebrate this as a festival to the LORD for seven days each year. This is to be a lasting ordinance for the generations to come; celebrate it in the seventh month. 42Live in booths for seven days: All native-born Israelites are to live in booths 43so your descendants will know that I had the Israelites live in booths when I brought them out of Egypt. I am the LORD your God.' "

44So Moses announced to the Israelites the appointed feasts of the LORD.

Oil and Bread Set Before the LORD

24 The LORD said to Moses, 2"Command the Israelites to bring you clear oil of pressed olives for the light so that the lamps may be kept burning continually. 3Outside the curtain of the Testimony in the Tent of Meeting, Aaron is to tend the lamps before the LORD from evening till morning, continually. This is to be a lasting ordinance for the generations to come. 4The lamps on the pure gold lampstand before the LORD must be tended continually.

5"Take fine flour and bake twelve loaves of bread, using two-tenths of an ephah*b* for each loaf. 6Set them in two rows, six in each row, on the table of pure gold before the LORD. 7Along each row put some pure incense as a memorial portion to represent the bread and to be an offering made to the LORD by fire. 8This bread is to be set out before the LORD

regularly, Sabbath after Sabbath, on behalf of the Israelites, as a lasting covenant. 9It belongs to Aaron and his sons, who are to eat it in a holy place, because it is a most holy part of their regular share of the offerings made to the LORD by fire."

A Blasphemer Stoned

10Now the son of an Israelite mother and an Egyptian father went out among the Israelites, and a fight broke out in the camp between him and an Israelite. 11The son of the Israelite woman blasphemed the Name with a curse; so they brought him to Moses. (His mother's name was Shelomith, the daughter of Dibri the Danite.) 12They put him in custody until the will of the LORD should be made clear to them.

13Then the LORD said to Moses: 14"Take the blasphemer outside the camp. All those who heard him are to lay their hands on his head, and the entire assembly is to stone him. 15Say to the Israelites: 'If anyone curses his God, he will be held responsible; 16anyone who blasphemes the name of the LORD must be put to death. The entire assembly must stone him. Whether an alien or native-born, when he blasphemes the Name, he must be put to death.

17" 'If anyone takes the life of a human being, he must be put to death. 18Anyone who takes the life of someone's animal must make restitution—life for life. 19If anyone injures his neighbor, whatever he has done must be done to him: 20fracture for fracture, eye for eye, tooth for tooth. As he has injured the other, so he is to be injured. 21Whoever kills an animal must make restitution, but whoever kills a man must be put to death. 22You are to have the same law for the alien and the native-born. I am the LORD your God.' "

23Then Moses spoke to the Israelites, and they took the blasphemer outside the camp and stoned him. The Israelites did as the LORD commanded Moses.

The Sabbath Year

25 The LORD said to Moses on Mount Sinai, 2"Speak to the Israelites and

---

*a*38 Or *These feasts are in addition to the LORD's Sabbaths, and these offerings are*   *b*5 That is, probably about 4 quarts (about 4.5 liters) say to them: 'When you enter the land I am going to give you, the land itself must observe a sabbath to the LORD. ³For six years sow your fields, and for six years prune your vineyards and gather their crops. ⁴But in the seventh year the land is to have a sabbath of rest, a sabbath to the LORD. Do not sow your fields or prune your vineyards. ⁵Do not reap what grows of itself or harvest the grapes of your untended vines. The land is to have a year of rest. ⁶Whatever the land yields during the sabbath year will be food for you—for yourself, your manservant and maidservant, and the hired worker and temporary resident who live among you, ⁷as well as for your livestock and the wild animals in your land. Whatever the land produces may be eaten.

The Year of Jubilee

8 " 'Count off seven sabbaths of years— seven times seven years—so that the seven sabbaths of years amount to a period of forty-nine years. ⁹Then have the trumpet sounded everywhere on the tenth day of the seventh month; on the Day of Atonement sound the trumpet throughout your land. ¹⁰Consecrate the fiftieth year and proclaim liberty throughout the land to all its inhabitants. It shall be a jubilee for you; each one of you is to return to his family property and each to his own clan. ¹¹The fiftieth year shall be a jubilee for you; do not sow and do not reap what grows of itself or harvest the untended vines. ¹²For it is a jubilee and is to be holy for you; eat only what is taken directly from the fields.

13 " 'In this Year of Jubilee everyone is to return to his own property.

14 " 'If you sell land to one of your countrymen or buy any from him, do not take advantage of each other. ¹⁵You are to buy from your countryman on the basis of the number of years since the Jubilee. And he is to sell to you on the basis of the number of years left for harvesting crops. ¹⁶When the years are many, you are to increase the price, and when the years are few, you are to decrease the price, because what he is really selling you is the number of crops. ¹⁷Do not take advantage of each other, but fear your God. I am the LORD your God.

18 " 'Follow my decrees and be careful to obey my laws, and you will live safely in the land. ¹⁹Then the land will yield its fruit, and you will eat your fill and live there in safety. ²⁰You may ask, "What will we eat in the seventh year if we do not plant or harvest our crops?" ²¹I will send you such a blessing in the sixth year that the land will yield enough for three years. ²²While you plant during the eighth year, you will eat from the old crop and will continue to eat from it until the harvest of the ninth year comes in.

23 " 'The land must not be sold permanently, because the land is mine and you are but aliens and my tenants. ²⁴Throughout the country that you hold as a possession, you must provide for the redemption of the land.

25 " 'If one of your countrymen becomes poor and sells some of his property, his nearest relative is to come and redeem what his countryman has sold. ²⁶If, however, a man has no one to redeem it for him but he himself prospers and acquires sufficient means to redeem it, ²⁷he is to determine the value for the years since he sold it and refund the balance to the man to whom he sold it; he can then go back to his own property. ²⁸But if he does not acquire the means to repay him, what he sold will remain in the possession of the buyer until the Year of Jubilee. It will be returned in the Jubilee, and he can then go back to his property.

29 " 'If a man sells a house in a walled city, he retains the right of redemption a full year after its sale. During that time he may redeem it. ³⁰If it is not redeemed before a full year has passed, the house in the walled city shall belong permanently to the buyer and his descendants. It is not to be returned in the Jubilee. ³¹But houses in villages without walls around them are to be considered as open country. They can be redeemed, and they are to be returned in the Jubilee.

32 " 'The Levites always have the right to redeem their houses in the Levitical towns, which they possess. ³³So the property of the Levites is redeemable—that is, a house sold in any town they hold—and is to be returned in the Jubilee, because the houses in the towns of the Levites are their property among the Israelites. ³⁴But the pastureland belonging to their towns

must not be sold; it is their permanent possession.

³⁵" 'If one of your countrymen becomes poor and is unable to support himself among you, help him as you would an alien or a temporary resident, so he can continue to live among you. ³⁶Do not take interest of any kind*a* from him, but fear your God, so that your countryman may continue to live among you. ³⁷You must not lend him money at interest or sell him food at a profit. ³⁸I am the LORD your God, who brought you out of Egypt to give you the land of Canaan and to be your God.

³⁹" 'If one of your countrymen becomes poor among you and sells himself to you, do not make him work as a slave. ⁴⁰He is to be treated as a hired worker or a temporary resident among you; he is to work for you until the Year of Jubilee. ⁴¹Then he and his children are to be released, and he will go back to his own clan and to the property of his forefathers. ⁴²Because the Israelites are my servants, whom I brought out of Egypt, they must not be sold as slaves. ⁴³Do not rule over them ruthlessly, but fear your God.

⁴⁴" 'Your male and female slaves are to come from the nations around you; from them you may buy slaves. ⁴⁵You may also buy some of the temporary residents living among you and members of their clans born in your country, and they will become your property. ⁴⁶You can will them to your children as inherited property and can make them slaves for life, but you must not rule over your fellow Israelites ruthlessly.

⁴⁷" 'If an alien or a temporary resident among you becomes rich and one of your countrymen becomes poor and sells himself to the alien living among you or to a member of the alien's clan, ⁴⁸he retains the right of redemption after he has sold himself. One of his relatives may redeem him: ⁴⁹An uncle or a cousin or any blood relative in his clan may redeem him. Or if he prospers, he may redeem himself. ⁵⁰He and his buyer are to count the time from the year he sold himself up to the Year of Jubilee. The price for his release is to be based on the rate paid to a hired man for that number of years. ⁵¹If many years remain, he must pay for his redemption a larger share of the price paid for him. ⁵²If only a few years remain until the Year of Jubilee, he is to compute that and pay for his redemption accordingly. ⁵³He is to be treated as a man hired from year to year; you must see to it that his owner does not rule over him ruthlessly.

⁵⁴" 'Even if he is not redeemed in any of these ways, he and his children are to be released in the Year of Jubilee, ⁵⁵for the Israelites belong to me as servants. They are my servants, whom I brought out of Egypt. I am the LORD your God.

Reward for Obedience

26 " 'Do not make idols or set up an image or a sacred stone for yourselves, and do not place a carved stone in your land to bow down before it. I am the LORD your God.

² " 'Observe my Sabbaths and have reverence for my sanctuary. I am the LORD.

³ " 'If you follow my decrees and are careful to obey my commands, ⁴I will send you rain in its season, and the ground will yield its crops and the trees of the field their fruit. ⁵Your threshing will continue until grape harvest and the grape harvest will continue until planting, and you will eat all the food you want and live in safety in your land.

⁶ ' I will grant peace in the land, and you will lie down and no one will make you afraid. I will remove savage beasts from the land, and the sword will not pass through your country. ⁷You will pursue your enemies, and they will fall by the sword before you. ⁸Five of you will chase a hundred, and a hundred of you will chase ten thousand, and your enemies will fall by the sword before you.

⁹ " 'I will look on you with favor and make you fruitful and increase your numbers, and I will keep my covenant with you. ¹⁰You will still be eating last year's harvest when you will have to move it out to make room for the new. ¹¹I will put my dwelling place*b* among you, and I will not abhor you. ¹²I will walk among you and be your God, and you will be my people. ¹³I am the LORD your God, who brought you out of Egypt so that you would no longer be slaves to the Egyptians; I broke the bars of your yoke and

---

a 36 Or *take excessive interest*; similarly in verse 37
b 11 Or *my tabernacle*

enabled you to walk with heads held high.

Punishment for Disobedience

14 " 'But if you will not listen to me and carry out all these commands, 15and if you reject my decrees and abhor my laws and fail to carry out all my commands and so violate my covenant, 16then I will do this to you: I will bring upon you sudden terror, wasting diseases and fever that will destroy your sight and drain away your life. You will plant seed in vain, because your enemies will eat it. 17I will set my face against you so that you will be defeated by your enemies; those who hate you will rule over you, and you will flee even when no one is pursuing you.

18 " 'If after all this you will not listen to me, I will punish you for your sins seven times over. 19I will break down your stubborn pride and make the sky above you like iron and the ground beneath you like bronze. 20Your strength will be spent in vain, because your soil will not yield its crops, nor will the trees of the land yield their fruit.

21 " 'If you remain hostile toward me and refuse to listen to me, I will multiply your afflictions seven times over, as your sins deserve. 22I will send wild animals against you, and they will rob you of your children, destroy your cattle and make you so few in number that your roads will be deserted.

23 " 'If in spite of these things you do not accept my correction but continue to be hostile toward me, 24I myself will be hostile toward you and will afflict you for your sins seven times over. 25And I will bring the sword upon you to avenge the breaking of the covenant. When you withdraw into your cities, I will send a plague among you, and you will be given into enemy hands. 26When I cut off your supply of bread, ten women will be able to bake your bread in one oven, and they will dole out the bread by weight. You will eat, but you will not be satisfied.

27 " 'If in spite of this you still do not listen to me but continue to be hostile toward me, 28then in my anger I will be hostile toward you, and I myself will punish you for your sins seven times over.

The Choice Is Yours

Quiet TIMES
with each other

LEVITICUS 26:3 In the traditional wedding liturgy, couples vow to stay together "for better or for worse." While the casual observer might think, "You never know—maybe this marriage will be good but then again maybe it won't," the road to marital success is one of effort and work. Good marriages don't just happen. Often our choices influence whether our marriage falls into the "for better" or "for worse" category.

The principles God sets forth in Leviticus 26 are still being played out in our world today. A life lived with self-discipline, moderation and wise moral choices brings its own reward. Just apply for life insurance or car insurance and notice that a healthy lifestyle will be rewarded with cheaper rates.

In looking back over the thirty-five plus years we have been married, we realize that good choices and bad choices we made correlate to the times when our marriage was "for better" or "for worse." Over the years we have worked at developing more self-discipline and making wise choices involving our health, finances and time management.

Of course, within the context of an imperfect world, with imperfect people, God does not guarantee the absence of problems. But he does promise his peace. And in the midst of problems, you can experience God's favor in your marriage when you choose obedience—and hard work!

—*Dave & Claudia*

*W*Weekend Warm-up *In the years you've been together, what have been your "for better" and "for worse" times?*

Go to page 145 for your next devotional reading.

²⁹You will eat the flesh of your sons and the flesh of your daughters. ³⁰I will destroy your high places, cut down your incense altars and pile your dead bodies on the lifeless forms of your idols, and I will abhor you. ³¹I will turn your cities into ruins and lay waste your sanctuaries, and I will take no delight in the pleasing aroma of your offerings. ³²I will lay waste the land, so that your enemies who live there will be appalled. ³³I will scatter you among the nations and will draw out my sword and pursue you. Your land will be laid waste, and your cities will lie in ruins. ³⁴Then the land will enjoy its sabbath years all the time that it lies desolate and you are in the country of your enemies; then the land will rest and enjoy its sabbaths. ³⁵All the time that it lies desolate, the land will have the rest it did not have during the sabbaths you lived in it.

³⁶" 'As for those of you who are left, I will make their hearts so fearful in the lands of their enemies that the sound of a windblown leaf will put them to flight. They will run as though fleeing from the sword, and they will fall, even though no one is pursuing them. ³⁷They will stumble over one another as though fleeing from the sword, even though no one is pursuing them. So you will not be able to stand before your enemies. ³⁸You will perish among the nations; the land of your enemies will devour you. ³⁹Those of you who are left will waste away in the lands of their enemies because of their sins; also because of their fathers' sins they will waste away.

⁴⁰" 'But if they will confess their sins and the sins of their fathers—their treachery against me and their hostility toward me, ⁴¹which made me hostile toward them so that I sent them into the land of their enemies—then when their uncircumcised hearts are humbled and they pay for their sin, ⁴²I will remember my covenant with Jacob and my covenant with Isaac and my covenant with Abraham, and I will remember the land. ⁴³For the land will be deserted by them and will enjoy its sabbaths while it lies desolate without them. They will pay for their sins because they rejected my laws and abhorred my decrees. ⁴⁴Yet in spite of this, when they are in the land of their enemies, I will not reject them or abhor them so as to destroy

them completely, breaking my covenant with them. I am the LORD their God. ⁴⁵But for their sake I will remember the covenant with their ancestors whom I brought out of Egypt in the sight of the nations to be their God. I am the LORD.' "

⁴⁶These are the decrees, the laws and the regulations that the LORD established on Mount Sinai between himself and the Israelites through Moses.

Redeeming What Is the LORD's

27 The LORD said to Moses, ²"Speak to the Israelites and say to them: 'If anyone makes a special vow to dedicate persons to the LORD by giving equivalent values, ³set the value of a male between the ages of twenty and sixty at fifty shekels*ᵃ* of silver, according to the sanctuary shekel*ᵇ*; ⁴and if it is a female, set her value at thirty shekels.*ᶜ* ⁵If it is a person between the ages of five and twenty, set the value of a male at twenty shekels*ᵈ* and of a female at ten shekels.*ᵉ* ⁶If it is a person between one month and five years, set the value of a male at five shekels*ᶠ* of silver and that of a female at three shekels*ᵍ* of silver. ⁷If it is a person sixty years old or more, set the value of a male at fifteen shekels*ʰ* and of a female at ten shekels. ⁸If anyone making the vow is too poor to pay the specified amount, he is to present the person to the priest, who will set the value for him according to what the man making the vow can afford.

⁹" 'If what he vowed is an animal that is acceptable as an offering to the LORD, such an animal given to the LORD becomes holy. ¹⁰He must not exchange it or substitute a good one for a bad one, or a bad one for a good one; if he should substitute one animal for another, both it and the substitute become holy. ¹¹If what he vowed is a ceremonially unclean animal—one that is not acceptable as an offering to the LORD—the animal must be presented to the priest, ¹²who will judge

---

ᵃ3 That is, about 1 1/4 pounds (about 0.6 kilogram); also in verse 16   *ᵇ3* That is, about 2/5 ounce (about 11.5 grams); also in verse 25   *ᶜ4* That is, about 12 ounces (about 0.3 kilogram)   *ᵈ5* That is, about 8 ounces (about 0.2 kilogram)   *ᵉ5* That is, about 4 ounces (about 110 grams); also in verse 7   *ᶠ6* That is, about 2 ounces (about 55 grams)   *ᵍ6* That is, about 1 1/4 ounces (about 35 grams)   *ʰ7* That is, about 6 ounces (about 170 grams) its quality as good or bad. Whatever value the priest then sets, that is what it will be. ¹³If the owner wishes to redeem the animal, he must add a fifth to its value.

¹⁴" 'If a man dedicates his house as something holy to the LORD, the priest will judge its quality as good or bad. Whatever value the priest then sets, so it will remain. ¹⁵If the man who dedicates his house redeems it, he must add a fifth to its value, and the house will again become his.

¹⁶" 'If a man dedicates to the LORD part of his family land, its value is to be set according to the amount of seed required for it—fifty shekels of silver to a homer*a* of barley seed. ¹⁷If he dedicates his field during the Year of Jubilee, the value that has been set remains. ¹⁸But if he dedicates his field after the Jubilee, the priest will determine the value according to the number of years that remain until the next Year of Jubilee, and its set value will be reduced. ¹⁹If the man who dedicates the field wishes to redeem it, he must add a fifth to its value, and the field will again become his. ²⁰If, however, he does not redeem the field, or if he has sold it to someone else, it can never be redeemed. ²¹When the field is released in the Jubilee, it will become holy, like a field devoted to the LORD; it will become the property of the priests.*b*

²²" 'If a man dedicates to the LORD a field he has bought, which is not part of his family land, ²³the priest will determine its value up to the Year of Jubilee, and the man must pay its value on that day as something holy to the LORD. ²⁴In the Year of Jubilee the field will revert to the person from whom he bought it, the one whose land it was. ²⁵Every value is to be set according to the sanctuary shekel, twenty gerahs to the shekel.

²⁶" 'No one, however, may dedicate the firstborn of an animal, since the firstborn already belongs to the LORD; whether an ox*c* or a sheep, it is the LORD's. ²⁷If it is one of the unclean animals, he may buy it back at its set value, adding a fifth of the value to it. If he does not redeem it, it is to be sold at its set value.

²⁸" 'But nothing that a man owns and devotes*d* to the LORD—whether man or animal or family land—may be sold or redeemed; everything so devoted is most holy to the LORD.

²⁹" 'No person devoted to destruction*e* may be ransomed; he must be put to death.

³⁰" 'A tithe of everything from the land, whether grain from the soil or fruit from the trees, belongs to the LORD; it is holy to the LORD. ³¹If a man redeems any of his tithe, he must add a fifth of the value to it. ³²The entire tithe of the herd and flock—every tenth animal that passes under the shepherd's rod—will be holy to the LORD. ³³He must not pick out the good from the bad or make any substitution. If he does make a substitution, both the animal and its substitute become holy and cannot be redeemed.' "

³⁴These are the commands the LORD gave Moses on Mount Sinai for the Israelites.

*a*16 That is, probably about 6 bushels (about 220 liters)   *b*21 Or *priest*   *c*26 The Hebrew word can include both male and female.
*d*28 The Hebrew term refers to the irrevocable giving over of things or persons to the LORD.
*e*29 The Hebrew term refers to the irrevocable giving over of things or persons to the LORD, often by totally destroying them.

Numbers

"Follow the Leader" may be the name of a child's game, but for the Israelites, it was serious business. These people—a couple million of them—were stuck between captivity in Egypt and a new life in the Promised Land. For forty years they lived from day to day, not knowing where they were going. They felt lost, they acted lost, they grumbled and complained like they were lost . . . but they weren't lost.

God knew exactly where the Israelites were. He knew why they were there, how long they were going to be there and where they were going. God even provided them a huge cloud to follow during the day and a fireball to follow for late-night trips. Throughout the desert years, it became clear to the Israelites that God was always with them.

Following God every day in spite of feeling completely lost is the story of the book of Numbers. This is also what Jesus, God's precious Son, told his disciples—and us as well—to do. "Follow me," Jesus said. So when you feel like you're wandering in your own marriage "desert," remember that God is always with you and that he loves, forgives and provides for you—even when you wander.

The Census

1 The LORD spoke to Moses in the Tent of Meeting in the Desert of Sinai on the first day of the second month of the second year after the Israelites came out of Egypt. He said: 2"Take a census of the whole Israelite community by their clans and families, listing every man by name, one by one. 3You and Aaron are to number by their divisions all the men in Israel twenty years old or more who are able to serve in the army. 4One man from each tribe, each the head of his family, is to

help you. ⁵These are the names of the men who are to assist you:

from Reuben, Elizur son of Shedeur;

⁶from Simeon, Shelumiel son of Zurishaddai;

⁷from Judah, Nahshon son of Amminadab;

⁸from Issachar, Nethanel son of Zuar;

⁹from Zebulun, Eliab son of Helon;

¹⁰from the sons of Joseph:

from Ephraim, Elishama son of Ammihud;

from Manasseh, Gamaliel son of Pedahzur;

¹¹from Benjamin, Abidan son of Gideoni;

¹²from Dan, Ahiezer son of Ammishaddai;

¹³from Asher, Pagiel son of Ocran;

¹⁴from Gad, Eliasaph son of Deuel;

¹⁵from Naphtali, Ahira son of Enan."

¹⁶These were the men appointed from the community, the leaders of their ancestral tribes. They were the heads of the clans of Israel.

¹⁷Moses and Aaron took these men whose names had been given, ¹⁸and they called the whole community together on the first day of the second month. The people indicated their ancestry by their clans and families, and the men twenty years old or more were listed by name, one by one, ¹⁹as the LORD commanded Moses. And so he counted them in the Desert of Sinai:

²⁰From the descendants of Reuben the firstborn son of Israel:

All the men twenty years old or more who were able to serve in the army were listed by name, one by one, according to the records of their clans and families. ²¹The number from the tribe of Reuben was 46,500.

²²From the descendants of Simeon:

All the men twenty years old or more who were able to serve in the army were counted and listed by name, one by one, according to the records of their clans and families. ²³The number from the tribe of Simeon was 59,300.

²⁴From the descendants of Gad:

All the men twenty years old or more who were able to serve in the army were listed by name, according to the records of their clans and families. ²⁵The number from the tribe of Gad was 45,650.

²⁶From the descendants of Judah:

All the men twenty years old or more who were able to serve in the army were listed by name, according to the records of their clans and families. ²⁷The number from the tribe of Judah was 74,600.

²⁸From the descendants of Issachar:

All the men twenty years old or more who were able to serve in the army were listed by name, according to the records of their clans and families. ²⁹The number from the tribe of Issachar was 54,400.

³⁰From the descendants of Zebulun:

All the men twenty years old or more who were able to serve in the army were listed by name, according to the records of their clans and families. ³¹The number from the tribe of Zebulun was 57,400.

³²From the sons of Joseph:

From the descendants of Ephraim:

All the men twenty years old or more who were able to serve in the army were listed by name, according to the records of their clans and families. ³³The number from the tribe of Ephraim was 40,500.

³⁴From the descendants of Manasseh:

All the men twenty years old or more who were able to serve in the army were listed by name, according to the records of their clans and families. ³⁵The number from the tribe of Manasseh was 32,200.

³⁶From the descendants of Benjamin:
All the men twenty years old or more who were able to serve in the army were listed by name, according to the records of their clans and families. ³⁷The number from the tribe of Benjamin was 35,400.

³⁸From the descendants of Dan:
All the men twenty years old or more who were able to serve in the army were listed by name, according to the records of their clans and families. ³⁹The number from the tribe of Dan was 62,700.

⁴⁰From the descendants of Asher:
All the men twenty years old or more who were able to serve in the army were listed by name, according to the records of their clans and families. ⁴¹The number from the tribe of Asher was 41,500.

⁴²From the descendants of Naphtali:
All the men twenty years old or more who were able to serve in the army were listed by name, according to the records of their clans and families. ⁴³The number from the tribe of Naphtali was 53,400.

⁴⁴These were the men counted by Moses and Aaron and the twelve leaders of Israel, each one representing his family. ⁴⁵All the Israelites twenty years old or more who were able to serve in Israel's army were counted according to their families. ⁴⁶The total number was 603,550.

⁴⁷The families of the tribe of Levi, however, were not counted along with the others. ⁴⁸The LORD had said to Moses: ⁴⁹"You must not count the tribe of Levi or include them in the census of the other Israelites. ⁵⁰Instead, appoint the Levites to be in charge of the tabernacle of the Testimony—over all its furnishings and everything belonging to it. They are to carry the tabernacle and all its furnishings; they are to take care of it and encamp around it. ⁵¹Whenever the tabernacle is to move, the Levites are to take it down, and whenever the tabernacle is to be set up, the Levites shall do it. Anyone else who goes near it shall be put to death. ⁵²The Israelites are to set up their tents by divisions, each man in his own camp under his own standard. ⁵³The Levites, however, are to set up their tents around the tabernacle of the Testimony so that wrath will not fall on the Israelite community. The Levites are to be responsible for the care of the tabernacle of the Testimony."

⁵⁴The Israelites did all this just as the LORD commanded Moses.

The Arrangement of the Tribal Camps

2 The LORD said to Moses and Aaron: ²"The Israelites are to camp around the Tent of Meeting some distance from it, each man under his standard with the banners of his family."

³On the east, toward the sunrise, the divisions of the camp of Judah are to encamp under their standard. The leader of the people of Judah is Nahshon son of Amminadab. ⁴His division numbers 74,600.

⁵The tribe of Issachar will camp next to them. The leader of the people of Issachar is Nethanel son of Zuar. ⁶His division numbers 54,400.

⁷The tribe of Zebulun will be next. The leader of the people of Zebulun is Eliab son of Helon. ⁸His division numbers 57,400.

⁹All the men assigned to the camp of Judah, according to their divisions, number 186,400. They will set out first.

¹⁰On the south will be the divisions of the camp of Reuben under their standard. The leader of the people of Reuben is Elizur son of Shedeur. ¹¹His division numbers 46,500.

¹²The tribe of Simeon will camp next to them. The leader of the people of Simeon is Shelumiel son of Zurishaddai. ¹³His division numbers 59,300.

¹⁴The tribe of Gad will be next. The leader of the people of Gad is

Eliasaph son of Deuel.[a] [15]His division numbers 45,650.

[16]All the men assigned to the camp of Reuben, according to their divisions, number 151,450. They will set out second.

[17]Then the Tent of Meeting and the camp of the Levites will set out in the middle of the camps. They will set out in the same order as they encamp, each in his own place under his standard.

[18]On the west will be the divisions of the camp of Ephraim under their standard. The leader of the people of Ephraim is Elishama son of Ammihud. [19]His division numbers 40,500.
[20]The tribe of Manasseh will be next to them. The leader of the people of Manasseh is Gamaliel son of Pedahzur. [21]His division numbers 32,200.
[22]The tribe of Benjamin will be next. The leader of the people of Benjamin is Abidan son of Gideoni. [23]His division numbers 35,400.

[24]All the men assigned to the camp of Ephraim, according to their divisions, number 108,100. They will set out third.

[25]On the north will be the divisions of the camp of Dan, under their standard. The leader of the people of Dan is Ahiezer son of Ammishaddai. [26]His division numbers 62,700.
[27]The tribe of Asher will camp next to them. The leader of the people of Asher is Pagiel son of Ocran. [28]His division numbers 41,500.
[29]The tribe of Naphtali will be next. The leader of the people of Naphtali is Ahira son of Enan. [30]His division numbers 53,400.
[31]All the men assigned to the camp of Dan number 157,600. They will set out last, under their standards.

[32]These are the Israelites, counted according to their families. All those in the camps, by their divisions, number 603,550. [33]The Levites, however, were not counted along with the other Israelites, as the LORD commanded Moses.

[34]So the Israelites did everything the LORD commanded Moses; that is the way they encamped under their standards, and that is the way they set out, each with his clan and family.

The Levites

3 This is the account of the family of Aaron and Moses at the time the LORD talked with Moses on Mount Sinai.

[2]The names of the sons of Aaron were Nadab the firstborn and Abihu, Eleazar and Ithamar. [3]Those were the names of Aaron's sons, the anointed priests, who were ordained to serve as priests. [4]Nadab and Abihu, however, fell dead before the LORD when they made an offering with unauthorized fire before him in the Desert of Sinai. They had no sons; so only Eleazar and Ithamar served as priests during the lifetime of their father Aaron.

[5]The LORD said to Moses, [6]"Bring the tribe of Levi and present them to Aaron the priest to assist him. [7]They are to perform duties for him and for the whole community at the Tent of Meeting by doing the work of the tabernacle. [8]They are to take care of all the furnishings of the Tent of Meeting, fulfilling the obligations of the Israelites by doing the work of the tabernacle. [9]Give the Levites to Aaron and his sons; they are the Israelites who are to be given wholly to him.[b] [10]Appoint Aaron and his sons to serve as priests; anyone else who approaches the sanctuary must be put to death."

[11]The LORD also said to Moses, [12]"I have taken the Levites from among the Israelites in place of the first male offspring of every Israelite woman. The Levites are mine, [13]for all the firstborn are mine. When I struck down all the firstborn in Egypt, I set apart for myself every firstborn in Israel, whether man or animal. They are to be mine. I am the LORD."

[14]The LORD said to Moses in the Desert of Sinai, [15]"Count the Levites by their

---

[a]14 Many manuscripts of the Masoretic Text, Samaritan Pentateuch and Vulgate (see also Num. 1:14); most manuscripts of the Masoretic Text *Reuel* [b]9 Most manuscripts of the Masoretic Text; some manuscripts of the Masoretic Text, Samaritan Pentateuch and Septuagint (see also Num. 8:16) *to me*

families and clans. Count every male a month old or more." ¹⁶So Moses counted them, as he was commanded by the word of the LORD.

¹⁷These were the names of the sons of Levi:

Gershon, Kohath and Merari.

¹⁸These were the names of the Gershonite clans:

Libni and Shimei.

¹⁹The Kohathite clans:

Amram, Izhar, Hebron and Uzziel.

²⁰The Merarite clans:

Mahli and Mushi.

These were the Levite clans, according to their families.

²¹To Gershon belonged the clans of the Libnites and Shimeites; these were the Gershonite clans. ²²The number of all the males a month old or more who were counted was 7,500. ²³The Gershonite clans were to camp on the west, behind the tabernacle. ²⁴The leader of the families of the Gershonites was Eliasaph son of Lael. ²⁵At the Tent of Meeting the Gershonites were responsible for the care of the tabernacle and tent, its coverings, the curtain at the entrance to the Tent of Meeting, ²⁶the curtains of the courtyard, the curtain at the entrance to the courtyard surrounding the tabernacle and altar, and the ropes—and everything related to their use.

²⁷To Kohath belonged the clans of the Amramites, Izharites, Hebronites and Uzzielites; these were the Kohathite clans. ²⁸The number of all the males a month old or more was 8,600.ᵃ The Kohathites were responsible for the care of the sanctuary. ²⁹The Kohathite clans were to camp on the south side of the tabernacle. ³⁰The leader of the families of the Kohathite clans was Elizaphan son of Uzziel. ³¹They were responsible for the care of the ark, the table, the lampstand, the altars, the articles of the sanctuary used in ministering, the curtain, and everything related to their use. ³²The chief leader of the Levites was Eleazar son of Aaron, the priest. He was appointed over those who were responsible for the care of the sanctuary.

³³To Merari belonged the clans of the Mahlites and the Mushites; these were the Merarite clans. ³⁴The number of all the males a month old or more who were counted was 6,200. ³⁵The leader of the families of the Merarite clans was Zuriel son of Abihail; they were to camp on the north side of the tabernacle. ³⁶The Merarites were appointed to take care of the frames of the tabernacle, its crossbars, posts, bases, all its equipment, and everything related to their use, ³⁷as well as the posts of the surrounding courtyard with their bases, tent pegs and ropes.

³⁸Moses and Aaron and his sons were to camp to the east of the tabernacle, toward the sunrise, in front of the Tent of Meeting. They were responsible for the care of the sanctuary on behalf of the Israelites. Anyone else who approached the sanctuary was to be put to death.

³⁹The total number of Levites counted at the LORD's command by Moses and Aaron according to their clans, including every male a month old or more, was 22,000.

⁴⁰The LORD said to Moses, "Count all the firstborn Israelite males who are a month old or more and make a list of their names. ⁴¹Take the Levites for me in place of all the firstborn of the Israelites, and the livestock of the Levites in place of all the firstborn of the livestock of the Israelites. I am the LORD."

⁴²So Moses counted all the firstborn of the Israelites, as the LORD commanded him. ⁴³The total number of firstborn males a month old or more, listed by name, was 22,273.

⁴⁴The LORD also said to Moses, ⁴⁵"Take the Levites in place of all the firstborn of Israel, and the livestock of the Levites in place of their livestock. The Levites are to be mine. I am the LORD. ⁴⁶To redeem the 273 firstborn Israelites who exceed the number of the Levites, ⁴⁷collect five shekelsᵇ for each one, according to the sanctuary shekel, which weighs twenty gerahs. ⁴⁸Give the money for the redemption of the additional Israelites to Aaron and his sons."

ᵃ28 Hebrew; some Septuagint manuscripts 8,300
ᵇ47 That is, about 2 ounces (about 55 grams)

⁴⁹So Moses collected the redemption money from those who exceeded the number redeemed by the Levites. ⁵⁰From the firstborn of the Israelites he collected silver weighing 1,365 shekels,ᵃ according to the sanctuary shekel. ⁵¹Moses gave the redemption money to Aaron and his sons, as he was commanded by the word of the LORD.

The Kohathites

4 The LORD said to Moses and Aaron: ²"Take a census of the Kohathite branch of the Levites by their clans and families. ³Count all the men from thirty to fifty years of age who come to serve in the work in the Tent of Meeting.

⁴"This is the work of the Kohathites in the Tent of Meeting: the care of the most holy things. ⁵When the camp is to move, Aaron and his sons are to go in and take down the shielding curtain and cover the ark of the Testimony with it. ⁶Then they are to cover this with hides of sea cows,ᵇ spread a cloth of solid blue over that and put the poles in place.

⁷"Over the table of the Presence they are to spread a blue cloth and put on it the plates, dishes and bowls, and the jars for drink offerings; the bread that is continually there is to remain on it. ⁸Over these they are to spread a scarlet cloth, cover that with hides of sea cows and put its poles in place.

⁹"They are to take a blue cloth and cover the lampstand that is for light, together with its lamps, its wick trimmers and trays, and all its jars for the oil used to supply it. ¹⁰Then they are to wrap it and all its accessories in a covering of hides of sea cows and put it on a carrying frame.

¹¹"Over the gold altar they are to spread a blue cloth and cover that with hides of sea cows and put its poles in place.

¹²"They are to take all the articles used for ministering in the sanctuary, wrap them in a blue cloth, cover that with hides of sea cows and put them on a carrying frame.

¹³"They are to remove the ashes from the bronze altar and spread a purple cloth over it. ¹⁴Then they are to place on it all the utensils used for ministering at the altar, including the firepans, meat forks, shovels and sprinkling bowls. Over it they are to spread a covering of hides of sea cows and put its poles in place.

¹⁵"After Aaron and his sons have finished covering the holy furnishings and all the holy articles, and when the camp is ready to move, the Kohathites are to come to do the carrying. But they must not touch the holy things or they will die. The Kohathites are to carry those things that are in the Tent of Meeting.

¹⁶"Eleazar son of Aaron, the priest, is to have charge of the oil for the light, the fragrant incense, the regular grain offering and the anointing oil. He is to be in charge of the entire tabernacle and everything in it, including its holy furnishings and articles."

¹⁷The LORD said to Moses and Aaron, ¹⁸"See that the Kohathite tribal clans are not cut off from the Levites. ¹⁹So that they may live and not die when they come near the most holy things, do this for them: Aaron and his sons are to go into the sanctuary and assign to each man his work and what he is to carry. ²⁰But the Kohathites must not go in to look at the holy things, even for a moment, or they will die."

The Gershonites

²¹The LORD said to Moses, ²²"Take a census also of the Gershonites by their families and clans. ²³Count all the men from thirty to fifty years of age who come to serve in the work at the Tent of Meeting.

²⁴"This is the service of the Gershonite clans as they work and carry burdens: ²⁵They are to carry the curtains of the tabernacle, the Tent of Meeting, its covering and the outer covering of hides of sea cows, the curtains for the entrance to the Tent of Meeting, ²⁶the curtains of the courtyard surrounding the tabernacle and altar, the curtain for the entrance, the ropes and all the equipment used in its service. The Gershonites are to do all that needs to be done with these things. ²⁷All their service, whether carrying or doing other work, is to be done under the direc-

---

ᵃ50 That is, about 35 pounds (about 15.5 kilograms)   ᵇ6 That is, dugongs; also in verses 8, 10, 11, 12, 14 and 25 tion of Aaron and his sons. You shall assign to them as their responsibility all they are to carry. ²⁸This is the service of the Gershonite clans at the Tent of Meeting. Their duties are to be under the direction of Ithamar son of Aaron, the priest.

The Merarites

²⁹"Count the Merarites by their clans and families. ³⁰Count all the men from thirty to fifty years of age who come to serve in the work at the Tent of Meeting. ³¹This is their duty as they perform service at the Tent of Meeting: to carry the frames of the tabernacle, its crossbars, posts and bases, ³²as well as the posts of the surrounding courtyard with their bases, tent pegs, ropes, all their equipment and everything related to their use. Assign to each man the specific things he is to carry. ³³This is the service of the Merarite clans as they work at the Tent of Meeting under the direction of Ithamar son of Aaron, the priest."

The Numbering of the Levite Clans

³⁴Moses, Aaron and the leaders of the community counted the Kohathites by their clans and families. ³⁵All the men from thirty to fifty years of age who came to serve in the work in the Tent of Meeting, ³⁶counted by clans, were 2,750. ³⁷This was the total of all those in the Kohathite clans who served in the Tent of Meeting. Moses and Aaron counted them according to the LORD's command through Moses.

³⁸The Gershonites were counted by their clans and families. ³⁹All the men from thirty to fifty years of age who came to serve in the work at the Tent of Meeting, ⁴⁰counted by their clans and families, were 2,630. ⁴¹This was the total of those in the Gershonite clans who served at the Tent of Meeting. Moses and Aaron counted them according to the LORD's command.

⁴²The Merarites were counted by their clans and families. ⁴³All the men from thirty to fifty years of age who came to serve in the work at the Tent of Meeting, ⁴⁴counted by their clans, were 3,200. ⁴⁵This was the total of those in the Merarite clans. Moses and Aaron counted them

according to the LORD's command through Moses.

⁴⁶So Moses, Aaron and the leaders of Israel counted all the Levites by their clans and families. ⁴⁷All the men from thirty to fifty years of age who came to do the work of serving and carrying the Tent of Meeting ⁴⁸numbered 8,580. ⁴⁹At the LORD's command through Moses, each was assigned his work and told what to carry.

Thus they were counted, as the LORD commanded Moses.

The Purity of the Camp

5 The LORD said to Moses, ²"Command the Israelites to send away from the camp anyone who has an infectious skin disease[a] or a discharge of any kind, or who is ceremonially unclean because of a dead body. ³Send away male and female alike; send them outside the camp so they will not defile their camp, where I dwell among them." ⁴The Israelites did this; they sent them outside the camp. They did just as the LORD had instructed Moses.

Restitution for Wrongs

⁵The LORD said to Moses, ⁶"Say to the Israelites: 'When a man or woman wrongs another in any way[b] and so is unfaithful to the LORD, that person is guilty ⁷and must confess the sin he has committed. He must make full restitution for his wrong, add one fifth to it and give it all to the person he has wronged. ⁸But if that person has no close relative to whom restitution can be made for the wrong, the restitution belongs to the LORD and must be given to the priest, along with the ram with which atonement is made for him. ⁹All the sacred contributions the Israelites bring to a priest will belong to him. ¹⁰Each man's sacred gifts are his own, but what he gives to the priest will belong to the priest.' "

The Test for an Unfaithful Wife

¹¹Then the LORD said to Moses, ¹²"Speak to the Israelites and say to them: 'If a man's wife goes astray and is unfaithful to him ¹³by sleeping with another

---

a2 Traditionally *leprosy*; the Hebrew word was used for various diseases affecting the skin—not necessarily leprosy.   *b6* Or *woman commits any wrong common to mankind* man, and this is hidden from her husband and her impurity is undetected (since there is no witness against her and she has not been caught in the act), [14]and if feelings of jealousy come over her husband and he suspects his wife and she is impure—or if he is jealous and suspects her even though she is not impure— [15]then he is to take his wife to the priest. He must also take an offering of a tenth of an ephah[a] of barley flour on her behalf. He must not pour oil on it or put incense on it, because it is a grain offering for jealousy, a reminder offering to draw attention to guilt.

[16]" 'The priest shall bring her and have her stand before the LORD. [17]Then he shall take some holy water in a clay jar and put some dust from the tabernacle floor into the water. [18]After the priest has had the woman stand before the LORD, he shall loosen her hair and place in her hands the reminder offering, the grain offering for jealousy, while he himself holds the bitter water that brings a curse. [19]Then the priest shall put the woman under oath and say to her, "If no other man has slept with you and you have not gone astray and become impure while married to your husband, may this bitter water that brings a curse not harm you. [20]But if you have gone astray while married to your husband and you have defiled yourself by sleeping with a man other than your husband"— [21]here the priest is to put the woman under this curse of the oath— "may the LORD cause your people to curse and denounce you when he causes your thigh to waste away and your abdomen to swell.[b] [22]May this water that brings a curse enter your body so that your abdomen swells and your thigh wastes away.[c]"

" 'Then the woman is to say, "Amen. So be it."

[23]" 'The priest is to write these curses on a scroll and then wash them off into the bitter water. [24]He shall have the woman drink the bitter water that brings a curse, and this water will enter her and cause bitter suffering. [25]The priest is to take from her hands the grain offering for jealousy, wave it before the LORD and bring it to the altar. [26]The priest is then to take a handful of the grain offering as a memorial offering and burn it on the altar; after that, he is to have the woman

drink the water. [27]If she has defiled herself and been unfaithful to her husband, then when she is made to drink the water that brings a curse, it will go into her and cause bitter suffering; her abdomen will swell and her thigh waste away,[d] and she will become accursed among her people. [28]If, however, the woman has not defiled herself and is free from impurity, she will be cleared of guilt and will be able to have children.

[29]" 'This, then, is the law of jealousy when a woman goes astray and defiles herself while married to her husband, [30]or when feelings of jealousy come over a man because he suspects his wife. The priest is to have her stand before the LORD and is to apply this entire law to her. [31]The husband will be innocent of any wrongdoing, but the woman will bear the consequences of her sin.' "

The Nazirite

6 The LORD said to Moses, [2]"Speak to the Israelites and say to them: 'If a man or woman wants to make a special vow, a vow of separation to the LORD as a Nazirite, [3]he must abstain from wine and other fermented drink and must not drink vinegar made from wine or from other fermented drink. He must not drink grape juice or eat grapes or raisins. [4]As long as he is a Nazirite, he must not eat anything that comes from the grapevine, not even the seeds or skins.

[5]" 'During the entire period of his vow of separation no razor may be used on his head. He must be holy until the period of his separation to the LORD is over; he must let the hair of his head grow long. [6]Throughout the period of his separation to the LORD he must not go near a dead body. [7]Even if his own father or mother or brother or sister dies, he must not make himself ceremonially unclean on account of them, because the symbol of his separation to God is on his head. [8]Throughout the period of his separation he is consecrated to the LORD.

[9]" 'If someone dies suddenly in his

---

[a]15 That is, probably about 2 quarts (about 2 liters)   [b]21 Or causes you to have a miscarrying womb and barrenness   [c]22 Or body and cause you to be barren and have a miscarrying womb   [d]27 Or suffering; she will have barrenness and a miscarrying womb

presence, thus defiling the hair he has dedicated, he must shave his head on the day of his cleansing—the seventh day. ¹⁰Then on the eighth day he must bring two doves or two young pigeons to the priest at the entrance to the Tent of Meeting. ¹¹The priest is to offer one as a sin offering and the other as a burnt offering to make atonement for him because he sinned by being in the presence of the dead body. That same day he is to consecrate his head. ¹²He must dedicate himself to the LORD for the period of his separation and must bring a year-old male lamb as a guilt offering. The previous days do not count, because he became defiled during his separation.

¹³" 'Now this is the law for the Nazirite when the period of his separation is over. He is to be brought to the entrance to the Tent of Meeting. ¹⁴There he is to present his offerings to the LORD: a year-old male lamb without defect for a burnt offering, a year-old ewe lamb without defect for a sin offering, a ram without defect for a fellowship offering,^a ¹⁵together with their grain offerings and drink offerings, and a basket of bread made without yeast—cakes made of fine flour mixed with oil, and wafers spread with oil.

¹⁶" 'The priest is to present them before the LORD and make the sin offering and the burnt offering. ¹⁷He is to present the basket of unleavened bread and is to sacrifice the ram as a fellowship offering to the LORD, together with its grain offering and drink offering.

¹⁸" 'Then at the entrance to the Tent of Meeting, the Nazirite must shave off the hair that he dedicated. He is to take the hair and put it in the fire that is under the sacrifice of the fellowship offering.

¹⁹" 'After the Nazirite has shaved off the hair of his dedication, the priest is to place in his hands a boiled shoulder of the ram, and a cake and a wafer from the basket, both made without yeast. ²⁰The priest shall then wave them before the LORD as a wave offering; they are holy and belong to the priest, together with the breast that was waved and the thigh that was presented. After that, the Nazirite may drink wine.

²¹" 'This is the law of the Nazirite who vows his offering to the LORD in accordance with his separation, in addition to

whatever else he can afford. He must fulfill the vow he has made, according to the law of the Nazirite.' "

The Priestly Blessing

²²The LORD said to Moses, ²³"Tell Aaron and his sons, 'This is how you are to bless the Israelites. Say to them:

²⁴" ' "The LORD bless you
    and keep you;
²⁵the LORD make his face shine upon
        you
    and be gracious to you;
²⁶the LORD turn his face toward you
    and give you peace." '

²⁷"So they will put my name on the Israelites, and I will bless them."

Offerings at the Dedication of the Tabernacle

7 When Moses finished setting up the tabernacle, he anointed it and consecrated it and all its furnishings. He also anointed and consecrated the altar and all its utensils. ²Then the leaders of Israel, the heads of families who were the tribal leaders in charge of those who were counted, made offerings. ³They brought as their gifts before the LORD six covered carts and twelve oxen—an ox from each leader and a cart from every two. These they presented before the tabernacle.

⁴The LORD said to Moses, ⁵"Accept these from them, that they may be used in the work at the Tent of Meeting. Give them to the Levites as each man's work requires."

⁶So Moses took the carts and oxen and gave them to the Levites. ⁷He gave two carts and four oxen to the Gershonites, as their work required, ⁸and he gave four carts and eight oxen to the Merarites, as their work required. They were all under the direction of Ithamar son of Aaron, the priest. ⁹But Moses did not give any to the Kohathites, because they were to carry on their shoulders the holy things, for which they were responsible.

¹⁰When the altar was anointed, the leaders brought their offerings for its dedication and presented them before the altar. ¹¹For the LORD had said to Moses,

^a14 Traditionally *peace offering*; also in verses 17 and 18

"Each day one leader is to bring his offering for the dedication of the altar."

[12]The one who brought his offering on the first day was Nahshon son of Amminadab of the tribe of Judah.

[13]His offering was one silver plate weighing a hundred and thirty shekels,[a] and one silver sprinkling bowl weighing seventy shekels,[b] both according to the sanctuary shekel, each filled with fine flour mixed with oil as a grain offering; [14]one gold dish weighing ten shekels,[c] filled with incense; [15]one young bull, one ram and one male lamb a year old, for a burnt offering; [16]one male goat for a sin offering; [17]and two oxen, five rams, five male goats and five male lambs a year old, to be sacrificed as a fellowship offering.[d] This was the offering of Nahshon son of Amminadab.

[18]On the second day Nethanel son of Zuar, the leader of Issachar, brought his offering.

[19]The offering he brought was one silver plate weighing a hundred and thirty shekels, and one silver sprinkling bowl weighing seventy shekels, both according to the sanctuary shekel, each filled with fine flour mixed with oil as a grain offering; [20]one gold dish weighing ten shekels, filled with incense; [21]one young bull, one ram and one male lamb a year old, for a burnt offering; [22]one male goat for a sin offering; [23]and two oxen, five rams, five male goats and five male lambs a year old, to be sacrificed as a fellowship offering.

[a]13 That is, about 3 1/4 pounds (about 1.5 kilograms); also elsewhere in this chapter
[b]13 That is, about 1 3/4 pounds (about 0.8 kilogram); also elsewhere in this chapter
[c]14 That is, about 4 ounces (about 110 grams); also elsewhere in this chapter
[d]17 Traditionally *peace offering*; also elsewhere in this chapter

The Blessing

Monday

NUMBERS 6:22–27 "Take the afternoon off. I'll drive the carpool." "Why don't you sit down with your favorite book? I'll do the dishes and get the kids in bed." "The kids are spending the night with your parents. The whole house is ours for the evening!"

How do you feel when you hear words like these? Surprised? Delighted? Loved? Now think about how your spouse might feel if words like these came out of your mouth. The words we speak to each other can build up or tear down. They give encouragement or discouragement. If we had the choice, we'd choose to hear encouraging words.

In this passage, called the "Priestly Blessing," you can hear God's encouraging words to you. He wants to bless you and make his face shine upon you and give you peace. Then as you experience God's blessing, you will naturally want to bless your mate. It could be something as simple as taking the dishes from the dining room to the kitchen without saying a word, putting the shoes in the closet, putting the cap back on the toothpaste, or running a bath for your tired spouse and lighting candles.

We have used the "Priestly Blessing" as a model for encouraging each other and for thanking God for his blessings on our marriage. Let us share our personal prayer with you:

"The LORD bless our marriage
and help us remain true to each other;
The LORD make his face shine upon our
    marriage
and help us experience his grace;
The LORD turn his face toward each of us
    and our marital union
and give us his peace."

You can practice the peace of the Lord by committing your marriage to him and asking him to help you grow in your love for him and for each other!

—Dave & Claudia

Go to page 152 for your next devotional reading.

This was the offering of Nethanel son of Zuar.

²⁴On the third day, Eliab son of Helon, the leader of the people of Zebulun, brought his offering.

²⁵His offering was one silver plate weighing a hundred and thirty shekels, and one silver sprinkling bowl weighing seventy shekels, both according to the sanctuary shekel, each filled with fine flour mixed with oil as a grain offering; ²⁶one gold dish weighing ten shekels, filled with incense; ²⁷one young bull, one ram and one male lamb a year old, for a burnt offering; ²⁸one male goat for a sin offering; ²⁹and two oxen, five rams, five male goats and five male lambs a year old, to be sacrificed as a fellowship offering. This was the offering of Eliab son of Helon.

³⁰On the fourth day Elizur son of Shedeur, the leader of the people of Reuben, brought his offering.

³¹His offering was one silver plate weighing a hundred and thirty shekels, and one silver sprinkling bowl weighing seventy shekels, both according to the sanctuary shekel, each filled with fine flour mixed with oil as a grain offering; ³²one gold dish weighing ten shekels, filled with incense; ³³one young bull, one ram and one male lamb a year old, for a burnt offering; ³⁴one male goat for a sin offering; ³⁵and two oxen, five rams, five male goats and five male lambs a year old, to be sacrificed as a fellowship offering. This was the offering of Elizur son of Shedeur.

³⁶On the fifth day Shelumiel son of Zurishaddai, the leader of the people of Simeon, brought his offering.

³⁷His offering was one silver plate weighing a hundred and thirty shekels, and one silver sprinkling bowl weighing seventy shekels, both according to the sanctuary shekel, each filled with fine flour mixed with oil as a grain offering; ³⁸one gold dish weighing ten shekels, filled with incense; ³⁹one young bull, one ram and one male lamb a year old, for a burnt offering; ⁴⁰one male goat for a sin offering; ⁴¹and two oxen, five rams, five male goats and five male lambs a year old, to be sacrificed as a fellowship offering. This was the offering of Shelumiel son of Zurishaddai.

⁴²On the sixth day Eliasaph son of Deuel, the leader of the people of Gad, brought his offering.

⁴³His offering was one silver plate weighing a hundred and thirty shekels, and one silver sprinkling bowl weighing seventy shekels, both according to the sanctuary shekel, each filled with fine flour mixed with oil as a grain offering; ⁴⁴one gold dish weighing ten shekels, filled with incense; ⁴⁵one young bull, one ram and one male lamb a year old, for a burnt offering; ⁴⁶one male goat for a sin offering; ⁴⁷and two oxen, five rams, five male goats and five male lambs a year old, to be sacrificed as a fellowship offering. This was the offering of Eliasaph son of Deuel.

⁴⁸On the seventh day Elishama son of Ammihud, the leader of the people of Ephraim, brought his offering.

⁴⁹His offering was one silver plate weighing a hundred and thirty shekels, and one silver sprinkling bowl weighing seventy shekels, both according to the sanctuary shekel, each filled with fine flour mixed with oil as a grain offering; ⁵⁰one gold dish weighing ten shekels, filled with incense; ⁵¹one young bull, one ram and one male lamb a year old, for a burnt offering; ⁵²one male goat for a sin offering; ⁵³and two oxen, five rams, five male goats and five male lambs a year old, to be sacrificed as a fellowship offering. This was the offering of Elishama son of Ammihud.

⁵⁴On the eighth day Gamaliel son of Pedahzur, the leader of the people of Manasseh, brought his offering.

⁵⁵His offering was one silver plate weighing a hundred and thirty shekels, and one silver sprinkling bowl

weighing seventy shekels, both according to the sanctuary shekel, each filled with fine flour mixed with oil as a grain offering; ⁵⁶one gold dish weighing ten shekels, filled with incense; ⁵⁷one young bull, one ram and one male lamb a year old, for a burnt offering; ⁵⁸one male goat for a sin offering; ⁵⁹and two oxen, five rams, five male goats and five male lambs a year old, to be sacrificed as a fellowship offering. This was the offering of Gamaliel son of Pedahzur.

⁶⁰On the ninth day Abidan son of Gideoni, the leader of the people of Benjamin, brought his offering.

⁶¹His offering was one silver plate weighing a hundred and thirty shekels, and one silver sprinkling bowl weighing seventy shekels, both according to the sanctuary shekel, each filled with fine flour mixed with oil as a grain offering; ⁶²one gold dish weighing ten shekels, filled with incense; ⁶³one young bull, one ram and one male lamb a year old, for a burnt offering; ⁶⁴one male goat for a sin offering; ⁶⁵and two oxen, five rams, five male goats and five male lambs a year old, to be sacrificed as a fellowship offering. This was the offering of Abidan son of Gideoni.

⁶⁶On the tenth day Ahiezer son of Ammishaddai, the leader of the people of Dan, brought his offering.

⁶⁷His offering was one silver plate weighing a hundred and thirty shekels, and one silver sprinkling bowl weighing seventy shekels, both according to the sanctuary shekel, each filled with fine flour mixed with oil as a grain offering; ⁶⁸one gold dish weighing ten shekels, filled with incense; ⁶⁹one young bull, one ram and one male lamb a year old, for a burnt offering; ⁷⁰one male goat for a sin offering; ⁷¹and two oxen, five rams, five male goats and five male lambs a year old, to be sacrificed as a fellowship offering. This was the offering of Ahiezer son of Ammishaddai.

⁷²On the eleventh day Pagiel son of Ocran, the leader of the people of Asher, brought his offering.

⁷³His offering was one silver plate weighing a hundred and thirty shekels, and one silver sprinkling bowl weighing seventy shekels, both according to the sanctuary shekel, each filled with fine flour mixed with oil as a grain offering; ⁷⁴one gold dish weighing ten shekels, filled with incense; ⁷⁵one young bull, one ram and one male lamb a year old, for a burnt offering; ⁷⁶one male goat for a sin offering; ⁷⁷and two oxen, five rams, five male goats and five male lambs a year old, to be sacrificed as a fellowship offering. This was the offering of Pagiel son of Ocran.

⁷⁸On the twelfth day Ahira son of Enan, the leader of the people of Naphtali, brought his offering.

⁷⁹His offering was one silver plate weighing a hundred and thirty shekels, and one silver sprinkling bowl weighing seventy shekels, both according to the sanctuary shekel, each filled with fine flour mixed with oil as a grain offering; ⁸⁰one gold dish weighing ten shekels, filled with incense; ⁸¹one young bull, one ram and one male lamb a year old, for a burnt offering; ⁸²one male goat for a sin offering; ⁸³and two oxen, five rams, five male goats and five male lambs a year old, to be sacrificed as a fellowship offering. This was the offering of Ahira son of Enan.

⁸⁴These were the offerings of the Israelite leaders for the dedication of the altar when it was anointed: twelve silver plates, twelve silver sprinkling bowls and twelve gold dishes. ⁸⁵Each silver plate weighed a hundred and thirty shekels, and each sprinkling bowl seventy shekels. Altogether, the silver dishes weighed two thousand four hundred shekels,ᵃ according to the sanctuary shekel. ⁸⁶The

---

ᵃ85 That is, about 60 pounds (about 28 kilograms)

twelve gold dishes filled with incense weighed ten shekels each, according to the sanctuary shekel. Altogether, the gold dishes weighed a hundred and twenty shekels.[a] 87The total number of animals for the burnt offering came to twelve young bulls, twelve rams and twelve male lambs a year old, together with their grain offering. Twelve male goats were used for the sin offering. 88The total number of animals for the sacrifice of the fellowship offering came to twenty-four oxen, sixty rams, sixty male goats and sixty male lambs a year old. These were the offerings for the dedication of the altar after it was anointed.

89When Moses entered the Tent of Meeting to speak with the LORD, he heard the voice speaking to him from between the two cherubim above the atonement cover on the ark of the Testimony. And he spoke with him.

Setting Up the Lamps

8 The LORD said to Moses, 2"Speak to Aaron and say to him, 'When you set up the seven lamps, they are to light the area in front of the lampstand.' "

3Aaron did so; he set up the lamps so that they faced forward on the lampstand, just as the LORD commanded Moses. 4This is how the lampstand was made: It was made of hammered gold—from its base to its blossoms. The lampstand was made exactly like the pattern the LORD had shown Moses.

The Setting Apart of the Levites

5The LORD said to Moses: 6"Take the Levites from among the other Israelites and make them ceremonially clean. 7To purify them, do this: Sprinkle the water of cleansing on them; then have them shave their whole bodies and wash their clothes, and so purify themselves. 8Have them take a young bull with its grain offering of fine flour mixed with oil; then you are to take a second young bull for a sin offering. 9Bring the Levites to the front of the Tent of Meeting and assemble the whole Israelite community. 10You are to bring the Levites before the LORD, and the Israelites are to lay their hands on them. 11Aaron is to present the Levites before

the LORD as a wave offering from the Israelites, so that they may be ready to do the work of the LORD.

12"After the Levites lay their hands on the heads of the bulls, use the one for a sin offering to the LORD and the other for a burnt offering, to make atonement for the Levites. 13Have the Levites stand in front of Aaron and his sons and then present them as a wave offering to the LORD. 14In this way you are to set the Levites apart from the other Israelites, and the Levites will be mine.

15"After you have purified the Levites and presented them as a wave offering, they are to come to do their work at the Tent of Meeting. 16They are the Israelites who are to be given wholly to me. I have taken them as my own in place of the firstborn, the first male offspring from every Israelite woman. 17Every firstborn male in Israel, whether man or animal, is mine. When I struck down all the firstborn in Egypt, I set them apart for myself. 18And I have taken the Levites in place of all the firstborn sons in Israel. 19Of all the Israelites, I have given the Levites as gifts to Aaron and his sons to do the work at the Tent of Meeting on behalf of the Israelites and to make atonement for them so that no plague will strike the Israelites when they go near the sanctuary."

20Moses, Aaron and the whole Israelite community did with the Levites just as the LORD commanded Moses. 21The Levites purified themselves and washed their clothes. Then Aaron presented them as a wave offering before the LORD and made atonement for them to purify them. 22After that, the Levites came to do their work at the Tent of Meeting under the supervision of Aaron and his sons. They did with the Levites just as the LORD commanded Moses.

23The LORD said to Moses, 24"This applies to the Levites: Men twenty-five years old or more shall come to take part in the work at the Tent of Meeting, 25but at the age of fifty, they must retire from their regular service and work no longer. 26They may assist their brothers in performing their duties at the Tent of Meeting, but they themselves must not do the

---

[a]86 That is, about 3 pounds (about 1.4 kilograms)

work. This, then, is how you are to assign the responsibilities of the Levites."

The Passover

9 The LORD spoke to Moses in the Desert of Sinai in the first month of the second year after they came out of Egypt. He said, ²"Have the Israelites celebrate the Passover at the appointed time. ³Celebrate it at the appointed time, at twilight on the fourteenth day of this month, in accordance with all its rules and regulations."

⁴So Moses told the Israelites to celebrate the Passover, ⁵and they did so in the Desert of Sinai at twilight on the fourteenth day of the first month. The Israelites did everything just as the LORD commanded Moses.

⁶But some of them could not celebrate the Passover on that day because they were ceremonially unclean on account of a dead body. So they came to Moses and Aaron that same day ⁷and said to Moses, "We have become unclean because of a dead body, but why should we be kept from presenting the LORD's offering with the other Israelites at the appointed time?"

⁸Moses answered them, "Wait until I find out what the LORD commands concerning you."

⁹Then the LORD said to Moses, ¹⁰"Tell the Israelites: 'When any of you or your descendants are unclean because of a dead body or are away on a journey, they may still celebrate the LORD's Passover. ¹¹They are to celebrate it on the fourteenth day of the second month at twilight. They are to eat the lamb, together with unleavened bread and bitter herbs. ¹²They must not leave any of it till morning or break any of its bones. When they celebrate the Passover, they must follow all the regulations. ¹³But if a man who is ceremonially clean and not on a journey fails to celebrate the Passover, that person must be cut off from his people because he did not present the LORD's offering at the appointed time. That man will bear the consequences of his sin.

¹⁴" 'An alien living among you who wants to celebrate the LORD's Passover must do so in accordance with its rules and regulations. You must have the same regulations for the alien and the native-born.' "

The Cloud Above the Tabernacle

¹⁵On the day the tabernacle, the Tent of the Testimony, was set up, the cloud covered it. From evening till morning the cloud above the tabernacle looked like fire. ¹⁶That is how it continued to be; the cloud covered it, and at night it looked like fire. ¹⁷Whenever the cloud lifted from above the Tent, the Israelites set out; wherever the cloud settled, the Israelites encamped. ¹⁸At the LORD's command the Israelites set out, and at his command they encamped. As long as the cloud stayed over the tabernacle, they remained in camp. ¹⁹When the cloud remained over the tabernacle a long time, the Israelites obeyed the LORD's order and did not set out. ²⁰Sometimes the cloud was over the tabernacle only a few days; at the LORD's command they would encamp, and then at his command they would set out. ²¹Sometimes the cloud stayed only from evening till morning, and when it lifted in the morning, they set out. Whether by day or by night, whenever the cloud lifted, they set out. ²²Whether the cloud stayed over the tabernacle for two days or a month or a year, the Israelites would remain in camp and not set out; but when it lifted, they would set out. ²³At the LORD's command they encamped, and at the LORD's command they set out. They obeyed the LORD's order, in accordance with his command through Moses.

The Silver Trumpets

10 The LORD said to Moses: ²"Make two trumpets of hammered silver, and use them for calling the community together and for having the camps set out. ³When both are sounded, the whole community is to assemble before you at the entrance to the Tent of Meeting. ⁴If only one is sounded, the leaders—the heads of the clans of Israel—are to assemble before you. ⁵When a trumpet blast is sounded, the tribes camping on the east are to set out. ⁶At the sounding of a second blast, the camps on the south are to set out. The blast will be the signal for setting out. ⁷To gather the assembly, blow the trumpets, but not with the same signal.

⁸"The sons of Aaron, the priests, are to blow the trumpets. This is to be a lasting ordinance for you and the generations to

come. [9]When you go into battle in your own land against an enemy who is oppressing you, sound a blast on the trumpets. Then you will be remembered by the LORD your God and rescued from your enemies. [10]Also at your times of rejoicing—your appointed feasts and New Moon festivals—you are to sound the trumpets over your burnt offerings and fellowship offerings,[a] and they will be a memorial for you before your God. I am the LORD your God."

The Israelites Leave Sinai

[11]On the twentieth day of the second month of the second year, the cloud lifted from above the tabernacle of the Testimony. [12]Then the Israelites set out from the Desert of Sinai and traveled from place to place until the cloud came to rest in the Desert of Paran. [13]They set out, this first time, at the LORD's command through Moses.

[14]The divisions of the camp of Judah went first, under their standard. Nahshon son of Amminadab was in command. [15]Nethanel son of Zuar was over the division of the tribe of Issachar, [16]and Eliab son of Helon was over the division of the tribe of Zebulun. [17]Then the tabernacle was taken down, and the Gershonites and Merarites, who carried it, set out.

[18]The divisions of the camp of Reuben went next, under their standard. Elizur son of Shedeur was in command. [19]Shelumiel son of Zurishaddai was over the division of the tribe of Simeon, [20]and Eliasaph son of Deuel was over the division of the tribe of Gad. [21]Then the Kohathites set out, carrying the holy things. The tabernacle was to be set up before they arrived.

[22]The divisions of the camp of Ephraim went next, under their standard. Elishama son of Ammihud was in command. [23]Gamaliel son of Pedahzur was over the division of the tribe of Manasseh, [24]and Abidan son of Gideoni was over the division of the tribe of Benjamin.

[25]Finally, as the rear guard for all the units, the divisions of the camp of Dan set out, under their standard. Ahiezer son of Ammishaddai was in command. [26]Pagiel son of Ocran was over the division of the tribe of Asher, [27]and Ahira son of Enan was over the division of the tribe of Naphtali. [28]This was the order of march for the Israelite divisions as they set out.

[29]Now Moses said to Hobab son of Reuel the Midianite, Moses' father-in-law, "We are setting out for the place about which the LORD said, 'I will give it to you.' Come with us and we will treat you well, for the LORD has promised good things to Israel."

[30]He answered, "No, I will not go; I am going back to my own land and my own people."

[31]But Moses said, "Please do not leave us. You know where we should camp in the desert, and you can be our eyes. [32]If you come with us, we will share with you whatever good things the LORD gives us."

[33]So they set out from the mountain of the LORD and traveled for three days. The ark of the covenant of the LORD went before them during those three days to find them a place to rest. [34]The cloud of the LORD was over them by day when they set out from the camp.

[35]Whenever the ark set out, Moses said,

"Rise up, O LORD!
 May your enemies be scattered;
 may your foes flee before you."

[36]Whenever it came to rest, he said,

"Return, O LORD,
 to the countless thousands of
 Israel."

Fire From the LORD

11 Now the people complained about their hardships in the hearing of the LORD, and when he heard them his anger was aroused. Then fire from the LORD burned among them and consumed some of the outskirts of the camp. [2]When the people cried out to Moses, he prayed to the LORD and the fire died down. [3]So that place was called Taberah,[b] because fire from the LORD had burned among them.

Quail From the LORD

[4]The rabble with them began to crave other food, and again the Israelites started wailing and said, "If only we had meat to eat! [5]We remember the fish we ate in

---

[a]10 Traditionally *peace offerings*   [b]3 *Taberah* means *burning.*

Egypt at no cost—also the cucumbers, melons, leeks, onions and garlic. 6But now we have lost our appetite; we never see anything but this manna!"

7The manna was like coriander seed and looked like resin. 8The people went around gathering it, and then ground it in a handmill or crushed it in a mortar. They cooked it in a pot or made it into cakes. And it tasted like something made with olive oil. 9When the dew settled on the camp at night, the manna also came down.

10Moses heard the people of every family wailing, each at the entrance to his tent. The LORD became exceedingly angry, and Moses was troubled. 11He asked the LORD, "Why have you brought this trouble on your servant? What have I done to displease you that you put the burden of all these people on me? 12Did I conceive all these people? Did I give them birth? Why do you tell me to carry them in my arms, as a nurse carries an infant, to the land you promised on oath to their forefathers? 13Where can I get meat for all these people? They keep wailing to me, 'Give us meat to eat!' 14I cannot carry all these people by myself; the burden is too heavy for me. 15If this is how you are going to treat me, put me to death right now—if I have found favor in your eyes—and do not let me face my own ruin."

16The LORD said to Moses: "Bring me seventy of Israel's elders who are known to you as leaders and officials among the people. Have them come to the Tent of Meeting, that they may stand there with you. 17I will come down and speak with you there, and I will take of the Spirit that is on you and put the Spirit on them. They will help you carry the burden of the people so that you will not have to carry it alone.

18"Tell the people: 'Consecrate yourselves in preparation for tomorrow, when you will eat meat. The LORD heard you when you wailed, "If only we had meat to eat! We were better off in Egypt!" Now the LORD will give you meat, and you will eat it. 19You will not eat it for just one day, or two days, or five, ten or twenty days, 20but for a whole month—until it comes out of your nostrils and you loathe it—because you have rejected the LORD, who is among

you, and have wailed before him, saying, "Why did we ever leave Egypt?" ' "

21But Moses said, "Here I am among six hundred thousand men on foot, and you say, 'I will give them meat to eat for a whole month!' 22Would they have enough if flocks and herds were slaughtered for them? Would they have enough if all the fish in the sea were caught for them?"

23The LORD answered Moses, "Is the LORD's arm too short? You will now see whether or not what I say will come true for you."

24So Moses went out and told the people what the LORD had said. He brought together seventy of their elders and had them stand around the Tent. 25Then the LORD came down in the cloud and spoke with him, and he took of the Spirit that was on him and put the Spirit on the seventy elders. When the Spirit rested on them, they prophesied, but they did not do so again.a

26However, two men, whose names were Eldad and Medad, had remained in the camp. They were listed among the elders, but did not go out to the Tent. Yet the Spirit also rested on them, and they prophesied in the camp. 27A young man ran and told Moses, "Eldad and Medad are prophesying in the camp."

28Joshua son of Nun, who had been Moses' aide since youth, spoke up and said, "Moses, my lord, stop them!"

29But Moses replied, "Are you jealous for my sake? I wish that all the LORD's people were prophets and that the LORD would put his Spirit on them!" 30Then Moses and the elders of Israel returned to the camp.

31Now a wind went out from the LORD and drove quail in from the sea. It brought themb down all around the camp to about three feetc above the ground, as far as a day's walk in any direction. 32All that day and night and all the next day the people went out and gathered quail. No one gathered less than ten homers.d Then they spread them out all around the camp. 33But while the meat was still between their teeth and before it

a25 Or prophesied and continued to do so   b31 Or They flew   c31 Hebrew two cubits (about 1 meter)   d32 That is, probably about 60 bushels (about 2.2 kiloliters) could be consumed, the anger of the LORD burned against the people, and he struck them with a severe plague. ³⁴Therefore the place was named Kibroth Hattaavah,ᵃ because there they buried the people who had craved other food.

³⁵From Kibroth Hattaavah the people traveled to Hazeroth and stayed there.

Miriam and Aaron Oppose Moses

12 Miriam and Aaron began to talk against Moses because of his Cushite wife, for he had married a Cushite. ²"Has the LORD spoken only through Moses?" they asked. "Hasn't he also spoken through us?" And the LORD heard this.

³(Now Moses was a very humble man, more humble than anyone else on the face of the earth.)

⁴At once the LORD said to Moses, Aaron and Miriam, "Come out to the Tent of Meeting, all three of you." So the three of them came out. ⁵Then the LORD came down in a pillar of cloud; he stood at the entrance to the Tent and summoned Aaron and Miriam. When both of them stepped forward, ⁶he said, "Listen to my words:

"When a prophet of the LORD is
    among you,
I reveal myself to him in visions,
I speak to him in dreams.
⁷But this is not true of my servant
    Moses;
he is faithful in all my house.
⁸With him I speak face to face,
    clearly and not in riddles;
he sees the form of the LORD.
Why then were you not afraid
    to speak against my servant Moses?"

⁹The anger of the LORD burned against them, and he left them.

¹⁰When the cloud lifted from above the Tent, there stood Miriam—leprous,ᵇ like snow. Aaron turned toward her and saw that she had leprosy; ¹¹and he said to Moses, "Please, my lord, do not hold against us the sin we have so foolishly committed. ¹²Do not let her be like a stillborn infant coming from its mother's womb with its flesh half eaten away."

¹³So Moses cried out to the LORD, "O God, please heal her!"

¹⁴The LORD replied to Moses, "If her father had spit in her face, would she not have been in disgrace for seven days? Confine her outside the camp for seven days; after that she can be brought back." ¹⁵So Miriam was confined outside the

---

ᵃ34 *Kibroth Hattaavah* means *graves of craving.*
ᵇ10 The Hebrew word was used for various diseases affecting the skin—not necessarily leprosy.

Conflict Resolution

Tuesday

NUMBERS 12 The marriage of two different people means two different sets of ideas. No one can prepare us enough for the challenges we face in a marriage where two people are so different, even opposite in many areas. For example, Rosemary and I disagree dramatically about what makes a great Friday night. Having been out of the house all week, I prefer to stay at home. Rosemary, on the other hand, prefers to get out of the house she's been in all week and participate in a social activity.

Acknowledging differing opinions is the beginning of growth. And dealing with conflicting ideas and thoughts is the road toward growth together as a couple.

Believe it or not, conflicts in marriage can be helpful. But they are only helpful if handled the proper way. Talking about the conflict is a must. We need to talk about it *together*, rather than behind each other's backs.

Consider the way God handled the conflict in Numbers 12. Miriam and Aaron criticized Moses' choice of spouse. At once God brought Moses, Miriam and Aaron into the Tent of Meeting so he could spend time alone with them. The principle of confrontation is the key to observe here in this passage. Everyone involved was brought together to work out the problem.

—***Bob & Rosemary***

Go to page 161 for your next devotional reading.

camp for seven days, and the people did not move on till she was brought back.

¹⁶After that, the people left Hazeroth and encamped in the Desert of Paran.

Exploring Canaan

13 The LORD said to Moses, ²"Send some men to explore the land of Canaan, which I am giving to the Israelites. From each ancestral tribe send one of its leaders."

³So at the LORD's command Moses sent them out from the Desert of Paran. All of them were leaders of the Israelites. ⁴These are their names:

> from the tribe of Reuben, Shammua son of Zaccur;
> ⁵from the tribe of Simeon, Shaphat son of Hori;
> ⁶from the tribe of Judah, Caleb son of Jephunneh;
> ⁷from the tribe of Issachar, Igal son of Joseph;
> ⁸from the tribe of Ephraim, Hoshea son of Nun;
> ⁹from the tribe of Benjamin, Palti son of Raphu;
> ¹⁰from the tribe of Zebulun, Gaddiel son of Sodi;
> ¹¹from the tribe of Manasseh (a tribe of Joseph), Gaddi son of Susi;
> ¹²from the tribe of Dan, Ammiel son of Gemalli;
> ¹³from the tribe of Asher, Sethur son of Michael;
> ¹⁴from the tribe of Naphtali, Nahbi son of Vophsi;
> ¹⁵from the tribe of Gad, Geuel son of Maki.

¹⁶These are the names of the men Moses sent to explore the land. (Moses gave Hoshea son of Nun the name Joshua.)

¹⁷When Moses sent them to explore Canaan, he said, "Go up through the Negev and on into the hill country. ¹⁸See what the land is like and whether the people who live there are strong or weak, few or many. ¹⁹What kind of land do they live in? Is it good or bad? What kind of towns do they live in? Are they unwalled or fortified? ²⁰How is the soil? Is it fertile or poor? Are there trees on it or not? Do your best to bring back some of the fruit of the land." (It was the season for the first ripe grapes.)

²¹So they went up and explored the land from the Desert of Zin as far as Rehob, toward Lebo[a] Hamath. ²²They went up through the Negev and came to Hebron, where Ahiman, Sheshai and Talmai, the descendants of Anak, lived. (Hebron had been built seven years before Zoan in Egypt.) ²³When they reached the Valley of Eshcol,[b] they cut off a branch bearing a single cluster of grapes. Two of them carried it on a pole between them, along with some pomegranates and figs. ²⁴That place was called the Valley of Eshcol because of the cluster of grapes the Israelites cut off there. ²⁵At the end of forty days they returned from exploring the land.

Report on the Exploration

²⁶They came back to Moses and Aaron and the whole Israelite community at Kadesh in the Desert of Paran. There they reported to them and to the whole assembly and showed them the fruit of the land. ²⁷They gave Moses this account: "We went into the land to which you sent us, and it does flow with milk and honey! Here is its fruit. ²⁸But the people who live there are powerful, and the cities are fortified and very large. We even saw descendants of Anak there. ²⁹The Amalekites live in the Negev; the Hittites, Jebusites and Amorites live in the hill country; and the Canaanites live near the sea and along the Jordan."

³⁰Then Caleb silenced the people before Moses and said, "We should go up and take possession of the land, for we can certainly do it."

³¹But the men who had gone up with him said, "We can't attack those people; they are stronger than we are." ³²And they spread among the Israelites a bad report about the land they had explored. They said, "The land we explored devours those living in it. All the people we saw there are of great size. ³³We saw the Nephilim there (the descendants of Anak come from the Nephilim). We seemed like grasshoppers in our own eyes, and we looked the same to them."

ᵃ21 Or *toward the entrance to*   ᵇ23 *Eshcol* means *cluster;* also in verse 24.

The People Rebel

14 That night all the people of the community raised their voices and wept aloud. ²All the Israelites grumbled against Moses and Aaron, and the whole assembly said to them, "If only we had died in Egypt! Or in this desert! ³Why is the LORD bringing us to this land only to let us fall by the sword? Our wives and children will be taken as plunder. Wouldn't it be better for us to go back to Egypt?" ⁴And they said to each other, "We should choose a leader and go back to Egypt."

⁵Then Moses and Aaron fell facedown in front of the whole Israelite assembly gathered there. ⁶Joshua son of Nun and Caleb son of Jephunneh, who were among those who had explored the land, tore their clothes ⁷and said to the entire Israelite assembly, "The land we passed through and explored is exceedingly good. ⁸If the LORD is pleased with us, he will lead us into that land, a land flowing with milk and honey, and will give it to us. ⁹Only do not rebel against the LORD. And do not be afraid of the people of the land, because we will swallow them up. Their protection is gone, but the LORD is with us. Do not be afraid of them."

¹⁰But the whole assembly talked about stoning them. Then the glory of the LORD appeared at the Tent of Meeting to all the Israelites. ¹¹The LORD said to Moses, "How long will these people treat me with contempt? How long will they refuse to believe in me, in spite of all the miraculous signs I have performed among them? ¹²I will strike them down with a plague and destroy them, but I will make you into a nation greater and stronger than they."

¹³Moses said to the LORD, "Then the Egyptians will hear about it! By your power you brought these people up from among them. ¹⁴And they will tell the inhabitants of this land about it. They have already heard that you, O LORD, are with these people and that you, O LORD, have been seen face to face, that your cloud stays over them, and that you go before them in a pillar of cloud by day and a pillar of fire by night. ¹⁵If you put these people to death all at one time, the nations who have heard this report about you will say, ¹⁶'The LORD was not able to bring these people into the land he promised them on oath; so he slaughtered them in the desert.'

¹⁷"Now may the Lord's strength be displayed, just as you have declared: ¹⁸'The LORD is slow to anger, abounding in love and forgiving sin and rebellion. Yet he does not leave the guilty unpunished; he punishes the children for the sin of the fathers to the third and fourth generation.' ¹⁹In accordance with your great love, forgive the sin of these people, just as you have pardoned them from the time they left Egypt until now."

²⁰The LORD replied, "I have forgiven them, as you asked. ²¹Nevertheless, as surely as I live and as surely as the glory of the LORD fills the whole earth, ²²not one of the men who saw my glory and the miraculous signs I performed in Egypt and in the desert but who disobeyed me and tested me ten times— ²³not one of them will ever see the land I promised on oath to their forefathers. No one who has treated me with contempt will ever see it. ²⁴But because my servant Caleb has a different spirit and follows me wholeheartedly, I will bring him into the land he went to, and his descendants will inherit it. ²⁵Since the Amalekites and Canaanites are living in the valleys, turn back tomorrow and set out toward the desert along the route to the Red Sea. *a*"

²⁶The LORD said to Moses and Aaron: ²⁷"How long will this wicked community grumble against me? I have heard the complaints of these grumbling Israelites. ²⁸So tell them, 'As surely as I live, declares the LORD, I will do to you the very things I heard you say: ²⁹In this desert your bodies will fall—every one of you twenty years old or more who was counted in the census and who has grumbled against me. ³⁰Not one of you will enter the land I swore with uplifted hand to make your home, except Caleb son of Jephunneh and Joshua son of Nun. ³¹As for your children that you said would be taken as plunder, I will bring them in to enjoy the land you have rejected. ³²But you—your bodies will fall in this desert. ³³Your children will be shepherds here for forty years, suffering for your unfaithfulness,

a25 Hebrew *Yam Suph*; that is, Sea of Reeds

until the last of your bodies lies in the desert. ³⁴For forty years—one year for each of the forty days you explored the land—you will suffer for your sins and know what it is like to have me against you.' ³⁵I, the LORD, have spoken, and I will surely do these things to this whole wicked community, which has banded together against me. They will meet their end in this desert; here they will die."

³⁶So the men Moses had sent to explore the land, who returned and made the whole community grumble against him by spreading a bad report about it—³⁷these men responsible for spreading the bad report about the land were struck down and died of a plague before the LORD. ³⁸Of the men who went to explore the land, only Joshua son of Nun and Caleb son of Jephunneh survived.

³⁹When Moses reported this to all the Israelites, they mourned bitterly. ⁴⁰Early the next morning they went up toward the high hill country. "We have sinned," they said. "We will go up to the place the LORD promised."

⁴¹But Moses said, "Why are you disobeying the LORD's command? This will not succeed! ⁴²Do not go up, because the LORD is not with you. You will be defeated by your enemies, ⁴³for the Amalekites and Canaanites will face you there. Because you have turned away from the LORD, he will not be with you and you will fall by the sword."

⁴⁴Nevertheless, in their presumption they went up toward the high hill country, though neither Moses nor the ark of the LORD's covenant moved from the camp. ⁴⁵Then the Amalekites and Canaanites who lived in that hill country came down and attacked them and beat them down all the way to Hormah.

Supplementary Offerings

15 The LORD said to Moses, ²"Speak to the Israelites and say to them: 'After you enter the land I am giving you as a home ³and you present to the LORD offerings made by fire, from the herd or the flock, as an aroma pleasing to the LORD—whether burnt offerings or sacrifices, for special vows or freewill offerings or festival offerings— ⁴then the one who brings his offering shall present to the LORD a grain offering of a tenth of an ephah^a of fine flour mixed with a quarter of a hin^b of oil. ⁵With each lamb for the burnt offering or the sacrifice, prepare a quarter of a hin of wine as a drink offering.

⁶" 'With a ram prepare a grain offering of two-tenths of an ephah^c of fine flour mixed with a third of a hin^d of oil, ⁷and a third of a hin of wine as a drink offering. Offer it as an aroma pleasing to the LORD.

⁸" 'When you prepare a young bull as a burnt offering or sacrifice, for a special vow or a fellowship offering^e to the LORD, ⁹bring with the bull a grain offering of three-tenths of an ephah^f of fine flour mixed with half a hin^g of oil. ¹⁰Also bring half a hin of wine as a drink offering. It will be an offering made by fire, an aroma pleasing to the LORD. ¹¹Each bull or ram, each lamb or young goat, is to be prepared in this manner. ¹²Do this for each one, for as many as you prepare.

¹³" 'Everyone who is native-born must do these things in this way when he brings an offering made by fire as an aroma pleasing to the LORD. ¹⁴For the generations to come, whenever an alien or anyone else living among you presents an offering made by fire as an aroma pleasing to the LORD, he must do exactly as you do. ¹⁵The community is to have the same rules for you and for the alien living among you; this is a lasting ordinance for the generations to come. You and the alien shall be the same before the LORD: ¹⁶The same laws and regulations will apply both to you and to the alien living among you.' "

¹⁷The LORD said to Moses, ¹⁸"Speak to the Israelites and say to them: 'When you enter the land to which I am taking you ¹⁹and you eat the food of the land, present a portion as an offering to the LORD. ²⁰Present a cake from the first of your ground meal and present it as an offering from the threshing floor. ²¹Throughout the generations to come

---

^a4 That is, probably about 2 quarts (about 2 liters)   ^b4 That is, probably about 1 quart (about 1 liter); also in verse 5   ^c6 That is, probably about 4 quarts (about 4.5 liters)   ^d6 That is, probably about 1 1/4 quarts (about 1.2 liters); also in verse 7   ^e8 Traditionally *peace offering*   ^f9 That is, probably about 6 quarts (about 6.5 liters)   ^g9 That is, probably about 2 quarts (about 2 liters); also in verse 10 you are to give this offering to the LORD from the first of your ground meal.

Offerings for Unintentional Sins

22 " 'Now if you unintentionally fail to keep any of these commands the LORD gave Moses— 23any of the LORD's commands to you through him, from the day the LORD gave them and continuing through the generations to come— 24and if this is done unintentionally without the community being aware of it, then the whole community is to offer a young bull for a burnt offering as an aroma pleasing to the LORD, along with its prescribed grain offering and drink offering, and a male goat for a sin offering. 25The priest is to make atonement for the whole Israelite community, and they will be forgiven, for it was not intentional and they have brought to the LORD for their wrong an offering made by fire and a sin offering. 26The whole Israelite community and the aliens living among them will be forgiven, because all the people were involved in the unintentional wrong.

27 " 'But if just one person sins unintentionally, he must bring a year-old female goat for a sin offering. 28The priest is to make atonement before the LORD for the one who erred by sinning unintentionally, and when atonement has been made for him, he will be forgiven. 29One and the same law applies to everyone who sins unintentionally, whether he is a native-born Israelite or an alien.

30 " 'But anyone who sins defiantly, whether native-born or alien, blasphemes the LORD, and that person must be cut off from his people. 31Because he has despised the LORD's word and broken his commands, that person must surely be cut off; his guilt remains on him.' "

The Sabbath-Breaker Put to Death

32While the Israelites were in the desert, a man was found gathering wood on the Sabbath day. 33Those who found him gathering wood brought him to Moses and Aaron and the whole assembly, 34and they kept him in custody, because it was not clear what should be done to him. 35Then the LORD said to Moses, "The man must die. The whole assembly must stone him outside the camp." 36So the as-

sembly took him outside the camp and stoned him to death, as the LORD commanded Moses.

Tassels on Garments

37The LORD said to Moses, 38"Speak to the Israelites and say to them: 'Throughout the generations to come you are to make tassels on the corners of your garments, with a blue cord on each tassel. 39You will have these tassels to look at and so you will remember all the commands of the LORD, that you may obey them and not prostitute yourselves by going after the lusts of your own hearts and eyes. 40Then you will remember to obey all my commands and will be consecrated to your God. 41I am the LORD your God, who brought you out of Egypt to be your God. I am the LORD your God.' "

Korah, Dathan and Abiram

16 Korah son of Izhar, the son of Kohath, the son of Levi, and certain Reubenites—Dathan and Abiram, sons of Eliab, and On son of Peleth—became insolent[a] 2and rose up against Moses. With them were 250 Israelite men, well-known community leaders who had been appointed members of the council. 3They came as a group to oppose Moses and Aaron and said to them, "You have gone too far! The whole community is holy, every one of them, and the LORD is with them. Why then do you set yourselves above the LORD's assembly?"

4When Moses heard this, he fell face-down. 5Then he said to Korah and all his followers: "In the morning the LORD will show who belongs to him and who is holy, and he will have that person come near him. The man he chooses he will cause to come near him. 6You, Korah, and all your followers are to do this: Take censers 7and tomorrow put fire and incense in them before the LORD. The man the LORD chooses will be the one who is holy. You Levites have gone too far!"

8Moses also said to Korah, "Now listen, you Levites! 9Isn't it enough for you that the God of Israel has separated you from the rest of the Israelite community and brought you near himself to do the

a1 Or Peleth—took ⌐men⌐

work at the LORD's tabernacle and to stand before the community and minister to them? ¹⁰He has brought you and all your fellow Levites near himself, but now you are trying to get the priesthood too. ¹¹It is against the LORD that you and all your followers have banded together. Who is Aaron that you should grumble against him?"

¹²Then Moses summoned Dathan and Abiram, the sons of Eliab. But they said, "We will not come! ¹³Isn't it enough that you have brought us up out of a land flowing with milk and honey to kill us in the desert? And now you also want to lord it over us? ¹⁴Moreover, you haven't brought us into a land flowing with milk and honey or given us an inheritance of fields and vineyards. Will you gouge out the eyes of*a* these men? No, we will not come!"

¹⁵Then Moses became very angry and said to the LORD, "Do not accept their offering. I have not taken so much as a donkey from them, nor have I wronged any of them."

¹⁶Moses said to Korah, "You and all your followers are to appear before the LORD tomorrow—you and they and Aaron. ¹⁷Each man is to take his censer and put incense in it—250 censers in all—and present it before the LORD. You and Aaron are to present your censers also." ¹⁸So each man took his censer, put fire and incense in it, and stood with Moses and Aaron at the entrance to the Tent of Meeting. ¹⁹When Korah had gathered all his followers in opposition to them at the entrance to the Tent of Meeting, the glory of the LORD appeared to the entire assembly. ²⁰The LORD said to Moses and Aaron, ²¹"Separate yourselves from this assembly so I can put an end to them at once."

²²But Moses and Aaron fell facedown and cried out, "O God, God of the spirits of all mankind, will you be angry with the entire assembly when only one man sins?"

²³Then the LORD said to Moses, ²⁴"Say to the assembly, 'Move away from the tents of Korah, Dathan and Abiram.' "

²⁵Moses got up and went to Dathan and Abiram, and the elders of Israel followed him. ²⁶He warned the assembly, "Move back from the tents of these wicked men! Do not touch anything belonging to them, or you will be swept away

because of all their sins." ²⁷So they moved away from the tents of Korah, Dathan and Abiram. Dathan and Abiram had come out and were standing with their wives, children and little ones at the entrances to their tents.

²⁸Then Moses said, "This is how you will know that the LORD has sent me to do all these things and that it was not my idea: ²⁹If these men die a natural death and experience only what usually happens to men, then the LORD has not sent me. ³⁰But if the LORD brings about something totally new, and the earth opens its mouth and swallows them, with everything that belongs to them, and they go down alive into the grave,*b* then you will know that these men have treated the LORD with contempt."

³¹As soon as he finished saying all this, the ground under them split apart ³²and the earth opened its mouth and swallowed them, with their households and all Korah's men and all their possessions. ³³They went down alive into the grave, with everything they owned; the earth closed over them, and they perished and were gone from the community. ³⁴At their cries, all the Israelites around them fled, shouting, "The earth is going to swallow us too!"

³⁵And fire came out from the LORD and consumed the 250 men who were offering the incense.

³⁶The LORD said to Moses, ³⁷"Tell Eleazar son of Aaron, the priest, to take the censers out of the smoldering remains and scatter the coals some distance away, for the censers are holy— ³⁸the censers of the men who sinned at the cost of their lives. Hammer the censers into sheets to overlay the altar, for they were presented before the LORD and have become holy. Let them be a sign to the Israelites."

³⁹So Eleazar the priest collected the bronze censers brought by those who had been burned up, and he had them hammered out to overlay the altar, ⁴⁰as the LORD directed him through Moses. This was to remind the Israelites that no one except a descendant of Aaron should come to burn incense before the LORD, or

a14 Or *you make slaves of;* or *you deceive*
b30 Hebrew *Sheol;* also in verse 33

he would become like Korah and his followers.

⁴¹The next day the whole Israelite community grumbled against Moses and Aaron. "You have killed the LORD's people," they said.

⁴²But when the assembly gathered in opposition to Moses and Aaron and turned toward the Tent of Meeting, suddenly the cloud covered it and the glory of the LORD appeared. ⁴³Then Moses and Aaron went to the front of the Tent of Meeting, ⁴⁴and the LORD said to Moses, ⁴⁵"Get away from this assembly so I can put an end to them at once." And they fell facedown.

⁴⁶Then Moses said to Aaron, "Take your censer and put incense in it, along with fire from the altar, and hurry to the assembly to make atonement for them. Wrath has come out from the LORD; the plague has started." ⁴⁷So Aaron did as Moses said, and ran into the midst of the assembly. The plague had already started among the people, but Aaron offered the incense and made atonement for them. ⁴⁸He stood between the living and the dead, and the plague stopped. ⁴⁹But 14,700 people died from the plague, in addition to those who had died because of Korah. ⁵⁰Then Aaron returned to Moses at the entrance to the Tent of Meeting, for the plague had stopped.

The Budding of Aaron's Staff

17 The LORD said to Moses, ²"Speak to the Israelites and get twelve staffs from them, one from the leader of each of their ancestral tribes. Write the name of each man on his staff. ³On the staff of Levi write Aaron's name, for there must be one staff for the head of each ancestral tribe. ⁴Place them in the Tent of Meeting in front of the Testimony, where I meet with you. ⁵The staff belonging to the man I choose will sprout, and I will rid myself of this constant grumbling against you by the Israelites."

⁶So Moses spoke to the Israelites, and their leaders gave him twelve staffs, one for the leader of each of their ancestral tribes, and Aaron's staff was among them. ⁷Moses placed the staffs before the LORD in the Tent of the Testimony.

⁸The next day Moses entered the Tent of the Testimony and saw that Aaron's staff, which represented the house of Levi, had not only sprouted but had budded, blossomed and produced almonds. ⁹Then Moses brought out all the staffs from the LORD's presence to all the Israelites. They looked at them, and each man took his own staff.

¹⁰The LORD said to Moses, "Put back Aaron's staff in front of the Testimony, to be kept as a sign to the rebellious. This will put an end to their grumbling against me, so that they will not die." ¹¹Moses did just as the LORD commanded him.

¹²The Israelites said to Moses, "We will die! We are lost, we are all lost! ¹³Anyone who even comes near the tabernacle of the LORD will die. Are we all going to die?"

Duties of Priests and Levites

18 The LORD said to Aaron, "You, your sons and your father's family are to bear the responsibility for offenses against the sanctuary, and you and your sons alone are to bear the responsibility for offenses against the priesthood. ²Bring your fellow Levites from your ancestral tribe to join you and assist you when you and your sons minister before the Tent of the Testimony. ³They are to be responsible to you and are to perform all the duties of the Tent, but they must not go near the furnishings of the sanctuary or the altar, or both they and you will die. ⁴They are to join you and be responsible for the care of the Tent of Meeting—all the work at the Tent—and no one else may come near where you are.

⁵"You are to be responsible for the care of the sanctuary and the altar, so that wrath will not fall on the Israelites again. ⁶I myself have selected your fellow Levites from among the Israelites as a gift to you, dedicated to the LORD to do the work at the Tent of Meeting. ⁷But only you and your sons may serve as priests in connection with everything at the altar and inside the curtain. I am giving you the service of the priesthood as a gift. Anyone else who comes near the sanctuary must be put to death."

Offerings for Priests and Levites

⁸Then the LORD said to Aaron, "I myself have put you in charge of the offer-

ings presented to me; all the holy offerings the Israelites give me I give to you and your sons as your portion and regular share. ⁹You are to have the part of the most holy offerings that is kept from the fire. From all the gifts they bring me as most holy offerings, whether grain or sin or guilt offerings, that part belongs to you and your sons. ¹⁰Eat it as something most holy; every male shall eat it. You must regard it as holy.

¹¹"This also is yours: whatever is set aside from the gifts of all the wave offerings of the Israelites. I give this to you and your sons and daughters as your regular share. Everyone in your household who is ceremonially clean may eat it.

¹²"I give you all the finest olive oil and all the finest new wine and grain they give the LORD as the firstfruits of their harvest. ¹³All the land's firstfruits that they bring to the LORD will be yours. Everyone in your household who is ceremonially clean may eat it.

¹⁴"Everything in Israel that is devoted*ᵃ* to the LORD is yours. ¹⁵The first offspring of every womb, both man and animal, that is offered to the LORD is yours. But you must redeem every firstborn son and every firstborn male of unclean animals. ¹⁶When they are a month old, you must redeem them at the redemption price set at five shekels*ᵇ* of silver, according to the sanctuary shekel, which weighs twenty gerahs.

¹⁷"But you must not redeem the firstborn of an ox, a sheep or a goat; they are holy. Sprinkle their blood on the altar and burn their fat as an offering made by fire, an aroma pleasing to the LORD. ¹⁸Their meat is to be yours, just as the breast of the wave offering and the right thigh are yours. ¹⁹Whatever is set aside from the holy offerings the Israelites present to the LORD I give to you and your sons and daughters as your regular share. It is an everlasting covenant of salt before the LORD for both you and your offspring."

²⁰The LORD said to Aaron, "You will have no inheritance in their land, nor will you have any share among them; I am your share and your inheritance among the Israelites.

²¹"I give to the Levites all the tithes in Israel as their inheritance in return for the work they do while serving at the Tent of Meeting. ²²From now on the Israelites must not go near the Tent of Meeting, or they will bear the consequences of their sin and will die. ²³It is the Levites who are to do the work at the Tent of Meeting and bear the responsibility for offenses against it. This is a lasting ordinance for the generations to come. They will receive no inheritance among the Israelites. ²⁴Instead, I give to the Levites as their inheritance the tithes that the Israelites present as an offering to the LORD. That is why I said concerning them: 'They will have no inheritance among the Israelites.' "

²⁵The LORD said to Moses, ²⁶"Speak to the Levites and say to them: 'When you receive from the Israelites the tithe I give you as your inheritance, you must present a tenth of that tithe as the LORD's offering. ²⁷Your offering will be reckoned to you as grain from the threshing floor or juice from the winepress. ²⁸In this way you also will present an offering to the LORD from all the tithes you receive from the Israelites. From these tithes you must give the LORD's portion to Aaron the priest. ²⁹You must present as the LORD's portion the best and holiest part of everything given to you.'

³⁰"Say to the Levites: 'When you present the best part, it will be reckoned to you as the product of the threshing floor or the winepress. ³¹You and your households may eat the rest of it anywhere, for it is your wages for your work at the Tent of Meeting. ³²By presenting the best part of it you will not be guilty in this matter; then you will not defile the holy offerings of the Israelites, and you will not die.' "

The Water of Cleansing

19 The LORD said to Moses and Aaron: ²"This is a requirement of the law that the LORD has commanded: Tell the Israelites to bring you a red heifer without defect or blemish and that has never been under a yoke. ³Give it to Eleazar the priest; it is to be taken outside the camp and slaughtered in his presence. ⁴Then Eleazar the priest is to take some of its blood on his finger and sprinkle it seven

ᵃ14 The Hebrew term refers to the irrevocable giving over of things or persons to the LORD.
ᵇ16 That is, about 2 ounces (about 55 grams)

times toward the front of the Tent of Meeting. ⁵While he watches, the heifer is to be burned—its hide, flesh, blood and offal. ⁶The priest is to take some cedar wood, hyssop and scarlet wool and throw them onto the burning heifer. ⁷After that, the priest must wash his clothes and bathe himself with water. He may then come into the camp, but he will be ceremonially unclean till evening. ⁸The man who burns it must also wash his clothes and bathe with water, and he too will be unclean till evening.

⁹"A man who is clean shall gather up the ashes of the heifer and put them in a ceremonially clean place outside the camp. They shall be kept by the Israelite community for use in the water of cleansing; it is for purification from sin. ¹⁰The man who gathers up the ashes of the heifer must also wash his clothes, and he too will be unclean till evening. This will be a lasting ordinance both for the Israelites and for the aliens living among them.

¹¹"Whoever touches the dead body of anyone will be unclean for seven days. ¹²He must purify himself with the water on the third day and on the seventh day; then he will be clean. But if he does not purify himself on the third and seventh days, he will not be clean. ¹³Whoever touches the dead body of anyone and fails to purify himself defiles the LORD's tabernacle. That person must be cut off from Israel. Because the water of cleansing has not been sprinkled on him, he is unclean; his uncleanness remains on him.

¹⁴"This is the law that applies when a person dies in a tent: Anyone who enters the tent and anyone who is in it will be unclean for seven days, ¹⁵and every open container without a lid fastened on it will be unclean.

¹⁶"Anyone out in the open who touches someone who has been killed with a sword or someone who has died a natural death, or anyone who touches a human bone or a grave, will be unclean for seven days.

¹⁷"For the unclean person, put some ashes from the burned purification offering into a jar and pour fresh water over them. ¹⁸Then a man who is ceremonially clean is to take some hyssop, dip it in the water and sprinkle the tent and all the furnishings and the people who were there. He must also sprinkle anyone who has touched a human bone or a grave or someone who has been killed or someone who has died a natural death. ¹⁹The man who is clean is to sprinkle the unclean person on the third and seventh days, and on the seventh day he is to purify him. The person being cleansed must wash his clothes and bathe with water, and that evening he will be clean. ²⁰But if a person who is unclean does not purify himself, he must be cut off from the community, because he has defiled the sanctuary of the LORD. The water of cleansing has not been sprinkled on him, and he is unclean. ²¹This is a lasting ordinance for them.

"The man who sprinkles the water of cleansing must also wash his clothes, and anyone who touches the water of cleansing will be unclean till evening. ²²Anything that an unclean person touches becomes unclean, and anyone who touches it becomes unclean till evening."

Water From the Rock

20 In the first month the whole Israelite community arrived at the Desert of Zin, and they stayed at Kadesh. There Miriam died and was buried.

²Now there was no water for the community, and the people gathered in opposition to Moses and Aaron. ³They quarreled with Moses and said, "If only we had died when our brothers fell dead before the LORD! ⁴Why did you bring the LORD's community into this desert, that we and our livestock should die here? ⁵Why did you bring us up out of Egypt to this terrible place? It has no grain or figs, grapevines or pomegranates. And there is no water to drink!"

⁶Moses and Aaron went from the assembly to the entrance to the Tent of Meeting and fell facedown, and the glory of the LORD appeared to them. ⁷The LORD said to Moses, ⁸"Take the staff, and you and your brother Aaron gather the assembly together. Speak to that rock before their eyes and it will pour out its water. You will bring water out of the rock for the community so they and their livestock can drink."

⁹So Moses took the staff from the

LORD's presence, just as he commanded him. ¹⁰He and Aaron gathered the assembly together in front of the rock and Moses said to them, "Listen, you rebels, must we bring you water out of this rock?" ¹¹Then Moses raised his arm and struck the rock twice with his staff. Water gushed out, and the community and their livestock drank.

¹²But the LORD said to Moses and Aaron, "Because you did not trust in me enough to honor me as holy in the sight of the Israelites, you will not bring this community into the land I give them."

¹³These were the waters of Meribah,ᵃ where the Israelites quarreled with the LORD and where he showed himself holy among them.

Edom Denies Israel Passage

¹⁴Moses sent messengers from Kadesh to the king of Edom, saying:

"This is what your brother Israel says: You know about all the hardships that have come upon us. ¹⁵Our forefathers went down into Egypt, and we lived there many years. The Egyptians mistreated us and our fathers, ¹⁶but when we cried out to the LORD, he heard our cry and sent an angel and brought us out of Egypt.

"Now we are here at Kadesh, a town on the edge of your territory. ¹⁷Please let us pass through your country. We will not go through any field or vineyard, or drink water from any well. We will travel along the king's highway and not turn to the right or to the left until we have passed through your territory."

¹⁸But Edom answered:

"You may not pass through here; if you try, we will march out and attack you with the sword."

ᵃ13 *Meribah* means *quarreling*.

Water From a Rock

Wednesday

NUMBERS 20 There are times in a marriage when we wonder whom it is we have married. We know the name and face, but everything else seems to have changed. There was so much potential during the dating stage. Then, over time, our spouse's attitude has hardened and that potential seems lost. For example, when we were dating, Bob seemed to enjoy spending hours talking together. During the early years of our marriage, however, he acted like he didn't want to be bothered.

Sometimes a spouse can become resistant to change or personal growth. We hear statements like, "This is just the way I am. Take it or leave it!" This hardened attitude can be discouraging for the other spouse who wants to grow in their relationship with each other and with God. Bob really didn't realize how important it was to keep talking after we got married.

What is a spouse to do in this situation? When a husband or wife refuses to grow or change, there are two options to take. The spouse can choose to become the molder and maker of the other's future by attempting to change and manipulate the partner. That's the option many well-meaning spouses take, but it's very discouraging. As Moses learned when he tried to force the rock to give water, God doesn't bless us when we try to do things our way (see verse 12). Trying to force something to happen will only cause the situation to become harder to live with.

The better second option is for one spouse to pray for and set an example for the other spouse—not a self-righteous example, but a loving, serving example. By praying and quietly setting an example, we can receive God's refreshing "water" out of a dry, hard rock. We begin to see change for the better. When I quit nagging Bob and instead asked God to teach me to be a better listener, God slowly opened the doors of communication in our marriage.

—Bob & Rosemary

Go to page 173 for your next devotional reading.

¹⁹The Israelites replied:

"We will go along the main road, and if we or our livestock drink any of your water, we will pay for it. We only want to pass through on foot—nothing else."

²⁰Again they answered:

"You may not pass through."

Then Edom came out against them with a large and powerful army. ²¹Since Edom refused to let them go through their territory, Israel turned away from them.

The Death of Aaron

²²The whole Israelite community set out from Kadesh and came to Mount Hor. ²³At Mount Hor, near the border of Edom, the LORD said to Moses and Aaron, ²⁴"Aaron will be gathered to his people. He will not enter the land I give the Israelites, because both of you rebelled against my command at the waters of Meribah. ²⁵Get Aaron and his son Eleazar and take them up Mount Hor. ²⁶Remove Aaron's garments and put them on his son Eleazar, for Aaron will be gathered to his people; he will die there."

²⁷Moses did as the LORD commanded: They went up Mount Hor in the sight of the whole community. ²⁸Moses removed Aaron's garments and put them on his son Eleazar. And Aaron died there on top of the mountain. Then Moses and Eleazar came down from the mountain, ²⁹and when the whole community learned that Aaron had died, the entire house of Israel mourned for him thirty days.

Arad Destroyed

21 When the Canaanite king of Arad, who lived in the Negev, heard that Israel was coming along the road to Atharim, he attacked the Israelites and captured some of them. ²Then Israel made this vow to the LORD: "If you will deliver these people into our hands, we will totally destroyᵃ their cities." ³The LORD listened to Israel's plea and gave the Canaanites over to them. They completely destroyed them and their towns; so the place was named Hormah.ᵇ

The Bronze Snake

⁴They traveled from Mount Hor along the route to the Red Sea,ᶜ to go around Edom. But the people grew impatient on the way; ⁵they spoke against God and against Moses, and said, "Why have you brought us up out of Egypt to die in the desert? There is no bread! There is no water! And we detest this miserable food!"

⁶Then the LORD sent venomous snakes among them; they bit the people and many Israelites died. ⁷The people came to Moses and said, "We sinned when we spoke against the LORD and against you. Pray that the LORD will take the snakes away from us." So Moses prayed for the people.

⁸The LORD said to Moses, "Make a snake and put it up on a pole; anyone who is bitten can look at it and live." ⁹So Moses made a bronze snake and put it up on a pole. Then when anyone was bitten by a snake and looked at the bronze snake, he lived.

The Journey to Moab

¹⁰The Israelites moved on and camped at Oboth. ¹¹Then they set out from Oboth and camped in Iye Abarim, in the desert that faces Moab toward the sunrise. ¹²From there they moved on and camped in the Zered Valley. ¹³They set out from there and camped alongside the Arnon, which is in the desert extending into Amorite territory. The Arnon is the border of Moab, between Moab and the Amorites. ¹⁴That is why the Book of the Wars of the LORD says:

". . . Waheb in Suphahᵈ and the ravines,
    the Arnon ¹⁵andᵉ the slopes of
        the ravines
that lead to the site of Ar
    and lie along the border of Moab."

¹⁶From there they continued on to Beer, the well where the LORD said to Moses,

---

ᵃ2 The Hebrew term refers to the irrevocable giving over of things or persons to the LORD, often by totally destroying them; also in verse 3.
ᵇ3 *Hormah* means *destruction*.   ᶜ4 Hebrew *Yam Suph*; that is, Sea of Reeds   ᵈ14 The meaning of the Hebrew for this phrase is uncertain.
ᵉ14,15 Or *"I have been given from Suphah and the ravines / of the Arnon* ¹⁵*to*

"Gather the people together and I will give them water."

[17]Then Israel sang this song:

"Spring up, O well!
  Sing about it,
[18]about the well that the princes dug,
    that the nobles of the people
      sank—
    the nobles with scepters and staffs."

Then they went from the desert to Mattanah, [19]from Mattanah to Nahaliel, from Nahaliel to Bamoth, [20]and from Bamoth to the valley in Moab where the top of Pisgah overlooks the wasteland.

Defeat of Sihon and Og

[21]Israel sent messengers to say to Sihon king of the Amorites:

[22]"Let us pass through your country. We will not turn aside into any field or vineyard, or drink water from any well. We will travel along the king's highway until we have passed through your territory."

[23]But Sihon would not let Israel pass through his territory. He mustered his entire army and marched out into the desert against Israel. When he reached Jahaz, he fought with Israel. [24]Israel, however, put him to the sword and took over his land from the Arnon to the Jabbok, but only as far as the Ammonites, because their border was fortified. [25]Israel captured all the cities of the Amorites and occupied them, including Heshbon and all its surrounding settlements. [26]Heshbon was the city of Sihon king of the Amorites, who had fought against the former king of Moab and had taken from him all his land as far as the Arnon.

[27]That is why the poets say:

"Come to Heshbon and let it be
    rebuilt;
  let Sihon's city be restored.

[28]"Fire went out from Heshbon,
    a blaze from the city of Sihon.
  It consumed Ar of Moab,
    the citizens of Arnon's heights.
[29]Woe to you, O Moab!
  You are destroyed, O people of
    Chemosh!
He has given up his sons as fugitives

and his daughters as captives
  to Sihon king of the Amorites.

[30]"But we have overthrown them;
  Heshbon is destroyed all the way
    to Dibon.
We have demolished them as far as
    Nophah,
  which extends to Medeba."

[31]So Israel settled in the land of the Amorites.

[32]After Moses had sent spies to Jazer, the Israelites captured its surrounding settlements and drove out the Amorites who were there. [33]Then they turned and went up along the road toward Bashan, and Og king of Bashan and his whole army marched out to meet them in battle at Edrei.

[34]The LORD said to Moses, "Do not be afraid of him, for I have handed him over to you, with his whole army and his land. Do to him what you did to Sihon king of the Amorites, who reigned in Heshbon."

[35]So they struck him down, together with his sons and his whole army, leaving them no survivors. And they took possession of his land.

Balak Summons Balaam

22 Then the Israelites traveled to the plains of Moab and camped along the Jordan across from Jericho.[a]

[2]Now Balak son of Zippor saw all that Israel had done to the Amorites, [3]and Moab was terrified because there were so many people. Indeed, Moab was filled with dread because of the Israelites.

[4]The Moabites said to the elders of Midian, "This horde is going to lick up everything around us, as an ox licks up the grass of the field."

So Balak son of Zippor, who was king of Moab at that time, [5]sent messengers to summon Balaam son of Beor, who was at Pethor, near the River,[b] in his native land. Balak said:

"A people has come out of Egypt;
  they cover the face of the land and
  have settled next to me. [6]Now come
  and put a curse on these people, because they are too powerful for me.

---

[a]1 Hebrew *Jordan of Jericho*; possibly an ancient name for the Jordan River   [b]5 That is, the Euphrates

Perhaps then I will be able to defeat them and drive them out of the country. For I know that those you bless are blessed, and those you curse are cursed."

7 The elders of Moab and Midian left, taking with them the fee for divination. When they came to Balaam, they told him what Balak had said.

8 "Spend the night here," Balaam said to them, "and I will bring you back the answer the LORD gives me." So the Moabite princes stayed with him.

9 God came to Balaam and asked, "Who are these men with you?"

10 Balaam said to God, "Balak son of Zippor, king of Moab, sent me this message: 11 'A people that has come out of Egypt covers the face of the land. Now come and put a curse on them for me. Perhaps then I will be able to fight them and drive them away.'"

12 But God said to Balaam, "Do not go with them. You must not put a curse on those people, because they are blessed."

13 The next morning Balaam got up and said to Balak's princes, "Go back to your own country, for the LORD has refused to let me go with you."

14 So the Moabite princes returned to Balak and said, "Balaam refused to come with us."

15 Then Balak sent other princes, more numerous and more distinguished than the first. 16 They came to Balaam and said:

"This is what Balak son of Zippor says: Do not let anything keep you from coming to me, 17 because I will reward you handsomely and do whatever you say. Come and put a curse on these people for me."

18 But Balaam answered them, "Even if Balak gave me his palace filled with silver and gold, I could not do anything great or small to go beyond the command of the LORD my God. 19 Now stay here tonight as the others did, and I will find out what else the LORD will tell me."

20 That night God came to Balaam and said, "Since these men have come to summon you, go with them, but do only what I tell you."

Balaam's Donkey

21 Balaam got up in the morning, saddled his donkey and went with the princes of Moab. 22 But God was very angry when he went, and the angel of the LORD stood in the road to oppose him. Balaam was riding on his donkey, and his two servants were with him. 23 When the donkey saw the angel of the LORD standing in the road with a drawn sword in his hand, she turned off the road into a field. Balaam beat her to get her back on the road.

24 Then the angel of the LORD stood in a narrow path between two vineyards, with walls on both sides. 25 When the donkey saw the angel of the LORD, she pressed close to the wall, crushing Balaam's foot against it. So he beat her again.

26 Then the angel of the LORD moved on ahead and stood in a narrow place where there was no room to turn, either to the right or to the left. 27 When the donkey saw the angel of the LORD, she lay down under Balaam, and he was angry and beat her with his staff. 28 Then the LORD opened the donkey's mouth, and she said to Balaam, "What have I done to you to make you beat me these three times?"

29 Balaam answered the donkey, "You have made a fool of me! If I had a sword in my hand, I would kill you right now."

30 The donkey said to Balaam, "Am I not your own donkey, which you have always ridden, to this day? Have I been in the habit of doing this to you?"

"No," he said.

31 Then the LORD opened Balaam's eyes, and he saw the angel of the LORD standing in the road with his sword drawn. So he bowed low and fell face-down.

32 The angel of the LORD asked him, "Why have you beaten your donkey these three times? I have come here to oppose you because your path is a reckless one before me.a 33 The donkey saw me and turned away from me these three times. If she had not turned away, I would certainly have killed you by now, but I would have spared her."

a 32 The meaning of the Hebrew for this clause is uncertain.

³⁴Balaam said to the angel of the LORD, "I have sinned. I did not realize you were standing in the road to oppose me. Now if you are displeased, I will go back."

³⁵The angel of the LORD said to Balaam, "Go with the men, but speak only what I tell you." So Balaam went with the princes of Balak.

³⁶When Balak heard that Balaam was coming, he went out to meet him at the Moabite town on the Arnon border, at the edge of his territory. ³⁷Balak said to Balaam, "Did I not send you an urgent summons? Why didn't you come to me? Am I really not able to reward you?"

³⁸"Well, I have come to you now," Balaam replied. "But can I say just anything? I must speak only what God puts in my mouth."

³⁹Then Balaam went with Balak to Kiriath Huzoth. ⁴⁰Balak sacrificed cattle and sheep, and gave some to Balaam and the princes who were with him. ⁴¹The next morning Balak took Balaam up to Bamoth Baal, and from there he saw part of the people.

Balaam's First Oracle

23 Balaam said, "Build me seven altars here, and prepare seven bulls and seven rams for me." ²Balak did as Balaam said, and the two of them offered a bull and a ram on each altar.

³Then Balaam said to Balak, "Stay here beside your offering while I go aside. Perhaps the LORD will come to meet with me. Whatever he reveals to me I will tell you." Then he went off to a barren height.

⁴God met with him, and Balaam said, "I have prepared seven altars, and on each altar I have offered a bull and a ram."

⁵The LORD put a message in Balaam's mouth and said, "Go back to Balak and give him this message."

⁶So he went back to him and found him standing beside his offering, with all the princes of Moab. ⁷Then Balaam uttered his oracle:

"Balak brought me from Aram,
　　the king of Moab from the eastern
　　　　mountains.
'Come,' he said, 'curse Jacob for me;
　　come, denounce Israel.'
⁸How can I curse
　　those whom God has not cursed?

How can I denounce
　　those whom the LORD has not
　　　　denounced?
⁹From the rocky peaks I see them,
　　from the heights I view them.
I see a people who live apart
　　and do not consider themselves
　　　　one of the nations.
¹⁰Who can count the dust of Jacob
　　or number the fourth part of
　　　　Israel?
Let me die the death of the righteous,
　　and may my end be like theirs!"

¹¹Balak said to Balaam, "What have you done to me? I brought you to curse my enemies, but you have done nothing but bless them!"

¹²He answered, "Must I not speak what the LORD puts in my mouth?"

Balaam's Second Oracle

¹³Then Balak said to him, "Come with me to another place where you can see them; you will see only a part but not all of them. And from there, curse them for me." ¹⁴So he took him to the field of Zophim on the top of Pisgah, and there he built seven altars and offered a bull and a ram on each altar.

¹⁵Balaam said to Balak, "Stay here beside your offering while I meet with him over there."

¹⁶The LORD met with Balaam and put a message in his mouth and said, "Go back to Balak and give him this message."

¹⁷So he went to him and found him standing beside his offering, with the princes of Moab. Balak asked him, "What did the LORD say?"

¹⁸Then he uttered his oracle:

"Arise, Balak, and listen;
　　hear me, son of Zippor.
¹⁹God is not a man, that he should lie,
　　nor a son of man, that he should
　　　　change his mind.
Does he speak and then not act?
　　Does he promise and not fulfill?
²⁰I have received a command to bless;
　　he has blessed, and I cannot
　　　　change it.

²¹"No misfortune is seen in Jacob,

no misery observed in Israel.ᵃ
The LORD their God is with them;
   the shout of the King is among
      them.
²²God brought them out of Egypt;
   they have the strength of a wild ox.
²³There is no sorcery against Jacob,
   no divination against Israel.
It will now be said of Jacob
   and of Israel, 'See what God has
      done!'
²⁴The people rise like a lioness;
   they rouse themselves like a lion
that does not rest till he devours his
      prey
   and drinks the blood of his
      victims."

²⁵Then Balak said to Balaam, "Neither curse them at all nor bless them at all!"

²⁶Balaam answered, "Did I not tell you I must do whatever the LORD says?"

Balaam's Third Oracle

²⁷Then Balak said to Balaam, "Come, let me take you to another place. Perhaps it will please God to let you curse them for me from there." ²⁸And Balak took Balaam to the top of Peor, overlooking the wasteland.

²⁹Balaam said, "Build me seven altars here, and prepare seven bulls and seven rams for me." ³⁰Balak did as Balaam had said, and offered a bull and a ram on each altar.

24 Now when Balaam saw that it pleased the LORD to bless Israel, he did not resort to sorcery as at other times, but turned his face toward the desert. ²When Balaam looked out and saw Israel encamped tribe by tribe, the Spirit of God came upon him ³and he uttered his oracle:

"The oracle of Balaam son of Beor,
   the oracle of one whose eye sees
      clearly,
⁴the oracle of one who hears the
      words of God,
   who sees a vision from the
      Almighty,ᵇ
who falls prostrate, and whose eyes
      are opened:

⁵"How beautiful are your tents,
      O Jacob,
   your dwelling places, O Israel!

⁶"Like valleys they spread out,
   like gardens beside a river,
like aloes planted by the LORD,
   like cedars beside the waters.
⁷Water will flow from their buckets;
   their seed will have abundant
      water.

"Their king will be greater than Agag;
   their kingdom will be exalted.

⁸"God brought them out of Egypt;
   they have the strength of a wild ox.
They devour hostile nations
   and break their bones in pieces;
   with their arrows they pierce them.
⁹Like a lion they crouch and lie down,
   like a lioness—who dares to rouse
      them?

"May those who bless you be blessed
   and those who curse you be
      cursed!"

¹⁰Then Balak's anger burned against Balaam. He struck his hands together and said to him, "I summoned you to curse my enemies, but you have blessed them these three times. ¹¹Now leave at once and go home! I said I would reward you handsomely, but the LORD has kept you from being rewarded."

¹²Balaam answered Balak, "Did I not tell the messengers you sent me, ¹³'Even if Balak gave me his palace filled with silver and gold, I could not do anything of my own accord, good or bad, to go beyond the command of the LORD—and I must say only what the LORD says'? ¹⁴Now I am going back to my people, but come, let me warn you of what this people will do to your people in days to come."

Balaam's Fourth Oracle

¹⁵Then he uttered his oracle:

"The oracle of Balaam son of Beor,
   the oracle of one whose eye sees
      clearly,
¹⁶the oracle of one who hears the
      words of God,
   who has knowledge from the Most
      High,
who sees a vision from the Almighty,

ᵃ21 Or He has not looked on Jacob's offenses / or on the wrongs found in Israel.   ᵇ4 Hebrew Shaddai; also in verse 16

who falls prostrate, and whose eyes
are opened:

[17]"I see him, but not now;
I behold him, but not near.
A star will come out of Jacob;
a scepter will rise out of Israel.
He will crush the foreheads of Moab,
the skulls[a] of[b] all the sons of
Sheth.[c]
[18]Edom will be conquered;
Seir, his enemy, will be conquered,
but Israel will grow strong.
[19]A ruler will come out of Jacob
and destroy the survivors of the
city."

Balaam's Final Oracles

[20]Then Balaam saw Amalek and uttered his oracle:

"Amalek was first among the nations,
but he will come to ruin at last."

[21]Then he saw the Kenites and uttered
his oracle:

"Your dwelling place is secure,
your nest is set in a rock;
[22]yet you Kenites will be destroyed
when Asshur takes you captive."

[23]Then he uttered his oracle:

"Ah, who can live when God does
this?[d]
[24]   Ships will come from the shores of
Kittim;
they will subdue Asshur and Eber,
but they too will come to ruin."

[25]Then Balaam got up and returned
home and Balak went his own way.

Moab Seduces Israel

25 While Israel was staying in Shittim,
the men began to indulge in sexual
immorality with Moabite women, [2]who
invited them to the sacrifices to their
gods. The people ate and bowed down
before these gods. [3]So Israel joined in
worshiping the Baal of Peor. And the
LORD's anger burned against them.
[4]The LORD said to Moses, "Take all the
leaders of these people, kill them and expose them in broad daylight before the
LORD, so that the LORD's fierce anger may
turn away from Israel."
[5]So Moses said to Israel's judges, "Each

of you must put to death those of your
men who have joined in worshiping the
Baal of Peor."
[6]Then an Israelite man brought to his
family a Midianite woman right before
the eyes of Moses and the whole assembly
of Israel while they were weeping at the
entrance to the Tent of Meeting. [7]When
Phinehas son of Eleazar, the son of Aaron, the priest, saw this, he left the assembly, took a spear in his hand [8]and followed the Israelite into the tent. He drove
the spear through both of them—through
the Israelite and into the woman's body.
Then the plague against the Israelites was
stopped; [9]but those who died in the
plague numbered 24,000.
[10]The LORD said to Moses, [11]"Phinehas
son of Eleazar, the son of Aaron, the
priest, has turned my anger away from the
Israelites; for he was as zealous as I am for
my honor among them, so that in my zeal
I did not put an end to them. [12]Therefore
tell him I am making my covenant of
peace with him. [13]He and his descendants
will have a covenant of a lasting priesthood, because he was zealous for the
honor of his God and made atonement
for the Israelites."
[14]The name of the Israelite who was
killed with the Midianite woman was
Zimri son of Salu, the leader of a Simeon-
ite family. [15]And the name of the Midianite woman who was put to death was
Cozbi daughter of Zur, a tribal chief of a
Midianite family.
[16]The LORD said to Moses, [17]"Treat the
Midianites as enemies and kill them,
[18]because they treated you as enemies
when they deceived you in the affair of
Peor and their sister Cozbi, the daughter
of a Midianite leader, the woman who
was killed when the plague came as a result of Peor."

The Second Census

26 After the plague the LORD said to
Moses and Eleazar son of Aaron,
the priest, [2]"Take a census of the whole
Israelite community by families—all those

---

[a]17 Samaritan Pentateuch (see also Jer. 48:45); the
meaning of the word in the Masoretic Text is
uncertain.   [b]17 Or possibly Moab, / batter
[c]17 Or all the noisy boasters   [d]23 Masoretic Text;
with a different word division of the Hebrew A
people will gather from the north.

twenty years old or more who are able to serve in the army of Israel." ³So on the plains of Moab by the Jordan across from Jericho,ᵃ Moses and Eleazar the priest spoke with them and said, ⁴"Take a census of the men twenty years old or more, as the LORD commanded Moses."

These were the Israelites who came out of Egypt:

⁵The descendants of Reuben, the firstborn son of Israel, were:

through Hanoch, the Hanochite clan;

through Pallu, the Palluite clan;

⁶through Hezron, the Hezronite clan;

through Carmi, the Carmite clan.

⁷These were the clans of Reuben; those numbered were 43,730.

⁸The son of Pallu was Eliab, ⁹and the sons of Eliab were Nemuel, Dathan and Abiram. The same Dathan and Abiram were the community officials who rebelled against Moses and Aaron and were among Korah's followers when they rebelled against the LORD. ¹⁰The earth opened its mouth and swallowed them along with Korah, whose followers died when the fire devoured the 250 men. And they served as a warning sign. ¹¹The line of Korah, however, did not die out.

¹²The descendants of Simeon by their clans were:

through Nemuel, the Nemuelite clan;

through Jamin, the Jaminite clan;

through Jakin, the Jakinite clan;

¹³through Zerah, the Zerahite clan;

through Shaul, the Shaulite clan.

¹⁴These were the clans of Simeon; there were 22,200 men.

¹⁵The descendants of Gad by their clans were:

through Zephon, the Zephonite clan;

through Haggi, the Haggite clan;

through Shuni, the Shunite clan;

¹⁶through Ozni, the Oznite clan;

through Eri, the Erite clan;

¹⁷through Arodi,ᵇ the Arodite clan;

through Areli, the Arelite clan.

¹⁸These were the clans of Gad; those numbered were 40,500.

¹⁹Er and Onan were sons of Judah, but they died in Canaan.

²⁰The descendants of Judah by their clans were:

through Shelah, the Shelanite clan;

through Perez, the Perezite clan;

through Zerah, the Zerahite clan.

²¹The descendants of Perez were:

through Hezron, the Hezronite clan;

through Hamul, the Hamulite clan.

²²These were the clans of Judah; those numbered were 76,500.

²³The descendants of Issachar by their clans were:

through Tola, the Tolaite clan;

through Puah, the Puiteᶜ clan;

²⁴through Jashub, the Jashubite clan;

through Shimron, the Shimronite clan.

²⁵These were the clans of Issachar; those numbered were 64,300.

²⁶The descendants of Zebulun by their clans were:

through Sered, the Seredite clan;

through Elon, the Elonite clan;

through Jahleel, the Jahleelite clan.

²⁷These were the clans of Zebulun; those numbered were 60,500.

²⁸The descendants of Joseph by their clans through Manasseh and Ephraim were:

²⁹The descendants of Manasseh:

through Makir, the Makirite clan (Makir was the father of Gilead);

through Gilead, the Gileadite clan.

³⁰These were the descendants of Gilead:

through Iezer, the Iezerite clan;

through Helek, the Helekite clan;

³¹through Asriel, the Asrielite clan;

through Shechem, the Shechemite clan;

³²through Shemida, the Shemidaite clan;

ᵃ3 Hebrew *Jordan of Jericho*; possibly an ancient name for the Jordan River; also in verse 63
ᵇ17 Samaritan Pentateuch and Syriac (see also Gen. 46:16); Masoretic Text *Arod*
ᶜ23 Samaritan Pentateuch, Septuagint, Vulgate and Syriac (see also 1 Chron. 7:1); Masoretic Text *through Puvah, the Punite*

through Hepher, the Hepherite clan.

33(Zelophehad son of Hepher had no sons; he had only daughters, whose names were Mahlah, Noah, Hoglah, Milcah and Tirzah.)

34These were the clans of Manasseh; those numbered were 52,700.

35These were the descendants of Ephraim by their clans:

through Shuthelah, the Shuthelahite clan;

through Beker, the Bekerite clan;

through Tahan, the Tahanite clan.

36These were the descendants of Shuthelah:

through Eran, the Eranite clan.

37These were the clans of Ephraim; those numbered were 32,500.

These were the descendants of Joseph by their clans.

38The descendants of Benjamin by their clans were:

through Bela, the Belaite clan;

through Ashbel, the Ashbelite clan;

through Ahiram, the Ahiramite clan;

39through Shupham,*a* the Shuphamite clan;

through Hupham, the Huphamite clan.

40The descendants of Bela through Ard and Naaman were:

through Ard,*b* the Ardite clan;

through Naaman, the Naamite clan.

41These were the clans of Benjamin; those numbered were 45,600.

42These were the descendants of Dan by their clans:

through Shuham, the Shuhamite clan.

These were the clans of Dan: 43All of them were Shuhamite clans; and those numbered were 64,400.

44The descendants of Asher by their clans were:

through Imnah, the Imnite clan;

through Ishvi, the Ishvite clan;

through Beriah, the Beriite clan;

45and through the descendants of Beriah:

through Heber, the Heberite clan;

through Malkiel, the Malkielite clan.

46(Asher had a daughter named Serah.)

47These were the clans of Asher; those numbered were 53,400.

48The descendants of Naphtali by their clans were:

through Jahzeel, the Jahzeelite clan;

through Guni, the Gunite clan;

49through Jezer, the Jezerite clan;

through Shillem, the Shillemite clan.

50These were the clans of Naphtali; those numbered were 45,400.

51The total number of the men of Israel was 601,730.

52The LORD said to Moses, 53"The land is to be allotted to them as an inheritance based on the number of names. 54To a larger group give a larger inheritance, and to a smaller group a smaller one; each is to receive its inheritance according to the number of those listed. 55Be sure that the land is distributed by lot. What each group inherits will be according to the names for its ancestral tribe. 56Each inheritance is to be distributed by lot among the larger and smaller groups."

57These were the Levites who were counted by their clans:

through Gershon, the Gershonite clan;

through Kohath, the Kohathite clan;

through Merari, the Merarite clan.

58These also were Levite clans:

the Libnite clan,

the Hebronite clan,

the Mahlite clan,

the Mushite clan,

the Korahite clan.

(Kohath was the forefather of Amram; 59the name of Amram's wife

---

a39 A few manuscripts of the Masoretic Text, Samaritan Pentateuch, Vulgate and Syriac (see also Septuagint); most manuscripts of the Masoretic Text *Shephupham*   *b40* Samaritan Pentateuch and Vulgate (see also Septuagint); Masoretic Text does not have *through Ard.*

was Jochebed, a descendant of Levi, who was born to the Levites[a] in Egypt. To Amram she bore Aaron, Moses and their sister Miriam. 60Aaron was the father of Nadab and Abihu, Eleazar and Ithamar. 61But Nadab and Abihu died when they made an offering before the LORD with unauthorized fire.)

62All the male Levites a month old or more numbered 23,000. They were not counted along with the other Israelites because they received no inheritance among them.

63These are the ones counted by Moses and Eleazar the priest when they counted the Israelites on the plains of Moab by the Jordan across from Jericho. 64Not one of them was among those counted by Moses and Aaron the priest when they counted the Israelites in the Desert of Sinai. 65For the LORD had told those Israelites they would surely die in the desert, and not one of them was left except Caleb son of Jephunneh and Joshua son of Nun.

Zelophehad's Daughters

27 The daughters of Zelophehad son of Hepher, the son of Gilead, the son of Makir, the son of Manasseh, belonged to the clans of Manasseh son of Joseph. The names of the daughters were Mahlah, Noah, Hoglah, Milcah and Tirzah. They approached 2the entrance to the Tent of Meeting and stood before Moses, Eleazar the priest, the leaders and the whole assembly, and said, 3"Our father died in the desert. He was not among Korah's followers, who banded together against the LORD, but he died for his own sin and left no sons. 4Why should our father's name disappear from his clan because he had no son? Give us property among our father's relatives."

5So Moses brought their case before the LORD 6and the LORD said to him, 7"What Zelophehad's daughters are saying is right. You must certainly give them property as an inheritance among their father's relatives and turn their father's inheritance over to them.

8"Say to the Israelites, 'If a man dies and leaves no son, turn his inheritance over to his daughter. 9If he has no daugh-

ter, give his inheritance to his brothers. 10If he has no brothers, give his inheritance to his father's brothers. 11If his father had no brothers, give his inheritance to the nearest relative in his clan, that he may possess it. This is to be a legal requirement for the Israelites, as the LORD commanded Moses.' "

Joshua to Succeed Moses

12Then the LORD said to Moses, "Go up this mountain in the Abarim range and see the land I have given the Israelites. 13After you have seen it, you too will be gathered to your people, as your brother Aaron was, 14for when the community rebelled at the waters in the Desert of Zin, both of you disobeyed my command to honor me as holy before their eyes." (These were the waters of Meribah Kadesh, in the Desert of Zin.)

15Moses said to the LORD, 16"May the LORD, the God of the spirits of all mankind, appoint a man over this community 17to go out and come in before them, one who will lead them out and bring them in, so the LORD's people will not be like sheep without a shepherd."

18So the LORD said to Moses, "Take Joshua son of Nun, a man in whom is the spirit,[b] and lay your hand on him. 19Have him stand before Eleazar the priest and the entire assembly and commission him in their presence. 20Give him some of your authority so the whole Israelite community will obey him. 21He is to stand before Eleazar the priest, who will obtain decisions for him by inquiring of the Urim before the LORD. At his command he and the entire community of the Israelites will go out, and at his command they will come in."

22Moses did as the LORD commanded him. He took Joshua and had him stand before Eleazar the priest and the whole assembly. 23Then he laid his hands on him and commissioned him, as the LORD instructed through Moses.

Daily Offerings

28 The LORD said to Moses, 2"Give this command to the Israelites and say to them: 'See that you present to me

a59 Or Jochebed, a daughter of Levi, who was born to Levi   b18 Or Spirit at the appointed time the food for my offerings made by fire, as an aroma pleasing to me.' ³Say to them: 'This is the offering made by fire that you are to present to the LORD: two lambs a year old without defect, as a regular burnt offering each day. ⁴Prepare one lamb in the morning and the other at twilight, ⁵together with a grain offering of a tenth of an ephah*a* of fine flour mixed with a quarter of a hin*b* of oil from pressed olives. ⁶This is the regular burnt offering instituted at Mount Sinai as a pleasing aroma, an offering made to the LORD by fire. ⁷The accompanying drink offering is to be a quarter of a hin of fermented drink with each lamb. Pour out the drink offering to the LORD at the sanctuary. ⁸Prepare the second lamb at twilight, along with the same kind of grain offering and drink offering that you prepare in the morning. This is an offering made by fire, an aroma pleasing to the LORD.

Sabbath Offerings

⁹" 'On the Sabbath day, make an offering of two lambs a year old without defect, together with its drink offering and a grain offering of two-tenths of an ephah*c* of fine flour mixed with oil. ¹⁰This is the burnt offering for every Sabbath, in addition to the regular burnt offering and its drink offering.

Monthly Offerings

¹¹" 'On the first of every month, present to the LORD a burnt offering of two young bulls, one ram and seven male lambs a year old, all without defect. ¹²With each bull there is to be a grain offering of three-tenths of an ephah*d* of fine flour mixed with oil; with the ram, a grain offering of two-tenths of an ephah of fine flour mixed with oil; ¹³and with each lamb, a grain offering of a tenth of an ephah of fine flour mixed with oil. This is for a burnt offering, a pleasing aroma, an offering made to the LORD by fire. ¹⁴With each bull there is to be a drink offering of half a hin*e* of wine; with the ram, a third of a hin*f*; and with each lamb, a quarter of a hin. This is the monthly burnt offering to be made at each new moon during the year. ¹⁵Besides the regular burnt offering with its drink

offering, one male goat is to be presented to the LORD as a sin offering.

The Passover

¹⁶" 'On the fourteenth day of the first month the LORD's Passover is to be held. ¹⁷On the fifteenth day of this month there is to be a festival; for seven days eat bread made without yeast. ¹⁸On the first day hold a sacred assembly and do no regular work. ¹⁹Present to the LORD an offering made by fire, a burnt offering of two young bulls, one ram and seven male lambs a year old, all without defect. ²⁰With each bull prepare a grain offering of three-tenths of an ephah of fine flour mixed with oil; with the ram, two-tenths; ²¹and with each of the seven lambs, one-tenth. ²²Include one male goat as a sin offering to make atonement for you. ²³Prepare these in addition to the regular morning burnt offering. ²⁴In this way prepare the food for the offering made by fire every day for seven days as an aroma pleasing to the LORD; it is to be prepared in addition to the regular burnt offering and its drink offering. ²⁵On the seventh day hold a sacred assembly and do no regular work.

Feast of Weeks

²⁶" 'On the day of firstfruits, when you present to the LORD an offering of new grain during the Feast of Weeks, hold a sacred assembly and do no regular work. ²⁷Present a burnt offering of two young bulls, one ram and seven male lambs a year old as an aroma pleasing to the LORD. ²⁸With each bull there is to be a grain offering of three-tenths of an ephah of fine flour mixed with oil; with the ram, two-tenths; ²⁹and with each of the seven lambs, one-tenth. ³⁰Include one male goat to make atonement for you. ³¹Prepare these together with their drink offerings, in addition to the regular burnt of-

a5 That is, probably about 2 quarts (about 2 liters); also in verses 13, 21 and 29   *b5* That is, probably about 1 quart (about 1 liter); also in verses 7 and 14   *c9* That is, probably about 4 quarts (about 4.5 liters); also in verses 12, 20 and 28   *d12* That is, probably about 6 quarts (about 6.5 liters); also in verses 20 and 28   *e14* That is, probably about 2 quarts (about 2 liters)   *f14* That is, probably about 1 1/4 quarts (about 1.2 liters) fering and its grain offering. Be sure the animals are without defect.

Feast of Trumpets

29 " 'On the first day of the seventh month hold a sacred assembly and do no regular work. It is a day for you to sound the trumpets. ²As an aroma pleasing to the LORD, prepare a burnt offering of one young bull, one ram and seven male lambs a year old, all without defect. ³With the bull prepare a grain offering of three-tenths of an ephah*ᵃ* of fine flour mixed with oil; with the ram, two-tenths*ᵇ*; ⁴and with each of the seven lambs, one-tenth.*ᶜ* ⁵Include one male goat as a sin offering to make atonement for you. ⁶These are in addition to the monthly and daily burnt offerings with their grain offerings and drink offerings as specified. They are offerings made to the LORD by fire—a pleasing aroma.

Day of Atonement

⁷" 'On the tenth day of this seventh month hold a sacred assembly. You must deny yourselves*ᵈ* and do no work. ⁸Present as an aroma pleasing to the LORD a burnt offering of one young bull, one ram and seven male lambs a year old, all without defect. ⁹With the bull prepare a grain offering of three-tenths of an ephah of fine flour mixed with oil; with the ram, two-tenths; ¹⁰and with each of the seven lambs, one-tenth. ¹¹Include one male goat as a sin offering, in addition to the sin offering for atonement and the regular burnt offering with its grain offering, and their drink offerings.

Feast of Tabernacles

¹²" 'On the fifteenth day of the seventh month, hold a sacred assembly and do no regular work. Celebrate a festival to the LORD for seven days. ¹³Present an offering made by fire as an aroma pleasing to the LORD, a burnt offering of thirteen young bulls, two rams and fourteen male lambs a year old, all without defect. ¹⁴With each of the thirteen bulls prepare a grain offering of three-tenths of an ephah of fine flour mixed with oil; with each of the two rams, two-tenths; ¹⁵and with each of the fourteen lambs, one-tenth. ¹⁶Include one male goat as a sin offering, in addition to

the regular burnt offering with its grain offering and drink offering.

¹⁷" 'On the second day prepare twelve young bulls, two rams and fourteen male lambs a year old, all without defect. ¹⁸With the bulls, rams and lambs, prepare their grain offerings and drink offerings according to the number specified. ¹⁹Include one male goat as a sin offering, in addition to the regular burnt offering with its grain offering, and their drink offerings.

²⁰" 'On the third day prepare eleven bulls, two rams and fourteen male lambs a year old, all without defect. ²¹With the bulls, rams and lambs, prepare their grain offerings and drink offerings according to the number specified. ²²Include one male goat as a sin offering, in addition to the regular burnt offering with its grain offering and drink offering.

²³" 'On the fourth day prepare ten bulls, two rams and fourteen male lambs a year old, all without defect. ²⁴With the bulls, rams and lambs, prepare their grain offerings and drink offerings according to the number specified. ²⁵Include one male goat as a sin offering, in addition to the regular burnt offering with its grain offering and drink offering.

²⁶" 'On the fifth day prepare nine bulls, two rams and fourteen male lambs a year old, all without defect. ²⁷With the bulls, rams and lambs, prepare their grain offerings and drink offerings according to the number specified. ²⁸Include one male goat as a sin offering, in addition to the regular burnt offering with its grain offering and drink offering.

²⁹" 'On the sixth day prepare eight bulls, two rams and fourteen male lambs a year old, all without defect. ³⁰With the bulls, rams and lambs, prepare their grain offerings and drink offerings according to the number specified. ³¹Include one male goat as a sin offering, in addition to the regular burnt offering with its grain offering and drink offering.

³²" 'On the seventh day prepare seven bulls, two rams and fourteen male lambs

---

ᵃ3 That is, probably about 6 quarts (about 6.5 liters); also in verses 9 and 14   *ᵇ3* That is, probably about 4 quarts (about 4.5 liters); also in verses 9 and 14   *ᶜ4* That is, probably about 2 quarts (about 2 liters); also in verses 10 and 15   *ᵈ7* Or *must fast* a year old, all without defect. ³³With the bulls, rams and lambs, prepare their grain offerings and drink offerings according to the number specified. ³⁴Include one male goat as a sin offering, in addition to the regular burnt offering with its grain offering and drink offering.

³⁵" 'On the eighth day hold an assembly and do no regular work. ³⁶Present an offering made by fire as an aroma pleasing to the LORD, a burnt offering of one bull, one ram and seven male lambs a year old, all without defect. ³⁷With the bull, the ram and the lambs, prepare their grain offerings and drink offerings according to the number specified. ³⁸Include one male goat as a sin offering, in addition to the regular burnt offering with its grain offering and drink offering.

³⁹" 'In addition to what you vow and your freewill offerings, prepare these for the LORD at your appointed feasts: your burnt offerings, grain offerings, drink offerings and fellowship offerings.ᵃ' "

⁴⁰Moses told the Israelites all that the LORD commanded him.

Vows

30 Moses said to the heads of the tribes of Israel: "This is what the LORD commands: ²When a man makes a vow to the LORD or takes an oath to obli-gate himself by a pledge, he must not break his word but must do everything he said.

³"When a young woman still living in her father's house makes a vow to the LORD or obligates herself by a pledge ⁴and her father hears about her vow or pledge but says nothing to her, then all her vows and every pledge by which she obligated herself will stand. ⁵But if her father forbids her when he hears about it, none of her vows or the pledges by which she obligated herself will stand; the LORD will release her because her father has forbidden her.

⁶"If she marries after she makes a vow or after her lips utter a rash promise by which she obligates herself ⁷and her husband hears about it but says nothing to her, then her vows or the pledges by which she obligated herself will stand. ⁸But if her husband forbids her when he hears about it, he nullifies the vow that obligates her or the rash promise by which she obligates herself, and the LORD will release her.

⁹"Any vow or obligation taken by a widow or divorced woman will be binding on her.

¹⁰"If a woman living with her husband

ᵃ39 Traditionally *peace offerings*

Guard Your Heart

Thursday

NUMBERS 30:1–2   Virtually every couple who takes their marriage vows seriously fully intends to keep them. On their wedding day, most couples are not thinking of the "poorer" or "sickness" part of their vows. They're filled with hopes, dreams and expectations. Eventually, of course, reality sets in, and they begin to live out the final phrase of the vows—sticking together until death parts them. That's when marriage needs protection.

When it comes to tough times, our natural tendency is to ask, "What's in it for me?" or "How will I benefit?" But the moment we ask these kinds of questions is the moment our heart becomes unprotected. It's like setting down a protective shield and opening our heart to be vulnerable to excessive self-indulgence. Our self-centered desires can sabotage our heart's capacity for commitment, and we instinctively look for the easy way out, the path of least resistance. And that path almost always leads to heartache.

No successful marriage has made it on the well-worn path of selfishness. Successful marriages occur when both spouses guard their hearts from selfish ways and forge a new and noble path of other-centeredness. For it is on this path that one finds "the wellspring of life."

—*Les & Leslie*

Go to page 189 for your next devotional reading.

makes a vow or obligates herself by a pledge under oath [11]and her husband hears about it but says nothing to her and does not forbid her, then all her vows or the pledges by which she obligated herself will stand. [12]But if her husband nullifies them when he hears about them, then none of the vows or pledges that came from her lips will stand. Her husband has nullified them, and the LORD will release her. [13]Her husband may confirm or nullify any vow she makes or any sworn pledge to deny herself. [14]But if her husband says nothing to her about it from day to day, then he confirms all her vows or the pledges binding on her. He confirms them by saying nothing to her when he hears about them. [15]If, however, he nullifies them some time after he hears about them, then he is responsible for her guilt."

[16]These are the regulations the LORD gave Moses concerning relationships between a man and his wife, and between a father and his young daughter still living in his house.

Vengeance on the Midianites

31 The LORD said to Moses, [2]"Take vengeance on the Midianites for the Israelites. After that, you will be gathered to your people."

[3]So Moses said to the people, "Arm some of your men to go to war against the Midianites and to carry out the LORD's vengeance on them. [4]Send into battle a thousand men from each of the tribes of Israel." [5]So twelve thousand men armed for battle, a thousand from each tribe, were supplied from the clans of Israel. [6]Moses sent them into battle, a thousand from each tribe, along with Phinehas son of Eleazar, the priest, who took with him articles from the sanctuary and the trumpets for signaling.

[7]They fought against Midian, as the LORD commanded Moses, and killed every man. [8]Among their victims were Evi, Rekem, Zur, Hur and Reba—the five kings of Midian. They also killed Balaam son of Beor with the sword. [9]The Israelites captured the Midianite women and children and took all the Midianite herds, flocks and goods as plunder. [10]They burned all the towns where the Midianites had set-

tled, as well as all their camps. [11]They took all the plunder and spoils, including the people and animals, [12]and brought the captives, spoils and plunder to Moses and Eleazar the priest and the Israelite assembly at their camp on the plains of Moab, by the Jordan across from Jericho.[a]

[13]Moses, Eleazar the priest and all the leaders of the community went to meet them outside the camp. [14]Moses was angry with the officers of the army—the commanders of thousands and commanders of hundreds—who returned from the battle.

[15]"Have you allowed all the women to live?" he asked them. [16]"They were the ones who followed Balaam's advice and were the means of turning the Israelites away from the LORD in what happened at Peor, so that a plague struck the LORD's people. [17]Now kill all the boys. And kill every woman who has slept with a man, [18]but save for yourselves every girl who has never slept with a man.

[19]"All of you who have killed anyone or touched anyone who was killed must stay outside the camp seven days. On the third and seventh days you must purify yourselves and your captives. [20]Purify every garment as well as everything made of leather, goat hair or wood."

[21]Then Eleazar the priest said to the soldiers who had gone into battle, "This is the requirement of the law that the LORD gave Moses: [22]Gold, silver, bronze, iron, tin, lead [23]and anything else that can withstand fire must be put through the fire, and then it will be clean. But it must also be purified with the water of cleansing. And whatever cannot withstand fire must be put through that water. [24]On the seventh day wash your clothes and you will be clean. Then you may come into the camp."

Dividing the Spoils

[25]The LORD said to Moses, [26]"You and Eleazar the priest and the family heads of the community are to count all the people and animals that were captured. [27]Divide the spoils between the soldiers who took part in the battle and the rest of the com-

*a12 Hebrew Jordan of Jericho; possibly an ancient name for the Jordan River munity. 28From the soldiers who fought in the battle, set apart as tribute for the LORD one out of every five hundred, whether persons, cattle, donkeys, sheep or goats. 29Take this tribute from their half share and give it to Eleazar the priest as the LORD's part. 30From the Israelites' half, select one out of every fifty, whether persons, cattle, donkeys, sheep, goats or other animals. Give them to the Levites, who are responsible for the care of the LORD's tabernacle." 31So Moses and Eleazar the priest did as the LORD commanded Moses.

32The plunder remaining from the spoils that the soldiers took was 675,000 sheep, 3372,000 cattle, 3461,000 donkeys 35and 32,000 women who had never slept with a man.

36The half share of those who fought in the battle was:

337,500 sheep, 37of which the tribute for the LORD was 675;
3836,000 cattle, of which the tribute for the LORD was 72;
3930,500 donkeys, of which the tribute for the LORD was 61;
4016,000 people, of which the tribute for the LORD was 32.

41Moses gave the tribute to Eleazar the priest as the LORD's part, as the LORD commanded Moses.

42The half belonging to the Israelites, which Moses set apart from that of the fighting men— 43the community's half— was 337,500 sheep, 4436,000 cattle, 4530,500 donkeys 46and 16,000 people. 47From the Israelites' half, Moses selected one out of every fifty persons and animals, as the LORD commanded him, and gave them to the Levites, who were responsible for the care of the LORD's tabernacle.

48Then the officers who were over the units of the army—the commanders of thousands and commanders of hundreds—went to Moses 49and said to him, "Your servants have counted the soldiers under our command, and not one is missing. 50So we have brought as an offering to the LORD the gold articles each of us acquired—armlets, bracelets, signet rings, earrings and necklaces—to make atonement for ourselves before the LORD." 51Moses and Eleazar the priest accepted

from them the gold—all the crafted articles. 52All the gold from the commanders of thousands and commanders of hundreds that Moses and Eleazar presented as a gift to the LORD weighed 16,750 shekels.ᵃ 53Each soldier had taken plunder for himself. 54Moses and Eleazar the priest accepted the gold from the commanders of thousands and commanders of hundreds and brought it into the Tent of Meeting as a memorial for the Israelites before the LORD.

The Transjordan Tribes

32 The Reubenites and Gadites, who had very large herds and flocks, saw that the lands of Jazer and Gilead were suitable for livestock. 2So they came to Moses and Eleazar the priest and to the leaders of the community, and said, 3"Ataroth, Dibon, Jazer, Nimrah, Heshbon, Elealeh, Sebam, Nebo and Beon— 4the land the LORD subdued before the people of Israel—are suitable for livestock, and your servants have livestock. 5If we have found favor in your eyes," they said, "let this land be given to your servants as our possession. Do not make us cross the Jordan."

6Moses said to the Gadites and Reubenites, "Shall your countrymen go to war while you sit here? 7Why do you discourage the Israelites from going over into the land the LORD has given them? 8This is what your fathers did when I sent them from Kadesh Barnea to look over the land. 9After they went up to the Valley of Eshcol and viewed the land, they discouraged the Israelites from entering the land the LORD had given them. 10The LORD's anger was aroused that day and he swore this oath: 11'Because they have not followed me wholeheartedly, not one of the men twenty years old or more who came up out of Egypt will see the land I promised on oath to Abraham, Isaac and Jacob— 12not one except Caleb son of Jephunneh the Kenizzite and Joshua son of Nun, for they followed the LORD wholeheartedly.' 13The LORD's anger burned against Israel and he made them wander in the desert forty years, until the whole

ᵃ52 That is, about 420 pounds (about 190 kilograms)

generation of those who had done evil in his sight was gone.

14"And here you are, a brood of sinners, standing in the place of your fathers and making the LORD even more angry with Israel. 15If you turn away from following him, he will again leave all this people in the desert, and you will be the cause of their destruction."

16Then they came up to him and said, "We would like to build pens here for our livestock and cities for our women and children. 17But we are ready to arm ourselves and go ahead of the Israelites until we have brought them to their place. Meanwhile our women and children will live in fortified cities, for protection from the inhabitants of the land. 18We will not return to our homes until every Israelite has received his inheritance. 19We will not receive any inheritance with them on the other side of the Jordan, because our inheritance has come to us on the east side of the Jordan."

20Then Moses said to them, "If you will do this—if you will arm yourselves before the LORD for battle, 21and if all of you will go armed over the Jordan before the LORD until he has driven his enemies out before him— 22then when the land is subdued before the LORD, you may return and be free from your obligation to the LORD and to Israel. And this land will be your possession before the LORD.

23"But if you fail to do this, you will be sinning against the LORD; and you may be sure that your sin will find you out. 24Build cities for your women and children, and pens for your flocks, but do what you have promised."

25The Gadites and Reubenites said to Moses, "We your servants will do as our lord commands. 26Our children and wives, our flocks and herds will remain here in the cities of Gilead. 27But your servants, every man armed for battle, will cross over to fight before the LORD, just as our lord says."

28Then Moses gave orders about them to Eleazar the priest and Joshua son of Nun and to the family heads of the Israelite tribes. 29He said to them, "If the Gadites and Reubenites, every man armed for battle, cross over the Jordan with you before the LORD, then when the land is subdued before you, give them the land of Gilead as their possession. 30But if they do not cross over with you armed, they must accept their possession with you in Canaan."

31The Gadites and Reubenites answered, "Your servants will do what the LORD has said. 32We will cross over before the LORD into Canaan armed, but the property we inherit will be on this side of the Jordan."

33Then Moses gave to the Gadites, the Reubenites and the half-tribe of Manasseh son of Joseph the kingdom of Sihon king of the Amorites and the kingdom of Og king of Bashan—the whole land with its cities and the territory around them.

34The Gadites built up Dibon, Ataroth, Aroer, 35Atroth Shophan, Jazer, Jogbehah, 36Beth Nimrah and Beth Haran as fortified cities, and built pens for their flocks. 37And the Reubenites rebuilt Heshbon, Elealeh and Kiriathaim, 38as well as Nebo and Baal Meon (these names were changed) and Sibmah. They gave names to the cities they rebuilt.

39The descendants of Makir son of Manasseh went to Gilead, captured it and drove out the Amorites who were there. 40So Moses gave Gilead to the Makirites, the descendants of Manasseh, and they settled there. 41Jair, a descendant of Manasseh, captured their settlements and called them Havvoth Jair.a 42And Nobah captured Kenath and its surrounding settlements and called it Nobah after himself.

Stages in Israel's Journey

33 Here are the stages in the journey of the Israelites when they came out of Egypt by divisions under the leadership of Moses and Aaron. 2At the LORD's command Moses recorded the stages in their journey. This is their journey by stages:

3The Israelites set out from Rameses on the fifteenth day of the first month, the day after the Passover. They marched out boldly in full view of all the Egyptians, 4who were burying all their firstborn, whom the LORD had struck down among

a41 Or them the settlements of Jair

them; for the LORD had brought judgment on their gods.

⁵The Israelites left Rameses and camped at Succoth. ⁶They left Succoth and camped at Etham, on the edge of the desert. ⁷They left Etham, turned back to Pi Hahiroth, to the east of Baal Zephon, and camped near Migdol. ⁸They left Pi Hahiroth*ᵃ* and passed through the sea into the desert, and when they had traveled for three days in the Desert of Etham, they camped at Marah. ⁹They left Marah and went to Elim, where there were twelve springs and seventy palm trees, and they camped there. ¹⁰They left Elim and camped by the Red Sea.*ᵇ* ¹¹They left the Red Sea and camped in the Desert of Sin. ¹²They left the Desert of Sin and camped at Dophkah. ¹³They left Dophkah and camped at Alush. ¹⁴They left Alush and camped at Rephidim, where there was no water for the people to drink. ¹⁵They left Rephidim and camped in the Desert of Sinai. ¹⁶They left the Desert of Sinai and camped at Kibroth Hattaavah. ¹⁷They left Kibroth Hattaavah and camped at Hazeroth. ¹⁸They left Hazeroth and camped at Rithmah. ¹⁹They left Rithmah and camped at Rimmon Perez. ²⁰They left Rimmon Perez and camped at Libnah. ²¹They left Libnah and camped at Rissah. ²²They left Rissah and camped at Kehelathah. ²³They left Kehelathah and camped at Mount Shepher. ²⁴They left Mount Shepher and camped at Haradah. ²⁵They left Haradah and camped at Makheloth. ²⁶They left Makheloth and camped at Tahath. ²⁷They left Tahath and camped at Terah.

²⁸They left Terah and camped at Mithcah. ²⁹They left Mithcah and camped at Hashmonah. ³⁰They left Hashmonah and camped at Moseroth. ³¹They left Moseroth and camped at Bene Jaakan. ³²They left Bene Jaakan and camped at Hor Haggidgad. ³³They left Hor Haggidgad and camped at Jotbathah. ³⁴They left Jotbathah and camped at Abronah. ³⁵They left Abronah and camped at Ezion Geber. ³⁶They left Ezion Geber and camped at Kadesh, in the Desert of Zin. ³⁷They left Kadesh and camped at Mount Hor, on the border of Edom. ³⁸At the LORD's command Aaron the priest went up Mount Hor, where he died on the first day of the fifth month of the fortieth year after the Israelites came out of Egypt. ³⁹Aaron was a hundred and twenty-three years old when he died on Mount Hor.

⁴⁰The Canaanite king of Arad, who lived in the Negev of Canaan, heard that the Israelites were coming.

⁴¹They left Mount Hor and camped at Zalmonah. ⁴²They left Zalmonah and camped at Punon. ⁴³They left Punon and camped at Oboth. ⁴⁴They left Oboth and camped at Iye Abarim, on the border of Moab. ⁴⁵They left Iyim*ᶜ* and camped at Dibon Gad. ⁴⁶They left Dibon Gad and camped at Almon Diblathaim. ⁴⁷They left Almon Diblathaim and camped in the mountains of Abarim, near Nebo. ⁴⁸They left the mountains of Abarim and camped on the plains of Moab by the Jordan across from Jeri-

---

ᵃ8 Many manuscripts of the Masoretic Text, Samaritan Pentateuch and Vulgate; most manuscripts of the Masoretic Text *left from before Hahiroth*   *ᵇ10* Hebrew *Yam Suph*; that is, Sea of Reeds; also in verse 11   *ᶜ45* That is, Iye Abarim cho.[a] 49There on the plains of Moab they camped along the Jordan from Beth Jeshimoth to Abel Shittim.

50On the plains of Moab by the Jordan across from Jericho the LORD said to Moses, 51"Speak to the Israelites and say to them: 'When you cross the Jordan into Canaan, 52drive out all the inhabitants of the land before you. Destroy all their carved images and their cast idols, and demolish all their high places. 53Take possession of the land and settle in it, for I have given you the land to possess. 54Distribute the land by lot, according to your clans. To a larger group give a larger inheritance, and to a smaller group a smaller one. Whatever falls to them by lot will be theirs. Distribute it according to your ancestral tribes.

55" 'But if you do not drive out the inhabitants of the land, those you allow to remain will become barbs in your eyes and thorns in your sides. They will give you trouble in the land where you will live. 56And then I will do to you what I plan to do to them.' "

Boundaries of Canaan

34 The LORD said to Moses, 2"Command the Israelites and say to them: 'When you enter Canaan, the land that will be allotted to you as an inheritance will have these boundaries:

3" 'Your southern side will include some of the Desert of Zin along the border of Edom. On the east, your southern boundary will start from the end of the Salt Sea,[b] 4cross south of Scorpion[c] Pass, continue on to Zin and go south of Kadesh Barnea. Then it will go to Hazar Addar and over to Azmon, 5where it will turn, join the Wadi of Egypt and end at the Sea.[d]

6" 'Your western boundary will be the coast of the Great Sea. This will be your boundary on the west.

7" 'For your northern boundary, run a line from the Great Sea to Mount Hor 8and from Mount Hor to Lebo[e] Hamath. Then the boundary will go to Zedad, 9continue to Ziphron and end at Hazar Enan. This will be your boundary on the north.

10" 'For your eastern boundary, run a line from Hazar Enan to Shepham. 11The boundary will go down from Shepham to Riblah on the east side of Ain and continue along the slopes east of the Sea of Kinnereth.[f] 12Then the boundary will go down along the Jordan and end at the Salt Sea.

" 'This will be your land, with its boundaries on every side.' "

13Moses commanded the Israelites: "Assign this land by lot as an inheritance. The LORD has ordered that it be given to the nine and a half tribes, 14because the families of the tribe of Reuben, the tribe of Gad and the half-tribe of Manasseh have received their inheritance. 15These two and a half tribes have received their inheritance on the east side of the Jordan of Jericho,[g] toward the sunrise."

16The LORD said to Moses, 17"These are the names of the men who are to assign the land for you as an inheritance: Eleazar the priest and Joshua son of Nun. 18And appoint one leader from each tribe to help assign the land. 19These are their names:

Caleb son of Jephunneh,
   from the tribe of Judah;
20Shemuel son of Ammihud,
   from the tribe of Simeon;
21Elidad son of Kislon,
   from the tribe of Benjamin;
22Bukki son of Jogli,
   the leader from the tribe of Dan;
23Hanniel son of Ephod,
   the leader from the tribe of Manasseh son of Joseph;
24Kemuel son of Shiphtan,
   the leader from the tribe of Ephraim son of Joseph;
25Elizaphan son of Parnach,
   the leader from the tribe of Zebulun;
26Paltiel son of Azzan,
   the leader from the tribe of Issachar;
27Ahihud son of Shelomi,

a48 Hebrew Jordan of Jericho; possibly an ancient name for the Jordan River; also in verse 50   b3 That is, the Dead Sea; also in verse 12   c4 Hebrew Akrabbim   d5 That is, the Mediterranean; also in verses 6 and 7   e8 Or to the entrance to   f11 That is, Galilee   g15 Jordan of Jericho was possibly an ancient name for the Jordan River.

the leader from the tribe of Asher;

²⁸Pedahel son of Ammihud,
the leader from the tribe of Naphtali."

²⁹These are the men the LORD commanded to assign the inheritance to the Israelites in the land of Canaan.

Towns for the Levites

35 On the plains of Moab by the Jordan across from Jericho,ᵃ the LORD said to Moses, ²"Command the Israelites to give the Levites towns to live in from the inheritance the Israelites will possess. And give them pasturelands around the towns. ³Then they will have towns to live in and pasturelands for their cattle, flocks and all their other livestock.

⁴"The pasturelands around the towns that you give the Levites will extend out fifteen hundred feetᵇ from the town wall. ⁵Outside the town, measure three thousand feetᶜ on the east side, three thousand on the south side, three thousand on the west and three thousand on the north, with the town in the center. They will have this area as pastureland for the towns.

Cities of Refuge

⁶"Six of the towns you give the Levites will be cities of refuge, to which a person who has killed someone may flee. In addition, give them forty-two other towns. ⁷In all you must give the Levites forty-eight towns, together with their pasturelands. ⁸The towns you give the Levites from the land the Israelites possess are to be given in proportion to the inheritance of each tribe: Take many towns from a tribe that has many, but few from one that has few."

⁹Then the LORD said to Moses: ¹⁰"Speak to the Israelites and say to them: 'When you cross the Jordan into Canaan, ¹¹select some towns to be your cities of refuge, to which a person who has killed someone accidentally may flee. ¹²They will be places of refuge from the avenger, so that a person accused of murder may not die before he stands trial before the assembly. ¹³These six towns you give will be your cities of refuge. ¹⁴Give three on this side of the Jordan and three in Ca-

naan as cities of refuge. ¹⁵These six towns will be a place of refuge for Israelites, aliens and any other people living among them, so that anyone who has killed another accidentally can flee there.

¹⁶"'If a man strikes someone with an iron object so that he dies, he is a murderer; the murderer shall be put to death. ¹⁷Or if anyone has a stone in his hand that could kill, and he strikes someone so that he dies, he is a murderer; the murderer shall be put to death. ¹⁸Or if anyone has a wooden object in his hand that could kill, and he hits someone so that he dies, he is a murderer; the murderer shall be put to death. ¹⁹The avenger of blood shall put the murderer to death; when he meets him, he shall put him to death. ²⁰If anyone with malice aforethought shoves another or throws something at him intentionally so that he dies ²¹or if in hostility he hits him with his fist so that he dies, that person shall be put to death; he is a murderer. The avenger of blood shall put the murderer to death when he meets him.

²²"'But if without hostility someone suddenly shoves another or throws something at him unintentionally ²³or, without seeing him, drops a stone on him that could kill him, and he dies, then since he was not his enemy and he did not intend to harm him, ²⁴the assembly must judge between him and the avenger of blood according to these regulations. ²⁵The assembly must protect the one accused of murder from the avenger of blood and send him back to the city of refuge to which he fled. He must stay there until the death of the high priest, who was anointed with the holy oil.

²⁶"'But if the accused ever goes outside the limits of the city of refuge to which he has fled ²⁷and the avenger of blood finds him outside the city, the avenger of blood may kill the accused without being guilty of murder. ²⁸The accused must stay in his city of refuge until the death of the high priest; only after the death of the high priest may he return to his own property.

²⁹"'These are to be legal requirements

ᵃ1 Hebrew *Jordan of Jericho*; possibly an ancient name for the Jordan River   ᵇ4 Hebrew *a thousand cubits* (about 450 meters)   ᶜ5 Hebrew *two thousand cubits* (about 900 meters) for you throughout the generations to come, wherever you live.

³⁰" 'Anyone who kills a person is to be put to death as a murderer only on the testimony of witnesses. But no one is to be put to death on the testimony of only one witness.

³¹" 'Do not accept a ransom for the life of a murderer, who deserves to die. He must surely be put to death.

³²" 'Do not accept a ransom for anyone who has fled to a city of refuge and so allow him to go back and live on his own land before the death of the high priest.

³³" 'Do not pollute the land where you are. Bloodshed pollutes the land, and atonement cannot be made for the land on which blood has been shed, except by the blood of the one who shed it. ³⁴Do not defile the land where you live and where I dwell, for I, the LORD, dwell among the Israelites.' "

Inheritance of Zelophehad's Daughters

36 The family heads of the clan of Gilead son of Makir, the son of Manasseh, who were from the clans of the descendants of Joseph, came and spoke before Moses and the leaders, the heads of the Israelite families. ²They said, "When the LORD commanded my lord to give the land as an inheritance to the Israelites by lot, he ordered you to give the inheritance of our brother Zelophehad to his daughters. ³Now suppose they marry men from other Israelite tribes; then their inheritance will be taken from our ancestral inheritance and added to that of the tribe they marry into. And so part of the

inheritance allotted to us will be taken away. ⁴When the Year of Jubilee for the Israelites comes, their inheritance will be added to that of the tribe into which they marry, and their property will be taken from the tribal inheritance of our forefathers."

⁵Then at the LORD's command Moses gave this order to the Israelites: "What the tribe of the descendants of Joseph is saying is right. ⁶This is what the LORD commands for Zelophehad's daughters: They may marry anyone they please as long as they marry within the tribal clan of their father. ⁷No inheritance in Israel is to pass from tribe to tribe, for every Israelite shall keep the tribal land inherited from his forefathers. ⁸Every daughter who inherits land in any Israelite tribe must marry someone in her father's tribal clan, so that every Israelite will possess the inheritance of his fathers. ⁹No inheritance may pass from tribe to tribe, for each Israelite tribe is to keep the land it inherits."

¹⁰So Zelophehad's daughters did as the LORD commanded Moses. ¹¹Zelophehad's daughters—Mahlah, Tirzah, Hoglah, Milcah and Noah—married their cousins on their father's side. ¹²They married within the clans of the descendants of Manasseh son of Joseph, and their inheritance remained in their father's clan and tribe.

¹³These are the commands and regulations the LORD gave through Moses to the Israelites on the plains of Moab by the Jordan across from Jericho.ᵃ

a13 Hebrew *Jordan of Jericho;* possibly an ancient name for the Jordan River

Deuteronomy

Life would be so much easier without rules. We could drive as fast as we wanted, we could forget about our loans, we could be as promiscuous as we felt, and we could tell our spouse to do whatever because that's what we were going to do. When you really think about this kind of life, it really doesn't sound like a good time at all, does it? Societies and families need rules to survive. Without them, chaos and unhappiness takes over.

The book of Deuteronomy was intended to be a guidebook for God's family, the Israelites. Sure, sometimes it may read like the tax code from the Internal Revenue Service, but every word is there for a good reason. People who live together—like the Israelites' and you and your spouse—need rules. You may not be applauded every time you enforce them, but guidelines make your marriage feel trustworthy and safe. Just ask a couple million people who wandered around in the desert for forty years.

The Command to Leave Horeb

1 These are the words Moses spoke to all Israel in the desert east of the Jordan—that is, in the Arabah—opposite Suph, between Paran and Tophel, Laban, Hazeroth and Dizahab. ²(It takes eleven days to go from Horeb to Kadesh Barnea by the Mount Seir road.)

³In the fortieth year, on the first day of the eleventh month, Moses proclaimed to the Israelites all that the LORD had commanded him concerning them. ⁴This was after he had defeated Sihon king of the Amorites, who reigned in Heshbon, and at Edrei had defeated Og king of Bashan, who reigned in Ashtaroth.

⁵East of the Jordan in the territory of Moab, Moses began to expound this law, saying:

⁶The LORD our God said to us at Horeb, "You have stayed long enough at this mountain. ⁷Break camp and advance into the hill country of the Amorites; go to all the neighboring peoples in the Arabah, in

the mountains, in the western foothills, in the Negev and along the coast, to the land of the Canaanites and to Lebanon, as far as the great river, the Euphrates. ⁸See, I have given you this land. Go in and take possession of the land that the LORD swore he would give to your fathers—to Abraham, Isaac and Jacob—and to their descendants after them."

The Appointment of Leaders

⁹At that time I said to you, "You are too heavy a burden for me to carry alone. ¹⁰The LORD your God has increased your numbers so that today you are as many as the stars in the sky. ¹¹May the LORD, the God of your fathers, increase you a thousand times and bless you as he has promised! ¹²But how can I bear your problems and your burdens and your disputes all by myself? ¹³Choose some wise, understanding and respected men from each of your tribes, and I will set them over you."

¹⁴You answered me, "What you propose to do is good."

¹⁵So I took the leading men of your tribes, wise and respected men, and appointed them to have authority over you—as commanders of thousands, of hundreds, of fifties and of tens and as tribal officials. ¹⁶And I charged your judges at that time: Hear the disputes between your brothers and judge fairly, whether the case is between brother Israelites or between one of them and an alien. ¹⁷Do not show partiality in judging; hear both small and great alike. Do not be afraid of any man, for judgment belongs to God. Bring me any case too hard for you, and I will hear it. ¹⁸And at that time I told you everything you were to do.

Spies Sent Out

¹⁹Then, as the LORD our God commanded us, we set out from Horeb and went toward the hill country of the Amorites through all that vast and dreadful desert that you have seen, and so we reached Kadesh Barnea. ²⁰Then I said to you, "You have reached the hill country of the Amorites, which the LORD our God is giving us. ²¹See, the LORD your God has given you the land. Go up and take possession of it as the LORD, the God of your

fathers, told you. Do not be afraid; do not be discouraged."

²²Then all of you came to me and said, "Let us send men ahead to spy out the land for us and bring back a report about the route we are to take and the towns we will come to."

²³The idea seemed good to me; so I selected twelve of you, one man from each tribe. ²⁴They left and went up into the hill country, and came to the Valley of Eshcol and explored it. ²⁵Taking with them some of the fruit of the land, they brought it down to us and reported, "It is a good land that the LORD our God is giving us."

Rebellion Against the LORD

²⁶But you were unwilling to go up; you rebelled against the command of the LORD your God. ²⁷You grumbled in your tents and said, "The LORD hates us; so he brought us out of Egypt to deliver us into the hands of the Amorites to destroy us. ²⁸Where can we go? Our brothers have made us lose heart. They say, 'The people are stronger and taller than we are; the cities are large, with walls up to the sky. We even saw the Anakites there.' "

²⁹Then I said to you, "Do not be terrified; do not be afraid of them. ³⁰The LORD your God, who is going before you, will fight for you, as he did for you in Egypt, before your very eyes, ³¹and in the desert. There you saw how the LORD your God carried you, as a father carries his son, all the way you went until you reached this place."

³²In spite of this, you did not trust in the LORD your God, ³³who went ahead of you on your journey, in fire by night and in a cloud by day, to search out places for you to camp and to show you the way you should go.

³⁴When the LORD heard what you said, he was angry and solemnly swore: ³⁵"Not a man of this evil generation shall see the good land I swore to give your forefathers, ³⁶except Caleb son of Jephunneh. He will see it, and I will give him and his descendants the land he set his feet on, because he followed the LORD wholeheartedly."

³⁷Because of you the LORD became angry with me also and said, "You shall not enter it, either. ³⁸But your assistant, Josh-

ua son of Nun, will enter it. Encourage him, because he will lead Israel to inherit it. [39]And the little ones that you said would be taken captive, your children who do not yet know good from bad—they will enter the land. I will give it to them and they will take possession of it. [40]But as for you, turn around and set out toward the desert along the route to the Red Sea.[a]"

[41]Then you replied, "We have sinned against the LORD. We will go up and fight, as the LORD our God commanded us." So every one of you put on his weapons, thinking it easy to go up into the hill country.

[42]But the LORD said to me, "Tell them, 'Do not go up and fight, because I will not be with you. You will be defeated by your enemies.'"

[43]So I told you, but you would not listen. You rebelled against the LORD's command and in your arrogance you marched up into the hill country. [44]The Amorites who lived in those hills came out against you; they chased you like a swarm of bees and beat you down from Seir all the way to Hormah. [45]You came back and wept before the LORD, but he paid no attention to your weeping and turned a deaf ear to you. [46]And so you stayed in Kadesh many days—all the time you spent there.

Wanderings in the Desert

2 Then we turned back and set out toward the desert along the route to the Red Sea,[a] as the LORD had directed me. For a long time we made our way around the hill country of Seir.

[2]Then the LORD said to me, [3]"You have made your way around this hill country long enough; now turn north. [4]Give the people these orders: 'You are about to pass through the territory of your brothers the descendants of Esau, who live in Seir. They will be afraid of you, but be very careful. [5]Do not provoke them to war, for I will not give you any of their land, not even enough to put your foot on. I have given Esau the hill country of Seir as his own. [6]You are to pay them in silver for the food you eat and the water you drink.'"

[7]The LORD your God has blessed you in all the work of your hands. He has watched over your journey through this vast desert. These forty years the LORD your God has been with you, and you have not lacked anything.

[8]So we went on past our brothers the descendants of Esau, who live in Seir. We turned from the Arabah road, which comes up from Elath and Ezion Geber, and traveled along the desert road of Moab.

[9]Then the LORD said to me, "Do not harass the Moabites or provoke them to war, for I will not give you any part of their land. I have given Ar to the descendants of Lot as a possession."

[10](The Emites used to live there—a people strong and numerous, and as tall as the Anakites. [11]Like the Anakites, they too were considered Rephaites, but the Moabites called them Emites. [12]Horites used to live in Seir, but the descendants of Esau drove them out. They destroyed the Horites from before them and settled in their place, just as Israel did in the land the LORD gave them as their possession.)

[13]And the LORD said, "Now get up and cross the Zered Valley." So we crossed the valley.

[14]Thirty-eight years passed from the time we left Kadesh Barnea until we crossed the Zered Valley. By then, that entire generation of fighting men had perished from the camp, as the LORD had sworn to them. [15]The LORD's hand was against them until he had completely eliminated them from the camp.

[16]Now when the last of these fighting men among the people had died, [17]the LORD said to me, [18]"Today you are to pass by the region of Moab at Ar. [19]When you come to the Ammonites, do not harass them or provoke them to war, for I will not give you possession of any land belonging to the Ammonites. I have given it as a possession to the descendants of Lot."

[20](That too was considered a land of the Rephaites, who used to live there; but the Ammonites called them Zamzummites. [21]They were a people strong and numerous, and as tall as the Anakites. The LORD destroyed them from before the Ammonites, who drove them out and settled in their place. [22]The LORD had done the same for the descendants of Esau,

[a]40,1 Hebrew *Yam Suph*; that is, Sea of Reeds

who lived in Seir, when he destroyed the Horites from before them. They drove them out and have lived in their place to this day. ²³And as for the Avvites who lived in villages as far as Gaza, the Caphtorites coming out from Caphtor[a] destroyed them and settled in their place.)

Defeat of Sihon King of Heshbon

²⁴"Set out now and cross the Arnon Gorge. See, I have given into your hand Sihon the Amorite, king of Heshbon, and his country. Begin to take possession of it and engage him in battle. ²⁵This very day I will begin to put the terror and fear of you on all the nations under heaven. They will hear reports of you and will tremble and be in anguish because of you."

²⁶From the desert of Kedemoth I sent messengers to Sihon king of Heshbon offering peace and saying, ²⁷"Let us pass through your country. We will stay on the main road; we will not turn aside to the right or to the left. ²⁸Sell us food to eat and water to drink for their price in silver. Only let us pass through on foot— ²⁹as the descendants of Esau, who live in Seir, and the Moabites, who live in Ar, did for us— until we cross the Jordan into the land the LORD our God is giving us." ³⁰But Sihon king of Heshbon refused to let us pass through. For the LORD your God had made his spirit stubborn and his heart obstinate in order to give him into your hands, as he has now done.

³¹The LORD said to me, "See, I have begun to deliver Sihon and his country over to you. Now begin to conquer and possess his land."

³²When Sihon and all his army came out to meet us in battle at Jahaz, ³³the LORD our God delivered him over to us and we struck him down, together with his sons and his whole army. ³⁴At that time we took all his towns and completely destroyed[b] them—men, women and children. We left no survivors. ³⁵But the livestock and the plunder from the towns we had captured we carried off for ourselves. ³⁶From Aroer on the rim of the Arnon Gorge, and from the town in the gorge, even as far as Gilead, not one town was too strong for us. The LORD our God gave us all of them. ³⁷But in accordance with the command of the LORD our God,

you did not encroach on any of the land of the Ammonites, neither the land along the course of the Jabbok nor that around the towns in the hills.

Defeat of Og King of Bashan

3 Next we turned and went up along the road toward Bashan, and Og king of Bashan with his whole army marched out to meet us in battle at Edrei. ²The LORD said to me, "Do not be afraid of him, for I have handed him over to you with his whole army and his land. Do to him what you did to Sihon king of the Amorites, who reigned in Heshbon."

³So the LORD our God also gave into our hands Og king of Bashan and all his army. We struck them down, leaving no survivors. ⁴At that time we took all his cities. There was not one of the sixty cities that we did not take from them—the whole region of Argob, Og's kingdom in Bashan. ⁵All these cities were fortified with high walls and with gates and bars, and there were also a great many unwalled villages. ⁶We completely destroyed[b] them, as we had done with Sihon king of Heshbon, destroying[b] every city—men, women and children. ⁷But all the livestock and the plunder from their cities we carried off for ourselves.

⁸So at that time we took from these two kings of the Amorites the territory east of the Jordan, from the Arnon Gorge as far as Mount Hermon. ⁹(Hermon is called Sirion by the Sidonians; the Amorites call it Senir.) ¹⁰We took all the towns on the plateau, and all Gilead, and all Bashan as far as Salecah and Edrei, towns of Og's kingdom in Bashan. ¹¹(Only Og king of Bashan was left of the remnant of the Rephaites. His bed[c] was made of iron and was more than thirteen feet long and six feet wide.[d] It is still in Rabbah of the Ammonites.)

Division of the Land

¹²Of the land that we took over at that time, I gave the Reubenites and the Gad-

---

a23 That is, Crete   *b34,6* The Hebrew term refers to the irrevocable giving over of things or persons to the LORD, often by totally destroying them.   *c11* Or *sarcophagus*   *d11* Hebrew *nine cubits long and four cubits wide* (about 4 meters long and 1.8 meters wide) ites the territory north of Aroer by the Arnon Gorge, including half the hill country of Gilead, together with its towns. ¹³The rest of Gilead and also all of Bashan, the kingdom of Og, I gave to the half tribe of Manasseh. (The whole region of Argob in Bashan used to be known as a land of the Rephaites. ¹⁴Jair, a descendant of Manasseh, took the whole region of Argob as far as the border of the Geshurites and the Maacathites; it was named after him, so that to this day Bashan is called Havvoth Jair.ᵃ) ¹⁵And I gave Gilead to Makir. ¹⁶But to the Reubenites and the Gadites I gave the territory extending from Gilead down to the Arnon Gorge (the middle of the gorge being the border) and out to the Jabbok River, which is the border of the Ammonites. ¹⁷Its western border was the Jordan in the Arabah, from Kinnereth to the Sea of the Arabah (the Salt Seaᵇ), below the slopes of Pisgah.

¹⁸I commanded you at that time: "The LORD your God has given you this land to take possession of it. But all your able-bodied men, armed for battle, must cross over ahead of your brother Israelites. ¹⁹However, your wives, your children and your livestock (I know you have much livestock) may stay in the towns I have given you, ²⁰until the LORD gives rest to your brothers as he has to you, and they too have taken over the land that the LORD your God is giving them, across the Jordan. After that, each of you may go back to the possession I have given you."

Moses Forbidden to Cross the Jordan

²¹At that time I commanded Joshua: "You have seen with your own eyes all that the LORD your God has done to these two kings. The LORD will do the same to all the kingdoms over there where you are going. ²²Do not be afraid of them; the LORD your God himself will fight for you."

²³At that time I pleaded with the LORD: ²⁴"O Sovereign LORD, you have begun to show to your servant your greatness and your strong hand. For what god is there in heaven or on earth who can do the deeds and mighty works you do? ²⁵Let me go over and see the good land beyond the Jordan—that fine hill country and Lebanon."

²⁶But because of you the LORD was angry with me and would not listen to me. "That is enough," the LORD said. "Do not speak to me anymore about this matter. ²⁷Go up to the top of Pisgah and look west and north and south and east. Look at the land with your own eyes, since you are not going to cross this Jordan. ²⁸But commission Joshua, and encourage and strengthen him, for he will lead this people across and will cause them to inherit the land that you will see." ²⁹So we stayed in the valley near Beth Peor.

Obedience Commanded

4 Hear now, O Israel, the decrees and laws I am about to teach you. Follow them so that you may live and may go in and take possession of the land that the LORD, the God of your fathers, is giving you. ²Do not add to what I command you and do not subtract from it, but keep the commands of the LORD your God that I give you.

³You saw with your own eyes what the LORD did at Baal Peor. The LORD your God destroyed from among you everyone who followed the Baal of Peor, ⁴but all of you who held fast to the LORD your God are still alive today.

⁵See, I have taught you decrees and laws as the LORD my God commanded me, so that you may follow them in the land you are entering to take possession of it. ⁶Observe them carefully, for this will show your wisdom and understanding to the nations, who will hear about all these decrees and say, "Surely this great nation is a wise and understanding people." ⁷What other nation is so great as to have their gods near them the way the LORD our God is near us whenever we pray to him? ⁸And what other nation is so great as to have such righteous decrees and laws as this body of laws I am setting before you today?

⁹Only be careful, and watch yourselves closely so that you do not forget the things your eyes have seen or let them slip from your heart as long as you live. Teach them to your children and to their children after them. ¹⁰Remember the day you stood before the LORD your God at Horeb,

ᵃ14 Or *called the settlements of Jair*   ᵇ17 That is, the Dead Sea when he said to me, "Assemble the people before me to hear my words so that they may learn to revere me as long as they live in the land and may teach them to their children." ¹¹You came near and stood at the foot of the mountain while it blazed with fire to the very heavens, with black clouds and deep darkness. ¹²Then the LORD spoke to you out of the fire. You heard the sound of words but saw no form; there was only a voice. ¹³He declared to you his covenant, the Ten Commandments, which he commanded you to follow and then wrote them on two stone tablets. ¹⁴And the LORD directed me at that time to teach you the decrees and laws you are to follow in the land that you are crossing the Jordan to possess.

Idolatry Forbidden

¹⁵You saw no form of any kind the day the LORD spoke to you at Horeb out of the fire. Therefore watch yourselves very carefully, ¹⁶so that you do not become corrupt and make for yourselves an idol, an image of any shape, whether formed like a man or a woman, ¹⁷or like any animal on earth or any bird that flies in the air, ¹⁸or like any creature that moves along the ground or any fish in the waters below. ¹⁹And when you look up to the sky and see the sun, the moon and the stars—all the heavenly array—do not be enticed into bowing down to them and worshiping things the LORD your God has apportioned to all the nations under heaven. ²⁰But as for you, the LORD took you and brought you out of the iron-smelting furnace, out of Egypt, to be the people of his inheritance, as you now are.

²¹The LORD was angry with me because of you, and he solemnly swore that I would not cross the Jordan and enter the good land the LORD your God is giving you as your inheritance. ²²I will die in this land; I will not cross the Jordan; but you are about to cross over and take possession of that good land. ²³Be careful not to forget the covenant of the LORD your God that he made with you; do not make for yourselves an idol in the form of anything the LORD your God has forbidden. ²⁴For the LORD your God is a consuming fire, a jealous God.

²⁵After you have had children and

grandchildren and have lived in the land a long time—if you then become corrupt and make any kind of idol, doing evil in the eyes of the LORD your God and provoking him to anger, ²⁶I call heaven and earth as witnesses against you this day that you will quickly perish from the land that you are crossing the Jordan to possess. You will not live there long but will certainly be destroyed. ²⁷The LORD will scatter you among the peoples, and only a few of you will survive among the nations to which the LORD will drive you. ²⁸There you will worship man-made gods of wood and stone, which cannot see or hear or eat or smell. ²⁹But if from there you seek the LORD your God, you will find him if you look for him with all your heart and with all your soul. ³⁰When you are in distress and all these things have happened to you, then in later days you will return to the LORD your God and obey him. ³¹For the LORD your God is a merciful God; he will not abandon or destroy you or forget the covenant with your forefathers, which he confirmed to them by oath.

The LORD Is God

³²Ask now about the former days, long before your time, from the day God created man on the earth; ask from one end of the heavens to the other. Has anything so great as this ever happened, or has anything like it ever been heard of? ³³Has any other people heard the voice of God*ᵃ* speaking out of fire, as you have, and lived? ³⁴Has any god ever tried to take for himself one nation out of another nation, by testings, by miraculous signs and wonders, by war, by a mighty hand and an outstretched arm, or by great and awesome deeds, like all the things the LORD your God did for you in Egypt before your very eyes?

³⁵You were shown these things so that you might know that the LORD is God; besides him there is no other. ³⁶From heaven he made you hear his voice to discipline you. On earth he showed you his great fire, and you heard his words from out of the fire. ³⁷Because he loved your forefathers and chose their descendants after them, he brought you out of

ᵃ33 Or *of a god*

Egypt by his Presence and his great strength, ³⁸to drive out before you nations greater and stronger than you and to bring you into their land to give it to you for your inheritance, as it is today.

³⁹Acknowledge and take to heart this day that the LORD is God in heaven above and on the earth below. There is no other. ⁴⁰Keep his decrees and commands, which I am giving you today, so that it may go well with you and your children after you and that you may live long in the land the LORD your God gives you for all time.

Cities of Refuge

⁴¹Then Moses set aside three cities east of the Jordan, ⁴²to which anyone who had killed a person could flee if he had unintentionally killed his neighbor without malice aforethought. He could flee into one of these cities and save his life. ⁴³The cities were these: Bezer in the desert plateau, for the Reubenites; Ramoth in Gilead, for the Gadites; and Golan in Bashan, for the Manassites.

Introduction to the Law

⁴⁴This is the law Moses set before the Israelites. ⁴⁵These are the stipulations, decrees and laws Moses gave them when they came out of Egypt ⁴⁶and were in the valley near Beth Peor east of the Jordan, in the land of Sihon king of the Amorites, who reigned in Heshbon and was defeated by Moses and the Israelites as they came out of Egypt. ⁴⁷They took possession of his land and the land of Og king of Bashan, the two Amorite kings east of the Jordan. ⁴⁸This land extended from Aroer on the rim of the Arnon Gorge to Mount Siyon^a (that is, Hermon), ⁴⁹and included all the Arabah east of the Jordan, as far as the Sea of the Arabah,^b below the slopes of Pisgah.

The Ten Commandments

5 Moses summoned all Israel and said:
Hear, O Israel, the decrees and laws I declare in your hearing today. Learn them and be sure to follow them. ²The LORD our God made a covenant with us at Horeb. ³It was not with our fathers that the LORD made this covenant, but with us, with all of us who are alive here today. ⁴The LORD spoke to you face to face out of

the fire on the mountain. ⁵(At that time I stood between the LORD and you to declare to you the word of the LORD, because you were afraid of the fire and did not go up the mountain.) And he said:

⁶"I am the LORD your God, who brought you out of Egypt, out of the land of slavery.

⁷"You shall have no other gods before^c me.

⁸"You shall not make for yourself an idol in the form of anything in heaven above or on the earth beneath or in the waters below. ⁹You shall not bow down to them or worship them; for I, the LORD your God, am a jealous God, punishing the children for the sin of the fathers to the third and fourth generation of those who hate me, ¹⁰but showing love to a thousand ⌊generations⌋ of those who love me and keep my commandments.

¹¹"You shall not misuse the name of the LORD your God, for the LORD will not hold anyone guiltless who misuses his name.

¹²"Observe the Sabbath day by keeping it holy, as the LORD your God has commanded you. ¹³Six days you shall labor and do all your work, ¹⁴but the seventh day is a Sabbath to the LORD your God. On it you shall not do any work, neither you, nor your son or daughter, nor your manservant or maidservant, nor your ox, your donkey or any of your animals, nor the alien within your gates, so that your manservant and maidservant may rest, as you do. ¹⁵Remember that you were slaves in Egypt and that the LORD your God brought you out of there with a mighty hand and an outstretched arm. Therefore the

^a48 Hebrew; Syriac (see also Deut. 3:9) *Sirion*   ^b49 That is, the Dead Sea   ^c7 Or *besides*

LORD your God has commanded you to observe the Sabbath day.

16 "Honor your father and your mother, as the LORD your God has commanded you, so that you may live long and that it may go well with you in the land the LORD your God is giving you.

17 "You shall not murder.

18 "You shall not commit adultery.

19 "You shall not steal.

20 "You shall not give false testimony against your neighbor.

21 "You shall not covet your neighbor's wife. You shall not set your desire on your neighbor's house or land, his manservant or maidservant, his ox or donkey, or anything that belongs to your neighbor."

22 These are the commandments the LORD proclaimed in a loud voice to your whole assembly there on the mountain from out of the fire, the cloud and the deep darkness; and he added nothing more. Then he wrote them on two stone tablets and gave them to me.

23 When you heard the voice out of the darkness, while the mountain was ablaze with fire, all the leading men of your tribes and your elders came to me. 24 And you said, "The LORD our God has shown us his glory and his majesty, and we have heard his voice from the fire. Today we have seen that a man can live even if God speaks with him. 25 But now, why should we die? This great fire will consume us, and we will die if we hear the voice of the LORD our God any longer. 26 For what mortal man has ever heard the voice of the living God speaking out of fire, as we have, and survived? 27 Go near and listen to all that the LORD our God says. Then tell us whatever the LORD our God tells you. We will listen and obey."

28 The LORD heard you when you spoke to me and the LORD said to me, "I have heard what this people said to you. Everything they said was good. 29 Oh, that their hearts would be inclined to fear me and keep all my commands always, so that it might go well with them and their children forever!

30 "Go, tell them to return to their tents. 31 But you stay here with me so that I may give you all the commands, decrees and laws you are to teach them to follow in the land I am giving them to possess."

32 So be careful to do what the LORD your God has commanded you; do not turn aside to the right or to the left. 33 Walk in all the way that the LORD your God has commanded you, so that you may live and prosper and prolong your days in the land that you will possess.

Love the LORD Your God

6 These are the commands, decrees and laws the LORD your God directed me to teach you to observe in the land that you are crossing the Jordan to possess, 2 so that you, your children and their children after them may fear the LORD your God as long as you live by keeping all his decrees and commands that I give you, and so that you may enjoy long life. 3 Hear, O Israel, and be careful to obey so that it may go well with you and that you may increase greatly in a land flowing with milk and honey, just as the LORD, the God of your fathers, promised you.

4 Hear, O Israel: The LORD our God, the LORD is one.[a] 5 Love the LORD your God with all your heart and with all your soul and with all your strength. 6 These commandments that I give you today are to be upon your hearts. 7 Impress them on your children. Talk about them when you sit at home and when you walk along the road, when you lie down and when you get up. 8 Tie them as symbols on your hands and bind them on your foreheads. 9 Write them on the doorframes of your houses and on your gates.

10 When the LORD your God brings you into the land he swore to your fathers, to Abraham, Isaac and Jacob, to give you—a land with large, flourishing cities you did not build, 11 houses filled with all kinds of good things you did not provide, wells you did not dig, and vineyards and olive groves you did not plant—then when you eat and are satisfied, 12 be careful that you do not forget the LORD, who brought

---

a4 Or The LORD our God is one LORD; or The LORD is our God, the LORD is one; or The LORD is our God, the LORD alone you out of Egypt, out of the land of slavery.

¹³Fear the LORD your God, serve him only and take your oaths in his name. ¹⁴Do not follow other gods, the gods of the peoples around you; ¹⁵for the LORD your God, who is among you, is a jealous God and his anger will burn against you, and he will destroy you from the face of the land. ¹⁶Do not test the LORD your God as you did at Massah. ¹⁷Be sure to keep the commands of the LORD your God and the stipulations and decrees he has given you. ¹⁸Do what is right and good in the LORD's sight, so that it may go well with you and you may go in and take over the good land that the LORD promised on oath to your forefathers, ¹⁹thrusting out all your enemies before you, as the LORD said.

²⁰In the future, when your son asks you, "What is the meaning of the stipulations, decrees and laws the LORD our God has commanded you?" ²¹tell him: "We were slaves of Pharaoh in Egypt, but the LORD brought us out of Egypt with a mighty hand. ²²Before our eyes the LORD sent miraculous signs and wonders—great and terrible—upon Egypt and Pharaoh and his whole household. ²³But he brought us out from there to bring us in and give us the land that he promised on oath to our forefathers. ²⁴The LORD commanded us to obey all these decrees and to fear the LORD our God, so that we might always prosper and be kept alive, as is the case today. ²⁵And if we are careful to obey all this law before the LORD our God, as he has commanded us, that will be our righteousness."

Driving Out the Nations

7 When the LORD your God brings you into the land you are entering to possess and drives out before you many nations—the Hittites, Girgashites, Amorites, Canaanites, Perizzites, Hivites and Jebusites, seven nations larger and stronger than you— ²and when the LORD your God has delivered them over to you and you have defeated them, then you must destroy them totally.ᵃ Make no treaty with them, and show them no mercy. ³Do not intermarry with them. Do not give your daughters to their sons or take their daughters for your sons, ⁴for they will turn your sons away from following me to serve other gods, and the LORD's anger

ᵃ2 The Hebrew term refers to the irrevocable giving over of things or persons to the LORD, often by totally destroying them; also in verse 26.

Generational Blessings

Friday

DEUTERONOMY 6:5–6 This passage challenges us to love God with all of our heart, soul and strength. Loving God with our heart involves our mind and our intellect as expressed through our personality. Loving God with our soul involves our will and our desires. When we love God with all our strength, we invest our energy.

If we really love God with such an active and consuming love, it naturally follows that we will talk about God with our children. And we can pass along the secret behind healthy marriages in the same way—when we love our spouse with our heart, soul and strength, our children will see our love in action.

During the active parenting years, we tried to let our children know how much we loved each other and, from time to time, solicited their help in expressing it. Once the boys helped me plan a surprise getaway for Claudia. Another time they helped Claudia put together a Father's Day slide show that featured our love story along with the birth of each child. Even today we still enjoy watching it. Amazingly, years later our three sons shared our slide show with three girls who are now our daughters-in-law!

Why not think about ways you can show your children how much you love their mom or dad? As they observe your love in action for God and for your mate, they will begin to realize how much you love them as well.

—*Dave & Claudia*

Go to page 190 for your next devotional reading.

will burn against you and will quickly destroy you. ⁵This is what you are to do to them: Break down their altars, smash their sacred stones, cut down their Asherah poles*a* and burn their idols in the fire. ⁶For you are a people holy to the LORD your God. The LORD your God has chosen you out of all the peoples on the face of the earth to be his people, his treasured possession.

⁷The LORD did not set his affection on you and choose you because you were more numerous than other peoples, for you were the fewest of all peoples. ⁸But it was because the LORD loved you and kept the oath he swore to your forefathers that he brought you out with a mighty hand and redeemed you from the land of slavery, from the power of Pharaoh king of Egypt. ⁹Know therefore that the LORD your God is God; he is the faithful God, keeping his covenant of love to a thousand generations of those who love him and keep his commands. ¹⁰But

> those who hate him he will repay to
> their face by destruction;
> he will not be slow to repay to
> their face those who hate
> him.

¹¹Therefore, take care to follow the commands, decrees and laws I give you today.

¹²If you pay attention to these laws and are careful to follow them, then the LORD your God will keep his covenant of love with you, as he swore to your forefathers. ¹³He will love you and bless you and increase your numbers. He will bless the fruit of your womb, the crops of your land—your grain, new wine and oil—the calves of your herds and the lambs of

---

a5 That is, symbols of the goddess Asherah; here and elsewhere in Deuteronomy

---

Unswerving Commitment

Quiet TIMES *with each other*

DEUTERONOMY 7:9 "It is easier in the United States to walk away from a marriage than from a commitment to purchase a used car," said an attorney at a conference we attended. "Most contracts cannot be unilaterally terminated; a marriage commitment, however, can be broken by practically anyone at any time, and without cause."

He is right. A friend of ours went to traffic court, where he heard two divorce decrees from the judge before his turn came. He dropped by our office later to tell us about his experience. He said, "I told my wife when I got home that we could have had a divorce any number of times if those reasons I heard in court were good enough for a legal separation."

The "till death do us part" of marriage, however, is not simply an ideal. It is a reality that is ensured by an unswerving commitment—an intentional agreement to keep love alive. "Do two walk together unless they have agreed to do so?" asked the prophet Amos (Amos 3:3). Commitment is the cerebral part of love, the part that comes more from our mind than our heart.

Why do so many marriage commitments fall flat these days? We believe it is because too many promises are made without the promises of God. We need to "hold unswervingly to the hope we profess, for he who promised is faithful" (Hebrews 10:23). Our commitment to each other in marriage is sustained by God's model of commitment, or faithfulness, to us. When a man and woman covenant with one another, God promises faithfulness to them (see 1 Corinthians 1:9). His faithfulness is woven throughout the Bible—from Genesis, where God initiates his rainbow promise of faithfulness, through Revelation, where John's vision depicts "a white horse, whose rider is called Faithful and True" (19:11).

—*Les & Leslie*

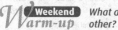

Weekend Warm-up *What are some signs or expressions of your unswerving commitment to each other?*

Go to page 192 for your next devotional reading.

your flocks in the land that he swore to your forefathers to give you. ¹⁴You will be blessed more than any other people; none of your men or women will be childless, nor any of your livestock without young. ¹⁵The LORD will keep you free from every disease. He will not inflict on you the horrible diseases you knew in Egypt, but he will inflict them on all who hate you. ¹⁶You must destroy all the peoples the LORD your God gives over to you. Do not look on them with pity and do not serve their gods, for that will be a snare to you.

¹⁷You may say to yourselves, "These nations are stronger than we are. How can we drive them out?" ¹⁸But do not be afraid of them; remember well what the LORD your God did to Pharaoh and to all Egypt. ¹⁹You saw with your own eyes the great trials, the miraculous signs and wonders, the mighty hand and outstretched arm, with which the LORD your God brought you out. The LORD your God will do the same to all the peoples you now fear. ²⁰Moreover, the LORD your God will send the hornet among them until even the survivors who hide from you have perished. ²¹Do not be terrified by them, for the LORD your God, who is among you, is a great and awesome God. ²²The LORD your God will drive out those nations before you, little by little. You will not be allowed to eliminate them all at once, or the wild animals will multiply around you. ²³But the LORD your God will deliver them over to you, throwing them into great confusion until they are destroyed. ²⁴He will give their kings into your hand, and you will wipe out their names from under heaven. No one will be able to stand up against you; you will destroy them. ²⁵The images of their gods you are to burn in the fire. Do not covet the silver and gold on them, and do not take it for yourselves, or you will be ensnared by it, for it is detestable to the LORD your God. ²⁶Do not bring a detestable thing into your house or you, like it, will be set apart for destruction. Utterly abhor and detest it, for it is set apart for destruction.

Do Not Forget the LORD

8 Be careful to follow every command I am giving you today, so that you may live and increase and may enter and possess the land that the LORD promised on oath to your forefathers. ²Remember how the LORD your God led you all the way in the desert these forty years, to humble you and to test you in order to know what was in your heart, whether or not you would keep his commands. ³He humbled you, causing you to hunger and then feeding you with manna, which neither you nor your fathers had known, to teach you that man does not live on bread alone but on every word that comes from the mouth of the LORD. ⁴Your clothes did not wear out and your feet did not swell during these forty years. ⁵Know then in your heart that as a man disciplines his son, so the LORD your God disciplines you.

⁶Observe the commands of the LORD your God, walking in his ways and revering him. ⁷For the LORD your God is bringing you into a good land—a land with streams and pools of water, with springs flowing in the valleys and hills; ⁸a land with wheat and barley, vines and fig trees, pomegranates, olive oil and honey; ⁹a land where bread will not be scarce and you will lack nothing; a land where the rocks are iron and you can dig copper out of the hills.

¹⁰When you have eaten and are satisfied, praise the LORD your God for the good land he has given you. ¹¹Be careful that you do not forget the LORD your God, failing to observe his commands, his laws and his decrees that I am giving you this day. ¹²Otherwise, when you eat and are satisfied, when you build fine houses and settle down, ¹³and when your herds and flocks grow large and your silver and gold increase and all you have is multiplied, ¹⁴then your heart will become proud and you will forget the LORD your God, who brought you out of Egypt, out of the land of slavery. ¹⁵He led you through the vast and dreadful desert, that thirsty and waterless land, with its venomous snakes and scorpions. He brought you water out of hard rock. ¹⁶He gave you manna to eat in the desert, something your fathers had never known, to humble and to test you so that in the end it might go well with you. ¹⁷You may say to yourself, "My power and the strength of my hands produced this wealth for me." ¹⁸But the LORD your God, for it is he

you the ability to produce wealth, and so confirms his covenant, which he swore to your forefathers, as it is today.

[19]If you ever forget the LORD your God and follow other gods and worship and bow down to them, I testify against you today that you will surely be destroyed. [20]Like the nations the LORD destroyed before you, so you will be destroyed for not obeying the LORD your God.

Not Because of Israel's Righteousness

9 Hear, O Israel. You are now about to cross the Jordan to go in and dispossess nations greater and stronger than you, with large cities that have walls up to the sky. [2]The people are strong and tall—Anakites! You know about them and have heard it said: "Who can stand up against the Anakites?" [3]But be assured today that the LORD your God is the one who goes across ahead of you like a devouring fire. He will destroy them; he will subdue them before you. And you will drive them out and annihilate them quickly, as the LORD has promised you.

[4]After the LORD your God has driven them out before you, do not say to yourself, "The LORD has brought me here to take possession of this land because of my righteousness." No, it is on account of the wickedness of these nations that the LORD is going to drive them out before you. [5]It is not because of your righteousness or your integrity that you are going in to take possession of their land; but on account of the wickedness of these nations, the LORD your God will drive them out before you, to accomplish what he swore to your fathers, to Abraham, Isaac and Jacob. [6]Understand, then, that it is not because of your righteousness that the LORD your God is giving you this good land to possess, for you are a stiff-necked people.

The Golden Calf

[7]Remember this and never forget how you provoked the LORD your God to anger in the desert. From the day you left Egypt until you arrived here, you have been rebellious against the LORD. [8]At Horeb you aroused the LORD's wrath so that

Pathetic Pride

Monday

DEUTERONOMY 8:10–18   What is it about human nature that so often makes us negligent about our relationship with God—especially when things are going well in our lives? When we are in difficult circumstances we have little or no control over, we are quick to run to God and beg for his intervention. At such times we know we need his control in our lives and marriages. During the best of times, however, we tend to act as if we are in control and don't *need* God.

Several years ago we were speaking together at a large marriage conference. It was one of those times when everything went perfectly and we were overwhelmed by the wonderful reception. On the flight home as we were congratulating ourselves, we stopped and suddenly realized our pathetic pride.

As God's created beings, we need to constantly remind ourselves that the good

times are a result of his blessings. God is the giver of every blessing—directly or indirectly. We are never in such a position of prosperity that we don't need his presence in our lives.

In Deuteronomy 8, God addresses our propensity to forget the blessing Giver. He tells us in verse 17 that our material, emotional and spiritual blessings do not come from our own strength and ability. Verse 18 reminds us that even the ability to earn a comfortable lifestyle is a gift from him. Our blessings are not a result of the way we have taken control of our lives. God is in control.

This is a much needed reminder for spouses. In both the good times and the difficult times, we should run quickly to the blessing Giver, for all blessings come from him.

—**Bob & Rosemary**

Go to page 198 for your next devotional reading.

he was angry enough to destroy you. [9]When I went up on the mountain to receive the tablets of stone, the tablets of the covenant that the LORD had made with you, I stayed on the mountain forty days and forty nights; I ate no bread and drank no water. [10]The LORD gave me two stone tablets inscribed by the finger of God. On them were all the commandments the LORD proclaimed to you on the mountain out of the fire, on the day of the assembly.

[11]At the end of the forty days and forty nights, the LORD gave me the two stone tablets, the tablets of the covenant. [12]Then the LORD told me, "Go down from here at once, because your people whom you brought out of Egypt have become corrupt. They have turned away quickly from what I commanded them and have made a cast idol for themselves."

[13]And the LORD said to me, "I have seen this people, and they are a stiff-necked people indeed! [14]Let me alone, so that I may destroy them and blot out their name from under heaven. And I will make you into a nation stronger and more numerous than they."

[15]So I turned and went down from the mountain while it was ablaze with fire. And the two tablets of the covenant were in my hands.[a] [16]When I looked, I saw that you had sinned against the LORD your God; you had made for yourselves an idol cast in the shape of a calf. You had turned aside quickly from the way that the LORD had commanded you. [17]So I took the two tablets and threw them out of my hands, breaking them to pieces before your eyes.

[18]Then once again I fell prostrate before the LORD for forty days and forty nights; I ate no bread and drank no water, because of all the sin you had committed, doing what was evil in the LORD's sight and so provoking him to anger. [19]I feared the anger and wrath of the LORD, for he was angry enough with you to destroy you. But again the LORD listened to me. [20]And the LORD was angry enough with Aaron to destroy him, but at that time I prayed for Aaron too. [21]Also I took that sinful thing of yours, the calf you had made, and burned it in the fire. Then I crushed it and ground it to powder as fine

JUST BETWEEN you & me

Pathetic Pride

Take a moment to answer each of these questions on your own. Then compare your answers to your spouse's.

Yes No Whenever I receive a blessing, I am quick to give God the credit.

Yes No Knowing that each blessing I receive is really from God, I share them with people around me.

Yes No The last time I received a blessing, I was so grateful to God that I gave away more than my usual portion.

Yes No When I look over my adult life, I would say that the blessings I have received have made me more of a giving person.

as dust and threw the dust into a stream that flowed down the mountain.

[22]You also made the LORD angry at Taberah, at Massah and at Kibroth Hattaavah.

[23]And when the LORD sent you out from Kadesh Barnea, he said, "Go up and take possession of the land I have given you." But you rebelled against the command of the LORD your God. You did not trust him or obey him. [24]You have been rebellious against the LORD ever since I have known you.

[25]I lay prostrate before the LORD those forty days and forty nights because the LORD had said he would destroy you. [26]I prayed to the LORD and said, "O Sovereign LORD, do not destroy your people, your own inheritance that you redeemed by your great power and brought out of Egypt with a mighty hand. [27]Remember your servants Abraham, Isaac and Jacob. Overlook the stubbornness of this people, their wickedness and their sin. [28]Otherwise, the country from which you brought us will say, 'Because the LORD was not able to take them into the land he had promised them, and because he hated them, he brought them out to put

a15 Or And I had the two tablets of the covenant with me, one in each hand them to death in the desert.' ²⁹But they are your people, your inheritance that you brought out by your great power and your outstretched arm."

Tablets Like the First Ones

10 At that time the LORD said to me, "Chisel out two stone tablets like the first ones and come up to me on the mountain. Also make a wooden chest.ᵃ ²I will write on the tablets the words that were on the first tablets, which you broke. Then you are to put them in the chest."

³So I made the ark out of acacia wood and chiseled out two stone tablets like the first ones, and I went up on the mountain with the two tablets in my hands. ⁴The LORD wrote on these tablets what he had written before, the Ten Commandments he had proclaimed to you on the mountain, out of the fire, on the day of the assembly. And the LORD gave them to me. ⁵Then I came back down the mountain and put the tablets in the ark I had made, as the LORD commanded me, and they are there now.

⁶(The Israelites traveled from the wells of the Jaakanites to Moserah. There Aaron died and was buried, and Eleazar his son succeeded him as priest. ⁷From there they traveled to Gudgodah and on to Jotbathah, a land with streams of water. ⁸At that time the LORD set apart the tribe of Levi to carry the ark of the covenant of the LORD, to stand before the LORD to minister and to pronounce blessings in his name, as they still do today. ⁹That is why the Levites have no share or inheritance among their brothers; the LORD is their inheritance, as the LORD your God told them.)

¹⁰Now I had stayed on the mountain forty days and nights, as I did the first time, and the LORD listened to me at this time also. It was not his will to destroy you. ¹¹"Go," the LORD said to me, "and lead the people on their way, so that they may enter and possess the land that I swore to their fathers to give them."

Fear the LORD

¹²And now, O Israel, what does the LORD your God ask of you but to fear the LORD your God, to walk in all his ways, to love him, to serve the LORD your God

with all your heart and with all your soul, ¹³and to observe the LORD's commands and decrees that I am giving you today for your own good?

¹⁴To the LORD your God belong the heavens, even the highest heavens, the earth and everything in it. ¹⁵Yet the LORD set his affection on your forefathers and loved them, and he chose you, their descendants, above all the nations, as it is today. ¹⁶Circumcise your hearts, therefore, and do not be stiff-necked any longer. ¹⁷For the LORD your God is God of gods and Lord of lords, the great God, mighty and awesome, who shows no partiality and accepts no bribes. ¹⁸He defends the cause of the fatherless and the widow, and loves the alien, giving him food and clothing. ¹⁹And you are to love those who are aliens, for you yourselves were aliens in Egypt. ²⁰Fear the LORD your God and serve him. Hold fast to him and take your oaths in his name. ²¹He is your praise; he is your God, who performed for you those great and awesome wonders you saw with your own eyes. ²²Your forefathers who went down into Egypt were seventy in all, and now the LORD your God has made you as numerous as the stars in the sky.

Love and Obey the LORD

11 Love the LORD your God and keep his requirements, his decrees, his laws and his commands always. ²Remember today that your children were not the ones who saw and experienced the discipline of the LORD your God: his majesty, his mighty hand, his outstretched arm; ³the signs he performed and the things he did in the heart of Egypt, both to Pharaoh king of Egypt and to his whole country; ⁴what he did to the Egyptian army, to its horses and chariots, how he overwhelmed them with the waters of the Red Seaᵇ as they were pursuing you, and how the LORD brought lasting ruin on them. ⁵It was not your children who saw what he did for you in the desert until you arrived at this place, ⁶and what he did to Dathan and Abiram, sons of Eliab the Reubenite, when the earth opened its mouth right in the middle of all Israel and swallowed

---

ᵃ1 That is, an ark   ᵇ4 Hebrew *Yam Suph*; that is, Sea of Reeds them up with their households, their tents and every living thing that belonged to them. ⁷But it was your own eyes that saw all these great things the LORD has done.

⁸Observe therefore all the commands I am giving you today, so that you may have the strength to go in and take over the land that you are crossing the Jordan to possess, ⁹and so that you may live long in the land that the LORD swore to your forefathers to give to them and their descendants, a land flowing with milk and honey. ¹⁰The land you are entering to take over is not like the land of Egypt, from which you have come, where you planted your seed and irrigated it by foot as in a vegetable garden. ¹¹But the land you are crossing the Jordan to take possession of is a land of mountains and valleys that drinks rain from heaven. ¹²It is a land the LORD your God cares for; the eyes of the LORD your God are continually on it from the beginning of the year to its end.

¹³So if you faithfully obey the commands I am giving you today—to love the LORD your God and to serve him with all your heart and with all your soul— ¹⁴then I will send rain on your land in its season, both autumn and spring rains, so that you may gather in your grain, new wine and oil. ¹⁵I will provide grass in the fields for your cattle, and you will eat and be satisfied.

¹⁶Be careful, or you will be enticed to turn away and worship other gods and bow down to them. ¹⁷Then the LORD's anger will burn against you, and he will shut the heavens so that it will not rain and the ground will yield no produce, and you will soon perish from the good land the LORD is giving you. ¹⁸Fix these words of mine in your hearts and minds; tie them as symbols on your hands and bind them on your foreheads. ¹⁹Teach them to your children, talking about them when you sit at home and when you walk along the road, when you lie down and when you get up. ²⁰Write them on the doorframes of your houses and on your gates, ²¹so that your days and the days of your children may be many in the land that the LORD swore to give your forefathers, as many as the days that the heavens are above the earth.

²²If you carefully observe all these commands I am giving you to follow—to love the LORD your God, to walk in all his ways and to hold fast to him— ²³then the LORD will drive out all these nations before you, and you will dispossess nations larger and stronger than you. ²⁴Every place where you set your foot will be yours: Your territory will extend from the desert to Lebanon, and from the Euphrates River to the western sea.ᵃ ²⁵No man will be able to stand against you. The LORD your God, as he promised you, will put the terror and fear of you on the whole land, wherever you go.

²⁶See, I am setting before you today a blessing and a curse— ²⁷the blessing if you obey the commands of the LORD your God that I am giving you today; ²⁸the curse if you disobey the commands of the LORD your God and turn from the way that I command you today by following other gods, which you have not known. ²⁹When the LORD your God has brought you into the land you are entering to possess, you are to proclaim on Mount Gerizim the blessings, and on Mount Ebal the curses. ³⁰As you know, these mountains are across the Jordan, west of the road,ᵇ toward the setting sun, near the great trees of Moreh, in the territory of those Canaanites living in the Arabah in the vicinity of Gilgal. ³¹You are about to cross the Jordan to enter and take possession of the land the LORD your God is giving you. When you have taken it over and are living there, ³²be sure that you obey all the decrees and laws I am setting before you today.

The One Place of Worship

12 These are the decrees and laws you must be careful to follow in the land that the LORD, the God of your fathers, has given you to possess—as long as you live in the land. ²Destroy completely all the places on the high mountains and on the hills and under every spreading tree where the nations you are dispossessing worship their gods. ³Break down their altars, smash their sacred stones and burn their Asherah poles in the fire; cut down the idols of their gods and wipe out their names from those places.

ᵃ24 That is, the Mediterranean   ᵇ30 Or *Jordan, westward*

⁴You must not worship the LORD your God in their way. ⁵But you are to seek the place the LORD your God will choose from among all your tribes to put his Name there for his dwelling. To that place you must go; ⁶there bring your burnt offerings and sacrifices, your tithes and special gifts, what you have vowed to give and your freewill offerings, and the firstborn of your herds and flocks. ⁷There, in the presence of the LORD your God, you and your families shall eat and shall rejoice in everything you have put your hand to, because the LORD your God has blessed you.

⁸You are not to do as we do here today, everyone as he sees fit, ⁹since you have not yet reached the resting place and the inheritance the LORD your God is giving you. ¹⁰But you will cross the Jordan and settle in the land the LORD your God is giving you as an inheritance, and he will give you rest from all your enemies around you so that you will live in safety. ¹¹Then to the place the LORD your God will choose as a dwelling for his Name—there you are to bring everything I command you: your burnt offerings and sacrifices, your tithes and special gifts, and all the choice possessions you have vowed to the LORD. ¹²And there rejoice before the LORD your God, you, your sons and daughters, your menservants and maidservants, and the Levites from your towns, who have no allotment or inheritance of their own. ¹³Be careful not to sacrifice your burnt offerings anywhere you please. ¹⁴Offer them only at the place the LORD will choose in one of your tribes, and there observe everything I command you.

¹⁵Nevertheless, you may slaughter your animals in any of your towns and eat as much of the meat as you want, as if it were gazelle or deer, according to the blessing the LORD your God gives you. Both the ceremonially unclean and the clean may eat it. ¹⁶But you must not eat the blood; pour it out on the ground like water. ¹⁷You must not eat in your own towns the tithe of your grain and new wine and oil, or the firstborn of your herds and flocks, or whatever you have vowed to give, or your freewill offerings or special gifts. ¹⁸Instead, you are to eat them in the presence of the LORD your

God at the place the LORD your God will choose—you, your sons and daughters, your menservants and maidservants, and the Levites from your towns—and you are to rejoice before the LORD your God in everything you put your hand to. ¹⁹Be careful not to neglect the Levites as long as you live in your land.

²⁰When the LORD your God has enlarged your territory as he promised you, and you crave meat and say, "I would like some meat," then you may eat as much of it as you want. ²¹If the place where the LORD your God chooses to put his Name is too far away from you, you may slaughter animals from the herds and flocks the LORD has given you, as I have commanded you, and in your own towns you may eat as much of them as you want. ²²Eat them as you would gazelle or deer. Both the ceremonially unclean and the clean may eat. ²³But be sure you do not eat the blood, because the blood is the life, and you must not eat the life with the meat. ²⁴You must not eat the blood; pour it out on the ground like water. ²⁵Do not eat it, so that it may go well with you and your children after you, because you will be doing what is right in the eyes of the LORD.

²⁶But take your consecrated things and whatever you have vowed to give, and go to the place the LORD will choose. ²⁷Present your burnt offerings on the altar of the LORD your God, both the meat and the blood. The blood of your sacrifices must be poured beside the altar of the LORD your God, but you may eat the meat. ²⁸Be careful to obey all these regulations I am giving you, so that it may always go well with you and your children after you, because you will be doing what is good and right in the eyes of the LORD your God.

²⁹The LORD your God will cut off before you the nations you are about to invade and dispossess. But when you have driven them out and settled in their land, ³⁰and after they have been destroyed before you, be careful not to be ensnared by inquiring about their gods, saying, "How do these nations serve their gods? We will do the same." ³¹You must not worship the LORD your God in their way, because in worshiping their gods, they do all kinds of detestable things the LORD hates. They

even burn their sons and daughters in the fire as sacrifices to their gods.

³²See that you do all I command you; do not add to it or take away from it.

Worshiping Other Gods

13 If a prophet, or one who foretells by dreams, appears among you and announces to you a miraculous sign or wonder, ²and if the sign or wonder of which he has spoken takes place, and he says, "Let us follow other gods" (gods you have not known) "and let us worship them," ³you must not listen to the words of that prophet or dreamer. The LORD your God is testing you to find out whether you love him with all your heart and with all your soul. ⁴It is the LORD your God you must follow, and him you must revere. Keep his commands and obey him; serve him and hold fast to him. ⁵That prophet or dreamer must be put to death, because he preached rebellion against the LORD your God, who brought you out of Egypt and redeemed you from the land of slavery; he has tried to turn you from the way the LORD your God commanded you to follow. You must purge the evil from among you.

⁶If your very own brother, or your son or daughter, or the wife you love, or your closest friend secretly entices you, saying, "Let us go and worship other gods" (gods that neither you nor your fathers have known, ⁷gods of the peoples around you, whether near or far, from one end of the land to the other), ⁸do not yield to him or listen to him. Show him no pity. Do not spare him or shield him. ⁹You must certainly put him to death. Your hand must be the first in putting him to death, and then the hands of all the people. ¹⁰Stone him to death, because he tried to turn you away from the LORD your God, who brought you out of Egypt, out of the land of slavery. ¹¹Then all Israel will hear and be afraid, and no one among you will do such an evil thing again.

¹²If you hear it said about one of the towns the LORD your God is giving you to live in ¹³that wicked men have arisen among you and have led the people of their town astray, saying, "Let us go and worship other gods" (gods you have not known), ¹⁴then you must inquire, probe and investigate it thoroughly. And if it is true and it has been proved that this detestable thing has been done among you, ¹⁵you must certainly put to the sword all who live in that town. Destroy it completely,ᵃ both its people and its livestock. ¹⁶Gather all the plunder of the town into the middle of the public square and completely burn the town and all its plunder as a whole burnt offering to the LORD your God. It is to remain a ruin forever, never to be rebuilt. ¹⁷None of those condemned thingsᵃ shall be found in your hands, so that the LORD will turn from his fierce anger; he will show you mercy, have compassion on you, and increase your numbers, as he promised on oath to your forefathers, ¹⁸because you obey the LORD your God, keeping all his commands that I am giving you today and doing what is right in his eyes.

Clean and Unclean Food

14 You are the children of the LORD your God. Do not cut yourselves or shave the front of your heads for the dead, ²for you are a people holy to the LORD your God. Out of all the peoples on the face of the earth, the LORD has chosen you to be his treasured possession.

³Do not eat any detestable thing. ⁴These are the animals you may eat: the ox, the sheep, the goat, ⁵the deer, the gazelle, the roe deer, the wild goat, the ibex, the antelope and the mountain sheep.ᵇ ⁶You may eat any animal that has a split hoof divided in two and that chews the cud. ⁷However, of those that chew the cud or that have a split hoof completely divided you may not eat the camel, the rabbit or the coney.ᶜ Although they chew the cud, they do not have a split hoof; they are ceremonially unclean for you. ⁸The pig is also unclean; although it has a split hoof, it does not chew the cud. You are not to eat their meat or touch their carcasses.

⁹Of all the creatures living in the water, you may eat any that has fins and scales. ¹⁰But anything that does not have fins

---

ᵃ15,17 The Hebrew term refers to the irrevocable giving over of things or persons to the LORD, often by totally destroying them.   ᵇ5 The precise identification of some of the birds and animals in this chapter is uncertain.   ᶜ7 That is, the hyrax or rock badger

JUST BETWEEN you & me

The Most Common "Other God"

Take a moment to answer each of these questions on your own. Then compare your answers to your spouse's.

Yes No Money is one of the top sources of conflict in our marriage.

Yes No Has money at times become like a "god" in our marriage?

Yes No I want to change the way we manage money in our home.

Yes No Am I more of a spender than a saver compared to my spouse?

Yes No I had good models of money management when I was growing up.

and scales you may not eat; for you it is unclean.

¹¹You may eat any clean bird. ¹²But these you may not eat: the eagle, the vulture, the black vulture, ¹³the red kite, the black kite, any kind of falcon, ¹⁴any kind of raven, ¹⁵the horned owl, the screech owl, the gull, any kind of hawk, ¹⁶the little owl, the great owl, the white owl, ¹⁷the desert owl, the osprey, the cormorant, ¹⁸the stork, any kind of heron, the hoopoe and the bat.

¹⁹All flying insects that swarm are unclean to you; do not eat them. ²⁰But any winged creature that is clean you may eat.

²¹Do not eat anything you find already dead. You may give it to an alien living in any of your towns, and he may eat it, or you may sell it to a foreigner. But you are a people holy to the LORD your God.

Do not cook a young goat in its mother's milk.

Tithes

²²Be sure to set aside a tenth of all that your fields produce each year. ²³Eat the tithe of your grain, new wine and oil, and the firstborn of your herds and flocks in the presence of the LORD your God at the place he will choose as a dwelling for his Name, so that you may learn to revere the LORD your God always. ²⁴But if that place is too distant and you have been blessed by the LORD your God and cannot carry your tithe (because the place where the LORD will choose to put his Name is so far away), ²⁵then exchange your tithe for silver, and take the silver with you and go to the place the LORD your God will choose. ²⁶Use the silver to buy whatever you like: cattle, sheep, wine or other fermented drink, or anything you wish. Then you and your household shall eat there in the presence of the LORD your God and rejoice. ²⁷And do not neglect the Levites living in your towns, for they have no allotment or inheritance of their own.

The Most Common "Other God"

Tuesday

DEUTERONOMY 13 Of all the "other gods" married couples are prone to follow, none can be more tempting than money. It's hard to admit, but most us are drawn to the promises and dreams of wealth. And, while money itself is not evil, the *love* of money is. For when we love money, it becomes a god (see 1 Timothy 6:10).

In spite of our fondness for money, research has shown that it is difficult for most couples to talk about it. Jesus spoke about money more frequently than any other subject except the kingdom of God. The range of his concern is startling—from teachings on

trust in Matthew 6 to teachings on the danger of wealth in Luke 6:24, from the parable of the sower (Matthew 13:22) to the parable of the rich farmer (Luke 12:16–21), from the encounter with the rich young ruler (Matthew 19:21) to the encounter with Zacchaeus (Luke 19). Maybe you and your spouse are not in danger of worshiping the "other god" of money. But if you don't talk about it, you might not see the danger signs.

—Les & Leslie

Go to page 199 for your next devotional reading.

²⁸At the end of every three years, bring all the tithes of that year's produce and store it in your towns, ²⁹so that the Levites (who have no allotment or inheritance of their own) and the aliens, the fatherless and the widows who live in your towns may come and eat and be satisfied, and so that the LORD your God may bless you in all the work of your hands.

The Year for Canceling Debts

15 At the end of every seven years you must cancel debts. ²This is how it is to be done: Every creditor shall cancel the loan he has made to his fellow Israelite. He shall not require payment from his fellow Israelite or brother, because the LORD's time for canceling debts has been proclaimed. ³You may require payment from a foreigner, but you must cancel any debt your brother owes you. ⁴However, there should be no poor among you, for in the land the LORD your God is giving you to possess as your inheritance, he will richly bless you, ⁵if only you fully obey the LORD your God and are careful to fol-

low all these commands I am giving you today. ⁶For the LORD your God will bless you as he has promised, and you will lend to many nations but will borrow from none. You will rule over many nations but none will rule over you.

⁷If there is a poor man among your brothers in any of the towns of the land that the LORD your God is giving you, do not be hardhearted or tightfisted toward your poor brother. ⁸Rather be openhanded and freely lend him whatever he needs. ⁹Be careful not to harbor this wicked thought: "The seventh year, the year for canceling debts, is near," so that you do not show ill will toward your needy brother and give him nothing. He may then appeal to the LORD against you, and you will be found guilty of sin. ¹⁰Give generously to him and do so without a grudging heart; then because of this the LORD your God will bless you in all your work and in everything you put your hand to. ¹¹There will always be poor people in the land. Therefore I command you to be openhanded toward your brothers

Canceling Debts

Wednesday

DEUTERONOMY 15:1   A central theme of the Bible is canceling debts, and the ultimate example is Jesus Christ who died on the cross, thereby canceling the debt and penalty of sin for all Christians. Realizing that Christ has paid our debt and forgiven us for our shortcomings should motivate us to do the same for our spouse.

When a long-term marriage crumbles, it's not usually the result of a major crisis or a one-time event, but more likely it's the result of little things that have built up over the years. We need to forgive each other daily. Letting go and forgiving injustices, hurts and disappointments will help build a healthy Christian marriage.

Our friend Peggy is married to Greg who is not the easiest person to live with. He is domineering, negative, critical, hard-driving and demanding—most people would have given up long ago, but not Peggy. We asked her to tell us her secret. "I never put a limit

on forgiveness," she said. "I can't control Greg, but I can control me. I had to stop asking myself, 'What do I deserve?' and instead ask, 'What can I give?' I've always tried to remember the best from the past and focus on the future. Because my marriage is so precious to me, I choose to give Greg a clean slate each morning. I just throw away the hurts from the previous day, forgive him and start over."

"And what about Greg?" we asked her.

"Over the years he has modified his behavior a little bit," she said. "For instance, he is actually beginning to spend less time at work and more time with me!"

If your spouse has accumulated debts, you can cancel them. Let them go, and follow another Biblical principle: "Let no debt remain outstanding, except the continuing debt to love one another" (Romans 13:8).

—**Dave & Claudia**

Go to page 208 for your next devotional reading.

and toward the poor and needy in your land.

Freeing Servants

12If a fellow Hebrew, a man or a woman, sells himself to you and serves you six years, in the seventh year you must let him go free. 13And when you release him, do not send him away empty-handed. 14Supply him liberally from your flock, your threshing floor and your winepress. Give to him as the LORD your God has blessed you. 15Remember that you were slaves in Egypt and the LORD your God redeemed you. That is why I give you this command today.

16But if your servant says to you, "I do not want to leave you," because he loves you and your family and is well off with you, 17then take an awl and push it through his ear lobe into the door, and he will become your servant for life. Do the same for your maidservant.

18Do not consider it a hardship to set your servant free, because his service to you these six years has been worth twice as much as that of a hired hand. And the LORD your God will bless you in everything you do.

The Firstborn Animals

19Set apart for the LORD your God every firstborn male of your herds and flocks. Do not put the firstborn of your oxen to work, and do not shear the firstborn of your sheep. 20Each year you and your family are to eat them in the presence of the LORD your God at the place he will choose. 21If an animal has a defect, is lame or blind, or has any serious flaw, you must not sacrifice it to the LORD your God. 22You are to eat it in your own towns. Both the ceremonially unclean and the clean may eat it, as if it were gazelle or deer. 23But you must not eat the blood; pour it out on the ground like water.

Passover

16 Observe the month of Abib and celebrate the Passover of the LORD your God, because in the month of Abib he brought you out of Egypt by night. 2Sacrifice as the Passover to the LORD your God an animal from your flock or herd at

the place the LORD will choose as a dwelling for his Name. 3Do not eat it with bread made with yeast, but for seven days eat unleavened bread, the bread of affliction, because you left Egypt in haste—so that all the days of your life you may remember the time of your departure from Egypt. 4Let no yeast be found in your possession in all your land for seven days. Do not let any of the meat you sacrifice on the evening of the first day remain until morning.

5You must not sacrifice the Passover in any town the LORD your God gives you 6except in the place he will choose as a dwelling for his Name. There you must sacrifice the Passover in the evening, when the sun goes down, on the anniversary*a* of your departure from Egypt. 7Roast it and eat it at the place the LORD your God will choose. Then in the morning return to your tents. 8For six days eat unleavened bread and on the seventh day hold an assembly to the LORD your God and do no work.

Feast of Weeks

9Count off seven weeks from the time you begin to put the sickle to the standing grain. 10Then celebrate the Feast of Weeks to the LORD your God by giving a freewill offering in proportion to the blessings the LORD your God has given you. 11And rejoice before the LORD your God at the place he will choose as a dwelling for his Name—you, your sons and daughters, your menservants and maidservants, the Levites in your towns, and the aliens, the fatherless and the widows living among you. 12Remember that you were slaves in Egypt, and follow carefully these decrees.

Feast of Tabernacles

13Celebrate the Feast of Tabernacles for seven days after you have gathered the produce of your threshing floor and your winepress. 14Be joyful at your Feast—you, your sons and daughters, your menservants and maidservants, and the Levites, the aliens, the fatherless and the widows who live in your towns. 15For seven days celebrate the Feast to the LORD your God at the place the LORD will choose. For the

a6 Or down, at the time of day

LORD your God will bless you in all your harvest and in all the work of your hands, and your joy will be complete.

¹⁶Three times a year all your men must appear before the LORD your God at the place he will choose: at the Feast of Unleavened Bread, the Feast of Weeks and the Feast of Tabernacles. No man should appear before the LORD empty-handed: ¹⁷Each of you must bring a gift in proportion to the way the LORD your God has blessed you.

Judges

¹⁸Appoint judges and officials for each of your tribes in every town the LORD your God is giving you, and they shall judge the people fairly. ¹⁹Do not pervert justice or show partiality. Do not accept a bribe, for a bribe blinds the eyes of the wise and twists the words of the righteous. ²⁰Follow justice and justice alone, so that you may live and possess the land the LORD your God is giving you.

Worshiping Other Gods

²¹Do not set up any wooden Asherah pole[a] beside the altar you build to the LORD your God, ²²and do not erect a sacred stone, for these the LORD your God hates.

17 Do not sacrifice to the LORD your God an ox or a sheep that has any defect or flaw in it, for that would be detestable to him.

²If a man or woman living among you in one of the towns the LORD gives you is found doing evil in the eyes of the LORD your God in violation of his covenant, ³and contrary to my command has worshiped other gods, bowing down to them or to the sun or the moon or the stars of the sky, ⁴and this has been brought to your attention, then you must investigate it thoroughly. If it is true and it has been proved that this detestable thing has been done in Israel, ⁵take the man or woman who has done this evil deed to your city gate and stone that person to death. ⁶On the testimony of two or three witnesses a man shall be put to death, but no one shall be put to death on the testimony of only one witness. ⁷The hands of the witnesses must be the first in putting him to death, and then the hands of all the people. You must purge the evil from among you.

Law Courts

⁸If cases come before your courts that are too difficult for you to judge—whether bloodshed, lawsuits or assaults—take them to the place the LORD your God will choose. ⁹Go to the priests, who are Levites, and to the judge who is in office at that time. Inquire of them and they will give you the verdict. ¹⁰You must act according to the decisions they give you at the place the LORD will choose. Be careful to do everything they direct you to do. ¹¹Act according to the law they teach you and the decisions they give you. Do not turn aside from what they tell you, to the right or to the left. ¹²The man who shows contempt for the judge or for the priest who stands ministering there to the LORD your God must be put to death. You must purge the evil from Israel. ¹³All the people will hear and be afraid, and will not be contemptuous again.

The King

¹⁴When you enter the land the LORD your God is giving you and have taken possession of it and settled in it, and you say, "Let us set a king over us like all the nations around us," ¹⁵be sure to appoint over you the king the LORD your God chooses. He must be from among your own brothers. Do not place a foreigner over you, one who is not a brother Israelite. ¹⁶The king, moreover, must not acquire great numbers of horses for himself or make the people return to Egypt to get more of them, for the LORD has told you, "You are not to go back that way again." ¹⁷He must not take many wives, or his heart will be led astray. He must not accumulate large amounts of silver and gold.

¹⁸When he takes the throne of his kingdom, he is to write for himself on a scroll a copy of this law, taken from that of the priests, who are Levites. ¹⁹It is to be with him, and he is to read it all the days of his life so that he may learn to revere the LORD his God and follow carefully all the words of this law and these decrees ²⁰and not consider himself better than his

---

a 21 Or Do not plant any tree dedicated to Asherah

brothers and turn from the law to the right or to the left. Then he and his descendants will reign a long time over his kingdom in Israel.

Offerings for Priests and Levites

18 The priests, who are Levites—indeed the whole tribe of Levi—are to have no allotment or inheritance with Israel. They shall live on the offerings made to the LORD by fire, for that is their inheritance. ²They shall have no inheritance among their brothers; the LORD is their inheritance, as he promised them.

³This is the share due the priests from the people who sacrifice a bull or a sheep: the shoulder, the jowls and the inner parts. ⁴You are to give them the firstfruits of your grain, new wine and oil, and the first wool from the shearing of your sheep, ⁵for the LORD your God has chosen them and their descendants out of all your tribes to stand and minister in the LORD's name always.

⁶If a Levite moves from one of your towns anywhere in Israel where he is living, and comes in all earnestness to the place the LORD will choose, ⁷he may minister in the name of the LORD his God like all his fellow Levites who serve there in the presence of the LORD. ⁸He is to share equally in their benefits, even though he has received money from the sale of family possessions.

Detestable Practices

⁹When you enter the land the LORD your God is giving you, do not learn to imitate the detestable ways of the nations there. ¹⁰Let no one be found among you who sacrifices his son or daughter in*a* the fire, who practices divination or sorcery, interprets omens, engages in witchcraft, ¹¹or casts spells, or who is a medium or spiritist or who consults the dead. ¹²Anyone who does these things is detestable to the LORD, and because of these detestable practices the LORD your God will drive out those nations before you. ¹³You must be blameless before the LORD your God.

The Prophet

¹⁴The nations you will dispossess listen to those who practice sorcery or divina-tion. But as for you, the LORD your God has not permitted you to do so. ¹⁵The LORD your God will raise up for you a prophet like me from among your own brothers. You must listen to him. ¹⁶For this is what you asked of the LORD your God at Horeb on the day of the assembly when you said, "Let us not hear the voice of the LORD our God nor see this great fire anymore, or we will die."

¹⁷The LORD said to me: "What they say is good. ¹⁸I will raise up for them a prophet like you from among their brothers; I will put my words in his mouth, and he will tell them everything I command him. ¹⁹If anyone does not listen to my words that the prophet speaks in my name, I myself will call him to account. ²⁰But a prophet who presumes to speak in my name anything I have not commanded him to say, or a prophet who speaks in the name of other gods, must be put to death."

²¹You may say to yourselves, "How can we know when a message has not been spoken by the LORD?" ²²If what a prophet proclaims in the name of the LORD does not take place or come true, that is a message the LORD has not spoken. That prophet has spoken presumptuously. Do not be afraid of him.

Cities of Refuge

19 When the LORD your God has destroyed the nations whose land he is giving you, and when you have driven them out and settled in their towns and houses, ²then set aside for yourselves three cities centrally located in the land the LORD your God is giving you to possess. ³Build roads to them and divide into three parts the land the LORD your God is giving you as an inheritance, so that anyone who kills a man may flee there.

⁴This is the rule concerning the man who kills another and flees there to save his life—one who kills his neighbor unintentionally, without malice aforethought. ⁵For instance, a man may go into the forest with his neighbor to cut wood, and as he swings his ax to fell a tree, the head may fly off and hit his neighbor and kill him. That man may flee to one of these cities and save his life. ⁶Otherwise, the

a 10 Or who makes his son or daughter pass through

avenger of blood might pursue him in a rage, overtake him if the distance is too great, and kill him even though he is not deserving of death, since he did it to his neighbor without malice aforethought. 7This is why I command you to set aside for yourselves three cities.

8If the LORD your God enlarges your territory, as he promised on oath to your forefathers, and gives you the whole land he promised them, 9because you carefully follow all these laws I command you today—to love the LORD your God and to walk always in his ways—then you are to set aside three more cities. 10Do this so that innocent blood will not be shed in your land, which the LORD your God is giving you as your inheritance, and so that you will not be guilty of bloodshed.

11But if a man hates his neighbor and lies in wait for him, assaults and kills him, and then flees to one of these cities, 12the elders of his town shall send for him, bring him back from the city, and hand him over to the avenger of blood to die. 13Show him no pity. You must purge from Israel the guilt of shedding innocent blood, so that it may go well with you.

14Do not move your neighbor's boundary stone set up by your predecessors in the inheritance you receive in the land the LORD your God is giving you to possess.

Witnesses

15One witness is not enough to convict a man accused of any crime or offense he may have committed. A matter must be established by the testimony of two or three witnesses.

16If a malicious witness takes the stand to accuse a man of a crime, 17the two men involved in the dispute must stand in the presence of the LORD before the priests and the judges who are in office at the time. 18The judges must make a thorough investigation, and if the witness proves to be a liar, giving false testimony against his brother, 19then do to him as he intended to do to his brother. You must purge the evil from among you. 20The rest of the people will hear of this and be afraid, and never again will such an evil thing be done among you. 21Show no pity: life for

life, eye for eye, tooth for tooth, hand for hand, foot for foot.

Going to War

20 When you go to war against your enemies and see horses and chariots and an army greater than yours, do not be afraid of them, because the LORD your God, who brought you up out of Egypt, will be with you. 2When you are about to go into battle, the priest shall come forward and address the army. 3He shall say: "Hear, O Israel, today you are going into battle against your enemies. Do not be fainthearted or afraid; do not be terrified or give way to panic before them. 4For the LORD your God is the one who goes with you to fight for you against your enemies to give you victory."

5The officers shall say to the army: "Has anyone built a new house and not dedicated it? Let him go home, or he may die in battle and someone else may dedicate it. 6Has anyone planted a vineyard and not begun to enjoy it? Let him go home, or he may die in battle and someone else enjoy it. 7Has anyone become pledged to a woman and not married her? Let him go home, or he may die in battle and someone else marry her." 8Then the officers shall add, "Is any man afraid or fainthearted? Let him go home so that his brothers will not become disheartened too." 9When the officers have finished speaking to the army, they shall appoint commanders over it.

10When you march up to attack a city, make its people an offer of peace. 11If they accept and open their gates, all the people in it shall be subject to forced labor and shall work for you. 12If they refuse to make peace and they engage you in battle, lay siege to that city. 13When the LORD your God delivers it into your hand, put to the sword all the men in it. 14As for the women, the children, the livestock and everything else in the city, you may take these as plunder for yourselves. And you may use the plunder the LORD your God gives you from your enemies. 15This is how you are to treat all the cities that are at a distance from you and do not belong to the nations nearby.

16However, in the cities of the nations

the LORD your God is giving you as an inheritance, do not leave alive anything that breathes. [17]Completely destroy[a] them—the Hittites, Amorites, Canaanites, Perizzites, Hivites and Jebusites—as the LORD your God has commanded you. [18]Otherwise, they will teach you to follow all the detestable things they do in worshiping their gods, and you will sin against the LORD your God.

[19]When you lay siege to a city for a long time, fighting against it to capture it, do not destroy its trees by putting an ax to them, because you can eat their fruit. Do not cut them down. Are the trees of the field people, that you should besiege them?[b] [20]However, you may cut down trees that you know are not fruit trees and use them to build siege works until the city at war with you falls.

Atonement for an Unsolved Murder

21 If a man is found slain, lying in a field in the land the LORD your God is giving you to possess, and it is not known who killed him, [2]your elders and judges shall go out and measure the distance from the body to the neighboring towns. [3]Then the elders of the town nearest the body shall take a heifer that has never been worked and has never worn a yoke [4]and lead her down to a valley that has not been plowed or planted and where there is a flowing stream. There in the valley they are to break the heifer's neck. [5]The priests, the sons of Levi, shall step forward, for the LORD your God has chosen them to minister and to pronounce blessings in the name of the LORD and to decide all cases of dispute and assault. [6]Then all the elders of the town nearest the body shall wash their hands over the heifer whose neck was broken in the valley, [7]and they shall declare: "Our hands did not shed this blood, nor did our eyes see it done. [8]Accept this atonement for your people Israel, whom you have redeemed, O LORD, and do not hold your people guilty of the blood of an innocent man." And the bloodshed will be atoned for. [9]So you will purge from yourselves the guilt of shedding innocent blood, since you have done what is right in the eyes of the LORD.

Marrying a Captive Woman

[10]When you go to war against your enemies and the LORD your God delivers them into your hands and you take captives, [11]if you notice among the captives a beautiful woman and are attracted to her, you may take her as your wife. [12]Bring her into your home and have her shave her head, trim her nails [13]and put aside the clothes she was wearing when captured. After she has lived in your house and mourned her father and mother for a full month, then you may go to her and be her husband and she shall be your wife. [14]If you are not pleased with her, let her go wherever she wishes. You must not sell her or treat her as a slave, since you have dishonored her.

The Right of the Firstborn

[15]If a man has two wives, and he loves one but not the other, and both bear him sons but the firstborn is the son of the wife he does not love, [16]when he wills his property to his sons, he must not give the rights of the firstborn to the son of the wife he loves in preference to his actual firstborn, the son of the wife he does not love. [17]He must acknowledge the son of his unloved wife as the firstborn by giving him a double share of all he has. That son is the first sign of his father's strength. The right of the firstborn belongs to him.

A Rebellious Son

[18]If a man has a stubborn and rebellious son who does not obey his father and mother and will not listen to them when they discipline him, [19]his father and mother shall take hold of him and bring him to the elders at the gate of his town. [20]They shall say to the elders, "This son of ours is stubborn and rebellious. He will not obey us. He is a profligate and a drunkard." [21]Then all the men of his town shall stone him to death. You must purge the evil from among you. All Israel will hear of it and be afraid.

---

[a]17 The Hebrew term refers to the irrevocable giving over of things or persons to the LORD, often by totally destroying them.   [b]19 Or *down to use in the siege, for the fruit trees are for the benefit of man.*

Various Laws

²²If a man guilty of a capital offense is put to death and his body is hung on a tree, ²³you must not leave his body on the tree overnight. Be sure to bury him that same day, because anyone who is hung on a tree is under God's curse. You must not desecrate the land the LORD your God is giving you as an inheritance.

22 If you see your brother's ox or sheep straying, do not ignore it but be sure to take it back to him. ²If the brother does not live near you or if you do not know who he is, take it home with you and keep it until he comes looking for it. Then give it back to him. ³Do the same if you find your brother's donkey or his cloak or anything he loses. Do not ignore it.

⁴If you see your brother's donkey or his ox fallen on the road, do not ignore it. Help him get it to its feet.

⁵A woman must not wear men's clothing, nor a man wear women's clothing, for the LORD your God detests anyone who does this.

⁶If you come across a bird's nest beside the road, either in a tree or on the ground, and the mother is sitting on the young or on the eggs, do not take the mother with the young. ⁷You may take the young, but be sure to let the mother go, so that it may go well with you and you may have a long life.

⁸When you build a new house, make a parapet around your roof so that you may not bring the guilt of bloodshed on your house if someone falls from the roof.

⁹Do not plant two kinds of seed in your vineyard; if you do, not only the crops you plant but also the fruit of the vineyard will be defiled.ᵃ

¹⁰Do not plow with an ox and a donkey yoked together.

¹¹Do not wear clothes of wool and linen woven together.

¹²Make tassels on the four corners of the cloak you wear.

Marriage Violations

¹³If a man takes a wife and, after lying with her, dislikes her ¹⁴and slanders her and gives her a bad name, saying, "I married this woman, but when I approached her, I did not find proof of her virginity,"

¹⁵then the girl's father and mother shall bring proof that she was a virgin to the town elders at the gate. ¹⁶The girl's father will say to the elders, "I gave my daughter in marriage to this man, but he dislikes her. ¹⁷Now he has slandered her and said, 'I did not find your daughter to be a virgin.' But here is the proof of my daughter's virginity." Then her parents shall display the cloth before the elders of the town, ¹⁸and the elders shall take the man and punish him. ¹⁹They shall fine him a hundred shekels of silverᵇ and give them to the girl's father, because this man has given an Israelite virgin a bad name. She shall continue to be his wife; he must not divorce her as long as he lives.

²⁰If, however, the charge is true and no proof of the girl's virginity can be found, ²¹she shall be brought to the door of her father's house and there the men of her town shall stone her to death. She has done a disgraceful thing in Israel by being promiscuous while still in her father's house. You must purge the evil from among you.

²²If a man is found sleeping with another man's wife, both the man who slept with her and the woman must die. You must purge the evil from Israel.

²³If a man happens to meet in a town a virgin pledged to be married and he sleeps with her, ²⁴you shall take both of them to the gate of that town and stone them to death—the girl because she was in a town and did not scream for help, and the man because he violated another man's wife. You must purge the evil from among you.

²⁵But if out in the country a man happens to meet a girl pledged to be married and rapes her, only the man who has done this shall die. ²⁶Do nothing to the girl; she has committed no sin deserving death. This case is like that of someone who attacks and murders his neighbor, ²⁷for the man found the girl out in the country, and though the betrothed girl screamed, there was no one to rescue her.

²⁸If a man happens to meet a virgin who is not pledged to be married and rapes her and they are discovered, ²⁹he shall pay the girl's father fifty shekels of

ᵃ9 Or *be forfeited to the sanctuary*   ᵇ19 That is, about 2 1/2 pounds (about 1 kilogram) silver.[a] He must marry the girl, for he has violated her. He can never divorce her as long as he lives.

30A man is not to marry his father's wife; he must not dishonor his father's bed.

Exclusion from the Assembly

23 No one who has been emasculated by crushing or cutting may enter the assembly of the LORD.

2No one born of a forbidden marriage[b] nor any of his descendants may enter the assembly of the LORD, even down to the tenth generation.

3No Ammonite or Moabite or any of his descendants may enter the assembly of the LORD, even down to the tenth generation. 4For they did not come to meet you with bread and water on your way when you came out of Egypt, and they hired Balaam son of Beor from Pethor in Aram Naharaim[c] to pronounce a curse on you. 5However, the LORD your God would not listen to Balaam but turned the curse into a blessing for you, because the LORD your God loves you. 6Do not seek a treaty of friendship with them as long as you live.

7Do not abhor an Edomite, for he is your brother. Do not abhor an Egyptian, because you lived as an alien in his country. 8The third generation of children born to them may enter the assembly of the LORD.

Uncleanness in the Camp

9When you are encamped against your enemies, keep away from everything impure. 10If one of your men is unclean because of a nocturnal emission, he is to go outside the camp and stay there. 11But as evening approaches he is to wash himself, and at sunset he may return to the camp.

12Designate a place outside the camp where you can go to relieve yourself. 13As part of your equipment have something to dig with, and when you relieve yourself, dig a hole and cover up your excrement. 14For the LORD your God moves about in your camp to protect you and to deliver your enemies to you. Your camp must be holy, so that he will not see among you anything indecent and turn away from you.

Miscellaneous Laws

15If a slave has taken refuge with you, do not hand him over to his master. 16Let him live among you wherever he likes and in whatever town he chooses. Do not oppress him.

17No Israelite man or woman is to become a shrine prostitute. 18You must not bring the earnings of a female prostitute or of a male prostitute[d] into the house of the LORD your God to pay any vow, because the LORD your God detests them both.

19Do not charge your brother interest, whether on money or food or anything else that may earn interest. 20You may charge a foreigner interest, but not a brother Israelite, so that the LORD your God may bless you in everything you put your hand to in the land you are entering to possess.

21If you make a vow to the LORD your God, do not be slow to pay it, for the LORD your God will certainly demand it of you and you will be guilty of sin. 22But if you refrain from making a vow, you will not be guilty. 23Whatever your lips utter you must be sure to do, because you made your vow freely to the LORD your God with your own mouth.

24If you enter your neighbor's vineyard, you may eat all the grapes you want, but do not put any in your basket. 25If you enter your neighbor's grainfield, you may pick kernels with your hands, but you must not put a sickle to his standing grain.

24 If a man marries a woman who becomes displeasing to him because he finds something indecent about her, and he writes her a certificate of divorce, gives it to her and sends her from his house, 2and if after she leaves his house she becomes the wife of another man, 3and her second husband dislikes her and writes her a certificate of divorce, gives it to her and sends her from his house, or if he dies, 4then her first husband, who divorced her, is not allowed to marry her again after she has been defiled. That would be detestable in the eyes of the

a29 That is, about 1 1/4 pounds (about 0.6 kilogram)   b2 Or one of illegitimate birth
c4 That is, Northwest Mesopotamia
d18 Hebrew of a dog

LORD. Do not bring sin upon the land the LORD your God is giving you as an inheritance.

5If a man has recently married, he must not be sent to war or have any other duty laid on him. For one year he is to be free to stay at home and bring happiness to the wife he has married.

6Do not take a pair of millstones—not even the upper one—as security for a debt, because that would be taking a man's livelihood as security.

7If a man is caught kidnapping one of his brother Israelites and treats him as a slave or sells him, the kidnapper must die. You must purge the evil from among you.

8In cases of leprous*a* diseases be very careful to do exactly as the priests, who are Levites, instruct you. You must follow carefully what I have commanded them. 9Remember what the LORD your God did to Miriam along the way after you came out of Egypt.

10When you make a loan of any kind to your neighbor, do not go into his house to get what he is offering as a pledge. 11Stay outside and let the man to whom you are making the loan bring the pledge out to you. 12If the man is poor, do not go to sleep with his pledge in your possession. 13Return his cloak to him by sunset so that he may sleep in it. Then he will thank you, and it will be regarded as a righteous act in the sight of the LORD your God.

14Do not take advantage of a hired man who is poor and needy, whether he is a brother Israelite or an alien living in one of your towns. 15Pay him his wages each day before sunset, because he is poor and is counting on it. Otherwise he may cry to the LORD against you, and you will be guilty of sin.

16Fathers shall not be put to death for their children, nor children put to death for their fathers; each is to die for his own sin.

17Do not deprive the alien or the fatherless of justice, or take the cloak of the widow as a pledge. 18Remember that you were slaves in Egypt and the LORD your God redeemed you from there. That is why I command you to do this.

19When you are harvesting in your field and you overlook a sheaf, do not go back to get it. Leave it for the alien, the fatherless and the widow, so that the LORD your God may bless you in all the work of your hands. 20When you beat the olives from your trees, do not go over the branches a second time. Leave what remains for the alien, the fatherless and the widow. 21When you harvest the grapes in your vineyard, do not go over the vines again. Leave what remains for the alien, the fatherless and the widow. 22Remember that you were slaves in Egypt. That is why I command you to do this.

25 When men have a dispute, they are to take it to court and the judges will decide the case, acquitting the innocent and condemning the guilty. 2If the guilty man deserves to be beaten, the judge shall make him lie down and have him flogged in his presence with the number of lashes his crime deserves, 3but he must not give him more than forty lashes. If he is flogged more than that, your brother will be degraded in your eyes.

4Do not muzzle an ox while it is treading out the grain.

5If brothers are living together and one of them dies without a son, his widow must not marry outside the family. Her husband's brother shall take her and marry her and fulfill the duty of a brother-in-law to her. 6The first son she bears shall carry on the name of the dead brother so that his name will not be blotted out from Israel.

7However, if a man does not want to marry his brother's wife, she shall go to the elders at the town gate and say, "My husband's brother refuses to carry on his brother's name in Israel. He will not fulfill the duty of a brother-in-law to me." 8Then the elders of his town shall summon him and talk to him. If he persists in saying, "I do not want to marry her," 9his brother's widow shall go up to him in the presence of the elders, take off one of his sandals, spit in his face and say, "This is what is done to the man who will not build up his brother's family line." 10That man's line shall be known in Israel as The Family of the Unsandaled.

---

a8 The Hebrew word was used for various diseases affecting the skin—not necessarily leprosy.

¹¹If two men are fighting and the wife of one of them comes to rescue her husband from his assailant, and she reaches out and seizes him by his private parts, ¹²you shall cut off her hand. Show her no pity.

¹³Do not have two differing weights in your bag—one heavy, one light. ¹⁴Do not have two differing measures in your house—one large, one small. ¹⁵You must have accurate and honest weights and measures, so that you may live long in the land the LORD your God is giving you. ¹⁶For the LORD your God detests anyone who does these things, anyone who deals dishonestly.

¹⁷Remember what the Amalekites did to you along the way when you came out of Egypt. ¹⁸When you were weary and worn out, they met you on your journey and cut off all who were lagging behind; they had no fear of God. ¹⁹When the LORD your God gives you rest from all the enemies around you in the land he is giving you to possess as an inheritance, you shall blot out the memory of Amalek from under heaven. Do not forget!

Firstfruits and Tithes

26 When you have entered the land the LORD your God is giving you as an inheritance and have taken possession of it and settled in it, ²take some of the firstfruits of all that you produce from the soil of the land the LORD your God is giving you and put them in a basket. Then go to the place the LORD your God will choose as a dwelling for his Name ³and say to the priest in office at the time, "I declare today to the LORD your God that I have come to the land the LORD swore to our forefathers to give us." ⁴The priest shall take the basket from your hands and set it down in front of the altar of the LORD your God. ⁵Then you shall declare before the LORD your God: "My father was a wandering Aramean, and he went down into Egypt with a few people and lived there and became a great nation, powerful and numerous. ⁶But the Egyptians mistreated us and made us suffer, putting us to hard labor. ⁷Then we cried out to the LORD, the God of our fathers, and the LORD heard our voice and saw our misery, toil and oppression. ⁸So the LORD brought us out of Egypt with a mighty hand and an outstretched arm, with great terror and with miraculous signs and wonders. ⁹He brought us to this place and gave us this land, a land flowing with milk and honey; ¹⁰and now I bring the firstfruits of the soil that you, O LORD, have given me." Place the basket before the LORD your God and bow down before him. ¹¹And you and the Levites and the aliens among you shall rejoice in all the

A Marriage Tithe

Thursday

DEUTERONOMY 26:1–2 For years Claudia had a vegetable garden. It was great therapy when we had three adolescents. If you've ever had a vegetable garden, you know the thrill you experience when the first produce is ready to harvest. Nothing tastes quite as good as fresh-snapped beans, a tomato sandwich or a bowl of strawberries! Imagine the sacrifice when the Israelites were told to tithe to the Lord the firstfruits from their crop.

Too often today we tithe with what is left over after everything else is budgeted out. But in Deuteronomy 26:1, God admonished his people and told them to give him the first fruits of their harvest because it demonstrated a thankful spirit and confidence that God would continue to bless their harvest—that he would supply all of their needs. Tithing the firstfruits was also a visible act of putting God first.

After putting God first, our next priority is to put our spouse first. It's probably impossible to tithe ten percent of our time, but we can take the "firstfruits" of the free time we do have to give to our spouse. By doing this, you will demonstrate a grateful spirit and reveal your trust and confidence in each other that your relationship will continue to grow.

—**Dave & Claudia**

Go to page 215 for your next devotional reading.

good things the LORD your God has given to you and your household.

¹²When you have finished setting aside a tenth of all your produce in the third year, the year of the tithe, you shall give it to the Levite, the alien, the fatherless and the widow, so that they may eat in your towns and be satisfied. ¹³Then say to the LORD your God: "I have removed from my house the sacred portion and have given it to the Levite, the alien, the fatherless and the widow, according to all you commanded. I have not turned aside from your commands nor have I forgotten any of them. ¹⁴I have not eaten any of the sacred portion while I was in mourning, nor have I removed any of it while I was unclean, nor have I offered any of it to the dead. I have obeyed the LORD my God; I have done everything you commanded me. ¹⁵Look down from heaven, your holy dwelling place, and bless your people Israel and the land you have given us as you promised on oath to our forefathers, a land flowing with milk and honey."

Follow the LORD's Commands

¹⁶The LORD your God commands you this day to follow these decrees and laws; carefully observe them with all your heart and with all your soul. ¹⁷You have declared this day that the LORD is your God and that you will walk in his ways, that you will keep his decrees, commands and laws, and that you will obey him. ¹⁸And the LORD has declared this day that you are his people, his treasured possession as he promised, and that you are to keep all his commands. ¹⁹He has declared that he will set you in praise, fame and honor high above all the nations he has made and that you will be a people holy to the LORD your God, as he promised.

The Altar on Mount Ebal

27 Moses and the elders of Israel commanded the people: "Keep all these commands that I give you today. ²When you have crossed the Jordan into the land the LORD your God is giving you, set up some large stones and coat them with plaster. ³Write on them all the words of this law when you have crossed over to enter the land the LORD your God is giv-

ing you, a land flowing with milk and honey, just as the LORD, the God of your fathers, promised you. ⁴And when you have crossed the Jordan, set up these stones on Mount Ebal, as I command you today, and coat them with plaster. ⁵Build there an altar to the LORD your God, an altar of stones. Do not use any iron tool upon them. ⁶Build the altar of the LORD your God with fieldstones and offer burnt offerings on it to the LORD your God. ⁷Sacrifice fellowship offerings*a* there, eating them and rejoicing in the presence of the LORD your God. ⁸And you shall write very clearly all the words of this law on these stones you have set up."

Curses From Mount Ebal

⁹Then Moses and the priests, who are Levites, said to all Israel, "Be silent, O Israel, and listen! You have now become the people of the LORD your God. ¹⁰Obey the LORD your God and follow his commands and decrees that I give you today."

¹¹On the same day Moses commanded the people:

¹²When you have crossed the Jordan, these tribes shall stand on Mount Gerizim to bless the people: Simeon, Levi, Judah, Issachar, Joseph and Benjamin. ¹³And these tribes shall stand on Mount Ebal to pronounce curses: Reuben, Gad, Asher, Zebulun, Dan and Naphtali.

¹⁴The Levites shall recite to all the people of Israel in a loud voice:

¹⁵"Cursed is the man who carves an image or casts an idol—a thing detestable to the LORD, the work of the craftsman's hands—and sets it up in secret."

Then all the people shall say, "Amen!"

¹⁶"Cursed is the man who dishonors his father or his mother."

Then all the people shall say, "Amen!"

¹⁷"Cursed is the man who moves his neighbor's boundary stone."

Then all the people shall say, "Amen!"

¹⁸"Cursed is the man who leads the blind astray on the road."

a7 Traditionally *peace offerings*

Then all the people shall say, "Amen!"

¹⁹"Cursed is the man who withholds justice from the alien, the fatherless or the widow."

Then all the people shall say, "Amen!"

²⁰"Cursed is the man who sleeps with his father's wife, for he dishonors his father's bed."

Then all the people shall say, "Amen!"

²¹"Cursed is the man who has sexual relations with any animal."

Then all the people shall say, "Amen!"

²²"Cursed is the man who sleeps with his sister, the daughter of his father or the daughter of his mother."

Then all the people shall say, "Amen!"

²³"Cursed is the man who sleeps with his mother-in-law."

Then all the people shall say, "Amen!"

²⁴"Cursed is the man who kills his neighbor secretly."

Then all the people shall say, "Amen!"

²⁵"Cursed is the man who accepts a bribe to kill an innocent person."

Then all the people shall say, "Amen!"

²⁶"Cursed is the man who does not uphold the words of this law by carrying them out."

Then all the people shall say, "Amen!"

Blessings for Obedience

28 If you fully obey the Lord your God and carefully follow all his commands I give you today, the Lord your God will set you high above all the nations on earth. ²All these blessings will come upon you and accompany you if you obey the Lord your God:

³You will be blessed in the city and blessed in the country.

⁴The fruit of your womb will be blessed, and the crops of your land and the young of your livestock—the calves of your herds and the lambs of your flocks.

⁵Your basket and your kneading trough will be blessed.

⁶You will be blessed when you come in and blessed when you go out.

⁷The Lord will grant that the enemies who rise up against you will be defeated before you. They will come at you from one direction but flee from you in seven.

⁸The Lord will send a blessing on your barns and on everything you put your hand to. The Lord your God will bless you in the land he is giving you.

⁹The Lord will establish you as his holy people, as he promised you on oath, if you keep the commands of the Lord your God and walk in his ways. ¹⁰Then all the peoples on earth will see that you are called by the name of the Lord, and they will fear you. ¹¹The Lord will grant you abundant prosperity—in the fruit of your womb, the young of your livestock and the crops of your ground—in the land he swore to your forefathers to give you.

¹²The Lord will open the heavens, the storehouse of his bounty, to send rain on your land in season and to bless all the work of your hands. You will lend to many nations but will borrow from none. ¹³The Lord will make you the head, not the tail. If you pay attention to the commands of the Lord your God that I give you this day and carefully follow them, you will always be at the top, never at the bottom. ¹⁴Do not turn aside from any of the commands I give you today, to the right or to the left, following other gods and serving them.

Curses for Disobedience

¹⁵However, if you do not obey the Lord your God and do not carefully follow all his commands and decrees I am giving you today, all these curses will come upon you and overtake you:

¹⁶You will be cursed in the city and cursed in the country.

¹⁷Your basket and your kneading trough will be cursed.

¹⁸The fruit of your womb will be cursed, and the crops of your land, and the calves of your herds and the lambs of your flocks.

¹⁹You will be cursed when you

come in and cursed when you go out.

20The LORD will send on you curses, confusion and rebuke in everything you put your hand to, until you are destroyed and come to sudden ruin because of the evil you have done in forsaking him.[a] 21The LORD will plague you with diseases until he has destroyed you from the land you are entering to possess. 22The LORD will strike you with wasting disease, with fever and inflammation, with scorching heat and drought, with blight and mildew, which will plague you until you perish. 23The sky over your head will be bronze, the ground beneath you iron. 24The LORD will turn the rain of your country into dust and powder; it will come down from the skies until you are destroyed.

25The LORD will cause you to be defeated before your enemies. You will come at them from one direction but flee from them in seven, and you will become a thing of horror to all the kingdoms on earth. 26Your carcasses will be food for all the birds of the air and the beasts of the earth, and there will be no one to frighten them away. 27The LORD will afflict you with the boils of Egypt and with tumors, festering sores and the itch, from which you cannot be cured. 28The LORD will afflict you with madness, blindness and confusion of mind. 29At midday you will grope about like a blind man in the dark. You will be unsuccessful in everything you do; day after day you will be oppressed and robbed, with no one to rescue you.

30You will be pledged to be married to a woman, but another will take her and ravish her. You will build a house, but you will not live in it. You will plant a vineyard, but you will not even begin to enjoy its fruit. 31Your ox will be slaughtered before your eyes, but you will eat none of it. Your donkey will be forcibly taken from you and will not be returned. Your sheep will be given to your enemies, and no one will rescue them. 32Your sons and daughters will be given to another nation, and you will wear out your eyes watching for them day after day, powerless to lift a hand. 33A people that you do not know will eat what your land and

labor produce, and you will have nothing but cruel oppression all your days. 34The sights you see will drive you mad. 35The LORD will afflict your knees and legs with painful boils that cannot be cured, spreading from the soles of your feet to the top of your head.

36The LORD will drive you and the king you set over you to a nation unknown to you or your fathers. There you will worship other gods, gods of wood and stone. 37You will become a thing of horror and an object of scorn and ridicule to all the nations where the LORD will drive you.

38You will sow much seed in the field but you will harvest little, because locusts will devour it. 39You will plant vineyards and cultivate them but you will not drink the wine or gather the grapes, because worms will eat them. 40You will have olive trees throughout your country but you will not use the oil, because the olives will drop off. 41You will have sons and daughters but you will not keep them, because they will go into captivity. 42Swarms of locusts will take over all your trees and the crops of your land.

43The alien who lives among you will rise above you higher and higher, but you will sink lower and lower. 44He will lend to you, but you will not lend to him. He will be the head, but you will be the tail.

45All these curses will come upon you. They will pursue you and overtake you until you are destroyed, because you did not obey the LORD your God and observe the commands and decrees he gave you. 46They will be a sign and a wonder to you and your descendants forever. 47Because you did not serve the LORD your God joyfully and gladly in the time of prosperity, 48therefore in hunger and thirst, in nakedness and dire poverty, you will serve the enemies the LORD sends against you. He will put an iron yoke on your neck until he has destroyed you.

49The LORD will bring a nation against you from far away, from the ends of the earth, like an eagle swooping down, a nation whose language you will not understand, 50a fierce-looking nation without respect for the old or pity for the young. 51They will devour the young of your livestock and the crops of your land until you

a20 Hebrew me

are destroyed. They will leave you no grain, new wine or oil, nor any calves of your herds or lambs of your flocks until you are ruined. 52They will lay siege to all the cities throughout your land until the high fortified walls in which you trust fall down. They will besiege all the cities throughout the land the LORD your God is giving you.

53Because of the suffering that your enemy will inflict on you during the siege, you will eat the fruit of the womb, the flesh of the sons and daughters the LORD your God has given you. 54Even the most gentle and sensitive man among you will have no compassion on his own brother or the wife he loves or his surviving children, 55and he will not give to one of them any of the flesh of his children that he is eating. It will be all he has left because of the suffering your enemy will inflict on you during the siege of all your cities. 56The most gentle and sensitive woman among you—so sensitive and gentle that she would not venture to touch the ground with the sole of her foot—will begrudge the husband she loves and her own son or daughter 57the afterbirth from her womb and the children she bears. For she intends to eat them secretly during the siege and in the distress that your enemy will inflict on you in your cities.

58If you do not carefully follow all the words of this law, which are written in this book, and do not revere this glorious and awesome name—the LORD your God— 59the LORD will send fearful plagues on you and your descendants, harsh and prolonged disasters, and severe and lingering illnesses. 60He will bring upon you all the diseases of Egypt that you dreaded, and they will cling to you. 61The LORD will also bring on you every kind of sickness and disaster not recorded in this Book of the Law, until you are destroyed. 62You who were as numerous as the stars in the sky will be left but few in number, because you did not obey the LORD your God. 63Just as it pleased the LORD to make you prosper and increase in number, so it will please him to ruin and destroy you. You will be uprooted from the land you are entering to possess.

64Then the LORD will scatter you among all nations, from one end of the earth to the other. There you will worship other gods—gods of wood and stone, which neither you nor your fathers have known. 65Among those nations you will find no repose, no resting place for the sole of your foot. There the LORD will give you an anxious mind, eyes weary with longing, and a despairing heart. 66You will live in constant suspense, filled with dread both night and day, never sure of your life. 67In the morning you will say, "If only it were evening!" and in the evening, "If only it were morning!"—because of the terror that will fill your hearts and the sights that your eyes will see. 68The LORD will send you back in ships to Egypt on a journey I said you should never make again. There you will offer yourselves for sale to your enemies as male and female slaves, but no one will buy you.

Renewal of the Covenant

29 These are the terms of the covenant the LORD commanded Moses to make with the Israelites in Moab, in addition to the covenant he had made with them at Horeb.

2Moses summoned all the Israelites and said to them:

Your eyes have seen all that the LORD did in Egypt to Pharaoh, to all his officials and to all his land. 3With your own eyes you saw those great trials, those miraculous signs and great wonders. 4But to this day the LORD has not given you a mind that understands or eyes that see or ears that hear. 5During the forty years that I led you through the desert, your clothes did not wear out, nor did the sandals on your feet. 6You ate no bread and drank no wine or other fermented drink. I did this so that you might know that I am the LORD your God.

7When you reached this place, Sihon king of Heshbon and Og king of Bashan came out to fight against us, but we defeated them. 8We took their land and gave it as an inheritance to the Reubenites, the Gadites and the half-tribe of Manasseh.

9Carefully follow the terms of this covenant, so that you may prosper in everything you do. 10All of you are standing today in the presence of the LORD your God—your leaders and chief men, your elders and officials, and all the other men of Israel, [11]together with your children and your wives, and the aliens living in your camps who chop your wood and carry your water. [12]You are standing here in order to enter into a covenant with the LORD your God, a covenant the LORD is making with you this day and sealing with an oath, [13]to confirm you this day as his people, that he may be your God as he promised you and as he swore to your fathers, Abraham, Isaac and Jacob. [14]I am making this covenant, with its oath, not only with you [15]who are standing here with us today in the presence of the LORD our God but also with those who are not here today.

[16]You yourselves know how we lived in Egypt and how we passed through the countries on the way here. [17]You saw among them their detestable images and idols of wood and stone, of silver and gold. [18]Make sure there is no man or woman, clan or tribe among you today whose heart turns away from the LORD our God to go and worship the gods of those nations; make sure there is no root among you that produces such bitter poison.

[19]When such a person hears the words of this oath, he invokes a blessing on himself and therefore thinks, "I will be safe, even though I persist in going my own way." This will bring disaster on the watered land as well as the dry.[a] [20]The LORD will never be willing to forgive him; his wrath and zeal will burn against that man. All the curses written in this book will fall upon him, and the LORD will blot out his name from under heaven. [21]The LORD will single him out from all the tribes of Israel for disaster, according to all the curses of the covenant written in this Book of the Law.

[22]Your children who follow you in later generations and foreigners who come from distant lands will see the calamities that have fallen on the land and the diseases with which the LORD has afflicted it. [23]The whole land will be a burning waste of salt and sulfur—nothing planted, nothing sprouting, no vegetation growing on it. It will be like the destruction of Sodom and Gomorrah, Admah and Zeboiim, which the LORD overthrew in fierce anger. [24]All the nations will ask: "Why has the LORD done this to this land? Why this fierce, burning anger?"

[25]And the answer will be: "It is because this people abandoned the covenant of the LORD, the God of their fathers, the covenant he made with them when he brought them out of Egypt. [26]They went off and worshiped other gods and bowed down to them, gods they did not know, gods he had not given them. [27]Therefore the LORD's anger burned against this land, so that he brought on it all the curses written in this book. [28]In furious anger and in great wrath the LORD uprooted them from their land and thrust them into another land, as it is now."

[29]The secret things belong to the LORD our God, but the things revealed belong to us and to our children forever, that we may follow all the words of this law.

Prosperity After Turning to the LORD

30 When all these blessings and curses I have set before you come upon you and you take them to heart wherever the LORD your God disperses you among the nations, [2]and when you and your children return to the LORD your God and obey him with all your heart and with all your soul according to everything I command you today, [3]then the LORD your God will restore your fortunes[b] and have compassion on you and gather you again from all the nations where he scattered you. [4]Even if you have been banished to the most distant land under the heavens, from there the LORD your God will gather you and bring you back. [5]He will bring you to the land that belonged to your fathers, and you will take possession of it. He will make you more prosperous and numerous than your fathers. [6]The LORD your God will circumcise your hearts and the hearts of your descendants, so that you may love him with all your heart and with all your soul, and live. [7]The LORD your God will put all these curses on your enemies who hate and persecute you. [8]You will again obey the LORD and follow all his commands I am giving you today. [9]Then the LORD your God will make you most prosperous in all the work of your hands and in the fruit of your womb, the

[a]19 Or way, in order to add drunkenness to thirst."
[b]3 Or will bring you back from captivity

young of your livestock and the crops of your land. The LORD will again delight in you and make you prosperous, just as he delighted in your fathers, [10]if you obey the LORD your God and keep his commands and decrees that are written in this Book of the Law and turn to the LORD your God with all your heart and with all your soul.

The Offer of Life or Death

[11]Now what I am commanding you today is not too difficult for you or beyond your reach. [12]It is not up in heaven, so that you have to ask, "Who will ascend into heaven to get it and proclaim it to us so we may obey it?" [13]Nor is it beyond the sea, so that you have to ask, "Who will cross the sea to get it and proclaim it to us so we may obey it?" [14]No, the word is very near you; it is in your mouth and in your heart so you may obey it.

[15]See, I set before you today life and prosperity, death and destruction. [16]For I command you today to love the LORD your God, to walk in his ways, and to keep his commands, decrees and laws; then you will live and increase, and the LORD your God will bless you in the land you are entering to possess.

[17]But if your heart turns away and you are not obedient, and if you are drawn away to bow down to other gods and worship them, [18]I declare to you this day that you will certainly be destroyed. You will not live long in the land you are crossing the Jordan to enter and possess. [19]This day I call heaven and earth as witnesses against you that I have set before you life and death, blessings and curses. Now choose life, so that you and your children may live [20]and that you may love the LORD your God, listen to his voice, and hold fast to him. For the LORD is your life, and he will give you many years in the land he swore to give to your fathers, Abraham, Isaac and Jacob.

Joshua to Succeed Moses

31 Then Moses went out and spoke these words to all Israel: [2]"I am now a hundred and twenty years old and I am no longer able to lead you. The LORD has said to me, 'You shall not cross the Jordan.' [3]The LORD your God himself will cross over ahead of you. He will destroy these nations before you, and you will take possession of their land. Joshua also will cross over ahead of you, as the LORD said. [4]And the LORD will do to them what he did to Sihon and Og, the kings of the Amorites, whom he destroyed along with their land. [5]The LORD will deliver them to you, and you must do to them all that I have commanded you. [6]Be strong and courageous. Do not be afraid or terrified because of them, for the LORD your God goes with you; he will never leave you nor forsake you."

[7]Then Moses summoned Joshua and said to him in the presence of all Israel, "Be strong and courageous, for you must go with this people into the land that the LORD swore to their forefathers to give them, and you must divide it among them as their inheritance. [8]The LORD himself goes before you and will be with you; he will never leave you nor forsake you. Do not be afraid; do not be discouraged."

The Reading of the Law

[9]So Moses wrote down this law and gave it to the priests, the sons of Levi, who carried the ark of the covenant of the LORD, and to all the elders of Israel. [10]Then Moses commanded them: "At the end of every seven years, in the year for canceling debts, during the Feast of Tabernacles, [11]when all Israel comes to appear before the LORD your God at the place he will choose, you shall read this law before them in their hearing. [12]Assemble the people—men, women and children, and the aliens living in your towns—so they can listen and learn to fear the LORD your God and follow carefully all the words of this law. [13]Their children, who do not know this law, must hear it and learn to fear the LORD your God as long as you live in the land you are crossing the Jordan to possess."

Israel's Rebellion Predicted

[14]The LORD said to Moses, "Now the day of your death is near. Call Joshua and present yourselves at the Tent of Meeting, where I will commission him." So Moses and Joshua came and presented themselves at the Tent of Meeting. [15]Then the LORD appeared at the Tent

in a pillar of cloud, and the cloud stood over the entrance to the Tent. ¹⁶And the LORD said to Moses: "You are going to rest with your fathers, and these people will soon prostitute themselves to the foreign gods of the land they are entering. They will forsake me and break the covenant I made with them. ¹⁷On that day I will become angry with them and forsake them; I will hide my face from them, and they will be destroyed. Many disasters and difficulties will come upon them, and on that day they will ask, 'Have not these disasters come upon us because our God is not with us?' ¹⁸And I will certainly hide my face on that day because of all their wickedness in turning to other gods.

¹⁹"Now write down for yourselves this song and teach it to the Israelites and have them sing it, so that it may be a witness for me against them. ²⁰When I have brought them into the land flowing with milk and honey, the land I promised on oath to their forefathers, and when they eat their fill and thrive, they will turn to other gods and worship them, rejecting

me and breaking my covenant. ²¹And when many disasters and difficulties come upon them, this song will testify against them, because it will not be forgotten by their descendants. I know what they are disposed to do, even before I bring them into the land I promised them on oath." ²²So Moses wrote down this song that day and taught it to the Israelites.

²³The LORD gave this command to Joshua son of Nun: "Be strong and courageous, for you will bring the Israelites into the land I promised them on oath, and I myself will be with you."

²⁴After Moses finished writing in a book the words of this law from beginning to end, ²⁵he gave this command to the Levites who carried the ark of the covenant of the LORD: ²⁶"Take this Book of the Law and place it beside the ark of the covenant of the LORD your God. There it will remain as a witness against you. ²⁷For I know how rebellious and stiff-necked you are. If you have been rebellious against the LORD while I am still alive and

God Will Go Before You

Friday

DEUTERONOMY 31:6–8 Joshua faced a huge job. How would you like to be the one to fill Moses' shoes? But God promised not only to be with Joshua but also to go before him, never leaving or forsaking him.

That same promise of God's abiding presence holds true today for you and for your spouse. At times when your marriage must cross "the Jordan," when you feel overwhelmed, remember God is the One who strengthens you and gives you courage. He will never leave you or forsake you, and he will keep going before you and make a path for you to follow.

I (Claudia) remember a time when God made "a path" for me. Tears rolled down my cheeks as I sat on the back doorstep, unsuccessfully trying to force a pill down Sam's throat. Sam was our new little Christmas beagle who had run away and gotten hurt in a fight with another dog—that's why he needed the pill. Sick myself, this was more than I could handle. The boys and I had been

sharing a stomach virus in twelve-hour shifts. *Where was the father of this family? Off on another business trip. Why was Dave always gone when I really needed him?* Alone, discouraged and desperate, I sat there staring at Sam's pill.

At the point of my greatest need, the phone rang. My friend Margaret said, "I've had you on my mind all day. I just made a big pot of vegetable soup. Would you like some?" There was the path God made for me through the forest of my troubles in order to send encouragement!

When stressful times come, you can choose to trust and not be afraid. In a culture where divorce runs rampant and some view "starter marriages" like "starter homes," you can surmount each challenge in your marriage with the confidence that the Lord not only is with you but is actually going before you.

—*Dave & Claudia*

Go to page 222 for your next devotional reading.

with you, how much more will you rebel after I die! ²⁸Assemble before me all the elders of your tribes and all your officials, so that I can speak these words in their hearing and call heaven and earth to testify against them. ²⁹For I know that after my death you are sure to become utterly corrupt and to turn from the way I have commanded you. In days to come, disaster will fall upon you because you will do evil in the sight of the LORD and provoke him to anger by what your hands have made."

The Song of Moses

³⁰And Moses recited the words of this song from beginning to end in the hearing of the whole assembly of Israel:

32 Listen, O heavens, and I will speak;
  hear, O earth, the words of my
    mouth.
²Let my teaching fall like rain
  and my words descend like dew,
like showers on new grass,
  like abundant rain on tender
    plants.

³I will proclaim the name of the LORD.
  Oh, praise the greatness of our
    God!
⁴He is the Rock, his works are perfect,
  and all his ways are just.
A faithful God who does no wrong,
  upright and just is he.

⁵They have acted corruptly toward
    him;
  to their shame they are no longer
    his children,
  but a warped and crooked
    generation.ᵃ
⁶Is this the way you repay the LORD,
  O foolish and unwise people?
Is he not your Father, your Creator,ᵇ
  who made you and formed you?

⁷Remember the days of old;
  consider the generations long past.
Ask your father and he will tell you,
  your elders, and they will explain
    to you.
⁸When the Most High gave the nations
    their inheritance,
  when he divided all mankind,
he set up boundaries for the peoples

according to the number of the
    sons of Israel.ᶜ
⁹For the LORD's portion is his people,
  Jacob his allotted inheritance.

¹⁰In a desert land he found him,
  in a barren and howling waste.
He shielded him and cared for him;
  he guarded him as the apple of his
    eye,
¹¹like an eagle that stirs up its nest
  and hovers over its young,
that spreads its wings to catch them
  and carries them on its pinions.
¹²The LORD alone led him;
  no foreign god was with him.

¹³He made him ride on the heights of
    the land
  and fed him with the fruit of the
    fields.
He nourished him with honey from
    the rock,
  and with oil from the flinty crag,
¹⁴with curds and milk from herd and
    flock
  and with fattened lambs and goats,
with choice rams of Bashan
  and the finest kernels of wheat.
You drank the foaming blood of the
    grape.

¹⁵Jeshurunᵈ grew fat and kicked;
  filled with food, he became heavy
    and sleek.
He abandoned the God who made
    him
  and rejected the Rock his Savior.
¹⁶They made him jealous with their
    foreign gods
  and angered him with their
    detestable idols.
¹⁷They sacrificed to demons, which are
    not God—
  gods they had not known,
  gods that recently appeared,
  gods your fathers did not fear.
¹⁸You deserted the Rock, who fathered
    you;
  you forgot the God who gave you
    birth.

¹⁹The LORD saw this and rejected them

ᵃ5 Or Corrupt are they and not his children, / a
generation warped and twisted to their shame
ᵇ6 Or Father, who bought you   ᶜ8 Masoretic Text;
Dead Sea Scrolls (see also Septuagint) sons of God
ᵈ15 Jeshurun means the upright one, that is, Israel.

because he was angered by his sons
　　and daughters.
20 "I will hide my face from them," he
　　said,
　　"and see what their end will be;
for they are a perverse generation,
　　children who are unfaithful.
21 They made me jealous by what is no
　　god
　　and angered me with their
　　　worthless idols.
I will make them envious by those
　　who are not a people;
I will make them angry by a nation
　　that has no understanding.
22 For a fire has been kindled by my
　　wrath,
　　one that burns to the realm of
　　　death[a] below.
It will devour the earth and its
　　harvests
　　and set afire the foundations of the
　　　mountains.

23 "I will heap calamities upon them
　　and spend my arrows against them.
24 I will send wasting famine against
　　them,
　　consuming pestilence and deadly
　　　plague;
I will send against them the fangs of
　　wild beasts,
　　the venom of vipers that glide in
　　　the dust.
25 In the street the sword will make
　　them childless;
　　in their homes terror will reign.
Young men and young women will
　　perish,
　　infants and gray-haired men.
26 I said I would scatter them
　　and blot out their memory from
　　　mankind,
27 but I dreaded the taunt of the enemy,
　　lest the adversary misunderstand
and say, 'Our hand has triumphed;
　　the LORD has not done all this.' "

28 They are a nation without sense,
　　there is no discernment in them.
29 If only they were wise and would
　　understand this
　　and discern what their end will be!
30 How could one man chase a
　　thousand,
　　or two put ten thousand to flight,
unless their Rock had sold them,

unless the LORD had given them
　　up?
31 For their rock is not like our Rock,
　　as even our enemies concede.
32 Their vine comes from the vine of
　　Sodom
　　and from the fields of Gomorrah.
Their grapes are filled with poison,
　　and their clusters with bitterness.
33 Their wine is the venom of serpents,
　　the deadly poison of cobras.

34 "Have I not kept this in reserve
　　and sealed it in my vaults?
35 It is mine to avenge; I will repay.
　　In due time their foot will slip;
their day of disaster is near
　　and their doom rushes upon them."

36 The LORD will judge his people
　　and have compassion on his
　　　servants
when he sees their strength is gone
　　and no one is left, slave or free.
37 He will say: "Now where are their
　　gods,
　　the rock they took refuge in,
38 the gods who ate the fat of their
　　sacrifices
　　and drank the wine of their drink
　　　offerings?
Let them rise up to help you!
　　Let them give you shelter!

39 "See now that I myself am He!
　　There is no god besides me.
I put to death and I bring to life,
　　I have wounded and I will heal,
　　and no one can deliver out of my
　　　hand.
40 I lift my hand to heaven and declare:
　　As surely as I live forever,
41 when I sharpen my flashing sword
　　and my hand grasps it in
　　　judgment,
I will take vengeance on my
　　adversaries
　　and repay those who hate me.
42 I will make my arrows drunk with
　　blood,
　　while my sword devours flesh:
the blood of the slain and the
　　captives,
　　the heads of the enemy leaders."

a 22 Hebrew to Sheol

43Rejoice, O nations, with his
        people,*a, b*
    for he will avenge the blood of his
        servants;
    he will take vengeance on his enemies
        and make atonement for his land
        and people.

44Moses came with Joshua*c* son of
Nun and spoke all the words of this song
in the hearing of the people. 45When Moses finished reciting all these words to all
Israel, 46he said to them, "Take to heart
all the words I have solemnly declared to
you this day, so that you may command
your children to obey carefully all the
words of this law. 47They are not just idle
words for you—they are your life. By them
you will live long in the land you are
crossing the Jordan to possess."

Moses to Die on Mount Nebo

48On that same day the LORD told Moses, 49"Go up into the Abarim Range to
Mount Nebo in Moab, across from Jericho, and view Canaan, the land I am giving the Israelites as their own possession.
50There on the mountain that you have
climbed you will die and be gathered to
your people, just as your brother Aaron
died on Mount Hor and was gathered to
his people. 51This is because both of you
broke faith with me in the presence of the
Israelites at the waters of Meribah Kadesh
in the Desert of Zin and because you did
not uphold my holiness among the Israelites. 52Therefore, you will see the land
only from a distance; you will not enter
the land I am giving to the people of Israel."

Moses Blesses the Tribes

33 This is the blessing that Moses the
man of God pronounced on the Israelites before his death. 2He said:

    "The LORD came from Sinai
        and dawned over them from Seir;
        he shone forth from Mount Paran.
    He came with*d* myriads of holy ones
        from the south, from his mountain
            slopes.*e*
3Surely it is you who love the people;
        all the holy ones are in your hand.
    At your feet they all bow down,
        and from you receive instruction,

4the law that Moses gave us,
        the possession of the assembly of
            Jacob.
5He was king over Jeshurun*f*
    when the leaders of the people
        assembled,
    along with the tribes of Israel.

6"Let Reuben live and not die,
    nor*g* his men be few."

7And this he said about Judah:

"Hear, O LORD, the cry of Judah;
    bring him to his people.
With his own hands he defends his
        cause.
    Oh, be his help against his foes!"

8About Levi he said:

"Your Thummim and Urim belong
        to the man you favored.
You tested him at Massah;
    you contended with him at the
        waters of Meribah.
9He said of his father and mother,
    'I have no regard for them.'
He did not recognize his brothers
    or acknowledge his own children,
but he watched over your word
    and guarded your covenant.
10He teaches your precepts to Jacob
    and your law to Israel.
He offers incense before you
    and whole burnt offerings on your
        altar.
11Bless all his skills, O LORD,
    and be pleased with the work of
        his hands.
Smite the loins of those who rise up
        against him;
    strike his foes till they rise no
        more."

12About Benjamin he said:

"Let the beloved of the LORD rest
        secure in him,
    for he shields him all day long,
    and the one the LORD loves rests
        between his shoulders."

---

*a*43 Or *Make his people rejoice, O nations*
*b*43 Masoretic Text; Dead Sea Scrolls (see also
Septuagint) *people, / and let all the angels worship
him /*   *c*44 Hebrew *Hoshea,* a variant of *Joshua*
*d*2 Or *from*   *e*2 The meaning of the Hebrew for
this phrase is uncertain.   *f*5 *Jeshurun* means the
upright one, that is, Israel; also in verse 26.
*g*6 Or *but let*

¹³About Joseph he said:

"May the LORD bless his land
   with the precious dew from heaven
      above
   and with the deep waters that lie
      below;
¹⁴with the best the sun brings forth
   and the finest the moon can yield;
¹⁵with the choicest gifts of the ancient
      mountains
   and the fruitfulness of the
      everlasting hills;
¹⁶with the best gifts of the earth and its
      fullness
   and the favor of him who dwelt in
      the burning bush.
Let all these rest on the head of
      Joseph,
   on the brow of the prince among[a]
      his brothers.
¹⁷In majesty he is like a firstborn bull;
   his horns are the horns of a wild
      ox.
With them he will gore the nations,
   even those at the ends of the earth.
Such are the ten thousands of
      Ephraim;
   such are the thousands of
      Manasseh."

¹⁸About Zebulun he said:

"Rejoice, Zebulun, in your going out,
   and you, Issachar, in your tents.
¹⁹They will summon peoples to the
      mountain
   and there offer sacrifices of
      righteousness;
they will feast on the abundance of
      the seas,
   on the treasures hidden in the
      sand."

²⁰About Gad he said:

"Blessed is he who enlarges Gad's
      domain!
Gad lives there like a lion,
   tearing at arm or head.
²¹He chose the best land for himself;
   the leader's portion was kept for
      him.
When the heads of the people
      assembled,
   he carried out the LORD's righteous
      will,

and his judgments concerning
      Israel."

²²About Dan he said:

"Dan is a lion's cub,
   springing out of Bashan."

²³About Naphtali he said:

"Naphtali is abounding with the
      favor of the LORD
   and is full of his blessing;
he will inherit southward to the
      lake."

²⁴About Asher he said:

"Most blessed of sons is Asher;
   let him be favored by his brothers,
   and let him bathe his feet in oil.
²⁵The bolts of your gates will be iron
      and bronze,
   and your strength will equal your
      days.

²⁶"There is no one like the God of
      Jeshurun,
   who rides on the heavens to help
      you
   and on the clouds in his majesty.
²⁷The eternal God is your refuge,
   and underneath are the everlasting
      arms.
He will drive out your enemy before
      you,
   saying, 'Destroy him!'
²⁸So Israel will live in safety alone;
   Jacob's spring is secure
in a land of grain and new wine,
   where the heavens drop dew.
²⁹Blessed are you, O Israel!
   Who is like you,
   a people saved by the LORD?
He is your shield and helper
   and your glorious sword.
Your enemies will cower before you,
   and you will trample down their
      high places.[b]"

The Death of Moses

34 Then Moses climbed Mount Nebo from the plains of Moab to the top of Pisgah, across from Jericho. There the LORD showed him the whole land—from Gilead to Dan, ²all of Naphtali, the terri-

---

[a]16 Or of the one separated from   [b]29 Or will
tread upon their bodies

tory of Ephraim and Manasseh, all the land of Judah as far as the western sea,[a] [3]the Negev and the whole region from the Valley of Jericho, the City of Palms, as far as Zoar. [4]Then the LORD said to him, "This is the land I promised on oath to Abraham, Isaac and Jacob when I said, 'I will give it to your descendants.' I have let you see it with your eyes, but you will not cross over into it."

[5]And Moses the servant of the LORD died there in Moab, as the LORD had said. [6]He buried him[b] in Moab, in the valley opposite Beth Peor, but to this day no one knows where his grave is. [7]Moses was a hundred and twenty years old when he died, yet his eyes were not weak nor his strength gone. [8]The Israelites grieved for Moses in the plains of Moab thirty days, until the time of weeping and mourning was over.

[9]Now Joshua son of Nun was filled with the spirit[c] of wisdom because Moses had laid his hands on him. So the Israelites listened to him and did what the LORD had commanded Moses.

[10]Since then, no prophet has risen in Israel like Moses, whom the LORD knew face to face, [11]who did all those miraculous signs and wonders the LORD sent him to do in Egypt—to Pharaoh and to all his officials and to his whole land. [12]For no one has ever shown the mighty power or performed the awesome deeds that Moses did in the sight of all Israel.

[a]2 That is, the Mediterranean   [b]6 Or *He was buried*   [c]9 Or *Spirit*

Joshua

*There may be
no more thrilling words* for a spouse to hear
than, "I'm so glad you're home!" Whether it's been a full
day away at work or a week-long business trip, there really
is no place like home. Having been away from home for a
few hundred years, the Israelites had been on a fairly significant journey. But now they were back in Canaan, the land
of their forefathers, the land in which God had promised
them they would resettle.

Imagine the celebration when Joshua stood in front of
the Israelites and shouted, "Welcome home!" These people,
who had for generations only heard about this wonderful
place, were now going to be able to settle down. They
would have their own land, their own possessions, a place
that they and their families could now call "home." Can you
imagine the joy? The book of Joshua contains the celebration of this precious place—a place of protection and
security for the children of Israel . . . and for you.

The Lord Commands Joshua

1 After the death of Moses the servant of
the Lord, the Lord said to Joshua son
of Nun, Moses' aide: ²"Moses my servant
is dead. Now then, you and all these people, get ready to cross the Jordan River
into the land I am about to give to them—
to the Israelites. ³I will give you every
place where you set your foot, as I promised Moses. ⁴Your territory will extend
from the desert to Lebanon, and from the
great river, the Euphrates—all the Hittite

country—to the Great Sea*a* on the west.
⁵No one will be able to stand up against
you all the days of your life. As I was with
Moses, so I will be with you; I will never
leave you nor forsake you.

⁶"Be strong and courageous, because
you will lead these people to inherit the
land I swore to their forefathers to give
them. ⁷Be strong and very courageous. Be
careful to obey all the law my servant Moses gave you; do not turn from it to the

a4 That is, the Mediterranean

right or to the left, that you may be successful wherever you go. ⁸Do not let this Book of the Law depart from your mouth; meditate on it day and night, so that you may be careful to do everything written in it. Then you will be prosperous and successful. ⁹Have I not commanded you? Be strong and courageous. Do not be terrified; do not be discouraged, for the LORD your God will be with you wherever you go."

¹⁰So Joshua ordered the officers of the people: ¹¹"Go through the camp and tell the people, 'Get your supplies ready. Three days from now you will cross the Jordan here to go in and take possession of the land the LORD your God is giving you for your own.' "

¹²But to the Reubenites, the Gadites and the half-tribe of Manasseh, Joshua said, ¹³"Remember the command that Moses the servant of the LORD gave you: 'The LORD your God is giving you rest and has granted you this land.' ¹⁴Your wives, your children and your livestock may stay in the land that Moses gave you east of the Jordan, but all your fighting men, fully armed, must cross over ahead of your brothers. You are to help your brothers ¹⁵until the LORD gives them rest, as he has done for you, and until they too have taken possession of the land that the LORD your God is giving them. After that, you may go back and occupy your own land, which Moses the servant of the LORD gave you east of the Jordan toward the sunrise."

¹⁶Then they answered Joshua, "Whatever you have commanded us we will do, and wherever you send us we will go. ¹⁷Just as we fully obeyed Moses, so we will obey you. Only may the LORD your God be with you as he was with Moses. ¹⁸Whoever rebels against your word and does not obey your words, whatever you may command them, will be put to death. Only be strong and courageous!"

Rahab and the Spies

2 Then Joshua son of Nun secretly sent two spies from Shittim. "Go, look over the land," he said, "especially Jericho." So they went and entered the house of a prostitute[a] named Rahab and stayed there.

ᵃ1 Or possibly *an innkeeper*

Staying the Course

Qu̇iet TIMES *with each other*

JOSHUA 1 God repeatedly reminded Joshua to keep his goals in mind. A new leader starting out on a journey, Joshua was told to keep focused. He was told not to veer off in any other direction—a good thing to keep in mind as we think about the marriage relationship.

At the time of the wedding, a couple vows to find happiness by loving and cherishing each other. But it doesn't take long before we can get sidetracked by other things or people who we think will bring us happiness.

For example, friends of ours have moved from house to house every few years. The next house is always going to be in the "perfect" location and "exactly" what they want. After each move, however, they find that the happiness they were pursuing has moved somewhere else!

Joshua was warned not to veer to the right or the left but to stay on the original path. No matter what distractions the Promised Land brought, more than once he was instructed to stay on the course set out for him. Similarly, the original marriage vow is the course set out for each of us in our marriages. It is important to ponder those vows often and make sure we haven't veered away from them.

—Bob & Rosemary

Weekend Warm-up *Turn your thoughts to your marriage vows—what did they mean then, and what do they mean now?*

Go to page 224 for your next devotional reading.

²The king of Jericho was told, "Look! Some of the Israelites have come here tonight to spy out the land." ³So the king of Jericho sent this message to Rahab: "Bring out the men who came to you and entered your house, because they have come to spy out the whole land."

⁴But the woman had taken the two men and hidden them. She said, "Yes, the men came to me, but I did not know where they had come from. ⁵At dusk, when it was time to close the city gate, the men left. I don't know which way they went. Go after them quickly. You may catch up with them." ⁶(But she had taken them up to the roof and hidden them under the stalks of flax she had laid out on the roof.) ⁷So the men set out in pursuit of the spies on the road that leads to the fords of the Jordan, and as soon as the pursuers had gone out, the gate was shut.

⁸Before the spies lay down for the night, she went up on the roof ⁹and said to them, "I know that the LORD has given this land to you and that a great fear of you has fallen on us, so that all who live in this country are melting in fear because of you. ¹⁰We have heard how the LORD dried up the water of the Red Sea[a] for you when you came out of Egypt, and what you did to Sihon and Og, the two kings of the Amorites east of the Jordan, whom you completely destroyed.[b] ¹¹When we heard of it, our hearts melted and everyone's courage failed because of you, for the LORD your God is God in heaven above and on the earth below. ¹²Now then, please swear to me by the LORD that you will show kindness to my family, because I have shown kindness to you. Give me a sure sign ¹³that you will spare the lives of my father and mother, my brothers and sisters, and all who belong to them, and that you will save us from death."

¹⁴"Our lives for your lives!" the men assured her. "If you don't tell what we are doing, we will treat you kindly and faithfully when the LORD gives us the land."

¹⁵So she let them down by a rope through the window, for the house she lived in was part of the city wall. ¹⁶Now she had said to them, "Go to the hills so the pursuers will not find you. Hide yourselves there three days until they return, and then go on your way."

¹⁷The men said to her, "This oath you made us swear will not be binding on us ¹⁸unless, when we enter the land, you have tied this scarlet cord in the window through which you let us down, and unless you have brought your father and mother, your brothers and all your family into your house. ¹⁹If anyone goes outside your house into the street, his blood will be on his own head; we will not be responsible. As for anyone who is in the house with you, his blood will be on our head if a hand is laid on him. ²⁰But if you tell what we are doing, we will be released from the oath you made us swear."

²¹"Agreed," she replied. "Let it be as you say." So she sent them away and they departed. And she tied the scarlet cord in the window.

²²When they left, they went into the hills and stayed there three days, until the pursuers had searched all along the road and returned without finding them. ²³Then the two men started back. They went down out of the hills, forded the river and came to Joshua son of Nun and told him everything that had happened to them. ²⁴They said to Joshua, "The LORD has surely given the whole land into our hands; all the people are melting in fear because of us."

Crossing the Jordan

3 Early in the morning Joshua and all the Israelites set out from Shittim and went to the Jordan, where they camped before crossing over. ²After three days the officers went throughout the camp, ³giving orders to the people: "When you see the ark of the covenant of the LORD your God, and the priests, who are Levites, carrying it, you are to move out from your positions and follow it. ⁴Then you will know which way to go, since you have never been this way before. But keep a distance of about a thousand yards[c] between you and the ark; do not go near it."

⁵Joshua told the people, "Consecrate yourselves, for tomorrow the LORD will do amazing things among you."

⁶Joshua said to the priests, "Take up

---

[a]10 Hebrew *Yam Suph*; that is, Sea of Reeds
[b]10 The Hebrew term refers to the irrevocable giving over of things or persons to the LORD, often by totally destroying them.   [c]4 Hebrew *about two thousand cubits* (about 900 meters)

the ark of the covenant and pass on ahead of the people." So they took it up and went ahead of them.

⁷And the LORD said to Joshua, "Today I will begin to exalt you in the eyes of all Israel, so they may know that I am with you as I was with Moses. ⁸Tell the priests who carry the ark of the covenant: 'When you reach the edge of the Jordan's waters, go and stand in the river.' "

⁹Joshua said to the Israelites, "Come here and listen to the words of the LORD your God. ¹⁰This is how you will know that the living God is among you and that he will certainly drive out before you the Canaanites, Hittites, Hivites, Perizzites, Girgashites, Amorites and Jebusites. ¹¹See, the ark of the covenant of the Lord of all the earth will go into the Jordan ahead of you. ¹²Now then, choose twelve men from the tribes of Israel, one from each tribe. ¹³And as soon as the priests who carry the ark of the LORD—the Lord of all the earth—set foot in the Jordan, its waters flowing downstream will be cut off and stand up in a heap."

¹⁴So when the people broke camp to cross the Jordan, the priests carrying the ark of the covenant went ahead of them. ¹⁵Now the Jordan is at flood stage all during harvest. Yet as soon as the priests who carried the ark reached the Jordan and their feet touched the water's edge, ¹⁶the water from upstream stopped flowing. It piled up in a heap a great distance away, at a town called Adam in the vicinity of Zarethan, while the water flowing down to the Sea of the Arabah (the Salt Sea ᵃ) was completely cut off. So the people crossed over opposite Jericho. ¹⁷The priests who carried the ark of the covenant of the LORD stood firm on dry ground in the middle of the Jordan, while all Israel passed by until the whole nation had completed the crossing on dry ground.

4 When the whole nation had finished crossing the Jordan, the LORD said to Joshua, ²"Choose twelve men from among the people, one from each tribe, ³and tell them to take up twelve stones from the middle of the Jordan from right

ᵃ16 That is, the Dead Sea

Milestones of Marriage

JOSHUA 4:21 Crossing the Jordan was definitely a milestone for the Israelites. Imagine what it must have been like to see God miraculously provide a dry path for them to cross the Jordan and march into the Promised Land. Certainly the Israelites would remember this day forever. So why did Joshua instruct them to take twelve stones from the middle of the Jordan River as a memorial? Could it be that he knew the tendency of God's people to forget God's past miracles when faced with the problems and challenges of the present?

What problems and challenges are you facing today in your marriage? Are you on a survival treadmill? You're working hard in your job; you're trying to be a good parent; but the constant daily demands are beating you down. You'd like to experience a few miracles—like no bills or sniffly colds this month. If only you could have twenty-four hours alone with your spouse. Life seems so daily, and it seems like it's been this way forever.

Stop! You may not have a literal stone memorial like the Israelites, but you can reflect on God's goodness and past provisions. Revisit the milestones of your marriage. Think back to how God brought the two of you together. Remember your wedding day and the first year of your marriage? Remember your first rented apartment or getting your first house mortgage? The birth of a baby, a breakthrough in your communication, resolving a major conflict—milestones include those times when God steps in and empowers you to love each other in a deeper way and together surmount challenges that, without his intervention, would have been too huge. Keep collecting the milestones. They will encourage you when life throws its challenges at you.

—*Dave & Claudia*

Go to page 227 for your next devotional reading.

where the priests stood and to carry them over with you and put them down at the place where you stay tonight."

⁴So Joshua called together the twelve men he had appointed from the Israelites, one from each tribe, ⁵and said to them, "Go over before the ark of the LORD your God into the middle of the Jordan. Each of you is to take up a stone on his shoulder, according to the number of the tribes of the Israelites, ⁶to serve as a sign among you. In the future, when your children ask you, 'What do these stones mean?' ⁷tell them that the flow of the Jordan was cut off before the ark of the covenant of the LORD. When it crossed the Jordan, the waters of the Jordan were cut off. These stones are to be a memorial to the people of Israel forever."

⁸So the Israelites did as Joshua commanded them. They took twelve stones from the middle of the Jordan, according to the number of the tribes of the Israelites, as the LORD had told Joshua; and they carried them over with them to their camp, where they put them down. ⁹Joshua set up the twelve stones that had beenᵃ in the middle of the Jordan at the spot where the priests who carried the ark of the covenant had stood. And they are there to this day.

¹⁰Now the priests who carried the ark remained standing in the middle of the Jordan until everything the LORD had commanded Joshua was done by the people, just as Moses had directed Joshua. The people hurried over, ¹¹and as soon as all of them had crossed, the ark of the LORD and the priests came to the other side while the people watched. ¹²The men of Reuben, Gad and the half-tribe of Manasseh crossed over, armed, in front of the Israelites, as Moses had directed them. ¹³About forty thousand armed for battle crossed over before the LORD to the plains of Jericho for war.

¹⁴That day the LORD exalted Joshua in the sight of all Israel; and they revered him all the days of his life, just as they had revered Moses.

¹⁵Then the LORD said to Joshua, ¹⁶"Command the priests carrying the ark of the Testimony to come up out of the Jordan."

¹⁷So Joshua commanded the priests, "Come up out of the Jordan."

JUST BETWEEN *you & me*

Milestones of Marriage

What are some of the milestones of your marriage? A milestone is any special event or situation that influences the direction of your lives together. Start by thinking about when you first met and fell in love. A milestone might be:

- Your first date
- Your wedding day
- Your honeymoon
- Birth of each child
- Moves you have made
- Crisis times you have weathered together
- Times of Celebration

For this check-up, choose a time when you will not be rushed, and a place where you can talk quietly. Take along paper and pen and note your marriage milestones. One of the nicest things about sharing your marriage milestones is that your memories are uniquely yours and sharing them can create intimacy and renew excitement. You'll be glad you took the time to remember and to focus on what is so important to both of you.

¹⁸And the priests came up out of the river carrying the ark of the covenant of the LORD. No sooner had they set their feet on the dry ground than the waters of the Jordan returned to their place and ran at flood stage as before.

¹⁹On the tenth day of the first month the people went up from the Jordan and camped at Gilgal on the eastern border of Jericho. ²⁰And Joshua set up at Gilgal the twelve stones they had taken out of the Jordan. ²¹He said to the Israelites, "In the future when your descendants ask their fathers, 'What do these stones mean?' ²²tell them, 'Israel crossed the Jordan on dry ground.' ²³For the LORD your God dried up the Jordan before you until you had crossed over. The LORD your God did to the Jordan just what he had done

ᵃ9 Or *Joshua also set up twelve stones*

to the Red Sea[a] when he dried it up before us until we had crossed over. [24]He did this so that all the peoples of the earth might know that the hand of the LORD is powerful and so that you might always fear the LORD your God."

Circumcision at Gilgal

5 Now when all the Amorite kings west of the Jordan and all the Canaanite kings along the coast heard how the LORD had dried up the Jordan before the Israelites until we had crossed over, their hearts melted and they no longer had the courage to face the Israelites.

[2]At that time the LORD said to Joshua, "Make flint knives and circumcise the Israelites again." [3]So Joshua made flint knives and circumcised the Israelites at Gibeath Haaraloth.[b]

[4]Now this is why he did so: All those who came out of Egypt—all the men of military age—died in the desert on the way after leaving Egypt. [5]All the people that came out had been circumcised, but all the people born in the desert during the journey from Egypt had not. [6]The Israelites had moved about in the desert forty years until all the men who were of military age when they left Egypt had died, since they had not obeyed the LORD. For the LORD had sworn to them that they would not see the land that he had solemnly promised their fathers to give us, a land flowing with milk and honey. [7]So he raised up their sons in their place, and these were the ones Joshua circumcised. They were still uncircumcised because they had not been circumcised on the way. [8]And after the whole nation had been circumcised, they remained where they were in camp until they were healed.

[9]Then the LORD said to Joshua, "Today I have rolled away the reproach of Egypt from you." So the place has been called Gilgal[c] to this day.

[10]On the evening of the fourteenth day of the month, while camped at Gilgal on the plains of Jericho, the Israelites celebrated the Passover. [11]The day after the Passover, that very day, they ate some of the produce of the land: unleavened bread and roasted grain. [12]The manna stopped the day after[d] they ate this food from the land; there was no longer any manna for the Israelites, but that year they ate of the produce of Canaan.

The Fall of Jericho

[13]Now when Joshua was near Jericho, he looked up and saw a man standing in front of him with a drawn sword in his hand. Joshua went up to him and asked, "Are you for us or for our enemies?"

[14]"Neither," he replied, "but as commander of the army of the LORD I have now come." Then Joshua fell facedown to the ground in reverence, and asked him, "What message does my Lord[e] have for his servant?"

[15]The commander of the LORD's army replied, "Take off your sandals, for the place where you are standing is holy." And Joshua did so.

6 Now Jericho was tightly shut up because of the Israelites. No one went out and no one came in.

[2]Then the LORD said to Joshua, "See, I have delivered Jericho into your hands, along with its king and its fighting men. [3]March around the city once with all the armed men. Do this for six days. [4]Have seven priests carry trumpets of rams' horns in front of the ark. On the seventh day, march around the city seven times, with the priests blowing the trumpets. [5]When you hear them sound a long blast on the trumpets, have all the people give a loud shout; then the wall of the city will collapse and the people will go up, every man straight in."

[6]So Joshua son of Nun called the priests and said to them, "Take up the ark of the covenant of the LORD and have seven priests carry trumpets in front of it." [7]And he ordered the people, "Advance! March around the city, with the armed guard going ahead of the ark of the LORD."

[8]When Joshua had spoken to the people, the seven priests carrying the seven trumpets before the LORD went forward, blowing their trumpets, and the ark of the LORD's covenant followed them. [9]The armed guard marched ahead of the priests who blew the trumpets, and the rear guard followed the ark. All this time the

---

[a]23 Hebrew *Yam Suph*; that is, Sea of Reeds
[b]3 *Gibeath Haaraloth* means *hill of foreskins.*
[c]9 *Gilgal* sounds like the Hebrew for *roll.*
[d]12 Or *the day*   [e]14 Or *lord*

trumpets were sounding. ¹⁰But Joshua had commanded the people, "Do not give a war cry, do not raise your voices, do not say a word until the day I tell you to shout. Then shout!" ¹¹So he had the ark of the LORD carried around the city, circling it once. Then the people returned to camp and spent the night there.

¹²Joshua got up early the next morning and the priests took up the ark of the LORD. ¹³The seven priests carrying the seven trumpets went forward, marching before the ark of the LORD and blowing the trumpets. The armed men went ahead of them and the rear guard followed the ark of the LORD, while the trumpets kept sounding. ¹⁴So on the second day they marched around the city once and returned to the camp. They did this for six days.

¹⁵On the seventh day, they got up at daybreak and marched around the city seven times in the same manner, except that on that day they circled the city seven times. ¹⁶The seventh time around, when the priests sounded the trumpet blast, Joshua commanded the people, "Shout! For the LORD has given you the city! ¹⁷The city and all that is in it are to be devoted*a* to the LORD. Only Rahab the prostitute*b*

and all who are with her in her house shall be spared, because she hid the spies we sent. ¹⁸But keep away from the devoted things, so that you will not bring about your own destruction by taking any of them. Otherwise you will make the camp of Israel liable to destruction and bring trouble on it. ¹⁹All the silver and gold and the articles of bronze and iron are sacred to the LORD and must go into his treasury."

²⁰When the trumpets sounded, the people shouted, and at the sound of the trumpet, when the people gave a loud shout, the wall collapsed; so every man charged straight in, and they took the city. ²¹They devoted the city to the LORD and destroyed with the sword every living thing in it—men and women, young and old, cattle, sheep and donkeys.

²²Joshua said to the two men who had spied out the land, "Go into the prostitute's house and bring her out and all who belong to her, in accordance with your oath to her." ²³So the young men who had done the spying went in and brought

*a*17 The Hebrew term refers to the irrevocable giving over of things or persons to the LORD, often by totally destroying them; also in verses 18 and 21.   *b*17 Or possibly *innkeeper*; also in verses 22 and 25

Boundless Love

Tuesday

JOSHUA 6 Reading about the battle of Jericho reminded us of a story we heard some time ago. A man who made his living by raising ducks had a problem. He only had one pond for several different kinds of ducks that tended to quack and peck at each other. Wanting to keep the different species separate, the man ran fences right through the water. When he was finished, he had fences crisscrossing in every direction. *Now,* he thought, *all the ducks will feel safe in their own sections.*

Sometimes couples do the same thing. We build fences and walls around parts of ourselves to keep from getting hurt (or quacked at). If that's a description of your marriage, it's time to consider doing something about those walls.

One day the man who raised the ducks

discovered that they weren't doing so well. Some seemed feeble because they didn't have enough room. The man didn't know what to do. It would be a messy job ripping out all those fences. Then it hit him. He came up with a solution: raise the level of the water. The fences were eventually submerged by the water, and the ducks had plenty of room to swim and interact, as well as to keep their distance.

You have the same option in your marriage. You might be tempted to tear down your spouse's fence, but take care. Nobody likes somebody else adjusting his or her boundaries. On the other hand, you can raise the level of love in your marriage until the fences disappear.

—Les & Leslie

Go to page 244 for your next devotional reading.

out Rahab, her father and mother and brothers and all who belonged to her. They brought out her entire family and put them in a place outside the camp of Israel.

²⁴Then they burned the whole city and everything in it, but they put the silver and gold and the articles of bronze and iron into the treasury of the LORD's house. ²⁵But Joshua spared Rahab the prostitute, with her family and all who belonged to her, because she hid the men Joshua had sent as spies to Jericho—and she lives among the Israelites to this day.

²⁶At that time Joshua pronounced this solemn oath: "Cursed before the LORD is the man who undertakes to rebuild this city, Jericho:

"At the cost of his firstborn son
    will he lay its foundations;
at the cost of his youngest
    will he set up its gates."

²⁷So the LORD was with Joshua, and his fame spread throughout the land.

Achan's Sin

7 But the Israelites acted unfaithfully in regard to the devoted things[a]; Achan son of Carmi, the son of Zimri,[b] the son of Zerah, of the tribe of Judah, took some of them. So the LORD's anger burned against Israel.

²Now Joshua sent men from Jericho to Ai, which is near Beth Aven to the east of Bethel, and told them, "Go up and spy out the region." So the men went up and spied out Ai. ³When they returned to Joshua, they said, "Not all the people will have to go up against Ai. Send two or three thousand men to take it and do not weary all the people, for only a few men are there." ⁴So about three thousand men went up; but they were routed by the men of Ai, ⁵who killed about thirty-six of them. They chased the Israelites from the city gate as far as the stone quarries[c] and struck them down on the slopes. At this the hearts of the people melted and became like water.

⁶Then Joshua tore his clothes and fell facedown to the ground before the ark of the LORD, remaining there till evening. The elders of Israel did the same, and

sprinkled dust on their heads. ⁷And Joshua said, "Ah, Sovereign LORD, why did you ever bring this people across the Jordan to deliver us into the hands of the Amorites to destroy us? If only we had been content to stay on the other side of the Jordan! ⁸O Lord, what can I say, now that Israel has been routed by its enemies? ⁹The Canaanites and the other people of the country will hear about this and they will surround us and wipe out our name from the earth. What then will you do for your own great name?"

¹⁰The LORD said to Joshua, "Stand up! What are you doing down on your face? ¹¹Israel has sinned; they have violated my covenant, which I commanded them to keep. They have taken some of the devoted things; they have stolen, they have lied, they have put them with their own possessions. ¹²That is why the Israelites cannot stand against their enemies; they turn their backs and run because they have been made liable to destruction. I will not be with you anymore unless you destroy whatever among you is devoted to destruction.

¹³"Go, consecrate the people. Tell them, 'Consecrate yourselves in preparation for tomorrow; for this is what the LORD, the God of Israel, says: That which is devoted is among you, O Israel. You cannot stand against your enemies until you remove it.

¹⁴"'In the morning, present yourselves tribe by tribe. The tribe that the LORD takes shall come forward clan by clan; the clan that the LORD takes shall come forward family by family; and the family that the LORD takes shall come forward man by man. ¹⁵He who is caught with the devoted things shall be destroyed by fire, along with all that belongs to him. He has violated the covenant of the LORD and has done a disgraceful thing in Israel!'"

¹⁶Early the next morning Joshua had Israel come forward by tribes, and Judah was taken. ¹⁷The clans of Judah came forward, and he took the Zerahites. He had the clan of the Zerahites come forward by

---

a1 The Hebrew term refers to the irrevocable giving over of things or persons to the LORD, often by totally destroying them; also in verses 11, 12, 13 and 15.   b1 See Septuagint and 1 Chron. 2:6; Hebrew *Zabdi*; also in verses 17 and 18.   c5 Or *as far as Shebarim* families, and Zimri was taken. ¹⁸Joshua had his family come forward man by man, and Achan son of Carmi, the son of Zimri, the son of Zerah, of the tribe of Judah, was taken.

¹⁹Then Joshua said to Achan, "My son, give glory to the LORD,ᵃ the God of Israel, and give him the praise.ᵇ Tell me what you have done; do not hide it from me."

²⁰Achan replied, "It is true! I have sinned against the LORD, the God of Israel. This is what I have done: ²¹When I saw in the plunder a beautiful robe from Babylonia,ᶜ two hundred shekelsᵈ of silver and a wedge of gold weighing fifty shekels,ᵉ I coveted them and took them. They are hidden in the ground inside my tent, with the silver underneath."

²²So Joshua sent messengers, and they ran to the tent, and there it was, hidden in his tent, with the silver underneath. ²³They took the things from the tent, brought them to Joshua and all the Israelites and spread them out before the LORD.

²⁴Then Joshua, together with all Israel, took Achan son of Zerah, the silver, the robe, the gold wedge, his sons and daughters, his cattle, donkeys and sheep, his tent and all that he had, to the Valley of Achor. ²⁵Joshua said, "Why have you brought this trouble on us? The LORD will bring trouble on you today."

Then all Israel stoned him, and after they had stoned the rest, they burned them. ²⁶Over Achan they heaped up a large pile of rocks, which remains to this day. Then the LORD turned from his fierce anger. Therefore that place has been called the Valley of Achorᶠ ever since.

Ai Destroyed

8 Then the LORD said to Joshua, "Do not be afraid; do not be discouraged. Take the whole army with you, and go up and attack Ai. For I have delivered into your hands the king of Ai, his people, his city and his land. ²You shall do to Ai and its king as you did to Jericho and its king, except that you may carry off their plunder and livestock for yourselves. Set an ambush behind the city."

³So Joshua and the whole army moved out to attack Ai. He chose thirty thousand of his best fighting men and sent them out at night ⁴with these orders: "Listen carefully. You are to set an ambush behind the city. Don't go very far from it. All of you be on the alert. ⁵I and all those with me will advance on the city, and when the men come out against us, as they did before, we will flee from them. ⁶They will pursue us until we have lured them away from the city, for they will say, 'They are running away from us as they did before.' So when we flee from them, ⁷you are to rise up from ambush and take the city. The LORD your God will give it into your hand. ⁸When you have taken the city, set it on fire. Do what the LORD has commanded. See to it; you have my orders."

⁹Then Joshua sent them off, and they went to the place of ambush and lay in wait between Bethel and Ai, to the west of Ai—but Joshua spent that night with the people.

¹⁰Early the next morning Joshua mustered his men, and he and the leaders of Israel marched before them to Ai. ¹¹The entire force that was with him marched up and approached the city and arrived in front of it. They set up camp north of Ai, with the valley between them and the city. ¹²Joshua had taken about five thousand men and set them in ambush between Bethel and Ai, to the west of the city. ¹³They had the soldiers take up their positions—all those in the camp to the north of the city and the ambush to the west of it. That night Joshua went into the valley.

¹⁴When the king of Ai saw this, he and all the men of the city hurried out early in the morning to meet Israel in battle at a certain place overlooking the Arabah. But he did not know that an ambush had been set against him behind the city. ¹⁵Joshua and all Israel let themselves be driven back before them, and they fled toward the desert. ¹⁶All the men of Ai were called to pursue them, and they pursued Joshua and were lured away from the city. ¹⁷Not a man remained in Ai or Bethel who did not go after Israel. They

---

ᵃ19 A solemn charge to tell the truth   ᵇ19 Or *and confess to him*   ᶜ21 Hebrew *Shinar*   ᵈ21 That is, about 5 pounds (about 2.3 kilograms)   ᵉ21 That is, about 1 1/4 pounds (about 0.6 kilogram)   ᶠ26 *Achor* means *trouble*.

left the city open and went in pursuit of Israel.

[18]Then the LORD said to Joshua, "Hold out toward Ai the javelin that is in your hand, for into your hand I will deliver the city." So Joshua held out his javelin toward Ai. [19]As soon as he did this, the men in the ambush rose quickly from their position and rushed forward. They entered the city and captured it and quickly set it on fire.

[20]The men of Ai looked back and saw the smoke of the city rising against the sky, but they had no chance to escape in any direction, for the Israelites who had been fleeing toward the desert had turned back against their pursuers. [21]For when Joshua and all Israel saw that the ambush had taken the city and that smoke was going up from the city, they turned around and attacked the men of Ai. [22]The men of the ambush also came out of the city against them, so that they were caught in the middle, with Israelites on both sides. Israel cut them down, leaving them neither survivors nor fugitives. [23]But they took the king of Ai alive and brought him to Joshua.

[24]When Israel had finished killing all the men of Ai in the fields and in the desert where they had chased them, and when every one of them had been put to the sword, all the Israelites returned to Ai and killed those who were in it. [25]Twelve thousand men and women fell that day— all the people of Ai. [26]For Joshua did not draw back the hand that held out his javelin until he had destroyed[a] all who lived in Ai. [27]But Israel did carry off for themselves the livestock and plunder of this city, as the LORD had instructed Joshua.

[28]So Joshua burned Ai and made it a permanent heap of ruins, a desolate place to this day. [29]He hung the king of Ai on a tree and left him there until evening. At sunset, Joshua ordered them to take his body from the tree and throw it down at the entrance of the city gate. And they raised a large pile of rocks over it, which remains to this day.

The Covenant Renewed at Mount Ebal

[30]Then Joshua built on Mount Ebal an altar to the LORD, the God of Israel, [31]as Moses the servant of the LORD had com-

manded the Israelites. He built it according to what is written in the Book of the Law of Moses—an altar of uncut stones, on which no iron tool had been used. On it they offered to the LORD burnt offerings and sacrificed fellowship offerings.[b] [32]There, in the presence of the Israelites, Joshua copied on stones the law of Moses, which he had written. [33]All Israel, aliens and citizens alike, with their elders, officials and judges, were standing on both sides of the ark of the covenant of the LORD, facing those who carried it—the priests, who were Levites. Half of the people stood in front of Mount Gerizim and half of them in front of Mount Ebal, as Moses the servant of the LORD had formerly commanded when he gave instructions to bless the people of Israel.

[34]Afterward, Joshua read all the words of the law—the blessings and the curses— just as it is written in the Book of the Law. [35]There was not a word of all that Moses had commanded that Joshua did not read to the whole assembly of Israel, including the women and children, and the aliens who lived among them.

The Gibeonite Deception

9 Now when all the kings west of the Jordan heard about these things— those in the hill country, in the western foothills, and along the entire coast of the Great Sea[c] as far as Lebanon (the kings of the Hittites, Amorites, Canaanites, Perizzites, Hivites and Jebusites)— [2]they came together to make war against Joshua and Israel.

[3]However, when the people of Gibeon heard what Joshua had done to Jericho and Ai, [4]they resorted to a ruse: They went as a delegation whose donkeys were loaded[d] with worn-out sacks and old wineskins, cracked and mended. [5]The men put worn and patched sandals on their feet and wore old clothes. All the bread of their food supply was dry and moldy. [6]Then they went to Joshua in the camp at

[a]26 The Hebrew term refers to the irrevocable giving over of things or persons to the LORD, often by totally destroying them.   [b]31 Traditionally *peace offerings*   [c]1 That is, the Mediterranean   [d]4 Most Hebrew manuscripts; some Hebrew manuscripts, Vulgate and Syriac (see also Septuagint) *They prepared provisions and loaded their donkeys*

Gilgal and said to him and the men of Israel, "We have come from a distant country; make a treaty with us."

⁷The men of Israel said to the Hivites, "But perhaps you live near us. How then can we make a treaty with you?"

⁸"We are your servants," they said to Joshua.

But Joshua asked, "Who are you and where do you come from?"

⁹They answered: "Your servants have come from a very distant country because of the fame of the LORD your God. For we have heard reports of him: all that he did in Egypt, ¹⁰and all that he did to the two kings of the Amorites east of the Jordan—Sihon king of Heshbon, and Og king of Bashan, who reigned in Ashtaroth. ¹¹And our elders and all those living in our country said to us, 'Take provisions for your journey; go and meet them and say to them, "We are your servants; make a treaty with us." ' ¹²This bread of ours was warm when we packed it at home on the day we left to come to you. But now see how dry and moldy it is. ¹³And these wineskins that we filled were new, but see how cracked they are. And our clothes and sandals are worn out by the very long journey."

¹⁴The men of Israel sampled their provisions but did not inquire of the LORD. ¹⁵Then Joshua made a treaty of peace with them to let them live, and the leaders of the assembly ratified it by oath.

¹⁶Three days after they made the treaty with the Gibeonites, the Israelites heard that they were neighbors, living near them. ¹⁷So the Israelites set out and on the third day came to their cities: Gibeon, Kephirah, Beeroth and Kiriath Jearim. ¹⁸But the Israelites did not attack them, because the leaders of the assembly had sworn an oath to them by the LORD, the God of Israel.

The whole assembly grumbled against the leaders, ¹⁹but all the leaders answered, "We have given them our oath by the LORD, the God of Israel, and we cannot touch them now. ²⁰This is what we will do to them: We will let them live, so that wrath will not fall on us for breaking the oath we swore to them." ²¹They continued, "Let them live, but let them be woodcutters and water carriers for the entire com-munity." So the leaders' promise to them was kept.

²²Then Joshua summoned the Gibeon-ites and said, "Why did you deceive us by saying, 'We live a long way from you,' while actually you live near us? ²³You are now under a curse: You will never cease to serve as woodcutters and water carriers for the house of my God."

²⁴They answered Joshua, "Your ser-vants were clearly told how the LORD your God had commanded his servant Moses to give you the whole land and to wipe out all its inhabitants from before you. So we feared for our lives because of you, and that is why we did this. ²⁵We are now in your hands. Do to us whatever seems good and right to you."

²⁶So Joshua saved them from the Isra-elites, and they did not kill them. ²⁷That day he made the Gibeonites woodcutters and water carriers for the community and for the altar of the LORD at the place the LORD would choose. And that is what they are to this day.

The Sun Stands Still

10 Now Adoni-Zedek king of Jerusa-lem heard that Joshua had taken Ai and totally destroyed*a* it, doing to Ai and its king as he had done to Jericho and its king, and that the people of Gibeon had made a treaty of peace with Israel and were living near them. ²He and his people were very much alarmed at this, because Gibeon was an important city, like one of the royal cities; it was larger than Ai, and all its men were good fighters. ³So Adoni-Zedek king of Jerusalem appealed to Ho-ham king of Hebron, Piram king of Jar-muth, Japhia king of Lachish and Debir king of Eglon. ⁴"Come up and help me attack Gibeon," he said, "because it has made peace with Joshua and the Israel-ites."

⁵Then the five kings of the Amorites—the kings of Jerusalem, Hebron, Jarmuth, Lachish and Eglon—joined forces. They moved up with all their troops and took up positions against Gibeon and at-tacked it.

---

a1 The Hebrew term refers to the irrevocable giving over of things or persons to the LORD, often by totally destroying them; also in verses 28, 35, 37, 39 and 40.

6The Gibeonites then sent word to Joshua in the camp at Gilgal: "Do not abandon your servants. Come up to us quickly and save us! Help us, because all the Amorite kings from the hill country have joined forces against us."

7So Joshua marched up from Gilgal with his entire army, including all the best fighting men. 8The LORD said to Joshua, "Do not be afraid of them; I have given them into your hand. Not one of them will be able to withstand you."

9After an all-night march from Gilgal, Joshua took them by surprise. 10The LORD threw them into confusion before Israel, who defeated them in a great victory at Gibeon. Israel pursued them along the road going up to Beth Horon and cut them down all the way to Azekah and Makkedah. 11As they fled before Israel on the road down from Beth Horon to Azekah, the LORD hurled large hailstones down on them from the sky, and more of them died from the hailstones than were killed by the swords of the Israelites.

12On the day the LORD gave the Amorites over to Israel, Joshua said to the LORD in the presence of Israel:

"O sun, stand still over Gibeon,
    O moon, over the Valley of
        Aijalon."
13So the sun stood still,
    and the moon stopped,
    till the nation avenged itself on[a]
        its enemies,

as it is written in the Book of Jashar.

The sun stopped in the middle of the sky and delayed going down about a full day. 14There has never been a day like it before or since, a day when the LORD listened to a man. Surely the LORD was fighting for Israel!

15Then Joshua returned with all Israel to the camp at Gilgal.

Five Amorite Kings Killed

16Now the five kings had fled and hidden in the cave at Makkedah. 17When Joshua was told that the five kings had been found hiding in the cave at Makkedah, 18he said, "Roll large rocks up to the mouth of the cave, and post some men there to guard it. 19But don't stop! Pursue your enemies, attack them from the rear

and don't let them reach their cities, for the LORD your God has given them into your hand."

20So Joshua and the Israelites destroyed them completely—almost to a man—but the few who were left reached their fortified cities. 21The whole army then returned safely to Joshua in the camp at Makkedah, and no one uttered a word against the Israelites.

22Joshua said, "Open the mouth of the cave and bring those five kings out to me." 23So they brought the five kings out of the cave—the kings of Jerusalem, Hebron, Jarmuth, Lachish and Eglon. 24When they had brought these kings to Joshua, he summoned all the men of Israel and said to the army commanders who had come with him, "Come here and put your feet on the necks of these kings." So they came forward and placed their feet on their necks.

25Joshua said to them, "Do not be afraid; do not be discouraged. Be strong and courageous. This is what the LORD will do to all the enemies you are going to fight." 26Then Joshua struck and killed the kings and hung them on five trees, and they were left hanging on the trees until evening.

27At sunset Joshua gave the order and they took them down from the trees and threw them into the cave where they had been hiding. At the mouth of the cave they placed large rocks, which are there to this day.

28That day Joshua took Makkedah. He put the city and its king to the sword and totally destroyed everyone in it. He left no survivors. And he did to the king of Makkedah as he had done to the king of Jericho.

Southern Cities Conquered

29Then Joshua and all Israel with him moved on from Makkedah to Libnah and attacked it. 30The LORD also gave that city and its king into Israel's hand. The city and everyone in it Joshua put to the sword. He left no survivors there. And he did to its king as he had done to the king of Jericho.

31Then Joshua and all Israel with him moved on from Libnah to Lachish; he

a13 Or *nation triumphed over*

took up positions against it and attacked it. ³²The LORD handed Lachish over to Israel, and Joshua took it on the second day. The city and everyone in it he put to the sword, just as he had done to Libnah. ³³Meanwhile, Horam king of Gezer had come up to help Lachish, but Joshua defeated him and his army—until no survivors were left.

³⁴Then Joshua and all Israel with him moved on from Lachish to Eglon; they took up positions against it and attacked it. ³⁵They captured it that same day and put it to the sword and totally destroyed everyone in it, just as they had done to Lachish.

³⁶Then Joshua and all Israel with him went up from Eglon to Hebron and attacked it. ³⁷They took the city and put it to the sword, together with its king, its villages and everyone in it. They left no survivors. Just as at Eglon, they totally destroyed it and everyone in it.

³⁸Then Joshua and all Israel with him turned around and attacked Debir. ³⁹They took the city, its king and its villages, and put them to the sword. Everyone in it they totally destroyed. They left no survivors. They did to Debir and its king as they had done to Libnah and its king and to Hebron.

⁴⁰So Joshua subdued the whole region, including the hill country, the Negev, the western foothills and the mountain slopes, together with all their kings. He left no survivors. He totally destroyed all who breathed, just as the LORD, the God of Israel, had commanded. ⁴¹Joshua subdued them from Kadesh Barnea to Gaza and from the whole region of Goshen to Gibeon. ⁴²All these kings and their lands Joshua conquered in one campaign, because the LORD, the God of Israel, fought for Israel.

⁴³Then Joshua returned with all Israel to the camp at Gilgal.

Northern Kings Defeated

11 When Jabin king of Hazor heard of this, he sent word to Jobab king of Madon, to the kings of Shimron and Acshaph, ²and to the northern kings who were in the mountains, in the Arabah south of Kinnereth, in the western foothills and in Naphoth Dor*a* on the west;

³to the Canaanites in the east and west; to the Amorites, Hittites, Perizzites and Jebusites in the hill country; and to the Hivites below Hermon in the region of Mizpah. ⁴They came out with all their troops and a large number of horses and chariots—a huge army, as numerous as the sand on the seashore. ⁵All these kings joined forces and made camp together at the Waters of Merom, to fight against Israel.

⁶The LORD said to Joshua, "Do not be afraid of them, because by this time tomorrow I will hand all of them over to Israel, slain. You are to hamstring their horses and burn their chariots."

⁷So Joshua and his whole army came against them suddenly at the Waters of Merom and attacked them, ⁸and the LORD gave them into the hand of Israel. They defeated them and pursued them all the way to Greater Sidon, to Misrephoth Maim, and to the Valley of Mizpah on the east, until no survivors were left. ⁹Joshua did to them as the LORD had directed: He hamstrung their horses and burned their chariots.

¹⁰At that time Joshua turned back and captured Hazor and put its king to the sword. (Hazor had been the head of all these kingdoms.) ¹¹Everyone in it they put to the sword. They totally destroyed*b* them, not sparing anything that breathed, and he burned up Hazor itself.

¹²Joshua took all these royal cities and their kings and put them to the sword. He totally destroyed them, as Moses the servant of the LORD had commanded. ¹³Yet Israel did not burn any of the cities built on their mounds—except Hazor, which Joshua burned. ¹⁴The Israelites carried off for themselves all the plunder and livestock of these cities, but all the people they put to the sword until they completely destroyed them, not sparing anyone that breathed. ¹⁵As the LORD commanded his servant Moses, so Moses commanded Joshua, and Joshua did it; he left nothing undone of all that the LORD commanded Moses.

¹⁶So Joshua took this entire land: the hill country, all the Negev, the whole re-

---

a2 Or *in the heights of Dor*   *b11* The Hebrew term refers to the irrevocable giving over of things or persons to the LORD, often by totally destroying them; also in verses 12, 20 and 21.

gion of Goshen, the western foothills, the Arabah and the mountains of Israel with their foothills, [17]from Mount Halak, which rises toward Seir, to Baal Gad in the Valley of Lebanon below Mount Hermon. He captured all their kings and struck them down, putting them to death. [18]Joshua waged war against all these kings for a long time. [19]Except for the Hivites living in Gibeon, not one city made a treaty of peace with the Israelites, who took them all in battle. [20]For it was the LORD himself who hardened their hearts to wage war against Israel, so that he might destroy them totally, exterminating them without mercy, as the LORD had commanded Moses.

[21]At that time Joshua went and destroyed the Anakites from the hill country: from Hebron, Debir and Anab, from all the hill country of Judah, and from all the hill country of Israel. Joshua totally destroyed them and their towns. [22]No Anakites were left in Israelite territory; only in Gaza, Gath and Ashdod did any survive. [23]So Joshua took the entire land, just as the LORD had directed Moses, and he gave it as an inheritance to Israel according to their tribal divisions.

Then the land had rest from war.

List of Defeated Kings

12 These are the kings of the land whom the Israelites had defeated and whose territory they took over east of the Jordan, from the Arnon Gorge to Mount Hermon, including all the eastern side of the Arabah:

[2]Sihon king of the Amorites,
who reigned in Heshbon. He ruled from Aroer on the rim of the Arnon Gorge—from the middle of the gorge—to the Jabbok River, which is the border of the Ammonites. This included half of Gilead. [3]He also ruled over the eastern Arabah from the Sea of Kinnereth[a] to the Sea of the Arabah (the Salt Sea[b]), to Beth Jeshimoth, and then southward below the slopes of Pisgah.

[4]And the territory of Og king of Bashan, one of the last of the Rephaites, who reigned in Ashtaroth and Edrei. [5]He ruled over Mount Hermon, Salecah, all of Bashan to the border of the people of Geshur and Maacah, and half of Gilead to the border of Sihon king of Heshbon.

[6]Moses, the servant of the LORD, and the Israelites conquered them. And Moses the servant of the LORD gave their land to the Reubenites, the Gadites and the half-tribe of Manasseh to be their possession.

[7]These are the kings of the land that Joshua and the Israelites conquered on the west side of the Jordan, from Baal Gad in the Valley of Lebanon to Mount Halak, which rises toward Seir (their lands Joshua gave as an inheritance to the tribes of Israel according to their tribal divisions— [8]the hill country, the western foothills, the Arabah, the mountain slopes, the desert and the Negev—the lands of the Hittites, Amorites, Canaanites, Perizzites, Hivites and Jebusites):

[9]the king of Jericho	one
the king of Ai (near Bethel)	one
[10]the king of Jerusalem	one
the king of Hebron	one
[11]the king of Jarmuth	one
the king of Lachish	one
[12]the king of Eglon	one
the king of Gezer	one
[13]the king of Debir	one
the king of Geder	one
[14]the king of Hormah	one
the king of Arad	one
[15]the king of Libnah	one
the king of Adullam	one
[16]the king of Makkedah	one
the king of Bethel	one
[17]the king of Tappuah	one
the king of Hepher	one
[18]the king of Aphek	one
the king of Lasharon	one
[19]the king of Madon	one
the king of Hazor	one
[20]the king of Shimron Meron	one
the king of Acshaph	one
[21]the king of Taanach	one
the king of Megiddo	one
[22]the king of Kedesh	one
the king of Jokneam in Carmel	one

a3 That is, Galilee   *b3* That is, the Dead Sea

²³the king of Dor (in Naphoth
Dor^a)   one
the king of Goyim in Gilgal   one
²⁴the king of Tirzah   one
thirty-one kings in all.

Land Still to Be Taken

13 When Joshua was old and well advanced in years, the LORD said to
him, "You are very old, and there are still
very large areas of land to be taken over.

²"This is the land that remains: all
the regions of the Philistines and
Geshurites: ³from the Shihor River
on the east of Egypt to the territory
of Ekron on the north, all of it
counted as Canaanite (the territory
of the five Philistine rulers in Gaza,
Ashdod, Ashkelon, Gath and Ek-
ron—that of the Avvites); ⁴from the
south, all the land of the Canaanites, from Arah of the Sidonians as
far as Aphek, the region of the Amo-
rites, ⁵the area of the Gebalites^b;
and all Lebanon to the east, from
Baal Gad below Mount Hermon to
Lebo^c Hamath.

⁶"As for all the inhabitants of the
mountain regions from Lebanon to Misrephoth Maim, that is, all the Sidonians,
I myself will drive them out before the
Israelites. Be sure to allocate this land to
Israel for an inheritance, as I have instructed you, ⁷and divide it as an inheritance among the nine tribes and half of
the tribe of Manasseh."

Division of the Land East of the Jordan

⁸The other half of Manasseh,^d the Reu-
benites and the Gadites had received the
inheritance that Moses had given them
east of the Jordan, as he, the servant of the
LORD, had assigned it to them.

⁹It extended from Aroer on the rim
of the Arnon Gorge, and from the
town in the middle of the gorge, and
included the whole plateau of Medeba as far as Dibon, ¹⁰and all the
towns of Sihon king of the Amo-
rites, who ruled in Heshbon, out to
the border of the Ammonites. ¹¹It
also included Gilead, the territory of
the people of Geshur and Maacah,
all of Mount Hermon and all Ba-

shan as far as Salecah— ¹²that is, the
whole kingdom of Og in Bashan,
who had reigned in Ashtaroth and
Edrei and had survived as one of the
last of the Rephaites. Moses had defeated them and taken over their
land. ¹³But the Israelites did not
drive out the people of Geshur and
Maacah, so they continue to live
among the Israelites to this day.

¹⁴But to the tribe of Levi he gave no
inheritance, since the offerings made by
fire to the LORD, the God of Israel, are
their inheritance, as he promised them.

¹⁵This is what Moses had given to the
tribe of Reuben, clan by clan:

¹⁶The territory from Aroer on the
rim of the Arnon Gorge, and from
the town in the middle of the gorge,
and the whole plateau past Medeba
¹⁷to Heshbon and all its towns on
the plateau, including Dibon, Ba-
moth Baal, Beth Baal Meon, ¹⁸Jahaz,
Kedemoth, Mephaath, ¹⁹Kiriathaim,
Sibmah, Zereth Shahar on the hill in
the valley, ²⁰Beth Peor, the slopes of
Pisgah, and Beth Jeshimoth ²¹—all
the towns on the plateau and the
entire realm of Sihon king of the
Amorites, who ruled at Heshbon.
Moses had defeated him and the
Midianite chiefs, Evi, Rekem, Zur,
Hur and Reba—princes allied with
Sihon—who lived in that country.
²²In addition to those slain in battle,
the Israelites had put to the sword
Balaam son of Beor, who practiced
divination. ²³The boundary of the
Reubenites was the bank of the Jor-
dan. These towns and their villages
were the inheritance of the Reuben-
ites, clan by clan.

²⁴This is what Moses had given to the
tribe of Gad, clan by clan:

²⁵The territory of Jazer, all the towns
of Gilead and half the Ammonite
country as far as Aroer, near Rabbah;
²⁶and from Heshbon to Ramath
Mizpah and Betonim, and from Ma-

^a23 Or in the heights of Dor   ^b5 That is, the
area of Byblos   ^c5 Or to the entrance to
^d8 Hebrew With it (that is, with the other half of
Manasseh)

hanaim to the territory of Debir;
²⁷and in the valley, Beth Haram,
Beth Nimrah, Succoth and Zaphon
with the rest of the realm of Sihon
king of Heshbon (the east side of
the Jordan, the territory up to the
end of the Sea of Kinnereth*a*).
²⁸These towns and their villages
were the inheritance of the Gadites,
clan by clan.

²⁹This is what Moses had given to the
half-tribe of Manasseh, that is, to half the
family of the descendants of Manasseh,
clan by clan:

³⁰The territory extending from Mahanaim and including all of Bashan,
the entire realm of Og king of Bashan—all the settlements of Jair in
Bashan, sixty towns, ³¹half of Gilead, and Ashtaroth and Edrei (the
royal cities of Og in Bashan). This
was for the descendants of Makir
son of Manasseh—for half of the
sons of Makir, clan by clan.

³²This is the inheritance Moses had giv-
en when he was in the plains of Moab
across the Jordan east of Jericho. ³³But to
the tribe of Levi, Moses had given no inheritance; the LORD, the God of Israel, is
their inheritance, as he promised them.

Division of the Land West of the Jordan

14 Now these are the areas the Israelites received as an inheritance in the
land of Canaan, which Eleazar the priest,
Joshua son of Nun and the heads of the
tribal clans of Israel allotted to them.
²Their inheritances were assigned by lot
to the nine-and-a-half tribes, as the LORD
had commanded through Moses. ³Moses
had granted the two-and-a-half tribes
their inheritance east of the Jordan but
had not granted the Levites an inheritance
among the rest, ⁴for the sons of Joseph
had become two tribes—Manasseh and
Ephraim. The Levites received no share of
the land but only towns to live in, with
pasturelands for their flocks and herds.
⁵So the Israelites divided the land, just as
the LORD had commanded Moses.

Hebron Given to Caleb

⁶Now the men of Judah approached
Joshua at Gilgal, and Caleb son of Je-

phunneh the Kenizzite said to him, "You
know what the LORD said to Moses the
man of God at Kadesh Barnea about you
and me. ⁷I was forty years old when Moses the servant of the LORD sent me from
Kadesh Barnea to explore the land. And I
brought him back a report according to
my convictions, ⁸but my brothers who
went up with me made the hearts of the
people melt with fear. I, however, followed the LORD my God wholeheartedly.
⁹So on that day Moses swore to me, 'The
land on which your feet have walked will
be your inheritance and that of your children forever, because you have followed
the LORD my God wholeheartedly.'*b*

¹⁰"Now then, just as the LORD promised, he has kept me alive for forty-five
years since the time he said this to Moses,
while Israel moved about in the desert. So
here I am today, eighty-five years old! ¹¹I
am still as strong today as the day Moses
sent me out; I'm just as vigorous to go out
to battle now as I was then. ¹²Now give
me this hill country that the LORD promised me that day. You yourself heard then
that the Anakites were there and their cities were large and fortified, but, the LORD
helping me, I will drive them out just as
he said."

¹³Then Joshua blessed Caleb son of Jephunneh and gave him Hebron as his inheritance. ¹⁴So Hebron has belonged to
Caleb son of Jephunneh the Kenizzite
ever since, because he followed the LORD,
the God of Israel, wholeheartedly. ¹⁵(Hebron used to be called Kiriath Arba after
Arba, who was the greatest man among
the Anakites.)

Then the land had rest from war.

Allotment for Judah

15 The allotment for the tribe of Judah,
clan by clan, extended down to the
territory of Edom, to the Desert of Zin in
the extreme south.

²Their southern boundary started
from the bay at the southern end
of the Salt Sea,*c* ³crossed south of
Scorpion*d* Pass, continued on to
Zin and went over to the south of
Kadesh Barnea. Then it ran past

---

*a*27 That is, Galilee　　*b*9 Deut. 1:36　　*c*2 That
is, the Dead Sea; also in verse 5　　*d*3 Hebrew
Akrabbim

Hezron up to Addar and curved around to Karka. ⁴It then passed along to Azmon and joined the Wadi of Egypt, ending at the sea. This is their*ᵃ* southern boundary.

⁵The eastern boundary is the Salt Sea as far as the mouth of the Jordan.

The northern boundary started from the bay of the sea at the mouth of the Jordan, ⁶went up to Beth Hoglah and continued north of Beth Arabah to the Stone of Bohan son of Reuben. ⁷The boundary then went up to Debir from the Valley of Achor and turned north to Gilgal, which faces the Pass of Adummim south of the gorge. It continued along to the waters of En Shemesh and came out at En Rogel. ⁸Then it ran up the Valley of Ben Hinnom along the southern slope of the Jebusite city (that is, Jerusalem). From there it climbed to the top of the hill west of the Hinnom Valley at the northern end of the Valley of Rephaim. ⁹From the hilltop the boundary headed toward the spring of the waters of Nephtoah, came out at the towns of Mount Ephron and went down toward Baalah (that is, Kiriath Jearim). ¹⁰Then it curved westward from Baalah to Mount Seir, ran along the northern slope of Mount Jearim (that is, Kesalon), continued down to Beth Shemesh and crossed to Timnah. ¹¹It went to the northern slope of Ekron, turned toward Shikkeron, passed along to Mount Baalah and reached Jabneel. The boundary ended at the sea.

¹²The western boundary is the coastline of the Great Sea.*ᵇ*

These are the boundaries around the people of Judah by their clans.

¹³In accordance with the LORD's command to him, Joshua gave to Caleb son of Jephunneh a portion in Judah—Kiriath Arba, that is, Hebron. (Arba was the forefather of Anak.) ¹⁴From Hebron Caleb drove out the three Anakites—Sheshai, Ahiman and Talmai—descendants of Anak. ¹⁵From there he marched against the people living in Debir (formerly called Kiriath Sepher). ¹⁶And Caleb said,

"I will give my daughter Acsah in marriage to the man who attacks and captures Kiriath Sepher." ¹⁷Othniel son of Kenaz, Caleb's brother, took it; so Caleb gave his daughter Acsah to him in marriage.

¹⁸One day when she came to Othniel, she urged him*ᶜ* to ask her father for a field. When she got off her donkey, Caleb asked her, "What can I do for you?"

¹⁹She replied, "Do me a special favor. Since you have given me land in the Negev, give me also springs of water." So Caleb gave her the upper and lower springs.

²⁰This is the inheritance of the tribe of Judah, clan by clan:

²¹The southernmost towns of the tribe of Judah in the Negev toward the boundary of Edom were:

Kabzeel, Eder, Jagur, ²²Kinah, Dimonah, Adadah, ²³Kedesh, Hazor, Ithnan, ²⁴Ziph, Telem, Bealoth, ²⁵Hazor Hadattah, Kerioth Hezron (that is, Hazor), ²⁶Amam, Shema, Moladah, ²⁷Hazar Gaddah, Heshmon, Beth Pelet, ²⁸Hazar Shual, Beersheba, Biziothiah, ²⁹Baalah, Iim, Ezem, ³⁰Eltolad, Kesil, Hormah, ³¹Ziklag, Madmannah, Sansannah, ³²Lebaoth, Shilhim, Ain and Rimmon—a total of twenty-nine towns and their villages.

³³In the western foothills:

Eshtaol, Zorah, Ashnah, ³⁴Zanoah, En Gannim, Tappuah, Enam, ³⁵Jarmuth, Adullam, Socoh, Azekah, ³⁶Shaaraim, Adithaim and Gederah (or Gederothaim)*ᵈ*—fourteen towns and their villages.

³⁷Zenan, Hadashah, Migdal Gad, ³⁸Dilean, Mizpah, Joktheel, ³⁹Lachish, Bozkath, Eglon, ⁴⁰Cabbon, Lahmas, Kitlish, ⁴¹Gederoth, Beth Dagon, Naamah and Makkedah—sixteen towns and their villages.

⁴²Libnah, Ether, Ashan, ⁴³Iphtah, Ashnah, Nezib, ⁴⁴Keilah, Aczib and Mareshah—nine towns and their villages.

⁴⁵Ekron, with its surrounding set-

ᵃ4 Hebrew *your*   *ᵇ12* That is, the Mediterranean; also in verse 47   *ᶜ18* Hebrew and some Septuagint manuscripts; other Septuagint manuscripts (see also note at Judges 1:14) *Othniel, he urged her*   *ᵈ36* Or *Gederah and Gederothaim* tlements and villages; [46]west of Ekron, all that were in the vicinity of Ashdod, together with their villages; [47]Ashdod, its surrounding settlements and villages; and Gaza, its settlements and villages, as far as the Wadi of Egypt and the coastline of the Great Sea.

[48]In the hill country:

Shamir, Jattir, Socoh, [49]Dannah, Kiriath Sannah (that is, Debir), [50]Anab, Eshtemoh, Anim, [51]Goshen, Holon and Giloh—eleven towns and their villages.

[52]Arab, Dumah, Eshan, [53]Janim, Beth Tappuah, Aphekah, [54]Humtah, Kiriath Arba (that is, Hebron) and Zior—nine towns and their villages.

[55]Maon, Carmel, Ziph, Juttah, [56]Jezreel, Jokdeam, Zanoah, [57]Kain, Gibeah and Timnah—ten towns and their villages.

[58]Halhul, Beth Zur, Gedor, [59]Maarath, Beth Anoth and Eltekon—six towns and their villages.

[60]Kiriath Baal (that is, Kiriath Jearim) and Rabbah—two towns and their villages.

[61]In the desert:

Beth Arabah, Middin, Secacah, [62]Nibshan, the City of Salt and En Gedi—six towns and their villages.

[63]Judah could not dislodge the Jebusites, who were living in Jerusalem; to this day the Jebusites live there with the people of Judah.

Allotment for Ephraim and Manasseh

16 The allotment for Joseph began at the Jordan of Jericho,[a] east of the waters of Jericho, and went up from there through the desert into the hill country of Bethel. [2]It went on from Bethel (that is, Luz),[b] crossed over to the territory of the Arkites in Ataroth, [3]descended westward to the territory of the Japhletites as far as the region of Lower Beth Horon and on to Gezer, ending at the sea.

[4]So Manasseh and Ephraim, the descendants of Joseph, received their inheritance.

[5]This was the territory of Ephraim, clan by clan:

The boundary of their inheritance went from Ataroth Addar in the east to Upper Beth Horon [6]and continued to the sea. From Micmethath on the north it curved eastward to Taanath Shiloh, passing by it to Janoah on the east. [7]Then it went down from Janoah to Ataroth and Naarah, touched Jericho and came out at the Jordan. [8]From Tappuah the border went west to the Kanah Ravine and ended at the sea. This was the inheritance of the tribe of the Ephraimites, clan by clan. [9]It also included all the towns and their villages that were set aside for the Ephraimites within the inheritance of the Manassites.

[10]They did not dislodge the Canaanites living in Gezer; to this day the Canaanites live among the people of Ephraim but are required to do forced labor.

17 This was the allotment for the tribe of Manasseh as Joseph's firstborn, that is, for Makir, Manasseh's firstborn. Makir was the ancestor of the Gileadites, who had received Gilead and Bashan because the Makirites were great soldiers. [2]So this allotment was for the rest of the people of Manasseh—the clans of Abiezer, Helek, Asriel, Shechem, Hepher and Shemida. These are the other male descendants of Manasseh son of Joseph by their clans.

[3]Now Zelophehad son of Hepher, the son of Gilead, the son of Makir, the son of Manasseh, had no sons but only daughters, whose names were Mahlah, Noah, Hoglah, Milcah and Tirzah. [4]They went to Eleazar the priest, Joshua son of Nun, and the leaders and said, "The LORD commanded Moses to give us an inheritance among our brothers." So Joshua gave them an inheritance along with the brothers of their father, according to the LORD's command. [5]Manasseh's share consisted of ten tracts of land besides Gilead and Bashan east of the Jordan, [6]because the daughters of the tribe of Manasseh received an inheritance among the sons.

---

[a]1 *Jordan of Jericho* was possibly an ancient name for the Jordan River.   [b]2 Septuagint; Hebrew *Bethel to Luz*

The land of Gilead belonged to the rest of the descendants of Manasseh.

⁷The territory of Manasseh extended from Asher to Micmethath east of Shechem. The boundary ran southward from there to include the people living at En Tappuah. ⁸(Manasseh had the land of Tappuah, but Tappuah itself, on the boundary of Manasseh, belonged to the Ephraimites.) ⁹Then the boundary continued south to the Kanah Ravine. There were towns belonging to Ephraim lying among the towns of Manasseh, but the boundary of Manasseh was the northern side of the ravine and ended at the sea. ¹⁰On the south the land belonged to Ephraim, on the north to Manasseh. The territory of Manasseh reached the sea and bordered Asher on the north and Issachar on the east.

¹¹Within Issachar and Asher, Manasseh also had Beth Shan, Ibleam and the people of Dor, Endor, Taanach and Megiddo, together with their surrounding settlements (the third in the list is Naphoth*a*).

¹²Yet the Manassites were not able to occupy these towns, for the Canaanites were determined to live in that region. ¹³However, when the Israelites grew stronger, they subjected the Canaanites to forced labor but did not drive them out completely.

¹⁴The people of Joseph said to Joshua, "Why have you given us only one allotment and one portion for an inheritance? We are a numerous people and the LORD has blessed us abundantly."

¹⁵"If you are so numerous," Joshua answered, "and if the hill country of Ephraim is too small for you, go up into the forest and clear land for yourselves there in the land of the Perizzites and Rephaites."

¹⁶The people of Joseph replied, "The hill country is not enough for us, and all the Canaanites who live in the plain have iron chariots, both those in Beth Shan and its settlements and those in the Valley of Jezreel."

¹⁷But Joshua said to the house of Joseph—to Ephraim and Manasseh—"You are numerous and very powerful. You will have not only one allotment ¹⁸but the forested hill country as well. Clear it, and its farthest limits will be yours; though the Canaanites have iron chariots and though they are strong, you can drive them out."

Division of the Rest of the Land

18 The whole assembly of the Israelites gathered at Shiloh and set up the Tent of Meeting there. The country was brought under their control, ²but there were still seven Israelite tribes who had not yet received their inheritance.

³So Joshua said to the Israelites: "How long will you wait before you begin to take possession of the land that the LORD, the God of your fathers, has given you? ⁴Appoint three men from each tribe. I will send them out to make a survey of the land and to write a description of it, according to the inheritance of each. Then they will return to me. ⁵You are to divide the land into seven parts. Judah is to remain in its territory on the south and the house of Joseph in its territory on the north. ⁶After you have written descriptions of the seven parts of the land, bring them here to me and I will cast lots for you in the presence of the LORD our God. ⁷The Levites, however, do not get a portion among you, because the priestly service of the LORD is their inheritance. And Gad, Reuben and the half-tribe of Manasseh have already received their inheritance on the east side of the Jordan. Moses the servant of the LORD gave it to them."

⁸As the men started on their way to map out the land, Joshua instructed them, "Go and make a survey of the land and write a description of it. Then return to me, and I will cast lots for you here at Shiloh in the presence of the LORD." ⁹So the men left and went through the land. They wrote its description on a scroll, town by town, in seven parts, and returned to Joshua in the camp at Shiloh. ¹⁰Joshua then cast lots for them in Shiloh in the presence of the LORD, and there he distributed the land to the Israelites according to their tribal divisions.

a 11 That is, Naphoth Dor

Allotment for Benjamin

[11]The lot came up for the tribe of Benjamin, clan by clan. Their allotted territory lay between the tribes of Judah and Joseph:

[12]On the north side their boundary began at the Jordan, passed the northern slope of Jericho and headed west into the hill country, coming out at the desert of Beth Aven. [13]From there it crossed to the south slope of Luz (that is, Bethel) and went down to Ataroth Addar on the hill south of Lower Beth Horon.

[14]From the hill facing Beth Horon on the south the boundary turned south along the western side and came out at Kiriath Baal (that is, Kiriath Jearim), a town of the people of Judah. This was the western side.

[15]The southern side began at the outskirts of Kiriath Jearim on the west, and the boundary came out at the spring of the waters of Nephtoah. [16]The boundary went down to the foot of the hill facing the Valley of Ben Hinnom, north of the Valley of Rephaim. It continued down the Hinnom Valley along the southern slope of the Jebusite city and so to En Rogel. [17]It then curved north, went to En Shemesh, continued to Geliloth, which faces the Pass of Adummim, and ran down to the Stone of Bohan son of Reuben. [18]It continued to the northern slope of Beth Arabah[a] and on down into the Arabah. [19]It then went to the northern slope of Beth Hoglah and came out at the northern bay of the Salt Sea,[b] at the mouth of the Jordan in the south. This was the southern boundary.

[20]The Jordan formed the boundary on the eastern side.

These were the boundaries that marked out the inheritance of the clans of Benjamin on all sides.

[21]The tribe of Benjamin, clan by clan, had the following cities:

Jericho, Beth Hoglah, Emek Keziz, [22]Beth Arabah, Zemaraim, Bethel, [23]Avvim, Parah, Ophrah, [24]Kephar Ammoni, Ophni and Geba—twelve towns and their villages.

[25]Gibeon, Ramah, Beeroth, [26]Mizpah, Kephirah, Mozah, [27]Rekem, Irpeel, Taralah, [28]Zelah, Haeleph, the Jebusite city (that is, Jerusalem), Gibeah and Kiriath—fourteen towns and their villages.

This was the inheritance of Benjamin for its clans.

Allotment for Simeon

19 The second lot came out for the tribe of Simeon, clan by clan. Their inheritance lay within the territory of Judah. [2]It included:

Beersheba (or Sheba),[c] Moladah, [3]Hazar Shual, Balah, Ezem, [4]Eltolad, Bethul, Hormah, [5]Ziklag, Beth Marcaboth, Hazar Susah, [6]Beth Lebaoth and Sharuhen—thirteen towns and their villages;

[7]Ain, Rimmon, Ether and Ashan—four towns and their villages— [8]and all the villages around these towns as far as Baalath Beer (Ramah in the Negev).

This was the inheritance of the tribe of the Simeonites, clan by clan. [9]The inheritance of the Simeonites was taken from the share of Judah, because Judah's portion was more than they needed. So the Simeonites received their inheritance within the territory of Judah.

Allotment for Zebulun

[10]The third lot came up for Zebulun, clan by clan:

The boundary of their inheritance went as far as Sarid. [11]Going west it ran to Maralah, touched Dabbesheth, and extended to the ravine near Jokneam. [12]It turned east from Sarid toward the sunrise to the territory of Kisloth Tabor and went on to Daberath and up to Japhia. [13]Then it continued eastward to Gath Hepher and Eth Kazin; it came out at Rimmon and turned toward Neah. [14]There the boundary went around on the north to Hannathon and

---

[a]18 Septuagint; Hebrew *slope facing the Arabah*
[b]19 That is, the Dead Sea   [c]2 Or *Beersheba, Sheba*; 1 Chron. 4:28 does not have *Sheba*.

ended at the Valley of Iphtah El. [15] Included were Kattath, Nahalal, Shimron, Idalah and Bethlehem. There were twelve towns and their villages.

[16] These towns and their villages were the inheritance of Zebulun, clan by clan.

Allotment for Issachar

[17] The fourth lot came out for Issachar, clan by clan. [18] Their territory included:

Jezreel, Kesulloth, Shunem, [19] Hapharaim, Shion, Anaharath, [20] Rabbith, Kishion, Ebez, [21] Remeth, En Gannim, En Haddah and Beth Pazzez. [22] The boundary touched Tabor, Shahazumah and Beth Shemesh, and ended at the Jordan. There were sixteen towns and their villages.

[23] These towns and their villages were the inheritance of the tribe of Issachar, clan by clan.

Allotment for Asher

[24] The fifth lot came out for the tribe of Asher, clan by clan. [25] Their territory included:

Helkath, Hali, Beten, Acshaph, [26] Allammelech, Amad and Mishal. On the west the boundary touched Carmel and Shihor Libnath. [27] It then turned east toward Beth Dagon, touched Zebulun and the Valley of Iphtah El, and went north to Beth Emek and Neiel, passing Cabul on the left. [28] It went to Abdon,[a] Rehob, Hammon and Kanah, as far as Greater Sidon. [29] The boundary then turned back toward Ramah and went to the fortified city of Tyre, turned toward Hosah and came out at the sea in the region of Aczib, [30] Ummah, Aphek and Rehob. There were twenty-two towns and their villages.

[31] These towns and their villages were the inheritance of the tribe of Asher, clan by clan.

Allotment for Naphtali

[32] The sixth lot came out for Naphtali, clan by clan:

[33] Their boundary went from Heleph and the large tree in Zaanannim, passing Adami Nekeb and Jabneel to Lakkum and ending at the Jordan. [34] The boundary ran west through Aznoth Tabor and came out at Hukkok. It touched Zebulun on the south, Asher on the west and the Jordan[b] on the east. [35] The fortified cities were Ziddim, Zer, Hammath, Rakkath, Kinnereth, [36] Adamah, Ramah, Hazor, [37] Kedesh, Edrei, En Hazor, [38] Iron, Migdal El, Horem, Beth Anath and Beth Shemesh. There were nineteen towns and their villages.

[39] These towns and their villages were the inheritance of the tribe of Naphtali, clan by clan.

Allotment for Dan

[40] The seventh lot came out for the tribe of Dan, clan by clan. [41] The territory of their inheritance included:

Zorah, Eshtaol, Ir Shemesh, [42] Shaalabbin, Aijalon, Ithlah, [43] Elon, Timnah, Ekron, [44] Eltekeh, Gibbethon, Baalath, [45] Jehud, Bene Berak, Gath Rimmon, [46] Me Jarkon and Rakkon, with the area facing Joppa.

[47] (But the Danites had difficulty taking possession of their territory, so they went up and attacked Leshem, took it, put it to the sword and occupied it. They settled in Leshem and named it Dan after their forefather.)

[48] These towns and their villages were the inheritance of the tribe of Dan, clan by clan.

Allotment for Joshua

[49] When they had finished dividing the land into its allotted portions, the Israelites gave Joshua son of Nun an inheritance among them, [50] as the LORD had commanded. They gave him the town he asked for—Timnath Serah[c] in the hill country of Ephraim. And he built up the town and settled there.

[51] These are the territories that Eleazar the priest, Joshua son of Nun and the heads of the tribal clans of Israel assigned

---

[a]28 Some Hebrew manuscripts (see also Joshua 21:30); most Hebrew manuscripts *Ebron*
[b]34 Septuagint; Hebrew *west, and Judah, the Jordan,*
[c]50 Also known as *Timnath Heres* (see Judges 2:9)

by lot at Shiloh in the presence of the LORD at the entrance to the Tent of Meeting. And so they finished dividing the land.

Cities of Refuge

20 Then the LORD said to Joshua: ²"Tell the Israelites to designate the cities of refuge, as I instructed you through Moses, ³so that anyone who kills a person accidentally and unintentionally may flee there and find protection from the avenger of blood.

⁴"When he flees to one of these cities, he is to stand in the entrance of the city gate and state his case before the elders of that city. Then they are to admit him into their city and give him a place to live with them. ⁵If the avenger of blood pursues him, they must not surrender the one accused, because he killed his neighbor unintentionally and without malice aforethought. ⁶He is to stay in that city until he has stood trial before the assembly and until the death of the high priest who is serving at that time. Then he may go back to his own home in the town from which he fled."

⁷So they set apart Kedesh in Galilee in the hill country of Naphtali, Shechem in the hill country of Ephraim, and Kiriath Arba (that is, Hebron) in the hill country of Judah. ⁸On the east side of the Jordan of Jericho[a] they designated Bezer in the desert on the plateau in the tribe of Reuben, Ramoth in Gilead in the tribe of Gad, and Golan in Bashan in the tribe of Manasseh. ⁹Any of the Israelites or any alien living among them who killed someone accidentally could flee to these designated cities and not be killed by the avenger of blood prior to standing trial before the assembly.

Towns for the Levites

21 Now the family heads of the Levites approached Eleazar the priest, Joshua son of Nun, and the heads of the other tribal families of Israel ²at Shiloh in Canaan and said to them, "The LORD commanded through Moses that you give us towns to live in, with pasturelands for our livestock." ³So, as the LORD had commanded, the Israelites gave the Levites the fol-

lowing towns and pasturelands out of their own inheritance:

⁴The first lot came out for the Kohathites, clan by clan. The Levites who were descendants of Aaron the priest were allotted thirteen towns from the tribes of Judah, Simeon and Benjamin. ⁵The rest of Kohath's descendants were allotted ten towns from the clans of the tribes of Ephraim, Dan and half of Manasseh.

⁶The descendants of Gershon were allotted thirteen towns from the clans of the tribes of Issachar, Asher, Naphtali and the half-tribe of Manasseh in Bashan.

⁷The descendants of Merari, clan by clan, received twelve towns from the tribes of Reuben, Gad and Zebulun.

⁸So the Israelites allotted to the Levites these towns and their pasturelands, as the LORD had commanded through Moses.

⁹From the tribes of Judah and Simeon they allotted the following towns by name ¹⁰(these towns were assigned to the descendants of Aaron who were from the Kohathite clans of the Levites, because the first lot fell to them):

¹¹They gave them Kiriath Arba (that is, Hebron), with its surrounding pastureland, in the hill country of Judah. (Arba was the forefather of Anak.) ¹²But the fields and villages around the city they had given to Caleb son of Jephunneh as his possession.

¹³So to the descendants of Aaron the priest they gave Hebron (a city of refuge for one accused of murder), Libnah, ¹⁴Jattir, Eshtemoa, ¹⁵Holon, Debir, ¹⁶Ain, Juttah and Beth Shemesh, together with their pasturelands—nine towns from these two tribes.

¹⁷And from the tribe of Benjamin they gave them Gibeon, Geba, ¹⁸Anathoth and Almon, together with their pasturelands—four towns.

¹⁹All the towns for the priests, the descendants of Aaron, were thirteen, together with their pasturelands.

²⁰The rest of the Kohathite clans of the Levites were allotted towns from the tribe of Ephraim:

---

[a] 8 *Jordan of Jericho* was possibly an ancient name for the Jordan River.

²¹In the hill country of Ephraim they were given Shechem (a city of refuge for one accused of murder) and Gezer, ²²Kibzaim and Beth Horon, together with their pasturelands—four towns.

²³Also from the tribe of Dan they received Eltekeh, Gibbethon, ²⁴Aijalon and Gath Rimmon, together with their pasturelands—four towns.

²⁵From half the tribe of Manasseh they received Taanach and Gath Rimmon, together with their pasturelands—two towns.

²⁶All these ten towns and their pasturelands were given to the rest of the Kohathite clans.

²⁷The Levite clans of the Gershonites were given:

from the half-tribe of Manasseh,
Golan in Bashan (a city of refuge for one accused of murder) and Be Eshtarah, together with their pasturelands—two towns;

²⁸from the tribe of Issachar,
Kishion, Daberath, ²⁹Jarmuth and En Gannim, together with their pasturelands—four towns;

³⁰from the tribe of Asher,
Mishal, Abdon, ³¹Helkath and Rehob, together with their pasturelands—four towns;

³²from the tribe of Naphtali,
Kedesh in Galilee (a city of refuge for one accused of murder), Hammoth Dor and Kartan, together with their pasturelands—three towns.

³³All the towns of the Gershonite clans were thirteen, together with their pasturelands.

³⁴The Merarite clans (the rest of the Levites) were given:

from the tribe of Zebulun,
Jokneam, Kartah, ³⁵Dimnah and Nahalal, together with their pasturelands—four towns;

³⁶from the tribe of Reuben,
Bezer, Jahaz, ³⁷Kedemoth and Mephaath, together with their pasturelands—four towns;

³⁸from the tribe of Gad,
Ramoth in Gilead (a city of refuge for one accused of murder), Mahanaim, ³⁹Heshbon and Jazer, together with their pasturelands—four towns in all.

⁴⁰All the towns allotted to the Merarite clans, who were the rest of the Levites, were twelve.

⁴¹The towns of the Levites in the territory held by the Israelites were forty-eight in all, together with their pasturelands. ⁴²Each of these towns had pasturelands surrounding it; this was true for all these towns.

⁴³So the LORD gave Israel all the land he had sworn to give their forefathers, and they took possession of it and settled there. ⁴⁴The LORD gave them rest on every side, just as he had sworn to their forefathers. Not one of their enemies withstood them; the LORD handed all their enemies over to them. ⁴⁵Not one of all the LORD's good promises to the house of Israel failed; every one was fulfilled.

Eastern Tribes Return Home

22 Then Joshua summoned the Reubenites, the Gadites and the half-tribe of Manasseh ²and said to them, "You have done all that Moses the servant of the LORD commanded, and you have obeyed me in everything I commanded. ³For a long time now—to this very day—you have not deserted your brothers but have carried out the mission the LORD your God gave you. ⁴Now that the LORD your God has given your brothers rest as he promised, return to your homes in the land that Moses the servant of the LORD gave you on the other side of the Jordan. ⁵But be very careful to keep the commandment and the law that Moses the servant of the LORD gave you: to love the LORD your God, to walk in all his ways, to obey his commands, to hold fast to him and to serve him with all your heart and all your soul."

⁶Then Joshua blessed them and sent them away, and they went to their homes. ⁷(To the half-tribe of Manasseh Moses had given land in Bashan, and to the other half of the tribe Joshua gave land on the west side of the Jordan with their brothers.) When Joshua sent them home, he blessed them, ⁸saying, "Return to your homes with your great wealth—with large herds of livestock, with silver, gold, bronze and iron, and a great quantity of

clothing—and divide with your brothers the plunder from your enemies."

⁹So the Reubenites, the Gadites and the half-tribe of Manasseh left the Israelites at Shiloh in Canaan to return to Gilead, their own land, which they had acquired in accordance with the command of the LORD through Moses.

¹⁰When they came to Geliloth near the Jordan in the land of Canaan, the Reubenites, the Gadites and the half-tribe of Manasseh built an imposing altar there by the Jordan. ¹¹And when the Israelites heard that they had built the altar on the border of Canaan at Geliloth near the Jordan on the Israelite side, ¹²the whole assembly of Israel gathered at Shiloh to go to war against them.

¹³So the Israelites sent Phinehas son of Eleazar, the priest, to the land of Gilead—to Reuben, Gad and the half-tribe of Manasseh. ¹⁴With him they sent ten of the chief men, one for each of the tribes of Israel, each the head of a family division among the Israelite clans.

¹⁵When they went to Gilead—to Reuben, Gad and the half-tribe of Manasseh— they said to them: ¹⁶"The whole assembly of the LORD says: 'How could you break faith with the God of Israel like this? How

could you turn away from the LORD and build yourselves an altar in rebellion against him now? ¹⁷Was not the sin of Peor enough for us? Up to this very day we have not cleansed ourselves from that sin, even though a plague fell on the community of the LORD! ¹⁸And are you now turning away from the LORD?

"'If you rebel against the LORD today, tomorrow he will be angry with the whole community of Israel. ¹⁹If the land you possess is defiled, come over to the LORD's land, where the LORD's tabernacle stands, and share the land with us. But do not rebel against the LORD or against us by building an altar for yourselves, other than the altar of the LORD our God. ²⁰When Achan son of Zerah acted unfaithfully regarding the devoted things,ᵃ did not wrath come upon the whole community of Israel? He was not the only one who died for his sin.'"

²¹Then Reuben, Gad and the half-tribe of Manasseh replied to the heads of the clans of Israel: ²²"The Mighty One, God, the LORD! The Mighty One, God, the LORD! He knows! And let Israel know! If

ᵃ20 The Hebrew term refers to the irrevocable giving over of things or persons to the LORD, often by totally destroying them.

Trust and Talk

JOSHUA 22 It's amazing how quickly one spouse can jump to conclusions about the other spouse. Early in our marriage, we were learning to share a checkbook. On more than one occasion, Rosemary would notice a check that had been written for an unusual amount of money. The first thing she thought was that I had purchased something that violated what we had previously agreed to. She was mad before we even had time to discuss it.

The armies of Joshua made the same mistake. They jumped to conclusions. They went into action against their brothers before they bothered to find out what really happened. The new altar that the eastern tribes built appeared to Joshua to be something completely different from what it was. It seemed to be an altar that was competing

with God, when in reality it was only built to remind the tribes of the very same God that the western tribes worshiped. Joshua and his people chose to prepare for war rather than to prepare to talk.

When it comes to building a healthy marriage, we must decide to trust before we decide to get angry and accuse. The love passage in 1 Corinthians 13 (see page 1252) offers a list of things we need to do to truly show love to another person. Verse 7 says that love always trusts. When it seems that something has been done that violates the trust of the marriage relationship, first choose to trust your spouse and then talk about it.

—*Bob & Rosemary*

Go to page 247 for your next devotional reading.

this has been in rebellion or disobedience to the LORD, do not spare us this day. ²³If we have built our own altar to turn away from the LORD and to offer burnt offerings and grain offerings, or to sacrifice fellowship offerings[a] on it, may the LORD himself call us to account.

²⁴"No! We did it for fear that some day your descendants might say to ours, 'What do you have to do with the LORD, the God of Israel? ²⁵The LORD has made the Jordan a boundary between us and you—you Reubenites and Gadites! You have no share in the LORD.' So your descendants might cause ours to stop fearing the LORD.

²⁶"That is why we said, 'Let us get ready and build an altar—but not for burnt offerings or sacrifices.' ²⁷On the contrary, it is to be a witness between us and you and the generations that follow, that we will worship the LORD at his sanctuary with our burnt offerings, sacrifices and fellowship offerings. Then in the future your descendants will not be able to say to ours, 'You have no share in the LORD.'

²⁸"And we said, 'If they ever say this to us, or to our descendants, we will answer: Look at the replica of the LORD's altar, which our fathers built, not for burnt offerings and sacrifices, but as a witness between us and you.'

²⁹"Far be it from us to rebel against the LORD and turn away from him today by building an altar for burnt offerings, grain offerings and sacrifices, other than the altar of the LORD our God that stands before his tabernacle."

³⁰When Phinehas the priest and the leaders of the community—the heads of the clans of the Israelites—heard what Reuben, Gad and Manasseh had to say, they were pleased. ³¹And Phinehas son of Eleazar, the priest, said to Reuben, Gad and Manasseh, "Today we know that the LORD is with us, because you have not acted unfaithfully toward the LORD in this matter. Now you have rescued the Israelites from the LORD's hand."

³²Then Phinehas son of Eleazar, the priest, and the leaders returned to Canaan from their meeting with the Reubenites and Gadites in Gilead and reported to the Israelites. ³³They were glad to hear the report and praised God. And they talked

no more about going to war against them to devastate the country where the Reubenites and the Gadites lived.

³⁴And the Reubenites and the Gadites gave the altar this name: A Witness Between Us that the LORD is God.

Joshua's Farewell to the Leaders

23 After a long time had passed and the LORD had given Israel rest from all their enemies around them, Joshua, by then old and well advanced in years, ²summoned all Israel—their elders, leaders, judges and officials—and said to them: "I am old and well advanced in years. ³You yourselves have seen everything the LORD your God has done to all these nations for your sake; it was the LORD your God who fought for you. ⁴Remember how I have allotted as an inheritance for your tribes all the land of the nations that remain—the nations I conquered—between the Jordan and the Great Sea[b] in the west. ⁵The LORD your God himself will drive them out of your way. He will push them out before you, and you will take possession of their land, as the LORD your God promised you.

⁶"Be very strong; be careful to obey all

---

a23 Traditionally *peace offerings*; also in verse 27
b4 That is, the Mediterranean

JUST BETWEEN
you & me

Trust and Talk

Take a moment to answer each of these questions on your own. Then compare your answers to your spouse's.

Yes No When my spouse is late, my mind tends to fear the worst.

Yes No When there is something wrong with the finances, I tend to wonder if my spouse is doing something behind my back.

Yes No When I see my spouse talking to a member of the opposite sex, I tend to become jealous.

Yes No There are things that happen that make me feel insecure about our marriage.

that is written in the Book of the Law of
Moses, without turning aside to the right
or to the left. [7]Do not associate with these
nations that remain among you; do not
invoke the names of their gods or swear
by them. You must not serve them or bow
down to them. [8]But you are to hold fast
to the LORD your God, as you have until
now.

[9]"The LORD has driven out before you
great and powerful nations; to this day
no one has been able to withstand you.
[10]One of you routs a thousand, because
the LORD your God fights for you, just as
he promised. [11]So be very careful to love
the LORD your God.

[12]"But if you turn away and ally yourselves with the survivors of these nations
that remain among you and if you intermarry with them and associate with
them, [13]then you may be sure that the
LORD your God will no longer drive out
these nations before you. Instead, they
will become snares and traps for you,
whips on your backs and thorns in your
eyes, until you perish from this good
land, which the LORD your God has given
you.

[14]"Now I am about to go the way of all
the earth. You know with all your heart
and soul that not one of all the good
promises the LORD your God gave you has
failed. Every promise has been fulfilled;
not one has failed. [15]But just as every
good promise of the LORD your God has
come true, so the LORD will bring on you
all the evil he has threatened, until he has
destroyed you from this good land he has
given you. [16]If you violate the covenant of
the LORD your God, which he commanded you, and go and serve other gods and
bow down to them, the LORD's anger will
burn against you, and you will quickly
perish from the good land he has given
you."

The Covenant Renewed at Shechem

24 Then Joshua assembled all the
tribes of Israel at Shechem. He
summoned the elders, leaders, judges and
officials of Israel, and they presented
themselves before God.

[2]Joshua said to all the people, "This is
what the LORD, the God of Israel, says:
'Long ago your forefathers, including Terah the father of Abraham and Nahor,
lived beyond the River[a] and worshiped
other gods. [3]But I took your father Abraham from the land beyond the River and
led him throughout Canaan and gave
him many descendants. I gave him Isaac,
[4]and to Isaac I gave Jacob and Esau. I
assigned the hill country of Seir to Esau,
but Jacob and his sons went down to
Egypt.

[5]" 'Then I sent Moses and Aaron, and
I afflicted the Egyptians by what I did
there, and I brought you out. [6]When I
brought your fathers out of Egypt, you
came to the sea, and the Egyptians pursued them with chariots and horsemen[b]
as far as the Red Sea.[c] [7]But they cried to
the LORD for help, and he put darkness
between you and the Egyptians; he
brought the sea over them and covered
them. You saw with your own eyes what
I did to the Egyptians. Then you lived in
the desert for a long time.

[8]" 'I brought you to the land of the
Amorites who lived east of the Jordan.
They fought against you, but I gave them
into your hands. I destroyed them from
before you, and you took possession of
their land. [9]When Balak son of Zippor,
the king of Moab, prepared to fight
against Israel, he sent for Balaam son of
Beor to put a curse on you. [10]But I would
not listen to Balaam, so he blessed you
again and again, and I delivered you out
of his hand.

[11]" 'Then you crossed the Jordan and
came to Jericho. The citizens of Jericho
fought against you, as did also the Amorites, Perizzites, Canaanites, Hittites, Girgashites, Hivites and Jebusites, but I gave
them into your hands. [12]I sent the hornet
ahead of you, which drove them out before you—also the two Amorite kings. You
did not do it with your own sword and
bow. [13]So I gave you a land on which you
did not toil and cities you did not build;
and you live in them and eat from vineyards and olive groves that you did not
plant.'

[14]"Now fear the LORD and serve him
with all faithfulness. Throw away the gods

---

[a]2 That is, the Euphrates; also in verses 3, 14 and
15   [b]6 Or *charioteers*   [c]6 Hebrew *Yam Suph*;
that is, Sea of Reeds

your forefathers worshiped beyond the River and in Egypt, and serve the LORD. ¹⁵But if serving the LORD seems undesirable to you, then choose for yourselves this day whom you will serve, whether the gods your forefathers served beyond the River, or the gods of the Amorites, in whose land you are living. But as for me and my household, we will serve the LORD."

¹⁶Then the people answered, "Far be it from us to forsake the LORD to serve other gods! ¹⁷It was the LORD our God himself who brought us and our fathers up out of Egypt, from that land of slavery, and performed those great signs before our eyes. He protected us on our entire journey and among all the nations through which we traveled. ¹⁸And the LORD drove out before us all the nations, including the Amorites, who lived in the land. We too will serve the LORD, because he is our God."

¹⁹Joshua said to the people, "You are not able to serve the LORD. He is a holy God; he is a jealous God. He will not forgive your rebellion and your sins. ²⁰If you forsake the LORD and serve foreign gods, he will turn and bring disaster on you and make an end of you, after he has been good to you."

²¹But the people said to Joshua, "No! We will serve the LORD."

²²Then Joshua said, "You are witnesses against yourselves that you have chosen to serve the LORD."

"Yes, we are witnesses," they replied.

²³"Now then," said Joshua, "throw away the foreign gods that are among you and yield your hearts to the LORD, the God of Israel."

²⁴And the people said to Joshua, "We will serve the LORD our God and obey him."

²⁵On that day Joshua made a covenant for the people, and there at Shechem he drew up for them decrees and laws. ²⁶And Joshua recorded these things in the Book of the Law of God. Then he took a large stone and set it up there under the oak near the holy place of the LORD.

²⁷"See!" he said to all the people. "This stone will be a witness against us. It has heard all the words the LORD has said to us. It will be a witness against you if you are untrue to your God."

Buried in the Promised Land

²⁸Then Joshua sent the people away, each to his own inheritance.

²⁹After these things, Joshua son of

Who Will You Serve?

Thursday

JOSHUA 24 There are certain areas in our lives in which we must make a decisive choice. One of those key areas is the direction our families are going to take. Are we, as a family, going to follow Jesus Christ and live the lifestyle that's promoted in God's Word? Or are we going to be swayed by the constantly shifting ideas and opinions presented by our society?

Joshua and the people of Israel were faced with that very decision in this passage. Joshua boldly asked each family to decide *who* they were going to follow. Were they going to go back to worshiping the gods of their past? Or were they going to make a new commitment? They were challenged to follow only Jehovah, the One true God. Joshua himself mentored the people by stating with great clarity, "But as for me and my household, we will serve the LORD" (verse 15).

If we desire to make that same strong commitment as families today, we need to spend time deciding to live this out in visible, practical ways. How do we become a family that "serves the LORD"? What behaviors, actions and traditions should we adopt that would show it? Though it was often difficult for our children to understand, we took a stand on what types of movies we watched at the theater and videos we rented. We also selected a time devoted to reading God's Word as a family. Jesus himself said, "No one can serve two masters" (Matthew 6:24). Who or what is your master? And does your family life reflect who you've chosen to serve?   **—Bob & Rosemary**

Go to page 275 for your next devotional reading.

Nun, the servant of the LORD, died at the
age of a hundred and ten. ³⁰And they buried him in the land of his inheritance, at
Timnath Serah*a* in the hill country of
Ephraim, north of Mount Gaash.

³¹Israel served the LORD throughout
the lifetime of Joshua and of the elders
who outlived him and who had experienced everything the LORD had done for
Israel.

³²And Joseph's bones, which the Israelites had brought up from Egypt, were bur-

ied at Shechem in the tract of land that
Jacob bought for a hundred pieces of silver*b* from the sons of Hamor, the father
of Shechem. This became the inheritance
of Joseph's descendants.

³³And Eleazar son of Aaron died and
was buried at Gibeah, which had been
allotted to his son Phinehas in the hill
country of Ephraim.

a30 Also known as *Timnath Heres* (see Judges 2:9)
b32 Hebrew *hundred kesitahs;* a kesitah was a unit
of money of unknown weight and value.

Judges

If Joshua recounts an "up" time for the people of Israel, then Judges recounts some of the "down" times. In fact, this period in Israel's history is like a roller coaster ride. Israel repeatedly falls away from God, a situation in which "Israel had no king; everyone did as he saw fit" (17:6). Eventually the Israelites become desperate and beg God to save them. God sends a judge to lead them out of trouble; things go better for a while, but then the cycle starts again.

Marriage is like a roller coaster ride too. There are "up" times and "down" times. Most (if not all) of the "down" times are the result of wanting to do it our way, without anyone else's help—even God's. We want to do as we see fit. This book clearly shows what happens when we try to get along without God—and what can happen when we turn around and trust God again.

Israel Fights the Remaining Canaanites

1 After the death of Joshua, the Israelites asked the LORD, "Who will be the first to go up and fight for us against the Canaanites?"

²The LORD answered, "Judah is to go; I have given the land into their hands."

³Then the men of Judah said to the Simeonites their brothers, "Come up with us into the territory allotted to us, to fight against the Canaanites. We in turn will go with you into yours." So the Simeonites went with them.

⁴When Judah attacked, the LORD gave the Canaanites and Perizzites into their hands and they struck down ten thousand men at Bezek. ⁵It was there that they found Adoni-Bezek and fought against him, putting to rout the Canaanites and Perizzites. ⁶Adoni-Bezek fled, but they chased him and caught him, and cut off his thumbs and big toes.

⁷Then Adoni-Bezek said, "Seventy kings with their thumbs and big toes cut off have picked up scraps under my table. Now God has paid me back for what I did to them." They brought him to Jerusalem, and he died there.

⁸The men of Judah attacked Jerusalem also and took it. They put the city to the sword and set it on fire.

⁹After that, the men of Judah went down to fight against the Canaanites living in the hill country, the Negev and the western foothills. ¹⁰They advanced against the Canaanites living in Hebron (formerly called Kiriath Arba) and defeated Sheshai, Ahiman and Talmai.

¹¹From there they advanced against the people living in Debir (formerly called Kiriath Sepher). ¹²And Caleb said, "I will give my daughter Acsah in marriage to the man who attacks and captures Kiriath Sepher." ¹³Othniel son of Kenaz, Caleb's younger brother, took it; so Caleb gave his daughter Acsah to him in marriage.

¹⁴One day when she came to Othniel, she urged him*a* to ask her father for a field. When she got off her donkey, Caleb asked her, "What can I do for you?"

¹⁵She replied, "Do me a special favor. Since you have given me land in the Negev, give me also springs of water." Then Caleb gave her the upper and lower springs.

¹⁶The descendants of Moses' father-in-law, the Kenite, went up from the City of Palms*b* with the men of Judah to live among the people of the Desert of Judah in the Negev near Arad.

¹⁷Then the men of Judah went with the Simeonites their brothers and attacked the Canaanites living in Zephath, and they totally destroyed*c* the city. Therefore it was called Hormah.*d* ¹⁸The men of Judah also took*e* Gaza, Ashkelon and Ekron—each city with its territory.

¹⁹The LORD was with the men of Judah. They took possession of the hill country, but they were unable to drive the people from the plains, because they had iron chariots. ²⁰As Moses had promised, Hebron was given to Caleb, who drove from it the three sons of Anak. ²¹The Benjamites, however, failed to dislodge the Jebusites, who were living in Jerusalem; to this day the Jebusites live there with the Benjamites.

²²Now the house of Joseph attacked Bethel, and the LORD was with them. ²³When they sent men to spy out Bethel (formerly called Luz), ²⁴the spies saw a man coming out of the city and they said to him, "Show us how to get into the city and we will see that you are treated well." ²⁵So he showed them, and they put the city to the sword but spared the man and his whole family. ²⁶He then went to the land of the Hittites, where he built a city and called it Luz, which is its name to this day.

²⁷But Manasseh did not drive out the people of Beth Shan or Taanach or Dor or Ibleam or Megiddo and their surrounding settlements, for the Canaanites were determined to live in that land. ²⁸When Israel became strong, they pressed the Canaanites into forced labor but never drove them out completely. ²⁹Nor did Ephraim drive out the Canaanites living in Gezer, but the Canaanites continued to live there among them. ³⁰Neither did Zebulun drive out the Canaanites living in Kitron or Nahalol, who remained among them; but they did subject them to forced labor. ³¹Nor did Asher drive out those living in Acco or Sidon or Ahlab or Aczib or Helbah or Aphek or Rehob, ³²and because of this the people of Asher lived among the Canaanite inhabitants of the land. ³³Neither did Naphtali drive out those living in Beth Shemesh or Beth Anath; but the Naphtalites too lived among the Canaanite inhabitants of the land, and those living in Beth Shemesh and Beth Anath became forced laborers for them. ³⁴The Amorites confined the Danites to the hill country, not allowing them to come down into the plain. ³⁵And the Amorites were determined also to hold out in Mount Heres, Aijalon and Shaalbim, but when the power of the house of Joseph increased, they too were pressed into forced labor. ³⁶The boundary of the Amorites was from Scorpion*f* Pass to Sela and beyond.

The Angel of the LORD at Bokim

2 The angel of the LORD went up from Gilgal to Bokim and said, "I brought you up out of Egypt and led you into the land that I swore to give to your forefathers. I said, 'I will never break my covenant with you, ²and you shall not make a covenant with the people of this land, but you shall break down their altars.' Yet

---

a14 Hebrew; Septuagint and Vulgate *Othniel, he urged her*   *b16* That is, Jericho
c17 The Hebrew term refers to the irrevocable giving over of things or persons to the LORD, often by totally destroying them.   *d17 Hormah* means *destruction.*   *e18* Hebrew; Septuagint *Judah did not take*   *f36* Hebrew *Akrabbim*

you have disobeyed me. Why have you done this? ³Now therefore I tell you that I will not drive them out before you; they will be ˹thorns˼ in your sides and their gods will be a snare to you."

⁴When the angel of the LORD had spoken these things to all the Israelites, the people wept aloud, ⁵and they called that place Bokim.*ᵃ There they offered sacrifices to the LORD.

Disobedience and Defeat

⁶After Joshua had dismissed the Israelites, they went to take possession of the land, each to his own inheritance. ⁷The people served the LORD throughout the lifetime of Joshua and of the elders who outlived him and who had seen all the great things the LORD had done for Israel.

⁸Joshua son of Nun, the servant of the LORD, died at the age of a hundred and ten. ⁹And they buried him in the land of his inheritance, at Timnath Heres*ᵇ in the hill country of Ephraim, north of Mount Gaash.

¹⁰After that whole generation had been gathered to their fathers, another generation grew up, who knew neither the LORD nor what he had done for Israel. ¹¹Then the Israelites did evil in the eyes of the LORD and served the Baals. ¹²They forsook the LORD, the God of their fathers, who had brought them out of Egypt. They followed and worshiped various gods of the peoples around them. They provoked the LORD to anger ¹³because they forsook him and served Baal and the Ashtoreths. ¹⁴In his anger against Israel the LORD handed them over to raiders who plundered them. He sold them to their enemies all around, whom they were no longer able to resist. ¹⁵Whenever Israel went out to fight, the hand of the LORD was against them to defeat them, just as he had sworn to them. They were in great distress.

¹⁶Then the LORD raised up judges,*ᶜ who saved them out of the hands of these raiders. ¹⁷Yet they would not listen to their judges but prostituted themselves to other gods and worshiped them. Unlike their fathers, they quickly turned from the way in which their fathers had walked, the way of obedience to the LORD's commands. ¹⁸Whenever the LORD raised up a judge for them, he was with the judge and saved them out of the hands of their enemies as long as the judge lived; for the LORD had compassion on them as they groaned under those who oppressed and afflicted them. ¹⁹But when the judge died, the people returned to ways even more corrupt than those of their fathers, following other gods and serving and worshiping them. They refused to give up their evil practices and stubborn ways.

²⁰Therefore the LORD was very angry with Israel and said, "Because this nation has violated the covenant that I laid down for their forefathers and has not listened to me, ²¹I will no longer drive out before them any of the nations Joshua left when he died. ²²I will use them to test Israel and see whether they will keep the way of the LORD and walk in it as their forefathers did." ²³The LORD had allowed those nations to remain; he did not drive them out at once by giving them into the hands of Joshua.

3 These are the nations the LORD left to test all those Israelites who had not experienced any of the wars in Canaan ²(he did this only to teach warfare to the descendants of the Israelites who had not had previous battle experience): ³the five rulers of the Philistines, all the Canaanites, the Sidonians, and the Hivites living in the Lebanon mountains from Mount Baal Hermon to Lebo*ᵈ Hamath. ⁴They were left to test the Israelites to see whether they would obey the LORD's commands, which he had given their forefathers through Moses.

⁵The Israelites lived among the Canaanites, Hittites, Amorites, Perizzites, Hivites and Jebusites. ⁶They took their daughters in marriage and gave their own daughters to their sons, and served their gods.

Othniel

⁷The Israelites did evil in the eyes of the LORD; they forgot the LORD their God and served the Baals and the Asherahs. ⁸The anger of the LORD burned against Israel so that he sold them into the hands of Cushan-Rishathaim king of Aram Na-

ᵃ5 *Bokim* means *weepers.*   ᵇ9 Also known as *Timnath Serah* (see Joshua 19:50 and 24:30)   ᶜ16 Or *leaders;* similarly in verses 17-19   ᵈ3 Or *to the entrance to* haraim,[a] to whom the Israelites were subject for eight years. [9]But when they cried out to the LORD, he raised up for them a deliverer, Othniel son of Kenaz, Caleb's younger brother, who saved them. [10]The Spirit of the LORD came upon him, so that he became Israel's judge[b] and went to war. The LORD gave Cushan-Rishathaim king of Aram into the hands of Othniel, who overpowered him. [11]So the land had peace for forty years, until Othniel son of Kenaz died.

Ehud

[12]Once again the Israelites did evil in the eyes of the LORD, and because they did this evil the LORD gave Eglon king of Moab power over Israel. [13]Getting the Ammonites and Amalekites to join him, Eglon came and attacked Israel, and they took possession of the City of Palms.[c] [14]The Israelites were subject to Eglon king of Moab for eighteen years.

[15]Again the Israelites cried out to the LORD, and he gave them a deliverer— Ehud, a left-handed man, the son of Gera the Benjamite. The Israelites sent him with tribute to Eglon king of Moab. [16]Now Ehud had made a double-edged sword about a foot and a half[d] long, which he strapped to his right thigh under his clothing. [17]He presented the tribute to Eglon king of Moab, who was a very fat man. [18]After Ehud had presented the tribute, he sent on their way the men who had carried it. [19]At the idols[e] near Gilgal he himself turned back and said, "I have a secret message for you, O king."

The king said, "Quiet!" And all his attendants left him.

[20]Ehud then approached him while he was sitting alone in the upper room of his summer palace[f] and said, "I have a message from God for you." As the king rose from his seat, [21]Ehud reached with his left hand, drew the sword from his right thigh and plunged it into the king's belly. [22]Even the handle sank in after the blade, which came out his back. Ehud did not pull the sword out, and the fat closed in over it. [23]Then Ehud went out to the porch[g]; he shut the doors of the upper room behind him and locked them.

[24]After he had gone, the servants came and found the doors of the upper room locked. They said, "He must be relieving himself in the inner room of the house." [25]They waited to the point of embarrassment, but when he did not open the doors of the room, they took a key and unlocked them. There they saw their lord fallen to the floor, dead.

[26]While they waited, Ehud got away. He passed by the idols and escaped to Seirah. [27]When he arrived there, he blew a trumpet in the hill country of Ephraim, and the Israelites went down with him from the hills, with him leading them.

[28]"Follow me," he ordered, "for the LORD has given Moab, your enemy, into your hands." So they followed him down and, taking possession of the fords of the Jordan that led to Moab, they allowed no one to cross over. [29]At that time they struck down about ten thousand Moabites, all vigorous and strong; not a man escaped. [30]That day Moab was made subject to Israel, and the land had peace for eighty years.

Shamgar

[31]After Ehud came Shamgar son of Anath, who struck down six hundred Philistines with an oxgoad. He too saved Israel.

Deborah

4 After Ehud died, the Israelites once again did evil in the eyes of the LORD. [2]So the LORD sold them into the hands of Jabin, a king of Canaan, who reigned in Hazor. The commander of his army was Sisera, who lived in Harosheth Haggoyim. [3]Because he had nine hundred iron chariots and had cruelly oppressed the Israelites for twenty years, they cried to the LORD for help.

[4]Deborah, a prophetess, the wife of Lappidoth, was leading[h] Israel at that time. [5]She held court under the Palm of Deborah between Ramah and Bethel in the hill country of Ephraim, and the Israelites came to her to have their disputes decided. [6]She sent for Barak son of Abino-

---

[a]8 That is, Northwest Mesopotamia　　[b]10 Or leader　　[c]13 That is, Jericho　　[d]16 Hebrew a cubit (about 0.5 meter)　　[e]19 Or the stone quarries; also in verse 26　　[f]20 The meaning of the Hebrew for this phrase is uncertain.　　[g]23 The meaning of the Hebrew for this word is uncertain.　　[h]4 Traditionally judging

am from Kedesh in Naphtali and said to him, "The LORD, the God of Israel, commands you: 'Go, take with you ten thousand men of Naphtali and Zebulun and lead the way to Mount Tabor. 7I will lure Sisera, the commander of Jabin's army, with his chariots and his troops to the Kishon River and give him into your hands.' "

8Barak said to her, "If you go with me, I will go; but if you don't go with me, I won't go."

9"Very well," Deborah said, "I will go with you. But because of the way you are going about this,[a] the honor will not be yours, for the LORD will hand Sisera over to a woman." So Deborah went with Barak to Kedesh, 10where he summoned Zebulun and Naphtali. Ten thousand men followed him, and Deborah also went with him.

11Now Heber the Kenite had left the other Kenites, the descendants of Hobab, Moses' brother-in-law,[b] and pitched his tent by the great tree in Zaanannim near Kedesh.

12When they told Sisera that Barak son of Abinoam had gone up to Mount Tabor, 13Sisera gathered together his nine hundred iron chariots and all the men with him, from Harosheth Haggoyim to the Kishon River.

14Then Deborah said to Barak, "Go! This is the day the LORD has given Sisera into your hands. Has not the LORD gone ahead of you?" So Barak went down Mount Tabor, followed by ten thousand men. 15At Barak's advance, the LORD routed Sisera and all his chariots and army by the sword, and Sisera abandoned his chariot and fled on foot. 16But Barak pursued the chariots and army as far as Harosheth Haggoyim. All the troops of Sisera fell by the sword; not a man was left.

17Sisera, however, fled on foot to the tent of Jael, the wife of Heber the Kenite, because there were friendly relations between Jabin king of Hazor and the clan of Heber the Kenite.

18Jael went out to meet Sisera and said to him, "Come, my lord, come right in. Don't be afraid." So he entered her tent, and she put a covering over him.

19"I'm thirsty," he said. "Please give me some water." She opened a skin of milk, gave him a drink, and covered him up.

20"Stand in the doorway of the tent," he told her. "If someone comes by and asks you, 'Is anyone here?' say 'No.' "

21But Jael, Heber's wife, picked up a tent peg and a hammer and went quietly to him while he lay fast asleep, exhausted. She drove the peg through his temple into the ground, and he died.

22Barak came by in pursuit of Sisera, and Jael went out to meet him. "Come," she said, "I will show you the man you're looking for." So he went in with her, and there lay Sisera with the tent peg through his temple—dead.

23On that day God subdued Jabin, the Canaanite king, before the Israelites. 24And the hand of the Israelites grew stronger and stronger against Jabin, the Canaanite king, until they destroyed him.

The Song of Deborah

5 On that day Deborah and Barak son of Abinoam sang this song:

2"When the princes in Israel take the
       lead,
    when the people willingly offer
       themselves—
    praise the LORD!

3"Hear this, you kings! Listen, you
       rulers!
    I will sing to[c] the LORD, I will
       sing;
    I will make music to[d] the LORD,
       the God of Israel.

4"O LORD, when you went out from
       Seir,
    when you marched from the land
       of Edom,
 the earth shook, the heavens poured,
    the clouds poured down water.
5The mountains quaked before the
       LORD, the One of Sinai,
    before the LORD, the God of Israel.

6"In the days of Shamgar son of
       Anath,
    in the days of Jael, the roads were
       abandoned;
    travelers took to winding paths.
7Village life[e] in Israel ceased,
    ceased until I,[f] Deborah, arose,

---

a9 Or But on the expedition you are undertaking
b11 Or father-in-law   c3 Or of   d3 Or / with
song I will praise   e7 Or Warriors   f7 Or you

arose a mother in Israel.
8When they chose new gods,
    war came to the city gates,
and not a shield or spear was seen
    among forty thousand in Israel.
9My heart is with Israel's princes,
    with the willing volunteers among
        the people.
    Praise the LORD!

10"You who ride on white donkeys,
    sitting on your saddle blankets,
    and you who walk along the road,
consider 11the voice of the singers*a*
    at the watering places.
    They recite the righteous acts of the
        LORD,
    the righteous acts of his warriors*b*
        in Israel.

"Then the people of the LORD
    went down to the city gates.
12'Wake up, wake up, Deborah!
    Wake up, wake up, break out in
        song!
    Arise, O Barak!
    Take captive your captives, O son
        of Abinoam.'

13"Then the men who were left
    came down to the nobles;
    the people of the LORD
    came to me with the mighty.
14Some came from Ephraim, whose
        roots were in Amalek;
    Benjamin was with the people who
        followed you.
From Makir captains came down,
    from Zebulun those who bear a
        commander's staff.
15The princes of Issachar were with
        Deborah;
    yes, Issachar was with Barak,
    rushing after him into the valley.
In the districts of Reuben
    there was much searching of heart.
16Why did you stay among the
        campfires*c*
    to hear the whistling for the flocks?
In the districts of Reuben
    there was much searching of heart.
17Gilead stayed beyond the Jordan.
    And Dan, why did he linger by the
        ships?
Asher remained on the coast
    and stayed in his coves.

18The people of Zebulun risked their
        very lives;
    so did Naphtali on the heights of
        the field.

19"Kings came, they fought;
    the kings of Canaan fought
at Taanach by the waters of Megiddo,
    but they carried off no silver, no
        plunder.
20From the heavens the stars fought,
    from their courses they fought
        against Sisera.
21The river Kishon swept them away,
    the age-old river, the river Kishon.
    March on, my soul; be strong!
22Then thundered the horses' hoofs—
    galloping, galloping go his mighty
        steeds.
23'Curse Meroz,' said the angel of the
        LORD.
    'Curse its people bitterly,
because they did not come to help
        the LORD,
    to help the LORD against the
        mighty.'

24"Most blessed of women be Jael,
    the wife of Heber the Kenite,
    most blessed of tent-dwelling
        women.
25He asked for water, and she gave him
        milk;
    in a bowl fit for nobles she
        brought him curdled milk.
26Her hand reached for the tent peg,
    her right hand for the workman's
        hammer.
She struck Sisera, she crushed his
        head,
    she shattered and pierced his
        temple.
27At her feet he sank,
    he fell; there he lay.
At her feet he sank, he fell;
    where he sank, there he fell—dead.

28"Through the window peered Sisera's
        mother;
    behind the lattice she cried out,
'Why is his chariot so long in
        coming?

---

*a*11 Or *archers*; the meaning of the Hebrew for this
word is uncertain.   *b*11 Or *villagers*   *c*16 Or
saddlebags

Why is the clatter of his chariots
   delayed?'
²⁹The wisest of her ladies answer her;
   indeed, she keeps saying to herself,
³⁰'Are they not finding and dividing the
      spoils:
   a girl or two for each man,
   colorful garments as plunder for
      Sisera,
   colorful garments embroidered,
   highly embroidered garments for
      my neck—
all this as plunder?'

³¹"So may all your enemies perish,
      O LORD!
   But may they who love you be like
      the sun
   when it rises in its strength."

Then the land had peace forty years.

Gideon

6 Again the Israelites did evil in the eyes of the LORD, and for seven years he gave them into the hands of the Midianites. ²Because the power of Midian was so oppressive, the Israelites prepared shelters for themselves in mountain clefts, caves and strongholds. ³Whenever the Israelites planted their crops, the Midianites, Amalekites and other eastern peoples invaded the country. ⁴They camped on the land and ruined the crops all the way to Gaza and did not spare a living thing for Israel, neither sheep nor cattle nor donkeys. ⁵They came up with their livestock and their tents like swarms of locusts. It was impossible to count the men and their camels; they invaded the land to ravage it. ⁶Midian so impoverished the Israelites that they cried out to the LORD for help.

⁷When the Israelites cried to the LORD because of Midian, ⁸he sent them a prophet, who said, "This is what the LORD, the God of Israel, says: I brought you up out of Egypt, out of the land of slavery. ⁹I snatched you from the power of Egypt and from the hand of all your oppressors. I drove them from before you and gave you their land. ¹⁰I said to you, 'I am the LORD your God; do not worship the gods of the Amorites, in whose land you live.' But you have not listened to me."

¹¹The angel of the LORD came and sat down under the oak in Ophrah that belonged to Joash the Abiezrite, where his son Gideon was threshing wheat in a winepress to keep it from the Midianites. ¹²When the angel of the LORD appeared to Gideon, he said, "The LORD is with you, mighty warrior."

¹³"But sir," Gideon replied, "if the LORD is with us, why has all this happened to us? Where are all his wonders that our fathers told us about when they said, 'Did not the LORD bring us up out of Egypt?' But now the LORD has abandoned us and put us into the hand of Midian."

¹⁴The LORD turned to him and said, "Go in the strength you have and save Israel out of Midian's hand. Am I not sending you?"

¹⁵"But Lord,^a" Gideon asked, "how can I save Israel? My clan is the weakest in Manasseh, and I am the least in my family."

¹⁶The LORD answered, "I will be with you, and you will strike down all the Midianites together."

¹⁷Gideon replied, "If now I have found favor in your eyes, give me a sign that it is really you talking to me. ¹⁸Please do not go away until I come back and bring my offering and set it before you."

And the LORD said, "I will wait until you return."

¹⁹Gideon went in, prepared a young goat, and from an ephah^b of flour he made bread without yeast. Putting the meat in a basket and its broth in a pot, he brought them out and offered them to him under the oak.

²⁰The angel of God said to him, "Take the meat and the unleavened bread, place them on this rock, and pour out the broth." And Gideon did so. ²¹With the tip of the staff that was in his hand, the angel of the LORD touched the meat and the unleavened bread. Fire flared from the rock, consuming the meat and the bread. And the angel of the LORD disappeared. ²²When Gideon realized that it was the angel of the LORD, he exclaimed, "Ah, Sovereign LORD! I have seen the angel of the LORD face to face!"

²³But the LORD said to him, "Peace! Do not be afraid. You are not going to die."

---

^a15 Or sir   ^b19 That is, probably about 3/5 bushel (about 22 liters)

²⁴So Gideon built an altar to the LORD there and called it The LORD is Peace. To this day it stands in Ophrah of the Abiezrites.

²⁵That same night the LORD said to him, "Take the second bull from your father's herd, the one seven years old.ᵃ Tear down your father's altar to Baal and cut down the Asherah poleᵇ beside it. ²⁶Then build a proper kind ofᶜ altar to the LORD your God on the top of this height. Using the wood of the Asherah pole that you cut down, offer the secondᵈ bull as a burnt offering."

²⁷So Gideon took ten of his servants and did as the LORD told him. But because he was afraid of his family and the men of the town, he did it at night rather than in the daytime.

²⁸In the morning when the men of the town got up, there was Baal's altar, demolished, with the Asherah pole beside it cut down and the second bull sacrificed on the newly built altar!

²⁹They asked each other, "Who did this?"

When they carefully investigated, they were told, "Gideon son of Joash did it."

³⁰The men of the town demanded of Joash, "Bring out your son. He must die, because he has broken down Baal's altar and cut down the Asherah pole beside it."

³¹But Joash replied to the hostile crowd around him, "Are you going to plead Baal's cause? Are you trying to save him? Whoever fights for him shall be put to death by morning! If Baal really is a god, he can defend himself when someone breaks down his altar." ³²So that day they called Gideon "Jerub-Baal,ᵉ" saying, "Let Baal contend with him," because he broke down Baal's altar.

³³Now all the Midianites, Amalekites and other eastern peoples joined forces and crossed over the Jordan and camped in the Valley of Jezreel. ³⁴Then the Spirit of the LORD came upon Gideon, and he blew a trumpet, summoning the Abiezrites to follow him. ³⁵He sent messengers throughout Manasseh, calling them to arms, and also into Asher, Zebulun and Naphtali, so that they too went up to meet them.

³⁶Gideon said to God, "If you will save Israel by my hand as you have promised— ³⁷look, I will place a wool fleece on the threshing floor. If there is dew only on the fleece and all the ground is dry, then I will know that you will save Israel by my hand, as you said." ³⁸And that is what happened. Gideon rose early the next day; he squeezed the fleece and wrung out the dew—a bowlful of water.

³⁹Then Gideon said to God, "Do not be angry with me. Let me make just one more request. Allow me one more test with the fleece. This time make the fleece dry and the ground covered with dew." ⁴⁰That night God did so. Only the fleece was dry; all the ground was covered with dew.

Gideon Defeats the Midianites

7 Early in the morning, Jerub-Baal (that is, Gideon) and all his men camped at the spring of Harod. The camp of Midian was north of them in the valley near the hill of Moreh. ²The LORD said to Gideon, "You have too many men for me to deliver Midian into their hands. In order that Israel may not boast against me that her own strength has saved her, ³announce now to the people, 'Anyone who trembles with fear may turn back and leave Mount Gilead.' " So twenty-two thousand men left, while ten thousand remained.

⁴But the LORD said to Gideon, "There are still too many men. Take them down to the water, and I will sift them for you there. If I say, 'This one shall go with you,' he shall go; but if I say, 'This one shall not go with you,' he shall not go."

⁵So Gideon took the men down to the water. There the LORD told him, "Separate those who lap the water with their tongues like a dog from those who kneel down to drink." ⁶Three hundred men lapped with their hands to their mouths. All the rest got down on their knees to drink.

⁷The LORD said to Gideon, "With the three hundred men that lapped I will save you and give the Midianites into your hands. Let all the other men go, each to his own place." ⁸So Gideon sent the rest of the Israelites to their tents but kept the

---

ᵃ25 Or *Take a full-grown, mature bull from your father's herd*   ᵇ25 That is, a symbol of the goddess Asherah; here and elsewhere in Judges   ᶜ26 Or *build with layers of stone an*   ᵈ26 Or *full-grown*; also in verse 28   ᵉ32 *Jerub-Baal* means *let Baal contend*.

three hundred, who took over the provisions and trumpets of the others.

Now the camp of Midian lay below him in the valley. ⁹During that night the LORD said to Gideon, "Get up, go down against the camp, because I am going to give it into your hands. ¹⁰If you are afraid to attack, go down to the camp with your servant Purah ¹¹and listen to what they are saying. Afterward, you will be encouraged to attack the camp." So he and Purah his servant went down to the outposts of the camp. ¹²The Midianites, the Amalekites and all the other eastern peoples had settled in the valley, thick as locusts. Their camels could no more be counted than the sand on the seashore.

¹³Gideon arrived just as a man was telling a friend his dream. "I had a dream," he was saying. "A round loaf of barley bread came tumbling into the Midianite camp. It struck the tent with such force that the tent overturned and collapsed."

¹⁴His friend responded, "This can be nothing other than the sword of Gideon son of Joash, the Israelite. God has given the Midianites and the whole camp into his hands."

¹⁵When Gideon heard the dream and its interpretation, he worshiped God. He returned to the camp of Israel and called out, "Get up! The LORD has given the Midianite camp into your hands." ¹⁶Dividing the three hundred men into three companies, he placed trumpets and empty jars in the hands of all of them, with torches inside.

¹⁷"Watch me," he told them. "Follow my lead. When I get to the edge of the camp, do exactly as I do. ¹⁸When I and all who are with me blow our trumpets, then from all around the camp blow yours and shout, 'For the LORD and for Gideon.' "

¹⁹Gideon and the hundred men with him reached the edge of the camp at the beginning of the middle watch, just after they had changed the guard. They blew their trumpets and broke the jars that were in their hands. ²⁰The three companies blew the trumpets and smashed the jars. Grasping the torches in their left hands and holding in their right hands the trumpets they were to blow, they shouted, "A sword for the LORD and for Gideon!" ²¹While each man held his position around the camp, all the Midianites ran, crying out as they fled.

²²When the three hundred trumpets sounded, the LORD caused the men throughout the camp to turn on each other with their swords. The army fled to Beth Shittah toward Zererah as far as the border of Abel Meholah near Tabbath. ²³Israelites from Naphtali, Asher and all Manasseh were called out, and they pursued the Midianites. ²⁴Gideon sent messengers throughout the hill country of Ephraim, saying, "Come down against the Midianites and seize the waters of the Jordan ahead of them as far as Beth Barah."

So all the men of Ephraim were called out and they took the waters of the Jordan as far as Beth Barah. ²⁵They also captured two of the Midianite leaders, Oreb and Zeeb. They killed Oreb at the rock of Oreb, and Zeeb at the winepress of Zeeb. They pursued the Midianites and brought the heads of Oreb and Zeeb to Gideon, who was by the Jordan.

Zebah and Zalmunna

8 Now the Ephraimites asked Gideon, "Why have you treated us like this? Why didn't you call us when you went to fight Midian?" And they criticized him sharply.

²But he answered them, "What have I accomplished compared to you? Aren't the gleanings of Ephraim's grapes better than the full grape harvest of Abiezer? ³God gave Oreb and Zeeb, the Midianite leaders, into your hands. What was I able to do compared to you?" At this, their resentment against him subsided.

⁴Gideon and his three hundred men, exhausted yet keeping up the pursuit, came to the Jordan and crossed it. ⁵He said to the men of Succoth, "Give my troops some bread; they are worn out, and I am still pursuing Zebah and Zalmunna, the kings of Midian."

⁶But the officials of Succoth said, "Do you already have the hands of Zebah and Zalmunna in your possession? Why should we give bread to your troops?"

⁷Then Gideon replied, "Just for that, when the LORD has given Zebah and Zalmunna into my hand, I will tear your flesh with desert thorns and briers."

⁸From there he went up to Peniel[a] and made the same request of them, but they answered as the men of Succoth had. ⁹So he said to the men of Peniel, "When I return in triumph, I will tear down this tower."

¹⁰Now Zebah and Zalmunna were in Karkor with a force of about fifteen thousand men, all that were left of the armies of the eastern peoples; a hundred and twenty thousand swordsmen had fallen. ¹¹Gideon went up by the route of the nomads east of Nobah and Jogbehah and fell upon the unsuspecting army. ¹²Zebah and Zalmunna, the two kings of Midian, fled, but he pursued them and captured them, routing their entire army.

¹³Gideon son of Joash then returned from the battle by the Pass of Heres. ¹⁴He caught a young man of Succoth and questioned him, and the young man wrote down for him the names of the seventy-seven officials of Succoth, the elders of the town. ¹⁵Then Gideon came and said to the men of Succoth, "Here are Zebah and Zalmunna, about whom you taunted me by saying, 'Do you already have the hands of Zebah and Zalmunna in your possession? Why should we give bread to your exhausted men?'" ¹⁶He took the elders of the town and taught the men of Succoth a lesson by punishing them with desert thorns and briers. ¹⁷He also pulled down the tower of Peniel and killed the men of the town.

¹⁸Then he asked Zebah and Zalmunna, "What kind of men did you kill at Tabor?"

"Men like you," they answered, "each one with the bearing of a prince."

¹⁹Gideon replied, "Those were my brothers, the sons of my own mother. As surely as the LORD lives, if you had spared their lives, I would not kill you." ²⁰Turning to Jether, his oldest son, he said, "Kill them!" But Jether did not draw his sword, because he was only a boy and was afraid.

²¹Zebah and Zalmunna said, "Come, do it yourself. 'As is the man, so is his strength.'" So Gideon stepped forward and killed them, and took the ornaments off their camels' necks.

Gideon's Ephod

²²The Israelites said to Gideon, "Rule over us—you, your son and your grand-son—because you have saved us out of the hand of Midian."

²³But Gideon told them, "I will not rule over you, nor will my son rule over you. The LORD will rule over you." ²⁴And he said, "I do have one request, that each of you give me an earring from your share of the plunder." (It was the custom of the Ishmaelites to wear gold earrings.)

²⁵They answered, "We'll be glad to give them." So they spread out a garment, and each man threw a ring from his plunder onto it. ²⁶The weight of the gold rings he asked for came to seventeen hundred shekels,[b] not counting the ornaments, the pendants and the purple garments worn by the kings of Midian or the chains that were on their camels' necks. ²⁷Gideon made the gold into an ephod, which he placed in Ophrah, his town. All Israel prostituted themselves by worshiping it there, and it became a snare to Gideon and his family.

Gideon's Death

²⁸Thus Midian was subdued before the Israelites and did not raise its head again. During Gideon's lifetime, the land enjoyed peace forty years.

²⁹Jerub-Baal son of Joash went back home to live. ³⁰He had seventy sons of his own, for he had many wives. ³¹His concubine, who lived in Shechem, also bore him a son, whom he named Abimelech. ³²Gideon son of Joash died at a good old age and was buried in the tomb of his father Joash in Ophrah of the Abiezrites.

³³No sooner had Gideon died than the Israelites again prostituted themselves to the Baals. They set up Baal-Berith as their god and ³⁴did not remember the LORD their God, who had rescued them from the hands of all their enemies on every side. ³⁵They also failed to show kindness to the family of Jerub-Baal (that is, Gideon) for all the good things he had done for them.

Abimelech

9 Abimelech son of Jerub-Baal went to his mother's brothers in Shechem and said to them and to all his mother's clan,

---

a8 Hebrew *Penuel*, a variant of *Peniel*; also in verses 9 and 17   *b26* That is, about 43 pounds (about 19.5 kilograms)

2"Ask all the citizens of Shechem, 'Which is better for you: to have all seventy of Jerub-Baal's sons rule over you, or just one man?' Remember, I am your flesh and blood."

3When the brothers repeated all this to the citizens of Shechem, they were inclined to follow Abimelech, for they said, "He is our brother." 4They gave him seventy shekels[a] of silver from the temple of Baal-Berith, and Abimelech used it to hire reckless adventurers, who became his followers. 5He went to his father's home in Ophrah and on one stone murdered his seventy brothers, the sons of Jerub-Baal. But Jotham, the youngest son of Jerub-Baal, escaped by hiding. 6Then all the citizens of Shechem and Beth Millo gathered beside the great tree at the pillar in Shechem to crown Abimelech king.

7When Jotham was told about this, he climbed up on the top of Mount Gerizim and shouted to them, "Listen to me, citizens of Shechem, so that God may listen to you. 8One day the trees went out to anoint a king for themselves. They said to the olive tree, 'Be our king.'

9"But the olive tree answered, 'Should I give up my oil, by which both gods and men are honored, to hold sway over the trees?'

10"Next, the trees said to the fig tree, 'Come and be our king.'

11"But the fig tree replied, 'Should I give up my fruit, so good and sweet, to hold sway over the trees?'

12"Then the trees said to the vine, 'Come and be our king.'

13"But the vine answered, 'Should I give up my wine, which cheers both gods and men, to hold sway over the trees?'

14"Finally all the trees said to the thornbush, 'Come and be our king.'

15"The thornbush said to the trees, 'If you really want to anoint me king over you, come and take refuge in my shade; but if not, then let fire come out of the thornbush and consume the cedars of Lebanon!'

16"Now if you have acted honorably and in good faith when you made Abimelech king, and if you have been fair to Jerub-Baal and his family, and if you have treated him as he deserves— 17and to think that my father fought for you, risked his life to rescue you from the hand of Midian 18(but today you have revolted against my father's family, murdered his seventy sons on a single stone, and made Abimelech, the son of his slave girl, king over the citizens of Shechem because he is your brother)— 19if then you have acted honorably and in good faith toward Jerub-Baal and his family today, may Abimelech be your joy, and may you be his, too! 20But if you have not, let fire come out from Abimelech and consume you, citizens of Shechem and Beth Millo, and let fire come out from you, citizens of Shechem and Beth Millo, and consume Abimelech!"

21Then Jotham fled, escaping to Beer, and he lived there because he was afraid of his brother Abimelech.

22After Abimelech had governed Israel three years, 23God sent an evil spirit between Abimelech and the citizens of Shechem, who acted treacherously against Abimelech. 24God did this in order that the crime against Jerub-Baal's seventy sons, the shedding of their blood, might be avenged on their brother Abimelech and on the citizens of Shechem, who had helped him murder his brothers. 25In opposition to him these citizens of Shechem set men on the hilltops to ambush and rob everyone who passed by, and this was reported to Abimelech.

26Now Gaal son of Ebed moved with his brothers into Shechem, and its citizens put their confidence in him. 27After they had gone out into the fields and gathered the grapes and trodden them, they held a festival in the temple of their god. While they were eating and drinking, they cursed Abimelech. 28Then Gaal son of Ebed said, "Who is Abimelech, and who is Shechem, that we should be subject to him? Isn't he Jerub-Baal's son, and isn't Zebul his deputy? Serve the men of Hamor, Shechem's father! Why should we serve Abimelech? 29If only this people were under my command! Then I would get rid of him. I would say to Abimelech, 'Call out your whole army!' "[b]

30When Zebul the governor of the city heard what Gaal son of Ebed said, he was very angry. 31Under cover he sent messen-

a4 That is, about 1 3/4 pounds (about 0.8 kilogram)   b29 Septuagint; Hebrew him." Then he said to Abimelech, "Call out your whole army!"

gers to Abimelech, saying, "Gaal son of Ebed and his brothers have come to Shechem and are stirring up the city against you. ³²Now then, during the night you and your men should come and lie in wait in the fields. ³³In the morning at sunrise, advance against the city. When Gaal and his men come out against you, do whatever your hand finds to do."

³⁴So Abimelech and all his troops set out by night and took up concealed positions near Shechem in four companies. ³⁵Now Gaal son of Ebed had gone out and was standing at the entrance to the city gate just as Abimelech and his soldiers came out from their hiding place.

³⁶When Gaal saw them, he said to Zebul, "Look, people are coming down from the tops of the mountains!"

Zebul replied, "You mistake the shadows of the mountains for men."

³⁷But Gaal spoke up again: "Look, people are coming down from the center of the land, and a company is coming from the direction of the soothsayers' tree."

³⁸Then Zebul said to him, "Where is your big talk now, you who said, 'Who is Abimelech that we should be subject to him?' Aren't these the men you ridiculed? Go out and fight them!"

³⁹So Gaal led outᵃ the citizens of Shechem and fought Abimelech. ⁴⁰Abimelech chased him, and many fell wounded in the flight—all the way to the entrance to the gate. ⁴¹Abimelech stayed in Arumah, and Zebul drove Gaal and his brothers out of Shechem.

⁴²The next day the people of Shechem went out to the fields, and this was reported to Abimelech. ⁴³So he took his men, divided them into three companies and set an ambush in the fields. When he saw the people coming out of the city, he rose to attack them. ⁴⁴Abimelech and the companies with him rushed forward to a position at the entrance to the city gate. Then two companies rushed upon those in the fields and struck them down. ⁴⁵All that day Abimelech pressed his attack against the city until he had captured it and killed its people. Then he destroyed the city and scattered salt over it.

⁴⁶On hearing this, the citizens in the tower of Shechem went into the stronghold of the temple of El-Berith. ⁴⁷When Abimelech heard that they had assembled there, ⁴⁸he and all his men went up Mount Zalmon. He took an ax and cut off some branches, which he lifted to his shoulders. He ordered the men with him, "Quick! Do what you have seen me do!" ⁴⁹So all the men cut branches and followed Abimelech. They piled them against the stronghold and set it on fire over the people inside. So all the people in the tower of Shechem, about a thousand men and women, also died.

⁵⁰Next Abimelech went to Thebez and besieged it and captured it. ⁵¹Inside the city, however, was a strong tower, to which all the men and women—all the people of the city—fled. They locked themselves in and climbed up on the tower roof. ⁵²Abimelech went to the tower and stormed it. But as he approached the entrance to the tower to set it on fire, ⁵³a woman dropped an upper millstone on his head and cracked his skull.

⁵⁴Hurriedly he called to his armor-bearer, "Draw your sword and kill me, so that they can't say, 'A woman killed him.' " So his servant ran him through, and he died. ⁵⁵When the Israelites saw that Abimelech was dead, they went home.

⁵⁶Thus God repaid the wickedness that Abimelech had done to his father by murdering his seventy brothers. ⁵⁷God also made the men of Shechem pay for all their wickedness. The curse of Jotham son of Jerub-Baal came on them.

Tola

10 After the time of Abimelech a man of Issachar, Tola son of Puah, the son of Dodo, rose to save Israel. He lived in Shamir, in the hill country of Ephraim. ²He ledᵇ Israel twenty-three years; then he died, and was buried in Shamir.

Jair

³He was followed by Jair of Gilead, who led Israel twenty-two years. ⁴He had thirty sons, who rode thirty donkeys. They controlled thirty towns in Gilead, which to this day are called Havvoth Jair.ᶜ ⁵When Jair died, he was buried in Kamon.

ᵃ39 Or Gaal went out in the sight of
ᵇ2 Traditionally judged; also in verse 3   ᶜ4 Or called the settlements of Jair

Jephthah

⁶Again the Israelites did evil in the eyes of the LORD. They served the Baals and the Ashtoreths, and the gods of Aram, the gods of Sidon, the gods of Moab, the gods of the Ammonites and the gods of the Philistines. And because the Israelites forsook the LORD and no longer served him, ⁷he became angry with them. He sold them into the hands of the Philistines and the Ammonites, ⁸who that year shattered and crushed them. For eighteen years they oppressed all the Israelites on the east side of the Jordan in Gilead, the land of the Amorites. ⁹The Ammonites also crossed the Jordan to fight against Judah, Benjamin and the house of Ephraim; and Israel was in great distress. ¹⁰Then the Israelites cried out to the LORD, "We have sinned against you, forsaking our God and serving the Baals."

¹¹The LORD replied, "When the Egyptians, the Amorites, the Ammonites, the Philistines, ¹²the Sidonians, the Amalekites and the Maonites*a* oppressed you and you cried to me for help, did I not save you from their hands? ¹³But you have forsaken me and served other gods, so I will no longer save you. ¹⁴Go and cry out to the gods you have chosen. Let them save you when you are in trouble!"

¹⁵But the Israelites said to the LORD, "We have sinned. Do with us whatever you think best, but please rescue us now." ¹⁶Then they got rid of the foreign gods among them and served the LORD. And he could bear Israel's misery no longer.

¹⁷When the Ammonites were called to arms and camped in Gilead, the Israelites assembled and camped at Mizpah. ¹⁸The leaders of the people of Gilead said to each other, "Whoever will launch the attack against the Ammonites will be the head of all those living in Gilead."

11 Jephthah the Gileadite was a mighty warrior. His father was Gilead; his mother was a prostitute. ²Gilead's wife also bore him sons, and when they were grown up, they drove Jephthah away. "You are not going to get any inheritance in our family," they said, "because you are the son of another woman." ³So Jephthah fled from his brothers and settled in the land of Tob, where a group of adventurers gathered around him and followed him.

⁴Some time later, when the Ammonites made war on Israel, ⁵the elders of Gilead went to get Jephthah from the land of Tob. ⁶"Come," they said, "be our commander, so we can fight the Ammonites."

⁷Jephthah said to them, "Didn't you hate me and drive me from my father's house? Why do you come to me now, when you're in trouble?"

⁸The elders of Gilead said to him, "Nevertheless, we are turning to you now; come with us to fight the Ammonites, and you will be our head over all who live in Gilead."

⁹Jephthah answered, "Suppose you take me back to fight the Ammonites and the LORD gives them to me—will I really be your head?"

¹⁰The elders of Gilead replied, "The LORD is our witness; we will certainly do as you say." ¹¹So Jephthah went with the elders of Gilead, and the people made him head and commander over them. And he repeated all his words before the LORD in Mizpah.

¹²Then Jephthah sent messengers to the Ammonite king with the question: "What do you have against us that you have attacked our country?"

¹³The king of the Ammonites answered Jephthah's messengers, "When Israel came up out of Egypt, they took away my land from the Arnon to the Jabbok, all the way to the Jordan. Now give it back peaceably."

¹⁴Jephthah sent back messengers to the Ammonite king, ¹⁵saying:

"This is what Jephthah says: Israel did not take the land of Moab or the land of the Ammonites. ¹⁶But when they came up out of Egypt, Israel went through the desert to the Red Sea*b* and on to Kadesh. ¹⁷Then Israel sent messengers to the king of Edom, saying, 'Give us permission to go through your country,' but the king of Edom would not listen. They sent also to the king of Moab, and he refused. So Israel stayed at Kadesh.

¹⁸"Next they traveled through the desert, skirted the lands of Edom

a12 Hebrew; some Septuagint manuscripts *Midianites*   *b16* Hebrew *Yam Suph*; that is, Sea of Reeds and Moab, passed along the eastern side of the country of Moab, and camped on the other side of the Arnon. They did not enter the territory of Moab, for the Arnon was its border.

¹⁹"Then Israel sent messengers to Sihon king of the Amorites, who ruled in Heshbon, and said to him, 'Let us pass through your country to our own place.' ²⁰Sihon, however, did not trust Israel*a* to pass through his territory. He mustered all his men and encamped at Jahaz and fought with Israel.

²¹"Then the LORD, the God of Israel, gave Sihon and all his men into Israel's hands, and they defeated them. Israel took over all the land of the Amorites who lived in that country, ²²capturing all of it from the Arnon to the Jabbok and from the desert to the Jordan.

²³"Now since the LORD, the God of Israel, has driven the Amorites out before his people Israel, what right have you to take it over? ²⁴Will you not take what your god Chemosh gives you? Likewise, whatever the LORD our God has given us, we will possess. ²⁵Are you better than Balak son of Zippor, king of Moab? Did he ever quarrel with Israel or fight with them? ²⁶For three hundred years Israel occupied Heshbon, Aroer, the surrounding settlements and all the towns along the Arnon. Why didn't you retake them during that time? ²⁷I have not wronged you, but you are doing me wrong by waging war against me. Let the LORD, the Judge,*b* decide the dispute this day between the Israelites and the Ammonites.'"

²⁸The king of Ammon, however, paid no attention to the message Jephthah sent him.

²⁹Then the Spirit of the LORD came upon Jephthah. He crossed Gilead and Manasseh, passed through Mizpah of Gilead, and from there he advanced against the Ammonites. ³⁰And Jephthah made a vow to the LORD: "If you give the Ammonites into my hands, ³¹whatever comes out of the door of my house to meet me when I return in triumph from the Ammonites will be the LORD's, and I will sacrifice it as a burnt offering."

³²Then Jephthah went over to fight the Ammonites, and the LORD gave them into his hands. ³³He devastated twenty towns from Aroer to the vicinity of Minnith, as far as Abel Keramim. Thus Israel subdued Ammon.

³⁴When Jephthah returned to his home in Mizpah, who should come out to meet him but his daughter, dancing to the sound of tambourines! She was an only child. Except for her he had neither son nor daughter. ³⁵When he saw her, he tore his clothes and cried, "Oh! My daughter! You have made me miserable and wretched, because I have made a vow to the LORD that I cannot break."

³⁶"My father," she replied, "you have given your word to the LORD. Do to me just as you promised, now that the LORD has avenged you of your enemies, the Ammonites. ³⁷But grant me this one request," she said. "Give me two months to roam the hills and weep with my friends, because I will never marry."

³⁸"You may go," he said. And he let her go for two months. She and the girls went into the hills and wept because she would never marry. ³⁹After the two months, she returned to her father and he did to her as he had vowed. And she was a virgin.

From this comes the Israelite custom ⁴⁰that each year the young women of Israel go out for four days to commemorate the daughter of Jephthah the Gileadite.

Jephthah and Ephraim

12 The men of Ephraim called out their forces, crossed over to Zaphon and said to Jephthah, "Why did you go to fight the Ammonites without calling us to go with you? We're going to burn down your house over your head."

²Jephthah answered, "I and my people were engaged in a great struggle with the Ammonites, and although I called, you didn't save me out of their hands. ³When I saw that you wouldn't help, I took my life in my hands and crossed over to fight the Ammonites, and the LORD gave me

a20 Or *however, would not make an agreement for Israel*   *b27* Or *Ruler* the victory over them. Now why have you come up today to fight me?"

⁴Jephthah then called together the men of Gilead and fought against Ephraim. The Gileadites struck them down because the Ephraimites had said, "You Gileadites are renegades from Ephraim and Manasseh." ⁵The Gileadites captured the fords of the Jordan leading to Ephraim, and whenever a survivor of Ephraim said, "Let me cross over," the men of Gilead asked him, "Are you an Ephraimite?" If he replied, "No," ⁶they said, "All right, say 'Shibboleth.' " If he said, "Sibboleth," because he could not pronounce the word correctly, they seized him and killed him at the fords of the Jordan. Forty-two thousand Ephraimites were killed at that time.

⁷Jephthah led^a Israel six years. Then Jephthah the Gileadite died, and was buried in a town in Gilead.

Ibzan, Elon and Abdon

⁸After him, Ibzan of Bethlehem led Israel. ⁹He had thirty sons and thirty daughters. He gave his daughters away in marriage to those outside his clan, and for his sons he brought in thirty young women as wives from outside his clan. Ibzan led Israel seven years. ¹⁰Then Ibzan died, and was buried in Bethlehem.

¹¹After him, Elon the Zebulunite led Israel ten years. ¹²Then Elon died, and was buried in Aijalon in the land of Zebulun.

¹³After him, Abdon son of Hillel, from Pirathon, led Israel. ¹⁴He had forty sons and thirty grandsons, who rode on seventy donkeys. He led Israel eight years. ¹⁵Then Abdon son of Hillel died, and was buried at Pirathon in Ephraim, in the hill country of the Amalekites.

The Birth of Samson

13 Again the Israelites did evil in the eyes of the LORD, so the LORD delivered them into the hands of the Philistines for forty years.

²A certain man of Zorah, named Manoah, from the clan of the Danites, had a wife who was sterile and remained childless. ³The angel of the LORD appeared to her and said, "You are sterile and childless, but you are going to conceive and have a son. ⁴Now see to it that you drink no wine or other fermented drink and that you do not eat anything unclean, ⁵because you will conceive and give birth to a son. No razor may be used on his head, because the boy is to be a Nazirite, set apart to God from birth, and he will begin the deliverance of Israel from the hands of the Philistines."

⁶Then the woman went to her husband and told him, "A man of God came to me. He looked like an angel of God, very awesome. I didn't ask him where he came from, and he didn't tell me his name. ⁷But he said to me, 'You will conceive and give birth to a son. Now then, drink no wine or other fermented drink and do not eat anything unclean, because the boy will be a Nazirite of God from birth until the day of his death.' "

⁸Then Manoah prayed to the LORD: "O Lord, I beg you, let the man of God you sent to us come again to teach us how to bring up the boy who is to be born."

⁹God heard Manoah, and the angel of God came again to the woman while she was out in the field; but her husband Manoah was not with her. ¹⁰The woman hurried to tell her husband, "He's here! The man who appeared to me the other day!"

¹¹Manoah got up and followed his wife. When he came to the man, he said, "Are you the one who talked to my wife?" "I am," he said.

¹²So Manoah asked him, "When your words are fulfilled, what is to be the rule for the boy's life and work?"

¹³The angel of the LORD answered, "Your wife must do all that I have told her. ¹⁴She must not eat anything that comes from the grapevine, nor drink any wine or other fermented drink nor eat anything unclean. She must do everything I have commanded her."

¹⁵Manoah said to the angel of the LORD, "We would like you to stay until we prepare a young goat for you."

¹⁶The angel of the LORD replied, "Even though you detain me, I will not eat any of your food. But if you prepare a burnt offering, offer it to the LORD." (Manoah did not realize that it was the angel of the LORD.)

¹⁷Then Manoah inquired of the angel

^a 7 Traditionally *judged*; also in verses 8-14

Manoah and his wife

JUDGES 13:1–24 Manoah and his wife, as most married couples, wanted to be parents. But like many couples today, they had to deal with infertility. Add to the fertility issue being in bondage to the Philistines, and you can imagine the stress they experienced in their marriage. Both Manoah and his wife trusted God, but both were surprised when an angel of the Lord appeared to Manoah's wife and announced that, although she was sterile and childless, she would conceive and have a son. When the angel returned, they prepared a burnt offering to the Lord. Perhaps worshiping God together was one of the things that kept their marriage strong. They named their son Samson. Knowing the story of Samson, we can just imagine the added challenge of building their marriage while parenting a strong-willed child!

If you are dealing with infertility in your own marriage, you can be encouraged by their example and, as they did, you can seek God's answer. God answered Manoah and his wife by giving them a special son. For others the answer is different. However God answers you, you can know that he is willing to reveal himself to you and to strengthen your marriage.

of the LORD, "What is your name, so that we may honor you when your word comes true?"

¹⁸He replied, "Why do you ask my name? It is beyond understanding.ᵃ"

¹⁹Then Manoah took a young goat, together with the grain offering, and sacrificed it on a rock to the LORD. And the LORD did an amazing thing while Manoah and his wife watched: ²⁰As the flame blazed up from the altar toward heaven, the angel of the LORD ascended in the flame. Seeing this, Manoah and his wife fell with their faces to the ground. ²¹When the angel of the LORD did not show himself again to Manoah and his wife, Manoah realized that it was the angel of the LORD.

²²"We are doomed to die!" he said to his wife. "We have seen God!"

²³But his wife answered, "If the LORD had meant to kill us, he would not have accepted a burnt offering and grain offering from our hands, nor shown us all these things or now told us this."

²⁴The woman gave birth to a boy and named him Samson. He grew and the LORD blessed him, ²⁵and the Spirit of the LORD began to stir him while he was in Mahaneh Dan, between Zorah and Eshtaol.

Samson's Marriage

14 Samson went down to Timnah and saw there a young Philistine woman. ²When he returned, he said to his father and mother, "I have seen a Philistine woman in Timnah; now get her for me as my wife."

³His father and mother replied, "Isn't there an acceptable woman among your relatives or among all our people? Must you go to the uncircumcised Philistines to get a wife?"

But Samson said to his father, "Get her for me. She's the right one for me." ⁴(His parents did not know that this was from the LORD, who was seeking an occasion to confront the Philistines; for at that time they were ruling over Israel.) ⁵Samson went down to Timnah together with his father and mother. As they approached the vineyards of Timnah, suddenly a young lion came roaring toward him. ⁶The Spirit of the LORD came upon him in power so that he tore the lion apart with his bare hands as he might have torn a young goat. But he told neither his father nor his mother what he had done. ⁷Then he went down and talked with the woman, and he liked her.

⁸Some time later, when he went back to marry her, he turned aside to look at the lion's carcass. In it was a swarm of bees and some honey, ⁹which he scooped out with his hands and ate as he went along. When he rejoined his parents, he gave them some, and they too ate it. But he did not tell them that he had taken the honey from the lion's carcass.

¹⁰Now his father went down to see the woman. And Samson made a feast there,

ᵃ18 Or *is wonderful*

as was customary for bridegrooms.
¹¹When he appeared, he was given thirty
companions.

¹²"Let me tell you a riddle," Samson
said to them. "If you can give me the
answer within the seven days of the feast,
I will give you thirty linen garments and
thirty sets of clothes. ¹³If you can't tell me
the answer, you must give me thirty linen
garments and thirty sets of clothes."

"Tell us your riddle," they said. "Let's
hear it."

¹⁴He replied,

"Out of the eater, something to eat;
    out of the strong, something sweet."

For three days they could not give the
answer.

¹⁵On the fourth*ª* day, they said to
Samson's wife, "Coax your husband into
explaining the riddle for us, or we will
burn you and your father's household to
death. Did you invite us here to rob us?"

¹⁶Then Samson's wife threw herself on
him, sobbing, "You hate me! You don't
really love me. You've given my people a
riddle, but you haven't told me the answer."

"I haven't even explained it to my father or mother," he replied, "so why
should I explain it to you?" ¹⁷She cried the
whole seven days of the feast. So on the
seventh day he finally told her, because
she continued to press him. She in turn
explained the riddle to her people.

¹⁸Before sunset on the seventh day the
men of the town said to him,

"What is sweeter than honey?
    What is stronger than a lion?"

Samson said to them,

"If you had not plowed with my
    heifer,
  you would not have solved my
    riddle."

¹⁹Then the Spirit of the LORD came
upon him in power. He went down to
Ashkelon, struck down thirty of their
men, stripped them of their belongings
and gave their clothes to those who had
explained the riddle. Burning with anger,
he went up to his father's house. ²⁰And
Samson's wife was given to the friend
who had attended him at his wedding.

Samson's Vengeance on the Philistines

15 Later on, at the time of wheat harvest, Samson took a young goat and
went to visit his wife. He said, "I'm going
to my wife's room." But her father would
not let him go in.

²"I was so sure you thoroughly hated
her," he said, "that I gave her to your
friend. Isn't her younger sister more attractive? Take her instead."

³Samson said to them, "This time I
have a right to get even with the Philistines; I will really harm them." ⁴So he went
out and caught three hundred foxes and
tied them tail to tail in pairs. He then
fastened a torch to every pair of tails, ⁵lit
the torches and let the foxes loose in the
standing grain of the Philistines. He
burned up the shocks and standing grain,
together with the vineyards and olive
groves.

⁶When the Philistines asked, "Who did
this?" they were told, "Samson, the Tim-
nite's son-in-law, because his wife was
given to his friend."

So the Philistines went up and burned
her and her father to death. ⁷Samson said
to them, "Since you've acted like this, I
won't stop until I get my revenge on you."
⁸He attacked them viciously and slaughtered many of them. Then he went down
and stayed in a cave in the rock of Etam.

⁹The Philistines went up and camped
in Judah, spreading out near Lehi. ¹⁰The
men of Judah asked, "Why have you
come to fight us?"

"We have come to take Samson prisoner," they answered, "to do to him as he
did to us."

¹¹Then three thousand men from Judah went down to the cave in the rock of
Etam and said to Samson, "Don't you
realize that the Philistines are rulers over
us? What have you done to us?"

He answered, "I merely did to them
what they did to me."

¹²They said to him, "We've come to tie
you up and hand you over to the Philistines."

Samson said, "Swear to me that you
won't kill me yourselves."

¹³"Agreed," they answered. "We will
only tie you up and hand you over to

*ª15 Some Septuagint manuscripts and Syriac;
Hebrew* seventh

them. We will not kill you." So they bound him with two new ropes and led him up from the rock. [14]As he approached Lehi, the Philistines came toward him shouting. The Spirit of the LORD came upon him in power. The ropes on his arms became like charred flax, and the bindings dropped from his hands. [15]Finding a fresh jawbone of a donkey, he grabbed it and struck down a thousand men.

[16]Then Samson said,

"With a donkey's jawbone
    I have made donkeys of them.[a]
With a donkey's jawbone
    I have killed a thousand men."

[17]When he finished speaking, he threw away the jawbone; and the place was called Ramath Lehi.[b]

[18]Because he was very thirsty, he cried out to the LORD, "You have given your servant this great victory. Must I now die of thirst and fall into the hands of the uncircumcised?" [19]Then God opened up the hollow place in Lehi, and water came out of it. When Samson drank, his strength returned and he revived. So the spring was called En Hakkore,[c] and it is still there in Lehi.

[20]Samson led[d] Israel for twenty years in the days of the Philistines.

Samson and Delilah

16 One day Samson went to Gaza, where he saw a prostitute. He went in to spend the night with her. [2]The people of Gaza were told, "Samson is here!" So they surrounded the place and lay in wait for him all night at the city gate. They made no move during the night, saying, "At dawn we'll kill him."

[3]But Samson lay there only until the middle of the night. Then he got up and took hold of the doors of the city gate, together with the two posts, and tore them loose, bar and all. He lifted them to his shoulders and carried them to the top of the hill that faces Hebron.

[4]Some time later, he fell in love with a woman in the Valley of Sorek whose name was Delilah. [5]The rulers of the Philistines went to her and said, "See if you can lure him into showing you the secret of his great strength and how we can overpower him so we may tie him up and

subdue him. Each one of us will give you eleven hundred shekels[e] of silver."

[6]So Delilah said to Samson, "Tell me the secret of your great strength and how you can be tied up and subdued."

[7]Samson answered her, "If anyone ties me with seven fresh thongs[f] that have not been dried, I'll become as weak as any other man."

[8]Then the rulers of the Philistines brought her seven fresh thongs that had not been dried, and she tied him with them. [9]With men hidden in the room, she called to him, "Samson, the Philistines are upon you!" But he snapped the thongs as easily as a piece of string snaps when it comes close to a flame. So the secret of his strength was not discovered.

[10]Then Delilah said to Samson, "You have made a fool of me; you lied to me. Come now, tell me how you can be tied."

[11]He said, "If anyone ties me securely with new ropes that have never been used, I'll become as weak as any other man."

[12]So Delilah took new ropes and tied him with them. Then, with men hidden in the room, she called to him, "Samson, the Philistines are upon you!" But he snapped the ropes off his arms as if they were threads.

[13]Delilah then said to Samson, "Until now, you have been making a fool of me and lying to me. Tell me how you can be tied."

He replied, "If you weave the seven braids of my head into the fabric ⌊on the loom⌋ and tighten it with the pin, I'll become as weak as any other man." So while he was sleeping, Delilah took the seven braids of his head, wove them into the fabric [14]and[g] tightened it with the pin.

Again she called to him, "Samson, the Philistines are upon you!" He awoke from his sleep and pulled up the pin and the loom, with the fabric.

[15]Then she said to him, "How can you say, 'I love you,' when you won't confide

---

[a]16 Or *made a heap or two*; the Hebrew for *donkey* sounds like the Hebrew for *heap*.   [b]17 *Ramath Lehi* means *jawbone hill*.   [c]19 *En Hakkore* means *caller's spring*.   [d]20 Traditionally *judged*
[e]5 That is, about 28 pounds (about 13 kilograms)
[f]7 Or *bowstrings*; also in verses 8 and 9
[g]13,14 Some Septuagint manuscripts; Hebrew "*⌊I can⌋ if you weave the seven braids of my head into the fabric ⌊on the loom⌋.*" [14]*So she*

in me? This is the third time you have made a fool of me and haven't told me the secret of your great strength." ¹⁶With such nagging she prodded him day after day until he was tired to death.

¹⁷So he told her everything. "No razor has ever been used on my head," he said, "because I have been a Nazirite set apart to God since birth. If my head were shaved, my strength would leave me, and I would become as weak as any other man."

¹⁸When Delilah saw that he had told her everything, she sent word to the rulers of the Philistines, "Come back once more; he has told me everything." So the rulers of the Philistines returned with the silver in their hands. ¹⁹Having put him to sleep on her lap, she called a man to shave off the seven braids of his hair, and so began to subdue him.ᵃ And his strength left him.

²⁰Then she called, "Samson, the Philistines are upon you!"

He awoke from his sleep and thought, "I'll go out as before and shake myself free." But he did not know that the LORD had left him.

²¹Then the Philistines seized him, gouged out his eyes and took him down to Gaza. Binding him with bronze shackles, they set him to grinding in the prison. ²²But the hair on his head began to grow again after it had been shaved.

The Death of Samson

²³Now the rulers of the Philistines assembled to offer a great sacrifice to Dagon their god and to celebrate, saying, "Our god has delivered Samson, our enemy, into our hands."

²⁴When the people saw him, they praised their god, saying,

"Our god has delivered our enemy
    into our hands,
the one who laid waste our land
    and multiplied our slain."

²⁵While they were in high spirits, they shouted, "Bring out Samson to entertain us." So they called Samson out of the prison, and he performed for them.

When they stood him among the pillars, ²⁶Samson said to the servant who held his hand, "Put me where I can feel

Samson and Delilah

JUDGES 16:1–22 Although few would choose Samson as their favorite character from the Bible, unfortunately many can identify with his self-centeredness and self-seeking attitude. Judges 14 and the following chapters tell the story of this man who was controlled far more by passion than by will or by the laws of God. Samson wanted what he wanted when he wanted it, and he used his strength and stubbornness to get it.

COUPLES IN THE BIBLE

The marriage of Samson and Delilah was no match made in heaven. Going against his parent's wishes, Samson insisted on having this Philistine for his bride. This marriage was everything a dysfunctional marriage could be, involving lust, unfaithfulness, anger, rage and betrayal.

A modern day marriage can learn much from Samson and Delilah. For example, we can observe that a marriage built on self-centeredness and deception is doomed. Looking at a dysfunctional relationship like this one can help you avoid pitfalls in your own marriage.

While we might not personally identify with the dysfunction of Samson and Delilah's marriage, we can see our selfishness in the little things we do, like choosing a video we like, knowing that our spouse won't.

Now picture a marriage the opposite of Samson and Delilah's. Characteristics that would describe such a marriage are other-centered, faithful, self controlled, trustworthy, intimate, unified, unselfish and so on. How many of these characteristics describe your marriage?

the pillars that support the temple, so that I may lean against them." ²⁷Now the temple was crowded with men and women; all the rulers of the Philistines were there, and on the roof were about three thousand men and women watching Samson perform. ²⁸Then Samson prayed to the LORD, "O Sovereign LORD, remember me.

ᵃ19 Hebrew; some Septuagint manuscripts *and he began to weaken*

O God, please strengthen me just once more, and let me with one blow get revenge on the Philistines for my two eyes." ²⁹Then Samson reached toward the two central pillars on which the temple stood. Bracing himself against them, his right hand on the one and his left hand on the other, ³⁰Samson said, "Let me die with the Philistines!" Then he pushed with all his might, and down came the temple on the rulers and all the people in it. Thus he killed many more when he died than while he lived.

³¹Then his brothers and his father's whole family went down to get him. They brought him back and buried him between Zorah and Eshtaol in the tomb of Manoah his father. He had led*ᵃ* Israel twenty years.

Micah's Idols

17 Now a man named Micah from the hill country of Ephraim ²said to his mother, "The eleven hundred shekels*ᵇ* of silver that were taken from you and about which I heard you utter a curse—I have that silver with me; I took it."

Then his mother said, "The LORD bless you, my son!"

³When he returned the eleven hundred shekels of silver to his mother, she said, "I solemnly consecrate my silver to the LORD for my son to make a carved image and a cast idol. I will give it back to you."

⁴So he returned the silver to his mother, and she took two hundred shekels*ᶜ* of silver and gave them to a silversmith, who made them into the image and the idol. And they were put in Micah's house.

⁵Now this man Micah had a shrine, and he made an ephod and some idols and installed one of his sons as his priest. ⁶In those days Israel had no king; everyone did as he saw fit.

⁷A young Levite from Bethlehem in Judah, who had been living within the clan of Judah, ⁸left that town in search of some other place to stay. On his way*ᵈ* he came to Micah's house in the hill country of Ephraim.

⁹Micah asked him, "Where are you from?"

"I'm a Levite from Bethlehem in Judah," he said, "and I'm looking for a place to stay."

¹⁰Then Micah said to him, "Live with me and be my father and priest, and I'll give you ten shekels*ᵉ* of silver a year, your clothes and your food." ¹¹So the Levite agreed to live with him, and the young man was to him like one of his sons. ¹²Then Micah installed the Levite, and the young man became his priest and lived in his house. ¹³And Micah said, "Now I know that the LORD will be good to me, since this Levite has become my priest."

Danites Settle in Laish

18 In those days Israel had no king.
And in those days the tribe of the Danites was seeking a place of their own where they might settle, because they had not yet come into an inheritance among the tribes of Israel. ²So the Danites sent five warriors from Zorah and Eshtaol to spy out the land and explore it. These men represented all their clans. They told them, "Go, explore the land."

The men entered the hill country of Ephraim and came to the house of Micah, where they spent the night. ³When they were near Micah's house, they recognized the voice of the young Levite; so they turned in there and asked him, "Who brought you here? What are you doing in this place? Why are you here?"

⁴He told them what Micah had done for him, and said, "He has hired me and I am his priest."

⁵Then they said to him, "Please inquire of God to learn whether our journey will be successful."

⁶The priest answered them, "Go in peace. Your journey has the LORD's approval."

⁷So the five men left and came to Laish, where they saw that the people were living in safety, like the Sidonians, unsuspecting and secure. And since their land lacked nothing, they were prosperous.*ᶠ* Also, they lived a long way from the Sidonians and had no relationship with anyone else.*ᵍ*

ᵃ31 Traditionally *judged*　　*ᵇ2* That is, about 28 pounds (about 13 kilograms)　　*ᶜ4* That is, about 5 pounds (about 2.3 kilograms)　　*ᵈ8* Or *To carry on his profession*　　*ᵉ10* That is, about 4 ounces (about 110 grams)　　*ᶠ7* The meaning of the Hebrew for this clause is uncertain.　　*ᵍ7* Hebrew; some Septuagint manuscripts *with the Arameans*

[8]When they returned to Zorah and Eshtaol, their brothers asked them, "How did you find things?"

[9]They answered, "Come on, let's attack them! We have seen that the land is very good. Aren't you going to do something? Don't hesitate to go there and take it over. [10]When you get there, you will find an unsuspecting people and a spacious land that God has put into your hands, a land that lacks nothing whatever."

[11]Then six hundred men from the clan of the Danites, armed for battle, set out from Zorah and Eshtaol. [12]On their way they set up camp near Kiriath Jearim in Judah. This is why the place west of Kiriath Jearim is called Mahaneh Dan[a] to this day. [13]From there they went on to the hill country of Ephraim and came to Micah's house.

[14]Then the five men who had spied out the land of Laish said to their brothers, "Do you know that one of these houses has an ephod, other household gods, a carved image and a cast idol? Now you know what to do." [15]So they turned in there and went to the house of the young Levite at Micah's place and greeted him. [16]The six hundred Danites, armed for battle, stood at the entrance to the gate. [17]The five men who had spied out the land went inside and took the carved image, the ephod, the other household gods and the cast idol while the priest and the six hundred armed men stood at the entrance to the gate.

[18]When these men went into Micah's house and took the carved image, the ephod, the other household gods and the cast idol, the priest said to them, "What are you doing?"

[19]They answered him, "Be quiet! Don't say a word. Come with us, and be our father and priest. Isn't it better that you serve a tribe and clan in Israel as priest rather than just one man's household?" [20]Then the priest was glad. He took the ephod, the other household gods and the carved image and went along with the people. [21]Putting their little children, their livestock and their possessions in front of them, they turned away and left.

[22]When they had gone some distance from Micah's house, the men who lived near Micah were called together and overtook the Danites. [23]As they shouted after them, the Danites turned and said to Micah, "What's the matter with you that you called out your men to fight?"

[24]He replied, "You took the gods I made, and my priest, and went away. What else do I have? How can you ask, 'What's the matter with you?'"

[25]The Danites answered, "Don't argue with us, or some hot-tempered men will attack you, and you and your family will lose your lives." [26]So the Danites went their way, and Micah, seeing that they were too strong for him, turned around and went back home.

[27]Then they took what Micah had made, and his priest, and went on to Laish, against a peaceful and unsuspecting people. They attacked them with the sword and burned down their city. [28]There was no one to rescue them because they lived a long way from Sidon and had no relationship with anyone else. The city was in a valley near Beth Rehob.

The Danites rebuilt the city and settled there. [29]They named it Dan after their forefather Dan, who was born to Israel—though the city used to be called Laish. [30]There the Danites set up for themselves the idols, and Jonathan son of Gershom, the son of Moses,[b] and his sons were priests for the tribe of Dan until the time of the captivity of the land. [31]They continued to use the idols Micah had made, all the time the house of God was in Shiloh.

A Levite and His Concubine

19 In those days Israel had no king.

Now a Levite who lived in a remote area in the hill country of Ephraim took a concubine from Bethlehem in Judah. [2]But she was unfaithful to him. She left him and went back to her father's house in Bethlehem, Judah. After she had been there four months, [3]her husband went to her to persuade her to return. He had with him his servant and two donkeys. She took him into her father's house, and when her father saw him, he gladly welcomed him. [4]His father-in-law, the girl's

---

[a]12 Mahaneh Dan means Dan's camp.
[b]30 An ancient Hebrew scribal tradition, some Septuagint manuscripts and Vulgate; Masoretic Text Manasseh

father, prevailed upon him to stay; so he remained with him three days, eating and drinking, and sleeping there.

⁵On the fourth day they got up early and he prepared to leave, but the girl's father said to his son-in-law, "Refresh yourself with something to eat; then you can go." ⁶So the two of them sat down to eat and drink together. Afterward the girl's father said, "Please stay tonight and enjoy yourself." ⁷And when the man got up to go, his father-in-law persuaded him, so he stayed there that night. ⁸On the morning of the fifth day, when he rose to go, the girl's father said, "Refresh yourself. Wait till afternoon!" So the two of them ate together.

⁹Then when the man, with his concubine and his servant, got up to leave, his father-in-law, the girl's father, said, "Now look, it's almost evening. Spend the night here; the day is nearly over. Stay and enjoy yourself. Early tomorrow morning you can get up and be on your way home." ¹⁰But, unwilling to stay another night, the man left and went toward Jebus (that is, Jerusalem), with his two saddled donkeys and his concubine.

¹¹When they were near Jebus and the day was almost gone, the servant said to his master, "Come, let's stop at this city of the Jebusites and spend the night."

¹²His master replied, "No. We won't go into an alien city, whose people are not Israelites. We will go on to Gibeah." ¹³He added, "Come, let's try to reach Gibeah or Ramah and spend the night in one of those places." ¹⁴So they went on, and the sun set as they neared Gibeah in Benjamin. ¹⁵There they stopped to spend the night. They went and sat in the city square, but no one took them into his home for the night.

¹⁶That evening an old man from the hill country of Ephraim, who was living in Gibeah (the men of the place were Benjamites), came in from his work in the fields. ¹⁷When he looked and saw the traveler in the city square, the old man asked, "Where are you going? Where did you come from?"

¹⁸He answered, "We are on our way from Bethlehem in Judah to a remote area in the hill country of Ephraim where I live. I have been to Bethlehem in Judah and now I am going to the house of the LORD. No one has taken me into his house. ¹⁹We have both straw and fodder for our donkeys and bread and wine for ourselves your servants—me, your maidservant, and the young man with us. We don't need anything."

²⁰"You are welcome at my house," the old man said. "Let me supply whatever you need. Only don't spend the night in the square." ²¹So he took him into his house and fed his donkeys. After they had washed their feet, they had something to eat and drink.

²²While they were enjoying themselves, some of the wicked men of the city surrounded the house. Pounding on the door, they shouted to the old man who owned the house, "Bring out the man who came to your house so we can have sex with him."

²³The owner of the house went outside and said to them, "No, my friends, don't be so vile. Since this man is my guest, don't do this disgraceful thing. ²⁴Look, here is my virgin daughter, and his concubine. I will bring them out to you now, and you can use them and do to them whatever you wish. But to this man, don't do such a disgraceful thing."

²⁵But the men would not listen to him. So the man took his concubine and sent her outside to them, and they raped her and abused her throughout the night, and at dawn they let her go. ²⁶At daybreak the woman went back to the house where her master was staying, fell down at the door and lay there until daylight.

²⁷When her master got up in the morning and opened the door of the house and stepped out to continue on his way, there lay his concubine, fallen in the doorway of the house, with her hands on the threshold. ²⁸He said to her, "Get up; let's go." But there was no answer. Then the man put her on his donkey and set out for home.

²⁹When he reached home, he took a knife and cut up his concubine, limb by limb, into twelve parts and sent them into all the areas of Israel. ³⁰Everyone who saw it said, "Such a thing has never been seen or done, not since the day the Israelites came up out of Egypt. Think about it! Consider it! Tell us what to do!"

Israelites Fight the Benjamites

20 Then all the Israelites from Dan to Beersheba and from the land of Gilead came out as one man and assembled before the LORD in Mizpah. ²The leaders of all the people of the tribes of Israel took their places in the assembly of the people of God, four hundred thousand soldiers armed with swords. ³(The Benjamites heard that the Israelites had gone up to Mizpah.) Then the Israelites said, "Tell us how this awful thing happened."

⁴So the Levite, the husband of the murdered woman, said, "I and my concubine came to Gibeah in Benjamin to spend the night. ⁵During the night the men of Gibeah came after me and surrounded the house, intending to kill me. They raped my concubine, and she died. ⁶I took my concubine, cut her into pieces and sent one piece to each region of Israel's inheritance, because they committed this lewd and disgraceful act in Israel. ⁷Now, all you Israelites, speak up and give your verdict."

⁸All the people rose as one man, saying, "None of us will go home. No, not one of us will return to his house. ⁹But now this is what we'll do to Gibeah: We'll go up against it as the lot directs. ¹⁰We'll take ten men out of every hundred from all the tribes of Israel, and a hundred from a thousand, and a thousand from ten thousand, to get provisions for the army. Then, when the army arrives at Gibeah[a] in Benjamin, it can give them what they deserve for all this vileness done in Israel." ¹¹So all the men of Israel got together and united as one man against the city.

¹²The tribes of Israel sent men throughout the tribe of Benjamin, saying, "What about this awful crime that was committed among you? ¹³Now surrender those wicked men of Gibeah so that we may put them to death and purge the evil from Israel."

But the Benjamites would not listen to their fellow Israelites. ¹⁴From their towns they came together at Gibeah to fight against the Israelites. ¹⁵At once the Benjamites mobilized twenty-six thousand swordsmen from their towns, in addition to seven hundred chosen men from those living in Gibeah. ¹⁶Among all these soldiers there were seven hundred chosen men who were left-handed, each of whom could sling a stone at a hair and not miss.

¹⁷Israel, apart from Benjamin, mustered four hundred thousand swordsmen, all of them fighting men.

¹⁸The Israelites went up to Bethel[b] and inquired of God. They said, "Who of us shall go first to fight against the Benjamites?"

The LORD replied, "Judah shall go first."

¹⁹The next morning the Israelites got up and pitched camp near Gibeah. ²⁰The men of Israel went out to fight the Benjamites and took up battle positions against them at Gibeah. ²¹The Benjamites came out of Gibeah and cut down twenty-two thousand Israelites on the battlefield that day. ²²But the men of Israel encouraged one another and again took up their positions where they had stationed themselves the first day. ²³The Israelites went up and wept before the LORD until evening, and they inquired of the LORD. They said, "Shall we go up again to battle against the Benjamites, our brothers?"

The LORD answered, "Go up against them."

²⁴Then the Israelites drew near to Benjamin the second day. ²⁵This time, when the Benjamites came out from Gibeah to oppose them, they cut down another eighteen thousand Israelites, all of them armed with swords.

²⁶Then the Israelites, all the people, went up to Bethel, and there they sat weeping before the LORD. They fasted that day until evening and presented burnt offerings and fellowship offerings[c] to the LORD. ²⁷And the Israelites inquired of the LORD. (In those days the ark of the covenant of God was there, ²⁸with Phinehas son of Eleazar, the son of Aaron, ministering before it.) They asked, "Shall we go up again to battle with Benjamin our brother, or not?"

The LORD responded, "Go, for tomorrow I will give them into your hands."

²⁹Then Israel set an ambush around Gibeah. ³⁰They went up against the Benjamites on the third day and took up posi-

---

a10 One Hebrew manuscript; most Hebrew manuscripts *Geba,* a variant of *Gibeah*   b18 Or *to the house of God;* also in verse 26   c26 Traditionally *peace offerings* tions against Gibeah as they had done before. [31]The Benjamites came out to meet them and were drawn away from the city. They began to inflict casualties on the Israelites as before, so that about thirty men fell in the open field and on the roads—the one leading to Bethel and the other to Gibeah.

[32]While the Benjamites were saying, "We are defeating them as before," the Israelites were saying, "Let's retreat and draw them away from the city to the roads."

[33]All the men of Israel moved from their places and took up positions at Baal Tamar, and the Israelite ambush charged out of its place on the west[a] of Gibeah.[b] [34]Then ten thousand of Israel's finest men made a frontal attack on Gibeah. The fighting was so heavy that the Benjamites did not realize how near disaster was. [35]The LORD defeated Benjamin before Israel, and on that day the Israelites struck down 25,100 Benjamites, all armed with swords. [36]Then the Benjamites saw that they were beaten.

Now the men of Israel had given way before Benjamin, because they relied on the ambush they had set near Gibeah. [37]The men who had been in ambush made a sudden dash into Gibeah, spread out and put the whole city to the sword. [38]The men of Israel had arranged with the ambush that they should send up a great cloud of smoke from the city, [39]and then the men of Israel would turn in the battle.

The Benjamites had begun to inflict casualties on the men of Israel (about thirty), and they said, "We are defeating them as in the first battle." [40]But when the column of smoke began to rise from the city, the Benjamites turned and saw the smoke of the whole city going up into the sky. [41]Then the men of Israel turned on them, and the men of Benjamin were terrified, because they realized that disaster had come upon them. [42]So they fled before the Israelites in the direction of the desert, but they could not escape the battle. And the men of Israel who came out of the towns cut them down there. [43]They surrounded the Benjamites, chased them and easily[c] overran them in the vicinity of Gibeah on the east. [44]Eighteen thousand Benjamites fell, all of them valiant fighters. [45]As they turned and fled toward

the desert to the rock of Rimmon, the Israelites cut down five thousand men along the roads. They kept pressing after the Benjamites as far as Gidom and struck down two thousand more.

[46]On that day twenty-five thousand Benjamite swordsmen fell, all of them valiant fighters. [47]But six hundred men turned and fled into the desert to the rock of Rimmon, where they stayed four months. [48]The men of Israel went back to Benjamin and put all the towns to the sword, including the animals and everything else they found. All the towns they came across they set on fire.

Wives for the Benjamites

21 The men of Israel had taken an oath at Mizpah: "Not one of us will give his daughter in marriage to a Benjamite."

[2]The people went to Bethel,[d] where they sat before God until evening, raising their voices and weeping bitterly. [3]"O LORD, the God of Israel," they cried, "why has this happened to Israel? Why should one tribe be missing from Israel today?"

[4]Early the next day the people built an altar and presented burnt offerings and fellowship offerings.[e]

[5]Then the Israelites asked, "Who from all the tribes of Israel has failed to assemble before the LORD?" For they had taken a solemn oath that anyone who failed to assemble before the LORD at Mizpah should certainly be put to death.

[6]Now the Israelites grieved for their brothers, the Benjamites. "Today one tribe is cut off from Israel," they said. [7]"How can we provide wives for those who are left, since we have taken an oath by the LORD not to give them any of our daughters in marriage?" [8]Then they asked, "Which one of the tribes of Israel failed to assemble before the LORD at Mizpah?" They discovered that no one from Jabesh Gilead had come to the camp for the assembly. [9]For when they counted the people, they found that none of the people of Jabesh Gilead were there.

---

[a]33 Some Septuagint manuscripts and Vulgate; the meaning of the Hebrew for this word is uncertain.
[b]33 Hebrew *Geba*, a variant of *Gibeah*
[c]43 The meaning of the Hebrew for this word is uncertain.   [d]2 Or *to the house of God*
[e]4 Traditionally *peace offerings*

¹⁰So the assembly sent twelve thousand fighting men with instructions to go to Jabesh Gilead and put to the sword those living there, including the women and children. ¹¹"This is what you are to do," they said. "Kill every male and every woman who is not a virgin." ¹²They found among the people living in Jabesh Gilead four hundred young women who had never slept with a man, and they took them to the camp at Shiloh in Canaan.

¹³Then the whole assembly sent an offer of peace to the Benjamites at the rock of Rimmon. ¹⁴So the Benjamites returned at that time and were given the women of Jabesh Gilead who had been spared. But there were not enough for all of them.

¹⁵The people grieved for Benjamin, because the LORD had made a gap in the tribes of Israel. ¹⁶And the elders of the assembly said, "With the women of Benjamin destroyed, how shall we provide wives for the men who are left? ¹⁷The Benjamite survivors must have heirs," they said, "so that a tribe of Israel will not be wiped out. ¹⁸We can't give them our daughters as wives, since we Israelites have taken this oath: 'Cursed be anyone who gives a wife to a Benjamite.' ¹⁹But look, there is the annual festival of the LORD in Shiloh, to the north of Bethel, and east of the road that goes from Bethel to Shechem, and to the south of Lebonah."

²⁰So they instructed the Benjamites, saying, "Go and hide in the vineyards ²¹and watch. When the girls of Shiloh come out to join in the dancing, then rush from the vineyards and each of you seize a wife from the girls of Shiloh and go to the land of Benjamin. ²²When their fathers or brothers complain to us, we will say to them, 'Do us a kindness by helping them, because we did not get wives for them during the war, and you are innocent, since you did not give your daughters to them.'"

²³So that is what the Benjamites did. While the girls were dancing, each man caught one and carried her off to be his wife. Then they returned to their inheritance and rebuilt the towns and settled in them.

²⁴At that time the Israelites left that place and went home to their tribes and clans, each to his own inheritance.

²⁵In those days Israel had no king; everyone did as he saw fit.

Ruth

*Marriage can
be a real challenge.* Not only are there the daily
hazards of living in harmony with your spouse, but there are
also the challenges of coping with extended family—your
parents and siblings and their families, and your spouse's
parents and siblings and their families. If you have children,
you have the added joys and dangers of being (or of
someday becoming) an in-law!

It's no small feat to keep all of these connections
intact. Happily, tucked away in the book of Ruth is the
tender account of a family who successfully negotiated the
potentially treacherous waters of living in an extended
family. Even though keeping your marriage—and every
family relationship—strong is difficult, it can be done. And it
can be very rewarding. This book gives us some important
evidence.

Naomi and Ruth

1 In the days when the judges ruled,[a] there was a famine in the land, and a man from Bethlehem in Judah, together with his wife and two sons, went to live for a while in the country of Moab. ²The man's name was Elimelech, his wife's name Naomi, and the names of his two sons were Mahlon and Kilion. They were Ephrathites from Bethlehem, Judah. And they went to Moab and lived there.

³Now Elimelech, Naomi's husband, died, and she was left with her two sons. ⁴They married Moabite women, one named Orpah and the other Ruth. After they had lived there about ten years, ⁵both Mahlon and Kilion also died, and Naomi was left without her two sons and her husband.

⁶When she heard in Moab that the LORD had come to the aid of his people by providing food for them, Naomi and her daughters-in-law prepared to return home from there. ⁷With her two daughters-in-law she left the place where she had been living and set out on the road that would take them back to the land of Judah.

⁸Then Naomi said to her two

a1 Traditionally judged

daughters-in-law, "Go back, each of you, to your mother's home. May the LORD show kindness to you, as you have shown to your dead and to me. ⁹May the LORD grant that each of you will find rest in the home of another husband."

Then she kissed them and they wept aloud ¹⁰and said to her, "We will go back with you to your people."

¹¹But Naomi said, "Return home, my daughters. Why would you come with me? Am I going to have any more sons, who could become your husbands? ¹²Return home, my daughters; I am too old to have another husband. Even if I thought there was still hope for me—even if I had a husband tonight and then gave birth to sons— ¹³would you wait until they grew up? Would you remain unmarried for them? No, my daughters. It is more bitter for me than for you, because the LORD's hand has gone out against me!"

¹⁴At this they wept again. Then Orpah kissed her mother-in-law good-by, but Ruth clung to her.

¹⁵"Look," said Naomi, "your sister-in-law is going back to her people and her gods. Go back with her."

¹⁶But Ruth replied, "Don't urge me to leave you or to turn back from you. Where you go I will go, and where you stay I will stay. Your people will be my people and your God my God. ¹⁷Where you die I will die, and there I will be buried. May the LORD deal with me, be it ever so severely, if anything but death separates you and me." ¹⁸When Naomi realized that Ruth was determined to go with her, she stopped urging her.

¹⁹So the two women went on until they came to Bethlehem. When they arrived in Bethlehem, the whole town was stirred because of them, and the women exclaimed, "Can this be Naomi?"

²⁰"Don't call me Naomi,ᵃ" she told them. "Call me Mara,ᵇ because the Almightyᶜ has made my life very bitter. ²¹I went away full, but the LORD has brought me back empty. Why call me Naomi? The LORD has afflictedᵈ me; the Almighty has brought misfortune upon me."

²²So Naomi returned from Moab accompanied by Ruth the Moabitess, her daughter-in-law, arriving in Bethlehem as the barley harvest was beginning.

ᵃ20 Naomi means pleasant; also in verse 21.
ᵇ20 Mara means bitter.   ᶜ20 Hebrew Shaddai;
also in verse 21   ᵈ21 Or has testified against

A Picture of Mature Love

Friday

RUTH 1   The first chapter of Ruth describes one of the Bible's most beautiful pictures of selfless love. Ruth chose to give up the life she had always known and accompany her mother-in-law Naomi to a foreign land. Ruth's unselfish focus on the welfare of Naomi is a model of mature love.

So often we approach our marriage relationship, wondering what *we* will get out of it, rather than what we can give to it. Although Naomi and Ruth obviously were not married, they treated each other with the same great love and concern that we need to show to our spouse.

In verses 8 and 15, we see Naomi pleading with Ruth to return to Ruth's childhood home rather than accompany Naomi on her journey to her homeland. This would be a dangerous journey for an older woman alone on a treacherous road. Yet Naomi's first concern was the welfare of her daughter-in-law. She knew that Ruth would be more welcomed by her own countrymen than by strangers.

In verses 16 and 17, Ruth gives an equally unselfish response. She tells Naomi that she will share in whatever Naomi's lot in life is when she arrives back in Israel. In that culture and time, a widow without sons was virtually a beggar. Naomi had nothing to offer Ruth but hardship. Ruth's beautiful response illustrates for us a love that is focused on the other person rather than circumstances or selfish concern. When we love with that kind of selfless maturity, we will bring to our marriage relationship an enriching love.

—*Bob & Rosemary*

Go to page 276 for your next devotional reading.

Ruth Meets Boaz

2 Now Naomi had a relative on her husband's side, from the clan of Elimelech, a man of standing, whose name was Boaz.

²And Ruth the Moabitess said to Naomi, "Let me go to the fields and pick up the leftover grain behind anyone in whose eyes I find favor."

Naomi said to her, "Go ahead, my daughter." ³So she went out and began to glean in the fields behind the harvesters. As it turned out, she found herself working in a field belonging to Boaz, who was from the clan of Elimelech.

⁴Just then Boaz arrived from Bethlehem and greeted the harvesters, "The LORD be with you!"

"The LORD bless you!" they called back.

⁵Boaz asked the foreman of his harvesters, "Whose young woman is that?"

⁶The foreman replied, "She is the Moabitess who came back from Moab with Naomi. ⁷She said, 'Please let me glean and gather among the sheaves behind the harvesters.' She went into the field and has worked steadily from morning till now, except for a short rest in the shelter."

⁸So Boaz said to Ruth, "My daughter, listen to me. Don't go and glean in another field and don't go away from here. Stay here with my servant girls. ⁹Watch the field where the men are harvesting, and follow along after the girls. I have told the men not to touch you. And whenever you are thirsty, go and get a drink from the water jars the men have filled."

¹⁰At this, she bowed down with her face to the ground. She exclaimed, "Why have I found such favor in your eyes that you notice me—a foreigner?"

¹¹Boaz replied, "I've been told all about what you have done for your mother-in-law since the death of your husband—how you left your father and mother and your homeland and came to live with a people you did not know be-

---

The In-law Factor

RUTH 4:13–15 Ruth's first marriage ended when her husband, Naomi's son, died. But Ruth was not willing to leave Naomi; her commitment to family went deeper than her own short marriage.

Quiet TIMES with each other

Because of her love and concern for Naomi, Ruth met and married Boaz. Through her unselfishness she found a new husband. Ruth is esteemed even today as part of the lineage of Christ. And of her relationship to her mother-in-law, we read that Ruth loved Naomi and was better to her than seven sons. Would your in-laws make similar comments about you?

My mother would have. During the eight years she lived after my father passed away, I watched as Dave demonstrated to her a "Ruth" kind of love. Without ever complaining, he took care of her financial business, kept up with her car and home maintenance and showed his thoughtfulness in many other ways such as calling her often just to say hello and chat. He was never too busy to stop and listen to her and hear with empathy. Once he took the initiative in arranging to fly her and her sister to Minneapolis for a family gathering. Many times I kidded him, "Mother loves you the best!" Dave certainly lived out the principles from this passage.

Perhaps there is something you can do to build more positive in-law relationships. You will experience God's favor as you seek to serve that special person who gave you one of your most precious gifts—your spouse!
—Dave & Claudia

Weekend Warm-up *What are a few ways you can encourage each other when it comes to the in-laws?*

Go to page 281 for your next devotional reading.

fore. ¹²May the LORD repay you for what
you have done. May you be richly rewarded by the LORD, the God of Israel, under
whose wings you have come to take refuge."

¹³"May I continue to find favor in your
eyes, my lord," she said. "You have given
me comfort and have spoken kindly to
your servant—though I do not have the
standing of one of your servant girls."

¹⁴At mealtime Boaz said to her, "Come
over here. Have some bread and dip it in
the wine vinegar."

When she sat down with the harvesters, he offered her some roasted grain. She
ate all she wanted and had some left over.
¹⁵As she got up to glean, Boaz gave orders
to his men, "Even if she gathers among
the sheaves, don't embarrass her. ¹⁶Rath-
er, pull out some stalks for her from the
bundles and leave them for her to pick
up, and don't rebuke her."

¹⁷So Ruth gleaned in the field until evening. Then she threshed the barley she
had gathered, and it amounted to about
an ephah.ᵃ ¹⁸She carried it back to town,
and her mother-in-law saw how much
she had gathered. Ruth also brought out
and gave her what she had left over after
she had eaten enough.

¹⁹Her mother-in-law asked her,
"Where did you glean today? Where did
you work? Blessed be the man who took
notice of you!"

Then Ruth told her mother-in-law
about the one at whose place she had
been working. "The name of the man I
worked with today is Boaz," she said.

²⁰"The LORD bless him!" Naomi said
to her daughter-in-law. "He has not
stopped showing his kindness to the living and the dead." She added, "That man
is our close relative; he is one of our
kinsman-redeemers."

²¹Then Ruth the Moabitess said, "He
even said to me, 'Stay with my workers
until they finish harvesting all my grain.'"

²²Naomi said to Ruth her daughter-in-
law, "It will be good for you, my daughter, to go with his girls, because in someone else's field you might be harmed."

²³So Ruth stayed close to the servant
girls of Boaz to glean until the barley and
wheat harvests were finished. And she
lived with her mother-in-law.

The In-law Factor

Naomi and Ruth have a wonderful mother-
in-law/daughter-in-law relationship. How is
your relationship with your in-laws? Take a
few minutes and evaluate your present in-
law relationships. Think about how you can
be a blessing in the lives of your in-laws.

1. Is the amount of contact you have with
   your in-law
   a. Too little
   b. Too much
   c. About right

2. Are you satisfied with the way your in-
   law relates to you?
   a. They help when needed
   b. They give encouragement
   c. Other

3. How do you help and encourage your
   in-law?
   a. Call often
   b. Express gratitude
   c. Invite them to visit
   d. Other

5. Do you maintain clear and open communication? Yes___ No___

Choose one thing you can do to improve your
relationship.

Ruth and Boaz at the Threshing Floor

3 One day Naomi her mother-in-law
said to her, "My daughter, should I
not try to find a homeᵇ for you, where
you will be well provided for? ²Is not
Boaz, with whose servant girls you have
been, a kinsman of ours? Tonight he will
be winnowing barley on the threshing
floor. ³Wash and perfume yourself, and
put on your best clothes. Then go down
to the threshing floor, but don't let him
know you are there until he has finished
eating and drinking. ⁴When he lies down,
note the place where he is lying. Then go
and uncover his feet and lie down. He
will tell you what to do."

⁵"I will do whatever you say," Ruth an-

ᵃ17 That is, probably about 3/5 bushel (about 22
liters)   ᵇ1 Hebrew *find rest* (see Ruth 1:9)

Boaz and Ruth

RUTH 4:1–12 The level of success or failure in second marriages often depends on the level of success in the first marriage. Divorce tends to run in families where people learn that the first separation is harder than the second or third. But in relationships that are characterized by love and understanding, being married again after an appropriate time of grief is often fulfilling.

COUPLES IN THE BIBLE

Such is the story of Boaz and Ruth. After the death of her husband, Ruth set out for Bethlehem with her mother-in-law Naomi, also widowed. God blessed Ruth's loving concern and loyalty for Naomi through Boaz, the owner of a field where the two women were gleaning grain. Eventually he married Ruth and took Naomi into his care as well. She eventually became the loving grandmother to their little boy Obed, who had the special honor of being part of the lineage of Jesus Christ.

swered. ⁶So she went down to the threshing floor and did everything her mother-in-law told her to do.

⁷When Boaz had finished eating and drinking and was in good spirits, he went over to lie down at the far end of the grain pile. Ruth approached quietly, uncovered his feet and lay down. ⁸In the middle of the night something startled the man, and he turned and discovered a woman lying at his feet.

⁹"Who are you?" he asked.

"I am your servant Ruth," she said. "Spread the corner of your garment over me, since you are a kinsman-redeemer."

¹⁰"The LORD bless you, my daughter," he replied. "This kindness is greater than that which you showed earlier: You have not run after the younger men, whether rich or poor. ¹¹And now, my daughter, don't be afraid. I will do for you all you ask. All my fellow townsmen know that you are a woman of noble character. ¹²Although it is true that I am near of kin, there is a kinsman-redeemer nearer than I. ¹³Stay here for the night, and in the morning if he wants to redeem, good; let him redeem. But if he is not willing, as

surely as the LORD lives I will do it. Lie here until morning."

¹⁴So she lay at his feet until morning, but got up before anyone could be recognized; and he said, "Don't let it be known that a woman came to the threshing floor."

¹⁵He also said, "Bring me the shawl you are wearing and hold it out." When she did so, he poured into it six measures of barley and put it on her. Then he*a* went back to town.

¹⁶When Ruth came to her mother-in-law, Naomi asked, "How did it go, my daughter?"

Then she told her everything Boaz had done for her ¹⁷and added, "He gave me these six measures of barley, saying, 'Don't go back to your mother-in-law empty-handed.' "

¹⁸Then Naomi said, "Wait, my daughter, until you find out what happens. For the man will not rest until the matter is settled today."

Boaz Marries Ruth

4 Meanwhile Boaz went up to the town gate and sat there. When the kinsman-redeemer he had mentioned came along, Boaz said, "Come over here, my friend, and sit down." So he went over and sat down.

²Boaz took ten of the elders of the town and said, "Sit here," and they did so. ³Then he said to the kinsman-redeemer, "Naomi, who has come back from Moab, is selling the piece of land that belonged to our brother Elimelech. ⁴I thought I should bring the matter to your attention and suggest that you buy it in the presence of these seated here and in the presence of the elders of my people. If you will redeem it, do so. But if you*b* will not, tell me, so I will know. For no one has the right to do it except you, and I am next in line."

"I will redeem it," he said.

⁵Then Boaz said, "On the day you buy the land from Naomi and from Ruth the Moabitess, you acquire*c* the dead man's

---

*a*15 Most Hebrew manuscripts; many Hebrew manuscripts, Vulgate and Syriac *she*   *b*4 Many Hebrew manuscripts, Septuagint, Vulgate and Syriac; most Hebrew manuscripts *he*
*c*5 Hebrew; Vulgate and Syriac *Naomi, you acquire Ruth the Moabitess,*

widow, in order to maintain the name of the dead with his property."

⁶At this, the kinsman-redeemer said, "Then I cannot redeem it because I might endanger my own estate. You redeem it yourself. I cannot do it."

⁷(Now in earlier times in Israel, for the redemption and transfer of property to become final, one party took off his sandal and gave it to the other. This was the method of legalizing transactions in Israel.)

⁸So the kinsman-redeemer said to Boaz, "Buy it yourself." And he removed his sandal.

⁹Then Boaz announced to the elders and all the people, "Today you are witnesses that I have bought from Naomi all the property of Elimelech, Kilion and Mahlon. ¹⁰I have also acquired Ruth the Moabitess, Mahlon's widow, as my wife, in order to maintain the name of the dead with his property, so that his name will not disappear from among his family or from the town records. Today you are witnesses!"

¹¹Then the elders and all those at the gate said, "We are witnesses. May the LORD make the woman who is coming into your home like Rachel and Leah, who together built up the house of Israel. May you have standing in Ephrathah and be famous in Bethlehem. ¹²Through the offspring the LORD gives you by this young woman, may your family be like that of Perez, whom Tamar bore to Judah."

The Genealogy of David

¹³So Boaz took Ruth and she became his wife. Then he went to her, and the LORD enabled her to conceive, and she gave birth to a son. ¹⁴The women said to Naomi: "Praise be to the LORD, who this day has not left you without a kinsman-redeemer. May he become famous throughout Israel! ¹⁵He will renew your life and sustain you in your old age. For your daughter-in-law, who loves you and who is better to you than seven sons, has given him birth."

¹⁶Then Naomi took the child, laid him in her lap and cared for him. ¹⁷The women living there said, "Naomi has a son." And they named him Obed. He was the father of Jesse, the father of David.

¹⁸This, then, is the family line of Perez:

Perez was the father of Hezron,
¹⁹Hezron the father of Ram,
    Ram the father of Amminadab,
²⁰Amminadab the father of Nahshon,
    Nahshon the father of Salmon,ᵃ
²¹Salmon the father of Boaz,
    Boaz the father of Obed,
²²Obed the father of Jesse,
    and Jesse the father of David.

ᵃ20 A few Hebrew manuscripts, some Septuagint manuscripts and Vulgate (see also verse 21 and Septuagint of 1 Chron. 2:11); most Hebrew manuscripts *Salma*

1 Samuel

First Samuel is a story of contrast between a man who abandons God and a man who abandons his life to God. Written by the prophet Samuel, the book focuses on Israel's first two kings, Saul and David. Saul, the first anointed king of Israel, decides to disobey God's directions. Tormented by his sin, he is finally rejected as ruler of Israel. In contrast, his successor David dedicates himself fully to the Lord, and God rewards him greatly.

As you read 1 Samuel, consider how you've experienced rejection and pain, like Saul did, as a result of disobedience to God's directions and guidance. Allow the stirring stories of David and Saul to inspire you to follow God wholeheartedly in your marriage relationship and beyond.

The Birth of Samuel

1 There was a certain man from Ramathaim, a Zuphite*a* from the hill country of Ephraim, whose name was Elkanah son of Jeroham, the son of Elihu, the son of Tohu, the son of Zuph, an Ephraimite. ²He had two wives; one was called Hannah and the other Peninnah. Peninnah had children, but Hannah had none.

³Year after year this man went up from his town to worship and sacrifice to the LORD Almighty at Shiloh, where Hophni and Phinehas, the two sons of Eli, were priests of the LORD. ⁴Whenever the day came for Elkanah to sacrifice, he would give portions of the meat to his wife Peninnah and to all her sons and daughters. ⁵But to Hannah he gave a double portion because he loved her, and the LORD had closed her womb. ⁶And because the LORD had closed her womb, her rival kept provoking her in order to irritate her. ⁷This went on year after year. Whenever Hannah went up to the house of the LORD, her rival provoked her till she wept and would not eat. ⁸Elkanah her husband would say to her, "Hannah, why are you weeping? Why don't you eat? Why are you downhearted? Don't I mean more to you than ten sons?"

⁹Once when they had finished eating and drinking in Shiloh, Hannah stood up. Now Eli the priest was sitting on a chair by the doorpost of the LORD's tem-

a1 Or from Ramathaim Zuphim

ple.[a] [10]In bitterness of soul Hannah wept much and prayed to the LORD. [11]And she made a vow, saying, "O LORD Almighty, if you will only look upon your servant's misery and remember me, and not forget your servant but give her a son, then I will give him to the LORD for all the days of his life, and no razor will ever be used on his head."

[12]As she kept on praying to the LORD, Eli observed her mouth. [13]Hannah was praying in her heart, and her lips were moving but her voice was not heard. Eli thought she was drunk [14]and said to her, "How long will you keep on getting drunk? Get rid of your wine."

[15]"Not so, my lord," Hannah replied, "I am a woman who is deeply troubled. I have not been drinking wine or beer; I was pouring out my soul to the LORD. [16]Do not take your servant for a wicked woman; I have been praying here out of my great anguish and grief."

[17]Eli answered, "Go in peace, and may the God of Israel grant you what you have asked of him."

[18]She said, "May your servant find favor in your eyes." Then she went her way and ate something, and her face was no longer downcast.

[19]Early the next morning they arose and worshiped before the LORD and then went back to their home at Ramah. Elkanah lay with Hannah his wife, and the LORD remembered her. [20]So in the course of time Hannah conceived and gave birth to a son. She named him Samuel,[b] saying, "Because I asked the LORD for him."

Hannah Dedicates Samuel

[21]When the man Elkanah went up with all his family to offer the annual sacrifice to the LORD and to fulfill his vow, [22]Hannah did not go. She said to her husband, "After the boy is weaned, I will take him and present him before the LORD, and he will live there always."

[23]"Do what seems best to you," Elkanah her husband told her. "Stay here until you have weaned him; only may the LORD make good his[c] word." So the woman stayed at home and nursed her son until she had weaned him.

[24]After he was weaned, she took the boy with her, young as he was, along with a three-year-old bull,[d] an ephah[e] of flour and a skin of wine, and brought him to the house of the LORD at Shiloh. [25]When they had slaughtered the bull, they brought the boy to Eli, [26]and she said to him, "As surely as you live, my lord, I am the woman who stood here beside

[a]9 That is, tabernacle   [b]20 Samuel sounds like the Hebrew for heard of God.   [c]23 Masoretic Text; Dead Sea Scrolls, Septuagint and Syriac your   [d]24 Dead Sea Scrolls, Septuagint and Syriac; Masoretic Text with three bulls   [e]24 That is, probably about 3/5 bushel (about 22 liters)

Hannah's Prayer

Monday

1 SAMUEL 1:10 Half of all American couples who try to get pregnant have trouble doing so. One in six couples face the crisis of infertility. Most of these couples will undergo an extremely expensive medical evaluation, intrusive medical procedures or forms of drug therapy—all with no guarantees about the outcome. Additionally, many couples will experience profound loss through miscarriage. About fifty percent of those couples eventually will conceive and bear a child, while the remaining couples will go on to grapple with adoption procedures or make a decision not to have children.

If a woman who can't have a child prays like Hannah, will she be blessed with a baby? We don't know. But we do know that Hannah reached a point where she was willing to give up her baby before he was even conceived. She promised to give her child back to God if he would only grant her wish.

If you happen to be struggling with infertility, take comfort in Hannah's prayer. It will help you remember that God is able to answer your prayer for a child.

—**Les & Leslie**

Go to page 297 for your next devotional reading.

Elkanah, Peninnah and Hannah

1 SAMUEL 1:1–23 From to-day's perspective, no marriage is big enough for two wives—Elkanah and Hannah's marriage was a case in point.

COUPLES IN THE BIBLE

Peninnah provoked her rival Hannah until Hannah would weep and not eat. While Peninnah had given Elkanah many children, she knew he loved Hannah the most. Imagine what it would feel like if you desperately wanted to have a child and couldn't. Then add Peninnah's taunting. What an impossible situation for Hannah!

Each year at the time of sacrifice, Hannah would pray at the temple for God to give her a son. One year God answered, and Samuel was born. When Hannah gave Samuel to God's service, Elkanah respected and supported her decision. Their relationship appears to be more of a partnership than some of the other couples in the Bible.

After Samuel, Elkanah and Hannah had three more sons and two daughters. Like parents today, they surely faced the challenge of building their marriage while parenting their children.

you praying to the LORD. ²⁷I prayed for this child, and the LORD has granted me what I asked of him. ²⁸So now I give him to the LORD. For his whole life he will be given over to the LORD." And he worshiped the LORD there.

Hannah's Prayer

2 Then Hannah prayed and said:

"My heart rejoices in the LORD;
   in the LORD my horn*a* is lifted
      high.
My mouth boasts over my enemies,
   for I delight in your deliverance.

²"There is no one holy*b* like the
      LORD;
   there is no one besides you;
   there is no Rock like our God.

³"Do not keep talking so proudly
   or let your mouth speak such
      arrogance,

for the LORD is a God who knows,
   and by him deeds are weighed.

⁴"The bows of the warriors are broken,
   but those who stumbled are armed
      with strength.
⁵Those who were full hire themselves
      out for food,
   but those who were hungry hunger
      no more.
She who was barren has borne seven
      children,
   but she who has had many sons
      pines away.

⁶"The LORD brings death and makes
      alive;
   he brings down to the grave*c* and
      raises up.
⁷The LORD sends poverty and wealth;
   he humbles and he exalts.
⁸He raises the poor from the dust
   and lifts the needy from the ash
      heap;
he seats them with princes
   and has them inherit a throne of
      honor.

"For the foundations of the earth are
      the LORD's;
   upon them he has set the world.
⁹He will guard the feet of his saints,
   but the wicked will be silenced in
      darkness.

"It is not by strength that one
      prevails;
10   those who oppose the LORD will be
      shattered.
He will thunder against them from
      heaven;
   the LORD will judge the ends of the
      earth.

"He will give strength to his king
   and exalt the horn of his anointed."

¹¹Then Elkanah went home to Ramah, but the boy ministered before the LORD under Eli the priest.

Eli's Wicked Sons

¹²Eli's sons were wicked men; they had no regard for the LORD. ¹³Now it was the practice of the priests with the people that whenever anyone offered a sacrifice and

---

*a*1 *Horn* here symbolizes strength; also in verse 10.
*b*2 Or *no Holy One*   *c*6 Hebrew *Sheol*

while the meat was being boiled, the servant of the priest would come with a three-pronged fork in his hand. ¹⁴He would plunge it into the pan or kettle or caldron or pot, and the priest would take for himself whatever the fork brought up. This is how they treated all the Israelites who came to Shiloh. ¹⁵But even before the fat was burned, the servant of the priest would come and say to the man who was sacrificing, "Give the priest some meat to roast; he won't accept boiled meat from you, but only raw."

¹⁶If the man said to him, "Let the fat be burned up first, and then take whatever you want," the servant would then answer, "No, hand it over now; if you don't, I'll take it by force."

¹⁷This sin of the young men was very great in the LORD's sight, for they*a* were treating the LORD's offering with contempt.

¹⁸But Samuel was ministering before the LORD—a boy wearing a linen ephod. ¹⁹Each year his mother made him a little robe and took it to him when she went up with her husband to offer the annual sacrifice. ²⁰Eli would bless Elkanah and his wife, saying, "May the LORD give you children by this woman to take the place of the one she prayed for and gave to the LORD." Then they would go home. ²¹And the LORD was gracious to Hannah; she conceived and gave birth to three sons and two daughters. Meanwhile, the boy Samuel grew up in the presence of the LORD.

²²Now Eli, who was very old, heard about everything his sons were doing to all Israel and how they slept with the women who served at the entrance to the Tent of Meeting. ²³So he said to them, "Why do you do such things? I hear from all the people about these wicked deeds of yours. ²⁴No, my sons; it is not a good report that I hear spreading among the LORD's people. ²⁵If a man sins against another man, God*b* may mediate for him; but if a man sins against the LORD, who will intercede for him?" His sons, however, did not listen to their father's rebuke, for it was the LORD's will to put them to death.

²⁶And the boy Samuel continued to grow in stature and in favor with the LORD and with men.

Prophecy Against the House of Eli

²⁷Now a man of God came to Eli and said to him, "This is what the LORD says: 'Did I not clearly reveal myself to your father's house when they were in Egypt under Pharaoh? ²⁸I chose your father out of all the tribes of Israel to be my priest, to go up to my altar, to burn incense, and to wear an ephod in my presence. I also gave your father's house all the offerings made with fire by the Israelites. ²⁹Why do you*c* scorn my sacrifice and offering that I prescribed for my dwelling? Why do you honor your sons more than me by fattening yourselves on the choice parts of every offering made by my people Israel?'

³⁰"Therefore the LORD, the God of Israel, declares: 'I promised that your house and your father's house would minister before me forever.' But now the LORD declares: 'Far be it from me! Those who honor me I will honor, but those who despise me will be disdained. ³¹The time is coming when I will cut short your strength and the strength of your father's house, so that there will not be an old man in your family line ³²and you will see distress in my dwelling. Although good will be done to Israel, in your family line there will never be an old man. ³³Every one of you that I do not cut off from my altar will be spared only to blind your eyes with tears and to grieve your heart, and all your descendants will die in the prime of life.

³⁴"'And what happens to your two sons, Hophni and Phinehas, will be a sign to you—they will both die on the same day. ³⁵I will raise up for myself a faithful priest, who will do according to what is in my heart and mind. I will firmly establish his house, and he will minister before my anointed one always. ³⁶Then everyone left in your family line will come and bow down before him for a piece of silver and a crust of bread and plead, "Appoint me to some priestly office so I can have food to eat." ' "

The LORD Calls Samuel

3 The boy Samuel ministered before the LORD under Eli. In those days the

---

*a*17 Or *men*   *b*25 Or *the judges*
*c*29 The Hebrew is plural.

word of the LORD was rare; there were not many visions.

2One night Eli, whose eyes were becoming so weak that he could barely see, was lying down in his usual place. 3The lamp of God had not yet gone out, and Samuel was lying down in the temple[a] of the LORD, where the ark of God was. 4Then the LORD called Samuel.

Samuel answered, "Here I am." 5And he ran to Eli and said, "Here I am; you called me."

But Eli said, "I did not call; go back and lie down." So he went and lay down.

6Again the LORD called, "Samuel!" And Samuel got up and went to Eli and said, "Here I am; you called me."

"My son," Eli said, "I did not call; go back and lie down."

7Now Samuel did not yet know the LORD: The word of the LORD had not yet been revealed to him.

8The LORD called Samuel a third time, and Samuel got up and went to Eli and said, "Here I am; you called me."

Then Eli realized that the LORD was calling the boy. 9So Eli told Samuel, "Go and lie down, and if he calls you, say, 'Speak, LORD, for your servant is listening.' " So Samuel went and lay down in his place.

10The LORD came and stood there, calling as at the other times, "Samuel! Samuel!"

Then Samuel said, "Speak, for your servant is listening."

11And the LORD said to Samuel: "See, I am about to do something in Israel that will make the ears of everyone who hears of it tingle. 12At that time I will carry out against Eli everything I spoke against his family—from beginning to end. 13For I told him that I would judge his family forever because of the sin he knew about; his sons made themselves contemptible,[b] and he failed to restrain them. 14Therefore, I swore to the house of Eli, 'The guilt of Eli's house will never be atoned for by sacrifice or offering.' "

15Samuel lay down until morning and then opened the doors of the house of the LORD. He was afraid to tell Eli the vision, 16but Eli called him and said, "Samuel, my son."

Samuel answered, "Here I am."

17"What was it he said to you?" Eli asked. "Do not hide it from me. May God deal with you, be it ever so severely, if you hide from me anything he told you." 18So Samuel told him everything, hiding nothing from him. Then Eli said, "He is the LORD; let him do what is good in his eyes."

19The LORD was with Samuel as he grew up, and he let none of his words fall to the ground. 20And all Israel from Dan to Beersheba recognized that Samuel was attested as a prophet of the LORD. 21The LORD continued to appear at Shiloh, and there he revealed himself to Samuel through his word.

4 And Samuel's word came to all Israel.

The Philistines Capture the Ark

Now the Israelites went out to fight against the Philistines. The Israelites camped at Ebenezer, and the Philistines at Aphek. 2The Philistines deployed their forces to meet Israel, and as the battle spread, Israel was defeated by the Philistines, who killed about four thousand of them on the battlefield. 3When the soldiers returned to camp, the elders of Israel asked, "Why did the LORD bring defeat upon us today before the Philistines? Let us bring the ark of the LORD's covenant from Shiloh, so that it[c] may go with us and save us from the hand of our enemies."

4So the people sent men to Shiloh, and they brought back the ark of the covenant of the LORD Almighty, who is enthroned between the cherubim. And Eli's two sons, Hophni and Phinehas, were there with the ark of the covenant of God.

5When the ark of the LORD's covenant came into the camp, all Israel raised such a great shout that the ground shook. 6Hearing the uproar, the Philistines asked, "What's all this shouting in the Hebrew camp?"

When they learned that the ark of the LORD had come into the camp, 7the Philistines were afraid. "A god has come into the camp," they said. "We're in trouble! Nothing like this has happened before. 8Woe to us! Who will deliver us from the hand of these mighty gods? They are the gods who struck the Egyptians with all

---

a3 That is, tabernacle   b13 Masoretic Text; an ancient Hebrew scribal tradition and Septuagint *sons blasphemed God*   c3 Or *he* kinds of plagues in the desert. 9Be strong, Philistines! Be men, or you will be subject to the Hebrews, as they have been to you. Be men, and fight!"

10So the Philistines fought, and the Israelites were defeated and every man fled to his tent. The slaughter was very great; Israel lost thirty thousand foot soldiers. 11The ark of God was captured, and Eli's two sons, Hophni and Phinehas, died.

Death of Eli

12That same day a Benjamite ran from the battle line and went to Shiloh, his clothes torn and dust on his head. 13When he arrived, there was Eli sitting on his chair by the side of the road, watching, because his heart feared for the ark of God. When the man entered the town and told what had happened, the whole town sent up a cry.

14Eli heard the outcry and asked, "What is the meaning of this uproar?"

The man hurried over to Eli, 15who was ninety-eight years old and whose eyes were set so that he could not see. 16He told Eli, "I have just come from the battle line; I fled from it this very day."

Eli asked, "What happened, my son?"

17The man who brought the news replied, "Israel fled before the Philistines, and the army has suffered heavy losses. Also your two sons, Hophni and Phinehas, are dead, and the ark of God has been captured."

18When he mentioned the ark of God, Eli fell backward off his chair by the side of the gate. His neck was broken and he died, for he was an old man and heavy. He had led*a* Israel forty years.

19His daughter-in-law, the wife of Phinehas, was pregnant and near the time of delivery. When she heard the news that the ark of God had been captured and that her father-in-law and her husband were dead, she went into labor and gave birth, but was overcome by her labor pains. 20As she was dying, the women attending her said, "Don't despair; you have given birth to a son." But she did not respond or pay any attention.

21She named the boy Ichabod,*b* saying, "The glory has departed from Israel"— because of the capture of the ark of God and the deaths of her father-in-law and her husband. 22She said, "The glory has departed from Israel, for the ark of God has been captured."

The Ark in Ashdod and Ekron

5 After the Philistines had captured the ark of God, they took it from Ebenezer to Ashdod. 2Then they carried the ark into Dagon's temple and set it beside Dagon. 3When the people of Ashdod rose early the next day, there was Dagon, fallen on his face on the ground before the ark of the LORD! They took Dagon and put him back in his place. 4But the following morning when they rose, there was Dagon, fallen on his face on the ground before the ark of the LORD! His head and hands had been broken off and were lying on the threshold; only his body remained. 5That is why to this day neither the priests of Dagon nor any others who enter Dagon's temple at Ashdod step on the threshold.

6The LORD's hand was heavy upon the people of Ashdod and its vicinity; he brought devastation upon them and afflicted them with tumors.*c* 7When the men of Ashdod saw what was happening, they said, "The ark of the god of Israel must not stay here with us, because his hand is heavy upon us and upon Dagon our god." 8So they called together all the rulers of the Philistines and asked them, "What shall we do with the ark of the god of Israel?"

They answered, "Have the ark of the god of Israel moved to Gath." So they moved the ark of the God of Israel.

9But after they had moved it, the LORD's hand was against that city, throwing it into a great panic. He afflicted the people of the city, both young and old, with an outbreak of tumors.*d* 10So they sent the ark of God to Ekron.

As the ark of God was entering Ekron, the people of Ekron cried out, "They have brought the ark of the god of Israel around to us to kill us and our people." 11So they called together all the rulers of the Philistines and said, "Send the ark of the god of Israel away; let it go back to its

a18 Traditionally *judged*   *b21* *Ichabod* means *no glory.*   *c6* Hebrew; Septuagint and Vulgate *tumors. And rats appeared in their land, and death and destruction were throughout the city*   *d9* Or *with tumors in the groin* (see Septuagint) own place, or it[a] will kill us and our people." For death had filled the city with panic; God's hand was very heavy upon it. [12]Those who did not die were afflicted with tumors, and the outcry of the city went up to heaven.

The Ark Returned to Israel

6 When the ark of the LORD had been in Philistine territory seven months, [2]the Philistines called for the priests and the diviners and said, "What shall we do with the ark of the LORD? Tell us how we should send it back to its place."

[3]They answered, "If you return the ark of the god of Israel, do not send it away empty, but by all means send a guilt offering to him. Then you will be healed, and you will know why his hand has not been lifted from you."

[4]The Philistines asked, "What guilt offering should we send to him?"

They replied, "Five gold tumors and five gold rats, according to the number of the Philistine rulers, because the same plague has struck both you and your rulers. [5]Make models of the tumors and of the rats that are destroying the country, and pay honor to Israel's god. Perhaps he will lift his hand from you and your gods and your land. [6]Why do you harden your hearts as the Egyptians and Pharaoh did? When he[b] treated them harshly, did they not send the Israelites out so they could go on their way?

[7]"Now then, get a new cart ready, with two cows that have calved and have never been yoked. Hitch the cows to the cart, but take their calves away and pen them up. [8]Take the ark of the LORD and put it on the cart, and in a chest beside it put the gold objects you are sending back to him as a guilt offering. Send it on its way, [9]but keep watching it. If it goes up to its own territory, toward Beth Shemesh, then the LORD has brought this great disaster on us. But if it does not, then we will know that it was not his hand that struck us and that it happened to us by chance."

[10]So they did this. They took two such cows and hitched them to the cart and penned up their calves. [11]They placed the ark of the LORD on the cart and along with it the chest containing the gold rats and the models of the tumors. [12]Then the cows went straight up toward Beth Shemesh, keeping on the road and lowing all the way; they did not turn to the right or to the left. The rulers of the Philistines followed them as far as the border of Beth Shemesh.

[13]Now the people of Beth Shemesh were harvesting their wheat in the valley, and when they looked up and saw the ark, they rejoiced at the sight. [14]The cart came to the field of Joshua of Beth Shemesh, and there it stopped beside a large rock. The people chopped up the wood of the cart and sacrificed the cows as a burnt offering to the LORD. [15]The Levites took down the ark of the LORD, together with the chest containing the gold objects, and placed them on the large rock. On that day the people of Beth Shemesh offered burnt offerings and made sacrifices to the LORD. [16]The five rulers of the Philistines saw all this and then returned that same day to Ekron.

[17]These are the gold tumors the Philistines sent as a guilt offering to the LORD—one each for Ashdod, Gaza, Ashkelon, Gath and Ekron. [18]And the number of the gold rats was according to the number of Philistine towns belonging to the five rulers—the fortified towns with their country villages. The large rock, on which[c] they set the ark of the LORD, is a witness to this day in the field of Joshua of Beth Shemesh.

[19]But God struck down some of the men of Beth Shemesh, putting seventy[d] of them to death because they had looked into the ark of the LORD. The people mourned because of the heavy blow the LORD had dealt them, [20]and the men of Beth Shemesh asked, "Who can stand in the presence of the LORD, this holy God? To whom will the ark go up from here?"

[21]Then they sent messengers to the people of Kiriath Jearim, saying, "The Philistines have returned the ark of the LORD. Come down and take it up to your **7** place." [1]So the men of Kiriath Jearim came and took up the ark of the LORD. They took it to Abinadab's house on the

---

a11 Or *he*　　*b6* That is, God　　*c18* A few Hebrew manuscripts (see also Septuagint); most Hebrew manuscripts *villages as far as Greater Abel, where*　　*d19* A few Hebrew manuscripts; most Hebrew manuscripts and Septuagint *50,070* hill and consecrated Eleazar his son to guard the ark of the LORD.

Samuel Subdues the Philistines at Mizpah

²It was a long time, twenty years in all, that the ark remained at Kiriath Jearim, and all the people of Israel mourned and sought after the LORD. ³And Samuel said to the whole house of Israel, "If you are returning to the LORD with all your hearts, then rid yourselves of the foreign gods and the Ashtoreths and commit yourselves to the LORD and serve him only, and he will deliver you out of the hand of the Philistines." ⁴So the Israelites put away their Baals and Ashtoreths, and served the LORD only.

⁵Then Samuel said, "Assemble all Israel at Mizpah and I will intercede with the LORD for you." ⁶When they had assembled at Mizpah, they drew water and poured it out before the LORD. On that day they fasted and there they confessed, "We have sinned against the LORD." And Samuel was leaderᵃ of Israel at Mizpah.

⁷When the Philistines heard that Israel had assembled at Mizpah, the rulers of the Philistines came up to attack them. And when the Israelites heard of it, they were afraid because of the Philistines. ⁸They said to Samuel, "Do not stop crying out to the LORD our God for us, that he may rescue us from the hand of the Philistines." ⁹Then Samuel took a suckling lamb and offered it up as a whole burnt offering to the LORD. He cried out to the LORD on Israel's behalf, and the LORD answered him.

¹⁰While Samuel was sacrificing the burnt offering, the Philistines drew near to engage Israel in battle. But that day the LORD thundered with loud thunder against the Philistines and threw them into such a panic that they were routed before the Israelites. ¹¹The men of Israel rushed out of Mizpah and pursued the Philistines, slaughtering them along the way to a point below Beth Car.

¹²Then Samuel took a stone and set it up between Mizpah and Shen. He named it Ebenezer,ᵇ saying, "Thus far has the LORD helped us." ¹³So the Philistines were subdued and did not invade Israelite territory again.

Throughout Samuel's lifetime, the hand of the LORD was against the Philistines. ¹⁴The towns from Ekron to Gath that the Philistines had captured from Israel were restored to her, and Israel delivered the neighboring territory from the power of the Philistines. And there was peace between Israel and the Amorites.

¹⁵Samuel continued as judge over Israel all the days of his life. ¹⁶From year to year he went on a circuit from Bethel to Gilgal to Mizpah, judging Israel in all those places. ¹⁷But he always went back to Ramah, where his home was, and there he also judged Israel. And he built an altar there to the LORD.

Israel Asks for a King

8 When Samuel grew old, he appointed his sons as judges for Israel. ²The name of his firstborn was Joel and the name of his second was Abijah, and they served at Beersheba. ³But his sons did not walk in his ways. They turned aside after dishonest gain and accepted bribes and perverted justice.

⁴So all the elders of Israel gathered together and came to Samuel at Ramah. ⁵They said to him, "You are old, and your sons do not walk in your ways; now appoint a king to leadᶜ us, such as all the other nations have."

⁶But when they said, "Give us a king to lead us," this displeased Samuel; so he prayed to the LORD. ⁷And the LORD told him: "Listen to all that the people are saying to you; it is not you they have rejected, but they have rejected me as their king. ⁸As they have done from the day I brought them up out of Egypt until this day, forsaking me and serving other gods, so they are doing to you. ⁹Now listen to them; but warn them solemnly and let them know what the king who will reign over them will do."

¹⁰Samuel told all the words of the LORD to the people who were asking him for a king. ¹¹He said, "This is what the king who will reign over you will do: He will take your sons and make them serve with his chariots and horses, and they will run in front of his chariots. ¹²Some he will assign to be commanders of thousands

---

ᵃ6 Traditionally *judge*   ᵇ12 *Ebenezer* means *stone of help.*   ᶜ5 Traditionally *judge*; also in verses 6 and 20

and commanders of fifties, and others to
plow his ground and reap his harvest, and
still others to make weapons of war and
equipment for his chariots. ¹³He will take
your daughters to be perfumers and cooks
and bakers. ¹⁴He will take the best of your
fields and vineyards and olive groves and
give them to his attendants. ¹⁵He will take
a tenth of your grain and of your vintage
and give it to his officials and attendants.
¹⁶Your menservants and maidservants
and the best of your cattle*a* and donkeys
he will take for his own use. ¹⁷He will take
a tenth of your flocks, and you yourselves
will become his slaves. ¹⁸When that day
comes, you will cry out for relief from the
king you have chosen, and the LORD will
not answer you in that day."

¹⁹But the people refused to listen to
Samuel. "No!" they said. "We want a king
over us. ²⁰Then we will be like all the
other nations, with a king to lead us and
to go out before us and fight our battles."

²¹When Samuel heard all that the people said, he repeated it before the LORD.
²²The LORD answered, "Listen to them
and give them a king."

Then Samuel said to the men of Israel,
"Everyone go back to his town."

Samuel Anoints Saul

9 There was a Benjamite, a man of
standing, whose name was Kish son
of Abiel, the son of Zeror, the son of Beco-
rath, the son of Aphiah of Benjamin. ²He
had a son named Saul, an impressive
young man without equal among the Israelites—a head taller than any of the
others.

³Now the donkeys belonging to Saul's
father Kish were lost, and Kish said to his
son Saul, "Take one of the servants with
you and go and look for the donkeys." ⁴So
he passed through the hill country of
Ephraim and through the area around
Shalisha, but they did not find them.
They went on into the district of Shaalim,
but the donkeys were not there. Then he
passed through the territory of Benjamin,
but they did not find them.

⁵When they reached the district of
Zuph, Saul said to the servant who was
with him, "Come, let's go back, or my
father will stop thinking about the donkeys and start worrying about us."

⁶But the servant replied, "Look, in this
town there is a man of God; he is highly
respected, and everything he says comes
true. Let's go there now. Perhaps he will
tell us what way to take."

⁷Saul said to his servant, "If we go,
what can we give the man? The food in
our sacks is gone. We have no gift to take
to the man of God. What do we have?"

⁸The servant answered him again.
"Look," he said, "I have a quarter of a
shekel*b* of silver. I will give it to the man
of God so that he will tell us what way to
take." ⁹(Formerly in Israel, if a man went
to inquire of God, he would say, "Come,
let us go to the seer," because the prophet
of today used to be called a seer.)

¹⁰"Good," Saul said to his servant.
"Come, let's go." So they set out for the
town where the man of God was.

¹¹As they were going up the hill to the
town, they met some girls coming out to
draw water, and they asked them, "Is the
seer here?"

¹²"He is," they answered. "He's ahead
of you. Hurry now; he has just come to
our town today, for the people have a
sacrifice at the high place. ¹³As soon as
you enter the town, you will find him
before he goes up to the high place to eat.
The people will not begin eating until he
comes, because he must bless the sacrifice; afterward, those who are invited will
eat. Go up now; you should find him
about this time."

¹⁴They went up to the town, and as
they were entering it, there was Samuel,
coming toward them on his way up to the
high place.

¹⁵Now the day before Saul came, the
LORD had revealed this to Samuel:
¹⁶"About this time tomorrow I will send
you a man from the land of Benjamin.
Anoint him leader over my people Israel;
he will deliver my people from the hand
of the Philistines. I have looked upon my
people, for their cry has reached me."

¹⁷When Samuel caught sight of Saul,
the LORD said to him, "This is the man I
spoke to you about; he will govern my
people."

¹⁸Saul approached Samuel in the gate-

---

*a*16 Septuagint; Hebrew *young men*   *b*8 That is,
about 1/10 ounce (about 3 grams)

way and asked, "Would you please tell me where the seer's house is?"

[19]"I am the seer," Samuel replied. "Go up ahead of me to the high place, for today you are to eat with me, and in the morning I will let you go and will tell you all that is in your heart. [20]As for the donkeys you lost three days ago, do not worry about them; they have been found. And to whom is all the desire of Israel turned, if not to you and all your father's family?"

[21]Saul answered, "But am I not a Benjamite, from the smallest tribe of Israel, and is not my clan the least of all the clans of the tribe of Benjamin? Why do you say such a thing to me?"

[22]Then Samuel brought Saul and his servant into the hall and seated them at the head of those who were invited—about thirty in number. [23]Samuel said to the cook, "Bring the piece of meat I gave you, the one I told you to lay aside."

[24]So the cook took up the leg with what was on it and set it in front of Saul. Samuel said, "Here is what has been kept for you. Eat, because it was set aside for you for this occasion, from the time I said, 'I have invited guests.' " And Saul dined with Samuel that day.

[25]After they came down from the high place to the town, Samuel talked with Saul on the roof of his house. [26]They rose about daybreak and Samuel called to Saul on the roof, "Get ready, and I will send you on your way." When Saul got ready, he and Samuel went outside together. [27]As they were going down to the edge of the town, Samuel said to Saul, "Tell the servant to go on ahead of us"—and the servant did so—"but you stay here awhile, so that I may give you a message from God."

10 Then Samuel took a flask of oil and poured it on Saul's head and kissed him, saying, "Has not the LORD anointed you leader over his inheritance?[a] [2]When you leave me today, you will meet two men near Rachel's tomb, at Zelzah on the border of Benjamin. They will say to you, 'The donkeys you set out to look for have been found. And now your father has stopped thinking about them and is worried about you. He is asking, "What shall I do about my son?" '

[3]"Then you will go on from there until you reach the great tree of Tabor. Three men going up to God at Bethel will meet

you there. One will be carrying three young goats, another three loaves of bread, and another a skin of wine. [4]They will greet you and offer you two loaves of bread, which you will accept from them.

[5]"After that you will go to Gibeah of God, where there is a Philistine outpost. As you approach the town, you will meet a procession of prophets coming down from the high place with lyres, tambourines, flutes and harps being played before them, and they will be prophesying. [6]The Spirit of the LORD will come upon you in power, and you will prophesy with them; and you will be changed into a different person. [7]Once these signs are fulfilled, do whatever your hand finds to do, for God is with you.

[8]"Go down ahead of me to Gilgal. I will surely come down to you to sacrifice burnt offerings and fellowship offerings,[b] but you must wait seven days until I come to you and tell you what you are to do."

Saul Made King

[9]As Saul turned to leave Samuel, God changed Saul's heart, and all these signs were fulfilled that day. [10]When they arrived at Gibeah, a procession of prophets met him; the Spirit of God came upon him in power, and he joined in their prophesying. [11]When all those who had formerly known him saw him prophesying with the prophets, they asked each other, "What is this that has happened to the son of Kish? Is Saul also among the prophets?"

[12]A man who lived there answered, "And who is their father?" So it became a saying: "Is Saul also among the prophets?" [13]After Saul stopped prophesying, he went to the high place.

[14]Now Saul's uncle asked him and his servant, "Where have you been?"

"Looking for the donkeys," he said. "But when we saw they were not to be found, we went to Samuel."

[15]Saul's uncle said, "Tell me what Samuel said to you."

---

a1 Hebrew; Septuagint and Vulgate *over his people Israel? You will reign over the LORD's people and save them from the power of their enemies round about. And this will be a sign to you that the LORD has anointed you leader over his inheritance:*
b8 Traditionally *peace offerings*

¹⁶Saul replied, "He assured us that the donkeys had been found." But he did not tell his uncle what Samuel had said about the kingship.

¹⁷Samuel summoned the people of Israel to the LORD at Mizpah ¹⁸and said to them, "This is what the LORD, the God of Israel, says: 'I brought Israel up out of Egypt, and I delivered you from the power of Egypt and all the kingdoms that oppressed you.' ¹⁹But you have now rejected your God, who saves you out of all your calamities and distresses. And you have said, 'No, set a king over us.' So now present yourselves before the LORD by your tribes and clans."

²⁰When Samuel brought all the tribes of Israel near, the tribe of Benjamin was chosen. ²¹Then he brought forward the tribe of Benjamin, clan by clan, and Matri's clan was chosen. Finally Saul son of Kish was chosen. But when they looked for him, he was not to be found. ²²So they inquired further of the LORD, "Has the man come here yet?"

And the LORD said, "Yes, he has hidden himself among the baggage."

²³They ran and brought him out, and as he stood among the people he was a head taller than any of the others. ²⁴Samuel said to all the people, "Do you see the man the LORD has chosen? There is no one like him among all the people."

Then the people shouted, "Long live the king!"

²⁵Samuel explained to the people the regulations of the kingship. He wrote them down on a scroll and deposited it before the LORD. Then Samuel dismissed the people, each to his own home.

²⁶Saul also went to his home in Gibeah, accompanied by valiant men whose hearts God had touched. ²⁷But some troublemakers said, "How can this fellow save us?" They despised him and brought him no gifts. But Saul kept silent.

Saul Rescues the City of Jabesh

11 Nahash the Ammonite went up and besieged Jabesh Gilead. And all the men of Jabesh said to him, "Make a treaty with us, and we will be subject to you."

²But Nahash the Ammonite replied, "I will make a treaty with you only on the condition that I gouge out the right eye of every one of you and so bring disgrace on all Israel."

³The elders of Jabesh said to him, "Give us seven days so we can send messengers throughout Israel; if no one comes to rescue us, we will surrender to you."

⁴When the messengers came to Gibeah of Saul and reported these terms to the people, they all wept aloud. ⁵Just then Saul was returning from the fields, behind his oxen, and he asked, "What is wrong with the people? Why are they weeping?" Then they repeated to him what the men of Jabesh had said.

⁶When Saul heard their words, the Spirit of God came upon him in power, and he burned with anger. ⁷He took a pair of oxen, cut them into pieces, and sent the pieces by messengers throughout Israel, proclaiming, "This is what will be done to the oxen of anyone who does not follow Saul and Samuel." Then the terror of the LORD fell on the people, and they turned out as one man. ⁸When Saul mustered them at Bezek, the men of Israel numbered three hundred thousand and the men of Judah thirty thousand.

⁹They told the messengers who had come, "Say to the men of Jabesh Gilead, 'By the time the sun is hot tomorrow, you will be delivered.' " When the messengers went and reported this to the men of Jabesh, they were elated. ¹⁰They said to the Ammonites, "Tomorrow we will surrender to you, and you can do to us whatever seems good to you."

¹¹The next day Saul separated his men into three divisions; during the last watch of the night they broke into the camp of the Ammonites and slaughtered them until the heat of the day. Those who survived were scattered, so that no two of them were left together.

Saul Confirmed as King

¹²The people then said to Samuel, "Who was it that asked, 'Shall Saul reign over us?' Bring these men to us and we will put them to death."

¹³But Saul said, "No one shall be put to death today, for this day the LORD has rescued Israel."

¹⁴Then Samuel said to the people, "Come, let us go to Gilgal and there reaf-

firm the kingship." ¹⁵So all the people went to Gilgal and confirmed Saul as king in the presence of the LORD. There they sacrificed fellowship offerings[a] before the LORD, and Saul and all the Israelites held a great celebration.

Samuel's Farewell Speech

12 Samuel said to all Israel, "I have listened to everything you said to me and have set a king over you. ²Now you have a king as your leader. As for me, I am old and gray, and my sons are here with you. I have been your leader from my youth until this day. ³Here I stand. Testify against me in the presence of the LORD and his anointed. Whose ox have I taken? Whose donkey have I taken? Whom have I cheated? Whom have I oppressed? From whose hand have I accepted a bribe to make me shut my eyes? If I have done any of these, I will make it right."

⁴"You have not cheated or oppressed us," they replied. "You have not taken anything from anyone's hand."

⁵Samuel said to them, "The LORD is witness against you, and also his anointed is witness this day, that you have not found anything in my hand."

"He is witness," they said.

⁶Then Samuel said to the people, "It is the LORD who appointed Moses and Aaron and brought your forefathers up out of Egypt. ⁷Now then, stand here, because I am going to confront you with evidence before the LORD as to all the righteous acts performed by the LORD for you and your fathers.

⁸"After Jacob entered Egypt, they cried to the LORD for help, and the LORD sent Moses and Aaron, who brought your forefathers out of Egypt and settled them in this place.

⁹"But they forgot the LORD their God; so he sold them into the hand of Sisera, the commander of the army of Hazor, and into the hands of the Philistines and the king of Moab, who fought against them. ¹⁰They cried out to the LORD and said, 'We have sinned; we have forsaken the LORD and served the Baals and the Ashtoreths. But now deliver us from the hands of our enemies, and we will serve you.' ¹¹Then the LORD sent Jerub-Baal,[b]

Barak,[c] Jephthah and Samuel,[d] and he delivered you from the hands of your enemies on every side, so that you lived securely.

¹²"But when you saw that Nahash king of the Ammonites was moving against you, you said to me, 'No, we want a king to rule over us'—even though the LORD your God was your king. ¹³Now here is the king you have chosen, the one you asked for; see, the LORD has set a king over you. ¹⁴If you fear the LORD and serve and obey him and do not rebel against his commands, and if both you and the king who reigns over you follow the LORD your God—good! ¹⁵But if you do not obey the LORD, and if you rebel against his commands, his hand will be against you, as it was against your fathers.

¹⁶"Now then, stand still and see this great thing the LORD is about to do before your eyes! ¹⁷Is it not wheat harvest now? I will call upon the LORD to send thunder and rain. And you will realize what an evil thing you did in the eyes of the LORD when you asked for a king."

¹⁸Then Samuel called upon the LORD, and that same day the LORD sent thunder and rain. So all the people stood in awe of the LORD and of Samuel.

¹⁹The people all said to Samuel, "Pray to the LORD your God for your servants so that we will not die, for we have added to all our other sins the evil of asking for a king."

²⁰"Do not be afraid," Samuel replied. "You have done all this evil; yet do not turn away from the LORD, but serve the LORD with all your heart. ²¹Do not turn away after useless idols. They can do you no good, nor can they rescue you, because they are useless. ²²For the sake of his great name the LORD will not reject his people, because the LORD was pleased to make you his own. ²³As for me, far be it from me that I should sin against the LORD by failing to pray for you. And I will teach you the way that is good and right. ²⁴But be sure to fear the LORD and serve him faithfully with all your heart; consider what great things he has done for you.

---

a 15 Traditionally *peace offerings*   *b 11* Also called *Gideon*   *c 11* Some Septuagint manuscripts and Syriac; Hebrew *Bedan*   *d 11* Hebrew; some Septuagint manuscripts and Syriac *Samson*

[25]Yet if you persist in doing evil, both you and your king will be swept away."

Samuel Rebukes Saul

13 Saul was ⌊thirty⌋[a] years old when he became king, and he reigned over Israel ⌊forty-⌋[b] two years.

[2]Saul[c] chose three thousand men from Israel; two thousand were with him at Micmash and in the hill country of Bethel, and a thousand were with Jonathan at Gibeah in Benjamin. The rest of the men he sent back to their homes.

[3]Jonathan attacked the Philistine outpost at Geba, and the Philistines heard about it. Then Saul had the trumpet blown throughout the land and said, "Let the Hebrews hear!" [4]So all Israel heard the news: "Saul has attacked the Philistine outpost, and now Israel has become a stench to the Philistines." And the people were summoned to join Saul at Gilgal.

[5]The Philistines assembled to fight Israel, with three thousand[d] chariots, six thousand charioteers, and soldiers as numerous as the sand on the seashore. They went up and camped at Micmash, east of Beth Aven. [6]When the men of Israel saw that their situation was critical and that their army was hard pressed, they hid in caves and thickets, among the rocks, and in pits and cisterns. [7]Some Hebrews even crossed the Jordan to the land of Gad and Gilead.

Saul remained at Gilgal, and all the troops with him were quaking with fear. [8]He waited seven days, the time set by Samuel; but Samuel did not come to Gilgal, and Saul's men began to scatter. [9]So he said, "Bring me the burnt offering and the fellowship offerings.[e]" And Saul offered up the burnt offering. [10]Just as he finished making the offering, Samuel arrived, and Saul went out to greet him.

[11]"What have you done?" asked Samuel.

Saul replied, "When I saw that the men were scattering, and that you did not come at the set time, and that the Philistines were assembling at Micmash, [12]I thought, 'Now the Philistines will come down against me at Gilgal, and I have not sought the LORD's favor.' So I felt compelled to offer the burnt offering."

[13]"You acted foolishly," Samuel said.

"You have not kept the command the LORD your God gave you; if you had, he would have established your kingdom over Israel for all time. [14]But now your kingdom will not endure; the LORD has sought out a man after his own heart and appointed him leader of his people, because you have not kept the LORD's command."

[15]Then Samuel left Gilgal[f] and went up to Gibeah in Benjamin, and Saul counted the men who were with him. They numbered about six hundred.

Israel Without Weapons

[16]Saul and his son Jonathan and the men with them were staying in Gibeah[g] in Benjamin, while the Philistines camped at Micmash. [17]Raiding parties went out from the Philistine camp in three detachments. One turned toward Ophrah in the vicinity of Shual, [18]another toward Beth Horon, and the third toward the borderland overlooking the Valley of Zeboim facing the desert.

[19]Not a blacksmith could be found in the whole land of Israel, because the Philistines had said, "Otherwise the Hebrews will make swords or spears!" [20]So all Israel went down to the Philistines to have their plowshares, mattocks, axes and sickles[h] sharpened. [21]The price was two thirds of a shekel[i] for sharpening plowshares and mattocks, and a third of a shekel[j] for sharpening forks and axes and for repointing goads.

[22]So on the day of the battle not a soldier with Saul and Jonathan had a sword or spear in his hand; only Saul and his son Jonathan had them.

Jonathan Attacks the Philistines

[23]Now a detachment of Philistines had

---

[a]1 A few late manuscripts of the Septuagint; Hebrew does not have *thirty*.   [b]1 See the round number in Acts 13:21; Hebrew does not have *forty-*.   [c]1,2 Or *and when he had reigned over Israel two years,* [2]he   [d]5 Some Septuagint manuscripts and Syriac; Hebrew *thirty thousand*   [e]9 Traditionally *peace offerings*   [f]15 Hebrew; Septuagint *Gilgal and went his way; the rest of the people went after Saul to meet the army, and they went out of Gilgal*   [g]16 Two Hebrew manuscripts; most Hebrew manuscripts *Geba,* a variant of *Gibeah*   [h]20 Septuagint; Hebrew *plowshares*   [i]21 Hebrew *pim*; that is, about 1/4 ounce (about 8 grams)   [j]21 That is, about 1/8 ounce (about 4 grams)

14

gone out to the pass at Micmash. [1]One day Jonathan son of Saul said to the young man bearing his armor, "Come, let's go over to the Philistine outpost on the other side." But he did not tell his father.

[2]Saul was staying on the outskirts of Gibeah under a pomegranate tree in Migron. With him were about six hundred men, [3]among whom was Ahijah, who was wearing an ephod. He was a son of Ichabod's brother Ahitub son of Phinehas, the son of Eli, the LORD's priest in Shiloh. No one was aware that Jonathan had left.

[4]On each side of the pass that Jonathan intended to cross to reach the Philistine outpost was a cliff; one was called Bozez, and the other Seneh. [5]One cliff stood to the north toward Micmash, the other to the south toward Geba.

[6]Jonathan said to his young armorbearer, "Come, let's go over to the outpost of those uncircumcised fellows. Perhaps the LORD will act in our behalf. Nothing can hinder the LORD from saving, whether by many or by few."

[7]"Do all that you have in mind," his armor-bearer said. "Go ahead; I am with you heart and soul."

[8]Jonathan said, "Come, then; we will cross over toward the men and let them see us. [9]If they say to us, 'Wait there until we come to you,' we will stay where we are and not go up to them. [10]But if they say, 'Come up to us,' we will climb up, because that will be our sign that the LORD has given them into our hands."

[11]So both of them showed themselves to the Philistine outpost. "Look!" said the Philistines. "The Hebrews are crawling out of the holes they were hiding in." [12]The men of the outpost shouted to Jonathan and his armor-bearer, "Come up to us and we'll teach you a lesson."

So Jonathan said to his armor-bearer, "Climb up after me; the LORD has given them into the hand of Israel."

[13]Jonathan climbed up, using his hands and feet, with his armor-bearer right behind him. The Philistines fell before Jonathan, and his armor-bearer followed and killed behind him. [14]In that first attack Jonathan and his armor-bearer killed some twenty men in an area of about half an acre.[a]

Israel Routs the Philistines

[15]Then panic struck the whole army—those in the camp and field, and those in the outposts and raiding parties—and the ground shook. It was a panic sent by God.[b]

[16]Saul's lookouts at Gibeah in Benjamin saw the army melting away in all directions. [17]Then Saul said to the men who were with him, "Muster the forces and see who has left us." When they did, it was Jonathan and his armor-bearer who were not there.

[18]Saul said to Ahijah, "Bring the ark of God." (At that time it was with the Israelites.)[c] [19]While Saul was talking to the priest, the tumult in the Philistine camp increased more and more. So Saul said to the priest, "Withdraw your hand."

[20]Then Saul and all his men assembled and went to the battle. They found the Philistines in total confusion, striking each other with their swords. [21]Those Hebrews who had previously been with the Philistines and had gone up with them to their camp went over to the Israelites who were with Saul and Jonathan. [22]When all the Israelites who had hidden in the hill country of Ephraim heard that the Philistines were on the run, they joined the battle in hot pursuit. [23]So the LORD rescued Israel that day, and the battle moved on beyond Beth Aven.

Jonathan Eats Honey

[24]Now the men of Israel were in distress that day, because Saul had bound the people under an oath, saying, "Cursed be any man who eats food before evening comes, before I have avenged myself on my enemies!" So none of the troops tasted food.

[25]The entire army[d] entered the woods, and there was honey on the ground. [26]When they went into the woods, they saw the honey oozing out, yet no one put his hand to his mouth, because they feared the oath. [27]But Jonathan had not heard that his father had bound the people with the oath, so he

---

[a]14 Hebrew half a yoke; a "yoke" was the land plowed by a yoke of oxen in one day.   [b]15 Or a terrible panic   [c]18 Hebrew; Septuagint "Bring the ephod." (At that time he wore the ephod before the Israelites.)   [d]25 Or Now all the people of the land

reached out the end of the staff that was in his hand and dipped it into the honeycomb. He raised his hand to his mouth, and his eyes brightened.[a] 28Then one of the soldiers told him, "Your father bound the army under a strict oath, saying, 'Cursed be any man who eats food today!' That is why the men are faint."

29Jonathan said, "My father has made trouble for the country. See how my eyes brightened[b] when I tasted a little of this honey. 30How much better it would have been if the men had eaten today some of the plunder they took from their enemies. Would not the slaughter of the Philistines have been even greater?"

31That day, after the Israelites had struck down the Philistines from Micmash to Aijalon, they were exhausted. 32They pounced on the plunder and, taking sheep, cattle and calves, they butchered them on the ground and ate them, together with the blood. 33Then someone said to Saul, "Look, the men are sinning against the LORD by eating meat that has blood in it."

"You have broken faith," he said. "Roll a large stone over here at once." 34Then he said, "Go out among the men and tell them, 'Each of you bring me your cattle and sheep, and slaughter them here and eat them. Do not sin against the LORD by eating meat with blood still in it.' "

So everyone brought his ox that night and slaughtered it there. 35Then Saul built an altar to the LORD; it was the first time he had done this.

36Saul said, "Let us go down after the Philistines by night and plunder them till dawn, and let us not leave one of them alive."

"Do whatever seems best to you," they replied.

But the priest said, "Let us inquire of God here."

37So Saul asked God, "Shall I go down after the Philistines? Will you give them into Israel's hand?" But God did not answer him that day.

38Saul therefore said, "Come here, all you who are leaders of the army, and let us find out what sin has been committed today. 39As surely as the LORD who rescues Israel lives, even if it lies with my son Jonathan, he must die." But not one of the men said a word.

40Saul then said to all the Israelites, "You stand over there; I and Jonathan my son will stand over here."

"Do what seems best to you," the men replied.

41Then Saul prayed to the LORD, the God of Israel, "Give me the right answer."[c] And Jonathan and Saul were taken by lot, and the men were cleared. 42Saul said, "Cast the lot between me and Jonathan my son." And Jonathan was taken.

43Then Saul said to Jonathan, "Tell me what you have done."

So Jonathan told him, "I merely tasted a little honey with the end of my staff. And now must I die?"

44Saul said, "May God deal with me, be it ever so severely, if you do not die, Jonathan."

45But the men said to Saul, "Should Jonathan die—he who has brought about this great deliverance in Israel? Never! As surely as the LORD lives, not a hair of his head will fall to the ground, for he did this today with God's help." So the men rescued Jonathan, and he was not put to death.

46Then Saul stopped pursuing the Philistines, and they withdrew to their own land.

47After Saul had assumed rule over Israel, he fought against their enemies on every side: Moab, the Ammonites, Edom, the kings[d] of Zobah, and the Philistines. Wherever he turned, he inflicted punishment on them.[e] 48He fought valiantly and defeated the Amalekites, delivering Israel from the hands of those who had plundered them.

Saul's family

49Saul's sons were Jonathan, Ishvi and Malki-Shua. The name of his older daughter was Merab, and that of the younger was Michal. 50His wife's name was Ahinoam daughter of Ahimaaz. The name of the commander of Saul's army

a27 Or his strength was renewed   b29 Or my strength was renewed   c41 Hebrew; Septuagint "Why have you not answered your servant today? If the fault is in me or my son Jonathan, respond with Urim, but if the men of Israel are at fault, respond with Thummim."   d47 Masoretic Text; Dead Sea Scrolls and Septuagint king   e47 Hebrew; Septuagint he was victorious was Abner son of Ner, and Ner was Saul's uncle. ⁵¹Saul's father Kish and Abner's father Ner were sons of Abiel.

⁵²All the days of Saul there was bitter war with the Philistines, and whenever Saul saw a mighty or brave man, he took him into his service.

The Lord Rejects Saul as King

15 Samuel said to Saul, "I am the one the Lord sent to anoint you king over his people Israel; so listen now to the message from the Lord. ²This is what the Lord Almighty says: 'I will punish the Amalekites for what they did to Israel when they waylaid them as they came up from Egypt. ³Now go, attack the Amalekites and totally destroy*ᵃ* everything that belongs to them. Do not spare them; put to death men and women, children and infants, cattle and sheep, camels and donkeys.'"

⁴So Saul summoned the men and mustered them at Telaim—two hundred thousand foot soldiers and ten thousand men from Judah. ⁵Saul went to the city of Amalek and set an ambush in the ravine. ⁶Then he said to the Kenites, "Go away, leave the Amalekites so that I do not destroy you along with them; for you showed kindness to all the Israelites when they came up out of Egypt." So the Kenites moved away from the Amalekites.

⁷Then Saul attacked the Amalekites all the way from Havilah to Shur, to the east of Egypt. ⁸He took Agag king of the Amalekites alive, and all his people he totally destroyed with the sword. ⁹But Saul and the army spared Agag and the best of the sheep and cattle, the fat calves*ᵇ* and lambs—everything that was good. These they were unwilling to destroy completely, but everything that was despised and weak they totally destroyed.

¹⁰Then the word of the Lord came to Samuel: ¹¹"I am grieved that I have made Saul king, because he has turned away from me and has not carried out my instructions." Samuel was troubled, and he cried out to the Lord all that night.

¹²Early in the morning Samuel got up and went to meet Saul, but he was told, "Saul has gone to Carmel. There he has set up a monument in his own honor and has turned and gone on down to Gilgal."

¹³When Samuel reached him, Saul said, "The Lord bless you! I have carried out the Lord's instructions."

¹⁴But Samuel said, "What then is this bleating of sheep in my ears? What is this lowing of cattle that I hear?"

¹⁵Saul answered, "The soldiers brought them from the Amalekites; they spared the best of the sheep and cattle to sacrifice to the Lord your God, but we totally destroyed the rest."

¹⁶"Stop!" Samuel said to Saul. "Let me tell you what the Lord said to me last night."

"Tell me," Saul replied.

¹⁷Samuel said, "Although you were once small in your own eyes, did you not become the head of the tribes of Israel? The Lord anointed you king over Israel. ¹⁸And he sent you on a mission, saying, 'Go and completely destroy those wicked people, the Amalekites; make war on them until you have wiped them out.' ¹⁹Why did you not obey the Lord? Why did you pounce on the plunder and do evil in the eyes of the Lord?"

²⁰"But I did obey the Lord," Saul said. "I went on the mission the Lord assigned me. I completely destroyed the Amalekites and brought back Agag their king. ²¹The soldiers took sheep and cattle from the plunder, the best of what was devoted to God, in order to sacrifice them to the Lord your God at Gilgal."

²²But Samuel replied:

"Does the Lord delight in burnt
         offerings and sacrifices
    as much as in obeying the voice of
         the Lord?
To obey is better than sacrifice,
    and to heed is better than the fat
         of rams.
²³For rebellion is like the sin of
         divination,
    and arrogance like the evil of
         idolatry.
Because you have rejected the word of
         the Lord,
    he has rejected you as king."

ᵃ3 The Hebrew term refers to the irrevocable giving over of things or persons to the Lord, often by totally destroying them; also in verses 8, 9, 15, 18, 20 and 21.   *ᵇ9* Or *the grown bulls*; the meaning of the Hebrew for this phrase is uncertain.

²⁴Then Saul said to Samuel, "I have sinned. I violated the LORD's command and your instructions. I was afraid of the people and so I gave in to them. ²⁵Now I beg you, forgive my sin and come back with me, so that I may worship the LORD."

²⁶But Samuel said to him, "I will not go back with you. You have rejected the word of the LORD, and the LORD has rejected you as king over Israel!"

²⁷As Samuel turned to leave, Saul caught hold of the hem of his robe, and it tore. ²⁸Samuel said to him, "The LORD has torn the kingdom of Israel from you today and has given it to one of your neighbors—to one better than you. ²⁹He who is the Glory of Israel does not lie or change his mind; for he is not a man, that he should change his mind."

³⁰Saul replied, "I have sinned. But please honor me before the elders of my people and before Israel; come back with me, so that I may worship the LORD your God." ³¹So Samuel went back with Saul, and Saul worshiped the LORD.

³²Then Samuel said, "Bring me Agag king of the Amalekites."

Agag came to him confidently,ᵃ thinking, "Surely the bitterness of death is past."

³³But Samuel said,

"As your sword has made women childless,
　　so will your mother be childless
　　　among women."

And Samuel put Agag to death before the LORD at Gilgal.

³⁴Then Samuel left for Ramah, but Saul went up to his home in Gibeah of Saul. ³⁵Until the day Samuel died, he did not go to see Saul again, though Samuel mourned for him. And the LORD was grieved that he had made Saul king over Israel.

Samuel Anoints David

16 The LORD said to Samuel, "How long will you mourn for Saul, since I have rejected him as king over Israel? Fill your horn with oil and be on your way; I am sending you to Jesse of Bethlehem. I have chosen one of his sons to be king."

²But Samuel said, "How can I go? Saul will hear about it and kill me."

The LORD said, "Take a heifer with you and say, 'I have come to sacrifice to the LORD.' ³Invite Jesse to the sacrifice, and I will show you what to do. You are to anoint for me the one I indicate."

⁴Samuel did what the LORD said. When he arrived at Bethlehem, the elders of the town trembled when they met him. They asked, "Do you come in peace?"

⁵Samuel replied, "Yes, in peace; I have come to sacrifice to the LORD. Consecrate yourselves and come to the sacrifice with me." Then he consecrated Jesse and his sons and invited them to the sacrifice.

⁶When they arrived, Samuel saw Eliab and thought, "Surely the LORD's anointed stands here before the LORD."

⁷But the LORD said to Samuel, "Do not consider his appearance or his height, for I have rejected him. The LORD does not look at the things man looks at. Man looks at the outward appearance, but the LORD looks at the heart."

⁸Then Jesse called Abinadab and had him pass in front of Samuel. But Samuel said, "The LORD has not chosen this one either." ⁹Jesse then had Shammah pass by, but Samuel said, "Nor has the LORD chosen this one." ¹⁰Jesse had seven of his sons pass before Samuel, but Samuel said to him, "The LORD has not chosen these." ¹¹So he asked Jesse, "Are these all the sons you have?"

"There is still the youngest," Jesse answered, "but he is tending the sheep."

Samuel said, "Send for him; we will not sit downᵇ until he arrives."

¹²So he sent and had him brought in. He was ruddy, with a fine appearance and handsome features.

Then the LORD said, "Rise and anoint him; he is the one."

¹³So Samuel took the horn of oil and anointed him in the presence of his brothers, and from that day on the Spirit of the LORD came upon David in power. Samuel then went to Ramah.

David in Saul's Service

¹⁴Now the Spirit of the LORD had departed from Saul, and an evilᶜ spirit from the LORD tormented him.

ᵃ32 Or *him trembling, yet*　　ᵇ11 Some Septuagint manuscripts; Hebrew *not gather around*　　ᶜ14 Or *injurious*; also in verses 15, 16 and 23

¹⁵Saul's attendants said to him, "See, an evil spirit from God is tormenting you. ¹⁶Let our lord command his servants here to search for someone who can play the harp. He will play when the evil spirit from God comes upon you, and you will feel better."

¹⁷So Saul said to his attendants, "Find someone who plays well and bring him to me."

¹⁸One of the servants answered, "I have seen a son of Jesse of Bethlehem who knows how to play the harp. He is a brave man and a warrior. He speaks well and is a fine-looking man. And the LORD is with him."

¹⁹Then Saul sent messengers to Jesse and said, "Send me your son David, who is with the sheep." ²⁰So Jesse took a donkey loaded with bread, a skin of wine and a young goat and sent them with his son David to Saul.

²¹David came to Saul and entered his service. Saul liked him very much, and David became one of his armor-bearers. ²²Then Saul sent word to Jesse, saying, "Allow David to remain in my service, for I am pleased with him."

²³Whenever the spirit from God came upon Saul, David would take his harp and play. Then relief would come to Saul; he would feel better, and the evil spirit would leave him.

David and Goliath

17 Now the Philistines gathered their forces for war and assembled at Socoh in Judah. They pitched camp at Ephes Dammim, between Socoh and Azekah. ²Saul and the Israelites assembled and camped in the Valley of Elah and drew up their battle line to meet the Philistines. ³The Philistines occupied one hill and the Israelites another, with the valley between them.

⁴A champion named Goliath, who was from Gath, came out of the Philistine camp. He was over nine feet[a] tall. ⁵He had a bronze helmet on his head and wore a coat of scale armor of bronze weighing five thousand shekels[b]; ⁶on his legs he wore bronze greaves, and a bronze javelin was slung on his back. ⁷His spear shaft was like a weaver's rod, and its iron point weighed six hundred shekels.[c] His shield bearer went ahead of him.

⁸Goliath stood and shouted to the ranks of Israel, "Why do you come out

---

[a]4 Hebrew *was six cubits and a span* (about 3 meters)   [b]5 That is, about 125 pounds (about 57 kilograms)   [c]7 That is, about 15 pounds (about 7 kilograms)

Taking the Right Advice

Tuesday

1 SAMUEL 17   David was very successful when he faced the giant Goliath. One reason he defeated Goliath was because he was careful about what advice he took. King Saul advised him to use the royal armor, and his brothers advised him to just go home. But David didn't see their advice as coming from God. He knew the strengths God had blessed him with. He even talked about how God had prepared him in the use of the sling.

Are you facing "giants" in your life as a couple? Is there a "giant" of poor health, financial burdens, problems with the children or a job? At some point, we all face a giant. Often as we face difficulties as couples, people are quick to give advice or comment on our problem. Sometimes the advice they give is advice that fits them, but it may not be the best for our marriage. A friend of ours discovered that her husband had been unfaithful. Well-meaning advisers urged her to divorce him. She knew this might be the solution for others but that God wanted her to work for reconciliation.

A couple must decide who they will take advice from and how they will determine if it is God's advice. God desires to give us the wisdom and strength we need to fight the giants. David knew what each of us needs to know. No matter what giant we face, God knows what equipment we should be using.

—Bob & Rosemary

Go to page 300 for your next devotional reading.

and line up for battle? Am I not a Philistine, and are you not the servants of Saul? Choose a man and have him come down to me. ⁹If he is able to fight and kill me, we will become your subjects; but if I overcome him and kill him, you will become our subjects and serve us." ¹⁰Then the Philistine said, "This day I defy the ranks of Israel! Give me a man and let us fight each other." ¹¹On hearing the Philistine's words, Saul and all the Israelites were dismayed and terrified.

¹²Now David was the son of an Ephrathite named Jesse, who was from Bethlehem in Judah. Jesse had eight sons, and in Saul's time he was old and well advanced in years. ¹³Jesse's three oldest sons had followed Saul to the war: The firstborn was Eliab; the second, Abinadab; and the third, Shammah. ¹⁴David was the youngest. The three oldest followed Saul, ¹⁵but David went back and forth from Saul to tend his father's sheep at Bethlehem.

¹⁶For forty days the Philistine came forward every morning and evening and took his stand.

¹⁷Now Jesse said to his son David, "Take this ephah*a* of roasted grain and these ten loaves of bread for your brothers and hurry to their camp. ¹⁸Take along these ten cheeses to the commander of their unit.*b* See how your brothers are and bring back some assurance*c* from them. ¹⁹They are with Saul and all the men of Israel in the Valley of Elah, fighting against the Philistines."

²⁰Early in the morning David left the flock with a shepherd, loaded up and set out, as Jesse had directed. He reached the camp as the army was going out to its battle positions, shouting the war cry. ²¹Israel and the Philistines were drawing up their lines facing each other. ²²David left his things with the keeper of supplies, ran to the battle lines and greeted his brothers. ²³As he was talking with them, Goliath, the Philistine champion from Gath, stepped out from his lines and shouted his usual defiance, and David heard it. ²⁴When the Israelites saw the man, they all ran from him in great fear. ²⁵Now the Israelites had been saying, "Do you see how this man keeps coming out? He comes out to defy Israel. The king will give great wealth to the man who kills

him. He will also give him his daughter in marriage and will exempt his father's family from taxes in Israel."

²⁶David asked the men standing near him, "What will be done for the man who kills this Philistine and removes this disgrace from Israel? Who is this uncircumcised Philistine that he should defy the armies of the living God?"

²⁷They repeated to him what they had been saying and told him, "This is what will be done for the man who kills him."

²⁸When Eliab, David's oldest brother, heard him speaking with the men, he burned with anger at him and asked, "Why have you come down here? And with whom did you leave those few sheep in the desert? I know how conceited you are and how wicked your heart is; you came down only to watch the battle."

²⁹"Now what have I done?" said David. "Can't I even speak?" ³⁰He then turned away to someone else and brought up the same matter, and the men answered him as before. ³¹What David said was overheard and reported to Saul, and Saul sent for him.

³²David said to Saul, "Let no one lose heart on account of this Philistine; your servant will go and fight him."

³³Saul replied, "You are not able to go out against this Philistine and fight him; you are only a boy, and he has been a fighting man from his youth."

³⁴But David said to Saul, "Your servant has been keeping his father's sheep. When a lion or a bear came and carried off a sheep from the flock, ³⁵I went after it, struck it and rescued the sheep from its mouth. When it turned on me, I seized it by its hair, struck it and killed it. ³⁶Your servant has killed both the lion and the bear; this uncircumcised Philistine will be like one of them, because he has defied the armies of the living God. ³⁷The Lord who delivered me from the paw of the lion and the paw of the bear will deliver me from the hand of this Philistine."

Saul said to David, "Go, and the Lord be with you."

³⁸Then Saul dressed David in his own tunic. He put a coat of armor on him and a bronze helmet on his head. ³⁹David fas-

---

a17 That is, probably about 3/5 bushel (about 22 liters)   *b18* Hebrew *thousand*   *c18* Or *some token; or some pledge of spoils* tened on his sword over the tunic and tried walking around, because he was not used to them.

"I cannot go in these," he said to Saul, "because I am not used to them." So he took them off. ⁴⁰Then he took his staff in his hand, chose five smooth stones from the stream, put them in the pouch of his shepherd's bag and, with his sling in his hand, approached the Philistine.

⁴¹Meanwhile, the Philistine, with his shield bearer in front of him, kept coming closer to David. ⁴²He looked David over and saw that he was only a boy, ruddy and handsome, and he despised him. ⁴³He said to David, "Am I a dog, that you come at me with sticks?" And the Philistine cursed David by his gods. ⁴⁴"Come here," he said, "and I'll give your flesh to the birds of the air and the beasts of the field!"

⁴⁵David said to the Philistine, "You come against me with sword and spear and javelin, but I come against you in the name of the LORD Almighty, the God of the armies of Israel, whom you have defied. ⁴⁶This day the LORD will hand you over to me, and I'll strike you down and cut off your head. Today I will give the carcasses of the Philistine army to the birds of the air and the beasts of the earth, and the whole world will know that there is a God in Israel. ⁴⁷All those gathered here will know that it is not by sword or spear that the LORD saves; for the battle is the LORD's, and he will give all of you into our hands."

⁴⁸As the Philistine moved closer to attack him, David ran quickly toward the battle line to meet him. ⁴⁹Reaching into his bag and taking out a stone, he slung it and struck the Philistine on the forehead. The stone sank into his forehead, and he fell facedown on the ground.

⁵⁰So David triumphed over the Philistine with a sling and a stone; without a sword in his hand he struck down the Philistine and killed him.

⁵¹David ran and stood over him. He took hold of the Philistine's sword and drew it from the scabbard. After he killed him, he cut off his head with the sword.

When the Philistines saw that their hero was dead, they turned and ran. ⁵²Then the men of Israel and Judah surged forward with a shout and pursued the Philistines to the entrance of Gath*ᵃ*

and to the gates of Ekron. Their dead were strewn along the Shaaraim road to Gath and Ekron. ⁵³When the Israelites returned from chasing the Philistines, they plundered their camp. ⁵⁴David took the Philistine's head and brought it to Jerusalem, and he put the Philistine's weapons in his own tent.

⁵⁵As Saul watched David going out to meet the Philistine, he said to Abner, commander of the army, "Abner, whose son is that young man?"

Abner replied, "As surely as you live, O king, I don't know."

⁵⁶The king said, "Find out whose son this young man is."

⁵⁷As soon as David returned from killing the Philistine, Abner took him and brought him before Saul, with David still holding the Philistine's head.

⁵⁸"Whose son are you, young man?" Saul asked him.

David said, "I am the son of your servant Jesse of Bethlehem."

Saul's Jealousy of David

18 After David had finished talking with Saul, Jonathan became one in spirit with David, and he loved him as himself. ²From that day Saul kept David with him and did not let him return to his father's house. ³And Jonathan made a covenant with David because he loved him as himself. ⁴Jonathan took off the robe he was wearing and gave it to David, along with his tunic, and even his sword, his bow and his belt.

⁵Whatever Saul sent him to do, David did it so successfully*ᵇ* that Saul gave him a high rank in the army. This pleased all the people, and Saul's officers as well.

⁶When the men were returning home after David had killed the Philistine, the women came out from all the towns of Israel to meet King Saul with singing and dancing, with joyful songs and with tambourines and lutes. ⁷As they danced, they sang:

"Saul has slain his thousands,
    and David his tens of thousands."

⁸Saul was very angry; this refrain galled him. "They have credited David with tens

---

ᵃ52 Some Septuagint manuscripts; Hebrew *a valley*
ᵇ5 Or *wisely*

of thousands," he thought, "but me with only thousands. What more can he get but the kingdom?" 9And from that time on Saul kept a jealous eye on David.

10The next day an evil[a] spirit from God came forcefully upon Saul. He was prophesying in his house, while David was playing the harp, as he usually did. Saul had a spear in his hand 11and he hurled it, saying to himself, "I'll pin David to the wall." But David eluded him twice.

12Saul was afraid of David, because the LORD was with David but had left Saul. 13So he sent David away from him and gave him command over a thousand men, and David led the troops in their campaigns. 14In everything he did he had great success,[b] because the LORD was with him. 15When Saul saw how successful[c] he was, he was afraid of him. 16But all Israel and Judah loved David, because he led them in their campaigns.

17Saul said to David, "Here is my older daughter Merab. I will give her to you in marriage; only serve me bravely and fight the battles of the LORD." For Saul said to himself, "I will not raise a hand against him. Let the Philistines do that!"

18But David said to Saul, "Who am I, and what is my family or my father's clan in Israel, that I should become the king's son-in-law?" 19So[d] when the time came for Merab, Saul's daughter, to be given to David, she was given in marriage to Adriel of Meholah.

20Now Saul's daughter Michal was in love with David, and when they told Saul about it, he was pleased. 21"I will give her to him," he thought, "so that she may be a snare to him and so that the hand of the Philistines may be against him." So Saul said to David, "Now you have a second opportunity to become my son-in-law."

22Then Saul ordered his attendants: "Speak to David privately and say, 'Look, the king is pleased with you, and his attendants all like you; now become his son-in-law.' "

23They repeated these words to David. But David said, "Do you think it is a small matter to become the king's son-in-law? I'm only a poor man and little known."

24When Saul's servants told him what David had said, 25Saul replied, "Say to David, 'The king wants no other price for the bride than a hundred Philistine foreskins, to take revenge on his enemies.' " Saul's plan was to have David fall by the hands of the Philistines.

a10 Or injurious   b14 Or he was very wise
c15 Or wise   d19 Or However,

Envy Alert

Wednesday

1 SAMUEL 18:8-9 With whom do you empathize in this passage—David or Saul? Be honest. Doesn't at least a small part of you understand Saul's jealousy? All of us have at one time or another been jealous of a sibling, a friend, a stranger—even our spouse. And what did it get you? Most likely it got you into trouble.

Jealousy and its cousin envy are downright lethal to a marriage. Why does a person "turn green" with envy? Perhaps jealously is the most sickening of all sins. Envy, unlike some of the seven deadly sins of gluttony, lust and pride, isn't even pleasurable. Envy is a tortuous, tormenting, even murderous emotion. Cain murdered Abel, remember, because Abel's sacrifice was more pleasing to the Lord. The Bible is filled with stories of envy: Jacob and Esau, Leah and Rachel, Joseph and his brothers. Envy feeds on itself and rots the bones. In *Paradise Lost*, Milton was right in identifying it as the devil's own emotion. Satan, seeing Adam and Eve in love in paradise, envies them and plots their fall. As we all know but can easily forget, jealousy and envy have no positive goal whatsoever.

As this passage makes clear, no matter who is envied and who does the envying, it is a destructive emotion that can hurt both parties. So to protect your marriage, steer clear of envy.

—*Les & Leslie*

Go to page 312 for your next devotional reading.

26When the attendants told David these things, he was pleased to become the king's son-in-law. So before the allotted time elapsed, 27David and his men went out and killed two hundred Philistines. He brought their foreskins and presented the full number to the king so that he might become the king's son-in-law. Then Saul gave him his daughter Michal in marriage.

28When Saul realized that the LORD was with David and that his daughter Michal loved David, 29Saul became still more afraid of him, and he remained his enemy the rest of his days.

30The Philistine commanders continued to go out to battle, and as often as they did, David met with more success*a* than the rest of Saul's officers, and his name became well known.

Saul Tries to Kill David

19 Saul told his son Jonathan and all the attendants to kill David. But Jonathan was very fond of David 2and warned him, "My father Saul is looking for a chance to kill you. Be on your guard tomorrow morning; go into hiding and stay there. 3I will go out and stand with my father in the field where you are. I'll speak to him about you and will tell you what I find out."

4Jonathan spoke well of David to Saul his father and said to him, "Let not the king do wrong to his servant David; he has not wronged you, and what he has done has benefited you greatly. 5He took his life in his hands when he killed the Philistine. The LORD won a great victory for all Israel, and you saw it and were glad. Why then would you do wrong to an innocent man like David by killing him for no reason?"

6Saul listened to Jonathan and took this oath: "As surely as the LORD lives, David will not be put to death."

7So Jonathan called David and told him the whole conversation. He brought him to Saul, and David was with Saul as before.

8Once more war broke out, and David went out and fought the Philistines. He struck them with such force that they fled before him.

9But an evil*b* spirit from the LORD

Just Between you & me

Envy Alert

Take a moment to answer each of these questions on your own. Then compare your answers to your spouse's.

Yes No Jealousy is sometimes good.

Yes No From time to time, am I jealous of others?

Yes No I have been jealous of my spouse.

Yes No Do I know of times when my spouse has been jealous?

Yes No I can point to ways in which I have worked at not being jealous.

came upon Saul as he was sitting in his house with his spear in his hand. While David was playing the harp, 10Saul tried to pin him to the wall with his spear, but David eluded him as Saul drove the spear into the wall. That night David made good his escape.

11Saul sent men to David's house to watch it and to kill him in the morning. But Michal, David's wife, warned him, "If you don't run for your life tonight, tomorrow you'll be killed." 12So Michal let David down through a window, and he fled and escaped. 13Then Michal took an idol*c* and laid it on the bed, covering it with a garment and putting some goats' hair at the head.

14When Saul sent the men to capture David, Michal said, "He is ill."

15Then Saul sent the men back to see David and told them, "Bring him up to me in his bed so that I may kill him." 16But when the men entered, there was the idol in the bed, and at the head was some goats' hair.

17Saul said to Michal, "Why did you deceive me like this and send my enemy away so that he escaped?"

Michal told him, "He said to me, 'Let me get away. Why should I kill you?'"

18When David had fled and made his

---

*a*30 Or *David acted more wisely*   *b*9 Or *injurious*
*c*13 Hebrew *teraphim*; also in verse 16

David and Michal

1 SAMUEL 18:20–30 The story of David and Michal is one of the most dramatic love stories in the Bible. The drama begins with this: "Now Saul's daughter Michal was in love with David…" Sadly, it ends with this: "She despised him in her heart."

COUPLES IN THE BIBLE

Too often today marriages start with love and commitment but tragically end with hurt, pain, hatred and bitterness. What causes a marriage to fail? What went wrong with the relationship between David and Michal? For starters, after their wedding, Michal continued to be influenced by her father King Saul, who hated David and tried to kill him. While she chose to protect David from Saul, her father still greatly influenced her. Michal ignored Genesis 2:24 and never truly "left" her family of origin to "cleave" to her spouse. Unfortunately, over 2000 years later, scheming in-laws and misplaced priorities still hurt many marriages.

Besides in-law problems, David and Michal came from radically different backgrounds. He was a shepherd boy and grew up near Bethlehem. She was a princess and grew up among royalty. Also, Michal was jealous of David's love for and devotion to God.

As we consider this couple, we quickly realize that love and passion are not enough to keep a marriage healthy and growing. In the end what started as love ended as hate. Michal, daughter of a king and wife of a king, became embittered. As you think about the example of David and Michal, you can help your own marriage by avoiding their mistakes.

escape, he went to Samuel at Ramah and told him all that Saul had done to him. Then he and Samuel went to Naioth and stayed there. ¹⁹Word came to Saul: "David is in Naioth at Ramah"; ²⁰so he sent men to capture him. But when they saw a group of prophets prophesying, with Samuel standing there as their leader, the Spirit of God came upon Saul's men and they also prophesied. ²¹Saul was told

about it, and he sent more men, and they prophesied too. Saul sent men a third time, and they also prophesied. ²²Finally, he himself left for Ramah and went to the great cistern at Secu. And he asked, "Where are Samuel and David?"

"Over in Naioth at Ramah," they said.

²³So Saul went to Naioth at Ramah. But the Spirit of God came even upon him, and he walked along prophesying until he came to Naioth. ²⁴He stripped off his robes and also prophesied in Samuel's presence. He lay that way all that day and night. This is why people say, "Is Saul also among the prophets?"

David and Jonathan

20 Then David fled from Naioth at Ramah and went to Jonathan and asked, "What have I done? What is my crime? How have I wronged your father, that he is trying to take my life?"

²"Never!" Jonathan replied. "You are not going to die! Look, my father doesn't do anything, great or small, without confiding in me. Why would he hide this from me? It's not so!"

³But David took an oath and said, "Your father knows very well that I have found favor in your eyes, and he has said to himself, 'Jonathan must not know this or he will be grieved.' Yet as surely as the LORD lives and as you live, there is only a step between me and death."

⁴Jonathan said to David, "Whatever you want me to do, I'll do for you."

⁵So David said, "Look, tomorrow is the New Moon festival, and I am supposed to dine with the king; but let me go and hide in the field until the evening of the day after tomorrow. ⁶If your father misses me at all, tell him, 'David earnestly asked my permission to hurry to Bethlehem, his hometown, because an annual sacrifice is being made there for his whole clan.' ⁷If he says, 'Very well,' then your servant is safe. But if he loses his temper, you can be sure that he is determined to harm me. ⁸As for you, show kindness to your servant, for you have brought him into a covenant with you before the LORD. If I am guilty, then kill me yourself! Why hand me over to your father?"

⁹"Never!" Jonathan said. "If I had the least inkling that my father was deter-

mined to harm you, wouldn't I tell you?"

¹⁰David asked, "Who will tell me if your father answers you harshly?"

¹¹"Come," Jonathan said, "let's go out into the field." So they went there together.

¹²Then Jonathan said to David: "By the LORD, the God of Israel, I will surely sound out my father by this time the day after tomorrow! If he is favorably disposed toward you, will I not send you word and let you know? ¹³But if my father is inclined to harm you, may the LORD deal with me, be it ever so severely, if I do not let you know and send you away safely. May the LORD be with you as he has been with my father. ¹⁴But show me unfailing kindness like that of the LORD as long as I live, so that I may not be killed, ¹⁵and do not ever cut off your kindness from my family—not even when the LORD has cut off every one of David's enemies from the face of the earth."

¹⁶So Jonathan made a covenant with the house of David, saying, "May the LORD call David's enemies to account." ¹⁷And Jonathan had David reaffirm his oath out of love for him, because he loved him as he loved himself.

¹⁸Then Jonathan said to David: "Tomorrow is the New Moon festival. You will be missed, because your seat will be empty. ¹⁹The day after tomorrow, toward evening, go to the place where you hid when this trouble began, and wait by the stone Ezel. ²⁰I will shoot three arrows to the side of it, as though I were shooting at a target. ²¹Then I will send a boy and say, 'Go, find the arrows.' If I say to him, 'Look, the arrows are on this side of you; bring them here,' then come, because, as surely as the LORD lives, you are safe; there is no danger. ²²But if I say to the boy, 'Look, the arrows are beyond you,' then you must go, because the LORD has sent you away. ²³And about the matter you and I discussed—remember, the LORD is witness between you and me forever."

²⁴So David hid in the field, and when the New Moon festival came, the king sat down to eat. ²⁵He sat in his customary place by the wall, opposite Jonathan,ᵃ and Abner sat next to Saul, but David's place was empty. ²⁶Saul said nothing that day, for he thought, "Something must have happened to David to make him ceremonially unclean—surely he is unclean."

²⁷But the next day, the second day of the month, David's place was empty again. Then Saul said to his son Jonathan, "Why hasn't the son of Jesse come to the meal, either yesterday or today?"

²⁸Jonathan answered, "David earnestly asked me for permission to go to Bethlehem. ²⁹He said, 'Let me go, because our family is observing a sacrifice in the town and my brother has ordered me to be there. If I have found favor in your eyes, let me get away to see my brothers.' That is why he has not come to the king's table."

³⁰Saul's anger flared up at Jonathan and he said to him, "You son of a perverse and rebellious woman! Don't I know that you have sided with the son of Jesse to your own shame and to the shame of the mother who bore you? ³¹As long as the son of Jesse lives on this earth, neither you nor your kingdom will be established. Now send and bring him to me, for he must die!"

³²"Why should he be put to death? What has he done?" Jonathan asked his father. ³³But Saul hurled his spear at him to kill him. Then Jonathan knew that his father intended to kill David.

³⁴Jonathan got up from the table in fierce anger; on that second day of the month he did not eat, because he was grieved at his father's shameful treatment of David.

³⁵In the morning Jonathan went out to the field for his meeting with David. He had a small boy with him, ³⁶and he said to the boy, "Run and find the arrows I shoot." As the boy ran, he shot an arrow beyond him. ³⁷When the boy came to the place where Jonathan's arrow had fallen, Jonathan called out after him, "Isn't the arrow beyond you?" ³⁸Then he shouted, "Hurry! Go quickly! Don't stop!" The boy picked up the arrow and returned to his master. ³⁹(The boy knew nothing of all this; only Jonathan and David knew.) ⁴⁰Then Jonathan gave his weapons to the boy and said, "Go, carry them back to town."

⁴¹After the boy had gone, David got up from the south side ⌊of the stone⌋ and bowed down before Jonathan three times, with his face to the ground. Then

ᵃ25 Septuagint; Hebrew *wall. Jonathan arose*

they kissed each other and wept together—but David wept the most.

42 Jonathan said to David, "Go in peace, for we have sworn friendship with each other in the name of the LORD, saying, 'The LORD is witness between you and me, and between your descendants and my descendants forever.'" Then David left, and Jonathan went back to the town.

David at Nob

21 David went to Nob, to Ahimelech the priest. Ahimelech trembled when he met him, and asked, "Why are you alone? Why is no one with you?"

2 David answered Ahimelech the priest, "The king charged me with a certain matter and said to me, 'No one is to know anything about your mission and your instructions.' As for my men, I have told them to meet me at a certain place. 3 Now then, what do you have on hand? Give me five loaves of bread, or whatever you can find."

4 But the priest answered David, "I don't have any ordinary bread on hand; however, there is some consecrated bread here—provided the men have kept themselves from women."

5 David replied, "Indeed women have been kept from us, as usual whenever[a] I set out. The men's things[b] are holy even on missions that are not holy. How much more so today!" 6 So the priest gave him the consecrated bread, since there was no bread there except the bread of the Presence that had been removed from before the LORD and replaced by hot bread on the day it was taken away.

7 Now one of Saul's servants was there that day, detained before the LORD; he was Doeg the Edomite, Saul's head shepherd.

8 David asked Ahimelech, "Don't you have a spear or a sword here? I haven't brought my sword or any other weapon, because the king's business was urgent."

9 The priest replied, "The sword of Goliath the Philistine, whom you killed in the Valley of Elah, is here; it is wrapped in a cloth behind the ephod. If you want it, take it; there is no sword here but that one."

David said, "There is none like it; give it to me."

David at Gath

10 That day David fled from Saul and went to Achish king of Gath. 11 But the servants of Achish said to him, "Isn't this David, the king of the land? Isn't he the one they sing about in their dances:

" 'Saul has slain his thousands,
    and David his tens of thousands'?"

12 David took these words to heart and was very much afraid of Achish king of Gath. 13 So he pretended to be insane in their presence; and while he was in their hands he acted like a madman, making marks on the doors of the gate and letting saliva run down his beard.

14 Achish said to his servants, "Look at the man! He is insane! Why bring him to me? 15 Am I so short of madmen that you have to bring this fellow here to carry on like this in front of me? Must this man come into my house?"

David at Adullam and Mizpah

22 David left Gath and escaped to the cave of Adullam. When his brothers and his father's household heard about it, they went down to him there. 2 All those who were in distress or in debt or discontented gathered around him, and he became their leader. About four hundred men were with him.

3 From there David went to Mizpah in Moab and said to the king of Moab, "Would you let my father and mother come and stay with you until I learn what God will do for me?" 4 So he left them with the king of Moab, and they stayed with him as long as David was in the stronghold.

5 But the prophet Gad said to David, "Do not stay in the stronghold. Go into the land of Judah." So David left and went to the forest of Hereth.

Saul Kills the Priests of Nob

6 Now Saul heard that David and his men had been discovered. And Saul, spear in hand, was seated under the tamarisk tree on the hill at Gibeah, with all his officials standing around him. 7 Saul said to them, "Listen, men of Benjamin! Will

---

a 5 Or *from us in the past few days since*   b 5 Or *bodies* the son of Jesse give all of you fields and vineyards? Will he make all of you commanders of thousands and commanders of hundreds? ⁸Is that why you have all conspired against me? No one tells me when my son makes a covenant with the son of Jesse. None of you is concerned about me or tells me that my son has incited my servant to lie in wait for me, as he does today."

⁹But Doeg the Edomite, who was standing with Saul's officials, said, "I saw the son of Jesse come to Ahimelech son of Ahitub at Nob. ¹⁰Ahimelech inquired of the LORD for him; he also gave him provisions and the sword of Goliath the Philistine."

¹¹Then the king sent for the priest Ahimelech son of Ahitub and his father's whole family, who were the priests at Nob, and they all came to the king. ¹²Saul said, "Listen now, son of Ahitub."

"Yes, my lord," he answered.

¹³Saul said to him, "Why have you conspired against me, you and the son of Jesse, giving him bread and a sword and inquiring of God for him, so that he has rebelled against me and lies in wait for me, as he does today?"

¹⁴Ahimelech answered the king, "Who of all your servants is as loyal as David, the king's son-in-law, captain of your bodyguard and highly respected in your household? ¹⁵Was that day the first time I inquired of God for him? Of course not! Let not the king accuse your servant or any of his father's family, for your servant knows nothing at all about this whole affair."

¹⁶But the king said, "You will surely die, Ahimelech, you and your father's whole family."

¹⁷Then the king ordered the guards at his side: "Turn and kill the priests of the LORD, because they too have sided with David. They knew he was fleeing, yet they did not tell me."

But the king's officials were not willing to raise a hand to strike the priests of the LORD.

¹⁸The king then ordered Doeg, "You turn and strike down the priests." So Doeg the Edomite turned and struck them down. That day he killed eighty-five men who wore the linen ephod. ¹⁹He also put to the sword Nob, the town of the priests,

with its men and women, its children and infants, and its cattle, donkeys and sheep.

²⁰But Abiathar, a son of Ahimelech son of Ahitub, escaped and fled to join David. ²¹He told David that Saul had killed the priests of the LORD. ²²Then David said to Abiathar: "That day, when Doeg the Edomite was there, I knew he would be sure to tell Saul. I am responsible for the death of your father's whole family. ²³Stay with me; don't be afraid; the man who is seeking your life is seeking mine also. You will be safe with me."

David Saves Keilah

23 When David was told, "Look, the Philistines are fighting against Keilah and are looting the threshing floors," ²he inquired of the LORD, saying, "Shall I go and attack these Philistines?"

The LORD answered him, "Go, attack the Philistines and save Keilah."

³But David's men said to him, "Here in Judah we are afraid. How much more, then, if we go to Keilah against the Philistine forces!"

⁴Once again David inquired of the LORD, and the LORD answered him, "Go down to Keilah, for I am going to give the Philistines into your hand." ⁵So David and his men went to Keilah, fought the Philistines and carried off their livestock. He inflicted heavy losses on the Philistines and saved the people of Keilah. ⁶(Now Abiathar son of Ahimelech had brought the ephod down with him when he fled to David at Keilah.)

Saul Pursues David

⁷Saul was told that David had gone to Keilah, and he said, "God has handed him over to me, for David has imprisoned himself by entering a town with gates and bars." ⁸And Saul called up all his forces for battle, to go down to Keilah to besiege David and his men.

⁹When David learned that Saul was plotting against him, he said to Abiathar the priest, "Bring the ephod." ¹⁰David said, "O LORD, God of Israel, your servant has heard definitely that Saul plans to come to Keilah and destroy the town on account of me. ¹¹Will the citizens of Keilah surrender me to him? Will Saul come down, as your servant has heard?

O LORD, God of Israel, tell your servant."
And the LORD said, "He will."

¹²Again David asked, "Will the citizens of Keilah surrender me and my men to Saul?"

And the LORD said, "They will."

¹³So David and his men, about six hundred in number, left Keilah and kept moving from place to place. When Saul was told that David had escaped from Keilah, he did not go there.

¹⁴David stayed in the desert strongholds and in the hills of the Desert of Ziph. Day after day Saul searched for him, but God did not give David into his hands.

¹⁵While David was at Horesh in the Desert of Ziph, he learned that Saul had come out to take his life. ¹⁶And Saul's son Jonathan went to David at Horesh and helped him find strength in God. ¹⁷"Don't be afraid," he said. "My father Saul will not lay a hand on you. You will be king over Israel, and I will be second to you. Even my father Saul knows this." ¹⁸The two of them made a covenant before the LORD. Then Jonathan went home, but David remained at Horesh.

¹⁹The Ziphites went up to Saul at Gibeah and said, "Is not David hiding among us in the strongholds at Horesh, on the hill of Hakilah, south of Jeshimon? ²⁰Now, O king, come down whenever it pleases you to do so, and we will be responsible for handing him over to the king."

²¹Saul replied, "The LORD bless you for your concern for me. ²²Go and make further preparation. Find out where David usually goes and who has seen him there. They tell me he is very crafty. ²³Find out about all the hiding places he uses and come back to me with definite information.ᵃ Then I will go with you; if he is in the area, I will track him down among all the clans of Judah."

²⁴So they set out and went to Ziph ahead of Saul. Now David and his men were in the Desert of Maon, in the Arabah south of Jeshimon. ²⁵Saul and his men began the search, and when David was told about it, he went down to the rock and stayed in the Desert of Maon. When Saul heard this, he went into the Desert of Maon in pursuit of David.

²⁶Saul was going along one side of the mountain, and David and his men were on the other side, hurrying to get away from Saul. As Saul and his forces were closing in on David and his men to capture them, ²⁷a messenger came to Saul, saying, "Come quickly! The Philistines are raiding the land." ²⁸Then Saul broke off his pursuit of David and went to meet the Philistines. That is why they call this place Sela Hammahlekoth.ᵇ ²⁹And David went up from there and lived in the strongholds of En Gedi.

David Spares Saul's Life

24 After Saul returned from pursuing the Philistines, he was told, "David is in the Desert of En Gedi." ²So Saul took three thousand chosen men from all Israel and set out to look for David and his men near the Crags of the Wild Goats.

³He came to the sheep pens along the way; a cave was there, and Saul went in to relieve himself. David and his men were far back in the cave. ⁴The men said, "This is the day the LORD spoke of when he saidᶜ to you, 'I will give your enemy into your hands for you to deal with as you wish.' " Then David crept up unnoticed and cut off a corner of Saul's robe.

⁵Afterward, David was conscience-stricken for having cut off a corner of his robe. ⁶He said to his men, "The LORD forbid that I should do such a thing to my master, the LORD's anointed, or lift my hand against him; for he is the anointed of the LORD." ⁷With these words David rebuked his men and did not allow them to attack Saul. And Saul left the cave and went his way.

⁸Then David went out of the cave and called out to Saul, "My lord the king!" When Saul looked behind him, David bowed down and prostrated himself with his face to the ground. ⁹He said to Saul, "Why do you listen when men say, 'David is bent on harming you'? ¹⁰This day you have seen with your own eyes how the LORD delivered you into my hands in the cave. Some urged me to kill you, but I spared you; I said, 'I will not lift my hand against my master, because he is the LORD's anointed.' ¹¹See, my father, look at

---

ᵃ23 Or me at Nacon means *rock of parting.*   ᵇ28 *Sela Hammahlekoth*   ᶜ4 Or *"Today the LORD is saying* this piece of your robe in my hand! I cut off the corner of your robe but did not kill you. Now understand and recognize that I am not guilty of wrongdoing or rebellion. I have not wronged you, but you are hunting me down to take my life. ¹²May the LORD judge between you and me. And may the LORD avenge the wrongs you have done to me, but my hand will not touch you. ¹³As the old saying goes, 'From evildoers come evil deeds,' so my hand will not touch you.

¹⁴"Against whom has the king of Israel come out? Whom are you pursuing? A dead dog? A flea? ¹⁵May the LORD be our judge and decide between us. May he consider my cause and uphold it; may he vindicate me by delivering me from your hand."

¹⁶When David finished saying this, Saul asked, "Is that your voice, David my son?" And he wept aloud. ¹⁷"You are more righteous than I," he said. "You have treated me well, but I have treated you badly. ¹⁸You have just now told me of the good you did to me; the LORD delivered me into your hands, but you did not kill me. ¹⁹When a man finds his enemy, does he let him get away unharmed? May the LORD reward you well for the way you treated me today. ²⁰I know that you will surely be king and that the kingdom of Israel will be established in your hands. ²¹Now swear to me by the LORD that you will not cut off my descendants or wipe out my name from my father's family."

²²So David gave his oath to Saul. Then Saul returned home, but David and his men went up to the stronghold.

David, Nabal and Abigail

25 Now Samuel died, and all Israel assembled and mourned for him; and they buried him at his home in Ramah.

Then David moved down into the Desert of Maon.ᵃ ²A certain man in Maon, who had property there at Carmel, was very wealthy. He had a thousand goats and three thousand sheep, which he was shearing in Carmel. ³His name was Nabal and his wife's name was Abigail. She was an intelligent and beautiful woman, but her husband, a Calebite, was surly and mean in his dealings.

⁴While David was in the desert, he heard that Nabal was shearing sheep. ⁵So he sent ten young men and said to them, "Go up to Nabal at Carmel and greet him in my name. ⁶Say to him: 'Long life to you! Good health to you and your household! And good health to all that is yours!

⁷" 'Now I hear that it is sheep-shearing time. When your shepherds were with us, we did not mistreat them, and the whole time they were at Carmel nothing of theirs was missing. ⁸Ask your own servants and they will tell you. Therefore be favorable toward my young men, since we come at a festive time. Please give your servants and your son David whatever you can find for them.' "

⁹When David's men arrived, they gave Nabal this message in David's name. Then they waited.

¹⁰Nabal answered David's servants, "Who is this David? Who is this son of Jesse? Many servants are breaking away from their masters these days. ¹¹Why should I take my bread and water, and the meat I have slaughtered for my shearers, and give it to men coming from who knows where?"

¹²David's men turned around and went back. When they arrived, they reported every word. ¹³David said to his men, "Put on your swords!" So they put on their swords, and David put on his. About four hundred men went up with David, while two hundred stayed with the supplies.

¹⁴One of the servants told Nabal's wife Abigail: "David sent messengers from the desert to give our master his greetings, but he hurled insults at them. ¹⁵Yet these men were very good to us. They did not mistreat us, and the whole time we were out in the fields near them nothing was missing. ¹⁶Night and day they were a wall around us all the time we were herding our sheep near them. ¹⁷Now think it over and see what you can do, because disaster is hanging over our master and his whole household. He is such a wicked man that no one can talk to him."

¹⁸Abigail lost no time. She took two hundred loaves of bread, two skins of

---

ᵃ1 Some Septuagint manuscripts; Hebrew *Paran*

wine, five dressed sheep, five seahs[a] of roasted grain, a hundred cakes of raisins and two hundred cakes of pressed figs, and loaded them on donkeys. [19]Then she told her servants, "Go on ahead; I'll follow you." But she did not tell her husband Nabal.

[20]As she came riding her donkey into a mountain ravine, there were David and his men descending toward her, and she met them. [21]David had just said, "It's been useless—all my watching over this fellow's property in the desert so that nothing of his was missing. He has paid me back evil for good. [22]May God deal with David,[b] be it ever so severely, if by morning I leave alive one male of all who belong to him!"

[23]When Abigail saw David, she quickly got off her donkey and bowed down before David with her face to the ground. [24]She fell at his feet and said: "My lord, let the blame be on me alone. Please let your servant speak to you; hear what your servant has to say. [25]May my lord pay no attention to that wicked man Nabal. He is just like his name—his name is Fool, and folly goes with him. But as for me, your servant, I did not see the men my master sent.

[26]"Now since the LORD has kept you, my master, from bloodshed and from avenging yourself with your own hands, as surely as the LORD lives and as you live, may your enemies and all who intend to harm my master be like Nabal. [27]And let this gift, which your servant has brought to my master, be given to the men who follow you. [28]Please forgive your servant's offense, for the LORD will certainly make a lasting dynasty for my master, because he fights the LORD's battles. Let no wrongdoing be found in you as long as you live. [29]Even though someone is pursuing you to take your life, the life of my master will be bound securely in the bundle of the living by the LORD your God. But the lives of your enemies he will hurl away as from the pocket of a sling. [30]When the LORD has done for my master every good thing he promised concerning him and has appointed him leader over Israel, [31]my master will not have on his conscience the staggering burden of needless bloodshed or of having avenged himself. And when

the LORD has brought my master success, remember your servant."

[32]David said to Abigail, "Praise be to the LORD, the God of Israel, who has sent you today to meet me. [33]May you be blessed for your good judgment and for keeping me from bloodshed this day and from avenging myself with my own hands. [34]Otherwise, as surely as the LORD, the God of Israel, lives, who has kept me from harming you, if you had not come quickly to meet me, not one male belonging to Nabal would have been left alive by daybreak."

[35]Then David accepted from her hand what she had brought him and said, "Go home in peace. I have heard your words and granted your request."

[36]When Abigail went to Nabal, he was in the house holding a banquet like that of a king. He was in high spirits and very drunk. So she told him nothing until daybreak. [37]Then in the morning, when Nabal was sober, his wife told him all these things, and his heart failed him and he became like a stone. [38]About ten days later, the LORD struck Nabal and he died.

[39]When David heard that Nabal was dead, he said, "Praise be to the LORD, who has upheld my cause against Nabal for treating me with contempt. He has kept his servant from doing wrong and has brought Nabal's wrongdoing down on his own head."

Then David sent word to Abigail, asking her to become his wife. [40]His servants went to Carmel and said to Abigail, "David has sent us to you to take you to become his wife."

[41]She bowed down with her face to the ground and said, "Here is your maidservant, ready to serve you and wash the feet of my master's servants." [42]Abigail quickly got on a donkey and, attended by her five maids, went with David's messengers and became his wife. [43]David had also married Ahinoam of Jezreel, and they both were his wives. [44]But Saul had given his daughter Michal, David's wife, to Paltiel[c] son of Laish, who was from Gallim.

[a]18 That is, probably about a bushel (about 37 liters)　　[b]22 Some Septuagint manuscripts; Hebrew *with David's enemies*　　[c]44 Hebrew *Palti*, a variant of *Paltiel*

David Again Spares Saul's Life

26 The Ziphites went to Saul at Gibeah and said, "Is not David hiding on the hill of Hakilah, which faces Jeshimon?"

²So Saul went down to the Desert of Ziph, with his three thousand chosen men of Israel, to search there for David. ³Saul made his camp beside the road on the hill of Hakilah facing Jeshimon, but David stayed in the desert. When he saw that Saul had followed him there, ⁴he sent out scouts and learned that Saul had definitely arrived. *a*

⁵Then David set out and went to the place where Saul had camped. He saw where Saul and Abner son of Ner, the commander of the army, had lain down. Saul was lying inside the camp, with the army encamped around him.

⁶David then asked Ahimelech the Hittite and Abishai son of Zeruiah, Joab's brother, "Who will go down into the camp with me to Saul?"

"I'll go with you," said Abishai.

⁷So David and Abishai went to the army by night, and there was Saul, lying asleep inside the camp with his spear stuck in the ground near his head. Abner and the soldiers were lying around him.

⁸Abishai said to David, "Today God has delivered your enemy into your hands. Now let me pin him to the ground with one thrust of my spear; I won't strike him twice."

⁹But David said to Abishai, "Don't destroy him! Who can lay a hand on the LORD's anointed and be guiltless? ¹⁰As surely as the LORD lives," he said, "the LORD himself will strike him; either his time will come and he will die, or he will go into battle and perish. ¹¹But the LORD forbid that I should lay a hand on the LORD's anointed. Now get the spear and water jug that are near his head, and let's go."

¹²So David took the spear and water jug near Saul's head, and they left. No one saw or knew about it, nor did anyone wake up. They were all sleeping, because the LORD had put them into a deep sleep.

¹³Then David crossed over to the other side and stood on top of the hill some distance away; there was a wide space between them. ¹⁴He called out to the army

Nabal and Abigail

1 SAMUEL 25 Every marriage is not always a good match. Certainly Nabal and Abigail seemed totally mismatched. Though Nabal was a wealthy man, he was surly and mean in his dealings. Abigail was just the opposite. She was intelligent and beautiful and cared deeply for the welfare of others. We don't know how they got together in the first place, but we do know about the dedication and energy that Abigail invested in their dysfunctional marriage. She seemed to do all the giving and Nabal seemed to do all the taking. But Abigail trusted God to protect her, meet her needs and help her through difficult situations. God showed himself strong in her behalf.

For instance, David had sent several men to Nabal asking for supplies, but Nabal was rude and refused to help. Abigail intervened and prevented a disastrous confrontation. She took the initiative and provided for David and his men. And she went the extra mile by taking responsibility for her husband's unkind actions. David accepted her gifts and thanked her for preventing bloodshed. And where was her husband? Home drunk. What a terrible situation! Ten days later God struck Nabal and he died. Later Abigail married David. From Abigail we can learn that, when faced with a difficult situation, we can trust God to lead us and care for us.

and to Abner son of Ner, "Aren't you going to answer me, Abner?"

Abner replied, "Who are you who calls to the king?"

¹⁵David said, "You're a man, aren't you? And who is like you in Israel? Why didn't you guard your lord the king? Someone came to destroy your lord the king. ¹⁶What you have done is not good. As surely as the LORD lives, you and your men deserve to die, because you did not guard your master, the LORD's anointed. Look around you. Where are the king's

---

a4 Or had come to Nacon

spear and water jug that were near his head?"

[17]Saul recognized David's voice and said, "Is that your voice, David my son?"

David replied, "Yes it is, my lord the king." [18]And he added, "Why is my lord pursuing his servant? What have I done, and what wrong am I guilty of? [19]Now let my lord the king listen to his servant's words. If the LORD has incited you against me, then may he accept an offering. If, however, men have done it, may they be cursed before the LORD! They have now driven me from my share in the LORD's inheritance and have said, 'Go, serve other gods.' [20]Now do not let my blood fall to the ground far from the presence of the LORD. The king of Israel has come out to look for a flea—as one hunts a partridge in the mountains."

[21]Then Saul said, "I have sinned. Come back, David my son. Because you considered my life precious today, I will not try to harm you again. Surely I have acted like a fool and have erred greatly."

[22]"Here is the king's spear," David answered. "Let one of your young men come over and get it. [23]The LORD rewards every man for his righteousness and faithfulness. The LORD delivered you into my hands today, but I would not lay a hand on the LORD's anointed. [24]As surely as I valued your life today, so may the LORD value my life and deliver me from all trouble."

[25]Then Saul said to David, "May you be blessed, my son David; you will do great things and surely triumph."

So David went on his way, and Saul returned home.

David Among the Philistines

27 But David thought to himself, "One of these days I will be destroyed by the hand of Saul. The best thing I can do is to escape to the land of the Philistines. Then Saul will give up searching for me anywhere in Israel, and I will slip out of his hand."

[2]So David and the six hundred men with him left and went over to Achish son of Maoch king of Gath. [3]David and his men settled in Gath with Achish. Each man had his family with him, and David had his two wives: Ahinoam of Jezreel

and Abigail of Carmel, the widow of Nabal. [4]When Saul was told that David had fled to Gath, he no longer searched for him.

[5]Then David said to Achish, "If I have found favor in your eyes, let a place be assigned to me in one of the country towns, that I may live there. Why should your servant live in the royal city with you?"

[6]So on that day Achish gave him Ziklag, and it has belonged to the kings of Judah ever since. [7]David lived in Philistine territory a year and four months.

[8]Now David and his men went up and raided the Geshurites, the Girzites and the Amalekites. (From ancient times these peoples had lived in the land extending to Shur and Egypt.) [9]Whenever David attacked an area, he did not leave a man or woman alive, but took sheep and cattle, donkeys and camels, and clothes. Then he returned to Achish.

[10]When Achish asked, "Where did you go raiding today?" David would say, "Against the Negev of Judah" or "Against the Negev of Jerahmeel" or "Against the Negev of the Kenites." [11]He did not leave a man or woman alive to be brought to Gath, for he thought, "They might inform on us and say, 'This is what David did.' " And such was his practice as long as he lived in Philistine territory. [12]Achish trusted David and said to himself, "He has become so odious to his people, the Israelites, that he will be my servant forever."

Saul and the Witch of Endor

28 In those days the Philistines gathered their forces to fight against Israel. Achish said to David, "You must understand that you and your men will accompany me in the army."

[2]David said, "Then you will see for yourself what your servant can do."

Achish replied, "Very well, I will make you my bodyguard for life."

[3]Now Samuel was dead, and all Israel had mourned for him and buried him in his own town of Ramah. Saul had expelled the mediums and spiritists from the land.

[4]The Philistines assembled and came and set up camp at Shunem, while Saul gathered all the Israelites and set up camp

at Gilboa. [5]When Saul saw the Philistine army, he was afraid; terror filled his heart. [6]He inquired of the LORD, but the LORD did not answer him by dreams or Urim or prophets. [7]Saul then said to his attendants, "Find me a woman who is a medium, so I may go and inquire of her."

"There is one in Endor," they said.

[8]So Saul disguised himself, putting on other clothes, and at night he and two men went to the woman. "Consult a spirit for me," he said, "and bring up for me the one I name."

[9]But the woman said to him, "Surely you know what Saul has done. He has cut off the mediums and spiritists from the land. Why have you set a trap for my life to bring about my death?"

[10]Saul swore to her by the LORD, "As surely as the LORD lives, you will not be punished for this."

[11]Then the woman asked, "Whom shall I bring up for you?"

"Bring up Samuel," he said.

[12]When the woman saw Samuel, she cried out at the top of her voice and said to Saul, "Why have you deceived me? You are Saul!"

[13]The king said to her, "Don't be afraid. What do you see?"

The woman said, "I see a spirit[a] coming up out of the ground."

[14]"What does he look like?" he asked.

"An old man wearing a robe is coming up," she said.

Then Saul knew it was Samuel, and he bowed down and prostrated himself with his face to the ground.

[15]Samuel said to Saul, "Why have you disturbed me by bringing me up?"

"I am in great distress," Saul said. "The Philistines are fighting against me, and God has turned away from me. He no longer answers me, either by prophets or by dreams. So I have called on you to tell me what to do."

[16]Samuel said, "Why do you consult me, now that the LORD has turned away from you and become your enemy? [17]The LORD has done what he predicted through me. The LORD has torn the kingdom out of your hands and given it to one of your neighbors—to David. [18]Because you did not obey the LORD or carry out his fierce wrath against the Amalekites, the LORD has done this to you today. [19]The LORD will hand over both Israel and you to the Philistines, and tomorrow you and your sons will be with me. The LORD will also hand over the army of Israel to the Philistines."

[20]Immediately Saul fell full length on the ground, filled with fear because of Samuel's words. His strength was gone, for he had eaten nothing all that day and night.

[21]When the woman came to Saul and saw that he was greatly shaken, she said, "Look, your maidservant has obeyed you. I took my life in my hands and did what you told me to do. [22]Now please listen to your servant and let me give you some food so you may eat and have the strength to go on your way."

[23]He refused and said, "I will not eat."

But his men joined the woman in urging him, and he listened to them. He got up from the ground and sat on the couch.

[24]The woman had a fattened calf at the house, which she butchered at once. She took some flour, kneaded it and baked bread without yeast. [25]Then she set it before Saul and his men, and they ate. That same night they got up and left.

Achish Sends David Back to Ziklag

29 The Philistines gathered all their forces at Aphek, and Israel camped by the spring in Jezreel. [2]As the Philistine rulers marched with their units of hundreds and thousands, David and his men were marching at the rear with Achish. [3]The commanders of the Philistines asked, "What about these Hebrews?"

Achish replied, "Is this not David, who was an officer of Saul king of Israel? He has already been with me for over a year, and from the day he left Saul until now, I have found no fault in him."

[4]But the Philistine commanders were angry with him and said, "Send the man back, that he may return to the place you assigned him. He must not go with us into battle, or he will turn against us during the fighting. How better could he regain his master's favor than by taking the

a13 Or see spirits; or see gods

heads of our own men? [5]Isn't this the David they sang about in their dances:

" 'Saul has slain his thousands,
    and David his tens of thousands'?"

[6]So Achish called David and said to him, "As surely as the LORD lives, you have been reliable, and I would be pleased to have you serve with me in the army. From the day you came to me until now, I have found no fault in you, but the rulers don't approve of you. [7]Turn back and go in peace; do nothing to displease the Philistine rulers."

[8]"But what have I done?" asked David. "What have you found against your servant from the day I came to you until now? Why can't I go and fight against the enemies of my lord the king?"

[9]Achish answered, "I know that you have been as pleasing in my eyes as an angel of God; nevertheless, the Philistine commanders have said, 'He must not go up with us into battle.' [10]Now get up early, along with your master's servants who have come with you, and leave in the morning as soon as it is light."

[11]So David and his men got up early in the morning to go back to the land of the Philistines, and the Philistines went up to Jezreel.

David Destroys the Amalekites

30 David and his men reached Ziklag on the third day. Now the Amalekites had raided the Negev and Ziklag. They had attacked Ziklag and burned it, [2]and had taken captive the women and all who were in it, both young and old. They killed none of them, but carried them off as they went on their way.

[3]When David and his men came to Ziklag, they found it destroyed by fire and their wives and sons and daughters taken captive. [4]So David and his men wept aloud until they had no strength left to weep. [5]David's two wives had been captured—Ahinoam of Jezreel and Abigail, the widow of Nabal of Carmel. [6]David was greatly distressed because the men were talking of stoning him; each one was bitter in spirit because of his sons and daughters. But David found strength in the LORD his God.

[7]Then David said to Abiathar the

Teamwork

Thursday

1 SAMUEL 30   From reading 1 Samuel, we know that David was a great leader and valiant warrior, but he wasn't a solo army. As he faced the Amalekites, his army was 600 strong, but only 400 were sent into battle. The other 200 were exhausted, so they stayed behind with the baggage. After winning the battle, David's 400 warriors did not want to share the spoils with the other 200, but he insisted that the spoils went equally to all.

Marriage is like an army of two. Sometimes in our marriages, one spouse may be more up front than the other, but both need to share equally. The spouse who works to put the other through medical school, or the one who stays home to nurture and love the children, shares equally in the spoils. From time to time roles may switch, but one spouse is never more important than the other. When both esteem and value the other, they live out their commitment to each other. They are truly one in Christ.

When our children were young, Claudia was the primary care giver. Over the years we moved wherever I needed to be professionally. Imagine Claudia's surprise when one day as we were walking, I said, "For the first thirty years of our marriage we have lived where it was best for me. For the next thirty years, I think we should live wherever it is best for you." This was the catalyst for many conversations and for exploring various options. In the end the decision to remain in Knoxville was best for both of us—but it was Claudia's choice.

Over the years roles may change, but in a healthy marriage both the husband and wife invest their talents and energy for the benefit of their partnership.

—Dave & Claudia

Go to page 322 for your next devotional reading.

COUPLE MINUTES

priest, the son of Ahimelech, "Bring me the ephod." Abiathar brought it to him, [8]and David inquired of the LORD, "Shall I pursue this raiding party? Will I overtake them?"

"Pursue them," he answered. "You will certainly overtake them and succeed in the rescue."

[9]David and the six hundred men with him came to the Besor Ravine, where some stayed behind, [10]for two hundred men were too exhausted to cross the ravine. But David and four hundred men continued the pursuit.

[11]They found an Egyptian in a field and brought him to David. They gave him water to drink and food to eat— [12]part of a cake of pressed figs and two cakes of raisins. He ate and was revived, for he had not eaten any food or drunk any water for three days and three nights.

[13]David asked him, "To whom do you belong, and where do you come from?"

He said, "I am an Egyptian, the slave of an Amalekite. My master abandoned me when I became ill three days ago. [14]We raided the Negev of the Kerethites and the territory belonging to Judah and the Negev of Caleb. And we burned Ziklag."

[15]David asked him, "Can you lead me down to this raiding party?"

He answered, "Swear to me before God that you will not kill me or hand me over to my master, and I will take you down to them."

[16]He led David down, and there they were, scattered over the countryside, eating, drinking and reveling because of the great amount of plunder they had taken from the land of the Philistines and from Judah. [17]David fought them from dusk until the evening of the next day, and none of them got away, except four hundred young men who rode off on camels and fled. [18]David recovered everything the Amalekites had taken, including his two wives. [19]Nothing was missing: young or old, boy or girl, plunder or anything else they had taken. David brought everything back. [20]He took all the flocks and herds, and his men drove them ahead of the other livestock, saying, "This is David's plunder."

[21]Then David came to the two hundred men who had been too exhausted to follow him and who were left behind at the Besor Ravine. They came out to meet David and the people with him. As David and his men approached, he greeted them. [22]But all the evil men and troublemakers among David's followers said, "Because they did not go out with us, we will not share with them the plunder we recovered. However, each man may take his wife and children and go."

[23]David replied, "No, my brothers, you must not do that with what the LORD has given us. He has protected us and handed over to us the forces that came against us. [24]Who will listen to what you say? The share of the man who stayed with the supplies is to be the same as that of him who went down to the battle. All will share alike." [25]David made this a statute and ordinance for Israel from that day to this.

[26]When David arrived in Ziklag, he sent some of the plunder to the elders of Judah, who were his friends, saying, "Here is a present for you from the plunder of the LORD's enemies."

[27]He sent it to those who were in Bethel, Ramoth Negev and Jattir; [28]to those in Aroer, Siphmoth, Eshtemoa [29]and Racal; to those in the towns of the Jerahmeelites and the Kenites; [30]to those in Hormah, Bor Ashan, Athach [31]and Hebron; and to those in all the other places where David and his men had roamed.

Saul Takes His Life

31 Now the Philistines fought against Israel; the Israelites fled before them, and many fell slain on Mount Gilboa. [2]The Philistines pressed hard after Saul and his sons, and they killed his sons Jonathan, Abinadab and Malki-Shua. [3]The fighting grew fierce around Saul, and when the archers overtook him, they wounded him critically.

[4]Saul said to his armor-bearer, "Draw your sword and run me through, or these uncircumcised fellows will come and run me through and abuse me."

But his armor-bearer was terrified and would not do it; so Saul took his own sword and fell on it. [5]When the armor-bearer saw that Saul was dead, he too fell on his sword and died with him. [6]So Saul and his three sons and his armor-bearer and all his men died together that same day.

⁷When the Israelites along the valley and those across the Jordan saw that the Israelite army had fled and that Saul and his sons had died, they abandoned their towns and fled. And the Philistines came and occupied them.

⁸The next day, when the Philistines came to strip the dead, they found Saul and his three sons fallen on Mount Gilboa. ⁹They cut off his head and stripped off his armor, and they sent messengers throughout the land of the Philistines to proclaim the news in the temple of their idols and among their people. ¹⁰They put his armor in the temple of the Ashtoreths and fastened his body to the wall of Beth Shan.

¹¹When the people of Jabesh Gilead heard of what the Philistines had done to Saul, ¹²all their valiant men journeyed through the night to Beth Shan. They took down the bodies of Saul and his sons from the wall of Beth Shan and went to Jabesh, where they burned them. ¹³Then they took their bones and buried them under a tamarisk tree at Jabesh, and they fasted seven days.

2 Samuel

What does it mean to be a person "after [God's] own heart" (1 Samuel 13:14)? Look at David's life. David's greatness resided in his response to his failures as well as in his many successes. After David's shameful sin with Bathsheba, the terrible consequences of his sin were felt both in his family and in his relationship with God. But David turned back to God with honesty and humility.

From David we learn that God's favor doesn't depend on our perfection but on his. As you read 2 Samuel, follow David's example: Go to the Lord, regardless of the imperfect condition of your life, and lay it down before him—watch his redeeming power work in your life and the life of your spouse.

David Hears of Saul's Death

1 After the death of Saul, David returned from defeating the Amalekites and stayed in Ziklag two days. ²On the third day a man arrived from Saul's camp, with his clothes torn and with dust on his head. When he came to David, he fell to the ground to pay him honor.

³"Where have you come from?" David asked him.

He answered, "I have escaped from the Israelite camp."

⁴"What happened?" David asked. "Tell me."

He said, "The men fled from the battle. Many of them fell and died. And Saul and his son Jonathan are dead."

⁵Then David said to the young man who brought him the report, "How do you know that Saul and his son Jonathan are dead?"

⁶"I happened to be on Mount Gilboa," the young man said, "and there was Saul, leaning on his spear, with the chariots and riders almost upon him. ⁷When he turned around and saw me, he called out to me, and I said, 'What can I do?'

⁸"He asked me, 'Who are you?'

" 'An Amalekite,' I answered.

⁹"Then he said to me, 'Stand over me and kill me! I am in the throes of death, but I'm still alive.'

¹⁰"So I stood over him and killed him, because I knew that after he had fallen he could not survive. And I took the crown that was on his head and the band on his

arm and have brought them here to my lord."

¹¹Then David and all the men with him took hold of their clothes and tore them. ¹²They mourned and wept and fasted till evening for Saul and his son Jonathan, and for the army of the LORD and the house of Israel, because they had fallen by the sword.

¹³David said to the young man who brought him the report, "Where are you from?"

"I am the son of an alien, an Amalekite," he answered.

¹⁴David asked him, "Why were you not afraid to lift your hand to destroy the LORD's anointed?"

¹⁵Then David called one of his men and said, "Go, strike him down!" So he struck him down, and he died. ¹⁶For David had said to him, "Your blood be on your own head. Your own mouth testified against you when you said, 'I killed the LORD's anointed.' "

David's Lament for Saul and Jonathan

¹⁷David took up this lament concerning Saul and his son Jonathan, ¹⁸and ordered that the men of Judah be taught this lament of the bow (it is written in the Book of Jashar):

¹⁹"Your glory, O Israel, lies slain on
        your heights.
   How the mighty have fallen!

²⁰"Tell it not in Gath,
        proclaim it not in the streets of
           Ashkelon,
   lest the daughters of the Philistines be
        glad,
        lest the daughters of the
           uncircumcised rejoice.

²¹"O mountains of Gilboa,
        may you have neither dew nor
           rain,
        nor fields that yield offerings ⌞of
           grain⌟.
   For there the shield of the mighty was
        defiled,
        the shield of Saul—no longer
           rubbed with oil.
²²From the blood of the slain,
        from the flesh of the mighty,
   the bow of Jonathan did not turn
        back,

   the sword of Saul did not return
        unsatisfied.

²³"Saul and Jonathan—
        in life they were loved and
           gracious,
   and in death they were not parted.
   They were swifter than eagles,
        they were stronger than lions.

²⁴"O daughters of Israel,
        weep for Saul,
   who clothed you in scarlet and finery,
        who adorned your garments with
           ornaments of gold.

²⁵"How the mighty have fallen in
           battle!
   Jonathan lies slain on your heights.
²⁶I grieve for you, Jonathan my brother;
        you were very dear to me.
   Your love for me was wonderful,
        more wonderful than that of
           women.

²⁷"How the mighty have fallen!
   The weapons of war have perished!"

David Anointed King Over Judah

2 In the course of time, David inquired of the LORD. "Shall I go up to one of the towns of Judah?" he asked.

The LORD said, "Go up."

David asked, "Where shall I go?"

"To Hebron," the LORD answered.

²So David went up there with his two wives, Ahinoam of Jezreel and Abigail, the widow of Nabal of Carmel. ³David also took the men who were with him, each with his family, and they settled in Hebron and its towns. ⁴Then the men of Judah came to Hebron and there they anointed David king over the house of Judah.

When David was told that it was the men of Jabesh Gilead who had buried Saul, ⁵he sent messengers to the men of Jabesh Gilead to say to them, "The LORD bless you for showing this kindness to Saul your master by burying him. ⁶May the LORD now show you kindness and faithfulness, and I too will show you the same favor because you have done this. ⁷Now then, be strong and brave, for Saul your master is dead, and the house of Judah has anointed me king over them."

War Between the Houses of David and Saul

⁸Meanwhile, Abner son of Ner, the commander of Saul's army, had taken Ish-Bosheth son of Saul and brought him over to Mahanaim. ⁹He made him king over Gilead, Ashuri*a* and Jezreel, and also over Ephraim, Benjamin and all Israel.

¹⁰Ish-Bosheth son of Saul was forty years old when he became king over Israel, and he reigned two years. The house of Judah, however, followed David. ¹¹The length of time David was king in Hebron over the house of Judah was seven years and six months.

¹²Abner son of Ner, together with the men of Ish-Bosheth son of Saul, left Mahanaim and went to Gibeon. ¹³Joab son of Zeruiah and David's men went out and met them at the pool of Gibeon. One group sat down on one side of the pool and one group on the other side.

¹⁴Then Abner said to Joab, "Let's have some of the young men get up and fight hand to hand in front of us."

"All right, let them do it," Joab said.

¹⁵So they stood up and were counted off—twelve men for Benjamin and Ish-Bosheth son of Saul, and twelve for David. ¹⁶Then each man grabbed his opponent by the head and thrust his dagger into his opponent's side, and they fell down together. So that place in Gibeon was called Helkath Hazzurim.*b*

¹⁷The battle that day was very fierce, and Abner and the men of Israel were defeated by David's men.

¹⁸The three sons of Zeruiah were there: Joab, Abishai and Asahel. Now Asahel was as fleet-footed as a wild gazelle. ¹⁹He chased Abner, turning neither to the right nor to the left as he pursued him. ²⁰Abner looked behind him and asked, "Is that you, Asahel?"

"It is," he answered.

²¹Then Abner said to him, "Turn aside to the right or to the left; take on one of the young men and strip him of his weapons." But Asahel would not stop chasing him.

²²Again Abner warned Asahel, "Stop chasing me! Why should I strike you down? How could I look your brother Joab in the face?"

²³But Asahel refused to give up the pursuit; so Abner thrust the butt of his spear into Asahel's stomach, and the spear came out through his back. He fell there and died on the spot. And every man stopped when he came to the place where Asahel had fallen and died.

²⁴But Joab and Abishai pursued Abner, and as the sun was setting, they came to the hill of Ammah, near Giah on the way to the wasteland of Gibeon. ²⁵Then the men of Benjamin rallied behind Abner. They formed themselves into a group and took their stand on top of a hill.

²⁶Abner called out to Joab, "Must the sword devour forever? Don't you realize that this will end in bitterness? How long before you order your men to stop pursuing their brothers?"

²⁷Joab answered, "As surely as God lives, if you had not spoken, the men would have continued the pursuit of their brothers until morning.*c*"

²⁸So Joab blew the trumpet, and all the men came to a halt; they no longer pursued Israel, nor did they fight anymore.

²⁹All that night Abner and his men marched through the Arabah. They crossed the Jordan, continued through the whole Bithron*d* and came to Mahanaim.

³⁰Then Joab returned from pursuing Abner and assembled all his men. Besides Asahel, nineteen of David's men were found missing. ³¹But David's men had killed three hundred and sixty Benjamites who were with Abner. ³²They took Asahel and buried him in his father's tomb at Bethlehem. Then Joab and his men marched all night and arrived at Hebron by daybreak.

3 The war between the house of Saul and the house of David lasted a long time. David grew stronger and stronger, while the house of Saul grew weaker and weaker.

²Sons were born to David in Hebron:

His firstborn was Amnon the son of Ahinoam of Jezreel;

---

a9 Or *Asher*   *b16 Helkath Hazzurim* means *field of daggers* or *field of hostilities.*   *c27* Or *spoken this morning, the men would not have taken up the pursuit of their brothers;* or *spoken, the men would have given up the pursuit of their brothers by morning*   *d29* Or *morning;* or *ravine;* the meaning of the Hebrew for this word is uncertain.

³his second, Kileab the son of Abigail the widow of Nabal of Carmel;

the third, Absalom the son of Maacah daughter of Talmai king of Geshur;

⁴the fourth, Adonijah the son of Haggith;

the fifth, Shephatiah the son of Abital;

⁵and the sixth, Ithream the son of David's wife Eglah.

These were born to David in Hebron.

Abner Goes Over to David

⁶During the war between the house of Saul and the house of David, Abner had been strengthening his own position in the house of Saul. ⁷Now Saul had had a concubine named Rizpah daughter of Aiah. And Ish-Bosheth said to Abner, "Why did you sleep with my father's concubine?"

⁸Abner was very angry because of what Ish-Bosheth said and he answered, "Am I a dog's head—on Judah's side? This very day I am loyal to the house of your father Saul and to his family and friends. I haven't handed you over to David. Yet now you accuse me of an offense involving this woman! ⁹May God deal with Abner, be it ever so severely, if I do not do for David what the LORD promised him on oath ¹⁰and transfer the kingdom from the house of Saul and establish David's throne over Israel and Judah from Dan to Beersheba." ¹¹Ish-Bosheth did not dare to say another word to Abner, because he was afraid of him.

¹²Then Abner sent messengers on his behalf to say to David, "Whose land is it? Make an agreement with me, and I will help you bring all Israel over to you."

¹³"Good," said David. "I will make an agreement with you. But I demand one thing of you: Do not come into my presence unless you bring Michal daughter of Saul when you come to see me." ¹⁴Then David sent messengers to Ish-Bosheth son of Saul, demanding, "Give me my wife Michal, whom I betrothed to myself for the price of a hundred Philistine foreskins."

¹⁵So Ish-Bosheth gave orders and had her taken away from her husband Paltiel son of Laish. ¹⁶Her husband, however, went with her, weeping behind her all the way to Bahurim. Then Abner said to him, "Go back home!" So he went back.

¹⁷Abner conferred with the elders of Israel and said, "For some time you have wanted to make David your king. ¹⁸Now do it! For the LORD promised David, 'By my servant David I will rescue my people Israel from the hand of the Philistines and from the hand of all their enemies.' "

¹⁹Abner also spoke to the Benjamites in person. Then he went to Hebron to tell David everything that Israel and the whole house of Benjamin wanted to do. ²⁰When Abner, who had twenty men with him, came to David at Hebron, David prepared a feast for him and his men. ²¹Then Abner said to David, "Let me go at once and assemble all Israel for my lord the king, so that they may make a compact with you, and that you may rule over all that your heart desires." So David sent Abner away, and he went in peace.

Joab Murders Abner

²²Just then David's men and Joab returned from a raid and brought with them a great deal of plunder. But Abner was no longer with David in Hebron, because David had sent him away, and he had gone in peace. ²³When Joab and all the soldiers with him arrived, he was told that Abner son of Ner had come to the king and that the king had sent him away and that he had gone in peace.

²⁴So Joab went to the king and said, "What have you done? Look, Abner came to you. Why did you let him go? Now he is gone! ²⁵You know Abner son of Ner; he came to deceive you and observe your movements and find out everything you are doing."

²⁶Joab then left David and sent messengers after Abner, and they brought him back from the well of Sirah. But David did not know it. ²⁷Now when Abner returned to Hebron, Joab took him aside into the gateway, as though to speak with him privately. And there, to avenge the blood of his brother Asahel, Joab stabbed him in the stomach, and he died.

²⁸Later, when David heard about this, he said, "I and my kingdom are forever

innocent before the LORD concerning the blood of Abner son of Ner. ²⁹May his blood fall upon the head of Joab and upon all his father's house! May Joab's house never be without someone who has a running sore or leprosy*a* or who leans on a crutch or who falls by the sword or who lacks food."

³⁰(Joab and his brother Abishai murdered Abner because he had killed their brother Asahel in the battle at Gibeon.)

³¹Then David said to Joab and all the people with him, "Tear your clothes and put on sackcloth and walk in mourning in front of Abner." King David himself walked behind the bier. ³²They buried Abner in Hebron, and the king wept aloud at Abner's tomb. All the people wept also.

³³The king sang this lament for Abner:

"Should Abner have died as the
        lawless die?
³⁴   Your hands were not bound,
        your feet were not fettered.
    You fell as one falls before wicked
        men."

And all the people wept over him again.

³⁵Then they all came and urged David to eat something while it was still day; but David took an oath, saying, "May God deal with me, be it ever so severely, if I taste bread or anything else before the sun sets!"

³⁶All the people took note and were pleased; indeed, everything the king did pleased them. ³⁷So on that day all the people and all Israel knew that the king had no part in the murder of Abner son of Ner.

³⁸Then the king said to his men, "Do you not realize that a prince and a great man has fallen in Israel this day? ³⁹And today, though I am the anointed king, I am weak, and these sons of Zeruiah are too strong for me. May the LORD repay the evildoer according to his evil deeds!"

Ish-Bosheth Murdered

4 When Ish-Bosheth son of Saul heard that Abner had died in Hebron, he lost courage, and all Israel became alarmed. ²Now Saul's son had two men who were leaders of raiding bands. One

was named Baanah and the other Recab; they were sons of Rimmon the Beerothite from the tribe of Benjamin—Beeroth is considered part of Benjamin, ³because the people of Beeroth fled to Gittaim and have lived there as aliens to this day.

⁴(Jonathan son of Saul had a son who was lame in both feet. He was five years old when the news about Saul and Jonathan came from Jezreel. His nurse picked him up and fled, but as she hurried to leave, he fell and became crippled. His name was Mephibosheth.)

⁵Now Recab and Baanah, the sons of Rimmon the Beerothite, set out for the house of Ish-Bosheth, and they arrived there in the heat of the day while he was taking his noonday rest. ⁶They went into the inner part of the house as if to get some wheat, and they stabbed him in the stomach. Then Recab and his brother Baanah slipped away.

⁷They had gone into the house while he was lying on the bed in his bedroom. After they stabbed and killed him, they cut off his head. Taking it with them, they traveled all night by way of the Arabah. ⁸They brought the head of Ish-Bosheth to David at Hebron and said to the king, "Here is the head of Ish-Bosheth son of Saul, your enemy, who tried to take your life. This day the LORD has avenged my lord the king against Saul and his offspring."

⁹David answered Recab and his brother Baanah, the sons of Rimmon the Beerothite, "As surely as the LORD lives, who has delivered me out of all trouble, ¹⁰when a man told me, 'Saul is dead,' and thought he was bringing good news, I seized him and put him to death in Ziklag. That was the reward I gave him for his news! ¹¹How much more—when wicked men have killed an innocent man in his own house and on his own bed—should I not now demand his blood from your hand and rid the earth of you!"

¹²So David gave an order to his men, and they killed them. They cut off their hands and feet and hung the bodies by the pool in Hebron. But they took the head of Ish-Bosheth and buried it in Abner's tomb at Hebron.

---

a29 The Hebrew word was used for various diseases affecting the skin—not necessarily leprosy.

David Becomes King Over Israel

5 All the tribes of Israel came to David at Hebron and said, "We are your own flesh and blood. ²In the past, while Saul was king over us, you were the one who led Israel on their military campaigns. And the LORD said to you, 'You will shepherd my people Israel, and you will become their ruler.' "

³When all the elders of Israel had come to King David at Hebron, the king made a compact with them at Hebron before the LORD, and they anointed David king over Israel.

⁴David was thirty years old when he became king, and he reigned forty years. ⁵In Hebron he reigned over Judah seven years and six months, and in Jerusalem he reigned over all Israel and Judah thirty-three years.

David Conquers Jerusalem

⁶The king and his men marched to Jerusalem to attack the Jebusites, who lived there. The Jebusites said to David, "You will not get in here; even the blind and the lame can ward you off." They thought, "David cannot get in here." ⁷Nevertheless, David captured the fortress of Zion, the City of David.

⁸On that day, David said, "Anyone who conquers the Jebusites will have to use the water shaft*a* to reach those 'lame and blind' who are David's enemies.*b*" That is why they say, "The 'blind and lame' will not enter the palace."

⁹David then took up residence in the fortress and called it the City of David. He built up the area around it, from the supporting terraces*c* inward. ¹⁰And he became more and more powerful, because the LORD God Almighty was with him.

¹¹Now Hiram king of Tyre sent messengers to David, along with cedar logs and carpenters and stonemasons, and they built a palace for David. ¹²And David knew that the LORD had established him as king over Israel and had exalted his kingdom for the sake of his people Israel.

¹³After he left Hebron, David took more concubines and wives in Jerusalem, and more sons and daughters were born to him. ¹⁴These are the names of the children born to him there: Shammua, Shobab, Nathan, Solomon, ¹⁵Ibhar, Elishua,

Nepheg, Japhia, ¹⁶Elishama, Eliada and Eliphelet.

David Defeats the Philistines

¹⁷When the Philistines heard that David had been anointed king over Israel, they went up in full force to search for him, but David heard about it and went down to the stronghold. ¹⁸Now the Philistines had come and spread out in the Valley of Rephaim; ¹⁹so David inquired of the LORD, "Shall I go and attack the Philistines? Will you hand them over to me?"

The LORD answered him, "Go, for I will surely hand the Philistines over to you."

²⁰So David went to Baal Perazim, and there he defeated them. He said, "As waters break out, the LORD has broken out against my enemies before me." So that place was called Baal Perazim.*d* ²¹The Philistines abandoned their idols there, and David and his men carried them off.

²²Once more the Philistines came up and spread out in the Valley of Rephaim; ²³so David inquired of the LORD, and he answered, "Do not go straight up, but circle around behind them and attack them in front of the balsam trees. ²⁴As soon as you hear the sound of marching in the tops of the balsam trees, move quickly, because that will mean the LORD has gone out in front of you to strike the Philistine army." ²⁵So David did as the LORD commanded him, and he struck down the Philistines all the way from Gibeon*e* to Gezer.

The Ark Brought to Jerusalem

6 David again brought together out of Israel chosen men, thirty thousand in all. ²He and all his men set out from Baalah of Judah*f* to bring up from there the ark of God, which is called by the Name,*g* the name of the LORD Almighty, who is enthroned between the cherubim that are on the ark. ³They set the ark of God on a new cart and brought it from the house of Abinadab, which was on the

---

*a*8 Or *use scaling hooks*   *b*8 Or *are hated by David*   *c*9 Or *the Millo*   *d*20 *Baal Perazim* means *the lord who breaks out.*   *e*25 Septuagint (see also 1 Chron. 14:16); Hebrew *Geba* *f*2 That is, Kiriath Jearim; Hebrew *Baale Judah*, a variant of *Baalah of Judah*   *g*2 Hebrew; Septuagint and Vulgate do not have *the Name.*

hill. Uzzah and Ahio, sons of Abinadab, were guiding the new cart [4]with the ark of God on it,[a] and Ahio was walking in front of it. [5]David and the whole house of Israel were celebrating with all their might before the LORD, with songs[b] and with harps, lyres, tambourines, sistrums and cymbals.

[6]When they came to the threshing floor of Nacon, Uzzah reached out and took hold of the ark of God, because the oxen stumbled. [7]The LORD's anger burned against Uzzah because of his irreverent act; therefore God struck him down and he died there beside the ark of God.

[8]Then David was angry because the LORD's wrath had broken out against Uzzah, and to this day that place is called Perez Uzzah.[c]

[9]David was afraid of the LORD that day and said, "How can the ark of the LORD ever come to me?" [10]He was not willing to take the ark of the LORD to be with him in the City of David. Instead, he took it aside to the house of Obed-Edom the Gittite. [11]The ark of the LORD remained in the house of Obed-Edom the Gittite for three months, and the LORD blessed him and his entire household.

[12]Now King David was told, "The LORD has blessed the household of Obed-Edom and everything he has, because of the ark of God." So David went down and brought up the ark of God from the house of Obed-Edom to the City of David with rejoicing. [13]When those who were carrying the ark of the LORD had taken six steps, he sacrificed a bull and a fattened calf. [14]David, wearing a linen ephod, danced before the LORD with all his might, [15]while he and the entire house of Israel brought up the ark of the LORD with shouts and the sound of trumpets.

[16]As the ark of the LORD was entering the City of David, Michal daughter of Saul watched from a window. And when she saw King David leaping and dancing before the LORD, she despised him in her heart.

[17]They brought the ark of the LORD and set it in its place inside the tent that David had pitched for it, and David sacrificed burnt offerings and fellowship offerings[d] before the LORD. [18]After he had finished sacrificing the burnt offerings and fellowship offerings, he blessed the people in the name of the LORD Almighty. [19]Then he gave a loaf of bread, a cake of dates and a cake of raisins to each person in the whole crowd of Israelites, both men and women. And all the people went to their homes.

[20]When David returned home to bless his household, Michal daughter of Saul came out to meet him and said, "How the king of Israel has distinguished himself today, disrobing in the sight of the slave girls of his servants as any vulgar fellow would!"

[21]David said to Michal, "It was before the LORD, who chose me rather than your father or anyone from his house when he appointed me ruler over the LORD's people Israel—I will celebrate before the LORD. [22]I will become even more undignified than this, and I will be humiliated in my own eyes. But by these slave girls you spoke of, I will be held in honor."

[23]And Michal daughter of Saul had no children to the day of her death.

God's Promise to David

7 After the king was settled in his palace and the LORD had given him rest from all his enemies around him, [2]he said to Nathan the prophet, "Here I am, living in a palace of cedar, while the ark of God remains in a tent."

[3]Nathan replied to the king, "Whatever you have in mind, go ahead and do it, for the LORD is with you."

[4]That night the word of the LORD came to Nathan, saying:

[5]"Go and tell my servant David, 'This is what the LORD says: Are you the one to build me a house to dwell in? [6]I have not dwelt in a house from the day I brought the Israelites up out of Egypt to this day. I have been moving from place to place with a tent as my dwelling. [7]Wherever I have moved with all the Israelites, did I ever say to any of their

---

[a]3,4 Dead Sea Scrolls and some Septuagint manuscripts; Masoretic Text *cart* [4]*and they brought it with the ark of God from the house of Abinadab, which was on the hill*   [b]5 See Dead Sea Scrolls, Septuagint and 1 Chronicles 13:8; Masoretic Text *celebrating before the LORD with all kinds of instruments made of pine.*   [c]8 *Perez Uzzah* means *outbreak against Uzzah.*   [d]17 Traditionally *peace offerings*; also in verse 18

rulers whom I commanded to shepherd my people Israel, "Why have you not built me a house of cedar?" '

⁸"Now then, tell my servant David, 'This is what the LORD Almighty says: I took you from the pasture and from following the flock to be ruler over my people Israel. ⁹I have been with you wherever you have gone, and I have cut off all your enemies from before you. Now I will make your name great, like the names of the greatest men of the earth. ¹⁰And I will provide a place for my people Israel and will plant them so that they can have a home of their own and no longer be disturbed. Wicked people will not oppress them anymore, as they did at the beginning ¹¹and have done ever since the time I appointed leaders^a over my people Israel. I will also give you rest from all your enemies.

" 'The LORD declares to you that the LORD himself will establish a house for you: ¹²When your days are over and you rest with your fathers, I will raise up your offspring to succeed you, who will come from your own body, and I will establish his kingdom. ¹³He is the one who will build a house for my Name, and I will establish the throne of his kingdom forever. ¹⁴I will be his father, and he will be my son. When he does wrong, I will punish him with the rod of men, with floggings inflicted by men. ¹⁵But my love will never be taken away from him, as I took it away from Saul, whom I removed from before you. ¹⁶Your house and your kingdom will endure forever before me^b; your throne will be established forever.' "

¹⁷Nathan reported to David all the words of this entire revelation.

David's Prayer

¹⁸Then King David went in and sat before the LORD, and he said:

"Who am I, O Sovereign LORD, and what is my family, that you have brought me this far? ¹⁹And as if this were not enough in your sight, O Sovereign LORD, you have also spoken about the future of the house of your servant. Is this your usual way of dealing with man, O Sovereign LORD?

²⁰"What more can David say to you? For you know your servant, O Sovereign LORD. ²¹For the sake of your word and according to your will, you have done this great thing and made it known to your servant. ²²"How great you are, O Sover-

---

^a 11 Traditionally *judges*　^b 16 Some Hebrew manuscripts and Septuagint; most Hebrew manuscripts *you*

Bringing Us This Far

Friday

2 SAMUEL 7:18 Dave and I have been working on our marriage for almost four decades, and, as we reflect on our marriage journey, we are amazed at how far God has brought us. We've journeyed from the early years of trying to change each other to the present where we now accept each other as a package deal—from living through the active parenting years to the second half of our marriage with our growing family which includes three wonderful daughters-in-law and our incredibly talented grandchildren. Years ago our journey included supporting each other in very different roles to now sharing the same profession. It is easy for us to identify with David's praise to the Lord: "Who am I, O Sovereign LORD, and what is my family, that you have brought me this far?"

Take the time to thank God for your spouse and how he uses your mate to help shape you into the image of Christ. Thank him for the way your mate's strengths balance some of your weaknesses. If you have children, thank him for this marriage miracle. Thank him for bringing you this far.

—Dave & Claudia

Go to page 324 for your next devotional reading.

eign LORD! There is no one like you, and there is no God but you, as we have heard with our own ears. ²³And who is like your people Israel—the one nation on earth that God went out to redeem as a people for himself, and to make a name for himself, and to perform great and awesome wonders by driving out nations and their gods from before your people, whom you redeemed from Egypt?ᵃ ²⁴You have established your people Israel as your very own forever, and you, O LORD, have become their God.

²⁵"And now, LORD God, keep forever the promise you have made concerning your servant and his house. Do as you promised, ²⁶so that your name will be great forever. Then men will say, 'The LORD Almighty is God over Israel!' And the house of your servant David will be established before you.

²⁷"O LORD Almighty, God of Israel, you have revealed this to your servant, saying, 'I will build a house for you.' So your servant has found courage to offer you this prayer. ²⁸O Sovereign LORD, you are God! Your words are trustworthy, and you have promised these good things to your servant. ²⁹Now be pleased to bless the house of your servant, that it may continue forever in your sight; for you, O Sovereign LORD, have spoken, and with your blessing the house of your servant will be blessed forever."

David's Victories

8 In the course of time, David defeated the Philistines and subdued them, and he took Metheg Ammah from the control of the Philistines.

²David also defeated the Moabites. He made them lie down on the ground and measured them off with a length of cord. Every two lengths of them were put to death, and the third length was allowed to live. So the Moabites became subject to David and brought tribute.

³Moreover, David fought Hadadezer son of Rehob, king of Zobah, when he went to restore his control along the Eu-

phrates River. ⁴David captured a thousand of his chariots, seven thousand charioteersᵇ and twenty thousand foot soldiers. He hamstrung all but a hundred of the chariot horses.

⁵When the Arameans of Damascus came to help Hadadezer king of Zobah, David struck down twenty-two thousand of them. ⁶He put garrisons in the Aramean kingdom of Damascus, and the Arameans became subject to him and brought tribute. The LORD gave David victory wherever he went.

⁷David took the gold shields that belonged to the officers of Hadadezer and brought them to Jerusalem. ⁸From Tebahᶜ and Berothai, towns that belonged to Hadadezer, King David took a great quantity of bronze.

⁹When Touᵈ king of Hamath heard that David had defeated the entire army of Hadadezer, ¹⁰he sent his son Joramᵉ to King David to greet him and congratulate him on his victory in battle over Hadadezer, who had been at war with Tou. Joram brought with him articles of silver and gold and bronze.

¹¹King David dedicated these articles to the LORD, as he had done with the silver and gold from all the nations he had subdued: ¹²Edomᶠ and Moab, the Ammonites and the Philistines, and Amalek. He also dedicated the plunder taken from Hadadezer son of Rehob, king of Zobah.

¹³And David became famous after he returned from striking down eighteen thousand Edomitesᵍ in the Valley of Salt.

¹⁴He put garrisons throughout Edom, and all the Edomites became subject to David. The LORD gave David victory wherever he went.

ᵃ23 See Septuagint and 1 Chron. 17:21; Hebrew *wonders for your land and before your people, whom you redeemed from Egypt, from the nations and their gods.* ᵇ4 Septuagint (see also Dead Sea Scrolls and 1 Chron. 18:4); Masoretic Text *captured seventeen hundred of his charioteers* ᶜ8 See some Septuagint manuscripts (see also 1 Chron. 18:8); Hebrew *Betah.* ᵈ9 Hebrew *Toi,* a variant of *Tou;* also in verse 10 ᵉ10 A variant of *Hadoram* ᶠ12 Some Hebrew manuscripts, Septuagint and Syriac (see also 1 Chron. 18:11); most Hebrew manuscripts *Aram* ᵍ13 A few Hebrew manuscripts, Septuagint and Syriac (see also 1 Chron. 18:12); most Hebrew manuscripts *Aram* (that is, Arameans)

David's Officials

¹⁵David reigned over all Israel, doing what was just and right for all his people. ¹⁶Joab son of Zeruiah was over the army; Jehoshaphat son of Ahilud was recorder; ¹⁷Zadok son of Ahitub and Ahimelech son of Abiathar were priests; Seraiah was secretary; ¹⁸Benaiah son of Jehoiada was over the Kerethites and Pelethites; and David's sons were royal advisers. *a*

David and Mephibosheth

9 David asked, "Is there anyone still left of the house of Saul to whom I can show kindness for Jonathan's sake?"

²Now there was a servant of Saul's household named Ziba. They called him to appear before David, and the king said to him, "Are you Ziba?"

"Your servant," he replied.

³The king asked, "Is there no one still left of the house of Saul to whom I can show God's kindness?"

Ziba answered the king, "There is still a son of Jonathan; he is crippled in both feet."

⁴"Where is he?" the king asked.

Ziba answered, "He is at the house of Makir son of Ammiel in Lo Debar."

⁵So King David had him brought from Lo Debar, from the house of Makir son of Ammiel.

⁶When Mephibosheth son of Jonathan, the son of Saul, came to David, he bowed down to pay him honor.

David said, "Mephibosheth!"

"Your servant," he replied.

⁷"Don't be afraid," David said to him, "for I will surely show you kindness for the sake of your father Jonathan. I will restore to you all the land that belonged to your grandfather Saul, and you will always eat at my table."

⁸Mephibosheth bowed down and said, "What is your servant, that you should notice a dead dog like me?"

⁹Then the king summoned Ziba, Saul's servant, and said to him, "I have given your master's grandson everything that belonged to Saul and his family. ¹⁰You and your sons and your servants are to farm the land for him and bring in the crops, so that your master's grandson may

a18 Or were priests

Giving Generously

Quiet TIMES

with each other

2 SAMUEL 9 David is very gracious toward Mephibosheth, a relative of David's best friend Jonathan. David's loving response to this crippled man is a picture of God's grace in our lives. Like Mephibosheth, we are crippled with nothing to offer God, our King. And like Mephibosheth, we are given an inheritance and treated as a son of the king. David wanted to give this man grace, just as God had given David grace.

God has bestowed the same generous grace upon us and made us part of his family, even though we have nothing to give him in return (see Ephesians 2:6–7, page 1281). So often in marriage, we keep track of the hurts and respond accordingly. Unfortunately our focus tends to be, "What can I get out of this marriage? How will it meet my needs or make me happy?" Our attitudes often reflect a self-centered attitude.

David's example offers much to each marriage partner. Following David's example, we can each change our marital focus, choosing to bless and give generously to one another, just as God has given to us.

Why should we bring joy and happiness to our spouse? Because so much has been given to us when we didn't deserve it, we can do nothing other than be quick to give generously to our spouse.

—Bob & Rosemary

Weekend Warm-up *When was a time you showed grace to each other?*

Go to page 326 for your next devotional reading.

be provided for. And Mephibosheth, grandson of your master, will always eat at my table." (Now Ziba had fifteen sons and twenty servants.)

¹¹Then Ziba said to the king, "Your servant will do whatever my lord the king commands his servant to do." So Mephibosheth ate at David's*ᵃ table like one of the king's sons.

¹²Mephibosheth had a young son named Mica, and all the members of Ziba's household were servants of Mephibosheth. ¹³And Mephibosheth lived in Jerusalem, because he always ate at the king's table, and he was crippled in both feet.

David Defeats the Ammonites

10 In the course of time, the king of the Ammonites died, and his son Hanun succeeded him as king. ²David thought, "I will show kindness to Hanun son of Nahash, just as his father showed kindness to me." So David sent a delegation to express his sympathy to Hanun concerning his father.

When David's men came to the land of the Ammonites, ³the Ammonite nobles said to Hanun their lord, "Do you think David is honoring your father by sending men to you to express sympathy? Hasn't David sent them to you to explore the city and spy it out and overthrow it?" ⁴So Hanun seized David's men, shaved off half of each man's beard, cut off their garments in the middle at the buttocks, and sent them away.

⁵When David was told about this, he sent messengers to meet the men, for they were greatly humiliated. The king said, "Stay at Jericho till your beards have grown, and then come back."

⁶When the Ammonites realized that they had become a stench in David's nostrils, they hired twenty thousand Aramean foot soldiers from Beth Rehob and Zobah, as well as the king of Maacah with a thousand men, and also twelve thousand men from Tob.

⁷On hearing this, David sent Joab out with the entire army of fighting men. ⁸The Ammonites came out and drew up in battle formation at the entrance to their city gate, while the Arameans of Zobah and Rehob and the men of Tob and

JUST BETWEEN you & me

Giving Generously

Take a moment to answer each of these questions on your own. Then compare your answers to your spouse's.

Yes　No In times of conflict, do you try to listen to your spouse's opinion rather than battle to express your own?

Yes　No When it comes to personal activities, do you plan for your enjoyment or do you try to plan things your spouse will enjoy?

Yes　No Do you view your sexual relationship as an opportunity to give happiness to your spouse?

Yes　No Do you try to think about life through the eyes of your spouse?

Maacah were by themselves in the open country.

⁹Joab saw that there were battle lines in front of him and behind him; so he selected some of the best troops in Israel and deployed them against the Arameans. ¹⁰He put the rest of the men under the command of Abishai his brother and deployed them against the Ammonites. ¹¹Joab said, "If the Arameans are too strong for me, then you are to come to my rescue; but if the Ammonites are too strong for you, then I will come to rescue you. ¹²Be strong and let us fight bravely for our people and the cities of our God. The LORD will do what is good in his sight."

¹³Then Joab and the troops with him advanced to fight the Arameans, and they fled before him. ¹⁴When the Ammonites saw that the Arameans were fleeing, they fled before Abishai and went inside the city. So Joab returned from fighting the Ammonites and came to Jerusalem.

¹⁵After the Arameans saw that they had been routed by Israel, they regrouped. ¹⁶Hadadezer had Arameans brought from beyond the Riverᵇ; they went to Helam,

ᵃ11 Septuagint; Hebrew *my*　ᵇ16 That is, the Euphrates

with Shobach the commander of Hadadezer's army leading them.

¹⁷When David was told of this, he gathered all Israel, crossed the Jordan and went to Helam. The Arameans formed their battle lines to meet David and fought against him. ¹⁸But they fled before Israel, and David killed seven hundred of their charioteers and forty thousand of their foot soldiers.*ᵃ* He also struck down Shobach the commander of their army, and he died there. ¹⁹When all the kings who were vassals of Hadadezer saw that they had been defeated by Israel, they made peace with the Israelites and became subject to them.

So the Arameans were afraid to help the Ammonites anymore.

David and Bathsheba

11 In the spring, at the time when kings go off to war, David sent Joab out with the king's men and the whole Israelite army. They destroyed the Ammonites and besieged Rabbah. But David remained in Jerusalem.

²One evening David got up from his bed and walked around on the roof of the palace. From the roof he saw a woman bathing. The woman was very beautiful, ³and David sent someone to find out about her. The man said, "Isn't this Bathsheba, the daughter of Eliam and the wife of Uriah the Hittite?" ⁴Then David sent messengers to get her. She came to him, and he slept with her. (She had purified herself from her uncleanness.) Thenᵇ she went back home. ⁵The woman conceived and sent word to David, saying, "I am pregnant."

⁶So David sent this word to Joab: "Send me Uriah the Hittite." And Joab sent him to David. ⁷When Uriah came to him, David asked him how Joab was, how the soldiers were and how the war was going. ⁸Then David said to Uriah, "Go down to your house and wash your feet." So Uriah left the palace, and a gift from the king was sent after him. ⁹But Uriah slept at the entrance to the palace with all his master's servants and did not go down to his house.

¹⁰When David was told, "Uriah did not go home," he asked him, "Haven't you just come from a distance? Why didn't you go home?"

¹¹Uriah said to David, "The ark and Israel and Judah are staying in tents, and my master Joab and my lord's men are

ᵃ18 Some Septuagint manuscripts (see also 1 Chron. 19:18); Hebrew *horsemen*   *ᵇ4* Or *with her. When she purified herself from her uncleanness,*

The Grass Isn't Greener

Monday

2 SAMUEL 11   Who doesn't know the story of David and Bathsheba? It has been told and retold in countless ways since the day it happened. It's talked about in church school classes and depicted in Hollywood movies. In fact, almost everyone knows a modern day equivalent of David and Bathsheba. The question is, What have you learned from the story?

For example, have you considered David's options? When he saw Bathsheba, he could have looked away or even left his rooftop perch. He could have gone out with his troops. He could have contacted Nathan or other godly friends for support. He could have talked with them about his struggle with lust. How different events could have been if only he had avoided this temptation.

Unfortunately, David decided to give in to his selfish desires—and he paid for his choice for the rest of his life.

The lesson seems obvious: We need to resist the temptation of adultery altogether. Whenever we find ourselves in a risky situation and are thinking about sinning, we need to run the opposite way. We need to talk about it with godly friends. We need to hold ourselves accountable.

Few temptations are more deceptive than adultery. So take a lesson from David and Bathsheba: Don't let yourself believe the grass-is-greener lie or it could ruin your marriage.

—Les & Leslie

Go to page 348 for your next devotional reading.

camped in the open fields. How could I go to my house to eat and drink and lie with my wife? As surely as you live, I will not do such a thing!"

¹²Then David said to him, "Stay here one more day, and tomorrow I will send you back." So Uriah remained in Jerusalem that day and the next. ¹³At David's invitation, he ate and drank with him, and David made him drunk. But in the evening Uriah went out to sleep on his mat among his master's servants; he did not go home.

¹⁴In the morning David wrote a letter to Joab and sent it with Uriah. ¹⁵In it he wrote, "Put Uriah in the front line where the fighting is fiercest. Then withdraw from him so he will be struck down and die."

¹⁶So while Joab had the city under siege, he put Uriah at a place where he knew the strongest defenders were. ¹⁷When the men of the city came out and fought against Joab, some of the men in David's army fell; moreover, Uriah the Hittite died.

¹⁸Joab sent David a full account of the battle. ¹⁹He instructed the messenger: "When you have finished giving the king this account of the battle, ²⁰the king's anger may flare up, and he may ask you, 'Why did you get so close to the city to fight? Didn't you know they would shoot arrows from the wall? ²¹Who killed Abimelech son of Jerub-Besheth*? Didn't a woman throw an upper millstone on him from the wall, so that he died in Thebez? Why did you get so close to the wall?' If he asks you this, then say to him, 'Also, your servant Uriah the Hittite is dead.' "

²²The messenger set out, and when he arrived he told David everything Joab had sent him to say. ²³The messenger said to David, "The men overpowered us and came out against us in the open, but we drove them back to the entrance to the city gate. ²⁴Then the archers shot arrows at your servants from the wall, and some of the king's men died. Moreover, your servant Uriah the Hittite is dead."

²⁵David told the messenger, "Say this to Joab: 'Don't let this upset you; the sword devours one as well as another. Press the attack against the city and destroy it.' Say this to encourage Joab."

²⁶When Uriah's wife heard that her

David and Bathsheba

2 SAMUEL 11   King David was overtaken with Bathsheba's beauty. But there was one problem—she was married. Instead of respecting the union of this woman with her husband, David succeeded in destroying it. He gave in to his flesh and slept with Bathsheba, and she became pregnant with his child. David took advantage of his power as king and had Uriah sent to the front line of battle to let his foes do his dirty work. Sure enough, Uriah was killed—a cruel way to manipulate fate. Needless to say, this was not a good way to build a solid foundation for their future marriage.

Although David was dearly loved by God and was truly remorseful for his affair with Bathsheba (see Psalm 51, page 596), his life became riddled with suffering and trouble. They lost the baby. And, although they were later blessed with baby Solomon, their family life was filled with dysfunction including rape and even murder (see 2 Samuel 13, page 329). If only David had not given in to his temptation! Having self-control is difficult. But it is a cornerstone when building a healthy marriage.

husband was dead, she mourned for him. ²⁷After the time of mourning was over, David had her brought to his house, and she became his wife and bore him a son. But the thing David had done displeased the LORD.

Nathan Rebukes David

12 The LORD sent Nathan to David. When he came to him, he said, "There were two men in a certain town, one rich and the other poor. ²The rich man had a very large number of sheep and cattle, ³but the poor man had nothing except one little ewe lamb he had bought. He raised it, and it grew up with him and his children. It shared his food, drank from his cup and even slept in his arms. It was like a daughter to him.

*21 Also known as *Jerub-Baal* (that is, Gideon)

⁴"Now a traveler came to the rich man, but the rich man refrained from taking one of his own sheep or cattle to prepare a meal for the traveler who had come to him. Instead, he took the ewe lamb that belonged to the poor man and prepared it for the one who had come to him."

⁵David burned with anger against the man and said to Nathan, "As surely as the LORD lives, the man who did this deserves to die! ⁶He must pay for that lamb four times over, because he did such a thing and had no pity."

⁷Then Nathan said to David, "You are the man! This is what the LORD, the God of Israel, says: 'I anointed you king over Israel, and I delivered you from the hand of Saul. ⁸I gave your master's house to you, and your master's wives into your arms. I gave you the house of Israel and Judah. And if all this had been too little, I would have given you even more. ⁹Why did you despise the word of the LORD by doing what is evil in his eyes? You struck down Uriah the Hittite with the sword and took his wife to be your own. You killed him with the sword of the Ammonites. ¹⁰Now, therefore, the sword will never depart from your house, because you despised me and took the wife of Uriah the Hittite to be your own.'

¹¹"This is what the LORD says: 'Out of your own household I am going to bring calamity upon you. Before your very eyes I will take your wives and give them to one who is close to you, and he will lie with your wives in broad daylight. ¹²You did it in secret, but I will do this thing in broad daylight before all Israel.' "

¹³Then David said to Nathan, "I have sinned against the LORD."

Nathan replied, "The LORD has taken away your sin. You are not going to die. ¹⁴But because by doing this you have made the enemies of the LORD show utter contempt,ᵃ the son born to you will die."

¹⁵After Nathan had gone home, the LORD struck the child that Uriah's wife had borne to David, and he became ill. ¹⁶David pleaded with God for the child. He fasted and went into his house and spent the nights lying on the ground. ¹⁷The elders of his household stood beside him to get him up from the ground, but he refused, and he would not eat any food with them.

¹⁸On the seventh day the child died. David's servants were afraid to tell him that the child was dead, for they thought, "While the child was still living, we spoke to David but he would not listen to us. How can we tell him the child is dead? He may do something desperate."

¹⁹David noticed that his servants were whispering among themselves and he realized the child was dead. "Is the child dead?" he asked.

"Yes," they replied, "he is dead."

²⁰Then David got up from the ground. After he had washed, put on lotions and changed his clothes, he went into the house of the LORD and worshiped. Then he went to his own house, and at his request they served him food, and he ate.

²¹His servants asked him, "Why are you acting this way? While the child was alive, you fasted and wept, but now that the child is dead, you get up and eat!"

²²He answered, "While the child was still alive, I fasted and wept. I thought, 'Who knows? The LORD may be gracious to me and let the child live.' ²³But now that he is dead, why should I fast? Can I bring him back again? I will go to him, but he will not return to me."

²⁴Then David comforted his wife Bathsheba, and he went to her and lay with her. She gave birth to a son, and they named him Solomon. The LORD loved him; ²⁵and because the LORD loved him, he sent word through Nathan the prophet to name him Jedidiah.ᵇ

²⁶Meanwhile Joab fought against Rabbah of the Ammonites and captured the royal citadel. ²⁷Joab then sent messengers to David, saying, "I have fought against Rabbah and taken its water supply. ²⁸Now muster the rest of the troops and besiege the city and capture it. Otherwise I will take the city, and it will be named after me."

²⁹So David mustered the entire army and went to Rabbah, and attacked and captured it. ³⁰He took the crown from the head of their kingᶜ—its weight was a talentᵈ of gold, and it was set with precious stones—and it was placed on David's

---

ᵃ14 Masoretic Text; an ancient Hebrew scribal tradition *this you have shown utter contempt for the LORD*　ᵇ25 *Jedidiah* means *loved by the LORD.*　ᶜ30 Or *of Milcom* (that is, Molech)　ᵈ30 That is, about 75 pounds (about 34 kilograms) head. He took a great quantity of plunder from the city ³¹and brought out the people who were there, consigning them to labor with saws and with iron picks and axes, and he made them work at brickmaking.ᵃ He did this to all the Ammonite towns. Then David and his entire army returned to Jerusalem.

Amnon and Tamar

13 In the course of time, Amnon son of David fell in love with Tamar, the beautiful sister of Absalom son of David.

²Amnon became frustrated to the point of illness on account of his sister Tamar, for she was a virgin, and it seemed impossible for him to do anything to her.

³Now Amnon had a friend named Jonadab son of Shimeah, David's brother. Jonadab was a very shrewd man. ⁴He asked Amnon, "Why do you, the king's son, look so haggard morning after morning? Won't you tell me?"

Amnon said to him, "I'm in love with Tamar, my brother Absalom's sister."

⁵"Go to bed and pretend to be ill," Jonadab said. "When your father comes to see you, say to him, 'I would like my sister Tamar to come and give me something to eat. Let her prepare the food in my sight so I may watch her and then eat it from her hand.' "

⁶So Amnon lay down and pretended to be ill. When the king came to see him, Amnon said to him, "I would like my sister Tamar to come and make some special bread in my sight, so I may eat from her hand."

⁷David sent word to Tamar at the palace: "Go to the house of your brother Amnon and prepare some food for him." ⁸So Tamar went to the house of her brother Amnon, who was lying down. She took some dough, kneaded it, made the bread in his sight and baked it. ⁹Then she took the pan and served him the bread, but he refused to eat.

"Send everyone out of here," Amnon said. So everyone left him. ¹⁰Then Amnon said to Tamar, "Bring the food here into my bedroom so I may eat from your hand." And Tamar took the bread she had prepared and brought it to her brother Amnon in his bedroom. ¹¹But when she

took it to him to eat, he grabbed her and said, "Come to bed with me, my sister."

¹²"Don't, my brother!" she said to him. "Don't force me. Such a thing should not be done in Israel! Don't do this wicked thing. ¹³What about me? Where could I get rid of my disgrace? And what about you? You would be like one of the wicked fools in Israel. Please speak to the king; he will not keep me from being married to you." ¹⁴But he refused to listen to her, and since he was stronger than she, he raped her.

¹⁵Then Amnon hated her with intense hatred. In fact, he hated her more than he had loved her. Amnon said to her, "Get up and get out!"

¹⁶"No!" she said to him. "Sending me away would be a greater wrong than what you have already done to me."

But he refused to listen to her. ¹⁷He called his personal servant and said, "Get this woman out of here and bolt the door after her." ¹⁸So his servant put her out and bolted the door after her. She was wearing a richly ornamentedᵇ robe, for this was the kind of garment the virgin daughters of the king wore. ¹⁹Tamar put ashes on her head and tore the ornamentedᶜ robe she was wearing. She put her hand on her head and went away, weeping aloud as she went.

²⁰Her brother Absalom said to her, "Has that Amnon, your brother, been with you? Be quiet now, my sister; he is your brother. Don't take this thing to heart." And Tamar lived in her brother Absalom's house, a desolate woman.

²¹When King David heard all this, he was furious. ²²Absalom never said a word to Amnon, either good or bad; he hated Amnon because he had disgraced his sister Tamar.

Absalom Kills Amnon

²³Two years later, when Absalom's sheepshearers were at Baal Hazor near the border of Ephraim, he invited all the king's sons to come there. ²⁴Absalom went to the king and said, "Your servant

ᵃ31 The meaning of the Hebrew for this clause is uncertain.   ᵇ18 The meaning of the Hebrew for this phrase is uncertain.   ᶜ19 The meaning of the Hebrew for this word is uncertain.

has had shearers come. Will the king and his officials please join me?"

²⁵"No, my son," the king replied. "All of us should not go; we would only be a burden to you." Although Absalom urged him, he still refused to go, but gave him his blessing.

²⁶Then Absalom said, "If not, please let my brother Amnon come with us."

The king asked him, "Why should he go with you?" ²⁷But Absalom urged him, so he sent with him Amnon and the rest of the king's sons.

²⁸Absalom ordered his men, "Listen! When Amnon is in high spirits from drinking wine and I say to you, 'Strike Amnon down,' then kill him. Don't be afraid. Have not I given you this order? Be strong and brave." ²⁹So Absalom's men did to Amnon what Absalom had ordered. Then all the king's sons got up, mounted their mules and fled.

³⁰While they were on their way, the report came to David: "Absalom has struck down all the king's sons; not one of them is left." ³¹The king stood up, tore his clothes and lay down on the ground; and all his servants stood by with their clothes torn.

³²But Jonadab son of Shimeah, David's brother, said, "My lord should not think that they killed all the princes; only Amnon is dead. This has been Absalom's expressed intention ever since the day Amnon raped his sister Tamar. ³³My lord the king should not be concerned about the report that all the king's sons are dead. Only Amnon is dead."

³⁴Meanwhile, Absalom had fled.

Now the man standing watch looked up and saw many people on the road west of him, coming down the side of the hill. The watchman went and told the king, "I see men in the direction of Horonaim, on the side of the hill."ᵃ

³⁵Jonadab said to the king, "See, the king's sons are here; it has happened just as your servant said."

³⁶As he finished speaking, the king's sons came in, wailing loudly. The king, too, and all his servants wept very bitterly.

³⁷Absalom fled and went to Talmai son of Ammihud, the king of Geshur. But King David mourned for his son every day.

³⁸After Absalom fled and went to Ge-shur, he stayed there three years. ³⁹And the spirit of the kingᵇ longed to go to Absalom, for he was consoled concerning Amnon's death.

Absalom Returns to Jerusalem

14 Joab son of Zeruiah knew that the king's heart longed for Absalom. ²So Joab sent someone to Tekoa and had a wise woman brought from there. He said to her, "Pretend you are in mourning. Dress in mourning clothes, and don't use any cosmetic lotions. Act like a woman who has spent many days grieving for the dead. ³Then go to the king and speak these words to him." And Joab put the words in her mouth.

⁴When the woman from Tekoa wentᶜ to the king, she fell with her face to the ground to pay him honor, and she said, "Help me, O king!"

⁵The king asked her, "What is troubling you?"

She said, "I am indeed a widow; my husband is dead. ⁶I your servant had two sons. They got into a fight with each other in the field, and no one was there to separate them. One struck the other and killed him. ⁷Now the whole clan has risen up against your servant; they say, 'Hand over the one who struck his brother down, so that we may put him to death for the life of his brother whom he killed; then we will get rid of the heir as well.' They would put out the only burning coal I have left, leaving my husband neither name nor descendant on the face of the earth."

⁸The king said to the woman, "Go home, and I will issue an order in your behalf."

⁹But the woman from Tekoa said to him, "My lord the king, let the blame rest on me and on my father's family, and let the king and his throne be without guilt."

¹⁰The king replied, "If anyone says anything to you, bring him to me, and he will not bother you again."

¹¹She said, "Then let the king invoke the Lord his God to prevent the avenger

---

ᵃ34 Septuagint; Hebrew does not have this sentence.   ᵇ39 Dead Sea Scrolls and some Septuagint manuscripts; Masoretic Text *But ⌊the spirit of⌋ David the king*   ᶜ4 Many Hebrew manuscripts, Septuagint, Vulgate and Syriac; most Hebrew manuscripts *spoke* of blood from adding to the destruction, so that my son will not be destroyed."

"As surely as the LORD lives," he said, "not one hair of your son's head will fall to the ground."

[12]Then the woman said, "Let your servant speak a word to my lord the king."

"Speak," he replied.

[13]The woman said, "Why then have you devised a thing like this against the people of God? When the king says this, does he not convict himself, for the king has not brought back his banished son? [14]Like water spilled on the ground, which cannot be recovered, so we must die. But God does not take away life; instead, he devises ways so that a banished person may not remain estranged from him.

[15]"And now I have come to say this to my lord the king because the people have made me afraid. Your servant thought, 'I will speak to the king; perhaps he will do what his servant asks. [16]Perhaps the king will agree to deliver his servant from the hand of the man who is trying to cut off both me and my son from the inheritance God gave us.'

[17]"And now your servant says, 'May the word of my lord the king bring me rest, for my lord the king is like an angel of God in discerning good and evil. May the LORD your God be with you.' "

[18]Then the king said to the woman, "Do not keep from me the answer to what I am going to ask you."

"Let my lord the king speak," the woman said.

[19]The king asked, "Isn't the hand of Joab with you in all this?"

The woman answered, "As surely as you live, my lord the king, no one can turn to the right or to the left from anything my lord the king says. Yes, it was your servant Joab who instructed me to do this and who put all these words into the mouth of your servant. [20]Your servant Joab did this to change the present situation. My lord has wisdom like that of an angel of God—he knows everything that happens in the land."

[21]The king said to Joab, "Very well, I will do it. Go, bring back the young man Absalom."

[22]Joab fell with his face to the ground to pay him honor, and he blessed the king. Joab said, "Today your servant knows that he has found favor in your eyes, my lord the king, because the king has granted his servant's request."

[23]Then Joab went to Geshur and brought Absalom back to Jerusalem. [24]But the king said, "He must go to his own house; he must not see my face." So Absalom went to his own house and did not see the face of the king.

[25]In all Israel there was not a man so highly praised for his handsome appearance as Absalom. From the top of his head to the sole of his foot there was no blemish in him. [26]Whenever he cut the hair of his head—he used to cut his hair from time to time when it became too heavy for him—he would weigh it, and its weight was two hundred shekels[a] by the royal standard.

[27]Three sons and a daughter were born to Absalom. The daughter's name was Tamar, and she became a beautiful woman.

[28]Absalom lived two years in Jerusalem without seeing the king's face. [29]Then Absalom sent for Joab in order to send him to the king, but Joab refused to come to him. So he sent a second time, but he refused to come. [30]Then he said to his servants, "Look, Joab's field is next to mine, and he has barley there. Go and set it on fire." So Absalom's servants set the field on fire.

[31]Then Joab did go to Absalom's house and he said to him, "Why have your servants set my field on fire?"

[32]Absalom said to Joab, "Look, I sent word to you and said, 'Come here so I can send you to the king to ask, "Why have I come from Geshur? It would be better for me if I were still there!" ' Now then, I want to see the king's face, and if I am guilty of anything, let him put me to death."

[33]So Joab went to the king and told him this. Then the king summoned Absalom, and he came in and bowed down with his face to the ground before the king. And the king kissed Absalom.

Absalom's Conspiracy

15 In the course of time, Absalom provided himself with a chariot and horses and with fifty men to run ahead of him. [2]He would get up early and stand by the side of the road leading to the city

---

[a]26 That is, about 5 pounds (about 2.3 kilograms)

gate. Whenever anyone came with a complaint to be placed before the king for a decision, Absalom would call out to him, "What town are you from?" He would answer, "Your servant is from one of the tribes of Israel." [3]Then Absalom would say to him, "Look, your claims are valid and proper, but there is no representative of the king to hear you." [4]And Absalom would add, "If only I were appointed judge in the land! Then everyone who has a complaint or case could come to me and I would see that he gets justice."

[5]Also, whenever anyone approached him to bow down before him, Absalom would reach out his hand, take hold of him and kiss him. [6]Absalom behaved in this way toward all the Israelites who came to the king asking for justice, and so he stole the hearts of the men of Israel.

[7]At the end of four[a] years, Absalom said to the king, "Let me go to Hebron and fulfill a vow I made to the LORD. [8]While your servant was living at Geshur in Aram, I made this vow: 'If the LORD takes me back to Jerusalem, I will worship the LORD in Hebron.[b]' "

[9]The king said to him, "Go in peace." So he went to Hebron.

[10]Then Absalom sent secret messengers throughout the tribes of Israel to say, "As soon as you hear the sound of the trumpets, then say, 'Absalom is king in Hebron.' " [11]Two hundred men from Jerusalem had accompanied Absalom. They had been invited as guests and went quite innocently, knowing nothing about the matter. [12]While Absalom was offering sacrifices, he also sent for Ahithophel the Gilonite, David's counselor, to come from Giloh, his hometown. And so the conspiracy gained strength, and Absalom's following kept on increasing.

David Flees

[13]A messenger came and told David, "The hearts of the men of Israel are with Absalom."

[14]Then David said to all his officials who were with him in Jerusalem, "Come! We must flee, or none of us will escape from Absalom. We must leave immediately, or he will move quickly to overtake us and bring ruin upon us and put the city to the sword."

[15]The king's officials answered him, "Your servants are ready to do whatever our lord the king chooses."

[16]The king set out, with his entire household following him; but he left ten concubines to take care of the palace. [17]So the king set out, with all the people following him, and they halted at a place some distance away. [18]All his men marched past him, along with all the Kerethites and Pelethites; and all the six hundred Gittites who had accompanied him from Gath marched before the king.

[19]The king said to Ittai the Gittite, "Why should you come along with us? Go back and stay with King Absalom. You are a foreigner, an exile from your homeland. [20]You came only yesterday. And today shall I make you wander about with us, when I do not know where I am going? Go back, and take your countrymen. May kindness and faithfulness be with you."

[21]But Ittai replied to the king, "As surely as the LORD lives, and as my lord the king lives, wherever my lord the king may be, whether it means life or death, there will your servant be."

[22]David said to Ittai, "Go ahead, march on." So Ittai the Gittite marched on with all his men and the families that were with him.

[23]The whole countryside wept aloud as all the people passed by. The king also crossed the Kidron Valley, and all the people moved on toward the desert.

[24]Zadok was there, too, and all the Levites who were with him were carrying the ark of the covenant of God. They set down the ark of God, and Abiathar offered sacrifices[c] until all the people had finished leaving the city.

[25]Then the king said to Zadok, "Take the ark of God back into the city. If I find favor in the LORD's eyes, he will bring me back and let me see it and his dwelling place again. [26]But if he says, 'I am not pleased with you,' then I am ready; let him do to me whatever seems good to him."

[27]The king also said to Zadok the priest, "Aren't you a seer? Go back to the

city in peace, with your son Ahimaaz and Jonathan son of Abiathar. You and Abiathar take your two sons with you. 28I will wait at the fords in the desert until word comes from you to inform me." 29So Zadok and Abiathar took the ark of God back to Jerusalem and stayed there.

30But David continued up the Mount of Olives, weeping as he went; his head was covered and he was barefoot. All the people with him covered their heads too and were weeping as they went up. 31Now David had been told, "Ahithophel is among the conspirators with Absalom." So David prayed, "O LORD, turn Ahithophel's counsel into foolishness."

32When David arrived at the summit, where people used to worship God, Hushai the Arkite was there to meet him, his robe torn and dust on his head. 33David said to him, "If you go with me, you will be a burden to me. 34But if you return to the city and say to Absalom, 'I will be your servant, O king; I was your father's servant in the past, but now I will be your servant,' then you can help me by frustrating Ahithophel's advice. 35Won't the priests Zadok and Abiathar be there with you? Tell them anything you hear in the king's palace. 36Their two sons, Ahimaaz son of Zadok and Jonathan son of Abiathar, are there with them. Send them to me with anything you hear."

37So David's friend Hushai arrived at Jerusalem as Absalom was entering the city.

David and Ziba

16 When David had gone a short distance beyond the summit, there was Ziba, the steward of Mephibosheth, waiting to meet him. He had a string of donkeys saddled and loaded with two hundred loaves of bread, a hundred cakes of raisins, a hundred cakes of figs and a skin of wine.

2The king asked Ziba, "Why have you brought these?"

Ziba answered, "The donkeys are for the king's household to ride on, the bread and fruit are for the men to eat, and the wine is to refresh those who become exhausted in the desert."

3The king then asked, "Where is your master's grandson?"

Ziba said to him, "He is staying in Jerusalem, because he thinks, 'Today the house of Israel will give me back my grandfather's kingdom.' "

4Then the king said to Ziba, "All that belonged to Mephibosheth is now yours."

"I humbly bow," Ziba said. "May I find favor in your eyes, my lord the king."

Shimei Curses David

5As King David approached Bahurim, a man from the same clan as Saul's family came out from there. His name was Shimei son of Gera, and he cursed as he came out. 6He pelted David and all the king's officials with stones, though all the troops and the special guard were on David's right and left. 7As he cursed, Shimei said, "Get out, get out, you man of blood, you scoundrel! 8The LORD has repaid you for all the blood you shed in the household of Saul, in whose place you have reigned. The LORD has handed the kingdom over to your son Absalom. You have come to ruin because you are a man of blood!"

9Then Abishai son of Zeruiah said to the king, "Why should this dead dog curse my lord the king? Let me go over and cut off his head."

10But the king said, "What do you and I have in common, you sons of Zeruiah? If he is cursing because the LORD said to him, 'Curse David,' who can ask, 'Why do you do this?' "

11David then said to Abishai and all his officials, "My son, who is of my own flesh, is trying to take my life. How much more, then, this Benjamite! Leave him alone; let him curse, for the LORD has told him to. 12It may be that the LORD will see my distress and repay me with good for the cursing I am receiving today."

13So David and his men continued along the road while Shimei was going along the hillside opposite him, cursing as he went and throwing stones at him and showering him with dirt. 14The king and all the people with him arrived at their destination exhausted. And there he refreshed himself.

The Advice of Hushai and Ahithophel

15Meanwhile, Absalom and all the men of Israel came to Jerusalem, and Ahithophel was with him. 16Then Hushai the Arkite, David's friend, went to Absalom and said to him, "Long live the king! Long live the king!"

17Absalom asked Hushai, "Is this the love you show your friend? Why didn't you go with your friend?"

18Hushai said to Absalom, "No, the one chosen by the LORD, by these people, and by all the men of Israel—his I will be, and I will remain with him. 19Furthermore, whom should I serve? Should I not serve the son? Just as I served your father, so I will serve you."

20Absalom said to Ahithophel, "Give us your advice. What should we do?"

21Ahithophel answered, "Lie with your father's concubines whom he left to take care of the palace. Then all Israel will hear that you have made yourself a stench in your father's nostrils, and the hands of everyone with you will be strengthened." 22So they pitched a tent for Absalom on the roof, and he lay with his father's concubines in the sight of all Israel.

23Now in those days the advice Ahithophel gave was like that of one who inquires of God. That was how both David and Absalom regarded all of Ahithophel's advice.

17 Ahithophel said to Absalom, "I woulda choose twelve thousand men and set out tonight in pursuit of David. 2I wouldb attack him while he is weary and weak. I wouldb strike him with terror, and then all the people with him will flee. I wouldb strike down only the king 3and bring all the people back to you. The death of the man you seek will mean the return of all; all the people will be unharmed." 4This plan seemed good to Absalom and to all the elders of Israel.

5But Absalom said, "Summon also Hushai the Arkite, so we can hear what he has to say." 6When Hushai came to him, Absalom said, "Ahithophel has given this advice. Should we do what he says? If not, give us your opinion."

7Hushai replied to Absalom, "The advice Ahithophel has given is not good this time. 8You know your father and his men; they are fighters, and as fierce as a wild bear robbed of her cubs. Besides, your father is an experienced fighter; he will not spend the night with the troops. 9Even now, he is hidden in a cave or some other place. If he should attack your

troops first,c whoever hears about it will say, 'There has been a slaughter among the troops who follow Absalom.' 10Then even the bravest soldier, whose heart is like the heart of a lion, will melt with fear, for all Israel knows that your father is a fighter and that those with him are brave.

11"So I advise you: Let all Israel, from Dan to Beersheba—as numerous as the sand on the seashore—be gathered to you, with you yourself leading them into battle. 12Then we will attack him wherever he may be found, and we will fall on him as dew settles on the ground. Neither he nor any of his men will be left alive. 13If he withdraws into a city, then all Israel will bring ropes to that city, and we will drag it down to the valley until not even a piece of it can be found."

14Absalom and all the men of Israel said, "The advice of Hushai the Arkite is better than that of Ahithophel." For the LORD had determined to frustrate the good advice of Ahithophel in order to bring disaster on Absalom.

15Hushai told Zadok and Abiathar, the priests, "Ahithophel has advised Absalom and the elders of Israel to do such and such, but I have advised them to do so and so. 16Now send a message immediately and tell David, 'Do not spend the night at the fords in the desert; cross over without fail, or the king and all the people with him will be swallowed up.' "

17Jonathan and Ahimaaz were staying at En Rogel. A servant girl was to go and inform them, and they were to go and tell King David, for they could not risk being seen entering the city. 18But a young man saw them and told Absalom. So the two of them left quickly and went to the house of a man in Bahurim. He had a well in his courtyard, and they climbed down into it. 19His wife took a covering and spread it out over the opening of the well and scattered grain over it. No one knew anything about it.

20When Absalom's men came to the woman at the house, they asked, "Where are Ahimaaz and Jonathan?"

The woman answered them, "They crossed over the brook."d The men

---

a1 Or Let me   b2 Or will   c9 Or When some of the men fall at the first attack   d20 Or "They passed by the sheep pen toward the water."

searched but found no one, so they returned to Jerusalem.

²¹After the men had gone, the two climbed out of the well and went to inform King David. They said to him, "Set out and cross the river at once; Ahithophel has advised such and such against you." ²²So David and all the people with him set out and crossed the Jordan. By daybreak, no one was left who had not crossed the Jordan.

²³When Ahithophel saw that his advice had not been followed, he saddled his donkey and set out for his house in his hometown. He put his house in order and then hanged himself. So he died and was buried in his father's tomb.

²⁴David went to Mahanaim, and Absalom crossed the Jordan with all the men of Israel. ²⁵Absalom had appointed Amasa over the army in place of Joab. Amasa was the son of a man named Jether,ᵃ an Israeliteᵇ who had married Abigail,ᶜ the daughter of Nahash and sister of Zeruiah the mother of Joab. ²⁶The Israelites and Absalom camped in the land of Gilead.

²⁷When David came to Mahanaim, Shobi son of Nahash from Rabbah of the Ammonites, and Makir son of Ammiel from Lo Debar, and Barzillai the Gileadite from Rogelim ²⁸brought bedding and bowls and articles of pottery. They also brought wheat and barley, flour and roasted grain, beans and lentils,ᵈ ²⁹honey and curds, sheep, and cheese from cows' milk for David and his people to eat. For they said, "The people have become hungry and tired and thirsty in the desert."

Absalom's Death

18 David mustered the men who were with him and appointed over them commanders of thousands and commanders of hundreds. ²David sent the troops out—a third under the command of Joab, a third under Joab's brother Abishai son of Zeruiah, and a third under Ittai the Gittite. The king told the troops, "I myself will surely march out with you."

³But the men said, "You must not go out; if we are forced to flee, they won't care about us. Even if half of us die, they won't care; but you are worth ten thou-

sand of us.ᵉ It would be better now for you to give us support from the city."

⁴The king answered, "I will do whatever seems best to you."

So the king stood beside the gate while all the men marched out in units of hundreds and of thousands. ⁵The king commanded Joab, Abishai and Ittai, "Be gentle with the young man Absalom for my sake." And all the troops heard the king giving orders concerning Absalom to each of the commanders.

⁶The army marched into the field to fight Israel, and the battle took place in the forest of Ephraim. ⁷There the army of Israel was defeated by David's men, and the casualties that day were great—twenty thousand men. ⁸The battle spread out over the whole countryside, and the forest claimed more lives that day than the sword.

⁹Now Absalom happened to meet David's men. He was riding his mule, and as the mule went under the thick branches of a large oak, Absalom's head got caught in the tree. He was left hanging in midair, while the mule he was riding kept on going.

¹⁰When one of the men saw this, he told Joab, "I just saw Absalom hanging in an oak tree."

¹¹Joab said to the man who had told him this, "What! You saw him? Why didn't you strike him to the ground right there? Then I would have had to give you ten shekelsᶠ of silver and a warrior's belt."

¹²But the man replied, "Even if a thousand shekelsᵍ were weighed out into my hands, I would not lift my hand against the king's son. In our hearing the king commanded you and Abishai and Ittai, 'Protect the young man Absalom for my sake.'ʰ ¹³And if I had put my life in jeop-

ᵃ25 Hebrew *Ithra,* a variant of *Jether*
ᵇ25 Hebrew and some Septuagint manuscripts; other Septuagint manuscripts (see also 1 Chron. 2:17) *Ishmaelite* or *Jezreelite*   ᶜ25 Hebrew *Abigal,* a variant of *Abigail*   ᵈ28 Most Septuagint manuscripts and Syriac; Hebrew *lentils, and roasted grain*   ᵉ3 Two Hebrew manuscripts, some Septuagint manuscripts and Vulgate; most Hebrew manuscripts *care; for now there are ten thousand like us*   ᶠ11 That is, about 4 ounces (about 115 grams)   ᵍ12 That is, about 25 pounds (about 11 kilograms)   ʰ12 A few Hebrew manuscripts, Septuagint, Vulgate and Syriac; most Hebrew manuscripts may be translated *Absalom, whoever you may be.*

ardy[a]—and nothing is hidden from the king—you would have kept your distance from me."

[14]Joab said, "I'm not going to wait like this for you." So he took three javelins in his hand and plunged them into Absalom's heart while Absalom was still alive in the oak tree. [15]And ten of Joab's armor-bearers surrounded Absalom, struck him and killed him.

[16]Then Joab sounded the trumpet, and the troops stopped pursuing Israel, for Joab halted them. [17]They took Absalom, threw him into a big pit in the forest and piled up a large heap of rocks over him. Meanwhile, all the Israelites fled to their homes.

[18]During his lifetime Absalom had taken a pillar and erected it in the King's Valley as a monument to himself, for he thought, "I have no son to carry on the memory of my name." He named the pillar after himself, and it is called Absalom's Monument to this day.

David Mourns

[19]Now Ahimaaz son of Zadok said, "Let me run and take the news to the king that the LORD has delivered him from the hand of his enemies."

[20]"You are not the one to take the news today," Joab told him. "You may take the news another time, but you must not do so today, because the king's son is dead."

[21]Then Joab said to a Cushite, "Go, tell the king what you have seen." The Cushite bowed down before Joab and ran off.

[22]Ahimaaz son of Zadok again said to Joab, "Come what may, please let me run behind the Cushite."

But Joab replied, "My son, why do you want to go? You don't have any news that will bring you a reward."

[23]He said, "Come what may, I want to run."

So Joab said, "Run!" Then Ahimaaz ran by way of the plain[b] and outran the Cushite.

[24]While David was sitting between the inner and outer gates, the watchman went up to the roof of the gateway by the wall. As he looked out, he saw a man running alone. [25]The watchman called out to the king and reported it.

The king said, "If he is alone, he must have good news." And the man came closer and closer.

[26]Then the watchman saw another man running, and he called down to the gatekeeper, "Look, another man running alone!"

The king said, "He must be bringing good news, too."

[27]The watchman said, "It seems to me that the first one runs like Ahimaaz son of Zadok."

"He's a good man," the king said. "He comes with good news."

[28]Then Ahimaaz called out to the king, "All is well!" He bowed down before the king with his face to the ground and said, "Praise be to the LORD your God! He has delivered up the men who lifted their hands against my lord the king."

[29]The king asked, "Is the young man Absalom safe?"

Ahimaaz answered, "I saw great confusion just as Joab was about to send the king's servant and me, your servant, but I don't know what it was."

[30]The king said, "Stand aside and wait here." So he stepped aside and stood there.

[31]Then the Cushite arrived and said, "My lord the king, hear the good news! The LORD has delivered you today from all who rose up against you."

[32]The king asked the Cushite, "Is the young man Absalom safe?"

The Cushite replied, "May the enemies of my lord the king and all who rise up to harm you be like that young man."

[33]The king was shaken. He went up to the room over the gateway and wept. As he went, he said: "O my son Absalom! My son, my son Absalom! If only I had died instead of you—O Absalom, my son, my son!"

19 Joab was told, "The king is weeping and mourning for Absalom." [2]And for the whole army the victory that day was turned into mourning, because on that day the troops heard it said, "The king is grieving for his son." [3]The men stole into the city that day as men steal in who are ashamed when they flee from battle. [4]The king covered his face and

---

[a]13 Or *Otherwise, if I had acted treacherously toward him*   [b]23 That is, the plain of the Jordan

cried aloud, "O my son Absalom! O Absalom, my son, my son!"

⁵Then Joab went into the house to the king and said, "Today you have humiliated all your men, who have just saved your life and the lives of your sons and daughters and the lives of your wives and concubines. ⁶You love those who hate you and hate those who love you. You have made it clear today that the commanders and their men mean nothing to you. I see that you would be pleased if Absalom were alive today and all of us were dead. ⁷Now go out and encourage your men. I swear by the LORD that if you don't go out, not a man will be left with you by nightfall. This will be worse for you than all the calamities that have come upon you from your youth till now."

⁸So the king got up and took his seat in the gateway. When the men were told, "The king is sitting in the gateway," they all came before him.

David Returns to Jerusalem

Meanwhile, the Israelites had fled to their homes. ⁹Throughout the tribes of Israel, the people were all arguing with each other, saying, "The king delivered us from the hand of our enemies; he is the one who rescued us from the hand of the Philistines. But now he has fled the country because of Absalom; ¹⁰and Absalom, whom we anointed to rule over us, has died in battle. So why do you say nothing about bringing the king back?"

¹¹King David sent this message to Zadok and Abiathar, the priests: "Ask the elders of Judah, 'Why should you be the last to bring the king back to his palace, since what is being said throughout Israel has reached the king at his quarters? ¹²You are my brothers, my own flesh and blood. So why should you be the last to bring back the king?' ¹³And say to Amasa, 'Are you not my own flesh and blood? May God deal with me, be it ever so severely, if from now on you are not the commander of my army in place of Joab.'"

¹⁴He won over the hearts of all the men of Judah as though they were one man. They sent word to the king, "Return, you and all your men." ¹⁵Then the king returned and went as far as the Jordan.

Now the men of Judah had come to Gilgal to go out and meet the king and bring him across the Jordan. ¹⁶Shimei son of Gera, the Benjamite from Bahurim, hurried down with the men of Judah to meet King David. ¹⁷With him were a thousand Benjamites, along with Ziba, the steward of Saul's household, and his fifteen sons and twenty servants. They rushed to the Jordan, where the king was. ¹⁸They crossed at the ford to take the king's household over and to do whatever he wished.

When Shimei son of Gera crossed the Jordan, he fell prostrate before the king ¹⁹and said to him, "May my lord not hold me guilty. Do not remember how your servant did wrong on the day my lord the king left Jerusalem. May the king put it out of his mind. ²⁰For I your servant know that I have sinned, but today I have come here as the first of the whole house of Joseph to come down and meet my lord the king."

²¹Then Abishai son of Zeruiah said, "Shouldn't Shimei be put to death for this? He cursed the LORD's anointed."

²²David replied, "What do you and I have in common, you sons of Zeruiah? This day you have become my adversaries! Should anyone be put to death in Israel today? Do I not know that today I am king over Israel?" ²³So the king said to Shimei, "You shall not die." And the king promised him on oath.

²⁴Mephibosheth, Saul's grandson, also went down to meet the king. He had not taken care of his feet or trimmed his mustache or washed his clothes from the day the king left until the day he returned safely. ²⁵When he came from Jerusalem to meet the king, the king asked him, "Why didn't you go with me, Mephibosheth?"

²⁶He said, "My lord the king, since I your servant am lame, I said, 'I will have my donkey saddled and will ride on it, so I can go with the king.' But Ziba my servant betrayed me. ²⁷And he has slandered your servant to my lord the king. My lord the king is like an angel of God; so do whatever pleases you. ²⁸All my grandfather's descendants deserved nothing but death from my lord the king, but you gave your servant a place among those who eat at your table. So what right do I have to make any more appeals to the king?"

²⁹The king said to him, "Why say more? I order you and Ziba to divide the fields."

³⁰Mephibosheth said to the king, "Let him take everything, now that my lord the king has arrived home safely."

³¹Barzillai the Gileadite also came down from Rogelim to cross the Jordan with the king and to send him on his way from there. ³²Now Barzillai was a very old man, eighty years of age. He had provided for the king during his stay in Mahanaim, for he was a very wealthy man. ³³The king said to Barzillai, "Cross over with me and stay with me in Jerusalem, and I will provide for you."

³⁴But Barzillai answered the king, "How many more years will I live, that I should go up to Jerusalem with the king? ³⁵I am now eighty years old. Can I tell the difference between what is good and what is not? Can your servant taste what he eats and drinks? Can I still hear the voices of men and women singers? Why should your servant be an added burden to my lord the king? ³⁶Your servant will cross over the Jordan with the king for a short distance, but why should the king reward me in this way? ³⁷Let your servant return, that I may die in my own town near the tomb of my father and mother. But here is your servant Kimham. Let him cross over with my lord the king. Do for him whatever pleases you."

³⁸The king said, "Kimham shall cross over with me, and I will do for him whatever pleases you. And anything you desire from me I will do for you."

³⁹So all the people crossed the Jordan, and then the king crossed over. The king kissed Barzillai and gave him his blessing, and Barzillai returned to his home.

⁴⁰When the king crossed over to Gilgal, Kimham crossed with him. All the troops of Judah and half the troops of Israel had taken the king over.

⁴¹Soon all the men of Israel were coming to the king and saying to him, "Why did our brothers, the men of Judah, steal the king away and bring him and his household across the Jordan, together with all his men?"

⁴²All the men of Judah answered the men of Israel, "We did this because the king is closely related to us. Why are you angry about it? Have we eaten any of the king's provisions? Have we taken anything for ourselves?"

⁴³Then the men of Israel answered the men of Judah, "We have ten shares in the king; and besides, we have a greater claim on David than you have. So why do you treat us with contempt? Were we not the first to speak of bringing back our king?"

But the men of Judah responded even more harshly than the men of Israel.

Sheba Rebels Against David

20 Now a troublemaker named Sheba son of Bicri, a Benjamite, happened to be there. He sounded the trumpet and shouted,

"We have no share in David,
  no part in Jesse's son!
Every man to his tent, O Israel!"

²So all the men of Israel deserted David to follow Sheba son of Bicri. But the men of Judah stayed by their king all the way from the Jordan to Jerusalem.

³When David returned to his palace in Jerusalem, he took the ten concubines he had left to take care of the palace and put them in a house under guard. He provided for them, but did not lie with them. They were kept in confinement till the day of their death, living as widows.

⁴Then the king said to Amasa, "Summon the men of Judah to come to me within three days, and be here yourself." ⁵But when Amasa went to summon Judah, he took longer than the time the king had set for him.

⁶David said to Abishai, "Now Sheba son of Bicri will do us more harm than Absalom did. Take your master's men and pursue him, or he will find fortified cities and escape from us." ⁷So Joab's men and the Kerethites and Pelethites and all the mighty warriors went out under the command of Abishai. They marched out from Jerusalem to pursue Sheba son of Bicri.

⁸While they were at the great rock in Gibeon, Amasa came to meet them. Joab was wearing his military tunic, and strapped over it at his waist was a belt with a dagger in its sheath. As he stepped forward, it dropped out of its sheath.

⁹Joab said to Amasa, "How are you, my brother?" Then Joab took Amasa by the beard with his right hand to kiss him.

¹⁰Amasa was not on his guard against the dagger in Joab's hand, and Joab plunged it into his belly, and his intestines spilled out on the ground. Without being stabbed again, Amasa died. Then Joab and his brother Abishai pursued Sheba son of Bicri.

¹¹One of Joab's men stood beside Amasa and said, "Whoever favors Joab, and whoever is for David, let him follow Joab!" ¹²Amasa lay wallowing in his blood in the middle of the road, and the man saw that all the troops came to a halt there. When he realized that everyone who came up to Amasa stopped, he dragged him from the road into a field and threw a garment over him. ¹³After Amasa had been removed from the road, all the men went on with Joab to pursue Sheba son of Bicri.

¹⁴Sheba passed through all the tribes of Israel to Abel Beth Maacah[a] and through the entire region of the Berites, who gathered together and followed him. ¹⁵All the troops with Joab came and besieged Sheba in Abel Beth Maacah. They built a siege ramp up to the city, and it stood against the outer fortifications. While they were battering the wall to bring it down, ¹⁶a wise woman called from the city, "Listen! Listen! Tell Joab to come here so I can speak to him." ¹⁷He went toward her, and she asked, "Are you Joab?"

"I am," he answered.

She said, "Listen to what your servant has to say."

"I'm listening," he said.

¹⁸She continued, "Long ago they used to say, 'Get your answer at Abel,' and that settled it. ¹⁹We are the peaceful and faithful in Israel. You are trying to destroy a city that is a mother in Israel. Why do you want to swallow up the LORD's inheritance?"

²⁰"Far be it from me!" Joab replied, "Far be it from me to swallow up or destroy! ²¹That is not the case. A man named Sheba son of Bicri, from the hill country of Ephraim, has lifted up his hand against the king, against David. Hand over this one man, and I'll withdraw from the city."

The woman said to Joab, "His head will be thrown to you from the wall."

²²Then the woman went to all the people with her wise advice, and they cut off the head of Sheba son of Bicri and threw it to Joab. So he sounded the trumpet, and his men dispersed from the city, each returning to his home. And Joab went back to the king in Jerusalem.

²³Joab was over Israel's entire army; Benaiah son of Jehoiada was over the Kerethites and Pelethites; ²⁴Adoniram[b] was in charge of forced labor; Jehoshaphat son of Ahilud was recorder; ²⁵Sheva was secretary; Zadok and Abiathar were priests; ²⁶and Ira the Jairite was David's priest.

The Gibeonites Avenged

21 During the reign of David, there was a famine for three successive years; so David sought the face of the LORD. The LORD said, "It is on account of Saul and his blood-stained house; it is because he put the Gibeonites to death."

²The king summoned the Gibeonites and spoke to them. (Now the Gibeonites were not a part of Israel but were survivors of the Amorites; the Israelites had sworn to ⌊spare⌋ them, but Saul in his zeal for Israel and Judah had tried to annihilate them.) ³David asked the Gibeonites, "What shall I do for you? How shall I make amends so that you will bless the LORD's inheritance?"

⁴The Gibeonites answered him, "We have no right to demand silver or gold from Saul or his family, nor do we have the right to put anyone in Israel to death."

"What do you want me to do for you?" David asked.

⁵They answered the king, "As for the man who destroyed us and plotted against us so that we have been decimated and have no place anywhere in Israel, ⁶let seven of his male descendants be given to us to be killed and exposed before the LORD at Gibeah of Saul—the LORD's chosen one."

So the king said, "I will give them to you."

⁷The king spared Mephibosheth son of Jonathan, the son of Saul, because of the oath before the LORD between David and Jonathan son of Saul. ⁸But the king took Armoni and Mephibosheth, the two sons of Aiah's daughter Rizpah, whom she had

---

a 14 Or *Abel, even Beth Maacah*; also in verse 15
b 24 Some Septuagint manuscripts (see also 1 Kings 4:6 and 5:14); Hebrew *Adoram*

borne to Saul, together with the five sons of Saul's daughter Merab,[a] whom she had borne to Adriel son of Barzillai the Meholathite. [9]He handed them over to the Gibeonites, who killed and exposed them on a hill before the LORD. All seven of them fell together; they were put to death during the first days of the harvest, just as the barley harvest was beginning.

[10]Rizpah daughter of Aiah took sackcloth and spread it out for herself on a rock. From the beginning of the harvest till the rain poured down from the heavens on the bodies, she did not let the birds of the air touch them by day or the wild animals by night. [11]When David was told what Aiah's daughter Rizpah, Saul's concubine, had done, [12]he went and took the bones of Saul and his son Jonathan from the citizens of Jabesh Gilead. (They had taken them secretly from the public square at Beth Shan, where the Philistines had hung them after they struck Saul down on Gilboa.) [13]David brought the bones of Saul and his son Jonathan from there, and the bones of those who had been killed and exposed were gathered up.

[14]They buried the bones of Saul and his son Jonathan in the tomb of Saul's father Kish, at Zela in Benjamin, and did everything the king commanded. After that, God answered prayer in behalf of the land.

Wars Against the Philistines

[15]Once again there was a battle between the Philistines and Israel. David went down with his men to fight against the Philistines, and he became exhausted. [16]And Ishbi-Benob, one of the descendants of Rapha, whose bronze spearhead weighed three hundred shekels[b] and who was armed with a new ⌞sword⌟, said he would kill David. [17]But Abishai son of Zeruiah came to David's rescue; he struck the Philistine down and killed him. Then David's men swore to him, saying, "Never again will you go out with us to battle, so that the lamp of Israel will not be extinguished."

[18]In the course of time, there was another battle with the Philistines, at Gob. At that time Sibbecai the Hushathite killed Saph, one of the descendants of Rapha.

[19]In another battle with the Philistines at Gob, Elhanan son of Jaare-Oregim[c] the Bethlehemite killed Goliath[d] the Gittite, who had a spear with a shaft like a weaver's rod.

[20]In still another battle, which took place at Gath, there was a huge man with six fingers on each hand and six toes on each foot—twenty-four in all. He also was descended from Rapha. [21]When he taunted Israel, Jonathan son of Shimeah, David's brother, killed him.

[22]These four were descendants of Rapha in Gath, and they fell at the hands of David and his men.

David's Song of Praise

22 David sang to the LORD the words of this song when the LORD delivered him from the hand of all his enemies and from the hand of Saul. [2]He said:

"The LORD is my rock, my fortress
    and my deliverer;
[3]   my God is my rock, in whom I
        take refuge,
    my shield and the horn[e] of my
        salvation.
He is my stronghold, my refuge and
        my savior—
    from violent men you save me.
[4]I call to the LORD, who is worthy of
        praise,
    and I am saved from my enemies.

[5]"The waves of death swirled about
        me;
    the torrents of destruction
        overwhelmed me.
[6]The cords of the grave[f] coiled
        around me;
    the snares of death confronted me.
[7]In my distress I called to the LORD;
    I called out to my God.
From his temple he heard my voice;
    my cry came to his ears.

[8]"The earth trembled and quaked,

---

[a]8 Two Hebrew manuscripts, some Septuagint manuscripts and Syriac (see also 1 Samuel 18:19); most Hebrew and Septuagint manuscripts *Michal*   [b]16 That is, about 7 1/2 pounds (about 3.5 kilograms)   [c]19 Or *son of Jair the weaver*   [d]19 Hebrew and Septuagint; 1 Chron. 20:5 *son of Jair killed Lahmi the brother of Goliath*   [e]3 *Horn* here symbolizes strength.   [f]6 Hebrew *Sheol*

the foundations of the heavens[a]
　shook;
they trembled because he was
　angry.
⁹Smoke rose from his nostrils;
　consuming fire came from his
　　mouth,
　burning coals blazed out of it.
¹⁰He parted the heavens and came
　　down;
　dark clouds were under his feet.
¹¹He mounted the cherubim and flew;
　he soared[b] on the wings of the
　　wind.
¹²He made darkness his canopy around
　　him—
　the dark[c] rain clouds of the sky.
¹³Out of the brightness of his presence
　bolts of lightning blazed forth.
¹⁴The LORD thundered from heaven;
　the voice of the Most High
　　resounded.
¹⁵He shot arrows and scattered ⌊the
　　enemies⌋,
　bolts of lightning and routed them.
¹⁶The valleys of the sea were exposed
　and the foundations of the earth
　　laid bare
　at the rebuke of the LORD,
　at the blast of breath from his
　　nostrils.

¹⁷"He reached down from on high and
　　took hold of me;
　he drew me out of deep waters.
¹⁸He rescued me from my powerful
　　enemy,
　from my foes, who were too strong
　　for me.
¹⁹They confronted me in the day of my
　　disaster,
　but the LORD was my support.
²⁰He brought me out into a spacious
　　place;
　he rescued me because he
　　delighted in me.

²¹"The LORD has dealt with me
　　according to my
　　righteousness,
　according to the cleanness of my
　　hands he has rewarded me.
²²For I have kept the ways of the LORD;
　I have not done evil by turning
　　from my God.
²³All his laws are before me;

I have not turned away from his
　decrees.
²⁴I have been blameless before him
　and have kept myself from sin.
²⁵The LORD has rewarded me according
　　to my righteousness,
　according to my cleanness[d] in his
　　sight.

²⁶"To the faithful you show yourself
　　faithful,
　to the blameless you show yourself
　　blameless,
²⁷to the pure you show yourself pure,
　but to the crooked you show
　　yourself shrewd.
²⁸You save the humble,
　but your eyes are on the haughty
　　to bring them low.
²⁹You are my lamp, O LORD;
　the LORD turns my darkness into
　　light.
³⁰With your help I can advance against
　　a troop[e];
　with my God I can scale a wall.

³¹"As for God, his way is perfect;
　the word of the LORD is flawless.
He is a shield
　for all who take refuge in him.
³²For who is God besides the LORD?
　And who is the Rock except our
　　God?
³³It is God who arms me with
　　strength[f]
　and makes my way perfect.
³⁴He makes my feet like the feet of a
　　deer;
　he enables me to stand on the
　　heights.
³⁵He trains my hands for battle;
　my arms can bend a bow of
　　bronze.
³⁶You give me your shield of victory;
　you stoop down to make me
　　great.

a8 Hebrew; Vulgate and Syriac (see also Psalm
18:7) *mountains*   *b11* Many Hebrew
manuscripts (see also Psalm 18:10); most Hebrew
manuscripts *appeared*   *c12* Septuagint and
Vulgate (see also Psalm 18:11); Hebrew *massed*
d25 Hebrew; Septuagint and Vulgate (see also
Psalm 18:24) *to the cleanness of my hands*
e30 Or *can run through a barricade*   *f33* Dead
Sea Scrolls, some Septuagint manuscripts, Vulgate
and Syriac (see also Psalm 18:32); Masoretic Text
who is my strong refuge

³⁷You broaden the path beneath me,
so that my ankles do not turn.
³⁸"I pursued my enemies and crushed
them;
I did not turn back till they were
destroyed.
³⁹I crushed them completely, and they
could not rise;
they fell beneath my feet.
⁴⁰You armed me with strength for
battle;
you made my adversaries bow at
my feet.
⁴¹You made my enemies turn their
backs in flight,
and I destroyed my foes.
⁴²They cried for help, but there was no
one to save them—
to the LORD, but he did not
answer.
⁴³I beat them as fine as the dust of the
earth;
I pounded and trampled them like
mud in the streets.

⁴⁴"You have delivered me from the
attacks of my people;
you have preserved me as the head
of nations.
People I did not know are subject to
me,
⁴⁵   and foreigners come cringing to
me;
as soon as they hear me, they obey
me.
⁴⁶They all lose heart;
they come trembling*ᵃ* from their
strongholds.

⁴⁷"The LORD lives! Praise be to my
Rock!
Exalted be God, the Rock, my
Savior!
⁴⁸He is the God who avenges me,
who puts the nations under me,
⁴⁹   who sets me free from my enemies.
You exalted me above my foes;
from violent men you rescued me.
⁵⁰Therefore I will praise you, O LORD,
among the nations;
I will sing praises to your name.
⁵¹He gives his king great victories;
he shows unfailing kindness to his
anointed,
to David and his descendants
forever."

The Last Words of David

23 These are the last words of David:

"The oracle of David son of Jesse,
the oracle of the man exalted by
the Most High,
the man anointed by the God of
Jacob,
Israel's singer of songs*ᵇ*:

²"The Spirit of the LORD spoke
through me;
his word was on my tongue.
³The God of Israel spoke,
the Rock of Israel said to me:
'When one rules over men in
righteousness,
when he rules in the fear of God,
⁴he is like the light of morning at
sunrise
on a cloudless morning,
like the brightness after rain
that brings the grass from the
earth.'

⁵"Is not my house right with God?
Has he not made with me an
everlasting covenant,
arranged and secured in every
part?
Will he not bring to fruition my
salvation
and grant me my every desire?
⁶But evil men are all to be cast aside
like thorns,
which are not gathered with the
hand.
⁷Whoever touches thorns
uses a tool of iron or the shaft of a
spear;
they are burned up where they lie."

David's Mighty Men

⁸These are the names of David's
mighty men:
Josheb-Basshebeth,*ᶜ* a Tahkemonite,*ᵈ*
was chief of the Three; he raised his

ᵃ46 Some Septuagint manuscripts and Vulgate (see
also Psalm 18:45); Masoretic Text *they arm
themselves.*   *ᵇ1* Or *Israel's beloved singer*
ᶜ8 Hebrew; some Septuagint manuscripts suggest
Ish-Bosheth, that is, *Esh-Baal* (see also 1 Chron.
11:11 *Jashobeam*).   *ᵈ8* Probably a variant of
Hacmonite (see 1 Chron. 11:11)

spear against eight hundred men, whom he killed[a] in one encounter.

[9]Next to him was Eleazar son of Dodai the Ahohite. As one of the three mighty men, he was with David when they taunted the Philistines gathered ⌊at Pas Dammim⌋[b] for battle. Then the men of Israel retreated, [10]but he stood his ground and struck down the Philistines till his hand grew tired and froze to the sword. The LORD brought about a great victory that day. The troops returned to Eleazar, but only to strip the dead.

[11]Next to him was Shammah son of Agee the Hararite. When the Philistines banded together at a place where there was a field full of lentils, Israel's troops fled from them. [12]But Shammah took his stand in the middle of the field. He defended it and struck the Philistines down, and the LORD brought about a great victory.

[13]During harvest time, three of the thirty chief men came down to David at the cave of Adullam, while a band of Philistines was encamped in the Valley of Rephaim. [14]At that time David was in the stronghold, and the Philistine garrison was at Bethlehem. [15]David longed for water and said, "Oh, that someone would get me a drink of water from the well near the gate of Bethlehem!" [16]So the three mighty men broke through the Philistine lines, drew water from the well near the gate of Bethlehem and carried it back to David. But he refused to drink it; instead, he poured it out before the LORD. [17]"Far be it from me, O LORD, to do this!" he said. "Is it not the blood of men who went at the risk of their lives?" And David would not drink it.

Such were the exploits of the three mighty men.

[18]Abishai the brother of Joab son of Zeruiah was chief of the Three.[c] He raised his spear against three hundred men, whom he killed, and so he became as famous as the Three. [19]Was he not held in greater honor than the Three? He became their commander, even though he was not included among them.

[20]Benaiah son of Jehoiada was a valiant fighter from Kabzeel, who performed great exploits. He struck down two of Moab's best men. He also went down into a pit on a snowy day and killed a lion.

[21]And he struck down a huge Egyptian. Although the Egyptian had a spear in his hand, Benaiah went against him with a club. He snatched the spear from the Egyptian's hand and killed him with his own spear. [22]Such were the exploits of Benaiah son of Jehoiada; he too was as famous as the three mighty men. [23]He was held in greater honor than any of the Thirty, but he was not included among the Three. And David put him in charge of his bodyguard.

[24]Among the Thirty were:

Asahel the brother of Joab,
Elhanan son of Dodo from Bethlehem,
[25]Shammah the Harodite,
Elika the Harodite,
[26]Helez the Paltite,
Ira son of Ikkesh from Tekoa,
[27]Abiezer from Anathoth,
Mebunnai[d] the Hushathite,
[28]Zalmon the Ahohite,
Maharai the Netophathite,
[29]Heled[e] son of Baanah the Netophathite,
Ithai son of Ribai from Gibeah in Benjamin,
[30]Benaiah the Pirathonite,
Hiddai[f] from the ravines of Gaash,
[31]Abi-Albon the Arbathite,
Azmaveth the Barhumite,
[32]Eliahba the Shaalbonite,
the sons of Jashen,
Jonathan [33]son of[g] Shammah the Hararite,
Ahiam son of Sharar[h] the Hararite,
[34]Eliphelet son of Ahasbai the Maacathite,

---

[a]8 Some Septuagint manuscripts (see also 1 Chron. 11:11); Hebrew and other Septuagint manuscripts Three; it was Adino the Eznite who killed eight hundred men   [b]9 See 1 Chron. 11:13; Hebrew gathered there.   [c]18 Most Hebrew manuscripts (see also 1 Chron. 11:20); two Hebrew manuscripts and Syriac Thirty   [d]27 Hebrew; some Septuagint manuscripts (see also 1 Chron. 11:29) Sibbecai   [e]29 Some Hebrew manuscripts and Vulgate (see also 1 Chron. 11:30); most Hebrew manuscripts Heleb   [f]30 Hebrew; some Septuagint manuscripts (see also 1 Chron. 11:32) Hurai   [g]33 Some Septuagint manuscripts (see also 1 Chron. 11:34); Hebrew does not have son of.   [h]33 Hebrew; some Septuagint manuscripts (see also 1 Chron. 11:35) Sacar

Eliam son of Ahithophel the Gilonite,
[35]Hezro the Carmelite,
Paarai the Arbite,
[36]Igal son of Nathan from Zobah,
the son of Hagri,[a]
[37]Zelek the Ammonite,
Naharai the Beerothite, the
armor-bearer of Joab son of
Zeruiah,
[38]Ira the Ithrite,
Gareb the Ithrite
[39]and Uriah the Hittite.
There were thirty-seven in all.

David Counts the Fighting Men

24 Again the anger of the LORD burned against Israel, and he incited David against them, saying, "Go and take a census of Israel and Judah."

[2]So the king said to Joab and the army commanders[b] with him, "Go throughout the tribes of Israel from Dan to Beersheba and enroll the fighting men, so that I may know how many there are."

[3]But Joab replied to the king, "May the LORD your God multiply the troops a hundred times over, and may the eyes of my lord the king see it. But why does my lord the king want to do such a thing?"

[4]The king's word, however, overruled Joab and the army commanders; so they left the presence of the king to enroll the fighting men of Israel.

[5]After crossing the Jordan, they camped near Aroer, south of the town in the gorge, and then went through Gad and on to Jazer. [6]They went to Gilead and the region of Tahtim Hodshi, and on to Dan Jaan and around toward Sidon. [7]Then they went toward the fortress of Tyre and all the towns of the Hivites and Canaanites. Finally, they went on to Beersheba in the Negev of Judah.

[8]After they had gone through the entire land, they came back to Jerusalem at the end of nine months and twenty days.

[9]Joab reported the number of the fighting men to the king: In Israel there were eight hundred thousand able-bodied men who could handle a sword, and in Judah five hundred thousand.

[10]David was conscience-stricken after he had counted the fighting men, and he said to the LORD, "I have sinned greatly in what I have done. Now, O LORD, I beg you, take away the guilt of your servant. I have done a very foolish thing."

[11]Before David got up the next morning, the word of the LORD had come to Gad the prophet, David's seer: [12]"Go and tell David, 'This is what the LORD says: I am giving you three options. Choose one of them for me to carry out against you.'"

[13]So Gad went to David and said to him, "Shall there come upon you three[c] years of famine in your land? Or three months of fleeing from your enemies while they pursue you? Or three days of plague in your land? Now then, think it over and decide how I should answer the one who sent me."

[14]David said to Gad, "I am in deep distress. Let us fall into the hands of the LORD, for his mercy is great; but do not let me fall into the hands of men."

[15]So the LORD sent a plague on Israel from that morning until the end of the time designated, and seventy thousand of the people from Dan to Beersheba died. [16]When the angel stretched out his hand to destroy Jerusalem, the LORD was grieved because of the calamity and said to the angel who was afflicting the people, "Enough! Withdraw your hand." The angel of the LORD was then at the threshing floor of Araunah the Jebusite.

[17]When David saw the angel who was striking down the people, he said to the LORD, "I am the one who has sinned and done wrong. These are but sheep. What have they done? Let your hand fall upon me and my family."

David Builds an Altar

[18]On that day Gad went to David and said to him, "Go up and build an altar to the LORD on the threshing floor of Araunah the Jebusite." [19]So David went up, as the LORD had commanded through Gad. [20]When Araunah looked and saw the king and his men coming toward him, he went out and bowed down before the king with his face to the ground.

[a]36 Some Septuagint manuscripts (see also
1 Chron. 11:38); Hebrew *Haggadi*
[b]2 Septuagint (see also verse 4 and 1 Chron. 21:2);
Hebrew *Joab the army commander*
[c]13 Septuagint (see also 1 Chron. 21:12); Hebrew
seven

²¹Araunah said, "Why has my lord the king come to his servant?"

"To buy your threshing floor," David answered, "so I can build an altar to the LORD, that the plague on the people may be stopped."

²²Araunah said to David, "Let my lord the king take whatever pleases him and offer it up. Here are oxen for the burnt offering, and here are threshing sledges and ox yokes for the wood. ²³O king, Araunah gives all this to the king." Araunah also said to him, "May the LORD your God accept you."

²⁴But the king replied to Araunah, "No, I insist on paying you for it. I will not sacrifice to the LORD my God burnt offerings that cost me nothing."

So David bought the threshing floor and the oxen and paid fifty shekels[a] of silver for them. ²⁵David built an altar to the LORD there and sacrificed burnt offerings and fellowship offerings.[b] Then the LORD answered prayer in behalf of the land, and the plague on Israel was stopped.

[a]24 That is, about 1 1/4 pounds (about 0.6 kilogram)　[b]25 Traditionally *peace offerings*

1 Kings

First Kings *evaluates the kings* of Israel and Judah and how faithfully they serve God. Some of them worship the Lord faithfully; others disregard him completely. Probably the highest standards for leadership are set by King Solomon and the prophet Elijah. Solomon is known as the wisest man who ever lived; in 1 Kings we see the impact of his leadership on the entire ancient world. And Elijah's total dedication to God distinguishes him as a model leader for all times. Consider their positive examples as you seek to serve God in your marriage.

Adonijah Sets Himself Up as King

1 When King David was old and well advanced in years, he could not keep warm even when they put covers over him. ²So his servants said to him, "Let us look for a young virgin to attend the king and take care of him. She can lie beside him so that our lord the king may keep warm."

³Then they searched throughout Israel for a beautiful girl and found Abishag, a Shunammite, and brought her to the king. ⁴The girl was very beautiful; she took care of the king and waited on him, but the king had no intimate relations with her.

⁵Now Adonijah, whose mother was Haggith, put himself forward and said, "I will be king." So he got chariots and horses*a* ready, with fifty men to run ahead of him. ⁶(His father had never interfered with him by asking, "Why do you behave as you do?" He was also very handsome and was born next after Absalom.)

⁷Adonijah conferred with Joab son of Zeruiah and with Abiathar the priest, and they gave him their support. ⁸But Zadok the priest, Benaiah son of Jehoiada, Nathan the prophet, Shimei and Rei*b* and David's special guard did not join Adonijah.

⁹Adonijah then sacrificed sheep, cattle and fattened calves at the Stone of Zoheleth near En Rogel. He invited all his brothers, the king's sons, and all the men of Judah who were royal officials, ¹⁰but he did not invite Nathan the prophet or Benaiah or the special guard or his brother Solomon.

¹¹Then Nathan asked Bathsheba, Solomon's mother, "Have you not heard that Adonijah, the son of Haggith, has become king without our lord David's knowing it?

*a*5 Or *charioteers*   *b*8 Or *and his friends*

12Now then, let me advise you how you can save your own life and the life of your son Solomon. 13Go in to King David and say to him, 'My lord the king, did you not swear to me your servant: "Surely Solomon your son shall be king after me, and he will sit on my throne"? Why then has Adonijah become king?' 14While you are still there talking to the king, I will come in and confirm what you have said."

15So Bathsheba went to see the aged king in his room, where Abishag the Shunammite was attending him. 16Bathsheba bowed low and knelt before the king.

"What is it you want?" the king asked.

17She said to him, "My lord, you yourself swore to me your servant by the LORD your God: 'Solomon your son shall be king after me, and he will sit on my throne.' 18But now Adonijah has become king, and you, my lord the king, do not know about it. 19He has sacrificed great numbers of cattle, fattened calves, and sheep, and has invited all the king's sons, Abiathar the priest and Joab the commander of the army, but he has not invited Solomon your servant. 20My lord the king, the eyes of all Israel are on you, to learn from you who will sit on the throne of my lord the king after him. 21Otherwise, as soon as my lord the king is laid to rest with his fathers, I and my son Solomon will be treated as criminals."

22While she was still speaking with the king, Nathan the prophet arrived. 23And they told the king, "Nathan the prophet is here." So he went before the king and bowed with his face to the ground.

24Nathan said, "Have you, my lord the king, declared that Adonijah shall be king after you, and that he will sit on your throne? 25Today he has gone down and sacrificed great numbers of cattle, fattened calves, and sheep. He has invited all the king's sons, the commanders of the army and Abiathar the priest. Right now they are eating and drinking with him and saying, 'Long live King Adonijah!' 26But me your servant, and Zadok the priest, and Benaiah son of Jehoiada, and your servant Solomon he did not invite. 27Is this something my lord the king has done without letting his servants know who should sit on the throne of my lord the king after him?"

David Makes Solomon King

28Then King David said, "Call in Bathsheba." So she came into the king's presence and stood before him.

29The king then took an oath: "As surely as the LORD lives, who has delivered me out of every trouble, 30I will surely carry out today what I swore to you by the LORD, the God of Israel: Solomon your son shall be king after me, and he will sit on my throne in my place."

31Then Bathsheba bowed low with her face to the ground and, kneeling before the king, said, "May my lord King David live forever!"

32King David said, "Call in Zadok the priest, Nathan the prophet and Benaiah son of Jehoiada." When they came before the king, 33he said to them: "Take your lord's servants with you and set Solomon my son on my own mule and take him down to Gihon. 34There have Zadok the priest and Nathan the prophet anoint him king over Israel. Blow the trumpet and shout, 'Long live King Solomon!' 35Then you are to go up with him, and he is to come and sit on my throne and reign in my place. I have appointed him ruler over Israel and Judah."

36Benaiah son of Jehoiada answered the king, "Amen! May the LORD, the God of my lord the king, so declare it. 37As the LORD was with my lord the king, so may he be with Solomon to make his throne even greater than the throne of my lord King David!"

38So Zadok the priest, Nathan the prophet, Benaiah son of Jehoiada, the Kerethites and the Pelethites went down and put Solomon on King David's mule and escorted him to Gihon. 39Zadok the priest took the horn of oil from the sacred tent and anointed Solomon. Then they sounded the trumpet and all the people shouted, "Long live King Solomon!" 40And all the people went up after him, playing flutes and rejoicing greatly, so that the ground shook with the sound.

41Adonijah and all the guests who were with him heard it as they were finishing their feast. On hearing the sound of the trumpet, Joab asked, "What's the meaning of all the noise in the city?"

42Even as he was speaking, Jonathan

son of Abiathar the priest arrived. Adonijah said, "Come in. A worthy man like you must be bringing good news."

⁴³"Not at all!" Jonathan answered. "Our lord King David has made Solomon king. ⁴⁴The king has sent with him Zadok the priest, Nathan the prophet, Benaiah son of Jehoiada, the Kerethites and the Pelethites, and they have put him on the king's mule, ⁴⁵and Zadok the priest and Nathan the prophet have anointed him king at Gihon. From there they have gone up cheering, and the city resounds with it. That's the noise you hear. ⁴⁶Moreover, Solomon has taken his seat on the royal throne. ⁴⁷Also, the royal officials have come to congratulate our lord King David, saying, 'May your God make Solomon's name more famous than yours and his throne greater than yours!' And the king bowed in worship on his bed ⁴⁸and said, 'Praise be to the LORD, the God of Israel, who has allowed my eyes to see a successor on my throne today.'"

⁴⁹At this, all Adonijah's guests rose in alarm and dispersed. ⁵⁰But Adonijah, in fear of Solomon, went and took hold of the horns of the altar. ⁵¹Then Solomon was told, "Adonijah is afraid of King Solomon and is clinging to the horns of the altar. He says, 'Let King Solomon swear to me today that he will not put his servant to death with the sword.'"

⁵²Solomon replied, "If he shows himself to be a worthy man, not a hair of his head will fall to the ground; but if evil is found in him, he will die." ⁵³Then King Solomon sent men, and they brought him down from the altar. And Adonijah came and bowed down to King Solomon, and Solomon said, "Go to your home."

David's Charge to Solomon

2 When the time drew near for David to die, he gave a charge to Solomon his son.

²"I am about to go the way of all the earth," he said. "So be strong, show yourself a man, ³and observe what the LORD your God requires: Walk in his ways, and keep his decrees and commands, his laws and requirements, as written in the Law of Moses, so that you may prosper in all you do and wherever you go, ⁴and that the LORD may keep his promise to me: 'If your descendants watch how they live, and if they walk faithfully before me with all their heart and soul, you will never fail to have a man on the throne of Israel.'

⁵"Now you yourself know what Joab son of Zeruiah did to me—what he did to the two commanders of Israel's armies,

Passing the Torch

Tuesday

1 KINGS 2:1-5 How great it would be to know and actually plan for the time we "pass the torch" to the next generation; however, few know the time of their death or are lucid enough to pass on a charge to their children. But if you did know it was time, what would you say?

We've thought about what we would say to our children—especially concerning their marriage. We would encourage them to love their wives, to date, laugh, have some fun and make their relationship a priority; make time for each other in the midst of parenting our grandchildren; to keep on leaving, cleaving and being one; and to grow closer to each other and to God.

We could even write a book and include a challenge for "passing the torch." But the cold fact is that our sons may or may not read our books, but we can be sure they will read our lives. Hopefully they see our love for and dedication to each other. Over the years they watched us work out our marriage in the laboratory of life. They've heard us argue—but also apologize and forgive each other. They laughed and joined us in many of the fun times in our marriage. They've seen us on our knees in prayer. They've walked with us through the death of three of our parents. Each day we continue to live out our life book.

If the only charge you are able to leave is the book you write with your life, what legacy will you pass on?

—*Dave & Claudia*

Go to page 350 for your next devotional reading.

Abner son of Ner and Amasa son of Jether. He killed them, shedding their blood in peacetime as if in battle, and with that blood stained the belt around his waist and the sandals on his feet. 6Deal with him according to your wisdom, but do not let his gray head go down to the grave*a* in peace.

7"But show kindness to the sons of Barzillai of Gilead and let them be among those who eat at your table. They stood by me when I fled from your brother Absalom.

8"And remember, you have with you Shimei son of Gera, the Benjamite from Bahurim, who called down bitter curses on me the day I went to Mahanaim. When he came down to meet me at the Jordan, I swore to him by the LORD: 'I will not put you to death by the sword.' 9But now, do not consider him innocent. You are a man of wisdom; you will know what to do to him. Bring his gray head down to the grave in blood."

10Then David rested with his fathers and was buried in the City of David. 11He had reigned forty years over Israel—seven years in Hebron and thirty-three in Jerusalem. 12So Solomon sat on the throne of his father David, and his rule was firmly established.

Solomon's Throne Established

13Now Adonijah, the son of Haggith, went to Bathsheba, Solomon's mother. Bathsheba asked him, "Do you come peacefully?"

He answered, "Yes, peacefully." 14Then he added, "I have something to say to you."

"You may say it," she replied.

15"As you know," he said, "the kingdom was mine. All Israel looked to me as their king. But things changed, and the kingdom has gone to my brother; for it has come to him from the LORD. 16Now I have one request to make of you. Do not refuse me."

"You may make it," she said.

17So he continued, "Please ask King Solomon—he will not refuse you—to give me Abishag the Shunammite as my wife."

18"Very well," Bathsheba replied, "I will speak to the king for you."

19When Bathsheba went to King Solomon to speak to him for Adonijah, the king stood up to meet her, bowed down to her and sat down on his throne. He had a throne brought for the king's mother, and she sat down at his right hand.

20"I have one small request to make of you," she said. "Do not refuse me."

The king replied, "Make it, my mother; I will not refuse you."

21So she said, "Let Abishag the Shunammite be given in marriage to your brother Adonijah."

22King Solomon answered his mother, "Why do you request Abishag the Shunammite for Adonijah? You might as well request the kingdom for him—after all, he is my older brother—yes, for him and for Abiathar the priest and Joab son of Zeruiah!"

23Then King Solomon swore by the LORD: "May God deal with me, be it ever so severely, if Adonijah does not pay with his life for this request! 24And now, as surely as the LORD lives—he who has established me securely on the throne of my father David and has founded a dynasty for me as he promised—Adonijah shall be put to death today!" 25So King Solomon gave orders to Benaiah son of Jehoiada, and he struck down Adonijah and he died.

26To Abiathar the priest the king said, "Go back to your fields in Anathoth. You deserve to die, but I will not put you to death now, because you carried the ark of the Sovereign LORD before my father David and shared all my father's hardships." 27So Solomon removed Abiathar from the priesthood of the LORD, fulfilling the word the LORD had spoken at Shiloh about the house of Eli.

28When the news reached Joab, who had conspired with Adonijah though not with Absalom, he fled to the tent of the LORD and took hold of the horns of the altar. 29King Solomon was told that Joab had fled to the tent of the LORD and was beside the altar. Then Solomon ordered Benaiah son of Jehoiada, "Go, strike him down!"

30So Benaiah entered the tent of the LORD and said to Joab, "The king says, 'Come out!'"

But he answered, "No, I will die here."

a6 Hebrew Sheol; also in verse 9

Benaiah reported to the king, "This is how Joab answered me."

³¹Then the king commanded Benaiah, "Do as he says. Strike him down and bury him, and so clear me and my father's house of the guilt of the innocent blood that Joab shed. ³²The LORD will repay him for the blood he shed, because without the knowledge of my father David he attacked two men and killed them with the sword. Both of them—Abner son of Ner, commander of Israel's army, and Amasa son of Jether, commander of Judah's army—were better men and more upright than he. ³³May the guilt of their blood rest on the head of Joab and his descendants forever. But on David and his descendants, his house and his throne, may there be the LORD's peace forever."

³⁴So Benaiah son of Jehoiada went up and struck down Joab and killed him, and he was buried on his own land*a* in the desert. ³⁵The king put Benaiah son of Jehoiada over the army in Joab's position and replaced Abiathar with Zadok the priest.

³⁶Then the king sent for Shimei and said to him, "Build yourself a house in Jerusalem and live there, but do not go anywhere else. ³⁷The day you leave and cross the Kidron Valley, you can be sure you will die; your blood will be on your own head."

³⁸Shimei answered the king, "What you say is good. Your servant will do as my lord the king has said." And Shimei stayed in Jerusalem for a long time.

³⁹But three years later, two of Shimei's slaves ran off to Achish son of Maacah, king of Gath, and Shimei was told, "Your slaves are in Gath." ⁴⁰At this, he saddled his donkey and went to Achish at Gath in search of his slaves. So Shimei went away and brought the slaves back from Gath.

⁴¹When Solomon was told that Shimei had gone from Jerusalem to Gath and had returned, ⁴²the king summoned Shimei and said to him, "Did I not make you swear by the LORD and warn you, 'On the day you leave to go anywhere else, you can be sure you will die'? At that time you said to me, 'What you say is good. I will obey.' ⁴³Why then did you not keep your oath to the LORD and obey the command I gave you?"

⁴⁴The king also said to Shimei, "You know in your heart all the wrong you did to my father David. Now the LORD will repay you for your wrongdoing. ⁴⁵But King Solomon will be blessed, and David's throne will remain secure before the LORD forever."

⁴⁶Then the king gave the order to Benaiah son of Jehoiada, and he went out and struck Shimei down and killed him.

The kingdom was now firmly established in Solomon's hands.

Solomon Asks for Wisdom

3 Solomon made an alliance with Pharaoh king of Egypt and married his daughter. He brought her to the City of

a34 Or buried in his tomb

Asking for Wisdom

Wednesday

1 KINGS 3 Marriage comes with a built-in reality check. We ask questions of our spouse like, "Do you think I sounded too flippant when John asked me about my job?" or "Do you think I don't smile enough?" And sometimes our partner says things like, "Honey, you tend to jump to conclusions at times" or "Do you realize how much you worry about that?" Questions and comments like these emerge naturally in a healthy marriage, and they can be a source for personal growth and wisdom.

Maybe that's what Solomon meant by a discerning heart. Instead of asking God for riches and honor, he asked for wisdom. That's not a bad idea for couples. When was the last time you asked God for wisdom in your marriage? If you are like most couples, it may have been a while. Read how the Lord responded to Solomon's request (see verses 10–14). God would like to do the same for you.

—Les & Leslie

Go to page 359 for your next devotional reading.

David until he finished building his palace and the temple of the LORD, and the wall around Jerusalem. ²The people, however, were still sacrificing at the high places, because a temple had not yet been built for the Name of the LORD. ³Solomon showed his love for the LORD by walking according to the statutes of his father David, except that he offered sacrifices and burned incense on the high places.

⁴The king went to Gibeon to offer sacrifices, for that was the most important high place, and Solomon offered a thousand burnt offerings on that altar. ⁵At Gibeon the LORD appeared to Solomon during the night in a dream, and God said, "Ask for whatever you want me to give you."

⁶Solomon answered, "You have shown great kindness to your servant, my father David, because he was faithful to you and righteous and upright in heart. You have continued this great kindness to him and have given him a son to sit on his throne this very day.

⁷"Now, O LORD my God, you have made your servant king in place of my father David. But I am only a little child and do not know how to carry out my duties. ⁸Your servant is here among the people you have chosen, a great people, too numerous to count or number. ⁹So give your servant a discerning heart to govern your people and to distinguish between right and wrong. For who is able to govern this great people of yours?"

¹⁰The Lord was pleased that Solomon had asked for this. ¹¹So God said to him, "Since you have asked for this and not for long life or wealth for yourself, nor have asked for the death of your enemies but for discernment in administering justice, ¹²I will do what you have asked. I will give you a wise and discerning heart, so that there will never have been anyone like you, nor will there ever be. ¹³Moreover, I will give you what you have not asked for—both riches and honor—so that in your lifetime you will have no equal among kings. ¹⁴And if you walk in my ways and obey my statutes and commands as David your father did, I will give you a long life." ¹⁵Then Solomon awoke—and he realized it had been a dream.

He returned to Jerusalem, stood before the ark of the Lord's covenant and sacrificed burnt offerings and fellowship offerings.ᵃ Then he gave a feast for all his court.

A Wise Ruling

¹⁶Now two prostitutes came to the king and stood before him. ¹⁷One of them said, "My lord, this woman and I live in the same house. I had a baby while she was there with me. ¹⁸The third day after my child was born, this woman also had a baby. We were alone; there was no one in the house but the two of us.

¹⁹"During the night this woman's son died because she lay on him. ²⁰So she got up in the middle of the night and took my son from my side while I your servant was asleep. She put him by her breast and put her dead son by my breast. ²¹The next morning, I got up to nurse my son—and he was dead! But when I looked at him closely in the morning light, I saw that it wasn't the son I had borne."

²²The other woman said, "No! The living one is my son; the dead one is yours."

But the first one insisted, "No! The dead one is yours; the living one is mine." And so they argued before the king.

²³The king said, "This one says, 'My son is alive and your son is dead,' while that one says, 'No! Your son is dead and mine is alive.' "

²⁴Then the king said, "Bring me a sword." So they brought a sword for the king. ²⁵He then gave an order: "Cut the living child in two and give half to one and half to the other."

²⁶The woman whose son was alive was filled with compassion for her son and said to the king, "Please, my lord, give her the living baby! Don't kill him!"

But the other said, "Neither I nor you shall have him. Cut him in two!"

²⁷Then the king gave his ruling: "Give the living baby to the first woman. Do not kill him; she is his mother."

²⁸When all Israel heard the verdict the king had given, they held the king in awe, because they saw that he had wisdom from God to administer justice.

ᵃ15 Traditionally *peace offerings*

Solomon's Officials and Governors

4 So King Solomon ruled over all Israel. ²And these were his chief officials:

Azariah son of Zadok—the priest;
³Elihoreph and Ahijah, sons of Shisha—secretaries;
Jehoshaphat son of Ahilud—recorder;
⁴Benaiah son of Jehoiada—commander in chief;
Zadok and Abiathar—priests;
⁵Azariah son of Nathan—in charge of the district officers;
Zabud son of Nathan—a priest and personal adviser to the king;
⁶Ahishar—in charge of the palace;
Adoniram son of Abda—in charge of forced labor.

⁷Solomon also had twelve district governors over all Israel, who supplied provisions for the king and the royal household. Each one had to provide supplies for one month in the year. ⁸These are their names:

Ben-Hur—in the hill country of Ephraim;
⁹Ben-Deker—in Makaz, Shaalbim, Beth Shemesh and Elon Bethhanan;
¹⁰Ben-Hesed—in Arubboth (Socoh and all the land of Hepher were his);
¹¹Ben-Abinadab—in Naphoth Dor*ᵃ* (he was married to Taphath daughter of Solomon);
¹²Baana son of Ahilud—in Taanach and Megiddo, and in all of Beth Shan next to Zarethan below Jezreel, from Beth Shan to Abel Meholah across to Jokmeam;
¹³Ben-Geber—in Ramoth Gilead (the settlements of Jair son of Manasseh in Gilead were his, as well as the district of Argob in Bashan and its sixty large walled cities with bronze gate bars);
¹⁴Ahinadab son of Iddo—in Mahanaim;
¹⁵Ahimaaz—in Naphtali (he had married Basemath daughter of Solomon);
¹⁶Baana son of Hushai—in Asher and in Aloth;
¹⁷Jehoshaphat son of Paruah—in Issachar;
¹⁸Shimei son of Ela—in Benjamin;
¹⁹Geber son of Uri—in Gilead (the country of Sihon king of the Amorites and the country of Og king of Bashan). He was the only governor over the district.

Solomon's Daily Provisions

²⁰The people of Judah and Israel were as numerous as the sand on the seashore; they ate, they drank and they were happy. ²¹And Solomon ruled over all the kingdoms from the River*ᵇ* to the land of the Philistines, as far as the border of Egypt. These countries brought tribute and were Solomon's subjects all his life.

²²Solomon's daily provisions were thirty cors*ᶜ* of fine flour and sixty cors*ᵈ* of meal, ²³ten head of stall-fed cattle, twenty of pasture-fed cattle and a hundred sheep and goats, as well as deer, gazelles, roebucks and choice fowl. ²⁴For he ruled over all the kingdoms west of the River, from Tiphsah to Gaza, and had peace on all sides. ²⁵During Solomon's lifetime Judah and Israel, from Dan to Beersheba, lived in safety, each man under his own vine and fig tree.

²⁶Solomon had four*ᵉ* thousand stalls for chariot horses, and twelve thousand horses.*ᶠ*

²⁷The district officers, each in his month, supplied provisions for King Solomon and all who came to the king's table. They saw to it that nothing was lacking. ²⁸They also brought to the proper place their quotas of barley and straw for the chariot horses and the other horses.

Solomon's Wisdom

²⁹God gave Solomon wisdom and very great insight, and a breadth of understanding as measureless as the sand on the seashore. ³⁰Solomon's wisdom was greater than the wisdom of all the men of the East, and greater than all the wisdom of Egypt. ³¹He was wiser than any other

---

ᵃ11 Or *in the heights of Dor*   *ᵇ21* That is, the Euphrates; also in verse 24   *ᶜ22* That is, probably about 185 bushels (about 6.6 kiloliters)   *ᵈ22* That is, probably about 375 bushels (about 13.2 kiloliters)   *ᵉ26* Some Septuagint manuscripts (see also 2 Chron. 9:25); Hebrew *forty*   *ᶠ26* Or *charioteers* man, including Ethan the Ezrahite—wiser than Heman, Calcol and Darda, the sons of Mahol. And his fame spread to all the surrounding nations. ³²He spoke three thousand proverbs and his songs numbered a thousand and five. ³³He described plant life, from the cedar of Lebanon to the hyssop that grows out of walls. He also taught about animals and birds, reptiles and fish. ³⁴Men of all nations came to listen to Solomon's wisdom, sent by all the kings of the world, who had heard of his wisdom.

Preparations for Building the Temple

5 When Hiram king of Tyre heard that Solomon had been anointed king to succeed his father David, he sent his envoys to Solomon, because he had always been on friendly terms with David. ²Solomon sent back this message to Hiram:

³"You know that because of the wars waged against my father David from all sides, he could not build a temple for the Name of the LORD his God until the LORD put his enemies under his feet. ⁴But now the LORD my God has given me rest on every side, and there is no adversary or disaster. ⁵I intend, therefore, to build a temple for the Name of the LORD my God, as the LORD told my father David, when he said, 'Your son whom I will put on the throne in your place will build the temple for my Name.'

⁶"So give orders that cedars of Lebanon be cut for me. My men will work with yours, and I will pay you for your men whatever wages you set. You know that we have no one so skilled in felling timber as the Sidonians."

⁷When Hiram heard Solomon's message, he was greatly pleased and said, "Praise be to the LORD today, for he has given David a wise son to rule over this great nation."

⁸So Hiram sent word to Solomon:

"I have received the message you sent me and will do all you want in providing the cedar and pine logs. ⁹My men will haul them down from Lebanon to the sea, and I will float them in rafts by sea to the place you specify. There I will separate them and you can take them away. And you are to grant my wish by providing food for my royal household."

¹⁰In this way Hiram kept Solomon supplied with all the cedar and pine logs he wanted, ¹¹and Solomon gave Hiram twenty thousand cors*a* of wheat as food for his household, in addition to twenty thousand baths*b,c* of pressed olive oil. Solomon continued to do this for Hiram year after year. ¹²The LORD gave Solomon wisdom, just as he had promised him. There were peaceful relations between Hiram and Solomon, and the two of them made a treaty.

¹³King Solomon conscripted laborers from all Israel—thirty thousand men. ¹⁴He sent them off to Lebanon in shifts of ten thousand a month, so that they spent one month in Lebanon and two months at home. Adoniram was in charge of the forced labor. ¹⁵Solomon had seventy thousand carriers and eighty thousand stonecutters in the hills, ¹⁶as well as thirty-three hundred*d* foremen who supervised the project and directed the workmen. ¹⁷At the king's command they removed from the quarry large blocks of quality stone to provide a foundation of dressed stone for the temple. ¹⁸The craftsmen of Solomon and Hiram and the men of Gebal*e* cut and prepared the timber and stone for the building of the temple.

Solomon Builds the Temple

6 In the four hundred and eightieth*f* year after the Israelites had come out of Egypt, in the fourth year of Solomon's reign over Israel, in the month of Ziv, the second month, he began to build the temple of the LORD.

²The temple that King Solomon built for the LORD was sixty cubits long, twenty

---

a 11 That is, probably about 125,000 bushels (about 4,400 kiloliters)   *b 11* Septuagint (see also 2 Chron. 2:10); Hebrew *twenty cors*
c 11 That is, about 115,000 gallons (about 440 kiloliters)   *d 16* Hebrew; some Septuagint manuscripts (see also 2 Chron. 2:2, 18) *thirty-six hundred*   *e 18* That is, Byblos   *f 1* Hebrew; Septuagint *four hundred and fortieth*

wide and thirty high.*a* ³The portico at the front of the main hall of the temple extended the width of the temple, that is twenty cubits,*b* and projected ten cubits*c* from the front of the temple. ⁴He made narrow clerestory windows in the temple. ⁵Against the walls of the main hall and inner sanctuary he built a structure around the building, in which there were side rooms. ⁶The lowest floor was five cubits*d* wide, the middle floor six cubits*e* and the third floor seven.*f* He made offset ledges around the outside of the temple so that nothing would be inserted into the temple walls.

⁷In building the temple, only blocks dressed at the quarry were used, and no hammer, chisel or any other iron tool was heard at the temple site while it was being built.

⁸The entrance to the lowest*g* floor was on the south side of the temple; a stairway led up to the middle level and from there to the third. ⁹So he built the temple and completed it, roofing it with beams and cedar planks. ¹⁰And he built the side rooms all along the temple. The height of each was five cubits, and they were attached to the temple by beams of cedar.

¹¹The word of the LORD came to Solomon: ¹²"As for this temple you are building, if you follow my decrees, carry out my regulations and keep all my commands and obey them, I will fulfill through you the promise I gave to David your father. ¹³And I will live among the Israelites and will not abandon my people Israel."

¹⁴So Solomon built the temple and completed it. ¹⁵He lined its interior walls with cedar boards, paneling them from the floor of the temple to the ceiling, and covered the floor of the temple with planks of pine. ¹⁶He partitioned off twenty cubits*b* at the rear of the temple with cedar boards from floor to ceiling to form within the temple an inner sanctuary, the Most Holy Place. ¹⁷The main hall in front of this room was forty cubits*h* long. ¹⁸The inside of the temple was cedar, carved with gourds and open flowers. Everything was cedar; no stone was to be seen.

¹⁹He prepared the inner sanctuary within the temple to set the ark of the covenant of the LORD there. ²⁰The inner sanctuary was twenty cubits long, twenty wide and twenty high.*i* He overlaid the inside with pure gold, and he also overlaid the altar of cedar. ²¹Solomon covered the inside of the temple with pure gold, and he extended gold chains across the front of the inner sanctuary, which was overlaid with gold. ²²So he overlaid the whole interior with gold. He also overlaid with gold the altar that belonged to the inner sanctuary.

²³In the inner sanctuary he made a pair of cherubim of olive wood, each ten cubits*c* high. ²⁴One wing of the first cherub was five cubits long, and the other wing five cubits—ten cubits from wing tip to wing tip. ²⁵The second cherub also measured ten cubits, for the two cherubim were identical in size and shape. ²⁶The height of each cherub was ten cubits. ²⁷He placed the cherubim inside the innermost room of the temple, with their wings spread out. The wing of one cherub touched one wall, while the wing of the other touched the other wall, and their wings touched each other in the middle of the room. ²⁸He overlaid the cherubim with gold.

²⁹On the walls all around the temple, in both the inner and outer rooms, he carved cherubim, palm trees and open flowers. ³⁰He also covered the floors of both the inner and outer rooms of the temple with gold.

³¹For the entrance of the inner sanctuary he made doors of olive wood with five-sided jambs. ³²And on the two olive wood doors he carved cherubim, palm trees and open flowers, and overlaid the cherubim and palm trees with beaten gold. ³³In the same way he made four-sided jambs of olive wood for the entrance to the main hall. ³⁴He also made two pine doors, each having two leaves that turned in sockets. ³⁵He carved cheru-

---

a2 That is, about 90 feet (about 27 meters) long and 30 feet (about 9 meters) wide and 45 feet (about 13.5 meters) high   *b3,16* That is, about 30 feet (about 9 meters)   *c3,23* That is, about 15 feet (about 4.5 meters)   *d6* That is, about 7 1/2 feet (about 2.3 meters); also in verses 10 and 24   *e6* That is, about 9 feet (about 2.7 meters)   *f6* That is, about 10 1/2 feet (about 3.1 meters)   *g8* Septuagint; Hebrew *middle*   *h17* That is, about 60 feet (about 18 meters)   *i20* That is, about 30 feet (about 9 meters) long, wide and high bim, palm trees and open flowers on them and overlaid them with gold hammered evenly over the carvings.

[36] And he built the inner courtyard of three courses of dressed stone and one course of trimmed cedar beams.

[37] The foundation of the temple of the LORD was laid in the fourth year, in the month of Ziv. [38] In the eleventh year in the month of Bul, the eighth month, the temple was finished in all its details according to its specifications. He had spent seven years building it.

Solomon Builds His Palace

7 It took Solomon thirteen years, however, to complete the construction of his palace. [2] He built the Palace of the Forest of Lebanon a hundred cubits long, fifty wide and thirty high,[a] with four rows of cedar columns supporting trimmed cedar beams. [3] It was roofed with cedar above the beams that rested on the columns—forty-five beams, fifteen to a row. [4] Its windows were placed high in sets of three, facing each other. [5] All the doorways had rectangular frames; they were in the front part in sets of three, facing each other.[b]

[6] He made a colonnade fifty cubits long and thirty wide.[c] In front of it was a portico, and in front of that were pillars and an overhanging roof.

[7] He built the throne hall, the Hall of Justice, where he was to judge, and he covered it with cedar from floor to ceiling.[d] [8] And the palace in which he was to live, set farther back, was similar in design. Solomon also made a palace like this hall for Pharaoh's daughter, whom he had married.

[9] All these structures, from the outside to the great courtyard and from foundation to eaves, were made of blocks of high-grade stone cut to size and trimmed with a saw on their inner and outer faces. [10] The foundations were laid with large stones of good quality, some measuring ten cubits[e] and some eight.[f] [11] Above were high-grade stones, cut to size, and cedar beams. [12] The great courtyard was surrounded by a wall of three courses of dressed stone and one course of trimmed cedar beams, as was the inner courtyard of the temple of the LORD with its portico.

The Temple's Furnishings

[13] King Solomon sent to Tyre and brought Huram,[g] [14] whose mother was a widow from the tribe of Naphtali and whose father was a man of Tyre and a craftsman in bronze. Huram was highly skilled and experienced in all kinds of bronze work. He came to King Solomon and did all the work assigned to him.

[15] He cast two bronze pillars, each eighteen cubits high and twelve cubits around,[h] by line. [16] He also made two capitals of cast bronze to set on the tops of the pillars; each capital was five cubits[i] high. [17] A network of interwoven chains festooned the capitals on top of the pillars, seven for each capital. [18] He made pomegranates in two rows[j] encircling each network to decorate the capitals on top of the pillars.[k] He did the same for each capital. [19] The capitals on top of the pillars in the portico were in the shape of lilies, four cubits[l] high. [20] On the capitals of both pillars, above the bowl-shaped part next to the network, were the two hundred pomegranates in rows all around. [21] He erected the pillars at the portico of the temple. The pillar to the south he named Jakin[m] and the one to the north Boaz.[n] [22] The capitals on top were in the shape of lilies. And so the work on the pillars was completed.

[23] He made the Sea of cast metal, circular in shape, measuring ten cubits[e] from rim to rim and five cubits high. It took a line of thirty cubits[o] to measure around it. [24] Below the rim, gourds encircled it—

a2 That is, about 150 feet (about 46 meters) long, 75 feet (about 23 meters) wide and 45 feet (about 13.5 meters) high   b5 The meaning of the Hebrew for this verse is uncertain.   c6 That is, about 75 feet (about 23 meters) long and 45 feet (about 13.5 meters) wide   d7 Vulgate and Syriac; Hebrew *floor*   e10,23 That is, about 15 feet (about 4.5 meters)   f10 That is, about 12 feet (about 3.6 meters)   g13 Hebrew *Hiram*, a variant of *Huram*; also in verses 40 and 45   h15 That is, about 27 feet (about 8.1 meters) high and 18 feet (about 5.4 meters) around   i16 That is, about 7 1/2 feet (about 2.3 meters); also in verse 23   j18 Two Hebrew manuscripts and Septuagint; most Hebrew manuscripts *made the pillars, and there were two rows*   k18 Many Hebrew manuscripts and Syriac; most Hebrew manuscripts *pomegranates*   l19 That is, about 6 feet (about 1.8 meters); also in verse 38   m21 *Jakin* probably means *he establishes*.   n21 *Boaz* probably means *in him is strength*.   o23 That is, about 45 feet (about 13.5 meters) ten to a cubit. The gourds were cast in two rows in one piece with the Sea.

^{25}The Sea stood on twelve bulls, three facing north, three facing west, three facing south and three facing east. The Sea rested on top of them, and their hindquarters were toward the center. ^{26}It was a handbreadth^a in thickness, and its rim was like the rim of a cup, like a lily blossom. It held two thousand baths.^{b}

^{27}He also made ten movable stands of bronze; each was four cubits long, four wide and three high.^{c} ^{28}This is how the stands were made: They had side panels attached to uprights. ^{29}On the panels between the uprights were lions, bulls and cherubim—and on the uprights as well. Above and below the lions and bulls were wreaths of hammered work. ^{30}Each stand had four bronze wheels with bronze axles, and each had a basin resting on four supports, cast with wreaths on each side. ^{31}On the inside of the stand there was an opening that had a circular frame one cubit^d deep. This opening was round, and with its basework it measured a cubit and a half.^{e} Around its opening there was engraving. The panels of the stands were square, not round. ^{32}The four wheels were under the panels, and the axles of the wheels were attached to the stand. The diameter of each wheel was a cubit and a half. ^{33}The wheels were made like chariot wheels; the axles, rims, spokes and hubs were all of cast metal.

^{34}Each stand had four handles, one on each corner, projecting from the stand. ^{35}At the top of the stand there was a circular band half a cubit^f deep. The supports and panels were attached to the top of the stand. ^{36}He engraved cherubim, lions and palm trees on the surfaces of the supports and on the panels, in every available space, with wreaths all around. ^{37}This is the way he made the ten stands. They were all cast in the same molds and were identical in size and shape.

^{38}He then made ten bronze basins, each holding forty baths^g and measuring four cubits across, one basin to go on each of the ten stands. ^{39}He placed five of the stands on the south side of the temple and five on the north. He placed the Sea on the south side, at the southeast corner of the temple. ^{40}He also made the basins and shovels and sprinkling bowls.

So Huram finished all the work he had undertaken for King Solomon in the temple of the LORD:

^{41}the two pillars;

the two bowl-shaped capitals on top of the pillars;

the two sets of network decorating the two bowl-shaped capitals on top of the pillars;

^{42}the four hundred pomegranates for the two sets of network (two rows of pomegranates for each network, decorating the bowl-shaped capitals on top of the pillars);

^{43}the ten stands with their ten basins;

^{44}the Sea and the twelve bulls under it;

^{45}the pots, shovels and sprinkling bowls.

All these objects that Huram made for King Solomon for the temple of the LORD were of burnished bronze. ^{46}The king had them cast in clay molds in the plain of the Jordan between Succoth and Zarethan. ^{47}Solomon left all these things unweighed, because there were so many; the weight of the bronze was not determined.

^{48}Solomon also made all the furnishings that were in the LORD's temple:

the golden altar;

the golden table on which was the bread of the Presence;

^{49}the lampstands of pure gold (five on the right and five on the left, in front of the inner sanctuary);

the gold floral work and lamps and tongs;

^{50}the pure gold basins, wick trimmers, sprinkling bowls, dishes and censers;

and the gold sockets for the doors of the innermost room, the Most Holy Place, and also for the doors of the main hall of the temple.

$^a26$ That is, about 3 inches (about 8 centimeters)
$^b26$ That is, probably about 11,500 gallons (about 44 kiloliters); the Septuagint does not have this sentence.　$^c27$ That is, about 6 feet (about 1.8 meters) long and wide and about 4 1/2 feet (about 1.3 meters) high　$^d31$ That is, about 1 1/2 feet (about 0.5 meter)　$^e31$ That is, about 2 1/4 feet (about 0.7 meter); also in verse 32　$^f35$ That is, about 3/4 foot (about 0.2 meter)　$^g38$ That is, about 230 gallons (about 880 liters)

[51]When all the work King Solomon had done for the temple of the LORD was finished, he brought in the things his father David had dedicated—the silver and gold and the furnishings—and he placed them in the treasuries of the LORD's temple.

The Ark Brought to the Temple

8 Then King Solomon summoned into his presence at Jerusalem the elders of Israel, all the heads of the tribes and the chiefs of the Israelite families, to bring up the ark of the LORD's covenant from Zion, the City of David. [2]All the men of Israel came together to King Solomon at the time of the festival in the month of Ethanim, the seventh month.

[3]When all the elders of Israel had arrived, the priests took up the ark, [4]and they brought up the ark of the LORD and the Tent of Meeting and all the sacred furnishings in it. The priests and Levites carried them up, [5]and King Solomon and the entire assembly of Israel that had gathered about him were before the ark, sacrificing so many sheep and cattle that they could not be recorded or counted.

[6]The priests then brought the ark of the LORD's covenant to its place in the inner sanctuary of the temple, the Most Holy Place, and put it beneath the wings of the cherubim. [7]The cherubim spread their wings over the place of the ark and overshadowed the ark and its carrying poles. [8]These poles were so long that their ends could be seen from the Holy Place in front of the inner sanctuary, but not from outside the Holy Place; and they are still there today. [9]There was nothing in the ark except the two stone tablets that Moses had placed in it at Horeb, where the LORD made a covenant with the Israelites after they came out of Egypt.

[10]When the priests withdrew from the Holy Place, the cloud filled the temple of the LORD. [11]And the priests could not perform their service because of the cloud, for the glory of the LORD filled his temple. [12]Then Solomon said, "The LORD has said that he would dwell in a dark cloud; [13]I have indeed built a magnificent temple for you, a place for you to dwell forever."

[14]While the whole assembly of Israel was standing there, the king turned around and blessed them. [15]Then he said:

"Praise be to the LORD, the God of Israel, who with his own hand has fulfilled what he promised with his own mouth to my father David. For he said, [16]'Since the day I brought my people Israel out of Egypt, I have not chosen a city in any tribe of Israel to have a temple built for my Name to be there, but I have chosen David to rule my people Israel.'

[17]"My father David had it in his heart to build a temple for the Name of the LORD, the God of Israel. [18]But the LORD said to my father David, 'Because it was in your heart to build a temple for my Name, you did well to have this in your heart. [19]Nevertheless, you are not the one to build the temple, but your son, who is your own flesh and blood— he is the one who will build the temple for my Name.'

[20]"The LORD has kept the promise he made: I have succeeded David my father and now I sit on the throne of Israel, just as the LORD promised, and I have built the temple for the Name of the LORD, the God of Israel. [21]I have provided a place there for the ark, in which is the covenant of the LORD that he made with our fathers when he brought them out of Egypt."

Solomon's Prayer of Dedication

[22]Then Solomon stood before the altar of the LORD in front of the whole assembly of Israel, spread out his hands toward heaven [23]and said:

"O LORD, God of Israel, there is no God like you in heaven above or on earth below—you who keep your covenant of love with your servants who continue wholeheartedly in your way. [24]You have kept your promise to your servant David my father; with your mouth you have promised and with your hand you have fulfilled it—as it is today.

[25]"Now LORD, God of Israel, keep for your servant David my father the

promises you made to him when you said, 'You shall never fail to have a man to sit before me on the throne of Israel, if only your sons are careful in all they do to walk before me as you have done.' 26And now, O God of Israel, let your word that you promised your servant David my father come true.

27"But will God really dwell on earth? The heavens, even the highest heaven, cannot contain you. How much less this temple I have built! 28Yet give attention to your servant's prayer and his plea for mercy, O LORD my God. Hear the cry and the prayer that your servant is praying in your presence this day. 29May your eyes be open toward this temple night and day, this place of which you said, 'My Name shall be there,' so that you will hear the prayer your servant prays toward this place. 30Hear the supplication of your servant and of your people Israel when they pray toward this place. Hear from heaven, your dwelling place, and when you hear, forgive.

31"When a man wrongs his neighbor and is required to take an oath and he comes and swears the oath before your altar in this temple, 32then hear from heaven and act. Judge between your servants, condemning the guilty and bringing down on his own head what he has done. Declare the innocent not guilty, and so establish his innocence.

33"When your people Israel have been defeated by an enemy because they have sinned against you, and when they turn back to you and confess your name, praying and making supplication to you in this temple, 34then hear from heaven and forgive the sin of your people Israel and bring them back to the land you gave to their fathers.

35"When the heavens are shut up and there is no rain because your people have sinned against you, and when they pray toward this place and confess your name and turn from their sin because you have af-

flicted them, 36then hear from heaven and forgive the sin of your servants, your people Israel. Teach them the right way to live, and send rain on the land you gave your people for an inheritance.

37"When famine or plague comes to the land, or blight or mildew, locusts or grasshoppers, or when an enemy besieges them in any of their cities, whatever disaster or disease may come, 38and when a prayer or plea is made by any of your people Israel—each one aware of the afflictions of his own heart, and spreading out his hands toward this temple— 39then hear from heaven, your dwelling place. Forgive and act; deal with each man according to all he does, since you know his heart (for you alone know the hearts of all men), 40so that they will fear you all the time they live in the land you gave our fathers.

41"As for the foreigner who does not belong to your people Israel but has come from a distant land because of your name— 42for men will hear of your great name and your mighty hand and your outstretched arm—when he comes and prays toward this temple, 43then hear from heaven, your dwelling place, and do whatever the foreigner asks of you, so that all the peoples of the earth may know your name and fear you, as do your own people Israel, and may know that this house I have built bears your Name.

44"When your people go to war against their enemies, wherever you send them, and when they pray to the LORD toward the city you have chosen and the temple I have built for your Name, 45then hear from heaven their prayer and their plea, and uphold their cause.

46"When they sin against you— for there is no one who does not sin—and you become angry with them and give them over to the enemy, who takes them captive to his own land, far away or near; 47and if they have a change of heart in the land where they are held captive, and repent and plead with you in the land of their conquerors and say, 'We have sinned, we have done wrong, we have acted wickedly'; ⁴⁸and if they turn back to you with all their heart and soul in the land of their enemies who took them captive, and pray to you toward the land you gave their fathers, toward the city you have chosen and the temple I have built for your Name; ⁴⁹then from heaven, your dwelling place, hear their prayer and their plea, and uphold their cause. ⁵⁰And forgive your people, who have sinned against you; forgive all the offenses they have committed against you, and cause their conquerors to show them mercy; ⁵¹for they are your people and your inheritance, whom you brought out of Egypt, out of that iron-smelting furnace.

⁵² "May your eyes be open to your servant's plea and to the plea of your people Israel, and may you listen to them whenever they cry out to you. ⁵³For you singled them out from all the nations of the world to be your own inheritance, just as you declared through your servant Moses when you, O Sovereign LORD, brought our fathers out of Egypt."

⁵⁴When Solomon had finished all these prayers and supplications to the LORD, he rose from before the altar of the LORD, where he had been kneeling with his hands spread out toward heaven. ⁵⁵He stood and blessed the whole assembly of Israel in a loud voice, saying:

⁵⁶ "Praise be to the LORD, who has given rest to his people Israel just as he promised. Not one word has failed of all the good promises he gave through his servant Moses. ⁵⁷May the LORD our God be with us as he was with our fathers; may he never leave us nor forsake us. ⁵⁸May

Bless This House

Thursday

1 KINGS 8:56–61 The second half of marriage brings many changes—one of ours was moving from our two-story suburban family home into our empty-nest condo. While moving can be unsettling, we wanted our new home to be filled with God's love. So when movers and packing boxes were history and we were reasonable settled, we asked God's blessing on our home and on those who would live and visit within its walls.

Joined by our children, grandchildren and close friends, we asked our pastor Rev. John Wood to dedicate our new home. Starting outside our front door, John asked God's peace to be granted to all who entered—that they might experience God's grace, forgiveness, love, compassion and joy.

We opened the door and went inside. In the living room John prayed for those who would come to share our lives—that in this room, we might rejoice with those who rejoice, weep with those who weep and, in the quiet moments, know the pleasure of God's presence.

In the kitchen he acknowledged God's provisions and presence for all who would sit at our table. As he prayed we pictured grandchildren putting sprinkles on cookies, conversations with friends over a cup of tea, or just the two of us eating a simple meal together. In the master bedroom, our pastor acknowledged how Jesus Christ had pursued us with his love and prayed that we would celebrate our love and also find rest and renewal in sleep.

After he gave each room a specific blessing, John asked God to fill it with his loving presence. After the formal dedication of our home, we gathered in the dining room for brunch and a time a celebration.

We thought about how Solomon dedicated the temple to God's name. Obviously God could not be contained within a building, but he could be present in a special way as he was with us on that day.

—*Dave & Claudia*

Go to page 371 for your next devotional reading.

he turn our hearts to him, to walk in all his ways and to keep the commands, decrees and regulations he gave our fathers. 59And may these words of mine, which I have prayed before the LORD, be near to the LORD our God day and night, that he may uphold the cause of his servant and the cause of his people Israel according to each day's need, 60so that all the peoples of the earth may know that the LORD is God and that there is no other. 61But your hearts must be fully committed to the LORD our God, to live by his decrees and obey his commands, as at this time."

The Dedication of the Temple

62Then the king and all Israel with him offered sacrifices before the LORD. 63Solomon offered a sacrifice of fellowship offerings*a* to the LORD: twenty-two thousand cattle and a hundred and twenty thousand sheep and goats. So the king and all the Israelites dedicated the temple of the LORD.

64On that same day the king consecrated the middle part of the courtyard in front of the temple of the LORD, and there he offered burnt offerings, grain offerings and the fat of the fellowship offerings, because the bronze altar before the LORD was too small to hold the burnt offerings, the grain offerings and the fat of the fellowship offerings.

65So Solomon observed the festival at that time, and all Israel with him—a vast assembly, people from Lebo*b* Hamath to the Wadi of Egypt. They celebrated it before the LORD our God for seven days and seven days more, fourteen days in all. 66On the following day he sent the people away. They blessed the king and then went home, joyful and glad in heart for all the good things the LORD had done for his servant David and his people Israel.

The LORD Appears to Solomon

9 When Solomon had finished building the temple of the LORD and the royal palace, and had achieved all he had desired to do, 2the LORD appeared to him a second time, as he had appeared to him at Gibeon. 3The LORD said to him:

"I have heard the prayer and plea you have made before me; I have consecrated this temple, which you have built, by putting my Name there forever. My eyes and my heart will always be there.

4"As for you, if you walk before me in integrity of heart and uprightness, as David your father did, and do all I command and observe my decrees and laws, 5I will establish your royal throne over Israel forever, as I promised David your father when I said, 'You shall never fail to have a man on the throne of Israel.'

6"But if you*c* or your sons turn away from me and do not observe the commands and decrees I have given you*c* and go off to serve other gods and worship them, 7then I will cut off Israel from the land I have given them and will reject this temple I have consecrated for my Name. Israel will then become a byword and an object of ridicule among all peoples. 8And though this temple is now imposing, all who pass by will be appalled and will scoff and say, 'Why has the LORD done such a thing to this land and to this temple?' 9People will answer, 'Because they have forsaken the LORD their God, who brought their fathers out of Egypt, and have embraced other gods, worshiping and serving them—that is why the LORD brought all this disaster on them.'"

Solomon's Other Activities

10At the end of twenty years, during which Solomon built these two buildings—the temple of the LORD and the royal palace— 11King Solomon gave twenty towns in Galilee to Hiram king of Tyre, because Hiram had supplied him with all the cedar and pine and gold he wanted. 12But when Hiram went from Tyre to see the towns that Solomon had given him, he was not pleased with them. 13"What

---

*a*63 Traditionally *peace offerings*; also in verse 64
*b*65 Or *from the entrance to*   *c*6 The Hebrew is plural.

kind of towns are these you have given me, my brother?" he asked. And he called them the Land of Cabul,[a] a name they have to this day. [14]Now Hiram had sent to the king 120 talents[b] of gold.

[15]Here is the account of the forced labor King Solomon conscripted to build the LORD's temple, his own palace, the supporting terraces,[c] the wall of Jerusalem, and Hazor, Megiddo and Gezer. [16](Pharaoh king of Egypt had attacked and captured Gezer. He had set it on fire. He killed its Canaanite inhabitants and then gave it as a wedding gift to his daughter, Solomon's wife. [17]And Solomon rebuilt Gezer.) He built up Lower Beth Horon, [18]Baalath, and Tadmor[d] in the desert, within his land, [19]as well as all his store cities and the towns for his chariots and for his horses[e]—whatever he desired to build in Jerusalem, in Lebanon and throughout all the territory he ruled.

[20]All the people left from the Amorites, Hittites, Perizzites, Hivites and Jebusites (these peoples were not Israelites), [21]that is, their descendants remaining in the land, whom the Israelites could not exterminate[f]—these Solomon conscripted for his slave labor force, as it is to this day. [22]But Solomon did not make slaves of any of the Israelites; they were his fighting men, his government officials, his officers, his captains, and the commanders of his chariots and charioteers. [23]They were also the chief officials in charge of Solomon's projects—550 officials supervising the men who did the work.

[24]After Pharaoh's daughter had come up from the City of David to the palace Solomon had built for her, he constructed the supporting terraces.

[25]Three times a year Solomon sacrificed burnt offerings and fellowship offerings[g] on the altar he had built for the LORD, burning incense before the LORD along with them, and so fulfilled the temple obligations.

[26]King Solomon also built ships at Ezion Geber, which is near Elath in Edom, on the shore of the Red Sea.[h] [27]And Hiram sent his men—sailors who knew the sea—to serve in the fleet with Solomon's men. [28]They sailed to Ophir and brought back 420 talents[i] of gold, which they delivered to King Solomon.

The Queen of Sheba Visits Solomon

10 When the queen of Sheba heard about the fame of Solomon and his relation to the name of the LORD, she came to test him with hard questions. [2]Arriving at Jerusalem with a very great caravan—with camels carrying spices, large quantities of gold, and precious stones—she came to Solomon and talked with him about all that she had on her mind. [3]Solomon answered all her questions; nothing was too hard for the king to explain to her. [4]When the queen of Sheba saw all the wisdom of Solomon and the palace he had built, [5]the food on his table, the seating of his officials, the attending servants in their robes, his cupbearers, and the burnt offerings he made at[j] the temple of the LORD, she was overwhelmed.

[6]She said to the king, "The report I heard in my own country about your achievements and your wisdom is true. [7]But I did not believe these things until I came and saw with my own eyes. Indeed, not even half was told me; in wisdom and wealth you have far exceeded the report I heard. [8]How happy your men must be! How happy your officials, who continually stand before you and hear your wisdom! [9]Praise be to the LORD your God, who has delighted in you and placed you on the throne of Israel. Because of the LORD's eternal love for Israel, he has made you king, to maintain justice and righteousness."

[10]And she gave the king 120 talents[b] of gold, large quantities of spices, and precious stones. Never again were so many spices brought in as those the queen of Sheba gave to King Solomon.

[11](Hiram's ships brought gold from Ophir; and from there they brought great cargoes of almugwood[k] and precious

---

[a]13 *Cabul* sounds like the Hebrew for *good-for-nothing.*   [b]14,10 That is, about 4 1/2 tons (about 4 metric tons)   [c]15 Or *the Millo;* also in verse 24   [d]18 The Hebrew may also be read *Tamar.*   [e]19 Or *charioteers*   [f]21 The Hebrew term refers to the irrevocable giving over of things or persons to the LORD, often by totally destroying them.   [g]25 Traditionally *peace offerings*   [h]26 Hebrew *Yam Suph;* that is, Sea of Reeds   [i]28 That is, about 16 tons (about 14.5 metric tons)   [j]5 Or *the ascent by which he went up to*   [k]11 Probably a variant of *algumwood;* also in verse 12

stones. ¹²The king used the almugwood to make supports for the temple of the LORD and for the royal palace, and to make harps and lyres for the musicians. So much almugwood has never been imported or seen since that day.)

¹³King Solomon gave the queen of Sheba all she desired and asked for, besides what he had given her out of his royal bounty. Then she left and returned with her retinue to her own country.

Solomon's Splendor

¹⁴The weight of the gold that Solomon received yearly was 666 talents,ᵃ ¹⁵not including the revenues from merchants and traders and from all the Arabian kings and the governors of the land.

¹⁶King Solomon made two hundred large shields of hammered gold; six hundred bekasᵇ of gold went into each shield. ¹⁷He also made three hundred small shields of hammered gold, with three minasᶜ of gold in each shield. The king put them in the Palace of the Forest of Lebanon.

¹⁸Then the king made a great throne inlaid with ivory and overlaid with fine gold. ¹⁹The throne had six steps, and its back had a rounded top. On both sides of the seat were armrests, with a lion standing beside each of them. ²⁰Twelve lions stood on the six steps, one at either end of each step. Nothing like it had ever been made for any other kingdom. ²¹All King Solomon's goblets were gold, and all the household articles in the Palace of the Forest of Lebanon were pure gold. Nothing was made of silver, because silver was considered of little value in Solomon's days. ²²The king had a fleet of trading shipsᵈ at sea along with the ships of Hiram. Once every three years it returned, carrying gold, silver and ivory, and apes and baboons.

²³King Solomon was greater in riches and wisdom than all the other kings of the earth. ²⁴The whole world sought audience with Solomon to hear the wisdom God had put in his heart. ²⁵Year after year, everyone who came brought a gift—articles of silver and gold, robes, weapons and spices, and horses and mules.

²⁶Solomon accumulated chariots and horses; he had fourteen hundred chariots

and twelve thousand horses,ᵉ which he kept in the chariot cities and also with him in Jerusalem. ²⁷The king made silver as common in Jerusalem as stones, and cedar as plentiful as sycamore-fig trees in the foothills. ²⁸Solomon's horses were imported from Egyptᶠ and from Kueᵍ—the royal merchants purchased them from Kue. ²⁹They imported a chariot from Egypt for six hundred shekelsʰ of silver, and a horse for a hundred and fifty.ᶜ They also exported them to all the kings of the Hittites and of the Arameans.

Solomon's Wives

11 King Solomon, however, loved many foreign women besides Pharaoh's daughter—Moabites, Ammonites, Edomites, Sidonians and Hittites. ²They were from nations about which the LORD had told the Israelites, "You must not intermarry with them, because they will surely turn your hearts after their gods." Nevertheless, Solomon held fast to them in love. ³He had seven hundred wives of royal birth and three hundred concubines, and his wives led him astray. ⁴As Solomon grew old, his wives turned his heart after other gods, and his heart was not fully devoted to the LORD his God, as the heart of David his father had been. ⁵He followed Ashtoreth the goddess of the Sidonians, and Molechⁱ the detestable god of the Ammonites. ⁶So Solomon did evil in the eyes of the LORD; he did not follow the LORD completely, as David his father had done.

⁷On a hill east of Jerusalem, Solomon built a high place for Chemosh the detestable god of Moab, and for Molech the detestable god of the Ammonites. ⁸He did the same for all his foreign wives, who burned incense and offered sacrifices to their gods.

⁹The LORD became angry with Solomon because his heart had turned away from the LORD, the God of Israel, who

---

ᵃ14 That is, about 25 tons (about 23 metric tons)   ᵇ16 That is, about 7 1/2 pounds (about 3.5 kilograms)   ᶜ17,29 That is, about 3 3/4 pounds (about 1.7 kilograms)   ᵈ22 Hebrew *of ships of Tarshish*   ᵉ26 Or *charioteers*   ᶠ28 Or possibly *Muzur, a region in Cilicia; also in verse 29*   ᵍ28 Probably *Cilicia*   ʰ29 That is, about 15 pounds (about 7 kilograms)   ⁱ5 Hebrew *Milcom; also in verse 33* had appeared to him twice. 10Although he had forbidden Solomon to follow other gods, Solomon did not keep the LORD's command. 11So the LORD said to Solomon, "Since this is your attitude and you have not kept my covenant and my decrees, which I commanded you, I will most certainly tear the kingdom away from you and give it to one of your subordinates. 12Nevertheless, for the sake of David your father, I will not do it during your lifetime. I will tear it out of the hand of your son. 13Yet I will not tear the whole kingdom from him, but will give him one tribe for the sake of David my servant and for the sake of Jerusalem, which I have chosen."

Solomon's Adversaries

14Then the LORD raised up against Solomon an adversary, Hadad the Edomite, from the royal line of Edom. 15Earlier when David was fighting with Edom, Joab the commander of the army, who had gone up to bury the dead, had struck down all the men in Edom. 16Joab and all the Israelites stayed there for six months, until they had destroyed all the men in Edom. 17But Hadad, still only a boy, fled to Egypt with some Edomite officials who had served his father. 18They set out from Midian and went to Paran. Then taking men from Paran with them, they went to Egypt, to Pharaoh king of Egypt, who gave Hadad a house and land and provided him with food.

19Pharaoh was so pleased with Hadad that he gave him a sister of his own wife, Queen Tahpenes, in marriage. 20The sister of Tahpenes bore him a son named Genubath, whom Tahpenes brought up in the royal palace. There Genubath lived with Pharaoh's own children.

21While he was in Egypt, Hadad heard that David rested with his fathers and that Joab the commander of the army was also dead. Then Hadad said to Pharaoh, "Let me go, that I may return to my own country."

22"What have you lacked here that you want to go back to your own country?" Pharaoh asked.

"Nothing," Hadad replied, "but do let me go!"

23And God raised up against Solomon another adversary, Rezon son of Eliada, who had fled from his master, Hadadezer king of Zobah. 24He gathered men around him and became the leader of a band of rebels when David destroyed the forces[a] ⌊of Zobah⌋; the rebels went to Damascus, where they settled and took control. 25Rezon was Israel's adversary as long as Solomon lived, adding to the trouble caused by Hadad. So Rezon ruled in Aram and was hostile toward Israel.

Jeroboam Rebels Against Solomon

26Also, Jeroboam son of Nebat rebelled against the king. He was one of Solomon's officials, an Ephraimite from Zeredah, and his mother was a widow named Zeruah.

27Here is the account of how he rebelled against the king: Solomon had built the supporting terraces[b] and had filled in the gap in the wall of the city of David his father. 28Now Jeroboam was a man of standing, and when Solomon saw how well the young man did his work, he put him in charge of the whole labor force of the house of Joseph.

29About that time Jeroboam was going out of Jerusalem, and Ahijah the prophet of Shiloh met him on the way, wearing a new cloak. The two of them were alone out in the country, 30and Ahijah took hold of the new cloak he was wearing and tore it into twelve pieces. 31Then he said to Jeroboam, "Take ten pieces for yourself, for this is what the LORD, the God of Israel, says: 'See, I am going to tear the kingdom out of Solomon's hand and give you ten tribes. 32But for the sake of my servant David and the city of Jerusalem, which I have chosen out of all the tribes of Israel, he will have one tribe. 33I will do this because they have[c] forsaken me and worshiped Ashtoreth the goddess of the Sidonians, Chemosh the god of the Moabites, and Molech the god of the Ammonites, and have not walked in my ways, nor done what is right in my eyes, nor kept my statutes and laws as David, Solomon's father, did.

34 'But I will not take the whole kingdom out of Solomon's hand; I have made

a24 Hebrew destroyed them   b27 Or the Millo
c33 Hebrew; Septuagint, Vulgate and Syriac because he has

him ruler all the days of his life for the sake of David my servant, whom I chose and who observed my commands and statutes. [35]I will take the kingdom from his son's hands and give you ten tribes. [36]I will give one tribe to his son so that David my servant may always have a lamp before me in Jerusalem, the city where I chose to put my Name. [37]However, as for you, I will take you, and you will rule over all that your heart desires; you will be king over Israel. [38]If you do whatever I command you and walk in my ways and do what is right in my eyes by keeping my statutes and commands, as David my servant did, I will be with you. I will build you a dynasty as enduring as the one I built for David and will give Israel to you. [39]I will humble David's descendants because of this, but not forever.'"

[40]Solomon tried to kill Jeroboam, but Jeroboam fled to Egypt, to Shishak the king, and stayed there until Solomon's death.

Solomon's Death

[41]As for the other events of Solomon's reign—all he did and the wisdom he displayed—are they not written in the book of the annals of Solomon? [42]Solomon reigned in Jerusalem over all Israel forty years. [43]Then he rested with his fathers and was buried in the city of David his father. And Rehoboam his son succeeded him as king.

Israel Rebels Against Rehoboam

12 Rehoboam went to Shechem, for all the Israelites had gone there to make him king. [2]When Jeroboam son of Nebat heard this (he was still in Egypt, where he had fled from King Solomon), he returned from[a] Egypt. [3]So they sent for Jeroboam, and he and the whole assembly of Israel went to Rehoboam and said to him: [4]"Your father put a heavy yoke on us, but now lighten the harsh labor and the heavy yoke he put on us, and we will serve you."

[5]Rehoboam answered, "Go away for three days and then come back to me." So the people went away.

[6]Then King Rehoboam consulted the elders who had served his father Solomon during his lifetime. "How would you advise me to answer these people?" he asked.

[7]They replied, "If today you will be a servant to these people and serve them and give them a favorable answer, they will always be your servants."

[8]But Rehoboam rejected the advice the elders gave him and consulted the young men who had grown up with him and were serving him. [9]He asked them, "What is your advice? How should we answer these people who say to me, 'Lighten the yoke your father put on us'?"

[10]The young men who had grown up with him replied, "Tell these people who have said to you, 'Your father put a heavy yoke on us, but make our yoke lighter'—tell them, 'My little finger is thicker than my father's waist. [11]My father laid on you a heavy yoke; I will make it even heavier. My father scourged you with whips; I will scourge you with scorpions.'"

[12]Three days later Jeroboam and all the people returned to Rehoboam, as the king had said, "Come back to me in three days." [13]The king answered the people harshly. Rejecting the advice given him by the elders, [14]he followed the advice of the young men and said, "My father made your yoke heavy; I will make it even heavier. My father scourged you with whips; I will scourge you with scorpions." [15]So the king did not listen to the people, for this turn of events was from the LORD, to fulfill the word the LORD had spoken to Jeroboam son of Nebat through Ahijah the Shilonite.

[16]When all Israel saw that the king refused to listen to them, they answered the king:

"What share do we have in David,
    what part in Jesse's son?
To your tents, O Israel!
    Look after your own house,
        O David!"

So the Israelites went home. [17]But as for the Israelites who were living in the towns of Judah, Rehoboam still ruled over them.

[18]King Rehoboam sent out Adoniram,[b] who was in charge of forced labor, but all Israel stoned him to death. King

---

[a]2 Or *he remained in*   [b]18 Some Septuagint manuscripts and Syriac (see also 1 Kings 4:6 and 5:14); Hebrew *Adoram*

Rehoboam, however, managed to get into his chariot and escape to Jerusalem. ¹⁹So Israel has been in rebellion against the house of David to this day.

²⁰When all the Israelites heard that Jeroboam had returned, they sent and called him to the assembly and made him king over all Israel. Only the tribe of Judah remained loyal to the house of David.

²¹When Rehoboam arrived in Jerusalem, he mustered the whole house of Judah and the tribe of Benjamin—a hundred and eighty thousand fighting men—to make war against the house of Israel and to regain the kingdom for Rehoboam son of Solomon.

²²But this word of God came to Shemaiah the man of God: ²³"Say to Rehoboam son of Solomon king of Judah, to the whole house of Judah and Benjamin, and to the rest of the people, ²⁴'This is what the LORD says: Do not go up to fight against your brothers, the Israelites. Go home, every one of you, for this is my doing.' " So they obeyed the word of the LORD and went home again, as the LORD had ordered.

Golden Calves at Bethel and Dan

²⁵Then Jeroboam fortified Shechem in the hill country of Ephraim and lived there. From there he went out and built up Peniel.ᵃ

²⁶Jeroboam thought to himself, "The kingdom will now likely revert to the house of David. ²⁷If these people go up to offer sacrifices at the temple of the LORD in Jerusalem, they will again give their allegiance to their lord, Rehoboam king of Judah. They will kill me and return to King Rehoboam."

²⁸After seeking advice, the king made two golden calves. He said to the people, "It is too much for you to go up to Jerusalem. Here are your gods, O Israel, who brought you up out of Egypt." ²⁹One he set up in Bethel, and the other in Dan. ³⁰And this thing became a sin; the people went even as far as Dan to worship the one there.

³¹Jeroboam built shrines on high places and appointed priests from all sorts of people, even though they were not Levites. ³²He instituted a festival on the fifteenth day of the eighth month, like

the festival held in Judah, and offered sacrifices on the altar. This he did in Bethel, sacrificing to the calves he had made. And at Bethel he also installed priests at the high places he had made. ³³On the fifteenth day of the eighth month, a month of his own choosing, he offered sacrifices on the altar he had built at Bethel. So he instituted the festival for the Israelites and went up to the altar to make offerings.

The Man of God From Judah

13 By the word of the LORD a man of God came from Judah to Bethel, as Jeroboam was standing by the altar to make an offering. ²He cried out against the altar by the word of the LORD: "O altar, altar! This is what the LORD says: 'A son named Josiah will be born to the house of David. On you he will sacrifice the priests of the high places who now make offerings here, and human bones will be burned on you.' " ³That same day the man of God gave a sign: "This is the sign the LORD has declared: The altar will be split apart and the ashes on it will be poured out."

⁴When King Jeroboam heard what the man of God cried out against the altar at Bethel, he stretched out his hand from the altar and said, "Seize him!" But the hand he stretched out toward the man shriveled up, so that he could not pull it back. ⁵Also, the altar was split apart and its ashes poured out according to the sign given by the man of God by the word of the LORD.

⁶Then the king said to the man of God, "Intercede with the LORD your God and pray for me that my hand may be restored." So the man of God interceded with the LORD, and the king's hand was restored and became as it was before.

⁷The king said to the man of God, "Come home with me and have something to eat, and I will give you a gift."

⁸But the man of God answered the king, "Even if you were to give me half your possessions, I would not go with you, nor would I eat bread or drink water here. ⁹For I was commanded by the word of the LORD: 'You must not eat bread or drink water or return by the way you came.' " ¹⁰So he took another road and did

ᵃ25 Hebrew *Penuel*, a variant of *Peniel*

not return by the way he had come to Bethel.

[11]Now there was a certain old prophet living in Bethel, whose sons came and told him all that the man of God had done there that day. They also told their father what he had said to the king. [12]Their father asked them, "Which way did he go?" And his sons showed him which road the man of God from Judah had taken. [13]So he said to his sons, "Saddle the donkey for me." And when they had saddled the donkey for him, he mounted it [14]and rode after the man of God. He found him sitting under an oak tree and asked, "Are you the man of God who came from Judah?"

"I am," he replied.

[15]So the prophet said to him, "Come home with me and eat."

[16]The man of God said, "I cannot turn back and go with you, nor can I eat bread or drink water with you in this place. [17]I have been told by the word of the LORD: 'You must not eat bread or drink water there or return by the way you came.' "

[18]The old prophet answered, "I too am a prophet, as you are. And an angel said to me by the word of the LORD: 'Bring him back with you to your house so that he may eat bread and drink water.' " (But he was lying to him.) [19]So the man of God returned with him and ate and drank in his house.

[20]While they were sitting at the table, the word of the LORD came to the old prophet who had brought him back. [21]He cried out to the man of God who had come from Judah, "This is what the LORD says: 'You have defied the word of the LORD and have not kept the command the LORD your God gave you. [22]You came back and ate bread and drank water in the place where he told you not to eat or drink. Therefore your body will not be buried in the tomb of your fathers.' "

[23]When the man of God had finished eating and drinking, the prophet who had brought him back saddled his donkey for him. [24]As he went on his way, a lion met him on the road and killed him, and his body was thrown down on the road, with both the donkey and the lion standing beside it. [25]Some people who passed by saw the body thrown down there, with the lion standing beside the body, and they went and reported it in the city where the old prophet lived.

[26]When the prophet who had brought him back from his journey heard of it, he said, "It is the man of God who defied the word of the LORD. The LORD has given him over to the lion, which has mauled him and killed him, as the word of the LORD had warned him."

[27]The prophet said to his sons, "Saddle the donkey for me," and they did so. [28]Then he went out and found the body thrown down on the road, with the donkey and the lion standing beside it. The lion had neither eaten the body nor mauled the donkey. [29]So the prophet picked up the body of the man of God, laid it on the donkey, and brought it back to his own city to mourn for him and bury him. [30]Then he laid the body in his own tomb, and they mourned over him and said, "Oh, my brother!"

[31]After burying him, he said to his sons, "When I die, bury me in the grave where the man of God is buried; lay my bones beside his bones. [32]For the message he declared by the word of the LORD against the altar in Bethel and against all the shrines on the high places in the towns of Samaria will certainly come true."

[33]Even after this, Jeroboam did not change his evil ways, but once more appointed priests for the high places from all sorts of people. Anyone who wanted to become a priest he consecrated for the high places. [34]This was the sin of the house of Jeroboam that led to its downfall and to its destruction from the face of the earth.

Ahijah's Prophecy Against Jeroboam

14 At that time Abijah son of Jeroboam became ill, [2]and Jeroboam said to his wife, "Go, disguise yourself, so you won't be recognized as the wife of Jeroboam. Then go to Shiloh. Ahijah the prophet is there—the one who told me I would be king over this people. [3]Take ten loaves of bread with you, some cakes and a jar of honey, and go to him. He will tell you what will happen to the boy." [4]So Jeroboam's wife did what he said and went to Ahijah's house in Shiloh.

Now Ahijah could not see; his sight was gone because of his age. [5]But the

LORD had told Ahijah, "Jeroboam's wife is coming to ask you about her son, for he is ill, and you are to give her such and such an answer. When she arrives, she will pretend to be someone else."

⁶So when Ahijah heard the sound of her footsteps at the door, he said, "Come in, wife of Jeroboam. Why this pretense? I have been sent to you with bad news. ⁷Go, tell Jeroboam that this is what the LORD, the God of Israel, says: 'I raised you up from among the people and made you a leader over my people Israel. ⁸I tore the kingdom away from the house of David and gave it to you, but you have not been like my servant David, who kept my commands and followed me with all his heart, doing only what was right in my eyes. ⁹You have done more evil than all who lived before you. You have made for yourself other gods, idols made of metal; you have provoked me to anger and thrust me behind your back.

¹⁰" 'Because of this, I am going to bring disaster on the house of Jeroboam. I will cut off from Jeroboam every last male in Israel—slave or free. I will burn up the house of Jeroboam as one burns dung, until it is all gone. ¹¹Dogs will eat those belonging to Jeroboam who die in the city, and the birds of the air will feed on those who die in the country. The LORD has spoken!'

¹²"As for you, go back home. When you set foot in your city, the boy will die. ¹³All Israel will mourn for him and bury him. He is the only one belonging to Jeroboam who will be buried, because he is the only one in the house of Jeroboam in whom the LORD, the God of Israel, has found anything good.

¹⁴"The LORD will raise up for himself a king over Israel who will cut off the family of Jeroboam. This is the day! What? Yes, even now.ᵃ ¹⁵And the LORD will strike Israel, so that it will be like a reed swaying in the water. He will uproot Israel from this good land that he gave to their forefathers and scatter them beyond the River,ᵇ because they provoked the LORD to anger by making Asherah poles.ᶜ ¹⁶And he will give Israel up because of the sins Jeroboam has committed and has caused Israel to commit."

¹⁷Then Jeroboam's wife got up and left and went to Tirzah. As soon as she stepped over the threshold of the house, the boy died. ¹⁸They buried him, and all Israel mourned for him, as the LORD had said through his servant the prophet Ahijah.

¹⁹The other events of Jeroboam's reign, his wars and how he ruled, are written in the book of the annals of the kings of Israel. ²⁰He reigned for twenty-two years and then rested with his fathers. And Nadab his son succeeded him as king.

Rehoboam King of Judah

²¹Rehoboam son of Solomon was king in Judah. He was forty-one years old when he became king, and he reigned seventeen years in Jerusalem, the city the LORD had chosen out of all the tribes of Israel in which to put his Name. His mother's name was Naamah; she was an Ammonite.

²²Judah did evil in the eyes of the LORD. By the sins they committed they stirred up his jealous anger more than their fathers had done. ²³They also set up for themselves high places, sacred stones and Asherah poles on every high hill and under every spreading tree. ²⁴There were even male shrine prostitutes in the land; the people engaged in all the detestable practices of the nations the LORD had driven out before the Israelites.

²⁵In the fifth year of King Rehoboam, Shishak king of Egypt attacked Jerusalem. ²⁶He carried off the treasures of the temple of the LORD and the treasures of the royal palace. He took everything, including all the gold shields Solomon had made. ²⁷So King Rehoboam made bronze shields to replace them and assigned these to the commanders of the guard on duty at the entrance to the royal palace. ²⁸Whenever the king went to the LORD's temple, the guards bore the shields, and afterward they returned them to the guardroom.

²⁹As for the other events of Rehoboam's reign, and all he did, are they not written in the book of the annals of the kings of Judah? ³⁰There was continual warfare between Rehoboam and Jerobo-

---

ᵃ14 The meaning of the Hebrew for this sentence is uncertain.   ᵇ15 That is, the Euphrates
ᶜ15 That is, symbols of the goddess Asherah; here and elsewhere in 1 Kings

am. [31]And Rehoboam rested with his fathers and was buried with them in the City of David. His mother's name was Naamah; she was an Ammonite. And Abijah[a] his son succeeded him as king.

Abijah King of Judah

15 In the eighteenth year of the reign of Jeroboam son of Nebat, Abijah[b] became king of Judah, [2]and he reigned in Jerusalem three years. His mother's name was Maacah daughter of Abishalom.[c]

[3]He committed all the sins his father had done before him; his heart was not fully devoted to the LORD his God, as the heart of David his forefather had been. [4]Nevertheless, for David's sake the LORD his God gave him a lamp in Jerusalem by raising up a son to succeed him and by making Jerusalem strong. [5]For David had done what was right in the eyes of the LORD and had not failed to keep any of the LORD's commands all the days of his life—except in the case of Uriah the Hittite.

[6]There was war between Rehoboam[d] and Jeroboam throughout ⌊Abijah's⌋ lifetime. [7]As for the other events of Abijah's reign, and all he did, are they not written in the book of the annals of the kings of Judah? There was war between Abijah and Jeroboam. [8]And Abijah rested with his fathers and was buried in the City of David. And Asa his son succeeded him as king.

Asa King of Judah

[9]In the twentieth year of Jeroboam king of Israel, Asa became king of Judah, [10]and he reigned in Jerusalem forty-one years. His grandmother's name was Maacah daughter of Abishalom.

[11]Asa did what was right in the eyes of the LORD, as his father David had done. [12]He expelled the male shrine prostitutes from the land and got rid of all the idols his fathers had made. [13]He even deposed his grandmother Maacah from her position as queen mother, because she had made a repulsive Asherah pole. Asa cut the pole down and burned it in the Kidron Valley. [14]Although he did not remove the high places, Asa's heart was fully committed to the LORD all his life. [15]He brought into the temple of the LORD the silver and gold and the articles that he and his father had dedicated.

[16]There was war between Asa and Baasha king of Israel throughout their reigns. [17]Baasha king of Israel went up against Judah and fortified Ramah to prevent anyone from leaving or entering the territory of Asa king of Judah.

[18]Asa then took all the silver and gold that was left in the treasuries of the LORD's temple and of his own palace. He entrusted it to his officials and sent them to Ben-Hadad son of Tabrimmon, the son of Hezion, the king of Aram, who was ruling in Damascus. [19]"Let there be a treaty between me and you," he said, "as there was between my father and your father. See, I am sending you a gift of silver and gold. Now break your treaty with Baasha king of Israel so he will withdraw from me."

[20]Ben-Hadad agreed with King Asa and sent the commanders of his forces against the towns of Israel. He conquered Ijon, Dan, Abel Beth Maacah and all Kinnereth in addition to Naphtali. [21]When Baasha heard this, he stopped building Ramah and withdrew to Tirzah. [22]Then King Asa issued an order to all Judah—no one was exempt—and they carried away from Ramah the stones and timber Baasha had been using there. With them King Asa built up Geba in Benjamin, and also Mizpah.

[23]As for all the other events of Asa's reign, all his achievements, all he did and the cities he built, are they not written in the book of the annals of the kings of Judah? In his old age, however, his feet became diseased. [24]Then Asa rested with his fathers and was buried with them in the city of his father David. And Jehoshaphat his son succeeded him as king.

Nadab King of Israel

[25]Nadab son of Jeroboam became king of Israel in the second year of Asa king of Judah, and he reigned over Israel two

[a]31 Some Hebrew manuscripts and Septuagint (see also 2 Chron. 12:16); most Hebrew manuscripts Abijam   [b]1 Some Hebrew manuscripts and Septuagint (see also 2 Chron. 12:16); most Hebrew manuscripts Abijam; also in verses 7 and 8   [c]2 A variant of Absalom; also in verse 10   [d]6 Most Hebrew manuscripts; some Hebrew manuscripts and Syriac Abijam (that is, Abijah)

years. ²⁶He did evil in the eyes of the LORD, walking in the ways of his father and in his sin, which he had caused Israel to commit.

²⁷Baasha son of Ahijah of the house of Issachar plotted against him, and he struck him down at Gibbethon, a Philistine town, while Nadab and all Israel were besieging it. ²⁸Baasha killed Nadab in the third year of Asa king of Judah and succeeded him as king.

²⁹As soon as he began to reign, he killed Jeroboam's whole family. He did not leave Jeroboam anyone that breathed, but destroyed them all, according to the word of the LORD given through his servant Ahijah the Shilonite— ³⁰because of the sins Jeroboam had committed and had caused Israel to commit, and because he provoked the LORD, the God of Israel, to anger.

³¹As for the other events of Nadab's reign, and all he did, are they not written in the book of the annals of the kings of Israel? ³²There was war between Asa and Baasha king of Israel throughout their reigns.

Baasha King of Israel

³³In the third year of Asa king of Judah, Baasha son of Ahijah became king of all Israel in Tirzah, and he reigned twenty-four years. ³⁴He did evil in the eyes of the LORD, walking in the ways of Jeroboam and in his sin, which he had caused Israel to commit.

16 Then the word of the LORD came to Jehu son of Hanani against Baasha: ²"I lifted you up from the dust and made you leader of my people Israel, but you walked in the ways of Jeroboam and caused my people Israel to sin and to provoke me to anger by their sins. ³So I am about to consume Baasha and his house, and I will make your house like that of Jeroboam son of Nebat. ⁴Dogs will eat those belonging to Baasha who die in the city, and the birds of the air will feed on those who die in the country."

⁵As for the other events of Baasha's reign, what he did and his achievements, are they not written in the book of the annals of the kings of Israel? ⁶Baasha rested with his fathers and was buried in Tirzah. And Elah his son succeeded him as king.

⁷Moreover, the word of the LORD came through the prophet Jehu son of Hanani to Baasha and his house, because of all the evil he had done in the eyes of the LORD, provoking him to anger by the things he did, and becoming like the house of Jeroboam—and also because he destroyed it.

Elah King of Israel

⁸In the twenty-sixth year of Asa king of Judah, Elah son of Baasha became king of Israel, and he reigned in Tirzah two years.

⁹Zimri, one of his officials, who had command of half his chariots, plotted against him. Elah was in Tirzah at the time, getting drunk in the home of Arza, the man in charge of the palace at Tirzah. ¹⁰Zimri came in, struck him down and killed him in the twenty-seventh year of Asa king of Judah. Then he succeeded him as king.

¹¹As soon as he began to reign and was seated on the throne, he killed off Baasha's whole family. He did not spare a single male, whether relative or friend. ¹²So Zimri destroyed the whole family of Baasha, in accordance with the word of the LORD spoken against Baasha through the prophet Jehu— ¹³because of all the sins Baasha and his son Elah had committed and had caused Israel to commit, so that they provoked the LORD, the God of Israel, to anger by their worthless idols.

¹⁴As for the other events of Elah's reign, and all he did, are they not written in the book of the annals of the kings of Israel?

Zimri King of Israel

¹⁵In the twenty-seventh year of Asa king of Judah, Zimri reigned in Tirzah seven days. The army was encamped near Gibbethon, a Philistine town. ¹⁶When the Israelites in the camp heard that Zimri had plotted against the king and murdered him, they proclaimed Omri, the commander of the army, king over Israel that very day there in the camp. ¹⁷Then Omri and all the Israelites with him withdrew from Gibbethon and laid siege to Tirzah. ¹⁸When Zimri saw that the city was taken, he went into the citadel of the royal palace and set the palace on fire

around him. So he died, ¹⁹because of the sins he had committed, doing evil in the eyes of the LORD and walking in the ways of Jeroboam and in the sin he had committed and had caused Israel to commit.

²⁰As for the other events of Zimri's reign, and the rebellion he carried out, are they not written in the book of the annals of the kings of Israel?

Omri King of Israel

²¹Then the people of Israel were split into two factions; half supported Tibni son of Ginath for king, and the other half supported Omri. ²²But Omri's followers proved stronger than those of Tibni son of Ginath. So Tibni died and Omri became king.

²³In the thirty-first year of Asa king of Judah, Omri became king of Israel, and he reigned twelve years, six of them in Tirzah. ²⁴He bought the hill of Samaria from Shemer for two talents*a* of silver and built a city on the hill, calling it Samaria, after Shemer, the name of the former owner of the hill.

²⁵But Omri did evil in the eyes of the LORD and sinned more than all those before him. ²⁶He walked in all the ways of Jeroboam son of Nebat and in his sin, which he had caused Israel to commit, so that they provoked the LORD, the God of Israel, to anger by their worthless idols.

²⁷As for the other events of Omri's reign, what he did and the things he achieved, are they not written in the book of the annals of the kings of Israel? ²⁸Omri rested with his fathers and was buried in Samaria. And Ahab his son succeeded him as king.

Ahab Becomes King of Israel

²⁹In the thirty-eighth year of Asa king of Judah, Ahab son of Omri became king of Israel, and he reigned in Samaria over Israel twenty-two years. ³⁰Ahab son of Omri did more evil in the eyes of the LORD than any of those before him. ³¹He not only considered it trivial to commit the sins of Jeroboam son of Nebat, but he also married Jezebel daughter of Ethbaal king of the Sidonians, and began to serve Baal and worship him. ³²He set up an altar for Baal in the temple of Baal that he built in Samaria. ³³Ahab also made an Asherah pole and did more to provoke the LORD, the God of Israel, to anger than did all the kings of Israel before him.

³⁴In Ahab's time, Hiel of Bethel rebuilt Jericho. He laid its foundations at the cost of his firstborn son Abiram, and he set up its gates at the cost of his youngest son Segub, in accordance with the word of the LORD spoken by Joshua son of Nun.

Elijah Fed by Ravens

17 Now Elijah the Tishbite, from Tishbe*b* in Gilead, said to Ahab, "As the LORD, the God of Israel, lives, whom I serve, there will be neither dew nor rain in the next few years except at my word."

²Then the word of the LORD came to Elijah: ³"Leave here, turn eastward and hide in the Kerith Ravine, east of the Jordan. ⁴You will drink from the brook, and I have ordered the ravens to feed you there."

⁵So he did what the LORD had told him. He went to the Kerith Ravine, east of the Jordan, and stayed there. ⁶The ravens brought him bread and meat in the morning and bread and meat in the evening, and he drank from the brook.

The Widow at Zarephath

⁷Some time later the brook dried up because there had been no rain in the land. ⁸Then the word of the LORD came to him: ⁹"Go at once to Zarephath of Sidon and stay there. I have commanded a widow in that place to supply you with food." ¹⁰So he went to Zarephath. When he came to the town gate, a widow was there gathering sticks. He called to her and asked, "Would you bring me a little water in a jar so I may have a drink?" ¹¹As she was going to get it, he called, "And bring me, please, a piece of bread."

¹²"As surely as the LORD your God lives," she replied, "I don't have any bread—only a handful of flour in a jar and a little oil in a jug. I am gathering a few sticks to take home and make a meal for myself and my son, that we may eat it—and die."

¹³Elijah said to her, "Don't be afraid. Go home and do as you have said. But first make a small cake of bread for me

a24 That is, about 150 pounds (about 70 kilograms)　　*b1* Or *Tishbite, of the settlers* from what you have and bring it to me, and then make something for yourself and your son. ¹⁴For this is what the LORD, the God of Israel, says: 'The jar of flour will not be used up and the jug of oil will not run dry until the day the LORD gives rain on the land.' "

¹⁵She went away and did as Elijah had told her. So there was food every day for Elijah and for the woman and her family. ¹⁶For the jar of flour was not used up and the jug of oil did not run dry, in keeping with the word of the LORD spoken by Elijah.

¹⁷Some time later the son of the woman who owned the house became ill. He grew worse and worse, and finally stopped breathing. ¹⁸She said to Elijah, "What do you have against me, man of God? Did you come to remind me of my sin and kill my son?"

¹⁹"Give me your son," Elijah replied. He took him from her arms, carried him to the upper room where he was staying, and laid him on his bed. ²⁰Then he cried out to the LORD, "O LORD my God, have you brought tragedy also upon this widow I am staying with, by causing her son to die?" ²¹Then he stretched himself out on

the boy three times and cried to the LORD, "O LORD my God, let this boy's life return to him!"

²²The LORD heard Elijah's cry, and the boy's life returned to him, and he lived. ²³Elijah picked up the child and carried him down from the room into the house. He gave him to his mother and said, "Look, your son is alive!"

²⁴Then the woman said to Elijah, "Now I know that you are a man of God and that the word of the LORD from your mouth is the truth."

Elijah and Obadiah

18 After a long time, in the third year, the word of the LORD came to Elijah: "Go and present yourself to Ahab, and I will send rain on the land." ²So Elijah went to present himself to Ahab.

Now the famine was severe in Samaria, ³and Ahab had summoned Obadiah, who was in charge of his palace. (Obadiah was a devout believer in the LORD. ⁴While Jezebel was killing off the LORD's prophets, Obadiah had taken a hundred prophets and hidden them in two caves, fifty in each, and had supplied them with food and water.) ⁵Ahab had said to Oba-

---

Marriages Can Be Lifelines

Friday

1 KINGS 17 Elijah had a need. He was hungry. But Elijah also saw a ministry opportunity. When the draught in the land deprived Elijah of food, God sent him to stay with a widow in Zarephath. He found a family in a worse condition than he was in, and he ministered to them. He realized that the purpose of his hunger was to bring him to the point of ministering to others.

We all have needs in our marriages. Striving to get them met can become all consuming—so consuming that it can overshadow our purpose for existence which is to love God and love our neighbors (see Matthew 22:37–39, page 1057). To allow a self-centered focus would cause us to miss a great opportunity. There are couples around us with greater needs than our own. Like the widow Elijah stayed with, people

around us are curious to see how we, as Christians, respond to personal adversity. And they want to see how we respond to their adversity.

Our marriages present a great tool for God to use. He wants to use our marriage relationship as a way of illustrating trust in him. God can also use our marriages as a tool to reach out to other couples when they are in pain.

Marriages are not put together simply for our own happiness. Marriages are the winding together of two separate cords around a center cord. Then, with God at the center, the cord becomes three strands woven together, creating great strength—strength that can become a lifeline to others in need.

—*Bob & Rosemary*

Go to page 384 for your next devotional reading.

diah, "Go through the land to all the springs and valleys. Maybe we can find some grass to keep the horses and mules alive so we will not have to kill any of our animals." ⁶So they divided the land they were to cover, Ahab going in one direction and Obadiah in another.

⁷As Obadiah was walking along, Elijah met him. Obadiah recognized him, bowed down to the ground, and said, "Is it really you, my lord Elijah?"

⁸"Yes," he replied. "Go tell your master, 'Elijah is here.' "

⁹"What have I done wrong," asked Obadiah, "that you are handing your servant over to Ahab to be put to death? ¹⁰As surely as the LORD your God lives, there is not a nation or kingdom where my master has not sent someone to look for you. And whenever a nation or kingdom claimed you were not there, he made them swear they could not find you. ¹¹But now you tell me to go to my master and say, 'Elijah is here.' ¹²I don't know where the Spirit of the LORD may carry you when I leave you. If I go and tell Ahab and he doesn't find you, he will kill me. Yet I your servant have worshiped the LORD since my youth. ¹³Haven't you heard, my lord, what I did while Jezebel was killing the prophets of the LORD? I hid a hundred of the LORD's prophets in two caves, fifty in each, and supplied them with food and water. ¹⁴And now you tell me to go to my master and say, 'Elijah is here.' He will kill me!"

¹⁵Elijah said, "As the LORD Almighty lives, whom I serve, I will surely present myself to Ahab today."

Elijah on Mount Carmel

¹⁶So Obadiah went to meet Ahab and told him, and Ahab went to meet Elijah. ¹⁷When he saw Elijah, he said to him, "Is that you, you troubler of Israel?"

¹⁸"I have not made trouble for Israel," Elijah replied. "But you and your father's family have. You have abandoned the LORD's commands and have followed the Baals. ¹⁹Now summon the people from all over Israel to meet me on Mount Carmel. And bring the four hundred and fifty prophets of Baal and the four hundred prophets of Asherah, who eat at Jezebel's table."

²⁰So Ahab sent word throughout all Israel and assembled the prophets on Mount Carmel. ²¹Elijah went before the people and said, "How long will you waver between two opinions? If the LORD is God, follow him; but if Baal is God, follow him."

But the people said nothing.

²²Then Elijah said to them, "I am the only one of the LORD's prophets left, but Baal has four hundred and fifty prophets. ²³Get two bulls for us. Let them choose one for themselves, and let them cut it into pieces and put it on the wood but not set fire to it. I will prepare the other bull and put it on the wood but not set fire to it. ²⁴Then you call on the name of your god, and I will call on the name of the LORD. The god who answers by fire—he is God."

Then all the people said, "What you say is good."

²⁵Elijah said to the prophets of Baal, "Choose one of the bulls and prepare it first, since there are so many of you. Call on the name of your god, but do not light the fire." ²⁶So they took the bull given them and prepared it.

Then they called on the name of Baal from morning till noon. "O Baal, answer us!" they shouted. But there was no response; no one answered. And they danced around the altar they had made.

²⁷At noon Elijah began to taunt them. "Shout louder!" he said. "Surely he is a god! Perhaps he is deep in thought, or busy, or traveling. Maybe he is sleeping and must be awakened." ²⁸So they shouted louder and slashed themselves with swords and spears, as was their custom, until their blood flowed. ²⁹Midday passed, and they continued their frantic prophesying until the time for the evening sacrifice. But there was no response, no one answered, no one paid attention.

³⁰Then Elijah said to all the people, "Come here to me." They came to him, and he repaired the altar of the LORD, which was in ruins. ³¹Elijah took twelve stones, one for each of the tribes descended from Jacob, to whom the word of the LORD had come, saying, "Your name shall be Israel." ³²With the stones he built an altar in the name of the LORD, and he dug a trench around it large enough to hold

two seahs*a* of seed. ³³He arranged the wood, cut the bull into pieces and laid it on the wood. Then he said to them, "Fill four large jars with water and pour it on the offering and on the wood."

³⁴"Do it again," he said, and they did it again.

"Do it a third time," he ordered, and they did it the third time. ³⁵The water ran down around the altar and even filled the trench.

³⁶At the time of sacrifice, the prophet Elijah stepped forward and prayed: "O LORD, God of Abraham, Isaac and Israel, let it be known today that you are God in Israel and that I am your servant and have done all these things at your command. ³⁷Answer me, O LORD, answer me, so these people will know that you, O LORD, are God, and that you are turning their hearts back again."

³⁸Then the fire of the LORD fell and burned up the sacrifice, the wood, the stones and the soil, and also licked up the water in the trench.

³⁹When all the people saw this, they fell prostrate and cried, "The LORD—he is God! The LORD—he is God!"

⁴⁰Then Elijah commanded them, "Seize the prophets of Baal. Don't let anyone get away!" They seized them, and Elijah had them brought down to the Kishon Valley and slaughtered there.

⁴¹And Elijah said to Ahab, "Go, eat and drink, for there is the sound of a heavy rain." ⁴²So Ahab went off to eat and drink, but Elijah climbed to the top of Carmel, bent down to the ground and put his face between his knees.

⁴³"Go and look toward the sea," he told his servant. And he went up and looked.

"There is nothing there," he said.

Seven times Elijah said, "Go back."

⁴⁴The seventh time the servant reported, "A cloud as small as a man's hand is rising from the sea."

So Elijah said, "Go and tell Ahab, 'Hitch up your chariot and go down before the rain stops you.' "

⁴⁵Meanwhile, the sky grew black with clouds, the wind rose, a heavy rain came on and Ahab rode off to Jezreel. ⁴⁶The power of the LORD came upon Elijah and, tucking his cloak into his belt, he ran ahead of Ahab all the way to Jezreel.

Elijah Flees to Horeb

19 Now Ahab told Jezebel everything Elijah had done and how he had killed all the prophets with the sword. ²So Jezebel sent a messenger to Elijah to say, "May the gods deal with me, be it ever so severely, if by this time tomorrow I do not make your life like that of one of them."

³Elijah was afraid*b* and ran for his life. When he came to Beersheba in Judah, he left his servant there, ⁴while he himself went a day's journey into the desert. He came to a broom tree, sat down under it and prayed that he might die. "I have had enough, LORD," he said. "Take my life; I am no better than my ancestors." ⁵Then he lay down under the tree and fell asleep.

All at once an angel touched him and said, "Get up and eat." ⁶He looked around, and there by his head was a cake of bread baked over hot coals, and a jar of water. He ate and drank and then lay down again.

⁷The angel of the LORD came back a second time and touched him and said, "Get up and eat, for the journey is too much for you." ⁸So he got up and ate and drank. Strengthened by that food, he traveled forty days and forty nights until he reached Horeb, the mountain of God. ⁹There he went into a cave and spent the night.

The LORD Appears to Elijah

And the word of the LORD came to him: "What are you doing here, Elijah?"

¹⁰He replied, "I have been very zealous for the LORD God Almighty. The Israelites have rejected your covenant, broken down your altars, and put your prophets to death with the sword. I am the only one left, and now they are trying to kill me too."

¹¹The LORD said, "Go out and stand on the mountain in the presence of the LORD, for the LORD is about to pass by."

Then a great and powerful wind tore the mountains apart and shattered the rocks before the LORD, but the LORD was not in the wind. After the wind there was an earthquake, but the LORD was not in the earthquake. ¹²After the earthquake

a32 That is, probably about 13 quarts (about 15 liters)   *b3* Or *Elijah saw* came a fire, but the LORD was not in the fire. And after the fire came a gentle whisper. [13]When Elijah heard it, he pulled his cloak over his face and went out and stood at the mouth of the cave.

Then a voice said to him, "What are you doing here, Elijah?"

[14]He replied, "I have been very zealous for the LORD God Almighty. The Israelites have rejected your covenant, broken down your altars, and put your prophets to death with the sword. I am the only one left, and now they are trying to kill me too."

[15]The LORD said to him, "Go back the way you came, and go to the Desert of Damascus. When you get there, anoint Hazael king over Aram. [16]Also, anoint Jehu son of Nimshi king over Israel, and anoint Elisha son of Shaphat from Abel Meholah to succeed you as prophet. [17]Jehu will put to death any who escape the sword of Hazael, and Elisha will put to death any who escape the sword of Jehu. [18]Yet I reserve seven thousand in Israel—all whose knees have not bowed down to Baal and all whose mouths have not kissed him."

The Call of Elisha

[19]So Elijah went from there and found Elisha son of Shaphat. He was plowing with twelve yoke of oxen, and he himself was driving the twelfth pair. Elijah went up to him and threw his cloak around him. [20]Elisha then left his oxen and ran after Elijah. "Let me kiss my father and mother good-by," he said, "and then I will come with you."

"Go back," Elijah replied. "What have I done to you?"

[21]So Elisha left him and went back. He took his yoke of oxen and slaughtered them. He burned the plowing equipment to cook the meat and gave it to the people, and they ate. Then he set out to follow Elijah and became his attendant.

Ben-Hadad Attacks Samaria

20 Now Ben-Hadad king of Aram mustered his entire army. Accompanied by thirty-two kings with their horses and chariots, he went up and besieged Samaria and attacked it. [2]He sent messengers into the city to Ahab king of Israel, saying, "This is what Ben-Hadad says: [3]'Your silver and gold are mine, and the best of your wives and children are mine.' "

[4]The king of Israel answered, "Just as you say, my lord the king. I and all I have are yours."

[5]The messengers came again and said, "This is what Ben-Hadad says: 'I sent to demand your silver and gold, your wives and your children. [6]But about this time tomorrow I am going to send my officials to search your palace and the houses of your officials. They will seize everything you value and carry it away.' "

[7]The king of Israel summoned all the elders of the land and said to them, "See how this man is looking for trouble! When he sent for my wives and my children, my silver and my gold, I did not refuse him."

[8]The elders and the people all answered, "Don't listen to him or agree to his demands."

[9]So he replied to Ben-Hadad's messengers, "Tell my lord the king, 'Your servant will do all you demanded the first time, but this demand I cannot meet.' " They left and took the answer back to Ben-Hadad.

[10]Then Ben-Hadad sent another message to Ahab: "May the gods deal with me, be it ever so severely, if enough dust remains in Samaria to give each of my men a handful."

[11]The king of Israel answered, "Tell him: 'One who puts on his armor should not boast like one who takes it off.' "

[12]Ben-Hadad heard this message while he and the kings were drinking in their tents,[a] and he ordered his men: "Prepare to attack." So they prepared to attack the city.

Ahab Defeats Ben-Hadad

[13]Meanwhile a prophet came to Ahab king of Israel and announced, "This is what the LORD says: 'Do you see this vast army? I will give it into your hand today, and then you will know that I am the LORD.' "

[14]"But who will do this?" asked Ahab.

The prophet replied, "This is what the LORD says: 'The young officers of the provincial commanders will do it.' "

---

a12 Or *in Succoth;* also in verse 16

"And who will start the battle?" he asked.

The prophet answered, "You will."

¹⁵So Ahab summoned the young officers of the provincial commanders, 232 men. Then he assembled the rest of the Israelites, 7,000 in all. ¹⁶They set out at noon while Ben-Hadad and the 32 kings allied with him were in their tents getting drunk. ¹⁷The young officers of the provincial commanders went out first.

Now Ben-Hadad had dispatched scouts, who reported, "Men are advancing from Samaria."

¹⁸He said, "If they have come out for peace, take them alive; if they have come out for war, take them alive."

¹⁹The young officers of the provincial commanders marched out of the city with the army behind them ²⁰and each one struck down his opponent. At that, the Arameans fled, with the Israelites in pursuit. But Ben-Hadad king of Aram escaped on horseback with some of his horsemen. ²¹The king of Israel advanced and overpowered the horses and chariots and inflicted heavy losses on the Arameans.

²²Afterward, the prophet came to the king of Israel and said, "Strengthen your position and see what must be done, because next spring the king of Aram will attack you again."

²³Meanwhile, the officials of the king of Aram advised him, "Their gods are gods of the hills. That is why they were too strong for us. But if we fight them on the plains, surely we will be stronger than they. ²⁴Do this: Remove all the kings from their commands and replace them with other officers. ²⁵You must also raise an army like the one you lost—horse for horse and chariot for chariot—so we can fight Israel on the plains. Then surely we will be stronger than they." He agreed with them and acted accordingly.

²⁶The next spring Ben-Hadad mustered the Arameans and went up to Aphek to fight against Israel. ²⁷When the Israelites were also mustered and given provisions, they marched out to meet them. The Israelites camped opposite them like two small flocks of goats, while the Arameans covered the countryside.

²⁸The man of God came up and told the king of Israel, "This is what the LORD says: 'Because the Arameans think the LORD is a god of the hills and not a god of the valleys, I will deliver this vast army into your hands, and you will know that I am the LORD.' "

²⁹For seven days they camped opposite each other, and on the seventh day the battle was joined. The Israelites inflicted a hundred thousand casualties on the Aramean foot soldiers in one day. ³⁰The rest of them escaped to the city of Aphek, where the wall collapsed on twenty-seven thousand of them. And Ben-Hadad fled to the city and hid in an inner room.

³¹His officials said to him, "Look, we have heard that the kings of the house of Israel are merciful. Let us go to the king of Israel with sackcloth around our waists and ropes around our heads. Perhaps he will spare your life."

³²Wearing sackcloth around their waists and ropes around their heads, they went to the king of Israel and said, "Your servant Ben-Hadad says: 'Please let me live.' "

The king answered, "Is he still alive? He is my brother."

³³The men took this as a good sign and were quick to pick up his word. "Yes, your brother Ben-Hadad!" they said.

"Go and get him," the king said. When Ben-Hadad came out, Ahab had him come up into his chariot.

³⁴"I will return the cities my father took from your father," Ben-Hadad offered. "You may set up your own market areas in Damascus, as my father did in Samaria."

⌐Ahab said,⌐ "On the basis of a treaty I will set you free." So he made a treaty with him, and let him go.

A Prophet Condemns Ahab

³⁵By the word of the LORD one of the sons of the prophets said to his companion, "Strike me with your weapon," but the man refused.

³⁶So the prophet said, "Because you have not obeyed the LORD, as soon as you leave me a lion will kill you." And after the man went away, a lion found him and killed him.

³⁷The prophet found another man and said, "Strike me, please." So the man struck him and wounded him. ³⁸Then the

prophet went and stood by the road waiting for the king. He disguised himself with his headband down over his eyes. ³⁹As the king passed by, the prophet called out to him, "Your servant went into the thick of the battle, and someone came to me with a captive and said, 'Guard this man. If he is missing, it will be your life for his life, or you must pay a talent^a of silver.' ⁴⁰While your servant was busy here and there, the man disappeared."

"That is your sentence," the king of Israel said. "You have pronounced it yourself."

⁴¹Then the prophet quickly removed the headband from his eyes, and the king of Israel recognized him as one of the prophets. ⁴²He said to the king, "This is what the LORD says: 'You have set free a man I had determined should die.^b Therefore it is your life for his life, your people for his people.' " ⁴³Sullen and angry, the king of Israel went to his palace in Samaria.

Naboth's Vineyard

21 Some time later there was an incident involving a vineyard belonging to Naboth the Jezreelite. The vineyard was in Jezreel, close to the palace of Ahab king of Samaria. ²Ahab said to Naboth, "Let me have your vineyard to use for a vegetable garden, since it is close to my palace. In exchange I will give you a better vineyard or, if you prefer, I will pay you whatever it is worth."

³But Naboth replied, "The LORD forbid that I should give you the inheritance of my fathers."

⁴So Ahab went home, sullen and angry because Naboth the Jezreelite had said, "I will not give you the inheritance of my fathers." He lay on his bed sulking and refused to eat.

⁵His wife Jezebel came in and asked him, "Why are you so sullen? Why won't you eat?"

⁶He answered her, "Because I said to Naboth the Jezreelite, 'Sell me your vineyard; or if you prefer, I will give you another vineyard in its place.' But he said, 'I will not give you my vineyard.' "

⁷Jezebel his wife said, "Is this how you act as king over Israel? Get up and eat! Cheer up. I'll get you the vineyard of Naboth the Jezreelite."

⁸So she wrote letters in Ahab's name, placed his seal on them, and sent them to the elders and nobles who lived in Naboth's city with him. ⁹In those letters she wrote:

> "Proclaim a day of fasting and seat Naboth in a prominent place among the people. ¹⁰But seat two scoundrels opposite him and have them testify that he has cursed both God and the king. Then take him out and stone him to death."

¹¹So the elders and nobles who lived in Naboth's city did as Jezebel directed in the letters she had written to them. ¹²They proclaimed a fast and seated Naboth in a prominent place among the people. ¹³Then two scoundrels came and sat opposite him and brought charges against Naboth before the people, saying, "Naboth has cursed both God and the king." So they took him outside the city and stoned him to death. ¹⁴Then they sent word to Jezebel: "Naboth has been stoned and is dead."

¹⁵As soon as Jezebel heard that Naboth had been stoned to death, she said to Ahab, "Get up and take possession of the vineyard of Naboth the Jezreelite that he refused to sell you. He is no longer alive, but dead." ¹⁶When Ahab heard that Naboth was dead, he got up and went down to take possession of Naboth's vineyard.

¹⁷Then the word of the LORD came to Elijah the Tishbite: ¹⁸"Go down to meet Ahab king of Israel, who rules in Samaria. He is now in Naboth's vineyard, where he has gone to take possession of it. ¹⁹Say to him, 'This is what the LORD says: Have you not murdered a man and seized his property?' Then say to him, 'This is what the LORD says: In the place where dogs licked up Naboth's blood, dogs will lick up your blood—yes, yours!' "

²⁰Ahab said to Elijah, "So you have found me, my enemy!"

"I have found you," he answered, "because you have sold yourself to do evil in the eyes of the LORD. ²¹I am going to

---

^a39 That is, about 75 pounds (about 34 kilograms)   ^b42 The Hebrew term refers to the irrevocable giving over of things or persons to the LORD, often by totally destroying them.

bring disaster on you. I will consume your descendants and cut off from Ahab every last male in Israel—slave or free. 22I will make your house like that of Jeroboam son of Nebat and that of Baasha son of Ahijah, because you have provoked me to anger and have caused Israel to sin.'

23"And also concerning Jezebel the LORD says: 'Dogs will devour Jezebel by the wall of^a Jezreel.'

24"Dogs will eat those belonging to Ahab who die in the city, and the birds of the air will feed on those who die in the country."

25(There was never a man like Ahab, who sold himself to do evil in the eyes of the LORD, urged on by Jezebel his wife. 26He behaved in the vilest manner by going after idols, like the Amorites the LORD drove out before Israel.)

27When Ahab heard these words, he tore his clothes, put on sackcloth and fasted. He lay in sackcloth and went around meekly.

28Then the word of the LORD came to Elijah the Tishbite: 29"Have you noticed how Ahab has humbled himself before me? Because he has humbled himself, I will not bring this disaster in his day, but I will bring it on his house in the days of his son."

Micaiah Prophesies Against Ahab

22 For three years there was no war between Aram and Israel. 2But in the third year Jehoshaphat king of Judah went down to see the king of Israel. 3The king of Israel had said to his officials, "Don't you know that Ramoth Gilead belongs to us and yet we are doing nothing to retake it from the king of Aram?"

4So he asked Jehoshaphat, "Will you go with me to fight against Ramoth Gilead?"

Jehoshaphat replied to the king of Israel, "I am as you are, my people as your people, my horses as your horses." 5But Jehoshaphat also said to the king of Israel, "First seek the counsel of the LORD."

6So the king of Israel brought together the prophets—about four hundred men—and asked them, "Shall I go to war against Ramoth Gilead, or shall I refrain?"

"Go," they answered, "for the Lord will give it into the king's hand."

Ahab and Jezebel

1 KINGS 21 The story of this couple is a study in manipulation. When Ahab wanted to own a vineyard adjoining his, Jezebel went to work on a secret scheme to put Naboth, the owner of the property, in an untenable position of being disloyal to the king and blaspheming God. Her lies helped Ahab possess the vineyard, but not before Naboth was stoned to death.

Ahab and Jezebel complemented one another, but not as a godly couple. Scripture sums up their relationship this way: "There was never a man like Ahab, who sold himself to do evil in the eyes of the LORD, urged on by Jezebel his wife" (verse 25).

7But Jehoshaphat asked, "Is there not a prophet of the LORD here whom we can inquire of?"

8The king of Israel answered Jehoshaphat, "There is still one man through whom we can inquire of the LORD, but I hate him because he never prophesies anything good about me, but always bad. He is Micaiah son of Imlah."

"The king should not say that," Jehoshaphat replied.

9So the king of Israel called one of his officials and said, "Bring Micaiah son of Imlah at once."

10Dressed in their royal robes, the king of Israel and Jehoshaphat king of Judah were sitting on their thrones at the threshing floor by the entrance of the gate of Samaria, with all the prophets prophesying before them. 11Now Zedekiah son of Kenaanah had made iron horns and he declared, "This is what the LORD says: 'With these you will gore the Arameans until they are destroyed.' "

12All the other prophets were prophesying the same thing. "Attack Ramoth Gilead and be victorious," they said, "for the LORD will give it into the king's hand."

13The messenger who had gone to summon Micaiah said to him, "Look, as one man the other prophets are predict-

^a23 Most Hebrew manuscripts; a few Hebrew manuscripts, Vulgate and Syriac (see also 2 Kings 9:26) *the plot of ground at*

ing success for the king. Let your word agree with theirs, and speak favorably."

¹⁴But Micaiah said, "As surely as the LORD lives, I can tell him only what the LORD tells me."

¹⁵When he arrived, the king asked him, "Micaiah, shall we go to war against Ramoth Gilead, or shall I refrain?"

"Attack and be victorious," he answered, "for the LORD will give it into the king's hand."

¹⁶The king said to him, "How many times must I make you swear to tell me nothing but the truth in the name of the LORD?"

¹⁷Then Micaiah answered, "I saw all Israel scattered on the hills like sheep without a shepherd, and the LORD said, 'These people have no master. Let each one go home in peace.' "

¹⁸The king of Israel said to Jehoshaphat, "Didn't I tell you that he never prophesies anything good about me, but only bad?"

¹⁹Micaiah continued, "Therefore hear the word of the LORD: I saw the LORD sitting on his throne with all the host of heaven standing around him on his right and on his left. ²⁰And the LORD said, 'Who will entice Ahab into attacking Ramoth Gilead and going to his death there?'

"One suggested this, and another that. ²¹Finally, a spirit came forward, stood before the LORD and said, 'I will entice him.'

²²" 'By what means?' the LORD asked.

" 'I will go out and be a lying spirit in the mouths of all his prophets,' he said.

" 'You will succeed in enticing him,' said the LORD. 'Go and do it.'

²³"So now the LORD has put a lying spirit in the mouths of all these prophets of yours. The LORD has decreed disaster for you."

²⁴Then Zedekiah son of Kenaanah went up and slapped Micaiah in the face. "Which way did the spirit from*a* the LORD go when he went from me to speak to you?" he asked.

²⁵Micaiah replied, "You will find out on the day you go to hide in an inner room."

²⁶The king of Israel then ordered, "Take Micaiah and send him back to Amon the ruler of the city and to Joash the king's son ²⁷and say, 'This is what the

king says: Put this fellow in prison and give him nothing but bread and water until I return safely.' "

²⁸Micaiah declared, "If you ever return safely, the LORD has not spoken through me." Then he added, "Mark my words, all you people!"

Ahab Killed at Ramoth Gilead

²⁹So the king of Israel and Jehoshaphat king of Judah went up to Ramoth Gilead. ³⁰The king of Israel said to Jehoshaphat, "I will enter the battle in disguise, but you wear your royal robes." So the king of Israel disguised himself and went into battle.

³¹Now the king of Aram had ordered his thirty-two chariot commanders, "Do not fight with anyone, small or great, except the king of Israel." ³²When the chariot commanders saw Jehoshaphat, they thought, "Surely this is the king of Israel." So they turned to attack him, but when Jehoshaphat cried out, ³³the chariot commanders saw that he was not the king of Israel and stopped pursuing him.

³⁴But someone drew his bow at random and hit the king of Israel between the sections of his armor. The king told his chariot driver, "Wheel around and get me out of the fighting. I've been wounded." ³⁵All day long the battle raged, and the king was propped up in his chariot facing the Arameans. The blood from his wound ran onto the floor of the chariot, and that evening he died. ³⁶As the sun was setting, a cry spread through the army: "Every man to his town; everyone to his land!"

³⁷So the king died and was brought to Samaria, and they buried him there. ³⁸They washed the chariot at a pool in Samaria (where the prostitutes bathed),*b* and the dogs licked up his blood, as the word of the LORD had declared.

³⁹As for the other events of Ahab's reign, including all he did, the palace he built and inlaid with ivory, and the cities he fortified, are they not written in the book of the annals of the kings of Israel? ⁴⁰Ahab rested with his fathers. And Ahaziah his son succeeded him as king.

a24 Or *Spirit of*   *b38* Or *Samaria and cleaned the weapons*

Jehoshaphat King of Judah

41Jehoshaphat son of Asa became king of Judah in the fourth year of Ahab king of Israel. **42**Jehoshaphat was thirty-five years old when he became king, and he reigned in Jerusalem twenty-five years. His mother's name was Azubah daughter of Shilhi. **43**In everything he walked in the ways of his father Asa and did not stray from them; he did what was right in the eyes of the LORD. The high places, however, were not removed, and the people continued to offer sacrifices and burn incense there. **44**Jehoshaphat was also at peace with the king of Israel.

45As for the other events of Jehoshaphat's reign, the things he achieved and his military exploits, are they not written in the book of the annals of the kings of Judah? **46**He rid the land of the rest of the male shrine prostitutes who remained there even after the reign of his father Asa. **47**There was then no king in Edom; a deputy ruled.

48Now Jehoshaphat built a fleet of trading ships*a* to go to Ophir for gold, but they never set sail—they were wrecked at Ezion Geber. **49**At that time Ahaziah son of Ahab said to Jehoshaphat, "Let my men sail with your men," but Jehoshaphat refused.

50Then Jehoshaphat rested with his fathers and was buried with them in the city of David his father. And Jehoram his son succeeded him.

Ahaziah King of Israel

51Ahaziah son of Ahab became king of Israel in Samaria in the seventeenth year of Jehoshaphat king of Judah, and he reigned over Israel two years. **52**He did evil in the eyes of the LORD, because he walked in the ways of his father and mother and in the ways of Jeroboam son of Nebat, who caused Israel to sin. **53**He served and worshiped Baal and provoked the LORD, the God of Israel, to anger, just as his father had done.

a48 Hebrew *of ships of Tarshish*

2 Kings

The book of
2 Kings continues the saga of men and nations,
most of them disobedient to God's laws and unaffected by
the inevitable repetition of the past. Because so many of
these foolish people refused to learn from those who had
gone before them, they found themselves living the same
tragedy. This is a book about learning from mistakes or
suffering the consequences of repeating them.

Consider how this applies to marriage. The longer you
are married, the more mistakes you make—hurtful words
are spoken, "little" lies are told, perhaps even serious
verbal wounds are inflicted. Hopefully you've learned from
the mistakes. But sometimes people simply refuse to learn
lessons from the past and they destroy their marriages,
their lives and the lives of their loved ones. Why? Good
question. Your parents made mistakes. But they probably
did more than a few things right as well. And they could
have said the same about their parents. The key is to pass
along the things you did right . . .

The Lord's Judgment on Ahaziah

1 After Ahab's death, Moab rebelled against Israel. ²Now Ahaziah had fallen through the lattice of his upper room in Samaria and injured himself. So he sent messengers, saying to them, "Go and consult Baal-Zebub, the god of Ekron, to see if I will recover from this injury."

³But the angel of the LORD said to Elijah the Tishbite, "Go up and meet the messengers of the king of Samaria and ask them, 'Is it because there is no God in Israel that you are going off to consult Baal-Zebub, the god of Ekron?' ⁴Therefore this is what the LORD says: 'You will not leave the bed you are lying on. You will certainly die!' " So Elijah went.

⁵When the messengers returned to the king, he asked them, "Why have you come back?"

⁶"A man came to meet us," they replied. "And he said to us, 'Go back to the king

who sent you and tell him, "This is what the LORD says: Is it because there is no God in Israel that you are sending men to consult Baal-Zebub, the god of Ekron? Therefore you will not leave the bed you are lying on. You will certainly die!' ' "

7The king asked them, "What kind of man was it who came to meet you and told you this?"

8They replied, "He was a man with a garment of hair and with a leather belt around his waist."

The king said, "That was Elijah the Tishbite."

9Then he sent to Elijah a captain with his company of fifty men. The captain went up to Elijah, who was sitting on the top of a hill, and said to him, "Man of God, the king says, 'Come down!' "

10Elijah answered the captain, "If I am a man of God, may fire come down from heaven and consume you and your fifty men!" Then fire fell from heaven and consumed the captain and his men.

11At this the king sent to Elijah another captain with his fifty men. The captain said to him, "Man of God, this is what the king says, 'Come down at once!' "

12"If I am a man of God," Elijah replied, "may fire come down from heaven and consume you and your fifty men!" Then the fire of God fell from heaven and consumed him and his fifty men.

13So the king sent a third captain with his fifty men. This third captain went up and fell on his knees before Elijah. "Man of God," he begged, "please have respect for my life and the lives of these fifty men, your servants! 14See, fire has fallen from heaven and consumed the first two captains and all their men. But now have respect for my life!"

15The angel of the LORD said to Elijah, "Go down with him; do not be afraid of him." So Elijah got up and went down with him to the king.

16He told the king, "This is what the LORD says: Is it because there is no God in Israel for you to consult that you have sent messengers to consult Baal-Zebub, the god of Ekron? Because you have done this, you will never leave the bed you are lying on. You will certainly die!" 17So he died, according to the word of the LORD that Elijah had spoken.

Because Ahaziah had no son, Joram*a*

succeeded him as king in the second year of Jehoram son of Jehoshaphat king of Judah. 18As for all the other events of Ahaziah's reign, and what he did, are they not written in the book of the annals of the kings of Israel?

Elijah Taken Up to Heaven

2 When the LORD was about to take Elijah up to heaven in a whirlwind, Elijah and Elisha were on their way from Gilgal. 2Elijah said to Elisha, "Stay here; the LORD has sent me to Bethel."

But Elisha said, "As surely as the LORD lives and as you live, I will not leave you." So they went down to Bethel.

3The company of the prophets at Bethel came out to Elisha and asked, "Do you know that the LORD is going to take your master from you today?"

"Yes, I know," Elisha replied, "but do not speak of it."

4Then Elijah said to him, "Stay here, Elisha; the LORD has sent me to Jericho."

And he replied, "As surely as the LORD lives and as you live, I will not leave you." So they went to Jericho.

5The company of the prophets at Jericho went up to Elisha and asked him, "Do you know that the LORD is going to take your master from you today?"

"Yes, I know," he replied, "but do not speak of it."

6Then Elijah said to him, "Stay here; the LORD has sent me to the Jordan."

And he replied, "As surely as the LORD lives and as you live, I will not leave you." So the two of them walked on.

7Fifty men of the company of the prophets went and stood at a distance, facing the place where Elijah and Elisha had stopped at the Jordan. 8Elijah took his cloak, rolled it up and struck the water with it. The water divided to the right and to the left, and the two of them crossed over on dry ground.

9When they had crossed, Elijah said to Elisha, "Tell me, what can I do for you before I am taken from you?"

"Let me inherit a double portion of your spirit," Elisha replied.

10"You have asked a difficult thing," Elijah said, "yet if you see me when I am

a17 Hebrew Jehoram, a variant of Joram

taken from you, it will be yours—otherwise not."

¹¹As they were walking along and talking together, suddenly a chariot of fire and horses of fire appeared and separated the two of them, and Elijah went up to heaven in a whirlwind. ¹²Elisha saw this and cried out, "My father! My father! The chariots and horsemen of Israel!" And Elisha saw him no more. Then he took hold of his own clothes and tore them apart.

¹³He picked up the cloak that had fallen from Elijah and went back and stood on the bank of the Jordan. ¹⁴Then he took the cloak that had fallen from him and struck the water with it. "Where now is the LORD, the God of Elijah?" he asked. When he struck the water, it divided to the right and to the left, and he crossed over.

¹⁵The company of the prophets from Jericho, who were watching, said, "The spirit of Elijah is resting on Elisha." And they went to meet him and bowed to the ground before him. ¹⁶"Look," they said, "we your servants have fifty able men. Let them go and look for your master. Perhaps the Spirit of the LORD has picked him up and set him down on some mountain or in some valley."

"No," Elisha replied, "do not send them."

¹⁷But they persisted until he was too ashamed to refuse. So he said, "Send them." And they sent fifty men, who searched for three days but did not find him. ¹⁸When they returned to Elisha, who was staying in Jericho, he said to them, "Didn't I tell you not to go?"

Healing of the Water

¹⁹The men of the city said to Elisha, "Look, our lord, this town is well situated, as you can see, but the water is bad and the land is unproductive."

²⁰"Bring me a new bowl," he said, "and put salt in it." So they brought it to him.

²¹Then he went out to the spring and threw the salt into it, saying, "This is what the LORD says: 'I have healed this water. Never again will it cause death or make the land unproductive.'" ²²And the water has remained wholesome to this day, according to the word Elisha had spoken.

Elisha Is Jeered

²³From there Elisha went up to Bethel. As he was walking along the road, some youths came out of the town and jeered at him. "Go on up, you baldhead!" they said. "Go on up, you baldhead!" ²⁴He turned around, looked at them and called down a curse on them in the name of the LORD. Then two bears came out of the woods and mauled forty-two of the youths. ²⁵And he went on to Mount Carmel and from there returned to Samaria.

Moab Revolts

3 Joram[a] son of Ahab became king of Israel in Samaria in the eighteenth year of Jehoshaphat king of Judah, and he reigned twelve years. ²He did evil in the eyes of the LORD, but not as his father and mother had done. He got rid of the sacred stone of Baal that his father had made. ³Nevertheless he clung to the sins of Jeroboam son of Nebat, which he had caused Israel to commit; he did not turn away from them.

⁴Now Mesha king of Moab raised sheep, and he had to supply the king of Israel with a hundred thousand lambs and with the wool of a hundred thousand rams. ⁵But after Ahab died, the king of Moab rebelled against the king of Israel. ⁶So at that time King Joram set out from Samaria and mobilized all Israel. ⁷He also sent this message to Jehoshaphat king of Judah: "The king of Moab has rebelled against me. Will you go with me to fight against Moab?"

"I will go with you," he replied. "I am as you are, my people as your people, my horses as your horses."

⁸"By what route shall we attack?" he asked.

"Through the Desert of Edom," he answered.

⁹So the king of Israel set out with the king of Judah and the king of Edom. After a roundabout march of seven days, the army had no more water for themselves or for the animals with them.

¹⁰"What!" exclaimed the king of Israel. "Has the LORD called us three kings together only to hand us over to Moab?"

---

a1 Hebrew *Jehoram*, a variant of *Joram*; also in verse 6

¹¹But Jehoshaphat asked, "Is there no prophet of the LORD here, that we may inquire of the LORD through him?"

An officer of the king of Israel answered, "Elisha son of Shaphat is here. He used to pour water on the hands of Elijah.ᵃ"

¹²Jehoshaphat said, "The word of the LORD is with him." So the king of Israel and Jehoshaphat and the king of Edom went down to him.

¹³Elisha said to the king of Israel, "What do we have to do with each other? Go to the prophets of your father and the prophets of your mother."

"No," the king of Israel answered, "because it was the LORD who called us three kings together to hand us over to Moab."

¹⁴Elisha said, "As surely as the LORD Almighty lives, whom I serve, if I did not have respect for the presence of Jehoshaphat king of Judah, I would not look at you or even notice you. ¹⁵But now bring me a harpist."

While the harpist was playing, the hand of the LORD came upon Elisha ¹⁶and he said, "This is what the LORD says: Make this valley full of ditches. ¹⁷For this is what the LORD says: You will see neither wind nor rain, yet this valley will be filled with water, and you, your cattle and your other animals will drink. ¹⁸This is an easy thing in the eyes of the LORD; he will also hand Moab over to you. ¹⁹You will overthrow every fortified city and every major town. You will cut down every good tree, stop up all the springs, and ruin every good field with stones."

²⁰The next morning, about the time for offering the sacrifice, there it was—water flowing from the direction of Edom! And the land was filled with water.

²¹Now all the Moabites had heard that the kings had come to fight against them; so every man, young and old, who could bear arms was called up and stationed on the border. ²²When they got up early in the morning, the sun was shining on the water. To the Moabites across the way, the water looked red—like blood. ²³"That's blood!" they said. "Those kings must have fought and slaughtered each other. Now to the plunder, Moab!"

²⁴But when the Moabites came to the camp of Israel, the Israelites rose up and fought them until they fled. And the Israelites invaded the land and slaughtered the Moabites. ²⁵They destroyed the towns, and each man threw a stone on every good field until it was covered. They stopped up all the springs and cut down every good tree. Only Kir Hareseth was left with its stones in place, but men armed with slings surrounded it and attacked it as well.

²⁶When the king of Moab saw that the battle had gone against him, he took with him seven hundred swordsmen to break through to the king of Edom, but they failed. ²⁷Then he took his firstborn son, who was to succeed him as king, and offered him as a sacrifice on the city wall. The fury against Israel was great; they withdrew and returned to their own land.

The Widow's Oil

4 The wife of a man from the company of the prophets cried out to Elisha, "Your servant my husband is dead, and you know that he revered the LORD. But now his creditor is coming to take my two boys as his slaves."

²Elisha replied to her, "How can I help you? Tell me, what do you have in your house?"

"Your servant has nothing there at all," she said, "except a little oil."

³Elisha said, "Go around and ask all your neighbors for empty jars. Don't ask for just a few. ⁴Then go inside and shut the door behind you and your sons. Pour oil into all the jars, and as each is filled, put it to one side."

⁵She left him and afterward shut the door behind her and her sons. They brought the jars to her and she kept pouring. ⁶When all the jars were full, she said to her son, "Bring me another one."

But he replied, "There is not a jar left." Then the oil stopped flowing.

⁷She went and told the man of God, and he said, "Go, sell the oil and pay your debts. You and your sons can live on what is left."

The Shunammite's Son Restored to Life

⁸One day Elisha went to Shunem. And a well-to-do woman was there, who

---

ᵃ11 That is, he was Elijah's personal servant.

urged him to stay for a meal. So whenever he came by, he stopped there to eat. ⁹She said to her husband, "I know that this man who often comes our way is a holy man of God. ¹⁰Let's make a small room on the roof and put in it a bed and a table, a chair and a lamp for him. Then he can stay there whenever he comes to us."

¹¹One day when Elisha came, he went up to his room and lay down there. ¹²He said to his servant Gehazi, "Call the Shunammite." So he called her, and she stood before him. ¹³Elisha said to him, "Tell her, 'You have gone to all this trouble for us. Now what can be done for you? Can we speak on your behalf to the king or the commander of the army?' "

She replied, "I have a home among my own people."

¹⁴"What can be done for her?" Elisha asked.

Gehazi said, "Well, she has no son and her husband is old."

¹⁵Then Elisha said, "Call her." So he called her, and she stood in the doorway.

¹⁶"About this time next year," Elisha said, "you will hold a son in your arms."

"No, my lord," she objected. "Don't mislead your servant, O man of God!"

¹⁷But the woman became pregnant, and the next year about that same time she gave birth to a son, just as Elisha had told her.

¹⁸The child grew, and one day he went out to his father, who was with the reapers. ¹⁹"My head! My head!" he said to his father.

His father told a servant, "Carry him to his mother." ²⁰After the servant had lifted him up and carried him to his mother, the boy sat on her lap until noon, and then he died. ²¹She went up and laid him on the bed of the man of God, then shut the door and went out.

²²She called her husband and said, "Please send me one of the servants and a donkey so I can go to the man of God quickly and return."

²³"Why go to him today?" he asked. "It's not the New Moon or the Sabbath."

God Provides

Qu**i**et TIMES *with each other*

2 KINGS 4:1–7 God delights in supplying all of our needs, but he often provides in the most unusual ways. Consider the widow who only had a little oil and was at the mercy of her creditors. Elisha's instruction to the widow to collect empty jars seemed strange. Then he told her to pour the oil into the bottles one at a time. Only as she poured the oil into each jar did she experience God's provisions. And after filling many jars, she was able to sell the oil and repay her debtors.

Sometimes God works in our lives in ways we wouldn't expect. When Dave and I joined the staff of Campus Crusade for Christ, our discretionary income was greatly reduced. I remember really wanting a new rug for our living room. Just when we had saved enough money to begin looking for a rug, the unexpected happened. A throbbing toothache required a root canal job. There went the money we been saving for a rug! But God had another plan. The next week our friends Don and Pattie asked us if we knew anyone who needed a rug. We'll always remember that gold and beige shag rug. It was just the right size and color for our living room!

A couple of years later when we moved to Inzlingen, Germany, our shag rug went with us—again just the right size and color for our living room in Germany. When we moved again, we gave our rug to another missionary family. Over the years, that rug never seemed to wear out and, like the widow's oil, was a reminder of God's goodness.

—Dave & Claudia

Weekend Warm-up *Do you have a "shag rug" story you've shared together?*

Go to page 386 for your next devotional reading.

"It's all right," she said.

24She saddled the donkey and said to her servant, "Lead on; don't slow down for me unless I tell you." 25So she set out and came to the man of God at Mount Carmel.

When he saw her in the distance, the man of God said to his servant Gehazi, "Look! There's the Shunammite! 26Run to meet her and ask her, 'Are you all right? Is your husband all right? Is your child all right?' "

"Everything is all right," she said.

27When she reached the man of God at the mountain, she took hold of his feet. Gehazi came over to push her away, but the man of God said, "Leave her alone! She is in bitter distress, but the LORD has hidden it from me and has not told me why."

28"Did I ask you for a son, my lord?" she said. "Didn't I tell you, 'Don't raise my hopes'?"

29Elisha said to Gehazi, "Tuck your cloak into your belt, take my staff in your hand and run. If you meet anyone, do not greet him, and if anyone greets you, do not answer. Lay my staff on the boy's face."

30But the child's mother said, "As surely as the LORD lives and as you live, I will not leave you." So he got up and followed her.

31Gehazi went on ahead and laid the staff on the boy's face, but there was no sound or response. So Gehazi went back to meet Elisha and told him, "The boy has not awakened."

32When Elisha reached the house, there was the boy lying dead on his couch. 33He went in, shut the door on the two of them and prayed to the LORD. 34Then he got on the bed and lay upon the boy, mouth to mouth, eyes to eyes, hands to hands. As he stretched himself out upon him, the boy's body grew warm. 35Elisha turned away and walked back and forth in the room and then got on the bed and stretched out upon him once more. The boy sneezed seven times and opened his eyes.

36Elisha summoned Gehazi and said, "Call the Shunammite." And he did. When she came, he said, "Take your son." 37She came in, fell at his feet and bowed to the ground. Then she took her son and went out.

Death in the Pot

38Elisha returned to Gilgal and there was a famine in that region. While the company of the prophets was meeting with him, he said to his servant, "Put on the large pot and cook some stew for these men."

39One of them went out into the fields to gather herbs and found a wild vine. He gathered some of its gourds and filled the fold of his cloak. When he returned, he cut them up into the pot of stew, though no one knew what they were. 40The stew was poured out for the men, but as they began to eat it, they cried out, "O man of God, there is death in the pot!" And they could not eat it.

41Elisha said, "Get some flour." He put it into the pot and said, "Serve it to the people to eat." And there was nothing harmful in the pot.

Feeding of a Hundred

42A man came from Baal Shalishah, bringing the man of God twenty loaves of barley bread baked from the first ripe grain, along with some heads of new grain. "Give it to the people to eat," Elisha said.

43"How can I set this before a hundred men?" his servant asked.

But Elisha answered, "Give it to the people to eat. For this is what the LORD says: 'They will eat and have some left over.' " 44Then he set it before them, and they ate and had some left over, according to the word of the LORD.

Naaman Healed of Leprosy

5 Now Naaman was commander of the army of the king of Aram. He was a great man in the sight of his master and highly regarded, because through him the LORD had given victory to Aram. He was a valiant soldier, but he had leprosy.[a]

2Now bands from Aram had gone out and had taken captive a young girl from Israel, and she served Naaman's wife. 3She said to her mistress, "If only my

---

a1 The Hebrew word was used for various diseases affecting the skin—not necessarily leprosy; also in verses 3, 6, 7, 11 and 27.

master would see the prophet who is in Samaria! He would cure him of his leprosy."

⁴Naaman went to his master and told him what the girl from Israel had said. ⁵"By all means, go," the king of Aram replied. "I will send a letter to the king of Israel." So Naaman left, taking with him ten talents*ᵃ* of silver, six thousand shekels*ᵇ* of gold and ten sets of clothing. ⁶The letter that he took to the king of Israel read: "With this letter I am sending my servant Naaman to you so that you may cure him of his leprosy."

⁷As soon as the king of Israel read the letter, he tore his robes and said, "Am I God? Can I kill and bring back to life? Why does this fellow send someone to me to be cured of his leprosy? See how he is trying to pick a quarrel with me!"

⁸When Elisha the man of God heard that the king of Israel had torn his robes, he sent him this message: "Why have you torn your robes? Have the man come to me and he will know that there is a prophet in Israel." ⁹So Naaman went with his horses and chariots and stopped at the door of Elisha's house. ¹⁰Elisha sent a messenger to say to him, "Go, wash yourself seven times in the Jordan, and your flesh will be restored and you will be cleansed."

¹¹But Naaman went away angry and said, "I thought that he would surely come out to me and stand and call on the name of the LORD his God, wave his hand over the spot and cure me of my leprosy. ¹²Are not Abana and Pharpar, the rivers of Damascus, better than any of the waters of Israel? Couldn't I wash in them and be cleansed?" So he turned and went off in a rage.

¹³Naaman's servants went to him and said, "My father, if the prophet had told you to do some great thing, would you not have done it? How much more, then, when he tells you, 'Wash and be cleansed'!" ¹⁴So he went down and dipped himself in the Jordan seven times, as the man of God had told him, and his flesh was restored and became clean like that of a young boy.

¹⁵Then Naaman and all his attendants went back to the man of God. He stood before him and said, "Now I know that there is no God in all the world except in

ᵃ5 That is, about 750 pounds (about 340 kilograms)   *ᵇ5* That is, about 150 pounds (about 70 kilograms)

My Way Versus God's Way

Monday

2 KINGS 5   What a challenge Naaman had to deal with! He was a man who had everything, yet something was out of his control. With all his wealth and power, he had leprosy.

Searching for a cure, he visited the great man of God in Israel, Elisha. The cure, to go and immerse himself in the Jordan River seven times, was something he never expected. It just wasn't what Naaman had pictured in his mind. It was far too easy and nowhere near extravagant enough. After all, Naaman was a man of considerable position. He had even brought with him some of that wealth, hoping to be treated with great respect. He desperately wanted to be healed, but he wanted it done his way. Finally, the people around Naaman convinced him to trust the plan.

Far too often we come to God, or representatives of God, and present our marriage difficulties. When they call us to a greater personal faith and trust, rather than "six steps to happiness," we become disenchanted. Immersing ourselves in God's love is not what we were looking for. Yet trusting God and following him is the only road to cure "leprosy" in a marriage. Yes, in many marriages, there might be details in the relationship that must be overcome. But ultimately, the total cure will depend on the One who originally created the marriage relationship. Ask yourself, *Will I resist and attempt to find a cure my own way, or will I do it God's way?*

—Bob & Rosemary

Go to page 405 for your next devotional reading.

Israel. Please accept now a gift from your servant."

¹⁶The prophet answered, "As surely as the LORD lives, whom I serve, I will not accept a thing." And even though Naaman urged him, he refused.

¹⁷"If you will not," said Naaman, "please let me, your servant, be given as much earth as a pair of mules can carry, for your servant will never again make burnt offerings and sacrifices to any other god but the LORD. ¹⁸But may the LORD forgive your servant for this one thing: When my master enters the temple of Rimmon to bow down and he is leaning on my arm and I bow there also—when I bow down in the temple of Rimmon, may the LORD forgive your servant for this."

¹⁹"Go in peace," Elisha said.

After Naaman had traveled some distance, ²⁰Gehazi, the servant of Elisha the man of God, said to himself, "My master was too easy on Naaman, this Aramean, by not accepting from him what he brought. As surely as the LORD lives, I will run after him and get something from him."

²¹So Gehazi hurried after Naaman. When Naaman saw him running toward him, he got down from the chariot to meet him. "Is everything all right?" he asked.

²²"Everything is all right," Gehazi answered. "My master sent me to say, 'Two young men from the company of the prophets have just come to me from the hill country of Ephraim. Please give them a talent*ᵃ* of silver and two sets of clothing.'"

²³"By all means, take two talents," said Naaman. He urged Gehazi to accept them, and then tied up the two talents of silver in two bags, with two sets of clothing. He gave them to two of his servants, and they carried them ahead of Gehazi. ²⁴When Gehazi came to the hill, he took the things from the servants and put them away in the house. He sent the men away and they left. ²⁵Then he went in and stood before his master Elisha.

"Where have you been, Gehazi?" Elisha asked.

"Your servant didn't go anywhere," Gehazi answered.

²⁶But Elisha said to him, "Was not my

Naaman and his wife

2 KINGS 5:1–14 Naaman was the commander of the army of the king of Aram. He was highly regarded and a valiant soldier, but he had leprosy. Fortunately his wife stood by him in sickness and took the initiative in seeking help. When her Israelite servant suggested that Naaman go see the prophet Elisha, she relayed the suggestion to her husband. Their relationship must have been one of open communication and trust, because he took her advice.

Maintaining a healthy marriage then and now is hard work—especially in the middle of health problems. If you put yourself in the place of Naaman's wife, would you be as supportive as she was? Other wives in the Bible, like Job's wife, weren't.

Think about how hard it must have been for Naaman and his wife to deal with his illness. He was a public figure, and everyone would have been aware of his leprosy. Consider what would be the equivalent today. For example, what if through a blood transfusion your spouse contracted AIDs? Would you be as supportive as Naaman's wife was? Naaman's story had a happy ending. He went to Elisha, was healed of leprosy and found a new faith in God.

God can bring blessings out of difficult situations. If you are facing health problems or another difficult situation, follow the example of Naaman's wife. Be future focused, be positive and talk about it. You can trust God to meet your needs as you support each other.

spirit with you when the man got down from his chariot to meet you? Is this the time to take money, or to accept clothes, olive groves, vineyards, flocks, herds, or menservants and maidservants? ²⁷Naaman's leprosy will cling to you and to your descendants forever." Then Gehazi went from Elisha's presence and he was leprous, as white as snow.

ᵃ22 That is, about 75 pounds (about 34 kilograms)

An Axhead Floats

6 The company of the prophets said to Elisha, "Look, the place where we meet with you is too small for us. ²Let us go to the Jordan, where each of us can get a pole; and let us build a place there for us to live."

And he said, "Go."

³Then one of them said, "Won't you please come with your servants?"

"I will," Elisha replied. ⁴And he went with them.

They went to the Jordan and began to cut down trees. ⁵As one of them was cutting down a tree, the iron axhead fell into the water. "Oh, my lord," he cried out, "it was borrowed!"

⁶The man of God asked, "Where did it fall?" When he showed him the place, Elisha cut a stick and threw it there, and made the iron float. ⁷"Lift it out," he said. Then the man reached out his hand and took it.

Elisha Traps Blinded Arameans

⁸Now the king of Aram was at war with Israel. After conferring with his officers, he said, "I will set up my camp in such and such a place."

⁹The man of God sent word to the king of Israel: "Beware of passing that place, because the Arameans are going down there." ¹⁰So the king of Israel checked on the place indicated by the man of God. Time and again Elisha warned the king, so that he was on his guard in such places.

¹¹This enraged the king of Aram. He summoned his officers and demanded of them, "Will you not tell me which of us is on the side of the king of Israel?"

¹²"None of us, my lord the king," said one of his officers, "but Elisha, the prophet who is in Israel, tells the king of Israel the very words you speak in your bedroom."

¹³"Go, find out where he is," the king ordered, "so I can send men and capture him." The report came back: "He is in Dothan." ¹⁴Then he sent horses and chariots and a strong force there. They went by night and surrounded the city.

¹⁵When the servant of the man of God got up and went out early the next morning, an army with horses and chariots had surrounded the city. "Oh, my lord, what shall we do?" the servant asked.

¹⁶"Don't be afraid," the prophet answered. "Those who are with us are more than those who are with them."

¹⁷And Elisha prayed, "O Lord, open his eyes so he may see." Then the Lord opened the servant's eyes, and he looked and saw the hills full of horses and chariots of fire all around Elisha.

¹⁸As the enemy came down toward him, Elisha prayed to the Lord, "Strike these people with blindness." So he struck them with blindness, as Elisha had asked.

¹⁹Elisha told them, "This is not the road and this is not the city. Follow me, and I will lead you to the man you are looking for." And he led them to Samaria.

²⁰After they entered the city, Elisha said, "Lord, open the eyes of these men so they can see." Then the Lord opened their eyes and they looked, and there they were, inside Samaria.

²¹When the king of Israel saw them, he asked Elisha, "Shall I kill them, my father? Shall I kill them?"

²²"Do not kill them," he answered. "Would you kill men you have captured with your own sword or bow? Set food and water before them so that they may eat and drink and then go back to their master." ²³So he prepared a great feast for them, and after they had finished eating and drinking, he sent them away, and they returned to their master. So the bands from Aram stopped raiding Israel's territory.

Famine in Besieged Samaria

²⁴Some time later, Ben-Hadad king of Aram mobilized his entire army and marched up and laid siege to Samaria. ²⁵There was a great famine in the city; the siege lasted so long that a donkey's head sold for eighty shekels*ᵃ* of silver, and a quarter of a cab*ᵇ* of seed pods*ᶜ* for five shekels.*ᵈ*

²⁶As the king of Israel was passing by on the wall, a woman cried to him, "Help me, my lord the king!"

²⁷The king replied, "If the Lord does

ᵃ25 That is, about 2 pounds (about 1 kilogram)
ᵇ25 That is, probably about 1/2 pint (about 0.3 liter)   *ᶜ25* Or *of dove's dung*   *ᵈ25* That is, about 2 ounces (about 55 grams)

not help you, where can I get help for you? From the threshing floor? From the winepress?" 28Then he asked her, "What's the matter?"

She answered, "This woman said to me, 'Give up your son so we may eat him today, and tomorrow we'll eat my son.' 29So we cooked my son and ate him. The next day I said to her, 'Give up your son so we may eat him,' but she had hidden him."

30When the king heard the woman's words, he tore his robes. As he went along the wall, the people looked, and there, underneath, he had sackcloth on his body. 31He said, "May God deal with me, be it ever so severely, if the head of Elisha son of Shaphat remains on his shoulders today!"

32Now Elisha was sitting in his house, and the elders were sitting with him. The king sent a messenger ahead, but before he arrived, Elisha said to the elders, "Don't you see how this murderer is sending someone to cut off my head? Look, when the messenger comes, shut the door and hold it shut against him. Is not the sound of his master's footsteps behind him?"

33While he was still talking to them, the messenger came down to him. And ˪the king ˩ said, "This disaster is from the LORD. Why should I wait for the LORD any longer?"

7 Elisha said, "Hear the word of the LORD. This is what the LORD says: About this time tomorrow, a seah[a] of flour will sell for a shekel[b] and two seahs[c] of barley for a shekel at the gate of Samaria."

2The officer on whose arm the king was leaning said to the man of God, "Look, even if the LORD should open the floodgates of the heavens, could this happen?"

"You will see it with your own eyes," answered Elisha, "but you will not eat any of it!"

The Siege Lifted

3Now there were four men with leprosy[d] at the entrance of the city gate. They said to each other, "Why stay here until we die? 4If we say, 'We'll go into the city'— the famine is there, and we will die. And if we stay here, we will die. So let's go over to the camp of the Arameans and surrender. If they spare us, we live; if they kill us, then we die."

5At dusk they got up and went to the camp of the Arameans. When they reached the edge of the camp, not a man was there, 6for the Lord had caused the Arameans to hear the sound of chariots and horses and a great army, so that they said to one another, "Look, the king of Israel has hired the Hittite and Egyptian kings to attack us!" 7So they got up and fled in the dusk and abandoned their tents and their horses and donkeys. They left the camp as it was and ran for their lives.

8The men who had leprosy reached the edge of the camp and entered one of the tents. They ate and drank, and carried away silver, gold and clothes, and went off and hid them. They returned and entered another tent and took some things from it and hid them also.

9Then they said to each other, "We're not doing right. This is a day of good news and we are keeping it to ourselves. If we wait until daylight, punishment will overtake us. Let's go at once and report this to the royal palace."

10So they went and called out to the city gatekeepers and told them, "We went into the Aramean camp and not a man was there—not a sound of anyone—only tethered horses and donkeys, and the tents left just as they were." 11The gatekeepers shouted the news, and it was reported within the palace.

12The king got up in the night and said to his officers, "I will tell you what the Arameans have done to us. They know we are starving; so they have left the camp to hide in the countryside, thinking, 'They will surely come out, and then we will take them alive and get into the city.' "

13One of his officers answered, "Have some men take five of the horses that are left in the city. Their plight will be like that of all the Israelites left here—yes, they will only be like all these Israelites who

---

a1 That is, probably about 7 quarts (about 7.3 liters); also in verses 16 and 18   b1 That is, about 2/5 ounce (about 11 grams); also in verses 16 and 18   c1 That is, probably about 13 quarts (about 15 liters); also in verses 16 and 18   d3 The Hebrew word is used for various diseases affecting the skin—not necessarily leprosy; also in verse 8.

are doomed. So let us send them to find out what happened."

[14]So they selected two chariots with their horses, and the king sent them after the Aramean army. He commanded the drivers, "Go and find out what has happened." [15]They followed them as far as the Jordan, and they found the whole road strewn with the clothing and equipment the Arameans had thrown away in their headlong flight. So the messengers returned and reported to the king. [16]Then the people went out and plundered the camp of the Arameans. So a seah of flour sold for a shekel, and two seahs of barley sold for a shekel, as the LORD had said.

[17]Now the king had put the officer on whose arm he leaned in charge of the gate, and the people trampled him in the gateway, and he died, just as the man of God had foretold when the king came down to his house. [18]It happened as the man of God had said to the king: "About this time tomorrow, a seah of flour will sell for a shekel and two seahs of barley for a shekel at the gate of Samaria."

[19]The officer had said to the man of God, "Look, even if the LORD should open the floodgates of the heavens, could this happen?" The man of God had replied, "You will see it with your own eyes, but you will not eat any of it!" [20]And that is exactly what happened to him, for the people trampled him in the gateway, and he died.

The Shunammite's Land Restored

8 Now Elisha had said to the woman whose son he had restored to life, "Go away with your family and stay for a while wherever you can, because the LORD has decreed a famine in the land that will last seven years." [2]The woman proceeded to do as the man of God said. She and her family went away and stayed in the land of the Philistines seven years.

[3]At the end of the seven years she came back from the land of the Philistines and went to the king to beg for her house and land. [4]The king was talking to Gehazi, the servant of the man of God, and had said, "Tell me about all the great things Elisha has done." [5]Just as Gehazi was telling the king how Elisha had restored the dead to life, the woman whose son Elisha had

brought back to life came to beg the king for her house and land.

Gehazi said, "This is the woman, my lord the king, and this is her son whom Elisha restored to life." [6]The king asked the woman about it, and she told him.

Then he assigned an official to her case and said to him, "Give back everything that belonged to her, including all the income from her land from the day she left the country until now."

Hazael Murders Ben-Hadad

[7]Elisha went to Damascus, and Ben-Hadad king of Aram was ill. When the king was told, "The man of God has come all the way up here," [8]he said to Hazael, "Take a gift with you and go to meet the man of God. Consult the LORD through him; ask him, 'Will I recover from this illness?' "

[9]Hazael went to meet Elisha, taking with him as a gift forty camel-loads of all the finest wares of Damascus. He went in and stood before him, and said, "Your son Ben-Hadad king of Aram has sent me to ask, 'Will I recover from this illness?' "

[10]Elisha answered, "Go and say to him, 'You will certainly recover'; but[a] the LORD has revealed to me that he will in fact die." [11]He stared at him with a fixed gaze until Hazael felt ashamed. Then the man of God began to weep.

[12]"Why is my lord weeping?" asked Hazael.

"Because I know the harm you will do to the Israelites," he answered. "You will set fire to their fortified places, kill their young men with the sword, dash their little children to the ground, and rip open their pregnant women."

[13]Hazael said, "How could your servant, a mere dog, accomplish such a feat?"

"The LORD has shown me that you will become king of Aram," answered Elisha.

[14]Then Hazael left Elisha and returned to his master. When Ben-Hadad asked, "What did Elisha say to you?" Hazael replied, "He told me that you would certainly recover." [15]But the next day he took a thick cloth, soaked it in water and spread it over the king's face, so that he died. Then Hazael succeeded him as king.

---

[a]10 The Hebrew may also be read *Go and say, 'You will certainly not recover,' for.*

Jehoram King of Judah

16In the fifth year of Joram son of Ahab king of Israel, when Jehoshaphat was king of Judah, Jehoram son of Jehoshaphat began his reign as king of Judah. 17He was thirty-two years old when he became king, and he reigned in Jerusalem eight years. 18He walked in the ways of the kings of Israel, as the house of Ahab had done, for he married a daughter of Ahab. He did evil in the eyes of the LORD. 19Nevertheless, for the sake of his servant David, the LORD was not willing to destroy Judah. He had promised to maintain a lamp for David and his descendants forever.

20In the time of Jehoram, Edom rebelled against Judah and set up its own king. 21So Jehoram*a* went to Zair with all his chariots. The Edomites surrounded him and his chariot commanders, but he rose up and broke through by night; his army, however, fled back home. 22To this day Edom has been in rebellion against Judah. Libnah revolted at the same time.

23As for the other events of Jehoram's reign, and all he did, are they not written in the book of the annals of the kings of Judah? 24Jehoram rested with his fathers and was buried with them in the City of David. And Ahaziah his son succeeded him as king.

Ahaziah King of Judah

25In the twelfth year of Joram son of Ahab king of Israel, Ahaziah son of Jehoram king of Judah began to reign. 26Ahaziah was twenty-two years old when he became king, and he reigned in Jerusalem one year. His mother's name was Athaliah, a granddaughter of Omri king of Israel. 27He walked in the ways of the house of Ahab and did evil in the eyes of the LORD, as the house of Ahab had done, for he was related by marriage to Ahab's family.

28Ahaziah went with Joram son of Ahab to war against Hazael king of Aram at Ramoth Gilead. The Arameans wounded Joram; 29so King Joram returned to Jezreel to recover from the wounds the Arameans had inflicted on him at Ramoth*b* in his battle with Hazael king of Aram.

Then Ahaziah son of Jehoram king of Judah went down to Jezreel to see Joram son of Ahab, because he had been wounded.

Jehu Anointed King of Israel

9 The prophet Elisha summoned a man from the company of the prophets and said to him, "Tuck your cloak into your belt, take this flask of oil with you and go to Ramoth Gilead. 2When you get there, look for Jehu son of Jehoshaphat, the son of Nimshi. Go to him, get him away from his companions and take him into an inner room. 3Then take the flask and pour the oil on his head and declare, 'This is what the LORD says: I anoint you king over Israel.' Then open the door and run; don't delay!"

4So the young man, the prophet, went to Ramoth Gilead. 5When he arrived, he found the army officers sitting together. "I have a message for you, commander," he said.

"For which of us?" asked Jehu.

"For you, commander," he replied.

6Jehu got up and went into the house. Then the prophet poured the oil on Jehu's head and declared, "This is what the LORD, the God of Israel, says: 'I anoint you king over the LORD's people Israel. 7You are to destroy the house of Ahab your master, and I will avenge the blood of my servants the prophets and the blood of all the LORD's servants shed by Jezebel. 8The whole house of Ahab will perish. I will cut off from Ahab every last male in Israel—slave or free. 9I will make the house of Ahab like the house of Jeroboam son of Nebat and like the house of Baasha son of Ahijah. 10As for Jezebel, dogs will devour her on the plot of ground at Jezreel, and no one will bury her.' " Then he opened the door and ran.

11When Jehu went out to his fellow officers, one of them asked him, "Is everything all right? Why did this madman come to you?"

"You know the man and the sort of things he says," Jehu replied.

12"That's not true!" they said. "Tell us."

Jehu said, "Here is what he told me: 'This is what the LORD says: I anoint you king over Israel.' "

a21 Hebrew *Joram*, a variant of *Jehoram*; also in verses 23 and 24   *b29* Hebrew *Ramah*, a variant of *Ramoth*

13They hurried and took their cloaks and spread them under him on the bare steps. Then they blew the trumpet and shouted, "Jehu is king!"

Jehu Kills Joram and Ahaziah

14So Jehu son of Jehoshaphat, the son of Nimshi, conspired against Joram. (Now Joram and all Israel had been defending Ramoth Gilead against Hazael king of Aram, 15but King Joram*a* had returned to Jezreel to recover from the wounds the Arameans had inflicted on him in the battle with Hazael king of Aram.) Jehu said, "If this is the way you feel, don't let anyone slip out of the city to go and tell the news in Jezreel." 16Then he got into his chariot and rode to Jezreel, because Joram was resting there and Ahaziah king of Judah had gone down to see him.

17When the lookout standing on the tower in Jezreel saw Jehu's troops approaching, he called out, "I see some troops coming."

"Get a horseman," Joram ordered. "Send him to meet them and ask, 'Do you come in peace?'"

18The horseman rode off to meet Jehu and said, "This is what the king says: 'Do you come in peace?'"

"What do you have to do with peace?" Jehu replied. "Fall in behind me."

The lookout reported, "The messenger has reached them, but he isn't coming back."

19So the king sent out a second horseman. When he came to them he said, "This is what the king says: 'Do you come in peace?'"

Jehu replied, "What do you have to do with peace? Fall in behind me."

20The lookout reported, "He has reached them, but he isn't coming back either. The driving is like that of Jehu son of Nimshi—he drives like a madman."

21"Hitch up my chariot," Joram ordered. And when it was hitched up, Joram king of Israel and Ahaziah king of Judah rode out, each in his own chariot, to meet Jehu. They met him at the plot of ground that had belonged to Naboth the Jezreelite. 22When Joram saw Jehu he asked, "Have you come in peace, Jehu?"

"How can there be peace," Jehu replied,

"as long as all the idolatry and witchcraft of your mother Jezebel abound?"

23Joram turned about and fled, calling out to Ahaziah, "Treachery, Ahaziah!"

24Then Jehu drew his bow and shot Joram between the shoulders. The arrow pierced his heart and he slumped down in his chariot. 25Jehu said to Bidkar, his chariot officer, "Pick him up and throw him on the field that belonged to Naboth the Jezreelite. Remember how you and I were riding together in chariots behind Ahab his father when the LORD made this prophecy about him: 26'Yesterday I saw the blood of Naboth and the blood of his sons, declares the LORD, and I will surely make you pay for it on this plot of ground, declares the LORD.'*b* Now then, pick him up and throw him on that plot, in accordance with the word of the LORD."

27When Ahaziah king of Judah saw what had happened, he fled up the road to Beth Haggan.*c* Jehu chased him, shouting, "Kill him too!" They wounded him in his chariot on the way up to Gur near Ibleam, but he escaped to Megiddo and died there. 28His servants took him by chariot to Jerusalem and buried him with his fathers in his tomb in the City of David. 29(In the eleventh year of Joram son of Ahab, Ahaziah had become king of Judah.)

Jezebel Killed

30Then Jehu went to Jezreel. When Jezebel heard about it, she painted her eyes, arranged her hair and looked out of a window. 31As Jehu entered the gate, she asked, "Have you come in peace, Zimri, you murderer of your master?"*d*

32He looked up at the window and called out, "Who is on my side? Who?" Two or three eunuchs looked down at him. 33"Throw her down!" Jehu said. So they threw her down, and some of her blood spattered the wall and the horses as they trampled her underfoot.

34Jehu went in and ate and drank. "Take care of that cursed woman," he said, "and bury her, for she was a king's daughter." 35But when they went out to bury her,

---

*a*15 Hebrew *Jehoram*, a variant of *Joram*; also in verses 17 and 21-24   *b*26 See 1 Kings 21:19.
*c*27 Or *fled by way of the garden house*   *d*31 Or *"Did Zimri have peace, who murdered his master?"*

they found nothing except her skull, her feet and her hands. ³⁶They went back and told Jehu, who said, "This is the word of the LORD that he spoke through his servant Elijah the Tishbite: On the plot of ground at Jezreel dogs will devour Jezebel's flesh.ᵃ ³⁷Jezebel's body will be like refuse on the ground in the plot at Jezreel, so that no one will be able to say, 'This is Jezebel.' "

Ahab's Family Killed

10 Now there were in Samaria seventy sons of the house of Ahab. So Jehu wrote letters and sent them to Samaria: to the officials of Jezreel,ᵇ to the elders and to the guardians of Ahab's children. He said, ²"As soon as this letter reaches you, since your master's sons are with you and you have chariots and horses, a fortified city and weapons, ³choose the best and most worthy of your master's sons and set him on his father's throne. Then fight for your master's house."

⁴But they were terrified and said, "If two kings could not resist him, how can we?"

⁵So the palace administrator, the city governor, the elders and the guardians sent this message to Jehu: "We are your servants and we will do anything you say. We will not appoint anyone as king; you do whatever you think best."

⁶Then Jehu wrote them a second letter, saying, "If you are on my side and will obey me, take the heads of your master's sons and come to me in Jezreel by this time tomorrow."

Now the royal princes, seventy of them, were with the leading men of the city, who were rearing them. ⁷When the letter arrived, these men took the princes and slaughtered all seventy of them. They put their heads in baskets and sent them to Jehu in Jezreel. ⁸When the messenger arrived, he told Jehu, "They have brought the heads of the princes."

Then Jehu ordered, "Put them in two piles at the entrance of the city gate until morning."

⁹The next morning Jehu went out. He stood before all the people and said, "You are innocent. It was I who conspired against my master and killed him, but who killed all these? ¹⁰Know then, that not a word the LORD has spoken against the house of Ahab will fail. The LORD has done what he promised through his servant Elijah." ¹¹So Jehu killed everyone in Jezreel who remained of the house of Ahab, as well as all his chief men, his close friends and his priests, leaving him no survivor.

¹²Jehu then set out and went toward Samaria. At Beth Eked of the Shepherds, ¹³he met some relatives of Ahaziah king of Judah and asked, "Who are you?"

They said, "We are relatives of Ahaziah, and we have come down to greet the families of the king and of the queen mother."

¹⁴"Take them alive!" he ordered. So they took them alive and slaughtered them by the well of Beth Eked—forty-two men. He left no survivor.

¹⁵After he left there, he came upon Jehonadab son of Recab, who was on his way to meet him. Jehu greeted him and said, "Are you in accord with me, as I am with you?"

"I am," Jehonadab answered.

"If so," said Jehu, "give me your hand." So he did, and Jehu helped him up into the chariot. ¹⁶Jehu said, "Come with me and see my zeal for the LORD." Then he had him ride along in his chariot.

¹⁷When Jehu came to Samaria, he killed all who were left there of Ahab's family; he destroyed them, according to the word of the LORD spoken to Elijah.

Ministers of Baal Killed

¹⁸Then Jehu brought all the people together and said to them, "Ahab served Baal a little; Jehu will serve him much. ¹⁹Now summon all the prophets of Baal, all his ministers and all his priests. See that no one is missing, because I am going to hold a great sacrifice for Baal. Anyone who fails to come will no longer live." But Jehu was acting deceptively in order to destroy the ministers of Baal.

²⁰Jehu said, "Call an assembly in honor of Baal." So they proclaimed it. ²¹Then he sent word throughout Israel, and all the ministers of Baal came; not one stayed away. They crowded into the temple of Baal until it was full from one end to the

ᵃ36 See 1 Kings 21:23.   ᵇ1 Hebrew; some Septuagint manuscripts and Vulgate *of the city* other. 22And Jehu said to the keeper of the wardrobe, "Bring robes for all the ministers of Baal." So he brought out robes for them.

23Then Jehu and Jehonadab son of Recab went into the temple of Baal. Jehu said to the ministers of Baal, "Look around and see that no servants of the LORD are here with you—only ministers of Baal." 24So they went in to make sacrifices and burnt offerings. Now Jehu had posted eighty men outside with this warning: "If one of you lets any of the men I am placing in your hands escape, it will be your life for his life."

25As soon as Jehu had finished making the burnt offering, he ordered the guards and officers: "Go in and kill them; let no one escape." So they cut them down with the sword. The guards and officers threw the bodies out and then entered the inner shrine of the temple of Baal. 26They brought the sacred stone out of the temple of Baal and burned it. 27They demolished the sacred stone of Baal and tore down the temple of Baal, and people have used it for a latrine to this day.

28So Jehu destroyed Baal worship in Israel. 29However, he did not turn away from the sins of Jeroboam son of Nebat, which he had caused Israel to commit— the worship of the golden calves at Bethel and Dan.

30The LORD said to Jehu, "Because you have done well in accomplishing what is right in my eyes and have done to the house of Ahab all I had in mind to do, your descendants will sit on the throne of Israel to the fourth generation." 31Yet Jehu was not careful to keep the law of the LORD, the God of Israel, with all his heart. He did not turn away from the sins of Jeroboam, which he had caused Israel to commit.

32In those days the LORD began to reduce the size of Israel. Hazael overpowered the Israelites throughout their territory 33east of the Jordan in all the land of Gilead (the region of Gad, Reuben and Manasseh), from Aroer by the Arnon Gorge through Gilead to Bashan.

34As for the other events of Jehu's reign, all he did, and all his achievements, are they not written in the book of the annals of the kings of Israel?

35Jehu rested with his fathers and was buried in Samaria. And Jehoahaz his son succeeded him as king. 36The time that Jehu reigned over Israel in Samaria was twenty-eight years.

Athaliah and Joash

11 When Athaliah the mother of Ahaziah saw that her son was dead, she proceeded to destroy the whole royal family. 2But Jehosheba, the daughter of King Jehoram*a* and sister of Ahaziah, took Joash son of Ahaziah and stole him away from among the royal princes, who were about to be murdered. She put him and his nurse in a bedroom to hide him from Athaliah; so he was not killed. 3He remained hidden with his nurse at the temple of the LORD for six years while Athaliah ruled the land.

4In the seventh year Jehoiada sent for the commanders of units of a hundred, the Carites and the guards and had them brought to him at the temple of the LORD. He made a covenant with them and put them under oath at the temple of the LORD. Then he showed them the king's son. 5He commanded them, saying, "This is what you are to do: You who are in the three companies that are going on duty on the Sabbath—a third of you guarding the royal palace, 6a third at the Sur Gate, and a third at the gate behind the guard, who take turns guarding the temple— 7and you who are in the other two companies that normally go off Sabbath duty are all to guard the temple for the king. 8Station yourselves around the king, each man with his weapon in his hand. Anyone who approaches your ranks*b* must be put to death. Stay close to the king wherever he goes."

9The commanders of units of a hundred did just as Jehoiada the priest ordered. Each one took his men—those who were going on duty on the Sabbath and those who were going off duty—and came to Jehoiada the priest. 10Then he gave the commanders the spears and shields that had belonged to King David and that were in the temple of the LORD. 11The guards, each with his weapon in his hand, stationed themselves around the king— near the altar and the temple, from the

a2 Hebrew *Joram*, a variant of *Jehoram*   *b8* Or *approaches the precincts* south side to the north side of the temple.

¹²Jehoiada brought out the king's son and put the crown on him; he presented him with a copy of the covenant and proclaimed him king. They anointed him, and the people clapped their hands and shouted, "Long live the king!"

¹³When Athaliah heard the noise made by the guards and the people, she went to the people at the temple of the LORD. ¹⁴She looked and there was the king, standing by the pillar, as the custom was. The officers and the trumpeters were beside the king, and all the people of the land were rejoicing and blowing trumpets. Then Athaliah tore her robes and called out, "Treason! Treason!"

¹⁵Jehoiada the priest ordered the commanders of units of a hundred, who were in charge of the troops: "Bring her out between the ranks[a] and put to the sword anyone who follows her." For the priest had said, "She must not be put to death in the temple of the LORD." ¹⁶So they seized her as she reached the place where the horses enter the palace grounds, and there she was put to death.

¹⁷Jehoiada then made a covenant between the LORD and the king and people that they would be the LORD's people. He also made a covenant between the king and the people. ¹⁸All the people of the land went to the temple of Baal and tore it down. They smashed the altars and idols to pieces and killed Mattan the priest of Baal in front of the altars.

Then Jehoiada the priest posted guards at the temple of the LORD. ¹⁹He took with him the commanders of hundreds, the Carites, the guards and all the people of the land, and together they brought the king down from the temple of the LORD and went into the palace, entering by way of the gate of the guards. The king then took his place on the royal throne, ²⁰and all the people of the land rejoiced. And the city was quiet, because Athaliah had been slain with the sword at the palace.

²¹Joash[b] was seven years old when he began to reign.

Joash Repairs the Temple

12 In the seventh year of Jehu, Joash[c] became king, and he reigned in Jerusalem forty years. His mother's name was Zibiah; she was from Beersheba. ²Joash did what was right in the eyes of the LORD all the years Jehoiada the priest instructed him. ³The high places, however, were not removed; the people continued to offer sacrifices and burn incense there.

⁴Joash said to the priests, "Collect all the money that is brought as sacred offerings to the temple of the LORD—the money collected in the census, the money received from personal vows and the money brought voluntarily to the temple. ⁵Let every priest receive the money from one of the treasurers, and let it be used to repair whatever damage is found in the temple."

⁶But by the twenty-third year of King Joash the priests still had not repaired the temple. ⁷Therefore King Joash summoned Jehoiada the priest and the other priests and asked them, "Why aren't you repairing the damage done to the temple? Take no more money from your treasurers, but hand it over for repairing the temple." ⁸The priests agreed that they would not collect any more money from the people and that they would not repair the temple themselves.

⁹Jehoiada the priest took a chest and bored a hole in its lid. He placed it beside the altar, on the right side as one enters the temple of the LORD. The priests who guarded the entrance put into the chest all the money that was brought to the temple of the LORD. ¹⁰Whenever they saw that there was a large amount of money in the chest, the royal secretary and the high priest came, counted the money that had been brought into the temple of the LORD and put it into bags. ¹¹When the amount had been determined, they gave the money to the men appointed to supervise the work on the temple. With it they paid those who worked on the temple of the LORD—the carpenters and builders, ¹²the masons and stonecutters. They purchased timber and dressed stone for the repair of the temple of the LORD, and met all the other expenses of restoring the temple.

¹³The money brought into the temple was not spent for making silver basins, wick trimmers, sprinkling bowls, trum-

---

a15 Or *out from the precincts*   *b21* Hebrew *Jehoash,* a variant of *Joash*   *c1* Hebrew *Jehoash,* a variant of *Joash;* also in verses 2, 4, 6, 7 and 18 pets or any other articles of gold or silver for the temple of the LORD; ¹⁴it was paid to the workmen, who used it to repair the temple. ¹⁵They did not require an accounting from those to whom they gave the money to pay the workers, because they acted with complete honesty. ¹⁶The money from the guilt offerings and sin offerings was not brought into the temple of the LORD; it belonged to the priests.

¹⁷About this time Hazael king of Aram went up and attacked Gath and captured it. Then he turned to attack Jerusalem. ¹⁸But Joash king of Judah took all the sacred objects dedicated by his fathers—Jehoshaphat, Jehoram and Ahaziah, the kings of Judah—and the gifts he himself had dedicated and all the gold found in the treasuries of the temple of the LORD and of the royal palace, and he sent them to Hazael king of Aram, who then withdrew from Jerusalem.

¹⁹As for the other events of the reign of Joash, and all he did, are they not written in the book of the annals of the kings of Judah? ²⁰His officials conspired against him and assassinated him at Beth Millo, on the road down to Silla. ²¹The officials who murdered him were Jozabad son of Shimeath and Jehozabad son of Shomer. He died and was buried with his fathers in the City of David. And Amaziah his son succeeded him as king.

Jehoahaz King of Israel

13 In the twenty-third year of Joash son of Ahaziah king of Judah, Jehoahaz son of Jehu became king of Israel in Samaria, and he reigned seventeen years. ²He did evil in the eyes of the LORD by following the sins of Jeroboam son of Nebat, which he had caused Israel to commit, and he did not turn away from them. ³So the LORD's anger burned against Israel, and for a long time he kept them under the power of Hazael king of Aram and Ben-Hadad his son.

⁴Then Jehoahaz sought the LORD's favor, and the LORD listened to him, for he saw how severely the king of Aram was oppressing Israel. ⁵The LORD provided a deliverer for Israel, and they escaped from the power of Aram. So the Israelites lived in their own homes as they had before. ⁶But they did not turn away from the sins

of the house of Jeroboam, which he had caused Israel to commit; they continued in them. Also, the Asherah pole^a remained standing in Samaria.

⁷Nothing had been left of the army of Jehoahaz except fifty horsemen, ten chariots and ten thousand foot soldiers, for the king of Aram had destroyed the rest and made them like the dust at threshing time.

⁸As for the other events of the reign of Jehoahaz, all he did and his achievements, are they not written in the book of the annals of the kings of Israel? ⁹Jehoahaz rested with his fathers and was buried in Samaria. And Jehoash^b his son succeeded him as king.

Jehoash King of Israel

¹⁰In the thirty-seventh year of Joash king of Judah, Jehoash son of Jehoahaz became king of Israel in Samaria, and he reigned sixteen years. ¹¹He did evil in the eyes of the LORD and did not turn away from any of the sins of Jeroboam son of Nebat, which he had caused Israel to commit; he continued in them.

¹²As for the other events of the reign of Jehoash, all he did and his achievements, including his war against Amaziah king of Judah, are they not written in the book of the annals of the kings of Israel? ¹³Jehoash rested with his fathers, and Jeroboam succeeded him on the throne. Jehoash was buried in Samaria with the kings of Israel.

¹⁴Now Elisha was suffering from the illness from which he died. Jehoash king of Israel went down to see him and wept over him. "My father! My father!" he cried. "The chariots and horsemen of Israel!"

¹⁵Elisha said, "Get a bow and some arrows," and he did so. ¹⁶"Take the bow in your hands," he said to the king of Israel. When he had taken it, Elisha put his hands on the king's hands.

¹⁷"Open the east window," he said, and he opened it. "Shoot!" Elisha said, and he shot. "The LORD's arrow of victory, the arrow of victory over Aram!" Elisha declared. "You will completely destroy the Arameans at Aphek."

^a6 That is, a symbol of the goddess Asherah; here and elsewhere in 2 Kings   ^b9 Hebrew Joash, a variant of Jehoash; also in verses 12–14 and 25

[18]Then he said, "Take the arrows," and the king took them. Elisha told him, "Strike the ground." He struck it three times and stopped. [19]The man of God was angry with him and said, "You should have struck the ground five or six times; then you would have defeated Aram and completely destroyed it. But now you will defeat it only three times."

[20]Elisha died and was buried.

Now Moabite raiders used to enter the country every spring. [21]Once while some Israelites were burying a man, suddenly they saw a band of raiders; so they threw the man's body into Elisha's tomb. When the body touched Elisha's bones, the man came to life and stood up on his feet.

[22]Hazael king of Aram oppressed Israel throughout the reign of Jehoahaz. [23]But the LORD was gracious to them and had compassion and showed concern for them because of his covenant with Abraham, Isaac and Jacob. To this day he has been unwilling to destroy them or banish them from his presence.

[24]Hazael king of Aram died, and Ben-Hadad his son succeeded him as king. [25]Then Jehoash son of Jehoahaz recaptured from Ben-Hadad son of Hazael the towns he had taken in battle from his father Jehoahaz. Three times Jehoash defeated him, and so he recovered the Israelite towns.

Amaziah King of Judah

14 In the second year of Jehoash[a] son of Jehoahaz king of Israel, Amaziah son of Joash king of Judah began to reign. [2]He was twenty-five years old when he became king, and he reigned in Jerusalem twenty-nine years. His mother's name was Jehoaddin; she was from Jerusalem. [3]He did what was right in the eyes of the LORD, but not as his father David had done. In everything he followed the example of his father Joash. [4]The high places, however, were not removed; the people continued to offer sacrifices and burn incense there.

[5]After the kingdom was firmly in his grasp, he executed the officials who had murdered his father the king. [6]Yet he did not put the sons of the assassins to death, in accordance with what is written in the Book of the Law of Moses where the LORD commanded: "Fathers shall not be put to death for their children, nor children put to death for their fathers; each is to die for his own sins."[b]

[7]He was the one who defeated ten thousand Edomites in the Valley of Salt and captured Sela in battle, calling it Joktheel, the name it has to this day.

[8]Then Amaziah sent messengers to Jehoash son of Jehoahaz, the son of Jehu, king of Israel, with the challenge: "Come, meet me face to face."

[9]But Jehoash king of Israel replied to Amaziah king of Judah: "A thistle in Lebanon sent a message to a cedar in Lebanon, 'Give your daughter to my son in marriage.' Then a wild beast in Lebanon came along and trampled the thistle underfoot. [10]You have indeed defeated Edom and now you are arrogant. Glory in your victory, but stay at home! Why ask for trouble and cause your own downfall and that of Judah also?"

[11]Amaziah, however, would not listen, so Jehoash king of Israel attacked. He and Amaziah king of Judah faced each other at Beth Shemesh in Judah. [12]Judah was routed by Israel, and every man fled to his home. [13]Jehoash king of Israel captured Amaziah king of Judah, the son of Joash, the son of Ahaziah, at Beth Shemesh. Then Jehoash went to Jerusalem and broke down the wall of Jerusalem from the Ephraim Gate to the Corner Gate—a section about six hundred feet long.[c] [14]He took all the gold and silver and all the articles found in the temple of the LORD and in the treasuries of the royal palace. He also took hostages and returned to Samaria.

[15]As for the other events of the reign of Jehoash, what he did and his achievements, including his war against Amaziah king of Judah, are they not written in the book of the annals of the kings of Israel? [16]Jehoash rested with his fathers and was buried in Samaria with the kings of Israel. And Jeroboam his son succeeded him as king.

[17]Amaziah son of Joash king of Judah lived for fifteen years after the death of Jehoash son of Jehoahaz king of Israel.

---

[a]1 Hebrew *Joash,* a variant of *Jehoash;* also in verses 13, 23 and 27   [b]6 Deut. 24:16
[c]13 Hebrew *four hundred cubits* (about 180 meters)

¹⁸As for the other events of Amaziah's reign, are they not written in the book of the annals of the kings of Judah?

¹⁹They conspired against him in Jerusalem, and he fled to Lachish, but they sent men after him to Lachish and killed him there. ²⁰He was brought back by horse and was buried in Jerusalem with his fathers, in the City of David.

²¹Then all the people of Judah took Azariah,ᵃ who was sixteen years old, and made him king in place of his father Amaziah. ²²He was the one who rebuilt Elath and restored it to Judah after Amaziah rested with his fathers.

Jeroboam II King of Israel

²³In the fifteenth year of Amaziah son of Joash king of Judah, Jeroboam son of Jehoash king of Israel became king in Samaria, and he reigned forty-one years. ²⁴He did evil in the eyes of the LORD and did not turn away from any of the sins of Jeroboam son of Nebat, which he had caused Israel to commit. ²⁵He was the one who restored the boundaries of Israel from Leboᵇ Hamath to the Sea of the Arabah,ᶜ in accordance with the word of the LORD, the God of Israel, spoken through his servant Jonah son of Amittai, the prophet from Gath Hepher.

²⁶The LORD had seen how bitterly everyone in Israel, whether slave or free, was suffering; there was no one to help them. ²⁷And since the LORD had not said he would blot out the name of Israel from under heaven, he saved them by the hand of Jeroboam son of Jehoash.

²⁸As for the other events of Jeroboam's reign, all he did, and his military achievements, including how he recovered for Israel both Damascus and Hamath, which had belonged to Yaudi,ᵈ are they not written in the book of the annals of the kings of Israel? ²⁹Jeroboam rested with his fathers, the kings of Israel. And Zechariah his son succeeded him as king.

Azariah King of Judah

15 In the twenty-seventh year of Jeroboam king of Israel, Azariah son of Amaziah king of Judah began to reign. ²He was sixteen years old when he became king, and he reigned in Jerusalem fifty-two years. His mother's name was Jecoliah; she was from Jerusalem. ³He did what was right in the eyes of the LORD, just as his father Amaziah had done. ⁴The high places, however, were not removed; the people continued to offer sacrifices and burn incense there.

⁵The LORD afflicted the king with leprosyᵉ until the day he died, and he lived in a separate house.ᶠ Jotham the king's son had charge of the palace and governed the people of the land.

⁶As for the other events of Azariah's reign, and all he did, are they not written in the book of the annals of the kings of Judah? ⁷Azariah rested with his fathers and was buried near them in the City of David. And Jotham his son succeeded him as king.

Zechariah King of Israel

⁸In the thirty-eighth year of Azariah king of Judah, Zechariah son of Jeroboam became king of Israel in Samaria, and he reigned six months. ⁹He did evil in the eyes of the LORD, as his fathers had done. He did not turn away from the sins of Jeroboam son of Nebat, which he had caused Israel to commit.

¹⁰Shallum son of Jabesh conspired against Zechariah. He attacked him in front of the people,ᵍ assassinated him and succeeded him as king. ¹¹The other events of Zechariah's reign are written in the book of the annals of the kings of Israel. ¹²So the word of the LORD spoken to Jehu was fulfilled: "Your descendants will sit on the throne of Israel to the fourth generation."ʰ

Shallum King of Israel

¹³Shallum son of Jabesh became king in the thirty-ninth year of Uzziah king of Judah, and he reigned in Samaria one month. ¹⁴Then Menahem son of Gadi went from Tirzah up to Samaria. He attacked Shallum son of Jabesh in Samaria, assassinated him and succeeded him as king.

ᵃ21 Also called *Uzziah*   ᵇ25 Or *from the entrance to*   ᶜ25 That is, the Dead Sea   ᵈ28 Or *Judah*   ᵉ5 The Hebrew word was used for various diseases affecting the skin—not necessarily leprosy.   ᶠ5 Or *in a house where he was relieved of responsibility*   ᵍ10 Hebrew; some Septuagint manuscripts *in Ibleam*   ʰ12 2 Kings 10:30

¹⁵The other events of Shallum's reign, and the conspiracy he led, are written in the book of the annals of the kings of Israel.

¹⁶At that time Menahem, starting out from Tirzah, attacked Tiphsah and everyone in the city and its vicinity, because they refused to open their gates. He sacked Tiphsah and ripped open all the pregnant women.

Menahem King of Israel

¹⁷In the thirty-ninth year of Azariah king of Judah, Menahem son of Gadi became king of Israel, and he reigned in Samaria ten years. ¹⁸He did evil in the eyes of the LORD. During his entire reign he did not turn away from the sins of Jeroboam son of Nebat, which he had caused Israel to commit.

¹⁹Then Pul[a] king of Assyria invaded the land, and Menahem gave him a thousand talents[b] of silver to gain his support and strengthen his own hold on the kingdom. ²⁰Menahem exacted this money from Israel. Every wealthy man had to contribute fifty shekels[c] of silver to be given to the king of Assyria. So the king of Assyria withdrew and stayed in the land no longer.

²¹As for the other events of Menahem's reign, and all he did, are they not written in the book of the annals of the kings of Israel? ²²Menahem rested with his fathers. And Pekahiah his son succeeded him as king.

Pekahiah King of Israel

²³In the fiftieth year of Azariah king of Judah, Pekahiah son of Menahem became king of Israel in Samaria, and he reigned two years. ²⁴Pekahiah did evil in the eyes of the LORD. He did not turn away from the sins of Jeroboam son of Nebat, which he had caused Israel to commit. ²⁵One of his chief officers, Pekah son of Remaliah, conspired against him. Taking fifty men of Gilead with him, he assassinated Pekahiah, along with Argob and Arieh, in the citadel of the royal palace at Samaria. So Pekah killed Pekahiah and succeeded him as king.

²⁶The other events of Pekahiah's reign, and all he did, are written in the book of the annals of the kings of Israel.

Pekah King of Israel

²⁷In the fifty-second year of Azariah king of Judah, Pekah son of Remaliah became king of Israel in Samaria, and he reigned twenty years. ²⁸He did evil in the eyes of the LORD. He did not turn away from the sins of Jeroboam son of Nebat, which he had caused Israel to commit.

²⁹In the time of Pekah king of Israel, Tiglath-Pileser king of Assyria came and took Ijon, Abel Beth Maacah, Janoah, Kedesh and Hazor. He took Gilead and Galilee, including all the land of Naphtali, and deported the people to Assyria. ³⁰Then Hoshea son of Elah conspired against Pekah son of Remaliah. He attacked and assassinated him, and then succeeded him as king in the twentieth year of Jotham son of Uzziah.

³¹As for the other events of Pekah's reign, and all he did, are they not written in the book of the annals of the kings of Israel?

Jotham King of Judah

³²In the second year of Pekah son of Remaliah king of Israel, Jotham son of Uzziah king of Judah began to reign. ³³He was twenty-five years old when he became king, and he reigned in Jerusalem sixteen years. His mother's name was Jerusha daughter of Zadok. ³⁴He did what was right in the eyes of the LORD, just as his father Uzziah had done. ³⁵The high places, however, were not removed; the people continued to offer sacrifices and burn incense there. Jotham rebuilt the Upper Gate of the temple of the LORD.

³⁶As for the other events of Jotham's reign, and what he did, are they not written in the book of the annals of the kings of Judah? ³⁷(In those days the LORD began to send Rezin king of Aram and Pekah son of Remaliah against Judah.) ³⁸Jotham rested with his fathers and was buried with them in the City of David, the city of his father. And Ahaz his son succeeded him as king.

---

a19 Also called *Tiglath-Pileser*   *b19* That is, about 37 tons (about 34 metric tons)   *c20* That is, about 1 1/4 pounds (about 0.6 kilogram)

Ahaz King of Judah

16 In the seventeenth year of Pekah son of Remaliah, Ahaz son of Jotham king of Judah began to reign. ²Ahaz was twenty years old when he became king, and he reigned in Jerusalem sixteen years. Unlike David his father, he did not do what was right in the eyes of the LORD his God. ³He walked in the ways of the kings of Israel and even sacrificed his son in*ª* the fire, following the detestable ways of the nations the LORD had driven out before the Israelites. ⁴He offered sacrifices and burned incense at the high places, on the hilltops and under every spreading tree.

⁵Then Rezin king of Aram and Pekah son of Remaliah king of Israel marched up to fight against Jerusalem and besieged Ahaz, but they could not overpower him. ⁶At that time, Rezin king of Aram recovered Elath for Aram by driving out the men of Judah. Edomites then moved into Elath and have lived there to this day.

⁷Ahaz sent messengers to say to Tiglath-Pileser king of Assyria, "I am your servant and vassal. Come up and save me out of the hand of the king of Aram and of the king of Israel, who are attacking me." ⁸And Ahaz took the silver and gold found in the temple of the LORD and in the treasuries of the royal palace and sent it as a gift to the king of Assyria. ⁹The king of Assyria complied by attacking Damascus and capturing it. He deported its inhabitants to Kir and put Rezin to death.

¹⁰Then King Ahaz went to Damascus to meet Tiglath-Pileser king of Assyria. He saw an altar in Damascus and sent to Uriah the priest a sketch of the altar, with detailed plans for its construction. ¹¹So Uriah the priest built an altar in accordance with all the plans that King Ahaz had sent from Damascus and finished it before King Ahaz returned. ¹²When the king came back from Damascus and saw the altar, he approached it and presented offerings*ᵇ* on it. ¹³He offered up his burnt offering and grain offering, poured out his drink offering, and sprinkled the blood of his fellowship offerings*ᶜ* on the [altar]. ¹⁴The bronze altar that stood before [the LORD] he brought from the front of the [temple—] from between the new altar and

the temple of the LORD—and put it on the north side of the new altar.

¹⁵King Ahaz then gave these orders to Uriah the priest: "On the large new altar, offer the morning burnt offering and the evening grain offering, the king's burnt offering and his grain offering, and the burnt offering of all the people of the land, and their grain offering and their drink offering. Sprinkle on the altar all the blood of the burnt offerings and sacrifices. But I will use the bronze altar for seeking guidance." ¹⁶And Uriah the priest did just as King Ahaz had ordered.

¹⁷King Ahaz took away the side panels and removed the basins from the movable stands. He removed the Sea from the bronze bulls that supported it and set it on a stone base. ¹⁸He took away the Sabbath canopy*ᵈ* that had been built at the temple and removed the royal entryway outside the temple of the LORD, in deference to the king of Assyria.

¹⁹As for the other events of the reign of Ahaz, and what he did, are they not written in the book of the annals of the kings of Judah? ²⁰Ahaz rested with his fathers and was buried with them in the City of David. And Hezekiah his son succeeded him as king.

Hoshea Last King of Israel

17 In the twelfth year of Ahaz king of Judah, Hoshea son of Elah became king of Israel in Samaria, and he reigned nine years. ²He did evil in the eyes of the LORD, but not like the kings of Israel who preceded him.

³Shalmaneser king of Assyria came up to attack Hoshea, who had been Shalmaneser's vassal and had paid him tribute. ⁴But the king of Assyria discovered that Hoshea was a traitor, for he had sent envoys to So*ᵉ* king of Egypt, and he no longer paid tribute to the king of Assyria, as he had done year by year. Therefore Shalmaneser seized him and put him in prison. ⁵The king of Assyria invaded the entire land, marched against Samaria and laid siege to it for three years. ⁶In the ninth year of Hoshea, the king of Assyria

---

ª3 Or even made his son pass through   *ᵇ12 Or and went up*   *ᶜ13 Traditionally peace offerings*   *ᵈ18 Or the dais of his throne (see Septuagint)*   *ᵉ4 Or to Sais, to the; So is possibly an abbreviation for Osorkon.*

captured Samaria and deported the Israelites to Assyria. He settled them in Halah, in Gozan on the Habor River and in the towns of the Medes.

Israel Exiled Because of Sin

7All this took place because the Israelites had sinned against the LORD their God, who had brought them up out of Egypt from under the power of Pharaoh king of Egypt. They worshiped other gods 8and followed the practices of the nations the LORD had driven out before them, as well as the practices that the kings of Israel had introduced. 9The Israelites secretly did things against the LORD their God that were not right. From watchtower to fortified city they built themselves high places in all their towns. 10They set up sacred stones and Asherah poles on every high hill and under every spreading tree. 11At every high place they burned incense, as the nations whom the LORD had driven out before them had done. They did wicked things that provoked the LORD to anger. 12They worshiped idols, though the LORD had said, "You shall not do this."a 13The LORD warned Israel and Judah through all his prophets and seers: "Turn from your evil ways. Observe my commands and decrees, in accordance with the entire Law that I commanded your fathers to obey and that I delivered to you through my servants the prophets."

14But they would not listen and were as stiff-necked as their fathers, who did not trust in the LORD their God. 15They rejected his decrees and the covenant he had made with their fathers and the warnings he had given them. They followed worthless idols and themselves became worthless. They imitated the nations around them although the LORD had ordered them, "Do not do as they do," and they did the things the LORD had forbidden them to do.

16They forsook all the commands of the LORD their God and made for themselves two idols cast in the shape of calves, and an Asherah pole. They bowed down to all the starry hosts, and they worshiped Baal. 17They sacrificed their sons and daughters inb the fire. They practiced divination and sorcery and sold

themselves to do evil in the eyes of the LORD, provoking him to anger.

18So the LORD was very angry with Israel and removed them from his presence. Only the tribe of Judah was left, 19and even Judah did not keep the commands of the LORD their God. They followed the practices Israel had introduced. 20Therefore the LORD rejected all the people of Israel; he afflicted them and gave them into the hands of plunderers, until he thrust them from his presence.

21When he tore Israel away from the house of David, they made Jeroboam son of Nebat their king. Jeroboam enticed Israel away from following the LORD and caused them to commit a great sin. 22The Israelites persisted in all the sins of Jeroboam and did not turn away from them 23until the LORD removed them from his presence, as he had warned through all his servants the prophets. So the people of Israel were taken from their homeland into exile in Assyria, and they are still there.

Samaria Resettled

24The king of Assyria brought people from Babylon, Cuthah, Avva, Hamath and Sepharvaim and settled them in the towns of Samaria to replace the Israelites. They took over Samaria and lived in its towns. 25When they first lived there, they did not worship the LORD; so he sent lions among them and they killed some of the people. 26It was reported to the king of Assyria: "The people you deported and resettled in the towns of Samaria do not know what the god of that country requires. He has sent lions among them, which are killing them off, because the people do not know what he requires."

27Then the king of Assyria gave this order: "Have one of the priests you took captive from Samaria go back to live there and teach the people what the god of the land requires." 28So one of the priests who had been exiled from Samaria came to live in Bethel and taught them how to worship the LORD.

29Nevertheless, each national group made its own gods in the several towns where they settled, and set them up in the

a12 Exodus 20:4, 5   b17 Or *They made their sons and daughters pass through* shrines the people of Samaria had made at the high places. ³⁰The men from Babylon made Succoth Benoth, the men from Cuthah made Nergal, and the men from Hamath made Ashima; ³¹the Avvites made Nibhaz and Tartak, and the Sepharvites burned their children in the fire as sacrifices to Adrammelech and Anammelech, the gods of Sepharvaim. ³²They worshiped the LORD, but they also appointed all sorts of their own people to officiate for them as priests in the shrines at the high places. ³³They worshiped the LORD, but they also served their own gods in accordance with the customs of the nations from which they had been brought.

³⁴To this day they persist in their former practices. They neither worship the LORD nor adhere to the decrees and ordinances, the laws and commands that the LORD gave the descendants of Jacob, whom he named Israel. ³⁵When the LORD made a covenant with the Israelites, he commanded them: "Do not worship any other gods or bow down to them, serve them or sacrifice to them. ³⁶But the LORD, who brought you up out of Egypt with mighty power and outstretched arm, is the one you must worship. To him you shall bow down and to him offer sacrifices. ³⁷You must always be careful to keep the decrees and ordinances, the laws and commands he wrote for you. Do not worship other gods. ³⁸Do not forget the covenant I have made with you, and do not worship other gods. ³⁹Rather, worship the LORD your God; it is he who will deliver you from the hand of all your enemies."

⁴⁰They would not listen, however, but persisted in their former practices. ⁴¹Even while these people were worshiping the LORD, they were serving their idols. To this day their children and grandchildren continue to do as their fathers did.

Hezekiah King of Judah

18 In the third year of Hoshea son of Elah king of Israel, Hezekiah son of Ahaz king of Judah began to reign. ²He was twenty-five years old when he became king, and he reigned in Jerusalem twenty-nine years. His mother's name was Abijah[a] daughter of Zechariah. ³He did what was right in the eyes of the LORD,

just as his father David had done. ⁴He removed the high places, smashed the sacred stones and cut down the Asherah poles. He broke into pieces the bronze snake Moses had made, for up to that time the Israelites had been burning incense to it. (It was called[b] Nehushtan.[c])

⁵Hezekiah trusted in the LORD, the God of Israel. There was no one like him among all the kings of Judah, either before him or after him. ⁶He held fast to the LORD and did not cease to follow him; he kept the commands the LORD had given Moses. ⁷And the LORD was with him; he was successful in whatever he undertook. He rebelled against the king of Assyria and did not serve him. ⁸From watchtower to fortified city, he defeated the Philistines, as far as Gaza and its territory.

⁹In King Hezekiah's fourth year, which was the seventh year of Hoshea son of Elah king of Israel, Shalmaneser king of Assyria marched against Samaria and laid siege to it. ¹⁰At the end of three years the Assyrians took it. So Samaria was captured in Hezekiah's sixth year, which was the ninth year of Hoshea king of Israel. ¹¹The king of Assyria deported Israel to Assyria and settled them in Halah, in Gozan on the Habor River and in towns of the Medes. ¹²This happened because they had not obeyed the LORD their God, but had violated his covenant—all that Moses the servant of the LORD commanded. They neither listened to the commands nor carried them out.

¹³In the fourteenth year of King Hezekiah's reign, Sennacherib king of Assyria attacked all the fortified cities of Judah and captured them. ¹⁴So Hezekiah king of Judah sent this message to the king of Assyria at Lachish: "I have done wrong. Withdraw from me, and I will pay whatever you demand of me." The king of Assyria exacted from Hezekiah king of Judah three hundred talents[d] of silver and thirty talents[e] of gold. ¹⁵So Hezekiah gave him all the silver that was found in the temple of the LORD and in the treasuries of the royal palace.

---

a2 Hebrew *Abi*, a variant of *Abijah*   b4 Or *He called it*   c4 *Nehushtan* sounds like the Hebrew for *bronze* and *snake* and *unclean thing.*
d14 That is, about 11 tons (about 10 metric tons)
e14 That is, about 1 ton (about 1 metric ton)

¹⁶At this time Hezekiah king of Judah stripped off the gold with which he had covered the doors and doorposts of the temple of the LORD, and gave it to the king of Assyria.

Sennacherib Threatens Jerusalem

¹⁷The king of Assyria sent his supreme commander, his chief officer and his field commander with a large army, from Lachish to King Hezekiah at Jerusalem. They came up to Jerusalem and stopped at the aqueduct of the Upper Pool, on the road to the Washerman's Field. ¹⁸They called for the king; and Eliakim son of Hilkiah the palace administrator, Shebna the secretary, and Joah son of Asaph the recorder went out to them.

¹⁹The field commander said to them, "Tell Hezekiah:

" 'This is what the great king, the king of Assyria, says: On what are you basing this confidence of yours? ²⁰You say you have strategy and military strength—but you speak only empty words. On whom are you depending, that you rebel against me? ²¹Look now, you are depending on Egypt, that splintered reed of a staff, which pierces a man's hand and wounds him if he leans on it! Such is Pharaoh king of Egypt to all who depend on him. ²²And if you say to me, "We are depending on the LORD our God"—isn't he the one whose high places and altars Hezekiah removed, saying to Judah and Jerusalem, "You must worship before this altar in Jerusalem"?

²³ " 'Come now, make a bargain with my master, the king of Assyria: I will give you two thousand horses—if you can put riders on them! ²⁴How can you repulse one officer of the least of my master's officials, even though you are depending on Egypt for chariots and horsemen*a*? ²⁵Furthermore, have I come to attack and destroy this place without word from the LORD? The LORD himself told me to march against this country and destroy it.' "

²⁶Then Eliakim son of Hilkiah, and Shebna and Joah said to the field commander, "Please speak to your servants in Aramaic, since we understand it. Don't speak to us in Hebrew in the hearing of the people on the wall."

²⁷But the commander replied, "Was it only to your master and you that my master sent me to say these things, and not to the men sitting on the wall—who, like you, will have to eat their own filth and drink their own urine?"

²⁸Then the commander stood and called out in Hebrew: "Hear the word of the great king, the king of Assyria! ²⁹This is what the king says: Do not let Hezekiah deceive you. He cannot deliver you from my hand. ³⁰Do not let Hezekiah persuade you to trust in the LORD when he says, 'The LORD will surely deliver us; this city will not be given into the hand of the king of Assyria.'

³¹"Do not listen to Hezekiah. This is what the king of Assyria says: Make peace with me and come out to me. Then every one of you will eat from his own vine and fig tree and drink water from his own cistern, ³²until I come and take you to a land like your own, a land of grain and new wine, a land of bread and vineyards, a land of olive trees and honey. Choose life and not death!

"Do not listen to Hezekiah, for he is misleading you when he says, 'The LORD will deliver us.' ³³Has the god of any nation ever delivered his land from the hand of the king of Assyria? ³⁴Where are the gods of Hamath and Arpad? Where are the gods of Sepharvaim, Hena and Ivvah? Have they rescued Samaria from my hand? ³⁵Who of all the gods of these countries has been able to save his land from me? How then can the LORD deliver Jerusalem from my hand?"

³⁶But the people remained silent and said nothing in reply, because the king had commanded, "Do not answer him."

³⁷Then Eliakim son of Hilkiah the palace administrator, Shebna the secretary and Joah son of Asaph the recorder went to Hezekiah, with their clothes torn, and told him what the field commander had said.

a 24 Or charioteers

Jerusalem's Deliverance Foretold

19 When King Hezekiah heard this, he tore his clothes and put on sackcloth and went into the temple of the LORD. ²He sent Eliakim the palace administrator, Shebna the secretary and the leading priests, all wearing sackcloth, to the prophet Isaiah son of Amoz. ³They told him, "This is what Hezekiah says: This day is a day of distress and rebuke and disgrace, as when children come to the point of birth and there is no strength to deliver them. ⁴It may be that the LORD your God will hear all the words of the field commander, whom his master, the king of Assyria, has sent to ridicule the living God, and that he will rebuke him for the words the LORD your God has heard. Therefore pray for the remnant that still survives.'"

⁵When King Hezekiah's officials came to Isaiah, ⁶Isaiah said to them, "Tell your master, 'This is what the LORD says: Do not be afraid of what you have heard—those words with which the underlings of the king of Assyria have blasphemed me. ⁷Listen! I am going to put such a spirit in him that when he hears a certain report, he will return to his own country, and there I will have him cut down with the sword.'"

⁸When the field commander heard that the king of Assyria had left Lachish, he withdrew and found the king fighting against Libnah.

⁹Now Sennacherib received a report that Tirhakah, the Cushite[a] king ˻of Egypt˼, was marching out to fight against him. So he again sent messengers to Hezekiah with this word: ¹⁰"Say to Hezekiah king of Judah: Do not let the god you depend on deceive you when he says, 'Jerusalem will not be handed over to the king of Assyria.' ¹¹Surely you have heard what the kings of Assyria have done to all the countries, destroying them completely. And will you be delivered? ¹²Did the gods of the nations that were destroyed by my forefathers deliver them: the gods of Gozan, Haran, Rezeph and the people of Eden who were in Tel Assar? ¹³Where is the king of Hamath, the king of Arpad, the king of the city of Sepharvaim, or of Hena or Ivvah?"

Hezekiah's Prayer

¹⁴Hezekiah received the letter from the messengers and read it. Then he went up to the temple of the LORD and spread it out before the LORD. ¹⁵And Hezekiah prayed to the LORD: "O LORD, God of Israel, enthroned between the cherubim, you alone are God over all the kingdoms of the earth. You have made heaven and earth. ¹⁶Give ear, O LORD, and hear; open your eyes, O LORD, and see; listen to the words Sennacherib has sent to insult the living God.

¹⁷"It is true, O LORD, that the Assyrian kings have laid waste these nations and their lands. ¹⁸They have thrown their gods into the fire and destroyed them, for they were not gods but only wood and stone, fashioned by men's hands. ¹⁹Now, O LORD our God, deliver us from his hand, so that all kingdoms on earth may know that you alone, O LORD, are God."

Isaiah Prophesies Sennacherib's Fall

²⁰Then Isaiah son of Amoz sent a message to Hezekiah: "This is what the LORD, the God of Israel, says: I have heard your prayer concerning Sennacherib king of Assyria. ²¹This is the word that the LORD has spoken against him:

" 'The Virgin Daughter of Zion
    despises you and mocks you.
The Daughter of Jerusalem
    tosses her head as you flee.
²²Who is it you have insulted and
        blasphemed?
    Against whom have you raised
        your voice
and lifted your eyes in pride?
    Against the Holy One of Israel!
²³By your messengers
    you have heaped insults on the
        Lord.
And you have said,
    "With my many chariots
I have ascended the heights of the
        mountains,
    the utmost heights of Lebanon.
I have cut down its tallest cedars,
    the choicest of its pines.
I have reached its remotest parts,
    the finest of its forests.
²⁴I have dug wells in foreign lands

a9 That is, from the upper Nile region

and drunk the water there.
With the soles of my feet
   I have dried up all the streams of
      Egypt."

25 " 'Have you not heard?
   Long ago I ordained it.
In days of old I planned it;
   now I have brought it to pass,
that you have turned fortified cities
   into piles of stone.
26 Their people, drained of power,
   are dismayed and put to shame.
They are like plants in the field,
   like tender green shoots,
like grass sprouting on the roof,
   scorched before it grows up.

27 " 'But I know where you stay
   and when you come and go
   and how you rage against me.
28 Because you rage against me
   and your insolence has reached my
      ears,
I will put my hook in your nose
   and my bit in your mouth,

and I will make you return
   by the way you came.'

29 "This will be the sign for you,
O Hezekiah:

"This year you will eat what grows by
     itself,
   and the second year what springs
     from that.
But in the third year sow and reap,
   plant vineyards and eat their fruit.
30 Once more a remnant of the house of
     Judah
   will take root below and bear fruit
     above.
31 For out of Jerusalem will come a
     remnant,
   and out of Mount Zion a band of
     survivors.

The zeal of the LORD Almighty will accomplish this.

32 "Therefore this is what the LORD says
concerning the king of Assyria:

Growing a Marriage

Tuesday

2 KINGS 19:29–31 Marriage, like life, is progressive. You can't build a life or a marriage in one day, one week or one year. In this passage God answers Hezekiah's prayer and promises a sign of provision and growth. God also provides for us today. Consider God's answer to Hezekiah through the filter of marriage.

   "This year you will eat what grows by it-self . . . "—As a newlywed couple, God often provides for you through others. For instance, we benefited from those we met along the way. We remember an older couple who befriended us. We were still in college and they generously took us out to eat each Sunday after church. Another time God's provision came through a book that just happened to answer a specific need, and through a sermon that encouraged us.

   "The second year what springs from that . . . " Life reproduces itself. Being faithful to learn what God wants to teach you will result in more growth in the future. When you invest in your marriage and in your walk with God, you will reap great dividends. For instance, developing the habit of regular dates and joining a marriage growth group helped keep our relationship growing.

   "In the third year sow and reap, plant vineyards and eat their fruit . . . " Growth multiplies as you become more established in your marriage and in your relationship with God. Your roots will draw deeply from God's love, and you can bear much fruit. You will be able to give to others. You might feel called to lead a couple's Bible study or prayer group where you can encourage others. Or maybe you'll take advantage of more spontaneous opportunities like lending a listening ear to a young husband or wife—even if it's in the checkout line at the store—or writing a short note or calling a friend whom you know is struggling.

   But the good news is it isn't all up to you. Verse 31 reminds us, "The zeal of the LORD Almighty will accomplish this."

—Dave & Claudia

Go to page 416 for your next devotional reading.

"He will not enter this city
or shoot an arrow here.
He will not come before it with
shield
or build a siege ramp against it.
³³By the way that he came he will
return;
he will not enter this city,
declares the LORD.
³⁴I will defend this city and save it,
for my sake and for the sake of
David my servant."

³⁵That night the angel of the LORD went out and put to death a hundred and eighty-five thousand men in the Assyrian camp. When the people got up the next morning—there were all the dead bodies! ³⁶So Sennacherib king of Assyria broke camp and withdrew. He returned to Nineveh and stayed there.

³⁷One day, while he was worshiping in the temple of his god Nisroch, his sons Adrammelech and Sharezer cut him down with the sword, and they escaped to the land of Ararat. And Esarhaddon his son succeeded him as king.

Hezekiah's Illness

20 In those days Hezekiah became ill and was at the point of death. The prophet Isaiah son of Amoz went to him and said, "This is what the LORD says: Put your house in order, because you are going to die; you will not recover."

²Hezekiah turned his face to the wall and prayed to the LORD, ³"Remember, O LORD, how I have walked before you faithfully and with wholehearted devotion and have done what is good in your eyes." And Hezekiah wept bitterly.

⁴Before Isaiah had left the middle court, the word of the LORD came to him: ⁵"Go back and tell Hezekiah, the leader of my people, 'This is what the LORD, the God of your father David, says: I have heard your prayer and seen your tears; I will heal you. On the third day from now you will go up to the temple of the LORD. ⁶I will add fifteen years to your life. And I will deliver you and this city from the hand of the king of Assyria. I will defend this city for my sake and for the sake of my servant David.' "

⁷Then Isaiah said, "Prepare a poultice of figs." They did so and applied it to the boil, and he recovered.

⁸Hezekiah had asked Isaiah, "What will be the sign that the LORD will heal me and that I will go up to the temple of the LORD on the third day from now?"

⁹Isaiah answered, "This is the LORD's sign to you that the LORD will do what he has promised: Shall the shadow go forward ten steps, or shall it go back ten steps?"

¹⁰"It is a simple matter for the shadow to go forward ten steps," said Hezekiah. "Rather, have it go back ten steps."

¹¹Then the prophet Isaiah called upon the LORD, and the LORD made the shadow go back the ten steps it had gone down on the stairway of Ahaz.

Envoys From Babylon

¹²At that time Merodach-Baladan son of Baladan king of Babylon sent Hezekiah letters and a gift, because he had heard of Hezekiah's illness. ¹³Hezekiah received the messengers and showed them all that was in his storehouses—the silver, the gold, the spices and the fine oil—his armory and everything found among his treasures. There was nothing in his palace or in all his kingdom that Hezekiah did not show them.

¹⁴Then Isaiah the prophet went to King Hezekiah and asked, "What did those men say, and where did they come from?"

"From a distant land," Hezekiah replied. "They came from Babylon."

¹⁵The prophet asked, "What did they see in your palace?"

"They saw everything in my palace," Hezekiah said. "There is nothing among my treasures that I did not show them."

¹⁶Then Isaiah said to Hezekiah, "Hear the word of the LORD: ¹⁷The time will surely come when everything in your palace, and all that your fathers have stored up until this day, will be carried off to Babylon. Nothing will be left, says the LORD. ¹⁸And some of your descendants, your own flesh and blood, that will be born to you, will be taken away, and they will become eunuchs in the palace of the king of Babylon."

¹⁹"The word of the LORD you have spoken is good," Hezekiah replied. For he

thought, "Will there not be peace and security in my lifetime?"

²⁰As for the other events of Hezekiah's reign, all his achievements and how he made the pool and the tunnel by which he brought water into the city, are they not written in the book of the annals of the kings of Judah? ²¹Hezekiah rested with his fathers. And Manasseh his son succeeded him as king.

Manasseh King of Judah

21 Manasseh was twelve years old when he became king, and he reigned in Jerusalem fifty-five years. His mother's name was Hephzibah. ²He did evil in the eyes of the LORD, following the detestable practices of the nations the LORD had driven out before the Israelites. ³He rebuilt the high places his father Hezekiah had destroyed; he also erected altars to Baal and made an Asherah pole, as Ahab king of Israel had done. He bowed down to all the starry hosts and worshiped them. ⁴He built altars in the temple of the LORD, of which the LORD had said, "In Jerusalem I will put my Name." ⁵In both courts of the temple of the LORD, he built altars to all the starry hosts. ⁶He sacrificed his own son in*ᵃ* the fire, practiced sorcery and divination, and consulted mediums and spiritists. He did much evil in the eyes of the LORD, provoking him to anger.

⁷He took the carved Asherah pole he had made and put it in the temple, of which the LORD had said to David and to his son Solomon, "In this temple and in Jerusalem, which I have chosen out of all the tribes of Israel, I will put my Name forever. ⁸I will not again make the feet of the Israelites wander from the land I gave their forefathers, if only they will be careful to do everything I commanded them and will keep the whole Law that my servant Moses gave them." ⁹But the people did not listen. Manasseh led them astray, so that they did more evil than the nations the LORD had destroyed before the Israelites.

¹⁰The LORD said through his servants the prophets: ¹¹"Manasseh king of Judah has committed these detestable sins. He has done more evil than the Amorites who preceded him and has led Judah into sin with his idols. ¹²Therefore this is what the LORD, the God of Israel, says: I am going to bring such disaster on Jerusalem and Judah that the ears of everyone who hears of it will tingle. ¹³I will stretch out over Jerusalem the measuring line used against Samaria and the plumb line used against the house of Ahab. I will wipe out Jerusalem as one wipes a dish, wiping it and turning it upside down. ¹⁴I will forsake the remnant of my inheritance and hand them over to their enemies. They will be looted and plundered by all their foes, ¹⁵because they have done evil in my eyes and have provoked me to anger from the day their forefathers came out of Egypt until this day."

¹⁶Moreover, Manasseh also shed so much innocent blood that he filled Jerusalem from end to end—besides the sin that he had caused Judah to commit, so that they did evil in the eyes of the LORD.

¹⁷As for the other events of Manasseh's reign, and all he did, including the sin he committed, are they not written in the book of the annals of the kings of Judah? ¹⁸Manasseh rested with his fathers and was buried in his palace garden, the garden of Uzza. And Amon his son succeeded him as king.

Amon King of Judah

¹⁹Amon was twenty-two years old when he became king, and he reigned in Jerusalem two years. His mother's name was Meshullemeth daughter of Haruz; she was from Jotbah. ²⁰He did evil in the eyes of the LORD, as his father Manasseh had done. ²¹He walked in all the ways of his father; he worshiped the idols his father had worshiped, and bowed down to them. ²²He forsook the LORD, the God of his fathers, and did not walk in the way of the LORD.

²³Amon's officials conspired against him and assassinated the king in his palace. ²⁴Then the people of the land killed all who had plotted against King Amon, and they made Josiah his son king in his place.

²⁵As for the other events of Amon's reign, and what he did, are they not written in the book of the annals of the kings of Judah? ²⁶He was buried in his grave in

ᵃ6 Or He made his own son pass through

the garden of Uzza. And Josiah his son succeeded him as king.

The Book of the Law Found

22 Josiah was eight years old when he became king, and he reigned in Jerusalem thirty-one years. His mother's name was Jedidah daughter of Adaiah; she was from Bozkath. ²He did what was right in the eyes of the LORD and walked in all the ways of his father David, not turning aside to the right or to the left.

³In the eighteenth year of his reign, King Josiah sent the secretary, Shaphan son of Azaliah, the son of Meshullam, to the temple of the LORD. He said: ⁴"Go up to Hilkiah the high priest and have him get ready the money that has been brought into the temple of the LORD, which the doorkeepers have collected from the people. ⁵Have them entrust it to the men appointed to supervise the work on the temple. And have these men pay the workers who repair the temple of the LORD— ⁶the carpenters, the builders and the masons. Also have them purchase timber and dressed stone to repair the temple. ⁷But they need not account for the money entrusted to them, because they are acting faithfully."

⁸Hilkiah the high priest said to Shaphan the secretary, "I have found the Book of the Law in the temple of the LORD." He gave it to Shaphan, who read it. ⁹Then Shaphan the secretary went to the king and reported to him: "Your officials have paid out the money that was in the temple of the LORD and have entrusted it to the workers and supervisors at the temple." ¹⁰Then Shaphan the secretary informed the king, "Hilkiah the priest has given me a book." And Shaphan read from it in the presence of the king.

¹¹When the king heard the words of the Book of the Law, he tore his robes. ¹²He gave these orders to Hilkiah the priest, Ahikam son of Shaphan, Acbor son of Micaiah, Shaphan the secretary and Asaiah the king's attendant: ¹³"Go and inquire of the LORD for me and for the people and for all Judah about what is written in this book that has been found. Great is the LORD's anger that burns against us because our fathers have not obeyed the words of this book; they

have not acted in accordance with all that is written there concerning us."

¹⁴Hilkiah the priest, Ahikam, Acbor, Shaphan and Asaiah went to speak to the prophetess Huldah, who was the wife of Shallum son of Tikvah, the son of Harhas, keeper of the wardrobe. She lived in Jerusalem, in the Second District.

¹⁵She said to them, "This is what the LORD, the God of Israel, says: Tell the man who sent you to me, ¹⁶'This is what the LORD says: I am going to bring disaster on this place and its people, according to everything written in the book the king of Judah has read. ¹⁷Because they have forsaken me and burned incense to other gods and provoked me to anger by all the idols their hands have made,ᵃ my anger will burn against this place and will not be quenched.' ¹⁸Tell the king of Judah, who sent you to inquire of the LORD, 'This is what the LORD, the God of Israel, says concerning the words you heard: ¹⁹Because your heart was responsive and you humbled yourself before the LORD when you heard what I have spoken against this place and its people, that they would become accursed and laid waste, and because you tore your robes and wept in my presence, I have heard you, declares the LORD. ²⁰Therefore I will gather you to your fathers, and you will be buried in peace. Your eyes will not see all the disaster I am going to bring on this place.' "

So they took her answer back to the king.

Josiah Renews the Covenant

23 Then the king called together all the elders of Judah and Jerusalem. ²He went up to the temple of the LORD with the men of Judah, the people of Jerusalem, the priests and the prophets—all the people from the least to the greatest. He read in their hearing all the words of the Book of the Covenant, which had been found in the temple of the LORD. ³The king stood by the pillar and renewed the covenant in the presence of the LORD— to follow the LORD and keep his commands, regulations and decrees with all his heart and all his soul, thus confirming the words of the covenant written in this

ᵃ17 Or *by everything they have done*

book. Then all the people pledged themselves to the covenant.

⁴The king ordered Hilkiah the high priest, the priests next in rank and the doorkeepers to remove from the temple of the LORD all the articles made for Baal and Asherah and all the starry hosts. He burned them outside Jerusalem in the fields of the Kidron Valley and took the ashes to Bethel. ⁵He did away with the pagan priests appointed by the kings of Judah to burn incense on the high places of the towns of Judah and on those around Jerusalem—those who burned incense to Baal, to the sun and moon, to the constellations and to all the starry hosts. ⁶He took the Asherah pole from the temple of the LORD to the Kidron Valley outside Jerusalem and burned it there. He ground it to powder and scattered the dust over the graves of the common people. ⁷He also tore down the quarters of the male shrine prostitutes, which were in the temple of the LORD and where women did weaving for Asherah.

⁸Josiah brought all the priests from the towns of Judah and desecrated the high places, from Geba to Beersheba, where the priests had burned incense. He broke down the shrines*a* at the gates—at the entrance to the Gate of Joshua, the city governor, which is on the left of the city gate. ⁹Although the priests of the high places did not serve at the altar of the LORD in Jerusalem, they ate unleavened bread with their fellow priests.

¹⁰He desecrated Topheth, which was in the Valley of Ben Hinnom, so no one could use it to sacrifice his son or daughter in*b* the fire to Molech. ¹¹He removed from the entrance to the temple of the LORD the horses that the kings of Judah had dedicated to the sun. They were in the court near the room of an official named Nathan-Melech. Josiah then burned the chariots dedicated to the sun.

¹²He pulled down the altars the kings of Judah had erected on the roof near the upper room of Ahaz, and the altars Manasseh had built in the two courts of the temple of the LORD. He removed them from there, smashed them to pieces and threw the rubble into the Kidron Valley. ¹³The king also desecrated the high places that were east of Jerusalem on the south of the Hill of Corruption—the ones Solomon king of Israel had built for Ashtoreth the vile goddess of the Sidonians, for Chemosh the vile god of Moab, and for Molech*c* the detestable god of the people of Ammon. ¹⁴Josiah smashed the sacred stones and cut down the Asherah poles and covered the sites with human bones.

¹⁵Even the altar at Bethel, the high place made by Jeroboam son of Nebat, who had caused Israel to sin—even that altar and high place he demolished. He burned the high place and ground it to powder, and burned the Asherah pole also. ¹⁶Then Josiah looked around, and when he saw the tombs that were there on the hillside, he had the bones removed from them and burned on the altar to defile it, in accordance with the word of the LORD proclaimed by the man of God who foretold these things.

¹⁷The king asked, "What is that tombstone I see?"

The men of the city said, "It marks the tomb of the man of God who came from Judah and pronounced against the altar of Bethel the very things you have done to it."

¹⁸"Leave it alone," he said. "Don't let anyone disturb his bones." So they spared his bones and those of the prophet who had come from Samaria.

¹⁹Just as he had done at Bethel, Josiah removed and defiled all the shrines at the high places that the kings of Israel had built in the towns of Samaria that had provoked the LORD to anger. ²⁰Josiah slaughtered all the priests of those high places on the altars and burned human bones on them. Then he went back to Jerusalem.

²¹The king gave this order to all the people: "Celebrate the Passover to the LORD your God, as it is written in this Book of the Covenant." ²²Not since the days of the judges who led Israel, nor throughout the days of the kings of Israel and the kings of Judah, had any such Passover been observed. ²³But in the eighteenth year of King Josiah, this Passover was celebrated to the LORD in Jerusalem.

²⁴Furthermore, Josiah got rid of the mediums and spiritists, the household gods, the idols and all the other detest-

a8 Or *high places*   *b10* Or *to make his son or daughter pass through*   *c13* Hebrew *Milcom* able things seen in Judah and Jerusalem. This he did to fulfill the requirements of the law written in the book that Hilkiah the priest had discovered in the temple of the LORD. 25Neither before nor after Josiah was there a king like him who turned to the LORD as he did—with all his heart and with all his soul and with all his strength, in accordance with all the Law of Moses.

26Nevertheless, the LORD did not turn away from the heat of his fierce anger, which burned against Judah because of all that Manasseh had done to provoke him to anger. 27So the LORD said, "I will remove Judah also from my presence as I removed Israel, and I will reject Jerusalem, the city I chose, and this temple, about which I said, 'There shall my Name be.'a"

28As for the other events of Josiah's reign, and all he did, are they not written in the book of the annals of the kings of Judah?

29While Josiah was king, Pharaoh Neco king of Egypt went up to the Euphrates River to help the king of Assyria. King Josiah marched out to meet him in battle, but Neco faced him and killed him at Megiddo. 30Josiah's servants brought his body in a chariot from Megiddo to Jerusalem and buried him in his own tomb. And the people of the land took Jehoahaz son of Josiah and anointed him and made him king in place of his father.

Jehoahaz King of Judah

31Jehoahaz was twenty-three years old when he became king, and he reigned in Jerusalem three months. His mother's name was Hamutal daughter of Jeremiah; she was from Libnah. 32He did evil in the eyes of the LORD, just as his fathers had done. 33Pharaoh Neco put him in chains at Riblah in the land of Hamathb so that he might not reign in Jerusalem, and he imposed on Judah a levy of a hundred talentsc of silver and a talentd of gold. 34Pharaoh Neco made Eliakim son of Josiah king in place of his father Josiah and changed Eliakim's name to Jehoiakim. But he took Jehoahaz and carried him off to Egypt, and there he died. 35Jehoiakim paid Pharaoh Neco the silver and gold he demanded. In order to do so, he taxed the land and exacted the silver and gold from the people of the land according to their assessments.

Jehoiakim King of Judah

36Jehoiakim was twenty-five years old when he became king, and he reigned in Jerusalem eleven years. His mother's name was Zebidah daughter of Pedaiah; she was from Rumah. 37And he did evil in the eyes of the LORD, just as his fathers had done.

24 During Jehoiakim's reign, Nebuchadnezzar king of Babylon invaded the land, and Jehoiakim became his vassal for three years. But then he changed his mind and rebelled against Nebuchadnezzar. 2The LORD sent Babylonian,e Aramean, Moabite and Ammonite raiders against him. He sent them to destroy Judah, in accordance with the word of the LORD proclaimed by his servants the prophets. 3Surely these things happened to Judah according to the LORD's command, in order to remove them from his presence because of the sins of Manasseh and all he had done, 4including the shedding of innocent blood. For he had filled Jerusalem with innocent blood, and the LORD was not willing to forgive.

5As for the other events of Jehoiakim's reign, and all he did, are they not written in the book of the annals of the kings of Judah? 6Jehoiakim rested with his fathers. And Jehoiachin his son succeeded him as king.

7The king of Egypt did not march out from his own country again, because the king of Babylon had taken all his territory, from the Wadi of Egypt to the Euphrates River.

Jehoiachin King of Judah

8Jehoiachin was eighteen years old when he became king, and he reigned in Jerusalem three months. His mother's name was Nehushta daughter of Elnathan; she was from Jerusalem. 9He did

a27 1 Kings 8:29   b33 Hebrew; Septuagint (see also 2 Chron. 36:3) Neco at Riblah in Hamath removed him   c33 That is, about 3 3/4 tons (about 3.4 metric tons)   d33 That is, about 75 pounds (about 34 kilograms)   e2 Or Chaldean evil in the eyes of the LORD, just as his father had done.

¹⁰At that time the officers of Nebuchadnezzar king of Babylon advanced on Jerusalem and laid siege to it, ¹¹and Nebuchadnezzar himself came up to the city while his officers were besieging it. ¹²Jehoiachin king of Judah, his mother, his attendants, his nobles and his officials all surrendered to him.

In the eighth year of the reign of the king of Babylon, he took Jehoiachin prisoner. ¹³As the LORD had declared, Nebuchadnezzar removed all the treasures from the temple of the LORD and from the royal palace, and took away all the gold articles that Solomon king of Israel had made for the temple of the LORD. ¹⁴He carried into exile all Jerusalem: all the officers and fighting men, and all the craftsmen and artisans—a total of ten thousand. Only the poorest people of the land were left.

¹⁵Nebuchadnezzar took Jehoiachin captive to Babylon. He also took from Jerusalem to Babylon the king's mother, his wives, his officials and the leading men of the land. ¹⁶The king of Babylon also deported to Babylon the entire force of seven thousand fighting men, strong and fit for war, and a thousand craftsmen and artisans. ¹⁷He made Mattaniah, Jehoiachin's uncle, king in his place and changed his name to Zedekiah.

Zedekiah King of Judah

¹⁸Zedekiah was twenty-one years old when he became king, and he reigned in Jerusalem eleven years. His mother's name was Hamutal daughter of Jeremiah; she was from Libnah. ¹⁹He did evil in the eyes of the LORD, just as Jehoiakim had done. ²⁰It was because of the LORD's anger that all this happened to Jerusalem and Judah, and in the end he thrust them from his presence.

The Fall of Jerusalem

Now Zedekiah rebelled against the king of Babylon.

25 So in the ninth year of Zedekiah's reign, on the tenth day of the tenth month, Nebuchadnezzar king of Babylon marched against Jerusalem with his whole army. He encamped outside the city and built siege works all around it. ²The city was kept under siege until the eleventh year of King Zedekiah. ³By the ninth day of the ⌊fourth⌋ᵃ month the famine in the city had become so severe that there was no food for the people to eat. ⁴Then the city wall was broken through, and the whole army fled at night through the gate between the two walls near the king's garden, though the Babyloniansᵇ were surrounding the city. They fled toward the Arabah,ᶜ ⁵but the Babylonianᵈ army pursued the king and overtook him in the plains of Jericho. All his soldiers were separated from him and scattered, ⁶and he was captured. He was taken to the king of Babylon at Riblah, where sentence was pronounced on him. ⁷They killed the sons of Zedekiah before his eyes. Then they put out his eyes, bound him with bronze shackles and took him to Babylon.

⁸On the seventh day of the fifth month, in the nineteenth year of Nebuchadnezzar king of Babylon, Nebuzaradan commander of the imperial guard, an official of the king of Babylon, came to Jerusalem. ⁹He set fire to the temple of the LORD, the royal palace and all the houses of Jerusalem. Every important building he burned down. ¹⁰The whole Babylonian army, under the commander of the imperial guard, broke down the walls around Jerusalem. ¹¹Nebuzaradan the commander of the guard carried into exile the people who remained in the city, along with the rest of the populace and those who had gone over to the king of Babylon. ¹²But the commander left behind some of the poorest people of the land to work the vineyards and fields.

¹³The Babylonians broke up the bronze pillars, the movable stands and the bronze Sea that were at the temple of the LORD and they carried the bronze to Babylon. ¹⁴They also took away the pots, shovels, wick trimmers, dishes and all the bronze articles used in the temple service. ¹⁵The commander of the imperial guard took away the censers and sprinkling bowls—all that were made of pure gold or silver.

ᵃ3 See Jer. 52:6.   ᵇ4 Or Chaldeans; also in verses 13, 25 and 26   ᶜ4 Or the Jordan Valley   ᵈ5 Or Chaldean; also in verses 10 and 24

[16]The bronze from the two pillars, the Sea and the movable stands, which Solomon had made for the temple of the LORD, was more than could be weighed. [17]Each pillar was twenty-seven feet[a] high. The bronze capital on top of one pillar was four and a half feet[b] high and was decorated with a network and pomegranates of bronze all around. The other pillar, with its network, was similar.

[18]The commander of the guard took as prisoners Seraiah the chief priest, Zephaniah the priest next in rank and the three doorkeepers. [19]Of those still in the city, he took the officer in charge of the fighting men and five royal advisers. He also took the secretary who was chief officer in charge of conscripting the people of the land and sixty of his men who were found in the city. [20]Nebuzaradan the commander took them all and brought them to the king of Babylon at Riblah. [21]There at Riblah, in the land of Hamath, the king had them executed.

So Judah went into captivity, away from her land.

[22]Nebuchadnezzar king of Babylon appointed Gedaliah son of Ahikam, the son of Shaphan, to be over the people he had left behind in Judah. [23]When all the army officers and their men heard that the king of Babylon had appointed Gedaliah as governor, they came to Gedaliah at Mizpah—Ishmael son of Nethaniah, Johanan son of Kareah, Seraiah son of Tanhumeth the Netophathite, Jaazaniah the son of the Maacathite, and their men. [24]Gedaliah took an oath to reassure them and their men. "Do not be afraid of the Babylonian officials," he said. "Settle down in the land and serve the king of Babylon, and it will go well with you."

[25]In the seventh month, however, Ishmael son of Nethaniah, the son of Elishama, who was of royal blood, came with ten men and assassinated Gedaliah and also the men of Judah and the Babylonians who were with him at Mizpah. [26]At this, all the people from the least to the greatest, together with the army officers, fled to Egypt for fear of the Babylonians.

Jehoiachin Released

[27]In the thirty-seventh year of the exile of Jehoiachin king of Judah, in the year Evil-Merodach[c] became king of Babylon, he released Jehoiachin from prison on the twenty-seventh day of the twelfth month. [28]He spoke kindly to him and gave him a seat of honor higher than those of the other kings who were with him in Babylon. [29]So Jehoiachin put aside his prison clothes and for the rest of his life ate regularly at the king's table. [30]Day by day the king gave Jehoiachin a regular allowance as long as he lived.

[a]17 Hebrew eighteen cubits (about 8.1 meters)
[b]17 Hebrew three cubits (about 1.3 meters)
[c]27 Also called Amel-Marduk

1 Chronicles

When we get discouraged with ourselves because of our sin, it's easy to lose sight of God's love for us. Sometimes we need to be reminded that God is always with us and that he wants to show us he is faithful. The books of Chronicles were written to reconnect the Babylonian exiles with their history as a people beloved and chosen by God.

There may be a point in your life when you ask the same question the exiles might have: *Is God still interested in me?* You may wonder if he understands what hardships you endure. *What's the point of all this? Why can't I be a better husband or wife? Where is God?*—Be open to hearing God's answer as you read 1 and 2 Chronicles.

Historical Records From Adam to Abraham

To Noah's Sons

1 Adam, Seth, Enosh, ²Kenan, Mahalalel, Jared, ³Enoch, Methuselah, Lamech, Noah.

⁴The sons of Noah:ᵃ
Shem, Ham and Japheth.

The Japhethites

⁵The sonsᵇ of Japheth:
Gomer, Magog, Madai, Javan, Tubal, Meshech and Tiras.
⁶The sons of Gomer:
Ashkenaz, Riphathᶜ and Togarmah.
⁷The sons of Javan:

Elishah, Tarshish, the Kittim and the Rodanim.

The Hamites

⁸The sons of Ham:
Cush, Mizraim,ᵈ Put and Canaan.
⁹The sons of Cush:
Seba, Havilah, Sabta, Raamah and Sabteca.
The sons of Raamah:
Sheba and Dedan.

ᵃ4 Septuagint; Hebrew does not have *The sons of Noah:* ᵇ5 *Sons* may mean *descendants* or *successors* or *nations*; also in verses 6-10, 17 and 20. ᶜ6 Many Hebrew manuscripts and Vulgate (see also Septuagint and Gen. 10:3); most Hebrew manuscripts *Diphath* ᵈ8 That is, Egypt; also in verse 11

10Cush was the father*a* of
Nimrod, who grew to be a
mighty warrior on earth.
11Mizraim was the father of
the Ludites, Anamites, Leha-
bites, Naphtuhites, **12**Pathru-
sites, Casluhites (from whom
the Philistines came) and Caphtorites.
13Canaan was the father of
Sidon his firstborn,*b* and of the
Hittites, **14**Jebusites, Amorites,
Girgashites, **15**Hivites, Arkites,
Sinites, **16**Arvadites, Zemarites
and Hamathites.

The Semites

17The sons of Shem:
Elam, Asshur, Arphaxad, Lud
and Aram.
The sons of Aram*c*:
Uz, Hul, Gether and Meshech.
18Arphaxad was the father of Shelah,
and Shelah the father of Eber.
19Two sons were born to Eber:
One was named Peleg,*d* because in his time the earth was
divided; his brother was named
Joktan.
20Joktan was the father of
Almodad, Sheleph, Hazarmaveth, Jerah, **21**Hadoram, Uzal,
Diklah, **22**Obal,*e* Abimael, Sheba, **23**Ophir, Havilah and Jobab.
All these were sons of Joktan.

24Shem, Arphaxad,*f* Shelah,
25Eber, Peleg, Reu,
26Serug, Nahor, Terah
27and Abram (that is, Abraham).

The Family of Abraham

28The sons of Abraham:
Isaac and Ishmael.

Descendants of Hagar

29These were their descendants:
Nebaioth the firstborn of Ishmael, Kedar, Adbeel, Mibsam,
30Mishma, Dumah, Massa, Hadad, Tema, **31**Jetur, Naphish and
Kedemah. These were the sons
of Ishmael.

Descendants of Keturah

32The sons born to Keturah, Abraham's concubine:
Zimran, Jokshan, Medan, Midian, Ishbak and Shuah.
The sons of Jokshan:
Sheba and Dedan.
33The sons of Midian:
Ephah, Epher, Hanoch, Abida
and Eldaah.
All these were descendants of Keturah.

Descendants of Sarah

34Abraham was the father of Isaac.
The sons of Isaac:
Esau and Israel.

Esau's Sons

35The sons of Esau:
Eliphaz, Reuel, Jeush, Jalam and
Korah.
36The sons of Eliphaz:
Teman, Omar, Zepho,*g* Gatam
and Kenaz;
by Timna: Amalek.*h*
37The sons of Reuel:
Nahath, Zerah, Shammah and
Mizzah.

The People of Seir in Edom

38The sons of Seir:
Lotan, Shobal, Zibeon, Anah,
Dishon, Ezer and Dishan.
39The sons of Lotan:
Hori and Homam. Timna was
Lotan's sister.
40The sons of Shobal:

---

a 10 Father may mean *ancestor* or *predecessor* or
founder; also in verses 11, 13, 18 and 20.
b 13 Or *of the Sidonians, the foremost*   *c 17* One
Hebrew manuscript and some Septuagint
manuscripts (see also Gen. 10:23); most Hebrew
manuscripts do not have this line.   *d 19 Peleg*
means *division*.   *e 22* Some Hebrew manuscripts
and Syriac (see also Gen. 10:28); most Hebrew
manuscripts *Ebal*   *f 24* Hebrew; some Septuagint
manuscripts *Arphaxad, Cainan* (see also note at
Gen. 11:10)   *g 36* Many Hebrew manuscripts,
some Septuagint manuscripts and Syriac (see also
Gen. 36:11); most Hebrew manuscripts *Zephi*
h 36 Some Septuagint manuscripts (see also Gen.
36:12); Hebrew *Gatam, Kenaz, Timna and Amalek*

Alvan,[a] Manahath, Ebal, Shepho and Onam.
The sons of Zibeon:
Aiah and Anah.
⁴¹The son of Anah:
Dishon.
The sons of Dishon:
Hemdan,[b] Eshban, Ithran and Keran.
⁴²The sons of Ezer:
Bilhan, Zaavan and Akan.[c]
The sons of Dishan[d]:
Uz and Aran.

The Rulers of Edom

⁴³These were the kings who reigned in Edom before any Israelite king reigned[e]:
Bela son of Beor, whose city was named Dinhabah.
⁴⁴When Bela died, Jobab son of Zerah from Bozrah succeeded him as king.
⁴⁵When Jobab died, Husham from the land of the Temanites succeeded him as king.
⁴⁶When Husham died, Hadad son of Bedad, who defeated Midian in the country of Moab, succeeded him as king. His city was named Avith.
⁴⁷When Hadad died, Samlah from Masrekah succeeded him as king.
⁴⁸When Samlah died, Shaul from Rehoboth on the river[f] succeeded him as king.
⁴⁹When Shaul died, Baal-Hanan son of Acbor succeeded him as king.
⁵⁰When Baal-Hanan died, Hadad succeeded him as king. His city was named Pau,[g] and his wife's name was Mehetabel daughter of Matred, the daughter of Me-Zahab. ⁵¹Hadad also died.

The chiefs of Edom were:
Timna, Alvah, Jetheth, ⁵²Oholibamah, Elah, Pinon, ⁵³Kenaz, Teman, Mibzar, ⁵⁴Magdiel and Iram. These were the chiefs of Edom.

Israel's Sons

2 These were the sons of Israel:
Reuben, Simeon, Levi, Judah, Issachar, Zebulun, ²Dan, Joseph, Benjamin, Naphtali, Gad and Asher.

Judah

To Hezron's Sons

³The sons of Judah:
Er, Onan and Shelah. These three were born to him by a Canaanite woman, the daughter of Shua. Er, Judah's firstborn, was wicked in the LORD's sight; so the LORD put him to death. ⁴Tamar, Judah's daughter-in-law, bore him Perez and Zerah. Judah had five sons in all.

⁵The sons of Perez:
Hezron and Hamul.
⁶The sons of Zerah:
Zimri, Ethan, Heman, Calcol and Darda[h]—five in all.
⁷The son of Carmi:
Achar,[i] who brought trouble on Israel by violating the ban on taking devoted things.[j]
⁸The son of Ethan:
Azariah.
⁹The sons born to Hezron were:
Jerahmeel, Ram and Caleb.[k]

From Ram Son of Hezron

¹⁰Ram was the father of
Amminadab, and Amminadab the father of Nahshon, the

---

a40 Many Hebrew manuscripts and some Septuagint manuscripts (see also Gen. 36:23); most Hebrew manuscripts *Alian*   b41 Many Hebrew manuscripts and some Septuagint manuscripts (see also Gen. 36:26); most Hebrew manuscripts *Hamran*   c42 Many Hebrew and Septuagint manuscripts (see also Gen. 36:27); most Hebrew manuscripts *Zaavan, Jaakan*   d42 Hebrew *Dishon*, a variant of *Dishan*   e43 Or *before an Israelite king reigned over them*   f48 Possibly the Euphrates   g50 Many Hebrew manuscripts, some Septuagint manuscripts, Vulgate and Syriac (see also Gen. 36:39); most Hebrew manuscripts *Pai*   h6 Many Hebrew manuscripts, some Septuagint manuscripts and Syriac (see also 1 Kings 4:31); most Hebrew manuscripts *Dara*   i7 *Achar* means *trouble*; *Achar* is called *Achan* in Joshua.   j7 The Hebrew term refers to the irrevocable giving over of things or persons to the LORD, often by totally destroying them.   k9 Hebrew *Kelubai*, a variant of *Caleb* leader of the people of Judah. [11]Nahshon was the father of Salmon,[a] Salmon the father of Boaz, [12]Boaz the father of Obed and Obed the father of Jesse.

[13]Jesse was the father of
Eliab his firstborn; the second son was Abinadab, the third Shimea, [14]the fourth Nethanel, the fifth Raddai, [15]the sixth Ozem and the seventh David. [16]Their sisters were Zeruiah and Abigail. Zeruiah's three sons were Abishai, Joab and Asahel. [17]Abigail was the mother of Amasa, whose father was Jether the Ishmaelite.

Caleb Son of Hezron

[18]Caleb son of Hezron had children by his wife Azubah (and by Jerioth). These were her sons: Jesher, Shobab and Ardon.

[19]When Azubah died, Caleb married Ephrath, who bore him Hur. [20]Hur was the father of Uri, and Uri the father of Bezalel.

[21]Later, Hezron lay with the daughter of Makir the father of Gilead (he had married her when he was sixty years old), and she bore him Segub. [22]Segub was the father of Jair, who controlled twenty-three towns in Gilead. [23](But Geshur and Aram captured Havvoth Jair,[b] as well as Kenath with its surrounding settlements—sixty towns.) All these were descendants of Makir the father of Gilead.

[24]After Hezron died in Caleb Ephrathah, Abijah the wife of Hezron

---

[a]11 Septuagint (see also Ruth 4:21); Hebrew *Salma*   [b]23 Or *captured the settlements of Jair*

From Generation to Generation

1 CHRONICLES 2 When we read the Bible, sometimes we feel like skipping over a chapter that just gives us a list of generations. After all, it's just a list of names. Of what significance can a list of names be?

Sometimes we've become so focused on the here and now that we forget we are "planting seeds" for the future. A marriage is much more than just a relationship for spouses. It's the soil for families—future generations—to grow in. Future generations will get their emotional, relational and, most significantly, their spiritual roots from the families they come out of. For example, some parents of the past believed they should never disagree in front of the children. But the children need to see how their parents handle their disagreements. We need to show our children how to deal with inevitable conflict by talking through the issues even at the dinner table.

What our generation believes to be important should be planted in the next gen-

eration. But divorces or relationship problems that have been passed on from past generations should be cut off and passed on no more. Statistics indicate that those who come from dysfunctional homes stand a greater chance of experiencing the same difficulties in their own homes. No one, however, should feel doomed by statistics. With God's guidance, we can go through our family's soil and "pull the weeds." We can create a more enriched soil in which to "plant" good "seeds" for the future.

It's important to have a "future generation" mind set. The things we do in our own marriages today will help set the course for the marriages of tomorrow. The commitment level of our children and grandchildren's marriages starts right here with our own marriages. What kind of marriage soil are you tilling for them?

—*Bob & Rosemary*

Go to page 428 for your next devotional reading.

bore him Ashhur the father*a* of Tekoa.

Jerahmeel Son of Hezron

25The sons of Jerahmeel the firstborn of Hezron:

Ram his firstborn, Bunah, Oren, Ozem and*b* Ahijah. 26Jerahmeel had another wife, whose name was Atarah; she was the mother of Onam.

27The sons of Ram the firstborn of Jerahmeel:

Maaz, Jamin and Eker.

28The sons of Onam:

Shammai and Jada.

The sons of Shammai:

Nadab and Abishur.

29Abishur's wife was named Abihail, who bore him Ahban and Molid.

30The sons of Nadab:

Seled and Appaim. Seled died without children.

31The son of Appaim:

Ishi, who was the father of Sheshan.

Sheshan was the father of Ahlai.

32The sons of Jada, Shammai's brother:

Jether and Jonathan. Jether died without children.

33The sons of Jonathan:

Peleth and Zaza.

These were the descendants of Jerahmeel.

34Sheshan had no sons—only daughters.

He had an Egyptian servant named Jarha. 35Sheshan gave his daughter in marriage to his servant Jarha, and she bore him Attai.

36Attai was the father of Nathan, Nathan the father of Zabad,

37Zabad the father of Ephlal, Ephlal the father of Obed,

38Obed the father of Jehu, Jehu the father of Azariah,

39Azariah the father of Helez, Helez the father of Eleasah,

40Eleasah the father of Sismai, Sismai the father of Shallum,

41Shallum the father of Jekamiah, and Jekamiah the father of Elishama.

The Clans of Caleb

42The sons of Caleb the brother of Jerahmeel:

Mesha his firstborn, who was the father of Ziph, and his son Mareshah,*c* who was the father of Hebron.

43The sons of Hebron:

Korah, Tappuah, Rekem and Shema. 44Shema was the father of Raham, and Raham the father of Jorkeam. Rekem was the father of Shammai. 45The son of Shammai was Maon, and Maon was the father of Beth Zur.

46Caleb's concubine Ephah was the mother of Haran, Moza and Gazez. Haran was the father of Gazez.

47The sons of Jahdai:

Regem, Jotham, Geshan, Pelet, Ephah and Shaaph.

48Caleb's concubine Maacah was the mother of Sheber and Tirhanah. 49She also gave birth to Shaaph the father of Madmannah and to Sheva the father of Macbenah and Gibea. Caleb's daughter was Acsah. 50These were the descendants of Caleb.

The sons of Hur the firstborn of Ephrathah:

Shobal the father of Kiriath Jearim, 51Salma the father of Bethlehem, and Hareph the father of Beth Gader.

52The descendants of Shobal the father of Kiriath Jearim were:

Haroeh, half the Manahathites, 53and the clans of Kiriath Jearim: the Ithrites, Puthites, Shumathites and Mishraites. From these descended the Zorathites and Eshtaolites.

54The descendants of Salma:

Bethlehem, the Netophathites, Atroth Beth Joab, half the Manahathites, the Zorites, 55and the clans of scribes*d* who lived at

---

*a*24 *Father* may mean *civic leader* or *military leader*; also in verses 42, 45, 49-52 and possibly elsewhere. *b*25 Or *Oren and Ozem, by*   *c*42 The meaning of the Hebrew for this phrase is uncertain. *d*55 Or *of the Sopherites*

Jabez: the Tirathites, Shimeath-
ites and Sucathites. These are the
Kenites who came from Hammath, the father of the house of
Recab.ᵃ

The Sons of David

3 These were the sons of David born to
him in Hebron:
The firstborn was Amnon the
son of Ahinoam of Jezreel;
the second, Daniel the son of
Abigail of Carmel;
²the third, Absalom the son of
Maacah daughter of Talmai king
of Geshur;
the fourth, Adonijah the son of
Haggith;
³the fifth, Shephatiah the son of
Abital;
and the sixth, Ithream, by his
wife Eglah.
⁴These six were born to David in
Hebron, where he reigned seven
years and six months.
David reigned in Jerusalem thirty-three
years, ⁵and these were the children born
to him there:
Shammua,ᵇ Shobab, Nathan
and Solomon. These four were
by Bathshebaᶜ daughter of Ammiel. ⁶There were also Ibhar, Elishua,ᵈ Eliphelet, ⁷Nogah, Nepheg, Japhia, ⁸Elishama, Eliada
and Eliphelet—nine in all. ⁹All
these were the sons of David, besides his sons by his concubines.
And Tamar was their sister.

The Kings of Judah

¹⁰Solomon's son was Rehoboam,
Abijah his son,
Asa his son,
Jehoshaphat his son,
¹¹Jehoramᵉ his son,
Ahaziah his son,
Joash his son,
¹²Amaziah his son,
Azariah his son,
Jotham his son,
¹³Ahaz his son,
Hezekiah his son,
Manasseh his son,
¹⁴Amon his son,
Josiah his son.
¹⁵The sons of Josiah:

Johanan the firstborn,
Jehoiakim the second son,
Zedekiah the third,
Shallum the fourth.
¹⁶The successors of Jehoiakim:
Jehoiachinᶠ his son,
and Zedekiah.

The Royal Line After the Exile

¹⁷The descendants of Jehoiachin the
captive:
Shealtiel his son, ¹⁸Malkiram,
Pedaiah, Shenazzar, Jekamiah,
Hoshama and Nedabiah.
¹⁹The sons of Pedaiah:
Zerubbabel and Shimei.
The sons of Zerubbabel:
Meshullam and Hananiah.
Shelomith was their sister.
²⁰There were also five others:
Hashubah, Ohel, Berekiah, Has-
adiah and Jushab-Hesed.
²¹The descendants of Hananiah:
Pelatiah and Jeshaiah, and the
sons of Rephaiah, of Arnan, of
Obadiah and of Shecaniah.
²²The descendants of Shecaniah:
Shemaiah and his sons:
Hattush, Igal, Bariah, Neariah
and Shaphat—six in all.
²³The sons of Neariah:
Elioenai, Hizkiah and Azrikam—
three in all.
²⁴The sons of Elioenai:
Hodaviah, Eliashib, Pelaiah, Akkub, Johanan, Delaiah and Ana-
ni—seven in all.

Other Clans of Judah

4 The descendants of Judah:
Perez, Hezron, Carmi, Hur and
Shobal.
²Reaiah son of Shobal was the father
of Jahath, and Jahath the father
of Ahumai and Lahad. These
were the clans of the Zorathites.
³These were the sonsᵍ of Etam:

ᵃ55 Or *father of Beth Recab*   ᵇ5 Hebrew *Shimea,*
a variant of *Shammua*   ᶜ5 One Hebrew
manuscript and Vulgate (see also Septuagint and
2 Samuel 11:3); most Hebrew manuscripts
Bathshua   ᵈ6 Two Hebrew manuscripts (see also
2 Samuel 5:15 and 1 Chron. 14:5); most Hebrew
manuscripts *Elishama*   ᵉ11 Hebrew *Joram,* a
variant of *Jehoram*   ᶠ16 Hebrew *Jeconiah,* a
variant of *Jehoiachin;* also in verse 17   ᵍ3 Some
Septuagint manuscripts (see also Vulgate); Hebrew
father

Jezreel, Ishma and Idbash. Their sister was named Hazzelelponi. ⁴Penuel was the father of Gedor, and Ezer the father of Hushah.

These were the descendants of Hur, the firstborn of Ephrathah and father*ᵃ* of Bethlehem.

⁵Ashhur the father of Tekoa had two wives, Helah and Naarah.

⁶Naarah bore him Ahuzzam, Hepher, Temeni and Haahashtari. These were the descendants of Naarah.

⁷The sons of Helah:

Zereth, Zohar, Ethnan, ⁸and Koz, who was the father of Anub and Hazzobebah and of the clans of Aharhel son of Harum.

⁹Jabez was more honorable than his brothers. His mother had named him Jabez,*ᵇ* saying, "I gave birth to him in pain." ¹⁰Jabez cried out to the God of Israel, "Oh, that you would bless me and enlarge my territory! Let your hand be with me, and keep me from harm so that I will be free from pain." And God granted his request.

¹¹Kelub, Shuhah's brother, was the father of Mehir, who was the father of Eshton. ¹²Eshton was the father of Beth Rapha, Paseah and Tehinnah the father of Ir Nahash.*ᶜ* These were the men of Recah.

¹³The sons of Kenaz:

Othniel and Seraiah.

The sons of Othniel:

Hathath and Meonothai.*ᵈ* ¹⁴Meonothai was the father of Ophrah.

Seraiah was the father of Joab,

the father of Ge Harashim.*ᵉ* It was called this because its people were craftsmen.

¹⁵The sons of Caleb son of Jephunneh:

Iru, Elah and Naam.

The son of Elah:

Kenaz.

¹⁶The sons of Jehallelel:

Ziph, Ziphah, Tiria and Asarel.

¹⁷The sons of Ezrah:

Jether, Mered, Epher and Jalon.

One of Mered's wives gave birth to Miriam, Shammai and Ishbah the father of Eshtemoa. ¹⁸(His Judean wife gave birth to Jered the father of Gedor, Heber the father of Soco, and Jekuthiel the father of Zanoah.) These were the children of Pharaoh's daughter Bithiah, whom Mered had married.

¹⁹The sons of Hodiah's wife, the sister of Naham:

the father of Keilah the Garmite, and Eshtemoa the Maacathite.

²⁰The sons of Shimon:

Amnon, Rinnah, Ben-Hanan and Tilon.

The descendants of Ishi:

Zoheth and Ben-Zoheth.

²¹The sons of Shelah son of Judah:

Er the father of Lecah, Laadah the father of Mareshah and the clans of the linen workers at Beth Ashbea, ²²Jokim, the men of Cozeba, and Joash and Saraph, who ruled in Moab and Jashubi Lehem. (These records are from ancient times.) ²³They were the potters who lived at Netaim and Gederah; they stayed there and worked for the king.

Simeon

²⁴The descendants of Simeon:

Nemuel, Jamin, Jarib, Zerah and Shaul;

²⁵Shallum was Shaul's son, Mibsam his son and Mishma his son.

²⁶The descendants of Mishma:

Hammuel his son, Zaccur his son and Shimei his son.

²⁷Shimei had sixteen sons and six daughters, but his brothers did not have many children; so their entire clan did not become as numerous as the people of Judah. ²⁸They lived in Beersheba, Moladah, Hazar Shual, ²⁹Bilhah, Ezem, Tolad, ³⁰Bethuel, Hormah, Ziklag, ³¹Beth Marcaboth, Hazar Susim, Beth Biri and Shaara-

---

ᵃ4 *Father* may mean *civic leader* or *military leader;* also in verses 12, 14, 17, 18 and possibly elsewhere.   *ᵇ9* *Jabez* sounds like the Hebrew for *pain.*   *ᶜ12* Or *of the city of Nahash*   *ᵈ13* Some Septuagint manuscripts and Vulgate; Hebrew does not have *and Meonothai.*   *ᵉ14* *Ge Harashim* means *valley of craftsmen.*

im. These were their towns until the reign of David. 32Their surrounding villages were Etam, Ain, Rimmon, Token and Ashan—five towns— 33and all the villages around these towns as far as Baalath.*a* These were their settlements. And they kept a genealogical record.

34Meshobab, Jamlech, Joshah son of Amaziah, 35Joel, Jehu son of Joshibiah, the son of Seraiah, the son of Asiel, 36also Elioenai, Jaakobah, Jeshohaiah, Asaiah, Adiel, Jesimiel, Benaiah, 37and Ziza son of Shiphi, the son of Allon, the son of Jedaiah, the son of Shimri, the son of Shemaiah.

38The men listed above by name were leaders of their clans. Their families increased greatly, 39and they went to the outskirts of Gedor to the east of the valley in search of pasture for their flocks. 40They found rich, good pasture, and the land was spacious, peaceful and quiet. Some Hamites had lived there formerly.

41The men whose names were listed came in the days of Hezekiah king of Judah. They attacked the Hamites in their dwellings and also the Meunites who were there and completely destroyed*b* them, as is evident to this day. Then they settled in their place, because there was pasture for their flocks. 42And five hundred of these Simeonites, led by Pelatiah, Neariah, Rephaiah and Uzziel, the sons of Ishi, invaded the hill country of Seir. 43They killed the remaining Amalekites who had escaped, and they have lived there to this day.

Reuben

5 The sons of Reuben the firstborn of Israel (he was the firstborn, but when he defiled his father's marriage bed, his rights as firstborn were given to the sons of Joseph son of Israel; so he could not be listed in the genealogical record in accordance with his birthright, 2and though Judah was the strongest of his brothers and a ruler came from him, the rights of the firstborn belonged to Joseph)— 3the sons of Reuben the firstborn of Israel:

Hanoch, Pallu, Hezron and Carmi.
4The descendants of Joel:
Shemaiah his son, Gog his son,

Shimei his son, 5Micah his son, Reaiah his son, Baal his son, 6and Beerah his son, whom Tiglath-Pileser*c* king of Assyria took into exile. Beerah was a leader of the Reubenites.

7Their relatives by clans, listed according to their genealogical records:
Jeiel the chief, Zechariah, 8and Bela son of Azaz, the son of Shema, the son of Joel. They settled in the area from Aroer to Nebo and Baal Meon. 9To the east they occupied the land up to the edge of the desert that extends to the Euphrates River, because their livestock had increased in Gilead.

10During Saul's reign they waged war against the Hagrites, who were defeated at their hands; they occupied the dwellings of the Hagrites throughout the entire region east of Gilead.

Gad

11The Gadites lived next to them in Bashan, as far as Salecah:
12Joel was the chief, Shapham the second, then Janai and Shaphat, in Bashan.
13Their relatives, by families, were:
Michael, Meshullam, Sheba, Jorai, Jacan, Zia and Eber—seven in all.
14These were the sons of Abihail son of Huri, the son of Jaroah, the son of Gilead, the son of Michael, the son of Jeshishai, the son of Jahdo, the son of Buz.
15Ahi son of Abdiel, the son of Guni, was head of their family.
16The Gadites lived in Gilead, in Bashan and its outlying villages, and on all the pasturelands of Sharon as far as they extended.
17All these were entered in the genealogical records during the reigns of Jo-

a33 Some Septuagint manuscripts (see also Joshua 19:8); Hebrew *Baal*   *b41* The Hebrew term refers to the irrevocable giving over of things or persons to the LORD, often by totally destroying them.   *c6* Hebrew *Tilgath-Pilneser,* a variant of *Tiglath-Pileser;* also in verse 26 tham king of Judah and Jeroboam king of Israel.

¹⁸The Reubenites, the Gadites and the half-tribe of Manasseh had 44,760 men ready for military service—able-bodied men who could handle shield and sword, who could use a bow, and who were trained for battle. ¹⁹They waged war against the Hagrites, Jetur, Naphish and Nodab. ²⁰They were helped in fighting them, and God handed the Hagrites and all their allies over to them, because they cried out to him during the battle. He answered their prayers, because they trusted in him. ²¹They seized the livestock of the Hagrites—fifty thousand camels, two hundred fifty thousand sheep and two thousand donkeys. They also took one hundred thousand people captive, ²²and many others fell slain, because the battle was God's. And they occupied the land until the exile.

The Half-Tribe of Manasseh

²³The people of the half-tribe of Manasseh were numerous; they settled in the land from Bashan to Baal Hermon, that is, to Senir (Mount Hermon). ²⁴These were the heads of their families: Epher, Ishi, Eliel, Azriel, Jeremiah, Hodaviah and Jahdiel. They were brave warriors, famous men, and heads of their families. ²⁵But they were unfaithful to the God of their fathers and prostituted themselves to the gods of the peoples of the land, whom God had destroyed before them. ²⁶So the God of Israel stirred up the spirit of Pul king of Assyria (that is, Tiglath-Pileser king of Assyria), who took the Reubenites, the Gadites and the half-tribe of Manasseh into exile. He took them to Halah, Habor, Hara and the river of Gozan, where they are to this day.

Levi

6 The sons of Levi:
Gershon, Kohath and Merari.
²The sons of Kohath:
Amram, Izhar, Hebron and Uzziel.
³The children of Amram:
Aaron, Moses and Miriam.
The sons of Aaron:
Nadab, Abihu, Eleazar and Ithamar.

⁴Eleazar was the father of Phinehas,
Phinehas the father of Abishua,
⁵Abishua the father of Bukki,
Bukki the father of Uzzi,
⁶Uzzi the father of Zerahiah,
Zerahiah the father of Meraioth,
⁷Meraioth the father of Amariah,
Amariah the father of Ahitub,
⁸Ahitub the father of Zadok,
Zadok the father of Ahimaaz,
⁹Ahimaaz the father of Azariah,
Azariah the father of Johanan,
¹⁰Johanan the father of Azariah (it was he who served as priest in the temple Solomon built in Jerusalem),
¹¹Azariah the father of Amariah,
Amariah the father of Ahitub,
¹²Ahitub the father of Zadok,
Zadok the father of Shallum,
¹³Shallum the father of Hilkiah,
Hilkiah the father of Azariah,
¹⁴Azariah the father of Seraiah,
and Seraiah the father of Jehozadak.

¹⁵Jehozadak was deported when the LORD sent Judah and Jerusalem into exile by the hand of Nebuchadnezzar.

¹⁶The sons of Levi:
Gershon,ᵃ Kohath and Merari.
¹⁷These are the names of the sons of Gershon:
Libni and Shimei.
¹⁸The sons of Kohath:
Amram, Izhar, Hebron and Uzziel.
¹⁹The sons of Merari:
Mahli and Mushi.
These are the clans of the Levites listed according to their fathers:
²⁰Of Gershon:
Libni his son, Jehath his son,
Zimmah his son, ²¹Joah his son,
Iddo his son, Zerah his son
and Jeatherai his son.
²²The descendants of Kohath:
Amminadab his son, Korah his son,
Assir his son, ²³Elkanah his son,
Ebiasaph his son, Assir his son,
²⁴Tahath his son, Uriel his son,

ᵃ16 Hebrew *Gershom*, a variant of *Gershon*; also in verses 17, 20, 43, 62 and 71

Uzziah his son and Shaul his son.

25The descendants of Elkanah:
Amasai, Ahimoth,
26Elkanah his son,[a] Zophai his son,
Nahath his son, 27Eliab his son,
Jeroham his son, Elkanah his son
and Samuel his son.[b]
28The sons of Samuel:
Joel[c] the firstborn
and Abijah the second son.
29The descendants of Merari:
Mahli, Libni his son,
Shimei his son, Uzzah his son,
30Shimea his son, Haggiah his son
and Asaiah his son.

The Temple Musicians

31These are the men David put in charge of the music in the house of the LORD after the ark came to rest there. 32They ministered with music before the tabernacle, the Tent of Meeting, until Solomon built the temple of the LORD in Jerusalem. They performed their duties according to the regulations laid down for them.

33Here are the men who served, together with their sons:

From the Kohathites:
Heman, the musician,
the son of Joel, the son of Samuel,
34the son of Elkanah, the son of Jeroham,
the son of Eliel, the son of Toah,
35the son of Zuph, the son of Elkanah,
the son of Mahath, the son of Amasai,
36the son of Elkanah, the son of Joel,
the son of Azariah, the son of Zephaniah,
37the son of Tahath, the son of Assir,
the son of Ebiasaph, the son of Korah,
38the son of Izhar, the son of Kohath,
the son of Levi, the son of Israel;
39and Heman's associate Asaph, who served at his right hand:

Asaph son of Berekiah, the son of Shimea,
40the son of Michael, the son of Baaseiah,[d]
the son of Malkijah, 41the son of Ethni,
the son of Zerah, the son of Adaiah,
42the son of Ethan, the son of Zimmah,
the son of Shimei, 43the son of Jahath,
the son of Gershon, the son of Levi;
44and from their associates, the Merarites, at his left hand:
Ethan son of Kishi, the son of Abdi,
the son of Malluch, 45the son of Hashabiah,
the son of Amaziah, the son of Hilkiah,
46the son of Amzi, the son of Bani,
the son of Shemer, 47the son of Mahli,
the son of Mushi, the son of Merari,
the son of Levi.

48Their fellow Levites were assigned to all the other duties of the tabernacle, the house of God. 49But Aaron and his descendants were the ones who presented offerings on the altar of burnt offering and on the altar of incense in connection with all that was done in the Most Holy Place, making atonement for Israel, in accordance with all that Moses the servant of God had commanded.

50These were the descendants of Aaron:
Eleazar his son, Phinehas his son,
Abishua his son, 51Bukki his son,
Uzzi his son, Zerahiah his son,

a26 Some Hebrew manuscripts, Septuagint and Syriac; most Hebrew manuscripts Ahimoth 26and Elkanah. The sons of Elkanah: b27 Some Septuagint manuscripts (see also 1 Samuel 1:19,20 and 1 Chron. 6:33,34); Hebrew does not have and Samuel his son. c28 Some Septuagint manuscripts and Syriac (see also 1 Samuel 8:2 and 1 Chron. 6:33); Hebrew does not have Joel. d40 Most Hebrew manuscripts; some Hebrew manuscripts, one Septuagint manuscript and Syriac Maaseiah

⁵²Meraioth his son, Amariah his son,

Ahitub his son, ⁵³Zadok his son and Ahimaaz his son.

⁵⁴These were the locations of their settlements allotted as their territory (they were assigned to the descendants of Aaron who were from the Kohathite clan, because the first lot was for them): ⁵⁵They were given Hebron in Judah with its surrounding pasturelands. ⁵⁶But the fields and villages around the city were given to Caleb son of Jephunneh. ⁵⁷So the descendants of Aaron were given Hebron (a city of refuge), and Libnah,ᵃ Jattir, Eshtemoa, ⁵⁸Hilen, Debir, ⁵⁹Ashan, Juttahᵇ and Beth Shemesh, together with their pasturelands. ⁶⁰And from the tribe of Benjamin they were given Gibeon,ᶜ Geba, Alemeth and Anathoth, together with their pasturelands.

These towns, which were distributed among the Kohathite clans, were thirteen in all.

⁶¹The rest of Kohath's descendants were allotted ten towns from the clans of half the tribe of Manasseh.

⁶²The descendants of Gershon, clan by clan, were allotted thirteen towns from the tribes of Issachar, Asher and Naphtali, and from the part of the tribe of Manasseh that is in Bashan.

⁶³The descendants of Merari, clan by clan, were allotted twelve towns from the tribes of Reuben, Gad and Zebulun.

⁶⁴So the Israelites gave the Levites these towns and their pasturelands. ⁶⁵From the tribes of Judah, Simeon and Benjamin they allotted the previously named towns.

⁶⁶Some of the Kohathite clans were given as their territory towns from the tribe of Ephraim.

⁶⁷In the hill country of Ephraim they were given Shechem (a city of refuge), and Gezer,ᵈ ⁶⁸Jokmeam, Beth Horon, ⁶⁹Aijalon and Gath Rimmon, together with their pasturelands.

⁷⁰And from half the tribe of Manasseh the Israelites gave Aner and Bileam, together with their pasture-

lands, to the rest of the Kohathite clans.

⁷¹The Gershonites received the following:

From the clan of the half-tribe of Manasseh
they received Golan in Bashan and also Ashtaroth, together with their pasturelands;

⁷²from the tribe of Issachar
they received Kedesh, Daberath, ⁷³Ramoth and Anem, together with their pasturelands;

⁷⁴from the tribe of Asher
they received Mashal, Abdon, ⁷⁵Hukok and Rehob, together with their pasturelands;

⁷⁶and from the tribe of Naphtali
they received Kedesh in Galilee, Hammon and Kiriathaim, together with their pasturelands.

⁷⁷The Merarites (the rest of the Levites) received the following:

From the tribe of Zebulun
they received Jokneam, Kartah,ᵉ Rimmono and Tabor, together with their pasturelands;

⁷⁸from the tribe of Reuben across the Jordan east of Jericho
they received Bezer in the desert, Jahzah, ⁷⁹Kedemoth and Mephaath, together with their pasturelands;

⁸⁰and from the tribe of Gad
they received Ramoth in Gilead, Mahanaim, ⁸¹Heshbon and Jazer, together with their pasturelands.

Issachar

7 The sons of Issachar:
Tola, Puah, Jashub and Shimron—four in all.

²The sons of Tola:
Uzzi, Rephaiah, Jeriel, Jahmai, Ibsam and Samuel—heads of their families. During the reign

ᵃ57 See Joshua 21:13; Hebrew *given the cities of refuge: Hebron, Libnah.* ᵇ59 Syriac (see also Septuagint and Joshua 21:16); Hebrew does not have *Juttah.* ᶜ60 See Joshua 21:17; Hebrew does not have *Gibeon.* ᵈ67 See Joshua 21:21; Hebrew *given the cities of refuge: Shechem, Gezer.* ᵉ77 See Septuagint and Joshua 21:34; Hebrew does not have *Jokneam, Kartah.*

of David, the descendants of
Tola listed as fighting men in
their genealogy numbered
22,600.
³The son of Uzzi:
Izrahiah.

The sons of Izrahiah:
Michael, Obadiah, Joel and Isshiah. All five of them were
chiefs. ⁴According to their family
genealogy, they had 36,000 men
ready for battle, for they had
many wives and children.
⁵The relatives who were fighting
men belonging to all the clans of
Issachar, as listed in their genealogy, were 87,000 in all.

Benjamin

⁶Three sons of Benjamin:
Bela, Beker and Jediael.
⁷The sons of Bela:
Ezbon, Uzzi, Uzziel, Jerimoth
and Iri, heads of families—five
in all. Their genealogical record
listed 22,034 fighting men.
⁸The sons of Beker:
Zemirah, Joash, Eliezer, Elioenai, Omri, Jeremoth, Abijah, Anathoth and Alemeth. All these
were the sons of Beker. ⁹Their
genealogical record listed the
heads of families and 20,200
fighting men.
¹⁰The son of Jediael:
Bilhan.

The sons of Bilhan:
Jeush, Benjamin, Ehud, Kenaa-
nah, Zethan, Tarshish and
Ahishahar. ¹¹All these sons of
Jediael were heads of families.
There were 17,200 fighting men
ready to go out to war.
¹²The Shuppites and Huppites were
the descendants of Ir, and the
Hushites the descendants of
Aher.

Naphtali

¹³The sons of Naphtali:
Jahziel, Guni, Jezer and Shil-
lemᵃ—the descendants of Bilhah.

Manasseh

¹⁴The descendants of Manasseh:
Asriel was his descendant
through his Aramean concubine.
She gave birth to Makir the father
of Gilead. ¹⁵Makir took a wife from
among the Huppites and Shuppites. His sister's name was Maacah.

Another descendant was named
Zelophehad, who had only daughters.
¹⁶Makir's wife Maacah gave birth
to a son and named him Peresh.
His brother was named Sheresh,
and his sons were Ulam and Ra-
kem.
¹⁷The son of Ulam:
Bedan.

These were the sons of Gilead son
of Makir, the son of Manasseh.
¹⁸His sister Hammoleketh gave
birth to Ishhod, Abiezer and
Mahlah.
¹⁹The sons of Shemida were:
Ahian, Shechem, Likhi and
Aniam.

Ephraim

²⁰The descendants of Ephraim:
Shuthelah, Bered his son,
Tahath his son, Eleadah his son,
Tahath his son, ²¹Zabad his son
and Shuthelah his son.

Ezer and Elead were killed by the
native-born men of Gath, when
they went down to seize their livestock. ²²Their father Ephraim
mourned for them many days, and
his relatives came to comfort him.
²³Then he lay with his wife again,
and she became pregnant and gave
birth to a son. He named him Beriah,ᵇ because there had been misfortune in his family. ²⁴His daughter was Sheerah, who built Lower
and Upper Beth Horon as well as
Uzzen Sheerah.

ᵃ13 Some Hebrew and Septuagint manuscripts
(see also Gen. 46:24 and Num. 26:49); most
Hebrew manuscripts *Shallum*   ᵇ23 *Beriah*
sounds like the Hebrew for *misfortune.*

25Rephah was his son, Resheph his son,[a]
Telah his son, Tahan his son,
26Ladan his son, Ammihud his son,
Elishama his son, 27Nun his son and Joshua his son.

28Their lands and settlements included Bethel and its surrounding villages, Naaran to the east, Gezer and its villages to the west, and Shechem and its villages all the way to Ayyah and its villages. 29Along the borders of Manasseh were Beth Shan, Taanach, Megiddo and Dor, together with their villages. The descendants of Joseph son of Israel lived in these towns.

Asher

30The sons of Asher:
Imnah, Ishvah, Ishvi and Beriah.
Their sister was Serah.
31The sons of Beriah:
Heber and Malkiel, who was the father of Birzaith.
32Heber was the father of Japhlet, Shomer and Hotham and of their sister Shua.
33The sons of Japhlet:
Pasach, Bimhal and Ashvath.
These were Japhlet's sons.
34The sons of Shomer:
Ahi, Rohgah,[b] Hubbah and Aram.
35The sons of his brother Helem:
Zophah, Imna, Shelesh and Amal.
36The sons of Zophah:
Suah, Harnepher, Shual, Beri, Imrah, 37Bezer, Hod, Shamma, Shilshah, Ithran[c] and Beera.
38The sons of Jether:
Jephunneh, Pispah and Ara.
39The sons of Ulla:
Arah, Hanniel and Rizia.

40All these were descendants of Asher—heads of families, choice men, brave warriors and outstanding leaders. The number of men ready for battle, as listed in their genealogy, was 26,000.

The Genealogy of Saul the Benjamite

8 Benjamin was the father of Bela his firstborn,
Ashbel the second son, Aharah the third,
2Nohah the fourth and Rapha the fifth.
3The sons of Bela were:
Addar, Gera, Abihud,[d] 4Abishua, Naaman, Ahoah, 5Gera, Shephuphan and Huram.

6These were the descendants of Ehud, who were heads of families of those living in Geba and were deported to Manahath:
7Naaman, Ahijah, and Gera, who deported them and who was the father of Uzza and Ahihud.

8Sons were born to Shaharaim in Moab after he had divorced his wives Hushim and Baara. 9By his wife Hodesh he had Jobab, Zibia, Mesha, Malcam, 10Jeuz, Sakia and Mirmah. These were his sons, heads of families. 11By Hushim he had Abitub and Elpaal.

12The sons of Elpaal:
Eber, Misham, Shemed (who built Ono and Lod with its surrounding villages), 13and Beriah and Shema, who were heads of families of those living in Aijalon and who drove out the inhabitants of Gath.

14Ahio, Shashak, Jeremoth, 15Zebadiah, Arad, Eder, 16Michael, Ishpah and Joha were the sons of Beriah.

17Zebadiah, Meshullam, Hizki, Heber, 18Ishmerai, Izliah and Jobab were the sons of Elpaal.

19Jakim, Zicri, Zabdi, 20Elienai, Zillethai, Eliel, 21Adaiah, Beraiah and Shimrath were the sons of Shimei.

22Ishpan, Eber, Eliel, 23Abdon, Zicri, Hanan, 24Hananiah, Elam, Anthothijah, 25Iphdeiah and Penuel were the sons of Shashak.

26Shamsherai, Shehariah, Athaliah, 27Jaareshiah, Elijah and Zicri were the sons of Jeroham.

28All these were heads of families, chiefs as listed in their genealogy, and they lived in Jerusalem.

---

a25 Some Septuagint manuscripts; Hebrew does not have *his son.*   b34 Or *of his brother Shomer: Rohgah*   c37 Possibly a variant of *Jether*   d3 Or *Gera the father of Ehud*

²⁹Jeiel[a] the father[b] of Gibeon lived in Gibeon.

His wife's name was Maacah, ³⁰and his firstborn son was Abdon, followed by Zur, Kish, Baal, Ner,[c] Nadab, ³¹Gedor, Ahio, Zeker ³²and Mikloth, who was the father of Shimeah. They too lived near their relatives in Jerusalem.

³³Ner was the father of Kish, Kish the father of Saul, and Saul the father of Jonathan, Malki-Shua, Abinadab and Esh-Baal.[d]

³⁴The son of Jonathan:

Merib-Baal,[e] who was the father of Micah.

³⁵The sons of Micah:

Pithon, Melech, Tarea and Ahaz.

³⁶Ahaz was the father of Jehoaddah, Jehoaddah was the father of Alemeth, Azmaveth and Zimri, and Zimri was the father of Moza. ³⁷Moza was the father of Binea; Raphah was his son, Eleasah his son and Azel his son.

³⁸Azel had six sons, and these were their names:

Azrikam, Bokeru, Ishmael, Sheariah, Obadiah and Hanan. All these were the sons of Azel.

³⁹The sons of his brother Eshek:

Ulam his firstborn, Jeush the second son and Eliphelet the third. ⁴⁰The sons of Ulam were brave warriors who could handle the bow. They had many sons and grandsons—150 in all.

All these were the descendants of Benjamin.

9 All Israel was listed in the genealogies recorded in the book of the kings of Israel.

The People in Jerusalem

The people of Judah were taken captive to Babylon because of their unfaithfulness. ²Now the first to resettle on their own property in their own towns were some Israelites, priests, Levites and temple servants.

³Those from Judah, from Benjamin, and from Ephraim and Manasseh who lived in Jerusalem were:

⁴Uthai son of Ammihud, the son of Omri, the son of Imri, the son of Bani, a descendant of Perez son of Judah.

⁵Of the Shilonites:

Asaiah the firstborn and his sons.

⁶Of the Zerahites:

Jeuel.

The people from Judah numbered 690.

⁷Of the Benjamites:

Sallu son of Meshullam, the son of Hodaviah, the son of Hassenuah;

⁸Ibneiah son of Jeroham; Elah son of Uzzi, the son of Micri; and Meshullam son of Shephatiah, the son of Reuel, the son of Ibnijah.

⁹The people from Benjamin, as listed in their genealogy, numbered 956. All these men were heads of their families.

¹⁰Of the priests:

Jedaiah; Jehoiarib; Jakin;

¹¹Azariah son of Hilkiah, the son of Meshullam, the son of Zadok, the son of Meraioth, the son of Ahitub, the official in charge of the house of God;

¹²Adaiah son of Jeroham, the son of Pashhur, the son of Malkijah; and Maasai son of Adiel, the son of Jahzerah, the son of Meshullam, the son of Meshillemith, the son of Immer.

¹³The priests, who were heads of families, numbered 1,760. They were able men, responsible for ministering in the house of God.

¹⁴Of the Levites:

Shemaiah son of Hasshub, the son of Azrikam, the son of Hashabiah, a Merarite; ¹⁵Bakbakkar, Heresh, Galal and Mattaniah son of Mica, the son of Zicri, the son of Asaph; ¹⁶Obadiah son of Shemaiah, the son of Galal, the son of Jeduthun; and Berekiah

---

a29 Some Septuagint manuscripts (see also
1 Chron. 9:35); Hebrew does not have *Jeiel.*
b29 *Father* may mean *civic leader* or *military leader.*
c30 Some Septuagint manuscripts (see also
1 Chron. 9:36); Hebrew does not have *Ner.*
d33 Also known as *Ish-Bosheth*   e34 Also
known as *Mephibosheth*

son of Asa, the son of Elkanah, who lived in the villages of the Netophathites.

17The gatekeepers:

Shallum, Akkub, Talmon, Ahiman and their brothers, Shallum their chief 18being stationed at the King's Gate on the east, up to the present time. These were the gatekeepers belonging to the camp of the Levites. 19Shallum son of Kore, the son of Ebiasaph, the son of Korah, and his fellow gatekeepers from his family (the Korahites) were responsible for guarding the thresholds of the Tent*a* just as their fathers had been responsible for guarding the entrance to the dwelling of the LORD. 20In earlier times Phinehas son of Eleazar was in charge of the gatekeepers, and the LORD was with him. 21Zechariah son of Meshelemiah was the gatekeeper at the entrance to the Tent of Meeting.

22Altogether, those chosen to be gatekeepers at the thresholds numbered 212. They were registered by genealogy in their villages. The gatekeepers had been assigned to their positions of trust by David and Samuel the seer. 23They and their descendants were in charge of guarding the gates of the house of the LORD—the house called the Tent. 24The gatekeepers were on the four sides: east, west, north and south. 25Their brothers in their villages had to come from time to time and share their duties for seven-day periods. 26But the four principal gatekeepers, who were Levites, were entrusted with the responsibility for the rooms and treasuries in the house of God. 27They would spend the night stationed around the house of God, because they had to guard it; and they had charge of the key for opening it each morning.

28Some of them were in charge of the articles used in the temple service; they counted them when they were brought in and when they were taken out. 29Others were assigned to take care of the furnishings and all the other articles of the sanctuary, as well as the flour and wine, and the oil, incense and spices. 30But some of the priests took care of mixing the spices.

31A Levite named Mattithiah, the firstborn son of Shallum the Korahite, was entrusted with the responsibility for baking the offering bread. 32Some of their Kohathite brothers were in charge of preparing for every Sabbath the bread set out on the table.

33Those who were musicians, heads of Levite families, stayed in the rooms of the temple and were exempt from other duties because they were responsible for the work day and night.

34All these were heads of Levite families, chiefs as listed in their genealogy, and they lived in Jerusalem.

The Genealogy of Saul

35Jeiel the father*b* of Gibeon lived in Gibeon.

His wife's name was Maacah, 36and his firstborn son was Abdon, followed by Zur, Kish, Baal, Ner, Nadab, 37Gedor, Ahio, Zechariah and Mikloth. 38Mikloth was the father of Shimeam. They too lived near their relatives in Jerusalem.

39Ner was the father of Kish, Kish the father of Saul, and Saul the father of Jonathan, Malki-Shua, Abinadab and Esh-Baal.*c*

40The son of Jonathan:

Merib-Baal,*d* who was the father of Micah.

41The sons of Micah:

Pithon, Melech, Tahrea and Ahaz.*e*

42Ahaz was the father of Jadah, Jadah*f* was the father of Alemeth, Azmaveth and Zimri, and Zimri was the father of Moza. 43Moza was the father of Binea; Rephaiah was his son, Eleasah his son and Azel his son.

44Azel had six sons, and these were their names:

Azrikam, Bokeru, Ishmael, Shea-

---

*a19 That is, the temple; also in verses 21 and 23
*b35 Father may mean civic leader or military leader.
*c39 Also known as Ish-Bosheth   *d40 Also known as Mephibosheth   *e41 Vulgate and Syriac (see also Septuagint and 1 Chron. 8:35); Hebrew does not have and Ahaz.   *f42 Some Hebrew manuscripts and Septuagint (see also 1 Chron. 8:36); most Hebrew manuscripts Jarah, Jarah

riah, Obadiah and Hanan. These were the sons of Azel.

Saul Takes His Life

10 Now the Philistines fought against Israel; the Israelites fled before them, and many fell slain on Mount Gilboa. ²The Philistines pressed hard after Saul and his sons, and they killed his sons Jonathan, Abinadab and Malki-Shua. ³The fighting grew fierce around Saul, and when the archers overtook him, they wounded him.

⁴Saul said to his armor-bearer, "Draw your sword and run me through, or these uncircumcised fellows will come and abuse me."

But his armor-bearer was terrified and would not do it; so Saul took his own sword and fell on it. ⁵When the armor-bearer saw that Saul was dead, he too fell on his sword and died. ⁶So Saul and his three sons died, and all his house died together.

⁷When all the Israelites in the valley saw that the army had fled and that Saul and his sons had died, they abandoned their towns and fled. And the Philistines came and occupied them.

⁸The next day, when the Philistines came to strip the dead, they found Saul and his sons fallen on Mount Gilboa. ⁹They stripped him and took his head and his armor, and sent messengers throughout the land of the Philistines to proclaim the news among their idols and their people. ¹⁰They put his armor in the temple of their gods and hung up his head in the temple of Dagon.

¹¹When all the inhabitants of Jabesh Gilead heard of everything the Philistines had done to Saul, ¹²all their valiant men went and took the bodies of Saul and his sons and brought them to Jabesh. Then they buried their bones under the great tree in Jabesh, and they fasted seven days.

¹³Saul died because he was unfaithful to the LORD; he did not keep the word of the LORD and even consulted a medium

Family Gatekeepers

Thursday

1 CHRONICLES 9:23-24 Gatekeepers had the job of guarding the temple doors. One of their tasks was to watch everything that went into the temple. A gatekeeper was stationed at each of the four gates. What happened if the gatekeepers disagreed with each other? What if an eastern gatekeeper thought a western gatekeeper was wrong for letting something or someone come into the temple? Certainly they would have had to discuss their differences of opinion or take their differences to a higher authority.

The marriage partnership is the "gatekeeper" for today's family. Many inappropriate things attempt to enter and pollute our homes. Television programs, videos and other worldly materials find easy access into the hearts and minds of today's families. For example, there have been times when one of us thinks a particular television program is too violent but the other disagrees. As perceptive as they are, the children learn who is the more lenient "gatekeeper."

The temple gatekeeper's role was to see to it that everything entering the temple glorified God. He never opened the doors and walked away, leaving them unguarded. Yet today some families provide very little watchfulness over what enters in. The door to many families has been flung open so wide that ungodly things walk right in. The role of the husband and wife includes looking at everything that is "knocking" at their door and evaluating whether it glorifies God.

Certainly when it comes to acceptable forms of entertainment, there will be times when one spouse will disagree with the other. In our own home, we ask ourselves important questions before deciding what we allow. When we just can't seem to agree, we need to remember to ask, "Will this glorify God?"

—*Bob & Rosemary*

Go to page 434 for your next devotional reading.

for guidance, ¹⁴and did not inquire of the LORD. So the LORD put him to death and turned the kingdom over to David son of Jesse.

David Becomes King Over Israel

11 All Israel came together to David at Hebron and said, "We are your own flesh and blood. ²In the past, even while Saul was king, you were the one who led Israel on their military campaigns. And the LORD your God said to you, 'You will shepherd my people Israel, and you will become their ruler.' "

³When all the elders of Israel had come to King David at Hebron, he made a compact with them at Hebron before the LORD, and they anointed David king over Israel, as the LORD had promised through Samuel.

David Conquers Jerusalem

⁴David and all the Israelites marched to Jerusalem (that is, Jebus). The Jebusites who lived there ⁵said to David, "You will not get in here." Nevertheless, David captured the fortress of Zion, the City of David.

⁶David had said, "Whoever leads the attack on the Jebusites will become commander-in-chief." Joab son of Zeruiah went up first, and so he received the command.

⁷David then took up residence in the fortress, and so it was called the City of David. ⁸He built up the city around it, from the supporting terraces*a* to the surrounding wall, while Joab restored the rest of the city. ⁹And David became more and more powerful, because the LORD Almighty was with him.

David's Mighty Men

¹⁰These were the chiefs of David's mighty men—they, together with all Israel, gave his kingship strong support to extend it over the whole land, as the LORD had promised— ¹¹this is the list of David's mighty men:

Jashobeam,*b* a Hacmonite, was chief of the officers*c*; he raised his spear against three hundred men, whom he killed in one encounter.

¹²Next to him was Eleazar son of Dodai the Ahohite, one of the three mighty men.

¹³He was with David at Pas Dammim when the Philistines gathered there for battle. At a place where there was a field full of barley, the troops fled from the Philistines. ¹⁴But they took their stand in the middle of the field. They defended it and struck the Philistines down, and the LORD brought about a great victory.

¹⁵Three of the thirty chiefs came down to David to the rock at the cave of Adullam, while a band of Philistines was encamped in the Valley of Rephaim. ¹⁶At that time David was in the stronghold, and the Philistine garrison was at Bethlehem. ¹⁷David longed for water and said, "Oh, that someone would get me a drink of water from the well near the gate of Bethlehem!" ¹⁸So the Three broke through the Philistine lines, drew water from the well near the gate of Bethlehem and carried it back to David. But he refused to drink it; instead, he poured it out before the LORD. ¹⁹"God forbid that I should do this!" he said. "Should I drink the blood of these men who went at the risk of their lives?" Because they risked their lives to bring it back, David would not drink it.

Such were the exploits of the three mighty men.

²⁰Abishai the brother of Joab was chief

---

a8 Or *the Millo*   *b11* Possibly a variant of *Jashob-Baal*   *c11* Or *Thirty*; some Septuagint manuscripts *Three* (see also 2 Samuel 23:8) of the Three. He raised his spear against three hundred men, whom he killed, and so he became as famous as the Three. ²¹He was doubly honored above the Three and became their commander, even though he was not included among them.

²²Benaiah son of Jehoiada was a valiant fighter from Kabzeel, who performed great exploits. He struck down two of Moab's best men. He also went down into a pit on a snowy day and killed a lion. ²³And he struck down an Egyptian who was seven and a half feet*a* tall. Although the Egyptian had a spear like a weaver's rod in his hand, Benaiah went against him with a club. He snatched the spear from the Egyptian's hand and killed him with his own spear. ²⁴Such were the exploits of Benaiah son of Jehoiada; he too was as famous as the three mighty men. ²⁵He was held in greater honor than any of the Thirty, but he was not included among the Three. And David put him in charge of his bodyguard.

²⁶The mighty men were:
Asahel the brother of Joab,
Elhanan son of Dodo from Bethlehem,
²⁷Shammoth the Harorite,
Helez the Pelonite,
²⁸Ira son of Ikkesh from Tekoa,
Abiezer from Anathoth,
²⁹Sibbecai the Hushathite,
Ilai the Ahohite,
³⁰Maharai the Netophathite,
Heled son of Baanah the Netophathite,
³¹Ithai son of Ribai from Gibeah in Benjamin,
Benaiah the Pirathonite,
³²Hurai from the ravines of Gaash,
Abiel the Arbathite,
³³Azmaveth the Baharumite,
Eliahba the Shaalbonite,
³⁴the sons of Hashem the Gizonite,
Jonathan son of Shagee the Hararite,
³⁵Ahiam son of Sacar the Hararite,
Eliphal son of Ur,
³⁶Hepher the Mekerathite,
Ahijah the Pelonite,
³⁷Hezro the Carmelite,
Naarai son of Ezbai,
³⁸Joel the brother of Nathan,

Mibhar son of Hagri,
³⁹Zelek the Ammonite,
Naharai the Berothite, the armor-bearer of Joab son of Zeruiah,
⁴⁰Ira the Ithrite,
Gareb the Ithrite,
⁴¹Uriah the Hittite,
Zabad son of Ahlai,
⁴²Adina son of Shiza the Reubenite, who was chief of the Reubenites, and the thirty with him,
⁴³Hanan son of Maacah,
Joshaphat the Mithnite,
⁴⁴Uzzia the Ashterathite,
Shama and Jeiel the sons of Hotham the Aroerite,
⁴⁵Jediael son of Shimri,
his brother Joha the Tizite,
⁴⁶Eliel the Mahavite,
Jeribai and Joshaviah the sons of Elnaam,
Ithmah the Moabite,
⁴⁷Eliel, Obed and Jaasiel the Mezobaite.

Warriors Join David

12 These were the men who came to David at Ziklag, while he was banished from the presence of Saul son of Kish (they were among the warriors who helped him in battle; ²they were armed with bows and were able to shoot arrows or to sling stones right-handed or left-handed; they were kinsmen of Saul from the tribe of Benjamin):

³Ahiezer their chief and Joash the sons of Shemaah the Gibeathite; Jeziel and Pelet the sons of Azmaveth; Beracah, Jehu the Anathothite, ⁴and Ishmaiah the Gibeonite, a mighty man among the Thirty, who was a leader of the Thirty; Jeremiah, Jahaziel, Johanan, Jozabad the Gederathite, ⁵Eluzai, Jerimoth, Bealiah, Shemariah and Shephatiah the Haruphite; ⁶Elkanah, Isshiah, Azarel, Joezer and Jashobeam the Korahites; ⁷and Joelah and Zebadiah the sons of Jeroham from Gedor.

⁸Some Gadites defected to David at his stronghold in the desert. They were brave warriors, ready for battle and able to han-

a23 Hebrew *five cubits* (about 2.3 meters)

dle the shield and spear. Their faces were the faces of lions, and they were as swift as gazelles in the mountains.

⁹Ezer was the chief,
   Obadiah the second in command,
      Eliab the third,
¹⁰Mishmannah the fourth, Jeremiah the fifth,
¹¹Attai the sixth, Eliel the seventh,
¹²Johanan the eighth, Elzabad the ninth,
¹³Jeremiah the tenth and Macbannai the eleventh.

¹⁴These Gadites were army commanders; the least was a match for a hundred, and the greatest for a thousand. ¹⁵It was they who crossed the Jordan in the first month when it was overflowing all its banks, and they put to flight everyone living in the valleys, to the east and to the west.

¹⁶Other Benjamites and some men from Judah also came to David in his stronghold. ¹⁷David went out to meet them and said to them, "If you have come to me in peace, to help me, I am ready to have you unite with me. But if you have come to betray me to my enemies when my hands are free from violence, may the God of our fathers see it and judge you."

¹⁸Then the Spirit came upon Amasai, chief of the Thirty, and he said:

   "We are yours, O David!
      We are with you, O son of Jesse!
   Success, success to you,
      and success to those who help you,
         for your God will help you."

So David received them and made them leaders of his raiding bands.

¹⁹Some of the men of Manasseh defected to David when he went with the Philistines to fight against Saul. (He and his men did not help the Philistines because, after consultation, their rulers sent him away. They said, "It will cost us our heads if he deserts to his master Saul.") ²⁰When David went to Ziklag, these were the men of Manasseh who defected to him: Adnah, Jozabad, Jediael, Michael, Jozabad, Elihu and Zillethai, leaders of units of a thousand in Manasseh. ²¹They helped David against raiding bands, for all of them were brave warriors, and they were commanders in his army. ²²Day after day men came to help David, until he had a great army, like the army of God.ᵃ

Others Join David at Hebron

²³These are the numbers of the men armed for battle who came to David at Hebron to turn Saul's kingdom over to him, as the LORD had said:

²⁴men of Judah, carrying shield and spear—6,800 armed for battle;

²⁵men of Simeon, warriors ready for battle—7,100;

²⁶men of Levi—4,600, ²⁷including Jehoiada, leader of the family of Aaron, with 3,700 men, ²⁸and Zadok, a brave young warrior, with 22 officers from his family;

²⁹men of Benjamin, Saul's kinsmen—3,000, most of whom had remained loyal to Saul's house until then;

³⁰men of Ephraim, brave warriors, famous in their own clans—20,800;

³¹men of half the tribe of Manasseh, designated by name to come and make David king—18,000;

³²men of Issachar, who understood the times and knew what Israel should do—200 chiefs, with all their relatives under their command;

³³men of Zebulun, experienced soldiers prepared for battle with every type of weapon, to help David with undivided loyalty—50,000;

³⁴men of Naphtali—1,000 officers, together with 37,000 men carrying shields and spears;

³⁵men of Dan, ready for battle—28,600;

³⁶men of Asher, experienced soldiers prepared for battle—40,000;

³⁷and from east of the Jordan, men of Reuben, Gad and the half-tribe of Manasseh, armed with every type of weapon—120,000.

³⁸All these were fighting men who volunteered to serve in the ranks. They came to Hebron fully determined to make David king over all Israel. All the rest of the Israelites were also of one mind to make David king. ³⁹The men spent three days

ᵃ22 Or *a great and mighty army*

there with David, eating and drinking, for their families had supplied provisions for them. ⁴⁰Also, their neighbors from as far away as Issachar, Zebulun and Naphtali came bringing food on donkeys, camels, mules and oxen. There were plentiful supplies of flour, fig cakes, raisin cakes, wine, oil, cattle and sheep, for there was joy in Israel.

Bringing Back the Ark

13 David conferred with each of his officers, the commanders of thousands and commanders of hundreds. ²He then said to the whole assembly of Israel, "If it seems good to you and if it is the will of the LORD our God, let us send word far and wide to the rest of our brothers throughout the territories of Israel, and also to the priests and Levites who are with them in their towns and pasturelands, to come and join us. ³Let us bring the ark of our God back to us, for we did not inquire of ᵃ it ᵇ during the reign of Saul." ⁴The whole assembly agreed to do this, because it seemed right to all the people.

⁵So David assembled all the Israelites, from the Shihor River in Egypt to Lebo ᶜ Hamath, to bring the ark of God from Kiriath Jearim. ⁶David and all the Israelites with him went to Baalah of Judah (Kiriath Jearim) to bring up from there the ark of God the LORD, who is enthroned between the cherubim—the ark that is called by the Name.

⁷They moved the ark of God from Abinadab's house on a new cart, with Uzzah and Ahio guiding it. ⁸David and all the Israelites were celebrating with all their might before God, with songs and with harps, lyres, tambourines, cymbals and trumpets.

⁹When they came to the threshing floor of Kidon, Uzzah reached out his hand to steady the ark, because the oxen stumbled. ¹⁰The LORD's anger burned against Uzzah, and he struck him down because he had put his hand on the ark. So he died there before God.

¹¹Then David was angry because the LORD's wrath had broken out against Uzzah, and to this day that place is called Perez Uzzah. ᵈ

¹²David was afraid of God that day and asked, "How can I ever bring the ark of God to me?" ¹³He did not take the ark to be with him in the City of David. Instead, he took it aside to the house of Obed-Edom the Gittite. ¹⁴The ark of God remained with the family of Obed-Edom in his house for three months, and the LORD blessed his household and everything he had.

David's House and Family

14 Now Hiram king of Tyre sent messengers to David, along with cedar logs, stonemasons and carpenters to build a palace for him. ²And David knew that the LORD had established him as king over Israel and that his kingdom had been highly exalted for the sake of his people Israel.

³In Jerusalem David took more wives and became the father of more sons and daughters. ⁴These are the names of the children born to him there: Shammua, Shobab, Nathan, Solomon, ⁵Ibhar, Elishua, Elpelet, ⁶Nogah, Nepheg, Japhia, ⁷Elishama, Beeliada ᵉ and Eliphelet.

David Defeats the Philistines

⁸When the Philistines heard that David had been anointed king over all Israel, they went up in full force to search for him, but David heard about it and went out to meet them. ⁹Now the Philistines had come and raided the Valley of Rephaim; ¹⁰so David inquired of God: "Shall I go and attack the Philistines? Will you hand them over to me?"

The LORD answered him, "Go, I will hand them over to you."

¹¹So David and his men went up to Baal Perazim, and there he defeated them. He said, "As waters break out, God has broken out against my enemies by my hand." So that place was called Baal Perazim. ᶠ ¹²The Philistines had abandoned their gods there, and David gave orders to burn them in the fire.

¹³Once more the Philistines raided the valley; ¹⁴so David inquired of God again, and God answered him, "Do not go straight up, but circle around them and

---

ᵃ3 Or we neglected   ᵇ3 Or him   ᶜ5 Or to the entrance to   ᵈ11 Perez Uzzah means outbreak against Uzzah.   ᵉ7 A variant of Eliada   ᶠ11 Baal Perazim means the lord who breaks out.

attack them in front of the balsam trees. [15]As soon as you hear the sound of marching in the tops of the balsam trees, move out to battle, because that will mean God has gone out in front of you to strike the Philistine army." [16]So David did as God commanded him, and they struck down the Philistine army, all the way from Gibeon to Gezer.

[17]So David's fame spread throughout every land, and the LORD made all the nations fear him.

The Ark Brought to Jerusalem

15 After David had constructed buildings for himself in the City of David, he prepared a place for the ark of God and pitched a tent for it. [2]Then David said, "No one but the Levites may carry the ark of God, because the LORD chose them to carry the ark of the LORD and to minister before him forever."

[3]David assembled all Israel in Jerusalem to bring up the ark of the LORD to the place he had prepared for it. [4]He called together the descendants of Aaron and the Levites:

[5]From the descendants of Kohath,
Uriel the leader and 120 relatives;

[6]from the descendants of Merari,
Asaiah the leader and 220 relatives;

[7]from the descendants of Gershon,[a]
Joel the leader and 130 relatives;

[8]from the descendants of Elizaphan,
Shemaiah the leader and 200 relatives;

[9]from the descendants of Hebron,
Eliel the leader and 80 relatives;

[10]from the descendants of Uzziel,
Amminadab the leader and 112 relatives.

[11]Then David summoned Zadok and Abiathar the priests, and Uriel, Asaiah, Joel, Shemaiah, Eliel and Amminadab the Levites. [12]He said to them, "You are the heads of the Levitical families; you and your fellow Levites are to consecrate yourselves and bring up the ark of the LORD, the God of Israel, to the place I have prepared for it. [13]It was because you, the Levites, did not bring it up the first time that the LORD our God broke out in anger

against us. We did not inquire of him about how to do it in the prescribed way." [14]So the priests and Levites consecrated themselves in order to bring up the ark of the LORD, the God of Israel. [15]And the Levites carried the ark of God with the poles on their shoulders, as Moses had commanded in accordance with the word of the LORD.

[16]David told the leaders of the Levites to appoint their brothers as singers to sing joyful songs, accompanied by musical instruments: lyres, harps and cymbals.

[17]So the Levites appointed Heman son of Joel; from his brothers, Asaph son of Berekiah; and from their brothers the Merarites, Ethan son of Kushaiah; [18]and with them their brothers next in rank: Zechariah,[b] Jaaziel, Shemiramoth, Jehiel, Unni, Eliab, Benaiah, Maaseiah, Mattithiah, Eliphelehu, Mikneiah, Obed-Edom and Jeiel,[c] the gatekeepers.

[19]The musicians Heman, Asaph and Ethan were to sound the bronze cymbals; [20]Zechariah, Aziel, Shemiramoth, Jehiel, Unni, Eliab, Maaseiah and Benaiah were to play the lyres according to *alamoth*,[d] [21]and Mattithiah, Eliphelehu, Mikneiah, Obed-Edom, Jeiel and Azaziah were to play the harps, directing according to *sheminith*.[d] [22]Kenaniah the head Levite was in charge of the singing; that was his responsibility because he was skillful at it.

[23]Berekiah and Elkanah were to be doorkeepers for the ark. [24]Shebaniah, Joshaphat, Nethanel, Amasai, Zechariah, Benaiah and Eliezer the priests were to blow trumpets before the ark of God. Obed-Edom and Jehiah were also to be doorkeepers for the ark.

[25]So David and the elders of Israel and the commanders of units of a thousand went to bring up the ark of the covenant of the LORD from the house of Obed-Edom, with rejoicing. [26]Because God had helped the Levites who were carrying the ark of the covenant of the LORD, seven bulls and seven rams were sacrificed.

---

a7 Hebrew *Gershom,* a variant of *Gershon*
b18 Three Hebrew manuscripts and most Septuagint manuscripts (see also verse 20 and 1 Chron. 16:5); most Hebrew manuscripts *Zechariah son and* or *Zechariah, Ben and*
c18 Hebrew; Septuagint (see also verse 21) *Jeiel and Azaziah*   *d20,21* Probably a musical term

²⁷Now David was clothed in a robe of fine linen, as were all the Levites who were carrying the ark, and as were the singers, and Kenaniah, who was in charge of the singing of the choirs. David also wore a linen ephod. ²⁸So all Israel brought up the ark of the covenant of the LORD with shouts, with the sounding of rams' horns and trumpets, and of cymbals, and the playing of lyres and harps.

²⁹As the ark of the covenant of the LORD was entering the City of David, Michal daughter of Saul watched from a window. And when she saw King David dancing and celebrating, she despised him in her heart.

16 They brought the ark of God and set it inside the tent that David had pitched for it, and they presented burnt offerings and fellowship offerings*ᵃ* before God. ²After David had finished sacrificing the burnt offerings and fellowship offerings, he blessed the people in the name of the LORD. ³Then he gave a loaf of bread, a cake of dates and a cake of raisins to each Israelite man and woman.

⁴He appointed some of the Levites to minister before the ark of the LORD, to make petition, to give thanks, and to praise the LORD, the God of Israel: ⁵Asaph was the chief, Zechariah second, then Jeiel, Shemiramoth, Jehiel, Mattithiah, Eliab, Benaiah, Obed-Edom and Jeiel. They were to play the lyres and harps, Asaph was to sound the cymbals, ⁶and Benaiah and Jahaziel the priests were to blow the trumpets regularly before the ark of the covenant of God.

David's Psalm of Thanks

⁷That day David first committed to Asaph and his associates this psalm of thanks to the LORD:

⁸Give thanks to the LORD, call on his name;
    make known among the nations
        what he has done.
⁹Sing to him, sing praise to him;
    tell of all his wonderful acts.
¹⁰Glory in his holy name;
    let the hearts of those who seek the
        LORD rejoice.
¹¹Look to the LORD and his strength;
    seek his face always.
¹²Remember the wonders he has done,
    his miracles, and the judgments he
        pronounced,
¹³O descendants of Israel his servant,
    O sons of Jacob, his chosen ones.

¹⁴He is the LORD our God;
    his judgments are in all the earth.

ᵃ1 Traditionally *peace offerings*; also in verse 2

In His Strength

Friday

1 CHRONICLES 16:11–12 Ted and Jan had been trying to get out of debt for years. Just as they were making real progress, their car died. Discouraged and broke, as hard as it was, they needed to keep looking to the Lord and rely on his strength.

It's easy for us to let our mind dwell on the negatives, like the time I (Dave) didn't get the raise. Or the time I forgot Claudia's birthday. Or when one of our sons brought home all Cs and Ds because he didn't apply himself.

Dwelling on past failures and disappointments steals our peace and joy, but we can learn from our failures. Scripture tells us again and again to look to the Lord for strength and to remember his wonders and miracles. Considering what God has done for me and Claudia in the past gives us courage to face the future—even when we fail.

Think about how God has given you strength in the midst of difficulties—both large and small—like the rainbow you saw on the way home from work, the surprise check you received in the mail, the Bible verse that was just what you needed, or the dinner your neighbor brought over after you two came home with a precious, new baby. When you need strength to carry on, don't rely on your own limited supply. Instead look to the Lord.

—Dave & Claudia

Go to page 456 for your next devotional reading.

¹⁵He remembers*a* his covenant forever,
  the word he commanded, for a
  thousand generations,
¹⁶the covenant he made with Abraham,
  the oath he swore to Isaac.
¹⁷He confirmed it to Jacob as a decree,
  to Israel as an everlasting covenant:
¹⁸"To you I will give the land of
  Canaan
  as the portion you will inherit."

¹⁹When they were but few in number,
  few indeed, and strangers in it,
²⁰they*b* wandered from nation to
  nation,
  from one kingdom to another.
²¹He allowed no man to oppress them;
  for their sake he rebuked kings:
²²"Do not touch my anointed ones;
  do my prophets no harm."

²³Sing to the LORD, all the earth;
  proclaim his salvation day after
  day.
²⁴Declare his glory among the nations,
  his marvelous deeds among all
  peoples.
²⁵For great is the LORD and most
  worthy of praise;
  he is to be feared above all gods.
²⁶For all the gods of the nations are
  idols,
  but the LORD made the heavens.
²⁷Splendor and majesty are before him;
  strength and joy in his dwelling
  place.
²⁸Ascribe to the LORD, O families of
  nations,
  ascribe to the LORD glory and
  strength,
²⁹   ascribe to the LORD the glory due
  his name.
  Bring an offering and come before
  him;
  worship the LORD in the splendor
  of his*c* holiness.
³⁰Tremble before him, all the earth!
  The world is firmly established; it
  cannot be moved.
³¹Let the heavens rejoice, let the earth
  be glad;
  let them say among the nations,
  "The LORD reigns!"
³²Let the sea resound, and all that is in
  it;
  let the fields be jubilant, and
  everything in them!

³³Then the trees of the forest will sing,
  they will sing for joy before the
  LORD,
  for he comes to judge the earth.

³⁴Give thanks to the LORD, for he is
  good;
  his love endures forever.
³⁵Cry out, "Save us, O God our Savior;
  gather us and deliver us from the
  nations,
  that we may give thanks to your holy
  name,
  that we may glory in your praise."
³⁶Praise be to the LORD, the God of
  Israel,
  from everlasting to everlasting.

Then all the people said "Amen" and
"Praise the LORD."

³⁷David left Asaph and his associates
before the ark of the covenant of the LORD
to minister there regularly, according to
each day's requirements. ³⁸He also left
Obed-Edom and his sixty-eight associates to minister with them. Obed-Edom
son of Jeduthun, and also Hosah, were
gatekeepers.

³⁹David left Zadok the priest and his
fellow priests before the tabernacle of the
LORD at the high place in Gibeon ⁴⁰to
present burnt offerings to the LORD on the
altar of burnt offering regularly, morning
and evening, in accordance with everything written in the Law of the LORD,
which he had given Israel. ⁴¹With them
were Heman and Jeduthun and the rest of
those chosen and designated by name to
give thanks to the LORD, "for his love
endures forever." ⁴²Heman and Jeduthun
were responsible for the sounding of the
trumpets and cymbals and for the playing
of the other instruments for sacred song.
The sons of Jeduthun were stationed at
the gate.

⁴³Then all the people left, each for his
own home, and David returned home to
bless his family.

a15 Some Septuagint manuscripts (see also Psalm
105:8); Hebrew *Remember*   *b18-20* One Hebrew
manuscript, Septuagint and Vulgate (see also
Psalm 105:12); most Hebrew manuscripts *inherit,* /
¹⁹*though you are but few in number,* / *few indeed, and
strangers in it."* / ²⁰*They*   *c29* Or LORD *with the
splendor of*

God's Promise to David

17 After David was settled in his palace, he said to Nathan the prophet, "Here I am, living in a palace of cedar, while the ark of the covenant of the LORD is under a tent."

²Nathan replied to David, "Whatever you have in mind, do it, for God is with you."

³That night the word of God came to Nathan, saying:

⁴"Go and tell my servant David, 'This is what the LORD says: You are not the one to build me a house to dwell in. ⁵I have not dwelt in a house from the day I brought Israel up out of Egypt to this day. I have moved from one tent site to another, from one dwelling place to another. ⁶Wherever I have moved with all the Israelites, did I ever say to any of their leaders*a* whom I commanded to shepherd my people, "Why have you not built me a house of cedar?" '

⁷"Now then, tell my servant David, 'This is what the LORD Almighty says: I took you from the pasture and from following the flock, to be ruler over my people Israel. ⁸I have been with you wherever you have gone, and I have cut off all your enemies from before you. Now I will make your name like the names of the greatest men of the earth. ⁹And I will provide a place for my people Israel and will plant them so that they can have a home of their own and no longer be disturbed. Wicked people will not oppress them anymore, as they did at the beginning ¹⁰and have done ever since the time I appointed leaders over my people Israel. I will also subdue all your enemies.

" 'I declare to you that the LORD will build a house for you: ¹¹When your days are over and you go to be with your fathers, I will raise up your offspring to succeed you, one of your own sons, and I will establish his kingdom. ¹²He is the one who will build a house for me, and I will establish his throne forever. ¹³I will be his father, and he will be my son. I will never take my love away from him, as I took it away from your predecessor. ¹⁴I will set him over my house and my kingdom forever; his throne will be established forever.' "

¹⁵Nathan reported to David all the words of this entire revelation.

David's Prayer

¹⁶Then King David went in and sat before the LORD, and he said:

"Who am I, O LORD God, and what is my family, that you have brought me this far? ¹⁷And as if this were not enough in your sight, O God, you have spoken about the future of the house of your servant. You have looked on me as though I were the most exalted of men, O LORD God.

¹⁸"What more can David say to you for honoring your servant? For you know your servant, ¹⁹O LORD. For the sake of your servant and according to your will, you have done this great thing and made known all these great promises.

²⁰"There is no one like you, O LORD, and there is no God but you, as we have heard with our own ears. ²¹And who is like your people Israel—the one nation on earth whose God went out to redeem a people for himself, and to make a name for yourself, and to perform great and awesome wonders by driving out nations from before your people, whom you redeemed from Egypt? ²²You made your people Israel your very own forever, and you, O LORD, have become their God.

²³"And now, LORD, let the promise you have made concerning your servant and his house be established forever. Do as you promised, ²⁴so that it will be established and that your name will be great forever. Then men will say, 'The LORD Almighty, the God over Israel, is Israel's God!' And the house of your servant David will be established before you.

a6 Traditionally *judges*; also in verse 10

25 "You, my God, have revealed to your servant that you will build a house for him. So your servant has found courage to pray to you. 26O LORD, you are God! You have promised these good things to your servant. 27Now you have been pleased to bless the house of your servant, that it may continue forever in your sight; for you, O LORD, have blessed it, and it will be blessed forever."

David's Victories

18 In the course of time, David defeated the Philistines and subdued them, and he took Gath and its surrounding villages from the control of the Philistines.

2David also defeated the Moabites, and they became subject to him and brought tribute.

3Moreover, David fought Hadadezer king of Zobah, as far as Hamath, when he went to establish his control along the Euphrates River. 4David captured a thousand of his chariots, seven thousand charioteers and twenty thousand foot soldiers. He hamstrung all but a hundred of the chariot horses.

5When the Arameans of Damascus came to help Hadadezer king of Zobah, David struck down twenty-two thousand of them. 6He put garrisons in the Aramean kingdom of Damascus, and the Arameans became subject to him and brought tribute. The LORD gave David victory everywhere he went.

7David took the gold shields carried by the officers of Hadadezer and brought them to Jerusalem. 8From Tebah*a* and Cun, towns that belonged to Hadadezer, David took a great quantity of bronze, which Solomon used to make the bronze Sea, the pillars and various bronze articles.

9When Tou king of Hamath heard that David had defeated the entire army of Hadadezer king of Zobah, 10he sent his son Hadoram to King David to greet him and congratulate him on his victory in battle over Hadadezer, who had been at war with Tou. Hadoram brought all kinds of articles of gold and silver and bronze.

11King David dedicated these articles to the LORD, as he had done with the silver and gold he had taken from all these nations: Edom and Moab, the Ammonites and the Philistines, and Amalek.

12Abishai son of Zeruiah struck down eighteen thousand Edomites in the Valley of Salt. 13He put garrisons in Edom, and all the Edomites became subject to David. The LORD gave David victory everywhere he went.

David's Officials

14David reigned over all Israel, doing what was just and right for all his people. 15Joab son of Zeruiah was over the army; Jehoshaphat son of Ahilud was recorder; 16Zadok son of Ahitub and Ahimelech*b* son of Abiathar were priests; Shavsha was secretary; 17Benaiah son of Jehoiada was over the Kerethites and Pelethites; and David's sons were chief officials at the king's side.

The Battle Against the Ammonites

19 In the course of time, Nahash king of the Ammonites died, and his son succeeded him as king. 2David thought, "I will show kindness to Hanun son of Nahash, because his father showed kindness to me." So David sent a delegation to express his sympathy to Hanun concerning his father.

When David's men came to Hanun in the land of the Ammonites to express sympathy to him, 3the Ammonite nobles said to Hanun, "Do you think David is honoring your father by sending men to you to express sympathy? Haven't his men come to you to explore and spy out the country and overthrow it?" 4So Hanun seized David's men, shaved them, cut off their garments in the middle at the buttocks, and sent them away.

5When someone came and told David about the men, he sent messengers to meet them, for they were greatly humiliated. The king said, "Stay at Jericho till your beards have grown, and then come back."

6When the Ammonites realized that they had become a stench in David's nos-

---

a8 Hebrew *Tibhath,* a variant of *Tebah*
b16 Some Hebrew manuscripts, Vulgate and Syriac (see also 2 Samuel 8:17); most Hebrew manuscripts *Abimelech*

trils, Hanun and the Ammonites sent a thousand talents[a] of silver to hire chariots and charioteers from Aram Naharaim,[b] Aram Maacah and Zobah. [7]They hired thirty-two thousand chariots and charioteers, as well as the king of Maacah with his troops, who came and camped near Medeba, while the Ammonites were mustered from their towns and moved out for battle.

[8]On hearing this, David sent Joab out with the entire army of fighting men. [9]The Ammonites came out and drew up in battle formation at the entrance to their city, while the kings who had come were by themselves in the open country.

[10]Joab saw that there were battle lines in front of him and behind him; so he selected some of the best troops in Israel and deployed them against the Arameans. [11]He put the rest of the men under the command of Abishai his brother, and they were deployed against the Ammonites. [12]Joab said, "If the Arameans are too strong for me, then you are to rescue me; but if the Ammonites are too strong for you, then I will rescue you. [13]Be strong and let us fight bravely for our people and the cities of our God. The LORD will do what is good in his sight."

[14]Then Joab and the troops with him advanced to fight the Arameans, and they fled before him. [15]When the Ammonites saw that the Arameans were fleeing, they too fled before his brother Abishai and went inside the city. So Joab went back to Jerusalem.

[16]After the Arameans saw that they had been routed by Israel, they sent messengers and had Arameans brought from beyond the River,[c] with Shophach the commander of Hadadezer's army leading them.

[17]When David was told of this, he gathered all Israel and crossed the Jordan; he advanced against them and formed his battle lines opposite them. David formed his lines to meet the Arameans in battle, and they fought against him. [18]But they fled before Israel, and David killed seven thousand of their charioteers and forty thousand of their foot soldiers. He also killed Shophach the commander of their army.

[19]When the vassals of Hadadezer saw that they had been defeated by Israel, they made peace with David and became subject to him.

So the Arameans were not willing to help the Ammonites anymore.

The Capture of Rabbah

20 In the spring, at the time when kings go off to war, Joab led out the armed forces. He laid waste the land of the Ammonites and went to Rabbah and besieged it, but David remained in Jerusalem. Joab attacked Rabbah and left it in ruins. [2]David took the crown from the head of their king[d]—its weight was found to be a talent[e] of gold, and it was set with precious stones—and it was placed on David's head. He took a great quantity of plunder from the city [3]and brought out the people who were there, consigning them to labor with saws and with iron picks and axes. David did this to all the Ammonite towns. Then David and his entire army returned to Jerusalem.

War With the Philistines

[4]In the course of time, war broke out with the Philistines, at Gezer. At that time Sibbecai the Hushathite killed Sippai, one of the descendants of the Rephaites, and the Philistines were subjugated.

[5]In another battle with the Philistines, Elhanan son of Jair killed Lahmi the brother of Goliath the Gittite, who had a spear with a shaft like a weaver's rod.

[6]In still another battle, which took place at Gath, there was a huge man with six fingers on each hand and six toes on each foot—twenty-four in all. He also was descended from Rapha. [7]When he taunted Israel, Jonathan son of Shimea, David's brother, killed him.

[8]These were descendants of Rapha in Gath, and they fell at the hands of David and his men.

David Numbers the Fighting Men

21 Satan rose up against Israel and incited David to take a census of Israel. [2]So David said to Joab and the commanders of the troops, "Go and count the

[a]6 That is, about 37 tons (about 34 metric tons)   [b]6 That is, Northwest Mesopotamia   [c]16 That is, the Euphrates   [d]2 Or of Milcom, that is, Molech   [e]2 That is, about 75 pounds (about 34 kilograms)

Israelites from Beersheba to Dan. Then report back to me so that I may know how many there are."

³But Joab replied, "May the LORD multiply his troops a hundred times over. My lord the king, are they not all my lord's subjects? Why does my lord want to do this? Why should he bring guilt on Israel?"

⁴The king's word, however, overruled Joab; so Joab left and went throughout Israel and then came back to Jerusalem. ⁵Joab reported the number of the fighting men to David: In all Israel there were one million one hundred thousand men who could handle a sword, including four hundred and seventy thousand in Judah.

⁶But Joab did not include Levi and Benjamin in the numbering, because the king's command was repulsive to him. ⁷This command was also evil in the sight of God; so he punished Israel.

⁸Then David said to God, "I have sinned greatly by doing this. Now, I beg you, take away the guilt of your servant. I have done a very foolish thing."

⁹The LORD said to Gad, David's seer, ¹⁰"Go and tell David, 'This is what the LORD says: I am giving you three options. Choose one of them for me to carry out against you.'"

¹¹So Gad went to David and said to him, "This is what the LORD says: 'Take your choice: ¹²three years of famine, three months of being swept away*ᵃ* before your enemies, with their swords overtaking you, or three days of the sword of the LORD—days of plague in the land, with the angel of the LORD ravaging every part of Israel.' Now then, decide how I should answer the one who sent me."

¹³David said to Gad, "I am in deep distress. Let me fall into the hands of the LORD, for his mercy is very great; but do not let me fall into the hands of men."

¹⁴So the LORD sent a plague on Israel, and seventy thousand men of Israel fell dead. ¹⁵And God sent an angel to destroy Jerusalem. But as the angel was doing so, the LORD saw it and was grieved because of the calamity and said to the angel who was destroying the people, "Enough! Withdraw your hand." The angel of the LORD was then standing at the threshing floor of Araunah*ᵇ* the Jebusite.

¹⁶David looked up and saw the angel of the LORD standing between heaven and earth, with a drawn sword in his hand extended over Jerusalem. Then David and the elders, clothed in sackcloth, fell facedown.

¹⁷David said to God, "Was it not I who ordered the fighting men to be counted? I am the one who has sinned and done wrong. These are but sheep. What have they done? O LORD my God, let your hand fall upon me and my family, but do not let this plague remain on your people."

¹⁸Then the angel of the LORD ordered Gad to tell David to go up and build an altar to the LORD on the threshing floor of Araunah the Jebusite. ¹⁹So David went up in obedience to the word that Gad had spoken in the name of the LORD.

²⁰While Araunah was threshing wheat, he turned and saw the angel; his four sons who were with him hid themselves. ²¹Then David approached, and when Araunah looked and saw him, he left the threshing floor and bowed down before David with his face to the ground.

²²David said to him, "Let me have the site of your threshing floor so I can build an altar to the LORD, that the plague on the people may be stopped. Sell it to me at the full price."

²³Araunah said to David, "Take it! Let my lord the king do whatever pleases him. Look, I will give the oxen for the burnt offerings, the threshing sledges for the wood, and the wheat for the grain offering. I will give all this."

²⁴But King David replied to Araunah, "No, I insist on paying the full price. I will not take for the LORD what is yours, or sacrifice a burnt offering that costs me nothing."

²⁵So David paid Araunah six hundred shekels*ᶜ* of gold for the site. ²⁶David built an altar to the LORD there and sacrificed burnt offerings and fellowship offerings.*ᵈ* He called on the LORD, and the LORD answered him with fire from heaven on the altar of burnt offering.

²⁷Then the LORD spoke to the angel, and he put his sword back into its sheath. ²⁸At that time, when David saw that the LORD had answered him on the threshing

ᵃ12 Hebrew; Septuagint and Vulgate (see also 2 Samuel 24:13) *of fleeing*   *ᵇ15* Hebrew *Ornan*, a variant of *Araunah*; also in verses 18-28   *ᶜ25* That is, about 15 pounds (about 7 kilograms)   *ᵈ26* Traditionally *peace offerings* floor of Araunah the Jebusite, he offered sacrifices there. ²⁹The tabernacle of the LORD, which Moses had made in the desert, and the altar of burnt offering were at that time on the high place at Gibeon. ³⁰But David could not go before it to inquire of God, because he was afraid of the sword of the angel of the LORD.

22 Then David said, "The house of the LORD God is to be here, and also the altar of burnt offering for Israel."

Preparations for the Temple

²So David gave orders to assemble the aliens living in Israel, and from among them he appointed stonecutters to prepare dressed stone for building the house of God. ³He provided a large amount of iron to make nails for the doors of the gateways and for the fittings, and more bronze than could be weighed. ⁴He also provided more cedar logs than could be counted, for the Sidonians and Tyrians had brought large numbers of them to David.

⁵David said, "My son Solomon is young and inexperienced, and the house to be built for the LORD should be of great magnificence and fame and splendor in the sight of all the nations. Therefore I will make preparations for it." So David made extensive preparations before his death.

⁶Then he called for his son Solomon and charged him to build a house for the LORD, the God of Israel. ⁷David said to Solomon: "My son, I had it in my heart to build a house for the Name of the LORD my God. ⁸But this word of the LORD came to me: 'You have shed much blood and have fought many wars. You are not to build a house for my Name, because you have shed much blood on the earth in my sight. ⁹But you will have a son who will be a man of peace and rest, and I will give him rest from all his enemies on every side. His name will be Solomon,^a and I will grant Israel peace and quiet during his reign. ¹⁰He is the one who will build a house for my Name. He will be my son, and I will be his father. And I will establish the throne of his kingdom over Israel forever.'

¹¹"Now, my son, the LORD be with you, and may you have success and build

the house of the LORD your God, as he said you would. ¹²May the LORD give you discretion and understanding when he puts you in command over Israel, so that you may keep the law of the LORD your God. ¹³Then you will have success if you are careful to observe the decrees and laws that the LORD gave Moses for Israel. Be strong and courageous. Do not be afraid or discouraged.

¹⁴"I have taken great pains to provide for the temple of the LORD a hundred thousand talents^b of gold, a million talents^c of silver, quantities of bronze and iron too great to be weighed, and wood and stone. And you may add to them. ¹⁵You have many workmen: stonecutters, masons and carpenters, as well as men skilled in every kind of work ¹⁶in gold and silver, bronze and iron—craftsmen beyond number. Now begin the work, and the LORD be with you."

¹⁷Then David ordered all the leaders of Israel to help his son Solomon. ¹⁸He said to them, "Is not the LORD your God with you? And has he not granted you rest on every side? For he has handed the inhabitants of the land over to me, and the land is subject to the LORD and to his people. ¹⁹Now devote your heart and soul to seeking the LORD your God. Begin to build the sanctuary of the LORD God, so that you may bring the ark of the covenant of the LORD and the sacred articles belonging to God into the temple that will be built for the Name of the LORD."

The Levites

23 When David was old and full of years, he made his son Solomon king over Israel.

²He also gathered together all the leaders of Israel, as well as the priests and Levites. ³The Levites thirty years old or more were counted, and the total number of men was thirty-eight thousand. ⁴David said, "Of these, twenty-four thousand are to supervise the work of the temple of the LORD and six thousand are to be officials and judges. ⁵Four thousand are to be gatekeepers and four thousand are to praise

^a9 *Solomon* sounds like and may be derived from the Hebrew for *peace.*   ^b14 That is, about 3,750 tons (about 3,450 metric tons)   ^c14 That is, about 37,500 tons (about 34,500 metric tons)

the LORD with the musical instruments I have provided for that purpose."

6David divided the Levites into groups corresponding to the sons of Levi: Gershon, Kohath and Merari.

Gershonites

7Belonging to the Gershonites:
Ladan and Shimei.
8The sons of Ladan:
Jehiel the first, Zetham and Joel—three in all.
9The sons of Shimei:
Shelomoth, Haziel and Haran—three in all.
These were the heads of the families of Ladan.
10And the sons of Shimei:
Jahath, Ziza,a Jeush and Beriah.
These were the sons of Shimei—four in all.
11Jahath was the first and Ziza the second, but Jeush and Beriah did not have many sons; so they were counted as one family with one assignment.

Kohathites

12The sons of Kohath:
Amram, Izhar, Hebron and Uzziel—four in all.
13The sons of Amram:
Aaron and Moses.
Aaron was set apart, he and his descendants forever, to consecrate the most holy things, to offer sacrifices before the LORD, to minister before him and to pronounce blessings in his name forever. 14The sons of Moses the man of God were counted as part of the tribe of Levi.
15The sons of Moses:
Gershom and Eliezer.
16The descendants of Gershom:
Shubael was the first.
17The descendants of Eliezer:
Rehabiah was the first.
Eliezer had no other sons, but the sons of Rehabiah were very numerous.
18The sons of Izhar:
Shelomith was the first.
19The sons of Hebron:
Jeriah the first, Amariah the second, Jahaziel the third and Jekameam the fourth.
20The sons of Uzziel:
Micah the first and Isshiah the second.

Merarites

21The sons of Merari:
Mahli and Mushi.
The sons of Mahli:
Eleazar and Kish.
22Eleazar died without having sons: he had only daughters. Their cousins, the sons of Kish, married them.
23The sons of Mushi:
Mahli, Eder and Jerimoth—three in all.

24These were the descendants of Levi by their families—the heads of families as they were registered under their names and counted individually, that is, the workers twenty years old or more who served in the temple of the LORD. 25For David had said, "Since the LORD, the God of Israel, has granted rest to his people and has come to dwell in Jerusalem forever, 26the Levites no longer need to carry the tabernacle or any of the articles used in its service." 27According to the last instructions of David, the Levites were counted from those twenty years old or more.

28The duty of the Levites was to help Aaron's descendants in the service of the temple of the LORD: to be in charge of the courtyards, the side rooms, the purification of all sacred things and the performance of other duties at the house of God. 29They were in charge of the bread set out on the table, the flour for the grain offerings, the unleavened wafers, the baking and the mixing, and all measurements of quantity and size. 30They were also to stand every morning to thank and praise the LORD. They were to do the same in the evening 31and whenever burnt offerings were presented to the LORD on Sabbaths and at New Moon festivals and at appointed feasts. They were to serve before the LORD regularly in the proper number and in the way prescribed for them.

a10 One Hebrew manuscript, Septuagint and Vulgate (see also verse 11); most Hebrew manuscripts Zina

³²And so the Levites carried out their responsibilities for the Tent of Meeting, for the Holy Place and, under their brothers the descendants of Aaron, for the service of the temple of the LORD.

The Divisions of Priests

24 These were the divisions of the sons of Aaron:

The sons of Aaron were Nadab, Abihu, Eleazar and Ithamar. ²But Nadab and Abihu died before their father did, and they had no sons; so Eleazar and Ithamar served as the priests. ³With the help of Zadok a descendant of Eleazar and Ahimelech a descendant of Ithamar, David separated them into divisions for their appointed order of ministering. ⁴A larger number of leaders were found among Eleazar's descendants than among Ithamar's, and they were divided accordingly: sixteen heads of families from Eleazar's descendants and eight heads of families from Ithamar's descendants. ⁵They divided them impartially by drawing lots, for there were officials of the sanctuary and officials of God among the descendants of both Eleazar and Ithamar.

⁶The scribe Shemaiah son of Nethanel, a Levite, recorded their names in the presence of the king and of the officials: Zadok the priest, Ahimelech son of Abiathar and the heads of families of the priests and of the Levites—one family being taken from Eleazar and then one from Ithamar.

⁷The first lot fell to Jehoiarib,
  the second to Jedaiah,
⁸the third to Harim,
  the fourth to Seorim,
⁹the fifth to Malkijah,
  the sixth to Mijamin,
¹⁰the seventh to Hakkoz,
  the eighth to Abijah,
¹¹the ninth to Jeshua,
  the tenth to Shecaniah,
¹²the eleventh to Eliashib,
  the twelfth to Jakim,
¹³the thirteenth to Huppah,
  the fourteenth to Jeshebeab,
¹⁴the fifteenth to Bilgah,
  the sixteenth to Immer,
¹⁵the seventeenth to Hezir,
  the eighteenth to Happizzez,
¹⁶the nineteenth to Pethahiah,
  the twentieth to Jehezkel,
¹⁷the twenty-first to Jakin,
  the twenty-second to Gamul,
¹⁸the twenty-third to Delaiah
  and the twenty-fourth to Maaziah.

¹⁹This was their appointed order of ministering when they entered the temple of the LORD, according to the regulations prescribed for them by their forefather Aaron, as the LORD, the God of Israel, had commanded him.

The Rest of the Levites

²⁰As for the rest of the descendants of Levi:

  from the sons of Amram: Shubael;
    from the sons of Shubael: Jehdeiah.
  ²¹As for Rehabiah, from his sons: Isshiah was the first.
²²From the Izharites: Shelomoth;
    from the sons of Shelomoth: Jahath.
²³The sons of Hebron: Jeriah the first,ᵃ Amariah the second, Jahaziel the third and Jekameam the fourth.
²⁴The son of Uzziel: Micah;
    from the sons of Micah: Shamir.
  ²⁵The brother of Micah: Isshiah;
    from the sons of Isshiah: Zechariah.
²⁶The sons of Merari: Mahli and Mushi.
    The son of Jaaziah: Beno.
²⁷The sons of Merari:
    from Jaaziah: Beno, Shoham, Zaccur and Ibri.
²⁸From Mahli: Eleazar, who had no sons.
²⁹From Kish: the son of Kish: Jerahmeel.
³⁰And the sons of Mushi: Mahli, Eder and Jerimoth.

These were the Levites, according to their families. ³¹They also cast lots, just as their brothers the descendants of Aaron did, in the presence of King David and of Zadok, Ahimelech, and the heads of families of the priests and of the Levites. The families of the oldest brother were treated the same as those of the youngest.

ᵃ23 Two Hebrew manuscripts and some Septuagint manuscripts (see also 1 Chron. 23:19); most Hebrew manuscripts *The sons of Jeriah:*

The Singers

25 David, together with the commanders of the army, set apart some of the sons of Asaph, Heman and Jeduthun for the ministry of prophesying, accompanied by harps, lyres and cymbals. Here is the list of the men who performed this service:

2From the sons of Asaph:
Zaccur, Joseph, Nethaniah and Asarelah. The sons of Asaph were under the supervision of Asaph, who prophesied under the king's supervision.

3As for Jeduthun, from his sons:
Gedaliah, Zeri, Jeshaiah, Shimei,*a* Hashabiah and Mattithiah, six in all, under the supervision of their father Jeduthun, who prophesied, using the harp in thanking and praising the LORD.

4As for Heman, from his sons:
Bukkiah, Mattaniah, Uzziel, Shubael and Jerimoth; Hananiah, Hanani, Eliathah, Giddalti and Romamti-Ezer; Joshbekashah, Mallothi, Hothir and Mahazioth. 5All these were sons of Heman the king's seer. They were given him through the promises of God to exalt him.*b* God gave Heman fourteen sons and three daughters.

6All these men were under the supervision of their fathers for the music of the temple of the LORD, with cymbals, lyres and harps, for the ministry at the house of God. Asaph, Jeduthun and Heman were under the supervision of the king. 7Along with their relatives—all of them trained and skilled in music for the LORD—they numbered 288. 8Young and old alike, teacher as well as student, cast lots for their duties.

9The first lot, which was for Asaph, fell to Joseph,
his sons and relatives,*c*   12*d*
the second to Gedaliah,
he and his relatives and sons,   12
10the third to Zaccur,
his sons and relatives,   12
11the fourth to Izri,*e*
his sons and relatives,   12

12the fifth to Nethaniah,
his sons and relatives,   12
13the sixth to Bukkiah,
his sons and relatives,   12
14the seventh to Jesarelah,*f*
his sons and relatives,   12
15the eighth to Jeshaiah,
his sons and relatives,   12
16the ninth to Mattaniah,
his sons and relatives,   12
17the tenth to Shimei,
his sons and relatives,   12
18the eleventh to Azarel,*g*
his sons and relatives,   12
19the twelfth to Hashabiah,
his sons and relatives,   12
20the thirteenth to Shubael,
his sons and relatives,   12
21the fourteenth to Mattithiah,
his sons and relatives,   12
22the fifteenth to Jerimoth,
his sons and relatives,   12
23the sixteenth to Hananiah,
his sons and relatives,   12
24the seventeenth to Joshbekashah,
his sons and relatives,   12
25the eighteenth to Hanani,
his sons and relatives,   12
26the nineteenth to Mallothi,
his sons and relatives,   12
27the twentieth to Eliathah,
his sons and relatives,   12
28the twenty-first to Hothir,
his sons and relatives,   12
29the twenty-second to Giddalti,
his sons and relatives,   12
30the twenty-third to Mahazioth,
his sons and relatives,   12
31the twenty-fourth to Romamti-Ezer,
his sons and relatives,   12

---

a3 One Hebrew manuscript and some Septuagint manuscripts (see also verse 17); most Hebrew manuscripts do not have *Shimei*.   *b5* Hebrew *exalt the horn*   *c9* See Septuagint; Hebrew does not have *his sons and relatives*.   *d9* See the total in verse 7; Hebrew does not have *twelve*.   *e11* A variant of *Zeri*   *f14* A variant of *Asarelah*   *g18* A variant of *Uzziel*

The Gatekeepers

26
The divisions of the gatekeepers:

From the Korahites: Meshelemiah son of Kore, one of the sons of Asaph.
[2]Meshelemiah had sons:
Zechariah the firstborn,
Jediael the second,
Zebadiah the third,
Jathniel the fourth,
[3]Elam the fifth,
Jehohanan the sixth
and Eliehoenai the seventh.
[4]Obed-Edom also had sons:
Shemaiah the firstborn,
Jehozabad the second,
Joah the third,
Sacar the fourth,
Nethanel the fifth,
[5]Ammiel the sixth,
Issachar the seventh
and Peullethai the eighth.
(For God had blessed Obed-Edom.)

[6]His son Shemaiah also had sons, who were leaders in their father's family because they were very capable men. [7]The sons of Shemaiah: Othni, Rephael, Obed and Elzabad; his relatives Elihu and Semakiah were also able men. [8]All these were descendants of Obed-Edom; they and their sons and their relatives were capable men with the strength to do the work—descendants of Obed-Edom, 62 in all.
[9]Meshelemiah had sons and relatives, who were able men—18 in all.

[10]Hosah the Merarite had sons: Shimri the first (although he was not the firstborn, his father had appointed him the first), [11]Hilkiah the second, Tabaliah the third and Zechariah the fourth. The sons and relatives of Hosah were 13 in all.
[12]These divisions of the gatekeepers, through their chief men, had duties for ministering in the temple of the LORD, just as their relatives had. [13]Lots were cast for each gate, according to their families, young and old alike.

[14]The lot for the East Gate fell to Shelemiah.[a] Then lots were cast for his son Zechariah, a wise counselor, and the lot for the North Gate fell to him. [15]The lot for the South Gate fell to Obed-Edom, and the lot for the storehouse fell to his sons. [16]The lots for the West Gate and the Shalleketh Gate on the upper road fell to Shuppim and Hosah.

Guard was alongside of guard: [17]There were six Levites a day on the east, four a day on the north, four a day on the south and two at a time at the storehouse. [18]As for the court to the west, there were four at the road and two at the court itself.

[19]These were the divisions of the gatekeepers who were descendants of Korah and Merari.

The Treasurers and Other Officials

[20]Their fellow Levites were[b] in charge of the treasuries of the house of God and the treasuries for the dedicated things.
[21]The descendants of Ladan, who were Gershonites through Ladan and who were heads of families belonging to Ladan the Gershonite, were Jehieli, [22]the sons of Jehieli, Zetham and his brother Joel. They were in charge of the treasuries of the temple of the LORD.
[23]From the Amramites, the Izharites, the Hebronites and the Uzzielites:

[24]Shubael, a descendant of Gershom son of Moses, was the officer in charge of the treasuries. [25]His relatives through Eliezer: Rehabiah his son, Jeshaiah his son, Joram his son, Zicri his son and Shelomith his son. [26]Shelomith and his relatives were in charge of all the treasuries for the things dedicated by King David, by the heads of families who were the commanders of thousands and commanders of hundreds, and by the other army commanders. [27]Some of the plunder taken in battle they dedicated for the repair of the temple of the LORD. [28]And everything dedicated by

---

[a]14 A variant of *Meshelemiah*   [b]20 Septuagint; Hebrew *As for the Levites, Ahijah was*

Samuel the seer and by Saul son of Kish, Abner son of Ner and Joab son of Zeruiah, and all the other dedicated things were in the care of Shelomith and his relatives.

²⁹From the Izharites: Kenaniah and his sons were assigned duties away from the temple, as officials and judges over Israel.

³⁰From the Hebronites: Hashabiah and his relatives—seventeen hundred able men—were responsible in Israel west of the Jordan for all the work of the LORD and for the king's service. ³¹As for the Hebronites, Jeriah was their chief according to the genealogical records of their families. In the fortieth year of David's reign a search was made in the records, and capable men among the Hebronites were found at Jazer in Gilead. ³²Jeriah had twenty-seven hundred relatives, who were able men and heads of families, and King David put them in charge of the Reubenites, the Gadites and the half-tribe of Manasseh for every matter pertaining to God and for the affairs of the king.

Army Divisions

27 This is the list of the Israelites—heads of families, commanders of thousands and commanders of hundreds, and their officers, who served the king in all that concerned the army divisions that were on duty month by month throughout the year. Each division consisted of 24,000 men.

²In charge of the first division, for the first month, was Jashobeam son of Zabdiel. There were 24,000 men in his division. ³He was a descendant of Perez and chief of all the army officers for the first month.

⁴In charge of the division for the second month was Dodai the Ahohite; Mikloth was the leader of his division. There were 24,000 men in his division.

⁵The third army commander, for the third month, was Benaiah son of Jehoiada the priest. He was chief and there were 24,000 men in his division. ⁶This was the Benaiah who was a mighty man among the Thirty and was over the Thirty. His son Ammizabad was in charge of his division.

⁷The fourth, for the fourth month, was Asahel the brother of Joab; his son Zebadiah was his successor. There were 24,000 men in his division.

⁸The fifth, for the fifth month, was the commander Shamhuth the Izrahite. There were 24,000 men in his division.

⁹The sixth, for the sixth month, was Ira the son of Ikkesh the Tekoite. There were 24,000 men in his division.

¹⁰The seventh, for the seventh month, was Helez the Pelonite, an Ephraimite. There were 24,000 men in his division.

¹¹The eighth, for the eighth month, was Sibbecai the Hushathite, a Zerahite. There were 24,000 men in his division.

¹²The ninth, for the ninth month, was Abiezer the Anathothite, a Benjamite. There were 24,000 men in his division.

¹³The tenth, for the tenth month, was Maharai the Netophathite, a Zerahite. There were 24,000 men in his division.

¹⁴The eleventh, for the eleventh month, was Benaiah the Pirathonite, an Ephraimite. There were 24,000 men in his division.

¹⁵The twelfth, for the twelfth month, was Heldai the Netophathite, from the family of Othniel. There were 24,000 men in his division.

Officers of the Tribes

¹⁶The officers over the tribes of Israel:

over the Reubenites: Eliezer son of Zicri;

over the Simeonites: Shephatiah son of Maacah;

¹⁷over Levi: Hashabiah son of Kemuel;

over Aaron: Zadok;

¹⁸over Judah: Elihu, a brother of David;

over Issachar: Omri son of Michael;

[19]over Zebulun: Ishmaiah son of Obadiah;

over Naphtali: Jerimoth son of Azriel;

[20]over the Ephraimites: Hoshea son of Azaziah;

over half the tribe of Manasseh: Joel son of Pedaiah;

[21]over the half-tribe of Manasseh in Gilead: Iddo son of Zechariah;

over Benjamin: Jaasiel son of Abner;

[22]over Dan: Azarel son of Jeroham.

These were the officers over the tribes of Israel.

[23]David did not take the number of the men twenty years old or less, because the LORD had promised to make Israel as numerous as the stars in the sky. [24]Joab son of Zeruiah began to count the men but did not finish. Wrath came on Israel on account of this numbering, and the number was not entered in the book[a] of the annals of King David.

The King's Overseers

[25]Azmaveth son of Adiel was in charge of the royal storehouses.

Jonathan son of Uzziah was in charge of the storehouses in the outlying districts, in the towns, the villages and the watchtowers.

[26]Ezri son of Kelub was in charge of the field workers who farmed the land.

[27]Shimei the Ramathite was in charge of the vineyards.

Zabdi the Shiphmite was in charge of the produce of the vineyards for the wine vats.

[28]Baal-Hanan the Gederite was in charge of the olive and sycamore-fig trees in the western foothills.

Joash was in charge of the supplies of olive oil.

[29]Shitrai the Sharonite was in charge of the herds grazing in Sharon.

Shaphat son of Adlai was in charge of the herds in the valleys.

[30]Obil the Ishmaelite was in charge of the camels.

Jehdeiah the Meronothite was in charge of the donkeys.

[31]Jaziz the Hagrite was in charge of the flocks.

All these were the officials in charge of King David's property.

[32]Jonathan, David's uncle, was a counselor, a man of insight and a scribe. Jehiel son of Hacmoni took care of the king's sons.

[33]Ahithophel was the king's counselor. Hushai the Arkite was the king's friend. [34]Ahithophel was succeeded by Jehoiada son of Benaiah and by Abiathar.

Joab was the commander of the royal army.

David's Plans for the Temple

28 David summoned all the officials of Israel to assemble at Jerusalem: the officers over the tribes, the commanders of the divisions in the service of the king, the commanders of thousands and commanders of hundreds, and the officials in charge of all the property and livestock belonging to the king and his sons, together with the palace officials, the mighty men and all the brave warriors.

[2]King David rose to his feet and said: "Listen to me, my brothers and my people. I had it in my heart to build a house as a place of rest for the ark of the covenant of the LORD, for the footstool of our God, and I made plans to build it. [3]But God said to me, 'You are not to build a house for my Name, because you are a warrior and have shed blood.'

[4]"Yet the LORD, the God of Israel, chose me from my whole family to be king over Israel forever. He chose Judah as leader, and from the house of Judah he chose my family, and from my father's sons he was pleased to make me king over all Israel. [5]Of all my sons—and the LORD has given me many—he has chosen my son Solomon to sit on the throne of the kingdom of the LORD over Israel. [6]He said to me: 'Solomon your son is the one who will build my house and my courts, for I have chosen him to be my son, and I will be his father. [7]I will establish his kingdom forever if he is unswerving in carrying out my commands and laws, as is being done at this time.'

[8]"So now I charge you in the sight of all Israel and of the assembly of the LORD, and in the hearing of our God: Be careful

[a]24 Septuagint; Hebrew *number*

to follow all the commands of the LORD your God, that you may possess this good land and pass it on as an inheritance to your descendants forever.

⁹"And you, my son Solomon, acknowledge the God of your father, and serve him with wholehearted devotion and with a willing mind, for the LORD searches every heart and understands every motive behind the thoughts. If you seek him, he will be found by you; but if you forsake him, he will reject you forever. ¹⁰Consider now, for the LORD has chosen you to build a temple as a sanctuary. Be strong and do the work."

¹¹Then David gave his son Solomon the plans for the portico of the temple, its buildings, its storerooms, its upper parts, its inner rooms and the place of atonement. ¹²He gave him the plans of all that the Spirit had put in his mind for the courts of the temple of the LORD and all the surrounding rooms, for the treasuries of the temple of God and for the treasuries for the dedicated things. ¹³He gave him instructions for the divisions of the priests and Levites, and for all the work of serving in the temple of the LORD, as well as for all the articles to be used in its service. ¹⁴He designated the weight of gold for all the gold articles to be used in various kinds of service, and the weight of silver for all the silver articles to be used in various kinds of service: ¹⁵the weight of gold for the gold lampstands and their lamps, with the weight for each lampstand and its lamps; and the weight of silver for each silver lampstand and its lamps, according to the use of each lampstand; ¹⁶the weight of gold for each table for consecrated bread; the weight of silver for the silver tables; ¹⁷the weight of pure gold for the forks, sprinkling bowls and pitchers; the weight of gold for each gold dish; the weight of silver for each silver dish; ¹⁸and the weight of the refined gold for the altar of incense. He also gave him the plan for the chariot, that is, the cherubim of gold that spread their wings and shelter the ark of the covenant of the LORD.

¹⁹"All this," David said, "I have in writing from the hand of the LORD upon me, and he gave me understanding in all the details of the plan."

²⁰David also said to Solomon his son,

"Be strong and courageous, and do the work. Do not be afraid or discouraged, for the LORD God, my God, is with you. He will not fail you or forsake you until all the work for the service of the temple of the LORD is finished. ²¹The divisions of the priests and Levites are ready for all the work on the temple of God, and every willing man skilled in any craft will help you in all the work. The officials and all the people will obey your every command."

Gifts for Building the Temple

29 Then King David said to the whole assembly: "My son Solomon, the one whom God has chosen, is young and inexperienced. The task is great, because this palatial structure is not for man but for the LORD God. ²With all my resources I have provided for the temple of my God—gold for the gold work, silver for the silver, bronze for the bronze, iron for the iron and wood for the wood, as well as onyx for the settings, turquoise,ᵃ stones of various colors, and all kinds of fine stone and marble—all of these in large quantities. ³Besides, in my devotion to the temple of my God I now give my personal treasures of gold and silver for the temple of my God, over and above everything I have provided for this holy temple: ⁴three thousand talentsᵇ of gold (gold of Ophir) and seven thousand talentsᶜ of refined silver, for the overlaying of the walls of the buildings, ⁵for the gold work and the silver work, and for all the work to be done by the craftsmen. Now, who is willing to consecrate himself today to the LORD?"

⁶Then the leaders of families, the officers of the tribes of Israel, the commanders of thousands and commanders of hundreds, and the officials in charge of the king's work gave willingly. ⁷They gave toward the work on the temple of God five thousand talentsᵈ and ten thousand daricsᵉ of gold, ten thousand talentsᶠ

ᵃ2 The meaning of the Hebrew for this word is uncertain.   ᵇ4 That is, about 110 tons (about 100 metric tons)   ᶜ4 That is, about 260 tons (about 240 metric tons)   ᵈ7 That is, about 190 tons (about 170 metric tons)   ᵉ7 That is, about 185 pounds (about 84 kilograms)   ᶠ7 That is, about 375 tons (about 345 metric tons) of silver, eighteen thousand talents*a* of bronze and a hundred thousand talents*b* of iron. ⁸Any who had precious stones gave them to the treasury of the temple of the LORD in the custody of Jehiel the Gershonite. ⁹The people rejoiced at the willing response of their leaders, for they had given freely and wholeheartedly to the LORD. David the king also rejoiced greatly.

David's Prayer

¹⁰David praised the LORD in the presence of the whole assembly, saying,

"Praise be to you, O LORD,
    God of our father Israel,
    from everlasting to everlasting.
¹¹Yours, O LORD, is the greatness and
        the power
    and the glory and the majesty and
        the splendor,
    for everything in heaven and earth
        is yours.
Yours, O LORD, is the kingdom;
    you are exalted as head over all.
¹²Wealth and honor come from you;
    you are the ruler of all things.
In your hands are strength and power
    to exalt and give strength to all.
¹³Now, our God, we give you thanks,
    and praise your glorious name.

¹⁴"But who am I, and who are my people, that we should be able to give as generously as this? Everything comes from you, and we have given you only what comes from your hand. ¹⁵We are aliens and strangers in your sight, as were all our forefathers. Our days on earth are like a shadow, without hope. ¹⁶O LORD our God, as for all this abundance that we have provided for building you a temple for your Holy Name, it comes from your hand, and all of it belongs to you. ¹⁷I know, my God, that you test the heart and are pleased with integrity. All these things have I given willingly and with honest intent. And now I have seen with joy how willingly your people who are here have given to you. ¹⁸O LORD, God of our fathers Abraham, Isaac and Israel, keep this desire in the hearts of your people forever, and keep their hearts loyal to you. ¹⁹And give my son Solomon the wholehearted devotion to keep your commands, requirements and decrees and to do everything to build the palatial structure for which I have provided."

²⁰Then David said to the whole assembly, "Praise the LORD your God." So they all praised the LORD, the God of their fathers; they bowed low and fell prostrate before the LORD and the king.

Solomon Acknowledged as King

²¹The next day they made sacrifices to the LORD and presented burnt offerings to him: a thousand bulls, a thousand rams and a thousand male lambs, together with their drink offerings, and other sacrifices in abundance for all Israel. ²²They ate and drank with great joy in the presence of the LORD that day.

Then they acknowledged Solomon son of David as king a second time, anointing him before the LORD to be ruler and Zadok to be priest. ²³So Solomon sat on the throne of the LORD as king in place of his father David. He prospered and all Israel obeyed him. ²⁴All the officers and mighty men, as well as all of King David's sons, pledged their submission to King Solomon.

²⁵The LORD highly exalted Solomon in the sight of all Israel and bestowed on him royal splendor such as no king over Israel ever had before.

The Death of David

²⁶David son of Jesse was king over all Israel. ²⁷He ruled over Israel forty years—seven in Hebron and thirty-three in Jerusalem. ²⁸He died at a good old age, having enjoyed long life, wealth and honor. His son Solomon succeeded him as king.

²⁹As for the events of King David's reign, from beginning to end, they are written in the records of Samuel the seer, the records of Nathan the prophet and the records of Gad the seer, ³⁰together with the details of his reign and power, and the circumstances that surrounded him and Israel and the kingdoms of all the other lands.

a7 That is, about 675 tons (about 610 metric tons)   *b7* That is, about 3,750 tons (about 3,450 metric tons)

2 Chronicles

Life is full of "if's" and "then's." If you pay attention to your spouse, then he or she will be happy. If you exercise three or four times a week, then your heart will stay strong. If you keep your car in good repair, then it won't rust and break down. If you take this medicine, then your backache will subside. If you invest conservatively, then you'll be less likely to lose everything overnight.

Second Chronicles offers one of the most important "if-then" promises ever made. The God of the universe expressed it to Solomon in the dead of night: "If my people, who are called by my name, will humble themselves and pray and seek my face and turn from their wicked ways, then will I hear from heaven and will forgive their sin and will heal their land" (7:14). This was true in the tenth century before Christ, and it's true for every tribe, every nation and every family today . . . including yours.

Solomon Asks for Wisdom

1 Solomon son of David established himself firmly over his kingdom, for the LORD his God was with him and made him exceedingly great.

²Then Solomon spoke to all Israel—to the commanders of thousands and commanders of hundreds, to the judges and to all the leaders in Israel, the heads of families— ³and Solomon and the whole assembly went to the high place at Gibeon, for God's Tent of Meeting was there, which Moses the LORD's servant had made in the desert. ⁴Now David had brought up the ark of God from Kiriath Jearim to the place he had prepared for it, because he had pitched a tent for it in Jerusalem. ⁵But the bronze altar that Bezalel son of Uri, the son of Hur, had made was in Gibeon in front of the tabernacle of the LORD; so Solomon and the assembly inquired of him there. ⁶Solomon went up to the bronze altar before the LORD in the Tent of Meeting and offered a thousand burnt offerings on it.

⁷That night God appeared to Solomon and said to him, "Ask for whatever you want me to give you."

⁸Solomon answered God, "You have shown great kindness to David my father and have made me king in his place. ⁹Now, LORD God, let your promise to my father David be confirmed, for you have made me king over a people who are as numerous as the dust of the earth. ¹⁰Give me wisdom and knowledge, that I may lead this people, for who is able to govern this great people of yours?"

¹¹God said to Solomon, "Since this is your heart's desire and you have not asked for wealth, riches or honor, nor for the death of your enemies, and since you have not asked for a long life but for wisdom and knowledge to govern my people over whom I have made you king, ¹²therefore wisdom and knowledge will be given you. And I will also give you wealth, riches and honor, such as no king who was before you ever had and none after you will have."

¹³Then Solomon went to Jerusalem from the high place at Gibeon, from before the Tent of Meeting. And he reigned over Israel.

¹⁴Solomon accumulated chariots and horses; he had fourteen hundred chariots and twelve thousand horses,ᵃ which he kept in the chariot cities and also with him in Jerusalem. ¹⁵The king made silver and gold as common in Jerusalem as stones, and cedar as plentiful as sycamore-fig trees in the foothills. ¹⁶Solomon's horses were imported from Egyptᵇ and from Kueᶜ—the royal merchants purchased them from Kue. ¹⁷They imported a chariot from Egypt for six hundred shekelsᵈ of silver, and a horse for a hundred and fifty.ᵉ They also exported them to all the kings of the Hittites and of the Arameans.

Preparations for Building the Temple

2 Solomon gave orders to build a temple for the Name of the LORD and a royal palace for himself. ²He conscripted seventy thousand men as carriers and eighty thousand as stonecutters in the hills and thirty-six hundred as foremen over them.

³Solomon sent this message to Hiramᶠ king of Tyre:

"Send me cedar logs as you did for my father David when you sent

him cedar to build a palace to live in. ⁴Now I am about to build a temple for the Name of the LORD my God and to dedicate it to him for burning fragrant incense before him, for setting out the consecrated bread regularly, and for making burnt offerings every morning and evening and on Sabbaths and New Moons and at the appointed feasts of the LORD our God. This is a lasting ordinance for Israel.

⁵"The temple I am going to build will be great, because our God is greater than all other gods. ⁶But who is able to build a temple for him, since the heavens, even the highest heavens, cannot contain him? Who then am I to build a temple for him, except as a place to burn sacrifices before him?

⁷"Send me, therefore, a man skilled to work in gold and silver, bronze and iron, and in purple, crimson and blue yarn, and experienced in the art of engraving, to work in Judah and Jerusalem with my skilled craftsmen, whom my father David provided.

⁸"Send me also cedar, pine and algumᵍ logs from Lebanon, for I know that your men are skilled in cutting timber there. My men will work with yours ⁹to provide me with plenty of lumber, because the temple I build must be large and magnificent. ¹⁰I will give your servants, the woodsmen who cut the timber, twenty thousand corsʰ of ground wheat, twenty thousand cors of barley, twenty thousand bathsⁱ of wine and twenty thousand baths of olive oil."

¹¹Hiram king of Tyre replied by letter to Solomon:

ᵃ14 Or charioteers   ᵇ16 Or possibly Muzur, a region in Cilicia; also in verse 17   ᶜ16 Probably Cilicia   ᵈ17 That is, about 15 pounds (about 7 kilograms)   ᵉ17 That is, about 3 3/4 pounds (about 1.7 kilograms)   ᶠ3 Hebrew Huram, a variant of Hiram; also in verses 11 and 12   ᵍ8 Probably a variant of almug; possibly juniper   ʰ10 That is, probably about 125,000 bushels (about 4,400 kiloliters)   ⁱ10 That is, probably about 115,000 gallons (about 440 kiloliters)

"Because the LORD loves his people, he has made you their king."

12And Hiram added:

"Praise be to the LORD, the God of Israel, who made heaven and earth! He has given King David a wise son, endowed with intelligence and discernment, who will build a temple for the LORD and a palace for himself.

13"I am sending you Huram-Abi, a man of great skill, 14whose mother was from Dan and whose father was from Tyre. He is trained to work in gold and silver, bronze and iron, stone and wood, and with purple and blue and crimson yarn and fine linen. He is experienced in all kinds of engraving and can execute any design given to him. He will work with your craftsmen and with those of my lord, David your father.

15"Now let my lord send his servants the wheat and barley and the olive oil and wine he promised, 16and we will cut all the logs from Lebanon that you need and will float them in rafts by sea down to Joppa. You can then take them up to Jerusalem."

17Solomon took a census of all the aliens who were in Israel, after the census his father David had taken; and they were found to be 153,600. 18He assigned 70,000 of them to be carriers and 80,000 to be stonecutters in the hills, with 3,600 foremen over them to keep the people working.

Solomon Builds the Temple

3 Then Solomon began to build the temple of the LORD in Jerusalem on Mount Moriah, where the LORD had appeared to his father David. It was on the threshing floor of Araunah[a] the Jebusite, the place provided by David. 2He began building on the second day of the second month in the fourth year of his reign.

3The foundation Solomon laid for building the temple of God was sixty cubits long and twenty cubits wide[b] (using the cubit of the old standard). 4The portico at the front of the temple was twenty

cubits[c] long across the width of the building and twenty cubits[d] high. He overlaid the inside with pure gold. 5He paneled the main hall with pine and covered it with fine gold and decorated it with palm tree and chain designs. 6He adorned the temple with precious stones. And the gold he used was gold of Parvaim. 7He overlaid the ceiling beams, doorframes, walls and doors of the temple with gold, and he carved cherubim on the walls.

8He built the Most Holy Place, its length corresponding to the width of the temple—twenty cubits long and twenty cubits wide. He overlaid the inside with six hundred talents[e] of fine gold. 9The gold nails weighed fifty shekels.[f] He also overlaid the upper parts with gold.

10In the Most Holy Place he made a pair of sculptured cherubim and overlaid them with gold. 11The total wingspan of the cherubim was twenty cubits. One wing of the first cherub was five cubits[g] long and touched the temple wall, while its other wing, also five cubits long, touched the wing of the other cherub. 12Similarly one wing of the second cherub was five cubits long and touched the other temple wall, and its other wing, also five cubits long, touched the wing of the first cherub. 13The wings of these cherubim extended twenty cubits. They stood on their feet, facing the main hall.[h]

14He made the curtain of blue, purple and crimson yarn and fine linen, with cherubim worked into it.

15In the front of the temple he made two pillars, which ⌞together⌟ were thirty-five cubits[i] long, each with a capital on top measuring five cubits. 16He made interwoven chains[j] and put them on top of the pillars. He also made a hundred pomegranates and attached them to the

a1 Hebrew *Ornan*, a variant of *Araunah*
b3 That is, about 90 feet (about 27 meters) long and 30 feet (about 9 meters) wide   c4 That is, about 30 feet (about 9 meters); also in verses 8, 11 and 13   d4 Some Septuagint and Syriac manuscripts; Hebrew *and a hundred and twenty*   e8 That is, about 23 tons (about 21 metric tons)   f9 That is, about 1 1/4 pounds (about 0.6 kilogram)   g11 That is, about 7 1/2 feet (about 2.3 meters); also in verse 15   h13 Or *facing inward*   i15 That is, about 52 feet (about 16 meters)   j16 Or possibly *made chains in the inner sanctuary*; the meaning of the Hebrew for this phrase is uncertain.

chains. [17]He erected the pillars in the front of the temple, one to the south and one to the north. The one to the south he named Jakin[a] and the one to the north Boaz.[b]

The Temple's Furnishings

4 He made a bronze altar twenty cubits long, twenty cubits wide and ten cubits high.[c] [2]He made the Sea of cast metal, circular in shape, measuring ten cubits from rim to rim and five cubits[d] high. It took a line of thirty cubits[e] to measure around it. [3]Below the rim, figures of bulls encircled it—ten to a cubit.[f] The bulls were cast in two rows in one piece with the Sea.

[4]The Sea stood on twelve bulls, three facing north, three facing west, three facing south and three facing east. The Sea rested on top of them, and their hindquarters were toward the center. [5]It was a handbreadth[g] in thickness, and its rim was like the rim of a cup, like a lily blossom. It held three thousand baths.[h]

[6]He then made ten basins for washing and placed five on the south side and five on the north. In them the things to be used for the burnt offerings were rinsed, but the Sea was to be used by the priests for washing.

[7]He made ten gold lampstands according to the specifications for them and placed them in the temple, five on the south side and five on the north.

[8]He made ten tables and placed them in the temple, five on the south side and five on the north. He also made a hundred gold sprinkling bowls.

[9]He made the courtyard of the priests, and the large court and the doors for the court, and overlaid the doors with bronze. [10]He placed the Sea on the south side, at the southeast corner.

[11]He also made the pots and shovels and sprinkling bowls.

So Huram finished the work he had undertaken for King Solomon in the temple of God:

[12]the two pillars;

the two bowl-shaped capitals on top of the pillars;

the two sets of network decorating the two bowl-shaped capitals on top of the pillars;

[13]the four hundred pomegranates for the two sets of network (two rows of pomegranates for each network, decorating the bowl-shaped capitals on top of the pillars);

[14]the stands with their basins;

[15]the Sea and the twelve bulls under it;

[16]the pots, shovels, meat forks and all related articles.

All the objects that Huram-Abi made for King Solomon for the temple of the LORD were of polished bronze. [17]The king had them cast in clay molds in the plain of the Jordan between Succoth and Zarethan.[i] [18]All these things that Solomon made amounted to so much that the weight of the bronze was not determined.

[19]Solomon also made all the furnishings that were in God's temple:

the golden altar;

the tables on which was the bread of the Presence;

[20]the lampstands of pure gold with their lamps, to burn in front of the inner sanctuary as prescribed;

[21]the gold floral work and lamps and tongs (they were solid gold);

[22]the pure gold wick trimmers, sprinkling bowls, dishes and censers; and the gold doors of the temple: the inner doors to the Most Holy Place and the doors of the main hall.

5 When all the work Solomon had done for the temple of the LORD was finished, he brought in the things his father David had dedicated—the silver and gold and all the furnishings—and he placed them in the treasuries of God's temple.

---

[a]17 Jakin probably means he establishes.   [b]17 Boaz probably means in him is strength.   [c]1 That is, about 30 feet (about 9 meters) long and wide, and about 15 feet (about 4.5 meters) high   [d]2 That is, about 7 1/2 feet (about 2.3 meters)   [e]2 That is, about 45 feet (about 13.5 meters)   [f]3 That is, about 1 1/2 feet (about 0.5 meter)   [g]5 That is, about 3 inches (about 8 centimeters)   [h]5 That is, about 17,500 gallons (about 66 kiloliters)   [i]17 Hebrew Zeredatha, a variant of Zarethan

The Ark Brought to the Temple

²Then Solomon summoned to Jerusalem the elders of Israel, all the heads of the tribes and the chiefs of the Israelite families, to bring up the ark of the LORD's covenant from Zion, the City of David. ³And all the men of Israel came together to the king at the time of the festival in the seventh month.

⁴When all the elders of Israel had arrived, the Levites took up the ark, ⁵and they brought up the ark and the Tent of Meeting and all the sacred furnishings in it. The priests, who were Levites, carried them up; ⁶and King Solomon and the entire assembly of Israel that had gathered about him were before the ark, sacrificing so many sheep and cattle that they could not be recorded or counted.

⁷The priests then brought the ark of the LORD's covenant to its place in the inner sanctuary of the temple, the Most Holy Place, and put it beneath the wings of the cherubim. ⁸The cherubim spread their wings over the place of the ark and covered the ark and its carrying poles. ⁹These poles were so long that their ends, extending from the ark, could be seen from in front of the inner sanctuary, but not from outside the Holy Place; and they are still there today. ¹⁰There was nothing in the ark except the two tablets that Moses had placed in it at Horeb, where the LORD made a covenant with the Israelites after they came out of Egypt.

¹¹The priests then withdrew from the Holy Place. All the priests who were there had consecrated themselves, regardless of their divisions. ¹²All the Levites who were musicians—Asaph, Heman, Jeduthun and their sons and relatives—stood on the east side of the altar, dressed in fine linen and playing cymbals, harps and lyres. They were accompanied by 120 priests sounding trumpets. ¹³The trumpeters and singers joined in unison, as with one voice, to give praise and thanks to the LORD. Accompanied by trumpets, cymbals and other instruments, they raised their voices in praise to the LORD and sang:

"He is good;
   his love endures forever."

Then the temple of the LORD was filled with a cloud, ¹⁴and the priests could not perform their service because of the cloud, for the glory of the LORD filled the temple of God.

6 Then Solomon said, "The LORD has said that he would dwell in a dark cloud; ²I have built a magnificent temple for you, a place for you to dwell forever."

³While the whole assembly of Israel was standing there, the king turned around and blessed them. ⁴Then he said:

"Praise be to the LORD, the God of Israel, who with his hands has fulfilled what he promised with his mouth to my father David. For he said, ⁵'Since the day I brought my people out of Egypt, I have not chosen a city in any tribe of Israel to have a temple built for my Name to be there, nor have I chosen anyone to be the leader over my people Israel. ⁶But now I have chosen Jerusalem for my Name to be there, and I have chosen David to rule my people Israel.'

⁷"My father David had it in his heart to build a temple for the Name of the LORD, the God of Israel. ⁸But the LORD said to my father David, 'Because it was in your heart to build a temple for my Name, you did well to have this in your heart. ⁹Nevertheless, you are not the one to build the temple, but your son, who is your own flesh and blood—he is the one who will build the temple for my Name.'

¹⁰"The LORD has kept the promise he made. I have succeeded David my father and now I sit on the throne of Israel, just as the LORD promised, and I have built the temple for the Name of the LORD, the God of Israel. ¹¹There I have placed the ark, in which is the covenant of the LORD that he made with the people of Israel."

Solomon's Prayer of Dedication

¹²Then Solomon stood before the altar of the LORD in front of the whole assembly of Israel and spread out his hands. ¹³Now he had made a bronze platform, five cubits*a* long, five cubits wide and

---

a13 That is, about 7 1/2 feet (about 2.3 meters)

three cubits*a* high, and had placed it in the center of the outer court. He stood on the platform and then knelt down before the whole assembly of Israel and spread out his hands toward heaven. 14He said:

"O LORD, God of Israel, there is no God like you in heaven or on earth—you who keep your covenant of love with your servants who continue wholeheartedly in your way. 15You have kept your promise to your servant David my father; with your mouth you have promised and with your hand you have fulfilled it—as it is today.

16"Now LORD, God of Israel, keep for your servant David my father the promises you made to him when you said, 'You shall never fail to have a man to sit before me on the throne of Israel, if only your sons are careful in all they do to walk before me according to my law, as you have done.' 17And now, O LORD, God of Israel, let your word that you promised your servant David come true.

18"But will God really dwell on earth with men? The heavens, even the highest heavens, cannot contain you. How much less this temple I have built! 19Yet give attention to your servant's prayer and his plea for mercy, O LORD my God. Hear the cry and the prayer that your servant is praying in your presence. 20May your eyes be open toward this temple day and night, this place of which you said you would put your Name there. May you hear the prayer your servant prays toward this place. 21Hear the supplications of your servant and of your people Israel when they pray toward this place. Hear from heaven, your dwelling place; and when you hear, forgive.

22"When a man wrongs his neighbor and is required to take an oath and he comes and swears the oath before your altar in this temple, 23then hear from heaven and act. Judge between your servants, repaying the guilty by bringing down on his own head what he has done.

Declare the innocent not guilty and so establish his innocence.

24"When your people Israel have been defeated by an enemy because they have sinned against you and when they turn back and confess your name, praying and making supplication before you in this temple, 25then hear from heaven and forgive the sin of your people Israel and bring them back to the land you gave to them and their fathers.

26"When the heavens are shut up and there is no rain because your people have sinned against you, and when they pray toward this place and confess your name and turn from their sin because you have afflicted them, 27then hear from heaven and forgive the sin of your servants, your people Israel. Teach them the right way to live, and send rain on the land you gave your people for an inheritance.

28"When famine or plague comes to the land, or blight or mildew, locusts or grasshoppers, or when enemies besiege them in any of their cities, whatever disaster or disease may come, 29and when a prayer or plea is made by any of your people Israel—each one aware of his afflictions and pains, and spreading out his hands toward this temple—30then hear from heaven, your dwelling place. Forgive, and deal with each man according to all he does, since you know his heart (for you alone know the hearts of men), 31so that they will fear you and walk in your ways all the time they live in the land you gave our fathers.

32"As for the foreigner who does not belong to your people Israel but has come from a distant land because of your great name and your mighty hand and your outstretched arm—when he comes and prays toward this temple, 33then hear from heaven, your dwelling place, and do whatever the foreigner asks of you, so that all the peoples of the earth may know your name and fear you, as do your own people Israel, and

a13 That is, about 4 1/2 feet (about 1.3 meters)

may know that this house I have built bears your Name.

³⁴"When your people go to war against their enemies, wherever you send them, and when they pray to you toward this city you have chosen and the temple I have built for your Name, ³⁵then hear from heaven their prayer and their plea, and uphold their cause.

³⁶"When they sin against you—for there is no one who does not sin—and you become angry with them and give them over to the enemy, who takes them captive to a land far away or near; ³⁷and if they have a change of heart in the land where they are held captive, and repent and plead with you in the land of their captivity and say, 'We have sinned, we have done wrong and acted wickedly'; ³⁸and if they turn back to you with all their heart and soul in the land of their captivity where they were taken, and pray toward the land you gave their fathers, toward the city you have chosen and toward the temple I have built for your Name; ³⁹then from heaven, your dwelling place, hear their prayer and their pleas, and uphold their cause. And forgive your people, who have sinned against you.

⁴⁰"Now, my God, may your eyes be open and your ears attentive to the prayers offered in this place.

⁴¹"Now arise, O Lᴏʀᴅ God, and
   come to your resting place,
   you and the ark of your
      might.
May your priests, O Lᴏʀᴅ God,
   be clothed with
      salvation,
   may your saints rejoice in
      your goodness.
⁴²O Lᴏʀᴅ God, do not reject your
   anointed one.
   Remember the great love
      promised to David your
      servant."

The Dedication of the Temple

7 When Solomon finished praying, fire came down from heaven and con-

sumed the burnt offering and the sacrifices, and the glory of the Lᴏʀᴅ filled the temple. ²The priests could not enter the temple of the Lᴏʀᴅ because the glory of the Lᴏʀᴅ filled it. ³When all the Israelites saw the fire coming down and the glory of the Lᴏʀᴅ above the temple, they knelt on the pavement with their faces to the ground, and they worshiped and gave thanks to the Lᴏʀᴅ, saying,

"He is good;
   his love endures forever."

⁴Then the king and all the people offered sacrifices before the Lᴏʀᴅ. ⁵And King Solomon offered a sacrifice of twenty-two thousand head of cattle and a hundred and twenty thousand sheep and goats. So the king and all the people dedicated the temple of God. ⁶The priests took their positions, as did the Levites with the Lᴏʀᴅ's musical instruments, which King David had made for praising the Lᴏʀᴅ and which were used when he gave thanks, saying, "His love endures forever." Opposite the Levites, the priests blew their trumpets, and all the Israelites were standing.

⁷Solomon consecrated the middle part of the courtyard in front of the temple of the Lᴏʀᴅ, and there he offered burnt offerings and the fat of the fellowship offerings,ᵃ because the bronze altar he had made could not hold the burnt offerings, the grain offerings and the fat portions.

⁸So Solomon observed the festival at that time for seven days, and all Israel with him—a vast assembly, people from Leboᵇ Hamath to the Wadi of Egypt. ⁹On the eighth day they held an assembly, for they had celebrated the dedication of the altar for seven days and the festival for seven days more. ¹⁰On the twenty-third day of the seventh month he sent the people to their homes, joyful and glad in heart for the good things the Lᴏʀᴅ had done for David and Solomon and for his people Israel.

The Lᴏʀᴅ Appears to Solomon

¹¹When Solomon had finished the temple of the Lᴏʀᴅ and the royal palace, and had succeeded in carrying out all he

ᵃ7 Traditionally *peace offerings*   ᵇ8 Or *from the entrance to* had in mind to do in the temple of the LORD and in his own palace, ¹²the LORD appeared to him at night and said:

"I have heard your prayer and have chosen this place for myself as a temple for sacrifices.

¹³"When I shut up the heavens so that there is no rain, or command locusts to devour the land or send a plague among my people, ¹⁴if my people, who are called by my name, will humble themselves and pray and seek my face and turn from their wicked ways, then will I hear from heaven and will forgive their sin and will heal their land. ¹⁵Now my eyes will be open and my ears attentive to the prayers offered in this place. ¹⁶I have chosen and consecrated this temple so that my Name may be there forever. My eyes and my heart will always be there.

¹⁷"As for you, if you walk before me as David your father did, and do all I command, and observe my de-

crees and laws, ¹⁸I will establish your royal throne, as I covenanted with David your father when I said, 'You shall never fail to have a man to rule over Israel.'

¹⁹"But if you*a* turn away and forsake the decrees and commands I have given you*a* and go off to serve other gods and worship them, ²⁰then I will uproot Israel from my land, which I have given them, and will reject this temple I have consecrated for my Name. I will make it a byword and an object of ridicule among all peoples. ²¹And though this temple is now so imposing, all who pass by will be appalled and say, 'Why has the LORD done such a thing to this land and to this temple?' ²²People will answer, 'Because they have forsaken the LORD, the God of their fathers, who brought them out of Egypt, and have embraced other gods, worshiping and

---

a19 The Hebrew is plural.

Getting My Needs Met

2 CHRONICLES 7:14 The trigger word to this famous verse about prayer is the word *humble*. God said he would meet the needs of Israel if his people would pray, seek him and turn from their sins. It all starts with the proper perspective, however. Who could meet the needs that Israel had? Only God. No matter how hard they tried, the people couldn't meet their own needs. No matter how much they demanded, they couldn't find someone else who could meet their needs. Only God can meet our most basic needs.

Meeting needs has become a significant demand in today's marriage relationship. For example, people have come to expect that marriage will meet their emotional, sexual, recreational and financial needs, just

to mention a few. But this is an impossible task. No one is able to meet all the needs of another. Very early in our own marriage, it became evident that Bob could never meet all my emotional needs. I was looking in the wrong direction. I needed to develop more of a personal prayer life and look to God.

Understanding that God, not a spouse, is the only One who can meet our most significant needs is the first step toward happiness. The next step is very important. We are called to humble ourselves, pray, worship and turn from our selfishness. Then God will hear, forgive and heal. But it all starts with a humble heart and admitting that we have needs that only God can meet.

—Bob & Rosemary

Weekend Warm-up   *What are some of your most significant needs?*

Go to page 466 for your next devotional reading.

serving them—that is why he brought all this disaster on them.' "

Solomon's Other Activities

8 At the end of twenty years, during which Solomon built the temple of the LORD and his own palace, ²Solomon rebuilt the villages that Hiram*ᵃ* had given him, and settled Israelites in them. ³Solomon then went to Hamath Zobah and captured it. ⁴He also built up Tadmor in the desert and all the store cities he had built in Hamath. ⁵He rebuilt Upper Beth Horon and Lower Beth Horon as fortified cities, with walls and with gates and bars, ⁶as well as Baalath and all his store cities, and all the cities for his chariots and for his horses*ᵇ*—whatever he desired to build in Jerusalem, in Lebanon and throughout all the territory he ruled.

⁷All the people left from the Hittites, Amorites, Perizzites, Hivites and Jebusites (these peoples were not Israelites), ⁸that is, their descendants remaining in the land, whom the Israelites had not destroyed—these Solomon conscripted for his slave labor force, as it is to this day. ⁹But Solomon did not make slaves of the Israelites for his work; they were his fighting men, commanders of his captains, and commanders of his chariots and charioteers. ¹⁰They were also King Solomon's chief officials—two hundred and fifty officials supervising the men.

¹¹Solomon brought Pharaoh's daughter up from the City of David to the palace he had built for her, for he said, "My wife must not live in the palace of David king of Israel, because the places the ark of the LORD has entered are holy."

¹²On the altar of the LORD that he had built in front of the portico, Solomon sacrificed burnt offerings to the LORD, ¹³according to the daily requirement for offerings commanded by Moses for Sabbaths, New Moons and the three annual feasts—the Feast of Unleavened Bread, the Feast of Weeks and the Feast of Tabernacles. ¹⁴In keeping with the ordinance of his father David, he appointed the divisions of the priests for their duties, and the Levites to lead the praise and to assist the priests according to each day's requirement. He also appointed the gatekeepers by divisions for the various gates, because

this was what David the man of God had ordered. ¹⁵They did not deviate from the king's commands to the priests or to the Levites in any matter, including that of the treasuries.

¹⁶All Solomon's work was carried out, from the day the foundation of the temple of the LORD was laid until its completion. So the temple of the LORD was finished.

¹⁷Then Solomon went to Ezion Geber and Elath on the coast of Edom. ¹⁸And Hiram sent him ships commanded by his own officers, men who knew the sea. These, with Solomon's men, sailed to Ophir and brought back four hundred and fifty talents*ᶜ* of gold, which they delivered to King Solomon.

The Queen of Sheba Visits Solomon

9 When the queen of Sheba heard of Solomon's fame, she came to Jerusalem to test him with hard questions. Arriving with a very great caravan—with camels carrying spices, large quantities of gold, and precious stones—she came to Solomon and talked with him about all she had on her mind. ²Solomon answered all her questions; nothing was too hard for him to explain to her. ³When the queen of Sheba saw the wisdom of Solomon, as well as the palace he had built, ⁴the food on his table, the seating of his officials, the attending servants in their robes, the cupbearers in their robes and the burnt offerings he made at*ᵈ* the temple of the LORD, she was overwhelmed.

⁵She said to the king, "The report I heard in my own country about your achievements and your wisdom is true. ⁶But I did not believe what they said until I came and saw with my own eyes. Indeed, not even half the greatness of your wisdom was told me; you have far exceeded the report I heard. ⁷How happy your men must be! How happy your officials, who continually stand before you and hear your wisdom! ⁸Praise be to the LORD your God, who has delighted in you and placed you on his throne as king to rule for the LORD your God. Because of the

ᵃ2 Hebrew *Huram,* a variant of *Hiram;* also in verse 18   *ᵇ6* Or *charioteers*   *ᶜ18* That is, about 17 tons (about 16 metric tons)   *ᵈ4* Or *the ascent by which he went up to* love of your God for Israel and his desire to uphold them forever, he has made you king over them, to maintain justice and righteousness."

⁹Then she gave the king 120 talents*a* of gold, large quantities of spices, and precious stones. There had never been such spices as those the queen of Sheba gave to King Solomon.

¹⁰(The men of Hiram and the men of Solomon brought gold from Ophir; they also brought algumwood*b* and precious stones. ¹¹The king used the algumwood to make steps for the temple of the LORD and for the royal palace, and to make harps and lyres for the musicians. Nothing like them had ever been seen in Judah.)

¹²King Solomon gave the queen of Sheba all she desired and asked for; he gave her more than she had brought to him. Then she left and returned with her retinue to her own country.

Solomon's Splendor

¹³The weight of the gold that Solomon received yearly was 666 talents,*c* ¹⁴not including the revenues brought in by merchants and traders. Also all the kings of Arabia and the governors of the land brought gold and silver to Solomon.

¹⁵King Solomon made two hundred large shields of hammered gold; six hundred bekas*d* of hammered gold went into each shield. ¹⁶He also made three hundred small shields of hammered gold, with three hundred bekas*e* of gold in each shield. The king put them in the Palace of the Forest of Lebanon.

¹⁷Then the king made a great throne inlaid with ivory and overlaid with pure gold. ¹⁸The throne had six steps, and a footstool of gold was attached to it. On both sides of the seat were armrests, with a lion standing beside each of them. ¹⁹Twelve lions stood on the six steps, one at either end of each step. Nothing like it had ever been made for any other kingdom. ²⁰All King Solomon's goblets were gold, and all the household articles in the Palace of the Forest of Lebanon were pure gold. Nothing was made of silver, because silver was considered of little value in Solomon's day. ²¹The king had a fleet of trading ships*f* manned by Hiram's*g* men.

Once every three years it returned, carrying gold, silver and ivory, and apes and baboons.

²²King Solomon was greater in riches and wisdom than all the other kings of the earth. ²³All the kings of the earth sought audience with Solomon to hear the wisdom God had put in his heart. ²⁴Year after year, everyone who came brought a gift—articles of silver and gold, and robes, weapons and spices, and horses and mules.

²⁵Solomon had four thousand stalls for horses and chariots, and twelve thousand horses,*h* which he kept in the chariot cities and also with him in Jerusalem. ²⁶He ruled over all the kings from the River*i* to the land of the Philistines, as far as the border of Egypt. ²⁷The king made silver as common in Jerusalem as stones, and cedar as plentiful as sycamore-fig trees in the foothills. ²⁸Solomon's horses were imported from Egypt*j* and from all other countries.

Solomon's Death

²⁹As for the other events of Solomon's reign, from beginning to end, are they not written in the records of Nathan the prophet, in the prophecy of Ahijah the Shilonite and in the visions of Iddo the seer concerning Jeroboam son of Nebat? ³⁰Solomon reigned in Jerusalem over all Israel forty years. ³¹Then he rested with his fathers and was buried in the city of David his father. And Rehoboam his son succeeded him as king.

Israel Rebels Against Rehoboam

10 Rehoboam went to Shechem, for all the Israelites had gone there to make him king. ²When Jeroboam son of Nebat heard this (he was in Egypt, where he had fled from King Solomon), he returned from Egypt. ³So they sent for Jeroboam, and he and all Israel went to Reho-

---

*a*9 That is, about 4 1/2 tons (about 4 metric tons)
*b*10 Probably a variant of *almugwood*　　*c*13 That is, about 25 tons (about 23 metric tons)
*d*15 That is, about 7 1/2 pounds (about 3.5 kilograms)　　*e*16 That is, about 3 3/4 pounds (about 1.7 kilograms)　　*f*21 Hebrew *of ships that could go to Tarshish*　　*g*21 Hebrew *Huram*, a variant of *Hiram*　　*h*25 Or *charioteers*
*i*26 That is, the Euphrates　　*j*28 Or possibly *Muzur*, a region in Cilicia

boam and said to him: [4]"Your father put a heavy yoke on us, but now lighten the harsh labor and the heavy yoke he put on us, and we will serve you."

[5]Rehoboam answered, "Come back to me in three days." So the people went away.

[6]Then King Rehoboam consulted the elders who had served his father Solomon during his lifetime. "How would you advise me to answer these people?" he asked.

[7]They replied, "If you will be kind to these people and please them and give them a favorable answer, they will always be your servants."

[8]But Rehoboam rejected the advice the elders gave him and consulted the young men who had grown up with him and were serving him. [9]He asked them, "What is your advice? How should we answer these people who say to me, 'Lighten the yoke your father put on us'?"

[10]The young men who had grown up with him replied, "Tell the people who have said to you, 'Your father put a heavy yoke on us, but make our yoke lighter'— tell them, 'My little finger is thicker than my father's waist. [11]My father laid on you a heavy yoke; I will make it even heavier. My father scourged you with whips; I will scourge you with scorpions.'"

[12]Three days later Jeroboam and all the people returned to Rehoboam, as the king had said, "Come back to me in three days." [13]The king answered them harshly. Rejecting the advice of the elders, [14]he followed the advice of the young men and said, "My father made your yoke heavy; I will make it even heavier. My father scourged you with whips; I will scourge you with scorpions." [15]So the king did not listen to the people, for this turn of events was from God, to fulfill the word the LORD had spoken to Jeroboam son of Nebat through Ahijah the Shilonite.

[16]When all Israel saw that the king refused to listen to them, they answered the king:

"What share do we have in David,
    what part in Jesse's son?
To your tents, O Israel!
    Look after your own house,
        O David!"

So all the Israelites went home. [17]But as

for the Israelites who were living in the towns of Judah, Rehoboam still ruled over them.

[18]King Rehoboam sent out Adoniram,[a] who was in charge of forced labor, but the Israelites stoned him to death. King Rehoboam, however, managed to get into his chariot and escape to Jerusalem. [19]So Israel has been in rebellion against the house of David to this day.

11 When Rehoboam arrived in Jerusalem, he mustered the house of Judah and Benjamin—a hundred and eighty thousand fighting men—to make war against Israel and to regain the kingdom for Rehoboam.

[2]But this word of the LORD came to Shemaiah the man of God: [3]"Say to Rehoboam son of Solomon king of Judah and to all the Israelites in Judah and Benjamin, [4]'This is what the LORD says: Do not go up to fight against your brothers. Go home, every one of you, for this is my doing.'" So they obeyed the words of the LORD and turned back from marching against Jeroboam.

Rehoboam Fortifies Judah

[5]Rehoboam lived in Jerusalem and built up towns for defense in Judah: [6]Bethlehem, Etam, Tekoa, [7]Beth Zur, Soco, Adullam, [8]Gath, Mareshah, Ziph, [9]Adoraim, Lachish, Azekah, [10]Zorah, Aijalon and Hebron. These were fortified cities in Judah and Benjamin. [11]He strengthened their defenses and put commanders in them, with supplies of food, olive oil and wine. [12]He put shields and spears in all the cities, and made them very strong. So Judah and Benjamin were his.

[13]The priests and Levites from all their districts throughout Israel sided with him. [14]The Levites even abandoned their pasturelands and property, and came to Judah and Jerusalem because Jeroboam and his sons had rejected them as priests of the LORD. [15]And he appointed his own priests for the high places and for the goat and calf idols he had made. [16]Those from every tribe of Israel who set their hearts on seeking the LORD, the God of Israel, followed the Levites to Jerusalem to offer sacrifices to the LORD, the God of their fathers. [17]They strengthened the kingdom

---

[a]18 Hebrew *Hadoram*, a variant of *Adoniram*

of Judah and supported Rehoboam son of Solomon three years, walking in the ways of David and Solomon during this time.

Rehoboam's Family

[18]Rehoboam married Mahalath, who was the daughter of David's son Jerimoth and of Abihail, the daughter of Jesse's son Eliab. [19]She bore him sons: Jeush, Shemariah and Zaham. [20]Then he married Maacah daughter of Absalom, who bore him Abijah, Attai, Ziza and Shelomith. [21]Rehoboam loved Maacah daughter of Absalom more than any of his other wives and concubines. In all, he had eighteen wives and sixty concubines, twenty-eight sons and sixty daughters.

[22]Rehoboam appointed Abijah son of Maacah to be the chief prince among his brothers, in order to make him king. [23]He acted wisely, dispersing some of his sons throughout the districts of Judah and Benjamin, and to all the fortified cities. He gave them abundant provisions and took many wives for them.

Shishak Attacks Jerusalem

12 After Rehoboam's position as king was established and he had become strong, he and all Israel[a] with him abandoned the law of the LORD. [2]Because they had been unfaithful to the LORD, Shishak king of Egypt attacked Jerusalem in the fifth year of King Rehoboam. [3]With twelve hundred chariots and sixty thousand horsemen and the innumerable troops of Libyans, Sukkites and Cushites[b] that came with him from Egypt, [4]he captured the fortified cities of Judah and came as far as Jerusalem.

[5]Then the prophet Shemaiah came to Rehoboam and to the leaders of Judah who had assembled in Jerusalem for fear of Shishak, and he said to them, "This is what the LORD says, 'You have abandoned me; therefore, I now abandon you to Shishak.' "

[6]The leaders of Israel and the king humbled themselves and said, "The LORD is just."

[7]When the LORD saw that they humbled themselves, this word of the LORD came to Shemaiah: "Since they have humbled themselves, I will not destroy them but will soon give them deliverance.

My wrath will not be poured out on Jerusalem through Shishak. [8]They will, however, become subject to him, so that they may learn the difference between serving me and serving the kings of other lands."

[9]When Shishak king of Egypt attacked Jerusalem, he carried off the treasures of the temple of the LORD and the treasures of the royal palace. He took everything, including the gold shields Solomon had made. [10]So King Rehoboam made bronze shields to replace them and assigned these to the commanders of the guard on duty at the entrance to the royal palace. [11]Whenever the king went to the LORD's temple, the guards went with him, bearing the shields, and afterward they returned them to the guardroom.

[12]Because Rehoboam humbled himself, the LORD's anger turned from him, and he was not totally destroyed. Indeed, there was some good in Judah.

[13]King Rehoboam established himself firmly in Jerusalem and continued as king. He was forty-one years old when he became king, and he reigned seventeen years in Jerusalem, the city the LORD had chosen out of all the tribes of Israel in which to put his Name. His mother's name was Naamah; she was an Ammonite. [14]He did evil because he had not set his heart on seeking the LORD.

[15]As for the events of Rehoboam's reign, from beginning to end, are they not written in the records of Shemaiah the prophet and of Iddo the seer that deal with genealogies? There was continual warfare between Rehoboam and Jeroboam. [16]Rehoboam rested with his fathers and was buried in the City of David. And Abijah his son succeeded him as king.

Abijah King of Judah

13 In the eighteenth year of the reign of Jeroboam, Abijah became king of Judah, [2]and he reigned in Jerusalem three years. His mother's name was Maacah,[c] a daughter[d] of Uriel of Gibeah.

There was war between Abijah and Jeroboam. [3]Abijah went into battle with a force of four hundred thousand able

---

[a]1 That is, Judah, as frequently in 2 Chronicles
[b]3 That is, people from the upper Nile region
[c]2 Most Septuagint manuscripts and Syriac (see also 2 Chron. 11:20 and 1 Kings 15:2); Hebrew *Micaiah*   [d]2 Or *granddaughter*

fighting men, and Jeroboam drew up a battle line against him with eight hundred thousand able troops.

⁴Abijah stood on Mount Zemaraim, in the hill country of Ephraim, and said, "Jeroboam and all Israel, listen to me! ⁵Don't you know that the LORD, the God of Israel, has given the kingship of Israel to David and his descendants forever by a covenant of salt? ⁶Yet Jeroboam son of Nebat, an official of Solomon son of David, rebelled against his master. ⁷Some worthless scoundrels gathered around him and opposed Rehoboam son of Solomon when he was young and indecisive and not strong enough to resist them.

⁸"And now you plan to resist the kingdom of the LORD, which is in the hands of David's descendants. You are indeed a vast army and have with you the golden calves that Jeroboam made to be your gods. ⁹But didn't you drive out the priests of the LORD, the sons of Aaron, and the Levites, and make priests of your own as the peoples of other lands do? Whoever comes to consecrate himself with a young bull and seven rams may become a priest of what are not gods.

¹⁰"As for us, the LORD is our God, and we have not forsaken him. The priests who serve the LORD are sons of Aaron, and the Levites assist them. ¹¹Every morning and evening they present burnt offerings and fragrant incense to the LORD. They set out the bread on the ceremonially clean table and light the lamps on the gold lampstand every evening. We are observing the requirements of the LORD our God. But you have forsaken him. ¹²God is with us; he is our leader. His priests with their trumpets will sound the battle cry against you. Men of Israel, do not fight against the LORD, the God of your fathers, for you will not succeed."

¹³Now Jeroboam had sent troops around to the rear, so that while he was in front of Judah the ambush was behind them. ¹⁴Judah turned and saw that they were being attacked at both front and rear. Then they cried out to the LORD. The priests blew their trumpets ¹⁵and the men of Judah raised the battle cry. At the sound of their battle cry, God routed Jeroboam and all Israel before Abijah and Judah. ¹⁶The Israelites fled before Judah, and God delivered them into their hands.

¹⁷Abijah and his men inflicted heavy losses on them, so that there were five hundred thousand casualties among Israel's able men. ¹⁸The men of Israel were subdued on that occasion, and the men of Judah were victorious because they relied on the LORD, the God of their fathers.

¹⁹Abijah pursued Jeroboam and took from him the towns of Bethel, Jeshanah and Ephron, with their surrounding villages. ²⁰Jeroboam did not regain power during the time of Abijah. And the LORD struck him down and he died.

²¹But Abijah grew in strength. He married fourteen wives and had twenty-two sons and sixteen daughters.

²²The other events of Abijah's reign, what he did and what he said, are written in the annotations of the prophet Iddo.

14 And Abijah rested with his fathers and was buried in the City of David. Asa his son succeeded him as king, and in his days the country was at peace for ten years.

Asa King of Judah

²Asa did what was good and right in the eyes of the LORD his God. ³He removed the foreign altars and the high places, smashed the sacred stones and cut down the Asherah poles.ᵃ ⁴He commanded Judah to seek the LORD, the God of their fathers, and to obey his laws and commands. ⁵He removed the high places and incense altars in every town in Judah, and the kingdom was at peace under him. ⁶He built up the fortified cities of Judah, since the land was at peace. No one was at war with him during those years, for the LORD gave him rest.

⁷"Let us build up these towns," he said to Judah, "and put walls around them, with towers, gates and bars. The land is still ours, because we have sought the LORD our God; we sought him and he has given us rest on every side." So they built and prospered.

⁸Asa had an army of three hundred thousand men from Judah, equipped with large shields and with spears, and two hundred and eighty thousand from Benjamin, armed with small shields and

---

ᵃ3 That is, symbols of the goddess Asherah; here and elsewhere in 2 Chronicles with bows. All these were brave fighting men.

⁹Zerah the Cushite marched out against them with a vast army*a* and three hundred chariots, and came as far as Mareshah. ¹⁰Asa went out to meet him, and they took up battle positions in the Valley of Zephathah near Mareshah.

¹¹Then Asa called to the LORD his God and said, "LORD, there is no one like you to help the powerless against the mighty. Help us, O LORD our God, for we rely on you, and in your name we have come against this vast army. O LORD, you are our God; do not let man prevail against you."

¹²The LORD struck down the Cushites before Asa and Judah. The Cushites fled, ¹³and Asa and his army pursued them as far as Gerar. Such a great number of Cushites fell that they could not recover; they were crushed before the LORD and his forces. The men of Judah carried off a large amount of plunder. ¹⁴They destroyed all the villages around Gerar, for the terror of the LORD had fallen upon them. They plundered all these villages, since there was much booty there. ¹⁵They also attacked the camps of the herdsmen and carried off droves of sheep and goats and camels. Then they returned to Jerusalem.

Asa's Reform

15 The Spirit of God came upon Azariah son of Oded. ²He went out to meet Asa and said to him, "Listen to me, Asa and all Judah and Benjamin. The LORD is with you when you are with him. If you seek him, he will be found by you, but if you forsake him, he will forsake you. ³For a long time Israel was without the true God, without a priest to teach and without the law. ⁴But in their distress they turned to the LORD, the God of Israel, and sought him, and he was found by them. ⁵In those days it was not safe to travel about, for all the inhabitants of the lands were in great turmoil. ⁶One nation was being crushed by another and one city by another, because God was troubling them with every kind of distress. ⁷But as for you, be strong and do not give up, for your work will be rewarded."

⁸When Asa heard these words and the

prophecy of Azariah son of*b* Oded the prophet, he took courage. He removed the detestable idols from the whole land of Judah and Benjamin and from the towns he had captured in the hills of Ephraim. He repaired the altar of the LORD that was in front of the portico of the LORD's temple.

⁹Then he assembled all Judah and Benjamin and the people from Ephraim, Manasseh and Simeon who had settled among them, for large numbers had come over to him from Israel when they saw that the LORD his God was with him.

¹⁰They assembled at Jerusalem in the third month of the fifteenth year of Asa's reign. ¹¹At that time they sacrificed to the LORD seven hundred head of cattle and seven thousand sheep and goats from the plunder they had brought back. ¹²They entered into a covenant to seek the LORD, the God of their fathers, with all their heart and soul. ¹³All who would not seek the LORD, the God of Israel, were to be put to death, whether small or great, man or woman. ¹⁴They took an oath to the LORD with loud acclamation, with shouting and with trumpets and horns. ¹⁵All Judah rejoiced about the oath because they had sworn it wholeheartedly. They sought God eagerly, and he was found by them. So the LORD gave them rest on every side.

¹⁶King Asa also deposed his grandmother Maacah from her position as queen mother, because she had made a repulsive Asherah pole. Asa cut the pole down, broke it up and burned it in the Kidron Valley. ¹⁷Although he did not remove the high places from Israel, Asa's heart was fully committed ⌊to the LORD⌋ all his life. ¹⁸He brought into the temple of God the silver and gold and the articles that he and his father had dedicated.

¹⁹There was no more war until the thirty-fifth year of Asa's reign.

Asa's Last Years

16 In the thirty-sixth year of Asa's reign Baasha king of Israel went up against Judah and fortified Ramah to pre-

---

a 9 Hebrew *with an army of a thousand thousands* or *with an army of thousands upon thousands*
b 8 Vulgate and Syriac (see also Septuagint and verse 1); Hebrew does not have *Azariah son of.*

vent anyone from leaving or entering the territory of Asa king of Judah.

²Asa then took the silver and gold out of the treasuries of the LORD's temple and of his own palace and sent it to Ben-Hadad king of Aram, who was ruling in Damascus. ³"Let there be a treaty between me and you," he said, "as there was between my father and your father. See, I am sending you silver and gold. Now break your treaty with Baasha king of Israel so he will withdraw from me."

⁴Ben-Hadad agreed with King Asa and sent the commanders of his forces against the towns of Israel. They conquered Ijon, Dan, Abel Maim*a* and all the store cities of Naphtali. ⁵When Baasha heard this, he stopped building Ramah and abandoned his work. ⁶Then King Asa brought all the men of Judah, and they carried away from Ramah the stones and timber Baasha had been using. With them he built up Geba and Mizpah.

⁷At that time Hanani the seer came to Asa king of Judah and said to him: "Because you relied on the king of Aram and not on the LORD your God, the army of the king of Aram has escaped from your hand. ⁸Were not the Cushites*b* and Libyans a mighty army with great numbers of chariots and horsemen*c*? Yet when you relied on the LORD, he delivered them into your hand. ⁹For the eyes of the LORD range throughout the earth to strengthen those whose hearts are fully committed to him. You have done a foolish thing, and from now on you will be at war."

¹⁰Asa was angry with the seer because of this; he was so enraged that he put him in prison. At the same time Asa brutally oppressed some of the people.

¹¹The events of Asa's reign, from beginning to end, are written in the book of the kings of Judah and Israel. ¹²In the thirty-ninth year of his reign Asa was afflicted with a disease in his feet. Though his disease was severe, even in his illness he did not seek help from the LORD, but only from the physicians. ¹³Then in the forty-first year of his reign Asa died and rested with his fathers. ¹⁴They buried him in the tomb that he had cut out for himself in the City of David. They laid him on a bier covered with spices and various blended perfumes, and they made a huge fire in his honor.

Jehoshaphat King of Judah

17 Jehoshaphat his son succeeded him as king and strengthened himself against Israel. ²He stationed troops in all the fortified cities of Judah and put garrisons in Judah and in the towns of Ephraim that his father Asa had captured.

³The LORD was with Jehoshaphat because in his early years he walked in the ways his father David had followed. He did not consult the Baals ⁴but sought the God of his father and followed his commands rather than the practices of Israel. ⁵The LORD established the kingdom under his control; and all Judah brought gifts to Jehoshaphat, so that he had great wealth and honor. ⁶His heart was devoted to the ways of the LORD; furthermore, he removed the high places and the Asherah poles from Judah.

⁷In the third year of his reign he sent his officials Ben-Hail, Obadiah, Zechariah, Nethanel and Micaiah to teach in the towns of Judah. ⁸With them were certain Levites—Shemaiah, Nethaniah, Zebadiah, Asahel, Shemiramoth, Jehonathan, Adonijah, Tobijah and Tob-Adonijah—and the priests Elishama and Jehoram. ⁹They taught throughout Judah, taking with them the Book of the Law of the LORD; they went around to all the towns of Judah and taught the people.

¹⁰The fear of the LORD fell on all the kingdoms of the lands surrounding Judah, so that they did not make war with Jehoshaphat. ¹¹Some Philistines brought Jehoshaphat gifts and silver as tribute, and the Arabs brought him flocks: seven thousand seven hundred rams and seven thousand seven hundred goats.

¹²Jehoshaphat became more and more powerful; he built forts and store cities in Judah ¹³and had large supplies in the towns of Judah. He also kept experienced fighting men in Jerusalem. ¹⁴Their enrollment by families was as follows:

From Judah, commanders of units of 1,000:
Adnah the commander, with 300,000 fighting men;

a4 Also known as *Abel Beth Maacah*   *b8* That is, people from the upper Nile region   *c8* Or *charioteers*

15next, Jehohanan the commander,
with 280,000;

16next, Amasiah son of Zicri, who
volunteered himself for the
service of the LORD, with
200,000.

17From Benjamin:

Eliada, a valiant soldier, with
200,000 men armed with
bows and shields;

18next, Jehozabad, with 180,000
men armed for battle.

19These were the men who served the
king, besides those he stationed in the
fortified cities throughout Judah.

Micaiah Prophesies Against Ahab

18 Now Jehoshaphat had great wealth
and honor, and he allied himself
with Ahab by marriage. 2Some years later
he went down to visit Ahab in Samaria.
Ahab slaughtered many sheep and cattle
for him and the people with him and
urged him to attack Ramoth Gilead.
3Ahab king of Israel asked Jehoshaphat
king of Judah, "Will you go with me
against Ramoth Gilead?"

Jehoshaphat replied, "I am as you are,
and my people as your people; we will
join you in the war." 4But Jehoshaphat also
said to the king of Israel, "First seek the
counsel of the LORD."

5So the king of Israel brought together
the prophets—four hundred men—and
asked them, "Shall we go to war against
Ramoth Gilead, or shall I refrain?"

"Go," they answered, "for God will give
it into the king's hand."

6But Jehoshaphat asked, "Is there not a
prophet of the LORD here whom we can
inquire of?"

7The king of Israel answered Jehoshaphat, "There is still one man through
whom we can inquire of the LORD, but
I hate him because he never prophesies
anything good about me, but always bad.
He is Micaiah son of Imlah."

"The king should not say that," Jehoshaphat replied.

8So the king of Israel called one of his
officials and said, "Bring Micaiah son of
Imlah at once."

9Dressed in their royal robes, the king
of Israel and Jehoshaphat king of Judah
were sitting on their thrones at the threshing floor by the entrance to the gate of
Samaria, with all the prophets prophesying before them. 10Now Zedekiah son of
Kenaanah had made iron horns, and he
declared, "This is what the LORD says:
'With these you will gore the Arameans
until they are destroyed.' "

11All the other prophets were prophesying the same thing. "Attack Ramoth
Gilead and be victorious," they said, "for
the LORD will give it into the king's hand."

12The messenger who had gone to
summon Micaiah said to him, "Look, as
one man the other prophets are predict-
ing success for the king. Let your word
agree with theirs, and speak favorably."

13But Micaiah said, "As surely as the
LORD lives, I can tell him only what my
God says."

14When he arrived, the king asked him,
"Micaiah, shall we go to war against Ramoth Gilead, or shall I refrain?"

"Attack and be victorious," he answered, "for they will be given into your
hand."

15The king said to him, "How many
times must I make you swear to tell me
nothing but the truth in the name of the
LORD?"

16Then Micaiah answered, "I saw all
Israel scattered on the hills like sheep
without a shepherd, and the LORD said,
'These people have no master. Let each
one go home in peace.' "

17The king of Israel said to Jehoshaphat, "Didn't I tell you that he never
prophesies anything good about me, but
only bad?"

18Micaiah continued, "Therefore hear
the word of the LORD: I saw the LORD
sitting on his throne with all the host of
heaven standing on his right and on his
left. 19And the LORD said, 'Who will entice
Ahab king of Israel into attacking Ramoth
Gilead and going to his death there?'

"One suggested this, and another that.
20Finally, a spirit came forward, stood before the LORD and said, 'I will entice him.'

" 'By what means?' the LORD asked.

21 " 'I will go and be a lying spirit in the
mouths of all his prophets,' he said.

" 'You will succeed in enticing him,'
said the LORD. 'Go and do it.'

22"So now the LORD has put a lying
spirit in the mouths of these prophets of

yours. The LORD has decreed disaster for you."

²³Then Zedekiah son of Kenaanah went up and slapped Micaiah in the face. "Which way did the spirit from*ᵃ* the LORD go when he went from me to speak to you?" he asked.

²⁴Micaiah replied, "You will find out on the day you go to hide in an inner room."

²⁵The king of Israel then ordered, "Take Micaiah and send him back to Amon the ruler of the city and to Joash the king's son, ²⁶and say, 'This is what the king says: Put this fellow in prison and give him nothing but bread and water until I return safely.' "

²⁷Micaiah declared, "If you ever return safely, the LORD has not spoken through me." Then he added, "Mark my words, all you people!"

Ahab Killed at Ramoth Gilead

²⁸So the king of Israel and Jehoshaphat king of Judah went up to Ramoth Gilead. ²⁹The king of Israel said to Jehoshaphat, "I will enter the battle in disguise, but you wear your royal robes." So the king of Israel disguised himself and went into battle.

³⁰Now the king of Aram had ordered his chariot commanders, "Do not fight with anyone, small or great, except the king of Israel." ³¹When the chariot commanders saw Jehoshaphat, they thought, "This is the king of Israel." So they turned to attack him, but Jehoshaphat cried out, and the LORD helped him. God drew them away from him, ³²for when the chariot commanders saw that he was not the king of Israel, they stopped pursuing him.

³³But someone drew his bow at random and hit the king of Israel between the sections of his armor. The king told the chariot driver, "Wheel around and get me out of the fighting. I've been wounded." ³⁴All day long the battle raged, and the king of Israel propped himself up in his chariot facing the Arameans until evening. Then at sunset he died.

19 When Jehoshaphat king of Judah returned safely to his palace in Jerusalem, ²Jehu the seer, the son of Hanani, went out to meet him and said to the king, "Should you help the wicked and love*ᵇ* those who hate the LORD? Because of this, the wrath of the LORD is upon you. ³There is, however, some good in you, for you have rid the land of the Asherah poles and have set your heart on seeking God."

Jehoshaphat Appoints Judges

⁴Jehoshaphat lived in Jerusalem, and he went out again among the people from Beersheba to the hill country of Ephraim and turned them back to the LORD, the God of their fathers. ⁵He appointed judges in the land, in each of the fortified cities of Judah. ⁶He told them, "Consider carefully what you do, because you are not judging for man but for the LORD, who is with you whenever you give a verdict. ⁷Now let the fear of the LORD be upon you. Judge carefully, for with the LORD our God there is no injustice or partiality or bribery."

⁸In Jerusalem also, Jehoshaphat appointed some of the Levites, priests and heads of Israelite families to administer the law of the LORD and to settle disputes. And they lived in Jerusalem. ⁹He gave them these orders: "You must serve faithfully and wholeheartedly in the fear of the LORD. ¹⁰In every case that comes before you from your fellow countrymen who live in the cities—whether bloodshed or other concerns of the law, commands, decrees or ordinances—you are to warn them not to sin against the LORD; otherwise his wrath will come on you and your brothers. Do this, and you will not sin.

¹¹"Amariah the chief priest will be over you in any matter concerning the LORD, and Zebadiah son of Ishmael, the leader of the tribe of Judah, will be over you in any matter concerning the king, and the Levites will serve as officials before you. Act with courage, and may the LORD be with those who do well."

Jehoshaphat Defeats Moab and Ammon

20 After this, the Moabites and Ammonites with some of the Meunites*ᶜ* came to make war on Jehoshaphat.

²Some men came and told Jehosha-

ᵃ23 Or *Spirit of*   *ᵇ2* Or *and make alliances with*
ᶜ1 Some Septuagint manuscripts; Hebrew *Ammonites*

phat, "A vast army is coming against you from Edom,ᵃ from the other side of the Sea.ᵇ It is already in Hazazon Tamar" (that is, En Gedi). ³Alarmed, Jehoshaphat resolved to inquire of the LORD, and he proclaimed a fast for all Judah. ⁴The people of Judah came together to seek help from the LORD; indeed, they came from every town in Judah to seek him.

⁵Then Jehoshaphat stood up in the assembly of Judah and Jerusalem at the temple of the LORD in the front of the new courtyard ⁶and said:

"O LORD, God of our fathers, are you not the God who is in heaven? You rule over all the kingdoms of the nations. Power and might are in your hand, and no one can withstand you. ⁷O our God, did you not drive out the inhabitants of this land before your people Israel and give it forever to the descendants of Abraham your friend? ⁸They have lived in it and have built in it a sanctuary for your Name, saying, ⁹'If calamity comes upon us, whether the sword of judgment, or plague or famine, we will stand in your presence before this temple that bears your Name and will cry out to you in our distress, and you will hear us and save us.'

¹⁰"But now here are men from Ammon, Moab and Mount Seir, whose territory you would not allow Israel to invade when they came from Egypt; so they turned away from them and did not destroy them. ¹¹See how they are repaying us by coming to drive us out of the possession you gave us as an inheritance. ¹²O our God, will you not judge them? For we have no power to face this vast army that is attacking us. We do not know what to do, but our eyes are upon you."

¹³All the men of Judah, with their wives and children and little ones, stood there before the LORD.

¹⁴Then the Spirit of the LORD came upon Jahaziel son of Zechariah, the son of Benaiah, the son of Jeiel, the son of Mattaniah, a Levite and descendant of Asaph, as he stood in the assembly.

¹⁵He said: "Listen, King Jehoshaphat and all who live in Judah and Jerusalem! This is what the LORD says to you: 'Do not be afraid or discouraged because of this vast army. For the battle is not yours, but God's. ¹⁶Tomorrow march down against

ᵃ2 One Hebrew manuscript; most Hebrew manuscripts, Septuagint and Vulgate *Aram*
ᵇ2 That is, the Dead Sea

Whose Battle Is It?

Monday

2 CHRONICLES 20:15–17 In this passage a vast army was ready to attack the Israelites. They were outnumbered, and they had no great war plan. They had no idea what they should do. It would've been tempting to panic or hide, complain or blame others, or beg for mercy; but the Israelites did something completely different. They admitted their lack of power and lack of plan, and they confessed their belief in God's power and chose to keep their eyes on him. Rather than focusing on the problem, they focused on the problem solver.

If we look at this passage through a marriage lens, there is a lesson here for spouses. At times we all face situations that seem hopeless when disaster is on the horizon—marital problems, relational disharmony, loneliness or maybe uncontrollable children.

At times like this we need to remember 2 Chronicles 20 and admit to God that we don't know what to do but are promising to keep our eyes on him anyway. We can take the Lord's response to the Israelites and claim it for our own marriages and personal situations. Just as God provided a miracle for the Israelites, when you keep your eyes on him, whatever happens, his miraculous love and care will see you through.

—Dave & Claudia

Go to page 481 for your next devotional reading.

them. They will be climbing up by the Pass of Ziz, and you will find them at the end of the gorge in the Desert of Jeruel. ¹⁷You will not have to fight this battle. Take up your positions; stand firm and see the deliverance the LORD will give you, O Judah and Jerusalem. Do not be afraid; do not be discouraged. Go out to face them tomorrow, and the LORD will be with you.' "

¹⁸Jehoshaphat bowed with his face to the ground, and all the people of Judah and Jerusalem fell down in worship before the LORD. ¹⁹Then some Levites from the Kohathites and Korahites stood up and praised the LORD, the God of Israel, with very loud voice.

²⁰Early in the morning they left for the Desert of Tekoa. As they set out, Jehoshaphat stood and said, "Listen to me, Judah and people of Jerusalem! Have faith in the LORD your God and you will be upheld; have faith in his prophets and you will be successful." ²¹After consulting the people, Jehoshaphat appointed men to sing to the LORD and to praise him for the splendor of his*a* holiness as they went out at the head of the army, saying:

"Give thanks to the LORD,
   for his love endures forever."

²²As they began to sing and praise, the LORD set ambushes against the men of Ammon and Moab and Mount Seir who were invading Judah, and they were defeated. ²³The men of Ammon and Moab rose up against the men from Mount Seir to destroy and annihilate them. After they finished slaughtering the men from Seir, they helped to destroy one another.

²⁴When the men of Judah came to the place that overlooks the desert and looked toward the vast army, they saw only dead bodies lying on the ground; no one had escaped. ²⁵So Jehoshaphat and his men went to carry off their plunder, and they found among them a great amount of equipment and clothing*b* and also articles of value—more than they could take away. There was so much plunder that it took three days to collect it. ²⁶On the fourth day they assembled in the Valley of Beracah, where they praised the LORD. This is why it is called the Valley of Beracah*c* to this day.

²⁷Then, led by Jehoshaphat, all the men of Judah and Jerusalem returned joyfully to Jerusalem, for the LORD had given them cause to rejoice over their enemies. ²⁸They entered Jerusalem and went to the temple of the LORD with harps and lutes and trumpets.

²⁹The fear of God came upon all the kingdoms of the countries when they heard how the LORD had fought against the enemies of Israel. ³⁰And the kingdom of Jehoshaphat was at peace, for his God had given him rest on every side.

The End of Jehoshaphat's Reign

³¹So Jehoshaphat reigned over Judah. He was thirty-five years old when he became king of Judah, and he reigned in Jerusalem twenty-five years. His mother's name was Azubah daughter of Shilhi. ³²He walked in the ways of his father Asa and did not stray from them; he did what was right in the eyes of the LORD. ³³The high places, however, were not removed, and the people still had not set their hearts on the God of their fathers.

³⁴The other events of Jehoshaphat's reign, from beginning to end, are written in the annals of Jehu son of Hanani, which are recorded in the book of the kings of Israel.

³⁵Later, Jehoshaphat king of Judah made an alliance with Ahaziah king of Israel, who was guilty of wickedness. ³⁶He agreed with him to construct a fleet of trading ships.*d* After these were built at Ezion Geber, ³⁷Eliezer son of Dodavahu of Mareshah prophesied against Jehoshaphat, saying, "Because you have made an alliance with Ahaziah, the LORD will destroy what you have made." The ships were wrecked and were not able to set sail to trade.*e*

21 Then Jehoshaphat rested with his fathers and was buried with them in the City of David. And Jehoram his son succeeded him as king. ²Jehoram's brothers, the sons of Jehoshaphat, were Azariah, Jehiel, Zechariah, Azariahu, Michael and Shephatiah. All these were sons of Jehoshaphat king of Israel.*f* ³Their fa-

---

*a*21 Or *him with the splendor of*   *b*25 Some Hebrew manuscripts and Vulgate; most Hebrew manuscripts *corpses*   *c*26 *Beracah* means *praise.*   *d*36 Hebrew *of ships that could go to Tarshish*   *e*37 Hebrew *sail for Tarshish*   *f*2 That is, Judah, as frequently in 2 Chronicles ther had given them many gifts of silver and gold and articles of value, as well as fortified cities in Judah, but he had given the kingdom to Jehoram because he was his firstborn son.

Jehoram King of Judah

⁴When Jehoram established himself firmly over his father's kingdom, he put all his brothers to the sword along with some of the princes of Israel. ⁵Jehoram was thirty-two years old when he became king, and he reigned in Jerusalem eight years. ⁶He walked in the ways of the kings of Israel, as the house of Ahab had done, for he married a daughter of Ahab. He did evil in the eyes of the LORD. ⁷Nevertheless, because of the covenant the LORD had made with David, the LORD was not willing to destroy the house of David. He had promised to maintain a lamp for him and his descendants forever.

⁸In the time of Jehoram, Edom rebelled against Judah and set up its own king. ⁹So Jehoram went there with his officers and all his chariots. The Edomites surrounded him and his chariot commanders, but he rose up and broke through by night. ¹⁰To this day Edom has been in rebellion against Judah.

Libnah revolted at the same time, because Jehoram had forsaken the LORD, the God of his fathers. ¹¹He had also built high places on the hills of Judah and had caused the people of Jerusalem to prostitute themselves and had led Judah astray.

¹²Jehoram received a letter from Elijah the prophet, which said:

"This is what the LORD, the God of your father David, says: 'You have not walked in the ways of your father Jehoshaphat or of Asa king of Judah. ¹³But you have walked in the ways of the kings of Israel, and you have led Judah and the people of Jerusalem to prostitute themselves, just as the house of Ahab did. You have also murdered your own brothers, members of your father's house, men who were better than you. ¹⁴So now the LORD is about to strike your people, your sons, your wives and everything that is yours, with a heavy blow. ¹⁵You yourself will be very ill with a lingering dis-

ease of the bowels, until the disease causes your bowels to come out.' "

¹⁶The LORD aroused against Jehoram the hostility of the Philistines and of the Arabs who lived near the Cushites. ¹⁷They attacked Judah, invaded it and carried off all the goods found in the king's palace, together with his sons and wives. Not a son was left to him except Ahaziah,^a the youngest.

¹⁸After all this, the LORD afflicted Jehoram with an incurable disease of the bowels. ¹⁹In the course of time, at the end of the second year, his bowels came out because of the disease, and he died in great pain. His people made no fire in his honor, as they had for his fathers.

²⁰Jehoram was thirty-two years old when he became king, and he reigned in Jerusalem eight years. He passed away, to no one's regret, and was buried in the City of David, but not in the tombs of the kings.

Ahaziah King of Judah

22 The people of Jerusalem made Ahaziah, Jehoram's youngest son, king in his place, since the raiders, who came with the Arabs into the camp, had killed all the older sons. So Ahaziah son of Jehoram king of Judah began to reign.

²Ahaziah was twenty-two^b years old when he became king, and he reigned in Jerusalem one year. His mother's name was Athaliah, a granddaughter of Omri.

³He too walked in the ways of the house of Ahab, for his mother encouraged him in doing wrong. ⁴He did evil in the eyes of the LORD, as the house of Ahab had done, for after his father's death they became his advisers, to his undoing. ⁵He also followed their counsel when he went with Joram^c son of Ahab king of Israel to war against Hazael king of Aram at Ramoth Gilead. The Arameans wounded Joram; ⁶so he returned to Jezreel to recover from the wounds they had inflicted on him at Ramoth^d in his battle with Hazael king of Aram.

---

^a17 Hebrew *Jehoahaz*, a variant of *Ahaziah*
^b2 Some Septuagint manuscripts and Syriac (see also 2 Kings 8:26); Hebrew *forty-two*
^c5 Hebrew *Jehoram*, a variant of *Joram*; also in verses 6 and 7   ^d6 Hebrew *Ramah*, a variant of *Ramoth*

Then Ahaziah[a] son of Jehoram king of Judah went down to Jezreel to see Joram son of Ahab because he had been wounded.

⁷Through Ahaziah's visit to Joram, God brought about Ahaziah's downfall. When Ahaziah arrived, he went out with Joram to meet Jehu son of Nimshi, whom the LORD had anointed to destroy the house of Ahab. ⁸While Jehu was executing judgment on the house of Ahab, he found the princes of Judah and the sons of Ahaziah's relatives, who had been attending Ahaziah, and he killed them. ⁹He then went in search of Ahaziah, and his men captured him while he was hiding in Samaria. He was brought to Jehu and put to death. They buried him, for they said, "He was a son of Jehoshaphat, who sought the LORD with all his heart." So there was no one in the house of Ahaziah powerful enough to retain the kingdom.

Athaliah and Joash

¹⁰When Athaliah the mother of Ahaziah saw that her son was dead, she proceeded to destroy the whole royal family of the house of Judah. ¹¹But Jehosheba,[b] the daughter of King Jehoram, took Joash son of Ahaziah and stole him away from among the royal princes who were about to be murdered and put him and his nurse in a bedroom. Because Jehosheba,[b] the daughter of King Jehoram and wife of the priest Jehoiada, was Ahaziah's sister, she hid the child from Athaliah so she could not kill him. ¹²He remained hidden with them at the temple of God for six years while Athaliah ruled the land.

23 In the seventh year Jehoiada showed his strength. He made a covenant with the commanders of units of a hundred: Azariah son of Jeroham, Ishmael son of Jehohanan, Azariah son of Obed, Maaseiah son of Adaiah, and Elishaphat son of Zicri. ²They went throughout Judah and gathered the Levites and the heads of Israelite families from all the towns. When they came to Jerusalem, ³the whole assembly made a covenant with the king at the temple of God.

Jehoiada said to them, "The king's son shall reign, as the LORD promised concerning the descendants of David. ⁴Now this is what you are to do: A third of you

priests and Levites who are going on duty on the Sabbath are to keep watch at the doors, ⁵a third of you at the royal palace and a third at the Foundation Gate, and all the other men are to be in the courtyards of the temple of the LORD. ⁶No one is to enter the temple of the LORD except the priests and Levites on duty; they may enter because they are consecrated, but all the other men are to guard what the LORD has assigned to them.[c] ⁷The Levites are to station themselves around the king, each man with his weapons in his hand. Anyone who enters the temple must be put to death. Stay close to the king wherever he goes."

⁸The Levites and all the men of Judah did just as Jehoiada the priest ordered. Each one took his men—those who were going on duty on the Sabbath and those who were going off duty—for Jehoiada the priest had not released any of the divisions. ⁹Then he gave the commanders of units of a hundred the spears and the large and small shields that had belonged to King David and that were in the temple of God. ¹⁰He stationed all the men, each with his weapon in his hand, around the king—near the altar and the temple, from the south side to the north side of temple.

¹¹Jehoiada and his sons brought out the king's son and put the crown on him; they presented him with a copy of the covenant and proclaimed him king. They anointed him and shouted, "Long live the king!"

¹²When Athaliah heard the noise of the people running and cheering the king, she went to them at the temple of the LORD. ¹³She looked, and there was the king, standing by his pillar at the entrance. The officers and the trumpeters were beside the king, and all the people of the land were rejoicing and blowing trumpets, and singers with musical instruments were leading the praises. Then Athaliah tore her robes and shouted, "Treason! Treason!"

¹⁴Jehoiada the priest sent out the commanders of units of a hundred, who were

---

a 6 Some Hebrew manuscripts, Septuagint, Vulgate and Syriac (see also 2 Kings 8:29); most Hebrew manuscripts *Azariah*   b 11 Hebrew *Jehoshabeath*, a variant of *Jehosheba*   c 6 Or *to observe the LORD's command ⌊not to enter⌋*

in charge of the troops, and said to them: "Bring her out between the ranks[a] and put to the sword anyone who follows her." For the priest had said, "Do not put her to death at the temple of the LORD." [15]So they seized her as she reached the entrance of the Horse Gate on the palace grounds, and there they put her to death.

[16]Jehoiada then made a covenant that he and the people and the king[b] would be the LORD's people. [17]All the people went to the temple of Baal and tore it down. They smashed the altars and idols and killed Mattan the priest of Baal in front of the altars.

[18]Then Jehoiada placed the oversight of the temple of the LORD in the hands of the priests, who were Levites, to whom David had made assignments in the temple, to present the burnt offerings of the LORD as written in the Law of Moses, with rejoicing and singing, as David had ordered. [19]He also stationed doorkeepers at the gates of the LORD's temple so that no one who was in any way unclean might enter.

[20]He took with him the commanders of hundreds, the nobles, the rulers of the people and all the people of the land and brought the king down from the temple of the LORD. They went into the palace through the Upper Gate and seated the king on the royal throne, [21]and all the people of the land rejoiced. And the city was quiet, because Athaliah had been slain with the sword.

Joash Repairs the Temple

24 Joash was seven years old when he became king, and he reigned in Jerusalem forty years. His mother's name was Zibiah; she was from Beersheba. [2]Joash did what was right in the eyes of the LORD all the years of Jehoiada the priest. [3]Jehoiada chose two wives for him, and he had sons and daughters.

[4]Some time later Joash decided to restore the temple of the LORD. [5]He called together the priests and Levites and said to them, "Go to the towns of Judah and collect the money due annually from all Israel, to repair the temple of your God. Do it now." But the Levites did not act at once.

[6]Therefore the king summoned Jehoiada the chief priest and said to him, "Why haven't you required the Levites to bring in from Judah and Jerusalem the tax imposed by Moses the servant of the LORD and by the assembly of Israel for the Tent of the Testimony?"

[7]Now the sons of that wicked woman Athaliah had broken into the temple of God and had used even its sacred objects for the Baals.

[8]At the king's command, a chest was made and placed outside, at the gate of the temple of the LORD. [9]A proclamation was then issued in Judah and Jerusalem that they should bring to the LORD the tax that Moses the servant of God had required of Israel in the desert. [10]All the officials and all the people brought their contributions gladly, dropping them into the chest until it was full. [11]Whenever the chest was brought in by the Levites to the king's officials and they saw that there was a large amount of money, the royal secretary and the officer of the chief priest would come and empty the chest and carry it back to its place. They did this regularly and collected a great amount of money. [12]The king and Jehoiada gave it to the men who carried out the work required for the temple of the LORD. They hired masons and carpenters to restore the LORD's temple, and also workers in iron and bronze to repair the temple.

[13]The men in charge of the work were diligent, and the repairs progressed under them. They rebuilt the temple of God according to its original design and reinforced it. [14]When they had finished, they brought the rest of the money to the king and Jehoiada, and with it were made articles for the LORD's temple: articles for the service and for the burnt offerings, and also dishes and other objects of gold and silver. As long as Jehoiada lived, burnt offerings were presented continually in the temple of the LORD.

[15]Now Jehoiada was old and full of years, and he died at the age of a hundred and thirty. [16]He was buried with the kings in the City of David, because of the good he had done in Israel for God and his temple.

a14 Or out from the precincts   b16 Or covenant between ⌊the LORD⌋ and the people and the king that they (see 2 Kings 11:17)

The Wickedness of Joash

¹⁷After the death of Jehoiada, the officials of Judah came and paid homage to the king, and he listened to them. ¹⁸They abandoned the temple of the LORD, the God of their fathers, and worshiped Asherah poles and idols. Because of their guilt, God's anger came upon Judah and Jerusalem. ¹⁹Although the LORD sent prophets to the people to bring them back to him, and though they testified against them, they would not listen.

²⁰Then the Spirit of God came upon Zechariah son of Jehoiada the priest. He stood before the people and said, "This is what God says: 'Why do you disobey the LORD's commands? You will not prosper. Because you have forsaken the LORD, he has forsaken you.' "

²¹But they plotted against him, and by order of the king they stoned him to death in the courtyard of the LORD's temple. ²²King Joash did not remember the kindness Zechariah's father Jehoiada had shown him but killed his son, who said as he lay dying, "May the LORD see this and call you to account."

²³At the turn of the year,^a the army of Aram marched against Joash; it invaded Judah and Jerusalem and killed all the leaders of the people. They sent all the plunder to their king in Damascus. ²⁴Although the Aramean army had come with only a few men, the LORD delivered into their hands a much larger army. Because Judah had forsaken the LORD, the God of their fathers, judgment was executed on Joash. ²⁵When the Arameans withdrew, they left Joash severely wounded. His officials conspired against him for murdering the son of Jehoiada the priest, and they killed him in his bed. So he died and was buried in the City of David, but not in the tombs of the kings.

²⁶Those who conspired against him were Zabad,^b son of Shimeath an Ammonite woman, and Jehozabad, son of Shimrith^c a Moabite woman. ²⁷The account of his sons, the many prophecies about him, and the record of the restoration of the temple of God are written in the annotations on the book of the kings. And Amaziah his son succeeded him as king.

Amaziah King of Judah

25 Amaziah was twenty-five years old when he became king, and he reigned in Jerusalem twenty-nine years. His mother's name was Jehoaddin^d; she was from Jerusalem. ²He did what was right in the eyes of the LORD, but not wholeheartedly. ³After the kingdom was firmly in his control, he executed the officials who had murdered his father the king. ⁴Yet he did not put their sons to death, but acted in accordance with what is written in the Law, in the Book of Moses, where the LORD commanded: "Fathers shall not be put to death for their children, nor children put to death for their fathers; each is to die for his own sins."^e

⁵Amaziah called the people of Judah together and assigned them according to their families to commanders of thousands and commanders of hundreds for all Judah and Benjamin. He then mustered those twenty years old or more and found that there were three hundred thousand men ready for military service, able to handle the spear and shield. ⁶He also hired a hundred thousand fighting men from Israel for a hundred talents^f of silver.

⁷But a man of God came to him and said, "O king, these troops from Israel must not march with you, for the LORD is not with Israel—not with any of the people of Ephraim. ⁸Even if you go and fight courageously in battle, God will overthrow you before the enemy, for God has the power to help or to overthrow."

⁹Amaziah asked the man of God, "But what about the hundred talents I paid for these Israelite troops?"

The man of God replied, "The LORD can give you much more than that."

¹⁰So Amaziah dismissed the troops who had come to him from Ephraim and sent them home. They were furious with Judah and left for home in a great rage.

¹¹Amaziah then marshaled his strength and led his army to the Valley of Salt, where he killed ten thousand men of Seir.

^a23 Probably in the spring   ^b26 A variant of Jozabad   ^c26 A variant of *Shomer*   ^d1 Hebrew *Jehoaddan*, a variant of *Jehoaddin*   ^e4 Deut. 24:16   ^f6 That is, about 3 3/4 tons (about 3.4 metric tons); also in verse 9

¹²The army of Judah also captured ten thousand men alive, took them to the top of a cliff and threw them down so that all were dashed to pieces.

¹³Meanwhile the troops that Amaziah had sent back and had not allowed to take part in the war raided Judean towns from Samaria to Beth Horon. They killed three thousand people and carried off great quantities of plunder.

¹⁴When Amaziah returned from slaughtering the Edomites, he brought back the gods of the people of Seir. He set them up as his own gods, bowed down to them and burned sacrifices to them. ¹⁵The anger of the LORD burned against Amaziah, and he sent a prophet to him, who said, "Why do you consult this people's gods, which could not save their own people from your hand?"

¹⁶While he was still speaking, the king said to him, "Have we appointed you an adviser to the king? Stop! Why be struck down?"

So the prophet stopped but said, "I know that God has determined to destroy you, because you have done this and have not listened to my counsel."

¹⁷After Amaziah king of Judah consulted his advisers, he sent this challenge to Jehoash[a] son of Jehoahaz, the son of Jehu, king of Israel: "Come, meet me face to face."

¹⁸But Jehoash king of Israel replied to Amaziah king of Judah: "A thistle in Lebanon sent a message to a cedar in Lebanon, 'Give your daughter to my son in marriage.' Then a wild beast in Lebanon came along and trampled the thistle underfoot. ¹⁹You say to yourself that you have defeated Edom, and now you are arrogant and proud. But stay at home! Why ask for trouble and cause your own downfall and that of Judah also?"

²⁰Amaziah, however, would not listen, for God so worked that he might hand them over to ⌊Jehoash⌋, because they sought the gods of Edom. ²¹So Jehoash king of Israel attacked. He and Amaziah king of Judah faced each other at Beth Shemesh in Judah. ²²Judah was routed by Israel, and every man fled to his home. ²³Jehoash king of Israel captured Amaziah king of Judah, the son of Joash, the son of Ahaziah,[b] at Beth Shemesh. Then Jehoash brought him to Jerusalem and broke

down the wall of Jerusalem from the Ephraim Gate to the Corner Gate—a section about six hundred feet[c] long. ²⁴He took all the gold and silver and all the articles found in the temple of God that had been in the care of Obed-Edom, together with the palace treasures and the hostages, and returned to Samaria.

²⁵Amaziah son of Joash king of Judah lived for fifteen years after the death of Jehoash son of Jehoahaz king of Israel. ²⁶As for the other events of Amaziah's reign, from beginning to end, are they not written in the book of the kings of Judah and Israel? ²⁷From the time that Amaziah turned away from following the LORD, they conspired against him in Jerusalem and he fled to Lachish, but they sent men after him to Lachish and killed him there. ²⁸He was brought back by horse and was buried with his fathers in the City of Judah.

Uzziah King of Judah

26 Then all the people of Judah took Uzziah,[d] who was sixteen years old, and made him king in place of his father Amaziah. ²He was the one who rebuilt Elath and restored it to Judah after Amaziah rested with his fathers.

³Uzziah was sixteen years old when he became king, and he reigned in Jerusalem fifty-two years. His mother's name was Jecoliah; she was from Jerusalem. ⁴He did what was right in the eyes of the LORD, just as his father Amaziah had done. ⁵He sought God during the days of Zechariah, who instructed him in the fear[e] of God. As long as he sought the LORD, God gave him success.

⁶He went to war against the Philistines and broke down the walls of Gath, Jabneh and Ashdod. He then rebuilt towns near Ashdod and elsewhere among the Philistines. ⁷God helped him against the Philistines and against the Arabs who lived in Gur Baal and against the Meunites. ⁸The Ammonites brought tribute to Uzziah, and his fame spread as far as the

---

a17 Hebrew *Joash,* a variant of *Jehoash;* also in verses 18, 21, 23 and 25   *b23* Hebrew *Jehoahaz,* a variant of *Ahaziah*   *c23* Hebrew *four hundred cubits* (about 180 meters)   *d1* Also called *Azariah*   *e5* Many Hebrew manuscripts, Septuagint and Syriac; other Hebrew manuscripts *vision* border of Egypt, because he had become very powerful.

⁹Uzziah built towers in Jerusalem at the Corner Gate, at the Valley Gate and at the angle of the wall, and he fortified them. ¹⁰He also built towers in the desert and dug many cisterns, because he had much livestock in the foothills and in the plain. He had people working his fields and vineyards in the hills and in the fertile lands, for he loved the soil.

¹¹Uzziah had a well-trained army, ready to go out by divisions according to their numbers as mustered by Jeiel the secretary and Maaseiah the officer under the direction of Hananiah, one of the royal officials. ¹²The total number of family leaders over the fighting men was 2,600. ¹³Under their command was an army of 307,500 men trained for war, a powerful force to support the king against his enemies. ¹⁴Uzziah provided shields, spears, helmets, coats of armor, bows and slingstones for the entire army. ¹⁵In Jerusalem he made machines designed by skillful men for use on the towers and on the corner defenses to shoot arrows and hurl large stones. His fame spread far and wide, for he was greatly helped until he became powerful.

¹⁶But after Uzziah became powerful, his pride led to his downfall. He was unfaithful to the LORD his God, and entered the temple of the LORD to burn incense on the altar of incense. ¹⁷Azariah the priest with eighty other courageous priests of the LORD followed him in. ¹⁸They confronted him and said, "It is not right for you, Uzziah, to burn incense to the LORD. That is for the priests, the descendants of Aaron, who have been consecrated to burn incense. Leave the sanctuary, for you have been unfaithful; and you will not be honored by the LORD God."

¹⁹Uzziah, who had a censer in his hand ready to burn incense, became angry. While he was raging at the priests in their presence before the incense altar in the LORD's temple, leprosy[a] broke out on his forehead. ²⁰When Azariah the chief priest and all the other priests looked at him, they saw that he had leprosy on his forehead, so they hurried him out. Indeed, he himself was eager to leave, because the LORD had afflicted him.

²¹King Uzziah had leprosy until the day he died. He lived in a separate house[b]—leprous, and excluded from the temple of the LORD. Jotham his son had charge of the palace and governed the people of the land.

²²The other events of Uzziah's reign, from beginning to end, are recorded by the prophet Isaiah son of Amoz. ²³Uzziah rested with his fathers and was buried near them in a field for burial that belonged to the kings, for people said, "He had leprosy." And Jotham his son succeeded him as king.

Jotham King of Judah

27 Jotham was twenty-five years old when he became king, and he reigned in Jerusalem sixteen years. His mother's name was Jerusha daughter of Zadok. ²He did what was right in the eyes of the LORD, just as his father Uzziah had done, but unlike him he did not enter the temple of the LORD. The people, however, continued their corrupt practices. ³Jotham rebuilt the Upper Gate of the temple of the LORD and did extensive work on the wall at the hill of Ophel. ⁴He built towns in the Judean hills and forts and towers in the wooded areas.

⁵Jotham made war on the king of the Ammonites and conquered them. That year the Ammonites paid him a hundred talents[c] of silver, ten thousand cors[d] of wheat and ten thousand cors of barley. The Ammonites brought him the same amount also in the second and third years.

⁶Jotham grew powerful because he walked steadfastly before the LORD his God.

⁷The other events in Jotham's reign, including all his wars and the other things he did, are written in the book of the kings of Israel and Judah. ⁸He was twenty-five years old when he became king, and he reigned in Jerusalem sixteen years. ⁹Jotham rested with his fathers and was buried in the City of David. And Ahaz his son succeeded him as king.

---

a19 The Hebrew word was used for various diseases affecting the skin—not necessarily leprosy; also in verses 20, 21 and 23.   b21 Or *in a house where he was relieved of responsibilities*   c5 That is, about 3 3/4 tons (about 3.4 metric tons)   d5 That is, probably about 62,000 bushels (about 2,200 kiloliters)

Ahaz King of Judah

28 Ahaz was twenty years old when he became king, and he reigned in Jerusalem sixteen years. Unlike David his father, he did not do what was right in the eyes of the LORD. ²He walked in the ways of the kings of Israel and also made cast idols for worshiping the Baals. ³He burned sacrifices in the Valley of Ben Hinnom and sacrificed his sons in the fire, following the detestable ways of the nations the LORD had driven out before the Israelites. ⁴He offered sacrifices and burned incense at the high places, on the hilltops and under every spreading tree.

⁵Therefore the LORD his God handed him over to the king of Aram. The Arameans defeated him and took many of his people as prisoners and brought them to Damascus.

He was also given into the hands of the king of Israel, who inflicted heavy casualties on him. ⁶In one day Pekah son of Remaliah killed a hundred and twenty thousand soldiers in Judah—because Judah had forsaken the LORD, the God of their fathers. ⁷Zicri, an Ephraimite warrior, killed Maaseiah the king's son, Azrikam the officer in charge of the palace, and Elkanah, second to the king. ⁸The Israelites took captive from their kinsmen two hundred thousand wives, sons and daughters. They also took a great deal of plunder, which they carried back to Samaria.

⁹But a prophet of the LORD named Oded was there, and he went out to meet the army when it returned to Samaria. He said to them, "Because the LORD, the God of your fathers, was angry with Judah, he gave them into your hand. But you have slaughtered them in a rage that reaches to heaven. ¹⁰And now you intend to make the men and women of Judah and Jerusalem your slaves. But aren't you also guilty of sins against the LORD your God? ¹¹Now listen to me! Send back your fellow countrymen you have taken as prisoners, for the LORD's fierce anger rests on you."

¹²Then some of the leaders in Ephraim—Azariah son of Jehohanan, Berekiah son of Meshillemoth, Jehizkiah son of Shallum, and Amasa son of Hadlai—confronted those who were arriving from the war. ¹³"You must not bring those prisoners here," they said, "or we will be guilty before the LORD. Do you intend to add to our sin and guilt? For our guilt is already great, and his fierce anger rests on Israel."

¹⁴So the soldiers gave up the prisoners and plunder in the presence of the officials and all the assembly. ¹⁵The men designated by name took the prisoners, and from the plunder they clothed all who were naked. They provided them with clothes and sandals, food and drink, and healing balm. All those who were weak they put on donkeys. So they took them back to their fellow countrymen at Jericho, the City of Palms, and returned to Samaria.

¹⁶At that time King Ahaz sent to the king*a* of Assyria for help. ¹⁷The Edomites had again come and attacked Judah and carried away prisoners, ¹⁸while the Philistines had raided towns in the foothills and in the Negev of Judah. They captured and occupied Beth Shemesh, Aijalon and Gederoth, as well as Soco, Timnah and Gimzo, with their surrounding villages. ¹⁹The LORD had humbled Judah because of Ahaz king of Israel,*b* for he had promoted wickedness in Judah and had been most unfaithful to the LORD. ²⁰Tiglath-Pileser*c* king of Assyria came to him, but he gave him trouble instead of help. ²¹Ahaz took some of the things from the temple of the LORD and from the royal palace and from the princes and presented them to the king of Assyria, but that did not help him.

²²In his time of trouble King Ahaz became even more unfaithful to the LORD. ²³He offered sacrifices to the gods of Damascus, who had defeated him; for he thought, "Since the gods of the kings of Aram have helped them, I will sacrifice to them so they will help me." But they were his downfall and the downfall of all Israel.

²⁴Ahaz gathered together the furnishings from the temple of God and took them away.*d* He shut the doors of the LORD's temple and set up altars at every street corner in Jerusalem. ²⁵In every town

---

a16 One Hebrew manuscript, Septuagint and Vulgate (see also 2 Kings 16:7); most Hebrew manuscripts *kings* *b19* That is, Judah, as frequently in 2 Chronicles *c20* Hebrew *Tilgath-Pilneser,* a variant of *Tiglath-Pileser* *d24* Or *and cut them up* in Judah he built high places to burn sacrifices to other gods and provoked the LORD, the God of his fathers, to anger.

²⁶The other events of his reign and all his ways, from beginning to end, are written in the book of the kings of Judah and Israel. ²⁷Ahaz rested with his fathers and was buried in the city of Jerusalem, but he was not placed in the tombs of the kings of Israel. And Hezekiah his son succeeded him as king.

Hezekiah Purifies the Temple

29 Hezekiah was twenty-five years old when he became king, and he reigned in Jerusalem twenty-nine years. His mother's name was Abijah daughter of Zechariah. ²He did what was right in the eyes of the LORD, just as his father David had done.

³In the first month of the first year of his reign, he opened the doors of the temple of the LORD and repaired them. ⁴He brought in the priests and the Levites, assembled them in the square on the east side ⁵and said: "Listen to me, Levites! Consecrate yourselves now and consecrate the temple of the LORD, the God of your fathers. Remove all defilement from the sanctuary. ⁶Our fathers were unfaithful; they did evil in the eyes of the LORD our God and forsook him. They turned their faces away from the LORD's dwelling place and turned their backs on him. ⁷They also shut the doors of the portico and put out the lamps. They did not burn incense or present any burnt offerings at the sanctuary to the God of Israel. ⁸Therefore, the anger of the LORD has fallen on Judah and Jerusalem; he has made them an object of dread and horror and scorn, as you can see with your own eyes. ⁹This is why our fathers have fallen by the sword and why our sons and daughters and our wives are in captivity. ¹⁰Now I intend to make a covenant with the LORD, the God of Israel, so that his fierce anger will turn away from us. ¹¹My sons, do not be negligent now, for the LORD has chosen you to stand before him and serve him, to minister before him and to burn incense."

¹²Then these Levites set to work:
from the Kohathites,

Mahath son of Amasai and Joel son of Azariah;
from the Merarites,
Kish son of Abdi and Azariah son of Jehallelel;
from the Gershonites,
Joah son of Zimmah and Eden son of Joah;
¹³from the descendants of Elizaphan, Shimri and Jeiel;
from the descendants of Asaph, Zechariah and Mattaniah;
¹⁴from the descendants of Heman, Jehiel and Shimei;
from the descendants of Jeduthun, Shemaiah and Uzziel.

¹⁵When they had assembled their brothers and consecrated themselves, they went in to purify the temple of the LORD, as the king had ordered, following the word of the LORD. ¹⁶The priests went into the sanctuary of the LORD to purify it. They brought out to the courtyard of the LORD's temple everything unclean that they found in the temple of the LORD. The Levites took it and carried it out to the Kidron Valley. ¹⁷They began the consecration on the first day of the first month, and by the eighth day of the month they reached the portico of the LORD. For eight more days they consecrated the temple of the LORD itself, finishing on the sixteenth day of the first month.

¹⁸Then they went in to King Hezekiah and reported: "We have purified the entire temple of the LORD, the altar of burnt offering with all its utensils, and the table for setting out the consecrated bread, with all its articles. ¹⁹We have prepared and consecrated all the articles that King Ahaz removed in his unfaithfulness while he was king. They are now in front of the LORD's altar."

²⁰Early the next morning King Hezekiah gathered the city officials together and went up to the temple of the LORD. ²¹They brought seven bulls, seven rams, seven male lambs and seven male goats as a sin offering for the kingdom, for the sanctuary and for Judah. The king commanded the priests, the descendants of Aaron, to offer these on the altar of the LORD. ²²So they slaughtered the bulls, and the priests took the blood and sprinkled it on the altar; next they slaughtered the rams and sprinkled their blood on the altar; then

they slaughtered the lambs and sprinkled their blood on the altar. ²³The goats for the sin offering were brought before the king and the assembly, and they laid their hands on them. ²⁴The priests then slaughtered the goats and presented their blood on the altar for a sin offering to atone for all Israel, because the king had ordered the burnt offering and the sin offering for all Israel.

²⁵He stationed the Levites in the temple of the LORD with cymbals, harps and lyres in the way prescribed by David and Gad the king's seer and Nathan the prophet; this was commanded by the LORD through his prophets. ²⁶So the Levites stood ready with David's instruments, and the priests with their trumpets.

²⁷Hezekiah gave the order to sacrifice the burnt offering on the altar. As the offering began, singing to the LORD began also, accompanied by trumpets and the instruments of David king of Israel. ²⁸The whole assembly bowed in worship, while the singers sang and the trumpeters played. All this continued until the sacrifice of the burnt offering was completed.

²⁹When the offerings were finished, the king and everyone present with him knelt down and worshiped. ³⁰King Hezekiah and his officials ordered the Levites to praise the LORD with the words of David and of Asaph the seer. So they sang praises with gladness and bowed their heads and worshiped.

³¹Then Hezekiah said, "You have now dedicated yourselves to the LORD. Come and bring sacrifices and thank offerings to the temple of the LORD." So the assembly brought sacrifices and thank offerings, and all whose hearts were willing brought burnt offerings.

³²The number of burnt offerings the assembly brought was seventy bulls, a hundred rams and two hundred male lambs—all of them for burnt offerings to the LORD. ³³The animals consecrated as sacrifices amounted to six hundred bulls and three thousand sheep and goats. ³⁴The priests, however, were too few to skin all the burnt offerings; so their kinsmen the Levites helped them until the task was finished and until other priests had been consecrated, for the Levites had been more conscientious in consecrating themselves than the priests had been. ³⁵There were burnt offerings in abundance, together with the fat of the fellowship offerings[a] and the drink offerings that accompanied the burnt offerings.

So the service of the temple of the LORD was reestablished. ³⁶Hezekiah and all the people rejoiced at what God had brought about for his people, because it was done so quickly.

Hezekiah Celebrates the Passover

30 Hezekiah sent word to all Israel and Judah and also wrote letters to Ephraim and Manasseh, inviting them to come to the temple of the LORD in Jerusalem and celebrate the Passover to the LORD, the God of Israel. ²The king and his officials and the whole assembly in Jerusalem decided to celebrate the Passover in the second month. ³They had not been able to celebrate it at the regular time because not enough priests had consecrated themselves and the people had not assembled in Jerusalem. ⁴The plan seemed right both to the king and to the whole assembly. ⁵They decided to send a proclamation throughout Israel, from Beersheba to Dan, calling the people to come to Jerusalem and celebrate the Passover to the LORD, the God of Israel. It had not been celebrated in large numbers according to what was written.

⁶At the king's command, couriers went throughout Israel and Judah with letters from the king and from his officials, which read:

"People of Israel, return to the LORD, the God of Abraham, Isaac and Israel, that he may return to you who are left, who have escaped from the hand of the kings of Assyria. ⁷Do not be like your fathers and brothers, who were unfaithful to the LORD, the God of their fathers, so that he made them an object of horror, as you see. ⁸Do not be stiffnecked, as your fathers were; submit to the LORD. Come to the sanctuary, which he has consecrated forever. Serve the LORD your God, so that his fierce anger will turn away from you. ⁹If you return to the LORD, then

^a35 Traditionally *peace offerings*

your brothers and your children will be shown compassion by their captors and will come back to this land, for the LORD your God is gracious and compassionate. He will not turn his face from you if you return to him."

¹⁰The couriers went from town to town in Ephraim and Manasseh, as far as Zebulun, but the people scorned and ridiculed them. ¹¹Nevertheless, some men of Asher, Manasseh and Zebulun humbled themselves and went to Jerusalem. ¹²Also in Judah the hand of God was on the people to give them unity of mind to carry out what the king and his officials had ordered, following the word of the LORD.

¹³A very large crowd of people assembled in Jerusalem to celebrate the Feast of Unleavened Bread in the second month. ¹⁴They removed the altars in Jerusalem and cleared away the incense altars and threw them into the Kidron Valley.

¹⁵They slaughtered the Passover lamb on the fourteenth day of the second month. The priests and the Levites were ashamed and consecrated themselves and brought burnt offerings to the temple of the LORD. ¹⁶Then they took up their regular positions as prescribed in the Law of Moses the man of God. The priests sprinkled the blood handed to them by the Levites. ¹⁷Since many in the crowd had not consecrated themselves, the Levites had to kill the Passover lambs for all those who were not ceremonially clean and could not consecrate ⌊their lambs⌋ to the LORD. ¹⁸Although most of the many people who came from Ephraim, Manasseh, Issachar and Zebulun had not purified themselves, yet they ate the Passover, contrary to what was written. But Hezekiah prayed for them, saying, "May the LORD, who is good, pardon everyone ¹⁹who sets his heart on seeking God—the LORD, the God of his fathers—even if he is not clean according to the rules of the sanctuary." ²⁰And the LORD heard Hezekiah and healed the people.

²¹The Israelites who were present in Jerusalem celebrated the Feast of Unleavened Bread for seven days with great rejoicing, while the Levites and priests sang to the LORD every day, accompanied by the LORD's instruments of praise. ᵃ

²²Hezekiah spoke encouragingly to all the Levites, who showed good understanding of the service of the LORD. For the seven days they ate their assigned portion and offered fellowship offerings ᵇ and praised the LORD, the God of their fathers.

²³The whole assembly then agreed to celebrate the festival seven more days; so for another seven days they celebrated joyfully. ²⁴Hezekiah king of Judah provided a thousand bulls and seven thousand sheep and goats for the assembly, and the officials provided them with a thousand bulls and ten thousand sheep and goats. A great number of priests consecrated themselves. ²⁵The entire assembly of Judah rejoiced, along with the priests and Levites and all who had assembled from Israel, including the aliens who had come from Israel and those who lived in Judah. ²⁶There was great joy in Jerusalem, for since the days of Solomon son of David king of Israel there had been nothing like this in Jerusalem. ²⁷The priests and the Levites stood to bless the people, and God heard them, for their prayer reached heaven, his holy dwelling place.

31 When all this had ended, the Israelites who were there went out to the towns of Judah, smashed the sacred stones and cut down the Asherah poles. They destroyed the high places and the altars throughout Judah and Benjamin and in Ephraim and Manasseh. After they had destroyed all of them, the Israelites returned to their own towns and to their own property.

Contributions for Worship

²Hezekiah assigned the priests and Levites to divisions—each of them according to their duties as priests or Levites—to offer burnt offerings and fellowship offerings, ᵇ to minister, to give thanks and to sing praises at the gates of the LORD's dwelling. ³The king contributed from his own possessions for the morning and evening burnt offerings and for the burnt offerings on the Sabbaths, New Moons and appointed feasts as written in the Law of the LORD. ⁴He ordered the people liv-

---

ᵃ21 Or *priests praised the* LORD *every day with resounding instruments belonging to the* LORD
ᵇ22,2 Traditionally *peace offerings*

ing in Jerusalem to give the portion due the priests and Levites so they could devote themselves to the Law of the LORD. [5]As soon as the order went out, the Israelites generously gave the firstfruits of their grain, new wine, oil and honey and all that the fields produced. They brought a great amount, a tithe of everything. [6]The men of Israel and Judah who lived in the towns of Judah also brought a tithe of their herds and flocks and a tithe of the holy things dedicated to the LORD their God, and they piled them in heaps. [7]They began doing this in the third month and finished in the seventh month. [8]When Hezekiah and his officials came and saw the heaps, they praised the LORD and blessed his people Israel.

[9]Hezekiah asked the priests and Levites about the heaps; [10]and Azariah the chief priest, from the family of Zadok, answered, "Since the people began to bring their contributions to the temple of the LORD, we have had enough to eat and plenty to spare, because the LORD has blessed his people, and this great amount is left over."

[11]Hezekiah gave orders to prepare storerooms in the temple of the LORD, and this was done. [12]Then they faithfully brought in the contributions, tithes and dedicated gifts. Conaniah, a Levite, was in charge of these things, and his brother Shimei was next in rank. [13]Jehiel, Azaziah, Nahath, Asahel, Jerimoth, Jozabad, Eliel, Ismakiah, Mahath and Benaiah were supervisors under Conaniah and Shimei his brother, by appointment of King Hezekiah and Azariah the official in charge of the temple of God.

[14]Kore son of Imnah the Levite, keeper of the East Gate, was in charge of the freewill offerings given to God, distributing the contributions made to the LORD and also the consecrated gifts. [15]Eden, Miniamin, Jeshua, Shemaiah, Amariah and Shecaniah assisted him faithfully in the towns of the priests, distributing to their fellow priests according to their divisions, old and young alike.

[16]In addition, they distributed to the males three years old or more whose names were in the genealogical records—all who would enter the temple of the LORD to perform the daily duties of their various tasks, according to their respon-

sibilities and their divisions. [17]And they distributed to the priests enrolled by their families in the genealogical records and likewise to the Levites twenty years old or more, according to their responsibilities and their divisions. [18]They included all the little ones, the wives, and the sons and daughters of the whole community listed in these genealogical records. For they were faithful in consecrating themselves.

[19]As for the priests, the descendants of Aaron, who lived on the farm lands around their towns or in any other towns, men were designated by name to distribute portions to every male among them and to all who were recorded in the genealogies of the Levites.

[20]This is what Hezekiah did throughout Judah, doing what was good and right and faithful before the LORD his God. [21]In everything that he undertook in the service of God's temple and in obedience to the law and the commands, he sought his God and worked wholeheartedly. And so he prospered.

Sennacherib Threatens Jerusalem

32 After all that Hezekiah had so faithfully done, Sennacherib king of Assyria came and invaded Judah. He laid siege to the fortified cities, thinking to conquer them for himself. [2]When Hezekiah saw that Sennacherib had come and that he intended to make war on Jerusalem, [3]he consulted with his officials and military staff about blocking off the water from the springs outside the city, and they helped him. [4]A large force of men assembled, and they blocked all the springs and the stream that flowed through the land. "Why should the kings[a] of Assyria come and find plenty of water?" they said. [5]Then he worked hard repairing all the broken sections of the wall and building towers on it. He built another wall outside that one and reinforced the supporting terraces[b] of the City of David. He also made large numbers of weapons and shields.

[6]He appointed military officers over the people and assembled them before him in the square at the city gate and encouraged them with these words: [7]"Be

*a4 Hebrew; Septuagint and Syriac king   *b5 Or the Millo

strong and courageous. Do not be afraid or discouraged because of the king of Assyria and the vast army with him, for there is a greater power with us than with him. [8]With him is only the arm of flesh, but with us is the LORD our God to help us and to fight our battles." And the people gained confidence from what Hezekiah the king of Judah said.

[9]Later, when Sennacherib king of Assyria and all his forces were laying siege to Lachish, he sent his officers to Jerusalem with this message for Hezekiah king of Judah and for all the people of Judah who were there:

[10]"This is what Sennacherib king of Assyria says: On what are you basing your confidence, that you remain in Jerusalem under siege? [11]When Hezekiah says, 'The LORD our God will save us from the hand of the king of Assyria,' he is misleading you, to let you die of hunger and thirst. [12]Did not Hezekiah himself remove this god's high places and altars, saying to Judah and Jerusalem, 'You must worship before one altar and burn sacrifices on it'?

[13]"Do you not know what I and my fathers have done to all the peoples of the other lands? Were the gods of those nations ever able to deliver their land from my hand? [14]Who of all the gods of these nations that my fathers destroyed has been able to save his people from me? How then can your god deliver you from my hand? [15]Now do not let Hezekiah deceive you and mislead you like this. Do not believe him, for no god of any nation or kingdom has been able to deliver his people from my hand or the hand of my fathers. How much less will your god deliver you from my hand!"

[16]Sennacherib's officers spoke further against the LORD God and against his servant Hezekiah. [17]The king also wrote letters insulting the LORD, the God of Israel, and saying this against him: "Just as the gods of the peoples of the other lands did not rescue their people from my hand, so the god of Hezekiah will not rescue his people from my hand." [18]Then they called out in Hebrew to the people of Jerusalem who were on the wall, to terrify them and make them afraid in order to capture the city. [19]They spoke about the God of Jerusalem as they did about the gods of the other peoples of the world—the work of men's hands.

[20]King Hezekiah and the prophet Isaiah son of Amoz cried out in prayer to heaven about this. [21]And the LORD sent an angel, who annihilated all the fighting men and the leaders and officers in the camp of the Assyrian king. So he withdrew to his own land in disgrace. And when he went into the temple of his god, some of his sons cut him down with the sword.

[22]So the LORD saved Hezekiah and the people of Jerusalem from the hand of Sennacherib king of Assyria and from the hand of all others. He took care of them[a] on every side. [23]Many brought offerings to Jerusalem for the LORD and valuable gifts for Hezekiah king of Judah. From then on he was highly regarded by all the nations.

Hezekiah's Pride, Success and Death

[24]In those days Hezekiah became ill and was at the point of death. He prayed to the LORD, who answered him and gave him a miraculous sign. [25]But Hezekiah's heart was proud and he did not respond to the kindness shown him; therefore the LORD's wrath was on him and on Judah and Jerusalem. [26]Then Hezekiah repented of the pride of his heart, as did the people of Jerusalem; therefore the LORD's wrath did not come upon them during the days of Hezekiah.

[27]Hezekiah had very great riches and honor, and he made treasuries for his silver and gold and for his precious stones, spices, shields and all kinds of valuables. [28]He also made buildings to store the harvest of grain, new wine and oil; and he made stalls for various kinds of cattle, and pens for the flocks. [29]He built villages and acquired great numbers of flocks and herds, for God had given him very great riches.

[30]It was Hezekiah who blocked the upper outlet of the Gihon spring and chan-

---

a22 Hebrew; Septuagint and Vulgate *He gave them rest*

neled the water down to the west side of the City of David. He succeeded in everything he undertook. ³¹But when envoys were sent by the rulers of Babylon to ask him about the miraculous sign that had occurred in the land, God left him to test him and to know everything that was in his heart.

³²The other events of Hezekiah's reign and his acts of devotion are written in the vision of the prophet Isaiah son of Amoz in the book of the kings of Judah and Israel. ³³Hezekiah rested with his fathers and was buried on the hill where the tombs of David's descendants are. All Judah and the people of Jerusalem honored him when he died. And Manasseh his son succeeded him as king.

Manasseh King of Judah

33 Manasseh was twelve years old when he became king, and he reigned in Jerusalem fifty-five years. ²He did evil in the eyes of the LORD, following the detestable practices of the nations the LORD had driven out before the Israelites. ³He rebuilt the high places his father Hezekiah had demolished; he also erected altars to the Baals and made Asherah poles. He bowed down to all the starry hosts and worshiped them. ⁴He built altars in the temple of the LORD, of which the LORD had said, "My Name will remain in Jerusalem forever." ⁵In both courts of the temple of the LORD, he built altars to all the starry hosts. ⁶He sacrificed his sons in*a* the fire in the Valley of Ben Hinnom, practiced sorcery, divination and witchcraft, and consulted mediums and spiritists. He did much evil in the eyes of the LORD, provoking him to anger.

⁷He took the carved image he had made and put it in God's temple, of which God had said to David and to his son Solomon, "In this temple and in Jerusalem, which I have chosen out of all the tribes of Israel, I will put my Name forever. ⁸I will not again make the feet of the Israelites leave the land I assigned to your forefathers, if only they will be careful to do everything I commanded them concerning all the laws, decrees and ordinances given through Moses." ⁹But Manasseh led Judah and the people of Jerusalem astray, so that they did more evil than the nations the LORD had destroyed before the Israelites.

¹⁰The LORD spoke to Manasseh and his people, but they paid no attention. ¹¹So the LORD brought against them the army commanders of the king of Assyria, who took Manasseh prisoner, put a hook in his nose, bound him with bronze shackles and took him to Babylon. ¹²In his distress he sought the favor of the LORD his God and humbled himself greatly before the God of his fathers. ¹³And when he prayed to him, the LORD was moved by his entreaty and listened to his plea; so he brought him back to Jerusalem and to his kingdom. Then Manasseh knew that the LORD is God.

¹⁴Afterward he rebuilt the outer wall of the City of David, west of the Gihon spring in the valley, as far as the entrance of the Fish Gate and encircling the hill of Ophel; he also made it much higher. He stationed military commanders in all the fortified cities in Judah.

¹⁵He got rid of the foreign gods and removed the image from the temple of the LORD, as well as all the altars he had built on the temple hill and in Jerusalem; and he threw them out of the city. ¹⁶Then he restored the altar of the LORD and sacrificed fellowship offerings*b* and thank offerings on it, and told Judah to serve the LORD, the God of Israel. ¹⁷The people, however, continued to sacrifice at the high places, but only to the LORD their God.

¹⁸The other events of Manasseh's reign, including his prayer to his God and the words the seers spoke to him in the name of the LORD, the God of Israel, are written in the annals of the kings of Israel.*c* ¹⁹His prayer and how God was moved by his entreaty, as well as all his sins and unfaithfulness, and the sites where he built high places and set up Asherah poles and idols before he humbled himself—all are written in the records of the seers.*d* ²⁰Manasseh rested with his fathers and was buried in his palace. And Amon his son succeeded him as king.

a6 Or *He made his sons pass through*
b16 Traditionally *peace offerings*   *c18* That is, Judah, as frequently in 2 Chronicles   *d19* One Hebrew manuscript and Septuagint; most Hebrew manuscripts *of Hozai*

Amon King of Judah

²¹Amon was twenty-two years old when he became king, and he reigned in Jerusalem two years. ²²He did evil in the eyes of the LORD, as his father Manasseh had done. Amon worshiped and offered sacrifices to all the idols Manasseh had made. ²³But unlike his father Manasseh, he did not humble himself before the LORD; Amon increased his guilt.

²⁴Amon's officials conspired against him and assassinated him in his palace. ²⁵Then the people of the land killed all who had plotted against King Amon, and they made Josiah his son king in his place.

Josiah's Reforms

34 Josiah was eight years old when he became king, and he reigned in Jerusalem thirty-one years. ²He did what was right in the eyes of the LORD and walked in the ways of his father David, not turning aside to the right or to the left.

³In the eighth year of his reign, while he was still young, he began to seek the God of his father David. In his twelfth year he began to purge Judah and Jerusalem of high places, Asherah poles, carved idols and cast images. ⁴Under his direction the altars of the Baals were torn down; he cut to pieces the incense altars that were above them, and smashed the Asherah poles, the idols and the images. These he broke to pieces and scattered over the graves of those who had sacrificed to them. ⁵He burned the bones of the priests on their altars, and so he purged Judah and Jerusalem. ⁶In the towns of Manasseh, Ephraim and Simeon, as far as Naphtali, and in the ruins around them, ⁷he tore down the altars and the Asherah poles and crushed the idols to powder and cut to pieces all the incense altars throughout Israel. Then he went back to Jerusalem.

⁸In the eighteenth year of Josiah's reign, to purify the land and the temple, he sent Shaphan son of Azaliah and Maaseiah the ruler of the city, with Joah son of Joahaz, the recorder, to repair the temple of the LORD his God.

⁹They went to Hilkiah the high priest

Getting Back on Track

Tuesday

2 CHRONICLES 34   The Israelites had allowed the culture around them to make them dull to sin. Rather than be a light in the darkness, they had gradually walked away from their focus on God. They had even begun worshiping other gods (see verse 3).

If we allow our relationship with God to become tedious and routine, our faith will become boring and lifeless. We will inevitably begin looking for other things to fill our hearts and minds. A marriage that drifts away from its original love for God is doomed to gradual demise.

This passage offers an action plan for returning to God. The first step in getting a marriage or an individual back into a vibrant relationship with God is to go back to the faith you had when you were excited about it.

Consider Josiah. He was young and excited about following in the faith of his "father" David, and he sought his nation's revival in his youthful way. Josiah's next step was to remove anything from his nation that was ungodly. Is there anything you have brought into your home that is ungodly? Anything that has eroded your faith?

Over a period of time have you become immune to what's ungodly? Josiah asked these questions of himself and destroyed whatever he found that was ungodly.

Many times couples allow their culture, rather than God, to define for them what is acceptable. Culturally acceptable things such as treating Sunday like every other day of the week need to be purged from our homes because of the ungodly impact they have on our marriage and our children. We need to take our lead from Josiah and purge ourselves of the ungodly things that have crept in.

—*Bob & Rosemary*

Go to page 489 for your next devotional reading.

and gave him the money that had been brought into the temple of God, which the Levites who were the doorkeepers had collected from the people of Manasseh, Ephraim and the entire remnant of Israel and from all the people of Judah and Benjamin and the inhabitants of Jerusalem. [10]Then they entrusted it to the men appointed to supervise the work on the LORD's temple. These men paid the workers who repaired and restored the temple. [11]They also gave money to the carpenters and builders to purchase dressed stone, and timber for joists and beams for the buildings that the kings of Judah had allowed to fall into ruin.

[12]The men did the work faithfully. Over them to direct them were Jahath and Obadiah, Levites descended from Merari, and Zechariah and Meshullam, descended from Kohath. The Levites—all who were skilled in playing musical instruments— [13]had charge of the laborers and supervised all the workers from job to job. Some of the Levites were secretaries, scribes and doorkeepers.

The Book of the Law Found

[14]While they were bringing out the money that had been taken into the temple of the LORD, Hilkiah the priest found the Book of the Law of the LORD that had been given through Moses. [15]Hilkiah said to Shaphan the secretary, "I have found the Book of the Law in the temple of the LORD." He gave it to Shaphan.

[16]Then Shaphan took the book to the king and reported to him: "Your officials are doing everything that has been committed to them. [17]They have paid out the money that was in the temple of the LORD and have entrusted it to the supervisors and workers." [18]Then Shaphan the secretary informed the king, "Hilkiah the priest has given me a book." And Shaphan read from it in the presence of the king.

[19]When the king heard the words of the Law, he tore his robes. [20]He gave these orders to Hilkiah, Ahikam son of Shaphan, Abdon son of Micah,[a] Shaphan the secretary and Asaiah the king's attendant: [21]"Go and inquire of the LORD for me and for the remnant in Israel and Judah about what is written in this book that has been found. Great is the LORD's

anger that is poured out on us because our fathers have not kept the word of the LORD; they have not acted in accordance with all that is written in this book."

[22]Hilkiah and those the king had sent with him[b] went to speak to the prophetess Huldah, who was the wife of Shallum son of Tokhath,[c] the son of Hasrah,[d] keeper of the wardrobe. She lived in Jerusalem, in the Second District.

[23]She said to them, "This is what the LORD, the God of Israel, says: Tell the man who sent you to me, [24]'This is what the LORD says: I am going to bring disaster on this place and its people—all the curses written in the book that has been read in the presence of the king of Judah. [25]Because they have forsaken me and burned incense to other gods and provoked me to anger by all that their hands have made,[e] my anger will be poured out on this place and will not be quenched.' [26]Tell the king of Judah, who sent you to inquire of the LORD, 'This is what the LORD, the God of Israel, says concerning the words you heard: [27]Because your heart was responsive and you humbled yourself before God when you heard what he spoke against this place and its people, and because you humbled yourself before me and tore your robes and wept in my presence, I have heard you, declares the LORD. [28]Now I will gather you to your fathers, and you will be buried in peace. Your eyes will not see all the disaster I am going to bring on this place and on those who live here.' "

So they took her answer back to the king.

[29]Then the king called together all the elders of Judah and Jerusalem. [30]He went up to the temple of the LORD with the men of Judah, the people of Jerusalem, the priests and the Levites—all the people from the least to the greatest. He read in their hearing all the words of the Book of the Covenant, which had been found in the temple of the LORD. [31]The king stood by his pillar and renewed the covenant in the presence of the LORD—to follow the

[a]20 Also called Acbor son of Micaiah   [b]22 One Hebrew manuscript, Vulgate and Syriac; most Hebrew manuscripts do not have had sent with him.   [c]22 Also called Tikvah   [d]22 Also called Harhas   [e]25 Or by everything they have done

LORD and keep his commands, regulations and decrees with all his heart and all his soul, and to obey the words of the covenant written in this book.

³²Then he had everyone in Jerusalem and Benjamin pledge themselves to it; the people of Jerusalem did this in accordance with the covenant of God, the God of their fathers.

³³Josiah removed all the detestable idols from all the territory belonging to the Israelites, and he had all who were present in Israel serve the LORD their God. As long as he lived, they did not fail to follow the LORD, the God of their fathers.

Josiah Celebrates the Passover

35 Josiah celebrated the Passover to the LORD in Jerusalem, and the Passover lamb was slaughtered on the fourteenth day of the first month. ²He appointed the priests to their duties and encouraged them in the service of the LORD's temple. ³He said to the Levites, who instructed all Israel and who had been consecrated to the LORD: "Put the sacred ark in the temple that Solomon son of David king of Israel built. It is not to be carried about on your shoulders. Now serve the LORD your God and his people Israel. ⁴Prepare yourselves by families in your divisions, according to the directions written by David king of Israel and by his son Solomon.

⁵"Stand in the holy place with a group of Levites for each subdivision of the families of your fellow countrymen, the lay people. ⁶Slaughter the Passover lambs, consecrate yourselves and prepare ⌐the lambs⌐ for your fellow countrymen, doing what the LORD commanded through Moses."

⁷Josiah provided for all the lay people who were there a total of thirty thousand sheep and goats for the Passover offerings, and also three thousand cattle—all from the king's own possessions.

⁸His officials also contributed voluntarily to the people and the priests and Levites. Hilkiah, Zechariah and Jehiel, the administrators of God's temple, gave the priests twenty-six hundred Passover offerings and three hundred cattle. ⁹Also Coniah along with Shemaiah and Nethanel, his brothers, and Hashabiah, Jeiel and Jozabad, the leaders of the Levites, provided five thousand Passover offerings and five hundred head of cattle for the Levites.

¹⁰The service was arranged and the priests stood in their places with the Levites in their divisions as the king had ordered. ¹¹The Passover lambs were slaughtered, and the priests sprinkled the blood handed to them, while the Levites skinned the animals. ¹²They set aside the burnt offerings to give them to the subdivisions of the families of the people to offer to the LORD, as is written in the Book of Moses. They did the same with the cattle. ¹³They roasted the Passover animals over the fire as prescribed, and boiled the holy offerings in pots, caldrons and pans and served them quickly to all the people. ¹⁴After this, they made preparations for themselves and for the priests, because the priests, the descendants of Aaron, were sacrificing the burnt offerings and the fat portions until nightfall. So the Levites made preparations for themselves and for the Aaronic priests.

¹⁵The musicians, the descendants of Asaph, were in the places prescribed by David, Asaph, Heman and Jeduthun the king's seer. The gatekeepers at each gate did not need to leave their posts, because their fellow Levites made the preparations for them.

¹⁶So at that time the entire service of the LORD was carried out for the celebration of the Passover and the offering of burnt offerings on the altar of the LORD, as King Josiah had ordered. ¹⁷The Israelites who were present celebrated the Passover at that time and observed the Feast of Unleavened Bread for seven days. ¹⁸The Passover had not been observed like this in Israel since the days of the prophet Samuel; and none of the kings of Israel had ever celebrated such a Passover as did Josiah, with the priests, the Levites and all Judah and Israel who were there with the people of Jerusalem. ¹⁹This Passover was celebrated in the eighteenth year of Josiah's reign.

The Death of Josiah

²⁰After all this, when Josiah had set the temple in order, Neco king of Egypt went up to fight at Carchemish on the Euphra-

tes, and Josiah marched out to meet him in battle. ²¹But Neco sent messengers to him, saying, "What quarrel is there between you and me, O king of Judah? It is not you I am attacking at this time, but the house with which I am at war. God has told me to hurry; so stop opposing God, who is with me, or he will destroy you."

²²Josiah, however, would not turn away from him, but disguised himself to engage him in battle. He would not listen to what Neco had said at God's command but went to fight him on the plain of Megiddo.

²³Archers shot King Josiah, and he told his officers, "Take me away; I am badly wounded." ²⁴So they took him out of his chariot, put him in the other chariot he had and brought him to Jerusalem, where he died. He was buried in the tombs of his fathers, and all Judah and Jerusalem mourned for him.

²⁵Jeremiah composed laments for Josiah, and to this day all the men and women singers commemorate Josiah in the laments. These became a tradition in Israel and are written in the Laments.

²⁶The other events of Josiah's reign and his acts of devotion, according to what is written in the Law of the LORD— ²⁷all the events, from beginning to end, are written in the book of the kings of Israel and **36** Judah. ¹And the people of the land took Jehoahaz son of Josiah and made him king in Jerusalem in place of his father.

Jehoahaz King of Judah

²Jehoahaz*ᵃ* was twenty-three years old when he became king, and he reigned in Jerusalem three months. ³The king of Egypt dethroned him in Jerusalem and imposed on Judah a levy of a hundred talents*ᵇ* of silver and a talent*ᶜ* of gold. ⁴The king of Egypt made Eliakim, a brother of Jehoahaz, king over Judah and Jerusalem and changed Eliakim's name to Jehoiakim. But Neco took Eliakim's brother Jehoahaz and carried him off to Egypt.

Jehoiakim King of Judah

⁵Jehoiakim was twenty-five years old when he became king, and he reigned in Jerusalem eleven years. He did evil in the

eyes of the LORD his God. ⁶Nebuchadnezzar king of Babylon attacked him and bound him with bronze shackles to take him to Babylon. ⁷Nebuchadnezzar also took to Babylon articles from the temple of the LORD and put them in his temple*ᵈ* there.

⁸The other events of Jehoiakim's reign, the detestable things he did and all that was found against him, are written in the book of the kings of Israel and Judah. And Jehoiachin his son succeeded him as king.

Jehoiachin King of Judah

⁹Jehoiachin was eighteen*ᵉ* years old when he became king, and he reigned in Jerusalem three months and ten days. He did evil in the eyes of the LORD. ¹⁰In the spring, King Nebuchadnezzar sent for him and brought him to Babylon, together with articles of value from the temple of the LORD, and he made Jehoiachin's uncle,*ᶠ* Zedekiah, king over Judah and Jerusalem.

Zedekiah King of Judah

¹¹Zedekiah was twenty-one years old when he became king, and he reigned in Jerusalem eleven years. ¹²He did evil in the eyes of the LORD his God and did not humble himself before Jeremiah the prophet, who spoke the word of the LORD. ¹³He also rebelled against King Nebuchadnezzar, who had made him take an oath in God's name. He became stiff-necked and hardened his heart and would not turn to the LORD, the God of Israel. ¹⁴Furthermore, all the leaders of the priests and the people became more and more unfaithful, following all the detestable practices of the nations and defiling the temple of the LORD, which he had consecrated in Jerusalem.

The Fall of Jerusalem

¹⁵The LORD, the God of their fathers, sent word to them through his messengers again and again, because he had pity

---

ᵃ2 Hebrew *Joahaz,* a variant of *Jehoahaz;* also in verse 4   *ᵇ3* That is, about 3 3/4 tons (about 3.4 metric tons)   *ᶜ3* That is, about 75 pounds (about 34 kilograms)   *ᵈ7* Or *palace*   *ᵉ9* One Hebrew manuscript, some Septuagint manuscripts and Syriac (see also 2 Kings 24:8); most Hebrew manuscripts *eight*   *ᶠ10* Hebrew *brother,* that is, relative (see 2 Kings 24:17) on his people and on his dwelling place. [16]But they mocked God's messengers, despised his words and scoffed at his prophets until the wrath of the LORD was aroused against his people and there was no remedy. [17]He brought up against them the king of the Babylonians,[a] who killed their young men with the sword in the sanctuary, and spared neither young man nor young woman, old man or aged. God handed all of them over to Nebuchadnezzar. [18]He carried to Babylon all the articles from the temple of God, both large and small, and the treasures of the LORD's temple and the treasures of the king and his officials. [19]They set fire to God's temple and broke down the wall of Jerusalem; they burned all the palaces and destroyed everything of value there.

[20]He carried into exile to Babylon the remnant, who escaped from the sword, and they became servants to him and his sons until the kingdom of Persia came to power. [21]The land enjoyed its sabbath rests; all the time of its desolation it rested, until the seventy years were completed in fulfillment of the word of the LORD spoken by Jeremiah.

[22]In the first year of Cyrus king of Persia, in order to fulfill the word of the LORD spoken by Jeremiah, the LORD moved the heart of Cyrus king of Persia to make a proclamation throughout his realm and to put it in writing:

[23]"This is what Cyrus king of Persia says:

" 'The LORD, the God of heaven, has given me all the kingdoms of the earth and he has appointed me to build a temple for him at Jerusalem in Judah. Anyone of his people among you—may the LORD his God be with him, and let him go up.' "

[a]17 Or *Chaldeans*

Ezra

In the book of Ezra, the Israelites' situation takes an upward swing. After a long exile in Babylon, they are allowed to return to Judah and rebuild the temple. What's more, God raises up a new leader in Ezra, a man devoted to studying and teaching the Law. While under Ezra's dynamic leadership, the temple is rebuilt and dedicated, and the people celebrate and renew their commitment to faithfulness and purity. The Israelites rejoice in the God who gives his people a second chance to trust and follow him.

Is your marriage in need of a second chance? Are there areas that you need to recommit to God and to each other? Rejoice—God is the God of second chances!

Cyrus Helps the Exiles to Return

1 In the first year of Cyrus king of Persia, in order to fulfill the word of the LORD spoken by Jeremiah, the LORD moved the heart of Cyrus king of Persia to make a proclamation throughout his realm and to put it in writing:

²"This is what Cyrus king of Persia says:

" 'The LORD, the God of heaven, has given me all the kingdoms of the earth and he has appointed me to build a temple for him at Jerusalem in Judah. ³Anyone of his people among you—may his God be with him, and let him go up to Jerusalem in Judah and build the temple of the LORD, the God of Israel, the God who is in Jerusalem. ⁴And the people of any place where survivors may now be living are to provide him with silver and gold, with goods and livestock, and with freewill offerings for the temple of God in Jerusalem.' "

⁵Then the family heads of Judah and Benjamin, and the priests and Levites—everyone whose heart God had moved—prepared to go up and build the house of the LORD in Jerusalem. ⁶All their neighbors assisted them with articles of silver and gold, with goods and livestock, and with valuable gifts, in addition to all the freewill offerings. ⁷Moreover, King Cyrus brought out the articles belonging to the temple of the LORD, which Nebuchadnezzar had carried away from Jerusalem and

had placed in the temple of his god.[a]
[8]Cyrus king of Persia had them brought
by Mithredath the treasurer, who counted
them out to Sheshbazzar the prince of
Judah.

[9]This was the inventory:

gold dishes	30
silver dishes	1,000
silver pans[b]	29
[10]gold bowls	30
matching silver bowls	410
other articles	1,000

[11]In all, there were 5,400 articles of
gold and of silver. Sheshbazzar brought
all these along when the exiles came up
from Babylon to Jerusalem.

The List of the Exiles Who Returned

2 Now these are the people of the province who came up from the captivity
of the exiles, whom Nebuchadnezzar king
of Babylon had taken captive to Babylon
(they returned to Jerusalem and Judah,
each to his own town, [2]in company with
Zerubbabel, Jeshua, Nehemiah, Seraiah,
Reelaiah, Mordecai, Bilshan, Mispar, Bigvai, Rehum and Baanah):

The list of the men of the people of
Israel:

[3]the descendants of Parosh	2,172
[4]of Shephatiah	372
[5]of Arah	775
[6]of Pahath-Moab (through the line of Jeshua and Joab)	2,812
[7]of Elam	1,254
[8]of Zattu	945
[9]of Zaccai	760
[10]of Bani	642
[11]of Bebai	623
[12]of Azgad	1,222
[13]of Adonikam	666
[14]of Bigvai	2,056
[15]of Adin	454
[16]of Ater (through Hezekiah)	98
[17]of Bezai	323
[18]of Jorah	112
[19]of Hashum	223
[20]of Gibbar	95
[21]the men of Bethlehem	123
[22]of Netophah	56
[23]of Anathoth	128
[24]of Azmaveth	42
[25]of Kiriath Jearim,[c] Kephirah and Beeroth	743
[26]of Ramah and Geba	621
[27]of Micmash	122
[28]of Bethel and Ai	223
[29]of Nebo	52
[30]of Magbish	156
[31]of the other Elam	1,254
[32]of Harim	320
[33]of Lod, Hadid and Ono	725
[34]of Jericho	345
[35]of Senaah	3,630

[36]The priests:

the descendants of Jedaiah (through the family of Jeshua)	973
[37]of Immer	1,052
[38]of Pashhur	1,247
[39]of Harim	1,017

[40]The Levites:

the descendants of Jeshua and Kadmiel (through the line of Hodaviah)	74

[41]The singers:

the descendants of Asaph	128

[42]The gatekeepers of the temple:

the descendants of Shallum, Ater, Talmon, Akkub, Hatita and Shobai	139

[43]The temple servants:

the descendants of
Ziha, Hasupha, Tabbaoth,
[44]Keros, Siaha, Padon,
[45]Lebanah, Hagabah, Akkub,
[46]Hagab, Shalmai, Hanan,
[47]Giddel, Gahar, Reaiah,
[48]Rezin, Nekoda, Gazzam,
[49]Uzza, Paseah, Besai,
[50]Asnah, Meunim, Nephussim,
[51]Bakbuk, Hakupha, Harhur,
[52]Bazluth, Mehida, Harsha,
[53]Barkos, Sisera, Temah,
[54]Neziah and Hatipha

[55]The descendants of the servants of
Solomon:

---

[a]7 Or *gods*   [b]9 The meaning of the Hebrew for
this word is uncertain.   [c]25 See Septuagint (see
also Neh. 7:29); Hebrew *Kiriath Arim.*

the descendants of
 Sotai, Hassophereth, Peruda,
 56Jaala, Darkon, Giddel,
 57Shephatiah, Hattil,
 Pokereth-Hazzebaim and Ami

58The temple servants and the
 descendants of the servants
 of Solomon   392

59The following came up from
the towns of Tel Melah, Tel Harsha,
Kerub, Addon and Immer, but they
could not show that their families
were descended from Israel:

60The descendants of
 Delaiah, Tobiah and
 Nekoda   652

61And from among the priests:

The descendants of
 Hobaiah, Hakkoz and
 Barzillai (a man who had
 married a daughter of Barzillai
 the Gileadite and was called
 by that name).
 62These searched for their family
records, but they could not find
them and so were excluded from the
priesthood as unclean. 63The governor ordered them not to eat any of
the most sacred food until there was
a priest ministering with the Urim
and Thummim.

64The whole company numbered
42,360, 65besides their 7,337 menservants and maidservants; and they
also had 200 men and women singers. 66They had 736 horses, 245
mules, 67435 camels and 6,720 donkeys.

68When they arrived at the house of the
LORD in Jerusalem, some of the heads of
the families gave freewill offerings toward
the rebuilding of the house of God on its
site. 69According to their ability they gave
to the treasury for this work 61,000 drachmas*a* of gold, 5,000 minas*b* of silver
and 100 priestly garments.
70The priests, the Levites, the singers,
the gatekeepers and the temple servants
settled in their own towns, along with
some of the other people, and the rest of
the Israelites settled in their towns.

Rebuilding the Altar

3 When the seventh month came and
the Israelites had settled in their
towns, the people assembled as one man
in Jerusalem. 2Then Jeshua son of Jozadak
and his fellow priests and Zerubbabel son
of Shealtiel and his associates began to
build the altar of the God of Israel to sacrifice burnt offerings on it, in accordance
with what is written in the Law of Moses
the man of God. 3Despite their fear of the
peoples around them, they built the altar
on its foundation and sacrificed burnt offerings on it to the LORD, both the morning and evening sacrifices. 4Then in accordance with what is written, they
celebrated the Feast of Tabernacles with
the required number of burnt offerings
prescribed for each day. 5After that, they
presented the regular burnt offerings, the
New Moon sacrifices and the sacrifices
for all the appointed sacred feasts of the
LORD, as well as those brought as freewill
offerings to the LORD. 6On the first day of
the seventh month they began to offer
burnt offerings to the LORD, though the
foundation of the LORD's temple had not
yet been laid.

Rebuilding the Temple

7Then they gave money to the masons
and carpenters, and gave food and drink
and oil to the people of Sidon and Tyre,
so that they would bring cedar logs by sea
from Lebanon to Joppa, as authorized by
Cyrus king of Persia.
8In the second month of the second
year after their arrival at the house of God
in Jerusalem, Zerubbabel son of Shealtiel,
Jeshua son of Jozadak and the rest of their
brothers (the priests and the Levites and
all who had returned from the captivity to
Jerusalem) began the work, appointing
Levites twenty years of age and older to
supervise the building of the house of the
LORD. 9Jeshua and his sons and brothers
and Kadmiel and his sons (descendants
of Hodaviah*c*) and the sons of Henadad
and their sons and brothers—all Levites—
joined together in supervising those
working on the house of God.

a69 That is, about 1,100 pounds (about 500
kilograms)   *b69* That is, about 3 tons (about
2.9 metric tons)   *c9* Hebrew *Yehudah*, probably
a variant of *Hodaviah*

[10]When the builders laid the foundation of the temple of the LORD, the priests in their vestments and with trumpets, and the Levites (the sons of Asaph) with cymbals, took their places to praise the LORD, as prescribed by David king of Israel. [11]With praise and thanksgiving they sang to the LORD:

"He is good;
    his love to Israel endures forever."

And all the people gave a great shout of praise to the LORD, because the foundation of the house of the LORD was laid. [12]But many of the older priests and Levites and family heads, who had seen the former temple, wept aloud when they saw the foundation of this temple being laid, while many others shouted for joy. [13]No one could distinguish the sound of the shouts of joy from the sound of weeping, because the people made so much noise. And the sound was heard far away.

Opposition to the Rebuilding

4 When the enemies of Judah and Benjamin heard that the exiles were building a temple for the LORD, the God of Israel, [2]they came to Zerubbabel and to the heads of the families and said, "Let us help you build because, like you, we seek your God and have been sacrificing to him since the time of Esarhaddon king of Assyria, who brought us here."

[3]But Zerubbabel, Jeshua and the rest of the heads of the families of Israel answered, "You have no part with us in building a temple to our God. We alone will build it for the LORD, the God of Israel, as King Cyrus, the king of Persia, commanded us."

[4]Then the peoples around them set out to discourage the people of Judah and make them afraid to go on building.[a] [5]They hired counselors to work against them and frustrate their plans during the entire reign of Cyrus king of Persia and down to the reign of Darius king of Persia.

Later Opposition Under Xerxes and Artaxerxes

[6]At the beginning of the reign of Xerxes,[b] they lodged an accusation against the people of Judah and Jerusalem.

[7]And in the days of Artaxerxes king of Persia, Bishlam, Mithredath, Tabeel and the rest of his associates wrote a letter to Artaxerxes. The letter was written in Aramaic script and in the Aramaic language.[c, d]

[8]Rehum the commanding officer and Shimshai the secretary wrote a letter against Jerusalem to Artaxerxes the king as follows:

[9]Rehum the commanding officer

---

[a]4 Or *and troubled them as they built*
[b]6 Hebrew *Ahasuerus,* a variant of Xerxes' Persian name   [c]7 Or *written in Aramaic and translated*
[d]7 The text of Ezra 4:8—6:18 is in Aramaic.

When Discouragement Leads to Defeat

Wednesday

EZRA 4:4   Have you ever felt like the people of Judah in verse 4? Discouraged? Afraid? Close to giving up? Tim and Janet sure did. They came to us after three years of marriage, because they were ready to call it quits. Talking with us was their last-ditch effort to save a sinking marriage. Soon into our first counseling session we understood why this young couple was already going to throw in the towel. They were pessimists—defeated, disappointed and depressed. They never expected their marriage to get any better. All they could see were problems with no solu-

tions. So they had given up hope. Nothing is more lethal to a marriage than negative thinking, especially in its most alluring form of pessimism. In fact, if couples could be given a vaccine against pessimistic thinking, we would probably see the divorce rate all but drop off. In a sense, you can protect your marriage against this virus. All it takes is a good shot of optimism—rising above your circumstances and maintaining hope for your future.

—Les & Leslie

Go to page 500 for your next devotional reading.

and Shimshai the secretary, together with the rest of their associates—the judges and officials over the men from Tripolis, Persia,[a] Erech and Babylon, the Elamites of Susa, [10]and the other people whom the great and honorable Ashurbanipal[b] deported and settled in the city of Samaria and elsewhere in Trans-Euphrates.

[11](This is a copy of the letter they sent him.)

To King Artaxerxes,

From your servants, the men of Trans-Euphrates:

[12]The king should know that the Jews who came up to us from you have gone to Jerusalem and are rebuilding that rebellious and wicked city. They are restoring the walls and repairing the foundations.

[13]Furthermore, the king should know that if this city is built and its walls are restored, no more taxes, tribute or duty will be paid, and the royal revenues will suffer. [14]Now since we are under obligation to the palace and it is not proper for us to see the king dishonored, we are sending this message to inform the king, [15]so that a search may be made in the archives of your predecessors. In these records you will find that this city is a rebellious city, troublesome to kings and provinces, a place of rebellion from ancient times. That is why this city was destroyed. [16]We inform the king that if this city is built and its walls are restored, you will be left with nothing in Trans-Euphrates.

[17]The king sent this reply:

To Rehum the commanding officer, Shimshai the secretary and the rest of their associates living in Samaria and elsewhere in Trans-Euphrates:

Greetings.

[18]The letter you sent us has been read and translated in my presence. [19]I issued an order and a search was made, and it was found that this city

has a long history of revolt against kings and has been a place of rebellion and sedition. [20]Jerusalem has had powerful kings ruling over the whole of Trans-Euphrates, and taxes, tribute and duty were paid to them. [21]Now issue an order to these men to stop work, so that this city will not be rebuilt until I so order. [22]Be careful not to neglect this matter. Why let this threat grow, to the detriment of the royal interests?

[23]As soon as the copy of the letter of King Artaxerxes was read to Rehum and Shimshai the secretary and their associates, they went immediately to the Jews in Jerusalem and compelled them by force to stop.

[24]Thus the work on the house of God in Jerusalem came to a standstill until the second year of the reign of Darius king of Persia.

Tattenai's Letter to Darius

5 Now Haggai the prophet and Zechariah the prophet, a descendant of Iddo, prophesied to the Jews in Judah and Jerusalem in the name of the God of Israel, who was over them. [2]Then Zerubbabel son of Shealtiel and Jeshua son of Jozadak set to work to rebuild the house of God in Jerusalem. And the prophets of God were with them, helping them.

[3]At that time Tattenai, governor of Trans-Euphrates, and Shethar-Bozenai and their associates went to them and asked, "Who authorized you to rebuild this temple and restore this structure?" [4]They also asked, "What are the names of the men constructing this building?"[c] [5]But the eye of their God was watching over the elders of the Jews, and they were not stopped until a report could go to Darius and his written reply be received.

[6]This is a copy of the letter that Tattenai, governor of Trans-Euphrates, and Shethar-Bozenai and their associates, the officials of Trans-Euphrates, sent to King

---

[a]9 Or officials, magistrates and governors over the men from   [b]10 Aramaic Osnappar, a variant of Ashurbanipal   [c]4 See Septuagint; Aramaic [4]We told them the names of the men constructing this building.

Darius. ⁷The report they sent him read as follows:

To King Darius:

Cordial greetings.

⁸The king should know that we went to the district of Judah, to the temple of the great God. The people are building it with large stones and placing the timbers in the walls. The work is being carried on with diligence and is making rapid progress under their direction.

⁹We questioned the elders and asked them, "Who authorized you to rebuild this temple and restore this structure?" ¹⁰We also asked them their names, so that we could write down the names of their leaders for your information.

¹¹This is the answer they gave us:

"We are the servants of the God of heaven and earth, and we are rebuilding the temple that was built many years ago, one that a great king of Israel built and finished. ¹²But because our fathers angered the God of heaven, he handed them over to Nebuchadnezzar the Chaldean, king of Babylon, who destroyed this temple and deported the people to Babylon.

¹³"However, in the first year of Cyrus king of Babylon, King Cyrus issued a decree to rebuild this house of God. ¹⁴He even removed from the temple*ᵃ* of Babylon the gold and silver articles of the house of God, which Nebuchadnezzar had taken from the temple in Jerusalem and brought to the temple*ᵃ* in Babylon.

"Then King Cyrus gave them to a man named Sheshbazzar, whom he had appointed governor, ¹⁵and he told him, 'Take these articles and go and deposit them in the temple in Jerusalem. And rebuild the house of God on its site.' ¹⁶So this Sheshbazzar came and laid the foundations of the house of God in Jerusalem. From that day to the present it has been under construction but is not yet finished."

¹⁷Now if it pleases the king, let a search be made in the royal archives of Babylon to see if King Cyrus did in fact issue a decree to rebuild this house of God in Jerusalem. Then let the king send us his decision in this matter.

The Decree of Darius

6 King Darius then issued an order, and they searched in the archives stored in the treasury at Babylon. ²A scroll was found in the citadel of Ecbatana in the province of Media, and this was written on it:

Memorandum:

³In the first year of King Cyrus, the king issued a decree concerning the temple of God in Jerusalem:

Let the temple be rebuilt as a place to present sacrifices, and let its foundations be laid. It is to be ninety feet*ᵇ* high and ninety feet wide, ⁴with three courses of large stones and one of timbers. The costs are to be paid by the royal treasury. ⁵Also, the gold and silver articles of the house of God, which Nebuchadnezzar took from the temple in Jerusalem and brought to Babylon, are to be returned to their places in the temple in Jerusalem; they are to be deposited in the house of God.

⁶Now then, Tattenai, governor of Trans-Euphrates, and Shethar-Bozenai and you, their fellow officials of that province, stay away from there. ⁷Do not interfere with the work on this temple of God. Let the governor of the Jews and the Jewish elders rebuild this house of God on its site.

⁸Moreover, I hereby decree what you are to do for these elders of the Jews in the construction of this house of God:

The expenses of these men are to be fully paid out of the royal treasury, from the revenues of Trans-Euphrates, so that the work will not

ᵃ14 Or *palace*   *ᵇ3* Aramaic *sixty cubits* (about 27 meters) stop. ⁹Whatever is needed—young bulls, rams, male lambs for burnt offerings to the God of heaven, and wheat, salt, wine and oil, as requested by the priests in Jerusalem—must be given them daily without fail, ¹⁰so that they may offer sacrifices pleasing to the God of heaven and pray for the well-being of the king and his sons.

¹¹Furthermore, I decree that if anyone changes this edict, a beam is to be pulled from his house and he is to be lifted up and impaled on it. And for this crime his house is to be made a pile of rubble. ¹²May God, who has caused his Name to dwell there, overthrow any king or people who lifts a hand to change this decree or to destroy this temple in Jerusalem.

I Darius have decreed it. Let it be carried out with diligence.

Completion and Dedication of the Temple

¹³Then, because of the decree King Darius had sent, Tattenai, governor of Trans-Euphrates, and Shethar-Bozenai and their associates carried it out with diligence. ¹⁴So the elders of the Jews continued to build and prosper under the preaching of Haggai the prophet and Zechariah, a descendant of Iddo. They finished building the temple according to the command of the God of Israel and the decrees of Cyrus, Darius and Artaxerxes, kings of Persia. ¹⁵The temple was completed on the third day of the month Adar, in the sixth year of the reign of King Darius.

¹⁶Then the people of Israel—the priests, the Levites and the rest of the exiles—celebrated the dedication of the house of God with joy. ¹⁷For the dedication of this house of God they offered a hundred bulls, two hundred rams, four hundred male lambs and, as a sin offering for all Israel, twelve male goats, one for each of the tribes of Israel. ¹⁸And they installed the priests in their divisions and the Levites in their groups for the service of God at Jerusalem, according to what is written in the Book of Moses.

The Passover

¹⁹On the fourteenth day of the first month, the exiles celebrated the Passover. ²⁰The priests and Levites had purified themselves and were all ceremonially clean. The Levites slaughtered the Passover lamb for all the exiles, for their brothers the priests and for themselves. ²¹So the Israelites who had returned from the exile ate it, together with all who had separated themselves from the unclean practices of their Gentile neighbors in order to seek the LORD, the God of Israel. ²²For seven days they celebrated with joy the Feast of Unleavened Bread, because the LORD had filled them with joy by changing the attitude of the king of Assyria, so that he assisted them in the work on the house of God, the God of Israel.

Ezra Comes to Jerusalem

7 After these things, during the reign of Artaxerxes king of Persia, Ezra son of Seraiah, the son of Azariah, the son of Hilkiah, ²the son of Shallum, the son of Zadok, the son of Ahitub, ³the son of Amariah, the son of Azariah, the son of Meraioth, ⁴the son of Zerahiah, the son of Uzzi, the son of Bukki, ⁵the son of Abishua, the son of Phinehas, the son of Eleazar, the son of Aaron the chief priest— ⁶this Ezra came up from Babylon. He was a teacher well versed in the Law of Moses, which the LORD, the God of Israel, had given. The king had granted him everything he asked, for the hand of the LORD his God was on him. ⁷Some of the Israelites, including priests, Levites, singers, gatekeepers and temple servants, also came up to Jerusalem in the seventh year of King Artaxerxes.

⁸Ezra arrived in Jerusalem in the fifth month of the seventh year of the king. ⁹He had begun his journey from Babylon on the first day of the first month, and he arrived in Jerusalem on the first day of the fifth month, for the gracious hand of his God was on him. ¹⁰For Ezra had devoted himself to the study and observance of the Law of the LORD, and to teaching its decrees and laws in Israel.

King Artaxerxes' Letter to Ezra

¹¹This is a copy of the letter King Artaxerxes had given to Ezra the priest and teacher, a man learned in matters con-

cerning the commands and decrees of the LORD for Israel:

[12a]Artaxerxes, king of kings,

To Ezra the priest, a teacher of the Law of the God of heaven:

Greetings.

[13]Now I decree that any of the Israelites in my kingdom, including priests and Levites, who wish to go to Jerusalem with you, may go. [14]You are sent by the king and his seven advisers to inquire about Judah and Jerusalem with regard to the Law of your God, which is in your hand. [15]Moreover, you are to take with you the silver and gold that the king and his advisers have freely given to the God of Israel, whose dwelling is in Jerusalem, [16]together with all the silver and gold you may obtain from the province of Babylon, as well as the freewill offerings of the people and priests for the temple of their God in Jerusalem. [17]With this money be sure to buy bulls, rams and male lambs, together with their grain offerings and drink offerings, and sacrifice them on the altar of the temple of your God in Jerusalem.

[18]You and your brother Jews may then do whatever seems best with the rest of the silver and gold, in accordance with the will of your God. [19]Deliver to the God of Jerusalem all the articles entrusted to you for worship in the temple of your God. [20]And anything else needed for the temple of your God that you may have occasion to supply, you may provide from the royal treasury.

[21]Now I, King Artaxerxes, order all the treasurers of Trans-Euphrates to provide with diligence whatever Ezra the priest, a teacher of the Law of the God of heaven, may ask of you— [22]up to a hundred talents[b] of silver, a hundred cors[c] of wheat, a hundred baths[d] of wine, a hundred baths[d] of olive oil, and salt without limit. [23]Whatever the God of heaven has prescribed, let it be done with diligence for the temple of the God of heaven. Why should there be

wrath against the realm of the king and of his sons? [24]You are also to know that you have no authority to impose taxes, tribute or duty on any of the priests, Levites, singers, gatekeepers, temple servants or other workers at this house of God.

[25]And you, Ezra, in accordance with the wisdom of your God, which you possess, appoint magistrates and judges to administer justice to all the people of Trans-Euphrates—all who know the laws of your God. And you are to teach any who do not know them. [26]Whoever does not obey the law of your God and the law of the king must surely be punished by death, banishment, confiscation of property, or imprisonment.

[27]Praise be to the LORD, the God of our fathers, who has put it into the king's heart to bring honor to the house of the LORD in Jerusalem in this way [28]and who has extended his good favor to me before the king and his advisers and all the king's powerful officials. Because the hand of the LORD my God was on me, I took courage and gathered leading men from Israel to go up with me.

List of the Family Heads Returning With Ezra

8 These are the family heads and those registered with them who came up with me from Babylon during the reign of King Artaxerxes:

[2]of the descendants of Phinehas, Gershom;
of the descendants of Ithamar, Daniel;
of the descendants of David, Hattush [3]of the descendants of Shecaniah;

of the descendants of Parosh, Zechariah, and with him were registered 150 men;
[4]of the descendants of Pahath-Moab, Eliehoenai son of Zerahiah, and with him 200 men;

---

[a]12 The text of Ezra 7:12-26 is in Aramaic.
[b]22 That is, about 3 3/4 tons (about 3.4 metric tons)   [c]22 That is, probably about 600 bushels (about 22 kiloliters)   [d]22 That is, probably about 600 gallons (about 2.2 kiloliters)

⁵of the descendants of Zattu,ᵃ Shecaniah son of Jahaziel, and with him 300 men;

⁶of the descendants of Adin, Ebed son of Jonathan, and with him 50 men;

⁷of the descendants of Elam, Jeshaiah son of Athaliah, and with him 70 men;

⁸of the descendants of Shephatiah, Zebadiah son of Michael, and with him 80 men;

⁹of the descendants of Joab, Obadiah son of Jehiel, and with him 218 men;

¹⁰of the descendants of Bani,ᵇ Shelomith son of Josiphiah, and with him 160 men;

¹¹of the descendants of Bebai, Zechariah son of Bebai, and with him 28 men;

¹²of the descendants of Azgad, Johanan son of Hakkatan, and with him 110 men;

¹³of the descendants of Adonikam, the last ones, whose names were Eliphelet, Jeuel and Shemaiah, and with them 60 men;

¹⁴of the descendants of Bigvai, Uthai and Zaccur, and with them 70 men.

The Return to Jerusalem

¹⁵I assembled them at the canal that flows toward Ahava, and we camped there three days. When I checked among the people and the priests, I found no Levites there. ¹⁶So I summoned Eliezer, Ariel, Shemaiah, Elnathan, Jarib, Elnathan, Nathan, Zechariah and Meshullam, who were leaders, and Joiarib and Elnathan, who were men of learning, ¹⁷and I sent them to Iddo, the leader in Casiphia. I told them what to say to Iddo and his kinsmen, the temple servants in Casiphia, so that they might bring attendants to us for the house of our God. ¹⁸Because the gracious hand of our God was on us, they brought us Sherebiah, a capable man, from the descendants of Mahli son of Levi, the son of Israel, and Sherebiah's sons and brothers, 18 men; ¹⁹and Hashabiah, together with Jeshaiah from the descendants of Merari, and his brothers and nephews, 20 men. ²⁰They also brought 220 of the temple servants—a body that David and the officials had established to assist the Levites. All were registered by name.

²¹There, by the Ahava Canal, I proclaimed a fast, so that we might humble ourselves before our God and ask him for a safe journey for us and our children, with all our possessions. ²²I was ashamed to ask the king for soldiers and horsemen to protect us from enemies on the road, because we had told the king, "The gracious hand of our God is on everyone who looks to him, but his great anger is against all who forsake him." ²³So we fasted and petitioned our God about this, and he answered our prayer.

²⁴Then I set apart twelve of the leading priests, together with Sherebiah, Hashabiah and ten of their brothers, ²⁵and I weighed out to them the offering of silver and gold and the articles that the king, his advisers, his officials and all Israel present there had donated for the house of our God. ²⁶I weighed out to them 650 talentsᶜ of silver, silver articles weighing 100 talents,ᵈ 100 talentsᵈ of gold, ²⁷20 bowls of gold valued at 1,000 darics,ᵉ and two fine articles of polished bronze, as precious as gold.

²⁸I said to them, "You as well as these articles are consecrated to the LORD. The silver and gold are a freewill offering to the LORD, the God of your fathers. ²⁹Guard them carefully until you weigh them out in the chambers of the house of the LORD in Jerusalem before the leading priests and the Levites and the family heads of Israel." ³⁰Then the priests and Levites received the silver and gold and sacred articles that had been weighed out to be taken to the house of our God in Jerusalem.

³¹On the twelfth day of the first month we set out from the Ahava Canal to go to Jerusalem. The hand of our God was on us, and he protected us from enemies and bandits along the way. ³²So we arrived in Jerusalem, where we rested three days.

ᵃ5 Some Septuagint manuscripts (also 1 Esdras 8:32); Hebrew does not have *Zattu*.   ᵇ10 Some Septuagint manuscripts (also 1 Esdras 8:36); Hebrew does not have *Bani*.   ᶜ26 That is, about 25 tons (about 22 metric tons)   ᵈ26 That is, about 3 3/4 tons (about 3.4 metric tons)   ᵉ27 That is, about 19 pounds (about 8.5 kilograms)

³³On the fourth day, in the house of our God, we weighed out the silver and gold and the sacred articles into the hands of Meremoth son of Uriah, the priest. Eleazar son of Phinehas was with him, and so were the Levites Jozabad son of Jeshua and Noadiah son of Binnui. ³⁴Everything was accounted for by number and weight, and the entire weight was recorded at that time.

³⁵Then the exiles who had returned from captivity sacrificed burnt offerings to the God of Israel: twelve bulls for all Israel, ninety-six rams, seventy-seven male lambs and, as a sin offering, twelve male goats. All this was a burnt offering to the LORD. ³⁶They also delivered the king's orders to the royal satraps and to the governors of Trans-Euphrates, who then gave assistance to the people and to the house of God.

Ezra's Prayer About Intermarriage

9 After these things had been done, the leaders came to me and said, "The people of Israel, including the priests and the Levites, have not kept themselves separate from the neighboring peoples with their detestable practices, like those of the Canaanites, Hittites, Perizzites, Jebusites, Ammonites, Moabites, Egyptians and Amorites. ²They have taken some of their daughters as wives for themselves and their sons, and have mingled the holy race with the peoples around them. And the leaders and officials have led the way in this unfaithfulness."

³When I heard this, I tore my tunic and cloak, pulled hair from my head and beard and sat down appalled. ⁴Then everyone who trembled at the words of the God of Israel gathered around me because of this unfaithfulness of the exiles. And I sat there appalled until the evening sacrifice.

⁵Then, at the evening sacrifice, I rose from my self-abasement, with my tunic and cloak torn, and fell on my knees with my hands spread out to the LORD my God ⁶and prayed:

"O my God, I am too ashamed and disgraced to lift up my face to you, my God, because our sins are higher than our heads and our guilt has reached to the heavens. ⁷From the days of our forefathers until now, our guilt has been great. Because of our sins, we and our kings and our priests have been subjected to the sword and captivity, to pillage and humiliation at the hand of foreign kings, as it is today.

⁸"But now, for a brief moment, the LORD our God has been gracious in leaving us a remnant and giving us a firm place in his sanctuary, and so our God gives light to our eyes and a little relief in our bondage. ⁹Though we are slaves, our God has not deserted us in our bondage. He has shown us kindness in the sight of the kings of Persia: He has granted us new life to rebuild the house of our God and repair its ruins, and he has given us a wall of protection in Judah and Jerusalem.

¹⁰"But now, O our God, what can we say after this? For we have disregarded the commands ¹¹you gave through your servants the prophets when you said: 'The land you are entering to possess is a land polluted by the corruption of its peoples. By their detestable practices they have filled it with their impurity from one end to the other. ¹²Therefore, do not give your daughters in marriage to their sons or take their daughters for your sons. Do not seek a treaty of friendship with them at any time, that you may be strong and eat the good things of the land and leave it to your children as an everlasting inheritance.'

¹³"What has happened to us is a result of our evil deeds and our great guilt, and yet, our God, you have punished us less than our sins have deserved and have given us a remnant like this. ¹⁴Shall we again break your commands and intermarry with the peoples who commit such detestable practices? Would you not be angry enough with us to destroy us, leaving us no remnant or survivor? ¹⁵O LORD, God of Israel, you are righteous! We are left this day as a remnant. Here we are before you in our guilt, though because of it not one of us can stand in your presence."

The People's Confession of Sin

10 While Ezra was praying and confessing, weeping and throwing himself down before the house of God, a large crowd of Israelites—men, women and children—gathered around him. They too wept bitterly. ²Then Shecaniah son of Jehiel, one of the descendants of Elam, said to Ezra, "We have been unfaithful to our God by marrying foreign women from the peoples around us. But in spite of this, there is still hope for Israel. ³Now let us make a covenant before our God to send away all these women and their children, in accordance with the counsel of my lord and of those who fear the commands of our God. Let it be done according to the Law. ⁴Rise up; this matter is in your hands. We will support you, so take courage and do it."

⁵So Ezra rose up and put the leading priests and Levites and all Israel under oath to do what had been suggested. And they took the oath. ⁶Then Ezra withdrew from before the house of God and went to the room of Jehohanan son of Eliashib. While he was there, he ate no food and drank no water, because he continued to mourn over the unfaithfulness of the exiles.

⁷A proclamation was then issued throughout Judah and Jerusalem for all the exiles to assemble in Jerusalem. ⁸Anyone who failed to appear within three days would forfeit all his property, in accordance with the decision of the officials and elders, and would himself be expelled from the assembly of the exiles.

⁹Within the three days, all the men of Judah and Benjamin had gathered in Jerusalem. And on the twentieth day of the ninth month, all the people were sitting in the square before the house of God, greatly distressed by the occasion and because of the rain. ¹⁰Then Ezra the priest stood up and said to them, "You have been unfaithful; you have married foreign women, adding to Israel's guilt. ¹¹Now make confession to the LORD, the God of your fathers, and do his will. Separate yourselves from the peoples around you and from your foreign wives."

¹²The whole assembly responded with a loud voice: "You are right! We must do as you say. ¹³But there are many people here and it is the rainy season; so we cannot stand outside. Besides, this matter cannot be taken care of in a day or two, because we have sinned greatly in this thing. ¹⁴Let our officials act for the whole assembly. Then let everyone in our towns who has married a foreign woman come at a set time, along with the elders and judges of each town, until the fierce anger of our God in this matter is turned away from us." ¹⁵Only Jonathan son of Asahel and Jahzeiah son of Tikvah, supported by Meshullam and Shabbethai the Levite, opposed this.

¹⁶So the exiles did as was proposed. Ezra the priest selected men who were family heads, one from each family division, and all of them designated by name. On the first day of the tenth month they sat down to investigate the cases, ¹⁷and by the first day of the first month they finished dealing with all the men who had married foreign women.

Those Guilty of Intermarriage

¹⁸Among the descendants of the priests, the following had married foreign women:

From the descendants of Jeshua son of Jozadak, and his brothers: Maaseiah, Eliezer, Jarib and Gedaliah. ¹⁹(They all gave their hands in pledge to put away their wives, and for their guilt they each presented a ram from the flock as a guilt offering.)

²⁰From the descendants of Immer: Hanani and Zebadiah.

²¹From the descendants of Harim: Maaseiah, Elijah, Shemaiah, Jehiel and Uzziah.

²²From the descendants of Pashhur: Elioenai, Maaseiah, Ishmael, Nethanel, Jozabad and Elasah.

²³Among the Levites:

Jozabad, Shimei, Kelaiah (that is, Kelita), Pethahiah, Judah and Eliezer.

²⁴From the singers: Eliashib.

From the gatekeepers: Shallum, Telem and Uri.

²⁵And among the other Israelites:

From the descendants of Parosh:
Ramiah, Izziah, Malkijah, Mija-
min, Eleazar, Malkijah and Be-
naiah.
26From the descendants of Elam:
Mattaniah, Zechariah, Jehiel,
Abdi, Jeremoth and Elijah.
27From the descendants of Zattu:
Elioenai, Eliashib, Mattaniah,
Jeremoth, Zabad and Aziza.
28From the descendants of Bebai:
Jehohanan, Hananiah, Zabbai
and Athlai.
29From the descendants of Bani:
Meshullam, Malluch, Adaiah, Ja-
shub, Sheal and Jeremoth.
30From the descendants of Pahath-
Moab:
Adna, Kelal, Benaiah, Maaseiah,
Mattaniah, Bezalel, Binnui and
Manasseh.
31From the descendants of Harim:
Eliezer, Ishijah, Malkijah, She-
maiah, Shimeon, 32Benjamin,
Malluch and Shemariah.

33From the descendants of Hashum:
Mattenai, Mattattah, Zabad,
Eliphelet, Jeremai, Manasseh
and Shimei.
34From the descendants of Bani:
Maadai, Amram, Uel, 35Benaiah,
Bedeiah, Keluhi, 36Vaniah, Mere-
moth, Eliashib, 37Mattaniah,
Mattenai and Jaasu.
38From the descendants of Binnui:[a]
Shimei, 39Shelemiah, Nathan,
Adaiah, 40Macnadebai, Shashai,
Sharai, 41Azarel, Shelemiah,
Shemariah, 42Shallum, Amariah
and Joseph.
43From the descendants of Nebo:
Jeiel, Mattithiah, Zabad, Zebina,
Jaddai, Joel and Benaiah.

44All these had married foreign wom-
en, and some of them had children by
these wives.[b]

---

[a]37,38 See Septuagint (also 1 Esdras 9:34); Hebrew
Jaasu 38and Bani and Binnui,   [b]44 Or and they
sent them away with their children

Nehemiah

Do you remember chanting "Sticks and stones may break my bones, but words will never hurt me"—or do you hear your children chant it now? Somehow the phrase seems to take the sting out of hurtful words. Words have a powerful and sometimes devastating effect. They can encourage, literally issuing strength to the hearer. They can also discourage, leaving the recipient feeling defeated.

Nehemiah's story is one of a courageous leader who risks a prestigious job to ask his superior, the King of Persia, to give him a leave of absence and allow him to organize the rebuilding of Jerusalem's walls. Given permission, Nehemiah sets out to accomplish this huge project. But right in the middle of the work, hecklers show up. The people are discouraged, but Nehemiah speaks words of assurance that revive and empower them. Good words restore tired and frustrated people. This includes, of course, spouses.

Nehemiah's Prayer

1 The words of Nehemiah son of Hacaliah:

In the month of Kislev in the twentieth year, while I was in the citadel of Susa, ²Hanani, one of my brothers, came from Judah with some other men, and I questioned them about the Jewish remnant that survived the exile, and also about Jerusalem.

³They said to me, "Those who survived the exile and are back in the province are in great trouble and disgrace. The wall of Jerusalem is broken down, and its gates have been burned with fire."

⁴When I heard these things, I sat down and wept. For some days I mourned and fasted and prayed before the God of heaven. ⁵Then I said:

"O LORD, God of heaven, the great and awesome God, who keeps his covenant of love with those who love him and obey his commands,

⁶let your ear be attentive and your eyes open to hear the prayer your servant is praying before you day and night for your servants, the people of Israel. I confess the sins we Israelites, including myself and my father's house, have committed against you. ⁷We have acted very wickedly toward you. We have not obeyed the commands, decrees and laws you gave your servant Moses.

⁸"Remember the instruction you gave your servant Moses, saying, 'If you are unfaithful, I will scatter you among the nations, ⁹but if you return to me and obey my commands, then even if your exiled people are at the farthest horizon, I will gather them from there and bring them to the place I have chosen as a dwelling for my Name.'

¹⁰"They are your servants and your people, whom you redeemed by your great strength and your mighty hand. ¹¹O Lord, let your ear be attentive to the prayer of this your servant and to the prayer of your servants who delight in revering your name. Give your servant success today by granting him favor in the presence of this man."

I was cupbearer to the king.

Artaxerxes Sends Nehemiah to Jerusalem

2 In the month of Nisan in the twentieth year of King Artaxerxes, when wine was brought for him, I took the wine and gave it to the king. I had not been sad in his presence before; ²so the king asked me, "Why does your face look so sad when you are not ill? This can be nothing but sadness of heart."

I was very much afraid, ³but I said to the king, "May the king live forever! Why should my face not look sad when the city where my fathers are buried lies in ruins, and its gates have been destroyed by fire?"

⁴The king said to me, "What is it you want?"

Then I prayed to the God of heaven, ⁵and I answered the king, "If it pleases the king and if your servant has found favor in his sight, let him send me to the city in Judah where my fathers are buried so that I can rebuild it."

⁶Then the king, with the queen sitting beside him, asked me, "How long will your journey take, and when will you get back?" It pleased the king to send me; so I set a time.

⁷I also said to him, "If it pleases the king, may I have letters to the governors of Trans-Euphrates, so that they will provide me safe-conduct until I arrive in Judah? ⁸And may I have a letter to Asaph, keeper of the king's forest, so he will give me timber to make beams for the gates of the citadel by the temple and for the city wall and for the residence I will occupy?" And because the gracious hand of my God was upon me, the king granted my requests. ⁹So I went to the governors of Trans-Euphrates and gave them the king's letters. The king had also sent army officers and cavalry with me.

¹⁰When Sanballat the Horonite and Tobiah the Ammonite official heard about this, they were very much disturbed that someone had come to promote the welfare of the Israelites.

Nehemiah Inspects Jerusalem's Walls

¹¹I went to Jerusalem, and after staying there three days ¹²I set out during the night with a few men. I had not told anyone what my God had put in my heart to do for Jerusalem. There were no mounts with me except the one I was riding on. ¹³By night I went out through the Valley Gate toward the Jackal[a] Well and the Dung Gate, examining the walls of Jerusalem, which had been broken down, and its gates, which had been destroyed by fire. ¹⁴Then I moved on toward the Fountain Gate and the King's Pool, but there was not enough room for my mount to get through; ¹⁵so I went up the valley by night, examining the wall. Finally, I turned back and reentered through the Valley Gate. ¹⁶The officials did not know where I had gone or what I was doing, because as yet I had said nothing to the Jews or the priests or nobles or officials or any others who would be doing the work. ¹⁷Then I said to them, "You see the trouble we are in: Jerusalem lies in ruins, and its gates have been burned with fire. Come, let us rebuild the wall of Jerusalem, and we will no longer be in disgrace."

a 13 Or *Serpent* or *Fig*

¹⁸I also told them about the gracious hand of my God upon me and what the king had said to me.

They replied, "Let us start rebuilding." So they began this good work.

¹⁹But when Sanballat the Horonite, Tobiah the Ammonite official and Geshem the Arab heard about it, they mocked and ridiculed us. "What is this you are doing?" they asked. "Are you rebelling against the king?"

²⁰I answered them by saying, "The God of heaven will give us success. We his servants will start rebuilding, but as for you, you have no share in Jerusalem or any claim or historic right to it."

Builders of the Wall

3 Eliashib the high priest and his fellow priests went to work and rebuilt the Sheep Gate. They dedicated it and set its doors in place, building as far as the Tower of the Hundred, which they dedicated, and as far as the Tower of Hananel. ²The men of Jericho built the adjoining section, and Zaccur son of Imri built next to them.

³The Fish Gate was rebuilt by the sons of Hassenaah. They laid its beams and put its doors and bolts and bars in place. ⁴Meremoth son of Uriah, the son of Hakkoz, repaired the next section. Next to him Meshullam son of Berekiah, the son of Meshezabel, made repairs, and next to him Zadok son of Baana also made repairs. ⁵The next section was repaired by the men of Tekoa, but their nobles would not put their shoulders to the work under their supervisors.ᵃ

⁶The Jeshanahᵇ Gate was repaired by Joiada son of Paseah and Meshullam son of Besodeiah. They laid its beams and put its doors and bolts and bars in place. ⁷Next to them, repairs were made by men from Gibeon and Mizpah—Melatiah of Gibeon and Jadon of Meronoth—places under the authority of the governor of Trans-Euphrates. ⁸Uzziel son of Harha-

ᵃ5 Or *their Lord* or *the governor*   ᵇ6 Or *Old*

One Flesh

Thursday

NEHEMIAH 3 Rebuilding the walls of Jerusalem—what an immense task! It was a success because the Israelites worked together. One thing that doesn't appear to be part of this chapter is "complaining." The people seem so focused on doing their part that they aren't focused on their neighbor's responsibilities. They stand next to each other, shoulder to shoulder, focusing only on their own sections. A view from the sky would probably have made them look like one body, working in concert, to complete the huge task.

There's a great principle here for the marriage relationship. Difficult tasks face each marriage. Some spouses have medical difficulties, while others have incredible parenting challenges. Serious financial difficulties seem to plague marriage relationships. Still other couples face a circumstance that has deflated trust in their marriage. Every marriage has a "wall" that has crumbled and needs to be rebuilt.

When it came to disciplining our children, Rosemary and I thought we were so different that we wouldn't be able to agree. She leans toward warmth and relationship. I am heavy on the side of structure and rules. After much discussion and understanding, however, we came to realize that together we made the structured bricks and soft mortar necessary to build our discipline system.

God reveals his amazing omniscience when we take the time to look at the spouse he has given us. Oftentimes one spouse will have the gifts to overcome the difficulty but not have the patience to endure. Yet it seems that God has linked that spouse, shoulder to shoulder, with a marriage partner who has that patience. Alone they would never be able to complete the task that lies before them. But working together, as one flesh, they find that they can.

—**Bob & Rosemary**

Go to page 506 for your next devotional reading.

iah, one of the goldsmiths, repaired the next section; and Hananiah, one of the perfume-makers, made repairs next to that. They restored[a] Jerusalem as far as the Broad Wall. ⁹Rephaiah son of Hur, ruler of a half-district of Jerusalem, repaired the next section. ¹⁰Adjoining this, Jedaiah son of Harumaph made repairs opposite his house, and Hattush son of Hashabneiah made repairs next to him. ¹¹Malkijah son of Harim and Hasshub son of Pahath-Moab repaired another section and the Tower of the Ovens. ¹²Shallum son of Hallohesh, ruler of a half-district of Jerusalem, repaired the next section with the help of his daughters.

¹³The Valley Gate was repaired by Hanun and the residents of Zanoah. They rebuilt it and put its doors and bolts and bars in place. They also repaired five hundred yards[b] of the wall as far as the Dung Gate.

¹⁴The Dung Gate was repaired by Malkijah son of Recab, ruler of the district of Beth Hakkerem. He rebuilt it and put its doors and bolts and bars in place.

¹⁵The Fountain Gate was repaired by Shallun son of Col-Hozeh, ruler of the district of Mizpah. He rebuilt it, roofing it over and putting its doors and bolts and bars in place. He also repaired the wall of the Pool of Siloam,[c] by the King's Garden, as far as the steps going down from the City of David. ¹⁶Beyond him, Nehemiah son of Azbuk, ruler of a half-district of Beth Zur, made repairs up to a point opposite the tombs[d] of David, as far as the artificial pool and the House of the Heroes.

¹⁷Next to him, the repairs were made by the Levites under Rehum son of Bani. Beside him, Hashabiah, ruler of half the district of Keilah, carried out repairs for his district. ¹⁸Next to him, the repairs were made by their countrymen under Binnui[e] son of Henadad, ruler of the other half-district of Keilah. ¹⁹Next to him, Ezer son of Jeshua, ruler of Mizpah, repaired another section, from a point facing the ascent to the armory as far as the angle. ²⁰Next to him, Baruch son of Zabbai zealously repaired another section, from the angle to the entrance of the house of Eliashib the high priest. ²¹Next to him, Meremoth son of Uriah, the son of Hakkoz, repaired another section, from the entrance of Eliashib's house to the end of it.

²²The repairs next to him were made by the priests from the surrounding region. ²³Beyond them, Benjamin and Hasshub made repairs in front of their house; and next to them, Azariah son of Maaseiah, the son of Ananiah, made repairs beside his house. ²⁴Next to him, Binnui son of Henadad repaired another section, from Azariah's house to the angle and the corner, ²⁵and Palal son of Uzai worked opposite the angle and the tower projecting from the upper palace near the court of the guard. Next to him, Pedaiah son of Parosh ²⁶and the temple servants living on the hill of Ophel made repairs up to a point opposite the Water Gate toward the east and the projecting tower. ²⁷Next to them, the men of Tekoa repaired another section, from the great projecting tower to the wall of Ophel.

²⁸Above the Horse Gate, the priests made repairs, each in front of his own house. ²⁹Next to them, Zadok son of Immer made repairs opposite his house. Next to him, Shemaiah son of Shecaniah, the guard at the East Gate, made repairs. ³⁰Next to him, Hananiah son of Shelemiah, and Hanun, the sixth son of Zalaph, repaired another section. Next to them, Meshullam son of Berekiah made repairs opposite his living quarters. ³¹Next to him, Malkijah, one of the goldsmiths, made repairs as far as the house of the temple servants and the merchants, opposite the Inspection Gate, and as far as the room above the corner; ³²and between the room above the corner and the Sheep Gate the goldsmiths and merchants made repairs.

Opposition to the Rebuilding

4 When Sanballat heard that we wer[e] rebuilding the wall, he became ang[ry] and was greatly incensed. He ridiculed t[he]

---

[a]8 Or *They left out part of*   [b]13 Hebrew *a thousand cubits* (about 450 meters)   [c]15 Heb[rew] *Shelah*, a variant of *Shiloah*, that is, Siloam   [d]16 Hebrew; Septuagint, some Vulgate manus[cripts] and Syriac *tomb*   [e]18 Two Hebrew manus[cripts] and Syriac (see also Septuagint and verse 24)[;] Hebrew manuscripts *Bavvai*

Jews, ²and in the presence of his associates and the army of Samaria, he said, "What are those feeble Jews doing? Will they restore their wall? Will they offer sacrifices? Will they finish in a day? Can they bring the stones back to life from those heaps of rubble—burned as they are?"

³Tobiah the Ammonite, who was at his side, said, "What they are building—if even a fox climbed up on it, he would break down their wall of stones!"

⁴Hear us, O our God, for we are despised. Turn their insults back on their own heads. Give them over as plunder in a land of captivity. ⁵Do not cover up their guilt or blot out their sins from your sight, for they have thrown insults in the face of ᵃ the builders.

⁶So we rebuilt the wall till all of it reached half its height, for the people worked with all their heart.

⁷But when Sanballat, Tobiah, the Arabs, the Ammonites and the men of Ashdod heard that the repairs to Jerusalem's walls had gone ahead and that the gaps were being closed, they were very angry. ⁸They all plotted together to come and fight against Jerusalem and stir up trouble against it. ⁹But we prayed to our God and posted a guard day and night to meet this threat.

¹⁰Meanwhile, the people in Judah said, "The strength of the laborers is giving out, and there is so much rubble that we cannot rebuild the wall."

¹¹Also our enemies said, "Before they know it or see us, we will be right there among them and will kill them and put an end to the work."

¹²Then the Jews who lived near them came and told us ten times over, "Wherever you turn, they will attack us."

¹³Therefore I stationed some of the people behind the lowest points of the wall at the exposed places, posting them by families, with their swords, spears and bows. ¹⁴After I looked things over, I stood up and said to the nobles, the officials and the rest of the people, "Don't be afraid of them. Remember the Lord, who is great and awesome, and fight for your brothers, your sons and your daughters, our wives and your homes."

¹⁵When our enemies heard that we were aware of their plot and that God had frustrated it, we all returned to the wall, each to his own work.

¹⁶From that day on, half of my men did the work, while the other half were equipped with spears, shields, bows and armor. The officers posted themselves behind all the people of Judah ¹⁷who were building the wall. Those who carried materials did their work with one hand and held a weapon in the other, ¹⁸and each of the builders wore his sword at his side as he worked. But the man who sounded the trumpet stayed with me.

¹⁹Then I said to the nobles, the officials and the rest of the people, "The work is extensive and spread out, and we are widely separated from each other along the wall. ²⁰Wherever you hear the sound of the trumpet, join us there. Our God will fight for us!"

²¹So we continued the work with half the men holding spears, from the first light of dawn till the stars came out. ²²At that time I also said to the people, "Have every man and his helper stay inside Jerusalem at night, so they can serve us as guards by night and workmen by day." ²³Neither I nor my brothers nor my men nor the guards with me took off our clothes; each had his weapon, even when he went for water.ᵇ

Nehemiah Helps the Poor

5 Now the men and their wives raised a great outcry against their Jewish brothers. ²Some were saying, "We and our sons and daughters are numerous; in order for us to eat and stay alive, we must get grain."

³Others were saying, "We are mortgaging our fields, our vineyards and our homes to get grain during the famine."

⁴Still others were saying, "We have had to borrow money to pay the king's tax on our fields and vineyards. ⁵Although we are of the same flesh and blood as our countrymen and though our sons are as good as theirs, yet we have to subject our sons and daughters to slavery. Some of our daughters have already been enslaved, but we are powerless, because our fields and our vineyards belong to others."

ᵃ5 Or *have provoked you to anger before*
ᵇ23 The meaning of the Hebrew for this clause is uncertain.

⁶When I heard their outcry and these charges, I was very angry. ⁷I pondered them in my mind and then accused the nobles and officials. I told them, "You are exacting usury from your own countrymen!" So I called together a large meeting to deal with them ⁸and said: "As far as possible, we have bought back our Jewish brothers who were sold to the Gentiles. Now you are selling your brothers, only for them to be sold back to us!" They kept quiet, because they could find nothing to say.

⁹So I continued, "What you are doing is not right. Shouldn't you walk in the fear of our God to avoid the reproach of our Gentile enemies? ¹⁰I and my brothers and my men are also lending the people money and grain. But let the exacting of usury stop! ¹¹Give back to them immediately their fields, vineyards, olive groves and houses, and also the usury you are charging them—the hundredth part of the money, grain, new wine and oil."

¹²"We will give it back," they said. "And we will not demand anything more from them. We will do as you say."

Then I summoned the priests and made the nobles and officials take an oath to do what they had promised. ¹³I also shook out the folds of my robe and said, "In this way may God shake out of his house and possessions every man who does not keep this promise. So may such a man be shaken out and emptied!"

At this the whole assembly said, "Amen," and praised the LORD. And the people did as they had promised.

¹⁴Moreover, from the twentieth year of King Artaxerxes, when I was appointed to be their governor in the land of Judah, until his thirty-second year—twelve years—neither I nor my brothers ate the food allotted to the governor. ¹⁵But the earlier governors—those preceding me—placed a heavy burden on the people and took forty shekels*ᵃ* of silver from them in addition to food and wine. Their assistants also lorded it over the people. But out of reverence for God I did not act like that. ¹⁶Instead, I devoted myself to the work on this wall. All my men were assembled there for the work; we*ᵇ* did not acquire any land.

¹⁷Furthermore, a hundred and fifty Jews and officials ate at my table, as well as those who came to us from the surrounding nations. ¹⁸Each day one ox, six choice sheep and some poultry were prepared for me, and every ten days an abundant supply of wine of all kinds. In spite of all this, I never demanded the food allotted to the governor, because the demands were heavy on these people.

¹⁹Remember me with favor, O my God, for all I have done for these people.

Further Opposition to the Rebuilding

6 When word came to Sanballat, Tobiah, Geshem the Arab and the rest of our enemies that I had rebuilt the wall and not a gap was left in it—though up to that time I had not set the doors in the gates— ²Sanballat and Geshem sent me this message: "Come, let us meet together in one of the villages*ᶜ* on the plain of Ono."

But they were scheming to harm me; ³so I sent messengers to them with this reply: "I am carrying on a great project and cannot go down. Why should the work stop while I leave it and go down to you?" ⁴Four times they sent me the same message, and each time I gave them the same answer.

⁵Then, the fifth time, Sanballat sent his aide to me with the same message, and in his hand was an unsealed letter ⁶in which was written:

"It is reported among the nations—and Geshem*ᵈ* says it is true—that you and the Jews are plotting to revolt, and therefore you are building the wall. Moreover, according to these reports you are about to become their king ⁷and have even appointed prophets to make this proclamation about you in Jerusalem: 'There is a king in Judah!' Now this report will get back to the king; so come, let us confer together."

⁸I sent him this reply: "Nothing like what you are saying is happening; you are just making it up out of your head."

⁹They were all trying to frighten us, thinking, "Their hands will get too weak

---

*ᵃ*15 That is, about 1 pound (about 0.5 kilogram)
*ᵇ*16 Most Hebrew manuscripts; some Hebrew manuscripts, Septuagint, Vulgate and Syriac *I*
*ᶜ*2 Or *in Kephirim*   *ᵈ*6 Hebrew *Gashmu*, a variant of *Geshem*

for the work, and it will not be completed."

⌊But I prayed,⌋ "Now strengthen my hands."

¹⁰One day I went to the house of Shemaiah son of Delaiah, the son of Mehetabel, who was shut in at his home. He said, "Let us meet in the house of God, inside the temple, and let us close the temple doors, because men are coming to kill you—by night they are coming to kill you." ¹¹But I said, "Should a man like me run away? Or should one like me go into the temple to save his life? I will not go!" ¹²I realized that God had not sent him, but that he had prophesied against me because Tobiah and Sanballat had hired him. ¹³He had been hired to intimidate me so that I would commit a sin by doing this, and then they would give me a bad name to discredit me.

¹⁴Remember Tobiah and Sanballat, O my God, because of what they have done; remember also the prophetess Noadiah and the rest of the prophets who have been trying to intimidate me.

The Completion of the Wall

¹⁵So the wall was completed on the twenty-fifth of Elul, in fifty-two days. ¹⁶When all our enemies heard about this, all the surrounding nations were afraid and lost their self-confidence, because they realized that this work had been done with the help of our God.

¹⁷Also, in those days the nobles of Judah were sending many letters to Tobiah, and replies from Tobiah kept coming to them. ¹⁸For many in Judah were under oath to him, since he was son-in-law to Shecaniah son of Arah, and his son Jehohanan had married the daughter of Meshullam son of Berekiah. ¹⁹Moreover, they kept reporting to me his good deeds and then telling him what I said. And Tobiah sent letters to intimidate me.

7 After the wall had been rebuilt and I had set the doors in place, the gatekeepers and the singers and the Levites were appointed. ²I put in charge of Jerusalem my brother Hanani, along with*a* Hananiah the commander of the citadel, because he was a man of integrity and feared God more than most men do. ³I said to them, "The gates of Jerusalem are

not to be opened until the sun is hot. While the gatekeepers are still on duty, have them shut the doors and bar them. Also appoint residents of Jerusalem as guards, some at their posts and some near their own houses."

The List of the Exiles Who Returned

⁴Now the city was large and spacious, but there were few people in it, and the houses had not yet been rebuilt. ⁵So my God put it into my heart to assemble the nobles, the officials and the common people for registration by families. I found the genealogical record of those who had been the first to return. This is what I found written there:

⁶These are the people of the province who came up from the captivity of the exiles whom Nebuchadnezzar king of Babylon had taken captive (they returned to Jerusalem and Judah, each to his own town, ⁷in company with Zerubbabel, Jeshua, Nehemiah, Azariah, Raamiah, Nahamani, Mordecai, Bilshan, Mispereth, Bigvai, Nehum and Baanah):

The list of the men of Israel:

⁸the descendants of Parosh	2,172
⁹of Shephatiah	372
¹⁰of Arah	652
¹¹of Pahath-Moab (through the line of Jeshua and Joab)	2,818
¹²of Elam	1,254
¹³of Zattu	845
¹⁴of Zaccai	760
¹⁵of Binnui	648
¹⁶of Bebai	628
¹⁷of Azgad	2,322
¹⁸of Adonikam	667
¹⁹of Bigvai	2,067
²⁰of Adin	655
²¹of Ater (through Hezekiah)	98
²²of Hashum	328
²³of Bezai	324
²⁴of Hariph	112
²⁵of Gibeon	95
²⁶the men of Bethlehem and Netophah	188
²⁷of Anathoth	128

a2 Or Hanani, that is,

²⁸of Beth Azmaveth   42
²⁹of Kiriath Jearim,
     Kephirah and Beeroth   743
³⁰of Ramah and Geba   621
³¹of Micmash   122
³²of Bethel and Ai   123
³³of the other Nebo   52
³⁴of the other Elam   1,254
³⁵of Harim   320
³⁶of Jericho   345
³⁷of Lod, Hadid and Ono   721
³⁸of Senaah   3,930

³⁹The priests:

the descendants of Jedaiah
     (through the family of
     Jeshua)   973
⁴⁰of Immer   1,052
⁴¹of Pashhur   1,247
⁴²of Harim   1,017

⁴³The Levites:

the descendants of Jeshua
     (through Kadmiel through
     the line of Hodaviah)   74

⁴⁴The singers:

the descendants of Asaph   148

⁴⁵The gatekeepers:

the descendants of
     Shallum, Ater, Talmon,
     Akkub, Hatita and
     Shobai   138

⁴⁶The temple servants:

the descendants of
     Ziha, Hasupha, Tabbaoth,
⁴⁷Keros, Sia, Padon,
⁴⁸Lebana, Hagaba, Shalmai,
⁴⁹Hanan, Giddel, Gahar,
⁵⁰Reaiah, Rezin, Nekoda,
⁵¹Gazzam, Uzza, Paseah,
⁵²Besai, Meunim, Nephussim,
⁵³Bakbuk, Hakupha, Harhur,
⁵⁴Bazluth, Mehida, Harsha,
⁵⁵Barkos, Sisera, Temah,
⁵⁶Neziah and Hatipha

⁵⁷The descendants of the servants of
Solomon:

the descendants of
     Sotai, Sophereth, Perida,
⁵⁸Jaala, Darkon, Giddel,
⁵⁹Shephatiah, Hattil,

Pokereth-Hazzebaim and
Amon

⁶⁰The temple servants and the
     descendants of the servants
     of Solomon   392

⁶¹The following came up from
the towns of Tel Melah, Tel Harsha,
Kerub, Addon and Immer, but they
could not show that their families
were descended from Israel:

⁶²the descendants of
     Delaiah, Tobiah and
     Nekoda   642

⁶³And from among the priests:

the descendants of
     Hobaiah, Hakkoz and
     Barzillai (a man who had
     married a daughter of Barzillai
     the Gileadite and was called
     by that name).
⁶⁴These searched for their family
records, but they could not find
them and so were excluded from the
priesthood as unclean. ⁶⁵The governor, therefore, ordered them not to
eat any of the most sacred food until
there should be a priest ministering
with the Urim and Thummim.

⁶⁶The whole company numbered
42,360, ⁶⁷besides their 7,337 menservants and maidservants; and they
also had 245 men and women singers. ⁶⁸There were 736 horses, 245
mules,ᵃ ⁶⁹435 camels and 6,720
donkeys.

⁷⁰Some of the heads of the families contributed to the work. The
governor gave to the treasury 1,000
drachmasᵇ of gold, 50 bowls and
530 garments for priests. ⁷¹Some of
the heads of the families gave to the
treasury for the work 20,000 drach-
masᶜ of gold and 2,200 minasᵈ of
silver. ⁷²The total given by the rest of
the people was 20,000 drachmas

ᵃ68 Some Hebrew manuscripts (see also Ezra
2:66); most Hebrew manuscripts do not have this
verse.   ᵇ70 That is, about 19 pounds (about 8.5
kilograms)   ᶜ71 That is, about 375 pounds
(about 170 kilograms); also in verse 72
ᵈ71 That is, about 1 1/3 tons (about 1.2 metric
tons)

of gold, 2,000 minas[a] of silver and 67 garments for priests.

[73] The priests, the Levites, the gatekeepers, the singers and the temple servants, along with certain of the people and the rest of the Israelites, settled in their own towns.

Ezra Reads the Law

When the seventh month came and the Israelites had settled in their towns, **8** [1] all the people assembled as one man in the square before the Water Gate. They told Ezra the scribe to bring out the Book of the Law of Moses, which the LORD had commanded for Israel.

[2] So on the first day of the seventh month Ezra the priest brought the Law before the assembly, which was made up of men and women and all who were able to understand. [3] He read it aloud from daybreak till noon as he faced the square before the Water Gate in the presence of the men, women and others who could understand. And all the people listened attentively to the Book of the Law.

[4] Ezra the scribe stood on a high wooden platform built for the occasion. Beside him on his right stood Mattithiah, Shema, Anaiah, Uriah, Hilkiah and Maaseiah; and on his left were Pedaiah, Misha-el, Malkijah, Hashum, Hashbaddanah, Zechariah and Meshullam.

[5] Ezra opened the book. All the people could see him because he was standing above them; and as he opened it, the people all stood up. [6] Ezra praised the LORD, the great God; and all the people lifted their hands and responded, "Amen! Amen!" Then they bowed down and worshiped the LORD with their faces to the ground.

[7] The Levites—Jeshua, Bani, Sherebiah, Jamin, Akkub, Shabbethai, Hodiah, Maaseiah, Kelita, Azariah, Jozabad, Hanan and Pelaiah—instructed the people in the Law while the people were standing there. [8] They read from the Book of the Law of God, making it clear[b] and giving the meaning so that the people could understand what was being read.

[9] Then Nehemiah the governor, Ezra the priest and scribe, and the Levites who were instructing the people said to them all, "This day is sacred to the LORD your God. Do not mourn or weep." For all the people had been weeping as they listened to the words of the Law.

[10] Nehemiah said, "Go and enjoy

---

[a]72 That is, about 1 1/4 tons (about 1.1 metric tons)   [b]8 Or God, translating it

---

Tears and Joy

Friday

NEHEMIAH 8:10 "How could you go over our credit limit without telling me?" she cried. "Do you know how embarrassing it was at the grocery store to be told my card was over its limit and to have to leave empty-handed with all my groceries still on the checkout counter and people staring at me?" He said nothing but silently thought, *I'm a failure. She hates me. I let her down. I let God down too.*

In this passage the Israelites also felt like failures. After completing the wall, they listened to Ezra as he read Scripture to them. Realizing how they had failed to live up to God's law, they were grief stricken. But Nehemiah's response demonstrates God's grace. He told them not to grieve but to be joyful. Because God is forgiving and loving, they could rejoice and find strength in the joy of the Lord.

Our strength doesn't come from doing everything right and never making mistakes; it comes from God who, through his grace, forgives us and grants us new mercies every day. Then we can extend this same love and grace to each other.

Maybe situations exist right now with your spouse that are causing hurt, and tears are more prevalent than joy. Are you willing to ask for forgiveness and to begin to focus on God's love and grace and how you can extend new mercies to your mate? The good comes with the bad. No one is perfect.

—*Dave & Claudia*

Go to page 525 for your next devotional reading.

choice food and sweet drinks, and send some to those who have nothing prepared. This day is sacred to our Lord. Do not grieve, for the joy of the LORD is your strength."

¹¹The Levites calmed all the people, saying, "Be still, for this is a sacred day. Do not grieve."

¹²Then all the people went away to eat and drink, to send portions of food and to celebrate with great joy, because they now understood the words that had been made known to them.

¹³On the second day of the month, the heads of all the families, along with the priests and the Levites, gathered around Ezra the scribe to give attention to the words of the Law. ¹⁴They found written in the Law, which the LORD had commanded through Moses, that the Israelites were to live in booths during the feast of the seventh month ¹⁵and that they should proclaim this word and spread it throughout their towns and in Jerusalem: "Go out into the hill country and bring back branches from olive and wild olive trees, and from myrtles, palms and shade trees, to make booths"—as it is written.ᵃ

¹⁶So the people went out and brought back branches and built themselves booths on their own roofs, in their courtyards, in the courts of the house of God and in the square by the Water Gate and the one by the Gate of Ephraim. ¹⁷The whole company that had returned from exile built booths and lived in them. From the days of Joshua son of Nun until that day, the Israelites had not celebrated it like this. And their joy was very great.

¹⁸Day after day, from the first day to the last, Ezra read from the Book of the Law of God. They celebrated the feast for seven days, and on the eighth day, in accordance with the regulation, there was an assembly.

The Israelites Confess Their Sins

9 On the twenty-fourth day of the same month, the Israelites gathered together, fasting and wearing sackcloth and having dust on their heads. ²Those of Israelite descent had separated themselves from all foreigners. They stood in their places and confessed their sins and the wickedness of their fathers. ³They stood where

they were and read from the Book of the Law of the LORD their God for a quarter of the day, and spent another quarter in confession and in worshiping the LORD their God. ⁴Standing on the stairs were the Levites—Jeshua, Bani, Kadmiel, Shebaniah, Bunni, Sherebiah, Bani and Kenani—who called with loud voices to the LORD their God. ⁵And the Levites—Jeshua, Kadmiel, Bani, Hashabneiah, Sherebiah, Hodiah, Shebaniah and Pethahiah—said: "Stand up and praise the LORD your God, who is from everlasting to everlasting.ᵇ"

"Blessed be your glorious name, and may it be exalted above all blessing and praise. ⁶You alone are the LORD. You made the heavens, even the highest heavens, and all their starry host, the earth and all that is on it, the seas and all that is in them. You give life to everything, and the multitudes of heaven worship you.

⁷"You are the LORD God, who chose Abram and brought him out of Ur of the Chaldeans and named him Abraham. ⁸You found his heart faithful to you, and you made a covenant with him to give to his descendants the land of the Canaanites, Hittites, Amorites, Perizzites, Jebusites and Girgashites. You have kept your promise because you are righteous.

⁹"You saw the suffering of our forefathers in Egypt; you heard their cry at the Red Sea.ᶜ ¹⁰You sent miraculous signs and wonders against Pharaoh, against all his officials and all the people of his land, for you knew how arrogantly the Egyptians treated them. You made a name for yourself, which remains to this day. ¹¹You divided the sea before them, so that they passed through it on dry ground, but you hurled their pursuers into the depths, like a stone into mighty waters. ¹²By day you led them with a pillar of cloud, and by night with a pillar of fire to give them light on the way they were to take.

ᵃ15 See Lev. 23:37-40.   ᵇ5 Or God for ever and ever   ᶜ9 Hebrew Yam Suph; that is, Sea of Reeds

13 "You came down on Mount Sinai; you spoke to them from heaven. You gave them regulations and laws that are just and right, and decrees and commands that are good. 14 You made known to them your holy Sabbath and gave them commands, decrees and laws through your servant Moses. 15 In their hunger you gave them bread from heaven and in their thirst you brought them water from the rock; you told them to go in and take possession of the land you had sworn with uplifted hand to give them.

16 "But they, our forefathers, became arrogant and stiff-necked, and did not obey your commands. 17 They refused to listen and failed to remember the miracles you performed among them. They became stiff-necked and in their rebellion appointed a leader in order to return to their slavery. But you are a forgiving God, gracious and compassionate, slow to anger and abounding in love. Therefore you did not desert them, 18 even when they cast for themselves an image of a calf and said, 'This is your god, who brought you up out of Egypt,' or when they committed awful blasphemies.

19 "Because of your great compassion you did not abandon them in the desert. By day the pillar of cloud did not cease to guide them on their path, nor the pillar of fire by night to shine on the way they were to take. 20 You gave your good Spirit to instruct them. You did not withhold your manna from their mouths, and you gave them water for their thirst. 21 For forty years you sustained them in the desert; they lacked nothing, their clothes did not wear out nor did their feet become swollen.

22 "You gave them kingdoms and nations, allotting to them even the remotest frontiers. They took over the country of Sihon*a* king of Heshbon and the country of Og king of Bashan. 23 You made their sons as numerous as the stars in the sky, and you brought them into the land that you told their fathers to enter and possess. 24 Their sons went in and took possession of the land. You subdued before them the Canaanites, who lived in the land; you handed the Canaanites over to them, along with their kings and the peoples of the land, to deal with them as they pleased. 25 They captured fortified cities and fertile land; they took possession of houses filled with all kinds of good things, wells already dug, vineyards, olive groves and fruit trees in abundance. They ate to the full and were well-nourished; they reveled in your great goodness.

26 "But they were disobedient and rebelled against you; they put your law behind their backs. They killed your prophets, who had admonished them in order to turn them back to you; they committed awful blasphemies. 27 So you handed them over to their enemies, who oppressed them. But when they were oppressed they cried out to you. From heaven you heard them, and in your great compassion you gave them deliverers, who rescued them from the hand of their enemies.

28 "But as soon as they were at rest, they again did what was evil in your sight. Then you abandoned them to the hand of their enemies so that they ruled over them. And when they cried out to you again, you heard from heaven, and in your compassion you delivered them time after time.

29 "You warned them to return to your law, but they became arrogant and disobeyed your commands. They sinned against your ordinances, by which a man will live if he obeys them. Stubbornly they turned their backs on you, became stiff-necked and refused to listen. 30 For many years you were patient with them. By your Spirit you admonished them through your prophets. Yet they paid no attention, so you handed them over to

---

*a*22 One Hebrew manuscript and Septuagint; most Hebrew manuscripts *Sihon, that is, the country of the*

the neighboring peoples. ³¹But in your great mercy you did not put an end to them or abandon them, for you are a gracious and merciful God.

³²"Now therefore, O our God, the great, mighty and awesome God, who keeps his covenant of love, do not let all this hardship seem trifling in your eyes—the hardship that has come upon us, upon our kings and leaders, upon our priests and prophets, upon our fathers and all your people, from the days of the kings of Assyria until today. ³³In all that has happened to us, you have been just; you have acted faithfully, while we did wrong. ³⁴Our kings, our leaders, our priests and our fathers did not follow your law; they did not pay attention to your commands or the warnings you gave them. ³⁵Even while they were in their kingdom, enjoying your great goodness to them in the spacious and fertile land you gave them, they did not serve you or turn from their evil ways.

³⁶"But see, we are slaves today, slaves in the land you gave our forefathers so they could eat its fruit and the other good things it produces. ³⁷Because of our sins, its abundant harvest goes to the kings you have placed over us. They rule over our bodies and our cattle as they please. We are in great distress.

The Agreement of the People

³⁸"In view of all this, we are making a binding agreement, putting it in writing, and our leaders, our Levites and our priests are affixing their seals to it."

10 Those who sealed it were:

Nehemiah the governor, the son of Hacaliah.

Zedekiah, ²Seraiah, Azariah, Jeremiah,
³Pashhur, Amariah, Malkijah,
⁴Hattush, Shebaniah, Malluch,
⁵Harim, Meremoth, Obadiah,
⁶Daniel, Ginnethon, Baruch,
⁷Meshullam, Abijah, Mijamin,

⁸Maaziah, Bilgai and Shemaiah.
These were the priests.

⁹The Levites:

Jeshua son of Azaniah, Binnui of the sons of Henadad, Kadmiel,
¹⁰and their associates: Shebaniah, Hodiah, Kelita, Pelaiah, Hanan,
¹¹Mica, Rehob, Hashabiah,
¹²Zaccur, Sherebiah, Shebaniah,
¹³Hodiah, Bani and Beninu.

¹⁴The leaders of the people:

Parosh, Pahath-Moab, Elam, Zattu, Bani,
¹⁵Bunni, Azgad, Bebai,
¹⁶Adonijah, Bigvai, Adin,
¹⁷Ater, Hezekiah, Azzur,
¹⁸Hodiah, Hashum, Bezai,
¹⁹Hariph, Anathoth, Nebai,
²⁰Magpiash, Meshullam, Hezir,
²¹Meshezabel, Zadok, Jaddua,
²²Pelatiah, Hanan, Anaiah,
²³Hoshea, Hananiah, Hasshub,
²⁴Hallohesh, Pilha, Shobek,
²⁵Rehum, Hashabnah, Maaseiah,
²⁶Ahiah, Hanan, Anan,
²⁷Malluch, Harim and Baanah.

²⁸"The rest of the people—priests, Levites, gatekeepers, singers, temple servants and all who separated themselves from the neighboring peoples for the sake of the Law of God, together with their wives and all their sons and daughters who are able to understand— ²⁹all these now join their brothers the nobles, and bind themselves with a curse and an oath to follow the Law of God given through Moses the servant of God and to obey carefully all the commands, regulations and decrees of the LORD our Lord.

³⁰"We promise not to give our daughters in marriage to the peoples around us or take their daughters for our sons.

³¹"When the neighboring peoples bring merchandise or grain to sell on the Sabbath, we will not buy from them on the Sabbath or on any holy day. Every seventh year we will forgo working the land and will cancel all debts.

³²"We assume the responsibility for carrying out the commands to give a third of a shekel[a] each year for the service of the house of our God: ³³for the bread set out on the table; for the regular grain offerings and burnt offerings; for the offerings on the Sabbaths, New Moon festivals and appointed feasts; for the holy offerings; for sin offerings to make atonement for Israel; and for all the duties of the house of our God.

³⁴"We—the priests, the Levites and the people—have cast lots to determine when each of our families is to bring to the house of our God at set times each year a contribution of wood to burn on the altar of the LORD our God, as it is written in the Law.

³⁵"We also assume responsibility for bringing to the house of the LORD each year the firstfruits of our crops and of every fruit tree.

³⁶"As it is also written in the Law, we will bring the firstborn of our sons and of our cattle, of our herds and of our flocks to the house of our God, to the priests ministering there.

³⁷"Moreover, we will bring to the storerooms of the house of our God, to the priests, the first of our ground meal, of our ⌞grain⌟ offerings, of the fruit of all our trees and of our new wine and oil. And we will bring a tithe of our crops to the Levites, for it is the Levites who collect the tithes in all the towns where we work. ³⁸A priest descended from Aaron is to accompany the Levites when they receive the tithes, and the Levites are to bring a tenth of the tithes up to the house of our God, to the storerooms of the treasury. ³⁹The people of Israel, including the Levites, are to bring their contributions of grain, new wine and oil to the storerooms where the articles for the sanctuary are kept and where the ministering priests, the gatekeepers and the singers stay.

"We will not neglect the house of our God."

The New Residents of Jerusalem

11 Now the leaders of the people settled in Jerusalem, and the rest of the people cast lots to bring one out of every ten to live in Jerusalem, the holy city, while the remaining nine were to stay in their own towns. ²The people commended all the men who volunteered to live in Jerusalem.

³These are the provincial leaders who settled in Jerusalem (now some Israelites, priests, Levites, temple servants and descendants of Solomon's servants lived in the towns of Judah, each on his own property in the various towns, ⁴while other people from both Judah and Benjamin lived in Jerusalem):

From the descendants of Judah:

Athaiah son of Uzziah, the son of Zechariah, the son of Amariah, the son of Shephatiah, the son of Mahalalel, a descendant of Perez; ⁵and Maaseiah son of Baruch, the son of Col-Hozeh, the son of Hazaiah, the son of Adaiah, the son of Joiarib, the son of Zechariah, a descendant of Shelah. ⁶The descendants of Perez who lived in Jerusalem totaled 468 able men.

⁷From the descendants of Benjamin:

Sallu son of Meshullam, the son of Joed, the son of Pedaiah, the son of Kolaiah, the son of Maaseiah, the son of Ithiel, the son of Jeshaiah, ⁸and his followers, Gabbai and Sallai—928 men. ⁹Joel son of Zicri was their chief officer, and Judah son of Hassenuah was over the Second District of the city.

¹⁰From the priests:

Jedaiah; the son of Joiarib; Jakin; ¹¹Seraiah son of Hilkiah, the son of Meshullam, the son of Zadok, the son of Meraioth, the son of Ahitub, supervisor in the house of God, ¹²and their associates, who carried on work for the temple—822 men; Adaiah son of Jeroham, the son of Pelaliah, the son of Amzi, the son of Zechariah, the son of Pashhur, the son of Malkijah, ¹³and his associ-

---

a 32 That is, about 1/8 ounce (about 4 grams)

ates, who were heads of families—242 men; Amashsai son of Azarel, the son of Ahzai, the son of Meshillemoth, the son of Immer, [14]and his[a] associates, who were able men—128. Their chief officer was Zabdiel son of Haggedolim.

[15]From the Levites:

Shemaiah son of Hasshub, the son of Azrikam, the son of Hashabiah, the son of Bunni; [16]Shabbethai and Jozabad, two of the heads of the Levites, who had charge of the outside work of the house of God; [17]Mattaniah son of Mica, the son of Zabdi, the son of Asaph, the director who led in thanksgiving and prayer; Bakbukiah, second among his associates; and Abda son of Shammua, the son of Galal, the son of Jeduthun. [18]The Levites in the holy city totaled 284.

[19]The gatekeepers:

Akkub, Talmon and their associates, who kept watch at the gates—172 men.

[20]The rest of the Israelites, with the priests and Levites, were in all the towns of Judah, each on his ancestral property.

[21]The temple servants lived on the hill of Ophel, and Ziha and Gishpa were in charge of them.

[22]The chief officer of the Levites in Jerusalem was Uzzi son of Bani, the son of Hashabiah, the son of Mattaniah, the son of Mica. Uzzi was one of Asaph's descendants, who were the singers responsible for the service of the house of God. [23]The singers were under the king's orders, which regulated their daily activity.

[24]Pethahiah son of Meshezabel, one of the descendants of Zerah son of Judah, was the king's agent in all affairs relating to the people.

[25]As for the villages with their fields, some of the people of Judah lived in Kiriath Arba and its surrounding settlements, in Dibon and its settlements, in Jekabzeel and its villages, [26]in Jeshua, in Moladah, in Beth Pelet, [27]in Hazar Shual, in Beersheba and its settlements, [28]in Ziklag, in Meconah and its settlements, [29]in En Rimmon, in Zorah, in Jarmuth, [30]Zanoah, Adullam and their villages, in Lachish

and its fields, and in Azekah and its settlements. So they were living all the way from Beersheba to the Valley of Hinnom.

[31]The descendants of the Benjamites from Geba lived in Micmash, Aija, Bethel and its settlements, [32]in Anathoth, Nob and Ananiah, [33]in Hazor, Ramah and Gittaim, [34]in Hadid, Zeboim and Neballat, [35]in Lod and Ono, and in the Valley of the Craftsmen.

[36]Some of the divisions of the Levites of Judah settled in Benjamin.

Priests and Levites

12 These were the priests and Levites who returned with Zerubbabel son of Shealtiel and with Jeshua:

Seraiah, Jeremiah, Ezra,
[2]Amariah, Malluch, Hattush,
[3]Shecaniah, Rehum, Meremoth,
[4]Iddo, Ginnethon,[b] Abijah,
[5]Mijamin,[c] Moadiah, Bilgah,
[6]Shemaiah, Joiarib, Jedaiah,
[7]Sallu, Amok, Hilkiah and Jedaiah.

These were the leaders of the priests and their associates in the days of Jeshua.

[8]The Levites were Jeshua, Binnui, Kadmiel, Sherebiah, Judah, and also Mattaniah, who, together with his associates, was in charge of the songs of thanksgiving. [9]Bakbukiah and Unni, their associates, stood opposite them in the services.

[10]Jeshua was the father of Joiakim, Joiakim the father of Eliashib, Eliashib the father of Joiada, [11]Joiada the father of Jonathan, and Jonathan the father of Jaddua.

[12]In the days of Joiakim, these were the heads of the priestly families:

of Seraiah's family, Meraiah;
of Jeremiah's, Hananiah;
[13]of Ezra's, Meshullam;
of Amariah's, Jehohanan;
[14]of Malluch's, Jonathan;
of Shecaniah's,[d] Joseph;
[15]of Harim's, Adna;
of Meremoth's,[e] Helkai;
[16]of Iddo's, Zechariah;

---

[a]14 Most Septuagint manuscripts; Hebrew *their*
[b]4 Many Hebrew manuscripts and Vulgate (see also Neh. 12:16); most Hebrew manuscripts *Ginnethoi*   [c]5 A variant of *Miniamin*
[d]14 Very many Hebrew manuscripts, some Septuagint manuscripts and Syriac (see also Neh. 12:3); most Hebrew manuscripts *Shebaniah's*
[e]15 Some Septuagint manuscripts (see also Neh. 12:3); Hebrew *Meraioth's*

of Ginnethon's, Meshullam;
¹⁷of Abijah's, Zicri;
of Miniamin's and of Moadiah's, Piltai;
¹⁸of Bilgah's, Shammua;
of Shemaiah's, Jehonathan;
¹⁹of Joiarib's, Mattenai;
of Jedaiah's, Uzzi;
²⁰of Sallu's, Kallai;
of Amok's, Eber;
²¹of Hilkiah's, Hashabiah;
of Jedaiah's, Nethanel.

²²The family heads of the Levites in the days of Eliashib, Joiada, Johanan and Jaddua, as well as those of the priests, were recorded in the reign of Darius the Persian. ²³The family heads among the descendants of Levi up to the time of Johanan son of Eliashib were recorded in the book of the annals. ²⁴And the leaders of the Levites were Hashabiah, Sherebiah, Jeshua son of Kadmiel, and their associates, who stood opposite them to give praise and thanksgiving, one section responding to the other, as prescribed by David the man of God.

²⁵Mattaniah, Bakbukiah, Obadiah, Meshullam, Talmon and Akkub were gatekeepers who guarded the storerooms at the gates. ²⁶They served in the days of Joiakim son of Jeshua, the son of Jozadak, and in the days of Nehemiah the governor and of Ezra the priest and scribe.

Dedication of the Wall of Jerusalem

²⁷At the dedication of the wall of Jerusalem, the Levites were sought out from where they lived and were brought to Jerusalem to celebrate joyfully the dedication with songs of thanksgiving and with the music of cymbals, harps and lyres. ²⁸The singers also were brought together from the region around Jerusalem—from the villages of the Netophathites, ²⁹from Beth Gilgal, and from the area of Geba and Azmaveth, for the singers had built villages for themselves around Jerusalem. ³⁰When the priests and Levites had purified themselves ceremonially, they purified the people, the gates and the wall.

³¹I had the leaders of Judah go up on top[a] of the wall. I also assigned two large choirs to give thanks. One was to proceed on top[b] of the wall to the right, toward the Dung Gate. ³²Hoshaiah and half the leaders of Judah followed them, ³³along with Azariah, Ezra, Meshullam, ³⁴Judah, Benjamin, Shemaiah, Jeremiah, ³⁵as well as some priests with trumpets, and also Zechariah son of Jonathan, the son of Shemaiah, the son of Mattaniah, the son of Micaiah, the son of Zaccur, the son of Asaph, ³⁶and his associates—Shemaiah, Azarel, Milalai, Gilalai, Maai, Nethanel, Judah and Hanani—with musical instruments ⌊ prescribed by⌋ David the man of God. Ezra the scribe led the procession. ³⁷At the Fountain Gate they continued directly up the steps of the City of David on the ascent to the wall and passed above the house of David to the Water Gate on the east.

³⁸The second choir proceeded in the opposite direction. I followed them on top[c] of the wall, together with half the people—past the Tower of the Ovens to the Broad Wall, ³⁹over the Gate of Ephraim, the Jeshanah[d] Gate, the Fish Gate, the Tower of Hananel and the Tower of the Hundred, as far as the Sheep Gate. At the Gate of the Guard they stopped.

⁴⁰The two choirs that gave thanks then took their places in the house of God; so did I, together with half the officials, ⁴¹as well as the priests—Eliakim, Maaseiah, Miniamin, Micaiah, Elioenai, Zechariah and Hananiah with their trumpets— ⁴²and also Maaseiah, Shemaiah, Eleazar, Uzzi, Jehohanan, Malkijah, Elam and Ezer. The choirs sang under the direction of Jezrahiah. ⁴³And on that day they offered great sacrifices, rejoicing because God had given them great joy. The women and children also rejoiced. The sound of rejoicing in Jerusalem could be heard far away.

⁴⁴At that time men were appointed to be in charge of the storerooms for the contributions, firstfruits and tithes. From the fields around the towns they were to bring into the storerooms the portions required by the Law for the priests and the Levites, for Judah was pleased with the ministering priests and Levites. ⁴⁵They performed the service of their God and the service of purification, as did also the singers and gatekeepers, according to the commands of David and his son Solo-

---

*a*31 Or *go alongside*   *b*31 Or *proceed alongside*
*c*38 Or *them alongside*   *d*39 Or *Old*

mon. [46]For long ago, in the days of David and Asaph, there had been directors for the singers and for the songs of praise and thanksgiving to God. [47]So in the days of Zerubbabel and of Nehemiah, all Israel contributed the daily portions for the singers and gatekeepers. They also set aside the portion for the other Levites, and the Levites set aside the portion for the descendants of Aaron.

Nehemiah's Final Reforms

13 On that day the Book of Moses was read aloud in the hearing of the people and there it was found written that no Ammonite or Moabite should ever be admitted into the assembly of God, [2]because they had not met the Israelites with food and water but had hired Balaam to call a curse down on them. (Our God, however, turned the curse into a blessing.) [3]When the people heard this law, they excluded from Israel all who were of foreign descent.

[4]Before this, Eliashib the priest had been put in charge of the storerooms of the house of our God. He was closely associated with Tobiah, [5]and he had provided him with a large room formerly used to store the grain offerings and incense and temple articles, and also the tithes of grain, new wine and oil prescribed for the Levites, singers and gatekeepers, as well as the contributions for the priests.

[6]But while all this was going on, I was not in Jerusalem, for in the thirty-second year of Artaxerxes king of Babylon I had returned to the king. Some time later I asked his permission [7]and came back to Jerusalem. Here I learned about the evil thing Eliashib had done in providing Tobiah a room in the courts of the house of God. [8]I was greatly displeased and threw all Tobiah's household goods out of the room. [9]I gave orders to purify the rooms, and then I put back into them the equipment of the house of God, with the grain offerings and the incense.

[10]I also learned that the portions assigned to the Levites had not been given to them, and that all the Levites and singers responsible for the service had gone back to their own fields. [11]So I rebuked the officials and asked them, "Why is the house of God neglected?" Then I called them together and stationed them at their posts.

[12]All Judah brought the tithes of grain, new wine and oil into the storerooms. [13]I put Shelemiah the priest, Zadok the scribe, and a Levite named Pedaiah in charge of the storerooms and made Hanan son of Zaccur, the son of Mattaniah, their assistant, because these men were considered trustworthy. They were made responsible for distributing the supplies to their brothers.

[14]Remember me for this, O my God, and do not blot out what I have so faithfully done for the house of my God and its services.

[15]In those days I saw men in Judah treading winepresses on the Sabbath and bringing in grain and loading it on donkeys, together with wine, grapes, figs and all other kinds of loads. And they were bringing all this into Jerusalem on the Sabbath. Therefore I warned them against selling food on that day. [16]Men from Tyre who lived in Jerusalem were bringing in fish and all kinds of merchandise and selling them in Jerusalem on the Sabbath to the people of Judah. [17]I rebuked the nobles of Judah and said to them, "What is this wicked thing you are doing—desecrating the Sabbath day? [18]Didn't your forefathers do the same things, so that our God brought all this calamity upon us and upon this city? Now you are stirring up more wrath against Israel by desecrating the Sabbath."

[19]When evening shadows fell on the gates of Jerusalem before the Sabbath, I ordered the doors to be shut and not opened until the Sabbath was over. I stationed some of my own men at the gates so that no load could be brought in on the Sabbath day. [20]Once or twice the merchants and sellers of all kinds of goods spent the night outside Jerusalem. [21]But I warned them and said, "Why do you spend the night by the wall? If you do this again, I will lay hands on you." From that time on they no longer came on the Sabbath. [22]Then I commanded the Levites to purify themselves and go and guard the gates in order to keep the Sabbath day holy.

Remember me for this also, O my God, and show mercy to me according to your great love.

23Moreover, in those days I saw men of Judah who had married women from Ashdod, Ammon and Moab. 24Half of their children spoke the language of Ashdod or the language of one of the other peoples, and did not know how to speak the language of Judah. 25I rebuked them and called curses down on them. I beat some of the men and pulled out their hair. I made them take an oath in God's name and said: "You are not to give your daughters in marriage to their sons, nor are you to take their daughters in marriage for your sons or for yourselves. 26Was it not because of marriages like these that Solomon king of Israel sinned? Among the many nations there was no king like him. He was loved by his God,

and God made him king over all Israel, but even he was led into sin by foreign women. 27Must we hear now that you too are doing all this terrible wickedness and are being unfaithful to our God by marrying foreign women?"

28One of the sons of Joiada son of Eliashib the high priest was son-in-law to Sanballat the Horonite. And I drove him away from me.

29Remember them, O my God, because they defiled the priestly office and the covenant of the priesthood and of the Levites.

30So I purified the priests and the Levites of everything foreign, and assigned them duties, each to his own task. 31I also made provision for contributions of wood at designated times, and for the firstfruits.

Remember me with favor, O my God.

Esther

Intrigue,
deception, romance, power struggles—all these can
be found in the book of Esther. Esther is a beautiful Jewish
girl chosen by King Xerxes of Persia to be his queen. The
book of Esther vividly recounts the deliverance of the Jewish
people after they are sentenced to annihilation. It highlights
the courage and effectiveness of the intrepid queen and
her steadfast uncle Mordecai as the two of them take a
stand against the forces of hatred and bigotry. Although
God's name isn't specifically mentioned in the book, the
events of this fascinating story clearly reveal his power and
his care for his people, even bringing good out of evil.

In our marriage, we have the opportunity to take a
stand against hatred and bigotry too. Consider what you can
do as a couple to bring good out of evil.

Queen Vashti Deposed

1 This is what happened during the time of Xerxes,[a] the Xerxes who ruled over 127 provinces stretching from India to Cush[b]: [2]At that time King Xerxes reigned from his royal throne in the citadel of Susa, [3]and in the third year of his reign he gave a banquet for all his nobles and officials. The military leaders of Persia and Media, the princes, and the nobles of the provinces were present.

[4]For a full 180 days he displayed the vast wealth of his kingdom and the splendor and glory of his majesty. [5]When these days were over, the king gave a banquet, lasting seven days, in the enclosed garden of the king's palace, for all the people from the least to the greatest, who were in the citadel of Susa. [6]The garden had hangings of white and blue linen, fastened with cords of white linen and purple material to silver rings on marble pillars. There were couches of gold and silver on a mosaic pavement of porphyry, marble, mother-of-pearl and other costly stones. [7]Wine was served in goblets of gold, each one different from the other, and the royal wine was abundant, in keeping with the king's liberality. [8]By the king's command each guest was allowed to drink in his own way, for the king instructed all

a1 Hebrew *Ahasuerus,* a variant of Xerxes' Persian name; here and throughout Esther   b1 That is, the upper Nile region the wine stewards to serve each man what he wished.

⁹Queen Vashti also gave a banquet for the women in the royal palace of King Xerxes.

¹⁰On the seventh day, when King Xerxes was in high spirits from wine, he commanded the seven eunuchs who served him—Mehuman, Biztha, Harbona, Bigtha, Abagtha, Zethar and Carcas— ¹¹to bring before him Queen Vashti, wearing her royal crown, in order to display her beauty to the people and nobles, for she was lovely to look at. ¹²But when the attendants delivered the king's command, Queen Vashti refused to come. Then the king became furious and burned with anger.

¹³Since it was customary for the king to consult experts in matters of law and justice, he spoke with the wise men who understood the times ¹⁴and were closest to the king—Carshena, Shethar, Admatha, Tarshish, Meres, Marsena and Memucan, the seven nobles of Persia and Media who had special access to the king and were highest in the kingdom.

¹⁵"According to law, what must be done to Queen Vashti?" he asked. "She has not obeyed the command of King Xerxes that the eunuchs have taken to her."

¹⁶Then Memucan replied in the presence of the king and the nobles, "Queen Vashti has done wrong, not only against the king but also against all the nobles and the peoples of all the provinces of King Xerxes. ¹⁷For the queen's conduct will become known to all the women, and so they will despise their husbands and say, 'King Xerxes commanded Queen Vashti to be brought before him, but she would not come.' ¹⁸This very day the Persian and Median women of the nobility who have heard about the queen's conduct will respond to all the king's nobles in the same way. There will be no end of disrespect and discord.

¹⁹"Therefore, if it pleases the king, let him issue a royal decree and let it be written in the laws of Persia and Media, which cannot be repealed, that Vashti is never again to enter the presence of King Xerxes. Also let the king give her royal position to someone else who is better than she. ²⁰Then when the king's edict is proclaimed throughout all his vast realm, all

the women will respect their husbands, from the least to the greatest."

²¹The king and his nobles were pleased with this advice, so the king did as Memucan proposed. ²²He sent dispatches to all parts of the kingdom, to each province in its own script and to each people in its own language, proclaiming in each people's tongue that every man should be ruler over his own household.

Esther Made Queen

2 Later when the anger of King Xerxes had subsided, he remembered Vashti and what she had done and what he had decreed about her. ²Then the king's personal attendants proposed, "Let a search be made for beautiful young virgins for the king. ³Let the king appoint commissioners in every province of his realm to bring all these beautiful girls into the harem at the citadel of Susa. Let them be placed under the care of Hegai, the king's eunuch, who is in charge of the women; and let beauty treatments be given to them. ⁴Then let the girl who pleases the king be queen instead of Vashti." This advice appealed to the king, and he followed it.

⁵Now there was in the citadel of Susa a Jew of the tribe of Benjamin, named Mordecai son of Jair, the son of Shimei, the son of Kish, ⁶who had been carried into exile from Jerusalem by Nebuchadnezzar king of Babylon, among those taken captive with Jehoiachin[a] king of Judah. ⁷Mordecai had a cousin named Hadassah, whom he had brought up because she had neither father nor mother. This girl, who was also known as Esther, was lovely in form and features, and Mordecai had taken her as his own daughter when her father and mother died.

⁸When the king's order and edict had been proclaimed, many girls were brought to the citadel of Susa and put under the care of Hegai. Esther also was taken to the king's palace and entrusted to Hegai, who had charge of the harem. ⁹The girl pleased him and won his favor. Immediately he provided her with her beauty treatments and special food. He assigned to her seven maids selected from

---

ᵃ6 Hebrew *Jeconiah*, a variant of *Jehoiachin*

the king's palace and moved her and her maids into the best place in the harem.

[10]Esther had not revealed her nationality and family background, because Mordecai had forbidden her to do so. [11]Every day he walked back and forth near the courtyard of the harem to find out how Esther was and what was happening to her.

[12]Before a girl's turn came to go in to King Xerxes, she had to complete twelve months of beauty treatments prescribed for the women, six months with oil of myrrh and six with perfumes and cosmetics. [13]And this is how she would go to the king: Anything she wanted was given her to take with her from the harem to the king's palace. [14]In the evening she would go there and in the morning return to another part of the harem to the care of Shaashgaz, the king's eunuch who was in charge of the concubines. She would not return to the king unless he was pleased with her and summoned her by name.

[15]When the turn came for Esther (the girl Mordecai had adopted, the daughter of his uncle Abihail) to go to the king, she asked for nothing other than what Hegai, the king's eunuch who was in charge of the harem, suggested. And Esther won the favor of everyone who saw her. [16]She was taken to King Xerxes in the royal residence in the tenth month, the month of Tebeth, in the seventh year of his reign.

[17]Now the king was attracted to Esther more than to any of the other women, and she won his favor and approval more than any of the other virgins. So he set a royal crown on her head and made her queen instead of Vashti. [18]And the king gave a great banquet, Esther's banquet, for all his nobles and officials. He proclaimed a holiday throughout the provinces and distributed gifts with royal liberality.

Mordecai Uncovers a Conspiracy

[19]When the virgins were assembled a second time, Mordecai was sitting at the king's gate. [20]But Esther had kept secret her family background and nationality just as Mordecai had told her to do, for she continued to follow Mordecai's instructions as she had done when he was bringing her up.

[21]During the time Mordecai was sitting at the king's gate, Bigthana[a] and Teresh, two of the king's officers who guarded the doorway, became angry and conspired to assassinate King Xerxes. [22]But Mordecai found out about the plot and told Queen Esther, who in turn reported it to the king, giving credit to Mordecai. [23]And when the report was investigated and found to be true, the two officials were hanged on a gallows.[b] All this was recorded in the book of the annals in the presence of the king.

Haman's Plot to Destroy the Jews

3 After these events, King Xerxes honored Haman son of Hammedatha, the Agagite, elevating him and giving him a seat of honor higher than that of all the other nobles. [2]All the royal officials at the king's gate knelt down and paid honor to Haman, for the king had commanded this concerning him. But Mordecai would not kneel down or pay him honor.

[3]Then the royal officials at the king's gate asked Mordecai, "Why do you disobey the king's command?" [4]Day after day they spoke to him but he refused to comply. Therefore they told Haman about it to see whether Mordecai's behavior would be tolerated, for he had told them he was a Jew.

[5]When Haman saw that Mordecai would not kneel down or pay him honor, he was enraged. [6]Yet having learned who Mordecai's people were, he scorned the idea of killing only Mordecai. Instead Haman looked for a way to destroy all Mordecai's people, the Jews, throughout the whole kingdom of Xerxes.

[7]In the twelfth year of King Xerxes, in the first month, the month of Nisan, they cast the *pur* (that is, the lot) in the presence of Haman to select a day and month. And the lot fell on[c] the twelfth month, the month of Adar.

[8]Then Haman said to King Xerxes, "There is a certain people dispersed and scattered among the peoples in all the provinces of your kingdom whose customs are different from those of all other

---

[a]21 Hebrew *Bigthan*, a variant of *Bigthana*
[b]23 Or *were hung* (or *impaled*) *on poles*; similarly elsewhere in Esther   [c]7 Septuagint; Hebrew does not have *And the lot fell on.*

people and who do not obey the king's laws; it is not in the king's best interest to tolerate them. ⁹If it pleases the king, let a decree be issued to destroy them, and I will put ten thousand talents*a* of silver into the royal treasury for the men who carry out this business."

¹⁰So the king took his signet ring from his finger and gave it to Haman son of Hammedatha, the Agagite, the enemy of the Jews. ¹¹"Keep the money," the king said to Haman, "and do with the people as you please."

¹²Then on the thirteenth day of the first month the royal secretaries were summoned. They wrote out in the script of each province and in the language of each people all Haman's orders to the king's satraps, the governors of the various provinces and the nobles of the various peoples. These were written in the name of King Xerxes himself and sealed with his own ring. ¹³Dispatches were sent by couriers to all the king's provinces with the order to destroy, kill and annihilate all the Jews—young and old, women and little children—on a single day, the thirteenth day of the twelfth month, the month of Adar, and to plunder their goods. ¹⁴A copy of the text of the edict was to be issued as law in every province and made known to the people of every nationality so they would be ready for that day.

¹⁵Spurred on by the king's command, the couriers went out, and the edict was issued in the citadel of Susa. The king and Haman sat down to drink, but the city of Susa was bewildered.

Mordecai Persuades Esther to Help

4 When Mordecai learned of all that had been done, he tore his clothes, put on sackcloth and ashes, and went out into the city, wailing loudly and bitterly. ²But he went only as far as the king's gate, because no one clothed in sackcloth was allowed to enter it. ³In every province to which the edict and order of the king came, there was great mourning among the Jews, with fasting, weeping and wailing. Many lay in sackcloth and ashes.

⁴When Esther's maids and eunuchs came and told her about Mordecai, she was in great distress. She sent clothes for

him to put on instead of his sackcloth, but he would not accept them. ⁵Then Esther summoned Hathach, one of the king's eunuchs assigned to attend her, and ordered him to find out what was troubling Mordecai and why.

⁶So Hathach went out to Mordecai in the open square of the city in front of the king's gate. ⁷Mordecai told him everything that had happened to him, including the exact amount of money Haman had promised to pay into the royal treasury for the destruction of the Jews. ⁸He also gave him a copy of the text of the edict for their annihilation, which had been published in Susa, to show to Esther and explain it to her, and he told him to urge her to go into the king's presence to beg for mercy and plead with him for her people.

⁹Hathach went back and reported to Esther what Mordecai had said. ¹⁰Then she instructed him to say to Mordecai, ¹¹"All the king's officials and the people of the royal provinces know that for any man or woman who approaches the king in the inner court without being summoned the king has but one law: that he be put to death. The only exception to this is for the king to extend the gold scepter to him and spare his life. But thirty days have passed since I was called to go to the king."

¹²When Esther's words were reported to Mordecai, ¹³he sent back this answer: "Do not think that because you are in the king's house you alone of all the Jews will escape. ¹⁴For if you remain silent at this time, relief and deliverance for the Jews will arise from another place, but you and your father's family will perish. And who knows but that you have come to royal position for such a time as this?"

¹⁵Then Esther sent this reply to Mordecai: ¹⁶"Go, gather together all the Jews who are in Susa, and fast for me. Do not eat or drink for three days, night or day. I and my maids will fast as you do. When this is done, I will go to the king, even though it is against the law. And if I perish, I perish."

¹⁷So Mordecai went away and carried out all of Esther's instructions.

---

a9 That is, about 375 tons (about 345 metric tons)

Esther's Request to the King

5 On the third day Esther put on her royal robes and stood in the inner court of the palace, in front of the king's hall. The king was sitting on his royal throne in the hall, facing the entrance. ²When he saw Queen Esther standing in the court, he was pleased with her and held out to her the gold scepter that was in his hand. So Esther approached and touched the tip of the scepter.

³Then the king asked, "What is it, Queen Esther? What is your request? Even up to half the kingdom, it will be given you."

⁴"If it pleases the king," replied Esther, "let the king, together with Haman, come today to a banquet I have prepared for him."

⁵"Bring Haman at once," the king said, "so that we may do what Esther asks."

So the king and Haman went to the banquet Esther had prepared. ⁶As they were drinking wine, the king again asked Esther, "Now what is your petition? It will be given you. And what is your request? Even up to half the kingdom, it will be granted."

⁷Esther replied, "My petition and my request is this: ⁸If the king regards me with favor and if it pleases the king to grant my petition and fulfill my request, let the king and Haman come tomorrow to the banquet I will prepare for them. Then I will answer the king's question."

Haman's Rage Against Mordecai

⁹Haman went out that day happy and in high spirits. But when he saw Mordecai at the king's gate and observed that he neither rose nor showed fear in his presence, he was filled with rage against Mordecai. ¹⁰Nevertheless, Haman restrained himself and went home.

Calling together his friends and Zeresh, his wife, ¹¹Haman boasted to them about his vast wealth, his many sons, and all the ways the king had honored him and how he had elevated him above the other nobles and officials. ¹²"And that's not all," Haman added. "I'm the only person Queen Esther invited to accompany the king to the banquet she gave. And she has invited me along with the king tomorrow. ¹³But all this gives me no satisfaction as

---

Xerxes and Esther

ESTHER 5   They must have made a striking couple— Xerxes, the king of Persia, and Esther, the extraordinarily beautiful Jewish Persian queen.
Perhaps you remember the story. King Xerxes selected Esther as his queen, not realizing her Jewish heritage. Then when her people were threatened by a plot by the evil Haman, she bravely confronted the king. But she took time to prepare and approached Xerxes in the best possible way. What a great lesson for spouses today. While today's marriages are much more democratic—most wives don't put their life on the line when they initiate a conversation with their husbands—we can still learn much from the example of Xerxes and Esther.

What do you do when you have a grave and important issue to discuss with your spouse? Consider Esther's example. First, she prepared. We would imagine all the time she was preparing herself and dressing in her royal robes, she was also considering what she would say and how she would say it. Second, she chose the timing carefully. Third, she was willing to take the risk, knowing that things might not work out the way she wanted them to and that she could actually lose her life. Her famous declaration, "If I perish, I perish" revealed her total commitment to be the woman God wanted her to be. From time to time in your marriage, you will need to take the risk to approach your spouse about an important but difficult issue. Remember Esther.

---

long as I see that Jew Mordecai sitting at the king's gate."

¹⁴His wife Zeresh and all his friends said to him, "Have a gallows built, seventy-five feet*a* high, and ask the king in the morning to have Mordecai hanged on it. Then go with the king to the dinner and be happy." This suggestion delighted Haman, and he had the gallows built.

---

a14 Hebrew *fifty cubits* (about 23 meters)

Mordecai Honored

6 That night the king could not sleep; so he ordered the book of the chronicles, the record of his reign, to be brought in and read to him. ²It was found recorded there that Mordecai had exposed Bigthana and Teresh, two of the king's officers who guarded the doorway, who had conspired to assassinate King Xerxes.

³"What honor and recognition has Mordecai received for this?" the king asked.

"Nothing has been done for him," his attendants answered.

⁴The king said, "Who is in the court?" Now Haman had just entered the outer court of the palace to speak to the king about hanging Mordecai on the gallows he had erected for him.

⁵His attendants answered, "Haman is standing in the court."

"Bring him in," the king ordered.

⁶When Haman entered, the king asked him, "What should be done for the man the king delights to honor?"

Now Haman thought to himself, "Who is there that the king would rather honor than me?" ⁷So he answered the king, "For the man the king delights to honor, ⁸have them bring a royal robe the king has worn and a horse the king has ridden, one with a royal crest placed on its head. ⁹Then let the robe and horse be entrusted to one of the king's most noble princes. Let them robe the man the king delights to honor, and lead him on the horse through the city streets, proclaiming before him, 'This is what is done for the man the king delights to honor!' "

¹⁰"Go at once," the king commanded Haman. "Get the robe and the horse and do just as you have suggested for Mordecai the Jew, who sits at the king's gate. Do not neglect anything you have recommended."

¹¹So Haman got the robe and the horse. He robed Mordecai, and led him on horseback through the city streets, proclaiming before him, "This is what is done for the man the king delights to honor!"

¹²Afterward Mordecai returned to the king's gate. But Haman rushed home, with his head covered in grief, ¹³and told Zeresh his wife and all his friends everything that had happened to him.

His advisers and his wife Zeresh said to him, "Since Mordecai, before whom your downfall has started, is of Jewish origin, you cannot stand against him—you will surely come to ruin!" ¹⁴While they were still talking with him, the king's eunuchs arrived and hurried Haman away to the banquet Esther had prepared.

Haman Hanged

7 So the king and Haman went to dine with Queen Esther, ²and as they were drinking wine on that second day, the king again asked, "Queen Esther, what is your petition? It will be given you. What is your request? Even up to half the kingdom, it will be granted."

³Then Queen Esther answered, "If I have found favor with you, O king, and if it pleases your majesty, grant me my life—this is my petition. And spare my people—this is my request. ⁴For I and my people have been sold for destruction and slaughter and annihilation. If we had merely been sold as male and female slaves, I would have kept quiet, because no such distress would justify disturbing the king.ᵃ"

⁵King Xerxes asked Queen Esther, "Who is he? Where is the man who has dared to do such a thing?"

⁶Esther said, "The adversary and enemy is this vile Haman."

Then Haman was terrified before the king and queen. ⁷The king got up in a rage, left his wine and went out into the palace garden. But Haman, realizing that the king had already decided his fate, stayed behind to beg Queen Esther for his life.

⁸Just as the king returned from the palace garden to the banquet hall, Haman was falling on the couch where Esther was reclining.

The king exclaimed, "Will he even molest the queen while she is with me in the house?"

As soon as the word left the king's mouth, they covered Haman's face. ⁹Then Harbona, one of the eunuchs attending the king, said, "A gallows seventy-five

ᵃ4 Or quiet, but the compensation our adversary offers cannot be compared with the loss the king would suffer feet[a] high stands by Haman's house. He had it made for Mordecai, who spoke up to help the king."

The king said, "Hang him on it!" [10]So they hanged Haman on the gallows he had prepared for Mordecai. Then the king's fury subsided.

The King's Edict in Behalf of the Jews

8 That same day King Xerxes gave Queen Esther the estate of Haman, the enemy of the Jews. And Mordecai came into the presence of the king, for Esther had told how he was related to her. [2]The king took off his signet ring, which he had reclaimed from Haman, and presented it to Mordecai. And Esther appointed him over Haman's estate.

[3]Esther again pleaded with the king, falling at his feet and weeping. She begged him to put an end to the evil plan of Haman the Agagite, which he had devised against the Jews. [4]Then the king extended the gold scepter to Esther and she arose and stood before him.

[5]"If it pleases the king," she said, "and if he regards me with favor and thinks it the right thing to do, and if he is pleased with me, let an order be written overruling the dispatches that Haman son of Hammedatha, the Agagite, devised and wrote to destroy the Jews in all the king's provinces. [6]For how can I bear to see disaster fall on my people? How can I bear to see the destruction of my family?"

[7]King Xerxes replied to Queen Esther and to Mordecai the Jew, "Because Haman attacked the Jews, I have given his estate to Esther, and they have hanged him on the gallows. [8]Now write another decree in the king's name in behalf of the Jews as seems best to you, and seal it with the king's signet ring—for no document written in the king's name and sealed with his ring can be revoked."

[9]At once the royal secretaries were summoned—on the twenty-third day of the third month, the month of Sivan. They wrote out all Mordecai's orders to the Jews, and to the satraps, governors and nobles of the 127 provinces stretching from India to Cush.[b] These orders were written in the script of each province and the language of each people and also to the Jews in their own script and language. [10]Mordecai wrote in the name of King Xerxes, sealed the dispatches with the king's signet ring, and sent them by mounted couriers, who rode fast horses especially bred for the king.

[11]The king's edict granted the Jews in every city the right to assemble and protect themselves; to destroy, kill and annihilate any armed force of any nationality or province that might attack them and their women and children; and to plunder the property of their enemies. [12]The day appointed for the Jews to do this in all the provinces of King Xerxes was the thirteenth day of the twelfth month, the month of Adar. [13]A copy of the text of the edict was to be issued as law in every province and made known to the people of every nationality so that the Jews would be ready on that day to avenge themselves on their enemies.

[14]The couriers, riding the royal horses, raced out, spurred on by the king's command. And the edict was also issued in the citadel of Susa.

[15]Mordecai left the king's presence wearing royal garments of blue and white, a large crown of gold and a purple robe of fine linen. And the city of Susa held a joyous celebration. [16]For the Jews it was a time of happiness and joy, gladness and honor. [17]In every province and in every city, wherever the edict of the king went, there was joy and gladness among the Jews, with feasting and celebrating. And many people of other nationalities became Jews because fear of the Jews had seized them.

Triumph of the Jews

9 On the thirteenth day of the twelfth month, the month of Adar, the edict commanded by the king was to be carried out. On this day the enemies of the Jews had hoped to overpower them, but now the tables were turned and the Jews got the upper hand over those who hated them. [2]The Jews assembled in their cities in all the provinces of King Xerxes to attack those seeking their destruction. No one could stand against them, because the people of all the other nationalities were afraid of them. [3]And all the nobles

---

a9 Hebrew *fifty cubits* (about 23 meters)
b9 That is, the upper Nile region

of the provinces, the satraps, the governors and the king's administrators helped the Jews, because fear of Mordecai had seized them. ⁴Mordecai was prominent in the palace; his reputation spread throughout the provinces, and he became more and more powerful.

⁵The Jews struck down all their enemies with the sword, killing and destroying them, and they did what they pleased to those who hated them. ⁶In the citadel of Susa, the Jews killed and destroyed five hundred men. ⁷They also killed Parshandatha, Dalphon, Aspatha, ⁸Poratha, Adalia, Aridatha, ⁹Parmashta, Arisai, Aridai and Vaizatha, ¹⁰the ten sons of Haman son of Hammedatha, the enemy of the Jews. But they did not lay their hands on the plunder.

¹¹The number of those slain in the citadel of Susa was reported to the king that same day. ¹²The king said to Queen Esther, "The Jews have killed and destroyed five hundred men and the ten sons of Haman in the citadel of Susa. What have they done in the rest of the king's provinces? Now what is your petition? It will be given you. What is your request? It will also be granted."

¹³"If it pleases the king," Esther answered, "give the Jews in Susa permission to carry out this day's edict tomorrow also, and let Haman's ten sons be hanged on gallows."

¹⁴So the king commanded that this be done. An edict was issued in Susa, and they hanged the ten sons of Haman. ¹⁵The Jews in Susa came together on the fourteenth day of the month of Adar, and they put to death in Susa three hundred men, but they did not lay their hands on the plunder.

¹⁶Meanwhile, the remainder of the Jews who were in the king's provinces also assembled to protect themselves and get relief from their enemies. They killed seventy-five thousand of them but did not lay their hands on the plunder. ¹⁷This happened on the thirteenth day of the month of Adar, and on the fourteenth they rested and made it a day of feasting and joy.

Purim Celebrated

¹⁸The Jews in Susa, however, had assembled on the thirteenth and fourteenth, and then on the fifteenth they rested and made it a day of feasting and joy.

¹⁹That is why rural Jews—those living in villages—observe the fourteenth of the month of Adar as a day of joy and feasting, a day for giving presents to each other.

²⁰Mordecai recorded these events, and he sent letters to all the Jews throughout the provinces of King Xerxes, near and far, ²¹to have them celebrate annually the fourteenth and fifteenth days of the month of Adar ²²as the time when the Jews got relief from their enemies, and as the month when their sorrow was turned into joy and their mourning into a day of celebration. He wrote them to observe the days as days of feasting and joy and giving presents of food to one another and gifts to the poor.

²³So the Jews agreed to continue the celebration they had begun, doing what Mordecai had written to them. ²⁴For Haman son of Hammedatha, the Agagite, the enemy of all the Jews, had plotted against the Jews to destroy them and had cast the *pur* (that is, the lot) for their ruin and destruction. ²⁵But when the plot came to the king's attention,[a] he issued written orders that the evil scheme Haman had devised against the Jews should come back onto his own head, and that he and his sons should be hanged on the gallows. ²⁶(Therefore these days were called Purim, from the word *pur*.) Because of everything written in this letter and because of what they had seen and what had happened to them, ²⁷the Jews took it upon themselves to establish the custom that they and their descendants and all who join them should without fail observe these two days every year, in the way prescribed and at the time appointed. ²⁸These days should be remembered and observed in every generation by every family, and in every province and in every city. And these days of Purim should never cease to be celebrated by the Jews, nor should the memory of them die out among their descendants.

²⁹So Queen Esther, daughter of Abi-

---

a25 Or when Esther came before the king

hail, along with Mordecai the Jew, wrote with full authority to confirm this second letter concerning Purim. [30]And Mordecai sent letters to all the Jews in the 127 provinces of the kingdom of Xerxes—words of goodwill and assurance— [31]to establish these days of Purim at their designated times, as Mordecai the Jew and Queen Esther had decreed for them, and as they had established for themselves and their descendants in regard to their times of fasting and lamentation. [32]Esther's decree confirmed these regulations about Purim, and it was written down in the records.

The Greatness of Mordecai

10 King Xerxes imposed tribute throughout the empire, to its distant shores. [2]And all his acts of power and might, together with a full account of the greatness of Mordecai to which the king had raised him, are they not written in the book of the annals of the kings of Media and Persia? [3]Mordecai the Jew was second in rank to King Xerxes, preeminent among the Jews, and held in high esteem by his many fellow Jews, because he worked for the good of his people and spoke up for the welfare of all the Jews.

Job

Where is God when we hurt?

Why would a wise, just, loving God allow suffering to stalk a man like Job who seemed to do all the right things? Because he lost everything—wealth, family and health—Job wondered about these same questions and struggled to make sense of his own misery in the light of God's justice. But after the crying, the reasoning and the questioning, he still trusted God.

How has God been at work in your life after you've experienced tragedy and testing? Although we may never fully understand Job's suffering or our own, God is always in control. God restored to Job his health, blessed him materially and gave him a new family. God can take the worst of situations and turn them around.

Prologue

1 In the land of Uz there lived a man whose name was Job. This man was blameless and upright; he feared God and shunned evil. ²He had seven sons and three daughters, ³and he owned seven thousand sheep, three thousand camels, five hundred yoke of oxen and five hundred donkeys, and had a large number of servants. He was the greatest man among all the people of the East.

⁴His sons used to take turns holding feasts in their homes, and they would invite their three sisters to eat and drink with them. ⁵When a period of feasting had run its course, Job would send and have them purified. Early in the morning he would sacrifice a burnt offering for each of them, thinking, "Perhaps my children have sinned and cursed God in their hearts." This was Job's regular custom.

Job's First Test

⁶One day the angels*a* came to present themselves before the LORD, and Satan*b* also came with them. ⁷The LORD said to Satan, "Where have you come from?"

Satan answered the LORD, "From roaming through the earth and going back and forth in it."

⁸Then the LORD said to Satan, "Have

---

a6 Hebrew *the sons of God*   *b6 Satan* means *accuser.*

you considered my servant Job? There is no one on earth like him; he is blameless and upright, a man who fears God and shuns evil."

9"Does Job fear God for nothing?" Satan replied. 10"Have you not put a hedge around him and his household and everything he has? You have blessed the work of his hands, so that his flocks and herds are spread throughout the land. 11But stretch out your hand and strike everything he has, and he will surely curse you to your face."

12The LORD said to Satan, "Very well, then, everything he has is in your hands, but on the man himself do not lay a finger."

Then Satan went out from the presence of the LORD.

13One day when Job's sons and daughters were feasting and drinking wine at the oldest brother's house, 14a messenger came to Job and said, "The oxen were plowing and the donkeys were grazing nearby, 15and the Sabeans attacked and carried them off. They put the servants to the sword, and I am the only one who has escaped to tell you!"

16While he was still speaking, another messenger came and said, "The fire of God fell from the sky and burned up the sheep and the servants, and I am the only one who has escaped to tell you!"

17While he was still speaking, another messenger came and said, "The Chaldeans formed three raiding parties and swept down on your camels and carried them off. They put the servants to the sword, and I am the only one who has escaped to tell you!"

18While he was still speaking, yet another messenger came and said, "Your sons and daughters were feasting and drinking wine at the oldest brother's house, 19when suddenly a mighty wind swept in from the desert and struck the four corners of the house. It collapsed on them and they are dead, and I am the only one who has escaped to tell you!"

20At this, Job got up and tore his robe and shaved his head. Then he fell to the ground in worship 21and said:

Living Past Expectations

JOB 1:21 Job certainly had dreams and goals in life. He could have never accomplished all that he had without them. But these expectations came to an abrupt halt when his circumstances took a very tragic turn. The lesson taught in this book is not the story of Job's difficulties, but the way Job responded to those difficulties.

Marriages rarely go the direction of our original dreams and expectations. The wedding and all that leads up to it is surrounded by incredible expectations of living happily ever after in blissful compatibility . . . It's all very dreamy. Then sometime after the wedding is over, we wake up from those dreams. Our lives and marriages sometimes don't end up the way we expected. The key is how

we deal with dashed expectations. In Job's case, he chose not to focus on his problems but rather on the Fixer of all problems. Instead of moping and whining about all he had lost, Job focused on who God is (see verses 20–21).

It is futile to try to control uncontrollable circumstances. And it's just as futile to expect a spouse to respond to us exactly the way we have dreamed and hoped for. But what's not futile is deciding how we individually will respond to circumstances. We must press on past our unmet expectations rather than bemoan them. After all, we know we can't trust circumstances of life to be everything we dreamed, but we can completely trust God.

—*Bob & Rosemary*

 Weekend Warm-up *How can you help each other press on past unmet expectations?*

Go to page 534 for your next devotional reading.

Job and His Wife

JOB 2:7–10 Job was one of the richest men in the Middle East. His cattle, numbering in the thousands, covered the floor of the valley. Suddenly, without warning, Job's life turned for the worse. At a time when Job desperately needed the support of his wife, it seemed she was barely present. In the midst of it all, Job was able to trust God because he believed all that happened to him was in God's hands. But like many people today who are faced with sudden hardship that doesn't seem to go away, Job's wife questioned her husband's trust in God. Her advice for him was to curse God and die. Bad advice.

"Naked I came from my mother's
        womb,
    and naked I will depart.*a*
The Lord gave and the Lord has
        taken away;
    may the name of the Lord be
        praised."

²²In all this, Job did not sin by charging God with wrongdoing.

Job's Second Test

2 On another day the angels*b* came to present themselves before the Lord, and Satan also came with them to present himself before him. ²And the Lord said to Satan, "Where have you come from?"

Satan answered the Lord, "From roaming through the earth and going back and forth in it."

³Then the Lord said to Satan, "Have you considered my servant Job? There is no one on earth like him; he is blameless and upright, a man who fears God and shuns evil. And he still maintains his integrity, though you incited me against him to ruin him without any reason."

⁴"Skin for skin!" Satan replied. "A man will give all he has for his own life. ⁵But stretch out your hand and strike his flesh and bones, and he will surely curse you to your face."

⁶The Lord said to Satan, "Very well, then, he is in your hands; but you must spare his life."

⁷So Satan went out from the presence of the Lord and afflicted Job with painful sores from the soles of his feet to the top of his head. ⁸Then Job took a piece of broken pottery and scraped himself with it as he sat among the ashes.

⁹His wife said to him, "Are you still holding on to your integrity? Curse God and die!"

¹⁰He replied, "You are talking like a foolish*c* woman. Shall we accept good from God, and not trouble?"

In all this, Job did not sin in what he said.

Job's Three Friends

¹¹When Job's three friends, Eliphaz the Temanite, Bildad the Shuhite and Zophar the Naamathite, heard about all the troubles that had come upon him, they set out from their homes and met together by agreement to go and sympathize with him and comfort him. ¹²When they saw him from a distance, they could hardly recognize him; they began to weep aloud, and they tore their robes and sprinkled dust on their heads. ¹³Then they sat on the ground with him for seven days and seven nights. No one said a word to him, because they saw how great his suffering was.

Job Speaks

3 After this, Job opened his mouth and cursed the day of his birth. ²He said:

³"May the day of my birth perish,
    and the night it was said, 'A boy is
        born!'
⁴That day—may it turn to darkness;
    may God above not care about it;
    may no light shine upon it.
⁵May darkness and deep shadow*d*
        claim it once more;
    may a cloud settle over it;
    may blackness overwhelm its light.
⁶That night—may thick darkness seize
        it;

---

a21 Or *will return there*   *b1* Hebrew *the sons of God*   *c10* The Hebrew word rendered *foolish* denotes moral deficiency.   *d5* Or *and the shadow of death*

may it not be included among the
    days of the year
nor be entered in any of the
    months.
7May that night be barren;
    may no shout of joy be heard in it.
8May those who curse days*a* curse
    that day,
    those who are ready to rouse
        Leviathan.
9May its morning stars become dark;
    may it wait for daylight in vain
    and not see the first rays of dawn,
10for it did not shut the doors of the
    womb on me
    to hide trouble from my eyes.

11"Why did I not perish at birth,
    and die as I came from the womb?
12Why were there knees to receive me
    and breasts that I might be nursed?
13For now I would be lying down in
    peace;
    I would be asleep and at rest
14with kings and counselors of the
    earth,
    who built for themselves places
        now lying in ruins,
15with rulers who had gold,
    who filled their houses with silver.
16Or why was I not hidden in the
    ground like a stillborn child,
    like an infant who never saw the
        light of day?
17There the wicked cease from turmoil,
    and there the weary are at rest.
18Captives also enjoy their ease;
    they no longer hear the slave
        driver's shout.
19The small and the great are there,
    and the slave is freed from his
        master.

20"Why is light given to those in
    misery,
    and life to the bitter of soul,
21to those who long for death that does
    not come,
    who search for it more than for
        hidden treasure,
22who are filled with gladness
    and rejoice when they reach the
        grave?
23Why is life given to a man
    whose way is hidden,
    whom God has hedged in?

24For sighing comes to me instead of
    food;
    my groans pour out like water.
25What I feared has come upon me;
    what I dreaded has happened to
        me.
26I have no peace, no quietness;
    I have no rest, but only turmoil."

Eliphaz

4 Then Eliphaz the Temanite replied:

2"If someone ventures a word with
    you, will you be impatient?
    But who can keep from speaking?
3Think how you have instructed many,
    how you have strengthened feeble
        hands.
4Your words have supported those
    who stumbled;
    you have strengthened faltering
        knees.
5But now trouble comes to you, and
    you are discouraged;
    it strikes you, and you are
        dismayed.
6Should not your piety be your
    confidence
    and your blameless ways your
        hope?

7"Consider now: Who, being innocent,
    has ever perished?
    Where were the upright ever
        destroyed?
8As I have observed, those who plow
    evil
    and those who sow trouble reap it.
9At the breath of God they are
    destroyed;
    at the blast of his anger they
        perish.
10The lions may roar and growl,
    yet the teeth of the great lions are
        broken.
11The lion perishes for lack of prey,
    and the cubs of the lioness are
        scattered.

12"A word was secretly brought to me,
    my ears caught a whisper of it.
13Amid disquieting dreams in the night,
    when deep sleep falls on men,
14fear and trembling seized me
    and made all my bones shake.

a8 Or *the sea*

¹⁵A spirit glided past my face,
>   and the hair on my body stood on
>   end.
¹⁶It stopped,
>   but I could not tell what it was.
> A form stood before my eyes,
>   and I heard a hushed voice:
¹⁷'Can a mortal be more righteous than
>   God?
>   Can a man be more pure than his
>   Maker?
¹⁸If God places no trust in his servants,
>   if he charges his angels with error,
¹⁹how much more those who live in
>   houses of clay,
>   whose foundations are in the dust,
>   who are crushed more readily than
>   a moth!
²⁰Between dawn and dusk they are
>   broken to pieces;
>   unnoticed, they perish forever.
²¹Are not the cords of their tent pulled
>   up,
>   so that they die without
>   wisdom?'^a

5 "Call if you will, but who will
>   answer you?
>   To which of the holy ones will you
>   turn?
²Resentment kills a fool,
>   and envy slays the simple.
³I myself have seen a fool taking root,
>   but suddenly his house was cursed.
⁴His children are far from safety,
>   crushed in court without a
>   defender.
⁵The hungry consume his harvest,
>   taking it even from among thorns,
>   and the thirsty pant after his
>   wealth.
⁶For hardship does not spring from
>   the soil,
>   nor does trouble sprout from the
>   ground.
⁷Yet man is born to trouble
>   as surely as sparks fly upward.

⁸"But if it were I, I would appeal to
>   God;
>   I would lay my cause before him.
⁹He performs wonders that cannot be
>   fathomed,
>   miracles that cannot be counted.
¹⁰He bestows rain on the earth;
>   he sends water upon the
>   countryside.

¹¹The lowly he sets on high,
>   and those who mourn are lifted to
>   safety.
¹²He thwarts the plans of the crafty,
>   so that their hands achieve no
>   success.
¹³He catches the wise in their craftiness,
>   and the schemes of the wily are
>   swept away.
¹⁴Darkness comes upon them in the
>   daytime;
>   at noon they grope as in the night.
¹⁵He saves the needy from the sword in
>   their mouth;
>   he saves them from the clutches of
>   the powerful.
¹⁶So the poor have hope,
>   and injustice shuts its mouth.

¹⁷"Blessed is the man whom God
>   corrects;
>   so do not despise the discipline of
>   the Almighty.^b
¹⁸For he wounds, but he also binds up;
>   he injures, but his hands also heal.
¹⁹From six calamities he will rescue
>   you;
>   in seven no harm will befall you.
²⁰In famine he will ransom you from
>   death,
>   and in battle from the stroke of the
>   sword.
²¹You will be protected from the lash
>   of the tongue,
>   and need not fear when destruction
>   comes.
²²You will laugh at destruction and
>   famine,
>   and need not fear the beasts of the
>   earth.
²³For you will have a covenant with the
>   stones of the field,
>   and the wild animals will be at
>   peace with you.
²⁴You will know that your tent is
>   secure;
>   you will take stock of your
>   property and find nothing
>   missing.
²⁵You will know that your children will
>   be many,
>   and your descendants like the grass
>   of the earth.

^a21 Some interpreters end the quotation after
verse 17.   ^b17 Hebrew *Shaddai*; here and
throughout Job

26You will come to the grave in full
vigor,
like sheaves gathered in season.

27"We have examined this, and it is
true.
So hear it and apply it to yourself."

Job

6 Then Job replied:

2"If only my anguish could be
weighed
and all my misery be placed on the
scales!
3It would surely outweigh the sand of
the seas—
no wonder my words have been
impetuous.
4The arrows of the Almighty are in me,
my spirit drinks in their poison;
God's terrors are marshaled against
me.
5Does a wild donkey bray when it has
grass,
or an ox bellow when it has
fodder?
6Is tasteless food eaten without salt,
or is there flavor in the white of an
egg*a*?
7I refuse to touch it;
such food makes me ill.

8"Oh, that I might have my request,
that God would grant what I hope
for,
9that God would be willing to crush
me,
to let loose his hand and cut me
off!
10Then I would still have this
consolation—
my joy in unrelenting pain—
that I had not denied the words of
the Holy One.

11"What strength do I have, that I
should still hope?
What prospects, that I should be
patient?
12Do I have the strength of stone?
Is my flesh bronze?
13Do I have any power to help myself,
now that success has been driven
from me?

14"A despairing man should have the
devotion of his friends,
even though he forsakes the fear of
the Almighty.
15But my brothers are as undependable
as intermittent streams,
as the streams that overflow
16when darkened by thawing ice
and swollen with melting snow,
17but that cease to flow in the dry
season,
and in the heat vanish from their
channels.
18Caravans turn aside from their routes;
they go up into the wasteland and
perish.
19The caravans of Tema look for water,
the traveling merchants of Sheba
look in hope.
20They are distressed, because they had
been confident;
they arrive there, only to be
disappointed.
21Now you too have proved to be of no
help;
you see something dreadful and are
afraid.
22Have I ever said, 'Give something on
my behalf,
pay a ransom for me from your
wealth,
23deliver me from the hand of the
enemy,
ransom me from the clutches of
the ruthless'?

24"Teach me, and I will be quiet;
show me where I have been wrong.
25How painful are honest words!
But what do your arguments
prove?
26Do you mean to correct what I say,
and treat the words of a despairing
man as wind?
27You would even cast lots for the
fatherless
and barter away your friend.

28"But now be so kind as to look at
me.
Would I lie to your face?
29Relent, do not be unjust;
reconsider, for my integrity is at
stake.*b*

---

*a*6 The meaning of the Hebrew for this phrase is
uncertain.   *b*29 Or *my righteousness still stands*

[30]Is there any wickedness on my lips?
  Can my mouth not discern malice?

7

"Does not man have hard service
    on earth?
  Are not his days like those of a
    hired man?
[2]Like a slave longing for the evening
    shadows,
  or a hired man waiting eagerly for
    his wages,
[3]so I have been allotted months of
    futility,
  and nights of misery have been
    assigned to me.
[4]When I lie down I think, 'How long
    before I get up?'
  The night drags on, and I toss till
    dawn.
[5]My body is clothed with worms and
    scabs,
  my skin is broken and festering.

[6]"My days are swifter than a weaver's
    shuttle,
  and they come to an end without
    hope.
[7]Remember, O God, that my life is but
    a breath;
  my eyes will never see happiness
    again.
[8]The eye that now sees me will see me
    no longer;
  you will look for me, but I will be
    no more.
[9]As a cloud vanishes and is gone,
  so he who goes down to the
    grave[a] does not return.
[10]He will never come to his house
    again;
  his place will know him no more.

[11]"Therefore I will not keep silent;
  I will speak out in the anguish of
    my spirit,
  I will complain in the bitterness of
    my soul.
[12]Am I the sea, or the monster of the
    deep,
  that you put me under guard?
[13]When I think my bed will comfort
    me
  and my couch will ease my
    complaint,
[14]even then you frighten me with
    dreams
  and terrify me with visions,

[15]so that I prefer strangling and death,
  rather than this body of mine.
[16]I despise my life; I would not live
    forever.
  Let me alone; my days have no
    meaning.

[17]"What is man that you make so
    much of him,
  that you give him so much
    attention,
[18]that you examine him every morning
  and test him every moment?
[19]Will you never look away from me,
  or let me alone even for an
    instant?
[20]If I have sinned, what have I done to
    you,
  O watcher of men?
  Why have you made me your target?
  Have I become a burden to you?[b]
[21]Why do you not pardon my offenses
  and forgive my sins?
  For I will soon lie down in the dust;
  you will search for me, but I will
    be no more."

Bildad

8

Then Bildad the Shuhite replied:

[2]"How long will you say such things?
  Your words are a blustering wind.
[3]Does God pervert justice?
  Does the Almighty pervert what is
    right?
[4]When your children sinned against
    him,
  he gave them over to the penalty
    of their sin.
[5]But if you will look to God
  and plead with the Almighty,
[6]if you are pure and upright,
  even now he will rouse himself on
    your behalf
  and restore you to your rightful
    place.
[7]Your beginnings will seem humble,
  so prosperous will your future be.

[8]"Ask the former generations
  and find out what their fathers
    learned,

---

[a]9 Hebrew *Sheol*   [b]20 A few manuscripts of the
Masoretic Text, an ancient Hebrew scribal tradition
and Septuagint; most manuscripts of the Masoretic
Text *I have become a burden to myself.*

⁹for we were born only yesterday and
      know nothing,
    and our days on earth are but a
      shadow.
¹⁰Will they not instruct you and tell
      you?
    Will they not bring forth words
      from their understanding?
¹¹Can papyrus grow tall where there is
      no marsh?
    Can reeds thrive without water?
¹²While still growing and uncut,
    they wither more quickly than
      grass.
¹³Such is the destiny of all who forget
      God;
    so perishes the hope of the godless.
¹⁴What he trusts in is fragile*a*;
    what he relies on is a spider's web.
¹⁵He leans on his web, but it gives way;
    he clings to it, but it does not
      hold.
¹⁶He is like a well-watered plant in the
      sunshine,
    spreading its shoots over the
      garden;
¹⁷it entwines its roots around a pile of
      rocks
    and looks for a place among the
      stones.
¹⁸But when it is torn from its spot,
    that place disowns it and says, 'I
      never saw you.'
¹⁹Surely its life withers away,
    and*b* from the soil other plants
      grow.

²⁰"Surely God does not reject a
      blameless man
    or strengthen the hands of
      evildoers.
²¹He will yet fill your mouth with
      laughter
    and your lips with shouts of joy.
²²Your enemies will be clothed in
      shame,
    and the tents of the wicked will be
      no more."

Job

9

Then Job replied:

²"Indeed, I know that this is true.
    But how can a mortal be righteous
      before God?

³Though one wished to dispute with
      him,
    he could not answer him one time
      out of a thousand.
⁴His wisdom is profound, his power is
      vast.
    Who has resisted him and come
      out unscathed?
⁵He moves mountains without their
      knowing it
    and overturns them in his anger.
⁶He shakes the earth from its place
    and makes its pillars tremble.
⁷He speaks to the sun and it does not
      shine;
    he seals off the light of the stars.
⁸He alone stretches out the heavens
    and treads on the waves of the sea.
⁹He is the Maker of the Bear and
      Orion,
    the Pleiades and the constellations
      of the south.
¹⁰He performs wonders that cannot be
      fathomed,
    miracles that cannot be counted.
¹¹When he passes me, I cannot see
      him;
    when he goes by, I cannot perceive
      him.
¹²If he snatches away, who can stop
      him?
    Who can say to him, 'What are
      you doing?'
¹³God does not restrain his anger;
    even the cohorts of Rahab cowered
      at his feet.

¹⁴"How then can I dispute with him?
    How can I find words to argue
      with him?
¹⁵Though I were innocent, I could not
      answer him;
    I could only plead with my Judge
      for mercy.
¹⁶Even if I summoned him and he
      responded,
    I do not believe he would give me
      a hearing.
¹⁷He would crush me with a storm
    and multiply my wounds for no
      reason.
¹⁸He would not let me regain my
      breath

a14 The meaning of the Hebrew for this word is
uncertain.   *b19* Or *Surely all the joy it has / is
that*

but would overwhelm me with
misery.
19If it is a matter of strength, he is
mighty!
And if it is a matter of justice, who
will summon him*a*?
20Even if I were innocent, my mouth
would condemn me;
if I were blameless, it would
pronounce me guilty.

21"Although I am blameless,
I have no concern for myself;
I despise my own life.
22It is all the same; that is why I say,
'He destroys both the blameless
and the wicked.'
23When a scourge brings sudden death,
he mocks the despair of the
innocent.
24When a land falls into the hands of
the wicked,
he blindfolds its judges.
If it is not he, then who is it?

25"My days are swifter than a runner;
they fly away without a glimpse of
joy.
26They skim past like boats of papyrus,
like eagles swooping down on their
prey.
27If I say, 'I will forget my complaint,
I will change my expression, and
smile,'
28I still dread all my sufferings,
for I know you will not hold me
innocent.
29Since I am already found guilty,
why should I struggle in vain?
30Even if I washed myself with soap*b*
and my hands with washing soda,
31you would plunge me into a slime pit
so that even my clothes would
detest me.

32"He is not a man like me that I
might answer him,
that we might confront each other
in court.
33If only there were someone to
arbitrate between us,
to lay his hand upon us both,
34someone to remove God's rod from
me,
so that his terror would frighten
me no more.

35Then I would speak up without fear
of him,
but as it now stands with me, I
cannot.

10 "I loathe my very life;
therefore I will give free rein to
my complaint
and speak out in the bitterness of
my soul.
2I will say to God: Do not condemn
me,
but tell me what charges you have
against me.
3Does it please you to oppress me,
to spurn the work of your hands,
while you smile on the schemes of
the wicked?
4Do you have eyes of flesh?
Do you see as a mortal sees?
5Are your days like those of a mortal
or your years like those of a man,
6that you must search out my faults
and probe after my sin—
7though you know that I am not guilty
and that no one can rescue me
from your hand?

8"Your hands shaped me and made
me.
Will you now turn and destroy me?
9Remember that you molded me like
clay.
Will you now turn me to dust
again?
10Did you not pour me out like milk
and curdle me like cheese,
11clothe me with skin and flesh
and knit me together with bones
and sinews?
12You gave me life and showed me
kindness,
and in your providence watched
over my spirit.

13"But this is what you concealed in
your heart,
and I know that this was in your
mind:
14If I sinned, you would be watching
me
and would not let my offense go
unpunished.
15If I am guilty—woe to me!

a19 See Septuagint; Hebrew me.   b30 Or snow

Even if I am innocent, I cannot lift
my head,
for I am full of shame
and drowned in*a* my affliction.
16If I hold my head high, you stalk me
like a lion
and again display your awesome
power against me.
17You bring new witnesses against me
and increase your anger toward me;
your forces come against me wave
upon wave.

18"Why then did you bring me out of
the womb?
I wish I had died before any eye
saw me.
19If only I had never come into being,
or had been carried straight from
the womb to the grave!
20Are not my few days almost over?
Turn away from me so I can have a
moment's joy
21before I go to the place of no return,
to the land of gloom and deep
shadow,*b*
22to the land of deepest night,
of deep shadow and disorder,
where even the light is like
darkness."

Zophar

11 Then Zophar the Naamathite replied:

2"Are all these words to go
unanswered?
Is this talker to be vindicated?
3Will your idle talk reduce men to
silence?
Will no one rebuke you when you
mock?
4You say to God, 'My beliefs are
flawless
and I am pure in your sight.'
5Oh, how I wish that God would
speak,
that he would open his lips against
you
6and disclose to you the secrets of
wisdom,
for true wisdom has two sides.
Know this: God has even forgotten
some of your sin.

7"Can you fathom the mysteries of
God?
Can you probe the limits of the
Almighty?
8They are higher than the heavens—
what can you do?
They are deeper than the depths of
the grave*c*—what can you
know?
9Their measure is longer than the earth
and wider than the sea.

10"If he comes along and confines you
in prison
and convenes a court, who can
oppose him?
11Surely he recognizes deceitful men;
and when he sees evil, does he not
take note?
12But a witless man can no more
become wise
than a wild donkey's colt can be
born a man.*d*

13"Yet if you devote your heart to him
and stretch out your hands to him,
14if you put away the sin that is in your
hand
and allow no evil to dwell in your
tent,
15then you will lift up your face
without shame;
you will stand firm and without
fear.
16You will surely forget your trouble,
recalling it only as waters gone by.
17Life will be brighter than noonday,
and darkness will become like
morning.
18You will be secure, because there is
hope;
you will look about you and take
your rest in safety.
19You will lie down, with no one to
make you afraid,
and many will court your favor.
20But the eyes of the wicked will fail,
and escape will elude them;
their hope will become a dying
gasp."

---

*a*15 Or *and aware of*   *b*21 Or *and the shadow of
death*; also in verse 22   *c*8 Hebrew *than Sheol*
*d*12 Or *wild donkey can be born tame*

Job

12 Then Job replied:

2 "Doubtless you are the people,
   and wisdom will die with you!
3 But I have a mind as well as you;
   I am not inferior to you.
   Who does not know all these
     things?

4 "I have become a laughingstock to
     my friends,
   though I called upon God and he
     answered—
   a mere laughingstock, though
     righteous and blameless!
5 Men at ease have contempt for
     misfortune
   as the fate of those whose feet are
     slipping.
6 The tents of marauders are
     undisturbed,
   and those who provoke God are
     secure—
   those who carry their god in their
     hands.[a]

7 "But ask the animals, and they will
     teach you,
   or the birds of the air, and they
     will tell you;
8 or speak to the earth, and it will
     teach you,
   or let the fish of the sea inform
     you.
9 Which of all these does not know
   that the hand of the LORD has
     done this?
10 In his hand is the life of every
     creature
   and the breath of all mankind.
11 Does not the ear test words
   as the tongue tastes food?
12 Is not wisdom found among the aged?
   Does not long life bring
     understanding?

13 "To God belong wisdom and power;
   counsel and understanding are his.
14 What he tears down cannot be
     rebuilt;
   the man he imprisons cannot be
     released.
15 If he holds back the waters, there is
     drought;
   if he lets them loose, they devastate
     the land.

The Wisdom of Marriage Mentors

Monday

JOB 12:12 Chaim Potok's novel, *The Chosen*, tells the story of a young boy born to a Hasidic rabbi and his wife. As the boy matures, his father recognizes that his child is especially clever and gifted and already a little arrogant and impatient. Knowing that his boy is likely to become the rabbi of his people, the father makes a mysterious and difficult decision to raise the boy in silence. The boy grows up in a home without the security of a speaking relationship with his father.

As the story draws to a close, Potok reveals that the father has chosen this unconventional path of parenthood because he wanted to instill in his son the capacity for empathy and compassion. He wanted him to minister from a heart that knows pain and can feel the pain of others. The father feared that his son's analytical brilliance and arrogance would rob him of the capacity to love.

The father in Potok's novel intuitively understood how keen, analytical abilities unsoftened by emotional tenderness can lead to manipulation rather than ministry, how they can lead to control rather than compassion. You may not agree with this rabbi's methods, but it is difficult to dispute his insight.

The story of this powerful novel has reminded us as a couple to consider the "wisdom found among the aged." God's wisdom often comes from those who have traveled the path before us. For this reason, we do not take marriage mentors for granted. How about you?

—Les & Leslie

Go to page 544 for your next devotional reading.

¹⁶To him belong strength and victory;
   both deceived and deceiver are his.
¹⁷He leads counselors away stripped
   and makes fools of judges.
¹⁸He takes off the shackles put on by
     kings
   and ties a loincloth*a* around their
     waist.
¹⁹He leads priests away stripped
   and overthrows men long
     established.
²⁰He silences the lips of trusted advisers
   and takes away the discernment of
     elders.
²¹He pours contempt on nobles
   and disarms the mighty.
²²He reveals the deep things of
     darkness
   and brings deep shadows into the
     light.
²³He makes nations great, and destroys
     them;
   he enlarges nations, and disperses
     them.
²⁴He deprives the leaders of the earth
     of their reason;
   he sends them wandering through
     a trackless waste.
²⁵They grope in darkness with no light;
   he makes them stagger like
     drunkards.

13 "My eyes have seen all this,
   my ears have heard and
     understood it.
²What you know, I also know;
   I am not inferior to you.
³But I desire to speak to the Almighty
   and to argue my case with God.
⁴You, however, smear me with lies;
   you are worthless physicians, all of
     you!
⁵If only you would be altogether
     silent!
   For you, that would be wisdom.
⁶Hear now my argument;
   listen to the plea of my lips.
⁷Will you speak wickedly on God's
     behalf?
   Will you speak deceitfully for him?
⁸Will you show him partiality?
   Will you argue the case for God?
⁹Would it turn out well if he examined
     you?
   Could you deceive him as you
     might deceive men?

JUST BETWEEN *you* & *me*

Marriage Mentors

Take a moment to answer each of these questions on your own. Then compare your answers to your spouse's.

Yes No We have a mentor couple outside of our family that invests in our marriage with us.

Yes No I would like to mentor another couple who is just getting started.

Yes No To be a good marriage mentor couple, we don't have to be perfect or have all the answers.

Yes No I think marriage mentors can teach and model things about marriage that a mom and dad, for example, can't.

Yes No Should every married couple have a marriage mentor couple?

¹⁰He would surely rebuke you
   if you secretly showed partiality.
¹¹Would not his splendor terrify you?
   Would not the dread of him fall
     on you?
¹²Your maxims are proverbs of ashes;
   your defenses are defenses of clay.

¹³"Keep silent and let me speak;
   then let come to me what may.
¹⁴Why do I put myself in jeopardy
   and take my life in my hands?
¹⁵Though he slay me, yet will I hope in
     him;
   I will surely*b* defend my ways to
     his face.
¹⁶Indeed, this will turn out for my
     deliverance,
   for no godless man would dare
     come before him!
¹⁷Listen carefully to my words;
   let your ears take in what I say.
¹⁸Now that I have prepared my case,
   I know I will be vindicated.
¹⁹Can anyone bring charges against me?
   If so, I will be silent and die.

---

a18 Or *shackles of kings / and ties a belt*   *b15* Or
He will surely slay me; I have no hope — / yet I will

²⁰"Only grant me these two things,
  O God,
  and then I will not hide from you:
²¹Withdraw your hand far from me,
  and stop frightening me with your
  terrors.
²²Then summon me and I will answer,
  or let me speak, and you reply.
²³How many wrongs and sins have I
  committed?
  Show me my offense and my sin.
²⁴Why do you hide your face
  and consider me your enemy?
²⁵Will you torment a windblown leaf?
  Will you chase after dry chaff?
²⁶For you write down bitter things
  against me
  and make me inherit the sins of
  my youth.
²⁷You fasten my feet in shackles;
  you keep close watch on all my
  paths
  by putting marks on the soles of
  my feet.

²⁸"So man wastes away like something
  rotten,
  like a garment eaten by moths.

14 "Man born of woman
  is of few days and full of trouble.
²He springs up like a flower and
  withers away;
  like a fleeting shadow, he does not
  endure.
³Do you fix your eye on such a one?
  Will you bring him*ᵃ* before you
  for judgment?
⁴Who can bring what is pure from the
  impure?
  No one!
⁵Man's days are determined;
  you have decreed the number of
  his months
  and have set limits he cannot
  exceed.
⁶So look away from him and let him
  alone,
  till he has put in his time like a
  hired man.

⁷"At least there is hope for a tree:
  If it is cut down, it will sprout
  again,
  and its new shoots will not fail.

⁸Its roots may grow old in the ground
  and its stump die in the soil,
⁹yet at the scent of water it will bud
  and put forth shoots like a plant.
¹⁰But man dies and is laid low;
  he breathes his last and is no
  more.
¹¹As water disappears from the sea
  or a riverbed becomes parched and
  dry,
¹²so man lies down and does not rise;
  till the heavens are no more, men
  will not awake
  or be roused from their sleep.

¹³"If only you would hide me in the
  grave*ᵇ*
  and conceal me till your anger has
  passed!
  If only you would set me a time
  and then remember me!
¹⁴If a man dies, will he live again?
  All the days of my hard service
  I will wait for my renewal*ᶜ* to
  come.
¹⁵You will call and I will answer you;
  you will long for the creature your
  hands have made.
¹⁶Surely then you will count my steps
  but not keep track of my sin.
¹⁷My offenses will be sealed up in a
  bag;
  you will cover over my sin.

¹⁸"But as a mountain erodes and
  crumbles
  and as a rock is moved from its
  place,
¹⁹as water wears away stones
  and torrents wash away the soil,
  so you destroy man's hope.
²⁰You overpower him once for all, and
  he is gone;
  you change his countenance and
  send him away.
²¹If his sons are honored, he does not
  know it;
  if they are brought low, he does
  not see it.
²²He feels but the pain of his own
  body
  and mourns only for himself."

ᵃ3 Septuagint, Vulgate and Syriac; Hebrew *me*
ᵇ13 Hebrew *Sheol*   *ᶜ14* Or *release*

Eliphaz

15

Then Eliphaz the Temanite replied:

2 "Would a wise man answer with
      empty notions
   or fill his belly with the hot east
      wind?
3 Would he argue with useless words,
   with speeches that have no value?
4 But you even undermine piety
   and hinder devotion to God.
5 Your sin prompts your mouth;
   you adopt the tongue of the crafty.
6 Your own mouth condemns you, not
      mine;
   your own lips testify against you.

7 "Are you the first man ever born?
   Were you brought forth before the
      hills?
8 Do you listen in on God's council?
   Do you limit wisdom to yourself?
9 What do you know that we do not
      know?
   What insights do you have that we
      do not have?
10 The gray-haired and the aged are on
      our side,
   men even older than your father.
11 Are God's consolations not enough
      for you,
   words spoken gently to you?
12 Why has your heart carried you away,
   and why do your eyes flash,
13 so that you vent your rage against
      God
   and pour out such words from
      your mouth?

14 "What is man, that he could be pure,
   or one born of woman, that he
      could be righteous?
15 If God places no trust in his holy
      ones,
   if even the heavens are not pure in
      his eyes,
16 how much less man, who is vile and
      corrupt,
   who drinks up evil like water!

17 "Listen to me and I will explain to
      you;
   let me tell you what I have seen,
18 what wise men have declared,
   hiding nothing received from their
      fathers
19 (to whom alone the land was given

when no alien passed among
      them):
20 All his days the wicked man suffers
      torment,
   the ruthless through all the years
      stored up for him.
21 Terrifying sounds fill his ears;
   when all seems well, marauders
      attack him.
22 He despairs of escaping the darkness;
   he is marked for the sword.
23 He wanders about—food for
      vultures[a];
   he knows the day of darkness is at
      hand.
24 Distress and anguish fill him with
      terror;
   they overwhelm him, like a king
      poised to attack,
25 because he shakes his fist at God
   and vaunts himself against the
      Almighty,
26 defiantly charging against him
   with a thick, strong shield.

27 "Though his face is covered with fat
   and his waist bulges with flesh,
28 he will inhabit ruined towns
   and houses where no one lives,
   houses crumbling to rubble.
29 He will no longer be rich and his
      wealth will not endure,
   nor will his possessions spread
      over the land.
30 He will not escape the darkness;
   a flame will wither his shoots,
   and the breath of God's mouth will
      carry him away.
31 Let him not deceive himself by
      trusting what is worthless,
   for he will get nothing in return.
32 Before his time he will be paid in
      full,
   and his branches will not flourish.
33 He will be like a vine stripped of its
      unripe grapes,
   like an olive tree shedding its
      blossoms.
34 For the company of the godless will
      be barren,
   and fire will consume the tents of
      those who love bribes.

a23 Or *about, looking for food*

35They conceive trouble and give birth
     to evil;
  their womb fashions deceit."

Job

16 Then Job replied:

2"I have heard many things like these;
  miserable comforters are you all!
3Will your long-winded speeches never
     end?
  What ails you that you keep on
     arguing?
4I also could speak like you,
  if you were in my place;
  I could make fine speeches against
     you
  and shake my head at you.
5But my mouth would encourage you;
  comfort from my lips would bring
     you relief.

6"Yet if I speak, my pain is not
     relieved;
  and if I refrain, it does not go
     away.
7Surely, O God, you have worn me
     out;
  you have devastated my entire
     household.
8You have bound me—and it has
     become a witness;
  my gauntness rises up and testifies
     against me.
9God assails me and tears me in his
     anger
  and gnashes his teeth at me;
  my opponent fastens on me his
     piercing eyes.
10Men open their mouths to jeer at me;
  they strike my cheek in scorn
  and unite together against me.
11God has turned me over to evil men
  and thrown me into the clutches of
     the wicked.
12All was well with me, but he
     shattered me;
  he seized me by the neck and
     crushed me.
  He has made me his target;
13   his archers surround me.
  Without pity, he pierces my kidneys
  and spills my gall on the ground.
14Again and again he bursts upon me;
  he rushes at me like a warrior.

15"I have sewed sackcloth over my skin
  and buried my brow in the dust.
16My face is red with weeping,
  deep shadows ring my eyes;
17yet my hands have been free of
     violence
  and my prayer is pure.

18"O earth, do not cover my blood;
  may my cry never be laid to rest!
19Even now my witness is in heaven;
  my advocate is on high.
20My intercessor is my frienda
  as my eyes pour out tears to God;
21on behalf of a man he pleads with
     God
  as a man pleads for his friend.

22"Only a few years will pass
  before I go on the journey of no
     return.

17 1My spirit is broken,
  my days are cut short,
  the grave awaits me.
2Surely mockers surround me;
  my eyes must dwell on their
     hostility.

3"Give me, O God, the pledge you
     demand.
  Who else will put up security for
     me?
4You have closed their minds to
     understanding;
  therefore you will not let them
     triumph.
5If a man denounces his friends for
     reward,
  the eyes of his children will fail.

6"God has made me a byword to
     everyone,
  a man in whose face people spit.
7My eyes have grown dim with grief;
  my whole frame is but a shadow.
8Upright men are appalled at this;
  the innocent are aroused against
     the ungodly.
9Nevertheless, the righteous will hold
     to their ways,
  and those with clean hands will
     grow stronger.

10"But come on, all of you, try again!
  I will not find a wise man among
     you.

a20 Or *My friends treat me with scorn*

¹¹My days have passed, my plans are
      shattered,
   and so are the desires of my heart.
¹²These men turn night into day;
   in the face of darkness they say,
      'Light is near.'
¹³If the only home I hope for is the
      grave,^a
   if I spread out my bed in darkness,
¹⁴if I say to corruption, 'You are my
      father,'
   and to the worm, 'My mother' or
      'My sister,'
¹⁵where then is my hope?
   Who can see any hope for me?
¹⁶Will it go down to the gates of
      death^a?
   Will we descend together into the
      dust?"

Bildad

18 Then Bildad the Shuhite replied:

²"When will you end these speeches?
   Be sensible, and then we can talk.
³Why are we regarded as cattle
   and considered stupid in your
      sight?
⁴You who tear yourself to pieces in
      your anger,
   is the earth to be abandoned for
      your sake?
   Or must the rocks be moved from
      their place?

⁵"The lamp of the wicked is snuffed
      out;
   the flame of his fire stops burning.
⁶The light in his tent becomes dark;
   the lamp beside him goes out.
⁷The vigor of his step is weakened;
   his own schemes throw him down.
⁸His feet thrust him into a net
   and he wanders into its mesh.
⁹A trap seizes him by the heel;
   a snare holds him fast.
¹⁰A noose is hidden for him on the
      ground;
   a trap lies in his path.
¹¹Terrors startle him on every side
   and dog his every step.
¹²Calamity is hungry for him;
   disaster is ready for him when he
      falls.
¹³It eats away parts of his skin;
   death's firstborn devours his limbs.

¹⁴He is torn from the security of his
      tent
   and marched off to the king of
      terrors.
¹⁵Fire resides^b in his tent;
   burning sulfur is scattered over his
      dwelling.
¹⁶His roots dry up below
   and his branches wither above.
¹⁷The memory of him perishes from
      the earth;
   he has no name in the land.
¹⁸He is driven from light into darkness
   and is banished from the world.
¹⁹He has no offspring or descendants
      among his people,
   no survivor where once he lived.
²⁰Men of the west are appalled at his
      fate;
   men of the east are seized with
      horror.
²¹Surely such is the dwelling of an evil
      man;
   such is the place of one who
      knows not God."

Job

19 Then Job replied:

²"How long will you torment me
   and crush me with words?
³Ten times now you have reproached
      me;
   shamelessly you attack me.
⁴If it is true that I have gone astray,
   my error remains my concern
      alone.
⁵If indeed you would exalt yourselves
      above me
   and use my humiliation against
      me,
⁶then know that God has wronged me
   and drawn his net around me.

⁷"Though I cry, 'I've been wronged!' I
      get no response;
   though I call for help, there is no
      justice.
⁸He has blocked my way so I cannot
      pass;
   he has shrouded my paths in
      darkness.
⁹He has stripped me of my honor

^a13,16 Hebrew *Sheol*   ^b15 Or *Nothing he had*
remains

and removed the crown from my
    head.
[10]He tears me down on every side till I
    am gone;
  he uproots my hope like a tree.
[11]His anger burns against me;
  he counts me among his enemies.
[12]His troops advance in force;
  they build a siege ramp against me
    and encamp around my tent.

[13]"He has alienated my brothers from
    me;
  my acquaintances are completely
    estranged from me.
[14]My kinsmen have gone away;
  my friends have forgotten me.
[15]My guests and my maidservants count
    me a stranger;
  they look upon me as an alien.
[16]I summon my servant, but he does
    not answer,
  though I beg him with my own
    mouth.
[17]My breath is offensive to my wife;
  I am loathsome to my own
    brothers.
[18]Even the little boys scorn me;
  when I appear, they ridicule me.
[19]All my intimate friends detest me;
  those I love have turned against
    me.
[20]I am nothing but skin and bones;
  I have escaped with only the skin
    of my teeth.[a]

[21]"Have pity on me, my friends, have
    pity,
  for the hand of God has struck me.
[22]Why do you pursue me as God does?
  Will you never get enough of my
    flesh?

[23]"Oh, that my words were recorded,
  that they were written on a scroll,
[24]that they were inscribed with an iron
    tool on[b] lead,
  or engraved in rock forever!
[25]I know that my Redeemer[c] lives,
  and that in the end he will stand
    upon the earth.[d]
[26]And after my skin has been destroyed,
  yet[e] in[f] my flesh I will see God;
[27]I myself will see him
  with my own eyes—I, and not
    another.
  How my heart yearns within me!

[28]"If you say, 'How we will hound
    him,
  since the root of the trouble lies in
    him,[g]'
[29]you should fear the sword yourselves;
  for wrath will bring punishment by
    the sword,
  and then you will know that there
    is judgment.[h]"

Zophar

20 Then Zophar the Naamathite re-
    plied:

[2]"My troubled thoughts prompt me to
    answer
  because I am greatly disturbed.
[3]I hear a rebuke that dishonors me,
  and my understanding inspires me
    to reply.

[4]"Surely you know how it has been
    from of old,
  ever since man[i] was placed on
    the earth,
[5]that the mirth of the wicked is brief,
  the joy of the godless lasts but a
    moment.
[6]Though his pride reaches to the
    heavens
  and his head touches the clouds,
[7]he will perish forever, like his own
    dung;
  those who have seen him will say,
    'Where is he?'
[8]Like a dream he flies away, no more
    to be found,
  banished like a vision of the night.
[9]The eye that saw him will not see
    him again;
  his place will look on him no
    more.
[10]His children must make amends to
    the poor;
  his own hands must give back his
    wealth.
[11]The youthful vigor that fills his bones
  will lie with him in the dust.

[12]"Though evil is sweet in his mouth

---

[a]20 Or *only my gums*   [b]24 Or *and*   [c]25 Or
defender   [d]25 Or *upon my grave*   [e]26 Or *And
after I awake, / though this ⸤body⸥ has been destroyed, /
then*   [f]26 Or */ apart from*   [g]28 Many
Hebrew manuscripts, Septuagint and Vulgate; most
Hebrew manuscripts *me*   [h]29 Or */ that you may
come to know the Almighty*   [i]4 Or *Adam*

and he hides it under his tongue,
13though he cannot bear to let it go
and keeps it in his mouth,
14yet his food will turn sour in his
stomach;
it will become the venom of
serpents within him.
15He will spit out the riches he
swallowed;
God will make his stomach vomit
them up.
16He will suck the poison of serpents;
the fangs of an adder will kill him.
17He will not enjoy the streams,
the rivers flowing with honey and
cream.
18What he toiled for he must give back
uneaten;
he will not enjoy the profit from
his trading.
19For he has oppressed the poor and
left them destitute;
he has seized houses he did not
build.

20"Surely he will have no respite from
his craving;
he cannot save himself by his
treasure.
21Nothing is left for him to devour;
his prosperity will not endure.
22In the midst of his plenty, distress
will overtake him;
the full force of misery will come
upon him.
23When he has filled his belly,
God will vent his burning anger
against him
and rain down his blows upon
him.
24Though he flees from an iron
weapon,
a bronze-tipped arrow pierces him.
25He pulls it out of his back,
the gleaming point out of his liver.
Terrors will come over him;
26   total darkness lies in wait for his
treasures.
A fire unfanned will consume him
and devour what is left in his tent.
27The heavens will expose his guilt;
the earth will rise up against him.
28A flood will carry off his house,
rushing watersª on the day of
God's wrath.

29Such is the fate God allots the
wicked,
the heritage appointed for them by
God."

Job

21 Then Job replied:

2"Listen carefully to my words;
let this be the consolation you give
me.
3Bear with me while I speak,
and after I have spoken, mock on.

4"Is my complaint directed to man?
Why should I not be impatient?
5Look at me and be astonished;
clap your hand over your mouth.
6When I think about this, I am
terrified;
trembling seizes my body.
7Why do the wicked live on,
growing old and increasing in
power?
8They see their children established
around them,
their offspring before their eyes.
9Their homes are safe and free from
fear;
the rod of God is not upon them.
10Their bulls never fail to breed;
their cows calve and do not
miscarry.
11They send forth their children as a
flock;
their little ones dance about.
12They sing to the music of tambourine
and harp;
they make merry to the sound of
the flute.
13They spend their years in prosperity
and go down to the graveᵇ in
peace.ᶜ
14Yet they say to God, 'Leave us alone!
We have no desire to know your
ways.
15Who is the Almighty, that we should
serve him?
What would we gain by praying to
him?'
16But their prosperity is not in their
own hands,

ª28 Or *The possessions in his house will be carried off,
/ washed away*   ᵇ13 Hebrew *Sheol*   ᶜ13 Or *in
an instant*

so I stand aloof from the counsel
of the wicked.

17 "Yet how often is the lamp of the
wicked snuffed out?
How often does calamity come
upon them,
the fate God allots in his anger?
18 How often are they like straw before
the wind,
like chaff swept away by a gale?
19 It is said, 'God stores up a man's
punishment for his sons.'
Let him repay the man himself, so
that he will know it!
20 Let his own eyes see his destruction;
let him drink of the wrath of the
Almighty.[a]
21 For what does he care about the
family he leaves behind
when his allotted months come to
an end?

22 "Can anyone teach knowledge to
God,
since he judges even the highest?
23 One man dies in full vigor,
completely secure and at ease,
24 his body[b] well nourished,
his bones rich with marrow.
25 Another man dies in bitterness of
soul,
never having enjoyed anything
good.
26 Side by side they lie in the dust,
and worms cover them both.

27 "I know full well what you are
thinking,
the schemes by which you would
wrong me.
28 You say, 'Where now is the great
man's house,
the tents where wicked men lived?'
29 Have you never questioned those who
travel?
Have you paid no regard to their
accounts—
30 that the evil man is spared from the
day of calamity,
that he is delivered from[c] the day
of wrath?
31 Who denounces his conduct to his
face?
Who repays him for what he has
done?
32 He is carried to the grave,

and watch is kept over his tomb.
33 The soil in the valley is sweet to him;
all men follow after him,
and a countless throng goes[d]
before him.

34 "So how can you console me with
your nonsense?
Nothing is left of your answers but
falsehood!"

Eliphaz

22 Then Eliphaz the Temanite replied:

2 "Can a man be of benefit to God?
Can even a wise man benefit him?
3 What pleasure would it give the
Almighty if you were
righteous?
What would he gain if your ways
were blameless?

4 "Is it for your piety that he rebukes
you
and brings charges against you?
5 Is not your wickedness great?
Are not your sins endless?
6 You demanded security from your
brothers for no reason;
you stripped men of their clothing,
leaving them naked.
7 You gave no water to the weary
and you withheld food from the
hungry,
8 though you were a powerful man,
owning land—
an honored man, living on it.
9 And you sent widows away
empty-handed
and broke the strength of the
fatherless.
10 That is why snares are all around you,
why sudden peril terrifies you,
11 why it is so dark you cannot see,
and why a flood of water covers
you.

12 "Is not God in the heights of heaven?
And see how lofty are the highest
stars!
13 Yet you say, 'What does God know?

---

a17-20 Verses 17 and 18 may be taken as
exclamations and 19 and 20 as declarations.
b24 The meaning of the Hebrew for this word is
uncertain.   c30 Or man is reserved for the day of
calamity, / that he is brought forth to   d33 Or / as
a countless throng went

Does he judge through such
darkness?
¹⁴Thick clouds veil him, so he does not
see us
as he goes about in the vaulted
heavens.'
¹⁵Will you keep to the old path
that evil men have trod?
¹⁶They were carried off before their
time,
their foundations washed away by
a flood.
¹⁷They said to God, 'Leave us alone!
What can the Almighty do to us?'
¹⁸Yet it was he who filled their houses
with good things,
so I stand aloof from the counsel
of the wicked.

¹⁹"The righteous see their ruin and
rejoice;
the innocent mock them, saying,
²⁰'Surely our foes are destroyed,
and fire devours their wealth.'

²¹"Submit to God and be at peace with
him;
in this way prosperity will come to
you.
²²Accept instruction from his mouth
and lay up his words in your heart.
²³If you return to the Almighty, you
will be restored:
If you remove wickedness far from
your tent
²⁴and assign your nuggets to the dust,
your gold of Ophir to the rocks in
the ravines,
²⁵then the Almighty will be your gold,
the choicest silver for you.
²⁶Surely then you will find delight in
the Almighty
and will lift up your face to God.
²⁷You will pray to him, and he will
hear you,
and you will fulfill your vows.
²⁸What you decide on will be done,
and light will shine on your ways.
²⁹When men are brought low and you
say, 'Lift them up!'
then he will save the downcast.
³⁰He will deliver even one who is not
innocent,
who will be delivered through the
cleanness of your hands."

Job
23
Then Job replied:

²"Even today my complaint is bitter;
his hand[a] is heavy in spite of[b]
my groaning.
³If only I knew where to find him;
if only I could go to his dwelling!
⁴I would state my case before him
and fill my mouth with arguments.
⁵I would find out what he would
answer me,
and consider what he would say.
⁶Would he oppose me with great
power?
No, he would not press charges
against me.
⁷There an upright man could present
his case before him,
and I would be delivered forever
from my judge.

⁸"But if I go to the east, he is not
there;
if I go to the west, I do not find
him.
⁹When he is at work in the north, I do
not see him;
when he turns to the south, I catch
no glimpse of him.
¹⁰But he knows the way that I take;
when he has tested me, I will come
forth as gold.
¹¹My feet have closely followed his
steps;
I have kept to his way without
turning aside.
¹²I have not departed from the
commands of his lips;
I have treasured the words of his
mouth more than my daily
bread.

¹³"But he stands alone, and who can
oppose him?
He does whatever he pleases.
¹⁴He carries out his decree against me,
and many such plans he still has in
store.
¹⁵That is why I am terrified before him;
when I think of all this, I fear him.
¹⁶God has made my heart faint;
the Almighty has terrified me.

---

a2 Septuagint and Syriac; Hebrew / *the hand on me*
b2 Or *heavy on me in*

¹⁷Yet I am not silenced by the darkness,
by the thick darkness that covers
my face.

24 "Why does the Almighty not set
times for judgment?
Why must those who know him
look in vain for such days?
²Men move boundary stones;
they pasture flocks they have
stolen.
³They drive away the orphan's donkey
and take the widow's ox in pledge.
⁴They thrust the needy from the path
and force all the poor of the land
into hiding.
⁵Like wild donkeys in the desert,
the poor go about their labor of
foraging food;
the wasteland provides food for
their children.
⁶They gather fodder in the fields
and glean in the vineyards of the
wicked.
⁷Lacking clothes, they spend the night
naked;

they have nothing to cover
themselves in the cold.
⁸They are drenched by mountain rains
and hug the rocks for lack of
shelter.
⁹The fatherless child is snatched from
the breast;
the infant of the poor is seized for
a debt.
¹⁰Lacking clothes, they go about naked;
they carry the sheaves, but still go
hungry.
¹¹They crush olives among the
terraces*ᵃ*;
they tread the winepresses, yet
suffer thirst.
¹²The groans of the dying rise from the
city,
and the souls of the wounded cry
out for help.
But God charges no one with
wrongdoing.

*ᵃ11 Or olives between the millstones; the meaning of
the Hebrew for this word is uncertain.*

Getting What I Deserve

Tuesday

JOB 23   "What did I do to deserve this?" Job must have wondered why he was suffering since he had done nothing wrong. Somehow we have come to believe that there is a check and balance system. Like walking through an airport metal detector, we walk through the "righteousness detector." If the beep goes off, we have obviously done something wrong. If we are good enough, there is no beep—no difficulties.

Much of the time the difficulties people experience in their marriages have nothing to do with how righteous the husband and wife are. Tragic circumstances attack many marriages. We live in the world where bad things just sometimes happen.

When difficulties strike a marriage, it's important to get past the "we don't deserve this" mentality. It's not a matter of asking, "Do we really deserve this in our life?" No one really wants what he or she deserves because we deserve far worse than the cir-

cumstances we go through. Just prior to the birth of our first child, Rosemary became very ill and experienced a seizure. The doctor informed me that she might not make it through the night. I sat in the waiting room feeling sorry for myself, wondering what we had done to deserve this strange twist in our lives. Like Job, we had to understand that our difficult circumstance had nothing to do with what we deserved.

Whatever circumstances have come into your marriage, choose to live with the knowledge that we really deserve far worse. But Jesus Christ gave up his life for our sake, so that we would not have to face what we really deserve (see Romans 6:23, page 1225). In gratitude, we need to live like Job, showing everyone around us that, no matter what comes into our lives, we will trust him.

—Bob & Rosemary

Go to page 560 for your next devotional reading.

13"There are those who rebel against
the light,
who do not know its ways
or stay in its paths.
14When daylight is gone, the murderer
rises up
and kills the poor and needy;
in the night he steals forth like a
thief.
15The eye of the adulterer watches for
dusk;
he thinks, 'No eye will see me,'
and he keeps his face concealed.
16In the dark, men break into houses,
but by day they shut themselves in;
they want nothing to do with the
light.
17For all of them, deep darkness is their
morning*a*;
they make friends with the terrors
of darkness.*b*

18"Yet they are foam on the surface of
the water;
their portion of the land is cursed,
so that no one goes to the
vineyards.
19As heat and drought snatch away the
melted snow,
so the grave*c* snatches away those
who have sinned.
20The womb forgets them,
the worm feasts on them;
evil men are no longer remembered
but are broken like a tree.
21They prey on the barren and childless
woman,
and to the widow show no
kindness.
22But God drags away the mighty by
his power;
though they become established,
they have no assurance of life.
23He may let them rest in a feeling of
security,
but his eyes are on their ways.
24For a little while they are exalted, and
then they are gone;
they are brought low and gathered
up like all others;
they are cut off like heads of grain.

25"If this is not so, who can prove me
false
and reduce my words to nothing?"

Bildad

25 Then Bildad the Shuhite replied:

2"Dominion and awe belong to God;
he establishes order in the heights
of heaven.
3Can his forces be numbered?
Upon whom does his light not
rise?
4How then can a man be righteous
before God?
How can one born of woman be
pure?
5If even the moon is not bright
and the stars are not pure in his
eyes,
6how much less man, who is but a
maggot—
a son of man, who is only a
worm!"

Job

26 Then Job replied:

2"How you have helped the
powerless!
How you have saved the arm that
is feeble!
3What advice you have offered to one
without wisdom!
And what great insight you have
displayed!
4Who has helped you utter these
words?
And whose spirit spoke from your
mouth?

5"The dead are in deep anguish,
those beneath the waters and all
that live in them.
6Death*c* is naked before God;
Destruction*d* lies uncovered.
7He spreads out the northern ⌐skies⌐
over empty space;
he suspends the earth over
nothing.
8He wraps up the waters in his clouds,
yet the clouds do not burst under
their weight.
9He covers the face of the full moon,
spreading his clouds over it.

*a*17 Or them, their morning is like the shadow of
death   *b*17 Or of the shadow of death
*c*19,6 Hebrew Sheol   *d*6 Hebrew Abaddon

¹⁰He marks out the horizon on the face
of the waters
for a boundary between light and
darkness.
¹¹The pillars of the heavens quake,
aghast at his rebuke.
¹²By his power he churned up the sea;
by his wisdom he cut Rahab to
pieces.
¹³By his breath the skies became fair;
his hand pierced the gliding
serpent.
¹⁴And these are but the outer fringe of
his works;
how faint the whisper we hear of
him!
Who then can understand the
thunder of his power?"

27 And Job continued his discourse:

²"As surely as God lives, who has
denied me justice,
the Almighty, who has made me
taste bitterness of soul,
³as long as I have life within me,
the breath of God in my nostrils,
⁴my lips will not speak wickedness,
and my tongue will utter no deceit.
⁵I will never admit you are in the
right;
till I die, I will not deny my
integrity.
⁶I will maintain my righteousness and
never let go of it;
my conscience will not reproach
me as long as I live.

⁷"May my enemies be like the wicked,
my adversaries like the unjust!
⁸For what hope has the godless when
he is cut off,
when God takes away his life?
⁹Does God listen to his cry
when distress comes upon him?
¹⁰Will he find delight in the Almighty?
Will he call upon God at all times?

¹¹"I will teach you about the power of
God;
the ways of the Almighty I will not
conceal.
¹²You have all seen this yourselves.
Why then this meaningless talk?

¹³"Here is the fate God allots to the
wicked,
the heritage a ruthless man receives
from the Almighty:
¹⁴However many his children, their fate
is the sword;
his offspring will never have
enough to eat.
¹⁵The plague will bury those who
survive him,
and their widows will not weep for
them.
¹⁶Though he heaps up silver like dust
and clothes like piles of clay,
¹⁷what he lays up the righteous will
wear,
and the innocent will divide his
silver.
¹⁸The house he builds is like a moth's
cocoon,
like a hut made by a watchman.
¹⁹He lies down wealthy, but will do so
no more;
when he opens his eyes, all is
gone.
²⁰Terrors overtake him like a flood;
a tempest snatches him away in the
night.
²¹The east wind carries him off, and he
is gone;
it sweeps him out of his place.
²²It hurls itself against him without
mercy
as he flees headlong from its
power.
²³It claps its hands in derision
and hisses him out of his place.

28 "There is a mine for silver
and a place where gold is refined.
²Iron is taken from the earth,
and copper is smelted from ore.
³Man puts an end to the darkness;
he searches the farthest recesses
for ore in the blackest darkness.
⁴Far from where people dwell he cuts
a shaft,
in places forgotten by the foot of
man;
far from men he dangles and
sways.
⁵The earth, from which food comes,
is transformed below as by fire;
⁶sapphires[a] come from its rocks,
and its dust contains nuggets of
gold.

_a6_ Or _lapis lazuli_; also in verse 16

7No bird of prey knows that hidden
    path,
  no falcon's eye has seen it.
8Proud beasts do not set foot on it,
  and no lion prowls there.
9Man's hand assaults the flinty rock
  and lays bare the roots of the
    mountains.
10He tunnels through the rock;
  his eyes see all its treasures.
11He searches*a* the sources of the rivers
  and brings hidden things to light.

12"But where can wisdom be found?
  Where does understanding dwell?
13Man does not comprehend its worth;
  it cannot be found in the land of
    the living.
14The deep says, 'It is not in me';
  the sea says, 'It is not with me.'
15It cannot be bought with the finest
    gold,
  nor can its price be weighed in
    silver.
16It cannot be bought with the gold of
    Ophir,
  with precious onyx or sapphires.
17Neither gold nor crystal can compare
    with it,
  nor can it be had for jewels of
    gold.
18Coral and jasper are not worthy of
    mention;
  the price of wisdom is beyond
    rubies.
19The topaz of Cush cannot compare
    with it;
  it cannot be bought with pure
    gold.

20"Where then does wisdom come
    from?
  Where does understanding dwell?
21It is hidden from the eyes of every
    living thing,
  concealed even from the birds of
    the air.
22Destruction*b* and Death say,
  'Only a rumor of it has reached
    our ears.'
23God understands the way to it
  and he alone knows where it
    dwells,
24for he views the ends of the earth
  and sees everything under the
    heavens.

25When he established the force of the
    wind
  and measured out the waters,
26when he made a decree for the rain
  and a path for the thunderstorm,
27then he looked at wisdom and
    appraised it;
  he confirmed it and tested it.
28And he said to man,
  'The fear of the Lord—that is
    wisdom,
  and to shun evil is understanding.' "

29 Job continued his discourse:

2"How I long for the months gone by,
  for the days when God watched
    over me,
3when his lamp shone upon my head
  and by his light I walked through
    darkness!
4Oh, for the days when I was in my
    prime,
  when God's intimate friendship
    blessed my house,
5when the Almighty was still with me
  and my children were around me,
6when my path was drenched with
    cream
  and the rock poured out for me
    streams of olive oil.

7"When I went to the gate of the city
  and took my seat in the public
    square,
8the young men saw me and stepped
    aside
  and the old men rose to their feet;
9the chief men refrained from speaking
  and covered their mouths with
    their hands;
10the voices of the nobles were hushed,
  and their tongues stuck to the roof
    of their mouths.
11Whoever heard me spoke well of me,
  and those who saw me
    commended me,
12because I rescued the poor who cried
    for help,
  and the fatherless who had none to
    assist him.
13The man who was dying blessed me;
  I made the widow's heart sing.
14I put on righteousness as my clothing;

a 11 Septuagint, Aquila and Vulgate; Hebrew *He
dams up*   *b 22* Hebrew *Abaddon*

justice was my robe and my
turban.
¹⁵I was eyes to the blind
and feet to the lame.
¹⁶I was a father to the needy;
I took up the case of the stranger.
¹⁷I broke the fangs of the wicked
and snatched the victims from their
teeth.

¹⁸"I thought, 'I will die in my own
house,
my days as numerous as the grains
of sand.
¹⁹My roots will reach to the water,
and the dew will lie all night on
my branches.
²⁰My glory will remain fresh in me,
the bow ever new in my hand.'

²¹"Men listened to me expectantly,
waiting in silence for my counsel.
²²After I had spoken, they spoke no
more;
my words fell gently on their ears.
²³They waited for me as for showers
and drank in my words as the
spring rain.
²⁴When I smiled at them, they scarcely
believed it;
the light of my face was precious
to them.^a
²⁵I chose the way for them and sat as
their chief;
I dwelt as a king among his troops;
I was like one who comforts
mourners.

30 "But now they mock me,
men younger than I,
whose fathers I would have disdained
to put with my sheep dogs.
²Of what use was the strength of their
hands to me,
since their vigor had gone from
them?
³Haggard from want and hunger,
they roamed^b the parched land
in desolate wastelands at night.
⁴In the brush they gathered salt herbs,
and their food^c was the root of
the broom tree.
⁵They were banished from their fellow
men,
shouted at as if they were thieves.
⁶They were forced to live in the dry
stream beds,

among the rocks and in holes in
the ground.
⁷They brayed among the bushes
and huddled in the undergrowth.
⁸A base and nameless brood,
they were driven out of the land.

⁹"And now their sons mock me in
song;
I have become a byword among
them.
¹⁰They detest me and keep their
distance;
they do not hesitate to spit in my
face.
¹¹Now that God has unstrung my bow
and afflicted me,
they throw off restraint in my
presence.
¹²On my right the tribe^d attacks;
they lay snares for my feet,
they build their siege ramps against
me.
¹³They break up my road;
they succeed in destroying me—
without anyone's helping them.^e
¹⁴They advance as through a gaping
breach;
amid the ruins they come rolling
in.
¹⁵Terrors overwhelm me;
my dignity is driven away as by the
wind,
my safety vanishes like a cloud.

¹⁶"And now my life ebbs away;
days of suffering grip me.
¹⁷Night pierces my bones;
my gnawing pains never rest.
¹⁸In his great power ⌞God⌟ becomes like
clothing to me^f;
he binds me like the neck of my
garment.
¹⁹He throws me into the mud,
and I am reduced to dust and
ashes.

²⁰"I cry out to you, O God, but you do
not answer;
I stand up, but you merely look at
me.
²¹You turn on me ruthlessly;

^a24 The meaning of the Hebrew for this clause is
uncertain.   ^b3 Or gnawed   ^c4 Or fuel
^d12 The meaning of the Hebrew for this word is
uncertain.   ^e13 Or me. / 'No one can help him,'
⌞they say⌟.   ^f18 Hebrew; Septuagint ⌞God⌟ grasps
my clothing

with the might of your hand you
    attack me.
²²You snatch me up and drive me
    before the wind;
    you toss me about in the storm.
²³I know you will bring me down to
    death,
    to the place appointed for all the
    living.

²⁴"Surely no one lays a hand on a
    broken man
    when he cries for help in his
    distress.
²⁵Have I not wept for those in trouble?
    Has not my soul grieved for the
    poor?
²⁶Yet when I hoped for good, evil
    came;
    when I looked for light, then came
    darkness.
²⁷The churning inside me never stops;
    days of suffering confront me.
²⁸I go about blackened, but not by the
    sun;
    I stand up in the assembly and cry
    for help.
²⁹I have become a brother of jackals,
    a companion of owls.
³⁰My skin grows black and peels;
    my body burns with fever.
³¹My harp is tuned to mourning,
    and my flute to the sound of
    wailing.

31 "I made a covenant with my eyes
    not to look lustfully at a girl.
²For what is man's lot from God
    above,
    his heritage from the Almighty on
    high?
³Is it not ruin for the wicked,
    disaster for those who do wrong?
⁴Does he not see my ways
    and count my every step?

⁵"If I have walked in falsehood
    or my foot has hurried after
    deceit—
⁶let God weigh me in honest scales
    and he will know that I am
    blameless—
⁷if my steps have turned from the
    path,
    if my heart has been led by my
    eyes,
    or if my hands have been defiled,

⁸then may others eat what I have
    sown,
    and may my crops be uprooted.

⁹"If my heart has been enticed by a
    woman,
    or if I have lurked at my neighbor's
    door,
¹⁰then may my wife grind another
    man's grain,
    and may other men sleep with her.
¹¹For that would have been shameful,
    a sin to be judged.
¹²It is a fire that burns to
    Destruction*ᵃ*;
    it would have uprooted my harvest.

¹³"If I have denied justice to my
    menservants and maidservants
    when they had a grievance against
    me,
¹⁴what will I do when God confronts
    me?
    What will I answer when called to
    account?
¹⁵Did not he who made me in the
    womb make them?
    Did not the same one form us
    both within our mothers?

¹⁶"If I have denied the desires of the
    poor
    or let the eyes of the widow grow
    weary,
¹⁷if I have kept my bread to myself,
    not sharing it with the fatherless—
¹⁸but from my youth I reared him as
    would a father,
    and from my birth I guided the
    widow—
¹⁹if I have seen anyone perishing for
    lack of clothing,
    or a needy man without a garment,
²⁰and his heart did not bless me
    for warming him with the fleece
    from my sheep,
²¹if I have raised my hand against the
    fatherless,
    knowing that I had influence in
    court,
²²then let my arm fall from the
    shoulder,
    let it be broken off at the joint.
²³For I dreaded destruction from God,

ᵃ12 Hebrew *Abaddon*

and for fear of his splendor I could
    not do such things.

24"If I have put my trust in gold
    or said to pure gold, 'You are my
        security,'
25if I have rejoiced over my great
    wealth,
    the fortune my hands had gained,
26if I have regarded the sun in its
    radiance
    or the moon moving in splendor,
27so that my heart was secretly enticed
    and my hand offered them a kiss
        of homage,
28then these also would be sins to be
    judged,
    for I would have been unfaithful to
        God on high.

29"If I have rejoiced at my enemy's
    misfortune
    or gloated over the trouble that
        came to him—
30I have not allowed my mouth to sin
    by invoking a curse against his
        life—
31if the men of my household have
    never said,
    'Who has not had his fill of Job's
        meat?'—
32but no stranger had to spend the
    night in the street,
    for my door was always open to
        the traveler—
33if I have concealed my sin as men
    do,*a*
    by hiding my guilt in my heart
34because I so feared the crowd
    and so dreaded the contempt of
        the clans
    that I kept silent and would not go
        outside
35("Oh, that I had someone to hear
    me!
    I sign now my defense—let the
        Almighty answer me;
    let my accuser put his indictment
        in writing.
36Surely I would wear it on my
    shoulder,
    I would put it on like a crown.
37I would give him an account of my
    every step;
    like a prince I would approach
        him.)—

38"if my land cries out against me
    and all its furrows are wet with
        tears,
39if I have devoured its yield without
    payment
    or broken the spirit of its tenants,
40then let briers come up instead of
    wheat
    and weeds instead of barley."

The words of Job are ended.

Elihu

32 So these three men stopped answering Job, because he was righteous in his own eyes. 2But Elihu son of
Barakel the Buzite, of the family of Ram,
became very angry with Job for justifying
himself rather than God. 3He was also
angry with the three friends, because they
had found no way to refute Job, and yet
had condemned him.*b* 4Now Elihu had
waited before speaking to Job because
they were older than he. 5But when he
saw that the three men had nothing more
to say, his anger was aroused.

6So Elihu son of Barakel the Buzite
said:

"I am young in years,
    and you are old;
    that is why I was fearful,
        not daring to tell you what I know.
7I thought, 'Age should speak;
    advanced years should teach
        wisdom.'
8But it is the spirit*c* in a man,
    the breath of the Almighty, that
        gives him understanding.
9It is not only the old*d* who are wise,
    not only the aged who understand
        what is right.

10"Therefore I say: Listen to me;
    I too will tell you what I know.
11I waited while you spoke,
    I listened to your reasoning;
    while you were searching for words,
12   I gave you my full attention.
    But not one of you has proved Job
        wrong;
    none of you has answered his
        arguments.

a33 Or *as Adam did*   *b3* Masoretic Text; an
ancient Hebrew scribal tradition *Job, and so had
condemned God*   *c8* Or *Spirit;* also in verse 18
d9 Or *many;* or *great*

¹³Do not say, 'We have found wisdom;
  let God refute him, not man.'
¹⁴But Job has not marshaled his words
      against me,
  and I will not answer him with
      your arguments.

¹⁵"They are dismayed and have no
      more to say;
  words have failed them.
¹⁶Must I wait, now that they are silent,
  now that they stand there with no
      reply?
¹⁷I too will have my say;
  I too will tell what I know.
¹⁸For I am full of words,
  and the spirit within me compels
      me;
¹⁹inside I am like bottled-up wine,
  like new wineskins ready to burst.
²⁰I must speak and find relief;
  I must open my lips and reply.
²¹I will show partiality to no one,
  nor will I flatter any man;
²²for if I were skilled in flattery,
  my Maker would soon take me
      away.

33 "But now, Job, listen to my
          words;
  pay attention to everything I say.
²I am about to open my mouth;
  my words are on the tip of my
      tongue.
³My words come from an upright
      heart;
  my lips sincerely speak what I
      know.
⁴The Spirit of God has made me;
  the breath of the Almighty gives
      me life.
⁵Answer me then, if you can;
  prepare yourself and confront me.
⁶I am just like you before God;
  I too have been taken from clay.
⁷No fear of me should alarm you,
  nor should my hand be heavy
      upon you.

⁸"But you have said in my hearing—
  I heard the very words—
⁹'I am pure and without sin;
  I am clean and free from guilt.
¹⁰Yet God has found fault with me;
  he considers me his enemy.
¹¹He fastens my feet in shackles;

he keeps close watch on all my
      paths.'

¹²"But I tell you, in this you are not
      right,
  for God is greater than man.
¹³Why do you complain to him
  that he answers none of man's
      words ᵃ?
¹⁴For God does speak—now one way,
      now another—
  though man may not perceive it.
¹⁵In a dream, in a vision of the night,
  when deep sleep falls on men
  as they slumber in their beds,
¹⁶he may speak in their ears
  and terrify them with warnings,
¹⁷to turn man from wrongdoing
  and keep him from pride,
¹⁸to preserve his soul from the pit, ᵇ
  his life from perishing by the
      sword. ᶜ
¹⁹Or a man may be chastened on a bed
      of pain
  with constant distress in his bones,
²⁰so that his very being finds food
      repulsive
  and his soul loathes the choicest
      meal.
²¹His flesh wastes away to nothing,
  and his bones, once hidden, now
      stick out.
²²His soul draws near to the pit, ᵈ
  and his life to the messengers of
      death. ᵉ

²³"Yet if there is an angel on his side
  as a mediator, one out of a
      thousand,
  to tell a man what is right for him,
²⁴to be gracious to him and say,
  'Spare him from going down to
      the pit ᶠ;
  I have found a ransom for him'—
²⁵then his flesh is renewed like a
      child's;
  it is restored as in the days of his
      youth.
²⁶He prays to God and finds favor with
      him,
  he sees God's face and shouts for
      joy;

ᵃ13 Or that he does not answer for any of his actions
ᵇ18 Or preserve him from the grave   ᶜ18 Or from
crossing the River   ᵈ22 Or He draws near to the
grave   ᵉ22 Or to the dead   ᶠ24 Or grave

he is restored by God to his
righteous state.
²⁷Then he comes to men and says,
'I sinned, and perverted what was
right,
but I did not get what I deserved.
²⁸He redeemed my soul from going
down to the pit,ᵃ
and I will live to enjoy the light.'

²⁹"God does all these things to a man—
twice, even three times—
³⁰to turn back his soul from the pit,ᵇ
that the light of life may shine on
him.

³¹"Pay attention, Job, and listen to me;
be silent, and I will speak.
³²If you have anything to say, answer
me;
speak up, for I want you to be
cleared.
³³But if not, then listen to me;
be silent, and I will teach you
wisdom."

34 Then Elihu said:

²"Hear my words, you wise men;
listen to me, you men of learning.
³For the ear tests words
as the tongue tastes food.
⁴Let us discern for ourselves what is
right;
let us learn together what is good.

⁵"Job says, 'I am innocent,
but God denies me justice.
⁶Although I am right,
I am considered a liar;
although I am guiltless,
his arrow inflicts an incurable
wound.'
⁷What man is like Job,
who drinks scorn like water?
⁸He keeps company with evildoers;
he associates with wicked men.
⁹For he says, 'It profits a man nothing
when he tries to please God.'

¹⁰"So listen to me, you men of
understanding.
Far be it from God to do evil,
from the Almighty to do wrong.
¹¹He repays a man for what he has
done;
he brings upon him what his
conduct deserves.

¹²It is unthinkable that God would do
wrong,
that the Almighty would pervert
justice.
¹³Who appointed him over the earth?
Who put him in charge of the
whole world?
¹⁴If it were his intention
and he withdrew his spiritᶜ and
breath,
¹⁵all mankind would perish together
and man would return to the dust.

¹⁶"If you have understanding, hear this;
listen to what I say.
¹⁷Can he who hates justice govern?
Will you condemn the just and
mighty One?
¹⁸Is he not the One who says to kings,
'You are worthless,'
and to nobles, 'You are wicked,'
¹⁹who shows no partiality to princes
and does not favor the rich over
the poor,
for they are all the work of his
hands?
²⁰They die in an instant, in the middle
of the night;
the people are shaken and they
pass away;
the mighty are removed without
human hand.

²¹"His eyes are on the ways of men;
he sees their every step.
²²There is no dark place, no deep
shadow,
where evildoers can hide.
²³God has no need to examine men
further,
that they should come before him
for judgment.
²⁴Without inquiry he shatters the
mighty
and sets up others in their place.
²⁵Because he takes note of their deeds,
he overthrows them in the night
and they are crushed.
²⁶He punishes them for their
wickedness
where everyone can see them,
²⁷because they turned from following
him

ᵃ28 Or *redeemed me from going down to the grave*
ᵇ30 Or *turn him back from the grave*   ᶜ14 Or
Spirit

and had no regard for any of his ways.
²⁸They caused the cry of the poor to come before him,
so that he heard the cry of the needy.
²⁹But if he remains silent, who can condemn him?
If he hides his face, who can see him?
Yet he is over man and nation alike,
³⁰   to keep a godless man from ruling,
from laying snares for the people.

³¹"Suppose a man says to God,
'I am guilty but will offend no more.
³²Teach me what I cannot see;
if I have done wrong, I will not do so again.'
³³Should God then reward you on your terms,
when you refuse to repent?
You must decide, not I;
so tell me what you know.

³⁴"Men of understanding declare,
wise men who hear me say to me,
³⁵'Job speaks without knowledge;
his words lack insight.'
³⁶Oh, that Job might be tested to the utmost
for answering like a wicked man!
³⁷To his sin he adds rebellion;
scornfully he claps his hands among us
and multiplies his words against God."

35 Then Elihu said:

²"Do you think this is just?
You say, 'I will be cleared by God.'ᵃ
³Yet you ask him, 'What profit is it to me,ᵇ
and what do I gain by not sinning?'

⁴"I would like to reply to you
and to your friends with you.
⁵Look up at the heavens and see;
gaze at the clouds so high above you.
⁶If you sin, how does that affect him?
If your sins are many, what does that do to him?
⁷If you are righteous, what do you give to him,
or what does he receive from your hand?
⁸Your wickedness affects only a man like yourself,
and your righteousness only the sons of men.

⁹"Men cry out under a load of oppression;
they plead for relief from the arm of the powerful.
¹⁰But no one says, 'Where is God my Maker,
who gives songs in the night,
¹¹who teaches more to us than toᶜ the beasts of the earth
and makes us wiser thanᵈ the birds of the air?'
¹²He does not answer when men cry out
because of the arrogance of the wicked.
¹³Indeed, God does not listen to their empty plea;
the Almighty pays no attention to it.
¹⁴How much less, then, will he listen
when you say that you do not see him,
that your case is before him
and you must wait for him,
¹⁵and further, that his anger never punishes
and he does not take the least notice of wickedness.ᵉ
¹⁶So Job opens his mouth with empty talk;
without knowledge he multiplies words."

36 Elihu continued:

²"Bear with me a little longer and I will show you
that there is more to be said in God's behalf.
³I get my knowledge from afar;
I will ascribe justice to my Maker.
⁴Be assured that my words are not false;

ᵃ2 Or *My righteousness is more than God's*   ᵇ3 Or *you*   ᶜ11 Or *teaches us by*   ᵈ11 Or *us wise by*   ᵉ15 Symmachus, Theodotion and Vulgate; the meaning of the Hebrew for this word is uncertain.

one perfect in knowledge is with
    you.

⁵"God is mighty, but does not despise
    men;
  he is mighty, and firm in his
    purpose.
⁶He does not keep the wicked alive
  but gives the afflicted their rights.
⁷He does not take his eyes off the
    righteous;
  he enthrones them with kings
  and exalts them forever.
⁸But if men are bound in chains,
  held fast by cords of affliction,
⁹he tells them what they have done—
  that they have sinned arrogantly.
¹⁰He makes them listen to correction
  and commands them to repent of
    their evil.
¹¹If they obey and serve him,
  they will spend the rest of their
    days in prosperity
  and their years in contentment.
¹²But if they do not listen,
  they will perish by the sword*a*
  and die without knowledge.

¹³"The godless in heart harbor
    resentment;
  even when he fetters them, they do
    not cry for help.
¹⁴They die in their youth,
  among male prostitutes of the
    shrines.
¹⁵But those who suffer he delivers in
    their suffering;
  he speaks to them in their
    affliction.

¹⁶"He is wooing you from the jaws of
    distress
  to a spacious place free from
    restriction,
  to the comfort of your table laden
    with choice food.
¹⁷But now you are laden with the
    judgment due the wicked;
  judgment and justice have taken
    hold of you.
¹⁸Be careful that no one entices you by
    riches;
  do not let a large bribe turn you
    aside.
¹⁹Would your wealth
  or even all your mighty efforts

sustain you so you would not be
    in distress?
²⁰Do not long for the night,
  to drag people away from their
    homes.*b*
²¹Beware of turning to evil,
  which you seem to prefer to
    affliction.

²²"God is exalted in his power.
  Who is a teacher like him?
²³Who has prescribed his ways for him,
  or said to him, 'You have done
    wrong'?
²⁴Remember to extol his work,
  which men have praised in song.
²⁵All mankind has seen it;
  men gaze on it from afar.
²⁶How great is God—beyond our
    understanding!
  The number of his years is past
    finding out.

²⁷"He draws up the drops of water,
  which distill as rain to the
    streams*c*;
²⁸the clouds pour down their moisture
  and abundant showers fall on
    mankind.
²⁹Who can understand how he spreads
    out the clouds,
  how he thunders from his
    pavilion?
³⁰See how he scatters his lightning
    about him,
  bathing the depths of the sea.
³¹This is the way he governs*d* the
    nations
  and provides food in abundance.
³²He fills his hands with lightning
  and commands it to strike its
    mark.
³³His thunder announces the coming
    storm;
  even the cattle make known its
    approach.*e*

37 "At this my heart pounds
    and leaps from its place.
²Listen! Listen to the roar of his voice,
  to the rumbling that comes from
    his mouth.

---

a12 Or *will cross the River*   *b20* The meaning of
the Hebrew for verses 18-20 is uncertain.
c27 Or *distill from the mist as rain*   *d31* Or
nourishes   *e33* Or *announces his coming—* / *the
One zealous against evil*

³He unleashes his lightning beneath
  the whole heaven
and sends it to the ends of the
  earth.
⁴After that comes the sound of his
  roar;
he thunders with his majestic
  voice.
  When his voice resounds,
  he holds nothing back.
⁵God's voice thunders in marvelous
  ways;
he does great things beyond our
  understanding.
⁶He says to the snow, 'Fall on the
  earth,'
and to the rain shower, 'Be a
  mighty downpour.'
⁷So that all men he has made may
  know his work,
he stops every man from his
  labor.ᵃ
⁸The animals take cover;
  they remain in their dens.
⁹The tempest comes out from its
  chamber,
the cold from the driving winds.
¹⁰The breath of God produces ice,
  and the broad waters become
  frozen.
¹¹He loads the clouds with moisture;
  he scatters his lightning through
  them.
¹²At his direction they swirl around
  over the face of the whole earth
  to do whatever he commands
  them.
¹³He brings the clouds to punish men,
  or to water his earthᵇ and show
  his love.

¹⁴"Listen to this, Job;
  stop and consider God's wonders.
¹⁵Do you know how God controls the
  clouds
and makes his lightning flash?
¹⁶Do you know how the clouds hang
  poised,
those wonders of him who is
  perfect in knowledge?
¹⁷You who swelter in your clothes
  when the land lies hushed under
  the south wind,
¹⁸can you join him in spreading out the
  skies,
hard as a mirror of cast bronze?

¹⁹"Tell us what we should say to him;
  we cannot draw up our case
  because of our darkness.
²⁰Should he be told that I want to
  speak?
Would any man ask to be
  swallowed up?
²¹Now no one can look at the sun,
  bright as it is in the skies
after the wind has swept them
  clean.
²²Out of the north he comes in golden
  splendor;
God comes in awesome majesty.
²³The Almighty is beyond our reach
  and exalted in power;
in his justice and great
  righteousness, he does not
  oppress.
²⁴Therefore, men revere him,
  for does he not have regard for all
  the wise in heart?ᶜ"

The LORD Speaks

38 Then the LORD answered Job out of
the storm. He said:

²"Who is this that darkens my counsel
  with words without knowledge?
³Brace yourself like a man;
  I will question you,
  and you shall answer me.

⁴"Where were you when I laid the
  earth's foundation?
Tell me, if you understand.
⁵Who marked off its dimensions?
  Surely you know!
Who stretched a measuring line
  across it?
⁶On what were its footings set,
  or who laid its cornerstone—
⁷while the morning stars sang together
  and all the angelsᵈ shouted for
  joy?

⁸"Who shut up the sea behind doors
  when it burst forth from the
  womb,
⁹when I made the clouds its garment
  and wrapped it in thick darkness,
¹⁰when I fixed limits for it
  and set its doors and bars in place,

ᵃ7 Or / he fills all men with fear by his power
ᵇ13 Or to favor them   ᶜ24 Or for he does not
have regard for any who think they are wise.
ᵈ7 Hebrew the sons of God

¹¹when I said, 'This far you may come
and no farther;
here is where your proud waves
halt'?

¹²"Have you ever given orders to the
morning,
or shown the dawn its place,
¹³that it might take the earth by the
edges
and shake the wicked out of it?
¹⁴The earth takes shape like clay under
a seal;
its features stand out like those of
a garment.
¹⁵The wicked are denied their light,
and their upraised arm is broken.

¹⁶"Have you journeyed to the springs
of the sea
or walked in the recesses of the
deep?
¹⁷Have the gates of death been shown
to you?
Have you seen the gates of the
shadow of death^a?
¹⁸Have you comprehended the vast
expanses of the earth?
Tell me, if you know all this.

¹⁹"What is the way to the abode of
light?
And where does darkness reside?
²⁰Can you take them to their places?
Do you know the paths to their
dwellings?
²¹Surely you know, for you were
already born!
You have lived so many years!

²²"Have you entered the storehouses of
the snow
or seen the storehouses of the hail,
²³which I reserve for times of trouble,
for days of war and battle?
²⁴What is the way to the place where
the lightning is dispersed,
or the place where the east winds
are scattered over the earth?
²⁵Who cuts a channel for the torrents
of rain,
and a path for the thunderstorm,
²⁶to water a land where no man lives,
a desert with no one in it,
²⁷to satisfy a desolate wasteland
and make it sprout with grass?
²⁸Does the rain have a father?
Who fathers the drops of dew?

²⁹From whose womb comes the ice?
Who gives birth to the frost from
the heavens
³⁰when the waters become hard as
stone,
when the surface of the deep is
frozen?

³¹"Can you bind the beautiful^b
Pleiades?
Can you loose the cords of Orion?
³²Can you bring forth the constellations
in their seasons^c
or lead out the Bear^d with its
cubs?
³³Do you know the laws of the
heavens?
Can you set up ⌊God's^e⌋ dominion
over the earth?

³⁴"Can you raise your voice to the
clouds
and cover yourself with a flood of
water?
³⁵Do you send the lightning bolts on
their way?
Do they report to you, 'Here we
are'?
³⁶Who endowed the heart^f with
wisdom
or gave understanding to the
mind^f?
³⁷Who has the wisdom to count the
clouds?
Who can tip over the water jars of
the heavens
³⁸when the dust becomes hard
and the clods of earth stick
together?

³⁹"Do you hunt the prey for the lioness
and satisfy the hunger of the lions
⁴⁰when they crouch in their dens
or lie in wait in a thicket?
⁴¹Who provides food for the raven
when its young cry out to God
and wander about for lack of food?

39 "Do you know when the
mountain goats give birth?
Do you watch when the doe bears
her fawn?

---

^a17 Or *gates of deep shadows*   ^b31 Or *the*
twinkling; or *the chains of the*   ^c32 Or *the*
morning star in its season   ^d32 Or *out Leo*
^e33 Or *his;* or *their*   ^f36 The meaning of the
Hebrew for this word is uncertain.

²Do you count the months till they
    bear?
  Do you know the time they give
    birth?
³They crouch down and bring forth
    their young;
  their labor pains are ended.
⁴Their young thrive and grow strong in
    the wilds;
  they leave and do not return.

⁵"Who let the wild donkey go free?
  Who untied his ropes?
⁶I gave him the wasteland as his
    home,
  the salt flats as his habitat.
⁷He laughs at the commotion in the
    town;
  he does not hear a driver's shout.
⁸He ranges the hills for his pasture
  and searches for any green thing.

⁹"Will the wild ox consent to serve
    you?
  Will he stay by your manger at
    night?
¹⁰Can you hold him to the furrow with
    a harness?
  Will he till the valleys behind you?
¹¹Will you rely on him for his great
    strength?
  Will you leave your heavy work to
    him?
¹²Can you trust him to bring in your
    grain
  and gather it to your threshing
    floor?

¹³"The wings of the ostrich flap
    joyfully,
  but they cannot compare with the
    pinions and feathers of the
    stork.
¹⁴She lays her eggs on the ground
  and lets them warm in the sand,
¹⁵unmindful that a foot may crush
    them,
  that some wild animal may
    trample them.
¹⁶She treats her young harshly, as if
    they were not hers;
  she cares not that her labor was in
    vain,
¹⁷for God did not endow her with
    wisdom
  or give her a share of good sense.

¹⁸Yet when she spreads her feathers to
    run,
  she laughs at horse and rider.

¹⁹"Do you give the horse his strength
  or clothe his neck with a flowing
    mane?
²⁰Do you make him leap like a locust,
  striking terror with his proud
    snorting?
²¹He paws fiercely, rejoicing in his
    strength,
  and charges into the fray.
²²He laughs at fear, afraid of nothing;
  he does not shy away from the
    sword.
²³The quiver rattles against his side,
  along with the flashing spear and
    lance.
²⁴In frenzied excitement he eats up the
    ground;
  he cannot stand still when the
    trumpet sounds.
²⁵At the blast of the trumpet he snorts,
    'Aha!'
  He catches the scent of battle from
    afar,
  the shout of commanders and the
    battle cry.

²⁶"Does the hawk take flight by your
    wisdom
  and spread his wings toward the
    south?
²⁷Does the eagle soar at your command
  and build his nest on high?
²⁸He dwells on a cliff and stays there at
    night;
  a rocky crag is his stronghold.
²⁹From there he seeks out his food;
  his eyes detect it from afar.
³⁰His young ones feast on blood,
  and where the slain are, there is
    he."

40

The LORD said to Job:

²"Will the one who contends with the
    Almighty correct him?
  Let him who accuses God answer
    him!"

³Then Job answered the LORD:

⁴"I am unworthy—how can I reply to
    you?
  I put my hand over my mouth.

⁵I spoke once, but I have no answer—
    twice, but I will say no more."

⁶Then the LORD spoke to Job out of the
storm:

⁷"Brace yourself like a man;
    I will question you,
    and you shall answer me.

⁸"Would you discredit my justice?
    Would you condemn me to justify
        yourself?
⁹Do you have an arm like God's,
    and can your voice thunder like
        his?
¹⁰Then adorn yourself with glory and
        splendor,
    and clothe yourself in honor and
        majesty.
¹¹Unleash the fury of your wrath,
    look at every proud man and bring
        him low,
¹²look at every proud man and humble
        him,
    crush the wicked where they stand.
¹³Bury them all in the dust together;
    shroud their faces in the grave.
¹⁴Then I myself will admit to you
    that your own right hand can save
        you.

¹⁵"Look at the behemoth,ᵃ
    which I made along with you
    and which feeds on grass like an
        ox.
¹⁶What strength he has in his loins,
    what power in the muscles of his
        belly!
¹⁷His tailᵇ sways like a cedar;
    the sinews of his thighs are
        close-knit.
¹⁸His bones are tubes of bronze,
    his limbs like rods of iron.
¹⁹He ranks first among the works of
        God,
    yet his Maker can approach him
        with his sword.
²⁰The hills bring him their produce,
    and all the wild animals play
        nearby.
²¹Under the lotus plants he lies,
    hidden among the reeds in the
        marsh.
²²The lotuses conceal him in their
        shadow;
    the poplars by the stream surround
        him.

²³When the river rages, he is not
        alarmed;
    he is secure, though the Jordan
        should surge against his
        mouth.
²⁴Can anyone capture him by the
        eyes,ᶜ
    or trap him and pierce his nose?

41

    "Can you pull in the leviathanᵈ
        with a fishhook
    or tie down his tongue with a
        rope?
²Can you put a cord through his nose
    or pierce his jaw with a hook?
³Will he keep begging you for mercy?
    Will he speak to you with gentle
        words?
⁴Will he make an agreement with you
    for you to take him as your slave
        for life?
⁵Can you make a pet of him like a
        bird
    or put him on a leash for your
        girls?
⁶Will traders barter for him?
    Will they divide him up among the
        merchants?
⁷Can you fill his hide with harpoons
    or his head with fishing spears?
⁸If you lay a hand on him,
    you will remember the struggle and
        never do it again!
⁹Any hope of subduing him is false;
    the mere sight of him is
        overpowering.
¹⁰No one is fierce enough to rouse him.
    Who then is able to stand against
        me?
¹¹Who has a claim against me that I
        must pay?
    Everything under heaven belongs
        to me.

¹²"I will not fail to speak of his limbs,
    his strength and his graceful form.
¹³Who can strip off his outer coat?
    Who would approach him with a
        bridle?
¹⁴Who dares open the doors of his
        mouth,
    ringed about with his fearsome
        teeth?

ᵃ15 Possibly the hippopotamus or the elephant
ᵇ17 Possibly trunk   ᶜ24 Or by a water hole
ᵈ1 Possibly the crocodile

¹⁵His back has[a] rows of shields
     tightly sealed together;
¹⁶each is so close to the next
     that no air can pass between.
¹⁷They are joined fast to one another;
     they cling together and cannot be
     parted.
¹⁸His snorting throws out flashes of
     light;
     his eyes are like the rays of dawn.
¹⁹Firebrands stream from his mouth;
     sparks of fire shoot out.
²⁰Smoke pours from his nostrils
     as from a boiling pot over a fire of
     reeds.
²¹His breath sets coals ablaze,
     and flames dart from his mouth.
²²Strength resides in his neck;
     dismay goes before him.
²³The folds of his flesh are tightly
     joined;
     they are firm and immovable.
²⁴His chest is hard as rock,
     hard as a lower millstone.
²⁵When he rises up, the mighty are
     terrified;
     they retreat before his thrashing.
²⁶The sword that reaches him has no
     effect,
     nor does the spear or the dart or
     the javelin.
²⁷Iron he treats like straw
     and bronze like rotten wood.
²⁸Arrows do not make him flee;
     slingstones are like chaff to him.
²⁹A club seems to him but a piece of
     straw;
     he laughs at the rattling of the
     lance.
³⁰His undersides are jagged potsherds,
     leaving a trail in the mud like a
     threshing sledge.
³¹He makes the depths churn like a
     boiling caldron
     and stirs up the sea like a pot of
     ointment.
³²Behind him he leaves a glistening
     wake;
     one would think the deep had
     white hair.
³³Nothing on earth is his equal—
     a creature without fear.
³⁴He looks down on all that are
     haughty;
     he is king over all that are proud."

Job

42

Then Job replied to the LORD:

²"I know that you can do all things;
     no plan of yours can be thwarted.
³⌊You asked,⌋ 'Who is this that obscures
          my counsel without
          knowledge?'
     Surely I spoke of things I did not
          understand,
     things too wonderful for me to
          know.
⁴⌊"You said,⌋ 'Listen now, and I will
          speak;
     I will question you,
          and you shall answer me.'
⁵My ears had heard of you
     but now my eyes have seen you.
⁶Therefore I despise myself
     and repent in dust and ashes."

Epilogue

⁷After the LORD had said these things to Job, he said to Eliphaz the Temanite, "I am angry with you and your two friends, because you have not spoken of me what is right, as my servant Job has. ⁸So now take seven bulls and seven rams and go to my servant Job and sacrifice a burnt offering for yourselves. My servant Job will pray for you, and I will accept his prayer and not deal with you according to your folly. You have not spoken of me what is right, as my servant Job has." ⁹So Eliphaz the Temanite, Bildad the Shuhite and Zophar the Naamathite did what the LORD told them; and the LORD accepted Job's prayer.

¹⁰After Job had prayed for his friends, the LORD made him prosperous again and gave him twice as much as he had before. ¹¹All his brothers and sisters and everyone who had known him before came and ate with him in his house. They comforted and consoled him over all the trouble the LORD had brought upon him, and each one gave him a piece of silver[b] and a gold ring.

¹²The LORD blessed the latter part of Job's life more than the first. He had four-

---

[a]15 Or *His pride is his*   [b]11 Hebrew *him a kesitah;* a kesitah was a unit of money of unknown weight and value.

teen thousand sheep, six thousand camels, a thousand yoke of oxen and a thousand donkeys. ¹³And he also had seven sons and three daughters. ¹⁴The first daughter he named Jemimah, the second Keziah and the third Keren-Happuch. ¹⁵Nowhere in all the land were there found women as beautiful as Job's daughters, and their father granted them an inheritance along with their brothers.

¹⁶After this, Job lived a hundred and forty years; he saw his children and their children to the fourth generation. ¹⁷And so he died, old and full of years.

Desperate Situations

Wednesday

JOB 42:2 Some time ago we went to visit our friends Jim and Felicia; they live in Germany where Jim directs the work for Athletes in Action. Their three active and delightful, small children kept us laughing and reminded us of our early parenting years.

A couple months later we stared at the email on our computer screen, not wanting to believe it. Jim, who always had always been articulate, started to have difficulty speaking and suddenly began to experience excruciating headaches. Tests confirmed the worst—a brain tumor. Surgery and chemotherapy followed. Still he suffers. Felicia, unlike Job's wife, continues to be a strong support for Jim. Both acknowledge that God is in control. Through their example and witness, many have found faith in Christ. But Jim is still suffering.

We ask ourselves how we would respond in such a desperate situation. Even in lesser situations, Dave and I haven't always started with the right response. Several years ago when faced with a potential medical crisis, my first response was fear. Before knowing the results were negative, God gave me his peace . . . but it didn't happen automatically. Neither did Job immediately accept his fate as being from God. When bad things began to happen to Job, he was convinced God was angry with him. He cursed the day he was born and demanded an explanation. He wanted vindication.

What would change if we really believed God was in control? Perhaps we would complain less and trust more. That's the choice Job made . . . and the one Jim and Felicia are presently making. —**Dave & Claudia**

Go to page 562 for your next devotional reading.

Psalms

*Perhaps nothing
reflects who we are* as much as the way in which we
express our most intimate thoughts about God. He deserves
our most honest and sincere worship. Psalms is a collection
of prayers and songs written by a variety of authors who
voice a wide range of human emotion—joy, excitement,
compassion, love, anger, grief, depression.

The psalms help us discover what it means to be "real"
with God, for we often hear our own emotions reflected in
these timeless songs. Through the psalms we discover what
it means to "worship [him] in spirit and in truth" (John
4:24). Select a psalm that expresses your thoughts about
God. Now read that psalm aloud to your spouse as a way to
be "real" with God, together.

BOOK I

Psalms 1–41

Psalm 1

¹Blessed is the man
  who does not walk in the counsel
    of the wicked
or stand in the way of sinners
  or sit in the seat of mockers.
²But his delight is in the law of the
    LORD,
  and on his law he meditates day
    and night.
³He is like a tree planted by streams of
    water,
which yields its fruit in season
and whose leaf does not wither.
  Whatever he does prospers.

⁴Not so the wicked!
  They are like chaff
    that the wind blows away.
⁵Therefore the wicked will not stand in
    the judgment,
  nor sinners in the assembly of the
    righteous.

⁶For the LORD watches over the way of
    the righteous,
  but the way of the wicked will
    perish.

Psalm 2

[1] Why do the nations conspire[a]
  and the peoples plot in vain?
[2] The kings of the earth take their stand
  and the rulers gather together
against the LORD
  and against his Anointed One.[b]
[3] "Let us break their chains," they say,
  "and throw off their fetters."

[4] The One enthroned in heaven laughs;
  the Lord scoffs at them.
[5] Then he rebukes them in his anger
  and terrifies them in his wrath,
    saying,
[6] "I have installed my King[c]
  on Zion, my holy hill."

[7] I will proclaim the decree of the LORD:

He said to me, "You are my Son[d];
  today I have become your Father.[e]
[8] Ask of me,

and I will make the nations your
    inheritance,
  the ends of the earth your
    possession.
[9] You will rule them with an iron
    scepter[f];
  you will dash them to pieces like
    pottery."

[10] Therefore, you kings, be wise;
  be warned, you rulers of the earth.
[11] Serve the LORD with fear
  and rejoice with trembling.
[12] Kiss the Son, lest he be angry
  and you be destroyed in your way,
for his wrath can flare up in a
    moment.
  Blessed are all who take refuge in
    him.

[a] 1 Hebrew; Septuagint *rage*   [b] 2 Or *anointed one*
[c] 6 Or *king*   [d] 7 Or *son*; also in verse 12
[e] 7 Or *have begotten you*   [f] 9 Or *will break them
with a rod of iron*

How to be Prosperous

Thursday

PSALM 1 Every married couple wants to be blessed and prosperous. We want our lives to be fruitful and successful. This psalm tells us how to be blessed. However, it gives us instruction on how to be prosperous and successful from God's perspective, rather than ours. Our culture tells us that success is measured by the accumulation of things, position and influence. But that kind of prosperity brings nothing lasting. It's very elusive and hard to hold on to.

If we are to be successful from God's standpoint, we must be careful of the counsel we receive. If we surround ourselves with people who live Godless lives, we will receive advice and an outlook that will result in emptiness. I (Bob) personally thought that success would be achieved by working long hours and accepting every extra opportunity I was offered. However, the longer I worked, the more I was away from home, and the less successful I felt. There was certainly more money . . . but much less fulfillment.

The ideas of our culture can change from one minute to the next. Like a feather, a couple can be blown from one direction to another, changing with the winds of each new fad. A feather never stays long in one place, and its future is always unstable. True happiness and prosperity never come to those who float from one thing to the next.

In contrast, if couples meditate on the consistent and anchoring Word of God, they will find true prosperity and live fruitful lives. I finally woke up and realized that God rather than the ever-changing culture defined success. I still do work hard, but I put in fewer hours. My primary focus has changed to God and home. The principles of God will ground us and bring the proper approach to life. Taking time each day, as a couple, to read and meditate on God's Word is an important way to ground ourselves in God's blessings.

—Bob & Rosemary

Go to page 564 for your next devotional reading.

Psalm 3

*A psalm of David. When he fled from
his son Absalom.*

[1] O LORD, how many are my foes!
How many rise up against me!
[2] Many are saying of me,
"God will not deliver him." *Selah*[a]

[3] But you are a shield around me,
O LORD;
you bestow glory on me and lift[b]
up my head.
[4] To the LORD I cry aloud,
and he answers me from his holy
hill. *Selah*

[5] I lie down and sleep;
I wake again, because the LORD
sustains me.
[6] I will not fear the tens of thousands
drawn up against me on every side.

[7] Arise, O LORD!
Deliver me, O my God!
Strike all my enemies on the jaw;
break the teeth of the wicked.

[8] From the LORD comes deliverance.
May your blessing be on your
people. *Selah*

Psalm 4

*For the director of music. With stringed
instruments. A psalm of David.*

[1] Answer me when I call to you,
O my righteous God.
Give me relief from my distress;
be merciful to me and hear my
prayer.

[2] How long, O men, will you turn my
glory into shame[c]?
How long will you love delusions
and seek false gods[d]? *Selah*
[3] Know that the LORD has set apart the
godly for himself;
the LORD will hear when I call to
him.

[4] In your anger do not sin;
when you are on your beds,
search your hearts and be silent.
Selah

[5] Offer right sacrifices
and trust in the LORD.

[6] Many are asking, "Who can show us
any good?"
Let the light of your face shine
upon us, O LORD.
[7] You have filled my heart with greater
joy
than when their grain and new
wine abound.
[8] I will lie down and sleep in peace,
for you alone, O LORD,
make me dwell in safety.

Psalm 5

*For the director of music. For flutes.
A psalm of David.*

[1] Give ear to my words, O LORD,
consider my sighing.
[2] Listen to my cry for help,
my King and my God,
for to you I pray.
[3] In the morning, O LORD, you hear my
voice;
in the morning I lay my requests
before you
and wait in expectation.

[4] You are not a God who takes pleasure
in evil;
with you the wicked cannot dwell.
[5] The arrogant cannot stand in your
presence;
you hate all who do wrong.
[6] You destroy those who tell lies;
bloodthirsty and deceitful men
the LORD abhors.

[7] But I, by your great mercy,
will come into your house;
in reverence will I bow down
toward your holy temple.
[8] Lead me, O LORD, in your
righteousness
because of my enemies—
make straight your way before me.

[9] Not a word from their mouth can be
trusted;
their heart is filled with
destruction.
Their throat is an open grave;
with their tongue they speak deceit.

---

[a]2 A word of uncertain meaning, occurring
frequently in the Psalms; possibly a musical term
[b]3 Or LORD, / my Glorious One, who lifts   [c]2 Or
you dishonor my Glorious One   [d]2 Or seek lies

¹⁰Declare them guilty, O God!
　Let their intrigues be their
　　downfall.
Banish them for their many sins,
　for they have rebelled against you.

¹¹But let all who take refuge in you be
　　glad;
　let them ever sing for joy.
Spread your protection over them,
　that those who love your name
　　may rejoice in you.
¹²For surely, O LORD, you bless the
　　righteous;
　you surround them with your favor
　　as with a shield.

Psalm 6

For the director of music. With stringed
instruments. According to *sheminith.* ᵃ
A psalm of David.

¹O LORD, do not rebuke me in your
　　anger
　or discipline me in your wrath.

²Be merciful to me, LORD, for I am
　　faint;
　O LORD, heal me, for my bones are
　　in agony.
³My soul is in anguish.
　How long, O LORD, how long?

⁴Turn, O LORD, and deliver me;
　save me because of your unfailing
　　love.
⁵No one remembers you when he is
　　dead.
　Who praises you from the grave ᵇ ?

⁶I am worn out from groaning;
　all night long I flood my bed with
　　weeping
　and drench my couch with tears.
⁷My eyes grow weak with sorrow;
　they fail because of all my foes.

⁸Away from me, all you who do evil,
　for the LORD has heard my
　　weeping.

ᵃTitle: Probably a musical term   ᵇ5 Hebrew
Sheol

Is Anger Bad?

Friday

PSALM 4:4 When we get angry and blow our top, we often sin against our spouse and against God. But it doesn't have to be that way—not if we follow King David's wise counsel.

The first part of this passage acknowledges that we do get angry. Anger is a God-given emotion. It's how we automatically respond either to fear or frustration. So anger isn't the real villain—it's how we express it that can be the problem. Anger can actually improve your marriage if you channel it correctly.

The key to making anger a positive force in your marriage is to decide beforehand that, when you get angry, you will attack the problem and not your mate. We learned the importance of not attacking each other after our "gas war" experience.

"Dave," I said. "Don't we need to stop for gas?" With our gas gauge near empty, Dave kept driving. "We're going to run out of gas!" I insisted.

Dave didn't perceive my questions as nagging until I had repeated them several times. You see, there was a gas war going on and gas was one or two cents per gallon cheaper at each station we passed. Dave was waiting for the best deal.

"You'd better stop," I repeated. "The price is going back up." But Dave kept driving. Our anger flared. We attacked each other with harsh words. By the time we stopped for gas, the price had gone up another ten cents a gallon; but the real cost that day wasn't the extra two dollars for a tank of gas—it was our hurt feelings.

After that experience, we made a contract with each other. We agreed to let the other know when we first begin to realize we are getting angry, and we agreed not to vent our anger at each other. Instead we would ask for the other's help. Consider making some sort of agreement like this with your spouse. It could turn a bad situation into something good (see Ephesians 4:26, page 1283).   **—Dave & Claudia**

Go to page 570 for your next devotional reading.

⁹The LORD has heard my cry for mercy;
   the LORD accepts my prayer.
¹⁰All my enemies will be ashamed and
     dismayed;
   they will turn back in sudden
     disgrace.

Psalm 7

A *shiggaion*ᵃ of David, which he sang
   to the LORD concerning Cush,
   a Benjamite.

¹O LORD my God, I take refuge in you;
   save and deliver me from all who
     pursue me,
²or they will tear me like a lion
   and rip me to pieces with no one
     to rescue me.

³O LORD my God, if I have done this
   and there is guilt on my hands—
⁴if I have done evil to him who is at
     peace with me
   or without cause have robbed my
     foe—
⁵then let my enemy pursue and
     overtake me;
   let him trample my life to the
     ground
   and make me sleep in the dust.
          Selah

⁶Arise, O LORD, in your anger;
   rise up against the rage of my
     enemies.
   Awake, my God; decree justice.
⁷Let the assembled peoples gather
     around you.
   Rule over them from on high;
⁸   let the LORD judge the peoples.
  Judge me, O LORD, according to my
     righteousness,
   according to my integrity, O Most
     High.
⁹O righteous God,
   who searches minds and hearts,
  bring to an end the violence of the
     wicked
   and make the righteous secure.

¹⁰My shieldᵇ is God Most High,
   who saves the upright in heart.
¹¹God is a righteous judge,
   a God who expresses his wrath
     every day.
¹²If he does not relent,
   heᶜ will sharpen his sword;

JUST BETWEEN you & me

Is Anger Bad?

How can you deal with your anger so that, in your anger, you do not sin? (See Psalm 4:4). It is possible to deal with anger in a positive way.

1. Think back to the last time you were angry and reflect on the following:

   • How did I feel when I was angry?
   • What did I do when I was angry?

2. Now think about what you wish you had done the last time you were angry.

3. Decide now what you want to do the next time you get angry. I will:

  ___ Resist attacking my spouse.
  ___ Resist defending myself.
  ___ Use "I" statements and let the statement reflect back on me. For instance, "I am angry because I feel ignored. Is it a good time for us to talk? If not, when can we talk?"
  ___ Avoid "why" questions that tend to be attacking and counter-productive.

Choose to attack the problem, not each other! Then you will be able to process your anger without sinning.

---

   he will bend and string his bow.
¹³He has prepared his deadly weapons;
   he makes ready his flaming arrows.

¹⁴He who is pregnant with evil
   and conceives trouble gives birth to
     disillusionment.
¹⁵He who digs a hole and scoops it out
   falls into the pit he has made.
¹⁶The trouble he causes recoils on
     himself;
   his violence comes down on his
     own head.

¹⁷I will give thanks to the LORD because
   of his righteousness
   and will sing praise to the name of
     the LORD Most High.

ᵃTitle: Probably a literary or musical term
ᵇ10 Or *sovereign*   ᶜ12 Or *If a man does not repent, / God*

Psalm 8

For the director of music. According to gittith.ᵃ A psalm of David.

¹O LORD, our Lord,
  how majestic is your name in all
    the earth!

You have set your glory
  above the heavens.
²From the lips of children and infants
  you have ordained praiseᵇ
because of your enemies,
  to silence the foe and the avenger.

³When I consider your heavens,
  the work of your fingers,
the moon and the stars,
  which you have set in place,
⁴what is man that you are mindful of
    him,
  the son of man that you care for
    him?
⁵You made him a little lower than the
    heavenly beingsᶜ
  and crowned him with glory and
    honor.

⁶You made him ruler over the works
    of your hands;
  you put everything under his feet:
⁷all flocks and herds,
  and the beasts of the field,
⁸the birds of the air,
  and the fish of the sea,
  all that swim the paths of the seas.

⁹O LORD, our Lord,
  how majestic is your name in all
    the earth!

Psalm 9ᵈ

For the director of music. To ⌊the tune of⌋ "The Death of the Son." A psalm of David.

¹I will praise you, O LORD, with all my
    heart;
  I will tell of all your wonders.
²I will be glad and rejoice in you;
  I will sing praise to your name,
    O Most High.

³My enemies turn back;
  they stumble and perish before
    you.

⁴For you have upheld my right and my
    cause;
  you have sat on your throne,
    judging righteously.
⁵You have rebuked the nations and
    destroyed the wicked;
  you have blotted out their name
    for ever and ever.
⁶Endless ruin has overtaken the
    enemy,
  you have uprooted their cities;
  even the memory of them has
    perished.

⁷The LORD reigns forever;
  he has established his throne for
    judgment.
⁸He will judge the world in
    righteousness;
  he will govern the peoples with
    justice.
⁹The LORD is a refuge for the
    oppressed,
  a stronghold in times of trouble.
¹⁰Those who know your name will trust
    in you,
  for you, LORD, have never forsaken
    those who seek you.

¹¹Sing praises to the LORD, enthroned
    in Zion;
  proclaim among the nations what
    he has done.
¹²For he who avenges blood
    remembers;
  he does not ignore the cry of the
    afflicted.

¹³O LORD, see how my enemies
    persecute me!
  Have mercy and lift me up from
    the gates of death,
¹⁴that I may declare your praises
  in the gates of the Daughter of
    Zion
  and there rejoice in your salvation.
¹⁵The nations have fallen into the pit
    they have dug;
  their feet are caught in the net they
    have hidden.

ᵃTitle: Probably a musical term   ᵇ2 Or *strength*
ᶜ5 Or *than God*   ᵈPsalms 9 and 10 may have
been originally a single acrostic poem, the stanzas
of which begin with the successive letters of the
Hebrew alphabet. In the Septuagint they constitute
one psalm.

¹⁶The Lord is known by his justice;
　the wicked are ensnared by the
　　work of their hands.
　　　　　　Higgaion.ᵃ Selah
¹⁷The wicked return to the grave,ᵇ
　all the nations that forget God.
¹⁸But the needy will not always be
　　forgotten,
　nor the hope of the afflicted ever
　　perish.

¹⁹Arise, O Lord, let not man triumph;
　let the nations be judged in your
　　presence.
²⁰Strike them with terror, O Lord;
　let the nations know they are but
　　men.　　　　　　　*Selah*

Psalm 10ᶜ

¹Why, O Lord, do you stand far off?
　Why do you hide yourself in times
　　of trouble?

²In his arrogance the wicked man
　　hunts down the weak,
　who are caught in the schemes he
　　devises.
³He boasts of the cravings of his heart;
　he blesses the greedy and reviles
　　the Lord.
⁴In his pride the wicked does not seek
　　him;
　in all his thoughts there is no
　　room for God.
⁵His ways are always prosperous;
　he is haughty and your laws are far
　　from him;
　he sneers at all his enemies.
⁶He says to himself, "Nothing will
　　shake me;
　I'll always be happy and never
　　have trouble."
⁷His mouth is full of curses and lies
　　and threats;
　trouble and evil are under his
　　tongue.
⁸He lies in wait near the villages;
　from ambush he murders the
　　innocent,
　watching in secret for his victims.
⁹He lies in wait like a lion in cover;
　he lies in wait to catch the
　　helpless;
　he catches the helpless and drags
　　them off in his net.

¹⁰His victims are crushed, they collapse;
　they fall under his strength.
¹¹He says to himself, "God has
　　forgotten;
　he covers his face and never sees."

¹²Arise, Lord! Lift up your hand,
　　O God.
　Do not forget the helpless.
¹³Why does the wicked man revile
　　God?
　Why does he say to himself,
　"He won't call me to account"?
¹⁴But you, O God, do see trouble and
　　grief;
　you consider it to take it in hand.
The victim commits himself to you;
　you are the helper of the fatherless.
¹⁵Break the arm of the wicked and evil
　　man;
　call him to account for his
　　wickedness
　that would not be found out.

¹⁶The Lord is King for ever and ever;
　the nations will perish from his
　　land.
¹⁷You hear, O Lord, the desire of the
　　afflicted;
　you encourage them, and you
　　listen to their cry,
¹⁸defending the fatherless and the
　　oppressed,
　in order that man, who is of the
　　earth, may terrify no more.

Psalm 11

For the director of music. Of David.

¹In the Lord I take refuge.
　How then can you say to me:
　"Flee like a bird to your mountain.
²For look, the wicked bend their bows;
　they set their arrows against the
　　strings
to shoot from the shadows
　at the upright in heart.

ᵃ16 Or *Meditation*; possibly a musical notation
ᵇ17 Hebrew *Sheol*　ᶜPsalms 9 and 10 may have
been originally a single acrostic poem, the stanzas
of which begin with the successive letters of the
Hebrew alphabet. In the Septuagint they constitute
one psalm.

³When the foundations are being
destroyed,
what can the righteous do*a*?"

⁴The LORD is in his holy temple;
the LORD is on his heavenly throne.
He observes the sons of men;
his eyes examine them.
⁵The LORD examines the righteous,
but the wicked*b* and those who
love violence
his soul hates.
⁶On the wicked he will rain
fiery coals and burning sulfur;
a scorching wind will be their lot.

⁷For the LORD is righteous,
he loves justice;
upright men will see his face.

Psalm 12

For the director of music. According to
*sheminith.*ᶜ A psalm of David.

¹Help, LORD, for the godly are no
more;
the faithful have vanished from
among men.
²Everyone lies to his neighbor;
their flattering lips speak with
deception.

³May the LORD cut off all flattering lips
and every boastful tongue
⁴that says, "We will triumph with our
tongues;
we own our lips*d*—who is our
master?"

⁵"Because of the oppression of the
weak
and the groaning of the needy,
I will now arise," says the LORD.
"I will protect them from those
who malign them."
⁶And the words of the LORD are
flawless,
like silver refined in a furnace of
clay,
purified seven times.

⁷O LORD, you will keep us safe
and protect us from such people
forever.
⁸The wicked freely strut about
when what is vile is honored
among men.

Psalm 13

For the director of music. A psalm
of David.

¹How long, O LORD? Will you forget
me forever?
How long will you hide your face
from me?
²How long must I wrestle with my
thoughts
and every day have sorrow in my
heart?
How long will my enemy triumph
over me?

³Look on me and answer, O LORD my
God.
Give light to my eyes, or I will
sleep in death;
⁴my enemy will say, "I have overcome
him,"
and my foes will rejoice when I fall.

⁵But I trust in your unfailing love;
my heart rejoices in your salvation.
⁶I will sing to the LORD,
for he has been good to me.

Psalm 14

For the director of music. Of David.

¹The fool*e* says in his heart,
"There is no God."
They are corrupt, their deeds are vile;
there is no one who does good.

²The LORD looks down from heaven
on the sons of men
to see if there are any who
understand,
any who seek God.
³All have turned aside,
they have together become corrupt;
there is no one who does good,
not even one.

⁴Will evildoers never learn—
those who devour my people as
men eat bread
and who do not call on the LORD?

---

*a*3 Or *what is the Righteous One doing*   *b*5 Or *The
LORD, the Righteous One, examines the wicked,* /
*c*Title: Probably a musical term   *d*4 Or / *our lips
are our plowshares*   *e*1 The Hebrew words
rendered *fool* in Psalms denote one who is morally
deficient.

⁵There they are, overwhelmed with
dread,
　for God is present in the company
　of the righteous.
⁶You evildoers frustrate the plans of
the poor,
　but the LORD is their refuge.

⁷Oh, that salvation for Israel would
come out of Zion!
　When the LORD restores the
　fortunes of his people,
　let Jacob rejoice and Israel be glad!

Psalm 15

A psalm of David.

¹LORD, who may dwell in your
sanctuary?
　Who may live on your holy hill?

²He whose walk is blameless
　and who does what is righteous,
who speaks the truth from his heart
³　and has no slander on his tongue,
who does his neighbor no wrong
　and casts no slur on his
　fellowman,
⁴who despises a vile man
　but honors those who fear the
　LORD,
who keeps his oath
　even when it hurts,
⁵who lends his money without usury
　and does not accept a bribe against
　the innocent.

He who does these things
　will never be shaken.

Psalm 16

A miktam ᵃ of David.

¹Keep me safe, O God,
　for in you I take refuge.

²I said to the LORD, "You are my Lord;
　apart from you I have no good
　thing."
³As for the saints who are in the land,
　they are the glorious ones in whom
　is all my delight. ᵇ
⁴The sorrows of those will increase
　who run after other gods.

I will not pour out their libations of
blood
　or take up their names on my lips.

⁵LORD, you have assigned me my
portion and my cup;
　you have made my lot secure.
⁶The boundary lines have fallen for
me in pleasant places;
　surely I have a delightful
　inheritance.

⁷I will praise the LORD, who counsels
me;
　even at night my heart instructs
　me.
⁸I have set the LORD always before me.
　Because he is at my right hand,
　I will not be shaken.

⁹Therefore my heart is glad and my
tongue rejoices;
　my body also will rest secure,
¹⁰because you will not abandon me to
the grave, ᶜ
　nor will you let your Holy One ᵈ
　see decay.
¹¹You have made ᵉ known to me the
path of life;
　you will fill me with joy in your
　presence,
　with eternal pleasures at your right
　hand.

Psalm 17

A prayer of David.

¹Hear, O LORD, my righteous plea;
　listen to my cry.
　Give ear to my prayer—
　it does not rise from deceitful lips.
²May my vindication come from you;
　may your eyes see what is right.

³Though you probe my heart and
examine me at night,
　though you test me, you will find
　nothing;
　I have resolved that my mouth will
　not sin.
⁴As for the deeds of men—
　by the word of your lips

ᵃTitle: Probably a literary or musical term
ᵇ3 Or *As for the pagan priests who are in the land /
and the nobles in whom all delight, I said:*
ᶜ10 Hebrew *Sheol*　　ᵈ10 Or *your faithful one*
ᵉ11 Or *You will make*

I have kept myself
  from the ways of the violent.
⁵My steps have held to your paths;
  my feet have not slipped.

⁶I call on you, O God, for you will
      answer me;
  give ear to me and hear my prayer.
⁷Show the wonder of your great love,
  you who save by your right hand
  those who take refuge in you from
      their foes.
⁸Keep me as the apple of your eye;
  hide me in the shadow of your
      wings
⁹from the wicked who assail me,
  from my mortal enemies who
      surround me.

¹⁰They close up their callous hearts,
  and their mouths speak with
      arrogance.

¹¹They have tracked me down, they
      now surround me,
  with eyes alert, to throw me to the
      ground.
¹²They are like a lion hungry for prey,
  like a great lion crouching in cover.

¹³Rise up, O LORD, confront them,
      bring them down;
  rescue me from the wicked by your
      sword.
¹⁴O LORD, by your hand save me from
      such men,
  from men of this world whose
      reward is in this life.

You still the hunger of those you
      cherish;
  their sons have plenty,
  and they store up wealth for their
      children.
¹⁵And I—in righteousness I will see your
      face;

My Father Knows About This

PSALM 16:5-6 Marriage brings the unexpected into our lives. The blessings we receive in marriage make us feel loved by God, but the tragedies often make us feel alone.

When our first child Torrey was a year old, she had two years of neurological problems. Night after night we worried about our daughter's health and future. In the isolation of pain, we began to wonder if God knew what we were going through. Was God busy someplace else? Would we get through this? Worse yet, would we go through this alone?

David reminds us that God has assigned each of his children the portions and cups in life. Whether today's cup runs over with blessings, or it's a cup that we would ask to have removed, God knows. He will keep us secure even in the midst of storms. He has established the boundaries so that nothing can be poured into our cup that is more than

we can endure. Nothing can come into our cup that he has not allowed or isn't aware of.

Going from one doctor to the next, looking for answers, made for a long two years of worry. But over and over, during our deepest moments of fear, we saw the hand of God come to our rescue.

All of us must deal with the difficulties of today, but we are not alone. God is with us; he has established our inheritance. He knows the rest of our story. Best of all, the Lord's prayer reminds us that our God in heaven is also our Father. That title Father indicates that he is more than just an observer. He is our Father and will take care of us as such. No matter what the circumstances, we need to focus on the fact that God our Father knows all about our life—no matter what cup we receive.

—*Bob & Rosemary*

 Weekend Warm-up   *When have you experienced God's love as that of a father?*

Go to page 574 for your next devotional reading.

when I awake, I will be satisfied
with seeing your likeness.

Psalm 18

For the director of music. Of David the
servant of the LORD. He sang to the
LORD the words of this song when the
LORD delivered him from the hand of
all his enemies and from the hand
of Saul. He said:

¹I love you, O LORD, my strength.

²The LORD is my rock, my fortress and
my deliverer;
my God is my rock, in whom I
take refuge.
He is my shield and the horn*ᵃ* of
my salvation, my stronghold.
³I call to the LORD, who is worthy of
praise,
and I am saved from my enemies.

⁴The cords of death entangled me;
the torrents of destruction
overwhelmed me.
⁵The cords of the grave*ᵇ* coiled
around me;
the snares of death confronted me.
⁶In my distress I called to the LORD;
I cried to my God for help.
From his temple he heard my voice;
my cry came before him, into his
ears.

⁷The earth trembled and quaked,
and the foundations of the
mountains shook;
they trembled because he was
angry.
⁸Smoke rose from his nostrils;
consuming fire came from his
mouth,
burning coals blazed out of it.
⁹He parted the heavens and came
down;
dark clouds were under his feet.
¹⁰He mounted the cherubim and flew;
he soared on the wings of the
wind.
¹¹He made darkness his covering, his
canopy around him —
the dark rain clouds of the sky.
¹²Out of the brightness of his presence
clouds advanced,
with hailstones and bolts of
lightning.

¹³The LORD thundered from heaven;
the voice of the Most High
resounded.*ᶜ*
¹⁴He shot his arrows and scattered ⌊the
enemies⌋,
great bolts of lightning and routed
them.
¹⁵The valleys of the sea were exposed
and the foundations of the earth
laid bare
at your rebuke, O LORD,
at the blast of breath from your
nostrils.

¹⁶He reached down from on high and
took hold of me;
he drew me out of deep waters.
¹⁷He rescued me from my powerful
enemy,
from my foes, who were too strong
for me.
¹⁸They confronted me in the day of my
disaster,
but the LORD was my support.
¹⁹He brought me out into a spacious
place;
he rescued me because he
delighted in me.

²⁰The LORD has dealt with me
according to my
righteousness;
according to the cleanness of my
hands he has rewarded me.
²¹For I have kept the ways of the LORD;
I have not done evil by turning
from my God.
²²All his laws are before me;
I have not turned away from his
decrees.
²³I have been blameless before him
and have kept myself from sin.
²⁴The LORD has rewarded me according
to my righteousness,
according to the cleanness of my
hands in his sight.

²⁵To the faithful you show yourself
faithful,
to the blameless you show yourself
blameless,
²⁶to the pure you show yourself pure,

*ᵃ2 Horn here symbolizes strength.   ᵇ5 Hebrew
Sheol   ᶜ13 Some Hebrew manuscripts and
Septuagint (see also 2 Samuel 22:14); most
Hebrew manuscripts resounded, / amid hailstones
and bolts of lightning*

but to the crooked you show
    yourself shrewd.
²⁷You save the humble
    but bring low those whose eyes are
        haughty.
²⁸You, O LORD, keep my lamp burning;
    my God turns my darkness into
        light.
²⁹With your help I can advance against
    a troop*a*;
    with my God I can scale a wall.

³⁰As for God, his way is perfect;
    the word of the LORD is flawless.
He is a shield
    for all who take refuge in him.
³¹For who is God besides the LORD?
    And who is the Rock except our
        God?
³²It is God who arms me with strength
    and makes my way perfect.
³³He makes my feet like the feet of a
        deer;
    he enables me to stand on the
        heights.
³⁴He trains my hands for battle;
    my arms can bend a bow of
        bronze.
³⁵You give me your shield of victory,
    and your right hand sustains me;
    you stoop down to make me great.
³⁶You broaden the path beneath me,
    so that my ankles do not turn.

³⁷I pursued my enemies and overtook
        them;
    I did not turn back till they were
        destroyed.
³⁸I crushed them so that they could not
        rise;
    they fell beneath my feet.
³⁹You armed me with strength for
        battle;
    you made my adversaries bow at
        my feet.
⁴⁰You made my enemies turn their
        backs in flight,
    and I destroyed my foes.
⁴¹They cried for help, but there was no
        one to save them—
    to the LORD, but he did not
        answer.
⁴²I beat them as fine as dust borne on
        the wind;
    I poured them out like mud in the
        streets.

⁴³You have delivered me from the
        attacks of the people;
    you have made me the head of
        nations;
    people I did not know are subject
        to me.
⁴⁴As soon as they hear me, they obey
        me;
    foreigners cringe before me.
⁴⁵They all lose heart;
    they come trembling from their
        strongholds.

⁴⁶The LORD lives! Praise be to my Rock!
    Exalted be God my Savior!
⁴⁷He is the God who avenges me,
    who subdues nations under me,
⁴⁸   who saves me from my enemies.
You exalted me above my foes;
    from violent men you rescued me.
⁴⁹Therefore I will praise you among the
    nations, O LORD;
    I will sing praises to your name.
⁵⁰He gives his king great victories;
    he shows unfailing kindness to his
        anointed,
    to David and his descendants
        forever.

Psalm 19

For the director of music. A psalm
of David.

¹The heavens declare the glory of God;
    the skies proclaim the work of his
        hands.
²Day after day they pour forth speech;
    night after night they display
        knowledge.
³There is no speech or language
    where their voice is not heard.*b*
⁴Their voice*c* goes out into all the
        earth,
    their words to the ends of the
        world.

In the heavens he has pitched a tent
    for the sun,
⁵   which is like a bridegroom coming
        forth from his pavilion,
    like a champion rejoicing to run
        his course.

a29 Or *can run through a barricade*   *b3* Or *They
have no speech, there are no words; / no sound is heard
from them*   *c4* Septuagint, Jerome and Syriac;
Hebrew *line*

⁶It rises at one end of the heavens
  and makes its circuit to the
    other;
  nothing is hidden from its heat.

⁷The law of the LORD is perfect,
  reviving the soul.
The statutes of the LORD are
    trustworthy,
  making wise the simple.
⁸The precepts of the LORD are right,
  giving joy to the heart.
The commands of the LORD are
    radiant,
  giving light to the eyes.
⁹The fear of the LORD is pure,
  enduring forever.
The ordinances of the LORD are sure
  and altogether righteous.
¹⁰They are more precious than gold,
  than much pure gold;
  they are sweeter than honey,
  than honey from the comb.
¹¹By them is your servant warned;
  in keeping them there is great
    reward.

¹²Who can discern his errors?
  Forgive my hidden faults.
¹³Keep your servant also from willful
    sins;
  may they not rule over me.
Then will I be blameless,
  innocent of great transgression.

¹⁴May the words of my mouth and the
    meditation of my heart
  be pleasing in your sight,
  O LORD, my Rock and my
    Redeemer.

Psalm 20

*For the director of music. A psalm
of David.*

¹May the LORD answer you when you
    are in distress;
  may the name of the God of Jacob
    protect you.
²May he send you help from the
    sanctuary
  and grant you support from Zion.
³May he remember all your sacrifices
  and accept your burnt offerings.
                                    Selah

⁴May he give you the desire of your
    heart
  and make all your plans succeed.
⁵We will shout for joy when you are
    victorious
  and will lift up our banners in the
    name of our God.
May the LORD grant all your requests.

⁶Now I know that the LORD saves his
    anointed;
  he answers him from his holy
    heaven
  with the saving power of his right
    hand.
⁷Some trust in chariots and some in
    horses,
  but we trust in the name of the
    LORD our God.
⁸They are brought to their knees and
    fall,
  but we rise up and stand firm.

⁹O LORD, save the king!
  Answer*ᵃ* us when we call!

Psalm 21

*For the director of music. A psalm
of David.*

¹O LORD, the king rejoices in your
    strength.
  How great is his joy in the victories
    you give!
²You have granted him the desire of
    his heart
  and have not withheld the request
    of his lips.   *Selah*
³You welcomed him with rich
    blessings
  and placed a crown of pure gold
    on his head.
⁴He asked you for life, and you gave it
    to him—
  length of days, for ever and ever.
⁵Through the victories you gave, his
    glory is great;
  you have bestowed on him
    splendor and majesty.
⁶Surely you have granted him eternal
    blessings
  and made him glad with the joy of
    your presence.
⁷For the king trusts in the LORD;

ᵃ9 Or *save! / O King, answer*

through the unfailing love of the
Most High
he will not be shaken.

8Your hand will lay hold on all your
enemies;
your right hand will seize your
foes.
9At the time of your appearing
you will make them like a fiery
furnace.
In his wrath the LORD will swallow
them up,
and his fire will consume them.
10You will destroy their descendants
from the earth,
their posterity from mankind.
11Though they plot evil against you
and devise wicked schemes, they
cannot succeed;
12for you will make them turn their
backs
when you aim at them with drawn
bow.

13Be exalted, O LORD, in your strength;
we will sing and praise your might.

Psalm 22

For the director of music. To ⌞the tune
of⌟ "The Doe of the Morning." A psalm
of David.

1My God, my God, why have you
forsaken me?
Why are you so far from saving
me,
so far from the words of my
groaning?
2O my God, I cry out by day, but you
do not answer,
by night, and am not silent.

3Yet you are enthroned as the Holy
One;
you are the praise of Israel.*a*
4In you our fathers put their trust;
they trusted and you delivered
them.
5They cried to you and were saved;
in you they trusted and were not
disappointed.

*a3 Or Yet you are holy, / enthroned on the praises of
Israel*

Marriage Goals

Monday

PSALM 20:4 Wouldn't it be great if all of our plans succeeded and we always got our heart's desire? While trusting God doesn't guarantee success, wise couples plan and set goals for their marriage. No matter how long you have been married, taking an annual check-up and setting goals is a smart thing to do.

First, look at your marriage as it is now. In your relationship, which of your heart desires have you already experienced? Second, consider what areas in your relationship need some work. Think about what you can do to strengthen these and choose one to start with. End your check-up by looking toward the future. What are your hopes and dreams—what are you looking forward to?

Marriage check-ups don't have to be complicated. You can have one almost anywhere. Once we did a check-up on a paper place mat over potato skins and two glasses of iced tea. Actually, as we write this devo-

tion, we are sitting in a small Austrian restaurant, sipping cups of coffee and sharing a piece of Sacher Torte (our favorite Viennese cake); we just took our own marriage check-up. We talked about some of the positive aspects of our marriage such as our good communication, flexibility, sense of adventure, ability to laugh together and our love life. Next we discussed areas we need to work on and picked one—getting more exercise—to start with. Last, we talked about things we are looking forward to this next year. We proclaimed that this year we are going to reorganize—starting with a bedroom make over (without a television).

Now it's your turn. Look at the questions next to this devotion. Then ask for God's blessing on your goals and be open to how he may adapt them to fit your true needs.

—*Dave & Claudia*

Go to page 576 for your next devotional reading.

⁶But I am a worm and not a man,
   scorned by men and despised by
      the people.
⁷All who see me mock me;
   they hurl insults, shaking their
      heads:
⁸"He trusts in the LORD;
   let the LORD rescue him.
 Let him deliver him,
   since he delights in him."

⁹Yet you brought me out of the
      womb;
   you made me trust in you
   even at my mother's breast.
¹⁰From birth I was cast upon you;
   from my mother's womb you have
      been my God.
¹¹Do not be far from me,
   for trouble is near
   and there is no one to help.

¹²Many bulls surround me;
   strong bulls of Bashan encircle me.
¹³Roaring lions tearing their prey
   open their mouths wide against
      me.
¹⁴I am poured out like water,
   and all my bones are out of joint.
 My heart has turned to wax;
   it has melted away within me.
¹⁵My strength is dried up like a
      potsherd,
   and my tongue sticks to the roof of
      my mouth;
 you lay me^a in the dust of death.
¹⁶Dogs have surrounded me;
   a band of evil men has encircled
      me,
   they have pierced^b my hands and
      my feet.
¹⁷I can count all my bones;
   people stare and gloat over me.
¹⁸They divide my garments among
      them
   and cast lots for my clothing.

¹⁹But you, O LORD, be not far off;
   O my Strength, come quickly to
      help me.
²⁰Deliver my life from the sword,
   my precious life from the power of
      the dogs.
²¹Rescue me from the mouth of the
      lions;

Marriage Goals

God's desires your marriage to succeed and to be successful. He is committed to you and to your marriage. How committed are you to your spouse? To evaluate where you are in your marriage, answer the following questions:

1. What are three things that are positive about my marriage?

2. What are two things about my marriage that are OK but could be better?

3. What is one thing I could (on my own) do to improve my marriage?

   save^c me from the horns of the
      wild oxen.

²²I will declare your name to my
      brothers;
   in the congregation I will praise
      you.
²³You who fear the LORD, praise him!
   All you descendants of Jacob,
      honor him!
 Revere him, all you descendants of
      Israel!
²⁴For he has not despised or disdained
   the suffering of the afflicted one;
 he has not hidden his face from him
   but has listened to his cry for help.

²⁵From you comes the theme of my
      praise in the great assembly;
   before those who fear you^d will I
      fulfill my vows.
²⁶The poor will eat and be satisfied;
   they who seek the LORD will praise
      him—
   may your hearts live forever!
²⁷All the ends of the earth
   will remember and turn to the
      LORD,
 and all the families of the nations
   will bow down before him,

^a15 Or / I am laid   ^b16 Some Hebrew
manuscripts, Septuagint and Syriac; most Hebrew
manuscripts / like the lion,   ^c21 Or / you have
heard   ^d25 Hebrew him

²⁸for dominion belongs to the LORD
and he rules over the nations.
²⁹All the rich of the earth will feast and
worship;
all who go down to the dust will
kneel before him—
those who cannot keep themselves
alive.
³⁰Posterity will serve him;
future generations will be told
about the Lord.
³¹They will proclaim his righteousness
to a people yet unborn—
for he has done it.

Psalm 23

A psalm of David.

¹The LORD is my shepherd, I shall not
be in want.
²   He makes me lie down in green
pastures,
he leads me beside quiet waters,
³   he restores my soul.
He guides me in paths of
righteousness
for his name's sake.
⁴Even though I walk
through the valley of the shadow
of death, ᵃ

I will fear no evil,
for you are with me;
your rod and your staff,
they comfort me.

⁵You prepare a table before me
in the presence of my enemies.
You anoint my head with oil;
my cup overflows.
⁶Surely goodness and love will follow
me
all the days of my life,
and I will dwell in the house of the
LORD
forever.

Psalm 24

Of David. A psalm.

¹The earth is the LORD's, and
everything in it,
the world, and all who live in it;
²for he founded it upon the seas
and established it upon the waters.

³Who may ascend the hill of the LORD?
Who may stand in his holy place?

ᵃ4 Or *through the darkest valley*

A Significant Need

Tuesday

PSALM 23 During the first year of our marriage, a marriage book uncovered a secret neither of us wanted to face. It showed us how we were each counting on the other person to make us feel significant. At a subconscious level, I (Les) was saying, "I need to feel important. I expect you to meet that need by respecting me no matter how I behave and by supporting me in whatever I choose to do. I want you to treat me as the most important person in the world. My goal in marrying you was to find my significance through you." Leslie had a similar unconscious message: "I have never felt as deeply loved as my nature requires. I am expecting you to meet that need through gentle affection even when I'm in a bad mood or not being sensitive to what you need. Don't let me down."

This was hard to swallow, but it was true. We each desperately wanted the other person to meet our need for significance, even though this was an unrealistic expectation for any person.

So are we stuck, forever floundering between fleeting moments of relational fulfillment? Fortunately not. While our earthly relationships will let us down time and again, our relationship with God can genuinely and fully meet our deepest need for significance. And Psalm 23 stands as a poetic reminder to every married person that, no matter how difficult loving your spouse can be, you can rely on the Lord as your Shepherd to restore your soul, comfort you and meet your deepest needs.

—Les & Leslie

Go to page 578 for your next devotional reading.

4He who has clean hands and a pure
heart,
who does not lift up his soul to an
idol
or swear by what is false. *a*
5He will receive blessing from the
LORD
and vindication from God his
Savior.
6Such is the generation of those who
seek him,
who seek your face, O God of
Jacob. *b*   Selah

7Lift up your heads, O you gates;
be lifted up, you ancient doors,
that the King of glory may come
in.
8Who is this King of glory?
The LORD strong and mighty,
the LORD mighty in battle.
9Lift up your heads, O you gates;
lift them up, you ancient doors,
that the King of glory may come
in.
10Who is he, this King of glory?
The LORD Almighty—
he is the King of glory.   Selah

Psalm 25 *c*

Of David.

1To you, O LORD, I lift up my soul;
2 in you I trust, O my God.
Do not let me be put to shame,
nor let my enemies triumph over
me.
3No one whose hope is in you
will ever be put to shame,
but they will be put to shame
who are treacherous without
excuse.

4Show me your ways, O LORD,
teach me your paths;
5guide me in your truth and teach me,
for you are God my Savior,
and my hope is in you all day
long.
6Remember, O LORD, your great mercy
and love,
for they are from of old.
7Remember not the sins of my youth
and my rebellious ways;

according to your love remember me,
for you are good, O LORD.

8Good and upright is the LORD;
therefore he instructs sinners in his
ways.
9He guides the humble in what is right
and teaches them his way.
10All the ways of the LORD are loving
and faithful
for those who keep the demands of
his covenant.
11For the sake of your name, O LORD,
forgive my iniquity, though it is
great.
12Who, then, is the man that fears the
LORD?
He will instruct him in the way
chosen for him.
13He will spend his days in prosperity,
and his descendants will inherit the
land.
14The LORD confides in those who fear
him;
he makes his covenant known to
them.
15My eyes are ever on the LORD,
for only he will release my feet
from the snare.

16Turn to me and be gracious to me,
for I am lonely and afflicted.
17The troubles of my heart have
multiplied;
free me from my anguish.
18Look upon my affliction and my
distress
and take away all my sins.
19See how my enemies have increased
and how fiercely they hate me!
20Guard my life and rescue me;
let me not be put to shame,
for I take refuge in you.
21May integrity and uprightness protect
me,
because my hope is in you.

22Redeem Israel, O God,
from all their troubles!

a4 Or *swear falsely*   b6 Two Hebrew
manuscripts and Syriac (see also Septuagint); most
Hebrew manuscripts *face, Jacob*   cThis psalm is
an acrostic poem, the verses of which begin with
the successive letters of the Hebrew alphabet.

Psalm 26

Of David.

[1] Vindicate me, O LORD,
for I have led a blameless life;
I have trusted in the LORD
without wavering.
[2] Test me, O LORD, and try me,
examine my heart and my mind;
[3] for your love is ever before me,
and I walk continually in your
truth.
[4] I do not sit with deceitful men,
nor do I consort with hypocrites;
[5] I abhor the assembly of evildoers
and refuse to sit with the wicked.
[6] I wash my hands in innocence,
and go about your altar, O LORD,
[7] proclaiming aloud your praise
and telling of all your wonderful
deeds.
[8] I love the house where you live,
O LORD,
the place where your glory dwells.

[9] Do not take away my soul along with
sinners,
my life with bloodthirsty men,
[10] in whose hands are wicked schemes,
whose right hands are full of
bribes.
[11] But I lead a blameless life;
redeem me and be merciful to me.

[12] My feet stand on level ground;
in the great assembly I will praise
the LORD.

Psalm 27

Of David.

[1] The LORD is my light and my
salvation—
whom shall I fear?
The LORD is the stronghold of my
life—
of whom shall I be afraid?
[2] When evil men advance against me

Getting Past Land Mines

Wednesday

PSALM 25:15 We had been married for five years when Rosemary got pregnant with our first child. Even though there had been plenty of time to prepare for this child, we were not prepared financially. The fact that we were both in graduate school meant that we had no medical insurance. Everywhere we turned there was another new expense, and it became overwhelming. I was so worried about the finances that I began to isolate myself in fear. I didn't want to cause Rosemary to worry, so I kept it all to myself.

Sometimes it seems as if life is a minefield of loneliness. It seems that everywhere a person steps, a lonely, isolating moment explodes in his or her face. The stress of one problem after another can make a person feel very much alone. The question is, How does one walk through this minefield?

In this psalm David is talking about more than feeling lonely. He's talking about a time in his life when everyone around him seemed to be against him. Even though he

probably had others with him, he felt lonely and afflicted. Anywhere he stepped, a land mine was waiting to explode.

When job difficulties, financial problems, health issues or other challenges of life press in on husbands and wives, we need to guide each other through the minefield. Though the oppressed spouse might be weighed down with the problems, the guiding spouse needs to help the other focus on the one thing that will get them through the explosions—God.

Fixing the immediate problem is only a temporary solution. Just as soon as one mine is deactivated, another will inevitably appear. Work on the problems, but also fix your eyes on God. Minefields or not, in good times or bad, God needs to be the focus of our lives. When your spouse is in a minefield situation, come alongside him or her to help regain that focus.

—Bob & Rosemary

Go to page 582 for your next devotional reading.

to devour my flesh,[a]
when my enemies and my foes attack
me,
they will stumble and fall.
[3]Though an army besiege me,
my heart will not fear;
though war break out against me,
even then will I be confident.

[4]One thing I ask of the LORD,
this is what I seek:
that I may dwell in the house of the
LORD
all the days of my life,
to gaze upon the beauty of the LORD
and to seek him in his temple.
[5]For in the day of trouble
he will keep me safe in his
dwelling;
he will hide me in the shelter of his
tabernacle
and set me high upon a rock.
[6]Then my head will be exalted
above the enemies who surround
me;
at his tabernacle will I sacrifice with
shouts of joy;
I will sing and make music to the
LORD.

[7]Hear my voice when I call, O LORD;
be merciful to me and answer me.
[8]My heart says of you, "Seek his[b]
face!"
Your face, LORD, I will seek.
[9]Do not hide your face from me,
do not turn your servant away in
anger;
you have been my helper.
Do not reject me or forsake me,
O God my Savior.
[10]Though my father and mother forsake
me,
the LORD will receive me.
[11]Teach me your way, O LORD;
lead me in a straight path
because of my oppressors.
[12]Do not turn me over to the desire of
my foes,
for false witnesses rise up against
me,
breathing out violence.

[13]I am still confident of this:
I will see the goodness of the LORD
in the land of the living.
[14]Wait for the LORD;

JUST BETWEEN you & me

Getting Past Land Mines

Take a moment to answer each of these
questions on your own. Then compare your
answers to your spouse's.

Yes No When a conflict arises, do you
take time before you take action?

Yes No Do you respond carefully rather
than react emotionally?

Yes No Do you attack the problem rather
than the person?

Yes No When discussing the conflict, is
your goal to restore the relationship rather than win an argument?

be strong and take heart
and wait for the LORD.

Psalm 28

Of David.

[1]To you I call, O LORD my Rock;
do not turn a deaf ear to me.
For if you remain silent,
I will be like those who have gone
down to the pit.
[2]Hear my cry for mercy
as I call to you for help,
as I lift up my hands
toward your Most Holy Place.

[3]Do not drag me away with the
wicked,
with those who do evil,
who speak cordially with their
neighbors
but harbor malice in their hearts.
[4]Repay them for their deeds
and for their evil work;
repay them for what their hands have
done
and bring back upon them what
they deserve.
[5]Since they show no regard for the
works of the LORD

[a]2 Or to slander me   [b]8 Or To you, O my heart,
he has said, "Seek my

and what his hands have done,
he will tear them down
and never build them up again.

[6]Praise be to the LORD,
for he has heard my cry for mercy.
[7]The LORD is my strength and my
shield;
my heart trusts in him, and I am
helped.
My heart leaps for joy
and I will give thanks to him in
song.

[8]The LORD is the strength of his
people,
a fortress of salvation for his
anointed one.
[9]Save your people and bless your
inheritance;
be their shepherd and carry them
forever.

Psalm 29

A psalm of David.

[1]Ascribe to the LORD, O mighty ones,
ascribe to the LORD glory and
strength.
[2]Ascribe to the LORD the glory due his
name;
worship the LORD in the splendor
of his[a] holiness.

[3]The voice of the LORD is over the
waters;
the God of glory thunders,
the LORD thunders over the mighty
waters.
[4]The voice of the LORD is powerful;
the voice of the LORD is majestic.
[5]The voice of the LORD breaks the
cedars;
the LORD breaks in pieces the
cedars of Lebanon.
[6]He makes Lebanon skip like a calf,
Sirion[b] like a young wild ox.
[7]The voice of the LORD strikes
with flashes of lightning.
[8]The voice of the LORD shakes the
desert;
the LORD shakes the Desert of
Kadesh.
[9]The voice of the LORD twists the
oaks[c]

and strips the forests bare.
And in his temple all cry, "Glory!"

[10]The LORD sits[d] enthroned over the
flood;
the LORD is enthroned as King
forever.
[11]The LORD gives strength to his people;
the LORD blesses his people with
peace.

Psalm 30

A psalm. A song. For the dedication of
the temple.[e] Of David.

[1]I will exalt you, O LORD,
for you lifted me out of the depths
and did not let my enemies gloat
over me.
[2]O LORD my God, I called to you for
help
and you healed me.
[3]O LORD, you brought me up from the
grave[f];
you spared me from going down
into the pit.

[4]Sing to the LORD, you saints of his;
praise his holy name.
[5]For his anger lasts only a moment,
but his favor lasts a lifetime;
weeping may remain for a night,
but rejoicing comes in the
morning.

[6]When I felt secure, I said,
"I will never be shaken."
[7]O LORD, when you favored me,
you made my mountain[g] stand
firm;
but when you hid your face,
I was dismayed.

[8]To you, O LORD, I called;
to the Lord I cried for mercy:
[9]"What gain is there in my
destruction,[h]
in my going down into the pit?
Will the dust praise you?
Will it proclaim your faithfulness?
[10]Hear, O LORD, and be merciful to me;
O LORD, be my help."

---

[a]2 Or LORD with the splendor of   [b]6 That is,
Mount Hermon   [c]9 Or LORD makes the deer give
birth   [d]10 Or sat   [e]Title: Or palace
[f]3 Hebrew Sheol   [g]7 Or hill country   [h]9 Or
there if I am silenced

¹¹You turned my wailing into dancing;
you removed my sackcloth and
clothed me with joy,
¹²that my heart may sing to you and
not be silent.
O Lord my God, I will give you
thanks forever.

Psalm 31

For the director of music. A psalm
of David.

¹In you, O Lord, I have taken refuge;
let me never be put to shame;
deliver me in your righteousness.
²Turn your ear to me,
come quickly to my rescue;
be my rock of refuge,
a strong fortress to save me.
³Since you are my rock and my
fortress,
for the sake of your name lead and
guide me.
⁴Free me from the trap that is set for
me,
for you are my refuge.
⁵Into your hands I commit my spirit;
redeem me, O Lord, the God of
truth.

⁶I hate those who cling to worthless
idols;
I trust in the Lord.
⁷I will be glad and rejoice in your
love,
for you saw my affliction
and knew the anguish of my soul.
⁸You have not handed me over to the
enemy
but have set my feet in a spacious
place.

⁹Be merciful to me, O Lord, for I am
in distress;
my eyes grow weak with sorrow,
my soul and my body with grief.
¹⁰My life is consumed by anguish
and my years by groaning;
my strength fails because of my
affliction,ᵃ
and my bones grow weak.
¹¹Because of all my enemies,
I am the utter contempt of my
neighbors;

I am a dread to my friends—
those who see me on the street flee
from me.
¹²I am forgotten by them as though I
were dead;
I have become like broken pottery.
¹³For I hear the slander of many;
there is terror on every side;
they conspire against me
and plot to take my life.

¹⁴But I trust in you, O Lord;
I say, "You are my God."
¹⁵My times are in your hands;
deliver me from my enemies
and from those who pursue me.
¹⁶Let your face shine on your servant;
save me in your unfailing love.
¹⁷Let me not be put to shame, O Lord,
for I have cried out to you;
but let the wicked be put to shame
and lie silent in the grave.ᵇ
¹⁸Let their lying lips be silenced,
for with pride and contempt
they speak arrogantly against the
righteous.

¹⁹How great is your goodness,
which you have stored up for those
who fear you,
which you bestow in the sight of men
on those who take refuge in you.
²⁰In the shelter of your presence you
hide them
from the intrigues of men;
in your dwelling you keep them safe
from accusing tongues.

²¹Praise be to the Lord,
for he showed his wonderful love
to me
when I was in a besieged city.
²²In my alarm I said,
"I am cut off from your sight!"
Yet you heard my cry for mercy
when I called to you for help.

²³Love the Lord, all his saints!
The Lord preserves the faithful,
but the proud he pays back in full.
²⁴Be strong and take heart,
all you who hope in the Lord.

ᵃ10 Or guilt   ᵇ17 Hebrew Sheol

Psalm 32

Of David. A *maskil.* ^a

¹Blessed is he
　　whose transgressions are forgiven,
　　whose sins are covered.
²Blessed is the man
　　whose sin the LORD does not count
　　　against him
　　and in whose spirit is no deceit.

³When I kept silent,
　　my bones wasted away
　　through my groaning all day long.
⁴For day and night
　　your hand was heavy upon me;
　my strength was sapped
　　as in the heat of summer.　　*Selah*
⁵Then I acknowledged my sin to you
　　and did not cover up my iniquity.
　I said, "I will confess
　　my transgressions to the LORD"—

and you forgave
　　the guilt of my sin.　　*Selah*

⁶Therefore let everyone who is godly
　　pray to you
　　while you may be found;
　surely when the mighty waters rise,
　　they will not reach him.
⁷You are my hiding place;
　　you will protect me from trouble
　　and surround me with songs of
　　　deliverance.　　*Selah*

⁸I will instruct you and teach you in
　　the way you should go;
　I will counsel you and watch over
　　you.
⁹Do not be like the horse or the mule,
　　which have no understanding
　but must be controlled by bit and
　　bridle
　　or they will not come to you.

---

^aTitle: Probably a literary or musical term

Good for the Bones

Thursday

PSALM 32:1–2 One of the loneliest times in a marriage is when there is unresolved conflict. Feelings of pain, misunderstanding and guilt can build walls between two people who love each other. David reminds us that when we are forgiven by God and by our spouse, our sin is not counted against us.

Asking for forgiveness and granting forgiveness are some of the most healing experiences we can have. Forgiveness is the beginning of resolving a conflict. It's the beginning of breaking down the walls between two people. We will always make mistakes, because no one is perfect. Spouses will hurt each other, whether it's intentional or unintentional. So it's important to decide ahead of time to be quick to forgive and quick to ask sincerely for forgiveness.

During the first few years of our marriage, sports leagues were very important to me (Bob). During softball season I scheduled myself into as many games as I could. It was something that was robbing my marriage of time, but I didn't realize it. During

one game, as I looked over to the sidelines and saw my sweet wife sitting alone watching me play, it hit me how selfish I had become. Later that night as we were talking, I decided it was time for me to devote my energy to our marriage. I asked Rosemary to forgive my selfishness, and this began a new stage in our marriage relationship.

Psalm 32:3–4 describes the distress a person feels when confession has not been made. Confession and forgiveness don't just heal the marriage relationship; they also heal the individual. The inner turmoil of David feeling as if his bones were wasting away because he kept silent graphically describes a person experiencing tremendous emotional pain. Not being forgiven can consume and hurt us as individuals and as couples. As difficult as it may be to admit wrong or forgive wrong, it is mandatory for our well being. Sincere confession and forgiveness should be practiced so regularly that they become a healthy cleansing habit in our lives.　　**—Bob & Rosemary**

Go to page 584 for your next devotional reading.

¹⁰Many are the woes of the wicked,
  but the LORD's unfailing love
  surrounds the man who trusts in
  him.

¹¹Rejoice in the LORD and be glad, you
  righteous;
  sing, all you who are upright in
  heart!

Psalm 33

¹Sing joyfully to the LORD, you
  righteous;
  it is fitting for the upright to praise
  him.
²Praise the LORD with the harp;
  make music to him on the
  ten-stringed lyre.
³Sing to him a new song;
  play skillfully, and shout for joy.

⁴For the word of the LORD is right and
  true;
  he is faithful in all he does.
⁵The LORD loves righteousness and
  justice;
  the earth is full of his unfailing
  love.

⁶By the word of the LORD were the
  heavens made,
  their starry host by the breath of
  his mouth.
⁷He gathers the waters of the sea into
  jars*a*;
  he puts the deep into storehouses.
⁸Let all the earth fear the LORD;
  let all the people of the world
  revere him.
⁹For he spoke, and it came to be;
  he commanded, and it stood firm.
¹⁰The LORD foils the plans of the
  nations;
  he thwarts the purposes of the
  peoples.
¹¹But the plans of the LORD stand firm
  forever,
  the purposes of his heart through
  all generations.

¹²Blessed is the nation whose God is
  the LORD,
  the people he chose for his
  inheritance.
¹³From heaven the LORD looks down
  and sees all mankind;
¹⁴from his dwelling place he watches

all who live on earth—
¹⁵he who forms the hearts of all,
  who considers everything they do.
¹⁶No king is saved by the size of his
  army;
  no warrior escapes by his great
  strength.
¹⁷A horse is a vain hope for
  deliverance;
  despite all its great strength it
  cannot save.
¹⁸But the eyes of the LORD are on those
  who fear him,
  on those whose hope is in his
  unfailing love,
¹⁹to deliver them from death
  and keep them alive in famine.

²⁰We wait in hope for the LORD;
  he is our help and our shield.
²¹In him our hearts rejoice,
  for we trust in his holy name.
²²May your unfailing love rest upon us,
  O LORD,
  even as we put our hope in you.

Psalm 34*b*

Of David. When he pretended to be
insane before Abimelech, who drove
  him away, and he left.

¹I will extol the LORD at all times;
  his praise will always be on my
  lips.
²My soul will boast in the LORD;
  let the afflicted hear and rejoice.
³Glorify the LORD with me;
  let us exalt his name together.

⁴I sought the LORD, and he answered
  me;
  he delivered me from all my fears.
⁵Those who look to him are radiant;
  their faces are never covered with
  shame.
⁶This poor man called, and the LORD
  heard him;
  he saved him out of all his
  troubles.
⁷The angel of the LORD encamps
  around those who fear him,
  and he delivers them.

---

*a*7 Or *sea as into a heap*   *b*This psalm is an
acrostic poem, the verses of which begin with the
successive letters of the Hebrew alphabet.

⁸Taste and see that the LORD is good;
　　blessed is the man who takes
　　　refuge in him.
⁹Fear the LORD, you his saints,
　　for those who fear him lack
　　　nothing.
¹⁰The lions may grow weak and
　　　hungry,
　　but those who seek the LORD lack
　　　no good thing.

¹¹Come, my children, listen to me;
　　I will teach you the fear of the
　　　LORD.
¹²Whoever of you loves life
　　and desires to see many good days,
¹³keep your tongue from evil
　　and your lips from speaking lies.
¹⁴Turn from evil and do good;
　　seek peace and pursue it.

¹⁵The eyes of the LORD are on the
　　　righteous
　　and his ears are attentive to their
　　　cry;
¹⁶the face of the LORD is against those
　　who do evil,
　　to cut off the memory of them
　　　from the earth.

¹⁷The righteous cry out, and the LORD
　　hears them;
　　he delivers them from all their
　　　troubles.

¹⁸The LORD is close to the
　　brokenhearted
　　and saves those who are crushed in
　　　spirit.

¹⁹A righteous man may have many
　　　troubles,
　　but the LORD delivers him from
　　　them all;
²⁰he protects all his bones,
　　not one of them will be broken.

²¹Evil will slay the wicked;
　　the foes of the righteous will be
　　condemned.
²²The LORD redeems his servants;
　　no one will be condemned who
　　　takes refuge in him.

Psalm 35

Of David.

¹Contend, O LORD, with those who
　　contend with me;
　　fight against those who fight
　　against me.
²Take up shield and buckler;
　　arise and come to my aid.
³Brandish spear and javelin*ᵃ*
　　against those who pursue me.

ᵃ3 Or and block the way

Your Holy Calling

Friday

PSALM 34:3 Marriage is a mystery—a wonderful mystery with a unique, holy calling. You can live out your marriage in such a way that it will show others what God is like. What we need today is a widespread movement of Christian marriages that show others how to love and serve each other.

Our friends Paul and Phyllis Stanley have been great models. Paul is an international vice-president of the Navigator ministry. As newlyweds they chose Psalm 34:3 as their marriage verse. Throughout the decades we have known Paul and Phyllis, they have consistently lived out this verse. We remember the first time we were in their home in Vienna, Austria, in 1976. Our conversation centered on how we could live out our calling by helping marriages and families. A couple of years later when they were living in Bonn, Germany, they sponsored one of our very first Marriage Alive seminars. Throughout the years they have encouraged us by their words and by living out their holy calling.

Can we do less? Won't you join with us, the Stanleys and others? Today accept the challenge to "glorify God and exalt his name together."

—Dave & Claudia

Go to page 586 for your next devotional reading.

Say to my soul,
"I am your salvation."

⁴May those who seek my life
be disgraced and put to shame;
may those who plot my ruin
be turned back in dismay.
⁵May they be like chaff before the
wind,
with the angel of the LORD driving
them away;
⁶may their path be dark and slippery,
with the angel of the LORD
pursuing them.
⁷Since they hid their net for me
without cause
and without cause dug a pit for
me,
⁸may ruin overtake them by surprise—
may the net they hid entangle
them,
may they fall into the pit, to their
ruin.
⁹Then my soul will rejoice in the LORD
and delight in his salvation.
¹⁰My whole being will exclaim,
"Who is like you, O LORD?
You rescue the poor from those too
strong for them,
the poor and needy from those
who rob them."

¹¹Ruthless witnesses come forward;
they question me on things I know
nothing about.
¹²They repay me evil for good
and leave my soul forlorn.
¹³Yet when they were ill, I put on
sackcloth
and humbled myself with fasting.
When my prayers returned to me
unanswered,
14   I went about mourning
as though for my friend or brother.
I bowed my head in grief
as though weeping for my mother.
¹⁵But when I stumbled, they gathered
in glee;
attackers gathered against me when
I was unaware.
They slandered me without ceasing.
¹⁶Like the ungodly they maliciously
mockedᵃ;
they gnashed their teeth at me.

¹⁷O Lord, how long will you look on?
Rescue my life from their ravages,
my precious life from these lions.
¹⁸I will give you thanks in the great
assembly;
among throngs of people I will
praise you.

¹⁹Let not those gloat over me
who are my enemies without
cause;
let not those who hate me without
reason
maliciously wink the eye.
²⁰They do not speak peaceably,
but devise false accusations
against those who live quietly in
the land.
²¹They gape at me and say, "Aha! Aha!
With our own eyes we have seen it."

²²O LORD, you have seen this; be not
silent.
Do not be far from me, O Lord.
²³Awake, and rise to my defense!
Contend for me, my God and
Lord.
²⁴Vindicate me in your righteousness,
O LORD my God;
do not let them gloat over me.
²⁵Do not let them think, "Aha, just
what we wanted!"
or say, "We have swallowed him
up."

²⁶May all who gloat over my distress
be put to shame and confusion;
may all who exalt themselves over me
be clothed with shame and
disgrace.
²⁷May those who delight in my
vindication
shout for joy and gladness;
may they always say, "The LORD be
exalted,
who delights in the well-being of
his servant."
²⁸My tongue will speak of your
righteousness
and of your praises all day long.

ᵃ16 Septuagint; Hebrew may mean *ungodly circle of
mockers.*

Psalm 36

For the director of music. Of David the servant of the LORD.

¹An oracle is within my heart
  concerning the sinfulness of the
  wicked:*ᵃ*
 There is no fear of God
  before his eyes.
²For in his own eyes he flatters himself
  too much to detect or hate his
  sin.
³The words of his mouth are wicked
  and deceitful;
  he has ceased to be wise and to do
  good.
⁴Even on his bed he plots evil;
  he commits himself to a sinful
  course
  and does not reject what is wrong.

⁵Your love, O LORD, reaches to the
  heavens,
  your faithfulness to the skies.
⁶Your righteousness is like the mighty
  mountains,
  your justice like the great deep.

O LORD, you preserve both man and
  beast.
⁷ How priceless is your unfailing
  love!
 Both high and low among men
  find*ᵇ* refuge in the shadow of
  your wings.
⁸They feast on the abundance of your
  house;
  you give them drink from your
  river of delights.
⁹For with you is the fountain of life;
  in your light we see light.

¹⁰Continue your love to those who
  know you,
  your righteousness to the upright
  in heart.
¹¹May the foot of the proud not come
  against me,
  nor the hand of the wicked drive
  me away.
¹²See how the evildoers lie fallen—
  thrown down, not able to rise!

ᵃ1 Or heart: / Sin proceeds from the wicked.   *ᵇ7 Or
love, O God! / Men find; or love! / Both heavenly beings
and men / find*

The True Desires of the Heart

PSALM 37:4 Sometimes we think we know exactly what we want. We think we even know what we desire most in our relationships. Our list of wants may be formulated by observing other people, from listening to clever advertising, and so on. We can become convinced that our deepest desires are things that are on the surface and temporary.

Some people look to their spouse to bring contentment. *If only he or she would do this or respond to me in that way,* we think, *then I would finally be happy and the desires of my heart would be met.* But it's unfair and unrealistic to place our happiness in the hands of another individual, no matter how loving that person may be.

God, the One who made us, truly under-stands the deepest needs in our lives. He knows that ful-filling surface desires only brings temporary satisfaction. The true desire of the heart can only be fulfilled through a relationship with God. The psalmist instructs us to do this by choosing to "delight in the LORD" by mak-ing him our top priority and spending time with him in prayer. Each of us can further de-light in him by studying the Bible, his Word. Then, as we know him better, he will bless us with fulfilled desires that truly satisfy . . . peace, his comfort and a joy that's not de-pendent on circumstances.

When we delight in the Lord, our desires change, and we begin to experience the lasting joys that are fulfilled only by a rela-tionship with him.   **—Bob & Rosemary**

Weekend Warm-up   *In whose hands do you place your happiness?*

Go to page 588 for your next devotional reading.

Psalm 37[a]

Of David.

[1]Do not fret because of evil men
 or be envious of those who do
  wrong;
[2]for like the grass they will soon
  wither,
 like green plants they will soon die
  away.

[3]Trust in the LORD and do good;
 dwell in the land and enjoy safe
  pasture.
[4]Delight yourself in the LORD
 and he will give you the desires of
  your heart.

[5]Commit your way to the LORD;
 trust in him and he will do this:
[6]He will make your righteousness
  shine like the dawn,
 the justice of your cause like the
  noonday sun.

[7]Be still before the LORD and wait
  patiently for him;
 do not fret when men succeed in
  their ways,
 when they carry out their wicked
  schemes.

[8]Refrain from anger and turn from
  wrath;
 do not fret—it leads only to evil.
[9]For evil men will be cut off,
 but those who hope in the LORD
  will inherit the land.

[10]A little while, and the wicked will be
  no more;
 though you look for them, they
  will not be found.
[11]But the meek will inherit the land
 and enjoy great peace.

[12]The wicked plot against the righteous
 and gnash their teeth at them;
[13]but the Lord laughs at the wicked,
 for he knows their day is coming.

[14]The wicked draw the sword
 and bend the bow
 to bring down the poor and needy,
 to slay those whose ways are
  upright.

[15]But their swords will pierce their own
  hearts,
 and their bows will be broken.

[16]Better the little that the righteous
  have
 than the wealth of many wicked;
[17]for the power of the wicked will be
  broken,
 but the LORD upholds the
  righteous.

[18]The days of the blameless are known
  to the LORD,
 and their inheritance will endure
  forever.
[19]In times of disaster they will not
  wither;
 in days of famine they will enjoy
  plenty.

[20]But the wicked will perish:
 The LORD's enemies will be like the
  beauty of the fields,
 they will vanish—vanish like
  smoke.

[a]This psalm is an acrostic poem, the stanzas of which begin with the successive letters of the Hebrew alphabet.

²¹The wicked borrow and do not repay,
    but the righteous give generously;
²²those the LORD blesses will inherit the
    land,
    but those he curses will be cut off.

²³If the LORD delights in a man's way,
    he makes his steps firm;
²⁴though he stumble, he will not fall,
    for the LORD upholds him with his
    hand.

²⁵I was young and now I am old,
    yet I have never seen the righteous
    forsaken
    or their children begging bread.
²⁶They are always generous and lend
    freely;
    their children will be blessed.

²⁷Turn from evil and do good;
    then you will dwell in the land
    forever.
²⁸For the LORD loves the just
    and will not forsake his faithful
    ones.

They will be protected forever,
    but the offspring of the wicked will
    be cut off;

²⁹the righteous will inherit the land
    and dwell in it forever.

³⁰The mouth of the righteous man
    utters wisdom,
    and his tongue speaks what is just.
³¹The law of his God is in his heart;
    his feet do not slip.

³²The wicked lie in wait for the
    righteous,
    seeking their very lives;
³³but the LORD will not leave them in
    their power
    or let them be condemned when
    brought to trial.

³⁴Wait for the LORD
    and keep his way.
He will exalt you to inherit the land;
    when the wicked are cut off, you
    will see it.

³⁵I have seen a wicked and ruthless
    man
    flourishing like a green tree in its
    native soil,
³⁶but he soon passed away and was no
    more;
    though I looked for him, he could
    not be found.

God Is Faithful

Monday

PSALM 37:25–26   Age has its privileges. One privilege for us is to have experienced God's long-term faithfulness in our marriage. In this passage the psalmist writes, "I was young and now I am old, yet I have never seen the righteous forsaken or their children begging bread." In verse 26 we read that their children will be blessed—isn't that every parent's dream? If you make your marriage a priority and together trust God, your children will benefit.

    Knowing that God is trustworthy and faithful takes the edge off life even when we let each other down—like the time Claudia got her hair cut too short. Rather than console her, I responded, "Makes you look older, doesn't it?" Or the time I procrastinated and missed an important IRS deadline and Claudia responded, "How could you be so careless? You let both of us down this time."

God's faithfulness is a great backdrop for dealing with marital irritations. And even when you walk through more difficult situations like the loss of a job, a child's serious illness or a serious disagreement, he will give you the courage to work through them. You can choose to grow and adapt to each other over the years, to take the risk to resolve hard issues. You can work through your problems instead of going around them.

    Life rushes by. For us, in each passing decade, time seems to accelerate. The less of life there is to waste, the more precious it becomes and the more we need to rely upon God and his faithfulness to help our marriage grow.

                        —Dave & Claudia

Go to page 597 for your next devotional reading.

37Consider the blameless, observe the
    upright;
  there is a future[a] for the man of
    peace.
38But all sinners will be destroyed;
  the future[b] of the wicked will be
    cut off.

39The salvation of the righteous comes
    from the LORD;
  he is their stronghold in time of
    trouble.
40The LORD helps them and delivers
    them;
  he delivers them from the wicked
    and saves them,
  because they take refuge in him.

Psalm 38

A psalm of David. A petition.

1O LORD, do not rebuke me in your
    anger
  or discipline me in your wrath.
2For your arrows have pierced me,
  and your hand has come down
    upon me.
3Because of your wrath there is no
    health in my body;
  my bones have no soundness
    because of my sin.
4My guilt has overwhelmed me
  like a burden too heavy to bear.

5My wounds fester and are loathsome
  because of my sinful folly.
6I am bowed down and brought very
    low;
  all day long I go about mourning.
7My back is filled with searing pain;
  there is no health in my body.
8I am feeble and utterly crushed;
  I groan in anguish of heart.

9All my longings lie open before you,
    O Lord;
  my sighing is not hidden from
    you.
10My heart pounds, my strength fails
    me;
  even the light has gone from my
    eyes.
11My friends and companions avoid me
    because of my wounds;
  my neighbors stay far away.

12Those who seek my life set their
    traps,
  those who would harm me talk of
    my ruin;
  all day long they plot deception.

13I am like a deaf man, who cannot
    hear,
  like a mute, who cannot open his
    mouth;
14I have become like a man who does
    not hear,
  whose mouth can offer no reply.
15I wait for you, O LORD;
  you will answer, O Lord my God.
16For I said, "Do not let them gloat
  or exalt themselves over me when
    my foot slips."

17For I am about to fall,
  and my pain is ever with me.
18I confess my iniquity;
  I am troubled by my sin.
19Many are those who are my vigorous
    enemies;
  those who hate me without reason
    are numerous.
20Those who repay my good with evil
  slander me when I pursue what is
    good.

21O LORD, do not forsake me;
  be not far from me, O my God.
22Come quickly to help me,
  O Lord my Savior.

Psalm 39

For the director of music. For Jeduthun.
A psalm of David.

1I said, "I will watch my ways
  and keep my tongue from sin;
  I will put a muzzle on my mouth
  as long as the wicked are in my
    presence."
2But when I was silent and still,
  not even saying anything good,
  my anguish increased.
3My heart grew hot within me,
  and as I meditated, the fire burned;
  then I spoke with my tongue:

4"Show me, O LORD, my life's end
  and the number of my days;

---

a37 Or there will be posterity   b38 Or posterity

let me know how fleeting is my
  life.
⁵You have made my days a mere
    handbreadth;
  the span of my years is as nothing
    before you.
  Each man's life is but a breath.
                                    Selah
⁶Man is a mere phantom as he goes to
    and fro:
  He bustles about, but only in vain;
  he heaps up wealth, not knowing
    who will get it.

⁷"But now, Lord, what do I look for?
  My hope is in you.
⁸Save me from all my transgressions;
  do not make me the scorn of fools.
⁹I was silent; I would not open my
    mouth,
  for you are the one who has done
    this.
¹⁰Remove your scourge from me;
  I am overcome by the blow of your
    hand.
¹¹You rebuke and discipline men for
    their sin;
  you consume their wealth like a
    moth—
  each man is but a breath.   *Selah*

¹²"Hear my prayer, O LORD,
  listen to my cry for help;
  be not deaf to my weeping.
  For I dwell with you as an alien,
  a stranger, as all my fathers were.
¹³Look away from me, that I may
    rejoice again
  before I depart and am no more."

Psalm 40

For the director of music. Of David.
A psalm.

¹I waited patiently for the LORD;
  he turned to me and heard my cry.
²He lifted me out of the slimy pit,
  out of the mud and mire;
  he set my feet on a rock
  and gave me a firm place to stand.
³He put a new song in my mouth,
  a hymn of praise to our God.
  Many will see and fear
  and put their trust in the LORD.

⁴Blessed is the man
  who makes the LORD his trust,

who does not look to the proud,
  to those who turn aside to false
    gods.ᵃ
⁵Many, O LORD my God,
  are the wonders you have done.
  The things you planned for us
  no one can recount to you;
  were I to speak and tell of them,
  they would be too many to declare.

⁶Sacrifice and offering you did not
    desire,
  but my ears you have piercedᵇ,ᶜ;
  burnt offerings and sin offerings
  you did not require.
⁷Then I said, "Here I am, I have
    come—
  it is written about me in the
    scroll.ᵈ
⁸I desire to do your will, O my God;
  your law is within my heart."

⁹I proclaim righteousness in the great
    assembly;
  I do not seal my lips,
  as you know, O LORD.
¹⁰I do not hide your righteousness in
    my heart;
  I speak of your faithfulness and
    salvation.
  I do not conceal your love and your
    truth
  from the great assembly.

¹¹Do not withhold your mercy from
    me, O LORD;
  may your love and your truth
  always protect me.
¹²For troubles without number
    surround me;
  my sins have overtaken me, and I
    cannot see.
  They are more than the hairs of my
    head,
  and my heart fails within me.

¹³Be pleased, O LORD, to save me;
  O LORD, come quickly to help me.
¹⁴May all who seek to take my life
  be put to shame and confusion;
  may all who desire my ruin
  be turned back in disgrace.
¹⁵May those who say to me, "Aha!
    Aha!"

ᵃ4 Or *to falsehood*   ᵇ6 Hebrew; Septuagint *but a
body you have prepared for me* (see also Symmachus
and Theodotion)   ᶜ6 Or *opened*   ᵈ7 Or *come
/ with the scroll written for me*

be appalled at their own shame.
¹⁶But may all who seek you
    rejoice and be glad in you;
may those who love your salvation
    always say,
    "The LORD be exalted!"

¹⁷Yet I am poor and needy;
    may the Lord think of me.
You are my help and my deliverer;
    O my God, do not delay.

Psalm 41

For the director of music. A psalm
of David.

¹Blessed is he who has regard for the
    weak;
    the LORD delivers him in times of
        trouble.
²The LORD will protect him and
    preserve his life;
he will bless him in the land
    and not surrender him to the
        desire of his foes.
³The LORD will sustain him on his
    sickbed
    and restore him from his bed of
        illness.

⁴I said, "O LORD, have mercy on me;
    heal me, for I have sinned against
        you."
⁵My enemies say of me in malice,
    "When will he die and his name
        perish?"
⁶Whenever one comes to see me,
    he speaks falsely, while his heart
        gathers slander;
then he goes out and spreads it
    abroad.

⁷All my enemies whisper together
    against me;
    they imagine the worst for me,
        saying,
⁸"A vile disease has beset him;
    he will never get up from the place
        where he lies."
⁹Even my close friend, whom I trusted,
    he who shared my bread,
    has lifted up his heel against me.

¹⁰But you, O LORD, have mercy on me;
    raise me up, that I may repay
        them.
¹¹I know that you are pleased with me,

for my enemy does not triumph
    over me.
¹²In my integrity you uphold me
    and set me in your presence
        forever.

¹³Praise be to the LORD, the God of
    Israel,
from everlasting to everlasting.
    Amen and Amen.

BOOK II

Psalms 42–72

Psalm 42 ^a

For the director of music. A *maskil*^b of
the Sons of Korah.

¹As the deer pants for streams of
    water,
    so my soul pants for you, O God.
²My soul thirsts for God, for the living
    God.
    When can I go and meet with
        God?
³My tears have been my food
    day and night,
while men say to me all day long,
    "Where is your God?"
⁴These things I remember
    as I pour out my soul:
how I used to go with the multitude,
    leading the procession to the house
        of God,
with shouts of joy and thanksgiving
    among the festive throng.

⁵Why are you downcast, O my soul?
    Why so disturbed within me?
Put your hope in God,
    for I will yet praise him,
    my Savior and ⁶my God.

My^c soul is downcast within me;
    therefore I will remember you
from the land of the Jordan,
    the heights of Hermon—from
        Mount Mizar.
⁷Deep calls to deep
    in the roar of your waterfalls;

^aIn many Hebrew manuscripts Psalms 42 and 43
constitute one psalm.   ^bTitle: Probably a literary
or musical term   ^c5,6 A few Hebrew
manuscripts, Septuagint and Syriac; most Hebrew
manuscripts *praise him for his saving help.* / ⁶O my
God, my

all your waves and breakers
  have swept over me.

[8]By day the LORD directs his love,
  at night his song is with me—
  a prayer to the God of my life.

[9]I say to God my Rock,
  "Why have you forgotten me?
Why must I go about mourning,
  oppressed by the enemy?"
[10]My bones suffer mortal agony
  as my foes taunt me,
saying to me all day long,
  "Where is your God?"

[11]Why are you downcast, O my soul?
  Why so disturbed within me?
Put your hope in God,
  for I will yet praise him,
  my Savior and my God.

Psalm 43[a]

[1]Vindicate me, O God,
  and plead my cause against an
    ungodly nation;
  rescue me from deceitful and
    wicked men.
[2]You are God my stronghold.
  Why have you rejected me?
Why must I go about mourning,
  oppressed by the enemy?
[3]Send forth your light and your truth,
  let them guide me;
let them bring me to your holy
    mountain,
  to the place where you dwell.
[4]Then will I go to the altar of God,
  to God, my joy and my delight.
I will praise you with the harp,
  O God, my God.

[5]Why are you downcast, O my soul?
  Why so disturbed within me?
Put your hope in God,
  for I will yet praise him,
  my Savior and my God.

Psalm 44

For the director of music. Of the Sons of
Korah. A maskil.[b]

[1]We have heard with our ears, O God;
  our fathers have told us
what you did in their days,
  in days long ago.

[2]With your hand you drove out the
    nations
  and planted our fathers;
you crushed the peoples
  and made our fathers flourish.
[3]It was not by their sword that they
    won the land,
  nor did their arm bring them
    victory;
it was your right hand, your arm,
  and the light of your face, for you
    loved them.

[4]You are my King and my God,
  who decrees[c] victories for Jacob.
[5]Through you we push back our
    enemies;
  through your name we trample our
    foes.
[6]I do not trust in my bow,
  my sword does not bring me
    victory;
[7]but you give us victory over our
    enemies,
  you put our adversaries to shame.
[8]In God we make our boast all day
    long,
  and we will praise your name
    forever.   *Selah*

[9]But now you have rejected and
    humbled us;
  you no longer go out with our
    armies.
[10]You made us retreat before the
    enemy,
  and our adversaries have plundered
    us.
[11]You gave us up to be devoured like
    sheep
  and have scattered us among the
    nations.
[12]You sold your people for a pittance,
  gaining nothing from their sale.

[13]You have made us a reproach to our
    neighbors,
  the scorn and derision of those
    around us.
[14]You have made us a byword among
    the nations;
  the peoples shake their heads at us.
[15]My disgrace is before me all day long,

---

[a]In many Hebrew manuscripts Psalms 42 and 43
constitute one psalm.   [b]Title: Probably a literary
or musical term   [c]4 Septuagint, Aquila and
Syriac; Hebrew *King, O God; / command*

and my face is covered with shame
¹⁶at the taunts of those who reproach
and revile me,
because of the enemy, who is bent
on revenge.

¹⁷All this happened to us,
though we had not forgotten you
or been false to your covenant.
¹⁸Our hearts had not turned back;
our feet had not strayed from your
path.
¹⁹But you crushed us and made us a
haunt for jackals
and covered us over with deep
darkness.

²⁰If we had forgotten the name of our
God
or spread out our hands to a
foreign god,
²¹would not God have discovered it,
since he knows the secrets of the
heart?
²²Yet for your sake we face death all
day long;
we are considered as sheep to be
slaughtered.

²³Awake, O Lord! Why do you sleep?
Rouse yourself! Do not reject us
forever.
²⁴Why do you hide your face
and forget our misery and
oppression?

²⁵We are brought down to the dust;
our bodies cling to the ground.
²⁶Rise up and help us;
redeem us because of your
unfailing love.

Psalm 45

For the director of music. To ⌊the tune
of⌋ "Lilies." Of the Sons of Korah. A
maskil. ᵃ A wedding song.

¹My heart is stirred by a noble theme
as I recite my verses for the king;
my tongue is the pen of a skillful
writer.

²You are the most excellent of men
and your lips have been anointed
with grace,
since God has blessed you forever.
³Gird your sword upon your side,
O mighty one;

clothe yourself with splendor and
majesty.
⁴In your majesty ride forth victoriously
in behalf of truth, humility and
righteousness;
let your right hand display
awesome deeds.
⁵Let your sharp arrows pierce the
hearts of the king's enemies;
let the nations fall beneath your
feet.
⁶Your throne, O God, will last for ever
and ever;
a scepter of justice will be the
scepter of your kingdom.
⁷You love righteousness and hate
wickedness;
therefore God, your God, has set
you above your companions
by anointing you with the oil of
joy.
⁸All your robes are fragrant with myrrh
and aloes and cassia;
from palaces adorned with ivory
the music of the strings makes you
glad.
⁹Daughters of kings are among your
honored women;
at your right hand is the royal
bride in gold of Ophir.

¹⁰Listen, O daughter, consider and give
ear:
Forget your people and your
father's house.
¹¹The king is enthralled by your beauty;
honor him, for he is your lord.
¹²The Daughter of Tyre will come with
a gift, ᵇ
men of wealth will seek your favor.

¹³All glorious is the princess within ⌊her
chamber⌋;
her gown is interwoven with gold.
¹⁴In embroidered garments she is led to
the king;
her virgin companions follow her
and are brought to you.
¹⁵They are led in with joy and gladness;
they enter the palace of the king.

¹⁶Your sons will take the place of your
fathers;
you will make them princes
throughout the land.

ᵃTitle: Probably a literary or musical term
ᵇ12 Or *A Tyrian robe is among the gifts*

17I will perpetuate your memory
  through all generations;
therefore the nations will praise
  you for ever and ever.

Psalm 46

For the director of music. Of the Sons of
Korah. According to *alamoth.*[a] A song.

1God is our refuge and strength,
  an ever-present help in trouble.
2Therefore we will not fear, though the
    earth give way
  and the mountains fall into the
    heart of the sea,
3though its waters roar and foam
  and the mountains quake with
    their surging.   *Selah*

4There is a river whose streams make
    glad the city of God,
  the holy place where the Most
    High dwells.
5God is within her, she will not fall;
  God will help her at break of day.
6Nations are in uproar, kingdoms fall;
  he lifts his voice, the earth melts.

7The LORD Almighty is with us;
  the God of Jacob is our fortress.
                          Selah

8Come and see the works of the LORD,
  the desolations he has brought on
    the earth.
9He makes wars cease to the ends of
    the earth;
  he breaks the bow and shatters the
    spear,
  he burns the shields[b] with fire.
10"Be still, and know that I am God;
  I will be exalted among the
    nations,
  I will be exalted in the earth."

11The LORD Almighty is with us;
  the God of Jacob is our fortress.
                          Selah

Psalm 47

For the director of music. Of the Sons of
Korah. A psalm.

1Clap your hands, all you nations;
  shout to God with cries of joy.

2How awesome is the LORD Most
    High,
  the great King over all the earth!
3He subdued nations under us,
  peoples under our feet.
4He chose our inheritance for us,
  the pride of Jacob, whom he loved.
                          Selah

5God has ascended amid shouts of joy,
  the LORD amid the sounding of
    trumpets.
6Sing praises to God, sing praises;
  sing praises to our King, sing
    praises.

7For God is the King of all the earth;
  sing to him a psalm[c] of praise.
8God reigns over the nations;
  God is seated on his holy throne.
9The nobles of the nations assemble
  as the people of the God of
    Abraham,
for the kings[d] of the earth belong to
    God;
  he is greatly exalted.

Psalm 48

A song. A psalm of the Sons of Korah.

1Great is the LORD, and most worthy
    of praise,
  in the city of our God, his holy
    mountain.
2It is beautiful in its loftiness,
  the joy of the whole earth.
Like the utmost heights of Zaphon[e]
  is Mount Zion,
  the[f] city of the Great King.
3God is in her citadels;
  he has shown himself to be her
    fortress.

4When the kings joined forces,
  when they advanced together,
5they saw ⌞her⌟ and were astounded;
  they fled in terror.
6Trembling seized them there,
  pain like that of a woman in labor.

---

aTitle: Probably a musical term   b9 Or *chariots*
c7 Or *a maskil* (probably a literary or musical
term)   d9 Or *shields*   e2 *Zaphon* can refer to
a sacred mountain or the direction north.
f2 Or *earth, / Mount Zion, on the northern side /
of the*

⁷You destroyed them like ships of
    Tarshish
    shattered by an east wind.

⁸As we have heard,
    so have we seen
in the city of the LORD Almighty,
    in the city of our God:
    God makes her secure forever.
                                    Selah

⁹Within your temple, O God,
    we meditate on your unfailing
        love.
¹⁰Like your name, O God,
    your praise reaches to the ends of
        the earth;
    your right hand is filled with
        righteousness.
¹¹Mount Zion rejoices,
    the villages of Judah are glad
    because of your judgments.

¹²Walk about Zion, go around her,
    count her towers,
¹³consider well her ramparts,
    view her citadels,
    that you may tell of them to the
        next generation.
¹⁴For this God is our God for ever and
        ever;
    he will be our guide even to the
        end.

Psalm 49

For the director of music. Of the Sons of
    Korah. A psalm.

¹Hear this, all you peoples;
    listen, all who live in this world,
²both low and high,
    rich and poor alike:
³My mouth will speak words of
        wisdom;
    the utterance from my heart will
        give understanding.
⁴I will turn my ear to a proverb;
    with the harp I will expound my
        riddle:

⁵Why should I fear when evil days
        come,
    when wicked deceivers surround
        me—
⁶those who trust in their wealth
    and boast of their great riches?

⁷No man can redeem the life of
    another
    or give to God a ransom for him—
⁸the ransom for a life is costly,
    no payment is ever enough—
⁹that he should live on forever
    and not see decay.

¹⁰For all can see that wise men die;
    the foolish and the senseless alike
        perish
    and leave their wealth to others.
¹¹Their tombs will remain their
        houses*ᵃ* forever,
    their dwellings for endless
        generations,
    though they had*ᵇ* named lands
        after themselves.

¹²But man, despite his riches, does not
        endure;
    he is*ᶜ* like the beasts that perish.

¹³This is the fate of those who trust in
        themselves,
    and of their followers, who
        approve their sayings.   *Selah*
¹⁴Like sheep they are destined for the
        grave,*ᵈ*
    and death will feed on them.
The upright will rule over them in the
        morning;
    their forms will decay in the
        grave,*ᵈ*
    far from their princely mansions.
¹⁵But God will redeem my life*ᵉ* from
        the grave;
    he will surely take me to himself.
                                    Selah

¹⁶Do not be overawed when a man
        grows rich,
    when the splendor of his house
        increases;
¹⁷for he will take nothing with him
        when he dies,
    his splendor will not descend with
        him.
¹⁸Though while he lived he counted
        himself blessed—
    and men praise you when you
        prosper—

ᵃ11 Septuagint and Syriac; Hebrew *In their thoughts
their houses will remain*   *ᵇ11* Or / *for they have*
ᶜ12 Hebrew; Septuagint and Syriac read verse 12
the same as verse 20.   *ᵈ14* Hebrew *Sheol*; also
in verse 15   *ᵉ15* Or *soul*

¹⁹he will join the generation of his
    fathers,
  who will never see the light ⌐of life⌐.

²⁰A man who has riches without
    understanding
  is like the beasts that perish.

Psalm 50

A psalm of Asaph.

¹The Mighty One, God, the LORD,
  speaks and summons the earth
  from the rising of the sun to the
    place where it sets.
²From Zion, perfect in beauty,
  God shines forth.
³Our God comes and will not be
    silent;
  a fire devours before him,
  and around him a tempest rages.
⁴He summons the heavens above,
  and the earth, that he may judge
    his people:
⁵"Gather to me my consecrated ones,
  who made a covenant with me by
    sacrifice."
⁶And the heavens proclaim his
    righteousness,
  for God himself is judge.   *Selah*

⁷"Hear, O my people, and I will
    speak,
  O Israel, and I will testify against
    you:
  I am God, your God.
⁸I do not rebuke you for your
    sacrifices
  or your burnt offerings, which are
    ever before me.
⁹I have no need of a bull from your
    stall
  or of goats from your pens,
¹⁰for every animal of the forest is mine,
  and the cattle on a thousand hills.
¹¹I know every bird in the mountains,
  and the creatures of the field are
    mine.
¹²If I were hungry I would not tell you,
  for the world is mine, and all that
    is in it.
¹³Do I eat the flesh of bulls
  or drink the blood of goats?
¹⁴Sacrifice thank offerings to God,
  fulfill your vows to the Most High,

¹⁵and call upon me in the day of
    trouble;
  I will deliver you, and you will
    honor me."

¹⁶But to the wicked, God says:

  "What right have you to recite my
    laws
  or take my covenant on your lips?
¹⁷You hate my instruction
  and cast my words behind you.
¹⁸When you see a thief, you join with
    him;
  you throw in your lot with
    adulterers.
¹⁹You use your mouth for evil
  and harness your tongue to deceit.
²⁰You speak continually against your
    brother
  and slander your own mother's
    son.
²¹These things you have done and I
    kept silent;
  you thought I was altogether*ᵃ* like
    you.
  But I will rebuke you
  and accuse you to your face.

²²"Consider this, you who forget God,
  or I will tear you to pieces, with
    none to rescue:
²³He who sacrifices thank offerings
    honors me,
  and he prepares the way
  so that I may show him*ᵇ* the
    salvation of God."

Psalm 51

*For the director of music. A psalm of
David. When the prophet Nathan came
to him after David had committed
adultery with Bathsheba.*

¹Have mercy on me, O God,
  according to your unfailing love;
according to your great compassion
  blot out my transgressions.
²Wash away all my iniquity
  and cleanse me from my sin.

³For I know my transgressions,
  and my sin is always before me.
⁴Against you, you only, have I sinned
  and done what is evil in your sight,

ᵃ21 Or thought the 'I AM' was   *ᵇ23 Or and to
him who considers his way / I will show*

so that you are proved right when
   you speak
   and justified when you judge.
[5] Surely I was sinful at birth,
   sinful from the time my mother
      conceived me.
[6] Surely you desire truth in the inner
      parts[a];
   you teach[b] me wisdom in the
      inmost place.

[7] Cleanse me with hyssop, and I will be
      clean;
   wash me, and I will be whiter than
      snow.
[8] Let me hear joy and gladness;
   let the bones you have crushed
      rejoice.
[9] Hide your face from my sins
   and blot out all my iniquity.

[10] Create in me a pure heart, O God,
   and renew a steadfast spirit within
      me.
[11] Do not cast me from your presence
   or take your Holy Spirit from me.
[12] Restore to me the joy of your
      salvation
   and grant me a willing spirit, to
      sustain me.

[13] Then I will teach transgressors your
      ways,
   and sinners will turn back to you.
[14] Save me from bloodguilt, O God,
   the God who saves me,
   and my tongue will sing of your
      righteousness.
[15] O Lord, open my lips,
   and my mouth will declare your
      praise.
[16] You do not delight in sacrifice, or I
      would bring it;
   you do not take pleasure in burnt
      offerings.
[17] The sacrifices of God are[c] a broken
      spirit;
   a broken and contrite heart,
   O God, you will not despise.

[18] In your good pleasure make Zion
      prosper;
   build up the walls of Jerusalem.
[19] Then there will be righteous sacrifices,
   whole burnt offerings to delight
      you;

[a]6 The meaning of the Hebrew for this phrase is
uncertain.   [b]6 Or you desired . . . ; / you taught
[c]17 Or My sacrifice, O God, is

Empty Your Suitcase

PSALM 51 Linda was sexually active before she became a Christian . . . and before she was married. She agonized over the fact that she had violated God's plan for her life. Though she continually asked God for forgiveness, she continued to carry her heavy suitcase of guilt. The guilt she carried was damaging her walk with God, her personal growth and her marriage.

The heavy burden of guilt is overwhelming. Many spouses walk through life carrying baggage from the past—things we feel guilty about, sins from previous relationships, difficulties from the dating years, transgressions from a previous marriage. A suitcase full of all our wrongs is weighing us down.

Some have grown up in homes where parents remind them of that suitcase. They use guilt as a behavior motivator—as a way to control their child. That child becomes an adult and arrives at the marriage altar lugging that heavy load.

God holds the key to that suitcase of guilt. Only God can open it up and empty it out. He doesn't want us walking bent over, trying to live life carrying all the guilt. It is his desire to take it from each of us, and he sent his Son to do just that (see verses 10–12).

Each spouse must decide whether to let God open his or her own "suitcase" and then confess each incident to him. God will take the guilt and shame, and we will be burdened no more. We will be forgiven. God has taken the burden of our sin and guilt. Like David, we need to praise God for taking our guilt away.

—Bob & Rosemary

Go to page 599 for your next devotional reading.

then bulls will be offered on your
    altar.

Psalm 52

For the director of music. A *maskil*[a]
of David. When Doeg the Edomite had
gone to Saul and told him: "David has
gone to the house of Ahimelech."

[1]Why do you boast of evil, you mighty
    man?
  Why do you boast all day long,
  you who are a disgrace in the eyes
    of God?
[2]Your tongue plots destruction;
  it is like a sharpened razor,
  you who practice deceit.
[3]You love evil rather than good,
  falsehood rather than speaking the
    truth.   *Selah*
[4]You love every harmful word,
  O you deceitful tongue!

[5]Surely God will bring you down to
    everlasting ruin:
  He will snatch you up and tear you
    from your tent;
  he will uproot you from the land
    of the living.   *Selah*
[6]The righteous will see and fear;
  they will laugh at him, saying,
[7]"Here now is the man
  who did not make God his
    stronghold
 but trusted in his great wealth
  and grew strong by destroying
    others!"

[8]But I am like an olive tree
  flourishing in the house of God;
I trust in God's unfailing love
  for ever and ever.
[9]I will praise you forever for what you
    have done;
  in your name I will hope, for your
    name is good.
  I will praise you in the presence of
    your saints.

Psalm 53

For the director of music. According to
mahalath.[b] A *maskil*[a] of David.

[1]The fool says in his heart,
  "There is no God."

They are corrupt, and their ways are
    vile;
  there is no one who does good.

[2]God looks down from heaven
  on the sons of men
to see if there are any who
    understand,
  any who seek God.
[3]Everyone has turned away,
  they have together become corrupt;
there is no one who does good,
  not even one.

[4]Will the evildoers never learn—
  those who devour my people as
    men eat bread
  and who do not call on God?
[5]There they were, overwhelmed with
    dread,
  where there was nothing to dread.
God scattered the bones of those who
    attacked you;
  you put them to shame, for God
    despised them.

[6]Oh, that salvation for Israel would
    come out of Zion!
  When God restores the fortunes of
    his people,
  let Jacob rejoice and Israel be glad!

Psalm 54

For the director of music. With stringed
instruments. A *maskil*[a] of David. When
the Ziphites had gone to Saul and said,
"Is not David hiding among us?"

[1]Save me, O God, by your name;
  vindicate me by your might.
[2]Hear my prayer, O God;
  listen to the words of my mouth.

[3]Strangers are attacking me;
  ruthless men seek my life—
  men without regard for God.   *Selah*

[4]Surely God is my help;
  the Lord is the one who sustains
    me.

[5]Let evil recoil on those who slander
    me;
  in your faithfulness destroy them.

---

[a]Title: Probably a literary or musical term
[b]Title: Probably a musical term

⁶I will sacrifice a freewill offering to
    you;
  I will praise your name, O LORD,
    for it is good.
⁷For he has delivered me from all my
    troubles,
  and my eyes have looked in
    triumph on my foes.

Psalm 55

For the director of music. With stringed
instruments. A *maskil*ᵃ of David.

¹Listen to my prayer, O God,
  do not ignore my plea;
² hear me and answer me.
My thoughts trouble me and I am
    distraught
³ at the voice of the enemy,
  at the stares of the wicked;
for they bring down suffering upon
    me
  and revile me in their anger.

⁴My heart is in anguish within me;
  the terrors of death assail me.
⁵Fear and trembling have beset me;

horror has overwhelmed me.
⁶I said, "Oh, that I had the wings of a
    dove!
  I would fly away and be at rest—
⁷I would flee far away
  and stay in the desert;   *Selah*
⁸I would hurry to my place of shelter,
  far from the tempest and storm."

⁹Confuse the wicked, O Lord,
    confound their speech,
  for I see violence and strife in the
    city.
¹⁰Day and night they prowl about on
    its walls;
  malice and abuse are within it.
¹¹Destructive forces are at work in the
    city;
  threats and lies never leave its
    streets.

¹²If an enemy were insulting me,
  I could endure it;
if a foe were raising himself against
    me,
  I could hide from him.

ᵃTitle: Probably a literary or musical term

Criticism spells O-u-c-h

Wednesday

PSALM 55:12–14 Some years ago
a team of psychologists did a study
of a mill town in New England.
Among the many facets of their
study was a concern surrounding
criticism among the people who
lived and worked so closely together.
They found, first of all, that everyone in the
community was guilty of criticizing everyone else. This was really no surprise. But
they were really surprised to learn that
everyone in the community was scandal-
ized whenever they heard that they themselves were the object of criticism. It was
okay to criticize other people, but it was
against the rules to be criticized.

Many sermons have been preached
against criticism and its awful relatives.
Many books have been written on the subject too. But you will probably be hard
pressed to find any helpful advice on how

to respond in a marriage relationship when you, at some point, become the object of your spouse's
criticism.

What couple can't relate to the
words of these verses? After all,
there is little you can do to escape
being criticized by the one who sees you up
close, who knows how you live seven days
a week. Being married naturally opens you
up to criticism. Sooner or later, whether intending to be critical or not, your partner
will off-handedly critique something you do
(or don't do). That's when we say with the
psalmist, "If an enemy were insulting me, I
could endure it . . ." But you?! My soulmate?!

These moments are a test of how well
we practice verse 22: "Cast your cares on the
LORD and he will sustain you."

—*Les & Leslie*

Go to page 665 for your next devotional reading.

¹³But it is you, a man like myself,
my companion, my close friend,
¹⁴with whom I once enjoyed sweet
fellowship
as we walked with the throng at
the house of God.

¹⁵Let death take my enemies by
surprise;
let them go down alive to the
grave,ᵃ
for evil finds lodging among them.

¹⁶But I call to God,
and the LORD saves me.
¹⁷Evening, morning and noon
I cry out in distress,
and he hears my voice.
¹⁸He ransoms me unharmed
from the battle waged against me,
even though many oppose me.
¹⁹God, who is enthroned forever,
will hear them and afflict them—
Selah
men who never change their ways
and have no fear of God.

²⁰My companion attacks his friends;
he violates his covenant.
²¹His speech is smooth as butter,
yet war is in his heart;
his words are more soothing than oil,
yet they are drawn swords.

²²Cast your cares on the LORD
and he will sustain you;
he will never let the righteous fall.
²³But you, O God, will bring down the
wicked
into the pit of corruption;
bloodthirsty and deceitful men
will not live out half their days.

But as for me, I trust in you.

Psalm 56

For the director of music. To ⌊the tune
of⌋ "A Dove on Distant Oaks." Of David.
A *miktam.*ᵇ When the Philistines had
seized him in Gath.

¹Be merciful to me, O God, for men
hotly pursue me;
all day long they press their attack.
²My slanderers pursue me all day long;
many are attacking me in their
pride.

³When I am afraid,
I will trust in you.
⁴In God, whose word I praise,
in God I trust; I will not be afraid.
What can mortal man do to me?

⁵All day long they twist my words;
they are always plotting to harm
me.
⁶They conspire, they lurk,
they watch my steps,
eager to take my life.

⁷On no account let them escape;
in your anger, O God, bring down
the nations.
⁸Record my lament;
list my tears on your scrollᶜ—
are they not in your record?

⁹Then my enemies will turn back
when I call for help.
By this I will know that God is for
me.
¹⁰In God, whose word I praise,
in the LORD, whose word I praise—
¹¹in God I trust; I will not be afraid.
What can man do to me?

¹²I am under vows to you, O God;
I will present my thank offerings to
you.
¹³For you have delivered meᵈ from
death
and my feet from stumbling,
that I may walk before God
in the light of life.ᵉ

Psalm 57

For the director of music. ⌊To the tune
of⌋ "Do Not Destroy." Of David. A
*miktam.*ᵇ When he had fled from Saul
into the cave.

¹Have mercy on me, O God, have
mercy on me,
for in you my soul takes refuge.
I will take refuge in the shadow of
your wings
until the disaster has passed.

²I cry out to God Most High,
to God, who fulfills ⌊his purpose⌋
for me.

ᵃ15 Hebrew *Sheol*   ᵇTitle: Probably a literary or
musical term   ᶜ8 Or / *put my tears in your
wineskin*   ᵈ13 Or *my soul*   ᵉ13 Or *the land of
the living*

³He sends from heaven and saves me,
  rebuking those who hotly pursue
    me;   *Selah*
  God sends his love and his
    faithfulness.

⁴I am in the midst of lions;
  I lie among ravenous beasts—
men whose teeth are spears and
    arrows,
  whose tongues are sharp swords.

⁵Be exalted, O God, above the
    heavens;
  let your glory be over all the earth.

⁶They spread a net for my feet—
  I was bowed down in distress.
They dug a pit in my path—
  but they have fallen into it
    themselves.   *Selah*

⁷My heart is steadfast, O God,
  my heart is steadfast;
  I will sing and make music.
⁸Awake, my soul!
  Awake, harp and lyre!
  I will awaken the dawn.

⁹I will praise you, O Lord, among the
    nations;
  I will sing of you among the
    peoples.
¹⁰For great is your love, reaching to the
    heavens;
  your faithfulness reaches to the
    skies.

¹¹Be exalted, O God, above the
    heavens;
  let your glory be over all the earth.

Psalm 58

For the director of music. ⌊To the tune
  of⌋ "Do Not Destroy." Of David.
      A *miktam.* ᵃ

¹Do you rulers indeed speak justly?
  Do you judge uprightly among
    men?
²No, in your heart you devise injustice,
  and your hands mete out violence
    on the earth.
³Even from birth the wicked go astray;
  from the womb they are wayward
    and speak lies.
⁴Their venom is like the venom of a
    snake,

like that of a cobra that has
    stopped its ears,
⁵that will not heed the tune of the
    charmer,
  however skillful the enchanter may
    be.

⁶Break the teeth in their mouths,
    O God;
  tear out, O Lᴏʀᴅ, the fangs of the
    lions!
⁷Let them vanish like water that flows
    away;
  when they draw the bow, let their
    arrows be blunted.
⁸Like a slug melting away as it moves
    along,
  like a stillborn child, may they not
    see the sun.

⁹Before your pots can feel ⌊the heat of⌋
    the thorns—
  whether they be green or dry—the
    wicked will be swept away. ᵇ
¹⁰The righteous will be glad when they
    are avenged,
  when they bathe their feet in the
    blood of the wicked.
¹¹Then men will say,
  "Surely the righteous still are
    rewarded;
  surely there is a God who judges
    the earth."

Psalm 59

For the director of music. ⌊To the tune
  of⌋ "Do Not Destroy." Of David. A
    miktam. ᵃ When Saul had sent men
    to watch David's house in order
        to kill him.

¹Deliver me from my enemies, O God;
  protect me from those who rise up
    against me.
²Deliver me from evildoers
  and save me from bloodthirsty
    men.

³See how they lie in wait for me!
  Fierce men conspire against me
for no offense or sin of mine,
    O Lᴏʀᴅ.
⁴I have done no wrong, yet they are
  ready to attack me.

ᵃTitle: Probably a literary or musical term
ᵇ9 The meaning of the Hebrew for this verse is
uncertain.

Arise to help me; look on my
plight!
[5]O Lord God Almighty, the God of
Israel,
rouse yourself to punish all the
nations;
show no mercy to wicked traitors.
Selah

[6]They return at evening,
snarling like dogs,
and prowl about the city.
[7]See what they spew from their
mouths—
they spew out swords from their
lips,
and they say, "Who can hear us?"
[8]But you, O Lord, laugh at them;
you scoff at all those nations.

[9]O my Strength, I watch for you;
you, O God, are my fortress, [10]my
loving God.

God will go before me
and will let me gloat over those
who slander me.
[11]But do not kill them, O Lord our
shield,[a]
or my people will forget.
In your might make them wander
about,
and bring them down.
[12]For the sins of their mouths,
for the words of their lips,
let them be caught in their pride.
For the curses and lies they utter,
[13]   consume them in wrath,
consume them till they are no
more.
Then it will be known to the ends of
the earth
that God rules over Jacob.   *Selah*

[14]They return at evening,
snarling like dogs,
and prowl about the city.
[15]They wander about for food
and howl if not satisfied.
[16]But I will sing of your strength,
in the morning I will sing of your
love;
for you are my fortress,
my refuge in times of trouble.

[17]O my Strength, I sing praise to you;
you, O God, are my fortress, my
loving God.

Psalm 60

For the director of music. To ⌐the tune
of⌐ "The Lily of the Covenant." A
miktam[b] of David. For teaching. When
he fought Aram Naharaim[c] and Aram
Zobah,[d] and when Joab returned and
struck down twelve thousand Edomites
in the Valley of Salt.

[1]You have rejected us, O God, and
burst forth upon us;
you have been angry—now restore
us!
[2]You have shaken the land and torn it
open;
mend its fractures, for it is quaking.
[3]You have shown your people
desperate times;
you have given us wine that makes
us stagger.

[4]But for those who fear you, you have
raised a banner
to be unfurled against the bow.
Selah

[5]Save us and help us with your right
hand,
that those you love may be
delivered.
[6]God has spoken from his sanctuary:
"In triumph I will parcel out
Shechem
and measure off the Valley of
Succoth.
[7]Gilead is mine, and Manasseh is
mine;
Ephraim is my helmet,
Judah my scepter.
[8]Moab is my washbasin,
upon Edom I toss my sandal;
over Philistia I shout in triumph."

[9]Who will bring me to the fortified
city?
Who will lead me to Edom?
[10]Is it not you, O God, you who have
rejected us
and no longer go out with our
armies?
[11]Give us aid against the enemy,
for the help of man is worthless.
[12]With God we will gain the victory,

---

[a]11 Or *sovereign*   [b]Title: Probably a literary or
musical term   [c]Title: That is, Arameans of
Northwest Mesopotamia   [d]Title: That is,
Arameans of central Syria

and he will trample down our
    enemies.

Psalm 61

For the director of music. With stringed
    instruments. Of David.

¹Hear my cry, O God;
    listen to my prayer.

²From the ends of the earth I call to
        you,
    I call as my heart grows faint;
    lead me to the rock that is higher
        than I.
³For you have been my refuge,
    a strong tower against the foe.

⁴I long to dwell in your tent forever
    and take refuge in the shelter of
        your wings.   *Selah*
⁵For you have heard my vows, O God;
    you have given me the heritage of
        those who fear your name.

⁶Increase the days of the king's life,
    his years for many generations.
⁷May he be enthroned in God's
        presence forever;
    appoint your love and faithfulness
        to protect him.

⁸Then will I ever sing praise to your
        name
    and fulfill my vows day after day.

Psalm 62

For the director of music. For Jeduthun.
    A psalm of David.

¹My soul finds rest in God alone;
    my salvation comes from him.
²He alone is my rock and my
        salvation;
    he is my fortress, I will never be
        shaken.

³How long will you assault a man?
    Would all of you throw him
        down—
    this leaning wall, this tottering
        fence?
⁴They fully intend to topple him
    from his lofty place;
    they take delight in lies.
With their mouths they bless,
    but in their hearts they curse.   *Selah*

⁵Find rest, O my soul, in God alone;
    my hope comes from him.
⁶He alone is my rock and my
        salvation;
    he is my fortress, I will not be
        shaken.
⁷My salvation and my honor depend
        on God[a];
    he is my mighty rock, my refuge.
⁸Trust in him at all times, O people;
    pour out your hearts to him,
    for God is our refuge.   *Selah*

⁹Lowborn men are but a breath,
    the highborn are but a lie;
    if weighed on a balance, they are
        nothing;
    together they are only a breath.
¹⁰Do not trust in extortion
    or take pride in stolen goods;
    though your riches increase,
    do not set your heart on them.

¹¹One thing God has spoken,
    two things have I heard:
    that you, O God, are strong,
¹²   and that you, O Lord, are loving.
    Surely you will reward each person
        according to what he has done.

Psalm 63

A psalm of David. When he was in the
    Desert of Judah.

¹O God, you are my God,
    earnestly I seek you;
    my soul thirsts for you,
    my body longs for you,
    in a dry and weary land
    where there is no water.

²I have seen you in the sanctuary
    and beheld your power and your
        glory.
³Because your love is better than life,
    my lips will glorify you.
⁴I will praise you as long as I live,
    and in your name I will lift up my
        hands.
⁵My soul will be satisfied as with the
        richest of foods;
    with singing lips my mouth will
        praise you.

⁶On my bed I remember you;

a7 Or / *God Most High is my salvation and my honor*

I think of you through the watches
of the night.
⁷Because you are my help,
I sing in the shadow of your wings.
⁸My soul clings to you;
your right hand upholds me.

⁹They who seek my life will be
destroyed;
they will go down to the depths of
the earth.
¹⁰They will be given over to the sword
and become food for jackals.

¹¹But the king will rejoice in God;
all who swear by God's name will
praise him,
while the mouths of liars will be
silenced.

Psalm 64

For the director of music. A psalm
of David.

¹Hear me, O God, as I voice my
complaint;
protect my life from the threat of
the enemy.
²Hide me from the conspiracy of the
wicked,
from that noisy crowd of evildoers.

³They sharpen their tongues like
swords
and aim their words like deadly
arrows.
⁴They shoot from ambush at the
innocent man;
they shoot at him suddenly,
without fear.

⁵They encourage each other in evil
plans,
they talk about hiding their snares;
they say, "Who will see them*a*?"
⁶They plot injustice and say,
"We have devised a perfect plan!"
Surely the mind and heart of man
are cunning.

⁷But God will shoot them with arrows;
suddenly they will be struck down.
⁸He will turn their own tongues
against them
and bring them to ruin;
all who see them will shake their
heads in scorn.

⁹All mankind will fear;
they will proclaim the works of
God
and ponder what he has done.
¹⁰Let the righteous rejoice in the LORD
and take refuge in him;
let all the upright in heart praise
him!

Psalm 65

For the director of music. A psalm
of David. A song.

¹Praise awaits*b* you, O God, in Zion;
to you our vows will be fulfilled.
²O you who hear prayer,
to you all men will come.
³When we were overwhelmed by sins,
you forgave*c* our transgressions.
⁴Blessed are those you choose
and bring near to live in your
courts!
We are filled with the good things of
your house,
of your holy temple.

⁵You answer us with awesome deeds
of righteousness,
O God our Savior,
the hope of all the ends of the earth
and of the farthest seas,
⁶who formed the mountains by your
power,
having armed yourself with
strength,
⁷who stilled the roaring of the seas,
the roaring of their waves,
and the turmoil of the nations.
⁸Those living far away fear your
wonders;
where morning dawns and evening
fades
you call forth songs of joy.

⁹You care for the land and water it;
you enrich it abundantly.
The streams of God are filled with
water
to provide the people with grain,
for so you have ordained it.*d*
¹⁰You drench its furrows
and level its ridges;

---

*a*5 Or *us*   *b*1 Or *befits*; the meaning of the
Hebrew for this word is uncertain.   *c*3 Or *made
atonement for*   *d*9 Or *for that is how you prepare
the land*

you soften it with showers
and bless its crops.
11 You crown the year with your bounty,
and your carts overflow with
abundance.
12 The grasslands of the desert overflow;
the hills are clothed with gladness.
13 The meadows are covered with flocks
and the valleys are mantled with
grain;
they shout for joy and sing.

Psalm 66

For the director of music. A song.
A psalm.

1 Shout with joy to God, all the earth!
2   Sing the glory of his name;
make his praise glorious!
3 Say to God, "How awesome are your
deeds!
So great is your power
that your enemies cringe before
you.
4 All the earth bows down to you;
they sing praise to you,
they sing praise to your name." *Selah*

5 Come and see what God has done,
how awesome his works in man's
behalf!
6 He turned the sea into dry land,
they passed through the waters on
foot—
come, let us rejoice in him.
7 He rules forever by his power,
his eyes watch the nations—
let not the rebellious rise up
against him.   *Selah*

8 Praise our God, O peoples,
let the sound of his praise be
heard;
9 he has preserved our lives
and kept our feet from slipping.
10 For you, O God, tested us;
you refined us like silver.
11 You brought us into prison
and laid burdens on our backs.
12 You let men ride over our heads;
we went through fire and water,
but you brought us to a place of
abundance.

13 I will come to your temple with burnt
offerings
and fulfill my vows to you—
14 vows my lips promised and my
mouth spoke
when I was in trouble.
15 I will sacrifice fat animals to you

Enjoying God's Creation

PSALM 65   Our God is an awesome God, and his awesomeness is revealed in nature. Just look around and you can observe God's strength. The mountains were formed by his power. He is the One who stills the roaring of the sea and the waves. He cares for the land and waters it. He makes the crops grow strong and lush.

In our busy lives, it's easy to overlook all the evidence around us of the majesty of God. So each December Dave and I try to slow down a bit. Whenever we have the opportunity, we head for our favorite writing hide-a-way tucked away in the Austrian Alps. That's where we are right now. We just returned from a wonderful walk in the snow. As we walked through the silent woods, the trees laden with snow and the

Alps towering in the background, we thanked God for helping us through another year and for giving us this moment of peace and tranquility. Now sitting in front of a roaring fire, we realize how special these times are for us. It's when we get back in touch with nature, with God and with each other.

Let us encourage you wherever you are to pause and appreciate God's wonderful creation. Look at the trees, the flowers, the mountains, the bubbling brook. Consider how only God can transform a seed into a flourishing tree. If God's power is so awesome in nature, we can also trust him with our lives and with our marriage.

—Dave & Claudia

Go to page 611 for your next devotional reading.

and an offering of rams;
    I will offer bulls and goats.   *Selah*

¹⁶Come and listen, all you who fear
    God;
    let me tell you what he has done
      for me.
¹⁷I cried out to him with my mouth;
    his praise was on my tongue.
¹⁸If I had cherished sin in my heart,
    the Lord would not have listened;
¹⁹but God has surely listened
    and heard my voice in prayer.
²⁰Praise be to God,
    who has not rejected my prayer
    or withheld his love from me!

Psalm 67

For the director of music. With stringed
instruments. A psalm. A song.

¹May God be gracious to us and bless
    us
    and make his face shine upon us,
                        Selah
²that your ways may be known on
    earth,
    your salvation among all nations.

³May the peoples praise you, O God;
    may all the peoples praise you.
⁴May the nations be glad and sing for
    joy,
    for you rule the peoples justly
    and guide the nations of the earth.
                        Selah
⁵May the peoples praise you, O God;
    may all the peoples praise you.

⁶Then the land will yield its harvest,
    and God, our God, will bless us.
⁷God will bless us,
    and all the ends of the earth will
      fear him.

Psalm 68

For the director of music. Of David.
A psalm. A song.

¹May God arise, may his enemies be
    scattered;
    may his foes flee before him.
²As smoke is blown away by the wind,
    may you blow them away;
  as wax melts before the fire,
    may the wicked perish before God.

³But may the righteous be glad
    and rejoice before God;
    may they be happy and joyful.

⁴Sing to God, sing praise to his name,
    extol him who rides on the
      clouds^{*a*}—
  his name is the LORD—
    and rejoice before him.
⁵A father to the fatherless, a defender
    of widows,
    is God in his holy dwelling.
⁶God sets the lonely in families,^{*b*}
    he leads forth the prisoners with
      singing;
    but the rebellious live in a
      sun-scorched land.

⁷When you went out before your
    people, O God,
    when you marched through the
      wasteland,   *Selah*
⁸the earth shook,
    the heavens poured down rain,
  before God, the One of Sinai,
    before God, the God of Israel.
⁹You gave abundant showers, O God;
    you refreshed your weary
      inheritance.
¹⁰Your people settled in it,
    and from your bounty, O God, you
      provided for the poor.

¹¹The Lord announced the word,
    and great was the company of
      those who proclaimed it:
¹²"Kings and armies flee in haste;
    in the camps men divide the
      plunder.
¹³Even while you sleep among the
    campfires,^{*c*}
    the wings of ⌐my¬ dove are sheathed
      with silver,
    its feathers with shining gold."
¹⁴When the Almighty^{*d*} scattered the
    kings in the land,
    it was like snow fallen on Zalmon.

¹⁵The mountains of Bashan are majestic
    mountains;
    rugged are the mountains of
      Bashan.
¹⁶Why gaze in envy, O rugged
    mountains,

a4 Or / *prepare the way for him who rides through the
deserts*   *b6* Or *the desolate in a homeland*
c13 Or *saddlebags*   *d14* Hebrew *Shaddai*

at the mountain where God
  chooses to reign,
where the LORD himself will dwell
  forever?
¹⁷The chariots of God are tens of
    thousands
  and thousands of thousands;
  the Lord ⌊has come⌋ from Sinai into
    his sanctuary.
¹⁸When you ascended on high,
  you led captives in your train;
  you received gifts from men,
even from ᵃ the rebellious—
  that you,ᵇ O LORD God, might
    dwell there.

¹⁹Praise be to the Lord, to God our
    Savior,
  who daily bears our burdens.   *Selah*
²⁰Our God is a God who saves;
  from the Sovereign LORD comes
    escape from death.

²¹Surely God will crush the heads of his
    enemies,
  the hairy crowns of those who go
    on in their sins.
²²The Lord says, "I will bring them
    from Bashan;
  I will bring them from the depths
    of the sea,
²³that you may plunge your feet in the
    blood of your foes,
  while the tongues of your dogs
    have their share."

²⁴Your procession has come into view,
    O God,
  the procession of my God and
    King into the sanctuary.
²⁵In front are the singers, after them the
    musicians;
  with them are the maidens playing
    tambourines.
²⁶Praise God in the great congregation;
  praise the LORD in the assembly of
    Israel.
²⁷There is the little tribe of Benjamin,
    leading them,
  there the great throng of Judah's
    princes,
  and there the princes of Zebulun
    and of Naphtali.

²⁸Summon your power, O Godᶜ;
  show us your strength, O God, as
    you have done before.
²⁹Because of your temple at Jerusalem

kings will bring you gifts.
³⁰Rebuke the beast among the reeds,
  the herd of bulls among the calves
    of the nations.
  Humbled, may it bring bars of silver.
  Scatter the nations who delight in
    war.
³¹Envoys will come from Egypt;
  Cushᵈ will submit herself to God.

³²Sing to God, O kingdoms of the
    earth,
  sing praise to the Lord,   *Selah*
³³to him who rides the ancient skies
    above,
  who thunders with mighty voice.
³⁴Proclaim the power of God,
  whose majesty is over Israel,
  whose power is in the skies.
³⁵You are awesome, O God, in your
    sanctuary;
  the God of Israel gives power and
    strength to his people.

Praise be to God!

Psalm 69

For the director of music. To ⌊the tune
of⌋ "Lilies." Of David.

¹Save me, O God,
  for the waters have come up to my
    neck.
²I sink in the miry depths,
  where there is no foothold.
I have come into the deep waters;
  the floods engulf me.
³I am worn out calling for help;
  my throat is parched.
My eyes fail,
  looking for my God.
⁴Those who hate me without reason
  outnumber the hairs of my head;
many are my enemies without cause,
  those who seek to destroy me.
I am forced to restore
  what I did not steal.

⁵You know my folly, O God;
  my guilt is not hidden from you.

⁶May those who hope in you

ᵃ18 Or *gifts for men, / even*   ᵇ18 Or *they*
ᶜ28 Many Hebrew manuscripts, Septuagint and
Syriac; most Hebrew manuscripts *Your God has
summoned power for you*   ᵈ31 That is, the upper
Nile region

not be disgraced because of me,
O Lord, the LORD Almighty;
may those who seek you
not be put to shame because of
me,
O God of Israel.
⁷For I endure scorn for your sake,
and shame covers my face.
⁸I am a stranger to my brothers,
an alien to my own mother's sons;
⁹for zeal for your house consumes me,
and the insults of those who insult
you fall on me.
¹⁰When I weep and fast,
I must endure scorn;
¹¹when I put on sackcloth,
people make sport of me.
¹²Those who sit at the gate mock me,
and I am the song of the
drunkards.

¹³But I pray to you, O LORD,
in the time of your favor;
in your great love, O God,
answer me with your sure
salvation.
¹⁴Rescue me from the mire,
do not let me sink;
deliver me from those who hate me,
from the deep waters.
¹⁵Do not let the floodwaters engulf me
or the depths swallow me up
or the pit close its mouth over me.
¹⁶Answer me, O LORD, out of the
goodness of your love;
in your great mercy turn to me.
¹⁷Do not hide your face from your
servant;
answer me quickly, for I am in
trouble.
¹⁸Come near and rescue me;
redeem me because of my foes.

¹⁹You know how I am scorned,
disgraced and shamed;
all my enemies are before you.
²⁰Scorn has broken my heart
and has left me helpless;
I looked for sympathy, but there was
none,
for comforters, but I found none.
²¹They put gall in my food
and gave me vinegar for my thirst.

²²May the table set before them become
a snare;

may it become retribution and*ᵃ* a
trap.
²³May their eyes be darkened so they
cannot see,
and their backs be bent forever.
²⁴Pour out your wrath on them;
let your fierce anger overtake them.
²⁵May their place be deserted;
let there be no one to dwell in
their tents.
²⁶For they persecute those you wound
and talk about the pain of those
you hurt.
²⁷Charge them with crime upon crime;
do not let them share in your
salvation.
²⁸May they be blotted out of the book
of life
and not be listed with the
righteous.

²⁹I am in pain and distress;
may your salvation, O God, protect
me.

³⁰I will praise God's name in song
and glorify him with thanksgiving.
³¹This will please the LORD more than
an ox,
more than a bull with its horns
and hoofs.
³²The poor will see and be glad—
you who seek God, may your
hearts live!
³³The LORD hears the needy
and does not despise his captive
people.

³⁴Let heaven and earth praise him,
the seas and all that move in them,
³⁵for God will save Zion
and rebuild the cities of Judah.
Then people will settle there and
possess it;
³⁶   the children of his servants will
inherit it,
and those who love his name will
dwell there.

Psalm 70

For the director of music. Of David.
A petition.

¹Hasten, O God, to save me;
O LORD, come quickly to help me.

ᵃ22 Or snare / and their fellowship become

²May those who seek my life
  be put to shame and confusion;
may all who desire my ruin
  be turned back in disgrace.
³May those who say to me, "Aha!
    Aha!"
  turn back because of their shame.
⁴But may all who seek you
  rejoice and be glad in you;
may those who love your salvation
    always say,
  "Let God be exalted!"

⁵Yet I am poor and needy;
  come quickly to me, O God.
You are my help and my deliverer;
  O LORD, do not delay.

Psalm 71

¹In you, O LORD, I have taken refuge;
  let me never be put to shame.
²Rescue me and deliver me in your
    righteousness;
  turn your ear to me and save me.
³Be my rock of refuge,
  to which I can always go;
give the command to save me,
  for you are my rock and my
    fortress.
⁴Deliver me, O my God, from the
    hand of the wicked,
  from the grasp of evil and cruel
    men.

⁵For you have been my hope,
    O Sovereign LORD,
  my confidence since my youth.
⁶From birth I have relied on you;
  you brought me forth from my
    mother's womb.
  I will ever praise you.
⁷I have become like a portent to many,
  but you are my strong refuge.
⁸My mouth is filled with your praise,
  declaring your splendor all day
    long.

⁹Do not cast me away when I am old;
  do not forsake me when my
    strength is gone.
¹⁰For my enemies speak against me;
  those who wait to kill me conspire
    together.
¹¹They say, "God has forsaken him;
  pursue him and seize him,
  for no one will rescue him."

¹²Be not far from me, O God;
  come quickly, O my God, to help
    me.
¹³May my accusers perish in shame;
  may those who want to harm me
  be covered with scorn and disgrace.

¹⁴But as for me, I will always have
    hope;
  I will praise you more and more.
¹⁵My mouth will tell of your
    righteousness,
  of your salvation all day long,
  though I know not its measure.
¹⁶I will come and proclaim your mighty
    acts, O Sovereign LORD;
  I will proclaim your righteousness,
    yours alone.
¹⁷Since my youth, O God, you have
    taught me,
  and to this day I declare your
    marvelous deeds.
¹⁸Even when I am old and gray,
  do not forsake me, O God,
till I declare your power to the next
    generation,
  your might to all who are to come.

¹⁹Your righteousness reaches to the
    skies, O God,
  you who have done great things.
  Who, O God, is like you?
²⁰Though you have made me see
    troubles, many and bitter,
  you will restore my life again;
from the depths of the earth
  you will again bring me up.
²¹You will increase my honor
  and comfort me once again.

²²I will praise you with the harp
  for your faithfulness, O my God;
I will sing praise to you with the
    lyre,
  O Holy One of Israel.
²³My lips will shout for joy
  when I sing praise to you—
  I, whom you have redeemed.
²⁴My tongue will tell of your righteous
    acts
  all day long,
for those who wanted to harm me
  have been put to shame and
    confusion.

Psalm 72

Of Solomon.

¹Endow the king with your justice,
   O God,
   the royal son with your
      righteousness.
²He will*a* judge your people in
      righteousness,
   your afflicted ones with justice.
³The mountains will bring prosperity
      to the people,
   the hills the fruit of righteousness.
⁴He will defend the afflicted among
      the people
   and save the children of the needy;
   he will crush the oppressor.

⁵He will endure*b* as long as the sun,
   as long as the moon, through all
      generations.
⁶He will be like rain falling on a
      mown field,
   like showers watering the earth.
⁷In his days the righteous will flourish;
   prosperity will abound till the
      moon is no more.

⁸He will rule from sea to sea
   and from the River*c* to the ends
      of the earth.*d*
⁹The desert tribes will bow before him
   and his enemies will lick the dust.
¹⁰The kings of Tarshish and of distant
      shores
   will bring tribute to him;
   the kings of Sheba and Seba
   will present him gifts.
¹¹All kings will bow down to him
   and all nations will serve him.

¹²For he will deliver the needy who cry
      out,
   the afflicted who have no one to
      help.
¹³He will take pity on the weak and the
      needy
   and save the needy from death.
¹⁴He will rescue them from oppression
      and violence,
   for precious is their blood in his
      sight.

¹⁵Long may he live!
   May gold from Sheba be given
      him.
   May people ever pray for him

and bless him all day long.
¹⁶Let grain abound throughout the
      land;
   on the tops of the hills may it
      sway.
   Let its fruit flourish like Lebanon;
   let it thrive like the grass of the
      field.
¹⁷May his name endure forever;
   may it continue as long as the sun.

   All nations will be blessed through
      him,
   and they will call him blessed.

¹⁸Praise be to the LORD God, the God
      of Israel,
   who alone does marvelous deeds.
¹⁹Praise be to his glorious name
      forever;
   may the whole earth be filled with
      his glory.
         Amen and Amen.

²⁰This concludes the prayers of David
   son of Jesse.

BOOK III
Psalms 73–89

Psalm 73

A psalm of Asaph.

¹Surely God is good to Israel,
   to those who are pure in heart.

²But as for me, my feet had almost
      slipped;
   I had nearly lost my foothold.
³For I envied the arrogant
   when I saw the prosperity of the
      wicked.

⁴They have no struggles;
   their bodies are healthy and
      strong.*e*
⁵They are free from the burdens
      common to man;
   they are not plagued by human
      ills.

a2 Or *May he;* similarly in verses 3-11 and 17
b5 Septuagint; Hebrew *You will be feared*
c8 That is, the Euphrates   *d8* Or *the end of the
land*   *e4* With a different word division of the
Hebrew; Masoretic Text *struggles at their death; /
their bodies are healthy*

⁶Therefore pride is their necklace;
  they clothe themselves with
    violence.
⁷From their callous hearts comes
    iniquity^a;
  the evil conceits of their minds
    know no limits.
⁸They scoff, and speak with malice;
  in their arrogance they threaten
    oppression.
⁹Their mouths lay claim to heaven,
  and their tongues take possession
    of the earth.
¹⁰Therefore their people turn to them
  and drink up waters in
    abundance.^b
¹¹They say, "How can God know?
  Does the Most High have
    knowledge?"

¹²This is what the wicked are like—
  always carefree, they increase in
    wealth.
¹³Surely in vain have I kept my heart
    pure;
  in vain have I washed my hands in
    innocence.
¹⁴All day long I have been plagued;
  I have been punished every
    morning.

¹⁵If I had said, "I will speak thus,"
  I would have betrayed your
    children.

¹⁶When I tried to understand all this,
  it was oppressive to me
¹⁷till I entered the sanctuary of God;
  then I understood their final
    destiny.

¹⁸Surely you place them on slippery
    ground;
  you cast them down to ruin.
¹⁹How suddenly are they destroyed,
  completely swept away by terrors!
²⁰As a dream when one awakes,
  so when you arise, O Lord,
  you will despise them as fantasies.

²¹When my heart was grieved
  and my spirit embittered,
²²I was senseless and ignorant;
  I was a brute beast before you.

²³Yet I am always with you;
  you hold me by my right hand.
²⁴You guide me with your counsel,
  and afterward you will take me
    into glory.
²⁵Whom have I in heaven but you?
  And earth has nothing I desire
    besides you.
²⁶My flesh and my heart may fail,
  but God is the strength of my heart
  and my portion forever.

^a7 Syriac (see also Septuagint); Hebrew *Their eyes bulge with fat*   ^b10 The meaning of the Hebrew for this verse is uncertain.

When Life Seems Unfair

Friday

PSALM 73   As an academic over-achiever mom, I have been known in the past to ask, "Why do my friends' children bring home all As and my child gets Bs?" Another favorite question of mine is, "How can she eat everything she wants to and not gain an ounce!"

What are your secret questions? Have you ever had thoughts like, *Our marriage would be better if we had as much money as the Jones have!* or *Why does my child have allergies?* or *How can everything go so great for them when they don't give God a second thought?*

Life quickly gets out of focus when we question God. How easy it is to let jealousy and envy creep into our hearts. Because we don't see the whole picture, it can seem like success has absolutely nothing to do with trusting God. We can easily become dissatisfied with our life when we focus on what others have that we don't.

Years ago the psalmist struggled with similar questions until he "went to God's temple" and focused on the eternal rather than the temporary. Then he understood. In light of eternity, things like good luck, fame, fortune and success are not important. What's important are relationships—especially our relationship with God.

—*Dave & Claudia*

Go to page 620 for your next devotional reading.

27Those who are far from you will
    perish;
  you destroy all who are unfaithful
    to you.
28But as for me, it is good to be near
    God.
  I have made the Sovereign LORD
    my refuge;
  I will tell of all your deeds.

Psalm 74

A *maskil*[a] of Asaph.

1Why have you rejected us forever,
    O God?
  Why does your anger smolder
    against the sheep of your
    pasture?
2Remember the people you purchased
    of old,
  the tribe of your inheritance,
    whom you redeemed—
  Mount Zion, where you dwelt.
3Turn your steps toward these
    everlasting ruins,
  all this destruction the enemy has
    brought on the sanctuary.

4Your foes roared in the place where
    you met with us;
  they set up their standards as
    signs.
5They behaved like men wielding
    axes
  to cut through a thicket of trees.
6They smashed all the carved paneling
    with their axes and hatchets.
7They burned your sanctuary to the
    ground;
  they defiled the dwelling place of
    your Name.
8They said in their hearts, "We will
    crush them completely!"
  They burned every place where
    God was worshiped in the
    land.
9We are given no miraculous signs;
    no prophets are left,
  and none of us knows how long
    this will be.

10How long will the enemy mock you,
    O God?
  Will the foe revile your name
    forever?

11Why do you hold back your hand,
    your right hand?
  Take it from the folds of your
    garment and destroy them!

12But you, O God, are my king from of
    old;
  you bring salvation upon the earth.
13It was you who split open the sea by
    your power;
  you broke the heads of the
    monster in the waters.
14It was you who crushed the heads of
    Leviathan
  and gave him as food to the
    creatures of the desert.
15It was you who opened up springs
    and streams;
  you dried up the ever flowing
    rivers.
16The day is yours, and yours also the
    night;
  you established the sun and moon.
17It was you who set all the boundaries
    of the earth;
  you made both summer and
    winter.

18Remember how the enemy has
    mocked you, O LORD,
  how foolish people have reviled
    your name.
19Do not hand over the life of your
    dove to wild beasts;
  do not forget the lives of your
    afflicted people forever.
20Have regard for your covenant,
  because haunts of violence fill the
    dark places of the land.
21Do not let the oppressed retreat in
    disgrace;
  may the poor and needy praise
    your name.

22Rise up, O God, and defend your
    cause;
  remember how fools mock you all
    day long.
23Do not ignore the clamor of your
    adversaries,
  the uproar of your enemies, which
    rises continually.

*a*Title: Probably a literary or musical term

Psalm 75

For the director of music. ⌊To the tune
of⌋ "Do Not Destroy." A psalm of Asaph.
A song.

¹We give thanks to you, O God,
  we give thanks, for your Name is
    near;
  men tell of your wonderful deeds.

²You say, "I choose the appointed
    time;
  it is I who judge uprightly.
³When the earth and all its people
    quake,
  it is I who hold its pillars firm.
                                    Selah

⁴To the arrogant I say, 'Boast no
    more,'
  and to the wicked, 'Do not lift up
    your horns.
⁵Do not lift your horns against heaven;
  do not speak with outstretched
    neck.' "

⁶No one from the east or the west
  or from the desert can exalt a man.
⁷But it is God who judges:
  He brings one down, he exalts
    another.
⁸In the hand of the LORD is a cup
  full of foaming wine mixed with
    spices;
  he pours it out, and all the wicked of
    the earth
  drink it down to its very dregs.

⁹As for me, I will declare this forever;
  I will sing praise to the God of
    Jacob.
¹⁰I will cut off the horns of all the
    wicked,
  but the horns of the righteous will
    be lifted up.

Psalm 76

For the director of music. With stringed
instruments. A psalm of Asaph. A song.

¹In Judah God is known;
  his name is great in Israel.
²His tent is in Salem,
  his dwelling place in Zion.
³There he broke the flashing arrows,
  the shields and the swords, the
    weapons of war.   *Selah*

⁴You are resplendent with light,
  more majestic than mountains rich
    with game.
⁵Valiant men lie plundered,
  they sleep their last sleep;
  not one of the warriors
  can lift his hands.
⁶At your rebuke, O God of Jacob,
  both horse and chariot lie still.
⁷You alone are to be feared.
  Who can stand before you when
    you are angry?
⁸From heaven you pronounced
    judgment,
  and the land feared and was
    quiet—
⁹when you, O God, rose up to judge,
  to save all the afflicted of the land.
                                    Selah
¹⁰Surely your wrath against men brings
    you praise,
  and the survivors of your wrath are
    restrained.ᵃ

¹¹Make vows to the LORD your God and
    fulfill them;
  let all the neighboring lands
  bring gifts to the One to be feared.
¹²He breaks the spirit of rulers;
  he is feared by the kings of the
    earth.

Psalm 77

For the director of music. For Jeduthun.
Of Asaph. A psalm.

¹I cried out to God for help;
  I cried out to God to hear me.
²When I was in distress, I sought the
    Lord;
  at night I stretched out untiring
    hands
  and my soul refused to be
    comforted.

³I remembered you, O God, and I
    groaned;
  I mused, and my spirit grew faint.
                                    Selah

⁴You kept my eyes from closing;
  I was too troubled to speak.

ᵃ 10 Or *Surely the wrath of men brings you praise,* /
and with the remainder of wrath you arm yourself

⁵I thought about the former days,
  the years of long ago;
⁶I remembered my songs in the night.
  My heart mused and my spirit
    inquired:

⁷"Will the Lord reject forever?
  Will he never show his favor again?
⁸Has his unfailing love vanished
    forever?
  Has his promise failed for all
    time?
⁹Has God forgotten to be merciful?
  Has he in anger withheld his
    compassion?"   *Selah*

¹⁰Then I thought, "To this I will
    appeal:
  the years of the right hand of the
    Most High."
¹¹I will remember the deeds of the
    LORD;
  yes, I will remember your miracles
    of long ago.
¹²I will meditate on all your works
  and consider all your mighty
    deeds.

¹³Your ways, O God, are holy.
  What god is so great as our God?
¹⁴You are the God who performs
    miracles;
  you display your power among the
    peoples.
¹⁵With your mighty arm you redeemed
    your people,
  the descendants of Jacob and
    Joseph.   *Selah*

¹⁶The waters saw you, O God,
  the waters saw you and writhed;
  the very depths were convulsed.
¹⁷The clouds poured down water,
  the skies resounded with thunder;
  your arrows flashed back and forth.
¹⁸Your thunder was heard in the
    whirlwind,
  your lightning lit up the world;
  the earth trembled and quaked.
¹⁹Your path led through the sea,
  your way through the mighty
    waters,
  though your footprints were not
    seen.

²⁰You led your people like a flock
  by the hand of Moses and Aaron.

Psalm 78

A *maskil*ᵃ of Asaph.

¹O my people, hear my teaching;
  listen to the words of my mouth.
²I will open my mouth in parables,
  I will utter hidden things, things
    from of old—
³what we have heard and known,
  what our fathers have told us.
⁴We will not hide them from their
    children;
  we will tell the next generation
  the praiseworthy deeds of the LORD,
    his power, and the wonders he has
    done.
⁵He decreed statutes for Jacob
  and established the law in Israel,
  which he commanded our forefathers
    to teach their children,
⁶so the next generation would know
    them,
  even the children yet to be born,
  and they in turn would tell their
    children.
⁷Then they would put their trust in
    God
  and would not forget his deeds
  but would keep his commands.
⁸They would not be like their
    forefathers—
  a stubborn and rebellious
    generation,
  whose hearts were not loyal to God,
  whose spirits were not faithful to
    him.

⁹The men of Ephraim, though armed
    with bows,
  turned back on the day of battle;
¹⁰they did not keep God's covenant
  and refused to live by his law.
¹¹They forgot what he had done,
  the wonders he had shown them.
¹²He did miracles in the sight of their
    fathers
  in the land of Egypt, in the region
    of Zoan.
¹³He divided the sea and led them
    through;
  he made the water stand firm like
    a wall.
¹⁴He guided them with the cloud by
    day

ᵃTitle: Probably a literary or musical term

and with light from the fire all
night.
¹⁵He split the rocks in the desert
and gave them water as abundant
as the seas;
¹⁶he brought streams out of a rocky
crag
and made water flow down like
rivers.

¹⁷But they continued to sin against
him,
rebelling in the desert against the
Most High.
¹⁸They willfully put God to the test
by demanding the food they
craved.
¹⁹They spoke against God, saying,
"Can God spread a table in the
desert?
²⁰When he struck the rock, water
gushed out,
and streams flowed abundantly.
But can he also give us food?
Can he supply meat for his people?"
²¹When the LORD heard them, he was
very angry;
his fire broke out against Jacob,
and his wrath rose against Israel,
²²for they did not believe in God
or trust in his deliverance.
²³Yet he gave a command to the skies
above
and opened the doors of the
heavens;
²⁴he rained down manna for the people
to eat,
he gave them the grain of heaven.
²⁵Men ate the bread of angels;
he sent them all the food they
could eat.
²⁶He let loose the east wind from the
heavens
and led forth the south wind by
his power.
²⁷He rained meat down on them like
dust,
flying birds like sand on the
seashore.
²⁸He made them come down inside
their camp,
all around their tents.
²⁹They ate till they had more than
enough,
for he had given them what they
craved.

³⁰But before they turned from the food
they craved,
even while it was still in their
mouths,
³¹God's anger rose against them;
he put to death the sturdiest
among them,
cutting down the young men of
Israel.

³²In spite of all this, they kept on
sinning;
in spite of his wonders, they did
not believe.
³³So he ended their days in futility
and their years in terror.
³⁴Whenever God slew them, they would
seek him;
they eagerly turned to him again.
³⁵They remembered that God was their
Rock,
that God Most High was their
Redeemer.
³⁶But then they would flatter him with
their mouths,
lying to him with their tongues;
³⁷their hearts were not loyal to him,
they were not faithful to his
covenant.
³⁸Yet he was merciful;
he forgave their iniquities
and did not destroy them.
Time after time he restrained his
anger
and did not stir up his full wrath.
³⁹He remembered that they were but
flesh,
a passing breeze that does not
return.

⁴⁰How often they rebelled against him
in the desert
and grieved him in the wasteland!
⁴¹Again and again they put God to the
test;
they vexed the Holy One of Israel.
⁴²They did not remember his power—
the day he redeemed them from
the oppressor,
⁴³the day he displayed his miraculous
signs in Egypt,
his wonders in the region of Zoan.
⁴⁴He turned their rivers to blood;
they could not drink from their
streams.
⁴⁵He sent swarms of flies that devoured
them,

and frogs that devastated them.
⁴⁶He gave their crops to the
      grasshopper,
   their produce to the locust.
⁴⁷He destroyed their vines with hail
   and their sycamore-figs with sleet.
⁴⁸He gave over their cattle to the hail,
   their livestock to bolts of lightning.
⁴⁹He unleashed against them his hot
      anger,
   his wrath, indignation and
      hostility—
   a band of destroying angels.
⁵⁰He prepared a path for his anger;
   he did not spare them from death
   but gave them over to the plague.
⁵¹He struck down all the firstborn of
      Egypt,
   the firstfruits of manhood in the
      tents of Ham.
⁵²But he brought his people out like a
      flock;
   he led them like sheep through the
      desert.
⁵³He guided them safely, so they were
      unafraid;
   but the sea engulfed their enemies.
⁵⁴Thus he brought them to the border
      of his holy land,
   to the hill country his right hand
      had taken.
⁵⁵He drove out nations before them
   and allotted their lands to them as
      an inheritance;
   he settled the tribes of Israel in
      their homes.

⁵⁶But they put God to the test
   and rebelled against the Most
      High;
   they did not keep his statutes.
⁵⁷Like their fathers they were disloyal
      and faithless,
   as unreliable as a faulty bow.
⁵⁸They angered him with their high
      places;
   they aroused his jealousy with their
      idols.
⁵⁹When God heard them, he was very
      angry;
   he rejected Israel completely.
⁶⁰He abandoned the tabernacle of
      Shiloh,
   the tent he had set up among men.
⁶¹He sent ˻the ark of˼ his might into
      captivity,

his splendor into the hands of the
      enemy.
⁶²He gave his people over to the sword;
   he was very angry with his
      inheritance.
⁶³Fire consumed their young men,
   and their maidens had no wedding
      songs;
⁶⁴their priests were put to the sword,
   and their widows could not weep.

⁶⁵Then the Lord awoke as from sleep,
   as a man wakes from the stupor of
      wine.
⁶⁶He beat back his enemies;
   he put them to everlasting shame.
⁶⁷Then he rejected the tents of Joseph,
   he did not choose the tribe of
      Ephraim;
⁶⁸but he chose the tribe of Judah,
   Mount Zion, which he loved.
⁶⁹He built his sanctuary like the
      heights,
   like the earth that he established
      forever.
⁷⁰He chose David his servant
   and took him from the sheep pens;
⁷¹from tending the sheep he brought
      him
   to be the shepherd of his people
      Jacob,
   of Israel his inheritance.
⁷²And David shepherded them with
      integrity of heart;
   with skillful hands he led them.

Psalm 79

A psalm of Asaph.

¹O God, the nations have invaded
      your inheritance;
   they have defiled your holy temple,
   they have reduced Jerusalem to
      rubble.
²They have given the dead bodies of
      your servants
   as food to the birds of the air,
   the flesh of your saints to the
      beasts of the earth.
³They have poured out blood like
      water
   all around Jerusalem,
   and there is no one to bury the
      dead.

⁴We are objects of reproach to our
    neighbors,
  of scorn and derision to those
    around us.

⁵How long, O LORD? Will you be
    angry forever?
  How long will your jealousy burn
    like fire?
⁶Pour out your wrath on the nations
  that do not acknowledge you,
on the kingdoms
  that do not call on your name;
⁷for they have devoured Jacob
  and destroyed his homeland.
⁸Do not hold against us the sins of the
    fathers;
  may your mercy come quickly to
    meet us,
for we are in desperate need.

⁹Help us, O God our Savior,
  for the glory of your name;
deliver us and forgive our sins
  for your name's sake.
¹⁰Why should the nations say,
  "Where is their God?"
Before our eyes, make known among
    the nations
  that you avenge the outpoured
    blood of your servants.
¹¹May the groans of the prisoners come
    before you;
  by the strength of your arm
  preserve those condemned to die.

¹²Pay back into the laps of our
    neighbors seven times
  the reproach they have hurled at
    you, O Lord.
¹³Then we your people, the sheep of
    your pasture,
  will praise you forever;
from generation to generation
  we will recount your praise.

Psalm 80

For the director of music. To ⌐the tune
of⌐ "The Lilies of the Covenant."
Of Asaph. A psalm.

¹Hear us, O Shepherd of Israel,
  you who lead Joseph like a flock;
you who sit enthroned between the
    cherubim, shine forth
2   before Ephraim, Benjamin and
    Manasseh.

Awaken your might;
  come and save us.

³Restore us, O God;
  make your face shine upon us,
  that we may be saved.

⁴O LORD God Almighty,
  how long will your anger smolder
  against the prayers of your people?
⁵You have fed them with the bread of
    tears;
  you have made them drink tears by
    the bowlful.
⁶You have made us a source of
    contention to our neighbors,
  and our enemies mock us.

⁷Restore us, O God Almighty;
  make your face shine upon us,
  that we may be saved.

⁸You brought a vine out of Egypt;
  you drove out the nations and
    planted it.
⁹You cleared the ground for it,
  and it took root and filled the
    land.
¹⁰The mountains were covered with its
    shade,
  the mighty cedars with its
    branches.
¹¹It sent out its boughs to the Sea,ᵃ
  its shoots as far as the River.ᵇ

¹²Why have you broken down its walls
  so that all who pass by pick its
    grapes?
¹³Boars from the forest ravage it
  and the creatures of the field feed
    on it.
¹⁴Return to us, O God Almighty!
  Look down from heaven and see!
Watch over this vine,
15   the root your right hand has
    planted,
  the sonᶜ you have raised up for
    yourself.

¹⁶Your vine is cut down, it is burned
    with fire;
  at your rebuke your people perish.
¹⁷Let your hand rest on the man at
    your right hand,
  the son of man you have raised up
    for yourself.

ᵃ11 Probably the Mediterranean   ᵇ11 That is,
the Euphrates   ᶜ15 Or branch

¹⁸Then we will not turn away from
    you;
  revive us, and we will call on your
    name.

¹⁹Restore us, O LORD God Almighty;
  make your face shine upon us,
  that we may be saved.

Psalm 81

For the director of music. According to
  *gittith.*ᵃ Of Asaph.

¹Sing for joy to God our strength;
  shout aloud to the God of Jacob!
²Begin the music, strike the
    tambourine,
  play the melodious harp and lyre.

³Sound the ram's horn at the New
    Moon,
  and when the moon is full, on the
    day of our Feast;
⁴this is a decree for Israel,
  an ordinance of the God of Jacob.
⁵He established it as a statute for
    Joseph
  when he went out against Egypt,
  where we heard a language we did
    not understand.ᵇ

⁶He says, "I removed the burden from
    their shoulders;
  their hands were set free from the
    basket.
⁷In your distress you called and I
    rescued you,
  I answered you out of a
    thundercloud;
  I tested you at the waters of
    Meribah.   *Selah*

⁸"Hear, O my people, and I will warn
    you—
  if you would but listen to me,
    O Israel!
⁹You shall have no foreign god among
    you;
  you shall not bow down to an
    alien god.
¹⁰I am the LORD your God,
  who brought you up out of Egypt.
  Open wide your mouth and I will
    fill it.

¹¹"But my people would not listen to
    me;
  Israel would not submit to me.

¹²So I gave them over to their stubborn
    hearts
  to follow their own devices.

¹³"If my people would but listen to
    me,
  if Israel would follow my ways,
¹⁴how quickly would I subdue their
    enemies
  and turn my hand against their
    foes!
¹⁵Those who hate the LORD would
    cringe before him,
  and their punishment would last
    forever.
¹⁶But you would be fed with the finest
    of wheat;
  with honey from the rock I would
    satisfy you."

Psalm 82

A psalm of Asaph.

¹God presides in the great assembly;
  he gives judgment among the
    "gods":

²"How long will youᶜ defend the
    unjust
  and show partiality to the wicked?
                              Selah
³Defend the cause of the weak and
    fatherless;
  maintain the rights of the poor and
    oppressed.
⁴Rescue the weak and needy;
  deliver them from the hand of the
    wicked.

⁵"They know nothing, they understand
    nothing.
  They walk about in darkness;
  all the foundations of the earth are
    shaken.

⁶"I said, 'You are "gods";
  you are all sons of the Most High.'
⁷But you will die like mere men;
  you will fall like every other ruler."

⁸Rise up, O God, judge the earth,
  for all the nations are your
    inheritance.

ᵃTitle: Probably a musical term   ᵇ5 Or / and we
heard a voice we had not known   ᶜ2 The Hebrew
is plural.

Psalm 83

A song. A psalm of Asaph.

¹O God, do not keep silent;
  be not quiet, O God, be not still.
²See how your enemies are astir,
  how your foes rear their heads.
³With cunning they conspire against
      your people;
  they plot against those you cherish.
⁴"Come," they say, "let us destroy
      them as a nation,
  that the name of Israel be
      remembered no more."

⁵With one mind they plot together;
  they form an alliance against you—
⁶the tents of Edom and the
      Ishmaelites,
  of Moab and the Hagrites,
⁷Gebal,ᵃ Ammon and Amalek,
  Philistia, with the people of Tyre.
⁸Even Assyria has joined them
  to lend strength to the descendants
      of Lot.   *Selah*

⁹Do to them as you did to Midian,
  as you did to Sisera and Jabin at
      the river Kishon,
¹⁰who perished at Endor
  and became like refuse on the
      ground.
¹¹Make their nobles like Oreb and
      Zeeb,
  all their princes like Zebah and
      Zalmunna,
¹²who said, "Let us take possession
  of the pasturelands of God."

¹³Make them like tumbleweed, O my
      God,
  like chaff before the wind.
¹⁴As fire consumes the forest
  or a flame sets the mountains
      ablaze,
¹⁵so pursue them with your tempest
  and terrify them with your storm.
¹⁶Cover their faces with shame
  so that men will seek your name,
      O LORD.

¹⁷May they ever be ashamed and
      dismayed;
  may they perish in disgrace.
¹⁸Let them know that you, whose name
      is the LORD—

that you alone are the Most High
  over all the earth.

Psalm 84

*For the director of music. According to
gittith.ᵇ Of the Sons of Korah. A psalm.*

¹How lovely is your dwelling place,
  O LORD Almighty!
²My soul yearns, even faints,
  for the courts of the LORD;
my heart and my flesh cry out
  for the living God.

³Even the sparrow has found a home,
  and the swallow a nest for herself,
  where she may have her young—
a place near your altar,
  O LORD Almighty, my King and my
      God.
⁴Blessed are those who dwell in your
      house;
  they are ever praising you.   *Selah*

⁵Blessed are those whose strength is in
      you,
  who have set their hearts on
      pilgrimage.
⁶As they pass through the Valley of
      Baca,
  they make it a place of springs;
  the autumn rains also cover it with
      pools.ᶜ
⁷They go from strength to strength,
  till each appears before God in
      Zion.

⁸Hear my prayer, O LORD God
      Almighty;
  listen to me, O God of Jacob. *Selah*
⁹Look upon our shield,ᵈ O God;
  look with favor on your anointed
      one.

¹⁰Better is one day in your courts
  than a thousand elsewhere;
I would rather be a doorkeeper in the
      house of my God
  than dwell in the tents of the
      wicked.
¹¹For the LORD God is a sun and shield;
  the LORD bestows favor and honor;
no good thing does he withhold
  from those whose walk is
      blameless.

ᵃ7 That is, Byblos   ᵇTitle: Probably a musical
term   ᶜ6 Or *blessings*   ᵈ9 Or *sovereign*

¹²O Lᴏʀᴅ Almighty,
     blessed is the man who trusts in
          you.

Psalm 85

For the director of music. Of the Sons of
     Korah. A psalm.

¹You showed favor to your land,
     O Lᴏʀᴅ;
     you restored the fortunes of Jacob.
²You forgave the iniquity of your
          people
     and covered all their sins.   *Selah*
³You set aside all your wrath
     and turned from your fierce anger.

⁴Restore us again, O God our Savior,
     and put away your displeasure
          toward us.
⁵Will you be angry with us forever?
     Will you prolong your anger
          through all generations?
⁶Will you not revive us again,
     that your people may rejoice in
          you?

⁷Show us your unfailing love, O Lᴏʀᴅ,
     and grant us your salvation.

⁸I will listen to what God the Lᴏʀᴅ
     will say;
     he promises peace to his people,
          his saints—
     but let them not return to folly.
⁹Surely his salvation is near those who
          fear him,
     that his glory may dwell in our
          land.

¹⁰Love and faithfulness meet together;
     righteousness and peace kiss each
          other.
¹¹Faithfulness springs forth from the
          earth,
     and righteousness looks down
          from heaven.
¹²The Lᴏʀᴅ will indeed give what is
          good,
     and our land will yield its harvest.
¹³Righteousness goes before him
     and prepares the way for his
          steps.

Low Batteries

Quiet TIMES *with each other*

PSALM 84   "Dave, where did you put the power source for the computer?" I asked. Dave's perplexed look was all the answer I needed to know we were in trouble. Our bags were unpacked, and I was ready to write. Unfortunately, on that day my writing time was numbered—without the power source connector, the computer battery would only last a couple of hours. It was back in Knoxville. We forgot to pack it. So there I sat—with our powerful laptop with all that data—but with no way to tap into it. I was frustrated with Dave and with myself.

When our own spiritual battery is running low and we are too tired to work on our marriage, we need to tap into God's power source. He is willing and able to give us his strength. Verse 5 reminds us, "Blessed are those whose strength is in you, who have set their hearts on pilgrimage." Where do you find your source of strength? For us, it's usually an act of the will to "set our hearts" on doing things God's way and not our way.

When we left our computer connector in Knoxville, we had to stop blaming each other and look to God to help us find a solution. Once we calmed down, we realized we could call Dianne, our office manager, and have her send the power attachment to us. And while we waited for it to arrive, we could choose to focus on something else rather than blaming each other.

—Dave & Claudia

Weekend Warm-up   *When you consider your spiritual life together, how "charged" is it?*

Go to page 621 for your next devotional reading.

Psalm 86

A prayer of David.

¹Hear, O LORD, and answer me,
  for I am poor and needy.
²Guard my life, for I am devoted to
    you.
  You are my God; save your servant
  who trusts in you.
³Have mercy on me, O Lord,
  for I call to you all day long.
⁴Bring joy to your servant,
  for to you, O Lord,
  I lift up my soul.

⁵You are forgiving and good, O Lord,
  abounding in love to all who call
    to you.
⁶Hear my prayer, O LORD;
  listen to my cry for mercy.
⁷In the day of my trouble I will call to
    you,
  for you will answer me.

⁸Among the gods there is none like
    you, O Lord;
  no deeds can compare with yours.
⁹All the nations you have made

will come and worship before you,
    O Lord;
  they will bring glory to your name.
¹⁰For you are great and do marvelous
    deeds;
  you alone are God.

¹¹Teach me your way, O LORD,
  and I will walk in your truth;
  give me an undivided heart,
  that I may fear your name.
¹²I will praise you, O Lord my God,
    with all my heart;
  I will glorify your name forever.
¹³For great is your love toward me;
  you have delivered me from the
    depths of the grave.ᵃ

¹⁴The arrogant are attacking me,
    O God;
  a band of ruthless men seeks my
    life—
  men without regard for you.
¹⁵But you, O Lord, are a compassionate
    and gracious God,
  slow to anger, abounding in love
    and faithfulness.
¹⁶Turn to me and have mercy on me;

ᵃ13 Hebrew *Sheol*

Residue or Realization

Monday

PSALM 86:11 Faith must be tested before faith can be trusted. Whether it's David's faith as he was fleeing those who would try to kill him or the faith of a spouse when her marriage is encountering deep troubles, we will never know how precious God is until he's all we have.

Phyllis went through several years of pain in her marriage. She had always believed in the Lord, but she "never really needed him in a significant way" until her nightmare. After four years of marriage, she found out that her husband had not been faithful to her since the beginning. Initially, she was devastated and spent weeks in tears. But eventually she learned to focus on God and trust him completely with the situation. The way she grew to handle this pain became so remarkable that it was a great example for the people around her.

Now as she looks back on that decade from the other side, Phyllis is able to make an incredible statement: "I'd go through it all again if for no other reason than I learned how wonderful and trustworthy God is." Her pain gave her the privilege of learning to walk in the truth of who God really is. She learned to have an undivided heart by focusing on God.

Difficulty is like an erupting volcano. Some walk away with bitterness and distrust that lingers on them like a residue of ashes. Some, like Phyllis, wash off the ashes of bitterness with the power of realizing who God is. He is the great Comforter in our times of need (see verse 17). As Phyllis grew to understand this truth, she became a mentor to all those around her.

—Bob & Rosemary

Go to page 625 for your next devotional reading.

grant your strength to your servant
and save the son of your
   maidservant.[a]
[17]Give me a sign of your goodness,
that my enemies may see it and be
   put to shame,
for you, O LORD, have helped me
and comforted me.

Psalm 87

Of the Sons of Korah. A psalm. A song.

[1]He has set his foundation on the holy
   mountain;
[2] the LORD loves the gates of Zion
more than all the dwellings of
   Jacob.
[3]Glorious things are said of you,
O city of God: Selah
[4]"I will record Rahab[b] and Babylon
among those who acknowledge
   me—
Philistia too, and Tyre, along with
   Cush[c]—
and will say, 'This[d] one was born
in Zion.' "

[5]Indeed, of Zion it will be said,
"This one and that one were born
   in her,
and the Most High himself will
   establish her."
[6]The LORD will write in the register of
   the peoples:
"This one was born in Zion."   Selah
[7]As they make music they will sing,
"All my fountains are in you."

Psalm 88

A song. A psalm of the Sons of Korah.
For the director of music. According to
mahalath leannoth.[e] A *maskil*[f] of
Heman the Ezrahite.

[1]O LORD, the God who saves me,
day and night I cry out before you.
[2]May my prayer come before you;
turn your ear to my cry.

[3]For my soul is full of trouble
and my life draws near the grave.[g]
[4]I am counted among those who go
   down to the pit;
I am like a man without strength.

[5]I am set apart with the dead,
like the slain who lie in the grave,
whom you remember no more,
who are cut off from your care.

[6]You have put me in the lowest pit,
in the darkest depths.
[7]Your wrath lies heavily upon me;
you have overwhelmed me with all
   your waves.   Selah
[8]You have taken from me my closest
   friends
and have made me repulsive to
   them.
I am confined and cannot escape;
[9] my eyes are dim with grief.

I call to you, O LORD, every day;
I spread out my hands to you.
[10]Do you show your wonders to the
   dead?
Do those who are dead rise up and
   praise you?   Selah
[11]Is your love declared in the grave,
your faithfulness in Destruction[h]?
[12]Are your wonders known in the place
   of darkness,
or your righteous deeds in the land
   of oblivion?

[13]But I cry to you for help, O LORD;
in the morning my prayer comes
   before you.
[14]Why, O LORD, do you reject me
and hide your face from me?

[15]From my youth I have been afflicted
and close to death;
I have suffered your terrors and am
   in despair.
[16]Your wrath has swept over me;
your terrors have destroyed me.
[17]All day long they surround me like a
   flood;
they have completely engulfed me.
[18]You have taken my companions and
   loved ones from me;
the darkness is my closest friend.

---

[a]16 Or *save your faithful son*   [b]4 A poetic name
for Egypt   [c]4 That is, the upper Nile region
[d]4 Or *"O Rahab and Babylon, / Philistia, Tyre and
Cush, / I will record concerning those who acknowledge
me: / 'This*   [e]Title: Possibly a tune, "The
Suffering of Affliction"   [f]Title: Probably a literary
or musical term   [g]3 Hebrew *Sheol*
[h]11 Hebrew *Abaddon*

Psalm 89

A maskil[a] of Ethan the Ezrahite.

[1] I will sing of the LORD's great love
forever;
　with my mouth I will make your
　faithfulness known through
　all generations.
[2] I will declare that your love stands
firm forever,
　that you established your
　faithfulness in heaven itself.

[3] You said, "I have made a covenant
with my chosen one,
　I have sworn to David my servant,
[4] 'I will establish your line forever
　and make your throne firm
　through all generations.' " *Selah*

[5] The heavens praise your wonders,
O LORD,
　your faithfulness too, in the
　assembly of the holy ones.
[6] For who in the skies above can
compare with the LORD?
　Who is like the LORD among the
　heavenly beings?
[7] In the council of the holy ones God
is greatly feared;
　he is more awesome than all who
　surround him.
[8] O LORD God Almighty, who is like
you?
　You are mighty, O LORD, and your
　faithfulness surrounds you.

[9] You rule over the surging sea;
　when its waves mount up, you still
　them.
[10] You crushed Rahab like one of the
slain;
　with your strong arm you scattered
　your enemies.
[11] The heavens are yours, and yours also
the earth;
　you founded the world and all that
　is in it.
[12] You created the north and the south;
　Tabor and Hermon sing for joy at
　your name.
[13] Your arm is endued with power;
　your hand is strong, your right
　hand exalted.

[14] Righteousness and justice are the
foundation of your throne;
　love and faithfulness go before
　you.
[15] Blessed are those who have learned to
acclaim you,
　who walk in the light of your
　presence, O LORD.
[16] They rejoice in your name all day
long;
　they exult in your righteousness.
[17] For you are their glory and strength,
　and by your favor you exalt our
　horn.[b]
[18] Indeed, our shield[c] belongs to the
LORD,
　our king to the Holy One of Israel.

[19] Once you spoke in a vision,
　to your faithful people you said:
"I have bestowed strength on a
warrior;
　I have exalted a young man from
　among the people.
[20] I have found David my servant;
　with my sacred oil I have anointed
　him.
[21] My hand will sustain him;
　surely my arm will strengthen him.
[22] No enemy will subject him to tribute;
　no wicked man will oppress him.
[23] I will crush his foes before him
　and strike down his adversaries.
[24] My faithful love will be with him,
　and through my name his horn[d]
　will be exalted.
[25] I will set his hand over the sea,
　his right hand over the rivers.
[26] He will call out to me, 'You are my
Father,
　my God, the Rock my Savior.'
[27] I will also appoint him my firstborn,
　the most exalted of the kings of the
　earth.
[28] I will maintain my love to him
forever,
　and my covenant with him will
　never fail.
[29] I will establish his line forever,
　his throne as long as the heavens
　endure.

[30] "If his sons forsake my law
　and do not follow my statutes,
[31] if they violate my decrees

---

*a*Title: Probably a literary or musical term
*b*17 *Horn* here symbolizes strong one.　　*c*18 Or
sovereign　　*d*24 *Horn* here symbolizes strength.

and fail to keep my commands,
³²I will punish their sin with the rod,
    their iniquity with flogging;
³³but I will not take my love from him,
    nor will I ever betray my
        faithfulness.
³⁴I will not violate my covenant
    or alter what my lips have uttered.
³⁵Once for all, I have sworn by my
        holiness—
    and I will not lie to David—
³⁶that his line will continue forever
    and his throne endure before me
        like the sun;
³⁷it will be established forever like the
        moon,
    the faithful witness in the sky."
                                    Selah

³⁸But you have rejected, you have
        spurned,
    you have been very angry with
        your anointed one.
³⁹You have renounced the covenant
        with your servant
    and have defiled his crown in the
        dust.
⁴⁰You have broken through all his walls
    and reduced his strongholds to
        ruins.
⁴¹All who pass by have plundered him;
    he has become the scorn of his
        neighbors.
⁴²You have exalted the right hand of
        his foes;
    you have made all his enemies
        rejoice.
⁴³You have turned back the edge of his
        sword
    and have not supported him in
        battle.
⁴⁴You have put an end to his splendor
    and cast his throne to the ground.
⁴⁵You have cut short the days of his
        youth;
    you have covered him with a
        mantle of shame.   *Selah*

⁴⁶How long, O LORD? Will you hide
        yourself forever?
    How long will your wrath burn
        like fire?
⁴⁷Remember how fleeting is my life.
    For what futility you have created
        all men!
⁴⁸What man can live and not see death,

or save himself from the power of
    the grave*ᵃ*?   *Selah*
⁴⁹O Lord, where is your former great
        love,
    which in your faithfulness you
        swore to David?
⁵⁰Remember, Lord, how your servant
        has*ᵇ* been mocked,
    how I bear in my heart the taunts
        of all the nations,
⁵¹the taunts with which your enemies
        have mocked, O LORD,
    with which they have mocked
        every step of your anointed
        one.

⁵²Praise be to the LORD forever!
    Amen and Amen.

BOOK IV
Psalms 90–106

Psalm 90

A prayer of Moses the man of God.

¹Lord, you have been our dwelling
        place
    throughout all generations.
²Before the mountains were born
    or you brought forth the earth and
        the world,
    from everlasting to everlasting you
        are God.

³You turn men back to dust,
    saying, "Return to dust, O sons of
        men."
⁴For a thousand years in your sight
    are like a day that has just gone by,
    or like a watch in the night.
⁵You sweep men away in the sleep of
        death;
    they are like the new grass of the
        morning—
⁶though in the morning it springs up
        new,
    by evening it is dry and withered.

⁷We are consumed by your anger
    and terrified by your indignation.
⁸You have set our iniquities before
        you,
    our secret sins in the light of your
        presence.

ᵃ48 Hebrew *Sheol*   *ᵇ50* Or *your servants have*

⁹All our days pass away under your
    wrath;
  we finish our years with a moan.
¹⁰The length of our days is seventy
    years—
  or eighty, if we have the strength;
  yet their span^a is but trouble and
    sorrow,
  for they quickly pass, and we fly
    away.

¹¹Who knows the power of your anger?
  For your wrath is as great as the
    fear that is due you.
¹²Teach us to number our days aright,
  that we may gain a heart of
    wisdom.

¹³Relent, O Lord! How long will it be?
  Have compassion on your servants.
¹⁴Satisfy us in the morning with your
    unfailing love,
  that we may sing for joy and be
    glad all our days.
¹⁵Make us glad for as many days as you
    have afflicted us,
  for as many years as we have seen
    trouble.
¹⁶May your deeds be shown to your
    servants,
  your splendor to their children.

¹⁷May the favor^b of the Lord our God
    rest upon us;

establish the work of our hands for
    us—
yes, establish the work of our
    hands.

Psalm 91

¹He who dwells in the shelter of the
    Most High
will rest in the shadow of the
    Almighty.^c
²I will say^d of the Lord, "He is my
    refuge and my fortress,
my God, in whom I trust."

³Surely he will save you from the
    fowler's snare
and from the deadly pestilence.
⁴He will cover you with his feathers,
  and under his wings you will find
    refuge;
his faithfulness will be your shield
    and rampart.
⁵You will not fear the terror of night,
  nor the arrow that flies by day,
⁶nor the pestilence that stalks in the
    darkness,
  nor the plague that destroys at
    midday.
⁷A thousand may fall at your side,
  ten thousand at your right hand,

^a10 Or yet the best of them   ^b17 Or beauty
^c1 Hebrew Shaddai   ^d2 Or He says

Seize the Day

Tuesday

PSALM 90 One wise couple literally numbered their days. If at age 40 they lived until age 85, they had 45 years left to live—or 540 months— or 16,425 days! Realizing the brevity of life motivated them to take time for their marriage now. They took practical steps to make their days count; they set aside one day a week for a date night, one week a year for a couple vacation and fifteen minutes each day for couple devotions and prayer.

Sixty seconds makes a minute. Sixty minutes make an hour and hours turn into days. Days disappear into years. Life zips by faster than you may think. The psalmist was well aware of how fast time goes by when he challenged us to "number our days" (verse 12) and to use wisely the time we have.

How our marriages need time! But too often our spouse gets put on hold. We think we'll focus on our marriage once that urgent project at work is finished . . . once the baby sleeps through the night . . . or is potty-trained . . . or starts school . . . or when we get through those difficult adolescent years.

Maybe it's time you stop, take a break, do a little math and number your days. It may be later than you think!

—*Dave & Claudia*

Go to page 628 for your next devotional reading.

but it will not come near you.
⁸You will only observe with your eyes
    and see the punishment of the
    wicked.

⁹If you make the Most High your
    dwelling—
    even the LORD, who is my refuge—
¹⁰then no harm will befall you,
    no disaster will come near your
    tent.
¹¹For he will command his angels
    concerning you
    to guard you in all your ways;
¹²they will lift you up in their hands,
    so that you will not strike your
    foot against a stone.
¹³You will tread upon the lion and the
    cobra;
    you will trample the great lion and
    the serpent.

¹⁴"Because he loves me," says the LORD,
    "I will rescue him;
    I will protect him, for he
    acknowledges my name.
¹⁵He will call upon me, and I will
    answer him;
    I will be with him in trouble,
    I will deliver him and honor him.
¹⁶With long life will I satisfy him
    and show him my salvation."

Psalm 92

A psalm. A song. For the Sabbath day.

¹It is good to praise the LORD
    and make music to your name,
    O Most High,
²to proclaim your love in the morning
    and your faithfulness at night,
³to the music of the ten-stringed lyre
    and the melody of the harp.

⁴For you make me glad by your deeds,
    O LORD;
    I sing for joy at the works of your
    hands.
⁵How great are your works, O LORD,
    how profound your thoughts!
⁶The senseless man does not know,
    fools do not understand,
⁷that though the wicked spring up like
    grass

and all evildoers flourish,
    they will be forever destroyed.

⁸But you, O LORD, are exalted forever.

⁹For surely your enemies, O LORD,
    surely your enemies will perish;
    all evildoers will be scattered.
¹⁰You have exalted my horn*ᵃ* like that
    of a wild ox;
    fine oils have been poured upon
    me.
¹¹My eyes have seen the defeat of my
    adversaries;
    my ears have heard the rout of my
    wicked foes.

¹²The righteous will flourish like a
    palm tree,
    they will grow like a cedar of
    Lebanon;
¹³planted in the house of the LORD,
    they will flourish in the courts of
    our God.
¹⁴They will still bear fruit in old age,
    they will stay fresh and green,
¹⁵proclaiming, "The LORD is upright;
    he is my Rock, and there is no
    wickedness in him."

Psalm 93

¹The LORD reigns, he is robed in
    majesty;
    the LORD is robed in majesty
    and is armed with strength.
The world is firmly established;
    it cannot be moved.
²Your throne was established long ago;
    you are from all eternity.

³The seas have lifted up, O LORD,
    the seas have lifted up their voice;
    the seas have lifted up their
    pounding waves.
⁴Mightier than the thunder of the great
    waters,
    mightier than the breakers of the
    sea—
    the LORD on high is mighty.

⁵Your statutes stand firm;
    holiness adorns your house
    for endless days, O LORD.

ᵃ 10 Horn here symbolizes strength.

Psalm 94

1O Lord, the God who avenges,
  O God who avenges, shine forth.
2Rise up, O Judge of the earth;
  pay back to the proud what they
    deserve.
3How long will the wicked, O Lord,
  how long will the wicked be
    jubilant?

4They pour out arrogant words;
  all the evildoers are full of
    boasting.
5They crush your people, O Lord;
  they oppress your inheritance.
6They slay the widow and the alien;
  they murder the fatherless.
7They say, "The Lord does not see;
  the God of Jacob pays no heed."

8Take heed, you senseless ones among
    the people;
  you fools, when will you become
    wise?
9Does he who implanted the ear not
    hear?
  Does he who formed the eye not
    see?
10Does he who disciplines nations not
    punish?
  Does he who teaches man lack
    knowledge?
11The Lord knows the thoughts of
    man;
  he knows that they are futile.

12Blessed is the man you discipline,
    O Lord,
  the man you teach from your law;
13you grant him relief from days of
    trouble,
  till a pit is dug for the wicked.
14For the Lord will not reject his
    people;
  he will never forsake his
    inheritance.
15Judgment will again be founded on
    righteousness,
  and all the upright in heart will
    follow it.

16Who will rise up for me against the
    wicked?
  Who will take a stand for me
    against evildoers?
17Unless the Lord had given me help,
  I would soon have dwelt in the
    silence of death.
18When I said, "My foot is slipping,"
  your love, O Lord, supported me.
19When anxiety was great within me,
  your consolation brought joy to
    my soul.

20Can a corrupt throne be allied with
    you—
  one that brings on misery by its
    decrees?
21They band together against the
    righteous
  and condemn the innocent to
    death.
22But the Lord has become my fortress,
  and my God the rock in whom I
    take refuge.
23He will repay them for their sins
  and destroy them for their
    wickedness;
  the Lord our God will destroy
    them.

Psalm 95

1Come, let us sing for joy to the Lord;
  let us shout aloud to the Rock of
    our salvation.
2Let us come before him with
    thanksgiving
  and extol him with music and
    song.

3For the Lord is the great God,
  the great King above all gods.
4In his hand are the depths of the
    earth,
  and the mountain peaks belong to
    him.
5The sea is his, for he made it,
  and his hands formed the dry land.

6Come, let us bow down in worship,
  let us kneel before the Lord our
    Maker;
7for he is our God
  and we are the people of his
    pasture,
  the flock under his care.

Today, if you hear his voice,
8   do not harden your hearts as you
      did at Meribah, a

a8 Meribah means quarreling.

as you did that day at Massah[a] in
the desert,
[9]where your fathers tested and tried
me,
though they had seen what I did.
[10]For forty years I was angry with that
generation;
I said, "They are a people whose
hearts go astray,
and they have not known my ways."
[11]So I declared on oath in my anger,
"They shall never enter my rest."

Psalm 96

[1]Sing to the LORD a new song;
sing to the LORD, all the earth.
[2]Sing to the LORD, praise his name;
proclaim his salvation day after
day.
[3]Declare his glory among the nations,
his marvelous deeds among all
peoples.

[4]For great is the LORD and most
worthy of praise;
he is to be feared above all gods.
[5]For all the gods of the nations are
idols,
but the LORD made the heavens.

[6]Splendor and majesty are before him;
strength and glory are in his
sanctuary.

[7]Ascribe to the LORD, O families of
nations,
ascribe to the LORD glory and
strength.
[8]Ascribe to the LORD the glory due his
name;
bring an offering and come into
his courts.
[9]Worship the LORD in the splendor of
his[b] holiness;
tremble before him, all the earth.

[10]Say among the nations, "The LORD
reigns."
The world is firmly established, it
cannot be moved;
he will judge the peoples with
equity.
[11]Let the heavens rejoice, let the earth
be glad;
let the sea resound, and all that is
in it;

---

[a]8 *Massah* means *testing.*   [b]9 Or LORD *with the*
splendor of

To Go or Not to Go

Wednesday

PSALM 95:6 A friend of ours told us
a funny story about two guys who
were fishing fanatics. On a recent
Sunday morning they woke up at
4:00 A.M. and drove more than one
hundred miles into the mountains
expecting to catch trout in their favorite secluded stream—they had kept its
location secret for years. After hiking two
miles in from the road, their enthusiasm
vanished when they saw how muddy the
waters were (because of recent flooding).
Muddy water made fishing impractical. With
disgust, one said to the other, "You might as
well have stayed home and gone to church,"
to which his companion retorted with a
straight face, "Oh, I can't go to church any-
how; my wife is sick."

Some people find an excuse to miss
church whenever they can. Others can't do
without it. We fall into the latter camp. The

church where we worship is a place
of support and spiritual refueling.
Singing hymns, learning from
Scripture, worshiping God and
meeting with friends who share
our spiritual quest are all comforting and inspiring. Worshiping together
buoys our relationship and helps the week
ahead feel more meaningful.

How we choose to incorporate the
church into our marriage is critically important in becoming soul mates. Paul recognized the idea of the church as being God's
family when he said we are "members of
God's household" (Ephesians 2:19). When
Jesus taught his disciples to pray, he did not
say "my Father"; he said, "our Father." We
cannot live the Christian life in isolation.
Even couples need a community of worship.

—Les & Leslie

Go to page 640 for your next devotional reading.

12 let the fields be jubilant, and
everything in them.
Then all the trees of the forest will
sing for joy;
13 they will sing before the LORD, for
he comes,
he comes to judge the earth.
He will judge the world in
righteousness
and the peoples in his truth.

Psalm 97

¹The LORD reigns, let the earth be glad;
let the distant shores rejoice.

²Clouds and thick darkness surround
him;
righteousness and justice are the
foundation of his throne.
³Fire goes before him
and consumes his foes on every
side.
⁴His lightning lights up the world;
the earth sees and trembles.
⁵The mountains melt like wax before
the LORD,
before the Lord of all the earth.
⁶The heavens proclaim his
righteousness,
and all the peoples see his glory.

⁷All who worship images are put to
shame,
those who boast in idols—
worship him, all you gods!

⁸Zion hears and rejoices
and the villages of Judah are glad
because of your judgments,
O LORD.
⁹For you, O LORD, are the Most High
over all the earth;
you are exalted far above all gods.

¹⁰Let those who love the LORD hate
evil,
for he guards the lives of his
faithful ones
and delivers them from the hand
of the wicked.
¹¹Light is shed upon the righteous
and joy on the upright in heart.
¹²Rejoice in the LORD, you who are
righteous,
and praise his holy name.

Psalm 98

A psalm.

¹Sing to the LORD a new song,
for he has done marvelous things;
his right hand and his holy arm
have worked salvation for him.
²The LORD has made his salvation
known
and revealed his righteousness to
the nations.
³He has remembered his love
and his faithfulness to the house of
Israel;
all the ends of the earth have seen
the salvation of our God.

⁴Shout for joy to the LORD, all the
earth,
burst into jubilant song with
music;
⁵make music to the LORD with the
harp,
with the harp and the sound of
singing,
⁶with trumpets and the blast of the
ram's horn—
shout for joy before the LORD, the
King.

⁷Let the sea resound, and everything in
it,
the world, and all who live in it.
⁸Let the rivers clap their hands,
let the mountains sing together for
joy;
⁹let them sing before the LORD,
for he comes to judge the earth.
He will judge the world in
righteousness
and the peoples with equity.

Psalm 99

¹The LORD reigns,
let the nations tremble;
he sits enthroned between the
cherubim,
let the earth shake.
²Great is the LORD in Zion;
he is exalted over all the nations.
³Let them praise your great and
awesome name—
he is holy.

⁴The King is mighty, he loves justice—
you have established equity;

in Jacob you have done
  what is just and right.
[5]Exalt the LORD our God
  and worship at his footstool;
  he is holy.

[6]Moses and Aaron were among his
    priests,
  Samuel was among those who
    called on his name;
they called on the LORD
  and he answered them.
[7]He spoke to them from the pillar of
    cloud;
  they kept his statutes and the
    decrees he gave them.

[8]O LORD our God,
  you answered them;
you were to Israel[a] a forgiving God,
  though you punished their
    misdeeds.[b]
[9]Exalt the LORD our God
  and worship at his holy mountain,
  for the LORD our God is holy.

Psalm 100

A psalm. For giving thanks.

[1]Shout for joy to the LORD, all the
    earth.
[2] Worship the LORD with gladness;
  come before him with joyful songs.
[3]Know that the LORD is God.
  It is he who made us, and we are
    his[c];
  we are his people, the sheep of his
    pasture.

[4]Enter his gates with thanksgiving
  and his courts with praise;
  give thanks to him and praise his
    name.
[5]For the LORD is good and his love
    endures forever;
  his faithfulness continues through
    all generations.

Psalm 101

Of David. A psalm.

[1]I will sing of your love and justice;
  to you, O LORD, I will sing praise.
[2]I will be careful to lead a blameless
    life—
  when will you come to me?

I will walk in my house
  with blameless heart.
[3]I will set before my eyes
  no vile thing.

The deeds of faithless men I hate;
  they will not cling to me.
[4]Men of perverse heart shall be far
    from me;
  I will have nothing to do with evil.

[5]Whoever slanders his neighbor in
    secret,
  him will I put to silence;
whoever has haughty eyes and a
    proud heart,
  him will I not endure.

[6]My eyes will be on the faithful in the
    land,
  that they may dwell with me;
  he whose walk is blameless
    will minister to me.

[7]No one who practices deceit
  will dwell in my house;
no one who speaks falsely
  will stand in my presence.

[8]Every morning I will put to silence
  all the wicked in the land;
I will cut off every evildoer
  from the city of the LORD.

Psalm 102

*A prayer of an afflicted man. When he is
faint and pours out his lament
before the LORD.*

[1]Hear my prayer, O LORD;
  let my cry for help come to you.
[2]Do not hide your face from me
  when I am in distress.
Turn your ear to me;
  when I call, answer me quickly.

[3]For my days vanish like smoke;
  my bones burn like glowing
    embers.
[4]My heart is blighted and withered like
    grass;
  I forget to eat my food.
[5]Because of my loud groaning
  I am reduced to skin and bones.
[6]I am like a desert owl,
  like an owl among the ruins.

[a]8 Hebrew *them* [b]8 Or / *an avenger of the
wrongs done to them* [c]3 Or *and not we ourselves*

⁷I lie awake; I have become
  like a bird alone on a roof.
⁸All day long my enemies taunt me;
  those who rail against me use my
    name as a curse.
⁹For I eat ashes as my food
  and mingle my drink with tears
¹⁰because of your great wrath,
  for you have taken me up and
    thrown me aside.
¹¹My days are like the evening shadow;
  I wither away like grass.

¹²But you, O LORD, sit enthroned
    forever;
  your renown endures through all
    generations.
¹³You will arise and have compassion
    on Zion,
  for it is time to show favor to her;
  the appointed time has come.
¹⁴For her stones are dear to your
    servants;
  her very dust moves them to pity.
¹⁵The nations will fear the name of the
    LORD,
  all the kings of the earth will revere
    your glory.
¹⁶For the LORD will rebuild Zion
  and appear in his glory.
¹⁷He will respond to the prayer of the
    destitute;
  he will not despise their plea.

¹⁸Let this be written for a future
    generation,
  that a people not yet created may
    praise the LORD:
¹⁹"The LORD looked down from his
    sanctuary on high,
  from heaven he viewed the earth,
²⁰to hear the groans of the prisoners
  and release those condemned to
    death."
²¹So the name of the LORD will be
    declared in Zion
  and his praise in Jerusalem
²²when the peoples and the kingdoms
  assemble to worship the LORD.

²³In the course of my life[a] he broke
    my strength;
  he cut short my days.
²⁴So I said:
  "Do not take me away, O my God,
    in the midst of my days;

your years go on through all
    generations.
²⁵In the beginning you laid the
    foundations of the earth,
  and the heavens are the work of
    your hands.
²⁶They will perish, but you remain;
  they will all wear out like a
    garment.
Like clothing you will change them
  and they will be discarded.
²⁷But you remain the same,
  and your years will never end.
²⁸The children of your servants will live
    in your presence;
  their descendants will be
    established before you."

Psalm 103

Of David.

¹Praise the LORD, O my soul;
  all my inmost being, praise his
    holy name.
²Praise the LORD, O my soul,
  and forget not all his benefits—
³who forgives all your sins
  and heals all your diseases,
⁴who redeems your life from the pit
  and crowns you with love and
    compassion,
⁵who satisfies your desires with good
    things
  so that your youth is renewed like
    the eagle's.

⁶The LORD works righteousness
  and justice for all the oppressed.

⁷He made known his ways to Moses,
  his deeds to the people of Israel:
⁸The LORD is compassionate and
    gracious,
  slow to anger, abounding in love.
⁹He will not always accuse,
  nor will he harbor his anger
    forever;
¹⁰he does not treat us as our sins
    deserve
  or repay us according to our
    iniquities.
¹¹For as high as the heavens are above
    the earth,

---

a23 Or By his power

so great is his love for those who
fear him;
¹²as far as the east is from the west,
so far has he removed our
transgressions from us.
¹³As a father has compassion on his
children,
so the LORD has compassion on
those who fear him;
¹⁴for he knows how we are formed,
he remembers that we are dust.
¹⁵As for man, his days are like grass,
he flourishes like a flower of the
field;
¹⁶the wind blows over it and it is gone,
and its place remembers it no
more.
¹⁷But from everlasting to everlasting
the LORD's love is with those who
fear him,
and his righteousness with their
children's children—
¹⁸with those who keep his covenant
and remember to obey his
precepts.

¹⁹The LORD has established his throne
in heaven,
and his kingdom rules over all.

²⁰Praise the LORD, you his angels,
you mighty ones who do his
bidding,
who obey his word.
²¹Praise the LORD, all his heavenly
hosts,
you his servants who do his will.
²²Praise the LORD, all his works
everywhere in his dominion.

Praise the LORD, O my soul.

Psalm 104

¹Praise the LORD, O my soul.

O LORD my God, you are very great;
you are clothed with splendor and
majesty.
²He wraps himself in light as with a
garment;
he stretches out the heavens like a
tent
³   and lays the beams of his upper
chambers on their waters.
He makes the clouds his chariot
and rides on the wings of the
wind.

⁴He makes winds his messengers,ᵃ
flames of fire his servants.

⁵He set the earth on its foundations;
it can never be moved.
⁶You covered it with the deep as with
a garment;
the waters stood above the
mountains.
⁷But at your rebuke the waters fled,
at the sound of your thunder they
took to flight;
⁸they flowed over the mountains,
they went down into the valleys,
to the place you assigned for them.
⁹You set a boundary they cannot cross;
never again will they cover the
earth.

¹⁰He makes springs pour water into the
ravines;
it flows between the mountains.
¹¹They give water to all the beasts of
the field;
the wild donkeys quench their
thirst.
¹²The birds of the air nest by the
waters;
they sing among the branches.
¹³He waters the mountains from his
upper chambers;
the earth is satisfied by the fruit of
his work.
¹⁴He makes grass grow for the cattle,
and plants for man to cultivate—
bringing forth food from the earth:
¹⁵wine that gladdens the heart of man,
oil to make his face shine,
and bread that sustains his heart.
¹⁶The trees of the LORD are well
watered,
the cedars of Lebanon that he
planted.
¹⁷There the birds make their nests;
the stork has its home in the pine
trees.
¹⁸The high mountains belong to the
wild goats;
the crags are a refuge for the
coneys.ᵇ

¹⁹The moon marks off the seasons,
and the sun knows when to go
down.
²⁰You bring darkness, it becomes night,

ᵃ4 Or angels   ᵇ18 That is, the hyrax or rock
badger

and all the beasts of the forest
  prowl.
21The lions roar for their prey
  and seek their food from God.
22The sun rises, and they steal away;
  they return and lie down in their
    dens.
23Then man goes out to his work,
  to his labor until evening.

24How many are your works, O LORD!
  In wisdom you made them all;
  the earth is full of your creatures.
25There is the sea, vast and spacious,
  teeming with creatures beyond
    number—
  living things both large and small.
26There the ships go to and fro,
  and the leviathan, which you
    formed to frolic there.

27These all look to you
  to give them their food at the
    proper time.
28When you give it to them,
  they gather it up;
  when you open your hand,
  they are satisfied with good things.
29When you hide your face,
  they are terrified;
  when you take away their breath,
  they die and return to the dust.
30When you send your Spirit,
  they are created,
  and you renew the face of the
    earth.

31May the glory of the LORD endure
    forever;
  may the LORD rejoice in his works—
32he who looks at the earth, and it
    trembles,
  who touches the mountains, and
    they smoke.

33I will sing to the LORD all my life;
  I will sing praise to my God as
    long as I live.
34May my meditation be pleasing to
    him,
  as I rejoice in the LORD.
35But may sinners vanish from the
    earth
  and the wicked be no more.

Praise the LORD, O my soul.

Praise the LORD.[a]

Psalm 105

1Give thanks to the LORD, call on his
    name;
  make known among the nations
    what he has done.
2Sing to him, sing praise to him;
  tell of all his wonderful acts.
3Glory in his holy name;
  let the hearts of those who seek the
    LORD rejoice.
4Look to the LORD and his strength;
  seek his face always.

5Remember the wonders he has done,
  his miracles, and the judgments he
    pronounced,
6O descendants of Abraham his
    servant,
  O sons of Jacob, his chosen ones.
7He is the LORD our God;
  his judgments are in all the earth.

8He remembers his covenant forever,
  the word he commanded, for a
    thousand generations,
9the covenant he made with Abraham,
  the oath he swore to Isaac.
10He confirmed it to Jacob as a decree,
  to Israel as an everlasting covenant:
11"To you I will give the land of
    Canaan
  as the portion you will inherit."

12When they were but few in number,
  few indeed, and strangers in it,
13they wandered from nation to nation,
  from one kingdom to another.
14He allowed no one to oppress them;
  for their sake he rebuked kings:
15"Do not touch my anointed ones;
  do my prophets no harm."

16He called down famine on the land
  and destroyed all their supplies of
    food;
17and he sent a man before them—
  Joseph, sold as a slave.
18They bruised his feet with shackles,
  his neck was put in irons,
19till what he foretold came to pass,
  till the word of the LORD proved
    him true.
20The king sent and released him,
  the ruler of peoples set him free.

a35 Hebrew Hallelu Yah; in the Septuagint this
line stands at the beginning of Psalm 105.

²¹He made him master of his
household,
ruler over all he possessed,
²²to instruct his princes as he pleased
and teach his elders wisdom.

²³Then Israel entered Egypt;
Jacob lived as an alien in the land
of Ham.
²⁴The LORD made his people very
fruitful;
he made them too numerous for
their foes,
²⁵whose hearts he turned to hate his
people,
to conspire against his servants.
²⁶He sent Moses his servant,
and Aaron, whom he had chosen.
²⁷They performed his miraculous signs
among them,
his wonders in the land of Ham.
²⁸He sent darkness and made the land
dark—
for had they not rebelled against
his words?
²⁹He turned their waters into blood,
causing their fish to die.
³⁰Their land teemed with frogs,
which went up into the bedrooms
of their rulers.
³¹He spoke, and there came swarms of
flies,
and gnats throughout their country.
³²He turned their rain into hail,
with lightning throughout their
land;
³³he struck down their vines and fig
trees
and shattered the trees of their
country.
³⁴He spoke, and the locusts came,
grasshoppers without number;
³⁵they ate up every green thing in their
land,
ate up the produce of their soil.
³⁶Then he struck down all the firstborn
in their land,
the firstfruits of all their manhood.

³⁷He brought out Israel, laden with
silver and gold,
and from among their tribes no
one faltered.
³⁸Egypt was glad when they left,
because dread of Israel had fallen
on them.
³⁹He spread out a cloud as a covering,

and a fire to give light at night.
⁴⁰They asked, and he brought them
quail
and satisfied them with the bread
of heaven.
⁴¹He opened the rock, and water
gushed out;
like a river it flowed in the desert.

⁴²For he remembered his holy promise
given to his servant Abraham.
⁴³He brought out his people with
rejoicing,
his chosen ones with shouts of joy;
⁴⁴he gave them the lands of the
nations,
and they fell heir to what others
had toiled for—
⁴⁵that they might keep his precepts
and observe his laws.

Praise the LORD.ᵃ

Psalm 106

¹Praise the LORD.ᵇ

Give thanks to the LORD, for he is
good;
his love endures forever.
²Who can proclaim the mighty acts of
the LORD
or fully declare his praise?
³Blessed are they who maintain justice,
who constantly do what is right.
⁴Remember me, O LORD, when you
show favor to your people,
come to my aid when you save
them,
⁵that I may enjoy the prosperity of
your chosen ones,
that I may share in the joy of your
nation
and join your inheritance in giving
praise.

⁶We have sinned, even as our fathers
did;
we have done wrong and acted
wickedly.
⁷When our fathers were in Egypt,
they gave no thought to your
miracles;
they did not remember your many
kindnesses,

ᵃ45 Hebrew Hallelu Yah   ᵇ1 Hebrew Hallelu
Yah; also in verse 48

and they rebelled by the sea, the
Red Sea.^a

⁸Yet he saved them for his name's
sake,
to make his mighty power known.

⁹He rebuked the Red Sea, and it dried
up;
he led them through the depths as
through a desert.

¹⁰He saved them from the hand of the
foe;
from the hand of the enemy he
redeemed them.

¹¹The waters covered their adversaries;
not one of them survived.

¹²Then they believed his promises
and sang his praise.

¹³But they soon forgot what he had
done
and did not wait for his counsel.

¹⁴In the desert they gave in to their
craving;
in the wasteland they put God to
the test.

¹⁵So he gave them what they asked for,
but sent a wasting disease upon
them.

¹⁶In the camp they grew envious of
Moses
and of Aaron, who was consecrated
to the LORD.

¹⁷The earth opened up and swallowed
Dathan;
it buried the company of Abiram.

¹⁸Fire blazed among their followers;
a flame consumed the wicked.

¹⁹At Horeb they made a calf
and worshiped an idol cast from
metal.

²⁰They exchanged their Glory
for an image of a bull, which eats
grass.

²¹They forgot the God who saved them,
who had done great things in
Egypt,

²²miracles in the land of Ham
and awesome deeds by the Red
Sea.

²³So he said he would destroy them—
had not Moses, his chosen one,
stood in the breach before him
to keep his wrath from destroying
them.

²⁴Then they despised the pleasant land;

they did not believe his promise.

²⁵They grumbled in their tents
and did not obey the LORD.

²⁶So he swore to them with uplifted
hand
that he would make them fall in
the desert,

²⁷make their descendants fall among
the nations
and scatter them throughout the
lands.

²⁸They yoked themselves to the Baal of
Peor
and ate sacrifices offered to lifeless
gods;

²⁹they provoked the LORD to anger by
their wicked deeds,
and a plague broke out among
them.

³⁰But Phinehas stood up and
intervened,
and the plague was checked.

³¹This was credited to him as
righteousness
for endless generations to come.

³²By the waters of Meribah they
angered the LORD,
and trouble came to Moses because
of them;

³³for they rebelled against the Spirit of
God,
and rash words came from Moses'
lips.^b

³⁴They did not destroy the peoples
as the LORD had commanded them,

³⁵but they mingled with the nations
and adopted their customs.

³⁶They worshiped their idols,
which became a snare to them.

³⁷They sacrificed their sons
and their daughters to demons.

³⁸They shed innocent blood,
the blood of their sons and
daughters,
whom they sacrificed to the idols of
Canaan,
and the land was desecrated by
their blood.

³⁹They defiled themselves by what they
did;

---

a7 Hebrew *Yam Suph*; that is, Sea of Reeds; also in
verses 9 and 22   *b33* Or *against his spirit, / and
rash words came from his lips*

by their deeds they prostituted
   themselves.

⁴⁰Therefore the LORD was angry with
   his people
   and abhorred his inheritance.
⁴¹He handed them over to the nations,
   and their foes ruled over them.
⁴²Their enemies oppressed them
   and subjected them to their power.
⁴³Many times he delivered them,
   but they were bent on rebellion
   and they wasted away in their sin.

⁴⁴But he took note of their distress
   when he heard their cry;
⁴⁵for their sake he remembered his
   covenant
   and out of his great love he
   relented.
⁴⁶He caused them to be pitied
   by all who held them captive.

⁴⁷Save us, O LORD our God,
   and gather us from the nations,
   that we may give thanks to your holy
   name
   and glory in your praise.

⁴⁸Praise be to the LORD, the God of
   Israel,
   from everlasting to everlasting.
Let all the people say, "Amen!"

Praise the LORD.

BOOK V

Psalms 107–150

Psalm 107

¹Give thanks to the LORD, for he is
   good;
   his love endures forever.
²Let the redeemed of the LORD say
   this—
   those he redeemed from the hand
   of the foe,
³those he gathered from the lands,
   from east and west, from north
   and south.ᵃ

⁴Some wandered in desert wastelands,
   finding no way to a city where they
   could settle.
⁵They were hungry and thirsty,
   and their lives ebbed away.

⁶Then they cried out to the LORD in
   their trouble,
   and he delivered them from their
   distress.
⁷He led them by a straight way
   to a city where they could settle.
⁸Let them give thanks to the LORD for
   his unfailing love
   and his wonderful deeds for men,
⁹for he satisfies the thirsty
   and fills the hungry with good
   things.

¹⁰Some sat in darkness and the deepest
   gloom,
   prisoners suffering in iron chains,
¹¹for they had rebelled against the
   words of God
   and despised the counsel of the
   Most High.
¹²So he subjected them to bitter labor;
   they stumbled, and there was no
   one to help.
¹³Then they cried to the LORD in their
   trouble,
   and he saved them from their
   distress.
¹⁴He brought them out of darkness and
   the deepest gloom
   and broke away their chains.
¹⁵Let them give thanks to the LORD for
   his unfailing love
   and his wonderful deeds for men,
¹⁶for he breaks down gates of bronze
   and cuts through bars of iron.

¹⁷Some became fools through their
   rebellious ways
   and suffered affliction because of
   their iniquities.
¹⁸They loathed all food
   and drew near the gates of death.
¹⁹Then they cried to the LORD in their
   trouble,
   and he saved them from their
   distress.
²⁰He sent forth his word and healed
   them;
   he rescued them from the grave.
²¹Let them give thanks to the LORD for
   his unfailing love
   and his wonderful deeds for men.
²²Let them sacrifice thank offerings
   and tell of his works with songs of
   joy.

ᵃ3 Hebrew *north and the sea*

23Others went out on the sea in ships;
  they were merchants on the mighty
    waters.
24They saw the works of the LORD,
  his wonderful deeds in the deep.
25For he spoke and stirred up a tempest
  that lifted high the waves.
26They mounted up to the heavens and
    went down to the depths;
  in their peril their courage melted
    away.
27They reeled and staggered like
    drunken men;
  they were at their wits' end.
28Then they cried out to the LORD in
    their trouble,
  and he brought them out of their
    distress.
29He stilled the storm to a whisper;
  the waves of the sea were hushed.
30They were glad when it grew calm,
  and he guided them to their
    desired haven.
31Let them give thanks to the LORD for
    his unfailing love
  and his wonderful deeds for men.
32Let them exalt him in the assembly of
    the people
  and praise him in the council of
    the elders.

33He turned rivers into a desert,
  flowing springs into thirsty ground,
34and fruitful land into a salt waste,
  because of the wickedness of those
    who lived there.
35He turned the desert into pools of
    water
  and the parched ground into
    flowing springs;
36there he brought the hungry to live,
  and they founded a city where they
    could settle.
37They sowed fields and planted
    vineyards
  that yielded a fruitful harvest;
38he blessed them, and their numbers
    greatly increased,
  and he did not let their herds
    diminish.

39Then their numbers decreased, and
    they were humbled
  by oppression, calamity and
    sorrow;
40he who pours contempt on nobles

made them wander in a trackless
    waste.
41But he lifted the needy out of their
    affliction
  and increased their families like
    flocks.
42The upright see and rejoice,
  but all the wicked shut their
    mouths.

43Whoever is wise, let him heed these
    things
  and consider the great love of the
    LORD.

Psalm 108

A song. A psalm of David.

1My heart is steadfast, O God;
  I will sing and make music with all
    my soul.
2Awake, harp and lyre!
  I will awaken the dawn.
3I will praise you, O LORD, among the
    nations;
  I will sing of you among the
    peoples.
4For great is your love, higher than the
    heavens;
  your faithfulness reaches to the
    skies.
5Be exalted, O God, above the
    heavens,
  and let your glory be over all the
    earth.

6Save us and help us with your right
    hand,
  that those you love may be
    delivered.
7God has spoken from his sanctuary:
  "In triumph I will parcel out
    Shechem
  and measure off the Valley of
    Succoth.
8Gilead is mine, Manasseh is mine;
  Ephraim is my helmet,
    Judah my scepter.
9Moab is my washbasin,
  upon Edom I toss my sandal;
  over Philistia I shout in triumph."

10Who will bring me to the fortified
    city?
  Who will lead me to Edom?

¹¹Is it not you, O God, you who have
      rejected us
   and no longer go out with our
      armies?
¹²Give us aid against the enemy,
   for the help of man is worthless.
¹³With God we will gain the victory,
   and he will trample down our
      enemies.

Psalm 109

*For the director of music. Of David.
A psalm.*

¹O God, whom I praise,
   do not remain silent,
²for wicked and deceitful men
      have opened their mouths against
      me;
   they have spoken against me with
      lying tongues.
³With words of hatred they surround
      me;
   they attack me without cause.
⁴In return for my friendship they
      accuse me,
   but I am a man of prayer.
⁵They repay me evil for good,
   and hatred for my friendship.

⁶Appoint*ᵃ* an evil man*ᵇ* to oppose
      him;
   let an accuser*ᶜ* stand at his right
      hand.
⁷When he is tried, let him be found
      guilty,
   and may his prayers condemn him.
⁸May his days be few;
   may another take his place of
      leadership.
⁹May his children be fatherless
   and his wife a widow.
¹⁰May his children be wandering
      beggars;
   may they be driven*ᵈ* from their
      ruined homes.
¹¹May a creditor seize all he has;
   may strangers plunder the fruits of
      his labor.
¹²May no one extend kindness to him
   or take pity on his fatherless
      children.
¹³May his descendants be cut off,
   their names blotted out from the
      next generation.

¹⁴May the iniquity of his fathers be
      remembered before the LORD;
   may the sin of his mother never be
      blotted out.
¹⁵May their sins always remain before
      the LORD,
   that he may cut off the memory of
      them from the earth.
¹⁶For he never thought of doing a
      kindness,
   but hounded to death the poor
   and the needy and the
      brokenhearted.
¹⁷He loved to pronounce a curse—
      may it*ᵉ* come on him;
   he found no pleasure in blessing—
      may it be*ᶠ* far from him.
¹⁸He wore cursing as his garment;
   it entered into his body like water,
      into his bones like oil.
¹⁹May it be like a cloak wrapped about
      him,
   like a belt tied forever around him.
²⁰May this be the LORD's payment to
      my accusers,
   to those who speak evil of me.

²¹But you, O Sovereign LORD,
      deal well with me for your name's
      sake;
   out of the goodness of your love,
      deliver me.
²²For I am poor and needy,
   and my heart is wounded within
      me.
²³I fade away like an evening shadow;
   I am shaken off like a locust.
²⁴My knees give way from fasting;
   my body is thin and gaunt.
²⁵I am an object of scorn to my
      accusers;
   when they see me, they shake their
      heads.

²⁶Help me, O LORD my God;
   save me in accordance with your
      love.
²⁷Let them know that it is your hand,
   that you, O LORD, have done it.
²⁸They may curse, but you will bless;

ᵃ6 Or ⸢*They say:*⸥ *"Appoint* (with quotation marks at
the end of verse 19)   *ᵇ6* Or *the Evil One*
ᶜ6 Or *let Satan*   *ᵈ10* Septuagint; Hebrew *sought*
ᵉ17 Or *curse,* / *and it has*   *ᶠ17* Or *blessing,* / *and
it is*

when they attack they will be put
  to shame,
but your servant will rejoice.
29My accusers will be clothed with
    disgrace
  and wrapped in shame as in a
    cloak.
30With my mouth I will greatly extol
    the LORD;
  in the great throng I will praise
    him.
31For he stands at the right hand of the
    needy one,
  to save his life from those who
    condemn him.

Psalm 110

Of David. A psalm.

1The LORD says to my Lord:
  "Sit at my right hand
until I make your enemies
  a footstool for your feet."

2The LORD will extend your mighty
    scepter from Zion;
  you will rule in the midst of your
    enemies.
3Your troops will be willing
  on your day of battle.
Arrayed in holy majesty,
  from the womb of the dawn
  you will receive the dew of your
    youth.*a*

4The LORD has sworn
  and will not change his mind:
"You are a priest forever,
  in the order of Melchizedek."

5The Lord is at your right hand;
  he will crush kings on the day of
    his wrath.
6He will judge the nations, heaping up
    the dead
  and crushing the rulers of the
    whole earth.
7He will drink from a brook beside the
    way*b*;
  therefore he will lift up his head.

Psalm 111 *c*

1Praise the LORD.*d*

I will extol the LORD with all my
    heart

in the council of the upright and
  in the assembly.

2Great are the works of the LORD;
  they are pondered by all who
    delight in them.
3Glorious and majestic are his deeds,
  and his righteousness endures
    forever.
4He has caused his wonders to be
    remembered;
  the LORD is gracious and
    compassionate.
5He provides food for those who fear
    him;
  he remembers his covenant forever.
6He has shown his people the power
    of his works,
  giving them the lands of other
    nations.
7The works of his hands are faithful
    and just;
  all his precepts are trustworthy.
8They are steadfast for ever and ever,
  done in faithfulness and
    uprightness.
9He provided redemption for his
    people;
  he ordained his covenant forever—
  holy and awesome is his name.

10The fear of the LORD is the beginning
    of wisdom;
  all who follow his precepts have
    good understanding.
  To him belongs eternal praise.

Psalm 112 *c*

1Praise the LORD.*d*

Blessed is the man who fears the
    LORD,
  who finds great delight in his
    commands.

2His children will be mighty in the
    land;
  the generation of the upright will
    be blessed.
3Wealth and riches are in his house,

---

a3 Or / *your young men will come to you like the dew*
b7 Or / *The One who grants succession will set him in
authority*   *c*This psalm is an acrostic poem, the
lines of which begin with the successive letters of
the Hebrew alphabet.   *d1* Hebrew *Hallelu Yah*

and his righteousness endures
  forever.
⁴Even in darkness light dawns for the
    upright,
  for the gracious and compassionate
    and righteous man.ᵃ
⁵Good will come to him who is
    generous and lends freely,
  who conducts his affairs with
    justice.
⁶Surely he will never be shaken;
  a righteous man will be
    remembered forever.
⁷He will have no fear of bad news;
  his heart is steadfast, trusting in the
    LORD.
⁸His heart is secure, he will have no
    fear;
  in the end he will look in triumph
    on his foes.
⁹He has scattered abroad his gifts to
    the poor,
  his righteousness endures forever;
  his hornᵇ will be lifted high in
    honor.

¹⁰The wicked man will see and be
    vexed,
  he will gnash his teeth and waste
    away;
  the longings of the wicked will
    come to nothing.

Psalm 113

¹Praise the LORD.ᶜ

  Praise, O servants of the LORD,
  praise the name of the LORD.
²Let the name of the LORD be praised,
  both now and forevermore.
³From the rising of the sun to the
    place where it sets,
  the name of the LORD is to be
    praised.

⁴The LORD is exalted over all the
    nations,
  his glory above the heavens.

ᵃ4 Or | for ⌊the LORD⌋ is gracious and compassionate
and righteous   ᵇ9 Horn here symbolizes dignity.
ᶜ1 Hebrew Hallelu Yah; also in verse 9

The Steadfast Marriage

Thursday

PSALM 112:4-7 Just a routine check-up with the dermatologist didn't seem like anything to worry about. Removing a small mole was preventative—that's how the doctor explained it. Then the phone call came. Words like "melanoma" and "malignancy" left Rick confused, scared and riddled with anxiety. As we talked with Rick and his wife Patti, we sensed what a hard time this was for them. With two teenage sons giving them fits, we knew they were already under a lot of stress. Now this. Facing surgery and an uncertain future, it was all they could do to hang on.

Have you been there? Sometimes we must solely rely on God to get us through the rough times because we've done all we can do. All of us from time to time face news that is less than thrilling, but in this passage we read that "Even in the darkness light dawns for the upright." The difference is that the one who is trusting in the Lord knows, even during tragedy, God will see him or her through.

Rick, with Patti at his side, managed to get through the next few weeks. During the surgery, the doctor removed the lymph nodes, and we all prayed that the cancer had been caught in time. At times Rick was strong. Other times when fear crept back in, Patti carried the load and had to be the strong one. Waiting for all lab reports—which took several weeks to get—was a dark time for both of them. But God was there with them. We rejoiced with them when all the reports came back negative.

Sometimes things work out well, as in Rick and Patti's situation. Sometimes God changes the circumstances; at other times he gives comfort in the midst of the problem. Whatever your situation, if you choose to focus on God and trust him, you don't have to live in fear. The darkness of your situation will dawn into a new day filled with renewed hope.

—*Dave & Claudia*

Go to page 644 for your next devotional reading.

5Who is like the LORD our God,
　　the One who sits enthroned on
　　　high,
6who stoops down to look
　　on the heavens and the earth?

7He raises the poor from the dust
　　and lifts the needy from the ash
　　　heap;
8he seats them with princes,
　　with the princes of their people.
9He settles the barren woman in her
　　　home
　　as a happy mother of children.

　　Praise the LORD.

Psalm 114

1When Israel came out of Egypt,
　　the house of Jacob from a people
　　　of foreign tongue,
2Judah became God's sanctuary,
　　Israel his dominion.

3The sea looked and fled,
　　the Jordan turned back;
4the mountains skipped like rams,
　　the hills like lambs.

5Why was it, O sea, that you fled,
　　O Jordan, that you turned back,
6you mountains, that you skipped like
　　　rams,
　　you hills, like lambs?

7Tremble, O earth, at the presence of
　　　the Lord,
　　at the presence of the God of
　　　Jacob,
8who turned the rock into a pool,
　　the hard rock into springs of water.

Psalm 115

1Not to us, O LORD, not to us
　　but to your name be the glory,
　　because of your love and
　　　faithfulness.

2Why do the nations say,
　　"Where is their God?"
3Our God is in heaven;
　　he does whatever pleases him.
4But their idols are silver and gold,
　　made by the hands of men.
5They have mouths, but cannot speak,
　　eyes, but they cannot see;
6they have ears, but cannot hear,

The Steadfast Marriage

To have a steadfast marriage, you need to
maintain a steadfast, positive attitude. Take
a few moments and check your own attitude. How do you look at the future? Reflect
on the following questions:

1. What are you looking forward to in
   the future?

2. What obstacles might you need to
   overcome?

3. How has God comforted you in the
   past?

4. What are the positive qualities of
   your marriage relationship?

List three things that you appreciate about
your spouse.

noses, but they cannot smell;
7they have hands, but cannot feel,
　　feet, but they cannot walk;
　　nor can they utter a sound with
　　　their throats.
8Those who make them will be like
　　　them,
　　and so will all who trust in them.

9O house of Israel, trust in the LORD—
　　he is their help and shield.
10O house of Aaron, trust in the LORD—
　　he is their help and shield.
11You who fear him, trust in the LORD—
　　he is their help and shield.

12The LORD remembers us and will
　　　bless us:
　　He will bless the house of Israel,
　　he will bless the house of Aaron,
13he will bless those who fear the
　　　LORD—
　　small and great alike.

14May the LORD make you increase,
　　both you and your children.
15May you be blessed by the LORD,
　　the Maker of heaven and earth.

16The highest heavens belong to the
　　　LORD,
　　but the earth he has given to man.

17It is not the dead who praise the
   LORD,
   those who go down to silence;
18it is we who extol the LORD,
   both now and forevermore.

Praise the LORD.[a]

Psalm 116

1I love the LORD, for he heard my
   voice;
   he heard my cry for mercy.
2Because he turned his ear to me,
   I will call on him as long as I live.

3The cords of death entangled me,
   the anguish of the grave[b] came
      upon me;
   I was overcome by trouble and
      sorrow.
4Then I called on the name of the
   LORD:
   "O LORD, save me!"

5The LORD is gracious and righteous;
   our God is full of compassion.
6The LORD protects the simplehearted;
   when I was in great need, he saved
      me.

7Be at rest once more, O my soul,
   for the LORD has been good to you.

8For you, O LORD, have delivered my
      soul from death,
   my eyes from tears,
   my feet from stumbling,
9that I may walk before the LORD
   in the land of the living.
10I believed; therefore[c] I said,
   "I am greatly afflicted."
11And in my dismay I said,
   "All men are liars."

12How can I repay the LORD
   for all his goodness to me?
13I will lift up the cup of salvation
   and call on the name of the LORD.
14I will fulfill my vows to the LORD
   in the presence of all his people.

15Precious in the sight of the LORD
   is the death of his saints.
16O LORD, truly I am your servant;
   I am your servant, the son of your
      maidservant[d];
   you have freed me from my chains.

17I will sacrifice a thank offering to you

and call on the name of the LORD.
18I will fulfill my vows to the LORD
   in the presence of all his people,
19in the courts of the house of the
   LORD—
   in your midst, O Jerusalem.

Praise the LORD.[a]

Psalm 117

1Praise the LORD, all you nations;
   extol him, all you peoples.
2For great is his love toward us,
   and the faithfulness of the LORD
      endures forever.

Praise the LORD.[a]

Psalm 118

1Give thanks to the LORD, for he is
      good;
   his love endures forever.

2Let Israel say:
   "His love endures forever."
3Let the house of Aaron say:
   "His love endures forever."
4Let those who fear the LORD say:
   "His love endures forever."

5In my anguish I cried to the LORD,
   and he answered by setting me
      free.
6The LORD is with me; I will not be
      afraid.
   What can man do to me?
7The LORD is with me; he is my helper.
   I will look in triumph on my
      enemies.

8It is better to take refuge in the LORD
   than to trust in man.
9It is better to take refuge in the LORD
   than to trust in princes.

10All the nations surrounded me,
   but in the name of the LORD I cut
      them off.
11They surrounded me on every side,
   but in the name of the LORD I cut
      them off.
12They swarmed around me like bees,
   but they died out as quickly as
      burning thorns;

a18,19,2 Hebrew Hallelu Yah   b3 Hebrew Sheol
c10 Or believed even when   d16 Or servant, your
faithful son

in the name of the LORD I cut
them off.

13I was pushed back and about to fall,
but the LORD helped me.
14The LORD is my strength and my
song;
he has become my salvation.

15Shouts of joy and victory
resound in the tents of the
righteous:
"The LORD's right hand has done
mighty things!
16   The LORD's right hand is lifted
high;
the LORD's right hand has done
mighty things!"

17I will not die but live,
and will proclaim what the LORD
has done.
18The LORD has chastened me severely,
but he has not given me over to
death.

19Open for me the gates of
righteousness;
I will enter and give thanks to the
LORD.
20This is the gate of the LORD
through which the righteous may
enter.
21I will give you thanks, for you
answered me;
you have become my salvation.

22The stone the builders rejected
has become the capstone;
23the LORD has done this,
and it is marvelous in our eyes.
24This is the day the LORD has made;
let us rejoice and be glad in it.

25O LORD, save us;
O LORD, grant us success.
26Blessed is he who comes in the name
of the LORD.
From the house of the LORD we
bless you.a
27The LORD is God,
and he has made his light shine
upon us.
With boughs in hand, join in the
festal procession
upb to the horns of the altar.

28You are my God, and I will give you
thanks;

you are my God, and I will exalt
you.

29Give thanks to the LORD, for he is
good;
his love endures forever.

Psalm 119 c

א   Aleph

1Blessed are they whose ways are
blameless,
who walk according to the law of
the LORD.
2Blessed are they who keep his statutes
and seek him with all their heart.
3They do nothing wrong;
they walk in his ways.
4You have laid down precepts
that are to be fully obeyed.
5Oh, that my ways were steadfast
in obeying your decrees!
6Then I would not be put to shame
when I consider all your
commands.
7I will praise you with an upright heart
as I learn your righteous laws.
8I will obey your decrees;
do not utterly forsake me.

ב   Beth

9How can a young man keep his way
pure?
By living according to your word.
10I seek you with all my heart;
do not let me stray from your
commands.
11I have hidden your word in my heart
that I might not sin against you.
12Praise be to you, O LORD;
teach me your decrees.
13With my lips I recount
all the laws that come from your
mouth.
14I rejoice in following your statutes
as one rejoices in great riches.
15I meditate on your precepts
and consider your ways.
16I delight in your decrees;
I will not neglect your word.

---

a26 The Hebrew is plural.   b27 Or Bind the
festal sacrifice with ropes / and take it   cThis
psalm is an acrostic poem; the verses of each
stanza begin with the same letter of the Hebrew
alphabet.

ג   Gimel

¹⁷Do good to your servant, and I will
      live;
   I will obey your word.
¹⁸Open my eyes that I may see
   wonderful things in your law.
¹⁹I am a stranger on earth;
   do not hide your commands from
      me.
²⁰My soul is consumed with longing
   for your laws at all times.
²¹You rebuke the arrogant, who are
      cursed
   and who stray from your
      commands.
²²Remove from me scorn and
      contempt,
   for I keep your statutes.
²³Though rulers sit together and slander
      me,
   your servant will meditate on your
      decrees.
²⁴Your statutes are my delight;
   they are my counselors.

ד   Daleth

²⁵I am laid low in the dust;
   preserve my life according to your
      word.
²⁶I recounted my ways and you
      answered me;
   teach me your decrees.
²⁷Let me understand the teaching of
   your precepts;

then I will meditate on your
   wonders.
²⁸My soul is weary with sorrow;
   strengthen me according to your
      word.
²⁹Keep me from deceitful ways;
   be gracious to me through your
      law.
³⁰I have chosen the way of truth;
   I have set my heart on your laws.
³¹I hold fast to your statutes, O LORD;
   do not let me be put to shame.
³²I run in the path of your commands,
   for you have set my heart free.

ה   He

³³Teach me, O LORD, to follow your
      decrees;
   then I will keep them to the end.
³⁴Give me understanding, and I will
      keep your law
   and obey it with all my heart.
³⁵Direct me in the path of your
      commands,
   for there I find delight.
³⁶Turn my heart toward your statutes
   and not toward selfish gain.
³⁷Turn my eyes away from worthless
      things;
   preserve my life according to your
      word.[a]

[a]37 Two manuscripts of the Masoretic Text and
Dead Sea Scrolls; most manuscripts of the
Masoretic Text *life in your way*

Wearing the Right Glasses

Friday

PSALM 119:33–37 How is a person to know what's okay and what's not okay? Those around us, even some in church, act in a way that indicates that there are really no true guidelines. It's confusing! Is it okay to flirt? Is it okay as long as it goes no further than talking? Is it okay to cheat on our taxes if we disagree with what the government is doing? What harm is there? Everybody is doing it anyway . . .

What "glasses" can we look through to see the truth of how to live pure lives? The culture around us says everything's okay as long as no one gets hurt. But the ideas of this same culture cause deep hurt through the high rate of divorce. An ever-changing culture cannot be allowed to set our standards. On the other hand, God has the "glasses" for each of us to look through when deciding what is acceptable. His view remains consistent and has our best interests at heart. The cultural glasses are murky and constantly changing. God's glasses have been clean, clear and consistent since the beginning of time. When deciding what is acceptable, choose to wear the lenses of the Word as you look at each situation.

—*Bob & Rosemary*

Go to page 650 for your next devotional reading.

³⁸Fulfill your promise to your servant,
  so that you may be feared.
³⁹Take away the disgrace I dread,
  for your laws are good.
⁴⁰How I long for your precepts!
  Preserve my life in your
    righteousness.

ו   Waw

⁴¹May your unfailing love come to me,
    O LORD,
  your salvation according to your
    promise;
⁴²then I will answer the one who taunts
    me,
  for I trust in your word.
⁴³Do not snatch the word of truth from
    my mouth,
  for I have put my hope in your
    laws.
⁴⁴I will always obey your law,
  for ever and ever.
⁴⁵I will walk about in freedom,
  for I have sought out your
    precepts.
⁴⁶I will speak of your statutes before
    kings
  and will not be put to shame,
⁴⁷for I delight in your commands
  because I love them.
⁴⁸I lift up my hands to^a your
    commands, which I love,
  and I meditate on your decrees.

ז   Zayin

⁴⁹Remember your word to your servant,
  for you have given me hope.
⁵⁰My comfort in my suffering is this:
  Your promise preserves my life.
⁵¹The arrogant mock me without
    restraint,
  but I do not turn from your law.
⁵²I remember your ancient laws,
    O LORD,
  and I find comfort in them.
⁵³Indignation grips me because of the
    wicked,
  who have forsaken your law.
⁵⁴Your decrees are the theme of my
    song
  wherever I lodge.
⁵⁵In the night I remember your name,
    O LORD,
  and I will keep your law.
⁵⁶This has been my practice:
  I obey your precepts.

ח   Heth

⁵⁷You are my portion, O LORD;
  I have promised to obey your
    words.
⁵⁸I have sought your face with all my
    heart;
  be gracious to me according to
    your promise.
⁵⁹I have considered my ways
  and have turned my steps to your
    statutes.
⁶⁰I will hasten and not delay
  to obey your commands.
⁶¹Though the wicked bind me with
    ropes,
  I will not forget your law.
⁶²At midnight I rise to give you thanks
  for your righteous laws.
⁶³I am a friend to all who fear you,
  to all who follow your precepts.
⁶⁴The earth is filled with your love,
    O LORD;
  teach me your decrees.

ט   Teth

⁶⁵Do good to your servant
  according to your word, O LORD.
⁶⁶Teach me knowledge and good
    judgment,
  for I believe in your commands.
⁶⁷Before I was afflicted I went astray,
  but now I obey your word.
⁶⁸You are good, and what you do is
    good;
  teach me your decrees.
⁶⁹Though the arrogant have smeared
    me with lies,
  I keep your precepts with all my
    heart.
⁷⁰Their hearts are callous and unfeeling,
  but I delight in your law.
⁷¹It was good for me to be afflicted
  so that I might learn your decrees.
⁷²The law from your mouth is more
    precious to me
  than thousands of pieces of silver
    and gold.

י   Yodh

⁷³Your hands made me and formed me;
  give me understanding to learn
    your commands.

^a48 Or for

74May those who fear you rejoice when
  they see me,
    for I have put my hope in your
      word.
75I know, O LORD, that your laws are
  righteous,
    and in faithfulness you have
      afflicted me.
76May your unfailing love be my
  comfort,
    according to your promise to your
      servant.
77Let your compassion come to me that
  I may live,
    for your law is my delight.
78May the arrogant be put to shame for
  wronging me without cause;
    but I will meditate on your
      precepts.
79May those who fear you turn to me,
  those who understand your
    statutes.
80May my heart be blameless toward
  your decrees,
    that I may not be put to shame.

 כ   Kaph

81My soul faints with longing for your
  salvation,
    but I have put my hope in your
      word.
82My eyes fail, looking for your
  promise;
    I say, "When will you comfort
      me?"
83Though I am like a wineskin in the
  smoke,
    I do not forget your decrees.
84How long must your servant wait?
  When will you punish my
    persecutors?
85The arrogant dig pitfalls for me,
  contrary to your law.
86All your commands are trustworthy;
  help me, for men persecute me
    without cause.
87They almost wiped me from the
  earth,
    but I have not forsaken your
      precepts.
88Preserve my life according to your
  love,
    and I will obey the statutes of your
      mouth.

ל   Lamedh

89Your word, O LORD, is eternal;
  it stands firm in the heavens.
90Your faithfulness continues through
  all generations;
    you established the earth, and it
      endures.
91Your laws endure to this day,
  for all things serve you.
92If your law had not been my delight,
  I would have perished in my
    affliction.
93I will never forget your precepts,
  for by them you have preserved my
    life.
94Save me, for I am yours;
  I have sought out your precepts.
95The wicked are waiting to destroy me,
  but I will ponder your statutes.
96To all perfection I see a limit;
  but your commands are boundless.

מ   Mem

97Oh, how I love your law!
  I meditate on it all day long.
98Your commands make me wiser than
  my enemies,
    for they are ever with me.
99I have more insight than all my
  teachers,
    for I meditate on your statutes.
100I have more understanding than the
  elders,
    for I obey your precepts.
101I have kept my feet from every evil
  path
    so that I might obey your word.
102I have not departed from your laws,
  for you yourself have taught me.
103How sweet are your words to my
  taste,
    sweeter than honey to my mouth!
104I gain understanding from your
  precepts;
    therefore I hate every wrong path.

נ   Nun

105Your word is a lamp to my feet
  and a light for my path.
106I have taken an oath and
  confirmed it,
    that I will follow your righteous
      laws.
107I have suffered much;

preserve my life, O LORD, according
to your word.
108Accept, O LORD, the willing praise of
my mouth,
and teach me your laws.
109Though I constantly take my life in
my hands,
I will not forget your law.
110The wicked have set a snare for me,
but I have not strayed from your
precepts.
111Your statutes are my heritage forever;
they are the joy of my heart.
112My heart is set on keeping your
decrees
to the very end.

ס   Samekh

113I hate double-minded men,
but I love your law.
114You are my refuge and my shield;
I have put my hope in your word.
115Away from me, you evildoers,
that I may keep the commands of
my God!
116Sustain me according to your
promise, and I will live;
do not let my hopes be dashed.
117Uphold me, and I will be delivered;
I will always have regard for your
decrees.
118You reject all who stray from your
decrees,
for their deceitfulness is in vain.
119All the wicked of the earth you
discard like dross;
therefore I love your statutes.
120My flesh trembles in fear of you;
I stand in awe of your laws.

ע   Ayin

121I have done what is righteous and
just;
do not leave me to my oppressors.
122Ensure your servant's well-being;
let not the arrogant oppress me.
123My eyes fail, looking for your
salvation,
looking for your righteous promise.
124Deal with your servant according to
your love
and teach me your decrees.
125I am your servant; give me
discernment
that I may understand your
statutes.

126It is time for you to act, O LORD;
your law is being broken.
127Because I love your commands
more than gold, more than pure
gold,
128and because I consider all your
precepts right,
I hate every wrong path.

פ   Pe

129Your statutes are wonderful;
therefore I obey them.
130The unfolding of your words gives
light;
it gives understanding to the
simple.
131I open my mouth and pant,
longing for your commands.
132Turn to me and have mercy on me,
as you always do to those who
love your name.
133Direct my footsteps according to
your word;
let no sin rule over me.
134Redeem me from the oppression of
men,
that I may obey your precepts.
135Make your face shine upon your
servant
and teach me your decrees.
136Streams of tears flow from my eyes,
for your law is not obeyed.

צ   Tsadhe

137Righteous are you, O LORD,
and your laws are right.
138The statutes you have laid down are
righteous;
they are fully trustworthy.
139My zeal wears me out,
for my enemies ignore your words.
140Your promises have been thoroughly
tested,
and your servant loves them.
141Though I am lowly and despised,
I do not forget your precepts.
142Your righteousness is everlasting
and your law is true.
143Trouble and distress have come
upon me,
but your commands are my
delight.
144Your statutes are forever right;
give me understanding that I may
live.

ק   Qoph

145I call with all my heart; answer me,
        O LORD,
    and I will obey your decrees.
146I call out to you; save me
    and I will keep your statutes.
147I rise before dawn and cry for help;
    I have put my hope in your word.
148My eyes stay open through the
        watches of the night,
    that I may meditate on your
        promises.
149Hear my voice in accordance with
        your love;
    preserve my life, O LORD, according
        to your laws.
150Those who devise wicked schemes
        are near,
    but they are far from your law.
151Yet you are near, O LORD,
    and all your commands are true.
152Long ago I learned from your
        statutes
    that you established them to last
        forever.

ר   Resh

153Look upon my suffering and
        deliver me,
    for I have not forgotten your law.
154Defend my cause and redeem me;
    preserve my life according to your
        promise.
155Salvation is far from the wicked,
    for they do not seek out your
        decrees.
156Your compassion is great, O LORD;
    preserve my life according to your
        laws.
157Many are the foes who persecute me,
    but I have not turned from your
        statutes.
158I look on the faithless with loathing,
    for they do not obey your word.
159See how I love your precepts;
    preserve my life, O LORD, according
        to your love.
160All your words are true;
    all your righteous laws are eternal.

ש   Sin and Shin

161Rulers persecute me without cause,
    but my heart trembles at your
        word.
162I rejoice in your promise

like one who finds great spoil.
163I hate and abhor falsehood
    but I love your law.
164Seven times a day I praise you
    for your righteous laws.
165Great peace have they who love your
        law,
    and nothing can make them
        stumble.
166I wait for your salvation, O LORD,
    and I follow your commands.
167I obey your statutes,
    for I love them greatly.
168I obey your precepts and your
        statutes,
    for all my ways are known to you.

ת   Taw

169May my cry come before you,
        O LORD;
    give me understanding according to
        your word.
170May my supplication come before
        you;
    deliver me according to your
        promise.
171May my lips overflow with praise,
    for you teach me your decrees.
172May my tongue sing of your word,
    for all your commands are
        righteous.
173May your hand be ready to help me,
    for I have chosen your precepts.
174I long for your salvation, O LORD,
    and your law is my delight.
175Let me live that I may praise you,
    and may your laws sustain me.
176I have strayed like a lost sheep.
    Seek your servant,
    for I have not forgotten your
        commands.

Psalm 120

A song of ascents.

1I call on the LORD in my distress,
    and he answers me.
2Save me, O LORD, from lying lips
    and from deceitful tongues.

3What will he do to you,
    and what more besides, O deceitful
        tongue?
4He will punish you with a warrior's
        sharp arrows,

with burning coals of the broom
tree.

⁵Woe to me that I dwell in Meshech,
that I live among the tents of
Kedar!
⁶Too long have I lived
among those who hate peace.
⁷I am a man of peace;
but when I speak, they are for war.

Psalm 121

A song of ascents.

¹I lift up my eyes to the hills—
where does my help come from?
²My help comes from the LORD,
the Maker of heaven and earth.

³He will not let your foot slip—
he who watches over you will not
slumber;
⁴indeed, he who watches over Israel
will neither slumber nor sleep.

⁵The LORD watches over you—
the LORD is your shade at your
right hand;
⁶the sun will not harm you by day,
nor the moon by night.

⁷The LORD will keep you from all
harm—
he will watch over your life;
⁸the LORD will watch over your coming
and going
both now and forevermore.

Psalm 122

A song of ascents. Of David.

¹I rejoiced with those who said to me,
"Let us go to the house of the
LORD."
²Our feet are standing
in your gates, O Jerusalem.

³Jerusalem is built like a city
that is closely compacted together.
⁴That is where the tribes go up,
the tribes of the LORD,
to praise the name of the LORD
according to the statute given to
Israel.
⁵There the thrones for judgment stand,
the thrones of the house of David.

⁶Pray for the peace of Jerusalem:
"May those who love you be
secure.
⁷May there be peace within your walls
and security within your citadels."
⁸For the sake of my brothers and
friends,
I will say, "Peace be within you."
⁹For the sake of the house of the LORD
our God,
I will seek your prosperity.

Psalm 123

A song of ascents.

¹I lift up my eyes to you,
to you whose throne is in heaven.
²As the eyes of slaves look to the hand
of their master,
as the eyes of a maid look to the
hand of her mistress,
so our eyes look to the LORD our
God,
till he shows us his mercy.

³Have mercy on us, O LORD, have
mercy on us,
for we have endured much
contempt.
⁴We have endured much ridicule from
the proud,
much contempt from the arrogant.

Psalm 124

A song of ascents. Of David.

¹If the LORD had not been on our
side—
let Israel say—
²if the LORD had not been on our side
when men attacked us,
³when their anger flared against us,
they would have swallowed us
alive;
⁴the flood would have engulfed us,
the torrent would have swept over
us,
⁵the raging waters
would have swept us away.

⁶Praise be to the LORD,
who has not let us be torn by their
teeth.
⁷We have escaped like a bird
out of the fowler's snare;

the snare has been broken,
　　and we have escaped.
[8]Our help is in the name of the LORD,
　　the Maker of heaven and earth.

Psalm 125

A song of ascents.

[1]Those who trust in the LORD are like
　　Mount Zion,
　which cannot be shaken but
　　endures forever.
[2]As the mountains surround Jerusalem,
　so the LORD surrounds his people
　　both now and forevermore.

[3]The scepter of the wicked will not
　　remain
　over the land allotted to the
　　righteous,
for then the righteous might use
　their hands to do evil.

[4]Do good, O LORD, to those who are
　　good,
　to those who are upright in
　　heart.

[5]But those who turn to crooked
　　ways
　the LORD will banish with the
　　evildoers.

Peace be upon Israel.

Psalm 126

A song of ascents.

[1]When the LORD brought back the
　　captives to[a] Zion,
　we were like men who dreamed.[b]
[2]Our mouths were filled with laughter,
　our tongues with songs of joy.
Then it was said among the nations,
　　"The LORD has done great things
　　　for them."
[3]The LORD has done great things for
　　us,
　and we are filled with joy.

[4]Restore our fortunes,[c] O LORD,
　like streams in the Negev.

[a]1 Or LORD restored the fortunes of   [b]1 Or men restored to health   [c]4 Or Bring back our captives

What Plans Are You Using?

PSALM 127 It would be foolish to build a model car using a dress pattern for instructions. Yet we often attempt to build a family without consulting the "blue prints" of the great Architect, God. We find ourselves formulating the plans for improving our marriages based on our culture instead of the eternal truths of God. For example, our culture encourages us to pursue meeting our own needs, not the needs of others. In our marriage, Bob and I had to choose to follow God's Word by doing just the opposite—submitting to each other rather than demanding from each other (see Ephesians 5:21).

God is the designer of the family. It was his plan that he formulated at the beginning of time. He knows the make-up of each individual and the needs of every family. A family without God cannot experience the spiritual bond God brings to relationships.

We would be wise to make a study of God's Word to understand his principles for building a home. We need to measure the ideas from our culture with God's ideas for the family. A home without the foundation of God's unchanging principles of the family will be unstable in the winds of changing ideas. God must be the firm foundation of our lives. Make God your highest priority, and let him do the building.

—Bob & Rosemary

Weekend Warm-up *Have you experienced a time of spiritual bonding?*

Go to page 652 for your next devotional reading.

⁵Those who sow in tears
    will reap with songs of joy.
⁶He who goes out weeping,
    carrying seed to sow,
will return with songs of joy,
    carrying sheaves with him.

Psalm 127

A song of ascents. Of Solomon.

¹Unless the LORD builds the house,
    its builders labor in vain.
Unless the LORD watches over the
    city,
    the watchmen stand guard in vain.
²In vain you rise early
    and stay up late,
toiling for food to eat—
    for he grants sleep to*ᵃ* those he
      loves.

³Sons are a heritage from the LORD,
    children a reward from him.
⁴Like arrows in the hands of a warrior
    are sons born in one's youth.
⁵Blessed is the man
    whose quiver is full of them.
They will not be put to shame
    when they contend with their
      enemies in the gate.

Psalm 128

A song of ascents.

¹Blessed are all who fear the LORD,
    who walk in his ways.
²You will eat the fruit of your labor;
    blessings and prosperity will be
      yours.
³Your wife will be like a fruitful vine
    within your house;
your sons will be like olive shoots
    around your table.
⁴Thus is the man blessed
    who fears the LORD.

⁵May the LORD bless you from Zion
    all the days of your life;
may you see the prosperity of
      Jerusalem,
⁶   and may you live to see your
      children's children.

Peace be upon Israel.

JUST BETWEEN you & me

What Plans Are You Using?

Take a moment to answer each of these questions on your own. Then compare your answers to your spouse's.

Yes No   I spend much of my time think-ing about my finances and de-pending on them for my future security.

Yes No   The success of my children is at the center of my daily thoughts and planning.

Yes No   I look to my parents or friends for affirmation that I am success-ful.

Yes No   When making decisions, I ask myself the question, "What would God want me to do here?"

Psalm 129

A song of ascents.

¹They have greatly oppressed me from
    my youth—
    let Israel say—
²they have greatly oppressed me from
    my youth,
    but they have not gained the
      victory over me.
³Plowmen have plowed my back
    and made their furrows long.
⁴But the LORD is righteous;
    he has cut me free from the cords
      of the wicked.

⁵May all who hate Zion
    be turned back in shame.
⁶May they be like grass on the roof,
    which withers before it can grow;
⁷with it the reaper cannot fill his
    hands,
    nor the one who gathers fill his
      arms.
⁸May those who pass by not say,
    "The blessing of the LORD be upon
      you;
    we bless you in the name of the
      LORD."

---

a2 Or eat— / for while they sleep he provides for

Psalm 130

A song of ascents.

[1] Out of the depths I cry to you,
O LORD;
[2]   O Lord, hear my voice.
Let your ears be attentive
to my cry for mercy.

[3] If you, O LORD, kept a record of sins,
O Lord, who could stand?
[4] But with you there is forgiveness;
therefore you are feared.

[5] I wait for the LORD, my soul waits,
and in his word I put my hope.
[6] My soul waits for the Lord
more than watchmen wait for the
morning,
more than watchmen wait for the
morning.

[7] O Israel, put your hope in the LORD,
for with the LORD is unfailing love
and with him is full redemption.
[8] He himself will redeem Israel
from all their sins.

Psalm 131

A song of ascents. Of David.

[1] My heart is not proud, O LORD,
my eyes are not haughty;

I do not concern myself with great
matters
or things too wonderful for me.
[2] But I have stilled and quieted my
soul;
like a weaned child with its
mother,
like a weaned child is my soul
within me.

[3] O Israel, put your hope in the LORD
both now and forevermore.

Psalm 132

A song of ascents.

[1] O LORD, remember David
and all the hardships he endured.

[2] He swore an oath to the LORD
and made a vow to the Mighty
One of Jacob:
[3] "I will not enter my house
or go to my bed—
[4] I will allow no sleep to my eyes,
no slumber to my eyelids,
[5] till I find a place for the LORD,
a dwelling for the Mighty One of
Jacob."

[6] We heard it in Ephrathah,

Let Contentment Rule

Monday

PSALM 131 Purchasing a new house is exciting. The wait before moving in seems to take a lifetime. We think about finally having more space . . . enough to last forever. When the day finally arrives, the effort of moving is worth it. After all, this is a dream come true, right?

Months later, when visiting a friend in his new house, we start to feel different. The friend's house has the extra garage or laundry room that you really wanted in your house. The house you loved when you first moved in is no longer quite as wonderful. What happened?

It might be a house, a car or any other once-desired possession. It might even be a

marriage relationship. Once the first rush of emotion is over, we need to find contentment. Contentment is a choice that is made despite the temptation to be ruled by feelings. Feelings can change overnight, especially when we compare our lives with what other people have. Verse 2 indicates that contentment is also an action. Having a still and quieted soul is what the psalmist has chosen.

But contentment is an ongoing choice to be happy with what we have. And it will bring long-term happiness.

—Bob & Rosemary

Go to page 656 for your next devotional reading.

we came upon it in the fields of
Jaar[a; b]
7 "Let us go to his dwelling place;
let us worship at his footstool —
8 arise, O LORD, and come to your
resting place,
you and the ark of your might.
9 May your priests be clothed with
righteousness;
may your saints sing for joy."

10 For the sake of David your servant,
do not reject your anointed one.

11 The LORD swore an oath to David,
a sure oath that he will not revoke:
"One of your own descendants
I will place on your throne —
12 if your sons keep my covenant
and the statutes I teach them,
then their sons will sit
on your throne for ever and ever."

13 For the LORD has chosen Zion,
he has desired it for his dwelling:
14 "This is my resting place for ever and
ever;
here I will sit enthroned, for I have
desired it —
15 I will bless her with abundant
provisions;
her poor will I satisfy with food.
16 I will clothe her priests with salvation,
and her saints will ever sing for
joy.

17 "Here I will make a horn[c] grow for
David
and set up a lamp for my anointed
one.
18 I will clothe his enemies with shame,
but the crown on his head will be
resplendent."

Psalm 133

A song of ascents. Of David.

1 How good and pleasant it is
when brothers live together in
unity!
2 It is like precious oil poured on the
head,
running down on the beard,
running down on Aaron's beard,
down upon the collar of his robes.
3 It is as if the dew of Hermon
were falling on Mount Zion.

For there the LORD bestows his
blessing,
even life forevermore.

Psalm 134

A song of ascents.

1 Praise the LORD, all you servants of
the LORD
who minister by night in the house
of the LORD.
2 Lift up your hands in the sanctuary
and praise the LORD.

3 May the LORD, the Maker of heaven
and earth,
bless you from Zion.

Psalm 135

1 Praise the LORD.[d]

Praise the name of the LORD;
praise him, you servants of the
LORD,
2 you who minister in the house of the
LORD,
in the courts of the house of our
God.

3 Praise the LORD, for the LORD is good;
sing praise to his name, for that is
pleasant.
4 For the LORD has chosen Jacob to be
his own,
Israel to be his treasured
possession.

5 I know that the LORD is great,
that our Lord is greater than all
gods.
6 The LORD does whatever pleases him,
in the heavens and on the earth,
in the seas and all their depths.
7 He makes clouds rise from the ends
of the earth;
he sends lightning with the rain
and brings out the wind from his
storehouses.

8 He struck down the firstborn of
Egypt,
the firstborn of men and animals.

---

a6 That is, Kiriath Jearim   b6 Or *heard of it in
Ephrathah, / we found it in the fields of Jaar.* (And no
quotes around verses 7-9)   c17 *Horn* here
symbolizes strong one, that is, king.
d1 Hebrew *Hallelu Yah;* also in verses 3 and 21

⁹He sent his signs and wonders into
   your midst, O Egypt,
   against Pharaoh and all his
   servants.
¹⁰He struck down many nations
   and killed mighty kings—
¹¹Sihon king of the Amorites,
   Og king of Bashan
   and all the kings of Canaan—
¹²and he gave their land as an
      inheritance,
   an inheritance to his people Israel.

¹³Your name, O LORD, endures forever,
   your renown, O LORD, through all
      generations.
¹⁴For the LORD will vindicate his people
   and have compassion on his
      servants.

¹⁵The idols of the nations are silver and
      gold,
   made by the hands of men.
¹⁶They have mouths, but cannot speak,
   eyes, but they cannot see;
¹⁷they have ears, but cannot hear,
   nor is there breath in their mouths.
¹⁸Those who make them will be like
      them,
   and so will all who trust in them.

¹⁹O house of Israel, praise the LORD;
   O house of Aaron, praise the LORD;
²⁰O house of Levi, praise the LORD;
   you who fear him, praise the LORD.
²¹Praise be to the LORD from Zion,
   to him who dwells in Jerusalem.

   Praise the LORD.

Psalm 136

¹Give thanks to the LORD, for he is
      good.
      His love endures forever.
²Give thanks to the God of gods.
      His love endures forever.
³Give thanks to the Lord of lords:
      His love endures forever.

⁴to him who alone does great
      wonders,
      His love endures forever.
⁵who by his understanding made the
      heavens,
      His love endures forever.
⁶who spread out the earth upon the
      waters,
      His love endures forever.

⁷who made the great lights—
      His love endures forever.
⁸the sun to govern the day,
      His love endures forever.
⁹the moon and stars to govern the
      night;
      His love endures forever.

¹⁰to him who struck down the firstborn
      of Egypt
      His love endures forever.
¹¹and brought Israel out from among
      them
      His love endures forever.
¹²with a mighty hand and outstretched
      arm;
      His love endures forever.

¹³to him who divided the Red Sea*ᵃ*
      asunder
      His love endures forever.
¹⁴and brought Israel through the midst
      of it,
      His love endures forever.
¹⁵but swept Pharaoh and his army into
      the Red Sea;
      His love endures forever.

¹⁶to him who led his people through
      the desert,
      His love endures forever.
¹⁷who struck down great kings,
      His love endures forever.
¹⁸and killed mighty kings—
      His love endures forever.
¹⁹Sihon king of the Amorites
      His love endures forever.
²⁰and Og king of Bashan—
      His love endures forever.
²¹and gave their land as an inheritance,
      His love endures forever.
²²an inheritance to his servant Israel;
      His love endures forever.

²³to the One who remembered us in
      our low estate
      His love endures forever.
²⁴and freed us from our enemies,
      His love endures forever.
²⁵and who gives food to every creature.
      His love endures forever.

²⁶Give thanks to the God of heaven.
      His love endures forever.

ᵃ13 Hebrew *Yam Suph*; that is, Sea of Reeds; also
in verse 15

Psalm 137

¹By the rivers of Babylon we sat and
wept
when we remembered Zion.
²There on the poplars
we hung our harps,
³for there our captors asked us for
songs,
our tormentors demanded songs of
joy;
they said, "Sing us one of the
songs of Zion!"

⁴How can we sing the songs of the
LORD
while in a foreign land?
⁵If I forget you, O Jerusalem,
may my right hand forget ⌐its skill⌐.
⁶May my tongue cling to the roof of
my mouth
if I do not remember you,
if I do not consider Jerusalem
my highest joy.

⁷Remember, O LORD, what the
Edomites did
on the day Jerusalem fell.
"Tear it down," they cried,
"tear it down to its foundations!"

⁸O Daughter of Babylon, doomed to
destruction,
happy is he who repays you
for what you have done to us—
⁹he who seizes your infants
and dashes them against the rocks.

Psalm 138

Of David.

¹I will praise you, O LORD, with all my
heart;
before the "gods" I will sing your
praise.
²I will bow down toward your holy
temple
and will praise your name
for your love and your faithfulness,
for you have exalted above all things
your name and your word.
³When I called, you answered me;
you made me bold and
stouthearted.

⁴May all the kings of the earth praise
you, O LORD,

when they hear the words of your
mouth.
⁵May they sing of the ways of the
LORD,
for the glory of the LORD is great.

⁶Though the LORD is on high, he looks
upon the lowly,
but the proud he knows from afar.
⁷Though I walk in the midst of
trouble,
you preserve my life;
you stretch out your hand against the
anger of my foes,
with your right hand you save me.
⁸The LORD will fulfill ⌐his purpose⌐ for
me;
your love, O LORD, endures
forever—
do not abandon the works of your
hands.

Psalm 139

For the director of music. Of David.
A psalm.

¹O LORD, you have searched me
and you know me.
²You know when I sit and when I rise;
you perceive my thoughts from
afar.
³You discern my going out and my
lying down;
you are familiar with all my ways.
⁴Before a word is on my tongue
you know it completely, O LORD.

⁵You hem me in—behind and before;
you have laid your hand upon me.
⁶Such knowledge is too wonderful for
me,
too lofty for me to attain.

⁷Where can I go from your Spirit?
Where can I flee from your
presence?
⁸If I go up to the heavens, you are
there;
if I make my bed in the depths,ᵃ
you are there.
⁹If I rise on the wings of the dawn,
if I settle on the far side of the sea,
¹⁰even there your hand will guide me,
your right hand will hold me fast.

ᵃ8 Hebrew *Sheol*

11If I say, "Surely the darkness will hide
          me
      and the light become night around
          me,"
12even the darkness will not be dark to
          you;
      the night will shine like the day,
      for darkness is as light to you.

13For you created my inmost being;
      you knit me together in my
          mother's womb.
14I praise you because I am fearfully
          and wonderfully made;
      your works are wonderful,
      I know that full well.
15My frame was not hidden from you
      when I was made in the secret
          place.
   When I was woven together in the
          depths of the earth,
16   your eyes saw my unformed body.
   All the days ordained for me
      were written in your book
      before one of them came to be.

17How precious to*a* me are your
          thoughts, O God!
      How vast is the sum of them!

18Were I to count them,
      they would outnumber the grains
          of sand.
   When I awake,
      I am still with you.

19If only you would slay the wicked,
          O God!
      Away from me, you bloodthirsty
          men!
20They speak of you with evil intent;
      your adversaries misuse your name.
21Do I not hate those who hate you,
          O LORD,
      and abhor those who rise up
          against you?
22I have nothing but hatred for them;
      I count them my enemies.

23Search me, O God, and know my
          heart;
      test me and know my anxious
          thoughts.
24See if there is any offensive way in
          me,
      and lead me in the way everlasting.

a17 Or *concerning*

Unity in Diversity

Tuesday

PSALM 139 As the children's song goes, "You are something special. You're the only one of your kind!" God is the One who crafted your uniqueness—even before you were born. And even now, God knows each intimate detail of your life—your personality, your secret fantasies, and even your hidden motives.

God knows your spouse just as well, and, in the midst of your individual uniqueness, God wants to mold you together and help you complement each other; he wants to shape your marriage into something special.

One spring we spent several months at the United Nations in Vienna, Austria, interviewing families to learn what they were doing right in their families and how they were passing on traditions and values to the next generations. Often our interviews would include talking about their marriage relationship.

We remember one lady in particular. She was from Brazil and was married to a German. Talk about different cultures! They had a real opportunity to let their differences bring out the best in each other. But we sensed that they had a very healthy marriage. "My husband and his German ways brings needed structure to our marriage," she told us. Then, with a twinkle in her eye, she added, "I bring fun and spontaneity—I liven things up!"

Think about how you bring out the best in your spouse. The ways you are different can be a foundation for a great marriage partnership. Strive for unity in your diversity, and you can celebrate your God-given uniqueness—"*Vive la différence!*"

—Dave & Claudia

Go to page 662 for your next devotional reading.

Psalm 140

For the director of music. A psalm
of David.

[1]Rescue me, O LORD, from evil men;
  protect me from men of violence,
[2]who devise evil plans in their hearts
  and stir up war every day.
[3]They make their tongues as sharp as a
    serpent's;
  the poison of vipers is on their
      lips.   *Selah*

[4]Keep me, O LORD, from the hands of
    the wicked;
  protect me from men of violence
  who plan to trip my feet.
[5]Proud men have hidden a snare for
    me;
  they have spread out the cords of
    their net
  and have set traps for me along my
      path.   *Selah*

[6]O LORD, I say to you, "You are my
    God."
  Hear, O LORD, my cry for mercy.
[7]O Sovereign LORD, my strong
    deliverer,
  who shields my head in the day of
    battle—
[8]do not grant the wicked their desires,
    O LORD;
  do not let their plans succeed,
  or they will become proud.   *Selah*

[9]Let the heads of those who surround
    me
  be covered with the trouble their
    lips have caused.
[10]Let burning coals fall upon them;
  may they be thrown into the fire,
  into miry pits, never to rise.
[11]Let slanderers not be established in
    the land;
  may disaster hunt down men of
    violence.

[12]I know that the LORD secures justice
    for the poor
  and upholds the cause of the
    needy.
[13]Surely the righteous will praise your
    name
  and the upright will live before
    you.

JUST BETWEEN *you* & *me*

Unity in Diversity

Spouses tend to react to their differences.
Instead of reacting, let Psalm 139 help you
appreciate how God made each unique and
together how you can reflect his image (see
verses 13–14).

1. In what ways are you different?
   Identify those that apply: (Put an H
   for husband and W for wife.)

___ Spontaneous   ___ Planner
___ Time-oriented   ___ Not Time-oriented
___ Public   ___ Private
___ Night Owl   ___ Day Lark
___ Feelings   ___ Facts

3. In what ways do your differences give
   balance?

4. What differences do you need to accept
   and learn to appreciate?

5. In what ways are your similar?

6. What are the strengths of your marriage partnership? Celebrate them.
   You are wonderfully made—and that
   includes your marriage.

Psalm 141

A psalm of David.

[1]O LORD, I call to you; come quickly
    to me.
  Hear my voice when I call to you.
[2]May my prayer be set before you like
    incense;
  may the lifting up of my hands be
    like the evening sacrifice.

[3]Set a guard over my mouth, O LORD;
  keep watch over the door of my
    lips.
[4]Let not my heart be drawn to what is
    evil,
  to take part in wicked deeds
with men who are evildoers;
  let me not eat of their delicacies.

[5]Let a righteous man[a] strike me—it is
    a kindness;

a5 Or Let the Righteous One

let him rebuke me—it is oil on my
    head.
My head will not refuse it.

Yet my prayer is ever against the
    deeds of evildoers;
6   their rulers will be thrown down
        from the cliffs,
    and the wicked will learn that my
        words were well spoken.
7⌊They will say,⌋ "As one plows and
        breaks up the earth,
    so our bones have been scattered at
        the mouth of the grave. *a* "

8But my eyes are fixed on you,
    O Sovereign LORD;
    in you I take refuge—do not give
        me over to death.
9Keep me from the snares they have
        laid for me,
    from the traps set by evildoers.
10Let the wicked fall into their own
        nets,
    while I pass by in safety.

Psalm 142

A *maskil*b of David. When he was in
    the cave. A prayer.

1I cry aloud to the LORD;
    I lift up my voice to the LORD for
        mercy.
2I pour out my complaint before him;
    before him I tell my trouble.

3When my spirit grows faint within
        me,
    it is you who know my way.
In the path where I walk
    men have hidden a snare for me.
4Look to my right and see;
    no one is concerned for me.
I have no refuge;
    no one cares for my life.

5I cry to you, O LORD;
    I say, "You are my refuge,
    my portion in the land of the
        living."
6Listen to my cry,
    for I am in desperate need;
rescue me from those who pursue
        me,
    for they are too strong for me.
7Set me free from my prison,
    that I may praise your name.

Then the righteous will gather about
        me
    because of your goodness to me.

Psalm 143

A psalm of David.

1O LORD, hear my prayer,
    listen to my cry for mercy;
in your faithfulness and righteousness
    come to my relief.
2Do not bring your servant into
        judgment,
    for no one living is righteous
        before you.

3The enemy pursues me,
    he crushes me to the ground;
he makes me dwell in darkness
    like those long dead.
4So my spirit grows faint within me;
    my heart within me is dismayed.

5I remember the days of long ago;
    I meditate on all your works
    and consider what your hands have
        done.
6I spread out my hands to you;
    my soul thirsts for you like a
        parched land.   *Selah*

7Answer me quickly, O LORD;
    my spirit fails.
Do not hide your face from me
    or I will be like those who go
        down to the pit.
8Let the morning bring me word of
        your unfailing love,
    for I have put my trust in you.
Show me the way I should go,
    for to you I lift up my soul.
9Rescue me from my enemies, O LORD,
    for I hide myself in you.
10Teach me to do your will,
    for you are my God;
may your good Spirit
    lead me on level ground.

11For your name's sake, O LORD,
    preserve my life;
    in your righteousness, bring me out
        of trouble.
12In your unfailing love, silence my
        enemies;

---

*a*7 Hebrew *Sheol*   *b*Title: Probably a literary or
musical term

destroy all my foes,
for I am your servant.

Psalm 144

Of David.

[1]Praise be to the LORD my Rock,
who trains my hands for war,
my fingers for battle.
[2]He is my loving God and my fortress,
my stronghold and my deliverer,
my shield, in whom I take refuge,
who subdues peoples[a] under me.

[3]O LORD, what is man that you care
for him,
the son of man that you think of
him?
[4]Man is like a breath;
his days are like a fleeting shadow.

[5]Part your heavens, O LORD, and come
down;
touch the mountains, so that they
smoke.
[6]Send forth lightning and scatter ⌐the
enemies¬;
shoot your arrows and rout them.
[7]Reach down your hand from on high;
deliver me and rescue me
from the mighty waters,
from the hands of foreigners
[8]whose mouths are full of lies,
whose right hands are deceitful.

[9]I will sing a new song to you, O God;
on the ten-stringed lyre I will make
music to you,
[10]to the One who gives victory to kings,
who delivers his servant David
from the deadly sword.

[11]Deliver me and rescue me
from the hands of foreigners
whose mouths are full of lies,
whose right hands are deceitful.

[12]Then our sons in their youth
will be like well-nurtured plants,
and our daughters will be like pillars
carved to adorn a palace.
[13]Our barns will be filled
with every kind of provision.
Our sheep will increase by thousands,
by tens of thousands in our fields;
[14]   our oxen will draw heavy loads.[b]
There will be no breaching of walls,

no going into captivity,
no cry of distress in our streets.
[15]Blessed are the people of whom this
is true;
blessed are the people whose God
is the LORD.

Psalm 145[c]

A psalm of praise. Of David.

[1]I will exalt you, my God the King;
I will praise your name for ever
and ever.
[2]Every day I will praise you
and extol your name for ever and
ever.

[3]Great is the LORD and most worthy of
praise;
his greatness no one can fathom.
[4]One generation will commend your
works to another;
they will tell of your mighty acts.
[5]They will speak of the glorious
splendor of your majesty,
and I will meditate on your
wonderful works.[d]
[6]They will tell of the power of your
awesome works,
and I will proclaim your great
deeds.
[7]They will celebrate your abundant
goodness
and joyfully sing of your
righteousness.

[8]The LORD is gracious and
compassionate,
slow to anger and rich in love.
[9]The LORD is good to all;
he has compassion on all he has
made.
[10]All you have made will praise you,
O LORD;
your saints will extol you.

a2 Many manuscripts of the Masoretic Text, Dead
Sea Scrolls, Aquila, Jerome and Syriac; most
manuscripts of the Masoretic Text *subdues my people*
b14 Or *our chieftains will be firmly established*
*c*This psalm is an acrostic poem, the verses of
which (including verse 13b) begin with the
successive letters of the Hebrew alphabet.
d5 Dead Sea Scrolls and Syriac (see also
Septuagint); Masoretic Text *On the glorious splendor
of your majesty / and on your wonderful works I will
meditate*

¹¹They will tell of the glory of your
kingdom
and speak of your might,
¹²so that all men may know of your
mighty acts
and the glorious splendor of your
kingdom.
¹³Your kingdom is an everlasting
kingdom,
and your dominion endures
through all generations.

The LORD is faithful to all his
promises
and loving toward all he has
made.ª
¹⁴The LORD upholds all those who fall
and lifts up all who are bowed
down.
¹⁵The eyes of all look to you,
and you give them their food at
the proper time.
¹⁶You open your hand
and satisfy the desires of every
living thing.

¹⁷The LORD is righteous in all his ways
and loving toward all he has made.
¹⁸The LORD is near to all who call on
him,
to all who call on him in truth.
¹⁹He fulfills the desires of those who
fear him;
he hears their cry and saves them.
²⁰The LORD watches over all who love
him,
but all the wicked he will destroy.

²¹My mouth will speak in praise of the
LORD.
Let every creature praise his holy
name
for ever and ever.

Psalm 146

¹Praise the LORD.ᵇ

Praise the LORD, O my soul.
²   I will praise the LORD all my life;
I will sing praise to my God as
long as I live.

³Do not put your trust in princes,
in mortal men, who cannot save.
⁴When their spirit departs, they return
to the ground;
on that very day their plans come
to nothing.

⁵Blessed is he whose help is the God
of Jacob,
whose hope is in the LORD his
God,
⁶the Maker of heaven and earth,
the sea, and everything in them—
the LORD, who remains faithful
forever.
⁷He upholds the cause of the
oppressed
and gives food to the hungry.
The LORD sets prisoners free,
⁸   the LORD gives sight to the blind,
the LORD lifts up those who are
bowed down,
the LORD loves the righteous.
⁹The LORD watches over the alien
and sustains the fatherless and the
widow,
but he frustrates the ways of the
wicked.

¹⁰The LORD reigns forever,
your God, O Zion, for all
generations.

Praise the LORD.

Psalm 147

¹Praise the LORD.ᶜ

How good it is to sing praises to our
God,
how pleasant and fitting to praise
him!

²The LORD builds up Jerusalem;
he gathers the exiles of Israel.
³He heals the brokenhearted
and binds up their wounds.
⁴He determines the number of the
stars
and calls them each by name.
⁵Great is our Lord and mighty in
power;
his understanding has no limit.
⁶The LORD sustains the humble
but casts the wicked to the ground.

⁷Sing to the LORD with thanksgiving;

ª13 One manuscript of the Masoretic Text, Dead
Sea Scrolls and Syriac (see also Septuagint); most
manuscripts of the Masoretic Text do not have the
last two lines of verse 13.   ᵇ1 Hebrew *Hallelu
Yah*; also in verse 10   ᶜ1 Hebrew *Hallelu Yah*;
also in verse 20

make music to our God on the
　　harp.
8He covers the sky with clouds;
　　he supplies the earth with rain
　　and makes grass grow on the hills.
9He provides food for the cattle
　　and for the young ravens when
　　　they call.

10His pleasure is not in the strength of
　　　the horse,
　　nor his delight in the legs of a
　　　man;
11the LORD delights in those who fear
　　　him,
　　who put their hope in his unfailing
　　　love.

12Extol the LORD, O Jerusalem;
　　praise your God, O Zion,
13for he strengthens the bars of your
　　　gates
　　and blesses your people within
　　　you.
14He grants peace to your borders
　　and satisfies you with the finest of
　　　wheat.

15He sends his command to the earth;
　　his word runs swiftly.
16He spreads the snow like wool
　　and scatters the frost like ashes.
17He hurls down his hail like pebbles.
　　Who can withstand his icy blast?
18He sends his word and melts them;
　　he stirs up his breezes, and the
　　　waters flow.

19He has revealed his word to Jacob,
　　his laws and decrees to Israel.
20He has done this for no other nation;
　　they do not know his laws.

Praise the LORD.

Psalm 148

1Praise the LORD.[a]

Praise the LORD from the heavens,
　　praise him in the heights above.
2Praise him, all his angels,
　　praise him, all his heavenly hosts.
3Praise him, sun and moon,
　　praise him, all you shining stars.
4Praise him, you highest heavens
　　and you waters above the skies.
5Let them praise the name of the
　　　LORD,

for he commanded and they were
　　created.
6He set them in place for ever and
　　ever;
　　he gave a decree that will never
　　　pass away.

7Praise the LORD from the earth,
　　you great sea creatures and all
　　　ocean depths,
8lightning and hail, snow and clouds,
　　stormy winds that do his bidding,
9you mountains and all hills,
　　fruit trees and all cedars,
10wild animals and all cattle,
　　small creatures and flying birds,
11kings of the earth and all nations,
　　you princes and all rulers on earth,
12young men and maidens,
　　old men and children.

13Let them praise the name of the
　　　LORD,
　　for his name alone is exalted;
　　his splendor is above the earth and
　　　the heavens.
14He has raised up for his people a
　　　horn,[b]
　　the praise of all his saints,
　　of Israel, the people close to his
　　　heart.

Praise the LORD.

Psalm 149

1Praise the LORD.[c]

Sing to the LORD a new song,
　　his praise in the assembly of the
　　　saints.

2Let Israel rejoice in their Maker;
　　let the people of Zion be glad in
　　　their King.
3Let them praise his name with
　　　dancing
　　and make music to him with
　　　tambourine and harp.
4For the LORD takes delight in his
　　　people;
　　he crowns the humble with
　　　salvation.
5Let the saints rejoice in this honor
　　and sing for joy on their beds.

a1 Hebrew Hallelu Yah; also in verse 14
b14 Horn here symbolizes strong one, that is, king.
c1 Hebrew Hallelu Yah; also in verse 9

⁶May the praise of God be in their
    mouths
    and a double-edged sword in their
      hands,
⁷to inflict vengeance on the nations
    and punishment on the peoples,
⁸to bind their kings with fetters,
    their nobles with shackles of iron,
⁹to carry out the sentence written
    against them.
    This is the glory of all his saints.

Praise the LORD.

Psalm 150

¹Praise the LORD.ᵃ

Praise God in his sanctuary;
    praise him in his mighty heavens.

²Praise him for his acts of power;
    praise him for his surpassing
      greatness.
³Praise him with the sounding of the
    trumpet,
    praise him with the harp and lyre,
⁴praise him with tambourine and
    dancing,
    praise him with the strings and
      flute,
⁵praise him with the clash of cymbals,
    praise him with resounding
      cymbals.

⁶Let everything that has breath praise
    the LORD.

Praise the LORD.

ᵃ1 Hebrew *Hallelu Yah*; also in verse 6

Father's Day Every Day

Wednesday

PSALM 150   Father's Day is an important holiday. It's a time to pay tribute to the father figures in our lives. More significantly, it's a time for a child to stop and give thanks for his or her own father and the good things he's done. In some homes there's a tradition of giving the greatest gift of all. The children individually "unwrap" the verbal gift of praise to their dad. They state how much they love him and give him praise for some of the specific things he has done.

Each Father's Day at our dinner table, our children take turns giving one- or two-sentence tributes to Dad. It's a time I (Bob) really look forward to!

When it comes to our heavenly Father, this is even more important. Sometimes we focus only on what we don't have. We fail to see all that God has done for us. This final psalm helps us to remember all that the Father has done in our lives and marriages—it focuses on gratitude rather than on needs. Consider saying this praise to God: "Thank you Father for all the wonderful things you have done in my life. As I take a second look at the events of days past, I am reminded of what you are doing in my life and marriage."

—Bob & Rosemary

Go to page 666 for your next devotional reading.

Proverbs

Sometimes the deepest truths are contained in simple sayings. The book of Proverbs is like that—simple sentences, yet full of wisdom and truth. Proverbs was written so that its readers might gain wisdom for avoiding some of the most common pitfalls of life.

Do you need guidance in making decisions? Are you trying to shape a balanced and fulfilling life and marriage? Would you like to understand what it means to "fear the LORD"? Proverbs offers a wealth of practical advice on the art of living—wisdom that works and insights that won't wear out.

Prologue: Purpose and Theme

1 The proverbs of Solomon son of David, king of Israel:

2for attaining wisdom and discipline;
    for understanding words of insight;
3for acquiring a disciplined and
        prudent life,
    doing what is right and just and
        fair;
4for giving prudence to the simple,
    knowledge and discretion to the
        young—
5let the wise listen and add to their
        learning,
    and let the discerning get
        guidance—
6for understanding proverbs and
        parables,
    the sayings and riddles of the
        wise.

7The fear of the LORD is the beginning
        of knowledge,
    but fools*a* despise wisdom and
        discipline.

Exhortations to Embrace Wisdom

Warning Against Enticement

8Listen, my son, to your father's
        instruction
    and do not forsake your mother's
        teaching.
9They will be a garland to grace your
        head
    and a chain to adorn your neck.

10My son, if sinners entice you,
    do not give in to them.

a7 The Hebrew words rendered fool *in Proverbs, and often elsewhere in the Old Testament, denote one who is morally deficient.*

[11]If they say, "Come along with us;
  let's lie in wait for someone's
    blood,
  let's waylay some harmless soul;
[12]let's swallow them alive, like the
    grave,[a]
  and whole, like those who go
    down to the pit;
[13]we will get all sorts of valuable things
  and fill our houses with plunder;
[14]throw in your lot with us,
  and we will share a common
    purse"—
[15]my son, do not go along with them,
  do not set foot on their paths;
[16]for their feet rush into sin,
  they are swift to shed blood.
[17]How useless to spread a net
  in full view of all the birds!
[18]These men lie in wait for their own
    blood;
  they waylay only themselves!
[19]Such is the end of all who go after
    ill-gotten gain;
  it takes away the lives of those who
    get it.

Warning Against Rejecting Wisdom

[20]Wisdom calls aloud in the street,
  she raises her voice in the public
    squares;
[21]at the head of the noisy streets[b] she
    cries out,
  in the gateways of the city she
    makes her speech:

[22]"How long will you simple ones[c]
    love your simple ways?
  How long will mockers delight in
    mockery
  and fools hate knowledge?
[23]If you had responded to my rebuke,
  I would have poured out my heart
    to you
  and made my thoughts known to
    you.
[24]But since you rejected me when I
    called
  and no one gave heed when I
    stretched out my hand,
[25]since you ignored all my advice
  and would not accept my rebuke,
[26]I in turn will laugh at your disaster;
  I will mock when calamity
    overtakes you—

[27]when calamity overtakes you like a
    storm,
  when disaster sweeps over you like
    a whirlwind,
  when distress and trouble
    overwhelm you.

[28]"Then they will call to me but I will
    not answer;
  they will look for me but will not
    find me.
[29]Since they hated knowledge
  and did not choose to fear the
    LORD,
[30]since they would not accept my
    advice
  and spurned my rebuke,
[31]they will eat the fruit of their ways
  and be filled with the fruit of their
    schemes.
[32]For the waywardness of the simple
    will kill them,
  and the complacency of fools will
    destroy them;
[33]but whoever listens to me will live in
    safety
  and be at ease, without fear of
    harm."

Moral Benefits of Wisdom

2 My son, if you accept my words
    and store up my commands within
      you,
[2]turning your ear to wisdom
  and applying your heart to
    understanding,
[3]and if you call out for insight
  and cry aloud for understanding,
[4]and if you look for it as for silver
  and search for it as for hidden
    treasure,
[5]then you will understand the fear of
    the LORD
  and find the knowledge of God.
[6]For the LORD gives wisdom,
  and from his mouth come
    knowledge and
      understanding.
[7]He holds victory in store for the
    upright,
  he is a shield to those whose walk
    is blameless,

[a]12 Hebrew Sheol   [b]21 Hebrew; Septuagint / on
the tops of the walls   [c]22 The Hebrew word
rendered simple in Proverbs generally denotes one
without moral direction and inclined to evil.

⁸for he guards the course of the just
  and protects the way of his faithful
    ones.

⁹Then you will understand what is
    right and just
  and fair—every good path.
¹⁰For wisdom will enter your heart,
  and knowledge will be pleasant to
    your soul.
¹¹Discretion will protect you,
  and understanding will guard you.

¹²Wisdom will save you from the ways
    of wicked men,
  from men whose words are
    perverse,
¹³who leave the straight paths
  to walk in dark ways,
¹⁴who delight in doing wrong
  and rejoice in the perverseness of
    evil,
¹⁵whose paths are crooked
  and who are devious in their ways.

¹⁶It will save you also from the
    adulteress,
  from the wayward wife with her
    seductive words,
¹⁷who has left the partner of her youth
  and ignored the covenant she
    made before God.ᵃ
¹⁸For her house leads down to death
  and her paths to the spirits of the
    dead.
¹⁹None who go to her return
  or attain the paths of life.

²⁰Thus you will walk in the ways of
    good men
  and keep to the paths of the
    righteous.
²¹For the upright will live in the land,
  and the blameless will remain in it;
²²but the wicked will be cut off from
    the land,
  and the unfaithful will be torn
    from it.

Further Benefits of Wisdom

3 My son, do not forget my teaching,
  but keep my commands in your
    heart,
²for they will prolong your life many
    years
  and bring you prosperity.

³Let love and faithfulness never leave
    you;
  bind them around your neck,
  write them on the tablet of your
    heart.
⁴Then you will win favor and a good
    name
  in the sight of God and man.

⁵Trust in the LORD with all your heart
  and lean not on your own
    understanding;
⁶in all your ways acknowledge him,
  and he will make your paths
    straight.ᵇ

⁷Do not be wise in your own eyes;
  fear the LORD and shun evil.
⁸This will bring health to your body
  and nourishment to your bones.

⁹Honor the LORD with your wealth,
  with the firstfruits of all your crops;
¹⁰then your barns will be filled to
    overflowing,
  and your vats will brim over with
    new wine.

¹¹My son, do not despise the LORD's
    discipline
  and do not resent his rebuke,
¹²because the LORD disciplines those he
    loves,
  as a fatherᶜ the son he delights in.

¹³Blessed is the man who finds
    wisdom,
  the man who gains understanding,
¹⁴for she is more profitable than silver
  and yields better returns than gold.
¹⁵She is more precious than rubies;
  nothing you desire can compare
    with her.
¹⁶Long life is in her right hand;
  in her left hand are riches and
    honor.
¹⁷Her ways are pleasant ways,
  and all her paths are peace.
¹⁸She is a tree of life to those who
    embrace her;
  those who lay hold of her will be
    blessed.

¹⁹By wisdom the LORD laid the earth's
    foundations,

ᵃ17 Or covenant of her God   ᵇ6 Or will direct
your paths   ᶜ12 Hebrew; Septuagint / and he
punishes

by understanding he set the
　　heavens in place;
20by his knowledge the deeps were
　　divided,
　　and the clouds let drop the dew.

21My son, preserve sound judgment and
　　discernment,
　　do not let them out of your sight;
22they will be life for you,
　　an ornament to grace your neck.
23Then you will go on your way in
　　safety,
　　and your foot will not stumble;
24when you lie down, you will not be
　　afraid;
　　when you lie down, your sleep will
　　be sweet.
25Have no fear of sudden disaster
　　or of the ruin that overtakes the
　　wicked,
26for the LORD will be your confidence
　　and will keep your foot from being
　　snared.

27Do not withhold good from those
　　who deserve it,
　　when it is in your power to act.
28Do not say to your neighbor,
　　"Come back later; I'll give it
　　tomorrow"—
　　when you now have it with you.

29Do not plot harm against your
　　neighbor,
　　who lives trustfully near you.
30Do not accuse a man for no reason—
　　when he has done you no harm.

31Do not envy a violent man
　　or choose any of his ways,
32for the LORD detests a perverse man
　　but takes the upright into his
　　confidence.

33The LORD's curse is on the house of
　　the wicked,
　　but he blesses the home of the
　　righteous.
34He mocks proud mockers
　　but gives grace to the humble.
35The wise inherit honor,
　　but fools he holds up to shame.

Wisdom Is Supreme

4 Listen, my sons, to a father's
　　instruction;
　　pay attention and gain
　　understanding.
2I give you sound learning,
　　so do not forsake my teaching.
3When I was a boy in my father's
　　house,
　　still tender, and an only child of
　　my mother,
4he taught me and said,

No-fault Marriage

Thursday

COUPLE · MINUTES

PROVERBS 3:30　Many couples we see in therapy are interested in what, or who, caused their problems; they're looking for a place to lay blame. What they do not understand about problems in marriage, technically speaking, is that finding fault—in the truest sense—is not easy. Why? Because the problem cannot be caused by just one thing or one person.

It's one of the most profound secrets of human relationships we know: Causality is circular. In a marital problem, choosing the point at which the chain begins is pointless and arbitrary, because there is no one single cause for any problem in marriage.

Does that make you feel uneasy? Most of us are far more comfortable with a linear cause-effect approach in which an unhappy childhood or bad nerves can be used to explain undesirable behavior. The truth is that human relationships are not that simple. A better approach is to focus not only on what goes on inside a person, but also on what takes place between two persons.

The point is that no one is really to blame in a faltering marriage relationship. Both of you have helped to establish your routine. And by heightening your self-awareness of the patterns in your relationship, you will learn how to improve your marriage—without playing the blame game.

—Les & Leslie

Go to page 668 for your next devotional reading.

"Lay hold of my words with all
　　your heart;
　keep my commands and you will
　　live.
⁵Get wisdom, get understanding;
　do not forget my words or swerve
　　from them.
⁶Do not forsake wisdom, and she will
　　protect you;
　love her, and she will watch over
　　you.
⁷Wisdom is supreme; therefore get
　　wisdom.
　Though it cost all you have, *a* get
　　understanding.
⁸Esteem her, and she will exalt you;
　embrace her, and she will honor
　　you.
⁹She will set a garland of grace on
　　your head
　and present you with a crown of
　　splendor."

¹⁰Listen, my son, accept what I say,
　and the years of your life will be
　　many.
¹¹I guide you in the way of wisdom
　and lead you along straight paths.
¹²When you walk, your steps will not
　　be hampered;
　when you run, you will not
　　stumble.
¹³Hold on to instruction, do not let it
　　go;
　guard it well, for it is your life.
¹⁴Do not set foot on the path of the
　　wicked
　or walk in the way of evil men.
¹⁵Avoid it, do not travel on it;
　turn from it and go on your way.
¹⁶For they cannot sleep till they do evil;
　they are robbed of slumber till they
　　make someone fall.
¹⁷They eat the bread of wickedness
　and drink the wine of violence.

¹⁸The path of the righteous is like the
　　first gleam of dawn,
　shining ever brighter till the full
　　light of day.
¹⁹But the way of the wicked is like deep
　　darkness;
　they do not know what makes
　　them stumble.

²⁰My son, pay attention to what I say;
　listen closely to my words.

No-fault Marriage

Take a moment to answer each of these
questions on your own. Then compare your
answers to your spouse's.

Yes　No　I think there is truth to the idea
　　　　　that we have become a culture
　　　　　of blame.

Yes　No　I am prone to blame others
　　　　　rather than own up to my mis-
　　　　　takes or faults.

Yes　No　Blame impacts how I treat my
　　　　　spouse.

Yes　No　I work in specific ways not to
　　　　　blame my spouse for things I
　　　　　am really more responsible for.

Yes　No　Is blame sometimes a good thing
　　　　　in marriage?

²¹Do not let them out of your sight,
　keep them within your heart;
²²for they are life to those who find
　　them
　　and health to a man's whole body.
²³Above all else, guard your heart,
　for it is the wellspring of life.
²⁴Put away perversity from your mouth;
　keep corrupt talk far from your
　　lips.
²⁵Let your eyes look straight ahead,
　fix your gaze directly before you.
²⁶Make level *b* paths for your feet
　and take only ways that are firm.
²⁷Do not swerve to the right or the left;
　keep your foot from evil.

Warning Against Adultery

5 My son, pay attention to my
　　wisdom,
　listen well to my words of insight,
²that you may maintain discretion
　and your lips may preserve
　　knowledge.
³For the lips of an adulteress drip
　　honey,
　and her speech is smoother than
　　oil;
⁴but in the end she is bitter as gall,

---

a7 Or *Whatever else you get*　　*b26* Or *Consider the*

sharp as a double-edged sword.
⁵Her feet go down to death;
    her steps lead straight to the
        grave.ᵃ
⁶She gives no thought to the way of
        life;
    her paths are crooked, but she
        knows it not.

⁷Now then, my sons, listen to me;
    do not turn aside from what I say.
⁸Keep to a path far from her,
    do not go near the door of her
        house,
⁹lest you give your best strength to
        others
    and your years to one who is cruel,
¹⁰lest strangers feast on your wealth
    and your toil enrich another man's
        house.
¹¹At the end of your life you will groan,
    when your flesh and body are
        spent.
¹²You will say, "How I hated
        discipline!
    How my heart spurned correction!
¹³I would not obey my teachers

or listen to my instructors.
¹⁴I have come to the brink of utter ruin
    in the midst of the whole
        assembly."

¹⁵Drink water from your own cistern,
    running water from your own well.
¹⁶Should your springs overflow in the
        streets,
    your streams of water in the public
        squares?
¹⁷Let them be yours alone,
    never to be shared with strangers.
¹⁸May your fountain be blessed,
    and may you rejoice in the wife of
        your youth.
¹⁹A loving doe, a graceful deer—
    may her breasts satisfy you always,
    may you ever be captivated by her
        love.
²⁰Why be captivated, my son, by an
        adulteress?
    Why embrace the bosom of
        another man's wife?

ᵃ5 Hebrew *Sheol*

The Purpose-driven Marriage

Friday

PROVERBS 4:25-26   We recently celebrated a wedding anniversary in the mountains of Colorado. This was not a camping trip, however. We were going deluxe—a late morning brunch, a lazy afternoon by the pool, maybe a little window shopping and then a gourmet dinner. Well, that was the first day. When the second morning rolled around, we were ready for a change of pace. We wanted activity, an outdoor adventure. The night before, on our stroll through town, we had spotted a mountain bike rental shop. It was filled with dozens of bikes with fat, knobby tires for traversing rocky terrain. So after a quick breakfast, we bee-lined it for the bikes, mapped out a route and took off for the wilderness.

One thing we didn't consider, however, was the impact of the high altitude on our breathing. Add to that the steep inclines, muddy patches and crooked trails, and you

COUPLE · MINUTES

can probably figure out that we did not get too far on our journey. We ended up returning to town and riding our bikes on paved, flat roads along the river. Ah, the serenity of a level path. No more huffing and puffing.

Proverbs has a lot to say about the benefits of traveling on a straight and level path. Of course, no marriage is exempt from a few steep inclines and some rocky terrain. They are a part of every marriage relationship. But generally speaking, we can do more than we think we can to smooth out the journey.

Proverbs speaks about "looking straight ahead" and "fixing our gaze." This is the talk of having a purpose, of having a mission. Have you ever written a purpose statement? More to the point, have you ever considered creating a mission statement unique to you as a married couple?   **—Les & Leslie**

Go to page 669 for your next devotional reading.

²¹For a man's ways are in full view of
the LORD,
and he examines all his paths.
²²The evil deeds of a wicked man
ensnare him;
the cords of his sin hold him fast.
²³He will die for lack of discipline,
led astray by his own great folly.

Warnings Against Folly

6 My son, if you have put up security
for your neighbor,
if you have struck hands in pledge
for another,
²if you have been trapped by what you
said,
ensnared by the words of your
mouth,
³then do this, my son, to free yourself,
since you have fallen into your
neighbor's hands:
Go and humble yourself;
press your plea with your
neighbor!
⁴Allow no sleep to your eyes,

no slumber to your eyelids.
⁵Free yourself, like a gazelle from the
hand of the hunter,
like a bird from the snare of the
fowler.

⁶Go to the ant, you sluggard;
consider its ways and be wise!
⁷It has no commander,
no overseer or ruler,
⁸yet it stores its provisions in summer
and gathers its food at harvest.

⁹How long will you lie there, you
sluggard?
When will you get up from your
sleep?
¹⁰A little sleep, a little slumber,
a little folding of the hands to
rest—
¹¹and poverty will come on you like a
bandit
and scarcity like an armed man. ᵃ

¹²A scoundrel and villain,

ᵃ 11 Or *like a vagrant / and scarcity like a beggar*

Sex and Passion

PROVERBS 5:18–19 God created sex and placed passion
deep within our hearts to be
expressed in the context of a
loving marriage. And he created sex for our pleasure. In
this passage, two God-given
benefits of the sexual relationship—pleasure and intimacy—are mentioned. While procreation is one purpose of
sex, God designed our bodies to experience
pleasure, enjoyment, closeness and intimacy as we share our love with each other. And
he was quite descriptive about it: "May your
fountain be blessed, and may you rejoice in
the wife of your youth. A loving doe, a graceful deer—may her breasts satisfy you always, may you ever be captivated by her
love."

How are you doing at loving each other?
One of the most difficult things about stay-

ing in love and growing closer
together is learning how to
keep intimacy alive. Love and
intimacy in a marriage grow
by stages, but if we ignore
our sexual relationship at any
stage, it can fade.

For centuries the attitude among
Christians was to avoid discussing sex.
Only in recent years has this begun to
change, but for many married couples it's
still difficult to say the "S" word. If we don't
talk about our love life, we won't be able
to develop true intimacy. Two of the most
important lovemaking skills and enhancers
to romance are listening with your heart and
talking to your spouse about your sexual
relationship.

Remember it's with God's blessing that
you are to be captivated by each other's
love!   **—Dave & Claudia**

Weekend Warm-up *What would be your ideal romantic evening with each other?*

Go to page 674 for your next devotional reading.

who goes about with a corrupt
    mouth,
13 who winks with his eye,
    signals with his feet
    and motions with his fingers,
14 who plots evil with deceit in his
        heart—
    he always stirs up dissension.
15Therefore disaster will overtake him
        in an instant;
    he will suddenly be destroyed—
        without remedy.

16There are six things the LORD hates,
    seven that are detestable to him:
17   haughty eyes,
        a lying tongue,
        hands that shed innocent blood,
18   a heart that devises wicked
            schemes,
        feet that are quick to rush into
            evil,
19   a false witness who pours out
            lies
        and a man who stirs up
            dissension among brothers.

Warning Against Adultery

20My son, keep your father's commands
    and do not forsake your mother's
        teaching.
21Bind them upon your heart forever;
    fasten them around your neck.
22When you walk, they will guide you;
    when you sleep, they will watch
        over you;
    when you awake, they will speak to
        you.
23For these commands are a lamp,
    this teaching is a light,
    and the corrections of discipline
    are the way to life,
24keeping you from the immoral
        woman,
    from the smooth tongue of the
        wayward wife.
25Do not lust in your heart after her
        beauty
    or let her captivate you with her
        eyes,
26for the prostitute reduces you to a
        loaf of bread,
    and the adulteress preys upon your
        very life.
27Can a man scoop fire into his lap
    without his clothes being burned?

28Can a man walk on hot coals
    without his feet being scorched?
29So is he who sleeps with another
        man's wife;
    no one who touches her will go
        unpunished.

30Men do not despise a thief if he steals
    to satisfy his hunger when he is
        starving.
31Yet if he is caught, he must pay
        sevenfold,
    though it costs him all the wealth
        of his house.
32But a man who commits adultery
        lacks judgment;
    whoever does so destroys himself.
33Blows and disgrace are his lot,
    and his shame will never be wiped
        away;
34for jealousy arouses a husband's fury,
    and he will show no mercy when
        he takes revenge.
35He will not accept any compensation;
    he will refuse the bribe, however
        great it is.

Warning Against the Adulteress

7 My son, keep my words
    and store up my commands within
        you.
2Keep my commands and you will
        live;
    guard my teachings as the apple of
        your eye.
3Bind them on your fingers;
    write them on the tablet of your
        heart.
4Say to wisdom, "You are my sister,"
    and call understanding your
        kinsman;
5they will keep you from the
        adulteress,
    from the wayward wife with her
        seductive words.

6At the window of my house
    I looked out through the lattice.
7I saw among the simple,
    I noticed among the young men,
    a youth who lacked judgment.
8He was going down the street near
        her corner,
    walking along in the direction of
        her house

⁹at twilight, as the day was fading,
  as the dark of night set in.

¹⁰Then out came a woman to meet
    him,
  dressed like a prostitute and with
    crafty intent.
¹¹(She is loud and defiant,
  her feet never stay at home;
¹²now in the street, now in the squares,
  at every corner she lurks.)
¹³She took hold of him and kissed him
  and with a brazen face she said:

¹⁴"I have fellowship offerings*a* at
    home;
  today I fulfilled my vows.
¹⁵So I came out to meet you;
  I looked for you and have found
    you!
¹⁶I have covered my bed
  with colored linens from Egypt.
¹⁷I have perfumed my bed
  with myrrh, aloes and cinnamon.
¹⁸Come, let's drink deep of love till
    morning;
  let's enjoy ourselves with love!
¹⁹My husband is not at home;
  he has gone on a long journey.
²⁰He took his purse filled with money
  and will not be home till full
    moon."

²¹With persuasive words she led him
    astray;
  she seduced him with her smooth
    talk.
²²All at once he followed her
  like an ox going to the slaughter,
  like a deer*b* stepping into a noose*c*
²³ till an arrow pierces his liver,
  like a bird darting into a snare,
    little knowing it will cost him his
      life.

²⁴Now then, my sons, listen to me;
  pay attention to what I say.
²⁵Do not let your heart turn to her
    ways
  or stray into her paths.
²⁶Many are the victims she has brought
    down;
  her slain are a mighty throng.
²⁷Her house is a highway to the
    grave,*d*
  leading down to the chambers of
    death.

Wisdom's Call

8 Does not wisdom call out?
  Does not understanding raise her
    voice?
²On the heights along the way,
  where the paths meet, she takes her
    stand;
³beside the gates leading into the city,
  at the entrances, she cries aloud:
⁴"To you, O men, I call out;
  I raise my voice to all mankind.
⁵You who are simple, gain prudence;
  you who are foolish, gain
    understanding.
⁶Listen, for I have worthy things to
    say;
  I open my lips to speak what is
    right.
⁷My mouth speaks what is true,
  for my lips detest wickedness.
⁸All the words of my mouth are just;
  none of them is crooked or
    perverse.
⁹To the discerning all of them are
    right;
  they are faultless to those who
    have knowledge.
¹⁰Choose my instruction instead of
    silver,
  knowledge rather than choice gold,
¹¹for wisdom is more precious than
    rubies,
  and nothing you desire can
    compare with her.

¹²"I, wisdom, dwell together with
    prudence;
  I possess knowledge and discretion.
¹³To fear the LORD is to hate evil;
  I hate pride and arrogance,
    evil behavior and perverse speech.
¹⁴Counsel and sound judgment are
    mine;
  I have understanding and power.
¹⁵By me kings reign
  and rulers make laws that are just;
¹⁶by me princes govern,
  and all nobles who rule on
    earth.*e*
¹⁷I love those who love me,

---

a14 Traditionally *peace offerings*   *b22* Syriac (see
also Septuagint); Hebrew *fool*   *c22* The meaning
of the Hebrew for this line is uncertain.
d27 Hebrew *Sheol*   *e16* Many Hebrew
manuscripts and Septuagint; most Hebrew
manuscripts *and nobles—all righteous rulers*

and those who seek me find me.
¹⁸With me are riches and honor,
    enduring wealth and prosperity.
¹⁹My fruit is better than fine gold;
    what I yield surpasses choice silver.
²⁰I walk in the way of righteousness,
    along the paths of justice,
²¹bestowing wealth on those who love
    me
    and making their treasuries full.

²²"The LORD brought me forth as the
    first of his works,[a, b]
    before his deeds of old;
²³I was appointed[c] from eternity,
    from the beginning, before the
    world began.
²⁴When there were no oceans, I was
    given birth,
    when there were no springs
    abounding with water;
²⁵before the mountains were settled in
    place,
    before the hills, I was given birth,
²⁶before he made the earth or its fields
    or any of the dust of the world.
²⁷I was there when he set the heavens
    in place,
    when he marked out the horizon
    on the face of the deep,
²⁸when he established the clouds above
    and fixed securely the fountains of
    the deep,
²⁹when he gave the sea its boundary
    so the waters would not overstep
    his command,
    and when he marked out the
    foundations of the earth.
³⁰   Then I was the craftsman at his
    side.
    I was filled with delight day after day,
    rejoicing always in his presence,
³¹rejoicing in his whole world
    and delighting in mankind.

³²"Now then, my sons, listen to me;
    blessed are those who keep my
    ways.
³³Listen to my instruction and be wise;
    do not ignore it.
³⁴Blessed is the man who listens to me,
    watching daily at my doors,
    waiting at my doorway.
³⁵For whoever finds me finds life
    and receives favor from the LORD.

³⁶But whoever fails to find me harms
    himself;
    all who hate me love death."

Invitations of Wisdom and of Folly

9 Wisdom has built her house;
    she has hewn out its seven pillars.
²She has prepared her meat and mixed
    her wine;
    she has also set her table.
³She has sent out her maids, and she
    calls
    from the highest point of the city.
⁴"Let all who are simple come in here!"
    she says to those who lack
    judgment.
⁵"Come, eat my food
    and drink the wine I have mixed.
⁶Leave your simple ways and you will
    live;
    walk in the way of understanding.

⁷"Whoever corrects a mocker invites
    insult;
    whoever rebukes a wicked man
    incurs abuse.
⁸Do not rebuke a mocker or he will
    hate you;
    rebuke a wise man and he will
    love you.
⁹Instruct a wise man and he will be
    wiser still;
    teach a righteous man and he will
    add to his learning.

¹⁰"The fear of the LORD is the
    beginning of wisdom,
    and knowledge of the Holy One is
    understanding.
¹¹For through me your days will be
    many,
    and years will be added to your
    life.
¹²If you are wise, your wisdom will
    reward you;
    if you are a mocker, you alone will
    suffer."

¹³The woman Folly is loud;
    she is undisciplined and without
    knowledge.
¹⁴She sits at the door of her house,

---

[a]22 Or *way;* or *dominion*   [b]22 Or *The* LORD
possessed me at the beginning of his work; or *The* LORD
brought me forth at the beginning of his work
[c]23 Or *fashioned*

on a seat at the highest point of
the city,
15 calling out to those who pass by,
who go straight on their way.
16 "Let all who are simple come in here!"
she says to those who lack
judgment.
17 "Stolen water is sweet;
food eaten in secret is delicious!"
18 But little do they know that the dead
are there,
that her guests are in the depths of
the grave. [a]

Proverbs of Solomon

10
The proverbs of Solomon:

A wise son brings joy to his father,
but a foolish son grief to his
mother.

2 Ill-gotten treasures are of no value,
but righteousness delivers from
death.

3 The LORD does not let the righteous
go hungry
but he thwarts the craving of the
wicked.

4 Lazy hands make a man poor,
but diligent hands bring wealth.

5 He who gathers crops in summer is a
wise son,
but he who sleeps during harvest is
a disgraceful son.

6 Blessings crown the head of the
righteous,
but violence overwhelms the
mouth of the wicked. [b]

7 The memory of the righteous will be
a blessing,
but the name of the wicked will
rot.

8 The wise in heart accept commands,
but a chattering fool comes to ruin.

9 The man of integrity walks securely,
but he who takes crooked paths
will be found out.

10 He who winks maliciously causes
grief,
and a chattering fool comes to
ruin.

11 The mouth of the righteous is a
fountain of life,
but violence overwhelms the
mouth of the wicked.

12 Hatred stirs up dissension,
but love covers over all wrongs.

13 Wisdom is found on the lips of the
discerning,
but a rod is for the back of him
who lacks judgment.

14 Wise men store up knowledge,
but the mouth of a fool invites
ruin.

15 The wealth of the rich is their
fortified city,
but poverty is the ruin of the poor.

16 The wages of the righteous bring
them life,
but the income of the wicked
brings them punishment.

17 He who heeds discipline shows the
way to life,
but whoever ignores correction
leads others astray.

18 He who conceals his hatred has lying
lips,
and whoever spreads slander is a
fool.

19 When words are many, sin is not
absent,
but he who holds his tongue is
wise.

20 The tongue of the righteous is choice
silver,
but the heart of the wicked is of
little value.

21 The lips of the righteous nourish
many,
but fools die for lack of judgment.

22 The blessing of the LORD brings
wealth,
and he adds no trouble to it.

23 A fool finds pleasure in evil conduct,
but a man of understanding
delights in wisdom.

24 What the wicked dreads will overtake
him;

---

[a]18 Hebrew *Sheol*   [b]6 Or *but the mouth of the
wicked conceals violence*; also in verse 11

what the righteous desire will be
　　granted.

25When the storm has swept by, the
　　wicked are gone,
　　but the righteous stand firm
　　　forever.

26As vinegar to the teeth and smoke to
　　the eyes,
　　so is a sluggard to those who send
　　　him.

27The fear of the LORD adds length to
　　life,
　　but the years of the wicked are cut
　　　short.

28The prospect of the righteous is joy,
　　but the hopes of the wicked come
　　　to nothing.

29The way of the LORD is a refuge for
　　the righteous,

but it is the ruin of those who do
　　evil.

30The righteous will never be uprooted,
　　but the wicked will not remain in
　　　the land.

31The mouth of the righteous brings
　　forth wisdom,
　　but a perverse tongue will be cut
　　　out.

32The lips of the righteous know what
　　is fitting,
　　but the mouth of the wicked only
　　　what is perverse.

11 The LORD abhors dishonest scales,
　　but accurate weights are his
　　　delight.

2When pride comes, then comes
　　disgrace,
　　but with humility comes wisdom.

Haven't Got Time for the Pain

Monday

PROVERBS 10:12 It hadn't been a good morning. Just before breakfast they had blown up at each other.

"You are so self-centered and insensitive," she told him.

"Well, you overreact to everything," he retorted.

She wanted to take some time to talk about the situation. He couldn't get out of there fast enough. Before they hopped into separate cars to drive to work, each got in a few final jabs on the fly.

Truth be known, the argument had been building up over several weeks, maybe even months. She thought about all the times he was preoccupied with his job, his friends, his hobbies, his favorite team—anything other than her. She began to wonder, *Does he really love me anymore? If he really loved me, would he treat me this way?*

He was irritable when he got to work that morning. *What's gotten into her?* he wondered. *She's really turned into a nag—just like her mother!*

That morning both Ron and Linda felt terribly alone. They both wondered if they were going to make it as a couple. With their hurts running so deep, marriage loomed over them like an endurance contest.

Have you ever felt that way? If not, you have certainly felt the stinging pain, if only briefly, of something your spouse said or did. With marriage inevitably comes pain. It's part of the package. And, whenever we are hurt, we usually see ourselves as innocent victims. Someone has done us an injustice, and now we're left to pick up the pieces. While it's true we may be victims, we are not *helpless* victims. We can choose how we'll respond. We can either choose to be angry and resentful, or we can choose to rise above the negativity, forgive whoever has hurt us and move on.

That's what this proverb is all about—forgiveness. Unless we live in total denial, it's the only way to cover over all wrongs. And it begins when we free ourselves from any desire to hurt back. "Never pay back evil for evil . . . do not seek revenge," says Paul in Romans (12:17–19).

—Les & Leslie

Go to page 675 for your next devotional reading.

³The integrity of the upright guides
them,
but the unfaithful are destroyed by
their duplicity.

⁴Wealth is worthless in the day of
wrath,
but righteousness delivers from
death.

⁵The righteousness of the blameless
makes a straight way for
them,
but the wicked are brought down
by their own wickedness.

⁶The righteousness of the upright
delivers them,
but the unfaithful are trapped by
evil desires.

⁷When a wicked man dies, his hope
perishes;
all he expected from his power
comes to nothing.

⁸The righteous man is rescued from
trouble,
and it comes on the wicked
instead.

⁹With his mouth the godless destroys
his neighbor,
but through knowledge the
righteous escape.

¹⁰When the righteous prosper, the city
rejoices;
when the wicked perish, there are
shouts of joy.

¹¹Through the blessing of the upright a
city is exalted,
but by the mouth of the wicked it
is destroyed.

¹²A man who lacks judgment derides
his neighbor,
but a man of understanding holds
his tongue.

¹³A gossip betrays a confidence,
but a trustworthy man keeps a
secret.

¹⁴For lack of guidance a nation falls,
but many advisers make victory
sure.

¹⁵He who puts up security for another
will surely suffer,
but whoever refuses to strike hands
in pledge is safe.

¹⁶A kindhearted woman gains respect,
but ruthless men gain only wealth.

¹⁷A kind man benefits himself,
but a cruel man brings trouble on
himself.

¹⁸The wicked man earns deceptive
wages,
but he who sows righteousness
reaps a sure reward.

¹⁹The truly righteous man attains life,

Give and Take

Tuesday

PROVERBS 11:2 "It's my way or the highway." Ever felt like that? If we are honest, we have all had times where we wanted something done our way while our spouse wanted it done another.

Make way for compromise—not one of my favorite words. I (Leslie) view it much the way I view such things as sit-ups and checkbook balancing: necessary but evil.

Some people start out marriage with the belief that they shouldn't have to negotiate because they should agree on everything. That's because during courtship they *seem* to agree on everything. But over time, different needs and issues are brought to bear.

And if a husband and wife don't learn to eat a little humble pie and make some concessions now and then, they might as well give up. Marriage cannot survive without a little give and take.

Arriving at a mutually pleasing agreement doesn't just solve an immediate, specific problem; it ushers in a spirit of humility to the marriage. Selfish pride is the primary barrier to negotiating in marriage. No wonder Proverbs says that when pride enters the picture, it's a disgrace. But humility cultivates wisdom.

—Les & Leslie

Go to page 677 for your next devotional reading.

but he who pursues evil goes to his
   death.

²⁰The LORD detests men of perverse
   heart
   but he delights in those whose
   ways are blameless.

²¹Be sure of this: The wicked will not
   go unpunished,
   but those who are righteous will go
   free.

²²Like a gold ring in a pig's snout
   is a beautiful woman who shows
   no discretion.

²³The desire of the righteous ends only
   in good,
   but the hope of the wicked only in
   wrath.

²⁴One man gives freely, yet gains even
   more;
   another withholds unduly, but
   comes to poverty.

²⁵A generous man will prosper;
   he who refreshes others will
   himself be refreshed.

²⁶People curse the man who hoards
   grain,
   but blessing crowns him who is
   willing to sell.

²⁷He who seeks good finds goodwill,
   but evil comes to him who
   searches for it.

²⁸Whoever trusts in his riches will fall,
   but the righteous will thrive like a
   green leaf.

²⁹He who brings trouble on his family
   will inherit only wind,
   and the fool will be servant to the
   wise.

³⁰The fruit of the righteous is a tree of
   life,
   and he who wins souls is wise.

³¹If the righteous receive their due on
   earth,
   how much more the ungodly and
   the sinner!

12 Whoever loves discipline loves
   knowledge,
but he who hates correction is
   stupid.

²A good man obtains favor from the
   LORD,
   but the LORD condemns a crafty
   man.

³A man cannot be established through
   wickedness,
   but the righteous cannot be
   uprooted.

⁴A wife of noble character is her
   husband's crown,
   but a disgraceful wife is like decay
   in his bones.

⁵The plans of the righteous are just,
   but the advice of the wicked is
   deceitful.

⁶The words of the wicked lie in wait
   for blood,
   but the speech of the upright
   rescues them.

⁷Wicked men are overthrown and are
   no more,
   but the house of the righteous
   stands firm.

⁸A man is praised according to his
   wisdom,
   but men with warped minds are
   despised.

⁹Better to be a nobody and yet have a
   servant
   than pretend to be somebody and
   have no food.

¹⁰A righteous man cares for the needs
   of his animal,
   but the kindest acts of the wicked
   are cruel.

¹¹He who works his land will have
   abundant food,
   but he who chases fantasies lacks
   judgment.

¹²The wicked desire the plunder of evil
   men,
   but the root of the righteous
   flourishes.

¹³An evil man is trapped by his sinful
   talk,
   but a righteous man escapes
   trouble.

¹⁴From the fruit of his lips a man is
   filled with good things

as surely as the work of his hands
rewards him.

¹⁵The way of a fool seems right to him,
but a wise man listens to advice.

¹⁶A fool shows his annoyance at once,
but a prudent man overlooks an
insult.

¹⁷A truthful witness gives honest
testimony,
but a false witness tells lies.

¹⁸Reckless words pierce like a sword,
but the tongue of the wise brings
healing.

¹⁹Truthful lips endure forever,
but a lying tongue lasts only a
moment.

²⁰There is deceit in the hearts of those
who plot evil,
but joy for those who promote
peace.

²¹No harm befalls the righteous,
but the wicked have their fill of
trouble.

²²The LORD detests lying lips,
but he delights in men who are
truthful.

²³A prudent man keeps his knowledge
to himself,
but the heart of fools blurts out
folly.

²⁴Diligent hands will rule,
but laziness ends in slave labor.

²⁵An anxious heart weighs a man
down,
but a kind word cheers him up.

²⁶A righteous man is cautious in
friendship, *ᵃ*
but the way of the wicked leads
them astray.

²⁷The lazy man does not roast *ᵇ* his
game,
but the diligent man prizes his
possessions.

²⁸In the way of righteousness there is
life;
along that path is immortality.

13 A wise son heeds his father's
instruction,
but a mocker does not listen to
rebuke.

ᵃ26 Or man is a guide to his neighbor
*ᵇ27 The meaning of the Hebrew for this word is
uncertain.*

A Kinder Word Does Wonders

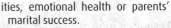

Wednesday

PROVERBS 12:25 Spouses routine-
ly underestimate the importance
of a kind word. We're not talking
about elaborate praise or a heartfelt poem, as wonderful as these
things are. We're talking about the
simple, everyday kindness of small
talk, such as "Thanks" or "You're great" or
"I missed you today."

Les and I think the small, day-to-day
things spouses say to each other are more
important than any of the overarching communication issues. Most marriage experts
agree. Thomas Holman is a professor of
family sciences at Brigham Young University. He studies ways to increase marital
quality and has found that making time
for small talk is at least as important to a
couple's happiness as agreeing on values
and role expectations, demographic similar-

ities, emotional health or parents'
marital success.

When a couple is just sitting
around talking, one of the things
they are saying is, "You are important enough to me just to sit here
with you." It's what Dr. Holman calls a
"Maxwell House moment" because it is the
kind of casual exchange that usually takes
place over a cup of coffee. The subject isn't
relevant, but the kind words expressed are.

The next time your spouse has a heavy
heart, remember the wise words of this
Proverb: "An anxious heart weighs a man
down, but a kind word cheers him up." You
don't have to throw a party, buy presents or
hire a singing telegram. All you need is to
say a kind word.

—Les & Leslie

Go to page 681 for your next devotional reading.

²From the fruit of his lips a man
enjoys good things,
but the unfaithful have a craving
for violence.

³He who guards his lips guards his
life,
but he who speaks rashly will
come to ruin.

⁴The sluggard craves and gets nothing,
but the desires of the diligent are
fully satisfied.

⁵The righteous hate what is false,
but the wicked bring shame and
disgrace.

⁶Righteousness guards the man of
integrity,
but wickedness overthrows the
sinner.

⁷One man pretends to be rich, yet has
nothing;
another pretends to be poor, yet
has great wealth.

⁸A man's riches may ransom his life,
but a poor man hears no threat.

⁹The light of the righteous shines
brightly,
but the lamp of the wicked is
snuffed out.

¹⁰Pride only breeds quarrels,
but wisdom is found in those who
take advice.

¹¹Dishonest money dwindles away,
but he who gathers money little by
little makes it grow.

¹²Hope deferred makes the heart sick,
but a longing fulfilled is a tree of
life.

¹³He who scorns instruction will pay
for it,
but he who respects a command is
rewarded.

¹⁴The teaching of the wise is a fountain
of life,
turning a man from the snares of
death.

¹⁵Good understanding wins favor,
but the way of the unfaithful is
hard.ᵃ

¹⁶Every prudent man acts out of
knowledge,
but a fool exposes his folly.

¹⁷A wicked messenger falls into trouble,
but a trustworthy envoy brings
healing.

¹⁸He who ignores discipline comes to
poverty and shame,
but whoever heeds correction is
honored.

¹⁹A longing fulfilled is sweet to the
soul,
but fools detest turning from evil.

²⁰He who walks with the wise grows
wise,
but a companion of fools suffers
harm.

²¹Misfortune pursues the sinner,
but prosperity is the reward of the
righteous.

²²A good man leaves an inheritance for
his children's children,
but a sinner's wealth is stored up
for the righteous.

²³A poor man's field may produce
abundant food,
but injustice sweeps it away.

²⁴He who spares the rod hates his son,
but he who loves him is careful to
discipline him.

²⁵The righteous eat to their hearts'
content,
but the stomach of the wicked goes
hungry.

14 The wise woman builds her
house,
but with her own hands the
foolish one tears hers down.

²He whose walk is upright fears the
LORD,
but he whose ways are devious
despises him.

³A fool's talk brings a rod to his back,
but the lips of the wise protect
them.

⁴Where there are no oxen, the manger
is empty,

ᵃ15 Or unfaithful does not endure

but from the strength of an ox
  comes an abundant harvest.

⁵A truthful witness does not deceive,
  but a false witness pours out lies.

⁶The mocker seeks wisdom and finds
    none,
  but knowledge comes easily to the
    discerning.

⁷Stay away from a foolish man,
  for you will not find knowledge on
    his lips.

⁸The wisdom of the prudent is to give
    thought to their ways,
  but the folly of fools is deception.

⁹Fools mock at making amends for
    sin,
  but goodwill is found among the
    upright.

¹⁰Each heart knows its own bitterness,
  and no one else can share its joy.

¹¹The house of the wicked will be
    destroyed,
  but the tent of the upright will
    flourish.

¹²There is a way that seems right to a
    man,
  but in the end it leads to death.

¹³Even in laughter the heart may ache,
  and joy may end in grief.

¹⁴The faithless will be fully repaid for
    their ways,
  and the good man rewarded for
    his.

¹⁵A simple man believes anything,
  but a prudent man gives thought
    to his steps.

¹⁶A wise man fears the LORD and shuns
    evil,
  but a fool is hotheaded and
    reckless.

¹⁷A quick-tempered man does foolish
    things,
  and a crafty man is hated.

¹⁸The simple inherit folly,
  but the prudent are crowned with
    knowledge.

¹⁹Evil men will bow down in the
    presence of the good,

and the wicked at the gates of the
  righteous.

²⁰The poor are shunned even by their
    neighbors,
  but the rich have many friends.

²¹He who despises his neighbor sins,
  but blessed is he who is kind to
    the needy.

²²Do not those who plot evil go astray?
  But those who plan what is good
    findᵃ love and faithfulness.

²³All hard work brings a profit,
  but mere talk leads only to
    poverty.

²⁴The wealth of the wise is their crown,
  but the folly of fools yields folly.

²⁵A truthful witness saves lives,
  but a false witness is deceitful.

²⁶He who fears the LORD has a secure
    fortress,
  and for his children it will be a
    refuge.

²⁷The fear of the LORD is a fountain of
    life,
  turning a man from the snares of
    death.

²⁸A large population is a king's glory,
  but without subjects a prince is
    ruined.

²⁹A patient man has great
    understanding,
  but a quick-tempered man displays
    folly.

³⁰A heart at peace gives life to the
    body,
  but envy rots the bones.

³¹He who oppresses the poor shows
    contempt for their Maker,
  but whoever is kind to the needy
    honors God.

³²When calamity comes, the wicked are
    brought down,
  but even in death the righteous
    have a refuge.

³³Wisdom reposes in the heart of the
    discerning

ᵃ22 Or show

and even among fools she lets
    herself be known.[a]

³⁴Righteousness exalts a nation,
    but sin is a disgrace to any people.

³⁵A king delights in a wise servant,
    but a shameful servant incurs his
        wrath.

15 A gentle answer turns away wrath,
    but a harsh word stirs up anger.

²The tongue of the wise commends
        knowledge,
    but the mouth of the fool gushes
        folly.

³The eyes of the LORD are everywhere,
    keeping watch on the wicked and
        the good.

⁴The tongue that brings healing is a
        tree of life,
    but a deceitful tongue crushes the
        spirit.

⁵A fool spurns his father's discipline,
    but whoever heeds correction
        shows prudence.

⁶The house of the righteous contains
        great treasure,
    but the income of the wicked
        brings them trouble.

⁷The lips of the wise spread
        knowledge;
    not so the hearts of fools.

⁸The LORD detests the sacrifice of the
        wicked,
    but the prayer of the upright
        pleases him.

⁹The LORD detests the way of the
        wicked
    but he loves those who pursue
        righteousness.

¹⁰Stern discipline awaits him who
        leaves the path;
    he who hates correction will die.

¹¹Death and Destruction[b] lie open
        before the LORD—
    how much more the hearts of
        men!

¹²A mocker resents correction;
    he will not consult the wise.

¹³A happy heart makes the face
        cheerful,
    but heartache crushes the spirit.

¹⁴The discerning heart seeks knowledge,
    but the mouth of a fool feeds on
        folly.

¹⁵All the days of the oppressed are
        wretched,
    but the cheerful heart has a
        continual feast.

¹⁶Better a little with the fear of the
        LORD
    than great wealth with turmoil.

¹⁷Better a meal of vegetables where
        there is love
    than a fattened calf with hatred.

¹⁸A hot-tempered man stirs up
        dissension,
    but a patient man calms a quarrel.

¹⁹The way of the sluggard is blocked
        with thorns,
    but the path of the upright is a
        highway.

²⁰A wise son brings joy to his father,
    but a foolish man despises his
        mother.

²¹Folly delights a man who lacks
        judgment,
    but a man of understanding keeps
        a straight course.

²²Plans fail for lack of counsel,
    but with many advisers they
        succeed.

²³A man finds joy in giving an apt
        reply—
    and how good is a timely word!

²⁴The path of life leads upward for the
        wise
    to keep him from going down to
        the grave.[c]

²⁵The LORD tears down the proud
        man's house
    but he keeps the widow's
        boundaries intact.

²⁶The LORD detests the thoughts of the
        wicked,

[a]33 Hebrew; Septuagint and Syriac / but in the
heart of fools she is not known   [b]11 Hebrew Sheol
and Abaddon   [c]24 Hebrew Sheol

but those of the pure are pleasing
    to him.

²⁷A greedy man brings trouble to his
    family,
  but he who hates bribes will live.

²⁸The heart of the righteous weighs its
    answers,
  but the mouth of the wicked
    gushes evil.

²⁹The LORD is far from the wicked
  but he hears the prayer of the
    righteous.

³⁰A cheerful look brings joy to the
    heart,
  and good news gives health to the
    bones.

³¹He who listens to a life-giving rebuke
  will be at home among the wise.

³²He who ignores discipline despises
    himself,
  but whoever heeds correction gains
    understanding.

³³The fear of the LORD teaches a man
    wisdom, ᵃ
  and humility comes before honor.

16 To man belong the plans of the
    heart,
  but from the LORD comes the reply
    of the tongue.

²All a man's ways seem innocent to
    him,
  but motives are weighed by the
    LORD.

³Commit to the LORD whatever you
    do,
  and your plans will succeed.

⁴The LORD works out everything for
    his own ends—
  even the wicked for a day of
    disaster.

⁵The LORD detests all the proud of
    heart.
  Be sure of this: They will not go
    unpunished.

⁶Through love and faithfulness sin is
    atoned for;
  through the fear of the LORD a man
    avoids evil.

⁷When a man's ways are pleasing to
    the LORD,
  he makes even his enemies live at
    peace with him.

⁸Better a little with righteousness
  than much gain with injustice.

⁹In his heart a man plans his course,
  but the LORD determines his steps.

ᵃ33 Or *Wisdom teaches the fear of the* LORD

Reclaiming Table Time

Thursday

PROVERBS 15:17 "Pass the corn."
    "Where's the salt?"
    "Move over."
    "Do you have to crunch your ice
so loud?"

This is common conversation
around many family dinner tables.
Pleasant, huh? And too bad. Mealtime offers
one of the best opportunities for human connection and companionship—especially for
couples. Culinary writer M. F. Fisher is known
for saying, "Sharing food with another
human being is an intimate act that should
not be indulged in lightly."

Think about it. The usual scenario is that
two people reunite at dinnertime and exchange portions of events from their day:
"Traffic was terrible on the way
home tonight." "Did you pick up
my dry cleaning?" "Your mother
called again." "I need the car
tonight." Or, even worse, they flip
on the television and eat without
saying a word.

If you want to reclaim table time with
your spouse, make it a time both of you look
forward to. You don't have to cook like Julia
Childs or set a table like Martha Stewart to
make mealtimes pleasurable. What matters
most is the focus of your conversation: "Let
your conversation be always full of grace,
seasoned with salt . . ." (Colossians 4:6).

—**Les & Leslie**

Go to page 689 for your next devotional reading.

[10]The lips of a king speak as an oracle,
and his mouth should not betray
justice.

[11]Honest scales and balances are from
the LORD;
all the weights in the bag are of his
making.

[12]Kings detest wrongdoing,
for a throne is established through
righteousness.

[13]Kings take pleasure in honest lips;
they value a man who speaks the
truth.

[14]A king's wrath is a messenger of
death,
but a wise man will appease it.

[15]When a king's face brightens, it
means life;
his favor is like a rain cloud in
spring.

[16]How much better to get wisdom than
gold,
to choose understanding rather
than silver!

[17]The highway of the upright avoids
evil;
he who guards his way guards his
life.

[18]Pride goes before destruction,
a haughty spirit before a fall.

[19]Better to be lowly in spirit and
among the oppressed
than to share plunder with the
proud.

[20]Whoever gives heed to instruction
prospers,
and blessed is he who trusts in the
LORD.

[21]The wise in heart are called
discerning,
and pleasant words promote
instruction.[a]

[22]Understanding is a fountain of life to
those who have it,
but folly brings punishment to
fools.

[23]A wise man's heart guides his mouth,
and his lips promote instruction.[b]

[24]Pleasant words are a honeycomb,
sweet to the soul and healing to
the bones.

[25]There is a way that seems right to a
man,
but in the end it leads to death.

[26]The laborer's appetite works for him;
his hunger drives him on.

[27]A scoundrel plots evil,
and his speech is like a scorching
fire.

[28]A perverse man stirs up dissension,
and a gossip separates close
friends.

[29]A violent man entices his neighbor
and leads him down a path that is
not good.

[30]He who winks with his eye is plotting
perversity;
he who purses his lips is bent on
evil.

[31]Gray hair is a crown of splendor;
it is attained by a righteous life.

[32]Better a patient man than a warrior,
a man who controls his temper
than one who takes a city.

[33]The lot is cast into the lap,
but its every decision is from the
LORD.

17 Better a dry crust with peace and
quiet
than a house full of feasting,[c]
with strife.

[2]A wise servant will rule over a
disgraceful son,
and will share the inheritance as
one of the brothers.

[3]The crucible for silver and the furnace
for gold,
but the LORD tests the heart.

[4]A wicked man listens to evil lips;
a liar pays attention to a malicious
tongue.

[5]He who mocks the poor shows
contempt for their Maker;

---

*a21 Or words make a man persuasive   b23 Or
mouth / and makes his lips persuasive   c1 Hebrew
sacrifices*

whoever gloats over disaster will
not go unpunished.

⁶Children's children are a crown to the
aged,
and parents are the pride of their
children.

⁷Arrogant*ᵃ* lips are unsuited to a
fool—
how much worse lying lips to a
ruler!

⁸A bribe is a charm to the one who
gives it;
wherever he turns, he succeeds.

⁹He who covers over an offense
promotes love,
but whoever repeats the matter
separates close friends.

¹⁰A rebuke impresses a man of
discernment
more than a hundred lashes a fool.

¹¹An evil man is bent only on
rebellion;
a merciless official will be sent
against him.

¹²Better to meet a bear robbed of her
cubs
than a fool in his folly.

¹³If a man pays back evil for good,
evil will never leave his house.

¹⁴Starting a quarrel is like breaching a
dam;
so drop the matter before a dispute
breaks out.

¹⁵Acquitting the guilty and condemning
the innocent—
the LORD detests them both.

¹⁶Of what use is money in the hand of
a fool,
since he has no desire to get
wisdom?

¹⁷A friend loves at all times,
and a brother is born for adversity.

¹⁸A man lacking in judgment strikes
hands in pledge
and puts up security for his
neighbor.

¹⁹He who loves a quarrel loves sin;
he who builds a high gate invites
destruction.

²⁰A man of perverse heart does not
prosper;
he whose tongue is deceitful falls
into trouble.

²¹To have a fool for a son brings grief;
there is no joy for the father of a
fool.

²²A cheerful heart is good medicine,
but a crushed spirit dries up the
bones.

²³A wicked man accepts a bribe in
secret
to pervert the course of justice.

²⁴A discerning man keeps wisdom in
view,
but a fool's eyes wander to the
ends of the earth.

²⁵A foolish son brings grief to his father
and bitterness to the one who bore
him.

²⁶It is not good to punish an innocent
man,
or to flog officials for their
integrity.

²⁷A man of knowledge uses words with
restraint,
and a man of understanding is
even-tempered.

²⁸Even a fool is thought wise if he
keeps silent,
and discerning if he holds his
tongue.

18 An unfriendly man pursues selfish
ends;
he defies all sound judgment.

²A fool finds no pleasure in
understanding
but delights in airing his own
opinions.

³When wickedness comes, so does
contempt,
and with shame comes disgrace.

⁴The words of a man's mouth are deep
waters,
but the fountain of wisdom is a
bubbling brook.

⁵It is not good to be partial to the
wicked

ᵃ7 Or Eloquent

or to deprive the innocent of
justice.

6A fool's lips bring him strife,
and his mouth invites a beating.

7A fool's mouth is his undoing,
and his lips are a snare to his soul.

8The words of a gossip are like choice
morsels;
they go down to a man's inmost
parts.

9One who is slack in his work
is brother to one who destroys.

10The name of the LORD is a strong
tower;
the righteous run to it and are safe.

11The wealth of the rich is their
fortified city;
they imagine it an unscalable wall.

12Before his downfall a man's heart is
proud,
but humility comes before honor.

13He who answers before listening—
that is his folly and his shame.

14A man's spirit sustains him in
sickness,
but a crushed spirit who can bear?

15The heart of the discerning acquires
knowledge;
the ears of the wise seek it out.

16A gift opens the way for the giver
and ushers him into the presence
of the great.

17The first to present his case seems
right,
till another comes forward and
questions him.

18Casting the lot settles disputes
and keeps strong opponents apart.

19An offended brother is more
unyielding than a fortified
city,
and disputes are like the barred
gates of a citadel.

20From the fruit of his mouth a man's
stomach is filled;
with the harvest from his lips he is
satisfied.

21The tongue has the power of life and
death,
and those who love it will eat its
fruit.

22He who finds a wife finds what is
good
and receives favor from the LORD.

23A poor man pleads for mercy,
but a rich man answers harshly.

24A man of many companions may
come to ruin,
but there is a friend who sticks
closer than a brother.

19 Better a poor man whose walk is
blameless
than a fool whose lips are perverse.

2It is not good to have zeal without
knowledge,
nor to be hasty and miss the way.

3A man's own folly ruins his life,
yet his heart rages against the
LORD.

4Wealth brings many friends,
but a poor man's friend deserts
him.

5A false witness will not go
unpunished,
and he who pours out lies will not
go free.

6Many curry favor with a ruler,
and everyone is the friend of a
man who gives gifts.

7A poor man is shunned by all his
relatives—
how much more do his friends
avoid him!
Though he pursues them with
pleading,
they are nowhere to be found.a

8He who gets wisdom loves his own
soul;
he who cherishes understanding
prospers.

9A false witness will not go
unpunished,
and he who pours out lies will
perish.

a7 The meaning of the Hebrew for this sentence is
uncertain.

¹⁰It is not fitting for a fool to live in
luxury—
how much worse for a slave to rule
over princes!

¹¹A man's wisdom gives him patience;
it is to his glory to overlook an
offense.

¹²A king's rage is like the roar of a lion,
but his favor is like dew on the
grass.

¹³A foolish son is his father's ruin,
and a quarrelsome wife is like a
constant dripping.

¹⁴Houses and wealth are inherited from
parents,
but a prudent wife is from the
LORD.

¹⁵Laziness brings on deep sleep,
and the shiftless man goes hungry.

¹⁶He who obeys instructions guards his
life,
but he who is contemptuous of his
ways will die.

¹⁷He who is kind to the poor lends to
the LORD,
and he will reward him for what
he has done.

¹⁸Discipline your son, for in that there
is hope;
do not be a willing party to his
death.

¹⁹A hot-tempered man must pay the
penalty;
if you rescue him, you will have to
do it again.

²⁰Listen to advice and accept
instruction,
and in the end you will be wise.

²¹Many are the plans in a man's heart,
but it is the LORD's purpose that
prevails.

²²What a man desires is unfailing
love*ᵃ*;
better to be poor than a liar.

²³The fear of the LORD leads to life:
Then one rests content, untouched
by trouble.

²⁴The sluggard buries his hand in the
dish;

he will not even bring it back to
his mouth!

²⁵Flog a mocker, and the simple will
learn prudence;
rebuke a discerning man, and he
will gain knowledge.

²⁶He who robs his father and drives out
his mother
is a son who brings shame and
disgrace.

²⁷Stop listening to instruction, my son,
and you will stray from the words
of knowledge.

²⁸A corrupt witness mocks at justice,
and the mouth of the wicked gulps
down evil.

²⁹Penalties are prepared for mockers,
and beatings for the backs of fools.

20 Wine is a mocker and beer a
brawler;
whoever is led astray by them is
not wise.

²A king's wrath is like the roar of a
lion;
he who angers him forfeits his life.

³It is to a man's honor to avoid strife,
but every fool is quick to quarrel.

⁴A sluggard does not plow in season;
so at harvest time he looks but
finds nothing.

⁵The purposes of a man's heart are
deep waters,
but a man of understanding draws
them out.

⁶Many a man claims to have unfailing
love,
but a faithful man who can find?

⁷The righteous man leads a blameless
life;
blessed are his children after him.

⁸When a king sits on his throne to
judge,
he winnows out all evil with his
eyes.

⁹Who can say, "I have kept my heart
pure;
I am clean and without sin"?

ᵃ22 Or A man's greed is his shame

¹⁰Differing weights and differing
measures—
the LORD detests them both.

¹¹Even a child is known by his actions,
by whether his conduct is pure and
right.

¹²Ears that hear and eyes that see—
the LORD has made them both.

¹³Do not love sleep or you will grow
poor;
stay awake and you will have food
to spare.

¹⁴"It's no good, it's no good!" says the
buyer;
then off he goes and boasts about
his purchase.

¹⁵Gold there is, and rubies in
abundance,
but lips that speak knowledge are a
rare jewel.

¹⁶Take the garment of one who puts up
security for a stranger;
hold it in pledge if he does it for a
wayward woman.

¹⁷Food gained by fraud tastes sweet to a
man,
but he ends up with a mouth full
of gravel.

¹⁸Make plans by seeking advice;
if you wage war, obtain guidance.

¹⁹A gossip betrays a confidence;
so avoid a man who talks too
much.

²⁰If a man curses his father or mother,
his lamp will be snuffed out in
pitch darkness.

²¹An inheritance quickly gained at the
beginning
will not be blessed at the end.

²²Do not say, "I'll pay you back for this
wrong!"
Wait for the LORD, and he will
deliver you.

²³The LORD detests differing weights,
and dishonest scales do not please
him.

²⁴A man's steps are directed by the
LORD.

How then can anyone understand
his own way?

²⁵It is a trap for a man to dedicate
something rashly
and only later to consider his
vows.

²⁶A wise king winnows out the wicked;
he drives the threshing wheel over
them.

²⁷The lamp of the LORD searches the
spirit of a man^a;
it searches out his inmost being.

²⁸Love and faithfulness keep a king
safe;
through love his throne is made
secure.

²⁹The glory of young men is their
strength,
gray hair the splendor of the old.

³⁰Blows and wounds cleanse away evil,
and beatings purge the inmost
being.

21 The king's heart is in the hand of
the LORD;
he directs it like a watercourse
wherever he pleases.

²All a man's ways seem right to him,
but the LORD weighs the heart.

³To do what is right and just
is more acceptable to the LORD
than sacrifice.

⁴Haughty eyes and a proud heart,
the lamp of the wicked, are sin!

⁵The plans of the diligent lead to
profit
as surely as haste leads to poverty.

⁶A fortune made by a lying tongue
is a fleeting vapor and a deadly
snare.^b

⁷The violence of the wicked will drag
them away,
for they refuse to do what is right.

⁸The way of the guilty is devious,
but the conduct of the innocent is
upright.

^a27 Or *The spirit of man is the LORD's lamp*
^b6 Some Hebrew manuscripts, Septuagint and
Vulgate; most Hebrew manuscripts *vapor for those
who seek death*

⁹Better to live on a corner of the roof
than share a house with a
quarrelsome wife.

¹⁰The wicked man craves evil;
his neighbor gets no mercy from
him.

¹¹When a mocker is punished, the
simple gain wisdom;
when a wise man is instructed, he
gets knowledge.

¹²The Righteous One*ᵃ* takes note of
the house of the wicked
and brings the wicked to ruin.

¹³If a man shuts his ears to the cry of
the poor,
he too will cry out and not be
answered.

¹⁴A gift given in secret soothes anger,
and a bribe concealed in the cloak
pacifies great wrath.

¹⁵When justice is done, it brings joy to
the righteous
but terror to evildoers.

¹⁶A man who strays from the path of
understanding
comes to rest in the company of
the dead.

¹⁷He who loves pleasure will become
poor;
whoever loves wine and oil will
never be rich.

¹⁸The wicked become a ransom for the
righteous,
and the unfaithful for the upright.

¹⁹Better to live in a desert
than with a quarrelsome and
ill-tempered wife.

²⁰In the house of the wise are stores of
choice food and oil,
but a foolish man devours all he
has.

²¹He who pursues righteousness and
love
finds life, prosperity*ᵇ* and honor.

²²A wise man attacks the city of the
mighty
and pulls down the stronghold in
which they trust.

²³He who guards his mouth and his
tongue
keeps himself from calamity.

²⁴The proud and arrogant man—
"Mocker" is his name;
he behaves with overweening
pride.

²⁵The sluggard's craving will be the
death of him,
because his hands refuse to work.

²⁶All day long he craves for more,
but the righteous give without
sparing.

²⁷The sacrifice of the wicked is
detestable—
how much more so when brought
with evil intent!

²⁸A false witness will perish,
and whoever listens to him will be
destroyed forever.*ᶜ*

²⁹A wicked man puts up a bold front,
but an upright man gives thought
to his ways.

³⁰There is no wisdom, no insight, no
plan
that can succeed against the LORD.

³¹The horse is made ready for the day
of battle,
but victory rests with the LORD.

22 A good name is more desirable
than great riches;
to be esteemed is better than silver
or gold.

²Rich and poor have this in common:
The LORD is the Maker of them all.

³A prudent man sees danger and takes
refuge,
but the simple keep going and
suffer for it.

⁴Humility and the fear of the LORD
bring wealth and honor and life.

⁵In the paths of the wicked lie thorns
and snares,
but he who guards his soul stays
far from them.

ᵃ12 Or *The righteous man*   *ᵇ21* Or *righteousness*
ᶜ28 Or / *but the words of an obedient man will
live on*

⁶Train*a* a child in the way he should
    go,
  and when he is old he will not
      turn from it.

⁷The rich rule over the poor,
  and the borrower is servant to the
      lender.

⁸He who sows wickedness reaps
      trouble,
  and the rod of his fury will be
      destroyed.

⁹A generous man will himself be
      blessed,
  for he shares his food with the
      poor.

¹⁰Drive out the mocker, and out goes
      strife;
  quarrels and insults are ended.

¹¹He who loves a pure heart and whose
      speech is gracious
  will have the king for his friend.

¹²The eyes of the LORD keep watch over
      knowledge,
  but he frustrates the words of the
      unfaithful.

¹³The sluggard says, "There is a lion
      outside!"
  or, "I will be murdered in the
      streets!"

¹⁴The mouth of an adulteress is a deep
      pit;
  he who is under the LORD's wrath
      will fall into it.

¹⁵Folly is bound up in the heart of a
      child,
  but the rod of discipline will drive
      it far from him.

¹⁶He who oppresses the poor to
      increase his wealth
  and he who gives gifts to the rich—
      both come to poverty.

Sayings of the Wise

¹⁷Pay attention and listen to the sayings
      of the wise;
  apply your heart to what I teach,
¹⁸for it is pleasing when you keep them
      in your heart
  and have all of them ready on your
      lips.

¹⁹So that your trust may be in the
      LORD,
  I teach you today, even you.
²⁰Have I not written thirty*b* sayings for
      you,
  sayings of counsel and knowledge,
²¹teaching you true and reliable words,
  so that you can give sound answers
      to him who sent you?

²²Do not exploit the poor because they
      are poor
  and do not crush the needy in
      court,
²³for the LORD will take up their case
  and will plunder those who
      plunder them.

²⁴Do not make friends with a
      hot-tempered man,
  do not associate with one easily
      angered,
²⁵or you may learn his ways
  and get yourself ensnared.

²⁶Do not be a man who strikes hands
      in pledge
  or puts up security for debts;
²⁷if you lack the means to pay,
  your very bed will be snatched
      from under you.

²⁸Do not move an ancient boundary
      stone
  set up by your forefathers.

²⁹Do you see a man skilled in his
      work?
  He will serve before kings;
  he will not serve before obscure
      men.

23 When you sit to dine with a
    ruler,
  note well what*c* is before you,
²and put a knife to your throat
  if you are given to gluttony.
³Do not crave his delicacies,
  for that food is deceptive.

⁴Do not wear yourself out to get rich;
  have the wisdom to show restraint.
⁵Cast but a glance at riches, and they
      are gone,
  for they will surely sprout wings
  and fly off to the sky like an eagle.

*a6 Or Start   b20 Or not formerly written; or not
written excellent   c1 Or who*

⁶Do not eat the food of a stingy man,
　　do not crave his delicacies;
⁷for he is the kind of man
　　who is always thinking about the
　　　cost. *ᵃ*
"Eat and drink," he says to you,
　　but his heart is not with you.
⁸You will vomit up the little you have
　　eaten
　　and will have wasted your
　　　compliments.

⁹Do not speak to a fool,
　　for he will scorn the wisdom of
　　　your words.

¹⁰Do not move an ancient boundary
　　stone
　　or encroach on the fields of the
　　　fatherless,
¹¹for their Defender is strong;
　　he will take up their case against
　　　you.

¹²Apply your heart to instruction
　　and your ears to words of
　　　knowledge.

¹³Do not withhold discipline from a
　　child;
　　if you punish him with the rod, he
　　　will not die.
¹⁴Punish him with the rod
　　and save his soul from death. *ᵇ*

¹⁵My son, if your heart is wise,
　　then my heart will be glad;
¹⁶my inmost being will rejoice
　　when your lips speak what is right.

¹⁷Do not let your heart envy sinners,
　　but always be zealous for the fear
　　　of the LORD.
¹⁸There is surely a future hope for you,
　　and your hope will not be cut off.

*ᵃ7 Or for as he thinks within himself, / so he is; or for
as he puts on a feast, / so he is*　　ᵇ14 Hebrew *Sheol*

Paying the Price

Friday

PROVERBS 23:6-7   "No, really, go
ahead. Order whatever you want,"
I told Leslie.

　　We were sitting in an upscale
restaurant perusing the menu
when she said something about the
grilled Mahi tuna looking pretty good.
I hope you're not being serious, I thought
to myself. *That dish is the most expensive
thing on the menu!* I didn't want to come
off as miserly in such a nice place, but I also
didn't want to break the bank on a single
meal.

　　I was desperate. So, in the meekest tone
I could manage, I asked, "Are you sure you
wouldn't like one of the pasta dishes?"

　　I kept my eyes fixed on the menu as I
asked the question, but I could feel Leslie
eyeing me to get a read on my unspoken intentions.

　　"Sure, the pasta primavera looks pretty
good too," she said without revealing a
twinge of disappointment.

　　Phew, I could relax again. It looked like I
was in the clear and wasn't going to have to
fork over *too* much money. It was about that
time, however, that the waiter arrived:

　　"Can I start you off with something
to drink?" he asked.

　　"Just water for me," I blurted out,
hoping Leslie would catch the cue.
"You know," Leslie told the server,
"I think I'd like an iced tea."

　　"What?!" I exclaimed as soon as the
waiter was out of earshot. "Do you know
how much that's going to cost?"

　　"I thought you said to order whatever I
wanted," Leslie innocently replied.

　　She caught me red-handed. I did say
that. The problem was I didn't mean it. I
didn't mean it at all. I wanted her to order
the cheapest thing she could find. And once
my selfish wishes were exposed, I felt
like crawling under the linen draped table
where we were seated.

　　Have you ever felt that way? I didn't want
to be stingy. I wanted to be a nice guy. I just
didn't want to pay the price, that's all. The
problem is that being generous always requires paying a price. Are you willing to pay
the price?

—Les & Leslie

Go to page 691 for your next devotional reading.

¹⁹Listen, my son, and be wise,
and keep your heart on the right
path.
²⁰Do not join those who drink too
much wine
or gorge themselves on meat,
²¹for drunkards and gluttons become
poor,
and drowsiness clothes them in
rags.

²²Listen to your father, who gave you
life,
and do not despise your mother
when she is old.
²³Buy the truth and do not sell it;
get wisdom, discipline and
understanding.
²⁴The father of a righteous man has
great joy;
he who has a wise son delights in
him.
²⁵May your father and mother be glad;
may she who gave you birth
rejoice!

²⁶My son, give me your heart
and let your eyes keep to my ways,
²⁷for a prostitute is a deep pit
and a wayward wife is a narrow
well.
²⁸Like a bandit she lies in wait,
and multiplies the unfaithful
among men.

²⁹Who has woe? Who has sorrow?
Who has strife? Who has
complaints?
Who has needless bruises? Who
has bloodshot eyes?
³⁰Those who linger over wine,
who go to sample bowls of mixed
wine.
³¹Do not gaze at wine when it is red,
when it sparkles in the cup,
when it goes down smoothly!
³²In the end it bites like a snake
and poisons like a viper.
³³Your eyes will see strange sights
and your mind imagine confusing
things.
³⁴You will be like one sleeping on the
high seas,
lying on top of the rigging.
³⁵"They hit me," you will say, "but I'm
not hurt!
They beat me, but I don't feel it!

When will I wake up
so I can find another drink?"

24 Do not envy wicked men,
do not desire their company;
²for their hearts plot violence,
and their lips talk about making
trouble.

³By wisdom a house is built,
and through understanding it is
established;
⁴through knowledge its rooms are
filled
with rare and beautiful treasures.

⁵A wise man has great power,
and a man of knowledge increases
strength;
⁶for waging war you need guidance,
and for victory many advisers.

⁷Wisdom is too high for a fool;
in the assembly at the gate he has
nothing to say.

⁸He who plots evil
will be known as a schemer.
⁹The schemes of folly are sin,
and men detest a mocker.

¹⁰If you falter in times of trouble,
how small is your strength!

¹¹Rescue those being led away to death;
hold back those staggering toward
slaughter.
¹²If you say, "But we knew nothing
about this,"
does not he who weighs the heart
perceive it?
Does not he who guards your life
know it?
Will he not repay each person
according to what he has
done?

¹³Eat honey, my son, for it is good;
honey from the comb is sweet to
your taste.
¹⁴Know also that wisdom is sweet to
your soul;
if you find it, there is a future hope
for you,
and your hope will not be cut off.

¹⁵Do not lie in wait like an outlaw
against a righteous man's
house,
do not raid his dwelling place;

¹⁶for though a righteous man falls
        seven times, he rises again,
    but the wicked are brought down
        by calamity.

¹⁷Do not gloat when your enemy falls;
    when he stumbles, do not let your
        heart rejoice,
¹⁸or the LORD will see and disapprove
    and turn his wrath away from him.

¹⁹Do not fret because of evil men
    or be envious of the wicked,
²⁰for the evil man has no future hope,
    and the lamp of the wicked will be
        snuffed out.

²¹Fear the LORD and the king, my son,
    and do not join with the
        rebellious,

²²for those two will send sudden
        destruction upon them,
    and who knows what calamities
        they can bring?

Further Sayings of the Wise

²³These also are sayings of the wise:

To show partiality in judging is not
        good:
²⁴Whoever says to the guilty, "You are
        innocent"—
    peoples will curse him and nations
        denounce him.
²⁵But it will go well with those who
        convict the guilty,
    and rich blessing will come upon
        them.

Wise Up

Quiet TIMES *with each other*

PROVERBS 24:3–4 In Cincinnati, a man hired a helicopter to drop 2,500 carnations and 10,000 love letters onto the lawn of a woman he loved. Apparently the woman failed to share this man's affection and had him charged with littering. She told reporters he had "lost his mind."

Losing one's mind is a common danger in new love. The compelling, emotional force of love can override the capacity to think clearly and drive one to become "crazy in love." And what's more, when a person's romantic passions are appreciated and returned by another, wisdom is all but put on ice. Once the spark of attraction between two people catches fire, love can quickly turn into a raging, uncontrollable blaze. Engulfed by its heat, the couple can become oblivious to many things—especially sound judgment.

But even after the heat dies down and a couple settles into the comfort and warmth of a healthy marriage, there is no guarantee of sound judgment returning. For this reason, God calls every couple to wise up. The Hebrew root word translated as "wise" or "wisdom" occurs more than 300 times in the Old Testament. And in the Greek New Testament, *wisdom* is found more than 60 times. It is a word that implies having special knowledge and sound judgment: A wise carpenter knows his trade well and makes good decisions. A wise couple knows marriage well and works together on important decisions such as financial management and child rearing. According to the *American Heritage Dictionary*, wisdom is "a common sense understanding of what is true, right and lasting." Did you catch that? It is built on common sense.

There is a small church in our neighborhood that understands the source of wisdom. Every year around Christmas time they display a rather shabby sign with an insightful message: "Wise men still seek him." So do wise couples.   **—Les & Leslie**

*W*arm-up **Weekend** *When was a time you were "lost in love," and how did you break out of it?*

Go to page 694 for your next devotional reading.

²⁶An honest answer
    is like a kiss on the lips.

²⁷Finish your outdoor work
    and get your fields ready;
    after that, build your house.

²⁸Do not testify against your neighbor
    without cause,
    or use your lips to deceive.
²⁹Do not say, "I'll do to him as he has
    done to me;
    I'll pay that man back for what he
    did."

³⁰I went past the field of the sluggard,
    past the vineyard of the man who
    lacks judgment;
³¹thorns had come up everywhere,
    the ground was covered with
    weeds,
    and the stone wall was in ruins.
³²I applied my heart to what I observed
    and learned a lesson from what I
    saw:
³³A little sleep, a little slumber,
    a little folding of the hands to
    rest—
³⁴and poverty will come on you like a
    bandit
    and scarcity like an armed man. *a*

More Proverbs of Solomon

25 These are more proverbs of Solomon, copied by the men of Hezekiah king of Judah:

²It is the glory of God to conceal a
    matter;
    to search out a matter is the glory
    of kings.

³As the heavens are high and the earth
    is deep,
    so the hearts of kings are
    unsearchable.

⁴Remove the dross from the silver,
    and out comes material for *b* the
    silversmith;
⁵remove the wicked from the king's
    presence,
    and his throne will be established
    through righteousness.

⁶Do not exalt yourself in the king's
    presence,
    and do not claim a place among
    great men;

⁷it is better for him to say to you,
    "Come up here,"
    than for him to humiliate you
    before a nobleman.

What you have seen with your eyes
⁸   do not bring *c* hastily to court,
    for what will you do in the end
    if your neighbor puts you to
    shame?

⁹If you argue your case with a
    neighbor,
    do not betray another man's
    confidence,
¹⁰or he who hears it may shame you
    and you will never lose your bad
    reputation.

¹¹A word aptly spoken
    is like apples of gold in settings of
    silver.

¹²Like an earring of gold or an
    ornament of fine gold
    is a wise man's rebuke to a
    listening ear.

¹³Like the coolness of snow at harvest
    time
    is a trustworthy messenger to those
    who send him;
    he refreshes the spirit of his
    masters.

¹⁴Like clouds and wind without rain
    is a man who boasts of gifts he
    does not give.

¹⁵Through patience a ruler can be
    persuaded,
    and a gentle tongue can break a
    bone.

¹⁶If you find honey, eat just enough—
    too much of it, and you will
    vomit.
¹⁷Seldom set foot in your neighbor's
    house—
    too much of you, and he will hate
    you.

¹⁸Like a club or a sword or a sharp
    arrow
    is the man who gives false
    testimony against his
    neighbor.

---

a 34 Or like a vagrant / and scarcity like a beggar
b 4 Or comes a vessel from   *c 7,8 Or nobleman / on*
whom you had set your eyes. / 8 Do not go

¹⁹Like a bad tooth or a lame foot
  is reliance on the unfaithful in
    times of trouble.

²⁰Like one who takes away a garment
    on a cold day,
  or like vinegar poured on soda,
  is one who sings songs to a heavy
    heart.

²¹If your enemy is hungry, give him
    food to eat;
  if he is thirsty, give him water to
    drink.

²²In doing this, you will heap burning
    coals on his head,
  and the LORD will reward you.

²³As a north wind brings rain,
  so a sly tongue brings angry looks.

²⁴Better to live on a corner of the roof
  than share a house with a
    quarrelsome wife.

²⁵Like cold water to a weary soul
  is good news from a distant land.

²⁶Like a muddied spring or a polluted
    well
  is a righteous man who gives way
    to the wicked.

²⁷It is not good to eat too much honey,
  nor is it honorable to seek one's
    own honor.

²⁸Like a city whose walls are broken
    down
  is a man who lacks self-control.

26 Like snow in summer or rain in
    harvest,
  honor is not fitting for a fool.

²Like a fluttering sparrow or a darting
    swallow,
  an undeserved curse does not come
    to rest.

³A whip for the horse, a halter for the
    donkey,
  and a rod for the backs of fools!

⁴Do not answer a fool according to his
    folly,
  or you will be like him yourself.

⁵Answer a fool according to his folly,
  or he will be wise in his own eyes.

⁶Like cutting off one's feet or drinking
    violence
is the sending of a message by the
    hand of a fool.

⁷Like a lame man's legs that hang limp
  is a proverb in the mouth of a
    fool.

⁸Like tying a stone in a sling
  is the giving of honor to a fool.

⁹Like a thornbush in a drunkard's
    hand
  is a proverb in the mouth of a
    fool.

¹⁰Like an archer who wounds at
    random
  is he who hires a fool or any
    passer-by.

¹¹As a dog returns to its vomit,
  so a fool repeats his folly.

¹²Do you see a man wise in his own
    eyes?
  There is more hope for a fool than
    for him.

¹³The sluggard says, "There is a lion in
    the road,
  a fierce lion roaming the streets!"

¹⁴As a door turns on its hinges,
  so a sluggard turns on his bed.

¹⁵The sluggard buries his hand in the
    dish;
  he is too lazy to bring it back to
    his mouth.

¹⁶The sluggard is wiser in his own eyes
  than seven men who answer
    discreetly.

¹⁷Like one who seizes a dog by the ears
  is a passer-by who meddles in a
    quarrel not his own.

¹⁸Like a madman shooting
    firebrands or deadly arrows
¹⁹is a man who deceives his neighbor
  and says, "I was only joking!"

²⁰Without wood a fire goes out;
  without gossip a quarrel dies
    down.

²¹As charcoal to embers and as wood to
    fire,
  so is a quarrelsome man for
    kindling strife.

²²The words of a gossip are like choice morsels;
    they go down to a man's inmost parts.

²³Like a coating of glaze*a* over earthenware
    are fervent lips with an evil heart.

²⁴A malicious man disguises himself with his lips,
    but in his heart he harbors deceit.
²⁵Though his speech is charming, do not believe him,
    for seven abominations fill his heart.
²⁶His malice may be concealed by deception,
    but his wickedness will be exposed in the assembly.

²⁷If a man digs a pit, he will fall into it;
    if a man rolls a stone, it will roll back on him.

²⁸A lying tongue hates those it hurts,
    and a flattering mouth works ruin.

27 Do not boast about tomorrow,
    for you do not know what a day may bring forth.

²Let another praise you, and not your own mouth;
    someone else, and not your own lips.

³Stone is heavy and sand a burden,
    but provocation by a fool is heavier than both.

⁴Anger is cruel and fury overwhelming,
    but who can stand before jealousy?

⁵Better is open rebuke
    than hidden love.

⁶Wounds from a friend can be trusted,
    but an enemy multiplies kisses.

⁷He who is full loathes honey,
    but to the hungry even what is bitter tastes sweet.

a23 With a different word division of the Hebrew; Masoretic Text *of silver dross*

The Gossip Chain

Monday

PROVERBS 26:20 "You told Rich what!?" Leslie exclaimed in shock.

"Oh, he doesn't care if you lost fifty dollars," I said defensively. "If you didn't want me to tell him, you should have told me it was private."

"Excuse me," Leslie retorted. "But can't you just assume I don't want everyone to know my stupid mistakes?"

Good point. All of us talk with friends about our marriages—whether we tell our best friend everything or simply throw into our conversation an occasional, "I know what you mean—he does that too." But what you *don't* tell your friends about your marriage is just as important as what you *do* tell them.

Protecting your spouse's confidence and keeping a secret are critical to building a trustworthy marriage. Unfortunately, some couples become hooked into gossip—not shop gossip or party gossip but gossip behind a partner's back about the state of your relationship. Does any of this sound familiar: "I probably shouldn't even be telling you this but . . ." "Sarah would kill me if she knew I told you this . . ." "You won't tell Bob I mentioned this, will you?"

Whatever the reasons, gossip—no doubt about it—is evil. The apostle Paul warns about the destructive power of gossip and the condemnation that comes to "gossips and busybodies" who say "things they ought not to" say (1 Timothy 5:13). But this doesn't stop a gossip. They don't even realize the damage they are doing to themselves, their spouse and their marriage.

Think of the remarkable energy that would be restored to their marriage if they "gossiped" about good things instead of bad. If, for example, she had only confided in a friend how sweet her husband had been to clean up the dirty kitchen. Or instead of telling him that she wastes money, he could've told his friend how generous his wife was in giving to the needy.

—Les & Leslie

Go to page 696 for your next devotional reading.

⁸Like a bird that strays from its nest
is a man who strays from his
home.

⁹Perfume and incense bring joy to the
heart,
and the pleasantness of one's
friend springs from his
earnest counsel.

¹⁰Do not forsake your friend and the
friend of your father,
and do not go to your brother's
house when disaster strikes
you—
better a neighbor nearby than a
brother far away.

¹¹Be wise, my son, and bring joy to my
heart;
then I can answer anyone who
treats me with contempt.

¹²The prudent see danger and take
refuge,
but the simple keep going and
suffer for it.

¹³Take the garment of one who puts up
security for a stranger;
hold it in pledge if he does it for a
wayward woman.

¹⁴If a man loudly blesses his neighbor
early in the morning,
it will be taken as a curse.

¹⁵A quarrelsome wife is like
a constant dripping on a rainy day;
¹⁶restraining her is like restraining the
wind
or grasping oil with the hand.

¹⁷As iron sharpens iron,
so one man sharpens another.

¹⁸He who tends a fig tree will eat its
fruit,
and he who looks after his master
will be honored.

¹⁹As water reflects a face,
so a man's heart reflects the man.

²⁰Death and Destruction*a* are never
satisfied,
and neither are the eyes of man.

²¹The crucible for silver and the furnace
for gold,
but man is tested by the praise he
receives.

²²Though you grind a fool in a mortar,
grinding him like grain with a
pestle,
you will not remove his folly from
him.

²³Be sure you know the condition of
your flocks,
give careful attention to your herds;
²⁴for riches do not endure forever,
and a crown is not secure for all
generations.
²⁵When the hay is removed and new
growth appears
and the grass from the hills is
gathered in,
²⁶the lambs will provide you with
clothing,
and the goats with the price of a
field.
²⁷You will have plenty of goats' milk
to feed you and your family
and to nourish your servant girls.

28 The wicked man flees though no
one pursues,
but the righteous are as bold as a
lion.

²When a country is rebellious, it has
many rulers,
but a man of understanding and
knowledge maintains order.

³A ruler*b* who oppresses the poor
is like a driving rain that leaves no
crops.

⁴Those who forsake the law praise the
wicked,
but those who keep the law resist
them.

⁵Evil men do not understand justice,
but those who seek the LORD
understand it fully.

⁶Better a poor man whose walk is
blameless
than a rich man whose ways are
perverse.

⁷He who keeps the law is a discerning
son,
but a companion of gluttons
disgraces his father.

a20 Hebrew *Sheol and Abaddon*   *b3* Or *A poor
man*

⁸He who increases his wealth by
     exorbitant interest
amasses it for another, who will be
     kind to the poor.

⁹If anyone turns a deaf ear to the law,
     even his prayers are detestable.

¹⁰He who leads the upright along an
     evil path
will fall into his own trap,
     but the blameless will receive a
     good inheritance.

¹¹A rich man may be wise in his own
     eyes,
     but a poor man who has
     discernment sees through
     him.

¹²When the righteous triumph, there is
     great elation;
     but when the wicked rise to power,
     men go into hiding.

¹³He who conceals his sins does not
     prosper,

but whoever confesses and
     renounces them finds mercy.

¹⁴Blessed is the man who always fears
     the LORD,
     but he who hardens his heart falls
     into trouble.

¹⁵Like a roaring lion or a charging bear
     is a wicked man ruling over a
     helpless people.

¹⁶A tyrannical ruler lacks judgment,
     but he who hates ill-gotten gain
     will enjoy a long life.

¹⁷A man tormented by the guilt of
     murder
will be a fugitive till death;
     let no one support him.

¹⁸He whose walk is blameless is kept
     safe,
     but he whose ways are perverse
     will suddenly fall.

¹⁹He who works his land will have
     abundant food,

Right Here, Right Now

Tuesday

PROVERBS 27:1 For six years of graduate school, I (Les) had a small sign pinned on a corkboard above the desk where I spent most of my time. It was a quote from Abraham Maslow: "Some people spend their entire lives indefinitely preparing to live."

Hardly a week went by that I did not ponder that statement and try desperately to avoid the temptation of focusing all of my energy on the future. I needed that little reminder because I often felt as though my life was on hold—like someone had pushed the pause button—until I completed my degree. *After graduation,* I would tell myself, *we'll move into a bigger apartment . . . we'll take a long vacation . . . I'll have a real job with normal hours . . . we'll eat better . . . we'll go out on more dates . . .*

After graduation, however, it wasn't long before I found myself saying, *Once I get tenure as a professor . . . once I finish writing this book . . . once we own our own house . . .* and on and on.

Yes, the future holds many exciting possibilities. But when we focus most all our attention on what is around the corner, we miss out on what we have right now. And that is especially true in marriage.

We often plan for the perfect romantic evening in an elegant, candlelit restaurant, for example, and miss out on the loving moment (even in the glaring sunshine) on our own doorstep. Marriage experts say that the greetings and good-byes we have with our mates are the most important moments of the day. When a husband and wife come together after an absence—upon waking, getting home from work or returning from a trip—the first few minutes will set the stage for how the rest of the time will go.

So boast about tomorrow if you must, dream big dreams about your future, but don't forsake the right here and now.

—Les & Leslie

Go to page 699 for your next devotional reading.

but the one who chases fantasies
    will have his fill of poverty.

²⁰A faithful man will be richly blessed,
    but one eager to get rich will not
        go unpunished.

²¹To show partiality is not good—
    yet a man will do wrong for a
        piece of bread.

²²A stingy man is eager to get rich
    and is unaware that poverty awaits
        him.

²³He who rebukes a man will in the
        end gain more favor
    than he who has a flattering
        tongue.

²⁴He who robs his father or mother
    and says, "It's not wrong"—
    he is partner to him who destroys.

²⁵A greedy man stirs up dissension,
    but he who trusts in the LORD will
        prosper.

²⁶He who trusts in himself is a fool,
    but he who walks in wisdom is
        kept safe.

²⁷He who gives to the poor will lack
        nothing,
    but he who closes his eyes to them
        receives many curses.

²⁸When the wicked rise to power,
        people go into hiding;
    but when the wicked perish, the
        righteous thrive.

29
A man who remains stiff-necked
    after many rebukes
will suddenly be destroyed—
    without remedy.

²When the righteous thrive, the people
        rejoice;
    when the wicked rule, the people
        groan.

³A man who loves wisdom brings joy
        to his father,
    but a companion of prostitutes
        squanders his wealth.

⁴By justice a king gives a country
        stability,
    but one who is greedy for bribes
        tears it down.

Right Here, Right Now

Take a moment to answer each of these
questions on your own. Then compare your
answers to your spouse's.

Yes   No   I believe every marriage can
             benefit from thinking about the
             future and setting specific goals.

Yes   No   Do we have specific long-term
             goals for our marriage?

Yes   No   Do we have specific short-term
             goals for our marriage?

Yes   No   When we set goals for our rela-
             tionship, they are realistic.

Yes   No   I believe that part of setting
             good goals is building in a re-
             ward or celebration for meeting
             them.

---

⁵Whoever flatters his neighbor
    is spreading a net for his feet.

⁶An evil man is snared by his own sin,
    but a righteous one can sing and
        be glad.

⁷The righteous care about justice for
        the poor,
    but the wicked have no such
        concern.

⁸Mockers stir up a city,
    but wise men turn away anger.

⁹If a wise man goes to court with a
        fool,
    the fool rages and scoffs, and there
        is no peace.

¹⁰Bloodthirsty men hate a man of
        integrity
    and seek to kill the upright.

¹¹A fool gives full vent to his anger,
    but a wise man keeps himself
        under control.

¹²If a ruler listens to lies,
    all his officials become wicked.

¹³The poor man and the oppressor
        have this in common:
    The LORD gives sight to the eyes of
        both.

¹⁴If a king judges the poor with
fairness,
his throne will always be secure.

¹⁵The rod of correction imparts
wisdom,
but a child left to himself disgraces
his mother.

¹⁶When the wicked thrive, so does sin,
but the righteous will see their
downfall.

¹⁷Discipline your son, and he will give
you peace;
he will bring delight to your soul.

¹⁸Where there is no revelation, the
people cast off restraint;
but blessed is he who keeps the
law.

¹⁹A servant cannot be corrected by mere
words;
though he understands, he will not
respond.

²⁰Do you see a man who speaks in
haste?
There is more hope for a fool than
for him.

²¹If a man pampers his servant from
youth,
he will bring grief*ᵃ* in the end.

²²An angry man stirs up dissension,
and a hot-tempered one commits
many sins.

²³A man's pride brings him low,
but a man of lowly spirit gains
honor.

²⁴The accomplice of a thief is his own
enemy;
he is put under oath and dare not
testify.

²⁵Fear of man will prove to be a snare,
but whoever trusts in the LORD is
kept safe.

²⁶Many seek an audience with a ruler,
but it is from the LORD that man
gets justice.

²⁷The righteous detest the dishonest;
the wicked detest the upright.

Sayings of Agur

30 The sayings of Agur son of Jakeh—
an oracle*ᵇ*:

This man declared to Ithiel,
to Ithiel and to Ucal:*ᶜ*

²"I am the most ignorant of men;
I do not have a man's
understanding.
³I have not learned wisdom,
nor have I knowledge of the Holy
One.
⁴Who has gone up to heaven and
come down?
Who has gathered up the wind in
the hollow of his hands?
Who has wrapped up the waters in
his cloak?
Who has established all the ends of
the earth?
What is his name, and the name of
his son?
Tell me if you know!

⁵"Every word of God is flawless;
he is a shield to those who take
refuge in him.
⁶Do not add to his words,
or he will rebuke you and prove
you a liar.

⁷"Two things I ask of you, O LORD;
do not refuse me before I die:
⁸Keep falsehood and lies far from me;
give me neither poverty nor riches,
but give me only my daily bread.
⁹Otherwise, I may have too much and
disown you
and say, 'Who is the LORD?'
Or I may become poor and steal,
and so dishonor the name of my
God.

¹⁰"Do not slander a servant to his
master,
or he will curse you, and you will
pay for it.

¹¹"There are those who curse their
fathers
and do not bless their mothers;
¹²those who are pure in their own eyes

ᵃ21 The meaning of the Hebrew for this word is
uncertain.   *ᵇ1* Or *Jakeh of Massa*
ᶜ1 Masoretic Text; with a different word division
of the Hebrew *declared, "I am weary, O God; / I am
weary, O God, and faint.*

and yet are not cleansed of their
  filth;
¹³those whose eyes are ever so haughty,
  whose glances are so disdainful;
¹⁴those whose teeth are swords
  and whose jaws are set with knives
to devour the poor from the earth,
  the needy from among mankind.

¹⁵"The leech has two daughters.
  'Give! Give!' they cry.

"There are three things that are never
  satisfied,
four that never say, 'Enough!':
¹⁶the grave,ᵃ the barren womb,
  land, which is never satisfied with
  water,
and fire, which never says,
  'Enough!'

¹⁷"The eye that mocks a father,
  that scorns obedience to a mother,
will be pecked out by the ravens of
  the valley,
will be eaten by the vultures.

¹⁸"There are three things that are too
  amazing for me,

four that I do not understand:
¹⁹the way of an eagle in the sky,
  the way of a snake on a rock,
the way of a ship on the high seas,
  and the way of a man with a
  maiden.

²⁰"This is the way of an adulteress:
  She eats and wipes her mouth
  and says, 'I've done nothing
  wrong.'

²¹"Under three things the earth
  trembles,
under four it cannot bear up:
²²a servant who becomes king,
  a fool who is full of food,
²³an unloved woman who is married,
  and a maidservant who displaces
  her mistress.

²⁴"Four things on earth are small,
  yet they are extremely wise:
²⁵Ants are creatures of little strength,
  yet they store up their food in the
  summer;

ᵃ16 Hebrew *Sheol*

Building a Bridge

Wednesday

PROVERBS 30:18-19 Few relationship books in recent years
have been more popular than
John Gray's *Men Are from Mars,
Women Are from Venus.* And
few books have been able to distinguish some of the most fundamental differences between men and
women more clearly than this best seller.
When it comes to styles of interaction, for
example, it really can feel as though the
genders are from totally different planets.
"Not only do men and women communicate differently," writes Gray, "but they
think, feel, perceive, react, respond, love,
need and appreciate differently."

"Great," you say. "We're from different
planets. Why not just admit defeat and
throw in the towel?" Some do just that. But
other men and women, despite all the differences, manage to communicate quite
well with each other. What makes the difference?

The difference is found in understanding—and truly respecting—
our gender differences, the things
that make him or her unique and
different from ourself.

Of course, there are always ex-
ceptions, but research and experience
have revealed this fundamental difference
between the sexes: Men focus on achievement and women focus on relationships.
Sure, this is overly simplistic, but it's a place
to start.

In our own marriage, we have found that
when we come to understand and accept
our differences, we can avoid some of the
biggest pitfalls of marriage and instead
begin to reach out to each other in new
ways. The more we come to learn about and
understand our gender-uniqueness, the
more we can improve our communication.
—*Les & Leslie*

Go to page 703 for your next devotional reading.

²⁶coneys*a* are creatures of little power,
    yet they make their home in the
        crags;
²⁷locusts have no king,
    yet they advance together in ranks;
²⁸a lizard can be caught with the hand,
    yet it is found in kings' palaces.

²⁹"There are three things that are stately
        in their stride,
    four that move with stately bearing:
³⁰a lion, mighty among beasts,
    who retreats before nothing;
³¹a strutting rooster, a he-goat,
    and a king with his army around
        him.*b*

³²"If you have played the fool and
        exalted yourself,
    or if you have planned evil,
    clap your hand over your mouth!
³³For as churning the milk produces
        butter,
    and as twisting the nose produces
        blood,
    so stirring up anger produces strife."

Sayings of King Lemuel

31 The sayings of King Lemuel—an oracle*c* his mother taught him:

²"O my son, O son of my womb,
    O son of my vows,*d*
³do not spend your strength on
        women,
    your vigor on those who ruin
        kings.

⁴"It is not for kings, O Lemuel—
    not for kings to drink wine,
    not for rulers to crave beer,
⁵lest they drink and forget what the
        law decrees,
    and deprive all the oppressed of
        their rights.
⁶Give beer to those who are perishing,
    wine to those who are in anguish;
⁷let them drink and forget their
        poverty
    and remember their misery no
        more.

⁸"Speak up for those who cannot
        speak for themselves,
    for the rights of all who are
        destitute.

⁹Speak up and judge fairly;
    defend the rights of the poor and
        needy."

Epilogue: The Wife of Noble Character

¹⁰*e*A wife of noble character who can
        find?
    She is worth far more than rubies.
¹¹Her husband has full confidence in
        her
    and lacks nothing of value.
¹²She brings him good, not harm,
    all the days of her life.
¹³She selects wool and flax
    and works with eager hands.
¹⁴She is like the merchant ships,
    bringing her food from afar.
¹⁵She gets up while it is still dark;
    she provides food for her family
    and portions for her servant girls.
¹⁶She considers a field and buys it;
    out of her earnings she plants a
        vineyard.
¹⁷She sets about her work vigorously;
    her arms are strong for her tasks.
¹⁸She sees that her trading is profitable,
    and her lamp does not go out at
        night.
¹⁹In her hand she holds the distaff
    and grasps the spindle with her
        fingers.
²⁰She opens her arms to the poor
    and extends her hands to the
        needy.
²¹When it snows, she has no fear for
        her household;
    for all of them are clothed in
        scarlet.
²²She makes coverings for her bed;
    she is clothed in fine linen and
        purple.
²³Her husband is respected at the city
        gate,
    where he takes his seat among the
        elders of the land.
²⁴She makes linen garments and sells
        them,

---

*a*26 That is, the hyrax or rock badger   *b*31 Or
king secure against revolt   *c*1 Or *of Lemuel king of
Massa, which*   *d*2 Or / *the answer to my prayers*
*e*10 Verses 10-31 are an acrostic, each verse beginning
with a successive letter of the Hebrew alphabet.

and supplies the merchants with
sashes.
25She is clothed with strength and
dignity;
she can laugh at the days to
come.
26She speaks with wisdom,
and faithful instruction is on her
tongue.
27She watches over the affairs of her
household
and does not eat the bread of
idleness.

28Her children arise and call her
blessed;
her husband also, and he praises
her:
29"Many women do noble things,
but you surpass them all."
30Charm is deceptive, and beauty is
fleeting;
but a woman who fears the LORD
is to be praised.
31Give her the reward she has earned,
and let her works bring her praise
at the city gate.

Ecclesiastes

Imagine what
it would be like to look back over your life and
discover that everything you had done had been meaningless—all the time and effort you put into your marriage, all
those degrees or certifications or awards of excellence, all
the lessons you taught your children so they'd live a good
life. The writer of Ecclesiastes, most likely Solomon, faced
this very situation. Though he enjoyed more knowledge,
accomplishments, opulence and pleasure than many of us
could even dream of, he concludes that a life without God at
its very center is futile. He honestly confesses his struggles
with doubt and disillusionment.

As you read this book, think about your own sense of
purpose and how you can cultivate a God-centered life and
marriage.

Everything Is Meaningless

1 The words of the Teacher,[a] son of David, king in Jerusalem:

2 "Meaningless! Meaningless!"
  says the Teacher.
"Utterly meaningless!
  Everything is meaningless."

3 What does man gain from all his
    labor
  at which he toils under the sun?
4 Generations come and generations go,
  but the earth remains forever.
5 The sun rises and the sun sets,
  and hurries back to where it rises.
6 The wind blows to the south
  and turns to the north;

round and round it goes,
  ever returning on its course.
7 All streams flow into the sea,
  yet the sea is never full.
To the place the streams come from,
  there they return again.
8 All things are wearisome,
  more than one can say.
The eye never has enough of seeing,
  nor the ear its fill of hearing.
9 What has been will be again,
  what has been done will be done
    again;
  there is nothing new under the
    sun.

a1 Or *leader of the assembly*; also in verses 2 and 12

¹⁰Is there anything of which one can
say,
"Look! This is something new"?
It was here already, long ago;
it was here before our time.
¹¹There is no remembrance of men of
old,
and even those who are yet to
come
will not be remembered
by those who follow.

Wisdom Is Meaningless

¹²I, the Teacher, was king over Israel in Jerusalem. ¹³I devoted myself to study and to explore by wisdom all that is done under heaven. What a heavy burden God has laid on men! ¹⁴I have seen all the things that are done under the sun; all of them are meaningless, a chasing after the wind.

¹⁵What is twisted cannot be
straightened;
what is lacking cannot be counted.

¹⁶I thought to myself, "Look, I have grown and increased in wisdom more than anyone who has ruled over Jerusalem before me; I have experienced much

of wisdom and knowledge." ¹⁷Then I applied myself to the understanding of wisdom, and also of madness and folly, but I learned that this, too, is a chasing after the wind.

¹⁸For with much wisdom comes much
sorrow;
the more knowledge, the more
grief.

Pleasures Are Meaningless

2 I thought in my heart, "Come now, I will test you with pleasure to find out what is good." But that also proved to be meaningless. ²"Laughter," I said, "is foolish. And what does pleasure accomplish?" ³I tried cheering myself with wine, and embracing folly—my mind still guiding me with wisdom. I wanted to see what was worthwhile for men to do under heaven during the few days of their lives.

⁴I undertook great projects: I built houses for myself and planted vineyards. ⁵I made gardens and parks and planted all kinds of fruit trees in them. ⁶I made reservoirs to water groves of flourishing trees. ⁷I bought male and female slaves and had other slaves who were born in my house.

Chasing After the Wind

Thursday

ECCLESIASTES 2   There are parts of every marriage that are very unfulfilling. Changing diapers, washing dishes, going to work day after day to do the same job—these tasks can all put a damper on a positive attitude. Usually those routines were not included in the original expectations of what marriage was all about. What makes it harder is that no one hardly ever acknowledges our efforts. All this mundane work and no apparent appreciation for what we are doing makes us wonder, "Does anyone really care about the effort I'm putting in here?"

The mundane tasks that are a part of every marriage can frustrate us and cause us to ask, "Is this all there is? Is this what I got married for?" When our vision for our marriage has degraded to the point of seeing only dirty dishes and broken lawnmowers,

happiness and satisfaction can escape us. When the mundane rules over a marriage, happiness is like chasing after the wind. It can't be caught.

But the mundane tasks are *not* the marriage. The relationship we have with our spouse is the marriage. But if tasks are allowed to rule every moment or every thought, there will be no time left for relationship. Yes, we need to perform the *tasks* of marriage without expecting appreciation. But we shouldn't do those tasks at the cost of the marriage *relationship*. Set aside time for your relationship with your spouse. Appreciate the relationship. Chase after relationship. Chase after something that can be caught.

—*Bob & Rosemary*

Go to page 705 for your next devotional reading.

I also owned more herds and flocks than anyone in Jerusalem before me. [8]I amassed silver and gold for myself, and the treasure of kings and provinces. I acquired men and women singers, and a harem[a] as well—the delights of the heart of man. [9]I became greater by far than anyone in Jerusalem before me. In all this my wisdom stayed with me.

[10]I denied myself nothing my eyes
    desired;
    I refused my heart no pleasure.
My heart took delight in all my work,
    and this was the reward for all my
      labor.
[11]Yet when I surveyed all that my
      hands had done
    and what I had toiled to achieve,
everything was meaningless, a chasing
    after the wind;
    nothing was gained under the sun.

Wisdom and Folly Are Meaningless

[12]Then I turned my thoughts to
      consider wisdom,
    and also madness and folly.
What more can the king's successor
      do
    than what has already been done?
[13]I saw that wisdom is better than folly,
    just as light is better than darkness.
[14]The wise man has eyes in his head,
    while the fool walks in the
      darkness;
but I came to realize
    that the same fate overtakes them
      both.

[15]Then I thought in my heart,

"The fate of the fool will overtake me
    also.
    What then do I gain by being wise?"
I said in my heart,
    "This too is meaningless."
[16]For the wise man, like the fool, will
      not be long remembered;
    in days to come both will be
      forgotten.
Like the fool, the wise man too must
      die!

Toil Is Meaningless

[17]So I hated life, because the work that is done under the sun was grievous to me. All of it is meaningless, a chasing after the

wind. [18]I hated all the things I had toiled for under the sun, because I must leave them to the one who comes after me. [19]And who knows whether he will be a wise man or a fool? Yet he will have control over all the work into which I have poured my effort and skill under the sun. This too is meaningless. [20]So my heart began to despair over all my toilsome labor under the sun. [21]For a man may do his work with wisdom, knowledge and skill, and then he must leave all he owns to someone who has not worked for it. This too is meaningless and a great misfortune. [22]What does a man get for all the toil and anxious striving with which he labors under the sun? [23]All his days his work is pain and grief; even at night his mind does not rest. This too is meaningless.

[24]A man can do nothing better than to eat and drink and find satisfaction in his work. This too, I see, is from the hand of God, [25]for without him, who can eat or find enjoyment? [26]To the man who pleases him, God gives wisdom, knowledge and happiness, but to the sinner he gives the task of gathering and storing up wealth to hand it over to the one who pleases God. This too is meaningless, a chasing after the wind.

A Time for Everything

3 There is a time for everything,
    and a season for every activity
      under heaven:

[2]   a time to be born and a time to
      die,
  a time to plant and a time to
      uproot,
[3]   a time to kill and a time to heal,
  a time to tear down and a time to
      build,
[4]   a time to weep and a time to
      laugh,
  a time to mourn and a time to
      dance,
[5]   a time to scatter stones and a time
      to gather them,
  a time to embrace and a time to
      refrain,

---

[a]8 The meaning of the Hebrew for this phrase is uncertain.

6 a time to search and a time to give
   up,
   a time to keep and a time to throw
   away,
7 a time to tear and a time to mend,
   a time to be silent and a time to
   speak,
8 a time to love and a time to hate,
   a time for war and a time for
   peace.

⁹What does the worker gain from his toil? ¹⁰I have seen the burden God has laid on men. ¹¹He has made everything beautiful in its time. He has also set eternity in the hearts of men; yet they cannot fathom what God has done from beginning to end. ¹²I know that there is nothing better for men than to be happy and do good while they live. ¹³That everyone may eat and drink, and find satisfaction in all his toil—this is the gift of God. ¹⁴I know that everything God does will endure forever; nothing can be added to it and nothing taken from it. God does it so that men will revere him.

¹⁵Whatever is has already been,
   and what will be has been before;
   and God will call the past to
   account.ᵃ

¹⁶And I saw something else under the sun:

In the place of judgment—wickedness
   was there,
   in the place of justice—wickedness
   was there.

¹⁷I thought in my heart,

"God will bring to judgment
   both the righteous and the wicked,
for there will be a time for every
   activity,
   a time for every deed."

¹⁸I also thought, "As for men, God tests them so that they may see that they are like the animals. ¹⁹Man's fate is like that of the animals; the same fate awaits them both: As one dies, so dies the other.

ᵃ15 Or God calls back the past

Seasons of Marriage

Friday

ECCLESIASTES 3:1 "There is a time for everything . . . and a season for every activity under heaven"; who is kidding who? Solomon definitely did not live in the twenty-first century!

Time is one of the great limitations of life, but for your marriage to endure, you need to find time to invest in it. Start by realizing that marriage is lived in seasons. With each season of marriage come unique challenges and stress points. What season are you in? Have the wonderful discovery days of the first months and years of your marriage been replaced with the hectic toddler and preschool years? If so, your ultimate fantasy may be eight hours of uninterrupted sleep!

Or maybe you are living through the turbulent adolescent years, and your marriage is on hold. You are emotionally drained and desperately need some "adult time" with your spouse. Maybe you are facing the empty nest, and you aren't sure if you know

that other "bird" in your nest. It's time to reinvent your marriage relationship and rediscover your friendship potential.

We're in the empty nest and still have to work at making time for each other. When faced with a writing deadline, it's easy to just keep working straight through mealtimes and ignore taking breaks to relax and focus on each other. Luckily one of us usually realizes there's a problem and says, "Stop! We're doing just what we're telling other couples not to do. Let's stop working and go for a walk."

Whatever season you are in, you too can make time to invest in your marriage. If you need some motivation, just think about what kind of marriage model you want to pass on to your children and grandchildren. The legacy of a healthy, loving, growing Christian marriage is yours to give to the next generation.

—*Dave & Claudia*

Go to page 707 for your next devotional reading.

COUPLE
MINUTES

All have the same breath[a]; man has no advantage over the animal. Everything is meaningless. [20]All go to the same place; all come from dust, and to dust all return. [21]Who knows if the spirit of man rises upward and if the spirit of the animal[b] goes down into the earth?"

[22]So I saw that there is nothing better for a man than to enjoy his work, because that is his lot. For who can bring him to see what will happen after him?

Oppression, Toil, Friendlessness

4 Again I looked and saw all the oppression that was taking place under the sun:

I saw the tears of the oppressed—
  and they have no comforter;
power was on the side of their
    oppressors—
  and they have no comforter.
[2]And I declared that the dead,
  who had already died,
are happier than the living,
  who are still alive.
[3]But better than both
  is he who has not yet been,
who has not seen the evil
  that is done under the sun.

[4]And I saw that all labor and all achievement spring from man's envy of his neighbor. This too is meaningless, a chasing after the wind.

[5]The fool folds his hands
  and ruins himself.
[6]Better one handful with tranquillity
  than two handfuls with toil
  and chasing after the wind.

[7]Again I saw something meaningless under the sun:

[8]There was a man all alone;
  he had neither son nor brother.
There was no end to his toil,
  yet his eyes were not content with
    his wealth.
"For whom am I toiling," he asked,
  "and why am I depriving myself of
    enjoyment?"
This too is meaningless—
  a miserable business!

[9]Two are better than one,
because they have a good return
  for their work:
[10]If one falls down,
  his friend can help him up.
But pity the man who falls
  and has no one to help him up!
[11]Also, if two lie down together, they
    will keep warm.
But how can one keep warm
    alone?
[12]Though one may be overpowered,
  two can defend themselves.
A cord of three strands is not quickly
    broken.

Advancement Is Meaningless

[13]Better a poor but wise youth than an old but foolish king who no longer knows how to take warning. [14]The youth may have come from prison to the kingship, or he may have been born in poverty within his kingdom. [15]I saw that all who lived and walked under the sun followed the youth, the king's successor. [16]There was no end to all the people who were before them. But those who came later were not pleased with the successor. This too is meaningless, a chasing after the wind.

Stand in Awe of God

5 Guard your steps when you go to the house of God. Go near to listen rather than to offer the sacrifice of fools, who do not know that they do wrong.

[2]Do not be quick with your mouth,
  do not be hasty in your heart
    to utter anything before God.
God is in heaven
  and you are on earth,
  so let your words be few.
[3]As a dream comes when there are
    many cares,
  so the speech of a fool when there
    are many words.

[4]When you make a vow to God, do not delay in fulfilling it. He has no pleasure in fools; fulfill your vow. [5]It is better not to vow than to make a vow and not fulfill it. [6]Do not let your mouth lead you into sin. And do not protest to the ⌊temple⌋ mes-

---

[a]19 Or *spirit*   [b]21 Or *Who knows the spirit of man, which rises upward, or the spirit of the animal, which*

senger, "My vow was a mistake." Why should God be angry at what you say and destroy the work of your hands? ⁷Much dreaming and many words are meaningless. Therefore stand in awe of God.

Riches Are Meaningless

⁸If you see the poor oppressed in a district, and justice and rights denied, do not be surprised at such things; for one official is eyed by a higher one, and over them both are others higher still. ⁹The increase from the land is taken by all; the king himself profits from the fields.

¹⁰Whoever loves money never has
    money enough;
whoever loves wealth is never
    satisfied with his income.
This too is meaningless.

¹¹As goods increase,
    so do those who consume them.
And what benefit are they to the
    owner
    except to feast his eyes on them?

¹²The sleep of a laborer is sweet,
    whether he eats little or much,
but the abundance of a rich man
    permits him no sleep.

¹³I have seen a grievous evil under the sun:

wealth hoarded to the harm of its
    owner,
¹⁴   or wealth lost through some
        misfortune,
so that when he has a son
    there is nothing left for him.
¹⁵Naked a man comes from his
    mother's womb,

A Cord of Three Strands

ECCLESIASTES 4:9–12 A Christian marriage is like a cord of three strands—the husband, the wife and God. Our faith in Jesus Christ gives us a common focus and helps to keep our marriage cord strong.

Years ago we chose Ecclesiastes 4:9–12 as our marriage passage. When viewed through a marriage filter, these verses give a wonderful picture of a Christian marriage. It's not a perfect relationship. The husband and wife fall down from time to time, but they willingly help each other up again. And even more important is the third strand. When both of our strands are frayed, God keeps our marriage cord strong . . . like the time we were lost in the snow.

Deep in a conversation while on a hike, we strayed off the path and, before we realized it, we were lost. More threatening snow clouds overhead added to our anxiety. "Dave," I said crossly, "I thought you were watching the trail markers."

"You always do that," Dave barked back. Our two strands were becoming frayed.

Lost and scared, we instinctively turned to our third strand and asked God to hold us together, protect us and help us find the path again. Slowly we retraced our steps until we found a path—not the easy one we had started on—but a more difficult one that led back to where we were staying. At this point, we literally experienced another part of this passage: "If one falls down, his friend can help him up" (verse 10). We slipped and fell a number of times on the icy, snowy path; but each time we helped the other up.

Like us, from time to time you will probably fall and let each other down, but God will remain faithful when you have a cord of three stands. When life gets hard, we can cope much better when we have a spouse-friend who will help with the challenges of life.   —*Dave & Claudia*

Weekend Warm-up   *Is God woven into your marriage as the third strand?*

Go to page 715 for your next devotional reading.

and as he comes, so he departs.
He takes nothing from his labor
that he can carry in his hand.

¹⁶This too is a grievous evil:

As a man comes, so he departs,
and what does he gain,
since he toils for the wind?
¹⁷All his days he eats in darkness,
with great frustration, affliction and
anger.

¹⁸Then I realized that it is good and
proper for a man to eat and drink, and to
find satisfaction in his toilsome labor under the sun during the few days of life
God has given him—for this is his lot.
¹⁹Moreover, when God gives any man
wealth and possessions, and enables him
to enjoy them, to accept his lot and be
happy in his work—this is a gift of God.
²⁰He seldom reflects on the days of his
life, because God keeps him occupied
with gladness of heart.

6 I have seen another evil under the
sun, and it weighs heavily on men:
²God gives a man wealth, possessions and
honor, so that he lacks nothing his heart
desires, but God does not enable him to
enjoy them, and a stranger enjoys them
instead. This is meaningless, a grievous
evil.

³A man may have a hundred children
and live many years; yet no matter how
long he lives, if he cannot enjoy his prosperity and does not receive proper burial,
I say that a stillborn child is better off
than he. ⁴It comes without meaning, it
departs in darkness, and in darkness its
name is shrouded. ⁵Though it never saw
the sun or knew anything, it has more rest
than does that man— ⁶even if he lives a
thousand years twice over but fails to enjoy his prosperity. Do not all go to the
same place?

⁷All man's efforts are for his mouth,
yet his appetite is never satisfied.
⁸What advantage has a wise man
over a fool?
What does a poor man gain
by knowing how to conduct
himself before others?
⁹Better what the eye sees
than the roving of the appetite.
This too is meaningless,
a chasing after the wind.

¹⁰Whatever exists has already been
named,
and what man is has been known;
no man can contend
with one who is stronger than he.
¹¹The more the words,
the less the meaning,
and how does that profit anyone?

¹²For who knows what is good for a
man in life, during the few and meaningless days he passes through like a shadow? Who can tell him what will happen
under the sun after he is gone?

Wisdom

7 A good name is better than fine
perfume,
and the day of death better than
the day of birth.
²It is better to go to a house of
mourning
than to go to a house of feasting,
for death is the destiny of every man;
the living should take this to heart.
³Sorrow is better than laughter,
because a sad face is good for the
heart.
⁴The heart of the wise is in the house
of mourning,
but the heart of fools is in the
house of pleasure.
⁵It is better to heed a wise man's
rebuke
than to listen to the song of fools.
⁶Like the crackling of thorns under the
pot,
so is the laughter of fools.
This too is meaningless.

⁷Extortion turns a wise man into a
fool,
and a bribe corrupts the heart.
⁸The end of a matter is better than its
beginning,
and patience is better than pride.
⁹Do not be quickly provoked in your
spirit,
for anger resides in the lap of
fools.

¹⁰Do not say, "Why were the old days
better than these?"
For it is not wise to ask such
questions.

¹¹Wisdom, like an inheritance, is a
    good thing
  and benefits those who see the
    sun.
¹²Wisdom is a shelter
  as money is a shelter,
  but the advantage of knowledge is
    this:
  that wisdom preserves the life of its
    possessor.

¹³Consider what God has done:

Who can straighten
  what he has made crooked?
¹⁴When times are good, be happy;
  but when times are bad, consider:
God has made the one
  as well as the other.
Therefore, a man cannot discover
  anything about his future.

¹⁵In this meaningless life of mine I
have seen both of these:

a righteous man perishing in his
  righteousness,
  and a wicked man living long in
    his wickedness.
¹⁶Do not be overrighteous,
  neither be overwise—
  why destroy yourself?
¹⁷Do not be overwicked,
  and do not be a fool—
  why die before your time?
¹⁸It is good to grasp the one
  and not let go of the other.
  The man who fears God will avoid
    all ⌐extremes⌐.ᵃ

¹⁹Wisdom makes one wise man more
    powerful
  than ten rulers in a city.

²⁰There is not a righteous man on earth
  who does what is right and never
    sins.

²¹Do not pay attention to every word
  people say,
  or you may hear your servant
    cursing you—
²²for you know in your heart
  that many times you yourself have
    cursed others.

²³All this I tested by wisdom and I said,

"I am determined to be wise"—
  but this was beyond me.

²⁴Whatever wisdom may be,
  it is far off and most profound—
  who can discover it?
²⁵So I turned my mind to understand,
  to investigate and to search out
    wisdom and the scheme of
    things
and to understand the stupidity of
    wickedness
  and the madness of folly.

²⁶I find more bitter than death
  the woman who is a snare,
whose heart is a trap
  and whose hands are chains.
The man who pleases God will escape
    her,
  but the sinner she will ensnare.

²⁷"Look," says the Teacher,ᵇ "this is
what I have discovered:

"Adding one thing to another to
    discover the scheme of
    things—
²⁸ while I was still searching
    but not finding—
I found one ⌐upright⌐ man among a
    thousand,
  but not one ⌐upright⌐ woman
    among them all.
²⁹This only have I found:
  God made mankind upright,
  but men have gone in search of
    many schemes."

8 Who is like the wise man?
    Who knows the explanation of
    things?
Wisdom brightens a man's face
  and changes its hard appearance.

Obey the King

²Obey the king's command, I say, because you took an oath before God. ³Do
not be in a hurry to leave the king's presence. Do not stand up for a bad cause, for
he will do whatever he pleases. ⁴Since a
king's word is supreme, who can say to
him, "What are you doing?"

⁵Whoever obeys his command will
    come to no harm,
  and the wise heart will know the
    proper time and procedure.

ᵃ18 Or *will follow them both*   ᵇ27 Or *leader of
the assembly*

⁶For there is a proper time and
    procedure for every matter,
though a man's misery weighs
    heavily upon him.

⁷Since no man knows the future,
    who can tell him what is to come?
⁸No man has power over the wind to
    contain it*a*;
    so no one has power over the day
      of his death.
As no one is discharged in time of
    war,
    so wickedness will not release
      those who practice it.

⁹All this I saw, as I applied my mind to everything done under the sun. There is a time when a man lords it over others to his own*b* hurt. ¹⁰Then too, I saw the wicked buried—those who used to come and go from the holy place and receive praise*c* in the city where they did this. This too is meaningless.

¹¹When the sentence for a crime is not quickly carried out, the hearts of the people are filled with schemes to do wrong. ¹²Although a wicked man commits a hundred crimes and still lives a long time, I know that it will go better with God-fearing men, who are reverent before God. ¹³Yet because the wicked do not fear God, it will not go well with them, and their days will not lengthen like a shadow.

¹⁴There is something else meaningless that occurs on earth: righteous men who get what the wicked deserve, and wicked men who get what the righteous deserve. This too, I say, is meaningless. ¹⁵So I commend the enjoyment of life, because nothing is better for a man under the sun than to eat and drink and be glad. Then joy will accompany him in his work all the days of the life God has given him under the sun.

¹⁶When I applied my mind to know wisdom and to observe man's labor on earth—his eyes not seeing sleep day or night— ¹⁷then I saw all that God has done. No one can comprehend what goes on under the sun. Despite all his efforts to search it out, man cannot discover its meaning. Even if a wise man claims he knows, he cannot really comprehend it.

A Common Destiny for All

9 So I reflected on all this and concluded that the righteous and the wise and what they do are in God's hands, but no man knows whether love or hate awaits him. ²All share a common destiny—the righteous and the wicked, the good and the bad,*d* the clean and the unclean, those who offer sacrifices and those who do not.

As it is with the good man,
    so with the sinner;
as it is with those who take oaths,
    so with those who are afraid to
      take them.

³This is the evil in everything that happens under the sun: The same destiny overtakes all. The hearts of men, moreover, are full of evil and there is madness in their hearts while they live, and afterward they join the dead. ⁴Anyone who is among the living has hope*e*—even a live dog is better off than a dead lion!

⁵For the living know that they will die,
    but the dead know nothing;
they have no further reward,
    and even the memory of them is
      forgotten.
⁶Their love, their hate
    and their jealousy have long since
      vanished;
never again will they have a part
    in anything that happens under the
      sun.

⁷Go, eat your food with gladness, and drink your wine with a joyful heart, for it is now that God favors what you do. ⁸Always be clothed in white, and always anoint your head with oil. ⁹Enjoy life with your wife, whom you love, all the days of this meaningless life that God has given you under the sun—all your meaningless days. For this is your lot in life and in your toilsome labor under the sun. ¹⁰Whatever your hand finds to do, do it with all your might, for in the grave,*f* where you are going, there is neither

---

*a*8 Or *over his spirit to retain it*   *b*9 Or *to their*
*c*10 Some Hebrew manuscripts and Septuagint (Aquila); most Hebrew manuscripts *and are forgotten*   *d*2 Septuagint (Aquila), Vulgate and Syriac; Hebrew does not have *and the bad.*
*e*4 Or *What then is to be chosen? With all who live, there is hope*   *f*10 Hebrew *Sheol*

working nor planning nor knowledge nor
wisdom.

¹¹I have seen something else under the
sun:

The race is not to the swift
    or the battle to the strong,
nor does food come to the wise
    or wealth to the brilliant
    or favor to the learned;
but time and chance happen to them
    all.

¹²Moreover, no man knows when his
hour will come:

As fish are caught in a cruel net,
    or birds are taken in a snare,
so men are trapped by evil times
    that fall unexpectedly upon them.

Wisdom Better Than Folly

¹³I also saw under the sun this example
of wisdom that greatly impressed me:
¹⁴There was once a small city with only a
few people in it. And a powerful king
came against it, surrounded it and built
huge siegeworks against it. ¹⁵Now there
lived in that city a man poor but wise, and
he saved the city by his wisdom. But nobody remembered that poor man. ¹⁶So I
said, "Wisdom is better than strength." But
the poor man's wisdom is despised, and
his words are no longer heeded.

¹⁷The quiet words of the wise are more
    to be heeded
        than the shouts of a ruler of fools.
¹⁸Wisdom is better than weapons of
    war,
        but one sinner destroys much
            good.

10 As dead flies give perfume a bad
        smell,
    so a little folly outweighs wisdom
        and honor.
²The heart of the wise inclines to the
    right,
        but the heart of the fool to the left.
³Even as he walks along the road,
    the fool lacks sense
        and shows everyone how stupid he
            is.
⁴If a ruler's anger rises against you,
    do not leave your post;

calmness can lay great errors to
    rest.

⁵There is an evil I have seen under the
    sun,
        the sort of error that arises from a
            ruler:
⁶Fools are put in many high positions,
    while the rich occupy the low ones.
⁷I have seen slaves on horseback,
    while princes go on foot like
        slaves.

⁸Whoever digs a pit may fall into it;
    whoever breaks through a wall may
        be bitten by a snake.
⁹Whoever quarries stones may be
    injured by them;
        whoever splits logs may be
            endangered by them.

¹⁰If the ax is dull
    and its edge unsharpened,
more strength is needed
    but skill will bring success.

¹¹If a snake bites before it is charmed,
    there is no profit for the charmer.

¹²Words from a wise man's mouth are
    gracious,
        but a fool is consumed by his own
            lips.
¹³At the beginning his words are folly;
    at the end they are wicked
        madness—
¹⁴   and the fool multiplies words.

No one knows what is coming—
    who can tell him what will happen
        after him?

¹⁵A fool's work wearies him;
    he does not know the way to
        town.

¹⁶Woe to you, O land whose king was
    a servant[a]
        and whose princes feast in the
            morning.
¹⁷Blessed are you, O land whose king is
    of noble birth
        and whose princes eat at a proper
            time—
            for strength and not for
                drunkenness.

¹⁸If a man is lazy, the rafters sag;

ᵃ16 Or king is a child

if his hands are idle, the house
leaks.

¹⁹A feast is made for laughter,
and wine makes life merry,
but money is the answer for
everything.

²⁰Do not revile the king even in your
thoughts,
or curse the rich in your bedroom,
because a bird of the air may carry
your words,
and a bird on the wing may report
what you say.

Bread Upon the Waters

11 Cast your bread upon the waters,
for after many days you will find it
again.
²Give portions to seven, yes to eight,
for you do not know what disaster
may come upon the land.

³If clouds are full of water,
they pour rain upon the earth.
Whether a tree falls to the south or to
the north,
in the place where it falls, there
will it lie.
⁴Whoever watches the wind will not
plant;
whoever looks at the clouds will
not reap.

⁵As you do not know the path of the
wind,
or how the body is formed ᵃ in a
mother's womb,
so you cannot understand the work
of God,
the Maker of all things.

⁶Sow your seed in the morning,
and at evening let not your hands
be idle,
for you do not know which will
succeed,
whether this or that,
or whether both will do equally
well.

Remember Your Creator While Young

⁷Light is sweet,
and it pleases the eyes to see the
sun.
⁸However many years a man may live,
let him enjoy them all.

But let him remember the days of
darkness,
for they will be many.
Everything to come is meaningless.

⁹Be happy, young man, while you are
young,
and let your heart give you joy in
the days of your youth.
Follow the ways of your heart
and whatever your eyes see,
but know that for all these things
God will bring you to judgment.
¹⁰So then, banish anxiety from your
heart
and cast off the troubles of your
body,
for youth and vigor are
meaningless.

12 Remember your Creator
in the days of your youth,
before the days of trouble come
and the years approach when you
will say,
"I find no pleasure in them"—
²before the sun and the light
and the moon and the stars grow
dark,
and the clouds return after the
rain;
³when the keepers of the house
tremble,
and the strong men stoop,
when the grinders cease because they
are few,
and those looking through the
windows grow dim;
⁴when the doors to the street are
closed
and the sound of grinding fades;
when men rise up at the sound of
birds,
but all their songs grow faint;
⁵when men are afraid of heights
and of dangers in the streets;
when the almond tree blossoms
and the grasshopper drags himself
along
and desire no longer is stirred.
Then man goes to his eternal home
and mourners go about the streets.

⁶Remember him—before the silver cord
is severed,

ᵃ5 Or *know how life* (or *the spirit*) / *enters the body
being formed*

or the golden bowl is broken;
before the pitcher is shattered at the
    spring,
or the wheel broken at the well,
[7]and the dust returns to the ground it
    came from,
and the spirit returns to God who
    gave it.

[8]"Meaningless! Meaningless!" says the
    Teacher.[a]
"Everything is meaningless!"

The Conclusion of the Matter

[9]Not only was the Teacher wise, but
also he imparted knowledge to the people. He pondered and searched out and
set in order many proverbs. [10]The Teacher
searched to find just the right words, and
what he wrote was upright and true.

[11]The words of the wise are like goads,
their collected sayings like firmly embed-
ded nails—given by one Shepherd. [12]Be
warned, my son, of anything in addition
to them.

Of making many books there is no
end, and much study wearies the body.

[13]Now all has been heard;
    here is the conclusion of the
        matter:
Fear God and keep his
        commandments,
    for this is the whole ⌞duty⌟ of man.
[14]For God will bring every deed into
        judgment,
    including every hidden thing,
    whether it is good or evil.

[a]8 Or *the leader of the assembly*; also in verses 9
and 10

Song of Songs

Turn on the television or radio, walk into any bookstore or even down a city street and you'll be inundated with songs and images about romantic love. Often it seems as though nothing consumes us so much as the desire to experience intimacy with another person. So it stands to reason that the God who created us with these desires has something to say about love, intimacy and marriage.

Song of Songs acclaims the passion, delight and allure of married love. This book of the Bible is a celebration of the love between a man and a woman—one of God's choicest gifts. Rejoice in the fact that your spouse is God's gift to you.

1 Solomon's Song of Songs.

Beloved*a*

²Let him kiss me with the kisses of his
  mouth—
  for your love is more delightful
    than wine.
³Pleasing is the fragrance of your
    perfumes;
  your name is like perfume poured
    out.
  No wonder the maidens love you!
⁴Take me away with you—let us hurry!
  Let the king bring me into his
    chambers.

Friends

We rejoice and delight in you*b*;
  we will praise your love more than
    wine.

Beloved

How right they are to adore you!

⁵Dark am I, yet lovely,
  O daughters of Jerusalem,
  dark like the tents of Kedar,
  like the tent curtains of
    Solomon.*c*
⁶Do not stare at me because I am
    dark,
  because I am darkened by the sun.
  My mother's sons were angry with me
    and made me take care of the
      vineyards;

---

*a*Primarily on the basis of the gender of the Hebrew pronouns used, male and female speakers are indicated in the margins by the captions *Lover* and *Beloved* respectively. The words of others are marked *Friends*. In some instances the divisions and their captions are debatable.   *b*4 The Hebrew is masculine singular.   *c*5 Or *Salma*

my own vineyard I have neglected.
⁷Tell me, you whom I love, where you
graze your flock
and where you rest your sheep at
midday.
Why should I be like a veiled woman
beside the flocks of your friends?

Friends

⁸If you do not know, most beautiful of
women,
follow the tracks of the sheep
and graze your young goats
by the tents of the shepherds.

Lover

⁹I liken you, my darling, to a mare
harnessed to one of the chariots of
Pharaoh.
¹⁰Your cheeks are beautiful with
earrings,
your neck with strings of jewels.
¹¹We will make you earrings of gold,
studded with silver.

Beloved

¹²While the king was at his table,
my perfume spread its fragrance.
¹³My lover is to me a sachet of myrrh
resting between my breasts.

¹⁴My lover is to me a cluster of henna
blossoms
from the vineyards of En Gedi.

Lover

¹⁵How beautiful you are, my darling!
Oh, how beautiful!
Your eyes are doves.

Beloved

¹⁶How handsome you are, my lover!
Oh, how charming!
And our bed is verdant.

Lover

¹⁷The beams of our house are cedars;
our rafters are firs.

Belovedᵃ

2 I am a roseᵇ of Sharon,
a lily of the valleys.

Lover

²Like a lily among thorns
is my darling among the maidens.

ᵃ1 Or Lover   ᵇ1 Possibly a member of the
crocus family

Bedroom Sanctuary

Monday

SONG OF SONGS 1:17 In most homes the last room to get special attention is the master bedroom. It's the last place a visitor will ever see, so it's often the last place a couple decorates or cleans up. The living room gets a beautiful painting on the wall, but the bedroom is often the place where the laundry gets dumped for eventual folding.

This passage in Song of Songs gives us a visual picture of a marital sanctuary. Two lovers are walking outdoors, imagining that the "green field" is their bed and the "cedar trees" above are the beams of their house.

With hectic schedules and a myriad of children's activities to go to, is there a place like this in your marriage where you can find

peace, tranquility and relationship? Perhaps the bedroom should become just that place. Instead of a place to sleep and fold laundry, it can become a place to grow deeper in love.

Spend a few moments together each day sitting in that "wooded forest" of your sanctuary. It's not just a purchase of the right furniture or tranquil paintings that will transform the master bedroom into a sanctuary. Each couple must devote time for each other—listening, sharing, loving and praying. Take time together to sit in the "cedar forest" of your bedroom.

—Bob & Rosemary

Go to page 718 for your next devotional reading.

Beloved

³Like an apple tree among the trees of
        the forest
    is my lover among the young men.
I delight to sit in his shade,
    and his fruit is sweet to my taste.
⁴He has taken me to the banquet hall,
    and his banner over me is love.
⁵Strengthen me with raisins,
    refresh me with apples,
    for I am faint with love.
⁶His left arm is under my head,
    and his right arm embraces me.
⁷Daughters of Jerusalem, I charge you
    by the gazelles and by the does of
        the field:
Do not arouse or awaken love
    until it so desires.

⁸Listen! My lover!
    Look! Here he comes,
leaping across the mountains,
    bounding over the hills.
⁹My lover is like a gazelle or a young
        stag.
    Look! There he stands behind our
        wall,
    gazing through the windows,
        peering through the lattice.
¹⁰My lover spoke and said to me,
    "Arise, my darling,
    my beautiful one, and come with
        me.
¹¹See! The winter is past;
    the rains are over and gone.
¹²Flowers appear on the earth;
    the season of singing has come,
    the cooing of doves
        is heard in our land.
¹³The fig tree forms its early fruit;
    the blossoming vines spread their
        fragrance.
Arise, come, my darling;
    my beautiful one, come with me."

Lover

¹⁴My dove in the clefts of the rock,
    in the hiding places on the
        mountainside,
show me your face,
    let me hear your voice;
for your voice is sweet,
    and your face is lovely.
¹⁵Catch for us the foxes,
    the little foxes

that ruin the vineyards,
    our vineyards that are in bloom.

Beloved

¹⁶My lover is mine and I am his;
    he browses among the lilies.
¹⁷Until the day breaks
    and the shadows flee,
turn, my lover,
    and be like a gazelle
or like a young stag
    on the rugged hills. ᵃ

3 All night long on my bed
    I looked for the one my heart
        loves;
    I looked for him but did not find
        him.
²I will get up now and go about the
        city,
    through its streets and squares;
I will search for the one my heart
        loves.
    So I looked for him but did not
        find him.
³The watchmen found me
    as they made their rounds in the
        city.
    "Have you seen the one my heart
        loves?"
⁴Scarcely had I passed them
    when I found the one my heart
        loves.
I held him and would not let him go
    till I had brought him to my
        mother's house,
    to the room of the one who
        conceived me.
⁵Daughters of Jerusalem, I charge you
    by the gazelles and by the does of
        the field:
Do not arouse or awaken love
    until it so desires.

⁶Who is this coming up from the
        desert
    like a column of smoke,
perfumed with myrrh and incense
    made from all the spices of the
        merchant?
⁷Look! It is Solomon's carriage,
    escorted by sixty warriors,
    the noblest of Israel,
⁸all of them wearing the sword,
    all experienced in battle,

ᵃ17 Or *the hills of Bether*

each with his sword at his side,
 prepared for the terrors of the
  night.
⁹King Solomon made for himself the
 carriage;
 he made it of wood from Lebanon.
¹⁰Its posts he made of silver,
 its base of gold.
Its seat was upholstered with purple,
 its interior lovingly inlaid
 by*a* the daughters of Jerusalem.
¹¹Come out, you daughters of Zion,
 and look at King Solomon wearing
  the crown,
 the crown with which his mother
  crowned him
on the day of his wedding,
 the day his heart rejoiced.

Lover

4 How beautiful you are, my darling!
 Oh, how beautiful!
 Your eyes behind your veil are
  doves.
Your hair is like a flock of goats
 descending from Mount Gilead.
²Your teeth are like a flock of sheep
 just shorn,
 coming up from the washing.
Each has its twin;
 not one of them is alone.
³Your lips are like a scarlet ribbon;
 your mouth is lovely.
Your temples behind your veil
 are like the halves of a
  pomegranate.
⁴Your neck is like the tower of David,
 built with elegance*b*;
on it hang a thousand shields,
 all of them shields of warriors.
⁵Your two breasts are like two fawns,
 like twin fawns of a gazelle
 that browse among the lilies.
⁶Until the day breaks
 and the shadows flee,
I will go to the mountain of myrrh
 and to the hill of incense.
⁷All beautiful you are, my darling;
 there is no flaw in you.

⁸Come with me from Lebanon, my
 bride,
 come with me from Lebanon.
Descend from the crest of Amana,
 from the top of Senir, the summit
  of Hermon,

from the lions' dens
 and the mountain haunts of the
  leopards.
⁹You have stolen my heart, my sister,
 my bride;
you have stolen my heart
with one glance of your eyes,
 with one jewel of your necklace.
¹⁰How delightful is your love, my sister,
 my bride!
How much more pleasing is your
 love than wine,
 and the fragrance of your perfume
 than any spice!
¹¹Your lips drop sweetness as the
 honeycomb, my bride;
 milk and honey are under your
  tongue.
The fragrance of your garments is
 like that of Lebanon.
¹²You are a garden locked up, my sister,
 my bride;
 you are a spring enclosed, a sealed
  fountain.
¹³Your plants are an orchard of
 pomegranates
 with choice fruits,
 with henna and nard,
¹⁴ nard and saffron,
 calamus and cinnamon,
 with every kind of incense tree,
 with myrrh and aloes
 and all the finest spices.
¹⁵You are*c* a garden fountain,
 a well of flowing water
 streaming down from Lebanon.

Beloved

¹⁶Awake, north wind,
 and come, south wind!
Blow on my garden,
 that its fragrance may spread
  abroad.
Let my lover come into his garden
 and taste its choice fruits.

Lover

5 I have come into my garden, my
 sister, my bride;
 I have gathered my myrrh with my
  spice.

a10 Or *its inlaid interior a gift of love / from*
b4 The meaning of the Hebrew for this word is
uncertain.   *c15* Or *I am* (spoken by the *Beloved*)

I have eaten my honeycomb and my
    honey;
  I have drunk my wine and my milk.

Friends

  Eat, O friends, and drink;
    drink your fill, O lovers.

Beloved

²I slept but my heart was awake.
  Listen! My lover is knocking:
"Open to me, my sister, my darling,
  my dove, my flawless one.
My head is drenched with dew,
  my hair with the dampness of the
    night."
³I have taken off my robe—
  must I put it on again?
I have washed my feet—
  must I soil them again?
⁴My lover thrust his hand through the
    latch-opening;
  my heart began to pound for him.
⁵I arose to open for my lover,
  and my hands dripped with myrrh,
my fingers with flowing myrrh,
  on the handles of the lock.
⁶I opened for my lover,
  but my lover had left; he was gone.
  My heart sank at his departure.ᵃ

I looked for him but did not find him.
  I called him but he did not answer.
⁷The watchmen found me
  as they made their rounds in the
    city.
They beat me, they bruised me;
  they took away my cloak,
  those watchmen of the walls!
⁸O daughters of Jerusalem, I charge
    you—
if you find my lover,
  what will you tell him?
  Tell him I am faint with love.

Friends

⁹How is your beloved better than
    others,
  most beautiful of women?
How is your beloved better than
    others,
  that you charge us so?

Beloved

¹⁰My lover is radiant and ruddy,
  outstanding among ten thousand.
¹¹His head is purest gold;
  his hair is wavy
  and black as a raven.
¹²His eyes are like doves

ᵃ6 Or *heart had gone out to him when he spoke*

Your Love Life and Beyond

Tuesday

SONG OF SONGS 5:1 Do you realize
that one of the greatest fears
children have today is that Mommy and Daddy are going to get
a divorce? "It's all my fault!"
ten-year-old Billy told his mother.
"I'm the reason you're divorcing Dad,
aren't I?"

If you want to add to your children's security and prevent this fear of divorce, let
your child know your marriage is strong
and that you really love and are committed
to each other. Your children will sense
whether you have a strong love relationship with each other. Song of Songs is a
wonderful guide. This book of the Bible is
a timeless expression of the pleasure, joy
and intimacy of sex—our Creator's good gift
to all married couples.

Some wonder why the Bible would
include such a graphic picture
of sexual intimacy. While some
read it symbolically, others take
it at face value. Whatever your
approach, Song of Songs is a lovely
picture of the love relationship in a
marriage and acknowledges sex as part of
God's wonderful creation.

The author of this book—most think it
was King Solomon—understood the importance of having a love vocabulary. As you
read through this small book, think of it as
a great opportunity to increase your own
love vocabulary. You may want to read
these chapters out loud to each other. They
will energize your love life!

—Dave & Claudia

Go to page 721 for your next devotional reading.

by the water streams,
washed in milk,
  mounted like jewels.
13His cheeks are like beds of spice
  yielding perfume.
His lips are like lilies
  dripping with myrrh.
14His arms are rods of gold
  set with chrysolite.
His body is like polished ivory
  decorated with sapphires.*a*
15His legs are pillars of marble
  set on bases of pure gold.
His appearance is like Lebanon,
  choice as its cedars.
16His mouth is sweetness itself;
  he is altogether lovely.
This is my lover, this my friend,
  O daughters of Jerusalem.

Friends

6 Where has your lover gone,
  most beautiful of women?
Which way did your lover turn,
  that we may look for him with
    you?

Beloved

2My lover has gone down to his
    garden,
  to the beds of spices,
to browse in the gardens
  and to gather lilies.
3I am my lover's and my lover is mine;
  he browses among the lilies.

Lover

4You are beautiful, my darling, as
    Tirzah,
  lovely as Jerusalem,
  majestic as troops with banners.
5Turn your eyes from me;
  they overwhelm me.
Your hair is like a flock of goats
  descending from Gilead.
6Your teeth are like a flock of sheep
  coming up from the washing.
Each has its twin,
  not one of them is alone.
7Your temples behind your veil
  are like the halves of a
    pomegranate.
8Sixty queens there may be,
  and eighty concubines,
  and virgins beyond number;

9but my dove, my perfect one, is
    unique,
  the only daughter of her mother,
  the favorite of the one who bore
    her.
The maidens saw her and called her
    blessed;
  the queens and concubines praised
    her.

Friends

10Who is this that appears like the
    dawn,
  fair as the moon, bright as the sun,
  majestic as the stars in procession?

Lover

11I went down to the grove of nut trees
  to look at the new growth in the
    valley,
to see if the vines had budded
  or the pomegranates were in
    bloom.
12Before I realized it,
  my desire set me among the royal
    chariots of my people.*b*

Friends

13Come back, come back,
    O Shulammite;
come back, come back, that we
    may gaze on you!

Lover

Why would you gaze on the
    Shulammite
  as on the dance of Mahanaim?

7 How beautiful your sandaled feet,
  O prince's daughter!
Your graceful legs are like jewels,
  the work of a craftsman's hands.
2Your navel is a rounded goblet
  that never lacks blended wine.
Your waist is a mound of wheat
  encircled by lilies.
3Your breasts are like two fawns,
  twins of a gazelle.
4Your neck is like an ivory tower.
Your eyes are the pools of Heshbon
  by the gate of Bath Rabbim.

---

a 14 Or *lapis lazuli*   *b 12* Or *among the chariots of
Amminadab; or among the chariots of the people of the
prince*

Your nose is like the tower of
　　Lebanon
　　looking toward Damascus.
[5]Your head crowns you like Mount
　　Carmel.
　　Your hair is like royal tapestry;
　　the king is held captive by its
　　　tresses.
[6]How beautiful you are and how
　　pleasing,
　　O love, with your delights!
[7]Your stature is like that of the palm,
　　and your breasts like clusters of
　　　fruit.
[8]I said, "I will climb the palm tree;
　　I will take hold of its fruit."
　　May your breasts be like the clusters
　　　of the vine,
　　the fragrance of your breath like
　　　apples,
[9]　and your mouth like the best wine.

Beloved

　　May the wine go straight to my lover,
　　flowing gently over lips and
　　　teeth.[a]
[10]I belong to my lover,
　　and his desire is for me.
[11]Come, my lover, let us go to the
　　countryside,
　　let us spend the night in the
　　　villages.[b]
[12]Let us go early to the vineyards
　　to see if the vines have budded,
　　if their blossoms have opened,
　　and if the pomegranates are in
　　　bloom—
　　there I will give you my love.
[13]The mandrakes send out their
　　fragrance,
　　and at our door is every delicacy,
　　both new and old,
　　that I have stored up for you, my
　　　lover.

8 If only you were to me like a
　　brother,
　　who was nursed at my mother's
　　　breasts!
　　Then, if I found you outside,
　　I would kiss you,
　　and no one would despise me.
[2]I would lead you
　　and bring you to my mother's
　　　house—
　　she who has taught me.

I would give you spiced wine to
　　drink,
　　the nectar of my pomegranates.
[3]His left arm is under my head
　　and his right arm embraces me.
[4]Daughters of Jerusalem, I charge you:
　　Do not arouse or awaken love
　　until it so desires.

Friends

[5]Who is this coming up from the
　　desert
　　leaning on her lover?

Beloved

　　Under the apple tree I roused you;
　　there your mother conceived you,
　　there she who was in labor gave
　　　you birth.
[6]Place me like a seal over your heart,
　　like a seal on your arm;
　　for love is as strong as death,
　　its jealousy[c] unyielding as the
　　　grave.[d]
　　It burns like blazing fire,
　　like a mighty flame.[e]
[7]Many waters cannot quench love;
　　rivers cannot wash it away.
　　If one were to give
　　all the wealth of his house for love,
　　it[f] would be utterly scorned.

Friends

[8]We have a young sister,
　　and her breasts are not yet grown.
　　What shall we do for our sister
　　for the day she is spoken for?
[9]If she is a wall,
　　we will build towers of silver on
　　　her.
　　If she is a door,
　　we will enclose her with panels of
　　　cedar.

Beloved

[10]I am a wall,
　　and my breasts are like towers.
　　Thus I have become in his eyes
　　like one bringing contentment.

[a]9 Septuagint, Aquila, Vulgate and Syriac; Hebrew
lips of sleepers　[b]11 Or *henna bushes*　[c]6 Or
ardor　[d]6 Hebrew *Sheol*　[e]6 Or / *like the very
flame of the* LORD　[f]7 Or *he*

¹¹Solomon had a vineyard in Baal
    Hamon;
  he let out his vineyard to tenants.
Each was to bring for its fruit
  a thousand shekels[a] of silver.
¹²But my own vineyard is mine to give;
  the thousand shekels are for you,
    O Solomon,
  and two hundred[b] are for those
    who tend its fruit.

Lover

¹³You who dwell in the gardens

with friends in attendance,
  let me hear your voice!

Beloved

¹⁴Come away, my lover,
  and be like a gazelle
  or like a young stag
    on the spice-laden mountains.

---

a 11 That is, about 25 pounds (about 11.5 kilograms); also in verse 12   *b 12* That is, about 5 pounds (about 2.3 kilograms)

My Spouse, My Lover

Wednesday

SONG OF SONGS 8:4   The media, popular music and our own physical desires often lead us to believe that sex is something that one marriage partner gets from the other partner. Perhaps this is true in the biological sense. But sex is only part of the much more involved act of making love. A term that the Bible uses concerning a husband and wife making love is the word *union*. For example, Matthew 1:25 says that Joseph had no "union" with Mary until she gave birth to a son. In the original language the word *union* can also mean "to know"—to understand absolutely.

To know someone sexually is to take the time to understand him or her—to take the time to focus on our spouse's sexual needs, rather than impose our own desires. Making love is not something one *gets* from the marriage; it's something one *gives* to the

marriage. In our own marriage, I (Bob) have to work hard at viewing our sexual union as part of the ongoing relationship rather than separating the two. I had to quest after getting to know Rosemary—understanding her absolutely—before we could form the union God planned for us to have.

In order to give myself to my spouse, I must take the time to know her sexually: to hear her desires, to study her needs, to quest after her dreams. Obviously, really knowing each other sexually takes time and patience.

The physical act of sex in marriage might be something that one person gets from another person, but making love is a lifetime quest of patiently getting to know one another sexually.

—Bob & Rosemary

Go to page 731 for your next devotional reading.

Isaiah

Through the visions God gave him, Isaiah unveils the full dimensions of God's judgment against sin. These images of destruction and death are difficult to read and are even more difficult to think about. But the prophet also paints a picture of comfort, redemption and restoration for those who put their hope in God. Many of Isaiah's most stirring prophecies are those that predict the coming of the Messiah, the One who is to restore and redeem the earth—and his people—to the divine ideal so that the God of Israel will be praised and glorified.

As you read this book, feel what it's like to live without hope . . . and with hope through Jesus Christ. Attempt to infuse your marriage relationship with hope.

1 The vision concerning Judah and Jerusalem that Isaiah son of Amoz saw during the reigns of Uzziah, Jotham, Ahaz and Hezekiah, kings of Judah.

A Rebellious Nation

²Hear, O heavens! Listen, O earth!
  For the LORD has spoken:
"I reared children and brought them
    up,
  but they have rebelled against me.
³The ox knows his master,
  the donkey his owner's manger,
but Israel does not know,
  my people do not understand."

⁴Ah, sinful nation,
  a people loaded with guilt,
a brood of evildoers,
  children given to corruption!
They have forsaken the LORD;
  they have spurned the Holy One of
    Israel
  and turned their backs on him.

⁵Why should you be beaten anymore?
  Why do you persist in rebellion?
Your whole head is injured,
  your whole heart afflicted.
⁶From the sole of your foot to the top
    of your head
  there is no soundness—
only wounds and welts
  and open sores,
not cleansed or bandaged
  or soothed with oil.

⁷Your country is desolate,
  your cities burned with fire;

your fields are being stripped by
  foreigners
    right before you,
    laid waste as when overthrown by
      strangers.
8The Daughter of Zion is left
  like a shelter in a vineyard,
  like a hut in a field of melons,
  like a city under siege.
9Unless the LORD Almighty
  had left us some survivors,
  we would have become like Sodom,
  we would have been like
    Gomorrah.

10Hear the word of the LORD,
  you rulers of Sodom;
  listen to the law of our God,
  you people of Gomorrah!
11"The multitude of your sacrifices—
  what are they to me?" says the
    LORD.
  "I have more than enough of burnt
    offerings,
  of rams and the fat of fattened
    animals;
  I have no pleasure
    in the blood of bulls and lambs
      and goats.
12When you come to appear before me,
  who has asked this of you,
  this trampling of my courts?
13Stop bringing meaningless offerings!
  Your incense is detestable to me.
  New Moons, Sabbaths and
    convocations—
  I cannot bear your evil assemblies.
14Your New Moon festivals and your
    appointed feasts
  my soul hates.
  They have become a burden to me;
  I am weary of bearing them.
15When you spread out your hands in
    prayer,
  I will hide my eyes from you;
  even if you offer many prayers,
  I will not listen.
  Your hands are full of blood;
16   wash and make yourselves clean.
  Take your evil deeds
    out of my sight!
  Stop doing wrong,
17   learn to do right!
  Seek justice,
    encourage the oppressed.a

Defend the cause of the fatherless,
  plead the case of the widow.

18"Come now, let us reason together,"
  says the LORD.
  "Though your sins are like scarlet,
  they shall be as white as snow;
  though they are red as crimson,
  they shall be like wool.
19If you are willing and obedient,
  you will eat the best from the land;
20but if you resist and rebel,
  you will be devoured by the sword."
          For the mouth of the LORD
              has spoken.

21See how the faithful city
  has become a harlot!
  She once was full of justice;
  righteousness used to dwell in her—
  but now murderers!
22Your silver has become dross,
  your choice wine is diluted with
    water.
23Your rulers are rebels,
  companions of thieves;
  they all love bribes
  and chase after gifts.
  They do not defend the cause of the
    fatherless;
  the widow's case does not come
    before them.
24Therefore the Lord, the LORD
    Almighty,
  the Mighty One of Israel, declares:
  "Ah, I will get relief from my foes
  and avenge myself on my enemies.
25I will turn my hand against you;
  I will thoroughly purge away your
    dross
  and remove all your impurities.
26I will restore your judges as in days of
    old,
  your counselors as at the
    beginning.
  Afterward you will be called
    the City of Righteousness,
    the Faithful City."

27Zion will be redeemed with justice,
  her penitent ones with
    righteousness.
28But rebels and sinners will both be
    broken,

a17 Or / rebuke the oppressor

and those who forsake the LORD
will perish.

29"You will be ashamed because of the
sacred oaks
in which you have delighted;
you will be disgraced because of the
gardens
that you have chosen.
30You will be like an oak with fading
leaves,
like a garden without water.
31The mighty man will become tinder
and his work a spark;
both will burn together,
with no one to quench the fire."

The Mountain of the LORD

2 This is what Isaiah son of Amoz saw
concerning Judah and Jerusalem:

2In the last days

the mountain of the LORD's temple
will be established
as chief among the mountains;
it will be raised above the hills,
and all nations will stream to it.

3Many peoples will come and say,

"Come, let us go up to the mountain
of the LORD,
to the house of the God of Jacob.
He will teach us his ways,
so that we may walk in his paths."
The law will go out from Zion,
the word of the LORD from
Jerusalem.
4He will judge between the nations
and will settle disputes for many
peoples.
They will beat their swords into
plowshares
and their spears into pruning
hooks.
Nation will not take up sword against
nation,
nor will they train for war
anymore.

5Come, O house of Jacob,
let us walk in the light of the
LORD.

The Day of the LORD

6You have abandoned your people,
the house of Jacob.

They are full of superstitions from the
East;
they practice divination like the
Philistines
and clasp hands with pagans.
7Their land is full of silver and gold;
there is no end to their treasures.
Their land is full of horses;
there is no end to their chariots.
8Their land is full of idols;
they bow down to the work of
their hands,
to what their fingers have made.
9So man will be brought low
and mankind humbled—
do not forgive them.a

10Go into the rocks,
hide in the ground
from dread of the LORD
and the splendor of his majesty!
11The eyes of the arrogant man will be
humbled
and the pride of men brought low;
the LORD alone will be exalted in that
day.

12The LORD Almighty has a day in store
for all the proud and lofty,
for all that is exalted
(and they will be humbled),
13for all the cedars of Lebanon, tall and
lofty,
and all the oaks of Bashan,
14for all the towering mountains
and all the high hills,
15for every lofty tower
and every fortified wall,
16for every trading shipb
and every stately vessel.
17The arrogance of man will be brought
low
and the pride of men humbled;
the LORD alone will be exalted in that
day,
18   and the idols will totally disappear.

19Men will flee to caves in the rocks
and to holes in the ground
from dread of the LORD
and the splendor of his majesty,
when he rises to shake the earth.
20In that day men will throw away
to the rodents and bats
their idols of silver and idols of gold,

---

a9 Or not raise them up   b16 Hebrew every ship
of Tarshish

which they made to worship.
²¹They will flee to caverns in the rocks
  and to the overhanging crags
from dread of the LORD
  and the splendor of his majesty,
  when he rises to shake the earth.

²²Stop trusting in man,
  who has but a breath in his
    nostrils.
Of what account is he?

Judgment on Jerusalem and Judah

3 See now, the Lord,
    the LORD Almighty,
  is about to take from Jerusalem and
    Judah
    both supply and support:
  all supplies of food and all supplies
    of water,
² the hero and warrior,
  the judge and prophet,
    the soothsayer and elder,
³the captain of fifty and man of rank,
    the counselor, skilled craftsman
    and clever enchanter.

⁴I will make boys their officials;
    mere children will govern them.
⁵People will oppress each other—
  man against man, neighbor against
    neighbor.
The young will rise up against the
    old,
  the base against the honorable.

⁶A man will seize one of his brothers
    at his father's home, and say,
  "You have a cloak, you be our leader;
    take charge of this heap of ruins!"
⁷But in that day he will cry out,
  "I have no remedy.
I have no food or clothing in my
    house;
  do not make me the leader of the
    people."

⁸Jerusalem staggers,
  Judah is falling;
  their words and deeds are against the
    LORD,
  defying his glorious presence.
⁹The look on their faces testifies
    against them;
  they parade their sin like Sodom;
  they do not hide it.
Woe to them!

They have brought disaster upon
    themselves.

¹⁰Tell the righteous it will be well with
    them,
  for they will enjoy the fruit of their
    deeds.
¹¹Woe to the wicked! Disaster is upon
    them!
They will be paid back for what their
    hands have done.

¹²Youths oppress my people,
  women rule over them.
O my people, your guides lead you
    astray;
  they turn you from the path.

¹³The LORD takes his place in court;
  he rises to judge the people.
¹⁴The LORD enters into judgment
  against the elders and leaders of
    his people:
  "It is you who have ruined my
    vineyard;
  the plunder from the poor is in
    your houses.
¹⁵What do you mean by crushing my
    people
  and grinding the faces of the poor?"
            declares the Lord,
            the LORD Almighty.

¹⁶The LORD says,
  "The women of Zion are haughty,
  walking along with outstretched
    necks,
    flirting with their eyes,
  tripping along with mincing steps,
    with ornaments jingling on their
      ankles.
¹⁷Therefore the Lord will bring sores on
    the heads of the women of
    Zion;
  the LORD will make their scalps
    bald."

¹⁸In that day the Lord will snatch away
their finery: the bangles and headbands
and crescent necklaces, ¹⁹the earrings and
bracelets and veils, ²⁰the headdresses and
ankle chains and sashes, the perfume bottles and charms, ²¹the signet rings and
nose rings, ²²the fine robes and the capes
and cloaks, the purses ²³and mirrors, and
the linen garments and tiaras and shawls.

²⁴Instead of fragrance there will be a
    stench;

instead of a sash, a rope;
   instead of well-dressed hair, baldness;
     instead of fine clothing, sackcloth;
     instead of beauty, branding.
²⁵Your men will fall by the sword,
   your warriors in battle.
²⁶The gates of Zion will lament and
     mourn;
   destitute, she will sit on the
     ground.

4 In that day seven women
   will take hold of one man
and say, "We will eat our own food
   and provide our own clothes;
only let us be called by your name.
   Take away our disgrace!"

The Branch of the LORD

²In that day the Branch of the LORD will be beautiful and glorious, and the fruit of the land will be the pride and glory of the survivors in Israel. ³Those who are left in Zion, who remain in Jerusalem, will be called holy, all who are recorded among the living in Jerusalem. ⁴The Lord will wash away the filth of the women of Zion; he will cleanse the bloodstains from Jerusalem by a spirit[a] of judgment and a spirit[a] of fire. ⁵Then the LORD will create over all of Mount Zion and over those who assemble there a cloud of smoke by day and a glow of flaming fire by night; over all the glory will be a canopy. ⁶It will be a shelter and shade from the heat of the day, and a refuge and hiding place from the storm and rain.

The Song of the Vineyard

5 I will sing for the one I love
   a song about his vineyard:
My loved one had a vineyard
   on a fertile hillside.
²He dug it up and cleared it of stones
   and planted it with the choicest
     vines.
He built a watchtower in it
   and cut out a winepress as well.
Then he looked for a crop of good
     grapes,
   but it yielded only bad fruit.

³"Now you dwellers in Jerusalem and
     men of Judah,
   judge between me and my
     vineyard.

⁴What more could have been done for
     my vineyard
   than I have done for it?
When I looked for good grapes,
   why did it yield only bad?
⁵Now I will tell you
   what I am going to do to my
     vineyard:
I will take away its hedge,
   and it will be destroyed;
I will break down its wall,
   and it will be trampled.
⁶I will make it a wasteland,
   neither pruned nor cultivated,
   and briers and thorns will grow
     there.
I will command the clouds
   not to rain on it."

⁷The vineyard of the LORD Almighty
   is the house of Israel,
and the men of Judah
   are the garden of his delight.
And he looked for justice, but saw
     bloodshed;
   for righteousness, but heard cries
     of distress.

Woes and Judgments

⁸Woe to you who add house to house
   and join field to field
till no space is left
   and you live alone in the land.

⁹The LORD Almighty has declared in my hearing:

"Surely the great houses will become
     desolate,
   the fine mansions left without
     occupants.
¹⁰A ten-acre[b] vineyard will produce
   only a bath[c] of wine,
a homer[d] of seed only an
     ephah[e] of grain."

¹¹Woe to those who rise early in the
     morning
   to run after their drinks,
who stay up late at night
   till they are inflamed with wine.

---

a 4 Or *the Spirit*   *b 10* Hebrew *ten-yoke,* that is, the land plowed by 10 yoke of oxen in one day   *c 10* That is, probably about 6 gallons (about 22 liters)   *d 10* That is, probably about 6 bushels (about 220 liters)   *e 10* That is, probably about 3/5 bushel (about 22 liters)

¹²They have harps and lyres at their
banquets,
tambourines and flutes and wine,
but they have no regard for the deeds
of the LORD,
no respect for the work of his
hands.
¹³Therefore my people will go into exile
for lack of understanding;
their men of rank will die of hunger
and their masses will be parched
with thirst.
¹⁴Therefore the grave*a* enlarges its
appetite
and opens its mouth without limit;
into it will descend their nobles and
masses
with all their brawlers and revelers.
¹⁵So man will be brought low
and mankind humbled,
the eyes of the arrogant humbled.
¹⁶But the LORD Almighty will be exalted
by his justice,
and the holy God will show
himself holy by his
righteousness.
¹⁷Then sheep will graze as in their own
pasture;
lambs will feed*b* among the ruins
of the rich.

¹⁸Woe to those who draw sin along
with cords of deceit,
and wickedness as with cart ropes,
¹⁹to those who say, "Let God hurry,
let him hasten his work
so we may see it.
Let it approach,
let the plan of the Holy One of
Israel come,
so we may know it."

²⁰Woe to those who call evil good
and good evil,
who put darkness for light
and light for darkness,
who put bitter for sweet
and sweet for bitter.

²¹Woe to those who are wise in their
own eyes
and clever in their own sight.

²²Woe to those who are heroes at
drinking wine
and champions at mixing drinks,
²³who acquit the guilty for a bribe,
but deny justice to the innocent.

²⁴Therefore, as tongues of fire lick up
straw
and as dry grass sinks down in the
flames,
so their roots will decay
and their flowers blow away like
dust;
for they have rejected the law of the
LORD Almighty
and spurned the word of the Holy
One of Israel.
²⁵Therefore the LORD's anger burns
against his people;
his hand is raised and he strikes
them down.
The mountains shake,
and the dead bodies are like refuse
in the streets.

Yet for all this, his anger is not turned
away,
his hand is still upraised.

²⁶He lifts up a banner for the distant
nations,
he whistles for those at the ends of
the earth.
Here they come,
swiftly and speedily!
²⁷Not one of them grows tired or
stumbles,
not one slumbers or sleeps;
not a belt is loosened at the waist,
not a sandal thong is broken.
²⁸Their arrows are sharp,
all their bows are strung;
their horses' hoofs seem like flint,
their chariot wheels like a
whirlwind.
²⁹Their roar is like that of the lion,
they roar like young lions;
they growl as they seize their prey
and carry it off with no one to
rescue.
³⁰In that day they will roar over it
like the roaring of the sea.
And if one looks at the land,
he will see darkness and distress;
even the light will be darkened by
the clouds.

Isaiah's Commission

6 In the year that King Uzziah died, I
saw the Lord seated on a throne, high

---

*a*14 Hebrew *Sheol*   *b*17 Septuagint; Hebrew /
strangers will eat

and exalted, and the train of his robe filled the temple. [2]Above him were seraphs, each with six wings: With two wings they covered their faces, with two they covered their feet, and with two they were flying. [3]And they were calling to one another:

"Holy, holy, holy is the LORD
    Almighty;
the whole earth is full of his glory."

[4]At the sound of their voices the doorposts and thresholds shook and the temple was filled with smoke.

[5]"Woe to me!" I cried. "I am ruined! For I am a man of unclean lips, and I live among a people of unclean lips, and my eyes have seen the King, the LORD Almighty."

[6]Then one of the seraphs flew to me with a live coal in his hand, which he had taken with tongs from the altar. [7]With it he touched my mouth and said, "See, this has touched your lips; your guilt is taken away and your sin atoned for."

[8]Then I heard the voice of the Lord saying, "Whom shall I send? And who will go for us?"

And I said, "Here am I. Send me!"

[9]He said, "Go and tell this people:

" 'Be ever hearing, but never
        understanding;
    be ever seeing, but never
        perceiving.'
[10]Make the heart of this people
        calloused;
    make their ears dull
        and close their eyes.[a]
Otherwise they might see with their
        eyes,
    hear with their ears,
    understand with their hearts,
and turn and be healed."

[11]Then I said, "For how long, O Lord?"
And he answered:

"Until the cities lie ruined
    and without inhabitant,
until the houses are left deserted
    and the fields ruined and ravaged,
[12]until the LORD has sent everyone far
        away
    and the land is utterly forsaken.
[13]And though a tenth remains in the
        land,

it will again be laid waste.
But as the terebinth and oak
    leave stumps when they are cut
        down,
    so the holy seed will be the stump
        in the land."

The Sign of Immanuel

7 When Ahaz son of Jotham, the son of Uzziah, was king of Judah, King Rezin of Aram and Pekah son of Remaliah king of Israel marched up to fight against Jerusalem, but they could not overpower it.

[2]Now the house of David was told, "Aram has allied itself with[b] Ephraim"; so the hearts of Ahaz and his people were shaken, as the trees of the forest are shaken by the wind.

[3]Then the LORD said to Isaiah, "Go out, you and your son Shear-Jashub,[c] to meet Ahaz at the end of the aqueduct of the Upper Pool, on the road to the Washerman's Field. [4]Say to him, 'Be careful, keep calm and don't be afraid. Do not lose heart because of these two smoldering stubs of firewood—because of the fierce anger of Rezin and Aram and of the son of Remaliah. [5]Aram, Ephraim and Remaliah's son have plotted your ruin, saying, [6]"Let us invade Judah; let us tear it apart and divide it among ourselves, and make the son of Tabeel king over it." [7]Yet this is what the Sovereign LORD says:

" 'It will not take place,
    it will not happen,
[8]for the head of Aram is Damascus,
    and the head of Damascus is only
        Rezin.
Within sixty-five years
    Ephraim will be too shattered to be
        a people.
[9]The head of Ephraim is Samaria,
    and the head of Samaria is only
        Remaliah's son.
If you do not stand firm in your
        faith,
    you will not stand at all.' "

[10]Again the LORD spoke to Ahaz, [11]"Ask the LORD your God for a sign,

---

[a]9,10 Hebrew; Septuagint 'You will be ever hearing, but never understanding; / you will be ever seeing, but never perceiving.' / [10]This people's heart has become calloused; / they hardly hear with their ears, / and they have closed their eyes   [b]2 Or has set up camp in   [c]3 Shear-Jashub means a remnant will return.

whether in the deepest depths or in the highest heights."

¹²But Ahaz said, "I will not ask; I will not put the LORD to the test."

¹³Then Isaiah said, "Hear now, you house of David! Is it not enough to try the patience of men? Will you try the patience of my God also? ¹⁴Therefore the Lord himself will give you*a* a sign: The virgin will be with child and will give birth to a son, and*b* will call him Immanuel.*c* ¹⁵He will eat curds and honey when he knows enough to reject the wrong and choose the right. ¹⁶But before the boy knows enough to reject the wrong and choose the right, the land of the two kings you dread will be laid waste. ¹⁷The LORD will bring on you and on your people and on the house of your father a time unlike any since Ephraim broke away from Judah—he will bring the king of Assyria."

¹⁸In that day the LORD will whistle for flies from the distant streams of Egypt and for bees from the land of Assyria. ¹⁹They will all come and settle in the steep ravines and in the crevices in the rocks, on all the thornbushes and at all the water holes. ²⁰In that day the Lord will use a razor hired from beyond the River*d*—the king of Assyria—to shave your head and the hair of your legs, and to take off your beards also. ²¹In that day, a man will keep alive a young cow and two goats. ²²And because of the abundance of the milk they give, he will have curds to eat. All who remain in the land will eat curds and honey. ²³In that day, in every place where there were a thousand vines worth a thousand silver shekels,*e* there will be only briers and thorns. ²⁴Men will go there with bow and arrow, for the land will be covered with briers and thorns. ²⁵As for all the hills once cultivated by the hoe, you will no longer go there for fear of the briers and thorns; they will become places where cattle are turned loose and where sheep run.

Assyria, the LORD's Instrument

8 The LORD said to me, "Take a large scroll and write on it with an ordinary pen: Maher-Shalal-Hash-Baz.*f* ²And I will call in Uriah the priest and Zechariah son of Jeberekiah as reliable witnesses for me."

³Then I went to the prophetess, and she conceived and gave birth to a son. And the LORD said to me, "Name him Maher-Shalal-Hash-Baz. ⁴Before the boy knows how to say 'My father' or 'My mother,' the wealth of Damascus and the plunder of Samaria will be carried off by the king of Assyria."

⁵The LORD spoke to me again:

⁶"Because this people has rejected
    the gently flowing waters of
        Shiloah
  and rejoices over Rezin
    and the son of Remaliah,
⁷therefore the Lord is about to bring
        against them
  the mighty floodwaters of the
        River*d*—
  the king of Assyria with all his
        pomp.
It will overflow all its channels,
    run over all its banks
⁸and sweep on into Judah, swirling
        over it,
  passing through it and reaching up
        to the neck.
Its outspread wings will cover the
        breadth of your land,
  O Immanuel*c*!"

⁹Raise the war cry,*g* you nations, and
        be shattered!
  Listen, all you distant lands.
Prepare for battle, and be shattered!
  Prepare for battle, and be
        shattered!
¹⁰Devise your strategy, but it will be
        thwarted;
  propose your plan, but it will not
        stand,
  for God is with us.*h*

Fear God

¹¹The LORD spoke to me with his strong hand upon me, warning me not to follow the way of this people. He said:

¹²"Do not call conspiracy

---

*a*14 The Hebrew is plural.   *b*14 Masoretic Text; Dead Sea Scrolls *and he* or *and they*
*c*14,8 *Immanuel* means *God with us.*
*d*20,7 That is, the Euphrates   *e*23 That is, about 25 pounds (about 11.5 kilograms)
*f*1 *Maher-Shalal-Hash-Baz* means *quick to the plunder, swift to the spoil;* also in verse 3.   *g*9 Or *Do your worst*   *h*10 Hebrew *Immanuel*

everything that these people call
        conspiracy[a];
do not fear what they fear,
    and do not dread it.
[13]The LORD Almighty is the one you are
        to regard as holy,
    he is the one you are to fear,
    he is the one you are to dread,
[14]and he will be a sanctuary;
    but for both houses of Israel he
        will be
a stone that causes men to stumble
    and a rock that makes them fall.
And for the people of Jerusalem he
        will be
a trap and a snare.
[15]Many of them will stumble;
    they will fall and be broken,
    they will be snared and captured."

[16]Bind up the testimony
    and seal up the law among my
        disciples.
[17]I will wait for the LORD,
    who is hiding his face from the
        house of Jacob.
I will put my trust in him.

[18]Here am I, and the children the LORD
has given me. We are signs and symbols
in Israel from the LORD Almighty, who
dwells on Mount Zion.

[19]When men tell you to consult mediums and spiritists, who whisper and mutter, should not a people inquire of their
God? Why consult the dead on behalf of
the living? [20]To the law and to the testimony! If they do not speak according to
this word, they have no light of dawn.
[21]Distressed and hungry, they will roam
through the land; when they are famished, they will become enraged and,
looking upward, will curse their king and
their God. [22]Then they will look toward
the earth and see only distress and darkness and fearful gloom, and they will be
thrust into utter darkness.

To Us a Child Is Born

9 Nevertheless, there will be no more
    gloom for those who were in distress.
In the past he humbled the land of Zebulun and the land of Naphtali, but in the
future he will honor Galilee of the Gentiles, by the way of the sea, along the Jordan—

[2]The people walking in darkness
    have seen a great light;
on those living in the land of the
        shadow of death[b]
    a light has dawned.
[3]You have enlarged the nation
    and increased their joy;
they rejoice before you
    as people rejoice at the harvest,
as men rejoice
    when dividing the plunder.
[4]For as in the day of Midian's defeat,
    you have shattered
the yoke that burdens them,
    the bar across their shoulders,
    the rod of their oppressor.
[5]Every warrior's boot used in battle
    and every garment rolled in blood
will be destined for burning,
    will be fuel for the fire.
[6]For to us a child is born,
    to us a son is given,
    and the government will be on his
        shoulders.
And he will be called
    Wonderful Counselor,[c] Mighty
        God,
    Everlasting Father, Prince of Peace.
[7]Of the increase of his government
        and peace
    there will be no end.
He will reign on David's throne
    and over his kingdom,
establishing and upholding it
    with justice and righteousness
    from that time on and forever.
The zeal of the LORD Almighty
    will accomplish this.

The Lord's Anger Against Israel

[8]The Lord has sent a message against
        Jacob;
    it will fall on Israel.
[9]All the people will know it—
    Ephraim and the inhabitants of
        Samaria—
who say with pride
    and arrogance of heart,
[10]"The bricks have fallen down,
    but we will rebuild with dressed
        stone;
the fig trees have been felled,

---

[a]12 Or *Do not call for a treaty / every time these
people call for a treaty*   [b]2 Or *land of darkness*
[c]6 Or *Wonderful, Counselor*

but we will replace them with
cedars."
¹¹But the LORD has strengthened Rezin's
foes against them
and has spurred their enemies on.
¹²Arameans from the east and
Philistines from the west
have devoured Israel with open
mouth.

Yet for all this, his anger is not turned
away,
his hand is still upraised.

¹³But the people have not returned to
him who struck them,
nor have they sought the LORD
Almighty.
¹⁴So the LORD will cut off from Israel
both head and tail,
both palm branch and reed in a
single day;
¹⁵the elders and prominent men are the
head,
the prophets who teach lies are the
tail.
¹⁶Those who guide this people mislead
them,
and those who are guided are led
astray.
¹⁷Therefore the Lord will take no
pleasure in the young men,
nor will he pity the fatherless and
widows,
for everyone is ungodly and wicked,
every mouth speaks vileness.

Yet for all this, his anger is not turned
away,
his hand is still upraised.

¹⁸Surely wickedness burns like a fire;
it consumes briers and thorns,
it sets the forest thickets ablaze,
so that it rolls upward in a column
of smoke.
¹⁹By the wrath of the LORD Almighty
the land will be scorched
and the people will be fuel for the
fire;
no one will spare his brother.
²⁰On the right they will devour,
but still be hungry;
on the left they will eat,
but not be satisfied.
Each will feed on the flesh of his own
offspring*:
²¹   Manasseh will feed on Ephraim,
and Ephraim on Manasseh;
together they will turn against
Judah.

Yet for all this, his anger is not turned
away,
his hand is still upraised.

10 Woe to those who make unjust
laws,
to those who issue oppressive
decrees,
²to deprive the poor of their rights
and withhold justice from the
oppressed of my people,
making widows their prey
and robbing the fatherless.
³What will you do on the day of
reckoning,
when disaster comes from afar?

a20 Or arm

A Child Is Born

Thursday

ISAIAH 9:6 Modern scholars have studied this poetic prophecy of Isaiah in much the same way a botanist studies flowers, dissecting and analyzing every piece and part. They have determined that many of the passages in this book are among the finest in literature. And this verse in particular may be one of the most frequently quoted in the entire book. It is nearly impossible to go through the Christmas season and not hear this read or sung.

COUPLE MINUTES

As you discover the beauty of this book, consider the power of its prophecy. No matter what time of year you happen to be reading this, consider how the coming of the Messiah—"Wonderful Counselor, Mighty God, Everlasting Father, Prince of Peace"—has changed your life. In fact, you might find it helpful to talk with your spouse about what each of these descriptions of Jesus means to you.   **—Les & Leslie**

Go to page 734 for your next devotional reading.

To whom will you run for help?
  Where will you leave your riches?
⁴Nothing will remain but to cringe
    among the captives
  or fall among the slain.

Yet for all this, his anger is not turned
    away,
  his hand is still upraised.

God's Judgment on Assyria

⁵"Woe to the Assyrian, the rod of my
    anger,
  in whose hand is the club of my
    wrath!
⁶I send him against a godless nation,
  I dispatch him against a people
    who anger me,
  to seize loot and snatch plunder,
    and to trample them down like
      mud in the streets.
⁷But this is not what he intends,
    this is not what he has in mind;
  his purpose is to destroy,
    to put an end to many nations.
⁸'Are not my commanders all kings?'
    he says.
⁹   'Has not Calno fared like
      Carchemish?
  Is not Hamath like Arpad,
    and Samaria like Damascus?
¹⁰As my hand seized the kingdoms of
      the idols,
    kingdoms whose images excelled
      those of Jerusalem and
      Samaria—
¹¹shall I not deal with Jerusalem and
      her images
    as I dealt with Samaria and her
      idols?' "

¹²When the Lord has finished all his
work against Mount Zion and Jerusalem,
he will say, "I will punish the king of
Assyria for the willful pride of his heart
and the haughty look in his eyes. ¹³For he
says:

  " 'By the strength of my hand I have
      done this,
    and by my wisdom, because I have
      understanding.
  I removed the boundaries of nations,
    I plundered their treasures;
    like a mighty one I subdued*ᵃ*
      their kings.
¹⁴As one reaches into a nest,

so my hand reached for the wealth
    of the nations;
  as men gather abandoned eggs,
    so I gathered all the countries;
  not one flapped a wing,
    or opened its mouth to chirp.' "

¹⁵Does the ax raise itself above him
      who swings it,
    or the saw boast against him who
      uses it?
  As if a rod were to wield him who
      lifts it up,
    or a club brandish him who is not
      wood!
¹⁶Therefore, the Lord, the LORD
      Almighty,
    will send a wasting disease upon
      his sturdy warriors;
  under his pomp a fire will be kindled
    like a blazing flame.
¹⁷The Light of Israel will become a fire,
    their Holy One a flame;
  in a single day it will burn and
      consume
    his thorns and his briers.
¹⁸The splendor of his forests and fertile
      fields
    it will completely destroy,
    as when a sick man wastes away.
¹⁹And the remaining trees of his forests
      will be so few
    that a child could write them
      down.

The Remnant of Israel

²⁰In that day the remnant of Israel,
    the survivors of the house of Jacob,
  will no longer rely on him
    who struck them down
  but will truly rely on the LORD,
    the Holy One of Israel.
²¹A remnant will return,*ᵇ* a remnant of
      Jacob
    will return to the Mighty God.
²²Though your people, O Israel, be like
      the sand by the sea,
    only a remnant will return.
  Destruction has been decreed,
    overwhelming and righteous.
²³The Lord, the LORD Almighty, will
      carry out

ᵃ13 Or / I subdued the mighty,   *ᵇ21 Hebrew*
shear-jashub; also in verse 22

the destruction decreed upon the
whole land.

²⁴Therefore, this is what the Lord, the
LORD Almighty, says:

"O my people who live in Zion,
　do not be afraid of the Assyrians,
who beat you with a rod
　and lift up a club against you, as
　　Egypt did.
²⁵Very soon my anger against you will
　　end
　and my wrath will be directed to
　　their destruction."

²⁶The LORD Almighty will lash them
　　with a whip,
　as when he struck down Midian at
　　the rock of Oreb;
and he will raise his staff over the
　　waters,
　as he did in Egypt.
²⁷In that day their burden will be lifted
　　from your shoulders,
　their yoke from your neck;
the yoke will be broken
　because you have grown so fat.ᵃ

²⁸They enter Aiath;
　they pass through Migron;
　they store supplies at Micmash.
²⁹They go over the pass, and say,
　"We will camp overnight at Geba."
Ramah trembles;
　Gibeah of Saul flees.
³⁰Cry out, O Daughter of Gallim!
　Listen, O Laishah!
　Poor Anathoth!
³¹Madmenah is in flight;
　the people of Gebim take cover.
³²This day they will halt at Nob;
　they will shake their fist
at the mount of the Daughter of
　　Zion,
　at the hill of Jerusalem.

³³See, the Lord, the LORD Almighty,
　will lop off the boughs with great
　　power.
The lofty trees will be felled,
　the tall ones will be brought low.
³⁴He will cut down the forest thickets
　　with an ax;
Lebanon will fall before the Mighty
　　One.

The Branch From Jesse

11 A shoot will come up from the
　stump of Jesse;
　from his roots a Branch will bear
　　fruit.
²The Spirit of the LORD will rest on
　　him—
　the Spirit of wisdom and of
　　understanding,
　the Spirit of counsel and of power,
　the Spirit of knowledge and of the
　　fear of the LORD—
³and he will delight in the fear of the
　　LORD.

He will not judge by what he sees
　with his eyes,
　or decide by what he hears with
　　his ears;
⁴but with righteousness he will judge
　the needy,
　with justice he will give decisions
　　for the poor of the earth.
He will strike the earth with the rod
　of his mouth;
　with the breath of his lips he will
　　slay the wicked.
⁵Righteousness will be his belt
　and faithfulness the sash around
　　his waist.

⁶The wolf will live with the lamb,
　the leopard will lie down with the
　　goat,
the calf and the lion and the
　　yearlingᵇ together;
　and a little child will lead them.
⁷The cow will feed with the bear,
　their young will lie down together,
　and the lion will eat straw like the
　　ox.
⁸The infant will play near the hole of
　　the cobra,
　and the young child put his hand
　　into the viper's nest.
⁹They will neither harm nor destroy
　on all my holy mountain,
for the earth will be full of the
　　knowledge of the LORD
　as the waters cover the sea.

¹⁰In that day the Root of Jesse will
stand as a banner for the peoples; the nations will rally to him, and his place of

ᵃ27 Hebrew; Septuagint *broken / from your shoulders*
ᵇ6 Hebrew; Septuagint *lion will feed*

rest will be glorious. ¹¹In that day the Lord will reach out his hand a second time to reclaim the remnant that is left of his people from Assyria, from Lower Egypt, from Upper Egypt,*ᵃ* from Cush,*ᵇ* from Elam, from Babylonia,*ᶜ* from Hamath and from the islands of the sea.

¹²He will raise a banner for the nations
    and gather the exiles of Israel;
he will assemble the scattered people
        of Judah
    from the four quarters of the earth.
¹³Ephraim's jealousy will vanish,
    and Judah's enemies*ᵈ* will be cut
        off;
Ephraim will not be jealous of Judah,
    nor Judah hostile toward Ephraim.
¹⁴They will swoop down on the slopes
        of Philistia to the west;
together they will plunder the
        people to the east.
They will lay hands on Edom and
        Moab,
    and the Ammonites will be subject
        to them.
¹⁵The Lᴏʀᴅ will dry up
    the gulf of the Egyptian sea;

with a scorching wind he will sweep
        his hand
    over the Euphrates River.*ᵉ*
He will break it up into seven streams
    so that men can cross over in
        sandals.
¹⁶There will be a highway for the
        remnant of his people
    that is left from Assyria,
as there was for Israel
    when they came up from Egypt.

Songs of Praise

12 In that day you will say:

"I will praise you, O Lᴏʀᴅ.
    Although you were angry with me,
your anger has turned away
    and you have comforted me.
²Surely God is my salvation;
    I will trust and not be afraid.
The Lᴏʀᴅ, the Lᴏʀᴅ, is my strength
        and my song;
he has become my salvation."

ᵃ 11 Hebrew *from Pathros*   *ᵇ 11* That is, the upper Nile region   *ᶜ 11* Hebrew *Shinar*
ᵈ 13 Or *hostility*   *ᵉ 15* Hebrew *the River*

Thank You

Friday

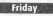

ISAIAH 12:4 Isaiah reminds us, "Give thanks to the Lᴏʀᴅ, call on his name; make known among the nations what he has done." What a great verse to apply to marriage. We hear so much negative news—divorce epidemics, spousal abuse, lonely husbands, lonely wives, dysfunctional homes and so on. Publicizing the positive can be a breath of fresh air in the stale world of reality. So start by thanking God for your spouse, for your children, for your health, for shelter, clothing and food.

During the years we lived in Vienna, Austria, Thanksgiving Day was not a national holiday. We didn't have extended family close by, but we built our own Thanksgiving traditions. To this day stuffed celery and pumpkin pie remind us to be thankful for family and all God has done for us—including our years in Vienna.

One Thanksgiving in Vienna stands out as

a time we realized how good God is. The snow was gently falling, and the trees looked as though they had been sprinkled with powdered sugar. Our friends Jody and Linda Dillow and their children joined us—as well as a pastor from Romania.

In the early 1980s, Christians in Romania experienced persecution and very hard times. Food was scarce. Things we take for granted like plenty of heat, hot water and warm clothes were luxuries to them. Our guest had few worldly possessions and many concerns, but he radiated a spirit of thankfulness. We felt God's presence in a special way on that Thanksgiving.

Pause with us and thank God for all the ways he has blessed you, your marriage and your family. Then tell others.

                        —**Dave & Claudia**

Go to page 747 for your next devotional reading.

³With joy you will draw water
  from the wells of salvation.

⁴In that day you will say:

"Give thanks to the LORD, call on his
      name;
  make known among the nations
      what he has done,
  and proclaim that his name is
      exalted.
⁵Sing to the LORD, for he has done
      glorious things;
  let this be known to all the world.
⁶Shout aloud and sing for joy, people
      of Zion,
  for great is the Holy One of Israel
      among you."

A Prophecy Against Babylon

13 An oracle concerning Babylon that
Isaiah son of Amoz saw:

²Raise a banner on a bare hilltop,
  shout to them;
beckon to them
  to enter the gates of the nobles.
³I have commanded my holy ones;
  I have summoned my warriors to
      carry out my wrath—
  those who rejoice in my triumph.

⁴Listen, a noise on the mountains,
  like that of a great multitude!
Listen, an uproar among the
      kingdoms,
  like nations massing together!
The LORD Almighty is mustering
  an army for war.
⁵They come from faraway lands,
  from the ends of the heavens—
the LORD and the weapons of his
      wrath—
  to destroy the whole country.

⁶Wail, for the day of the LORD is near;
  it will come like destruction from
      the Almighty.ª
⁷Because of this, all hands will go
      limp,
  every man's heart will melt.
⁸Terror will seize them,
  pain and anguish will grip them;
  they will writhe like a woman in
      labor.
They will look aghast at each other,
  their faces aflame.

Just Between you & me

Thank You

Everyone needs encouragement, so take a
few moments and focus on the positive.

1. Think about:
    - The ways God has blessed me
    - The ways God has blessed our
      marriage
    - The ways God has blessed our
      children (if it applies)

2. What do you especially appreciate
    about your spouse? Check those that
    apply and describe:

    ___ Character qualities, such as . . .
    ___ Talents and abilities, such as . . .
    ___ Spiritual gifts, such as . . .
    ___ An endearing quality, such as . . .

3. For the next week, give your mate and
    each child one honest compliment
    each day. Then watch how much they
    appreciate being appreciated.

⁹See, the day of the LORD is coming
  —a cruel day, with wrath and fierce
      anger—
to make the land desolate
  and destroy the sinners within it.
¹⁰The stars of heaven and their
      constellations
  will not show their light.
The rising sun will be darkened
  and the moon will not give its
      light.
¹¹I will punish the world for its evil,
  the wicked for their sins.
I will put an end to the arrogance of
      the haughty
  and will humble the pride of the
      ruthless.
¹²I will make man scarcer than pure
      gold,
  more rare than the gold of Ophir.
¹³Therefore I will make the heavens
      tremble;
  and the earth will shake from its
      place
at the wrath of the LORD Almighty,
  in the day of his burning anger.

ª6 Hebrew *Shaddai*

¹⁴Like a hunted gazelle,
  like sheep without a shepherd,
each will return to his own people,
  each will flee to his native land.
¹⁵Whoever is captured will be thrust
    through;
  all who are caught will fall by the
    sword.
¹⁶Their infants will be dashed to pieces
    before their eyes;
  their houses will be looted and
    their wives ravished.

¹⁷See, I will stir up against them the
    Medes,
  who do not care for silver
  and have no delight in gold.
¹⁸Their bows will strike down the
    young men;
  they will have no mercy on infants
  nor will they look with compassion
    on children.
¹⁹Babylon, the jewel of kingdoms,
  the glory of the Babylonians'ᵃ
    pride,
will be overthrown by God
  like Sodom and Gomorrah.
²⁰She will never be inhabited
  or lived in through all generations;
no Arab will pitch his tent there,
  no shepherd will rest his flocks
    there.
²¹But desert creatures will lie there,
  jackals will fill her houses;
there the owls will dwell,
  and there the wild goats will leap
    about.
²²Hyenas will howl in her strongholds,
  jackals in her luxurious palaces.
Her time is at hand,
  and her days will not be
    prolonged.

14 The LORD will have compassion
  on Jacob;
  once again he will choose Israel
  and will settle them in their own
    land.
Aliens will join them
  and unite with the house of Jacob.
²Nations will take them
  and bring them to their own place.
And the house of Israel will possess
    the nations
  as menservants and maidservants
    in the LORD's land.

They will make captives of their
    captors
  and rule over their oppressors.

³On the day the LORD gives you relief
from suffering and turmoil and cruel
bondage, ⁴you will take up this taunt
against the king of Babylon:

How the oppressor has come to an
    end!
  How his furyᵇ has ended!
⁵The LORD has broken the rod of the
    wicked,
  the scepter of the rulers,
⁶which in anger struck down peoples
  with unceasing blows,
and in fury subdued nations
  with relentless aggression.
⁷All the lands are at rest and at peace;
  they break into singing.
⁸Even the pine trees and the cedars of
    Lebanon
  exult over you and say,
"Now that you have been laid low,
  no woodsman comes to cut us
    down."

⁹The graveᶜ below is all astir
  to meet you at your coming;
it rouses the spirits of the departed to
    greet you—
  all those who were leaders in the
    world;
it makes them rise from their
    thrones—
  all those who were kings over the
    nations.
¹⁰They will all respond,
  they will say to you,
"You also have become weak, as we
    are;
  you have become like us."
¹¹All your pomp has been brought
    down to the grave,
  along with the noise of your harps;
maggots are spread out beneath you
  and worms cover you.

¹²How you have fallen from heaven,
  O morning star, son of the dawn!
You have been cast down to the
    earth,

ᵃ19 Or *Chaldeans'*   ᵇ4 Dead Sea Scrolls,
Septuagint and Syriac; the meaning of the word in
the Masoretic Text is uncertain.   ᶜ9 Hebrew
Sheol; also in verses 11 and 15

you who once laid low the
    nations!
13You said in your heart,
    "I will ascend to heaven;
I will raise my throne
    above the stars of God;
I will sit enthroned on the mount of
    assembly,
    on the utmost heights of the sacred
      mountain. *a*
14I will ascend above the tops of the
    clouds;
I will make myself like the Most
    High."
15But you are brought down to the
    grave,
    to the depths of the pit.

16Those who see you stare at you,
    they ponder your fate:
"Is this the man who shook the earth
    and made kingdoms tremble,
17the man who made the world a
    desert,
    who overthrew its cities
    and would not let his captives go
      home?"
18All the kings of the nations lie in
    state,
    each in his own tomb.
19But you are cast out of your tomb
    like a rejected branch;
you are covered with the slain,
    with those pierced by the sword,
    those who descend to the stones of
      the pit.
Like a corpse trampled underfoot,
20   you will not join them in burial,
for you have destroyed your land
    and killed your people.

The offspring of the wicked
    will never be mentioned again.
21Prepare a place to slaughter his sons
    for the sins of their forefathers;
they are not to rise to inherit the land
    and cover the earth with their
      cities.

22"I will rise up against them,"
    declares the LORD Almighty.
"I will cut off from Babylon her
    name and survivors,
    her offspring and descendants,"
        declares the LORD.
23"I will turn her into a place for owls

and into swampland;
I will sweep her with the broom of
    destruction,"
    declares the LORD Almighty.

A Prophecy Against Assyria

24The LORD Almighty has sworn,

"Surely, as I have planned, so it will
    be,
    and as I have purposed, so it will
      stand.
25I will crush the Assyrian in my land;
    on my mountains I will trample
      him down.
His yoke will be taken from my
    people,
    and his burden removed from their
      shoulders."

26This is the plan determined for the
    whole world;
    this is the hand stretched out over
      all nations.
27For the LORD Almighty has purposed,
    and who can thwart him?
    His hand is stretched out, and who
      can turn it back?

A Prophecy Against the Philistines

28This oracle came in the year King
Ahaz died:

29Do not rejoice, all you Philistines,
    that the rod that struck you is
      broken;
from the root of that snake will
      spring up a viper,
    its fruit will be a darting,
      venomous serpent.
30The poorest of the poor will find
    pasture,
    and the needy will lie down in
      safety.
But your root I will destroy by
    famine;
    it will slay your survivors.

31Wail, O gate! Howl, O city!
    Melt away, all you Philistines!
A cloud of smoke comes from the
    north,
    and there is not a straggler in its
      ranks.
32What answer shall be given

a13 Or *the north;* Hebrew *Zaphon*

to the envoys of that nation?
"The LORD has established Zion,
    and in her his afflicted people will
        find refuge."

A Prophecy Against Moab

15 An oracle concerning Moab:

Ar in Moab is ruined,
    destroyed in a night!
Kir in Moab is ruined,
    destroyed in a night!
[2]Dibon goes up to its temple,
    to its high places to weep;
Moab wails over Nebo and
        Medeba.
Every head is shaved
    and every beard cut off.
[3]In the streets they wear sackcloth;
    on the roofs and in the public
        squares
they all wail,
    prostrate with weeping.
[4]Heshbon and Elealeh cry out,
    their voices are heard all the way
        to Jahaz.
Therefore the armed men of Moab cry
        out,
    and their hearts are faint.

[5]My heart cries out over Moab;
    her fugitives flee as far as Zoar,
    as far as Eglath Shelishiyah.
They go up the way to Luhith,
    weeping as they go;
on the road to Horonaim
    they lament their destruction.
[6]The waters of Nimrim are dried up
    and the grass is withered;
the vegetation is gone
    and nothing green is left.
[7]So the wealth they have acquired and
        stored up
    they carry away over the Ravine of
        the Poplars.
[8]Their outcry echoes along the border
        of Moab;
    their wailing reaches as far as
        Eglaim,
    their lamentation as far as Beer
        Elim.
[9]Dimon's[a] waters are full of blood,
    but I will bring still more upon
        Dimon[a]—
a lion upon the fugitives of Moab

and upon those who remain in the
        land.

16 Send lambs as tribute
    to the ruler of the land,
from Sela, across the desert,
    to the mount of the Daughter of
        Zion.
[2]Like fluttering birds
    pushed from the nest,
so are the women of Moab
    at the fords of the Arnon.

[3]"Give us counsel,
    render a decision.
Make your shadow like night—
    at high noon.
Hide the fugitives,
    do not betray the refugees.
[4]Let the Moabite fugitives stay with
        you;
    be their shelter from the destroyer."

The oppressor will come to an end,
    and destruction will cease;
    the aggressor will vanish from the
        land.
[5]In love a throne will be established;
    in faithfulness a man will sit on
        it—
    one from the house[b] of David—
one who in judging seeks justice
    and speeds the cause of
        righteousness.

[6]We have heard of Moab's pride—
    her overweening pride and conceit,
her pride and her insolence—
    but her boasts are empty.
[7]Therefore the Moabites wail,
    they wail together for Moab.
Lament and grieve
    for the men[c] of Kir Hareseth.
[8]The fields of Heshbon wither,
    the vines of Sibmah also.
The rulers of the nations
    have trampled down the choicest
        vines,
which once reached Jazer
    and spread toward the desert.
Their shoots spread out
    and went as far as the sea.
[9]So I weep, as Jazer weeps,
    for the vines of Sibmah.

---

a9 Masoretic Text; Dead Sea Scrolls, some
Septuagint manuscripts and Vulgate *Dibon*
b5 Hebrew *tent*   *c7* Or *"raisin cakes,"* a wordplay

O Heshbon, O Elealeh,
  I drench you with tears!
The shouts of joy over your ripened
    fruit
  and over your harvests have been
    stilled.
¹⁰Joy and gladness are taken away from
    the orchards;
  no one sings or shouts in the
    vineyards;
  no one treads out wine at the presses,
  for I have put an end to the
    shouting.
¹¹My heart laments for Moab like a
    harp,
  my inmost being for Kir Hareseth.
¹²When Moab appears at her high
    place,
  she only wears herself out;
  when she goes to her shrine to pray,
    it is to no avail.

¹³This is the word the LORD has already spoken concerning Moab. ¹⁴But now the LORD says: "Within three years, as a servant bound by contract would count them, Moab's splendor and all her many people will be despised, and her survivors will be very few and feeble."

An Oracle Against Damascus

17 An oracle concerning Damascus:

"See, Damascus will no longer be a
    city
  but will become a heap of ruins.
²The cities of Aroer will be deserted
  and left to flocks, which will lie
    down,
  with no one to make them afraid.
³The fortified city will disappear from
    Ephraim,
  and royal power from Damascus;
  the remnant of Aram will be
  like the glory of the Israelites,"
      declares the LORD Almighty.

⁴"In that day the glory of Jacob will
    fade;
  the fat of his body will waste away.
⁵It will be as when a reaper gathers the
    standing grain
  and harvests the grain with his
    arm—
as when a man gleans heads of grain
  in the Valley of Rephaim.

⁶Yet some gleanings will remain,
  as when an olive tree is beaten,
leaving two or three olives on the
    topmost branches,
  four or five on the fruitful boughs,"
      declares the LORD, the God
          of Israel.

⁷In that day men will look to their
    Maker
  and turn their eyes to the Holy
    One of Israel.
⁸They will not look to the altars,
    the work of their hands,
  and they will have no regard for the
    Asherah poles[a]
  and the incense altars their fingers
    have made.

⁹In that day their strong cities, which they left because of the Israelites, will be like places abandoned to thickets and undergrowth. And all will be desolation.

¹⁰You have forgotten God your Savior;
  you have not remembered the
    Rock, your fortress.
Therefore, though you set out the
    finest plants
  and plant imported vines,
¹¹though on the day you set them out,
    you make them grow,
  and on the morning when you
    plant them, you bring them
      to bud,
yet the harvest will be as nothing
  in the day of disease and incurable
    pain.

¹²Oh, the raging of many nations—
  they rage like the raging sea!
Oh, the uproar of the peoples—
  they roar like the roaring of great
    waters!
¹³Although the peoples roar like the
    roar of surging waters,
  when he rebukes them they flee far
    away,
driven before the wind like chaff on
    the hills,
  like tumbleweed before a gale.
¹⁴In the evening, sudden terror!
  Before the morning, they are gone!
This is the portion of those who loot
    us,
  the lot of those who plunder us.

---

a8 That is, symbols of the goddess Asherah

A Prophecy Against Cush

18 Woe to the land of whirring
        wings[a]
    along the rivers of Cush,[b]
²which sends envoys by sea
    in papyrus boats over the water.

Go, swift messengers,
to a people tall and smooth-skinned,
    to a people feared far and wide,
an aggressive nation of strange
        speech,
    whose land is divided by rivers.

³All you people of the world,
    you who live on the earth,
when a banner is raised on the
        mountains,
    you will see it,
and when a trumpet sounds,
    you will hear it.
⁴This is what the LORD says to me:
    "I will remain quiet and will look
        on from my dwelling place,
like shimmering heat in the sunshine,
    like a cloud of dew in the heat of
        harvest."
⁵For, before the harvest, when the
        blossom is gone
    and the flower becomes a ripening
        grape,
he will cut off the shoots with
        pruning knives,
    and cut down and take away the
        spreading branches.
⁶They will all be left to the mountain
        birds of prey
    and to the wild animals;
the birds will feed on them all
        summer,
    the wild animals all winter.

⁷At that time gifts will be brought to
the LORD Almighty

from a people tall and
        smooth-skinned,
    from a people feared far and wide,
an aggressive nation of strange
        speech,
    whose land is divided by rivers—

the gifts will be brought to Mount Zion,
the place of the Name of the LORD Almighty.

A Prophecy About Egypt

19 An oracle concerning Egypt:

See, the LORD rides on a swift cloud
    and is coming to Egypt.
The idols of Egypt tremble before
        him,
    and the hearts of the Egyptians
        melt within them.

²"I will stir up Egyptian against
        Egyptian—
    brother will fight against brother,
    neighbor against neighbor,
    city against city,
    kingdom against kingdom.
³The Egyptians will lose heart,
    and I will bring their plans to
        nothing;
they will consult the idols and the
        spirits of the dead,
    the mediums and the spiritists.
⁴I will hand the Egyptians over
    to the power of a cruel master,
and a fierce king will rule over them,"
    declares the Lord, the LORD
        Almighty.

⁵The waters of the river will dry up,
    and the riverbed will be parched
        and dry.
⁶The canals will stink;
    the streams of Egypt will dwindle
        and dry up.
The reeds and rushes will wither,
⁷   also the plants along the Nile,
    at the mouth of the river.
Every sown field along the Nile
    will become parched, will blow
        away and be no more.
⁸The fishermen will groan and lament,
    all who cast hooks into the Nile;
those who throw nets on the water
    will pine away.
⁹Those who work with combed flax
        will despair,
    the weavers of fine linen will lose
        hope.
¹⁰The workers in cloth will be dejected,
    and all the wage earners will be
        sick at heart.

¹¹The officials of Zoan are nothing but
        fools;

a1 Or *of locusts*   b1 That is, the upper Nile
region

the wise counselors of Pharaoh
  give senseless advice.
How can you say to Pharaoh,
  "I am one of the wise men,
  a disciple of the ancient kings"?

¹²Where are your wise men now?
  Let them show you and make
    known
  what the LORD Almighty
    has planned against Egypt.
¹³The officials of Zoan have become
    fools,
  the leaders of Memphis*a* are
    deceived;
  the cornerstones of her peoples
    have led Egypt astray.
¹⁴The LORD has poured into them
    a spirit of dizziness;
  they make Egypt stagger in all that
    she does,
  as a drunkard staggers around in
    his vomit.
¹⁵There is nothing Egypt can do—
  head or tail, palm branch or reed.

¹⁶In that day the Egyptians will be like women. They will shudder with fear at the uplifted hand that the LORD Almighty raises against them. ¹⁷And the land of Judah will bring terror to the Egyptians; everyone to whom Judah is mentioned will be terrified, because of what the LORD Almighty is planning against them.

¹⁸In that day five cities in Egypt will speak the language of Canaan and swear allegiance to the LORD Almighty. One of them will be called the City of Destruction.*b*

¹⁹In that day there will be an altar to the LORD in the heart of Egypt, and a monument to the LORD at its border. ²⁰It will be a sign and witness to the LORD Almighty in the land of Egypt. When they cry out to the LORD because of their oppressors, he will send them a savior and defender, and he will rescue them. ²¹So the LORD will make himself known to the Egyptians, and in that day they will acknowledge the LORD. They will worship with sacrifices and grain offerings; they will make vows to the LORD and keep them. ²²The LORD will strike Egypt with a plague; he will strike them and heal them. They will turn to the LORD, and he will respond to their pleas and heal them.

²³In that day there will be a highway from Egypt to Assyria. The Assyrians will go to Egypt and the Egyptians to Assyria. The Egyptians and Assyrians will worship together. ²⁴In that day Israel will be the third, along with Egypt and Assyria, a blessing on the earth. ²⁵The LORD Almighty will bless them, saying, "Blessed be Egypt my people, Assyria my handiwork, and Israel my inheritance."

A Prophecy Against Egypt and Cush

20 In the year that the supreme commander, sent by Sargon king of Assyria, came to Ashdod and attacked and captured it— ²at that time the LORD spoke through Isaiah son of Amoz. He said to him, "Take off the sackcloth from your body and the sandals from your feet." And he did so, going around stripped and barefoot.

³Then the LORD said, "Just as my servant Isaiah has gone stripped and barefoot for three years, as a sign and portent against Egypt and Cush,*c* ⁴so the king of Assyria will lead away stripped and barefoot the Egyptian captives and Cushite exiles, young and old, with buttocks bared—to Egypt's shame. ⁵Those who trusted in Cush and boasted in Egypt will be afraid and put to shame. ⁶In that day the people who live on this coast will say, 'See what has happened to those we relied on, those we fled to for help and deliverance from the king of Assyria! How then can we escape?' "

A Prophecy Against Babylon

21 An oracle concerning the Desert by the Sea:

Like whirlwinds sweeping through the
    southland,
  an invader comes from the desert,
    from a land of terror.

²A dire vision has been shown to me:
  The traitor betrays, the looter takes
    loot.
Elam, attack! Media, lay siege!
  I will bring to an end all the
    groaning she caused.

---

a13 Hebrew *Noph*   *b18* Most manuscripts of the Masoretic Text; some manuscripts of the Masoretic Text, Dead Sea Scrolls and Vulgate *City of the Sun* (that is, Heliopolis)   *c3* That is, the upper Nile region; also in verse 5

³At this my body is racked with pain,
    pangs seize me, like those of a
        woman in labor;
I am staggered by what I hear,
    I am bewildered by what I see.
⁴My heart falters,
    fear makes me tremble;
the twilight I longed for
    has become a horror to me.

⁵They set the tables,
    they spread the rugs,
    they eat, they drink!
Get up, you officers,
    oil the shields!

⁶This is what the Lord says to me:

"Go, post a lookout
    and have him report what he sees.
⁷When he sees chariots
    with teams of horses,
riders on donkeys
    or riders on camels,
let him be alert,
    fully alert."

⁸And the lookout*ᵃ* shouted,

"Day after day, my lord, I stand on
      the watchtower;
every night I stay at my post.
⁹Look, here comes a man in a chariot
    with a team of horses.
And he gives back the answer:
    'Babylon has fallen, has fallen!
All the images of its gods
    lie shattered on the ground!' "

¹⁰O my people, crushed on the
      threshing floor,
    I tell you what I have heard
from the Lord Almighty,
    from the God of Israel.

A Prophecy Against Edom

¹¹An oracle concerning Dumah*ᵇ*:

Someone calls to me from Seir,
    "Watchman, what is left of the
      night?
Watchman, what is left of the
      night?"
¹²The watchman replies,
    "Morning is coming, but also the
      night.
If you would ask, then ask;
    and come back yet again."

A Prophecy Against Arabia

¹³An oracle concerning Arabia:

You caravans of Dedanites,
    who camp in the thickets of
      Arabia,
¹⁴   bring water for the thirsty;
you who live in Tema,
    bring food for the fugitives.
¹⁵They flee from the sword,
    from the drawn sword,
from the bent bow
    and from the heat of battle.

¹⁶This is what the Lord says to me:
"Within one year, as a servant bound by
contract would count it, all the pomp of
Kedar will come to an end. ¹⁷The survivors of the bowmen, the warriors of Kedar, will be few." The Lord, the God of
Israel, has spoken.

A Prophecy About Jerusalem

22 An oracle concerning the Valley of
Vision:

What troubles you now,
    that you have all gone up on the
      roofs,
²O town full of commotion,
    O city of tumult and revelry?
Your slain were not killed by the
      sword,
    nor did they die in battle.
³All your leaders have fled together;
    they have been captured without
      using the bow.
All you who were caught were taken
      prisoner together,
    having fled while the enemy was
      still far away.
⁴Therefore I said, "Turn away from
      me;
    let me weep bitterly.
Do not try to console me
    over the destruction of my people."

⁵The Lord, the Lord Almighty, has a
      day
of tumult and trampling and terror
    in the Valley of Vision,
a day of battering down walls
    and of crying out to the
      mountains.

ᵃ8 Dead Sea Scrolls and Syriac; Masoretic Text *A
lion*   *ᵇ11 Dumah* means *silence* or *stillness*, a
wordplay on *Edom*.

⁶Elam takes up the quiver,
  with her charioteers and horses;
  Kir uncovers the shield.
⁷Your choicest valleys are full of
    chariots,
  and horsemen are posted at the
    city gates;
⁸ the defenses of Judah are stripped
    away.

And you looked in that day
  to the weapons in the Palace of the
    Forest;
⁹you saw that the City of David
  had many breaches in its defenses;
you stored up water
  in the Lower Pool.
¹⁰You counted the buildings in
    Jerusalem
  and tore down houses to
    strengthen the wall.
¹¹You built a reservoir between the two
    walls
  for the water of the Old Pool,
but you did not look to the One who
    made it,
  or have regard for the One who
    planned it long ago.

¹²The Lord, the LORD Almighty,
  called you on that day
to weep and to wail,
  to tear out your hair and put on
    sackcloth.
¹³But see, there is joy and revelry,
  slaughtering of cattle and killing of
    sheep,
  eating of meat and drinking of
    wine!
"Let us eat and drink," you say,
  "for tomorrow we die!"

¹⁴The LORD Almighty has revealed this
in my hearing: "Till your dying day this
sin will not be atoned for," says the Lord,
the LORD Almighty.

¹⁵This is what the Lord, the LORD Almighty, says:

"Go, say to this steward,
  to Shebna, who is in charge of the
    palace:
¹⁶What are you doing here and who
    gave you permission
  to cut out a grave for yourself here,
hewing your grave on the height

and chiseling your resting place in
    the rock?

¹⁷"Beware, the LORD is about to take
    firm hold of you
  and hurl you away, O you mighty
    man.
¹⁸He will roll you up tightly like a ball
  and throw you into a large country.
There you will die
  and there your splendid chariots
    will remain—
  you disgrace to your master's
    house!
¹⁹I will depose you from your office,
  and you will be ousted from your
    position.

²⁰"In that day I will summon my servant, Eliakim son of Hilkiah. ²¹I will clothe him with your robe and fasten your sash around him and hand your authority over to him. He will be a father to those who live in Jerusalem and to the house of Judah. ²²I will place on his shoulder the key to the house of David; what he opens no one can shut, and what he shuts no one can open. ²³I will drive him like a peg into a firm place; he will be a seat*a* of honor for the house of his father. ²⁴All the glory of his family will hang on him: its offspring and offshoots—all its lesser vessels, from the bowls to all the jars.

²⁵"In that day," declares the LORD Almighty, "the peg driven into the firm place will give way; it will be sheared off and will fall, and the load hanging on it will be cut down." The LORD has spoken.

A Prophecy About Tyre

23 An oracle concerning Tyre:

Wail, O ships of Tarshish!
  For Tyre is destroyed
  and left without house or harbor.
From the land of Cyprus*b*
  word has come to them.

²Be silent, you people of the island
  and you merchants of Sidon,
  whom the seafarers have enriched.
³On the great waters
  came the grain of the Shihor;

a23 Or *throne*   *b1* Hebrew *Kittim*

the harvest of the Nile[a] was the
revenue of Tyre,
and she became the marketplace of
the nations.

[4] Be ashamed, O Sidon, and you,
O fortress of the sea,
for the sea has spoken:
"I have neither been in labor nor
given birth;
I have neither reared sons nor
brought up daughters."
[5] When word comes to Egypt,
they will be in anguish at the
report from Tyre.

[6] Cross over to Tarshish;
wail, you people of the island.
[7] Is this your city of revelry,
the old, old city,
whose feet have taken her
to settle in far-off lands?
[8] Who planned this against Tyre,
the bestower of crowns,
whose merchants are princes,
whose traders are renowned in the
earth?
[9] The LORD Almighty planned it,
to bring low the pride of all glory
and to humble all who are
renowned on the earth.

[10] Till[b] your land as along the Nile,
O Daughter of Tarshish,
for you no longer have a harbor.
[11] The LORD has stretched out his hand
over the sea
and made its kingdoms tremble.
He has given an order concerning
Phoenicia[c]
that her fortresses be destroyed.
[12] He said, "No more of your reveling,
O Virgin Daughter of Sidon, now
crushed!

"Up, cross over to Cyprus[d];
even there you will find no rest."
[13] Look at the land of the
Babylonians,[e]
this people that is now of no
account!
The Assyrians have made it
a place for desert creatures;
they raised up their siege towers,
they stripped its fortresses bare
and turned it into a ruin.

[14] Wail, you ships of Tarshish;
your fortress is destroyed!

[15] At that time Tyre will be forgotten for
seventy years, the span of a king's life. But
at the end of these seventy years, it will
happen to Tyre as in the song of the prostitute:

[16] "Take up a harp, walk through the
city,
O prostitute forgotten;
play the harp well, sing many a song,
so that you will be remembered."

[17] At the end of seventy years, the LORD
will deal with Tyre. She will return to her
hire as a prostitute and will ply her trade
with all the kingdoms on the face of the
earth. [18] Yet her profit and her earnings
will be set apart for the LORD; they will
not be stored up or hoarded. Her profits
will go to those who live before the LORD,
for abundant food and fine clothes.

The LORD's Devastation of the Earth

24 See, the LORD is going to lay
waste the earth
and devastate it;
he will ruin its face
and scatter its inhabitants—
[2] it will be the same
for priest as for people,
for master as for servant,
for mistress as for maid,
for seller as for buyer,
for borrower as for lender,
for debtor as for creditor.
[3] The earth will be completely laid
waste
and totally plundered.
The LORD has spoken
this word.

[4] The earth dries up and withers,
the world languishes and withers,
the exalted of the earth languish.
[5] The earth is defiled by its people;
they have disobeyed the laws,
violated the statutes

---

[a] 2,3 Masoretic Text; one Dead Sea Scroll *Sidon, /
who cross over the sea; / your envoys* [3] *are on the great
waters. / The grain of the Shihor, / the harvest of the
Nile,*   [b] 10 Dead Sea Scrolls and some
Septuagint manuscripts; Masoretic Text *Go through*
[c] 11 Hebrew *Canaan*   [d] 12 Hebrew *Kittim*
[e] 13 Or *Chaldeans*

and broken the everlasting
covenant.
⁶Therefore a curse consumes the earth;
its people must bear their guilt.
Therefore earth's inhabitants are
burned up,
and very few are left.
⁷The new wine dries up and the vine
withers;
all the merrymakers groan.
⁸The gaiety of the tambourines is
stilled,
the noise of the revelers has
stopped,
the joyful harp is silent.
⁹No longer do they drink wine with a
song;
the beer is bitter to its drinkers.
¹⁰The ruined city lies desolate;
the entrance to every house is
barred.
¹¹In the streets they cry out for wine;
all joy turns to gloom,
all gaiety is banished from the
earth.
¹²The city is left in ruins,
its gate is battered to pieces.
¹³So will it be on the earth
and among the nations,
as when an olive tree is beaten,
or as when gleanings are left after
the grape harvest.

¹⁴They raise their voices, they shout for
joy;
from the west they acclaim the
LORD's majesty.
¹⁵Therefore in the east give glory to the
LORD;
exalt the name of the LORD, the
God of Israel,
in the islands of the sea.
¹⁶From the ends of the earth we hear
singing:
"Glory to the Righteous One."

But I said, "I waste away, I waste
away!
Woe to me!
The treacherous betray!
With treachery the treacherous
betray!"
¹⁷Terror and pit and snare await you,
O people of the earth.
¹⁸Whoever flees at the sound of terror
will fall into a pit;

whoever climbs out of the pit
will be caught in a snare.

The floodgates of the heavens are
opened,
the foundations of the earth shake.
¹⁹The earth is broken up,
the earth is split asunder,
the earth is thoroughly shaken.
²⁰The earth reels like a drunkard,
it sways like a hut in the wind;
so heavy upon it is the guilt of its
rebellion
that it falls—never to rise again.

²¹In that day the LORD will punish
the powers in the heavens above
and the kings on the earth below.
²²They will be herded together
like prisoners bound in a dungeon;
they will be shut up in prison
and be punished[a] after many
days.
²³The moon will be abashed, the sun
ashamed;
for the LORD Almighty will reign
on Mount Zion and in Jerusalem,
and before its elders, gloriously.

Praise to the LORD

25 O LORD, you are my God;
I will exalt you and praise your
name,
for in perfect faithfulness
you have done marvelous things,
things planned long ago.
²You have made the city a heap of
rubble,
the fortified town a ruin,
the foreigners' stronghold a city no
more;
it will never be rebuilt.
³Therefore strong peoples will honor
you;
cities of ruthless nations will revere
you.
⁴You have been a refuge for the poor,
a refuge for the needy in his
distress,
a shelter from the storm
and a shade from the heat.
For the breath of the ruthless
is like a storm driving against a
wall
⁵ and like the heat of the desert.

a22 Or *released*

You silence the uproar of foreigners;
  as heat is reduced by the shadow
    of a cloud,
  so the song of the ruthless is
    stilled.
6On this mountain the LORD Almighty
    will prepare
  a feast of rich food for all peoples,
a banquet of aged wine—
  the best of meats and the finest of
    wines.
7On this mountain he will destroy
  the shroud that enfolds all peoples,
the sheet that covers all nations;
8   he will swallow up death forever.
The Sovereign LORD will wipe away
    the tears
  from all faces;
he will remove the disgrace of his
    people
  from all the earth.
          The LORD has spoken.

9In that day they will say,

"Surely this is our God;
  we trusted in him, and he saved
    us.
This is the LORD, we trusted in him;
  let us rejoice and be glad in his
    salvation."

10The hand of the LORD will rest on
    this mountain;
  but Moab will be trampled under
    him
  as straw is trampled down in the
    manure.
11They will spread out their hands in it,
  as a swimmer spreads out his
    hands to swim.
God will bring down their pride
  despite the cleverness*a* of their
    hands.
12He will bring down your high
    fortified walls
  and lay them low;
he will bring them down to the
    ground,
  to the very dust.

A Song of Praise

26 In that day this song will be sung in
the land of Judah:

We have a strong city;
  God makes salvation

its walls and ramparts.
2Open the gates
  that the righteous nation may
    enter,
  the nation that keeps faith.
3You will keep in perfect peace
  him whose mind is steadfast,
  because he trusts in you.
4Trust in the LORD forever,
  for the LORD, the LORD, is the Rock
    eternal.
5He humbles those who dwell on
    high,
  he lays the lofty city low;
he levels it to the ground
  and casts it down to the dust.
6Feet trample it down—
  the feet of the oppressed,
  the footsteps of the poor.

7The path of the righteous is level;
  O upright One, you make the way
    of the righteous smooth.
8Yes, LORD, walking in the way of your
    laws,*b*
  we wait for you;
your name and renown
  are the desire of our hearts.
9My soul yearns for you in the night;
  in the morning my spirit longs for
    you.
When your judgments come upon the
    earth,
  the people of the world learn
    righteousness.
10Though grace is shown to the wicked,
  they do not learn righteousness;
even in a land of uprightness they go
    on doing evil
  and regard not the majesty of the
    LORD.
11O LORD, your hand is lifted high,
  but they do not see it.
Let them see your zeal for your
    people and be put to shame;
  let the fire reserved for your
    enemies consume them.

12LORD, you establish peace for us;
  all that we have accomplished you
    have done for us.
13O LORD, our God, other lords besides
    you have ruled over us,

---

a 11 The meaning of the Hebrew for this word is
uncertain.   *b 8* Or *judgments*

but your name alone do we honor.
¹⁴They are now dead, they live no
    more;
   those departed spirits do not
       rise.
You punished them and brought
       them to ruin;
   you wiped out all memory of
       them.
¹⁵You have enlarged the nation,
       O Lord;
   you have enlarged the nation.
You have gained glory for yourself;
   you have extended all the borders
       of the land.

¹⁶Lord, they came to you in their
       distress;
   when you disciplined them,
   they could barely whisper a
       prayer.ᵃ
¹⁷As a woman with child and about to
       give birth
   writhes and cries out in her pain,
   so were we in your presence,
       O Lord.

¹⁸We were with child, we writhed in
       pain,
   but we gave birth to wind.
We have not brought salvation to the
       earth;
   we have not given birth to people
       of the world.

¹⁹But your dead will live;
   their bodies will rise.
You who dwell in the dust,
   wake up and shout for joy.
Your dew is like the dew of the
       morning;
   the earth will give birth to her
       dead.

²⁰Go, my people, enter your rooms
   and shut the doors behind you;
hide yourselves for a little while
   until his wrath has passed by.
²¹See, the Lord is coming out of his
       dwelling

ᵃ16 The meaning of the Hebrew for this clause is
uncertain.

Finding Perfect Peace

ISAIAH 26:3 As we write this devotional, we are bouncing around on an airplane in the middle of a storm somewhere between Louisville, Kentucky, and Atlanta, Georgia. Are we experiencing "perfect peace?" Not exactly!

Peace isn't something you crank out whenever you need it. God is the One who gives peace in difficult or turbulent times. Our part involves focusing on him with our mind and willingly choosing to trust him.

Isaiah 26:3, a great marriage and family verse, can be a soothing salve for chaotic times like when the skies are stormy, kids are fighting, the baby is crying or your spouse just called to say she'll be late for dinner—or a combination of all three.

Sometimes it takes a little "turbulence" to help us realize that God ultimately is the source of our peace. For instance, Sue and Daryl were arguing about which TV show to watch when the power suddenly went out. They both realized how pointless this argument had been, and the sudden silence was almost deafening. With no TV they began to talk about their relationship. They ended up enjoying the peace and quiet and decided in the future to limit their TV viewing and spend more time talking.

During times when we begin to worry or fret, we need to step back for a moment and focus on God and place our trust in him; we need to realize that he is the peace giver, not our spouse, our children or our circumstances. In the chaos of life, we can experience his perfect peace.

—*Dave & Claudia*

Quiet TIMES with each other

Weekend Warm-up *How do you deal with your moments of chaos?*

Go to page 755 for your next devotional reading.

to punish the people of the earth
    for their sins.
The earth will disclose the blood shed
    upon her;
    she will conceal her slain no
        longer.

Deliverance of Israel

27 In that day,

the LORD will punish with his sword,
    his fierce, great and powerful
        sword,
Leviathan the gliding serpent,
    Leviathan the coiling serpent;
he will slay the monster of the sea.

    2In that day—

"Sing about a fruitful vineyard:
3   I, the LORD, watch over it;
    I water it continually.
I guard it day and night
    so that no one may harm it.
4   I am not angry.
If only there were briers and thorns
    confronting me!
    I would march against them in
        battle;
    I would set them all on fire.
5Or else let them come to me for
    refuge;
    let them make peace with me,
    yes, let them make peace with me."

6In days to come Jacob will take root,
    Israel will bud and blossom
    and fill all the world with fruit.

7Has ⌊the LORD⌋ struck her
    as he struck down those who
        struck her?
Has she been killed
    as those were killed who killed
        her?
8By warfare[a] and exile you contend
    with her—
    with his fierce blast he drives her
        out,
    as on a day the east wind blows.
9By this, then, will Jacob's guilt be
    atoned for,
    and this will be the full fruitage of
        the removal of his sin:
When he makes all the altar stones
    to be like chalk stones crushed to
        pieces,

no Asherah poles[b] or incense altars
    will be left standing.
10The fortified city stands desolate,
    an abandoned settlement, forsaken
        like the desert;
there the calves graze,
    there they lie down;
    they strip its branches bare.
11When its twigs are dry, they are
        broken off
    and women come and make fires
        with them.
For this is a people without
    understanding;
    so their Maker has no compassion
        on them,
    and their Creator shows them no
        favor.

12In that day the LORD will thresh from
the flowing Euphrates[c] to the Wadi of
Egypt, and you, O Israelites, will be gathered up one by one. 13And in that day a
great trumpet will sound. Those who were
perishing in Assyria and those who were
exiled in Egypt will come and worship the
LORD on the holy mountain in Jerusalem.

Woe to Ephraim

28 Woe to that wreath, the pride of
       Ephraim's drunkards,
    to the fading flower, his glorious
        beauty,
set on the head of a fertile valley—
    to that city, the pride of those laid
        low by wine!
2See, the Lord has one who is
    powerful and strong.
    Like a hailstorm and a destructive
        wind,
like a driving rain and a flooding
    downpour,
    he will throw it forcefully to the
        ground.
3That wreath, the pride of Ephraim's
    drunkards,
    will be trampled underfoot.
4That fading flower, his glorious
    beauty,
    set on the head of a fertile valley,
will be like a fig ripe before harvest—

a8 See Septuagint; the meaning of the Hebrew for
this word is uncertain.   b9 That is, symbols of
the goddess Asherah   c12 Hebrew *River*

as soon as someone sees it and
  takes it in his hand,
  he swallows it.

⁵In that day the LORD Almighty
  will be a glorious crown,
a beautiful wreath
  for the remnant of his people.
⁶He will be a spirit of justice
  to him who sits in judgment,
a source of strength
  to those who turn back the battle
    at the gate.

⁷And these also stagger from wine
  and reel from beer:
Priests and prophets stagger from beer
  and are befuddled with wine;
they reel from beer,
  they stagger when seeing visions,
  they stumble when rendering
    decisions.
⁸All the tables are covered with vomit
  and there is not a spot without
    filth.

⁹"Who is it he is trying to teach?
  To whom is he explaining his
    message?
To children weaned from their milk,
  to those just taken from the breast?
¹⁰For it is:
  Do and do, do and do,
  rule on rule, rule on rule*ᵃ*;
  a little here, a little there."

¹¹Very well then, with foreign lips and
    strange tongues
  God will speak to this people,
¹²to whom he said,
  "This is the resting place, let the
    weary rest";
and, "This is the place of repose" —
  but they would not listen.
¹³So then, the word of the LORD to
    them will become:
  Do and do, do and do,
  rule on rule, rule on rule;
  a little here, a little there —
so that they will go and fall
    backward,
  be injured and snared and
    captured.

¹⁴Therefore hear the word of the LORD,
  you scoffers
  who rule this people in Jerusalem.

¹⁵You boast, "We have entered into a
    covenant with death,
  with the grave*ᵇ* we have made an
    agreement.
When an overwhelming scourge
    sweeps by,
  it cannot touch us,
for we have made a lie our refuge
  and falsehood*ᶜ* our hiding place."

¹⁶So this is what the Sovereign LORD
says:

"See, I lay a stone in Zion,
  a tested stone,
a precious cornerstone for a sure
    foundation;
  the one who trusts will never be
    dismayed.
¹⁷I will make justice the measuring line
  and righteousness the plumb line;
hail will sweep away your refuge, the
    lie,
  and water will overflow your
    hiding place.
¹⁸Your covenant with death will be
    annulled;
  your agreement with the grave will
    not stand.
When the overwhelming scourge
    sweeps by,
  you will be beaten down by it.
¹⁹As often as it comes it will carry you
    away;
  morning after morning, by day and
    by night,
  it will sweep through."

The understanding of this message
  will bring sheer terror.
²⁰The bed is too short to stretch out
    on,
  the blanket too narrow to wrap
    around you.
²¹The LORD will rise up as he did at
    Mount Perazim,
  he will rouse himself as in the
    Valley of Gibeon —
to do his work, his strange work,
  and perform his task, his alien
    task.
²²Now stop your mocking,

ᵃ10 Hebrew / sav lasav sav lasav / kav lakav kav
lakav (possibly meaningless sounds; perhaps a
mimicking of the prophet's words); also in
verse 13   ᵇ15 Hebrew Sheol; also in verse 18
ᶜ15 Or false gods

or your chains will become heavier;
the Lord, the LORD Almighty, has told
    me
of the destruction decreed against
    the whole land.

²³Listen and hear my voice;
    pay attention and hear what I say.
²⁴When a farmer plows for planting,
    does he plow continually?
Does he keep on breaking up and
    harrowing the soil?
²⁵When he has leveled the surface,
    does he not sow caraway and
        scatter cummin?
Does he not plant wheat in its
        place,ᵃ
    barley in its plot,ᵃ
    and spelt in its field?
²⁶His God instructs him
    and teaches him the right way.

²⁷Caraway is not threshed with a
        sledge,
    nor is a cartwheel rolled over
        cummin;
caraway is beaten out with a rod,
    and cummin with a stick.
²⁸Grain must be ground to make bread;
    so one does not go on threshing it
        forever.
Though he drives the wheels of his
        threshing cart over it,
    his horses do not grind it.
²⁹All this also comes from the LORD
        Almighty,
    wonderful in counsel and
        magnificent in wisdom.

Woe to David's City

29 Woe to you, Ariel, Ariel,
    the city where David settled!
Add year to year
    and let your cycle of festivals go
        on.
²Yet I will besiege Ariel;
    she will mourn and lament,
    she will be to me like an altar
        hearth.ᵇ
³I will encamp against you all around;
    I will encircle you with towers
    and set up my siege works against
        you.
⁴Brought low, you will speak from the
        ground;

your speech will mumble out of
        the dust.
Your voice will come ghostlike from
        the earth;
    out of the dust your speech will
        whisper.

⁵But your many enemies will become
        like fine dust,
    the ruthless hordes like blown
        chaff.
Suddenly, in an instant,
⁶   the LORD Almighty will come
with thunder and earthquake and
        great noise,
    with windstorm and tempest and
        flames of a devouring fire.
⁷Then the hordes of all the nations
        that fight against Ariel,
    that attack her and her fortress and
        besiege her,
will be as it is with a dream,
    with a vision in the night—
⁸as when a hungry man dreams that
        he is eating,
    but he awakens, and his hunger
        remains;
as when a thirsty man dreams that he
        is drinking,
    but he awakens faint, with his
        thirst unquenched.
So will it be with the hordes of all
        the nations
    that fight against Mount Zion.

⁹Be stunned and amazed,
    blind yourselves and be sightless;
be drunk, but not from wine,
    stagger, but not from beer.
¹⁰The LORD has brought over you a
        deep sleep:
    He has sealed your eyes (the
        prophets);
    he has covered your heads (the
        seers).

¹¹For you this whole vision is nothing
but words sealed in a scroll. And if you
give the scroll to someone who can read,
and say to him, "Read this, please," he will
answer, "I can't; it is sealed." ¹²Or if you
give the scroll to someone who cannot
read, and say, "Read this, please," he will
answer, "I don't know how to read."

ᵃ25 The meaning of the Hebrew for this word is
uncertain.   ᵇ2 The Hebrew for *altar hearth*
sounds like the Hebrew for *Ariel*.

13The Lord says:

"These people come near to me with
their mouth
and honor me with their lips,
but their hearts are far from me.
Their worship of me
is made up only of rules taught by
men.*a*
14Therefore once more I will astound
these people
with wonder upon wonder;
the wisdom of the wise will perish,
the intelligence of the intelligent
will vanish."
15Woe to those who go to great depths
to hide their plans from the LORD,
who do their work in darkness and
think,
"Who sees us? Who will know?"
16You turn things upside down,
as if the potter were thought to be
like the clay!
Shall what is formed say to him who
formed it,
"He did not make me"?
Can the pot say of the potter,
"He knows nothing"?

17In a very short time, will not Lebanon
be turned into a fertile field
and the fertile field seem like a
forest?
18In that day the deaf will hear the
words of the scroll,
and out of gloom and darkness
the eyes of the blind will see.
19Once more the humble will rejoice in
the LORD;
the needy will rejoice in the Holy
One of Israel.
20The ruthless will vanish,
the mockers will disappear,
and all who have an eye for evil
will be cut down—
21those who with a word make a man
out to be guilty,
who ensnare the defender in court
and with false testimony deprive
the innocent of justice.

22Therefore this is what the LORD, who
redeemed Abraham, says to the house of
Jacob:

"No longer will Jacob be ashamed;
no longer will their faces grow
pale.

23When they see among them their
children,
the work of my hands,
they will keep my name holy;
they will acknowledge the holiness
of the Holy One of Jacob,
and will stand in awe of the God
of Israel.
24Those who are wayward in spirit will
gain understanding;
those who complain will accept
instruction."

Woe to the Obstinate Nation

30 "Woe to the obstinate children,"
declares the LORD,
"to those who carry out plans that
are not mine,
forming an alliance, but not by my
Spirit,
heaping sin upon sin;
2who go down to Egypt
without consulting me;
who look for help to Pharaoh's
protection,
to Egypt's shade for refuge.
3But Pharaoh's protection will be to
your shame,
Egypt's shade will bring you
disgrace.
4Though they have officials in Zoan
and their envoys have arrived in
Hanes,
5everyone will be put to shame
because of a people useless to
them,
who bring neither help nor
advantage,
but only shame and disgrace."

6An oracle concerning the animals of
the Negev:

Through a land of hardship and
distress,
of lions and lionesses,
of adders and darting snakes,
the envoys carry their riches on
donkeys' backs,
their treasures on the humps of
camels,
to that unprofitable nation,
7 to Egypt, whose help is utterly
useless.

*a13 Hebrew; Septuagint They worship me in vain; /
their teachings are but rules taught by men*

Therefore I call her
  Rahab the Do-Nothing.

[8]Go now, write it on a tablet for them,
  inscribe it on a scroll,
that for the days to come
  it may be an everlasting witness.
[9]These are rebellious people, deceitful
    children,
  children unwilling to listen to the
    Lord's instruction.
[10]They say to the seers,
  "See no more visions!"
and to the prophets,
  "Give us no more visions of what
    is right!
Tell us pleasant things,
  prophesy illusions.
[11]Leave this way,
  get off this path,
and stop confronting us
  with the Holy One of Israel!"

[12]Therefore, this is what the Holy One
of Israel says:

"Because you have rejected this
    message,
  relied on oppression
  and depended on deceit,
[13]this sin will become for you
  like a high wall, cracked and
    bulging,
  that collapses suddenly, in an
    instant.
[14]It will break in pieces like pottery,
  shattered so mercilessly
that among its pieces not a fragment
    will be found
  for taking coals from a hearth
  or scooping water out of a cistern."

[15]This is what the Sovereign Lord, the
Holy One of Israel, says:

"In repentance and rest is your
    salvation,
  in quietness and trust is your
    strength,
  but you would have none of it.
[16]You said, 'No, we will flee on horses.'
  Therefore you will flee!
You said, 'We will ride off on swift
    horses.'
  Therefore your pursuers will be
    swift!
[17]A thousand will flee
  at the threat of one;

at the threat of five
  you will all flee away,
till you are left
  like a flagstaff on a mountaintop,
  like a banner on a hill."

[18]Yet the Lord longs to be gracious to
    you;
  he rises to show you compassion.
For the Lord is a God of justice.
  Blessed are all who wait for him!

[19]O people of Zion, who live in Jerusalem, you will weep no more. How gracious he will be when you cry for help! As soon as he hears, he will answer you. [20]Although the Lord gives you the bread of adversity and the water of affliction, your teachers will be hidden no more; with your own eyes you will see them. [21]Whether you turn to the right or to the left, your ears will hear a voice behind you, saying, "This is the way; walk in it." [22]Then you will defile your idols overlaid with silver and your images covered with gold; you will throw them away like a menstrual cloth and say to them, "Away with you!"

[23]He will also send you rain for the seed you sow in the ground, and the food that comes from the land will be rich and plentiful. In that day your cattle will graze in broad meadows. [24]The oxen and donkeys that work the soil will eat fodder and mash, spread out with fork and shovel. [25]In the day of great slaughter, when the towers fall, streams of water will flow on every high mountain and every lofty hill. [26]The moon will shine like the sun, and the sunlight will be seven times brighter, like the light of seven full days, when the Lord binds up the bruises of his people and heals the wounds he inflicted.

[27]See, the Name of the Lord comes
    from afar,
  with burning anger and dense
    clouds of smoke;
his lips are full of wrath,
  and his tongue is a consuming fire.
[28]His breath is like a rushing torrent,
  rising up to the neck.
He shakes the nations in the sieve of
    destruction;
  he places in the jaws of the
    peoples
  a bit that leads them astray.

²⁹And you will sing
   as on the night you celebrate a
     holy festival;
your hearts will rejoice
   as when people go up with flutes
to the mountain of the LORD,
   to the Rock of Israel.
³⁰The LORD will cause men to hear his
     majestic voice
   and will make them see his arm
     coming down
with raging anger and consuming fire,
   with cloudburst, thunderstorm and
     hail.
³¹The voice of the LORD will shatter
     Assyria;
   with his scepter he will strike them
     down.
³²Every stroke the LORD lays on them
   with his punishing rod
will be to the music of tambourines
     and harps,
   as he fights them in battle with the
     blows of his arm.
³³Topheth has long been prepared;
   it has been made ready for the
     king.
Its fire pit has been made deep and
     wide,
   with an abundance of fire and
     wood;
the breath of the LORD,
   like a stream of burning sulfur,
   sets it ablaze.

Woe to Those Who Rely on Egypt

31 Woe to those who go down to
     Egypt for help,
   who rely on horses,
who trust in the multitude of their
     chariots
   and in the great strength of their
     horsemen,
but do not look to the Holy One of
     Israel,
   or seek help from the LORD.
²Yet he too is wise and can bring
     disaster;
   he does not take back his words.
He will rise up against the house of
     the wicked,
   against those who help evildoers.
³But the Egyptians are men and not
     God;
   their horses are flesh and not spirit.

When the LORD stretches out his
     hand,
   he who helps will stumble,
   he who is helped will fall;
   both will perish together.

⁴This is what the LORD says to me:

"As a lion growls,
   a great lion over his prey—
and though a whole band of
     shepherds
is called together against him,
he is not frightened by their shouts
   or disturbed by their clamor—
so the LORD Almighty will come
     down
   to do battle on Mount Zion and
     on its heights.
⁵Like birds hovering overhead,
   the LORD Almighty will shield
     Jerusalem;
he will shield it and deliver it,
   he will 'pass over' it and will
     rescue it."

⁶Return to him you have so greatly revolted against, O Israelites. ⁷For in that
day every one of you will reject the idols
of silver and gold your sinful hands have
made.

⁸"Assyria will fall by a sword that is
     not of man;
   a sword, not of mortals, will
     devour them.
They will flee before the sword
   and their young men will be put to
     forced labor.
⁹Their stronghold will fall because of
     terror;
   at sight of the battle standard their
     commanders will panic,"
declares the LORD,
   whose fire is in Zion,
   whose furnace is in Jerusalem.

The Kingdom of Righteousness

32 See, a king will reign in
     righteousness
   and rulers will rule with justice.
²Each man will be like a shelter from
     the wind
   and a refuge from the storm,
like streams of water in the desert
   and the shadow of a great rock in
     a thirsty land.

³Then the eyes of those who see will
    no longer be closed,
  and the ears of those who hear will
    listen.
⁴The mind of the rash will know and
    understand,
  and the stammering tongue will be
    fluent and clear.
⁵No longer will the fool be called
    noble
  nor the scoundrel be highly
    respected.
⁶For the fool speaks folly,
  his mind is busy with evil:
He practices ungodliness
  and spreads error concerning the
    LORD;
the hungry he leaves empty
  and from the thirsty he withholds
    water.
⁷The scoundrel's methods are wicked,
  he makes up evil schemes
to destroy the poor with lies,
  even when the plea of the needy is
    just.
⁸But the noble man makes noble
    plans,
  and by noble deeds he stands.

The Women of Jerusalem

⁹You women who are so complacent,
    rise up and listen to me;
you daughters who feel secure,
    hear what I have to say!
¹⁰In little more than a year
    you who feel secure will tremble;
the grape harvest will fail,
    and the harvest of fruit will not
      come.
¹¹Tremble, you complacent women;
    shudder, you daughters who feel
      secure!
Strip off your clothes,
    put sackcloth around your waists.
¹²Beat your breasts for the pleasant
      fields,
    for the fruitful vines
¹³and for the land of my people,
    a land overgrown with thorns and
      briers—
yes, mourn for all houses of
      merriment
and for this city of revelry.
¹⁴The fortress will be abandoned,
    the noisy city deserted;

citadel and watchtower will become a
      wasteland forever,
  the delight of donkeys, a pasture
      for flocks,
¹⁵till the Spirit is poured upon us from
      on high,
  and the desert becomes a fertile
      field,
  and the fertile field seems like a
      forest.
¹⁶Justice will dwell in the desert
  and righteousness live in the fertile
      field.
¹⁷The fruit of righteousness will be
      peace;
  the effect of righteousness will be
      quietness and confidence
      forever.
¹⁸My people will live in peaceful
      dwelling places,
  in secure homes,
  in undisturbed places of rest.
¹⁹Though hail flattens the forest
  and the city is leveled completely,
²⁰how blessed you will be,
  sowing your seed by every stream,
  and letting your cattle and donkeys
      range free.

Distress and Help

33 Woe to you, O destroyer,
    you who have not been
      destroyed!
Woe to you, O traitor,
  you who have not been betrayed!
When you stop destroying,
  you will be destroyed;
when you stop betraying,
  you will be betrayed.

²O LORD, be gracious to us;
  we long for you.
Be our strength every morning,
  our salvation in time of distress.
³At the thunder of your voice, the
      peoples flee;
  when you rise up, the nations
      scatter.
⁴Your plunder, O nations, is harvested
      as by young locusts;
  like a swarm of locusts men
      pounce on it.

⁵The LORD is exalted, for he dwells on
      high;

he will fill Zion with justice and
   righteousness.
⁶He will be the sure foundation for
   your times,
  a rich store of salvation and
    wisdom and knowledge;
  the fear of the LORD is the key to
    this treasure.ᵃ

⁷Look, their brave men cry aloud in
   the streets;
  the envoys of peace weep bitterly.
⁸The highways are deserted,
  no travelers are on the roads.
The treaty is broken,
  its witnessesᵇ are despised,
  no one is respected.
⁹The land mournsᶜ and wastes away,
  Lebanon is ashamed and withers;
Sharon is like the Arabah,
  and Bashan and Carmel drop their
    leaves.

¹⁰"Now will I arise," says the LORD.
  "Now will I be exalted;
  now will I be lifted up.

¹¹You conceive chaff,
  you give birth to straw;
  your breath is a fire that consumes
    you.
¹²The peoples will be burned as if to
   lime;
  like cut thornbushes they will be
    set ablaze."

¹³You who are far away, hear what I
   have done;
  you who are near, acknowledge my
    power!
¹⁴The sinners in Zion are terrified;
  trembling grips the godless:
"Who of us can dwell with the
    consuming fire?
Who of us can dwell with
    everlasting burning?"
¹⁵He who walks righteously
  and speaks what is right,
who rejects gain from extortion

ᵃ6 Or *is a treasure from him*   ᵇ8 Dead Sea
Scrolls; Masoretic Text / *the cities*   ᶜ9 Or *dries up*

Beating the Odds

Monday

ISAIAH 32:18 The statisticians say the chances are five in ten that a marriage will end in divorce. If one or both partners are still teenagers, they say the odds for divorce are even higher. If either partner witnessed an unhappy marriage at home, the odds increase again. If one or both partners come from broken homes, the odds rise yet higher. If either partner has been divorced, the odds soar. If there has been regular sexual involvement before marriage, or if either or both partners abuse alcohol or drugs, the odds skyrocket.

Regardless of your marriage "odds," we have a soul-searching question for you that will help you beat them: *How would I like to be married to me?* That simple question can do more to help you ensure the success of your marriage and build a secure home than just about anything else. Think about it. How would you rate *you* as a marriage partner? Are you easy to live with? How do you enrich the relationship? What are the positive qualities you bring to your marriage?

Every marriage is unique, and, while there is not a definitive list of qualities that describes a good spouse, consider some of the traits that show up again and again in studies of life-long love. Research has shown that the partner who is easy to live with feels good about himself. He is not unduly concerned over the impression he makes on others. She can throw back her head, breathe deeply and enjoy life. This kind of person is described in Galatians 6:4: " . . . he can take pride in himself without comparing himself to somebody else." The person who makes a good, life-long marriage partner and helps to build a "peaceful dwelling place" also has a way of passing over minor offenses and injustices. In other words, he or she is not easily offended (see Romans 14:19, page 1234)—good things to keep in mind as you and your spouse work together to beat the odds.

—Les & Leslie

Go to page 764 for your next devotional reading.

and keeps his hand from accepting
    bribes,
who stops his ears against plots of
    murder
and shuts his eyes against
    contemplating evil—
¹⁶this is the man who will dwell on the
    heights,
whose refuge will be the mountain
    fortress.
His bread will be supplied,
    and water will not fail him.

¹⁷Your eyes will see the king in his
    beauty
and view a land that stretches afar.
¹⁸In your thoughts you will ponder the
    former terror:
"Where is that chief officer?
Where is the one who took the
    revenue?
Where is the officer in charge of
    the towers?"
¹⁹You will see those arrogant people no
    more,
those people of an obscure speech,
with their strange,
    incomprehensible tongue.

²⁰Look upon Zion, the city of our
    festivals;
your eyes will see Jerusalem,
a peaceful abode, a tent that will
    not be moved;
its stakes will never be pulled up,
    nor any of its ropes broken.
²¹There the LORD will be our Mighty
    One.
It will be like a place of broad
    rivers and streams.
No galley with oars will ride them,
    no mighty ship will sail them.
²²For the LORD is our judge,
    the LORD is our lawgiver,
the LORD is our king;
    it is he who will save us.

²³Your rigging hangs loose:
The mast is not held secure,
    the sail is not spread.
Then an abundance of spoils will be
    divided
and even the lame will carry off
    plunder.

²⁴No one living in Zion will say, "I am
    ill";
and the sins of those who dwell
    there will be forgiven.

Judgment Against the Nations

34 Come near, you nations, and
    listen;
    pay attention, you peoples!
Let the earth hear, and all that is in
    it,
the world, and all that comes out
    of it!
²The LORD is angry with all nations;
    his wrath is upon all their armies.
He will totally destroy[a] them,
    he will give them over to slaughter.
³Their slain will be thrown out,
    their dead bodies will send up a
        stench;
    the mountains will be soaked with
        their blood.
⁴All the stars of the heavens will be
    dissolved
and the sky rolled up like a scroll;
all the starry host will fall
    like withered leaves from the vine,
    like shriveled figs from the fig tree.

⁵My sword has drunk its fill in the
    heavens;
see, it descends in judgment on
    Edom,
the people I have totally destroyed.
⁶The sword of the LORD is bathed in
    blood,
    it is covered with fat—
the blood of lambs and goats,
    fat from the kidneys of rams.
For the LORD has a sacrifice in Bozrah
    and a great slaughter in Edom.
⁷And the wild oxen will fall with
    them,
    the bull calves and the great bulls.
Their land will be drenched with
    blood,
and the dust will be soaked with
    fat.

⁸For the LORD has a day of vengeance,
    a year of retribution, to uphold
        Zion's cause.

---

a2 The Hebrew term refers to the irrevocable
giving over of things or persons to the LORD, often
by totally destroying them; also in verse 5.

⁹Edom's streams will be turned into
  pitch,
    her dust into burning sulfur;
    her land will become blazing
      pitch!
¹⁰It will not be quenched night and
  day;
    its smoke will rise forever.
  From generation to generation it will
    lie desolate;
    no one will ever pass through it
      again.
¹¹The desert owl*a* and screech owl*a*
  will possess it;
    the great owl*a* and the raven will
      nest there.
  God will stretch out over Edom
    the measuring line of chaos
    and the plumb line of desolation.
¹²Her nobles will have nothing there to
  be called a kingdom,
    all her princes will vanish away.
¹³Thorns will overrun her citadels,
    nettles and brambles her
      strongholds.
  She will become a haunt for jackals,
    a home for owls.
¹⁴Desert creatures will meet with
  hyenas,
    and wild goats will bleat to each
      other;
  there the night creatures will also
    repose
    and find for themselves places of
      rest.
¹⁵The owl will nest there and lay eggs,
    she will hatch them, and care for
      her young under the shadow
      of her wings;
  there also the falcons will gather,
    each with its mate.

¹⁶Look in the scroll of the LORD and
read:

  None of these will be missing,
    not one will lack her mate.
  For it is his mouth that has given the
    order,
    and his Spirit will gather them
      together.
¹⁷He allots their portions;
    his hand distributes them by
      measure.
  They will possess it forever
    and dwell there from generation to
      generation.

Joy of the Redeemed

35 The desert and the parched land
      will be glad;
    the wilderness will rejoice and
      blossom.
  Like the crocus, ²it will burst into
    bloom;
    it will rejoice greatly and shout for
      joy.
  The glory of Lebanon will be given to
    it,
    the splendor of Carmel and
      Sharon;
  they will see the glory of the LORD,
    the splendor of our God.

³Strengthen the feeble hands,
    steady the knees that give way;
⁴say to those with fearful hearts,
    "Be strong, do not fear;
  your God will come,
    he will come with vengeance;
  with divine retribution
    he will come to save you."

⁵Then will the eyes of the blind be
    opened
    and the ears of the deaf unstopped.
⁶Then will the lame leap like a deer,
    and the mute tongue shout for
      joy.
  Water will gush forth in the
    wilderness
    and streams in the desert.
⁷The burning sand will become a pool,
    the thirsty ground bubbling
      springs.
  In the haunts where jackals once
    lay,
    grass and reeds and papyrus will
      grow.

⁸And a highway will be there;
    it will be called the Way of
      Holiness.
  The unclean will not journey on it;
    it will be for those who walk in
      that Way;
    wicked fools will not go about on
      it.*b*
⁹No lion will be there,

---

a 11 The precise identification of these birds is
uncertain.   *b 8* Or / *the simple will not stray
from it*

nor will any ferocious beast get up
on it;
they will not be found there.
But only the redeemed will walk
there,
10   and the ransomed of the LORD will
return.
They will enter Zion with singing;
everlasting joy will crown their
heads.
Gladness and joy will overtake them,
and sorrow and sighing will flee
away.

Sennacherib Threatens Jerusalem

36 In the fourteenth year of King Hezekiah's reign, Sennacherib king of
Assyria attacked all the fortified cities of
Judah and captured them. ²Then the king
of Assyria sent his field commander with
a large army from Lachish to King Hezekiah at Jerusalem. When the commander
stopped at the aqueduct of the Upper
Pool, on the road to the Washerman's
Field, ³Eliakim son of Hilkiah the palace
administrator, Shebna the secretary, and
Joah son of Asaph the recorder went out
to him.

⁴The field commander said to them,
"Tell Hezekiah,

" 'This is what the great king, the
king of Assyria, says: On what are
you basing this confidence of yours?
⁵You say you have strategy and military strength—but you speak only
empty words. On whom are you depending, that you rebel against me?
⁶Look now, you are depending on
Egypt, that splintered reed of a staff,
which pierces a man's hand and
wounds him if he leans on it! Such
is Pharaoh king of Egypt to all who
depend on him. ⁷And if you say to
me, "We are depending on the LORD
our God"—isn't he the one whose
high places and altars Hezekiah removed, saying to Judah and Jerusalem, "You must worship before this
altar"?

⁸ " 'Come now, make a bargain
with my master, the king of Assyria:
I will give you two thousand
horses—if you can put riders on
them! ⁹How then can you repulse

one officer of the least of my master's officials, even though you are
depending on Egypt for chariots and
horsemen? ¹⁰Furthermore, have I
come to attack and destroy this land
without the LORD? The LORD himself
told me to march against this country and destroy it.' "

¹¹Then Eliakim, Shebna and Joah said
to the field commander, "Please speak to
your servants in Aramaic, since we understand it. Don't speak to us in Hebrew in
the hearing of the people on the wall."

¹²But the commander replied, "Was it
only to your master and you that my master sent me to say these things, and not to
the men sitting on the wall—who, like
you, will have to eat their own filth and
drink their own urine?"

¹³Then the commander stood and
called out in Hebrew, "Hear the words of
the great king, the king of Assyria! ¹⁴This
is what the king says: Do not let Hezekiah
deceive you. He cannot deliver you! ¹⁵Do
not let Hezekiah persuade you to trust in
the LORD when he says, 'The LORD will
surely deliver us; this city will not be giv-
en into the hand of the king of Assyria.'

¹⁶"Do not listen to Hezekiah. This is
what the king of Assyria says: Make peace
with me and come out to me. Then every
one of you will eat from his own vine and
fig tree and drink water from his own cistern, ¹⁷until I come and take you to a land
like your own—a land of grain and new
wine, a land of bread and vineyards.

¹⁸"Do not let Hezekiah mislead you
when he says, 'The LORD will deliver us.'
Has the god of any nation ever delivered
his land from the hand of the king of
Assyria? ¹⁹Where are the gods of Hamath
and Arpad? Where are the gods of Sepharvaim? Have they rescued Samaria from
my hand? ²⁰Who of all the gods of these
countries has been able to save his land
from me? How then can the LORD deliver
Jerusalem from my hand?"

²¹But the people remained silent and
said nothing in reply, because the king
had commanded, "Do not answer him."

²²Then Eliakim son of Hilkiah the palace administrator, Shebna the secretary,
and Joah son of Asaph the recorder went
to Hezekiah, with their clothes torn, and

told him what the field commander had said.

Jerusalem's Deliverance Foretold

37 When King Hezekiah heard this, he tore his clothes and put on sackcloth and went into the temple of the LORD. ²He sent Eliakim the palace administrator, Shebna the secretary, and the leading priests, all wearing sackcloth, to the prophet Isaiah son of Amoz. ³They told him, "This is what Hezekiah says: This day is a day of distress and rebuke and disgrace, as when children come to the point of birth and there is no strength to deliver them. ⁴It may be that the LORD your God will hear the words of the field commander, whom his master, the king of Assyria, has sent to ridicule the living God, and that he will rebuke him for the words the LORD your God has heard. Therefore pray for the remnant that still survives."

⁵When King Hezekiah's officials came to Isaiah, ⁶Isaiah said to them, "Tell your master, 'This is what the LORD says: Do not be afraid of what you have heard— those words with which the underlings of the king of Assyria have blasphemed me. ⁷Listen! I am going to put a spirit in him so that when he hears a certain report, he will return to his own country, and there I will have him cut down with the sword.' "

⁸When the field commander heard that the king of Assyria had left Lachish, he withdrew and found the king fighting against Libnah.

⁹Now Sennacherib received a report that Tirhakah, the Cushite[a] king ⌞of Egypt⌟, was marching out to fight against him. When he heard it, he sent messengers to Hezekiah with this word: ¹⁰"Say to Hezekiah king of Judah: Do not let the god you depend on deceive you when he says, 'Jerusalem will not be handed over to the king of Assyria.' ¹¹Surely you have heard what the kings of Assyria have done to all the countries, destroying them completely. And will you be delivered? ¹²Did the gods of the nations that were destroyed by my forefathers deliver them— the gods of Gozan, Haran, Rezeph and the people of Eden who were in Tel Assar? ¹³Where is the king of Hamath, the king of Arpad, the king of the city of Sepharvaim, or of Hena or Ivvah?"

Hezekiah's Prayer

¹⁴Hezekiah received the letter from the messengers and read it. Then he went up to the temple of the LORD and spread it out before the LORD. ¹⁵And Hezekiah prayed to the LORD: ¹⁶"O LORD Almighty, God of Israel, enthroned between the cherubim, you alone are God over all the kingdoms of the earth. You have made heaven and earth. ¹⁷Give ear, O LORD, and hear; open your eyes, O LORD, and see; listen to all the words Sennacherib has sent to insult the living God.

¹⁸"It is true, O LORD, that the Assyrian kings have laid waste all these peoples and their lands. ¹⁹They have thrown their gods into the fire and destroyed them, for they were not gods but only wood and stone, fashioned by human hands. ²⁰Now, O LORD our God, deliver us from his hand, so that all kingdoms on earth may know that you alone, O LORD, are God.[b]"

Sennacherib's Fall

²¹Then Isaiah son of Amoz sent a message to Hezekiah: "This is what the LORD, the God of Israel, says: Because you have prayed to me concerning Sennacherib king of Assyria, ²²this is the word the LORD has spoken against him:

"The Virgin Daughter of Zion
    despises and mocks you.
The Daughter of Jerusalem
    tosses her head as you flee.
²³Who is it you have insulted and
      blasphemed?
    Against whom have you raised
      your voice
and lifted your eyes in pride?
    Against the Holy One of Israel!
²⁴By your messengers
    you have heaped insults on the
      Lord.
And you have said,
    'With my many chariots
I have ascended the heights of the
      mountains,
    the utmost heights of Lebanon.
I have cut down its tallest cedars,
    the choicest of its pines.

---

a9 That is, from the upper Nile region
b20 Dead Sea Scrolls (see also 2 Kings 19:19);
Masoretic Text *alone are the* LORD

I have reached its remotest heights,
the finest of its forests.
25I have dug wells in foreign lands*a*
and drunk the water there.
With the soles of my feet
I have dried up all the streams of
Egypt.'

26"Have you not heard?
Long ago I ordained it.
In days of old I planned it;
now I have brought it to pass,
that you have turned fortified cities
into piles of stone.
27Their people, drained of power,
are dismayed and put to shame.
They are like plants in the field,
like tender green shoots,
like grass sprouting on the roof,
scorched*b* before it grows up.

28"But I know where you stay
and when you come and go
and how you rage against me.
29Because you rage against me
and because your insolence has
reached my ears,
I will put my hook in your nose
and my bit in your mouth,
and I will make you return
by the way you came.

30"This will be the sign for you,
O Hezekiah:

"This year you will eat what grows by
itself,
and the second year what springs
from that.
But in the third year sow and reap,
plant vineyards and eat their fruit.
31Once more a remnant of the house of
Judah
will take root below and bear fruit
above.
32For out of Jerusalem will come a
remnant,
and out of Mount Zion a band of
survivors.
The zeal of the LORD Almighty
will accomplish this.

33"Therefore this is what the LORD says
concerning the king of Assyria:

"He will not enter this city
or shoot an arrow here.
He will not come before it with
shield

or build a siege ramp against it.
34By the way that he came he will
return;
he will not enter this city,"
declares the LORD.
35"I will defend this city and save it,
for my sake and for the sake of
David my servant!"

36Then the angel of the LORD went out
and put to death a hundred and eighty-
five thousand men in the Assyrian camp.
When the people got up the next morning—there were all the dead bodies! 37So
Sennacherib king of Assyria broke camp
and withdrew. He returned to Nineveh
and stayed there.

38One day, while he was worshiping in
the temple of his god Nisroch, his sons
Adrammelech and Sharezer cut him
down with the sword, and they escaped to
the land of Ararat. And Esarhaddon his
son succeeded him as king.

Hezekiah's Illness

38 In those days Hezekiah became ill
and was at the point of death. The
prophet Isaiah son of Amoz went to him
and said, "This is what the LORD says: Put
your house in order, because you are going to die; you will not recover."

2Hezekiah turned his face to the wall
and prayed to the LORD, 3"Remember,
O LORD, how I have walked before you
faithfully and with wholehearted devotion and have done what is good in your
eyes." And Hezekiah wept bitterly.

4Then the word of the LORD came to
Isaiah: 5"Go and tell Hezekiah, 'This is
what the LORD, the God of your father
David, says: I have heard your prayer and
seen your tears; I will add fifteen years to
your life. 6And I will deliver you and this
city from the hand of the king of Assyria.
I will defend this city.

7"'This is the LORD's sign to you that
the LORD will do what he has promised: 8I
will make the shadow cast by the sun go
back the ten steps it has gone down on

*a*25 Dead Sea Scrolls (see also 2 Kings 19:24);
Masoretic Text does not have *in foreign lands.*
*b*27 Some manuscripts of the Masoretic Text, Dead
Sea Scrolls and some Septuagint manuscripts (see
also 2 Kings 19:26); most manuscripts of the
Masoretic Text *roof / and terraced fields*

the stairway of Ahaz.'" So the sunlight went back the ten steps it had gone down.

⁹A writing of Hezekiah king of Judah after his illness and recovery:

¹⁰I said, "In the prime of my life
   must I go through the gates of
      death*a*
   and be robbed of the rest of my
      years?"
¹¹I said, "I will not again see the LORD,
   the LORD, in the land of the living;
no longer will I look on mankind,
   or be with those who now dwell in
      this world.*b*
¹²Like a shepherd's tent my house
   has been pulled down and taken
      from me.
Like a weaver I have rolled up my life,
   and he has cut me off from the
      loom;
   day and night you made an end of
      me.
¹³I waited patiently till dawn,
   but like a lion he broke all my
      bones;
   day and night you made an end of
      me.
¹⁴I cried like a swift or thrush,
   I moaned like a mourning dove.
My eyes grew weak as I looked to the
      heavens.
   I am troubled; O Lord, come to my
      aid!"

¹⁵But what can I say?
   He has spoken to me, and he
      himself has done this.
I will walk humbly all my years
   because of this anguish of my soul.
¹⁶Lord, by such things men live;
   and my spirit finds life in them
      too.
You restored me to health
   and let me live.
¹⁷Surely it was for my benefit
   that I suffered such anguish.
In your love you kept me
   from the pit of destruction;
you have put all my sins
   behind your back.
¹⁸For the grave*a* cannot praise you,
   death cannot sing your praise;
those who go down to the pit
   cannot hope for your faithfulness.
¹⁹The living, the living—they praise you,

as I am doing today;
fathers tell their children
   about your faithfulness.

²⁰The LORD will save me,
   and we will sing with stringed
      instruments
all the days of our lives
   in the temple of the LORD.

²¹Isaiah had said, "Prepare a poultice of figs and apply it to the boil, and he will recover." ²²Hezekiah had asked, "What will be the sign that I will go up to the temple of the LORD?"

Envoys From Babylon

39 At that time Merodach-Baladan son of Baladan king of Babylon sent Hezekiah letters and a gift, because he had heard of his illness and recovery. ²Hezekiah received the envoys gladly and showed them what was in his storehouses—the silver, the gold, the spices, the fine oil, his entire armory and everything found among his treasures. There was nothing in his palace or in all his kingdom that Hezekiah did not show them.

³Then Isaiah the prophet went to King Hezekiah and asked, "What did those men say, and where did they come from?"

"From a distant land," Hezekiah replied. "They came to me from Babylon."

⁴The prophet asked, "What did they see in your palace?"

"They saw everything in my palace," Hezekiah said. "There is nothing among my treasures that I did not show them."

⁵Then Isaiah said to Hezekiah, "Hear the word of the LORD Almighty: ⁶The time will surely come when everything in your palace, and all that your fathers have stored up until this day, will be carried off to Babylon. Nothing will be left, says the LORD. ⁷And some of your descendants, your own flesh and blood who will be born to you, will be taken away, and they will become eunuchs in the palace of the king of Babylon."

⁸"The word of the LORD you have spoken is good," Hezekiah replied. For he

a 10,18 Hebrew *Sheol*   *b 11* A few Hebrew manuscripts; most Hebrew manuscripts *in the place of cessation* thought, "There will be peace and security in my lifetime."

Comfort for God's People

40 Comfort, comfort my people,
says your God.
²Speak tenderly to Jerusalem,
and proclaim to her
that her hard service has been
completed,
that her sin has been paid for,
that she has received from the LORD's
hand
double for all her sins.

³A voice of one calling:
"In the desert prepare
the way for the LORD*ᵃ*;
make straight in the wilderness
a highway for our God.*ᵇ*
⁴Every valley shall be raised up,
every mountain and hill made low;
the rough ground shall become level,
the rugged places a plain.
⁵And the glory of the LORD will be
revealed,
and all mankind together will see
it.
For the mouth of the LORD
has spoken."

⁶A voice says, "Cry out."
And I said, "What shall I cry?"

"All men are like grass,
and all their glory is like the
flowers of the field.
⁷The grass withers and the flowers fall,
because the breath of the LORD
blows on them.
Surely the people are grass.
⁸The grass withers and the flowers fall,
but the word of our God stands
forever."

⁹You who bring good tidings to Zion,
go up on a high mountain.
You who bring good tidings to
Jerusalem,*ᶜ*
lift up your voice with a shout,
lift it up, do not be afraid;
say to the towns of Judah,
"Here is your God!"
¹⁰See, the Sovereign LORD comes with
power,
and his arm rules for him.
See, his reward is with him,

and his recompense accompanies
him.
¹¹He tends his flock like a shepherd:
He gathers the lambs in his arms
and carries them close to his heart;
he gently leads those that have
young.

¹²Who has measured the waters in the
hollow of his hand,
or with the breadth of his hand
marked off the heavens?
Who has held the dust of the earth in
a basket,
or weighed the mountains on the
scales
and the hills in a balance?
¹³Who has understood the mind*ᵈ* of
the LORD,
or instructed him as his counselor?
¹⁴Whom did the LORD consult to
enlighten him,
and who taught him the right way?
Who was it that taught him
knowledge
or showed him the path of
understanding?

¹⁵Surely the nations are like a drop in a
bucket;
they are regarded as dust on the
scales;
he weighs the islands as though
they were fine dust.
¹⁶Lebanon is not sufficient for altar
fires,
nor its animals enough for burnt
offerings.
¹⁷Before him all the nations are as
nothing;
they are regarded by him as
worthless
and less than nothing.

¹⁸To whom, then, will you compare
God?
What image will you compare him
to?
¹⁹As for an idol, a craftsman casts it,
and a goldsmith overlays it with
gold
and fashions silver chains for it.

*ᵃ3 Or A voice of one calling in the desert: / "Prepare
the way for the LORD   ᵇ3 Hebrew; Septuagint
make straight the paths of our God   ᶜ9 Or O Zion,
bringer of good tidings, / go up on a high mountain. /
O Jerusalem, bringer of good tidings   ᵈ13 Or
Spirit; or spirit*

²⁰A man too poor to present such an
        offering
    selects wood that will not rot.
He looks for a skilled craftsman
    to set up an idol that will not
        topple.

²¹Do you not know?
    Have you not heard?
Has it not been told you from the
        beginning?
    Have you not understood since the
        earth was founded?
²²He sits enthroned above the circle of
        the earth,
    and its people are like
        grasshoppers.
He stretches out the heavens like a
        canopy,
    and spreads them out like a tent to
        live in.
²³He brings princes to naught
    and reduces the rulers of this world
        to nothing.
²⁴No sooner are they planted,
    no sooner are they sown,
    no sooner do they take root in the
        ground,
than he blows on them and they
        wither,
    and a whirlwind sweeps them away
        like chaff.

²⁵"To whom will you compare me?
    Or who is my equal?" says the Holy
        One.
²⁶Lift your eyes and look to the
        heavens:
    Who created all these?
He who brings out the starry host one
        by one,
    and calls them each by name.
Because of his great power and
        mighty strength,
    not one of them is missing.

²⁷Why do you say, O Jacob,
    and complain, O Israel,
"My way is hidden from the LORD;
    my cause is disregarded by my
        God"?
²⁸Do you not know?
    Have you not heard?
The LORD is the everlasting God,
    the Creator of the ends of the
        earth.
He will not grow tired or weary,

and his understanding no one can
        fathom.
²⁹He gives strength to the weary
    and increases the power of the
        weak.
³⁰Even youths grow tired and weary,
    and young men stumble and fall;
³¹but those who hope in the LORD
    will renew their strength.
They will soar on wings like eagles;
    they will run and not grow weary,
    they will walk and not be faint.

The Helper of Israel

41 "Be silent before me, you islands!
        Let the nations renew their
            strength!
Let them come forward and speak;
    let us meet together at the place of
        judgment.

²"Who has stirred up one from the
        east,
    calling him in righteousness to his
        service*ᵃ*?
He hands nations over to him
    and subdues kings before him.
He turns them to dust with his
        sword,
    to windblown chaff with his bow.
³He pursues them and moves on
        unscathed,
    by a path his feet have not traveled
        before.
⁴Who has done this and carried it
        through,
    calling forth the generations from
        the beginning?
I, the LORD—with the first of them
    and with the last—I am he."

⁵The islands have seen it and fear;
    the ends of the earth tremble.
They approach and come forward;
⁶   each helps the other
    and says to his brother, "Be
        strong!"
⁷The craftsman encourages the
        goldsmith,
    and he who smooths with the
        hammer
    spurs on him who strikes the anvil.
He says of the welding, "It is good."
    He nails down the idol so it will
        not topple.

ᵃ2 Or / whom victory meets at every step

8"But you, O Israel, my servant,
  Jacob, whom I have chosen,
  you descendants of Abraham my
    friend,
9I took you from the ends of the earth,
  from its farthest corners I called
    you.
  I said, 'You are my servant';
  I have chosen you and have not
    rejected you.
10So do not fear, for I am with you;
  do not be dismayed, for I am your
    God.
  I will strengthen you and help you;
  I will uphold you with my
    righteous right hand.

11"All who rage against you
  will surely be ashamed and
    disgraced;
  those who oppose you
  will be as nothing and perish.
12Though you search for your enemies,
  you will not find them.
  Those who wage war against you
  will be as nothing at all.
13For I am the LORD, your God,
  who takes hold of your right hand
  and says to you, Do not fear;
  I will help you.
14Do not be afraid, O worm Jacob,
  O little Israel,
  for I myself will help you," declares
    the LORD,
  your Redeemer, the Holy One of
    Israel.

15"See, I will make you into a threshing
    sledge,
  new and sharp, with many teeth.
  You will thresh the mountains and
    crush them,
  and reduce the hills to chaff.
16You will winnow them, the wind will
    pick them up,
  and a gale will blow them away.
  But you will rejoice in the LORD
  and glory in the Holy One of
    Israel.

17"The poor and needy search for
    water,
  but there is none;
  their tongues are parched with
    thirst.
  But I the LORD will answer them;
  I, the God of Israel, will not
    forsake them.
18I will make rivers flow on barren
    heights,
  and springs within the valleys.
  I will turn the desert into pools of
    water,
  and the parched ground into
    springs.
19I will put in the desert
  the cedar and the acacia, the myrtle
    and the olive.
  I will set pines in the wasteland,
  the fir and the cypress together,
20so that people may see and know,
  may consider and understand,
  that the hand of the LORD has done
    this,

Marriage Renewal

Tuesday

ISAIAH 40:28–31 We have attended more marriage retreats than we can count. Some in hard-to-find, out-of-the-way, rustic settings. Others in posh hotels or resort getaways. No matter where they are or how they are structured, they always serve the same purpose—renewal.

Every couple, no matter how strong and secure, needs occasional renewal—a time to recharge emotional and relational batteries. And don't think that newlyweds still enjoying the "honeymoon phase" don't need the same thing: "Even youths grow

COUPLE MINUTES

tired and weary" (verse 30). No matter how far along we are in our marriage journey, all of us need to renew our strength— whether it is a full-blown retreat, a dinner without the kids or a quiet breakfast at home before the rest of the house begins to stir.

Take a moment to consider how you and your spouse can do just that. What can you do that will help the other soar on wings like eagles? On a personal level, what helps you run and not grow weary? —*Les & Leslie*

Go to page 768 for your next devotional reading.

that the Holy One of Israel has
  created it.

21 "Present your case," says the LORD.
  "Set forth your arguments," says
  Jacob's King.
22 "Bring in ⌊your idols⌋ to tell us
  what is going to happen.
Tell us what the former things were,
  so that we may consider them
  and know their final outcome.
Or declare to us the things to come,
23   tell us what the future holds,
  so we may know that you are gods.
Do something, whether good or bad,
  so that we will be dismayed and
  filled with fear.
24 But you are less than nothing
  and your works are utterly
  worthless;
  he who chooses you is detestable.

25 "I have stirred up one from the
  north, and he comes—
  one from the rising sun who calls
  on my name.
He treads on rulers as if they were
  mortar,
  as if he were a potter treading the
  clay.
26 Who told of this from the beginning,
  so we could know,
  or beforehand, so we could say,
  'He was right'?
No one told of this,
  no one foretold it,
  no one heard any words from you.
27 I was the first to tell Zion, 'Look, here
  they are!'
  I gave to Jerusalem a messenger of
  good tidings.
28 I look but there is no one—
  no one among them to give
  counsel,
  no one to give answer when I ask
  them.
29 See, they are all false!
  Their deeds amount to nothing;
  their images are but wind and
  confusion.

The Servant of the LORD

42 "Here is my servant, whom I
  uphold,
  my chosen one in whom I delight;
  I will put my Spirit on him

and he will bring justice to the
  nations.
2 He will not shout or cry out,
  or raise his voice in the streets.
3 A bruised reed he will not break,
  and a smoldering wick he will not
  snuff out.
In faithfulness he will bring forth
  justice;
4   he will not falter or be discouraged
till he establishes justice on earth.
  In his law the islands will put their
  hope."

5 This is what God the LORD says—
he who created the heavens and
  stretched them out,
  who spread out the earth and all
  that comes out of it,
who gives breath to its people,
  and life to those who walk on it:
6 "I, the LORD, have called you in
  righteousness;
  I will take hold of your hand.
I will keep you and will make you
  to be a covenant for the people
  and a light for the Gentiles,
7 to open eyes that are blind,

to free captives from prison
and to release from the dungeon
those who sit in darkness.

[8]"I am the LORD; that is my name!
I will not give my glory to another
or my praise to idols.
[9]See, the former things have taken
place,
and new things I declare;
before they spring into being
I announce them to you."

Song of Praise to the LORD

[10]Sing to the LORD a new song,
his praise from the ends of the
earth,
you who go down to the sea, and all
that is in it,
you islands, and all who live in
them.
[11]Let the desert and its towns raise their
voices;
let the settlements where Kedar
lives rejoice.
Let the people of Sela sing for joy;
let them shout from the
mountaintops.
[12]Let them give glory to the LORD
and proclaim his praise in the
islands.
[13]The LORD will march out like a
mighty man,
like a warrior he will stir up his
zeal;
with a shout he will raise the battle
cry
and will triumph over his enemies.

[14]"For a long time I have kept silent,
I have been quiet and held myself
back.
But now, like a woman in childbirth,
I cry out, I gasp and pant.
[15]I will lay waste the mountains and
hills
and dry up all their vegetation;
I will turn rivers into islands
and dry up the pools.
[16]I will lead the blind by ways they
have not known,
along unfamiliar paths I will guide
them;
I will turn the darkness into light
before them

and make the rough places
smooth.
These are the things I will do;
I will not forsake them.
[17]But those who trust in idols,
who say to images, 'You are our
gods,'
will be turned back in utter shame.

Israel Blind and Deaf

[18]"Hear, you deaf;
look, you blind, and see!
[19]Who is blind but my servant,
and deaf like the messenger I send?
Who is blind like the one committed
to me,
blind like the servant of the LORD?
[20]You have seen many things, but have
paid no attention;
your ears are open, but you hear
nothing."
[21]It pleased the LORD
for the sake of his righteousness
to make his law great and glorious.
[22]But this is a people plundered and
looted,
all of them trapped in pits
or hidden away in prisons.
They have become plunder,
with no one to rescue them;
they have been made loot,
with no one to say, "Send them
back."

[23]Which of you will listen to this
or pay close attention in time to
come?
[24]Who handed Jacob over to become
loot,
and Israel to the plunderers?
Was it not the LORD,
against whom we have sinned?
For they would not follow his ways;
they did not obey his law.
[25]So he poured out on them his
burning anger,
the violence of war.
It enveloped them in flames, yet they
did not understand;
it consumed them, but they did
not take it to heart.

Israel's Only Savior

43 But now, this is what the LORD
says—
he who created you, O Jacob,

he who formed you, O Israel:
"Fear not, for I have redeemed you;
  I have summoned you by name;
    you are mine.
2When you pass through the waters,
  I will be with you;
and when you pass through the
    rivers,
  they will not sweep over you.
When you walk through the fire,
  you will not be burned;
  the flames will not set you ablaze.
3For I am the LORD, your God,
  the Holy One of Israel, your
    Savior;
I give Egypt for your ransom,
  Cush*a* and Seba in your stead.
4Since you are precious and honored
    in my sight,
  and because I love you,
I will give men in exchange for you,
  and people in exchange for your
    life.
5Do not be afraid, for I am with you;
  I will bring your children from the
    east
  and gather you from the west.
6I will say to the north, 'Give them
    up!'
  and to the south, 'Do not hold
    them back.'
Bring my sons from afar
  and my daughters from the ends of
    the earth—
7everyone who is called by my name,
  whom I created for my glory,
  whom I formed and made."

8Lead out those who have eyes but are
    blind,
  who have ears but are deaf.
9All the nations gather together
  and the peoples assemble.
Which of them foretold this
  and proclaimed to us the former
    things?
Let them bring in their witnesses to
    prove they were right,
  so that others may hear and say,
    "It is true."
10"You are my witnesses," declares the
    LORD,
  "and my servant whom I have
    chosen,
so that you may know and believe
    me

and understand that I am he.
Before me no god was formed,
  nor will there be one after me.
11I, even I, am the LORD,
  and apart from me there is no
    savior.
12I have revealed and saved and
    proclaimed—
  I, and not some foreign god among
    you.
You are my witnesses," declares the
    LORD, "that I am God.
13   Yes, and from ancient days I am
    he.
No one can deliver out of my hand.
  When I act, who can reverse it?"

God's Mercy and Israel's Unfaithfulness

14This is what the LORD says—
  your Redeemer, the Holy One of
    Israel:
"For your sake I will send to Babylon
  and bring down as fugitives all the
    Babylonians,*b*
in the ships in which they took
    pride.
15I am the LORD, your Holy One,
  Israel's Creator, your King."

16This is what the LORD says—
  he who made a way through the
    sea,
  a path through the mighty waters,
17who drew out the chariots and
    horses,
  the army and reinforcements
    together,
and they lay there, never to rise again,
  extinguished, snuffed out like a
    wick:
18"Forget the former things;
  do not dwell on the past.
19See, I am doing a new thing!
  Now it springs up; do you not
    perceive it?
I am making a way in the desert
  and streams in the wasteland.
20The wild animals honor me,
  the jackals and the owls,
because I provide water in the desert
  and streams in the wasteland,
to give drink to my people, my
    chosen,

a3 That is, the upper Nile region   *b14* Or
Chaldeans

21 the people I formed for myself
   that they may proclaim my praise.

22 "Yet you have not called upon me,
    O Jacob,
   you have not wearied yourselves
    for me, O Israel.
23 You have not brought me sheep for
    burnt offerings,
   nor honored me with your
    sacrifices.
 I have not burdened you with grain
    offerings
   nor wearied you with demands for
    incense.
24 You have not bought any fragrant
    calamus for me,
   or lavished on me the fat of your
    sacrifices.
 But you have burdened me with your
    sins
   and wearied me with your offenses.

25 "I, even I, am he who blots out
   your transgressions, for my own
    sake,
   and remembers your sins no more.
26 Review the past for me,
   let us argue the matter together;
   state the case for your innocence.

27 Your first father sinned;
   your spokesmen rebelled against
    me.
28 So I will disgrace the dignitaries of
    your temple,
   and I will consign Jacob to
    destruction[a]
   and Israel to scorn.

Israel the Chosen

44 "But now listen, O Jacob, my
    servant,
 Israel, whom I have chosen.
2 This is what the LORD says—
   he who made you, who formed
    you in the womb,
   and who will help you:
 Do not be afraid, O Jacob, my
    servant,
   Jeshurun, whom I have chosen.
3 For I will pour water on the thirsty
    land,
   and streams on the dry ground;
 I will pour out my Spirit on your
    offspring,

[a]28 The Hebrew term refers to the irrevocable giving over of things or persons to the LORD, often by totally destroying them.

Pass It on

Wednesday

ISAIAH 44:3–5   A couple has no greater responsibility than to bring up children who love God and have faith in him. Most of us feel a tremendous burden and longing for our children to share the same commitment that we have to living fruitful, godly lives. This passage describes offspring that are healthy and flourishing. These descendants describe themselves as followers of God. Teaching our children to love God is an important goal for couples to set. But how can we accomplish such a lofty goal? First, make it a matter of prayer as a couple. Read Isaiah's beautiful description of committed offspring and ask God to make it a reality in the lives of your children. Ask the Father of us all for wisdom on how, as parents, we can help our children come to know God in a deeper way.

Second, be an example. Our children need to see us model lives that are nourished by God's Word—lives that show a desire to identify with the things of God. Third, we need to carve out time in our schedules when we can read the Bible and pray together as a family. Doing this as a family allows the Word of God to be further planted and understood in the hearts of the next generation—especially when parents take the time to illustrate how these truths have been real in their own lives.

Finally, provide opportunities for your children to be exposed to other godly truths and experiences such as church activities, youth groups, mission trips, etc. It is God's desire to pour out "[his] Spirit on your offspring."

—*Bob & Rosemary*

Go to page 771 for your next devotional reading.

and my blessing on your
  descendants.
⁴They will spring up like grass in a
  meadow,
  like poplar trees by flowing
    streams.
⁵One will say, 'I belong to the LORD';
  another will call himself by the
    name of Jacob;
  still another will write on his hand,
    'The LORD's,'
  and will take the name Israel.

The LORD, Not Idols

⁶"This is what the LORD says—
  Israel's King and Redeemer, the
    LORD Almighty:
  I am the first and I am the last;
    apart from me there is no God.
⁷Who then is like me? Let him
    proclaim it.
  Let him declare and lay out before
    me
  what has happened since I established
    my ancient people,
  and what is yet to come—
    yes, let him foretell what will
      come.
⁸Do not tremble, do not be afraid.
    Did I not proclaim this and foretell
      it long ago?
  You are my witnesses. Is there any
    God besides me?
  No, there is no other Rock; I know
    not one."

⁹All who make idols are nothing,
  and the things they treasure are
    worthless.
  Those who would speak up for them
    are blind;
  they are ignorant, to their own
    shame.
¹⁰Who shapes a god and casts an idol,
  which can profit him nothing?
¹¹He and his kind will be put to
    shame;
  craftsmen are nothing but men.
  Let them all come together and take
    their stand;
  they will be brought down to terror
    and infamy.

¹²The blacksmith takes a tool
  and works with it in the coals;
  he shapes an idol with hammers,

he forges it with the might of his
    arm.
  He gets hungry and loses his strength;
    he drinks no water and grows faint.
¹³The carpenter measures with a line
  and makes an outline with a
    marker;
  he roughs it out with chisels
    and marks it with compasses.
  He shapes it in the form of man,
    of man in all his glory,
    that it may dwell in a shrine.
¹⁴He cut down cedars,
  or perhaps took a cypress or oak.
  He let it grow among the trees of the
    forest,
  or planted a pine, and the rain
    made it grow.
¹⁵It is man's fuel for burning;
  some of it he takes and warms
    himself,
  he kindles a fire and bakes bread.
  But he also fashions a god and
    worships it;
  he makes an idol and bows down
    to it.
¹⁶Half of the wood he burns in the fire;
  over it he prepares his meal,
  he roasts his meat and eats his fill.
  He also warms himself and says,
    "Ah! I am warm; I see the fire."
¹⁷From the rest he makes a god, his
    idol;
  he bows down to it and worships.
  He prays to it and says,
    "Save me; you are my god."
¹⁸They know nothing, they understand
    nothing;
  their eyes are plastered over so they
    cannot see,
  and their minds closed so they
    cannot understand.
¹⁹No one stops to think,
  no one has the knowledge or
    understanding to say,
  "Half of it I used for fuel;
    I even baked bread over its coals,
    I roasted meat and I ate.
  Shall I make a detestable thing from
    what is left?
  Shall I bow down to a block of
    wood?"
²⁰He feeds on ashes, a deluded heart
    misleads him;
  he cannot save himself, or say,

"Is not this thing in my right hand
    a lie?"

21"Remember these things, O Jacob,
    for you are my servant, O Israel.
I have made you, you are my servant;
    O Israel, I will not forget you.
22I have swept away your offenses like a
    cloud,
    your sins like the morning mist.
Return to me,
    for I have redeemed you."

23Sing for joy, O heavens, for the LORD
    has done this;
    shout aloud, O earth beneath.
Burst into song, you mountains,
    you forests and all your trees,
for the LORD has redeemed Jacob,
    he displays his glory in Israel.

Jerusalem to Be Inhabited

24"This is what the LORD says—
    your Redeemer, who formed you in
    the womb:

I am the LORD,
    who has made all things,
who alone stretched out the heavens,
    who spread out the earth by myself,

25who foils the signs of false prophets
    and makes fools of diviners,
who overthrows the learning of the
    wise
    and turns it into nonsense,
26who carries out the words of his
    servants
    and fulfills the predictions of his
    messengers,

who says of Jerusalem, 'It shall be
    inhabited,'
    of the towns of Judah, 'They shall
    be built,'
    and of their ruins, 'I will restore
    them,'
27who says to the watery deep, 'Be dry,
    and I will dry up your streams,'
28who says of Cyrus, 'He is my
    shepherd
    and will accomplish all that I
    please;
he will say of Jerusalem, "Let it be
    rebuilt,"
    and of the temple, "Let its
    foundations be laid." '

45 "This is what the LORD says to
    his anointed,
    to Cyrus, whose right hand I take
    hold of
to subdue nations before him
    and to strip kings of their armor,
to open doors before him
    so that gates will not be shut:
2I will go before you
    and will level the mountainsª;
I will break down gates of bronze
    and cut through bars of iron.
3I will give you the treasures of
    darkness,
    riches stored in secret places,
so that you may know that I am the
    LORD,
    the God of Israel, who summons
    you by name.
4For the sake of Jacob my servant,
    of Israel my chosen,
I summon you by name
    and bestow on you a title of
    honor,
    though you do not acknowledge
    me.
5I am the LORD, and there is no other;
    apart from me there is no God.
I will strengthen you,
    though you have not acknowledged
    me,
6so that from the rising of the sun
    to the place of its setting
men may know there is none besides
    me.
I am the LORD, and there is no
    other.
7I form the light and create darkness,
    I bring prosperity and create
    disaster;
    I, the LORD, do all these things.

8"You heavens above, rain down
    righteousness;
    let the clouds shower it down.
Let the earth open wide,
    let salvation spring up,
let righteousness grow with it;
    I, the LORD, have created it.

9"Woe to him who quarrels with his
    Maker,

ª2 Dead Sea Scrolls and Septuagint; the meaning
of the word in the Masoretic Text is uncertain.

to him who is but a potsherd
    among the potsherds on the
    ground.
Does the clay say to the potter,
    'What are you making?'
Does your work say,
    'He has no hands'?
¹⁰Woe to him who says to his father,
    'What have you begotten?'
or to his mother,
    'What have you brought to
      birth?'

¹¹ "This is what the LORD says—
    the Holy One of Israel, and its
      Maker:
Concerning things to come,
    do you question me about my
      children,
    or give me orders about the work
      of my hands?
¹²It is I who made the earth
    and created mankind upon it.
My own hands stretched out the
      heavens;
    I marshaled their starry hosts.

¹³I will raise up Cyrus*ᵃ* in my
    righteousness:
    I will make all his ways straight.
He will rebuild my city
    and set my exiles free,
but not for a price or reward,
    says the LORD Almighty."

¹⁴This is what the LORD says:

"The products of Egypt and the
    merchandise of Cush,*ᵇ*
    and those tall Sabeans—
they will come over to you
    and will be yours;
they will trudge behind you,
    coming over to you in chains.
They will bow down before you
    and plead with you, saying,
'Surely God is with you, and there is
      no other;
    there is no other god.' "

¹⁵Truly you are a God who hides
    himself,

ᵃ13 Hebrew *him*   *ᵇ14* That is, the upper Nile
region

Leveling the Mountains

Thursday

ISAIAH 45:1–3   The day this passage became meaningful to us was on a Sunday in 1977. We were getting ready to move to Vienna, Austria. The week before the movers had packed up all our household goods. They called and said they had greatly underestimated our moving cost. The bill was almost double and our moving budget was already tight. I (Claudia) tossed and turned throughout the night worrying about our move. Not being able to sleep, I got up before daybreak and opened my Bible to where I was reading this passage in Isaiah. Isaiah 45 was a personal message for me and Dave. God was the One who would level the mountains and provide for our needs.

I (Dave) didn't sleep well either. When I got up, Claudia excitedly read this passage with me. Together we prayed and thanked God for "leveling our mountain" of fear, and we asked him to give us "riches stored in secret places" (verse 3) so we could pay the moving company. A few hours later at Sunday School, a couple came up to us and said how, the evening before, their family had decided they wanted to write a check for whatever we still needed for our moving expenses.

Our mountain had just been leveled! In verse 2, God told Cyrus, "I will go before you and will level the mountains." What a great verse to claim for your marriage—to know that the battle is not yours, but the Lord's and to put your trust in him.

Stop for a moment and evaluate the mountains in your marriage. Are finances tight? Maybe you are struggling with the awesome responsibility of parenting teenagers or caring for elderly parents. Whatever you're facing, let us encourage you to refocus on God. He will go before you and help you overcome the mountains in your marriage.

—***Dave & Claudia***

Go to page 784 for your next devotional reading.

O God and Savior of Israel.
¹⁶All the makers of idols will be put to
    shame and disgraced;
    they will go off into disgrace
        together.
¹⁷But Israel will be saved by the Lord
    with an everlasting salvation;
    you will never be put to shame or
        disgraced,
    to ages everlasting.

¹⁸For this is what the Lord says—
    he who created the heavens,
        he is God;
    he who fashioned and made the
        earth,
        he founded it;
    he did not create it to be empty,
        but formed it to be inhabited—
    he says:
    "I am the Lord,
        and there is no other.
¹⁹I have not spoken in secret,
        from somewhere in a land of
           darkness;
    I have not said to Jacob's
        descendants,
    'Seek me in vain.'
    I, the Lord, speak the truth;
        I declare what is right.

²⁰"Gather together and come;
        assemble, you fugitives from the
           nations.
    Ignorant are those who carry about
        idols of wood,
    who pray to gods that cannot save.
²¹Declare what is to be, present it—
        let them take counsel together.
    Who foretold this long ago,
        who declared it from the distant
           past?
    Was it not I, the Lord?
        And there is no God apart from
           me,
    a righteous God and a Savior;
        there is none but me.

²²"Turn to me and be saved,
        all you ends of the earth;
        for I am God, and there is no
           other.
²³By myself I have sworn,
        my mouth has uttered in all
           integrity
    a word that will not be revoked:
    Before me every knee will bow;

        by me every tongue will swear.
²⁴They will say of me, 'In the Lord
        alone
    are righteousness and strength.' "
    All who have raged against him
        will come to him and be put to
           shame.
²⁵But in the Lord all the descendants of
    Israel
    will be found righteous and will
        exult.

Gods of Babylon

46 Bel bows down, Nebo stoops
      low;
    their idols are borne by beasts of
        burden.ᵃ
The images that are carried about are
    burdensome,
    a burden for the weary.
²They stoop and bow down together;
    unable to rescue the burden,
    they themselves go off into
        captivity.

³"Listen to me, O house of Jacob,
    all you who remain of the house
        of Israel,
    you whom I have upheld since you
        were conceived,
    and have carried since your birth.
⁴Even to your old age and gray hairs
    I am he, I am he who will sustain
        you.
    I have made you and I will carry you;
    I will sustain you and I will rescue
        you.

⁵"To whom will you compare me or
        count me equal?
    To whom will you liken me that
        we may be compared?
⁶Some pour out gold from their bags
    and weigh out silver on the scales;
    they hire a goldsmith to make it into
        a god,
    and they bow down and worship
        it.
⁷They lift it to their shoulders and
        carry it;
    they set it up in its place, and there
        it stands.
    From that spot it cannot move.
    Though one cries out to it, it does not
        answer;

ᵃ1 Or *are but beasts and cattle*

it cannot save him from his
troubles.

8 "Remember this, fix it in mind,
take it to heart, you rebels.
9 Remember the former things, those of
long ago;
I am God, and there is no other;
I am God, and there is none like
me.
10 I make known the end from the
beginning,
from ancient times, what is still to
come.
I say: My purpose will stand,
and I will do all that I please.
11 From the east I summon a bird of
prey;
from a far-off land, a man to fulfill
my purpose.
What I have said, that will I bring
about;
what I have planned, that will I do.
12 Listen to me, you stubborn-hearted,
you who are far from
righteousness.
13 I am bringing my righteousness near,
it is not far away;
and my salvation will not be
delayed.
I will grant salvation to Zion,
my splendor to Israel.

The Fall of Babylon

47 "Go down, sit in the dust,
Virgin Daughter of Babylon;
sit on the ground without a throne,
Daughter of the Babylonians.*a*
No more will you be called
tender or delicate.
2 Take millstones and grind flour;
take off your veil.
Lift up your skirts, bare your legs,
and wade through the streams.
3 Your nakedness will be exposed
and your shame uncovered.
I will take vengeance;
I will spare no one."

4 Our Redeemer—the LORD Almighty is
his name—
is the Holy One of Israel.

5 "Sit in silence, go into darkness,
Daughter of the Babylonians;
no more will you be called
queen of kingdoms.

6 I was angry with my people
and desecrated my inheritance;
I gave them into your hand,
and you showed them no mercy.
Even on the aged
you laid a very heavy yoke.
7 You said, 'I will continue forever—
the eternal queen!'
But you did not consider these things
or reflect on what might happen.

8 "Now then, listen, you wanton
creature,
lounging in your security
and saying to yourself,
'I am, and there is none besides
me.
I will never be a widow
or suffer the loss of children.'
9 Both of these will overtake you
in a moment, on a single day:
loss of children and widowhood.
They will come upon you in full
measure,
in spite of your many sorceries
and all your potent spells.
10 You have trusted in your wickedness
and have said, 'No one sees me.'
Your wisdom and knowledge mislead
you
when you say to yourself,
'I am, and there is none besides
me.'
11 Disaster will come upon you,
and you will not know how to
conjure it away.
A calamity will fall upon you
that you cannot ward off with a
ransom;
a catastrophe you cannot foresee
will suddenly come upon you.

12 "Keep on, then, with your magic
spells
and with your many sorceries,
which you have labored at since
childhood.
Perhaps you will succeed,
perhaps you will cause terror.
13 All the counsel you have received has
only worn you out!
Let your astrologers come forward,
those stargazers who make predictions
month by month,

a1 Or Chaldeans; also in verse 5

let them save you from what is
　　coming upon you.
¹⁴Surely they are like stubble;
　　the fire will burn them up.
They cannot even save themselves
　　from the power of the flame.
Here are no coals to warm anyone;
　　here is no fire to sit by.
¹⁵That is all they can do for you—
　　these you have labored with
　　and trafficked with since
　　　childhood.
Each of them goes on in his error;
　　there is not one that can save you.

Stubborn Israel

48 "Listen to this, O house of Jacob,
　　you who are called by the name
　　　of Israel
and come from the line of Judah,
you who take oaths in the name of
　　the LORD
and invoke the God of Israel—
　　but not in truth or righteousness—
²you who call yourselves citizens of
　　the holy city
and rely on the God of Israel—
　　the LORD Almighty is his name:
³I foretold the former things long ago,
　　my mouth announced them and I
　　　made them known;
then suddenly I acted, and they
　　came to pass.
⁴For I knew how stubborn you were;
　　the sinews of your neck were iron,
　　your forehead was bronze.
⁵Therefore I told you these things long
　　ago;
before they happened I announced
　　them to you
so that you could not say,
　　'My idols did them;
my wooden image and metal god
　　ordained them.'
⁶You have heard these things; look at
　　them all.
Will you not admit them?

"From now on I will tell you of new
　　things,
of hidden things unknown to you.
⁷They are created now, and not long
　　ago;
you have not heard of them before
　　today.
So you cannot say,

'Yes, I knew of them.'
⁸You have neither heard nor
　　understood;
from of old your ear has not been
　　open.
Well do I know how treacherous you
　　are;
you were called a rebel from birth.
⁹For my own name's sake I delay my
　　wrath;
for the sake of my praise I hold it
　　back from you,
so as not to cut you off.
¹⁰See, I have refined you, though not as
　　silver;
I have tested you in the furnace of
　　affliction.
¹¹For my own sake, for my own sake, I
　　do this.
How can I let myself be defamed?
I will not yield my glory to
　　another.

Israel Freed

¹²"Listen to me, O Jacob,
　　Israel, whom I have called:
I am he;
　　I am the first and I am the last.
¹³My own hand laid the foundations of
　　the earth,
and my right hand spread out the
　　heavens;
when I summon them,
　　they all stand up together.

¹⁴"Come together, all of you, and
　　listen:
Which of ⌊the idols⌋ has foretold
　　these things?
The LORD's chosen ally
　　will carry out his purpose against
　　　Babylon;
his arm will be against the
　　Babylonians.ᵃ
¹⁵I, even I, have spoken;
　　yes, I have called him.
I will bring him,
　　and he will succeed in his mission.

¹⁶"Come near me and listen to this:

"From the first announcement I have
　　not spoken in secret;
at the time it happens, I am there."

ᵃ14 Or *Chaldeans*; also in verse 20

And now the Sovereign LORD has sent
    me,
  with his Spirit.

17This is what the LORD says—
  your Redeemer, the Holy One of
    Israel:
"I am the LORD your God,
  who teaches you what is best for
    you,
  who directs you in the way you
    should go.
18If only you had paid attention to my
    commands,
  your peace would have been like a
    river,
  your righteousness like the waves
    of the sea.
19Your descendants would have been
    like the sand,
  your children like its numberless
    grains;
  their name would never be cut off
    nor destroyed from before me."

20Leave Babylon,
  flee from the Babylonians!
Announce this with shouts of joy
  and proclaim it.
Send it out to the ends of the earth;
  say, "The LORD has redeemed his
    servant Jacob."
21They did not thirst when he led them
    through the deserts;
  he made water flow for them from
    the rock;
  he split the rock
    and water gushed out.

22"There is no peace," says the LORD,
  "for the wicked."

The Servant of the LORD

49 Listen to me, you islands;
  hear this, you distant nations:
Before I was born the LORD called me;
  from my birth he has made
    mention of my name.
2He made my mouth like a sharpened
    sword,
  in the shadow of his hand he hid
    me;
he made me into a polished arrow
  and concealed me in his quiver.
3He said to me, "You are my servant,
  Israel, in whom I will display my
    splendor."

4But I said, "I have labored to no
    purpose;
  I have spent my strength in vain
    and for nothing.
Yet what is due me is in the LORD's
    hand,
  and my reward is with my God."

5And now the LORD says—
  he who formed me in the womb
    to be his servant
to bring Jacob back to him
  and gather Israel to himself,
for I am honored in the eyes of the
    LORD
  and my God has been my
    strength—
6he says:
"It is too small a thing for you to be
    my servant
to restore the tribes of Jacob
  and bring back those of Israel I
    have kept.
I will also make you a light for the
    Gentiles,
  that you may bring my salvation to
    the ends of the earth."

7This is what the LORD says—
  the Redeemer and Holy One of
    Israel—
to him who was despised and
    abhorred by the nation,
  to the servant of rulers:
"Kings will see you and rise up,
  princes will see and bow down,
because of the LORD, who is faithful,
  the Holy One of Israel, who has
    chosen you."

Restoration of Israel

8This is what the LORD says:

"In the time of my favor I will
    answer you,
  and in the day of salvation I will
    help you;
I will keep you and will make you
  to be a covenant for the people,
to restore the land
  and to reassign its desolate
    inheritances,
9to say to the captives, 'Come out,'
  and to those in darkness, 'Be free!'

"They will feed beside the roads

and find pasture on every barren
hill.
¹⁰They will neither hunger nor thirst,
nor will the desert heat or the sun
beat upon them.
He who has compassion on them will
guide them
and lead them beside springs of
water.
¹¹I will turn all my mountains into
roads,
and my highways will be raised up.
¹²See, they will come from afar—
some from the north, some from
the west,
some from the region of Aswan.ᵃ "

¹³Shout for joy, O heavens;
rejoice, O earth;
burst into song, O mountains!
For the LORD comforts his people
and will have compassion on his
afflicted ones.

¹⁴But Zion said, "The LORD has
forsaken me,
the Lord has forgotten me."

¹⁵"Can a mother forget the baby at her
breast
and have no compassion on the
child she has borne?
Though she may forget,
I will not forget you!
¹⁶See, I have engraved you on the
palms of my hands;
your walls are ever before me.
¹⁷Your sons hasten back,
and those who laid you waste
depart from you.
¹⁸Lift up your eyes and look around;
all your sons gather and come to
you.
As surely as I live," declares the LORD,
"you will wear them all as
ornaments;
you will put them on, like a bride.

¹⁹"Though you were ruined and made
desolate
and your land laid waste,
now you will be too small for your
people,
and those who devoured you will
be far away.
²⁰The children born during your
bereavement

will yet say in your hearing,
'This place is too small for us;
give us more space to live in.'
²¹Then you will say in your heart,
'Who bore me these?
I was bereaved and barren;
I was exiled and rejected.
Who brought these up?
I was left all alone,
but these—where have they come
from?' "

²²This is what the Sovereign LORD says:

"See, I will beckon to the Gentiles,
I will lift up my banner to the
peoples;
they will bring your sons in their
arms
and carry your daughters on their
shoulders.
²³Kings will be your foster fathers,
and their queens your nursing
mothers.
They will bow down before you with
their faces to the ground;
they will lick the dust at your feet.
Then you will know that I am the
LORD;
those who hope in me will not be
disappointed."

²⁴Can plunder be taken from warriors,
or captives rescued from the
fierceᵇ ?

²⁵But this is what the LORD says:

"Yes, captives will be taken from
warriors,
and plunder retrieved from the
fierce;
I will contend with those who
contend with you,
and your children I will save.
²⁶I will make your oppressors eat their
own flesh;
they will be drunk on their own
blood, as with wine.
Then all mankind will know
that I, the LORD, am your Savior,
your Redeemer, the Mighty One of
Jacob."

ᵃ12 Dead Sea Scrolls; Masoretic Text *Sinim*
ᵇ24 Dead Sea Scrolls, Vulgate and Syriac (see also
Septuagint and verse 25); Masoretic Text *righteous*

Israel's Sin and the Servant's Obedience

50 This is what the LORD says:

"Where is your mother's certificate of
    divorce
  with which I sent her away?
Or to which of my creditors
  did I sell you?
Because of your sins you were sold;
  because of your transgressions your
    mother was sent away.
²When I came, why was there no one?
  When I called, why was there no
    one to answer?
Was my arm too short to ransom
    you?
  Do I lack the strength to rescue
    you?
By a mere rebuke I dry up the sea,
  I turn rivers into a desert;
their fish rot for lack of water
  and die of thirst.
³I clothe the sky with darkness
  and make sackcloth its covering."

⁴The Sovereign LORD has given me an
    instructed tongue,
  to know the word that sustains the
    weary.
He wakens me morning by morning,
  wakens my ear to listen like one
    being taught.
⁵The Sovereign LORD has opened my
    ears,
  and I have not been rebellious;
  I have not drawn back.
⁶I offered my back to those who beat
    me,
  my cheeks to those who pulled out
    my beard;
I did not hide my face
  from mocking and spitting.
⁷Because the Sovereign LORD helps me,
  I will not be disgraced.
Therefore have I set my face like flint,
  and I know I will not be put to
    shame.
⁸He who vindicates me is near.
  Who then will bring charges
    against me?
  Let us face each other!
Who is my accuser?
  Let him confront me!
⁹It is the Sovereign LORD who helps
    me.
  Who is he that will condemn me?

They will all wear out like a garment;
  the moths will eat them up.

¹⁰Who among you fears the LORD
  and obeys the word of his servant?
Let him who walks in the dark,
  who has no light,
trust in the name of the LORD
  and rely on his God.
¹¹But now, all you who light fires
  and provide yourselves with
    flaming torches,
go, walk in the light of your fires
  and of the torches you have set
    ablaze.
This is what you shall receive from
    my hand:
  You will lie down in torment.

Everlasting Salvation for Zion

51 "Listen to me, you who pursue
    righteousness
  and who seek the LORD:
Look to the rock from which you
    were cut
  and to the quarry from which you
    were hewn;
²look to Abraham, your father,
  and to Sarah, who gave you birth.
When I called him he was but one,
  and I blessed him and made him
    many.
³The LORD will surely comfort Zion
  and will look with compassion on
    all her ruins;
he will make her deserts like Eden,
  her wastelands like the garden of
    the LORD.
Joy and gladness will be found in her,
  thanksgiving and the sound of
    singing.

⁴"Listen to me, my people;
  hear me, my nation:
The law will go out from me;
  my justice will become a light to
    the nations.
⁵My righteousness draws near speedily,
  my salvation is on the way,
  and my arm will bring justice to
    the nations.
The islands will look to me
  and wait in hope for my arm.
⁶Lift up your eyes to the heavens,
  look at the earth beneath;
the heavens will vanish like smoke,

the earth will wear out like a
garment
and its inhabitants die like flies.
But my salvation will last forever,
my righteousness will never fail.

⁷"Hear me, you who know what is
right,
you people who have my law in
your hearts:
Do not fear the reproach of men
or be terrified by their insults.
⁸For the moth will eat them up like a
garment;
the worm will devour them like
wool.
But my righteousness will last forever,
my salvation through all
generations."

⁹Awake, awake! Clothe yourself with
strength,
O arm of the LORD;
awake, as in days gone by,
as in generations of old.
Was it not you who cut Rahab to
pieces,
who pierced that monster through?
¹⁰Was it not you who dried up the sea,
the waters of the great deep,
who made a road in the depths of the
sea
so that the redeemed might cross
over?
¹¹The ransomed of the LORD will
return.
They will enter Zion with singing;
everlasting joy will crown their
heads.
Gladness and joy will overtake them,
and sorrow and sighing will flee
away.

¹²"I, even I, am he who comforts you.
Who are you that you fear mortal
men,
the sons of men, who are but
grass,
¹³that you forget the LORD your Maker,
who stretched out the heavens
and laid the foundations of the
earth,
that you live in constant terror every
day
because of the wrath of the
oppressor,
who is bent on destruction?

For where is the wrath of the
oppressor?
¹⁴ The cowering prisoners will soon
be set free;
they will not die in their dungeon,
nor will they lack bread.
¹⁵For I am the LORD your God,
who churns up the sea so that its
waves roar—
the LORD Almighty is his name.
¹⁶I have put my words in your mouth
and covered you with the shadow
of my hand—
I who set the heavens in place,
who laid the foundations of the
earth,
and who say to Zion, 'You are my
people.' "

The Cup of the LORD's Wrath

¹⁷Awake, awake!
Rise up, O Jerusalem,
you who have drunk from the hand
of the LORD
the cup of his wrath,
you who have drained to its dregs
the goblet that makes men stagger.
¹⁸Of all the sons she bore
there was none to guide her;
of all the sons she reared
there was none to take her by the
hand.
¹⁹These double calamities have come
upon you—
who can comfort you?—
ruin and destruction, famine and
sword—
who can*ᵃ* console you?
²⁰Your sons have fainted;
they lie at the head of every street,
like antelope caught in a net.
They are filled with the wrath of the
LORD
and the rebuke of your God.

²¹Therefore hear this, you afflicted one,
made drunk, but not with wine.
²²This is what your Sovereign LORD
says,
your God, who defends his people:
"See, I have taken out of your hand
the cup that made you stagger;

ᵃ19 Dead Sea Scrolls, Septuagint, Vulgate and
Syriac; Masoretic Text / *how can I*

from that cup, the goblet of my
wrath,
you will never drink again.
²³I will put it into the hands of your
tormentors,
who said to you,
'Fall prostrate that we may walk
over you.'
And you made your back like the
ground,
like a street to be walked over."

52 Awake, awake, O Zion,
clothe yourself with strength.
Put on your garments of splendor,
O Jerusalem, the holy city.
The uncircumcised and defiled
will not enter you again.
²Shake off your dust;
rise up, sit enthroned, O Jerusalem.
Free yourself from the chains on your
neck,
O captive Daughter of Zion.

³For this is what the LORD says:

"You were sold for nothing,
and without money you will be
redeemed."

⁴For this is what the Sovereign LORD
says:

"At first my people went down to
Egypt to live;
lately, Assyria has oppressed them.

⁵"And now what do I have here?" declares the LORD.

"For my people have been taken
away for nothing,
and those who rule them mock,ᵃ "
declares the LORD.

"And all day long
my name is constantly
blasphemed.
⁶Therefore my people will know my
name;
therefore in that day they will
know
that it is I who foretold it.
Yes, it is I."

⁷How beautiful on the mountains
are the feet of those who bring
good news,
who proclaim peace,
who bring good tidings,

who proclaim salvation,
who say to Zion,
"Your God reigns!"
⁸Listen! Your watchmen lift up their
voices;
together they shout for joy.
When the LORD returns to Zion,
they will see it with their own eyes.
⁹Burst into songs of joy together,
you ruins of Jerusalem,
for the LORD has comforted his
people,
he has redeemed Jerusalem.
¹⁰The LORD will lay bare his holy arm
in the sight of all the nations,
and all the ends of the earth will see
the salvation of our God.

¹¹Depart, depart, go out from there!
Touch no unclean thing!
Come out from it and be pure,
you who carry the vessels of the
LORD.
¹²But you will not leave in haste
or go in flight;
for the LORD will go before you,
the God of Israel will be your rear
guard.

The Suffering and Glory of the Servant

¹³See, my servant will act wiselyᵇ;
he will be raised and lifted up and
highly exalted.
¹⁴Just as there were many who were
appalled at himᶜ—
his appearance was so disfigured
beyond that of any man
and his form marred beyond
human likeness—
¹⁵so will he sprinkle many nations,ᵈ
and kings will shut their mouths
because of him.
For what they were not told, they will
see,
and what they have not heard, they
will understand.

53 Who has believed our message
and to whom has the arm of the
LORD been revealed?
²He grew up before him like a tender
shoot,

ᵃ5 Dead Sea Scrolls and Vulgate; Masoretic Text
wail   ᵇ13 Or *will prosper*   ᶜ14 Hebrew *you*
ᵈ15 Hebrew; Septuagint *so will many nations marvel
at him*

and like a root out of dry ground.
He had no beauty or majesty to
    attract us to him,
  nothing in his appearance that we
    should desire him.
³He was despised and rejected by men,
  a man of sorrows, and familiar
    with suffering.
Like one from whom men hide their
    faces
  he was despised, and we esteemed
    him not.

⁴Surely he took up our infirmities
  and carried our sorrows,
yet we considered him stricken by
    God,
  smitten by him, and afflicted.
⁵But he was pierced for our
    transgressions,
  he was crushed for our iniquities;
the punishment that brought us peace
    was upon him,
  and by his wounds we are healed.
⁶We all, like sheep, have gone astray,
  each of us has turned to his own
    way;
and the Lord has laid on him
  the iniquity of us all.

⁷He was oppressed and afflicted,
  yet he did not open his mouth;
he was led like a lamb to the
    slaughter,
  and as a sheep before her shearers
    is silent,
so he did not open his mouth.
⁸By oppression ᵃ and judgment he
    was taken away.
  And who can speak of his
    descendants?
For he was cut off from the land of
    the living;
  for the transgression of my people
    he was stricken. ᵇ
⁹He was assigned a grave with the
    wicked,
  and with the rich in his death,
though he had done no violence,
  nor was any deceit in his mouth.

¹⁰Yet it was the Lord's will to crush
    him and cause him to suffer,
and though the Lord makes ᶜ his
    life a guilt offering,
he will see his offspring and prolong
    his days,

and the will of the Lord will
    prosper in his hand.
¹¹After the suffering of his soul,
  he will see the light ˌof lifeˌ ᵈ and
    be satisfied ᵉ;
by his knowledge ᶠ my righteous
    servant will justify many,
  and he will bear their iniquities.
¹²Therefore I will give him a portion
    among the great, ᵍ
  and he will divide the spoils with
    the strong, ʰ
because he poured out his life unto
    death,
  and was numbered with the
    transgressors.
For he bore the sin of many,
  and made intercession for the
    transgressors.

The Future Glory of Zion

54 "Sing, O barren woman,
  you who never bore a child;
burst into song, shout for joy,
  you who were never in labor;
because more are the children of the
    desolate woman
  than of her who has a husband,"
                    says the Lord.
²"Enlarge the place of your tent,
  stretch your tent curtains wide,
  do not hold back;
lengthen your cords,
  strengthen your stakes.
³For you will spread out to the right
    and to the left;
  your descendants will dispossess
    nations
  and settle in their desolate cities.

⁴"Do not be afraid; you will not suffer
    shame.
  Do not fear disgrace; you will not
    be humiliated.
You will forget the shame of your
    youth

ᵃ8 Or From arrest   ᵇ8 Or away. / Yet who of his
generation considered / that he was cut off from the
land of the living / for the transgression of my people, /
to whom the blow was due?   ᶜ10 Hebrew though
you make   ᵈ11 Dead Sea Scrolls (see also
Septuagint); Masoretic Text does not have the light
ˌof lifeˌ.   ᵉ11 Or (with Masoretic Text) ¹¹He will
see the result of the suffering of his soul / and be
satisfied   ᶠ11 Or by knowledge of him   ᵍ12 Or
many   ʰ12 Or numerous

and remember no more the
   reproach of your widowhood.
[5]For your Maker is your husband—
   the LORD Almighty is his name—
the Holy One of Israel is your
      Redeemer;
   he is called the God of all the
      earth.
[6]The LORD will call you back
   as if you were a wife deserted and
      distressed in spirit—
a wife who married young,
   only to be rejected," says your God.
[7]"For a brief moment I abandoned
      you,
   but with deep compassion I will
      bring you back.
[8]In a surge of anger
   I hid my face from you for a
      moment,
but with everlasting kindness
   I will have compassion on you,"
   says the LORD your Redeemer.

[9]"To me this is like the days of Noah,
   when I swore that the waters of
      Noah would never again
      cover the earth.
So now I have sworn not to be angry
      with you,
   never to rebuke you again.
[10]Though the mountains be shaken
      and the hills be removed,
yet my unfailing love for you will not
      be shaken
   nor my covenant of peace be
      removed,"
   says the LORD, who has
      compassion on you.

[11]"O afflicted city, lashed by storms
      and not comforted,
   I will build you with stones of
      turquoise,[a]
   your foundations with sapphires.[b]
[12]I will make your battlements of
      rubies,
   your gates of sparkling jewels,
   and all your walls of precious
      stones.
[13]All your sons will be taught by the
      LORD,
   and great will be your children's
      peace.
[14]In righteousness you will be
      established:

Tyranny will be far from you;
   you will have nothing to fear.
Terror will be far removed;
   it will not come near you.
[15]If anyone does attack you, it will not
      be my doing;
   whoever attacks you will surrender
      to you.

[16]"See, it is I who created the
      blacksmith
   who fans the coals into flame
   and forges a weapon fit for its
      work.
And it is I who have created the
      destroyer to work havoc;
[17]   no weapon forged against you will
      prevail,
   and you will refute every tongue
      that accuses you.
This is the heritage of the servants of
      the LORD,
   and this is their vindication from
      me,"
                  declares the LORD.

Invitation to the Thirsty

55 "Come, all you who are thirsty,
      come to the waters;
   and you who have no money,
      come, buy and eat!
Come, buy wine and milk
   without money and without cost.
[2]Why spend money on what is not
      bread,
   and your labor on what does not
      satisfy?
Listen, listen to me, and eat what is
      good,
   and your soul will delight in the
      richest of fare.
[3]Give ear and come to me;
   hear me, that your soul may live.
I will make an everlasting covenant
      with you,
   my faithful love promised to
      David.
[4]See, I have made him a witness to the
      peoples,
   a leader and commander of the
      peoples.

---

[a]11 The meaning of the Hebrew for this word is
uncertain.   [b]11 Or lapis lazuli

⁵Surely you will summon nations you
    know not,
    and nations that do not know you
        will hasten to you,
because of the LORD your God,
    the Holy One of Israel,
    for he has endowed you with
        splendor."

⁶Seek the LORD while he may be
    found;
    call on him while he is near.
⁷Let the wicked forsake his way
    and the evil man his thoughts.
Let him turn to the LORD, and he will
    have mercy on him,
    and to our God, for he will freely
        pardon.

⁸"For my thoughts are not your
    thoughts,
    neither are your ways my ways,"
                    declares the LORD.
⁹"As the heavens are higher than the
    earth,
    so are my ways higher than your
        ways
    and my thoughts than your
        thoughts.
¹⁰As the rain and the snow
    come down from heaven,
    and do not return to it
    without watering the earth
and making it bud and flourish,
    so that it yields seed for the sower
        and bread for the eater,
¹¹so is my word that goes out from my
    mouth:
    It will not return to me empty,
but will accomplish what I desire
    and achieve the purpose for which
        I sent it.
¹²You will go out in joy
    and be led forth in peace;
the mountains and hills
    will burst into song before you,
and all the trees of the field
    will clap their hands.
¹³Instead of the thornbush will grow
    the pine tree,
    and instead of briers the myrtle
        will grow.
This will be for the LORD's renown,
    for an everlasting sign,
    which will not be destroyed."

Salvation for Others

56 This is what the LORD says:

"Maintain justice
    and do what is right,
for my salvation is close at hand
    and my righteousness will soon be
        revealed.
²Blessed is the man who does this,
    the man who holds it fast,
who keeps the Sabbath without
    desecrating it,
    and keeps his hand from doing
        any evil."

³Let no foreigner who has bound
        himself to the LORD say,
    "The LORD will surely exclude me
        from his people."
And let not any eunuch complain,
    "I am only a dry tree."

⁴For this is what the LORD says:

"To the eunuchs who keep my
        Sabbaths,
    who choose what pleases me
    and hold fast to my covenant—
⁵to them I will give within my temple
        and its walls
    a memorial and a name
    better than sons and daughters;
I will give them an everlasting name
    that will not be cut off.
⁶And foreigners who bind themselves
        to the LORD
    to serve him,
to love the name of the LORD,
    and to worship him,
all who keep the Sabbath without
        desecrating it
    and who hold fast to my
        covenant—
⁷these I will bring to my holy
        mountain
    and give them joy in my house of
        prayer.
Their burnt offerings and sacrifices
    will be accepted on my altar;
for my house will be called
    a house of prayer for all nations."
⁸The Sovereign LORD declares—
    he who gathers the exiles of Israel:
"I will gather still others to them
    besides those already gathered."

God's Accusation Against the Wicked

9Come, all you beasts of the field,
come and devour, all you beasts of
the forest!
10Israel's watchmen are blind,
they all lack knowledge;
they are all mute dogs,
they cannot bark;
they lie around and dream,
they love to sleep.
11They are dogs with mighty appetites;
they never have enough.
They are shepherds who lack
understanding;
they all turn to their own way,
each seeks his own gain.
12"Come," each one cries, "let me get
wine!
Let us drink our fill of beer!
And tomorrow will be like today,
or even far better."

57 The righteous perish,
and no one ponders it in his
heart;
devout men are taken away,
and no one understands
that the righteous are taken away
to be spared from evil.
2Those who walk uprightly
enter into peace;
they find rest as they lie in death.

3"But you—come here, you sons of a
sorceress,
you offspring of adulterers and
prostitutes!
4Whom are you mocking?
At whom do you sneer
and stick out your tongue?
Are you not a brood of rebels,
the offspring of liars?
5You burn with lust among the oaks
and under every spreading tree;
you sacrifice your children in the
ravines
and under the overhanging crags.
6The idols among the smooth stones
of the ravines are your
portion;
they, they are your lot.
Yes, to them you have poured out
drink offerings
and offered grain offerings.
In the light of these things, should
I relent?

7You have made your bed on a high
and lofty hill;
there you went up to offer your
sacrifices.
8Behind your doors and your
doorposts
you have put your pagan symbols.
Forsaking me, you uncovered your
bed,
you climbed into it and opened it
wide;
you made a pact with those whose
beds you love,
and you looked on their
nakedness.
9You went to Molech*a* with olive oil
and increased your perfumes.
You sent your ambassadors*b* far
away;
you descended to the grave*c*
itself!
10You were wearied by all your ways,
but you would not say, 'It is
hopeless.'
You found renewal of your strength,
and so you did not faint.

11"Whom have you so dreaded and
feared
that you have been false to me,
and have neither remembered me
nor pondered this in your hearts?
Is it not because I have long been
silent
that you do not fear me?
12I will expose your righteousness and
your works,
and they will not benefit you.
13When you cry out for help,
let your collection ⌊of idols⌋ save
you!
The wind will carry all of them off,
a mere breath will blow them
away.
But the man who makes me his
refuge
will inherit the land
and possess my holy mountain."

Comfort for the Contrite

14And it will be said:

"Build up, build up, prepare the
road!

---

*a*9 Or *to the king*   *b*9 Or *idols*   *c*9 Hebrew
Sheol

Remove the obstacles out of the
way of my people."
¹⁵For this is what the high and lofty
One says—
he who lives forever, whose name
is holy:
"I live in a high and holy place,
but also with him who is contrite
and lowly in spirit,
to revive the spirit of the lowly
and to revive the heart of the
contrite.
¹⁶I will not accuse forever,
nor will I always be angry,
for then the spirit of man would grow
faint before me—
the breath of man that I have
created.
¹⁷I was enraged by his sinful greed;
I punished him, and hid my face
in anger,
yet he kept on in his willful
ways.
¹⁸I have seen his ways, but I will heal
him;
I will guide him and restore
comfort to him,

¹⁹ creating praise on the lips of the
mourners in Israel.
Peace, peace, to those far and near,"
says the LORD. "And I will heal
them."
²⁰But the wicked are like the tossing
sea,
which cannot rest,
whose waves cast up mire and
mud.
²¹"There is no peace," says my God,
"for the wicked."

True Fasting

58 "Shout it aloud, do not hold
back.
Raise your voice like a trumpet.
Declare to my people their rebellion
and to the house of Jacob their
sins.
²For day after day they seek me out;
they seem eager to know my ways,
as if they were a nation that does
what is right
and has not forsaken the
commands of its God.

Going Through the Motions

Friday

ISAIAH 58   Isaiah reminds the people of how sad it is to go through the motions of a fast but not really mean it. They were performing the outward signs of a fast, but there was nothing going on inside their hearts. The people weren't fasting in order to truly know God in a more intimate way.

Often this kind of thing happens in marriage. We get busy and find ourselves going through the motions. We talk *at* each other but not really *with* each other. Our purpose for talking is to make a point or give an opinion, rather than come to a greater understanding of our spouse's heart.

I will never forget one time when we were sitting in a restaurant with another couple. Rosemary and I had been married for seven years. I sat there listening to my wife explain one of her dreams for our future in such a dynamic way; I was amazed. "Why haven't you told me these things before?" I

asked later that night. To my surprise she replied, "I've tried, but you never want to really talk and listen anymore!"

The people in Isaiah's day were fasting to get what they wanted from God, but they were unwilling to do what was necessary to grow closer to God. Often we desire to get something from our marriage, but we fail to find the intimacy of a marital relationship. We want the blessing without the work, without the changed behavior.

Take this warning from the prophet. Find ways to fast to develop a closer intimacy with the one you love. Instead of going through the marital motions, take time to analyze your spouse's heart. Listen to his or her needs. Put aside your own wants, so that you can better understand your spouse.
—Bob & Rosemary

Go to page 786 for your next devotional reading.

They ask me for just decisions
　　and seem eager for God to come
　　　near them.
3'Why have we fasted,' they say,
　　'and you have not seen it?
Why have we humbled ourselves,
　　and you have not noticed?'

"Yet on the day of your fasting, you
　　do as you please
　　and exploit all your workers.
4Your fasting ends in quarreling and
　　strife,
　　and in striking each other with
　　　wicked fists.
You cannot fast as you do today
　　and expect your voice to be heard
　　　on high.
5Is this the kind of fast I have chosen,
　　only a day for a man to humble
　　　himself?
Is it only for bowing one's head like a
　　reed
　　and for lying on sackcloth and
　　　ashes?
Is that what you call a fast,
　　a day acceptable to the LORD?

6"Is not this the kind of fasting I have
　　chosen:
to loose the chains of injustice
　　and untie the cords of the yoke,
to set the oppressed free
　　and break every yoke?
7Is it not to share your food with the
　　hungry
　　and to provide the poor wanderer
　　　with shelter—
when you see the naked, to clothe
　　him,
　　and not to turn away from your
　　　own flesh and blood?
8Then your light will break forth like
　　the dawn,
　　and your healing will quickly
　　　appear;
then your righteousness[a] will go
　　before you,
　　and the glory of the LORD will be
　　　your rear guard.
9Then you will call, and the LORD will
　　answer;
　　you will cry for help, and he will
　　　say: Here am I.

"If you do away with the yoke of
　　oppression,

with the pointing finger and
　　malicious talk,
10and if you spend yourselves in behalf
　　of the hungry
　　and satisfy the needs of the
　　　oppressed,
then your light will rise in the
　　darkness,
　　and your night will become like
　　　the noonday.
11The LORD will guide you always;
　　he will satisfy your needs in a
　　　sun-scorched land
　　and will strengthen your frame.
You will be like a well-watered
　　garden,
　　like a spring whose waters never
　　　fail.
12Your people will rebuild the ancient
　　ruins
　　and will raise up the age-old
　　　foundations;
you will be called Repairer of Broken
　　Walls,
　　Restorer of Streets with Dwellings.

13"If you keep your feet from breaking
　　the Sabbath
　　and from doing as you please on
　　　my holy day,
if you call the Sabbath a delight
　　and the LORD's holy day honorable,
and if you honor it by not going your
　　own way
　　and not doing as you please or
　　　speaking idle words,
14then you will find your joy in the
　　LORD,
　　and I will cause you to ride on the
　　　heights of the land
　　and to feast on the inheritance of
　　　your father Jacob."
　　　　　The mouth of the LORD
　　　　　　　has spoken.

Sin, Confession and Redemption

59 Surely the arm of the LORD is not
　　too short to save,
　　nor his ear too dull to hear.
2But your iniquities have separated
　　you from your God;
　　your sins have hidden his face from
　　　you,

---

a8 Or *your righteous One*

so that he will not hear.
³For your hands are stained with
    blood,
    your fingers with guilt.
Your lips have spoken lies,
    and your tongue mutters wicked
        things.
⁴No one calls for justice;
    no one pleads his case with
        integrity.
They rely on empty arguments and
    speak lies;
    they conceive trouble and give
        birth to evil.
⁵They hatch the eggs of vipers
    and spin a spider's web.
Whoever eats their eggs will die,
    and when one is broken, an adder
        is hatched.
⁶Their cobwebs are useless for
    clothing;

they cannot cover themselves with
    what they make.
Their deeds are evil deeds,
    and acts of violence are in their
        hands.
⁷Their feet rush into sin;
    they are swift to shed innocent
        blood.
Their thoughts are evil thoughts;
    ruin and destruction mark their
        ways.
⁸The way of peace they do not know;
    there is no justice in their paths.
They have turned them into crooked
    roads;
    no one who walks in them will
        know peace.

⁹So justice is far from us,
    and righteousness does not reach
        us.

Turbo Talk

Quiet TIMES with each other

ISAIAH 59:3 The scene? Our counseling office. The clients? Rick and Amy, a couple married less than a year. "I hear the words coming out of your mouth, but I just don't understand what you mean!" Rick's frustration was unmistakable: "It's like you're speaking a foreign language." "Well, you're the only person I've ever known who didn't understand me when I talked," she replied angrily. "What you say sometimes just isn't logical," he countered. "I'm not like you, Rick, analyzing everything, picking apart every word." Amy was close to tears. "I know. I just wish you weren't so emotional when you talk. I can't get what you're saying. We just can't communicate."

That's it—the number one complaint in marriage: We just can't communicate. The truth is, every couple communicates whether they want to or not. Saying nothing is communicating. What most couples mean by this complaint is that they

don't understand each other.

Like this couple, many of us have a hard time talking with each other from time to time. In order to better understand and communicate more effectively with your spouse, you first have to slow down. Good communication takes time.

When we slow down, we are less likely to give hasty orders and solutions. We are more likely to listen to the emotions that underlie the words our mate is saying and pay more attention to the nonverbal messages. Truly listening will bring about true understanding.

So slow down. Allow your mate time to mull things over if need be. Don't rush to fill in the silences. Talking can happen on the run, but understanding takes more time. Listen to the wise message of Proverbs 29:20: "Do you see a man who speaks in haste? There is more hope for a fool than for him."

—*Les & Leslie*

Weekend Warm-up   *How are you doing at talking with each other?*

Go to page 789 for your next devotional reading.

We look for light, but all is darkness;
for brightness, but we walk in deep
shadows.
10Like the blind we grope along the
wall,
feeling our way like men without
eyes.
At midday we stumble as if it were
twilight;
among the strong, we are like the
dead.
11We all growl like bears;
we moan mournfully like doves.
We look for justice, but find none;
for deliverance, but it is far away.

12For our offenses are many in your
sight,
and our sins testify against us.
Our offenses are ever with us,
and we acknowledge our iniquities:
13rebellion and treachery against the
LORD,
turning our backs on our God,
fomenting oppression and revolt,
uttering lies our hearts have
conceived.
14So justice is driven back,
and righteousness stands at a
distance;
truth has stumbled in the streets,
honesty cannot enter.
15Truth is nowhere to be found,
and whoever shuns evil becomes a
prey.

The LORD looked and was displeased
that there was no justice.
16He saw that there was no one,
he was appalled that there was no
one to intervene;
so his own arm worked salvation for
him,
and his own righteousness
sustained him.
17He put on righteousness as his
breastplate,
and the helmet of salvation on his
head;
he put on the garments of vengeance
and wrapped himself in zeal as in
a cloak.
18According to what they have done,
so will he repay
wrath to his enemies
and retribution to his foes;
he will repay the islands their due.

19From the west, men will fear the
name of the LORD,
and from the rising of the sun,
they will revere his glory.
For he will come like a pent-up flood
that the breath of the LORD drives
along.[a]

20"The Redeemer will come to Zion,
to those in Jacob who repent of
their sins,"
declares the LORD.

21"As for me, this is my covenant with
them," says the LORD. "My Spirit, who is
on you, and my words that I have put in
your mouth will not depart from your
mouth, or from the mouths of your children, or from the mouths of their descendants from this time on and forever," says
the LORD.

The Glory of Zion

60 "Arise, shine, for your light has
come,
and the glory of the LORD rises
upon you.
2See, darkness covers the earth
and thick darkness is over the
peoples,
but the LORD rises upon you
and his glory appears over you.
3Nations will come to your light,
and kings to the brightness of your
dawn.

4"Lift up your eyes and look about
you:
All assemble and come to you;
your sons come from afar,
and your daughters are carried on
the arm.
5Then you will look and be radiant,
your heart will throb and swell
with joy;
the wealth on the seas will be
brought to you,
to you the riches of the nations
will come.
6Herds of camels will cover your land,
young camels of Midian and
Ephah.
And all from Sheba will come,
bearing gold and incense

[a]19 Or *When the enemy comes in like a flood, / the
Spirit of the LORD will put him to flight*

and proclaiming the praise of the
LORD.
⁷All Kedar's flocks will be gathered to
you,
the rams of Nebaioth will serve
you;
they will be accepted as offerings on
my altar,
and I will adorn my glorious
temple.

⁸"Who are these that fly along like
clouds,
like doves to their nests?
⁹Surely the islands look to me;
in the lead are the ships of
Tarshish,ᵃ
bringing your sons from afar,
with their silver and gold,
to the honor of the LORD your God,
the Holy One of Israel,
for he has endowed you with
splendor.

¹⁰"Foreigners will rebuild your walls,
and their kings will serve you.
Though in anger I struck you,
in favor I will show you
compassion.
¹¹Your gates will always stand open,
they will never be shut, day or
night,
so that men may bring you the
wealth of the nations—
their kings led in triumphal
procession.
¹²For the nation or kingdom that will
not serve you will perish;
it will be utterly ruined.

¹³"The glory of Lebanon will come to
you,
the pine, the fir and the cypress
together,
to adorn the place of my sanctuary;
and I will glorify the place of my
feet.
¹⁴The sons of your oppressors will
come bowing before you;
all who despise you will bow down
at your feet
and will call you the City of the
LORD,
Zion of the Holy One of Israel.

¹⁵"Although you have been forsaken
and hated,

with no one traveling through,
I will make you the everlasting pride
and the joy of all generations.
¹⁶You will drink the milk of nations
and be nursed at royal breasts.
Then you will know that I, the LORD,
am your Savior,
your Redeemer, the Mighty One of
Jacob.
¹⁷Instead of bronze I will bring you
gold,
and silver in place of iron.
Instead of wood I will bring you
bronze,
and iron in place of stones.
I will make peace your governor
and righteousness your ruler.
¹⁸No longer will violence be heard in
your land,
nor ruin or destruction within your
borders,
but you will call your walls Salvation
and your gates Praise.
¹⁹The sun will no more be your light
by day,
nor will the brightness of the
moon shine on you,
for the LORD will be your everlasting
light,
and your God will be your glory.
²⁰Your sun will never set again,
and your moon will wane no
more;
the LORD will be your everlasting
light,
and your days of sorrow will end.
²¹Then will all your people be
righteous
and they will possess the land
forever.
They are the shoot I have planted,
the work of my hands,
for the display of my splendor.
²²The least of you will become a
thousand,
the smallest a mighty nation.
I am the LORD;
in its time I will do this swiftly."

The Year of the LORD's Favor

61 The Spirit of the Sovereign LORD
is on me,
because the LORD has anointed me
to preach good news to the poor.

ᵃ9 Or *the trading ships*

He has sent me to bind up the
      brokenhearted,
   to proclaim freedom for the
      captives
   and release from darkness for the
      prisoners,[a]
²to proclaim the year of the LORD's
      favor
   and the day of vengeance of our
      God,
to comfort all who mourn,
³   and provide for those who grieve
      in Zion—
to bestow on them a crown of beauty
      instead of ashes,
the oil of gladness
      instead of mourning,
and a garment of praise
      instead of a spirit of despair.
They will be called oaks of
      righteousness,
   a planting of the LORD
   for the display of his splendor.

⁴They will rebuild the ancient ruins
   and restore the places long
      devastated;

they will renew the ruined cities
   that have been devastated for
      generations.
⁵Aliens will shepherd your flocks;
   foreigners will work your fields and
      vineyards.
⁶And you will be called priests of the
      LORD,
   you will be named ministers of our
      God.
You will feed on the wealth of
      nations,
   and in their riches you will boast.

⁷Instead of their shame
   my people will receive a double
      portion,
and instead of disgrace
   they will rejoice in their
      inheritance;
and so they will inherit a double
      portion in their land,
   and everlasting joy will be theirs.

⁸"For I, the LORD, love justice;
   I hate robbery and iniquity.

a1   Hebrew; Septuagint *the blind*

More than Worthy

Monday

ISAIAH 61   Barbara grew up in a home that was devoid of encouragement or praise. That background led her to feel as if she could do nothing of value with her life. This initially caused Barbara to shy away from using the wonderful gifts God had given her. It was her husband John who gave her the courage to discover these gifts.

Every marriage partner arrives at the altar with perspectives and experiences from the past. Many spouses carry baggage from their past that weighs them down with a sense of unworthiness. They carry words spoken, harsh actions or unfair attitudes displayed toward them. They have become prisoners of their thoughts and feelings of unworthiness.

What can be done to help release them from this prison? One step is to "bestow on them a crown of beauty instead of ashes" (verse 3)—in other words, to repeatedly point out their worthiness, to continually step into their moments of doubt and reaffirm your love.

The more significant step, however, is the step Isaiah takes. He tells us that the Lord is the One who affirms our value to himself. We are not weeds of inadequacy, but in him we are like "oaks of righteousness" (verse 3). Constantly help your spouse see herself as God sees her.

Though the world might contribute to feelings of unworthiness, we should "delight greatly in the LORD . . . for he has clothed [us] with garments of salvation" (verse 10). We should feel just as a "bridegroom adorns his head like a priest, and as a bride adorns herself with her jewels" (verse 10). God sees us as precious in his sight; he has made each of us more than worthy through Christ Jesus.

—Bob & Rosemary

Go to page 794 for your next devotional reading.

In my faithfulness I will reward them
    and make an everlasting covenant
        with them.
⁹Their descendants will be known
        among the nations
    and their offspring among the
        peoples.
All who see them will acknowledge
    that they are a people the LORD has
        blessed."

¹⁰I delight greatly in the LORD;
    my soul rejoices in my God.
For he has clothed me with garments
        of salvation
    and arrayed me in a robe of
        righteousness,
as a bridegroom adorns his head like
        a priest,
    and as a bride adorns herself with
        her jewels.
¹¹For as the soil makes the sprout come
        up
    and a garden causes seeds to grow,
so the Sovereign LORD will make
        righteousness and praise
spring up before all nations.

Zion's New Name

62 For Zion's sake I will not keep
        silent,
    for Jerusalem's sake I will not
        remain quiet,
till her righteousness shines out like
        the dawn,
    her salvation like a blazing torch.
²The nations will see your
        righteousness,
    and all kings your glory;
you will be called by a new name
    that the mouth of the LORD will
        bestow.
³You will be a crown of splendor in
        the LORD's hand,
    a royal diadem in the hand of your
        God.
⁴No longer will they call you Deserted,
    or name your land Desolate.
But you will be called Hephzibah,ᵃ
    and your land Beulahᵇ;
for the LORD will take delight in you,
    and your land will be married.
⁵As a young man marries a maiden,
    so will your sonsᶜ marry you;

as a bridegroom rejoices over his
        bride,
    so will your God rejoice over you.

⁶I have posted watchmen on your
        walls, O Jerusalem;
    they will never be silent day or
        night.
You who call on the LORD,
    give yourselves no rest,
⁷and give him no rest till he
        establishes Jerusalem
    and makes her the praise of the
        earth.

⁸The LORD has sworn by his right
        hand
    and by his mighty arm:
"Never again will I give your grain
        as food for your enemies,
    and never again will foreigners drink
        the new wine
    for which you have toiled;
⁹but those who harvest it will eat it
    and praise the LORD,
and those who gather the grapes will
        drink it
    in the courts of my sanctuary."

¹⁰Pass through, pass through the gates!
    Prepare the way for the people.
Build up, build up the highway!
    Remove the stones.
Raise a banner for the nations.

¹¹The LORD has made proclamation
    to the ends of the earth:
"Say to the Daughter of Zion,
    'See, your Savior comes!
See, his reward is with him,
    and his recompense accompanies
        him.' "
¹²They will be called the Holy People,
    the Redeemed of the LORD;
and you will be called Sought After,
    the City No Longer Deserted.

God's Day of Vengeance and Redemption

63 Who is this coming from Edom,
        from Bozrah, with his garments
            stained crimson?
Who is this, robed in splendor,
    striding forward in the greatness of
        his strength?

ᵃ4 Hephzibah means *my delight is in her.*
ᵇ4 Beulah means *married.*   ᶜ5 Or *Builder*

"It is I, speaking in righteousness,
  mighty to save."

²Why are your garments red,
  like those of one treading the
    winepress?

³"I have trodden the winepress alone;
  from the nations no one was with
    me.
I trampled them in my anger
  and trod them down in my wrath;
their blood spattered my garments,
  and I stained all my clothing.
⁴For the day of vengeance was in my
    heart,
  and the year of my redemption has
    come.
⁵I looked, but there was no one to
    help,
  I was appalled that no one gave
    support;
so my own arm worked salvation for
    me,
  and my own wrath sustained me.
⁶I trampled the nations in my anger;
  in my wrath I made them drunk
  and poured their blood on the
    ground."

Praise and Prayer

⁷I will tell of the kindnesses of the
    LORD,
  the deeds for which he is to be
    praised,
  according to all the LORD has done
    for us—
yes, the many good things he has
    done
  for the house of Israel,
  according to his compassion and
    many kindnesses.
⁸He said, "Surely they are my people,
  sons who will not be false to me";
  and so he became their Savior.
⁹In all their distress he too was
    distressed,
  and the angel of his presence saved
    them.
In his love and mercy he redeemed
    them;
  he lifted them up and carried them
    all the days of old.
¹⁰Yet they rebelled
  and grieved his Holy Spirit.
So he turned and became their enemy

and he himself fought against
    them.
¹¹Then his people recalled[a] the days
    of old,
  the days of Moses and his people—
where is he who brought them
    through the sea,
  with the shepherd of his flock?
Where is he who set
  his Holy Spirit among them,
¹²who sent his glorious arm of power
  to be at Moses' right hand,
who divided the waters before them,
  to gain for himself everlasting
    renown,
¹³who led them through the depths?
Like a horse in open country,
  they did not stumble;
¹⁴like cattle that go down to the plain,
  they were given rest by the Spirit of
    the LORD.
This is how you guided your people
  to make for yourself a glorious
    name.

¹⁵Look down from heaven and see
  from your lofty throne, holy and
    glorious.
Where are your zeal and your might?
  Your tenderness and compassion
  are withheld from us.
¹⁶But you are our Father,
  though Abraham does not know us
  or Israel acknowledge us;
you, O LORD, are our Father,
  our Redeemer from of old is your
    name.
¹⁷Why, O LORD, do you make us
    wander from your ways
  and harden our hearts so we do
    not revere you?
Return for the sake of your servants,
  the tribes that are your inheritance.
¹⁸For a little while your people
    possessed your holy place,
  but now our enemies have
    trampled down your
    sanctuary.
¹⁹We are yours from of old;
  but you have not ruled over them,
  they have not been called by your
    name.[b]

a 11 Or But may he recall   b 19 Or We are like
those you have never ruled, / like those never called by
your name

64

Oh, that you would rend the
heavens and come down,
that the mountains would tremble
before you!
[2] As when fire sets twigs ablaze
and causes water to boil,
come down to make your name
known to your enemies
and cause the nations to quake
before you!
[3] For when you did awesome things
that we did not expect,
you came down, and the
mountains trembled before
you.
[4] Since ancient times no one has heard,
no ear has perceived,
no eye has seen any God besides you,
who acts on behalf of those who
wait for him.
[5] You come to the help of those who
gladly do right,
who remember your ways.
But when we continued to sin against
them,
you were angry.
How then can we be saved?
[6] All of us have become like one who
is unclean,
and all our righteous acts are like
filthy rags;
we all shrivel up like a leaf,
and like the wind our sins sweep
us away.
[7] No one calls on your name
or strives to lay hold of you;
for you have hidden your face from
us
and made us waste away because of
our sins.

[8] Yet, O LORD, you are our Father.
We are the clay, you are the potter;
we are all the work of your hand.
[9] Do not be angry beyond measure,
O LORD;
do not remember our sins forever.
Oh, look upon us, we pray,
for we are all your people.
[10] Your sacred cities have become a
desert;
even Zion is a desert, Jerusalem a
desolation.
[11] Our holy and glorious temple, where
our fathers praised you,
has been burned with fire,

and all that we treasured lies in
ruins.
[12] After all this, O LORD, will you hold
yourself back?
Will you keep silent and punish us
beyond measure?

Judgment and Salvation

65

"I revealed myself to those who
did not ask for me;
I was found by those who did not
seek me.
To a nation that did not call on my
name,
I said, 'Here am I, here am I.'
[2] All day long I have held out my
hands
to an obstinate people,
who walk in ways not good,
pursuing their own imaginations—
[3] a people who continually provoke me
to my very face,
offering sacrifices in gardens
and burning incense on altars of
brick;
[4] who sit among the graves
and spend their nights keeping
secret vigil;
who eat the flesh of pigs,
and whose pots hold broth of
unclean meat;
[5] who say, 'Keep away; don't come
near me,
for I am too sacred for you!'
Such people are smoke in my nostrils,
a fire that keeps burning all day.

[6] "See, it stands written before me:
I will not keep silent but will pay
back in full;
I will pay it back into their laps—
[7] both your sins and the sins of your
fathers,"
says the LORD.
"Because they burned sacrifices on
the mountains
and defied me on the hills,
I will measure into their laps
the full payment for their former
deeds."

[8] This is what the LORD says:

"As when juice is still found in a
cluster of grapes
and men say, 'Don't destroy it,
there is yet some good in it,'

so will I do in behalf of my servants;
  I will not destroy them all.
9 I will bring forth descendants from
      Jacob,
  and from Judah those who will
      possess my mountains;
my chosen people will inherit them,
  and there will my servants live.
10 Sharon will become a pasture for
      flocks,
  and the Valley of Achor a resting
      place for herds,
  for my people who seek me.

11 "But as for you who forsake the LORD
  and forget my holy mountain,
who spread a table for Fortune
  and fill bowls of mixed wine for
      Destiny,
12 I will destine you for the sword,
  and you will all bend down for the
      slaughter;
  for I called but you did not answer,
  I spoke but you did not listen.
You did evil in my sight
  and chose what displeases me."

13 Therefore this is what the Sovereign
LORD says:

"My servants will eat,
  but you will go hungry;
my servants will drink,
  but you will go thirsty;
my servants will rejoice,
  but you will be put to shame.
14 My servants will sing
  out of the joy of their hearts,
but you will cry out
  from anguish of heart
  and wail in brokenness of spirit.
15 You will leave your name
  to my chosen ones as a curse;
the Sovereign LORD will put you to
      death,
  but to his servants he will give
      another name.
16 Whoever invokes a blessing in the
      land
  will do so by the God of truth;
he who takes an oath in the land
  will swear by the God of truth.
For the past troubles will be forgotten
  and hidden from my eyes.

New Heavens and a New Earth

17 "Behold, I will create

new heavens and a new earth.
The former things will not be
      remembered,
  nor will they come to mind.
18 But be glad and rejoice forever
  in what I will create,
for I will create Jerusalem to be a
      delight
  and its people a joy.
19 I will rejoice over Jerusalem
  and take delight in my people;
the sound of weeping and of
      crying
  will be heard in it no more.

20 "Never again will there be in it
  an infant who lives but a few
      days,
  or an old man who does not live
      out his years;
he who dies at a hundred
  will be thought a mere youth;
he who fails to reach*a* a hundred
  will be considered accursed.
21 They will build houses and dwell in
      them;
  they will plant vineyards and eat
      their fruit.
22 No longer will they build houses and
      others live in them,
  or plant and others eat.
For as the days of a tree,
  so will be the days of my people;
my chosen ones will long enjoy
  the works of their hands.
23 They will not toil in vain
  or bear children doomed to
      misfortune;
for they will be a people blessed by
      the LORD,
  they and their descendants with
      them.
24 Before they call I will answer;
  while they are still speaking I will
      hear.
25 The wolf and the lamb will feed
      together,
  and the lion will eat straw like the
      ox,
  but dust will be the serpent's food.
They will neither harm nor destroy
  on all my holy mountain,"
                              says the LORD.

a20 Or / *the sinner who reaches*

Judgment and Hope

66

This is what the LORD says:

"Heaven is my throne,
     and the earth is my footstool.
Where is the house you will build for
          me?
     Where will my resting place be?
²Has not my hand made all these
          things,
     and so they came into being?"
                              declares the LORD.

"This is the one I esteem:
     he who is humble and contrite in
          spirit,
     and trembles at my word.
³But whoever sacrifices a bull
     is like one who kills a man,
and whoever offers a lamb,
     like one who breaks a dog's neck;
whoever makes a grain offering
     is like one who presents pig's
          blood,
and whoever burns memorial incense,
     like one who worships an idol.
They have chosen their own ways,
     and their souls delight in their
          abominations;

⁴so I also will choose harsh treatment
          for them
     and will bring upon them what
          they dread.
For when I called, no one answered,
     when I spoke, no one listened.
They did evil in my sight
     and chose what displeases me."

⁵Hear the word of the LORD,
     you who tremble at his word:
"Your brothers who hate you,
     and exclude you because of my
          name, have said,
'Let the LORD be glorified,
     that we may see your joy!'
Yet they will be put to shame.
⁶Hear that uproar from the city,
     hear that noise from the temple!
It is the sound of the LORD
     repaying his enemies all they
          deserve.

⁷"Before she goes into labor,
     she gives birth;
before the pains come upon her,
     she delivers a son.
⁸Who has ever heard of such a thing?
     Who has ever seen such things?
Can a country be born in a day

A Humbling Priority

Tuesday

ISAIAH 66:2 Having two toddlers running underfoot was more exhausting than Diane could have imagined. Her husband Alan noticed her need and made a difficult decision. Even though he had been the captain of his college baseball team, even though he was the founder of the adult baseball league in his community, even though his friends would ridicule his decision, Alan decided to leave his weekend baseball to help his wife.

Isaiah tells us about the type of person God esteems: one who is humble in spirit and respects God's Word. This attitude of humility is one that must be shown both toward God and our fellow human beings. Perhaps there is no place where a lack of humility shows its face more than in the marriage relationship. The prevalent philosophy today is one that fosters self-preserva-

tion and making sure that one spouse does not take advantage of the other. Today's marriage priority is to get our own needs met.

In contrast, God's Word encourages us to be humble. A humble person is mindful of others and focuses on the needs of others, rather than demanding that his own needs be met. There is no more difficult place to exercise humility than in the marriage relationship. It's so easy to develop long mental lists of what we desire to "get" from the relationship, rather than concentrating on what we can give. Yet that is not what we are called to do. Are we willing to do the more difficult, yet fruitful task of being marriage partners who humble themselves before God and each other? That is what God esteems.

—Bob & Rosemary

Go to page 798 for your next devotional reading.

or a nation be brought forth in a
moment?
Yet no sooner is Zion in labor
than she gives birth to her
children.
⁹Do I bring to the moment of birth
and not give delivery?" says the
LORD.
"Do I close up the womb
when I bring to delivery?" says your
God.
¹⁰"Rejoice with Jerusalem and be glad
for her,
all you who love her;
rejoice greatly with her,
all you who mourn over her.
¹¹For you will nurse and be satisfied
at her comforting breasts;
you will drink deeply
and delight in her overflowing
abundance."

¹²For this is what the LORD says:

"I will extend peace to her like a
river,
and the wealth of nations like a
flooding stream;
you will nurse and be carried on her
arm
and dandled on her knees.
¹³As a mother comforts her child,
so will I comfort you;
and you will be comforted over
Jerusalem."

¹⁴When you see this, your heart will
rejoice
and you will flourish like grass;
the hand of the LORD will be made
known to his servants,
but his fury will be shown to his
foes.
¹⁵See, the LORD is coming with fire,
and his chariots are like a
whirlwind;
he will bring down his anger with
fury,
and his rebuke with flames of fire.
¹⁶For with fire and with his sword

the LORD will execute judgment
upon all men,
and many will be those slain by
the LORD.

¹⁷"Those who consecrate and purify
themselves to go into the gardens, following the one in the midst of[a] those who
eat the flesh of pigs and rats and other
abominable things—they will meet their
end together," declares the LORD.

¹⁸"And I, because of their actions and
their imaginations, am about to come[b]
and gather all nations and tongues, and
they will come and see my glory.

¹⁹"I will set a sign among them, and I
will send some of those who survive to
the nations—to Tarshish, to the Libyans[c]
and Lydians (famous as archers), to Tubal
and Greece, and to the distant islands that
have not heard of my fame or seen my
glory. They will proclaim my glory among
the nations. ²⁰And they will bring all your
brothers, from all the nations, to my holy
mountain in Jerusalem as an offering to
the LORD—on horses, in chariots and wagons, and on mules and camels," says the
LORD. "They will bring them, as the Israelites bring their grain offerings, to the
temple of the LORD in ceremonially clean
vessels. ²¹And I will select some of them
also to be priests and Levites," says the
LORD.

²²"As the new heavens and the new
earth that I make will endure before me,"
declares the LORD, "so will your name
and descendants endure. ²³From one
New Moon to another and from one Sabbath to another, all mankind will come
and bow down before me," says the LORD.
²⁴"And they will go out and look upon
the dead bodies of those who rebelled
against me; their worm will not die, nor
will their fire be quenched, and they will
be loathsome to all mankind."

a 17 Or *gardens behind one of your temples, and*
b 18 The meaning of the Hebrew for this clause is
uncertain.   c 19 Some Septuagint manuscripts
Put (Libyans); Hebrew *Pul*

Jeremiah

You have been called. God has an assignment for you that literally has your name—and no one else's name—on it. Your life is not accidental. Your vocation is holy. Your spouse is God's gift to you and you alone.

The book of Jeremiah opens with the affirmation that what is true about you and your special calling was also true for Jeremiah. God told this ordinary man, "Before you were formed in the womb I knew you, before you were born I set you apart" (1:5).

Certainly Jeremiah was aghast at the news. But as incredible as this was for the prophet to hear, this was not a one-time event. The Sovereign God says the same to you. You are called. Your assignments have been planned since before there were oceans. Listen carefully to Jeremiah when he speaks. Actually, he sounds like a man who has been told that he was "the man for the job"—the one who can do it best.

How are you doing with your charge?

---

1 The words of Jeremiah son of Hilkiah, one of the priests at Anathoth in the territory of Benjamin. ²The word of the LORD came to him in the thirteenth year of the reign of Josiah son of Amon king of Judah, ³and through the reign of Jehoiakim son of Josiah king of Judah, down to the fifth month of the eleventh year of Zedekiah son of Josiah king of Judah, when the people of Jerusalem went into exile.

The Call of Jeremiah

⁴The word of the LORD came to me, saying,

⁵"Before I formed you in the womb I
    knew[a] you,
    before you were born I set you apart;
I appointed you as a prophet to
    the nations."

a5 Or *chose*

⁶"Ah, Sovereign LORD," I said, "I do not know how to speak; I am only a child."

⁷But the LORD said to me, "Do not say, 'I am only a child.' You must go to everyone I send you to and say whatever I command you. ⁸Do not be afraid of them, for I am with you and will rescue you," declares the LORD.

⁹Then the LORD reached out his hand and touched my mouth and said to me, "Now, I have put my words in your mouth. ¹⁰See, today I appoint you over nations and kingdoms to uproot and tear down, to destroy and overthrow, to build and to plant."

¹¹The word of the LORD came to me: "What do you see, Jeremiah?"

"I see the branch of an almond tree," I replied.

¹²The LORD said to me, "You have seen correctly, for I am watching*a* to see that my word is fulfilled."

¹³The word of the LORD came to me again: "What do you see?"

"I see a boiling pot, tilting away from the north," I answered.

¹⁴The LORD said to me, "From the north disaster will be poured out on all who live in the land. ¹⁵I am about to summon all the peoples of the northern kingdoms," declares the LORD.

"Their kings will come and set up
    their thrones
  in the entrance of the gates of
    Jerusalem;
they will come against all her
    surrounding walls
  and against all the towns of Judah.
¹⁶I will pronounce my judgments on
    my people
  because of their wickedness in
    forsaking me,
in burning incense to other gods
  and in worshiping what their
    hands have made.

¹⁷"Get yourself ready! Stand up and say to them whatever I command you. Do not be terrified by them, or I will terrify you before them. ¹⁸Today I have made you a fortified city, an iron pillar and a bronze wall to stand against the whole land—against the kings of Judah, its officials, its priests and the people of the land. ¹⁹They will fight against you but will not overcome you, for I am with you and will rescue you," declares the LORD.

Israel Forsakes God

2 The word of the LORD came to me: ²"Go and proclaim in the hearing of Jerusalem:

" 'I remember the devotion of your
      youth,
  how as a bride you loved me
and followed me through the desert,
  through a land not sown.
³Israel was holy to the LORD,
  the firstfruits of his harvest;
all who devoured her were held
      guilty,
  and disaster overtook them,' "
                    declares the LORD.

⁴Hear the word of the LORD, O house
      of Jacob,
  all you clans of the house of Israel.

⁵This is what the LORD says:

"What fault did your fathers find in
      me,
  that they strayed so far from me?
They followed worthless idols
  and became worthless themselves.
⁶They did not ask, 'Where is the LORD,
  who brought us up out of Egypt
and led us through the barren
      wilderness,
  through a land of deserts and rifts,
a land of drought and darkness,*b*
  a land where no one travels and
      no one lives?'
⁷I brought you into a fertile land
  to eat its fruit and rich produce.
But you came and defiled my land
  and made my inheritance
      detestable.
⁸The priests did not ask,
  'Where is the LORD?'
Those who deal with the law did not
      know me;
  the leaders rebelled against me.
The prophets prophesied by Baal,
  following worthless idols.

⁹"Therefore I bring charges against you
      again,"
                    declares the LORD.

---

a 12 The Hebrew for *watching* sounds like the Hebrew for *almond tree.*   *b* 6 Or *and the shadow of death*

"And I will bring charges against
    your children's children.
¹⁰Cross over to the coasts of Kittim*a*
    and look,
send to Kedar*b* and observe
    closely;
see if there has ever been anything
    like this:
¹¹Has a nation ever changed its gods?
    (Yet they are not gods at all.)
But my people have exchanged
    their*c* Glory
for worthless idols.
¹²Be appalled at this, O heavens,
    and shudder with great horror,"
                declares the LORD.
¹³"My people have committed two
    sins:
They have forsaken me,
    the spring of living water,
and have dug their own cisterns,
    broken cisterns that cannot hold
    water.
¹⁴Is Israel a servant, a slave by birth?
    Why then has he become plunder?
¹⁵Lions have roared;
    they have growled at him.
They have laid waste his land;
    his towns are burned and deserted.
¹⁶Also, the men of Memphis*d* and
    Tahpanhes

have shaved the crown of your
    head.*e*
¹⁷Have you not brought this on
    yourselves
by forsaking the LORD your God
    when he led you in the way?
¹⁸Now why go to Egypt
    to drink water from the Shihor*f*?
And why go to Assyria
    to drink water from the River*g*?
¹⁹Your wickedness will punish you;
    your backsliding will rebuke you.
Consider then and realize
    how evil and bitter it is for you
when you forsake the LORD your God
    and have no awe of me,"
                declares the Lord,
                the LORD Almighty.

²⁰"Long ago you broke off your yoke
    and tore off your bonds;
you said, 'I will not serve you!'
Indeed, on every high hill
    and under every spreading tree
you lay down as a prostitute.

---

a10 That is, Cyprus and western coastlands
b10 The home of Bedouin tribes in the
Syro-Arabian desert   *c11* Masoretic Text; an
ancient Hebrew scribal tradition *my*
d16 Hebrew *Noph*   *e16* Or *have cracked your
skull*   *f18* That is, a branch of the Nile
g18 That is, the Euphrates

Remembering Young Love

Wednesday

JEREMIAH 2:1–2 We were so in love during the first months of our marriage that we would have followed each other through the desert! But as the months turned into years, we were unwilling to follow the other into the kitchen to help with the dishes, let alone brave a desert. So what happened to that initial devotion?

In the second chapter of Jeremiah, Israel is compared to a marriage in which the initial love and devotion have waned. As the house of Jacob forgot the Lord and his love, couples forget the intense love and devotion that brought them together. After married life settles in, and as we get busy with our careers, families and other interests, it's easy to put the marriage relationship aside. But boredom doesn't have to set in. You can add vigor and zest to your marriage and renew your love and commitment.

Remember that life and marriage are filled with many ups and downs. You can choose to rekindle your love at any point in your marriage. Spend some time remembering what drew you together, what great successes you have shared and what disappointments you have experienced in your relationship. Then join together in renewing your marriage vows and deciding what positive steps you can take to equip your marriage for future desert experiences. Finally, dream about what you want your marriage to be five and ten years from now.   **—Dave & Claudia**

Go to page 800 for your next devotional reading.

²¹I had planted you like a choice vine
    of sound and reliable stock.
How then did you turn against me
    into a corrupt, wild vine?
²²Although you wash yourself with
        soda
    and use an abundance of soap,
    the stain of your guilt is still before
        me,"
            declares the Sovereign LORD.
²³"How can you say, 'I am not defiled;
    I have not run after the Baals'?
See how you behaved in the valley;
    consider what you have done.
You are a swift she-camel
    running here and there,
²⁴a wild donkey accustomed to the
        desert,
    sniffing the wind in her craving—
    in her heat who can restrain her?
Any males that pursue her need not
        tire themselves;
    at mating time they will find her.
²⁵Do not run until your feet are bare
    and your throat is dry.
But you said, 'It's no use!
    I love foreign gods,
    and I must go after them.'

²⁶"As a thief is disgraced when he is
        caught,
    so the house of Israel is disgraced—
they, their kings and their officials,
    their priests and their prophets.
²⁷They say to wood, 'You are my
        father,'
    and to stone, 'You gave me birth.'
They have turned their backs to me
    and not their faces;
yet when they are in trouble, they say,
    'Come and save us!'
²⁸Where then are the gods you made
        for yourselves?
    Let them come if they can save you
        when you are in trouble!
For you have as many gods
    as you have towns, O Judah.

²⁹"Why do you bring charges against
        me?
    You have all rebelled against me,"
            declares the LORD.
³⁰"In vain I punished your people;
    they did not respond to correction.
Your sword has devoured your
        prophets
    like a ravening lion.

³¹"You of this generation, consider the
word of the LORD:

"Have I been a desert to Israel
    or a land of great darkness?
Why do my people say, 'We are free
        to roam;
    we will come to you no more'?
³²Does a maiden forget her jewelry,
    a bride her wedding ornaments?
Yet my people have forgotten me,
    days without number.
³³How skilled you are at pursuing love!
    Even the worst of women can learn
        from your ways.
³⁴On your clothes men find
    the lifeblood of the innocent poor,
    though you did not catch them
        breaking in.
Yet in spite of all this
³⁵   you say, 'I am innocent;
    he is not angry with me.'
But I will pass judgment on you
    because you say, 'I have not
        sinned.'
³⁶Why do you go about so much,
    changing your ways?
You will be disappointed by Egypt

as you were by Assyria.
³⁷You will also leave that place
    with your hands on your head,
for the LORD has rejected those you
        trust;
    you will not be helped by them.

3 "If a man divorces his wife
    and she leaves him and marries
        another man,
should he return to her again?
    Would not the land be completely
        defiled?
But you have lived as a prostitute
    with many lovers—
would you now return to me?"
                    declares the LORD.
² "Look up to the barren heights and
        see.
    Is there any place where you have
        not been ravished?
By the roadside you sat waiting for
        lovers,
    sat like a nomad*ᵃ* in the desert.
You have defiled the land

with your prostitution and
        wickedness.
³Therefore the showers have been
        withheld,
    and no spring rains have fallen.
Yet you have the brazen look of a
        prostitute;
    you refuse to blush with shame.
⁴Have you not just called to me:
    'My Father, my friend from my
        youth,
⁵will you always be angry?
    Will your wrath continue forever?'
This is how you talk,
    but you do all the evil you can."

Unfaithful Israel

⁶During the reign of King Josiah, the
LORD said to me, "Have you seen what
faithless Israel has done? She has gone up
on every high hill and under every spreading tree and has committed adultery
there. ⁷I thought that after she had done

ᵃ2 Or *an Arab*

Restoring a Relationship

Thursday

JEREMIAH 3:1-25   "I feel like I'm caught in a cross fire," Don wept as he unfolded to us the process of his divorce. "The bullets of pain, anger, loneliness and confusion seem to be coming from all directions. Going through this divorce is more painful than I could have ever imagined."

The pain and devastation of divorce are chronicled in this passage. Although this chapter is about Israel's adulterous turning away from God, the marriage relationship is used to paint the picture. In God's desire to receive his nation back, we see the perfect outline for restoration in a marriage.

God does not say that Israel can come back to him any way it chooses. He does not compromise the standards just because it is his chosen nation. The first thing God does in this passage is to point out Israel's sin. There can be no relationship if there is no standard against which the relationship is measured. God reveals how Israel has violated the covenant.

Secondly, God gives Israel the opportunity to choose its way. He does not force his chosen people to stay in a relationship with him. Finally, God offers his people the opportunity to return to him (see verse 12).

God wants the return of the love relationship, but only after his people acknowledge the sin they've committed. Once they confess their sin, God says, "I will frown on you no longer" (verse 12).

Repenting and finding restoration are difficult. Living within necessary marital boundaries also calls for personal sacrifice. But it's worth the effort. There's a structure to any relationship. Boundaries of trust must be upheld. The important issue is not that one of us would have a watchful eye for violations of the boundaries, but rather a forgiving heart. When heartfelt forgiveness is asked for, it should be given to the point where you can look on each other with favor again.

—Bob & Rosemary

Go to page 806 for your next devotional reading.

all this she would return to me but she did not, and her unfaithful sister Judah saw it. ⁸I gave faithless Israel her certificate of divorce and sent her away because of all her adulteries. Yet I saw that her unfaithful sister Judah had no fear; she also went out and committed adultery. ⁹Because Israel's immorality mattered so little to her, she defiled the land and committed adultery with stone and wood. ¹⁰In spite of all this, her unfaithful sister Judah did not return to me with all her heart, but only in pretense," declares the LORD.

¹¹The LORD said to me, "Faithless Israel is more righteous than unfaithful Judah. ¹²Go, proclaim this message toward the north:

" 'Return, faithless Israel,' declares the
      LORD,
   'I will frown on you no longer,
for I am merciful,' declares the LORD,
   'I will not be angry forever.
¹³Only acknowledge your guilt—
      you have rebelled against the LORD
         your God,
you have scattered your favors to
         foreign gods
      under every spreading tree,
      and have not obeyed me,' "
                        declares the LORD.

¹⁴"Return, faithless people," declares the LORD, "for I am your husband. I will choose you—one from a town and two from a clan—and bring you to Zion. ¹⁵Then I will give you shepherds after my own heart, who will lead you with knowledge and understanding. ¹⁶In those days, when your numbers have increased greatly in the land," declares the LORD, "men will no longer say, 'The ark of the covenant of the LORD.' It will never enter their minds or be remembered; it will not be missed, nor will another one be made. ¹⁷At that time they will call Jerusalem The Throne of the LORD, and all nations will gather in Jerusalem to honor the name of the LORD. No longer will they follow the stubbornness of their evil hearts. ¹⁸In those days the house of Judah will join the house of Israel, and together they will come from a northern land to the land I gave your forefathers as an inheritance.

¹⁹"I myself said,

Restoring a Relationship

Take a moment to answer each of these questions on your own. Then compare your answers to your spouse's.

Yes   No   When my spouse has done something to violate our trust, I focus on putting the relationship back together.

Yes   No   When confronting my spouse, I focus on the specific violation rather than attack the person.

Yes   No   If my spouse cannot see the problem with what they have done, I allow them the time and opportunity to think through the problem.

Yes   No   If my spouse asks for forgiveness, I move toward restoring the relationship.

Yes   No   When we discuss differences, my goal is always to grow closer to my spouse rather than judge him/her.

" 'How gladly would I treat you like
         sons
      and give you a desirable land,
      the most beautiful inheritance of
         any nation.'
I thought you would call me 'Father'
      and not turn away from following
         me.
²⁰But like a woman unfaithful to her
         husband,
      so you have been unfaithful to me,
         O house of Israel,"
                        declares the LORD.

²¹A cry is heard on the barren heights,
      the weeping and pleading of the
         people of Israel,
because they have perverted their
         ways
      and have forgotten the LORD their
         God.

²²"Return, faithless people;
      I will cure you of backsliding."

"Yes, we will come to you,
      for you are the LORD our God.

23Surely the ⸤idolatrous⸥ commotion on
    the hills
  and mountains is a deception;
surely in the LORD our God
  is the salvation of Israel.
24From our youth shameful gods have
    consumed
  the fruits of our fathers' labor—
their flocks and herds,
  their sons and daughters.
25Let us lie down in our shame,
  and let our disgrace cover us.
We have sinned against the LORD our
    God,
  both we and our fathers;
from our youth till this day
  we have not obeyed the LORD our
    God."

4 "If you will return, O Israel,
  return to me,"
                 declares the LORD.
"If you put your detestable idols out
    of my sight
  and no longer go astray,
2and if in a truthful, just and righteous
    way
  you swear, 'As surely as the LORD
    lives,'
then the nations will be blessed by
    him
  and in him they will glory."

3This is what the LORD says to the men
of Judah and to Jerusalem:

"Break up your unplowed ground
  and do not sow among thorns.
4Circumcise yourselves to the LORD,
  circumcise your hearts,
  you men of Judah and people of
    Jerusalem,
or my wrath will break out and burn
    like fire
  because of the evil you have done—
burn with no one to quench it.

Disaster From the North

5"Announce in Judah and proclaim in
    Jerusalem and say:
'Sound the trumpet throughout the
    land!'
Cry aloud and say:
'Gather together!
Let us flee to the fortified cities!'
6Raise the signal to go to Zion!

Flee for safety without delay!
For I am bringing disaster from the
    north,
  even terrible destruction."

7A lion has come out of his lair;
  a destroyer of nations has set out.
He has left his place
  to lay waste your land.
Your towns will lie in ruins
  without inhabitant.
8So put on sackcloth,
  lament and wail,
for the fierce anger of the LORD
  has not turned away from us.

9"In that day," declares the LORD,
  "the king and the officials will lose
    heart,
the priests will be horrified,
  and the prophets will be appalled."

10Then I said, "Ah, Sovereign LORD,
how completely you have deceived this
people and Jerusalem by saying, 'You will
have peace,' when the sword is at our
throats."

11At that time this people and Jerusalem will be told, "A scorching wind from
the barren heights in the desert blows toward my people, but not to winnow or
cleanse; 12a wind too strong for that
comes from me.*a* Now I pronounce my
judgments against them."

13Look! He advances like the clouds,
  his chariots come like a whirlwind,
his horses are swifter than eagles.
  Woe to us! We are ruined!
14O Jerusalem, wash the evil from your
    heart and be saved.
  How long will you harbor wicked
    thoughts?
15A voice is announcing from Dan,
  proclaiming disaster from the hills
    of Ephraim.
16"Tell this to the nations,
  proclaim it to Jerusalem:
'A besieging army is coming from a
    distant land,
  raising a war cry against the cities
    of Judah.
17They surround her like men guarding
    a field,

a12 Or comes at my command

because she has rebelled against
   me,' "
               declares the LORD.
18 "Your own conduct and actions
   have brought this upon you.
This is your punishment.
   How bitter it is!
   How it pierces to the heart!"

19 Oh, my anguish, my anguish!
   I writhe in pain.
Oh, the agony of my heart!
   My heart pounds within me,
   I cannot keep silent.
For I have heard the sound of the
     trumpet;
   I have heard the battle cry.
20 Disaster follows disaster;
   the whole land lies in ruins.
In an instant my tents are destroyed,
   my shelter in a moment.
21 How long must I see the battle
     standard
   and hear the sound of the
     trumpet?

22 "My people are fools;
   they do not know me.
They are senseless children;
   they have no understanding.
They are skilled in doing evil;
   they know not how to do good."

23 I looked at the earth,
   and it was formless and empty;
and at the heavens,
   and their light was gone.
24 I looked at the mountains,
   and they were quaking;
   all the hills were swaying.
25 I looked, and there were no people;
   every bird in the sky had flown
     away.
26 I looked, and the fruitful land was a
     desert;
   all its towns lay in ruins
   before the LORD, before his fierce
     anger.

27 This is what the LORD says:

"The whole land will be ruined,
   though I will not destroy it
     completely.
28 Therefore the earth will mourn
   and the heavens above grow dark,
because I have spoken and will not
     relent,

I have decided and will not turn
   back."

29 At the sound of horsemen and
     archers
   every town takes to flight.
Some go into the thickets;
   some climb up among the rocks.
All the towns are deserted;
   no one lives in them.

30 What are you doing, O devastated
     one?
Why dress yourself in scarlet
   and put on jewels of gold?
Why shade your eyes with paint?
   You adorn yourself in vain.
Your lovers despise you;
   they seek your life.

31 I hear a cry as of a woman in labor,
   a groan as of one bearing her first
     child—
the cry of the Daughter of Zion
   gasping for breath,
   stretching out her hands and
     saying,
"Alas! I am fainting;
   my life is given over to murderers."

Not One Is Upright

5 "Go up and down the streets of
     Jerusalem,
   look around and consider,
   search through her squares.
If you can find but one person
   who deals honestly and seeks the
     truth,
   I will forgive this city.
2 Although they say, 'As surely as the
     LORD lives,'
   still they are swearing falsely."

3 O LORD, do not your eyes look for
     truth?
   You struck them, but they felt no
     pain;
   you crushed them, but they refused
     correction.
They made their faces harder than
     stone
   and refused to repent.
4 I thought, "These are only the poor;
   they are foolish,
for they do not know the way of the
     LORD,
   the requirements of their God.

⁵So I will go to the leaders
  and speak to them;
surely they know the way of the
    LORD,
  the requirements of their God."
But with one accord they too had
    broken off the yoke
  and torn off the bonds.
⁶Therefore a lion from the forest will
    attack them,
  a wolf from the desert will ravage
    them,
a leopard will lie in wait near their
    towns
  to tear to pieces any who venture
    out,
for their rebellion is great
  and their backslidings many.

⁷"Why should I forgive you?
  Your children have forsaken me
  and sworn by gods that are not
    gods.
I supplied all their needs,
  yet they committed adultery
  and thronged to the houses of
    prostitutes.
⁸They are well-fed, lusty stallions,
  each neighing for another man's
    wife.
⁹Should I not punish them for this?"
    declares the LORD.
  "Should I not avenge myself
  on such a nation as this?

¹⁰"Go through her vineyards and
    ravage them,
  but do not destroy them
    completely.
Strip off her branches,
  for these people do not belong to
    the LORD.
¹¹The house of Israel and the house of
    Judah
  have been utterly unfaithful to me,"
      declares the LORD.

¹²They have lied about the LORD;
  they said, "He will do nothing!
No harm will come to us;
  we will never see sword or famine.
¹³The prophets are but wind
  and the word is not in them;
  so let what they say be done to
    them."

¹⁴Therefore this is what the LORD God
Almighty says:

"Because the people have spoken
    these words,
  I will make my words in your
    mouth a fire
  and these people the wood it
    consumes.
¹⁵O house of Israel," declares the LORD,
  "I am bringing a distant nation
    against you—
an ancient and enduring nation,
  a people whose language you do
    not know,
  whose speech you do not
    understand.
¹⁶Their quivers are like an open grave;
  all of them are mighty warriors.
¹⁷They will devour your harvests and
    food,
  devour your sons and daughters;
they will devour your flocks and
    herds,
  devour your vines and fig trees.
With the sword they will destroy
  the fortified cities in which you
    trust.

¹⁸"Yet even in those days," declares the
LORD, "I will not destroy you completely.
¹⁹And when the people ask, 'Why has the
LORD our God done all this to us?' you
will tell them, 'As you have forsaken me
and served foreign gods in your own land,
so now you will serve foreigners in a land
not your own.'

²⁰"Announce this to the house of Jacob
  and proclaim it in Judah:
²¹Hear this, you foolish and senseless
    people,
  who have eyes but do not see,
  who have ears but do not hear:
²²Should you not fear me?" declares the
    LORD.
  "Should you not tremble in my
    presence?
I made the sand a boundary for the
    sea,
  an everlasting barrier it cannot
    cross.
The waves may roll, but they cannot
    prevail;
  they may roar, but they cannot
    cross it.
²³But these people have stubborn and
    rebellious hearts;
  they have turned aside and gone
    away.

²⁴They do not say to themselves,
   'Let us fear the LORD our God,
who gives autumn and spring rains in
      season,
   who assures us of the regular weeks
      of harvest.'
²⁵Your wrongdoings have kept these
      away;
   your sins have deprived you of
      good.

²⁶"Among my people are wicked men
   who lie in wait like men who snare
      birds
   and like those who set traps to
      catch men.
²⁷Like cages full of birds,
   their houses are full of deceit;
they have become rich and powerful
²⁸   and have grown fat and sleek.
   Their evil deeds have no limit;
   they do not plead the case of the
      fatherless to win it,
   they do not defend the rights of
      the poor.
²⁹Should I not punish them for this?"
   declares the LORD.
   "Should I not avenge myself
      on such a nation as this?

³⁰"A horrible and shocking thing
   has happened in the land:
³¹The prophets prophesy lies,
   the priests rule by their own
      authority,
and my people love it this way.
   But what will you do in the end?

Jerusalem Under Siege

6 "Flee for safety, people of
      Benjamin!
   Flee from Jerusalem!
Sound the trumpet in Tekoa!
   Raise the signal over Beth
      Hakkerem!
For disaster looms out of the north,
   even terrible destruction.
²I will destroy the Daughter of Zion,
   so beautiful and delicate.
³Shepherds with their flocks will come
      against her;
   they will pitch their tents around
      her,
   each tending his own portion."

⁴"Prepare for battle against her!
   Arise, let us attack at noon!

But, alas, the daylight is fading,
   and the shadows of evening grow
      long.
⁵So arise, let us attack at night
   and destroy her fortresses!"

⁶This is what the LORD Almighty says:

"Cut down the trees
   and build siege ramps against
      Jerusalem.
This city must be punished;
   it is filled with oppression.
⁷As a well pours out its water,
   so she pours out her wickedness.
Violence and destruction resound in
      her;
   her sickness and wounds are ever
      before me.
⁸Take warning, O Jerusalem,
   or I will turn away from you
and make your land desolate
   so no one can live in it."

⁹This is what the LORD Almighty says:

"Let them glean the remnant of Israel
   as thoroughly as a vine;
pass your hand over the branches
      again,
   like one gathering grapes."

¹⁰To whom can I speak and give
      warning?
   Who will listen to me?
Their ears are closed[a]
   so they cannot hear.
The word of the LORD is offensive to
      them;
   they find no pleasure in it.
¹¹But I am full of the wrath of the
      LORD,
   and I cannot hold it in.

"Pour it out on the children in the
      street
   and on the young men gathered
      together;
both husband and wife will be caught
      in it,
   and the old, those weighed down
      with years.
¹²Their houses will be turned over to
      others,
   together with their fields and their
      wives,
when I stretch out my hand

---

^a*10* Hebrew *uncircumcised*

against those who live in the land,"
                                    declares the LORD.
¹³"From the least to the greatest,
    all are greedy for gain;
prophets and priests alike,
    all practice deceit.
¹⁴They dress the wound of my people
    as though it were not serious.
'Peace, peace,' they say,
    when there is no peace.
¹⁵Are they ashamed of their loathsome
        conduct?
    No, they have no shame at all;
    they do not even know how to
        blush.
So they will fall among the fallen;
    they will be brought down when I
        punish them,"
                        says the LORD.

¹⁶This is what the LORD says:

"Stand at the crossroads and look;
    ask for the ancient paths,
ask where the good way is, and walk
        in it,
    and you will find rest for your
        souls.

But you said, 'We will not walk in
        it.'
¹⁷I appointed watchmen over you and
        said,
    'Listen to the sound of the
        trumpet!'
    But you said, 'We will not listen.'
¹⁸Therefore hear, O nations;
    observe, O witnesses,
    what will happen to them.
¹⁹Hear, O earth:
I am bringing disaster on this people,
    the fruit of their schemes,
because they have not listened to my
        words
    and have rejected my law.
²⁰What do I care about incense from
        Sheba
    or sweet calamus from a distant
        land?
Your burnt offerings are not
        acceptable;
    your sacrifices do not please me."

²¹Therefore this is what the LORD says:

"I will put obstacles before this
        people.

Crossroads

Friday

JEREMIAH 6:16 The year 1976 stands out in our memory as our "crossroad" year. That was the year we explored the feasibility of working full-time in the field of marriage and family education. It was also the year we chose to remain in Europe and pursue it there. Without a doubt, it was the hardest year of our marriage.

If you've ever attempted to pioneer something new or make a major change of profession, you understand some of the stresses we encountered. An up-and-down roller coaster experience went on for months. During that year we felt so discouraged that many times we almost gave up our dream. Somehow we were each other's support system. When one was down, the other was up. We kept asking God for "the good way" and for his direction and, in the end, he answered with approval and with the support of our directors. The rest is his-tory. We helped pioneer marriage education in the German speaking countries and now, years later, are still leading marriage seminars in Europe.

Life involves choices, and it's up to us to choose the direction in which we walk. How can we find "the good way" for our marriage? Fortunately Biblical principles light our way along God's reliable path. Marital advice from "experts" changes from time to time and from culture to culture, but God's principles are eternal. And it's reassuring to know that others have traveled the marriage road; the ancient path is marked.

When you come to a "crossroads" in your marriage, look to your heavenly Father. He will guide you in the way you should go. You can trust the ancient paths. You can know that God's path is the best one to follow, and you will find rest in that.

—*Dave & Claudia*

Go to page 810 for your next devotional reading.

Fathers and sons alike will stumble
over them;
neighbors and friends will perish."

22This is what the LORD says:

"Look, an army is coming
from the land of the north;
a great nation is being stirred up
from the ends of the earth.
23They are armed with bow and spear;
they are cruel and show no mercy.
They sound like the roaring sea
as they ride on their horses;
they come like men in battle
formation
to attack you, O Daughter of Zion."

24We have heard reports about them,
and our hands hang limp.
Anguish has gripped us,
pain like that of a woman in labor.
25Do not go out to the fields
or walk on the roads,
for the enemy has a sword,
and there is terror on every side.
26O my people, put on sackcloth
and roll in ashes;
mourn with bitter wailing
as for an only son,
for suddenly the destroyer
will come upon us.

27"I have made you a tester of metals
and my people the ore,
that you may observe
and test their ways.
28They are all hardened rebels,
going about to slander.
They are bronze and iron;
they all act corruptly.
29The bellows blow fiercely
to burn away the lead with fire,
but the refining goes on in vain;
the wicked are not purged out.
30They are called rejected silver,
because the LORD has rejected
them."

False Religion Worthless

7 This is the word that came to Jeremiah from the LORD: 2"Stand at the gate
of the LORD's house and there proclaim
this message:
    " 'Hear the word of the LORD, all you
people of Judah who come through these
gates to worship the LORD. 3This is what
the LORD Almighty, the God of Israel,
says: Reform your ways and your actions,
and I will let you live in this place. 4Do
not trust in deceptive words and say,
"This is the temple of the LORD, the temple of the LORD, the temple of the LORD!"
5If you really change your ways and your
actions and deal with each other justly, 6if
you do not oppress the alien, the fatherless or the widow and do not shed innocent blood in this place, and if you do not
follow other gods to your own harm,
7then I will let you live in this place, in the
land I gave your forefathers for ever and
ever. 8But look, you are trusting in deceptive words that are worthless.

9" 'Will you steal and murder, commit
adultery and perjury,a burn incense to
Baal and follow other gods you have not
known, 10and then come and stand before me in this house, which bears my
Name, and say, "We are safe"—safe to do
all these detestable things? 11Has this
house, which bears my Name, become a
den of robbers to you? But I have been
watching! declares the LORD.

12" 'Go now to the place in Shiloh
where I first made a dwelling for my
Name, and see what I did to it because
of the wickedness of my people Israel.
13While you were doing all these things,
declares the LORD, I spoke to you again
and again, but you did not listen; I called
you, but you did not answer. 14Therefore,
what I did to Shiloh I will now do to the
house that bears my Name, the temple
you trust in, the place I gave to you and
your fathers. 15I will thrust you from my
presence, just as I did all your brothers,
the people of Ephraim.'

16"So do not pray for this people nor
offer any plea or petition for them; do not
plead with me, for I will not listen to you.
17Do you not see what they are doing in
the towns of Judah and in the streets of
Jerusalem? 18The children gather wood,
the fathers light the fire, and the women
knead the dough and make cakes of bread
for the Queen of Heaven. They pour out
drink offerings to other gods to provoke
me to anger. 19But am I the one they are
provoking? declares the LORD. Are they
not rather harming themselves, to their
own shame?

a9 Or and swear by false gods

20 " 'Therefore this is what the Sovereign LORD says: My anger and my wrath will be poured out on this place, on man and beast, on the trees of the field and on the fruit of the ground, and it will burn and not be quenched.

21 " 'This is what the LORD Almighty, the God of Israel, says: Go ahead, add your burnt offerings to your other sacrifices and eat the meat yourselves! 22For when I brought your forefathers out of Egypt and spoke to them, I did not just give them commands about burnt offerings and sacrifices, 23but I gave them this command: Obey me, and I will be your God and you will be my people. Walk in all the ways I command you, that it may go well with you. 24But they did not listen or pay attention; instead, they followed the stubborn inclinations of their evil hearts. They went backward and not forward. 25From the time your forefathers left Egypt until now, day after day, again and again I sent you my servants the prophets. 26But they did not listen to me or pay attention. They were stiff-necked and did more evil than their forefathers.'

27 "When you tell them all this, they will not listen to you; when you call to them, they will not answer. 28Therefore say to them, 'This is the nation that has not obeyed the LORD its God or responded to correction. Truth has perished; it has vanished from their lips. 29Cut off your hair and throw it away; take up a lament on the barren heights, for the LORD has rejected and abandoned this generation that is under his wrath.

The Valley of Slaughter

30 " 'The people of Judah have done evil in my eyes, declares the LORD. They have set up their detestable idols in the house that bears my Name and have defiled it. 31They have built the high places of Topheth in the Valley of Ben Hinnom to burn their sons and daughters in the fire—something I did not command, nor did it enter my mind. 32So beware, the days are coming, declares the LORD, when people will no longer call it Topheth or the Valley of Ben Hinnom, but the Valley of Slaughter, for they will bury the dead in Topheth until there is no more room. 33Then the carcasses of this people will become food for the birds of the air and the beasts of the earth, and there will be no one to frighten them away. 34I will bring an end to the sounds of joy and gladness and to the voices of bride and bridegroom in the towns of Judah and the streets of Jerusalem, for the land will become desolate.

8 " 'At that time, declares the LORD, the bones of the kings and officials of Judah, the bones of the priests and prophets, and the bones of the people of Jerusalem will be removed from their graves. 2They will be exposed to the sun and the moon and all the stars of the heavens, which they have loved and served and which they have followed and consulted and worshiped. They will not be gathered up or buried, but will be like refuse lying on the ground. 3Wherever I banish them, all the survivors of this evil nation will prefer death to life, declares the LORD Almighty.'

Sin and Punishment

4 "Say to them, 'This is what the LORD says:

" 'When men fall down, do they not
  get up?
When a man turns away, does he
  not return?
5Why then have these people turned
  away?
Why does Jerusalem always turn
  away?
They cling to deceit;
  they refuse to return.
6I have listened attentively,
  but they do not say what is right.
No one repents of his wickedness,
  saying, "What have I done?"
Each pursues his own course
  like a horse charging into battle.
7Even the stork in the sky
  knows her appointed seasons,
and the dove, the swift and the
    thrush
  observe the time of their migration.
But my people do not know
  the requirements of the LORD.

8 " 'How can you say, "We are wise,
  for we have the law of the LORD,"
when actually the lying pen of the
    scribes

has handled it falsely?
⁹The wise will be put to shame;
  they will be dismayed and trapped.
Since they have rejected the word of
    the LORD,
  what kind of wisdom do they
    have?
¹⁰Therefore I will give their wives to
    other men
  and their fields to new owners.
From the least to the greatest,
  all are greedy for gain;
prophets and priests alike,
  all practice deceit.
¹¹They dress the wound of my people
  as though it were not serious.
"Peace, peace," they say,
  when there is no peace.
¹²Are they ashamed of their loathsome
    conduct?
  No, they have no shame at all;
  they do not even know how to
    blush.
So they will fall among the fallen;
  they will be brought down when
    they are punished,
                          says the LORD.

¹³" 'I will take away their harvest,
                    declares the LORD.
  There will be no grapes on the
    vine.
There will be no figs on the tree,
  and their leaves will wither.
What I have given them
  will be taken from them.ᵃ' "

¹⁴"Why are we sitting here?
  Gather together!
Let us flee to the fortified cities
  and perish there!
For the LORD our God has doomed us
    to perish
  and given us poisoned water to
    drink,
  because we have sinned against
    him.
¹⁵We hoped for peace
  but no good has come,
for a time of healing
  but there was only terror.
¹⁶The snorting of the enemy's horses
  is heard from Dan;
at the neighing of their stallions
  the whole land trembles.
They have come to devour

the land and everything in it,
  the city and all who live there."

¹⁷"See, I will send venomous snakes
    among you,
  vipers that cannot be charmed,
  and they will bite you,"
                          declares the LORD.

¹⁸O my Comforterᵇ in sorrow,
  my heart is faint within me.
¹⁹Listen to the cry of my people
  from a land far away:
"Is the LORD not in Zion?
  Is her King no longer there?"

"Why have they provoked me to
    anger with their images,
  with their worthless foreign idols?"

²⁰"The harvest is past,
  the summer has ended,
  and we are not saved."

²¹Since my people are crushed, I am
    crushed;
  I mourn, and horror grips me.
²²Is there no balm in Gilead?
  Is there no physician there?
Why then is there no healing
  for the wound of my people?

9 ¹Oh, that my head were a spring of
      water
  and my eyes a fountain of tears!
I would weep day and night
  for the slain of my people.
²Oh, that I had in the desert
  a lodging place for travelers,
so that I might leave my people
  and go away from them;
for they are all adulterers,
  a crowd of unfaithful people.

³"They make ready their tongue
  like a bow, to shoot lies;
it is not by truth
  that they triumphᶜ in the land.
They go from one sin to another;
  they do not acknowledge me,"
                          declares the LORD.
⁴"Beware of your friends;
  do not trust your brothers.
For every brother is a deceiver,ᵈ
  and every friend a slanderer.
⁵Friend deceives friend,

ᵃ13 The meaning of the Hebrew for this sentence
is uncertain.   ᵇ18 The meaning of the Hebrew
for this word is uncertain.   ᶜ3 Or lies; / they are
not valiant for truth   ᵈ4 Or a deceiving Jacob

and no one speaks the truth.
They have taught their tongues to lie;
   they weary themselves with
      sinning.
[6]You[a] live in the midst of deception;
   in their deceit they refuse to
      acknowledge me,"
               declares the LORD.

[7]Therefore this is what the LORD Almighty says:

"See, I will refine and test them,
   for what else can I do
   because of the sin of my people?
[8]Their tongue is a deadly arrow;
   it speaks with deceit.
With his mouth each speaks cordially
     to his neighbor,
but in his heart he sets a trap for
     him.
[9]Should I not punish them for this?"
   declares the LORD.

"Should I not avenge myself
   on such a nation as this?"

[10]I will weep and wail for the
     mountains
   and take up a lament concerning
     the desert pastures.
They are desolate and untraveled,
   and the lowing of cattle is not
     heard.
The birds of the air have fled
   and the animals are gone.

[11]"I will make Jerusalem a heap of
     ruins,
   a haunt of jackals;
and I will lay waste the towns of
     Judah
   so no one can live there."

[12]What man is wise enough to under-

---

[a]6 That is, Jeremiah (the Hebrew is singular)

Affair-proofing Marriage

Quiet TIMES with each other

JEREMIAH 9:4 "She was my very best friend," Lisa sobbed. "Why would she have gone after my husband?"

It's important not to become so insecure about our marriage that we suspect everyone who befriends us. But it's also very important to be wise in evaluating our friendships. We have all heard the stories about someone whose spouse has an extra-marital affair with a person who was the other spouse's friend— even best friend. Beware of behavioral signs or inappropriate discussions that take place with the people or other couples you spend time with. The majority of those relationships are innocent friendships, but sometimes these friendships can become something more.

Our society often downplays the importance of purity in marriage. Flirting has become an acceptable form of socializing, and adultery is commonplace. Most of our entertainment is filled with infidelity. Both in church and out of church, there are those who find nothing wrong with pursuing the spouse of another.

Paranoia and constant jealousy about our friendships is not healthy. And fearing friendships with other couples is unwise. It is equally unwise, however, to assume that all friends maintain the same marital boundaries you do.

Together, you and your spouse need to establish marital boundaries. These boundaries should be discussed regularly. Ask each other, "Is there anyone we spend time with who steps dangerously close to violating our marital space?" This passage doesn't advise us to eliminate all friends. But, in a culture that has turned away from God, it can be interpreted as instructing us to be *careful* when forming friendships.

—*Bob & Rosemary*

Weekend Warm-up *Do you recall a "crossroad" year in your marriage?*

Go to page 820 for your next devotional reading.

stand this? Who has been instructed by the LORD and can explain it? Why has the land been ruined and laid waste like a desert that no one can cross?

¹³The LORD said, "It is because they have forsaken my law, which I set before them; they have not obeyed me or followed my law. ¹⁴Instead, they have followed the stubbornness of their hearts; they have followed the Baals, as their fathers taught them." ¹⁵Therefore, this is what the LORD Almighty, the God of Israel, says: "See, I will make this people eat bitter food and drink poisoned water. ¹⁶I will scatter them among nations that neither they nor their fathers have known, and I will pursue them with the sword until I have destroyed them."

¹⁷This is what the LORD Almighty says:

"Consider now! Call for the wailing
        women to come;
    send for the most skillful of them.
¹⁸Let them come quickly
        and wail over us
    till our eyes overflow with tears
        and water streams from our
            eyelids.
¹⁹The sound of wailing is heard from
            Zion:
    'How ruined we are!
    How great is our shame!
    We must leave our land
        because our houses are in ruins.' "

²⁰Now, O women, hear the word of the
            LORD;
    open your ears to the words of his
            mouth.
    Teach your daughters how to wail;
        teach one another a lament.
²¹Death has climbed in through our
            windows
        and has entered our fortresses;
    it has cut off the children from the
            streets
        and the young men from the
            public squares.

²²Say, "This is what the LORD declares:

" 'The dead bodies of men will lie
        like refuse on the open field,
    like cut grain behind the reaper,
        with no one to gather them.' "

²³This is what the LORD says:

"Let not the wise man boast of his
        wisdom
    or the strong man boast of his
        strength
    or the rich man boast of his riches,
²⁴but let him who boasts boast about
        this:
    that he understands and knows
        me,
    that I am the LORD, who exercises
        kindness,
    justice and righteousness on earth,
        for in these I delight,"
                    declares the LORD.

²⁵"The days are coming," declares the LORD, "when I will punish all who are circumcised only in the flesh— ²⁶Egypt, Judah, Edom, Ammon, Moab and all who live in the desert in distant places.ᵃ For all these nations are really uncircumcised, and even the whole house of Israel is uncircumcised in heart."

God and Idols

10 Hear what the LORD says to you, O house of Israel. ²This is what the LORD says:

"Do not learn the ways of the
        nations
    or be terrified by signs in the sky,
        though the nations are terrified by
            them.
³For the customs of the peoples are
        worthless;
    they cut a tree out of the forest,
        and a craftsman shapes it with his
            chisel.
⁴They adorn it with silver and gold;
        they fasten it with hammer and
            nails
    so it will not totter.
⁵Like a scarecrow in a melon patch,
        their idols cannot speak;
    they must be carried
        because they cannot walk.
Do not fear them;
        they can do no harm
    nor can they do any good."

⁶No one is like you, O LORD;
    you are great,
        and your name is mighty in power.
⁷Who should not revere you,

ᵃ26 Or *desert and who clip the hair by their foreheads*

O King of the nations?
This is your due.
Among all the wise men of the
nations
and in all their kingdoms,
there is no one like you.
⁸They are all senseless and foolish;
they are taught by worthless
wooden idols.
⁹Hammered silver is brought from
Tarshish
and gold from Uphaz.
What the craftsman and goldsmith
have made
is then dressed in blue and
purple—
all made by skilled workers.
¹⁰But the LORD is the true God;
he is the living God, the eternal
King.
When he is angry, the earth trembles;
the nations cannot endure his
wrath.

¹¹"Tell them this: 'These gods, who did
not make the heavens and the earth, will
perish from the earth and from under the
heavens.' "ᵃ

¹²But God made the earth by his
power;
he founded the world by his
wisdom
and stretched out the heavens by
his understanding.
¹³When he thunders, the waters in the
heavens roar;
he makes clouds rise from the ends
of the earth.
He sends lightning with the rain
and brings out the wind from his
storehouses.

¹⁴Everyone is senseless and without
knowledge;
every goldsmith is shamed by his
idols.
His images are a fraud;
they have no breath in them.
¹⁵They are worthless, the objects of
mockery;
when their judgment comes, they
will perish.
¹⁶He who is the Portion of Jacob is not
like these,
for he is the Maker of all things,

including Israel, the tribe of his
inheritance—
the LORD Almighty is his name.

Coming Destruction

¹⁷Gather up your belongings to leave
the land,
you who live under siege.
¹⁸For this is what the LORD says:
"At this time I will hurl out
those who live in this land;
I will bring distress on them
so that they may be captured."

¹⁹Woe to me because of my injury!
My wound is incurable!
Yet I said to myself,
"This is my sickness, and I must
endure it."
²⁰My tent is destroyed;
all its ropes are snapped.
My sons are gone from me and are
no more;
no one is left now to pitch my tent
or to set up my shelter.
²¹The shepherds are senseless
and do not inquire of the LORD;
so they do not prosper
and all their flock is scattered.
²²Listen! The report is coming—
a great commotion from the land
of the north!
It will make the towns of Judah
desolate,
a haunt of jackals.

Jeremiah's Prayer

²³I know, O LORD, that a man's life is
not his own;
it is not for man to direct his steps.
²⁴Correct me, LORD, but only with
justice—
not in your anger,
lest you reduce me to nothing.
²⁵Pour out your wrath on the nations
that do not acknowledge you,
on the peoples who do not call on
your name.
For they have devoured Jacob;
they have devoured him
completely
and destroyed his homeland.

ᵃ11 The text of this verse is in Aramaic.

The Covenant Is Broken

11 This is the word that came to Jeremiah from the LORD: ²"Listen to the terms of this covenant and tell them to the people of Judah and to those who live in Jerusalem. ³Tell them that this is what the LORD, the God of Israel, says: 'Cursed is the man who does not obey the terms of this covenant— ⁴the terms I commanded your forefathers when I brought them out of Egypt, out of the iron-smelting furnace.' I said, 'Obey me and do everything I command you, and you will be my people, and I will be your God. ⁵Then I will fulfill the oath I swore to your forefathers, to give them a land flowing with milk and honey'—the land you possess today."

I answered, "Amen, LORD."

⁶The LORD said to me, "Proclaim all these words in the towns of Judah and in the streets of Jerusalem: 'Listen to the terms of this covenant and follow them. ⁷From the time I brought your forefathers up from Egypt until today, I warned them again and again, saying, "Obey me." ⁸But they did not listen or pay attention; instead, they followed the stubbornness of their evil hearts. So I brought on them all the curses of the covenant I had commanded them to follow but that they did not keep.' "

⁹Then the LORD said to me, "There is a conspiracy among the people of Judah and those who live in Jerusalem. ¹⁰They have returned to the sins of their forefathers, who refused to listen to my words. They have followed other gods to serve them. Both the house of Israel and the house of Judah have broken the covenant I made with their forefathers. ¹¹Therefore this is what the LORD says: 'I will bring on them a disaster they cannot escape. Although they cry out to me, I will not listen to them. ¹²The towns of Judah and the people of Jerusalem will go and cry out to the gods to whom they burn incense, but they will not help them at all when disaster strikes. ¹³You have as many gods as you have towns, O Judah; and the altars you have set up to burn incense to that shameful god Baal are as many as the streets of Jerusalem.'

¹⁴"Do not pray for this people nor offer any plea or petition for them, because I will not listen when they call to me in the time of their distress.

¹⁵"What is my beloved doing in my temple
    as she works out her evil schemes
        with many?
    Can consecrated meat avert ⌐your
        punishment⌐?
When you engage in your wickedness,
    then you rejoice. ª"

¹⁶The LORD called you a thriving olive
        tree
    with fruit beautiful in form.
But with the roar of a mighty storm
    he will set it on fire,
    and its branches will be broken.

¹⁷The LORD Almighty, who planted you, has decreed disaster for you, because the house of Israel and the house of Judah have done evil and provoked me to anger by burning incense to Baal.

Plot Against Jeremiah

¹⁸Because the LORD revealed their plot to me, I knew it, for at that time he showed me what they were doing. ¹⁹I had been like a gentle lamb led to the slaughter; I did not realize that they had plotted against me, saying,

"Let us destroy the tree and its fruit;
    let us cut him off from the land of
        the living,
    that his name be remembered no
        more."
²⁰But, O LORD Almighty, you who
        judge righteously
    and test the heart and mind,
let me see your vengeance upon
        them,
    for to you I have committed my
        cause.

²¹"Therefore this is what the LORD says about the men of Anathoth who are seeking your life and saying, 'Do not prophesy in the name of the LORD or you will die by our hands'— ²²therefore this is what the LORD Almighty says: 'I will punish them. Their young men will die by the sword, their sons and daughters by famine. ²³Not even a remnant will be left to

---

ª15 Or *Could consecrated meat avert your
punishment? / Then you would rejoice*

them, because I will bring disaster on the men of Anathoth in the year of their punishment.' "

Jeremiah's Complaint

12 You are always righteous, O LORD,
　　when I bring a case before you.
　Yet I would speak with you about
　　　your justice:
　　Why does the way of the wicked
　　　prosper?
　　Why do all the faithless live at
　　　ease?
　²You have planted them, and they
　　　have taken root;
　　they grow and bear fruit.
　You are always on their lips
　　but far from their hearts.
　³Yet you know me, O LORD;
　　you see me and test my thoughts
　　　about you.
　Drag them off like sheep to be
　　　butchered!
　　Set them apart for the day of
　　　slaughter!
　⁴How long will the land lie parched*a*
　　and the grass in every field be
　　　withered?
　Because those who live in it are
　　　wicked,
　　the animals and birds have
　　　perished.
　Moreover, the people are saying,
　　"He will not see what happens to
　　　us."

God's Answer

　⁵"If you have raced with men on foot
　　and they have worn you out,
　　how can you compete with horses?
　If you stumble in safe country,*b*
　　how will you manage in the
　　　thickets by*c* the Jordan?
　⁶Your brothers, your own family—
　　even they have betrayed you;
　　they have raised a loud cry against
　　　you.
　Do not trust them,
　　though they speak well of you.

　⁷"I will forsake my house,
　　abandon my inheritance;
　I will give the one I love
　　into the hands of her enemies.
　⁸My inheritance has become to me
　　like a lion in the forest.

　She roars at me;
　　therefore I hate her.
　⁹Has not my inheritance become to
　　　me
　　like a speckled bird of prey
　　that other birds of prey surround
　　　and attack?
　Go and gather all the wild beasts;
　　bring them to devour.
　¹⁰Many shepherds will ruin my
　　　vineyard
　　and trample down my field;
　they will turn my pleasant field
　　into a desolate wasteland.
　¹¹It will be made a wasteland,
　　parched and desolate before me;
　the whole land will be laid waste
　　because there is no one who cares.
　¹²Over all the barren heights in the
　　　desert
　　destroyers will swarm,
　for the sword of the LORD will devour
　　from one end of the land to the
　　　other;
　　no one will be safe.
　¹³They will sow wheat but reap thorns;
　　they will wear themselves out but
　　　gain nothing.
　So bear the shame of your harvest
　　because of the LORD's fierce anger."

¹⁴This is what the LORD says: "As for all my wicked neighbors who seize the inheritance I gave my people Israel, I will uproot them from their lands and I will uproot the house of Judah from among them. ¹⁵But after I uproot them, I will again have compassion and will bring each of them back to his own inheritance and his own country. ¹⁶And if they learn well the ways of my people and swear by my name, saying, 'As surely as the LORD lives'—even as they once taught my people to swear by Baal—then they will be established among my people. ¹⁷But if any nation does not listen, I will completely uproot and destroy it," declares the LORD.

A Linen Belt

13 This is what the LORD said to me:
"Go and buy a linen belt and put it around your waist, but do not let it touch

----

a4 Or land mourn　　b5 Or If you put your trust in a land of safety　　c5 Or the flooding of water." ²So I bought a belt, as the LORD directed, and put it around my waist.

³Then the word of the LORD came to me a second time: ⁴"Take the belt you bought and are wearing around your waist, and go now to Perath*a* and hide it there in a crevice in the rocks." ⁵So I went and hid it at Perath, as the LORD told me.

⁶Many days later the LORD said to me, "Go now to Perath and get the belt I told you to hide there." ⁷So I went to Perath and dug up the belt and took it from the place where I had hidden it, but now it was ruined and completely useless.

⁸Then the word of the LORD came to me: ⁹"This is what the LORD says: 'In the same way I will ruin the pride of Judah and the great pride of Jerusalem. ¹⁰These wicked people, who refuse to listen to my words, who follow the stubbornness of their hearts and go after other gods to serve and worship them, will be like this belt—completely useless! ¹¹For as a belt is bound around a man's waist, so I bound the whole house of Israel and the whole house of Judah to me,' declares the LORD, 'to be my people for my renown and praise and honor. But they have not listened.'

Wineskins

¹²"Say to them: 'This is what the LORD, the God of Israel, says: Every wineskin should be filled with wine.' And if they say to you, 'Don't we know that every wineskin should be filled with wine?' ¹³then tell them, 'This is what the LORD says: I am going to fill with drunkenness all who live in this land, including the kings who sit on David's throne, the priests, the prophets and all those living in Jerusalem. ¹⁴I will smash them one against the other, fathers and sons alike, declares the LORD. I will allow no pity or mercy or compassion to keep me from destroying them.' "

Threat of Captivity

¹⁵Hear and pay attention,
    do not be arrogant,
    for the LORD has spoken.
¹⁶Give glory to the LORD your God
    before he brings the darkness,
    before your feet stumble
    on the darkening hills.

You hope for light,
    but he will turn it to thick darkness
    and change it to deep gloom.
¹⁷But if you do not listen,
    I will weep in secret
    because of your pride;
my eyes will weep bitterly,
    overflowing with tears,
    because the LORD's flock will be
        taken captive.

¹⁸Say to the king and to the queen
        mother,
    "Come down from your thrones,
for your glorious crowns
    will fall from your heads."
¹⁹The cities in the Negev will be shut
        up,
    and there will be no one to open
        them.
All Judah will be carried into exile,
    carried completely away.

²⁰Lift up your eyes and see
    those who are coming from the
        north.
Where is the flock that was entrusted
        to you,
    the sheep of which you boasted?
²¹What will you say when ⌊the LORD⌋
        sets over you
    those you cultivated as your special
        allies?
Will not pain grip you
    like that of a woman in labor?
²²And if you ask yourself,
    "Why has this happened to me?"—
it is because of your many sins
    that your skirts have been torn off
    and your body mistreated.
²³Can the Ethiopian*b* change his skin
    or the leopard its spots?
Neither can you do good
    who are accustomed to doing evil.

²⁴"I will scatter you like chaff
    driven by the desert wind.
²⁵This is your lot,
    the portion I have decreed for you,"
            declares the LORD,
    "because you have forgotten me
    and trusted in false gods.
²⁶I will pull up your skirts over your
        face

a4 Or possibly *the Euphrates*; also in verses 5-7
b23 Hebrew *Cushite* (probably a person from the upper Nile region)

that your shame may be seen—
27your adulteries and lustful neighings,
    your shameless prostitution!
I have seen your detestable acts
    on the hills and in the fields.
Woe to you, O Jerusalem!
    How long will you be unclean?"

Drought, Famine, Sword

14 This is the word of the LORD to Jeremiah concerning the drought:

2"Judah mourns,
    her cities languish;
they wail for the land,
    and a cry goes up from Jerusalem.
3The nobles send their servants for
        water;
    they go to the cisterns
    but find no water.
They return with their jars unfilled;
    dismayed and despairing,
    they cover their heads.
4The ground is cracked
    because there is no rain in the
        land;
the farmers are dismayed
    and cover their heads.
5Even the doe in the field
    deserts her newborn fawn
    because there is no grass.
6Wild donkeys stand on the barren
        heights
    and pant like jackals;
their eyesight fails
    for lack of pasture."

7Although our sins testify against us,
    O LORD, do something for the sake
        of your name.
For our backsliding is great;
    we have sinned against you.
8O Hope of Israel,
    its Savior in times of distress,
why are you like a stranger in the
        land,
    like a traveler who stays only a
        night?
9Why are you like a man taken by
        surprise,
    like a warrior powerless to save?
You are among us, O LORD,
    and we bear your name;
    do not forsake us!

10This is what the LORD says about this
people:

"They greatly love to wander;
    they do not restrain their feet.
So the LORD does not accept them;
    he will now remember their
        wickedness
    and punish them for their sins."

11Then the LORD said to me, "Do not
pray for the well-being of this people.
12Although they fast, I will not listen to
their cry; though they offer burnt offerings and grain offerings, I will not accept
them. Instead, I will destroy them with
the sword, famine and plague."

13But I said, "Ah, Sovereign LORD, the
prophets keep telling them, 'You will not
see the sword or suffer famine. Indeed, I
will give you lasting peace in this place.'"

14Then the LORD said to me, "The
prophets are prophesying lies in my
name. I have not sent them or appointed
them or spoken to them. They are prophesying to you false visions, divinations,
idolatries[a] and the delusions of their
own minds. 15Therefore, this is what the
LORD says about the prophets who are
prophesying in my name: I did not send
them, yet they are saying, 'No sword or
famine will touch this land.' Those same
prophets will perish by sword and famine. 16And the people they are prophesying to will be thrown out into the streets
of Jerusalem because of the famine and
sword. There will be no one to bury them
or their wives, their sons or their daughters. I will pour out on them the calamity
they deserve.

17"Speak this word to them:

" 'Let my eyes overflow with tears
    night and day without ceasing;
for my virgin daughter—my people—
    has suffered a grievous wound,
    a crushing blow.
18If I go into the country,
    I see those slain by the sword;
if I go into the city,
    I see the ravages of famine.
Both prophet and priest
    have gone to a land they know
        not.'"

19Have you rejected Judah completely?
    Do you despise Zion?
Why have you afflicted us

_____
a14 Or visions, worthless divinations

so that we cannot be healed?
We hoped for peace
    but no good has come,
for a time of healing
    but there is only terror.
²⁰O LORD, we acknowledge our
    wickedness
    and the guilt of our fathers;
    we have indeed sinned against you.
²¹For the sake of your name do not
    despise us;
    do not dishonor your glorious
    throne.
Remember your covenant with us
    and do not break it.
²²Do any of the worthless idols of the
    nations bring rain?
    Do the skies themselves send down
    showers?
No, it is you, O LORD our God.
    Therefore our hope is in you,
    for you are the one who does all
    this.

15 Then the LORD said to me: "Even if Moses and Samuel were to stand before me, my heart would not go out to this people. Send them away from my presence! Let them go! ²And if they ask you, 'Where shall we go?' tell them, 'This is what the LORD says:

    " 'Those destined for death, to death;
    those for the sword, to the sword;
    those for starvation, to starvation;
    those for captivity, to captivity.'

³"I will send four kinds of destroyers against them," declares the LORD, "the sword to kill and the dogs to drag away and the birds of the air and the beasts of the earth to devour and destroy. ⁴I will make them abhorrent to all the kingdoms of the earth because of what Manasseh son of Hezekiah king of Judah did in Jerusalem.

⁵"Who will have pity on you,
    O Jerusalem?
    Who will mourn for you?
    Who will stop to ask how you are?
⁶You have rejected me," declares the
    LORD.
    "You keep on backsliding.
So I will lay hands on you and
    destroy you;
    I can no longer show compassion.

⁷I will winnow them with a
    winnowing fork
    at the city gates of the land.
I will bring bereavement and
    destruction on my people,
    for they have not changed their
    ways.
⁸I will make their widows more
    numerous
    than the sand of the sea.
At midday I will bring a destroyer
    against the mothers of their young
    men;
    suddenly I will bring down on them
    anguish and terror.
⁹The mother of seven will grow faint
    and breathe her last.
Her sun will set while it is still day;
    she will be disgraced and
    humiliated.
I will put the survivors to the sword
    before their enemies,"
            declares the LORD.

¹⁰Alas, my mother, that you gave me
    birth,
    a man with whom the whole land
    strives and contends!
I have neither lent nor borrowed,
    yet everyone curses me.

¹¹The LORD said,

"Surely I will deliver you for a good
    purpose;
    surely I will make your enemies
    plead with you
    in times of disaster and times of
    distress.

¹²"Can a man break iron—
    iron from the north—or bronze?
¹³Your wealth and your treasures
    I will give as plunder, without
    charge,
    because of all your sins
    throughout your country.
¹⁴I will enslave you to your enemies
    in*ᵃ* a land you do not know,
for my anger will kindle a fire
    that will burn against you."

¹⁵You understand, O LORD;
    remember me and care for me.

ᵃ14 Some Hebrew manuscripts, Septuagint and Syriac (see also Jer. 17:4); most Hebrew manuscripts *I will cause your enemies to bring you / into*

Avenge me on my persecutors.
You are long-suffering—do not take
    me away;
  think of how I suffer reproach for
    your sake.
¹⁶When your words came, I ate them;
  they were my joy and my heart's
    delight,
for I bear your name,
  O LORD God Almighty.
¹⁷I never sat in the company of revelers,
  never made merry with them;
I sat alone because your hand was on
    me
  and you had filled me with
    indignation.
¹⁸Why is my pain unending
  and my wound grievous and
    incurable?
Will you be to me like a deceptive
    brook,
  like a spring that fails?

¹⁹Therefore this is what the LORD says:

"If you repent, I will restore you
  that you may serve me;
if you utter worthy, not worthless,
    words,
  you will be my spokesman.
Let this people turn to you,
  but you must not turn to them.
²⁰I will make you a wall to this people,
  a fortified wall of bronze;
they will fight against you
  but will not overcome you,
for I am with you
  to rescue and save you,"
               declares the LORD.
²¹"I will save you from the hands of
    the wicked
  and redeem you from the grasp of
    the cruel."

Day of Disaster

16 Then the word of the LORD came
to me: ²"You must not marry and
have sons or daughters in this place." ³For
this is what the LORD says about the sons
and daughters born in this land and
about the women who are their mothers
and the men who are their fathers: ⁴"They
will die of deadly diseases. They will not
be mourned or buried but will be like
refuse lying on the ground. They will perish by sword and famine, and their dead

bodies will become food for the birds of
the air and the beasts of the earth."

⁵For this is what the LORD says: "Do
not enter a house where there is a funeral
meal; do not go to mourn or show sympathy, because I have withdrawn my
blessing, my love and my pity from this
people," declares the LORD. ⁶"Both high
and low will die in this land. They will
not be buried or mourned, and no one
will cut himself or shave his head for
them. ⁷No one will offer food to comfort
those who mourn for the dead—not even
for a father or a mother—nor will anyone
give them a drink to console them.

⁸"And do not enter a house where
there is feasting and sit down to eat and
drink. ⁹For this is what the LORD Almighty, the God of Israel, says: Before
your eyes and in your days I will bring an
end to the sounds of joy and gladness and
to the voices of bride and bridegroom in
this place.

¹⁰"When you tell these people all this
and they ask you, 'Why has the LORD
decreed such a great disaster against us?
What wrong have we done? What sin
have we committed against the LORD our
God?' ¹¹then say to them, 'It is because
your fathers forsook me,' declares the
LORD, 'and followed other gods and
served and worshiped them. They forsook
me and did not keep my law. ¹²But you
have behaved more wickedly than your
fathers. See how each of you is following
the stubbornness of his evil heart instead
of obeying me. ¹³So I will throw you out
of this land into a land neither you nor
your fathers have known, and there you
will serve other gods day and night, for I
will show you no favor.'

¹⁴"However, the days are coming," declares the LORD, "when men will no longer say, 'As surely as the LORD lives, who
brought the Israelites up out of Egypt,'
¹⁵but they will say, 'As surely as the LORD
lives, who brought the Israelites up out of
the land of the north and out of all the
countries where he had banished them.'
For I will restore them to the land I gave
their forefathers.

¹⁶"But now I will send for many fishermen," declares the LORD, "and they will
catch them. After that I will send for many
hunters, and they will hunt them down
on every mountain and hill and from the

crevices of the rocks. ¹⁷My eyes are on all their ways; they are not hidden from me, nor is their sin concealed from my eyes. ¹⁸I will repay them double for their wickedness and their sin, because they have defiled my land with the lifeless forms of their vile images and have filled my inheritance with their detestable idols."

¹⁹O LORD, my strength and my fortress,
　　my refuge in time of distress,
to you the nations will come
　　from the ends of the earth and say,
"Our fathers possessed nothing but
　　　　false gods,
　　worthless idols that did them no
　　　　good.
²⁰Do men make their own gods?
　　Yes, but they are not gods!"

²¹"Therefore I will teach them—
　　this time I will teach them
　　my power and might.
Then they will know
　　that my name is the LORD.

17 "Judah's sin is engraved with an iron tool,
　　inscribed with a flint point,
on the tablets of their hearts
　　and on the horns of their altars.
²Even their children remember
　　their altars and Asherah poles^a
beside the spreading trees
　　and on the high hills.
³My mountain in the land
　　and your^b wealth and all your
　　　　treasures
I will give away as plunder,
　　together with your high places,
　　because of sin throughout your
　　　　country.
⁴Through your own fault you will lose
　　the inheritance I gave you.
I will enslave you to your enemies
　　in a land you do not know,
for you have kindled my anger,
　　and it will burn forever."

⁵This is what the LORD says:

"Cursed is the one who trusts in
　　　　man,
　　who depends on flesh for his
　　　　strength
and whose heart turns away from
　　the LORD.

⁶He will be like a bush in the
　　　　wastelands;
　　he will not see prosperity when it
　　　　comes.
He will dwell in the parched places of
　　the desert,
　　in a salt land where no one lives.

⁷"But blessed is the man who trusts in
　　the LORD,
　　whose confidence is in him.
⁸He will be like a tree planted by the
　　water
　　that sends out its roots by the
　　　　stream.
It does not fear when heat comes;
　　its leaves are always green.
It has no worries in a year of drought
　　and never fails to bear fruit."

⁹The heart is deceitful above all things
　　and beyond cure.
　　Who can understand it?

¹⁰"I the LORD search the heart
　　and examine the mind,
to reward a man according to his
　　　　conduct,
　　according to what his deeds
　　　　deserve."

¹¹Like a partridge that hatches eggs it
　　did not lay
　　is the man who gains riches by
　　　　unjust means.
When his life is half gone, they will
　　desert him,
　　and in the end he will prove to be
　　a fool.

¹²A glorious throne, exalted from the
　　beginning,
　　is the place of our sanctuary.
¹³O LORD, the hope of Israel,
　　all who forsake you will be put to
　　　　shame.
Those who turn away from you will
　　be written in the dust
　　because they have forsaken the
　　　　LORD,
　　the spring of living water.

¹⁴Heal me, O LORD, and I will be
　　healed;
　　save me and I will be saved,
　　for you are the one I praise.

---

^a2　That is, symbols of the goddess Asherah
^b2,3　Or hills / ³and the mountains of the land. / Your

¹⁵They keep saying to me,
    "Where is the word of the LORD?
    Let it now be fulfilled!"
¹⁶I have not run away from being your
      shepherd;
    you know I have not desired the
      day of despair.
    What passes my lips is open before
      you.
¹⁷Do not be a terror to me;
    you are my refuge in the day of
      disaster.
¹⁸Let my persecutors be put to shame,
    but keep me from shame;
   let them be terrified,
    but keep me from terror.
Bring on them the day of disaster;
    destroy them with double
      destruction.

Keeping the Sabbath Holy

¹⁹This is what the LORD said to me:

"Go and stand at the gate of the people, through which the kings of Judah go in and out; stand also at all the other gates of Jerusalem. ²⁰Say to them, 'Hear the word of the LORD, O kings of Judah and all people of Judah and everyone living in Jerusalem who come through these gates. ²¹This is what the LORD says: Be careful not to carry a load on the Sabbath day or bring it through the gates of Jerusalem. ²²Do not bring a load out of your houses or do any work on the Sabbath, but keep the Sabbath day holy, as I commanded your forefathers. ²³Yet they did not listen or pay attention; they were stiff-necked and would not listen or respond to discipline. ²⁴But if you are careful to obey me, declares the LORD, and bring no load through the gates of this city on the Sabbath, but keep the Sabbath day holy by not doing any work on it, ²⁵then kings who sit on David's throne will come through the gates of this city with their

How Do You Feel About Your Spouse?

Monday

JEREMIAH 17:9 Eight years of marriage and three babies had worn Nancy out. She was exhausted, and her feelings for her husband were numb. Then one day she found the listening ear of a stranger in an Internet chat room. She was getting to know this new Internet confidant, and escaping into the chat room with him felt so good. *How could this be wrong,* she asked herself, *if it feels so good?*

Feelings are often allowed to rule our lives. Our culture encourages us to act upon our feelings, as if they are a compass to direct our lives. We hear statements such as "do what feels right."

This verse, however, tells us something quite different. God wants us to understand how fickle our feelings can be. Feelings are transient and unreliable. They are affected by variables such as a physical condition, what happened at work or, as in Nancy's case, loneliness and exhaustion. Making relationship decisions impacted by such variables is unwise.

Our response to our spouse should be based on the foundation of the truth of God's

Word, on prayer and on communication. There are steps to take in order to get along with one another, particularly during times of emotional turmoil. First, analyze the source of your feelings. Is there something else affecting how you feel? Is there some underlying cause for your anger or hurt? It might be something totally unrelated to the present issue. Nancy and her husband had allowed family responsibilities to drain their marriage relationship.

Second, determine whether the emotion you are feeling is worth fighting about. If so, choose a neutral time and situation, then begin to communicate those feelings. Nancy had to tell her husband that she felt tired and lonely . . . that they need to work at finding some time to spend alone together.

Feelings should not rule us. In fact, we can take control of the way we respond to our feelings. Feelings of the heart must be handled wisely, unselfishly and prayerfully. If we express those feelings appropriately, we will deepen our relationships.

—Bob & Rosemary

Go to page 833 for your next devotional reading.

officials. They and their officials will come riding in chariots and on horses, accompanied by the men of Judah and those living in Jerusalem, and this city will be inhabited forever. ²⁶People will come from the towns of Judah and the villages around Jerusalem, from the territory of Benjamin and the western foothills, from the hill country and the Negev, bringing burnt offerings and sacrifices, grain offerings, incense and thank offerings to the house of the LORD. ²⁷But if you do not obey me to keep the Sabbath day holy by not carrying any load as you come through the gates of Jerusalem on the Sabbath day, then I will kindle an unquenchable fire in the gates of Jerusalem that will consume her fortresses.' "

At the Potter's House

18 This is the word that came to Jeremiah from the LORD: ²"Go down to the potter's house, and there I will give you my message." ³So I went down to the potter's house, and I saw him working at the wheel. ⁴But the pot he was shaping from the clay was marred in his hands; so the potter formed it into another pot, shaping it as seemed best to him.

⁵Then the word of the LORD came to me: ⁶"O house of Israel, can I not do with you as this potter does?" declares the LORD. "Like clay in the hand of the potter, so are you in my hand, O house of Israel. ⁷If at any time I announce that a nation or kingdom is to be uprooted, torn down and destroyed, ⁸and if that nation I warned repents of its evil, then I will relent and not inflict on it the disaster I had planned. ⁹And if at another time I announce that a nation or kingdom is to be built up and planted, ¹⁰and if it does evil in my sight and does not obey me, then I will reconsider the good I had intended to do for it.

¹¹"Now therefore say to the people of Judah and those living in Jerusalem, 'This is what the LORD says: Look! I am preparing a disaster for you and devising a plan against you. So turn from your evil ways, each one of you, and reform your ways and your actions.' ¹²But they will reply, 'It's no use. We will continue with our own plans; each of us will follow the stubbornness of his evil heart.' "

¹³Therefore this is what the LORD says:

"Inquire among the nations:
  Who has ever heard anything like
    this?
A most horrible thing has been done
  by Virgin Israel.
¹⁴Does the snow of Lebanon
  ever vanish from its rocky slopes?
Do its cool waters from distant
    sources
  ever cease to flow?ᵃ
¹⁵Yet my people have forgotten me;
  they burn incense to worthless
    idols,
which made them stumble in their
    ways
  and in the ancient paths.
They made them walk in bypaths
  and on roads not built up.
¹⁶Their land will be laid waste,
  an object of lasting scorn;
all who pass by will be appalled
  and will shake their heads.
¹⁷Like a wind from the east,
  I will scatter them before their
    enemies;
I will show them my back and not
    my face
  in the day of their disaster."

ᵃ14 The meaning of the Hebrew for this sentence is uncertain.

¹⁸They said, "Come, let's make plans against Jeremiah; for the teaching of the law by the priest will not be lost, nor will counsel from the wise, nor the word from the prophets. So come, let's attack him with our tongues and pay no attention to anything he says."

¹⁹Listen to me, O LORD;
hear what my accusers are saying!
²⁰Should good be repaid with evil?
Yet they have dug a pit for me.
Remember that I stood before you
and spoke in their behalf
to turn your wrath away from
them.
²¹So give their children over to famine;
hand them over to the power of
the sword.
Let their wives be made childless and
widows;
let their men be put to death,
their young men slain by the
sword in battle.
²²Let a cry be heard from their houses
when you suddenly bring invaders
against them,
for they have dug a pit to capture me
and have hidden snares for my
feet.
²³But you know, O LORD,
all their plots to kill me.
Do not forgive their crimes
or blot out their sins from your
sight.
Let them be overthrown before you;
deal with them in the time of your
anger.

19 This is what the LORD says: "Go and buy a clay jar from a potter. Take along some of the elders of the people and of the priests ²and go out to the Valley of Ben Hinnom, near the entrance of the Potsherd Gate. There proclaim the words I tell you, ³and say, 'Hear the word of the LORD, O kings of Judah and people of Jerusalem. This is what the LORD Almighty, the God of Israel, says: Listen! I am going to bring a disaster on this place that will make the ears of everyone who hears of it tingle. ⁴For they have forsaken me and made this a place of foreign gods; they have burned sacrifices in it to gods

that neither they nor their fathers nor the kings of Judah ever knew, and they have filled this place with the blood of the innocent. ⁵They have built the high places of Baal to burn their sons in the fire as offerings to Baal—something I did not command or mention, nor did it enter my mind. ⁶So beware, the days are coming, declares the LORD, when people will no longer call this place Topheth or the Valley of Ben Hinnom, but the Valley of Slaughter.

⁷"'In this place I will ruin*a* the plans of Judah and Jerusalem. I will make them fall by the sword before their enemies, at the hands of those who seek their lives, and I will give their carcasses as food to the birds of the air and the beasts of the earth. ⁸I will devastate this city and make it an object of scorn; all who pass by will be appalled and will scoff because of all its wounds. ⁹I will make them eat the flesh of their sons and daughters, and they will eat one another's flesh during the stress of the siege imposed on them by the enemies who seek their lives.'

¹⁰"Then break the jar while those who go with you are watching, ¹¹and say to them, 'This is what the LORD Almighty says: I will smash this nation and this city just as this potter's jar is smashed and cannot be repaired. They will bury the dead in Topheth until there is no more room. ¹²This is what I will do to this place and to those who live here, declares the LORD. I will make this city like Topheth. ¹³The houses in Jerusalem and those of the kings of Judah will be defiled like this place, Topheth—all the houses where they burned incense on the roofs to all the starry hosts and poured out drink offerings to other gods.'"

¹⁴Jeremiah then returned from Topheth, where the LORD had sent him to prophesy, and stood in the court of the LORD's temple and said to all the people, ¹⁵"This is what the LORD Almighty, the God of Israel, says: 'Listen! I am going to bring on this city and the villages around it every disaster I pronounced against them, because they were stiff-necked and would not listen to my words.'"

*a*7 The Hebrew for *ruin* sounds like the Hebrew for *jar* (see verses 1 and 10).

Jeremiah and Pashhur

20 When the priest Pashhur son of Immer, the chief officer in the temple of the LORD, heard Jeremiah prophesying these things, ²he had Jeremiah the prophet beaten and put in the stocks at the Upper Gate of Benjamin at the LORD's temple. ³The next day, when Pashhur released him from the stocks, Jeremiah said to him, "The LORD's name for you is not Pashhur, but Magor-Missabib.*ᵃ* ⁴For this is what the LORD says: 'I will make you a terror to yourself and to all your friends; with your own eyes you will see them fall by the sword of their enemies. I will hand all Judah over to the king of Babylon, who will carry them away to Babylon or put them to the sword. ⁵I will hand over to their enemies all the wealth of this city—all its products, all its valuables and all the treasures of the kings of Judah. They will take it away as plunder and carry it off to Babylon. ⁶And you, Pashhur, and all who live in your house will go into exile to Babylon. There you will die and be buried, you and all your friends to whom you have prophesied lies.' "

Jeremiah's Complaint

⁷O LORD, you deceived*ᵇ* me, and I
        was deceived*ᵇ*;
    you overpowered me and
        prevailed.
    I am ridiculed all day long;
        everyone mocks me.
⁸Whenever I speak, I cry out
        proclaiming violence and
        destruction.
    So the word of the LORD has brought
        me
    insult and reproach all day long.
⁹But if I say, "I will not mention him
        or speak any more in his name,"
    his word is in my heart like a fire,
        a fire shut up in my bones.
    I am weary of holding it in;
        indeed, I cannot.
¹⁰I hear many whispering,
        "Terror on every side!
        Report him! Let's report him!"
    All my friends
        are waiting for me to slip, saying,

"Perhaps he will be deceived;
        then we will prevail over him
        and take our revenge on him."

¹¹But the LORD is with me like a mighty
        warrior;
    so my persecutors will stumble and
        not prevail.
    They will fail and be thoroughly
        disgraced;
    their dishonor will never be
        forgotten.
¹²O LORD Almighty, you who examine
        the righteous
    and probe the heart and mind,
    let me see your vengeance upon
        them,
    for to you I have committed my
        cause.

¹³Sing to the LORD!
    Give praise to the LORD!
    He rescues the life of the needy
        from the hands of the wicked.

¹⁴Cursed be the day I was born!
    May the day my mother bore me
        not be blessed!
¹⁵Cursed be the man who brought my
        father the news,
    who made him very glad, saying,
    "A child is born to you—a son!"
¹⁶May that man be like the towns
        the LORD overthrew without pity.
    May he hear wailing in the morning,
        a battle cry at noon.
¹⁷For he did not kill me in the womb,
        with my mother as my grave,
        her womb enlarged forever.
¹⁸Why did I ever come out of the
        womb
    to see trouble and sorrow
        and to end my days in shame?

God Rejects Zedekiah's Request

21 The word came to Jeremiah from the LORD when King Zedekiah sent to him Pashhur son of Malkijah and the priest Zephaniah son of Maaseiah. They said: ²"Inquire now of the LORD for us because Nebuchadnezzar*ᶜ* king of Babylon is attacking us. Perhaps the LORD will

---

ᵃ3 *Magor-Missabib means* terror on every side.
ᵇ7 Or persuaded   *ᶜ2* Hebrew *Nebuchadrezzar,* of which *Nebuchadnezzar* is a variant; here and often in Jeremiah and Ezekiel

perform wonders for us as in times past so that he will withdraw from us."

[3]But Jeremiah answered them, "Tell Zedekiah, [4]'This is what the LORD, the God of Israel, says: I am about to turn against you the weapons of war that are in your hands, which you are using to fight the king of Babylon and the Babylonians[a] who are outside the wall besieging you. And I will gather them inside this city. [5]I myself will fight against you with an outstretched hand and a mighty arm in anger and fury and great wrath. [6]I will strike down those who live in this city—both men and animals—and they will die of a terrible plague. [7]After that, declares the LORD, I will hand over Zedekiah king of Judah, his officials and the people in this city who survive the plague, sword and famine, to Nebuchadnezzar king of Babylon and to their enemies who seek their lives. He will put them to the sword; he will show them no mercy or pity or compassion.'

[8]"Furthermore, tell the people, 'This is what the LORD says: See, I am setting before you the way of life and the way of death. [9]Whoever stays in this city will die by the sword, famine or plague. But whoever goes out and surrenders to the Babylonians who are besieging you will live; he will escape with his life. [10]I have determined to do this city harm and not good, declares the LORD. It will be given into the hands of the king of Babylon, and he will destroy it with fire.'

[11]"Moreover, say to the royal house of Judah, 'Hear the word of the LORD; [12]O house of David, this is what the LORD says:

" 'Administer justice every morning;
    rescue from the hand of his
      oppressor
    the one who has been robbed,
or my wrath will break out and burn
      like fire
    because of the evil you have done—
    burn with no one to quench it.
[13]I am against you, ⌞Jerusalem,⌟
    you who live above this valley
    on the rocky plateau,
            declares the LORD—
you who say, "Who can come against
      us?
    Who can enter our refuge?"

[14]I will punish you as your deeds
      deserve,
            declares the LORD.
I will kindle a fire in your forests
    that will consume everything
      around you.' "

Judgment Against Evil Kings

22 This is what the LORD says: "Go down to the palace of the king of Judah and proclaim this message there: [2]'Hear the word of the LORD, O king of Judah, you who sit on David's throne—you, your officials and your people who come through these gates. [3]This is what the LORD says: Do what is just and right. Rescue from the hand of his oppressor the one who has been robbed. Do no wrong or violence to the alien, the fatherless or the widow, and do not shed innocent blood in this place. [4]For if you are careful to carry out these commands, then kings who sit on David's throne will come through the gates of this palace, riding in chariots and on horses, accompanied by their officials and their people. [5]But if you do not obey these commands, declares the LORD, I swear by myself that this palace will become a ruin.' "

[6]For this is what the LORD says about the palace of the king of Judah:

"Though you are like Gilead to me,
    like the summit of Lebanon,
I will surely make you like a desert,
    like towns not inhabited.
[7]I will send destroyers against you,
    each man with his weapons,
and they will cut up your fine cedar
      beams
    and throw them into the fire.

[8]"People from many nations will pass by this city and will ask one another, 'Why has the LORD done such a thing to this great city?' [9]And the answer will be: 'Because they have forsaken the covenant of the LORD their God and have worshiped and served other gods.' "

[10]Do not weep for the dead ⌞king⌟ or
      mourn his loss;
    rather, weep bitterly for him who is
      exiled,

a4 Or Chaldeans; also in verse 9

because he will never return
nor see his native land again.

11For this is what the LORD says about Shallum[a] son of Josiah, who succeeded his father as king of Judah but has gone from this place: "He will never return. 12He will die in the place where they have led him captive; he will not see this land again."

13"Woe to him who builds his palace
by unrighteousness,
his upper rooms by injustice,
making his countrymen work for
nothing,
not paying them for their labor.
14He says, 'I will build myself a great
palace
with spacious upper rooms.'
So he makes large windows in it,
panels it with cedar
and decorates it in red.

15"Does it make you a king
to have more and more cedar?
Did not your father have food and
drink?
He did what was right and just,
so all went well with him.
16He defended the cause of the poor
and needy,
and so all went well.
Is that not what it means to know
me?"
declares the LORD.
17"But your eyes and your heart
are set only on dishonest gain,
on shedding innocent blood
and on oppression and extortion."

18Therefore this is what the LORD says about Jehoiakim son of Josiah king of Judah:

"They will not mourn for him:
'Alas, my brother! Alas, my sister!'
They will not mourn for him:
'Alas, my master! Alas, his
splendor!'
19He will have the burial of a donkey—
dragged away and thrown
outside the gates of Jerusalem."

20"Go up to Lebanon and cry out,
let your voice be heard in Bashan,
cry out from Abarim,
for all your allies are crushed.
21I warned you when you felt secure,

but you said, 'I will not listen!'
This has been your way from your
youth;
you have not obeyed me.
22The wind will drive all your
shepherds away,
and your allies will go into exile.
Then you will be ashamed and
disgraced
because of all your wickedness.
23You who live in 'Lebanon,'[b]
who are nestled in cedar buildings,
how you will groan when pangs come
upon you,
pain like that of a woman in labor!

24"As surely as I live," declares the LORD, "even if you, Jehoiachin[c] son of Jehoiakim king of Judah, were a signet ring on my right hand, I would still pull you off. 25I will hand you over to those who seek your life, those you fear—to Nebuchadnezzar king of Babylon and to the Babylonians.[d] 26I will hurl you and the mother who gave you birth into another country, where neither of you was born, and there you both will die. 27You will never come back to the land you long to return to."

28Is this man Jehoiachin a despised,
broken pot,
an object no one wants?
Why will he and his children be
hurled out,
cast into a land they do not know?
29O land, land, land,
hear the word of the LORD!
30This is what the LORD says:
"Record this man as if childless,
a man who will not prosper in his
lifetime,
for none of his offspring will prosper,
none will sit on the throne of
David
or rule anymore in Judah."

The Righteous Branch

23 "Woe to the shepherds who are destroying and scattering the sheep of my pasture!" declares the LORD. 2Therefore this is what the LORD, the God of Israel, says to the shepherds who tend my peo-

a11 Also called Jehoahaz   b23 That is, the palace in Jerusalem (see 1 Kings 7:2)
c24 Hebrew Coniah, a variant of Jehoiachin; also in verse 28   d25 Or Chaldeans

ple: "Because you have scattered my flock and driven them away and have not bestowed care on them, I will bestow punishment on you for the evil you have done," declares the LORD. ³"I myself will gather the remnant of my flock out of all the countries where I have driven them and will bring them back to their pasture, where they will be fruitful and increase in number. ⁴I will place shepherds over them who will tend them, and they will no longer be afraid or terrified, nor will any be missing," declares the LORD.

⁵"The days are coming," declares the
    LORD,
    "when I will raise up to Davidᵃ a
        righteous Branch,
a King who will reign wisely
    and do what is just and right in
        the land.
⁶In his days Judah will be saved
    and Israel will live in safety.
This is the name by which he will be
        called:
    The LORD Our Righteousness.

⁷"So then, the days are coming," declares the LORD, "when people will no longer say, 'As surely as the LORD lives, who brought the Israelites up out of Egypt,' ⁸but they will say, 'As surely as the LORD lives, who brought the descendants of Israel up out of the land of the north and out of all the countries where he had banished them.' Then they will live in their own land."

Lying Prophets

⁹Concerning the prophets:

My heart is broken within me;
    all my bones tremble.
I am like a drunken man,
    like a man overcome by wine,
because of the LORD
    and his holy words.
¹⁰The land is full of adulterers;
    because of the curseᵇ the land lies
        parchedᶜ
    and the pastures in the desert are
        withered.
The ⌊prophets⌋ follow an evil course
    and use their power unjustly.

¹¹"Both prophet and priest are godless;

even in my temple I find their
        wickedness,"
                                declares the LORD.
¹²"Therefore their path will become
        slippery;
    they will be banished to darkness
        and there they will fall.
I will bring disaster on them
    in the year they are punished,"
                                declares the LORD.

¹³"Among the prophets of Samaria
    I saw this repulsive thing:
They prophesied by Baal
    and led my people Israel astray.
¹⁴And among the prophets of Jerusalem
    I have seen something horrible:
    They commit adultery and live a
        lie.
They strengthen the hands of
        evildoers,
    so that no one turns from his
        wickedness.
They are all like Sodom to me;
    the people of Jerusalem are like
        Gomorrah."

¹⁵Therefore, this is what the LORD Almighty says concerning the prophets:

"I will make them eat bitter food
    and drink poisoned water,
because from the prophets of
        Jerusalem
    ungodliness has spread throughout
        the land."

¹⁶This is what the LORD Almighty says:

"Do not listen to what the prophets
    are prophesying to you;
    they fill you with false hopes.
They speak visions from their own
        minds,
    not from the mouth of the LORD.
¹⁷They keep saying to those who
        despise me,
    'The LORD says: You will have
        peace.'
And to all who follow the
        stubbornness of their hearts
    they say, 'No harm will come to
        you.'
¹⁸But which of them has stood in the
        council of the LORD
    to see or to hear his word?

ᵃ5 Or up from David's line   ᵇ10 Or because of
these things   ᶜ10 Or land mourns

Who has listened and heard his
word?
¹⁹See, the storm of the LORD
will burst out in wrath,
a whirlwind swirling down
on the heads of the wicked.
²⁰The anger of the LORD will not turn
back
until he fully accomplishes
the purposes of his heart.
In days to come
you will understand it clearly.
²¹I did not send these prophets,
yet they have run with their
message;
I did not speak to them,
yet they have prophesied.
²²But if they had stood in my council,
they would have proclaimed my
words to my people
and would have turned them from
their evil ways
and from their evil deeds.

²³"Am I only a God nearby,"
declares the LORD,
"and not a God far away?
²⁴Can anyone hide in secret places
so that I cannot see him?"
declares the LORD.
"Do not I fill heaven and earth?"
declares the LORD.

²⁵"I have heard what the prophets say
who prophesy lies in my name. They say,
'I had a dream! I had a dream!' ²⁶How
long will this continue in the hearts of
these lying prophets, who prophesy the
delusions of their own minds? ²⁷They
think the dreams they tell one another
will make my people forget my name, just
as their fathers forgot my name through
Baal worship. ²⁸Let the prophet who has
a dream tell his dream, but let the one
who has my word speak it faithfully. For
what has straw to do with grain?" declares
the LORD. ²⁹"Is not my word like fire," declares the LORD, "and like a hammer that
breaks a rock in pieces?

³⁰"Therefore," declares the LORD, "I am
against the prophets who steal from one
another words supposedly from me.
³¹Yes," declares the LORD, "I am against
the prophets who wag their own tongues
and yet declare, 'The LORD declares.' ³²In-
deed, I am against those who prophesy
false dreams," declares the LORD. "They

tell them and lead my people astray with
their reckless lies, yet I did not send or
appoint them. They do not benefit these
people in the least," declares the LORD.

False Oracles and False Prophets

³³"When these people, or a prophet or
a priest, ask you, 'What is the oracle[a] of
the LORD?' say to them, 'What oracle?[b] I
will forsake you, declares the LORD.' ³⁴If a
prophet or a priest or anyone else claims,
'This is the oracle of the LORD,' I will punish that man and his household. ³⁵This is
what each of you keeps on saying to his
friend or relative: 'What is the LORD's answer?' or 'What has the LORD spoken?'
³⁶But you must not mention 'the oracle of
the LORD' again, because every man's own
word becomes his oracle and so you distort the words of the living God, the LORD
Almighty, our God. ³⁷This is what you
keep saying to a prophet: 'What is the
LORD's answer to you?' or 'What has the
LORD spoken?' ³⁸Although you claim,
'This is the oracle of the LORD,' this is
what the LORD says: You used the words,
'This is the oracle of the LORD,' even
though I told you that you must not
claim, 'This is the oracle of the LORD.'
³⁹Therefore, I will surely forget you and
cast you out of my presence along with
the city I gave to you and your fathers. ⁴⁰I
will bring upon you everlasting disgrace—
everlasting shame that will not be forgotten."

Two Baskets of Figs

24 After Jehoiachin[c] son of Jehoiakim king of Judah and the officials,
the craftsmen and the artisans of Judah
were carried into exile from Jerusalem to
Babylon by Nebuchadnezzar king of Babylon, the LORD showed me two baskets of
figs placed in front of the temple of the
LORD. ²One basket had very good figs, like
those that ripen early; the other basket
had very poor figs, so bad they could not
be eaten.

³Then the LORD asked me, "What do
you see, Jeremiah?"

---

[a]33 Or burden (see Septuagint and Vulgate)
[b]33 Hebrew; Septuagint and Vulgate 'You are the
burden. (The Hebrew for oracle and burden is the
same.)   [c]1 Hebrew Jeconiah, a variant of
Jehoiachin

"Figs," I answered. "The good ones are very good, but the poor ones are so bad they cannot be eaten."

⁴Then the word of the LORD came to me: ⁵"This is what the LORD, the God of Israel, says: 'Like these good figs, I regard as good the exiles from Judah, whom I sent away from this place to the land of the Babylonians.ᵃ ⁶My eyes will watch over them for their good, and I will bring them back to this land. I will build them up and not tear them down; I will plant them and not uproot them. ⁷I will give them a heart to know me, that I am the LORD. They will be my people, and I will be their God, for they will return to me with all their heart.

⁸" 'But like the poor figs, which are so bad they cannot be eaten,' says the LORD, 'so will I deal with Zedekiah king of Judah, his officials and the survivors from Jerusalem, whether they remain in this land or live in Egypt. ⁹I will make them abhorrent and an offense to all the kingdoms of the earth, a reproach and a byword, an object of ridicule and cursing, wherever I banish them. ¹⁰I will send the sword, famine and plague against them until they are destroyed from the land I gave to them and their fathers.' "

Seventy Years of Captivity

25 The word came to Jeremiah concerning all the people of Judah in the fourth year of Jehoiakim son of Josiah king of Judah, which was the first year of Nebuchadnezzar king of Babylon. ²So Jeremiah the prophet said to all the people of Judah and to all those living in Jerusalem: ³For twenty-three years—from the thirteenth year of Josiah son of Amon king of Judah until this very day—the word of the LORD has come to me and I have spoken to you again and again, but you have not listened.

⁴And though the LORD has sent all his servants the prophets to you again and again, you have not listened or paid any attention. ⁵They said, "Turn now, each of you, from your evil ways and your evil practices, and you can stay in the land the LORD gave to you and your fathers for ever and ever. ⁶Do not follow other gods to serve and worship them; do not provoke

me to anger with what your hands have made. Then I will not harm you."

⁷"But you did not listen to me," declares the LORD, "and you have provoked me with what your hands have made, and you have brought harm to yourselves."

⁸Therefore the LORD Almighty says this: "Because you have not listened to my words, ⁹I will summon all the peoples of the north and my servant Nebuchadnezzar king of Babylon," declares the LORD, "and I will bring them against this land and its inhabitants and against all the surrounding nations. I will completely destroyᵇ them and make them an object of horror and scorn, and an everlasting ruin. ¹⁰I will banish from them the sounds of joy and gladness, the voices of bride and bridegroom, the sound of millstones and the light of the lamp. ¹¹This whole country will become a desolate wasteland, and these nations will serve the king of Babylon seventy years.

¹²"But when the seventy years are fulfilled, I will punish the king of Babylon and his nation, the land of the Babylonians,ᵃ for their guilt," declares the LORD, "and will make it desolate forever. ¹³I will bring upon that land all the things I have spoken against it, all that are written in this book and prophesied by Jeremiah against all the nations. ¹⁴They themselves will be enslaved by many nations and great kings; I will repay them according to their deeds and the work of their hands."

The Cup of God's Wrath

¹⁵This is what the LORD, the God of Israel, said to me: "Take from my hand this cup filled with the wine of my wrath and make all the nations to whom I send you drink it. ¹⁶When they drink it, they will stagger and go mad because of the sword I will send among them."

¹⁷So I took the cup from the LORD's hand and made all the nations to whom he sent me drink it: ¹⁸Jerusalem and the towns of Judah, its kings and officials, to make them a ruin and an object of horror and scorn and cursing, as they are today; ¹⁹Pharaoh king of Egypt, his attendants, his officials and all his people, ²⁰and all

ᵃ5,12 Or *Chaldeans*   ᵇ9 The Hebrew term refers to the irrevocable giving over of things or persons to the LORD, often by totally destroying them.

the foreign people there; all the kings of Uz; all the kings of the Philistines (those of Ashkelon, Gaza, Ekron, and the people left at Ashdod); ²¹Edom, Moab and Ammon; ²²all the kings of Tyre and Sidon; the kings of the coastlands across the sea; ²³Dedan, Tema, Buz and all who are in distant places^a; ²⁴all the kings of Arabia and all the kings of the foreign people who live in the desert; ²⁵all the kings of Zimri, Elam and Media; ²⁶and all the kings of the north, near and far, one after the other—all the kingdoms on the face of the earth. And after all of them, the king of Sheshach^b will drink it too.

²⁷"Then tell them, 'This is what the LORD Almighty, the God of Israel, says: Drink, get drunk and vomit, and fall to rise no more because of the sword I will send among you.' ²⁸But if they refuse to take the cup from your hand and drink, tell them, 'This is what the LORD Almighty says: You must drink it! ²⁹See, I am beginning to bring disaster on the city that bears my Name, and will you indeed go unpunished? You will not go unpunished, for I am calling down a sword upon all who live on the earth, declares the LORD Almighty.'

³⁰"Now prophesy all these words against them and say to them:

" 'The LORD will roar from on high;
he will thunder from his holy
dwelling
and roar mightily against his land.
He will shout like those who tread
the grapes,
shout against all who live on the
earth.
³¹The tumult will resound to the ends
of the earth,
for the LORD will bring charges
against the nations;
he will bring judgment on all
mankind
and put the wicked to the sword,' "
declares the LORD.

³²This is what the LORD Almighty says:

"Look! Disaster is spreading
from nation to nation;
a mighty storm is rising
from the ends of the earth."

³³At that time those slain by the LORD will be everywhere—from one end of the earth

to the other. They will not be mourned or gathered up or buried, but will be like refuse lying on the ground.

³⁴Weep and wail, you shepherds;
roll in the dust, you leaders of the
flock.
For your time to be slaughtered has
come;
you will fall and be shattered like
fine pottery.
³⁵The shepherds will have nowhere to
flee,
the leaders of the flock no place to
escape.
³⁶Hear the cry of the shepherds,
the wailing of the leaders of the
flock,
for the LORD is destroying their
pasture.
³⁷The peaceful meadows will be laid
waste
because of the fierce anger of the
LORD.
³⁸Like a lion he will leave his lair,
and their land will become
desolate
because of the sword^c of the
oppressor
and because of the LORD's fierce
anger.

Jeremiah Threatened With Death

26 Early in the reign of Jehoiakim son of Josiah king of Judah, this word came from the LORD: ²"This is what the LORD says: Stand in the courtyard of the LORD's house and speak to all the people of the towns of Judah who come to worship in the house of the LORD. Tell them everything I command you; do not omit a word. ³Perhaps they will listen and each will turn from his evil way. Then I will relent and not bring on them the disaster I was planning because of the evil they have done. ⁴Say to them, 'This is what the LORD says: If you do not listen to me and follow my law, which I have set before you, ⁵and if you do not listen to the words of my servants the prophets, whom I have sent to you again and again (though you

^a23 Or *who clip the hair by their foreheads*
^b26 *Sheshach* is a cryptogram for Babylon.
^c38 Some Hebrew manuscripts and Septuagint (see also Jer. 46:16 and 50:16); most Hebrew manuscripts *anger*

have not listened), [6]then I will make this house like Shiloh and this city an object of cursing among all the nations of the earth.' "

[7]The priests, the prophets and all the people heard Jeremiah speak these words in the house of the LORD. [8]But as soon as Jeremiah finished telling all the people everything the LORD had commanded him to say, the priests, the prophets and all the people seized him and said, "You must die! [9]Why do you prophesy in the LORD's name that this house will be like Shiloh and this city will be desolate and deserted?" And all the people crowded around Jeremiah in the house of the LORD.

[10]When the officials of Judah heard about these things, they went up from the royal palace to the house of the LORD and took their places at the entrance of the New Gate of the LORD's house. [11]Then the priests and the prophets said to the officials and all the people, "This man should be sentenced to death because he has prophesied against this city. You have heard it with your own ears!"

[12]Then Jeremiah said to all the officials and all the people: "The LORD sent me to prophesy against this house and this city all the things you have heard. [13]Now reform your ways and your actions and obey the LORD your God. Then the LORD will relent and not bring the disaster he has pronounced against you. [14]As for me, I am in your hands; do with me whatever you think is good and right. [15]Be assured, however, that if you put me to death, you will bring the guilt of innocent blood on yourselves and on this city and on those who live in it, for in truth the LORD has sent me to you to speak all these words in your hearing."

[16]Then the officials and all the people said to the priests and the prophets, "This man should not be sentenced to death! He has spoken to us in the name of the LORD our God."

[17]Some of the elders of the land stepped forward and said to the entire assembly of people, [18]"Micah of Moresheth prophesied in the days of Hezekiah king of Judah. He told all the people of Judah, 'This is what the LORD Almighty says:

" 'Zion will be plowed like a field,

Jerusalem will become a heap of rubble,
the temple hill a mound overgrown with thickets.'[a]

[19]"Did Hezekiah king of Judah or anyone else in Judah put him to death? Did not Hezekiah fear the LORD and seek his favor? And did not the LORD relent, so that he did not bring the disaster he pronounced against them? We are about to bring a terrible disaster on ourselves!"

[20](Now Uriah son of Shemaiah from Kiriath Jearim was another man who prophesied in the name of the LORD; he prophesied the same things against this city and this land as Jeremiah did. [21]When King Jehoiakim and all his officers and officials heard his words, the king sought to put him to death. But Uriah heard of it and fled in fear to Egypt. [22]King Jehoiakim, however, sent Elnathan son of Acbor to Egypt, along with some other men. [23]They brought Uriah out of Egypt and took him to King Jehoiakim, who had him struck down with a sword and his body thrown into the burial place of the common people.)

[24]Furthermore, Ahikam son of Shaphan supported Jeremiah, and so he was not handed over to the people to be put to death.

Judah to Serve Nebuchadnezzar

27 Early in the reign of Zedekiah[b] son of Josiah king of Judah, this word came to Jeremiah from the LORD: [2]This is what the LORD said to me: "Make a yoke out of straps and crossbars and put it on your neck. [3]Then send word to the kings of Edom, Moab, Ammon, Tyre and Sidon through the envoys who have come to Jerusalem to Zedekiah king of Judah. [4]Give them a message for their masters and say, 'This is what the LORD Almighty, the God of Israel, says: "Tell this to your masters: [5]With my great power and outstretched arm I made the earth and its people and the animals that are on it, and I give it to anyone I please. [6]Now I will hand all your countries over to my servant Nebuchadnezzar king of Babylon; I

---

[a]18 Micah 3:12   [b]1 A few Hebrew manuscripts and Syriac (see also Jer. 27:3, 12 and 28:1); most Hebrew manuscripts *Jehoiakim* (Most Septuagint manuscripts do not have this verse.)

will make even the wild animals subject to him. ⁷All nations will serve him and his son and his grandson until the time for his land comes; then many nations and great kings will subjugate him.

⁸" ' "If, however, any nation or kingdom will not serve Nebuchadnezzar king of Babylon or bow its neck under his yoke, I will punish that nation with the sword, famine and plague, declares the LORD, until I destroy it by his hand. ⁹So do not listen to your prophets, your diviners, your interpreters of dreams, your mediums or your sorcerers who tell you, 'You will not serve the king of Babylon.' ¹⁰They prophesy lies to you that will only serve to remove you far from your lands; I will banish you and you will perish. ¹¹But if any nation will bow its neck under the yoke of the king of Babylon and serve him, I will let that nation remain in its own land to till it and to live there, declares the LORD." ' "

¹²I gave the same message to Zedekiah king of Judah. I said, "Bow your neck under the yoke of the king of Babylon; serve him and his people, and you will live. ¹³Why will you and your people die by the sword, famine and plague with which the LORD has threatened any nation that will not serve the king of Babylon? ¹⁴Do not listen to the words of the prophets who say to you, 'You will not serve the king of Babylon,' for they are prophesying lies to you. ¹⁵'I have not sent them,' declares the LORD. 'They are prophesying lies in my name. Therefore, I will banish you and you will perish, both you and the prophets who prophesy to you.' "

¹⁶Then I said to the priests and all these people, "This is what the LORD says: Do not listen to the prophets who say, 'Very soon now the articles from the LORD's house will be brought back from Babylon.' They are prophesying lies to you. ¹⁷Do not listen to them. Serve the king of Babylon, and you will live. Why should this city become a ruin? ¹⁸If they are prophets and have the word of the LORD, let them plead with the LORD Almighty that the furnishings remaining in the house of the LORD and in the palace of the king of Judah and in Jerusalem not be taken to Babylon. ¹⁹For this is what the LORD Almighty says about the pillars, the

Sea, the movable stands and the other furnishings that are left in this city, ²⁰which Nebuchadnezzar king of Babylon did not take away when he carried Jehoiachin[a] son of Jehoiakim king of Judah into exile from Jerusalem to Babylon, along with all the nobles of Judah and Jerusalem— ²¹yes, this is what the LORD Almighty, the God of Israel, says about the things that are left in the house of the LORD and in the palace of the king of Judah and in Jerusalem: ²²'They will be taken to Babylon and there they will remain until the day I come for them,' declares the LORD. 'Then I will bring them back and restore them to this place.' "

The False Prophet Hananiah

28 In the fifth month of that same year, the fourth year, early in the reign of Zedekiah king of Judah, the prophet Hananiah son of Azzur, who was from Gibeon, said to me in the house of the LORD in the presence of the priests and all the people: ²"This is what the LORD Almighty, the God of Israel, says: 'I will break the yoke of the king of Babylon. ³Within two years I will bring back to this place all the articles of the LORD's house that Nebuchadnezzar king of Babylon removed from here and took to Babylon. ⁴I will also bring back to this place Jehoiachin[a] son of Jehoiakim king of Judah and all the other exiles from Judah who went to Babylon,' declares the LORD, 'for I will break the yoke of the king of Babylon.' "

⁵Then the prophet Jeremiah replied to the prophet Hananiah before the priests and all the people who were standing in the house of the LORD. ⁶He said, "Amen! May the LORD do so! May the LORD fulfill the words you have prophesied by bringing the articles of the LORD's house and all the exiles back to this place from Babylon. ⁷Nevertheless, listen to what I have to say in your hearing and in the hearing of all the people: ⁸From early times the prophets who preceded you and me have prophesied war, disaster and plague against many countries and great kingdoms. ⁹But the prophet who prophesies peace will be recognized as one truly sent

a20,4 Hebrew *Jeconiah*, a variant of *Jehoiachin*

by the LORD only if his prediction comes true."

¹⁰Then the prophet Hananiah took the yoke off the neck of the prophet Jeremiah and broke it, ¹¹and he said before all the people, "This is what the LORD says: 'In the same way will I break the yoke of Nebuchadnezzar king of Babylon off the neck of all the nations within two years.'" At this, the prophet Jeremiah went on his way.

¹²Shortly after the prophet Hananiah had broken the yoke off the neck of the prophet Jeremiah, the word of the LORD came to Jeremiah: ¹³"Go and tell Hananiah, 'This is what the LORD says: You have broken a wooden yoke, but in its place you will get a yoke of iron. ¹⁴This is what the LORD Almighty, the God of Israel, says: I will put an iron yoke on the necks of all these nations to make them serve Nebuchadnezzar king of Babylon, and they will serve him. I will even give him control over the wild animals.'"

¹⁵Then the prophet Jeremiah said to Hananiah the prophet, "Listen, Hananiah! The LORD has not sent you, yet you have persuaded this nation to trust in lies. ¹⁶Therefore, this is what the LORD says: 'I am about to remove you from the face of the earth. This very year you are going to die, because you have preached rebellion against the LORD.'"

¹⁷In the seventh month of that same year, Hananiah the prophet died.

A Letter to the Exiles

29 This is the text of the letter that the prophet Jeremiah sent from Jerusalem to the surviving elders among the exiles and to the priests, the prophets and all the other people Nebuchadnezzar had carried into exile from Jerusalem to Babylon. ²(This was after King Jehoiachin*ᵃ* and the queen mother, the court officials and the leaders of Judah and Jerusalem, the craftsmen and the artisans had gone into exile from Jerusalem.) ³He entrusted the letter to Elasah son of Shaphan and to Gemariah son of Hilkiah, whom Zedekiah king of Judah sent to King Nebuchadnezzar in Babylon. It said:

⁴This is what the LORD Almighty, the God of Israel, says to all those I carried into exile from Jerusalem to Babylon: ⁵"Build houses and settle down; plant gardens and eat what they produce. ⁶Marry and have sons and daughters; find wives for your sons and give your daughters in marriage, so that they too may have sons and daughters. Increase in number there; do not decrease. ⁷Also, seek the peace and prosperity of the city to which I have carried you into exile. Pray to the LORD for it, because if it prospers, you too will prosper." ⁸Yes, this is what the LORD Almighty, the God of Israel, says: "Do not let the prophets and diviners among you deceive you. Do not listen to the dreams you encourage them to have. ⁹They are prophesying lies to you in my name. I have not sent them," declares the LORD.

¹⁰This is what the LORD says: "When seventy years are completed for Babylon, I will come to you and fulfill my gracious promise to bring you back to this place. ¹¹For I know the plans I have for you," declares the LORD, "plans to prosper you and not to harm you, plans to give you hope and a future. ¹²Then you will call upon me and come and pray to me, and I will listen to you. ¹³You will seek me and find me when you seek me with all your heart. ¹⁴I will be found by you," declares the LORD, "and will bring you back from captivity.*ᵇ* I will gather you from all the nations and places where I have banished you," declares the LORD, "and will bring you back to the place from which I carried you into exile."

¹⁵You may say, "The LORD has raised up prophets for us in Babylon," ¹⁶but this is what the LORD says about the king who sits on David's throne and all the people who remain in this city, your countrymen who did not go with you into exile— ¹⁷yes, this is what the LORD Almighty says: "I will send the sword, famine and plague against them and I will make them like poor figs that are so bad they cannot be

---

ᵃ2 Hebrew *Jeconiah*, a variant of *Jehoiachin*
ᵇ14 Or *will restore your fortunes*

eaten. ¹⁸I will pursue them with the sword, famine and plague and will make them abhorrent to all the kingdoms of the earth and an object of cursing and horror, of scorn and reproach, among all the nations where I drive them. ¹⁹For they have not listened to my words," declares the LORD, "words that I sent to them again and again by my servants the prophets. And you exiles have not listened either," declares the LORD.

²⁰Therefore, hear the word of the LORD, all you exiles whom I have sent away from Jerusalem to Babylon. ²¹This is what the LORD Almighty, the God of Israel, says about Ahab son of Kolaiah and Zedekiah son of Maaseiah, who are prophesying lies to you in my name: "I will hand them over to Nebuchadnezzar king of Babylon, and he will put them to death before your very eyes. ²²Because of them, all the exiles from Judah who are in Babylon will use this curse: 'The LORD treat you like Zedekiah and Ahab, whom the king of Babylon burned in the fire.' ²³For they have done outrageous things in Israel; they have committed adultery with their neighbors' wives and in my name have spoken lies, which I did not tell them to do. I know it and am a witness to it," declares the LORD.

Message to Shemaiah

²⁴Tell Shemaiah the Nehelamite, ²⁵"This is what the LORD Almighty, the God of Israel, says: You sent letters in your own name to all the people in Jerusalem, to Zephaniah son of Maaseiah the priest, and to all the other priests. You said to Zephaniah, ²⁶'The LORD has appointed you priest in place of Jehoiada to be in charge of the house of the LORD; you should put any madman who acts like a prophet into the stocks and neck-irons. ²⁷So why have you not reprimanded Jeremiah from Anathoth, who poses as a prophet among you? ²⁸He has sent this message to us in Babylon: It will be a long time. Therefore build houses and settle down; plant gardens and eat what they produce.' "

²⁹Zephaniah the priest, however, read the letter to Jeremiah the prophet. ³⁰Then the word of the LORD came to Jeremiah:

The Ultimate Hope for Our Marriage

JEREMIAH 29:11 Spouses can get caught on the cultural treadmill—get married, pursue careers, buy a house, have kids . . . are we having fun yet? Before we know it, we are on the marriage treadmill, trying to jump through the culturally imposed hoops and often doing good things, but not necessarily the best things.

Rosemary and I got out of school and hit our careers running. We were married, but we were also in hot pursuit of God's plans for us individually. Isn't that what a spouse is supposed to do?

It's exciting to know that God has his plans for us on his mind. It's even more exciting to know that God's plans are specific for each of us, and they offer hope for our future. What could be more hopeful than knowing that the One who made us, made us for a purpose?

The key to a prospering marriage is to take the time to discover our Maker's plans. The typical marriage treadmill picks up the pace so quickly that couples often get distracted away from God. Rosemary and I needed to choose whether to consult others about our future or spend time consulting God. After years of trying to find ourselves individually and being pulled apart, we made a conscious choice. We were a couple, and we had to make our personal and professional decisions in light of that fact.

God has the perfect plan that he has laid out for each and every one of us. He already knows the plans he has for our lives and marriages. Why should we settle for anything less?

—*Bob & Rosemary*

Go to page 839 for your next devotional reading.

³¹"Send this message to all the exiles: 'This is what the LORD says about Shemaiah the Nehelamite: Because Shemaiah has prophesied to you, even though I did not send him, and has led you to believe a lie, ³²this is what the LORD says: I will surely punish Shemaiah the Nehelamite and his descendants. He will have no one left among this people, nor will he see the good things I will do for my people, declares the LORD, because he has preached rebellion against me.' "

Restoration of Israel

30 This is the word that came to Jeremiah from the LORD: ²"This is what the LORD, the God of Israel, says: 'Write in a book all the words I have spoken to you. ³The days are coming,' declares the LORD, 'when I will bring my people Israel and Judah back from captivity*ᵃ* and restore them to the land I gave their forefathers to possess,' says the LORD."

⁴These are the words the LORD spoke concerning Israel and Judah: ⁵"This is what the LORD says:

" 'Cries of fear are heard—
    terror, not peace.
⁶Ask and see:
    Can a man bear children?
Then why do I see every strong man
    with his hands on his stomach like
        a woman in labor,
    every face turned deathly pale?
⁷How awful that day will be!
    None will be like it.
It will be a time of trouble for Jacob,
    but he will be saved out of it.

⁸" 'In that day,' declares the LORD
        Almighty,
    'I will break the yoke off their
        necks
and will tear off their bonds;
    no longer will foreigners enslave
        them.
⁹Instead, they will serve the LORD their
        God
    and David their king,
    whom I will raise up for them.

¹⁰" 'So do not fear, O Jacob my
        servant;
    do not be dismayed, O Israel,'
                    declares the LORD.

'I will surely save you out of a distant
        place,
    your descendants from the land of
        their exile.
Jacob will again have peace and
        security,
    and no one will make him afraid.
¹¹I am with you and will save you,'
    declares the LORD.
'Though I completely destroy all the
        nations
    among which I scatter you,
    I will not completely destroy you.
I will discipline you but only with
        justice;
    I will not let you go entirely
        unpunished.'

¹²"This is what the LORD says:

" 'Your wound is incurable,
    your injury beyond healing.
¹³There is no one to plead your cause,
    no remedy for your sore,
    no healing for you.
¹⁴All your allies have forgotten you;
    they care nothing for you.
I have struck you as an enemy would
    and punished you as would the
        cruel,
because your guilt is so great
    and your sins so many.
¹⁵Why do you cry out over your
        wound,
    your pain that has no cure?
Because of your great guilt and many
        sins
    I have done these things to you.

¹⁶" 'But all who devour you will be
        devoured;
    all your enemies will go into exile.
Those who plunder you will be
        plundered;
    all who make spoil of you I will
        despoil.
¹⁷But I will restore you to health
    and heal your wounds,'
                    declares the LORD,
'because you are called an outcast,
    Zion for whom no one cares.'

¹⁸"This is what the LORD says:

" 'I will restore the fortunes of Jacob's
        tents

ᵃ3 Or *will restore the fortunes of my people Israel and Judah*

and have compassion on his
    dwellings;
the city will be rebuilt on her ruins,
    and the palace will stand in its
        proper place.
¹⁹From them will come songs of
        thanksgiving
    and the sound of rejoicing.
I will add to their numbers,
    and they will not be decreased;
I will bring them honor,
    and they will not be disdained.
²⁰Their children will be as in days of
        old,
    and their community will be
        established before me;
I will punish all who oppress
    them.
²¹Their leader will be one of their own;
    their ruler will arise from among
        them.
I will bring him near and he will
        come close to me,
    for who is he who will devote
        himself
    to be close to me?'
                            declares the LORD.
²²" 'So you will be my people,
    and I will be your God.' "

²³See, the storm of the LORD
    will burst out in wrath,
a driving wind swirling down
    on the heads of the wicked.
²⁴The fierce anger of the LORD will not
        turn back
    until he fully accomplishes
    the purposes of his heart.
In days to come
    you will understand this.

31 "At that time," declares the LORD, "I
    will be the God of all the clans of
Israel, and they will be my people."

²This is what the LORD says:

"The people who survive the sword
    will find favor in the desert;
    I will come to give rest to Israel."

³The LORD appeared to us in the
past,ᵃ saying:

"I have loved you with an everlasting
        love;
    I have drawn you with
        loving-kindness.
⁴I will build you up again

and you will be rebuilt, O Virgin
    Israel.
Again you will take up your
        tambourines
    and go out to dance with the
        joyful.
⁵Again you will plant vineyards
    on the hills of Samaria;
the farmers will plant them
    and enjoy their fruit.
⁶There will be a day when watchmen
        cry out
    on the hills of Ephraim,
'Come, let us go up to Zion,
    to the LORD our God.' "

⁷This is what the LORD says:

"Sing with joy for Jacob;
    shout for the foremost of the
        nations.
Make your praises heard, and say,
    'O LORD, save your people,
    the remnant of Israel.'
⁸See, I will bring them from the land
        of the north
    and gather them from the ends of
        the earth.
Among them will be the blind and
        the lame,
    expectant mothers and women in
        labor;
    a great throng will return.
⁹They will come with weeping;
    they will pray as I bring them back.
I will lead them beside streams of
        water
    on a level path where they will not
        stumble,
because I am Israel's father,
    and Ephraim is my firstborn son.

¹⁰"Hear the word of the LORD,
        O nations;
    proclaim it in distant coastlands:
'He who scattered Israel will gather
        them
    and will watch over his flock like a
        shepherd.'
¹¹For the LORD will ransom Jacob
    and redeem them from the hand of
        those stronger than they.
¹²They will come and shout for joy on
        the heights of Zion;

ᵃ3 Or LORD *has appeared to us from afar*

they will rejoice in the bounty of
    the LORD—
the grain, the new wine and the oil,
    the young of the flocks and herds.
They will be like a well-watered
    garden,
    and they will sorrow no more.
¹³Then maidens will dance and be glad,
    young men and old as well.
I will turn their mourning into
    gladness;
    I will give them comfort and joy
    instead of sorrow.
¹⁴I will satisfy the priests with
    abundance,
    and my people will be filled with
    my bounty,"
                declares the LORD.

¹⁵This is what the LORD says:

"A voice is heard in Ramah,
    mourning and great weeping,
Rachel weeping for her children
    and refusing to be comforted,
    because her children are no more."

¹⁶This is what the LORD says:

"Restrain your voice from weeping
    and your eyes from tears,
for your work will be rewarded,"
                declares the LORD.
    "They will return from the land of
    the enemy.
¹⁷So there is hope for your future,"
                declares the LORD.
    "Your children will return to their
    own land.

¹⁸"I have surely heard Ephraim's
    moaning:
'You disciplined me like an unruly
    calf,
    and I have been disciplined.
Restore me, and I will return,
    because you are the LORD my God.
¹⁹After I strayed,
    I repented;
after I came to understand,
    I beat my breast.
I was ashamed and humiliated
    because I bore the disgrace of my
    youth.'
²⁰Is not Ephraim my dear son,
    the child in whom I delight?
Though I often speak against him,
    I still remember him.

Therefore my heart yearns for him;
    I have great compassion for him,"
                declares the LORD.
²¹"Set up road signs;
    put up guideposts.
Take note of the highway,
    the road that you take.
Return, O Virgin Israel,
    return to your towns.
²²How long will you wander,
    O unfaithful daughter?
The LORD will create a new thing on
    earth—
    a woman will surround*ᵃ* a man."

²³This is what the LORD Almighty, the
God of Israel, says: "When I bring them
back from captivity,*ᵇ* the people in the
land of Judah and in its towns will once
again use these words: 'The LORD bless
you, O righteous dwelling, O sacred
mountain.' ²⁴People will live together in
Judah and all its towns—farmers and
those who move about with their flocks.
²⁵I will refresh the weary and satisfy the
faint."

²⁶At this I awoke and looked around.
My sleep had been pleasant to me.

²⁷"The days are coming," declares the
LORD, "when I will plant the house of
Israel and the house of Judah with the
offspring of men and of animals. ²⁸Just as
I watched over them to uproot and tear
down, and to overthrow, destroy and
bring disaster, so I will watch over them
to build and to plant," declares the LORD.
²⁹"In those days people will no longer
say,

'The fathers have eaten sour grapes,
    and the children's teeth are set on
    edge.'

³⁰Instead, everyone will die for his own
sin; whoever eats sour grapes—his own
teeth will be set on edge.

³¹"The time is coming," declares the
    LORD,
    "when I will make a new covenant
with the house of Israel
    and with the house of Judah.
³²It will not be like the covenant
    I made with their forefathers
when I took them by the hand

ᵃ22 Or *will go about ⸤seeking⸥*; or *will protect*
ᵇ23 Or *I restore their fortunes*

to lead them out of Egypt,
because they broke my covenant,
though I was a husband to[a]
them,[b]"
declares the LORD.

33"This is the covenant I will make
with the house of Israel
after that time," declares the LORD.
"I will put my law in their minds
and write it on their hearts.
I will be their God,
and they will be my people.
34No longer will a man teach his
neighbor,
or a man his brother, saying,
'Know the LORD,'
because they will all know me,
from the least of them to the
greatest,"
declares the LORD.
"For I will forgive their wickedness
and will remember their sins no
more."

35This is what the LORD says,

he who appoints the sun
to shine by day,
who decrees the moon and stars
to shine by night,
who stirs up the sea
so that its waves roar—
the LORD Almighty is his name:
36"Only if these decrees vanish from
my sight,"
declares the LORD,
"will the descendants of Israel ever
cease
to be a nation before me."

37This is what the LORD says:

"Only if the heavens above can be
measured
and the foundations of the earth
below be searched out
will I reject all the descendants of
Israel
because of all they have done,"
declares the LORD.

38"The days are coming," declares the
LORD, "when this city will be rebuilt for
me from the Tower of Hananel to the
Corner Gate. 39The measuring line will
stretch from there straight to the hill of
Gareb and then turn to Goah. 40The
whole valley where dead bodies and

ashes are thrown, and all the terraces out
to the Kidron Valley on the east as far as
the corner of the Horse Gate, will be holy
to the LORD. The city will never again be
uprooted or demolished."

Jeremiah Buys a Field

32 This is the word that came to Jeremiah from the LORD in the tenth
year of Zedekiah king of Judah, which
was the eighteenth year of Nebuchadnezzar. 2The army of the king of Babylon was
then besieging Jerusalem, and Jeremiah
the prophet was confined in the courtyard
of the guard in the royal palace of Judah.

3Now Zedekiah king of Judah had imprisoned him there, saying, "Why do you
prophesy as you do? You say, 'This is
what the LORD says: I am about to hand
this city over to the king of Babylon, and
he will capture it. 4Zedekiah king of Judah
will not escape out of the hands of the
Babylonians[c] but will certainly be handed over to the king of Babylon, and will
speak with him face to face and see him
with his own eyes. 5He will take Zedekiah
to Babylon, where he will remain until I
deal with him, declares the LORD. If you
fight against the Babylonians, you will
not succeed.' "

6Jeremiah said, "The word of the LORD
came to me: 7Hanamel son of Shallum
your uncle is going to come to you and
say, 'Buy my field at Anathoth, because as
nearest relative it is your right and duty to
buy it.'

8"Then, just as the LORD had said, my
cousin Hanamel came to me in the courtyard of the guard and said, 'Buy my field
at Anathoth in the territory of Benjamin.
Since it is your right to redeem it and
possess it, buy it for yourself.'

"I knew that this was the word of the
LORD; 9so I bought the field at Anathoth
from my cousin Hanamel and weighed
out for him seventeen shekels[d] of silver.
10I signed and sealed the deed, had it witnessed, and weighed out the silver on the
scales. 11I took the deed of purchase—the
sealed copy containing the terms and
conditions, as well as the unsealed copy—

---

[a]32 Hebrew; Septuagint and Syriac / *and I turned
away from*　　[b]32 Or *was their master*　　[c]4 Or
Chaldeans; also in verses 5, 24, 25, 28, 29 and 43
[d]9 *That is, about 7 ounces (about 200 grams)*

¹²and I gave this deed to Baruch son of Neriah, the son of Mahseiah, in the presence of my cousin Hanamel and of the witnesses who had signed the deed and of all the Jews sitting in the courtyard of the guard.

¹³"In their presence I gave Baruch these instructions: ¹⁴'This is what the LORD Almighty, the God of Israel, says: Take these documents, both the sealed and unsealed copies of the deed of purchase, and put them in a clay jar so they will last a long time. ¹⁵For this is what the LORD Almighty, the God of Israel, says: Houses, fields and vineyards will again be bought in this land.'

¹⁶"After I had given the deed of purchase to Baruch son of Neriah, I prayed to the LORD:

¹⁷"Ah, Sovereign LORD, you have made the heavens and the earth by your great power and outstretched arm. Nothing is too hard for you. ¹⁸You show love to thousands but bring the punishment for the fathers' sins into the laps of their children after them. O great and powerful God, whose name is the LORD Almighty, ¹⁹great are your purposes and mighty are your deeds. Your eyes are open to all the ways of men; you reward everyone according to his conduct and as his deeds deserve. ²⁰You performed miraculous signs and wonders in Egypt and have continued them to this day, both in Israel and among all mankind, and have gained the renown that is still yours. ²¹You brought your people Israel out of Egypt with signs and wonders, by a mighty hand and an outstretched arm and with great terror. ²²You gave them this land you had sworn to give their forefathers, a land flowing with milk and honey. ²³They came in and took possession of it, but they did not obey you or follow your law; they did not do what you commanded them to do. So you brought all this disaster upon them.

²⁴"See how the siege ramps are built up to take the city. Because of the sword, famine and plague, the city will be handed over to the Bab-

ylonians who are attacking it. What you said has happened, as you now see. ²⁵And though the city will be handed over to the Babylonians, you, O Sovereign LORD, say to me, 'Buy the field with silver and have the transaction witnessed.' "

²⁶Then the word of the LORD came to Jeremiah: ²⁷"I am the LORD, the God of all mankind. Is anything too hard for me? ²⁸Therefore, this is what the LORD says: I am about to hand this city over to the Babylonians and to Nebuchadnezzar king of Babylon, who will capture it. ²⁹The Babylonians who are attacking this city will come in and set it on fire; they will burn it down, along with the houses where the people provoked me to anger by burning incense on the roofs to Baal and by pouring out drink offerings to other gods.

³⁰"The people of Israel and Judah have done nothing but evil in my sight from their youth; indeed, the people of Israel have done nothing but provoke me with what their hands have made, declares the LORD. ³¹From the day it was built until now, this city has so aroused my anger and wrath that I must remove it from my sight. ³²The people of Israel and Judah have provoked me by all the evil they have done—they, their kings and officials, their priests and prophets, the men of Judah and the people of Jerusalem. ³³They turned their backs to me and not their faces; though I taught them again and again, they would not listen or respond to discipline. ³⁴They set up their abominable idols in the house that bears my Name and defiled it. ³⁵They built high places for Baal in the Valley of Ben Hinnom to sacrifice their sons and daughters[a] to Molech, though I never commanded, nor did it enter my mind, that they should do such a detestable thing and so make Judah sin.

³⁶"You are saying about this city, 'By the sword, famine and plague it will be handed over to the king of Babylon'; but this is what the LORD, the God of Israel, says: ³⁷I will surely gather them from all the lands where I banish them in my furious anger and great wrath; I will bring

[a]35 Or *to make their sons and daughters pass through the fire*

them back to this place and let them live in safety. ³⁸They will be my people, and I will be their God. ³⁹I will give them singleness of heart and action, so that they will always fear me for their own good and the good of their children after them. ⁴⁰I will make an everlasting covenant with them: I will never stop doing good to them, and I will inspire them to fear me, so that they will never turn away from me. ⁴¹I will rejoice in doing them good and will assuredly plant them in this land with all my heart and soul.

⁴²"This is what the LORD says: As I have brought all this great calamity on this people, so I will give them all the prosperity I have promised them. ⁴³Once more fields will be bought in this land of which you say, 'It is a desolate waste, without men or animals, for it has been handed over to the Babylonians.' ⁴⁴Fields will be bought for silver, and deeds will be signed, sealed and witnessed in the territory of Benjamin, in the villages around Jerusalem, in the towns of Judah and in the towns of the hill country, of the western foothills and of the Negev, because I will restore their fortunes,ᵃ declares the LORD."

Promise of Restoration

33 While Jeremiah was still confined in the courtyard of the guard, the word of the LORD came to him a second time: ²"This is what the LORD says, he who made the earth, the LORD who formed it and established it—the LORD is his name: ³'Call to me and I will answer you and tell you great and unsearchable things you do not know.' ⁴For this is what the LORD, the God of Israel, says about the houses in this city and the royal palaces of Judah that have been torn down to be

ᵃ44 Or will bring them back from captivity

Who Ya Gonna Call?

Wednesday

JEREMIAH 33:3 Too often God is last on our phone list. First we call our best friend, a neighbor, a parent or relative. Or we look for answers on the Internet, in popular magazines or books, or maybe even watch a self-help television program. But better help is available.

Jeremiah reminds us that God is ready to answer our call. What a reassuring verse this is for all soul-searching spouses! God is the One who can tell you great things you don't know—even about your marriage. He can restore, refresh and infuse your relationship with hope.

First, when we call on God we take the focus off our own difficulties and ourselves. At times, fearing the future robs us of enjoying the present. Instead, we can take comfort in trusting God's infinite wisdom and power.

Second, when we call on God we acknowledge that answers *will* come from him. Over our thirty-five plus years of marriage, we have encountered many roadblocks at which neither of us knew what to do. For example, right before one of our sons was born, Dave's director gave him a teaching assignment at a conference in West Virginia. Twenty-six years ago there was no quick way to get home in case the baby came early. We prayed, talked, pleaded with God to change Dave's director's mind. Still no resolution—just a brick wall. Dave finally decided that there would be many more conferences but no other opportunity to be present at the birth of our baby, so he told the director, "I'm not going to the conference—even if I run the risk of being fired."

We both felt God's peace and knew Dave had made the right decision for our situation. Amazingly, our son Jonathan was born early—during the time Dave would have been away from home. And just as amazingly, Dave's boss understood. Things don't always work out that well. We continue to encounter roadblocks. Thank goodness God refreshes our marriage and leads us to his answers. He will also lead you. He's waiting for your call.

—Dave & Claudia

Go to page 849 for your next devotional reading.

used against the siege ramps and the sword ⁵in the fight with the Babylonians[a]: 'They will be filled with the dead bodies of the men I will slay in my anger and wrath. I will hide my face from this city because of all its wickedness.

⁶" 'Nevertheless, I will bring health and healing to it; I will heal my people and will let them enjoy abundant peace and security. ⁷I will bring Judah and Israel back from captivity[b] and will rebuild them as they were before. ⁸I will cleanse them from all the sin they have committed against me and will forgive all their sins of rebellion against me. ⁹Then this city will bring me renown, joy, praise and honor before all nations on earth that hear of all the good things I do for it; and they will be in awe and will tremble at the abundant prosperity and peace I provide for it.'

¹⁰"This is what the LORD says: 'You say about this place, "It is a desolate waste, without men or animals." Yet in the towns of Judah and the streets of Jerusalem that are deserted, inhabited by neither men nor animals, there will be heard once more ¹¹the sounds of joy and gladness, the voices of bride and bridegroom, and the voices of those who bring thank offerings to the house of the LORD, saying,

"Give thanks to the LORD Almighty,
    for the LORD is good;
    his love endures forever."

For I will restore the fortunes of the land as they were before,' says the LORD.

¹²"This is what the LORD Almighty says: 'In this place, desolate and without men or animals—in all its towns there will again be pastures for shepherds to rest their flocks. ¹³In the towns of the hill country, of the western foothills and of the Negev, in the territory of Benjamin, in the villages around Jerusalem and in the towns of Judah, flocks will again pass under the hand of the one who counts them,' says the LORD.

¹⁴" 'The days are coming,' declares the LORD, 'when I will fulfill the gracious promise I made to the house of Israel and to the house of Judah.

¹⁵" 'In those days and at that time
    I will make a righteous Branch
        sprout from David's line;

he will do what is just and right in
    the land.
¹⁶In those days Judah will be saved
    and Jerusalem will live in safety.
This is the name by which it[c] will
        be called:
    The LORD Our Righteousness.'

¹⁷For this is what the LORD says: 'David will never fail to have a man to sit on the throne of the house of Israel, ¹⁸nor will the priests, who are Levites, ever fail to have a man to stand before me continually to offer burnt offerings, to burn grain offerings and to present sacrifices.' "

¹⁹The word of the LORD came to Jeremiah: ²⁰"This is what the LORD says: 'If you can break my covenant with the day and my covenant with the night, so that day and night no longer come at their appointed time, ²¹then my covenant with David my servant—and my covenant with the Levites who are priests ministering before me—can be broken and David will no longer have a descendant to reign on his throne. ²²I will make the descendants of David my servant and the Levites who minister before me as countless as the stars of the sky and as measureless as the sand on the seashore.' "

²³The word of the LORD came to Jeremiah: ²⁴"Have you not noticed that these people are saying, 'The LORD has rejected the two kingdoms[d] he chose'? So they despise my people and no longer regard them as a nation. ²⁵This is what the LORD says: 'If I have not established my covenant with day and night and the fixed laws of heaven and earth, ²⁶then I will reject the descendants of Jacob and David my servant and will not choose one of his sons to rule over the descendants of Abraham, Isaac and Jacob. For I will restore their fortunes[e] and have compassion on them.' "

Warning to Zedekiah

34 While Nebuchadnezzar king of Babylon and all his army and all the kingdoms and peoples in the empire he ruled were fighting against Jerusalem and all its surrounding towns, this word

---

[a]5 Or *Chaldeans*   [b]7 Or *will restore the fortunes of Judah and Israel*   [c]16 Or *he*   [d]24 Or *families*   [e]26 Or *will bring them back from captivity*

came to Jeremiah from the LORD: ²"This is what the LORD, the God of Israel, says: Go to Zedekiah king of Judah and tell him, 'This is what the LORD says: I am about to hand this city over to the king of Babylon, and he will burn it down. ³You will not escape from his grasp but will surely be captured and handed over to him. You will see the king of Babylon with your own eyes, and he will speak with you face to face. And you will go to Babylon.

⁴" 'Yet hear the promise of the LORD, O Zedekiah king of Judah. This is what the LORD says concerning you: You will not die by the sword; ⁵you will die peacefully. As people made a funeral fire in honor of your fathers, the former kings who preceded you, so they will make a fire in your honor and lament, "Alas, O master!" I myself make this promise, declares the LORD.' "

⁶Then Jeremiah the prophet told all this to Zedekiah king of Judah, in Jerusalem, ⁷while the army of the king of Babylon was fighting against Jerusalem and the other cities of Judah that were still holding out—Lachish and Azekah. These were the only fortified cities left in Judah.

Freedom for Slaves

⁸The word came to Jeremiah from the LORD after King Zedekiah had made a covenant with all the people in Jerusalem to proclaim freedom for the slaves. ⁹Everyone was to free his Hebrew slaves, both male and female; no one was to hold a fellow Jew in bondage. ¹⁰So all the officials and people who entered into this covenant agreed that they would free their male and female slaves and no longer hold them in bondage. They agreed, and set them free. ¹¹But afterward they changed their minds and took back the slaves they had freed and enslaved them again.

¹²Then the word of the LORD came to Jeremiah: ¹³"This is what the LORD, the God of Israel, says: I made a covenant with your forefathers when I brought them out of Egypt, out of the land of slavery. I said, ¹⁴'Every seventh year each of you must free any fellow Hebrew who has sold himself to you. After he has served you six years, you must let him go free.'ᵃ

Your fathers, however, did not listen to me or pay attention to me. ¹⁵Recently you repented and did what is right in my sight: Each of you proclaimed freedom to his countrymen. You even made a covenant before me in the house that bears my Name. ¹⁶But now you have turned around and profaned my name; each of you has taken back the male and female slaves you had set free to go where they wished. You have forced them to become your slaves again.

¹⁷"Therefore, this is what the LORD says: You have not obeyed me; you have not proclaimed freedom for your fellow countrymen. So I now proclaim 'freedom' for you, declares the LORD—'freedom' to fall by the sword, plague and famine. I will make you abhorrent to all the kingdoms of the earth. ¹⁸The men who have violated my covenant and have not fulfilled the terms of the covenant they made before me, I will treat like the calf they cut in two and then walked between its pieces. ¹⁹The leaders of Judah and Jerusalem, the court officials, the priests and all the people of the land who walked between the pieces of the calf, ²⁰I will hand over to their enemies who seek their lives. Their dead bodies will become food for the birds of the air and the beasts of the earth.

²¹"I will hand Zedekiah king of Judah and his officials over to their enemies who seek their lives, to the army of the king of Babylon, which has withdrawn from you. ²²I am going to give the order, declares the LORD, and I will bring them back to this city. They will fight against it, take it and burn it down. And I will lay waste the towns of Judah so no one can live there."

The Recabites

35 This is the word that came to Jeremiah from the LORD during the reign of Jehoiakim son of Josiah king of Judah: ²"Go to the Recabite family and invite them to come to one of the side rooms of the house of the LORD and give them wine to drink."

³So I went to get Jaazaniah son of Jeremiah, the son of Habazziniah, and his brothers and all his sons—the whole fami-

ᵃ14 Deut. 15:12

ly of the Recabites. ⁴I brought them into the house of the LORD, into the room of the sons of Hanan son of Igdaliah the man of God. It was next to the room of the officials, which was over that of Maaseiah son of Shallum the doorkeeper. ⁵Then I set bowls full of wine and some cups before the men of the Recabite family and said to them, "Drink some wine."

⁶But they replied, "We do not drink wine, because our forefather Jonadab son of Recab gave us this command: 'Neither you nor your descendants must ever drink wine. ⁷Also you must never build houses, sow seed or plant vineyards; you must never have any of these things, but must always live in tents. Then you will live a long time in the land where you are nomads.' ⁸We have obeyed everything our forefather Jonadab son of Recab commanded us. Neither we nor our wives nor our sons and daughters have ever drunk wine ⁹or built houses to live in or had vineyards, fields or crops. ¹⁰We have lived in tents and have fully obeyed everything our forefather Jonadab commanded us. ¹¹But when Nebuchadnezzar king of Babylon invaded this land, we said, 'Come, we must go to Jerusalem to escape the Babylonian*a* and Aramean armies.' So we have remained in Jerusalem."

¹²Then the word of the LORD came to Jeremiah, saying: ¹³"This is what the LORD Almighty, the God of Israel, says: Go and tell the men of Judah and the people of Jerusalem, 'Will you not learn a lesson and obey my words?' declares the LORD. ¹⁴'Jonadab son of Recab ordered his sons not to drink wine and this command has been kept. To this day they do not drink wine, because they obey their forefather's command. But I have spoken to you again and again, yet you have not obeyed me. ¹⁵Again and again I sent all my servants the prophets to you. They said, "Each of you must turn from your wicked ways and reform your actions; do not follow other gods to serve them. Then you will live in the land I have given to you and your fathers." But you have not paid attention or listened to me. ¹⁶The descendants of Jonadab son of Recab have carried out the command their forefather gave them, but these people have not obeyed me.'

¹⁷"Therefore, this is what the LORD God Almighty, the God of Israel, says: 'Listen! I am going to bring on Judah and on everyone living in Jerusalem every disaster I pronounced against them. I spoke to them, but they did not listen; I called to them, but they did not answer.' "

¹⁸Then Jeremiah said to the family of the Recabites, "This is what the LORD Almighty, the God of Israel, says: 'You have obeyed the command of your forefather Jonadab and have followed all his instructions and have done everything he ordered.' ¹⁹Therefore, this is what the LORD Almighty, the God of Israel, says: 'Jonadab son of Recab will never fail to have a man to serve me.' "

Jehoiakim Burns Jeremiah's Scroll

36 In the fourth year of Jehoiakim son of Josiah king of Judah, this word came to Jeremiah from the LORD: ²"Take a scroll and write on it all the words I have spoken to you concerning Israel, Judah and all the other nations from the time I began speaking to you in the reign of Josiah till now. ³Perhaps when the people of Judah hear about every disaster I plan to inflict on them, each of them will turn from his wicked way; then I will forgive their wickedness and their sin."

⁴So Jeremiah called Baruch son of Neriah, and while Jeremiah dictated all the words the LORD had spoken to him, Baruch wrote them on the scroll. ⁵Then Jeremiah told Baruch, "I am restricted; I cannot go to the LORD's temple. ⁶So you go to the house of the LORD on a day of fasting and read to the people from the scroll the words of the LORD that you wrote as I dictated. Read them to all the people of Judah who come in from their towns. ⁷Perhaps they will bring their petition before the LORD, and each will turn from his wicked ways, for the anger and wrath pronounced against this people by the LORD are great."

⁸Baruch son of Neriah did everything Jeremiah the prophet told him to do; at the LORD's temple he read the words of the LORD from the scroll. ⁹In the ninth month of the fifth year of Jehoiakim son of Josiah king of Judah, a time of fasting before the LORD was proclaimed for all the people in Jerusalem and those who

a 11 Or *Chaldean*

had come from the towns of Judah. [10]From the room of Gemariah son of Shaphan the secretary, which was in the upper courtyard at the entrance of the New Gate of the temple, Baruch read to all the people at the LORD's temple the words of Jeremiah from the scroll.

[11]When Micaiah son of Gemariah, the son of Shaphan, heard all the words of the LORD from the scroll, [12]he went down to the secretary's room in the royal palace, where all the officials were sitting: Elishama the secretary, Delaiah son of Shemaiah, Elnathan son of Acbor, Gemariah son of Shaphan, Zedekiah son of Hananiah, and all the other officials. [13]After Micaiah told them everything he had heard Baruch read to the people from the scroll, [14]all the officials sent Jehudi son of Nethaniah, the son of Shelemiah, the son of Cushi, to say to Baruch, "Bring the scroll from which you have read to the people and come." So Baruch son of Neriah went to them with the scroll in his hand. [15]They said to him, "Sit down, please, and read it to us."

So Baruch read it to them. [16]When they heard all these words, they looked at each other in fear and said to Baruch, "We must report all these words to the king." [17]Then they asked Baruch, "Tell us, how did you come to write all this? Did Jeremiah dictate it?"

[18]"Yes," Baruch replied, "he dictated all these words to me, and I wrote them in ink on the scroll."

[19]Then the officials said to Baruch, "You and Jeremiah, go and hide. Don't let anyone know where you are."

[20]After they put the scroll in the room of Elishama the secretary, they went to the king in the courtyard and reported everything to him. [21]The king sent Jehudi to get the scroll, and Jehudi brought it from the room of Elishama the secretary and read it to the king and all the officials standing beside him. [22]It was the ninth month and the king was sitting in the winter apartment, with a fire burning in the firepot in front of him. [23]Whenever Jehudi had read three or four columns of the scroll, the king cut them off with a scribe's knife and threw them into the firepot, until the entire scroll was burned in the fire. [24]The king and all his attendants who heard all these words showed no fear, nor did they

tear their clothes. [25]Even though Elnathan, Delaiah and Gemariah urged the king not to burn the scroll, he would not listen to them. [26]Instead, the king commanded Jerahmeel, a son of the king, Seraiah son of Azriel and Shelemiah son of Abdeel to arrest Baruch the scribe and Jeremiah the prophet. But the LORD had hidden them.

[27]After the king burned the scroll containing the words that Baruch had written at Jeremiah's dictation, the word of the LORD came to Jeremiah: [28]"Take another scroll and write on it all the words that were on the first scroll, which Jehoiakim king of Judah burned up. [29]Also tell Jehoiakim king of Judah, 'This is what the LORD says: You burned that scroll and said, "Why did you write on it that the king of Babylon would certainly come and destroy this land and cut off both men and animals from it?" [30]Therefore, this is what the LORD says about Jehoiakim king of Judah: He will have no one to sit on the throne of David; his body will be thrown out and exposed to the heat by day and the frost by night. [31]I will punish him and his children and his attendants for their wickedness; I will bring on them and those living in Jerusalem and the people of Judah every disaster I pronounced against them, because they have not listened.' "

[32]So Jeremiah took another scroll and gave it to the scribe Baruch son of Neriah, and as Jeremiah dictated, Baruch wrote on it all the words of the scroll that Jehoiakim king of Judah had burned in the fire. And many similar words were added to them.

Jeremiah in Prison

37 Zedekiah son of Josiah was made king of Judah by Nebuchadnezzar king of Babylon; he reigned in place of Jehoiachin[a] son of Jehoiakim. [2]Neither he nor his attendants nor the people of the land paid any attention to the words the LORD had spoken through Jeremiah the prophet.

[3]King Zedekiah, however, sent Jehucal son of Shelemiah with the priest Zephaniah son of Maaseiah to Jeremiah the

[a]1 Hebrew *Coniah*, a variant of *Jehoiachin*

prophet with this message: "Please pray to the LORD our God for us."

⁴Now Jeremiah was free to come and go among the people, for he had not yet been put in prison. ⁵Pharaoh's army had marched out of Egypt, and when the Babylonians*a* who were besieging Jerusalem heard the report about them, they withdrew from Jerusalem.

⁶Then the word of the LORD came to Jeremiah the prophet: ⁷"This is what the LORD, the God of Israel, says: Tell the king of Judah, who sent you to inquire of me, 'Pharaoh's army, which has marched out to support you, will go back to its own land, to Egypt. ⁸Then the Babylonians will return and attack this city; they will capture it and burn it down.'

⁹"This is what the LORD says: Do not deceive yourselves, thinking, 'The Babylonians will surely leave us.' They will not! ¹⁰Even if you were to defeat the entire Babylonian*b* army that is attacking you and only wounded men were left in their tents, they would come out and burn this city down."

¹¹After the Babylonian army had withdrawn from Jerusalem because of Pharaoh's army, ¹²Jeremiah started to leave the city to go to the territory of Benjamin to get his share of the property among the people there. ¹³But when he reached the Benjamin Gate, the captain of the guard, whose name was Irijah son of Shelemiah, the son of Hananiah, arrested him and said, "You are deserting to the Babylonians!"

¹⁴"That's not true!" Jeremiah said. "I am not deserting to the Babylonians." But Irijah would not listen to him; instead, he arrested Jeremiah and brought him to the officials. ¹⁵They were angry with Jeremiah and had him beaten and imprisoned in the house of Jonathan the secretary, which they had made into a prison.

¹⁶Jeremiah was put into a vaulted cell in a dungeon, where he remained a long time. ¹⁷Then King Zedekiah sent for him and had him brought to the palace, where he asked him privately, "Is there any word from the LORD?"

"Yes," Jeremiah replied, "you will be handed over to the king of Babylon."

¹⁸Then Jeremiah said to King Zedekiah, "What crime have I committed against you or your officials or this peo-

ple, that you have put me in prison? ¹⁹Where are your prophets who prophesied to you, 'The king of Babylon will not attack you or this land'? ²⁰But now, my lord the king, please listen. Let me bring my petition before you: Do not send me back to the house of Jonathan the secretary, or I will die there."

²¹King Zedekiah then gave orders for Jeremiah to be placed in the courtyard of the guard and given bread from the street of the bakers each day until all the bread in the city was gone. So Jeremiah remained in the courtyard of the guard.

Jeremiah Thrown Into a Cistern

38 Shephatiah son of Mattan, Gedaliah son of Pashhur, Jehucal*c* son of Shelemiah, and Pashhur son of Malkijah heard what Jeremiah was telling all the people when he said, ²"This is what the LORD says: 'Whoever stays in this city will die by the sword, famine or plague, but whoever goes over to the Babylonians*d* will live. He will escape with his life; he will live.' ³And this is what the LORD says: 'This city will certainly be handed over to the army of the king of Babylon, who will capture it.' "

⁴Then the officials said to the king, "This man should be put to death. He is discouraging the soldiers who are left in this city, as well as all the people, by the things he is saying to them. This man is not seeking the good of these people but their ruin."

⁵"He is in your hands," King Zedekiah answered. "The king can do nothing to oppose you."

⁶So they took Jeremiah and put him into the cistern of Malkijah, the king's son, which was in the courtyard of the guard. They lowered Jeremiah by ropes into the cistern; it had no water in it, only mud, and Jeremiah sank down into the mud.

⁷But Ebed-Melech, a Cushite,*e* an official*f* in the royal palace, heard that they had put Jeremiah into the cistern. While the king was sitting in the Benjamin Gate, ⁸Ebed-Melech went out of the

---

a5 Or *Chaldeans*; also in verses 8, 9, 13 and 14
b10 Or *Chaldean*; also in verse 11   *c1* Hebrew
Jucal, a variant of *Jehucal*   *d2* Or *Chaldeans*; also
in verses 18, 19 and 23   *e7* Probably from the
upper Nile region   *f7* Or *a eunuch*

palace and said to him, [9]"My lord the king, these men have acted wickedly in all they have done to Jeremiah the prophet. They have thrown him into a cistern, where he will starve to death when there is no longer any bread in the city."

[10]Then the king commanded Ebed-Melech the Cushite, "Take thirty men from here with you and lift Jeremiah the prophet out of the cistern before he dies."

[11]So Ebed-Melech took the men with him and went to a room under the treasury in the palace. He took some old rags and worn-out clothes from there and let them down with ropes to Jeremiah in the cistern. [12]Ebed-Melech the Cushite said to Jeremiah, "Put these old rags and worn-out clothes under your arms to pad the ropes." Jeremiah did so, [13]and they pulled him up with the ropes and lifted him out of the cistern. And Jeremiah remained in the courtyard of the guard.

Zedekiah Questions Jeremiah Again

[14]Then King Zedekiah sent for Jeremiah the prophet and had him brought to the third entrance to the temple of the LORD. "I am going to ask you something," the king said to Jeremiah. "Do not hide anything from me."

[15]Jeremiah said to Zedekiah, "If I give you an answer, will you not kill me? Even if I did give you counsel, you would not listen to me."

[16]But King Zedekiah swore this oath secretly to Jeremiah: "As surely as the LORD lives, who has given us breath, I will neither kill you nor hand you over to those who are seeking your life."

[17]Then Jeremiah said to Zedekiah, "This is what the LORD God Almighty, the God of Israel, says: 'If you surrender to the officers of the king of Babylon, your life will be spared and this city will not be burned down; you and your family will live. [18]But if you will not surrender to the officers of the king of Babylon, this city will be handed over to the Babylonians and they will burn it down; you yourself will not escape from their hands.'"

[19]King Zedekiah said to Jeremiah, "I am afraid of the Jews who have gone over to the Babylonians, for the Babylonians may hand me over to them and they will mistreat me."

[20]"They will not hand you over," Jeremiah replied. "Obey the LORD by doing what I tell you. Then it will go well with you, and your life will be spared. [21]But if you refuse to surrender, this is what the LORD has revealed to me: [22]All the women left in the palace of the king of Judah will be brought out to the officials of the king of Babylon. Those women will say to you:

" 'They misled you and overcame
        you—
    those trusted friends of yours.
Your feet are sunk in the mud;
    your friends have deserted you.'

[23]"All your wives and children will be brought out to the Babylonians. You yourself will not escape from their hands but will be captured by the king of Babylon; and this city will[a] be burned down."

[24]Then Zedekiah said to Jeremiah, "Do not let anyone know about this conversation, or you may die. [25]If the officials hear that I talked with you, and they come to you and say, 'Tell us what you said to the king and what the king said to you; do not hide it from us or we will kill you,' [26]then tell them, 'I was pleading with the king not to send me back to Jonathan's house to die there.'"

[27]All the officials did come to Jeremiah and question him, and he told them everything the king had ordered him to say. So they said no more to him, for no one had heard his conversation with the king.

[28]And Jeremiah remained in the courtyard of the guard until the day Jerusalem was captured.

The Fall of Jerusalem

39 This is how Jerusalem was taken: [1]In the ninth year of Zedekiah king of Judah, in the tenth month, Nebuchadnezzar king of Babylon marched against Jerusalem with his whole army and laid siege to it. [2]And on the ninth day of the fourth month of Zedekiah's eleventh year, the city wall was broken through. [3]Then all the officials of the king of Babylon came and took seats in the Middle Gate: Nergal-Sharezer of Samgar, Nebo-Sarsekim[b] a chief officer, Nergal-Sharezer a high official and all the other

a23 Or *and you will cause this city to*   b3 Or
Nergal-Sharezer, Samgar-Nebo, Sarsekim

officials of the king of Babylon. [4]When Zedekiah king of Judah and all the soldiers saw them, they fled; they left the city at night by way of the king's garden, through the gate between the two walls, and headed toward the Arabah. [a]

[5]But the Babylonian[b] army pursued them and overtook Zedekiah in the plains of Jericho. They captured him and took him to Nebuchadnezzar king of Babylon at Riblah in the land of Hamath, where he pronounced sentence on him. [6]There at Riblah the king of Babylon slaughtered the sons of Zedekiah before his eyes and also killed all the nobles of Judah. [7]Then he put out Zedekiah's eyes and bound him with bronze shackles to take him to Babylon.

[8]The Babylonians[c] set fire to the royal palace and the houses of the people and broke down the walls of Jerusalem. [9]Nebuzaradan commander of the imperial guard carried into exile to Babylon the people who remained in the city, along with those who had gone over to him, and the rest of the people. [10]But Nebuzaradan the commander of the guard left behind in the land of Judah some of the poor people, who owned nothing; and at that time he gave them vineyards and fields.

[11]Now Nebuchadnezzar king of Babylon had given these orders about Jeremiah through Nebuzaradan commander of the imperial guard: [12]"Take him and look after him; don't harm him but do for him whatever he asks." [13]So Nebuzaradan the commander of the guard, Nebushazban a chief officer, Nergal-Sharezer a high official and all the other officers of the king of Babylon [14]sent and had Jeremiah taken out of the courtyard of the guard. They turned him over to Gedaliah son of Ahikam, the son of Shaphan, to take him back to his home. So he remained among his own people.

[15]While Jeremiah had been confined in the courtyard of the guard, the word of the LORD came to him: [16]"Go and tell Ebed-Melech the Cushite, 'This is what the LORD Almighty, the God of Israel, says: I am about to fulfill my words against this city through disaster, not prosperity. At that time they will be fulfilled before your eyes. [17]But I will rescue you on that day, declares the LORD; you will not be handed over to those you fear. [18]I will save you; you will not fall by the sword but will escape with your life, because you trust in me, declares the LORD.' "

Jeremiah Freed

40 The word came to Jeremiah from the LORD after Nebuzaradan commander of the imperial guard had released him at Ramah. He had found Jeremiah bound in chains among all the captives from Jerusalem and Judah who were being carried into exile to Babylon. [2]When the commander of the guard found Jeremiah, he said to him, "The LORD your God decreed this disaster for this place. [3]And now the LORD has brought it about; he has done just as he said he would. All this happened because you people sinned against the LORD and did not obey him. [4]But today I am freeing you from the chains on your wrists. Come with me to Babylon, if you like, and I will look after you; but if you do not want to, then don't come. Look, the whole country lies before you; go wherever you please." [5]However, before Jeremiah turned to go,[d] Nebuzaradan added, "Go back to Gedaliah son of Ahikam, the son of Shaphan, whom the king of Babylon has appointed over the towns of Judah, and live with him among the people, or go anywhere else you please."

Then the commander gave him provisions and a present and let him go. [6]So Jeremiah went to Gedaliah son of Ahikam at Mizpah and stayed with him among the people who were left behind in the land.

Gedaliah Assassinated

[7]When all the army officers and their men who were still in the open country heard that the king of Babylon had appointed Gedaliah son of Ahikam as governor over the land and had put him in charge of the men, women and children who were the poorest in the land and who had not been carried into exile to Babylon, [8]they came to Gedaliah at Mizpah—Ishmael son of Nethaniah, Johanan and Jonathan the sons of Kareah, Seraiah son of Tanhumeth, the sons of Ephai the

[a]4 Or *the Jordan Valley*   [b]5 Or *Chaldean*
[c]8 Or *Chaldeans*   [d]5 Or *Jeremiah answered*

Netophathite, and Jaazaniah[a] the son of the Maacathite, and their men. 9Gedaliah son of Ahikam, the son of Shaphan, took an oath to reassure them and their men. "Do not be afraid to serve the Babylonians,[b]" he said. "Settle down in the land and serve the king of Babylon, and it will go well with you. 10I myself will stay at Mizpah to represent you before the Babylonians who come to us, but you are to harvest the wine, summer fruit and oil, and put them in your storage jars, and live in the towns you have taken over."

11When all the Jews in Moab, Ammon, Edom and all the other countries heard that the king of Babylon had left a remnant in Judah and had appointed Gedaliah son of Ahikam, the son of Shaphan, as governor over them, 12they all came back to the land of Judah, to Gedaliah at Mizpah, from all the countries where they had been scattered. And they harvested an abundance of wine and summer fruit.

13Johanan son of Kareah and all the army officers still in the open country came to Gedaliah at Mizpah 14and said to him, "Don't you know that Baalis king of the Ammonites has sent Ishmael son of Nethaniah to take your life?" But Gedaliah son of Ahikam did not believe them.

15Then Johanan son of Kareah said privately to Gedaliah in Mizpah, "Let me go and kill Ishmael son of Nethaniah, and no one will know it. Why should he take your life and cause all the Jews who are gathered around you to be scattered and the remnant of Judah to perish?"

16But Gedaliah son of Ahikam said to Johanan son of Kareah, "Don't do such a thing! What you are saying about Ishmael is not true."

41 In the seventh month Ishmael son of Nethaniah, the son of Elishama, who was of royal blood and had been one of the king's officers, came with ten men to Gedaliah son of Ahikam at Mizpah. While they were eating together there, 2Ishmael son of Nethaniah and the ten men who were with him got up and struck down Gedaliah son of Ahikam, the son of Shaphan, with the sword, killing the one whom the king of Babylon had appointed as governor over the land. 3Ishmael also killed all the Jews who were with Gedaliah at Mizpah, as well as the Babylonian[c] soldiers who were there.

4The day after Gedaliah's assassination, before anyone knew about it, 5eighty men who had shaved off their beards, torn their clothes and cut themselves came from Shechem, Shiloh and Samaria, bringing grain offerings and incense with them to the house of the LORD. 6Ishmael son of Nethaniah went out from Mizpah to meet them, weeping as he went. When he met them, he said, "Come to Gedaliah son of Ahikam." 7When they went into the city, Ishmael son of Nethaniah and the men who were with him slaughtered them and threw them into a cistern. 8But ten of them said to Ishmael, "Don't kill us! We have wheat and barley, oil and honey, hidden in a field." So he let them alone and did not kill them with the others. 9Now the cistern where he threw all the bodies of the men he had killed along with Gedaliah was the one King Asa had made as part of his defense against Baasha king of Israel. Ishmael son of Nethaniah filled it with the dead.

10Ishmael made captives of all the rest of the people who were in Mizpah—the king's daughters along with all the others who were left there, over whom Nebuzaradan commander of the imperial guard had appointed Gedaliah son of Ahikam. Ishmael son of Nethaniah took them captive and set out to cross over to the Ammonites.

11When Johanan son of Kareah and all the army officers who were with him heard about all the crimes Ishmael son of Nethaniah had committed, 12they took all their men and went to fight Ishmael son of Nethaniah. They caught up with him near the great pool in Gibeon. 13When all the people Ishmael had with him saw Johanan son of Kareah and the army officers who were with him, they were glad. 14All the people Ishmael had taken captive at Mizpah turned and went over to Johanan son of Kareah. 15But Ishmael son of Nethaniah and eight of his men escaped from Johanan and fled to the Ammonites.

Flight to Egypt

16Then Johanan son of Kareah and all

a8 Hebrew *Jezaniah*, a variant of *Jaazaniah*
b9 Or *Chaldeans*; also in verse 10   c3 Or
Chaldean

the army officers who were with him led away all the survivors from Mizpah whom he had recovered from Ishmael son of Nethaniah after he had assassinated Gedaliah son of Ahikam: the soldiers, women, children and court officials he had brought from Gibeon. [17]And they went on, stopping at Geruth Kimham near Bethlehem on their way to Egypt [18]to escape the Babylonians.[a] They were afraid of them because Ishmael son of Nethaniah had killed Gedaliah son of Ahikam, whom the king of Babylon had appointed as governor over the land.

42 Then all the army officers, including Johanan son of Kareah and Jezaniah[b] son of Hoshaiah, and all the people from the least to the greatest approached [2]Jeremiah the prophet and said to him, "Please hear our petition and pray to the LORD your God for this entire remnant. For as you now see, though we were once many, now only a few are left. [3]Pray that the LORD your God will tell us where we should go and what we should do."

[4]"I have heard you," replied Jeremiah the prophet. "I will certainly pray to the LORD your God as you have requested; I will tell you everything the LORD says and will keep nothing back from you."

[5]Then they said to Jeremiah, "May the LORD be a true and faithful witness against us if we do not act in accordance with everything the LORD your God sends you to tell us. [6]Whether it is favorable or unfavorable, we will obey the LORD our God, to whom we are sending you, so that it will go well with us, for we will obey the LORD our God."

[7]Ten days later the word of the LORD came to Jeremiah. [8]So he called together Johanan son of Kareah and all the army officers who were with him and all the people from the least to the greatest. [9]He said to them, "This is what the LORD, the God of Israel, to whom you sent me to present your petition, says: [10]'If you stay in this land, I will build you up and not tear you down; I will plant you and not uproot you, for I am grieved over the disaster I have inflicted on you. [11]Do not be afraid of the king of Babylon, whom you now fear. Do not be afraid of him, declares the LORD, for I am with you and will save you and deliver you from his

hands. [12]I will show you compassion so that he will have compassion on you and restore you to your land.'

[13]"However, if you say, 'We will not stay in this land,' and so disobey the LORD your God, [14]and if you say, 'No, we will go and live in Egypt, where we will not see war or hear the trumpet or be hungry for bread,' [15]then hear the word of the LORD, O remnant of Judah. This is what the LORD Almighty, the God of Israel, says: 'If you are determined to go to Egypt and you do go to settle there, [16]then the sword you fear will overtake you there, and the famine you dread will follow you into Egypt, and there you will die. [17]Indeed, all who are determined to go to Egypt to settle there will die by the sword, famine and plague; not one of them will survive or escape the disaster I will bring on them.' [18]This is what the LORD Almighty, the God of Israel, says: 'As my anger and wrath have been poured out on those who lived in Jerusalem, so will my wrath be poured out on you when you go to Egypt. You will be an object of cursing and horror, of condemnation and reproach; you will never see this place again.'

[19]"O remnant of Judah, the LORD has told you, 'Do not go to Egypt.' Be sure of this: I warn you today [20]that you made a fatal mistake[c] when you sent me to the LORD your God and said, 'Pray to the LORD our God for us; tell us everything he says and we will do it.' [21]I have told you today, but you still have not obeyed the LORD your God in all he sent me to tell you. [22]So now, be sure of this: You will die by the sword, famine and plague in the place where you want to go to settle."

43 When Jeremiah finished telling the people all the words of the LORD their God—everything the LORD had sent him to tell them— [2]Azariah son of Hoshaiah and Johanan son of Kareah and all the arrogant men said to Jeremiah, "You are lying! The LORD our God has not sent you to say, 'You must not go to Egypt to settle there.' [3]But Baruch son of Neriah is inciting you against us to hand us over to the

---

[a]18 Or *Chaldeans*   [b]1 Hebrew; Septuagint (see also 43:2) *Azariah*   [c]20 Or *you erred in your hearts*

Babylonians,[a] so they may kill us or carry us into exile to Babylon."

[4]So Johanan son of Kareah and all the army officers and all the people disobeyed the LORD's command to stay in the land of Judah. [5]Instead, Johanan son of Kareah and all the army officers led away all the remnant of Judah who had come back to live in the land of Judah from all the nations where they had been scattered. [6]They also led away all the men, women and children and the king's daughters whom Nebuzaradan commander of the imperial guard had left with Gedaliah son of Ahikam, the son of Shaphan, and Jeremiah the prophet and Baruch son of Neriah. [7]So they entered Egypt in disobedience to the LORD and went as far as Tahpanhes.

[8]In Tahpanhes the word of the LORD came to Jeremiah: [9]"While the Jews are watching, take some large stones with you and bury them in clay in the brick pavement at the entrance to Pharaoh's palace in Tahpanhes. [10]Then say to them, 'This is what the LORD Almighty, the God of Israel, says: I will send for my servant Nebuchadnezzar king of Babylon, and I will set his throne over these stones I have buried here; he will spread his royal canopy above them. [11]He will come and attack Egypt, bringing death to those destined for death, captivity to those destined for captivity, and the sword to those destined for the sword. [12]He[b] will set fire to the temples of the gods of Egypt; he will burn their temples and take their gods captive.

As a shepherd wraps his garment around him, so will he wrap Egypt around himself and depart from there unscathed. [13]There in the temple of the sun[c] in Egypt he will demolish the sacred pillars and will burn down the temples of the gods of Egypt.' "

Disaster Because of Idolatry

44 This word came to Jeremiah concerning all the Jews living in Lower Egypt—in Migdol, Tahpanhes and Memphis[d]—and in Upper Egypt[e]: [2]"This is what the LORD Almighty, the God of Israel, says: You saw the great disaster I brought on Jerusalem and on all the towns of Judah. Today they lie deserted and in ruins [3]because of the evil they have done. They provoked me to anger by burning incense and by worshiping other gods that neither they nor you nor your fathers ever knew. [4]Again and again I sent my servants the prophets, who said, 'Do not do this detestable thing that I hate!' [5]But they did not listen or pay attention; they did not turn from their wickedness or stop burning incense to other gods. [6]Therefore, my fierce anger was poured out; it raged against the towns of Judah and the streets of Jerusalem and made them the desolate ruins they are today.

[7]"Now this is what the LORD God Almighty, the God of Israel, says: Why bring such great disaster on yourselves by cut-

---

[a]3 Or *Chaldeans*   [b]12 Or *I*   [c]13 Or *in Heliopolis*   [d]1 Hebrew *Noph*   [e]1 Hebrew *in Pathros*

The Idolatry of Marriage

Thursday

COUPLE MINUTES

JEREMIAH 44:2–3 At first reading this passage, you may wonder what it might have to say especially to couples. After all, what does "idolatry" have to do with marriage?—in truth, a lot. Ever seen a couple who gets consumed by building their dream house? How about a couple who puts their careers on a pedestal? Any number of things can become an idol to us in marriage. Even our love life can take priority over worshiping God.

Sheldon and Davy Vanauken are living proof. In his gripping book, *A Severe Mercy*, Sheldon tells the story of his and Davy's romantic life together and how their love for one another superseded their love for God. It was only in the tragedy of Davy's death that Sheldon discovered how he had worshiped Davy and their relationship in place of worshiping God.

How about you? What "idols" are you prone to worship as a couple?

—Les & Leslie

Go to page 866 for your next devotional reading.

ting off from Judah the men and women, the children and infants, and so leave yourselves without a remnant? [8]Why provoke me to anger with what your hands have made, burning incense to other gods in Egypt, where you have come to live? You will destroy yourselves and make yourselves an object of cursing and reproach among all the nations on earth. [9]Have you forgotten the wickedness committed by your fathers and by the kings and queens of Judah and the wickedness committed by you and your wives in the land of Judah and the streets of Jerusalem? [10]To this day they have not humbled themselves or shown reverence, nor have they followed my law and the decrees I set before you and your fathers.

[11]"Therefore, this is what the LORD Almighty, the God of Israel, says: I am determined to bring disaster on you and to destroy all Judah. [12]I will take away the remnant of Judah who were determined to go to Egypt to settle there. They will all perish in Egypt; they will fall by the sword or die from famine. From the least to the greatest, they will die by sword or famine. They will become an object of cursing and horror, of condemnation and reproach. [13]I will punish those who live in Egypt with the sword, famine and plague, as I punished Jerusalem. [14]None of the remnant of Judah who have gone to live in Egypt will escape or survive to return to the land of Judah, to which they long to return and live; none will return except a few fugitives."

[15]Then all the men who knew that their wives were burning incense to other gods, along with all the women who were present—a large assembly—and all the people living in Lower and Upper Egypt,[a] said to Jeremiah, [16]"We will not listen to the message you have spoken to us in the name of the LORD! [17]We will certainly do everything we said we would: We will burn incense to the Queen of Heaven and will pour out drink offerings to her just as we and our fathers, our kings and our officials did in the towns of Judah and in the streets of Jerusalem. At that time we had plenty of food and were well off and suffered no harm. [18]But ever since we stopped burning incense to the Queen of Heaven and pouring out drink offerings to her, we have had nothing and

have been perishing by sword and famine."

[19]The women added, "When we burned incense to the Queen of Heaven and poured out drink offerings to her, did not our husbands know that we were making cakes like her image and pouring out drink offerings to her?"

[20]Then Jeremiah said to all the people, both men and women, who were answering him, [21]"Did not the LORD remember and think about the incense burned in the towns of Judah and the streets of Jerusalem by you and your fathers, your kings and your officials and the people of the land? [22]When the LORD could no longer endure your wicked actions and the detestable things you did, your land became an object of cursing and a desolate waste without inhabitants, as it is today. [23]Because you have burned incense and have sinned against the LORD and have not obeyed him or followed his law or his decrees or his stipulations, this disaster has come upon you, as you now see."

[24]Then Jeremiah said to all the people, including the women, "Hear the word of the LORD, all you people of Judah in Egypt. [25]This is what the LORD Almighty, the God of Israel, says: You and your wives have shown by your actions what you promised when you said, 'We will certainly carry out the vows we made to burn incense and pour out drink offerings to the Queen of Heaven.'

"Go ahead then, do what you promised! Keep your vows! [26]But hear the word of the LORD, all Jews living in Egypt: 'I swear by my great name,' says the LORD, 'that no one from Judah living anywhere in Egypt will ever again invoke my name or swear, "As surely as the Sovereign LORD lives." [27]For I am watching over them for harm, not for good; the Jews in Egypt will perish by sword and famine until they are all destroyed. [28]Those who escape the sword and return to the land of Judah from Egypt will be very few. Then the whole remnant of Judah who came to live in Egypt will know whose word will stand—mine or theirs.

[29]" 'This will be the sign to you that I will punish you in this place,' declares the LORD, 'so that you will know that my

[a]15 Hebrew in Egypt and Pathros

threats of harm against you will surely stand.' ³⁰This is what the LORD says: 'I am going to hand Pharaoh Hophra king of Egypt over to his enemies who seek his life, just as I handed Zedekiah king of Judah over to Nebuchadnezzar king of Babylon, the enemy who was seeking his life.' "

A Message to Baruch

45 This is what Jeremiah the prophet told Baruch son of Neriah in the fourth year of Jehoiakim son of Josiah king of Judah, after Baruch had written on a scroll the words Jeremiah was then dictating: ²"This is what the LORD, the God of Israel, says to you, Baruch: ³You said, 'Woe to me! The LORD has added sorrow to my pain; I am worn out with groaning and find no rest.' "

⁴ ⌊The LORD said,⌋ "Say this to him: 'This is what the LORD says: I will overthrow what I have built and uproot what I have planted, throughout the land. ⁵Should you then seek great things for yourself? Seek them not. For I will bring disaster on all people, declares the LORD, but wherever you go I will let you escape with your life.' "

A Message About Egypt

46 This is the word of the LORD that came to Jeremiah the prophet concerning the nations:

²Concerning Egypt:

This is the message against the army of Pharaoh Neco king of Egypt, which was defeated at Carchemish on the Euphrates River by Nebuchadnezzar king of Babylon in the fourth year of Jehoiakim son of Josiah king of Judah:

³ "Prepare your shields, both large and
  small,
  and march out for battle!
⁴Harness the horses,
  mount the steeds!
Take your positions
  with helmets on!
Polish your spears,
  put on your armor!
⁵What do I see?
  They are terrified,
  they are retreating,

their warriors are defeated.
They flee in haste
  without looking back,
  and there is terror on every side,"
      declares the LORD.
⁶ "The swift cannot flee
  nor the strong escape.
In the north by the River Euphrates
  they stumble and fall.

⁷ "Who is this that rises like the Nile,
  like rivers of surging waters?
⁸Egypt rises like the Nile,
  like rivers of surging waters.
She says, 'I will rise and cover the
    earth;
  I will destroy cities and their
    people.'
⁹Charge, O horses!
  Drive furiously, O charioteers!
March on, O warriors—
  men of Cush^a and Put who carry
    shields,
  men of Lydia who draw the bow.
¹⁰But that day belongs to the Lord, the
    LORD Almighty—
  a day of vengeance, for vengeance
    on his foes.
The sword will devour till it is
    satisfied,
  till it has quenched its thirst with
    blood.
For the Lord, the LORD Almighty, will
    offer sacrifice
  in the land of the north by the
    River Euphrates.

¹¹ "Go up to Gilead and get balm,
  O Virgin Daughter of Egypt.
But you multiply remedies in vain;
  there is no healing for you.
¹²The nations will hear of your shame;
  your cries will fill the earth.
One warrior will stumble over
    another;
  both will fall down together."

¹³This is the message the LORD spoke to Jeremiah the prophet about the coming of Nebuchadnezzar king of Babylon to attack Egypt:

¹⁴ "Announce this in Egypt, and
    proclaim it in Migdol;

---

a9 That is, the upper Nile region

proclaim it also in Memphis[a] and
Tahpanhes:
'Take your positions and get ready,
for the sword devours those
around you.'
15Why will your warriors be laid low?
They cannot stand, for the Lord
will push them down.
16They will stumble repeatedly;
they will fall over each other.
They will say, 'Get up, let us go back
to our own people and our native
lands,
away from the sword of the
oppressor.'
17There they will exclaim,
'Pharaoh king of Egypt is only a
loud noise;
he has missed his opportunity.'

18"As surely as I live," declares the King,
whose name is the Lord Almighty,
"one will come who is like Tabor
among the mountains,
like Carmel by the sea.
19Pack your belongings for exile,
you who live in Egypt,
for Memphis will be laid waste
and lie in ruins without inhabitant.

20"Egypt is a beautiful heifer,
but a gadfly is coming
against her from the north.
21The mercenaries in her ranks
are like fattened calves.
They too will turn and flee together,
they will not stand their ground,
for the day of disaster is coming upon
them,
the time for them to be punished.
22Egypt will hiss like a fleeing serpent
as the enemy advances in force;
they will come against her with axes,
like men who cut down trees.
23They will chop down her forest,"
declares the Lord,
"dense though it be.
They are more numerous than locusts,
they cannot be counted.
24The Daughter of Egypt will be put to
shame,
handed over to the people of the
north."

25The Lord Almighty, the God of Israel, says: "I am about to bring punishment
on Amon god of Thebes,[b] on Pharaoh,

on Egypt and her gods and her kings, and
on those who rely on Pharaoh. 26I will
hand them over to those who seek their
lives, to Nebuchadnezzar king of Babylon
and his officers. Later, however, Egypt will
be inhabited as in times past," declares the
Lord.

27"Do not fear, O Jacob my servant;
do not be dismayed, O Israel.
I will surely save you out of a distant
place,
your descendants from the land of
their exile.
Jacob will again have peace and
security,
and no one will make him afraid.
28Do not fear, O Jacob my servant,
for I am with you," declares the
Lord.
"Though I completely destroy all the
nations
among which I scatter you,
I will not completely destroy you.
I will discipline you but only with
justice;
I will not let you go entirely
unpunished."

A Message About the Philistines

47 This is the word of the Lord that
came to Jeremiah the prophet concerning the Philistines before Pharaoh attacked Gaza:

2This is what the Lord says:

"See how the waters are rising in the
north;
they will become an overflowing
torrent.
They will overflow the land and
everything in it,
the towns and those who live in
them.
The people will cry out;
all who dwell in the land will wail
3at the sound of the hoofs of galloping
steeds,
at the noise of enemy chariots
and the rumble of their wheels.
Fathers will not turn to help their
children;
their hands will hang limp.

a14 Hebrew Noph; also in verse 19
b25 Hebrew No

⁴For the day has come
　to destroy all the Philistines
and to cut off all survivors
　who could help Tyre and Sidon.
The LORD is about to destroy the
　　Philistines,
　the remnant from the coasts of
　　Caphtor.ᵃ
⁵Gaza will shave her head in
　　mourning;
　Ashkelon will be silenced.
O remnant on the plain,
　how long will you cut yourselves?

⁶" 'Ah, sword of the LORD,' ⌐you cry,⌐
　'how long till you rest?
Return to your scabbard;
　cease and be still.'
⁷But how can it rest
　when the LORD has commanded it,
when he has ordered it
　to attack Ashkelon and the coast?"

A Message About Moab

48 Concerning Moab:

This is what the LORD Almighty, the
God of Israel, says:

"Woe to Nebo, for it will be ruined.
　Kiriathaim will be disgraced and
　　captured;
　the strongholdᵇ will be disgraced
　　and shattered.
²Moab will be praised no more;
　in Heshbonᶜ men will plot her
　　downfall:
　'Come, let us put an end to that
　　nation.'
You too, O Madmen,ᵈ will be
　　silenced;
　the sword will pursue you.
³Listen to the cries from Horonaim,
　cries of great havoc and
　　destruction.
⁴Moab will be broken;
　her little ones will cry out.ᵉ
⁵They go up the way to Luhith,
　weeping bitterly as they go;
on the road down to Horonaim
　anguished cries over the
　　destruction are heard.
⁶Flee! Run for your lives;
　become like a bushᶠ in the desert.
⁷Since you trust in your deeds and
　　riches,

you too will be taken captive,
and Chemosh will go into exile,
　together with his priests and
　　officials.
⁸The destroyer will come against every
　　town,
　and not a town will escape.
The valley will be ruined
　and the plateau destroyed,
because the LORD has spoken.
⁹Put salt on Moab,
　for she will be laid wasteᵍ;
her towns will become desolate,
　with no one to live in them.

¹⁰"A curse on him who is lax in doing
　　the LORD's work!
A curse on him who keeps his
　　sword from bloodshed!

¹¹"Moab has been at rest from youth,
　like wine left on its dregs,
not poured from one jar to another—
　she has not gone into exile.
So she tastes as she did,
　and her aroma is unchanged.
¹²But days are coming,"
　declares the LORD,
"when I will send men who pour
　　from jars,
　and they will pour her out;
they will empty her jars
　and smash her jugs.
¹³Then Moab will be ashamed of
　　Chemosh,
　as the house of Israel was ashamed
　when they trusted in Bethel.

¹⁴"How can you say, 'We are warriors,
　men valiant in battle'?
¹⁵Moab will be destroyed and her
　　towns invaded;
　her finest young men will go down
　　in the slaughter,"
declares the King, whose name is
　　the LORD Almighty.
¹⁶"The fall of Moab is at hand;
　her calamity will come quickly.
¹⁷Mourn for her, all who live around
　　her,
　all who know her fame;

ᵃ4 That is, Crete   ᵇ1 Or / Misgab
ᶜ2 The Hebrew for Heshbon sounds like the
Hebrew for plot.   ᵈ2 The name of the Moabite
town Madmen sounds like the Hebrew for be
silenced.   ᵉ4 Hebrew; Septuagint / proclaim it to
Zoar   ᶠ6 Or like Aroer   ᵍ9 Or Give wings to
Moab, / for she will fly away

say, 'How broken is the mighty
    scepter,
how broken the glorious staff!'

18"Come down from your glory
    and sit on the parched ground,
O inhabitants of the Daughter of
    Dibon,
for he who destroys Moab
    will come up against you
    and ruin your fortified cities.
19Stand by the road and watch,
    you who live in Aroer.
Ask the man fleeing and the woman
    escaping,
    ask them, 'What has happened?'
20Moab is disgraced, for she is
    shattered.
    Wail and cry out!
Announce by the Arnon
    that Moab is destroyed.
21Judgment has come to the plateau—
    to Holon, Jahzah and Mephaath,
22   to Dibon, Nebo and Beth
    Diblathaim,
23   to Kiriathaim, Beth Gamul and
    Beth Meon,
24   to Kerioth and Bozrah—
    to all the towns of Moab, far and
    near.
25Moab's horn*a* is cut off;
    her arm is broken,"
                 declares the LORD.

26"Make her drunk,
    for she has defied the LORD.
Let Moab wallow in her vomit;
    let her be an object of ridicule.
27Was not Israel the object of your
    ridicule?
Was she caught among thieves,
that you shake your head in scorn
    whenever you speak of her?
28Abandon your towns and dwell
    among the rocks,
    you who live in Moab.
Be like a dove that makes its nest
    at the mouth of a cave.

29"We have heard of Moab's pride—
    her overweening pride and conceit,
her pride and arrogance
    and the haughtiness of her heart.
30I know her insolence but it is futile,"
                 declares the LORD,
  "and her boasts accomplish
    nothing.

31Therefore I wail over Moab,
    for all Moab I cry out,
    I moan for the men of Kir
    Hareseth.
32I weep for you, as Jazer weeps,
    O vines of Sibmah.
Your branches spread as far as the
    sea;
    they reached as far as the sea of
    Jazer.
The destroyer has fallen
    on your ripened fruit and grapes.
33Joy and gladness are gone
    from the orchards and fields of
    Moab.
I have stopped the flow of wine from
    the presses;
    no one treads them with shouts of
    joy.
Although there are shouts,
    they are not shouts of joy.

34"The sound of their cry rises
    from Heshbon to Elealeh and
    Jahaz,
from Zoar as far as Horonaim and
    Eglath Shelishiyah,
    for even the waters of Nimrim are
    dried up.
35In Moab I will put an end
    to those who make offerings on
    the high places
    and burn incense to their gods,"
                 declares the LORD.
36"So my heart laments for Moab like a
    flute;
    it laments like a flute for the men
    of Kir Hareseth.
The wealth they acquired is gone.
37Every head is shaved
    and every beard cut off;
every hand is slashed
    and every waist is covered with
    sackcloth.
38On all the roofs in Moab
    and in the public squares
there is nothing but mourning,
    for I have broken Moab
    like a jar that no one wants,"
                 declares the LORD.
39"How shattered she is! How they
    wail!
    How Moab turns her back in
    shame!

a25 Horn here symbolizes strength.

Moab has become an object of
ridicule,
an object of horror to all those
around her."

⁴⁰This is what the LORD says:

"Look! An eagle is swooping down,
spreading its wings over Moab.
⁴¹Kerioth*ᵃ* will be captured
and the strongholds taken.
In that day the hearts of Moab's
warriors
will be like the heart of a woman
in labor.
⁴²Moab will be destroyed as a nation
because she defied the LORD.
⁴³Terror and pit and snare await you,
O people of Moab,"
declares the LORD.
⁴⁴"Whoever flees from the terror
will fall into a pit,
whoever climbs out of the pit
will be caught in a snare;
for I will bring upon Moab
the year of her punishment,"
declares the LORD.

⁴⁵"In the shadow of Heshbon
the fugitives stand helpless,
for a fire has gone out from Heshbon,
a blaze from the midst of Sihon;
it burns the foreheads of Moab,
the skulls of the noisy boasters.
⁴⁶Woe to you, O Moab!
The people of Chemosh are
destroyed;
your sons are taken into exile
and your daughters into captivity.

⁴⁷"Yet I will restore the fortunes of
Moab
in days to come,"
declares the LORD.
Here ends the judgment on Moab.

A Message About Ammon

49 Concerning the Ammonites:

This is what the LORD says:

"Has Israel no sons?
Has she no heirs?
Why then has Molech*ᵇ* taken
possession of Gad?
Why do his people live in its
towns?

²But the days are coming,"
declares the LORD,
"when I will sound the battle cry
against Rabbah of the Ammonites;
it will become a mound of ruins,
and its surrounding villages will be
set on fire.
Then Israel will drive out
those who drove her out,"
says the LORD.
³"Wail, O Heshbon, for Ai is
destroyed!
Cry out, O inhabitants of Rabbah!
Put on sackcloth and mourn;
rush here and there inside the
walls,
for Molech will go into exile,
together with his priests and
officials.
⁴Why do you boast of your valleys,
boast of your valleys so fruitful?
O unfaithful daughter,
you trust in your riches and say,
'Who will attack me?'
⁵I will bring terror on you
from all those around you,"
declares the Lord,
the LORD Almighty.
"Every one of you will be driven
away,
and no one will gather the
fugitives.

⁶"Yet afterward, I will restore the
fortunes of the Ammonites,"
declares the LORD.

A Message About Edom

⁷Concerning Edom:

This is what the LORD Almighty says:

"Is there no longer wisdom in
Teman?
Has counsel perished from the
prudent?
Has their wisdom decayed?
⁸Turn and flee, hide in deep caves,
you who live in Dedan,
for I will bring disaster on Esau
at the time I punish him.
⁹If grape pickers came to you,
would they not leave a few grapes?
If thieves came during the night,

ᵃ41 Or *The cities*   *ᵇ1* Or *their king*; Hebrew
malcam; also in verse 3

would they not steal only as much
　　as they wanted?
¹⁰But I will strip Esau bare;
　　I will uncover his hiding places,
　　so that he cannot conceal himself.
　His children, relatives and neighbors
　　will perish,
　　and he will be no more.
¹¹Leave your orphans; I will protect
　　their lives.
　Your widows too can trust in me."

¹²This is what the LORD says: "If those
who do not deserve to drink the cup must
drink it, why should you go unpunished?
You will not go unpunished, but must
drink it. ¹³I swear by myself," declares the
LORD, "that Bozrah will become a ruin
and an object of horror, of reproach and
of cursing; and all its towns will be in
ruins forever."

¹⁴I have heard a message from the
　　LORD:
　An envoy was sent to the nations
　　to say,
　"Assemble yourselves to attack it!
　　Rise up for battle!"

¹⁵"Now I will make you small among
　　the nations,
　　despised among men.
¹⁶The terror you inspire
　　and the pride of your heart have
　　　deceived you,
　you who live in the clefts of the
　　rocks,
　　who occupy the heights of the hill.
　Though you build your nest as high
　　as the eagle's,
　　from there I will bring you down,"
　　　　　　　　declares the LORD.
¹⁷"Edom will become an object of
　　horror;
　　all who pass by will be appalled
　　　and will scoff
　　because of all its wounds.
¹⁸As Sodom and Gomorrah were
　　overthrown,
　　along with their neighboring
　　　towns,"
　　　　　　　　says the LORD,
　"so no one will live there;
　　no man will dwell in it.

¹⁹"Like a lion coming up from Jordan's
　　thickets
　　to a rich pastureland,

I will chase Edom from its land in an
　　instant.
　Who is the chosen one I will
　　appoint for this?
　Who is like me and who can
　　challenge me?
　　And what shepherd can stand
　　　against me?"
²⁰Therefore, hear what the LORD has
　　planned against Edom,
　what he has purposed against those
　　who live in Teman:
　The young of the flock will be
　　dragged away;
　　he will completely destroy their
　　　pasture because of them.
²¹At the sound of their fall the earth
　　will tremble;
　　their cry will resound to the Red
　　　Sea.ᵃ
²²Look! An eagle will soar and swoop
　　down,
　　spreading its wings over Bozrah.
　In that day the hearts of Edom's
　　warriors
　　will be like the heart of a woman
　　　in labor.

A Message About Damascus

²³Concerning Damascus:

"Hamath and Arpad are dismayed,
　　for they have heard bad news.
　They are disheartened,
　　troubled likeᵇ the restless sea.
²⁴Damascus has become feeble,
　　she has turned to flee
　　and panic has gripped her;
　anguish and pain have seized her,
　　pain like that of a woman in labor.
²⁵Why has the city of renown not been
　　abandoned,
　　the town in which I delight?
²⁶Surely, her young men will fall in the
　　streets;
　all her soldiers will be silenced in
　　that day,"
　　　　　　declares the LORD Almighty.
²⁷"I will set fire to the walls of
　　Damascus;
　　it will consume the fortresses of
　　　Ben-Hadad."

ᵃ21 Hebrew *Yam Suph*; that is, Sea of Reeds
ᵇ23 Hebrew *on* or *by*

A Message About Kedar and Hazor

²⁸Concerning Kedar and the kingdoms of Hazor, which Nebuchadnezzar king of Babylon attacked:

This is what the LORD says:

"Arise, and attack Kedar
    and destroy the people of the East.
²⁹Their tents and their flocks will be
        taken;
    their shelters will be carried off
    with all their goods and camels.
Men will shout to them,
    'Terror on every side!'

³⁰"Flee quickly away!
    Stay in deep caves, you who live in
        Hazor,"
                        declares the LORD.
"Nebuchadnezzar king of Babylon
        has plotted against you;
    he has devised a plan against you.

³¹"Arise and attack a nation at ease,
    which lives in confidence,"
                        declares the LORD,
"a nation that has neither gates nor
        bars;
    its people live alone.
³²Their camels will become plunder,
    and their large herds will be booty.
I will scatter to the winds those who
        are in distant places ͣ
    and will bring disaster on them
        from every side,"
                        declares the LORD.
³³"Hazor will become a haunt of
        jackals,
    a desolate place forever.
No one will live there;
    no man will dwell in it."

A Message About Elam

³⁴This is the word of the LORD that came to Jeremiah the prophet concerning Elam, early in the reign of Zedekiah king of Judah:

³⁵This is what the LORD Almighty says:

"See, I will break the bow of Elam,
    the mainstay of their might.
³⁶I will bring against Elam the four
        winds
    from the four quarters of the
        heavens;
I will scatter them to the four winds,

and there will not be a nation
    where Elam's exiles do not go.
³⁷I will shatter Elam before their foes,
    before those who seek their lives;
I will bring disaster upon them,
    even my fierce anger,"
                        declares the LORD.
"I will pursue them with the sword
    until I have made an end of them.
³⁸I will set my throne in Elam
    and destroy her king and officials,"
                        declares the LORD.

³⁹"Yet I will restore the fortunes of
        Elam
    in days to come,"
                        declares the LORD.

A Message About Babylon

50 This is the word the LORD spoke through Jeremiah the prophet concerning Babylon and the land of the Babylonians ᵇ:

²"Announce and proclaim among the
        nations,
    lift up a banner and proclaim it;
    keep nothing back, but say,
'Babylon will be captured;
    Bel will be put to shame,
    Marduk filled with terror.
Her images will be put to shame
    and her idols filled with terror.'
³A nation from the north will attack
        her
    and lay waste her land.
No one will live in it;
    both men and animals will flee
        away.

⁴"In those days, at that time,"
    declares the LORD,
"the people of Israel and the people
        of Judah together
    will go in tears to seek the LORD
        their God.
⁵They will ask the way to Zion
    and turn their faces toward it.
They will come and bind themselves
        to the LORD
    in an everlasting covenant
    that will not be forgotten.

⁶"My people have been lost sheep;

ͣ32 Or *who clip the hair by their foreheads*
ᵇ1 Or *Chaldeans*; also in verses 8, 25, 35 and 45

their shepherds have led them
astray
and caused them to roam on the
mountains.
They wandered over mountain and
hill
and forgot their own resting place.
⁷Whoever found them devoured them;
their enemies said, 'We are not
guilty,
for they sinned against the LORD, their
true pasture,
the LORD, the hope of their fathers.'

⁸"Flee out of Babylon;
leave the land of the Babylonians,
and be like the goats that lead the
flock.
⁹For I will stir up and bring against
Babylon
an alliance of great nations from
the land of the north.
They will take up their positions
against her,
and from the north she will be
captured.
Their arrows will be like skilled
warriors
who do not return empty-handed.
¹⁰So Babylonia*ᵃ* will be plundered;
all who plunder her will have their
fill,"
declares the LORD.

¹¹"Because you rejoice and are glad,
you who pillage my inheritance,
because you frolic like a heifer
threshing grain
and neigh like stallions,
¹²your mother will be greatly ashamed;
she who gave you birth will be
disgraced.
She will be the least of the nations—
a wilderness, a dry land, a desert.
¹³Because of the LORD's anger she will
not be inhabited
but will be completely desolate.
All who pass Babylon will be
horrified and scoff
because of all her wounds.

¹⁴"Take up your positions around
Babylon,
all you who draw the bow.
Shoot at her! Spare no arrows,
for she has sinned against the
LORD.

¹⁵Shout against her on every side!
She surrenders, her towers fall,
her walls are torn down.
Since this is the vengeance of the
LORD,
take vengeance on her;
do to her as she has done to
others.
¹⁶Cut off from Babylon the sower,
and the reaper with his sickle at
harvest.
Because of the sword of the oppressor
let everyone return to his own
people,
let everyone flee to his own land.

¹⁷"Israel is a scattered flock
that lions have chased away.
The first to devour him
was the king of Assyria;
the last to crush his bones
was Nebuchadnezzar king of
Babylon."

¹⁸Therefore this is what the LORD Almighty, the God of Israel, says:

"I will punish the king of Babylon
and his land
as I punished the king of Assyria.
¹⁹But I will bring Israel back to his own
pasture
and he will graze on Carmel and
Bashan;
his appetite will be satisfied
on the hills of Ephraim and
Gilead.
²⁰In those days, at that time,"
declares the LORD,
"search will be made for Israel's guilt,
but there will be none,
and for the sins of Judah,
but none will be found,
for I will forgive the remnant I
spare.

²¹"Attack the land of Merathaim
and those who live in Pekod.
Pursue, kill and completely destroy*ᵇ*
them,"
declares the LORD.
"Do everything I have commanded
you.
²²The noise of battle is in the land,

ᵃ10 Or *Chaldea*   ᵇ21 The Hebrew term refers to
the irrevocable giving over of things or persons to
the LORD, often by totally destroying them; also in
verse 26.

the noise of great destruction!
²³How broken and shattered
  is the hammer of the whole earth!
How desolate is Babylon
  among the nations!
²⁴I set a trap for you, O Babylon,
  and you were caught before you
    knew it;
you were found and captured
  because you opposed the LORD.
²⁵The LORD has opened his arsenal
  and brought out the weapons of
    his wrath,
for the Sovereign LORD Almighty has
    work to do
  in the land of the Babylonians.
²⁶Come against her from afar.
  Break open her granaries;
  pile her up like heaps of grain.
Completely destroy her
  and leave her no remnant.
²⁷Kill all her young bulls;
  let them go down to the slaughter!
Woe to them! For their day has come,
  the time for them to be punished.
²⁸Listen to the fugitives and refugees
    from Babylon
  declaring in Zion
how the LORD our God has taken
    vengeance,
  vengeance for his temple.

²⁹"Summon archers against Babylon,
  all those who draw the bow.
Encamp all around her;
  let no one escape.
Repay her for her deeds;
  do to her as she has done.
For she has defied the LORD,
  the Holy One of Israel.
³⁰Therefore, her young men will fall in
    the streets;
  all her soldiers will be silenced in
    that day,"
                    declares the LORD.
³¹"See, I am against you, O arrogant
    one,"
  declares the Lord, the LORD
    Almighty,
"for your day has come,
  the time for you to be punished.
³²The arrogant one will stumble and
    fall
  and no one will help her up;
I will kindle a fire in her towns

that will consume all who are
    around her."

³³This is what the LORD Almighty says:

"The people of Israel are oppressed,
  and the people of Judah as well.
All their captors hold them fast,
  refusing to let them go.
³⁴Yet their Redeemer is strong;
  the LORD Almighty is his name.
He will vigorously defend their cause
  so that he may bring rest to their
    land,
but unrest to those who live in
    Babylon.

³⁵"A sword against the Babylonians!"
  declares the LORD—
"against those who live in Babylon
  and against her officials and wise
    men!
³⁶A sword against her false prophets!
  They will become fools.
A sword against her warriors!
  They will be filled with terror.
³⁷A sword against her horses and
    chariots
  and all the foreigners in her ranks!
  They will become women.
A sword against her treasures!
  They will be plundered.
³⁸A drought onᵃ her waters!
  They will dry up.
For it is a land of idols,
  idols that will go mad with terror.

³⁹"So desert creatures and hyenas will
    live there,
  and there the owl will dwell.
It will never again be inhabited
  or lived in from generation to
    generation.
⁴⁰As God overthrew Sodom and
    Gomorrah
  along with their neighboring
    towns,"
                    declares the LORD,
"so no one will live there;
  no man will dwell in it.

⁴¹"Look! An army is coming from the
    north;
  a great nation and many kings
  are being stirred up from the ends
    of the earth.

ᵃ38 Or A sword against

⁴²They are armed with bows and
    spears;
  they are cruel and without mercy.
They sound like the roaring sea
  as they ride on their horses;
  they come like men in battle
    formation
  to attack you, O Daughter of
    Babylon.
⁴³The king of Babylon has heard
    reports about them,
  and his hands hang limp.
Anguish has gripped him,
  pain like that of a woman in labor.
⁴⁴Like a lion coming up from Jordan's
    thickets
  to a rich pastureland,
I will chase Babylon from its land in
    an instant.
  Who is the chosen one I will
    appoint for this?
Who is like me and who can
    challenge me?
  And what shepherd can stand
    against me?"
⁴⁵Therefore, hear what the LORD has
    planned against Babylon,
  what he has purposed against the
    land of the Babylonians:
The young of the flock will be
    dragged away;
  he will completely destroy their
    pasture because of them.
⁴⁶At the sound of Babylon's capture the
    earth will tremble;
  its cry will resound among the
    nations.

51 This is what the LORD says:

"See, I will stir up the spirit of a
    destroyer
  against Babylon and the people of
    Leb Kamai.ᵃ
²I will send foreigners to Babylon
  to winnow her and to devastate her
    land;
  they will oppose her on every side
  in the day of her disaster.
³Let not the archer string his bow,
  nor let him put on his armor.
Do not spare her young men;
  completely destroyᵇ her army.
⁴They will fall down slain in
    Babylon,ᶜ
  fatally wounded in her streets.

⁵For Israel and Judah have not been
    forsaken
  by their God, the LORD Almighty,
  though their landᵈ is full of guilt
  before the Holy One of Israel.

⁶"Flee from Babylon!
  Run for your lives!
  Do not be destroyed because of her
    sins.
It is time for the LORD's vengeance;
  he will pay her what she deserves.
⁷Babylon was a gold cup in the LORD's
    hand;
  she made the whole earth drunk.
The nations drank her wine;
  therefore they have now gone mad.
⁸Babylon will suddenly fall and be
    broken.
  Wail over her!
Get balm for her pain;
  perhaps she can be healed.

⁹" 'We would have healed Babylon,
  but she cannot be healed;
let us leave her and each go to his
    own land,
  for her judgment reaches to the
    skies,
  it rises as high as the clouds.'

¹⁰" 'The LORD has vindicated us;
  come, let us tell in Zion
  what the LORD our God has done.'

¹¹"Sharpen the arrows,
  take up the shields!
The LORD has stirred up the kings of
    the Medes,
  because his purpose is to destroy
    Babylon.
The LORD will take vengeance,
  vengeance for his temple.
¹²Lift up a banner against the walls of
    Babylon!
  Reinforce the guard,
station the watchmen,
  prepare an ambush!
The LORD will carry out his purpose,
  his decree against the people of
    Babylon.
¹³You who live by many waters
  and are rich in treasures,

ᵃ1 *Leb Kamai* is a cryptogram for Chaldea, that is,
Babylonia.   ᵇ3 The Hebrew term refers to the
irrevocable giving over of things or persons to the
LORD, often by totally destroying them.   ᶜ4 Or
Chaldea   ᵈ5 Or / *and the land* ⌊*of the Babylonians*⌋

your end has come,
    the time for you to be cut off.
¹⁴The LORD Almighty has sworn by
       himself:
    I will surely fill you with men, as
       with a swarm of locusts,
    and they will shout in triumph
       over you.

¹⁵"He made the earth by his power;
    he founded the world by his
       wisdom
    and stretched out the heavens by
       his understanding.
¹⁶When he thunders, the waters in the
       heavens roar;
    he makes clouds rise from the ends
       of the earth.
    He sends lightning with the rain
       and brings out the wind from his
       storehouses.

¹⁷"Every man is senseless and without
       knowledge;
    every goldsmith is shamed by his
       idols.
    His images are a fraud;
       they have no breath in them.
¹⁸They are worthless, the objects of
       mockery;
    when their judgment comes, they
       will perish.
¹⁹He who is the Portion of Jacob is not
       like these,
    for he is the Maker of all things,
    including the tribe of his inheritance—
       the LORD Almighty is his name.

²⁰"You are my war club,
    my weapon for battle—
  with you I shatter nations,
    with you I destroy kingdoms,
²¹with you I shatter horse and rider,
    with you I shatter chariot and
       driver,
²²with you I shatter man and woman,
    with you I shatter old man and
       youth,
    with you I shatter young man and
       maiden,
²³with you I shatter shepherd and flock,
    with you I shatter farmer and oxen,
    with you I shatter governors and
       officials.

²⁴"Before your eyes I will repay Babylon and all who live in Babylonia*ᵃ* for

all the wrong they have done in Zion,"
declares the LORD.

²⁵"I am against you, O destroying
       mountain,
    you who destroy the whole earth,"
             declares the LORD.
    "I will stretch out my hand against
       you,
    roll you off the cliffs,
    and make you a burned-out
       mountain.
²⁶No rock will be taken from you for a
       cornerstone,
    nor any stone for a foundation,
    for you will be desolate forever,"
             declares the LORD.

²⁷"Lift up a banner in the land!
    Blow the trumpet among the
       nations!
    Prepare the nations for battle against
       her;
    summon against her these
       kingdoms:
       Ararat, Minni and Ashkenaz.
    Appoint a commander against her;
    send up horses like a swarm of
       locusts.
²⁸Prepare the nations for battle against
       her—
    the kings of the Medes,
  their governors and all their officials,
    and all the countries they rule.
²⁹The land trembles and writhes,
    for the LORD's purposes against
       Babylon stand—
  to lay waste the land of Babylon
    so that no one will live there.
³⁰Babylon's warriors have stopped
       fighting;
    they remain in their strongholds.
    Their strength is exhausted;
    they have become like women.
    Her dwellings are set on fire;
    the bars of her gates are broken.
³¹One courier follows another
    and messenger follows messenger
  to announce to the king of Babylon
    that his entire city is captured,
³²the river crossings seized,
    the marshes set on fire,
    and the soldiers terrified."

ᵃ24 Or *Chaldea*; also in verse 35

³³This is what the LORD Almighty, the God of Israel, says:

"The Daughter of Babylon is like a
    threshing floor
  at the time it is trampled;
  the time to harvest her will soon
    come."

³⁴"Nebuchadnezzar king of Babylon
    has devoured us,
  he has thrown us into confusion,
  he has made us an empty jar.
Like a serpent he has swallowed us
  and filled his stomach with our
    delicacies,
  and then has spewed us out.
³⁵May the violence done to our flesh^a
    be upon Babylon,"
  say the inhabitants of Zion.
"May our blood be on those who live
    in Babylonia,"
  says Jerusalem.

³⁶Therefore, this is what the LORD says:

"See, I will defend your cause
    and avenge you;
I will dry up her sea
    and make her springs dry.
³⁷Babylon will be a heap of ruins,
    a haunt of jackals,
  an object of horror and scorn,
    a place where no one lives.
³⁸Her people all roar like young lions,
    they growl like lion cubs.
³⁹But while they are aroused,
    I will set out a feast for them
    and make them drunk,
  so that they shout with laughter—
    then sleep forever and not awake,"
        declares the LORD.
⁴⁰"I will bring them down
    like lambs to the slaughter,
    like rams and goats.

⁴¹"How Sheshach^b will be captured,
    the boast of the whole earth
      seized!
What a horror Babylon will be
    among the nations!
⁴²The sea will rise over Babylon;
    its roaring waves will cover her.
⁴³Her towns will be desolate,
    a dry and desert land,
  a land where no one lives,
    through which no man travels.

⁴⁴I will punish Bel in Babylon
    and make him spew out what he
      has swallowed.
The nations will no longer stream to
    him.
  And the wall of Babylon will fall.

⁴⁵"Come out of her, my people!
    Run for your lives!
  Run from the fierce anger of the
    LORD.
⁴⁶Do not lose heart or be afraid
    when rumors are heard in the
      land;
  one rumor comes this year, another
    the next,
  rumors of violence in the land
    and of ruler against ruler.
⁴⁷For the time will surely come
    when I will punish the idols of
      Babylon;
  her whole land will be disgraced
    and her slain will all lie fallen
      within her.
⁴⁸Then heaven and earth and all that is
    in them
  will shout for joy over Babylon,
for out of the north
    destroyers will attack her,"
        declares the LORD.

⁴⁹"Babylon must fall because of Israel's
    slain,
  just as the slain in all the earth
    have fallen because of Babylon.
⁵⁰You who have escaped the sword,
    leave and do not linger!
Remember the LORD in a distant land,
    and think on Jerusalem."

⁵¹"We are disgraced,
    for we have been insulted
    and shame covers our faces,
because foreigners have entered
    the holy places of the LORD's
      house."

⁵²"But days are coming," declares the
    LORD,
  "when I will punish her idols,
and throughout her land
    the wounded will groan.
⁵³Even if Babylon reaches the sky

---

^a35 Or *done to us and to our children*
^b41 *Sheshach* is a cryptogram for Babylon.

and fortifies her lofty stronghold,
   I will send destroyers against her,"
      declares the LORD.

54"The sound of a cry comes from
      Babylon,
   the sound of great destruction
      from the land of the
      Babylonians.*a*
55The LORD will destroy Babylon;
   he will silence her noisy din.
Waves ⌊of enemies⌋ will rage like great
      waters;
   the roar of their voices will
      resound.
56A destroyer will come against Babylon;
   her warriors will be captured,
   and their bows will be broken.
For the LORD is a God of retribution;
   he will repay in full.
57I will make her officials and wise
      men drunk,
   her governors, officers and warriors
      as well;
they will sleep forever and not awake,"
   declares the King, whose name is
      the LORD Almighty.

58This is what the LORD Almighty says:

"Babylon's thick wall will be leveled
   and her high gates set on fire;
the peoples exhaust themselves for
      nothing,
   the nations' labor is only fuel for
      the flames."

59This is the message Jeremiah gave to the staff officer Seraiah son of Neriah, the son of Mahseiah, when he went to Babylon with Zedekiah king of Judah in the fourth year of his reign. 60Jeremiah had written on a scroll about all the disasters that would come upon Babylon—all that had been recorded concerning Babylon. 61He said to Seraiah, "When you get to Babylon, see that you read all these words aloud. 62Then say, 'O LORD, you have said you will destroy this place, so that neither man nor animal will live in it; it will be desolate forever.' 63When you finish reading this scroll, tie a stone to it and throw it into the Euphrates. 64Then say, 'So will Babylon sink to rise no more because of the disaster I will bring upon her. And her people will fall.' "

The words of Jeremiah end here.

The Fall of Jerusalem

52 Zedekiah was twenty-one years old when he became king, and he reigned in Jerusalem eleven years. His mother's name was Hamutal daughter of Jeremiah; she was from Libnah. 2He did evil in the eyes of the LORD, just as Jehoiakim had done. 3It was because of the LORD's anger that all this happened to Jerusalem and Judah, and in the end he thrust them from his presence.

Now Zedekiah rebelled against the king of Babylon.

4So in the ninth year of Zedekiah's reign, on the tenth day of the tenth month, Nebuchadnezzar king of Babylon marched against Jerusalem with his whole army. They camped outside the city and built siege works all around it. 5The city was kept under siege until the eleventh year of King Zedekiah.

6By the ninth day of the fourth month the famine in the city had become so severe that there was no food for the people to eat. 7Then the city wall was broken through, and the whole army fled. They left the city at night through the gate between the two walls near the king's garden, though the Babylonians*b* were surrounding the city. They fled toward the Arabah,*c* 8but the Babylonian*d* army pursued King Zedekiah and overtook him in the plains of Jericho. All his soldiers were separated from him and scattered, 9and he was captured.

He was taken to the king of Babylon at Riblah in the land of Hamath, where he pronounced sentence on him. 10There at Riblah the king of Babylon slaughtered the sons of Zedekiah before his eyes; he also killed all the officials of Judah. 11Then he put out Zedekiah's eyes, bound him with bronze shackles and took him to Babylon, where he put him in prison till the day of his death.

12On the tenth day of the fifth month, in the nineteenth year of Nebuchadnezzar king of Babylon, Nebuzaradan commander of the imperial guard, who served the king of Babylon, came to Jerusalem. 13He set fire to the temple of the LORD, the royal palace and all the houses of Jerusa-

a54 Or *Chaldeans*   *b7* Or *Chaldeans; also in verse 17*   *c7* Or *the Jordan Valley*   *d8* Or *Chaldean; also in verse 14* lem. Every important building he burned down. [14]The whole Babylonian army under the commander of the imperial guard broke down all the walls around Jerusalem. [15]Nebuzaradan the commander of the guard carried into exile some of the poorest people and those who remained in the city, along with the rest of the craftsmen[a] and those who had gone over to the king of Babylon. [16]But Nebuzaradan left behind the rest of the poorest people of the land to work the vineyards and fields.

[17]The Babylonians broke up the bronze pillars, the movable stands and the bronze Sea that were at the temple of the LORD and they carried all the bronze to Babylon. [18]They also took away the pots, shovels, wick trimmers, sprinkling bowls, dishes and all the bronze articles used in the temple service. [19]The commander of the imperial guard took away the basins, censers, sprinkling bowls, pots, lampstands, dishes and bowls used for drink offerings—all that were made of pure gold or silver.

[20]The bronze from the two pillars, the Sea and the twelve bronze bulls under it, and the movable stands, which King Solomon had made for the temple of the LORD, was more than could be weighed. [21]Each of the pillars was eighteen cubits high and twelve cubits in circumference[b]; each was four fingers thick, and hollow. [22]The bronze capital on top of the one pillar was five cubits[c] high and was decorated with a network and pomegranates of bronze all around. The other pillar, with its pomegranates, was similar. [23]There were ninety-six pomegranates on the sides; the total number of pomegranates above the surrounding network was a hundred.

[24]The commander of the guard took as prisoners Seraiah the chief priest, Zephaniah the priest next in rank and the three doorkeepers. [25]Of those still in the city, he took the officer in charge of the fighting men, and seven royal advisers. He also took the secretary who was chief officer in charge of conscripting the people of the land and sixty of his men who were found in the city. [26]Nebuzaradan the commander took them all and brought them to the king of Babylon at Riblah. [27]There at Riblah, in the land of Hamath, the king had them executed.

So Judah went into captivity, away from her land. [28]This is the number of the people Nebuchadnezzar carried into exile:

in the seventh year, 3,023 Jews;
[29]in Nebuchadnezzar's eighteenth year,
832 people from Jerusalem;
[30]in his twenty-third year,
745 Jews taken into exile by Nebuzaradan the commander of the imperial guard.
There were 4,600 people in all.

Jehoiachin Released

[31]In the thirty-seventh year of the exile of Jehoiachin king of Judah, in the year Evil-Merodach[d] became king of Babylon, he released Jehoiachin king of Judah and freed him from prison on the twenty-fifth day of the twelfth month. [32]He spoke kindly to him and gave him a seat of honor higher than those of the other kings who were with him in Babylon. [33]So Jehoiachin put aside his prison clothes and for the rest of his life ate regularly at the king's table. [34]Day by day the king of Babylon gave Jehoiachin a regular allowance as long as he lived, till the day of his death.

[a]15 Or populace   [b]21 That is, about 27 feet (about 8.1 meters) high and 18 feet (about 5.4 meters) in circumference   [c]22 That is, about 7 1/2 feet (about 2.3 meters)   [d]31 Also called Amel-Marduk

Lamentations

Beloved Christian author, artist and speaker Joni Eareckson Tada has been a quadriplegic for over thirty years. It has been that long since she's had any sensation or movement in her hands or her feet. Imagine the despair of knowing that the rest of your life would hold confinement to a wheelchair and complete dependence on others . . . for everything.

In January of 1993, a pre-dawn earthquake rocked the Tadas' house. Joni's precious husband literally threw himself on top of his motionless wife to protect her from falling plaster. Moments later, Joni was sitting in her wheelchair on the back deck of her home. As she looked over the devastation, she began singing. At first, her notes were quiet and subdued, but soon they swelled to top-of-the-lungs decibels. "Our God is an awesome God," Joni sang, "He reigns from heaven above with wisdom, power, and love. Our God is an awesome God."

The prophet Jeremiah, who authored this book of Lamentations, and Joni would have been soul mates. Right in the middle of the most awful devastation he had ever seen, Jeremiah wrote the words, "Great is [God's] faithfulness" (3:23). Isn't that incredible? As you read through this short book, reflect on how our great God has shown his faithfulness to you.

1 *a* How deserted lies the city,
      once so full of people!
How like a widow is she,
      who once was great among the
      nations!
She who was queen among the
      provinces

*a*This chapter is an acrostic poem, the verses of which begin with the successive letters of the Hebrew alphabet.

has now become a slave.

²Bitterly she weeps at night,
    tears are upon her cheeks.
Among all her lovers
    there is none to comfort her.
All her friends have betrayed her;
    they have become her enemies.

³After affliction and harsh labor,
    Judah has gone into exile.
She dwells among the nations;
    she finds no resting place.
All who pursue her have overtaken
    her
    in the midst of her distress.

⁴The roads to Zion mourn,
    for no one comes to her appointed
      feasts.
All her gateways are desolate,
    her priests groan,
her maidens grieve,
    and she is in bitter anguish.

⁵Her foes have become her masters;
    her enemies are at ease.
The LORD has brought her grief
    because of her many sins.
Her children have gone into exile,
    captive before the foe.

⁶All the splendor has departed
    from the Daughter of Zion.
Her princes are like deer
    that find no pasture;

in weakness they have fled
    before the pursuer.

⁷In the days of her affliction and
      wandering
Jerusalem remembers all the
      treasures
    that were hers in days of old.
When her people fell into enemy
      hands,
    there was no one to help her.
Her enemies looked at her
    and laughed at her destruction.

⁸Jerusalem has sinned greatly
    and so has become unclean.
All who honored her despise
      her,
    for they have seen her nakedness;
she herself groans
    and turns away.

⁹Her filthiness clung to her skirts;
    she did not consider her future.
Her fall was astounding;
    there was none to comfort her.
"Look, O LORD, on my affliction,
    for the enemy has triumphed."

¹⁰The enemy laid hands
    on all her treasures;
she saw pagan nations
    enter her sanctuary—
those you had forbidden
    to enter your assembly.

Lonely Times

Friday

LAMENTATIONS 1:1–2 There are seasons of a marriage when the relationship can seem empty. Once it was so full of hope and excitement, but then things changed and each spouse felt alienated from the other. Although the couple is together, even sleeping in the same bed, spouses can still feel completely alone. He or she may wonder, *What happened to us?* And loneliness can grow into fear.

We can learn much from children. When our son Robey was a little boy, he was afraid of the dark. At night it didn't take much to turn his darkened bedroom into a frightening chamber of horrors. The one thing that would sustain him was knowing that we were close by. Some nights Robey would even call out for reassurance: "Daddy . . . are you there?"

We need to have childlike confidence in our heavenly Father. He knows about your fears. Nothing in a person's life catches him off guard. Nothing causes him to have to say, "Oops, I didn't know that was going to happen." Keep this in mind when you're going through a lonely marital season. No matter how lonely you feel, God is with you . . . always.

—Bob & Rosemary

Go to page 868 for your next devotional reading.

[11]All her people groan
    as they search for bread;
they barter their treasures for food
    to keep themselves alive.
"Look, O LORD, and consider,
    for I am despised."

[12]"Is it nothing to you, all you who
        pass by?
    Look around and see.
Is any suffering like my suffering
    that was inflicted on me,
that the LORD brought on me
    in the day of his fierce anger?

[13]"From on high he sent fire,
    sent it down into my bones.
He spread a net for my feet
    and turned me back.
He made me desolate,
    faint all the day long.

[14]"My sins have been bound into a
        yoke[a];
    by his hands they were woven
        together.
They have come upon my neck
    and the Lord has sapped my
        strength.
He has handed me over
    to those I cannot withstand.

[15]"The Lord has rejected
    all the warriors in my midst;
he has summoned an army against
        me
    to[b] crush my young men.
In his winepress the Lord has
        trampled
    the Virgin Daughter of Judah.

[16]"This is why I weep
    and my eyes overflow with tears.
No one is near to comfort me,
    no one to restore my spirit.
My children are destitute
    because the enemy has prevailed."

[17]Zion stretches out her hands,
    but there is no one to comfort her.
The LORD has decreed for Jacob
    that his neighbors become his foes;
Jerusalem has become
    an unclean thing among them.

[18]"The LORD is righteous,
    yet I rebelled against his command.
Listen, all you peoples;
    look upon my suffering.

My young men and maidens
    have gone into exile.

[19]"I called to my allies
    but they betrayed me.
My priests and my elders
    perished in the city
while they searched for food
    to keep themselves alive.

[20]"See, O LORD, how distressed I am!
    I am in torment within,
and in my heart I am disturbed,
    for I have been most rebellious.
Outside, the sword bereaves;
    inside, there is only death.

[21]"People have heard my groaning,
    but there is no one to comfort
        me.
All my enemies have heard of my
        distress;
    they rejoice at what you have done.
May you bring the day you have
        announced
    so they may become like me.

[22]"Let all their wickedness come before
        you;
    deal with them
as you have dealt with me
    because of all my sins.
My groans are many
    and my heart is faint."

2[c] How the Lord has covered the
        Daughter of Zion
    with the cloud of his anger[d]!
He has hurled down the splendor of
        Israel
    from heaven to earth;
he has not remembered his footstool
    in the day of his anger.

[2]Without pity the Lord has swallowed
        up
    all the dwellings of Jacob;
in his wrath he has torn down
    the strongholds of the Daughter of
        Judah.

---

[a]14 Most Hebrew manuscripts; Septuagint *He kept
watch over my sins*   [b]15 Or *has set a time for me /
when he will*   [c]This chapter is an acrostic poem,
the verses of which begin with the successive
letters of the Hebrew alphabet.   [d]1 Or *How the
Lord in his anger / has treated the Daughter of Zion
with contempt*

He has brought her kingdom and its
  princes
  down to the ground in dishonor.

³In fierce anger he has cut off
  every horn*a* of Israel.
He has withdrawn his right hand
  at the approach of the enemy.
He has burned in Jacob like a flaming
  fire
  that consumes everything around
    it.

⁴Like an enemy he has strung his
  bow;
  his right hand is ready.
Like a foe he has slain
  all who were pleasing to the eye;
he has poured out his wrath like fire
  on the tent of the Daughter of
    Zion.

⁵The Lord is like an enemy;
  he has swallowed up Israel.
He has swallowed up all her palaces
  and destroyed her strongholds.

He has multiplied mourning and
  lamentation
  for the Daughter of Judah.

⁶He has laid waste his dwelling like a
  garden;
  he has destroyed his place of
    meeting.
The LORD has made Zion forget
  her appointed feasts and her
    Sabbaths;
in his fierce anger he has spurned
  both king and priest.

⁷The Lord has rejected his altar
  and abandoned his sanctuary.
He has handed over to the enemy
  the walls of her palaces;
they have raised a shout in the house
  of the LORD
  as on the day of an appointed
    feast.

⁸The LORD determined to tear down

---

a3 Or / all the strength; or *every king; horn* here
symbolizes strength.

Raging Anger

LAMENTATIONS 1:20–21 Several years ago I (Les) was invited to a workshop for psychologists promoting a new therapeutic tool for helping people manage anger. It was a foam rubber bat designed for a person to hit something—or someone. The idea was that an angry person in the counseling office could blow off steam, or "vent" anger, without causing harm or pain. Instead of bottling up our anger, we needed to release our anger. That was the theory, anyway.

I have worked with enough angry people in therapy to know that, while helping them to get in touch with buried anger can serve a useful purpose, expressing anger frequently and openly neither removes the cause nor diminishes the frustrated feelings. In fact, plenty of research now shows that "ventilation" techniques for dealing with anger only reduce one's control over anger and instead encourage more frequent and aggressive forms of the behavior. Yikes!

When we practice letting angry feelings out, we become less able to control them the next time. Rather than "venting" the emotion and getting rid of it, we find it returning more frequently. And, as this passage makes clear, anger brings alienation.

Anger in marriage, especially when we nurse it, motivates us to hate, wound, damage, despise and humiliate our spouse. It guarantees "torment within." Thank goodness we don't have to surrender to anger. We can choose to rise above it.

—*Les & Leslie*

 What ways can you show more affection toward each other?

Go to page 871 for your next devotional reading.

the wall around the Daughter of
  Zion.
He stretched out a measuring line
  and did not withhold his hand
    from destroying.
He made ramparts and walls lament;
  together they wasted away.

⁹Her gates have sunk into the ground;
  their bars he has broken and
    destroyed.
Her king and her princes are exiled
    among the nations,
  the law is no more,
and her prophets no longer find
  visions from the LORD.

¹⁰The elders of the Daughter of Zion
  sit on the ground in silence;
they have sprinkled dust on their
    heads
  and put on sackcloth.
The young women of Jerusalem
  have bowed their heads to the
    ground.

¹¹My eyes fail from weeping,
  I am in torment within,
my heart is poured out on the ground
  because my people are destroyed,
because children and infants faint
  in the streets of the city.

¹²They say to their mothers,
  "Where is bread and wine?"
as they faint like wounded men
  in the streets of the city,
as their lives ebb away
  in their mothers' arms.

¹³What can I say for you?
  With what can I compare you,
  O Daughter of Jerusalem?
To what can I liken you,
  that I may comfort you,
  O Virgin Daughter of Zion?
Your wound is as deep as the sea.
  Who can heal you?

¹⁴The visions of your prophets
  were false and worthless;
they did not expose your sin
  to ward off your captivity.
The oracles they gave you
  were false and misleading.

¹⁵All who pass your way
  clap their hands at you;
they scoff and shake their heads

at the Daughter of Jerusalem:
"Is this the city that was called
  the perfection of beauty,
  the joy of the whole earth?"

¹⁶All your enemies open their mouths
  wide against you;
they scoff and gnash their teeth
  and say, "We have swallowed her
    up.
This is the day we have waited for;
  we have lived to see it."

¹⁷The LORD has done what he planned;
  he has fulfilled his word,
  which he decreed long ago.
He has overthrown you without pity,
  he has let the enemy gloat over
    you,
  he has exalted the horn*a* of your
    foes.

¹⁸The hearts of the people
  cry out to the Lord.
O wall of the Daughter of Zion,
  let your tears flow like a river
    day and night;
give yourself no relief,
  your eyes no rest.

---

a17 Horn here symbolizes strength.

¹⁹Arise, cry out in the night,
    as the watches of the night begin;
pour out your heart like water
    in the presence of the Lord.
Lift up your hands to him
    for the lives of your children,
who faint from hunger
    at the head of every street.

²⁰"Look, O LORD, and consider:
    Whom have you ever treated like
        this?
Should women eat their offspring,
    the children they have cared for?
Should priest and prophet be killed
    in the sanctuary of the Lord?

²¹"Young and old lie together
    in the dust of the streets;
my young men and maidens
    have fallen by the sword.
You have slain them in the day of
        your anger;
    you have slaughtered them without
        pity.

²²"As you summon to a feast day,
    so you summoned against me
        terrors on every side.
In the day of the LORD's anger
    no one escaped or survived;
those I cared for and reared,
    my enemy has destroyed."

3 ^a I am the man who has seen
        affliction
    by the rod of his wrath.
²He has driven me away and made me
        walk
    in darkness rather than light;
³indeed, he has turned his hand
        against me
    again and again, all day long.

⁴He has made my skin and my flesh
        grow old
    and has broken my bones.
⁵He has besieged me and surrounded
        me
    with bitterness and hardship.
⁶He has made me dwell in darkness
    like those long dead.

⁷He has walled me in so I cannot
        escape;
    he has weighed me down with
        chains.
⁸Even when I call out or cry for help,
    he shuts out my prayer.
⁹He has barred my way with blocks of
        stone;
    he has made my paths crooked.

¹⁰Like a bear lying in wait,
    like a lion in hiding,
¹¹he dragged me from the path and
        mangled me
    and left me without help.
¹²He drew his bow
    and made me the target for his
        arrows.

¹³He pierced my heart
    with arrows from his quiver.
¹⁴I became the laughingstock of all my
        people;
    they mock me in song all day long.
¹⁵He has filled me with bitter herbs
    and sated me with gall.

¹⁶He has broken my teeth with gravel;
    he has trampled me in the dust.
¹⁷I have been deprived of peace;
    I have forgotten what prosperity is.
¹⁸So I say, "My splendor is gone
    and all that I had hoped from the
        LORD."

¹⁹I remember my affliction and my
        wandering,
    the bitterness and the gall.
²⁰I well remember them,
    and my soul is downcast within
        me.
²¹Yet this I call to mind
    and therefore I have hope:

²²Because of the LORD's great love we
        are not consumed,
    for his compassions never fail.
²³They are new every morning;
    great is your faithfulness.
²⁴I say to myself, "The LORD is my
        portion;
    therefore I will wait for him."

²⁵The LORD is good to those whose
        hope is in him,
    to the one who seeks him;
²⁶it is good to wait quietly
    for the salvation of the LORD.
²⁷It is good for a man to bear the yoke
    while he is young.

---

^aThis chapter is an acrostic poem; the verses of
each stanza begin with the successive letters of the
Hebrew alphabet, and the verses within each
stanza begin with the same letter.

28Let him sit alone in silence,
  for the LORD has laid it on him.
29Let him bury his face in the dust—
  there may yet be hope.
30Let him offer his cheek to one who
     would strike him,
  and let him be filled with disgrace.

31For men are not cast off
  by the Lord forever.
32Though he brings grief, he will show
     compassion,
  so great is his unfailing love.
33For he does not willingly bring
     affliction
  or grief to the children of men.

34To crush underfoot
  all prisoners in the land,
35to deny a man his rights
  before the Most High,
36to deprive a man of justice—
  would not the Lord see such
     things?

37Who can speak and have it happen
  if the Lord has not decreed it?
38Is it not from the mouth of the Most
     High
  that both calamities and good
     things come?
39Why should any living man complain
  when punished for his sins?

40Let us examine our ways and test
     them,
  and let us return to the LORD.
41Let us lift up our hearts and our
     hands
  to God in heaven, and say:
42"We have sinned and rebelled
  and you have not forgiven.

43"You have covered yourself with
     anger and pursued us;
  you have slain without pity.
44You have covered yourself with a
     cloud
  so that no prayer can get through.
45You have made us scum and refuse
  among the nations.

46"All our enemies have opened their
     mouths
  wide against us.
47We have suffered terror and pitfalls,
  ruin and destruction."
48Streams of tears flow from my eyes
  because my people are destroyed.

49My eyes will flow unceasingly,
  without relief,
50until the LORD looks down
  from heaven and sees.
51What I see brings grief to my soul
  because of all the women of my
     city.

New Compassion

Monday

LAMENTATIONS 3:19–23 "Everyone has problems," our friend Bob told us. "Basically there are three kinds of problems—health issues, relationship issues and financial difficulties." At present, Bob's difficulties center around health issues. He and his wife Rebecca must daily deal with an asthmatic child. From time to time in the middle of the night when little Sarah has trouble breathing, they race to the emergency room. They must rely on God's faithfulness and compassion morning, noon and night.

Everyone needs God's compassion, especially when facing turbulent times in marriage. Jeremiah wrote this encouraging passage to the Israelites during a very dark and bleak time in the history of Jerusalem. The Holy City had been destroyed, and Jeremiah's own soul was downcast. Yet he chose to call on the Lord; and he held on to hope.

Whatever problems you are facing in your marriage, you have the unique opportunity to unite together as a couple and turn to God, to put your hope in him and experience his love and compassion daily. And it is especially appropriate to start the day together, acknowledging that God is waiting to bless you and direct your marriage as well as your individual lives. His compassions are new every morning.

—Dave & Claudia

Go to page 872 for your next devotional reading.

⁵²Those who were my enemies without
　　cause
　　hunted me like a bird.
⁵³They tried to end my life in a pit
　　and threw stones at me;
⁵⁴the waters closed over my head,
　　and I thought I was about to be
　　　cut off.

⁵⁵I called on your name, O LORD,
　　from the depths of the pit.
⁵⁶You heard my plea: "Do not close
　　　your ears
　　to my cry for relief."
⁵⁷You came near when I called you,
　　and you said, "Do not fear."

⁵⁸O Lord, you took up my case;
　　you redeemed my life.
⁵⁹You have seen, O LORD, the wrong
　　　done to me.
　　Uphold my cause!
⁶⁰You have seen the depth of their
　　vengeance,
　　all their plots against me.

⁶¹O LORD, you have heard their insults,
　　all their plots against me—
⁶²what my enemies whisper and mutter
　　against me all day long.

⁶³Look at them! Sitting or standing,
　　they mock me in their songs.

⁶⁴Pay them back what they deserve,
　　O LORD,
　　for what their hands have done.
⁶⁵Put a veil over their hearts,
　　and may your curse be on them!
⁶⁶Pursue them in anger and destroy
　　them
　　from under the heavens of the
　　　LORD.

4 ᵃ How the gold has lost its luster,
　　the fine gold become dull!
The sacred gems are scattered
　　at the head of every street.

²How the precious sons of Zion,
　　once worth their weight in gold,
are now considered as pots of clay,
　　the work of a potter's hands!

³Even jackals offer their breasts
　　to nurse their young,
but my people have become heartless
　　like ostriches in the desert.

⁴Because of thirst the infant's tongue

ᵃThis chapter is an acrostic poem, the verses of
which begin with the successive letters of the
Hebrew alphabet.

Time Together

Tuesday

LAMENTATIONS 4:1 After being conquered by the Babylonians, the
Jews found themselves mourning
the loss of everything they held
dear. In their time of suffering and
crisis, they learned what was of true
value in their lives. They realized how
quickly "gold become[s] dull" and "sacred
gems are scattered."

What an important reminder for us! So
often couples expend great energy thinking
about and planning for things that can so
quickly become dull and lost. In a mad dash
to "get ahead" and "live the good life," a
couple can forget to develop the truly important things—the things that bring lasting
joy and fulfillment. Scripture reminds us
over and over again that it's a relationship
with God and each other that will bring us
lasting joy.

There are some specific ways a couple can change the focus of their
lives. Begin by answering this
question: What is the direction our
family's currently traveling? Are we
truly reflecting a commitment to developing deeper relationships, or are
we swept up in a whirlwind of events without any goals? After answering this question, develop a plan to allow for time to
cultivate a bond with the ones you love. This
may mean reorganizing schedules or dropping activities. Commit to making family
relationships a top priority. Choose to fill
in the hours of busyness with periods of
significance. Spend time together.

—*Bob & Rosemary*

Go to page 874 for your next devotional reading.

sticks to the roof of its mouth;
the children beg for bread,
    but no one gives it to them.

5 Those who once ate delicacies
    are destitute in the streets.
Those nurtured in purple
    now lie on ash heaps.

6 The punishment of my people
    is greater than that of Sodom,
which was overthrown in a moment
    without a hand turned to help her.

7 Their princes were brighter than snow
    and whiter than milk,
their bodies more ruddy than rubies,
    their appearance like sapphires. *a*

8 But now they are blacker than soot;
    they are not recognized in the
        streets.
Their skin has shriveled on their
        bones;
    it has become as dry as a stick.

9 Those killed by the sword are better
        off
    than those who die of famine;
racked with hunger, they waste away
    for lack of food from the field.

10 With their own hands compassionate
        women
    have cooked their own children,
who became their food
    when my people were destroyed.

11 The LORD has given full vent to his
        wrath;
    he has poured out his fierce anger.
He kindled a fire in Zion
    that consumed her foundations.

12 The kings of the earth did not
        believe,
    nor did any of the world's people,
that enemies and foes could enter
    the gates of Jerusalem.

13 But it happened because of the sins
        of her prophets
    and the iniquities of her priests,
who shed within her
    the blood of the righteous.

14 Now they grope through the streets
    like men who are blind.
They are so defiled with blood
    that no one dares to touch their
        garments.

JUST BETWEEN
you **& *me***

Time Together

Take a moment to answer each of these
questions on your own. Then compare your
answers to your spouse's.

Yes   No   I spend some time each day
thinking about what I can do to
make my spouse's day better.

Yes   No   I call my spouse daily to ask how
the day is going.

Yes   No   I find myself looking for little extra things I can do for my spouse,
like I did when we were dating.

Yes   No   I listen to my spouse so that I can
better assess his or her personal
needs.

---

15 "Go away! You are unclean!" men cry
        to them.
    "Away! Away! Don't touch us!"
When they flee and wander about,
    people among the nations say,
    "They can stay here no longer."

16 The LORD himself has scattered them;
    he no longer watches over them.
The priests are shown no honor,
    the elders no favor.

17 Moreover, our eyes failed,
    looking in vain for help;
from our towers we watched
    for a nation that could not save us.

18 Men stalked us at every step,
    so we could not walk in our
        streets.
Our end was near, our days were
        numbered,
    for our end had come.

19 Our pursuers were swifter
    than eagles in the sky;
they chased us over the mountains
    and lay in wait for us in the desert.

20 The LORD's anointed, our very life
        breath,
    was caught in their traps.
We thought that under his shadow
    we would live among the nations.

a7 Or lapis lazuli

²¹Rejoice and be glad, O Daughter of
   Edom,
  you who live in the land of Uz.
  But to you also the cup will be
     passed;
  you will be drunk and stripped
     naked.

²²O Daughter of Zion, your
     punishment will end;
  he will not prolong your exile.
  But, O Daughter of Edom, he will
     punish your sin
  and expose your wickedness.

5 Remember, O LORD, what has
     happened to us;
  look, and see our disgrace.
²Our inheritance has been turned over
     to aliens,
  our homes to foreigners.
³We have become orphans and
     fatherless,
  our mothers like widows.
⁴We must buy the water we drink;
  our wood can be had only at a
     price.
⁵Those who pursue us are at our heels;
  we are weary and find no rest.
⁶We submitted to Egypt and Assyria

to get enough bread.
⁷Our fathers sinned and are no more,
  and we bear their punishment.
⁸Slaves rule over us,
  and there is none to free us from
     their hands.
⁹We get our bread at the risk of our
     lives
  because of the sword in the desert.
¹⁰Our skin is hot as an oven,
  feverish from hunger.
¹¹Women have been ravished in Zion,
  and virgins in the towns of Judah.
¹²Princes have been hung up by their
     hands;
  elders are shown no respect.
¹³Young men toil at the millstones;
  boys stagger under loads of wood.
¹⁴The elders are gone from the city
     gate;
  the young men have stopped their
     music.
¹⁵Joy is gone from our hearts;
  our dancing has turned to
     mourning.
¹⁶The crown has fallen from our head.
  Woe to us, for we have sinned!
¹⁷Because of this our hearts are faint,
  because of these things our eyes
     grow dim

Are We Preprogrammed?

Wednesday

LAMENTATIONS 5:7   When Jack's wife asked him why he frequently lost his temper when they had disagreements, Jack replied, "That's the way my father handled his problems; I never wanted to be like that, and yet I find myself responding in the very same way."

Are we doomed? Are we somehow genetically preprogrammed to handle the marriage relationship the same way our parents did? The Bible tells us that the sins of our fathers will be visited upon us, and we "bear their punishment."

We observe many attitudes and behaviors as we grow up. Some are incorrect or damaging behaviors. Observing misguided individuals or a dysfunctional marriage can have a significant impact on a young child. However, having an impact is very different

from being preprogrammed. Each of us chooses the way we will respond to life.

The Word of God offers us new direction for overcoming the mistakes of the past. The gentle guiding hand of the Holy Spirit helps us follow that direction. We are not prisoners of our past! The saving grace of Jesus Christ is able to rescue us from whatever we have experienced. We are not stopped from personal growth and happiness in our marriages by the marriages of our parents. But that new direction is a conscious choice we must make. Make a choice to step out of any generational pit you may be in, and look for the new direction God has to offer for your marriage.

—Bob & Rosemary

Go to page 884 for your next devotional reading.

¹⁸for Mount Zion, which lies desolate,
    with jackals prowling over it.

¹⁹You, O LORD, reign forever;
    your throne endures from
        generation to generation.
²⁰Why do you always forget us?

Why do you forsake us so long?
²¹Restore us to yourself, O LORD, that
        we may return;
    renew our days as of old
²²unless you have utterly rejected us
        and are angry with us beyond
        measure.

Ezekiel

In exile among his people, Ezekiel uses words, visions and "mini-dramas" as he communicates God's messages to his people. Even though the book was written when more than 3,000 Jews were in oppressive exile in Babylon, the main theme is hope. Although God has righteously judged his people, he hasn't forsaken them; he promises to remain with them in exile and return with them someday to their home. Through Ezekiel, God told the Jews to "know that I am the LORD" (6:14).

Wherever your marriage takes you—whether into dark times of uncertainty or blinding times of pain, God promises to be with us even in the most remote and unlikely places. He is faithful and will see you through.

The Living Creatures and the Glory of the LORD

1 In the^a thirtieth year, in the fourth month on the fifth day, while I was among the exiles by the Kebar River, the heavens were opened and I saw visions of God.

²On the fifth of the month—it was the fifth year of the exile of King Jehoiachin— ³the word of the LORD came to Ezekiel the priest, the son of Buzi,^b by the Kebar River in the land of the Babylonians.^c There the hand of the LORD was upon him.

⁴I looked, and I saw a windstorm coming out of the north—an immense cloud with flashing lightning and surrounded by brilliant light. The center of the fire looked like glowing metal, ⁵and in the fire was what looked like four living creatures. In appearance their form was that of a man, ⁶but each of them had four faces and four wings. ⁷Their legs were straight; their feet were like those of a calf and gleamed like burnished bronze. ⁸Under their wings on their four sides they had the hands of a man. All four of them had faces and wings, ⁹and their wings touched one another. Each one went straight ahead; they did not turn as they moved.

¹⁰Their faces looked like this: Each of the four had the face of a man, and on the right side each had the face of a lion, and on the left the face of an ox; each also had the face of an eagle. ¹¹Such were their

^a1 Or _my_ ^b3 Or *Ezekiel son of Buzi the priest* ^c3 Or *Chaldeans*

faces. Their wings were spread out upward; each had two wings, one touching the wing of another creature on either side, and two wings covering its body. [12]Each one went straight ahead. Wherever the spirit would go, they would go, without turning as they went. [13]The appearance of the living creatures was like burning coals of fire or like torches. Fire moved back and forth among the creatures; it was bright, and lightning flashed out of it. [14]The creatures sped back and forth like flashes of lightning.

[15]As I looked at the living creatures, I saw a wheel on the ground beside each creature with its four faces. [16]This was the appearance and structure of the wheels: They sparkled like chrysolite, and all four looked alike. Each appeared to be made like a wheel intersecting a wheel. [17]As they moved, they would go in any one of the four directions the creatures faced; the wheels did not turn about[a] as the creatures went. [18]Their rims were high and awesome, and all four rims were full of eyes all around.

[19]When the living creatures moved, the wheels beside them moved; and when the living creatures rose from the ground, the wheels also rose. [20]Wherever the spirit would go, they would go, and the wheels would rise along with them, because the spirit of the living creatures was in the wheels. [21]When the creatures moved, they also moved; when the creatures stood still, they also stood still; and when the creatures rose from the ground, the wheels rose along with them, because the spirit of the living creatures was in the wheels.

[22]Spread out above the heads of the living creatures was what looked like an expanse, sparkling like ice, and awesome. [23]Under the expanse their wings were stretched out one toward the other, and each had two wings covering its body. [24]When the creatures moved, I heard the sound of their wings, like the roar of rushing waters, like the voice of the Almighty,[b] like the tumult of an army. When they stood still, they lowered their wings.

[25]Then there came a voice from above the expanse over their heads as they stood with lowered wings. [26]Above the expanse over their heads was what looked like a throne of sapphire,[c] and high above on the throne was a figure like that of a man. [27]I saw that from what appeared to be his waist up he looked like glowing metal, as if full of fire, and that from there down he looked like fire; and brilliant light surrounded him. [28]Like the appearance of a rainbow in the clouds on a rainy day, so was the radiance around him.

This was the appearance of the likeness of the glory of the LORD. When I saw it, I fell facedown, and I heard the voice of one speaking.

Ezekiel's Call

2 He said to me, "Son of man, stand up on your feet and I will speak to you." [2]As he spoke, the Spirit came into me and raised me to my feet, and I heard him speaking to me.

[3]He said: "Son of man, I am sending you to the Israelites, to a rebellious nation that has rebelled against me; they and their fathers have been in revolt against me to this very day. [4]The people to whom I am sending you are obstinate and stubborn. Say to them, 'This is what the Sovereign LORD says.' [5]And whether they listen or fail to listen—for they are a rebellious house—they will know that a prophet has been among them. [6]And you, son of man, do not be afraid of them or their words. Do not be afraid, though briers and thorns are all around you and you live among scorpions. Do not be afraid of what they say or terrified by them, though they are a rebellious house. [7]You must speak my words to them, whether they listen or fail to listen, for they are rebellious. [8]But you, son of man, listen to what I say to you. Do not rebel like that rebellious house; open your mouth and eat what I give you."

[9]Then I looked, and I saw a hand stretched out to me. In it was a scroll, [10]which he unrolled before me. On both sides of it were written words of lament and mourning and woe.

3 And he said to me, "Son of man, eat what is before you, eat this scroll; then go and speak to the house of Israel." [2]So I opened my mouth, and he gave me the scroll to eat.

[a]17 Or *aside*   [b]24 Hebrew *Shaddai*   [c]26 Or *lapis lazuli*

³Then he said to me, "Son of man, eat this scroll I am giving you and fill your stomach with it." So I ate it, and it tasted as sweet as honey in my mouth.

⁴He then said to me: "Son of man, go now to the house of Israel and speak my words to them. ⁵You are not being sent to a people of obscure speech and difficult language, but to the house of Israel— ⁶not to many peoples of obscure speech and difficult language, whose words you cannot understand. Surely if I had sent you to them, they would have listened to you. ⁷But the house of Israel is not willing to listen to you because they are not willing to listen to me, for the whole house of Israel is hardened and obstinate. ⁸But I will make you as unyielding and hardened as they are. ⁹I will make your forehead like the hardest stone, harder than flint. Do not be afraid of them or terrified by them, though they are a rebellious house."

¹⁰And he said to me, "Son of man, listen carefully and take to heart all the words I speak to you. ¹¹Go now to your countrymen in exile and speak to them. Say to them, 'This is what the Sovereign LORD says,' whether they listen or fail to listen."

¹²Then the Spirit lifted me up, and I heard behind me a loud rumbling sound—May the glory of the LORD be praised in his dwelling place!— ¹³the sound of the wings of the living creatures brushing against each other and the sound of the wheels beside them, a loud rumbling sound. ¹⁴The Spirit then lifted me up and took me away, and I went in bitterness and in the anger of my spirit, with the strong hand of the LORD upon me. ¹⁵I came to the exiles who lived at Tel Abib near the Kebar River. And there, where they were living, I sat among them for seven days—overwhelmed.

Warning to Israel

¹⁶At the end of seven days the word of the LORD came to me: ¹⁷"Son of man, I have made you a watchman for the house of Israel; so hear the word I speak and give them warning from me. ¹⁸When I say to a wicked man, 'You will surely die,' and you do not warn him or speak out to dissuade him from his evil ways in order to save his life, that wicked man will die for[a] his sin, and I will hold you accountable for his blood. ¹⁹But if you do warn the wicked man and he does not turn from his wickedness or from his evil ways, he will die for his sin; but you will have saved yourself.

²⁰"Again, when a righteous man turns from his righteousness and does evil, and I put a stumbling block before him, he will die. Since you did not warn him, he will die for his sin. The righteous things he did will not be remembered, and I will hold you accountable for his blood. ²¹But if you do warn the righteous man not to sin and he does not sin, he will surely live because he took warning, and you will have saved yourself."

²²The hand of the LORD was upon me there, and he said to me, "Get up and go out to the plain, and there I will speak to you." ²³So I got up and went out to the plain. And the glory of the LORD was standing there, like the glory I had seen by the Kebar River, and I fell facedown.

²⁴Then the Spirit came into me and raised me to my feet. He spoke to me and said: "Go, shut yourself inside your house. ²⁵And you, son of man, they will tie with ropes; you will be bound so that you cannot go out among the people. ²⁶I will make your tongue stick to the roof of your mouth so that you will be silent and unable to rebuke them, though they are a rebellious house. ²⁷But when I speak to you, I will open your mouth and you shall say to them, 'This is what the Sovereign LORD says.' Whoever will listen let him listen, and whoever will refuse let him refuse; for they are a rebellious house.

Siege of Jerusalem Symbolized

4 "Now, son of man, take a clay tablet, put it in front of you and draw the city of Jerusalem on it. ²Then lay siege to it: Erect siege works against it, build a ramp up to it, set up camps against it and put battering rams around it. ³Then take an iron pan, place it as an iron wall between you and the city and turn your face toward it. It will be under siege, and you shall besiege it. This will be a sign to the house of Israel.

[a]18 Or *in*; also in verses 19 and 20

⁴"Then lie on your left side and put the sin of the house of Israel upon yourself.ᵃ You are to bear their sin for the number of days you lie on your side. ⁵I have assigned you the same number of days as the years of their sin. So for 390 days you will bear the sin of the house of Israel.

⁶"After you have finished this, lie down again, this time on your right side, and bear the sin of the house of Judah. I have assigned you 40 days, a day for each year. ⁷Turn your face toward the siege of Jerusalem and with bared arm prophesy against her. ⁸I will tie you up with ropes so that you cannot turn from one side to the other until you have finished the days of your siege.

⁹"Take wheat and barley, beans and lentils, millet and spelt; put them in a storage jar and use them to make bread for yourself. You are to eat it during the 390 days you lie on your side. ¹⁰Weigh out twenty shekelsᵇ of food to eat each day and eat it at set times. ¹¹Also measure out a sixth of a hinᶜ of water and drink it at set times. ¹²Eat the food as you would a barley cake; bake it in the sight of the people, using human excrement for fuel." ¹³The LORD said, "In this way the people of Israel will eat defiled food among the nations where I will drive them."

¹⁴Then I said, "Not so, Sovereign LORD! I have never defiled myself. From my youth until now I have never eaten anything found dead or torn by wild animals. No unclean meat has ever entered my mouth."

¹⁵"Very well," he said, "I will let you bake your bread over cow manure instead of human excrement."

¹⁶He then said to me: "Son of man, I will cut off the supply of food in Jerusalem. The people will eat rationed food in anxiety and drink rationed water in despair, ¹⁷for food and water will be scarce. They will be appalled at the sight of each other and will waste away because ofᵈ their sin.

5 "Now, son of man, take a sharp sword and use it as a barber's razor to shave your head and your beard. Then take a set of scales and divide up the hair. ²When the days of your siege come to an end, burn a third of the hair with fire inside the city. Take a third and strike it with the sword all around the city. And

scatter a third to the wind. For I will pursue them with drawn sword. ³But take a few strands of hair and tuck them away in the folds of your garment. ⁴Again, take a few of these and throw them into the fire and burn them up. A fire will spread from there to the whole house of Israel.

⁵"This is what the Sovereign LORD says: This is Jerusalem, which I have set in the center of the nations, with countries all around her. ⁶Yet in her wickedness she has rebelled against my laws and decrees more than the nations and countries around her. She has rejected my laws and has not followed my decrees.

⁷"Therefore this is what the Sovereign LORD says: You have been more unruly than the nations around you and have not followed my decrees or kept my laws. You have not evenᵉ conformed to the standards of the nations around you.

⁸"Therefore this is what the Sovereign LORD says: I myself am against you, Jerusalem, and I will inflict punishment on you in the sight of the nations. ⁹Because of all your detestable idols, I will do to you what I have never done before and will never do again. ¹⁰Therefore in your midst fathers will eat their children, and children will eat their fathers. I will inflict punishment on you and will scatter all your survivors to the winds. ¹¹Therefore as surely as I live, declares the Sovereign LORD, because you have defiled my sanctuary with all your vile images and detestable practices, I myself will withdraw my favor; I will not look on you with pity or spare you. ¹²A third of your people will die of the plague or perish by famine inside you; a third will fall by the sword outside your walls; and a third I will scatter to the winds and pursue with drawn sword.

¹³"Then my anger will cease and my wrath against them will subside, and I will be avenged. And when I have spent my wrath upon them, they will know that I the LORD have spoken in my zeal.

¹⁴"I will make you a ruin and a reproach among the nations around you, in the sight of all who pass by. ¹⁵You will be

ᵃ4 Or your side   ᵇ10 That is, about 8 ounces (about 0.2 kilogram)   ᶜ11 That is, about 2/3 quart (about 0.6 liter)   ᵈ17 Or away in ᵉ7 Most Hebrew manuscripts; some Hebrew manuscripts and Syriac You have a reproach and a taunt, a warning and an object of horror to the nations around you when I inflict punishment on you in anger and in wrath and with stinging rebuke. I the LORD have spoken. ¹⁶When I shoot at you with my deadly and destructive arrows of famine, I will shoot to destroy you. I will bring more and more famine upon you and cut off your supply of food. ¹⁷I will send famine and wild beasts against you, and they will leave you childless. Plague and bloodshed will sweep through you, and I will bring the sword against you. I the LORD have spoken."

A Prophecy Against the Mountains of Israel

6 The word of the LORD came to me: ²"Son of man, set your face against the mountains of Israel; prophesy against them ³and say: 'O mountains of Israel, hear the word of the Sovereign LORD. This is what the Sovereign LORD says to the mountains and hills, to the ravines and valleys: I am about to bring a sword against you, and I will destroy your high places. ⁴Your altars will be demolished and your incense altars will be smashed; and I will slay your people in front of your idols. ⁵I will lay the dead bodies of the Israelites in front of their idols, and I will scatter your bones around your altars. ⁶Wherever you live, the towns will be laid waste and the high places demolished, so that your altars will be laid waste and devastated, your idols smashed and ruined, your incense altars broken down, and what you have made wiped out. ⁷Your people will fall slain among you, and you will know that I am the LORD.

⁸" 'But I will spare some, for some of you will escape the sword when you are scattered among the lands and nations. ⁹Then in the nations where they have been carried captive, those who escape will remember me—how I have been grieved by their adulterous hearts, which have turned away from me, and by their eyes, which have lusted after their idols. They will loathe themselves for the evil they have done and for all their detestable practices. ¹⁰And they will know that I am the LORD; I did not threaten in vain to bring this calamity on them.

¹¹" 'This is what the Sovereign LORD says: Strike your hands together and stamp your feet and cry out "Alas!" because of all the wicked and detestable practices of the house of Israel, for they will fall by the sword, famine and plague. ¹²He that is far away will die of the plague, and he that is near will fall by the sword, and he that survives and is spared will die of famine. So will I spend my wrath upon them. ¹³And they will know that I am the LORD, when their people lie slain among their idols around their altars, on every high hill and on all the mountaintops, under every spreading tree and every leafy oak—places where they offered fragrant incense to all their idols. ¹⁴And I will stretch out my hand against them and make the land a desolate waste from the desert to Diblah[a]—wherever they live. Then they will know that I am the LORD.' "

The End Has Come

7 The word of the LORD came to me: ²"Son of man, this is what the Sovereign LORD says to the land of Israel: The end! The end has come upon the four corners of the land. ³The end is now upon you and I will unleash my anger against you. I will judge you according to your conduct and repay you for all your detestable practices. ⁴I will not look on you with pity or spare you; I will surely repay you for your conduct and the detestable practices among you. Then you will know that I am the LORD.

⁵"This is what the Sovereign LORD says: Disaster! An unheard-of[b] disaster is coming. ⁶The end has come! The end has come! It has roused itself against you. It has come! ⁷Doom has come upon you—you who dwell in the land. The time has come, the day is near; there is panic, not joy, upon the mountains. ⁸I am about to pour out my wrath on you and spend my anger against you; I will judge you according to your conduct and repay you for all your detestable practices. ⁹I will not look on you with pity or spare you; I will repay you in accordance with your conduct and the detestable practices among you. Then

---

[a]14 Most Hebrew manuscripts; a few Hebrew manuscripts *Riblah*   [b]5 Most Hebrew manuscripts; some Hebrew manuscripts and Syriac *Disaster after*

you will know that it is I the LORD who strikes the blow.

¹⁰"The day is here! It has come! Doom has burst forth, the rod has budded, arrogance has blossomed! ¹¹Violence has grown into[a] a rod to punish wickedness; none of the people will be left, none of that crowd—no wealth, nothing of value. ¹²The time has come, the day has arrived. Let not the buyer rejoice nor the seller grieve, for wrath is upon the whole crowd. ¹³The seller will not recover the land he has sold as long as both of them live, for the vision concerning the whole crowd will not be reversed. Because of their sins, not one of them will preserve his life. ¹⁴Though they blow the trumpet and get everything ready, no one will go into battle, for my wrath is upon the whole crowd.

¹⁵"Outside is the sword, inside are plague and famine; those in the country will die by the sword, and those in the city will be devoured by famine and plague. ¹⁶All who survive and escape will be in the mountains, moaning like doves of the valleys, each because of his sins. ¹⁷Every hand will go limp, and every knee will become as weak as water. ¹⁸They will put on sackcloth and be clothed with terror. Their faces will be covered with shame and their heads will be shaved. ¹⁹They will throw their silver into the streets, and their gold will be an unclean thing. Their silver and gold will not be able to save them in the day of the LORD's wrath. They will not satisfy their hunger or fill their stomachs with it, for it has made them stumble into sin. ²⁰They were proud of their beautiful jewelry and used it to make their detestable idols and vile images. Therefore I will turn these into an unclean thing for them. ²¹I will hand it all over as plunder to foreigners and as loot to the wicked of the earth, and they will defile it. ²²I will turn my face away from them, and they will desecrate my treasured place; robbers will enter it and desecrate it.

²³"Prepare chains, because the land is full of bloodshed and the city is full of violence. ²⁴I will bring the most wicked of the nations to take possession of their houses; I will put an end to the pride of the mighty, and their sanctuaries will be desecrated. ²⁵When terror comes, they will seek peace, but there will be none. ²⁶Calamity upon calamity will come, and rumor upon rumor. They will try to get a vision from the prophet; the teaching of the law by the priest will be lost, as will the counsel of the elders. ²⁷The king will mourn, the prince will be clothed with despair, and the hands of the people of the land will tremble. I will deal with them according to their conduct, and by their own standards I will judge them. Then they will know that I am the LORD."

Idolatry in the Temple

8 In the sixth year, in the sixth month on the fifth day, while I was sitting in my house and the elders of Judah were sitting before me, the hand of the Sovereign LORD came upon me there. ²I looked, and I saw a figure like that of a man.[b] From what appeared to be his waist down he was like fire, and from there up his appearance was as bright as glowing metal. ³He stretched out what looked like a hand and took me by the hair of my head. The Spirit lifted me up between earth and heaven and in visions of God he took me to Jerusalem, to the entrance to the north gate of the inner court, where the idol that provokes to jealousy stood. ⁴And there before me was the glory of the God of Israel, as in the vision I had seen in the plain.

⁵Then he said to me, "Son of man, look toward the north." So I looked, and in the entrance north of the gate of the altar I saw this idol of jealousy.

⁶And he said to me, "Son of man, do you see what they are doing—the utterly detestable things the house of Israel is doing here, things that will drive me far from my sanctuary? But you will see things that are even more detestable."

⁷Then he brought me to the entrance to the court. I looked, and I saw a hole in the wall. ⁸He said to me, "Son of man, now dig into the wall." So I dug into the wall and saw a doorway there.

⁹And he said to me, "Go in and see the wicked and detestable things they are doing here." ¹⁰So I went in and looked, and I saw portrayed all over the walls all kinds of crawling things and detestable animals

a11 Or The violent one has become   *b2 Or saw a fiery figure* and all the idols of the house of Israel. [11]In front of them stood seventy elders of the house of Israel, and Jaazaniah son of Shaphan was standing among them. Each had a censer in his hand, and a fragrant cloud of incense was rising.

[12]He said to me, "Son of man, have you seen what the elders of the house of Israel are doing in the darkness, each at the shrine of his own idol? They say, 'The LORD does not see us; the LORD has forsaken the land.' " [13]Again, he said, "You will see them doing things that are even more detestable."

[14]Then he brought me to the entrance to the north gate of the house of the LORD, and I saw women sitting there, mourning for Tammuz. [15]He said to me, "Do you see this, son of man? You will see things that are even more detestable than this."

[16]He then brought me into the inner court of the house of the LORD, and there at the entrance to the temple, between the portico and the altar, were about twenty-five men. With their backs toward the temple of the LORD and their faces toward the east, they were bowing down to the sun in the east.

[17]He said to me, "Have you seen this, son of man? Is it a trivial matter for the house of Judah to do the detestable things they are doing here? Must they also fill the land with violence and continually provoke me to anger? Look at them putting the branch to their nose! [18]Therefore I will deal with them in anger; I will not look on them with pity or spare them. Although they shout in my ears, I will not listen to them."

Idolaters Killed

9 Then I heard him call out in a loud voice, "Bring the guards of the city here, each with a weapon in his hand." [2]And I saw six men coming from the direction of the upper gate, which faces north, each with a deadly weapon in his hand. With them was a man clothed in linen who had a writing kit at his side. They came in and stood beside the bronze altar.

[3]Now the glory of the God of Israel went up from above the cherubim, where it had been, and moved to the threshold of the temple. Then the LORD called to the man clothed in linen who had the writing kit at his side [4]and said to him, "Go throughout the city of Jerusalem and put a mark on the foreheads of those who grieve and lament over all the detestable things that are done in it."

[5]As I listened, he said to the others, "Follow him through the city and kill, without showing pity or compassion. [6]Slaughter old men, young men and maidens, women and children, but do not touch anyone who has the mark. Begin at my sanctuary." So they began with the elders who were in front of the temple.

[7]Then he said to them, "Defile the temple and fill the courts with the slain. Go!" So they went out and began killing throughout the city. [8]While they were killing and I was left alone, I fell facedown, crying out, "Ah, Sovereign LORD! Are you going to destroy the entire remnant of Israel in this outpouring of your wrath on Jerusalem?"

[9]He answered me, "The sin of the house of Israel and Judah is exceedingly great; the land is full of bloodshed and the city is full of injustice. They say, 'The LORD has forsaken the land; the LORD does not see.' [10]So I will not look on them with pity or spare them, but I will bring down on their own heads what they have done."

[11]Then the man in linen with the writing kit at his side brought back word, saying, "I have done as you commanded."

The Glory Departs From the Temple

10 I looked, and I saw the likeness of a throne of sapphire[a] above the expanse that was over the heads of the cherubim. [2]The LORD said to the man clothed in linen, "Go in among the wheels beneath the cherubim. Fill your hands with burning coals from among the cherubim and scatter them over the city." And as I watched, he went in.

[3]Now the cherubim were standing on the south side of the temple when the man went in, and a cloud filled the inner court. [4]Then the glory of the LORD rose from above the cherubim and moved to the threshold of the temple. The cloud filled the temple, and the court was full of

---

[a]1 Or *lapis lazuli*

the radiance of the glory of the LORD. ⁵The sound of the wings of the cherubim could be heard as far away as the outer court, like the voice of God Almighty*a* when he speaks.

⁶When the LORD commanded the man in linen, "Take fire from among the wheels, from among the cherubim," the man went in and stood beside a wheel. ⁷Then one of the cherubim reached out his hand to the fire that was among them. He took up some of it and put it into the hands of the man in linen, who took it and went out. ⁸(Under the wings of the cherubim could be seen what looked like the hands of a man.)

⁹I looked, and I saw beside the cherubim four wheels, one beside each of the cherubim; the wheels sparkled like chrysolite. ¹⁰As for their appearance, the four of them looked alike; each was like a wheel intersecting a wheel. ¹¹As they moved, they would go in any one of the four directions the cherubim faced; the wheels did not turn about*b* as the cherubim went. The cherubim went in whatever direction the head faced, without turning as they went. ¹²Their entire bodies, including their backs, their hands and their wings, were completely full of eyes, as were their four wheels. ¹³I heard the wheels being called "the whirling wheels." ¹⁴Each of the cherubim had four faces: One face was that of a cherub, the second the face of a man, the third the face of a lion, and the fourth the face of an eagle.

¹⁵Then the cherubim rose upward. These were the living creatures I had seen by the Kebar River. ¹⁶When the cherubim moved, the wheels beside them moved; and when the cherubim spread their wings to rise from the ground, the wheels did not leave their side. ¹⁷When the cherubim stood still, they also stood still; and when the cherubim rose, they rose with them, because the spirit of the living creatures was in them.

¹⁸Then the glory of the LORD departed from over the threshold of the temple and stopped above the cherubim. ¹⁹While I watched, the cherubim spread their wings and rose from the ground, and as they went, the wheels went with them. They stopped at the entrance to the east gate of the LORD's house, and the glory of the God of Israel was above them.

²⁰These were the living creatures I had seen beneath the God of Israel by the Kebar River, and I realized that they were cherubim. ²¹Each had four faces and four wings, and under their wings was what looked like the hands of a man. ²²Their faces had the same appearance as those I had seen by the Kebar River. Each one went straight ahead.

Judgment on Israel's Leaders

11 Then the Spirit lifted me up and brought me to the gate of the house of the LORD that faces east. There at the entrance to the gate were twenty-five men, and I saw among them Jaazaniah son of Azzur and Pelatiah son of Benaiah, leaders of the people. ²The LORD said to me, "Son of man, these are the men who are plotting evil and giving wicked advice in this city. ³They say, 'Will it not soon be time to build houses?*c* This city is a cooking pot, and we are the meat.' ⁴Therefore prophesy against them; prophesy, son of man."

⁵Then the Spirit of the LORD came upon me, and he told me to say: "This is what the LORD says: That is what you are saying, O house of Israel, but I know what is going through your mind. ⁶You have killed many people in this city and filled its streets with the dead.

⁷"Therefore this is what the Sovereign LORD says: The bodies you have thrown there are the meat and this city is the pot, but I will drive you out of it. ⁸You fear the sword, and the sword is what I will bring against you, declares the Sovereign LORD. ⁹I will drive you out of the city and hand you over to foreigners and inflict punishment on you. ¹⁰You will fall by the sword, and I will execute judgment on you at the borders of Israel. Then you will know that I am the LORD. ¹¹This city will not be a pot for you, nor will you be the meat in it; I will execute judgment on you at the borders of Israel. ¹²And you will know that I am the LORD, for you have not followed my decrees or kept my laws but have conformed to the standards of the nations around you."

¹³Now as I was prophesying, Pelatiah son of Benaiah died. Then I fell facedown

---

a5 Hebrew *El-Shaddai*   *b11* Or *aside*   *c3* Or *This is not the time to build houses.*

and cried out in a loud voice, "Ah, Sovereign LORD! Will you completely destroy the remnant of Israel?"

[14]The word of the LORD came to me: [15]"Son of man, your brothers—your brothers who are your blood relatives[a] and the whole house of Israel—are those of whom the people of Jerusalem have said, 'They are[b] far away from the LORD; this land was given to us as our possession.'

Promised Return of Israel

[16]"Therefore say: 'This is what the Sovereign LORD says: Although I sent them far away among the nations and scattered them among the countries, yet for a little while I have been a sanctuary for them in the countries where they have gone.'

[17]"Therefore say: 'This is what the Sovereign LORD says: I will gather you from the nations and bring you back from the countries where you have been scattered, and I will give you back the land of Israel again.'

[18]"They will return to it and remove all its vile images and detestable idols. [19]I will give them an undivided heart and put a new spirit in them; I will remove from them their heart of stone and give them a heart of flesh. [20]Then they will follow my decrees and be careful to keep my laws. They will be my people, and I will be their God. [21]But as for those whose hearts are devoted to their 'vile images and detestable idols, I will bring down on their own heads what they have done, declares the Sovereign LORD."

[22]Then the cherubim, with the wheels beside them, spread their wings, and the glory of the God of Israel was above them. [23]The glory of the LORD went up from within the city and stopped above the mountain east of it. [24]The Spirit lifted me up and brought me to the exiles in Babylonia[c] in the vision given by the Spirit of God.

Then the vision I had seen went up from me, [25]and I told the exiles everything the LORD had shown me.

The Exile Symbolized

12 The word of the LORD came to me: [2]"Son of man, you are living among a rebellious people. They have eyes to see but do not see and ears to hear but do not hear, for they are a rebellious people.

[3]"Therefore, son of man, pack your belongings for exile and in the daytime, as they watch, set out and go from where you are to another place. Perhaps they will understand, though they are a rebellious house. [4]During the daytime, while they watch, bring out your belongings packed for exile. Then in the evening, while they are watching, go out like those who go into exile. [5]While they watch, dig

---

[a]15 Or *are in exile with you* (see Septuagint and Syriac)   [b]15 Or *those to whom the people of Jerusalem have said, 'Stay*   [c]24 Or *Chaldea*

Heart of Stone

Thursday

EZEKIEL 11:19 The human heart is a hard-working marvel. It beats 75 times a minute, 40 million times a year, or 2½ billion times in a lifetime of 70 years. At each beat, the average adult discharges about 4 ounces of blood. This amounts to 3,000 gallons a day or 650,000 gallons a year—enough to fill more than 81 car tanks of 8,000 gallons each. The heart does enough work in one hour to lift a 150-pound man to the top of a three-story building, and it exerts enough power in 70 years to lift the largest battleship completely out of the water.

In spite of the miraculous power of this vital human organ and what it represents in the human spirit, our heart—as this verse points out—can become divided and even turn to stone. The cause? It's not cholesterol or high blood pressure. It's "vile images and detestable idols" that cause our hearts to harden (verse 21). So, we ask you, what images and idols is your heart given to? Is there something that has hardened your heart?

—*Les & Leslie*

Go to page 885 for your next devotional reading.

through the wall and take your belongings out through it. ⁶Put them on your shoulder as they are watching and carry them out at dusk. Cover your face so that you cannot see the land, for I have made you a sign to the house of Israel."

⁷So I did as I was commanded. During the day I brought out my things packed for exile. Then in the evening I dug through the wall with my hands. I took my belongings out at dusk, carrying them on my shoulders while they watched.

⁸In the morning the word of the LORD came to me: ⁹"Son of man, did not that rebellious house of Israel ask you, 'What are you doing?'

¹⁰"Say to them, 'This is what the Sovereign LORD says: This oracle concerns the prince in Jerusalem and the whole house of Israel who are there.' ¹¹Say to them, 'I am a sign to you.'

"As I have done, so it will be done to them. They will go into exile as captives.

¹²"The prince among them will put his things on his shoulder at dusk and leave, and a hole will be dug in the wall for him to go through. He will cover his face so that he cannot see the land. ¹³I will spread my net for him, and he will be caught in my snare; I will bring him to Babylonia,

the land of the Chaldeans, but he will not see it, and there he will die. ¹⁴I will scatter to the winds all those around him—his staff and all his troops—and I will pursue them with drawn sword.

¹⁵"They will know that I am the LORD, when I disperse them among the nations and scatter them through the countries. ¹⁶But I will spare a few of them from the sword, famine and plague, so that in the nations where they go they may acknowledge all their detestable practices. Then they will know that I am the LORD."

¹⁷The word of the LORD came to me: ¹⁸"Son of man, tremble as you eat your food, and shudder in fear as you drink your water. ¹⁹Say to the people of the land: 'This is what the Sovereign LORD says about those living in Jerusalem and in the land of Israel: They will eat their food in anxiety and drink their water in despair, for their land will be stripped of everything in it because of the violence of all who live there. ²⁰The inhabited towns will be laid waste and the land will be desolate. Then you will know that I am the LORD.' "

²¹The word of the LORD came to me: ²²"Son of man, what is this proverb you have in the land of Israel: 'The days go by

Stop, Look and Listen

Friday

EZEKIEL 12:2 City traffic drives us crazy . . . like the time we were driving in six lanes of traffic with cars weaving in and out ahead of us. Caught in the fast lane, we missed our exit. How frustrating! The same thing happens in our life. When children come along and our careers take off, the lanes of our life multiply—we're partners, parents, professionals, friends, church members, in-laws and so on.

It's easy to get "caught in the fast lane" and miss each other. Sometimes in our relationship, Dave and I fall into the same camp of people Ezekiel described: having eyes but not seeing and ears but not hearing. At times it's like we both wear blinders and can't see the other's non-verbal messages such as, "I'm discouraged; a hug would really feel good right now."

Can you identify with us? Most of us desire an intimate, open and loving relationship with our spouse, but it's hard work. We have to stop, look and listen. From time to time we try to find a "rest area" and take a break. Then we can see the signs around us like each other's non-verbal communication. A major part of the message we send is communicated in the shrugs and glares, but also the tender glances.

Next we need to listen for the total message . . . especially our tone of voice. Words are only a small part of the total message. Think about whether you are getting your spouse's message, and what kind of message you are sending.

—Dave & Claudia

Go to page 900 for your next devotional reading.

and every vision comes to nothing'? ²³Say to them, 'This is what the Sovereign LORD says: I am going to put an end to this proverb, and they will no longer quote it in Israel.' Say to them, 'The days are near when every vision will be fulfilled. ²⁴For there will be no more false visions or flattering divinations among the people of Israel. ²⁵But I the LORD will speak what I will, and it shall be fulfilled without delay. For in your days, you rebellious house, I will fulfill whatever I say, declares the Sovereign LORD.' "

²⁶The word of the LORD came to me: ²⁷"Son of man, the house of Israel is saying, 'The vision he sees is for many years from now, and he prophesies about the distant future.'

²⁸"Therefore say to them, 'This is what the Sovereign LORD says: None of my words will be delayed any longer; whatever I say will be fulfilled, declares the Sovereign LORD.' "

False Prophets Condemned

13 The word of the LORD came to me: ²"Son of man, prophesy against the prophets of Israel who are now prophesying. Say to those who prophesy out of their own imagination: 'Hear the word of the LORD! ³This is what the Sovereign LORD says: Woe to the foolish[a] prophets who follow their own spirit and have seen nothing! ⁴Your prophets, O Israel, are like jackals among ruins. ⁵You have not gone up to the breaks in the wall to repair it for the house of Israel so that it will stand firm in the battle on the day of the LORD. ⁶Their visions are false and their divinations a lie. They say, "The LORD declares," when the LORD has not sent them; yet they expect their words to be fulfilled. ⁷Have you not seen false visions and uttered lying divinations when you say, "The LORD declares," though I have not spoken?

⁸" 'Therefore this is what the Sovereign LORD says: Because of your false words and lying visions, I am against you, declares the Sovereign LORD. ⁹My hand will be against the prophets who see false visions and utter lying divinations. They will not belong to the council of my people or be listed in the records of the house of Israel, nor will they enter the land of Israel. Then you will know that I am the Sovereign LORD.

¹⁰" 'Because they lead my people astray, saying, "Peace," when there is no peace, and because, when a flimsy wall is built, they cover it with whitewash, ¹¹therefore tell those who cover it with whitewash that it is going to fall. Rain will come in torrents, and I will send hailstones hurtling down, and violent winds will burst forth. ¹²When the wall collapses, will people not ask you, "Where is the whitewash you covered it with?"

¹³" 'Therefore this is what the Sovereign LORD says: In my wrath I will unleash a violent wind, and in my anger hailstones and torrents of rain will fall with destructive fury. ¹⁴I will tear down the wall you have covered with whitewash and will level it to the ground so that its foundation will be laid bare. When it[b] falls, you will be destroyed in it; and you will know that I am the LORD. ¹⁵So I will spend my wrath against the wall and against those who covered it with whitewash. I will say to you, "The wall is gone and so are those who whitewashed it, ¹⁶those prophets of Israel who prophesied to Jerusalem and saw visions of peace for her when there was no peace, declares the Sovereign LORD." '

¹⁷"Now, son of man, set your face against the daughters of your people who prophesy out of their own imagination. Prophesy against them ¹⁸and say, 'This is what the Sovereign LORD says: Woe to the women who sew magic charms on all their wrists and make veils of various lengths for their heads in order to ensnare people. Will you ensnare the lives of my people but preserve your own? ¹⁹You have profaned me among my people for a few handfuls of barley and scraps of bread. By lying to my people, who listen to lies, you have killed those who should not have died and have spared those who should not live.

²⁰" 'Therefore this is what the Sovereign LORD says: I am against your magic charms with which you ensnare people like birds and I will tear them from your arms; I will set free the people that you ensnare like birds. ²¹I will tear off your veils and save my people from your

---

a3 Or *wicked*   *b14* Or *the city*

hands, and they will no longer fall prey to your power. Then you will know that I am the LORD. ²²Because you disheartened the righteous with your lies, when I had brought them no grief, and because you encouraged the wicked not to turn from their evil ways and so save their lives, ²³therefore you will no longer see false visions or practice divination. I will save my people from your hands. And then you will know that I am the LORD.' "

Idolaters Condemned

14 Some of the elders of Israel came to me and sat down in front of me. ²Then the word of the LORD came to me: ³"Son of man, these men have set up idols in their hearts and put wicked stumbling blocks before their faces. Should I let them inquire of me at all? ⁴Therefore speak to them and tell them, 'This is what the Sovereign LORD says: When any Israelite sets up idols in his heart and puts a wicked stumbling block before his face and then goes to a prophet, I the LORD will answer him myself in keeping with his great idolatry. ⁵I will do this to recapture the hearts of the people of Israel, who have all deserted me for their idols.'

⁶"Therefore say to the house of Israel, 'This is what the Sovereign LORD says: Repent! Turn from your idols and renounce all your detestable practices!

⁷" 'When any Israelite or any alien living in Israel separates himself from me and sets up idols in his heart and puts a wicked stumbling block before his face and then goes to a prophet to inquire of me, I the LORD will answer him myself. ⁸I will set my face against that man and make him an example and a byword. I will cut him off from my people. Then you will know that I am the LORD.

⁹" 'And if the prophet is enticed to utter a prophecy, I the LORD have enticed that prophet, and I will stretch out my hand against him and destroy him from among my people Israel. ¹⁰They will bear their guilt—the prophet will be as guilty as the one who consults him. ¹¹Then the people of Israel will no longer stray from me, nor will they defile themselves anymore with all their sins. They will be my people, and I will be their God, declares the Sovereign LORD.' "

Judgment Inescapable

¹²The word of the LORD came to me: ¹³"Son of man, if a country sins against me by being unfaithful and I stretch out my hand against it to cut off its food supply and send famine upon it and kill its men and their animals, ¹⁴even if these three men—Noah, Daniel[a] and Job—were in it, they could save only themselves by their righteousness, declares the Sovereign LORD.

¹⁵"Or if I send wild beasts through that country and they leave it childless and it becomes desolate so that no one can pass through it because of the beasts, ¹⁶as surely as I live, declares the Sovereign LORD, even if these three men were in it, they could not save their own sons or daughters. They alone would be saved, but the land would be desolate.

¹⁷"Or if I bring a sword against that country and say, 'Let the sword pass throughout the land,' and I kill its men and their animals, ¹⁸as surely as I live, declares the Sovereign LORD, even if these three men were in it, they could not save their own sons or daughters. They alone would be saved.

¹⁹"Or if I send a plague into that land and pour out my wrath upon it through bloodshed, killing its men and their animals, ²⁰as surely as I live, declares the Sovereign LORD, even if Noah, Daniel and Job were in it, they could save neither son nor daughter. They would save only themselves by their righteousness.

²¹"For this is what the Sovereign LORD says: How much worse will it be when I send against Jerusalem my four dreadful judgments—sword and famine and wild beasts and plague—to kill its men and their animals! ²²Yet there will be some survivors—sons and daughters who will be brought out of it. They will come to you, and when you see their conduct and their actions, you will be consoled regarding the disaster I have brought upon Jerusalem—every disaster I have brought upon it. ²³You will be consoled when you see their conduct and their actions, for you will know that I have done nothing in

---

*a*14 Or *Danel*; the Hebrew spelling may suggest a person other than the prophet Daniel; also in verse 20.

it without cause, declares the Sovereign LORD."

Jerusalem, A Useless Vine

15 The word of the LORD came to me: ²"Son of man, how is the wood of a vine better than that of a branch on any of the trees in the forest? ³Is wood ever taken from it to make anything useful? Do they make pegs from it to hang things on? ⁴And after it is thrown on the fire as fuel and the fire burns both ends and chars the middle, is it then useful for anything? ⁵If it was not useful for anything when it was whole, how much less can it be made into something useful when the fire has burned it and it is charred?

⁶"Therefore this is what the Sovereign LORD says: As I have given the wood of the vine among the trees of the forest as fuel for the fire, so will I treat the people living in Jerusalem. ⁷I will set my face against them. Although they have come out of the fire, the fire will yet consume them. And when I set my face against them, you will know that I am the LORD. ⁸I will make the land desolate because they have been unfaithful, declares the Sovereign LORD."

An Allegory of Unfaithful Jerusalem

16 The word of the LORD came to me: ²"Son of man, confront Jerusalem with her detestable practices ³and say, 'This is what the Sovereign LORD says to Jerusalem: Your ancestry and birth were in the land of the Canaanites; your father was an Amorite and your mother a Hittite. ⁴On the day you were born your cord was not cut, nor were you washed with water to make you clean, nor were you rubbed with salt or wrapped in cloths. ⁵No one looked on you with pity or had compassion enough to do any of these things for you. Rather, you were thrown out into the open field, for on the day you were born you were despised.

⁶"'Then I passed by and saw you kicking about in your blood, and as you lay there in your blood I said to you, "Live!"ᵃ ⁷I made you grow like a plant of the field. You grew up and developed and became the most beautiful of jewels.ᵇ Your breasts were formed and your hair grew, you who were naked and bare.

⁸"'Later I passed by, and when I looked at you and saw that you were old enough for love, I spread the corner of my garment over you and covered your nakedness. I gave you my solemn oath and entered into a covenant with you, declares the Sovereign LORD, and you became mine.

⁹"'I bathedᶜ you with water and washed the blood from you and put ointments on you. ¹⁰I clothed you with an embroidered dress and put leather sandals on you. I dressed you in fine linen and covered you with costly garments. ¹¹I adorned you with jewelry: I put bracelets on your arms and a necklace around your neck, ¹²and I put a ring on your nose, earrings on your ears and a beautiful crown on your head. ¹³So you were adorned with gold and silver; your clothes were of fine linen and costly fabric and embroidered cloth. Your food was fine flour, honey and olive oil. You became very beautiful and rose to be a queen. ¹⁴And your fame spread among the nations on account of your beauty, because the splendor I had given you made your beauty perfect, declares the Sovereign LORD.

¹⁵"'But you trusted in your beauty and used your fame to become a prostitute. You lavished your favors on anyone who passed by and your beauty became his.ᵈ ¹⁶You took some of your garments to make gaudy high places, where you carried on your prostitution. Such things should not happen, nor should they ever occur. ¹⁷You also took the fine jewelry I gave you, the jewelry made of my gold and silver, and you made for yourself male idols and engaged in prostitution with them. ¹⁸And you took your embroidered clothes to put on them, and you offered my oil and incense before them. ¹⁹Also the food I provided for you—the fine flour, olive oil and honey I gave you to eat—you offered as fragrant incense before them. That is what happened, declares the Sovereign LORD.

²⁰"'And you took your sons and

ᵃ6 A few Hebrew manuscripts, Septuagint and Syriac; most Hebrew manuscripts *"Live!" And as you lay there in your blood I said to you, "Live!"*   ᵇ7 Or *became mature*   ᶜ9 Or *I had bathed*
ᵈ15 Most Hebrew manuscripts; one Hebrew manuscript (see some Septuagint manuscripts) *by. Such a thing should not happen*

daughters whom you bore to me and sacrificed them as food to the idols. Was your prostitution not enough? ²¹You slaughtered my children and sacrificed them*a* to the idols. ²²In all your detestable practices and your prostitution you did not remember the days of your youth, when you were naked and bare, kicking about in your blood.

²³" 'Woe! Woe to you, declares the Sovereign LORD. In addition to all your other wickedness, ²⁴you built a mound for yourself and made a lofty shrine in every public square. ²⁵At the head of every street you built your lofty shrines and degraded your beauty, offering your body with increasing promiscuity to anyone who passed by. ²⁶You engaged in prostitution with the Egyptians, your lustful neighbors, and provoked me to anger with your increasing promiscuity. ²⁷So I stretched out my hand against you and reduced your territory; I gave you over to the greed of your enemies, the daughters of the Philistines, who were shocked by your lewd conduct. ²⁸You engaged in prostitution with the Assyrians too, because you were insatiable; and even after that, you still were not satisfied. ²⁹Then you increased your promiscuity to include Babylonia,*b* a land of merchants, but even with this you were not satisfied.

³⁰" 'How weak-willed you are, declares the Sovereign LORD, when you do all these things, acting like a brazen prostitute! ³¹When you built your mounds at the head of every street and made your lofty shrines in every public square, you were unlike a prostitute, because you scorned payment.

³²" 'You adulterous wife! You prefer strangers to your own husband! ³³Every prostitute receives a fee, but you give gifts to all your lovers, bribing them to come to you from everywhere for your illicit favors. ³⁴So in your prostitution you are the opposite of others; no one runs after you for your favors. You are the very opposite, for you give payment and none is given to you.

³⁵" 'Therefore, you prostitute, hear the word of the LORD! ³⁶This is what the Sovereign LORD says: Because you poured out your wealth*c* and exposed your nakedness in your promiscuity with your lovers, and because of all your detestable idols, and because you gave them your children's blood, ³⁷therefore I am going to gather all your lovers, with whom you found pleasure, those you loved as well as those you hated. I will gather them against you from all around and will strip you in front of them, and they will see all your nakedness. ³⁸I will sentence you to the punishment of women who commit adultery and who shed blood; I will bring upon you the blood vengeance of my wrath and jealous anger. ³⁹Then I will hand you over to your lovers, and they will tear down your mounds and destroy your lofty shrines. They will strip you of your clothes and take your fine jewelry and leave you naked and bare. ⁴⁰They will bring a mob against you, who will stone you and hack you to pieces with their swords. ⁴¹They will burn down your houses and inflict punishment on you in the sight of many women. I will put a stop to your prostitution, and you will no longer pay your lovers. ⁴²Then my wrath against you will subside and my jealous anger will turn away from you; I will be calm and no longer angry.

⁴³" 'Because you did not remember the days of your youth but enraged me with all these things, I will surely bring down on your head what you have done, declares the Sovereign LORD. Did you not add lewdness to all your other detestable practices?

⁴⁴" 'Everyone who quotes proverbs will quote this proverb about you: "Like mother, like daughter." ⁴⁵You are a true daughter of your mother, who despised her husband and her children; and you are a true sister of your sisters, who despised their husbands and their children. Your mother was a Hittite and your father an Amorite. ⁴⁶Your older sister was Samaria, who lived to the north of you with her daughters; and your younger sister, who lived to the south of you with her daughters, was Sodom. ⁴⁷You not only walked in their ways and copied their detestable practices, but in all your ways you soon became more depraved than they. ⁴⁸As surely as I live, declares the Sovereign LORD, your sister Sodom and her daugh-

---

a21 Or *and made them pass through ⌊the fire⌋*
b29 Or *Chaldea*   *c36* Or *lust*

ters never did what you and your daughters have done.

49 " 'Now this was the sin of your sister Sodom: She and her daughters were arrogant, overfed and unconcerned; they did not help the poor and needy. 50They were haughty and did detestable things before me. Therefore I did away with them as you have seen. 51Samaria did not commit half the sins you did. You have done more detestable things than they, and have made your sisters seem righteous by all these things you have done. 52Bear your disgrace, for you have furnished some justification for your sisters. Because your sins were more vile than theirs, they appear more righteous than you. So then, be ashamed and bear your disgrace, for you have made your sisters appear righteous.

53 " 'However, I will restore the fortunes of Sodom and her daughters and of Samaria and her daughters, and your fortunes along with them, 54so that you may bear your disgrace and be ashamed of all you have done in giving them comfort. 55And your sisters, Sodom with her daughters and Samaria with her daughters, will return to what they were before; and you and your daughters will return to what you were before. 56You would not even mention your sister Sodom in the day of your pride, 57before your wickedness was uncovered. Even so, you are now scorned by the daughters of Edom*a* and all her neighbors and the daughters of the Philistines—all those around you who despise you. 58You will bear the consequences of your lewdness and your detestable practices, declares the LORD.

59 " 'This is what the Sovereign LORD says: I will deal with you as you deserve, because you have despised my oath by breaking the covenant. 60Yet I will remember the covenant I made with you in the days of your youth, and I will establish an everlasting covenant with you. 61Then you will remember your ways and be ashamed when you receive your sisters, both those who are older than you and those who are younger. I will give them to you as daughters, but not on the basis of my covenant with you. 62So I will establish my covenant with you, and you will know that I am the LORD. 63Then, when I make atonement for you for all

you have done, you will remember and be ashamed and never again open your mouth because of your humiliation, declares the Sovereign LORD.' "

Two Eagles and a Vine

17 The word of the LORD came to me: 2"Son of man, set forth an allegory and tell the house of Israel a parable. 3Say to them, 'This is what the Sovereign LORD says: A great eagle with powerful wings, long feathers and full plumage of varied colors came to Lebanon. Taking hold of the top of a cedar, 4he broke off its topmost shoot and carried it away to a land of merchants, where he planted it in a city of traders.

5 " 'He took some of the seed of your land and put it in fertile soil. He planted it like a willow by abundant water, 6and it sprouted and became a low, spreading vine. Its branches turned toward him, but its roots remained under it. So it became a vine and produced branches and put out leafy boughs.

7 " 'But there was another great eagle with powerful wings and full plumage. The vine now sent out its roots toward him from the plot where it was planted and stretched out its branches to him for water. 8It had been planted in good soil by abundant water so that it would produce branches, bear fruit and become a splendid vine.'

9 "Say to them, 'This is what the Sovereign LORD says: Will it thrive? Will it not be uprooted and stripped of its fruit so that it withers? All its new growth will wither. It will not take a strong arm or many people to pull it up by the roots. 10Even if it is transplanted, will it thrive? Will it not wither completely when the east wind strikes it—wither away in the plot where it grew?' "

11Then the word of the LORD came to me: 12"Say to this rebellious house, 'Do you not know what these things mean?' Say to them: 'The king of Babylon went to Jerusalem and carried off her king and her nobles, bringing them back with him to Babylon. 13Then he took a member of the royal family and made a treaty with him, putting him under oath. He also carried

---

a57 Many Hebrew manuscripts and Syriac; most Hebrew manuscripts, Septuagint and Vulgate *Aram*

away the leading men of the land, ¹⁴so
that the kingdom would be brought low,
unable to rise again, surviving only by
keeping his treaty. ¹⁵But the king rebelled
against him by sending his envoys to
Egypt to get horses and a large army. Will
he succeed? Will he who does such things
escape? Will he break the treaty and yet
escape?

¹⁶" 'As surely as I live, declares the Sovereign LORD, he shall die in Babylon, in
the land of the king who put him on
the throne, whose oath he despised and
whose treaty he broke. ¹⁷Pharaoh with his
mighty army and great horde will be of
no help to him in war, when ramps are
built and siege works erected to destroy
many lives. ¹⁸He despised the oath by
breaking the covenant. Because he had
given his hand in pledge and yet did all
these things, he shall not escape.

¹⁹" 'Therefore this is what the Sovereign LORD says: As surely as I live, I will
bring down on his head my oath that he
despised and my covenant that he broke.
²⁰I will spread my net for him, and he will
be caught in my snare. I will bring him to
Babylon and execute judgment upon him
there because he was unfaithful to me.
²¹All his fleeing troops will fall by the
sword, and the survivors will be scattered
to the winds. Then you will know that I
the LORD have spoken.

²²" 'This is what the Sovereign LORD
says: I myself will take a shoot from the
very top of a cedar and plant it; I will
break off a tender sprig from its topmost
shoots and plant it on a high and lofty
mountain. ²³On the mountain heights
of Israel I will plant it; it will produce
branches and bear fruit and become a
splendid cedar. Birds of every kind will
nest in it; they will find shelter in the
shade of its branches. ²⁴All the trees of the
field will know that I the LORD bring
down the tall tree and make the low tree
grow tall. I dry up the green tree and make
the dry tree flourish.

" 'I the LORD have spoken, and I will
do it.' "

The Soul Who Sins Will Die

18 The word of the LORD came to me:
²"What do you people mean by

quoting this proverb about the land of
Israel:

" 'The fathers eat sour grapes,
    and the children's teeth are set on
        edge'?

³"As surely as I live, declares the Sovereign LORD, you will no longer quote this
proverb in Israel. ⁴For every living soul
belongs to me, the father as well as the
son—both alike belong to me. The soul
who sins is the one who will die.

⁵"Suppose there is a righteous man
    who does what is just and right.
⁶He does not eat at the mountain
        shrines
    or look to the idols of the house of
        Israel.
He does not defile his neighbor's wife
    or lie with a woman during her
        period.
⁷He does not oppress anyone,
    but returns what he took in pledge
        for a loan.
He does not commit robbery
    but gives his food to the hungry
    and provides clothing for the
        naked.
⁸He does not lend at usury
    or take excessive interest.^a
He withholds his hand from doing
        wrong
    and judges fairly between man and
        man.
⁹He follows my decrees
    and faithfully keeps my laws.
That man is righteous;
    he will surely live,
            declares the Sovereign LORD.

¹⁰"Suppose he has a violent son, who
sheds blood or does any of these other
things^b ¹¹(though the father has done
none of them):

"He eats at the mountain shrines.
He defiles his neighbor's wife.
¹²He oppresses the poor and needy.
He commits robbery.
He does not return what he took in
        pledge.
He looks to the idols.
He does detestable things.

^a8 Or *take interest*; similarly in verses 13 and 17
^b10 Or *things to a brother*

¹³He lends at usury and takes excessive
  interest.

Will such a man live? He will not! Because he has done all these detestable
things, he will surely be put to death and
his blood will be on his own head.

¹⁴"But suppose this son has a son who
sees all the sins his father commits, and
though he sees them, he does not do such
things:

¹⁵"He does not eat at the mountain
  shrines
    or look to the idols of the house of
      Israel.
  He does not defile his neighbor's
    wife.
¹⁶He does not oppress anyone
    or require a pledge for a loan.
  He does not commit robbery
    but gives his food to the hungry
    and provides clothing for the
      naked.
¹⁷He withholds his hand from sin*a*
    and takes no usury or excessive
      interest.
  He keeps my laws and follows my
    decrees.

He will not die for his father's sin; he will
surely live. ¹⁸But his father will die for his
own sin, because he practiced extortion,
robbed his brother and did what was
wrong among his people.

¹⁹"Yet you ask, 'Why does the son not
share the guilt of his father?' Since the son
has done what is just and right and has
been careful to keep all my decrees, he
will surely live. ²⁰The soul who sins is the
one who will die. The son will not share
the guilt of the father, nor will the father
share the guilt of the son. The righteousness of the righteous man will be credited
to him, and the wickedness of the wicked
will be charged against him.

²¹"But if a wicked man turns away
from all the sins he has committed and
keeps all my decrees and does what is just
and right, he will surely live; he will not
die. ²²None of the offenses he has committed will be remembered against him.
Because of the righteous things he has
done, he will live. ²³Do I take any pleasure in the death of the wicked? declares
the Sovereign LORD. Rather, am I not

pleased when they turn from their ways
and live?

²⁴"But if a righteous man turns from
his righteousness and commits sin and
does the same detestable things the wicked man does, will he live? None of the
righteous things he has done will be remembered. Because of the unfaithfulness
he is guilty of and because of the sins he
has committed, he will die.

²⁵"Yet you say, 'The way of the Lord is
not just.' Hear, O house of Israel: Is my
way unjust? Is it not your ways that are
unjust? ²⁶If a righteous man turns from
his righteousness and commits sin, he
will die for it; because of the sin he has
committed he will die. ²⁷But if a wicked
man turns away from the wickedness he
has committed and does what is just and
right, he will save his life. ²⁸Because he
considers all the offenses he has committed and turns away from them, he will
surely live; he will not die. ²⁹Yet the house
of Israel says, 'The way of the Lord is not
just.' Are my ways unjust, O house of Israel? Is it not your ways that are unjust?

³⁰"Therefore, O house of Israel, I will
judge you, each one according to his
ways, declares the Sovereign LORD. Repent! Turn away from all your offenses;
then sin will not be your downfall. ³¹Rid
yourselves of all the offenses you have
committed, and get a new heart and a
new spirit. Why will you die, O house of
Israel? ³²For I take no pleasure in the
death of anyone, declares the Sovereign
LORD. Repent and live!

A Lament for Israel's Princes

19 "Take up a lament concerning the
princes of Israel ²and say:

" 'What a lioness was your mother
    among the lions!
  She lay down among the young lions
    and reared her cubs.
³She brought up one of her cubs,
    and he became a strong lion.
  He learned to tear the prey
    and he devoured men.
⁴The nations heard about him,
    and he was trapped in their pit.

a17 Septuagint (see also verse 8); Hebrew *from
the poor*

They led him with hooks
　　to the land of Egypt.

5 " 'When she saw her hope
　　　unfulfilled,
　　her expectation gone,
　she took another of her cubs
　　and made him a strong lion.
6 He prowled among the lions,
　　for he was now a strong lion.
He learned to tear the prey
　　and he devoured men.
7 He broke down[a] their strongholds
　　and devastated their towns.
The land and all who were in it
　　were terrified by his roaring.
8 Then the nations came against him,
　　those from regions round about.
They spread their net for him,
　　and he was trapped in their pit.
9 With hooks they pulled him into a
　　　cage
　　and brought him to the king of
　　　Babylon.
They put him in prison,
　　so his roar was heard no longer
　　on the mountains of Israel.

10 " 'Your mother was like a vine in
　　　your vineyard[b]
　　planted by the water;
　it was fruitful and full of branches
　　because of abundant water.
11 Its branches were strong,
　　fit for a ruler's scepter.
It towered high
　　above the thick foliage,
　conspicuous for its height
　　and for its many branches.
12 But it was uprooted in fury
　　and thrown to the ground.
The east wind made it shrivel,
　　it was stripped of its fruit;
　its strong branches withered
　　and fire consumed them.
13 Now it is planted in the desert,
　　in a dry and thirsty land.
14 Fire spread from one of its main[c]
　　　branches
　　and consumed its fruit.
No strong branch is left on it
　　fit for a ruler's scepter.'

This is a lament and is to be used as a
lament."

Rebellious Israel

20 In the seventh year, in the fifth
month on the tenth day, some of
the elders of Israel came to inquire of the
LORD, and they sat down in front of me.
² Then the word of the LORD came to
me: ³ "Son of man, speak to the elders of
Israel and say to them, 'This is what the
Sovereign LORD says: Have you come to
inquire of me? As surely as I live, I will not
let you inquire of me, declares the Sovereign LORD.'

⁴ "Will you judge them? Will you judge
them, son of man? Then confront them
with the detestable practices of their fathers ⁵ and say to them: 'This is what the
Sovereign LORD says: On the day I chose
Israel, I swore with uplifted hand to the
descendants of the house of Jacob and
revealed myself to them in Egypt. With
uplifted hand I said to them, "I am the
LORD your God." ⁶ On that day I swore
to them that I would bring them out of
Egypt into a land I had searched out for
them, a land flowing with milk and honey, the most beautiful of all lands. ⁷ And I
said to them, "Each of you, get rid of the
vile images you have set your eyes on, and
do not defile yourselves with the idols of
Egypt. I am the LORD your God."

⁸ "But they rebelled against me and
would not listen to me; they did not get
rid of the vile images they had set their
eyes on, nor did they forsake the idols of
Egypt. So I said I would pour out my
wrath on them and spend my anger
against them in Egypt. ⁹ But for the sake of
my name I did what would keep it from
being profaned in the eyes of the nations
they lived among and in whose sight I
had revealed myself to the Israelites by
bringing them out of Egypt. ¹⁰ Therefore I
led them out of Egypt and brought them
into the desert. ¹¹ I gave them my decrees
and made known to them my laws, for
the man who obeys them will live by
them. ¹² Also I gave them my Sabbaths as
a sign between us, so they would know
that I the LORD made them holy.

¹³ " 'Yet the people of Israel rebelled
against me in the desert. They did not
follow my decrees but rejected my laws—

---

a7 Targum (see Septuagint); Hebrew *He knew*
b10 Two Hebrew manuscripts; most Hebrew
manuscripts *your blood*   *c14* Or *from under its*

although the man who obeys them will live by them—and they utterly desecrated my Sabbaths. So I said I would pour out my wrath on them and destroy them in the desert. ¹⁴But for the sake of my name I did what would keep it from being profaned in the eyes of the nations in whose sight I had brought them out. ¹⁵Also with uplifted hand I swore to them in the desert that I would not bring them into the land I had given them—a land flowing with milk and honey, most beautiful of all lands— ¹⁶because they rejected my laws and did not follow my decrees and desecrated my Sabbaths. For their hearts were devoted to their idols. ¹⁷Yet I looked on them with pity and did not destroy them or put an end to them in the desert. ¹⁸I said to their children in the desert, "Do not follow the statutes of your fathers or keep their laws or defile yourselves with their idols. ¹⁹I am the LORD your God; follow my decrees and be careful to keep my laws. ²⁰Keep my Sabbaths holy, that they may be a sign between us. Then you will know that I am the LORD your God."

²¹" 'But the children rebelled against me: They did not follow my decrees, they were not careful to keep my laws—although the man who obeys them will live by them—and they desecrated my Sabbaths. So I said I would pour out my wrath on them and spend my anger against them in the desert. ²²But I withheld my hand, and for the sake of my name I did what would keep it from being profaned in the eyes of the nations in whose sight I had brought them out. ²³Also with uplifted hand I swore to them in the desert that I would disperse them among the nations and scatter them through the countries, ²⁴because they had not obeyed my laws but had rejected my decrees and desecrated my Sabbaths, and their eyes ⌞lusted⌟ after their fathers' idols. ²⁵I also gave them over to statutes that were not good and laws they could not live by; ²⁶I let them become defiled through their gifts—the sacrifice of every firstborn[a]—that I might fill them with horror so they would know that I am the LORD.'

²⁷"Therefore, son of man, speak to the people of Israel and say to them, 'This is what the Sovereign LORD says: In this also your fathers blasphemed me by forsaking

me: ²⁸When I brought them into the land I had sworn to give them and they saw any high hill or any leafy tree, there they offered their sacrifices, made offerings that provoked me to anger, presented their fragrant incense and poured out their drink offerings. ²⁹Then I said to them: What is this high place you go to?' " (It is called Bamah[b] to this day.)

Judgment and Restoration

³⁰"Therefore say to the house of Israel: 'This is what the Sovereign LORD says: Will you defile yourselves the way your fathers did and lust after their vile images? ³¹When you offer your gifts—the sacrifice of your sons in[c] the fire—you continue to defile yourselves with all your idols to this day. Am I to let you inquire of me, O house of Israel? As surely as I live, declares the Sovereign LORD, I will not let you inquire of me.

³²" 'You say, "We want to be like the nations, like the peoples of the world, who serve wood and stone." But what you have in mind will never happen. ³³As surely as I live, declares the Sovereign LORD, I will rule over you with a mighty hand and an outstretched arm and with outpoured wrath. ³⁴I will bring you from the nations and gather you from the countries where you have been scattered— with a mighty hand and an outstretched arm and with outpoured wrath. ³⁵I will bring you into the desert of the nations and there, face to face, I will execute judgment upon you. ³⁶As I judged your fathers in the desert of the land of Egypt, so I will judge you, declares the Sovereign LORD. ³⁷I will take note of you as you pass under my rod, and I will bring you into the bond of the covenant. ³⁸I will purge you of those who revolt and rebel against me. Although I will bring them out of the land where they are living, yet they will not enter the land of Israel. Then you will know that I am the LORD.

³⁹" 'As for you, O house of Israel, this is what the Sovereign LORD says: Go and serve your idols, every one of you! But afterward you will surely listen to me and no longer profane my holy name with

---

[a]26 Or —making every firstborn pass through ⌞the fire⌟
[b]29 Bamah means high place.   [c]31 Or —making your sons pass through

your gifts and idols. **40**For on my holy mountain, the high mountain of Israel, declares the Sovereign LORD, there in the land the entire house of Israel will serve me, and there I will accept them. There I will require your offerings and your choice gifts,*a* along with all your holy sacrifices. **41**I will accept you as fragrant incense when I bring you out from the nations and gather you from the countries where you have been scattered, and I will show myself holy among you in the sight of the nations. **42**Then you will know that I am the LORD, when I bring you into the land of Israel, the land I had sworn with uplifted hand to give to your fathers. **43**There you will remember your conduct and all the actions by which you have defiled yourselves, and you will loathe yourselves for all the evil you have done. **44**You will know that I am the LORD, when I deal with you for my name's sake and not according to your evil ways and your corrupt practices, O house of Israel, declares the Sovereign LORD.' "

Prophecy Against the South

45The word of the LORD came to me: **46**"Son of man, set your face toward the south; preach against the south and prophesy against the forest of the southland. **47**Say to the southern forest: 'Hear the word of the LORD. This is what the Sovereign LORD says: I am about to set fire to you, and it will consume all your trees, both green and dry. The blazing flame will not be quenched, and every face from south to north will be scorched by it. **48**Everyone will see that I the LORD have kindled it; it will not be quenched.' "

49Then I said, "Ah, Sovereign LORD! They are saying of me, 'Isn't he just telling parables?' "

Babylon, God's Sword of Judgment

21 The word of the LORD came to me: **2**"Son of man, set your face against Jerusalem and preach against the sanctuary. Prophesy against the land of Israel **3**and say to her: 'This is what the LORD says: I am against you. I will draw my sword from its scabbard and cut off from you both the righteous and the wicked. **4**Because I am going to cut off the righteous and the wicked, my sword will be unsheathed against everyone from south to north. **5**Then all people will know that I the LORD have drawn my sword from its scabbard; it will not return again.'

6"Therefore groan, son of man! Groan before them with broken heart and bitter grief. **7**And when they ask you, 'Why are you groaning?' you shall say, 'Because of the news that is coming. Every heart will melt and every hand go limp; every spirit will become faint and every knee become as weak as water.' It is coming! It will surely take place, declares the Sovereign LORD."

8The word of the LORD came to me: **9**"Son of man, prophesy and say, 'This is what the Lord says:

" 'A sword, a sword,
    sharpened and polished—
10sharpened for the slaughter,
    polished to flash like lightning!

" 'Shall we rejoice in the scepter of my son ⌊Judah⌋? The sword despises every such stick.

11" 'The sword is appointed to be
       polished,
    to be grasped with the hand;
  it is sharpened and polished,
    made ready for the hand of the
       slayer.
12Cry out and wail, son of man,
    for it is against my people;
    it is against all the princes of Israel.
They are thrown to the sword
    along with my people.
Therefore beat your breast.

13" 'Testing will surely come. And what if the scepter ⌊of Judah⌋, which the sword despises, does not continue? declares the Sovereign LORD.'

14"So then, son of man, prophesy
    and strike your hands together.
Let the sword strike twice,
    even three times.
It is a sword for slaughter—
    a sword for great slaughter,
    closing in on them from every side.
15So that hearts may melt
    and the fallen be many,

a40 Or and the gifts of your firstfruits

I have stationed the sword for
slaughter[a]
at all their gates.
Oh! It is made to flash like lightning,
it is grasped for slaughter.
16O sword, slash to the right,
then to the left,
wherever your blade is turned.
17I too will strike my hands together,
and my wrath will subside.
I the LORD have spoken."

18The word of the LORD came to me:
19"Son of man, mark out two roads for
the sword of the king of Babylon to take,
both starting from the same country.
Make a signpost where the road branches
off to the city. 20Mark out one road for the
sword to come against Rabbah of the Ammonites and another against Judah and
fortified Jerusalem. 21For the king of Babylon will stop at the fork in the road, at
the junction of the two roads, to seek an
omen: He will cast lots with arrows, he
will consult his idols, he will examine the
liver. 22Into his right hand will come the
lot for Jerusalem, where he is to set up
battering rams, to give the command to
slaughter, to sound the battle cry, to set
battering rams against the gates, to build
a ramp and to erect siege works. 23It will
seem like a false omen to those who have
sworn allegiance to him, but he will remind them of their guilt and take them
captive.

24"Therefore this is what the Sovereign
LORD says: 'Because you people have
brought to mind your guilt by your open
rebellion, revealing your sins in all that
you do—because you have done this, you
will be taken captive.

25" 'O profane and wicked prince of
Israel, whose day has come, whose time
of punishment has reached its climax,
26this is what the Sovereign LORD says:
Take off the turban, remove the crown. It
will not be as it was: The lowly will be
exalted and the exalted will be brought
low. 27A ruin! A ruin! I will make it a ruin!
It will not be restored until he comes to
whom it rightfully belongs; to him I will
give it.'

28"And you, son of man, prophesy and
say, 'This is what the Sovereign LORD says
about the Ammonites and their insults:

" 'A sword, a sword,

drawn for the slaughter,
polished to consume
and to flash like lightning!
29Despite false visions concerning you
and lying divinations about you,
it will be laid on the necks
of the wicked who are to be slain,
whose day has come,
whose time of punishment has
reached its climax.
30Return the sword to its scabbard.
In the place where you were
created,
in the land of your ancestry,
I will judge you.
31I will pour out my wrath upon you
and breathe out my fiery anger
against you;
I will hand you over to brutal men,
men skilled in destruction.
32You will be fuel for the fire,
your blood will be shed in your
land,
you will be remembered no more;
for I the LORD have spoken.' "

Jerusalem's Sins

22 The word of the LORD came to me:
2"Son of man, will you judge her?
Will you judge this city of bloodshed?
Then confront her with all her detestable
practices 3and say: 'This is what the Sovereign LORD says: O city that brings on herself doom by shedding blood in her midst
and defiles herself by making idols, 4you
have become guilty because of the blood
you have shed and have become defiled
by the idols you have made. You have
brought your days to a close, and the end
of your years has come. Therefore I will
make you an object of scorn to the nations and a laughingstock to all the countries. 5Those who are near and those who
are far away will mock you, O infamous
city, full of turmoil.

6" 'See how each of the princes of Israel who are in you uses his power to shed
blood. 7In you they have treated father
and mother with contempt; in you they
have oppressed the alien and mistreated
the fatherless and the widow. 8You have
despised my holy things and desecrated
my Sabbaths. 9In you are slanderous men

---

a15 Septuagint; the meaning of the Hebrew for
this word is uncertain.

bent on shedding blood; in you are those who eat at the mountain shrines and commit lewd acts. [10]In you are those who dishonor their fathers' bed; in you are those who violate women during their period, when they are ceremonially unclean. [11]In you one man commits a detestable offense with his neighbor's wife, another shamefully defiles his daughter-in-law, and another violates his sister, his own father's daughter. [12]In you men accept bribes to shed blood; you take usury and excessive interest[a] and make unjust gain from your neighbors by extortion. And you have forgotten me, declares the Sovereign LORD.

[13]" 'I will surely strike my hands together at the unjust gain you have made and at the blood you have shed in your midst. [14]Will your courage endure or your hands be strong in the day I deal with you? I the LORD have spoken, and I will do it. [15]I will disperse you among the nations and scatter you through the countries; and I will put an end to your uncleanness. [16]When you have been defiled[b] in the eyes of the nations, you will know that I am the LORD.' "

[17]Then the word of the LORD came to me: [18]"Son of man, the house of Israel has become dross to me; all of them are the copper, tin, iron and lead left inside a furnace. They are but the dross of silver. [19]Therefore this is what the Sovereign LORD says: 'Because you have all become dross, I will gather you into Jerusalem. [20]As men gather silver, copper, iron, lead and tin into a furnace to melt it with a fiery blast, so will I gather you in my anger and my wrath and put you inside the city and melt you. [21]I will gather you and I will blow on you with my fiery wrath, and you will be melted inside her. [22]As silver is melted in a furnace, so you will be melted inside her, and you will know that I the LORD have poured out my wrath upon you.' "

[23]Again the word of the LORD came to me: [24]"Son of man, say to the land, 'You are a land that has had no rain or showers[c] in the day of wrath.' [25]There is a conspiracy of her princes[d] within her like a roaring lion tearing its prey; they devour people, take treasures and precious things and make many widows within her. [26]Her priests do violence to

my law and profane my holy things; they do not distinguish between the holy and the common; they teach that there is no difference between the unclean and the clean; and they shut their eyes to the keeping of my Sabbaths, so that I am profaned among them. [27]Her officials within her are like wolves tearing their prey; they shed blood and kill people to make unjust gain. [28]Her prophets whitewash these deeds for them by false visions and lying divinations. They say, 'This is what the Sovereign LORD says'—when the LORD has not spoken. [29]The people of the land practice extortion and commit robbery; they oppress the poor and needy and mistreat the alien, denying them justice.

[30]"I looked for a man among them who would build up the wall and stand before me in the gap on behalf of the land so I would not have to destroy it, but I found none. [31]So I will pour out my wrath on them and consume them with my fiery anger, bringing down on their own heads all they have done, declares the Sovereign LORD."

Two Adulterous Sisters

23 The word of the LORD came to me: [2]"Son of man, there were two women, daughters of the same mother. [3]They became prostitutes in Egypt, engaging in prostitution from their youth. In that land their breasts were fondled and their virgin bosoms caressed. [4]The older was named Oholah, and her sister was Oholibah. They were mine and gave birth to sons and daughters. Oholah is Samaria, and Oholibah is Jerusalem.

[5]"Oholah engaged in prostitution while she was still mine; and she lusted after her lovers, the Assyrians—warriors [6]clothed in blue, governors and commanders, all of them handsome young men, and mounted horsemen. [7]She gave herself as a prostitute to all the elite of the Assyrians and defiled herself with all the idols of everyone she lusted after. [8]She did not give up the prostitution she began in Egypt, when during her youth men

---

[a]12 Or *usury and interest*   [b]16 Or *When I have allotted you your inheritance*   [c]24 Septuagint; Hebrew *has not been cleansed or rained on*   [d]25 Septuagint; Hebrew *prophets*

slept with her, caressed her virgin bosom and poured out their lust upon her.

9"Therefore I handed her over to her lovers, the Assyrians, for whom she lusted. 10They stripped her naked, took away her sons and daughters and killed her with the sword. She became a byword among women, and punishment was inflicted on her.

11"Her sister Oholibah saw this, yet in her lust and prostitution she was more depraved than her sister. 12She too lusted after the Assyrians—governors and commanders, warriors in full dress, mounted horsemen, all handsome young men. 13I saw that she too defiled herself; both of them went the same way.

14"But she carried her prostitution still further. She saw men portrayed on a wall, figures of Chaldeans*a* portrayed in red, 15with belts around their waists and flowing turbans on their heads; all of them looked like Babylonian chariot officers, natives of Chaldea.*b* 16As soon as she saw them, she lusted after them and sent messengers to them in Chaldea. 17Then the Babylonians came to her, to the bed of love, and in their lust they defiled her. After she had been defiled by them, she turned away from them in disgust. 18When she carried on her prostitution openly and exposed her nakedness, I turned away from her in disgust, just as I had turned away from her sister. 19Yet she became more and more promiscuous as she recalled the days of her youth, when she was a prostitute in Egypt. 20There she lusted after her lovers, whose genitals were like those of donkeys and whose emission was like that of horses. 21So you longed for the lewdness of your youth, when in Egypt your bosom was caressed and your young breasts fondled.*c*

22"Therefore, Oholibah, this is what the Sovereign LORD says: I will stir up your lovers against you, those you turned away from in disgust, and I will bring them against you from every side— 23the Babylonians and all the Chaldeans, the men of Pekod and Shoa and Koa, and all the Assyrians with them, handsome young men, all of them governors and commanders, chariot officers and men of high rank, all mounted on horses. 24They will come against you with weapons,*d* chariots and wagons and with a throng of peo-

ple; they will take up positions against you on every side with large and small shields and with helmets. I will turn you over to them for punishment, and they will punish you according to their standards. 25I will direct my jealous anger against you, and they will deal with you in fury. They will cut off your noses and your ears, and those of you who are left will fall by the sword. They will take away your sons and daughters, and those of you who are left will be consumed by fire. 26They will also strip you of your clothes and take your fine jewelry. 27So I will put a stop to the lewdness and prostitution you began in Egypt. You will not look on these things with longing or remember Egypt anymore.

28"For this is what the Sovereign LORD says: I am about to hand you over to those you hate, to those you turned away from in disgust. 29They will deal with you in hatred and take away everything you have worked for. They will leave you naked and bare, and the shame of your prostitution will be exposed. Your lewdness and promiscuity 30have brought this upon you, because you lusted after the nations and defiled yourself with their idols. 31You have gone the way of your sister; so I will put her cup into your hand.

32"This is what the Sovereign LORD says:

"You will drink your sister's cup,
    a cup large and deep;
it will bring scorn and derision,
    for it holds so much.
33You will be filled with drunkenness
        and sorrow,
    the cup of ruin and desolation,
    the cup of your sister Samaria.
34You will drink it and drain it dry;
    you will dash it to pieces
    and tear your breasts.

I have spoken, declares the Sovereign LORD.

35"Therefore this is what the Sovereign LORD says: Since you have forgotten me

---

a14 Or *Babylonians*   *b15* Or *Babylonia*; also
in verse 16   *c21* Syriac (see also verse 3);
Hebrew *caressed because of your young breasts*
d24 The meaning of the Hebrew for this word is
uncertain.

and thrust me behind your back, you must bear the consequences of your lewdness and prostitution."

36The LORD said to me: "Son of man, will you judge Oholah and Oholibah? Then confront them with their detestable practices, 37for they have committed adultery and blood is on their hands. They committed adultery with their idols; they even sacrificed their children, whom they bore to me,a as food for them. 38They have also done this to me: At that same time they defiled my sanctuary and desecrated my Sabbaths. 39On the very day they sacrificed their children to their idols, they entered my sanctuary and desecrated it. That is what they did in my house.

40"They even sent messengers for men who came from far away, and when they arrived you bathed yourself for them, painted your eyes and put on your jewelry. 41You sat on an elegant couch, with a table spread before it on which you had placed the incense and oil that belonged to me.

42"The noise of a carefree crowd was around her; Sabeansb were brought from the desert along with men from the rabble, and they put bracelets on the arms of the woman and her sister and beautiful crowns on their heads. 43Then I said about the one worn out by adultery, 'Now let them use her as a prostitute, for that is all she is.' 44And they slept with her. As men sleep with a prostitute, so they slept with those lewd women, Oholah and Oholibah. 45But righteous men will sentence them to the punishment of women who commit adultery and shed blood, because they are adulterous and blood is on their hands.

46"This is what the Sovereign LORD says: Bring a mob against them and give them over to terror and plunder. 47The mob will stone them and cut them down with their swords; they will kill their sons and daughters and burn down their houses.

48"So I will put an end to lewdness in the land, that all women may take warning and not imitate you. 49You will suffer the penalty for your lewdness and bear the consequences of your sins of idolatry. Then you will know that I am the Sovereign LORD."

The Cooking Pot

24 In the ninth year, in the tenth month on the tenth day, the word of the LORD came to me: 2"Son of man, record this date, this very date, because the king of Babylon has laid siege to Jerusalem this very day. 3Tell this rebellious house a parable and say to them: 'This is what the Sovereign LORD says:

" 'Put on the cooking pot; put it on
    and pour water into it.
4Put into it the pieces of meat,
    all the choice pieces—the leg and
        the shoulder.
Fill it with the best of these bones;
5   take the pick of the flock.
Pile wood beneath it for the bones;
    bring it to a boil
    and cook the bones in it.

6" 'For this is what the Sovereign LORD says:

" 'Woe to the city of bloodshed,
    to the pot now encrusted,
    whose deposit will not go away!
Empty it piece by piece
    without casting lots for them.

7" 'For the blood she shed is in her
       midst:
    She poured it on the bare rock;
she did not pour it on the ground,
    where the dust would cover it.
8To stir up wrath and take revenge
    I put her blood on the bare rock,
    so that it would not be covered.

9" 'Therefore this is what the Sovereign LORD says:

" 'Woe to the city of bloodshed!
    I, too, will pile the wood high.
10So heap on the wood
    and kindle the fire.
Cook the meat well,
    mixing in the spices;
    and let the bones be charred.
11Then set the empty pot on the coals
    till it becomes hot and its copper
       glows
so its impurities may be melted
    and its deposit burned away.
12It has frustrated all efforts;

a37 Or *even made the children they bore to me pass through* ⌞*the fire*⌟   b42 Or *drunkards*

its heavy deposit has not been
    removed,
not even by fire.

13 " 'Now your impurity is lewdness.
Because I tried to cleanse you but you
would not be cleansed from your impurity, you will not be clean again until my
wrath against you has subsided.

14 " 'I the LORD have spoken. The time
has come for me to act. I will not hold
back; I will not have pity, nor will I relent.
You will be judged according to your conduct and your actions, declares the Sovereign LORD.' "

Ezekiel's Wife Dies

15 The word of the LORD came to me:
16 "Son of man, with one blow I am about
to take away from you the delight of your
eyes. Yet do not lament or weep or shed
any tears. 17 Groan quietly; do not mourn
for the dead. Keep your turban fastened
and your sandals on your feet; do not
cover the lower part of your face or eat the
customary food ⌊of mourners⌋."

18 So I spoke to the people in the morning, and in the evening my wife died. The
next morning I did as I had been commanded.

19 Then the people asked me, "Won't
you tell us what these things have to do
with us?"

20 So I said to them, "The word of the
LORD came to me: 21 Say to the house of
Israel, 'This is what the Sovereign LORD
says: I am about to desecrate my sanctuary—the stronghold in which you take
pride, the delight of your eyes, the object
of your affection. The sons and daughters
you left behind will fall by the sword.
22 And you will do as I have done. You will
not cover the lower part of your face or eat
the customary food ⌊of mourners⌋. 23 You
will keep your turbans on your heads and
your sandals on your feet. You will not
mourn or weep but will waste away because of[a] your sins and groan among
yourselves. 24 Ezekiel will be a sign to you;
you will do just as he has done. When this

───

a23 Or away in

Seize the Day!

Quiet TIMES with each other

EZEKIEL 24:15–17   No one
is ever prepared to lose a
spouse—including Ezekiel.
God's purpose in taking Ezekiel's wife was to get his people's attention and to force
them to confront their sins.
Still, for Ezekiel it must have been
so painful, whatever the reason, to
have his wife taken away.

One thing we can learn from Ezekiel's experience is that each day together is a gift.
His story challenges us to appreciate the
time we do have with each other and to
never take the future for granted. Consider
Carlos and Genie, missionaries to Mexico,
who we met several years ago at our
church's missions conference. They lived in
Mexico City with their two young daughters
and were excited about trying one of our

small group resources at their
church. Returning to Mexico,
Carlos and Genie started a
marriage growth group with
several other couples. Between the sessions they arranged childcare so each couple could have a date. You can
imagine our utter shock the next year
when we heard that Genie had died suddenly of meningitis.

The Sunday before she died, Genie had a
wonderful date with Carlos—they didn't
know it was their last. "Tell other couples,"
Carlos told us with his voice breaking, "not
to take each other for granted, to seize the
day, to take time for their relationship now.
You just don't know how long you will have
with each other. I'm so glad I took the time
with Genie."   —Dave & Claudia

Weekend Warm-up   Are you getting each other's message? What kind of message are you
sending?

Go to page 912 for your next devotional reading.

happens, you will know that I am the Sovereign LORD.'

25"And you, son of man, on the day I take away their stronghold, their joy and glory, the delight of their eyes, their heart's desire, and their sons and daughters as well— 26on that day a fugitive will come to tell you the news. 27At that time your mouth will be opened; you will speak with him and will no longer be silent. So you will be a sign to them, and they will know that I am the LORD."

A Prophecy Against Ammon

25 The word of the LORD came to me: 2"Son of man, set your face against the Ammonites and prophesy against them. 3Say to them, 'Hear the word of the Sovereign LORD. This is what the Sovereign LORD says: Because you said "Aha!" over my sanctuary when it was desecrated and over the land of Israel when it was laid waste and over the people of Judah when they went into exile, 4therefore I am going to give you to the people of the East as a possession. They will set up their camps and pitch their tents among you; they will eat your fruit and drink your milk. 5I will turn Rabbah into a pasture for camels and Ammon into a resting place for sheep. Then you will know that I am the LORD. 6For this is what the Sovereign LORD says: Because you have clapped your hands and stamped your feet, rejoicing with all the malice of your heart against the land of Israel, 7therefore I will stretch out my hand against you and give you as plunder to the nations. I will cut you off from the nations and exterminate you from the countries. I will destroy you, and you will know that I am the LORD.' "

A Prophecy Against Moab

8"This is what the Sovereign LORD says: 'Because Moab and Seir said, "Look, the house of Judah has become like all the other nations," 9therefore I will expose the flank of Moab, beginning at its frontier towns—Beth Jeshimoth, Baal Meon and Kiriathaim—the glory of that land. 10I will give Moab along with the Ammonites to the people of the East as a possession, so that the Ammonites will not be remembered among the nations; 11and I will inflict punishment on Moab. Then they will know that I am the LORD.' "

A Prophecy Against Edom

12"This is what the Sovereign LORD says: 'Because Edom took revenge on the house of Judah and became very guilty by doing so, 13therefore this is what the Sovereign LORD says: I will stretch out my hand against Edom and kill its men and their animals. I will lay it waste, and from Teman to Dedan they will fall by the sword. 14I will take vengeance on Edom by the hand of my people Israel, and they will deal with Edom in accordance with my anger and my wrath; they will know my vengeance, declares the Sovereign LORD.' "

A Prophecy Against Philistia

15"This is what the Sovereign LORD says: 'Because the Philistines acted in vengeance and took revenge with malice in their hearts, and with ancient hostility sought to destroy Judah, 16therefore this is what the Sovereign LORD says: I am about to stretch out my hand against the Philistines, and I will cut off the Kerethites and destroy those remaining along the coast. 17I will carry out great vengeance on them and punish them in my wrath. Then they will know that I am the LORD, when I take vengeance on them.' "

A Prophecy Against Tyre

26 In the eleventh year, on the first day of the month, the word of the LORD came to me: 2"Son of man, because Tyre has said of Jerusalem, 'Aha! The gate to the nations is broken, and its doors have swung open to me; now that she lies in ruins I will prosper,' 3therefore this is what the Sovereign LORD says: I am against you, O Tyre, and I will bring many nations against you, like the sea casting up its waves. 4They will destroy the walls of Tyre and pull down her towers; I will scrape away her rubble and make her a bare rock. 5Out in the sea she will become a place to spread fishnets, for I have spoken, declares the Sovereign LORD. She will become plunder for the nations, 6and her settlements on the mainland will be ravaged by the sword. Then they will know that I am the LORD.

⁷"For this is what the Sovereign LORD says: From the north I am going to bring against Tyre Nebuchadnezzar[a] king of Babylon, king of kings, with horses and chariots, with horsemen and a great army. ⁸He will ravage your settlements on the mainland with the sword; he will set up siege works against you, build a ramp up to your walls and raise his shields against you. ⁹He will direct the blows of his battering rams against your walls and demolish your towers with his weapons. ¹⁰His horses will be so many that they will cover you with dust. Your walls will tremble at the noise of the war horses, wagons and chariots when he enters your gates as men enter a city whose walls have been broken through. ¹¹The hoofs of his horses will trample all your streets; he will kill your people with the sword, and your strong pillars will fall to the ground. ¹²They will plunder your wealth and loot your merchandise; they will break down your walls and demolish your fine houses and throw your stones, timber and rubble into the sea. ¹³I will put an end to your noisy songs, and the music of your harps will be heard no more. ¹⁴I will make you a bare rock, and you will become a place to spread fishnets. You will never be rebuilt, for I the LORD have spoken, declares the Sovereign LORD.

¹⁵"This is what the Sovereign LORD says to Tyre: Will not the coastlands tremble at the sound of your fall, when the wounded groan and the slaughter takes place in you? ¹⁶Then all the princes of the coast will step down from their thrones and lay aside their robes and take off their embroidered garments. Clothed with terror, they will sit on the ground, trembling every moment, appalled at you. ¹⁷Then they will take up a lament concerning you and say to you:

" 'How you are destroyed, O city of renown,
    peopled by men of the sea!
You were a power on the seas,
    you and your citizens;
you put your terror
    on all who lived there.
¹⁸Now the coastlands tremble
    on the day of your fall;
the islands in the sea
    are terrified at your collapse.'

¹⁹"This is what the Sovereign LORD says: When I make you a desolate city, like cities no longer inhabited, and when I bring the ocean depths over you and its vast waters cover you, ²⁰then I will bring you down with those who go down to the pit, to the people of long ago. I will make you dwell in the earth below, as in ancient ruins, with those who go down to the pit, and you will not return or take your place[b] in the land of the living. ²¹I will bring you to a horrible end and you will be no more. You will be sought, but you will never again be found, declares the Sovereign LORD."

A Lament for Tyre

27 The word of the LORD came to me: ²"Son of man, take up a lament concerning Tyre. ³Say to Tyre, situated at the gateway to the sea, merchant of peoples on many coasts, 'This is what the Sovereign LORD says:

" 'You say, O Tyre,
    "I am perfect in beauty."
⁴Your domain was on the high seas;
    your builders brought your beauty
        to perfection.
⁵They made all your timbers
    of pine trees from Senir[c];
they took a cedar from Lebanon
    to make a mast for you.
⁶Of oaks from Bashan
    they made your oars;
of cypress wood[d] from the coasts of
        Cyprus[e]
    they made your deck, inlaid with
        ivory.
⁷Fine embroidered linen from Egypt
        was your sail
    and served as your banner;
your awnings were of blue and purple
    from the coasts of Elishah.
⁸Men of Sidon and Arvad were your
        oarsmen;
    your skilled men, O Tyre, were
        aboard as your seamen.
⁹Veteran craftsmen of Gebal[f] were on
        board

---

[a]7 Hebrew *Nebuchadrezzar*, of which
Nebuchadnezzar is a variant; here and often in
Ezekiel and Jeremiah   [b]20 Septuagint; Hebrew
return, and I will give glory   [c]5 That is, Hermon
[d]6 Targum; the Masoretic Text has a different
division of the consonants.   [e]6 Hebrew *Kittim*
[f]9 That is, Byblos

as shipwrights to caulk your seams.
All the ships of the sea and their
    sailors
    came alongside to trade for your
        wares.

10" 'Men of Persia, Lydia and Put
    served as soldiers in your army.
They hung their shields and helmets
        on your walls,
    bringing you splendor.
11Men of Arvad and Helech
    manned your walls on every side;
men of Gammad
    were in your towers.
They hung their shields around your
        walls;
    they brought your beauty to
        perfection.

12" 'Tarshish did business with you because of your great wealth of goods; they
exchanged silver, iron, tin and lead for
your merchandise.
    13" 'Greece, Tubal and Meshech traded
with you; they exchanged slaves and articles of bronze for your wares.
    14" 'Men of Beth Togarmah exchanged
work horses, war horses and mules for
your merchandise.
    15" 'The men of Rhodes*a* traded with
you, and many coastlands were your customers; they paid you with ivory tusks
and ebony.
    16" 'Aram*b* did business with you be-
cause of your many products; they exchanged turquoise, purple fabric, embroidered work, fine linen, coral and rubies
for your merchandise.
    17" 'Judah and Israel traded with you;
they exchanged wheat from Minnith and
confections,*c* honey, oil and balm for
your wares.
    18" 'Damascus, because of your many
products and great wealth of goods, did
business with you in wine from Helbon
and wool from Zahar.
    19" 'Danites and Greeks from Uzal
bought your merchandise; they exchanged wrought iron, cassia and calamus for your wares.
    20" 'Dedan traded in saddle blankets
with you.
    21" 'Arabia and all the princes of Kedar
were your customers; they did business
with you in lambs, rams and goats.
    22" 'The merchants of Sheba and Raa-

mah traded with you; for your merchandise they exchanged the finest of all kinds
of spices and precious stones, and gold.
    23" 'Haran, Canneh and Eden and
merchants of Sheba, Asshur and Kilmad
traded with you. 24In your marketplace
they traded with you beautiful garments,
blue fabric, embroidered work and multi-
colored rugs with cords twisted and tightly knotted.

25" 'The ships of Tarshish serve
    as carriers for your wares.
You are filled with heavy cargo
    in the heart of the sea.
26Your oarsmen take you
    out to the high seas.
But the east wind will break you to
        pieces
    in the heart of the sea.
27Your wealth, merchandise and wares,
    your mariners, seamen and
        shipwrights,
    your merchants and all your soldiers,
    and everyone else on board
will sink into the heart of the sea
    on the day of your shipwreck.
28The shorelands will quake
    when your seamen cry out.
29All who handle the oars
    will abandon their ships;
the mariners and all the seamen
    will stand on the shore.
30They will raise their voice
    and cry bitterly over you;
they will sprinkle dust on their heads
    and roll in ashes.
31They will shave their heads because
        of you
    and will put on sackcloth.
They will weep over you with anguish
        of soul
    and with bitter mourning.
32As they wail and mourn over you,
    they will take up a lament
        concerning you:
"Who was ever silenced like Tyre,
    surrounded by the sea?"
33When your merchandise went out on
        the seas,
    you satisfied many nations;

*a*15 Septuagint; Hebrew *Dedan*   *b*16 Most
Hebrew manuscripts; some Hebrew manuscripts
and Syriac *Edom*   *c*17 The meaning of the
Hebrew for this word is uncertain.

with your great wealth and your
> wares
>> you enriched the kings of the
>> earth.
34Now you are shattered by the sea
> in the depths of the waters;
> your wares and all your company
>> have gone down with you.
35All who live in the coastlands
> are appalled at you;
> their kings shudder with horror
>> and their faces are distorted with
>> fear.
36The merchants among the nations
> hiss at you;
> you have come to a horrible end
> and will be no more.' "

A Prophecy Against the King of Tyre

28 The word of the LORD came to me:
2"Son of man, say to the ruler of
Tyre, 'This is what the Sovereign LORD
says:

" 'In the pride of your heart
> you say, "I am a god;
> I sit on the throne of a god
> in the heart of the seas."
> But you are a man and not a god,
>> though you think you are as wise
>> as a god.
3Are you wiser than Daniel*a*?
> Is no secret hidden from you?
4By your wisdom and understanding
> you have gained wealth for yourself
> and amassed gold and silver
> in your treasuries.
5By your great skill in trading
> you have increased your wealth,
> and because of your wealth
> your heart has grown proud.

6" 'Therefore this is what the Sovereign
LORD says:

" 'Because you think you are wise,
> as wise as a god,
7I am going to bring foreigners against
> you,
> the most ruthless of nations;
> they will draw their swords against
>> your beauty and wisdom
> and pierce your shining splendor.
8They will bring you down to the pit,
> and you will die a violent death
> in the heart of the seas.
9Will you then say, "I am a god,"

in the presence of those who kill
> you?
You will be but a man, not a god,
> in the hands of those who slay
> you.
10You will die the death of the
> uncircumcised
> at the hands of foreigners.

I have spoken, declares the Sovereign
LORD.' "

11The word of the LORD came to me:
12"Son of man, take up a lament concerning the king of Tyre and say to him: 'This is what the Sovereign LORD says:

" 'You were the model of perfection,
> full of wisdom and perfect in
> beauty.
13You were in Eden,
> the garden of God;
> every precious stone adorned you:
>> ruby, topaz and emerald,
>> chrysolite, onyx and jasper,
>> sapphire,*b* turquoise and beryl.*c*
Your settings and mountings*d* were
>> made of gold;
> on the day you were created they
>> were prepared.
14You were anointed as a guardian
> cherub,
> for so I ordained you.
You were on the holy mount of God;
> you walked among the fiery stones.
15You were blameless in your ways
> from the day you were created
> till wickedness was found in you.
16Through your widespread trade
> you were filled with violence,
> and you sinned.
So I drove you in disgrace from the
> mount of God,
> and I expelled you, O guardian
> cherub,
> from among the fiery stones.
17Your heart became proud
> on account of your beauty,
> and you corrupted your wisdom
> because of your splendor.
So I threw you to the earth;

a3 Or *Danel*; the Hebrew spelling may suggest a
person other than the prophet Daniel.   *b13* Or
lapis lazuli   *c13* The precise identification of
some of these precious stones is uncertain.
d13 The meaning of the Hebrew for this phrase is
uncertain.

I made a spectacle of you before
    kings.
18By your many sins and dishonest
    trade
    you have desecrated your
        sanctuaries.
So I made a fire come out from you,
    and it consumed you,
and I reduced you to ashes on the
    ground
    in the sight of all who were
        watching.
19All the nations who knew you
    are appalled at you;
you have come to a horrible end
    and will be no more.' "

A Prophecy Against Sidon

20The word of the LORD came to me:
21"Son of man, set your face against Sidon; prophesy against her 22and say: 'This
is what the Sovereign LORD says:

" 'I am against you, O Sidon,
    and I will gain glory within you.
They will know that I am the LORD,
    when I inflict punishment on her
    and show myself holy within her.
23I will send a plague upon her
    and make blood flow in her streets.
The slain will fall within her,
    with the sword against her on
        every side.
Then they will know that I am the
    LORD.

24" 'No longer will the people of Israel
have malicious neighbors who are painful briers and sharp thorns. Then they will
know that I am the Sovereign LORD.

25" 'This is what the Sovereign LORD
says: When I gather the people of Israel
from the nations where they have been
scattered, I will show myself holy among
them in the sight of the nations. Then
they will live in their own land, which I
gave to my servant Jacob. 26They will live
there in safety and will build houses and
plant vineyards; they will live in safety
when I inflict punishment on all their
neighbors who maligned them. Then they
will know that I am the LORD their God.' "

A Prophecy Against Egypt

29 In the tenth year, in the tenth month
on the twelfth day, the word of the

LORD came to me: 2"Son of man, set
your face against Pharaoh king of Egypt
and prophesy against him and against
all Egypt. 3Speak to him and say: 'This is
what the Sovereign LORD says:

" 'I am against you, Pharaoh king of
    Egypt,
    you great monster lying among
        your streams.
You say, "The Nile is mine;
    I made it for myself."
4But I will put hooks in your jaws
    and make the fish of your streams
        stick to your scales.
I will pull you out from among your
    streams,
    with all the fish sticking to your
        scales.
5I will leave you in the desert,
    you and all the fish of your
        streams.
You will fall on the open field
    and not be gathered or picked up.
I will give you as food
    to the beasts of the earth and the
        birds of the air.

6Then all who live in Egypt will know that
I am the LORD.

" 'You have been a staff of reed for the
house of Israel. 7When they grasped you
with their hands, you splintered and you
tore open their shoulders; when they
leaned on you, you broke and their backs
were wrenched.a

8" 'Therefore this is what the Sovereign
LORD says: I will bring a sword against
you and kill your men and their animals.
9Egypt will become a desolate wasteland.
Then they will know that I am the LORD.

" 'Because you said, "The Nile is mine;
I made it," 10therefore I am against you
and against your streams, and I will make
the land of Egypt a ruin and a desolate
waste from Migdol to Aswan, as far as the
border of Cush.b 11No foot of man or
animal will pass through it; no one will
live there for forty years. 12I will make the
land of Egypt desolate among devastated
lands, and her cities will lie desolate forty
years among ruined cities. And I will dis-

a7 Syriac (see also Septuagint and Vulgate);
Hebrew *and you caused their backs to stand*
b10 That is, the upper Nile region

perse the Egyptians among the nations and scatter them through the countries.

13 " 'Yet this is what the Sovereign LORD says: At the end of forty years I will gather the Egyptians from the nations where they were scattered. 14I will bring them back from captivity and return them to Upper Egypt, *a* the land of their ancestry. There they will be a lowly kingdom. 15It will be the lowliest of kingdoms and will never again exalt itself above the other nations. I will make it so weak that it will never again rule over the nations. 16Egypt will no longer be a source of confidence for the people of Israel but will be a reminder of their sin in turning to her for help. Then they will know that I am the Sovereign LORD.' "

17In the twenty-seventh year, in the first month on the first day, the word of the LORD came to me: 18"Son of man, Nebuchadnezzar king of Babylon drove his army in a hard campaign against Tyre; every head was rubbed bare and every shoulder made raw. Yet he and his army got no reward from the campaign he led against Tyre. 19Therefore this is what the Sovereign LORD says: I am going to give Egypt to Nebuchadnezzar king of Babylon, and he will carry off its wealth. He will loot and plunder the land as pay for his army. 20I have given him Egypt as a reward for his efforts because he and his army did it for me, declares the Sovereign LORD. 21"On that day I will make a horn*b* grow for the house of Israel, and I will open your mouth among them. Then they will know that I am the LORD."

A Lament for Egypt

30 The word of the LORD came to me: 2"Son of man, prophesy and say: 'This is what the Sovereign LORD says:

" 'Wail and say,
  "Alas for that day!"
3For the day is near,
  the day of the LORD is near—
a day of clouds,
  a time of doom for the nations.
4A sword will come against Egypt,
  and anguish will come upon
      Cush.*c*
When the slain fall in Egypt,

her wealth will be carried away
  and her foundations torn down.

5Cush and Put, Lydia and all Arabia, Libya*d* and the people of the covenant land will fall by the sword along with Egypt.

6 " 'This is what the LORD says:

" 'The allies of Egypt will fall
  and her proud strength will fail.
From Migdol to Aswan
  they will fall by the sword within
      her,
        declares the Sovereign LORD.
7 " 'They will be desolate
  among desolate lands,
and their cities will lie
  among ruined cities.
8Then they will know that I am the
      LORD,
  when I set fire to Egypt
  and all her helpers are crushed.

9 " 'On that day messengers will go out from me in ships to frighten Cush out of her complacency. Anguish will take hold of them on the day of Egypt's doom, for it is sure to come.

10 " 'This is what the Sovereign LORD says:

" 'I will put an end to the hordes of
      Egypt
  by the hand of Nebuchadnezzar
      king of Babylon.
11He and his army—the most ruthless of
      nations—
  will be brought in to destroy the
      land.
They will draw their swords against
      Egypt
  and fill the land with the slain.
12I will dry up the streams of the Nile
  and sell the land to evil men;
by the hand of foreigners
  I will lay waste the land and
      everything in it.

I the LORD have spoken.

13 " 'This is what the Sovereign LORD says:

" 'I will destroy the idols

---

a14 Hebrew *to Pathros*   *b21* *Horn* here symbolizes strength.   *c4* That is, the upper Nile region; also in verses 5 and 9   *d5* Hebrew *Cub*

and put an end to the images in
   Memphis.ᵃ
No longer will there be a prince in
   Egypt,
   and I will spread fear throughout
      the land.
¹⁴I will lay waste Upper Egypt,ᵇ
   set fire to Zoan
   and inflict punishment on
      Thebes.ᶜ
¹⁵I will pour out my wrath on
   Pelusium,ᵈ
   the stronghold of Egypt,
   and cut off the hordes of Thebes.
¹⁶I will set fire to Egypt;
   Pelusium will writhe in agony.
Thebes will be taken by storm;
   Memphis will be in constant
      distress.
¹⁷The young men of Heliopolisᵉ and
   Bubastisᶠ
   will fall by the sword,
   and the cities themselves will go
      into captivity.
¹⁸Dark will be the day at Tahpanhes
   when I break the yoke of Egypt;
   there her proud strength will come
      to an end.
She will be covered with clouds,
   and her villages will go into
      captivity.
¹⁹So I will inflict punishment on Egypt,
   and they will know that I am the
      Lord.' "

²⁰In the eleventh year, in the first
month on the seventh day, the word of
the Lord came to me: ²¹"Son of man, I
have broken the arm of Pharaoh king of
Egypt. It has not been bound up for healing or put in a splint so as to become
strong enough to hold a sword. ²²Therefore this is what the Sovereign Lord says:
I am against Pharaoh king of Egypt. I will
break both his arms, the good arm as well
as the broken one, and make the sword
fall from his hand. ²³I will disperse the
Egyptians among the nations and scatter
them through the countries. ²⁴I will
strengthen the arms of the king of Babylon and put my sword in his hand, but
I will break the arms of Pharaoh, and
he will groan before him like a mortally
wounded man. ²⁵I will strengthen the
arms of the king of Babylon, but the arms
of Pharaoh will fall limp. Then they will

know that I am the Lord, when I put my
sword into the hand of the king of Babylon and he brandishes it against Egypt.
²⁶I will disperse the Egyptians among the
nations and scatter them through the
countries. Then they will know that I am
the Lord."

A Cedar in Lebanon

31 In the eleventh year, in the third
month on the first day, the word of
the Lord came to me: ²"Son of man,
say to Pharaoh king of Egypt and to his
hordes:

   " 'Who can be compared with you in
      majesty?
³Consider Assyria, once a cedar in
   Lebanon,
   with beautiful branches
      overshadowing the forest;
it towered on high,
   its top above the thick foliage.
⁴The waters nourished it,
   deep springs made it grow tall;
   their streams flowed
   all around its base
and sent their channels
   to all the trees of the field.
⁵So it towered higher
   than all the trees of the field;
   its boughs increased
   and its branches grew long,
   spreading because of abundant
      waters.
⁶All the birds of the air
   nested in its boughs,
all the beasts of the field
   gave birth under its branches;
all the great nations
   lived in its shade.
⁷It was majestic in beauty,
   with its spreading boughs,
for its roots went down
   to abundant waters.
⁸The cedars in the garden of God
   could not rival it,
   nor could the pine trees
      equal its boughs,
   nor could the plane trees
      compare with its branches—

ᵃ13 Hebrew *Noph*; also in verse 16
ᵇ14 Hebrew *waste Pathros*   ᶜ14 Hebrew *No*; also
in verses 15 and 16   ᵈ15 Hebrew *Sin*; also in
verse 16   ᵉ17 Hebrew *Awen* (or *On*)
ᶠ17 Hebrew *Pi Beseth*

no tree in the garden of God
　　could match its beauty.
⁹I made it beautiful
　　with abundant branches,
the envy of all the trees of Eden
　　in the garden of God.

¹⁰" 'Therefore this is what the Sovereign LORD says: Because it towered on high, lifting its top above the thick foliage, and because it was proud of its height, ¹¹I handed it over to the ruler of the nations, for him to deal with according to its wickedness. I cast it aside, ¹²and the most ruthless of foreign nations cut it down and left it. Its boughs fell on the mountains and in all the valleys; its branches lay broken in all the ravines of the land. All the nations of the earth came out from under its shade and left it. ¹³All the birds of the air settled on the fallen tree, and all the beasts of the field were among its branches. ¹⁴Therefore no other trees by the waters are ever to tower proudly on high, lifting their tops above the thick foliage. No other trees so well-watered are ever to reach such a height; they are all destined for death, for the earth below, among mortal men, with those who go down to the pit.

¹⁵" 'This is what the Sovereign LORD says: On the day it was brought down to the grave[a] I covered the deep springs with mourning for it; I held back its streams, and its abundant waters were restrained. Because of it I clothed Lebanon with gloom, and all the trees of the field withered away. ¹⁶I made the nations tremble at the sound of its fall when I brought it down to the grave with those who go down to the pit. Then all the trees of Eden, the choicest and best of Lebanon, all the trees that were well-watered, were consoled in the earth below. ¹⁷Those who lived in its shade, its allies among the nations, had also gone down to the grave with it, joining those killed by the sword.

¹⁸" 'Which of the trees of Eden can be compared with you in splendor and majesty? Yet you, too, will be brought down with the trees of Eden to the earth below; you will lie among the uncircumcised, with those killed by the sword.

" 'This is Pharaoh and all his hordes, declares the Sovereign LORD.' "

A Lament for Pharaoh

32 In the twelfth year, in the twelfth month on the first day, the word of the LORD came to me: ²"Son of man, take up a lament concerning Pharaoh king of Egypt and say to him:

" 'You are like a lion among the
　　nations;
　　you are like a monster in the seas
thrashing about in your streams,
　　churning the water with your feet
　　and muddying the streams.

³" 'This is what the Sovereign LORD says:

" 'With a great throng of people
　　I will cast my net over you,
　　and they will haul you up in my
　　　net.
⁴I will throw you on the land
　　and hurl you on the open field.
I will let all the birds of the air settle
　　on you
　　and all the beasts of the earth
　　　gorge themselves on you.
⁵I will spread your flesh on the
　　mountains
　　and fill the valleys with your
　　remains.
⁶I will drench the land with your
　　flowing blood
　　all the way to the mountains,
　　and the ravines will be filled with
　　　your flesh.
⁷When I snuff you out, I will cover the
　　heavens
　　and darken their stars;
I will cover the sun with a cloud,
　　and the moon will not give its
　　　light.
⁸All the shining lights in the heavens
　　I will darken over you;
I will bring darkness over your
　　land,
　　　　declares the Sovereign LORD.
⁹I will trouble the hearts of many
　　peoples
　　when I bring about your
　　　destruction among the
　　　nations,

_____
[a]15 Hebrew *Sheol*; also in verses 16 and 17

among[a] lands you have not
known.
¹⁰I will cause many peoples to be
appalled at you,
and their kings will shudder with
horror because of you
when I brandish my sword before
them.
On the day of your downfall
each of them will tremble
every moment for his life.

¹¹ " 'For this is what the Sovereign
LORD says:

" 'The sword of the king of Babylon
will come against you.
¹²I will cause your hordes to fall
by the swords of mighty men—
the most ruthless of all nations.
They will shatter the pride of Egypt,
and all her hordes will be
overthrown.
¹³I will destroy all her cattle
from beside abundant waters
no longer to be stirred by the foot of
man
or muddied by the hoofs of cattle.
¹⁴Then I will let her waters settle
and make her streams flow like oil,
declares the Sovereign LORD.
¹⁵When I make Egypt desolate
and strip the land of everything in
it,
when I strike down all who live there,
then they will know that I am the
LORD.'

¹⁶"This is the lament they will chant
for her. The daughters of the nations will
chant it; for Egypt and all her hordes they
will chant it, declares the Sovereign LORD."

¹⁷In the twelfth year, on the fifteenth
day of the month, the word of the LORD
came to me: ¹⁸"Son of man, wail for the
hordes of Egypt and consign to the earth
below both her and the daughters of
mighty nations, with those who go down
to the pit. ¹⁹Say to them, 'Are you more
favored than others? Go down and be laid
among the uncircumcised.' ²⁰They will
fall among those killed by the sword. The
sword is drawn; let her be dragged off
with all her hordes. ²¹From within the
grave[b] the mighty leaders will say of
Egypt and her allies, 'They have come

down and they lie with the uncircumcised, with those killed by the sword.'

²²"Assyria is there with her whole
army; she is surrounded by the graves of
all her slain, all who have fallen by the
sword. ²³Their graves are in the depths
of the pit and her army lies around her
grave. All who had spread terror in the
land of the living are slain, fallen by the
sword.

²⁴"Elam is there, with all her hordes
around her grave. All of them are slain,
fallen by the sword. All who had spread
terror in the land of the living went down
uncircumcised to the earth below. They
bear their shame with those who go down
to the pit. ²⁵A bed is made for her among
the slain, with all her hordes around her
grave. All of them are uncircumcised,
killed by the sword. Because their terror
had spread in the land of the living, they
bear their shame with those who go down
to the pit; they are laid among the slain.

²⁶"Meshech and Tubal are there, with
all their hordes around their graves. All of
them are uncircumcised, killed by the
sword because they spread their terror in
the land of the living. ²⁷Do they not lie
with the other uncircumcised warriors
who have fallen, who went down to the
grave with their weapons of war, whose
swords were placed under their heads?
The punishment for their sins rested on
their bones, though the terror of these
warriors had stalked through the land of
the living.

²⁸"You too, O Pharaoh, will be broken
and will lie among the uncircumcised,
with those killed by the sword.

²⁹"Edom is there, her kings and all her
princes; despite their power, they are laid
with those killed by the sword. They lie
with the uncircumcised, with those who
go down to the pit.

³⁰"All the princes of the north and all
the Sidonians are there; they went down
with the slain in disgrace despite the terror caused by their power. They lie uncircumcised with those killed by the sword
and bear their shame with those who go
down to the pit.

³¹"Pharaoh—he and all his army—will

---

[a]9 Hebrew; Septuagint *bring you into captivity
among the nations,* / *to* [b]21 Hebrew *Sheol;* also
in verse 27

see them and he will be consoled for all his hordes that were killed by the sword, declares the Sovereign LORD. [32]Although I had him spread terror in the land of the living, Pharaoh and all his hordes will be laid among the uncircumcised, with those killed by the sword, declares the Sovereign LORD."

Ezekiel a Watchman

33 The word of the LORD came to me: [2]"Son of man, speak to your countrymen and say to them: 'When I bring the sword against a land, and the people of the land choose one of their men and make him their watchman, [3]and he sees the sword coming against the land and blows the trumpet to warn the people, [4]then if anyone hears the trumpet but does not take warning and the sword comes and takes his life, his blood will be on his own head. [5]Since he heard the sound of the trumpet but did not take warning, his blood will be on his own head. If he had taken warning, he would have saved himself. [6]But if the watchman sees the sword coming and does not blow the trumpet to warn the people and the sword comes and takes the life of one of them, that man will be taken away because of his sin, but I will hold the watchman accountable for his blood.'

[7]"Son of man, I have made you a watchman for the house of Israel; so hear the word I speak and give them warning from me. [8]When I say to the wicked, 'O wicked man, you will surely die,' and you do not speak out to dissuade him from his ways, that wicked man will die for[a] his sin, and I will hold you accountable for his blood. [9]But if you do warn the wicked man to turn from his ways and he does not do so, he will die for his sin, but you will have saved yourself.

[10]"Son of man, say to the house of Israel, 'This is what you are saying: "Our offenses and sins weigh us down, and we are wasting away because of[b] them. How then can we live?" ' [11]Say to them, 'As surely as I live, declares the Sovereign LORD, I take no pleasure in the death of the wicked, but rather that they turn from their ways and live. Turn! Turn from your evil ways! Why will you die, O house of Israel?'

[12]"Therefore, son of man, say to your countrymen, 'The righteousness of the righteous man will not save him when he disobeys, and the wickedness of the wicked man will not cause him to fall when he turns from it. The righteous man, if he sins, will not be allowed to live because of his former righteousness.' [13]If I tell the righteous man that he will surely live, but then he trusts in his righteousness and does evil, none of the righteous things he has done will be remembered; he will die for the evil he has done. [14]And if I say to the wicked man, 'You will surely die,' but he then turns away from his sin and does what is just and right— [15]if he gives back what he took in pledge for a loan, returns what he has stolen, follows the decrees that give life, and does no evil, he will surely live; he will not die. [16]None of the sins he has committed will be remembered against him. He has done what is just and right; he will surely live.

[17]"Yet your countrymen say, 'The way of the Lord is not just.' But it is their way that is not just. [18]If a righteous man turns from his righteousness and does evil, he will die for it. [19]And if a wicked man turns away from his wickedness and does what is just and right, he will live by doing so. [20]Yet, O house of Israel, you say, 'The way of the Lord is not just.' But I will judge each of you according to his own ways."

Jerusalem's Fall Explained

[21]In the twelfth year of our exile, in the tenth month on the fifth day, a man who had escaped from Jerusalem came to me and said, "The city has fallen!" [22]Now the evening before the man arrived, the hand of the LORD was upon me, and he opened my mouth before the man came to me in the morning. So my mouth was opened and I was no longer silent.

[23]Then the word of the LORD came to me: [24]"Son of man, the people living in those ruins in the land of Israel are saying, 'Abraham was only one man, yet he possessed the land. But we are many; surely the land has been given to us as our possession.' [25]Therefore say to them, 'This is what the Sovereign LORD says: Since you

---

[a]8 Or *in;* also in verse 9   [b]10 Or *away in*

eat meat with the blood still in it and look to your idols and shed blood, should you then possess the land? 26You rely on your sword, you do detestable things, and each of you defiles his neighbor's wife. Should you then possess the land?'

27"Say this to them: 'This is what the Sovereign LORD says: As surely as I live, those who are left in the ruins will fall by the sword, those out in the country I will give to the wild animals to be devoured, and those in strongholds and caves will die of a plague. 28I will make the land a desolate waste, and her proud strength will come to an end, and the mountains of Israel will become desolate so that no one will cross them. 29Then they will know that I am the LORD, when I have made the land a desolate waste because of all the detestable things they have done.'

30"As for you, son of man, your countrymen are talking together about you by the walls and at the doors of the houses, saying to each other, 'Come and hear the message that has come from the LORD.' 31My people come to you, as they usually do, and sit before you to listen to your words, but they do not put them into practice. With their mouths they express devotion, but their hearts are greedy for unjust gain. 32Indeed, to them you are nothing more than one who sings love songs with a beautiful voice and plays an instrument well, for they hear your words but do not put them into practice.

33"When all this comes true—and it surely will—then they will know that a prophet has been among them."

Shepherds and Sheep

34 The word of the LORD came to me: 2"Son of man, prophesy against the shepherds of Israel; prophesy and say to them: 'This is what the Sovereign LORD says: Woe to the shepherds of Israel who only take care of themselves! Should not shepherds take care of the flock? 3You eat the curds, clothe yourselves with the wool and slaughter the choice animals, but you do not take care of the flock. 4You have not strengthened the weak or healed the sick or bound up the injured. You have not brought back the strays or searched for the lost. You have ruled them harshly

and brutally. 5So they were scattered because there was no shepherd, and when they were scattered they became food for all the wild animals. 6My sheep wandered over all the mountains and on every high hill. They were scattered over the whole earth, and no one searched or looked for them.

7" 'Therefore, you shepherds, hear the word of the LORD: 8As surely as I live, declares the Sovereign LORD, because my flock lacks a shepherd and so has been plundered and has become food for all the wild animals, and because my shepherds did not search for my flock but cared for themselves rather than for my flock, 9therefore, O shepherds, hear the word of the LORD: 10This is what the Sovereign LORD says: I am against the shepherds and will hold them accountable for my flock. I will remove them from tending the flock so that the shepherds can no longer feed themselves. I will rescue my flock from their mouths, and it will no longer be food for them.

11" 'For this is what the Sovereign LORD says: I myself will search for my sheep and look after them. 12As a shepherd looks after his scattered flock when he is with them, so will I look after my sheep. I will rescue them from all the places where they were scattered on a day of clouds and darkness. 13I will bring them out from the nations and gather them from the countries, and I will bring them into their own land. I will pasture them on the mountains of Israel, in the ravines and in all the settlements in the land. 14I will tend them in a good pasture, and the mountain heights of Israel will be their grazing land. There they will lie down in good grazing land, and there they will feed in a rich pasture on the mountains of Israel. 15I myself will tend my sheep and have them lie down, declares the Sovereign LORD. 16I will search for the lost and bring back the strays. I will bind up the injured and strengthen the weak, but the sleek and the strong I will destroy. I will shepherd the flock with justice.

17" 'As for you, my flock, this is what the Sovereign LORD says: I will judge between one sheep and another, and between rams and goats. 18Is it not enough for you to feed on the good pasture? Must you also trample the rest of your pasture with your feet? Is it not enough for you to drink clear water? Must you also muddy the rest with your feet? ¹⁹Must my flock feed on what you have trampled and drink what you have muddied with your feet?

²⁰" 'Therefore this is what the Sovereign LORD says to them: See, I myself will judge between the fat sheep and the lean sheep. ²¹Because you shove with flank and shoulder, butting all the weak sheep with your horns until you have driven them away, ²²I will save my flock, and they will no longer be plundered. I will judge between one sheep and another. ²³I will place over them one shepherd, my servant David, and he will tend them; he will tend them and be their shepherd. ²⁴I the LORD will be their God, and my servant David will be prince among them. I the LORD have spoken.

²⁵" 'I will make a covenant of peace with them and rid the land of wild beasts so that they may live in the desert and sleep in the forests in safety. ²⁶I will bless them and the places surrounding my hill.ᵃ I will send down showers in season; there will be showers of blessing. ²⁷The trees of the field will yield their fruit and the ground will yield its crops; the people will be secure in their land. They will know that I am the LORD, when I break the bars of their yoke and rescue them from the hands of those who enslaved them. ²⁸They will no longer be plundered by the nations, nor will wild animals devour them. They will live in safety, and no one will make them afraid. ²⁹I will provide for them a land renowned for its crops, and they will no longer be victims of famine in the land or bear the scorn of the nations. ³⁰Then they will know that I, the LORD their God, am with them and that they, the house of Israel, are my people, declares the Sovereign LORD. ³¹You my sheep, the sheep of my

---

ᵃ26 Or I will make them and the places surrounding my hill a blessing

Showers of Blessing

Monday

EZEKIEL 34:26   In marriage, as with any area of life, we can lose the perspective of where our blessings come from. We can easily become preoccupied with what we have not yet obtained and thus forget what God has given us. Advertisers want us to focus on what we do not yet "have." It seems to be an American epidemic to become dissatisfied by focusing on what we have not yet obtained or accomplished. We also have the tendency to compare ourselves *up* rather than *down*. Instead of seeing the blessings we enjoy compared to the great majority of the rest of the world, we compare ourselves with those who have "more."

Our perspective should always be one of deep gratitude to the giver of blessings. God has blessed us immeasurably just by giving us life. We don't have an empty stomach, and we have a roof over our head. Our dissatisfaction or gratefulness depends on the perspective we choose.

Each year Christmas seems to bring out chronic dissatisfaction. Recently one of our home videos of an earlier Christmas changed that perspective for us forever. As we watched our first Christmas with children, we were moved by two scenes. The first scene showed us to be overwhelmed with happiness and emotion over a used microwave I had purchased for Rosemary. In those day an inexpensive gift seemed to bring us so much joy. The real blessing, however, soon came crawling into the video scene. As we watched our then baby girl, we were overcome with the realization of how "rich" God had made us in the blessings that money can't buy.

When you find yourself taking a blessing inventory, look at the things God has given you that no amount of money could ever buy. Surely we will all find that we are all showered with blessings.

—Bob & Rosemary

Go to page 930 for your next devotional reading.

pasture, are people, and I am your God, declares the Sovereign LORD.' "

A Prophecy Against Edom

35 The word of the LORD came to me: 2"Son of man, set your face against Mount Seir; prophesy against it 3and say: 'This is what the Sovereign LORD says: I am against you, Mount Seir, and I will stretch out my hand against you and make you a desolate waste. 4I will turn your towns into ruins and you will be desolate. Then you will know that I am the LORD.

5" 'Because you harbored an ancient hostility and delivered the Israelites over to the sword at the time of their calamity, the time their punishment reached its climax, 6therefore as surely as I live, declares the Sovereign LORD, I will give you over to bloodshed and it will pursue you. Since you did not hate bloodshed, bloodshed will pursue you. 7I will make Mount Seir a desolate waste and cut off from it all who come and go. 8I will fill your mountains with the slain; those killed by the sword will fall on your hills and in your valleys and in all your ravines. 9I will make you desolate forever; your towns will not be inhabited. Then you will know that I am the LORD.

10" 'Because you have said, "These two nations and countries will be ours and we will take possession of them," even though I the LORD was there, 11therefore as surely as I live, declares the Sovereign LORD, I will treat you in accordance with the anger and jealousy you showed in your hatred of them and I will make myself known among them when I judge you. 12Then you will know that I the LORD have heard all the contemptible things you have said against the mountains of Israel. You said, "They have been laid waste and have been given over to us to devour." 13You boasted against me and spoke against me without restraint, and I heard it. 14This is what the Sovereign LORD says: While the whole earth rejoices, I will make you desolate. 15Because you rejoiced when the inheritance of the house of Israel became desolate, that is how I will treat you. You will be desolate, O Mount Seir, you and all of Edom. Then they will know that I am the LORD.' "

A Prophecy to the Mountains of Israel

36 "Son of man, prophesy to the mountains of Israel and say, 'O mountains of Israel, hear the word of the LORD. 2This is what the Sovereign LORD says: The enemy said of you, "Aha! The ancient heights have become our possession." ' 3Therefore prophesy and say, 'This is what the Sovereign LORD says: Because they ravaged and hounded you from every side so that you became the possession of the rest of the nations and the object of people's malicious talk and slander, 4therefore, O mountains of Israel, hear the word of the Sovereign LORD: This is what the Sovereign LORD says to the mountains and hills, to the ravines and valleys, to the desolate ruins and the deserted towns that have been plundered and ridiculed by the rest of the nations around you— 5this is what the Sovereign LORD says: In my burning zeal I have spoken against the rest of the nations, and against all Edom, for with glee and with malice in their hearts they made my land their own possession so that they might plunder its pastureland.' 6Therefore prophesy concerning the land of Israel and say to the mountains and hills, to the ravines and valleys: 'This is what the Sovereign LORD says: I speak in my jealous wrath because you have suffered the scorn of the nations. 7Therefore this is what the Sovereign LORD says: I swear with uplifted hand that the nations around you will also suffer scorn.

8" 'But you, O mountains of Israel, will produce branches and fruit for my people Israel, for they will soon come home. 9I am concerned for you and will look on you with favor; you will be plowed and sown, 10and I will multiply the number of people upon you, even the whole house of Israel. The towns will be inhabited and the ruins rebuilt. 11I will increase the number of men and animals upon you, and they will be fruitful and become numerous. I will settle people on you as in the past and will make you prosper more than before. Then you will know that I am the LORD. 12I will cause people, my people Israel, to walk upon you. They will possess you, and you will be their inheritance; you will never again deprive them of their children.

13 " 'This is what the Sovereign LORD says: Because people say to you, "You devour men and deprive your nation of its children," 14therefore you will no longer devour men or make your nation childless, declares the Sovereign LORD. 15No longer will I make you hear the taunts of the nations, and no longer will you suffer the scorn of the peoples or cause your nation to fall, declares the Sovereign LORD.' "

16Again the word of the LORD came to me: 17"Son of man, when the people of Israel were living in their own land, they defiled it by their conduct and their actions. Their conduct was like a woman's monthly uncleanness in my sight. 18So I poured out my wrath on them because they had shed blood in the land and because they had defiled it with their idols. 19I dispersed them among the nations, and they were scattered through the countries; I judged them according to their conduct and their actions. 20And wherever they went among the nations they profaned my holy name, for it was said of them, 'These are the LORD's people, and yet they had to leave his land.' 21I had concern for my holy name, which the house of Israel profaned among the nations where they had gone.

22"Therefore say to the house of Israel, 'This is what the Sovereign LORD says: It is not for your sake, O house of Israel, that I am going to do these things, but for the sake of my holy name, which you have profaned among the nations where you have gone. 23I will show the holiness of my great name, which has been profaned among the nations, the name you have profaned among them. Then the nations will know that I am the LORD, declares the Sovereign LORD, when I show myself holy through you before their eyes.

24" 'For I will take you out of the nations; I will gather you from all the countries and bring you back into your own land. 25I will sprinkle clean water on you, and you will be clean; I will cleanse you from all your impurities and from all your idols. 26I will give you a new heart and put a new spirit in you; I will remove from you your heart of stone and give you a heart of flesh. 27And I will put my Spirit in you and move you to follow my decrees and be careful to keep my laws.

28You will live in the land I gave your forefathers; you will be my people, and I will be your God. 29I will save you from all your uncleanness. I will call for the grain and make it plentiful and will not bring famine upon you. 30I will increase the fruit of the trees and the crops of the field, so that you will no longer suffer disgrace among the nations because of famine. 31Then you will remember your evil ways and wicked deeds, and you will loathe yourselves for your sins and detestable practices. 32I want you to know that I am not doing this for your sake, declares the Sovereign LORD. Be ashamed and disgraced for your conduct, O house of Israel!

33" 'This is what the Sovereign LORD says: On the day I cleanse you from all your sins, I will resettle your towns, and the ruins will be rebuilt. 34The desolate land will be cultivated instead of lying desolate in the sight of all who pass through it. 35They will say, "This land that was laid waste has become like the garden of Eden; the cities that were lying in ruins, desolate and destroyed, are now fortified and inhabited." 36Then the nations around you that remain will know that I the LORD have rebuilt what was destroyed and have replanted what was desolate. I the LORD have spoken, and I will do it.'

37"This is what the Sovereign LORD says: Once again I will yield to the plea of the house of Israel and do this for them: I will make their people as numerous as sheep, 38as numerous as the flocks for offerings at Jerusalem during her appointed feasts. So will the ruined cities be filled with flocks of people. Then they will know that I am the LORD."

The Valley of Dry Bones

37 The hand of the LORD was upon me, and he brought me out by the Spirit of the LORD and set me in the middle of a valley; it was full of bones. 2He led me back and forth among them, and I saw a great many bones on the floor of the valley, bones that were very dry. 3He asked me, "Son of man, can these bones live?"

I said, "O Sovereign LORD, you alone know."

⁴Then he said to me, "Prophesy to these bones and say to them, 'Dry bones, hear the word of the LORD! ⁵This is what the Sovereign LORD says to these bones: I will make breath*ᵃ* enter you, and you will come to life. ⁶I will attach tendons to you and make flesh come upon you and cover you with skin; I will put breath in you, and you will come to life. Then you will know that I am the LORD.' "

⁷So I prophesied as I was commanded. And as I was prophesying, there was a noise, a rattling sound, and the bones came together, bone to bone. ⁸I looked, and tendons and flesh appeared on them and skin covered them, but there was no breath in them.

⁹Then he said to me, "Prophesy to the breath; prophesy, son of man, and say to it, 'This is what the Sovereign LORD says: Come from the four winds, O breath, and breathe into these slain, that they may live.' " ¹⁰So I prophesied as he commanded me, and breath entered them; they came to life and stood up on their feet—a vast army.

¹¹Then he said to me: "Son of man, these bones are the whole house of Israel. They say, 'Our bones are dried up and our hope is gone; we are cut off.' ¹²Therefore prophesy and say to them: 'This is what the Sovereign LORD says: O my people, I am going to open your graves and bring you up from them; I will bring you back to the land of Israel. ¹³Then you, my people, will know that I am the LORD, when I open your graves and bring you up from them. ¹⁴I will put my Spirit in you and you will live, and I will settle you in your own land. Then you will know that I the LORD have spoken, and I have done it, declares the LORD.' "

One Nation Under One King

¹⁵The word of the LORD came to me: ¹⁶"Son of man, take a stick of wood and write on it, 'Belonging to Judah and the Israelites associated with him.' Then take another stick of wood, and write on it, 'Ephraim's stick, belonging to Joseph and all the house of Israel associated with him.' ¹⁷Join them together into one stick so that they will become one in your hand.

¹⁸"When your countrymen ask you, 'Won't you tell us what you mean by this?' ¹⁹say to them, 'This is what the Sovereign LORD says: I am going to take the stick of Joseph—which is in Ephraim's hand—and of the Israelite tribes associated with him, and join it to Judah's stick, making them a single stick of wood, and they will become one in my hand.' ²⁰Hold before their eyes the sticks you have written on ²¹and say to them, 'This is what the Sovereign LORD says: I will take the Israelites out of the nations where they have gone. I will gather them from all around and bring them back into their own land. ²²I will make them one nation in the land, on the mountains of Israel. There will be one king over all of them and they will never again be two nations or be divided into two kingdoms. ²³They will no longer defile themselves with their idols and vile images or with any of their offenses, for I will save them from all their sinful backsliding,*ᵇ* and I will cleanse them. They will be my people, and I will be their God.

²⁴" 'My servant David will be king over them, and they will all have one shepherd. They will follow my laws and be careful to keep my decrees. ²⁵They will live in the land I gave to my servant Jacob, the land where your fathers lived. They and their children and their children's children will live there forever, and David my servant will be their prince forever. ²⁶I will make a covenant of peace with them; it will be an everlasting covenant. I will establish them and increase their numbers, and I will put my sanctuary among them forever. ²⁷My dwelling place will be with them; I will be their God, and they will be my people. ²⁸Then the nations will know that I the LORD make Israel holy, when my sanctuary is among them forever.' "

A Prophecy Against Gog

38 The word of the LORD came to me: ²"Son of man, set your face against Gog, of the land of Magog, the chief prince of*ᶜ* Meshech and Tubal; prophesy against him ³and say: 'This is what the

ᵃ5 The Hebrew for this word can also mean wind or spirit (see verses 6-14).   ᵇ23 Many Hebrew manuscripts (see also Septuagint); most Hebrew manuscripts all their dwelling places where they sinned   ᶜ2 Or the prince of Rosh,

Sovereign LORD says: I am against you, O Gog, chief prince of[a] Meshech and Tubal. [4]I will turn you around, put hooks in your jaws and bring you out with your whole army—your horses, your horsemen fully armed, and a great horde with large and small shields, all of them brandishing their swords. [5]Persia, Cush[b] and Put will be with them, all with shields and helmets, [6]also Gomer with all its troops, and Beth Togarmah from the far north with all its troops—the many nations with you.

[7]" 'Get ready; be prepared, you and all the hordes gathered about you, and take command of them. [8]After many days you will be called to arms. In future years you will invade a land that has recovered from war, whose people were gathered from many nations to the mountains of Israel, which had long been desolate. They had been brought out from the nations, and now all of them live in safety. [9]You and all your troops and the many nations with you will go up, advancing like a storm; you will be like a cloud covering the land.

[10]" 'This is what the Sovereign LORD says: On that day thoughts will come into your mind and you will devise an evil scheme. [11]You will say, "I will invade a land of unwalled villages; I will attack a peaceful and unsuspecting people—all of them living without walls and without gates and bars. [12]I will plunder and loot and turn my hand against the resettled ruins and the people gathered from the nations, rich in livestock and goods, living at the center of the land." [13]Sheba and Dedan and the merchants of Tarshish and all her villages[c] will say to you, "Have you come to plunder? Have you gathered your hordes to loot, to carry off silver and gold, to take away livestock and goods and to seize much plunder?" '

[14]"Therefore, son of man, prophesy and say to Gog: 'This is what the Sovereign LORD says: In that day, when my people Israel are living in safety, will you not take notice of it? [15]You will come from your place in the far north, you and many nations with you, all of them riding on horses, a great horde, a mighty army. [16]You will advance against my people Israel like a cloud that covers the land. In days to come, O Gog, I will bring you

against my land, so that the nations may know me when I show myself holy through you before their eyes.

[17]" 'This is what the Sovereign LORD says: Are you not the one I spoke of in former days by my servants the prophets of Israel? At that time they prophesied for years that I would bring you against them. [18]This is what will happen in that day: When Gog attacks the land of Israel, my hot anger will be aroused, declares the Sovereign LORD. [19]In my zeal and fiery wrath I declare that at that time there shall be a great earthquake in the land of Israel. [20]The fish of the sea, the birds of the air, the beasts of the field, every creature that moves along the ground, and all the people on the face of the earth will tremble at my presence. The mountains will be overturned, the cliffs will crumble and every wall will fall to the ground. [21]I will summon a sword against Gog on all my mountains, declares the Sovereign LORD. Every man's sword will be against his brother. [22]I will execute judgment upon him with plague and bloodshed; I will pour down torrents of rain, hailstones and burning sulfur on him and on his troops and on the many nations with him. [23]And so I will show my greatness and my holiness, and I will make myself known in the sight of many nations. Then they will know that I am the LORD.'

39 "Son of man, prophesy against Gog and say: 'This is what the Sovereign LORD says: I am against you, O Gog, chief prince of[a] Meshech and Tubal. [2]I will turn you around and drag you along. I will bring you from the far north and send you against the mountains of Israel. [3]Then I will strike your bow from your left hand and make your arrows drop from your right hand. [4]On the mountains of Israel you will fall, you and all your troops and the nations with you. I will give you as food to all kinds of carrion birds and to the wild animals. [5]You will fall in the open field, for I have spoken, declares the Sovereign LORD. [6]I will send fire on Magog and on those who live in safety in the coastlands, and they will know that I am the LORD.

[7]" 'I will make known my holy name

---

[a]3,1 Or *Gog, prince of Rosh,*   [b]5 That is, the upper Nile region   [c]13 Or *her strong lions*

among my people Israel. I will no longer let my holy name be profaned, and the nations will know that I the LORD am the Holy One in Israel. [8]It is coming! It will surely take place, declares the Sovereign LORD. This is the day I have spoken of.

[9]" 'Then those who live in the towns of Israel will go out and use the weapons for fuel and burn them up—the small and large shields, the bows and arrows, the war clubs and spears. For seven years they will use them for fuel. [10]They will not need to gather wood from the fields or cut it from the forests, because they will use the weapons for fuel. And they will plunder those who plundered them and loot those who looted them, declares the Sovereign LORD.

[11]" 'On that day I will give Gog a burial place in Israel, in the valley of those who travel east toward[a] the Sea.[b] It will block the way of travelers, because Gog and all his hordes will be buried there. So it will be called the Valley of Hamon Gog.[c]

[12]" 'For seven months the house of Israel will be burying them in order to cleanse the land. [13]All the people of the land will bury them, and the day I am glorified will be a memorable day for them, declares the Sovereign LORD.

[14]" 'Men will be regularly employed to cleanse the land. Some will go throughout the land and, in addition to them, others will bury those that remain on the ground. At the end of the seven months they will begin their search. [15]As they go through the land and one of them sees a human bone, he will set up a marker beside it until the gravediggers have buried it in the Valley of Hamon Gog. [16](Also a town called Hamonah[d] will be there.) And so they will cleanse the land.'

[17]"Son of man, this is what the Sovereign LORD says: Call out to every kind of bird and all the wild animals: 'Assemble and come together from all around to the sacrifice I am preparing for you, the great sacrifice on the mountains of Israel. There you will eat flesh and drink blood. [18]You will eat the flesh of mighty men and drink the blood of the princes of the earth as if they were rams and lambs, goats and bulls—all of them fattened animals from Bashan. [19]At the sacrifice I am preparing for you, you will eat fat till you are glutted

and drink blood till you are drunk. [20]At my table you will eat your fill of horses and riders, mighty men and soldiers of every kind,' declares the Sovereign LORD.

[21]"I will display my glory among the nations, and all the nations will see the punishment I inflict and the hand I lay upon them. [22]From that day forward the house of Israel will know that I am the LORD their God. [23]And the nations will know that the people of Israel went into exile for their sin, because they were unfaithful to me. So I hid my face from them and handed them over to their enemies, and they all fell by the sword. [24]I dealt with them according to their uncleanness and their offenses, and I hid my face from them.

[25]"Therefore this is what the Sovereign LORD says: I will now bring Jacob back from captivity[e] and will have compassion on all the people of Israel, and I will be zealous for my holy name. [26]They will forget their shame and all the unfaithfulness they showed toward me when they lived in safety in their land with no one to make them afraid. [27]When I have brought them back from the nations and have gathered them from the countries of their enemies, I will show myself holy through them in the sight of many nations. [28]Then they will know that I am the LORD their God, for though I sent them into exile among the nations, I will gather them to their own land, not leaving any behind. [29]I will no longer hide my face from them, for I will pour out my Spirit on the house of Israel, declares the Sovereign LORD."

The New Temple Area

40 In the twenty-fifth year of our exile, at the beginning of the year, on the tenth of the month, in the fourteenth year after the fall of the city—on that very day the hand of the LORD was upon me and he took me there. [2]In visions of God he took me to the land of Israel and set me on a very high mountain, on whose south side were some buildings that looked like a city. [3]He took me there, and I saw a man

---

[a]11 Or of   [b]11 That is, the Dead Sea
[c]11 Hamon Gog means hordes of Gog.
[d]16 Hamonah means horde.   [e]25 Or now restore the fortunes of Jacob

whose appearance was like bronze; he was standing in the gateway with a linen cord and a measuring rod in his hand. [4]The man said to me, "Son of man, look with your eyes and hear with your ears and pay attention to everything I am going to show you, for that is why you have been brought here. Tell the house of Israel everything you see."

The East Gate to the Outer Court

[5]I saw a wall completely surrounding the temple area. The length of the measuring rod in the man's hand was six long cubits, each of which was a cubit[a] and a handbreadth.[b] He measured the wall; it was one measuring rod thick and one rod high.

[6]Then he went to the gate facing east. He climbed its steps and measured the threshold of the gate; it was one rod deep.[c] [7]The alcoves for the guards were one rod long and one rod wide, and the projecting walls between the alcoves were five cubits thick. And the threshold of the gate next to the portico facing the temple was one rod deep.

[8]Then he measured the portico of the gateway; [9]it[d] was eight cubits deep and its jambs were two cubits thick. The portico of the gateway faced the temple.

[10]Inside the east gate were three alcoves on each side; the three had the same measurements, and the faces of the projecting walls on each side had the same measurements. [11]Then he measured the width of the entrance to the gateway; it was ten cubits and its length was thirteen cubits. [12]In front of each alcove was a wall one cubit high, and the alcoves were six cubits square. [13]Then he measured the gateway from the top of the rear wall of one alcove to the top of the opposite one; the distance was twenty-five cubits from one parapet opening to the opposite one. [14]He measured along the faces of the projecting walls all around the inside of the gateway—sixty cubits. The measurement was up to the portico[e] facing the courtyard.[f] [15]The distance from the entrance of the gateway to the far end of its portico was fifty cubits. [16]The alcoves and the projecting walls inside the gateway were surmounted by narrow parapet openings all around, as was the portico; the open-

ings all around faced inward. The faces of the projecting walls were decorated with palm trees.

The Outer Court

[17]Then he brought me into the outer court. There I saw some rooms and a pavement that had been constructed all around the court; there were thirty rooms along the pavement. [18]It abutted the sides of the gateways and was as wide as they were long; this was the lower pavement. [19]Then he measured the distance from the inside of the lower gateway to the outside of the inner court; it was a hundred cubits on the east side as well as on the north.

The North Gate

[20]Then he measured the length and width of the gate facing north, leading into the outer court. [21]Its alcoves—three on each side—its projecting walls and its portico had the same measurements as those of the first gateway. It was fifty cubits long and twenty-five cubits wide. [22]Its openings, its portico and its palm tree decorations had the same measurements as those of the gate facing east. Seven steps led up to it, with its portico opposite them. [23]There was a gate to the inner court facing the north gate, just as there was on the east. He measured from one gate to the opposite one; it was a hundred cubits.

The South Gate

[24]Then he led me to the south side and I saw a gate facing south. He measured its jambs and its portico, and they had the same measurements as the others. [25]The gateway and its portico had narrow openings all around, like the openings of the others. It was fifty cubits long and twenty-five cubits wide. [26]Seven steps led up to it, with its portico opposite them; it had palm tree decorations on the faces of the

a5 The common cubit was about 1 1/2 feet (about 0.5 meter).　　b5 That is, about 3 inches (about 8 centimeters)　　c6 Septuagint; Hebrew *deep, the first threshold, one rod deep*　　d8,9 Many Hebrew manuscripts, Septuagint, Vulgate and Syriac; most Hebrew manuscripts *gateway facing the temple; it was one rod deep. 9Then he measured the portico of the gateway; it*　　e14 Septuagint; Hebrew *projecting wall*　　f14 The meaning of the Hebrew for this verse is uncertain.

projecting walls on each side. ²⁷The inner court also had a gate facing south, and he measured from this gate to the outer gate on the south side; it was a hundred cubits.

Gates to the Inner Court

²⁸Then he brought me into the inner court through the south gate, and he measured the south gate; it had the same measurements as the others. ²⁹Its alcoves, its projecting walls and its portico had the same measurements as the others. The gateway and its portico had openings all around. It was fifty cubits long and twenty-five cubits wide. ³⁰(The porticoes of the gateways around the inner court were twenty-five cubits wide and five cubits deep.) ³¹Its portico faced the outer court; palm trees decorated its jambs, and eight steps led up to it.

³²Then he brought me to the inner court on the east side, and he measured the gateway; it had the same measurements as the others. ³³Its alcoves, its projecting walls and its portico had the same measurements as the others. The gateway and its portico had openings all around. It was fifty cubits long and twenty-five cubits wide. ³⁴Its portico faced the outer court; palm trees decorated the jambs on either side, and eight steps led up to it.

³⁵Then he brought me to the north gate and measured it. It had the same measurements as the others, ³⁶as did its alcoves, its projecting walls and its portico, and it had openings all around. It was fifty cubits long and twenty-five cubits wide. ³⁷Its portico^a faced the outer court; palm trees decorated the jambs on either side, and eight steps led up to it.

The Rooms for Preparing Sacrifices

³⁸A room with a doorway was by the portico in each of the inner gateways, where the burnt offerings were washed. ³⁹In the portico of the gateway were two tables on each side, on which the burnt offerings, sin offerings and guilt offerings were slaughtered. ⁴⁰By the outside wall of the portico of the gateway, near the steps at the entrance to the north gateway were two tables, and on the other side of the steps were two tables. ⁴¹So there were four tables on one side of the gateway and four on the other—eight tables in all—on which

the sacrifices were slaughtered. ⁴²There were also four tables of dressed stone for the burnt offerings, each a cubit and a half long, a cubit and a half wide and a cubit high. On them were placed the utensils for slaughtering the burnt offerings and the other sacrifices. ⁴³And double-pronged hooks, each a handbreadth long, were attached to the wall all around. The tables were for the flesh of the offerings.

Rooms for the Priests

⁴⁴Outside the inner gate, within the inner court, were two rooms, one^b at the side of the north gate and facing south, and another at the side of the south^c gate and facing north. ⁴⁵He said to me, "The room facing south is for the priests who have charge of the temple, ⁴⁶and the room facing north is for the priests who have charge of the altar. These are the sons of Zadok, who are the only Levites who may draw near to the LORD to minister before him."

⁴⁷Then he measured the court: It was square—a hundred cubits long and a hundred cubits wide. And the altar was in front of the temple.

The Temple

⁴⁸He brought me to the portico of the temple and measured the jambs of the portico; they were five cubits wide on either side. The width of the entrance was fourteen cubits and its projecting walls were^d three cubits wide on either side. ⁴⁹The portico was twenty cubits wide, and twelve^e cubits from front to back. It was reached by a flight of stairs,^f and there were pillars on each side of the jambs.

41 Then the man brought me to the outer sanctuary and measured the jambs; the width of the jambs was six cubits^g on each side.^h ²The entrance was ten cubits wide, and the projecting walls on each side of it were five cubits

---

^a37 Septuagint (see also verses 31 and 34); Hebrew *jambs*   ^b44 Septuagint; Hebrew *were rooms for singers, which were*   ^c44 Septuagint; Hebrew *east*   ^d48 Septuagint; Hebrew *entrance was*   ^e49 Septuagint; Hebrew *eleven*   ^f49 Hebrew; Septuagint *Ten steps led up to it*   ^g1 The common cubit was about 1 1/2 feet (about 0.5 meter).   ^h1 One Hebrew manuscript and Septuagint; most Hebrew manuscripts *side, the width of the tent*

wide. He also measured the outer sanctuary; it was forty cubits long and twenty cubits wide.

³Then he went into the inner sanctuary and measured the jambs of the entrance; each was two cubits wide. The entrance was six cubits wide, and the projecting walls on each side of it were seven cubits wide. ⁴And he measured the length of the inner sanctuary; it was twenty cubits, and its width was twenty cubits across the end of the outer sanctuary. He said to me, "This is the Most Holy Place."

⁵Then he measured the wall of the temple; it was six cubits thick, and each side room around the temple was four cubits wide. ⁶The side rooms were on three levels, one above another, thirty on each level. There were ledges all around the wall of the temple to serve as supports for the side rooms, so that the supports were not inserted into the wall of the temple. ⁷The side rooms all around the temple were wider at each successive level. The structure surrounding the temple was built in ascending stages, so that the rooms widened as one went upward. A stairway went up from the lowest floor to the top floor through the middle floor.

⁸I saw that the temple had a raised base all around it, forming the foundation of the side rooms. It was the length of the rod, six long cubits. ⁹The outer wall of the side rooms was five cubits thick. The open area between the side rooms of the temple ¹⁰and the ⌞priests'⌟ rooms was twenty cubits wide all around the temple. ¹¹There were entrances to the side rooms from the open area, one on the north and another on the south; and the base adjoining the open area was five cubits wide all around.

¹²The building facing the temple courtyard on the west side was seventy cubits wide. The wall of the building was five cubits thick all around, and its length was ninety cubits.

¹³Then he measured the temple; it was a hundred cubits long, and the temple courtyard and the building with its walls were also a hundred cubits long. ¹⁴The width of the temple courtyard on the east, including the front of the temple, was a hundred cubits.

¹⁵Then he measured the length of the building facing the courtyard at the rear of the temple, including its galleries on each side; it was a hundred cubits.

The outer sanctuary, the inner sanctuary and the portico facing the court, ¹⁶as well as the thresholds and the narrow windows and galleries around the three of them—everything beyond and including the threshold was covered with wood. The floor, the wall up to the windows, and the windows were covered. ¹⁷In the space above the outside of the entrance to the inner sanctuary and on the walls at regular intervals all around the inner and outer sanctuary ¹⁸were carved cherubim and palm trees. Palm trees alternated with cherubim. Each cherub had two faces: ¹⁹the face of a man toward the palm tree on one side and the face of a lion toward the palm tree on the other. They were carved all around the whole temple. ²⁰From the floor to the area above the entrance, cherubim and palm trees were carved on the wall of the outer sanctuary.

²¹The outer sanctuary had a rectangular doorframe, and the one at the front of the Most Holy Place was similar. ²²There was a wooden altar three cubits high and two cubits square*a*; its corners, its base*b* and its sides were of wood. The man said to me, "This is the table that is before the LORD." ²³Both the outer sanctuary and the Most Holy Place had double doors. ²⁴Each door had two leaves—two hinged leaves for each door. ²⁵And on the doors of the outer sanctuary were carved cherubim and palm trees like those carved on the walls, and there was a wooden overhang on the front of the portico. ²⁶On the sidewalls of the portico were narrow windows with palm trees carved on each side. The side rooms of the temple also had overhangs.

Rooms for the Priests

42 Then the man led me northward into the outer court and brought me to the rooms opposite the temple courtyard and opposite the outer wall on the north side. ²The building whose door faced north was a hundred cubits*c* long and fifty cubits wide. ³Both in the section twenty cubits from the inner court and in

a22 Septuagint; Hebrew *long*   *b22* Septuagint; Hebrew *length*   *c2* The common cubit was about 1 1/2 feet (about 0.5 meter).

the section opposite the pavement of the outer court, gallery faced gallery at the three levels. [4]In front of the rooms was an inner passageway ten cubits wide and a hundred cubits[a] long. Their doors were on the north. [5]Now the upper rooms were narrower, for the galleries took more space from them than from the rooms on the lower and middle floors of the building. [6]The rooms on the third floor had no pillars, as the courts had; so they were smaller in floor space than those on the lower and middle floors. [7]There was an outer wall parallel to the rooms and the outer court; it extended in front of the rooms for fifty cubits. [8]While the row of rooms on the side next to the outer court was fifty cubits long, the row on the side nearest the sanctuary was a hundred cubits long. [9]The lower rooms had an entrance on the east side as one enters them from the outer court.

[10]On the south side[b] along the length of the wall of the outer court, adjoining the temple courtyard and opposite the outer wall, were rooms [11]with a passageway in front of them. These were like the rooms on the north; they had the same length and width, with similar exits and dimensions. Similar to the doorways on the north [12]were the doorways of the rooms on the south. There was a doorway at the beginning of the passageway that was parallel to the corresponding wall extending eastward, by which one enters the rooms.

[13]Then he said to me, "The north and south rooms facing the temple courtyard are the priests' rooms, where the priests who approach the LORD will eat the most holy offerings. There they will put the most holy offerings—the grain offerings, the sin offerings and the guilt offerings—for the place is holy. [14]Once the priests enter the holy precincts, they are not to go into the outer court until they leave behind the garments in which they minister, for these are holy. They are to put on other clothes before they go near the places that are for the people."

[15]When he had finished measuring what was inside the temple area, he led me out by the east gate and measured the area all around: [16]He measured the east side with the measuring rod; it was five hundred cubits.[c] [17]He measured the north side; it was five hundred cubits[d] by the measuring rod. [18]He measured the south side; it was five hundred cubits by the measuring rod. [19]Then he turned to the west side and measured; it was five hundred cubits by the measuring rod. [20]So he measured the area on all four sides. It had a wall around it, five hundred cubits long and five hundred cubits wide, to separate the holy from the common.

The Glory Returns to the Temple

43 Then the man brought me to the gate facing east, [2]and I saw the glory of the God of Israel coming from the east. His voice was like the roar of rushing waters, and the land was radiant with his glory. [3]The vision I saw was like the vision I had seen when he[e] came to destroy the city and like the visions I had seen by the Kebar River, and I fell facedown. [4]The glory of the LORD entered the temple through the gate facing east. [5]Then the Spirit lifted me up and brought me into the inner court, and the glory of the LORD filled the temple.

[6]While the man was standing beside me, I heard someone speaking to me from inside the temple. [7]He said: "Son of man, this is the place of my throne and the place for the soles of my feet. This is where I will live among the Israelites forever. The house of Israel will never again defile my holy name—neither they nor their kings—by their prostitution[f] and the lifeless idols[g] of their kings at their high places. [8]When they placed their threshold next to my threshold and their doorposts beside my doorposts, with only a wall between me and them, they defiled my holy name by their detestable practices. So I destroyed them in my anger. [9]Now let them put away from me their prostitution and the lifeless idols of their kings, and I will live among them forever.

[10]"Son of man, describe the temple to the people of Israel, that they may be

---

[a]4 Septuagint and Syriac; Hebrew *and one cubit*
[b]10 Septuagint; Hebrew *Eastward*   [c]16 See Septuagint of verse 17; Hebrew *rods*; also in verses 18 and 19.   [d]17 Septuagint; Hebrew *rods*
[e]3 Some Hebrew manuscripts and Vulgate; most Hebrew manuscripts *I*   [f]7 Or *their spiritual adultery*; also in verse 9   [g]7 Or *the corpses*; also in verse 9

ashamed of their sins. Let them consider the plan, [11]and if they are ashamed of all they have done, make known to them the design of the temple—its arrangement, its exits and entrances—its whole design and all its regulations[a] and laws. Write these down before them so that they may be faithful to its design and follow all its regulations.

[12]"This is the law of the temple: All the surrounding area on top of the mountain will be most holy. Such is the law of the temple.

The Altar

[13]"These are the measurements of the altar in long cubits, that cubit being a cubit[b] and a handbreadth[c]: Its gutter is a cubit deep and a cubit wide, with a rim of one span[d] around the edge. And this is the height of the altar: [14]From the gutter on the ground up to the lower ledge it is two cubits high and a cubit wide, and from the smaller ledge up to the larger ledge it is four cubits high and a cubit wide. [15]The altar hearth is four cubits high, and four horns project upward from the hearth. [16]The altar hearth is square, twelve cubits long and twelve cubits wide. [17]The upper ledge also is square, fourteen cubits long and fourteen cubits wide, with a rim of half a cubit and a gutter of a cubit all around. The steps of the altar face east."

[18]Then he said to me, "Son of man, this is what the Sovereign LORD says: These will be the regulations for sacrificing burnt offerings and sprinkling blood upon the altar when it is built: [19]You are to give a young bull as a sin offering to the priests, who are Levites, of the family of Zadok, who come near to minister before me, declares the Sovereign LORD. [20]You are to take some of its blood and put it on the four horns of the altar and on the four corners of the upper ledge and all around the rim, and so purify the altar and make atonement for it. [21]You are to take the bull for the sin offering and burn it in the designated part of the temple area outside the sanctuary.

[22]"On the second day you are to offer a male goat without defect for a sin offering, and the altar is to be purified as it was purified with the bull. [23]When you have finished purifying it, you are to offer a young bull and a ram from the flock, both without defect. [24]You are to offer them before the LORD, and the priests are to sprinkle salt on them and sacrifice them as a burnt offering to the LORD.

[25]"For seven days you are to provide a male goat daily for a sin offering; you are also to provide a young bull and a ram from the flock, both without defect. [26]For seven days they are to make atonement for the altar and cleanse it; thus they will dedicate it. [27]At the end of these days, from the eighth day on, the priests are to present your burnt offerings and fellowship offerings[e] on the altar. Then I will accept you, declares the Sovereign LORD."

The Prince, the Levites, the Priests

44 Then the man brought me back to the outer gate of the sanctuary, the one facing east, and it was shut. [2]The LORD said to me, "This gate is to remain shut. It must not be opened; no one may enter through it. It is to remain shut because the LORD, the God of Israel, has entered through it. [3]The prince himself is the only one who may sit inside the gateway to eat in the presence of the LORD. He is to enter by way of the portico of the gateway and go out the same way."

[4]Then the man brought me by way of the north gate to the front of the temple. I looked and saw the glory of the LORD filling the temple of the LORD, and I fell facedown.

[5]The LORD said to me, "Son of man, look carefully, listen closely and give attention to everything I tell you concerning all the regulations regarding the temple of the LORD. Give attention to the entrance of the temple and all the exits of the sanctuary. [6]Say to the rebellious house of Israel, 'This is what the Sovereign LORD says: Enough of your detestable practices, O house of Israel! [7]In addition to all your other detestable practices, you brought foreigners uncircumcised in heart and flesh into my sanctuary, desecrating my temple while you offered me

---

[a]11 Some Hebrew manuscripts and Septuagint; most Hebrew manuscripts *regulations and its whole design*   [b]13 The common cubit was about 1 1/2 feet (about 0.5 meter).   [c]13 That is, about 3 inches (about 8 centimeters)   [d]13 That is, about 9 inches (about 22 centimeters)   [e]27 Traditionally *peace offerings*

food, fat and blood, and you broke my covenant. [8]Instead of carrying out your duty in regard to my holy things, you put others in charge of my sanctuary. [9]This is what the Sovereign LORD says: No foreigner uncircumcised in heart and flesh is to enter my sanctuary, not even the foreigners who live among the Israelites.

[10]" 'The Levites who went far from me when Israel went astray and who wandered from me after their idols must bear the consequences of their sin. [11]They may serve in my sanctuary, having charge of the gates of the temple and serving in it; they may slaughter the burnt offerings and sacrifices for the people and stand before the people and serve them. [12]But because they served them in the presence of their idols and made the house of Israel fall into sin, therefore I have sworn with uplifted hand that they must bear the consequences of their sin, declares the Sovereign LORD. [13]They are not to come near to serve me as priests or come near any of my holy things or my most holy offerings; they must bear the shame of their detestable practices. [14]Yet I will put them in charge of the duties of the temple and all the work that is to be done in it.

[15]" 'But the priests, who are Levites and descendants of Zadok and who faithfully carried out the duties of my sanctuary when the Israelites went astray from me, are to come near to minister before me; they are to stand before me to offer sacrifices of fat and blood, declares the Sovereign LORD. [16]They alone are to enter my sanctuary; they alone are to come near my table to minister before me and perform my service.

[17]" 'When they enter the gates of the inner court, they are to wear linen clothes; they must not wear any woolen garment while ministering at the gates of the inner court or inside the temple. [18]They are to wear linen turbans on their heads and linen undergarments around their waists. They must not wear anything that makes them perspire. [19]When they go out into the outer court where the people are, they are to take off the clothes they have been ministering in and are to leave them in the sacred rooms, and put on other clothes, so that they do not consecrate the people by means of their garments.

[20]" 'They must not shave their heads or let their hair grow long, but they are to keep the hair of their heads trimmed. [21]No priest is to drink wine when he enters the inner court. [22]They must not marry widows or divorced women; they may marry only virgins of Israelite descent or widows of priests. [23]They are to teach my people the difference between the holy and the common and show them how to distinguish between the unclean and the clean.

[24]" 'In any dispute, the priests are to serve as judges and decide it according to my ordinances. They are to keep my laws and my decrees for all my appointed feasts, and they are to keep my Sabbaths holy.

[25]" 'A priest must not defile himself by going near a dead person; however, if the dead person was his father or mother, son or daughter, brother or unmarried sister, then he may defile himself. [26]After he is cleansed, he must wait seven days. [27]On the day he goes into the inner court of the sanctuary to minister in the sanctuary, he is to offer a sin offering for himself, declares the Sovereign LORD.

[28]" 'I am to be the only inheritance the priests have. You are to give them no possession in Israel; I will be their possession. [29]They will eat the grain offerings, the sin offerings and the guilt offerings; and everything in Israel devoted[a] to the LORD will belong to them. [30]The best of all the firstfruits and of all your special gifts will belong to the priests. You are to give them the first portion of your ground meal so that a blessing may rest on your household. [31]The priests must not eat anything, bird or animal, found dead or torn by wild animals.

Division of the Land

45 " 'When you allot the land as an inheritance, you are to present to the LORD a portion of the land as a sacred district, 25,000 cubits long and 20,000[b] cubits wide; the entire area will be holy. [2]Of this, a section 500 cubits square is to be for the sanctuary, with 50 cubits around it for open land. [3]In the sacred

[a]29 The Hebrew term refers to the irrevocable giving over of things or persons to the LORD.
[b]1 Septuagint (see also verses 3 and 5 and 48:9); Hebrew *10,000*

district, measure off a section 25,000 cubits[a] long and 10,000 cubits[b] wide. In it will be the sanctuary, the Most Holy Place. [4]It will be the sacred portion of the land for the priests, who minister in the sanctuary and who draw near to minister before the LORD. It will be a place for their houses as well as a holy place for the sanctuary. [5]An area 25,000 cubits long and 10,000 cubits wide will belong to the Levites, who serve in the temple, as their possession for towns to live in.[c]

[6]" 'You are to give the city as its property an area 5,000 cubits wide and 25,000 cubits long, adjoining the sacred portion; it will belong to the whole house of Israel.

[7]" 'The prince will have the land bordering each side of the area formed by the sacred district and the property of the city. It will extend westward from the west side and eastward from the east side, running lengthwise from the western to the eastern border parallel to one of the tribal portions. [8]This land will be his possession in Israel. And my princes will no longer oppress my people but will allow the house of Israel to possess the land according to their tribes.

[9]" 'This is what the Sovereign LORD says: You have gone far enough, O princes of Israel! Give up your violence and oppression and do what is just and right. Stop dispossessing my people, declares the Sovereign LORD. [10]You are to use accurate scales, an accurate ephah[d] and an accurate bath.[e] [11]The ephah and the bath are to be the same size, the bath containing a tenth of a homer[f] and the ephah a tenth of a homer; the homer is to be the standard measure for both. [12]The shekel[g] is to consist of twenty gerahs. Twenty shekels plus twenty-five shekels plus fifteen shekels equal one mina.[h]

Offerings and Holy Days

[13]" 'This is the special gift you are to offer: a sixth of an ephah from each homer of wheat and a sixth of an ephah from each homer of barley. [14]The prescribed portion of oil, measured by the bath, is a tenth of a bath from each cor (which consists of ten baths or one homer, for ten baths are equivalent to a homer). [15]Also one sheep is to be taken from every flock of two hundred from the well-watered pastures of Israel. These will be used for the grain offerings, burnt offerings and fellowship offerings[i] to make atonement for the people, declares the Sovereign LORD. [16]All the people of the land will participate in this special gift for the use of the prince in Israel. [17]It will be the duty of the prince to provide the burnt offerings, grain offerings and drink offerings at the festivals, the New Moons and the Sabbaths—at all the appointed feasts of the house of Israel. He will provide the sin offerings, grain offerings, burnt offerings and fellowship offerings to make atonement for the house of Israel.

[18]" 'This is what the Sovereign LORD says: In the first month on the first day you are to take a young bull without defect and purify the sanctuary. [19]The priest is to take some of the blood of the sin offering and put it on the doorposts of the temple, on the four corners of the upper ledge of the altar and on the gateposts of the inner court. [20]You are to do the same on the seventh day of the month for anyone who sins unintentionally or through ignorance; so you are to make atonement for the temple.

[21]" 'In the first month on the fourteenth day you are to observe the Passover, a feast lasting seven days, during which you shall eat bread made without yeast. [22]On that day the prince is to provide a bull as a sin offering for himself and for all the people of the land. [23]Every day during the seven days of the Feast he is to provide seven bulls and seven rams without defect as a burnt offering to the LORD, and a male goat for a sin offering. [24]He is to provide as a grain offering an ephah for each bull and an ephah for each ram, along with a hin[j] of oil for each ephah.

[25]" 'During the seven days of the Feast, which begins in the seventh month on the fifteenth day, he is to make the same

[a]3 That is, about 7 miles (about 12 kilometers)
[b]3 That is, about 3 miles (about 5 kilometers)
[c]5 Septuagint; Hebrew *temple; they will have as their possession 20 rooms*   [d]10 An ephah was a dry measure.   [e]10 A bath was a liquid measure.
[f]11 A homer was a dry measure.   [g]12 A shekel weighed about 2/5 ounce (about 11.5 grams).
[h]12 That is, 60 shekels; the common mina was 50 shekels.   [i]15 Traditionally *peace offerings*; also in verse 17   [j]24 That is, probably about 4 quarts (about 4 liters)

provision for sin offerings, burnt offerings, grain offerings and oil.

46 " 'This is what the Sovereign LORD says: The gate of the inner court facing east is to be shut on the six working days, but on the Sabbath day and on the day of the New Moon it is to be opened. ²The prince is to enter from the outside through the portico of the gateway and stand by the gatepost. The priests are to sacrifice his burnt offering and his fellowship offerings.[a] He is to worship at the threshold of the gateway and then go out, but the gate will not be shut until evening. ³On the Sabbaths and New Moons the people of the land are to worship in the presence of the LORD at the entrance to that gateway. ⁴The burnt offering the prince brings to the LORD on the Sabbath day is to be six male lambs and a ram, all without defect. ⁵The grain offering given with the ram is to be an ephah,[b] and the grain offering with the lambs is to be as much as he pleases, along with a hin[c] of oil for each ephah. ⁶On the day of the New Moon he is to offer a young bull, six lambs and a ram, all without defect. ⁷He is to provide as a grain offering one ephah with the bull, one ephah with the ram, and with the lambs as much as he wants to give, along with a hin of oil with each ephah. ⁸When the prince enters, he is to go in through the portico of the gateway, and he is to come out the same way.

⁹" 'When the people of the land come before the LORD at the appointed feasts, whoever enters by the north gate to worship is to go out the south gate; and whoever enters by the south gate is to go out the north gate. No one is to return through the gate by which he entered, but each is to go out the opposite gate. ¹⁰The prince is to be among them, going in when they go in and going out when they go out.

¹¹" 'At the festivals and the appointed feasts, the grain offering is to be an ephah with a bull, an ephah with a ram, and with the lambs as much as one pleases, along with a hin of oil for each ephah. ¹²When the prince provides a freewill offering to the LORD—whether a burnt offering or fellowship offerings—the gate facing east is to be opened for him. He shall offer his burnt offering or his fellowship offerings as he does on the Sabbath day.

Then he shall go out, and after he has gone out, the gate will be shut.

¹³" 'Every day you are to provide a year-old lamb without defect for a burnt offering to the LORD; morning by morning you shall provide it. ¹⁴You are also to provide with it morning by morning a grain offering, consisting of a sixth of an ephah with a third of a hin of oil to moisten the flour. The presenting of this grain offering to the LORD is a lasting ordinance. ¹⁵So the lamb and the grain offering and the oil shall be provided morning by morning for a regular burnt offering.

¹⁶" 'This is what the Sovereign LORD says: If the prince makes a gift from his inheritance to one of his sons, it will also belong to his descendants; it is to be their property by inheritance. ¹⁷If, however, he makes a gift from his inheritance to one of his servants, the servant may keep it until the year of freedom; then it will revert to the prince. His inheritance belongs to his sons only; it is theirs. ¹⁸The prince must not take any of the inheritance of the people, driving them off their property. He is to give his sons their inheritance out of his own property, so that none of my people will be separated from his property.' "

¹⁹Then the man brought me through the entrance at the side of the gate to the sacred rooms facing north, which belonged to the priests, and showed me a place at the western end. ²⁰He said to me, "This is the place where the priests will cook the guilt offering and the sin offering and bake the grain offering, to avoid bringing them into the outer court and consecrating the people."

²¹He then brought me to the outer court and led me around to its four corners, and I saw in each corner another court. ²²In the four corners of the outer court were enclosed[d] courts, forty cubits long and thirty cubits wide; each of the courts in the four corners was the same size. ²³Around the inside of each of the four courts was a ledge of stone, with places for fire built all around under the ledge. ²⁴He said to me, "These are the

---

[a]2 Traditionally *peace offerings*; also in verse 12   [b]5 That is, probably about 3/5 bushel (about 22 liters)   [c]5 That is, probably about 4 quarts (about 4 liters)   [d]22 The meaning of the Hebrew for this word is uncertain.

kitchens where those who minister at the temple will cook the sacrifices of the people."

The River From the Temple

47 The man brought me back to the entrance of the temple, and I saw water coming out from under the threshold of the temple toward the east (for the temple faced east). The water was coming down from under the south side of the temple, south of the altar. ²He then brought me out through the north gate and led me around the outside to the outer gate facing east, and the water was flowing from the south side.

³As the man went eastward with a measuring line in his hand, he measured off a thousand cubits*a* and then led me through water that was ankle-deep. ⁴He measured off another thousand cubits and led me through water that was knee-deep. He measured off another thousand and led me through water that was up to the waist. ⁵He measured off another thousand, but now it was a river that I could not cross, because the water had risen and was deep enough to swim in—a river that no one could cross. ⁶He asked me, "Son of man, do you see this?"

Then he led me back to the bank of the river. ⁷When I arrived there, I saw a great number of trees on each side of the river. ⁸He said to me, "This water flows toward the eastern region and goes down into the Arabah,*b* where it enters the Sea.*c* When it empties into the Sea,*c* the water there becomes fresh. ⁹Swarms of living creatures will live wherever the river flows. There will be large numbers of fish, because this water flows there and makes the salt water fresh; so where the river flows everything will live. ¹⁰Fishermen will stand along the shore; from En Gedi to En Eglaim there will be places for spreading nets. The fish will be of many kinds—like the fish of the Great Sea.*d* ¹¹But the swamps and marshes will not become fresh; they will be left for salt. ¹²Fruit trees of all kinds will grow on both banks of the river. Their leaves will not wither, nor will their fruit fail. Every month they will bear, because the water from the sanctuary flows to them. Their fruit will serve for food and their leaves for healing."

The Boundaries of the Land

¹³This is what the Sovereign LORD says: "These are the boundaries by which you are to divide the land for an inheritance among the twelve tribes of Israel, with two portions for Joseph. ¹⁴You are to divide it equally among them. Because I swore with uplifted hand to give it to your forefathers, this land will become your inheritance.

¹⁵"This is to be the boundary of the land:

"On the north side it will run from the Great Sea by the Hethlon road past Lebo*e* Hamath to Zedad, ¹⁶Berothah*f* and Sibraim (which lies on the border between Damascus and Hamath), as far as Hazer Hatticon, which is on the border of Hauran. ¹⁷The boundary will extend from the sea to Hazar Enan,*g* along the northern border of Damascus, with the border of Hamath to the north. This will be the north boundary.

¹⁸"On the east side the boundary will run between Hauran and Damascus, along the Jordan between Gilead and the land of Israel, to the eastern sea and as far as Tamar.*h* This will be the east boundary.

¹⁹"On the south side it will run from Tamar as far as the waters of Meribah Kadesh, then along the Wadi ⌊of Egypt⌋ to the Great Sea. This will be the south boundary.

²⁰"On the west side, the Great Sea will be the boundary to a point opposite Lebo*i* Hamath. This will be the west boundary.

²¹"You are to distribute this land among yourselves according to the tribes

---

a3 That is, about 1,500 feet (about 450 meters)
b8 Or the Jordan Valley   *c8* That is, the Dead Sea   *d10* That is, the Mediterranean; also in verses 15, 19 and 20   *e15* Or *past the entrance to*   *f15,16* See Septuagint and Ezekiel 48:1; Hebrew *road to go into Zedad,* ¹⁶*Hamath, Berothah*   *g17* Hebrew *Enon,* a variant of *Enan*   *h18* Septuagint and Syriac; Hebrew *Israel. You will measure to the eastern sea*   *i20* Or *opposite the entrance to*

of Israel. [22]You are to allot it as an inheritance for yourselves and for the aliens who have settled among you and who have children. You are to consider them as native-born Israelites; along with you they are to be allotted an inheritance among the tribes of Israel. [23]In whatever tribe the alien settles, there you are to give him his inheritance," declares the Sovereign LORD.

The Division of the Land

48 "These are the tribes, listed by name: At the northern frontier, Dan will have one portion; it will follow the Hethlon road to Lebo[a] Hamath; Hazar Enan and the northern border of Damascus next to Hamath will be part of its border from the east side to the west side.

[2]"Asher will have one portion; it will border the territory of Dan from east to west.

[3]"Naphtali will have one portion; it will border the territory of Asher from east to west.

[4]"Manasseh will have one portion; it will border the territory of Naphtali from east to west.

[5]"Ephraim will have one portion; it will border the territory of Manasseh from east to west.

[6]"Reuben will have one portion; it will border the territory of Ephraim from east to west.

[7]"Judah will have one portion; it will border the territory of Reuben from east to west.

[8]"Bordering the territory of Judah from east to west will be the portion you are to present as a special gift. It will be 25,000 cubits[b] wide, and its length from east to west will equal one of the tribal portions; the sanctuary will be in the center of it.

[9]"The special portion you are to offer to the LORD will be 25,000 cubits long and 10,000 cubits[c] wide. [10]This will be the sacred portion for the priests. It will be 25,000 cubits long on the north side, 10,000 cubits wide on the west side, 10,000 cubits wide on the east side and 25,000 cubits long on the south side. In the center of it will be the sanctuary of the LORD. [11]This will be for the consecrated priests, the Zadokites, who were faithful in serving me and did not go astray as the Levites did when the Israelites went astray. [12]It will be a special gift to them from the sacred portion of the land, a most holy portion, bordering the territory of the Levites.

[13]"Alongside the territory of the priests, the Levites will have an allotment 25,000 cubits long and 10,000 cubits wide. Its total length will be 25,000 cubits and its width 10,000 cubits. [14]They must not sell or exchange any of it. This is the best of the land and must not pass into other hands, because it is holy to the LORD.

[15]"The remaining area, 5,000 cubits wide and 25,000 cubits long, will be for the common use of the city, for houses and for pastureland. The city will be in the center of it [16]and will have these measurements: the north side 4,500 cubits, the south side 4,500 cubits, the east side 4,500 cubits, and the west side 4,500 cubits. [17]The pastureland for the city will be 250 cubits on the north, 250 cubits on the south, 250 cubits on the east, and 250 cubits on the west. [18]What remains of the area, bordering on the sacred portion and running the length of it, will be 10,000 cubits on the east side and 10,000 cubits on the west side. Its produce will supply food for the workers of the city. [19]The workers from the city who farm it will come from all the tribes of Israel. [20]The entire portion will be a square, 25,000 cubits on each side. As a special gift you will set aside the sacred portion, along with the property of the city.

[21]"What remains on both sides of the area formed by the sacred portion and the city property will belong to the prince. It will extend eastward from the 25,000 cubits of the sacred portion to the eastern border, and westward from the 25,000 cubits to the western border. Both these areas running the length of the tribal portions will belong to the prince, and the sacred portion with the temple sanctuary will be in the center of them. [22]So the property of the Levites and the property of

*a*1 Or *to the entrance to*   *b*8 That is, about 7 miles (about 12 kilometers)   *c*9 That is, about 3 miles (about 5 kilometers) the city will lie in the center of the area that belongs to the prince. The area belonging to the prince will lie between the border of Judah and the border of Benjamin.

²³"As for the rest of the tribes: Benjamin will have one portion; it will extend from the east side to the west side.

²⁴"Simeon will have one portion; it will border the territory of Benjamin from east to west.

²⁵"Issachar will have one portion; it will border the territory of Simeon from east to west.

²⁶"Zebulun will have one portion; it will border the territory of Issachar from east to west.

²⁷"Gad will have one portion; it will border the territory of Zebulun from east to west.

²⁸"The southern boundary of Gad will run south from Tamar to the waters of Meribah Kadesh, then along the Wadi ⌊of Egypt⌋ to the Great Sea.ᵃ

²⁹"This is the land you are to allot as an inheritance to the tribes of Israel, and these will be their portions," declares the Sovereign LORD.

The Gates of the City

³⁰"These will be the exits of the city: Beginning on the north side, which is 4,500 cubits long, ³¹the gates of the city will be named after the tribes of Israel. The three gates on the north side will be the gate of Reuben, the gate of Judah and the gate of Levi.

³²"On the east side, which is 4,500 cubits long, will be three gates: the gate of Joseph, the gate of Benjamin and the gate of Dan.

³³"On the south side, which measures 4,500 cubits, will be three gates: the gate of Simeon, the gate of Issachar and the gate of Zebulun.

³⁴"On the west side, which is 4,500 cubits long, will be three gates: the gate of Gad, the gate of Asher and the gate of Naphtali.

³⁵"The distance all around will be 18,000 cubits.

"And the name of the city from that time on will be:

THE LORD IS THERE."

ᵃ28 That is, the Mediterranean

Daniel

*Fiery furnaces and
lions' dens, dreams* and visions—these are the
larger-than-life experiences recounted by Daniel. Yet even
greater than these events is the God who controlled them.
Daniel and his three friends—Shadrach, Meshach and
Abednego—live out their faith in amazing ways that reveal
God's power and his ability to save them (and us).

Holding out for what one believes in the face of
perilous consequences is no easy assignment. In fact,
bailing out just to avoid a little embarrassment happens all
too often. Who can blame us for not wanting to unneces-
sarily attract attention? "Live and let live," we think to
ourselves. But then there's Daniel and his friends.

Daniel's Training in Babylon

1 In the third year of the reign of Jehoiakim king of Judah, Nebuchadnezzar
king of Babylon came to Jerusalem and
besieged it. ²And the Lord delivered Jehoiakim king of Judah into his hand, along
with some of the articles from the temple
of God. These he carried off to the temple
of his god in Babylonia*a* and put in the
treasure house of his god.

³Then the king ordered Ashpenaz,
chief of his court officials, to bring in
some of the Israelites from the royal family and the nobility— ⁴young men without
any physical defect, handsome, showing
aptitude for every kind of learning, well
informed, quick to understand, and qualified to serve in the king's palace. He was
to teach them the language and literature
of the Babylonians.*b* ⁵The king assigned

them a daily amount of food and wine
from the king's table. They were to be
trained for three years, and after that they
were to enter the king's service.

⁶Among these were some from Judah:
Daniel, Hananiah, Mishael and Azariah.
⁷The chief official gave them new names:
to Daniel, the name Belteshazzar; to Hananiah, Shadrach; to Mishael, Meshach;
and to Azariah, Abednego.

⁸But Daniel resolved not to defile himself with the royal food and wine, and he
asked the chief official for permission not
to defile himself this way. ⁹Now God had
caused the official to show favor and sympathy to Daniel, ¹⁰but the official told
Daniel, "I am afraid of my lord the king,

a2 Hebrew *Shinar*   *b4* Or *Chaldeans*

who has assigned your*a* food and drink. Why should he see you looking worse than the other young men your age? The king would then have my head because of you."

11Daniel then said to the guard whom the chief official had appointed over Daniel, Hananiah, Mishael and Azariah, 12"Please test your servants for ten days: Give us nothing but vegetables to eat and water to drink. 13Then compare our appearance with that of the young men who eat the royal food, and treat your servants in accordance with what you see." 14So he agreed to this and tested them for ten days.

15At the end of the ten days they looked healthier and better nourished than any of the young men who ate the royal food. 16So the guard took away their choice food and the wine they were to drink and gave them vegetables instead.

17To these four young men God gave knowledge and understanding of all kinds of literature and learning. And Daniel could understand visions and dreams of all kinds.

18At the end of the time set by the king to bring them in, the chief official presented them to Nebuchadnezzar. 19The king talked with them, and he found none equal to Daniel, Hananiah, Mishael and Azariah; so they entered the king's service. 20In every matter of wisdom and understanding about which the king questioned them, he found them ten times better than all the magicians and enchanters in his whole kingdom.

21And Daniel remained there until the first year of King Cyrus.

Nebuchadnezzar's Dream

2 In the second year of his reign, Nebuchadnezzar had dreams; his mind was troubled and he could not sleep. 2So the king summoned the magicians, enchanters, sorcerers and astrologers*b* to tell him what he had dreamed. When they came in and stood before the king, 3he said to them, "I have had a dream that troubles me and I want to know what it means.*c*"

4Then the astrologers answered the king in Aramaic,*d* "O king, live forever! Tell your servants the dream, and we will interpret it."

5The king replied to the astrologers, "This is what I have firmly decided: If you do not tell me what my dream was and interpret it, I will have you cut into pieces and your houses turned into piles of rubble. 6But if you tell me the dream and

---

a10 The Hebrew for *your* and *you* in this verse is plural.   *b2* Or *Chaldeans;* also in verses 4, 5 and 10   *c3* Or *was*   *d4* The text from here through chapter 7 is in Aramaic.

Dare to Be Different!

DANIEL 1:17 Christian couples can be found at every level of society, so shouldn't they be impacting the marriages around them? Unfortunately, instead of being a positive influence on others, many Christian couples simply reflect the society in which they live. But why is this happening? Why are Christian couples not having more of an impact on others around them?

Consider Daniel. He lived in one of the most godless cultures. Yet, rather than being impacted by all the negative influences of his culture, he impacted the culture in an impressive way. His integrity, unswerving faith and courage to live out his convictions caused others to take notice.

Note that Daniel worked and prospered at the highest level of government. God knew his needs and gave him "knowledge and understanding" and even the ability to "understand visions and dreams."

The only accusation that could be brought against Daniel was that he continued to pray daily to his God.

Daniel lived out his convictions in an unfriendly culture, and we can too. When other couples see how we love and serve each other with God's love, we can create a thirst for godly relationships in a culture that tends to devalue the institution of marriage.

—*Dave & Claudia*

Go to page 938 for your next devotional reading.

explain it, you will receive from me gifts and rewards and great honor. So tell me the dream and interpret it for me."

7Once more they replied, "Let the king tell his servants the dream, and we will interpret it."

8Then the king answered, "I am certain that you are trying to gain time, because you realize that this is what I have firmly decided: 9If you do not tell me the dream, there is just one penalty for you. You have conspired to tell me misleading and wicked things, hoping the situation will change. So then, tell me the dream, and I will know that you can interpret it for me."

10The astrologers answered the king, "There is not a man on earth who can do what the king asks! No king, however great and mighty, has ever asked such a thing of any magician or enchanter or astrologer. 11What the king asks is too difficult. No one can reveal it to the king except the gods, and they do not live among men."

12This made the king so angry and furious that he ordered the execution of all the wise men of Babylon. 13So the decree was issued to put the wise men to death, and men were sent to look for Daniel and his friends to put them to death.

14When Arioch, the commander of the king's guard, had gone out to put to death the wise men of Babylon, Daniel spoke to him with wisdom and tact. 15He asked the king's officer, "Why did the king issue such a harsh decree?" Arioch then explained the matter to Daniel. 16At this, Daniel went in to the king and asked for time, so that he might interpret the dream for him.

17Then Daniel returned to his house and explained the matter to his friends Hananiah, Mishael and Azariah. 18He urged them to plead for mercy from the God of heaven concerning this mystery, so that he and his friends might not be executed with the rest of the wise men of Babylon. 19During the night the mystery was revealed to Daniel in a vision. Then Daniel praised the God of heaven 20and said:

"Praise be to the name of God for
        ever and ever;
    wisdom and power are his.

Dare to Be Different!

Are you willing, like Daniel, to go against the culture? This exercise will help you to see how you can set your marriage apart to honor God. Reflect on the following questions:

1. In what ways is your marriage different from the culture?

2. Are you satisfied with your witness to others? Yes___ No___

3. What are your present challenges as you live out your convictions in a culture that isn't marriage friendly?

4. How can you be salt and light? How can your marriage positively influence other marriages? (Check what you would be interested in pursuing):

    ___   Host a couples' Bible study
    ___   Organize a marriage growth
           group
    ___   Mentor a younger couple

5. In what ways are you working together as a couple to develop a deeper faith and Christian spirituality? (Check those that apply):

    ___   Pray together.
    ___   Study the Bible together.
    ___   Attend church and church
           school together.
    ___   Participate in a service project
           together.

Choose one thing you can do to honor God in your marriage.

21He changes times and seasons;
    he sets up kings and deposes them.
He gives wisdom to the wise
    and knowledge to the discerning.
22He reveals deep and hidden things;
    he knows what lies in darkness,
    and light dwells with him.
23I thank and praise you, O God of my
        fathers:
    You have given me wisdom and
        power,
    you have made known to me what
        we asked of you,
    you have made known to us the
        dream of the king."

Daniel Interprets the Dream

²⁴Then Daniel went to Arioch, whom the king had appointed to execute the wise men of Babylon, and said to him, "Do not execute the wise men of Babylon. Take me to the king, and I will interpret his dream for him."

²⁵Arioch took Daniel to the king at once and said, "I have found a man among the exiles from Judah who can tell the king what his dream means."

²⁶The king asked Daniel (also called Belteshazzar), "Are you able to tell me what I saw in my dream and interpret it?"

²⁷Daniel replied, "No wise man, enchanter, magician or diviner can explain to the king the mystery he has asked about, ²⁸but there is a God in heaven who reveals mysteries. He has shown King Nebuchadnezzar what will happen in days to come. Your dream and the visions that passed through your mind as you lay on your bed are these:

²⁹"As you were lying there, O king, your mind turned to things to come, and the revealer of mysteries showed you what is going to happen. ³⁰As for me, this mystery has been revealed to me, not because I have greater wisdom than other living men, but so that you, O king, may know the interpretation and that you may understand what went through your mind.

³¹"You looked, O king, and there before you stood a large statue—an enormous, dazzling statue, awesome in appearance. ³²The head of the statue was made of pure gold, its chest and arms of silver, its belly and thighs of bronze, ³³its legs of iron, its feet partly of iron and partly of baked clay. ³⁴While you were watching, a rock was cut out, but not by human hands. It struck the statue on its feet of iron and clay and smashed them. ³⁵Then the iron, the clay, the bronze, the silver and the gold were broken to pieces at the same time and became like chaff on a threshing floor in the summer. The wind swept them away without leaving a trace. But the rock that struck the statue became a huge mountain and filled the whole earth.

³⁶"This was the dream, and now we will interpret it to the king. ³⁷You, O king, are the king of kings. The God of heaven has given you dominion and power and might and glory; ³⁸in your hands he has placed mankind and the beasts of the field and the birds of the air. Wherever they live, he has made you ruler over them all. You are that head of gold.

³⁹"After you, another kingdom will rise, inferior to yours. Next, a third kingdom, one of bronze, will rule over the whole earth. ⁴⁰Finally, there will be a fourth kingdom, strong as iron—for iron breaks and smashes everything—and as iron breaks things to pieces, so it will crush and break all the others. ⁴¹Just as you saw that the feet and toes were partly of baked clay and partly of iron, so this will be a divided kingdom; yet it will have some of the strength of iron in it, even as you saw iron mixed with clay. ⁴²As the toes were partly iron and partly clay, so this kingdom will be partly strong and partly brittle. ⁴³And just as you saw the iron mixed with baked clay, so the people will be a mixture and will not remain united, any more than iron mixes with clay.

⁴⁴"In the time of those kings, the God of heaven will set up a kingdom that will never be destroyed, nor will it be left to another people. It will crush all those kingdoms and bring them to an end, but it will itself endure forever. ⁴⁵This is the meaning of the vision of the rock cut out of a mountain, but not by human hands— a rock that broke the iron, the bronze, the clay, the silver and the gold to pieces.

"The great God has shown the king what will take place in the future. The dream is true and the interpretation is trustworthy."

⁴⁶Then King Nebuchadnezzar fell prostrate before Daniel and paid him honor and ordered that an offering and incense be presented to him. ⁴⁷The king said to Daniel, "Surely your God is the God of gods and the Lord of kings and a revealer of mysteries, for you were able to reveal this mystery."

⁴⁸Then the king placed Daniel in a high position and lavished many gifts on him. He made him ruler over the entire province of Babylon and placed him in charge of all its wise men. ⁴⁹Moreover, at Daniel's request the king appointed Shadrach, Meshach and Abednego administrators over the province of Babylon,

while Daniel himself remained at the royal court.

The Image of Gold and the Fiery Furnace

3 King Nebuchadnezzar made an image of gold, ninety feet high and nine feet[a] wide, and set it up on the plain of Dura in the province of Babylon. [2]He then summoned the satraps, prefects, governors, advisers, treasurers, judges, magistrates and all the other provincial officials to come to the dedication of the image he had set up. [3]So the satraps, prefects, governors, advisers, treasurers, judges, magistrates and all the other provincial officials assembled for the dedication of the image that King Nebuchadnezzar had set up, and they stood before it.

[4]Then the herald loudly proclaimed, "This is what you are commanded to do, O peoples, nations and men of every language: [5]As soon as you hear the sound of the horn, flute, zither, lyre, harp, pipes and all kinds of music, you must fall down and worship the image of gold that King Nebuchadnezzar has set up. [6]Whoever does not fall down and worship will immediately be thrown into a blazing furnace."

[7]Therefore, as soon as they heard the sound of the horn, flute, zither, lyre, harp and all kinds of music, all the peoples, nations and men of every language fell down and worshiped the image of gold that King Nebuchadnezzar had set up.

[8]At this time some astrologers[b] came forward and denounced the Jews. [9]They said to King Nebuchadnezzar, "O king, live forever! [10]You have issued a decree, O king, that everyone who hears the sound of the horn, flute, zither, lyre, harp, pipes and all kinds of music must fall down and worship the image of gold, [11]and that whoever does not fall down and worship will be thrown into a blazing furnace. [12]But there are some Jews whom you have set over the affairs of the province of Babylon—Shadrach, Meshach and Abednego—who pay no attention to you, O king. They neither serve your gods nor worship the image of gold you have set up."

[13]Furious with rage, Nebuchadnezzar summoned Shadrach, Meshach and Abednego. So these men were brought before the king, [14]and Nebuchadnezzar said to them, "Is it true, Shadrach, Meshach and Abednego, that you do not serve my gods or worship the image of gold I have set up? [15]Now when you hear the sound of the horn, flute, zither, lyre, harp, pipes and all kinds of music, if you are ready to fall down and worship the image I made, very good. But if you do not worship it, you will be thrown immediately into a blazing furnace. Then what god will be able to rescue you from my hand?"

[16]Shadrach, Meshach and Abednego replied to the king, "O Nebuchadnezzar, we do not need to defend ourselves before you in this matter. [17]If we are thrown into the blazing furnace, the God we serve is able to save us from it, and he will rescue us from your hand, O king. [18]But even if he does not, we want you to know, O king, that we will not serve your gods or worship the image of gold you have set up."

[19]Then Nebuchadnezzar was furious with Shadrach, Meshach and Abednego, and his attitude toward them changed. He ordered the furnace heated seven times hotter than usual [20]and commanded some of the strongest soldiers in his army to tie up Shadrach, Meshach and Abednego and throw them into the blazing furnace. [21]So these men, wearing their robes, trousers, turbans and other clothes, were bound and thrown into the blazing furnace. [22]The king's command was so urgent and the furnace so hot that the flames of the fire killed the soldiers who took up Shadrach, Meshach and Abednego, [23]and these three men, firmly tied, fell into the blazing furnace.

[24]Then King Nebuchadnezzar leaped to his feet in amazement and asked his advisers, "Weren't there three men that we tied up and threw into the fire?"

They replied, "Certainly, O king."

[25]He said, "Look! I see four men walking around in the fire, unbound and unharmed, and the fourth looks like a son of the gods."

[26]Nebuchadnezzar then approached the opening of the blazing furnace and

---

a1 Aramaic *sixty cubits high and six cubits wide* (about 27 meters high and 2.7 meters wide)
b8 Or *Chaldeans*

shouted, "Shadrach, Meshach and Abednego, servants of the Most High God, come out! Come here!"

So Shadrach, Meshach and Abednego came out of the fire, 27and the satraps, prefects, governors and royal advisers crowded around them. They saw that the fire had not harmed their bodies, nor was a hair of their heads singed; their robes were not scorched, and there was no smell of fire on them.

28Then Nebuchadnezzar said, "Praise be to the God of Shadrach, Meshach and Abednego, who has sent his angel and rescued his servants! They trusted in him and defied the king's command and were willing to give up their lives rather than serve or worship any god except their own God. 29Therefore I decree that the people of any nation or language who say anything against the God of Shadrach, Meshach and Abednego be cut into pieces and their houses be turned into piles of rubble, for no other god can save in this way."

30Then the king promoted Shadrach, Meshach and Abednego in the province of Babylon.

Nebuchadnezzar's Dream of a Tree

4 King Nebuchadnezzar,

To the peoples, nations and men of every language, who live in all the world:

May you prosper greatly!

2It is my pleasure to tell you about the miraculous signs and wonders that the Most High God has performed for me.

3How great are his signs,
   how mighty his wonders!
His kingdom is an eternal
      kingdom;
   his dominion endures from
      generation to generation.

4I, Nebuchadnezzar, was at home in my palace, contented and prosperous. 5I had a dream that made me afraid. As I was lying in my bed, the images and visions that passed through my mind terrified me. 6So I commanded that all the wise men of Babylon be brought before me to interpret the dream for me. 7When the magicians, enchanters, astrologers[a] and diviners came, I told them the dream, but they could not interpret it for me. 8Finally, Daniel came into my presence and I told him the dream. (He is called Belteshazzar, after the name of my god, and the spirit of the holy gods is in him.)

9I said, "Belteshazzar, chief of the magicians, I know that the spirit of the holy gods is in you, and no mystery is too difficult for you. Here is my dream; interpret it for me. 10These are the visions I saw while lying in my bed: I looked, and there before me stood a tree in the middle of the land. Its height was enormous. 11The tree grew large and strong and its top touched the sky; it was visible to the ends of the earth. 12Its leaves were beautiful, its fruit abundant, and on it was food for all. Under it the beasts of the field found shelter, and the birds of the air lived in its branches; from it every creature was fed.

13"In the visions I saw while lying in my bed, I looked, and there before me was a messenger,[b] a holy one, coming down from heaven. 14He called in a loud voice: 'Cut down the tree and trim off its branches; strip off its leaves and scatter its fruit. Let the animals flee from under it and the birds from its branches. 15But let the stump and its roots, bound with iron and bronze, remain in the ground, in the grass of the field.

" 'Let him be drenched with the dew of heaven, and let him live with the animals among the plants of the earth. 16Let his mind be changed from that of a man and let him be given the mind of an animal, till seven times[c] pass by for him.

17" 'The decision is announced by messengers, the holy ones declare the verdict, so that the living

a7 Or Chaldeans   b13 Or watchman; also in verses 17 and 23   c16 Or years; also in verses 23, 25 and 32 may know that the Most High is sovereign over the kingdoms of men and gives them to anyone he wishes and sets over them the lowliest of men.'

18 "This is the dream that I, King Nebuchadnezzar, had. Now, Belteshazzar, tell me what it means, for none of the wise men in my kingdom can interpret it for me. But you can, because the spirit of the holy gods is in you."

Daniel Interprets the Dream

19 Then Daniel (also called Belteshazzar) was greatly perplexed for a time, and his thoughts terrified him. So the king said, "Belteshazzar, do not let the dream or its meaning alarm you."

Belteshazzar answered, "My lord, if only the dream applied to your enemies and its meaning to your adversaries! 20 The tree you saw, which grew large and strong, with its top touching the sky, visible to the whole earth, 21 with beautiful leaves and abundant fruit, providing food for all, giving shelter to the beasts of the field, and having nesting places in its branches for the birds of the air— 22 you, O king, are that tree! You have become great and strong; your greatness has grown until it reaches the sky, and your dominion extends to distant parts of the earth.

23 "You, O king, saw a messenger, a holy one, coming down from heaven and saying, 'Cut down the tree and destroy it, but leave the stump, bound with iron and bronze, in the grass of the field, while its roots remain in the ground. Let him be drenched with the dew of heaven; let him live like the wild animals, until seven times pass by for him.'

24 "This is the interpretation, O king, and this is the decree the Most High has issued against my lord the king: 25 You will be driven away from people and will live with the wild animals; you will eat grass like cattle and be drenched with the dew of heaven. Seven times will pass by for you until you acknowledge that the Most High is sovereign over the kingdoms of men and gives them to anyone he wishes. 26 The command to leave the stump of the tree with its roots means that your kingdom will be restored to you when you acknowledge that Heaven rules. 27 Therefore, O king, be pleased to accept my advice: Renounce your sins by doing what is right, and your wickedness by being kind to the oppressed. It may be that then your prosperity will continue."

The Dream Is Fulfilled

28 All this happened to King Nebuchadnezzar. 29 Twelve months later, as the king was walking on the roof of the royal palace of Babylon, 30 he said, "Is not this the great Babylon I have built as the royal residence, by my mighty power and for the glory of my majesty?"

31 The words were still on his lips when a voice came from heaven, "This is what is decreed for you, King Nebuchadnezzar: Your royal authority has been taken from you. 32 You will be driven away from people and will live with the wild animals; you will eat grass like cattle. Seven times will pass by for you until you acknowledge that the Most High is sovereign over the kingdoms of men and gives them to anyone he wishes."

33 Immediately what had been said about Nebuchadnezzar was fulfilled. He was driven away from people and ate grass like cattle. His body was drenched with the dew of heaven until his hair grew like the feathers of an eagle and his nails like the claws of a bird.

34 At the end of that time, I, Nebuchadnezzar, raised my eyes toward heaven, and my sanity was restored. Then I praised the Most High; I honored and glorified him who lives forever.

His dominion is an eternal dominion;
  his kingdom endures from
    generation to generation.

³⁵All the peoples of the earth
    are regarded as nothing.
He does as he pleases
    with the powers of heaven
    and the peoples of the earth.
No one can hold back his hand
    or say to him: "What have you
        done?"

    ³⁶At the same time that my sanity
was restored, my honor and splendor were returned to me for the glory of my kingdom. My advisers and
nobles sought me out, and I was
restored to my throne and became
even greater than before. ³⁷Now I,
Nebuchadnezzar, praise and exalt
and glorify the King of heaven, because everything he does is right and
all his ways are just. And those who
walk in pride he is able to humble.

The Writing on the Wall

5 King Belshazzar gave a great banquet
for a thousand of his nobles and
drank wine with them. ²While Belshazzar
was drinking his wine, he gave orders to
bring in the gold and silver goblets that
Nebuchadnezzar his father*ᵃ* had taken
from the temple in Jerusalem, so that the
king and his nobles, his wives and his
concubines might drink from them. ³So
they brought in the gold goblets that had
been taken from the temple of God in
Jerusalem, and the king and his nobles,
his wives and his concubines drank from
them. ⁴As they drank the wine, they
praised the gods of gold and silver, of
bronze, iron, wood and stone.

⁵Suddenly the fingers of a human hand
appeared and wrote on the plaster of the
wall, near the lampstand in the royal palace. The king watched the hand as it
wrote. ⁶His face turned pale and he was so
frightened that his knees knocked together and his legs gave way.

⁷The king called out for the enchanters,
astrologersᵇ and diviners to be brought
and said to these wise men of Babylon,
"Whoever reads this writing and tells me
what it means will be clothed in purple
and have a gold chain placed around his
neck, and he will be made the third highest ruler in the kingdom."

⁸Then all the king's wise men came in,
but they could not read the writing or tell
the king what it meant. ⁹So King Belshazzar became even more terrified and his
face grew more pale. His nobles were baffled.

¹⁰The queen,ᶜ hearing the voices of
the king and his nobles, came into the
banquet hall. "O king, live forever!" she
said. "Don't be alarmed! Don't look so
pale! ¹¹There is a man in your kingdom
who has the spirit of the holy gods in
him. In the time of your father he was
found to have insight and intelligence
and wisdom like that of the gods. King
Nebuchadnezzar your father—your father
the king, I say—appointed him chief of the
magicians, enchanters, astrologers and diviners. ¹²This man Daniel, whom the king
called Belteshazzar, was found to have a
keen mind and knowledge and understanding, and also the ability to interpret
dreams, explain riddles and solve difficult
problems. Call for Daniel, and he will tell
you what the writing means."

¹³So Daniel was brought before the
king, and the king said to him, "Are you
Daniel, one of the exiles my father the
king brought from Judah? ¹⁴I have heard
that the spirit of the gods is in you and
that you have insight, intelligence and
outstanding wisdom. ¹⁵The wise men
and enchanters were brought before me
to read this writing and tell me what it
means, but they could not explain it.
¹⁶Now I have heard that you are able to
give interpretations and to solve difficult
problems. If you can read this writing and
tell me what it means, you will be clothed
in purple and have a gold chain placed
around your neck, and you will be made
the third highest ruler in the kingdom."

¹⁷Then Daniel answered the king,
"You may keep your gifts for yourself and
give your rewards to someone else. Nevertheless, I will read the writing for the king
and tell him what it means.

¹⁸"O king, the Most High God gave
your father Nebuchadnezzar sovereignty
and greatness and glory and splendor.
¹⁹Because of the high position he gave
him, all the peoples and nations and men

ᵃ2 Or *ancestor;* or *predecessor;* also in verses 11, 13
and 18   ᵇ7 Or *Chaldeans;* also in verse 11
ᶜ10 Or *queen mother*

of every language dreaded and feared him. Those the king wanted to put to death, he put to death; those he wanted to spare, he spared; those he wanted to promote, he promoted; and those he wanted to humble, he humbled. 20But when his heart became arrogant and hardened with pride, he was deposed from his royal throne and stripped of his glory. 21He was driven away from people and given the mind of an animal; he lived with the wild donkeys and ate grass like cattle; and his body was drenched with the dew of heaven, until he acknowledged that the Most High God is sovereign over the kingdoms of men and sets over them anyone he wishes.

22"But you his son,[a] O Belshazzar, have not humbled yourself, though you knew all this. 23Instead, you have set yourself up against the Lord of heaven. You had the goblets from his temple brought to you, and you and your nobles, your wives and your concubines drank wine from them. You praised the gods of silver and gold, of bronze, iron, wood and stone, which cannot see or hear or understand. But you did not honor the God who holds in his hand your life and all your ways. 24Therefore he sent the hand that wrote the inscription.

25"This is the inscription that was written:

MENE, MENE, TEKEL, PARSIN[b]

26"This is what these words mean:

Mene[c]: God has numbered the days of your reign and brought it to an end.
27Tekel[d]: You have been weighed on the scales and found wanting.
28Peres[e]: Your kingdom is divided and given to the Medes and Persians."

29Then at Belshazzar's command, Daniel was clothed in purple, a gold chain was placed around his neck, and he was proclaimed the third highest ruler in the kingdom.

30That very night Belshazzar, king of the Babylonians,[f] was slain, 31and Darius the Mede took over the kingdom, at the age of sixty-two.

Daniel in the Den of Lions

6 It pleased Darius to appoint 120 satraps to rule throughout the kingdom, 2with three administrators over them, one of whom was Daniel. The satraps were made accountable to them so that the king might not suffer loss. 3Now Daniel so distinguished himself among the administrators and the satraps by his exceptional qualities that the king planned to set him over the whole kingdom. 4At this, the administrators and the satraps tried to find grounds for charges against Daniel in his conduct of government affairs, but they were unable to do so. They could find no corruption in him, because he was trustworthy and neither corrupt nor negligent. 5Finally these men said, "We will never find any basis for charges against this man Daniel unless it has something to do with the law of his God."

6So the administrators and the satraps went as a group to the king and said: "O King Darius, live forever! 7The royal administrators, prefects, satraps, advisers and governors have all agreed that the king should issue an edict and enforce the decree that anyone who prays to any god or man during the next thirty days, except to you, O king, shall be thrown into the lions' den. 8Now, O king, issue the decree and put it in writing so that it cannot be altered—in accordance with the laws of the Medes and Persians, which cannot be repealed." 9So King Darius put the decree in writing.

10Now when Daniel learned that the decree had been published, he went home to his upstairs room where the windows opened toward Jerusalem. Three times a day he got down on his knees and prayed, giving thanks to his God, just as he had done before. 11Then these men went as a group and found Daniel praying and asking God for help. 12So they went to the king and spoke to him about his royal decree: "Did you not publish a decree that during the next thirty days any-

---

a22 Or descendant; or successor   b25 Aramaic UPARSIN (that is, AND PARSIN)   c26 Mene can mean numbered or mina (a unit of money).   d27 Tekel can mean weighed or shekel.   e28 Peres (the singular of Parsin) can mean divided or Persia or a half mina or a half shekel.   f30 Or Chaldeans one who prays to any god or man except to you, O king, would be thrown into the lions' den?"

The king answered, "The decree stands—in accordance with the laws of the Medes and Persians, which cannot be repealed."

¹³Then they said to the king, "Daniel, who is one of the exiles from Judah, pays no attention to you, O king, or to the decree you put in writing. He still prays three times a day." ¹⁴When the king heard this, he was greatly distressed; he was determined to rescue Daniel and made every effort until sundown to save him.

¹⁵Then the men went as a group to the king and said to him, "Remember, O king, that according to the law of the Medes and Persians no decree or edict that the king issues can be changed."

¹⁶So the king gave the order, and they brought Daniel and threw him into the lions' den. The king said to Daniel, "May your God, whom you serve continually, rescue you!"

¹⁷A stone was brought and placed over the mouth of the den, and the king sealed it with his own signet ring and with the rings of his nobles, so that Daniel's situation might not be changed. ¹⁸Then the king returned to his palace and spent the night without eating and without any entertainment being brought to him. And he could not sleep.

¹⁹At the first light of dawn, the king got up and hurried to the lions' den. ²⁰When he came near the den, he called to Daniel in an anguished voice, "Daniel, servant of the living God, has your God, whom you serve continually, been able to rescue you from the lions?"

²¹Daniel answered, "O king, live forever! ²²My God sent his angel, and he shut the mouths of the lions. They have not hurt me, because I was found innocent in his sight. Nor have I ever done any wrong before you, O king."

²³The king was overjoyed and gave orders to lift Daniel out of the den. And when Daniel was lifted from the den, no wound was found on him, because he had trusted in his God.

²⁴At the king's command, the men who had falsely accused Daniel were brought in and thrown into the lions' den, along with their wives and children. And before they reached the floor of the den, the lions overpowered them and crushed all their bones.

²⁵Then King Darius wrote to all the peoples, nations and men of every language throughout the land:

"May you prosper greatly!

Your Steering Wheel or Spare Tire?

Wednesday

DANIEL 6:10 Prayer transports us to the deepest levels of the human spirit. It is in prayer that we begin to think God's thoughts and desire the things he desires. We believe that praying for each other is critically important. Corrie ten Boom once asked this question about prayer that every couple should answer: "Is prayer your steering wheel or your spare tire?"

The giants of the faith viewed prayer as the main source of direction in their lives. For example, Martin Luther declared, "I have so much business I cannot get on without spending three hours daily in prayer." John Wesley said, "God does nothing but in answer to prayer," and he backed up his conviction by devoting two hours daily to pray-

ing. And the words of Mark stand as a commentary on the lifestyle of Jesus: "Very early in the morning while it was still dark, Jesus got up, left the house and went off to a solitary place, where he prayed" (Mark 1:35).

You don't have to be a "giant of the faith" to pray daily. In fact, you may just be learning to pray. (Even the disciples had to learn; in Luke 11:1 they implored Jesus, "Lord teach us to pray.") As long as you are spending time in prayer—not with a "spare tire" approach but with a true desire for God to steer your life—you can be assured that God will make himself present in your life and in your marriage.   **—Les & Leslie**

Go to page 939 for your next devotional reading.

²⁶"I issue a decree that in every part of my kingdom people must fear and reverence the God of Daniel.

"For he is the living God
and he endures forever;
his kingdom will not be destroyed,
his dominion will never end.
²⁷He rescues and he saves;
he performs signs and wonders
in the heavens and on the earth.
He has rescued Daniel
from the power of the lions."

²⁸So Daniel prospered during the reign of Darius and the reign of Cyrus*a* the Persian.

Daniel's Dream of Four Beasts

7 In the first year of Belshazzar king of Babylon, Daniel had a dream, and visions passed through his mind as he was lying on his bed. He wrote down the substance of his dream.

²Daniel said: "In my vision at night I looked, and there before me were the four winds of heaven churning up the great sea. ³Four great beasts, each different from the others, came up out of the sea.

⁴"The first was like a lion, and it had the wings of an eagle. I watched until its wings were torn off and it was lifted from the ground so that it stood on two feet like a man, and the heart of a man was given to it.

⁵"And there before me was a second beast, which looked like a bear. It was raised up on one of its sides, and it had three ribs in its mouth between its teeth. It was told, 'Get up and eat your fill of flesh!'

⁶"After that, I looked, and there before me was another beast, one that looked like a leopard. And on its back it had four wings like those of a bird. This beast had four heads, and it was given authority to rule.

⁷"After that, in my vision at night I looked, and there before me was a fourth

a28 Or Darius, that is, the reign of Cyrus

Leaning on God

Thursday

DANIEL 6 Life forces us to deal with decisions we are not necessarily taught how to make. Sometimes we are faced with circumstances so far beyond us that we can do nothing but look to God for a solution. Standing in the lions' den, Daniel found himself totally dependent upon God. He couldn't possibly come up with a rescue plan of his own. Once that became apparent, Daniel was left with a choice. He could either focus, in total fear, on the jaws of the lions, or he could look up and focus on God. One focus brought terror; the other focus brought confidence.

The marriage journey brings with it many difficulties that we are responsible to work through. The process of blending two people together in the marriage is difficult. It can point out areas within each spouse that need improvement. But the journey also includes "jaws of the lions"—circumstances we personally cannot change.

I (Rosemary) quickly realized I would never be able to change the fact that Bob was so driven professionally that he felt it necessary to spend most of his waking hours at work. How could I battle with the jaws of the lion of success? After many seasons of praying that God would change Bob, I began to pray that God would change me—that God would make me into anything I needed to be, to help Bob become whatever God wanted my husband to be. After much time spent focusing on my own personal growth with God, the grip of the jaws of success that had almost consumed my husband were finally loosened and God rescued our marriage.

If we focus on the insurmountable circumstances, the "jaws" will be terrifying. We must leave the impossible up to God. Then we can find comfort in realizing that we aren't responsible to do the impossible.

—Bob & Rosemary

Go to page 949 for your next devotional reading.

beast—terrifying and frightening and very powerful. It had large iron teeth; it crushed and devoured its victims and trampled underfoot whatever was left. It was different from all the former beasts, and it had ten horns.

⁸"While I was thinking about the horns, there before me was another horn, a little one, which came up among them; and three of the first horns were uprooted before it. This horn had eyes like the eyes of a man and a mouth that spoke boastfully.

⁹"As I looked,

"thrones were set in place,
    and the Ancient of Days took his
        seat.
His clothing was as white as snow;
    the hair of his head was white like
        wool.
His throne was flaming with fire,
    and its wheels were all ablaze.
¹⁰A river of fire was flowing,
    coming out from before him.
Thousands upon thousands attended
        him;
    ten thousand times ten thousand
        stood before him.
The court was seated,
    and the books were opened.

¹¹"Then I continued to watch because of the boastful words the horn was speaking. I kept looking until the beast was slain and its body destroyed and thrown into the blazing fire. ¹²(The other beasts had been stripped of their authority, but were allowed to live for a period of time.)

¹³"In my vision at night I looked, and there before me was one like a son of man, coming with the clouds of heaven. He approached the Ancient of Days and was led into his presence. ¹⁴He was given authority, glory and sovereign power; all peoples, nations and men of every language worshiped him. His dominion is an everlasting dominion that will not pass away, and his kingdom is one that will never be destroyed.

The Interpretation of the Dream

¹⁵"I, Daniel, was troubled in spirit, and the visions that passed through my mind disturbed me. ¹⁶I approached one of those standing there and asked him the true meaning of all this.

"So he told me and gave me the interpretation of these things: ¹⁷'The four great beasts are four kingdoms that will rise from the earth. ¹⁸But the saints of the Most High will receive the kingdom and will possess it forever—yes, for ever and ever.'

¹⁹"Then I wanted to know the true meaning of the fourth beast, which was different from all the others and most terrifying, with its iron teeth and bronze claws—the beast that crushed and devoured its victims and trampled underfoot whatever was left. ²⁰I also wanted to know about the ten horns on its head and about the other horn that came up, before which three of them fell—the horn that looked more imposing than the others and that had eyes and a mouth that spoke boastfully. ²¹As I watched, this horn was waging war against the saints and defeating them, ²²until the Ancient of Days came and pronounced judgment in favor of the saints of the Most High, and the time came when they possessed the kingdom.

²³"He gave me this explanation: 'The fourth beast is a fourth kingdom that will appear on earth. It will be different from all the other kingdoms and will devour the whole earth, trampling it down and crushing it. ²⁴The ten horns are ten kings who will come from this kingdom. After them another king will arise, different from the earlier ones; he will subdue three kings. ²⁵He will speak against the Most High and oppress his saints and try to change the set times and the laws. The saints will be handed over to him for a time, times and half a time.ᵃ

²⁶" 'But the court will sit, and his power will be taken away and completely destroyed forever. ²⁷Then the sovereignty, power and greatness of the kingdoms under the whole heaven will be handed over to the saints, the people of the Most High. His kingdom will be an everlasting kingdom, and all rulers will worship and obey him.'

²⁸"This is the end of the matter. I, Daniel, was deeply troubled by my thoughts,

ᵃ25 Or *for a year, two years and half a year*

and my face turned pale, but I kept the matter to myself."

Daniel's Vision of a Ram and a Goat

8 In the third year of King Belshazzar's reign, I, Daniel, had a vision, after the one that had already appeared to me. ²In my vision I saw myself in the citadel of Susa in the province of Elam; in the vision I was beside the Ulai Canal. ³I looked up, and there before me was a ram with two horns, standing beside the canal, and the horns were long. One of the horns was longer than the other but grew up later. ⁴I watched the ram as he charged toward the west and the north and the south. No animal could stand against him, and none could rescue from his power. He did as he pleased and became great.

⁵As I was thinking about this, suddenly a goat with a prominent horn between his eyes came from the west, crossing the whole earth without touching the ground. ⁶He came toward the two-horned ram I had seen standing beside the canal and charged at him in great rage. ⁷I saw him attack the ram furiously, striking the ram and shattering his two horns. The ram was powerless to stand against him; the goat knocked him to the ground and trampled on him, and none could rescue the ram from his power. ⁸The goat became very great, but at the height of his power his large horn was broken off, and in its place four prominent horns grew up toward the four winds of heaven.

⁹Out of one of them came another horn, which started small but grew in power to the south and to the east and toward the Beautiful Land. ¹⁰It grew until it reached the host of the heavens, and it threw some of the starry host down to the earth and trampled on them. ¹¹It set itself up to be as great as the Prince of the host; it took away the daily sacrifice from him, and the place of his sanctuary was brought low. ¹²Because of rebellion, the host ⌊of the saints⌋ᵃ and the daily sacrifice were given over to it. It prospered in everything it did, and truth was thrown to the ground.

¹³Then I heard a holy one speaking, and another holy one said to him, "How long will it take for the vision to be fulfilled—the vision concerning the daily sac-

rifice, the rebellion that causes desolation, and the surrender of the sanctuary and of the host that will be trampled underfoot?"

¹⁴He said to me, "It will take 2,300 evenings and mornings; then the sanctuary will be reconsecrated."

The Interpretation of the Vision

¹⁵While I, Daniel, was watching the vision and trying to understand it, there before me stood one who looked like a man. ¹⁶And I heard a man's voice from the Ulai calling, "Gabriel, tell this man the meaning of the vision."

¹⁷As he came near the place where I was standing, I was terrified and fell prostrate. "Son of man," he said to me, "understand that the vision concerns the time of the end."

¹⁸While he was speaking to me, I was in a deep sleep, with my face to the ground. Then he touched me and raised me to my feet.

¹⁹He said: "I am going to tell you what will happen later in the time of wrath, because the vision concerns the appointed time of the end.ᵇ ²⁰The two-horned ram that you saw represents the kings of Media and Persia. ²¹The shaggy goat is the king of Greece, and the large horn between his eyes is the first king. ²²The four horns that replaced the one that was broken off represent four kingdoms that will emerge from his nation but will not have the same power.

²³"In the latter part of their reign, when rebels have become completely wicked, a stern-faced king, a master of intrigue, will arise. ²⁴He will become very strong, but not by his own power. He will cause astounding devastation and will succeed in whatever he does. He will destroy the mighty men and the holy people. ²⁵He will cause deceit to prosper, and he will consider himself superior. When they feel secure, he will destroy many and take his stand against the Prince of princes. Yet he will be destroyed, but not by human power.

²⁶"The vision of the evenings and mornings that has been given you is true,

---

ᵃ12 Or *rebellion, the armies*   ᵇ19 Or *because the end will be at the appointed time* but seal up the vision, for it concerns the distant future."

²⁷I, Daniel, was exhausted and lay ill for several days. Then I got up and went about the king's business. I was appalled by the vision; it was beyond understanding.

Daniel's Prayer

9 In the first year of Darius son of Xerxes[a] (a Mede by descent), who was made ruler over the Babylonian[b] kingdom— ²in the first year of his reign, I, Daniel, understood from the Scriptures, according to the word of the LORD given to Jeremiah the prophet, that the desolation of Jerusalem would last seventy years. ³So I turned to the Lord God and pleaded with him in prayer and petition, in fasting, and in sackcloth and ashes.

⁴I prayed to the LORD my God and confessed:

"O Lord, the great and awesome God, who keeps his covenant of love with all who love him and obey his commands, ⁵we have sinned and done wrong. We have been wicked and have rebelled; we have turned away from your commands and laws. ⁶We have not listened to your servants the prophets, who spoke in your name to our kings, our princes and our fathers, and to all the people of the land.

⁷"Lord, you are righteous, but this day we are covered with shame— the men of Judah and people of Jerusalem and all Israel, both near and far, in all the countries where you have scattered us because of our unfaithfulness to you. ⁸O LORD, we and our kings, our princes and our fathers are covered with shame because we have sinned against you. ⁹The Lord our God is merciful and forgiving, even though we have rebelled against him; ¹⁰we have not obeyed the LORD our God or kept the laws he gave us through his servants the prophets. ¹¹All Israel has transgressed your law and turned away, refusing to obey you.

"Therefore the curses and sworn judgments written in the Law of Moses, the servant of God, have been poured out on us, because we have sinned against you. ¹²You have fulfilled the words spoken against us and against our rulers by bringing upon us great disaster. Under the whole heaven nothing has ever been done like what has been done to Jerusalem. ¹³Just as it is written in the Law of Moses, all this disaster has come upon us, yet we have not sought the favor of the LORD our God by turning from our sins and giving attention to your truth. ¹⁴The LORD did not hesitate to bring the disaster upon us, for the LORD our God is righteous in everything he does; yet we have not obeyed him.

¹⁵"Now, O Lord our God, who brought your people out of Egypt with a mighty hand and who made for yourself a name that endures to this day, we have sinned, we have done wrong. ¹⁶O Lord, in keeping with all your righteous acts, turn away your anger and your wrath from Jerusalem, your city, your holy hill. Our sins and the iniquities of our fathers have made Jerusalem and your people an object of scorn to all those around us.

¹⁷"Now, our God, hear the prayers and petitions of your servant. For your sake, O Lord, look with favor on your desolate sanctuary. ¹⁸Give ear, O God, and hear; open your eyes and see the desolation of the city that bears your Name. We do not make requests of you because we are righteous, but because of your great mercy. ¹⁹O Lord, listen! O Lord, forgive! O Lord, hear and act! For your sake, O my God, do not delay, because your city and your people bear your Name."

The Seventy "Sevens"

²⁰While I was speaking and praying, confessing my sin and the sin of my people Israel and making my request to the LORD my God for his holy hill— ²¹while I was still in prayer, Gabriel, the man I had seen in the earlier vision, came to me in swift flight about the time of the evening

---

a 1 Hebrew *Ahasuerus*   *b* 1 Or *Chaldean*

sacrifice. [22]He instructed me and said to me, "Daniel, I have now come to give you insight and understanding. [23]As soon as you began to pray, an answer was given, which I have come to tell you, for you are highly esteemed. Therefore, consider the message and understand the vision:

[24]"Seventy 'sevens'[a] are decreed for your people and your holy city to finish[b] transgression, to put an end to sin, to atone for wickedness, to bring in everlasting righteousness, to seal up vision and prophecy and to anoint the most holy.[c]

[25]"Know and understand this: From the issuing of the decree[d] to restore and rebuild Jerusalem until the Anointed One,[e] the ruler, comes, there will be seven 'sevens,' and sixty-two 'sevens.' It will be rebuilt with streets and a trench, but in times of trouble. [26]After the sixty-two 'sevens,' the Anointed One will be cut off and will have nothing.[f] The people of the ruler who will come will destroy the city and the sanctuary. The end will come like a flood: War will continue until the end, and desolations have been decreed. [27]He will confirm a covenant with many for one 'seven.'[g] In the middle of the 'seven'[g] he will put an end to sacrifice and offering. And on a wing ⌐of the temple⌐ he will set up an abomination that causes desolation, until the end that is decreed is poured out on him.[h]"[i]

Daniel's Vision of a Man

10 In the third year of Cyrus king of Persia, a revelation was given to Daniel (who was called Belteshazzar). Its message was true and it concerned a great war.[j] The understanding of the message came to him in a vision.

[2]At that time I, Daniel, mourned for three weeks. [3]I ate no choice food; no meat or wine touched my lips; and I used no lotions at all until the three weeks were over.

[4]On the twenty-fourth day of the first month, as I was standing on the bank of the great river, the Tigris, [5]I looked up and there before me was a man dressed in linen, with a belt of the finest gold around his waist. [6]His body was like chrysolite, his face like lightning, his eyes like flaming torches, his arms and legs

like the gleam of burnished bronze, and his voice like the sound of a multitude.

[7]I, Daniel, was the only one who saw the vision; the men with me did not see it, but such terror overwhelmed them that they fled and hid themselves. [8]So I was left alone, gazing at this great vision; I had no strength left, my face turned deathly pale and I was helpless. [9]Then I heard him speaking, and as I listened to him, I fell into a deep sleep, my face to the ground.

[10]A hand touched me and set me trembling on my hands and knees. [11]He said, "Daniel, you who are highly esteemed, consider carefully the words I am about to speak to you, and stand up, for I have now been sent to you." And when he said this to me, I stood up trembling.

[12]Then he continued, "Do not be afraid, Daniel. Since the first day that you set your mind to gain understanding and to humble yourself before your God, your words were heard, and I have come in response to them. [13]But the prince of the Persian kingdom resisted me twenty-one days. Then Michael, one of the chief princes, came to help me, because I was detained there with the king of Persia. [14]Now I have come to explain to you what will happen to your people in the future, for the vision concerns a time yet to come."

[15]While he was saying this to me, I bowed with my face toward the ground and was speechless. [16]Then one who looked like a man[k] touched my lips, and I opened my mouth and began to speak. I said to the one standing before me, "I am overcome with anguish because of the vision, my lord, and I am helpless. [17]How can I, your servant, talk with you, my lord? My strength is gone and I can hardly breathe."

[18]Again the one who looked like a man touched me and gave me strength. [19]"Do

---

[a]24 Or 'weeks'; also in verses 25 and 26
[b]24 Or restrain   [c]24 Or Most Holy Place; or most holy One   [d]25 Or word   [e]25 Or an anointed one; also in verse 26   [f]26 Or off and will have no one; or off, but not for himself   [g]27 Or 'week'
[h]27 Or it   [i]27 Or And one who causes desolation will come upon the pinnacle of the abominable ⌐temple⌐, until the end that is decreed is poured out on the desolated ⌐city⌐   [j]1 Or true and burdensome
[k]16 Most manuscripts of the Masoretic Text; one manuscript of the Masoretic Text, Dead Sea Scrolls and Septuagint Then something that looked like a man's hand

not be afraid, O man highly esteemed," he said. "Peace! Be strong now; be strong."

When he spoke to me, I was strengthened and said, "Speak, my lord, since you have given me strength."

²⁰So he said, "Do you know why I have come to you? Soon I will return to fight against the prince of Persia, and when I go, the prince of Greece will come; ²¹but first I will tell you what is written in the Book of Truth. (No one supports me against them except Michael, your prince.

11 ¹And in the first year of Darius the Mede, I took my stand to support and protect him.)

The Kings of the South and the North

²"Now then, I tell you the truth: Three more kings will appear in Persia, and then a fourth, who will be far richer than all the others. When he has gained power by his wealth, he will stir up everyone against the kingdom of Greece. ³Then a mighty king will appear, who will rule with great power and do as he pleases. ⁴After he has appeared, his empire will be broken up and parceled out toward the four winds of heaven. It will not go to his descendants, nor will it have the power he exercised, because his empire will be uprooted and given to others.

⁵"The king of the South will become strong, but one of his commanders will become even stronger than he and will rule his own kingdom with great power. ⁶After some years, they will become allies. The daughter of the king of the South will go to the king of the North to make an alliance, but she will not retain her power, and he and his power*ᵃ* will not last. In those days she will be handed over, together with her royal escort and her father*ᵇ* and the one who supported her.

⁷"One from her family line will arise to take her place. He will attack the forces of the king of the North and enter his fortress; he will fight against them and be victorious. ⁸He will also seize their gods, their metal images and their valuable articles of silver and gold and carry them off to Egypt. For some years he will leave the king of the North alone. ⁹Then the king of the North will invade the realm of the king of the South but will retreat to his own country. ¹⁰His sons will prepare for war and assemble a great army, which will sweep on like an irresistible flood and carry the battle as far as his fortress.

¹¹"Then the king of the South will march out in a rage and fight against the king of the North, who will raise a large army, but it will be defeated. ¹²When the army is carried off, the king of the South will be filled with pride and will slaughter many thousands, yet he will not remain triumphant. ¹³For the king of the North will muster another army, larger than the first; and after several years, he will advance with a huge army fully equipped.

¹⁴"In those times many will rise against the king of the South. The violent men among your own people will rebel in fulfillment of the vision, but without success. ¹⁵Then the king of the North will come and build up siege ramps and will capture a fortified city. The forces of the South will be powerless to resist; even their best troops will not have the strength to stand. ¹⁶The invader will do as he pleases; no one will be able to stand against him. He will establish himself in the Beautiful Land and will have the power to destroy it. ¹⁷He will determine to come with the might of his entire kingdom and will make an alliance with the king of the South. And he will give him a daughter in marriage in order to overthrow the kingdom, but his plans*ᶜ* will not succeed or help him. ¹⁸Then he will turn his attention to the coastlands and will take many of them, but a commander will put an end to his insolence and will turn his insolence back upon him. ¹⁹After this, he will turn back toward the fortresses of his own country but will stumble and fall, to be seen no more.

²⁰"His successor will send out a tax collector to maintain the royal splendor. In a few years, however, he will be destroyed, yet not in anger or in battle.

²¹"He will be succeeded by a contemptible person who has not been given the honor of royalty. He will invade the kingdom when its people feel secure, and he will seize it through intrigue. ²²Then an overwhelming army will be swept away before him; both it and a prince of

---

ᵃ6 Or offspring   *ᵇ6 Or child (see Vulgate and Syriac)*   *ᶜ17 Or but she* the covenant will be destroyed. ²³After coming to an agreement with him, he will act deceitfully, and with only a few people he will rise to power. ²⁴When the richest provinces feel secure, he will invade them and will achieve what neither his fathers nor his forefathers did. He will distribute plunder, loot and wealth among his followers. He will plot the overthrow of fortresses—but only for a time.

²⁵"With a large army he will stir up his strength and courage against the king of the South. The king of the South will wage war with a large and very powerful army, but he will not be able to stand because of the plots devised against him. ²⁶Those who eat from the king's provisions will try to destroy him; his army will be swept away, and many will fall in battle. ²⁷The two kings, with their hearts bent on evil, will sit at the same table and lie to each other, but to no avail, because an end will still come at the appointed time. ²⁸The king of the North will return to his own country with great wealth, but his heart will be set against the holy covenant. He will take action against it and then return to his own country.

²⁹"At the appointed time he will invade the South again, but this time the outcome will be different from what it was before. ³⁰Ships of the western coastlands[a] will oppose him, and he will lose heart. Then he will turn back and vent his fury against the holy covenant. He will return and show favor to those who forsake the holy covenant.

³¹"His armed forces will rise up to desecrate the temple fortress and will abolish the daily sacrifice. Then they will set up the abomination that causes desolation. ³²With flattery he will corrupt those who have violated the covenant, but the people who know their God will firmly resist him.

³³"Those who are wise will instruct many, though for a time they will fall by the sword or be burned or captured or plundered. ³⁴When they fall, they will receive a little help, and many who are not sincere will join them. ³⁵Some of the wise will stumble, so that they may be refined, purified and made spotless until the time of the end, for it will still come at the appointed time.

The King Who Exalts Himself

³⁶"The king will do as he pleases. He will exalt and magnify himself above every god and will say unheard-of things against the God of gods. He will be successful until the time of wrath is completed, for what has been determined must take place. ³⁷He will show no regard for the gods of his fathers or for the one desired by women, nor will he regard any god, but will exalt himself above them all. ³⁸Instead of them, he will honor a god of fortresses; a god unknown to his fathers he will honor with gold and silver, with precious stones and costly gifts. ³⁹He will attack the mightiest fortresses with the help of a foreign god and will greatly honor those who acknowledge him. He will make them rulers over many people and will distribute the land at a price.[b]

⁴⁰"At the time of the end the king of the South will engage him in battle, and the king of the North will storm out against him with chariots and cavalry and a great fleet of ships. He will invade many countries and sweep through them like a flood. ⁴¹He will also invade the Beautiful Land. Many countries will fall, but Edom, Moab and the leaders of Ammon will be delivered from his hand. ⁴²He will extend his power over many countries; Egypt will not escape. ⁴³He will gain control of the treasures of gold and silver and all the riches of Egypt, with the Libyans and Nubians in submission. ⁴⁴But reports from the east and the north will alarm him, and he will set out in a great rage to destroy and annihilate many. ⁴⁵He will pitch his royal tents between the seas at[c] the beautiful holy mountain. Yet he will come to his end, and no one will help him.

The End Times

12 "At that time Michael, the great prince who protects your people, will arise. There will be a time of distress such as has not happened from the beginning of nations until then. But at that time your people—everyone whose name is found written in the book—will be delivered. ²Multitudes who sleep in the dust

---

a30 Hebrew *of Kittim* *b39* Or *land for a reward*
c45 Or *the sea and*

of the earth will awake: some to everlasting life, others to shame and everlasting contempt. ³Those who are wise*a* will shine like the brightness of the heavens, and those who lead many to righteousness, like the stars for ever and ever. ⁴But you, Daniel, close up and seal the words of the scroll until the time of the end. Many will go here and there to increase knowledge."

⁵Then I, Daniel, looked, and there before me stood two others, one on this bank of the river and one on the opposite bank. ⁶One of them said to the man clothed in linen, who was above the waters of the river, "How long will it be before these astonishing things are fulfilled?"

⁷The man clothed in linen, who was above the waters of the river, lifted his right hand and his left hand toward heaven, and I heard him swear by him who lives forever, saying, "It will be for a time, times and half a time.*b* When the power

of the holy people has been finally broken, all these things will be completed."

⁸I heard, but I did not understand. So I asked, "My lord, what will the outcome of all this be?"

⁹He replied, "Go your way, Daniel, because the words are closed up and sealed until the time of the end. ¹⁰Many will be purified, made spotless and refined, but the wicked will continue to be wicked. None of the wicked will understand, but those who are wise will understand.

¹¹"From the time that the daily sacrifice is abolished and the abomination that causes desolation is set up, there will be 1,290 days. ¹²Blessed is the one who waits for and reaches the end of the 1,335 days.

¹³"As for you, go your way till the end. You will rest, and then at the end of the days you will rise to receive your allotted inheritance."

---

*a*3 Or *who impart wisdom*   *b*7 Or *a year, two years and half a year*

Hosea

Sometimes God uses unexpected methods to teach us about himself; the prophet Hosea was a case in point. God told Hosea to marry a prostitute and then to forgive her unfaithfulness—more than once! Why? Because God wanted to create a vivid, living picture of his love for the people of Israel. The book of Hosea is a vignette of God as a lover who's been repeatedly abandoned, letting us see God's hurt and anger as well as his unrelenting devotion to his people and his willingness to forgive them time and again.

Whenever you feel discouraged about your spouse's mistakes—even the big ones—consider this passage. What can you do to stop the cycle of hurt and anger? Whom do you need to forgive? From whom do you need to seek forgiveness? Being faithful requires forgiveness and unrelenting love.

1 The word of the LORD that came to Hosea son of Beeri during the reigns of Uzziah, Jotham, Ahaz and Hezekiah, kings of Judah, and during the reign of Jeroboam son of Jehoash[a] king of Israel:

Hosea's Wife and Children

²When the LORD began to speak through Hosea, the LORD said to him, "Go, take to yourself an adulterous wife and children of unfaithfulness, because the land is guilty of the vilest adultery in departing from the LORD." ³So he married Gomer daughter of Diblaim, and she conceived and bore him a son.

⁴Then the LORD said to Hosea, "Call him Jezreel, because I will soon punish the house of Jehu for the massacre at Jezreel, and I will put an end to the kingdom of Israel. ⁵In that day I will break Israel's bow in the Valley of Jezreel."

⁶Gomer conceived again and gave birth to a daughter. Then the LORD said to Hosea, "Call her Lo-Ruhamah,[b] for I will no longer show love to the house of Israel, that I should at all forgive them. ⁷Yet I will show love to the house of Judah; and I will save them—not by bow,

---

*a*1 Hebrew *Joash,* a variant of *Jehoash*
*b*6 *Lo-Ruhamah* means *not loved.*

sword or battle, or by horses and horsemen, but by the LORD their God."

⁸After she had weaned Lo-Ruhamah, Gomer had another son. ⁹Then the LORD said, "Call him Lo-Ammi,ᵃ for you are not my people, and I am not your God.

¹⁰"Yet the Israelites will be like the sand on the seashore, which cannot be measured or counted. In the place where it was said to them, 'You are not my people,' they will be called 'sons of the living God.' ¹¹The people of Judah and the people of Israel will be reunited, and they will appoint one leader and will come up out of the land, for great will be the day of Jezreel.

2 "Say of your brothers, 'My people,' and of your sisters, 'My loved one.'

Israel Punished and Restored

²"Rebuke your mother, rebuke her,
    for she is not my wife,
    and I am not her husband.
Let her remove the adulterous look
      from her face
    and the unfaithfulness from
      between her breasts.
³Otherwise I will strip her naked
    and make her as bare as on the
      day she was born;
I will make her like a desert,
    turn her into a parched land,
    and slay her with thirst.
⁴I will not show my love to her
      children,
    because they are the children of
      adultery.
⁵Their mother has been unfaithful
    and has conceived them in
      disgrace.
She said, 'I will go after my lovers,
    who give me my food and my
      water,
    my wool and my linen, my oil and
      my drink.'
⁶Therefore I will block her path with
      thornbushes;
    I will wall her in so that she
      cannot find her way.
⁷She will chase after her lovers but not
      catch them;
    she will look for them but not find
      them.
Then she will say,

'I will go back to my husband as at
      first,
    for then I was better off than now.'
⁸She has not acknowledged that I was
      the one
    who gave her the grain, the new
      wine and oil,
who lavished on her the silver and
      gold—
    which they used for Baal.

⁹"Therefore I will take away my grain
      when it ripens,
    and my new wine when it is ready.
I will take back my wool and my
      linen,
    intended to cover her nakedness.
¹⁰So now I will expose her lewdness
    before the eyes of her lovers;
    no one will take her out of my
      hands.
¹¹I will stop all her celebrations:
    her yearly festivals, her New
      Moons,
    her Sabbath days—all her appointed
      feasts.
¹²I will ruin her vines and her fig trees,
    which she said were her pay from
      her lovers;
I will make them a thicket,
    and wild animals will devour
      them.
¹³I will punish her for the days
    she burned incense to the Baals;
she decked herself with rings and
      jewelry,
    and went after her lovers,
    but me she forgot,"
                declares the LORD.

¹⁴"Therefore I am now going to allure
      her;
    I will lead her into the desert
    and speak tenderly to her.
¹⁵There I will give her back her
      vineyards,
    and will make the Valley of
      Achorᵇ a door of hope.
There she will singᶜ as in the days of
      her youth,
    as in the day she came up out of
      Egypt.

¹⁶"In that day," declares the LORD,
    "you will call me 'my husband';

ᵃ9 *Lo-Ammi* means *not my people.*   ᵇ15 *Achor*
means *trouble.*   ᶜ15 Or *respond*

you will no longer call me 'my
    master.[a]'
[17]I will remove the names of the Baals
        from her lips;
    no longer will their names be
        invoked.
[18]In that day I will make a covenant for
        them
    with the beasts of the field and the
        birds of the air
    and the creatures that move along
        the ground.
Bow and sword and battle
    I will abolish from the land,
    so that all may lie down in safety.
[19]I will betroth you to me forever;
    I will betroth you in[b]
        righteousness and justice,
    in[c] love and compassion.
[20]I will betroth you in faithfulness,
    and you will acknowledge the
        LORD.

[21]"In that day I will respond,"
        declares the LORD—
    "I will respond to the skies,
        and they will respond to the earth;
[22]and the earth will respond to the
        grain,

the new wine and oil,
    and they will respond to Jezreel.[d]
[23]I will plant her for myself in the land;
    I will show my love to the one I
        called 'Not my loved one.'[e]
I will say to those called 'Not my
        people,[f]' 'You are my
        people';
    and they will say, 'You are my
        God.' "

Hosea's Reconciliation With His Wife

3 The LORD said to me, "Go, show your
love to your wife again, though she is
loved by another and is an adulteress.
Love her as the LORD loves the Israelites,
though they turn to other gods and love
the sacred raisin cakes."

[2]So I bought her for fifteen shekels[g] of
silver and about a homer and a lethek[h]
of barley. [3]Then I told her, "You are to
live with[i] me many days; you must not

---

[a]16 Hebrew *baal*   [b]19 Or *with*; also in verse 20
[c]19 Or *with*   [d]22 *Jezreel* means *God plants.*
[e]23 Hebrew *Lo-Ruhamah*   [f]23 Hebrew *Lo-Ammi*
[g]2 That is, about 6 ounces (about 170 grams)
[h]2 That is, probably about 10 bushels (about 330
liters)   [i]3 Or *wait for*

What Do You Deserve?

Friday

HOSEA 2:19-20   After all the stress
he had been going through at
work, Al sure thought he deserved
more than just a kiss good night.
But that's exactly what his wife
Vicky gave him. Once again she just
kissed him good night and went to
sleep. As Al laid in bed pondering his situation, that old phrase kept coming back: "I
deserve better."

Hosea never responded to his wife using
the "I deserve better" philosophy. Hosea
might have thought to himself that a marriage commitment certainly demanded
much more than his wife was giving, but
that never guided his reactions to her. He
chose to love her and forgive her no matter
what she had done. Hosea chose to view
his marriage the way God views his relationship with his people. Hosea's response
was one of faithfulness.

Marriage partners cannot allow the
thought of "I deserve better" to
creep into their marriage. There
are certainly commitments and
responsibilities that should be upheld in the marriage relationship,
but they aren't to be upheld because
of what one partner deserves. The reason
for the marriage commitment goes far beyond the actual marriage relationship. It's a
commitment for the sake of Jesus Christ's
glory. The level of commitment that one
spouse chooses to exhibit toward the marriage should have little to do with the response of the other spouse. It's not a matter
of what you think you deserve. It's realizing
what kind of marital commitment God deserves from you.

—Bob & Rosemary

Go to page 951 for your next devotional reading.

Hosea and Gomer

HOSEA 3:1–5 How did Hosea ever make it through the tragedy that ravaged his marriage? The blatant infidelity of his wife Gomer must have crushed his heart. Yet he was willing to take her back. He took her back because of his faithfulness to God rather than his commitment to his wife.

When you take your vows at the wedding, you bring a third Person into the union. That third Person is God. It changes the whole perspective of faithfulness. You are no longer pledging only to be faithful to each other. A couple is also making this vow to God. When Hosea took his wife back, after all she had done, he was doing it out of faithfulness and obedience to God.

Whether or not he wanted to take her back was not the issue. God wanted him to take Gomer back. Hosea faithfully obeyed God. God had big plans to use the story of Hosea's marriage. Your marriage is for more than your own happiness—it is for God's glory. Are you allowing him to use you in your journey of faithfulness?

be a prostitute or be intimate with any man, and I will live with*a* you."

⁴For the Israelites will live many days without king or prince, without sacrifice or sacred stones, without ephod or idol. ⁵Afterward the Israelites will return and seek the LORD their God and David their king. They will come trembling to the LORD and to his blessings in the last days.

The Charge Against Israel

4 Hear the word of the LORD, you Israelites,
    because the LORD has a charge to bring
    against you who live in the land:
"There is no faithfulness, no love,
    no acknowledgment of God in the land.
²There is only cursing,*b* lying and murder,
    stealing and adultery;
they break all bounds,
    and bloodshed follows bloodshed.

³Because of this the land mourns,*c*
    and all who live in it waste away;
the beasts of the field and the birds of the air
    and the fish of the sea are dying.

⁴"But let no man bring a charge,
    let no man accuse another,
for your people are like those
    who bring charges against a priest.
⁵You stumble day and night,
    and the prophets stumble with you.
So I will destroy your mother—
⁶   my people are destroyed from lack of knowledge.

"Because you have rejected knowledge,
    I also reject you as my priests;
because you have ignored the law of your God,
    I also will ignore your children.
⁷The more the priests increased,
    the more they sinned against me;
they exchanged*d* their*e* Glory for
    something disgraceful.
⁸They feed on the sins of my people
    and relish their wickedness.
⁹And it will be: Like people, like priests.
    I will punish both of them for their ways
    and repay them for their deeds.

¹⁰"They will eat but not have enough;
    they will engage in prostitution but not increase,
because they have deserted the LORD
    to give themselves ¹¹to prostitution,
to old wine and new,
    which take away the understanding ¹²of my people.
They consult a wooden idol
    and are answered by a stick of wood.
A spirit of prostitution leads them astray;
    they are unfaithful to their God.
¹³They sacrifice on the mountaintops
    and burn offerings on the hills,
under oak, poplar and terebinth,

---

a3 Or *wait for*   *b2* That is, to pronounce a curse upon   *c3* Or *dries up*   *d7* Syriac and an ancient Hebrew scribal tradition; Masoretic Text *I will exchange*   *e7* Masoretic Text; an ancient Hebrew scribal tradition *my*

where the shade is pleasant.
Therefore your daughters turn to
prostitution
and your daughters-in-law to
adultery.

14 "I will not punish your daughters
when they turn to prostitution,
nor your daughters-in-law
when they commit adultery,
because the men themselves consort
with harlots
and sacrifice with shrine
prostitutes—
a people without understanding
will come to ruin!

15 "Though you commit adultery,
O Israel,
let not Judah become guilty.

"Do not go to Gilgal;
do not go up to Beth Aven.*a*
And do not swear, 'As surely as the
LORD lives!'
16 The Israelites are stubborn,
like a stubborn heifer.
How then can the LORD pasture them
like lambs in a meadow?
17 Ephraim is joined to idols;

leave him alone!
18 Even when their drinks are gone,
they continue their prostitution;
their rulers dearly love shameful
ways.
19 A whirlwind will sweep them away,
and their sacrifices will bring them
shame.

Judgment Against Israel

5 "Hear this, you priests!
Pay attention, you Israelites!
Listen, O royal house!
This judgment is against you:
You have been a snare at Mizpah,
a net spread out on Tabor.
2 The rebels are deep in slaughter.
I will discipline all of them.
3 I know all about Ephraim;
Israel is not hidden from me.
Ephraim, you have now turned to
prostitution;
Israel is corrupt.

4 "Their deeds do not permit them
to return to their God.

---

a15 Beth Aven means *house of wickedness* (a name
for Bethel, which means *house of God*).

Keeping the Door Open

QuIet TIMES with each other

HOSEA 4:10–15 Hosea's tragic marriage is symbolic of God's love relationship with Israel. Israel was unfaithful to God, and he didn't overlook their sin; he said they would be judged. But God did want his people to know he was committed to them and loved them.

Marital love never means a denial of sin on the part of a spouse. To deny a sin such as adultery is, in a small way, to be an accomplice to that sin. For one spouse to act as if the other spouse is not involved in a violation of the marriage, or to refuse to confront it, is to facilitate that sin.

Sinful actions need to be confronted. Confronting sin doesn't close the door on the relationship. Confronting sin opens the door for restoration. It's like saying, "Yes, I know the sin exists and that repentance must take place." It is also an affirmation of the marriage commitment: "Yes, I want to do what is necessary to bind this marriage back together."

As despicable as Israel's behavior was, God was ready to receive his people back if only they would repent from their sin of worshiping false gods. Our responsibility in our marriages is to respond correctly to the trials of the relationship. We are to confront sin but leave the door of restoration open for repentant hearts. That's what love is.

—*Bob & Rosemary*

Weekend **Warm-up** How do you feel when you think of your marriage commitment foremost as a commitment to God?

Go to page 953 for your next devotional reading.

A spirit of prostitution is in their
　　heart;
　　they do not acknowledge the LORD.
5Israel's arrogance testifies against
　　them;
　　the Israelites, even Ephraim,
　　　stumble in their sin;
　　Judah also stumbles with them.
6When they go with their flocks and
　　herds
　　to seek the LORD,
　they will not find him;
　　he has withdrawn himself from
　　　them.
7They are unfaithful to the LORD;
　　they give birth to illegitimate
　　　children.
Now their New Moon festivals
　　will devour them and their fields.

8"Sound the trumpet in Gibeah,
　　the horn in Ramah.
Raise the battle cry in Beth Aven*a*;
　　lead on, O Benjamin.
9Ephraim will be laid waste
　　on the day of reckoning.
Among the tribes of Israel
　　I proclaim what is certain.
10Judah's leaders are like those
　　who move boundary stones.
I will pour out my wrath on them
　　like a flood of water.
11Ephraim is oppressed,
　　trampled in judgment,
　　intent on pursuing idols.*b*
12I am like a moth to Ephraim,
　　like rot to the people of Judah.

13"When Ephraim saw his sickness,
　　and Judah his sores,
　then Ephraim turned to Assyria,
　　and sent to the great king for help.
But he is not able to cure you,
　　not able to heal your sores.
14For I will be like a lion to Ephraim,
　　like a great lion to Judah.
I will tear them to pieces and go
　　away;
　I will carry them off, with no one
　　to rescue them.
15Then I will go back to my place
　　until they admit their guilt.
And they will seek my face;
　　in their misery they will earnestly
　　　seek me."

Israel Unrepentant

6 "Come, let us return to the LORD.
　　He has torn us to pieces
　　but he will heal us;
　he has injured us
　　but he will bind up our wounds.
2After two days he will revive us;
　　on the third day he will restore us,
　　that we may live in his presence.
3Let us acknowledge the LORD;
　　let us press on to acknowledge
　　　him.
As surely as the sun rises,
　　he will appear;
　he will come to us like the winter
　　rains,
　　like the spring rains that water the
　　　earth."

4"What can I do with you, Ephraim?
　　What can I do with you, Judah?
Your love is like the morning mist,
　　like the early dew that disappears.
5Therefore I cut you in pieces with my
　　prophets,
　I killed you with the words of my
　　mouth;
　my judgments flashed like
　　lightning upon you.
6For I desire mercy, not sacrifice,
　　and acknowledgment of God rather
　　than burnt offerings.
7Like Adam,*c* they have broken the
　　covenant—
　they were unfaithful to me there.
8Gilead is a city of wicked men,
　　stained with footprints of blood.
9As marauders lie in ambush for a
　　man,
　so do bands of priests;
　they murder on the road to Shechem,
　　committing shameful crimes.
10I have seen a horrible thing
　　in the house of Israel.
There Ephraim is given to prostitution
　　and Israel is defiled.

11"Also for you, Judah,
　　a harvest is appointed.

"Whenever I would restore the
　　fortunes of my people,

---

a8 Beth Aven means *house of wickedness* (a name for
Bethel, which means *house of God*).　*b11* The
meaning of the Hebrew for this word is uncertain.
c7 Or *As at Adam;* or *Like men*

7 ¹whenever I would heal Israel,
    the sins of Ephraim are exposed
    and the crimes of Samaria revealed.
They practice deceit,
    thieves break into houses,
    bandits rob in the streets;
²but they do not realize
    that I remember all their evil
        deeds.
Their sins engulf them;
    they are always before me.

³ "They delight the king with their
        wickedness,
    the princes with their lies.
⁴They are all adulterers,
    burning like an oven
whose fire the baker need not stir
    from the kneading of the dough till
        it rises.
⁵On the day of the festival of our king
    the princes become inflamed with
        wine,
    and he joins hands with the
        mockers.
⁶Their hearts are like an oven;
    they approach him with intrigue.
Their passion smolders all night;
    in the morning it blazes like a
        flaming fire.

⁷All of them are hot as an oven;
    they devour their rulers.
All their kings fall,
    and none of them calls on me.

⁸ "Ephraim mixes with the nations;
    Ephraim is a flat cake not turned
        over.
⁹Foreigners sap his strength,
    but he does not realize it.
His hair is sprinkled with gray,
    but he does not notice.
¹⁰Israel's arrogance testifies against him,
    but despite all this
he does not return to the LORD his
        God
    or search for him.

¹¹ "Ephraim is like a dove,
    easily deceived and senseless—
now calling to Egypt,
    now turning to Assyria.
¹²When they go, I will throw my net
        over them;
    I will pull them down like birds of
        the air.
When I hear them flocking together,
    I will catch them.
¹³Woe to them,
    because they have strayed from
        me!

Revive Us Again

Monday

HOSEA 6:1–3 You know the scenario; it happens over and over in the Bible. When in serious trouble, usually because they didn't obey God in the first place, the Israelites cried out to God for help. God answered their pleas and rescued the Israelites. Unfortunately, when the crisis was over, the Israelites usually forgot about what they had been through and what they had learned, so they returned to their old ways. God's long-suffering and willingness to forgive and restore his people again and again is simply amazing. The Israelites were God's chosen people; he loved them, and he chose to restore them continually.

In marriage, spouses can be much like the Israelites. Often after overcoming a crisis and working through difficult issues, we soon forget our promises and good inten-

tions and return to our old ways. We need continuous restoration to one another and to God. How reassuring it is to realize that, no matter how many times we let God down and disappoint each other, there is forgiveness. Shouldn't we extend the same principle of unlimited forgiveness and restoration to our spouse?

True restoration and refreshment come from the Lord, and he empowers us to forgive our spouse. Six of the most precious words a husband or wife can say are "I was wrong; please forgive me." Like a refreshing spring rain that clears the air and removes the fog, forgiveness cleanses and restores our relationship so that we can clearly see our love for and dedication to one another.

—**Dave & Claudia**

Go to page 954 for your next devotional reading.

Destruction to them,
>because they have rebelled against
>>me!
I long to redeem them
>but they speak lies against me.
[14]They do not cry out to me from their
>>hearts
>but wail upon their beds.
They gather together[a] for grain and
>>new wine
>but turn away from me.
[15]I trained them and strengthened
>>them,
>but they plot evil against me.
[16]They do not turn to the Most High;
>they are like a faulty bow.
Their leaders will fall by the sword
>because of their insolent words.
For this they will be ridiculed
>in the land of Egypt.

Israel to Reap the Whirlwind

8 "Put the trumpet to your lips!
>An eagle is over the house of the
>>LORD
because the people have broken my
>>covenant
>and rebelled against my law.
[2]Israel cries out to me,
>'O our God, we acknowledge you!'
[3]But Israel has rejected what is good;

an enemy will pursue him.
[4]They set up kings without my
>>consent;
>they choose princes without my
>>approval.
With their silver and gold
>they make idols for themselves
>to their own destruction.
[5]Throw out your calf-idol, O Samaria!
>My anger burns against them.
How long will they be incapable of
>>purity?
[6]   They are from Israel!
This calf—a craftsman has made it;
>it is not God.
It will be broken in pieces,
>that calf of Samaria.

[7]"They sow the wind
>and reap the whirlwind.
The stalk has no head;
>it will produce no flour.
Were it to yield grain,
>foreigners would swallow it up.
[8]Israel is swallowed up;
>now she is among the nations
>like a worthless thing.
[9]For they have gone up to Assyria

*a14 Most Hebrew manuscripts; some Hebrew
manuscripts and Septuagint They slash themselves*

Peace in the Whirlwind

Tuesday

HOSEA 8:7 In our fast-pace society, we are all in danger of sowing the wind and reaping the whirlwind that Hosea writes about. The telltale sign is stress—the kind that results in ulcers, high blood pressure and other physical symptoms. We carry the stress of the workaday world into our marriage. It creates tension in our relationship. If we can't take out our anger on the boss, for example, we might take it out on our spouse.

One sure way to prevent your stress from becoming debilitating is to respond to the call of Jesus Christ when he says, "Come to me . . . I will give you rest" (Matthew 11:28).

The most frequently overlooked dimension in stress management, even among Christians, is resting in God's presence. This is not always easy; even the great leader Moses had difficulty with it. He experienced unrelieved stress as he tried to keep two million Israelites happy as they wandered in the desert. In exasperation Moses turned to God with this plea: "Why have you brought this trouble on your servant? . . . I cannot carry all these people by myself; the burden is too heavy for me" (Numbers 11:11,14). But God called Moses to rest in God's wisdom, and soon Moses' burden and stress became more manageable. The same God who called Moses to rest is calling you and your spouse to relax with him—even in the midst of your "whirlwind."

—Les & Leslie

Go to page 959 for your next devotional reading.

like a wild donkey wandering
  alone.
Ephraim has sold herself to lovers.
¹⁰Although they have sold themselves
    among the nations,
  I will now gather them together.
They will begin to waste away
  under the oppression of the mighty
    king.
¹¹"Though Ephraim built many altars
    for sin offerings,
  these have become altars for
    sinning.
¹²I wrote for them the many things of
    my law,
  but they regarded them as
    something alien.
¹³They offer sacrifices given to me
  and they eat the meat,
  but the LORD is not pleased with
    them.
Now he will remember their
    wickedness
  and punish their sins:
  They will return to Egypt.
¹⁴Israel has forgotten his Maker
  and built palaces;
  Judah has fortified many towns.
But I will send fire upon their cities
  that will consume their fortresses."

Punishment for Israel

9 Do not rejoice, O Israel;
  do not be jubilant like the other
    nations.
For you have been unfaithful to your
    God;
  you love the wages of a prostitute
  at every threshing floor.
²Threshing floors and winepresses will
    not feed the people;
  the new wine will fail them.
³They will not remain in the LORD's
    land;
  Ephraim will return to Egypt
  and eat unclean*a* food in Assyria.
⁴They will not pour out wine offerings
    to the LORD,
  nor will their sacrifices please him.
Such sacrifices will be to them like
    the bread of mourners;
  all who eat them will be unclean.
This food will be for themselves;
  it will not come into the temple of
    the LORD.

⁵What will you do on the day of your
    appointed feasts,
  on the festival days of the LORD?
⁶Even if they escape from destruction,
  Egypt will gather them,
  and Memphis will bury them.
Their treasures of silver will be taken
    over by briers,
  and thorns will overrun their tents.
⁷The days of punishment are coming,
  the days of reckoning are at hand.
  Let Israel know this.
Because your sins are so many
  and your hostility so great,
the prophet is considered a fool,
  the inspired man a maniac.
⁸The prophet, along with my God,
  is the watchman over Ephraim,*b*
yet snares await him on all his paths,
  and hostility in the house of his
    God.
⁹They have sunk deep into corruption,
  as in the days of Gibeah.
God will remember their wickedness
  and punish them for their sins.

¹⁰"When I found Israel,
  it was like finding grapes in the
    desert;
when I saw your fathers,
  it was like seeing the early fruit on
    the fig tree.
But when they came to Baal Peor,
  they consecrated themselves to that
    shameful idol
and became as vile as the thing
    they loved.
¹¹Ephraim's glory will fly away like a
    bird—
  no birth, no pregnancy, no
    conception.
¹²Even if they rear children,
  I will bereave them of every one.
Woe to them
  when I turn away from them!
¹³I have seen Ephraim, like Tyre,
  planted in a pleasant place.
But Ephraim will bring out
  their children to the slayer."

¹⁴Give them, O LORD—
  what will you give them?

a3 That is, ceremonially unclean   *b8* Or *The
prophet is the watchman over Ephraim, / the people of
my God*

Give them wombs that miscarry
and breasts that are dry.

[15] "Because of all their wickedness in
Gilgal,
I hated them there.
Because of their sinful deeds,
I will drive them out of my house.
I will no longer love them;
all their leaders are rebellious.
[16]Ephraim is blighted,
their root is withered,
they yield no fruit.
Even if they bear children,
I will slay their cherished offspring."

[17]My God will reject them
because they have not obeyed him;
they will be wanderers among the
nations.

10 Israel was a spreading vine;
he brought forth fruit for himself.
As his fruit increased,
he built more altars;
as his land prospered,
he adorned his sacred stones.
[2]Their heart is deceitful,
and now they must bear their guilt.
The LORD will demolish their altars
and destroy their sacred stones.

[3]Then they will say, "We have no king
because we did not revere the
LORD.
But even if we had a king,
what could he do for us?"
[4]They make many promises,
take false oaths
and make agreements;
therefore lawsuits spring up
like poisonous weeds in a plowed
field.
[5]The people who live in Samaria fear
for the calf-idol of Beth Aven.[a]
Its people will mourn over it,
and so will its idolatrous priests,
those who had rejoiced over its
splendor,
because it is taken from them into
exile.
[6]It will be carried to Assyria
as tribute for the great king.
Ephraim will be disgraced;
Israel will be ashamed of its
wooden idols.[b]
[7]Samaria and its king will float away

like a twig on the surface of the
waters.
[8]The high places of wickedness[c] will
be destroyed—
it is the sin of Israel.
Thorns and thistles will grow up
and cover their altars.
Then they will say to the mountains,
"Cover us!"
and to the hills, "Fall on us!"

[9]"Since the days of Gibeah, you have
sinned, O Israel,
and there you have remained.[d]
Did not war overtake
the evildoers in Gibeah?
[10]When I please, I will punish them;
nations will be gathered against
them
to put them in bonds for their
double sin.
[11]Ephraim is a trained heifer
that loves to thresh;
so I will put a yoke
on her fair neck.
I will drive Ephraim,
Judah must plow,
and Jacob must break up the
ground.
[12]Sow for yourselves righteousness,
reap the fruit of unfailing love,
and break up your unplowed ground;
for it is time to seek the LORD,
until he comes
and showers righteousness on you.
[13]But you have planted wickedness,
you have reaped evil,
you have eaten the fruit of
deception.
Because you have depended on your
own strength
and on your many warriors,
[14]the roar of battle will rise against
your people,
so that all your fortresses will be
devastated—
as Shalman devastated Beth Arbel on
the day of battle,
when mothers were dashed to the
ground with their children.
[15]Thus will it happen to you, O Bethel,

---

[a]5 *Beth Aven* means *house of wickedness* (a name for
Bethel, which means *house of God*).   [b]6 Or *its
counsel*   [c]8 Hebrew *aven*, a reference to Beth
Aven (a derogatory name for Bethel)   [d]9 Or
there a stand was taken

because your wickedness is great.
When that day dawns,
    the king of Israel will be
        completely destroyed.

God's Love for Israel

11 "When Israel was a child, I loved
        him,
    and out of Egypt I called my son.
²But the more I[a] called Israel,
    the further they went from me.[b]
They sacrificed to the Baals
    and they burned incense to images.
³It was I who taught Ephraim to walk,
    taking them by the arms;
but they did not realize
    it was I who healed them.
⁴I led them with cords of human
        kindness,
    with ties of love;
I lifted the yoke from their neck
    and bent down to feed them.

⁵"Will they not return to Egypt
    and will not Assyria rule over them
because they refuse to repent?
⁶Swords will flash in their cities,
    will destroy the bars of their gates
    and put an end to their plans.
⁷My people are determined to turn
        from me.
    Even if they call to the Most High,
    he will by no means exalt them.

⁸"How can I give you up, Ephraim?
    How can I hand you over, Israel?
How can I treat you like Admah?
    How can I make you like Zeboiim?
My heart is changed within me;
    all my compassion is aroused.
⁹I will not carry out my fierce anger,
    nor will I turn and devastate
        Ephraim.
For I am God, and not man—
    the Holy One among you.
    I will not come in wrath.[c]
¹⁰They will follow the LORD;
    he will roar like a lion.
When he roars,
    his children will come trembling
        from the west.
¹¹They will come trembling
    like birds from Egypt,
    like doves from Assyria.
I will settle them in their homes,"
    declares the LORD.

Israel's Sin

¹²Ephraim has surrounded me with lies,
    the house of Israel with deceit.
And Judah is unruly against God,
    even against the faithful Holy One.

12 ¹Ephraim feeds on the wind;
        he pursues the east wind all day
    and multiplies lies and violence.
He makes a treaty with Assyria
    and sends olive oil to Egypt.
²The LORD has a charge to bring
        against Judah;
    he will punish Jacob[d] according
        to his ways
    and repay him according to his
        deeds.
³In the womb he grasped his brother's
        heel;
    as a man he struggled with God.
⁴He struggled with the angel and
        overcame him;
    he wept and begged for his favor.
He found him at Bethel
    and talked with him there—
⁵the LORD God Almighty,
    the LORD is his name of renown!
⁶But you must return to your God;
    maintain love and justice,
    and wait for your God always.

⁷The merchant uses dishonest scales;
    he loves to defraud.
⁸Ephraim boasts,
    "I am very rich; I have become
        wealthy.
With all my wealth they will not find
        in me
    any iniquity or sin."

⁹"I am the LORD your God,
    ⌊who brought you⌋ out of[e] Egypt;
I will make you live in tents again,
    as in the days of your appointed
        feasts.
¹⁰I spoke to the prophets,
    gave them many visions
    and told parables through them."

¹¹Is Gilead wicked?
    Its people are worthless!
    Do they sacrifice bulls in Gilgal?

---

[a]2 Some Septuagint manuscripts; Hebrew *they*
[b]2 Septuagint; Hebrew *them*   [c]9 Or *come against
any city*   [d]2 *Jacob* means *he grasps the heel*
(figuratively, *he deceives*).   [e]9 Or *God / ever since
you were in*

Their altars will be like piles of
        stones
    on a plowed field.
¹²Jacob fled to the country of Aram*a*;
    Israel served to get a wife,
    and to pay for her he tended
        sheep.
¹³The LORD used a prophet to bring
        Israel up from Egypt,
    by a prophet he cared for him.
¹⁴But Ephraim has bitterly provoked
        him to anger;
    his Lord will leave upon him the
        guilt of his bloodshed
    and will repay him for his
        contempt.

The LORD'S Anger Against Israel

13 When Ephraim spoke, men
        trembled;
    he was exalted in Israel.
    But he became guilty of Baal
        worship and died.
²Now they sin more and more;
    they make idols for themselves
        from their silver,
    cleverly fashioned images,
    all of them the work of craftsmen.
    It is said of these people,
    "They offer human sacrifice
    and kiss*b* the calf-idols."
³Therefore they will be like the
        morning mist,
    like the early dew that disappears,
    like chaff swirling from a threshing
        floor,
    like smoke escaping through a
        window.

⁴"But I am the LORD your God,
    ⌞who brought you⌟ out of*c* Egypt.
    You shall acknowledge no God but
        me,
    no Savior except me.
⁵I cared for you in the desert,
    in the land of burning heat.
⁶When I fed them, they were satisfied;
    when they were satisfied, they
        became proud;
    then they forgot me.
⁷So I will come upon them like a lion,
    like a leopard I will lurk by the
        path.
⁸Like a bear robbed of her cubs,
    I will attack them and rip them
        open.

Like a lion I will devour them;
    a wild animal will tear them apart.

⁹"You are destroyed, O Israel,
    because you are against me, against
        your helper.
¹⁰Where is your king, that he may save
        you?
    Where are your rulers in all your
        towns,
    of whom you said,
    'Give me a king and princes'?
¹¹So in my anger I gave you a king,
    and in my wrath I took him away.
¹²The guilt of Ephraim is stored up,
    his sins are kept on record.
¹³Pains as of a woman in childbirth
        come to him,
    but he is a child without wisdom;
    when the time arrives,
    he does not come to the opening
        of the womb.

¹⁴"I will ransom them from the power
        of the grave*d*;
    I will redeem them from death.
    Where, O death, are your plagues?
    Where, O grave,*d* is your
        destruction?

    "I will have no compassion,
¹⁵   even though he thrives among his
        brothers.
    An east wind from the LORD will
        come,
    blowing in from the desert;
    his spring will fail
    and his well dry up.
    His storehouse will be plundered
    of all its treasures.
¹⁶The people of Samaria must bear
        their guilt,
    because they have rebelled against
        their God.
    They will fall by the sword;
    their little ones will be dashed to
        the ground,
    their pregnant women ripped open."

Repentance to Bring Blessing

14 Return, O Israel, to the LORD your
        God.
    Your sins have been your downfall!
²Take words with you

---

*a*12 That is, Northwest Mesopotamia   *b*2 Or
"Men who sacrifice / kiss   *c*4 Or God / ever since
you were in   *d*14 Hebrew *Sheol*

and return to the LORD.
Say to him:
   "Forgive all our sins
and receive us graciously,
   that we may offer the fruit of our
      lips.*ᵃ*
³Assyria cannot save us;
   we will not mount war-horses.
We will never again say 'Our gods'
   to what our own hands have made,
   for in you the fatherless find
      compassion."

⁴"I will heal their waywardness
   and love them freely,
   for my anger has turned away from
      them.
⁵I will be like the dew to Israel;
   he will blossom like a lily.
Like a cedar of Lebanon
   he will send down his roots;
⁶   his young shoots will grow.
His splendor will be like an olive tree,

his fragrance like a cedar of
      Lebanon.
⁷Men will dwell again in his shade.
   He will flourish like the grain.
He will blossom like a vine,
   and his fame will be like the wine
      from Lebanon.
⁸O Ephraim, what more have I*ᵇ* to do
      with idols?
   I will answer him and care for him.
I am like a green pine tree;
   your fruitfulness comes from me."

⁹Who is wise? He will realize these
      things.
   Who is discerning? He will
      understand them.
The ways of the LORD are right;
   the righteous walk in them,
   but the rebellious stumble in them.

ᵃ2 Or offer our lips as sacrifices of bulls   *ᵇ8 Or What more has Ephraim*

What Is Repentance?

Wednesday

HOSEA 14:1–4 Repentance is an action that begins with pain and ends gloriously. When my children have done something wrong, they can hardly look me (Bob) in the eye. They know that they have done wrong and might even wonder if they can get away without getting caught. But they have "caught themselves." *They* know they've done something wrong, and it alienates or strains their relationship with me. As painful as it is to come to me and confess what they have done, it's the only way to re-establish the relationship. Then they can look me in the eye again . . . free from guilt.

In the marriage relationship, sincere repentance is both mandatory and difficult. It

is mandatory in order to keep the relationship healthy. Repentance requires more than words; it requires change. Real repentance requires a humble attitude, as well as removing the behavior that is causing the problem.

Once true repentance occurs, the relationship can move into a glorious stage of growth. The throbbing pain that had developed between the spouses will be gone. If true repentance has been offered and true forgiveness is given, the marriage relationship will be ready for a time of growth and intimacy.

—Bob & Rosemary

Go to page 961 for your next devotional reading.

Joel

Have you ever wondered if there is spiritual significance in natural disasters such as floods, hurricanes and earthquakes? The book of Joel may give you a clue. Joel views the plague of locusts as a catastrophic foretaste of God's judgment on people who are cold and indifferent toward him. Joel warns of the coming judgment for all nations, including the Israelites. He calls the nation to repent and paints a picture of the restoration and healing that will follow if they do.

Consider this as you read the book of Joel: In God's eyes, the worst disaster is a human heart that is closed to his love.

1 The word of the LORD that came to Joel son of Pethuel.

An Invasion of Locusts

²Hear this, you elders;
　listen, all who live in the land.
Has anything like this ever happened
　　in your days
　or in the days of your forefathers?
³Tell it to your children,
　　and let your children tell it to their
　　　children,
　and their children to the next
　　　generation.
⁴What the locust swarm has left
　　the great locusts have eaten;
what the great locusts have left
　　the young locusts have eaten;
what the young locusts have left
　　other locusts*ᵃ* have eaten.

⁵Wake up, you drunkards, and weep!

Wail, all you drinkers of wine;
wail because of the new wine,
　for it has been snatched from your
　　　lips.
⁶A nation has invaded my land,
　　powerful and without number;
it has the teeth of a lion,
　　the fangs of a lioness.
⁷It has laid waste my vines
　　and ruined my fig trees.
It has stripped off their bark
　　and thrown it away,
　　leaving their branches white.

⁸Mourn like a virgin*ᵇ* in sackcloth
　　grieving for the husband*ᶜ* of her
　　　youth.
⁹Grain offerings and drink offerings

ᵃ4 The precise meaning of the four Hebrew words used here for locusts is uncertain.　　*ᵇ8* Or *young woman*　　*ᶜ8* Or *betrothed*

are cut off from the house of the
    LORD.
The priests are in mourning,
    those who minister before the
    LORD.
¹⁰The fields are ruined,
    the ground is dried up*a*;
the grain is destroyed,
    the new wine is dried up,
    the oil fails.
¹¹Despair, you farmers,
    wail, you vine growers;
grieve for the wheat and the barley,
    because the harvest of the field is
    destroyed.
¹²The vine is dried up
    and the fig tree is withered;
the pomegranate, the palm and the
    apple tree—
all the trees of the field—are dried
    up.
Surely the joy of mankind
    is withered away.

A Call to Repentance

¹³Put on sackcloth, O priests, and
    mourn;
    wail, you who minister before the
    altar.
Come, spend the night in sackcloth,
    you who minister before my God;

for the grain offerings and drink
    offerings
    are withheld from the house of
    your God.
¹⁴Declare a holy fast;
    call a sacred assembly.
Summon the elders
    and all who live in the land
to the house of the LORD your God,
    and cry out to the LORD.

¹⁵Alas for that day!
    For the day of the LORD is near;
    it will come like destruction from
    the Almighty.*b*
¹⁶Has not the food been cut off
    before our very eyes—
joy and gladness
    from the house of our God?
¹⁷The seeds are shriveled
    beneath the clods.*c*
The storehouses are in ruins,
    the granaries have been broken
    down,
for the grain has dried up.
¹⁸How the cattle moan!
    The herds mill about
    because they have no pasture;

a10 Or *ground mourns*   *b15* Hebrew *Shaddai*
c17 The meaning of the Hebrew for this word is
uncertain.

Leaving a Legacy

Thursday

JOEL 1:3   How fortunate are those children whose parents take God's Word seriously and not only share the Scripture with their children but also live it out. Joel encourages us to start the tradition of passing on our spiritual heritage to future generations by telling the story of what God has meant to us—and this should also include our marriage story.

The older Claudia and I get, the more we realize how important it is to pass what we've learned along to our own children and grandchildren. After Claudia's mother died, we were sorting through her things and found a small devotional journal in which Claudia's grandmother had recorded her devotions and prayers. Claudia's mother had been given this journal and found com-

fort from it for years. Now we have passed it on to our own children and grandchildren.

Why not pass on your own "story?" Think about how meaningful it might be if someday your great-grandchildren could read your love story of God's grace. If you don't especially like to write, you could record history in other ways, such as videotaping, making photo albums or tape recording a message to future generations in your family. Talk with each other about the highlights of your marriage history and how God has walked with you through the pages of your marriage. Then record it. Someday it may be a legacy that your ancestors will appreciate.

—Dave & Claudia

Go to page 963 for your next devotional reading.

even the flocks of sheep are
  suffering.

¹⁹To you, O LORD, I call,
  for fire has devoured the open
    pastures
  and flames have burned up all the
    trees of the field.
²⁰Even the wild animals pant for you;
  the streams of water have dried up
  and fire has devoured the open
    pastures.

An Army of Locusts

2 Blow the trumpet in Zion;
  sound the alarm on my holy hill.
Let all who live in the land tremble,
  for the day of the LORD is coming.
It is close at hand—
²   a day of darkness and gloom,
  a day of clouds and blackness.
Like dawn spreading across the
    mountains
  a large and mighty army comes,
such as never was of old
  nor ever will be in ages to come.

³Before them fire devours,
  behind them a flame blazes.
Before them the land is like the
    garden of Eden,
  behind them, a desert waste—
  nothing escapes them.
⁴They have the appearance of horses;
  they gallop along like cavalry.
⁵With a noise like that of chariots
  they leap over the mountaintops,
like a crackling fire consuming
    stubble,
  like a mighty army drawn up for
    battle.

⁶At the sight of them, nations are in
    anguish;
  every face turns pale.
⁷They charge like warriors;
  they scale walls like soldiers.
They all march in line,
  not swerving from their course.
⁸They do not jostle each other;
  each marches straight ahead.
They plunge through defenses
  without breaking ranks.
⁹They rush upon the city;
  they run along the wall.
They climb into the houses;

like thieves they enter through the
    windows.

¹⁰Before them the earth shakes,
  the sky trembles,
the sun and moon are darkened,
  and the stars no longer shine.
¹¹The LORD thunders
  at the head of his army;
his forces are beyond number,
  and mighty are those who obey his
    command.
The day of the LORD is great;
  it is dreadful.
Who can endure it?

Rend Your Heart

¹²"Even now," declares the LORD,
  "return to me with all your heart,
  with fasting and weeping and
    mourning."

¹³Rend your heart
  and not your garments.
Return to the LORD your God,
  for he is gracious and
    compassionate,
slow to anger and abounding in love,
  and he relents from sending
    calamity.
¹⁴Who knows? He may turn and have
    pity
  and leave behind a blessing—
grain offerings and drink offerings
  for the LORD your God.

¹⁵Blow the trumpet in Zion,
  declare a holy fast,
  call a sacred assembly.
¹⁶Gather the people,
  consecrate the assembly;
bring together the elders,
  gather the children,
  those nursing at the breast.
Let the bridegroom leave his room
  and the bride her chamber.
¹⁷Let the priests, who minister before
    the LORD,
  weep between the temple porch
    and the altar.
Let them say, "Spare your people,
    O LORD.
Do not make your inheritance an
    object of scorn,
  a byword among the nations.

Why should they say among the
  peoples,
'Where is their God?' "

The Lord's Answer

18Then the LORD will be jealous for his
    land
  and take pity on his people.

19The LORD will reply[a] to them:

"I am sending you grain, new wine
    and oil,
  enough to satisfy you fully;
never again will I make you
  an object of scorn to the nations.

20"I will drive the northern army far
    from you,
  pushing it into a parched and
    barren land,
with its front columns going into the
    eastern sea[b]
and those in the rear into the
    western sea.[c]
And its stench will go up;
  its smell will rise."

Surely he has done great things.[d]
21   Be not afraid, O land;
  be glad and rejoice.
Surely the LORD has done great
    things.
22   Be not afraid, O wild animals,
  for the open pastures are becoming
    green.
The trees are bearing their fruit;
  the fig tree and the vine yield their
    riches.
23Be glad, O people of Zion,
  rejoice in the LORD your God,
for he has given you
  the autumn rains in
    righteousness.[e]
He sends you abundant showers,
  both autumn and spring rains, as
    before.
24The threshing floors will be filled
    with grain;

a18,19 Or LORD was jealous . . . / and took pity . . . /
19The LORD replied   b20 That is, the Dead Sea
c20 That is, the Mediterranean   d20 Or rise. /
Surely it has done great things."   e23 Or / the
teacher for righteousness:

Do You Dream What I Dream?

Friday

COUPLE MINUTES

JOEL 2:28-29 The musical play *Man of La Mancha* is one of our all-time favorites. It is the story of a crazy old man suffering from what we would now call senile dementia. The action takes place one hundred years after the age of chivalry, when there were no more knights. But, thinking he is one, Don Quixote puts on a strange suit of armor and rides into the world to battle evil and protect the weak. He brings along his funny little servant Sancho Panza. When they arrive at an old inn used by mule traders, Don Quixote calls the innkeeper the lord of a great castle. In the inn he meets the most miserable human being imaginable, an orphan girl who is degraded by the mule traders. Don Quixote pronounces this wretched girl the great lady Dulcinea and begs for her handkerchief as a token to carry with him into battle.

Everyone thinks Don Quixote is bonkers, but at the end of the play the old man who is now about to die is no longer suffering from these delusions. In a moving scene, all the people he has re-named appear at his bedside and beg him not to change. His ex-citement about their future has transformed them, and they have become the people that this insane visionary saw them to be.

The message of the play is simple: The dreams and hopes of the people around us powerfully shape our lives. And the mes-sage to married couples is that what you dream for each other will powerfully shape your marriage. What we consciously dream about, what we envision for our future to-gether, the goals we set for our partner-ship, determine the quality of our marriage in the present. For where there is no vision, a marriage will perish (see Proverbs 29:18, page 697). And if our dreams are worthy and filled with godly hope, they take us to heights we could never have imagined.

—Les & Leslie

Go to page 964 for your next devotional reading.

the vats will overflow with new
wine and oil.

25 "I will repay you for the years the
locusts have eaten—
the great locust and the young
locust,
the other locusts and the locust
swarm*a*—
my great army that I sent among
you.
26 You will have plenty to eat, until
you are full,
and you will praise the name of
the LORD your God,
who has worked wonders for you;
never again will my people be
shamed.
27 Then you will know that I am in
Israel,
that I am the LORD your God,
and that there is no other;

never again will my people be
shamed.

The Day of the LORD

28 "And afterward,
I will pour out my Spirit on all
people.
Your sons and daughters will
prophesy,
your old men will dream dreams,
your young men will see visions.
29 Even on my servants, both men and
women,
I will pour out my Spirit in those
days.
30 I will show wonders in the heavens
and on the earth,
blood and fire and billows of
smoke.

*a*25 The precise meaning of the four Hebrew
words used here for locusts is uncertain.

Preparing for Tomorrow

Qui et TIMES
with each other

JOEL 3:9   Our phone rang. On
the other end of the call an
attorney in Boston said, "You
don't know me, but I read
about your books in the
Bottom Line Newsletter. I
need your help." He continued,
"Last night my wife told me that
she doesn't love me anymore. I don't
know what I did that was so wrong. I've
never had affairs. We've both been good
parents, but now our children are growing
up and leaving home. And now my wife
says she's bored and wants to leave me.
I'm dumbfounded. By profession, I'm an
attorney; I fix things. Why didn't my wife
just tell me what she wanted? If she wanted conversation, all she had to do was ask.
If she wanted to go to a fancy restaurant, she
only had to tell me. There's a gap here I
wasn't aware of. If she'll tell me what I
need to do to fix it, fine, but I don't have
a clue!"

Unfortunately, we had no "quick fixes" to

offer this attorney. We did
challenge him, if his wife was
willing, to set some goals
with her for the future to
revitalize their relationship.
Perhaps if she saw him take
some initiative, she would
change her mind.

Just as God challenged the nations
through Joel to prepare and be protective, so
must we be proactive in our marriage. Now
is the time to be intentional. As Joel's
prophecy extends far into the future, we also
need to have a long-term view of our marriage. And like Joel, we need to prepare for
war—not against each other—but against
the forces that would attack and seek to
weaken our marriage such as indifference,
busyness, miscommunication or no communication. You can prepare and nurture the
fertile ground of your marriage for future
growth by being proactive. This is one war
that, together, you can win.

—*Dave & Claudia*

Weekend Warm-up   *In what ways are you shaping each other's lives?*

Go to page 969 for your next devotional reading.

³¹The sun will be turned to darkness
and the moon to blood
before the coming of the great and
dreadful day of the LORD.
³²And everyone who calls
on the name of the LORD will be
saved;
for on Mount Zion and in Jerusalem
there will be deliverance,
as the LORD has said,
among the survivors
whom the LORD calls.

The Nations Judged

3 "In those days and at that time,
when I restore the fortunes of
Judah and Jerusalem,
²I will gather all nations
and bring them down to the Valley
of Jehoshaphat.ᵃ
There I will enter into judgment
against them
concerning my inheritance, my
people Israel,
for they scattered my people among
the nations
and divided up my land.
³They cast lots for my people
and traded boys for prostitutes;
they sold girls for wine
that they might drink.

⁴"Now what have you against me,
O Tyre and Sidon and all you regions of
Philistia? Are you repaying me for something
I have done? If you are paying me
back, I will swiftly and speedily return on
your own heads what you have done. ⁵For
you took my silver and my gold and carried
off my finest treasures to your temples.
⁶You sold the people of Judah and
Jerusalem to the Greeks, that you might
send them far from their homeland.

⁷"See, I am going to rouse them out of
the places to which you sold them, and I
will return on your own heads what you
have done. ⁸I will sell your sons and
daughters to the people of Judah, and
they will sell them to the Sabeans, a nation
far away." The LORD has spoken.

⁹Proclaim this among the nations:
Prepare for war!
Rouse the warriors!
Let all the fighting men draw near
and attack.

JUST BETWEEN you & me

Preparing for Tomorrow

Having a future proactive marriage begins
with evaluating your marriage as it is today.
On a scale of one to five (one being "needs
improvement" and five being "awesome"),
rate your relationship the following areas:

Communication

Handling anger

Resolving conflict

Encouragement

Commitment

Humor

Goal setting

Spiritual intimacy

Sexual intimacy

Friendship

Choose an area that is ranked lower and
come up with your own proactive plan for
improvement. As you see progress, choose
another needy area. Continue this plan and
you will have a proactive marriage.

¹⁰Beat your plowshares into swords
and your pruning hooks into
spears.
Let the weakling say,
"I am strong!"
¹¹Come quickly, all you nations from
every side,
and assemble there.

Bring down your warriors, O LORD!

¹²"Let the nations be roused;
let them advance into the Valley of
Jehoshaphat,
for there I will sit
to judge all the nations on every
side.
¹³Swing the sickle,
for the harvest is ripe.
Come, trample the grapes,
for the winepress is full
and the vats overflow—
so great is their wickedness!"

ᵃ2 *Jehoshaphat* means *the LORD judges*; also in
verse 12.

¹⁴Multitudes, multitudes
   in the valley of decision!
  For the day of the LORD is near
   in the valley of decision.
¹⁵The sun and moon will be darkened,
   and the stars no longer shine.
¹⁶The LORD will roar from Zion
   and thunder from Jerusalem;
   the earth and the sky will tremble.
  But the LORD will be a refuge for his
   people,
   a stronghold for the people of
   Israel.

Blessings for God's People

¹⁷"Then you will know that I, the LORD
   your God,
   dwell in Zion, my holy hill.
  Jerusalem will be holy;
   never again will foreigners invade
   her.

¹⁸"In that day the mountains will drip
   new wine,
  and the hills will flow with milk;
   all the ravines of Judah will run
   with water.
  A fountain will flow out of the LORD's
   house
   and will water the valley of
   acacias. ^a
¹⁹But Egypt will be desolate,
   Edom a desert waste,
  because of violence done to the
   people of Judah,
   in whose land they shed innocent
   blood.
²⁰Judah will be inhabited forever
   and Jerusalem through all
   generations.
²¹Their bloodguilt, which I have not
   pardoned,
   I will pardon."

   The LORD dwells in Zion!

---

^a18 Or *Valley of Shittim*

Amos

If you would like to know one of the great secrets of the Bible, the book of Amos reveals it. Truth be known, it's not a secret at all. For centuries, scholars have argued over religion's minute details. But the great challenge of our faith is listening, understanding and obeying the things we fully understand.

Amos must have known all about this. He proved it by delivering a knockout punch to the bickering and wayward Jews: "The Sovereign LORD does nothing without revealing his plan" (3:7). Can you believe how mightily profound that is, how much that statement reveals about our heavenly Father? That kind of straightforward wisdom tells us a lot about Amos. What kind of plan might God be revealing to you in your marriage relationship?

1 The words of Amos, one of the shepherds of Tekoa—what he saw concerning Israel two years before the earthquake, when Uzziah was king of Judah and Jeroboam son of Jehoash[a] was king of Israel. ²He said:

"The LORD roars from Zion
and thunders from Jerusalem;
the pastures of the shepherds dry
up,[b]
and the top of Carmel withers."

Judgment on Israel's Neighbors

³This is what the LORD says:

"For three sins of Damascus,
even for four, I will not turn back
⌐my wrath⌐.
Because she threshed Gilead
with sledges having iron teeth,
⁴I will send fire upon the house of
Hazael
that will consume the fortresses of
Ben-Hadad.
⁵I will break down the gate of
Damascus;
I will destroy the king who is in[c]
the Valley of Aven[d]
and the one who holds the scepter in
Beth Eden.

---

[a]1 Hebrew *Joash*, a variant of *Jehoash*   [b]2 Or
shepherds mourn   [c]5 Or *the inhabitants of*
[d]5 *Aven* means *wickedness*.

The people of Aram will go into
  exile to Kir,"
  says the LORD.

⁶This is what the LORD says:

"For three sins of Gaza,
  even for four, I will not turn back
  ⌐my wrath⌐.
Because she took captive whole
  communities
and sold them to Edom,
⁷I will send fire upon the walls of
  Gaza
  that will consume her fortresses.
⁸I will destroy the king ᵃ of Ashdod
  and the one who holds the scepter
  in Ashkelon.
I will turn my hand against Ekron,
  till the last of the Philistines is
  dead,"
  says the Sovereign LORD.

⁹This is what the LORD says:

"For three sins of Tyre,
  even for four, I will not turn back
  ⌐my wrath⌐.
Because she sold whole communities
  of captives to Edom,
  disregarding a treaty of
  brotherhood,
¹⁰I will send fire upon the walls of Tyre
  that will consume her fortresses."

¹¹This is what the LORD says:

"For three sins of Edom,
  even for four, I will not turn back
  ⌐my wrath⌐.
Because he pursued his brother with a
  sword,
  stifling all compassion, ᵇ
because his anger raged continually
  and his fury flamed unchecked,
¹²I will send fire upon Teman
  that will consume the fortresses of
  Bozrah."

¹³This is what the LORD says:

"For three sins of Ammon,
  even for four, I will not turn back
  ⌐my wrath⌐.
Because he ripped open the pregnant
  women of Gilead
in order to extend his borders,
¹⁴I will set fire to the walls of Rabbah
  that will consume her fortresses
amid war cries on the day of battle,

amid violent winds on a stormy
  day.
¹⁵Her king ᶜ will go into exile,
  he and his officials together,"
  says the LORD.

2 This is what the LORD says:

"For three sins of Moab,
  even for four, I will not turn back
  ⌐my wrath⌐.
Because he burned, as if to lime,
  the bones of Edom's king,
²I will send fire upon Moab
  that will consume the fortresses of
  Kerioth. ᵈ
Moab will go down in great tumult
  amid war cries and the blast of the
  trumpet.
³I will destroy her ruler
  and kill all her officials with him,"
  says the LORD.

⁴This is what the LORD says:

"For three sins of Judah,
  even for four, I will not turn back
  ⌐my wrath⌐.
Because they have rejected the law of
  the LORD
  and have not kept his decrees,
because they have been led astray by
  false gods, ᵉ
  the gods ᶠ their ancestors followed,
⁵I will send fire upon Judah
  that will consume the fortresses of
  Jerusalem."

Judgment on Israel

⁶This is what the LORD says:

"For three sins of Israel,
  even for four, I will not turn back
  ⌐my wrath⌐.
They sell the righteous for silver,
  and the needy for a pair of sandals.
⁷They trample on the heads of the
  poor
  as upon the dust of the ground
  and deny justice to the oppressed.
Father and son use the same girl
  and so profane my holy name.
⁸They lie down beside every altar
  on garments taken in pledge.

ᵃ8 Or *inhabitants*   ᵇ11 Or *sword / and destroyed
his allies*   ᶜ15 Or */ Molech;* Hebrew *malcam*
ᵈ2 Or *of her cities*   ᵉ4 Or *by lies*   ᶠ4 Or *lies*

In the house of their god
    they drink wine taken as fines.

⁹"I destroyed the Amorite before
    them,
    though he was tall as the cedars
    and strong as the oaks.
I destroyed his fruit above
    and his roots below.

¹⁰"I brought you up out of Egypt,
    and I led you forty years in the
      desert
    to give you the land of the
      Amorites.
¹¹I also raised up prophets from among
      your sons
    and Nazirites from among your
      young men.
Is this not true, people of Israel?"
              declares the LORD.
¹²"But you made the Nazirites drink
      wine
    and commanded the prophets not
      to prophesy.

¹³"Now then, I will crush you
    as a cart crushes when loaded with
      grain.
¹⁴The swift will not escape,
    the strong will not muster their
      strength,

and the warrior will not save his
    life.
¹⁵The archer will not stand his ground,
    the fleet-footed soldier will not get
      away,
    and the horseman will not save his
      life.
¹⁶Even the bravest warriors
    will flee naked on that day,"
              declares the LORD.

Witnesses Summoned Against Israel

3 Hear this word the LORD has spoken
against you, O people of Israel—
against the whole family I brought up out
of Egypt:

²"You only have I chosen
    of all the families of the earth;
    therefore I will punish you
    for all your sins."

³Do two walk together
    unless they have agreed to do so?
⁴Does a lion roar in the thicket
    when he has no prey?
Does he growl in his den
    when he has caught nothing?
⁵Does a bird fall into a trap on the
      ground
    where no snare has been set?
Does a trap spring up from the earth

A Three-legged Race

Monday

AMOS 3:3   A three-legged race forces two different people to focus their efforts on one common goal. Standing side by side, facing the same direction, the inside legs of the two racers are bound together. The two people either work out a system of running with the same stride . . . or they fall. With each couple having the outside leg free and the inside leg tied, they must talk with each other about how to coordinate efforts.

    Marriage includes many challenges as husband and wife learn to walk as one. Each spouse has his or her own opinion concerning issues such as finances, parenting, sex and careers. These are only a few of the "races" that an individual must run. But marriage is like a three-legged race, and these

decisions can't be made independent of one another.

    The first step in the three-legged marriage race is to decide to run those races bound together and coordinated. Focus on the discussion rather than the destination. If one spouse decides to focus only on a personal destination, the other spouse will get dragged along and the race will be lost.

    Success in the three-legged marriage race means realizing that speed isn't as important as deliberate coordination. Communication and a desire to work together will help two different individuals function as one.

               —Bob & Rosemary

Go to page 971 for your next devotional reading.

when there is nothing to catch?
⁶When a trumpet sounds in a city,
   do not the people tremble?
When disaster comes to a city,
   has not the LORD caused it?

⁷Surely the Sovereign LORD does
     nothing
   without revealing his plan
   to his servants the prophets.

⁸The lion has roared—
   who will not fear?
The Sovereign LORD has spoken—
   who can but prophesy?

⁹Proclaim to the fortresses of Ashdod
   and to the fortresses of Egypt:
"Assemble yourselves on the
     mountains of Samaria;
   see the great unrest within her
   and the oppression among her
     people."

¹⁰"They do not know how to do right,"
   declares the LORD,
   "who hoard plunder and loot in
     their fortresses."

¹¹Therefore this is what the Sovereign
LORD says:

"An enemy will overrun the land;
   he will pull down your strongholds
   and plunder your fortresses."

¹²This is what the LORD says:

"As a shepherd saves from the lion's
     mouth
   only two leg bones or a piece of an
     ear,
so will the Israelites be saved,
those who sit in Samaria
   on the edge of their beds
   and in Damascus on their
     couches.ᵃ"

¹³"Hear this and testify against the
house of Jacob," declares the Lord, the
LORD God Almighty.

¹⁴"On the day I punish Israel for her
     sins,
   I will destroy the altars of Bethel;
the horns of the altar will be cut off
   and fall to the ground.
¹⁵I will tear down the winter house
   along with the summer house;
the houses adorned with ivory will be
     destroyed

and the mansions will be
   demolished,"
             declares the LORD.

Israel Has Not Returned to God

4 Hear this word, you cows of Bashan
   on Mount Samaria,
you women who oppress the poor
   and crush the needy
and say to your husbands, "Bring
   us some drinks!"
²The Sovereign LORD has sworn by his
     holiness:
"The time will surely come
when you will be taken away with
     hooks,
   the last of you with fishhooks.
³You will each go straight out
   through breaks in the wall,
   and you will be cast out toward
     Harmon,ᵇ"
             declares the LORD.
⁴"Go to Bethel and sin;
   go to Gilgal and sin yet more.
Bring your sacrifices every morning,
   your tithes every three years.ᶜ
⁵Burn leavened bread as a thank
     offering
   and brag about your freewill
     offerings—
boast about them, you Israelites,
   for this is what you love to do,"
        declares the Sovereign LORD.

⁶"I gave you empty stomachsᵈ in
     every city
and lack of bread in every town,
   yet you have not returned to me,"
           declares the LORD.

⁷"I also withheld rain from you
   when the harvest was still three
     months away.
I sent rain on one town,
   but withheld it from another.
One field had rain;
   another had none and dried up.
⁸People staggered from town to town
     for water
   but did not get enough to drink,
   yet you have not returned to me,"
           declares the LORD.

ᵃ12 The meaning of the Hebrew for this line is
uncertain.   ᵇ3 Masoretic Text; with a different
word division of the Hebrew (see Septuagint) *out,
O mountain of oppression*   ᶜ4 Or *tithes on the
third day*   ᵈ6 Hebrew *you cleanness of teeth*

⁹"Many times I struck your gardens
　　and vineyards,
　I struck them with blight and
　　mildew.
　Locusts devoured your fig and olive
　　trees,
　yet you have not returned to me,"
　　　　declares the LORD.

¹⁰"I sent plagues among you
　　as I did to Egypt.
　I killed your young men with the
　　sword,
　along with your captured horses.
　I filled your nostrils with the stench
　　of your camps,
　yet you have not returned to me,"
　　　　declares the LORD.

¹¹"I overthrew some of you
　　as I*a* overthrew Sodom and
　　Gomorrah.
　You were like a burning stick
　　snatched from the fire,
　yet you have not returned to me,"
　　　　declares the LORD.

¹²"Therefore this is what I will do to
　　you, Israel,
　and because I will do this to you,
　prepare to meet your God,
　　O Israel."

¹³He who forms the mountains,
　　creates the wind,
　and reveals his thoughts to man,
　he who turns dawn to darkness,
　　and treads the high places of the
　　　earth—
　the LORD God Almighty is his
　　name.

A Lament and Call to Repentance

5 Hear this word, O house of Israel, this
　　lament I take up concerning you:

²"Fallen is Virgin Israel,
　　never to rise again,
　deserted in her own land,
　　with no one to lift her up."

a 11 Hebrew *God*

Caring for Others

Tuesday

AMOS 4:1　As our family walked by an appliance store, I (Bob) looked in the window filled with new, hi-tech large screen televisions. *It's time,* I thought to myself, *that we had one of those entertainment centers.* As I proceeded to lead my family inside the store, I noticed my daughter Torrey looking at the largest of the screens. But she was looking at the program on the screen—a documentary about the plight of the homeless. Standing there next to her, I realized I had once again fallen into the trap of bigger and better, when there are those around me with little or nothing.

God severely rebuked the children of Israel for living in self-indulgent luxury while others around them were needy and in want. This passage can serve as a warning to us in a time when *we* live in comfort and luxury. It is a warning to check our attitudes concerning our own comfort. It is a warning to look at the needs of those

around us who are less fortunate. Is our focus, as a family, to continue to indulge ourselves with the "good things in life"? Is it to "build bigger barns"?

God has called us to focus on others rather than our own comfort. His desire is for us to trust him for our needs and have a deeper concern for the less fortunate around us. In Colossians 3:23 we are instructed to work hard (see page 1297). What a blessing we could be to our communities if every Christian family considered what they could share and give, rather than how they could accumulate more wealth.

As Christians, our perspective in every area of life should reflect the desires of God. May we be a blessing to the lives of others through our generosity rather than "cows of Bashan," thinking only of our own comfort.

　　　　　　　　　　　　　　　—Bob & Rosemary

Go to page 978 for your next devotional reading.

³This is what the Sovereign LORD says:

"The city that marches out a
    thousand strong for Israel
will have only a hundred left;
the town that marches out a hundred
    strong
will have only ten left."

⁴This is what the LORD says to the
house of Israel:

"Seek me and live;
5   do not seek Bethel,
do not go to Gilgal,
    do not journey to Beersheba.
For Gilgal will surely go into exile,
    and Bethel will be reduced to
        nothing.ᵃ"
⁶Seek the LORD and live,
    or he will sweep through the house
        of Joseph like a fire;
it will devour,
    and Bethel will have no one to
        quench it.

⁷You who turn justice into bitterness
    and cast righteousness to the
        ground
⁸(he who made the Pleiades and
        Orion,
    who turns blackness into dawn
    and darkens day into night,
who calls for the waters of the sea
    and pours them out over the face
        of the land—
    the LORD is his name—
⁹he flashes destruction on the
        stronghold
    and brings the fortified city to
        ruin),
¹⁰you hate the one who reproves in
        court
    and despise him who tells the
        truth.

¹¹You trample on the poor
    and force him to give you grain.
Therefore, though you have built
        stone mansions,
    you will not live in them;
though you have planted lush
        vineyards,
    you will not drink their wine.
¹²For I know how many are your
        offenses
    and how great your sins.

You oppress the righteous and take
        bribes
    and you deprive the poor of justice
        in the courts.
¹³Therefore the prudent man keeps
        quiet in such times,
    for the times are evil.

¹⁴Seek good, not evil,
    that you may live.
Then the LORD God Almighty will be
        with you,
    just as you say he is.
¹⁵Hate evil, love good;
    maintain justice in the courts.
Perhaps the LORD God Almighty will
        have mercy
    on the remnant of Joseph.

¹⁶Therefore this is what the Lord, the
LORD God Almighty, says:

"There will be wailing in all the streets
    and cries of anguish in every public
        square.
The farmers will be summoned to weep
    and the mourners to wail.
¹⁷There will be wailing in all the
        vineyards,
    for I will pass through your midst,"
                    says the LORD.

The Day of the LORD

¹⁸Woe to you who long
    for the day of the LORD!
Why do you long for the day of the
        LORD?
    That day will be darkness, not
        light.
¹⁹It will be as though a man fled from
        a lion
    only to meet a bear,
as though he entered his house
    and rested his hand on the wall
    only to have a snake bite him.
²⁰Will not the day of the LORD be
        darkness, not light—
    pitch-dark, without a ray of
        brightness?

²¹"I hate, I despise your religious feasts;
    I cannot stand your assemblies.
²²Even though you bring me burnt
        offerings and grain offerings,
    I will not accept them.

ᵃ5 Or grief; or wickedness; Hebrew aven, a reference
to Beth Aven (a derogatory name for Bethel)

Though you bring choice fellowship
offerings, [a]
I will have no regard for them.
23Away with the noise of your songs!
I will not listen to the music of
your harps.
24But let justice roll on like a river,
righteousness like a never-failing
stream!

25"Did you bring me sacrifices and
offerings
forty years in the desert, O house
of Israel?
26You have lifted up the shrine of your
king,
the pedestal of your idols,
the star of your god[b]—
which you made for yourselves.
27Therefore I will send you into exile
beyond Damascus,"
says the LORD, whose name is God
Almighty.

Woe to the Complacent

6 Woe to you who are complacent in
Zion,
and to you who feel secure on
Mount Samaria,
you notable men of the foremost
nation,
to whom the people of Israel
come!
2Go to Calneh and look at it;
go from there to great Hamath,
and then go down to Gath in
Philistia.
Are they better off than your two
kingdoms?
Is their land larger than yours?
3You put off the evil day
and bring near a reign of terror.
4You lie on beds inlaid with ivory
and lounge on your couches.
You dine on choice lambs
and fattened calves.
5You strum away on your harps like
David
and improvise on musical
instruments.
6You drink wine by the bowlful
and use the finest lotions,
but you do not grieve over the ruin
of Joseph.
7Therefore you will be among the first
to go into exile;

your feasting and lounging will
end.

The LORD Abhors the Pride of Israel

8The Sovereign LORD has sworn by
himself—the LORD God Almighty declares:

"I abhor the pride of Jacob
and detest his fortresses;
I will deliver up the city
and everything in it."

9If ten men are left in one house, they
too will die. 10And if a relative who is to
burn the bodies comes to carry them out
of the house and asks anyone still hiding
there, "Is anyone with you?" and he says,
"No," then he will say, "Hush! We must
not mention the name of the LORD."

11For the LORD has given the command,
and he will smash the great house
into pieces
and the small house into bits.

12Do horses run on the rocky crags?
Does one plow there with oxen?
But you have turned justice into
poison
and the fruit of righteousness into
bitterness—
13you who rejoice in the conquest of Lo
Debar[c]
and say, "Did we not take
Karnaim[d] by our own
strength?"

14For the LORD God Almighty declares,
"I will stir up a nation against you,
O house of Israel,
that will oppress you all the way
from Lebo[e] Hamath to the valley
of the Arabah."

Locusts, Fire and a Plumb Line

7 This is what the Sovereign LORD
showed me: He was preparing
swarms of locusts after the king's share
had been harvested and just as the second
crop was coming up. 2When they had

---

[a]22 Traditionally *peace offerings*   [b]26 Or *lifted
up Sakkuth your king / and Kaiwan your idols, / your
star-gods;* Septuagint *lifted up the shrine of Molech /
and the star of your god Rephan, / their idols*
[c]13 *Lo Debar* means *nothing.*   [d]13 *Karnaim*
means *horns;* horn here symbolizes strength.
[e]14 Or *from the entrance to*

stripped the land clean, I cried out, "Sovereign LORD, forgive! How can Jacob survive? He is so small!"

³So the LORD relented.

"This will not happen," the LORD said.

⁴This is what the Sovereign LORD showed me: The Sovereign LORD was calling for judgment by fire; it dried up the great deep and devoured the land. ⁵Then I cried out, "Sovereign LORD, I beg you, stop! How can Jacob survive? He is so small!"

⁶So the LORD relented.

"This will not happen either," the Sovereign LORD said.

⁷This is what he showed me: The Lord was standing by a wall that had been built true to plumb, with a plumb line in his hand. ⁸And the LORD asked me, "What do you see, Amos?"

"A plumb line," I replied.

Then the Lord said, "Look, I am setting a plumb line among my people Israel; I will spare them no longer.

⁹"The high places of Isaac will be
destroyed
and the sanctuaries of Israel will be
ruined;
with my sword I will rise against
the house of Jeroboam."

Amos and Amaziah

¹⁰Then Amaziah the priest of Bethel sent a message to Jeroboam king of Israel: "Amos is raising a conspiracy against you in the very heart of Israel. The land cannot bear all his words. ¹¹For this is what Amos is saying:

" 'Jeroboam will die by the sword,
and Israel will surely go into exile,
away from their native land.' "

¹²Then Amaziah said to Amos, "Get out, you seer! Go back to the land of Judah. Earn your bread there and do your prophesying there. ¹³Don't prophesy anymore at Bethel, because this is the king's sanctuary and the temple of the kingdom."

¹⁴Amos answered Amaziah, "I was neither a prophet nor a prophet's son, but I was a shepherd, and I also took care of sycamore-fig trees. ¹⁵But the LORD took me from tending the flock and said to me, 'Go, prophesy to my people Israel.'

¹⁶Now then, hear the word of the LORD. You say,

" 'Do not prophesy against Israel,
and stop preaching against the
house of Isaac.'

¹⁷"Therefore this is what the LORD says:

" 'Your wife will become a prostitute
in the city,
and your sons and daughters will
fall by the sword.
Your land will be measured and
divided up,
and you yourself will die in a
pagan[a] country.
And Israel will certainly go into exile,
away from their native land.' "

A Basket of Ripe Fruit

8 This is what the Sovereign LORD showed me: a basket of ripe fruit. ²"What do you see, Amos?" he asked.

"A basket of ripe fruit," I answered.

Then the LORD said to me, "The time is ripe for my people Israel; I will spare them no longer.

³"In that day," declares the Sovereign LORD, "the songs in the temple will turn to wailing.[b] Many, many bodies—flung everywhere! Silence!"

⁴Hear this, you who trample the needy
and do away with the poor of the
land,

⁵saying,

"When will the New Moon be over
that we may sell grain,
and the Sabbath be ended
that we may market wheat?"—
skimping the measure,
boosting the price
and cheating with dishonest scales,
⁶buying the poor with silver
and the needy for a pair of sandals,
selling even the sweepings with the
wheat.

⁷The LORD has sworn by the Pride of Jacob: "I will never forget anything they have done.

⁸"Will not the land tremble for this,
and all who live in it mourn?

---

[a]17 Hebrew an unclean   [b]3 Or "the temple singers will wail

The whole land will rise like the Nile;
　　it will be stirred up and then sink
　　like the river of Egypt.

⁹"In that day," declares the Sovereign
LORD,

"I will make the sun go down at
　　noon
　　and darken the earth in broad
　　　daylight.
¹⁰I will turn your religious feasts into
　　mourning
　　and all your singing into weeping.
I will make all of you wear sackcloth
　　and shave your heads.
I will make that time like mourning
　　for an only son
　　and the end of it like a bitter day.

¹¹"The days are coming," declares the
　　Sovereign LORD,
　　"when I will send a famine
　　　through the land—
not a famine of food or a thirst for
　　water,
　　but a famine of hearing the words
　　　of the LORD.
¹²Men will stagger from sea to sea
　　and wander from north to east,
searching for the word of the LORD,
　　but they will not find it.

¹³"In that day

"the lovely young women and strong
　　young men
　　will faint because of thirst.
¹⁴They who swear by the shame[a] of
　　Samaria,
　　or say, 'As surely as your god lives,
　　　O Dan,'
or, 'As surely as the god[b] of
　　Beersheba lives'—
they will fall,
　　never to rise again."

Israel to Be Destroyed

9 I saw the Lord standing by the altar,
and he said:

"Strike the tops of the pillars
　　so that the thresholds shake.
Bring them down on the heads of all
　　the people;
　　those who are left I will kill with
　　　the sword.
Not one will get away,

none will escape.
²Though they dig down to the depths
　　of the grave,[c]
　　from there my hand will take
　　　them.
Though they climb up to the heavens,
　　from there I will bring them down.
³Though they hide themselves on the
　　top of Carmel,
　　there I will hunt them down and
　　　seize them.
Though they hide from me at the
　　bottom of the sea,
　　there I will command the serpent
　　　to bite them.
⁴Though they are driven into exile by
　　their enemies,
　　there I will command the sword to
　　　slay them.
I will fix my eyes upon them
　　for evil and not for good."

⁵The Lord, the LORD Almighty,
　　he who touches the earth and it
　　　melts,
　　and all who live in it mourn—
the whole land rises like the Nile,
　　then sinks like the river of Egypt—
⁶he who builds his lofty palace[d] in
　　the heavens
　　and sets its foundation[e] on the
　　　earth,
who calls for the waters of the sea
　　and pours them out over the face
　　　of the land—
　　the LORD is his name.

⁷"Are not you Israelites
　　the same to me as the Cushites[f]?"
　　　　　　　　　　declares the LORD.
"Did I not bring Israel up from
　　Egypt,
　　the Philistines from Caphtor[g]
　　and the Arameans from Kir?

⁸"Surely the eyes of the Sovereign
　　LORD
　　are on the sinful kingdom.
I will destroy it
　　from the face of the earth—
　　yet I will not totally destroy

---

a14 Or *by Ashima*; or *by the idol*   *b14* Or *power*
c2 Hebrew *to Sheol*   *d6* The meaning of the
Hebrew for this phrase is uncertain.
e6 The meaning of the Hebrew for this word is
uncertain.   *f7* That is, people from the upper
Nile region   *g7* That is, Crete

the house of Jacob,"

declares the LORD.

9 "For I will give the command,
and I will shake the house of Israel
among all the nations
as grain is shaken in a sieve,
and not a pebble will reach the
ground.
10 All the sinners among my people
will die by the sword,
all those who say,
'Disaster will not overtake or meet
us.'

Israel's Restoration

11 "In that day I will restore
David's fallen tent.
I will repair its broken places,
restore its ruins,
and build it as it used to be,
12 so that they may possess the remnant
of Edom
and all the nations that bear my
name,[a]"

declares the LORD,
who will do these things.

13 "The days are coming," declares the
LORD,

"when the reaper will be overtaken
by the plowman
and the planter by the one treading
grapes.
New wine will drip from the
mountains
and flow from all the hills.
14 I will bring back my exiled[b] people
Israel;
they will rebuild the ruined cities
and live in them.
They will plant vineyards and drink
their wine;
they will make gardens and eat
their fruit.
15 I will plant Israel in their own land,
never again to be uprooted
from the land I have given
them,"

says the LORD your God.

---

a12 Hebrew; Septuagint *so that the remnant of men
/ and all the nations that bear my name may seek ⌞the
Lord⌟*   *b14* Or *will restore the fortunes of my*

Obadiah

Remember Jacob and Esau from Genesis? The Edomites (descendants of Esau) still haven't forgiven Jacob for stealing Esau's birthright. So they gloat when the Israelites (descendants of Jacob) are devastated by foreign powers. Then Obadiah enters the picture, rebuking the Edomites for their pride and announcing that they will be destroyed for their attitude and actions. Obadiah's searing message to Edom wasn't just for them.

The Bible is laced with this truth: If you're proud, you'll fall. God wants you to boast only in his power and might. Then his love will give you a quiet confidence and the humility to be the person he wants you to be—a spouse, a parent, a friend. Obadiah knew all about this.

¹The vision of Obadiah.

This is what the Sovereign LORD says about Edom—

We have heard a message from the
    LORD:
  An envoy was sent to the nations
    to say,
"Rise, and let us go against her for
    battle"—

²"See, I will make you small among
    the nations;
  you will be utterly despised.
³The pride of your heart has deceived
    you,
  you who live in the clefts of the
    rocks*a*

and make your home on the
    heights,
you who say to yourself,
  'Who can bring me down to the
    ground?'
⁴Though you soar like the eagle
  and make your nest among the
    stars,
  from there I will bring you down,"
          declares the LORD.
⁵"If thieves came to you,
  if robbers in the night—
Oh, what a disaster awaits you—
  would they not steal only as much
    as they wanted?
If grape pickers came to you,
  would they not leave a few grapes?

a3 Or of Sela

⁶But how Esau will be ransacked,
  his hidden treasures pillaged!
⁷All your allies will force you to the
    border;
  your friends will deceive and
    overpower you;
  those who eat your bread will set a
    trap for you,ᵃ
  but you will not detect it.

⁸"In that day," declares the LORD,
  "will I not destroy the wise men of
    Edom,
  men of understanding in the
    mountains of Esau?
⁹Your warriors, O Teman, will be
    terrified,
  and everyone in Esau's mountains
    will be cut down in the slaughter.
¹⁰Because of the violence against your
    brother Jacob,
  you will be covered with shame;
  you will be destroyed forever.
¹¹On the day you stood aloof
  while strangers carried off his
    wealth
  and foreigners entered his gates
    and cast lots for Jerusalem,
  you were like one of them.
¹²You should not look down on your
    brother
  in the day of his misfortune,
  nor rejoice over the people of Judah

in the day of their destruction,
  nor boast so much
  in the day of their trouble.
¹³You should not march through the
    gates of my people
  in the day of their disaster,
  nor look down on them in their
    calamity
  in the day of their disaster,
  nor seize their wealth
  in the day of their disaster.
¹⁴You should not wait at the crossroads
  to cut down their fugitives,
  nor hand over their survivors
  in the day of their trouble.

¹⁵"The day of the LORD is near
  for all nations.
  As you have done, it will be done to
    you;
  your deeds will return upon your
    own head.
¹⁶Just as you drank on my holy hill,
  so all the nations will drink
    continually;
  they will drink and drink
  and be as if they had never been.
¹⁷But on Mount Zion will be
    deliverance;
  it will be holy,

ᵃ7 The meaning of the Hebrew for this clause is
uncertain.

Proud—Who Me?

Wednesday

OBADIAH 3   Pride is deceptive—especially in a marriage relationship. Just when we think we have it all together, we realize we've only just begun. I remember the day Dave and I were writing a chapter on communication for our next book. We spent hours crafting the principles of positive communication into words and then connecting them with Biblical principles.

Then it happened. It was a simple question I asked with no malice intended: "Dave, when are you going to get around to paying our monthly bills?" Tired and exhausted from writing our chapter on positive communication, we quickly ignored all of our wonderful principles. These few, poorly cho-

sen words brought up Dave's mental computer with all the previous arguments we have had about this touchy subject. He served back a few choice words to me, and we were right back in an unproductive conversation. On this occasion we had forgotten to do what we know is right. We had to stop and confess that, once again, we had slipped and pridefully taken for granted our own need to think carefully about our own words.

Each day, if we keep our pride in check, it won't sneak up on us so quickly. We'll be able to make progress instead of going one step forward, then two steps back.

—Dave & Claudia

Go to page 981 for your next devotional reading.

and the house of Jacob
  will possess its inheritance.
¹⁸The house of Jacob will be a fire
  and the house of Joseph a flame;
the house of Esau will be stubble,
  and they will set it on fire and
    consume it.
There will be no survivors
  from the house of Esau."
      The LORD has spoken.

¹⁹People from the Negev will occupy
  the mountains of Esau,
and people from the foothills will
    possess
  the land of the Philistines.
They will occupy the fields of
  Ephraim and Samaria,
and Benjamin will possess Gilead.
²⁰This company of Israelite exiles who
    are in Canaan
  will possess ⌊the land⌋ as far as
    Zarephath;
the exiles from Jerusalem who are in
    Sepharad
  will possess the towns of the
    Negev.
²¹Deliverers will go up on ᵃ Mount
    Zion
  to govern the mountains of
    Esau.
And the kingdom will be the
  LORD's.

ᵃ21 Or *from*

Jonah

Have you ever been in a situation when you knew God wanted you to do something, but instead of obeying him, you tried to hide? If so, you're about the meet a guy who can relate. Jonah had tried to refuse God's call but later got angry when God didn't do what he expected. Despite Jonah's resistance, God used Jonah to demonstrate his mercy to Nineveh.

Through Jonah's story we see that God goes to great lengths to pursue his people and that he responds with compassion and forgiveness when they return to him. Think about the times in your marriage when you've tried to run away from God, when you tried to ignore what he was trying to tell you to do. What happened?

Jonah Flees From the Lord

1 The word of the LORD came to Jonah son of Amittai: ²"Go to the great city of Nineveh and preach against it, because its wickedness has come up before me."

³But Jonah ran away from the LORD and headed for Tarshish. He went down to Joppa, where he found a ship bound for that port. After paying the fare, he went aboard and sailed for Tarshish to flee from the LORD.

⁴Then the LORD sent a great wind on the sea, and such a violent storm arose that the ship threatened to break up. ⁵All the sailors were afraid and each cried out to his own god. And they threw the cargo into the sea to lighten the ship.

But Jonah had gone below deck, where he lay down and fell into a deep sleep. ⁶The captain went to him and said, "How can you sleep? Get up and call on your god! Maybe he will take notice of us, and we will not perish."

⁷Then the sailors said to each other, "Come, let us cast lots to find out who is responsible for this calamity." They cast lots and the lot fell on Jonah.

⁸So they asked him, "Tell us, who is responsible for making all this trouble for us? What do you do? Where do you come from? What is your country? From what people are you?"

⁹He answered, "I am a Hebrew and I worship the LORD, the God of heaven, who made the sea and the land."

¹⁰This terrified them and they asked, "What have you done?" (They knew he was running away from the LORD, because he had already told them so.)

¹¹The sea was getting rougher and

rougher. So they asked him, "What should we do to you to make the sea calm down for us?"

¹²"Pick me up and throw me into the sea," he replied, "and it will become calm. I know that it is my fault that this great storm has come upon you."

¹³Instead, the men did their best to row back to land. But they could not, for the sea grew even wilder than before. ¹⁴Then they cried to the LORD, "O LORD, please do not let us die for taking this man's life. Do not hold us accountable for killing an innocent man, for you, O LORD, have done as you pleased." ¹⁵Then they took Jonah and threw him overboard, and the raging sea grew calm. ¹⁶At this the men greatly feared the LORD, and they offered a sacrifice to the LORD and made vows to him.

¹⁷But the LORD provided a great fish to swallow Jonah, and Jonah was inside the fish three days and three nights.

Jonah's Prayer

2 From inside the fish Jonah prayed to the LORD his God. ²He said:

"In my distress I called to the LORD,

and he answered me.
From the depths of the grave*ᵃ* I
    called for help,
    and you listened to my cry.
³You hurled me into the deep,
    into the very heart of the seas,
    and the currents swirled about me;
all your waves and breakers
    swept over me.
⁴I said, 'I have been banished
    from your sight;
yet I will look again
    toward your holy temple.'
⁵The engulfing waters threatened
    me,*ᵇ*
    the deep surrounded me;
    seaweed was wrapped around my
        head.
⁶To the roots of the mountains I sank
        down;
    the earth beneath barred me in
        forever.
But you brought my life up from the
        pit,
    O LORD my God.

⁷"When my life was ebbing away,
    I remembered you, LORD,

ᵃ2 Hebrew *Sheol*   *ᵇ5* Or *waters were at my throat*

Desperate Measures

Thursday

JONAH 2:7   A long time ago while we were stationed in El Paso with the U.S. Army, we enjoyed many evenings walking across the Mexican border to Juarez.

Years later, when we were vacationing in San Diego, we decided to go across the Mexican border, just like old times. But this time we were eager to explore Tijuana. We took a cab into the city. Later when we were ready to go back to our hotel in San Diego, we looked for a cab but couldn't find one. We remembered how we had walked to and from Juarez years before, so we decided to walk back across the border.

Not smart. Before we could say "adventure," we were lost in a bad section of town. No street lights, no sidewalks, shady looking characters, you name it—it was a bad situation! Convinced that our lives were about to

be cut short, all we could do was to cry out to God for help. Eventually we found our way to the border, but we've never forgotten the sheer terror of that experience.

What do you do in desperate situations? Maybe you haven't been swallowed by a fish or lost in Tijuana, but perhaps your marriage is drowning from too many other demands or from extremely stressful circumstances. You may feel like Jonah did—hopeless, discouraged and frustrated. But in your distress, you can call on the Lord.

Even if you feel your relationship with your mate is too dysfunctional to ever be restored, let us encourage you to give God a chance to work at it. Remember the Lord and pray. He can—and still does—work miracles.

—Dave & Claudia

Go to page 982 for your next devotional reading.

and my prayer rose to you,
to your holy temple.

⁸"Those who cling to worthless idols
forfeit the grace that could be theirs.
⁹But I, with a song of thanksgiving,
will sacrifice to you.
What I have vowed I will make good.
Salvation comes from the LORD."

¹⁰And the LORD commanded the fish, and it vomited Jonah onto dry land.

Jonah Goes to Nineveh

3 Then the word of the LORD came to Jonah a second time: ²"Go to the great city of Nineveh and proclaim to it the message I give you."

³Jonah obeyed the word of the LORD and went to Nineveh. Now Nineveh was a very important city—a visit required three days. ⁴On the first day, Jonah started into the city. He proclaimed: "Forty more days and Nineveh will be overturned." ⁵The Ninevites believed God. They declared a fast, and all of them, from the greatest to the least, put on sackcloth.

⁶When the news reached the king of Nineveh, he rose from his throne, took off his royal robes, covered himself with sackcloth and sat down in the dust. ⁷Then he issued a proclamation in Nineveh:

"By the decree of the king and his nobles:

Do not let any man or beast, herd or flock, taste anything; do not let them eat or drink. ⁸But let man and beast be covered with sackcloth. Let everyone call urgently on God. Let them give up their evil ways and their violence. ⁹Who knows? God may yet relent and with compassion turn from his fierce anger so that we will not perish."

¹⁰When God saw what they did and how they turned from their evil ways, he had compassion and did not bring upon them the destruction he had threatened.

Jonah's Anger at the LORD's Compassion

4 But Jonah was greatly displeased and became angry. ²He prayed to the LORD, "O LORD, is this not what I said when I was still at home? That is why I was so quick to flee to Tarshish. I knew that you are a gracious and compassionate God, slow to anger and abounding in love, a God who relents from sending calamity. ³Now, O LORD, take away my life, for it is better for me to die than to live."

Letting Go of Revenge

Friday

JONAH 3:10—4:3 Jack and Judy had been married fifteen years. Theirs had been a rocky relationship due to Jack's drinking problem. After years of Judy's prayers and confrontation, Jack finally confessed his problem and started attending a support group at their church. He was actually getting help and his life was changing . . . but that just wasn't enough for Judy. She had years of pent-up frustration. *That's it?!* she asked herself. *Confess the problem, join a group and that's all he has to do?* She was finding it very difficult to forgive and then deal with all the pain she had gone through.

So often we feel like Jonah. When we have been wronged, we want the inflictors

of pain to suffer before we grant forgiveness. We have suffered, so they should suffer! It's a natural feeling to want revenge before restoration. But while those feelings may be very natural, they are very wrong.

Instead of giving our *natural* response, we need to give our *supernatural* response. If we ask, God will give us the supernatural strength to respond in a way that will please him. We are reminded in this passage that God is merciful and compassionate. He will give us that same spirit if we are willing to let go of revenge and choose to forgive.

—Bob & Rosemary

Go to page 989 for your next devotional reading.

⁴But the LORD replied, "Have you any right to be angry?"

⁵Jonah went out and sat down at a place east of the city. There he made himself a shelter, sat in its shade and waited to see what would happen to the city. ⁶Then the LORD God provided a vine and made it grow up over Jonah to give shade for his head to ease his discomfort, and Jonah was very happy about the vine. ⁷But at dawn the next day God provided a worm, which chewed the vine so that it withered. ⁸When the sun rose, God provided a scorching east wind, and the sun blazed on Jonah's head so that he grew faint. He wanted to die, and said, "It would be better for me to die than to live."

⁹But God said to Jonah, "Do you have a right to be angry about the vine?"

"I do," he said. "I am angry enough to die."

¹⁰But the LORD said, "You have been concerned about this vine, though you did not tend it or make it grow. It sprang up overnight and died overnight. ¹¹But Nineveh has more than a hundred and twenty thousand people who cannot tell their right hand from their left, and many cattle as well. Should I not be concerned about that great city?"

Micah

Nothing eats away at the fabric of a nation like social injustice and empty spirituality. When the rich get richer at the expense of the less powerful, when political leaders habitually accept bribes and when spiritual leaders lead others astray, God takes notice—and he isn't pleased. God does not make light of sin. The prophet Micah lived during a time when the Israelites experienced all these things, and his message to them resounds with judgment. Yet Micah also provides a message of hope—hope of deliverance, comfort and forgiveness through the coming Messiah.

Today, as we live in a culture that often doesn't respect the marriage institution—where affairs are commonplace and divorce is a fifty-fifty chance, lean on God and the hope, in his Son, that he will see you through.

1 The word of the LORD that came to Micah of Moresheth during the reigns of Jotham, Ahaz and Hezekiah, kings of Judah—the vision he saw concerning Samaria and Jerusalem.

²Hear, O peoples, all of you,
    listen, O earth and all who are in
      it,
  that the Sovereign LORD may witness
      against you,
    the Lord from his holy temple.

Judgment Against Samaria and Jerusalem

³Look! The LORD is coming from his
      dwelling place;

  he comes down and treads the
      high places of the earth.
⁴The mountains melt beneath him
    and the valleys split apart,
  like wax before the fire,
    like water rushing down a slope.
⁵All this is because of Jacob's
      transgression,
    because of the sins of the house of
      Israel.
  What is Jacob's transgression?
    Is it not Samaria?
  What is Judah's high place?
    Is it not Jerusalem?

⁶"Therefore I will make Samaria a
      heap of rubble,

a place for planting vineyards.
I will pour her stones into the valley
and lay bare her foundations.
⁷All her idols will be broken to pieces;
all her temple gifts will be burned
with fire;
I will destroy all her images.
Since she gathered her gifts from the
wages of prostitutes,
as the wages of prostitutes they will
again be used."

Weeping and Mourning

⁸Because of this I will weep and wail;
I will go about barefoot and naked.
I will howl like a jackal
and moan like an owl.
⁹For her wound is incurable;
it has come to Judah.
It*a* has reached the very gate of my
people,
even to Jerusalem itself.
¹⁰Tell it not in Gath*b*;
weep not at all.*c*
In Beth Ophrah*d*
roll in the dust.
¹¹Pass on in nakedness and shame,
you who live in Shaphir.*e*
Those who live in Zaanan*f*
will not come out.
Beth Ezel is in mourning;
its protection is taken from you.
¹²Those who live in Maroth*g* writhe in
pain,
waiting for relief,
because disaster has come from the
LORD,
even to the gate of Jerusalem.
¹³You who live in Lachish,*h*
harness the team to the chariot.
You were the beginning of sin
to the Daughter of Zion,
for the transgressions of Israel
were found in you.
¹⁴Therefore you will give parting gifts
to Moresheth Gath.
The town of Aczib*i* will prove
deceptive
to the kings of Israel.
¹⁵I will bring a conqueror against you
who live in Mareshah.*j*
He who is the glory of Israel
will come to Adullam.
¹⁶Shave your heads in mourning

for the children in whom you
delight;
make yourselves as bald as the
vulture,
for they will go from you into
exile.

Man's Plans and God's

2 Woe to those who plan iniquity,
to those who plot evil on their
beds!
At morning's light they carry it out
because it is in their power to do
it.
²They covet fields and seize them,
and houses, and take them.
They defraud a man of his home,
a fellowman of his inheritance.

³Therefore, the LORD says:

"I am planning disaster against this
people,
from which you cannot save
yourselves.
You will no longer walk proudly,
for it will be a time of calamity.
⁴In that day men will ridicule you;
they will taunt you with this
mournful song:
'We are utterly ruined;
my people's possession is divided
up.
He takes it from me!
He assigns our fields to traitors.' "

⁵Therefore you will have no one in the
assembly of the LORD
to divide the land by lot.

False Prophets

⁶"Do not prophesy," their prophets say.
"Do not prophesy about these
things;
disgrace will not overtake us."
⁷Should it be said, O house of Jacob:
"Is the Spirit of the LORD angry?
Does he do such things?"

---

*a*9 Or *He*   *b*10 *Gath* sounds like the Hebrew
for *tell.*   *c*10 Hebrew; Septuagint may suggest
not in Acco. The Hebrew for *in Acco* sounds like the
Hebrew for *weep.*   *d*10 *Beth Ophrah* means *house
of dust.*   *e*11 *Shaphir* means *pleasant.*
*f*11 *Zaanan* sounds like the Hebrew for *come out.*
*g*12 *Maroth* sounds like the Hebrew for *bitter.*
*h*13 *Lachish* sounds like the Hebrew for *team.*
*i*14 *Aczib* means *deception.*   *j*15 *Mareshah*
sounds like the Hebrew for *conqueror.*

"Do not my words do good
  to him whose ways are upright?
8Lately my people have risen up
  like an enemy.
You strip off the rich robe
  from those who pass by without a
    care,
  like men returning from battle.
9You drive the women of my people
  from their pleasant homes.
You take away my blessing
  from their children forever.
10Get up, go away!
  For this is not your resting place,
because it is defiled,
  it is ruined, beyond all remedy.
11If a liar and deceiver comes and says,
  'I will prophesy for you plenty of
    wine and beer,'
  he would be just the prophet for
    this people!

Deliverance Promised

12"I will surely gather all of you,
    O Jacob;
  I will surely bring together the
    remnant of Israel.
I will bring them together like sheep
    in a pen,
  like a flock in its pasture;
  the place will throng with people.
13One who breaks open the way will go
    up before them;
  they will break through the gate
    and go out.
Their king will pass through before
    them,
  the LORD at their head."

Leaders and Prophets Rebuked

3 Then I said,

"Listen, you leaders of Jacob,
  you rulers of the house of Israel.
Should you not know justice,
2   you who hate good and love evil;
who tear the skin from my people
  and the flesh from their bones;
3who eat my people's flesh,
  strip off their skin
  and break their bones in pieces;
who chop them up like meat for the
    pan,
  like flesh for the pot?"

4Then they will cry out to the LORD,

but he will not answer them.
At that time he will hide his face
    from them
  because of the evil they have done.

5This is what the LORD says:

"As for the prophets
  who lead my people astray,
if one feeds them,
  they proclaim 'peace';
if he does not,
  they prepare to wage war against
    him.
6Therefore night will come over you,
    without visions,
  and darkness, without divination.
The sun will set for the prophets,
  and the day will go dark for them.
7The seers will be ashamed
  and the diviners disgraced.
They will all cover their faces
  because there is no answer from
    God."

8But as for me, I am filled with power,
  with the Spirit of the LORD,
  and with justice and might,
to declare to Jacob his transgression,
  to Israel his sin.
9Hear this, you leaders of the house of
    Jacob,
  you rulers of the house of Israel,
who despise justice
  and distort all that is right;
10who build Zion with bloodshed,
  and Jerusalem with wickedness.
11Her leaders judge for a bribe,
  her priests teach for a price,
  and her prophets tell fortunes for
    money.
Yet they lean upon the LORD and say,
  "Is not the LORD among us?
  No disaster will come upon us."
12Therefore because of you,
  Zion will be plowed like a field,
Jerusalem will become a heap of
    rubble,
  the temple hill a mound
    overgrown with thickets.

The Mountain of the LORD

4 In the last days

the mountain of the LORD's temple
    will be established
  as chief among the mountains;

it will be raised above the hills,
  and peoples will stream to it.

²Many nations will come and say,

"Come, let us go up to the mountain
    of the LORD,
  to the house of the God of Jacob.
He will teach us his ways,
  so that we may walk in his paths."
The law will go out from Zion,
  the word of the LORD from
    Jerusalem.
³He will judge between many peoples
  and will settle disputes for strong
    nations far and wide.
They will beat their swords into
    plowshares
  and their spears into pruning
    hooks.
Nation will not take up sword against
    nation,
  nor will they train for war
    anymore.
⁴Every man will sit under his own vine
  and under his own fig tree,
and no one will make them afraid,
  for the LORD Almighty has spoken.
⁵All the nations may walk
  in the name of their gods;
we will walk in the name of the LORD
  our God for ever and ever.

The LORD's Plan

⁶"In that day," declares the LORD,

"I will gather the lame;
  I will assemble the exiles
  and those I have brought to grief.
⁷I will make the lame a remnant,
  those driven away a strong nation.
The LORD will rule over them in
    Mount Zion
  from that day and forever.
⁸As for you, O watchtower of the
    flock,
  O stronghold^a of the Daughter of
    Zion,
the former dominion will be restored
    to you;
  kingship will come to the Daughter
    of Jerusalem."

⁹Why do you now cry aloud—
  have you no king?
Has your counselor perished,

that pain seizes you like that of a
    woman in labor?
¹⁰Writhe in agony, O Daughter of Zion,
  like a woman in labor,
for now you must leave the city
  to camp in the open field.
You will go to Babylon;
  there you will be rescued.
There the LORD will redeem you
  out of the hand of your enemies.

¹¹But now many nations
  are gathered against you.
They say, "Let her be defiled,
  let our eyes gloat over Zion!"
¹²But they do not know
  the thoughts of the LORD;
they do not understand his plan,
  he who gathers them like sheaves
    to the threshing floor.
¹³"Rise and thresh, O Daughter of
    Zion,
  for I will give you horns of iron;
I will give you hoofs of bronze
  and you will break to pieces many
    nations."

You will devote their ill-gotten gains
    to the LORD,
  their wealth to the Lord of all the
    earth.

A Promised Ruler From Bethlehem

5 Marshal your troops, O city of
    troops,^{b}
  for a siege is laid against us.
They will strike Israel's ruler
  on the cheek with a rod.

²"But you, Bethlehem Ephrathah,
  though you are small among the
    clans^c of Judah,
out of you will come for me
  one who will be ruler over Israel,
whose origins^d are from of old,
  from ancient times.^{e}"

³Therefore Israel will be abandoned
  until the time when she who is in
    labor gives birth
and the rest of his brothers return
  to join the Israelites.

⁴He will stand and shepherd his flock

---

*^{a}8 Or hill ^{b}1 Or Strengthen your walls, O walled
city ^{c}2 Or rulers ^{d}2 Hebrew goings out
^{e}2 Or from days of eternity*

in the strength of the LORD,
in the majesty of the name of the
LORD his God.
And they will live securely, for then
his greatness
will reach to the ends of the earth.
5   And he will be their peace.

Deliverance and Destruction

When the Assyrian invades our land
and marches through our
fortresses,
we will raise against him seven
shepherds,
even eight leaders of men.
⁶They will rule*a* the land of Assyria
with the sword,
the land of Nimrod with drawn
sword.*b*
He will deliver us from the Assyrian
when he invades our land
and marches into our borders.

⁷The remnant of Jacob will be
in the midst of many peoples
like dew from the LORD,
like showers on the grass,
which do not wait for man
or linger for mankind.
⁸The remnant of Jacob will be among
the nations,
in the midst of many peoples,
like a lion among the beasts of the
forest,
like a young lion among flocks of
sheep,
which mauls and mangles as it goes,
and no one can rescue.
⁹Your hand will be lifted up in
triumph over your enemies,
and all your foes will be destroyed.

¹⁰"In that day," declares the LORD,

"I will destroy your horses from
among you
and demolish your chariots.
¹¹I will destroy the cities of your land
and tear down all your
strongholds.
¹²I will destroy your witchcraft
and you will no longer cast spells.
¹³I will destroy your carved images
and your sacred stones from
among you;
you will no longer bow down
to the work of your hands.

¹⁴I will uproot from among you your
Asherah poles*c*
and demolish your cities.
¹⁵I will take vengeance in anger and
wrath
upon the nations that have not
obeyed me."

The LORD's Case Against Israel

6 Listen to what the LORD says:

"Stand up, plead your case before the
mountains;
let the hills hear what you have to
say.
²Hear, O mountains, the LORD's
accusation;
listen, you everlasting foundations
of the earth.
For the LORD has a case against his
people;
he is lodging a charge against
Israel.

³"My people, what have I done to
you?
How have I burdened you? Answer
me.
⁴I brought you up out of Egypt
and redeemed you from the land
of slavery.
I sent Moses to lead you,
also Aaron and Miriam.
⁵My people, remember
what Balak king of Moab
counseled
and what Balaam son of Beor
answered.
Remember ⌞your journey⌟ from
Shittim to Gilgal,
that you may know the righteous
acts of the LORD."

⁶With what shall I come before the
LORD
and bow down before the exalted
God?
Shall I come before him with burnt
offerings,
with calves a year old?
⁷Will the LORD be pleased with
thousands of rams,

---

*a*6 Or *crush*   *b*6 Or *Nimrod in its gates*
*c*14 That is, symbols of the goddess Asherah

with ten thousand rivers of oil?
Shall I offer my firstborn for my
    transgression,
    the fruit of my body for the sin of
        my soul?
[8] He has showed you, O man, what is
    good.
    And what does the LORD require of
        you?
To act justly and to love mercy
    and to walk humbly with your
        God.

Israel's Guilt and Punishment

[9] Listen! The LORD is calling to the
    city—
    and to fear your name is wisdom—
    "Heed the rod and the One who
        appointed it. [a]
[10] Am I still to forget, O wicked house,
    your ill-gotten treasures
    and the short ephah, [b] which is
        accursed?

[11] Shall I acquit a man with dishonest
    scales,
    with a bag of false weights?
[12] Her rich men are violent;
    her people are liars
    and their tongues speak deceitfully.
[13] Therefore, I have begun to destroy
    you,
    to ruin you because of your sins.
[14] You will eat but not be satisfied;
    your stomach will still be empty. [c]
You will store up but save nothing,
    because what you save I will give
        to the sword.
[15] You will plant but not harvest;
    you will press olives but not use
        the oil on yourselves,
    you will crush grapes but not drink
        the wine.

[a] 9 The meaning of the Hebrew for this line is
uncertain.   [b] 10 An ephah was a dry measure.
[c] 14 The meaning of the Hebrew for this word is
uncertain.

Like a Child

Quiet TIMES
with each other

MICAH 6:8   The kitchen at Grammy's house was buzzing with Christmas preparation. Five-year-old Sophie and three-year-old Walker were diligently sharing assignments. While Sophie cracked the eggs, Walker sifted the flour. A sudden "poof" and flour was in the air and all over the floor.

"It's your fault, Walker!" Sophie cried indignantly as Walker looked helplessly at the mess on the floor. What just a moment before was pure Christmas joy was now spoiled by angry accusations.

Taking a deep breath, Grammy stepped in to help and knelt beside the frozen little boy and said, "Walker, the clean-up sponge is under the sink. While you're wiping up, I'll get the dustpan."

When Sophie's accusations persisted, Grammy reminded her that she may need to collect herself on the little chair just around the corner. Walker whispered, "I'm sorry, Grammy. I made a mess."

"I'm sorry too, Walker," Grammy lovingly responded. "But sometimes accidents happen when we try new things. This is just a kitchen floor; we can clean it."

Frowning, Sophie watched from the corner of the room as clean-up proceeded. As Grammy and Walker got underway once again, her heart changed. Whirling around, she hugged Grammy. "I love you, Grammy! Walker, let's sift the flour again."

Little children still have that sweet innocence to affirm justice and mercy when they see it happening around them. If only we could have a pure heart like a child, we would deeply understand this passage.
                                         —Dave & Claudia

Warm-up **Weekend** *Think of the children you know. How have they shown you their "pure hearts"?*

Go to page 990 for your next devotional reading.

¹⁶You have observed the statutes of
Omri
and all the practices of Ahab's
house,
and you have followed their
traditions.
Therefore I will give you over to ruin
and your people to derision;
you will bear the scorn of the
nations.ᵃ "

Israel's Misery

7 What misery is mine!
I am like one who gathers summer
fruit
at the gleaning of the vineyard;
there is no cluster of grapes to eat,
none of the early figs that I crave.
²The godly have been swept from the
land;
not one upright man remains.
All men lie in wait to shed blood;
each hunts his brother with a net.
³Both hands are skilled in doing evil;
the ruler demands gifts,
the judge accepts bribes,
the powerful dictate what they
desire—
they all conspire together.
⁴The best of them is like a brier,

the most upright worse than a
thorn hedge.
The day of your watchmen has come,
the day God visits you.
Now is the time of their confusion.
⁵Do not trust a neighbor;
put no confidence in a friend.
Even with her who lies in your
embrace
be careful of your words.
⁶For a son dishonors his father,
a daughter rises up against her
mother,
a daughter-in-law against her
mother-in-law—
a man's enemies are the members
of his own household.

⁷But as for me, I watch in hope for the
LORD,
I wait for God my Savior;
my God will hear me.

Israel Will Rise

⁸Do not gloat over me, my enemy!
Though I have fallen, I will rise.
Though I sit in darkness,
the LORD will be my light.

ᵃ16 Septuagint; Hebrew *scorn due my people*

In-law Dos and Don'ts

Monday

MICAH 7:6 Diane was newly married and had a very controlling mother-in-law. Even though her mother-in-law lived in a different city, Diane received a phone call from her every few days. Actually these phone calls were more like a phone survey, where her mother-in-law asked questions and then told her "how to do it right." This manipulative relationship was making Diane feel very discouraged as a wife. She found herself being drawn toward her controlling mother-in-law for answers instead of to God. The phone calls were becoming her report card.

It's often difficult to find the balance between honoring our parents versus being controlled by them. We cannot allow ourselves to build our homes on the foundations of our parents' ways. The bedrock of the family foundation is faith in the One who created family.

Diane had allowed her desire to please to manipulate her into responding to the wrong leadership. This young bride had to learn to honor her mother-in-law by receiving the phone calls. But her mother-in-law could not be allowed to direct her home. Every suggestion needed to be discussed with her husband and evaluated by God's plan.

If our focus is on pleasing God, if our trust is in God's plan, if our confidence is in God's sovereignty, we will be able to look at our in-laws differently. Their opinion will not be the foundation on which we try to build our homes.

—*Bob & Rosemary*

Go to page 993 for your next devotional reading.

⁹Because I have sinned against him,
  I will bear the LORD's wrath,
until he pleads my case
  and establishes my right.
He will bring me out into the light;
  I will see his righteousness.
¹⁰Then my enemy will see it
  and will be covered with shame,
she who said to me,
  "Where is the LORD your God?"
My eyes will see her downfall;
  even now she will be trampled
    underfoot
  like mire in the streets.

¹¹The day for building your walls will
    come,
  the day for extending your
    boundaries.
¹²In that day people will come to you
  from Assyria and the cities of
    Egypt,
  even from Egypt to the Euphrates
  and from sea to sea
  and from mountain to mountain.
¹³The earth will become desolate
    because of its inhabitants,
  as the result of their deeds.

Prayer and Praise

¹⁴Shepherd your people with your staff,
  the flock of your inheritance,
which lives by itself in a forest,
  in fertile pasturelands. *ᵃ*
Let them feed in Bashan and Gilead
  as in days long ago.

¹⁵"As in the days when you came out
    of Egypt,
  I will show them my wonders."

¹⁶Nations will see and be ashamed,
  deprived of all their power.
They will lay their hands on their
    mouths
  and their ears will become deaf.
¹⁷They will lick dust like a snake,
  like creatures that crawl on the
    ground.
They will come trembling out of their
    dens;
  they will turn in fear to the LORD
    our God
  and will be afraid of you.
¹⁸Who is a God like you,
  who pardons sin and forgives the
    transgression
  of the remnant of his inheritance?
You do not stay angry forever
  but delight to show mercy.
¹⁹You will again have compassion on
    us;
  you will tread our sins underfoot
  and hurl all our iniquities into the
    depths of the sea.
²⁰You will be true to Jacob,
  and show mercy to Abraham,
as you pledged on oath to our fathers
  in days long ago.

ᵃ14 Or *in the middle of Carmel*

Nahum

"Is God good?
Is God just and fair?" People have been asking
these questions from the dawn of time. We can grow
cynical about the goodness and justice of God when we look
at our world and when we think of the people who have
failed us or abused us.

The prophet Nahum answers our questions with an
emphatic, "Yes!" He says, "The LORD is good, a refuge in
times of trouble. He cares for those who trust in him, but . . .
he will pursue his foes into darkness" (1:7–8). God is always
good. He is always fair. He can be trusted. He will not disappoint us.

1 An oracle concerning Nineveh. The book of the vision of Nahum the El-koshite.

The LORD's Anger Against Nineveh

²The LORD is a jealous and avenging
God;
    the LORD takes vengeance and is
      filled with wrath.
The LORD takes vengeance on his foes
    and maintains his wrath against his
      enemies.
³The LORD is slow to anger and great
    in power;
    the LORD will not leave the guilty
      unpunished.
His way is in the whirlwind and the
    storm,
    and clouds are the dust of his feet.
⁴He rebukes the sea and dries it up;
    he makes all the rivers run dry.

Bashan and Carmel wither
    and the blossoms of Lebanon fade.
⁵The mountains quake before him
    and the hills melt away.
The earth trembles at his presence,
    the world and all who live in it.
⁶Who can withstand his indignation?
    Who can endure his fierce anger?
His wrath is poured out like fire;
    the rocks are shattered before him.

⁷The LORD is good,
    a refuge in times of trouble.
He cares for those who trust in him,
⁸   but with an overwhelming flood
he will make an end of ⌊Nineveh⌋;
    he will pursue his foes into
      darkness.

⁹Whatever they plot against the LORD
    he*ᵃ* will bring to an end;

ᵃ9 Or What do you foes plot against the LORD? / He

trouble will not come a second
time.
¹⁰They will be entangled among thorns
and drunk from their wine;
they will be consumed like dry
stubble. ᵃ
¹¹From you, ⌊O Nineveh,⌋ has one come
forth
who plots evil against the LORD
and counsels wickedness.

¹²This is what the LORD says:

"Although they have allies and are
numerous,
they will be cut off and pass away.
Although I have afflicted you,
⌊O Judah,⌋
I will afflict you no more.
¹³Now I will break their yoke from
your neck
and tear your shackles away."

¹⁴The LORD has given a command
concerning you, ⌊Nineveh⌋:
"You will have no descendants to
bear your name.
I will destroy the carved images and
cast idols
that are in the temple of your gods.
I will prepare your grave,
for you are vile."

¹⁵Look, there on the mountains,

the feet of one who brings good
news,
who proclaims peace!
Celebrate your festivals, O Judah,
and fulfill your vows.
No more will the wicked invade you;
they will be completely destroyed.

Nineveh to Fall

2 An attacker advances against you,
⌊Nineveh⌋.
Guard the fortress,
watch the road,
brace yourselves,
marshal all your strength!

²The LORD will restore the splendor of
Jacob
like the splendor of Israel,
though destroyers have laid them
waste
and have ruined their vines.

³The shields of his soldiers are red;
the warriors are clad in scarlet.
The metal on the chariots flashes
on the day they are made ready;
the spears of pine are
brandished. ᵇ

ᵃ10 The meaning of the Hebrew for this verse is
uncertain.   ᵇ3 Hebrew; Septuagint and Syriac /
the horsemen rush to and fro

Trust

Tuesday

NAHUM 1:7 Trust most often begins
to crumble in a marriage when little promises are broken, when little deceptions are discovered. And
the tragedy of most seemingly insignificant experiences of deception
is that they mushroom and ultimately
create a cloud of distrust that hovers over
the relationship. That's why the author of
Nahum reminds us that God cares for those
who trust in him.

Soul mates must have integrity. Without
it, Scripture says we will be despised and
destroyed (see Psalm 5:6; 63:11; 101:7;
Proverbs 11:3; 12:8; 19:1; Revelation 21:8).
Integrity means telling the truth, keeping
our promises, doing what we said we would
do, choosing to be accountable and taking

as our motto *semper fidelis*—the
promise to be *always faithful.*

Honesty, as a popular song
says, is such a lonely word. At
times it does seem that everyone is
so untrue. And it's been that way
ever since sin entered the world.
Consider these verses: "All men are liars"
(Psalm 116:11); "Friend deceives friend,
and no one speaks the truth" (Jeremiah 9:5).
The book of Proverbs asks, "Many a man
claims to have unfailing love, but a faithful
man who can find?" (Proverbs 20:6). The gift
of trust and integrity is so rare. But doesn't
your marriage deserve it?

—*Les & Leslie*

Go to page 994 for your next devotional reading.

⁴The chariots storm through the
    streets,
    rushing back and forth through the
      squares.
They look like flaming torches;
    they dart about like lightning.

⁵He summons his picked troops,
    yet they stumble on their way.
They dash to the city wall;
    the protective shield is put in
      place.
⁶The river gates are thrown open
    and the palace collapses.
⁷It is decreed ᵃ that ⌊the city⌋
    be exiled and carried away.
Its slave girls moan like doves
    and beat upon their breasts.
⁸Nineveh is like a pool,
    and its water is draining away.
"Stop! Stop!" they cry,
    but no one turns back.
⁹Plunder the silver!
    Plunder the gold!
The supply is endless,
    the wealth from all its treasures!
¹⁰She is pillaged, plundered, stripped!
    Hearts melt, knees give way,

bodies tremble, every face grows
    pale.
¹¹Where now is the lions' den,
    the place where they fed their
      young,
where the lion and lioness went,
    and the cubs, with nothing to fear?
¹²The lion killed enough for his cubs
    and strangled the prey for his mate,
filling his lairs with the kill
    and his dens with the prey.

¹³"I am against you,"
    declares the LORD Almighty.
"I will burn up your chariots in
      smoke,
    and the sword will devour your
      young lions.
I will leave you no prey on the earth.
The voices of your messengers
    will no longer be heard."

Woe to Nineveh

3 Woe to the city of blood,
    full of lies,

ᵃ7 The meaning of the Hebrew for this word is
uncertain.

Seduction

Wednesday

NAHUM 3:4 Seduction has an interesting power. When we are seduced, it is often by things that look good on the outside. The things that lure us away from what we know to be godly are things that give false promises. They promise to make us happy, powerful or more secure.

The world tries to seduce us with things that seem promising, but they ultimately end in false hope. It might be a job opportunity that offers more financial security but would mean an inordinate amount of time away from home. It might be a friendship across gender lines that seems to bring so much comfort but could ultimately undermine trust in the marriage. It could be a behavior that "everyone else" claims to derive pleasure from but could become a habit or addiction that enslaves us.

On the surface these seductions seem positive, even advantageous. But in our hearts we know they can destroy our family. The book of Nahum describes Nineveh as a seductive neighbor to other nations. This city befriended and seduced its neighbors, only to destroy and force them into slavery.

There is no power or happiness to be gained by giving in to the seductions of the world. They become enslaving. We must choose to protect our hearts from those things that seduce. The only sure protection from the temptations of the world is to put our faith in God. By trusting him, using his Word for guidance and being empowered by the Holy Spirit, we can resist the seductions that tear down the walls of our marriages.

                          —*Bob & Rosemary*

Go to page 998 for your next devotional reading.

full of plunder,
     never without victims!
²The crack of whips,
     the clatter of wheels,
galloping horses
     and jolting chariots!
³Charging cavalry,
     flashing swords
     and glittering spears!
Many casualties,
     piles of dead,
bodies without number,
     people stumbling over the corpses—
⁴all because of the wanton lust of a
          harlot,
     alluring, the mistress of sorceries,
who enslaved nations by her
          prostitution
     and peoples by her witchcraft.

⁵"I am against you," declares the LORD
          Almighty.
     "I will lift your skirts over your
          face.
I will show the nations your
          nakedness
     and the kingdoms your shame.
⁶I will pelt you with filth,
     I will treat you with contempt
     and make you a spectacle.
⁷All who see you will flee from you
          and say,
     'Nineveh is in ruins—who will
          mourn for her?'
Where can I find anyone to
     comfort you?"

⁸Are you better than Thebes,ᵃ
     situated on the Nile,
     with water around her?
The river was her defense,
     the waters her wall.
⁹Cushᵇ and Egypt were her boundless
          strength;
     Put and Libya were among her
          allies.
¹⁰Yet she was taken captive
     and went into exile.
Her infants were dashed to pieces
     at the head of every street.
Lots were cast for her nobles,
     and all her great men were put in
          chains.
¹¹You too will become drunk;

you will go into hiding
     and seek refuge from the enemy.

¹²All your fortresses are like fig trees
     with their first ripe fruit;
when they are shaken,
     the figs fall into the mouth of the
          eater.
¹³Look at your troops—
     they are all women!
The gates of your land
     are wide open to your enemies;
     fire has consumed their bars.

¹⁴Draw water for the siege,
     strengthen your defenses!
Work the clay,
     tread the mortar,
     repair the brickwork!
¹⁵There the fire will devour you;
     the sword will cut you down
     and, like grasshoppers, consume
          you.
Multiply like grasshoppers,
     multiply like locusts!
¹⁶You have increased the number of
          your merchants
     till they are more than the stars of
          the sky,
but like locusts they strip the land
     and then fly away.
¹⁷Your guards are like locusts,
     your officials like swarms of locusts
     that settle in the walls on a cold
          day—
but when the sun appears they fly
          away,
     and no one knows where.

¹⁸O king of Assyria, your shepherdsᶜ
          slumber;
     your nobles lie down to rest.
Your people are scattered on the
          mountains
     with no one to gather them.
¹⁹Nothing can heal your wound;
     your injury is fatal.
Everyone who hears the news about
          you
     claps his hands at your fall,
for who has not felt
     your endless cruelty?

ᵃ8 Hebrew *No Amon*   ᵇ9 That is, the upper
Nile region   ᶜ18 Or *rulers*

Habakkuk

*If you could
have a Q & A time* with God, what would you ask?
The prophet Habakkuk had such an opportunity. This book
is like a transcript of his conversation with God. Habakkuk
poses two questions that we still wonder about today:
(1) Why does God tolerate cruelty and injustice, and
(2) why is God silent when wicked people seem to be in
control?

God answers, declaring that when the time is right,
the wicked will be punished and the faithful rewarded. As
you and your spouse read this book, you might realize, as
Habakkuk did, that God is willing enough and powerful
enough to see justice done.

1 The oracle that Habakkuk the prophet received.

Habakkuk's Complaint

²How long, O LORD, must I call for
help,
but you do not listen?
Or cry out to you, "Violence!"
but you do not save?
³Why do you make me look at
injustice?
Why do you tolerate wrong?
Destruction and violence are before
me;
there is strife, and conflict
abounds.
⁴Therefore the law is paralyzed,
and justice never prevails.
The wicked hem in the righteous,
so that justice is perverted.

The LORD's Answer

⁵"Look at the nations and watch—
and be utterly amazed.
For I am going to do something in
your days
that you would not believe,
even if you were told.
⁶I am raising up the Babylonians,ᵃ
that ruthless and impetuous
people,
who sweep across the whole earth
to seize dwelling places not their
own.
⁷They are a feared and dreaded people;
they are a law to themselves
and promote their own honor.
⁸Their horses are swifter than leopards,
fiercer than wolves at dusk.

ᵃ6 Or *Chaldeans*

Their cavalry gallops headlong;
    their horsemen come from afar.
They fly like a vulture swooping to
    devour;
9   they all come bent on violence.
Their hordes*a* advance like a desert
    wind
    and gather prisoners like sand.
10They deride kings
    and scoff at rulers.
They laugh at all fortified cities;
    they build earthen ramps and
        capture them.
11Then they sweep past like the wind
    and go on—
    guilty men, whose own strength is
        their god."

Habakkuk's Second Complaint

12O LORD, are you not from everlasting?
    My God, my Holy One, we will
        not die.
O LORD, you have appointed them to
    execute judgment;
    O Rock, you have ordained them
        to punish.
13Your eyes are too pure to look on
    evil;
    you cannot tolerate wrong.
Why then do you tolerate the
    treacherous?
    Why are you silent while the
        wicked
    swallow up those more righteous
        than themselves?
14You have made men like fish in the
    sea,
    like sea creatures that have no
        ruler.
15The wicked foe pulls all of them up
    with hooks,
    he catches them in his net,
he gathers them up in his dragnet;
    and so he rejoices and is glad.
16Therefore he sacrifices to his net
    and burns incense to his dragnet,
for by his net he lives in luxury
    and enjoys the choicest food.
17Is he to keep on emptying his net,
    destroying nations without mercy?

2 I will stand at my watch
    and station myself on the ramparts;
I will look to see what he will say to
    me,

and what answer I am to give to
    this complaint.*b*

The LORD's Answer

2Then the LORD replied:

"Write down the revelation
    and make it plain on tablets
    so that a herald*c* may run with it.
3For the revelation awaits an
    appointed time;
    it speaks of the end
    and will not prove false.
Though it linger, wait for it;
    it*d* will certainly come and will
        not delay.

4"See, he is puffed up;
    his desires are not upright—
    but the righteous will live by his
        faith*e*—
5indeed, wine betrays him;
    he is arrogant and never at rest.
Because he is as greedy as the grave*f*
    and like death is never satisfied,
he gathers to himself all the nations
    and takes captive all the peoples.

6"Will not all of them taunt him with
ridicule and scorn, saying,

" 'Woe to him who piles up stolen
    goods
    and makes himself wealthy by
        extortion!
How long must this go on?'
7Will not your debtors*g* suddenly
    arise?
    Will they not wake up and make
        you tremble?
    Then you will become their victim.
8Because you have plundered many
    nations,
    the peoples who are left will
        plunder you.
For you have shed man's blood;
    you have destroyed lands and cities
        and everyone in them.

9"Woe to him who builds his realm
    by unjust gain
    to set his nest on high,
    to escape the clutches of ruin!

---

a9 The meaning of the Hebrew for this word is
uncertain.   *b1* Or *and what to answer when I am
rebuked*   *c2* Or *so that whoever reads it*   *d3* Or
Though he linger, wait for him; / he   *e4* Or
faithfulness   *f5* Hebrew *Sheol*   *g7* Or *creditors*

¹⁰You have plotted the ruin of many
    peoples,
shaming your own house and
    forfeiting your life.
¹¹The stones of the wall will cry out,
and the beams of the woodwork
    will echo it.

¹²"Woe to him who builds a city with
    bloodshed
and establishes a town by crime!
¹³Has not the Lord Almighty
    determined
that the people's labor is only fuel
    for the fire,
that the nations exhaust themselves
    for nothing?
¹⁴For the earth will be filled with the
    knowledge of the glory of the
    Lord,
as the waters cover the sea.

¹⁵"Woe to him who gives drink to his
    neighbors,
pouring it from the wineskin till
    they are drunk,

so that he can gaze on their naked
    bodies.
¹⁶You will be filled with shame instead
    of glory.
Now it is your turn! Drink and be
    exposed ᵃ!
The cup from the Lord's right hand is
    coming around to you,
and disgrace will cover your glory.
¹⁷The violence you have done to
    Lebanon will overwhelm you,
and your destruction of animals
    will terrify you.
For you have shed man's blood;
you have destroyed lands and cities
    and everyone in them.

¹⁸"Of what value is an idol, since a
    man has carved it?
Or an image that teaches lies?
For he who makes it trusts in his own
    creation;
he makes idols that cannot speak.

ᵃ16 Masoretic Text; Dead Sea Scrolls, Aquila,
Vulgate and Syriac (see also Septuagint) *and stagger*

The Marriage Watchtower

Thursday

HABAKKUK 2:1 At the time of Habakkuk, sin abounded. The people of Judah worshiped idols, sacrificed their children and basically ignored God. Yet, as he stood watch and stationed himself on the ramparts, Habakkuk pleaded for God's intervention.

Our society may not appear as decadent as Judah, but we still need to zealously guard our marriage from evil. We need to watch and pray. In Bible times, the watchmen in the watchtowers had two purposes: to guard against possible invasions and to watch for messengers. We can guard our marriages against attacks by making our marriage a priority. When Dave and I get too busy—even helping other couples build their marriages—it's easy to let down our own defenses and ignore our own marriage.

Take the time we had just finished presenting another program on dating. Exhausted, we sat in our car, glaring at each other. "Why do we do this to ourselves?" I

asked. "I don't know," Dave answered, "but something has got to change." Over the past several months, we'd had no dating life of our own. This night would be no different. We didn't even have time to stop for a coffee date on the way home—we still had to race to a FedEx box to mail an urgent package. We could easily rationalize that working with other couples keeps us developing our own marriage. Yet, as we headed for FedEx instead of our favorite coffee shop, we knew we were kidding ourselves.

Since that experience we've been more intentional about finding time for each other. From time to time, we turn off our computers, let voice mail take messages and go for a walk. Away from the pressure, we're able to see things more clearly and come up with a better plan for guarding our marriage. Consider what your plan is, or should be.

—Dave & Claudia

Go to page 1000 for your next devotional reading.

¹⁹Woe to him who says to wood,
'Come to life!'
Or to lifeless stone, 'Wake up!'
Can it give guidance?
It is covered with gold and silver;
there is no breath in it.
²⁰But the LORD is in his holy temple;
let all the earth be silent before
him."

Habakkuk's Prayer

3 A prayer of Habakkuk the prophet.
On *shigionoth.*ᵃ

²LORD, I have heard of your fame;
I stand in awe of your deeds,
O LORD.
Renew them in our day,
in our time make them known;
in wrath remember mercy.

³God came from Teman,
the Holy One from Mount Paran.
*Selah*ᵇ
His glory covered the heavens
and his praise filled the earth.
⁴His splendor was like the sunrise;
rays flashed from his hand,
where his power was hidden.
⁵Plague went before him;
pestilence followed his steps.
⁶He stood, and shook the earth;
he looked, and made the nations
tremble.
The ancient mountains crumbled
and the age-old hills collapsed.
His ways are eternal.
⁷I saw the tents of Cushan in distress,
the dwellings of Midian in anguish.

⁸Were you angry with the rivers,
O LORD?
Was your wrath against the
streams?
Did you rage against the sea
when you rode with your horses
and your victorious chariots?
⁹You uncovered your bow,
you called for many arrows. *Selah*
You split the earth with rivers;
¹⁰ the mountains saw you and
writhed.
Torrents of water swept by;
the deep roared
and lifted its waves on high.

The Marriage Watchtower

Just as Habakkuk guarded his city, you need to guard your marriage. Reflect on the following questions:

1. **What is attacking your marriage?** Check all that apply:
   ___ Over-commitment (job, hobbies, community activities and so on)
   ___ Too much television and/or videos
   ___ Lack of time alone to focus on your relationship
   ___ Too much stuff to take care of
   ___ Lack of energy; too tired to care

2. **How can you guard your marriage?** Check all that apply:
   ___ Invest more time in your relationship
   ___ Share responsibilities and work together
   ___ Pray together
   ___ Start couple devotions
   ___ Fellowship with other Christian couples

3. **Reflect on how God speaks to you as a couple and individually.**

¹¹Sun and moon stood still in the
heavens
at the glint of your flying arrows,
at the lightning of your flashing
spear.
¹²In wrath you strode through the earth
and in anger you threshed the
nations.
¹³You came out to deliver your people,
to save your anointed one.
You crushed the leader of the land of
wickedness,
you stripped him from head to
foot. *Selah*
¹⁴With his own spear you pierced his
head
when his warriors stormed out to
scatter us,
gloating as though about to devour

ᵃ1 Probably a literary or musical term
ᵇ3 A word of uncertain meaning; possibly a
musical term; also in verses 9 and 13

the wretched who were in hiding.
¹⁵You trampled the sea with your
  horses,
  churning the great waters.

¹⁶I heard and my heart pounded,
  my lips quivered at the sound;
decay crept into my bones,
  and my legs trembled.
Yet I will wait patiently for the day of
  calamity
  to come on the nation invading us.
¹⁷Though the fig tree does not bud
  and there are no grapes on the
    vines,

though the olive crop fails
  and the fields produce no food,
though there are no sheep in the pen
  and no cattle in the stalls,
¹⁸yet I will rejoice in the LORD,
  I will be joyful in God my Savior.

¹⁹The Sovereign LORD is my strength;
  he makes my feet like the feet of a
    deer,
  he enables me to go on the
    heights.

For the director of music. On my
  stringed instruments.

Going to New Heights

Friday

HABAKKUK 3:19 Pete's boss had just offered him the promotion of a lifetime. It was a great financial opportunity, but it meant he'd be away from home all week. Early on in their marriage, Pete and his wife had decided they wanted to raise their children together. Even though there were a lot of things they could do with that extra money, they knew Pete needed to turn down the opportunity. The alternative was going to mean much less income, but he knew it was the right thing for him to do. The question that weighed heavily on his heart was, *Can I do what God's calling me to do and still pay the bills?*

There are times when circumstances in our married life seem as frightening as hiking on the side of a rocky cliff. Every step seems to have hidden danger. One wrong step could end in disaster. In those desperate times, God reminds us that he is our strength and guide. If we shift our focus from the treacherous, rocky precipice to our solid

Rock, God will make our "feet like the feet of a deer."

A mountain goat's foot is perfectly designed for the rocky cliffs. It can find its way over dangerous crevices and precipices without fear of a wrong step. However, the mountain goat only focuses on the next step, not the whole mountain.

That is how God enables us to climb through the most dangerous circumstances we face. We learn to focus only on the next step when God guides us up "the mountain." As the passage goes on to say, God will enable us to go on to the heights. Instead of focusing on fear, discouragement or even exhaustion, when we focus on God and take the next step, we will find ourselves in new heights with a new perspective. When we trust God to be our strength, he will help us traverse dangerous ground and take us to new heights in our relationship.
                                                        —*Bob & Rosemary*

Go to page 1003 for your next devotional reading.

Zephaniah

*The day
of the Lord.* Sounds ominous. Although no one really
knows what it will be like, it's a safe bet we won't want to
experience it. Zephaniah's prophecy depicts the stark horror
of that ordeal, the force of God's anger against sin. But
Zephaniah doesn't stop there. While God does punish
people for their flagrant and deliberate sin, he's always
merciful to those who seek him with humility. As you read
Zephaniah, look for the note of hope—that God's judgment
will pave the way for a new day when all people will
worship the Lord.

1 The word of the LORD that came to
Zephaniah son of Cushi, the son of
Gedaliah, the son of Amariah, the son of
Hezekiah, during the reign of Josiah son
of Amon king of Judah:

Warning of Coming Destruction

2 "I will sweep away everything
 from the face of the earth,"
   declares the LORD.
3 "I will sweep away both men and
  animals;
 I will sweep away the birds of the
  air
 and the fish of the sea.
The wicked will have only heaps of
  rubble[a]
 when I cut off man from the face
  of the earth,"
   declares the LORD.

Against Judah

4 "I will stretch out my hand against
  Judah
 and against all who live in
  Jerusalem.
I will cut off from this place every
  remnant of Baal,
 the names of the pagan and the
  idolatrous priests—
5 those who bow down on the roofs
 to worship the starry host,
 those who bow down and swear by
  the LORD
 and who also swear by Molech,[b]
6 those who turn back from following
  the LORD
 and neither seek the LORD nor
  inquire of him.

[a]3 The meaning of the Hebrew for this line is
uncertain.   [b]5 Hebrew *Malcam*, that is, Milcom

⁷Be silent before the Sovereign LORD,
  for the day of the LORD is near.
The LORD has prepared a sacrifice;
  he has consecrated those he has
    invited.
⁸On the day of the LORD's sacrifice
  I will punish the princes
  and the king's sons
and all those clad
  in foreign clothes.
⁹On that day I will punish
  all who avoid stepping on the
    threshold,ᵃ
who fill the temple of their gods
  with violence and deceit.

¹⁰"On that day," declares the LORD,
  "a cry will go up from the Fish
    Gate,
  wailing from the New Quarter,
  and a loud crash from the hills.
¹¹Wail, you who live in the market
    districtᵇ;
  all your merchants will be wiped
    out,
  all who trade withᶜ silver will be
    ruined.
¹²At that time I will search Jerusalem
  with lamps
and punish those who are
  complacent,
  who are like wine left on its dregs,
who think, 'The LORD will do
  nothing,
  either good or bad.'
¹³Their wealth will be plundered,
  their houses demolished.
They will build houses
  but not live in them;
they will plant vineyards
  but not drink the wine.

The Great Day of the Lord

¹⁴"The great day of the LORD is near—
  near and coming quickly.
Listen! The cry on the day of the
  LORD will be bitter,
  the shouting of the warrior there.
¹⁵That day will be a day of wrath,
  a day of distress and anguish,
a day of trouble and ruin,
  a day of darkness and gloom,
  a day of clouds and blackness,
¹⁶a day of trumpet and battle cry
  against the fortified cities
  and against the corner towers.

¹⁷I will bring distress on the people
  and they will walk like blind men,
  because they have sinned against
    the LORD.
Their blood will be poured out like
  dust
  and their entrails like filth.
¹⁸Neither their silver nor their gold
  will be able to save them
  on the day of the LORD's wrath.
In the fire of his jealousy
  the whole world will be consumed,
for he will make a sudden end
  of all who live in the earth."

2 Gather together, gather together,
  O shameful nation,
²before the appointed time arrives
  and that day sweeps on like chaff,
before the fierce anger of the LORD
  comes upon you,
  before the day of the LORD's wrath
    comes upon you.
³Seek the LORD, all you humble of the
  land,
  you who do what he commands.
Seek righteousness, seek humility;
  perhaps you will be sheltered
  on the day of the LORD's anger.

Against Philistia

⁴Gaza will be abandoned
  and Ashkelon left in ruins.
At midday Ashdod will be emptied
  and Ekron uprooted.
⁵Woe to you who live by the sea,
  O Kerethite people;
the word of the LORD is against you,
  O Canaan, land of the Philistines.

"I will destroy you,
  and none will be left."

⁶The land by the sea, where the
  Kerethitesᵈ dwell,
  will be a place for shepherds and
    sheep pens.
⁷It will belong to the remnant of the
  house of Judah;
  there they will find pasture.
In the evening they will lie down
  in the houses of Ashkelon.

ᵃ9 See 1 Samuel 5:5.   ᵇ11 Or the Mortar
ᶜ11 Or in   ᵈ6 The meaning of the Hebrew for
this word is uncertain.

The LORD their God will care for
them;
he will restore their fortunes. [a]

Against Moab and Ammon

8 "I have heard the insults of Moab
and the taunts of the Ammonites,
who insulted my people
and made threats against their
land.
9 Therefore, as surely as I live,"
declares the LORD Almighty, the
God of Israel,
"surely Moab will become like
Sodom,
the Ammonites like Gomorrah—
a place of weeds and salt pits,
a wasteland forever.
The remnant of my people will
plunder them;
the survivors of my nation will
inherit their land."

10 This is what they will get in return for
their pride,

for insulting and mocking the
people of the LORD Almighty.
11 The LORD will be awesome to them
when he destroys all the gods of
the land.
The nations on every shore will
worship him,
every one in its own land.

Against Cush

12 "You too, O Cushites, [b]
will be slain by my sword."

Against Assyria

13 He will stretch out his hand against
the north
and destroy Assyria,
leaving Nineveh utterly desolate
and dry as the desert.
14 Flocks and herds will lie down there,
creatures of every kind.
The desert owl and the screech owl
will roost on her columns.

[a] 7 Or *will bring back their captives*   [b] 12 That is,
people from the upper Nile region

Taken for Granted?

Quiet TIMES *with each other*

ZEPHANIAH 2:2   The longer you hang around someone, the more you tend to take him or her for granted. Before you know it, you find yourself saying things to that person you would never say in public. The marriage can easily become a "taken for granted" relationship. You can slip into the sin of sarcasm or cutting statements so that it becomes a habit.

Sin is like that. A person can participate in it for so long that they get complacent about it—so complacent that they pick up speed, falling further and further into the habit of sin. Zephaniah reminds us that it's never too late to stop falling. An amazing thing about God is that he loves us so much that, though there will be judgment for sin, he has provided a rescue from our fall.

Zephaniah's warning is both frightening and wonderful. Frightening for those who don't seek God's forgiveness and become complacent about their sin. Yet it's wonderful for those who do seek God and realize he loves us so much that he has provided a rescue from the devastating judgment to come.

It's never too late to turn from sin. Though your spouse may continue taking your marriage for granted, you don't have to. You can choose to lead the way and take marriage seriously . . . like you did when you first got married. No matter how long the marriage has been in the "taken for granted" stage, God will provide a rescue for those who will turn to him.

—*Bob & Rosemary*

Weekend Warm-up *Do you cherish your marriage?*

Go to page 1005 for your next devotional reading.

Their calls will echo through the
windows,
rubble will be in the doorways,
the beams of cedar will be
exposed.
¹⁵This is the carefree city
that lived in safety.
She said to herself,
"I am, and there is none besides
me."
What a ruin she has become,
a lair for wild beasts!
All who pass by her scoff
and shake their fists.

The Future of Jerusalem

3 Woe to the city of oppressors,
rebellious and defiled!
²She obeys no one,
she accepts no correction.
She does not trust in the LORD,
she does not draw near to her God.
³Her officials are roaring lions,
her rulers are evening wolves,
who leave nothing for the
morning.
⁴Her prophets are arrogant;
they are treacherous men.
Her priests profane the sanctuary
and do violence to the law.
⁵The LORD within her is righteous;
he does no wrong.
Morning by morning he dispenses his
justice,
and every new day he does not fail,
yet the unrighteous know no
shame.

⁶"I have cut off nations;
their strongholds are demolished.
I have left their streets deserted,
with no one passing through.
Their cities are destroyed;
no one will be left—no one at all.
⁷I said to the city,
'Surely you will fear me
and accept correction!'
Then her dwelling would not be cut
off,
nor all my punishments come
upon her.
But they were still eager
to act corruptly in all they did.
⁸Therefore wait for me," declares the
LORD,

"for the day I will stand up to
testify.ᵃ
I have decided to assemble the
nations,
to gather the kingdoms
and to pour out my wrath on them—
all my fierce anger.
The whole world will be consumed
by the fire of my jealous anger.

⁹"Then will I purify the lips of the
peoples,
that all of them may call on the
name of the LORD
and serve him shoulder to
shoulder.
¹⁰From beyond the rivers of Cushᵇ
my worshipers, my scattered
people,
will bring me offerings.
¹¹On that day you will not be put to
shame
for all the wrongs you have done
to me,
because I will remove from this city
those who rejoice in their pride.
Never again will you be haughty
on my holy hill.
¹²But I will leave within you
the meek and humble,
who trust in the name of the LORD.
¹³The remnant of Israel will do no
wrong;
they will speak no lies,
nor will deceit be found in their
mouths.
They will eat and lie down
and no one will make them afraid."

¹⁴Sing, O Daughter of Zion;
shout aloud, O Israel!
Be glad and rejoice with all your
heart,
O Daughter of Jerusalem!
¹⁵The LORD has taken away your
punishment,
he has turned back your enemy.
The LORD, the King of Israel, is with
you;
never again will you fear any harm.
¹⁶On that day they will say to
Jerusalem,
"Do not fear, O Zion;
do not let your hands hang limp.

ᵃ8 Septuagint and Syriac; Hebrew *will rise up to
plunder*   ᵇ10 That is, the upper Nile region

¹⁷The LORD your God is with you,
he is mighty to save.
He will take great delight in you,
he will quiet you with his love,
he will rejoice over you with
singing."

¹⁸"The sorrows for the appointed feasts
I will remove from you;
they are a burden and a reproach
to you.ᵃ
¹⁹At that time I will deal
with all who oppressed you;
I will rescue the lame
and gather those who have been
scattered.

I will give them praise and honor
in every land where they were put
to shame.
²⁰At that time I will gather you;
at that time I will bring you
home.
I will give you honor and praise
among all the peoples of the
earth
when I restore your fortunesᵇ
before your very eyes,"
says the LORD.

ᵃ18 Or "I will gather you who mourn for the
appointed feasts; / your reproach is a burden to you
ᵇ20 Or I bring back your captives

Great Expectations

Monday

ZEPHANIAH 3:17 I (Rosemary) had very exciting expectations about marriage. I grew up watching romantic movies. This meant I expected that it would be natural for Bob to understand my intimate needs—my needs for romance, my desire for the right atmosphere, my expectation of poetic words flowing out of his mouth . . . the whole package. I just knew he would be the perfect composite of all the movies I had ever seen. Unfortunately Bob grew up watching westerns. Our expectations were very different.

Some people presume that their spouse has been sent to fulfill all the longings and desires in their heart. Some view their spouse as an escape from an unhappy childhood home. Others feel that their loved one will fulfill all of their needs in the areas of companionship, sexual gratification, romance or friendship. They dream that their spouse will be their greatest fan club and support in their endeavors of life. While it is

true that a spouse should attempt to satisfy some areas of need, it is unrealistic and unfair to expect a spouse to meet all our needs. As humans, we are not equipped to meet all the needs of another person.

Zephaniah reminds us that there is One who can, will and does meet all the needs of our hearts. God. He is with us at all times. He is aware of our every desire. Through his mighty power, God is able to save us and comfort us in our times of distress and weakness. When we feel the most unlovable and insecure, he assures us that he delights in us unconditionally. Just because of the fact that we are his children and belong to him, he rejoices. When we feel alone and disappointed, our gaze should be turned to the loving Father who will never disappoint us or leave our needs unmet.

—Bob & Rosemary

Go to page 1007 for your next devotional reading.

Haggai

We hear a lot of talk these days about priorities, and such talk is warranted. After all, whether we realize it or not, every daily activity we engage in reflects our priorities like a mirror. Some companies even set up workshops on this issue and pay their employees to attend.

Well, if Haggai had led one such workshop, he would have had a lesson prepared about priorities. Listen to what he said to the people coming back from years in captivity: "Don't take care of your own house," he warned. "Rebuild God's house first." Now, Haggai wasn't just talking about physical structures here. His references didn't only relate to bricks and mortar. He was telling the people to never put their personal desires, goals, aspirations or even their marriages and families ahead of God. What does your day planner look like? Listen for God's message to you, through Haggai, about your priorities.

A Call to Build the House of the Lord

1 In the second year of King Darius, on the first day of the sixth month, the word of the Lord came through the prophet Haggai to Zerubbabel son of Shealtiel, governor of Judah, and to Joshua*a* son of Jehozadak, the high priest:

²This is what the Lord Almighty says: "These people say, 'The time has not yet come for the Lord's house to be built.' "

³Then the word of the Lord came through the prophet Haggai: ⁴"Is it a time for you yourselves to be living in your paneled houses, while this house remains a ruin?"

⁵Now this is what the Lord Almighty says: "Give careful thought to your ways. ⁶You have planted much, but have harvested little. You eat, but never have enough. You drink, but never have your fill. You put on clothes, but are not warm. You earn wages, only to put them in a purse with holes in it."

⁷This is what the Lord Almighty says: "Give careful thought to your ways. ⁸Go

a1 A variant of Jeshua; here and elsewhere in Haggai

up into the mountains and bring down timber and build the house, so that I may take pleasure in it and be honored," says the LORD. ⁹"You expected much, but see, it turned out to be little. What you brought home, I blew away. Why?" declares the LORD Almighty. "Because of my house, which remains a ruin, while each of you is busy with his own house. ¹⁰Therefore, because of you the heavens have withheld their dew and the earth its crops. ¹¹I called for a drought on the fields and the mountains, on the grain, the new wine, the oil and whatever the ground produces, on men and cattle, and on the labor of your hands."

¹²Then Zerubbabel son of Shealtiel, Joshua son of Jehozadak, the high priest, and the whole remnant of the people obeyed the voice of the LORD their God and the message of the prophet Haggai, because the LORD their God had sent him. And the people feared the LORD.

¹³Then Haggai, the LORD's messenger, gave this message of the LORD to the people: "I am with you," declares the LORD. ¹⁴So the LORD stirred up the spirit of Zerubbabel son of Shealtiel, governor of Judah, and the spirit of Joshua son of Jehozadak, the high priest, and the spirit of the whole remnant of the people. They came and began to work on the house of the LORD Almighty, their God, ¹⁵on the twenty-fourth day of the sixth month in the second year of King Darius.

The Promised Glory of the New House

2 On the twenty-first day of the seventh month, the word of the LORD came through the prophet Haggai: ²"Speak to Zerubbabel son of Shealtiel, governor of Judah, to Joshua son of Jehozadak, the high priest, and to the remnant of the people. Ask them, ³'Who of you is left who saw this house in its former glory? How does it look to you now? Does it not seem to you like nothing? ⁴But now be strong, O Zerubbabel,' declares the LORD. 'Be strong, O Joshua son of Jehozadak, the high priest. Be strong, all you people of the land,' declares the LORD, 'and work. For I am with you,' declares the LORD Almighty. ⁵'This is what I covenanted with you when you came out of Egypt. And my Spirit remains among you. Do not fear.'

⁶"This is what the LORD Almighty says: 'In a little while I will once more shake the heavens and the earth, the sea and the dry land. ⁷I will shake all nations, and the desired of all nations will come, and I will fill this house with glory,' says the LORD

Just a Little Bit More

Tuesday

HAGGAI 1:6 No matter how much a couple has, they often believe they need a little bit more. In fact, studies have shown that most couples believe they would be happier if their income were 20 percent higher. Of course, 20 percent more would never satisfy, at least not for long. As our financial growth is absorbed into our living standard, expectations rise and the cycle repeats itself.

Above a certain subsistence level that varies with the life stage of each couple, happiness in marriage depends on the quality of the relationship. And this is true at all stages of life, for richer, for poorer. That's why this passage urges us to consider whether we will ever have enough. The writer of Ecclesiastes agrees: "Better one handful with tranquillity than two handfuls with toil and chasing after the wind" (Ecclesiastes 4:6; see also Proverbs 15:17 and 17:1, page 680).

So if you are living in a one-bedroom apartment praying that your monthly income will outlast the month, remember these wise words: "Do not wear yourself out to get rich; have the wisdom to show restraint. Cast but a glance at riches, and they are gone, for they will surely sprout wings and fly off to the sky like an eagle" (Proverbs 23:4–5). It is far more rewarding to put your hope in God, "who richly provides us with everything for our enjoyment" (1 Timothy 6:17).

—Les & Leslie

Go to page 1012 for your next devotional reading.

Almighty. 8'The silver is mine and the gold is mine,' declares the LORD Almighty. 9'The glory of this present house will be greater than the glory of the former house,' says the LORD Almighty. 'And in this place I will grant peace,' declares the LORD Almighty."

Blessings for a Defiled People

10On the twenty-fourth day of the ninth month, in the second year of Darius, the word of the LORD came to the prophet Haggai: 11"This is what the LORD Almighty says: 'Ask the priests what the law says: 12If a person carries consecrated meat in the fold of his garment, and that fold touches some bread or stew, some wine, oil or other food, does it become consecrated?' "

The priests answered, "No."

13Then Haggai said, "If a person defiled by contact with a dead body touches one of these things, does it become defiled?"

"Yes," the priests replied, "it becomes defiled."

14Then Haggai said, " 'So it is with this people and this nation in my sight,' declares the LORD. 'Whatever they do and whatever they offer there is defiled.

15" 'Now give careful thought to this from this day on*a*—consider how things were before one stone was laid on another in the LORD's temple. 16When anyone came to a heap of twenty measures, there were only ten. When anyone went to a wine vat to draw fifty measures, there were only twenty. 17I struck all the work of your hands with blight, mildew and hail, yet you did not turn to me,' declares the LORD. 18'From this day on, from this twenty-fourth day of the ninth month, give careful thought to the day when the foundation of the LORD's temple was laid. Give careful thought: 19Is there yet any seed left in the barn? Until now, the vine and the fig tree, the pomegranate and the olive tree have not borne fruit.

" 'From this day on I will bless you.' "

Zerubbabel the Lord's Signet Ring

20The word of the LORD came to Haggai a second time on the twenty-fourth day of the month: 21"Tell Zerubbabel governor of Judah that I will shake the heavens and the earth. 22I will overturn royal thrones and shatter the power of the foreign kingdoms. I will overthrow chariots and their drivers; horses and their riders will fall, each by the sword of his brother.

23" 'On that day,' declares the LORD Almighty, 'I will take you, my servant Zerubbabel son of Shealtiel,' declares the LORD, 'and I will make you like my signet ring, for I have chosen you,' declares the LORD Almighty."

a15 Or *to the days past*

Zechariah

Can you remember a time when you felt so discouraged that you didn't have the energy to move (either physically or emotionally)? You felt like you were totally powerless to act—as if you were stuck in the mud. What eventually lifted you up and got you moving ahead? The prophet Zechariah introduces us to an energy source that has great potential to provide power and comfort to human beings. It's encouragement.

The Jews to whom Zechariah spoke were devastated. They had been living in exile, and as they returned to their beloved city they saw its destruction. Their precious homes were lying in ruin. But Zechariah knew that a little encouragement goes a long way: "[The LORD] will return" he said, "and dwell in Jerusalem . . . The city streets will be filled with boys and girls playing there" (8:3, 5). Zechariah knew that a minute of reassurance was worth hours of hard work. Encouragement is a limitless resource. It's abundant, and it's free. Help yourself (and your spouse).

A Call to Return to the LORD

1 In the eighth month of the second year of Darius, the word of the LORD came to the prophet Zechariah son of Berekiah, the son of Iddo:

² "The LORD was very angry with your forefathers. ³Therefore tell the people: This is what the LORD Almighty says: 'Return to me,' declares the LORD Almighty, 'and I will return to you,' says the LORD Almighty. ⁴Do not be like your forefathers, to whom the earlier prophets proclaimed: This is what the LORD Almighty says: 'Turn from your evil ways and your evil practices.' But they would not listen or pay attention to me, declares the LORD. ⁵Where are your forefathers now? And the prophets, do they live forever? ⁶But did not my words and my decrees, which I commanded my servants the prophets, overtake your forefathers?

"Then they repented and said, 'The

LORD Almighty has done to us what our ways and practices deserve, just as he determined to do.' "

The Man Among the Myrtle Trees

⁷On the twenty-fourth day of the eleventh month, the month of Shebat, in the second year of Darius, the word of the LORD came to the prophet Zechariah son of Berekiah, the son of Iddo.

⁸During the night I had a vision—and there before me was a man riding a red horse! He was standing among the myrtle trees in a ravine. Behind him were red, brown and white horses.

⁹I asked, "What are these, my lord?"

The angel who was talking with me answered, "I will show you what they are."

¹⁰Then the man standing among the myrtle trees explained, "They are the ones the LORD has sent to go throughout the earth."

¹¹And they reported to the angel of the LORD, who was standing among the myrtle trees, "We have gone throughout the earth and found the whole world at rest and in peace."

¹²Then the angel of the LORD said, "LORD Almighty, how long will you withhold mercy from Jerusalem and from the towns of Judah, which you have been angry with these seventy years?" ¹³So the LORD spoke kind and comforting words to the angel who talked with me.

¹⁴Then the angel who was speaking to me said, "Proclaim this word: This is what the LORD Almighty says: 'I am very jealous for Jerusalem and Zion, ¹⁵but I am very angry with the nations that feel secure. I was only a little angry, but they added to the calamity.'

¹⁶"Therefore, this is what the LORD says: 'I will return to Jerusalem with mercy, and there my house will be rebuilt. And the measuring line will be stretched out over Jerusalem,' declares the LORD Almighty.

¹⁷"Proclaim further: This is what the LORD Almighty says: 'My towns will again overflow with prosperity, and the LORD will again comfort Zion and choose Jerusalem.' "

Four Horns and Four Craftsmen

¹⁸Then I looked up—and there before

me were four horns! ¹⁹I asked the angel who was speaking to me, "What are these?"

He answered me, "These are the horns that scattered Judah, Israel and Jerusalem."

²⁰Then the LORD showed me four craftsmen. ²¹I asked, "What are these coming to do?"

He answered, "These are the horns that scattered Judah so that no one could raise his head, but the craftsmen have come to terrify them and throw down these horns of the nations who lifted up their horns against the land of Judah to scatter its people."

A Man With a Measuring Line

2 Then I looked up—and there before me was a man with a measuring line in his hand! ²I asked, "Where are you going?"

He answered me, "To measure Jerusalem, to find out how wide and how long it is."

³Then the angel who was speaking to me left, and another angel came to meet him ⁴and said to him: "Run, tell that young man, 'Jerusalem will be a city without walls because of the great number of men and livestock in it. ⁵And I myself will be a wall of fire around it,' declares the LORD, 'and I will be its glory within.'

⁶"Come! Come! Flee from the land of the north," declares the LORD, "for I have scattered you to the four winds of heaven," declares the LORD.

⁷"Come, O Zion! Escape, you who live in the Daughter of Babylon!" ⁸For this is what the LORD Almighty says: "After he has honored me and has sent me against the nations that have plundered you—for whoever touches you touches the apple of his eye— ⁹I will surely raise my hand against them so that their slaves will plunder them.ᵃ Then you will know that the LORD Almighty has sent me.

¹⁰"Shout and be glad, O Daughter of Zion. For I am coming, and I will live among you," declares the LORD. ¹¹"Many nations will be joined with the LORD in that day and will become my people. I will live among you and you will know that the LORD Almighty has sent me to you. ¹²The LORD will inherit Judah as his

ᵃ8,9 Or says after . . . eye: 9"I . . . plunder them."

portion in the holy land and will again choose Jerusalem. ¹³Be still before the LORD, all mankind, because he has roused himself from his holy dwelling."

Clean Garments for the High Priest

3 Then he showed me Joshua*ᵃ* the high priest standing before the angel of the LORD, and Satan*ᵇ* standing at his right side to accuse him. ²The LORD said to Satan, "The LORD rebuke you, Satan! The LORD, who has chosen Jerusalem, rebuke you! Is not this man a burning stick snatched from the fire?"

³Now Joshua was dressed in filthy clothes as he stood before the angel. ⁴The angel said to those who were standing before him, "Take off his filthy clothes."

Then he said to Joshua, "See, I have taken away your sin, and I will put rich garments on you."

⁵Then I said, "Put a clean turban on his head." So they put a clean turban on his head and clothed him, while the angel of the LORD stood by.

⁶The angel of the LORD gave this charge to Joshua: ⁷"This is what the LORD Almighty says: 'If you will walk in my ways and keep my requirements, then you will govern my house and have charge of my courts, and I will give you a place among these standing here.

⁸"'Listen, O high priest Joshua and your associates seated before you, who are men symbolic of things to come: I am going to bring my servant, the Branch. ⁹See, the stone I have set in front of Joshua! There are seven eyes*ᶜ* on that one stone, and I will engrave an inscription on it,' says the LORD Almighty, 'and I will remove the sin of this land in a single day.

¹⁰"'In that day each of you will invite his neighbor to sit under his vine and fig tree,' declares the LORD Almighty."

The Gold Lampstand and the Two Olive Trees

4 Then the angel who talked with me returned and wakened me, as a man is wakened from his sleep. ²He asked me, "What do you see?"

I answered, "I see a solid gold lampstand with a bowl at the top and seven lights on it, with seven channels to the lights. ³Also there are two olive trees by it,

one on the right of the bowl and the other on its left."

⁴I asked the angel who talked with me, "What are these, my lord?"

⁵He answered, "Do you not know what these are?"

"No, my lord," I replied.

⁶So he said to me, "This is the word of the LORD to Zerubbabel: 'Not by might nor by power, but by my Spirit,' says the LORD Almighty.

⁷"What*ᵈ* are you, O mighty mountain? Before Zerubbabel you will become level ground. Then he will bring out the capstone to shouts of 'God bless it! God bless it!'"

⁸Then the word of the LORD came to me: ⁹"The hands of Zerubbabel have laid the foundation of this temple; his hands will also complete it. Then you will know that the LORD Almighty has sent me to you.

¹⁰"Who despises the day of small things? Men will rejoice when they see the plumb line in the hand of Zerubbabel.

"(These seven are the eyes of the LORD, which range throughout the earth.)"

¹¹Then I asked the angel, "What are these two olive trees on the right and the left of the lampstand?"

¹²Again I asked him, "What are these two olive branches beside the two gold pipes that pour out golden oil?"

¹³He replied, "Do you not know what these are?"

"No, my lord," I said.

¹⁴So he said, "These are the two who are anointed to*ᵉ* serve the Lord of all the earth."

The Flying Scroll

5 I looked again—and there before me was a flying scroll!

²He asked me, "What do you see?"

I answered, "I see a flying scroll, thirty feet long and fifteen feet wide.*ᶠ*"

³And he said to me, "This is the curse that is going out over the whole land; for according to what it says on one side, every thief will be banished, and according to what it says on the other, everyone who

---

ᵃ1 A variant of *Jeshua*; here and elsewhere in Zechariah　　*ᵇ1 Satan* means *accuser*.　　*ᶜ9* Or *facets*　　*ᵈ7* Or *Who*　　*ᵉ14* Or *two who bring oil and*　　*ᶠ2* Hebrew *twenty cubits long and ten cubits wide* (about 9 meters long and 4.5 meters wide) swears falsely will be banished. ⁴The LORD Almighty declares, 'I will send it out, and it will enter the house of the thief and the house of him who swears falsely by my name. It will remain in his house and destroy it, both its timbers and its stones.' "

The Woman in a Basket

⁵Then the angel who was speaking to me came forward and said to me, "Look up and see what this is that is appearing."

⁶I asked, "What is it?"

He replied, "It is a measuring basket.ᵃ" And he added, "This is the iniquityᵇ of the people throughout the land."

⁷Then the cover of lead was raised, and there in the basket sat a woman! ⁸He said, "This is wickedness," and he pushed her back into the basket and pushed the lead cover down over its mouth.

⁹Then I looked up—and there before me were two women, with the wind in their wings! They had wings like those of a stork, and they lifted up the basket between heaven and earth.

¹⁰"Where are they taking the basket?" I asked the angel who was speaking to me.

¹¹He replied, "To the country of Babyloniaᶜ to build a house for it. When it is ready, the basket will be set there in its place."

Four Chariots

6 I looked up again—and there before me were four chariots coming out from between two mountains—mountains of bronze! ²The first chariot had red horses, the second black, ³the third white, and the fourth dappled—all of them powerful. ⁴I asked the angel who was speaking to me, "What are these, my lord?"

⁵The angel answered me, "These are the four spiritsᵈ of heaven, going out from standing in the presence of the Lord of the whole world. ⁶The one with the black horses is going toward the north country, the one with the white horses toward the west,ᵉ and the one with the dappled horses toward the south."

⁷When the powerful horses went out, they were straining to go throughout the earth. And he said, "Go throughout the earth!" So they went throughout the earth.

⁸Then he called to me, "Look, those going toward the north country have given my Spiritᶠ rest in the land of the north."

A Crown for Joshua

⁹The word of the LORD came to me:

ᵃ6 Hebrew *an ephah*; also in verses 7-11   ᵇ6 Or *appearance*   ᶜ11 Hebrew *Shinar*   ᵈ5 Or *winds*   ᵉ6 Or *horses after them*   ᶠ8 Or *spirit*

Only God

Wednesday

ZECHARIAH 4:6 It is liberating to realize that the important things of life are not accomplished by our own might or power, but only by God. It relieves us from agonizing over every decision: the wife who is trying to find the perfect marriage seminar to get her husband to go to; or the husband who is toiling over the perfect approach to win his wife back to him after the flame has gone out. What if the speakers or writers say the wrong things? What if they make the wrong choice? Will it only serve to push their spouse further away?

Although we can fully trust God to help us make decisions, we still have to make an effort. During Zechariah's time, when it came to rebuilding the temple, each person had a job to do. Zechariah and the people trusted God, but they also worked hard to accomplish his will. Likewise in the marriage, each spouse has his or her own personal ingenuity. It is only God who can do the delicate work of mending a damaged heart. Only the Spirit of God can blend two different people into one powerful marriage bond. Neither our personal efforts nor someone else's counsel can accomplish that.

The sooner each spouse realizes that only God can bind two hearts together, the sooner we will be relieved of the burden of trying to control our marriages on our own.

—Bob & Rosemary

Go to page 1014 for your next devotional reading.

[10] "Take ⌐silver and gold¬ from the exiles Heldai, Tobijah and Jedaiah, who have arrived from Babylon. Go the same day to the house of Josiah son of Zephaniah. [11] Take the silver and gold and make a crown, and set it on the head of the high priest, Joshua son of Jehozadak. [12] Tell him this is what the LORD Almighty says: 'Here is the man whose name is the Branch, and he will branch out from his place and build the temple of the LORD. [13] It is he who will build the temple of the LORD, and he will be clothed with majesty and will sit and rule on his throne. And he will be a priest on his throne. And there will be harmony between the two.' [14] The crown will be given to Heldai,[a] Tobijah, Jedaiah and Hen[b] son of Zephaniah as a memorial in the temple of the LORD. [15] Those who are far away will come and help to build the temple of the LORD, and you will know that the LORD Almighty has sent me to you. This will happen if you diligently obey the LORD your God."

Justice and Mercy, Not Fasting

7 In the fourth year of King Darius, the word of the LORD came to Zechariah on the fourth day of the ninth month, the month of Kislev. [2] The people of Bethel had sent Sharezer and Regem-Melech, together with their men, to entreat the LORD [3] by asking the priests of the house of the LORD Almighty and the prophets, "Should I mourn and fast in the fifth month, as I have done for so many years?"

[4] Then the word of the LORD Almighty came to me: [5] "Ask all the people of the land and the priests, 'When you fasted and mourned in the fifth and seventh months for the past seventy years, was it really for me that you fasted? [6] And when you were eating and drinking, were you not just feasting for yourselves? [7] Are these not the words the LORD proclaimed through the earlier prophets when Jerusalem and its surrounding towns were at rest and prosperous, and the Negev and the western foothills were settled?' "

[8] And the word of the LORD came again to Zechariah: [9] "This is what the LORD Almighty says: 'Administer true justice; show mercy and compassion to one another. [10] Do not oppress the widow or the fatherless, the alien or the poor. In your hearts do not think evil of each other.'

[11] "But they refused to pay attention; stubbornly they turned their backs and stopped up their ears. [12] They made their hearts as hard as flint and would not listen to the law or to the words that the LORD Almighty had sent by his Spirit through the earlier prophets. So the LORD Almighty was very angry.

[13] " 'When I called, they did not listen; so when they called, I would not listen,' says the LORD Almighty. [14] 'I scattered them with a whirlwind among all the nations, where they were strangers. The land was left so desolate behind them that no one could come or go. This is how they made the pleasant land desolate.' "

The Lord Promises to Bless Jerusalem

8 Again the word of the LORD Almighty came to me. [2] This is what the LORD Almighty says: "I am very jealous for Zion; I am burning with jealousy for her."

[3] This is what the LORD says: "I will return to Zion and dwell in Jerusalem. Then Jerusalem will be called the City of Truth, and the mountain of the LORD Almighty will be called the Holy Mountain."

[4] This is what the LORD Almighty says: "Once again men and women of ripe old age will sit in the streets of Jerusalem, each with cane in hand because of his age. [5] The city streets will be filled with boys and girls playing there."

[6] This is what the LORD Almighty says: "It may seem marvelous to the remnant of this people at that time, but will it seem marvelous to me?" declares the LORD Almighty.

[7] This is what the LORD Almighty says: "I will save my people from the countries of the east and the west. [8] I will bring them back to live in Jerusalem; they will be my people, and I will be faithful and righteous to them as their God."

[9] This is what the LORD Almighty says: "You who now hear these words spoken by the prophets who were there when the foundation was laid for the house of the LORD Almighty, let your hands be strong so that the temple may be built. [10] Before that time there were no wages for man or

[a]14 Syriac; Hebrew *Helem*   [b]14 Or *and the gracious one, the*

beast. No one could go about his business safely because of his enemy, for I had turned every man against his neighbor. [11]But now I will not deal with the remnant of this people as I did in the past," declares the LORD Almighty.

[12]"The seed will grow well, the vine will yield its fruit, the ground will produce its crops, and the heavens will drop their dew. I will give all these things as an inheritance to the remnant of this people. [13]As you have been an object of cursing among the nations, O Judah and Israel, so will I save you, and you will be a blessing. Do not be afraid, but let your hands be strong."

[14]This is what the LORD Almighty says: "Just as I had determined to bring disaster upon you and showed no pity when your fathers angered me," says the LORD Almighty, [15]"so now I have determined to do good again to Jerusalem and Judah. Do not be afraid. [16]These are the things you are to do: Speak the truth to each other, and render true and sound judgment in your courts; [17]do not plot evil against your neighbor, and do not love to swear falsely. I hate all this," declares the LORD.

[18]Again the word of the LORD Almighty came to me. [19]This is what the LORD Almighty says: "The fasts of the fourth, fifth, seventh and tenth months will become joyful and glad occasions and happy festivals for Judah. Therefore love truth and peace."

[20]This is what the LORD Almighty says: "Many peoples and the inhabitants of many cities will yet come, [21]and the inhabitants of one city will go to another and say, 'Let us go at once to entreat the LORD and seek the LORD Almighty. I myself am going.' [22]And many peoples and powerful nations will come to Jerusalem to seek the LORD Almighty and to entreat him."

[23]This is what the LORD Almighty says: "In those days ten men from all languages and nations will take firm hold of one Jew by the hem of his robe and say, 'Let us go with you, because we have heard that God is with you.' "

Speaking the Truth

Thursday

ZECHARIAH 8:16 Every couple tells little white lies to one another once in awhile in an attempt to be more "loving." If we don't like our spouse's cooking, for example, we might say, "Oh, it tastes good." It's a little lie that couldn't hurt a flea, right? Wrong.

Consider Ron and Cindy who had been married only a few weeks when he cooked his "world famous BBQ hot ribs" on their brand new grill. As they were eating, Ron asked Cindy if she liked the ribs. Cindy knew Ron had worked hard to make them and was afraid that she would offend him if she was honest. "Oh yes," she told Ron. "They're great!"

Believing that Cindy really liked his famous dish, Ron began barbecuing quite regularly as a kind of family tradition, and there were always leftovers which had to be eaten. After awhile, Cindy could bear it no longer, and, in a moment of anger about something else, she blurted out that she hated Ron's ribs, that they made her gag, that she never wanted to see ribs on her table again! Ron was shocked and hurt. She had *lied* to him. "How can I ever believe you again?" he asked.

Should Cindy have told Ron right from the beginning that the ribs made her feel like gagging? No, honesty does not require brutality. Truth is "brutal" only when it is a partial truth or when it is meant to cause pain. If Cindy had said she hated the ribs, that would have been only part of the truth. To be honest, she could say something like, "I've never liked ribs barbecued on the grill—but I love seeing you have fun cooking them. We could have them as a side dish once in awhile. What do you think?"

The danger of deception is that it only gets worse with time and repeat offenses. Surely that's what was on Zechariah's mind when he wrote this passage.

—*Les & Leslie*

Go to page 1022 for your next devotional reading.

Judgment on Israel's Enemies

An Oracle

9 The word of the LORD is against the
        land of Hadrach
    and will rest upon Damascus—
for the eyes of men and all the tribes
        of Israel
    are on the LORD—[a]
²and upon Hamath too, which borders
        on it,
    and upon Tyre and Sidon, though
        they are very skillful.
³Tyre has built herself a stronghold;
    she has heaped up silver like dust,
    and gold like the dirt of the streets.
⁴But the Lord will take away her
        possessions
    and destroy her power on the sea,
    and she will be consumed by fire.
⁵Ashkelon will see it and fear;
    Gaza will writhe in agony,
    and Ekron too, for her hope will
        wither.
Gaza will lose her king
    and Ashkelon will be deserted.
⁶Foreigners will occupy Ashdod,
    and I will cut off the pride of the
        Philistines.
⁷I will take the blood from their
        mouths,
    the forbidden food from between
        their teeth.
Those who are left will belong to our
        God
    and become leaders in Judah,
    and Ekron will be like the
        Jebusites.
⁸But I will defend my house
    against marauding forces.
Never again will an oppressor overrun
        my people,
    for now I am keeping watch.

The Coming of Zion's King

⁹Rejoice greatly, O Daughter of Zion!
    Shout, Daughter of Jerusalem!
See, your king[b] comes to you,
    righteous and having salvation,
    gentle and riding on a donkey,
    on a colt, the foal of a donkey.
¹⁰I will take away the chariots from
        Ephraim
    and the war-horses from Jerusalem,
    and the battle bow will be broken.

He will proclaim peace to the
        nations.
    His rule will extend from sea to sea
    and from the River[c] to the ends
        of the earth.[d]
¹¹As for you, because of the blood of
        my covenant with you,
    I will free your prisoners from the
        waterless pit.
¹²Return to your fortress, O prisoners of
        hope;
    even now I announce that I will
        restore twice as much to you.
¹³I will bend Judah as I bend my bow
    and fill it with Ephraim.
I will rouse your sons, O Zion,
    against your sons, O Greece,
    and make you like a warrior's
        sword.

The LORD Will Appear

¹⁴Then the LORD will appear over them;
    his arrow will flash like lightning.

---

*a 1 Or Damascus. / For the eye of the LORD is on all
mankind, / as well as on the tribes of Israel,*
b 9 Or King   c 10 That is, the Euphrates
d 10 Or the end of the land

The Sovereign LORD will sound the
    trumpet;
  he will march in the storms of the
    south,
15 and the LORD Almighty will shield
    them.
They will destroy
  and overcome with slingstones.
They will drink and roar as with
    wine;
  they will be full like a bowl
  used for sprinkling*a* the corners of
    the altar.
16The LORD their God will save them
    on that day
  as the flock of his people.
They will sparkle in his land
  like jewels in a crown.
17How attractive and beautiful they will
    be!
  Grain will make the young men
    thrive,
  and new wine the young women.

The LORD Will Care for Judah

10 Ask the LORD for rain in the
    springtime;
  it is the LORD who makes the
    storm clouds.
He gives showers of rain to men,
  and plants of the field to everyone.
2The idols speak deceit,
  diviners see visions that lie;
they tell dreams that are false,
  they give comfort in vain.
Therefore the people wander like
    sheep
  oppressed for lack of a shepherd.

3"My anger burns against the
    shepherds,
  and I will punish the leaders;
for the LORD Almighty will care
  for his flock, the house of Judah,
  and make them like a proud horse
    in battle.
4From Judah will come the
    cornerstone,
  from him the tent peg,
  from him the battle bow,
  from him every ruler.
5Together they*b* will be like mighty
    men
  trampling the muddy streets in
    battle.
Because the LORD is with them,

they will fight and overthrow the
    horsemen.
6"I will strengthen the house of Judah
  and save the house of Joseph.
I will restore them
  because I have compassion on
    them.
They will be as though
  I had not rejected them,
for I am the LORD their God
  and I will answer them.
7The Ephraimites will become like
    mighty men,
  and their hearts will be glad as
    with wine.
Their children will see it and be
    joyful;
  their hearts will rejoice in the
    LORD.
8I will signal for them
  and gather them in.
Surely I will redeem them;
  they will be as numerous as before.
9Though I scatter them among the
    peoples,
  yet in distant lands they will
    remember me.
They and their children will survive,
  and they will return.
10I will bring them back from Egypt
  and gather them from Assyria.
I will bring them to Gilead and
    Lebanon,
  and there will not be room enough
    for them.
11They will pass through the sea of
    trouble;
  the surging sea will be subdued
  and all the depths of the Nile will
    dry up.
Assyria's pride will be brought down
  and Egypt's scepter will pass away.
12I will strengthen them in the LORD
  and in his name they will walk,"
                declares the LORD.

11 Open your doors, O Lebanon,
  so that fire may devour your
    cedars!
2Wail, O pine tree, for the cedar has
    fallen;
  the stately trees are ruined!
Wail, oaks of Bashan;

*a*15 Or *bowl,* / *like*   *b*4,5 Or *ruler, all of them
together.* / 5*They*

the dense forest has been cut
down!
3Listen to the wail of the shepherds;
their rich pastures are destroyed!
Listen to the roar of the lions;
the lush thicket of the Jordan is
ruined!

Two Shepherds

4This is what the LORD my God says:
"Pasture the flock marked for slaughter.
5Their buyers slaughter them and go unpunished. Those who sell them say,
'Praise the LORD, I am rich!' Their own
shepherds do not spare them. 6For I will
no longer have pity on the people of the
land," declares the LORD. "I will hand everyone over to his neighbor and his king.
They will oppress the land, and I will not
rescue them from their hands."

7So I pastured the flock marked for
slaughter, particularly the oppressed of
the flock. Then I took two staffs and
called one Favor and the other Union,
and I pastured the flock. 8In one month I
got rid of the three shepherds.

The flock detested me, and I grew weary of them 9and said, "I will not be your
shepherd. Let the dying die, and the perishing perish. Let those who are left eat
one another's flesh."

10Then I took my staff called Favor and
broke it, revoking the covenant I had
made with all the nations. 11It was revoked on that day, and so the afflicted of
the flock who were watching me knew it
was the word of the LORD.

12I told them, "If you think it best, give
me my pay; but if not, keep it." So they
paid me thirty pieces of silver.

13And the LORD said to me, "Throw
it to the potter"—the handsome price at
which they priced me! So I took the thirty
pieces of silver and threw them into the
house of the LORD to the potter.

14Then I broke my second staff called
Union, breaking the brotherhood between Judah and Israel.

15Then the LORD said to me, "Take
again the equipment of a foolish shepherd. 16For I am going to raise up a shepherd over the land who will not care for
the lost, or seek the young, or heal the
injured, or feed the healthy, but will eat

the meat of the choice sheep, tearing off
their hoofs.

17"Woe to the worthless shepherd,
who deserts the flock!
May the sword strike his arm and his
right eye!
May his arm be completely
withered,
his right eye totally blinded!"

Jerusalem's Enemies to Be Destroyed
An Oracle

12 This is the word of the LORD concerning Israel. The LORD, who
stretches out the heavens, who lays the
foundation of the earth, and who forms
the spirit of man within him, declares: 2"I
am going to make Jerusalem a cup that
sends all the surrounding peoples reeling.
Judah will be besieged as well as Jerusalem. 3On that day, when all the nations of
the earth are gathered against her, I will
make Jerusalem an immovable rock for
all the nations. All who try to move it will
injure themselves. 4On that day I will
strike every horse with panic and its rider
with madness," declares the LORD. "I will
keep a watchful eye over the house of Judah, but I will blind all the horses of the
nations. 5Then the leaders of Judah will
say in their hearts, 'The people of Jerusalem are strong, because the LORD Almighty is their God.'

6"On that day I will make the leaders
of Judah like a firepot in a woodpile, like
a flaming torch among sheaves. They will
consume right and left all the surrounding peoples, but Jerusalem will remain intact in her place.

7"The LORD will save the dwellings of
Judah first, so that the honor of the house
of David and of Jerusalem's inhabitants
may not be greater than that of Judah.
8On that day the LORD will shield those
who live in Jerusalem, so that the feeblest
among them will be like David, and the
house of David will be like God, like the
Angel of the LORD going before them. 9On
that day I will set out to destroy all the
nations that attack Jerusalem.

Mourning for the One They Pierced

10"And I will pour out on the house of
David and the inhabitants of Jerusalem a

spirit[a] of grace and supplication. They will look on[b] me, the one they have pierced, and they will mourn for him as one mourns for an only child, and grieve bitterly for him as one grieves for a first-born son. [11]On that day the weeping in Jerusalem will be great, like the weeping of Hadad Rimmon in the plain of Megiddo. [12]The land will mourn, each clan by itself, with their wives by themselves: the clan of the house of David and their wives, the clan of the house of Nathan and their wives, [13]the clan of the house of Levi and their wives, the clan of Shimei and their wives, [14]and all the rest of the clans and their wives.

Cleansing From Sin

13 "On that day a fountain will be opened to the house of David and the inhabitants of Jerusalem, to cleanse them from sin and impurity.

[2]"On that day, I will banish the names of the idols from the land, and they will be remembered no more," declares the LORD Almighty. "I will remove both the prophets and the spirit of impurity from the land. [3]And if anyone still prophesies, his father and mother, to whom he was born, will say to him, 'You must die, because you have told lies in the LORD's name.' When he prophesies, his own parents will stab him.

[4]"On that day every prophet will be ashamed of his prophetic vision. He will not put on a prophet's garment of hair in order to deceive. [5]He will say, 'I am not a prophet. I am a farmer; the land has been my livelihood since my youth.[c]' [6]If someone asks him, 'What are these wounds on your body[d]?' he will answer, 'The wounds I was given at the house of my friends.'

The Shepherd Struck, the Sheep Scattered

[7]"Awake, O sword, against my
        shepherd,
    against the man who is close to
        me!"
    declares the LORD Almighty.
"Strike the shepherd,
    and the sheep will be scattered,
    and I will turn my hand against
        the little ones.
[8]In the whole land," declares the LORD,

"two-thirds will be struck down
        and perish;
    yet one-third will be left in it.
[9]This third I will bring into the fire;
    I will refine them like silver
    and test them like gold.
They will call on my name
    and I will answer them;
I will say, 'They are my people,'
    and they will say, 'The LORD is our
        God.'"

The LORD Comes and Reigns

14 A day of the LORD is coming when your plunder will be divided among you.

[2]I will gather all the nations to Jerusalem to fight against it; the city will be captured, the houses ransacked, and the women raped. Half of the city will go into exile, but the rest of the people will not be taken from the city. [3]Then the LORD will go out and fight against those nations, as he fights in the day of battle. [4]On that day his feet will stand on the Mount of Olives, east of Jerusalem, and the Mount of Olives will be split in two from east to west, forming a great valley, with half of the mountain moving north and half moving south. [5]You will flee by my mountain valley, for it will extend to Azel. You will flee as you fled from the earthquake[e] in the days of Uzziah king of Judah. Then the LORD my God will come, and all the holy ones with him.

[6]On that day there will be no light, no cold or frost. [7]It will be a unique day, without daytime or nighttime—a day known to the LORD. When evening comes, there will be light.

[8]On that day living water will flow out from Jerusalem, half to the eastern sea[f] and half to the western sea,[g] in summer and in winter. [9]The LORD will be king over the whole earth. On that day there will be one LORD, and his name the only name.

[10]The whole land, from Geba to Rimmon, south of Jerusalem, will become

---

a 10 Or the Spirit   b 10 Or to   c 5 Or farmer; a man sold me in my youth   d 6 Or wounds between your hands   e 5 Or 5My mountain valley will be blocked and will extend to Azel. It will be blocked as it was blocked because of the earthquake   f 8 That is, the Dead Sea   g 8 That is, the Mediterranean like the Arabah. But Jerusalem will be raised up and remain in its place, from the Benjamin Gate to the site of the First Gate, to the Corner Gate, and from the Tower of Hananel to the royal winepresses. ¹¹It will be inhabited; never again will it be destroyed. Jerusalem will be secure.

¹²This is the plague with which the LORD will strike all the nations that fought against Jerusalem: Their flesh will rot while they are still standing on their feet, their eyes will rot in their sockets, and their tongues will rot in their mouths. ¹³On that day men will be stricken by the LORD with great panic. Each man will seize the hand of another, and they will attack each other. ¹⁴Judah too will fight at Jerusalem. The wealth of all the surrounding nations will be collected—great quantities of gold and silver and clothing. ¹⁵A similar plague will strike the horses and mules, the camels and donkeys, and all the animals in those camps.

¹⁶Then the survivors from all the nations that have attacked Jerusalem will go up year after year to worship the King, the LORD Almighty, and to celebrate the Feast of Tabernacles. ¹⁷If any of the peoples of the earth do not go up to Jerusalem to worship the King, the LORD Almighty, they will have no rain. ¹⁸If the Egyptian people do not go up and take part, they will have no rain. The LORD ᵃ will bring on them the plague he inflicts on the nations that do not go up to celebrate the Feast of Tabernacles. ¹⁹This will be the punishment of Egypt and the punishment of all the nations that do not go up to celebrate the Feast of Tabernacles.

²⁰On that day HOLY TO THE LORD will be inscribed on the bells of the horses, and the cooking pots in the LORD's house will be like the sacred bowls in front of the altar. ²¹Every pot in Jerusalem and Judah will be holy to the LORD Almighty, and all who come to sacrifice will take some of the pots and cook in them. And on that day there will no longer be a Canaaniteᵇ in the house of the LORD Almighty.

ᵃ18 Or part, then the LORD   ᵇ21 Or merchant

Malachi

Marriage involves a lot of promises. It is the promise of a lifetime for a lifetime. Malachi tells us that God hates divorce (2:16). He hates the pain and division it creates, because he makes two people one in body and spirit when they marry.

The marriage covenant mirrors God's covenant with his people. God is always faithful, but we often are not. Making a lifetime commitment isn't easy. But God's love, care and forgiveness are constant, and he wants us to be constant in keeping our promise to stay devoted for a lifetime.

1 An oracle: The word of the LORD to Israel through Malachi.*a*

Jacob Loved, Esau Hated

²"I have loved you," says the LORD.

"But you ask, 'How have you loved us?'

"Was not Esau Jacob's brother?" the LORD says. "Yet I have loved Jacob, ³but Esau I have hated, and I have turned his mountains into a wasteland and left his inheritance to the desert jackals."

⁴Edom may say, "Though we have been crushed, we will rebuild the ruins."

But this is what the LORD Almighty says: "They may build, but I will demolish. They will be called the Wicked Land, a people always under the wrath of the LORD. ⁵You will see it with your own eyes and say, 'Great is the LORD—even beyond the borders of Israel!'

Blemished Sacrifices

⁶"A son honors his father, and a servant his master. If I am a father, where is the honor due me? If I am a master, where is the respect due me?" says the LORD Almighty. "It is you, O priests, who show contempt for my name.

"But you ask, 'How have we shown contempt for your name?'

⁷"You place defiled food on my altar.

"But you ask, 'How have we defiled you?'

"By saying that the LORD's table is contemptible. ⁸When you bring blind animals for sacrifice, is that not wrong? When you sacrifice crippled or diseased animals, is that not wrong? Try offering them to your governor! Would he be pleased with you? Would he accept you?" says the LORD Almighty.

a 1 *Malachi* means *my messenger.*

⁹"Now implore God to be gracious to us. With such offerings from your hands, will he accept you?"—says the LORD Almighty.

¹⁰"Oh, that one of you would shut the temple doors, so that you would not light useless fires on my altar! I am not pleased with you," says the LORD Almighty, "and I will accept no offering from your hands. ¹¹My name will be great among the nations, from the rising to the setting of the sun. In every place incense and pure offerings will be brought to my name, because my name will be great among the nations," says the LORD Almighty.

¹²"But you profane it by saying of the Lord's table, 'It is defiled,' and of its food, 'It is contemptible.' ¹³And you say, 'What a burden!' and you sniff at it contemptuously," says the LORD Almighty.

"When you bring injured, crippled or diseased animals and offer them as sacrifices, should I accept them from your hands?" says the LORD. ¹⁴"Cursed is the cheat who has an acceptable male in his flock and vows to give it, but then sacrifices a blemished animal to the Lord. For I am a great king," says the LORD Almighty, "and my name is to be feared among the nations.

Admonition for the Priests

2 "And now this admonition is for you, O priests. ²If you do not listen, and if you do not set your heart to honor my name," says the LORD Almighty, "I will send a curse upon you, and I will curse your blessings. Yes, I have already cursed them, because you have not set your heart to honor me.

³"Because of you I will rebuke[a] your descendants[b]; I will spread on your faces the offal from your festival sacrifices, and you will be carried off with it. ⁴And you will know that I have sent you this admonition so that my covenant with Levi may continue," says the LORD Almighty. ⁵"My covenant was with him, a covenant of life and peace, and I gave them to him; this called for reverence and he revered me and stood in awe of my name. ⁶True instruction was in his mouth and nothing false was found on his lips. He walked with me in peace and uprightness, and turned many from sin.

⁷"For the lips of a priest ought to preserve knowledge, and from his mouth men should seek instruction—because he is the messenger of the LORD Almighty. ⁸But you have turned from the way and by your teaching have caused many to stumble; you have violated the covenant with Levi," says the LORD Almighty. ⁹"So I have caused you to be despised and humiliated before all the people, because you have not followed my ways but have shown partiality in matters of the law."

Judah Unfaithful

¹⁰Have we not all one Father[c]? Did not one God create us? Why do we profane the covenant of our fathers by breaking faith with one another?

¹¹Judah has broken faith. A detestable thing has been committed in Israel and in Jerusalem: Judah has desecrated the sanctuary the LORD loves, by marrying the daughter of a foreign god. ¹²As for the man who does this, whoever he may be, may the LORD cut him off from the tents of Jacob[d]—even though he brings offerings to the LORD Almighty.

¹³Another thing you do: You flood the LORD's altar with tears. You weep and wail because he no longer pays attention to your offerings or accepts them with pleasure from your hands. ¹⁴You ask, "Why?" It is because the LORD is acting as the witness between you and the wife of your youth, because you have broken faith with her, though she is your partner, the wife of your marriage covenant.

¹⁵Has not ⌊the LORD⌋ made them one? In flesh and spirit they are his. And why one? Because he was seeking godly offspring.[e] So guard yourself in your spirit, and do not break faith with the wife of your youth.

¹⁶"I hate divorce," says the LORD God of Israel, "and I hate a man's covering himself[f] with violence as well as with his garment," says the LORD Almighty.

---

[a]3 Or cut off (see Septuagint)   [b]3 Or will blight your grain   [c]10 Or father   [d]12 Or ¹²May the LORD cut off from the tents of Jacob anyone who gives testimony in behalf of the man who does this   [e]15 Or ¹⁵But the one ⌊who is our father⌋ did not do this, not as long as life remained in him. And what was he seeking? An offspring from God   [f]16 Or his wife

So guard yourself in your spirit, and do not break faith.

The Day of Judgment

[17]You have wearied the LORD with your words.

"How have we wearied him?" you ask.

By saying, "All who do evil are good in the eyes of the LORD, and he is pleased with them" or "Where is the God of justice?"

3 "See, I will send my messenger, who will prepare the way before me. Then suddenly the Lord you are seeking will come to his temple; the messenger of the covenant, whom you desire, will come," says the LORD Almighty.

[2]But who can endure the day of his coming? Who can stand when he appears? For he will be like a refiner's fire or a launderer's soap. [3]He will sit as a refiner and purifier of silver; he will purify the Levites and refine them like gold and silver. Then the LORD will have men who will bring offerings in righteousness, [4]and the offerings of Judah and Jerusalem will be acceptable to the LORD, as in days gone by, as in former years.

[5]"So I will come near to you for judgment. I will be quick to testify against sorcerers, adulterers and perjurers, against those who defraud laborers of their wages, who oppress the widows and the fatherless, and deprive aliens of justice, but do not fear me," says the LORD Almighty.

Robbing God

[6]"I the LORD do not change. So you, O descendants of Jacob, are not destroyed. [7]Ever since the time of your forefathers you have turned away from my decrees and have not kept them. Return to me, and I will return to you," says the LORD Almighty.

"But you ask, 'How are we to return?'

[8]"Will a man rob God? Yet you rob me.

"But you ask, 'How do we rob you?'

"In tithes and offerings. [9]You are under a curse—the whole nation of you—because you are robbing me. [10]Bring the whole tithe into the storehouse, that there may be food in my house. Test me in this," says the LORD Almighty, "and see if I will not throw open the floodgates of heaven and pour out so much blessing that you will not have room enough for it. [11]I will prevent pests from devouring your crops, and the vines in your fields will not cast their fruit," says the LORD Almighty. [12]"Then all the nations will call you blessed, for yours will be a delightful land," says the LORD Almighty.

[13]"You have said harsh things against me," says the LORD.

Cultivating Faithfulness

Friday

MALACHI 2:13–16 Tears, pleading and offerings can never replace faithfulness to your marriage covenant. Just ask anyone who has experienced the devastation of infidelity. As we've counseled couples who are dealing with infidelity, one thing is clear—in most cases they weren't focusing on cultivating faithfulness in their marriage.

In order to affair-proof your marriage, look again at the Bible's perspective of infidelity. God takes this seriously, and we should too. While this passage refers to divorce and breaking the vow of faithfulness, we have the opportunity to live out faithfulness daily in our marriages in little ways.

Faithfulness is not just achieved by avoiding affairs; it also involves being considerate—calling when you are going to be late, giving and receiving love and affection, getting up with the baby or waiting up for your night-owl teenager to come home.

With all life's stresses, it's easy to grow apart emotionally. You can get so busy with careers, children and other activities that you have little time and energy to invest in your marriage. Let us encourage you to invest in each other every day. Think about all the time, worry and energy you'll save if you don't have to battle with infidelity.

—Dave & Claudia

Go to page 1023 for your next devotional reading.

"Yet you ask, 'What have we said against you?'

¹⁴"You have said, 'It is futile to serve God. What did we gain by carrying out his requirements and going about like mourners before the LORD Almighty? ¹⁵But now we call the arrogant blessed. Certainly the evildoers prosper, and even those who challenge God escape.' "

¹⁶Then those who feared the LORD talked with each other, and the LORD listened and heard. A scroll of remembrance was written in his presence concerning those who feared the LORD and honored his name.

¹⁷"They will be mine," says the LORD Almighty, "in the day when I make up my treasured possession.ᵃ I will spare them, just as in compassion a man spares his son who serves him. ¹⁸And you will again see the distinction between the righteous and the wicked, between those who serve God and those who do not.

The Day of the LORD

4 "Surely the day is coming; it will burn like a furnace. All the arrogant and every evildoer will be stubble, and that day that is coming will set them on fire," says the LORD Almighty. "Not a root or a branch will be left to them. ²But for you who revere my name, the sun of righteousness will rise with healing in its wings. And you will go out and leap like calves released from the stall. ³Then you will trample down the wicked; they will be ashes under the soles of your feet on the day when I do these things," says the LORD Almighty.

⁴"Remember the law of my servant Moses, the decrees and laws I gave him at Horeb for all Israel.

⁵"See, I will send you the prophet Elijah before that great and dreadful day of the LORD comes. ⁶He will turn the hearts of the fathers to their children, and the hearts of the children to their fathers; or else I will come and strike the land with a curse."

ᵃ17 Or Almighty, "my treasured possession, in the day when I act

Conversion of the Purse

MALACHI 3:8–10 Religious reformer Martin Luther observed that there are three conversions necessary: the conversion of the heart, the mind and the purse. Of the three, the purse can be the most difficult. Agreeing on money matters can be tough, and, for many couples, agreeing on tithes and offerings presents a special challenge.

A fundamental shift in attitude toward giving took place in our home when we changed the question we were asking each other. Rather than, "How much of our money should we give to God," we learned to ask, "How much of God's money should we spend on ourselves?" The difference between these two questions was monumental for us. It helped us to remember that our financial resources are not partly ours and partly God's. Our income is *all* God's (see Exodus 19:5–6; Job 41:11; Psalm 24:1).

Although having this attitude is sometimes hard, especially when the bills pile up and the car needs to go the mechanic—again! But if we trust in God, he will surely provide what we need to pay the bills . . . and then again some.   —*Les & Leslie*

Weekend Warm-up   *Is tithing a priority for you?*

Go to page 1028 for your next devotional reading.

New
TESTAMENT

Matthew

*Have you
ever read a sequel* to a novel without having read
the original story? The book of Matthew picks up the story
line between the Old and New Testaments, helping us
understand how the life and teachings of Jesus build upon
what God had promised his people for centuries. The Jewish
people in Jesus' day had been waiting for the promised
Messiah to come to inaugurate God's kingdom on earth.
Matthew draws heavily from material from the Old
Testament, offering proof that Jesus is the One Israel has
been waiting for.

The Genealogy of Jesus

1 A record of the genealogy of Jesus Christ the son of David, the son of Abraham:

²Abraham was the father of Isaac,
Isaac the father of Jacob,
Jacob the father of Judah and his
brothers,
³Judah the father of Perez and
Zerah, whose mother was
Tamar,
Perez the father of Hezron,
Hezron the father of Ram,
⁴Ram the father of Amminadab,
Amminadab the father of Nah-
shon,
Nahshon the father of Salmon,
⁵Salmon the father of Boaz, whose
mother was Rahab,
Boaz the father of Obed, whose
mother was Ruth,
Obed the father of Jesse,
⁶and Jesse the father of King Da-
vid.

David was the father of Solomon,
whose mother had been Uriah's wife,
⁷Solomon the father of Rehoboam,
Rehoboam the father of Abijah,
Abijah the father of Asa,
⁸Asa the father of Jehoshaphat,
Jehoshaphat the father of Jehoram,
Jehoram the father of Uzziah,
⁹Uzziah the father of Jotham,
Jotham the father of Ahaz,
Ahaz the father of Hezekiah,
¹⁰Hezekiah the father of Manasseh,
Manasseh the father of Amon,
Amon the father of Josiah,
¹¹and Josiah the father of Jeconi-

ah[a] and his brothers at the time of the exile to Babylon.

¹²After the exile to Babylon:

Jeconiah was the father of Shealtiel,

Shealtiel the father of Zerubbabel,

¹³Zerubbabel the father of Abiud,

Abiud the father of Eliakim,

Eliakim the father of Azor,

¹⁴Azor the father of Zadok,

Zadok the father of Akim,

Akim the father of Eliud,

¹⁵Eliud the father of Eleazar,

Eleazar the father of Matthan,

Matthan the father of Jacob,

¹⁶and Jacob the father of Joseph, the husband of Mary, of whom was born Jesus, who is called Christ.

¹⁷Thus there were fourteen generations in all from Abraham to David, fourteen from David to the exile to Babylon, and fourteen from the exile to the Christ.[b]

The Birth of Jesus Christ

¹⁸This is how the birth of Jesus Christ came about: His mother Mary was pledged to be married to Joseph, but before they came together, she was found to be with child through the Holy Spirit. ¹⁹Because Joseph her husband was a righteous man and did not want to expose her to public disgrace, he had in mind to divorce her quietly.

²⁰But after he had considered this, an angel of the Lord appeared to him in a dream and said, "Joseph son of David, do not be afraid to take Mary home as your wife, because what is conceived in her is from the Holy Spirit. ²¹She will give birth to a son, and you are to give him the name Jesus,[c] because he will save his people from their sins."

²²All this took place to fulfill what the Lord had said through the prophet: ²³"The virgin will be with child and will give birth to a son, and they will call him Immanuel"[d]—which means, "God with us."

²⁴When Joseph woke up, he did what the angel of the Lord had commanded him and took Mary home as his wife. ²⁵But he had no union with her until she

---

[a]11 That is, Jehoiachin; also in verse 12
[b]17 Or *Messiah*. "The Christ" (Greek) and "the Messiah" (Hebrew) both mean "the Anointed One."
[c]21 *Jesus* is the Greek form of *Joshua*, which means the LORD *saves.*   [d]23 Isaiah 7:14

A Role Model

Monday

MATTHEW 1:18–19 In the beautiful story of our Lord's birth, there is a principal character who is often overlooked. While we often hear about the events of Mary's life, Joseph, the stepfather of Jesus, gets less attention. Yet we can learn much from this role model. In this passage we see Joseph wrestling with the difficult and painful decision of what to do about the unexpected pregnancy of Mary, the woman he was engaged to. Under the law there were several options available to him. Deuteronomy 22:23–24 describes the punishment for a woman who violates an engagement—she was to be stoned. Another option Joseph had was to quietly divorce her. He chose neither option.

The action Joseph chose revealed several character traits that are an example to

us all. First, he exhibited righteousness. His desire was to please God rather than do what was legally allowed. Second, we see in Joseph a deep sensitivity and compassion. In spite of the humiliation he undoubtedly thought he would be exposed to, he had concern for Mary. He was sensitive and compassionate to her feelings by not wanting her to be publicly disgraced. Finally, we see Joseph's obedience to God. When he received instructions from the angel of God, Joseph immediately did as he was told (see verses 20–21, 24). He did not hesitate. He obeyed.

Joseph serves as a wonderful example for us when we are faced with situations that don't always go as planned.

—**Bob and Rosemary**

Go to page 1033 for your next devotional reading.

gave birth to a son. And he gave him the name Jesus.

The Visit of the Magi

2 After Jesus was born in Bethlehem in Judea, during the time of King Herod, Magi[a] from the east came to Jerusalem [2]and asked, "Where is the one who has been born king of the Jews? We saw his star in the east[b] and have come to worship him."

[3]When King Herod heard this he was disturbed, and all Jerusalem with him. [4]When he had called together all the people's chief priests and teachers of the law, he asked them where the Christ[c] was to be born. [5]"In Bethlehem in Judea," they replied, "for this is what the prophet has written:

[6]" 'But you, Bethlehem, in the land of
     Judah,
   are by no means least among the
        rulers of Judah;
   for out of you will come a ruler
     who will be the shepherd of my
        people Israel.'[d] "

[7]Then Herod called the Magi secretly and found out from them the exact time the star had appeared. [8]He sent them to Bethlehem and said, "Go and make a careful search for the child. As soon as you find him, report to me, so that I too may go and worship him."

[9]After they had heard the king, they went on their way, and the star they had seen in the east[e] went ahead of them until it stopped over the place where the child was. [10]When they saw the star, they were overjoyed. [11]On coming to the house, they saw the child with his mother Mary, and they bowed down and worshiped him. Then they opened their treasures and presented him with gifts of gold and of incense and of myrrh. [12]And having been warned in a dream not to go back to Herod, they returned to their country by another route.

The Escape to Egypt

[13]When they had gone, an angel of the Lord appeared to Joseph in a dream. "Get up," he said, "take the child and his mother and escape to Egypt. Stay there until I tell you, for Herod is going to search for the child to kill him."

[14]So he got up, took the child and his mother during the night and left for Egypt, [15]where he stayed until the death of Herod. And so was fulfilled what the Lord had said through the prophet: "Out of Egypt I called my son."[f]

[16]When Herod realized that he had been outwitted by the Magi, he was furious, and he gave orders to kill all the boys in Bethlehem and its vicinity who were two years old and under, in accordance with the time he had learned from the Magi. [17]Then what was said through the prophet Jeremiah was fulfilled:

[18]"A voice is heard in Ramah,
     weeping and great mourning,
   Rachel weeping for her children
     and refusing to be comforted,
   because they are no more."[g]

The Return to Nazareth

[19]After Herod died, an angel of the Lord appeared in a dream to Joseph in Egypt [20]and said, "Get up, take the child and his mother and go to the land of Israel, for those who were trying to take the child's life are dead."

[21]So he got up, took the child and his mother and went to the land of Israel. [22]But when he heard that Archelaus was reigning in Judea in place of his father Herod, he was afraid to go there. Having been warned in a dream, he withdrew to the district of Galilee, [23]and he went and lived in a town called Nazareth. So was fulfilled what was said through the prophets: "He will be called a Nazarene."

John the Baptist Prepares the Way

3 In those days John the Baptist came, preaching in the Desert of Judea [2]and saying, "Repent, for the kingdom of heaven is near." [3]This is he who was spoken of through the prophet Isaiah:

"A voice of one calling in the desert,
   'Prepare the way for the Lord,
     make straight paths for him.' "[h]

---

[a]1 Traditionally *Wise Men*   [b]2 Or *star when it rose*   [c]4 Or *Messiah*   [d]6 Micah 5:2
[e]9 Or *seen when it rose*   [f]15 Hosea 11:1
[g]18 Jer. 31:15   [h]3 Isaiah 40:3

[4]John's clothes were made of camel's hair, and he had a leather belt around his waist. His food was locusts and wild honey. [5]People went out to him from Jerusalem and all Judea and the whole region of the Jordan. [6]Confessing their sins, they were baptized by him in the Jordan River.

[7]But when he saw many of the Pharisees and Sadducees coming to where he was baptizing, he said to them: "You brood of vipers! Who warned you to flee from the coming wrath? [8]Produce fruit in keeping with repentance. [9]And do not think you can say to yourselves, 'We have Abraham as our father.' I tell you that out of these stones God can raise up children for Abraham. [10]The ax is already at the root of the trees, and every tree that does not produce good fruit will be cut down and thrown into the fire.

[11]"I baptize you with[a] water for repentance. But after me will come one who is more powerful than I, whose sandals I am not fit to carry. He will baptize you with the Holy Spirit and with fire. [12]His winnowing fork is in his hand, and he will clear his threshing floor, gathering his wheat into the barn and burning up the chaff with unquenchable fire."

The Baptism of Jesus

[13]Then Jesus came from Galilee to the Jordan to be baptized by John. [14]But John tried to deter him, saying, "I need to be baptized by you, and do you come to me?"

[15]Jesus replied, "Let it be so now; it is proper for us to do this to fulfill all righteousness." Then John consented.

[16]As soon as Jesus was baptized, he went up out of the water. At that moment heaven was opened, and he saw the Spirit of God descending like a dove and lighting on him. [17]And a voice from heaven said, "This is my Son, whom I love; with him I am well pleased."

The Temptation of Jesus

4 Then Jesus was led by the Spirit into the desert to be tempted by the devil. [2]After fasting forty days and forty nights, he was hungry. [3]The tempter came to him and said, "If you are the Son of God, tell these stones to become bread."

[4]Jesus answered, "It is written: 'Man does not live on bread alone, but on every word that comes from the mouth of God.'[b]"

[5]Then the devil took him to the holy city and had him stand on the highest point of the temple. [6]"If you are the Son of God," he said, "throw yourself down. For it is written:

" 'He will command his angels
        concerning you,
    and they will lift you up in their
        hands,
so that you will not strike your foot
        against a stone.'[c]"

[7]Jesus answered him, "It is also written: 'Do not put the Lord your God to the test.'[d]"

[8]Again, the devil took him to a very high mountain and showed him all the kingdoms of the world and their splendor. [9]"All this I will give you," he said, "if you will bow down and worship me."

[10]Jesus said to him, "Away from me, Satan! For it is written: 'Worship the Lord your God, and serve him only.'[e]"

[11]Then the devil left him, and angels came and attended him.

Jesus Begins to Preach

[12]When Jesus heard that John had been put in prison, he returned to Galilee. [13]Leaving Nazareth, he went and lived in Capernaum, which was by the lake in the area of Zebulun and Naphtali— [14]to fulfill what was said through the prophet Isaiah:

[15]"Land of Zebulun and land of
        Naphtali,
    the way to the sea, along the
        Jordan,
    Galilee of the Gentiles—
[16]the people living in darkness
    have seen a great light;
on those living in the land of the
        shadow of death
    a light has dawned."[f]

[17]From that time on Jesus began to preach, "Repent, for the kingdom of heaven is near."

The Calling of the First Disciples

[18]As Jesus was walking beside the Sea

[a]11 Or in   [b]4 Deut. 8:3   [c]6 Psalm 91:11,12
[d]7 Deut. 6:16   [e]10 Deut. 6:13
[f]16 Isaiah 9:1,2

of Galilee, he saw two brothers, Simon called Peter and his brother Andrew. They were casting a net into the lake, for they were fishermen. ¹⁹"Come, follow me," Jesus said, "and I will make you fishers of men." ²⁰At once they left their nets and followed him.

²¹Going on from there, he saw two other brothers, James son of Zebedee and his brother John. They were in a boat with their father Zebedee, preparing their nets. Jesus called them, ²²and immediately they left the boat and their father and followed him.

Jesus Heals the Sick

²³Jesus went throughout Galilee, teaching in their synagogues, preaching the good news of the kingdom, and healing every disease and sickness among the people. ²⁴News about him spread all over Syria, and people brought to him all who were ill with various diseases, those suffering severe pain, the demon-possessed, those having seizures, and the paralyzed, and he healed them. ²⁵Large crowds from Galilee, the Decapolis,ᵃ Jerusalem, Judea and the region across the Jordan followed him.

The Beatitudes

5 Now when he saw the crowds, he went up on a mountainside and sat down. His disciples came to him, ²and he began to teach them, saying:

³"Blessed are the poor in spirit,
    for theirs is the kingdom of
        heaven.
⁴Blessed are those who mourn,
    for they will be comforted.
⁵Blessed are the meek,
    for they will inherit the earth.
⁶Blessed are those who hunger and
        thirst for righteousness,
    for they will be filled.
⁷Blessed are the merciful,
    for they will be shown mercy.
⁸Blessed are the pure in heart,
    for they will see God.
⁹Blessed are the peacemakers,
    for they will be called sons of God.
¹⁰Blessed are those who are persecuted
        because of righteousness,
    for theirs is the kingdom of
        heaven.

¹¹"Blessed are you when people insult you, persecute you and falsely say all kinds of evil against you because of me. ¹²Rejoice and be glad, because great is your reward in heaven, for in the same way they persecuted the prophets who were before you.

Salt and Light

¹³"You are the salt of the earth. But if the salt loses its saltiness, how can it be made salty again? It is no longer good for anything, except to be thrown out and trampled by men.

¹⁴"You are the light of the world. A city on a hill cannot be hidden. ¹⁵Neither do people light a lamp and put it under a bowl. Instead they put it on its stand, and it gives light to everyone in the house. ¹⁶In the same way, let your light shine before men, that they may see your good deeds and praise your Father in heaven.

The Fulfillment of the Law

¹⁷"Do not think that I have come to abolish the Law or the Prophets; I have not come to abolish them but to fulfill them. ¹⁸I tell you the truth, until heaven and earth disappear, not the smallest letter, not the least stroke of a pen, will by any means disappear from the Law until everything is accomplished. ¹⁹Anyone who breaks one of the least of these commandments and teaches others to do the same will be called least in the kingdom of heaven, but whoever practices and teaches these commands will be called great in the kingdom of heaven. ²⁰For I tell you that unless your righteousness surpasses that of the Pharisees and the teachers of the law, you will certainly not enter the kingdom of heaven.

Murder

²¹"You have heard that it was said to the people long ago, 'Do not murder,ᵇ and anyone who murders will be subject to judgment.' ²²But I tell you that anyone who is angry with his brotherᶜ will be subject to judgment. Again, anyone who says to his brother, 'Raca,ᵈ' is answer-

---

ᵃ25 That is, the Ten Cities   ᵇ21 Exodus 20:13
ᶜ22 Some manuscripts *brother without cause*
ᵈ22 An Aramaic term of contempt

able to the Sanhedrin. But anyone who says, 'You fool!' will be in danger of the fire of hell.

²³ "Therefore, if you are offering your gift at the altar and there remember that your brother has something against you, ²⁴leave your gift there in front of the altar. First go and be reconciled to your brother; then come and offer your gift.

²⁵ "Settle matters quickly with your adversary who is taking you to court. Do it while you are still with him on the way, or he may hand you over to the judge, and the judge may hand you over to the officer, and you may be thrown into prison. ²⁶I tell you the truth, you will not get out until you have paid the last penny.ᵃ

Adultery

²⁷ "You have heard that it was said, 'Do not commit adultery.'ᵇ ²⁸But I tell you that anyone who looks at a woman lustfully has already committed adultery with her in his heart. ²⁹If your right eye causes you to sin, gouge it out and throw it away. It is better for you to lose one part of your body than for your whole body to be thrown into hell. ³⁰And if your right hand causes you to sin, cut it off and throw it away. It is better for you to lose one part of your body than for your whole body to go into hell.

Divorce

³¹ "It has been said, 'Anyone who divorces his wife must give her a certificate of divorce.'ᶜ ³²But I tell you that anyone who divorces his wife, except for marital unfaithfulness, causes her to become an adulteress, and anyone who marries the divorced woman commits adultery.

Oaths

³³ "Again, you have heard that it was said to the people long ago, 'Do not break your oath, but keep the oaths you have made to the Lord.' ³⁴But I tell you, Do not swear at all: either by heaven, for it is God's throne; ³⁵or by the earth, for it is his footstool; or by Jerusalem, for it is the city of the Great King. ³⁶And do not swear by your head, for you cannot make even one hair white or black. ³⁷Simply let your 'Yes' be 'Yes,' and your 'No,' 'No'; anything beyond this comes from the evil one.

An Eye for an Eye

³⁸ "You have heard that it was said, 'Eye for eye, and tooth for tooth.'ᵈ ³⁹But I tell you, Do not resist an evil person. If someone strikes you on the right cheek, turn to him the other also. ⁴⁰And if someone wants to sue you and take your tunic, let him have your cloak as well. ⁴¹If someone forces you to go one mile, go with him two miles. ⁴²Give to the one who asks you, and do not turn away from the one who wants to borrow from you.

Love for Enemies

⁴³ "You have heard that it was said, 'Love your neighborᵉ and hate your enemy.' ⁴⁴But I tell you: Love your enemiesᶠ and pray for those who persecute you, ⁴⁵that you may be sons of your Father in heaven. He causes his sun to rise on the evil and the good, and sends rain on the righteous and the unrighteous. ⁴⁶If you love those who love you, what reward will you get? Are not even the tax collectors doing that? ⁴⁷And if you greet only your brothers, what are you doing more than others? Do not even pagans do that? ⁴⁸Be perfect, therefore, as your heavenly Father is perfect.

Giving to the Needy

6 "Be careful not to do your 'acts of righteousness' before men, to be seen by them. If you do, you will have no reward from your Father in heaven.

² "So when you give to the needy, do not announce it with trumpets, as the hypocrites do in the synagogues and on the streets, to be honored by men. I tell you the truth, they have received their reward in full. ³But when you give to the needy, do not let your left hand know what your right hand is doing, ⁴so that your giving may be in secret. Then your Father, who sees what is done in secret, will reward you.

Prayer

⁵ "And when you pray, do not be like

ᵃ26 Greek kodrantes   ᵇ27 Exodus 20:14
ᶜ31 Deut. 24:1   ᵈ38 Exodus 21:24; Lev. 24:20;
Deut. 19:21   ᵉ43 Lev. 19:18   ᶠ44 Some late
manuscripts enemies, bless those who curse you, do
good to those who hate you

the hypocrites, for they love to pray standing in the synagogues and on the street corners to be seen by men. I tell you the truth, they have received their reward in full. ⁶But when you pray, go into your room, close the door and pray to your Father, who is unseen. Then your Father, who sees what is done in secret, will reward you. ⁷And when you pray, do not keep on babbling like pagans, for they think they will be heard because of their many words. ⁸Do not be like them, for your Father knows what you need before you ask him.

⁹"This, then, is how you should pray:

" 'Our Father in heaven,
hallowed be your name,
¹⁰your kingdom come,
your will be done
    on earth as it is in heaven.

¹¹Give us today our daily bread.
¹²Forgive us our debts,
    as we also have forgiven our
        debtors.
¹³And lead us not into temptation,
    but deliver us from the evil one.ᵃ'

¹⁴For if you forgive men when they sin against you, your heavenly Father will also forgive you. ¹⁵But if you do not forgive men their sins, your Father will not forgive your sins.

Fasting

¹⁶"When you fast, do not look somber as the hypocrites do, for they disfigure their faces to show men they are fasting.

ᵃ13 Or *from evil*; some late manuscripts *one, / for yours is the kingdom and the power and the glory forever. Amen.*

The Extra-mile Marriage

Tuesday

MATTHEW 5:40–42 Perhaps the most shocking statement Jesus ever made holds enough power to revolutionize your marriage. He said, "If someone forces you to go one mile, go with him two miles" (verse 41).

Have you learned to apply the extra mile principle to your marriage? Every husband and wife knows how to walk the first mile. After all, our relationships couldn't survive without it. The first mile is what we know we have to do. It is taking out the trash, preparing dinner or balancing the checkbook because we said we would do it.

So what's the second mile? At the time Jesus made this statement, the Roman army had a pesky practice of forcing men and boys who were nearby to carry their soldier's packs. Being more civilized than other armies, the Romans limited the task to one mile. And every boy under Roman rule knew exactly how far that was. In fact, as a marker, most boys drove a stake into the ground precisely one mile from their house. This way, when a soldier required the task, the boy would walk exactly a mile down the road to the stake, set the pack on the other side and be done with it. That was all he was required, and nobody expected more.

Jesus used this illustration to point out that we sometimes do the same thing in our relationships. We measure out exactly how much is expected and do just that, nothing more. Let's face it—with our hectic pace most of us do just enough to squeak by even in the relationship that matters most. So, yes, we grumble and take out the trash, or we whine and make the meal, but only because we have to. Jesus, however, says there is a better way—to do more than the minimum.

The extra mile turns the ordinary into the extraordinary, the expected into to the unexpected. You walk the extra mile for your partner, for example, when you take out the trash with a smile or prepare a meal with a special touch. The extra mile turns responsibility into opportunity. When you are walking the extra mile in marriage, your attitude shifts from "have to" to "want to."
                              —Les and Leslie

Go to page 1034 for your next devotional reading.

I tell you the truth, they have received their reward in full. [17]But when you fast, put oil on your head and wash your face, [18]so that it will not be obvious to men that you are fasting, but only to your Father, who is unseen; and your Father, who sees what is done in secret, will reward you.

Treasures in Heaven

[19]"Do not store up for yourselves treasures on earth, where moth and rust destroy, and where thieves break in and steal. [20]But store up for yourselves treasures in heaven, where moth and rust do not destroy, and where thieves do not break in and steal. [21]For where your treasure is, there your heart will be also.

[22]"The eye is the lamp of the body. If your eyes are good, your whole body will be full of light. [23]But if your eyes are bad, your whole body will be full of darkness. If then the light within you is darkness, how great is that darkness!

[24]"No one can serve two masters. Either he will hate the one and love the other, or he will be devoted to the one and despise the other. You cannot serve both God and Money.

Do Not Worry

[25]"Therefore I tell you, do not worry about your life, what you will eat or drink; or about your body, what you will wear. Is not life more important than food, and the body more important than clothes? [26]Look at the birds of the air; they do not sow or reap or store away in barns, and yet your heavenly Father feeds them. Are you not much more valuable than they? [27]Who of you by worrying can add a single hour to his life[a]?

[28]"And why do you worry about clothes? See how the lilies of the field grow. They do not labor or spin. [29]Yet I tell you that not even Solomon in all his splendor was dressed like one of these. [30]If that is how God clothes the grass of the field, which is here today and tomorrow is thrown into the fire, will he not much more clothe you, O you of little faith? [31]So do not worry, saying, 'What shall we eat?' or 'What shall we drink?' or 'What shall we wear?' [32]For the pagans run after all these things, and your heavenly Father knows that you need them. [33]But seek first his kingdom and his righ-

[a]27 Or *single cubit to his height*

Money Matters

Wednesday

MATTHEW 6:19–21 "When my husband and I agreed that I should quit my job to stay home with our daughter," Jenny confided in us, "our income suffered an incredible hit. And at the beginning of each month, Dan and I nearly came to blows ourselves. As we faced a huge pile of unpaid bills, our arguments did nothing but escalate."

Sound familiar? Money is the number one thing couples fight about. Since financial decisions have to be made almost daily, they are frequent fodder for fights. Many underlying emotional issues can cause money battles. Sometimes it's power and control. Sometimes the fights stem from the couple's different family backgrounds. What's surprising to many couples is that money fights are not a function of how much money you have or don't have. It has more to do with the attitudes each of you brings to money itself. And the more important money is to you, the more you prize it—whether you are a hoarder or a spender—the more likely you are to have fights about it in your home.

Every marriage must protect itself against greed. One of the best ways to do this is to give money away. That's right, give it away. God has given us all that we have. And by giving a portion of what he has given us back to him, we help free ourselves from its tyranny. The Bible calls us to give money away (see Luke 12:33, page 1122). And to do that, we must take Christ's famous exhortation and apply it to our checkbooks: "Where your treasure is," Jesus said, "there your heart will be also" (verse 21).   **—Les and Leslie**

Go to page 1036 for your next devotional reading.

teousness, and all these things will be given to you as well. [34]Therefore do not worry about tomorrow, for tomorrow will worry about itself. Each day has enough trouble of its own.

Judging Others

7 "Do not judge, or you too will be judged. [2]For in the same way you judge others, you will be judged, and with the measure you use, it will be measured to you.

[3]"Why do you look at the speck of sawdust in your brother's eye and pay no attention to the plank in your own eye? [4]How can you say to your brother, 'Let me take the speck out of your eye,' when all the time there is a plank in your own eye? [5]You hypocrite, first take the plank out of your own eye, and then you will see clearly to remove the speck from your brother's eye.

[6]"Do not give dogs what is sacred; do not throw your pearls to pigs. If you do, they may trample them under their feet, and then turn and tear you to pieces.

Ask, Seek, Knock

[7]"Ask and it will be given to you; seek and you will find; knock and the door will be opened to you. [8]For everyone who asks receives; he who seeks finds; and to him who knocks, the door will be opened.

[9]"Which of you, if his son asks for bread, will give him a stone? [10]Or if he asks for a fish, will give him a snake? [11]If you, then, though you are evil, know how to give good gifts to your children, how much more will your Father in heaven give good gifts to those who ask him! [12]So in everything, do to others what you would have them do to you, for this sums up the Law and the Prophets.

The Narrow and Wide Gates

[13]"Enter through the narrow gate. For wide is the gate and broad is the road that leads to destruction, and many enter through it. [14]But small is the gate and narrow the road that leads to life, and only a few find it.

A Tree and Its Fruit

[15]"Watch out for false prophets. They come to you in sheep's clothing, but inwardly they are ferocious wolves. [16]By their fruit you will recognize them. Do people pick grapes from thornbushes, or figs from thistles? [17]Likewise every good tree bears good fruit, but a bad tree bears bad fruit. [18]A good tree cannot bear bad fruit, and a bad tree cannot bear good fruit. [19]Every tree that does not bear good fruit is cut down and thrown into the fire. [20]Thus, by their fruit you will recognize them.

[21]"Not everyone who says to me, 'Lord, Lord,' will enter the kingdom of heaven, but only he who does the will of my Father who is in heaven. [22]Many will say to me on that day, 'Lord, Lord, did we not prophesy in your name, and in your name drive out demons and perform many miracles?' [23]Then I will tell them plainly, 'I never knew you. Away from me, you evildoers!'

The Wise and Foolish Builders

[24]"Therefore everyone who hears these words of mine and puts them into practice is like a wise man who built his house on the rock. [25]The rain came down, the streams rose, and the winds blew and beat against that house; yet it did not fall, because it had its foundation on the rock. [26]But everyone who hears these words of mine and does not put them into practice is like a foolish man who built his house on sand. [27]The rain came down, the streams rose, and the winds blew and beat against that house, and it fell with a great crash."

[28]When Jesus had finished saying these things, the crowds were amazed at his teaching, [29]because he taught as one who had authority, and not as their teachers of the law.

The Man With Leprosy

8 When he came down from the mountainside, large crowds followed him. [2]A man with leprosy[a] came and knelt before him and said, "Lord, if you are willing, you can make me clean."

---

[a]2 The Greek word was used for various diseases affecting the skin—not necessarily leprosy.

[3]Jesus reached out his hand and touched the man. "I am willing," he said. "Be clean!" Immediately he was cured[a] of his leprosy. [4]Then Jesus said to him, "See that you don't tell anyone. But go, show yourself to the priest and offer the gift Moses commanded, as a testimony to them."

The Faith of the Centurion

[5]When Jesus had entered Capernaum, a centurion came to him, asking for help. [6]"Lord," he said, "my servant lies at home paralyzed and in terrible suffering."

[7]Jesus said to him, "I will go and heal him."

[8]The centurion replied, "Lord, I do not deserve to have you come under my roof. But just say the word, and my servant will be healed. [9]For I myself am a man under authority, with soldiers under me. I tell this one, 'Go,' and he goes; and that one, 'Come,' and he comes. I say to my servant, 'Do this,' and he does it."

[10]When Jesus heard this, he was astonished and said to those following him, "I tell you the truth, I have not found anyone in Israel with such great faith. [11]I say to you that many will come from the east and the west, and will take their places at the feast with Abraham, Isaac and Jacob in the kingdom of heaven. [12]But the subjects of the kingdom will be thrown outside, into the darkness, where there will be weeping and gnashing of teeth."

[13]Then Jesus said to the centurion, "Go! It will be done just as you believed it would." And his servant was healed at that very hour.

Jesus Heals Many

[14]When Jesus came into Peter's house, he saw Peter's mother-in-law lying in bed with a fever. [15]He touched her hand and the fever left her, and she got up and began to wait on him.

[16]When evening came, many who were demon-possessed were brought to him, and he drove out the spirits with a word and healed all the sick. [17]This was to ful-

a3 Greek made clean

Log Removal

Thursday

MATTHEW 7:3–5 Did you ever notice that some of the things that attracted you to each other before marriage became irritating after marriage? Claudia's whirlwind of energy simply tired me out, while my laid-back, easy-going disposition translated into boring evenings at home for Claudia.

Even after over thirty-five years of marriage, we still can respond inappropriately to each other's differences. For example, Claudia still gets upset when I "casually" pause to clip my fingernails when we are already late for a dinner date. And I get frustrated with Claudia's "endless" chatter when she tells me the same story over and over again.

At times like these we need to practice "log removal" by taking the log out of our own eye before we are critical of others (see verse 5). Start by making a list of your spouse's differences that trigger an inappropriate response in you. Perhaps your mate is not time oriented and tends to be late. Do you assume that he or she just doesn't care or is trying to annoy you by not being on time? What is your typical response? Do you lecture, sigh or give the silent treatment?

As you consider your own "logs," you may find that your responses are worse than your mate's differences. No relationship can thrive without forgiveness; we all blow it from time to time. So rather than flame the fires of anger and frustration, try to deal with inappropriate reactions. Ask your spouse for forgiveness and be willing to forgive when your spouse also reacts badly to your differences. Instead of trying to change your mate, concentrate on being the person your mate needs.

—Dave and Claudia

Go to page 1038 for your next devotional reading.

fill what was spoken through the prophet Isaiah:

> "He took up our infirmities
>   and carried our diseases." [a]

The Cost of Following Jesus

18When Jesus saw the crowd around him, he gave orders to cross to the other side of the lake. 19Then a teacher of the law came to him and said, "Teacher, I will follow you wherever you go."

20Jesus replied, "Foxes have holes and birds of the air have nests, but the Son of Man has no place to lay his head."

21Another disciple said to him, "Lord, first let me go and bury my father."

22But Jesus told him, "Follow me, and let the dead bury their own dead."

Jesus Calms the Storm

23Then he got into the boat and his disciples followed him. 24Without warning, a furious storm came up on the lake, so that the waves swept over the boat. But Jesus was sleeping. 25The disciples went and woke him, saying, "Lord, save us! We're going to drown!"

26He replied, "You of little faith, why are you so afraid?" Then he got up and rebuked the winds and the waves, and it was completely calm.

27The men were amazed and asked, "What kind of man is this? Even the winds and the waves obey him!"

The Healing of Two Demon-possessed Men

28When he arrived at the other side in the region of the Gadarenes,[b] two demon-possessed men coming from the tombs met him. They were so violent that no one could pass that way. 29"What do you want with us, Son of God?" they shouted. "Have you come here to torture us before the appointed time?"

30Some distance from them a large herd of pigs was feeding. 31The demons begged Jesus, "If you drive us out, send us into the herd of pigs."

32He said to them, "Go!" So they came out and went into the pigs, and the whole herd rushed down the steep bank into the lake and died in the water. 33Those tending the pigs ran off, went into the town and reported all this, including what had

JUST BETWEEN you & me

Log Removal

Often we are so concerned with our spouse's actions that we cannot see our own faults. To clear your vision, follow these steps:

1. Make two columns on a sheet of paper. In the left column, list your mate's perceived faults. In the right column, list your inappropriate responses to each. (You may find your responses are worse than your mate's faults.) For instance, if your mate is late, do you criticize, compare with others, get angry, nag or give the silent treatment?)

2. Admit to God your inappropriate response and attitudes. (Remember, emphasize your inappropriate responses and attitudes, not your mate's.)

3. Accept one of your mate's weaknesses or faults.

4. Ask your mate's forgiveness for your past negative responses.

5. Be willing to forgive your spouse—even when not asked.

happened to the demon-possessed men. 34Then the whole town went out to meet Jesus. And when they saw him, they pleaded with him to leave their region.

Jesus Heals a Paralytic

9 Jesus stepped into a boat, crossed over and came to his own town. 2Some men brought to him a paralytic, lying on a mat. When Jesus saw their faith, he said to the paralytic, "Take heart, son; your sins are forgiven."

3At this, some of the teachers of the law said to themselves, "This fellow is blaspheming!"

4Knowing their thoughts, Jesus said, "Why do you entertain evil thoughts in your hearts? 5Which is easier: to say, 'Your sins are forgiven,' or to say, 'Get up and walk'? 6But so that you may know that the Son of Man has authority on earth to forgive sins . . ." Then he said to the paralytic, "Get up, take your mat and

*a*17 Isaiah 53:4   *b*28 Some manuscripts *Gergesenes*; others *Gerasenes* go home." ⁷And the man got up and went home. ⁸When the crowd saw this, they were filled with awe; and they praised God, who had given such authority to men.

The Calling of Matthew

⁹As Jesus went on from there, he saw a man named Matthew sitting at the tax collector's booth. "Follow me," he told him, and Matthew got up and followed him.

¹⁰While Jesus was having dinner at Matthew's house, many tax collectors and "sinners" came and ate with him and his disciples. ¹¹When the Pharisees saw this, they asked his disciples, "Why does your teacher eat with tax collectors and 'sinners'?"

¹²On hearing this, Jesus said, "It is not the healthy who need a doctor, but the sick. ¹³But go and learn what this means: 'I desire mercy, not sacrifice.'ᵃ For I have not come to call the righteous, but sinners."

Jesus Questioned About Fasting

¹⁴Then John's disciples came and asked him, "How is it that we and the Pharisees fast, but your disciples do not fast?"

¹⁵Jesus answered, "How can the guests of the bridegroom mourn while he is with them? The time will come when the bridegroom will be taken from them; then they will fast.

¹⁶"No one sews a patch of unshrunk cloth on an old garment, for the patch will pull away from the garment, making the tear worse. ¹⁷Neither do men pour new wine into old wineskins. If they do, the skins will burst, the wine will run out and the wineskins will be ruined. No, they pour new wine into new wineskins, and both are preserved."

A Dead Girl and a Sick Woman

¹⁸While he was saying this, a ruler came and knelt before him and said, "My

ᵃ13 Hosea 6:6

Firm Foundations

Friday

MATTHEW 7:24–25 Foundations are interesting. You can't see them, yet you can't build anything that will last without one. Think of a house or an office building. It is built on top of a foundation of concrete and steel that can't even be seen. As far as the strength and stability of the structure is concerned, the foundation is the most important part. Even tornadoes and hurricanes can't shake a foundation. The shingles and windows—even the whole main floor—could be blown away. But the foundation will remain.

When we consider how this relates to our marriage relationship, it's not the outside appearances that hold the marriage together when the storms come . . . it's the foundation. Many couples build their marriages on shaky foundations that won't withstand the storms. Some count on growing careers or on the acquisition of things. Some even believe that having children will do the job of holding a marriage together when difficulties come. Only too late do couples find out that none of these things will withstand the hard times that blast into every marriage.

There's only one way to prepare a marriage for the storms of life: building on the foundation of a faith in Jesus Christ. Only this foundation of a growing faith in Jesus can help us weather the storms of life. When illness strikes one spouse, the couple must lean on God's strength. Financial difficulties, problems with a difficult teenager, a season when one mate needs to travel away from home —these are times when it's crucial to depend on Jesus and ask him for endurance.

As the storms are weathered, a person's faith is strengthened. Where all other foundations eventually crumble, a foundation built on Christ actually gets stronger. No other foundation can offer that guarantee.

—Bob and Rosemary

Go to page 1041 for your next devotional reading.

daughter has just died. But come and put your hand on her, and she will live." ¹⁹Jesus got up and went with him, and so did his disciples.

²⁰Just then a woman who had been subject to bleeding for twelve years came up behind him and touched the edge of his cloak. ²¹She said to herself, "If I only touch his cloak, I will be healed."

²²Jesus turned and saw her. "Take heart, daughter," he said, "your faith has healed you." And the woman was healed from that moment.

²³When Jesus entered the ruler's house and saw the flute players and the noisy crowd, ²⁴he said, "Go away. The girl is not dead but asleep." But they laughed at him. ²⁵After the crowd had been put outside, he went in and took the girl by the hand, and she got up. ²⁶News of this spread through all that region.

Jesus Heals the Blind and Mute

²⁷As Jesus went on from there, two blind men followed him, calling out, "Have mercy on us, Son of David!"

²⁸When he had gone indoors, the blind men came to him, and he asked them, "Do you believe that I am able to do this?"

"Yes, Lord," they replied.

²⁹Then he touched their eyes and said, "According to your faith will it be done to you"; ³⁰and their sight was restored. Jesus warned them sternly, "See that no one knows about this." ³¹But they went out and spread the news about him all over that region.

³²While they were going out, a man who was demon-possessed and could not talk was brought to Jesus. ³³And when the demon was driven out, the man who had been mute spoke. The crowd was amazed and said, "Nothing like this has ever been seen in Israel."

³⁴But the Pharisees said, "It is by the prince of demons that he drives out demons."

The Workers Are Few

³⁵Jesus went through all the towns and villages, teaching in their synagogues, preaching the good news of the kingdom and healing every disease and sickness. ³⁶When he saw the crowds, he had compassion on them, because they were harassed and helpless, like sheep without a shepherd. ³⁷Then he said to his disciples, "The harvest is plentiful but the workers are few. ³⁸Ask the Lord of the harvest, therefore, to send out workers into his harvest field."

Jesus Sends Out the Twelve

10 He called his twelve disciples to him and gave them authority to drive out evil*ᵃ* spirits and to heal every disease and sickness.

²These are the names of the twelve apostles: first, Simon (who is called Peter) and his brother Andrew; James son of Zebedee, and his brother John; ³Philip and Bartholomew; Thomas and Matthew the tax collector; James son of Alphaeus, and Thaddaeus; ⁴Simon the Zealot and Judas Iscariot, who betrayed him.

⁵These twelve Jesus sent out with the following instructions: "Do not go among the Gentiles or enter any town of the Samaritans. ⁶Go rather to the lost sheep of Israel. ⁷As you go, preach this message: 'The kingdom of heaven is near.' ⁸Heal the sick, raise the dead, cleanse those who have leprosy,*ᵇ* drive out demons. Freely you have received, freely give. ⁹Do not take along any gold or silver or copper in your belts; ¹⁰take no bag for the journey, or extra tunic, or sandals or a staff; for the worker is worth his keep.

¹¹"Whatever town or village you enter, search for some worthy person there and stay at his house until you leave. ¹²As you enter the home, give it your greeting. ¹³If the home is deserving, let your peace rest on it; if it is not, let your peace return to you. ¹⁴If anyone will not welcome you or listen to your words, shake the dust off your feet when you leave that home or town. ¹⁵I tell you the truth, it will be more bearable for Sodom and Gomorrah on the day of judgment than for that town. ¹⁶I am sending you out like sheep among wolves. Therefore be as shrewd as snakes and as innocent as doves.

¹⁷"Be on your guard against men; they will hand you over to the local councils and flog you in their synagogues. ¹⁸On

---

ᵃ1 Greek *unclean*   *ᵇ8* The Greek word was used for various diseases affecting the skin—not necessarily leprosy.

my account you will be brought before governors and kings as witnesses to them and to the Gentiles. ¹⁹But when they arrest you, do not worry about what to say or how to say it. At that time you will be given what to say, ²⁰for it will not be you speaking, but the Spirit of your Father speaking through you.

²¹"Brother will betray brother to death, and a father his child; children will rebel against their parents and have them put to death. ²²All men will hate you because of me, but he who stands firm to the end will be saved. ²³When you are persecuted in one place, flee to another. I tell you the truth, you will not finish going through the cities of Israel before the Son of Man comes.

²⁴"A student is not above his teacher, nor a servant above his master. ²⁵It is enough for the student to be like his teacher, and the servant like his master. If the head of the house has been called Beelzebub,ᵃ how much more the members of his household!

²⁶"So do not be afraid of them. There is nothing concealed that will not be disclosed, or hidden that will not be made known. ²⁷What I tell you in the dark, speak in the daylight; what is whispered in your ear, proclaim from the roofs. ²⁸Do not be afraid of those who kill the body but cannot kill the soul. Rather, be afraid of the One who can destroy both soul and body in hell. ²⁹Are not two sparrows sold for a pennyᵇ? Yet not one of them will fall to the ground apart from the will of your Father. ³⁰And even the very hairs of your head are all numbered. ³¹So don't be afraid; you are worth more than many sparrows.

³²"Whoever acknowledges me before men, I will also acknowledge him before my Father in heaven. ³³But whoever disowns me before men, I will disown him before my Father in heaven.

³⁴"Do not suppose that I have come to bring peace to the earth. I did not come to bring peace, but a sword. ³⁵For I have come to turn

" 'a man against his father,
     a daughter against her mother,
a daughter-in-law against her
          mother-in-law—

³⁶   a man's enemies will be the
        members of his own
        household.'ᶜ

³⁷"Anyone who loves his father or mother more than me is not worthy of me; anyone who loves his son or daughter more than me is not worthy of me; ³⁸and anyone who does not take his cross and follow me is not worthy of me. ³⁹Whoever finds his life will lose it, and whoever loses his life for my sake will find it.

⁴⁰"He who receives you receives me, and he who receives me receives the one who sent me. ⁴¹Anyone who receives a prophet because he is a prophet will receive a prophet's reward, and anyone who receives a righteous man because he is a righteous man will receive a righteous man's reward. ⁴²And if anyone gives even a cup of cold water to one of these little ones because he is my disciple, I tell you the truth, he will certainly not lose his reward."

Jesus and John the Baptist

11 After Jesus had finished instructing his twelve disciples, he went on from there to teach and preach in the towns of Galilee.ᵈ

²When John heard in prison what Christ was doing, he sent his disciples ³to ask him, "Are you the one who was to come, or should we expect someone else?"

⁴Jesus replied, "Go back and report to John what you hear and see: ⁵The blind receive sight, the lame walk, those who have leprosyᵉ are cured, the deaf hear, the dead are raised, and the good news is preached to the poor. ⁶Blessed is the man who does not fall away on account of me."

⁷As John's disciples were leaving, Jesus began to speak to the crowd about John: "What did you go out into the desert to see? A reed swayed by the wind? ⁸If not, what did you go out to see? A man dressed in fine clothes? No, those who wear fine clothes are in kings' palaces. ⁹Then what did you go out to see? A prophet? Yes, I tell you, and more than a

ᵃ25 Greek Beezeboul or Beelzeboul   ᵇ29 Greek an assarion   ᶜ36 Micah 7:6   ᵈ1 Greek in their towns   ᵉ5 The Greek word was used for various diseases affecting the skin—not necessarily leprosy.

prophet. ¹⁰This is the one about whom it is written:

" 'I will send my messenger ahead of
    you,
  who will prepare your way before
    you.'^a

¹¹I tell you the truth: Among those born of women there has not risen anyone greater than John the Baptist; yet he who is least in the kingdom of heaven is greater than he. ¹²From the days of John the Baptist until now, the kingdom of heaven has been forcefully advancing, and forceful men lay hold of it. ¹³For all the Prophets and the Law prophesied until John. ¹⁴And if you are willing to accept it, he is the Elijah who was to come. ¹⁵He who has ears, let him hear.

¹⁶"To what can I compare this generation? They are like children sitting in the marketplaces and calling out to others:

¹⁷" 'We played the flute for you,
    and you did not dance;
  we sang a dirge,
    and you did not mourn.'

¹⁸For John came neither eating nor drinking, and they say, 'He has a demon.' ¹⁹The Son of Man came eating and drinking, and they say, 'Here is a glutton and a drunkard, a friend of tax collectors and "sinners." ' But wisdom is proved right by her actions."

Woe on Unrepentant Cities

²⁰Then Jesus began to denounce the cities in which most of his miracles had been performed, because they did not repent. ²¹"Woe to you, Korazin! Woe to you, Bethsaida! If the miracles that were performed in you had been performed in Tyre and Sidon, they would have repented long ago in sackcloth and ashes. ²²But I tell you, it will be more bearable for Tyre and Sidon on the day of judgment than for you. ²³And you, Capernaum, will you be lifted up to the skies? No, you will go down to the depths.^b If the miracles that were performed in you had been performed in Sodom, it would have remained to this day. ²⁴But I tell you that it

^a10 Mal. 3:1   ^b23 Greek *Hades*

At Your Service

Quiet TIMES
with each other

MATTHEW 10:42 The most thirsty we've ever been was in Venice, Italy. Wandering through the narrow streets surrounded by canals filled with water, we couldn't find a drop to drink! As we tried to find our hotel, we looked for a water fountain, street café or market where we could buy a bottle of water . . . but to no avail.

If you've ever been that thirsty, you know how refreshing a cup of cold water can be. And if you are a parent, you're familiar with those exhausting words often heard in the middle of the night: "Mommy (or Daddy), I want a glass of water." Every human being needs water to sustain life. It's a basic need.

In this passage Jesus reminds us that giving cups of cold water to others, including a child, has its rewards. Serving others is an important part of the Christian life, and serving each other is one of the keys to a successful marriage. A question seldom asked by spouses is, "Honey, what can I do to serve you?"

You could be the first to offer to change the dirty diaper, mow the yard, do the laundry or clean the toilet. Why not make a list of ways you can serve, comfort and support your spouse? In so doing you'll express your love and meet your spouse's needs as simply and as refreshingly as a cup of cold water.
—***Dave and Claudia***

Weekend Warm-up *What are some ways you can serve your spouse in the coming week?*

Go to page 1042 for your next devotional reading.

will be more bearable for Sodom on the day of judgment than for you."

Rest for the Weary

²⁵At that time Jesus said, "I praise you, Father, Lord of heaven and earth, because you have hidden these things from the wise and learned, and revealed them to little children. ²⁶Yes, Father, for this was your good pleasure.

²⁷"All things have been committed to me by my Father. No one knows the Son except the Father, and no one knows the Father except the Son and those to whom the Son chooses to reveal him.

²⁸"Come to me, all you who are weary and burdened, and I will give you rest. ²⁹Take my yoke upon you and learn from me, for I am gentle and humble in heart, and you will find rest for your souls. ³⁰For my yoke is easy and my burden is light."

Lord of the Sabbath

12 At that time Jesus went through the grainfields on the Sabbath. His disciples were hungry and began to pick some heads of grain and eat them. ²When the Pharisees saw this, they said to him, "Look! Your disciples are doing what is unlawful on the Sabbath."

³He answered, "Haven't you read what

David did when he and his companions were hungry? ⁴He entered the house of God, and he and his companions ate the consecrated bread—which was not lawful for them to do, but only for the priests. ⁵Or haven't you read in the Law that on the Sabbath the priests in the temple desecrate the day and yet are innocent? ⁶I tell you that one*ᵃ* greater than the temple is here. ⁷If you had known what these words mean, 'I desire mercy, not sacrifice,'*ᵇ* you would not have condemned the innocent. ⁸For the Son of Man is Lord of the Sabbath."

⁹Going on from that place, he went into their synagogue, ¹⁰and a man with a shriveled hand was there. Looking for a reason to accuse Jesus, they asked him, "Is it lawful to heal on the Sabbath?"

¹¹He said to them, "If any of you has a sheep and it falls into a pit on the Sabbath, will you not take hold of it and lift it out? ¹²How much more valuable is a man than a sheep! Therefore it is lawful to do good on the Sabbath."

¹³Then he said to the man, "Stretch out your hand." So he stretched it out and it was completely restored, just as sound

---

ᵃ6 Or *something;* also in verses 41 and 42
ᵇ7 Hosea 6:6

United or Divided?

Monday

MATTHEW 12:25 "You did it again!" he said.

"What's the big deal? I only spent $28!"

There went another round in a continuing argument. Marla and George just didn't agree on how to handle their finances. George was a saver; Marla was a spender. Marla's solution was to buy anyway and hope George didn't notice. Oops. What Marla and George needed to do was to unite and come up with a financial plan they both could live with.

From our high school cheerleading and football days, we remember the cheer, "United we stand, divided we fall; come on team, and let's play ball!" That's a great cheer to remember for marriage—and it's

Biblical. But it wasn't always easy for Dave and me to live out this Biblical principle. While we don't usually struggle with differing spending styles like Marla and George, over the years we found our challenges in other areas such as our role as parents. I was the more cautious one; Dave was more daring. So when our sons wanted to go rock climbing in the rain, our unity as parents was tested.

If your partnership is out of balance, it's time to regroup. To check your own unity, you may want to go through the questions together on the next page. Remember that uniting together will make your marriage strong. **—Dave and Claudia**

Go to page 1051 for your next devotional reading.

as the other. ¹⁴But the Pharisees went out and plotted how they might kill Jesus.

God's Chosen Servant

¹⁵Aware of this, Jesus withdrew from that place. Many followed him, and he healed all their sick, ¹⁶warning them not to tell who he was. ¹⁷This was to fulfill what was spoken through the prophet Isaiah:

¹⁸"Here is my servant whom I have chosen,
the one I love, in whom I delight;
I will put my Spirit on him,
and he will proclaim justice to the nations.
¹⁹He will not quarrel or cry out;
no one will hear his voice in the streets.
²⁰A bruised reed he will not break,
and a smoldering wick he will not snuff out,
till he leads justice to victory.
²¹   In his name the nations will put their hope." *a*

Jesus and Beelzebub

²²Then they brought him a demon-possessed man who was blind and mute, and Jesus healed him, so that he could both talk and see. ²³All the people were astonished and said, "Could this be the Son of David?"

²⁴But when the Pharisees heard this, they said, "It is only by Beelzebub,*b* the prince of demons, that this fellow drives out demons."

²⁵Jesus knew their thoughts and said to them, "Every kingdom divided against itself will be ruined, and every city or household divided against itself will not stand. ²⁶If Satan drives out Satan, he is divided against himself. How then can his kingdom stand? ²⁷And if I drive out demons by Beelzebub, by whom do your people drive them out? So then, they will be your judges. ²⁸But if I drive out demons by the Spirit of God, then the kingdom of God has come upon you.

²⁹"Or again, how can anyone enter a strong man's house and carry off his possessions unless he first ties up the strong man? Then he can rob his house.

³⁰"He who is not with me is against me, and he who does not gather with me

JUST BETWEEN you & me

United or Divided?

How are you doing in building your own marriage partnership? Consider the following statements and check true or false.

True   False   We share household responsibilities.

True   False   We are united in our role as parents.

True   False   We plan our free time together.

True   False   We agree on how to relate with in-laws and extended family.

True   False   We worship God together, pray together and together serve others.

True   False   We make financial decisions together.

If you have any "false" ones circled, talk about how you can better partner together. What is a small first step like going over your budget—or making one?

scatters. ³¹And so I tell you, every sin and blasphemy will be forgiven men, but the blasphemy against the Spirit will not be forgiven. ³²Anyone who speaks a word against the Son of Man will be forgiven, but anyone who speaks against the Holy Spirit will not be forgiven, either in this age or in the age to come.

³³"Make a tree good and its fruit will be good, or make a tree bad and its fruit will be bad, for a tree is recognized by its fruit. ³⁴You brood of vipers, how can you who are evil say anything good? For out of the overflow of the heart the mouth speaks. ³⁵The good man brings good things out of the good stored up in him, and the evil man brings evil things out of the evil stored up in him. ³⁶But I tell you that men will have to give account on the day of judgment for every careless word they have spoken. ³⁷For by your words you will be acquitted, and by your words you will be condemned."

a21 Isaiah 42:1-4   *b24* Greek *Beezeboul* or *Beelzeboul*; also in verse 27

The Sign of Jonah

38Then some of the Pharisees and teachers of the law said to him, "Teacher, we want to see a miraculous sign from you."

39He answered, "A wicked and adulterous generation asks for a miraculous sign! But none will be given it except the sign of the prophet Jonah. **40**For as Jonah was three days and three nights in the belly of a huge fish, so the Son of Man will be three days and three nights in the heart of the earth. **41**The men of Nineveh will stand up at the judgment with this generation and condemn it; for they repented at the preaching of Jonah, and now one*a* greater than Jonah is here. **42**The Queen of the South will rise at the judgment with this generation and condemn it; for she came from the ends of the earth to listen to Solomon's wisdom, and now one greater than Solomon is here.

43"When an evil*b* spirit comes out of a man, it goes through arid places seeking rest and does not find it. **44**Then it says, 'I will return to the house I left.' When it arrives, it finds the house unoccupied, swept clean and put in order. **45**Then it goes and takes with it seven other spirits more wicked than itself, and they go in and live there. And the final condition of that man is worse than the first. That is how it will be with this wicked generation."

Jesus' Mother and Brothers

46While Jesus was still talking to the crowd, his mother and brothers stood outside, wanting to speak to him. **47**Someone told him, "Your mother and brothers are standing outside, wanting to speak to you."*c*

48He replied to him, "Who is my mother, and who are my brothers?" **49**Pointing to his disciples, he said, "Here are my mother and my brothers. **50**For whoever does the will of my Father in heaven is my brother and sister and mother."

The Parable of the Sower

13 That same day Jesus went out of the house and sat by the lake. **2**Such large crowds gathered around him that he got into a boat and sat in it, while all the people stood on the shore. **3**Then he told them many things in parables, saying: "A farmer went out to sow his seed. **4**As he was scattering the seed, some fell along the path, and the birds came and ate it up. **5**Some fell on rocky places, where it did not have much soil. It sprang up quickly, because the soil was shallow. **6**But when the sun came up, the plants were scorched, and they withered because they had no root. **7**Other seed fell among thorns, which grew up and choked the plants. **8**Still other seed fell on good soil, where it produced a crop—a hundred, sixty or thirty times what was sown. **9**He who has ears, let him hear."

10The disciples came to him and asked, "Why do you speak to the people in parables?"

11He replied, "The knowledge of the secrets of the kingdom of heaven has been given to you, but not to them. **12**Whoever has will be given more, and he will have an abundance. Whoever does not have, even what he has will be taken from him. **13**This is why I speak to them in parables:

"Though seeing, they do not see;
    though hearing, they do not hear
        or understand.

14In them is fulfilled the prophecy of Isaiah:

" 'You will be ever hearing but never
        understanding;
    you will be ever seeing but never
        perceiving.
15For this people's heart has become
        calloused;
    they hardly hear with their ears,
    and they have closed their eyes.
Otherwise they might see with their
        eyes,
    hear with their ears,
    understand with their hearts
and turn, and I would heal them.'*d*

16But blessed are your eyes because they see, and your ears because they hear. **17**For I tell you the truth, many prophets and righteous men longed to see what you see

---

a41 Or something; also in verse 42   *b43 Greek unclean*   *c47 Some manuscripts do not have verse 47.*   *d15 Isaiah 6:9,10* but did not see it, and to hear what you hear but did not hear it.

18 "Listen then to what the parable of the sower means: 19 When anyone hears the message about the kingdom and does not understand it, the evil one comes and snatches away what was sown in his heart. This is the seed sown along the path. 20 The one who received the seed that fell on rocky places is the man who hears the word and at once receives it with joy. 21 But since he has no root, he lasts only a short time. When trouble or persecution comes because of the word, he quickly falls away. 22 The one who received the seed that fell among the thorns is the man who hears the word, but the worries of this life and the deceitfulness of wealth choke it, making it unfruitful. 23 But the one who received the seed that fell on good soil is the man who hears the word and understands it. He produces a crop, yielding a hundred, sixty or thirty times what was sown."

The Parable of the Weeds

24 Jesus told them another parable: "The kingdom of heaven is like a man who sowed good seed in his field. 25 But while everyone was sleeping, his enemy came and sowed weeds among the wheat, and went away. 26 When the wheat sprouted and formed heads, then the weeds also appeared.

27 "The owner's servants came to him and said, 'Sir, didn't you sow good seed in your field? Where then did the weeds come from?'

28 " 'An enemy did this,' he replied.

"The servants asked him, 'Do you want us to go and pull them up?'

29 " 'No,' he answered, 'because while you are pulling the weeds, you may root up the wheat with them. 30 Let both grow together until the harvest. At that time I will tell the harvesters: First collect the weeds and tie them in bundles to be burned; then gather the wheat and bring it into my barn.' "

The Parables of the Mustard Seed and the Yeast

31 He told them another parable: "The kingdom of heaven is like a mustard seed, which a man took and planted in his field. 32 Though it is the smallest of all

your seeds, yet when it grows, it is the largest of garden plants and becomes a tree, so that the birds of the air come and perch in its branches."

33 He told them still another parable: "The kingdom of heaven is like yeast that a woman took and mixed into a large amount[a] of flour until it worked all through the dough."

34 Jesus spoke all these things to the crowd in parables; he did not say anything to them without using a parable. 35 So was fulfilled what was spoken through the prophet:

"I will open my mouth in parables,
I will utter things hidden since the
creation of the world."[b]

The Parable of the Weeds Explained

36 Then he left the crowd and went into the house. His disciples came to him and said, "Explain to us the parable of the weeds in the field."

37 He answered, "The one who sowed the good seed is the Son of Man. 38 The field is the world, and the good seed stands for the sons of the kingdom. The weeds are the sons of the evil one, 39 and the enemy who sows them is the devil. The harvest is the end of the age, and the harvesters are angels.

40 "As the weeds are pulled up and burned in the fire, so it will be at the end of the age. 41 The Son of Man will send out his angels, and they will weed out of his kingdom everything that causes sin and all who do evil. 42 They will throw them into the fiery furnace, where there will be weeping and gnashing of teeth. 43 Then the righteous will shine like the sun in the kingdom of their Father. He who has ears, let him hear.

The Parables of the Hidden Treasure and the Pearl

44 "The kingdom of heaven is like treasure hidden in a field. When a man found it, he hid it again, and then in his joy went and sold all he had and bought that field.

45 "Again, the kingdom of heaven is like a merchant looking for fine pearls. 46 When he found one of great value, he

---

a 33 Greek *three satas* (probably about 1/2 bushel or 22 liters) b 35 Psalm 78:2

went away and sold everything he had and bought it.

The Parable of the Net

47 "Once again, the kingdom of heaven is like a net that was let down into the lake and caught all kinds of fish. 48When it was full, the fishermen pulled it up on the shore. Then they sat down and collected the good fish in baskets, but threw the bad away. 49This is how it will be at the end of the age. The angels will come and separate the wicked from the righteous 50and throw them into the fiery furnace, where there will be weeping and gnashing of teeth.

51 "Have you understood all these things?" Jesus asked.

"Yes," they replied.

52He said to them, "Therefore every teacher of the law who has been instructed about the kingdom of heaven is like the owner of a house who brings out of his storeroom new treasures as well as old."

A Prophet Without Honor

53When Jesus had finished these parables, he moved on from there. 54Coming to his hometown, he began teaching the people in their synagogue, and they were amazed. "Where did this man get this wisdom and these miraculous powers?" they asked. 55 "Isn't this the carpenter's son? Isn't his mother's name Mary, and aren't his brothers James, Joseph, Simon and Judas? 56Aren't all his sisters with us? Where then did this man get all these things?" 57And they took offense at him.

But Jesus said to them, "Only in his hometown and in his own house is a prophet without honor."

58And he did not do many miracles there because of their lack of faith.

John the Baptist Beheaded

14 At that time Herod the tetrarch heard the reports about Jesus, 2and he said to his attendants, "This is John the Baptist; he has risen from the dead! That is why miraculous powers are at work in him."

3Now Herod had arrested John and bound him and put him in prison because of Herodias, his brother Philip's wife, 4for John had been saying to him: "It is not lawful for you to have her." 5Herod wanted to kill John, but he was afraid of the people, because they considered him a prophet.

6On Herod's birthday the daughter of Herodias danced for them and pleased Herod so much 7that he promised with an oath to give her whatever she asked. 8Prompted by her mother, she said, "Give me here on a platter the head of John the Baptist." 9The king was distressed, but because of his oaths and his dinner guests, he ordered that her request be granted 10and had John beheaded in the prison. 11His head was brought in on a platter and given to the girl, who carried it to her mother. 12John's disciples came and took his body and buried it. Then they went and told Jesus.

Jesus Feeds the Five Thousand

13When Jesus heard what had happened, he withdrew by boat privately to a solitary place. Hearing of this, the crowds followed him on foot from the towns. 14When Jesus landed and saw a large crowd, he had compassion on them and healed their sick.

15As evening approached, the disciples came to him and said, "This is a remote place, and it's already getting late. Send the crowds away, so they can go to the villages and buy themselves some food."

16Jesus replied, "They do not need to go away. You give them something to eat."

17 "We have here only five loaves of bread and two fish," they answered.

18 "Bring them here to me," he said. 19And he directed the people to sit down on the grass. Taking the five loaves and the two fish and looking up to heaven, he gave thanks and broke the loaves. Then he gave them to the disciples, and the disciples gave them to the people. 20They all ate and were satisfied, and the disciples picked up twelve basketfuls of broken pieces that were left over. 21The number of those who ate was about five thousand men, besides women and children.

Jesus Walks on the Water

22Immediately Jesus made the disciples get into the boat and go on ahead of him to the other side, while he dismissed the crowd. ²³After he had dismissed them, he went up on a mountainside by himself to pray. When evening came, he was there alone, ²⁴but the boat was already a considerable distance[a] from land, buffeted by the waves because the wind was against them.

²⁵During the fourth watch of the night Jesus went out to them, walking on the lake. ²⁶When the disciples saw him walking on the lake, they were terrified. "It's a ghost," they said, and cried out in fear.

²⁷But Jesus immediately said to them: "Take courage! It is I. Don't be afraid."

²⁸"Lord, if it's you," Peter replied, "tell me to come to you on the water."

²⁹"Come," he said.

Then Peter got down out of the boat, walked on the water and came toward Jesus. ³⁰But when he saw the wind, he was afraid and, beginning to sink, cried out, "Lord, save me!"

³¹Immediately Jesus reached out his hand and caught him. "You of little faith," he said, "why did you doubt?"

³²And when they climbed into the boat, the wind died down. ³³Then those who were in the boat worshiped him, saying, "Truly you are the Son of God."

³⁴When they had crossed over, they landed at Gennesaret. ³⁵And when the men of that place recognized Jesus, they sent word to all the surrounding country. People brought all their sick to him ³⁶and begged him to let the sick just touch the edge of his cloak, and all who touched him were healed.

Clean and Unclean

15 Then some Pharisees and teachers of the law came to Jesus from Jerusalem and asked, ²"Why do your disciples break the tradition of the elders? They don't wash their hands before they eat!"

³Jesus replied, "And why do you break the command of God for the sake of your tradition? ⁴For God said, 'Honor your father and mother'[b] and 'Anyone who curses his father or mother must be put to death.'[c] ⁵But you say that if a man says to his father or mother, 'Whatever help you might otherwise have received from me is a gift devoted to God,' ⁶he is not to

Herod and Herodias

MATTHEW 14:1-12 Listening to someone correct us is never easy. It can be especially difficult when it is spiritual correction, when someone talks to us about sin in our lives. It's what you do with those corrective statements that can change your life. Herod and his wife Herodias were in a sinful marriage and the preacher, John the Baptist, was willing to confront their sin. Even though John's sermons of correction were truthful, this couple was so furious that they would not listen to him.

It's easy for a couple to become so focused on the direction they are going that they are blinded to their sin. Then, all of the sudden, a sermon challenges their lifestyle and they are confronted by their sin. They have to decide how to handle this correction. Some leave the church, while others just get mad at the teacher. Herod and Herodias became so enraged that they chose to further their sin by eliminating the preacher all together.

When we are confronted by a prophetic word, it is important to take considerate pause before taking action. As difficult as the truth might be to handle, it is still the truth. It could be a turning point.

'honor his father[d]' with it. Thus you nullify the word of God for the sake of your tradition. ⁷You hypocrites! Isaiah was right when he prophesied about you:

⁸" 'These people honor me with their lips,
    but their hearts are far from me.
⁹They worship me in vain;
    their teachings are but rules taught by men.'[e]"

¹⁰Jesus called the crowd to him and said, "Listen and understand. ¹¹What goes into a man's mouth does not make him 'unclean,' but what comes out of his mouth, that is what makes him 'unclean.' "

---

[a]24 Greek *many stadia*   [b]4 Exodus 20:12; Deut. 5:16   [c]4 Exodus 21:17; Lev. 20:9   [d]6 Some manuscripts *father or his mother*   [e]9 Isaiah 29:13

¹²Then the disciples came to him and asked, "Do you know that the Pharisees were offended when they heard this?"

¹³He replied, "Every plant that my heavenly Father has not planted will be pulled up by the roots. ¹⁴Leave them; they are blind guides.ᵃ If a blind man leads a blind man, both will fall into a pit."

¹⁵Peter said, "Explain the parable to us."

¹⁶"Are you still so dull?" Jesus asked them. ¹⁷"Don't you see that whatever enters the mouth goes into the stomach and then out of the body? ¹⁸But the things that come out of the mouth come from the heart, and these make a man 'unclean.' ¹⁹For out of the heart come evil thoughts, murder, adultery, sexual immorality, theft, false testimony, slander. ²⁰These are what make a man 'unclean'; but eating with unwashed hands does not make him 'unclean.' "

The Faith of the Canaanite Woman

²¹Leaving that place, Jesus withdrew to the region of Tyre and Sidon. ²²A Canaanite woman from that vicinity came to him, crying out, "Lord, Son of David, have mercy on me! My daughter is suffering terribly from demon-possession."

²³Jesus did not answer a word. So his disciples came to him and urged him, "Send her away, for she keeps crying out after us."

²⁴He answered, "I was sent only to the lost sheep of Israel."

²⁵The woman came and knelt before him. "Lord, help me!" she said.

²⁶He replied, "It is not right to take the children's bread and toss it to their dogs."

²⁷"Yes, Lord," she said, "but even the dogs eat the crumbs that fall from their masters' table."

²⁸Then Jesus answered, "Woman, you have great faith! Your request is granted." And her daughter was healed from that very hour.

Jesus Feeds the Four Thousand

²⁹Jesus left there and went along the Sea of Galilee. Then he went up on a mountainside and sat down. ³⁰Great crowds came to him, bringing the lame, the blind, the crippled, the mute and many others, and laid them at his feet;

and he healed them. ³¹The people were amazed when they saw the mute speaking, the crippled made well, the lame walking and the blind seeing. And they praised the God of Israel.

³²Jesus called his disciples to him and said, "I have compassion for these people; they have already been with me three days and have nothing to eat. I do not want to send them away hungry, or they may collapse on the way."

³³His disciples answered, "Where could we get enough bread in this remote place to feed such a crowd?"

³⁴"How many loaves do you have?" Jesus asked.

"Seven," they replied, "and a few small fish."

³⁵He told the crowd to sit down on the ground. ³⁶Then he took the seven loaves and the fish, and when he had given thanks, he broke them and gave them to the disciples, and they in turn to the people. ³⁷They all ate and were satisfied. Afterward the disciples picked up seven basketfuls of broken pieces that were left over. ³⁸The number of those who ate was four thousand, besides women and children. ³⁹After Jesus had sent the crowd away, he got into the boat and went to the vicinity of Magadan.

The Demand for a Sign

16 The Pharisees and Sadducees came to Jesus and tested him by asking him to show them a sign from heaven.

²He replied,ᵇ "When evening comes, you say, 'It will be fair weather, for the sky is red,' ³and in the morning, 'Today it will be stormy, for the sky is red and overcast.' You know how to interpret the appearance of the sky, but you cannot interpret the signs of the times. ⁴A wicked and adulterous generation looks for a miraculous sign, but none will be given it except the sign of Jonah." Jesus then left them and went away.

The Yeast of the Pharisees and Sadducees

⁵When they went across the lake, the disciples forgot to take bread. ⁶"Be careful," Jesus said to them. "Be on your guard

ᵃ14 Some manuscripts *guides of the blind*
ᵇ2 Some early manuscripts do not have the rest of verse 2 and all of verse 3.

against the yeast of the Pharisees and Sadducees."

[7] They discussed this among themselves and said, "It is because we didn't bring any bread."

[8] Aware of their discussion, Jesus asked, "You of little faith, why are you talking among yourselves about having no bread? [9] Do you still not understand? Don't you remember the five loaves for the five thousand, and how many basketfuls you gathered? [10] Or the seven loaves for the four thousand, and how many basketfuls you gathered? [11] How is it you don't understand that I was not talking to you about bread? But be on your guard against the yeast of the Pharisees and Sadducees." [12] Then they understood that he was not telling them to guard against the yeast used in bread, but against the teaching of the Pharisees and Sadducees.

Peter's Confession of Christ

[13] When Jesus came to the region of Caesarea Philippi, he asked his disciples, "Who do people say the Son of Man is?"

[14] They replied, "Some say John the Baptist; others say Elijah; and still others, Jeremiah or one of the prophets."

[15] "But what about you?" he asked. "Who do you say I am?"

[16] Simon Peter answered, "You are the Christ,[a] the Son of the living God."

[17] Jesus replied, "Blessed are you, Simon son of Jonah, for this was not revealed to you by man, but by my Father in heaven. [18] And I tell you that you are Peter,[b] and on this rock I will build my church, and the gates of Hades[c] will not overcome it.[d] [19] I will give you the keys of the kingdom of heaven; whatever you bind on earth will be[e] bound in heaven, and whatever you loose on earth will be[e] loosed in heaven." [20] Then he warned his disciples not to tell anyone that he was the Christ.

Jesus Predicts His Death

[21] From that time on Jesus began to explain to his disciples that he must go to Jerusalem and suffer many things at the hands of the elders, chief priests and teachers of the law, and that he must be killed and on the third day be raised to life.

[22] Peter took him aside and began to rebuke him. "Never, Lord!" he said. "This shall never happen to you!"

[23] Jesus turned and said to Peter, "Get behind me, Satan! You are a stumbling block to me; you do not have in mind the things of God, but the things of men."

[24] Then Jesus said to his disciples, "If anyone would come after me, he must deny himself and take up his cross and follow me. [25] For whoever wants to save his life[f] will lose it, but whoever loses his life for me will find it. [26] What good will it be for a man if he gains the whole world, yet forfeits his soul? Or what can a man give in exchange for his soul? [27] For the Son of Man is going to come in his Father's glory with his angels, and then he will reward each person according to what he has done. [28] I tell you the truth, some who are standing here will not taste death before they see the Son of Man coming in his kingdom."

The Transfiguration

17 After six days Jesus took with him Peter, James and John the brother of James, and led them up a high mountain by themselves. [2] There he was transfigured before them. His face shone like the sun, and his clothes became as white as the light. [3] Just then there appeared before them Moses and Elijah, talking with Jesus.

[4] Peter said to Jesus, "Lord, it is good for us to be here. If you wish, I will put up three shelters—one for you, one for Moses and one for Elijah."

[5] While he was still speaking, a bright cloud enveloped them, and a voice from the cloud said, "This is my Son, whom I love; with him I am well pleased. Listen to him!"

[6] When the disciples heard this, they fell facedown to the ground, terrified. [7] But Jesus came and touched them. "Get up," he said. "Don't be afraid." [8] When they looked up, they saw no one except Jesus.

[9] As they were coming down the mountain, Jesus instructed them, "Don't tell

---

*a*16 Or *Messiah*; also in verse 20   *b*18 *Peter* means *rock*.   *c*18 Or *hell*   *d*18 Or *not prove stronger than it*   *e*19 Or *have been*   *f*25 The Greek word means either *life* or *soul*; also in verse 26.

anyone what you have seen, until the Son of Man has been raised from the dead."

[10] The disciples asked him, "Why then do the teachers of the law say that Elijah must come first?"

[11] Jesus replied, "To be sure, Elijah comes and will restore all things. [12] But I tell you, Elijah has already come, and they did not recognize him, but have done to him everything they wished. In the same way the Son of Man is going to suffer at their hands." [13] Then the disciples understood that he was talking to them about John the Baptist.

The Healing of a Boy With a Demon

[14] When they came to the crowd, a man approached Jesus and knelt before him. [15] "Lord, have mercy on my son," he said. "He has seizures and is suffering greatly. He often falls into the fire or into the water. [16] I brought him to your disciples, but they could not heal him."

[17] "O unbelieving and perverse generation," Jesus replied, "how long shall I stay with you? How long shall I put up with you? Bring the boy here to me." [18] Jesus rebuked the demon, and it came out of the boy, and he was healed from that moment.

[19] Then the disciples came to Jesus in private and asked, "Why couldn't we drive it out?"

[20] He replied, "Because you have so little faith. I tell you the truth, if you have faith as small as a mustard seed, you can say to this mountain, 'Move from here to there' and it will move. Nothing will be impossible for you.[a]"

[22] When they came together in Galilee, he said to them, "The Son of Man is going to be betrayed into the hands of men. [23] They will kill him, and on the third day he will be raised to life." And the disciples were filled with grief.

The Temple Tax

[24] After Jesus and his disciples arrived in Capernaum, the collectors of the two-drachma tax came to Peter and asked, "Doesn't your teacher pay the temple tax[b]?"

[25] "Yes, he does," he replied.

When Peter came into the house, Jesus was the first to speak. "What do you think, Simon?" he asked. "From whom do the kings of the earth collect duty and taxes—from their own sons or from others?"

[26] "From others," Peter answered.

"Then the sons are exempt," Jesus said to him. [27] "But so that we may not offend them, go to the lake and throw out your line. Take the first fish you catch; open its mouth and you will find a four-drachma coin. Take it and give it to them for my tax and yours."

The Greatest in the Kingdom of Heaven

18 At that time the disciples came to Jesus and asked, "Who is the greatest in the kingdom of heaven?"

[2] He called a little child and had him stand among them. [3] And he said: "I tell you the truth, unless you change and become like little children, you will never enter the kingdom of heaven. [4] Therefore, whoever humbles himself like this child is the greatest in the kingdom of heaven.

[5] "And whoever welcomes a little child like this in my name welcomes me. [6] But if anyone causes one of these little ones who believe in me to sin, it would be better for him to have a large millstone hung around his neck and to be drowned in the depths of the sea.

[7] "Woe to the world because of the things that cause people to sin! Such things must come, but woe to the man through whom they come! [8] If your hand or your foot causes you to sin, cut it off and throw it away. It is better for you to enter life maimed or crippled than to have two hands or two feet and be thrown into eternal fire. [9] And if your eye causes you to sin, gouge it out and throw it away. It is better for you to enter life with one eye than to have two eyes and be thrown into the fire of hell.

The Parable of the Lost Sheep

[10] "See that you do not look down on one of these little ones. For I tell you that their angels in heaven always see the face of my Father in heaven.[c]

[12] "What do you think? If a man owns

---

[a] 20 Some manuscripts *you.* 21 *But this kind does not go out except by prayer and fasting.*   [b] 24 Greek *the two drachmas*   [c] 10 Some manuscripts *heaven.* 11 *The Son of Man came to save what was lost.*

a hundred sheep, and one of them wanders away, will he not leave the ninety-nine on the hills and go to look for the one that wandered off? ¹³And if he finds it, I tell you the truth, he is happier about that one sheep than about the ninety-nine that did not wander off. ¹⁴In the same way your Father in heaven is not willing that any of these little ones should be lost.

A Brother Who Sins Against You

¹⁵"If your brother sins against you,[a] go and show him his fault, just between the two of you. If he listens to you, you have won your brother over. ¹⁶But if he will not listen, take one or two others along, so that 'every matter may be established by the testimony of two or three witnesses.'[b] ¹⁷If he refuses to listen to them, tell it to the church; and if he refuses to listen even to the church, treat him as you would a pagan or a tax collector.

¹⁸"I tell you the truth, whatever you bind on earth will be[c] bound in heaven, and whatever you loose on earth will be[c] loosed in heaven.

¹⁹"Again, I tell you that if two of you on earth agree about anything you ask for, it will be done for you by my Father in heaven. ²⁰For where two or three come together in my name, there am I with them."

The Parable of the Unmerciful Servant

²¹Then Peter came to Jesus and asked, "Lord, how many times shall I forgive my brother when he sins against me? Up to seven times?"

²²Jesus answered, "I tell you, not seven times, but seventy-seven times.[d]

²³"Therefore, the kingdom of heaven is like a king who wanted to settle accounts with his servants. ²⁴As he began the settle-

---

[a]15 Some manuscripts do not have *against you.*
[b]16 Deut. 19:15   [c]18 Or *have been*   [d]22 Or *seventy times seven*

Prayer for Two

Tuesday

MATTHEW 18:19–20 "A family that prays together stays together" and "Prayer changes things" are two popular sayings. They may be cute and catchy, but they are also profoundly true. We learn from this

passage that God does indeed hear and answer our prayers when we come to him.

Unfortunately, praying together as a couple can be very difficult. Keeping up with a personal prayer time is difficult enough, let alone finding time, and the desire, to pray as a couple. According to this passage, God desires us to pray together. Whatever the obstacles, we need to decide to make prayer a priority in our relationship. But we are not just called to pray together; we must deal with the issues we are presenting to God, so that we can be in agreement on them.

Agreeing on a direction for your relationship, your family or in an area of conflict can be a huge hurdle. There have been times in our own marriage when it was

hard to pray together about an issue because we disagreed so vehemently. One instance was when Rosemary and I had opposite opinions about whether or not to let one of our teenagers go to a party. It was hard to pray together because we each had our own ideas about what should be done. Difficult as it was, we stopped in the middle of the heat of the conflict and prayed. Doing this helped bring us back to our priorities.

Ironically, conflict offers an opportunity to strengthen marriage. When handled maturely, conflicts show us that we need to look to God for the answers. Then, as a team, we can present a unified petition to God—the only One who has all the right answers to begin with. At that point we will be drawing on that special strength when we join together in prayer as an agreeing, united force.

—Bob and Rosemary

Go to page 1052 for your next devotional reading.

ment, a man who owed him ten thousand talents[a] was brought to him. [25]Since he was not able to pay, the master ordered that he and his wife and his children and all that he had be sold to repay the debt.

[26]"The servant fell on his knees before him. 'Be patient with me,' he begged, 'and I will pay back everything.' [27]The servant's master took pity on him, canceled the debt and let him go.

[28]"But when that servant went out, he found one of his fellow servants who owed him a hundred denarii.[b] He grabbed him and began to choke him. 'Pay back what you owe me!' he demanded.

[29]"His fellow servant fell to his knees and begged him, 'Be patient with me, and I will pay you back.'

[30]"But he refused. Instead, he went off and had the man thrown into prison until he could pay the debt. [31]When the other servants saw what had happened, they were greatly distressed and went and told their master everything that had happened.

[32]"Then the master called the servant in. 'You wicked servant,' he said, 'I canceled all that debt of yours because you begged me to. [33]Shouldn't you have had mercy on your fellow servant just as I had on you?' [34]In anger his master turned him over to the jailers to be tortured, until he should pay back all he owed.

[35]"This is how my heavenly Father will treat each of you unless you forgive your brother from your heart."

Divorce

19 When Jesus had finished saying these things, he left Galilee and went into the region of Judea to the other side of the Jordan. [2]Large crowds followed him, and he healed them there.

[3]Some Pharisees came to him to test him. They asked, "Is it lawful for a man to divorce his wife for any and every reason?"

[4]"Haven't you read," he replied, "that at the beginning the Creator 'made them male and female,'[c] [5]and said, 'For this

---

[a]24 That is, millions of dollars   [b]28 That is, a few dollars   [c]4 Gen. 1:27

How's Your Sex Life?

Wednesday

MATTHEW 19:6 That's a fair question, isn't it? After all, sexuality is not something that somehow miraculously takes care of itself once we're married. It needs nurturing, tenderness, education and—are you ready for this?—religion.

It's a fact. According to some studies, religious faith is good for your sex life. As strange as it may sound, there is a strong link in marriage between spirituality and sexuality. Married couples who cultivate spiritual intimacy are far more likely to report higher satisfaction with their sex life than other couples.

This fact makes sense if you think about it. The mysteries, wonders and pleasures of sex in marriage are divine gifts to celebrate. Those who try to limit sex to procreation are simply ignoring the Bible. Scripture—right from the beginning—enthusiastically affirms sex within the bonds of marriage.

Consider the first chapter of the Bible. It contains a magnificent commentary on the meaning of sexuality in marriage. Our maleness and femaleness are not just an accidental arrangement of the human species. Our male and female sexuality is related to being created in the image of God. This point is echoed throughout Scripture. Jesus underscores a high view of sex in marriage when he refers to the Genesis passage and then adds, "So they are no longer two, but one. Therefore what God has joined together, let man not separate."

In the Old Testament and in the New Testament, in the Gospels and in the Epistles, we are called to celebrate sexuality in marriage. There is no denying that your spiritual growth helps enhance your sexual intimacy in marriage. So, we'll ask it again. How's your sex life?

—Les and Leslie

Go to page 1058 for your next devotional reading.

reason a man will leave his father and mother and be united to his wife, and the two will become one flesh'*? 6So they are no longer two, but one. Therefore what God has joined together, let man not separate."

7"Why then," they asked, "did Moses command that a man give his wife a certificate of divorce and send her away?"

8Jesus replied, "Moses permitted you to divorce your wives because your hearts were hard. But it was not this way from the beginning. 9I tell you that anyone who divorces his wife, except for marital unfaithfulness, and marries another woman commits adultery."

10The disciples said to him, "If this is the situation between a husband and wife, it is better not to marry."

11Jesus replied, "Not everyone can accept this word, but only those to whom it has been given. 12For some are eunuchs because they were born that way; others were made that way by men; and others have renounced marriage*b* because of the kingdom of heaven. The one who can accept this should accept it."

The Little Children and Jesus

13Then little children were brought to Jesus for him to place his hands on them and pray for them. But the disciples rebuked those who brought them.

14Jesus said, "Let the little children come to me, and do not hinder them, for the kingdom of heaven belongs to such as these." 15When he had placed his hands on them, he went on from there.

The Rich Young Man

16Now a man came up to Jesus and asked, "Teacher, what good thing must I do to get eternal life?"

17"Why do you ask me about what is good?" Jesus replied. "There is only One who is good. If you want to enter life, obey the commandments."

18"Which ones?" the man inquired.

Jesus replied, " 'Do not murder, do not commit adultery, do not steal, do not give false testimony, 19honor your father and mother,'*c* and 'love your neighbor as yourself.'*d* "

20"All these I have kept," the young man said. "What do I still lack?"

21Jesus answered, "If you want to be perfect, go, sell your possessions and give to the poor, and you will have treasure in heaven. Then come, follow me."

22When the young man heard this, he went away sad, because he had great wealth.

23Then Jesus said to his disciples, "I tell you the truth, it is hard for a rich man to enter the kingdom of heaven. 24Again I tell you, it is easier for a camel to go through the eye of a needle than for a rich man to enter the kingdom of God."

25When the disciples heard this, they were greatly astonished and asked, "Who then can be saved?"

26Jesus looked at them and said, "With man this is impossible, but with God all things are possible."

27Peter answered him, "We have left everything to follow you! What then will there be for us?"

28Jesus said to them, "I tell you the truth, at the renewal of all things, when the Son of Man sits on his glorious throne, you who have followed me will also sit on twelve thrones, judging the twelve tribes of Israel. 29And everyone who has left houses or brothers or sisters

a5 Gen. 2:24   *b12* Or *have made themselves eunuchs*   *c19* Exodus 20:12-16; Deut. 5:16-20   *d19* Lev. 19:18

or father or mother[a] or children or fields for my sake will receive a hundred times as much and will inherit eternal life. [30]But many who are first will be last, and many who are last will be first.

The Parable of the Workers in the Vineyard

20 "For the kingdom of heaven is like a landowner who went out early in the morning to hire men to work in his vineyard. [2]He agreed to pay them a denarius for the day and sent them into his vineyard.

[3]"About the third hour he went out and saw others standing in the market-place doing nothing. [4]He told them, 'You also go and work in my vineyard, and I will pay you whatever is right.' [5]So they went.

"He went out again about the sixth hour and the ninth hour and did the same thing. [6]About the eleventh hour he went out and found still others standing around. He asked them, 'Why have you been standing here all day long doing nothing?'

[7]" 'Because no one has hired us,' they answered.

"He said to them, 'You also go and work in my vineyard.'

[8]"When evening came, the owner of the vineyard said to his foreman, 'Call the workers and pay them their wages, beginning with the last ones hired and going on to the first.'

[9]"The workers who were hired about the eleventh hour came and each received a denarius. [10]So when those came who were hired first, they expected to receive more. But each one of them also received a denarius. [11]When they received it, they began to grumble against the landowner. [12]'These men who were hired last worked only one hour,' they said, 'and you have made them equal to us who have borne the burden of the work and the heat of the day.'

[13]"But he answered one of them, 'Friend, I am not being unfair to you. Didn't you agree to work for a denarius? [14]Take your pay and go. I want to give the man who was hired last the same as I gave you. [15]Don't I have the right to do what I want with my own money? Or are you envious because I am generous?'

[16]"So the last will be first, and the first will be last."

Jesus Again Predicts His Death

[17]Now as Jesus was going up to Jerusalem, he took the twelve disciples aside and said to them, [18]"We are going up to Jerusalem, and the Son of Man will be betrayed to the chief priests and the teachers of the law. They will condemn him to death [19]and will turn him over to the Gentiles to be mocked and flogged and crucified. On the third day he will be raised to life!"

A Mother's Request

[20]Then the mother of Zebedee's sons came to Jesus with her sons and, kneeling down, asked a favor of him.

[21]"What is it you want?" he asked.

She said, "Grant that one of these two sons of mine may sit at your right and the other at your left in your kingdom."

[22]"You don't know what you are asking," Jesus said to them. "Can you drink the cup I am going to drink?"

"We can," they answered.

[23]Jesus said to them, "You will indeed drink from my cup, but to sit at my right or left is not for me to grant. These places belong to those for whom they have been prepared by my Father."

[24]When the ten heard about this, they were indignant with the two brothers. [25]Jesus called them together and said, "You know that the rulers of the Gentiles lord it over them, and their high officials exercise authority over them. [26]Not so with you. Instead, whoever wants to become great among you must be your servant, [27]and whoever wants to be first must be your slave— [28]just as the Son of Man did not come to be served, but to serve, and to give his life as a ransom for many."

Two Blind Men Receive Sight

[29]As Jesus and his disciples were leaving Jericho, a large crowd followed him. [30]Two blind men were sitting by the roadside, and when they heard that Jesus was going by, they shouted, "Lord, Son of David, have mercy on us!"

[a]29 Some manuscripts *mother or wife*

31The crowd rebuked them and told them to be quiet, but they shouted all the louder, "Lord, Son of David, have mercy on us!"

32Jesus stopped and called them. "What do you want me to do for you?" he asked.

33"Lord," they answered, "we want our sight."

34Jesus had compassion on them and touched their eyes. Immediately they received their sight and followed him.

The Triumphal Entry

21 As they approached Jerusalem and came to Bethphage on the Mount of Olives, Jesus sent two disciples, 2saying to them, "Go to the village ahead of you, and at once you will find a donkey tied there, with her colt by her. Untie them and bring them to me. 3If anyone says anything to you, tell him that the Lord needs them, and he will send them right away."

4This took place to fulfill what was spoken through the prophet:

5"Say to the Daughter of Zion,
    'See, your king comes to you,
gentle and riding on a donkey,
    on a colt, the foal of a donkey.' " *a*

6The disciples went and did as Jesus had instructed them. 7They brought the donkey and the colt, placed their cloaks on them, and Jesus sat on them. 8A very large crowd spread their cloaks on the road, while others cut branches from the trees and spread them on the road. 9The crowds that went ahead of him and those that followed shouted,

"Hosanna*b* to the Son of David!"

"Blessed is he who comes in the
    name of the Lord!"*c*

"Hosanna*b* in the highest!"

10When Jesus entered Jerusalem, the whole city was stirred and asked, "Who is this?"

11The crowds answered, "This is Jesus, the prophet from Nazareth in Galilee."

Jesus at the Temple

12Jesus entered the temple area and drove out all who were buying and selling

there. He overturned the tables of the money changers and the benches of those selling doves. 13"It is written," he said to them, " 'My house will be called a house of prayer,'*d* but you are making it a 'den of robbers.'*e* "

14The blind and the lame came to him at the temple, and he healed them. 15But when the chief priests and the teachers of the law saw the wonderful things he did and the children shouting in the temple area, "Hosanna to the Son of David," they were indignant.

16"Do you hear what these children are saying?" they asked him.

"Yes," replied Jesus, "have you never read,

" 'From the lips of children and
        infants
    you have ordained praise'*f*?"

17And he left them and went out of the city to Bethany, where he spent the night.

The Fig Tree Withers

18Early in the morning, as he was on his way back to the city, he was hungry. 19Seeing a fig tree by the road, he went up to it but found nothing on it except leaves. Then he said to it, "May you never bear fruit again!" Immediately the tree withered.

20When the disciples saw this, they were amazed. "How did the fig tree wither so quickly?" they asked.

21Jesus replied, "I tell you the truth, if you have faith and do not doubt, not only can you do what was done to the fig tree, but also you can say to this mountain, 'Go, throw yourself into the sea,' and it will be done. 22If you believe, you will receive whatever you ask for in prayer."

The Authority of Jesus Questioned

23Jesus entered the temple courts, and, while he was teaching, the chief priests and the elders of the people came to him. "By what authority are you doing these things?" they asked. "And who gave you this authority?"

---

a5 Zech. 9:9   *b9* A Hebrew expression meaning
"Save!" which became an exclamation of praise;
also in verse 15   *c9* Psalm 118:26
d13 Isaiah 56:7   *e13* Jer. 7:11
f16 Psalm 8:2

24Jesus replied, "I will also ask you one question. If you answer me, I will tell you by what authority I am doing these things. 25John's baptism—where did it come from? Was it from heaven, or from men?"

They discussed it among themselves and said, "If we say, 'From heaven,' he will ask, 'Then why didn't you believe him?' 26But if we say, 'From men'—we are afraid of the people, for they all hold that John was a prophet."

27So they answered Jesus, "We don't know."

Then he said, "Neither will I tell you by what authority I am doing these things.

The Parable of the Two Sons

28"What do you think? There was a man who had two sons. He went to the first and said, 'Son, go and work today in the vineyard.'

29" 'I will not,' he answered, but later he changed his mind and went.

30"Then the father went to the other son and said the same thing. He answered, 'I will, sir,' but he did not go.

31"Which of the two did what his father wanted?"

"The first," they answered.

Jesus said to them, "I tell you the truth, the tax collectors and the prostitutes are entering the kingdom of God ahead of you. 32For John came to you to show you the way of righteousness, and you did not believe him, but the tax collectors and the prostitutes did. And even after you saw this, you did not repent and believe him.

The Parable of the Tenants

33"Listen to another parable: There was a landowner who planted a vineyard. He put a wall around it, dug a winepress in it and built a watchtower. Then he rented the vineyard to some farmers and went away on a journey. 34When the harvest time approached, he sent his servants to the tenants to collect his fruit.

35"The tenants seized his servants; they beat one, killed another, and stoned a third. 36Then he sent other servants to them, more than the first time, and the tenants treated them the same way. 37Last

of all, he sent his son to them. 'They will respect my son,' he said.

38"But when the tenants saw the son, they said to each other, 'This is the heir. Come, let's kill him and take his inheritance.' 39So they took him and threw him out of the vineyard and killed him.

40"Therefore, when the owner of the vineyard comes, what will he do to those tenants?"

41"He will bring those wretches to a wretched end," they replied, "and he will rent the vineyard to other tenants, who will give him his share of the crop at harvest time."

42Jesus said to them, "Have you never read in the Scriptures:

" 'The stone the builders rejected
  has become the capstone[a];
the Lord has done this,
  and it is marvelous in our eyes'[b]?

43"Therefore I tell you that the kingdom of God will be taken away from you and given to a people who will produce its fruit. 44He who falls on this stone will be broken to pieces, but he on whom it falls will be crushed."[c]

45When the chief priests and the Pharisees heard Jesus' parables, they knew he was talking about them. 46They looked for a way to arrest him, but they were afraid of the crowd because the people held that he was a prophet.

The Parable of the Wedding Banquet

22 Jesus spoke to them again in parables, saying: 2"The kingdom of heaven is like a king who prepared a wedding banquet for his son. 3He sent his servants to those who had been invited to the banquet to tell them to come, but they refused to come.

4"Then he sent some more servants and said, 'Tell those who have been invited that I have prepared my dinner: My oxen and fattened cattle have been butchered, and everything is ready. Come to the wedding banquet.'

5"But they paid no attention and went off—one to his field, another to his business. 6The rest seized his servants, mistreated them and killed them. 7The king

---

a42 Or cornerstone   b42 Psalm 118:22,23
c44 Some manuscripts do not have verse 44.

was enraged. He sent his army and destroyed those murderers and burned their city.

8"Then he said to his servants, 'The wedding banquet is ready, but those I invited did not deserve to come. 9Go to the street corners and invite to the banquet anyone you find.' 10So the servants went out into the streets and gathered all the people they could find, both good and bad, and the wedding hall was filled with guests.

11"But when the king came in to see the guests, he noticed a man there who was not wearing wedding clothes. 12'Friend,' he asked, 'how did you get in here without wedding clothes?' The man was speechless.

13"Then the king told the attendants, 'Tie him hand and foot, and throw him outside, into the darkness, where there will be weeping and gnashing of teeth.'

14"For many are invited, but few are chosen."

Paying Taxes to Caesar

15Then the Pharisees went out and laid plans to trap him in his words. 16They sent their disciples to him along with the Herodians. "Teacher," they said, "we know you are a man of integrity and that you teach the way of God in accordance with the truth. You aren't swayed by men, because you pay no attention to who they are. 17Tell us then, what is your opinion? Is it right to pay taxes to Caesar or not?"

18But Jesus, knowing their evil intent, said, "You hypocrites, why are you trying to trap me? 19Show me the coin used for paying the tax." They brought him a denarius, 20and he asked them, "Whose portrait is this? And whose inscription?"

21"Caesar's," they replied.

Then he said to them, "Give to Caesar what is Caesar's, and to God what is God's."

22When they heard this, they were amazed. So they left him and went away.

Marriage at the Resurrection

23That same day the Sadducees, who say there is no resurrection, came to him with a question. 24"Teacher," they said, "Moses told us that if a man dies without having children, his brother must marry

the widow and have children for him. 25Now there were seven brothers among us. The first one married and died, and since he had no children, he left his wife to his brother. 26The same thing happened to the second and third brother, right on down to the seventh. 27Finally, the woman died. 28Now then, at the resurrection, whose wife will she be of the seven, since all of them were married to her?"

29Jesus replied, "You are in error because you do not know the Scriptures or the power of God. 30At the resurrection people will neither marry nor be given in marriage; they will be like the angels in heaven. 31But about the resurrection of the dead—have you not read what God said to you, 32'I am the God of Abraham, the God of Isaac, and the God of Jacob'a? He is not the God of the dead but of the living."

33When the crowds heard this, they were astonished at his teaching.

The Greatest Commandment

34Hearing that Jesus had silenced the Sadducees, the Pharisees got together. 35One of them, an expert in the law, tested him with this question: 36"Teacher, which is the greatest commandment in the Law?"

37Jesus replied: "'Love the Lord your God with all your heart and with all your soul and with all your mind.'b 38This is the first and greatest commandment. 39And the second is like it: 'Love your neighbor as yourself.'c 40All the Law and the Prophets hang on these two commandments."

Whose Son Is the Christ?

41While the Pharisees were gathered together, Jesus asked them, 42"What do you think about the Christd? Whose son is he?"

"The son of David," they replied.

43He said to them, "How is it then that David, speaking by the Spirit, calls him 'Lord'? For he says,

44"'The Lord said to my Lord:
    "Sit at my right hand

a32 Exodus 3:6   b37 Deut. 6:5
c39 Lev. 19:18   d42 Or Messiah

until I put your enemies
    under your feet." ' a

45If then David calls him 'Lord,' how can
he be his son?" 46No one could say a word
in reply, and from that day on no one
dared to ask him any more questions.

Seven Woes

23 Then Jesus said to the crowds and
to his disciples: 2"The teachers of
the law and the Pharisees sit in Moses'
seat. 3So you must obey them and do everything they tell you. But do not do what
they do, for they do not practice what
they preach. 4They tie up heavy loads and
put them on men's shoulders, but they
themselves are not willing to lift a finger
to move them.

5"Everything they do is done for men
to see: They make their phylacteries b
wide and the tassels on their garments
long; 6they love the place of honor at banquets and the most important seats in the
synagogues; 7they love to be greeted in
the marketplaces and to have men call
them 'Rabbi.'

8"But you are not to be called 'Rabbi,'
for you have only one Master and you are
all brothers. 9And do not call anyone on
earth 'father,' for you have one Father,
and he is in heaven. 10Nor are you to be
called 'teacher,' for you have one Teacher,
the Christ. c 11The greatest among you
will be your servant. 12For whoever exalts
himself will be humbled, and whoever
humbles himself will be exalted.

13"Woe to you, teachers of the law and
Pharisees, you hypocrites! You shut the
kingdom of heaven in men's faces. You
yourselves do not enter, nor will you let
those enter who are trying to. d

15"Woe to you, teachers of the law and
Pharisees, you hypocrites! You travel over
land and sea to win a single convert, and
when he becomes one, you make him
twice as much a son of hell as you are.

---

a44 Psalm 110:1   b5 That is, boxes containing
Scripture verses, worn on forehead and arm
c10 Or Messiah   d13 Some manuscripts to.
14Woe to you, teachers of the law and Pharisees, you
hypocrites! You devour widows' houses and for a show
make lengthy prayers. Therefore you will be punished
more severely.

Love Your Closest Neighbor

Thursday

MATTHEW 22:36–39 These verses
took on a fresh, new meaning for
us when we applied them to our
marriage. The key word, *neighbor*,
means the person who is closest,
nearest and dearest to you. For any
married person, that is your spouse,
the one you chose to share life with at its
deepest and most intimate level. If we love
our marriage partner as we love ourselves,
we will have his or her best interests at
heart, we will want to serve instead of being served, and we will resist the urge to
manipulate or control each other. Our relationship will be based on love and trust.

Think about how often marital conflict
would be resolved if we put the other's interests before our own—if we just loved our
spouse as we love ourselves. We live in
such a me-centered world concerned about
everything being fair. But just the opposite
attitude promotes intimacy in a marriage.

One time that I especially remember

feeling really close to Dave was a
time he chose to be a servant. The
aftermath of my root canal left me
in much pain. The dentist had casually said to me, "Go home and
take two aspirin; you'll be just fine!"

Who was he kidding? While I still remember feeling oh so miserable, years
later what is foremost in my memory is
Dave bringing me Jell-O and simply sitting
by me and holding my hand.

Take a couple of minutes and think of
ways you can love your spouse as your closest neighbor. It could be little things, like
going out in the rain to get the paper or being the first to get up and make the coffee.
Or maybe it's something larger, like sacrificing your golf game for a much-needed
family outing or reprioritizing your budget
to provide resources for a weekend getaway.

—Dave and Claudia

Go to page 1062 for your next devotional reading.

16 "Woe to you, blind guides! You say, 'If anyone swears by the temple, it means nothing; but if anyone swears by the gold of the temple, he is bound by his oath.' 17 You blind fools! Which is greater: the gold, or the temple that makes the gold sacred? 18 You also say, 'If anyone swears by the altar, it means nothing; but if anyone swears by the gift on it, he is bound by his oath.' 19 You blind men! Which is greater: the gift, or the altar that makes the gift sacred? 20 Therefore, he who swears by the altar swears by it and by everything on it. 21 And he who swears by the temple swears by it and by the one who dwells in it. 22 And he who swears by heaven swears by God's throne and by the one who sits on it.

23 "Woe to you, teachers of the law and Pharisees, you hypocrites! You give a tenth of your spices—mint, dill and cummin. But you have neglected the more important matters of the law—justice, mercy and faithfulness. You should have practiced the latter, without neglecting the former. 24 You blind guides! You strain out a gnat but swallow a camel.

25 "Woe to you, teachers of the law and Pharisees, you hypocrites! You clean the outside of the cup and dish, but inside they are full of greed and self-indulgence. 26 Blind Pharisee! First clean the inside of the cup and dish, and then the outside also will be clean.

27 "Woe to you, teachers of the law and Pharisees, you hypocrites! You are like whitewashed tombs, which look beautiful on the outside but on the inside are full of dead men's bones and everything unclean. 28 In the same way, on the outside you appear to people as righteous but on the inside you are full of hypocrisy and wickedness.

29 "Woe to you, teachers of the law and Pharisees, you hypocrites! You build tombs for the prophets and decorate the graves of the righteous. 30 And you say, 'If we had lived in the days of our forefathers, we would not have taken part with them in shedding the blood of the prophets.' 31 So you testify against yourselves that you are the descendants of those who murdered the prophets. 32 Fill up, then, the measure of the sin of your forefathers!

33 "You snakes! You brood of vipers! How will you escape being condemned to hell? 34 Therefore I am sending you prophets and wise men and teachers. Some of them you will kill and crucify; others you will flog in your synagogues and pursue from town to town. 35 And so upon you will come all the righteous blood that has been shed on earth, from the blood of righteous Abel to the blood of Zechariah son of Berekiah, whom you murdered between the temple and the altar. 36 I tell you the truth, all this will come upon this generation.

37 "O Jerusalem, Jerusalem, you who kill the prophets and stone those sent to you, how often I have longed to gather your children together, as a hen gathers her chicks under her wings, but you were not willing. 38 Look, your house is left to you desolate. 39 For I tell you, you will not see me again until you say, 'Blessed is he who comes in the name of the Lord.' [a]"

Signs of the End of the Age

24 Jesus left the temple and was walking away when his disciples came up to him to call his attention to its buildings. 2 "Do you see all these things?" he asked. "I tell you the truth, not one stone here will be left on another; every one will be thrown down."

3 As Jesus was sitting on the Mount of Olives, the disciples came to him privately. "Tell us," they said, "when will this happen, and what will be the sign of your coming and of the end of the age?"

4 Jesus answered: "Watch out that no one deceives you. 5 For many will come in my name, claiming, 'I am the Christ,[b]' and will deceive many. 6 You will hear of wars and rumors of wars, but see to it that you are not alarmed. Such things must happen, but the end is still to come. 7 Nation will rise against nation, and kingdom against kingdom. There will be famines and earthquakes in various places. 8 All these are the beginning of birth pains.

9 "Then you will be handed over to be persecuted and put to death, and you will be hated by all nations because of me. 10 At that time many will turn away from the faith and will betray and hate each other, 11 and many false prophets will appear and deceive many people. 12 Because

a39 Psalm 118:26   b5 Or Messiah; also in verse 23

of the increase of wickedness, the love of most will grow cold, [13]but he who stands firm to the end will be saved. [14]And this gospel of the kingdom will be preached in the whole world as a testimony to all nations, and then the end will come.

[15]"So when you see standing in the holy place 'the abomination that causes desolation,'[a] spoken of through the prophet Daniel—let the reader understand— [16]then let those who are in Judea flee to the mountains. [17]Let no one on the roof of his house go down to take anything out of the house. [18]Let no one in the field go back to get his cloak. [19]How dreadful it will be in those days for pregnant women and nursing mothers! [20]Pray that your flight will not take place in winter or on the Sabbath. [21]For then there will be great distress, unequaled from the beginning of the world until now—and never to be equaled again. [22]If those days had not been cut short, no one would survive, but for the sake of the elect those days will be shortened. [23]At that time if anyone says to you, 'Look, here is the Christ!' or, 'There he is!' do not believe it. [24]For false Christs and false prophets will appear and perform great signs and miracles to deceive even the elect—if that were possible. [25]See, I have told you ahead of time.

[26]"So if anyone tells you, 'There he is, out in the desert,' do not go out; or, 'Here he is, in the inner rooms,' do not believe it. [27]For as lightning that comes from the east is visible even in the west, so will be the coming of the Son of Man. [28]Wherever there is a carcass, there the vultures will gather.

[29]"Immediately after the distress of those days

" 'the sun will be darkened,
    and the moon will not give its
        light;
  the stars will fall from the sky,
    and the heavenly bodies will be
        shaken.'[b]

[30]"At that time the sign of the Son of Man will appear in the sky, and all the nations of the earth will mourn. They will see the Son of Man coming on the clouds of the sky, with power and great glory. [31]And he will send his angels with a loud trumpet call, and they will gather his elect from the four winds, from one end of the heavens to the other.

[32]"Now learn this lesson from the fig tree: As soon as its twigs get tender and its leaves come out, you know that summer is near. [33]Even so, when you see all these things, you know that it[c] is near, right at the door. [34]I tell you the truth, this generation[d] will certainly not pass away until all these things have happened. [35]Heaven and earth will pass away, but my words will never pass away.

The Day and Hour Unknown

[36]"No one knows about that day or hour, not even the angels in heaven, nor the Son,[e] but only the Father. [37]As it was in the days of Noah, so it will be at the coming of the Son of Man. [38]For in the days before the flood, people were eating and drinking, marrying and giving in marriage, up to the day Noah entered the ark; [39]and they knew nothing about what would happen until the flood came and took them all away. That is how it will be at the coming of the Son of Man. [40]Two men will be in the field; one will be taken and the other left. [41]Two women will be grinding with a hand mill; one will be taken and the other left.

[42]"Therefore keep watch, because you do not know on what day your Lord will come. [43]But understand this: If the owner of the house had known at what time of night the thief was coming, he would have kept watch and would not have let his house be broken into. [44]So you also must be ready, because the Son of Man will come at an hour when you do not expect him.

[45]"Who then is the faithful and wise servant, whom the master has put in charge of the servants in his household to give them their food at the proper time? [46]It will be good for that servant whose master finds him doing so when he returns. [47]I tell you the truth, he will put him in charge of all his possessions. [48]But suppose that servant is wicked and says to himself, 'My master is staying away a long time,' [49]and he then begins to beat his

---

[a]15 Daniel 9:27; 11:31; 12:11   [b]29 Isaiah 13:10; 34:4   [c]33 Or *he*   [d]34 Or *race*
[e]36 Some manuscripts do not have *nor the Son.*

fellow servants and to eat and drink with drunkards. ⁵⁰The master of that servant will come on a day when he does not expect him and at an hour he is not aware of. ⁵¹He will cut him to pieces and assign him a place with the hypocrites, where there will be weeping and gnashing of teeth.

The Parable of the Ten Virgins

25 "At that time the kingdom of heaven will be like ten virgins who took their lamps and went out to meet the bridegroom. ²Five of them were foolish and five were wise. ³The foolish ones took their lamps but did not take any oil with them. ⁴The wise, however, took oil in jars along with their lamps. ⁵The bridegroom was a long time in coming, and they all became drowsy and fell asleep.

⁶"At midnight the cry rang out: 'Here's the bridegroom! Come out to meet him!'

⁷"Then all the virgins woke up and trimmed their lamps. ⁸The foolish ones said to the wise, 'Give us some of your oil; our lamps are going out.'

⁹"'No,' they replied, 'there may not be enough for both us and you. Instead, go to those who sell oil and buy some for yourselves.'

¹⁰"But while they were on their way to buy the oil, the bridegroom arrived. The virgins who were ready went in with him to the wedding banquet. And the door was shut.

¹¹"Later the others also came. 'Sir! Sir!' they said. 'Open the door for us!'

¹²"But he replied, 'I tell you the truth, I don't know you.'

¹³"Therefore keep watch, because you do not know the day or the hour.

The Parable of the Talents

¹⁴"Again, it will be like a man going on a journey, who called his servants and entrusted his property to them. ¹⁵To one he gave five talents*ᵃ* of money, to another two talents, and to another one talent, each according to his ability. Then he went on his journey. ¹⁶The man who had received the five talents went at once and put his money to work and gained five more. ¹⁷So also, the one with the two talents gained two more. ¹⁸But the man who had received the one talent went off, dug

a hole in the ground and hid his master's money.

¹⁹"After a long time the master of those servants returned and settled accounts with them. ²⁰The man who had received the five talents brought the other five. 'Master,' he said, 'you entrusted me with five talents. See, I have gained five more.'

²¹"His master replied, 'Well done, good and faithful servant! You have been faithful with a few things; I will put you in charge of many things. Come and share your master's happiness!'

²²"The man with the two talents also came. 'Master,' he said, 'you entrusted me with two talents; see, I have gained two more.'

²³"His master replied, 'Well done, good and faithful servant! You have been faithful with a few things; I will put you in charge of many things. Come and share your master's happiness!'

²⁴"Then the man who had received the one talent came. 'Master,' he said, 'I knew that you are a hard man, harvesting where you have not sown and gathering where you have not scattered seed. ²⁵So I was afraid and went out and hid your talent in the ground. See, here is what belongs to you.'

²⁶"His master replied, 'You wicked, lazy servant! So you knew that I harvest where I have not sown and gather where I have not scattered seed? ²⁷Well then, you should have put my money on deposit with the bankers, so that when I returned I would have received it back with interest.

²⁸"'Take the talent from him and give it to the one who has the ten talents. ²⁹For everyone who has will be given more, and he will have an abundance. Whoever does not have, even what he has will be taken from him. ³⁰And throw that worthless servant outside, into the darkness, where there will be weeping and gnashing of teeth.'

The Sheep and the Goats

³¹"When the Son of Man comes in his glory, and all the angels with him, he will sit on his throne in heavenly glory. ³²All

---

*ᵃ*15 A talent was worth more than a thousand dollars.

the nations will be gathered before him, and he will separate the people one from another as a shepherd separates the sheep from the goats. ³³He will put the sheep on his right and the goats on his left.

³⁴"Then the King will say to those on his right, 'Come, you who are blessed by my Father; take your inheritance, the kingdom prepared for you since the creation of the world. ³⁵For I was hungry and you gave me something to eat, I was thirsty and you gave me something to drink, I was a stranger and you invited me in, ³⁶I needed clothes and you clothed me, I was sick and you looked after me, I was in prison and you came to visit me.'

³⁷"Then the righteous will answer him, 'Lord, when did we see you hungry and feed you, or thirsty and give you something to drink? ³⁸When did we see you a stranger and invite you in, or needing clothes and clothe you? ³⁹When did we see you sick or in prison and go to visit you?'

⁴⁰"The King will reply, 'I tell you the truth, whatever you did for one of the least of these brothers of mine, you did for me.'

⁴¹"Then he will say to those on his left, 'Depart from me, you who are cursed, into the eternal fire prepared for the devil and his angels. ⁴²For I was hungry and you gave me nothing to eat, I was thirsty and you gave me nothing to drink, ⁴³I was a stranger and you did not invite me in, I needed clothes and you did not clothe me, I was sick and in prison and you did not look after me.'

⁴⁴"They also will answer, 'Lord, when did we see you hungry or thirsty or a stranger or needing clothes or sick or in prison, and did not help you?'

⁴⁵"He will reply, 'I tell you the truth, whatever you did not do for one of the least of these, you did not do for me.'

⁴⁶"Then they will go away to eternal punishment, but the righteous to eternal life."

The Plot Against Jesus

26 When Jesus had finished saying all these things, he said to his disciples, ²"As you know, the Passover is two days away—and the Son of Man will be handed over to be crucified."

Unique Talents

Friday

MATTHEW 25:14-30   God gives each of us unique gifts and talents designed to glorify him. The marriage relationship offers the perfect place to discover those individual talents. You may have put to use some of your talents while you were single, but now your spouse can give you insight and encouragement to develop your gifts.

Additionally, God has given each couple unique talents or gifts to use together. However, the uniqueness of each spouse's temperament and background makes for either conflict or a positive experience. We need to take on the responsibility of working through the different ways we each look at life's circumstances, so we can discover the talents and gifts God has entrusted to our unique union.

Shortly after we got married, it became apparent that Bob had gifts as a speaker and teacher. As his wife, I felt it was my role to help and encourage him. I had no desire to speak in public. Bob, on the other hand, believed that I too had a gift of teaching. I fought him on this for years and hid a God-given talent in the sand. Finally, after years of rejecting opportunities to speak at conferences and years of encouragement from Bob, I risked pulling out that buried gift. My initial fear was overwhelming, but God was faithful to bless my risk. Now Bob and I are even using this gift together. Though we teach with a very different style, we are told there is much more power when we speak together.

We hope you discover that using the gifts and talents God has given you in your marriage will bring you happiness and give God glory. —**Bob and Rosemary**

Go to page 1065 for your next devotional reading.

³Then the chief priests and the elders of the people assembled in the palace of the high priest, whose name was Caiaphas, ⁴and they plotted to arrest Jesus in some sly way and kill him. ⁵"But not during the Feast," they said, "or there may be a riot among the people."

Jesus Anointed at Bethany

⁶While Jesus was in Bethany in the home of a man known as Simon the Leper, ⁷a woman came to him with an alabaster jar of very expensive perfume, which she poured on his head as he was reclining at the table.

⁸When the disciples saw this, they were indignant. "Why this waste?" they asked. ⁹"This perfume could have been sold at a high price and the money given to the poor."

¹⁰Aware of this, Jesus said to them, "Why are you bothering this woman? She has done a beautiful thing to me. ¹¹The poor you will always have with you, but you will not always have me. ¹²When she poured this perfume on my body, she did it to prepare me for burial. ¹³I tell you the truth, wherever this gospel is preached throughout the world, what she has done will also be told, in memory of her."

Judas Agrees to Betray Jesus

¹⁴Then one of the Twelve—the one called Judas Iscariot—went to the chief priests ¹⁵and asked, "What are you willing to give me if I hand him over to you?" So they counted out for him thirty silver coins. ¹⁶From then on Judas watched for an opportunity to hand him over.

The Lord's Supper

¹⁷On the first day of the Feast of Unleavened Bread, the disciples came to Jesus and asked, "Where do you want us to make preparations for you to eat the Passover?"

¹⁸He replied, "Go into the city to a certain man and tell him, 'The Teacher says: My appointed time is near. I am going to celebrate the Passover with my disciples at your house.' " ¹⁹So the disciples did as Jesus had directed them and prepared the Passover.

²⁰When evening came, Jesus was reclining at the table with the Twelve. ²¹And while they were eating, he said, "I tell you the truth, one of you will betray me."

²²They were very sad and began to say to him one after the other, "Surely not I, Lord?"

²³Jesus replied, "The one who has dipped his hand into the bowl with me will betray me. ²⁴The Son of Man will go just as it is written about him. But woe to that man who betrays the Son of Man! It would be better for him if he had not been born."

²⁵Then Judas, the one who would betray him, said, "Surely not I, Rabbi?"

Jesus answered, "Yes, it is you."ᵃ

²⁶While they were eating, Jesus took bread, gave thanks and broke it, and gave it to his disciples, saying, "Take and eat; this is my body."

²⁷Then he took the cup, gave thanks and offered it to them, saying, "Drink from it, all of you. ²⁸This is my blood of theᵇ covenant, which is poured out for many for the forgiveness of sins. ²⁹I tell you, I will not drink of this fruit of the vine from now on until that day when I drink it anew with you in my Father's kingdom."

³⁰When they had sung a hymn, they went out to the Mount of Olives.

ᵃ25 Or "You yourself have said it"   ᵇ28 Some manuscripts the new

---

Jesus Predicts Peter's Denial

³¹Then Jesus told them, "This very night you will all fall away on account of me, for it is written:

" 'I will strike the shepherd,
    and the sheep of the flock will be
        scattered.'ᵃ

³²But after I have risen, I will go ahead of you into Galilee."

³³Peter replied, "Even if all fall away on account of you, I never will."

³⁴"I tell you the truth," Jesus answered, "this very night, before the rooster crows, you will disown me three times."

³⁵But Peter declared, "Even if I have to die with you, I will never disown you." And all the other disciples said the same.

Gethsemane

³⁶Then Jesus went with his disciples to a place called Gethsemane, and he said to them, "Sit here while I go over there and pray." ³⁷He took Peter and the two sons of Zebedee along with him, and he began to be sorrowful and troubled. ³⁸Then he said to them, "My soul is overwhelmed with sorrow to the point of death. Stay here and keep watch with me."

³⁹Going a little farther, he fell with his face to the ground and prayed, "My Father, if it is possible, may this cup be taken from me. Yet not as I will, but as you will."

⁴⁰Then he returned to his disciples and found them sleeping. "Could you men not keep watch with me for one hour?" he asked Peter. ⁴¹"Watch and pray so that you will not fall into temptation. The spirit is willing, but the body is weak."

⁴²He went away a second time and prayed, "My Father, if it is not possible for this cup to be taken away unless I drink it, may your will be done."

⁴³When he came back, he again found them sleeping, because their eyes were heavy. ⁴⁴So he left them and went away once more and prayed the third time, saying the same thing.

⁴⁵Then he returned to the disciples and said to them, "Are you still sleeping and resting? Look, the hour is near, and the Son of Man is betrayed into the hands of sinners. ⁴⁶Rise, let us go! Here comes my betrayer!"

Jesus Arrested

⁴⁷While he was still speaking, Judas, one of the Twelve, arrived. With him was a large crowd armed with swords and clubs, sent from the chief priests and the elders of the people. ⁴⁸Now the betrayer had arranged a signal with them: "The one I kiss is the man; arrest him." ⁴⁹Going at once to Jesus, Judas said, "Greetings, Rabbi!" and kissed him.

⁵⁰Jesus replied, "Friend, do what you came for."ᵇ

Then the men stepped forward, seized Jesus and arrested him. ⁵¹With that, one of Jesus' companions reached for his sword, drew it out and struck the servant of the high priest, cutting off his ear.

⁵²"Put your sword back in its place," Jesus said to him, "for all who draw the sword will die by the sword. ⁵³Do you think I cannot call on my Father, and he will at once put at my disposal more than twelve legions of angels? ⁵⁴But how then would the Scriptures be fulfilled that say it must happen in this way?"

⁵⁵At that time Jesus said to the crowd, "Am I leading a rebellion, that you have come out with swords and clubs to capture me? Every day I sat in the temple courts teaching, and you did not arrest me. ⁵⁶But this has all taken place that the writings of the prophets might be fulfilled." Then all the disciples deserted him and fled.

Before the Sanhedrin

⁵⁷Those who had arrested Jesus took him to Caiaphas, the high priest, where the teachers of the law and the elders had assembled. ⁵⁸But Peter followed him at a distance, right up to the courtyard of the high priest. He entered and sat down with the guards to see the outcome.

⁵⁹The chief priests and the whole Sanhedrin were looking for false evidence against Jesus so that they could put him to death. ⁶⁰But they did not find any, though many false witnesses came forward.

Finally two came forward ⁶¹and declared, "This fellow said, 'I am able to destroy the temple of God and rebuild it in three days.' "

ᵃ31 Zech. 13:7   ᵇ50 Or "Friend, why have you come?"

62Then the high priest stood up and said to Jesus, "Are you not going to answer? What is this testimony that these men are bringing against you?" 63But Jesus remained silent.

The high priest said to him, "I charge you under oath by the living God: Tell us if you are the Christ,ᵃ the Son of God."

64"Yes, it is as you say," Jesus replied. "But I say to all of you: In the future you will see the Son of Man sitting at the right hand of the Mighty One and coming on the clouds of heaven."

65Then the high priest tore his clothes and said, "He has spoken blasphemy! Why do we need any more witnesses? Look, now you have heard the blasphemy. 66What do you think?"

"He is worthy of death," they answered.

67Then they spit in his face and struck him with their fists. Others slapped him 68and said, "Prophesy to us, Christ. Who hit you?"

Peter Disowns Jesus

69Now Peter was sitting out in the courtyard, and a servant girl came to him. "You also were with Jesus of Galilee," she said.

70But he denied it before them all. "I don't know what you're talking about," he said.

71Then he went out to the gateway, where another girl saw him and said to the people there, "This fellow was with Jesus of Nazareth."

72He denied it again, with an oath: "I don't know the man!"

73After a little while, those standing there went up to Peter and said, "Surely

ᵃ63 Or Messiah; also in verse 68

Marital Life Preserver

Quiet TIMES with each other

MATTHEW 26:41 They argued at breakfast. No hugs and good-bye kisses. Disgruntled, they headed out the door. Then came a kind word from a co-worker; an innocent touch, eyes locking and forming an emotional connection.

Sexual temptation can be so subtle. It can sneak up when we least expect it. It lurks behind the shadows of dissatisfied spouses. How can you affair-proof your marriage?

One way is to never part angry. Even if things are not resolved, you can defuse anger by acknowledging it and by agreeing to work things out when you are together again. Following the commands of Jesus to watch and pray will enable you to be faithful to your spouse and build a marriage that will go the distance.

Another affair preventer is to develop the habit of praying together. Praying together not only protects your marriage but also promotes spiritual unity and intimacy. If you've struggled with praying together, talk about how God has answered your prayers in the past and the ways he has protected the integrity of your marriage. Make a prayer list, and ask God to protect the very core of your marriage.

Prayer has many benefits, among which is protection from giving in to temptation. In verses 40–41, Jesus found his disciples sleeping rather than praying. Even though they had proclaimed their allegiance to Jesus, in reality they became cowards and gave into temptation—even to the point of denying they knew Jesus.

Prayer in marriage can be a marital life preserver. To protect the spirit of your marriage, you must also protect the physical aspect of your marriage. To put it bluntly, you need the protection of prayer to prevent infidelity in your marriage.

—*Dave and Claudia*

 Weekend Warm-up *Have you prayed for your marriage to be strong?*

Go to page 1066 for your next devotional reading.

you are one of them, for your accent gives you away."

[74]Then he began to call down curses on himself and he swore to them, "I don't know the man!"

Immediately a rooster crowed. [75]Then Peter remembered the word Jesus had spoken: "Before the rooster crows, you will disown me three times." And he went outside and wept bitterly.

Judas Hangs Himself

27 Early in the morning, all the chief priests and the elders of the people came to the decision to put Jesus to death. [2]They bound him, led him away and handed him over to Pilate, the governor.

[3]When Judas, who had betrayed him, saw that Jesus was condemned, he was seized with remorse and returned the thirty silver coins to the chief priests and the elders. [4]"I have sinned," he said, "for I have betrayed innocent blood."

"What is that to us?" they replied. "That's your responsibility."

[5]So Judas threw the money into the temple and left. Then he went away and hanged himself.

[6]The chief priests picked up the coins and said, "It is against the law to put this into the treasury, since it is blood money." [7]So they decided to use the money to buy the potter's field as a burial place for foreigners. [8]That is why it has been called the Field of Blood to this day. [9]Then what was spoken by Jeremiah the prophet was fulfilled: "They took the thirty silver coins, the price set on him by the people of Israel, [10]and they used them to buy the potter's field, as the Lord commanded me."[a]

Jesus Before Pilate

[11]Meanwhile Jesus stood before the governor, and the governor asked him, "Are you the king of the Jews?"

"Yes, it is as you say," Jesus replied.

[12]When he was accused by the chief priests and the elders, he gave no answer.

[a]10 See Zech. 11:12,13; Jer. 19:1-13; 32:6-9.

Hope in the Darkest Hour

Monday

MATTHEW 27—28 The greatest story ever told is that of the death and resurrection of our Lord Jesus Christ. It's great to us because we know the outcome. But for the disciples, it was the greatest tragedy in their lives. They vividly saw Jesus' crucifixion and burial. What could have been worse than witnessing the crucifixion? There was no hope. All seemed lost. But they huddled together and waited on God.

There's a great lesson here in their actions. When a marriage comes up against a great loss, a terminal disease or any tragic circumstance, we learn from the disciples two important steps to take. When nothing more can be done, a couple should huddle together in their own "upper room"—a safe place of prayer and intimacy together. Then they need to wait for relief from God.

In our own life, when one of our children suddenly began suffering from frightening seizures, my inclination was to escape into activity. In my attempt to avoid dealing with, or even thinking about, the fact that I was unable to help my child, I tried to get busy with my work. Rosemary, however, knew we needed to huddle together and wait on God. She sat me down and confronted me about my "running away" from the pain. As I gave in and faced the fear of the unknown with her, I was forced to think about what I really believed in . . . where my confidence truly resided. It was at that time that God became my hope in the darkest hour. Huddled together, we found hope in trusting God for the future.

Relief in times of tragedy will only come when we deepen our relationship with Jesus Christ—the very relationship that was made possible by what is described in this passage. When there are no answers, wait together for his answer.

—Bob and Rosemary

Go to page 1069 for your next devotional reading.

¹³Then Pilate asked him, "Don't you hear the testimony they are bringing against you?" ¹⁴But Jesus made no reply, not even to a single charge—to the great amazement of the governor.

¹⁵Now it was the governor's custom at the Feast to release a prisoner chosen by the crowd. ¹⁶At that time they had a notorious prisoner, called Barabbas. ¹⁷So when the crowd had gathered, Pilate asked them, "Which one do you want me to release to you: Barabbas, or Jesus who is called Christ?" ¹⁸For he knew it was out of envy that they had handed Jesus over to him.

¹⁹While Pilate was sitting on the judge's seat, his wife sent him this message: "Don't have anything to do with that innocent man, for I have suffered a great deal today in a dream because of him."

²⁰But the chief priests and the elders persuaded the crowd to ask for Barabbas and to have Jesus executed.

²¹"Which of the two do you want me to release to you?" asked the governor.

"Barabbas," they answered.

²²"What shall I do, then, with Jesus who is called Christ?" Pilate asked.

They all answered, "Crucify him!"

²³"Why? What crime has he committed?" asked Pilate.

But they shouted all the louder, "Crucify him!"

²⁴When Pilate saw that he was getting nowhere, but that instead an uproar was starting, he took water and washed his hands in front of the crowd. "I am innocent of this man's blood," he said. "It is your responsibility!"

²⁵All the people answered, "Let his blood be on us and on our children!"

²⁶Then he released Barabbas to them. But he had Jesus flogged, and handed him over to be crucified.

The Soldiers Mock Jesus

²⁷Then the governor's soldiers took Jesus into the Praetorium and gathered the whole company of soldiers around him. ²⁸They stripped him and put a scarlet robe on him, ²⁹and then twisted together a crown of thorns and set it on his head. They put a staff in his right hand and knelt in front of him and mocked

Pilate and His Wife

MATTHEW 27:11–26 In verse 19 we are given a glimpse of Pilate's marriage. Pilate's wife was a quiet voice of advice in the middle of a screaming mob. She was advising him to do the opposite of what the public was demanding that he do. Pilate had to choose whether to listen to his wife or succumb to public pressure.

God has declared marriage to be a "one flesh" relationship. Among other things, that phrase indicates that we can have a unique oneness and understanding of each other. The marriage relationship is meant to foster such a close understanding between two people that one spouse can even detect the motives behind the actions of the other spouse. Our spouse often becomes our best advisor. That also makes our spouse the very person God can use to offer life-changing input. It is a wise person who takes his or her spouse's counsel very seriously. It just could be the counsel of God.

In Pilate's case, his wife made a statement that was more profound than she could possibly imagine. "Don't have anything to do with that innocent man" (verse 19), she said. His wife was used to state a great truth. There had never been, nor will there ever be, another "innocent man" such as Jesus. Unfortunately, Pilate listened to the wrong voice.

him. "Hail, king of the Jews!" they said. ³⁰They spit on him, and took the staff and struck him on the head again and again. ³¹After they had mocked him, they took off the robe and put his own clothes on him. Then they led him away to crucify him.

The Crucifixion

³²As they were going out, they met a man from Cyrene, named Simon, and they forced him to carry the cross. ³³They came to a place called Golgotha (which means The Place of the Skull). ³⁴There they offered Jesus wine to drink, mixed with gall; but after tasting it, he refused to

drink it. [35]When they had crucified him, they divided up his clothes by casting lots.[a] [36]And sitting down, they kept watch over him there. [37]Above his head they placed the written charge against him: THIS IS JESUS, THE KING OF THE JEWS. [38]Two robbers were crucified with him, one on his right and one on his left. [39]Those who passed by hurled insults at him, shaking their heads [40]and saying, "You who are going to destroy the temple and build it in three days, save yourself! Come down from the cross, if you are the Son of God!"

[41]In the same way the chief priests, the teachers of the law and the elders mocked him. [42]"He saved others," they said, "but he can't save himself! He's the King of Israel! Let him come down now from the cross, and we will believe in him. [43]He trusts in God. Let God rescue him now if he wants him, for he said, 'I am the Son of God.' " [44]In the same way the robbers who were crucified with him also heaped insults on him.

The Death of Jesus

[45]From the sixth hour until the ninth hour darkness came over all the land. [46]About the ninth hour Jesus cried out in a loud voice, "Eloi, Eloi,[b] lama sabachthani?"—which means, "My God, my God, why have you forsaken me?"[c]

[47]When some of those standing there heard this, they said, "He's calling Elijah." [48]Immediately one of them ran and got a sponge. He filled it with wine vinegar, put it on a stick, and offered it to Jesus to drink. [49]The rest said, "Now leave him alone. Let's see if Elijah comes to save him."

[50]And when Jesus had cried out again in a loud voice, he gave up his spirit.

[51]At that moment the curtain of the temple was torn in two from top to bottom. The earth shook and the rocks split. [52]The tombs broke open and the bodies of many holy people who had died were raised to life. [53]They came out of the tombs, and after Jesus' resurrection they went into the holy city and appeared to many people.

[54]When the centurion and those with him who were guarding Jesus saw the earthquake and all that had happened, they were terrified, and exclaimed, "Surely he was the Son[d] of God!"

[55]Many women were there, watching from a distance. They had followed Jesus from Galilee to care for his needs. [56]Among them were Mary Magdalene, Mary the mother of James and Joses, and the mother of Zebedee's sons.

The Burial of Jesus

[57]As evening approached, there came a rich man from Arimathea, named Joseph, who had himself become a disciple of Jesus. [58]Going to Pilate, he asked for Jesus' body, and Pilate ordered that it be given to him. [59]Joseph took the body, wrapped it in a clean linen cloth, [60]and placed it in his own new tomb that he had cut out of the rock. He rolled a big stone in front of the entrance to the tomb and went away. [61]Mary Magdalene and the other Mary were sitting there opposite the tomb.

The Guard at the Tomb

[62]The next day, the one after Preparation Day, the chief priests and the Pharisees went to Pilate. [63]"Sir," they said, "we remember that while he was still alive that deceiver said, 'After three days I will rise again.' [64]So give the order for the tomb to be made secure until the third day. Otherwise, his disciples may come and steal the body and tell the people that he has been raised from the dead. This last deception will be worse than the first."

[65]"Take a guard," Pilate answered. "Go, make the tomb as secure as you know how." [66]So they went and made the tomb secure by putting a seal on the stone and posting the guard.

The Resurrection

28 After the Sabbath, at dawn on the first day of the week, Mary Magdalene and the other Mary went to look at the tomb.

[2]There was a violent earthquake, for an angel of the Lord came down from heaven and, going to the tomb, rolled back the

---

[a]35 A few late manuscripts lots that the word spoken by the prophet might be fulfilled: "They divided my garments among themselves and cast lots for my clothing" (Psalm 22:18)　　[b]46 Some manuscripts Eli, Eli　　[c]46 Psalm 22:1　　[d]54 Or a son

stone and sat on it. ³His appearance was like lightning, and his clothes were white as snow. ⁴The guards were so afraid of him that they shook and became like dead men.

⁵The angel said to the women, "Do not be afraid, for I know that you are looking for Jesus, who was crucified. ⁶He is not here; he has risen, just as he said. Come and see the place where he lay. ⁷Then go quickly and tell his disciples: 'He has risen from the dead and is going ahead of you into Galilee. There you will see him.' Now I have told you."

⁸So the women hurried away from the tomb, afraid yet filled with joy, and ran to tell his disciples. ⁹Suddenly Jesus met them. "Greetings," he said. They came to him, clasped his feet and worshiped him. ¹⁰Then Jesus said to them, "Do not be afraid. Go and tell my brothers to go to Galilee; there they will see me."

The Guards' Report

¹¹While the women were on their way, some of the guards went into the city and reported to the chief priests everything that had happened. ¹²When the chief priests had met with the elders and de-

vised a plan, they gave the soldiers a large sum of money, ¹³telling them, "You are to say, 'His disciples came during the night and stole him away while we were asleep.' ¹⁴If this report gets to the governor, we will satisfy him and keep you out of trouble." ¹⁵So the soldiers took the money and did as they were instructed. And this story has been widely circulated among the Jews to this very day.

The Great Commission

¹⁶Then the eleven disciples went to Galilee, to the mountain where Jesus had told them to go. ¹⁷When they saw him, they worshiped him; but some doubted. ¹⁸Then Jesus came to them and said, "All authority in heaven and on earth has been given to me. ¹⁹Therefore go and make disciples of all nations, baptizing them in*ᵃ* the name of the Father and of the Son and of the Holy Spirit, ²⁰and teaching them to obey everything I have commanded you. And surely I am with you always, to the very end of the age."

ᵃ19 Or into; see Acts 8:16; 19:5; Romans 6:3; 1 Cor. 1:13; 10:2 and Gal. 3:27.

Passing the Torch

Tuesday

MATTHEW 28:19 Over the years couples like our (Dave and Claudia) dear friends and mentors Drs. David and Vera Mace modeled for us how to have a positive, growing and spiritually intimate marriage. We remember so many times they graciously answered our questions that must have seen so elementary to them. Whether it was a big issue such as future educational plans or questions about our relationship, the Maces become personally involved with us, and, by doing so, impacted our lives forever.

David and Vera's advice as to the academic track I (Dave) should take was invaluable. They encouraged me to pursue

graduate studies in the field of Social Work, which I did. Over the years that experience and credential has greatly benefited both of us and added to my credibility as a marriage educator.

On the strong foundation that the Maces and other concerned Christian couples built, we now are able to help others experience what they have passed on to us. Won't you join with us and help pass the torch to others? You will find that shared service promotes spiritual intimacy and is one way you can help to fulfill the Great Commission.

—Dave and Claudia

Go to page 1072 for your next devotional reading.

Mark

Mark was a young man — perhaps a teenager—when Jesus Christ walked planet Earth. Tradition tells us that he learned most of what he recorded from the apostle Peter's preaching. But when it came time for him to put pen to parchment, Mark doesn't even mention the Messiah's birth. Most teenage boys wouldn't pay close attention to the details of babies or lineage. So Mark's account is filled with the overwhelming emotion of a young man—observations from someone who was not an insider but whose life was radically changed by this man from Nazareth. Nearly half of Mark's book covers the final, incredible week before the Savior's crucifixion and resurrection.

Mark's writing ends after he records how Jesus revealed himself to his disciples and told them to share with the world what had happened. Having heard Peter's stories and seen Jesus' power to transform lives, Mark was probably packing his own bags, preparing to tell everyone what he knew, regardless of the consequences. Are you and your spouse eager to share Jesus' story?

John the Baptist Prepares the Way

1 The beginning of the gospel about Jesus Christ, the Son of God. *a*

²It is written in Isaiah the prophet:

"I will send my messenger ahead of you,
who will prepare your way" *b*—
³ "a voice of one calling in the desert,
'Prepare the way for the Lord,
make straight paths for him.' " *c*

⁴And so John came, baptizing in the desert region and preaching a baptism of repentance for the forgiveness of sins. ⁵The whole Judean countryside and all the people of Jerusalem went out to him.

a1 Some manuscripts do not have the Son of God.
b2 Mal. 3:1   c3 Isaiah 40:3

Confessing their sins, they were baptized by him in the Jordan River. ⁶John wore clothing made of camel's hair, with a leather belt around his waist, and he ate locusts and wild honey. ⁷And this was his message: "After me will come one more powerful than I, the thongs of whose sandals I am not worthy to stoop down and untie. ⁸I baptize you with*a* water, but he will baptize you with the Holy Spirit."

The Baptism and Temptation of Jesus

⁹At that time Jesus came from Nazareth in Galilee and was baptized by John in the Jordan. ¹⁰As Jesus was coming up out of the water, he saw heaven being torn open and the Spirit descending on him like a dove. ¹¹And a voice came from heaven: "You are my Son, whom I love; with you I am well pleased."

¹²At once the Spirit sent him out into the desert, ¹³and he was in the desert forty days, being tempted by Satan. He was with the wild animals, and angels attended him.

The Calling of the First Disciples

¹⁴After John was put in prison, Jesus went into Galilee, proclaiming the good news of God. ¹⁵"The time has come," he said. "The kingdom of God is near. Repent and believe the good news!"

¹⁶As Jesus walked beside the Sea of Galilee, he saw Simon and his brother Andrew casting a net into the lake, for they were fishermen. ¹⁷"Come, follow me," Jesus said, "and I will make you fishers of men." ¹⁸At once they left their nets and followed him.

¹⁹When he had gone a little farther, he saw James son of Zebedee and his brother John in a boat, preparing their nets. ²⁰Without delay he called them, and they left their father Zebedee in the boat with the hired men and followed him.

Jesus Drives Out an Evil Spirit

²¹They went to Capernaum, and when the Sabbath came, Jesus went into the synagogue and began to teach. ²²The people were amazed at his teaching, because he taught them as one who had authority, not as the teachers of the law. ²³Just then a man in their synagogue who was possessed by an evil*b* spirit cried out,

Zebedee and Salome

MARK 1:14–20 Ministry can either be a source of great stress or a blessing on family life. By all appearances Zebedee and Salome had done a good job of catching a vision for each family member's part in serving God. We hear no objections from Zebedee when his two sons were called to leave the family business and follow the Lord in ministry. In fact, we get the impression that Zebedee carried on the family business with his hired servants while James and John went off to serve. Salome was also involved in the ministry of Jesus Christ. Mark 15 and 16 tell us that she was even one of the women at the tomb. Everyone mentioned in this family seems to have worked toward the common effort of serving Christ. Salome and her two sons were in Christ's inner circle, while Zebedee made this possible by keeping the family business running.

Keeping your marriage and family focused on the right priority is a difficult task. It starts with the question, "Why are we really here?" Some families would send every able bodied worker out the door to make as much money as possible. But is that what we're here to do? No matter what form it may take, we are here to love and to serve Christ. If we don't coordinate those efforts, we will find each family member running in different directions. If we focus on understanding and supporting each other, our family ministry will be a blessing.

²⁴"What do you want with us, Jesus of Nazareth? Have you come to destroy us? I know who you are—the Holy One of God!"

²⁵"Be quiet!" said Jesus sternly. "Come out of him!" ²⁶The evil spirit shook the man violently and came out of him with a shriek.

²⁷The people were all so amazed that they asked each other, "What is this? A new teaching—and with authority! He

*a*8 Or *in*   *b*23 Greek *unclean*; also in verses 26 and 27 even gives orders to evil spirits and they obey him." [28]News about him spread quickly over the whole region of Galilee.

Jesus Heals Many

[29]As soon as they left the synagogue, they went with James and John to the home of Simon and Andrew. [30]Simon's mother-in-law was in bed with a fever, and they told Jesus about her. [31]So he went to her, took her hand and helped her up. The fever left her and she began to wait on them.

[32]That evening after sunset the people brought to Jesus all the sick and demon-possessed. [33]The whole town gathered at the door, [34]and Jesus healed many who had various diseases. He also drove out many demons, but he would not let the demons speak because they knew who he was.

Jesus Prays in a Solitary Place

[35]Very early in the morning, while it was still dark, Jesus got up, left the house and went off to a solitary place, where he prayed. [36]Simon and his companions went to look for him, [37]and when they

found him, they exclaimed: "Everyone is looking for you!"

[38]Jesus replied, "Let us go somewhere else—to the nearby villages—so I can preach there also. That is why I have come." [39]So he traveled throughout Galilee, preaching in their synagogues and driving out demons.

A Man With Leprosy

[40]A man with leprosy[a] came to him and begged him on his knees, "If you are willing, you can make me clean."

[41]Filled with compassion, Jesus reached out his hand and touched the man. "I am willing," he said. "Be clean!" [42]Immediately the leprosy left him and he was cured.

[43]Jesus sent him away at once with a strong warning: [44]"See that you don't tell this to anyone. But go, show yourself to the priest and offer the sacrifices that Moses commanded for your cleansing, as a testimony to them." [45]Instead he went out and began to talk freely, spreading the news. As a result, Jesus could no longer enter a town openly but stayed outside in

[a]40 The Greek word was used for various diseases affecting the skin—not necessarily leprosy.

The Value of a Tender Touch

Wednesday

MARK 1:41–42 In May, 1985, Brigitte Gerney was trapped beneath a 35-ton collapsed construction crane in New York City for 6 hours. Throughout her ordeal, she held the hand of rescue officer Paul Ragonese, who stayed by her side as heavy machinery moved the tons of twisted steel from her crushed legs. A stranger's touch gave her hope and the will to live.

Touch is one of the most powerful communication tools. From a mother's cradling embrace to a friend's comforting hug or a spouse's caress, touch has the special power to send messages of union and communion. Even a momentary and seemingly incidental touch on your spouse's shoulder or hand can strengthen the marital bond by conveying affirmation, comfort and security.

Scripture shows the value of touch as it conveys a blessing (see Genesis 27:26 and 48:9–14, page 29). The Old Testament priestly duties involved the laying on of hands. Moses laid his hands on Joshua to symbolize that he was giving Joshua authority over the people (see Numbers 27:18, page 170). And Jesus, of course, was a master of communicating love. He practiced the blessing of touch, often with children: "And he took the children in his arms, put his hands on them and blessed them" (Mark 10:16).

So consider the value of meaningful touch in your marriage. If a stranger's touch meant life to Brigitte Gerney, think of what a meaningful touch from you can do for your spouse. —*Les and Leslie*

Go to page 1076 for your next devotional reading.

lonely places. Yet the people still came to him from everywhere.

Jesus Heals a Paralytic

2 A few days later, when Jesus again entered Capernaum, the people heard that he had come home. ²So many gathered that there was no room left, not even outside the door, and he preached the word to them. ³Some men came, bringing to him a paralytic, carried by four of them. ⁴Since they could not get him to Jesus because of the crowd, they made an opening in the roof above Jesus and, after digging through it, lowered the mat the paralyzed man was lying on. ⁵When Jesus saw their faith, he said to the paralytic, "Son, your sins are forgiven."

⁶Now some teachers of the law were sitting there, thinking to themselves, ⁷"Why does this fellow talk like that? He's blaspheming! Who can forgive sins but God alone?"

⁸Immediately Jesus knew in his spirit that this was what they were thinking in their hearts, and he said to them, "Why are you thinking these things? ⁹Which is easier: to say to the paralytic, 'Your sins are forgiven,' or to say, 'Get up, take your mat and walk'? ¹⁰But that you may know that the Son of Man has authority on earth to forgive sins . . ." He said to the paralytic, ¹¹"I tell you, get up, take your mat and go home." ¹²He got up, took his mat and walked out in full view of them all. This amazed everyone and they praised God, saying, "We have never seen anything like this!"

The Calling of Levi

¹³Once again Jesus went out beside the lake. A large crowd came to him, and he began to teach them. ¹⁴As he walked along, he saw Levi son of Alphaeus sitting at the tax collector's booth. "Follow me," Jesus told him, and Levi got up and followed him.

¹⁵While Jesus was having dinner at Levi's house, many tax collectors and "sinners" were eating with him and his disciples, for there were many who followed him. ¹⁶When the teachers of the law who were Pharisees saw him eating with the "sinners" and tax collectors, they asked his disciples: "Why does he eat with tax collectors and 'sinners'?"

¹⁷On hearing this, Jesus said to them, "It is not the healthy who need a doctor, but the sick. I have not come to call the righteous, but sinners."

Jesus Questioned About Fasting

¹⁸Now John's disciples and the Pharisees were fasting. Some people came and asked Jesus, "How is it that John's disciples and the disciples of the Pharisees are fasting, but yours are not?"

¹⁹Jesus answered, "How can the guests of the bridegroom fast while he is with them? They cannot, so long as they have him with them. ²⁰But the time will come when the bridegroom will be taken from them, and on that day they will fast.

²¹"No one sews a patch of unshrunk cloth on an old garment. If he does, the new piece will pull away from the old, making the tear worse. ²²And no one pours new wine into old wineskins. If he does, the wine will burst the skins, and both the wine and the wineskins will be ruined. No, he pours new wine into new wineskins."

Lord of the Sabbath

²³One Sabbath Jesus was going through the grainfields, and as his disciples walked along, they began to pick some heads of grain. ²⁴The Pharisees said to him, "Look, why are they doing what is unlawful on the Sabbath?"

²⁵He answered, "Have you never read what David did when he and his companions were hungry and in need? ²⁶In the days of Abiathar the high priest, he entered the house of God and ate the consecrated bread, which is lawful only for priests to eat. And he also gave some to his companions."

²⁷Then he said to them, "The Sabbath was made for man, not man for the Sabbath. ²⁸So the Son of Man is Lord even of the Sabbath."

3 Another time he went into the synagogue, and a man with a shriveled hand was there. ²Some of them were looking for a reason to accuse Jesus, so they watched him closely to see if he would heal him on the Sabbath. ³Jesus

said to the man with the shriveled hand, "Stand up in front of everyone."

⁴Then Jesus asked them, "Which is lawful on the Sabbath: to do good or to do evil, to save life or to kill?" But they remained silent.

⁵He looked around at them in anger and, deeply distressed at their stubborn hearts, said to the man, "Stretch out your hand." He stretched it out, and his hand was completely restored. ⁶Then the Pharisees went out and began to plot with the Herodians how they might kill Jesus.

Crowds Follow Jesus

⁷Jesus withdrew with his disciples to the lake, and a large crowd from Galilee followed. ⁸When they heard all he was doing, many people came to him from Judea, Jerusalem, Idumea, and the regions across the Jordan and around Tyre and Sidon. ⁹Because of the crowd he told his disciples to have a small boat ready for him, to keep the people from crowding him. ¹⁰For he had healed many, so that those with diseases were pushing forward to touch him. ¹¹Whenever the evil*a* spirits saw him, they fell down before him and cried out, "You are the Son of God." ¹²But he gave them strict orders not to tell who he was.

The Appointing of the Twelve Apostles

¹³Jesus went up on a mountainside and called to him those he wanted, and they came to him. ¹⁴He appointed twelve—designating them apostles*b*—that they might be with him and that he might send them out to preach ¹⁵and to have authority to drive out demons. ¹⁶These are the twelve he appointed: Simon (to whom he gave the name Peter); ¹⁷James son of Zebedee and his brother John (to them he gave the name Boanerges, which means Sons of Thunder); ¹⁸Andrew, Philip, Bartholomew, Matthew, Thomas, James son of Alphaeus, Thaddaeus, Simon the Zealot ¹⁹and Judas Iscariot, who betrayed him.

Jesus and Beelzebub

²⁰Then Jesus entered a house, and again a crowd gathered, so that he and his disciples were not even able to eat. ²¹When his family heard about this, they went to take charge of him, for they said, "He is out of his mind."

²²And the teachers of the law who came down from Jerusalem said, "He is possessed by Beelzebub*c*! By the prince of demons he is driving out demons."

²³So Jesus called them and spoke to them in parables: "How can Satan drive out Satan? ²⁴If a kingdom is divided against itself, that kingdom cannot stand. ²⁵If a house is divided against itself, that house cannot stand. ²⁶And if Satan opposes himself and is divided, he cannot stand; his end has come. ²⁷In fact, no one can enter a strong man's house and carry off his possessions unless he first ties up the strong man. Then he can rob his house. ²⁸I tell you the truth, all the sins and blasphemies of men will be forgiven them. ²⁹But whoever blasphemes against the Holy Spirit will never be forgiven; he is guilty of an eternal sin."

³⁰He said this because they were saying, "He has an evil spirit."

Jesus' Mother and Brothers

³¹Then Jesus' mother and brothers arrived. Standing outside, they sent someone in to call him. ³²A crowd was sitting around him, and they told him, "Your mother and brothers are outside looking for you."

³³"Who are my mother and my brothers?" he asked.

³⁴Then he looked at those seated in a circle around him and said, "Here are my mother and my brothers! ³⁵Whoever does God's will is my brother and sister and mother."

The Parable of the Sower

4 Again Jesus began to teach by the lake. The crowd that gathered around him was so large that he got into a boat and sat in it out on the lake, while all the people were along the shore at the water's edge. ²He taught them many things by parables, and in his teaching said: ³"Listen! A farmer went out to sow his seed. ⁴As he was scattering the seed, some fell along the path, and the birds came and ate it up. ⁵Some fell on rocky places,

---

a 11 Greek *unclean*; also in verse 30   *b 14* Some manuscripts do not have *designating them apostles*. *c 22* Greek *Beezeboul* or *Beelzeboul* where it did not have much soil. It sprang up quickly, because the soil was shallow. [6]But when the sun came up, the plants were scorched, and they withered because they had no root. [7]Other seed fell among thorns, which grew up and choked the plants, so that they did not bear grain. [8]Still other seed fell on good soil. It came up, grew and produced a crop, multiplying thirty, sixty, or even a hundred times."

[9]Then Jesus said, "He who has ears to hear, let him hear."

[10]When he was alone, the Twelve and the others around him asked him about the parables. [11]He told them, "The secret of the kingdom of God has been given to you. But to those on the outside everything is said in parables [12]so that,

" 'they may be ever seeing but never
    perceiving,
    and ever hearing but never
        understanding;
otherwise they might turn and be
    forgiven!'[a] "

[13]Then Jesus said to them, "Don't you understand this parable? How then will you understand any parable? [14]The farmer sows the word. [15]Some people are like seed along the path, where the word is sown. As soon as they hear it, Satan comes and takes away the word that was sown in them. [16]Others, like seed sown on rocky places, hear the word and at once receive it with joy. [17]But since they have no root, they last only a short time. When trouble or persecution comes because of the word, they quickly fall away. [18]Still others, like seed sown among thorns, hear the word; [19]but the worries of this life, the deceitfulness of wealth and the desires for other things come in and choke the word, making it unfruitful. [20]Others, like seed sown on good soil, hear the word, accept it, and produce a crop—thirty, sixty or even a hundred times what was sown."

A Lamp on a Stand

[21]He said to them, "Do you bring in a lamp to put it under a bowl or a bed? Instead, don't you put it on its stand? [22]For whatever is hidden is meant to be disclosed, and whatever is concealed is meant to be brought out into the open.

[23]If anyone has ears to hear, let him hear."

[24]"Consider carefully what you hear," he continued. "With the measure you use, it will be measured to you—and even more. [25]Whoever has will be given more; whoever does not have, even what he has will be taken from him."

The Parable of the Growing Seed

[26]He also said, "This is what the kingdom of God is like. A man scatters seed on the ground. [27]Night and day, whether he sleeps or gets up, the seed sprouts and grows, though he does not know how. [28]All by itself the soil produces grain—first the stalk, then the head, then the full kernel in the head. [29]As soon as the grain is ripe, he puts the sickle to it, because the harvest has come."

The Parable of the Mustard Seed

[30]Again he said, "What shall we say the kingdom of God is like, or what parable shall we use to describe it? [31]It is like a mustard seed, which is the smallest seed you plant in the ground. [32]Yet when planted, it grows and becomes the largest of all garden plants, with such big branches that the birds of the air can perch in its shade."

[33]With many similar parables Jesus spoke the word to them, as much as they could understand. [34]He did not say anything to them without using a parable. But when he was alone with his own disciples, he explained everything.

Jesus Calms the Storm

[35]That day when evening came, he said to his disciples, "Let us go over to the other side." [36]Leaving the crowd behind, they took him along, just as he was, in the boat. There were also other boats with him. [37]A furious squall came up, and the waves broke over the boat, so that it was nearly swamped. [38]Jesus was in the stern, sleeping on a cushion. The disciples woke him and said to him, "Teacher, don't you care if we drown?"

[39]He got up, rebuked the wind and said to the waves, "Quiet! Be still!" Then the wind died down and it was completely calm.

[a]12 Isaiah 6:9,10

[40]He said to his disciples, "Why are you so afraid? Do you still have no faith?"

[41]They were terrified and asked each other, "Who is this? Even the wind and the waves obey him!"

The Healing of a Demon-possessed Man

5 They went across the lake to the region of the Gerasenes.[a] [2]When Jesus got out of the boat, a man with an evil[b] spirit came from the tombs to meet him. [3]This man lived in the tombs, and no one could bind him any more, not even with a chain. [4]For he had often been chained hand and foot, but he tore the chains apart and broke the irons on his feet. No one was strong enough to subdue him. [5]Night and day among the tombs and in the hills he would cry out and cut himself with stones.

[6]When he saw Jesus from a distance, he ran and fell on his knees in front of him. [7]He shouted at the top of his voice, "What do you want with me, Jesus, Son of the Most High God? Swear to God that you won't torture me!" [8]For Jesus had said to him, "Come out of this man, you evil spirit!"

[9]Then Jesus asked him, "What is your name?"

"My name is Legion," he replied, "for we are many." [10]And he begged Jesus again and again not to send them out of the area.

[11]A large herd of pigs was feeding on the nearby hillside. [12]The demons begged Jesus, "Send us among the pigs; allow us to go into them." [13]He gave them permission, and the evil spirits came out and went into the pigs. The herd, about two thousand in number, rushed down the steep bank into the lake and were drowned.

[14]Those tending the pigs ran off and reported this in the town and countryside, and the people went out to see what had happened. [15]When they came to Jesus, they saw the man who had been possessed by the legion of demons, sitting there, dressed and in his right mind; and they were afraid. [16]Those who had seen it told the people what had happened to the demon-possessed man—and told about the pigs as well. [17]Then the people began to plead with Jesus to leave their region.

[18]As Jesus was getting into the boat, the man who had been demon-possessed begged to go with him. [19]Jesus did not let him, but said, "Go home to your family and tell them how much the Lord has done for you, and how he has had mercy

---

[a]1 Some manuscripts *Gadarenes*; other manuscripts *Gergesenes*　　[b]2 Greek *unclean*; also in verses 8 and 13

Who's in the Driver's Seat?

Thursday

MARK 4:35–40 Recently we bought a new van. It was quite an upgrade from our previous vehicle and contained gadgets we had never seen before. When you've never had them or used them, they're hard to trust. While taking the first family trip with the new van, we got lost on some country roads. The harder I tried to get my bearings, the more lost we got. Finally, from the back seat my daughter Torrey suggested, "Push the button on the direction-finder-thing, Daddy!"

It was a button I had pushed before but only when showing it off in our driveway. Never had I used it in a moment of need. As usual, I was relying on my own skills to get us through the difficulty. These were skills I had gotten used to over the years—skills that were letting us down at the moment. Yet I had the help I needed right there in front of me. Many couples struggle through the storms of life because they react the same way as the disciples. The One who could calm the storm was on board, but they still wanted to handle it their way. Like couples today, the disciples had a decision to make: Would they trust Jesus to guide them through, or would they try to make it on their own?

Jesus doesn't want to be just a passenger in your marriage. He's waiting to be in the driver's seat, so he can help you find your way. **—Bob and Rosemary**

Go to page 1077 for your next devotional reading.

on you." ²⁰So the man went away and began to tell in the Decapolis*a* how much Jesus had done for him. And all the people were amazed.

A Dead Girl and a Sick Woman

²¹When Jesus had again crossed over by boat to the other side of the lake, a large crowd gathered around him while he was by the lake. ²²Then one of the synagogue rulers, named Jairus, came there. Seeing Jesus, he fell at his feet ²³and pleaded earnestly with him, "My little daughter is dying. Please come and put your hands on her so that she will be healed and live." ²⁴So Jesus went with him.

A large crowd followed and pressed around him. ²⁵And a woman was there who had been subject to bleeding for twelve years. ²⁶She had suffered a great deal under the care of many doctors and had spent all she had, yet instead of getting better she grew worse. ²⁷When she heard about Jesus, she came up behind him in the crowd and touched his cloak, ²⁸because she thought, "If I just touch his clothes, I will be healed." ²⁹Immediately her bleeding stopped and she felt in her body that she was freed from her suffering.

³⁰At once Jesus realized that power had gone out from him. He turned around in the crowd and asked, "Who touched my clothes?"

³¹"You see the people crowding against you," his disciples answered, "and yet you can ask, 'Who touched me?'"

³²But Jesus kept looking around to see who had done it. ³³Then the woman, knowing what had happened to her, came and fell at his feet and, trembling with fear, told him the whole truth. ³⁴He said to her, "Daughter, your faith has healed you. Go in peace and be freed from your suffering."

³⁵While Jesus was still speaking, some men came from the house of Jairus, the synagogue ruler. "Your daughter is dead," they said. "Why bother the teacher any more?"

³⁶Ignoring what they said, Jesus told the synagogue ruler, "Don't be afraid; just believe."

³⁷He did not let anyone follow him except Peter, James and John the brother

a20 That is, the Ten Cities

The Risk of Public Allegiance

Friday

MARK 5:21–43 There are two people at the center of this passage— a synagogue leader who was prominent in his town and a woman who was an outcast because she had been "unclean" for twelve years. Each had a need. At this point they had to decide if they really believed Jesus could meet their needs. Did they believe it enough to publicly bow before him? Just a quiet nod would not do.

To publicly announce his faith in Jesus meant that Jairus was risking his reputation. For the woman to come out in public and attempt to touch Jesus meant she was risking public ridicule or further rejection. This passage reveals two people who took the risk of making their faith in Jesus public.

In what or in who are you putting your faith? Jesus desires all of our allegiance—in public and in private. The marriage rela-

tionship offers many opportunities for a public declaration of where we are putting our trust. In times of family difficulty or tragedy, friends, well wishers and others in our community who are concerned need to hear us say that we are praying and counting on Jesus Christ for the outcome. In times of blessings, a promotion at work or the birth of a baby once again offers us the chance to be bold and give praise to Jesus. These events are not always just for our own use and growth. Sometimes they are intended to draw others to God.

In both tragedy and prosperity, bystanders will be watching to see how a couple handles the events of life—a great opportunity to be a godly example and witness to them! **—Bob and Rosemary**

Go to page 1079 for your next devotional reading.

Jairus and His Wife

MARK 5:35–43 At times God permits a tragedy to nurture our faith. When circumstances force us to the end of helping ourselves, we often find ourselves at the beginning of trusting God.

Jairus and his wife were people of great status in the large town of Capernaum. As president of the synagogue, Jairus was the most powerful layman of the region. It must have shocked the people to see him humble himself and fall at the feet of an itinerant preacher. Jairus and his wife had hit the end of their own means to help their only daughter. They were forced to trust more than a religion. They trusted Jesus, the Christ.

The partnership behind this decision is implied. While Jairus went for help, his wife stayed and ministered to their dying child. We can see in this situation that the wife of this religious leader was in accord with his decision to step out and trust Jesus. When Jesus walked into their home, he didn't have to work around the wife of Jairus because of any lack of faith. Jesus didn't tell her to wait outside with the other doubters (see verse 40). Instead he honored their faith by inviting them both into the room where the girl was to be healed. Jairus and his wife were equally yoked in their faith. This adversity caused them to humble themselves and unify their singular trust in Jesus Christ.

of James. ³⁸When they came to the home of the synagogue ruler, Jesus saw a commotion, with people crying and wailing loudly. ³⁹He went in and said to them, "Why all this commotion and wailing? The child is not dead but asleep." ⁴⁰But they laughed at him.

After he put them all out, he took the child's father and mother and the disciples who were with him, and went in where the child was. ⁴¹He took her by the hand and said to her, *"Talitha koum!"* (which means, "Little girl, I say to you, get up!"). ⁴²Immediately the girl stood up and walked around (she was twelve years old). At this they were completely aston-

ished. ⁴³He gave strict orders not to let anyone know about this, and told them to give her something to eat.

A Prophet Without Honor

6 Jesus left there and went to his hometown, accompanied by his disciples. ²When the Sabbath came, he began to teach in the synagogue, and many who heard him were amazed.

"Where did this man get these things?" they asked. "What's this wisdom that has been given him, that he even does miracles! ³Isn't this the carpenter? Isn't this Mary's son and the brother of James, Joseph,ᵃ Judas and Simon? Aren't his sisters here with us?" And they took offense at him.

⁴Jesus said to them, "Only in his hometown, among his relatives and in his own house is a prophet without honor." ⁵He could not do any miracles there, except lay his hands on a few sick people and heal them. ⁶And he was amazed at their lack of faith.

Jesus Sends Out the Twelve

Then Jesus went around teaching from village to village. ⁷Calling the Twelve to him, he sent them out two by two and gave them authority over evilᵇ spirits.

⁸These were his instructions: "Take nothing for the journey except a staff—no bread, no bag, no money in your belts. ⁹Wear sandals but not an extra tunic. ¹⁰Whenever you enter a house, stay there until you leave that town. ¹¹And if any place will not welcome you or listen to you, shake the dust off your feet when you leave, as a testimony against them."

¹²They went out and preached that people should repent. ¹³They drove out many demons and anointed many sick people with oil and healed them.

John the Baptist Beheaded

¹⁴King Herod heard about this, for Jesus' name had become well known. Some were saying,ᶜ "John the Baptist has been raised from the dead, and that is why miraculous powers are at work in him."

ᵃ3 Greek *Joses*, a variant of *Joseph*   ᵇ7 Greek *unclean*   ᶜ14 Some early manuscripts *He was saying*

¹⁵Others said, "He is Elijah."

And still others claimed, "He is a prophet, like one of the prophets of long ago."

¹⁶But when Herod heard this, he said, "John, the man I beheaded, has been raised from the dead!"

¹⁷For Herod himself had given orders to have John arrested, and he had him bound and put in prison. He did this because of Herodias, his brother Philip's wife, whom he had married. ¹⁸For John had been saying to Herod, "It is not lawful for you to have your brother's wife." ¹⁹So Herodias nursed a grudge against John and wanted to kill him. But she was not able to, ²⁰because Herod feared John and protected him, knowing him to be a righteous and holy man. When Herod heard John, he was greatly puzzled[a]; yet he liked to listen to him.

²¹Finally the opportune time came. On his birthday Herod gave a banquet for his high officials and military commanders and the leading men of Galilee. ²²When the daughter of Herodias came in and danced, she pleased Herod and his dinner guests.

The king said to the girl, "Ask me for anything you want, and I'll give it to you." ²³And he promised her with an oath, "Whatever you ask I will give you, up to half my kingdom."

²⁴She went out and said to her mother, "What shall I ask for?"

"The head of John the Baptist," she answered.

²⁵At once the girl hurried in to the king with the request: "I want you to give me right now the head of John the Baptist on a platter."

²⁶The king was greatly distressed, but

[a]20 Some early manuscripts *he did many things*

Get Some Rest

Quiet TIMES *with each other*

MARK 6:31 This passage sounds like a typical day straight out of the Arp journal—probably yours too. Nobody needs to take Jesus more seriously than we do when he says, "Come with me by yourselves to a quiet place and get some rest."

Are you weary? If you are married with small children, your answer is probably "yes." You may feel that the adjectives "weary, worn-out and tired" permanently describe this season of life. Yet Jesus encourages us to take time from our hectic life, to slow down and get some rest.

During the active parenting years, we helped each other find balance by agreeing to check with the other before we accepted a new commitment. I (Claudia) tend to be overly optimistic and spontaneous. Even today it's easy for me to take on too many challenges, so it's vital to check with Dave. So many times when we look at things together, we realize we are close to overload and can avoid approaching burn out by saying no or postponing a project.

If you have little ones, look for ways you can slow down and get some rest. Take a tip from our friend, Laura. Recruit some help. Laura often hires a neighbor to play with her two preschoolers while she collects her wits or gets dinner started. She has also learned not to compete with *House Beautiful*. She closes more doors and doesn't worry about the dust bunnies that live under her couch. She has given herself permission not to be perfect.

Remember that Jesus wants to give us spiritual refreshment and renew our perspective. If you feel your life is spinning out of control, look to your heavenly Father to help you figure out how to slow down.

—*Dave and Claudia*

Weekend **Warm-up** *Can you plan a time to relax with each other soon?*

Go to page 1086 for your next devotional reading.

because of his oaths and his dinner guests, he did not want to refuse her. ²⁷So he immediately sent an executioner with orders to bring John's head. The man went, beheaded John in the prison, ²⁸and brought back his head on a platter. He presented it to the girl, and she gave it to her mother. ²⁹On hearing of this, John's disciples came and took his body and laid it in a tomb.

Jesus Feeds the Five Thousand

³⁰The apostles gathered around Jesus and reported to him all they had done and taught. ³¹Then, because so many people were coming and going that they did not even have a chance to eat, he said to them, "Come with me by yourselves to a quiet place and get some rest."

³²So they went away by themselves in a boat to a solitary place. ³³But many who saw them leaving recognized them and ran on foot from all the towns and got there ahead of them. ³⁴When Jesus landed and saw a large crowd, he had compassion on them, because they were like sheep without a shepherd. So he began teaching them many things.

³⁵By this time it was late in the day, so his disciples came to him. "This is a remote place," they said, "and it's already very late. ³⁶Send the people away so they can go to the surrounding countryside and villages and buy themselves something to eat."

³⁷But he answered, "You give them something to eat."

They said to him, "That would take eight months of a man's wages[a]! Are we to go and spend that much on bread and give it to them to eat?"

³⁸"How many loaves do you have?" he asked. "Go and see."

When they found out, they said, "Five—and two fish."

³⁹Then Jesus directed them to have all the people sit down in groups on the green grass. ⁴⁰So they sat down in groups of hundreds and fifties. ⁴¹Taking the five loaves and the two fish and looking up to heaven, he gave thanks and broke the loaves. Then he gave them to his disciples to set before the people. He also divided the two fish among them all. ⁴²They all ate and were satisfied, ⁴³and the disciples picked up twelve basketfuls of broken pieces of bread and fish. ⁴⁴The number of the men who had eaten was five thousand.

Jesus Walks on the Water

⁴⁵Immediately Jesus made his disciples get into the boat and go on ahead of him to Bethsaida, while he dismissed the crowd. ⁴⁶After leaving them, he went up on a mountainside to pray.

⁴⁷When evening came, the boat was in the middle of the lake, and he was alone on land. ⁴⁸He saw the disciples straining at the oars, because the wind was against them. About the fourth watch of the night he went out to them, walking on the lake. He was about to pass by them, ⁴⁹but when they saw him walking on the lake, they thought he was a ghost. They cried out, ⁵⁰because they all saw him and were terrified.

Immediately he spoke to them and said, "Take courage! It is I. Don't be afraid." ⁵¹Then he climbed into the boat with them, and the wind died down. They were completely amazed, ⁵²for they had not understood about the loaves; their hearts were hardened.

⁵³When they had crossed over, they landed at Gennesaret and anchored there. ⁵⁴As soon as they got out of the boat, people recognized Jesus. ⁵⁵They ran throughout that whole region and carried the sick on mats to wherever they heard he was. ⁵⁶And wherever he went—into villages, towns or countryside—they placed the sick in the marketplaces. They begged him to let them touch even the edge of his cloak, and all who touched him were healed.

Clean and Unclean

7 The Pharisees and some of the teachers of the law who had come from Jerusalem gathered around Jesus and ²saw some of his disciples eating food with hands that were "unclean," that is, unwashed. ³(The Pharisees and all the Jews do not eat unless they give their hands a ceremonial washing, holding to the tradition of the elders. ⁴When they come from

---

a 37 Greek *take two hundred denarii*

the marketplace they do not eat unless they wash. And they observe many other traditions, such as the washing of cups, pitchers and kettles. [a])

[5] So the Pharisees and teachers of the law asked Jesus, "Why don't your disciples live according to the tradition of the elders instead of eating their food with 'unclean' hands?"

[6] He replied, "Isaiah was right when he prophesied about you hypocrites; as it is written:

" 'These people honor me with their
    lips,
but their hearts are far from me.
[7] They worship me in vain;
    their teachings are but rules taught
        by men.' [b]

[8] You have let go of the commands of God and are holding on to the traditions of men."

[9] And he said to them: "You have a fine way of setting aside the commands of God in order to observe [c] your own traditions! [10] For Moses said, 'Honor your father and your mother,' [d] and, 'Anyone who curses his father or mother must be put to death.' [e] [11] But you say that if a man says to his father or mother: 'Whatever help you might otherwise have received from me is Corban' (that is, a gift devoted to God), [12] then you no longer let him do anything for his father or mother. [13] Thus you nullify the word of God by your tradition that you have handed down. And you do many things like that."

[14] Again Jesus called the crowd to him and said, "Listen to me, everyone, and understand this. [15] Nothing outside a man can make him 'unclean' by going into him. Rather, it is what comes out of a man that makes him 'unclean.' [f]"

[17] After he had left the crowd and entered the house, his disciples asked him about this parable. [18] "Are you so dull?" he asked. "Don't you see that nothing that enters a man from the outside can make him 'unclean'? [19] For it doesn't go into his heart but into his stomach, and then out of his body." (In saying this, Jesus declared all foods "clean.")

[20] He went on: "What comes out of a man is what makes him 'unclean.' [21] For from within, out of men's hearts, come evil thoughts, sexual immorality, theft, murder, adultery, [22] greed, malice, deceit, lewdness, envy, slander, arrogance and folly. [23] All these evils come from inside and make a man 'unclean.' "

The Faith of a Syrophoenician Woman

[24] Jesus left that place and went to the vicinity of Tyre. [g] He entered a house and did not want anyone to know it; yet he could not keep his presence secret. [25] In fact, as soon as she heard about him, a woman whose little daughter was possessed by an evil [h] spirit came and fell at his feet. [26] The woman was a Greek, born in Syrian Phoenicia. She begged Jesus to drive the demon out of her daughter.

[27] "First let the children eat all they want," he told her, "for it is not right to take the children's bread and toss it to their dogs."

[28] "Yes, Lord," she replied, "but even the dogs under the table eat the children's crumbs."

[29] Then he told her, "For such a reply, you may go; the demon has left your daughter."

[30] She went home and found her child lying on the bed, and the demon gone.

The Healing of a Deaf and Mute Man

[31] Then Jesus left the vicinity of Tyre and went through Sidon, down to the Sea of Galilee and into the region of the Decapolis. [i] [32] There some people brought to him a man who was deaf and could hardly talk, and they begged him to place his hand on the man.

[33] After he took him aside, away from the crowd, Jesus put his fingers into the man's ears. Then he spit and touched the man's tongue. [34] He looked up to heaven and with a deep sigh said to him, "Ephphatha!" (which means, "Be opened!"). [35] At this, the man's ears were opened, his tongue was loosened and he began to speak plainly.

[36] Jesus commanded them not to tell anyone. But the more he did so, the more

---

a4 Some early manuscripts *pitchers, kettles and dining couches*   *b6,7* Isaiah 29:13   *c9* Some manuscripts *set up*   *d10* Exodus 20:12; Deut. 5:16   *e10* Exodus 21:17; Lev. 20:9
f15 Some early manuscripts *'unclean.'* *16If anyone has ears to hear, let him hear.*   *g24* Many early manuscripts *Tyre and Sidon*   *h25* Greek *unclean*   *i31* That is, the Ten Cities

they kept talking about it. [37]People were overwhelmed with amazement. "He has done everything well," they said. "He even makes the deaf hear and the mute speak."

Jesus Feeds the Four Thousand

8 During those days another large crowd gathered. Since they had nothing to eat, Jesus called his disciples to him and said, [2]"I have compassion for these people; they have already been with me three days and have nothing to eat. [3]If I send them home hungry, they will collapse on the way, because some of them have come a long distance."

[4]His disciples answered, "But where in this remote place can anyone get enough bread to feed them?"

[5]"How many loaves do you have?" Jesus asked.

"Seven," they replied.

[6]He told the crowd to sit down on the ground. When he had taken the seven loaves and given thanks, he broke them and gave them to his disciples to set before the people, and they did so. [7]They had a few small fish as well; he gave thanks for them also and told the disciples to distribute them. [8]The people ate and were satisfied. Afterward the disciples picked up seven basketfuls of broken pieces that were left over. [9]About four thousand men were present. And having sent them away, [10]he got into the boat with his disciples and went to the region of Dalmanutha.

[11]The Pharisees came and began to question Jesus. To test him, they asked him for a sign from heaven. [12]He sighed deeply and said, "Why does this generation ask for a miraculous sign? I tell you the truth, no sign will be given to it." [13]Then he left them, got back into the boat and crossed to the other side.

The Yeast of the Pharisees and Herod

[14]The disciples had forgotten to bring bread, except for one loaf they had with them in the boat. [15]"Be careful," Jesus warned them. "Watch out for the yeast of the Pharisees and that of Herod."

[16]They discussed this with one another and said, "It is because we have no bread."

[17]Aware of their discussion, Jesus asked them: "Why are you talking about having

no bread? Do you still not see or understand? Are your hearts hardened? [18]Do you have eyes but fail to see, and ears but fail to hear? And don't you remember? [19]When I broke the five loaves for the five thousand, how many basketfuls of pieces did you pick up?"

"Twelve," they replied.

[20]"And when I broke the seven loaves for the four thousand, how many basketfuls of pieces did you pick up?"

They answered, "Seven."

[21]He said to them, "Do you still not understand?"

The Healing of a Blind Man at Bethsaida

[22]They came to Bethsaida, and some people brought a blind man and begged Jesus to touch him. [23]He took the blind man by the hand and led him outside the village. When he had spit on the man's eyes and put his hands on him, Jesus asked, "Do you see anything?"

[24]He looked up and said, "I see people; they look like trees walking around."

[25]Once more Jesus put his hands on the man's eyes. Then his eyes were opened, his sight was restored, and he saw everything clearly. [26]Jesus sent him home, saying, "Don't go into the village. [a] "

Peter's Confession of Christ

[27]Jesus and his disciples went on to the villages around Caesarea Philippi. On the way he asked them, "Who do people say I am?"

[28]They replied, "Some say John the Baptist; others say Elijah; and still others, one of the prophets."

[29]"But what about you?" he asked. "Who do you say I am?"

Peter answered, "You are the Christ. [b] "

[30]Jesus warned them not to tell anyone about him.

Jesus Predicts His Death

[31]He then began to teach them that the Son of Man must suffer many things and be rejected by the elders, chief priests and teachers of the law, and that he must be

[a]26 Some manuscripts *Don't go and tell anyone in the village*   [b]29 Or *Messiah*. "The Christ" (Greek) and "the Messiah" (Hebrew) both mean "the Anointed One."

killed and after three days rise again. ³²He spoke plainly about this, and Peter took him aside and began to rebuke him.

³³But when Jesus turned and looked at his disciples, he rebuked Peter. "Get behind me, Satan!" he said. "You do not have in mind the things of God, but the things of men."

³⁴Then he called the crowd to him along with his disciples and said: "If anyone would come after me, he must deny himself and take up his cross and follow me. ³⁵For whoever wants to save his life*a* will lose it, but whoever loses his life for me and for the gospel will save it. ³⁶What good is it for a man to gain the whole world, yet forfeit his soul? ³⁷Or what can a man give in exchange for his soul? ³⁸If anyone is ashamed of me and my words in this adulterous and sinful generation, the Son of Man will be ashamed of him when he comes in his Father's glory with the holy angels."

9 And he said to them, "I tell you the truth, some who are standing here will not taste death before they see the kingdom of God come with power."

The Transfiguration

²After six days Jesus took Peter, James and John with him and led them up a high mountain, where they were all alone. There he was transfigured before them. ³His clothes became dazzling white, whiter than anyone in the world could bleach them. ⁴And there appeared before them Elijah and Moses, who were talking with Jesus.

⁵Peter said to Jesus, "Rabbi, it is good for us to be here. Let us put up three shelters—one for you, one for Moses and one for Elijah." ⁶(He did not know what to say, they were so frightened.)

⁷Then a cloud appeared and enveloped them, and a voice came from the cloud: "This is my Son, whom I love. Listen to him!"

⁸Suddenly, when they looked around, they no longer saw anyone with them except Jesus.

⁹As they were coming down the mountain, Jesus gave them orders not to tell anyone what they had seen until the Son of Man had risen from the dead. ¹⁰They

kept the matter to themselves, discussing what "rising from the dead" meant.

¹¹And they asked him, "Why do the teachers of the law say that Elijah must come first?"

¹²Jesus replied, "To be sure, Elijah does come first, and restores all things. Why then is it written that the Son of Man must suffer much and be rejected? ¹³But I tell you, Elijah has come, and they have done to him everything they wished, just as it is written about him."

The Healing of a Boy With an Evil Spirit

¹⁴When they came to the other disciples, they saw a large crowd around them and the teachers of the law arguing with them. ¹⁵As soon as all the people saw Jesus, they were overwhelmed with wonder and ran to greet him.

¹⁶"What are you arguing with them about?" he asked.

¹⁷A man in the crowd answered, "Teacher, I brought you my son, who is possessed by a spirit that has robbed him of speech. ¹⁸Whenever it seizes him, it throws him to the ground. He foams at the mouth, gnashes his teeth and becomes rigid. I asked your disciples to drive out the spirit, but they could not."

¹⁹"O unbelieving generation," Jesus replied, "how long shall I stay with you? How long shall I put up with you? Bring the boy to me."

²⁰So they brought him. When the spirit saw Jesus, it immediately threw the boy into a convulsion. He fell to the ground and rolled around, foaming at the mouth.

²¹Jesus asked the boy's father, "How long has he been like this?"

"From childhood," he answered. ²²"It has often thrown him into fire or water to kill him. But if you can do anything, take pity on us and help us."

²³"'If you can'?" said Jesus. "Everything is possible for him who believes."

²⁴Immediately the boy's father exclaimed, "I do believe; help me overcome my unbelief!"

²⁵When Jesus saw that a crowd was running to the scene, he rebuked the evil*b* spirit. "You deaf and mute spirit,"

a35 The Greek word means either life or soul; also in verse 36.   b25 Greek unclean he said, "I command you, come out of him and never enter him again."

²⁶The spirit shrieked, convulsed him violently and came out. The boy looked so much like a corpse that many said, "He's dead." ²⁷But Jesus took him by the hand and lifted him to his feet, and he stood up.

²⁸After Jesus had gone indoors, his disciples asked him privately, "Why couldn't we drive it out?"

²⁹He replied, "This kind can come out only by prayer.ᵃ"

³⁰They left that place and passed through Galilee. Jesus did not want anyone to know where they were, ³¹because he was teaching his disciples. He said to them, "The Son of Man is going to be betrayed into the hands of men. They will kill him, and after three days he will rise." ³²But they did not understand what he meant and were afraid to ask him about it.

Who Is the Greatest?

³³They came to Capernaum. When he was in the house, he asked them, "What were you arguing about on the road?" ³⁴But they kept quiet because on the way they had argued about who was the greatest.

³⁵Sitting down, Jesus called the Twelve and said, "If anyone wants to be first, he must be the very last, and the servant of all."

³⁶He took a little child and had him stand among them. Taking him in his arms, he said to them, ³⁷"Whoever welcomes one of these little children in my name welcomes me; and whoever welcomes me does not welcome me but the one who sent me."

Whoever Is Not Against Us Is for Us

³⁸"Teacher," said John, "we saw a man driving out demons in your name and we told him to stop, because he was not one of us."

³⁹"Do not stop him," Jesus said. "No one who does a miracle in my name can in the next moment say anything bad about me, ⁴⁰for whoever is not against us is for us. ⁴¹I tell you the truth, anyone who gives you a cup of water in my name because you belong to Christ will certainly not lose his reward.

Causing to Sin

⁴²"And if anyone causes one of these little ones who believe in me to sin, it would be better for him to be thrown into the sea with a large millstone tied around his neck. ⁴³If your hand causes you to sin, cut it off. It is better for you to enter life maimed than with two hands to go into hell, where the fire never goes out.ᵇ ⁴⁵And if your foot causes you to sin, cut it off. It is better for you to enter life crippled than to have two feet and be thrown into hell.ᶜ ⁴⁷And if your eye causes you to sin, pluck it out. It is better for you to enter the kingdom of God with one eye than to have two eyes and be thrown into hell, ⁴⁸where

  " 'their worm does not die,
    and the fire is not quenched.'ᵈ

⁴⁹Everyone will be salted with fire.

⁵⁰"Salt is good, but if it loses its saltiness, how can you make it salty again? Have salt in yourselves, and be at peace with each other."

Divorce

10 Jesus then left that place and went into the region of Judea and across the Jordan. Again crowds of people came to him, and as was his custom, he taught them.

²Some Pharisees came and tested him by asking, "Is it lawful for a man to divorce his wife?"

³"What did Moses command you?" he replied.

⁴They said, "Moses permitted a man to write a certificate of divorce and send her away."

⁵"It was because your hearts were hard that Moses wrote you this law," Jesus replied. ⁶"But at the beginning of creation God 'made them male and female.'ᵉ ⁷For this reason a man will leave his father and mother and be united to his

ᵃ29 Some manuscripts *prayer and fasting*
ᵇ43 Some manuscripts *out, ⁴⁴where / " 'their worm does not die, / and the fire is not quenched.'*
ᶜ45 Some manuscripts *hell, ⁴⁶where / " 'their worm does not die, / and the fire is not quenched.'*
ᵈ48 Isaiah 66:24   ᵉ6 Gen. 1:27

wife,[a] [8]and the two will become one flesh.'[b] So they are no longer two, but one. [9]Therefore what God has joined together, let man not separate."

[10]When they were in the house again, the disciples asked Jesus about this. [11]He answered, "Anyone who divorces his wife and marries another woman commits adultery against her. [12]And if she divorces her husband and marries another man, she commits adultery."

The Little Children and Jesus

[13]People were bringing little children to Jesus to have him touch them, but the disciples rebuked them. [14]When Jesus saw this, he was indignant. He said to them, "Let the little children come to me, and do not hinder them, for the kingdom of God belongs to such as these. [15]I tell you the truth, anyone who will not receive the kingdom of God like a little child will never enter it." [16]And he took the children in his arms, put his hands on them and blessed them.

The Rich Young Man

[17]As Jesus started on his way, a man ran up to him and fell on his knees before him. "Good teacher," he asked, "what must I do to inherit eternal life?"

[18]"Why do you call me good?" Jesus answered. "No one is good—except God alone. [19]You know the commandments: 'Do not murder, do not commit adultery, do not steal, do not give false testimony, do not defraud, honor your father and mother.'[c]"

[20]"Teacher," he declared, "all these I have kept since I was a boy."

[21]Jesus looked at him and loved him. "One thing you lack," he said. "Go, sell everything you have and give to the poor, and you will have treasure in heaven. Then come, follow me."

[22]At this the man's face fell. He went away sad, because he had great wealth.

[23]Jesus looked around and said to his disciples, "How hard it is for the rich to enter the kingdom of God!"

[24]The disciples were amazed at his words. But Jesus said again, "Children, how hard it is[d] to enter the kingdom of God! [25]It is easier for a camel to go

through the eye of a needle than for a rich man to enter the kingdom of God."

[26]The disciples were even more amazed, and said to each other, "Who then can be saved?"

[27]Jesus looked at them and said, "With man this is impossible, but not with God; all things are possible with God."

[28]Peter said to him, "We have left everything to follow you!"

[29]"I tell you the truth," Jesus replied, "no one who has left home or brothers or sisters or mother or father or children or fields for me and the gospel [30]will fail to receive a hundred times as much in this present age (homes, brothers, sisters, mothers, children and fields—and with them, persecutions) and in the age to come, eternal life. [31]But many who are first will be last, and the last first."

Jesus Again Predicts His Death

[32]They were on their way up to Jerusalem, with Jesus leading the way, and the disciples were astonished, while those who followed were afraid. Again he took the Twelve aside and told them what was going to happen to him. [33]"We are going up to Jerusalem," he said, "and the Son of Man will be betrayed to the chief priests and teachers of the law. They will condemn him to death and will hand him over to the Gentiles, [34]who will mock him and spit on him, flog him and kill him. Three days later he will rise."

The Request of James and John

[35]Then James and John, the sons of Zebedee, came to him. "Teacher," they said, "we want you to do for us whatever we ask."

[36]"What do you want me to do for you?" he asked.

[37]They replied, "Let one of us sit at your right and the other at your left in your glory."

[38]"You don't know what you are asking," Jesus said. "Can you drink the cup I drink or be baptized with the baptism I am baptized with?"

[39]"We can," they answered.

---

[a]7 Some early manuscripts do not have *and be united to his wife.*　　[b]8 Gen. 2:24
[c]19 Exodus 20:12-16; Deut. 5:16-20　　　[d]24 Some manuscripts *is for those who trust in riches*

Jesus said to them, "You will drink the cup I drink and be baptized with the baptism I am baptized with, ⁴⁰but to sit at my right or left is not for me to grant. These places belong to those for whom they have been prepared."

⁴¹When the ten heard about this, they became indignant with James and John. ⁴²Jesus called them together and said, "You know that those who are regarded as rulers of the Gentiles lord it over them, and their high officials exercise authority over them. ⁴³Not so with you. Instead, whoever wants to become great among you must be your servant, ⁴⁴and whoever wants to be first must be slave of all. ⁴⁵For even the Son of Man did not come to be served, but to serve, and to give his life as a ransom for many."

Blind Bartimaeus Receives His Sight

⁴⁶Then they came to Jericho. As Jesus and his disciples, together with a large crowd, were leaving the city, a blind man, Bartimaeus (that is, the Son of Timaeus), was sitting by the roadside begging. ⁴⁷When he heard that it was Jesus of Nazareth, he began to shout, "Jesus, Son of David, have mercy on me!"

⁴⁸Many rebuked him and told him to be quiet, but he shouted all the more, "Son of David, have mercy on me!"

⁴⁹Jesus stopped and said, "Call him."

So they called to the blind man, "Cheer up! On your feet! He's calling you." ⁵⁰Throwing his cloak aside, he jumped to his feet and came to Jesus.

⁵¹"What do you want me to do for you?" Jesus asked him.

The blind man said, "Rabbi, I want to see."

⁵²"Go," said Jesus, "your faith has healed you." Immediately he received his sight and followed Jesus along the road.

The Triumphal Entry

11 As they approached Jerusalem and came to Bethphage and Bethany at the Mount of Olives, Jesus sent two of his disciples, ²saying to them, "Go to the village ahead of you, and just as you enter it, you will find a colt tied there, which no one has ever ridden. Untie it and bring it here. ³If anyone asks you, 'Why are you doing this?' tell him, 'The Lord needs it and will send it back here shortly.' "

⁴They went and found a colt outside in the street, tied at a doorway. As they un-

Double Your Serve

Monday

MARK 10:43–45 We know of nothing else that can cultivate the intimacy of marriage more than reaching out to the world as a team. Doing good for others as a couple helps you transcend yourselves and become part of something larger.

God is committed to one major objective: helping us conform to the image of his Son (see Philippians 2:5–11, page 1288). And his Son, Scripture says, came not to be served, but to serve (Mark 10:45). It is as straightforward as that. God wants us to be a giving people. Galatians 5:13 says, " . . . serve one another in love." Philippians 2:4 says, " . . . look not only to your own interests, but also to the interests of others."

Marriage is a great means to becoming more like Christ. Paul says to " . . . spur one another on toward love and good deeds"

(Hebrews 10:24). Marriage helps us do that, and when we join our efforts in service together we are doubly blessed.

There are literally hundreds of ways to incorporate shared service into your marriage—offer hospitality in your home, volunteer at a shelter, sponsor a needy child, work in the church nursery. The key is to find something that fits your personal style. One of the ways Leslie and I enjoy reaching out as a couple is to do something anonymously. Even something small. We call it a mission of service in secret. It is an act of kindness that is concealed from everyone but the two of us. Our own sense of devotion and intimacy deepens as we secretly observe the results of our service.

—Les and Leslie

Go to page 1088 for your next devotional reading.

tied it, ⁵some people standing there asked, "What are you doing, untying that colt?" ⁶They answered as Jesus had told them to, and the people let them go. ⁷When they brought the colt to Jesus and threw their cloaks over it, he sat on it. ⁸Many people spread their cloaks on the road, while others spread branches they had cut in the fields. ⁹Those who went ahead and those who followed shouted,

"Hosanna!ᵃ"

"Blessed is he who comes in the
    name of the Lord!"ᵇ

¹⁰"Blessed is the coming kingdom of
    our father David!"

"Hosanna in the highest!"

¹¹Jesus entered Jerusalem and went to the temple. He looked around at everything, but since it was already late, he went out to Bethany with the Twelve.

Jesus Clears the Temple

¹²The next day as they were leaving Bethany, Jesus was hungry. ¹³Seeing in the distance a fig tree in leaf, he went to find out if it had any fruit. When he reached it, he found nothing but leaves, because it was not the season for figs. ¹⁴Then he said to the tree, "May no one ever eat fruit from you again." And his disciples heard him say it.

¹⁵On reaching Jerusalem, Jesus entered the temple area and began driving out those who were buying and selling there. He overturned the tables of the money changers and the benches of those selling doves, ¹⁶and would not allow anyone to carry merchandise through the temple courts. ¹⁷And as he taught them, he said, "Is it not written:

" 'My house will be called
    a house of prayer for all
        nations'ᶜ?

But you have made it 'a den of robbers.'ᵈ"

¹⁸The chief priests and the teachers of the law heard this and began looking for a way to kill him, for they feared him, because the whole crowd was amazed at his teaching.

¹⁹When evening came, theyᵉ went out of the city.

The Withered Fig Tree

²⁰In the morning, as they went along, they saw the fig tree withered from the roots. ²¹Peter remembered and said to Jesus, "Rabbi, look! The fig tree you cursed has withered!"

²²"Haveᶠ faith in God," Jesus answered. ²³"I tell you the truth, if anyone says to this mountain, 'Go, throw yourself into the sea,' and does not doubt in his heart but believes that what he says will happen, it will be done for him. ²⁴Therefore I tell you, whatever you ask for in prayer, believe that you have received it, and it will be yours. ²⁵And when you stand praying, if you hold anything against anyone, forgive him, so that your Father in heaven may forgive you your sins.ᵍ"

The Authority of Jesus Questioned

²⁷They arrived again in Jerusalem, and while Jesus was walking in the temple courts, the chief priests, the teachers of the law and the elders came to him. ²⁸"By what authority are you doing these things?" they asked. "And who gave you authority to do this?"

²⁹Jesus replied, "I will ask you one question. Answer me, and I will tell you by what authority I am doing these things. ³⁰John's baptism—was it from heaven, or from men? Tell me!"

³¹They discussed it among themselves and said, "If we say, 'From heaven,' he will ask, 'Then why didn't you believe him?' ³²But if we say, 'From men' . . ." (They feared the people, for everyone held that John really was a prophet.)

³³So they answered Jesus, "We don't know."

Jesus said, "Neither will I tell you by what authority I am doing these things."

The Parable of the Tenants

12 He then began to speak to them in parables: "A man planted a vine-

ᵃ9 A Hebrew expression meaning "Save!" which became an exclamation of praise; also in verse 10
ᵇ9 Psalm 118:25,26   ᶜ17 Isaiah 56:7
ᵈ17 Jer. 7:11   ᵉ19 Some early manuscripts he
ᶠ22 Some early manuscripts If you have
ᵍ25 Some manuscripts sins. ²⁶But if you do not forgive, neither will your Father who is in heaven forgive your sins.

yard. He put a wall around it, dug a pit for the winepress and built a watchtower. Then he rented the vineyard to some farmers and went away on a journey. ²At harvest time he sent a servant to the tenants to collect from them some of the fruit of the vineyard. ³But they seized him, beat him and sent him away empty-handed. ⁴Then he sent another servant to them; they struck this man on the head and treated him shamefully. ⁵He sent still another, and that one they killed. He sent many others; some of them they beat, others they killed.

⁶"He had one left to send, a son, whom he loved. He sent him last of all, saying, 'They will respect my son.'

⁷"But the tenants said to one another, 'This is the heir. Come, let's kill him, and the inheritance will be ours.' ⁸So they took him and killed him, and threw him out of the vineyard.

⁹"What then will the owner of the vineyard do? He will come and kill those tenants and give the vineyard to others. ¹⁰Haven't you read this scripture:

" 'The stone the builders rejected
has become the capstone*a*;
¹¹the Lord has done this,
and it is marvelous in our eyes'*b*?"

¹²Then they looked for a way to arrest him because they knew he had spoken the parable against them. But they were afraid of the crowd; so they left him and went away.

Paying Taxes to Caesar

¹³Later they sent some of the Pharisees and Herodians to Jesus to catch him in his words. ¹⁴They came to him and said, "Teacher, we know you are a man of integrity. You aren't swayed by men, because you pay no attention to who they are; but you teach the way of God in accordance with the truth. Is it right to pay taxes to Caesar or not? ¹⁵Should we pay or shouldn't we?"

But Jesus knew their hypocrisy. "Why are you trying to trap me?" he asked.

a 10 Or *cornerstone*   *b 11* Psalm 118:22,23

A Prayer . . . of Forgiveness

Tuesday

MARK 11:25 Have you ever tried praying for your spouse when you're holding a grudge? Be honest. If you are holding something against your partner, your first thought is probably not to pray. More likely you are thinking, *How can I get even?* or *I didn't deserve this and my spouse is going to know it!* It is this kind of thinking, no matter how natural, that guarantees more problems for you and your spouse.

So what's the alternative? Well, it's not to get down on your knees and put the tips of your fingers together and say a sanctimonious prayer. The solution—as Jesus points out in this verse—is found in forgiveness: ". . . if you hold anything against anyone, forgive him . . . " It's there in plain language. In this single verse, Jesus pinpoints a common marital problem and provides a succinct solution.

Yes, you say, *but how do I forgive?* Forgiveness begins when you put yourself in your spouse's shoes and see the world from his or her perspective. It begins when you sympathize as well as analyze. Bringing both your heart and your head into the situation is called empathy. And the best model of empathy is our Lord himself. If Jesus Christ had been merely sympathetic to our plight, he would have watched our struggles from afar, shaking his head and feeling bad. (Ever done that for your spouse?) If he had been merely analytical, he would have told us exactly what to do, stripping us of our freedom and solving our problems for us. Instead, the Son of God chose to become one of us (see John 1:14; Philippians 2:7; 1 Timothy 2:5).

If we are ever going to overcome a grudge against our spouse and offer a genuine prayer on his or her behalf, it is going to be because we practiced empathy and learned to forgive.

—Les and Leslie

Go to page 1091 for your next devotional reading.

"Bring me a denarius and let me look at it." [16]They brought the coin, and he asked them, "Whose portrait is this? And whose inscription?"

"Caesar's," they replied.

[17]Then Jesus said to them, "Give to Caesar what is Caesar's and to God what is God's."

And they were amazed at him.

Marriage at the Resurrection

[18]Then the Sadducees, who say there is no resurrection, came to him with a question. [19]"Teacher," they said, "Moses wrote for us that if a man's brother dies and leaves a wife but no children, the man must marry the widow and have children for his brother. [20]Now there were seven brothers. The first one married and died without leaving any children. [21]The second one married the widow, but he also died, leaving no child. It was the same with the third. [22]In fact, none of the seven left any children. Last of all, the woman died too. [23]At the resurrection[a] whose wife will she be, since the seven were married to her?"

[24]Jesus replied, "Are you not in error because you do not know the Scriptures or the power of God? [25]When the dead rise, they will neither marry nor be given in marriage; they will be like the angels in heaven. [26]Now about the dead rising—have you not read in the book of Moses, in the account of the bush, how God said to him, 'I am the God of Abraham, the God of Isaac, and the God of Jacob'[b]? [27]He is not the God of the dead, but of the living. You are badly mistaken!"

The Greatest Commandment

[28]One of the teachers of the law came and heard them debating. Noticing that Jesus had given them a good answer, he asked him, "Of all the commandments, which is the most important?"

[29]"The most important one," answered Jesus, "is this: 'Hear, O Israel, the Lord our God, the Lord is one.[c] [30]Love the Lord your God with all your heart and with all your soul and with all your mind and with all your strength.'[d] [31]The second is this: 'Love your neighbor as yourself.'[e] There is no commandment greater than these."

A Prayer . . . of Forgiveness

Take a moment to answer each of these questions on your own. Then compare your answers to your spouse's.

Yes	No	Do we value prayer together as a couple?
Yes	No	I am currently satisfied with how often we pray together.
Yes	No	I often share my prayer requests with my spouse.
Yes	No	Our marriage is undergirded with prayer.
Yes	No	I can recount ways God has answered our prayers in our marriage.

[32]"Well said, teacher," the man replied. "You are right in saying that God is one and there is no other but him. [33]To love him with all your heart, with all your understanding and with all your strength, and to love your neighbor as yourself is more important than all burnt offerings and sacrifices."

[34]When Jesus saw that he had answered wisely, he said to him, "You are not far from the kingdom of God." And from then on no one dared ask him any more questions.

Whose Son Is the Christ?

[35]While Jesus was teaching in the temple courts, he asked, "How is it that the teachers of the law say that the Christ[f] is the son of David? [36]David himself, speaking by the Holy Spirit, declared:

" 'The Lord said to my Lord:
  "Sit at my right hand
until I put your enemies
    under your feet." ' [g]

[37]David himself calls him 'Lord.' How then can he be his son?"

---

[a]23 Some manuscripts *resurrection, when men rise from the dead,*   [b]26 Exodus 3:6   [c]29 Or *the Lord our God is one Lord*   [d]30 Deut. 6:4,5   [e]31 Lev. 19:18   [f]35 Or *Messiah*   [g]36 Psalm 110:1

The large crowd listened to him with delight.

[38]As he taught, Jesus said, "Watch out for the teachers of the law. They like to walk around in flowing robes and be greeted in the marketplaces, [39]and have the most important seats in the synagogues and the places of honor at banquets. [40]They devour widows' houses and for a show make lengthy prayers. Such men will be punished most severely."

The Widow's Offering

[41]Jesus sat down opposite the place where the offerings were put and watched the crowd putting their money into the temple treasury. Many rich people threw in large amounts. [42]But a poor widow came and put in two very small copper coins,[a] worth only a fraction of a penny.[b]

[43]Calling his disciples to him, Jesus said, "I tell you the truth, this poor widow has put more into the treasury than all the others. [44]They all gave out of their wealth; but she, out of her poverty, put in everything—all she had to live on."

Signs of the End of the Age

13 As he was leaving the temple, one of his disciples said to him, "Look, Teacher! What massive stones! What magnificent buildings!"

[2]"Do you see all these great buildings?" replied Jesus. "Not one stone here will be left on another; every one will be thrown down."

[3]As Jesus was sitting on the Mount of Olives opposite the temple, Peter, James, John and Andrew asked him privately, [4]"Tell us, when will these things happen? And what will be the sign that they are all about to be fulfilled?"

[5]Jesus said to them: "Watch out that no one deceives you. [6]Many will come in my name, claiming, 'I am he,' and will deceive many. [7]When you hear of wars and rumors of wars, do not be alarmed. Such things must happen, but the end is still to come. [8]Nation will rise against nation, and kingdom against kingdom. There will be earthquakes in various places, and famines. These are the beginning of birth pains.

[9]"You must be on your guard. You will be handed over to the local councils and flogged in the synagogues. On account of me you will stand before governors and kings as witnesses to them. [10]And the gospel must first be preached to all nations. [11]Whenever you are arrested and brought to trial, do not worry beforehand about what to say. Just say whatever is given you at the time, for it is not you speaking, but the Holy Spirit.

[12]"Brother will betray brother to death, and a father his child. Children will rebel against their parents and have them put to death. [13]All men will hate you because of me, but he who stands firm to the end will be saved.

[14]"When you see 'the abomination that causes desolation'[c] standing where it[d] does not belong—let the reader understand—then let those who are in Judea flee to the mountains. [15]Let no one on the roof of his house go down or enter the house to take anything out. [16]Let no one in the field go back to get his cloak. [17]How dreadful it will be in those days for pregnant women and nursing mothers! [18]Pray that this will not take place in winter, [19]because those will be days of distress unequaled from the beginning, when God created the world, until now—and never to be equaled again. [20]If the Lord had not cut short those days, no one would survive. But for the sake of the elect, whom he has chosen, he has shortened them. [21]At that time if anyone says to you, 'Look, here is the Christ[e]!' or, 'Look, there he is!' do not believe it. [22]For false Christs and false prophets will appear and perform signs and miracles to deceive the elect—if that were possible. [23]So be on your guard; I have told you everything ahead of time.

[24]"But in those days, following that distress,

" 'the sun will be darkened,
     and the moon will not give its
         light;
[25]the stars will fall from the sky,
     and the heavenly bodies will be
         shaken.'[f]

---

[a]42 Greek *two lepta*   [b]42 Greek *kodrantes*
[c]14 Daniel 9:27; 11:31; 12:11   [d]14 Or *he;* also in verse 29   [e]21 Or *Messiah*
[f]25 Isaiah 13:10; 34:4

²⁶"At that time men will see the Son of Man coming in clouds with great power and glory. ²⁷And he will send his angels and gather his elect from the four winds, from the ends of the earth to the ends of the heavens.

²⁸"Now learn this lesson from the fig tree: As soon as its twigs get tender and its leaves come out, you know that summer is near. ²⁹Even so, when you see these things happening, you know that it is near, right at the door. ³⁰I tell you the truth, this generation*a* will certainly not pass away until all these things have happened. ³¹Heaven and earth will pass away, but my words will never pass away.

The Day and Hour Unknown

³²"No one knows about that day or hour, not even the angels in heaven, nor the Son, but only the Father. ³³Be on guard! Be alert*b*! You do not know when that time will come. ³⁴It's like a man going away: He leaves his house and puts his servants in charge, each with his as-signed task, and tells the one at the door to keep watch.

³⁵"Therefore keep watch because you do not know when the owner of the house will come back—whether in the evening, or at midnight, or when the rooster crows, or at dawn. ³⁶If he comes suddenly, do not let him find you sleeping. ³⁷What I say to you, I say to everyone: 'Watch!' "

Jesus Anointed at Bethany

14 Now the Passover and the Feast of Unleavened Bread were only two days away, and the chief priests and the teachers of the law were looking for some sly way to arrest Jesus and kill him. ²"But not during the Feast," they said, "or the people may riot."

³While he was in Bethany, reclining at the table in the home of a man known as Simon the Leper, a woman came with an alabaster jar of very expensive perfume,

*a*30 Or *race*   *b*33 Some manuscripts *alert and pray*

Lavishing Love

Wednesday

MARK 14:1–9 Extravagant love is an expression of love that is far beyond expectation. The woman who anointed Jesus expressed her love for him by doing something above and beyond the expectations of others. In fact, it was so extravagant that those observing her questioned the excess of her gesture. What they did not understand was that she was not fulfilling a need or hoping for something in return. She was pouring out a lavish expression of love. Her extravagance was so profound that Jesus declared her actions would be remembered wherever the gospel would be preached.

Love is not simply fulfilling marital responsibility. It is meant to go far beyond relational duty. Love has no boundaries of excess. It persists unconditionally. It is an outpouring of extravagant, sacrificial love.

To lavish love on one's spouse is to choose to do things that are beyond need or duty. For instance, Bob is very frugal. And he likes staying in his comfort zone. That means when we travel, his choice would be to stay in the same kind of inexpensive motel each night. But we don't. He does something that is way out of his comfort zone. When we travel, which we do frequently, Bob does some homework and makes reservations for us to stay at bed and breakfasts. Why does he do it? Why does he step way out of his comfort zone and spend the extra money? He does it only to lavish me with love.

Going beyond the ordinary expected or wanted actions shows incredible, "Christlike love" for our spouse—an expression of love so extraordinary that it cannot possibly go unnoticed. Extravagant love can only be motivated by a desire to please Christ. The woman with the alabaster jar found her expression of lavished love. The quest for each of us as spouses is to find ours.

—Bob and Rosemary

Go to page 1094 for your next devotional reading.

made of pure nard. She broke the jar and poured the perfume on his head.

[4]Some of those present were saying indignantly to one another, "Why this waste of perfume? [5]It could have been sold for more than a year's wages[a] and the money given to the poor." And they rebuked her harshly.

[6]"Leave her alone," said Jesus. "Why are you bothering her? She has done a beautiful thing to me. [7]The poor you will always have with you, and you can help them any time you want. But you will not always have me. [8]She did what she could. She poured perfume on my body beforehand to prepare for my burial. [9]I tell you the truth, wherever the gospel is preached throughout the world, what she has done will also be told, in memory of her."

[10]Then Judas Iscariot, one of the Twelve, went to the chief priests to betray Jesus to them. [11]They were delighted to hear this and promised to give him money. So he watched for an opportunity to hand him over.

The Lord's Supper

[12]On the first day of the Feast of Unleavened Bread, when it was customary to sacrifice the Passover lamb, Jesus' disciples asked him, "Where do you want us to go and make preparations for you to eat the Passover?"

[13]So he sent two of his disciples, telling them, "Go into the city, and a man carrying a jar of water will meet you. Follow him. [14]Say to the owner of the house he enters, 'The Teacher asks: Where is my guest room, where I may eat the Passover with my disciples?' [15]He will show you a large upper room, furnished and ready. Make preparations for us there."

[16]The disciples left, went into the city and found things just as Jesus had told them. So they prepared the Passover.

[17]When evening came, Jesus arrived with the Twelve. [18]While they were reclining at the table eating, he said, "I tell you the truth, one of you will betray me—one who is eating with me."

[19]They were saddened, and one by one they said to him, "Surely not I?"

[20]"It is one of the Twelve," he replied, "one who dips bread into the bowl with me. [21]The Son of Man will go just as it is

written about him. But woe to that man who betrays the Son of Man! It would be better for him if he had not been born."

[22]While they were eating, Jesus took bread, gave thanks and broke it, and gave it to his disciples, saying, "Take it; this is my body."

[23]Then he took the cup, gave thanks and offered it to them, and they all drank from it.

[24]"This is my blood of the[b] covenant, which is poured out for many," he said to them. [25]"I tell you the truth, I will not drink again of the fruit of the vine until that day when I drink it anew in the kingdom of God."

[26]When they had sung a hymn, they went out to the Mount of Olives.

Jesus Predicts Peter's Denial

[27]"You will all fall away," Jesus told them, "for it is written:

" 'I will strike the shepherd,
　　and the sheep will be scattered.'[c]

[28]But after I have risen, I will go ahead of you into Galilee."

[29]Peter declared, "Even if all fall away, I will not."

[30]"I tell you the truth," Jesus answered, "today—yes, tonight—before the rooster crows twice[d] you yourself will disown me three times."

[31]But Peter insisted emphatically, "Even if I have to die with you, I will never disown you." And all the others said the same.

Gethsemane

[32]They went to a place called Gethsemane, and Jesus said to his disciples, "Sit here while I pray." [33]He took Peter, James and John along with him, and he began to be deeply distressed and troubled. [34]"My soul is overwhelmed with sorrow to the point of death," he said to them. "Stay here and keep watch."

[35]Going a little farther, he fell to the ground and prayed that if possible the hour might pass from him. [36]"Abba,[e] Father," he said, "everything is possible

[a]5 Greek than three hundred denarii　　[b]24 Some manuscripts the new　　[c]27 Zech. 13:7
[d]30 Some early manuscripts do not have twice.
[e]36 Aramaic for Father

for you. Take this cup from me. Yet not what I will, but what you will."

37Then he returned to his disciples and found them sleeping. "Simon," he said to Peter, "are you asleep? Could you not keep watch for one hour? 38Watch and pray so that you will not fall into temptation. The spirit is willing, but the body is weak."

39Once more he went away and prayed the same thing. 40When he came back, he again found them sleeping, because their eyes were heavy. They did not know what to say to him.

41Returning the third time, he said to them, "Are you still sleeping and resting? Enough! The hour has come. Look, the Son of Man is betrayed into the hands of sinners. 42Rise! Let us go! Here comes my betrayer!"

Jesus Arrested

43Just as he was speaking, Judas, one of the Twelve, appeared. With him was a crowd armed with swords and clubs, sent from the chief priests, the teachers of the law, and the elders. 44Now the betrayer had arranged a signal with them: "The one I kiss is the man; arrest him and lead him away under guard." 45Going at once to Jesus, Judas said, "Rabbi!" and kissed him. 46The men seized Jesus and arrested him. 47Then one of those standing near drew his sword and struck the servant of the high priest, cutting off his ear.

48"Am I leading a rebellion," said Jesus, "that you have come out with swords and clubs to capture me? 49Every day I was with you, teaching in the temple courts, and you did not arrest me. But the Scriptures must be fulfilled." 50Then everyone deserted him and fled.

51A young man, wearing nothing but a linen garment, was following Jesus. When they seized him, 52he fled naked, leaving his garment behind.

Before the Sanhedrin

53They took Jesus to the high priest, and all the chief priests, elders and teachers of the law came together. 54Peter followed him at a distance, right into the courtyard of the high priest. There he sat with the guards and warmed himself at the fire.

55The chief priests and the whole Sanhedrin were looking for evidence against Jesus so that they could put him to death, but they did not find any. 56Many testified falsely against him, but their statements did not agree.

57Then some stood up and gave this false testimony against him: 58"We heard him say, 'I will destroy this man-made temple and in three days will build another, not made by man.' " 59Yet even then their testimony did not agree.

60Then the high priest stood up before them and asked Jesus, "Are you not going to answer? What is this testimony that these men are bringing against you?" 61But Jesus remained silent and gave no answer.

Again the high priest asked him, "Are you the Christ,*a* the Son of the Blessed One?"

62"I am," said Jesus. "And you will see the Son of Man sitting at the right hand of the Mighty One and coming on the clouds of heaven."

63The high priest tore his clothes. "Why do we need any more witnesses?" he asked. 64"You have heard the blasphemy. What do you think?"

They all condemned him as worthy of death. 65Then some began to spit at him; they blindfolded him, struck him with their fists, and said, "Prophesy!" And the guards took him and beat him.

Peter Disowns Jesus

66While Peter was below in the courtyard, one of the servant girls of the high priest came by. 67When she saw Peter warming himself, she looked closely at him.

"You also were with that Nazarene, Jesus," she said.

68But he denied it. "I don't know or understand what you're talking about," he said, and went out into the entryway.*b*

69When the servant girl saw him there, she said again to those standing around, "This fellow is one of them." 70Again he denied it.

After a little while, those standing near

*a*61 Or *Messiah*   *b*68 Some early manuscripts *entryway and the rooster crowed* said to Peter, "Surely you are one of them, for you are a Galilean."

⁷¹He began to call down curses on himself, and he swore to them, "I don't know this man you're talking about."

⁷²Immediately the rooster crowed the second time.*ᵃ* Then Peter remembered the word Jesus had spoken to him: "Before the rooster crows twice*ᵇ* you will disown me three times." And he broke down and wept.

Jesus Before Pilate

15 Very early in the morning, the chief priests, with the elders, the teachers of the law and the whole Sanhedrin, reached a decision. They bound Jesus, led him away and handed him over to Pilate.

²"Are you the king of the Jews?" asked Pilate.

"Yes, it is as you say," Jesus replied.

³The chief priests accused him of many things. ⁴So again Pilate asked him, "Aren't you going to answer? See how many things they are accusing you of."

⁵But Jesus still made no reply, and Pilate was amazed.

⁶Now it was the custom at the Feast to release a prisoner whom the people requested. ⁷A man called Barabbas was in prison with the insurrectionists who had committed murder in the uprising. ⁸The crowd came up and asked Pilate to do for them what he usually did.

⁹"Do you want me to release to you the king of the Jews?" asked Pilate, ¹⁰knowing it was out of envy that the chief priests had handed Jesus over to him. ¹¹But the chief priests stirred up the crowd to have Pilate release Barabbas instead.

¹²"What shall I do, then, with the one you call the king of the Jews?" Pilate asked them.

¹³"Crucify him!" they shouted.

¹⁴"Why? What crime has he committed?" asked Pilate.

But they shouted all the louder, "Crucify him!"

¹⁵Wanting to satisfy the crowd, Pilate released Barabbas to them. He had Jesus flogged, and handed him over to be crucified.

The Soldiers Mock Jesus

¹⁶The soldiers led Jesus away into the palace (that is, the Praetorium) and called together the whole company of soldiers. ¹⁷They put a purple robe on him, then

---

ᵃ72 Some early manuscripts do not have *the second time.*   *ᵇ72* Some early manuscripts do not have *twice.*

Present Pain, Future Glory

MARK 15 The amazing truth about this chapter is that Jesus did not have to choose the agony he went through. He endured this agony because of his great love for us that flowed out of his great love for the Father. Jesus was not focussing on the tremendous agony of the present. He was focussing on the Father's purposes for us.

The marriage relationship includes similar opportunities for sacrificial love. When our children were toddlers, it frustrated me that Rosemary never seemed to have time for us . . . for me. Even when I came home and pitched in to take the children off her hands so she could get some peace, she still fell asleep early most nights, before we could have our own time together. At first I got mad, but I had to remind myself to get focused—focused on the fact that this exhausting season would pass.

Don't allow yourself to become focused on the present pain. Present pain demands our attention, but it does not represent the future. Instead, try to imagine what your current sacrifice can lead to. The pain of the cross was so overwhelming that many could not watch it. Then came the glory of the empty tomb, a glory beyond our imagination. To release that glory, however, it took the most unfair sacrifice in the history of humankind. In comparison, how can we call the sacrifices of our marriages unfair!

—Bob and Rosemary

Go to page 1098 for your next devotional reading.

twisted together a crown of thorns and set it on him. ¹⁸And they began to call out to him, "Hail, king of the Jews!" ¹⁹Again and again they struck him on the head with a staff and spit on him. Falling on their knees, they paid homage to him. ²⁰And when they had mocked him, they took off the purple robe and put his own clothes on him. Then they led him out to crucify him.

The Crucifixion

²¹A certain man from Cyrene, Simon, the father of Alexander and Rufus, was passing by on his way in from the country, and they forced him to carry the cross. ²²They brought Jesus to the place called Golgotha (which means The Place of the Skull). ²³Then they offered him wine mixed with myrrh, but he did not take it. ²⁴And they crucified him. Dividing up his clothes, they cast lots to see what each would get.

²⁵It was the third hour when they crucified him. ²⁶The written notice of the charge against him read: THE KING OF THE JEWS. ²⁷They crucified two robbers with him, one on his right and one on his left.ᵃ ²⁹Those who passed by hurled insults at him, shaking their heads and saying, "So! You who are going to destroy the temple and build it in three days, ³⁰come down from the cross and save yourself!"

³¹In the same way the chief priests and the teachers of the law mocked him among themselves. "He saved others," they said, "but he can't save himself! ³²Let this Christ,ᵇ this King of Israel, come down now from the cross, that we may see and believe." Those crucified with him also heaped insults on him.

The Death of Jesus

³³At the sixth hour darkness came over the whole land until the ninth hour. ³⁴And at the ninth hour Jesus cried out in a loud voice, *"Eloi, Eloi, lama sabachthani?"*—which means, "My God, my God, why have you forsaken me?"ᶜ

³⁵When some of those standing near heard this, they said, "Listen, he's calling Elijah."

³⁶One man ran, filled a sponge with wine vinegar, put it on a stick, and offered it to Jesus to drink. "Now leave him alone. Let's see if Elijah comes to take him down," he said.

³⁷With a loud cry, Jesus breathed his last.

³⁸The curtain of the temple was torn in two from top to bottom. ³⁹And when the centurion, who stood there in front of Jesus, heard his cry andᵈ saw how he died, he said, "Surely this man was the Sonᵉ of God!"

⁴⁰Some women were watching from a distance. Among them were Mary Magdalene, Mary the mother of James the younger and of Joses, and Salome. ⁴¹In Galilee these women had followed him and cared for his needs. Many other women who had come up with him to Jerusalem were also there.

The Burial of Jesus

⁴²It was Preparation Day (that is, the day before the Sabbath). So as evening approached, ⁴³Joseph of Arimathea, a prominent member of the Council, who was himself waiting for the kingdom of God, went boldly to Pilate and asked for Jesus' body. ⁴⁴Pilate was surprised to hear that he was already dead. Summoning the centurion, he asked him if Jesus had already died. ⁴⁵When he learned from the centurion that it was so, he gave the body to Joseph. ⁴⁶So Joseph bought some linen cloth, took down the body, wrapped it in the linen, and placed it in a tomb cut out of rock. Then he rolled a stone against the entrance of the tomb. ⁴⁷Mary Magdalene and Mary the mother of Joses saw where he was laid.

The Resurrection

16 When the Sabbath was over, Mary Magdalene, Mary the mother of James, and Salome bought spices so that they might go to anoint Jesus' body. ²Very early on the first day of the week, just after sunrise, they were on their way to the tomb ³and they asked each other, "Who

---

ᵃ27 Some manuscripts *left,* ²⁸*and the scripture was fulfilled which says, "He was counted with the lawless ones"* (Isaiah 53:12)   ᵇ32 Or *Messiah*   ᶜ34 Psalm 22:1   ᵈ39 Some manuscripts do not have *heard his cry and*   ᵉ39 Or *a son* will roll the stone away from the entrance of the tomb?"

⁴But when they looked up, they saw that the stone, which was very large, had been rolled away. ⁵As they entered the tomb, they saw a young man dressed in a white robe sitting on the right side, and they were alarmed.

⁶"Don't be alarmed," he said. "You are looking for Jesus the Nazarene, who was crucified. He has risen! He is not here. See the place where they laid him. ⁷But go, tell his disciples and Peter, 'He is going ahead of you into Galilee. There you will see him, just as he told you.' "

⁸Trembling and bewildered, the women went out and fled from the tomb. They said nothing to anyone, because they were afraid.

[The earliest manuscripts and some other ancient witnesses do not have Mark 16:9–20.]

⁹When Jesus rose early on the first day of the week, he appeared first to Mary Magdalene, out of whom he had driven seven demons. ¹⁰She went and told those who had been with him and who were mourning and weeping. ¹¹When they heard that Jesus was alive and that she had seen him, they did not believe it.

¹²Afterward Jesus appeared in a different form to two of them while they were walking in the country. ¹³These returned and reported it to the rest; but they did not believe them either.

¹⁴Later Jesus appeared to the Eleven as they were eating; he rebuked them for their lack of faith and their stubborn refusal to believe those who had seen him after he had risen.

¹⁵He said to them, "Go into all the world and preach the good news to all creation. ¹⁶Whoever believes and is baptized will be saved, but whoever does not believe will be condemned. ¹⁷And these signs will accompany those who believe: In my name they will drive out demons; they will speak in new tongues; ¹⁸they will pick up snakes with their hands; and when they drink deadly poison, it will not hurt them at all; they will place their hands on sick people, and they will get well."

¹⁹After the Lord Jesus had spoken to them, he was taken up into heaven and he sat at the right hand of God. ²⁰Then the disciples went out and preached everywhere, and the Lord worked with them and confirmed his word by the signs that accompanied it.

Luke

One would fully expect a physician to tell the story of Jesus with compassion and with a gentle bedside manner that reveals the true heart of the Savior. Luke begins his story with the birth of John the Baptist, then provides us with the Bible's most thorough account of the conception and nativity of Jesus . . . exactly what you'd expect from a gifted doctor. And no Gospel account gives us more information about the women whose lives affected Jesus, women whose lives were transformed by the Savior. These things set the Gospel of Luke apart from the other three accounts of Jesus' life.

This story shows us what happened when the loving Messiah touched real people—people who were homeless, downtrodden, scorned, hurting. Luke knew the power of tenderness; his message is filled with the compassion of a man who spent his days surrounded by the needy and the sick. As you read on, you'll also see that the power of Jesus' teaching and miracles proclaims that he is God. More than any other Gospel, Luke demonstrates that Jesus is both God and man.

Introduction

1 Many have undertaken to draw up an account of the things that have been fulfilled[a] among us, ²just as they were handed down to us by those who from the first were eyewitnesses and servants of the word. ³Therefore, since I myself have carefully investigated everything from the beginning, it seemed good also to me to write an orderly account for you, most excellent Theophilus, ⁴so that you may know the certainty of the things you have been taught.

a1 Or been surely believed

The Birth of John the Baptist Foretold

⁵In the time of Herod king of Judea there was a priest named Zechariah, who belonged to the priestly division of Abijah; his wife Elizabeth was also a descendant of Aaron. ⁶Both of them were upright in the sight of God, observing all the Lord's commandments and regulations blamelessly. ⁷But they had no children, because Elizabeth was barren; and they were both well along in years.

⁸Once when Zechariah's division was on duty and he was serving as priest before God, ⁹he was chosen by lot, according to the custom of the priesthood, to go into the temple of the Lord and burn incense. ¹⁰And when the time for the burning of incense came, all the assembled worshipers were praying outside.

¹¹Then an angel of the Lord appeared to him, standing at the right side of the altar of incense. ¹²When Zechariah saw him, he was startled and was gripped with fear. ¹³But the angel said to him: "Do not be afraid, Zechariah; your prayer has been heard. Your wife Elizabeth will bear you a son, and you are to give him the name John. ¹⁴He will be a joy and delight to you, and many will rejoice because of his birth, ¹⁵for he will be great in the sight of the Lord. He is never to take wine or other fermented drink, and he will be filled with the Holy Spirit even from birth.[a] ¹⁶Many of the people of Israel he will bring back to the Lord their God. ¹⁷And he will go on before the Lord, in the spirit and power of Elijah, to turn the hearts of the fathers to their children and the disobedient to the wisdom of the righteous—to make ready a people prepared for the Lord."

¹⁸Zechariah asked the angel, "How can I be sure of this? I am an old man and my wife is well along in years."

¹⁹The angel answered, "I am Gabriel. I stand in the presence of God, and I have been sent to speak to you and to tell you this good news. ²⁰And now you will be silent and not able to speak until the day this happens, because you did not believe my words, which will come true at their proper time."

²¹Meanwhile, the people were waiting for Zechariah and wondering why he stayed so long in the temple. ²²When he came out, he could not speak to them. They realized he had seen a vision in the temple, for he kept making signs to them but remained unable to speak.

²³When his time of service was completed, he returned home. ²⁴After this his wife Elizabeth became pregnant and for five months remained in seclusion. ²⁵"The Lord has done this for me," she said. "In these days he has shown his favor and taken away my disgrace among the people."

The Birth of Jesus Foretold

²⁶In the sixth month, God sent the angel Gabriel to Nazareth, a town in Galilee, ²⁷to a virgin pledged to be married to a man named Joseph, a descendant of David. The virgin's name was Mary. ²⁸The

---

[a]15 Or *from his mother's womb*

A Christmas to Remember

Friday

LUKE 1—2 What's your favorite Christmas memory? Is it of a special gift as a child? Maybe it was seeing your own child open a wished-for present. Some think the gift-giving part of Christmas is spoiling the season. At times it is difficult to keep the "reason for the season" in mind while wading through an ocean of wrapping paper.

Christmas is not about what we find under the tree. No. Christmas commemorates the time when God came down the stairs of heaven with a baby in his arms. And that Gift is what the wonder of Christmas is all about.

As you study the first two chapters of Luke this Christmas season, consider—together as a couple—how you will seek what the Wise Men were looking for that night in Bethlehem.

—Les and Leslie

Go to page 1103 for your next devotional reading.

angel went to her and said, "Greetings, you who are highly favored! The Lord is with you."

²⁹Mary was greatly troubled at his words and wondered what kind of greeting this might be. ³⁰But the angel said to her, "Do not be afraid, Mary, you have found favor with God. ³¹You will be with child and give birth to a son, and you are to give him the name Jesus. ³²He will be great and will be called the Son of the Most High. The Lord God will give him the throne of his father David, ³³and he will reign over the house of Jacob forever; his kingdom will never end."

³⁴"How will this be," Mary asked the angel, "since I am a virgin?"

³⁵The angel answered, "The Holy Spirit will come upon you, and the power of the Most High will overshadow you. So the holy one to be born will be called*ᵃ* the Son of God. ³⁶Even Elizabeth your relative is going to have a child in her old age, and she who was said to be barren is in her sixth month. ³⁷For nothing is impossible with God."

³⁸"I am the Lord's servant," Mary answered. "May it be to me as you have said." Then the angel left her.

Mary Visits Elizabeth

³⁹At that time Mary got ready and hurried to a town in the hill country of Judea, ⁴⁰where she entered Zechariah's home and greeted Elizabeth. ⁴¹When Elizabeth heard Mary's greeting, the baby leaped in her womb, and Elizabeth was filled with the Holy Spirit. ⁴²In a loud voice she exclaimed: "Blessed are you among women, and blessed is the child you will bear! ⁴³But why am I so favored, that the mother of my Lord should come to me? ⁴⁴As soon as the sound of your greeting reached my ears, the baby in my womb leaped for joy. ⁴⁵Blessed is she who believed that what the Lord has said to her will be accomplished!"

Mary's Song

⁴⁶And Mary said:

"My soul glorifies the Lord
⁴⁷   and my spirit rejoices in God my Savior,
⁴⁸for he has been mindful
      of the humble state of his servant.

Zechariah and Elizabeth

LUKE 1:5–25 Zechariah and Elizabeth were without any children because she was barren. At that time in Israel, barrenness was considered a terrible disgrace. Together they most certainly agonized in prayer for a child. Now, at their advanced age, it could be assumed that all hope was lost. Though they might have given up hope for this prayer request, it is important to see that this couple never gave up faith in God. Verse 6 tells us that, regardless of this unanswered prayer, they were righteous before the Lord. God knew the desire of their hearts.

Our role as a couple is to bare our hearts before the Lord and trust that he knows best. His timing is perfect. His plans for us are better than we could ever have dreamed. Though this couple's wait was long, God eventually blessed them with an answer to their prayers that was greater than they could have dreamed or dare to ask for. They were selected to bring forth the child about whom the Lord himself would state: "Among those born of women there has not risen anyone greater than John the Baptist" (Matthew 11:11). This couple was blessed because their faith was in God, not in an answer to their prayer.

From now on all generations will call
      me blessed,
⁴⁹   for the Mighty One has done great
            things for me—
      holy is his name.
⁵⁰His mercy extends to those who fear
            him,
      from generation to generation.
⁵¹He has performed mighty deeds with
            his arm;
      he has scattered those who are
            proud in their inmost
            thoughts.
⁵²He has brought down rulers from
            their thrones
      but has lifted up the humble.
⁵³He has filled the hungry with good
            things

ᵃ35 Or *So the child to be born will be called holy,*

but has sent the rich away empty.
⁵⁴He has helped his servant Israel,
    remembering to be merciful
⁵⁵to Abraham and his descendants
        forever,
    even as he said to our fathers."

⁵⁶Mary stayed with Elizabeth for about three months and then returned home.

The Birth of John the Baptist

⁵⁷When it was time for Elizabeth to have her baby, she gave birth to a son. ⁵⁸Her neighbors and relatives heard that the Lord had shown her great mercy, and they shared her joy.

⁵⁹On the eighth day they came to circumcise the child, and they were going to name him after his father Zechariah, ⁶⁰but his mother spoke up and said, "No! He is to be called John."

⁶¹They said to her, "There is no one among your relatives who has that name."

⁶²Then they made signs to his father, to find out what he would like to name the child. ⁶³He asked for a writing tablet, and to everyone's astonishment he wrote, "His name is John." ⁶⁴Immediately his mouth was opened and his tongue was loosed, and he began to speak, praising God. ⁶⁵The neighbors were all filled with awe, and throughout the hill country of Judea people were talking about all these things. ⁶⁶Everyone who heard this wondered about it, asking, "What then is this child going to be?" For the Lord's hand was with him.

Zechariah's Song

⁶⁷His father Zechariah was filled with the Holy Spirit and prophesied:

⁶⁸"Praise be to the Lord, the God of
        Israel,
    because he has come and has
        redeemed his people.
⁶⁹He has raised up a horn[a] of
        salvation for us
    in the house of his servant David
⁷⁰(as he said through his holy prophets
        of long ago),
⁷¹salvation from our enemies
    and from the hand of all who hate
        us—
⁷²to show mercy to our fathers

and to remember his holy
        covenant,
⁷³   the oath he swore to our father
        Abraham:
⁷⁴to rescue us from the hand of our
        enemies,
    and to enable us to serve him
        without fear
⁷⁵   in holiness and righteousness
        before him all our days.

⁷⁶And you, my child, will be called a
        prophet of the Most High;
    for you will go on before the Lord
        to prepare the way for him,
⁷⁷to give his people the knowledge of
        salvation
    through the forgiveness of their
        sins,
⁷⁸because of the tender mercy of our
        God,
    by which the rising sun will come
        to us from heaven
⁷⁹to shine on those living in darkness
    and in the shadow of death,
    to guide our feet into the path of
        peace."

⁸⁰And the child grew and became strong in spirit; and he lived in the desert until he appeared publicly to Israel.

The Birth of Jesus

2 In those days Caesar Augustus issued a decree that a census should be taken of the entire Roman world. ²(This was the first census that took place while Quirinius was governor of Syria.) ³And everyone went to his own town to register.

⁴So Joseph also went up from the town of Nazareth in Galilee to Judea, to Bethlehem the town of David, because he belonged to the house and line of David. ⁵He went there to register with Mary, who was pledged to be married to him and was expecting a child. ⁶While they were there, the time came for the baby to be born, ⁷and she gave birth to her firstborn, a son. She wrapped him in cloths and placed him in a manger, because there was no room for them in the inn.

The Shepherds and the Angels

⁸And there were shepherds living out

ᵃ69 *Horn* here symbolizes strength.

in the fields nearby, keeping watch over their flocks at night. ⁹An angel of the Lord appeared to them, and the glory of the Lord shone around them, and they were terrified. ¹⁰But the angel said to them, "Do not be afraid. I bring you good news of great joy that will be for all the people. ¹¹Today in the town of David a Savior has been born to you; he is Christ*ᵃ* the Lord. ¹²This will be a sign to you: You will find a baby wrapped in cloths and lying in a manger."

¹³Suddenly a great company of the heavenly host appeared with the angel, praising God and saying,

¹⁴"Glory to God in the highest,
　　and on earth peace to men on
　　　　whom his favor rests."

¹⁵When the angels had left them and gone into heaven, the shepherds said to one another, "Let's go to Bethlehem and see this thing that has happened, which the Lord has told us about."

¹⁶So they hurried off and found Mary and Joseph, and the baby, who was lying in the manger. ¹⁷When they had seen him, they spread the word concerning what had been told them about this child, ¹⁸and all who heard it were amazed at what the shepherds said to them. ¹⁹But Mary treasured up all these things and pondered them in her heart. ²⁰The shepherds returned, glorifying and praising God for all the things they had heard and seen, which were just as they had been told.

Jesus Presented in the Temple

²¹On the eighth day, when it was time to circumcise him, he was named Jesus, the name the angel had given him before he had been conceived.

²²When the time of their purification according to the Law of Moses had been completed, Joseph and Mary took him to Jerusalem to present him to the Lord ²³(as it is written in the Law of the Lord, "Every firstborn male is to be consecrated to the Lord"*ᵇ*), ²⁴and to offer a sacrifice in keeping with what is said in the Law of the Lord: "a pair of doves or two young pigeons."*ᶜ*

²⁵Now there was a man in Jerusalem called Simeon, who was righteous and de-

Mary and Joseph

LUKE 2:1–20　　Few couples have had a more difficult beginning in their marriage than Mary and Joseph. First of all, she was pregnant; many may have wanted her to be stoned or at least call off the wedding. However, after the angel visited Joseph and explained that Mary was with child by the Holy Spirit, he had compassion on her. Second, Joseph's business was probably under financed when the decree went out from Caesar Augustus that all people were to be enrolled for a new taxing. Just what a young couple needed! Can you imagine what it must have been like for a girl in her mid-teens, more than eight months pregnant, to ride on the back of a donkey? On top of all this, there was no room in the inn!

Their rough beginning continued with an announcement that all boy babies under two would be slain. There were dozens of places where this new marriage could have wavered and fallen apart. But these two good people loved God and were determined to make their love secure.

vout. He was waiting for the consolation of Israel, and the Holy Spirit was upon him. ²⁶It had been revealed to him by the Holy Spirit that he would not die before he had seen the Lord's Christ. ²⁷Moved by the Spirit, he went into the temple courts. When the parents brought in the child Jesus to do for him what the custom of the Law required, ²⁸Simeon took him in his arms and praised God, saying:

²⁹"Sovereign Lord, as you have
　　　promised,
　　you now dismiss*ᵈ* your servant in
　　　peace.
³⁰For my eyes have seen your salvation,
³¹　which you have prepared in the
　　　sight of all people,
³²a light for revelation to the Gentiles
　　and for glory to your people Israel."

ᵃ11 Or *Messiah.* "The Christ" (Greek) and "the Messiah" (Hebrew) both mean "the Anointed One"; also in verse 26.　　*ᵇ23* Exodus 13:2,12　　*ᶜ24* Lev. 12:8　　*ᵈ29* Or *promised, / now dismiss*

33The child's father and mother marveled at what was said about him. 34Then Simeon blessed them and said to Mary, his mother: "This child is destined to cause the falling and rising of many in Israel, and to be a sign that will be spoken against, 35so that the thoughts of many hearts will be revealed. And a sword will pierce your own soul too."

36There was also a prophetess, Anna, the daughter of Phanuel, of the tribe of Asher. She was very old; she had lived with her husband seven years after her marriage, 37and then was a widow until she was eighty-four.*a* She never left the temple but worshiped night and day, fasting and praying. 38Coming up to them at that very moment, she gave thanks to God and spoke about the child to all who were looking forward to the redemption of Jerusalem.

39When Joseph and Mary had done everything required by the Law of the Lord, they returned to Galilee to their own town of Nazareth. 40And the child grew and became strong; he was filled with wisdom, and the grace of God was upon him.

The Boy Jesus at the Temple

41Every year his parents went to Jerusalem for the Feast of the Passover. 42When he was twelve years old, they went up to the Feast, according to the custom. 43After the Feast was over, while his parents were returning home, the boy Jesus stayed behind in Jerusalem, but they were unaware of it. 44Thinking he was in their company, they traveled on for a day. Then they began looking for him among their relatives and friends. 45When they did not find him, they went back to Jerusalem to look for him. 46After three days they found him in the temple courts, sitting among the teachers, listening to them and asking them questions. 47Everyone who heard him was amazed at his understanding and his answers. 48When his parents saw him, they were astonished. His mother said to him, "Son, why have you treated us like this? Your father and I have been anxiously searching for you."

49"Why were you searching for me?" he asked. "Didn't you know I had to be in my Father's house?" 50But they did not understand what he was saying to them.

51Then he went down to Nazareth with them and was obedient to them. But his mother treasured all these things in her heart. 52And Jesus grew in wisdom and stature, and in favor with God and men.

John the Baptist Prepares the Way

3 In the fifteenth year of the reign of Tiberius Caesar—when Pontius Pilate was governor of Judea, Herod tetrarch of Galilee, his brother Philip tetrarch of Iturea and Traconitis, and Lysanias tetrarch of Abilene— 2during the high priesthood of Annas and Caiaphas, the word of God came to John son of Zechariah in the desert. 3He went into all the country around the Jordan, preaching a baptism of repentance for the forgiveness of sins. 4As is written in the book of the words of Isaiah the prophet:

"A voice of one calling in the desert,
'Prepare the way for the Lord,
    make straight paths for him.
5Every valley shall be filled in,
    every mountain and hill made low.
The crooked roads shall become
        straight,
    the rough ways smooth.
6And all mankind will see God's
        salvation.' "*b*

7John said to the crowds coming out to be baptized by him, "You brood of vipers! Who warned you to flee from the coming wrath? 8Produce fruit in keeping with repentance. And do not begin to say to yourselves, 'We have Abraham as our father.' For I tell you that out of these stones God can raise up children for Abraham. 9The ax is already at the root of the trees, and every tree that does not produce good fruit will be cut down and thrown into the fire."

10"What should we do then?" the crowd asked.

11John answered, "The man with two tunics should share with him who has none, and the one who has food should do the same."

12Tax collectors also came to be bap-

a37 Or widow for eighty-four years
b6 Isaiah 40:3-5

tized. "Teacher," they asked, "what should we do?"

¹³"Don't collect any more than you are required to," he told them.

¹⁴Then some soldiers asked him, "And what should we do?"

He replied, "Don't extort money and don't accuse people falsely—be content with your pay."

¹⁵The people were waiting expectantly and were all wondering in their hearts if John might possibly be the Christ.ᵃ ¹⁶John answered them all, "I baptize you withᵇ water. But one more powerful than I will come, the thongs of whose sandals I am not worthy to untie. He will baptize you with the Holy Spirit and with fire. ¹⁷His winnowing fork is in his hand to clear his threshing floor and to gather the wheat into his barn, but he will burn up the chaff with unquenchable fire." ¹⁸And with many other words John ex-horted the people and preached the good news to them.

¹⁹But when John rebuked Herod the tetrarch because of Herodias, his brother's wife, and all the other evil things he had done, ²⁰Herod added this to them all: He locked John up in prison.

The Baptism and Genealogy of Jesus

²¹When all the people were being baptized, Jesus was baptized too. And as he was praying, heaven was opened ²²and the Holy Spirit descended on him in bodily form like a dove. And a voice came from heaven: "You are my Son, whom I love; with you I am well pleased."

²³Now Jesus himself was about thirty years old when he began his ministry. He was the son, so it was thought, of Joseph,

ᵃ15 Or Messiah   ᵇ16 Or in

Marriage Treasure Chest

LUKE 2:51–52 Mary was a wise mother. Whatever the stage of family life—from the discovery that a baby was coming to the challenges of parenting a self-willed twelve-year old—she took time to "treasure all these things in her heart."

In today's fast-paced world, time for reflection and treasuring the parenting process is rare. But if cultivated, this habit can enrich your family and your marriage. Your role as parent can enhance your role as partner.

As new parents, Dave and I remember gazing at our sleeping infant and suddenly realizing that this little one was a witness to our love for each other. As our three sons became toddlers, preschoolers and then entered the elementary years, they motivated us to be more creative in finding time for each other. They challenged our communication; when little ears were listening, we were more intentional in choosing our words. In the struggles of parenting adolescents, we found strength in our marriage relationship.

Now in the empty nest, our memories are precious. Many times it's the simple things we treasure the most. Taking a moment to enjoy a lovely sunset, the thrill of seeing the first spring daffodil, or recording some of the cute things a grandchild tells us over the phone all add to our treasure chest.

Appreciating the simple things in life will add to your own treasure chest of memories. Consider journaling some of the wonderful, ordinary and precious times you have together. Keep a log of your children's cute sayings and the funny things they do. Fill your own treasure chest.

—Dave and Claudia

Weekend **Warm-up** *Why not journal some of the wonderful, ordinary and precious times you have together.*

Go to page 1105 for your next devotional reading.

the son of Heli, ²⁴the son of Mat-
that,
the son of Levi, the son of Melki,
the son of Jannai, the son of Joseph,
²⁵the son of Mattathias, the son of
Amos,
the son of Nahum, the son of Esli,
the son of Naggai, ²⁶the son of Ma-
ath,
the son of Mattathias, the son of
Semein,
the son of Josech, the son of Joda,
²⁷the son of Joanan, the son of Rhesa,
the son of Zerubbabel, the son of
Shealtiel,
the son of Neri, ²⁸the son of Melki,
the son of Addi, the son of Cosam,
the son of Elmadam, the son of Er,
²⁹the son of Joshua, the son of Elie-
zer,
the son of Jorim, the son of Mat-
that,
the son of Levi, ³⁰the son of Simeon,
the son of Judah, the son of Joseph,
the son of Jonam, the son of Eliakim,
³¹the son of Melea, the son of Menna,
the son of Mattatha, the son of Na-
than,
the son of David, ³²the son of Jesse,
the son of Obed, the son of Boaz,
the son of Salmon,^a the son of
Nahshon,
³³the son of Amminadab, the son of
Ram,^b
the son of Hezron, the son of Perez,
the son of Judah, ³⁴the son of Jacob,
the son of Isaac, the son of Abraham,
the son of Terah, the son of Nahor,
³⁵the son of Serug, the son of Reu,
the son of Peleg, the son of Eber,
the son of Shelah, ³⁶the son of Cainan,
the son of Arphaxad, the son of
Shem,
the son of Noah, the son of Lamech,
³⁷the son of Methuselah, the son of
Enoch,
the son of Jared, the son of Mahalalel,

the son of Kenan, ³⁸the son of
Enosh,
the son of Seth, the son of Adam,
the son of God.

The Temptation of Jesus

4 Jesus, full of the Holy Spirit, returned
from the Jordan and was led by the
Spirit in the desert, ²where for forty days
he was tempted by the devil. He ate noth-
ing during those days, and at the end of
them he was hungry.

³The devil said to him, "If you are the
Son of God, tell this stone to become
bread."

⁴Jesus answered, "It is written: 'Man
does not live on bread alone.'^c"

⁵The devil led him up to a high place
and showed him in an instant all the
kingdoms of the world. ⁶And he said to
him, "I will give you all their authority
and splendor, for it has been given to me,
and I can give it to anyone I want to. ⁷So
if you worship me, it will all be yours."

⁸Jesus answered, "It is written: 'Wor-
ship the Lord your God and serve him
only.'^d"

⁹The devil led him to Jerusalem and
had him stand on the highest point of the
temple. "If you are the Son of God," he
said, "throw yourself down from here.
¹⁰For it is written:

" 'He will command his angels
        concerning you
    to guard you carefully;
¹¹they will lift you up in their hands,
    so that you will not strike your
        foot against a stone.'^e"

¹²Jesus answered, "It says: 'Do not put
the Lord your God to the test.'^f"

¹³When the devil had finished all this
tempting, he left him until an opportune
time.

Jesus Rejected at Nazareth

¹⁴Jesus returned to Galilee in the power
of the Spirit, and news about him spread
through the whole countryside. ¹⁵He

^a32 Some early manuscripts *Sala*   ^b33 Some
manuscripts *Amminadab, the son of Admin, the son
of Arni*; other manuscripts vary widely.
^c4 Deut. 8:3   ^d8 Deut. 6:13
^e11 Psalm 91:11,12   ^f12 Deut. 6:16

taught in their synagogues, and everyone praised him.

¹⁶He went to Nazareth, where he had been brought up, and on the Sabbath day he went into the synagogue, as was his custom. And he stood up to read. ¹⁷The scroll of the prophet Isaiah was handed to him. Unrolling it, he found the place where it is written:

¹⁸"The Spirit of the Lord is on me,
    because he has anointed me
    to preach good news to the poor.
He has sent me to proclaim freedom
        for the prisoners
    and recovery of sight for the blind,
to release the oppressed,
¹⁹   to proclaim the year of the Lord's
        favor."ᵃ

²⁰Then he rolled up the scroll, gave it back to the attendant and sat down. The eyes of everyone in the synagogue were fastened on him, ²¹and he began by saying to them, "Today this scripture is fulfilled in your hearing."

²²All spoke well of him and were amazed at the gracious words that came from his lips. "Isn't this Joseph's son?" they asked.

²³Jesus said to them, "Surely you will quote this proverb to me: 'Physician, heal yourself! Do here in your hometown what we have heard that you did in Capernaum.' "

²⁴"I tell you the truth," he continued, "no prophet is accepted in his hometown. ²⁵I assure you that there were many widows in Israel in Elijah's time, when the sky was shut for three and a half years and there was a severe famine throughout the land. ²⁶Yet Elijah was not sent to any of them, but to a widow in Zarephath in the region of Sidon. ²⁷And there were many in Israel with leprosyᵇ in the time of Elisha the prophet, yet not one of them was cleansed—only Naaman the Syrian."

²⁸All the people in the synagogue were furious when they heard this. ²⁹They got up, drove him out of the town, and took him to the brow of the hill on which the

ᵃ19 Isaiah 61:1,2   ᵇ27 The Greek word was used for various diseases affecting the skin—not necessarily leprosy.

Not by Bread Alone

Monday

LUKE 4:1–4 This passage reveals an intimate moment in the life of Christ. He is by himself in the desert, seeking the will of God. During this forty-day period, Jesus chooses to go without eating. Naturally Satan tempts Jesus with food, wanting to cause Jesus to make the needs of his body first priority.

There are seasons in a marriage when the needs of the body are not met. Not necessarily in terms of hunger for food, as was Jesus' case, but in terms of sexual intimacy. Sometimes long distance, medical problems or marital conflicts make sexual intimacy difficult or nonexistent. When physical and emotional intimacy break down between a husband and wife, temptation can become strong and we can try to make physical needs a priority no matter what the cost.

Early in our own marriage, there was a time when our sexual relationship got put on the back burner. Rosemary and I were both working full time jobs while in graduate school and neglected to take time for each other. During that season it was amazing how Satan would attempt to draw my eyes and thoughts in sinful directions. That was the season that this passage of Scripture became very meaningful to me.

When Satan tried to tempt Jesus into making his physical needs (hunger) the priority, Jesus responded by quoting scripture. His example of this dependence upon the Word of the Father is to teach us how to respond to the strong pull of temptation. It boils down to a decision. What are you going to trust? Will you trust the ever-changing cravings of your body or the never-changing instructions of your God?

—*Bob and Rosemary*

Go to page 1109 for your next devotional reading.

town was built, in order to throw him down the cliff. 30But he walked right through the crowd and went on his way.

Jesus Drives Out an Evil Spirit

31Then he went down to Capernaum, a town in Galilee, and on the Sabbath began to teach the people. 32They were amazed at his teaching, because his message had authority.

33In the synagogue there was a man possessed by a demon, an evila spirit. He cried out at the top of his voice, 34"Ha! What do you want with us, Jesus of Nazareth? Have you come to destroy us? I know who you are—the Holy One of God!"

35"Be quiet!" Jesus said sternly. "Come out of him!" Then the demon threw the man down before them all and came out without injuring him.

36All the people were amazed and said to each other, "What is this teaching? With authority and power he gives orders to evil spirits and they come out!" 37And the news about him spread throughout the surrounding area.

Jesus Heals Many

38Jesus left the synagogue and went to the home of Simon. Now Simon's mother-in-law was suffering from a high fever, and they asked Jesus to help her. 39So he bent over her and rebuked the fever, and it left her. She got up at once and began to wait on them.

40When the sun was setting, the people brought to Jesus all who had various kinds of sickness, and laying his hands on each one, he healed them. 41Moreover, demons came out of many people, shouting, "You are the Son of God!" But he rebuked them and would not allow them to speak, because they knew he was the Christ.b

42At daybreak Jesus went out to a solitary place. The people were looking for him and when they came to where he was, they tried to keep him from leaving them. 43But he said, "I must preach the good news of the kingdom of God to the other towns also, because that is why I was sent." 44And he kept on preaching in the synagogues of Judea.c

The Calling of the First Disciples

5 One day as Jesus was standing by the Lake of Gennesaret,d with the people crowding around him and listening to the word of God, 2he saw at the water's edge two boats, left there by the fishermen, who were washing their nets. 3He got into one of the boats, the one belonging to Simon, and asked him to put out a little from shore. Then he sat down and taught the people from the boat.

4When he had finished speaking, he said to Simon, "Put out into deep water, and let downe the nets for a catch."

5Simon answered, "Master, we've worked hard all night and haven't caught anything. But because you say so, I will let down the nets."

6When they had done so, they caught such a large number of fish that their nets began to break. 7So they signaled their partners in the other boat to come and help them, and they came and filled both boats so full that they began to sink.

8When Simon Peter saw this, he fell at Jesus' knees and said, "Go away from me, Lord; I am a sinful man!" 9For he and all his companions were astonished at the catch of fish they had taken, 10and so were James and John, the sons of Zebedee, Simon's partners.

Then Jesus said to Simon, "Don't be afraid; from now on you will catch men." 11So they pulled their boats up on shore, left everything and followed him.

The Man With Leprosy

12While Jesus was in one of the towns, a man came along who was covered with leprosy.f When he saw Jesus, he fell with his face to the ground and begged him, "Lord, if you are willing, you can make me clean."

13Jesus reached out his hand and touched the man. "I am willing," he said. "Be clean!" And immediately the leprosy left him.

14Then Jesus ordered him, "Don't tell anyone, but go, show yourself to the

---

a33 Greek unclean; also in verse 36   b41 Or Messiah   c44 Or the land of the Jews; some manuscripts Galilee   d1 That is, Sea of Galilee   e4 The Greek verb is plural.   f12 The Greek word was used for various diseases affecting the skin—not necessarily leprosy.

priest and offer the sacrifices that Moses commanded for your cleansing, as a testimony to them."

¹⁵Yet the news about him spread all the more, so that crowds of people came to hear him and to be healed of their sicknesses. ¹⁶But Jesus often withdrew to lonely places and prayed.

Jesus Heals a Paralytic

¹⁷One day as he was teaching, Pharisees and teachers of the law, who had come from every village of Galilee and from Judea and Jerusalem, were sitting there. And the power of the Lord was present for him to heal the sick. ¹⁸Some men came carrying a paralytic on a mat and tried to take him into the house to lay him before Jesus. ¹⁹When they could not find a way to do this because of the crowd, they went up on the roof and lowered him on his mat through the tiles into the middle of the crowd, right in front of Jesus.

²⁰When Jesus saw their faith, he said, "Friend, your sins are forgiven."

²¹The Pharisees and the teachers of the law began thinking to themselves, "Who is this fellow who speaks blasphemy? Who can forgive sins but God alone?"

²²Jesus knew what they were thinking and asked, "Why are you thinking these things in your hearts? ²³Which is easier: to say, 'Your sins are forgiven,' or to say, 'Get up and walk'? ²⁴But that you may know that the Son of Man has authority on earth to forgive sins . . ." He said to the paralyzed man, "I tell you, get up, take your mat and go home." ²⁵Immediately he stood up in front of them, took what he had been lying on and went home praising God. ²⁶Everyone was amazed and gave praise to God. They were filled with awe and said, "We have seen remarkable things today."

The Calling of Levi

²⁷After this, Jesus went out and saw a tax collector by the name of Levi sitting at his tax booth. "Follow me," Jesus said to him, ²⁸and Levi got up, left everything and followed him.

²⁹Then Levi held a great banquet for Jesus at his house, and a large crowd of tax collectors and others were eating with them. ³⁰But the Pharisees and the teachers of the law who belonged to their sect complained to his disciples, "Why do you eat and drink with tax collectors and 'sinners'?"

³¹Jesus answered them, "It is not the healthy who need a doctor, but the sick. ³²I have not come to call the righteous, but sinners to repentance."

Jesus Questioned About Fasting

³³They said to him, "John's disciples often fast and pray, and so do the disciples of the Pharisees, but yours go on eating and drinking."

³⁴Jesus answered, "Can you make the guests of the bridegroom fast while he is with them? ³⁵But the time will come when the bridegroom will be taken from them; in those days they will fast."

³⁶He told them this parable: "No one tears a patch from a new garment and sews it on an old one. If he does, he will have torn the new garment, and the patch from the new will not match the old. ³⁷And no one pours new wine into old wineskins. If he does, the new wine will burst the skins, the wine will run out and the wineskins will be ruined. ³⁸No, new wine must be poured into new wineskins. ³⁹And no one after drinking old wine wants the new, for he says, 'The old is better.' "

Lord of the Sabbath

6 One Sabbath Jesus was going through the grainfields, and his disciples began to pick some heads of grain, rub them in their hands and eat the kernels. ²Some of the Pharisees asked, "Why are you doing what is unlawful on the Sabbath?"

³Jesus answered them, "Have you never read what David did when he and his companions were hungry? ⁴He entered the house of God, and taking the consecrated bread, he ate what is lawful only for priests to eat. And he also gave some to his companions." ⁵Then Jesus said to them, "The Son of Man is Lord of the Sabbath."

⁶On another Sabbath he went into the synagogue and was teaching, and a man was there whose right hand was shriveled. ⁷The Pharisees and the teachers of the law were looking for a reason to accuse Jesus,

so they watched him closely to see if he would heal on the Sabbath. ⁸But Jesus knew what they were thinking and said to the man with the shriveled hand, "Get up and stand in front of everyone." So he got up and stood there.

⁹Then Jesus said to them, "I ask you, which is lawful on the Sabbath: to do good or to do evil, to save life or to destroy it?"

¹⁰He looked around at them all, and then said to the man, "Stretch out your hand." He did so, and his hand was completely restored. ¹¹But they were furious and began to discuss with one another what they might do to Jesus.

The Twelve Apostles

¹²One of those days Jesus went out to a mountainside to pray, and spent the night praying to God. ¹³When morning came, he called his disciples to him and chose twelve of them, whom he also designated apostles: ¹⁴Simon (whom he named Peter), his brother Andrew, James, John, Philip, Bartholomew, ¹⁵Matthew, Thomas, James son of Alphaeus, Simon who was called the Zealot, ¹⁶Judas son of James, and Judas Iscariot, who became a traitor.

Blessings and Woes

¹⁷He went down with them and stood on a level place. A large crowd of his disciples was there and a great number of people from all over Judea, from Jerusalem, and from the coast of Tyre and Sidon, ¹⁸who had come to hear him and to be healed of their diseases. Those troubled by evil[a] spirits were cured, ¹⁹and the people all tried to touch him, because power was coming from him and healing them all.

²⁰Looking at his disciples, he said:

"Blessed are you who are poor,
    for yours is the kingdom of God.
²¹Blessed are you who hunger now,
    for you will be satisfied.
Blessed are you who weep now,
    for you will laugh.
²²Blessed are you when men hate you,
    when they exclude you and insult
        you
    and reject your name as evil,
        because of the Son of Man.

²³"Rejoice in that day and leap for joy, because great is your reward in heaven. For that is how their fathers treated the prophets.

²⁴"But woe to you who are rich,
    for you have already received your
        comfort.
²⁵Woe to you who are well fed now,
    for you will go hungry.
Woe to you who laugh now,
    for you will mourn and weep.
²⁶Woe to you when all men speak well
        of you,
    for that is how their fathers treated
        the false prophets.

Love for Enemies

²⁷"But I tell you who hear me: Love your enemies, do good to those who hate you, ²⁸bless those who curse you, pray for those who mistreat you. ²⁹If someone strikes you on one cheek, turn to him the other also. If someone takes your cloak, do not stop him from taking your tunic. ³⁰Give to everyone who asks you, and if anyone takes what belongs to you, do not demand it back. ³¹Do to others as you would have them do to you.

³²"If you love those who love you, what credit is that to you? Even 'sinners' love those who love them. ³³And if you do good to those who are good to you, what credit is that to you? Even 'sinners' do that. ³⁴And if you lend to those from whom you expect repayment, what credit is that to you? Even 'sinners' lend to 'sinners,' expecting to be repaid in full. ³⁵But love your enemies, do good to them, and lend to them without expecting to get anything back. Then your reward will be great, and you will be sons of the Most High, because he is kind to the ungrateful and wicked. ³⁶Be merciful, just as your Father is merciful.

Judging Others

³⁷"Do not judge, and you will not be judged. Do not condemn, and you will not be condemned. Forgive, and you will be forgiven. ³⁸Give, and it will be given to you. A good measure, pressed down, shaken together and running over, will

a18 Greek *unclean*

be poured into your lap. For with the measure you use, it will be measured to you."

³⁹He also told them this parable: "Can a blind man lead a blind man? Will they not both fall into a pit? ⁴⁰A student is not above his teacher, but everyone who is fully trained will be like his teacher.

⁴¹"Why do you look at the speck of sawdust in your brother's eye and pay no attention to the plank in your own eye? ⁴²How can you say to your brother, 'Brother, let me take the speck out of your eye,' when you yourself fail to see the plank in your own eye? You hypocrite, first take the plank out of your eye, and then you will see clearly to remove the speck from your brother's eye.

A Tree and Its Fruit

⁴³"No good tree bears bad fruit, nor does a bad tree bear good fruit. ⁴⁴Each tree is recognized by its own fruit. People do not pick figs from thornbushes, or grapes from briers. ⁴⁵The good man brings good things out of the good stored up in his heart, and the evil man brings evil things out of the evil stored up in his heart. For out of the overflow of his heart his mouth speaks.

The Wise and Foolish Builders

⁴⁶"Why do you call me, 'Lord, Lord,' and do not do what I say? ⁴⁷I will show you what he is like who comes to me and hears my words and puts them into practice. ⁴⁸He is like a man building a house, who dug down deep and laid the foundation on rock. When a flood came, the torrent struck that house but could not shake it, because it was well built. ⁴⁹But the one who hears my words and does not put them into practice is like a man who built a house on the ground without a foundation. The moment the torrent struck that house, it collapsed and its destruction was complete."

The Faith of the Centurion

7 When Jesus had finished saying all this in the hearing of the people, he entered Capernaum. ²There a centurion's servant, whom his master valued highly, was sick and about to die. ³The centurion heard of Jesus and sent some elders of the Jews to him, asking him to come and heal his servant. ⁴When they came to Jesus, they pleaded earnestly with him, "This man deserves to have you do this, ⁵because he loves our nation and has built

---

Turning the Other Cheek

Tuesday

LUKE 6:29   Are you ready to discover and practice a relational principle that can revolutionize your marriage? Here it is: Turn the other cheek. Okay, okay, so you've heard this all your life. But do you know the difference it can make in your marriage? Here's when and how it works.

When you are injured by something your spouse has said or done, the pain you feel is understandable. Maybe you can talk to him or her as a reasonable adult and work through the problem without much fuss. If, on the other hand, the pain is causing you to want to hurt your spouse back, you are in need of the "other cheek" principle.

When a businessman that I know was recently fired, a mutual friend told me with a grim smile, "Well, there is justice in the world. If you wait long enough, things even out!" I asked him what he meant by that comment and found out that the man who had been fired had fired him. When I asked the businessman when this had occurred, he told me the firing had taken place fifteen years earlier, when they were both young executives!

It's been said that revenge "is a dish best eaten cold"—meaning that the longer you wait, the sweeter it is. We think it is a dish best not eaten at all. Storing it up, nurturing your pain, plotting revenge—all these punish you more than the person who has hurt you. So turn the other cheek. Surrender your right to hurt back and save your marriage in the process.

—Les and Leslie

Go to page 1110 for your next devotional reading.

our synagogue." ⁶So Jesus went with them.

He was not far from the house when the centurion sent friends to say to him: "Lord, don't trouble yourself, for I do not deserve to have you come under my roof. ⁷That is why I did not even consider myself worthy to come to you. But say the word, and my servant will be healed. ⁸For I myself am a man under authority, with soldiers under me. I tell this one, 'Go,' and he goes; and that one, 'Come,' and he comes. I say to my servant, 'Do this,' and he does it."

⁹When Jesus heard this, he was amazed at him, and turning to the crowd following him, he said, "I tell you, I have not found such great faith even in Israel." ¹⁰Then the men who had been sent returned to the house and found the servant well.

Jesus Raises a Widow's Son

¹¹Soon afterward, Jesus went to a town called Nain, and his disciples and a large crowd went along with him. ¹²As he approached the town gate, a dead person was being carried out—the only son of his mother, and she was a widow. And a large crowd from the town was with her. ¹³When the Lord saw her, his heart went out to her and he said, "Don't cry."

¹⁴Then he went up and touched the coffin, and those carrying it stood still. He said, "Young man, I say to you, get up!"

¹⁵The dead man sat up and began to talk, and Jesus gave him back to his mother.

¹⁶They were all filled with awe and praised God. "A great prophet has appeared among us," they said. "God has come to help his people." ¹⁷This news about Jesus spread throughout Judea[a] and the surrounding country.

Jesus and John the Baptist

¹⁸John's disciples told him about all these things. Calling two of them, ¹⁹he sent them to the Lord to ask, "Are you the one who was to come, or should we expect someone else?"

²⁰When the men came to Jesus, they said, "John the Baptist sent us to you to ask, 'Are you the one who was to come, or should we expect someone else?' "

²¹At that very time Jesus cured many who had diseases, sicknesses and evil spirits, and gave sight to many who were blind. ²²So he replied to the messengers, "Go back and report to John what you have seen and heard: The blind receive sight, the lame walk, those who have leprosy[b] are cured, the deaf hear, the dead are raised, and the good news is preached to the poor. ²³Blessed is the man who does not fall away on account of me."

²⁴After John's messengers left, Jesus began to speak to the crowd about John:

---

[a]17 Or *the land of the Jews*   [b]22 The Greek word was used for various diseases affecting the skin—not necessarily leprosy.

A Fruitful Marriage

Wednesday

LUKE 6:43 If your marriage were a fruit tree, what kind of tree would you like it to be? Some marriages are as sweet as peaches. Others are as sour as grapes. The Scriptures often use the analogy of fruit trees and fruit to illustrate spiritual principles. Good fruit is pleasantly sweet. It is health-giving and nutritious. Each fruit is also unique. No two apples are exactly alike, apples aren't like pears and pears are quite different from either oranges or figs. Likewise, marriages are unique and can be positive or negative, sweet or sour.

Claudia's father was an apple grower, so we know firsthand that good fruit doesn't just happen—a successful apple crop is the result of much hard work cultivating the orchards. Marriages also require cultivation. Good marriages cultivate the fruits of the Spirit like love, joy, peace, patience, kindness, gentleness and self-control (see Galatians 5:22, page 1277). What can you do today to produce "good fruit" in your marriage? Let your life and your marriage be rooted in God's love, and let his character be reflected in the way you love your spouse.   **—Dave and Claudia**

Go to page 1112 for your next devotional reading.

"What did you go out into the desert to see? A reed swayed by the wind? [25]If not, what did you go out to see? A man dressed in fine clothes? No, those who wear expensive clothes and indulge in luxury are in palaces. [26]But what did you go out to see? A prophet? Yes, I tell you, and more than a prophet. [27]This is the one about whom it is written:

" 'I will send my messenger ahead of
    you,
  who will prepare your way before
    you.'[a]

[28]I tell you, among those born of women there is no one greater than John; yet the one who is least in the kingdom of God is greater than he."

[29](All the people, even the tax collectors, when they heard Jesus' words, acknowledged that God's way was right, because they had been baptized by John. [30]But the Pharisees and experts in the law rejected God's purpose for themselves, because they had not been baptized by John.)

[31]"To what, then, can I compare the people of this generation? What are they like? [32]They are like children sitting in the marketplace and calling out to each other:

" 'We played the flute for you,
    and you did not dance;
  we sang a dirge,
    and you did not cry.'

[33]For John the Baptist came neither eating bread nor drinking wine, and you say, 'He has a demon.' [34]The Son of Man came eating and drinking, and you say, 'Here is a glutton and a drunkard, a friend of tax collectors and "sinners." ' [35]But wisdom is proved right by all her children."

Jesus Anointed by a Sinful Woman

[36]Now one of the Pharisees invited Jesus to have dinner with him, so he went to the Pharisee's house and reclined at the table. [37]When a woman who had lived a sinful life in that town learned that Jesus was eating at the Pharisee's house, she brought an alabaster jar of perfume, [38]and as she stood behind him at his feet weeping, she began to wet his feet with her tears. Then she wiped them with her hair,

kissed them and poured perfume on them.

[39]When the Pharisee who had invited him saw this, he said to himself, "If this man were a prophet, he would know who is touching him and what kind of woman she is—that she is a sinner."

[40]Jesus answered him, "Simon, I have something to tell you."

"Tell me, teacher," he said.

[41]"Two men owed money to a certain moneylender. One owed him five hundred denarii,[b] and the other fifty. [42]Neither of them had the money to pay him back, so he canceled the debts of both. Now which of them will love him more?"

[43]Simon replied, "I suppose the one who had the bigger debt canceled."

"You have judged correctly," Jesus said. [44]Then he turned toward the woman and said to Simon, "Do you see this woman? I came into your house. You did not give me any water for my feet, but she wet my feet with her tears and wiped them with her hair. [45]You did not give me a kiss, but this woman, from the time I entered, has not stopped kissing my feet. [46]You did not put oil on my head, but she has poured perfume on my feet. [47]Therefore, I tell you, her many sins have been forgiven—for she loved much. But he who has been forgiven little loves little."

[48]Then Jesus said to her, "Your sins are forgiven."

[49]The other guests began to say among themselves, "Who is this who even forgives sins?"

[50]Jesus said to the woman, "Your faith has saved you; go in peace."

The Parable of the Sower

8 After this, Jesus traveled about from one town and village to another, proclaiming the good news of the kingdom of God. The Twelve were with him, [2]and also some women who had been cured of evil spirits and diseases: Mary (called Magdalene) from whom seven demons had come out; [3]Joanna the wife of Cuza, the manager of Herod's household; Susanna; and many others. These women were helping to support them out of their own means.

a27 Mal. 3:1   b41 A denarius was a coin worth about a day's wages.

4While a large crowd was gathering and people were coming to Jesus from town after town, he told this parable: 5"A farmer went out to sow his seed. As he was scattering the seed, some fell along the path; it was trampled on, and the birds of the air ate it up. 6Some fell on rock, and when it came up, the plants withered because they had no moisture. 7Other seed fell among thorns, which grew up with it and choked the plants. 8Still other seed fell on good soil. It came up and yielded a crop, a hundred times more than was sown."

When he said this, he called out, "He who has ears to hear, let him hear."

9His disciples asked him what this parable meant. 10He said, "The knowledge of the secrets of the kingdom of God has been given to you, but to others I speak in parables, so that,

    " 'though seeing, they may not see;
       though hearing, they may not
          understand.'ᵃ

11"This is the meaning of the parable: The seed is the word of God. 12Those along the path are the ones who hear, and then the devil comes and takes away the word from their hearts, so that they may not believe and be saved. 13Those on the rock are the ones who receive the word with joy when they hear it, but they have no root. They believe for a while, but in the time of testing they fall away. 14The seed that fell among thorns stands for those who hear, but as they go on their way they are choked by life's worries, riches and pleasures, and they do not mature. 15But the seed on good soil stands for those with a noble and good heart, who hear the word, retain it, and by persevering produce a crop.

A Lamp on a Stand

16"No one lights a lamp and hides it in a jar or puts it under a bed. Instead, he puts it on a stand, so that those who come in can see the light. 17For there is nothing hidden that will not be disclosed, and nothing concealed that will not be known or brought out into the open. 18Therefore consider carefully how you listen. Whoever has will be given more; whoever does not have, even what he thinks he has will be taken from him."

Jesus' Mother and Brothers

19Now Jesus' mother and brothers came to see him, but they were not able

ᵃ10 Isaiah 6:9

Let Your Light Shine

Thursday

LUKE 8:16–17 As a little child, do you remember singing "This little light of mine, I'm going to let it shine"? That's not a bad theme song for couples who enjoy a solid Christian marriage. Strong couples can light the way for others. But unfortunately, our culture has a marital taboo—many feel their marriage is too private and personal to talk about. The result is a hesitancy to share. Then when other couples experience problems, these couples see no one who can "light their way."

Dr. John Gottman, marital researcher at the University of Washington, told us that the average couple waits six years before getting help for their marital problems. We can change that by sharing our marriage experiences—both the good and the bad—with other couples. And when we encourage other couples, the light of healthy Christian marriages can shine even brighter. What we need today is a widespread movement of Christian couples who, rather than hiding their valuable insights, are talking to others about marriage—what works and what doesn't.

Is there something more you could do for other married couples? Consider starting a marriage growth group, dating club or marriage mentoring group, or help to mentor a younger couple. If you're newly married, find an older couple who has a healthy Christian marriage to be your mentor.

—*Dave and Claudia*

Go to page 1115 for your next devotional reading.

to get near him because of the crowd. [20]Someone told him, "Your mother and brothers are standing outside, wanting to see you."

[21]He replied, "My mother and brothers are those who hear God's word and put it into practice."

Jesus Calms the Storm

[22]One day Jesus said to his disciples, "Let's go over to the other side of the lake." So they got into a boat and set out. [23]As they sailed, he fell asleep. A squall came down on the lake, so that the boat was being swamped, and they were in great danger.

[24]The disciples went and woke him, saying, "Master, Master, we're going to drown!"

He got up and rebuked the wind and the raging waters; the storm subsided, and all was calm. [25]"Where is your faith?" he asked his disciples.

In fear and amazement they asked one another, "Who is this? He commands even the winds and the water, and they obey him."

The Healing of a Demon-possessed Man

[26]They sailed to the region of the Gerasenes,[a] which is across the lake from Galilee. [27]When Jesus stepped ashore, he was met by a demon-possessed man from the town. For a long time this man had not worn clothes or lived in a house, but had lived in the tombs. [28]When he saw Jesus, he cried out and fell at his feet, shouting at the top of his voice, "What do you want with me, Jesus, Son of the Most High God? I beg you, don't torture me!" [29]For Jesus had commanded the evil[b] spirit to come out of the man. Many times it had seized him, and though he was chained hand and foot and kept under guard, he had broken his chains and had been driven by the demon into solitary places.

[30]Jesus asked him, "What is your name?"

"Legion," he replied, because many demons had gone into him. [31]And they begged him repeatedly not to order them to go into the Abyss.

[32]A large herd of pigs was feeding there on the hillside. The demons begged Jesus to let them go into them, and he gave them permission. [33]When the demons came out of the man, they went into the pigs, and the herd rushed down the steep bank into the lake and was drowned.

[34]When those tending the pigs saw what had happened, they ran off and reported this in the town and countryside, [35]and the people went out to see what had happened. When they came to Jesus, they found the man from whom the demons had gone out, sitting at Jesus' feet, dressed and in his right mind; and they were afraid. [36]Those who had seen it told the people how the demon-possessed man had been cured. [37]Then all the people of the region of the Gerasenes asked Jesus to leave them, because they were overcome with fear. So he got into the boat and left.

[38]The man from whom the demons had gone out begged to go with him, but Jesus sent him away, saying, [39]"Return home and tell how much God has done for you." So the man went away and told all over town how much Jesus had done for him.

A Dead Girl and a Sick Woman

[40]Now when Jesus returned, a crowd welcomed him, for they were all expecting him. [41]Then a man named Jairus, a ruler of the synagogue, came and fell at Jesus' feet, pleading with him to come to his house [42]because his only daughter, a girl of about twelve, was dying.

As Jesus was on his way, the crowds almost crushed him. [43]And a woman was there who had been subject to bleeding for twelve years,[c] but no one could heal her. [44]She came up behind him and touched the edge of his cloak, and immediately her bleeding stopped.

[45]"Who touched me?" Jesus asked.

When they all denied it, Peter said, "Master, the people are crowding and pressing against you."

[46]But Jesus said, "Someone touched me; I know that power has gone out from me."

[47]Then the woman, seeing that she

a26 Some manuscripts *Gadarenes*; other manuscripts *Gergesenes*; also in verse 37
b29 Greek *unclean*   c43 Many manuscripts years, *and she had spent all she had on doctors*

could not go unnoticed, came trembling and fell at his feet. In the presence of all the people, she told why she had touched him and how she had been instantly healed. ⁴⁸Then he said to her, "Daughter, your faith has healed you. Go in peace."

⁴⁹While Jesus was still speaking, someone came from the house of Jairus, the synagogue ruler. "Your daughter is dead," he said. "Don't bother the teacher any more."

⁵⁰Hearing this, Jesus said to Jairus, "Don't be afraid; just believe, and she will be healed."

⁵¹When he arrived at the house of Jairus, he did not let anyone go in with him except Peter, John and James, and the child's father and mother. ⁵²Meanwhile, all the people were wailing and mourning for her. "Stop wailing," Jesus said. "She is not dead but asleep."

⁵³They laughed at him, knowing that she was dead. ⁵⁴But he took her by the hand and said, "My child, get up!" ⁵⁵Her spirit returned, and at once she stood up. Then Jesus told them to give her something to eat. ⁵⁶Her parents were astonished, but he ordered them not to tell anyone what had happened.

Jesus Sends Out the Twelve

9 When Jesus had called the Twelve together, he gave them power and authority to drive out all demons and to cure diseases, ²and he sent them out to preach the kingdom of God and to heal the sick. ³He told them: "Take nothing for the journey—no staff, no bag, no bread, no money, no extra tunic. ⁴Whatever house you enter, stay there until you leave that town. ⁵If people do not welcome you, shake the dust off your feet when you leave their town, as a testimony against them." ⁶So they set out and went from village to village, preaching the gospel and healing people everywhere.

⁷Now Herod the tetrarch heard about all that was going on. And he was perplexed, because some were saying that John had been raised from the dead, ⁸others that Elijah had appeared, and still others that one of the prophets of long ago had come back to life. ⁹But Herod said, "I beheaded John. Who, then, is this I hear

such things about?" And he tried to see him.

Jesus Feeds the Five Thousand

¹⁰When the apostles returned, they reported to Jesus what they had done. Then he took them with him and they withdrew by themselves to a town called Bethsaida, ¹¹but the crowds learned about it and followed him. He welcomed them and spoke to them about the kingdom of God, and healed those who needed healing.

¹²Late in the afternoon the Twelve came to him and said, "Send the crowd away so they can go to the surrounding villages and countryside and find food and lodging, because we are in a remote place here."

¹³He replied, "You give them something to eat."

They answered, "We have only five loaves of bread and two fish—unless we go and buy food for all this crowd." ¹⁴(About five thousand men were there.)

But he said to his disciples, "Have them sit down in groups of about fifty each." ¹⁵The disciples did so, and everybody sat down. ¹⁶Taking the five loaves and the two fish and looking up to heaven, he gave thanks and broke them. Then he gave them to the disciples to set before the people. ¹⁷They all ate and were satisfied, and the disciples picked up twelve basketfuls of broken pieces that were left over.

Peter's Confession of Christ

¹⁸Once when Jesus was praying in private and his disciples were with him, he asked them, "Who do the crowds say I am?"

¹⁹They replied, "Some say John the Baptist; others say Elijah; and still others, that one of the prophets of long ago has come back to life."

²⁰"But what about you?" he asked. "Who do you say I am?"

Peter answered, "The Christ[a] of God."

²¹Jesus strictly warned them not to tell this to anyone. ²²And he said, "The Son of Man must suffer many things and be rejected by the elders, chief priests and

ᵃ20 Or Messiah

teachers of the law, and he must be killed and on the third day be raised to life."

²³Then he said to them all: "If anyone would come after me, he must deny himself and take up his cross daily and follow me. ²⁴For whoever wants to save his life will lose it, but whoever loses his life for me will save it. ²⁵What good is it for a man to gain the whole world, and yet lose or forfeit his very self? ²⁶If anyone is ashamed of me and my words, the Son of Man will be ashamed of him when he comes in his glory and in the glory of the Father and of the holy angels. ²⁷I tell you the truth, some who are standing here will not taste death before they see the kingdom of God."

The Transfiguration

²⁸About eight days after Jesus said this, he took Peter, John and James with him and went up onto a mountain to pray. ²⁹As he was praying, the appearance of his face changed, and his clothes became as bright as a flash of lightning. ³⁰Two men, Moses and Elijah, ³¹appeared in glorious splendor, talking with Jesus. They spoke about his departure, which he was about to bring to fulfillment at Jerusalem. ³²Peter and his companions were very sleepy, but when they became fully awake, they saw his glory and the two men standing with him. ³³As the men were leaving Jesus, Peter said to him, "Master, it is good for us to be here. Let us put up three shelters—one for you, one for Moses and one for Elijah." (He did not know what he was saying.)

³⁴While he was speaking, a cloud appeared and enveloped them, and they were afraid as they entered the cloud. ³⁵A voice came from the cloud, saying, "This is my Son, whom I have chosen; listen to him." ³⁶When the voice had spoken, they found that Jesus was alone. The disciples kept this to themselves, and told no one at that time what they had seen.

The Healing of a Boy With an Evil Spirit

³⁷The next day, when they came down from the mountain, a large crowd met him. ³⁸A man in the crowd called out,

---

Becoming a Basket Carrier

Friday

LUKE 9:12–17 "I just can't do it! It's beyond me to even consider it!" The disciples must have had these thoughts when they were called upon to carry the baskets of fishes and loaves to the people. They knew that feeding so many people with next-to-no-food was impossible. Why was Jesus even asking them to try it?

The marriage relationship sometimes makes similar demands. There are times when we are called to do things or adjust to things that seem beyond our ability. For example, Bob and I are so different. He's task oriented, putting everything out of his mind in order to get the job done. I, on the other hand, am relationship oriented. I find myself weighing every move to make sure I won't hurt anyone. Bob gets more done than anyone I've ever seen, but in the first decade of our marriage, my feelings were often left in his wake. I found myself having to continually do the impossible—talk to him about what had happened and then forgive him. This ongoing forgiveness initially seemed like an impossible assignment.

The disciples must have thought they just didn't have it in them to do what was being asked of them. They were right! They didn't have to perform a miracle; they just had to do what Jesus asked. When we are called upon to do what seems impossible, our job is to take one step at a time and just "carry the basket." Carrying the basket means doing our part and leaving what seems impossible up to God. Do your job in your marriage and depend on God to work the miracles. If you resist what seems to be the impossible task of "carrying the baskets," you will miss out on being a part of God's great miraculous plan.

—**Bob and Rosemary**

Go to page 1118 for your next devotional reading.

"Teacher, I beg you to look at my son, for he is my only child. ³⁹A spirit seizes him and he suddenly screams; it throws him into convulsions so that he foams at the mouth. It scarcely ever leaves him and is destroying him. ⁴⁰I begged your disciples to drive it out, but they could not."

⁴¹"O unbelieving and perverse generation," Jesus replied, "how long shall I stay with you and put up with you? Bring your son here."

⁴²Even while the boy was coming, the demon threw him to the ground in a convulsion. But Jesus rebuked the evil*a* spirit, healed the boy and gave him back to his father. ⁴³And they were all amazed at the greatness of God.

While everyone was marveling at all that Jesus did, he said to his disciples, ⁴⁴"Listen carefully to what I am about to tell you: The Son of Man is going to be betrayed into the hands of men." ⁴⁵But they did not understand what this meant. It was hidden from them, so that they did not grasp it, and they were afraid to ask him about it.

Who Will Be the Greatest?

⁴⁶An argument started among the disciples as to which of them would be the greatest. ⁴⁷Jesus, knowing their thoughts, took a little child and had him stand beside him. ⁴⁸Then he said to them, "Whoever welcomes this little child in my name welcomes me; and whoever welcomes me welcomes the one who sent me. For he who is least among you all—he is the greatest."

⁴⁹"Master," said John, "we saw a man driving out demons in your name and we tried to stop him, because he is not one of us."

⁵⁰"Do not stop him," Jesus said, "for whoever is not against you is for you."

Samaritan Opposition

⁵¹As the time approached for him to be taken up to heaven, Jesus resolutely set out for Jerusalem. ⁵²And he sent messengers on ahead, who went into a Samaritan village to get things ready for him; ⁵³but the people there did not welcome him, because he was heading for Jerusalem. ⁵⁴When the disciples James and John saw this, they asked, "Lord, do you want us to call fire down from heaven to destroy them*b*?" ⁵⁵But Jesus turned and rebuked them, ⁵⁶and*c* they went to another village.

The Cost of Following Jesus

⁵⁷As they were walking along the road, a man said to him, "I will follow you wherever you go."

⁵⁸Jesus replied, "Foxes have holes and birds of the air have nests, but the Son of Man has no place to lay his head."

⁵⁹He said to another man, "Follow me."

But the man replied, "Lord, first let me go and bury my father."

⁶⁰Jesus said to him, "Let the dead bury their own dead, but you go and proclaim the kingdom of God."

⁶¹Still another said, "I will follow you, Lord; but first let me go back and say good-by to my family."

⁶²Jesus replied, "No one who puts his hand to the plow and looks back is fit for service in the kingdom of God."

Jesus Sends Out the Seventy-two

10 After this the Lord appointed seventy-two*d* others and sent them two by two ahead of him to every town and place where he was about to go. ²He told them, "The harvest is plentiful, but the workers are few. Ask the Lord of the harvest, therefore, to send out workers into his harvest field. ³Go! I am sending you out like lambs among wolves. ⁴Do not take a purse or bag or sandals; and do not greet anyone on the road.

⁵"When you enter a house, first say, 'Peace to this house.' ⁶If a man of peace is there, your peace will rest on him; if not, it will return to you. ⁷Stay in that house, eating and drinking whatever they give you, for the worker deserves his wages. Do not move around from house to house.

⁸"When you enter a town and are welcomed, eat what is set before you. ⁹Heal the sick who are there and tell them, 'The

---

*a*42 Greek *unclean*   *b*54 Some manuscripts *them, even as Elijah did*   *c*55,56 Some manuscripts *them. And he said, "You do not know what kind of spirit you are of, for the Son of Man did not come to destroy men's lives, but to save them."* *⁵⁶And*   *d*1 Some manuscripts *seventy*; also in verse 17 kingdom of God is near you.' ¹⁰But when you enter a town and are not welcomed, go into its streets and say, ¹¹'Even the dust of your town that sticks to our feet we wipe off against you. Yet be sure of this: The kingdom of God is near.' ¹²I tell you, it will be more bearable on that day for Sodom than for that town.

¹³"Woe to you, Korazin! Woe to you, Bethsaida! For if the miracles that were performed in you had been performed in Tyre and Sidon, they would have repented long ago, sitting in sackcloth and ashes. ¹⁴But it will be more bearable for Tyre and Sidon at the judgment than for you. ¹⁵And you, Capernaum, will you be lifted up to the skies? No, you will go down to the depths.ᵃ

¹⁶"He who listens to you listens to me; he who rejects you rejects me; but he who rejects me rejects him who sent me."

¹⁷The seventy-two returned with joy and said, "Lord, even the demons submit to us in your name."

¹⁸He replied, "I saw Satan fall like lightning from heaven. ¹⁹I have given you authority to trample on snakes and scorpions and to overcome all the power of the enemy; nothing will harm you. ²⁰However, do not rejoice that the spirits submit to you, but rejoice that your names are written in heaven."

²¹At that time Jesus, full of joy through the Holy Spirit, said, "I praise you, Father, Lord of heaven and earth, because you have hidden these things from the wise and learned, and revealed them to little children. Yes, Father, for this was your good pleasure.

²²"All things have been committed to me by my Father. No one knows who the Son is except the Father, and no one knows who the Father is except the Son and those to whom the Son chooses to reveal him."

²³Then he turned to his disciples and said privately, "Blessed are the eyes that see what you see. ²⁴For I tell you that many prophets and kings wanted to see what you see but did not see it, and to hear what you hear but did not hear it."

The Parable of the Good Samaritan

²⁵On one occasion an expert in the law stood up to test Jesus. "Teacher," he asked, "what must I do to inherit eternal life?"

²⁶"What is written in the Law?" he replied. "How do you read it?"

²⁷He answered: " 'Love the Lord your God with all your heart and with all your soul and with all your strength and with all your mind'ᵇ; and, 'Love your neighbor as yourself.'ᶜ"

²⁸"You have answered correctly," Jesus replied. "Do this and you will live."

²⁹But he wanted to justify himself, so he asked Jesus, "And who is my neighbor?"

³⁰In reply Jesus said: "A man was going down from Jerusalem to Jericho, when he fell into the hands of robbers. They stripped him of his clothes, beat him and went away, leaving him half dead. ³¹A priest happened to be going down the same road, and when he saw the man, he passed by on the other side. ³²So too, a Levite, when he came to the place and saw him, passed by on the other side. ³³But a Samaritan, as he traveled, came where the man was; and when he saw him, he took pity on him. ³⁴He went to him and bandaged his wounds, pouring on oil and wine. Then he put the man on his own donkey, took him to an inn and took care of him. ³⁵The next day he took out two silver coinsᵈ and gave them to the innkeeper. 'Look after him,' he said, 'and when I return, I will reimburse you for any extra expense you may have.'

³⁶"Which of these three do you think was a neighbor to the man who fell into the hands of robbers?"

³⁷The expert in the law replied, "The one who had mercy on him."

Jesus told him, "Go and do likewise."

At the Home of Martha and Mary

³⁸As Jesus and his disciples were on their way, he came to a village where a woman named Martha opened her home to him. ³⁹She had a sister called Mary, who sat at the Lord's feet listening to what he said. ⁴⁰But Martha was distracted by all the preparations that had to be made. She came to him and asked, "Lord, don't you care that my sister has left me to do the work by myself? Tell her to help me!"

ᵃ15 Greek Hades　　ᵇ27 Deut. 6:5
ᶜ27 Lev. 19:18　　ᵈ35 Greek two denarii

⁴¹"Martha, Martha," the Lord answered, "you are worried and upset about many things, ⁴²but only one thing is needed.ᵃ Mary has chosen what is better, and it will not be taken away from her."

Jesus' Teaching on Prayer

11 One day Jesus was praying in a certain place. When he finished, one of his disciples said to him, "Lord, teach us to pray, just as John taught his disciples."

²He said to them, "When you pray, say:

" 'Father,ᵇ
hallowed be your name,
   your kingdom come.ᶜ
³Give us each day our daily bread.
⁴Forgive us our sins,
   for we also forgive everyone who
      sins against us.ᵈ
And lead us not into temptation.ᵉ' "

⁵Then he said to them, "Suppose one of you has a friend, and he goes to him at midnight and says, 'Friend, lend me three loaves of bread, ⁶because a friend of mine on a journey has come to me, and I have nothing to set before him.'

⁷"Then the one inside answers, 'Don't bother me. The door is already locked, and my children are with me in bed. I can't get up and give you anything.' ⁸I tell you, though he will not get up and give him the bread because he is his friend, yet because of the man's boldnessᶠ he will get up and give him as much as he needs.

⁹"So I say to you: Ask and it will be given to you; seek and you will find; knock and the door will be opened to you. ¹⁰For everyone who asks receives; he who seeks finds; and to him who knocks, the door will be opened.

¹¹"Which of you fathers, if your son asks forᵍ a fish, will give him a snake instead? ¹²Or if he asks for an egg, will give him a scorpion? ¹³If you then, though you are evil, know how to give good gifts to your children, how much

---

ᵃ42 Some manuscripts *but few things are needed—or only one*   ᵇ2 Some manuscripts *Our Father in heaven*   ᶜ2 Some manuscripts *come. May your will be done on earth as it is in heaven.*   ᵈ4 Greek *everyone who is indebted to us*   ᵉ4 Some manuscripts *temptation but deliver us from the evil one*   ᶠ8 Or *persistence*   ᵍ11 Some manuscripts *for bread, will give him a stone; or if he asks for*

A Good Kind of Love Triangle

LUKE 10:25–27 When we talk with other couples about what makes their relationship strong, we often hear responses like "having a shared faith in God and worshiping and praying together." In our own marriage, our common love for and faith in God are key to loving each other. He empowers us to love with our heart, soul, strength and mind.

Because God loves us unconditionally we can love each other in like manner even when one of us is less than lovable. I remember once when Claudia smelled coffee in our bedroom and accused me of spilling my coffee and trying to hide it. I just smiled lovingly without reacting and said, "Hon-

ey, look under your pillow."

Under the pillow, Claudia found a pound of her favorite Viennese blend coffee! The next time Claudia started to react, she caught herself and remembered my love gift.

Your love for God will help you to live out your love for each other. Faith in Christ should be the foundation of any Christian marriage. Picture marriage as a triangle with God at the top and the husband and wife at the other two corners. As you move closer to your heavenly Father, you will move closer to each other. Why not take a few minutes and talk about how your spiritual life enriches your love for each other?   **—Dave and Claudia**

***W**arm-up* **Weekend** *Why not take a few minutes and talk about how your spiritual life enriches your love for each other?*

Go to page 1120 for your next devotional reading.

more will your Father in heaven give the Holy Spirit to those who ask him!"

Jesus and Beelzebub

[14]Jesus was driving out a demon that was mute. When the demon left, the man who had been mute spoke, and the crowd was amazed. [15]But some of them said, "By Beelzebub,[a] the prince of demons, he is driving out demons." [16]Others tested him by asking for a sign from heaven.

[17]Jesus knew their thoughts and said to them: "Any kingdom divided against itself will be ruined, and a house divided against itself will fall. [18]If Satan is divided against himself, how can his kingdom stand? I say this because you claim that I drive out demons by Beelzebub. [19]Now if I drive out demons by Beelzebub, by whom do your followers drive them out? So then, they will be your judges. [20]But if I drive out demons by the finger of God, then the kingdom of God has come to you.

[21]"When a strong man, fully armed, guards his own house, his possessions are safe. [22]But when someone stronger attacks and overpowers him, he takes away the armor in which the man trusted and divides up the spoils.

[23]"He who is not with me is against me, and he who does not gather with me, scatters.

[24]"When an evil[b] spirit comes out of a man, it goes through arid places seeking rest and does not find it. Then it says, 'I will return to the house I left.' [25]When it arrives, it finds the house swept clean and put in order. [26]Then it goes and takes seven other spirits more wicked than itself, and they go in and live there. And the final condition of that man is worse than the first."

[27]As Jesus was saying these things, a woman in the crowd called out, "Blessed is the mother who gave you birth and nursed you."

[28]He replied, "Blessed rather are those who hear the word of God and obey it."

The Sign of Jonah

[29]As the crowds increased, Jesus said, "This is a wicked generation. It asks for a miraculous sign, but none will be given it except the sign of Jonah. [30]For as Jonah

was a sign to the Ninevites, so also will the Son of Man be to this generation. [31]The Queen of the South will rise at the judgment with the men of this generation and condemn them; for she came from the ends of the earth to listen to Solomon's wisdom, and now one[c] greater than Solomon is here. [32]The men of Nineveh will stand up at the judgment with this generation and condemn it; for they repented at the preaching of Jonah, and now one greater than Jonah is here.

The Lamp of the Body

[33]"No one lights a lamp and puts it in a place where it will be hidden, or under a bowl. Instead he puts it on its stand, so that those who come in may see the light. [34]Your eye is the lamp of your body.

---

[a]15 Greek *Beezeboul* or *Beelzeboul*; also in verses 18 and 19   [b]24 Greek *unclean*   [c]31 Or *something*; also in verse 32

When your eyes are good, your whole body also is full of light. But when they are bad, your body also is full of darkness. ³⁵See to it, then, that the light within you is not darkness. ³⁶Therefore, if your whole body is full of light, and no part of it dark, it will be completely lighted, as when the light of a lamp shines on you."

Six Woes

³⁷When Jesus had finished speaking, a Pharisee invited him to eat with him; so he went in and reclined at the table. ³⁸But the Pharisee, noticing that Jesus did not first wash before the meal, was surprised.

³⁹Then the Lord said to him, "Now then, you Pharisees clean the outside of the cup and dish, but inside you are full of greed and wickedness. ⁴⁰You foolish people! Did not the one who made the outside make the inside also? ⁴¹But give what is inside ⌊the dish⌋ᵃ to the poor, and everything will be clean for you.

⁴²"Woe to you Pharisees, because you give God a tenth of your mint, rue and all other kinds of garden herbs, but you neglect justice and the love of God. You should have practiced the latter without leaving the former undone.

⁴³"Woe to you Pharisees, because you love the most important seats in the synagogues and greetings in the marketplaces.

⁴⁴"Woe to you, because you are like unmarked graves, which men walk over without knowing it."

⁴⁵One of the experts in the law answered him, "Teacher, when you say these things, you insult us also."

⁴⁶Jesus replied, "And you experts in the law, woe to you, because you load people down with burdens they can hardly carry, and you yourselves will not lift one finger to help them.

⁴⁷"Woe to you, because you build tombs for the prophets, and it was your forefathers who killed them. ⁴⁸So you testify that you approve of what your forefathers did; they killed the prophets, and you build their tombs. ⁴⁹Because of this, God in his wisdom said, 'I will send them prophets and apostles, some of whom they will kill and others they will persecute.' ⁵⁰Therefore this generation will be

---

ᵃ41 Or *what you have*

Sloppy Agape

Monday

LUKE 10:38–42 Jan, married only a couple of years to Mike, came to us because she could never seem to please him. "I'm not blaming Mike," Jan confided. "I just wish I could be a better wife. I do a lot for him, but it never seems to be enough." Jan took all the responsibility for Mike's happiness. And if he was not perfectly content, she thought it was her fault!

Jan's marital happiness was at the mercy of her feelings. What's wrong with that? Well, when we use feelings to navigate our marriage, we end up *doing* loving things rather than *being* a loving person. We end up falling into a trap we call "sloppy agape."

This kind of love can look like the ultimate in selflessness, but it continually misses the mark. A classic Biblical example of sloppy agape is found in Jesus' friend Martha. Martha opened her home to Jesus and his disciples. She scurried about making preparations to serve the men, while her sister Mary simply sat and talked with Jesus.

Martha was more concerned with *doing* loving things in the kitchen than *being* a loving person in her relationship with Jesus. She was attending to everyone else's needs, but she did not recognize her own need to sit at the feet of Jesus. Only later, when her faith in Jesus had grown, was she able to put aside her own worries and trust him even in the worst of circumstances— when her beloved brother Lazarus had died.

Don't get caught in the sloppy agape trap. If you focus too much on your feelings, you will end up *doing* instead of *being*.
—Les and Leslie

Go to page 1122 for your next devotional reading.

held responsible for the blood of all the prophets that has been shed since the beginning of the world, [51]from the blood of Abel to the blood of Zechariah, who was killed between the altar and the sanctuary. Yes, I tell you, this generation will be held responsible for it all.

[52]"Woe to you experts in the law, because you have taken away the key to knowledge. You yourselves have not entered, and you have hindered those who were entering."

[53]When Jesus left there, the Pharisees and the teachers of the law began to oppose him fiercely and to besiege him with questions, [54]waiting to catch him in something he might say.

Warnings and Encouragements

12 Meanwhile, when a crowd of many thousands had gathered, so that they were trampling on one another, Jesus began to speak first to his disciples, saying: "Be on your guard against the yeast of the Pharisees, which is hypocrisy. [2]There is nothing concealed that will not be disclosed, or hidden that will not be made known. [3]What you have said in the dark will be heard in the daylight, and what you have whispered in the ear in the inner rooms will be proclaimed from the roofs.

[4]"I tell you, my friends, do not be afraid of those who kill the body and after that can do no more. [5]But I will show you whom you should fear: Fear him who, after the killing of the body, has power to throw you into hell. Yes, I tell you, fear him. [6]Are not five sparrows sold for two pennies[a]? Yet not one of them is forgotten by God. [7]Indeed, the very hairs of your head are all numbered. Don't be afraid; you are worth more than many sparrows.

[8]"I tell you, whoever acknowledges me before men, the Son of Man will also acknowledge him before the angels of God. [9]But he who disowns me before men will be disowned before the angels of God. [10]And everyone who speaks a word against the Son of Man will be forgiven, but anyone who blasphemes against the Holy Spirit will not be forgiven.

[11]"When you are brought before synagogues, rulers and authorities, do not worry about how you will defend yourselves or what you will say, [12]for the Holy Spirit will teach you at that time what you should say."

The Parable of the Rich Fool

[13]Someone in the crowd said to him, "Teacher, tell my brother to divide the inheritance with me."

[14]Jesus replied, "Man, who appointed me a judge or an arbiter between you?" [15]Then he said to them, "Watch out! Be on your guard against all kinds of greed; a man's life does not consist in the abundance of his possessions."

[16]And he told them this parable: "The ground of a certain rich man produced a good crop. [17]He thought to himself, 'What shall I do? I have no place to store my crops.'

[18]"Then he said, 'This is what I'll do. I will tear down my barns and build bigger ones, and there I will store all my grain and my goods. [19]And I'll say to myself, "You have plenty of good things laid up for many years. Take life easy; eat, drink and be merry." '

[20]"But God said to him, 'You fool! This very night your life will be demanded from you. Then who will get what you have prepared for yourself?'

[21]"This is how it will be with anyone who stores up things for himself but is not rich toward God."

Do Not Worry

[22]Then Jesus said to his disciples: "Therefore I tell you, do not worry about your life, what you will eat; or about your body, what you will wear. [23]Life is more than food, and the body more than clothes. [24]Consider the ravens: They do not sow or reap, they have no storeroom or barn; yet God feeds them. And how much more valuable you are than birds! [25]Who of you by worrying can add a single hour to his life[b]? [26]Since you cannot do this very little thing, why do you worry about the rest?

[27]"Consider how the lilies grow. They do not labor or spin. Yet I tell you, not even Solomon in all his splendor was dressed like one of these. [28]If that is how

a6 Greek *two assaria*   b25 Or *single cubit to his height*

God clothes the grass of the field, which is here today, and tomorrow is thrown into the fire, how much more will he clothe you, O you of little faith! ²⁹And do not set your heart on what you will eat or drink; do not worry about it. ³⁰For the pagan world runs after all such things, and your Father knows that you need them. ³¹But seek his kingdom, and these things will be given to you as well.

³²"Do not be afraid, little flock, for your Father has been pleased to give you the kingdom. ³³Sell your possessions and give to the poor. Provide purses for yourselves that will not wear out, a treasure in heaven that will not be exhausted, where no thief comes near and no moth destroys. ³⁴For where your treasure is, there your heart will be also.

Watchfulness

³⁵"Be dressed ready for service and keep your lamps burning, ³⁶like men waiting for their master to return from a wedding banquet, so that when he comes and knocks they can immediately open the door for him. ³⁷It will be good for those servants whose master finds them watching when he comes. I tell you the truth, he will dress himself to serve, will have them recline at the table and will come and wait on them. ³⁸It will be good for those servants whose master finds them ready, even if he comes in the second or third watch of the night. ³⁹But understand this: If the owner of the house had known at what hour the thief was coming, he would not have let his house be broken into. ⁴⁰You also must be ready, because the Son of Man will come at an hour when you do not expect him."

⁴¹Peter asked, "Lord, are you telling this parable to us, or to everyone?"

⁴²The Lord answered, "Who then is the faithful and wise manager, whom the master puts in charge of his servants to give them their food allowance at the proper time? ⁴³It will be good for that servant whom the master finds doing so when he returns. ⁴⁴I tell you the truth, he will put him in charge of all his posses-

No Worries

Tuesday

LUKE 12:22-26   A recent study determined that 60 percent of human worries are totally unwarranted. Of the remaining portion of our worries, 20 percent are about past activities completely beyond our control. And another 10 percent are so petty that they don't make much difference at all. Of the remaining 10 percent of our worries, only 4 to 5 percent are really justifiable. And even half of these viable worries are beyond our capacity to change! The final half, or 2 percent, of our worries that are real, can be solved easily, according to these researchers, "if we stop stewing and start doing!"

Whether or not these statistics are reliable doesn't really matter. The indisputable point is that most of our worries are not worth the stress they generate. How many times have the two of you let worry cloud your dinner conversation? How often do you lie awake at night consumed with an obsessive worry?

You don't need to let worrying contaminate your marriage. Jesus Christ came to give us eternal life, but also *abundant* life (see John 10:10, page 1159). He came to give us life to the fullest and to set us free from the harmful effects of worry. By the way, Jesus practiced what he preached. When faced with the hostility of Herod and the pressure of the public clamor for healing, for example, he had plenty to worry about. Instead, Scripture tells us that he and the disciples took rest. Jesus said to his disciples, "Come with me by yourselves to a quiet place and get some rest" (Mark 6:31).

So don't allow worrying to get a foothold in your marriage. Instead, help each other to "cast all your anxiety on him because he cares for you" (1 Peter 5:7).

—*Les and Leslie*

Go to page 1126 for your next devotional reading.

sions. ⁴⁵But suppose the servant says to himself, 'My master is taking a long time in coming,' and he then begins to beat the menservants and maidservants and to eat and drink and get drunk. ⁴⁶The master of that servant will come on a day when he does not expect him and at an hour he is not aware of. He will cut him to pieces and assign him a place with the unbelievers.

⁴⁷"That servant who knows his master's will and does not get ready or does not do what his master wants will be beaten with many blows. ⁴⁸But the one who does not know and does things deserving punishment will be beaten with few blows. From everyone who has been given much, much will be demanded; and from the one who has been entrusted with much, much more will be asked.

Not Peace but Division

⁴⁹"I have come to bring fire on the earth, and how I wish it were already kindled! ⁵⁰But I have a baptism to undergo, and how distressed I am until it is completed! ⁵¹Do you think I came to bring peace on earth? No, I tell you, but division. ⁵²From now on there will be five in one family divided against each other, three against two and two against three. ⁵³They will be divided, father against son and son against father, mother against daughter and daughter against mother, mother-in-law against daughter-in-law and daughter-in-law against mother-in-law."

Interpreting the Times

⁵⁴He said to the crowd: "When you see a cloud rising in the west, immediately you say, 'It's going to rain,' and it does. ⁵⁵And when the south wind blows, you say, 'It's going to be hot,' and it is. ⁵⁶Hypocrites! You know how to interpret the appearance of the earth and the sky. How is it that you don't know how to interpret this present time?

⁵⁷"Why don't you judge for yourselves what is right? ⁵⁸As you are going with your adversary to the magistrate, try hard to be reconciled to him on the way, or he may drag you off to the judge, and the judge turn you over to the officer, and the officer throw you into prison. ⁵⁹I tell you,

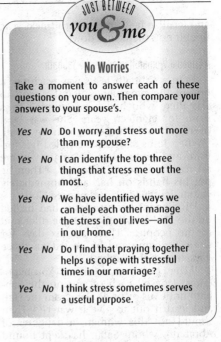

JUST BETWEEN you & me

No Worries

Take a moment to answer each of these questions on your own. Then compare your answers to your spouse's.

Yes No Do I worry and stress out more than my spouse?

Yes No I can identify the top three things that stress me out the most.

Yes No We have identified ways we can help each other manage the stress in our lives—and in our home.

Yes No Do I find that praying together helps us cope with stressful times in our marriage?

Yes No I think stress sometimes serves a useful purpose.

you will not get out until you have paid the last penny.ᵃ "

Repent or Perish

13 Now there were some present at that time who told Jesus about the Galileans whose blood Pilate had mixed with their sacrifices. ²Jesus answered, "Do you think that these Galileans were worse sinners than all the other Galileans because they suffered this way? ³I tell you, no! But unless you repent, you too will all perish. ⁴Or those eighteen who died when the tower in Siloam fell on them—do you think they were more guilty than all the others living in Jerusalem? ⁵I tell you, no! But unless you repent, you too will all perish."

⁶Then he told this parable: "A man had a fig tree, planted in his vineyard, and he went to look for fruit on it, but did not find any. ⁷So he said to the man who took care of the vineyard, 'For three years now I've been coming to look for fruit on this fig tree and haven't found any. Cut it down! Why should it use up the soil?'

⁸" 'Sir,' the man replied, 'leave it alone for one more year, and I'll dig around it

ᵃ59 Greek *lepton*

and fertilize it. ⁹If it bears fruit next year, fine! If not, then cut it down.' "

A Crippled Woman Healed on the Sabbath

¹⁰On a Sabbath Jesus was teaching in one of the synagogues, ¹¹and a woman was there who had been crippled by a spirit for eighteen years. She was bent over and could not straighten up at all. ¹²When Jesus saw her, he called her forward and said to her, "Woman, you are set free from your infirmity." ¹³Then he put his hands on her, and immediately she straightened up and praised God.

¹⁴Indignant because Jesus had healed on the Sabbath, the synagogue ruler said to the people, "There are six days for work. So come and be healed on those days, not on the Sabbath."

¹⁵The Lord answered him, "You hypocrites! Doesn't each of you on the Sabbath untie his ox or donkey from the stall and lead it out to give it water? ¹⁶Then should not this woman, a daughter of Abraham, whom Satan has kept bound for eighteen long years, be set free on the Sabbath day from what bound her?"

¹⁷When he said this, all his opponents were humiliated, but the people were delighted with all the wonderful things he was doing.

The Parables of the Mustard Seed and the Yeast

¹⁸Then Jesus asked, "What is the kingdom of God like? What shall I compare it to? ¹⁹It is like a mustard seed, which a man took and planted in his garden. It grew and became a tree, and the birds of the air perched in its branches."

²⁰Again he asked, "What shall I compare the kingdom of God to? ²¹It is like yeast that a woman took and mixed into a large amount^a of flour until it worked all through the dough."

The Narrow Door

²²Then Jesus went through the towns and villages, teaching as he made his way to Jerusalem. ²³Someone asked him, "Lord, are only a few people going to be saved?"

He said to them, ²⁴"Make every effort to enter through the narrow door, because many, I tell you, will try to enter and will not be able to. ²⁵Once the owner of the house gets up and closes the door, you will stand outside knocking and pleading, 'Sir, open the door for us.'

"But he will answer, 'I don't know you or where you come from.'

²⁶"Then you will say, 'We ate and drank with you, and you taught in our streets.'

²⁷"But he will reply, 'I don't know you or where you come from. Away from me, all you evildoers!'

²⁸"There will be weeping there, and gnashing of teeth, when you see Abraham, Isaac and Jacob and all the prophets in the kingdom of God, but you yourselves thrown out. ²⁹People will come from east and west and north and south, and will take their places at the feast in the kingdom of God. ³⁰Indeed there are those who are last who will be first, and first who will be last."

Jesus' Sorrow for Jerusalem

³¹At that time some Pharisees came to Jesus and said to him, "Leave this place and go somewhere else. Herod wants to kill you."

³²He replied, "Go tell that fox, 'I will drive out demons and heal people today and tomorrow, and on the third day I will reach my goal.' ³³In any case, I must keep going today and tomorrow and the next day—for surely no prophet can die outside Jerusalem!

³⁴"O Jerusalem, Jerusalem, you who kill the prophets and stone those sent to you, how often I have longed to gather your children together, as a hen gathers her chicks under her wings, but you were not willing! ³⁵Look, your house is left to you desolate. I tell you, you will not see me again until you say, 'Blessed is he who comes in the name of the Lord.'^{b} "

Jesus at a Pharisee's House

14 One Sabbath, when Jesus went to eat in the house of a prominent Pharisee, he was being carefully watched. ²There in front of him was a man suffering from dropsy. ³Jesus asked the Pharisees and experts in the law, "Is it lawful to heal on the Sabbath or not?" ⁴But they remained silent. So taking hold of the

---

^{a}21 Greek *three satas* (probably about 1/2 bushel or 22 liters) ^{b}35 Psalm 118:26

man, he healed him and sent him away.

⁵Then he asked them, "If one of you has a son*a* or an ox that falls into a well on the Sabbath day, will you not immediately pull him out?" ⁶And they had nothing to say.

⁷When he noticed how the guests picked the places of honor at the table, he told them this parable: ⁸"When someone invites you to a wedding feast, do not take the place of honor, for a person more distinguished than you may have been invited. ⁹If so, the host who invited both of you will come and say to you, 'Give this man your seat.' Then, humiliated, you will have to take the least important place. ¹⁰But when you are invited, take the lowest place, so that when your host comes, he will say to you, 'Friend, move up to a better place.' Then you will be honored in the presence of all your fellow guests. ¹¹For everyone who exalts himself will be humbled, and he who humbles himself will be exalted."

¹²Then Jesus said to his host, "When you give a luncheon or dinner, do not invite your friends, your brothers or relatives, or your rich neighbors; if you do, they may invite you back and so you will be repaid. ¹³But when you give a banquet, invite the poor, the crippled, the lame, the blind, ¹⁴and you will be blessed. Although they cannot repay you, you will be repaid at the resurrection of the righteous."

The Parable of the Great Banquet

¹⁵When one of those at the table with him heard this, he said to Jesus, "Blessed is the man who will eat at the feast in the kingdom of God."

¹⁶Jesus replied: "A certain man was preparing a great banquet and invited many guests. ¹⁷At the time of the banquet he sent his servant to tell those who had been invited, 'Come, for everything is now ready.'

¹⁸"But they all alike began to make excuses. The first said, 'I have just bought a field, and I must go and see it. Please excuse me.'

¹⁹"Another said, 'I have just bought five yoke of oxen, and I'm on my way to try them out. Please excuse me.'

²⁰"Still another said, 'I just got married, so I can't come.'

²¹"The servant came back and reported this to his master. Then the owner of the house became angry and ordered his servant, 'Go out quickly into the streets and alleys of the town and bring in the poor, the crippled, the blind and the lame.'

²²"'Sir,' the servant said, 'what you ordered has been done, but there is still room.'

²³"Then the master told his servant, 'Go out to the roads and country lanes and make them come in, so that my house will be full. ²⁴I tell you, not one of those men who were invited will get a taste of my banquet.' "

The Cost of Being a Disciple

²⁵Large crowds were traveling with Jesus, and turning to them he said: ²⁶"If anyone comes to me and does not hate his father and mother, his wife and children, his brothers and sisters—yes, even his own life—he cannot be my disciple. ²⁷And anyone who does not carry his cross and follow me cannot be my disciple.

²⁸"Suppose one of you wants to build a tower. Will he not first sit down and estimate the cost to see if he has enough money to complete it? ²⁹For if he lays the foundation and is not able to finish it, everyone who sees it will ridicule him, ³⁰saying, 'This fellow began to build and was not able to finish.'

³¹"Or suppose a king is about to go to war against another king. Will he not first sit down and consider whether he is able with ten thousand men to oppose the one coming against him with twenty thousand? ³²If he is not able, he will send a delegation while the other is still a long way off and will ask for terms of peace. ³³In the same way, any of you who does not give up everything he has cannot be my disciple.

³⁴"Salt is good, but if it loses its saltiness, how can it be made salty again? ³⁵It is fit neither for the soil nor for the manure pile; it is thrown out.

"He who has ears to hear, let him hear."

---

a5 Some manuscripts donkey

The Parable of the Lost Sheep

15 Now the tax collectors and "sinners" were all gathering around to hear him. ²But the Pharisees and the teachers of the law muttered, "This man welcomes sinners and eats with them."

³Then Jesus told them this parable: ⁴"Suppose one of you has a hundred sheep and loses one of them. Does he not leave the ninety-nine in the open country and go after the lost sheep until he finds it? ⁵And when he finds it, he joyfully puts it on his shoulders ⁶and goes home. Then he calls his friends and neighbors together and says, 'Rejoice with me; I have found my lost sheep.' ⁷I tell you that in the same way there will be more rejoicing in heaven over one sinner who repents than over ninety-nine righteous persons who do not need to repent.

The Parable of the Lost Coin

⁸"Or suppose a woman has ten silver coins*ᵃ* and loses one. Does she not light a lamp, sweep the house and search carefully until she finds it? ⁹And when she finds it, she calls her friends and neigh-

bors together and says, 'Rejoice with me; I have found my lost coin.' ¹⁰In the same way, I tell you, there is rejoicing in the presence of the angels of God over one sinner who repents."

The Parable of the Lost Son

¹¹Jesus continued: "There was a man who had two sons. ¹²The younger one said to his father, 'Father, give me my share of the estate.' So he divided his property between them.

¹³"Not long after that, the younger son got together all he had, set off for a distant country and there squandered his wealth in wild living. ¹⁴After he had spent everything, there was a severe famine in that whole country, and he began to be in need. ¹⁵So he went and hired himself out to a citizen of that country, who sent him to his fields to feed pigs. ¹⁶He longed to fill his stomach with the pods that the pigs were eating, but no one gave him anything.

¹⁷"When he came to his senses, he

ᵃ8 Greek ten drachmas, each worth about a day's wages

You're Invited

Wednesday

LUKE 14:15–23 A wedding often joins two people with very different ideas about what it means to have a marriage relationship. One person might be interested in developing a deep and intimate marriage, while the other spouse is moving on to the next project—maybe a new career or having children. When this happens in a marriage, the spouse desiring a deeper relationship can become discouraged and feel rejected. It might seem safer for the relationship-oriented spouse to quit trying to relate, but instead he or she must look past the rejection.

The key is to never quit pursuing the marriage relationship. Do more than just placidly maintain a vague open invitation. The relationship-oriented spouse must overcome the hurt of rejection and continue to issue specific invitations to spend time together and develop intimacy. The possi-

bility of drawing the non-relating spouse into a deeper relationship is worth risking the pain of rejection.

Make no assumptions that the non-relating spouse even knows how to initiate a relationship. The spouse who is not adept at relating might even desire more intimacy but not know how to get started.

In our own marriage, it was an eight-year journey of Rosemary attempting to initiate relationship. Not meaning to, I rejected her by rejecting her requests to just be together and talk. It was only years later that I found out how lonely she had been. But years later, because she never quit, we now have a wonderful, intimate marriage. Keep inviting relationship.

—**Bob and Rosemary**

Go to page 1128 for your next devotional reading.

said, 'How many of my father's hired men have food to spare, and here I am starving to death! ¹⁸I will set out and go back to my father and say to him: Father, I have sinned against heaven and against you. ¹⁹I am no longer worthy to be called your son; make me like one of your hired men.' ²⁰So he got up and went to his father.

"But while he was still a long way off, his father saw him and was filled with compassion for him; he ran to his son, threw his arms around him and kissed him.

²¹"The son said to him, 'Father, I have sinned against heaven and against you. I am no longer worthy to be called your son.'ᵃ'

²²"But the father said to his servants, 'Quick! Bring the best robe and put it on him. Put a ring on his finger and sandals on his feet. ²³Bring the fattened calf and kill it. Let's have a feast and celebrate. ²⁴For this son of mine was dead and is alive again; he was lost and is found.' So they began to celebrate.

²⁵"Meanwhile, the older son was in the field. When he came near the house, he heard music and dancing. ²⁶So he called one of the servants and asked him what was going on. ²⁷'Your brother has come,' he replied, 'and your father has killed the fattened calf because he has him back safe and sound.'

²⁸"The older brother became angry and refused to go in. So his father went out and pleaded with him. ²⁹But he answered his father, 'Look! All these years I've been slaving for you and never disobeyed your orders. Yet you never gave me even a young goat so I could celebrate with my friends. ³⁰But when this son of yours who has squandered your property with prostitutes comes home, you kill the fattened calf for him!'

³¹"'My son,' the father said, 'you are always with me, and everything I have is yours. ³²But we had to celebrate and be glad, because this brother of yours was dead and is alive again; he was lost and is found.' "

The Parable of the Shrewd Manager

16 Jesus told his disciples: "There was a rich man whose manager was ac-

You're Invited

Take a moment to answer each of these questions on your own. Then compare your answers to your spouse's.

Yes No I think that I am the one who works hardest at getting us to do things together as a couple.

Yes No I haven't slowed down or quit in the pursuit of marriage activities.

Yes No Generally I work to find things my spouse would like to do, as opposed to the things I would rather do.

Yes No When my spouse does these marriage activities with me, I go out of my way to show my appreciation.

cused of wasting his possessions. ²So he called him in and asked him, 'What is this I hear about you? Give an account of your management, because you cannot be manager any longer.'

³"The manager said to himself, 'What shall I do now? My master is taking away my job. I'm not strong enough to dig, and I'm ashamed to beg— ⁴I know what I'll do so that, when I lose my job here, people will welcome me into their houses.'

⁵"So he called in each one of his master's debtors. He asked the first, 'How much do you owe my master?'

⁶"'Eight hundred gallonsᵇ of olive oil,' he replied.

"The manager told him, 'Take your bill, sit down quickly, and make it four hundred.'

⁷"Then he asked the second, 'And how much do you owe?'

"'A thousand bushelsᶜ of wheat,' he replied.

"He told him, 'Take your bill and make it eight hundred.'

⁸"The master commended the dishon-

ᵃ21 Some early manuscripts son. Make me like one of your hired men.   ᵇ6 Greek one hundred batous (probably about 3 kiloliters)   ᶜ7 Greek one hundred korous (probably about 35 kiloliters) est manager because he had acted shrewdly. For the people of this world are more shrewd in dealing with their own kind than are the people of the light. ⁹I tell you, use worldly wealth to gain friends for yourselves, so that when it is gone, you will be welcomed into eternal dwellings.

¹⁰"Whoever can be trusted with very little can also be trusted with much, and whoever is dishonest with very little will also be dishonest with much. ¹¹So if you have not been trustworthy in handling worldly wealth, who will trust you with true riches? ¹²And if you have not been trustworthy with someone else's property, who will give you property of your own?

¹³"No servant can serve two masters. Either he will hate the one and love the other, or he will be devoted to the one and despise the other. You cannot serve both God and Money."

¹⁴The Pharisees, who loved money, heard all this and were sneering at Jesus. ¹⁵He said to them, "You are the ones who justify yourselves in the eyes of men, but God knows your hearts. What is highly valued among men is detestable in God's sight.

Additional Teachings

¹⁶"The Law and the Prophets were proclaimed until John. Since that time, the good news of the kingdom of God is being preached, and everyone is forcing his way into it. ¹⁷It is easier for heaven and earth to disappear than for the least stroke of a pen to drop out of the Law.

¹⁸"Anyone who divorces his wife and marries another woman commits adultery, and the man who marries a divorced woman commits adultery.

The Rich Man and Lazarus

¹⁹"There was a rich man who was dressed in purple and fine linen and lived in luxury every day. ²⁰At his gate was laid a beggar named Lazarus, covered with sores ²¹and longing to eat what fell from the rich man's table. Even the dogs came and licked his sores.

²²"The time came when the beggar died and the angels carried him to Abraham's side. The rich man also died and was buried. ²³In hell,ᵃ where he was in torment, he looked up and saw Abraham

ᵃ23 Greek Hades

The Prodigal Spouse

Thursday

LUKE 15:11–32 Broken promises, deception, infidelity—Nancy watched her marriage fall apart. Like the prodigal son, her husband Hal "set off for [another life] and squandered his wealth in wild living." Most of Nancy's friends advised her to divorce him, cut her losses and get on with her life. But like the father of the prodigal son in this passage, she refused to stop loving, caring and praying for Hal. She kept the porch light on—waiting for Hal to "come to his senses" (see verse 17).

God answered Nancy's prayers. Hal returned home repentant, remorseful and broken. "How could you let him walk all over you like this?" Nancy's friends asked. She answered, "Bring out the steaks. Light the grill. Let's celebrate! My marriage was dead; now it's alive again. My husband was lost and now he is found."

The reunion was only the beginning of this couple's efforts to rebuild their marriage and re-establish trust. There's no quick fix for a "prodigal" spouse. But Nancy and Hal would never have salvaged their relationship if she hadn't given him a second chance.

Whether or not you have lived through marital pain like Nancy and Hal, you've certainly felt wounded by your marriage partner at some point. Missed expectations, unfulfilled dreams, broken promises—these are a part of every marriage. What can you learn from the father of the prodigal son? Are you willing to let go of your own hurts and disappointments, to forgive your spouse and choose to focus on the future?

—**Dave and Claudia**

Go to page 1129 for your next devotional reading.

far away, with Lazarus by his side. ²⁴So he called to him, 'Father Abraham, have pity on me and send Lazarus to dip the tip of his finger in water and cool my tongue, because I am in agony in this fire.'

²⁵"But Abraham replied, 'Son, remember that in your lifetime you received your good things, while Lazarus received bad things, but now he is comforted here and you are in agony. ²⁶And besides all this, between us and you a great chasm has been fixed, so that those who want to go from here to you cannot, nor can anyone cross over from there to us.'

²⁷"He answered, 'Then I beg you, father, send Lazarus to my father's house, ²⁸for I have five brothers. Let him warn them, so that they will not also come to this place of torment.'

²⁹"Abraham replied, 'They have Moses and the Prophets; let them listen to them.'

³⁰" 'No, father Abraham,' he said, 'but if someone from the dead goes to them, they will repent.'

³¹"He said to him, 'If they do not listen to Moses and the Prophets, they will not be convinced even if someone rises from the dead.' "

Sin, Faith, Duty

17 Jesus said to his disciples: "Things that cause people to sin are bound to come, but woe to that person through whom they come. ²It would be better for him to be thrown into the sea with a millstone tied around his neck than for him to cause one of these little ones to sin. ³So watch yourselves.

"If your brother sins, rebuke him, and if he repents, forgive him. ⁴If he sins against you seven times in a day, and seven times comes back to you and says, 'I repent,' forgive him."

The Oil of Forgiveness

Friday

LUKE 17:3-4 "How many times should I forgive him?" a participant at one of our seminars asked us. "I forgive my husband for one thing, and then he just does something else. Tell me, how many times does it take? Isn't there a limit?" Her question hung in the room while the audience was silent.

Dave answered with compassion and sincerity: "No." Problems that took years to develop cannot be resolved in one day. Forgiveness is a gift we must give to our spouse over and over—as many times as it takes.

It's a difficult truth to swallow, but read again what Jesus said in this passage: "If your brother sins against you seven times in a day, and seven times comes back to you and says, 'I repent,' forgive him" (verse 4). That's a lot of forgiveness in just one day. If we multiply that by 365 days and then the 50 plus years we hope our marriage will last, it doesn't take a calculator to realize that Christ is calling us to a lifetime of forgiveness.

Forgiveness is a key element in healthy long-term marriages. It's the oil that soothes a love relationship, and it's an oil we need to use over and over again—as long as it takes! No spouse is perfect. Even when we are trying to please each other, we can mess up. Like the time I mailed our plane tickets (along with our bills) right before our flight. When Dave got to the Delta counter, he found me in tears. When I explained what I had done, he consoled me without placing blame or getting angry. Many times I've wondered if I would have responded the same way if he were the one that had snail-mailed our tickets by mistake.

Holding on to grudges will only prevent you from moving on in your relationship. If you are willing to keep on forgiving each other, you can handle disappointments that come your way. You can deepen your love and devotion for each other and renew your commitment to your marriage when you choose to forgive—for a lifetime!

—*Dave and Claudia*

Go to page 1131 for your next devotional reading.

⁵The apostles said to the Lord, "Increase our faith!"

⁶He replied, "If you have faith as small as a mustard seed, you can say to this mulberry tree, 'Be uprooted and planted in the sea,' and it will obey you.

⁷"Suppose one of you had a servant plowing or looking after the sheep. Would he say to the servant when he comes in from the field, 'Come along now and sit down to eat'? ⁸Would he not rather say, 'Prepare my supper, get yourself ready and wait on me while I eat and drink; after that you may eat and drink'? ⁹Would he thank the servant because he did what he was told to do? ¹⁰So you also, when you have done everything you were told to do, should say, 'We are unworthy servants; we have only done our duty.' "

Ten Healed of Leprosy

¹¹Now on his way to Jerusalem, Jesus traveled along the border between Samaria and Galilee. ¹²As he was going into a village, ten men who had leprosy*a* met him. They stood at a distance ¹³and called out in a loud voice, "Jesus, Master, have pity on us!"

¹⁴When he saw them, he said, "Go, show yourselves to the priests." And as they went, they were cleansed.

¹⁵One of them, when he saw he was healed, came back, praising God in a loud voice. ¹⁶He threw himself at Jesus' feet and thanked him—and he was a Samaritan.

¹⁷Jesus asked, "Were not all ten cleansed? Where are the other nine? ¹⁸Was no one found to return and give praise to God except this foreigner?" ¹⁹Then he said to him, "Rise and go; your faith has made you well."

The Coming of the Kingdom of God

²⁰Once, having been asked by the Pharisees when the kingdom of God would come, Jesus replied, "The kingdom of God does not come with your careful observation, ²¹nor will people say, 'Here it is,' or 'There it is,' because the kingdom of God is within*b* you."

²²Then he said to his disciples, "The time is coming when you will long to see one of the days of the Son of Man, but you will not see it. ²³Men will tell you, 'There he is!' or 'Here he is!' Do not go running off after them. ²⁴For the Son of Man in his day*c* will be like the lightning, which flashes and lights up the sky from one end to the other. ²⁵But first he must suffer many things and be rejected by this generation.

²⁶"Just as it was in the days of Noah, so also will it be in the days of the Son of Man. ²⁷People were eating, drinking, marrying and being given in marriage up to the day Noah entered the ark. Then the flood came and destroyed them all.

²⁸"It was the same in the days of Lot. People were eating and drinking, buying and selling, planting and building. ²⁹But the day Lot left Sodom, fire and sulfur rained down from heaven and destroyed them all.

³⁰"It will be just like this on the day the Son of Man is revealed. ³¹On that day no one who is on the roof of his house, with his goods inside, should go down to get them. Likewise, no one in the field should go back for anything. ³²Remember Lot's wife! ³³Whoever tries to keep his life will lose it, and whoever loses his life will preserve it. ³⁴I tell you, on that night two people will be in one bed; one will be taken and the other left. ³⁵Two women will be grinding grain together; one will be taken and the other left.*d* "

³⁷"Where, Lord?" they asked.

He replied, "Where there is a dead body, there the vultures will gather."

The Parable of the Persistent Widow

18 Then Jesus told his disciples a parable to show them that they should always pray and not give up. ²He said: "In a certain town there was a judge who neither feared God nor cared about men. ³And there was a widow in that town who kept coming to him with the plea, 'Grant me justice against my adversary.'

⁴"For some time he refused. But finally he said to himself, 'Even though I don't fear God or care about men, ⁵yet because this widow keeps bothering me, I will see that she gets justice, so that she won't

---

a12 The Greek word was used for various diseases affecting the skin—not necessarily leprosy.
b21 Or *among*   *c24* Some manuscripts do not have *in his day.*   *d35* Some manuscripts *left.*
36Two men will be in the field; one will be taken and the other left.

eventually wear me out with her coming!' "

⁶And the Lord said, "Listen to what the unjust judge says. ⁷And will not God bring about justice for his chosen ones, who cry out to him day and night? Will he keep putting them off? ⁸I tell you, he will see that they get justice, and quickly. However, when the Son of Man comes, will he find faith on the earth?"

The Parable of the Pharisee and the Tax Collector

⁹To some who were confident of their own righteousness and looked down on everybody else, Jesus told this parable: ¹⁰"Two men went up to the temple to pray, one a Pharisee and the other a tax collector. ¹¹The Pharisee stood up and prayed about[a] himself: 'God, I thank you that I am not like other men—robbers, evildoers, adulterers—or even like this tax collector. ¹²I fast twice a week and give a tenth of all I get.'

¹³"But the tax collector stood at a distance. He would not even look up to heaven, but beat his breast and said, 'God, have mercy on me, a sinner.'

¹⁴"I tell you that this man, rather than the other, went home justified before God. For everyone who exalts himself will be humbled, and he who humbles himself will be exalted."

The Little Children and Jesus

¹⁵People were also bringing babies to Jesus to have him touch them. When the

[a] 11 Or to

Seeking God's Touch

LUKE 18:15-17   Once we were in Austria when the Pope was making an official visit. Austria is, for the most part, a Catholic country; every television network covered this event. As we watched, we were fascinated by the great lengths to which the parents would go to have the Pope touch their babies and young children. As we talked about why parents would put forth such effort, we concluded that they wanted their children to be blessed.

Luke 18:15 depicts a similar scene—but the one touching and blessing is Jesus. Parents desperately wanted Jesus to touch, heal and bless their children. Even 2000 years later, parents still seek God's blessings for their children—and for their marriage. We desperately want to experience some form of God's touch.

One way God touches us is by encouraging us when we are discouraged. Years ago when we were pursuing working full-time in marriage and family education, we met many obstacles. At times when we were so discouraged that we were ready to give up and do something else, God encouraged us to continue. Once he urged us on through a letter from a coworker, and another encouragement came from a couple who we have helped to get their marriage back on track. Another time, a letter came from a prayer partner. Finally we got the "go-ahead" to begin to move into this new career path.

Twenty years later we are glad we didn't give up our pursuit. But we won't ever forget the long process that included times of discouragement. Actually we are stronger today because we have experienced God's encouraging touch during the hard times.

Perhaps you are in the midst of a difficult situation right now. Let Jesus touch you with encouragement and hope.

—*Dave and Claudia*

Weekend Warm-up   *Are you in the midst of a difficult situation right now? Let Jesus touch you both with encouragement and hope.*   Go to page 1133 for your next devotional reading.

disciples saw this, they rebuked them. [16]But Jesus called the children to him and said, "Let the little children come to me, and do not hinder them, for the kingdom of God belongs to such as these. [17]I tell you the truth, anyone who will not receive the kingdom of God like a little child will never enter it."

The Rich Ruler

[18]A certain ruler asked him, "Good teacher, what must I do to inherit eternal life?"

[19]"Why do you call me good?" Jesus answered. "No one is good—except God alone. [20]You know the commandments: 'Do not commit adultery, do not murder, do not steal, do not give false testimony, honor your father and mother.'[a]"

[21]"All these I have kept since I was a boy," he said.

[22]When Jesus heard this, he said to him, "You still lack one thing. Sell everything you have and give to the poor, and you will have treasure in heaven. Then come, follow me."

[23]When he heard this, he became very sad, because he was a man of great wealth. [24]Jesus looked at him and said, "How hard it is for the rich to enter the kingdom of God! [25]Indeed, it is easier for a camel to go through the eye of a needle than for a rich man to enter the kingdom of God."

[26]Those who heard this asked, "Who then can be saved?"

[27]Jesus replied, "What is impossible with men is possible with God."

[28]Peter said to him, "We have left all we had to follow you!"

[29]"I tell you the truth," Jesus said to them, "no one who has left home or wife or brothers or parents or children for the sake of the kingdom of God [30]will fail to receive many times as much in this age and, in the age to come, eternal life."

Jesus Again Predicts His Death

[31]Jesus took the Twelve aside and told them, "We are going up to Jerusalem, and everything that is written by the prophets about the Son of Man will be fulfilled. [32]He will be handed over to the Gentiles.

They will mock him, insult him, spit on him, flog him and kill him. [33]On the third day he will rise again."

[34]The disciples did not understand any of this. Its meaning was hidden from them, and they did not know what he was talking about.

A Blind Beggar Receives His Sight

[35]As Jesus approached Jericho, a blind man was sitting by the roadside begging. [36]When he heard the crowd going by, he asked what was happening. [37]They told him, "Jesus of Nazareth is passing by."

[38]He called out, "Jesus, Son of David, have mercy on me!"

[39]Those who led the way rebuked him and told him to be quiet, but he shouted all the more, "Son of David, have mercy on me!"

[40]Jesus stopped and ordered the man to be brought to him. When he came near, Jesus asked him, [41]"What do you want me to do for you?"

"Lord, I want to see," he replied.

[42]Jesus said to him, "Receive your sight; your faith has healed you." [43]Immediately he received his sight and followed Jesus, praising God. When all the people saw it, they also praised God.

Zacchaeus the Tax Collector

19 Jesus entered Jericho and was passing through. [2]A man was there by the name of Zacchaeus; he was a chief tax collector and was wealthy. [3]He wanted to see who Jesus was, but being a short man he could not, because of the crowd. [4]So he ran ahead and climbed a sycamore-fig tree to see him, since Jesus was coming that way.

[5]When Jesus reached the spot, he looked up and said to him, "Zacchaeus, come down immediately. I must stay at your house today." [6]So he came down at once and welcomed him gladly.

[7]All the people saw this and began to mutter, "He has gone to be the guest of a 'sinner.'"

[8]But Zacchaeus stood up and said to the Lord, "Look, Lord! Here and now I

---

a20 Exodus 20:12-16; Deut. 5:16-20

give half of my possessions to the poor, and if I have cheated anybody out of anything, I will pay back four times the amount."

⁹Jesus said to him, "Today salvation has come to this house, because this man, too, is a son of Abraham. ¹⁰For the Son of Man came to seek and to save what was lost."

The Parable of the Ten Minas

¹¹While they were listening to this, he went on to tell them a parable, because he was near Jerusalem and the people thought that the kingdom of God was going to appear at once. ¹²He said: "A man of noble birth went to a distant country to have himself appointed king and then to return. ¹³So he called ten of his servants and gave them ten minas.ᵃ 'Put this money to work,' he said, 'until I come back.'

¹⁴"But his subjects hated him and sent a delegation after him to say, 'We don't want this man to be our king.'

¹⁵"He was made king, however, and returned home. Then he sent for the servants to whom he had given the money, in order to find out what they had gained with it.

¹⁶"The first one came and said, 'Sir, your mina has earned ten more.'

¹⁷"'Well done, my good servant!' his master replied. 'Because you have been trustworthy in a very small matter, take charge of ten cities.'

¹⁸"The second came and said, 'Sir, your mina has earned five more.'

¹⁹"His master answered, 'You take charge of five cities.'

²⁰"Then another servant came and said, 'Sir, here is your mina; I have kept it laid away in a piece of cloth. ²¹I was afraid of you, because you are a hard man. You take out what you did not put in and reap what you did not sow.'

²²"His master replied, 'I will judge you by your own words, you wicked servant! You knew, did you, that I am a hard man, taking out what I did not put in, and reaping what I did not sow? ²³Why then didn't you put my money on deposit, so that when I came back, I could have collected it with interest?'

ᵃ13 A mina was about three months' wages.

A Wee Little Man

Monday

LUKE 19:1-10 "Zacchaeus was a wee little man . . . " If you grew up in the church as we did, you probably know this little song. Even as small children, many of us learned the story of this tax collector who took advantage of other people's money.

But the profound message of this man's conversion goes deep. Think about the scenario. Jesus knew all about Zacchaeus and his reputation. When he saw him up there in that sycamore tree, he could have pointed a finger of condemnation at him and ridiculed him in front of the crowd. But he didn't. He called Zacchaeus down from his perch and went to his home. The townspeople scoffed at Jesus, but he wasn't bothered by them.

What mattered was that Jesus removed the heavy blanket of condemnation from Zacchaeus's back and gave him an opportunity to change. No blame. No ridicule. No harsh words. In effect, Jesus was saying to this greedy little man, "I don't condemn you, but how would you like your life to be different?" And different it became! Zacchaeus made restitution for his misdeeds and more.

There is a lesson for every married couple in this story. It has to do with how we respond to our spouse when we could rightfully point at his or her faults. We somehow think that doing this will be the catalyst for change. But it won't be. True change only comes about when the heavy blanket of condemnation is removed and the guilty person has the opportunity to *choose* a different way—not out of fear or pressure—but because he or she wants to be a better person.

—Les and Leslie

Go to page 1136 for your next devotional reading.

COUPLE MINUTES

²⁴"Then he said to those standing by, 'Take his mina away from him and give it to the one who has ten minas.'

²⁵" 'Sir,' they said, 'he already has ten!'

²⁶"He replied, 'I tell you that to everyone who has, more will be given, but as for the one who has nothing, even what he has will be taken away. ²⁷But those enemies of mine who did not want me to be king over them—bring them here and kill them in front of me.' "

The Triumphal Entry

²⁸After Jesus had said this, he went on ahead, going up to Jerusalem. ²⁹As he approached Bethphage and Bethany at the hill called the Mount of Olives, he sent two of his disciples, saying to them, ³⁰"Go to the village ahead of you, and as you enter it, you will find a colt tied there, which no one has ever ridden. Untie it and bring it here. ³¹If anyone asks you, 'Why are you untying it?' tell him, 'The Lord needs it.' "

³²Those who were sent ahead went and found it just as he had told them. ³³As they were untying the colt, its owners asked them, "Why are you untying the colt?"

³⁴They replied, "The Lord needs it."

³⁵They brought it to Jesus, threw their cloaks on the colt and put Jesus on it. ³⁶As he went along, people spread their cloaks on the road.

³⁷When he came near the place where the road goes down the Mount of Olives, the whole crowd of disciples began joyfully to praise God in loud voices for all the miracles they had seen:

³⁸"Blessed is the king who comes in
    the name of the Lord!"ᵃ

"Peace in heaven and glory in the
    highest!"

³⁹Some of the Pharisees in the crowd said to Jesus, "Teacher, rebuke your disciples!"

⁴⁰"I tell you," he replied, "if they keep quiet, the stones will cry out."

⁴¹As he approached Jerusalem and saw the city, he wept over it ⁴²and said, "If you, even you, had only known on this day what would bring you peace—but now it is hidden from your eyes. ⁴³The days will come upon you when your ene-

mies will build an embankment against you and encircle you and hem you in on every side. ⁴⁴They will dash you to the ground, you and the children within your walls. They will not leave one stone on another, because you did not recognize the time of God's coming to you."

Jesus at the Temple

⁴⁵Then he entered the temple area and began driving out those who were selling. ⁴⁶"It is written," he said to them, " 'My house will be a house of prayer'ᵇ; but you have made it 'a den of robbers.'ᶜ "

⁴⁷Every day he was teaching at the temple. But the chief priests, the teachers of the law and the leaders among the people were trying to kill him. ⁴⁸Yet they could not find any way to do it, because all the people hung on his words.

The Authority of Jesus Questioned

20 One day as he was teaching the people in the temple courts and preaching the gospel, the chief priests and the teachers of the law, together with the elders, came up to him. ²"Tell us by what authority you are doing these things," they said. "Who gave you this authority?"

³He replied, "I will also ask you a question. Tell me, ⁴John's baptism—was it from heaven, or from men?"

⁵They discussed it among themselves and said, "If we say, 'From heaven,' he will ask, 'Why didn't you believe him?' ⁶But if we say, 'From men,' all the people will stone us, because they are persuaded that John was a prophet."

⁷So they answered, "We don't know where it was from."

⁸Jesus said, "Neither will I tell you by what authority I am doing these things."

The Parable of the Tenants

⁹He went on to tell the people this parable: "A man planted a vineyard, rented it to some farmers and went away for a long time. ¹⁰At harvest time he sent a servant to the tenants so they would give him some of the fruit of the vineyard. But the tenants beat him and sent him away empty-handed. ¹¹He sent another ser-

ᵃ38 Psalm 118:26   ᵇ46 Isaiah 56:7
ᶜ46 Jer. 7:11

vant, but that one also they beat and treated shamefully and sent away empty-handed. ¹²He sent still a third, and they wounded him and threw him out.

¹³"Then the owner of the vineyard said, 'What shall I do? I will send my son, whom I love; perhaps they will respect him.'

¹⁴"But when the tenants saw him, they talked the matter over. 'This is the heir,' they said. 'Let's kill him, and the inheritance will be ours.' ¹⁵So they threw him out of the vineyard and killed him.

"What then will the owner of the vineyard do to them? ¹⁶He will come and kill those tenants and give the vineyard to others."

When the people heard this, they said, "May this never be!"

¹⁷Jesus looked directly at them and asked, "Then what is the meaning of that which is written:

" 'The stone the builders rejected
　　has become the capstone[a]'[b]?

¹⁸Everyone who falls on that stone will be broken to pieces, but he on whom it falls will be crushed."

¹⁹The teachers of the law and the chief priests looked for a way to arrest him immediately, because they knew he had spoken this parable against them. But they were afraid of the people.

Paying Taxes to Caesar

²⁰Keeping a close watch on him, they sent spies, who pretended to be honest. They hoped to catch Jesus in something he said so that they might hand him over to the power and authority of the governor. ²¹So the spies questioned him: "Teacher, we know that you speak and teach what is right, and that you do not show partiality but teach the way of God in accordance with the truth. ²²Is it right for us to pay taxes to Caesar or not?"

²³He saw through their duplicity and said to them, ²⁴"Show me a denarius. Whose portrait and inscription are on it?"

²⁵"Caesar's," they replied.

He said to them, "Then give to Caesar what is Caesar's, and to God what is God's."

²⁶They were unable to trap him in what he had said there in public. And astonished by his answer, they became silent.

The Resurrection and Marriage

²⁷Some of the Sadducees, who say there is no resurrection, came to Jesus with a question. ²⁸"Teacher," they said, "Moses wrote for us that if a man's brother dies and leaves a wife but no children, the man must marry the widow and have children for his brother. ²⁹Now there were seven brothers. The first one married a woman and died childless. ³⁰The second ³¹and then the third married her, and in the same way the seven died, leaving no children. ³²Finally, the woman died too. ³³Now then, at the resurrection whose wife will she be, since the seven were married to her?"

³⁴Jesus replied, "The people of this age marry and are given in marriage. ³⁵But those who are considered worthy of taking part in that age and in the resurrection from the dead will neither marry nor be given in marriage, ³⁶and they can no longer die; for they are like the angels. They are God's children, since they are children of the resurrection. ³⁷But in the account of the bush, even Moses showed that the dead rise, for he calls the Lord 'the God of Abraham, and the God of Isaac, and the God of Jacob.'[c] ³⁸He is not the God of the dead, but of the living, for to him all are alive."

³⁹Some of the teachers of the law responded, "Well said, teacher!" ⁴⁰And no one dared to ask him any more questions.

Whose Son Is the Christ?

⁴¹Then Jesus said to them, "How is it that they say the Christ[d] is the Son of David? ⁴²David himself declares in the Book of Psalms:

" 'The Lord said to my Lord:
　　"Sit at my right hand
⁴³until I make your enemies
　　a footstool for your feet." '[e]

⁴⁴David calls him 'Lord.' How then can he be his son?"

⁴⁵While all the people were listening, Jesus said to his disciples, ⁴⁶"Beware of

---

ᵃ17 Or cornerstone　　ᵇ17 Psalm 118:22
ᶜ37 Exodus 3:6　　ᵈ41 Or Messiah
ᵉ43 Psalm 110:1

the teachers of the law. They like to walk around in flowing robes and love to be greeted in the marketplaces and have the most important seats in the synagogues and the places of honor at banquets. 47They devour widows' houses and for a show make lengthy prayers. Such men will be punished most severely."

The Widow's Offering

21 As he looked up, Jesus saw the rich putting their gifts into the temple treasury. 2He also saw a poor widow put in two very small copper coins.*a* 3"I tell you the truth," he said, "this poor widow has put in more than all the others. 4All these people gave their gifts out of their wealth; but she out of her poverty put in all she had to live on."

Signs of the End of the Age

5Some of his disciples were remarking about how the temple was adorned with beautiful stones and with gifts dedicated to God. But Jesus said, 6"As for what you see here, the time will come when not one stone will be left on another; every one of them will be thrown down."

7"Teacher," they asked, "when will these things happen? And what will be the sign that they are about to take place?"

8He replied: "Watch out that you are not deceived. For many will come in my name, claiming, 'I am he,' and, 'The time is near.' Do not follow them. 9When you hear of wars and revolutions, do not be frightened. These things must happen first, but the end will not come right away."

10Then he said to them: "Nation will rise against nation, and kingdom against kingdom. 11There will be great earthquakes, famines and pestilences in various places, and fearful events and great signs from heaven.

12"But before all this, they will lay hands on you and persecute you. They will deliver you to synagogues and prisons, and you will be brought before kings and governors, and all on account of my name. 13This will result in your being witnesses to them. 14But make up your mind not to worry beforehand how you will defend yourselves. 15For I will give you words and wisdom that none of your ad-

a2 Greek two lepta

Are You Keeping Score?

LUKE 21:1–4 In this passage Jesus pointed out to his disciples generous and sacrificial giving. The specific amount the widow gave was irrelevant to Jesus. He wanted the disciples to see what she had kept for herself—nothing. Her great sacrifice revealed her heart. The desire of her heart was to love God with everything she had and hold back nothing. God is more concerned about the motivation behind the act than the act itself. This generous widow can serve as a great example of the way to give within a marriage relationship.

Sometimes our motives for giving to one another are selfish. We give to the needs of our spouse in order to receive something in return. It's not sacrificial giving we're doing; it's investing so that we will receive a return. Like the husband who is very attentive to his wife . . . because it's

10:00 at night and they are about to go to bed. He's been watching television all evening, but now that it's almost bed time his thoughts have turned elsewhere . . . not to her needs but to his desires.

This kind of giving does not please God. It's not sacrificial; it's reciprocal. God desires for us to give with the right motive—to give without concern for ourselves. Our giving to one another should be motivated by the desire to serve and give as much as we can for the welfare of the other. Give to one another without calculating what you will receive. Follow the example of the widow in this passage: When your motive is pure, sacrificial generosity, you will receive the treasure of God's approval.

—**Bob and Rosemary**

Go to page 1139 for your next devotional reading.

versaries will be able to resist or contradict. ¹⁶You will be betrayed even by parents, brothers, relatives and friends, and they will put some of you to death. ¹⁷All men will hate you because of me. ¹⁸But not a hair of your head will perish. ¹⁹By standing firm you will gain life.

²⁰"When you see Jerusalem being surrounded by armies, you will know that its desolation is near. ²¹Then let those who are in Judea flee to the mountains, let those in the city get out, and let those in the country not enter the city. ²²For this is the time of punishment in fulfillment of all that has been written. ²³How dreadful it will be in those days for pregnant women and nursing mothers! There will be great distress in the land and wrath against this people. ²⁴They will fall by the sword and will be taken as prisoners to all the nations. Jerusalem will be trampled on by the Gentiles until the times of the Gentiles are fulfilled.

²⁵"There will be signs in the sun, moon and stars. On the earth, nations will be in anguish and perplexity at the roaring and tossing of the sea. ²⁶Men will faint from terror, apprehensive of what is coming on the world, for the heavenly bodies will be shaken. ²⁷At that time they will see the Son of Man coming in a cloud with power and great glory. ²⁸When these things begin to take place, stand up and lift up your heads, because your redemption is drawing near."

²⁹He told them this parable: "Look at the fig tree and all the trees. ³⁰When they sprout leaves, you can see for yourselves and know that summer is near. ³¹Even so, when you see these things happening, you know that the kingdom of God is near.

³²"I tell you the truth, this generation[a] will certainly not pass away until all these things have happened. ³³Heaven and earth will pass away, but my words will never pass away.

³⁴"Be careful, or your hearts will be weighed down with dissipation, drunkenness and the anxieties of life, and that day will close on you unexpectedly like a trap. ³⁵For it will come upon all those who live on the face of the whole earth. ³⁶Be always on the watch, and pray that you may be able to escape all that is about to happen, and that you may be able to stand before the Son of Man."

³⁷Each day Jesus was teaching at the temple, and each evening he went out to spend the night on the hill called the Mount of Olives, ³⁸and all the people came early in the morning to hear him at the temple.

Judas Agrees to Betray Jesus

22 Now the Feast of Unleavened Bread, called the Passover, was approaching, ²and the chief priests and the teachers of the law were looking for some way to get rid of Jesus, for they were afraid of the people. ³Then Satan entered Judas, called Iscariot, one of the Twelve. ⁴And Judas went to the chief priests and the officers of the temple guard and discussed with them how he might betray Jesus. ⁵They were delighted and agreed to give him money. ⁶He consented, and watched for an opportunity to hand Jesus over to them when no crowd was present.

The Last Supper

⁷Then came the day of Unleavened Bread on which the Passover lamb had to be sacrificed. ⁸Jesus sent Peter and John, saying, "Go and make preparations for us to eat the Passover."

⁹"Where do you want us to prepare for it?" they asked.

¹⁰He replied, "As you enter the city, a man carrying a jar of water will meet you. Follow him to the house that he enters, ¹¹and say to the owner of the house, 'The Teacher asks: Where is the guest room, where I may eat the Passover with my disciples?' ¹²He will show you a large upper room, all furnished. Make preparations there."

¹³They left and found things just as Jesus had told them. So they prepared the Passover.

¹⁴When the hour came, Jesus and his apostles reclined at the table. ¹⁵And he said to them, "I have eagerly desired to eat this Passover with you before I suffer. ¹⁶For I tell you, I will not eat it again until it finds fulfillment in the kingdom of God."

¹⁷After taking the cup, he gave thanks

a32 Or race

and said, "Take this and divide it among you. ¹⁸For I tell you I will not drink again of the fruit of the vine until the kingdom of God comes."

¹⁹And he took bread, gave thanks and broke it, and gave it to them, saying, "This is my body given for you; do this in remembrance of me."

²⁰In the same way, after the supper he took the cup, saying, "This cup is the new covenant in my blood, which is poured out for you. ²¹But the hand of him who is going to betray me is with mine on the table. ²²The Son of Man will go as it has been decreed, but woe to that man who betrays him." ²³They began to question among themselves which of them it might be who would do this.

²⁴Also a dispute arose among them as to which of them was considered to be greatest. ²⁵Jesus said to them, "The kings of the Gentiles lord it over them; and those who exercise authority over them call themselves Benefactors. ²⁶But you are not to be like that. Instead, the greatest among you should be like the youngest, and the one who rules like the one who serves. ²⁷For who is greater, the one who is at the table or the one who serves? Is it not the one who is at the table? But I am among you as one who serves. ²⁸You are those who have stood by me in my trials. ²⁹And I confer on you a kingdom, just as my Father conferred one on me, ³⁰so that you may eat and drink at my table in my kingdom and sit on thrones, judging the twelve tribes of Israel.

³¹"Simon, Simon, Satan has asked to sift you*ᵃ* as wheat. ³²But I have prayed for you, Simon, that your faith may not fail. And when you have turned back, strengthen your brothers."

³³But he replied, "Lord, I am ready to go with you to prison and to death."

³⁴Jesus answered, "I tell you, Peter, before the rooster crows today, you will deny three times that you know me."

³⁵Then Jesus asked them, "When I sent you without purse, bag or sandals, did you lack anything?"

"Nothing," they answered.

³⁶He said to them, "But now if you have a purse, take it, and also a bag; and if you don't have a sword, sell your cloak and buy one. ³⁷It is written: 'And he was numbered with the transgressors'ᵇ; and I tell you that this must be fulfilled in me. Yes, what is written about me is reaching its fulfillment."

³⁸The disciples said, "See, Lord, here are two swords."

"That is enough," he replied.

Jesus Prays on the Mount of Olives

³⁹Jesus went out as usual to the Mount of Olives, and his disciples followed him. ⁴⁰On reaching the place, he said to them, "Pray that you will not fall into temptation." ⁴¹He withdrew about a stone's throw beyond them, knelt down and prayed, ⁴²"Father, if you are willing, take this cup from me; yet not my will, but yours be done." ⁴³An angel from heaven appeared to him and strengthened him. ⁴⁴And being in anguish, he prayed more earnestly, and his sweat was like drops of blood falling to the ground.ᶜ

⁴⁵When he rose from prayer and went back to the disciples, he found them asleep, exhausted from sorrow. ⁴⁶"Why are you sleeping?" he asked them. "Get up and pray so that you will not fall into temptation."

Jesus Arrested

⁴⁷While he was still speaking a crowd came up, and the man who was called Judas, one of the Twelve, was leading them. He approached Jesus to kiss him, ⁴⁸but Jesus asked him, "Judas, are you betraying the Son of Man with a kiss?"

⁴⁹When Jesus' followers saw what was going to happen, they said, "Lord, should we strike with our swords?" ⁵⁰And one of them struck the servant of the high priest, cutting off his right ear.

⁵¹But Jesus answered, "No more of this!" And he touched the man's ear and healed him.

⁵²Then Jesus said to the chief priests, the officers of the temple guard, and the elders, who had come for him, "Am I leading a rebellion, that you have come with swords and clubs? ⁵³Every day I was with you in the temple courts, and you did not lay a hand on me. But this is your hour—when darkness reigns."

ᵃ31 The Greek is plural.   ᵇ37 Isaiah 53:12
ᶜ44 Some early manuscripts do not have verses 43 and 44.

Peter Disowns Jesus

⁵⁴Then seizing him, they led him away and took him into the house of the high priest. Peter followed at a distance. ⁵⁵But when they had kindled a fire in the middle of the courtyard and had sat down together, Peter sat down with them. ⁵⁶A servant girl saw him seated there in the firelight. She looked closely at him and said, "This man was with him."

⁵⁷But he denied it. "Woman, I don't know him," he said.

⁵⁸A little later someone else saw him and said, "You also are one of them."

"Man, I am not!" Peter replied.

⁵⁹About an hour later another asserted, "Certainly this fellow was with him, for he is a Galilean."

⁶⁰Peter replied, "Man, I don't know what you're talking about!" Just as he was speaking, the rooster crowed. ⁶¹The Lord turned and looked straight at Peter. Then Peter remembered the word the Lord had spoken to him: "Before the rooster crows today, you will disown me three times." ⁶²And he went outside and wept bitterly.

The Guards Mock Jesus

⁶³The men who were guarding Jesus began mocking and beating him. ⁶⁴They blindfolded him and demanded, "Prophesy! Who hit you?" ⁶⁵And they said many other insulting things to him.

Jesus Before Pilate and Herod

⁶⁶At daybreak the council of the elders of the people, both the chief priests and teachers of the law, met together, and Jesus was led before them. ⁶⁷"If you are the Christ,ᵃ" they said, "tell us."

Jesus answered, "If I tell you, you will not believe me, ⁶⁸and if I asked you, you would not answer. ⁶⁹But from now on, the Son of Man will be seated at the right hand of the mighty God."

⁷⁰They all asked, "Are you then the Son of God?"

He replied, "You are right in saying I am."

⁷¹Then they said, "Why do we need any more testimony? We have heard it from his own lips."

23 Then the whole assembly rose and led him off to Pilate. ²And they began to accuse him, saying, "We have found this man subverting our nation. He

ᵃ67 Or Messiah

Feeling Unappreciated

Wednesday

LUKE 22:54–62 There have been a few times in my life when I (Bob) spent a lot of energy feeling unappreciated by my wife. Trying to balance career, marriage and parenting meant dropping personal activities from my schedule. Seasons when personal opportunities for sports and recreation were impossible because of the other demands. *Does she really know how hard I work? Does she have any idea how much I sacrifice for the good of this family?* These very human thoughts can creep into a marriage, but they are very damaging.

In this passage we see how Jesus was not appreciated by those closest to him. In his hour of need, all his friends left him. After all he had done for them, he could have given up on his relationships. But he didn't.

Jesus' actions give us an example to follow when we feel unappreciated The first thing he did was to gently confront his disciples by showing them how they were taking him for granted. For Judas it was betrayal, for Peter it was denial and for all of them it was a preoccupation with self. Jesus began healing the relationships by talking to them about his hurt.

But Jesus didn't shut down and refuse to serve. He did just the opposite. Instead of quitting, he continued serving to such a great degree that it was unmistakable. He set an example for them. When we feel unappreciated, we can deal with those feelings of being taken for granted by serving to an even greater degree.

—Bob and Rosemary

Go to page 1145 for your next devotional reading.

opposes payment of taxes to Caesar and claims to be Christ,[a] a king."

[3]So Pilate asked Jesus, "Are you the king of the Jews?"

"Yes, it is as you say," Jesus replied.

[4]Then Pilate announced to the chief priests and the crowd, "I find no basis for a charge against this man."

[5]But they insisted, "He stirs up the people all over Judea[b] by his teaching. He started in Galilee and has come all the way here."

[6]On hearing this, Pilate asked if the man was a Galilean. [7]When he learned that Jesus was under Herod's jurisdiction, he sent him to Herod, who was also in Jerusalem at that time.

[8]When Herod saw Jesus, he was greatly pleased, because for a long time he had been wanting to see him. From what he had heard about him, he hoped to see him perform some miracle. [9]He plied him with many questions, but Jesus gave him no answer. [10]The chief priests and the teachers of the law were standing there, vehemently accusing him. [11]Then Herod and his soldiers ridiculed and mocked him. Dressing him in an elegant robe, they sent him back to Pilate. [12]That day Herod and Pilate became friends—before this they had been enemies.

[13]Pilate called together the chief priests, the rulers and the people, [14]and said to them, "You brought me this man as one who was inciting the people to rebellion. I have examined him in your presence and have found no basis for your charges against him. [15]Neither has Herod, for he sent him back to us; as you can see, he has done nothing to deserve death. [16]Therefore, I will punish him and then release him.[c]"

[18]With one voice they cried out, "Away with this man! Release Barabbas to us!" [19](Barabbas had been thrown into prison for an insurrection in the city, and for murder.)

[20]Wanting to release Jesus, Pilate appealed to them again. [21]But they kept shouting, "Crucify him! Crucify him!"

[22]For the third time he spoke to them: "Why? What crime has this man committed? I have found in him no grounds for the death penalty. Therefore I will have him punished and then release him."

[23]But with loud shouts they insistently demanded that he be crucified, and their shouts prevailed. [24]So Pilate decided to grant their demand. [25]He released the man who had been thrown into prison for insurrection and murder, the one they asked for, and surrendered Jesus to their will.

The Crucifixion

[26]As they led him away, they seized Simon from Cyrene, who was on his way in from the country, and put the cross on him and made him carry it behind Jesus. [27]A large number of people followed him, including women who mourned and wailed for him. [28]Jesus turned and said to them, "Daughters of Jerusalem, do not weep for me; weep for yourselves and for your children. [29]For the time will come when you will say, 'Blessed are the barren women, the wombs that never bore and the breasts that never nursed!' [30]Then

" 'they will say to the mountains,
    "Fall on us!"
  and to the hills, "Cover us!" '[d]

[31]For if men do these things when the tree is green, what will happen when it is dry?"

[32]Two other men, both criminals, were also led out with him to be executed. [33]When they came to the place called the Skull, there they crucified him, along with the criminals—one on his right, the other on his left. [34]Jesus said, "Father, forgive them, for they do not know what they are doing."[e] And they divided up his clothes by casting lots.

[35]The people stood watching, and the rulers even sneered at him. They said, "He saved others; let him save himself if he is the Christ of God, the Chosen One."

[36]The soldiers also came up and mocked him. They offered him wine vinegar [37]and said, "If you are the king of the Jews, save yourself."

[38]There was a written notice above him, which read: THIS IS THE KING OF THE JEWS.

[39]One of the criminals who hung there hurled insults at him: "Aren't you the Christ? Save yourself and us!"

[a]2 Or *Messiah*; also in verses 35 and 39   [b]5 Or *over the land of the Jews*   [c]16 *Some manuscripts him." [17]Now he was obliged to release one man to them at the Feast.*   [d]30 Hosea 10:8   [e]34 Some early manuscripts do not have this sentence.

⁴⁰But the other criminal rebuked him. "Don't you fear God," he said, "since you are under the same sentence? ⁴¹We are punished justly, for we are getting what our deeds deserve. But this man has done nothing wrong."

⁴²Then he said, "Jesus, remember me when you come into your kingdom.ᵃ"

⁴³Jesus answered him, "I tell you the truth, today you will be with me in paradise."

Jesus' Death

⁴⁴It was now about the sixth hour, and darkness came over the whole land until the ninth hour, ⁴⁵for the sun stopped shining. And the curtain of the temple was torn in two. ⁴⁶Jesus called out with a loud voice, "Father, into your hands I commit my spirit." When he had said this, he breathed his last.

⁴⁷The centurion, seeing what had happened, praised God and said, "Surely this was a righteous man." ⁴⁸When all the people who had gathered to witness this sight saw what took place, they beat their breasts and went away. ⁴⁹But all those who knew him, including the women who had followed him from Galilee, stood at a distance, watching these things.

Jesus' Burial

⁵⁰Now there was a man named Joseph, a member of the Council, a good and upright man, ⁵¹who had not consented to their decision and action. He came from the Judean town of Arimathea and he was waiting for the kingdom of God. ⁵²Going to Pilate, he asked for Jesus' body. ⁵³Then he took it down, wrapped it in linen cloth and placed it in a tomb cut in the rock, one in which no one had yet been laid. ⁵⁴It was Preparation Day, and the Sabbath was about to begin.

⁵⁵The women who had come with Jesus from Galilee followed Joseph and saw the tomb and how his body was laid in it. ⁵⁶Then they went home and prepared spices and perfumes. But they rested on the Sabbath in obedience to the commandment.

The Resurrection

24 On the first day of the week, very early in the morning, the women took the spices they had prepared and went to the tomb. ²They found the stone rolled away from the tomb, ³but when they entered, they did not find the body of the Lord Jesus. ⁴While they were wondering about this, suddenly two men in clothes that gleamed like lightning stood beside them. ⁵In their fright the women bowed down with their faces to the ground, but the men said to them, "Why do you look for the living among the dead? ⁶He is not here; he has risen! Remember how he told you, while he was still with you in Galilee: ⁷'The Son of Man must be delivered into the hands of sinful men, be crucified and on the third day be raised again.' " ⁸Then they remembered his words.

⁹When they came back from the tomb, they told all these things to the Eleven and to all the others. ¹⁰It was Mary Magdalene, Joanna, Mary the mother of James, and the others with them who told this to the apostles. ¹¹But they did not believe the women, because their words seemed to them like nonsense. ¹²Peter, however, got up and ran to the tomb. Bending over, he saw the strips of linen lying by themselves, and he went away, wondering to himself what had happened.

On the Road to Emmaus

¹³Now that same day two of them were going to a village called Emmaus, about seven milesᵇ from Jerusalem. ¹⁴They were talking with each other about everything that had happened. ¹⁵As they talked and discussed these things with each other, Jesus himself came up and walked along with them; ¹⁶but they were kept from recognizing him.

¹⁷He asked them, "What are you discussing together as you walk along?"

They stood still, their faces downcast. ¹⁸One of them, named Cleopas, asked him, "Are you only a visitor to Jerusalem and do not know the things that have happened there in these days?"

¹⁹"What things?" he asked.

"About Jesus of Nazareth," they replied.

ᵃ42 Some manuscripts *come with your kingly power*
ᵇ13 Greek *sixty stadia* (about 11 kilometers)

"He was a prophet, powerful in word and deed before God and all the people. ²⁰The chief priests and our rulers handed him over to be sentenced to death, and they crucified him; ²¹but we had hoped that he was the one who was going to redeem Israel. And what is more, it is the third day since all this took place. ²²In addition, some of our women amazed us. They went to the tomb early this morning ²³but didn't find his body. They came and told us that they had seen a vision of angels, who said he was alive. ²⁴Then some of our companions went to the tomb and found it just as the women had said, but him they did not see."

²⁵He said to them, "How foolish you are, and how slow of heart to believe all that the prophets have spoken! ²⁶Did not the Christ*a* have to suffer these things and then enter his glory?" ²⁷And beginning with Moses and all the Prophets, he explained to them what was said in all the Scriptures concerning himself.

²⁸As they approached the village to which they were going, Jesus acted as if he were going farther. ²⁹But they urged him strongly, "Stay with us, for it is nearly evening; the day is almost over." So he went in to stay with them.

³⁰When he was at the table with them, he took bread, gave thanks, broke it and began to give it to them. ³¹Then their eyes were opened and they recognized him, and he disappeared from their sight. ³²They asked each other, "Were not our hearts burning within us while he talked with us on the road and opened the Scriptures to us?"

³³They got up and returned at once to Jerusalem. There they found the Eleven and those with them, assembled together ³⁴and saying, "It is true! The Lord has risen and has appeared to Simon." ³⁵Then the two told what had happened on the way, and how Jesus was recognized by them when he broke the bread.

Jesus Appears to the Disciples

³⁶While they were still talking about this, Jesus himself stood among them and said to them, "Peace be with you."

³⁷They were startled and frightened, thinking they saw a ghost. ³⁸He said to them, "Why are you troubled, and why do doubts rise in your minds? ³⁹Look at my hands and my feet. It is I myself! Touch me and see; a ghost does not have flesh and bones, as you see I have."

⁴⁰When he had said this, he showed them his hands and feet. ⁴¹And while they still did not believe it because of joy and amazement, he asked them, "Do you have anything here to eat?" ⁴²They gave him a piece of broiled fish, ⁴³and he took it and ate it in their presence.

⁴⁴He said to them, "This is what I told you while I was still with you: Everything must be fulfilled that is written about me in the Law of Moses, the Prophets and the Psalms."

⁴⁵Then he opened their minds so they could understand the Scriptures. ⁴⁶He told them, "This is what is written: The Christ will suffer and rise from the dead on the third day, ⁴⁷and repentance and forgiveness of sins will be preached in his name to all nations, beginning at Jerusalem. ⁴⁸You are witnesses of these things. ⁴⁹I am going to send you what my Father has promised; but stay in the city until you have been clothed with power from on high."

The Ascension

⁵⁰When he had led them out to the vicinity of Bethany, he lifted up his hands and blessed them. ⁵¹While he was blessing them, he left them and was taken up into heaven. ⁵²Then they worshiped him and returned to Jerusalem with great joy. ⁵³And they stayed continually at the temple, praising God.

a26 Or *Messiah*; also in verse 46

John

*What was it
actually like to live* with Jesus—to walk with him,
to hear his words, to witness his emotions, to enjoy his
companionship, to feel his love? As "the disciple whom
Jesus loved" (13:23), John knew the answer to these questions. Given John's close friendship with the Savior, it's not
surprising that this account gives us the most thorough
chronology of the events of Jesus' life. And John lets the
story tell the message. Somehow he knew that if he would
simply let us in on what really happened during the years of
Jesus' earthly ministry, our lives would never be the same.

It's little wonder that the book of John is the best-
selling and most-often-reprinted portion of the Bible—the
best-selling book of all time. Do you and your spouse want
to know who Jesus was and what it was really like to be
face-to-face with the Creator of the universe? Read on.

The Word Became Flesh

1 In the beginning was the Word, and the Word was with God, and the Word was God. ²He was with God in the beginning.

³Through him all things were made; without him nothing was made that has been made. ⁴In him was life, and that life was the light of men. ⁵The light shines in the darkness, but the darkness has not understood*ᵃ* it.

⁶There came a man who was sent from God; his name was John. ⁷He came as a witness to testify concerning that light, so that through him all men might believe.

⁸He himself was not the light; he came only as a witness to the light. ⁹The true light that gives light to every man was coming into the world.*ᵇ*

¹⁰He was in the world, and though the world was made through him, the world did not recognize him. ¹¹He came to that which was his own, but his own did not receive him. ¹²Yet to all who received him, to those who believed in his name, he gave the right to become children of God— ¹³children born not of natural de-

---

ᵃ5 Or darkness, and the darkness has not overcome
ᵇ9 Or This was the true light that gives light to every man who comes into the world

scent,[a] nor of human decision or a husband's will, but born of God.

[14]The Word became flesh and made his dwelling among us. We have seen his glory, the glory of the One and Only,[b] who came from the Father, full of grace and truth.

[15]John testifies concerning him. He cries out, saying, "This was he of whom I said, 'He who comes after me has surpassed me because he was before me.' " [16]From the fullness of his grace we have all received one blessing after another. [17]For the law was given through Moses; grace and truth came through Jesus Christ. [18]No one has ever seen God, but God the One and Only,[b,c] who is at the Father's side, has made him known.

John the Baptist Denies Being the Christ

[19]Now this was John's testimony when the Jews of Jerusalem sent priests and Levites to ask him who he was. [20]He did not fail to confess, but confessed freely, "I am not the Christ.[d] "

[21]They asked him, "Then who are you? Are you Elijah?"

He said, "I am not."

"Are you the Prophet?"

He answered, "No."

[22]Finally they said, "Who are you? Give us an answer to take back to those who sent us. What do you say about yourself?"

[23]John replied in the words of Isaiah the prophet, "I am the voice of one calling in the desert, 'Make straight the way for the Lord.' "[e]

[24]Now some Pharisees who had been sent [25]questioned him, "Why then do you baptize if you are not the Christ, nor Elijah, nor the Prophet?"

[26]"I baptize with[f] water," John replied, "but among you stands one you do not know. [27]He is the one who comes after me, the thongs of whose sandals I am not worthy to untie."

[28]This all happened at Bethany on the other side of the Jordan, where John was baptizing.

Jesus the Lamb of God

[29]The next day John saw Jesus coming toward him and said, "Look, the Lamb of God, who takes away the sin of the world!

[30]This is the one I meant when I said, 'A man who comes after me has surpassed me because he was before me.' [31]I myself did not know him, but the reason I came baptizing with water was that he might be revealed to Israel."

[32]Then John gave this testimony: "I saw the Spirit come down from heaven as a dove and remain on him. [33]I would not have known him, except that the one who sent me to baptize with water told me, 'The man on whom you see the Spirit come down and remain is he who will baptize with the Holy Spirit.' [34]I have seen and I testify that this is the Son of God."

Jesus' First Disciples

[35]The next day John was there again with two of his disciples. [36]When he saw Jesus passing by, he said, "Look, the Lamb of God!"

[37]When the two disciples heard him say this, they followed Jesus. [38]Turning around, Jesus saw them following and asked, "What do you want?"

They said, "Rabbi" (which means Teacher), "where are you staying?"

[39]"Come," he replied, "and you will see."

So they went and saw where he was staying, and spent that day with him. It was about the tenth hour.

[40]Andrew, Simon Peter's brother, was one of the two who heard what John had said and who had followed Jesus. [41]The first thing Andrew did was to find his brother Simon and tell him, "We have found the Messiah" (that is, the Christ). [42]And he brought him to Jesus.

Jesus looked at him and said, "You are Simon son of John. You will be called Cephas" (which, when translated, is Peter[g]).

Jesus Calls Philip and Nathanael

[43]The next day Jesus decided to leave for Galilee. Finding Philip, he said to him, "Follow me."

---

[a]13 Greek of bloods   [b]14,18 Or the Only Begotten   [c]18 Some manuscripts but the only (or only begotten) Son   [d]20 Or Messiah. "The Christ" (Greek) and "the Messiah" (Hebrew) both mean "the Anointed One"; also in verse 25.
[e]23 Isaiah 40:3   [f]26 Or in; also in verses 31 and 33   [g]42 Both Cephas (Aramaic) and Peter (Greek) mean rock.

44Philip, like Andrew and Peter, was from the town of Bethsaida. 45Philip found Nathanael and told him, "We have found the one Moses wrote about in the Law, and about whom the prophets also wrote—Jesus of Nazareth, the son of Joseph."

46"Nazareth! Can anything good come from there?" Nathanael asked.

"Come and see," said Philip.

47When Jesus saw Nathanael approaching, he said of him, "Here is a true Israelite, in whom there is nothing false."

48"How do you know me?" Nathanael asked.

Jesus answered, "I saw you while you were still under the fig tree before Philip called you."

49Then Nathanael declared, "Rabbi, you are the Son of God; you are the King of Israel."

50Jesus said, "You believe*a* because I told you I saw you under the fig tree. You shall see greater things than that." 51He then added, "I tell you*b* the truth, you*b* shall see heaven open, and the angels of God ascending and descending on the Son of Man."

Jesus Changes Water to Wine

2 On the third day a wedding took place at Cana in Galilee. Jesus' mother was there, 2and Jesus and his disciples had also been invited to the wedding. 3When the wine was gone, Jesus' mother said to him, "They have no more wine."

4"Dear woman, why do you involve me?" Jesus replied. "My time has not yet come."

5His mother said to the servants, "Do whatever he tells you."

6Nearby stood six stone water jars, the kind used by the Jews for ceremonial washing, each holding from twenty to thirty gallons.*c*

7Jesus said to the servants, "Fill the jars with water"; so they filled them to the brim.

*a*50 Or *Do you believe . . . ?*   *b*51 The Greek is plural.   *c*6 Greek *two to three metretes* (probably about 75 to 115 liters)

The Miracle Wedding

Thursday

JOHN 2:1–11 Preparing for the wedding has been compared to readying for a trip into the wild unknown. The wedding dress and bride's trousseau, according to some, need to be as carefully selected as a compass pointed toward new territory. As Dr. Mary Roberts wrote in her 1912 book, *Why Women Are So*, "A trousseau was as essential to the prospective bride as an outfit to the explorer of arctic or tropical wilds . . . who knows what might be needed and yet unattainable in the great adventure upon which she was about to embark!" To prepare the trousseau, a prospective bride spent the final days of her engagement stitching linens and clothing. She sewed and shopped, packed and cleaned, sewed and packed some more. There was no time to spare. The process became her transition into wifehood, and she certainly wanted to come out of it looking her absolute best.

A century later, some of us may think

that modern women have moved beyond that. But the wedding dress and ceremony are still a big deal. The millions of dollars spent each year merely on magazines about weddings can attest to that fact.

In this passage Jesus is at a wedding in Cana where he and his mother probably knew the family. His disciples were also invited. What is interesting to note, say many commentators, is that the miracle he performed at this wedding was actually for his disciples. Few besides them saw it. The miracle signaled the unveiling of his glory, and his disciples put their faith in him (see verse 11). As you look back at your own wedding, is there a sign of Jesus' presence and glory that you recall? In the midst of preparing for the special ceremony, were you able to see the miracle God was performing in your own life?

—Les and Leslie

Go to page 1147 for your next devotional reading.

⁸Then he told them, "Now draw some out and take it to the master of the banquet."

They did so, ⁹and the master of the banquet tasted the water that had been turned into wine. He did not realize where it had come from, though the servants who had drawn the water knew. Then he called the bridegroom aside ¹⁰and said, "Everyone brings out the choice wine first and then the cheaper wine after the guests have had too much to drink; but you have saved the best till now."

¹¹This, the first of his miraculous signs, Jesus performed at Cana in Galilee. He thus revealed his glory, and his disciples put their faith in him.

Jesus Clears the Temple

¹²After this he went down to Capernaum with his mother and brothers and his disciples. There they stayed for a few days. ¹³When it was almost time for the Jewish Passover, Jesus went up to Jerusalem. ¹⁴In the temple courts he found men selling cattle, sheep and doves, and others sitting at tables exchanging money. ¹⁵So he made a whip out of cords, and drove all from the temple area, both sheep and cattle; he scattered the coins of the money changers and overturned their tables. ¹⁶To those who sold doves he said, "Get these out of here! How dare you turn my Father's house into a market!"

¹⁷His disciples remembered that it is written: "Zeal for your house will consume me."ᵃ

¹⁸Then the Jews demanded of him, "What miraculous sign can you show us to prove your authority to do all this?"

¹⁹Jesus answered them, "Destroy this temple, and I will raise it again in three days."

²⁰The Jews replied, "It has taken forty-six years to build this temple, and you are going to raise it in three days?" ²¹But the temple he had spoken of was his body. ²²After he was raised from the dead, his disciples recalled what he had said. Then they believed the Scripture and the words that Jesus had spoken.

²³Now while he was in Jerusalem at the Passover Feast, many people saw the miraculous signs he was doing and believed in his name.ᵇ ²⁴But Jesus would not entrust himself to them, for he knew all men. ²⁵He did not need man's testimony about man, for he knew what was in a man.

Jesus Teaches Nicodemus

3 Now there was a man of the Pharisees named Nicodemus, a member of the Jewish ruling council. ²He came to Jesus at night and said, "Rabbi, we know you are a teacher who has come from God. For no one could perform the miraculous signs you are doing if God were not with him."

³In reply Jesus declared, "I tell you the truth, no one can see the kingdom of God unless he is born again.ᶜ"

⁴"How can a man be born when he is old?" Nicodemus asked. "Surely he cannot enter a second time into his mother's womb to be born!"

⁵Jesus answered, "I tell you the truth, no one can enter the kingdom of God unless he is born of water and the Spirit. ⁶Flesh gives birth to flesh, but the Spiritᵈ gives birth to spirit. ⁷You should not be surprised at my saying, 'Youᵉ must be born again.' ⁸The wind blows wherever it pleases. You hear its sound, but you cannot tell where it comes from or where it is going. So it is with everyone born of the Spirit."

⁹"How can this be?" Nicodemus asked.

¹⁰"You are Israel's teacher," said Jesus, "and do you not understand these things? ¹¹I tell you the truth, we speak of what we know, and we testify to what we have seen, but still you people do not accept our testimony. ¹²I have spoken to you of earthly things and you do not believe; how then will you believe if I speak of heavenly things? ¹³No one has ever gone into heaven except the one who came from heaven—the Son of Man.ᶠ ¹⁴Just as Moses lifted up the snake in the desert, so the Son of Man must be lifted up, ¹⁵that everyone who believes in him may have eternal life.ᵍ

¹⁶"For God so loved the world that he

ᵃ17 Psalm 69:9   ᵇ23 Or and believed in him
ᶜ3 Or born from above; also in verse 7   ᵈ6 Or
but spirit   ᵉ7 The Greek is plural.   ᶠ13 Some
manuscripts Man, who is in heaven   ᵍ15 Or
believes may have eternal life in him

gave his one and only Son,[a] that whoever believes in him shall not perish but have eternal life. [17]For God did not send his Son into the world to condemn the world, but to save the world through him. [18]Whoever believes in him is not condemned, but whoever does not believe stands condemned already because he has not believed in the name of God's one and only Son.[b] [19]This is the verdict: Light has come into the world, but men loved darkness instead of light because their deeds were evil. [20]Everyone who does evil hates the light, and will not come into the light for fear that his deeds will be exposed. [21]But whoever lives by the truth comes into the light, so that it may be seen plainly that what he has done has been done through God."[c]

John the Baptist's Testimony About Jesus

[22]After this, Jesus and his disciples went out into the Judean countryside, where he spent some time with them, and baptized. [23]Now John also was baptizing at Aenon near Salim, because there was plenty of water, and people were constantly coming to be baptized. [24](This was before John was put in prison.) [25]An argument developed between some of John's disciples and a certain Jew[d] over the matter of ceremonial washing. [26]They came to John and said to him, "Rabbi, that man who was with you on the other side of the Jordan—the one you testified about—well, he is baptizing, and everyone is going to him."

[27]To this John replied, "A man can receive only what is given him from heaven. [28]You yourselves can testify that I said, 'I am not the Christ[e] but am sent ahead of him.' [29]The bride belongs to the bridegroom. The friend who attends the bridegroom waits and listens for him, and is full of joy when he hears the bridegroom's voice. That joy is mine, and it is now complete. [30]He must become greater; I must become less.

[31]"The one who comes from above is above all; the one who is from the earth belongs to the earth, and speaks as one from the earth. The one who comes from heaven is above all. [32]He testifies to what he has seen and heard, but no one accepts his testimony. [33]The man who has accepted it has certified that God is truthful. [34]For the one whom God has sent speaks the words of God, for God[f] gives the Spirit without limit. [35]The Father loves

[a]16 Or *his only begotten Son*   [b]18 Or *God's only begotten Son*   [c]21 Some interpreters end the quotation after verse 15.   [d]25 Some manuscripts *and certain Jews*   [e]28 Or *Messiah*   [f]34 Greek *he*

Never Alone

Friday

JOHN 3:16 Perhaps too many of us have memorized this great verse but never allowed it to settle into our hearts. It's a great verse of salvation through faith in the One who paid for our sins. But there's much more here. It's also a statement about how much we are each loved.

As we wake up to each morning, we can allow ourselves to feel very much alone. We're busy, and we're running to meet our own personal schedules. Even though we're in a marriage relationship, there are times when we feel isolated, lonely or unloved. That might be the way you feel from time to time, but it's not true. You are never alone and never unloved.

Don't make the mistake of reading this great verse as an impersonal message to the whole world. This is a statement made to each of us individually. We might read it this way: "For God specifically and individually loves (your name) so much that he paid the ultimate price in order to have a relationship with (your name) and spend eternity with (your name)."

As you go out the door today, are you feeling alone? Loneliness is a feeling, and feelings can be very deceptive. The Creator of the universe gave himself because of his great love for you; no matter what your circumstance, you are never alone.

—**Bob and Rosemary**

Go to page 1148 for your next devotional reading.

the Son and has placed everything in his hands. ³⁶Whoever believes in the Son has eternal life, but whoever rejects the Son will not see life, for God's wrath remains on him."ᵃ

Jesus Talks With a Samaritan Woman

4 The Pharisees heard that Jesus was gaining and baptizing more disciples than John, ²although in fact it was not Jesus who baptized, but his disciples. ³When the Lord learned of this, he left Judea and went back once more to Galilee.

⁴Now he had to go through Samaria. ⁵So he came to a town in Samaria called Sychar, near the plot of ground Jacob had given to his son Joseph. ⁶Jacob's well was there, and Jesus, tired as he was from the journey, sat down by the well. It was about the sixth hour.

⁷When a Samaritan woman came to draw water, Jesus said to her, "Will you give me a drink?" ⁸(His disciples had gone into the town to buy food.)

⁹The Samaritan woman said to him, "You are a Jew and I am a Samaritan woman. How can you ask me for a drink?" (For Jews do not associate with Samaritans.ᵇ)

¹⁰Jesus answered her, "If you knew the gift of God and who it is that asks you for a drink, you would have asked him and he would have given you living water."

¹¹"Sir," the woman said, "you have nothing to draw with and the well is deep. Where can you get this living water? ¹²Are you greater than our father Jacob, who gave us the well and drank from it himself, as did also his sons and his flocks and herds?"

¹³Jesus answered, "Everyone who drinks this water will be thirsty again, ¹⁴but whoever drinks the water I give him will never thirst. Indeed, the water I give him will become in him a spring of water welling up to eternal life."

¹⁵The woman said to him, "Sir, give me this water so that I won't get thirsty and have to keep coming here to draw water."

¹⁶He told her, "Go, call your husband and come back."

¹⁷"I have no husband," she replied.

Jesus said to her, "You are right when you say you have no husband. ¹⁸The fact is, you have had five husbands, and the

---

ᵃ36 Some interpreters end the quotation after verse 30.   ᵇ9 Or *do not use dishes Samaritans have used*

Living Water

JOHN 4:1–26 Did you ever notice how many times the Bible uses water in an analogy? Actually 436 verses contain the word "water." And it's central in Jesus' encounter with the Samaritan woman in this passage.

Quiet TIMES with each other

The Samaritan woman didn't understand Jesus' request for a drink of water. First, she got sidetracked with cultural issues: "You are a Jew and I am a Samaritan woman. How can you ask me for a drink?" (verse 9). She didn't realize that Jesus was offering her the living water—eternal life through faith in him.

Too many times we look to each other to meet our deepest needs. But we're drawing from the wrong well. Our well of compassion, understanding and refreshment will quickly run dry. Only Jesus can ultimately meet our needs, and he is the one who empowers us to serve each other. His "living water" can be found nowhere else. So let Jesus refresh your soul, and, in so doing, he will bring refreshment to your marriage. Together, drink from his well. Then you will experience a living and refreshing marriage.

—*Dave and Claudia*

 Weekend Warm-up *When was a time Jesus brought refreshment to your marriage?*

Go to page 1150 for your next devotional reading.

man you now have is not your husband. What you have just said is quite true."

[19]"Sir," the woman said, "I can see that you are a prophet. [20]Our fathers worshiped on this mountain, but you Jews claim that the place where we must worship is in Jerusalem."

[21]Jesus declared, "Believe me, woman, a time is coming when you will worship the Father neither on this mountain nor in Jerusalem. [22]You Samaritans worship what you do not know; we worship what we do know, for salvation is from the Jews. [23]Yet a time is coming and has now come when the true worshipers will worship the Father in spirit and truth, for they are the kind of worshipers the Father seeks. [24]God is spirit, and his worshipers must worship in spirit and in truth."

[25]The woman said, "I know that Messiah" (called Christ) "is coming. When he comes, he will explain everything to us."

[26]Then Jesus declared, "I who speak to you am he."

The Disciples Rejoin Jesus

[27]Just then his disciples returned and were surprised to find him talking with a woman. But no one asked, "What do you want?" or "Why are you talking with her?"

[28]Then, leaving her water jar, the woman went back to the town and said to the people, [29]"Come, see a man who told me everything I ever did. Could this be the Christ[a]?" [30]They came out of the town and made their way toward him.

[31]Meanwhile his disciples urged him, "Rabbi, eat something."

[32]But he said to them, "I have food to eat that you know nothing about."

[33]Then his disciples said to each other, "Could someone have brought him food?"

[34]"My food," said Jesus, "is to do the will of him who sent me and to finish his work. [35]Do you not say, 'Four months more and then the harvest'? I tell you, open your eyes and look at the fields! They are ripe for harvest. [36]Even now the reaper draws his wages, even now he harvests the crop for eternal life, so that the sower and the reaper may be glad together. [37]Thus the saying 'One sows and another reaps' is true. [38]I sent you to reap what you have not worked for. Others have done the hard work, and you have reaped the benefits of their labor."

Many Samaritans Believe

[39]Many of the Samaritans from that town believed in him because of the woman's testimony, "He told me everything I ever did." [40]So when the Samaritans came to him, they urged him to stay with them, and he stayed two days. [41]And because of his words many more became believers.

[42]They said to the woman, "We no longer believe just because of what you said; now we have heard for ourselves, and we know that this man really is the Savior of the world."

Jesus Heals the Official's Son

[43]After the two days he left for Galilee. [44](Now Jesus himself had pointed out that a prophet has no honor in his own country.) [45]When he arrived in Galilee, the Galileans welcomed him. They had seen all that he had done in Jerusalem at the Passover Feast, for they also had been there.

[46]Once more he visited Cana in Galilee, where he had turned the water into wine. And there was a certain royal official whose son lay sick at Capernaum. [47]When this man heard that Jesus had arrived in Galilee from Judea, he went to him and begged him to come and heal his son, who was close to death.

[48]"Unless you people see miraculous signs and wonders," Jesus told him, "you will never believe."

[49]The royal official said, "Sir, come down before my child dies."

[50]Jesus replied, "You may go. Your son will live."

The man took Jesus at his word and departed. [51]While he was still on the way, his servants met him with the news that his boy was living. [52]When he inquired as to the time when his son got better, they said to him, "The fever left him yesterday at the seventh hour."

[53]Then the father realized that this was the exact time at which Jesus had said to him, "Your son will live." So he and all his household believed.

[a]29 Or Messiah

⁵⁴This was the second miraculous sign that Jesus performed, having come from Judea to Galilee.

The Healing at the Pool

5 Some time later, Jesus went up to Jerusalem for a feast of the Jews. ²Now there is in Jerusalem near the Sheep Gate a pool, which in Aramaic is called Bethesda*ᵃ* and which is surrounded by five covered colonnades. ³Here a great number of disabled people used to lie—the blind, the lame, the paralyzed.*ᵇ* ⁵One who was there had been an invalid for thirty-eight years. ⁶When Jesus saw him lying there and learned that he had been in this condition for a long time, he asked him, "Do you want to get well?"

⁷"Sir," the invalid replied, "I have no one to help me into the pool when the water is stirred. While I am trying to get in, someone else goes down ahead of me."

⁸Then Jesus said to him, "Get up! Pick up your mat and walk." ⁹At once the man was cured; he picked up his mat and walked.

The day on which this took place was a Sabbath, ¹⁰and so the Jews said to the man who had been healed, "It is the Sabbath; the law forbids you to carry your mat."

¹¹But he replied, "The man who made me well said to me, 'Pick up your mat and walk.' "

¹²So they asked him, "Who is this fellow who told you to pick it up and walk?"

¹³The man who was healed had no idea who it was, for Jesus had slipped away into the crowd that was there.

¹⁴Later Jesus found him at the temple and said to him, "See, you are well again. Stop sinning or something worse may happen to you." ¹⁵The man went away and told the Jews that it was Jesus who had made him well.

Life Through the Son

¹⁶So, because Jesus was doing these things on the Sabbath, the Jews persecuted him. ¹⁷Jesus said to them, "My Father is always at his work to this very day, and

ᵃ2 Some manuscripts *Bethzatha*; other manuscripts *Bethsaida*   *ᵇ3* Some less important manuscripts *paralyzed—and they waited for the moving of the waters. ⁴From time to time an angel of the Lord would come down and stir up the waters. The first one into the pool after each such disturbance would be cured of whatever disease he had.*

Prescription for a Healthy Marriage

JOHN 5:1–8 Imagine going to a doctor and having him ask you, "Do you want to get well?" Yet that is the question Jesus asked the paralyzed man who had been an invalid for thirty-eight years.

As we lead marriage seminars around the country, we meet some couples whose marriages remind us of this paralyzed man. Their marriages have been crippled for many years. Like the man in this passage, they hang around the pool where other marriages are being healed, but they never seem to take action. So Jesus' question to the invalid also applies to the problem areas of our marriages. Do you *really* want to build a better marriage? Do you *really* want to improve your communication? Do you *really* want to resolve the conflicts?

Perhaps you're not sure your marriage

can be healed. The man had been disabled for almost four decades, but it wasn't too late for him. It's not too late for any of us who are willing to get up and do something. Like the man in this passage, we must take the first step.

Listen as Jesus says to you, "Get up! Pick up your mat and walk" (verse 8). Perhaps your "first step" is finding a Christian counselor who can help you look realistically at your marriage and help you design a plan for marital growth. Another step might be joining a marriage growth group so you will have other couples to encourage you in your marriage walk. But like the man at the pool, whether you take these first steps will depend on whether you *really* want your marriage to get well.

—Dave and Claudia

Go to page 1152 for your next devotional reading.

I, too, am working." ¹⁸For this reason the Jews tried all the harder to kill him; not only was he breaking the Sabbath, but he was even calling God his own Father, making himself equal with God.

¹⁹Jesus gave them this answer: "I tell you the truth, the Son can do nothing by himself; he can do only what he sees his Father doing, because whatever the Father does the Son also does. ²⁰For the Father loves the Son and shows him all he does. Yes, to your amazement he will show him even greater things than these. ²¹For just as the Father raises the dead and gives them life, even so the Son gives life to whom he is pleased to give it. ²²Moreover, the Father judges no one, but has entrusted all judgment to the Son, ²³that all may honor the Son just as they honor the Father. He who does not honor the Son does not honor the Father, who sent him.

²⁴"I tell you the truth, whoever hears my word and believes him who sent me has eternal life and will not be condemned; he has crossed over from death to life. ²⁵I tell you the truth, a time is coming and has now come when the dead will hear the voice of the Son of God and those who hear will live. ²⁶For as the Father has life in himself, so he has granted the Son to have life in himself. ²⁷And he has given him authority to judge because he is the Son of Man.

²⁸"Do not be amazed at this, for a time is coming when all who are in their graves will hear his voice ²⁹and come out—those who have done good will rise to live, and those who have done evil will rise to be condemned. ³⁰By myself I can do nothing; I judge only as I hear, and my judgment is just, for I seek not to please myself but him who sent me.

Testimonies About Jesus

³¹"If I testify about myself, my testimony is not valid. ³²There is another who testifies in my favor, and I know that his testimony about me is valid.

³³"You have sent to John and he has testified to the truth. ³⁴Not that I accept human testimony; but I mention it that you may be saved. ³⁵John was a lamp that burned and gave light, and you chose for a time to enjoy his light.

³⁶"I have testimony weightier than that of John. For the very work that the Father has given me to finish, and which I am doing, testifies that the Father has sent me. ³⁷And the Father who sent me has himself testified concerning me. You have never heard his voice nor seen his form, ³⁸nor does his word dwell in you, for you do not believe the one he sent. ³⁹You diligently study^a the Scriptures because you think that by them you possess eternal life. These are the Scriptures that testify about me, ⁴⁰yet you refuse to come to me to have life.

⁴¹"I do not accept praise from men, ⁴²but I know you. I know that you do not have the love of God in your hearts. ⁴³I have come in my Father's name, and you do not accept me; but if someone else comes in his own name, you will accept him. ⁴⁴How can you believe if you accept praise from one another, yet make no effort to obtain the praise that comes from the only God^b?

⁴⁵"But do not think I will accuse you before the Father. Your accuser is Moses, on whom your hopes are set. ⁴⁶If you believed Moses, you would believe me, for he wrote about me. ⁴⁷But since you do not believe what he wrote, how are you going to believe what I say?"

Jesus Feeds the Five Thousand

6 Some time after this, Jesus crossed to the far shore of the Sea of Galilee (that is, the Sea of Tiberias), ²and a great crowd of people followed him because they saw the miraculous signs he had performed on the sick. ³Then Jesus went up on a mountainside and sat down with his disciples. ⁴The Jewish Passover Feast was near.

⁵When Jesus looked up and saw a great crowd coming toward him, he said to Philip, "Where shall we buy bread for these people to eat?" ⁶He asked this only to test him, for he already had in mind what he was going to do.

⁷Philip answered him, "Eight months' wages^c would not buy enough bread for each one to have a bite!"

⁸Another of his disciples, Andrew, Simon Peter's brother, spoke up, ⁹"Here is

---

a39 Or *Study diligently* (the imperative)
b44 Some early manuscripts *the Only One*
c7 Greek *two hundred denarii*

a boy with five small barley loaves and two small fish, but how far will they go among so many?"

¹⁰Jesus said, "Have the people sit down." There was plenty of grass in that place, and the men sat down, about five thousand of them. ¹¹Jesus then took the loaves, gave thanks, and distributed to those who were seated as much as they wanted. He did the same with the fish.

¹²When they had all had enough to eat, he said to his disciples, "Gather the pieces that are left over. Let nothing be wasted." ¹³So they gathered them and filled twelve baskets with the pieces of the five barley loaves left over by those who had eaten.

¹⁴After the people saw the miraculous sign that Jesus did, they began to say, "Surely this is the Prophet who is to come into the world." ¹⁵Jesus, knowing that they intended to come and make him king by force, withdrew again to a mountain by himself.

Jesus Walks on the Water

¹⁶When evening came, his disciples went down to the lake, ¹⁷where they got into a boat and set off across the lake for Capernaum. By now it was dark, and Jesus had not yet joined them. ¹⁸A strong wind was blowing and the waters grew rough. ¹⁹When they had rowed three or three and a half miles,ᵃ they saw Jesus approaching the boat, walking on the water; and they were terrified. ²⁰But he said to them, "It is I; don't be afraid." ²¹Then they were willing to take him into the boat, and immediately the boat reached the shore where they were heading.

²²The next day the crowd that had stayed on the opposite shore of the lake realized that only one boat had been there, and that Jesus had not entered it with his disciples, but that they had gone away alone. ²³Then some boats from Tiberias landed near the place where the people had eaten the bread after the Lord had given thanks. ²⁴Once the crowd realized that neither Jesus nor his disciples were there, they got into the boats and went to Capernaum in search of Jesus.

Jesus the Bread of Life

²⁵When they found him on the other side of the lake, they asked him, "Rabbi, when did you get here?"

²⁶Jesus answered, "I tell you the truth,

ᵃ19 Greek *rowed twenty-five or thirty stadia* (about 5 or 6 kilometers)

Glue or Gunpowder?

Tuesday

JOHN 6:16–21 Financial hardship was one of the best things to happen to our marriage. During our newlywed years, finances were extremely tight. Initially, the thought of not being able to pay our bills scared me (Bob) to death. But that potential time of fear actually became a strong gluing element in our marriage.

Fear is an emotion, not an event. Fear is a reaction to events going on around us. Fear can be very destructive when an event enters a marriage and "blows the couple apart" from each other. The illness of a child, the loss of a job or the possibility of a disease can bring on fear. When each spouse deals with the difficulty alone, the night at sea becomes much more foreboding.

In their night at sea, the disciples had to learn three steps in dealing with their fear. They learned to pull together, to do their best and to look for Jesus. In our nights of fear we must do the same. A couple must "glue" together rather than allow the fear to blow them apart. Then as they pray and talk over their options, they must then do their best to deal with the difficulty. Most of all, each couple needs to know that Jesus will come to them. He may not come in the way you expect him or have requested him to come; but he will come to your aid. When a couple accepts that as fact, then they can avoid being debilitated by the emotion of fear. There is nothing to fear when we know that Jesus will rescue us.

—Bob and Rosemary

Go to page 1156 for your next devotional reading.

you are looking for me, not because you saw miraculous signs but because you ate the loaves and had your fill. 27Do not work for food that spoils, but for food that endures to eternal life, which the Son of Man will give you. On him God the Father has placed his seal of approval."

28Then they asked him, "What must we do to do the works God requires?"

29Jesus answered, "The work of God is this: to believe in the one he has sent."

30So they asked him, "What miraculous sign then will you give that we may see it and believe you? What will you do? 31Our forefathers ate the manna in the desert; as it is written: 'He gave them bread from heaven to eat.'a"

32Jesus said to them, "I tell you the truth, it is not Moses who has given you the bread from heaven, but it is my Father who gives you the true bread from heaven. 33For the bread of God is he who comes down from heaven and gives life to the world."

34"Sir," they said, "from now on give us this bread."

35Then Jesus declared, "I am the bread of life. He who comes to me will never go hungry, and he who believes in me will never be thirsty. 36But as I told you, you have seen me and still you do not believe. 37All that the Father gives me will come to me, and whoever comes to me I will never drive away. 38For I have come down from heaven not to do my will but to do the will of him who sent me. 39And this is the will of him who sent me, that I shall lose none of all that he has given me, but raise them up at the last day. 40For my Father's will is that everyone who looks to the Son and believes in him shall have eternal life, and I will raise him up at the last day."

41At this the Jews began to grumble about him because he said, "I am the bread that came down from heaven." 42They said, "Is this not Jesus, the son of Joseph, whose father and mother we know? How can he now say, 'I came down from heaven'?"

43"Stop grumbling among yourselves," Jesus answered. 44"No one can come to me unless the Father who sent me draws him, and I will raise him up at the last day. 45It is written in the Prophets: 'They will all be taught by God.'b Everyone who listens to the Father and learns from

him comes to me. 46No one has seen the Father except the one who is from God; only he has seen the Father. 47I tell you the truth, he who believes has everlasting life. 48I am the bread of life. 49Your forefathers ate the manna in the desert, yet they died. 50But here is the bread that comes down from heaven, which a man may eat and not die. 51I am the living bread that came down from heaven. If anyone eats of this bread, he will live forever. This bread is my flesh, which I will give for the life of the world."

52Then the Jews began to argue sharply among themselves, "How can this man give us his flesh to eat?"

53Jesus said to them, "I tell you the truth, unless you eat the flesh of the Son of Man and drink his blood, you have no life in you. 54Whoever eats my flesh and drinks my blood has eternal life, and I will raise him up at the last day. 55For my flesh is real food and my blood is real drink. 56Whoever eats my flesh and drinks my blood remains in me, and I in him. 57Just as the living Father sent me and I live because of the Father, so the one who feeds on me will live because of me. 58This is the bread that came down from heaven. Your forefathers ate manna and died, but he who feeds on this bread will live forever." 59He said this while teaching in the synagogue in Capernaum.

Many Disciples Desert Jesus

60On hearing it, many of his disciples said, "This is a hard teaching. Who can accept it?"

61Aware that his disciples were grumbling about this, Jesus said to them, "Does this offend you? 62What if you see the Son of Man ascend to where he was before! 63The Spirit gives life; the flesh counts for nothing. The words I have spoken to you are spiritc and they are life. 64Yet there are some of you who do not believe." For Jesus had known from the beginning which of them did not believe and who would betray him. 65He went on to say, "This is why I told you that no one can come to me unless the Father has enabled him."

66From this time many of his disciples

a31 Exodus 16:4; Neh. 9:15; Psalm 78:24,25
b45 Isaiah 54:13   c63 Or Spirit

turned back and no longer followed him.

⁶⁷"You do not want to leave too, do you?" Jesus asked the Twelve.

⁶⁸Simon Peter answered him, "Lord, to whom shall we go? You have the words of eternal life. ⁶⁹We believe and know that you are the Holy One of God."

⁷⁰Then Jesus replied, "Have I not chosen you, the Twelve? Yet one of you is a devil!" ⁷¹(He meant Judas, the son of Simon Iscariot, who, though one of the Twelve, was later to betray him.)

Jesus Goes to the Feast of Tabernacles

7 After this, Jesus went around in Galilee, purposely staying away from Judea because the Jews there were waiting to take his life. ²But when the Jewish Feast of Tabernacles was near, ³Jesus' brothers said to him, "You ought to leave here and go to Judea, so that your disciples may see the miracles you do. ⁴No one who wants to become a public figure acts in secret. Since you are doing these things, show yourself to the world." ⁵For even his own brothers did not believe in him.

⁶Therefore Jesus told them, "The right time for me has not yet come; for you any time is right. ⁷The world cannot hate you, but it hates me because I testify that what it does is evil. ⁸You go to the Feast. I am not yet*ᵃ* going up to this Feast, because for me the right time has not yet come." ⁹Having said this, he stayed in Galilee.

¹⁰However, after his brothers had left for the Feast, he went also, not publicly, but in secret. ¹¹Now at the Feast the Jews were watching for him and asking, "Where is that man?"

¹²Among the crowds there was widespread whispering about him. Some said, "He is a good man."

Others replied, "No, he deceives the people." ¹³But no one would say anything publicly about him for fear of the Jews.

Jesus Teaches at the Feast

¹⁴Not until halfway through the Feast did Jesus go up to the temple courts and begin to teach. ¹⁵The Jews were amazed and asked, "How did this man get such learning without having studied?"

¹⁶Jesus answered, "My teaching is not my own. It comes from him who sent me. ¹⁷If anyone chooses to do God's will, he will find out whether my teaching comes from God or whether I speak on my own. ¹⁸He who speaks on his own does so to gain honor for himself, but he who works for the honor of the one who sent him is a man of truth; there is nothing false about him. ¹⁹Has not Moses given you the law? Yet not one of you keeps the law. Why are you trying to kill me?"

²⁰"You are demon-possessed," the crowd answered. "Who is trying to kill you?"

²¹Jesus said to them, "I did one miracle, and you are all astonished. ²²Yet, because Moses gave you circumcision (though actually it did not come from Moses, but from the patriarchs), you circumcise a child on the Sabbath. ²³Now if a child can be circumcised on the Sabbath so that the law of Moses may not be broken, why are you angry with me for healing the whole man on the Sabbath? ²⁴Stop judging by mere appearances, and make a right judgment."

Is Jesus the Christ?

²⁵At that point some of the people of Jerusalem began to ask, "Isn't this the man they are trying to kill? ²⁶Here he is, speaking publicly, and they are not saying a word to him. Have the authorities really concluded that he is the Christ*ᵇ*? ²⁷But we know where this man is from; when the Christ comes, no one will know where he is from."

²⁸Then Jesus, still teaching in the temple courts, cried out, "Yes, you know me, and you know where I am from. I am not here on my own, but he who sent me is true. You do not know him, ²⁹but I know him because I am from him and he sent me."

³⁰At this they tried to seize him, but no one laid a hand on him, because his time had not yet come. ³¹Still, many in the crowd put their faith in him. They said, "When the Christ comes, will he do more miraculous signs than this man?"

³²The Pharisees heard the crowd whispering such things about him. Then the chief priests and the Pharisees sent temple guards to arrest him.

³³Jesus said, "I am with you for only a

ᵃ8 Some early manuscripts do not have *yet.*
ᵇ26 Or *Messiah;* also in verses 27, 31, 41 and 42

short time, and then I go to the one who sent me. 34You will look for me, but you will not find me; and where I am, you cannot come."

35The Jews said to one another, "Where does this man intend to go that we cannot find him? Will he go where our people live scattered among the Greeks, and teach the Greeks? 36What did he mean when he said, 'You will look for me, but you will not find me,' and 'Where I am, you cannot come'?"

37On the last and greatest day of the Feast, Jesus stood and said in a loud voice, "If anyone is thirsty, let him come to me and drink. 38Whoever believes in me, as[a] the Scripture has said, streams of living water will flow from within him." 39By this he meant the Spirit, whom those who believed in him were later to receive. Up to that time the Spirit had not been given, since Jesus had not yet been glorified.

40On hearing his words, some of the people said, "Surely this man is the Prophet."

41Others said, "He is the Christ."

Still others asked, "How can the Christ come from Galilee? 42Does not the Scripture say that the Christ will come from David's family[b] and from Bethlehem, the town where David lived?" 43Thus the people were divided because of Jesus. 44Some wanted to seize him, but no one laid a hand on him.

Unbelief of the Jewish Leaders

45Finally the temple guards went back to the chief priests and Pharisees, who asked them, "Why didn't you bring him in?"

46"No one ever spoke the way this man does," the guards declared.

47"You mean he has deceived you also?" the Pharisees retorted. 48"Has any of the rulers or of the Pharisees believed in him? 49No! But this mob that knows nothing of the law—there is a curse on them."

50Nicodemus, who had gone to Jesus earlier and who was one of their own number, asked, 51"Does our law condemn anyone without first hearing him to find out what he is doing?"

52They replied, "Are you from Galilee, too? Look into it, and you will find that a prophet[c] does not come out of Galilee."

[The earliest manuscripts and many other ancient witnesses do not have John 7:53–8:11.]

53Then each went to his own home.

8 But Jesus went to the Mount of Olives. 2At dawn he appeared again in the temple courts, where all the people gathered around him, and he sat down to teach them. 3The teachers of the law and the Pharisees brought in a woman caught in adultery. They made her stand before the group 4and said to Jesus, "Teacher, this woman was caught in the act of adultery. 5In the Law Moses commanded us to stone such women. Now what do you say?" 6They were using this question as a trap, in order to have a basis for accusing him.

But Jesus bent down and started to write on the ground with his finger. 7When they kept on questioning him, he straightened up and said to them, "If any one of you is without sin, let him be the first to throw a stone at her." 8Again he stooped down and wrote on the ground.

9At this, those who heard began to go away one at a time, the older ones first, until only Jesus was left, with the woman still standing there. 10Jesus straightened up and asked her, "Woman, where are they? Has no one condemned you?"

11"No one, sir," she said.

"Then neither do I condemn you," Jesus declared. "Go now and leave your life of sin."

The Validity of Jesus' Testimony

12When Jesus spoke again to the people, he said, "I am the light of the world. Whoever follows me will never walk in darkness, but will have the light of life."

13The Pharisees challenged him, "Here you are, appearing as your own witness; your testimony is not valid."

---

[a]37,38 Or / If anyone is thirsty, let him come to me. / And let him drink, 38who believes in me. / As [b]42 Greek seed [c]52 Two early manuscripts the Prophet

[14]Jesus answered, "Even if I testify on my own behalf, my testimony is valid, for I know where I came from and where I am going. But you have no idea where I come from or where I am going. [15]You judge by human standards; I pass judgment on no one. [16]But if I do judge, my decisions are right, because I am not alone. I stand with the Father, who sent me. [17]In your own Law it is written that the testimony of two men is valid. [18]I am one who testifies for myself; my other witness is the Father, who sent me."

[19]Then they asked him, "Where is your father?"

"You do not know me or my Father," Jesus replied. "If you knew me, you would know my Father also." [20]He spoke these words while teaching in the temple area near the place where the offerings were put. Yet no one seized him, because his time had not yet come.

[21]Once more Jesus said to them, "I am going away, and you will look for me, and you will die in your sin. Where I go, you cannot come."

[22]This made the Jews ask, "Will he kill himself? Is that why he says, 'Where I go, you cannot come'?"

[23]But he continued, "You are from be-low; I am from above. You are of this world; I am not of this world. [24]I told you that you would die in your sins; if you do not believe that I am ˪the one I claim to be˩,[a] you will indeed die in your sins."

[25]"Who are you?" they asked.

"Just what I have been claiming all along," Jesus replied. [26]"I have much to say in judgment of you. But he who sent me is reliable, and what I have heard from him I tell the world."

[27]They did not understand that he was telling them about his Father. [28]So Jesus said, "When you have lifted up the Son of Man, then you will know that I am ˪the one I claim to be˩ and that I do nothing on my own but speak just what the Father has taught me. [29]The one who sent me is with me; he has not left me alone, for I always do what pleases him." [30]Even as he spoke, many put their faith in him.

The Children of Abraham

[31]To the Jews who had believed him, Jesus said, "If you hold to my teaching, you are really my disciples. [32]Then you will know the truth, and the truth will set you free."

[a]24 Or *I am he*; also in verse 28

"I Don't Condemn You"

Wednesday

JOHN 8:1–11 Each of us is born with a judge and jury on the inside. We are in the courtroom daily, waiting to hear the verdict: "guilty" or "not guilty." Not that the decision has any bearing on the truth—our emotions, not reality, will determine the verdict. For at the root of self-imposed guilt is the idea that what you feel must be true. In other words, if you *feel* guilty, you think you must have *done* something wrong. However, emotions can lie because they are not products of reality but are our *interpretation* of reality. The psalmist alludes to this when he says, "For troubles without number surround me; my sins have overtaken me and I cannot see" (Psalm 40:12).

But then there are those times when guilt is real. And this passage is a clear ex-ample of it. This woman was "caught in the act." No doubt about it, she was guilty. But isn't it interesting how Jesus responds to her? Look at verse 11: "Then neither do I condemn you . . . Go now and leave your life of sin." We've often wondered if Jesus made a mistake when he said that. Shouldn't he have gotten her to promise to change *before* pronouncing his forgiveness? But that's not Christ's way of responding to guilt. Jesus did not want a co-erced confession motivated by fear. He wanted her to *choose* a better way of living in order to *be* a better person.

We all have the opportunity to do the same thing when our spouse is caught in the guilt trap. The question is, will we respond as Jesus did?   **—*Les and Leslie***

Go to page 1160 for your next devotional reading.

³³They answered him, "We are Abraham's descendants[a] and have never been slaves of anyone. How can you say that we shall be set free?"

³⁴Jesus replied, "I tell you the truth, everyone who sins is a slave to sin. ³⁵Now a slave has no permanent place in the family, but a son belongs to it forever. ³⁶So if the Son sets you free, you will be free indeed. ³⁷I know you are Abraham's descendants. Yet you are ready to kill me, because you have no room for my word. ³⁸I am telling you what I have seen in the Father's presence, and you do what you have heard from your father.[b]"

³⁹"Abraham is our father," they answered.

"If you were Abraham's children," said Jesus, "then you would[c] do the things Abraham did. ⁴⁰As it is, you are determined to kill me, a man who has told you the truth that I heard from God. Abraham did not do such things. ⁴¹You are doing the things your own father does."

"We are not illegitimate children," they protested. "The only Father we have is God himself."

The Children of the Devil

⁴²Jesus said to them, "If God were your Father, you would love me, for I came from God and now am here. I have not come on my own; but he sent me. ⁴³Why is my language not clear to you? Because you are unable to hear what I say. ⁴⁴You belong to your father, the devil, and you want to carry out your father's desire. He was a murderer from the beginning, not holding to the truth, for there is no truth in him. When he lies, he speaks his native language, for he is a liar and the father of lies. ⁴⁵Yet because I tell the truth, you do not believe me! ⁴⁶Can any of you prove me guilty of sin? If I am telling the truth, why don't you believe me? ⁴⁷He who belongs to God hears what God says. The reason you do not hear is that you do not belong to God."

The Claims of Jesus About Himself

⁴⁸The Jews answered him, "Aren't we right in saying that you are a Samaritan and demon-possessed?"

⁴⁹"I am not possessed by a demon," said Jesus, "but I honor my Father and you dishonor me. ⁵⁰I am not seeking glory for myself; but there is one who seeks it, and he is the judge. ⁵¹I tell you the truth, if anyone keeps my word, he will never see death."

⁵²At this the Jews exclaimed, "Now we know that you are demon-possessed! Abraham died and so did the prophets, yet you say that if anyone keeps your word, he will never taste death. ⁵³Are you greater than our father Abraham? He died, and so did the prophets. Who do you think you are?"

⁵⁴Jesus replied, "If I glorify myself, my glory means nothing. My Father, whom you claim as your God, is the one who glorifies me. ⁵⁵Though you do not know him, I know him. If I said I did not, I would be a liar like you, but I do know him and keep his word. ⁵⁶Your father Abraham rejoiced at the thought of seeing my day; he saw it and was glad."

⁵⁷"You are not yet fifty years old," the Jews said to him, "and you have seen Abraham!"

⁵⁸"I tell you the truth," Jesus answered, "before Abraham was born, I am!" ⁵⁹At this, they picked up stones to stone him, but Jesus hid himself, slipping away from the temple grounds.

Jesus Heals a Man Born Blind

9 As he went along, he saw a man blind from birth. ²His disciples asked him, "Rabbi, who sinned, this man or his parents, that he was born blind?"

³"Neither this man nor his parents sinned," said Jesus, "but this happened so that the work of God might be displayed in his life. ⁴As long as it is day, we must do the work of him who sent me. Night is coming, when no one can work. ⁵While I am in the world, I am the light of the world."

⁶Having said this, he spit on the ground, made some mud with the saliva, and put it on the man's eyes. ⁷"Go," he told him, "wash in the Pool of Siloam" (this word means Sent). So the man went and washed, and came home seeing.

⁸His neighbors and those who had for-

ᵃ33 Greek *seed*; also in verse 37   ᵇ38 Or *presence. Therefore do what you have heard from the Father.*   ᶜ39 Some early manuscripts *"If you are Abraham's children," said Jesus, "then* merly seen him begging asked, "Isn't this the same man who used to sit and beg?" ⁹Some claimed that he was.

Others said, "No, he only looks like him."

But he himself insisted, "I am the man."

¹⁰"How then were your eyes opened?" they demanded.

¹¹He replied, "The man they call Jesus made some mud and put it on my eyes. He told me to go to Siloam and wash. So I went and washed, and then I could see."

¹²"Where is this man?" they asked him.

"I don't know," he said.

The Pharisees Investigate the Healing

¹³They brought to the Pharisees the man who had been blind. ¹⁴Now the day on which Jesus had made the mud and opened the man's eyes was a Sabbath. ¹⁵Therefore the Pharisees also asked him how he had received his sight. "He put mud on my eyes," the man replied, "and I washed, and now I see."

¹⁶Some of the Pharisees said, "This man is not from God, for he does not keep the Sabbath."

But others asked, "How can a sinner do such miraculous signs?" So they were divided.

¹⁷Finally they turned again to the blind man, "What have you to say about him? It was your eyes he opened."

The man replied, "He is a prophet."

¹⁸The Jews still did not believe that he had been blind and had received his sight until they sent for the man's parents. ¹⁹"Is this your son?" they asked. "Is this the one you say was born blind? How is it that now he can see?"

²⁰"We know he is our son," the parents answered, "and we know he was born blind. ²¹But how he can see now, or who opened his eyes, we don't know. Ask him. He is of age; he will speak for himself."

²²His parents said this because they were afraid of the Jews, for already the Jews had decided that anyone who acknowledged that Jesus was the Christ*a* would be put out of the synagogue. ²³That was why his parents said, "He is of age; ask him."

²⁴A second time they summoned the man who had been blind. "Give glory to God,*b*" they said. "We know this man is a sinner."

²⁵He replied, "Whether he is a sinner or not, I don't know. One thing I do know. I was blind but now I see!"

²⁶Then they asked him, "What did he do to you? How did he open your eyes?"

²⁷He answered, "I have told you already and you did not listen. Why do you want to hear it again? Do you want to become his disciples, too?"

²⁸Then they hurled insults at him and said, "You are this fellow's disciple! We are disciples of Moses! ²⁹We know that God spoke to Moses, but as for this fellow, we don't even know where he comes from."

³⁰The man answered, "Now that is remarkable! You don't know where he comes from, yet he opened my eyes. ³¹We know that God does not listen to sinners. He listens to the godly man who does his will. ³²Nobody has ever heard of opening the eyes of a man born blind. ³³If this man were not from God, he could do nothing."

³⁴To this they replied, "You were steeped in sin at birth; how dare you lecture us!" And they threw him out.

Spiritual Blindness

³⁵Jesus heard that they had thrown him out, and when he found him, he said, "Do you believe in the Son of Man?"

³⁶"Who is he, sir?" the man asked. "Tell me so that I may believe in him."

³⁷Jesus said, "You have now seen him; in fact, he is the one speaking with you."

³⁸Then the man said, "Lord, I believe," and he worshiped him.

³⁹Jesus said, "For judgment I have come into this world, so that the blind will see and those who see will become blind."

⁴⁰Some Pharisees who were with him heard him say this and asked, "What? Are we blind too?"

⁴¹Jesus said, "If you were blind, you would not be guilty of sin; but now that you claim you can see, your guilt remains.

The Shepherd and His Flock

10 "I tell you the truth, the man who does not enter the sheep pen by the

---

*a*22 Or *Messiah*   *b*24 A solemn charge to tell the truth (see Joshua 7:19) gate, but climbs in by some other way, is a thief and a robber. [2]The man who enters by the gate is the shepherd of his sheep. [3]The watchman opens the gate for him, and the sheep listen to his voice. He calls his own sheep by name and leads them out. [4]When he has brought out all his own, he goes on ahead of them, and his sheep follow him because they know his voice. [5]But they will never follow a stranger; in fact, they will run away from him because they do not recognize a stranger's voice." [6]Jesus used this figure of speech, but they did not understand what he was telling them.

[7]Therefore Jesus said again, "I tell you the truth, I am the gate for the sheep. [8]All who ever came before me were thieves and robbers, but the sheep did not listen to them. [9]I am the gate; whoever enters through me will be saved.[a] He will come in and go out, and find pasture. [10]The thief comes only to steal and kill and destroy; I have come that they may have life, and have it to the full.

[11]"I am the good shepherd. The good shepherd lays down his life for the sheep. [12]The hired hand is not the shepherd who owns the sheep. So when he sees the wolf coming, he abandons the sheep and runs away. Then the wolf attacks the flock and scatters it. [13]The man runs away because he is a hired hand and cares nothing for the sheep.

[14]"I am the good shepherd; I know my sheep and my sheep know me— [15]just as the Father knows me and I know the Father—and I lay down my life for the sheep. [16]I have other sheep that are not of this sheep pen. I must bring them also. They too will listen to my voice, and there shall be one flock and one shepherd. [17]The reason my Father loves me is that I lay down my life—only to take it up again. [18]No one takes it from me, but I lay it down of my own accord. I have authority to lay it down and authority to take it up again. This command I received from my Father."

[19]At these words the Jews were again divided. [20]Many of them said, "He is demon-possessed and raving mad. Why listen to him?"

[21]But others said, "These are not the sayings of a man possessed by a demon. Can a demon open the eyes of the blind?"

The Unbelief of the Jews

[22]Then came the Feast of Dedication[b] at Jerusalem. It was winter, [23]and Jesus was in the temple area walking in Solomon's Colonnade. [24]The Jews gathered around him, saying, "How long will you keep us in suspense? If you are the Christ,[c] tell us plainly."

[25]Jesus answered, "I did tell you, but you do not believe. The miracles I do in my Father's name speak for me, [26]but you do not believe because you are not my sheep. [27]My sheep listen to my voice; I know them, and they follow me. [28]I give them eternal life, and they shall never perish; no one can snatch them out of my hand. [29]My Father, who has given them to me, is greater than all[d]; no one can snatch them out of my Father's hand. [30]I and the Father are one."

[31]Again the Jews picked up stones to stone him, [32]but Jesus said to them, "I have shown you many great miracles from the Father. For which of these do you stone me?"

[33]"We are not stoning you for any of these," replied the Jews, "but for blasphemy, because you, a mere man, claim to be God."

[34]Jesus answered them, "Is it not written in your Law, 'I have said you are gods'[e]? [35]If he called them 'gods,' to whom the word of God came—and the Scripture cannot be broken— [36]what about the one whom the Father set apart as his very own and sent into the world? Why then do you accuse me of blasphemy because I said, 'I am God's Son'? [37]Do not believe me unless I do what my Father does. [38]But if I do it, even though you do not believe me, believe the miracles, that you may know and understand that the Father is in me, and I in the Father." [39]Again they tried to seize him, but he escaped their grasp.

[40]Then Jesus went back across the Jordan to the place where John had been baptizing in the early days. Here he stayed [41]and many people came to him. They said, "Though John never performed a miraculous sign, all that John said about

[a]9 Or *kept safe*   [b]22 That is, Hanukkah
[c]24 Or *Messiah*   [d]29 Many early manuscripts
What my Father has given me is greater than all
[e]34 Psalm 82:6

this man was true." ⁴²And in that place many believed in Jesus.

The Death of Lazarus

11 Now a man named Lazarus was sick. He was from Bethany, the village of Mary and her sister Martha. ²This Mary, whose brother Lazarus now lay sick, was the same one who poured perfume on the Lord and wiped his feet with her hair. ³So the sisters sent word to Jesus, "Lord, the one you love is sick."

⁴When he heard this, Jesus said, "This sickness will not end in death. No, it is for God's glory so that God's Son may be glorified through it." ⁵Jesus loved Martha and her sister and Lazarus. ⁶Yet when he heard that Lazarus was sick, he stayed where he was two more days.

⁷Then he said to his disciples, "Let us go back to Judea."

⁸"But Rabbi," they said, "a short while ago the Jews tried to stone you, and yet you are going back there?"

⁹Jesus answered, "Are there not twelve hours of daylight? A man who walks by day will not stumble, for he sees by this world's light. ¹⁰It is when he walks by night that he stumbles, for he has no light."

¹¹After he had said this, he went on to tell them, "Our friend Lazarus has fallen asleep; but I am going there to wake him up."

¹²His disciples replied, "Lord, if he sleeps, he will get better." ¹³Jesus had been speaking of his death, but his disciples thought he meant natural sleep.

¹⁴So then he told them plainly, "Lazarus is dead, ¹⁵and for your sake I am glad I was not there, so that you may believe. But let us go to him."

¹⁶Then Thomas (called Didymus) said to the rest of the disciples, "Let us also go, that we may die with him."

Jesus Comforts the Sisters

¹⁷On his arrival, Jesus found that Lazarus had already been in the tomb for four days. ¹⁸Bethany was less than two miles[a] from Jerusalem, ¹⁹and many Jews had come to Martha and Mary to comfort them in the loss of their brother. ²⁰When Martha heard that Jesus was coming, she

ᵃ18 Greek *fifteen stadia* (about 3 kilometers)

Jesus Wept . . . and So Do I

Thursday

JOHN 11:35 It's the shortest verse in all of Scripture: "Jesus wept." These two words reveal volumes. They tell us that Jesus felt deeply, that his words sometimes failed him, that God values tears. Consider whom God chose to be his spokesperson at the most critical time in Israel's history—Jeremiah, "the weeping prophet!" Jeremiah didn't always have the words to describe his feelings, but his tears often served as his message. He was not ashamed to bury his head in his hands and sob aloud.

Research on crying has shown that tears contain chemicals related to stress. When a person cries, he or she is actually washing away harmful effects of stress. William Fry, in his book *Crying: The Mystery of Tears*, suggests that if women cry more frequently and openly, they may be able to excrete their "stress waste" more readily than men, who are conditioned to block this natural cleansing system.

Whatever the scientists have discovered about crying, God understood in the beginning. How about you? When your words fail, can you let the tears flow? Can you identify with the woman in the opening chapter of Lamentations: "Bitterly she weeps at night, tears are upon her cheeks" (1:2)? Can you identify with the prophet who said, "Streams of tears flow from my eyes because my people are destroyed. My eyes will flow unceasingly, without relief, until the Lord looks down from heaven and sees" (Lamentations 3:48–50)? How about with Jesus as he wept at the death of his friend Lazarus?

—*Les and Leslie*

Go to page 1164 for your next devotional reading.

went out to meet him, but Mary stayed at home.

²¹"Lord," Martha said to Jesus, "if you had been here, my brother would not have died. ²²But I know that even now God will give you whatever you ask."

²³Jesus said to her, "Your brother will rise again."

²⁴Martha answered, "I know he will rise again in the resurrection at the last day."

²⁵Jesus said to her, "I am the resurrection and the life. He who believes in me will live, even though he dies; ²⁶and whoever lives and believes in me will never die. Do you believe this?"

²⁷"Yes, Lord," she told him, "I believe that you are the Christ,ᵃ the Son of God, who was to come into the world."

²⁸And after she had said this, she went back and called her sister Mary aside. "The Teacher is here," she said, "and is asking for you." ²⁹When Mary heard this, she got up quickly and went to him. ³⁰Now Jesus had not yet entered the village, but was still at the place where Martha had met him. ³¹When the Jews who had been with Mary in the house, comforting her, noticed how quickly she got up and went out, they followed her, supposing she was going to the tomb to mourn there.

³²When Mary reached the place where Jesus was and saw him, she fell at his feet and said, "Lord, if you had been here, my brother would not have died."

³³When Jesus saw her weeping, and the Jews who had come along with her also weeping, he was deeply moved in spirit and troubled. ³⁴"Where have you laid him?" he asked.

"Come and see, Lord," they replied.

³⁵Jesus wept.

³⁶Then the Jews said, "See how he loved him!"

³⁷But some of them said, "Could not he who opened the eyes of the blind man have kept this man from dying?"

Jesus Raises Lazarus From the Dead

³⁸Jesus, once more deeply moved, came to the tomb. It was a cave with a stone laid across the entrance. ³⁹"Take away the stone," he said.

"But, Lord," said Martha, the sister of

Jesus Wept . . . and So Do I

Take a moment to answer each of these questions on your own. Then compare your answers to your spouse's.

Yes	No	I believe there is a balance between feeling too much and feeling too little.
Yes	No	Do I feel comfortable crying in front of my spouse?
Yes	No	I know which emotions are most difficult for me to manage.
Yes	No	Sometimes I "read" emotions on my spouse that aren't there.
Yes	No	Do I play a big role in determining how my spouse feels?

the dead man, "by this time there is a bad odor, for he has been there four days."

⁴⁰Then Jesus said, "Did I not tell you that if you believed, you would see the glory of God?"

⁴¹So they took away the stone. Then Jesus looked up and said, "Father, I thank you that you have heard me. ⁴²I knew that you always hear me, but I said this for the benefit of the people standing here, that they may believe that you sent me."

⁴³When he had said this, Jesus called in a loud voice, "Lazarus, come out!" ⁴⁴The dead man came out, his hands and feet wrapped with strips of linen, and a cloth around his face.

Jesus said to them, "Take off the grave clothes and let him go."

The Plot to Kill Jesus

⁴⁵Therefore many of the Jews who had come to visit Mary, and had seen what Jesus did, put their faith in him. ⁴⁶But some of them went to the Pharisees and told them what Jesus had done. ⁴⁷Then the chief priests and the Pharisees called a meeting of the Sanhedrin.

"What are we accomplishing?" they asked. "Here is this man performing many miraculous signs. ⁴⁸If we let him go on like this, everyone will believe in him,

ᵃ27 Or Messiah

and then the Romans will come and take away both our place*a* and our nation."

⁴⁹Then one of them, named Caiaphas, who was high priest that year, spoke up, "You know nothing at all! ⁵⁰You do not realize that it is better for you that one man die for the people than that the whole nation perish."

⁵¹He did not say this on his own, but as high priest that year he prophesied that Jesus would die for the Jewish nation, ⁵²and not only for that nation but also for the scattered children of God, to bring them together and make them one. ⁵³So from that day on they plotted to take his life.

⁵⁴Therefore Jesus no longer moved about publicly among the Jews. Instead he withdrew to a region near the desert, to a village called Ephraim, where he stayed with his disciples.

⁵⁵When it was almost time for the Jewish Passover, many went up from the country to Jerusalem for their ceremonial cleansing before the Passover. ⁵⁶They kept looking for Jesus, and as they stood in the temple area they asked one another, "What do you think? Isn't he coming to the Feast at all?" ⁵⁷But the chief priests and Pharisees had given orders that if anyone found out where Jesus was, he should report it so that they might arrest him.

Jesus Anointed at Bethany

12 Six days before the Passover, Jesus arrived at Bethany, where Lazarus lived, whom Jesus had raised from the dead. ²Here a dinner was given in Jesus' honor. Martha served, while Lazarus was among those reclining at the table with him. ³Then Mary took about a pint*b* of pure nard, an expensive perfume; she poured it on Jesus' feet and wiped his feet with her hair. And the house was filled with the fragrance of the perfume.

⁴But one of his disciples, Judas Iscariot, who was later to betray him, objected, ⁵"Why wasn't this perfume sold and the money given to the poor? It was worth a year's wages.*c*" ⁶He did not say this because he cared about the poor but because he was a thief; as keeper of the money bag, he used to help himself to what was put into it.

⁷"Leave her alone," Jesus replied. "˻It

was intended˼ that she should save this perfume for the day of my burial. ⁸You will always have the poor among you, but you will not always have me."

⁹Meanwhile a large crowd of Jews found out that Jesus was there and came, not only because of him but also to see Lazarus, whom he had raised from the dead. ¹⁰So the chief priests made plans to kill Lazarus as well, ¹¹for on account of him many of the Jews were going over to Jesus and putting their faith in him.

The Triumphal Entry

¹²The next day the great crowd that had come for the Feast heard that Jesus was on his way to Jerusalem. ¹³They took palm branches and went out to meet him, shouting,

"Hosanna!*d*"

"Blessed is he who comes in the
　　name of the Lord!"*e*

"Blessed is the King of Israel!"

¹⁴Jesus found a young donkey and sat upon it, as it is written,

¹⁵"Do not be afraid, O Daughter of
　　Zion;
　　see, your king is coming,
　　　seated on a donkey's colt."*f*

¹⁶At first his disciples did not understand all this. Only after Jesus was glorified did they realize that these things had been written about him and that they had done these things to him.

¹⁷Now the crowd that was with him when he called Lazarus from the tomb and raised him from the dead continued to spread the word. ¹⁸Many people, because they had heard that he had given this miraculous sign, went out to meet him. ¹⁹So the Pharisees said to one another, "See, this is getting us nowhere. Look how the whole world has gone after him!"

Jesus Predicts His Death

²⁰Now there were some Greeks among those who went up to worship at the

---

*a*48 Or *temple*   *b*3 Greek *a litra* (probably about 0.5 liter)   *c*5 Greek *three hundred denarii*
*d*13 A Hebrew expression meaning "Save!" which became an exclamation of praise
*e*13 Psalm 118:25, 26   *f*15 Zech. 9:9

Feast. [21]They came to Philip, who was from Bethsaida in Galilee, with a request. "Sir," they said, "we would like to see Jesus." [22]Philip went to tell Andrew; Andrew and Philip in turn told Jesus.

[23]Jesus replied, "The hour has come for the Son of Man to be glorified. [24]I tell you the truth, unless a kernel of wheat falls to the ground and dies, it remains only a single seed. But if it dies, it produces many seeds. [25]The man who loves his life will lose it, while the man who hates his life in this world will keep it for eternal life. [26]Whoever serves me must follow me; and where I am, my servant also will be. My Father will honor the one who serves me.

[27]"Now my heart is troubled, and what shall I say? 'Father, save me from this hour'? No, it was for this very reason I came to this hour. [28]Father, glorify your name!"

Then a voice came from heaven, "I have glorified it, and will glorify it again." [29]The crowd that was there and heard it said it had thundered; others said an angel had spoken to him.

[30]Jesus said, "This voice was for your benefit, not mine. [31]Now is the time for judgment on this world; now the prince of this world will be driven out. [32]But I, when I am lifted up from the earth, will draw all men to myself." [33]He said this to show the kind of death he was going to die.

[34]The crowd spoke up, "We have heard from the Law that the Christ[a] will remain forever, so how can you say, 'The Son of Man must be lifted up'? Who is this 'Son of Man'?"

[35]Then Jesus told them, "You are going to have the light just a little while longer. Walk while you have the light, before darkness overtakes you. The man who walks in the dark does not know where he is going. [36]Put your trust in the light while you have it, so that you may become sons of light." When he had finished speaking, Jesus left and hid himself from them.

The Jews Continue in Their Unbelief

[37]Even after Jesus had done all these miraculous signs in their presence, they still would not believe in him. [38]This was to fulfill the word of Isaiah the prophet:

"Lord, who has believed our message
and to whom has the arm of the
Lord been revealed?"[b]

[39]For this reason they could not believe, because, as Isaiah says elsewhere:

[40]"He has blinded their eyes
and deadened their hearts,
so they can neither see with their
eyes,
nor understand with their hearts,
nor turn—and I would heal them."[c]

[41]Isaiah said this because he saw Jesus' glory and spoke about him.

[42]Yet at the same time many even among the leaders believed in him. But because of the Pharisees they would not confess their faith for fear they would be put out of the synagogue; [43]for they loved praise from men more than praise from God.

[44]Then Jesus cried out, "When a man believes in me, he does not believe in me only, but in the one who sent me. [45]When he looks at me, he sees the one who sent me. [46]I have come into the world as a light, so that no one who believes in me should stay in darkness.

[47]"As for the person who hears my words but does not keep them, I do not judge him. For I did not come to judge the world, but to save it. [48]There is a judge for the one who rejects me and does not accept my words; that very word which I spoke will condemn him at the last day. [49]For I did not speak of my own accord, but the Father who sent me commanded me what to say and how to say it. [50]I know that his command leads to eternal life. So whatever I say is just what the Father has told me to say."

Jesus Washes His Disciples' Feet

13 It was just before the Passover Feast. Jesus knew that the time had come for him to leave this world and go to the Father. Having loved his own who were in the world, he now showed them the full extent of his love.[d]

[2]The evening meal was being served, and the devil had already prompted Judas

---

[a]34 Or Messiah   [b]38 Isaiah 53:1
[c]40 Isaiah 6:10   [d]1 Or he loved them to the last

Iscariot, son of Simon, to betray Jesus. [3]Jesus knew that the Father had put all things under his power, and that he had come from God and was returning to God; [4]so he got up from the meal, took off his outer clothing, and wrapped a towel around his waist. [5]After that, he poured water into a basin and began to wash his disciples' feet, drying them with the towel that was wrapped around him.

[6]He came to Simon Peter, who said to him, "Lord, are you going to wash my feet?"

[7]Jesus replied, "You do not realize now what I am doing, but later you will understand."

[8]"No," said Peter, "you shall never wash my feet."

Jesus answered, "Unless I wash you, you have no part with me."

[9]"Then, Lord," Simon Peter replied, "not just my feet but my hands and my head as well!"

[10]Jesus answered, "A person who has had a bath needs only to wash his feet; his whole body is clean. And you are clean, though not every one of you." [11]For he knew who was going to betray him, and that was why he said not every one was clean.

[12]When he had finished washing their feet, he put on his clothes and returned to his place. "Do you understand what I have done for you?" he asked them. [13]"You call me 'Teacher' and 'Lord,' and rightly so, for that is what I am. [14]Now that I, your Lord and Teacher, have washed your feet, you also should wash one another's feet. [15]I have set you an example that you should do as I have done for you. [16]I tell you the truth, no servant is greater than his master, nor is a messenger greater than the one who sent him. [17]Now that you know these things, you will be blessed if you do them.

Jesus Predicts His Betrayal

[18]"I am not referring to all of you; I know those I have chosen. But this is to fulfill the scripture: 'He who shares my bread has lifted up his heel against me.'[a]

[19]"I am telling you now before it happens, so that when it does happen you will believe that I am He. [20]I tell you the

[a]18 Psalm 41:9

"Honey, I'll Do the Dishes"

Friday

JOHN 13:1–17 Imagine being present at the Last Supper with Jesus and his disciples. And imagine the disciples' surprise when Jesus poured water into a basin and began to wash their feet.

Would you, like Peter, have protested? Or would you have understood the deeper meaning of Jesus' act of servanthood? In John 13:15, Jesus explained his action when he said, "I have set you an example that you should do as I have done for you."

What a difference it would make in our marriages if we continually had the mindset that we are here to serve each other. Jesus washed the disciples' feet. We just want someone to wash the dishes! If we followed Jesus' example, we would race to see who could first say, "Honey, I'll do the dishes!"

What can you do today to serve your husband or wife? Even without asking, you probably know of a couple of things that your spouse would like you to do that—if you actually took the initiative and did them—would improve your relationship.

At our house Dave is affectionately called "the kitchen elf." In our empty nest we are learning more about serving each other, and we're working harder at sharing tasks and responsibilities. For instance, I cook; Dave does the dishes. Dave usually takes out the trash; I make the bed each morning.

The key is to serve each other—without thought of reward and without keeping score. In the quietness of your devotional time, make a list of ways you can serve your mate. Not only will you follow Jesus' example, but you will also bless your spouse.

—**Dave and Claudia**

Go to page 1166 for your next devotional reading.

truth, whoever accepts anyone I send accepts me; and whoever accepts me accepts the one who sent me."

²¹After he had said this, Jesus was troubled in spirit and testified, "I tell you the truth, one of you is going to betray me."

²²His disciples stared at one another, at a loss to know which of them he meant. ²³One of them, the disciple whom Jesus loved, was reclining next to him. ²⁴Simon Peter motioned to this disciple and said, "Ask him which one he means."

²⁵Leaning back against Jesus, he asked him, "Lord, who is it?"

²⁶Jesus answered, "It is the one to whom I will give this piece of bread when I have dipped it in the dish." Then, dipping the piece of bread, he gave it to Judas Iscariot, son of Simon. ²⁷As soon as Judas took the bread, Satan entered into him.

"What you are about to do, do quickly," Jesus told him, ²⁸but no one at the meal understood why Jesus said this to him. ²⁹Since Judas had charge of the money, some thought Jesus was telling him to buy what was needed for the Feast, or to give something to the poor. ³⁰As soon as Judas had taken the bread, he went out. And it was night.

Jesus Predicts Peter's Denial

³¹When he was gone, Jesus said, "Now is the Son of Man glorified and God is glorified in him. ³²If God is glorified in him,ᵃ God will glorify the Son in himself, and will glorify him at once.

³³"My children, I will be with you only a little longer. You will look for me, and just as I told the Jews, so I tell you now: Where I am going, you cannot come.

³⁴"A new command I give you: Love one another. As I have loved you, so you must love one another. ³⁵By this all men will know that you are my disciples, if you love one another."

³⁶Simon Peter asked him, "Lord, where are you going?"

Jesus replied, "Where I am going, you cannot follow now, but you will follow later."

³⁷Peter asked, "Lord, why can't I follow you now? I will lay down my life for you."

³⁸Then Jesus answered, "Will you really lay down your life for me? I tell you

the truth, before the rooster crows, you will disown me three times!

Jesus Comforts His Disciples

14 "Do not let your hearts be troubled. Trust in God;ᵇ trust also in me. ²In my Father's house are many rooms; if it were not so, I would have told you. I am going there to prepare a place for you. ³And if I go and prepare a place for you, I will come back and take you to be with me that you also may be where I am. ⁴You know the way to the place where I am going."

Jesus the Way to the Father

⁵Thomas said to him, "Lord, we don't know where you are going, so how can we know the way?"

⁶Jesus answered, "I am the way and the truth and the life. No one comes to the Father except through me. ⁷If you really knew me, you would knowᶜ my Father as well. From now on, you do know him and have seen him."

⁸Philip said, "Lord, show us the Father and that will be enough for us."

⁹Jesus answered: "Don't you know me, Philip, even after I have been among you such a long time? Anyone who has seen me has seen the Father. How can you say, 'Show us the Father'? ¹⁰Don't you believe that I am in the Father, and that the Father is in me? The words I say to you are not just my own. Rather, it is the Father, living in me, who is doing his work. ¹¹Believe me when I say that I am in the Father and the Father is in me; or at least believe on the evidence of the miracles themselves. ¹²I tell you the truth, anyone who has faith in me will do what I have been doing. He will do even greater things than these, because I am going to the Father. ¹³And I will do whatever you ask in my name, so that the Son may bring glory to the Father. ¹⁴You may ask me for anything in my name, and I will do it.

Jesus Promises the Holy Spirit

¹⁵"If you love me, you will obey what

ᵃ32 Many early manuscripts do not have *If God is glorified in him.*   ᵇ1 Or *You trust in God*
ᶜ7 Some early manuscripts *If you really have known me, you will know*

I command. [16]And I will ask the Father, and he will give you another Counselor to be with you forever— [17]the Spirit of truth. The world cannot accept him, because it neither sees him nor knows him. But you know him, for he lives with you and will be[a] in you. [18]I will not leave you as orphans; I will come to you. [19]Before long, the world will not see me anymore, but you will see me. Because I live, you also will live. [20]On that day you will realize that I am in my Father, and you are in me, and I am in you. [21]Whoever has my commands and obeys them, he is the one who loves me. He who loves me will be loved by my Father, and I too will love him and show myself to him."

[22]Then Judas (not Judas Iscariot) said, "But, Lord, why do you intend to show yourself to us and not to the world?"

[23]Jesus replied, "If anyone loves me, he will obey my teaching. My Father will love him, and we will come to him and make our home with him. [24]He who does not love me will not obey my teaching. These words you hear are not my own; they belong to the Father who sent me.

[25]"All this I have spoken while still with you. [26]But the Counselor, the Holy Spirit, whom the Father will send in my name, will teach you all things and will remind you of everything I have said to you. [27]Peace I leave with you; my peace I give you. I do not give to you as the world gives. Do not let your hearts be troubled and do not be afraid.

[28]"You heard me say, 'I am going away and I am coming back to you.' If you loved me, you would be glad that I am going to the Father, for the Father is greater than I. [29]I have told you now before it happens, so that when it does happen you will believe. [30]I will not speak with you much longer, for the prince of this world is coming. He has no hold on me, [31]but the world must learn that I love the Father and that I do exactly what my Father has commanded me.

"Come now; let us leave.

[a]17 Some early manuscripts and is

Marriage Tune-ups

Quiet TIMES with each other

JOHN 14:26 Marital therapy, or just plain good counsel from a wise friend or mentor, isn't only for embattled spouses. What used to be a last resort, in fact, is now an increasingly popular option for any state of a marriage. Truth be known, counselors who used to focus exclusively on the make-or-break variety of interventions are now equipping themselves for doing basic marriage tune-ups on successful relationships. And with good reason. There is so much good research and information on marriage that is waiting for real-life couples to put to good use.

But while the stigma of going to counseling is lessening, far too many couples allow pride to stand in the way of receiving a bit of advice. It seems many couples would rather have their teeth cleaned than visit their local marriage counselor. I suppose this shouldn't be too surprising when you consider that therapy demands emotional vulnerability, not to mention admitting that you can't solve every problem by yourself. That's especially difficult for men. After all, men are often taught to repress feelings of hurt, shame or caring. Push a young boy into the playground dirt, and he knows it's his job to come back with a fistful of gravel rather than a face full of tears.

Whatever the aversion to counseling may appear to be, pride is almost always a factor. And that holds true when it comes to seeking help from the ultimate counselor—the Holy Spirit.　　**—Les and Leslie**

Weekend Warm-up　　_Is pride holding back any part of your relationship?_

Go to page 1170 for your next devotional reading.

The Vine and the Branches

15 "I am the true vine, and my Father is the gardener. ²He cuts off every branch in me that bears no fruit, while every branch that does bear fruit he prunes*a* so that it will be even more fruitful. ³You are already clean because of the word I have spoken to you. ⁴Remain in me, and I will remain in you. No branch can bear fruit by itself; it must remain in the vine. Neither can you bear fruit unless you remain in me.

⁵"I am the vine; you are the branches. If a man remains in me and I in him, he will bear much fruit; apart from me you can do nothing. ⁶If anyone does not remain in me, he is like a branch that is thrown away and withers; such branches are picked up, thrown into the fire and burned. ⁷If you remain in me and my words remain in you, ask whatever you wish, and it will be given you. ⁸This is to my Father's glory, that you bear much fruit, showing yourselves to be my disciples.

⁹"As the Father has loved me, so have I loved you. Now remain in my love. ¹⁰If you obey my commands, you will remain in my love, just as I have obeyed my Father's commands and remain in his love. ¹¹I have told you this so that my joy may be in you and that your joy may be complete. ¹²My command is this: Love each other as I have loved you. ¹³Greater love has no one than this, that he lay down his life for his friends. ¹⁴You are my friends if you do what I command. ¹⁵I no longer call you servants, because a servant does not know his master's business. Instead, I have called you friends, for everything that I learned from my Father I have made known to you. ¹⁶You did not choose me, but I chose you and appointed you to go and bear fruit—fruit that will last. Then the Father will give you whatever you ask in my name. ¹⁷This is my command: Love each other.

The World Hates the Disciples

¹⁸"If the world hates you, keep in mind that it hated me first. ¹⁹If you belonged to the world, it would love you as its own. As it is, you do not belong to the world, but I have chosen you out of the world. That is why the world hates you.

²⁰Remember the words I spoke to you: 'No servant is greater than his master.'*b* If they persecuted me, they will persecute you also. If they obeyed my teaching, they will obey yours also. ²¹They will treat you this way because of my name, for they do not know the One who sent me. ²²If I had not come and spoken to them, they would not be guilty of sin. Now, however, they have no excuse for their sin. ²³He who hates me hates my Father as well. ²⁴If I had not done among them what no one else did, they would not be guilty of sin. But now they have seen these miracles, and yet they have hated both me and my Father. ²⁵But this is to fulfill what is written in their Law: 'They hated me without reason.'*c*

²⁶"When the Counselor comes, whom I will send to you from the Father, the Spirit of truth who goes out from the Father, he will testify about me. ²⁷And you also must testify, for you have been with me from the beginning.

16 "All this I have told you so that you will not go astray. ²They will put you out of the synagogue; in fact, a time is coming when anyone who kills you will think he is offering a service to God. ³They will do such things because they have not known the Father or me. ⁴I told you this, so that when the time comes you will remember that I warned you. I did not tell you this at first because I was with you.

The Work of the Holy Spirit

⁵"Now I am going to him who sent me, yet none of you asks me, 'Where are you going?' ⁶Because I have said these things, you are filled with grief. ⁷But I tell you the truth: It is for your good that I am going away. Unless I go away, the Counselor will not come to you; but if I go, I will send him to you. ⁸When he comes, he will convict the world of guilt*d* in regard to sin and righteousness and judgment: ⁹in regard to sin, because men do not believe in me; ¹⁰in regard to righteousness, because I am going to the Father, where you can see me no longer; ¹¹and in regard to judgment, because the

a2 The Greek for *prunes* also means *cleans*.
b20 John 13:16 *c25* Psalms 35:19; 69:4
d8 Or *will expose the guilt of the world*

prince of this world now stands condemned.

12"I have much more to say to you, more than you can now bear. 13But when he, the Spirit of truth, comes, he will guide you into all truth. He will not speak on his own; he will speak only what he hears, and he will tell you what is yet to come. 14He will bring glory to me by taking from what is mine and making it known to you. 15All that belongs to the Father is mine. That is why I said the Spirit will take from what is mine and make it known to you.

16"In a little while you will see me no more, and then after a little while you will see me."

The Disciples' Grief Will Turn to Joy

17Some of his disciples said to one another, "What does he mean by saying, 'In a little while you will see me no more, and then after a little while you will see me,' and 'Because I am going to the Father'?" 18They kept asking, "What does he mean by 'a little while'? We don't understand what he is saying."

19Jesus saw that they wanted to ask him about this, so he said to them, "Are you asking one another what I meant when I said, 'In a little while you will see me no more, and then after a little while you will see me'? 20I tell you the truth, you will weep and mourn while the world rejoices. You will grieve, but your grief will turn to joy. 21A woman giving birth to a child has pain because her time has come; but when her baby is born she forgets the anguish because of her joy that a child is born into the world. 22So with you: Now is your time of grief, but I will see you again and you will rejoice, and no one will take away your joy. 23In that day you will no longer ask me anything. I tell you the truth, my Father will give you whatever you ask in my name. 24Until now you have not asked for anything in my name. Ask and you will receive, and your joy will be complete.

25"Though I have been speaking figuratively, a time is coming when I will no longer use this kind of language but will tell you plainly about my Father. 26In that day you will ask in my name. I am not saying that I will ask the Father on your behalf. 27No, the Father himself loves you because you have loved me and have believed that I came from God. 28I came from the Father and entered the world; now I am leaving the world and going back to the Father."

29Then Jesus' disciples said, "Now you are speaking clearly and without figures of speech. 30Now we can see that you know all things and that you do not even need to have anyone ask you questions. This makes us believe that you came from God."

31"You believe at last!"a Jesus answered. 32"But a time is coming, and has come, when you will be scattered, each to his own home. You will leave me all alone. Yet I am not alone, for my Father is with me.

33"I have told you these things, so that in me you may have peace. In this world you will have trouble. But take heart! I have overcome the world."

Jesus Prays for Himself

17 After Jesus said this, he looked toward heaven and prayed:

"Father, the time has come. Glorify your Son, that your Son may glorify you. 2For you granted him authority over all people that he might give eternal life to all those you have given him. 3Now this is eternal life: that they may know you, the only true God, and Jesus Christ, whom you have sent. 4I have brought you glory on earth by completing the work you gave me to do. 5And now, Father, glorify me in your presence with the glory I had with you before the world began.

Jesus Prays for His Disciples

6"I have revealed youb to those whom you gave me out of the world. They were yours; you gave them to me and they have obeyed your word. 7Now they know that everything you have given me comes from you. 8For I gave them the words you gave me and they accept-

---

a31 Or "Do you now believe?"   b6 Greek your name; also in verse 26 ed them. They knew with certainty that I came from you, and they believed that you sent me. ⁹I pray for them. I am not praying for the world, but for those you have given me, for they are yours. ¹⁰All I have is yours, and all you have is mine. And glory has come to me through them. ¹¹I will remain in the world no longer, but they are still in the world, and I am coming to you. Holy Father, protect them by the power of your name—the name you gave me—so that they may be one as we are one. ¹²While I was with them, I protected them and kept them safe by that name you gave me. None has been lost except the one doomed to destruction so that Scripture would be fulfilled.

¹³"I am coming to you now, but I say these things while I am still in the world, so that they may have the full measure of my joy within them. ¹⁴I have given them your word and the world has hated them, for they are not of the world any more than I am of the world. ¹⁵My prayer is not that you take them out of the world but that you protect them from the evil one. ¹⁶They are not of the world, even as I am not of it. ¹⁷Sanctify*a* them by the truth; your word is truth. ¹⁸As you sent me into the world, I have sent them into the world. ¹⁹For them I sanctify myself, that they too may be truly sanctified.

Jesus Prays for All Believers

²⁰"My prayer is not for them alone. I pray also for those who will believe in me through their message, ²¹that all of them may be one, Father, just as you are in me and I am in you. May they also be in us so that the world may believe that you have sent me. ²²I have given them the glory that you gave me, that they may be one as we are one: ²³I in them and you in me. May they be brought to complete unity to let the world know that you sent me and have loved them even as you have loved me.

²⁴"Father, I want those you have given me to be with me where I am, and to see my glory, the glory you have given me because you loved me before the creation of the world.

²⁵"Righteous Father, though the world does not know you, I know you, and they know that you have sent me. ²⁶I have made you known to them, and will continue to make you known in order that the love you have for me may be in them and that I myself may be in them."

Jesus Arrested

18 When he had finished praying, Jesus left with his disciples and crossed the Kidron Valley. On the other side there was an olive grove, and he and his disciples went into it.

²Now Judas, who betrayed him, knew the place, because Jesus had often met there with his disciples. ³So Judas came to the grove, guiding a detachment of soldiers and some officials from the chief priests and Pharisees. They were carrying torches, lanterns and weapons.

⁴Jesus, knowing all that was going to happen to him, went out and asked them, "Who is it you want?"

⁵"Jesus of Nazareth," they replied.

"I am he," Jesus said. (And Judas the traitor was standing there with them.) ⁶When Jesus said, "I am he," they drew back and fell to the ground.

⁷Again he asked them, "Who is it you want?"

And they said, "Jesus of Nazareth."

⁸"I told you that I am he," Jesus answered. "If you are looking for me, then let these men go." ⁹This happened so that the words he had spoken would be fulfilled: "I have not lost one of those you gave me."*b*

¹⁰Then Simon Peter, who had a sword, drew it and struck the high priest's servant, cutting off his right ear. (The servant's name was Malchus.)

¹¹Jesus commanded Peter, "Put your sword away! Shall I not drink the cup the Father has given me?"

---

a17 Greek *hagiazo (set apart for sacred use* or *make holy);* also in verse 19   *b9* John 6:39

JUST BETWEEN
you & *me*

Witnessing God's Love

In the past week I have:
(Check yes or no to all that apply)

Yes No offered to return the voice mail

Yes No shared the remote

Yes No hung up clothes left on the chair in the bedroom and/or bathroom

Yes No prayed with my spouse

Yes No worshiped with my spouse

Yes No given my mate an honest compliment

Yes No complimented my mate in front of our children

Think of one thing you can do today to show God's love to your spouse.

Jesus Taken to Annas

¹²Then the detachment of soldiers with its commander and the Jewish officials arrested Jesus. They bound him ¹³and brought him first to Annas, who was the father-in-law of Caiaphas, the high priest that year. ¹⁴Caiaphas was the one who had advised the Jews that it would be good if one man died for the people.

Peter's First Denial

¹⁵Simon Peter and another disciple were following Jesus. Because this disciple was known to the high priest, he went with Jesus into the high priest's courtyard, ¹⁶but Peter had to wait outside at the door. The other disciple, who was known to the high priest, came back, spoke to the girl on duty there and brought Peter in.

¹⁷"You are not one of his disciples, are you?" the girl at the door asked Peter.

He replied, "I am not."

¹⁸It was cold, and the servants and officials stood around a fire they had made to keep warm. Peter also was standing with them, warming himself.

The High Priest Questions Jesus

¹⁹Meanwhile, the high priest questioned Jesus about his disciples and his teaching.

²⁰"I have spoken openly to the world," Jesus replied. "I always taught in synagogues or at the temple, where all the Jews come together. I said nothing in secret. ²¹Why question me? Ask those who heard me. Surely they know what I said."

²²When Jesus said this, one of the officials nearby struck him in the face. "Is this the way you answer the high priest?" he demanded.

²³"If I said something wrong," Jesus replied, "testify as to what is wrong. But if

Witnessing God's Love

Monday

JOHN 17:23   Years ago when we served on the staff of Campus Crusade for Christ, we remember being introduced to one of our favorite songs, "They Will Know We Are Christians by Our Love." Hopefully the reality of that song is evident in our lives and ministry today.

Nowhere is it more important to show we are Christians by our love than in our marriages. In this passage, Jesus prays that we will be one and that we will experience spiritual unity so that the world can see, in a tangible way, the outworking of God's love in our lives.

If someone observed the way you relate to your spouse, would they assume that you are a Christian? Think about some of the concrete ways you demonstrate God's love—like making homemade chicken soup for your partner when a cold strikes, or volunteering to be the one to wait up for your teenager to get home.

United in love and grace, you can let those around you know you are Christians by the way you relate to each other. Through your witness perhaps others will be drawn to the ultimate expression of love—God's love.   **—Dave and Claudia**

Go to page 1171 for your next devotional reading.

I spoke the truth, why did you strike me?" [24]Then Annas sent him, still bound, to Caiaphas the high priest.[a]

Peter's Second and Third Denials

[25]As Simon Peter stood warming himself, he was asked, "You are not one of his disciples, are you?"

He denied it, saying, "I am not."

[26]One of the high priest's servants, a relative of the man whose ear Peter had cut off, challenged him, "Didn't I see you with him in the olive grove?" [27]Again Peter denied it, and at that moment a rooster began to crow.

Jesus Before Pilate

[28]Then the Jews led Jesus from Caiaphas to the palace of the Roman governor. By now it was early morning, and to avoid ceremonial uncleanness the Jews did not enter the palace; they wanted to be able to eat the Passover. [29]So Pilate came out to them and asked, "What charges are you bringing against this man?"

[30]"If he were not a criminal," they replied, "we would not have handed him over to you."

[31]Pilate said, "Take him yourselves and judge him by your own law."

"But we have no right to execute anyone," the Jews objected. [32]This happened so that the words Jesus had spoken indicating the kind of death he was going to die would be fulfilled.

[33]Pilate then went back inside the palace, summoned Jesus and asked him, "Are you the king of the Jews?"

[34]"Is that your own idea," Jesus asked, "or did others talk to you about me?"

[35]"Am I a Jew?" Pilate replied. "It was your people and your chief priests who handed you over to me. What is it you have done?"

[36]Jesus said, "My kingdom is not of this world. If it were, my servants would fight to prevent my arrest by the Jews. But now my kingdom is from another place."

[37]"You are a king, then!" said Pilate.

Jesus answered, "You are right in saying I am a king. In fact, for this reason I was born, and for this I came into the world, to testify to the truth. Everyone on the side of truth listens to me."

[38]"What is truth?" Pilate asked. With this he went out again to the Jews and said, "I find no basis for a charge against him. [39]But it is your custom for me to release to you one prisoner at the time of

[a]24 Or (Now Annas had sent him, still bound, to Caiaphas the high priest.)

Denying Christ
Tuesday

JOHN 18:15–17 In this passage of Scripture, we see Peter denying Christ with his words. Unfortunately, there are many ways to deny the Lord. We can deny him with our words, like Peter, or we can deny him through actions or attitudes. Another form of denial is disobedience—not following God's plan for our lives. In his Word God has shown us certain actions and attitudes that we are to exhibit in our marriages. For example, we know that God commands us to be faithful to our marriage vows (see Malachi 2:15 and 1 Corinthians 7:10–11). We are also to love each other sacrificially and unconditionally (see Ephesians 5:22–33). We are to encourage one another (see Hebrews 3:13) and to make the marriage relationship a priority in our lives (see Ephesians 5:31). When we blatantly ignore or disregard God's design for our lives and our marriages, we are, in a sense, denying Christ. We know of the remorse and regret that Peter felt after he verbally denied his Lord. We would feel the same sorrow if we were in a similar situation. We even wonder how Peter could have denied Christ so blatantly. Yet our lack of obedience in the way we handle our marriage is just as much of a denial of Christ's role in our life as our Lord. Through our marriage relationship, we can display our allegiance to him in word, attitude and action.   —*Bob and Rosemary*

Go to page 1173 for your next devotional reading.

the Passover. Do you want me to release 'the king of the Jews'?"

⁴⁰They shouted back, "No, not him! Give us Barabbas!" Now Barabbas had taken part in a rebellion.

Jesus Sentenced to Be Crucified

19 Then Pilate took Jesus and had him flogged. ²The soldiers twisted together a crown of thorns and put it on his head. They clothed him in a purple robe ³and went up to him again and again, saying, "Hail, king of the Jews!" And they struck him in the face.

⁴Once more Pilate came out and said to the Jews, "Look, I am bringing him out to you to let you know that I find no basis for a charge against him." ⁵When Jesus came out wearing the crown of thorns and the purple robe, Pilate said to them, "Here is the man!"

⁶As soon as the chief priests and their officials saw him, they shouted, "Crucify! Crucify!"

But Pilate answered, "You take him and crucify him. As for me, I find no basis for a charge against him."

⁷The Jews insisted, "We have a law, and according to that law he must die, because he claimed to be the Son of God."

⁸When Pilate heard this, he was even more afraid, ⁹and he went back inside the palace. "Where do you come from?" he asked Jesus, but Jesus gave him no answer. ¹⁰"Do you refuse to speak to me?" Pilate said. "Don't you realize I have power either to free you or to crucify you?"

¹¹Jesus answered, "You would have no power over me if it were not given to you from above. Therefore the one who handed me over to you is guilty of a greater sin."

¹²From then on, Pilate tried to set Jesus free, but the Jews kept shouting, "If you let this man go, you are no friend of Caesar. Anyone who claims to be a king opposes Caesar."

¹³When Pilate heard this, he brought Jesus out and sat down on the judge's seat at a place known as the Stone Pavement (which in Aramaic is Gabbatha). ¹⁴It was the day of Preparation of Passover Week, about the sixth hour.

"Here is your king," Pilate said to the Jews.

¹⁵But they shouted, "Take him away! Take him away! Crucify him!"

"Shall I crucify your king?" Pilate asked.

"We have no king but Caesar," the chief priests answered.

¹⁶Finally Pilate handed him over to them to be crucified.

The Crucifixion

So the soldiers took charge of Jesus. ¹⁷Carrying his own cross, he went out to the place of the Skull (which in Aramaic is called Golgotha). ¹⁸Here they crucified him, and with him two others—one on each side and Jesus in the middle.

¹⁹Pilate had a notice prepared and fastened to the cross. It read: JESUS OF NAZARETH, THE KING OF THE JEWS. ²⁰Many of the Jews read this sign, for the place where Jesus was crucified was near the city, and the sign was written in Aramaic, Latin and Greek. ²¹The chief priests of the Jews protested to Pilate, "Do not write 'The King of the Jews,' but that this man claimed to be king of the Jews."

²²Pilate answered, "What I have written, I have written."

²³When the soldiers crucified Jesus, they took his clothes, dividing them into four shares, one for each of them, with the undergarment remaining. This garment was seamless, woven in one piece from top to bottom.

²⁴"Let's not tear it," they said to one another. "Let's decide by lot who will get it."

This happened that the scripture might be fulfilled which said,

"They divided my garments among them
    and cast lots for my clothing." ᵃ

So this is what the soldiers did.

²⁵Near the cross of Jesus stood his mother, his mother's sister, Mary the wife of Clopas, and Mary Magdalene. ²⁶When Jesus saw his mother there, and the disciple whom he loved standing nearby, he said to his mother, "Dear woman, here is your son," ²⁷and to the disciple, "Here is your mother." From that time on, this disciple took her into his home.

ᵃ24 Psalm 22:18

The Death of Jesus

²⁸Later, knowing that all was now completed, and so that the Scripture would be fulfilled, Jesus said, "I am thirsty." ²⁹A jar of wine vinegar was there, so they soaked a sponge in it, put the sponge on a stalk of the hyssop plant, and lifted it to Jesus' lips. ³⁰When he had received the drink, Jesus said, "It is finished." With that, he bowed his head and gave up his spirit.

³¹Now it was the day of Preparation, and the next day was to be a special Sabbath. Because the Jews did not want the bodies left on the crosses during the Sabbath, they asked Pilate to have the legs broken and the bodies taken down. ³²The soldiers therefore came and broke the legs of the first man who had been crucified with Jesus, and then those of the other. ³³But when they came to Jesus and found that he was already dead, they did not break his legs. ³⁴Instead, one of the soldiers pierced Jesus' side with a spear, bringing a sudden flow of blood and water. ³⁵The man who saw it has given testimony, and his testimony is true. He knows that he tells the truth, and he testifies so that you also may believe. ³⁶These things happened so that the scripture would be fulfilled: "Not one of his bones will be broken," ᵃ ³⁷and, as another scripture says, "They will look on the one they have pierced." ᵇ

The Burial of Jesus

³⁸Later, Joseph of Arimathea asked Pilate for the body of Jesus. Now Joseph was a disciple of Jesus, but secretly because he feared the Jews. With Pilate's permission, he came and took the body away. ³⁹He was accompanied by Nicodemus, the man who earlier had visited Jesus at night. Nicodemus brought a mixture of myrrh and aloes, about seventy-five pounds.ᶜ ⁴⁰Taking Jesus' body, the two of them wrapped it, with the spices, in strips of linen. This was in accordance with Jewish burial customs. ⁴¹At the place where Jesus was crucified, there was a garden, and in the garden a new tomb, in which no one had ever been laid. ⁴²Because it was the Jewish day of Preparation and since the tomb was nearby, they laid Jesus there.

ᵃ36 Exodus 12:46; Num. 9:12; Psalm 34:20
ᵇ37 Zech. 12:10   ᶜ39 Greek *a hundred litrai*
(about 34 kilograms)

An Empty Tomb Brings Hope

Wednesday

JOHN 20:1 Easter is the celebration of the most significant event in history and in the life of every Christian. Easter commemorates the victory Jesus Christ won over death. The door of eternity is now open for those who believe in him. However, it's not only assurance for our future; Easter gives us hope for today. Christ's victory over sin on Easter morning gives us hope and power for day-to-day living.

There are times in every marriage when one or both spouses feel distraught, fearful or even hopeless—just as the disciples no doubt felt the day before Easter Sunday morning. We live in turbulent times when changes are all around us. Changes in ourselves, families and in society are a normal part of life. In our modern, mobile society, many of us feel disconnected from people and places that once provided a sense of stability and belonging. All of these things can contribute to a feeling of hopelessness.

Instead of feeling hopeless, we must confidently hope in God and his promises. That is what Easter represents. Through the darkness of fear and uncertainty on Good Friday came the gleam of hope on Easter. God's victorious plan for us in Jesus is a plan for us today. Jeremiah 29:11 (page 832) tells us that God's plan is to prosper us, give us hope and a future. In our moments of despair, our focus needs to be on the One who provides hope for today and triumphant life for tomorrow. The same God who raised Jesus from the grave can bring light and life into our marriage.

—Bob and Rosemary

Go to page 1174 for your next devotional reading.

The Empty Tomb

20 Early on the first day of the week, while it was still dark, Mary Magdalene went to the tomb and saw that the stone had been removed from the entrance. ²So she came running to Simon Peter and the other disciple, the one Jesus loved, and said, "They have taken the Lord out of the tomb, and we don't know where they have put him!"

³So Peter and the other disciple started for the tomb. ⁴Both were running, but the other disciple outran Peter and reached the tomb first. ⁵He bent over and looked in at the strips of linen lying there but did not go in. ⁶Then Simon Peter, who was behind him, arrived and went into the tomb. He saw the strips of linen lying there, ⁷as well as the burial cloth that had been around Jesus' head. The cloth was folded up by itself, separate from the linen. ⁸Finally the other disciple, who had reached the tomb first, also went inside. He saw and believed. ⁹(They still did not understand from Scripture that Jesus had to rise from the dead.)

Jesus Appears to Mary Magdalene

¹⁰Then the disciples went back to their homes, ¹¹but Mary stood outside the tomb crying. As she wept, she bent over to look into the tomb ¹²and saw two angels in white, seated where Jesus' body had been, one at the head and the other at the foot.

¹³They asked her, "Woman, why are you crying?"

"They have taken my Lord away," she said, "and I don't know where they have put him." ¹⁴At this, she turned around and saw Jesus standing there, but she did not realize that it was Jesus.

¹⁵"Woman," he said, "why are you crying? Who is it you are looking for?"

Thinking he was the gardener, she said, "Sir, if you have carried him away, tell me where you have put him, and I will get him."

¹⁶Jesus said to her, "Mary."

She turned toward him and cried out in Aramaic, "Rabboni!" (which means Teacher).

¹⁷Jesus said, "Do not hold on to me,

Catch Anything?

Thursday

JOHN 21:6 Even though they had seen Jesus after the crucifixion, the disciples really didn't know what to do. So they simply did what was familiar—they went fishing. If there is one thing the disciples knew how to do, it was to fish. But on this night they caught nothing.

We can imagine that they were discouraged and tired. Then Jesus, whom they did not recognize, called out to them from the shore and said, "Throw your net on the right side of the boat and you will find some" (verse 6).

Now, if we had been the disciples, we most likely would have been tempted to respond to the stranger, "Give us a break; we're the fishermen; we've fished all night and caught nothing; you don't know what you are talking about!" Yet, the disciples were willing to take this person's advice and try something different. You know the

story. When they threw out their nets once again—this time on the right side—they couldn't haul in the net because it held so many fish.

Maybe it's time to throw your marriage "net" on the other side. All marriages drift from time to time when you just aren't making progress in building your relationship, and you get discouraged and tired. Or maybe you are in a rut of "sameness," and your marriage has become boring. Explore new ways to grow in your relationship. Participate in a marriage seminar, take a course in communication, join a Bible study for couples or plan a getaway for just the two of you. As you step out in faith, Jesus may be standing on the shore, just waiting to bless your marriage with his presence.

—Dave and Claudia

Go to page 1176 for your next devotional reading.

for I have not yet returned to the Father. Go instead to my brothers and tell them, 'I am returning to my Father and your Father, to my God and your God.' "

¹⁸Mary Magdalene went to the disciples with the news: "I have seen the Lord!" And she told them that he had said these things to her.

Jesus Appears to His Disciples

¹⁹On the evening of that first day of the week, when the disciples were together, with the doors locked for fear of the Jews, Jesus came and stood among them and said, "Peace be with you!" ²⁰After he said this, he showed them his hands and side. The disciples were overjoyed when they saw the Lord.

²¹Again Jesus said, "Peace be with you! As the Father has sent me, I am sending you." ²²And with that he breathed on them and said, "Receive the Holy Spirit. ²³If you forgive anyone his sins, they are forgiven; if you do not forgive them, they are not forgiven."

Jesus Appears to Thomas

²⁴Now Thomas (called Didymus), one of the Twelve, was not with the disciples when Jesus came. ²⁵So the other disciples told him, "We have seen the Lord!"

But he said to them, "Unless I see the nail marks in his hands and put my finger where the nails were, and put my hand into his side, I will not believe it."

²⁶A week later his disciples were in the house again, and Thomas was with them. Though the doors were locked, Jesus came and stood among them and said, "Peace be with you!" ²⁷Then he said to Thomas, "Put your finger here; see my hands. Reach out your hand and put it into my side. Stop doubting and believe."

²⁸Thomas said to him, "My Lord and my God!"

²⁹Then Jesus told him, "Because you have seen me, you have believed; blessed are those who have not seen and yet have believed."

³⁰Jesus did many other miraculous signs in the presence of his disciples, which are not recorded in this book. ³¹But these are written that you may[a] believe that Jesus is the Christ, the Son of God,

---

JUST BETWEEN you & me

Catch Anything?

"Nothing ventured, nothing gained" goes the old saying. When applied to marriage, this could mean "Too much sameness, too predictable; no spontaneity, no growth." We grow when we step out of our comfort zone. See how willing you are to venture out. In the following areas, rate yourself on a scale of one to five (one being "very complacent" and five being "very venturesome"):

Sharing chores

Dealing with anger

Building a creative love life

Praying together

Growing spiritually

Managing finances

Parenting your children

Setting goals

Deepening communication

Having fun and building your friendship

Choose one area both of you can agree on and take the risk to venture out together.

---

and that by believing you may have life in his name.

Jesus and the Miraculous Catch of Fish

21 Afterward Jesus appeared again to his disciples, by the Sea of Tiberias.[b] It happened this way: ²Simon Peter, Thomas (called Didymus), Nathanael from Cana in Galilee, the sons of Zebedee, and two other disciples were together. ³"I'm going out to fish," Simon Peter told them, and they said, "We'll go with you." So they went out and got into the boat, but that night they caught nothing.

⁴Early in the morning, Jesus stood on the shore, but the disciples did not realize that it was Jesus.

⁵He called out to them, "Friends, haven't you any fish?"

---

*a31 Some manuscripts *may continue to*   *b1 That is, Sea of Galilee

"No," they answered.

[6]He said, "Throw your net on the right side of the boat and you will find some." When they did, they were unable to haul the net in because of the large number of fish.

[7]Then the disciple whom Jesus loved said to Peter, "It is the Lord!" As soon as Simon Peter heard him say, "It is the Lord," he wrapped his outer garment around him (for he had taken it off) and jumped into the water. [8]The other disciples followed in the boat, towing the net full of fish, for they were not far from shore, about a hundred yards.[a] [9]When they landed, they saw a fire of burning coals there with fish on it, and some bread.

[10]Jesus said to them, "Bring some of the fish you have just caught."

[11]Simon Peter climbed aboard and dragged the net ashore. It was full of large fish, 153, but even with so many the net was not torn. [12]Jesus said to them, "Come and have breakfast." None of the disciples dared ask him, "Who are you?" They knew it was the Lord. [13]Jesus came, took the bread and gave it to them, and did the same with the fish. [14]This was now the third time Jesus appeared to his disciples after he was raised from the dead.

Jesus Reinstates Peter

[15]When they had finished eating, Jesus said to Simon Peter, "Simon son of John, do you truly love me more than these?"

"Yes, Lord," he said, "you know that I love you."

Jesus said, "Feed my lambs."

[16]Again Jesus said, "Simon son of John, do you truly love me?"

He answered, "Yes, Lord, you know that I love you."

Jesus said, "Take care of my sheep."

[17]The third time he said to him, "Simon son of John, do you love me?"

Peter was hurt because Jesus asked him the third time, "Do you love me?" He said, "Lord, you know all things; you know that I love you."

Jesus said, "Feed my sheep. [18]I tell you the truth, when you were younger you dressed yourself and went where you wanted; but when you are old you will stretch out your hands, and someone else

[a]8 Greek *about two hundred cubits* (about 90 meters)

How to Love Jesus

JOHN 21:15 It is one thing to say you love Jesus; it is another thing to express that love by choosing to serve him by serving others. When Jesus appeared to Peter after the resurrection, Peter was given the opportunity of removing the cloud of his triple denial of Jesus. Jesus asked Peter three times if he loved him. Each time Peter responded that he did love Jesus, Peter was instructed to "feed my sheep." Jesus was giving Peter an opportunity to prove his love by being willing to love others.

We each have the opportunity to show our love for Jesus every day. We have an opportunity to care for and love those around us. Sometimes the most difficult people to love and serve are the ones closest to us—like our spouses. We are to "feed" or minister to our spouses. Think through ways to "feed' or minister to your spouse in the name of Jesus. What are some tangible ways to love him or her better? Being everywhere fifteen minutes early seems meaningless to me, but to Bob it's almost the law! Initially I used to balk at it and selfishly refused to be controlled by his temperament. After many arguments over punctuality, I realized this was a "sheep feeding" opportunity. No, it wasn't me caving in to Bob. Choosing to be ready to go places fifteen minutes early was my opportunity to show my love for Jesus Christ. I was feeding one of his very punctual sheep.

Jesus can turn our marital selfishness into selfless love for each other. Do you love Jesus? Then serve each other.

—Bob and Rosemary

Go to page 1179 for your next devotional reading.

will dress you and lead you where you do not want to go." [19]Jesus said this to indicate the kind of death by which Peter would glorify God. Then he said to him, "Follow me!"

[20]Peter turned and saw that the disciple whom Jesus loved was following them. (This was the one who had leaned back against Jesus at the supper and had said, "Lord, who is going to betray you?") [21]When Peter saw him, he asked, "Lord, what about him?"

[22]Jesus answered, "If I want him to remain alive until I return, what is that to you? You must follow me." [23]Because of this, the rumor spread among the brothers that this disciple would not die. But Jesus did not say that he would not die; he only said, "If I want him to remain alive until I return, what is that to you?"

[24]This is the disciple who testifies to these things and who wrote them down. We know that his testimony is true.

[25]Jesus did many other things as well. If every one of them were written down, I suppose that even the whole world would not have room for the books that would be written.

Acts

The book of Acts picks up the story of the embryonic church where the Gospel of Luke ends—with Jesus' ascension. In this book the physician Luke compresses a broad range of information about the development of the church after Jesus' ascension. He begins by telling how Jesus pours out the Holy Spirit on the believers assembled at Jerusalem. The Spirit, in turn, inspires them to spread the message of salvation from Jerusalem to Rome.

In his story Luke stresses how unity and love prevail in the church and how God protects the early believers from their enemies. The book of Acts is much more than an historical account—each chapter is illuminated with the power and grace of the Holy Spirit.

Jesus Taken Up Into Heaven

1 In my former book, Theophilus, I wrote about all that Jesus began to do and to teach ²until the day he was taken up to heaven, after giving instructions through the Holy Spirit to the apostles he had chosen. ³After his suffering, he showed himself to these men and gave many convincing proofs that he was alive. He appeared to them over a period of forty days and spoke about the kingdom of God. ⁴On one occasion, while he was eating with them, he gave them this command: "Do not leave Jerusalem, but wait for the gift my Father promised, which you have heard me speak about. ⁵For John baptized with*ᵃ* water, but in a few days you will be baptized with the Holy Spirit."

⁶So when they met together, they asked him, "Lord, are you at this time going to restore the kingdom to Israel?"

⁷He said to them: "It is not for you to know the times or dates the Father has set by his own authority. ⁸But you will receive power when the Holy Spirit comes on you; and you will be my witnesses in Jerusalem, and in all Judea and Samaria, and to the ends of the earth."

⁹After he said this, he was taken up before their very eyes, and a cloud hid him from their sight.

¹⁰They were looking intently up into

ᵃ5 Or in

the sky as he was going, when suddenly two men dressed in white stood beside them. ¹¹"Men of Galilee," they said, "why do you stand here looking into the sky? This same Jesus, who has been taken from you into heaven, will come back in the same way you have seen him go into heaven."

Matthias Chosen to Replace Judas

¹²Then they returned to Jerusalem from the hill called the Mount of Olives, a Sabbath day's walk*a* from the city. ¹³When they arrived, they went upstairs to the room where they were staying. Those present were Peter, John, James and Andrew; Philip and Thomas, Bartholomew and Matthew; James son of Alphaeus and Simon the Zealot, and Judas son of James. ¹⁴They all joined together constantly in prayer, along with the women and Mary the mother of Jesus, and with his brothers.

¹⁵In those days Peter stood up among the believers*b* (a group numbering about a hundred and twenty) ¹⁶and said,

"Brothers, the Scripture had to be fulfilled which the Holy Spirit spoke long ago through the mouth of David concerning Judas, who served as guide for those who arrested Jesus— ¹⁷he was one of our number and shared in this ministry."

¹⁸(With the reward he got for his wickedness, Judas bought a field; there he fell headlong, his body burst open and all his intestines spilled out. ¹⁹Everyone in Jerusalem heard about this, so they called that field in their language Akeldama, that is, Field of Blood.)

²⁰"For," said Peter, "it is written in the book of Psalms,

" 'May his place be deserted;
    let there be no one to dwell in
        it,'*c*

and,

" 'May another take his place of
    leadership.'*d*

---

a12 That is, about 3/4 mile (about 1,100 meters)
b15 Greek *brothers*   *c20* Psalm 69:25
d20 Psalm 109:8

Too Busy to Pray?

Quiet TIMES *with each other*

ACTS 1:14 Praying together is not easy for us. Oh, we pray as a couple before meals, and we pray together when there is a special need or crisis, but we aren't the kind of couple who kneels beside our bed each night. We might be better persons if we did, but we don't. I suppose we could blame our busy and unpredictable schedules, but the truth is that we just haven't developed the discipline to build a consistent shared prayer time into our lives.

We admire couples who do, and we want the type of rewards they surely reap. For as Jesus has said, " . . . if two of you on earth agree about anything you ask for, it will be done for you by my Father in heaven. For where two or three come together in my name, there am I with them" (Matthew 18:19–20).

Still, one thing we do every day is pray for each other, whether we are together or in separate cities. We made that commitment on our wedding day, and Leslie had the passage from Philippians 1:3–11 engraved inside my wedding band: "I thank my God every time I remember you . . . I always pray with joy because of your partnership in the gospel from the first day until now . . . "

Sometimes one of us will say to the other, "I'll be praying for you today," but most of the time there is just a quiet assurance that we are lifting each other up in prayer.
—Les and Leslie

Weekend Warm-up *What can you offer up for each other in prayer?*

Go to page 1180 for your next devotional reading.

²¹Therefore it is necessary to choose one of the men who have been with us the whole time the Lord Jesus went in and out among us, ²²beginning from John's baptism to the time when Jesus was taken up from us. For one of these must become a witness with us of his resurrection."

²³So they proposed two men: Joseph called Barsabbas (also known as Justus) and Matthias. ²⁴Then they prayed, "Lord, you know everyone's heart. Show us which of these two you have chosen ²⁵to take over this apostolic ministry, which Judas left to go where he belongs." ²⁶Then they cast lots, and the lot fell to Matthias; so he was added to the eleven apostles.

The Holy Spirit Comes at Pentecost

2 When the day of Pentecost came, they were all together in one place. ²Suddenly a sound like the blowing of a violent wind came from heaven and filled the whole house where they were sitting. ³They saw what seemed to be tongues of fire that separated and came to rest on each of them. ⁴All of them were filled with the Holy Spirit and began to speak in other tongues*ᵃ* as the Spirit enabled them.

⁵Now there were staying in Jerusalem God-fearing Jews from every nation under heaven. ⁶When they heard this sound, a crowd came together in bewilderment, because each one heard them speaking in his own language. ⁷Utterly amazed, they asked: "Are not all these men who are speaking Galileans? ⁸Then how is it that each of us hears them in his own native language? ⁹Parthians, Medes and Elamites; residents of Mesopotamia, Judea and Cappadocia, Pontus and Asia, ¹⁰Phrygia and Pamphylia, Egypt and the parts of Libya near Cyrene; visitors from Rome ¹¹(both Jews and converts to Judaism); Cretans and Arabs—we hear them declaring the wonders of God in our own tongues!" ¹²Amazed and perplexed, they asked one another, "What does this mean?"

¹³Some, however, made fun of them and said, "They have had too much wine.*ᵇ*"

Peter Addresses the Crowd

¹⁴Then Peter stood up with the Eleven, raised his voice and addressed the crowd: "Fellow Jews and all of you who live in

---

ᵃ4 Or *languages; also in verse 11*   *ᵇ13* Or *sweet wine*

A Marriage Partnership

Monday

ACTS 2:28 David is a great example of a man who pushed forward on the paths God had put before him. David didn't know the ultimate outcome of his journey. He didn't know all that God was going to do in the future through his lineage. But he did trust that following God would bring ultimate good in his life and the life of his descendants.

Unmentioned in this passage, however, is a behind-the-scenes partner in David's life. Though obviously not a spouse, Nathan fulfilled a pivotal advisory role in David's life. When it came to the building of the temple, David turned to Nathan and asked for his wisdom (see 2 Samuel 7:1–17, page 321). On another occasion, when Nathan wasn't asked for advice, he gave it anyway. Nathan knew David well enough to choose

the right moment to approach his friend about the sin with Bathsheba (see 2 Samuel 12:1–4). David depended on this complementary partner who offered a perspective different from his own.

By design, the marriage relationship offers this same opportunity for privileged advisory partnerships. Sometimes a spouse has to wait until advice is requested. Other times a spouse must prayerfully choose the right time to offer unsolicited input. This kind of partnership was a key to David's success.

A marriage partnership provides us with a spouse who lovingly offers godly input, whether solicited or not, and gives us opportunity to be an advisor too.

—**Bob and Rosemary**

Go to page 1182 for your next devotional reading.

Jerusalem, let me explain this to you; listen carefully to what I say. ¹⁵These men are not drunk, as you suppose. It's only nine in the morning! ¹⁶No, this is what was spoken by the prophet Joel:

¹⁷" 'In the last days, God says,
    I will pour out my Spirit on all
        people.
    Your sons and daughters will
        prophesy,
    your young men will see visions,
    your old men will dream dreams.
¹⁸Even on my servants, both men and
        women,
    I will pour out my Spirit in those
        days,
    and they will prophesy.
¹⁹I will show wonders in the heaven
        above
    and signs on the earth below,
    blood and fire and billows of
        smoke.
²⁰The sun will be turned to darkness
    and the moon to blood
    before the coming of the great and
        glorious day of the Lord.
²¹And everyone who calls
    on the name of the Lord will be
        saved.'ᵃ

²²"Men of Israel, listen to this: Jesus of Nazareth was a man accredited by God to you by miracles, wonders and signs, which God did among you through him, as you yourselves know. ²³This man was handed over to you by God's set purpose and foreknowledge; and you, with the help of wicked men,ᵇ put him to death by nailing him to the cross. ²⁴But God raised him from the dead, freeing him from the agony of death, because it was impossible for death to keep its hold on him. ²⁵David said about him:

" 'I saw the Lord always before me.
    Because he is at my right hand,
    I will not be shaken.
²⁶Therefore my heart is glad and my
        tongue rejoices;
    my body also will live in hope,
²⁷because you will not abandon me to
        the grave,
    nor will you let your Holy One see
        decay.
²⁸You have made known to me the
        paths of life;

A Marriage Partnership

Take a moment to answer each of these questions on your own. Then compare your answers to your spouse's.

Yes No I have found the balance of making my spouse feel loved by me and yet helping my spouse see an alternative viewpoint.

Yes No I have learned the time when my spouse is the most receptive to hearing that he or she might be wrong in a point of view.

Yes No My spouse and I have talked about and set up a game plan for offering this kind of difficult advice.

Yes No I might not like showing my spouse an alternative viewpoint that differs from his or hers, but I know it's my responsibility as a loving marriage partner.

---

    you will fill me with joy in your
        presence.'ᶜ

²⁹"Brothers, I can tell you confidently that the patriarch David died and was buried, and his tomb is here to this day. ³⁰But he was a prophet and knew that God had promised him on oath that he would place one of his descendants on his throne. ³¹Seeing what was ahead, he spoke of the resurrection of the Christ,ᵈ that he was not abandoned to the grave, nor did his body see decay. ³²God has raised this Jesus to life, and we are all witnesses of the fact. ³³Exalted to the right hand of God, he has received from the Father the promised Holy Spirit and has poured out what you now see and hear. ³⁴For David did not ascend to heaven, and yet he said,

" 'The Lord said to my Lord:
    "Sit at my right hand

ᵃ21 Joel 2:28-32   ᵇ23 Or *of those not having the law* (that is, Gentiles)   ᶜ28 Psalm 16:8-11
ᵈ31 Or *Messiah.* "The Christ" (Greek) and "the Messiah" (Hebrew) both mean "the Anointed One"; also in verse 36.

³⁵until I make your enemies
  a footstool for your feet." ᵃ

³⁶"Therefore let all Israel be assured of this: God has made this Jesus, whom you crucified, both Lord and Christ."

³⁷When the people heard this, they were cut to the heart and said to Peter and the other apostles, "Brothers, what shall we do?"

³⁸Peter replied, "Repent and be baptized, every one of you, in the name of Jesus Christ for the forgiveness of your sins. And you will receive the gift of the Holy Spirit. ³⁹The promise is for you and your children and for all who are far off— for all whom the Lord our God will call."

⁴⁰With many other words he warned them; and he pleaded with them, "Save yourselves from this corrupt generation." ⁴¹Those who accepted his message were baptized, and about three thousand were added to their number that day.

The Fellowship of the Believers

⁴²They devoted themselves to the apostles' teaching and to the fellowship, to the breaking of bread and to prayer. ⁴³Everyone was filled with awe, and many wonders and miraculous signs were done by the apostles. ⁴⁴All the believers were together and had everything in common. ⁴⁵Selling their possessions and goods, they gave to anyone as he had need. ⁴⁶Every day they continued to meet together in the temple courts. They broke bread in their homes and ate together with glad and sincere hearts, ⁴⁷praising God and enjoying the favor of all the people. And the Lord added to their number daily those who were being saved.

Peter Heals the Crippled Beggar

3 One day Peter and John were going up to the temple at the time of prayer—at three in the afternoon. ²Now a man crippled from birth was being carried to the temple gate called Beautiful, where he was put every day to beg from those going into the temple courts. ³When he saw Peter and John about to enter, he asked them for money. ⁴Peter

ᵃ35 Psalm 110:1

Becoming a Church "Family"

Tuesday

ACTS 2:42–47 A young woman approached me (Rosemary) at a conference and made an interesting comment. She said, "I am a new believer and need some direction. My husband and I both grew up in very dysfunctional homes, and I deeply desire to have a Christian one. But I don't even know where to begin. If only there was a way I could be a 'bug on the wall' and watch how a healthy Christian home functions. If I could watch how a husband and wife interact with one another in a godly way and see how the children fit in, I would have an idea of what to do."

The church family portrayed in Acts 2 would have provided for this young woman what she was seeking. This passage describes a church where people loved each other and shared all they had. Our churches are meant to be more than places where believers gather to worship. They can and should be our "families." Rather than leave the church building on Sundays, never to see each other again for a week, we too should be breaking bread together in our homes . . . like a big family. If one of us has a need, such as being a single mom, the church family should reach out to that person.

Our church families can be the parents, grandparents, siblings, aunts and uncles we need. In such a setting, a new believer can observe families functioning, not perfectly, but with the desire to honor God in their relationships. Broken, hurting families or single parent families can be integrated into family groups so they feel less isolated. There has never been a more important time for the church to be a functional family, a place where all hurting families can fellowship, break bread together and pray (see verse 42).

—Bob and Rosemary

Go to page 1184 for your next devotional reading.

looked straight at him, as did John. Then Peter said, "Look at us!" ⁵So the man gave them his attention, expecting to get something from them.

⁶Then Peter said, "Silver or gold I do not have, but what I have I give you. In the name of Jesus Christ of Nazareth, walk." ⁷Taking him by the right hand, he helped him up, and instantly the man's feet and ankles became strong. ⁸He jumped to his feet and began to walk. Then he went with them into the temple courts, walking and jumping, and praising God. ⁹When all the people saw him walking and praising God, ¹⁰they recognized him as the same man who used to sit begging at the temple gate called Beautiful, and they were filled with wonder and amazement at what had happened to him.

Peter Speaks to the Onlookers

¹¹While the beggar held on to Peter and John, all the people were astonished and came running to them in the place called Solomon's Colonnade. ¹²When Peter saw this, he said to them: "Men of Israel, why does this surprise you? Why do you stare at us as if by our own power or godliness we had made this man walk? ¹³The God of Abraham, Isaac and Jacob, the God of our fathers, has glorified his servant Jesus. You handed him over to be killed, and you disowned him before Pilate, though he had decided to let him go. ¹⁴You disowned the Holy and Righteous One and asked that a murderer be released to you. ¹⁵You killed the author of life, but God raised him from the dead. We are witnesses of this. ¹⁶By faith in the name of Jesus, this man whom you see and know was made strong. It is Jesus' name and the faith that comes through him that has given this complete healing to him, as you can all see.

¹⁷"Now, brothers, I know that you acted in ignorance, as did your leaders. ¹⁸But this is how God fulfilled what he had foretold through all the prophets, saying that his Christ[a] would suffer. ¹⁹Repent, then, and turn to God, so that your sins may be wiped out, that times of refreshing may come from the Lord, ²⁰and that he may send the Christ, who has been appointed for you—even Jesus. ²¹He must remain in heaven until the time comes for God to restore everything, as he promised long ago through his holy prophets. ²²For Moses said, 'The Lord your God will raise up for you a prophet like me from among your own people; you must listen to everything he tells you. ²³Anyone who does not listen to him will be completely cut off from among his people.'[b]

²⁴"Indeed, all the prophets from Samuel on, as many as have spoken, have foretold these days. ²⁵And you are heirs of the prophets and of the covenant God made with your fathers. He said to Abraham, 'Through your offspring all peoples on earth will be blessed.'[c] ²⁶When God raised up his servant, he sent him first to you to bless you by turning each of you from your wicked ways."

Peter and John Before the Sanhedrin

4 The priests and the captain of the temple guard and the Sadducees came up to Peter and John while they were speaking to the people. ²They were greatly disturbed because the apostles were teaching the people and proclaiming in Jesus the resurrection of the dead. ³They seized Peter and John, and because it was evening, they put them in jail until the next day. ⁴But many who heard the message believed, and the number of men grew to about five thousand.

⁵The next day the rulers, elders and teachers of the law met in Jerusalem. ⁶Annas the high priest was there, and so were Caiaphas, John, Alexander and the other men of the high priest's family. ⁷They had Peter and John brought before them and began to question them: "By what power or what name did you do this?"

⁸Then Peter, filled with the Holy Spirit, said to them: "Rulers and elders of the people! ⁹If we are being called to account today for an act of kindness shown to a cripple and are asked how he was healed, ¹⁰then know this, you and all the people of Israel: It is by the name of Jesus Christ of Nazareth, whom you crucified but whom God raised from the dead, that this man stands before you healed. ¹¹He is

" 'the stone you builders rejected,

---

a18 Or *Messiah*; also in verse 20
b23 Deut. 18:15,18,19   c25 Gen. 22:18; 26:4

which has become the
capstone.*a' b*

¹²Salvation is found in no one else, for there is no other name under heaven given to men by which we must be saved."

¹³When they saw the courage of Peter and John and realized that they were unschooled, ordinary men, they were astonished and they took note that these men had been with Jesus. ¹⁴But since they could see the man who had been healed standing there with them, there was nothing they could say. ¹⁵So they ordered them to withdraw from the Sanhedrin and then conferred together. ¹⁶"What are we going to do with these men?" they asked. "Everybody living in Jerusalem knows they have done an outstanding miracle, and we cannot deny it. ¹⁷But to stop this thing from spreading any further among the people, we must warn these men to speak no longer to anyone in this name."

¹⁸Then they called them in again and commanded them not to speak or teach at all in the name of Jesus. ¹⁹But Peter and John replied, "Judge for yourselves whether it is right in God's sight to obey you rather than God. ²⁰For we cannot help speaking about what we have seen and heard."

²¹After further threats they let them go. They could not decide how to punish them, because all the people were praising God for what had happened. ²²For the man who was miraculously healed was over forty years old.

The Believers' Prayer

²³On their release, Peter and John went back to their own people and reported all that the chief priests and elders had said to them. ²⁴When they heard this, they raised their voices together in prayer to God. "Sovereign Lord," they said, "you made the heaven and the earth and the sea, and everything in them. ²⁵You spoke by the Holy Spirit through the mouth of your servant, our father David:

" 'Why do the nations rage
    and the peoples plot in vain?
²⁶The kings of the earth take their stand
    and the rulers gather together
against the Lord
    and against his Anointed One.*c' d*

a 11 Or *cornerstone*　　*b 11* Psalm 118:22
c 26 That is, Christ or Messiah　　*d 26* Psalm 2:1,2

The Capstone

Wednesday

ACTS 4:11 One of the primary purposes of a capstone is to serve as an intersection. The capstone of a building is placed at the point where two walls intersect, binding them together. Another function is to commemorate origin. A capstone of a cornerstone is ceremoniously installed at the grand opening of the building.

What or who is the capstone of your marriage? What are you using to bind you and your spouse together into a strong unity? There is nothing that can more effectively bind two very different people together than the capstone mentioned in this passage: Jesus Christ. Nothing else—no career, living situation, financial condition, number of children or anything—can permanently bind a marriage together.

There is only this one true capstone of Jesus Christ.

A building might have an electronic billboard on the front, drawing people's attention with its continually changing message. But the inscription on the capstone is permanent. Similarly a marriage might be blessed with many exciting things that draw the admiration of onlookers, but these things aren't permanent; they come and go. The marriage needs to be built on a rock-solid faith in Jesus Christ. This permanent capstone will bind two people together and keep them focused on the vows they took at the "grand opening" of their marriage. Perhaps it is time to take a look at the capstone upon which your marriage is built. **—Bob and Rosemary**

Go to page 1185 for your next devotional reading.

²⁷Indeed Herod and Pontius Pilate met together with the Gentiles and the people*ᵃ* of Israel in this city to conspire against your holy servant Jesus, whom you anointed. ²⁸They did what your power and will had decided beforehand should happen. ²⁹Now, Lord, consider their threats and enable your servants to speak your word with great boldness. ³⁰Stretch out your hand to heal and perform miraculous signs and wonders through the name of your holy servant Jesus."

³¹After they prayed, the place where they were meeting was shaken. And they were all filled with the Holy Spirit and spoke the word of God boldly.

The Believers Share Their Possessions

³²All the believers were one in heart and mind. No one claimed that any of his possessions was his own, but they shared everything they had. ³³With great power the apostles continued to testify to the resurrection of the Lord Jesus, and much grace was upon them all. ³⁴There were no needy persons among them. For from time to time those who owned lands or houses sold them, brought the money from the sales ³⁵and put it at the apostles' feet, and it was distributed to anyone as he had need.

³⁶Joseph, a Levite from Cyprus, whom the apostles called Barnabas (which means Son of Encouragement), ³⁷sold a field he owned and brought the money and put it at the apostles' feet.

Ananias and Sapphira

5 Now a man named Ananias, together with his wife Sapphira, also sold a piece of property. ²With his wife's full knowledge he kept back part of the money for himself, but brought the rest and put it at the apostles' feet.

³Then Peter said, "Ananias, how is it that Satan has so filled your heart that you have lied to the Holy Spirit and have kept for yourself some of the money you received for the land? ⁴Didn't it belong to you before it was sold? And after it was sold, wasn't the money at your disposal? What made you think of doing such a thing? You have not lied to men but to God."

⁵When Ananias heard this, he fell down and died. And great fear seized all who heard what had happened. ⁶Then the young men came forward, wrapped up his body, and carried him out and buried him.

⁷About three hours later his wife came in, not knowing what had happened. ⁸Peter asked her, "Tell me, is this the price you and Ananias got for the land?"

"Yes," she said, "that is the price."

ᵃ27 The Greek is plural.

Dying for a Lie

Thursday

ACTS 5:1–11 Family businesses can be positive or negative experiences. For Ananias and Sapphira, it was deadly. They agreed to lie to the church about the purchase price of a piece of property. The issue wasn't what they did with their profit—they gave most of the money to the church—but that together they lied about it.

Ananias and Sapphira died because they lied. Certainly hypocrisy and deception are sinful and destructive, but who of us would be left if God were to strike dead everyone who misrepresented the truth? While this seemingly bizarre event does not appear to represent the norm even in the early church, it can be a warning for us today.

Be willing to challenge your marriage partner if he or she asks you to do something illegal or unethical. While we are to defer and submit to one another, there are limits. God never calls us to sin. There will be times when we slip, make unwise choices and sin anyway. But God's grace is abundant, and he will forgive us if we repent. But think twice before you get involved in a shady real estate deal!

—*Dave and Claudia*

Go to page 1191 for your next devotional reading.

Ananias and Sapphira

ACTS 5:1-11   Dishonesty forces a heavy decision upon a marriage. For example, if one spouse lies about the condition of their house when talking to a prospective buyer, this leaves the other spouse with a very difficult decision. Should they perpetuate their spouse's sin by backing up the story?

COUPLES IN THE BIBLE

We don't know all the details of the Ananias and Sapphira story found in Acts 5, but we do know it was tragic. Being a woman at that time, it is not likely that the wife took part in the transaction of their land sale. So we can surmise that the husband sold the property and convinced his wife to go along with the lie. In verse 9, Peter asks her how she could agree to go along with it.

When her husband asked her to perpetuate his sin, Sapphira had to choose. Had she refused to go along with his lie, had she confronted him in the sin, he might not have been struck dead. Jointly perpetuating sin resulted in death.

When our spouse sins, we need to love him or her enough to refuse to go along with it. It just might save our spouse and our marriage.

⁹Peter said to her, "How could you agree to test the Spirit of the Lord? Look! The feet of the men who buried your husband are at the door, and they will carry you out also."

¹⁰At that moment she fell down at his feet and died. Then the young men came in and, finding her dead, carried her out and buried her beside her husband. ¹¹Great fear seized the whole church and all who heard about these events.

The Apostles Heal Many

¹²The apostles performed many miraculous signs and wonders among the people. And all the believers used to meet together in Solomon's Colonnade. ¹³No one else dared join them, even though they were highly regarded by the people. ¹⁴Nevertheless, more and more men and women believed in the Lord and were added to their number. ¹⁵As a result, people brought the sick into the streets and laid them on beds and mats so that at least Peter's shadow might fall on some of them as he passed by. ¹⁶Crowds gathered also from the towns around Jerusalem, bringing their sick and those tormented by evil*ᵃ* spirits, and all of them were healed.

The Apostles Persecuted

¹⁷Then the high priest and all his associates, who were members of the party of the Sadducees, were filled with jealousy. ¹⁸They arrested the apostles and put them in the public jail. ¹⁹But during the night an angel of the Lord opened the doors of the jail and brought them out. ²⁰"Go, stand in the temple courts," he said, "and tell the people the full message of this new life."

²¹At daybreak they entered the temple courts, as they had been told, and began to teach the people.

When the high priest and his associates arrived, they called together the Sanhedrin—the full assembly of the elders of Israel—and sent to the jail for the apostles. ²²But on arriving at the jail, the officers did not find them there. So they went back and reported, ²³"We found the jail securely locked, with the guards standing at the doors; but when we opened them, we found no one inside." ²⁴On hearing this report, the captain of the temple guard and the chief priests were puzzled, wondering what would come of this.

²⁵Then someone came and said, "Look! The men you put in jail are standing in the temple courts teaching the people." ²⁶At that, the captain went with his officers and brought the apostles. They did not use force, because they feared that the people would stone them.

²⁷Having brought the apostles, they made them appear before the Sanhedrin to be questioned by the high priest. ²⁸"We gave you strict orders not to teach in this name," he said. "Yet you have filled Jerusalem with your teaching and are determined to make us guilty of this man's blood."

²⁹Peter and the other apostles replied: "We must obey God rather than men!

ᵃ16 Greek *unclean*

30The God of our fathers raised Jesus from the dead—whom you had killed by hanging him on a tree. 31God exalted him to his own right hand as Prince and Savior that he might give repentance and forgiveness of sins to Israel. 32We are witnesses of these things, and so is the Holy Spirit, whom God has given to those who obey him."

33When they heard this, they were furious and wanted to put them to death. 34But a Pharisee named Gamaliel, a teacher of the law, who was honored by all the people, stood up in the Sanhedrin and ordered that the men be put outside for a little while. 35Then he addressed them: "Men of Israel, consider carefully what you intend to do to these men. 36Some time ago Theudas appeared, claiming to be somebody, and about four hundred men rallied to him. He was killed, all his followers were dispersed, and it all came to nothing. 37After him, Judas the Galilean appeared in the days of the census and led a band of people in revolt. He too was killed, and all his followers were scattered. 38Therefore, in the present case I advise you: Leave these men alone! Let them go! For if their purpose or activity is of human origin, it will fail. 39But if it is from God, you will not be able to stop these men; you will only find yourselves fighting against God."

40His speech persuaded them. They called the apostles in and had them flogged. Then they ordered them not to speak in the name of Jesus, and let them go.

41The apostles left the Sanhedrin, rejoicing because they had been counted worthy of suffering disgrace for the Name. 42Day after day, in the temple courts and from house to house, they never stopped teaching and proclaiming the good news that Jesus is the Christ. [a]

The Choosing of the Seven

6 In those days when the number of disciples was increasing, the Grecian Jews among them complained against the Hebraic Jews because their widows were being overlooked in the daily distribution of food. 2So the Twelve gathered all the disciples together and said, "It would not be right for us to neglect the ministry of the word of God in order to wait on tables. 3Brothers, choose seven men from among you who are known to be full of the Spirit and wisdom. We will turn this responsibility over to them 4and will give our attention to prayer and the ministry of the word."

5This proposal pleased the whole group. They chose Stephen, a man full of faith and of the Holy Spirit; also Philip, Procorus, Nicanor, Timon, Parmenas, and Nicolas from Antioch, a convert to Judaism. 6They presented these men to the apostles, who prayed and laid their hands on them.

7So the word of God spread. The number of disciples in Jerusalem increased rapidly, and a large number of priests became obedient to the faith.

Stephen Seized

8Now Stephen, a man full of God's grace and power, did great wonders and miraculous signs among the people. 9Opposition arose, however, from members of the Synagogue of the Freedmen (as it was called)—Jews of Cyrene and Alexandria as well as the provinces of Cilicia and Asia. These men began to argue with Stephen, 10but they could not stand up against his wisdom or the Spirit by whom he spoke.

11Then they secretly persuaded some men to say, "We have heard Stephen speak words of blasphemy against Moses and against God."

12So they stirred up the people and the elders and the teachers of the law. They seized Stephen and brought him before the Sanhedrin. 13They produced false witnesses, who testified, "This fellow never stops speaking against this holy place and against the law. 14For we have heard him say that this Jesus of Nazareth will destroy this place and change the customs Moses handed down to us."

15All who were sitting in the Sanhedrin looked intently at Stephen, and they saw that his face was like the face of an angel.

Stephen's Speech to the Sanhedrin

7 Then the high priest asked him, "Are these charges true?"

a42 Or Messiah

²To this he replied: "Brothers and fathers, listen to me! The God of glory appeared to our father Abraham while he was still in Mesopotamia, before he lived in Haran. ³'Leave your country and your people,' God said, 'and go to the land I will show you.'ᵃ

⁴"So he left the land of the Chaldeans and settled in Haran. After the death of his father, God sent him to this land where you are now living. ⁵He gave him no inheritance here, not even a foot of ground. But God promised him that he and his descendants after him would possess the land, even though at that time Abraham had no child. ⁶God spoke to him in this way: 'Your descendants will be strangers in a country not their own, and they will be enslaved and mistreated four hundred years. ⁷But I will punish the nation they serve as slaves,' God said, 'and afterward they will come out of that country and worship me in this place.'ᵇ ⁸Then he gave Abraham the covenant of circumcision. And Abraham became the father of Isaac and circumcised him eight days after his birth. Later Isaac became the father of Jacob, and Jacob became the father of the twelve patriarchs.

⁹"Because the patriarchs were jealous of Joseph, they sold him as a slave into Egypt. But God was with him ¹⁰and rescued him from all his troubles. He gave Joseph wisdom and enabled him to gain the goodwill of Pharaoh king of Egypt; so he made him ruler over Egypt and all his palace.

¹¹"Then a famine struck all Egypt and Canaan, bringing great suffering, and our fathers could not find food. ¹²When Jacob heard that there was grain in Egypt, he sent our fathers on their first visit. ¹³On their second visit, Joseph told his brothers who he was, and Pharaoh learned about Joseph's family. ¹⁴After this, Joseph sent for his father Jacob and his whole family, seventy-five in all. ¹⁵Then Jacob went down to Egypt, where he and our fathers died. ¹⁶Their bodies were brought back to Shechem and placed in the tomb that Abraham had bought from the sons of Hamor at Shechem for a certain sum of money.

¹⁷"As the time drew near for God to fulfill his promise to Abraham, the num-ber of our people in Egypt greatly increased. ¹⁸Then another king, who knew nothing about Joseph, became ruler of Egypt. ¹⁹He dealt treacherously with our people and oppressed our forefathers by forcing them to throw out their newborn babies so that they would die.

²⁰"At that time Moses was born, and he was no ordinary child.ᶜ For three months he was cared for in his father's house. ²¹When he was placed outside, Pharaoh's daughter took him and brought him up as her own son. ²²Moses was educated in all the wisdom of the Egyptians and was powerful in speech and action.

²³"When Moses was forty years old, he decided to visit his fellow Israelites. ²⁴He saw one of them being mistreated by an Egyptian, so he went to his defense and avenged him by killing the Egyptian. ²⁵Moses thought that his own people would realize that God was using him to rescue them, but they did not. ²⁶The next day Moses came upon two Israelites who were fighting. He tried to reconcile them by saying, 'Men, you are brothers; why do you want to hurt each other?'

²⁷"But the man who was mistreating the other pushed Moses aside and said, 'Who made you ruler and judge over us? ²⁸Do you want to kill me as you killed the Egyptian yesterday?'ᵈ ²⁹When Moses heard this, he fled to Midian, where he settled as a foreigner and had two sons.

³⁰"After forty years had passed, an angel appeared to Moses in the flames of a burning bush in the desert near Mount Sinai. ³¹When he saw this, he was amazed at the sight. As he went over to look more closely, he heard the Lord's voice: ³²'I am the God of your fathers, the God of Abraham, Isaac and Jacob.'ᵉ Moses trembled with fear and did not dare to look.

³³"Then the Lord said to him, 'Take off your sandals; the place where you are standing is holy ground. ³⁴I have indeed seen the oppression of my people in Egypt. I have heard their groaning and have come down to set them free. Now come, I will send you back to Egypt.'ᶠ

³⁵"This is the same Moses whom they had rejected with the words, 'Who made

ᵃ3 Gen. 12:1   ᵇ7 Gen. 15:13,14   ᶜ20 Or *was fair in the sight of God*   ᵈ28 Exodus 2:14
ᵉ32 Exodus 3:6   ᶠ34 Exodus 3:5,7,8,10

you ruler and judge?' He was sent to be their ruler and deliverer by God himself, through the angel who appeared to him in the bush. 36He led them out of Egypt and did wonders and miraculous signs in Egypt, at the Red Sea*a* and for forty years in the desert.

37"This is that Moses who told the Israelites, 'God will send you a prophet like me from your own people.'*b* 38He was in the assembly in the desert, with the angel who spoke to him on Mount Sinai, and with our fathers; and he received living words to pass on to us.

39"But our fathers refused to obey him. Instead, they rejected him and in their hearts turned back to Egypt. 40They told Aaron, 'Make us gods who will go before us. As for this fellow Moses who led us out of Egypt—we don't know what has happened to him!'*c* 41That was the time they made an idol in the form of a calf. They brought sacrifices to it and held a celebration in honor of what their hands had made. 42But God turned away and gave them over to the worship of the heavenly bodies. This agrees with what is written in the book of the prophets:

" 'Did you bring me sacrifices and
        offerings
    forty years in the desert, O house
        of Israel?
43You have lifted up the shrine of
        Molech
    and the star of your god Rephan,
        the idols you made to worship.
Therefore I will send you into exile'*d*
        beyond Babylon.

44"Our forefathers had the tabernacle of the Testimony with them in the desert. It had been made as God directed Moses, according to the pattern he had seen. 45Having received the tabernacle, our fathers under Joshua brought it with them when they took the land from the nations God drove out before them. It remained in the land until the time of David, 46who enjoyed God's favor and asked that he might provide a dwelling place for the God of Jacob.*e* 47But it was Solomon who built the house for him.

48"However, the Most High does not live in houses made by men. As the prophet says:

49" 'Heaven is my throne,
        and the earth is my footstool.
    What kind of house will you build
        for me?
                    says the Lord.
    Or where will my resting place be?
50Has not my hand made all these
        things?'*f*

51"You stiff-necked people, with uncircumcised hearts and ears! You are just like your fathers: You always resist the Holy Spirit! 52Was there ever a prophet your fathers did not persecute? They even killed those who predicted the coming of the Righteous One. And now you have betrayed and murdered him— 53you who have received the law that was put into effect through angels but have not obeyed it."

The Stoning of Stephen

54When they heard this, they were furious and gnashed their teeth at him. 55But Stephen, full of the Holy Spirit, looked up to heaven and saw the glory of God, and Jesus standing at the right hand of God. 56"Look," he said, "I see heaven open and the Son of Man standing at the right hand of God."

57At this they covered their ears and, yelling at the top of their voices, they all rushed at him, 58dragged him out of the city and began to stone him. Meanwhile, the witnesses laid their clothes at the feet of a young man named Saul.

59While they were stoning him, Stephen prayed, "Lord Jesus, receive my spirit." 60Then he fell on his knees and cried out, "Lord, do not hold this sin against them." When he had said this, he fell asleep.

8 And Saul was there, giving approval to his death.

The Church Persecuted and Scattered

On that day a great persecution broke out against the church at Jerusalem, and all except the apostles were scattered throughout Judea and Samaria. 2Godly men buried Stephen and mourned deeply

*a*36 That is, Sea of Reeds   *b*37 Deut. 18:15
*c*40 Exodus 32:1   *d*43 Amos 5:25-27
*e*46 Some early manuscripts *the house of Jacob*
*f*50 Isaiah 66:1,2

for him. ³But Saul began to destroy the church. Going from house to house, he dragged off men and women and put them in prison.

Philip in Samaria

⁴Those who had been scattered preached the word wherever they went. ⁵Philip went down to a city in Samaria and proclaimed the Christ*a* there. ⁶When the crowds heard Philip and saw the miraculous signs he did, they all paid close attention to what he said. ⁷With shrieks, evil*b* spirits came out of many, and many paralytics and cripples were healed. ⁸So there was great joy in that city.

Simon the Sorcerer

⁹Now for some time a man named Simon had practiced sorcery in the city and amazed all the people of Samaria. He boasted that he was someone great, ¹⁰and all the people, both high and low, gave him their attention and exclaimed, "This man is the divine power known as the Great Power." ¹¹They followed him because he had amazed them for a long time with his magic. ¹²But when they believed Philip as he preached the good news of the kingdom of God and the name of Jesus Christ, they were baptized, both men and women. ¹³Simon himself believed and was baptized. And he followed Philip everywhere, astonished by the great signs and miracles he saw.

¹⁴When the apostles in Jerusalem heard that Samaria had accepted the word of God, they sent Peter and John to them. ¹⁵When they arrived, they prayed for them that they might receive the Holy Spirit, ¹⁶because the Holy Spirit had not yet come upon any of them; they had simply been baptized into*c* the name of the Lord Jesus. ¹⁷Then Peter and John placed their hands on them, and they received the Holy Spirit.

¹⁸When Simon saw that the Spirit was given at the laying on of the apostles' hands, he offered them money ¹⁹and said, "Give me also this ability so that everyone on whom I lay my hands may receive the Holy Spirit."

²⁰Peter answered: "May your money perish with you, because you thought you could buy the gift of God with money!

²¹You have no part or share in this ministry, because your heart is not right before God. ²²Repent of this wickedness and pray to the Lord. Perhaps he will forgive you for having such a thought in your heart. ²³For I see that you are full of bitterness and captive to sin."

²⁴Then Simon answered, "Pray to the Lord for me so that nothing you have said may happen to me."

²⁵When they had testified and proclaimed the word of the Lord, Peter and John returned to Jerusalem, preaching the gospel in many Samaritan villages.

Philip and the Ethiopian

²⁶Now an angel of the Lord said to Philip, "Go south to the road—the desert road—that goes down from Jerusalem to Gaza." ²⁷So he started out, and on his way he met an Ethiopian*d* eunuch, an important official in charge of all the treasury of Candace, queen of the Ethiopians. This man had gone to Jerusalem to worship, ²⁸and on his way home was sitting in his chariot reading the book of Isaiah the prophet. ²⁹The Spirit told Philip, "Go to that chariot and stay near it."

³⁰Then Philip ran up to the chariot and heard the man reading Isaiah the prophet. "Do you understand what you are reading?" Philip asked.

³¹"How can I," he said, "unless someone explains it to me?" So he invited Philip to come up and sit with him.

³²The eunuch was reading this passage of Scripture:

"He was led like a sheep to the
          slaughter,
     and as a lamb before the shearer is
          silent,
     so he did not open his mouth.
³³In his humiliation he was deprived of
          justice.
     Who can speak of his descendants?
     For his life was taken from the
          earth."*e*

³⁴The eunuch asked Philip, "Tell me, please, who is the prophet talking about, himself or someone else?" ³⁵Then Philip began with that very passage of Scripture

---

a5 Or *Messiah*   *b7* Greek *unclean*   *c16* Or *in*
d27 That is, from the upper Nile region
e33 Isaiah 53:7,8

and told him the good news about Jesus. ³⁶As they traveled along the road, they came to some water and the eunuch said, "Look, here is water. Why shouldn't I be baptized?"ᵃ ³⁸And he gave orders to stop the chariot. Then both Philip and the eunuch went down into the water and Philip baptized him. ³⁹When they came up out of the water, the Spirit of the Lord suddenly took Philip away, and the eunuch did not see him again, but went on his way rejoicing. ⁴⁰Philip, however, appeared at Azotus and traveled about, preaching the gospel in all the towns until he reached Caesarea.

Saul's Conversion

9 Meanwhile, Saul was still breathing out murderous threats against the Lord's disciples. He went to the high priest ²and asked him for letters to the synagogues in Damascus, so that if he found any there who belonged to the Way, whether men or women, he might take them as prisoners to Jerusalem. ³As he neared Damascus on his journey, suddenly a light from heaven flashed around him. ⁴He fell to the ground and heard a voice say to him, "Saul, Saul, why do you persecute me?"

⁵"Who are you, Lord?" Saul asked.

"I am Jesus, whom you are persecuting," he replied. ⁶"Now get up and go into the city, and you will be told what you must do."

⁷The men traveling with Saul stood there speechless; they heard the sound but did not see anyone. ⁸Saul got up from the ground, but when he opened his eyes he could see nothing. So they led him by the hand into Damascus. ⁹For three days he was blind, and did not eat or drink anything.

¹⁰In Damascus there was a disciple named Ananias. The Lord called to him in a vision, "Ananias!"

"Yes, Lord," he answered.

¹¹The Lord told him, "Go to the house of Judas on Straight Street and ask for a man from Tarsus named Saul, for he is praying. ¹²In a vision he has seen a man named Ananias come and place his hands on him to restore his sight."

¹³"Lord," Ananias answered, "I have heard many reports about this man and all the harm he has done to your saints in Jerusalem. ¹⁴And he has come here with

ᵃ36 Some late manuscripts *baptized?" 37Philip said, "If you believe with all your heart, you may."* The eunuch answered, *"I believe that Jesus Christ is the Son of God."*

Never Give Up Hope

Friday

ACTS 9 The shock of Saul's conversion caught many by surprise. After all the negative things believers had heard about Saul, his would have been the last conversion they expected. Many spouses find themselves in a similar situation. Perhaps one spouse becomes a Christian after marriage, but the other shows absolutely no inclination to do the same. In fact, like Saul, this spouse even exhibits hostility toward the gospel.

I (Bob) am living proof that you can never give up on anyone. Having never been in church, I was about as far away from Christ as I could be. Then in college I met a girl who was a Christian. She began sharing about her faith. I listened, but only to gain her attention. After several months of her sharing with me, I invited her to listen to a lecture by America's leading atheist. It was a lecture that I had looked forward to because it was titled "Why Atheism Makes Sense." As I listened to the talk, I realized that none of it made any sense at all. In the middle of the lecture, I got up and asked the girl I had invited to leave the auditorium with me.

We sat together on a bench outside the building, and, to her astonishment, I asked her to lead me to Christ. Five years later that young lady became my wife. Never give up hope and never stop praying for someone. You might be about to witness an astonishing "Damascus Road" conversion.
        —Bob and Rosemary

Go to page 1193 for your next devotional reading.

authority from the chief priests to arrest all who call on your name."

[15]But the Lord said to Ananias, "Go! This man is my chosen instrument to carry my name before the Gentiles and their kings and before the people of Israel. [16]I will show him how much he must suffer for my name."

[17]Then Ananias went to the house and entered it. Placing his hands on Saul, he said, "Brother Saul, the Lord—Jesus, who appeared to you on the road as you were coming here—has sent me so that you may see again and be filled with the Holy Spirit." [18]Immediately, something like scales fell from Saul's eyes, and he could see again. He got up and was baptized, [19]and after taking some food, he regained his strength.

Saul in Damascus and Jerusalem

Saul spent several days with the disciples in Damascus. [20]At once he began to preach in the synagogues that Jesus is the Son of God. [21]All those who heard him were astonished and asked, "Isn't he the man who raised havoc in Jerusalem among those who call on this name? And hasn't he come here to take them as prisoners to the chief priests?" [22]Yet Saul grew more and more powerful and baffled the Jews living in Damascus by proving that Jesus is the Christ.[a]

[23]After many days had gone by, the Jews conspired to kill him, [24]but Saul learned of their plan. Day and night they kept close watch on the city gates in order to kill him. [25]But his followers took him by night and lowered him in a basket through an opening in the wall.

[26]When he came to Jerusalem, he tried to join the disciples, but they were all afraid of him, not believing that he really was a disciple. [27]But Barnabas took him and brought him to the apostles. He told them how Saul on his journey had seen the Lord and that the Lord had spoken to him, and how in Damascus he had preached fearlessly in the name of Jesus. [28]So Saul stayed with them and moved about freely in Jerusalem, speaking boldly in the name of the Lord. [29]He talked and debated with the Grecian Jews, but they tried to kill him. [30]When the brothers

learned of this, they took him down to Caesarea and sent him off to Tarsus.

[31]Then the church throughout Judea, Galilee and Samaria enjoyed a time of peace. It was strengthened; and encouraged by the Holy Spirit, it grew in numbers, living in the fear of the Lord.

Aeneas and Dorcas

[32]As Peter traveled about the country, he went to visit the saints in Lydda. [33]There he found a man named Aeneas, a paralytic who had been bedridden for eight years. [34]"Aeneas," Peter said to him, "Jesus Christ heals you. Get up and take care of your mat." Immediately Aeneas got up. [35]All those who lived in Lydda and Sharon saw him and turned to the Lord.

[36]In Joppa there was a disciple named Tabitha (which, when translated, is Dorcas[b]), who was always doing good and helping the poor. [37]About that time she became sick and died, and her body was washed and placed in an upstairs room. [38]Lydda was near Joppa; so when the disciples heard that Peter was in Lydda, they sent two men to him and urged him, "Please come at once!"

[39]Peter went with them, and when he arrived he was taken upstairs to the room. All the widows stood around him, crying and showing him the robes and other clothing that Dorcas had made while she was still with them.

[40]Peter sent them all out of the room; then he got down on his knees and prayed. Turning toward the dead woman, he said, "Tabitha, get up." She opened her eyes, and seeing Peter she sat up. [41]He took her by the hand and helped her to her feet. Then he called the believers and the widows and presented her to them alive. [42]This became known all over Joppa, and many people believed in the Lord. [43]Peter stayed in Joppa for some time with a tanner named Simon.

Cornelius Calls for Peter

10 At Caesarea there was a man named Cornelius, a centurion in what was known as the Italian Regiment. [2]He and all his family were devout and God-fearing; he gave generously to those in

---

[a]22 Or *Messiah*   [b]36 Both *Tabitha* (Aramaic) and *Dorcas* (Greek) mean *gazelle.*

need and prayed to God regularly. ³One day at about three in the afternoon he had a vision. He distinctly saw an angel of God, who came to him and said, "Cornelius!"

⁴Cornelius stared at him in fear. "What is it, Lord?" he asked.

The angel answered, "Your prayers and gifts to the poor have come up as a memorial offering before God. ⁵Now send men to Joppa to bring back a man named Simon who is called Peter. ⁶He is staying with Simon the tanner, whose house is by the sea."

⁷When the angel who spoke to him had gone, Cornelius called two of his servants and a devout soldier who was one of his attendants. ⁸He told them everything that had happened and sent them to Joppa.

Peter's Vision

⁹About noon the following day as they were on their journey and approaching the city, Peter went up on the roof to pray. ¹⁰He became hungry and wanted something to eat, and while the meal was being prepared, he fell into a trance. ¹¹He saw heaven opened and something like a large sheet being let down to earth by its four corners. ¹²It contained all kinds of four-footed animals, as well as reptiles of the earth and birds of the air. ¹³Then a voice told him, "Get up, Peter. Kill and eat."

¹⁴"Surely not, Lord!" Peter replied. "I have never eaten anything impure or unclean."

¹⁵The voice spoke to him a second time, "Do not call anything impure that God has made clean."

¹⁶This happened three times, and immediately the sheet was taken back to heaven.

¹⁷While Peter was wondering about the meaning of the vision, the men sent by Cornelius found out where Simon's

Your Marriage Vision

Quiet TIMES with each other

ACTS 10 Cornelius was a devout, generous, God-fearing Italian centurion. He prayed regularly, and one day in the form of a vision, God dramatically answered his prayer. God used Cornelius to adopt a new paradigm so he could help Peter bring the good news of the gospel to the world. What if Peter had been unwilling to step out of his comfort zone?

Many times in our marriage, we notice that it's when we are willing to step out of our comfort zone and take an honest look at our marriage that we experience God's richest blessings. But it isn't easy. Today couples have greater expectations for their marriage. And with each new season of marriage come challenges to change and grow together—especially in the second half of marriage.

The challenge of building a deeper and more personal long-term marriage relationship could be compared to the challenge pilots faced when the aeronautics industry switched from piston-engine planes to jet-engine planes. The new planes were superior and could fly higher and faster, but they were more complicated to fly.

Similarly, marriage today is more complicated than in the past. Our culture does not tend to support the institution of marriage, and couples who want a "jet-engine marriage" need to first get off the ground by learning better relationship skills. Are you willing to learn how to communicate on a deeper level? Pray, and God can answer your deep longings for your marriage. He can send the help you need in order to love and glorify him—especially in your marriage.   **—Dave and Claudia**

Weekend Warm-up   *What is your comfort zone?*

Go to page 1196 for your next devotional reading.

house was and stopped at the gate. [18]They called out, asking if Simon who was known as Peter was staying there.

[19]While Peter was still thinking about the vision, the Spirit said to him, "Simon, three[a] men are looking for you. [20]So get up and go downstairs. Do not hesitate to go with them, for I have sent them."

[21]Peter went down and said to the men, "I'm the one you're looking for. Why have you come?"

[22]The men replied, "We have come from Cornelius the centurion. He is a righteous and God-fearing man, who is respected by all the Jewish people. A holy angel told him to have you come to his house so that he could hear what you have to say." [23]Then Peter invited the men into the house to be his guests.

Peter at Cornelius's House

The next day Peter started out with them, and some of the brothers from Joppa went along. [24]The following day he arrived in Caesarea. Cornelius was expecting them and had called together his relatives and close friends. [25]As Peter entered the house, Cornelius met him and fell at his feet in reverence. [26]But Peter made him get up. "Stand up," he said, "I am only a man myself."

[27]Talking with him, Peter went inside and found a large gathering of people. [28]He said to them: "You are well aware that it is against our law for a Jew to associate with a Gentile or visit him. But God has shown me that I should not call any man impure or unclean. [29]So when I was sent for, I came without raising any objection. May I ask why you sent for me?"

[30]Cornelius answered: "Four days ago I was in my house praying at this hour, at three in the afternoon. Suddenly a man in shining clothes stood before me [31]and said, 'Cornelius, God has heard your prayer and remembered your gifts to the poor. [32]Send to Joppa for Simon who is called Peter. He is a guest in the home of Simon the tanner, who lives by the sea.' [33]So I sent for you immediately, and it was good of you to come. Now we are all here in the presence of God to listen to everything the Lord has commanded you to tell us."

[34]Then Peter began to speak: "I now realize how true it is that God does not show favoritism [35]but accepts men from every nation who fear him and do what is right. [36]You know the message God sent to the people of Israel, telling the good news of peace through Jesus Christ, who is Lord of all. [37]You know what has happened throughout Judea, beginning in Galilee after the baptism that John preached— [38]how God anointed Jesus of Nazareth with the Holy Spirit and power, and how he went around doing good and healing all who were under the power of the devil, because God was with him.

[39]"We are witnesses of everything he did in the country of the Jews and in Jerusalem. They killed him by hanging him on a tree, [40]but God raised him from the dead on the third day and caused him to be seen. [41]He was not seen by all the people, but by witnesses whom God had already chosen—by us who ate and drank with him after he rose from the dead. [42]He commanded us to preach to the people and to testify that he is the one whom God appointed as judge of the living and the dead. [43]All the prophets testify about him that everyone who believes in him receives forgiveness of sins through his name."

[44]While Peter was still speaking these words, the Holy Spirit came on all who heard the message. [45]The circumcised believers who had come with Peter were astonished that the gift of the Holy Spirit had been poured out even on the Gentiles. [46]For they heard them speaking in tongues[b] and praising God.

Then Peter said, [47]"Can anyone keep these people from being baptized with water? They have received the Holy Spirit just as we have." [48]So he ordered that they be baptized in the name of Jesus Christ. Then they asked Peter to stay with them for a few days.

Peter Explains His Actions

11 The apostles and the brothers throughout Judea heard that the Gentiles also had received the word of God. [2]So when Peter went up to Jerusalem, the circumcised believers criticized

---

[a]19 One early manuscript *two*; other manuscripts do not have the number.   [b]46 Or *other languages*

him ³and said, "You went into the house of uncircumcised men and ate with them."

⁴Peter began and explained everything to them precisely as it had happened: ⁵"I was in the city of Joppa praying, and in a trance I saw a vision. I saw something like a large sheet being let down from heaven by its four corners, and it came down to where I was. ⁶I looked into it and saw four-footed animals of the earth, wild beasts, reptiles, and birds of the air. ⁷Then I heard a voice telling me, 'Get up, Peter. Kill and eat.'

⁸"I replied, 'Surely not, Lord! Nothing impure or unclean has ever entered my mouth.'

⁹"The voice spoke from heaven a second time, 'Do not call anything impure that God has made clean.' ¹⁰This happened three times, and then it was all pulled up to heaven again.

¹¹"Right then three men who had been sent to me from Caesarea stopped at the house where I was staying. ¹²The Spirit told me to have no hesitation about going with them. These six brothers also went with me, and we entered the man's house. ¹³He told us how he had seen an angel appear in his house and say, 'Send to Joppa for Simon who is called Peter. ¹⁴He will bring you a message through which you and all your household will be saved.'

¹⁵"As I began to speak, the Holy Spirit came on them as he had come on us at the beginning. ¹⁶Then I remembered what the Lord had said: 'John baptized with*a* water, but you will be baptized with the Holy Spirit.' ¹⁷So if God gave them the same gift as he gave us, who believed in the Lord Jesus Christ, who was I to think that I could oppose God?"

¹⁸When they heard this, they had no further objections and praised God, saying, "So then, God has granted even the Gentiles repentance unto life."

The Church in Antioch

¹⁹Now those who had been scattered by the persecution in connection with Stephen traveled as far as Phoenicia, Cyprus and Antioch, telling the message only to Jews. ²⁰Some of them, however, men from Cyprus and Cyrene, went to Antioch and began to speak to Greeks

also, telling them the good news about the Lord Jesus. ²¹The Lord's hand was with them, and a great number of people believed and turned to the Lord.

²²News of this reached the ears of the church at Jerusalem, and they sent Barnabas to Antioch. ²³When he arrived and saw the evidence of the grace of God, he was glad and encouraged them all to remain true to the Lord with all their hearts. ²⁴He was a good man, full of the Holy Spirit and faith, and a great number of people were brought to the Lord.

²⁵Then Barnabas went to Tarsus to look for Saul, ²⁶and when he found him, he brought him to Antioch. So for a whole year Barnabas and Saul met with the church and taught great numbers of people. The disciples were called Christians first at Antioch.

²⁷During this time some prophets came down from Jerusalem to Antioch. ²⁸One of them, named Agabus, stood up and through the Spirit predicted that a severe famine would spread over the entire Roman world. (This happened during the reign of Claudius.) ²⁹The disciples, each according to his ability, decided to provide help for the brothers living in Judea. ³⁰This they did, sending their gift to the elders by Barnabas and Saul.

Peter's Miraculous Escape From Prison

12 It was about this time that King Herod arrested some who belonged to the church, intending to persecute them. ²He had James, the brother of John, put to death with the sword. ³When he saw that this pleased the Jews, he proceeded to seize Peter also. This happened during the Feast of Unleavened Bread. ⁴After arresting him, he put him in prison, handing him over to be guarded by four squads of four soldiers each. Herod intended to bring him out for public trial after the Passover.

⁵So Peter was kept in prison, but the church was earnestly praying to God for him.

⁶The night before Herod was to bring him to trial, Peter was sleeping between two soldiers, bound with two chains, and sentries stood guard at the entrance. ⁷Sud-

a16 Or in

denly an angel of the Lord appeared and a light shone in the cell. He struck Peter on the side and woke him up. "Quick, get up!" he said, and the chains fell off Peter's wrists.

[8]Then the angel said to him, "Put on your clothes and sandals." And Peter did so. "Wrap your cloak around you and follow me," the angel told him. [9]Peter followed him out of the prison, but he had no idea that what the angel was doing was really happening; he thought he was seeing a vision. [10]They passed the first and second guards and came to the iron gate leading to the city. It opened for them by itself, and they went through it. When they had walked the length of one street, suddenly the angel left him.

[11]Then Peter came to himself and said, "Now I know without a doubt that the Lord sent his angel and rescued me from Herod's clutches and from everything the Jewish people were anticipating."

[12]When this had dawned on him, he went to the house of Mary the mother of John, also called Mark, where many people had gathered and were praying. [13]Peter knocked at the outer entrance, and a servant girl named Rhoda came to answer the door. [14]When she recognized Peter's voice, she was so overjoyed she ran back without opening it and exclaimed, "Peter is at the door!"

[15]"You're out of your mind," they told her. When she kept insisting that it was so, they said, "It must be his angel."

[16]But Peter kept on knocking, and when they opened the door and saw him, they were astonished. [17]Peter motioned with his hand for them to be quiet and described how the Lord had brought him out of prison. "Tell James and the brothers about this," he said, and then he left for another place.

[18]In the morning, there was no small commotion among the soldiers as to what had become of Peter. [19]After Herod had a thorough search made for him and did not find him, he cross-examined the guards and ordered that they be executed.

Herod's Death

Then Herod went from Judea to Caesarea and stayed there a while. [20]He had been quarreling with the people of Tyre and Sidon; they now joined together and sought an audience with him. Having secured the support of Blastus, a trusted personal servant of the king, they asked for peace, because they depended on the king's country for their food supply.

[21]On the appointed day Herod, wear-

Surprise!

Monday

ACTS 12 Have you ever prayed for something and then been surprised when God answered? That certainly happened to the disciples in Acts 12 when they prayed that Peter would be let out of prison. Suddenly, there he was at their doorstep! They literally didn't believe it. Before you are too critical of their lack of faith, ask yourself, "Would I be surprised if God answered my prayers?"

Sarah was. For a long time, she had been concerned about her relationship with John. The transition into the empty nest had not been an easy one, and she had often prayed that God would do something. Then one day when Sarah and John were talking about what they really wanted for the rest of their lives, John surprised her by saying,

"Sarah, I want our marriage to be better!"

Like the disciples, Sarah had to get over disbelief and realize that God indeed answers prayers—sometimes suddenly! This man who, in the past, had wanted freedom and space in their relationship, was now saying he wanted intimacy. John followed his declaration with a commitment to do whatever it took to build a closer relationship with his wife. And over the next ten years, through God's help and much hard work, John and Sarah achieved the emotional closeness Sarah had prayed for.

Is God knocking at the door of your marriage? Why not open the door and let him in?   —*Dave and Claudia*

Go to page 1201 for your next devotional reading.

ing his royal robes, sat on his throne and delivered a public address to the people. 22They shouted, "This is the voice of a god, not of a man." 23Immediately, because Herod did not give praise to God, an angel of the Lord struck him down, and he was eaten by worms and died.

24But the word of God continued to increase and spread.

25When Barnabas and Saul had finished their mission, they returned from[a] Jerusalem, taking with them John, also called Mark.

Barnabas and Saul Sent Off

13 In the church at Antioch there were prophets and teachers: Barnabas, Simeon called Niger, Lucius of Cyrene, Manaen (who had been brought up with Herod the tetrarch) and Saul. 2While they were worshiping the Lord and fasting, the Holy Spirit said, "Set apart for me Barnabas and Saul for the work to which I have called them." 3So after they had fasted and prayed, they placed their hands on them and sent them off.

On Cyprus

4The two of them, sent on their way by the Holy Spirit, went down to Seleucia and sailed from there to Cyprus. 5When they arrived at Salamis, they proclaimed the word of God in the Jewish synagogues. John was with them as their helper.

6They traveled through the whole island until they came to Paphos. There they met a Jewish sorcerer and false prophet named Bar-Jesus, 7who was an attendant of the proconsul, Sergius Paulus. The proconsul, an intelligent man, sent for Barnabas and Saul because he wanted to hear the word of God. 8But Elymas the sorcerer (for that is what his name means) opposed them and tried to turn the proconsul from the faith. 9Then Saul, who was also called Paul, filled with the Holy Spirit, looked straight at Elymas and said, 10"You are a child of the devil and an enemy of everything that is right! You are full of all kinds of deceit and trickery. Will you never stop perverting the right ways of the Lord? 11Now the hand of the Lord is against you. You are

going to be blind, and for a time you will be unable to see the light of the sun."

Immediately mist and darkness came over him, and he groped about, seeking someone to lead him by the hand. 12When the proconsul saw what had happened, he believed, for he was amazed at the teaching about the Lord.

In Pisidian Antioch

13From Paphos, Paul and his companions sailed to Perga in Pamphylia, where John left them to return to Jerusalem. 14From Perga they went on to Pisidian Antioch. On the Sabbath they entered the synagogue and sat down. 15After the reading from the Law and the Prophets, the synagogue rulers sent word to them, saying, "Brothers, if you have a message of encouragement for the people, please speak."

16Standing up, Paul motioned with his hand and said: "Men of Israel and you Gentiles who worship God, listen to me! 17The God of the people of Israel chose our fathers; he made the people prosper during their stay in Egypt, with mighty power he led them out of that country, 18he endured their conduct[b] for about forty years in the desert, 19he overthrew seven nations in Canaan and gave their land to his people as their inheritance. 20All this took about 450 years.

"After this, God gave them judges until the time of Samuel the prophet. 21Then the people asked for a king, and he gave them Saul son of Kish, of the tribe of Benjamin, who ruled forty years. 22After removing Saul, he made David their king. He testified concerning him: 'I have found David son of Jesse a man after my own heart; he will do everything I want him to do.'

23"From this man's descendants God has brought to Israel the Savior Jesus, as he promised. 24Before the coming of Jesus, John preached repentance and baptism to all the people of Israel. 25As John was completing his work, he said: 'Who do you think I am? I am not that one. No, but he is coming after me, whose sandals I am not worthy to untie.'

26"Brothers, children of Abraham, and

---

a25 Some manuscripts to   b18 Some manuscripts and cared for them you God-fearing Gentiles, it is to us that this message of salvation has been sent. [27]The people of Jerusalem and their rulers did not recognize Jesus, yet in condemning him they fulfilled the words of the prophets that are read every Sabbath. [28]Though they found no proper ground for a death sentence, they asked Pilate to have him executed. [29]When they had carried out all that was written about him, they took him down from the tree and laid him in a tomb. [30]But God raised him from the dead, [31]and for many days he was seen by those who had traveled with him from Galilee to Jerusalem. They are now his witnesses to our people.

[32]"We tell you the good news: What God promised our fathers [33]he has fulfilled for us, their children, by raising up Jesus. As it is written in the second Psalm:

" 'You are my Son;
    today I have become your
       Father.[a][b]

[34]The fact that God raised him from the dead, never to decay, is stated in these words:

" 'I will give you the holy and sure
      blessings promised to
      David.'[c]

[35]So it is stated elsewhere:

" 'You will not let your Holy One see
      decay.'[d]

[36]"For when David had served God's purpose in his own generation, he fell asleep; he was buried with his fathers and his body decayed. [37]But the one whom God raised from the dead did not see decay.

[38]"Therefore, my brothers, I want you to know that through Jesus the forgiveness of sins is proclaimed to you. [39]Through him everyone who believes is justified from everything you could not be justified from by the law of Moses. [40]Take care that what the prophets have said does not happen to you:

[41]" 'Look, you scoffers,
    wonder and perish,
  for I am going to do something in
      your days
    that you would never believe,
      even if someone told you.'[e] "

[42]As Paul and Barnabas were leaving the synagogue, the people invited them to speak further about these things on the next Sabbath. [43]When the congregation was dismissed, many of the Jews and devout converts to Judaism followed Paul and Barnabas, who talked with them and urged them to continue in the grace of God.

[44]On the next Sabbath almost the whole city gathered to hear the word of the Lord. [45]When the Jews saw the crowds, they were filled with jealousy and talked abusively against what Paul was saying.

[46]Then Paul and Barnabas answered them boldly: "We had to speak the word of God to you first. Since you reject it and do not consider yourselves worthy of eternal life, we now turn to the Gentiles. [47]For this is what the Lord has commanded us:

" 'I have made you[f] a light for the
      Gentiles,
    that you[f] may bring salvation to
      the ends of the earth.'[g] "

[48]When the Gentiles heard this, they were glad and honored the word of the Lord; and all who were appointed for eternal life believed.

[49]The word of the Lord spread through the whole region. [50]But the Jews incited the God-fearing women of high standing and the leading men of the city. They stirred up persecution against Paul and Barnabas, and expelled them from their region. [51]So they shook the dust from their feet in protest against them and went to Iconium. [52]And the disciples were filled with joy and with the Holy Spirit.

In Iconium

14 At Iconium Paul and Barnabas went as usual into the Jewish synagogue. There they spoke so effectively that a great number of Jews and Gentiles believed. [2]But the Jews who refused to believe stirred up the Gentiles and poisoned their minds against the brothers. [3]So Paul and Barnabas spent considerable time there, speaking boldly for the Lord, who con-

[a]33   Or *have begotten you*   [b]33   Psalm 2:7
[c]34   Isaiah 55:3   [d]35   Psalm 16:10
[e]41   Hab. 1:5   [f]47   The Greek is singular.
[g]47   Isaiah 49:6

firmed the message of his grace by enabling them to do miraculous signs and wonders. [4]The people of the city were divided; some sided with the Jews, others with the apostles. [5]There was a plot afoot among the Gentiles and Jews, together with their leaders, to mistreat them and stone them. [6]But they found out about it and fled to the Lycaonian cities of Lystra and Derbe and to the surrounding country, [7]where they continued to preach the good news.

In Lystra and Derbe

[8]In Lystra there sat a man crippled in his feet, who was lame from birth and had never walked. [9]He listened to Paul as he was speaking. Paul looked directly at him, saw that he had faith to be healed [10]and called out, "Stand up on your feet!" At that, the man jumped up and began to walk.

[11]When the crowd saw what Paul had done, they shouted in the Lycaonian language, "The gods have come down to us in human form!" [12]Barnabas they called Zeus, and Paul they called Hermes because he was the chief speaker. [13]The priest of Zeus, whose temple was just outside the city, brought bulls and wreaths to the city gates because he and the crowd wanted to offer sacrifices to them.

[14]But when the apostles Barnabas and Paul heard of this, they tore their clothes and rushed out into the crowd, shouting: [15]"Men, why are you doing this? We too are only men, human like you. We are bringing you good news, telling you to turn from these worthless things to the living God, who made heaven and earth and sea and everything in them. [16]In the past, he let all nations go their own way. [17]Yet he has not left himself without testimony: He has shown kindness by giving you rain from heaven and crops in their seasons; he provides you with plenty of food and fills your hearts with joy." [18]Even with these words, they had difficulty keeping the crowd from sacrificing to them.

[19]Then some Jews came from Antioch and Iconium and won the crowd over. They stoned Paul and dragged him outside the city, thinking he was dead. [20]But after the disciples had gathered around

him, he got up and went back into the city. The next day he and Barnabas left for Derbe.

The Return to Antioch in Syria

[21]They preached the good news in that city and won a large number of disciples. Then they returned to Lystra, Iconium and Antioch, [22]strengthening the disciples and encouraging them to remain true to the faith. "We must go through many hardships to enter the kingdom of God," they said. [23]Paul and Barnabas appointed elders[a] for them in each church and, with prayer and fasting, committed them to the Lord, in whom they had put their trust. [24]After going through Pisidia, they came into Pamphylia, [25]and when they had preached the word in Perga, they went down to Attalia.

[26]From Attalia they sailed back to Antioch, where they had been committed to the grace of God for the work they had now completed. [27]On arriving there, they gathered the church together and reported all that God had done through them and how he had opened the door of faith to the Gentiles. [28]And they stayed there a long time with the disciples.

The Council at Jerusalem

15 Some men came down from Judea to Antioch and were teaching the brothers: "Unless you are circumcised, according to the custom taught by Moses, you cannot be saved." [2]This brought Paul and Barnabas into sharp dispute and debate with them. So Paul and Barnabas were appointed, along with some other believers, to go up to Jerusalem to see the apostles and elders about this question. [3]The church sent them on their way, and as they traveled through Phoenicia and Samaria, they told how the Gentiles had been converted. This news made all the brothers very glad. [4]When they came to Jerusalem, they were welcomed by the church and the apostles and elders, to whom they reported everything God had done through them.

[5]Then some of the believers who be-

---

[a]23 Or *Barnabas ordained elders*; or *Barnabas had elders elected*

longed to the party of the Pharisees stood up and said, "The Gentiles must be circumcised and required to obey the law of Moses."

[6]The apostles and elders met to consider this question. [7]After much discussion, Peter got up and addressed them: "Brothers, you know that some time ago God made a choice among you that the Gentiles might hear from my lips the message of the gospel and believe. [8]God, who knows the heart, showed that he accepted them by giving the Holy Spirit to them, just as he did to us. [9]He made no distinction between us and them, for he purified their hearts by faith. [10]Now then, why do you try to test God by putting on the necks of the disciples a yoke that neither we nor our fathers have been able to bear? [11]No! We believe it is through the grace of our Lord Jesus that we are saved, just as they are."

[12]The whole assembly became silent as they listened to Barnabas and Paul telling about the miraculous signs and wonders God had done among the Gentiles through them. [13]When they finished, James spoke up: "Brothers, listen to me. [14]Simon[a] has described to us how God at first showed his concern by taking from the Gentiles a people for himself. [15]The words of the prophets are in agreement with this, as it is written:

[16] "'After this I will return
    and rebuild David's fallen tent.
  Its ruins I will rebuild,
    and I will restore it,
[17]that the remnant of men may seek
    the Lord,
  and all the Gentiles who bear my
    name,
  says the Lord, who does these
    things'[b]
[18] that have been known for ages.[c]

[19]"It is my judgment, therefore, that we should not make it difficult for the Gentiles who are turning to God. [20]Instead we should write to them, telling them to abstain from food polluted by idols, from sexual immorality, from the meat of strangled animals and from blood. [21]For Moses has been preached in every city from the earliest times and is read in the synagogues on every Sabbath."

The Council's Letter to Gentile Believers

[22]Then the apostles and elders, with the whole church, decided to choose some of their own men and send them to Antioch with Paul and Barnabas. They chose Judas (called Barsabbas) and Silas, two men who were leaders among the brothers. [23]With them they sent the following letter:

The apostles and elders, your brothers,

To the Gentile believers in Antioch, Syria and Cilicia:

Greetings.

[24]We have heard that some went out from us without our authorization and disturbed you, troubling your minds by what they said. [25]So we all agreed to choose some men and send them to you with our dear friends Barnabas and Paul— [26]men who have risked their lives for the name of our Lord Jesus Christ. [27]Therefore we are sending Judas and Silas to confirm by word of mouth what we are writing. [28]It seemed good to the Holy Spirit and to us not to burden you with anything beyond the following requirements: [29]You are to abstain from food sacrificed to idols, from blood, from the meat of strangled animals and from sexual immorality. You will do well to avoid these things.

Farewell.

[30]The men were sent off and went down to Antioch, where they gathered the church together and delivered the letter. [31]The people read it and were glad for its encouraging message. [32]Judas and Silas, who themselves were prophets, said much to encourage and strengthen the brothers. [33]After spending some time there, they were sent off by the brothers with the blessing of peace to return to those who had sent them.[d] [35]But Paul

---

[a]14 Greek *Simeon*, a variant of *Simon*; that is, Peter   [b]17 Amos 9:11,12   [c]17,18 Some manuscripts *things'— / 18known to the Lord for ages is his work*   [d]33 Some manuscripts *them, 34but Silas decided to remain there*

and Barnabas remained in Antioch, where they and many others taught and preached the word of the Lord.

Disagreement Between Paul and Barnabas

36Some time later Paul said to Barnabas, "Let us go back and visit the brothers in all the towns where we preached the word of the Lord and see how they are doing." 37Barnabas wanted to take John, also called Mark, with them, 38but Paul did not think it wise to take him, because he had deserted them in Pamphylia and had not continued with them in the work. 39They had such a sharp disagreement that they parted company. Barnabas took Mark and sailed for Cyprus, 40but Paul chose Silas and left, commended by the brothers to the grace of the Lord. 41He went through Syria and Cilicia, strengthening the churches.

Timothy Joins Paul and Silas

16 He came to Derbe and then to Lystra, where a disciple named Timothy lived, whose mother was a Jewess and a believer, but whose father was a Greek. 2The brothers at Lystra and Iconium spoke well of him. 3Paul wanted to take him along on the journey, so he circumcised him because of the Jews who lived in that area, for they all knew that his father was a Greek. 4As they traveled from town to town, they delivered the decisions reached by the apostles and elders in Jerusalem for the people to obey. 5So

the churches were strengthened in the faith and grew daily in numbers.

Paul's Vision of the Man of Macedonia

6Paul and his companions traveled throughout the region of Phrygia and Galatia, having been kept by the Holy Spirit from preaching the word in the province of Asia. 7When they came to the border of Mysia, they tried to enter Bithynia, but the Spirit of Jesus would not allow them to. 8So they passed by Mysia and went down to Troas. 9During the night Paul had a vision of a man of Macedonia standing and begging him, "Come over to Macedonia and help us." 10After Paul had seen the vision, we got ready at once to leave for Macedonia, concluding that God had called us to preach the gospel to them.

Lydia's Conversion in Philippi

11From Troas we put out to sea and sailed straight for Samothrace, and the next day on to Neapolis. 12From there we traveled to Philippi, a Roman colony and the leading city of that district of Macedonia. And we stayed there several days.

13On the Sabbath we went outside the city gate to the river, where we expected to find a place of prayer. We sat down and began to speak to the women who had gathered there. 14One of those listening was a woman named Lydia, a dealer in purple cloth from the city of Thyatira, who was a worshiper of God. The Lord opened her heart to respond to Paul's

An Encouraging Word

Tuesday

ACTS 15:32 Some marriage partners see every problem as interminable. They believe one problem will ruin everything. So they quit trying. They give up. They raise the white flag and surrender to the problems of life they could otherwise beat.

A different group of couples see their problems as mere obstacles, as challenges to overcome. They face a difficult situation at work or with a friend and try hard to work it out. They don't give up.

Research has shown time and again

that all it takes for many people to persevere in the midst of a difficulty is an encouraging word from their spouse: "I believe in you." "You have what it takes." "You are doing great." Seemingly small and insignificant, these simple statements might almost go unnoticed by a casual observer. But not by the person on the receiving end. Encouragement brings strength and can make the difference between a spouse who gives up and a spouse who perseveres.   **—Les and Leslie**

Go to page 1202 for your next devotional reading.

message. [15]When she and the members of her household were baptized, she invited us to her home. "If you consider me a believer in the Lord," she said, "come and stay at my house." And she persuaded us.

Paul and Silas in Prison

[16]Once when we were going to the place of prayer, we were met by a slave girl who had a spirit by which she predicted the future. She earned a great deal of money for her owners by fortune-telling. [17]This girl followed Paul and the rest of us, shouting, "These men are servants of the Most High God, who are telling you the way to be saved." [18]She kept this up for many days. Finally Paul became so troubled that he turned around and said to the spirit, "In the name of Jesus Christ I command you to come out of her!" At that moment the spirit left her.

[19]When the owners of the slave girl realized that their hope of making money was gone, they seized Paul and Silas and dragged them into the marketplace to face the authorities. [20]They brought them before the magistrates and said, "These men are Jews, and are throwing our city into an uproar [21]by advocating customs unlawful for us Romans to accept or practice."

[22]The crowd joined in the attack against Paul and Silas, and the magistrates ordered them to be stripped and beaten. [23]After they had been severely flogged, they were thrown into prison, and the jailer was commanded to guard them carefully. [24]Upon receiving such orders, he put them in the inner cell and fastened their feet in the stocks.

[25]About midnight Paul and Silas were praying and singing hymns to God, and the other prisoners were listening to them. [26]Suddenly there was such a violent earthquake that the foundations of the prison were shaken. At once all the prison doors flew open, and everybody's chains came loose. [27]The jailer woke up, and when he saw the prison doors open, he drew his sword and was about to kill himself because he thought the prisoners had escaped. [28]But Paul shouted, "Don't harm yourself! We are all here!"

[29]The jailer called for lights, rushed in and fell trembling before Paul and Silas. [30]He then brought them out and asked, "Sirs, what must I do to be saved?"

[31]They replied, "Believe in the Lord Jesus, and you will be saved—you and your household." [32]Then they spoke the word of the Lord to him and to all the others in his house. [33]At that hour of the night the jailer took them and washed their wounds; then immediately he and all his family were baptized. [34]The jailer brought them into his house and set a meal before them; he was filled with joy because he had come to believe in God—he and his whole family.

In the Face of Adversity

Wednesday

ACTS 16:25 Why were Paul and Silas singing instead of commiserating? How could they be singing in the face of the injustice done to them? They had done a good thing—casting a demon out of a girl. Yet her masters had them beaten, stripped and jailed without a trial.

The first thing Paul and Silas did in jail was pray. They didn't pray individually; they prayed together. They turned the questions they had about their circumstances over to God. Then they reaffirmed their faith in God by singing hymns to him. Together they found strength. This strength was not merely in their companionship; they were able to sing because they pointed each other toward God. They helped each other maintain focus on God's work in their lives.

When adversity hits, couples can either drag each other down or gently help each other focus on God. We may not be able to help each other understand the reasons behind our circumstances, but we can help each other focus on the One who has all of life's answers. We need to help each other focus on "who" rather than "why." Choose to focus on God and praise him in adversity, and see what he will do.   **—Bob and Rosemary**

Go to page 1205 for your next devotional reading.

35When it was daylight, the magistrates sent their officers to the jailer with the order: "Release those men." 36The jailer told Paul, "The magistrates have ordered that you and Silas be released. Now you can leave. Go in peace."

37But Paul said to the officers: "They beat us publicly without a trial, even though we are Roman citizens, and threw us into prison. And now do they want to get rid of us quietly? No! Let them come themselves and escort us out."

38The officers reported this to the magistrates, and when they heard that Paul and Silas were Roman citizens, they were alarmed. 39They came to appease them and escorted them from the prison, requesting them to leave the city. 40After Paul and Silas came out of the prison, they went to Lydia's house, where they met with the brothers and encouraged them. Then they left.

In Thessalonica

17 When they had passed through Amphipolis and Apollonia, they came to Thessalonica, where there was a Jewish synagogue. 2As his custom was, Paul went into the synagogue, and on three Sabbath days he reasoned with them from the Scriptures, 3explaining and proving that the Christ*a* had to suffer and rise from the dead. "This Jesus I am proclaiming to you is the Christ,*a*" he said. 4Some of the Jews were persuaded and joined Paul and Silas, as did a large number of God-fearing Greeks and not a few prominent women.

5But the Jews were jealous; so they rounded up some bad characters from the marketplace, formed a mob and started a riot in the city. They rushed to Jason's house in search of Paul and Silas in order to bring them out to the crowd.*b* 6But when they did not find them, they dragged Jason and some other brothers before the city officials, shouting: "These men who have caused trouble all over the world have now come here, 7and Jason has welcomed them into his house. They are all defying Caesar's decrees, saying that there is another king, one called Jesus." 8When they heard this, the crowd and the city officials were thrown into

turmoil. 9Then they made Jason and the others post bond and let them go.

In Berea

10As soon as it was night, the brothers sent Paul and Silas away to Berea. On arriving there, they went to the Jewish synagogue. 11Now the Bereans were of more noble character than the Thessalonians, for they received the message with great eagerness and examined the Scriptures every day to see if what Paul said was true. 12Many of the Jews believed, as did also a number of prominent Greek women and many Greek men.

13When the Jews in Thessalonica learned that Paul was preaching the word of God at Berea, they went there too, agitating the crowds and stirring them up. 14The brothers immediately sent Paul to the coast, but Silas and Timothy stayed at Berea. 15The men who escorted Paul brought him to Athens and then left with instructions for Silas and Timothy to join him as soon as possible.

In Athens

16While Paul was waiting for them in Athens, he was greatly distressed to see that the city was full of idols. 17So he reasoned in the synagogue with the Jews and the God-fearing Greeks, as well as in the marketplace day by day with those who happened to be there. 18A group of Epicurean and Stoic philosophers began to dispute with him. Some of them asked, "What is this babbler trying to say?" Others remarked, "He seems to be advocating foreign gods." They said this because Paul was preaching the good news about Jesus and the resurrection. 19Then they took him and brought him to a meeting of the Areopagus, where they said to him, "May we know what this new teaching is that you are presenting? 20You are bringing some strange ideas to our ears, and we want to know what they mean." 21(All the Athenians and the foreigners who lived there spent their time doing nothing but talking about and listening to the latest ideas.)

22Paul then stood up in the meeting of the Areopagus and said: "Men of Athens!

a3 Or *Messiah*   *b5* Or *the assembly of the people*

I see that in every way you are very religious. [23]For as I walked around and looked carefully at your objects of worship, I even found an altar with this inscription: TO AN UNKNOWN GOD. Now what you worship as something unknown I am going to proclaim to you.

[24]"The God who made the world and everything in it is the Lord of heaven and earth and does not live in temples built by hands. [25]And he is not served by human hands, as if he needed anything, because he himself gives all men life and breath and everything else. [26]From one man he made every nation of men, that they should inhabit the whole earth; and he determined the times set for them and the exact places where they should live. [27]God did this so that men would seek him and perhaps reach out for him and find him, though he is not far from each one of us. [28]'For in him we live and move and have our being.' As some of your own poets have said, 'We are his offspring.'

[29]"Therefore since we are God's offspring, we should not think that the divine being is like gold or silver or stone—an image made by man's design and skill. [30]In the past God overlooked such ignorance, but now he commands all people everywhere to repent. [31]For he has set a day when he will judge the world with justice by the man he has appointed. He has given proof of this to all men by raising him from the dead."

[32]When they heard about the resurrection of the dead, some of them sneered, but others said, "We want to hear you again on this subject." [33]At that, Paul left the Council. [34]A few men became followers of Paul and believed. Among them was Dionysius, a member of the Areopagus, also a woman named Damaris, and a number of others.

In Corinth

18 After this, Paul left Athens and went to Corinth. [2]There he met a Jew named Aquila, a native of Pontus, who had recently come from Italy with his wife Priscilla, because Claudius had ordered all the Jews to leave Rome. Paul went to see them, [3]and because he was a tentmaker as they were, he stayed and worked with them. [4]Every Sabbath he reasoned in the synagogue, trying to persuade Jews and Greeks.

[5]When Silas and Timothy came from Macedonia, Paul devoted himself exclusively to preaching, testifying to the Jews that Jesus was the Christ.[a] [6]But when the Jews opposed Paul and became abusive, he shook out his clothes in protest and said to them, "Your blood be on your own heads! I am clear of my responsibility. From now on I will go to the Gentiles."

[7]Then Paul left the synagogue and went next door to the house of Titius Justus, a worshiper of God. [8]Crispus, the synagogue ruler, and his entire household believed in the Lord; and many of the Corinthians who heard him believed and were baptized.

[9]One night the Lord spoke to Paul in a vision: "Do not be afraid; keep on speaking, do not be silent. [10]For I am with you, and no one is going to attack and harm you, because I have many people in this city." [11]So Paul stayed for a year and a half, teaching them the word of God.

[12]While Gallio was proconsul of Achaia, the Jews made a united attack on Paul and brought him into court. [13]"This man," they charged, "is persuading the people to worship God in ways contrary to the law."

[14]Just as Paul was about to speak, Gallio said to the Jews, "If you Jews were making a complaint about some misdemeanor or serious crime, it would be reasonable for me to listen to you. [15]But since it involves questions about words and names and your own law—settle the matter yourselves. I will not be a judge of such things." [16]So he had them ejected from the court. [17]Then they all turned on Sosthenes the synagogue ruler and beat him in front of the court. But Gallio showed no concern whatever.

Priscilla, Aquila and Apollos

[18]Paul stayed on in Corinth for some time. Then he left the brothers and sailed for Syria, accompanied by Priscilla and Aquila. Before he sailed, he had his hair cut off at Cenchrea because of a vow he had taken. [19]They arrived at Ephesus, where Paul left Priscilla and Aquila. He himself went into the synagogue and rea-

----

a5 Or *Messiah;* also in verse 28

soned with the Jews. ²⁰When they asked him to spend more time with them, he declined. ²¹But as he left, he promised, "I will come back if it is God's will." Then he set sail from Ephesus. ²²When he landed at Caesarea, he went up and greeted the church and then went down to Antioch.

²³After spending some time in Antioch, Paul set out from there and traveled from place to place throughout the region of Galatia and Phrygia, strengthening all the disciples.

²⁴Meanwhile a Jew named Apollos, a native of Alexandria, came to Ephesus. He was a learned man, with a thorough knowledge of the Scriptures. ²⁵He had been instructed in the way of the Lord, and he spoke with great fervor^a and taught about Jesus accurately, though he knew only the baptism of John. ²⁶He began to speak boldly in the synagogue. When Priscilla and Aquila heard him, they invited him to their home and explained to him the way of God more adequately.

²⁷When Apollos wanted to go to Achaia, the brothers encouraged him and wrote to the disciples there to welcome him. On arriving, he was a great help to those who by grace had believed. ²⁸For he vigorously refuted the Jews in public debate, proving from the Scriptures that Jesus was the Christ.

Paul in Ephesus

19 While Apollos was at Corinth, Paul took the road through the interior and arrived at Ephesus. There he found some disciples ²and asked them, "Did you receive the Holy Spirit when^b you believed?"

They answered, "No, we have not even heard that there is a Holy Spirit."

³So Paul asked, "Then what baptism did you receive?"

"John's baptism," they replied.

⁴Paul said, "John's baptism was a baptism of repentance. He told the people to believe in the one coming after him, that is, in Jesus." ⁵On hearing this, they were baptized into^c the name of the Lord Jesus. ⁶When Paul placed his hands on them, the Holy Spirit came on them, and they spoke in tongues^d and prophesied. ⁷There were about twelve men in all.

---

a25 Or *with fervor in the Spirit*   *b2* Or *after*
c5 Or *in*   *d6* Or *other languages*

Beacons of Light

Thursday

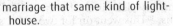

ACTS 18:24–26 How fortunate for Apollos that he met Priscilla and Aquila. At the synagogue Apollos spoke boldly but without full knowledge of God. Rather than being critical, this loving couple invited Apollos into their home where they explained to him more thoroughly the way of God.

Priscilla and Aquila chose to minister as a couple. They used their marriage and their home to illuminate God's truths to Apollos and to others. Is your home and marriage a lighthouse to others? Years ago when we (Dave and Claudia) came into a vital relationship with Christ, it was mostly through the love and care of other couples who befriended us and invited us into their homes. These couples modeled for us how to minister as a couple and, over the years, we have tried to make our own home and marriage that same kind of lighthouse.

As Christian couples, our marriages can be little beacons of light and can create in others a thirst for God and for a healthy Christian marriage. We agree with our friends and mentors, Drs. David and Vera Mace, when they said, "We believe that any married couple, at any stage in their life together, can restructure their relationship to bring it into line with the divine purpose."*

Our hurting and confused world needs to see Christian marriages where couples really love each other. It can be a joy to serve others together when you have a loving relationship.   **—Dave and Claudia**

Go to page 1215 for your next devotional reading.

*Mace, David and Vera. *Letters to a Retired Couple*. Valley Forge, PA: Judson, 1985 (p. 147).

Aquila and Priscilla

ACTS 18:18–28 Throughout Scripture Aquila and Priscilla are mentioned together—one is never named without the other. As lay ministers in the early church, they worked well as a husband-and-wife team. And they enjoyed a long relationship with Paul, sometimes following him on his missionary journeys. They held a special concern for ministering to other teachers in the church, wanting them to teach the full message of the gospel.

One of these teachers was Apollos, an eloquent speaker who needed a little help in understanding doctrine. Aquila and Priscilla gently took him aside and taught the teacher.

This couple serves as an example to any lay couple in the church today who has a gift for ministering to others through education—a much-needed skill still today!

[8] Paul entered the synagogue and spoke boldly there for three months, arguing persuasively about the kingdom of God. [9] But some of them became obstinate; they refused to believe and publicly maligned the Way. So Paul left them. He took the disciples with him and had discussions daily in the lecture hall of Tyrannus. [10] This went on for two years, so that all the Jews and Greeks who lived in the province of Asia heard the word of the Lord.

[11] God did extraordinary miracles through Paul, [12] so that even handkerchiefs and aprons that had touched him were taken to the sick, and their illnesses were cured and the evil spirits left them.

[13] Some Jews who went around driving out evil spirits tried to invoke the name of the Lord Jesus over those who were demon-possessed. They would say, "In the name of Jesus, whom Paul preaches, I command you to come out." [14] Seven sons of Sceva, a Jewish chief priest, were doing this. [15] ⌜One day⌝ the evil spirit answered them, "Jesus I know, and I know about Paul, but who are you?" [16] Then the man who had the evil spirit jumped on them and overpowered them all. He gave them such a beating that they ran out of the house naked and bleeding.

[17] When this became known to the Jews and Greeks living in Ephesus, they were all seized with fear, and the name of the Lord Jesus was held in high honor. [18] Many of those who believed now came and openly confessed their evil deeds. [19] A number who had practiced sorcery brought their scrolls together and burned them publicly. When they calculated the value of the scrolls, the total came to fifty thousand drachmas.[a] [20] In this way the word of the Lord spread widely and grew in power.

[21] After all this had happened, Paul decided to go to Jerusalem, passing through Macedonia and Achaia. "After I have been there," he said, "I must visit Rome also." [22] He sent two of his helpers, Timothy and Erastus, to Macedonia, while he stayed in the province of Asia a little longer.

The Riot in Ephesus

[23] About that time there arose a great disturbance about the Way. [24] A silversmith named Demetrius, who made silver shrines of Artemis, brought in no little business for the craftsmen. [25] He called them together, along with the workmen in related trades, and said: "Men, you know we receive a good income from this business. [26] And you see and hear how this fellow Paul has convinced and led astray large numbers of people here in Ephesus and in practically the whole province of Asia. He says that man-made gods are no gods at all. [27] There is danger not only that our trade will lose its good name, but also that the temple of the great goddess Artemis will be discredited, and the goddess herself, who is worshiped throughout the province of Asia and the world, will be robbed of her divine majesty."

[28] When they heard this, they were furious and began shouting: "Great is Artemis of the Ephesians!" [29] Soon the whole city was in an uproar. The people seized Gaius and Aristarchus, Paul's traveling companions from Macedonia, and rushed as one man into the theater.

---

[a] 19 A drachma was a silver coin worth about a day's wages.

³⁰Paul wanted to appear before the crowd, but the disciples would not let him. ³¹Even some of the officials of the province, friends of Paul, sent him a message begging him not to venture into the theater.

³²The assembly was in confusion: Some were shouting one thing, some another. Most of the people did not even know why they were there. ³³The Jews pushed Alexander to the front, and some of the crowd shouted instructions to him. He motioned for silence in order to make a defense before the people. ³⁴But when they realized he was a Jew, they all shouted in unison for about two hours: "Great is Artemis of the Ephesians!"

³⁵The city clerk quieted the crowd and said: "Men of Ephesus, doesn't all the world know that the city of Ephesus is the guardian of the temple of the great Artemis and of her image, which fell from heaven? ³⁶Therefore, since these facts are undeniable, you ought to be quiet and not do anything rash. ³⁷You have brought these men here, though they have neither robbed temples nor blasphemed our goddess. ³⁸If, then, Demetrius and his fellow craftsmen have a grievance against anybody, the courts are open and there are proconsuls. They can press charges. ³⁹If there is anything further you want to bring up, it must be settled in a legal assembly. ⁴⁰As it is, we are in danger of being charged with rioting because of today's events. In that case we would not be able to account for this commotion, since there is no reason for it." ⁴¹After he had said this, he dismissed the assembly.

Through Macedonia and Greece

20 When the uproar had ended, Paul sent for the disciples and, after encouraging them, said good-by and set out for Macedonia. ²He traveled through that area, speaking many words of encouragement to the people, and finally arrived in Greece, ³where he stayed three months. Because the Jews made a plot against him just as he was about to sail for Syria, he decided to go back through Macedonia. ⁴He was accompanied by Sopater son of Pyrrhus from Berea, Aristarchus and Secundus from Thessalonica, Gaius from

Derbe, Timothy also, and Tychicus and Trophimus from the province of Asia. ⁵These men went on ahead and waited for us at Troas. ⁶But we sailed from Philippi after the Feast of Unleavened Bread, and five days later joined the others at Troas, where we stayed seven days.

Eutychus Raised From the Dead at Troas

⁷On the first day of the week we came together to break bread. Paul spoke to the people and, because he intended to leave the next day, kept on talking until midnight. ⁸There were many lamps in the upstairs room where we were meeting. ⁹Seated in a window was a young man named Eutychus, who was sinking into a deep sleep as Paul talked on and on. When he was sound asleep, he fell to the ground from the third story and was picked up dead. ¹⁰Paul went down, threw himself on the young man and put his arms around him. "Don't be alarmed," he said. "He's alive!" ¹¹Then he went upstairs again and broke bread and ate. After talking until daylight, he left. ¹²The people took the young man home alive and were greatly comforted.

Paul's Farewell to the Ephesian Elders

¹³We went on ahead to the ship and sailed for Assos, where we were going to take Paul aboard. He had made this arrangement because he was going there on foot. ¹⁴When he met us at Assos, we took him aboard and went on to Mitylene. ¹⁵The next day we set sail from there and arrived off Kios. The day after that we crossed over to Samos, and on the following day arrived at Miletus. ¹⁶Paul had decided to sail past Ephesus to avoid spending time in the province of Asia, for he was in a hurry to reach Jerusalem, if possible, by the day of Pentecost.

¹⁷From Miletus, Paul sent to Ephesus for the elders of the church. ¹⁸When they arrived, he said to them: "You know how I lived the whole time I was with you, from the first day I came into the province of Asia. ¹⁹I served the Lord with great humility and with tears, although I was severely tested by the plots of the Jews. ²⁰You know that I have not hesitated to

preach anything that would be helpful to you but have taught you publicly and from house to house. 21I have declared to both Jews and Greeks that they must turn to God in repentance and have faith in our Lord Jesus.

22"And now, compelled by the Spirit, I am going to Jerusalem, not knowing what will happen to me there. 23I only know that in every city the Holy Spirit warns me that prison and hardships are facing me. 24However, I consider my life worth nothing to me, if only I may finish the race and complete the task the Lord Jesus has given me—the task of testifying to the gospel of God's grace.

25"Now I know that none of you among whom I have gone about preaching the kingdom will ever see me again. 26Therefore, I declare to you today that I am innocent of the blood of all men. 27For I have not hesitated to proclaim to you the whole will of God. 28Keep watch over yourselves and all the flock of which the Holy Spirit has made you overseers.*a* Be shepherds of the church of God,*b* which he bought with his own blood. 29I know that after I leave, savage wolves will come in among you and will not spare the flock. 30Even from your own number men will arise and distort the truth in order to draw away disciples after them. 31So be on your guard! Remember that for three years I never stopped warning each of you night and day with tears.

32"Now I commit you to God and to the word of his grace, which can build you up and give you an inheritance among all those who are sanctified. 33I have not coveted anyone's silver or gold or clothing. 34You yourselves know that these hands of mine have supplied my own needs and the needs of my companions. 35In everything I did, I showed you that by this kind of hard work we must help the weak, remembering the words the Lord Jesus himself said: 'It is more blessed to give than to receive.'"

36When he had said this, he knelt down with all of them and prayed. 37They all wept as they embraced him and kissed him. 38What grieved them most was his statement that they would never see his face again. Then they accompanied him to the ship.

On to Jerusalem

21 After we had torn ourselves away from them, we put out to sea and sailed straight to Cos. The next day we went to Rhodes and from there to Patara. 2We found a ship crossing over to Phoenicia, went on board and set sail. 3After sighting Cyprus and passing to the south of it, we sailed on to Syria. We landed at Tyre, where our ship was to unload its cargo. 4Finding the disciples there, we stayed with them seven days. Through the Spirit they urged Paul not to go on to Jerusalem. 5But when our time was up, we left and continued on our way. All the disciples and their wives and children accompanied us out of the city, and there on the beach we knelt to pray. 6After saying good-by to each other, we went aboard the ship, and they returned home.

7We continued our voyage from Tyre and landed at Ptolemais, where we greeted the brothers and stayed with them for a day. 8Leaving the next day, we reached Caesarea and stayed at the house of Philip the evangelist, one of the Seven. 9He had four unmarried daughters who prophesied.

10After we had been there a number of days, a prophet named Agabus came down from Judea. 11Coming over to us, he took Paul's belt, tied his own hands and feet with it and said, "The Holy Spirit says, 'In this way the Jews of Jerusalem will bind the owner of this belt and will hand him over to the Gentiles.'"

12When we heard this, we and the people there pleaded with Paul not to go up to Jerusalem. 13Then Paul answered, "Why are you weeping and breaking my heart? I am ready not only to be bound, but also to die in Jerusalem for the name of the Lord Jesus." 14When he would not be dissuaded, we gave up and said, "The Lord's will be done."

15After this, we got ready and went up to Jerusalem. 16Some of the disciples from Caesarea accompanied us and brought us to the home of Mnason, where we were to stay. He was a man from Cyprus and one of the early disciples.

a28 Traditionally *bishops*   *b28* Many manuscripts *of the Lord*

Paul's Arrival at Jerusalem

17When we arrived at Jerusalem, the brothers received us warmly. **18**The next day Paul and the rest of us went to see James, and all the elders were present. **19**Paul greeted them and reported in detail what God had done among the Gentiles through his ministry.

20When they heard this, they praised God. Then they said to Paul: "You see, brother, how many thousands of Jews have believed, and all of them are zealous for the law. **21**They have been informed that you teach all the Jews who live among the Gentiles to turn away from Moses, telling them not to circumcise their children or live according to our customs. **22**What shall we do? They will certainly hear that you have come, **23**so do what we tell you. There are four men with us who have made a vow. **24**Take these men, join in their purification rites and pay their expenses, so that they can have their heads shaved. Then everybody will know there is no truth in these reports about you, but that you yourself are living in obedience to the law. **25**As for the Gentile believers, we have written to them our decision that they should abstain from food sacrificed to idols, from blood, from the meat of strangled animals and from sexual immorality."

26The next day Paul took the men and purified himself along with them. Then he went to the temple to give notice of the date when the days of purification would end and the offering would be made for each of them.

Paul Arrested

27When the seven days were nearly over, some Jews from the province of Asia saw Paul at the temple. They stirred up the whole crowd and seized him, **28**shouting, "Men of Israel, help us! This is the man who teaches all men everywhere against our people and our law and this place. And besides, he has brought Greeks into the temple area and defiled this holy place." **29**(They had previously seen Trophimus the Ephesian in the city with Paul and assumed that Paul had brought him into the temple area.)

30The whole city was aroused, and the people came running from all directions.

Seizing Paul, they dragged him from the temple, and immediately the gates were shut. **31**While they were trying to kill him, news reached the commander of the Roman troops that the whole city of Jerusalem was in an uproar. **32**He at once took some officers and soldiers and ran down to the crowd. When the rioters saw the commander and his soldiers, they stopped beating Paul.

33The commander came up and arrested him and ordered him to be bound with two chains. Then he asked who he was and what he had done. **34**Some in the crowd shouted one thing and some another, and since the commander could not get at the truth because of the uproar, he ordered that Paul be taken into the barracks. **35**When Paul reached the steps, the violence of the mob was so great he had to be carried by the soldiers. **36**The crowd that followed kept shouting, "Away with him!"

Paul Speaks to the Crowd

37As the soldiers were about to take Paul into the barracks, he asked the commander, "May I say something to you?"

"Do you speak Greek?" he replied. **38**"Aren't you the Egyptian who started a revolt and led four thousand terrorists out into the desert some time ago?"

39Paul answered, "I am a Jew, from Tarsus in Cilicia, a citizen of no ordinary city. Please let me speak to the people."

40Having received the commander's permission, Paul stood on the steps and motioned to the crowd. When they were all silent, he said to them in Aramaic[a]:

22 **1**"Brothers and fathers, listen now to my defense." **2**When they heard him speak to them in Aramaic, they became very quiet.

Then Paul said: **3**"I am a Jew, born in Tarsus of Cilicia, but brought up in this city. Under Gamaliel I was thoroughly trained in the law of our fathers and was just as zealous for God as any of you are today. **4**I persecuted the followers of this Way to their death, arresting both men and women and throwing them into prison, **5**as also the high priest and all the Council can testify. I even obtained letters from them to their brothers in Damascus,

a40 Or possibly Hebrew; *also in 22:2*

and went there to bring these people as prisoners to Jerusalem to be punished.

⁶"About noon as I came near Damascus, suddenly a bright light from heaven flashed around me. ⁷I fell to the ground and heard a voice say to me, 'Saul! Saul! Why do you persecute me?'

⁸" 'Who are you, Lord?' I asked.

" 'I am Jesus of Nazareth, whom you are persecuting,' he replied. ⁹My companions saw the light, but they did not understand the voice of him who was speaking to me.

¹⁰" 'What shall I do, Lord?' I asked.

" 'Get up,' the Lord said, 'and go into Damascus. There you will be told all that you have been assigned to do.' ¹¹My companions led me by the hand into Damascus, because the brilliance of the light had blinded me.

¹²"A man named Ananias came to see me. He was a devout observer of the law and highly respected by all the Jews living there. ¹³He stood beside me and said, 'Brother Saul, receive your sight!' And at that very moment I was able to see him.

¹⁴"Then he said: 'The God of our fathers has chosen you to know his will and to see the Righteous One and to hear words from his mouth. ¹⁵You will be his witness to all men of what you have seen and heard. ¹⁶And now what are you waiting for? Get up, be baptized and wash your sins away, calling on his name.'

¹⁷"When I returned to Jerusalem and was praying at the temple, I fell into a trance ¹⁸and saw the Lord speaking. 'Quick!' he said to me. 'Leave Jerusalem immediately, because they will not accept your testimony about me.'

¹⁹" 'Lord,' I replied, 'these men know that I went from one synagogue to another to imprison and beat those who believe in you. ²⁰And when the blood of your martyr[a] Stephen was shed, I stood there giving my approval and guarding the clothes of those who were killing him.'

²¹"Then the Lord said to me, 'Go; I will send you far away to the Gentiles.' "

Paul the Roman Citizen

²²The crowd listened to Paul until he said this. Then they raised their voices and shouted, "Rid the earth of him! He's not fit to live!"

²³As they were shouting and throwing off their cloaks and flinging dust into the air, ²⁴the commander ordered Paul to be taken into the barracks. He directed that he be flogged and questioned in order to find out why the people were shouting at him like this. ²⁵As they stretched him out to flog him, Paul said to the centurion standing there, "Is it legal for you to flog a Roman citizen who hasn't even been found guilty?"

²⁶When the centurion heard this, he went to the commander and reported it. "What are you going to do?" he asked. "This man is a Roman citizen."

²⁷The commander went to Paul and asked, "Tell me, are you a Roman citizen?"

"Yes, I am," he answered.

²⁸Then the commander said, "I had to pay a big price for my citizenship."

"But I was born a citizen," Paul replied.

²⁹Those who were about to question him withdrew immediately. The commander himself was alarmed when he realized that he had put Paul, a Roman citizen, in chains.

Before the Sanhedrin

³⁰The next day, since the commander wanted to find out exactly why Paul was being accused by the Jews, he released him and ordered the chief priests and all the Sanhedrin to assemble. Then he brought Paul and had him stand before them.

23 Paul looked straight at the Sanhedrin and said, "My brothers, I have fulfilled my duty to God in all good conscience to this day." ²At this the high priest Ananias ordered those standing near Paul to strike him on the mouth. ³Then Paul said to him, "God will strike you, you whitewashed wall! You sit there to judge me according to the law, yet you yourself violate the law by commanding that I be struck!"

⁴Those who were standing near Paul said, "You dare to insult God's high priest?"

⁵Paul replied, "Brothers, I did not realize that he was the high priest; for it is written: 'Do not speak evil about the ruler of your people.'[b] "

⁶Then Paul, knowing that some of

them were Sadducees and the others Pharisees, called out in the Sanhedrin, "My brothers, I am a Pharisee, the son of a Pharisee. I stand on trial because of my hope in the resurrection of the dead." ⁷When he said this, a dispute broke out between the Pharisees and the Sadducees, and the assembly was divided. ⁸(The Sadducees say that there is no resurrection, and that there are neither angels nor spirits, but the Pharisees acknowledge them all.)

⁹There was a great uproar, and some of the teachers of the law who were Pharisees stood up and argued vigorously. "We find nothing wrong with this man," they said. "What if a spirit or an angel has spoken to him?" ¹⁰The dispute became so violent that the commander was afraid Paul would be torn to pieces by them. He ordered the troops to go down and take him away from them by force and bring him into the barracks.

¹¹The following night the Lord stood near Paul and said, "Take courage! As you have testified about me in Jerusalem, so you must also testify in Rome."

The Plot to Kill Paul

¹²The next morning the Jews formed a conspiracy and bound themselves with an oath not to eat or drink until they had killed Paul. ¹³More than forty men were involved in this plot. ¹⁴They went to the chief priests and elders and said, "We have taken a solemn oath not to eat anything until we have killed Paul. ¹⁵Now then, you and the Sanhedrin petition the commander to bring him before you on the pretext of wanting more accurate information about his case. We are ready to kill him before he gets here."

¹⁶But when the son of Paul's sister heard of this plot, he went into the barracks and told Paul.

¹⁷Then Paul called one of the centurions and said, "Take this young man to the commander; he has something to tell him." ¹⁸So he took him to the commander.

The centurion said, "Paul, the prisoner, sent for me and asked me to bring this young man to you because he has something to tell you."

¹⁹The commander took the young man by the hand, drew him aside and asked, "What is it you want to tell me?"

²⁰He said: "The Jews have agreed to ask you to bring Paul before the Sanhedrin tomorrow on the pretext of wanting more accurate information about him. ²¹Don't give in to them, because more than forty of them are waiting in ambush for him. They have taken an oath not to eat or drink until they have killed him. They are ready now, waiting for your consent to their request."

²²The commander dismissed the young man and cautioned him, "Don't tell anyone that you have reported this to me."

Paul Transferred to Caesarea

²³Then he called two of his centurions and ordered them, "Get ready a detachment of two hundred soldiers, seventy horsemen and two hundred spearmen*a* to go to Caesarea at nine tonight. ²⁴Provide mounts for Paul so that he may be taken safely to Governor Felix."

²⁵He wrote a letter as follows:

²⁶Claudius Lysias,

To His Excellency, Governor Felix:

Greetings.

²⁷This man was seized by the Jews and they were about to kill him, but I came with my troops and rescued him, for I had learned that he is a Roman citizen. ²⁸I wanted to know why they were accusing him, so I brought him to their Sanhedrin. ²⁹I found that the accusation had to do with questions about their law, but there was no charge against him that deserved death or imprisonment. ³⁰When I was informed of a plot to be carried out against the man, I sent him to you at once. I also ordered his accusers to present to you their case against him.

³¹So the soldiers, carrying out their orders, took Paul with them during the night and brought him as far as Antipatris. ³²The next day they let the cavalry go

---

a23 The meaning of the Greek for this word is uncertain.

on with him, while they returned to the barracks. 33When the cavalry arrived in Caesarea, they delivered the letter to the governor and handed Paul over to him. 34The governor read the letter and asked what province he was from. Learning that he was from Cilicia, 35he said, "I will hear your case when your accusers get here." Then he ordered that Paul be kept under guard in Herod's palace.

The Trial Before Felix

24 Five days later the high priest Ananias went down to Caesarea with some of the elders and a lawyer named Tertullus, and they brought their charges against Paul before the governor. 2When Paul was called in, Tertullus presented his case before Felix: "We have enjoyed a long period of peace under you, and your foresight has brought about reforms in this nation. 3Everywhere and in every way, most excellent Felix, we acknowledge this with profound gratitude. 4But in order not to weary you further, I would request that you be kind enough to hear us briefly.

5"We have found this man to be a troublemaker, stirring up riots among the Jews all over the world. He is a ringleader of the Nazarene sect 6and even tried to desecrate the temple; so we seized him. 8Bya examining him yourself you will be able to learn the truth about all these charges we are bringing against him."

9The Jews joined in the accusation, asserting that these things were true.

10When the governor motioned for him to speak, Paul replied: "I know that for a number of years you have been a judge over this nation; so I gladly make my defense. 11You can easily verify that no more than twelve days ago I went up to Jerusalem to worship. 12My accusers did not find me arguing with anyone at the temple, or stirring up a crowd in the synagogues or anywhere else in the city. 13And they cannot prove to you the charges they are now making against me. 14However, I admit that I worship the God of our fathers as a follower of the Way, which they call a sect. I believe everything that agrees with the Law and that is written in the Prophets, 15and I have the same hope in God as these men, that

there will be a resurrection of both the righteous and the wicked. 16So I strive always to keep my conscience clear before God and man.

17"After an absence of several years, I came to Jerusalem to bring my people gifts for the poor and to present offerings. 18I was ceremonially clean when they found me in the temple courts doing this. There was no crowd with me, nor was I involved in any disturbance. 19But there are some Jews from the province of Asia, who ought to be here before you and bring charges if they have anything against me. 20Or these who are here should state what crime they found in me when I stood before the Sanhedrin— 21unless it was this one thing I shouted as I stood in their presence: 'It is concerning the resurrection of the dead that I am on trial before you today.' "

22Then Felix, who was well acquainted with the Way, adjourned the proceedings. "When Lysias the commander comes," he said, "I will decide your case." 23He ordered the centurion to keep Paul under guard but to give him some freedom and permit his friends to take care of his needs.

24Several days later Felix came with his wife Drusilla, who was a Jewess. He sent for Paul and listened to him as he spoke about faith in Christ Jesus. 25As Paul discoursed on righteousness, self-control and the judgment to come, Felix was afraid and said, "That's enough for now! You may leave. When I find it convenient, I will send for you." 26At the same time he was hoping that Paul would offer him a bribe, so he sent for him frequently and talked with him.

27When two years had passed, Felix was succeeded by Porcius Festus, but because Felix wanted to grant a favor to the Jews, he left Paul in prison.

The Trial Before Festus

25 Three days after arriving in the province, Festus went up from Caesarea to Jerusalem, 2where the chief priests and Jewish leaders appeared be-

---

a6-8 Some manuscripts *him and wanted to judge him according to our law.* 7But the commander, Lysias, *came and with the use of much force snatched him from our hands* 8and ordered his accusers to come *before you. By* fore him and presented the charges against Paul. ³They urgently requested Festus, as a favor to them, to have Paul transferred to Jerusalem, for they were preparing an ambush to kill him along the way. ⁴Festus answered, "Paul is being held at Caesarea, and I myself am going there soon. ⁵Let some of your leaders come with me and press charges against the man there, if he has done anything wrong."

⁶After spending eight or ten days with them, he went down to Caesarea, and the next day he convened the court and ordered that Paul be brought before him. ⁷When Paul appeared, the Jews who had come down from Jerusalem stood around him, bringing many serious charges against him, which they could not prove.

⁸Then Paul made his defense: "I have done nothing wrong against the law of the Jews or against the temple or against Caesar."

⁹Festus, wishing to do the Jews a favor, said to Paul, "Are you willing to go up to Jerusalem and stand trial before me there on these charges?"

¹⁰Paul answered: "I am now standing before Caesar's court, where I ought to be tried. I have not done any wrong to the Jews, as you yourself know very well. ¹¹If, however, I am guilty of doing anything deserving death, I do not refuse to die. But if the charges brought against me by these Jews are not true, no one has the right to hand me over to them. I appeal to Caesar!"

¹²After Festus had conferred with his council, he declared: "You have appealed to Caesar. To Caesar you will go!"

Festus Consults King Agrippa

¹³A few days later King Agrippa and Bernice arrived at Caesarea to pay their respects to Festus. ¹⁴Since they were spending many days there, Festus discussed Paul's case with the king. He said: "There is a man here whom Felix left as a prisoner. ¹⁵When I went to Jerusalem, the chief priests and elders of the Jews brought charges against him and asked that he be condemned.

¹⁶"I told them that it is not the Roman custom to hand over any man before he has faced his accusers and has had an opportunity to defend himself against their charges. ¹⁷When they came here with me, I did not delay the case, but convened the court the next day and ordered the man to be brought in. ¹⁸When his accusers got up to speak, they did not charge him with any of the crimes I had expected. ¹⁹Instead, they had some points of dispute with him about their own religion and about a dead man named Jesus who Paul claimed was alive. ²⁰I was at a loss how to investigate such matters; so I asked if he would be willing to go to Jerusalem and stand trial there on these charges. ²¹When Paul made his appeal to be held over for the Emperor's decision, I ordered him held until I could send him to Caesar."

²²Then Agrippa said to Festus, "I would like to hear this man myself."

He replied, "Tomorrow you will hear him."

Paul Before Agrippa

²³The next day Agrippa and Bernice came with great pomp and entered the audience room with the high ranking officers and the leading men of the city. At the command of Festus, Paul was brought in. ²⁴Festus said: "King Agrippa, and all who are present with us, you see this man! The whole Jewish community has petitioned me about him in Jerusalem and here in Caesarea, shouting that he ought not to live any longer. ²⁵I found he had done nothing deserving of death, but because he made his appeal to the Emperor I decided to send him to Rome. ²⁶But I have nothing definite to write to His Majesty about him. Therefore I have brought him before all of you, and especially before you, King Agrippa, so that as a result of this investigation I may have something to write. ²⁷For I think it is unreasonable to send on a prisoner without specifying the charges against him."

26 Then Agrippa said to Paul, "You have permission to speak for yourself."

So Paul motioned with his hand and began his defense: ²"King Agrippa, I consider myself fortunate to stand before you today as I make my defense against all the accusations of the Jews, ³and especially so because you are well acquainted with all the Jewish customs and controversies.

Therefore, I beg you to listen to me patiently.

4 "The Jews all know the way I have lived ever since I was a child, from the beginning of my life in my own country, and also in Jerusalem. 5 They have known me for a long time and can testify, if they are willing, that according to the strictest sect of our religion, I lived as a Pharisee. 6 And now it is because of my hope in what God has promised our fathers that I am on trial today. 7 This is the promise our twelve tribes are hoping to see fulfilled as they earnestly serve God day and night. O king, it is because of this hope that the Jews are accusing me. 8 Why should any of you consider it incredible that God raises the dead?

9 "I too was convinced that I ought to do all that was possible to oppose the name of Jesus of Nazareth. 10 And that is just what I did in Jerusalem. On the authority of the chief priests I put many of the saints in prison, and when they were put to death, I cast my vote against them. 11 Many a time I went from one synagogue to another to have them punished, and I tried to force them to blaspheme. In my obsession against them, I even went to foreign cities to persecute them.

12 "On one of these journeys I was going to Damascus with the authority and commission of the chief priests. 13 About noon, O king, as I was on the road, I saw a light from heaven, brighter than the sun, blazing around me and my companions. 14 We all fell to the ground, and I heard a voice saying to me in Aramaic,ᵃ 'Saul, Saul, why do you persecute me? It is hard for you to kick against the goads.'

15 "Then I asked, 'Who are you, Lord?'

" 'I am Jesus, whom you are persecuting,' the Lord replied. 16 'Now get up and stand on your feet. I have appeared to you to appoint you as a servant and as a witness of what you have seen of me and what I will show you. 17 I will rescue you from your own people and from the Gentiles. I am sending you to them 18 to open their eyes and turn them from darkness to light, and from the power of Satan to God, so that they may receive forgiveness of sins and a place among those who are sanctified by faith in me.'

19 "So then, King Agrippa, I was not disobedient to the vision from heaven.

20 First to those in Damascus, then to those in Jerusalem and in all Judea, and to the Gentiles also, I preached that they should repent and turn to God and prove their repentance by their deeds. 21 That is why the Jews seized me in the temple courts and tried to kill me. 22 But I have had God's help to this very day, and so I stand here and testify to small and great alike. I am saying nothing beyond what the prophets and Moses said would happen— 23 that the Christᵇ would suffer and, as the first to rise from the dead, would proclaim light to his own people and to the Gentiles."

24 At this point Festus interrupted Paul's defense. "You are out of your mind, Paul!" he shouted. "Your great learning is driving you insane."

25 "I am not insane, most excellent Festus," Paul replied. "What I am saying is true and reasonable. 26 The king is familiar with these things, and I can speak freely to him. I am convinced that none of this has escaped his notice, because it was not done in a corner. 27 King Agrippa, do you believe the prophets? I know you do."

28 Then Agrippa said to Paul, "Do you think that in such a short time you can persuade me to be a Christian?"

29 Paul replied, "Short time or long—I pray God that not only you but all who are listening to me today may become what I am, except for these chains."

30 The king rose, and with him the governor and Bernice and those sitting with them. 31 They left the room, and while talking with one another, they said, "This man is not doing anything that deserves death or imprisonment."

32 Agrippa said to Festus, "This man could have been set free if he had not appealed to Caesar."

Paul Sails for Rome

27 When it was decided that we would sail for Italy, Paul and some other prisoners were handed over to a centurion named Julius, who belonged to the Imperial Regiment. 2 We boarded a ship from Adramyttium about to sail for ports along the coast of the province of Asia, and we put out to sea. Aristarchus, a Macedonian from Thessalonica, was with us.

ᵃ14 Or Hebrew　　ᵇ23 Or Messiah

³The next day we landed at Sidon; and Julius, in kindness to Paul, allowed him to go to his friends so they might provide for his needs. ⁴From there we put out to sea again and passed to the lee of Cyprus because the winds were against us. ⁵When we had sailed across the open sea off the coast of Cilicia and Pamphylia, we landed at Myra in Lycia. ⁶There the centurion found an Alexandrian ship sailing for Italy and put us on board. ⁷We made slow headway for many days and had difficulty arriving off Cnidus. When the wind did not allow us to hold our course, we sailed to the lee of Crete, opposite Salmone. ⁸We moved along the coast with difficulty and came to a place called Fair Havens, near the town of Lasea.

⁹Much time had been lost, and sailing had already become dangerous because by now it was after the Fast.ᵃ So Paul warned them, ¹⁰"Men, I can see that our voyage is going to be disastrous and bring great loss to ship and cargo, and to our own lives also." ¹¹But the centurion, instead of listening to what Paul said, followed the advice of the pilot and of the owner of the ship. ¹²Since the harbor was unsuitable to winter in, the majority decided that we should sail on, hoping to reach Phoenix and winter there. This was a harbor in Crete, facing both southwest and northwest.

The Storm

¹³When a gentle south wind began to blow, they thought they had obtained what they wanted; so they weighed anchor and sailed along the shore of Crete. ¹⁴Before very long, a wind of hurricane force, called the "northeaster," swept down from the island. ¹⁵The ship was caught by the storm and could not head into the wind; so we gave way to it and were driven along. ¹⁶As we passed to the lee of a small island called Cauda, we were hardly able to make the lifeboat secure. ¹⁷When the men had hoisted it aboard, they passed ropes under the ship itself to hold it together. Fearing that they would run aground on the sandbars of Syrtis, they lowered the sea anchor and let the ship be driven along. ¹⁸We took such a violent battering from the storm that the

ᵃ9 That is, the Day of Atonement (Yom Kippur)

Storm Warnings

Friday

ACTS 27:10-44 When you live in southern Florida like we do, you get used to hearing the local meteorologists give warnings about hurricanes. But even when a hurricane is imminent, it can be difficult to heed the warning. During the hours before a hurricane strikes, the skies can be clear and sunny. However, anyone who has lived here very long knows that these warnings need to be taken very seriously.

Similarly, there are warnings that surface in a marriage—warnings that need to be taken seriously to avoid a potentially damaging situation. Warnings can be found in attitudes. When we discover an attitude such as, "I deserve better than this," "if only I had . . ." or "just this one time . . ." we should take these thoughts as very serious warnings.

Eric was a husband who allowed these self-centered attitudes to slowly sail him into ungodly behaviors that were contradictory to the marriage commitment. He allowed himself to have lunch alone with female co-workers—something he vowed he would never do. A fellow Christian co-worker noticed and warned him about it, but Eric continued on anyway . . . until his marriage wrecked on the rocks of infidelity.

Warning signals offer an opportunity to evaluate what needs to be done to turn ourselves around before it's too late. Assess the source of any weaknesses and what can be done to repair the damage to your marriage. Every marriage has seasons when storm warnings occur. Will you take the warnings seriously or allow the storm to hit and bring devastation in its wake?

—Bob and Rosemary

Go to page 1220 for your next devotional reading.

next day they began to throw the cargo overboard. ¹⁹On the third day, they threw the ship's tackle overboard with their own hands. ²⁰When neither sun nor stars appeared for many days and the storm continued raging, we finally gave up all hope of being saved.

²¹After the men had gone a long time without food, Paul stood up before them and said: "Men, you should have taken my advice not to sail from Crete; then you would have spared yourselves this damage and loss. ²²But now I urge you to keep up your courage, because not one of you will be lost; only the ship will be destroyed. ²³Last night an angel of the God whose I am and whom I serve stood beside me ²⁴and said, 'Do not be afraid, Paul. You must stand trial before Caesar; and God has graciously given you the lives of all who sail with you.' ²⁵So keep up your courage, men, for I have faith in God that it will happen just as he told me. ²⁶Nevertheless, we must run aground on some island."

The Shipwreck

²⁷On the fourteenth night we were still being driven across the Adriatic[a] Sea, when about midnight the sailors sensed they were approaching land. ²⁸They took soundings and found that the water was a hundred and twenty feet[b] deep. A short time later they took soundings again and found it was ninety feet[c] deep. ²⁹Fearing that we would be dashed against the rocks, they dropped four anchors from the stern and prayed for daylight. ³⁰In an attempt to escape from the ship, the sailors let the lifeboat down into the sea, pretending they were going to lower some anchors from the bow. ³¹Then Paul said to the centurion and the soldiers, "Unless these men stay with the ship, you cannot be saved." ³²So the soldiers cut the ropes that held the lifeboat and let it fall away.

³³Just before dawn Paul urged them all to eat. "For the last fourteen days," he said, "you have been in constant suspense and have gone without food—you haven't eaten anything. ³⁴Now I urge you to take some food. You need it to survive. Not one of you will lose a single hair from his head." ³⁵After he said this, he took some bread and gave thanks to God in front of them all. Then he broke it and began to eat. ³⁶They were all encouraged and ate some food themselves. ³⁷Altogether there were 276 of us on board. ³⁸When they had eaten as much as they wanted, they lightened the ship by throwing the grain into the sea.

³⁹When daylight came, they did not recognize the land, but they saw a bay with a sandy beach, where they decided to run the ship aground if they could. ⁴⁰Cutting loose the anchors, they left them in the sea and at the same time untied the ropes that held the rudders. Then they hoisted the foresail to the wind and made for the beach. ⁴¹But the ship struck a sandbar and ran aground. The bow stuck fast and would not move, and the stern was broken to pieces by the pounding of the surf.

⁴²The soldiers planned to kill the prisoners to prevent any of them from swimming away and escaping. ⁴³But the centurion wanted to spare Paul's life and kept them from carrying out their plan. He ordered those who could swim to jump overboard first and get to land. ⁴⁴The rest were to get there on planks or on pieces of the ship. In this way everyone reached land in safety.

Ashore on Malta

28 Once safely on shore, we found out that the island was called Malta. ²The islanders showed us unusual kindness. They built a fire and welcomed us all because it was raining and cold. ³Paul gathered a pile of brushwood and, as he put it on the fire, a viper, driven out by the heat, fastened itself on his hand. ⁴When the islanders saw the snake hanging from his hand, they said to each other, "This man must be a murderer; for though he escaped from the sea, Justice has not allowed him to live." ⁵But Paul shook the snake off into the fire and suffered no ill effects. ⁶The people expected him to swell up or suddenly fall dead, but after waiting a long time and seeing nothing unusual happen to him, they changed their minds and said he was a god.

---

[a]27 In ancient times the name referred to an area extending well south of Italy.   [b]28 Greek *twenty orguias* (about 37 meters)   [c]28 Greek *fifteen orguias* (about 27 meters)

⁷There was an estate nearby that belonged to Publius, the chief official of the island. He welcomed us to his home and for three days entertained us hospitably. ⁸His father was sick in bed, suffering from fever and dysentery. Paul went in to see him and, after prayer, placed his hands on him and healed him. ⁹When this had happened, the rest of the sick on the island came and were cured. ¹⁰They honored us in many ways and when we were ready to sail, they furnished us with the supplies we needed.

Arrival at Rome

¹¹After three months we put out to sea in a ship that had wintered in the island. It was an Alexandrian ship with the figurehead of the twin gods Castor and Pollux. ¹²We put in at Syracuse and stayed there three days. ¹³From there we set sail and arrived at Rhegium. The next day the south wind came up, and on the following day we reached Puteoli. ¹⁴There we found some brothers who invited us to spend a week with them. And so we came to Rome. ¹⁵The brothers there had heard that we were coming, and they traveled as far as the Forum of Appius and the Three Taverns to meet us. At the sight of these men Paul thanked God and was encouraged. ¹⁶When we got to Rome, Paul was allowed to live by himself, with a soldier to guard him.

Paul Preaches at Rome Under Guard

¹⁷Three days later he called together the leaders of the Jews. When they had assembled, Paul said to them: "My brothers, although I have done nothing against our people or against the customs of our ancestors, I was arrested in Jerusalem and handed over to the Romans. ¹⁸They examined me and wanted to release me, because I was not guilty of any crime deserving death. ¹⁹But when the Jews objected, I was compelled to appeal to Caesar—not that I had any charge to bring against my own people. ²⁰For this reason I have asked to see you and talk with you. It is because of the hope of Israel that I am bound with this chain."

²¹They replied, "We have not received any letters from Judea concerning you, and none of the brothers who have come from there has reported or said anything bad about you. ²²But we want to hear what your views are, for we know that people everywhere are talking against this sect."

²³They arranged to meet Paul on a certain day, and came in even larger numbers to the place where he was staying. From morning till evening he explained and declared to them the kingdom of God and tried to convince them about Jesus from the Law of Moses and from the Prophets. ²⁴Some were convinced by what he said, but others would not believe. ²⁵They disagreed among themselves and began to leave after Paul had made this final statement: "The Holy Spirit spoke the truth to your forefathers when he said through Isaiah the prophet:

²⁶" 'Go to this people and say,
  "You will be ever hearing but never
      understanding;
    you will be ever seeing but never
      perceiving."
²⁷For this people's heart has become
      calloused;
    they hardly hear with their ears,
    and they have closed their eyes.
  Otherwise they might see with their
      eyes,
    hear with their ears,
    understand with their hearts
  and turn, and I would heal them.'ᵃ

²⁸"Therefore I want you to know that God's salvation has been sent to the Gentiles, and they will listen!"ᵇ

³⁰For two whole years Paul stayed there in his own rented house and welcomed all who came to see him. ³¹Boldly and without hindrance he preached the kingdom of God and taught about the Lord Jesus Christ.

ᵃ27 Isaiah 6:9,10   ᵇ28 Some manuscripts listen!"
²⁹After he said this, the Jews left, arguing vigorously among themselves.

Romans

Why do I struggle with sin even though I'm a Christian? Why do some people accept Jesus as Savior and Lord but others don't? How can a gracious and loving God judge and punish people?

If you've ever wanted answers for questions like these, you'll find a clear expression of Christian belief in lively, practical terms in the book of Romans. But be prepared! Reading this book has been a turning point for many, including Martin Luther and John Wesley. If you're hungry for spiritual renewal, read Romans—it's a great place to begin.

1 Paul, a servant of Christ Jesus, called to be an apostle and set apart for the gospel of God— ²the gospel he promised beforehand through his prophets in the Holy Scriptures ³regarding his Son, who as to his human nature was a descendant of David, ⁴and who through the Spirit*a* of holiness was declared with power to be the Son of God*b* by his resurrection from the dead: Jesus Christ our Lord. ⁵Through him and for his name's sake, we received grace and apostleship to call people from among all the Gentiles to the obedience that comes from faith. ⁶And you also are among those who are called to belong to Jesus Christ.

⁷To all in Rome who are loved by God and called to be saints:

Grace and peace to you from God our Father and from the Lord Jesus Christ.

Paul's Longing to Visit Rome

⁸First, I thank my God through Jesus Christ for all of you, because your faith is being reported all over the world. ⁹God, whom I serve with my whole heart in preaching the gospel of his Son, is my witness how constantly I remember you ¹⁰in my prayers at all times; and I pray that now at last by God's will the way may be opened for me to come to you.

¹¹I long to see you so that I may impart to you some spiritual gift to make you strong— ¹²that is, that you and I may be mutually encouraged by each other's faith. ¹³I do not want you to be unaware, brothers, that I planned many times to come to you (but have been prevented from doing so until now) in order that I

a4 Or *who as to his spirit*   *b4* Or *was appointed to be the Son of God with power* might have a harvest among you, just as I have had among the other Gentiles.

[14]I am obligated both to Greeks and non-Greeks, both to the wise and the foolish. [15]That is why I am so eager to preach the gospel also to you who are at Rome.

[16]I am not ashamed of the gospel, because it is the power of God for the salvation of everyone who believes: first for the Jew, then for the Gentile. [17]For in the gospel a righteousness from God is revealed, a righteousness that is by faith from first to last,[a] just as it is written: "The righteous will live by faith."[b]

God's Wrath Against Mankind

[18]The wrath of God is being revealed from heaven against all the godlessness and wickedness of men who suppress the truth by their wickedness, [19]since what may be known about God is plain to them, because God has made it plain to them. [20]For since the creation of the world God's invisible qualities—his eternal power and divine nature—have been clearly seen, being understood from what has been made, so that men are without excuse.

[21]For although they knew God, they neither glorified him as God nor gave thanks to him, but their thinking became futile and their foolish hearts were darkened. [22]Although they claimed to be wise, they became fools [23]and exchanged the glory of the immortal God for images made to look like mortal man and birds and animals and reptiles.

[24]Therefore God gave them over in the sinful desires of their hearts to sexual impurity for the degrading of their bodies with one another. [25]They exchanged the truth of God for a lie, and worshiped and served created things rather than the Creator—who is forever praised. Amen.

[26]Because of this, God gave them over to shameful lusts. Even their women exchanged natural relations for unnatural ones. [27]In the same way the men also abandoned natural relations with women and were inflamed with lust for one another. Men committed indecent acts with other men, and received in themselves the due penalty for their perversion.

[28]Furthermore, since they did not think it worthwhile to retain the knowledge of God, he gave them over to a depraved mind, to do what ought not to be done. [29]They have become filled with every kind of wickedness, evil, greed and depravity. They are full of envy, murder, strife, deceit and malice. They are gossips, [30]slanderers, God-haters, insolent, arrogant and boastful; they invent ways of doing evil; they disobey their parents; [31]they are senseless, faithless, heartless, ruthless. [32]Although they know God's righteous decree that those who do such things deserve death, they not only continue to do these very things but also approve of those who practice them.

God's Righteous Judgment

2 You, therefore, have no excuse, you who pass judgment on someone else, for at whatever point you judge the other, you are condemning yourself, because you who pass judgment do the same things. [2]Now we know that God's judgment against those who do such things is based on truth. [3]So when you, a mere man, pass judgment on them and yet do the same things, do you think you will escape God's judgment? [4]Or do you show contempt for the riches of his kindness, tolerance and patience, not realizing that God's kindness leads you toward repentance?

[5]But because of your stubbornness and your unrepentant heart, you are storing up wrath against yourself for the day of God's wrath, when his righteous judgment will be revealed. [6]God "will give to each person according to what he has done."[c] [7]To those who by persistence in doing good seek glory, honor and immortality, he will give eternal life. [8]But for those who are self-seeking and who reject the truth and follow evil, there will be wrath and anger. [9]There will be trouble and distress for every human being who does evil: first for the Jew, then for the Gentile; [10]but glory, honor and peace for everyone who does good: first for the Jew, then for the Gentile. [11]For God does not show favoritism.

[12]All who sin apart from the law will also perish apart from the law, and all

[a]17 Or is from faith to faith   [b]17 Hab. 2:4
[c]6 Psalm 62:12; Prov. 24:12

who sin under the law will be judged by the law. [13]For it is not those who hear the law who are righteous in God's sight, but it is those who obey the law who will be declared righteous. [14](Indeed, when Gentiles, who do not have the law, do by nature things required by the law, they are a law for themselves, even though they do not have the law, [15]since they show that the requirements of the law are written on their hearts, their consciences also bearing witness, and their thoughts now accusing, now even defending them.) [16]This will take place on the day when God will judge men's secrets through Jesus Christ, as my gospel declares.

The Jews and the Law

[17]Now you, if you call yourself a Jew; if you rely on the law and brag about your relationship to God; [18]if you know his will and approve of what is superior because you are instructed by the law; [19]if you are convinced that you are a guide for the blind, a light for those who are in the dark, [20]an instructor of the foolish, a teacher of infants, because you have in the law the embodiment of knowledge and truth— [21]you, then, who teach others, do you not teach yourself? You who preach against stealing, do you steal? [22]You who say that people should not commit adultery, do you commit adultery? You who abhor idols, do you rob temples? [23]You who brag about the law, do you dishonor God by breaking the law? [24]As it is written: "God's name is blasphemed among the Gentiles because of you."[a]

[25]Circumcision has value if you observe the law, but if you break the law, you have become as though you had not been circumcised. [26]If those who are not circumcised keep the law's requirements, will they not be regarded as though they were circumcised? [27]The one who is not circumcised physically and yet obeys the law will condemn you who, even though

[a]24 Isaiah 52:5; Ezek. 36:22

Don't Give Up

ROMANS 2:7 An African proverb says, "Perseverance is everything." The apostle Paul would certainly agree. As he makes clear in this verse, eternal life hinges on our capacity to persevere.

Ignacy Paderewski, the great Polish pianist, composer and statesman, was waiting to begin one of his recitals when an eight-year-old boy from the audience slid out of his seat and headed for the stage before his parents could stop him. The young man seated himself at the piano and began playing "Chopsticks." The audience scowled at this brash lad with his jarring sounds. From the side of the stage, however, Paderewski entered and quietly slid up behind the boy, reaching his long arms out to the right and left of the two small hands. Paderewski began to improvise on the "Chopsticks" theme. Suddenly the simple melody, played imperfectly, took on a sound of beauty, blessed with the master's approval and touch. The audience burst into applause. Everybody noticed that Paderewski kept whispering into the boy's ear. It was later revealed that he just kept saying, "Don't quit, don't quit."

We have a similar opportunity in marriage to keep one another keeping on. At those times when one partner is weak, the other can be strong. And when both husband and wife are losing strength, the Master always comes alongside to make our imperfections beautiful. God's voice saying, "Don't quit, don't quit" can keep us persevering.

—*Les and Leslie*.

Quiet TIMES with each other

Weekend Warm-up *Do either of you need help "keeping on" right now?*

Go to page 1222 for your next devotional reading.

you have the[a] written code and circumcision, are a lawbreaker.

²⁸A man is not a Jew if he is only one outwardly, nor is circumcision merely outward and physical. ²⁹No, a man is a Jew if he is one inwardly; and circumcision is circumcision of the heart, by the Spirit, not by the written code. Such a man's praise is not from men, but from God.

God's Faithfulness

3 What advantage, then, is there in being a Jew, or what value is there in circumcision? ²Much in every way! First of all, they have been entrusted with the very words of God.

³What if some did not have faith? Will their lack of faith nullify God's faithfulness? ⁴Not at all! Let God be true, and every man a liar. As it is written:

> "So that you may be proved right
>   when you speak
>   and prevail when you judge."[b]

⁵But if our unrighteousness brings out God's righteousness more clearly, what shall we say? That God is unjust in bringing his wrath on us? (I am using a human argument.) ⁶Certainly not! If that were so, how could God judge the world? ⁷Someone might argue, "If my falsehood enhances God's truthfulness and so increases his glory, why am I still condemned as a sinner?" ⁸Why not say— as we are being slanderously reported as saying and as some claim that we say— "Let us do evil that good may result"? Their condemnation is deserved.

No One Is Righteous

⁹What shall we conclude then? Are we any better[c]? Not at all! We have already made the charge that Jews and Gentiles alike are all under sin. ¹⁰As it is written:

> "There is no one righteous, not even
>   one;
> ¹¹   there is no one who understands,
>   no one who seeks God.
> ¹²All have turned away,
>   they have together become
>   worthless;
>   there is no one who does good,
>   not even one."[d]
> ¹³ "Their throats are open graves;

> their tongues practice deceit."[e]
> "The poison of vipers is on their
>   lips."[f]
> 14   "Their mouths are full of cursing
>   and bitterness."[g]
> ¹⁵"Their feet are swift to shed blood;
> 16   ruin and misery mark their ways,
> ¹⁷and the way of peace they do not
>   know."[h]
> 18   "There is no fear of God before
>   their eyes."[i]

¹⁹Now we know that whatever the law says, it says to those who are under the law, so that every mouth may be silenced and the whole world held accountable to God. ²⁰Therefore no one will be declared righteous in his sight by observing the law; rather, through the law we become conscious of sin.

Righteousness Through Faith

²¹But now a righteousness from God, apart from law, has been made known, to which the Law and the Prophets testify.

[a]27 Or who, by means of a   [b]4 Psalm 51:4
[c]9 Or worse   [d]12 Psalms 14:1-3; 53:1-3;
Eccles. 7:20   [e]13 Psalm 5:9
[f]13 Psalm 140:3   [g]14 Psalm 10:7
[h]17 Isaiah 59:7,8   [i]18 Psalm 36:1

²²This righteousness from God comes through faith in Jesus Christ to all who believe. There is no difference, ²³for all have sinned and fall short of the glory of God, ²⁴and are justified freely by his grace through the redemption that came by Christ Jesus. ²⁵God presented him as a sacrifice of atonement,[a] through faith in his blood. He did this to demonstrate his justice, because in his forbearance he had left the sins committed beforehand unpunished— ²⁶he did it to demonstrate his justice at the present time, so as to be just and the one who justifies those who have faith in Jesus.

²⁷Where, then, is boasting? It is excluded. On what principle? On that of observing the law? No, but on that of faith. ²⁸For we maintain that a man is justified by faith apart from observing the law. ²⁹Is God the God of Jews only? Is he not the God of Gentiles too? Yes, of Gentiles too, ³⁰since there is only one God, who will justify the circumcised by faith and the uncircumcised through that same faith. ³¹Do we, then, nullify the law by this faith? Not at all! Rather, we uphold the law.

Abraham Justified by Faith

4 What then shall we say that Abraham, our forefather, discovered in this mat-ter? ²If, in fact, Abraham was justified by works, he had something to boast about— but not before God. ³What does the Scripture say? "Abraham believed God, and it was credited to him as righteousness."[b]

⁴Now when a man works, his wages are not credited to him as a gift, but as an obligation. ⁵However, to the man who does not work but trusts God who justifies the wicked, his faith is credited as righteousness. ⁶David says the same thing when he speaks of the blessedness of the man to whom God credits righteousness apart from works:

⁷"Blessed are they
    whose transgressions are forgiven,
    whose sins are covered.
⁸Blessed is the man
    whose sin the Lord will never
        count against him."[c]

⁹Is this blessedness only for the circumcised, or also for the uncircumcised? We have been saying that Abraham's faith was credited to him as righteousness. ¹⁰Under what circumstances was it credited? Was it after he was circumcised, or

---

[a]25 Or *as the one who would turn aside his wrath, taking away sin*   [b]3 Gen. 15:6; also in verse 22
[c]8 Psalm 32:1,2

Law Versus Love

Monday

ROMANS 3:20 The early church struggled with legalism. Because Judaism emphasized keeping God's Law, the first Christians had to decide what place laws and rules would play in their new lives in Jesus Christ. In the book of Galatians, Paul goes to great lengths to convince new Christians that circumcision is not necessary for their salvation. Following the rules, keeping the old Jewish laws, will not save you. Only a relationship with Jesus Christ will bring you redemption.

Many contemporary Christians have never really felt too comfortable balancing rules and relationships. But if there were ever an earthly testing ground for this important task, it is in marriage. We've all

known of couples who became so uptight and rigid about the way things should be done in marriage that the relationship never stood a chance. It was too weighted down with rules. On the opposite end of the continuum is the so-called "open marriage" where anything goes and there is barely a rule to be found. So what's the balance?

Laws and rules have their place. We need them in our spiritual walk, we need them in society and we need them in marriage. But here's what rule-bound couples often forget: Rules turn sour when they become more important than relationships.

—Les and Leslie

Go to page 1224 for your next devotional reading.

before? It was not after, but before! ¹¹And he received the sign of circumcision, a seal of the righteousness that he had by faith while he was still uncircumcised. So then, he is the father of all who believe but have not been circumcised, in order that righteousness might be credited to them. ¹²And he is also the father of the circumcised who not only are circumcised but who also walk in the footsteps of the faith that our father Abraham had before he was circumcised.

¹³It was not through law that Abraham and his offspring received the promise that he would be heir of the world, but through the righteousness that comes by faith. ¹⁴For if those who live by law are heirs, faith has no value and the promise is worthless, ¹⁵because law brings wrath. And where there is no law there is no transgression.

¹⁶Therefore, the promise comes by faith, so that it may be by grace and may be guaranteed to all Abraham's offspring—not only to those who are of the law but also to those who are of the faith of Abraham. He is the father of us all. ¹⁷As it is written: "I have made you a father of many nations."ᵃ He is our father in the sight of God, in whom he believed—the God who gives life to the dead and calls things that are not as though they were.

¹⁸Against all hope, Abraham in hope believed and so became the father of many nations, just as it had been said to him, "So shall your offspring be."ᵇ ¹⁹Without weakening in his faith, he faced the fact that his body was as good as dead—since he was about a hundred years old—and that Sarah's womb was also dead. ²⁰Yet he did not waver through unbelief regarding the promise of God, but was strengthened in his faith and gave glory to God, ²¹being fully persuaded that God had power to do what he had promised. ²²This is why "it was credited to him as righteousness." ²³The words "it was credited to him" were written not for him alone, ²⁴but also for us, to whom God will credit righteousness—for us who believe in him who raised Jesus our Lord from the dead. ²⁵He was delivered over to death for our sins and was raised to life for our justification.

Abraham and Sarah

ROMANS 4:1–25 Few couples have shown their faith in God more clearly than Abraham and Sarah. But it was never easy. By faith, Abraham went to a place he would later receive as his inheritance, even though he did not know where he was going. Surviving famine, he and Sarah made the journey to Canaan, the Promised Land. When Abraham was ninety-nine and Sarah was ninety, God gave them a son Isaac—the heir God had promised.

COUPLES
IN THE
BIBLE

Can you imagine hearing that you would be entering parenthood at this old age? No doubt Abraham and Sarah had to make major adjustments to their nearly lifelong lifestyle as a twosome when little Isaac arrived on the scene. But that's not all.

When Isaac was a boy, God asked Abraham to sacrifice this cherished son upon an altar—an ultimate test of faith. Thankfully God provided a ram for the sacrifice instead of Isaac. Throughout all of these challenges, Abraham and Sarah listened to God and obeyed him. Surely their marriage endured hardships and confusion though all of these trials. But it stayed strong because their faith in God's plan for them stayed strong.

Peace and Joy

5 Therefore, since we have been justified through faith, weᶜ have peace with God through our Lord Jesus Christ, ²through whom we have gained access by faith into this grace in which we now stand. And weᶜ rejoice in the hope of the glory of God. ³Not only so, but weᶜ also rejoice in our sufferings, because we know that suffering produces perseverance; ⁴perseverance, character; and character, hope. ⁵And hope does not disappoint us, because God has poured out his love into our hearts by the Holy Spirit, whom he has given us.

⁶You see, at just the right time, when we were still powerless, Christ died for the

ᵃ17 Gen. 17:5   ᵇ18 Gen. 15:5   ᶜ1,2,3 Or let us

ungodly. 7Very rarely will anyone die for a righteous man, though for a good man someone might possibly dare to die. 8But God demonstrates his own love for us in this: While we were still sinners, Christ died for us.

9Since we have now been justified by his blood, how much more shall we be saved from God's wrath through him! 10For if, when we were God's enemies, we were reconciled to him through the death of his Son, how much more, having been reconciled, shall we be saved through his life! 11Not only is this so, but we also rejoice in God through our Lord Jesus Christ, through whom we have now received reconciliation.

Death Through Adam, Life Through Christ

12Therefore, just as sin entered the world through one man, and death through sin, and in this way death came to all men, because all sinned— 13for before the law was given, sin was in the world. But sin is not taken into account when there is no law. 14Nevertheless, death reigned from the time of Adam to the time of Moses, even over those who did not sin by breaking a command, as did Adam, who was a pattern of the one to come.

15But the gift is not like the trespass. For if the many died by the trespass of the one man, how much more did God's grace and the gift that came by the grace of the one man, Jesus Christ, overflow to the many! 16Again, the gift of God is not like the result of the one man's sin: The judgment followed one sin and brought condemnation, but the gift followed many trespasses and brought justification. 17For if, by the trespass of the one man, death reigned through that one man, how much more will those who receive God's abundant provision of grace and of the gift of righteousness reign in life through the one man, Jesus Christ.

18Consequently, just as the result of one trespass was condemnation for all men, so also the result of one act of righteousness was justification that brings life for all men. 19For just as through the disobedience of the one man the many were made sinners, so also through the obedi-

Holding on to Hope

Tuesday

ROMANS 5:3–5 We sat in a small German restaurant and listened to our friends, Roger and Kristin, as they told us the saga of the past fifteen years Kristin has struggled with her health. Living in and out of hospitals and enduring treatments— most of which have not been effective— have left Kristin weak and anemic. She still struggles with her health each day, and we were encouraged that she felt well enough to meet us at the restaurant.

Roger and Kristin have experienced far more than their share of suffering. Yet as we saw the loving, tender way Roger looked at Kristin, we were amazed at the depth of his love. Kristin was radiant as she told us all the ways God encourages her and gives her hope.

How different from another dinner engagement we had with Tim and Cathy. As they glared at each other across the table,

COUPLE MINUTES

Tim said, "It just didn't work out. After we got married, Cathy and I changed. We're too opposite. The divorce is final next week. We'll try to stay friends, but our marriage is over. We had hoped things would be different."

Tim and Cathy's hope was not the Biblical hope that Roger and Kristin claim. We all have problems, but God makes the difference in whether we are successful or not in solving them. Problems are simply the stage upon which we play out our lives.

While problems and suffering are not enjoyable, we can tap into God's resources, and he can make something positive out of the negative. That's the message of this passage. When we allow God to work, we can learn perseverance, develop character and experience hope.

—Dave and Claudia

Go to page 1230 for your next devotional reading.

ence of the one man the many will be made righteous.

²⁰The law was added so that the trespass might increase. But where sin increased, grace increased all the more, ²¹so that, just as sin reigned in death, so also grace might reign through righteousness to bring eternal life through Jesus Christ our Lord.

Dead to Sin, Alive in Christ

6 What shall we say, then? Shall we go on sinning so that grace may increase? ²By no means! We died to sin; how can we live in it any longer? ³Or don't you know that all of us who were baptized into Christ Jesus were baptized into his death? ⁴We were therefore buried with him through baptism into death in order that, just as Christ was raised from the dead through the glory of the Father, we too may live a new life.

⁵If we have been united with him like this in his death, we will certainly also be united with him in his resurrection. ⁶For we know that our old self was crucified with him so that the body of sin might be done away with,ᵃ that we should no longer be slaves to sin— ⁷because anyone who has died has been freed from sin.

⁸Now if we died with Christ, we believe that we will also live with him. ⁹For we know that since Christ was raised from the dead, he cannot die again; death no longer has mastery over him. ¹⁰The death he died, he died to sin once for all; but the life he lives, he lives to God.

¹¹In the same way, count yourselves dead to sin but alive to God in Christ Jesus. ¹²Therefore do not let sin reign in your mortal body so that you obey its evil desires. ¹³Do not offer the parts of your body to sin, as instruments of wickedness, but rather offer yourselves to God, as those who have been brought from death to life; and offer the parts of your body to him as instruments of righteousness. ¹⁴For sin shall not be your master, because you are not under law, but under grace.

Slaves to Righteousness

¹⁵What then? Shall we sin because we are not under law but under grace? By no means! ¹⁶Don't you know that when you

offer yourselves to someone to obey him as slaves, you are slaves to the one whom you obey—whether you are slaves to sin, which leads to death, or to obedience, which leads to righteousness? ¹⁷But thanks be to God that, though you used to be slaves to sin, you wholeheartedly obeyed the form of teaching to which you were entrusted. ¹⁸You have been set free from sin and have become slaves to righteousness.

¹⁹I put this in human terms because you are weak in your natural selves. Just as you used to offer the parts of your body in slavery to impurity and to ever-increasing wickedness, so now offer them in slavery to righteousness leading to holiness. ²⁰When you were slaves to sin, you were free from the control of righteousness. ²¹What benefit did you reap at that time from the things you are now ashamed of? Those things result in death! ²²But now that you have been set free from sin and have become slaves to God, the benefit you reap leads to holiness, and the result is eternal life. ²³For the wages of sin is death, but the gift of God is eternal life inᵇ Christ Jesus our Lord.

An Illustration From Marriage

7 Do you not know, brothers—for I am speaking to men who know the law— that the law has authority over a man only as long as he lives? ²For example, by law a married woman is bound to her husband as long as he is alive, but if her husband dies, she is released from the law of marriage. ³So then, if she marries another man while her husband is still alive, she is called an adulteress. But if her husband dies, she is released from that law and is not an adulteress, even though she marries another man.

⁴So, my brothers, you also died to the law through the body of Christ, that you might belong to another, to him who was raised from the dead, in order that we might bear fruit to God. ⁵For when we were controlled by the sinful nature,ᶜ the sinful passions aroused by the law were at work in our bodies, so that we bore fruit for death. ⁶But now, by dying to what once bound us, we have been re-

ᵃ6 Or *be rendered powerless*   ᵇ23 Or *through*
ᶜ5 Or *the flesh*; also in verse 25

leased from the law so that we serve in the new way of the Spirit, and not in the old way of the written code.

Struggling With Sin

⁷What shall we say, then? Is the law sin? Certainly not! Indeed I would not have known what sin was except through the law. For I would not have known what coveting really was if the law had not said, "Do not covet." *a* ⁸But sin, seizing the opportunity afforded by the commandment, produced in me every kind of covetous desire. For apart from law, sin is dead. ⁹Once I was alive apart from law; but when the commandment came, sin sprang to life and I died. ¹⁰I found that the very commandment that was intended to bring life actually brought death. ¹¹For sin, seizing the opportunity afforded by the commandment, deceived me, and through the commandment put me to death. ¹²So then, the law is holy, and the commandment is holy, righteous and good.

¹³Did that which is good, then, become death to me? By no means! But in order that sin might be recognized as sin, it produced death in me through what was good, so that through the commandment sin might become utterly sinful.

¹⁴We know that the law is spiritual; but I am unspiritual, sold as a slave to sin. ¹⁵I do not understand what I do. For what I want to do I do not do, but what I hate I do. ¹⁶And if I do what I do not want to do, I agree that the law is good. ¹⁷As it is, it is no longer I myself who do it, but it is sin living in me. ¹⁸I know that nothing good lives in me, that is, in my sinful nature. *b* For I have the desire to do what is good, but I cannot carry it out. ¹⁹For what I do is not the good I want to do; no, the evil I do not want to do—this I keep on doing. ²⁰Now if I do what I do not want to do, it is no longer I who do it, but it is sin living in me that does it.

²¹So I find this law at work: When I want to do good, evil is right there with me. ²²For in my inner being I delight in God's law; ²³but I see another law at work in the members of my body, waging war against the law of my mind and making me a prisoner of the law of sin at work within my members. ²⁴What a wretched

man I am! Who will rescue me from this body of death? ²⁵Thanks be to God—through Jesus Christ our Lord!

So then, I myself in my mind am a slave to God's law, but in the sinful nature a slave to the law of sin.

Life Through the Spirit

8 Therefore, there is now no condemnation for those who are in Christ Jesus, *c* ²because through Christ Jesus the law of the Spirit of life set me free from the law of sin and death. ³For what the law was powerless to do in that it was weakened by the sinful nature, *d* God did by sending his own Son in the likeness of sinful man to be a sin offering. *e* And so he condemned sin in sinful man, *f* ⁴in order that the righteous requirements of the law might be fully met in us, who do not live according to the sinful nature but according to the Spirit.

⁵Those who live according to the sinful nature have their minds set on what that nature desires; but those who live in accordance with the Spirit have their minds set on what the Spirit desires. ⁶The mind of sinful man *g* is death, but the mind controlled by the Spirit is life and peace; ⁷the sinful mind *h* is hostile to God. It does not submit to God's law, nor can it do so. ⁸Those controlled by the sinful nature cannot please God.

⁹You, however, are controlled not by the sinful nature but by the Spirit, if the Spirit of God lives in you. And if anyone does not have the Spirit of Christ, he does not belong to Christ. ¹⁰But if Christ is in you, your body is dead because of sin, yet your spirit is alive because of righteousness. ¹¹And if the Spirit of him who raised Jesus from the dead is living in you, he who raised Christ from the dead will also give life to your mortal bodies through his Spirit, who lives in you.

¹²Therefore, brothers, we have an obligation—but it is not to the sinful nature, to live according to it. ¹³For if you live according to the sinful nature, you will

---

a 7 Exodus 20:17; Deut. 5:21   *b* 18 Or *my flesh*
c 1 Some later manuscripts *Jesus, who do not live according to the sinful nature but according to the Spirit,*   *d* 3 Or *the flesh*; also in verses 4, 5, 8, 9, 12 and 13   *e* 3 Or *man, for sin*   *f* 3 Or *in the flesh*   *g* 6 Or *mind set on the flesh*   *h* 7 Or *the mind set on the flesh*

die; but if by the Spirit you put to death the misdeeds of the body, you will live, [14]because those who are led by the Spirit of God are sons of God. [15]For you did not receive a spirit that makes you a slave again to fear, but you received the Spirit of sonship.[a] And by him we cry, "Abba,[b] Father." [16]The Spirit himself testifies with our spirit that we are God's children. [17]Now if we are children, then we are heirs—heirs of God and co-heirs with Christ, if indeed we share in his sufferings in order that we may also share in his glory.

Future Glory

[18]I consider that our present sufferings are not worth comparing with the glory that will be revealed in us. [19]The creation waits in eager expectation for the sons of God to be revealed. [20]For the creation was subjected to frustration, not by its own choice, but by the will of the one who subjected it, in hope [21]that[c] the creation itself will be liberated from its bondage to decay and brought into the glorious freedom of the children of God.

[22]We know that the whole creation has been groaning as in the pains of childbirth right up to the present time. [23]Not only so, but we ourselves, who have the firstfruits of the Spirit, groan inwardly as we wait eagerly for our adoption as sons, the redemption of our bodies. [24]For in this hope we were saved. But hope that is seen is no hope at all. Who hopes for what he already has? [25]But if we hope for what we do not yet have, we wait for it patiently.

[26]In the same way, the Spirit helps us in our weakness. We do not know what we ought to pray for, but the Spirit himself intercedes for us with groans that words cannot express. [27]And he who searches our hearts knows the mind of the Spirit, because the Spirit intercedes for the saints in accordance with God's will.

More Than Conquerors

[28]And we know that in all things God works for the good of those who love him,[d] who[e] have been called according to his purpose. [29]For those God foreknew he also predestined to be conformed to the likeness of his Son, that he might

be the firstborn among many brothers. [30]And those he predestined, he also called; those he called, he also justified; those he justified, he also glorified.

[31]What, then, shall we say in response to this? If God is for us, who can be against us? [32]He who did not spare his own Son, but gave him up for us all—how will he not also, along with him, graciously give us all things? [33]Who will bring any charge against those whom God has chosen? It is God who justifies. [34]Who is he that condemns? Christ Jesus, who died—more than that, who was raised to life—is at the right hand of God and is also interceding for us. [35]Who shall separate us from the love of Christ? Shall trouble or hardship or persecution or famine or nakedness or danger or sword? [36]As it is written:

> "For your sake we face death all day
>   long;
>   we are considered as sheep to be
>   slaughtered."[f]

[37]No, in all these things we are more than conquerors through him who loved us. [38]For I am convinced that neither death nor life, neither angels nor demons,[g] neither the present nor the future, nor any powers, [39]neither height nor depth, nor anything else in all creation, will be able to separate us from the love of God that is in Christ Jesus our Lord.

God's Sovereign Choice

9 I speak the truth in Christ—I am not lying, my conscience confirms it in the Holy Spirit— [2]I have great sorrow and unceasing anguish in my heart. [3]For I could wish that I myself were cursed and cut off from Christ for the sake of my brothers, those of my own race, [4]the people of Israel. Theirs is the adoption as sons; theirs the divine glory, the covenants, the receiving of the law, the temple worship and the promises. [5]Theirs are the patriarchs, and from them is traced

---

[a]15 Or *adoption*   [b]15 Aramaic for *Father*
[c]20,21 Or *subjected it in hope.* [21]*For*   [d]28 Some manuscripts *And we know that all things work together for good to those who love God*   [e]28 Or *works together with those who love him to bring about what is good—with those who*   [f]36 Psalm 44:22
[g]38 Or *nor heavenly rulers*

the human ancestry of Christ, who is God over all, forever praised![a] Amen.

[6]It is not as though God's word had failed. For not all who are descended from Israel are Israel. [7]Nor because they are his descendants are they all Abraham's children. On the contrary, "It is through Isaac that your offspring will be reckoned."[b] [8]In other words, it is not the natural children who are God's children, but it is the children of the promise who are regarded as Abraham's offspring. [9]For this was how the promise was stated: "At the appointed time I will return, and Sarah will have a son."[c]

[10]Not only that, but Rebekah's children had one and the same father, our father Isaac. [11]Yet, before the twins were born or had done anything good or bad—in order that God's purpose in election might stand: [12]not by works but by him who calls—she was told, "The older will serve the younger."[d] [13]Just as it is written: "Jacob I loved, but Esau I hated."[e]

[14]What then shall we say? Is God unjust? Not at all! [15]For he says to Moses,

"I will have mercy on whom I have
        mercy,
  and I will have compassion on
        whom I have compassion."[f]

[16]It does not, therefore, depend on man's desire or effort, but on God's mercy. [17]For the Scripture says to Pharaoh: "I raised you up for this very purpose, that I might display my power in you and that my name might be proclaimed in all the earth."[g] [18]Therefore God has mercy on whom he wants to have mercy, and he hardens whom he wants to harden.

[19]One of you will say to me: "Then why does God still blame us? For who resists his will?" [20]But who are you, O man, to talk back to God? "Shall what is formed say to him who formed it, 'Why did you make me like this?' "[h] [21]Does not the potter have the right to make out of the same lump of clay some pottery for noble purposes and some for common use?

[22]What if God, choosing to show his wrath and make his power known, bore with great patience the objects of his wrath—prepared for destruction? [23]What if he did this to make the riches of his glory known to the objects of his mercy, whom he prepared in advance for glory— [24]even us, whom he also called, not only from the Jews but also from the Gentiles? [25]As he says in Hosea:

"I will call them 'my people' who are
        not my people;
  and I will call her 'my loved one'
        who is not my loved one,"[i]

[26]and,

"It will happen that in the very place
        where it was said to them,
  'You are not my people,'
  they will be called 'sons of the living
        God.' "[j]

[27]Isaiah cries out concerning Israel:

"Though the number of the Israelites
        be like the sand by the sea,
  only the remnant will be saved.
[28]For the Lord will carry out
  his sentence on earth with speed
        and finality."[k]

[29]It is just as Isaiah said previously:

"Unless the Lord Almighty
  had left us descendants,
  we would have become like Sodom,
  we would have been like
        Gomorrah."[l]

Israel's Unbelief

[30]What then shall we say? That the Gentiles, who did not pursue righteousness, have obtained it, a righteousness that is by faith; [31]but Israel, who pursued a law of righteousness, has not attained it. [32]Why not? Because they pursued it not by faith but as if it were by works. They stumbled over the "stumbling stone." [33]As it is written:

"See, I lay in Zion a stone that causes
        men to stumble
  and a rock that makes them fall,
  and the one who trusts in him will
        never be put to shame."[m]

[a]5 Or Christ, who is over all. God be forever praised! Or Christ. God who is over all be forever praised!
[b]7 Gen. 21:12   [c]9 Gen. 18:10,14
[d]12 Gen. 25:23   [e]13 Mal. 1:2,3
[f]15 Exodus 33:19   [g]17 Exodus 9:16
[h]20 Isaiah 29:16; 45:9   [i]25 Hosea 2:23
[j]26 Hosea 1:10   [k]28 Isaiah 10:22,23
[l]29 Isaiah 1:9   [m]33 Isaiah 8:14; 28:16

10 Brothers, my heart's desire and prayer to God for the Israelites is that they may be saved. ²For I can testify about them that they are zealous for God, but their zeal is not based on knowledge. ³Since they did not know the righteousness that comes from God and sought to establish their own, they did not submit to God's righteousness. ⁴Christ is the end of the law so that there may be righteousness for everyone who believes.

⁵Moses describes in this way the righteousness that is by the law: "The man who does these things will live by them."[a] ⁶But the righteousness that is by faith says: "Do not say in your heart, 'Who will ascend into heaven?'[b]" (that is, to bring Christ down) ⁷"or 'Who will descend into the deep?'[c]" (that is, to bring Christ up from the dead). ⁸But what does it say? "The word is near you; it is in your mouth and in your heart,"[d] that is, the word of faith we are proclaiming: ⁹That if you confess with your mouth, "Jesus is Lord," and believe in your heart that God raised him from the dead, you will be saved. ¹⁰For it is with your heart that you believe and are justified, and it is with your mouth that you confess and are saved. ¹¹As the Scripture says, "Anyone who trusts in him will never be put to shame."[e] ¹²For there is no difference between Jew and Gentile—the same Lord is Lord of all and richly blesses all who call on him, ¹³for, "Everyone who calls on the name of the Lord will be saved."[f]

¹⁴How, then, can they call on the one they have not believed in? And how can they believe in the one of whom they have not heard? And how can they hear without someone preaching to them? ¹⁵And how can they preach unless they are sent? As it is written, "How beautiful are the feet of those who bring good news!"[g]

¹⁶But not all the Israelites accepted the good news. For Isaiah says, "Lord, who has believed our message?"[h] ¹⁷Consequently, faith comes from hearing the message, and the message is heard through the word of Christ. ¹⁸But I ask: Did they not hear? Of course they did:

"Their voice has gone out into all the earth,

their words to the ends of the world."[i]

¹⁹Again I ask: Did Israel not understand? First, Moses says,

"I will make you envious by those
who are not a nation;
I will make you angry by a nation
that has no understanding."[j]

²⁰And Isaiah boldly says,

"I was found by those who did not
seek me;
I revealed myself to those who did
not ask for me."[k]

²¹But concerning Israel he says,

"All day long I have held out my
hands
to a disobedient and obstinate
people."[l]

The Remnant of Israel

11 I ask then: Did God reject his people? By no means! I am an Israelite myself, a descendant of Abraham, from the tribe of Benjamin. ²God did not reject his people, whom he foreknew. Don't you know what the Scripture says in the passage about Elijah—how he appealed to God against Israel: ³"Lord, they have killed your prophets and torn down your altars; I am the only one left, and they are trying to kill me"[m]? ⁴And what was God's answer to him? "I have reserved for myself seven thousand who have not bowed the knee to Baal."[n] ⁵So too, at the present time there is a remnant chosen by grace. ⁶And if by grace, then it is no longer by works; if it were, grace would no longer be grace.[o]

⁷What then? What Israel sought so earnestly it did not obtain, but the elect did. The others were hardened, ⁸as it is written:

"God gave them a spirit of stupor,

---

a5 Lev. 18:5   b6 Deut. 30:12
c7 Deut. 30:13   d8 Deut. 30:14
e11 Isaiah 28:16   f13 Joel 2:32
g15 Isaiah 52:7   h16 Isaiah 53:1
i18 Psalm 19:4   j19 Deut. 32:21
k20 Isaiah 65:1   l21 Isaiah 65:2
m3 1 Kings 19:10,14   n4 1 Kings 19:18
o6 Some manuscripts by grace. But if by works, then it is no longer grace; if it were, work would no longer be work.

eyes so that they could not see
and ears so that they could not
hear,
to this very day." [a]

[9]And David says:

"May their table become a snare and
a trap,
a stumbling block and a retribution
for them.
[10]May their eyes be darkened so they
cannot see,
and their backs be bent forever." [b]

Ingrafted Branches

[11]Again I ask: Did they stumble so as to
fall beyond recovery? Not at all! Rather,
because of their transgression, salvation
has come to the Gentiles to make Israel
envious. [12]But if their transgression
means riches for the world, and their loss
means riches for the Gentiles, how much
greater riches will their fullness bring!

[13]I am talking to you Gentiles. Inas-
much as I am the apostle to the Gentiles,
I make much of my ministry [14]in the hope
that I may somehow arouse my own people to envy and save some of them. [15]For
if their rejection is the reconciliation of
the world, what will their acceptance be
but life from the dead? [16]If the part of the
dough offered as firstfruits is holy, then
the whole batch is holy; if the root is holy,
so are the branches.

[17]If some of the branches have been
broken off, and you, though a wild olive
shoot, have been grafted in among the
others and now share in the nourishing
sap from the olive root, [18]do not boast
over those branches. If you do, consider
this: You do not support the root, but the
root supports you. [19]You will say then,
"Branches were broken off so that I could
be grafted in." [20]Granted. But they were
broken off because of unbelief, and you
stand by faith. Do not be arrogant, but be
afraid. [21]For if God did not spare the nat-

[a]8 Deut. 29:4; Isaiah 29:10
[b]10 Psalm 69:22,23

Built to Last

Wednesday

ROMANS 12:1-2 Within the pages
of Billy Graham's autobiography,
Just As I Am, are many wonderful
snapshots, but our favorite is the
picture of Ruth and Billy Graham
renewing their vows on their fiftieth wedding anniversary. Ruth is
wearing her fifty-year-old wedding dress.
As you observe the peace, love and joy
evidenced in this picture, you know that
they have lived out Romans 12:1-2 in their
lives and marriage.

They have resisted conforming to the
"pattern of this world." That's the pattern
that advocates philosophies like, "Meet my
needs," "I want to be first" and serial marriage—"If things don't work out, we'll just
divorce."

Instead, Billy and Ruth Graham have allowed God to continually transform them
by the renewing of their minds. Servanthood, sacrifice, unconditional love and
forgiveness are descriptive of their relationship that has been lived out over the

years, both in their private lives and
in the public eye. But it wasn't always easy for them. Dr. Graham
writes, "If Ruth had not been convinced that God had called her to
fulfill that side of our partnership
(the active parenting side), and had
not resorted constantly to God's Word for
instruction and to his grace for strength,
I don't see how she could have survived." [*]

Does Romans 12:1-2 reflect your marriage relationship? Why not let these verses
challenge you today to put aside negative
thoughts and let God renew your mind—
and your marriage. Start by listing areas in
which you would like to experience renewal, such as being a servant to your
spouse or being quicker to forgive and
expressing unconditional love. Like the
Grahams, you can build a marriage that
will last. **—Dave and Claudia**

Go to page 1232 for your next devotional reading.

[*]Graham, Billy. *Just As I Am.*
Grand Rapids, MI: Zondervan, 1997 (p. 704).

ural branches, he will not spare you either.

²²Consider therefore the kindness and sternness of God: sternness to those who fell, but kindness to you, provided that you continue in his kindness. Otherwise, you also will be cut off. ²³And if they do not persist in unbelief, they will be grafted in, for God is able to graft them in again. ²⁴After all, if you were cut out of an olive tree that is wild by nature, and contrary to nature were grafted into a cultivated olive tree, how much more readily will these, the natural branches, be grafted into their own olive tree!

All Israel Will Be Saved

²⁵I do not want you to be ignorant of this mystery, brothers, so that you may not be conceited: Israel has experienced a hardening in part until the full number of the Gentiles has come in. ²⁶And so all Israel will be saved, as it is written:

"The deliverer will come from Zion;
    he will turn godlessness away from
        Jacob.
²⁷And this is^a my covenant with them
    when I take away their sins."^b

²⁸As far as the gospel is concerned, they are enemies on your account; but as far as election is concerned, they are loved on account of the patriarchs, ²⁹for God's gifts and his call are irrevocable. ³⁰Just as you who were at one time disobedient to God have now received mercy as a result of their disobedience, ³¹so they too have now become disobedient in order that they too may now^c receive mercy as a result of God's mercy to you. ³²For God has bound all men over to disobedience so that he may have mercy on them all.

Doxology

³³Oh, the depth of the riches of the
        wisdom and^d knowledge of
        God!
    How unsearchable his judgments,
        and his paths beyond tracing out!
³⁴"Who has known the mind of the
        Lord?
    Or who has been his counselor?"^e
³⁵"Who has ever given to God,
    that God should repay him?"^f

Built to Last

On a scale of one to five (one being "low" and five being "high"), rate the following qualities needed for renewing your marriage:

Forgiveness

Service

Compassion

Unconditional love

Trust

Spirit of rejoicing

Optimism

Sacrifice

Choose an area and think of one practical thing you can do today to renew your marriage.

³⁶For from him and through him and
        to him are all things.
    To him be the glory forever! Amen.

Living Sacrifices

12 Therefore, I urge you, brothers, in view of God's mercy, to offer your bodies as living sacrifices, holy and pleasing to God—this is your spiritual^g act of worship. ²Do not conform any longer to the pattern of this world, but be transformed by the renewing of your mind. Then you will be able to test and approve what God's will is—his good, pleasing and perfect will.

³For by the grace given me I say to every one of you: Do not think of yourself more highly than you ought, but rather think of yourself with sober judgment, in accordance with the measure of faith God has given you. ⁴Just as each of us has one body with many members, and these members do not all have the same function, ⁵so in Christ we who are many form

---

^a27 Or will be   ^b27 Isaiah 59:20,21; 27:9;
Jer. 31:33,34   ^c31 Some manuscripts do not
have now.   ^d33 Or riches and the wisdom and the
^e34 Isaiah 40:13   ^f35 Job 41:11   ^g1 Or
reasonable

one body, and each member belongs to all the others. ⁶We have different gifts, according to the grace given us. If a man's gift is prophesying, let him use it in proportion to his*a* faith. ⁷If it is serving, let him serve; if it is teaching, let him teach; ⁸if it is encouraging, let him encourage; if it is contributing to the needs of others, let him give generously; if it is leadership, let him govern diligently; if it is showing mercy, let him do it cheerfully.

Love

⁹Love must be sincere. Hate what is evil; cling to what is good. ¹⁰Be devoted to one another in brotherly love. Honor one another above yourselves. ¹¹Never be lacking in zeal, but keep your spiritual fervor, serving the Lord. ¹²Be joyful in hope, patient in affliction, faithful in prayer. ¹³Share with God's people who are in need. Practice hospitality.

¹⁴Bless those who persecute you; bless and do not curse. ¹⁵Rejoice with those who rejoice; mourn with those who mourn. ¹⁶Live in harmony with one another. Do not be proud, but be willing to associate with people of low position.*b* Do not be conceited.

¹⁷Do not repay anyone evil for evil. Be careful to do what is right in the eyes of everybody. ¹⁸If it is possible, as far as it depends on you, live at peace with everyone. ¹⁹Do not take revenge, my friends, but leave room for God's wrath, for it is written: "It is mine to avenge; I will repay,"*c* says the Lord. ²⁰On the contrary:

> "If your enemy is hungry, feed him;
>   if he is thirsty, give him something
>   to drink.
> In doing this, you will heap burning
>   coals on his head."*d*

²¹Do not be overcome by evil, but overcome evil with good.

Submission to the Authorities

13 Everyone must submit himself to the governing authorities, for there is no authority except that which God has

a6 Or *in agreement with the*   *b16* Or *willing to do menial work*   *c19* Deut. 32:35
d20 Prov. 25:21,22

The Deadly Emotion of Anger

Thursday

ROMANS 12:17–21 It would be tough to find another emotion that has caused married couples more damage than anger. Why do we get angry at the person we love the most? Why do we allow ourselves to get angry when we know in advance that we will need to apologize? Why do we raise our voices when it does no good?

We have seen firsthand in our marriage counseling how different people use different means for dealing with their anger. Some try to deny it by calling it something else. They confuse anger with fatigue or feeling nervous or uptight. Others try to deal with their anger by suppressing it. They make every effort to keep it from showing. Still others try to spiritualize their anger by talking about anger that is righteous and anger that is unrighteous (which usually means "my anger is righteous and yours isn't"). We have even seen some relationships in which one partner flaunts anger: "This is the way God made me. You know what I am like so you just might as well get used to it. It's in my genes."

Well, anger is not inherited. It is learned and can be unlearned. And anger by any other name is still anger. Whether suppressed, spiritualized or flaunted, anger can damage even the best of marriages.

What matters is not whether or not you get angry but what you do with your anger once it kicks in. That's why Paul encourages us, "Be careful to do what is right . . . live at peace with everyone" (verses 17–18). He warns us, "Do not take revenge . . ." (verse 19). God will help us manage our anger when we ask.

—Les and Leslie

Go to page 1234 for your next devotional reading.

established. The authorities that exist have been established by God. ²Consequently, he who rebels against the authority is rebelling against what God has instituted, and those who do so will bring judgment on themselves. ³For rulers hold no terror for those who do right, but for those who do wrong. Do you want to be free from fear of the one in authority? Then do what is right and he will commend you. ⁴For he is God's servant to do you good. But if you do wrong, be afraid, for he does not bear the sword for nothing. He is God's servant, an agent of wrath to bring punishment on the wrongdoer. ⁵Therefore, it is necessary to submit to the authorities, not only because of possible punishment but also because of conscience.

⁶This is also why you pay taxes, for the authorities are God's servants, who give their full time to governing. ⁷Give everyone what you owe him: If you owe taxes, pay taxes; if revenue, then revenue; if respect, then respect; if honor, then honor.

Love, for the Day Is Near

⁸Let no debt remain outstanding, except the continuing debt to love one another, for he who loves his fellowman has fulfilled the law. ⁹The commandments, "Do not commit adultery," "Do not murder," "Do not steal," "Do not covet,"ᵃ and whatever other commandment there may be, are summed up in this one rule: "Love your neighbor as yourself."ᵇ ¹⁰Love does no harm to its neighbor. Therefore love is the fulfillment of the law.

¹¹And do this, understanding the present time. The hour has come for you to wake up from your slumber, because our salvation is nearer now than when we first believed. ¹²The night is nearly over; the day is almost here. So let us put aside the deeds of darkness and put on the armor of light. ¹³Let us behave decently, as in the daytime, not in orgies and drunkenness, not in sexual immorality and debauchery, not in dissension and jealousy. ¹⁴Rather, clothe yourselves with the Lord Jesus Christ, and do not think about how to gratify the desires of the sinful nature.ᶜ

The Weak and the Strong

14 Accept him whose faith is weak, without passing judgment on disputable matters. ²One man's faith allows him to eat everything, but another man, whose faith is weak, eats only vegetables. ³The man who eats everything must not look down on him who does not, and the man who does not eat everything must not condemn the man who does, for God has accepted him. ⁴Who are you to judge someone else's servant? To his own master he stands or falls. And he will stand, for the Lord is able to make him stand.

⁵One man considers one day more sacred than another; another man considers every day alike. Each one should be fully convinced in his own mind. ⁶He who regards one day as special, does so to the Lord. He who eats meat, eats to the Lord, for he gives thanks to God; and he who abstains, does so to the Lord and gives thanks to God. ⁷For none of us lives to himself alone and none of us dies to himself alone. ⁸If we live, we live to the Lord; and if we die, we die to the Lord. So, whether we live or die, we belong to the Lord.

⁹For this very reason, Christ died and returned to life so that he might be the Lord of both the dead and the living. ¹⁰You, then, why do you judge your brother? Or why do you look down on your brother? For we will all stand before God's judgment seat. ¹¹It is written:

" 'As surely as I live,' says the Lord,
'every knee will bow before me;
    every tongue will confess to
        God.' "ᵈ

¹²So then, each of us will give an account of himself to God.

¹³Therefore let us stop passing judgment on one another. Instead, make up your mind not to put any stumbling block or obstacle in your brother's way. ¹⁴As one who is in the Lord Jesus, I am fully convinced that no foodᵉ is unclean in itself. But if anyone regards something as unclean, then for him it is unclean. ¹⁵If your brother is distressed because of what

ᵃ9 Exodus 20:13-15,17; Deut. 5:17-19,21
ᵇ9 Lev. 19:18　　ᶜ14 Or the flesh
ᵈ11 Isaiah 45:23　　ᵉ14 Or that nothing

you eat, you are no longer acting in love. Do not by your eating destroy your brother for whom Christ died. ¹⁶Do not allow what you consider good to be spoken of as evil. ¹⁷For the kingdom of God is not a matter of eating and drinking, but of righteousness, peace and joy in the Holy Spirit, ¹⁸because anyone who serves Christ in this way is pleasing to God and approved by men.

¹⁹Let us therefore make every effort to do what leads to peace and to mutual edification. ²⁰Do not destroy the work of God for the sake of food. All food is clean, but it is wrong for a man to eat anything that causes someone else to stumble. ²¹It is better not to eat meat or drink wine or to do anything else that will cause your brother to fall.

²²So whatever you believe about these things keep between yourself and God. Blessed is the man who does not condemn himself by what he approves. ²³But the man who has doubts is condemned if he eats, because his eating is not from faith; and everything that does not come from faith is sin.

15 We who are strong ought to bear with the failings of the weak and not to please ourselves. ²Each of us should please his neighbor for his good, to build him up. ³For even Christ did not please himself but, as it is written: "The insults of those who insult you have fallen on me."ᵃ ⁴For everything that was written in the past was written to teach us, so that through endurance and the encouragement of the Scriptures we might have hope.

⁵May the God who gives endurance and encouragement give you a spirit of unity among yourselves as you follow Christ Jesus, ⁶so that with one heart and mouth you may glorify the God and Father of our Lord Jesus Christ.

⁷Accept one another, then, just as Christ accepted you, in order to bring praise to God. ⁸For I tell you that Christ has become a servant of the Jewsᵇ on behalf of God's truth, to confirm the promises made to the patriarchs ⁹so that

ᵃ3 Psalm 69:9   ᵇ8 Greek *circumcision*

You're Not the Boss of Me

Friday

ROMANS 14:10–13 When a person's head is not linked to his or her heart, real love is difficult to muster—especially in marriage. The result is a spouse we sometimes call "the controller."

Controllers, analytical by nature, typically use two powerful tools in gaining and maintaining control in their marriage. The first is fear. Controllers have refined the technique of "winning through intimidation." They have a hawk-like eye for their partner's weakness, and their partner knows it. Without so much as a peep, the controller can shoot fear and anxiety into his or her mate like Rambo fires a machine gun.

The second tool of control is guilt. A controlling husband can make his wife feel guilty for not having supper on the table at exactly 6:00. A controlling wife can maneuver her husband into performing tasks for which she is actually responsible by laying on a sense of obligation and guilt. Controllers needle the conscience of their partner to provoke them to do what they want done.

The disciple Peter, in his own bungling way, was a controller. He kept trying to tell Jesus what to do and what to say, to the point where Jesus rebuked him sharply: "Get behind me, Satan! You are a stumbling block to me; you do not have in mind the things of God, but the things of men" (Matthew 16:23). Finally, humbled by his denial of Jesus, Peter became an effective leader of the new church, even admitting his fault when Paul confronted him for forcing Gentiles to follow Jewish laws (Galatians 2:11–14).

The secret to not becoming a control freak is found in balancing your head with your heart.

—*Les and Leslie*

Go to page 1236 for your next devotional reading.

the Gentiles may glorify God for his mercy, as it is written:

"Therefore I will praise you among
   the Gentiles;
I will sing hymns to your name." [a]

[10]Again, it says,

"Rejoice, O Gentiles, with his
   people." [b]

[11]And again,

"Praise the Lord, all you Gentiles,
   and sing praises to him, all you
      peoples." [c]

[12]And again, Isaiah says,

"The Root of Jesse will spring up,
   one who will arise to rule over the
      nations;
the Gentiles will hope in him." [d]

[13]May the God of hope fill you with all joy and peace as you trust in him, so that you may overflow with hope by the power of the Holy Spirit.

Paul the Minister to the Gentiles

[14]I myself am convinced, my brothers, that you yourselves are full of goodness, complete in knowledge and competent to instruct one another. [15]I have written you quite boldly on some points, as if to remind you of them again, because of the grace God gave me [16]to be a minister of Christ Jesus to the Gentiles with the priestly duty of proclaiming the gospel of God, so that the Gentiles might become an offering acceptable to God, sanctified by the Holy Spirit.

[17]Therefore I glory in Christ Jesus in my service to God. [18]I will not venture to speak of anything except what Christ has accomplished through me in leading the Gentiles to obey God by what I have said and done— [19]by the power of signs and miracles, through the power of the Spirit. So from Jerusalem all the way around to Illyricum, I have fully proclaimed the gospel of Christ. [20]It has always been my ambition to preach the gospel where Christ was not known, so that I would not be building on someone else's foundation. [21]Rather, as it is written:

"Those who were not told about him
   will see,

You're Not the Boss of Me

Take a moment to answer each of these questions on your own. Then compare your answers to your spouse's.

Yes No I agree that criticism is like a poison to marriage.

Yes No Do I think there's a difference between criticizing and complaining in marriage?

Yes No Have I identified specific things I am most tempted to be critical of in our marriage relationship?

Yes No Do I know what to do to reduce criticism in our marriage?

Yes No Can I respond with maturity when I feel my spouse has been critical of me?

and those who have not heard will
   understand." [e]

[22]This is why I have often been hindered from coming to you.

Paul's Plan to Visit Rome

[23]But now that there is no more place for me to work in these regions, and since I have been longing for many years to see you, [24]I plan to do so when I go to Spain. I hope to visit you while passing through and to have you assist me on my journey there, after I have enjoyed your company for a while. [25]Now, however, I am on my way to Jerusalem in the service of the saints there. [26]For Macedonia and Achaia were pleased to make a contribution for the poor among the saints in Jerusalem. [27]They were pleased to do it, and indeed they owe it to them. For if the Gentiles have shared in the Jews' spiritual blessings, they owe it to the Jews to share with them their material blessings. [28]So after I have completed this task and have made sure that they have received this fruit, I will go to Spain and visit you on the way. [29]I know that when I come to you, I will

[a]9 2 Samuel 22:50; Psalm 18:49
[b]10 Deut. 32:43   [c]11 Psalm 117:1
[d]12 Isaiah 11:10   [e]21 Isaiah 52:15

come in the full measure of the blessing of Christ.

³⁰I urge you, brothers, by our Lord Jesus Christ and by the love of the Spirit, to join me in my struggle by praying to God for me. ³¹Pray that I may be rescued from the unbelievers in Judea and that my service in Jerusalem may be acceptable to the saints there, ³²so that by God's will I may come to you with joy and together with you be refreshed. ³³The God of peace be with you all. Amen.

Personal Greetings

16 I commend to you our sister Phoebe, a servant*ᵃ* of the church in Cenchrea. ²I ask you to receive her in the Lord in a way worthy of the saints and to give her any help she may need from you, for she has been a great help to many people, including me.

³Greet Priscilla*ᵇ* and Aquila, my fellow workers in Christ Jesus. ⁴They risked their lives for me. Not only I but all the churches of the Gentiles are grateful to them.

⁵Greet also the church that meets at their house.

Greet my dear friend Epenetus, who was the first convert to Christ in the province of Asia.

⁶Greet Mary, who worked very hard for you.

⁷Greet Andronicus and Junias, my relatives who have been in prison with me. They are outstanding among the apostles, and they were in Christ before I was.

⁸Greet Ampliatus, whom I love in the Lord.

⁹Greet Urbanus, our fellow worker in Christ, and my dear friend Stachys.

¹⁰Greet Apelles, tested and approved in Christ.

Greet those who belong to the household of Aristobulus.

¹¹Greet Herodion, my relative.

Greet those in the household of Narcissus who are in the Lord.

ᵃ1 Or *deaconess*　　*ᵇ3* Greek *Prisca*, a variant of *Priscilla*

Enduring Love

ROMANS 15:5 Disappointments, little irritating habits—every marriage has them. How well do you endure them? One trait of a successful, long-term marriage is the willingness to tolerate each other's idiosyncrasies and to accept each other as a package deal. We've been married over thirty-five years and have had many opportunities to test our enduring love. For instance, I continue to pick up Claudia's tissues she leaves behind, and Claudia continues to overlook the lint I leave on the carpet when I walk around the house in my socks.

One wife who faced more that just little irritating habits commented on how she chose to have enduring love in her marriage: "I've always tried to grab the best from the past and focus on the future. Because my marriage is so precious to me, I haven't been willing to throw it away just because 'I'm right' in a situation and my husband is wrong."

When we choose to endure, then God gives encouragement. Through the years spouses grow closer to each other through enduring the hard times and celebrating the good times. As you begin to accept each other as a package deal, you can live out the rest of this passage. With one heart and mouth you (and your marriage) will glorify the God and Father of our Lord Jesus Christ (see verse 6).

—Dave and Claudia

Weekend Warm-up *What is something you cherish about each other?*

Go to page 1239 for your next devotional reading.

¹²Greet Tryphena and Tryphosa, those women who work hard in the Lord. Greet my dear friend Persis, another woman who has worked very hard in the Lord. ¹³Greet Rufus, chosen in the Lord, and his mother, who has been a mother to me, too. ¹⁴Greet Asyncritus, Phlegon, Hermes, Patrobas, Hermas and the brothers with them. ¹⁵Greet Philologus, Julia, Nereus and his sister, and Olympas and all the saints with them. ¹⁶Greet one another with a holy kiss.

All the churches of Christ send greetings.

¹⁷I urge you, brothers, to watch out for those who cause divisions and put obstacles in your way that are contrary to the teaching you have learned. Keep away from them. ¹⁸For such people are not serving our Lord Christ, but their own appetites. By smooth talk and flattery they deceive the minds of naive people. ¹⁹Everyone has heard about your obedience, so I am full of joy over you; but I want you to be wise about what is good, and innocent about what is evil.

²⁰The God of peace will soon crush Satan under your feet.

The grace of our Lord Jesus be with you.

²¹Timothy, my fellow worker, sends his greetings to you, as do Lucius, Jason and Sosipater, my relatives.

²²I, Tertius, who wrote down this letter, greet you in the Lord.

²³Gaius, whose hospitality I and the whole church here enjoy, sends you his greetings.

Erastus, who is the city's director of public works, and our brother Quartus send you their greetings.[a]

²⁵Now to him who is able to establish you by my gospel and the proclamation of Jesus Christ, according to the revelation of the mystery hidden for long ages past, ²⁶but now revealed and made known through the prophetic writings by the command of the eternal God, so that all nations might believe and obey him— ²⁷to the only wise God be glory forever through Jesus Christ! Amen.

[a]23 Some manuscripts *their greetings.* ²⁴*May the grace of our Lord Jesus Christ be with all of you. Amen.*

1 Corinthians

There's a good chance that Corinth might have ranked first on the "Top 10" list for "The Ancient World's Most Wicked Cities." The Corinthian Christians faced the difficulty of following Jesus Christ in the midst of a contaminated culture. The church had to deal with problems such as sexual immorality, dissension among various groups, Christians suing Christians and misuse of spiritual gifts.

Paul's letter addresses these issues, but it also tackles some underlying spiritual issues—inspiring readers with a few words on love (chapter 13) and on the resurrection (chapter 15). Let this book inspire you to renew your efforts to follow Jesus as a married person while living in a worldly culture.

1 Paul, called to be an apostle of Christ Jesus by the will of God, and our brother Sosthenes,

²To the church of God in Corinth, to those sanctified in Christ Jesus and called to be holy, together with all those everywhere who call on the name of our Lord Jesus Christ—their Lord and ours:

³Grace and peace to you from God our Father and the Lord Jesus Christ.

Thanksgiving

⁴I always thank God for you because of his grace given you in Christ Jesus. ⁵For in him you have been enriched in every way—in all your speaking and in all your knowledge— ⁶because our testimony about Christ was confirmed in you. ⁷Therefore you do not lack any spiritual gift as you eagerly wait for our Lord Jesus Christ to be revealed. ⁸He will keep you strong to the end, so that you will be blameless on the day of our Lord Jesus Christ. ⁹God, who has called you into fellowship with his Son Jesus Christ our Lord, is faithful.

Divisions in the Church

¹⁰I appeal to you, brothers, in the name of our Lord Jesus Christ, that all of you agree with one another so that there may be no divisions among you and that you may be perfectly united in mind and thought. ¹¹My brothers, some from Chloe's household have informed me

that there are quarrels among you. [12]What I mean is this: One of you says, "I follow Paul"; another, "I follow Apollos"; another, "I follow Cephas[a]"; still another, "I follow Christ."

[13]Is Christ divided? Was Paul crucified for you? Were you baptized into[b] the name of Paul? [14]I am thankful that I did not baptize any of you except Crispus and Gaius, [15]so no one can say that you were baptized into my name. [16](Yes, I also baptized the household of Stephanas; beyond that, I don't remember if I baptized anyone else.) [17]For Christ did not send me to baptize, but to preach the gospel—not with words of human wisdom, lest the cross of Christ be emptied of its power.

Christ the Wisdom and Power of God

[18]For the message of the cross is foolishness to those who are perishing, but to us who are being saved it is the power of God. [19]For it is written:

> "I will destroy the wisdom of the wise;
> the intelligence of the intelligent I will frustrate."[c]

[20]Where is the wise man? Where is the scholar? Where is the philosopher of this age? Has not God made foolish the wisdom of the world? [21]For since in the wisdom of God the world through its wisdom did not know him, God was pleased through the foolishness of what was preached to save those who believe. [22]Jews demand miraculous signs and Greeks look for wisdom, [23]but we preach Christ crucified: a stumbling block to Jews and foolishness to Gentiles, [24]but to those whom God has called, both Jews and Greeks, Christ the power of God and the wisdom of God. [25]For the foolishness of God is wiser than man's wisdom, and the weakness of God is stronger than man's strength.

[26]Brothers, think of what you were when you were called. Not many of you were wise by human standards; not many were influential; not many were of noble birth. [27]But God chose the foolish things of the world to shame the wise; God chose the weak things of the world to shame the strong. [28]He chose the lowly things of this world and the despised things—and the things that are not—to

---

[a]12 That is, Peter   [b]13 Or in; also in verse 15
[c]19 Isaiah 29:14

Strong to the End

Monday

1 CORINTHIANS 1:8-9 Sam and Rita's fortieth anniversary party was a joyful, fun celebration and we were happy to participate. We always like being around Sam and Rita. Besides being a fun couple, they really seem to enjoy their marriage. Near the end of the party, we asked them the secret of their success.

Sam replied, "Our secret is two-fold. First, realizing God created marriage as a life-long commitment has kept us from giving up when we experienced difficulties. Second, I'm married to my best friend."

Rita added, "Even after forty years, we don't take each other for granted. We still try to add to the other's happiness by surprising each other with little gifts, a hug, a kiss, giving a compliment—or just being thoughtful."

Sam continued, "We know a Christian couple going through a divorce right now. They have been married for twenty-five years. This is very sobering. We know that we will always have to work at our marriage and never, ever assume that it will just last without any effort."

Marriage is a marathon—not a sprint. Each day we, like Sam and Rita, choose to invest in our relationship—to build our friendship. With our whole heart, we want to finish well. And to do that we must make our marriage a priority every day. With God's help, and this kind of intentionality, determination and hard work, you too can have a marriage that is strong to the end.
—Dave and Claudia

Go to page 1240 for your next devotional reading.

nullify the things that are, [29]so that no one may boast before him. [30]It is because of him that you are in Christ Jesus, who has become for us wisdom from God— that is, our righteousness, holiness and redemption. [31]Therefore, as it is written: "Let him who boasts boast in the Lord."[a]

2 When I came to you, brothers, I did not come with eloquence or superior wisdom as I proclaimed to you the testimony about God.[b] [2]For I resolved to know nothing while I was with you except Jesus Christ and him crucified. [3]I came to you in weakness and fear, and with much trembling. [4]My message and my preaching were not with wise and persuasive words, but with a demonstration of the Spirit's power, [5]so that your faith might not rest on men's wisdom, but on God's power.

Wisdom From the Spirit

[6]We do, however, speak a message of wisdom among the mature, but not the wisdom of this age or of the rulers of this age, who are coming to nothing. [7]No, we speak of God's secret wisdom, a wisdom that has been hidden and that God destined for our glory before time began.

[8]None of the rulers of this age understood it, for if they had, they would not have crucified the Lord of glory. [9]However, as it is written:

"No eye has seen,
  no ear has heard,
no mind has conceived
  what God has prepared for those
    who love him"[c]—

[10]but God has revealed it to us by his Spirit.

The Spirit searches all things, even the deep things of God. [11]For who among men knows the thoughts of a man except the man's spirit within him? In the same way no one knows the thoughts of God except the Spirit of God. [12]We have not received the spirit of the world but the Spirit who is from God, that we may understand what God has freely given us. [13]This is what we speak, not in words taught us by human wisdom but in words taught by the Spirit, expressing spiritual truths in spiritual words.[d] [14]The man

a31 Jer. 9:24   b1 Some manuscripts as I proclaimed to you God's mystery   c9 Isaiah 64:4   d13 Or Spirit, interpreting spiritual truths to spiritual men

Powerful Truth

Tuesday

1 CORINTHIANS 2:13 There are many books and seminars on the market that instruct people to speak boldly and directly, with commanding power. However, when you speak in a way that demands a person's attention, you can alienate the person to whom you are speaking. Sometimes in the marriage relationship we need to learn to be less forceful, especially in time of conflict. Focusing on building a strong, well-crafted argument is the wrong approach for this situation. The times of conflict in a marriage relationship are already volatile. Added forcefulness will only light the gunpowder.

Our Lord offers believers another "power" to call upon when dealing with conflict—the power of the Holy Spirit. Set aside some time to pray before difficult discussions. A quiet time of prayer, meditating

on God's Word and calling on him for help will allow God's Spirit to control us, so we can be fair and understanding.

Becoming one flesh in a marriage relationship means more than physical intimacy. It means growing together over a period of time so that a couple gets to know each other in greater and deeper intimacy. Cunning debate, forceful argument and a focus on "winning" will only push two people apart. Speaking the truth kindly and gently, empowered with the Holy Spirit, will tenderly knit a couple together. Speak the truth to each other; even speak it with power. But make sure it's the right power: the power of God wrapped in the love of God.

—Bob and Rosemary

Go to page 1242 for your next devotional reading.

without the Spirit does not accept the things that come from the Spirit of God, for they are foolishness to him, and he cannot understand them, because they are spiritually discerned. 15The spiritual man makes judgments about all things, but he himself is not subject to any man's judgment:

16 "For who has known the mind of the Lord
   that he may instruct him?"[a]

But we have the mind of Christ.

On Divisions in the Church

3 Brothers, I could not address you as spiritual but as worldly—mere infants in Christ. 2I gave you milk, not solid food, for you were not yet ready for it. Indeed, you are still not ready. 3You are still worldly. For since there is jealousy and quarreling among you, are you not worldly? Are you not acting like mere men? 4For when one says, "I follow Paul," and another, "I follow Apollos," are you not mere men?

5What, after all, is Apollos? And what is Paul? Only servants, through whom you came to believe—as the Lord has assigned to each his task. 6I planted the seed, Apollos watered it, but God made it grow. 7So neither he who plants nor he who waters is anything, but only God, who makes things grow. 8The man who plants and the man who waters have one purpose, and each will be rewarded according to his own labor. 9For we are God's fellow workers; you are God's field, God's building.

10By the grace God has given me, I laid a foundation as an expert builder, and someone else is building on it. But each one should be careful how he builds. 11For no one can lay any foundation other than the one already laid, which is Jesus Christ. 12If any man builds on this foundation using gold, silver, costly stones, wood, hay or straw, 13his work will be shown for what it is, because the Day will bring it to light. It will be revealed with fire, and the fire will test the quality of each man's work. 14If what he has built survives, he will receive his reward. 15If it is burned up, he will suffer

loss; he himself will be saved, but only as one escaping through the flames.

16Don't you know that you yourselves are God's temple and that God's Spirit lives in you? 17If anyone destroys God's temple, God will destroy him; for God's temple is sacred, and you are that temple.

18Do not deceive yourselves. If any one of you thinks he is wise by the standards of this age, he should become a "fool" so that he may become wise. 19For the wisdom of this world is foolishness in God's sight. As it is written: "He catches the wise in their craftiness"[b]; 20and again, "The Lord knows that the thoughts of the wise are futile."[c] 21So then, no more boasting about men! All things are yours, 22whether Paul or Apollos or Cephas[d] or the world or life or death or the present or the future—all are yours, 23and you are of Christ, and Christ is of God.

Apostles of Christ

4 So then, men ought to regard us as servants of Christ and as those entrusted with the secret things of God. 2Now it is required that those who have been given a trust must prove faithful. 3I care very little if I am judged by you or by any human court; indeed, I do not even judge myself. 4My conscience is clear, but that does not make me innocent. It is the Lord who judges me. 5Therefore judge nothing before the appointed time; wait till the Lord comes. He will bring to light what is hidden in darkness and will expose the motives of men's hearts. At that time each will receive his praise from God.

6Now, brothers, I have applied these things to myself and Apollos for your benefit, so that you may learn from us the meaning of the saying, "Do not go beyond what is written." Then you will not take pride in one man over against another. 7For who makes you different from anyone else? What do you have that you did not receive? And if you did receive it, why do you boast as though you did not?

8Already you have all you want! Already you have become rich! You have become kings—and that without us! How I wish that you really had become kings

a16 Isaiah 40:13   b19 Job 5:13
c20 Psalm 94:11   d22 That is, Peter

so that we might be kings with you! 9For it seems to me that God has put us apostles on display at the end of the procession, like men condemned to die in the arena. We have been made a spectacle to the whole universe, to angels as well as to men. 10We are fools for Christ, but you are so wise in Christ! We are weak, but you are strong! You are honored, we are dishonored! 11To this very hour we go hungry and thirsty, we are in rags, we are brutally treated, we are homeless. 12We work hard with our own hands. When we are cursed, we bless; when we are persecuted, we endure it; 13when we are slandered, we answer kindly. Up to this moment we have become the scum of the earth, the refuse of the world.

14I am not writing this to shame you, but to warn you, as my dear children. 15Even though you have ten thousand guardians in Christ, you do not have many fathers, for in Christ Jesus I became your father through the gospel. 16Therefore I urge you to imitate me. 17For this reason I am sending to you Timothy, my son whom I love, who is faithful in the Lord. He will remind you of my way of life in Christ Jesus, which agrees with what I teach everywhere in every church.

18Some of you have become arrogant, as if I were not coming to you. 19But I will come to you very soon, if the Lord is willing, and then I will find out not only how these arrogant people are talking, but what power they have. 20For the kingdom of God is not a matter of talk but of power. 21What do you prefer? Shall I come to you with a whip, or in love and with a gentle spirit?

Expel the Immoral Brother!

5 It is actually reported that there is sexual immorality among you, and of a kind that does not occur even among pagans: A man has his father's wife. 2And you are proud! Shouldn't you rather have been filled with grief and have put out of your fellowship the man who did this? 3Even though I am not physically present, I am with you in spirit. And I have already passed judgment on the one who did this, just as if I were present. 4When you are assembled in the name of our Lord Jesus and I am with you in spirit, and the power of our Lord Jesus is present, 5hand this man over to Satan, so that the sinful nature[a] may be destroyed and his spirit saved on the day of the Lord.

6Your boasting is not good. Don't you

---

a5 Or *that his body*; or *that the flesh*

God's Canopy

Wednesday

1 CORINTHIANS 4:2 Recently we attended a lovely wedding where the couple was married under a canopy. Flowers and ribbons graciously adorned the tulle canopy under which Cannon and Rachel stood to exchange their marriage vows. The canopy, taken from the Jewish wedding tradition, signified God's protective covering for Cannon and Rachel's marriage.

As we watched Cannon and Rachel exchange their wedding vows, we silently prayed that God's sacred canopy of love would protect and cover their marriage; that God would guide them; that they would remain faithful to their vows taken on this day; and that their marriage would always be distinctively Christian.

This passage gives the guiding principle for living out marital faithfulness. The apostle Paul reminds us "that those who have been given a trust must prove faithful." Do you remember your own wedding day and vowing to love each other "until death do you part?"

For us, in the beginning it seemed so simple. We didn't realize the work that would be involved in living it out. Each day we still need God's sacred canopy of protection. God has given each of us a trust and our part is to prove faithful. Ask him to place his holy canopy of love over your marriage.

—Dave and Claudia

Go to page 1244 for your next devotional reading.

know that a little yeast works through the whole batch of dough? [7]Get rid of the old yeast that you may be a new batch without yeast—as you really are. For Christ, our Passover lamb, has been sacrificed. [8]Therefore let us keep the Festival, not with the old yeast, the yeast of malice and wickedness, but with bread without yeast, the bread of sincerity and truth.

[9]I have written you in my letter not to associate with sexually immoral people— [10]not at all meaning the people of this world who are immoral, or the greedy and swindlers, or idolaters. In that case you would have to leave this world. [11]But now I am writing you that you must not associate with anyone who calls himself a brother but is sexually immoral or greedy, an idolater or a slanderer, a drunkard or a swindler. With such a man do not even eat.

[12]What business is it of mine to judge those outside the church? Are you not to judge those inside? [13]God will judge those outside. "Expel the wicked man from among you."[a]

Lawsuits Among Believers

6 If any of you has a dispute with another, dare he take it before the ungodly for judgment instead of before the saints? [2]Do you not know that the saints will judge the world? And if you are to judge the world, are you not competent to judge trivial cases? [3]Do you not know that we will judge angels? How much more the things of this life! [4]Therefore, if you have disputes about such matters, appoint as judges even men of little account in the church![b] [5]I say this to shame you. Is it possible that there is nobody among you wise enough to judge a dispute between believers? [6]But instead, one brother goes to law against another—and this in front of unbelievers!

[7]The very fact that you have lawsuits among you means you have been completely defeated already. Why not rather be wronged? Why not rather be cheated? [8]Instead, you yourselves cheat and do wrong, and you do this to your brothers.

[9]Do you not know that the wicked will not inherit the kingdom of God? Do not be deceived: Neither the sexually immoral nor idolaters nor adulterers nor male prostitutes nor homosexual offenders [10]nor thieves nor the greedy nor drunkards nor slanderers nor swindlers will inherit the kingdom of God. [11]And that is what some of you were. But you were washed, you were sanctified, you were justified in the name of the Lord Jesus Christ and by the Spirit of our God.

Sexual Immorality

[12]"Everything is permissible for me"— but not everything is beneficial. "Everything is permissible for me"—but I will not be mastered by anything. [13]"Food for the stomach and the stomach for food"—but God will destroy them both. The body is not meant for sexual immorality, but for the Lord, and the Lord for the body. [14]By his power God raised the Lord from the dead, and he will raise us also. [15]Do you not know that your bodies are members of Christ himself? Shall I then take the members of Christ and unite them with a prostitute? Never! [16]Do you not know that he who unites himself with a prostitute is one with her in body? For it is said, "The two will become one flesh."[c] [17]But he who unites himself with the Lord is one with him in spirit.

[18]Flee from sexual immorality. All other sins a man commits are outside his body, but he who sins sexually sins against his own body. [19]Do you not know that your body is a temple of the Holy Spirit, who is in you, whom you have received from God? You are not your own; [20]you were bought at a price. Therefore honor God with your body.

Marriage

7 Now for the matters you wrote about: It is good for a man not to marry.[d] [2]But since there is so much immorality, each man should have his own wife, and each woman her own husband. [3]The husband should fulfill his marital duty to his wife, and likewise the wife to her husband. [4]The wife's body does not belong to her alone but also to her husband. In the same way, the husband's body does

---

[a]13 Deut. 17:7; 19:19; 21:21; 22:21,24; 24:7
[b]4 Or matters, do you appoint as judges men of little account in the church?   [c]16 Gen. 2:24   [d]1 Or "It is good for a man not to have sexual relations with a woman."

not belong to him alone but also to his wife. ⁵Do not deprive each other except by mutual consent and for a time, so that you may devote yourselves to prayer. Then come together again so that Satan will not tempt you because of your lack of self-control. ⁶I say this as a concession, not as a command. ⁷I wish that all men were as I am. But each man has his own gift from God; one has this gift, another has that.

⁸Now to the unmarried and the widows I say: It is good for them to stay unmarried, as I am. ⁹But if they cannot control themselves, they should marry, for it is better to marry than to burn with passion.

¹⁰To the married I give this command (not I, but the Lord): A wife must not separate from her husband. ¹¹But if she does, she must remain unmarried or else be reconciled to her husband. And a husband must not divorce his wife.

¹²To the rest I say this (I, not the Lord): If any brother has a wife who is not a believer and she is willing to live with him, he must not divorce her. ¹³And if a woman has a husband who is not a believer and he is willing to live with her, she must not divorce him. ¹⁴For the unbelieving husband has been sanctified through his wife, and the unbelieving wife has been sanctified through her believing husband. Otherwise your children would be unclean, but as it is, they are holy.

¹⁵But if the unbeliever leaves, let him do so. A believing man or woman is not bound in such circumstances; God has called us to live in peace. ¹⁶How do you know, wife, whether you will save your husband? Or, how do you know, husband, whether you will save your wife?

¹⁷Nevertheless, each one should retain the place in life that the Lord assigned to him and to which God has called him. This is the rule I lay down in all the churches. ¹⁸Was a man already circumcised when he was called? He should not become uncircumcised. Was a man uncircumcised when he was called? He should not be circumcised. ¹⁹Circumcision is

Making Love

Thursday

1 CORINTHIANS 7 In many areas of life, we evaluate the events around us by what we get out of them: "If I do that, buy that, donate that or go there, what's in it for me?" In other words, "What will I get from the experience?" Sometimes we find this self-centered attitude present in our marriage relationship. When that happens, even the sexual part of the marriage relationship can suffer. When we focus on ourselves, we view sex as something we get from marriage rather than something we give to our spouse.

During the first decade of our marriage, I (Bob) honestly believed that sex was something we each took from each other. At first Rosemary also enjoyed the passion, but slowly she began to feel used by the whole experience. Due to the input of our culture and the media around us, we hadn't yet learned that sex was just part of the whole giving package in the marriage. It didn't take any effort on my part to *get* sex.

But it took a great deal of learning about relationship to *give* sexually. There is a major difference between having sex and making love. Having sex is a biological act. Making love is a relationship experience where the focus of each spouse is to give to the other. This giving "adventure" might include the biological act of sex; however, it involves a relationship of freely giving to each other. The sexual experience is not held back or traded for power. Lovemaking is offered to please the other person, whose happiness is the focal point rather than personal pleasure. Lovemaking is a give, not a get. That's why the word "love" forms part of the word. When a couple begins to experience the sexual relationship in their marriage as a wonderful offering that they look forward to giving to each other, they have graduated from having sex to making love.

—*Bob and Rosemary*

Go to page 1246 for your next devotional reading.

nothing and uncircumcision is nothing. Keeping God's commands is what counts. 20Each one should remain in the situation which he was in when God called him. 21Were you a slave when you were called? Don't let it trouble you—although if you can gain your freedom, do so. 22For he who was a slave when he was called by the Lord is the Lord's freedman; similarly, he who was a free man when he was called is Christ's slave. 23You were bought at a price; do not become slaves of men. 24Brothers, each man, as responsible to God, should remain in the situation God called him to.

25Now about virgins: I have no command from the Lord, but I give a judgment as one who by the Lord's mercy is trustworthy. 26Because of the present crisis, I think that it is good for you to remain as you are. 27Are you married? Do not seek a divorce. Are you unmarried? Do not look for a wife. 28But if you do marry, you have not sinned; and if a virgin marries, she has not sinned. But those who marry will face many troubles in this life, and I want to spare you this.

29What I mean, brothers, is that the time is short. From now on those who have wives should live as if they had none; 30those who mourn, as if they did not; those who are happy, as if they were not; those who buy something, as if it were not theirs to keep; 31those who use the things of the world, as if not engrossed in them. For this world in its present form is passing away.

32I would like you to be free from concern. An unmarried man is concerned about the Lord's affairs—how he can please the Lord. 33But a married man is concerned about the affairs of this world— how he can please his wife— 34and his interests are divided. An unmarried woman or virgin is concerned about the Lord's affairs: Her aim is to be devoted to the Lord in both body and spirit. But a married woman is concerned about the affairs of this world—how she can please her husband. 35I am saying this for your own good, not to restrict you, but that you may live in a right way in undivided devotion to the Lord.

36If anyone thinks he is acting improperly toward the virgin he is engaged to, and if she is getting along in years and he feels he ought to marry, he should do as he wants. He is not sinning. They should get married. 37But the man who has settled the matter in his own mind, who is under no compulsion but has control over his own will, and who has made up his mind not to marry the virgin—this man also does the right thing. 38So then, he who marries the virgin does right, but he who does not marry her does even better.a

39A woman is bound to her husband as long as he lives. But if her husband dies, she is free to marry anyone she wishes, but he must belong to the Lord. 40In my judgment, she is happier if she stays as she is—and I think that I too have the Spirit of God.

Food Sacrificed to Idols

8 Now about food sacrificed to idols: We know that we all possess knowledge.b Knowledge puffs up, but love builds up. 2The man who thinks he knows something does not yet know as he ought to know. 3But the man who loves God is known by God.

4So then, about eating food sacrificed to idols: We know that an idol is nothing at all in the world and that there is no God but one. 5For even if there are so-called gods, whether in heaven or on earth (as indeed there are many "gods" and many "lords"), 6yet for us there is but one God, the Father, from whom all things came and for whom we live; and there is but one Lord, Jesus Christ, through whom all things came and through whom we live.

7But not everyone knows this. Some people are still so accustomed to idols that when they eat such food they think of it as having been sacrificed to an idol, and since their conscience is weak, it is defiled. 8But food does not bring us near

a36-38 Or 36If anyone thinks he is not treating his daughter properly, and if she is getting along in years, and he feels she ought to marry, he should do as he wants. He is not sinning. He should let her get married. 37But the man who has settled the matter in his own mind, who is under no compulsion but has control over his own will, and who has made up his mind to keep the virgin unmarried—this man also does the right thing. 38So then, he who gives his virgin in marriage does right, but he who does not give her in marriage does even better.   b1 Or "We all possess knowledge," as you say to God; we are no worse if we do not eat, and no better if we do.

⁹Be careful, however, that the exercise of your freedom does not become a stumbling block to the weak. ¹⁰For if anyone with a weak conscience sees you who have this knowledge eating in an idol's temple, won't he be emboldened to eat what has been sacrificed to idols? ¹¹So this weak brother, for whom Christ died, is destroyed by your knowledge. ¹²When you sin against your brothers in this way and wound their weak conscience, you sin against Christ. ¹³Therefore, if what I eat causes my brother to fall into sin, I will never eat meat again, so that I will not cause him to fall.

The Rights of an Apostle

9 Am I not free? Am I not an apostle? Have I not seen Jesus our Lord? Are you not the result of my work in the Lord? ²Even though I may not be an apostle to others, surely I am to you! For you are the seal of my apostleship in the Lord.

³This is my defense to those who sit in judgment on me. ⁴Don't we have the right to food and drink? ⁵Don't we have the right to take a believing wife along with us, as do the other apostles and the Lord's brothers and Cephas*a*? ⁶Or is it only I and Barnabas who must work for a living? ⁷Who serves as a soldier at his own

expense? Who plants a vineyard and does not eat of its grapes? Who tends a flock and does not drink of the milk? ⁸Do I say this merely from a human point of view? Doesn't the Law say the same thing? ⁹For it is written in the Law of Moses: "Do not muzzle an ox while it is treading out the grain."*b* Is it about oxen that God is concerned? ¹⁰Surely he says this for us, doesn't he? Yes, this was written for us, because when the plowman plows and the thresher threshes, they ought to do so in the hope of sharing in the harvest. ¹¹If we have sown spiritual seed among you, is it too much if we reap a material harvest from you? ¹²If others have this right of support from you, shouldn't we have it all the more?

But we did not use this right. On the contrary, we put up with anything rather than hinder the gospel of Christ. ¹³Don't you know that those who work in the temple get their food from the temple, and those who serve at the altar share in what is offered on the altar? ¹⁴In the same way, the Lord has commanded that those who preach the gospel should receive their living from the gospel.

¹⁵But I have not used any of these rights. And I am not writing this in the hope that you will do such things for me.

a5 That is, Peter   *b9* Deut. 25:4

Eating Humble Pie

Friday

1 CORINTHIANS 8:1 I (Les) have a friend who has a saying I like. It always pops into my mind when I know I am wrong and should apologize: "Humble pie is the only pastry that's never tasty."

That goofy statement helps trigger my apology mechanism. After all, it's not easy to say "I'm sorry." Why? Because whenever we apologize we must first set aside our pride. Genuine regret is based on humility. There is no way around it. Paul understood this when he said "Knowledge puffs up, but love builds up." Perhaps he was echoing the wisdom of Proverbs: "When pride comes, then comes disgrace, but with humility comes wisdom"

(Proverbs 11:2; see also Proverbs 29:23, page 674).

I feel for the person married to someone who never says he or she is sorry. Without another piece of information about them, I can predict with confidence that their home is filled with conflict and quarrels. "Pride only breeds quarrels, but wisdom is found in those who take advice" (Proverbs 13:10).

So remember, the next time you do something stupid, the next time you are in the wrong, 'fess up. Eat a little humble pie. It won't taste good, but it's the only sure way to say you're sorry. —*Les and Leslie*

Go to page 1247 for your next devotional reading.

I would rather die than have anyone deprive me of this boast. ¹⁶Yet when I preach the gospel, I cannot boast, for I am compelled to preach. Woe to me if I do not preach the gospel! ¹⁷If I preach voluntarily, I have a reward; if not voluntarily, I am simply discharging the trust committed to me. ¹⁸What then is my reward? Just this: that in preaching the gospel I may offer it free of charge, and so not make use of my rights in preaching it.

¹⁹Though I am free and belong to no man, I make myself a slave to everyone, to win as many as possible. ²⁰To the Jews I became like a Jew, to win the Jews. To those under the law I became like one under the law (though I myself am not under the law), so as to win those under the law. ²¹To those not having the law I became like one not having the law (though I am not free from God's law but am under Christ's law), so as to win those not having the law. ²²To the weak I became weak, to win the weak. I have become all things to all men so that by all possible means I might save some. ²³I do all this for the sake of the gospel, that I may share in its blessings.

²⁴Do you not know that in a race all the runners run, but only one gets the prize? Run in such a way as to get the prize. ²⁵Everyone who competes in the games goes into strict training. They do it to get a crown that will not last; but we do it to get a crown that will last forever. ²⁶Therefore I do not run like a man running aimlessly; I do not fight like a man beating the air. ²⁷No, I beat my body and make it my slave so that after I have preached to others, I myself will not be disqualified for the prize.

Warnings From Israel's History

10 For I do not want you to be ignorant of the fact, brothers, that our forefa-

---

Too Busy?

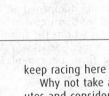

Qu[i]et TIMES *with each other*

1 CORINTHIANS 9:24 We remember leading a marriage seminar in North Carolina. We stayed at a lovely mountain bed and breakfast that was owned and operated by a couple from Atlanta; they had left the corporate world and life in the fast lane. Visions of simplifying their lives and working together lured them to the serenity of the North Carolina mountains and to owning and operating this particular bed and breakfast. But even there, they were still "too busy" for each other. We never saw them together. The wife told us, "We race through the day but basically work in shifts. Actually our life is a relay race."

If we want to receive God's crown for our marriage, we need to run together. And we need realistic goals. As with business, marriage thrives on goal setting. But few couples take time to set goals—they just keep racing here and there.

Why not take a few minutes and consider your own marriage goals? What steps are you taking to achieve them? We recently set a goal to keep our bodies in better physical condition as our health directly influences our marriage relationship. We agreed to take walks together at least three times each week and each year to have a "flu shot date" when we go together to get our flu shot and then go out to dinner.

Take a few minutes and set your own marriage goals. You might consider building a better relationship, finding private times for two, being a good witness for other marriages and passing on to your children a marriage model that glorifies God. These are marriage prizes worth running for . . .
—*Dave and Claudia*

Weekend Warm-up *How are you doing with your marriage goals?*

Go to page 1248 for your next devotional reading.

thers were all under the cloud and that they all passed through the sea. ²They were all baptized into Moses in the cloud and in the sea. ³They all ate the same spiritual food ⁴and drank the same spiritual drink; for they drank from the spiritual rock that accompanied them, and that rock was Christ. ⁵Nevertheless, God was not pleased with most of them; their bodies were scattered over the desert.

⁶Now these things occurred as examples[a] to keep us from setting our hearts on evil things as they did. ⁷Do not be idolaters, as some of them were; as it is written: "The people sat down to eat and drink and got up to indulge in pagan revelry."[b] ⁸We should not commit sexual immorality, as some of them did—and in one day twenty-three thousand of them died. ⁹We should not test the Lord, as some of them did—and were killed by snakes. ¹⁰And do not grumble, as some of them did—and were killed by the destroying angel.

¹¹These things happened to them as examples and were written down as warnings for us, on whom the fulfillment of the ages has come. ¹²So, if you think you are standing firm, be careful that you don't fall! ¹³No temptation has seized you except what is common to man. And God is faithful; he will not let you be tempted beyond what you can bear. But when you are tempted, he will also provide a way out so that you can stand up under it.

Idol Feasts and the Lord's Supper

¹⁴Therefore, my dear friends, flee from idolatry. ¹⁵I speak to sensible people; judge for yourselves what I say. ¹⁶Is not the cup of thanksgiving for which we give thanks a participation in the blood of Christ? And is not the bread that we break a participation in the body of Christ? ¹⁷Because there is one loaf, we, who are many, are one body, for we all partake of the one loaf.

¹⁸Consider the people of Israel: Do not those who eat the sacrifices participate in the altar? ¹⁹Do I mean then that a sacrifice offered to an idol is anything, or that an idol is anything? ²⁰No, but the sacrifices of pagans are offered to demons, not to God, and I do not want you to be participants with demons. ²¹You cannot drink

[a]6 Or types; also in verse 11   [b]7 Exodus 32:6

My Father-in-law

Monday

1 CORINTHIANS 10:31 Once a month my father in-law comes to visit. I don't know what it is about these visits, but I'm definitely different when he's in our home. I'm much nicer and more of a servant toward Rosemary. I'm conscious of this behavior, but that doesn't matter; I do it anyway. I want him to see how well I treat his daughter.

Some time ago a friend made a statement to me that greatly illuminated my thinking about fathers-in-law. He said, "You know, it hit me that God is not only my father, but my wife's father as well. I guess that makes him my father and my father-in-law."

Whether it's theologically correct or not, I don't know. But that statement had a great impact on me. In light of the fact that I am conscious about being more of a servant when my earthly father in-law is in my home, I began to reevaluate my behavior when he was not present. Although my earthly father-in-law may only come for a visit occasionally, my friend's statement helped me realize that my heavenly "Father in-law" is always in my home. He is always able to see how I am treating his child. In fact, he is even able to know what I am thinking concerning my spouse.

It is profound to realize that God is always observing how I treat Rosemary. Do I serve her in a way that would be pleasing to the Lord? Do I approach every day of my marriage to bring glory to God? Before I act, I need to remind myself that God is continually with me. I need to honor him in all I do.

—Bob and Rosemary

Go to page 1251 for your next devotional reading.

the cup of the Lord and the cup of demons too; you cannot have a part in both the Lord's table and the table of demons. 22Are we trying to arouse the Lord's jealousy? Are we stronger than he?

The Believer's Freedom

23"Everything is permissible"—but not everything is beneficial. "Everything is permissible"—but not everything is constructive. 24Nobody should seek his own good, but the good of others.

25Eat anything sold in the meat market without raising questions of conscience, 26for, "The earth is the Lord's, and everything in it."[a]

27If some unbeliever invites you to a meal and you want to go, eat whatever is put before you without raising questions of conscience. 28But if anyone says to you, "This has been offered in sacrifice," then do not eat it, both for the sake of the man who told you and for conscience' sake[b]— 29the other man's conscience, I mean, not yours. For why should my freedom be judged by another's conscience? 30If I take part in the meal with thankfulness, why am I denounced because of something I thank God for?

31So whether you eat or drink or whatever you do, do it all for the glory of God. 32Do not cause anyone to stumble, whether Jews, Greeks or the church of God— 33even as I try to please everybody in every way. For I am not seeking my own good but the good of many, so that **11** they may be saved. 1Follow my example, as I follow the example of Christ.

Propriety in Worship

2I praise you for remembering me in everything and for holding to the teachings,[c] just as I passed them on to you. 3Now I want you to realize that the head of every man is Christ, and the head of the woman is man, and the head of Christ is God. 4Every man who prays or prophesies with his head covered dishonors his head. 5And every woman who prays or prophesies with her head uncovered dishonors her head—it is just as though her head were shaved. 6If a woman does not cover her head, she should have her hair cut off; and if it is a disgrace

Just Between you & me

Married for God's Glory

Take a moment to answer each of these questions on your own. Then compare your answers to your spouse's.

Yes	No	I do the things I do for my spouse because I want to, not because I have to.
Yes	No	Most of the time I serve or help my spouse before being asked.
Yes	No	I don't do things for my spouse in order to get something in return.
Yes	No	When my spouse is under stress and very busy, I look for ways to serve without him/her even knowing it.

for a woman to have her hair cut or shaved off, she should cover her head. 7A man ought not to cover his head,[d] since he is the image and glory of God; but the woman is the glory of man. 8For man did not come from woman, but woman from man; 9neither was man created for woman, but woman for man. 10For this reason, and because of the angels, the woman ought to have a sign of authority on her head.

11In the Lord, however, woman is not independent of man, nor is man independent of woman. 12For as woman came from man, so also man is born of woman. But everything comes from God. 13Judge for yourselves: Is it proper for a woman to pray to God with her head uncovered? 14Does not the very nature of things teach you that if a man has long hair, it is a disgrace to him, 15but that if a woman has long hair, it is her glory? For long hair is given to her as a covering. 16If anyone wants to be contentious about this, we

---

a26 Psalm 24:1   b28 Some manuscripts conscience' sake, for "the earth is the Lord's and everything in it"   c2 Or traditions   d4-7 Or 4Every man who prays or prophesies with long hair dishonors his head. 5And every woman who prays or prophesies with no covering [of hair] on her head dishonors her head—she is just like one of the "shorn women." 6If a woman has no covering, let her be for now with short hair, but since it is a disgrace for a woman to have her hair shorn or shaved, she should grow it again. 7A man ought not to have long hair have no other practice—nor do the churches of God.

The Lord's Supper

[17]In the following directives I have no praise for you, for your meetings do more harm than good. [18]In the first place, I hear that when you come together as a church, there are divisions among you, and to some extent I believe it. [19]No doubt there have to be differences among you to show which of you have God's approval. [20]When you come together, it is not the Lord's Supper you eat, [21]for as you eat, each of you goes ahead without waiting for anybody else. One remains hungry, another gets drunk. [22]Don't you have homes to eat and drink in? Or do you despise the church of God and humiliate those who have nothing? What shall I say to you? Shall I praise you for this? Certainly not!

[23]For I received from the Lord what I also passed on to you: The Lord Jesus, on the night he was betrayed, took bread, [24]and when he had given thanks, he broke it and said, "This is my body, which is for you; do this in remembrance of me." [25]In the same way, after supper he took the cup, saying, "This cup is the new covenant in my blood; do this, whenever you drink it, in remembrance of me." [26]For whenever you eat this bread and drink this cup, you proclaim the Lord's death until he comes.

[27]Therefore, whoever eats the bread or drinks the cup of the Lord in an unworthy manner will be guilty of sinning against the body and blood of the Lord. [28]A man ought to examine himself before he eats of the bread and drinks of the cup. [29]For anyone who eats and drinks without recognizing the body of the Lord eats and drinks judgment on himself. [30]That is why many among you are weak and sick, and a number of you have fallen asleep. [31]But if we judged ourselves, we would not come under judgment. [32]When we are judged by the Lord, we are being disciplined so that we will not be condemned with the world.

[33]So then, my brothers, when you come together to eat, wait for each other. [34]If anyone is hungry, he should eat at home, so that when you meet together it may not result in judgment.

And when I come I will give further directions.

Spiritual Gifts

12 Now about spiritual gifts, brothers, I do not want you to be ignorant. [2]You know that when you were pagans, somehow or other you were influenced and led astray to mute idols. [3]Therefore I tell you that no one who is speaking by the Spirit of God says, "Jesus be cursed," and no one can say, "Jesus is Lord," except by the Holy Spirit.

[4]There are different kinds of gifts, but the same Spirit. [5]There are different kinds of service, but the same Lord. [6]There are different kinds of working, but the same God works all of them in all men.

[7]Now to each one the manifestation of the Spirit is given for the common good. [8]To one there is given through the Spirit the message of wisdom, to another the message of knowledge by means of the same Spirit, [9]to another faith by the same Spirit, to another gifts of healing by that one Spirit, [10]to another miraculous powers, to another prophecy, to another distinguishing between spirits, to another speaking in different kinds of tongues,[a] and to still another the interpretation of tongues.[a] [11]All these are the work of one and the same Spirit, and he gives them to each one, just as he determines.

One Body, Many Parts

[12]The body is a unit, though it is made up of many parts; and though all its parts are many, they form one body. So it is with Christ. [13]For we were all baptized by[b] one Spirit into one body—whether Jews or Greeks, slave or free—and we were all given the one Spirit to drink.

[14]Now the body is not made up of one part but of many. [15]If the foot should say, "Because I am not a hand, I do not belong to the body," it would not for that reason cease to be part of the body. [16]And if the ear should say, "Because I am not an eye, I do not belong to the body," it would not for that reason cease to be part

[a]10 Or *languages*; also in verse 28   [b]13 Or *with; or in*

of the body. [17]If the whole body were an eye, where would the sense of hearing be? If the whole body were an ear, where would the sense of smell be? [18]But in fact God has arranged the parts in the body, every one of them, just as he wanted them to be. [19]If they were all one part, where would the body be? [20]As it is, there are many parts, but one body.

[21]The eye cannot say to the hand, "I don't need you!" And the head cannot say to the feet, "I don't need you!" [22]On the contrary, those parts of the body that seem to be weaker are indispensable, [23]and the parts that we think are less honorable we treat with special honor. And the parts that are unpresentable are treated with special modesty, [24]while our presentable parts need no special treatment. But God has combined the members of the body and has given greater honor to the parts that lacked it, [25]so that there should be no division in the body, but that its parts should have equal concern for each other. [26]If one part suffers, every part suffers with it; if one part is honored, every part rejoices with it.

[27]Now you are the body of Christ, and each one of you is a part of it. [28]And in the church God has appointed first of all apostles, second prophets, third teachers, then workers of miracles, also those having gifts of healing, those able to help others, those with gifts of administration, and those speaking in different kinds of tongues. [29]Are all apostles? Are all prophets? Are all teachers? Do all work miracles? [30]Do all have gifts of healing? Do all speak in tongues[a]? Do all interpret? [31]But eagerly desire[b] the greater gifts.

Love

And now I will show you the most excellent way.

13 If I speak in the tongues[c] of men and of angels, but have not love, I am only a resounding gong or a clanging

[a]30 Or *other languages*   [b]31 Or *But you are eagerly desiring*   [c]1 Or *languages*

Unity in Diversity

Tuesday

1 CORINTHIANS 12:4-5 To build a strong marriage we must learn how to benefit from our different gifts. In other words, wise spouses appreciate the ways they are different. Paul tells us that there are different kinds of spiritual gifts, but the same Spirit. If God's Spirit is working in our marriage relationship, then shouldn't we be able to find unity in our diversity?

For the first few years of our marriage, we tried to change each other. It didn't work. I didn't understand why Claudia couldn't just "laugh things off" and loosen up a little. Claudia wanted me to be more introspective and analytical—take life more seriously. I wished Claudia weren't so tied to the clock, and Claudia just wanted me to occasionally pay attention to the alarm watch she had given me for my birthday.

Then we made a job change and part of the process was taking a battery of psychological tests. Through this process we began to realize that our differences could compliment each other and strengthen our marriage partnership. We began to affirm each other's spiritual gifts and natural abilities. For instance, Claudia's time-orientation keeps us on schedule while my people-orientation helps us to be sensitive to the people we meet along the way.

Think about your strengths as a couple and how you complement each other. Batteries of psychological tests are not required to determine your basic strengths and weaknesses; just make a list of the ways you are alike and the ways you are different.

Your unique abilities can help you balance each other out—especially if you appreciate those differences rather than feeling threatened or frustrated by them. In the areas where you have similar gifts, look for ways you can work together. Affirm your God-given talents, and you can find unity in your diversity.   **—Dave and Claudia**

Go to page 1252 for your next devotional reading.

cymbal. ²If I have the gift of prophecy and can fathom all mysteries and all knowledge, and if I have a faith that can move mountains, but have not love, I am nothing. ³If I give all I possess to the poor and surrender my body to the flames,ᵃ but have not love, I gain nothing.

⁴Love is patient, love is kind. It does not envy, it does not boast, it is not proud. ⁵It is not rude, it is not self-seeking, it is not easily angered, it keeps no record of wrongs. ⁶Love does not delight in evil but rejoices with the truth. ⁷It always protects, always trusts, always hopes, always perseveres.

⁸Love never fails. But where there are prophecies, they will cease; where there are tongues, they will be stilled; where there is knowledge, it will pass away. ⁹For we know in part and we prophesy in part, ¹⁰but when perfection comes, the imperfect disappears. ¹¹When I was a child, I talked like a child, I thought like a child, I reasoned like a child. When I became a man, I put childish ways behind me. ¹²Now we see but a poor reflection as in a mirror; then we shall see face to face. Now I know in part; then I shall know fully, even as I am fully known.

¹³And now these three remain: faith, hope and love. But the greatest of these is love.

Gifts of Prophecy and Tongues

14 Follow the way of love and eagerly desire spiritual gifts, especially the gift of prophecy. ²For anyone who speaks in a tongueᵇ does not speak to men but to God. Indeed, no one understands him; he utters mysteries with his spirit.ᶜ ³But everyone who prophesies speaks to men for their strengthening, encouragement and comfort. ⁴He who speaks in a tongue edifies himself, but he who prophesies edifies the church. ⁵I would like every one of you to speak in tongues,ᵈ but I would rather have you prophesy. He who prophesies is greater than one who speaks in tongues,ᵈ unless he interprets, so that the church may be edified.

⁶Now, brothers, if I come to you and speak in tongues, what good will I be to you, unless I bring you some revelation or knowledge or prophecy or word of instruction? ⁷Even in the case of lifeless things that make sounds, such as the flute or harp, how will anyone know what tune is being played unless there is a distinction in the notes? ⁸Again, if the trumpet does not sound a clear call, who will get

ᵃ3 Some early manuscripts *body that I may boast*
ᵇ2 Or *another language*; also in verses 4, 13, 14, 19, 26 and 27   *ᶜ2* Or *by the Spirit*   *ᵈ5* Or *other languages*; also in verses 6, 18, 22, 23 and 39

Saying "I Love You"

Wednesday

1 CORINTHIANS 13 Emily sat in our office weeping. She had come for counseling on her own, without telling her husband. "I am so hungry for affection," she confided in us. "We have been married for twenty-five years, and I know he is capable of tenderness. He shows it to the dog. But . . . " Emily's voice broke down and her tears began to flow. She reached for a tissue and quietly said, " . . . I'd just like to hear him say 'I love you.' "

These three simple words are so critical to marriage. We take these tender words for granted sometimes, but we have never known anyone who got tired of hearing "I love you" . . . before leaving the house in the morning . . . after a quick message on the answering machine . . . while working in the garden . . . before dozing off in bed. These little words are like vitamins to a marriage. Without a consistent dose of verbal expression, without saying and hearing those words, the heart of a spouse withers.

We have over 600,000 words in the English language and more synonyms per word than are found in any other language. However, we have only one word with which to express all the various shadings of love. Deficient as English is in this respect, we long to hear the familiar words, "I love you."

—**Les and Leslie**

Go to page 1254 for your next devotional reading.

ready for battle? 9So it is with you. Unless you speak intelligible words with your tongue, how will anyone know what you are saying? You will just be speaking into the air. 10Undoubtedly there are all sorts of languages in the world, yet none of them is without meaning. 11If then I do not grasp the meaning of what someone is saying, I am a foreigner to the speaker, and he is a foreigner to me. 12So it is with you. Since you are eager to have spiritual gifts, try to excel in gifts that build up the church.

13For this reason anyone who speaks in a tongue should pray that he may interpret what he says. 14For if I pray in a tongue, my spirit prays, but my mind is unfruitful. 15So what shall I do? I will pray with my spirit, but I will also pray with my mind; I will sing with my spirit, but I will also sing with my mind. 16If you are praising God with your spirit, how can one who finds himself among those who do not understand[a] say "Amen" to your thanksgiving, since he does not know what you are saying? 17You may be giving thanks well enough, but the other man is not edified.

18I thank God that I speak in tongues more than all of you. 19But in the church I would rather speak five intelligible words to instruct others than ten thousand words in a tongue.

20Brothers, stop thinking like children. In regard to evil be infants, but in your thinking be adults. 21In the Law it is written:

"Through men of strange tongues
    and through the lips of foreigners
I will speak to this people,
    but even then they will not listen
        to me,"[b]

says the Lord.

22Tongues, then, are a sign, not for believers but for unbelievers; prophecy, however, is for believers, not for unbelievers. 23So if the whole church comes together and everyone speaks in tongues, and some who do not understand[c] or some unbelievers come in, will they not say that you are out of your mind? 24But if an unbeliever or someone who does not understand[d] comes in while everybody is prophesying, he will be convinced by all that he is a sinner and will be

judged by all, 25and the secrets of his heart will be laid bare. So he will fall down and worship God, exclaiming, "God is really among you!"

Orderly Worship

26What then shall we say, brothers? When you come together, everyone has a hymn, or a word of instruction, a revelation, a tongue or an interpretation. All of these must be done for the strengthening of the church. 27If anyone speaks in a tongue, two—or at the most three—should speak, one at a time, and someone must interpret. 28If there is no interpreter, the speaker should keep quiet in the church and speak to himself and God.

29Two or three prophets should speak, and the others should weigh carefully what is said. 30And if a revelation comes to someone who is sitting down, the first speaker should stop. 31For you can all prophesy in turn so that everyone may be instructed and encouraged. 32The spirits of prophets are subject to the control of prophets. 33For God is not a God of disorder but of peace.

As in all the congregations of the saints, 34women should remain silent in the churches. They are not allowed to speak, but must be in submission, as the Law says. 35If they want to inquire about something, they should ask their own husbands at home; for it is disgraceful for a woman to speak in the church.

36Did the word of God originate with you? Or are you the only people it has reached? 37If anybody thinks he is a prophet or spiritually gifted, let him acknowledge that what I am writing to you is the Lord's command. 38If he ignores this, he himself will be ignored.[e]

39Therefore, my brothers, be eager to prophesy, and do not forbid speaking in tongues. 40But everything should be done in a fitting and orderly way.

The Resurrection of Christ

15 Now, brothers, I want to remind you of the gospel I preached to you,

---

a16 Or among the inquirers   b21 Isaiah 28:11,12
c23 Or some inquirers   d24 Or or some inquirer
e38 Some manuscripts If he is ignorant of this, let him be ignorant

which you received and on which you have taken your stand. ²By this gospel you are saved, if you hold firmly to the word I preached to you. Otherwise, you have believed in vain.

³For what I received I passed on to you as of first importance[a]: that Christ died for our sins according to the Scriptures, ⁴that he was buried, that he was raised on the third day according to the Scriptures, ⁵and that he appeared to Peter,[b] and then to the Twelve. ⁶After that, he appeared to more than five hundred of the brothers at the same time, most of whom are still living, though some have fallen asleep. ⁷Then he appeared to James, then to all the apostles, ⁸and last of all he appeared to me also, as to one abnormally born.

⁹For I am the least of the apostles and do not even deserve to be called an apostle, because I persecuted the church of God. ¹⁰But by the grace of God I am what I am, and his grace to me was not without effect. No, I worked harder than all of them—yet not I, but the grace of God that was with me. ¹¹Whether, then, it was I or they, this is what we preach, and this is what you believed.

The Resurrection of the Dead

¹²But if it is preached that Christ has been raised from the dead, how can some of you say that there is no resurrection of the dead? ¹³If there is no resurrection of the dead, then not even Christ has been raised. ¹⁴And if Christ has not been raised, our preaching is useless and so is your faith. ¹⁵More than that, we are then found to be false witnesses about God, for we have testified about God that he raised Christ from the dead. But he did not raise him if in fact the dead are not raised. ¹⁶For if the dead are not raised, then Christ has not been raised either. ¹⁷And if Christ has not been raised, your faith is futile; you are still in your sins. ¹⁸Then those also who have fallen asleep in Christ are lost. ¹⁹If only for this life we have hope in Christ, we are to be pitied more than all men.

²⁰But Christ has indeed been raised from the dead, the firstfruits of those who have fallen asleep. ²¹For since death came through a man, the resurrection of the dead comes also through a man. ²²For as in Adam all die, so in Christ all will be

[a]3 Or you at the first   [b]5 Greek Cephas

Getting Rid of Balls and Chains

Thursday

1 CORINTHIANS 15:10 "If it weren't for the way I was raised, my marriage would be doing so much better." Have you ever thought of that excuse? A behavior or thought process from the past keeps popping up, causing problems in the marriage. It could be a pattern of negative thinking as a result of your parents' influence. Or it could be repeating something your parents modeled that adversely affected their marriage. It has become so frequent in your own marriage that you've accepted it as a debilitating ball and chain around your ankle.

Paul acknowledges the fact that he persecuted the church in the past. He even indicates that his past caused him to have to work harder than others. And work he does! Paul admits that his past is a reality, but so is the grace of God.

That is the very same grace that covers our past and helps us triumph in the future. We each bring our flaws into the marriage relationship. Getting married won't cover them up. In fact, marriage tends to bring out flaws and negative habits. Like Paul, each of us must work hard to overcome things from our past, all the while trusting that we are not alone in the effort. Not only does God know about our past, but his grace has covered our flaws and has made our progress possible. Don't stall your progress in the marriage relationship by wallowing in thoughts like, "That's just the way I was raised." Work hard to grow, and praise God for his grace that makes it possible.

—*Bob and Rosemary*

Go to page 1256 for your next devotional reading.

made alive. ²³But each in his own turn: Christ, the firstfruits; then, when he comes, those who belong to him. ²⁴Then the end will come, when he hands over the kingdom to God the Father after he has destroyed all dominion, authority and power. ²⁵For he must reign until he has put all his enemies under his feet. ²⁶The last enemy to be destroyed is death. ²⁷For he "has put everything under his feet."*a* Now when it says that "everything" has been put under him, it is clear that this does not include God himself, who put everything under Christ. ²⁸When he has done this, then the Son himself will be made subject to him who put everything under him, so that God may be all in all.

²⁹Now if there is no resurrection, what will those do who are baptized for the dead? If the dead are not raised at all, why are people baptized for them? ³⁰And as for us, why do we endanger ourselves every hour? ³¹I die every day—I mean that, brothers—just as surely as I glory over you in Christ Jesus our Lord. ³²If I fought wild beasts in Ephesus for merely human reasons, what have I gained? If the dead are not raised,

"Let us eat and drink,
   for tomorrow we die."*b*

³³Do not be misled: "Bad company corrupts good character." ³⁴Come back to your senses as you ought, and stop sinning; for there are some who are ignorant of God—I say this to your shame.

The Resurrection Body

³⁵But someone may ask, "How are the dead raised? With what kind of body will they come?" ³⁶How foolish! What you sow does not come to life unless it dies. ³⁷When you sow, you do not plant the body that will be, but just a seed, perhaps of wheat or of something else. ³⁸But God gives it a body as he has determined, and to each kind of seed he gives its own body. ³⁹All flesh is not the same: Men have one kind of flesh, animals have another, birds another and fish another. ⁴⁰There are also heavenly bodies and there are earthly bodies; but the splendor of the heavenly bodies is one kind, and the splendor of the earthly bodies is an-

other. ⁴¹The sun has one kind of splendor, the moon another and the stars another; and star differs from star in splendor.

⁴²So will it be with the resurrection of the dead. The body that is sown is perishable, it is raised imperishable; ⁴³it is sown in dishonor, it is raised in glory; it is sown in weakness, it is raised in power; ⁴⁴it is sown a natural body, it is raised a spiritual body.

If there is a natural body, there is also a spiritual body. ⁴⁵So it is written: "The first man Adam became a living being"*c*; the last Adam, a life-giving spirit. ⁴⁶The spiritual did not come first, but the natural, and after that the spiritual. ⁴⁷The first man was of the dust of the earth, the second man from heaven. ⁴⁸As was the earthly man, so are those who are of the earth; and as is the man from heaven, so also are those who are of heaven. ⁴⁹And just as we have borne the likeness of the earthly man, so shall we*d* bear the likeness of the man from heaven.

⁵⁰I declare to you, brothers, that flesh and blood cannot inherit the kingdom of God, nor does the perishable inherit the imperishable. ⁵¹Listen, I tell you a mystery: We will not all sleep, but we will all be changed— ⁵²in a flash, in the twinkling of an eye, at the last trumpet. For the trumpet will sound, the dead will be raised imperishable, and we will be changed. ⁵³For the perishable must clothe itself with the imperishable, and the mortal with immortality. ⁵⁴When the perishable has been clothed with the imperishable, and the mortal with immortality, then the saying that is written will come true: "Death has been swallowed up in victory."*e*

⁵⁵"Where, O death, is your victory?
   Where, O death, is your sting?"*f*

⁵⁶The sting of death is sin, and the power of sin is the law. ⁵⁷But thanks be to God! He gives us the victory through our Lord Jesus Christ.

⁵⁸Therefore, my dear brothers, stand firm. Let nothing move you. Always give

---

a27 Psalm 8:6   *b32* Isaiah 22:13
c45 Gen. 2:7   *d49* Some early manuscripts *so let us*   *e54* Isaiah 25:8   *f55* Hosea 13:14

yourselves fully to the work of the Lord, because you know that your labor in the Lord is not in vain.

The Collection for God's People

16 Now about the collection for God's people: Do what I told the Galatian churches to do. ²On the first day of every week, each one of you should set aside a sum of money in keeping with his income, saving it up, so that when I come no collections will have to be made. ³Then, when I arrive, I will give letters of introduction to the men you approve and send them with your gift to Jerusalem. ⁴If it seems advisable for me to go also, they will accompany me.

Personal Requests

⁵After I go through Macedonia, I will come to you—for I will be going through Macedonia. ⁶Perhaps I will stay with you awhile, or even spend the winter, so that you can help me on my journey, wherever I go. ⁷I do not want to see you now and make only a passing visit; I hope to spend some time with you, if the Lord permits. ⁸But I will stay on at Ephesus until Pente-

cost, ⁹because a great door for effective work has opened to me, and there are many who oppose me.

¹⁰If Timothy comes, see to it that he has nothing to fear while he is with you, for he is carrying on the work of the Lord, just as I am. ¹¹No one, then, should refuse to accept him. Send him on his way in peace so that he may return to me. I am expecting him along with the brothers.

¹²Now about our brother Apollos: I strongly urged him to go to you with the brothers. He was quite unwilling to go now, but he will go when he has the opportunity.

¹³Be on your guard; stand firm in the faith; be men of courage; be strong. ¹⁴Do everything in love.

¹⁵You know that the household of Stephanas were the first converts in Achaia, and they have devoted themselves to the service of the saints. I urge you, brothers, ¹⁶to submit to such as these and to everyone who joins in the work, and labors at it. ¹⁷I was glad when Stephanas, Fortunatus and Achaicus arrived, because they have supplied what was lacking from you. ¹⁸For they refreshed my spirit and yours also. Such men deserve recognition.

Let Nothing Move You

Friday

1 CORINTHIANS 15:58 "I am so tired of all the effort I put into this marriage that sometimes I feel like I'm the only one who even cares. It would be so easy just to give in and give up. Nobody else seems to be staying together when things get difficult, so why should we?"

How often we have said this, or at least thought about it, at discouraging times. This passage has a strong message for us when we feel like quitting. First, it indicates that these feelings are very real. You are not alone when you feel like giving up in the tough times. If it were not a real problem that all of us experience in one way or another, the apostle Paul would not have addressed the issue. There is comfort in knowing that we are not alone in discouragement.

Second, Paul instructs us to stand firm and not be moved away from doing what we need to do. In other words, don't let discouragement keep you from doing the right thing. His third point gives us the "why." We are not to be discouraged from doing the right thing, because our efforts are not in vain. God sees every discouraged, tired effort we make. Though we might not see the results of our efforts on this side of eternity, we must never lose the perspective that God is pleased when we do what's right. If we can keep that "heavenly" perspective, even if we cannot see the results, our efforts will be worth it.

—Bob and Rosemary

Go to page 1259 for your next devotional reading.

Final Greetings

19The churches in the province of Asia send you greetings. Aquila and Priscilla*a* greet you warmly in the Lord, and so does the church that meets at their house. 20All the brothers here send you greetings. Greet one another with a holy kiss.

21I, Paul, write this greeting in my own hand.

22If anyone does not love the Lord—a curse be on him. Come, O Lord*b*!

23The grace of the Lord Jesus be with you.

24My love to all of you in Christ Jesus. Amen.*c*

a19 Greek *Prisca*, a variant of *Priscilla*
b22 In Aramaic the expression *Come, O Lord* is *Marana tha.* *c24* Some manuscripts do not have *Amen.*

2 Corinthians

> ## "Wait a minute!
> ## That's not what I said—and that's not who I am."
>
> Thoughts like these must have raced through Paul's mind after his character and ministry were attacked in Corinth. Among other things, false teachers were challenging Paul's authority as an apostle and accusing him of stealing church collection money. So it's not surprising that Paul gets emotional and seesaws between despair and joy as he writes. Yet even as he defends himself, he challenges the Corinthians (and his contemporary readers) to let themselves be controlled by Jesus' love when they face conflict and to rely on his grace when they're weak—a good thing to remember when we face arguments in our marriage relationship.

1 Paul, an apostle of Christ Jesus by the will of God, and Timothy our brother,

To the church of God in Corinth, together with all the saints throughout Achaia:

2Grace and peace to you from God our Father and the Lord Jesus Christ.

The God of All Comfort

3Praise be to the God and Father of our Lord Jesus Christ, the Father of compassion and the God of all comfort, 4who comforts us in all our troubles, so that we can comfort those in any trouble with the comfort we ourselves have received from God. 5For just as the sufferings of Christ flow over into our lives, so also through Christ our comfort overflows. 6If we are distressed, it is for your comfort and salvation; if we are comforted, it is for your comfort, which produces in you patient endurance of the same sufferings we suffer. 7And our hope for you is firm, because we know that just as you share in our sufferings, so also you share in our comfort.

8We do not want you to be uninformed, brothers, about the hardships we suffered in the province of Asia. We were under great pressure, far beyond our ability to endure, so that we despaired even of life. 9Indeed, in our hearts we felt the sentence of death. But this happened that we might not rely on ourselves but on God, who raises the dead. 10He has delivered us from such a deadly peril, and he will deliver us. On him we have set our hope that he will continue to deliver us, [11]as you help us by your prayers. Then many will give thanks on our[a] behalf for the gracious favor granted us in answer to the prayers of many.

Paul's Change of Plans

[12]Now this is our boast: Our conscience testifies that we have conducted ourselves in the world, and especially in our relations with you, in the holiness and sincerity that are from God. We have done so not according to worldly wisdom but according to God's grace. [13]For we do not write you anything you cannot read or understand. And I hope that, [14]as you have understood us in part, you will come to understand fully that you can boast of us just as we will boast of you in the day of the Lord Jesus.

[15]Because I was confident of this, I planned to visit you first so that you might benefit twice. [16]I planned to visit you on my way to Macedonia and to come back to you from Macedonia, and then to have you send me on my way to Judea. [17]When I planned this, did I do it lightly? Or do I make my plans in a worldly manner so that in the same breath I say, "Yes, yes" and "No, no"?

[18]But as surely as God is faithful, our message to you is not "Yes" and "No." [19]For the Son of God, Jesus Christ, who was preached among you by me and Silas[b] and Timothy, was not "Yes" and "No," but in him it has always been "Yes." [20]For no matter how many promises God has made, they are "Yes" in Christ. And so through him the "Amen" is spoken by us

[a]11 Many manuscripts *your*   [b]19 Greek *Silvanus,* a variant of *Silas*

Pass It On

Quiet TIMES
with each other

2 CORINTHIANS 1:3–5 Saying good-bye is difficult—especially when a loved one is dying. We have faced the death of three of our parents, but it was only with my (Claudia's) mother that we actually knew she was dying and had the opportunity to say our good-byes. Three months before her ninety-first birthday, she was diagnosed with cancer and died ten days later. During these days we experienced the reality of God's comfort. And we were able to pass that comfort on to my mom.

From our recent experience we can join with the apostle Paul and praise God for his compassion and comfort. For instance, the assurance of life after death allowed both me and Mother to face those days without fear. As I held my Mother's hand as she was dying, she peacefully listened as I read to her, "My peace I give you . . . Do not let your hearts be troubled and do not be afraid" (John 14:27). God's comfort gave both of us peace. And God is willing to do the same for you.

Perhaps you have not had to face the death of a parent, but you are probably suffering in other ways. Perhaps you're experiencing financial difficulties or your job is extremely stressful right now. Or maybe you're struggling with whether or not to start a family or can't seem to break away from depression.

Whether you face the death of a loved one or difficulties in your marriage, with your children or whatever, the Lord will be with you. You can experience God's peace, compassion and comfort. But one of the most important things you can learn about God's comfort and compassion is that it's not intended just for you—it's meant for you to pass on to others.

—Dave and Claudia

W **Weekend Warm-up** When you've lost a loved one, how have you supported each other? How can you improve?

Go to page 1260 for your next devotional reading.

to the glory of God. [21]Now it is God who makes both us and you stand firm in Christ. He anointed us, [22]set his seal of ownership on us, and put his Spirit in our hearts as a deposit, guaranteeing what is to come.

[23]I call God as my witness that it was in order to spare you that I did not return to Corinth. [24]Not that we lord it over your faith, but we work with you for your joy, because it is by faith you stand firm.

[1]So I made up my mind that I would not make another painful visit to you. [2]For if I grieve you, who is left to make me glad but you whom I have grieved? [3]I wrote as I did so that when I came I should not be distressed by those who ought to make me rejoice. I had confidence in all of you, that you would all share my joy. [4]For I wrote you out of great distress and anguish of heart and with many tears, not to grieve you but to let you know the depth of my love for you.

Forgiveness for the Sinner

[5]If anyone has caused grief, he has not so much grieved me as he has grieved all of you, to some extent—not to put it too severely. [6]The punishment inflicted on him by the majority is sufficient for him. [7]Now instead, you ought to forgive and comfort him, so that he will not be overwhelmed by excessive sorrow. [8]I urge you, therefore, to reaffirm your love for him. [9]The reason I wrote you was to see if you would stand the test and be obedient in everything. [10]If you forgive anyone, I also forgive him. And what I have forgiven—if there was anything to forgive—I have forgiven in the sight of Christ for your sake, [11]in order that Satan might not outwit us. For we are not unaware of his schemes.

Ministers of the New Covenant

[12]Now when I went to Troas to preach the gospel of Christ and found that the Lord had opened a door for me, [13]I still had no peace of mind, because I did not find my brother Titus there. So I said good-by to them and went on to Macedonia.

[14]But thanks be to God, who always leads us in triumphal procession in Christ and through us spreads everywhere the

Forgive and Forget?

Monday

2 CORINTHIANS 2:5–11 While we were living in Los Angeles, a friend of ours invited us to tour the Hollywood film studio where she worked. We rode across the lot on a handy golf cart and quietly ducked into sound stages to catch behind-the-scene glimpses of familiar faces. One of the highlights was watching the filming of the hit TV show "Thirtysomething." You may recall the series about the lives of seven friends in their thirties. The plots were typically peppered with mundane events depicting a kind of "yuppie angst" with all its fear, love and anxiety. The episode we stumbled into on our tour was, appropriately enough, called "Therapy." Our friend, observing our special interest in this particular show, later sent us the script (autographed by the cast). It featured Nancy and Elliot, a struggling married couple in an unguarded, if not brutal, counseling session that led Elliot to say, "I don't know if I love Nancy anymore . . . And no matter what she does, I can't seem to forgive her for that."

COUPLE MINUTES

Forgiveness lies at the heart of marriage. Two people living together, day after day, are bound to cause pain, sometimes innocently, sometimes not. And if forgiveness is not given to cleanse the marriage soul, condemnation hovers over the relationship. Resentment piles on top of resentment until we blame our partner not just for his or her wrongdoing, but also for our failure to forgive him or her.

The whole agonizing mess, of course, can be avoided when we put forgiveness into practice. Even though forgiving is easier said than done, it's worth the effort.

—*Les and Leslie*

Go to page 1262 for your next devotional reading.

fragrance of the knowledge of him. [15]For we are to God the aroma of Christ among those who are being saved and those who are perishing. [16]To the one we are the smell of death; to the other, the fragrance of life. And who is equal to such a task? [17]Unlike so many, we do not peddle the word of God for profit. On the contrary, in Christ we speak before God with sincerity, like men sent from God.

3 Are we beginning to commend ourselves again? Or do we need, like some people, letters of recommendation to you or from you? [2]You yourselves are our letter, written on our hearts, known and read by everybody. [3]You show that you are a letter from Christ, the result of our ministry, written not with ink but with the Spirit of the living God, not on tablets of stone but on tablets of human hearts.

[4]Such confidence as this is ours through Christ before God. [5]Not that we are competent in ourselves to claim anything for ourselves, but our competence comes from God. [6]He has made us competent as ministers of a new covenant— not of the letter but of the Spirit; for the letter kills, but the Spirit gives life.

The Glory of the New Covenant

[7]Now if the ministry that brought death, which was engraved in letters on stone, came with glory, so that the Israelites could not look steadily at the face of Moses because of its glory, fading though it was, [8]will not the ministry of the Spirit be even more glorious? [9]If the ministry that condemns men is glorious, how much more glorious is the ministry that brings righteousness! [10]For what was glorious has no glory now in comparison with the surpassing glory. [11]And if what was fading away came with glory, how much greater is the glory of that which lasts!

[12]Therefore, since we have such a hope, we are very bold. [13]We are not like Moses, who would put a veil over his face to keep the Israelites from gazing at it while the radiance was fading away. [14]But their minds were made dull, for to this day the same veil remains when the old covenant is read. It has not been removed, because only in Christ is it taken away. [15]Even to this day when Moses is read, a veil covers their hearts. [16]But whenever anyone turns to the Lord, the veil is taken away. [17]Now the Lord is the Spirit, and where the Spirit of the Lord is, there is freedom. [18]And we, who with unveiled faces all reflect[a] the Lord's glory, are being transformed into his likeness with ever-increasing glory, which comes from the Lord, who is the Spirit.

Treasures in Jars of Clay

4 Therefore, since through God's mercy we have this ministry, we do not lose heart. [2]Rather, we have renounced secret and shameful ways; we do not use deception, nor do we distort the word of God. On the contrary, by setting forth the truth plainly we commend ourselves to every man's conscience in the sight of God. [3]And even if our gospel is veiled, it is veiled to those who are perishing. [4]The god of this age has blinded the minds of unbelievers, so that they cannot see the light of the gospel of the glory of Christ, who is the image of God. [5]For we do not preach ourselves, but Jesus Christ as Lord, and ourselves as your servants for Jesus' sake. [6]For God, who said, "Let light shine out of darkness,"[b] made his light shine in our hearts to give us the light of the knowledge of the glory of God in the face of Christ.

[7]But we have this treasure in jars of clay to show that this all-surpassing power is from God and not from us. [8]We are hard pressed on every side, but not crushed; perplexed, but not in despair; [9]persecuted, but not abandoned; struck down, but not destroyed. [10]We always carry around in our body the death of Jesus, so that the life of Jesus may also be revealed in our body. [11]For we who are alive are always being given over to death for Jesus' sake, so that his life may be revealed in our mortal body. [12]So then, death is at work in us, but life is at work in you.

[13]It is written: "I believed; therefore I have spoken."[c] With that same spirit of faith we also believe and therefore speak, [14]because we know that the one who raised the Lord Jesus from the dead will also raise us with Jesus and present us

a18 Or contemplate   b6 Gen. 1:3
c13 Psalm 116:10

with you in his presence. [15]All this is for your benefit, so that the grace that is reaching more and more people may cause thanksgiving to overflow to the glory of God.

[16]Therefore we do not lose heart. Though outwardly we are wasting away, yet inwardly we are being renewed day by day. [17]For our light and momentary troubles are achieving for us an eternal glory that far outweighs them all. [18]So we fix our eyes not on what is seen, but on what is unseen. For what is seen is temporary, but what is unseen is eternal.

Our Heavenly Dwelling

5 Now we know that if the earthly tent we live in is destroyed, we have a building from God, an eternal house in heaven, not built by human hands. [2]Meanwhile we groan, longing to be clothed with our heavenly dwelling, [3]because when we are clothed, we will not be found naked. [4]For while we are in this tent, we groan and are burdened, because we do not wish to be unclothed but to be clothed with our heavenly dwelling, so that what is mortal may be swallowed up by life. [5]Now it is God who has made us for this very purpose and has given us the Spirit as a deposit, guaranteeing what is to come.

[6]Therefore we are always confident and know that as long as we are at home in the body we are away from the Lord. [7]We live by faith, not by sight. [8]We are confident, I say, and would prefer to be away from the body and at home with the Lord. [9]So we make it our goal to please him, whether we are at home in the body or away from it. [10]For we must all appear before the judgment seat of Christ, that each one may receive what is due him for the things done while in the body, whether good or bad.

The Ministry of Reconciliation

[11]Since, then, we know what it is to fear the Lord, we try to persuade men. What we are is plain to God, and I hope it is also plain to your conscience. [12]We are not trying to commend ourselves to you

Focus on Graduation

Tuesday

2 CORINTHIANS 4:16–18 When I was in college, there were times when I wondered why I was putting myself through the effort. Term papers, exams, no money, late nights studying—the list of drawbacks went on and on. I knew if I lost focus, I'd quit. I had to keep pushing myself forward because of the vision I had for the future. I knew there would come a time when it will all be over, a time when I would graduate and not have to put up with a student's life anymore. I didn't really know what awaited me after graduation, but I trusted the people who told me that life would be better when I finished this course of study.

That's what Paul is saying about life. We can't allow ourselves to fixate on the discouragements we face here and now. As hard as it is to deal with great difficulties, we must focus on an eternity with Jesus Christ and the glory that is to come. If we allow ourselves to focus only on the here and now, life's difficulties can lead us to become discouraged.

The day to day work of the marriage relationship can bring times of discouragement, struggle or despair. There will be days when keeping your heart in the relationship is an effort. When you hear your mind rehearsing the lines, "Is this all there is?" don't lose hope. As hard as it is to comprehend, this is not all there is. Life does not consist of only the present. There will be a time of "graduation." The things we tend to focus on for happiness are only temporary. Paul tells us that the way we face these day to day "courses" of life can bring eternal glory in the future. Fix your eyes not on the difficulties of your life and marriage, but on eternal glory to come. Eventually you will "graduate."

COUPLE MINUTES

—**Bob and Rosemary**

Go to page 1264 for your next devotional reading.

again, but are giving you an opportunity to take pride in us, so that you can answer those who take pride in what is seen rather than in what is in the heart. ¹³If we are out of our mind, it is for the sake of God; if we are in our right mind, it is for you. ¹⁴For Christ's love compels us, because we are convinced that one died for all, and therefore all died. ¹⁵And he died for all, that those who live should no longer live for themselves but for him who died for them and was raised again.

¹⁶So from now on we regard no one from a worldly point of view. Though we once regarded Christ in this way, we do so no longer. ¹⁷Therefore, if anyone is in Christ, he is a new creation; the old has gone, the new has come! ¹⁸All this is from God, who reconciled us to himself through Christ and gave us the ministry of reconciliation: ¹⁹that God was reconciling the world to himself in Christ, not counting men's sins against them. And he has committed to us the message of reconciliation. ²⁰We are therefore Christ's ambassadors, as though God were making his appeal through us. We implore you on Christ's behalf: Be reconciled to God. ²¹God made him who had no sin to be sin*a* for us, so that in him we might become the righteousness of God.

6 As God's fellow workers we urge you not to receive God's grace in vain. ²For he says,

"In the time of my favor I heard you,
    and in the day of salvation I
        helped you."*b*

I tell you, now is the time of God's favor, now is the day of salvation.

Paul's Hardships

³We put no stumbling block in anyone's path, so that our ministry will not be discredited. ⁴Rather, as servants of God we commend ourselves in every way: in great endurance; in troubles, hardships and distresses; ⁵in beatings, imprisonments and riots; in hard work, sleepless nights and hunger; ⁶in purity, understanding, patience and kindness; in the Holy Spirit and in sincere love; ⁷in truthful speech and in the power of God; with weapons of righteousness in the right hand and in the left; ⁸through glory and

dishonor, bad report and good report; genuine, yet regarded as impostors; ⁹known, yet regarded as unknown; dying, and yet we live on; beaten, and yet not killed; ¹⁰sorrowful, yet always rejoicing; poor, yet making many rich; having nothing, and yet possessing everything.

¹¹We have spoken freely to you, Corinthians, and opened wide our hearts to you. ¹²We are not withholding our affection from you, but you are withholding yours from us. ¹³As a fair exchange—I speak as to my children—open wide your hearts also.

Do Not Be Yoked With Unbelievers

¹⁴Do not be yoked together with unbelievers. For what do righteousness and wickedness have in common? Or what fellowship can light have with darkness? ¹⁵What harmony is there between Christ and Belial*c*? What does a believer have in common with an unbeliever? ¹⁶What agreement is there between the temple of God and idols? For we are the temple of the living God. As God has said: "I will live with them and walk among them, and I will be their God, and they will be my people."*d*

¹⁷"Therefore come out from them
        and be separate,
                    says the Lord.
Touch no unclean thing,
        and I will receive you."*e*
¹⁸"I will be a Father to you,
        and you will be my sons and
            daughters,
                    says the Lord Almighty."*f*

7 Since we have these promises, dear friends, let us purify ourselves from everything that contaminates body and spirit, perfecting holiness out of reverence for God.

Paul's Joy

²Make room for us in your hearts. We have wronged no one, we have corrupted no one, we have exploited no one. ³I do not say this to condemn you; I have said

---

a21 Or *be a sin offering*   *b2* Isaiah 49:8
c15 Greek *Beliar*, a variant of *Belial*
d16 Lev. 26:12; Jer. 32:38; Ezek. 37:27
e17 Isaiah 52:11; Ezek. 20:34,41
f18 2 Samuel 7:14; 7:8

before that you have such a place in our hearts that we would live or die with you. ⁴I have great confidence in you; I take great pride in you. I am greatly encouraged; in all our troubles my joy knows no bounds.

⁵For when we came into Macedonia, this body of ours had no rest, but we were harassed at every turn—conflicts on the outside, fears within. ⁶But God, who comforts the downcast, comforted us by the coming of Titus, ⁷and not only by his coming but also by the comfort you had given him. He told us about your longing for me, your deep sorrow, your ardent concern for me, so that my joy was greater than ever.

⁸Even if I caused you sorrow by my letter, I do not regret it. Though I did regret it—I see that my letter hurt you, but only for a little while— ⁹yet now I am happy, not because you were made sorry, but because your sorrow led you to repentance. For you became sorrowful as God intended and so were not harmed in any way by us. ¹⁰Godly sorrow brings repentance that leads to salvation and leaves no regret, but worldly sorrow brings death. ¹¹See what this godly sorrow has produced in you: what earnestness, what eagerness to clear yourselves, what indignation, what alarm, what longing, what concern, what readiness to see justice done. At every point you have proved

yourselves to be innocent in this matter. ¹²So even though I wrote to you, it was not on account of the one who did the wrong or of the injured party, but rather that before God you could see for yourselves how devoted to us you are. ¹³By all this we are encouraged.

In addition to our own encouragement, we were especially delighted to see how happy Titus was, because his spirit has been refreshed by all of you. ¹⁴I had boasted to him about you, and you have not embarrassed me. But just as everything we said to you was true, so our boasting about you to Titus has proved to be true as well. ¹⁵And his affection for you is all the greater when he remembers that you were all obedient, receiving him with fear and trembling. ¹⁶I am glad I can have complete confidence in you.

Generosity Encouraged

8 And now, brothers, we want you to know about the grace that God has given the Macedonian churches. ²Out of the most severe trial, their overflowing joy and their extreme poverty welled up in rich generosity. ³For I testify that they gave as much as they were able, and even beyond their ability. Entirely on their own, ⁴they urgently pleaded with us for the privilege of sharing in this service to the saints. ⁵And they did not do as we expected, but they gave themselves first to

Unequally Yoked

2 CORINTHIANS 6:14 When a Christian magazine asked its readers for advice to spouses who are married to a partner who does not possess a personal faith, the letters flowed in. They made suggestions about maintaining respect for your spouse when it isn't easy, laying off the guilt trap, finding common ground where possible, sticking strongly to your convictions, being a good model of Jesus and on and on. But one piece of advice was so consistent that it became predictable. Nearly every single letter urged people in this situation to pray.

A working mother with two toddlers

and a husband who is not a Christian was typical: "Our diverging spiritual paths greatly affect our relationship, and my answer has been found in a four-letter word: PRAY. I 'pray without ceasing' that my spouse will be filled with questions for which only God has answers; that our children will be drawn to the Lord; and that I will be strengthened and guided to be a good Christian role model for our family."

Prayer in its simplest definition is merely a wish turned Godward. So turn your wishes toward God. Raise your thoughts to heaven. **—Les and Leslie**

Go to page 1265 for your next devotional reading.

the Lord and then to us in keeping with God's will. ⁶So we urged Titus, since he had earlier made a beginning, to bring also to completion this act of grace on your part. ⁷But just as you excel in everything—in faith, in speech, in knowledge, in complete earnestness and in your love for us[a]—see that you also excel in this grace of giving.

⁸I am not commanding you, but I want to test the sincerity of your love by comparing it with the earnestness of others. ⁹For you know the grace of our Lord Jesus Christ, that though he was rich, yet for your sakes he became poor, so that you through his poverty might become rich.

¹⁰And here is my advice about what is best for you in this matter: Last year you were the first not only to give but also to have the desire to do so. ¹¹Now finish the work, so that your eager willingness to do it may be matched by your completion of it, according to your means. ¹²For if the willingness is there, the gift is acceptable according to what one has, not according to what he does not have.

¹³Our desire is not that others might be relieved while you are hard pressed, but

that there might be equality. ¹⁴At the present time your plenty will supply what they need, so that in turn their plenty will supply what you need. Then there will be equality, ¹⁵as it is written: "He who gathered much did not have too much, and he who gathered little did not have too little."[b]

Titus Sent to Corinth

¹⁶I thank God, who put into the heart of Titus the same concern I have for you. ¹⁷For Titus not only welcomed our appeal, but he is coming to you with much enthusiasm and on his own initiative. ¹⁸And we are sending along with him the brother who is praised by all the churches for his service to the gospel. ¹⁹What is more, he was chosen by the churches to accompany us as we carry the offering, which we administer in order to honor the Lord himself and to show our eagerness to help. ²⁰We want to avoid any criticism of the way we administer this liberal gift. ²¹For we are taking pains to do what

a7 Some manuscripts *in our love for you*
b15 Exodus 16:18

Godly Sorrow

Thursday

2 CORINTHIANS 7:9–10   Early Catholic guides for priests taking confessions warned about a type of person called "the scrupulous," an individual who held on to guilt no matter what. These people were "unrelieved confessors" who, in spite of all assurances, could not accept grace.

If you are "scrupulous," if you are holding on to your guilt like a security blanket, you can be assured that it is doing damage to your marriage. Guilt can be toxic to relationships. There is a better way. The secret is found in this passage, and it is called "godly sorrow"—as opposed to "worldly sorrow" or guilt.

While guilt and sorrow are sometimes seen as the same emotional experience, they could not be further apart. Sorrow, unlike guilt, does not wallow in self-punishment and self-abasement. Instead, it is usually grounded in a deep concern for re-

lationships and constructive change.

German reformer Martin Luther struggled with unbounded feelings of guilt early on when he became a monk. He expended great energy meeting the requirements of his religious order, confessing his sins repeatedly (and on one occasion for six hours straight). He was so obsessed with confessing even the tiniest sins that once his superior chided him by saying, "If you expect God to forgive you, come in to confession with something to forgive."

When we relate to God out of a guilty conscience rather than godly sorrow, we try to earn our worth by being severely critical of ourselves. We struggle to show God—and sometimes our spouse—how good we are, rather than relying on God's mercy.

—Les and Leslie

Go to page 1267 for your next devotional reading.

is right, not only in the eyes of the Lord but also in the eyes of men.

[22]In addition, we are sending with them our brother who has often proved to us in many ways that he is zealous, and now even more so because of his great confidence in you. [23]As for Titus, he is my partner and fellow worker among you; as for our brothers, they are representatives of the churches and an honor to Christ. [24]Therefore show these men the proof of your love and the reason for our pride in you, so that the churches can see it.

9 There is no need for me to write to you about this service to the saints. [2]For I know your eagerness to help, and I have been boasting about it to the Macedonians, telling them that since last year you in Achaia were ready to give; and your enthusiasm has stirred most of them to action. [3]But I am sending the brothers in order that our boasting about you in this matter should not prove hollow, but that you may be ready, as I said you would be. [4]For if any Macedonians come with me and find you unprepared, we—not to say anything about you—would be ashamed of having been so confident. [5]So I thought it necessary to urge the brothers to visit you in advance and finish the arrangements for the generous gift you had promised. Then it will be ready as a generous gift, not as one grudgingly given.

Sowing Generously

[6]Remember this: Whoever sows sparingly will also reap sparingly, and whoever sows generously will also reap generously. [7]Each man should give what he has decided in his heart to give, not reluctantly or under compulsion, for God loves a cheerful giver. [8]And God is able to make all grace abound to you, so that in all things at all times, having all that you need, you will abound in every good work. [9]As it is written:

"He has scattered abroad his gifts to
    the poor;
  his righteousness endures forever."[a]

[10]Now he who supplies seed to the sower and bread for food will also supply and increase your store of seed and will enlarge the harvest of your righteousness. [11]You will be made rich in every way so that you can be generous on every occasion, and through us your generosity will result in thanksgiving to God.

[12]This service that you perform is not only supplying the needs of God's people but is also overflowing in many expressions of thanks to God. [13]Because of the service by which you have proved yourselves, men will praise God for the obedience that accompanies your confession of the gospel of Christ, and for your generosity in sharing with them and with everyone else. [14]And in their prayers for you their hearts will go out to you, because of the surpassing grace God has given you. [15]Thanks be to God for his indescribable gift!

Paul's Defense of His Ministry

10 By the meekness and gentleness of Christ, I appeal to you—I, Paul, who am "timid" when face to face with you, but "bold" when away! [2]I beg you that when I come I may not have to be as bold as I expect to be toward some people who think that we live by the standards of this world. [3]For though we live in the world, we do not wage war as the world does. [4]The weapons we fight with are not the weapons of the world. On the contrary, they have divine power to demolish strongholds. [5]We demolish arguments and every pretension that sets itself up against the knowledge of God, and we take captive every thought to make it obedient to Christ. [6]And we will be ready to punish every act of disobedience, once your obedience is complete.

[7]You are looking only on the surface of things.[b] If anyone is confident that he belongs to Christ, he should consider again that we belong to Christ just as much as he. [8]For even if I boast somewhat freely about the authority the Lord gave us for building you up rather than pulling you down, I will not be ashamed of it. [9]I do not want to seem to be trying to frighten you with my letters. [10]For some say, "His letters are weighty and forceful, but in person he is unimpressive and his speaking amounts to nothing." [11]Such people should realize that what we are in our letters when we are absent, we will be in our actions when we are present.

[a]9 Psalm 112:9   [b]7 Or *Look at the obvious facts*

¹²We do not dare to classify or compare ourselves with some who commend themselves. When they measure themselves by themselves and compare themselves with themselves, they are not wise. ¹³We, however, will not boast beyond proper limits, but will confine our boasting to the field God has assigned to us, a field that reaches even to you. ¹⁴We are not going too far in our boasting, as would be the case if we had not come to you, for we did get as far as you with the gospel of Christ. ¹⁵Neither do we go beyond our limits by boasting of work done by others.ᵃ Our hope is that, as your faith continues to grow, our area of activity among you will greatly expand, ¹⁶so that we can preach the gospel in the regions beyond you. For we do not want to boast about work already done in another man's territory. ¹⁷But, "Let him who boasts boast in the Lord."ᵇ ¹⁸For it is not the one who commends himself who is approved, but the one whom the Lord commends.

Paul and the False Apostles

11 I hope you will put up with a little of my foolishness; but you are already doing that. ²I am jealous for you with a godly jealousy. I promised you to one husband, to Christ, so that I might present you as a pure virgin to him. ³But I am afraid that just as Eve was deceived by the serpent's cunning, your minds may somehow be led astray from your sincere and pure devotion to Christ. ⁴For if someone comes to you and preaches a Jesus other than the Jesus we preached, or if you receive a different spirit from the one you received, or a different gospel from the one you accepted, you put up with it easily enough. ⁵But I do not think I am in the least inferior to those "super-apostles." ⁶I may not be a trained speaker, but I do have knowledge. We have made this perfectly clear to you in every way.

⁷Was it a sin for me to lower myself in order to elevate you by preaching the gospel of God to you free of charge? ⁸I robbed other churches by receiving support from them so as to serve you. ⁹And when I was with you and needed something, I was not a burden to anyone, for

---

ᵃ13-15 Or ¹³We, however, will not boast about things that cannot be measured, but we will boast according to the standard of measurement that the God of measure has assigned us—a measurement that relates even to you. 14 . . . ¹⁵Neither do we boast about things that cannot be measured in regard to the work done by others.   ᵇ17 Jer. 9:24

Captive Thoughts

Friday

2 CORINTHIANS 10:5 Paul uses the strong word "captive" in regard to his thought life. He does not use the term "keep an eye on" or "be careful of." He would never have said, "I can handle such-and-such a thought without getting tempted because I'm a Christian." Paul chose to take responsibility for his every thought.

If that were true for a man who lived in a time of no television, videos or Internet, how much more profound is it for us today! In my own life as a man, early on I found out how dramatically my thought life could be polluted by visual stimuli.

Taken captive means there is no freedom for the thought life. What initially seems to be freedom insidiously becomes a harsh prison. What was just a one-time experimental thought becomes a demanding taskmaster. This wandering thought life isn't freedom; it's a prison designed by one who desires destruction for us and those we love.

We must choose to take our thoughts captive or they will certainly take us captive. One or the other will be in control. Develop a rule for your thoughts. Place a guard at the door of your mind. Ask yourself, *Are my thoughts pleasing to Christ? If he were sitting with me, would I be allowing my mind to wander?*

For me the "guard at the door" was to cancel any cable programming that delivered sexually explicit movies. I needed to learn to guard the door to my mind, so the temptation never got in "the door" to begin with.   **—Bob and Rosemary**

Go to page 1269 for your next devotional reading.

the brothers who came from Macedonia supplied what I needed. I have kept myself from being a burden to you in any way, and will continue to do so. ¹⁰As surely as the truth of Christ is in me, nobody in the regions of Achaia will stop this boasting of mine. ¹¹Why? Because I do not love you? God knows I do! ¹²And I will keep on doing what I am doing in order to cut the ground from under those who want an opportunity to be considered equal with us in the things they boast about.

¹³For such men are false apostles, deceitful workmen, masquerading as apostles of Christ. ¹⁴And no wonder, for Satan himself masquerades as an angel of light. ¹⁵It is not surprising, then, if his servants masquerade as servants of righteousness. Their end will be what their actions deserve.

Paul Boasts About His Sufferings

¹⁶I repeat: Let no one take me for a fool. But if you do, then receive me just as you would a fool, so that I may do a little boasting. ¹⁷In this self-confident boasting I am not talking as the Lord would, but as a fool. ¹⁸Since many are boasting in the way the world does, I too will boast. ¹⁹You gladly put up with fools since you are so wise! ²⁰In fact, you even put up with anyone who enslaves you or exploits you or takes advantage of you or pushes himself forward or slaps you in the face. ²¹To my shame I admit that we were too weak for that!

What anyone else dares to boast about—I am speaking as a fool—I also dare to boast about. ²²Are they Hebrews? So am I. Are they Israelites? So am I. Are they Abraham's descendants? So am I. ²³Are they servants of Christ? (I am out of my mind to talk like this.) I am more. I have worked much harder, been in prison more frequently, been flogged more severely, and been exposed to death again and again. ²⁴Five times I received from the Jews the forty lashes minus one. ²⁵Three times I was beaten with rods, once I was stoned, three times I was shipwrecked, I spent a night and a day in the open sea, ²⁶I have been constantly on the move. I have been in danger from rivers, in danger from bandits, in danger from my own

countrymen, in danger from Gentiles; in danger in the city, in danger in the country, in danger at sea; and in danger from false brothers. ²⁷I have labored and toiled and have often gone without sleep; I have known hunger and thirst and have often gone without food; I have been cold and naked. ²⁸Besides everything else, I face daily the pressure of my concern for all the churches. ²⁹Who is weak, and I do not feel weak? Who is led into sin, and I do not inwardly burn?

³⁰If I must boast, I will boast of the things that show my weakness. ³¹The God and Father of the Lord Jesus, who is to be praised forever, knows that I am not lying. ³²In Damascus the governor under King Aretas had the city of the Damascenes guarded in order to arrest me. ³³But I was lowered in a basket from a window in the wall and slipped through his hands.

Paul's Vision and His Thorn

12 I must go on boasting. Although there is nothing to be gained, I will go on to visions and revelations from the Lord. ²I know a man in Christ who fourteen years ago was caught up to the third heaven. Whether it was in the body or out of the body I do not know—God knows. ³And I know that this man—whether in the body or apart from the body I do not know, but God knows— ⁴was caught up to paradise. He heard inexpressible things, things that man is not permitted to tell. ⁵I will boast about a man like that, but I will not boast about myself, except about my weaknesses. ⁶Even if I should choose to boast, I would not be a fool, because I would be speaking the truth. But I refrain, so no one will think more of me than is warranted by what I do or say.

⁷To keep me from becoming conceited because of these surpassingly great revelations, there was given me a thorn in my flesh, a messenger of Satan, to torment me. ⁸Three times I pleaded with the Lord to take it away from me. ⁹But he said to me, "My grace is sufficient for you, for my power is made perfect in weakness." Therefore I will boast all the more gladly about my weaknesses, so that Christ's power may rest on me. ¹⁰That is why, for Christ's sake, I delight in weaknesses, in insults, in

hardships, in persecutions, in difficulties. For when I am weak, then I am strong.

Paul's Concern for the Corinthians

[11] I have made a fool of myself, but you drove me to it. I ought to have been commended by you, for I am not in the least inferior to the "super-apostles," even though I am nothing. [12] The things that mark an apostle—signs, wonders and miracles—were done among you with great perseverance. [13] How were you inferior to the other churches, except that I was never a burden to you? Forgive me this wrong!

[14] Now I am ready to visit you for the third time, and I will not be a burden to you, because what I want is not your possessions but you. After all, children should not have to save up for their parents, but parents for their children. [15] So I will very gladly spend for you everything I have and expend myself as well. If I love you more, will you love me less? [16] Be that as it may, I have not been a burden to you. Yet, crafty fellow that I am, I caught you by trickery! [17] Did I exploit you through any of the men I sent you? [18] I

urged Titus to go to you and I sent our brother with him. Titus did not exploit you, did he? Did we not act in the same spirit and follow the same course?

[19] Have you been thinking all along that we have been defending ourselves to you? We have been speaking in the sight of God as those in Christ; and everything we do, dear friends, is for your strengthening. [20] For I am afraid that when I come I may not find you as I want you to be, and you may not find me as you want me to be. I fear that there may be quarreling, jealousy, outbursts of anger, factions, slander, gossip, arrogance and disorder. [21] I am afraid that when I come again my God will humble me before you, and I will be grieved over many who have sinned earlier and have not repented of the impurity, sexual sin and debauchery in which they have indulged.

Final Warnings

13 This will be my third visit to you. "Every matter must be established by the testimony of two or three wit-

Perfectly Human

Quiet TIMES
with each other

2 CORINTHIANS 12:9 When a person wants to comfort a friend who has made a mistake, he or she will often say, "You're only human—you're supposed to make mistakes!" But the perfectionist doesn't agree. Perfectionists have unrealistic goals, and they ignore human weakness. They don't ever want to make a mistake or be seen as weak. And, as this verse makes clear, they are missing out on the power of God's grace.

Perfection is the ultimate illusion, for it simply does not exist on this earth. When people try to live under self-imposed, perfectionistic standards, they will forever be tormented by unnecessary guilt—not to mention driving their spouses nuts.

This does not mean we shouldn't aim for high standards. There is a difference between perfectionism and excellence. Thomas Peters and Robert Waterman, Jr., authors of the best-selling *In Search of Excellence*, describe excellence not as attaining an impossible, out-of-reach goal but as living up to your potential. Everyone, no matter how lowly, has the potential to attain excellence in his or her life.

When you wake up each morning, give yourself (and your spouse) permission to be wrong, to be weak. Strive for excellence but not perfection. And allow God's power to be made perfect in your weakness.

—Les and Leslie

Weekend Warm-up *Have you given each other permission to be less than perfect?*

Go to page 1270 for your next devotional reading.

nesses."*a ²I already gave you a warning when I was with you the second time. I now repeat it while absent: On my return I will not spare those who sinned earlier or any of the others, ³since you are demanding proof that Christ is speaking through me. He is not weak in dealing with you, but is powerful among you. ⁴For to be sure, he was crucified in weakness, yet he lives by God's power. Likewise, we are weak in him, yet by God's power we will live with him to serve you.

⁵Examine yourselves to see whether you are in the faith; test yourselves. Do you not realize that Christ Jesus is in you—unless, of course, you fail the test? ⁶And I trust that you will discover that we have not failed the test. ⁷Now we pray to God that you will not do anything wrong. Not that people will see that we have stood the test but that you will do what is right even though we may seem to have failed. ⁸For we cannot do anything against the truth, but only for the truth. ⁹We are glad whenever we are weak but you are strong; and our prayer is for your perfection. ¹⁰This is why I write these things when I am absent, that when I come I may not have to be harsh in my use of authority—the authority the Lord gave me for building you up, not for tearing you down.

Final Greetings

¹¹Finally, brothers, good-by. Aim for perfection, listen to my appeal, be of one mind, live in peace. And the God of love and peace will be with you.

¹²Greet one another with a holy kiss. ¹³All the saints send their greetings.

¹⁴May the grace of the Lord Jesus Christ, and the love of God, and the fellowship of the Holy Spirit be with you all.

*a*1 Deut. 19:15

Holy Kiss

Monday

2 CORINTHIANS 13:12 We were in the Black Forest of southern Germany for several months, working on a writing project. When we write we spend a lot of time walking and talking. One day as we climbed a path by a waterfall, we reminisced about a similar walk we had taken years earlier to Abram's Falls in the Smokey Mountains. One reason we remembered it was because on that day we had kissed a lot! Dave suggested that whenever we saw a waterfall, we should stop and kiss. Soon we were stopping at a stream, or even a puddle! We laugh about our "walk, talk and kiss" dates, but they help us put a little romance back into our relationship.

In our marriage seminars we encourage couples to have their own walk, talk and kiss dates. Also we suggest another way to enhance your love life: Kiss for ten seconds each time you say hello or goodbye. Try it. You may be surprised by how long ten seconds really is! By the way, we call it our "holy kiss."

—*Dave and Claudia*

Go to page 1272 for your next devotional reading.

Galatians

What if someone told you that this little collection of chapters—the book of Galatians—contained the unequivocal secret to living a successful, victorious, awe-inspiring Christian life? Well, these pages do contain the heretofore classified mystery of how to please your heavenly Father, how to lead others to faith, and how to set a godly example for your spouse, children and friends. In fact, let's cut to the chase and discover this enigmatic truth right now. Ready? Here it is.

You cannot, under any circumstances whatsoever, do any of the above. The secret to living a pure Christian life is coming to the full understanding that it is impossible to live a pure Christian life. God's Holy Spirit—his power released inside a person—does all this through us. Our challenge is not to plumb the depths of our abilities, to fine-tune our skills or to try harder. Our task is to admit our need for God's filling and to submit to his control. Paul lived a stellar Christian life because he discovered that he couldn't.

1 Paul, an apostle—sent not from men nor by man, but by Jesus Christ and God the Father, who raised him from the dead— ²and all the brothers with me,

To the churches in Galatia:

³Grace and peace to you from God our Father and the Lord Jesus Christ, ⁴who gave himself for our sins to rescue us from the present evil age, according to the will of our God and Father, ⁵to whom be glory for ever and ever. Amen.

No Other Gospel

⁶I am astonished that you are so quickly deserting the one who called you by the grace of Christ and are turning to a different gospel— ⁷which is really no gospel at all. Evidently some people are throwing you into confusion and are trying to per-

vert the gospel of Christ. 8But even if we or an angel from heaven should preach a gospel other than the one we preached to you, let him be eternally condemned! 9As we have already said, so now I say again: If anybody is preaching to you a gospel other than what you accepted, let him be eternally condemned!

10Am I now trying to win the approval of men, or of God? Or am I trying to please men? If I were still trying to please men, I would not be a servant of Christ.

Paul Called by God

11I want you to know, brothers, that the gospel I preached is not something that man made up. 12I did not receive it from any man, nor was I taught it; rather, I received it by revelation from Jesus Christ.

13For you have heard of my previous way of life in Judaism, how intensely I persecuted the church of God and tried to destroy it. 14I was advancing in Judaism beyond many Jews of my own age and was extremely zealous for the traditions of my fathers. 15But when God, who set me apart from birth*a* and called me by his grace, was pleased 16to reveal his Son in me so that I might preach him among the Gentiles, I did not consult any man, 17nor did I go up to Jerusalem to see those who were apostles before I was, but I went immediately into Arabia and later returned to Damascus.

18Then after three years, I went up to Jerusalem to get acquainted with Peter*b* and stayed with him fifteen days. 19I saw none of the other apostles—only James, the Lord's brother. 20I assure you before God that what I am writing you is no lie. 21Later I went to Syria and Cilicia. 22I was personally unknown to the churches of Judea that are in Christ. 23They only heard the report: "The man who formerly persecuted us is now preaching the faith he once tried to destroy." 24And they praised God because of me.

Paul Accepted by the Apostles

2 Fourteen years later I went up again to Jerusalem, this time with Barnabas. I took Titus along also. 2I went in response to a revelation and set before them the gospel that I preach among the Gentiles. But I did this privately to those who seemed to be leaders, for fear that I was running or had run my race in vain. 3Yet not even Titus, who was with me, was compelled to be circumcised, even though he was a Greek. 4This matter arose, because some false brothers had infiltrated our ranks to spy on the freedom we have in Christ Jesus and to make us

---

a15 Or *from my mother's womb*   *b18* Greek *Cephas*

Doing Versus Being

Tuesday

GALATIANS 1:10   Pulitzer prize-winning journalist Henry Byard Swope noted, "I cannot give you the formula for success, but I can give you the formula for failure: Try to please everybody." Sometimes this compulsion to please contaminates a marriage, and one spouse or the other walks around on eggshells attempting to do anything and everything to make the other happy. Unfortunately, these good intentions, no matter how sincere, are a formula for failure.

Whenever we place winning the approval of another person over our desire to win the approval of God, we fall into the trap of *doing* rather than *being.* We do loving things instead of being a loving person. We become more concerned with doing things right than doing the right thing. We become hungry for compliments. Like a periscope scanning the sea, we are on the lookout for the approval from our spouse (or anyone else) who will stroke our ego. We have one eye on our action and the other on our audience. That's another way of saying we aren't looking to God for much of anything. But the truth is, only God's love allows us to relax into *being* rather than *doing.*   —**Les and Leslie**

Go to page 1274 for your next devotional reading.

slaves. [5]We did not give in to them for a moment, so that the truth of the gospel might remain with you.

[6]As for those who seemed to be important—whatever they were makes no difference to me; God does not judge by external appearance—those men added nothing to my message. [7]On the contrary, they saw that I had been entrusted with the task of preaching the gospel to the Gentiles,[a] just as Peter had been to the Jews.[b] [8]For God, who was at work in the ministry of Peter as an apostle to the Jews, was also at work in my ministry as an apostle to the Gentiles. [9]James, Peter[c] and John, those reputed to be pillars, gave me and Barnabas the right hand of fellowship when they recognized the grace given to me. They agreed that we should go to the Gentiles, and they to the Jews. [10]All they asked was that we should continue to remember the poor, the very thing I was eager to do.

Paul Opposes Peter

[11]When Peter came to Antioch, I opposed him to his face, because he was clearly in the wrong. [12]Before certain men came from James, he used to eat with the Gentiles. But when they arrived, he began to draw back and separate himself from the Gentiles because he was afraid of those who belonged to the circumcision group. [13]The other Jews joined him in his hypocrisy, so that by their hypocrisy even Barnabas was led astray.

[14]When I saw that they were not acting in line with the truth of the gospel, I said to Peter in front of them all, "You are a Jew, yet you live like a Gentile and not like a Jew. How is it, then, that you force Gentiles to follow Jewish customs?

[15]"We who are Jews by birth and not 'Gentile sinners' [16]know that a man is not justified by observing the law, but by faith in Jesus Christ. So we, too, have put our faith in Christ Jesus that we may be justified by faith in Christ and not by observing the law, because by observing the law no one will be justified.

[17]"If, while we seek to be justified in Christ, it becomes evident that we ourselves are sinners, does that mean that Christ promotes sin? Absolutely not! [18]If I rebuild what I destroyed, I prove that I am a lawbreaker. [19]For through the law I died to the law so that I might live for God. [20]I have been crucified with Christ and I no longer live, but Christ lives in me. The life I live in the body, I live by faith in the Son of God, who loved me and gave himself for me. [21]I do not set aside the grace of God, for if righteousness could be gained through the law, Christ died for nothing!"[d]

Faith or Observance of the Law

3 You foolish Galatians! Who has bewitched you? Before your very eyes Jesus Christ was clearly portrayed as crucified. [2]I would like to learn just one thing from you: Did you receive the Spirit by observing the law, or by believing what you heard? [3]Are you so foolish? After beginning with the Spirit, are you now trying to attain your goal by human effort? [4]Have you suffered so much for nothing—if it really was for nothing? [5]Does God give you his Spirit and work miracles among you because you observe the law, or because you believe what you heard?

[6]Consider Abraham: "He believed God, and it was credited to him as righteousness."[e] [7]Understand, then, that those who believe are children of Abraham. [8]The Scripture foresaw that God would justify the Gentiles by faith, and announced the gospel in advance to Abraham: "All nations will be blessed through you."[f] [9]So those who have faith are blessed along with Abraham, the man of faith.

[10]All who rely on observing the law are under a curse, for it is written: "Cursed is everyone who does not continue to do everything written in the Book of the Law."[g] [11]Clearly no one is justified before God by the law, because, "The righteous will live by faith."[h] [12]The law is not based on faith; on the contrary, "The man who does these things will live by them."[i] [13]Christ redeemed us from the curse of the law by becoming a curse for us, for it is written: "Cursed is everyone who is

---

a7 Greek *uncircumcised*   *b7* Greek *circumcised*;
also in verses 8 and 9   *c9* Greek *Cephas*; also in
verses 11 and 14   *d21* Some interpreters end
the quotation after verse 14.   *e6* Gen. 15:6
f8 Gen. 12:3; 18:18; 22:18   *g10* Deut. 27:26
h11 Hab. 2:4   *i12* Lev. 18:5

hung on a tree."[a] [14]He redeemed us in order that the blessing given to Abraham might come to the Gentiles through Christ Jesus, so that by faith we might receive the promise of the Spirit.

The Law and the Promise

[15]Brothers, let me take an example from everyday life. Just as no one can set aside or add to a human covenant that has been duly established, so it is in this case. [16]The promises were spoken to Abraham and to his seed. The Scripture does not say "and to seeds," meaning many people, but "and to your seed,"[b] meaning one person, who is Christ. [17]What I mean is this: The law, introduced 430 years later, does not set aside the covenant previously established by God and thus do away with the promise. [18]For if the inheritance depends on the law, then it no longer depends on a promise; but God in his grace gave it to Abraham through a promise.

[19]What, then, was the purpose of the law? It was added because of transgressions until the Seed to whom the promise referred had come. The law was put into effect through angels by a mediator. [20]A mediator, however, does not represent just one party; but God is one.

[21]Is the law, therefore, opposed to the promises of God? Absolutely not! For if a law had been given that could impart life, then righteousness would certainly have come by the law. [22]But the Scripture declares that the whole world is a prisoner of sin, so that what was promised, being given through faith in Jesus Christ, might be given to those who believe.

[23]Before this faith came, we were held prisoners by the law, locked up until faith should be revealed. [24]So the law was put in charge to lead us to Christ[c] that we might be justified by faith. [25]Now that faith has come, we are no longer under the supervision of the law.

Sons of God

[26]You are all sons of God through faith in Christ Jesus, [27]for all of you who were baptized into Christ have clothed yourselves with Christ. [28]There is neither Jew nor Greek, slave nor free, male nor female, for you are all one in Christ Jesus. [29]If you belong to Christ, then you are Abraham's seed, and heirs according to the promise.

4 What I am saying is that as long as the heir is a child, he is no different from a slave, although he owns the whole es-

[a]13 Deut. 21:23   [b]16 Gen. 12:7; 13:15; 24:7
[c]24 Or *charge until Christ came*

Gender Wars

Wednesday

GALATIANS 3:28 Ed and Linda had been married for four years, and they were battling over which chores were appropriate for each other. Handling the finances was a key issue. Even though Linda had worked in a bank before they were married and was much more able to handle their money, Ed had a hard time letting go. He had grown up believing it was the man's place of power to handle the money and stay away from "the more womanly things" such as diapers and laundry. Their attitudes were damaging their marriage, as well as their finances.

Ed and Linda were in a gender war. Rather than work together and use each other's gifts to benefit the marriage, they

were defining themselves by stereotypes and drawing boundaries. Instead of developing a sensitivity toward each other's particular skills, they spent their time announcing what they would and wouldn't do for their marriage.

The marriage relationship shouldn't involve two people battling for status. It should be about two people battling to serve each other. Like Jesus Christ, who came from his throne in heaven, giving up everything, he served the needs of his bride, the church . . . even dying to meet those needs. We need to learn to serve like that.

—Bob and Rosemary

Go to page 1276 for your next devotional reading.

tate. ²He is subject to guardians and trustees until the time set by his father. ³So also, when we were children, we were in slavery under the basic principles of the world. ⁴But when the time had fully come, God sent his Son, born of a woman, born under law, ⁵to redeem those under law, that we might receive the full rights of sons. ⁶Because you are sons, God sent the Spirit of his Son into our hearts, the Spirit who calls out, *"Abba,ᵃ Father."* ⁷So you are no longer a slave, but a son; and since you are a son, God has made you also an heir.

Paul's Concern for the Galatians

⁸Formerly, when you did not know God, you were slaves to those who by nature are not gods. ⁹But now that you know God—or rather are known by God—how is it that you are turning back to those weak and miserable principles? Do you wish to be enslaved by them all over again? ¹⁰You are observing special days and months and seasons and years! ¹¹I fear for you, that somehow I have wasted my efforts on you.

¹²I plead with you, brothers, become like me, for I became like you. You have done me no wrong. ¹³As you know, it was because of an illness that I first preached the gospel to you. ¹⁴Even though my illness was a trial to you, you did not treat me with contempt or scorn. Instead, you welcomed me as if I were an angel of God, as if I were Christ Jesus himself. ¹⁵What has happened to all your joy? I can testify that, if you could have done so, you would have torn out your eyes and given them to me. ¹⁶Have I now become your enemy by telling you the truth?

¹⁷Those people are zealous to win you over, but for no good. What they want is to alienate you ⌊from us⌋, so that you may be zealous for them. ¹⁸It is fine to be zealous, provided the purpose is good, and to be so always and not just when I am with you. ¹⁹My dear children, for whom I am again in the pains of childbirth until Christ is formed in you, ²⁰how I wish I could be with you now and change my tone, because I am perplexed about you!

Hagar and Sarah

²¹Tell me, you who want to be under

Gender Wars

Take a moment to answer each of these questions on your own. Then compare your answers to your spouse's.

Yes   No   I am totally free from any preconceived ideas of what each gender's role is in a marriage relationship.

Yes   No   When it comes to dividing up the family chores, I don't have a problem doing things my parents would have seen as the other gender's responsibility.

Yes   No   I don't have a problem discussing this area of our marriage.

Yes   No   My actions indicate that my main focus is to help my spouse in any way I can.

---

the law, are you not aware of what the law says? ²²For it is written that Abraham had two sons, one by the slave woman and the other by the free woman. ²³His son by the slave woman was born in the ordinary way; but his son by the free woman was born as the result of a promise.

²⁴These things may be taken figuratively, for the women represent two covenants. One covenant is from Mount Sinai and bears children who are to be slaves: This is Hagar. ²⁵Now Hagar stands for Mount Sinai in Arabia and corresponds to the present city of Jerusalem, because she is in slavery with her children. ²⁶But the Jerusalem that is above is free, and she is our mother. ²⁷For it is written:

"Be glad, O barren woman,
    who bears no children;
break forth and cry aloud,
    you who have no labor pains;
because more are the children of the
        desolate woman
    than of her who has a husband."ᵇ

²⁸Now you, brothers, like Isaac, are children of promise. ²⁹At that time the son born in the ordinary way persecuted

ᵃ6 Aramaic for *Father*   ᵇ27 Isaiah 54:1

the son born by the power of the Spirit. It is the same now. ³⁰But what does the Scripture say? "Get rid of the slave woman and her son, for the slave woman's son will never share in the inheritance with the free woman's son."ᵃ ³¹Therefore, brothers, we are not children of the slave woman, but of the free woman.

Freedom in Christ

5 It is for freedom that Christ has set us free. Stand firm, then, and do not let yourselves be burdened again by a yoke of slavery.

²Mark my words! I, Paul, tell you that if you let yourselves be circumcised, Christ will be of no value to you at all. ³Again I declare to every man who lets himself be circumcised that he is obligated to obey the whole law. ⁴You who are trying to be justified by law have been alienated from Christ; you have fallen away from grace. ⁵But by faith we eagerly await through the Spirit the righteousness for which we hope. ⁶For in Christ Jesus neither circumcision nor uncircumcision has any value. The only thing that counts is faith expressing itself through love.

⁷You were running a good race. Who cut in on you and kept you from obeying the truth? ⁸That kind of persuasion does not come from the one who calls you. ⁹"A little yeast works through the whole batch of dough." ¹⁰I am confident in the Lord that you will take no other view. The one who is throwing you into confusion will pay the penalty, whoever he may be. ¹¹Brothers, if I am still preaching circumcision, why am I still being persecuted? In that case the offense of the cross has been abolished. ¹²As for those agitators, I wish they would go the whole way and emasculate themselves!

¹³You, my brothers, were called to be free. But do not use your freedom to indulge the sinful natureᵇ; rather, serve one another in love. ¹⁴The entire law is summed up in a single command: "Love your neighbor as yourself."ᶜ ¹⁵If you keep on biting and devouring each other, watch out or you will be destroyed by each other.

Life by the Spirit

¹⁶So I say, live by the Spirit, and you will not gratify the desires of the sinful nature. ¹⁷For the sinful nature desires

ᵃ30 Gen. 21:10   ᵇ13 Or *the flesh*; also in verses 16, 17, 19 and 24   ᶜ14 Lev. 19:18

The Fruit of Your Marriage

Thursday

GALATIANS 5:22–23   Building a strong Christian marriage is hard work. Unfortunately, God's love, joy, peace, patience, kindness, goodness, gentleness and self-control don't automatically come with the marriage license. The fruit of the Spirit must be cultivated.

It's usually not the big things that can wreck a marriage. Instead it's the unhealthy patterns that pile up on top of each other such as being negative, sarcastic, neglectful or critical. These are sure to quickly turn good fruit rotten.

How we invest in each other daily will influence our relationship. We can choose to be "other-centered," to be patient and to be kind. What little things are you doing today to cultivate the fruit of the spirit in your marriage?

Consider these suggestions from other Christian couples:
• "Never go to bed mad at each other."
• "Look for ways to compliment your mate."
• "Spend time talking together. Set a regular communication time and stick to it."
• "Take a thirty-minute walk together each evening after dinner."
• "Pray together each morning."
To these comments we would add, "Laugh together and don't take yourselves so seriously." Having a satisfying marriage is hard work, but the good fruit is there to enjoy if we help it grow.

—Dave and Claudia

Go to page 1277 for your next devotional reading.

what is contrary to the Spirit, and the Spirit what is contrary to the sinful nature. They are in conflict with each other, so that you do not do what you want. ¹⁸But if you are led by the Spirit, you are not under law.

¹⁹The acts of the sinful nature are obvious: sexual immorality, impurity and debauchery; ²⁰idolatry and witchcraft; hatred, discord, jealousy, fits of rage, selfish ambition, dissensions, factions ²¹and envy; drunkenness, orgies, and the like. I warn you, as I did before, that those who live like this will not inherit the kingdom of God.

²²But the fruit of the Spirit is love, joy, peace, patience, kindness, goodness, faithfulness, ²³gentleness and self-control. Against such things there is no law. ²⁴Those who belong to Christ Jesus have crucified the sinful nature with its passions and desires. ²⁵Since we live by the Spirit, let us keep in step with the Spirit. ²⁶Let us not become conceited, provoking and envying each other.

Doing Good to All

6 Brothers, if someone is caught in a sin, you who are spiritual should restore him gently. But watch yourself, or you also may be tempted. ²Carry each other's burdens, and in this way you will fulfill the law of Christ. ³If anyone thinks he is something when he is nothing, he deceives himself. ⁴Each one should test his own actions. Then he can take pride in himself, without comparing himself to somebody else, ⁵for each one should carry his own load.

⁶Anyone who receives instruction in the word must share all good things with his instructor.

⁷Do not be deceived: God cannot be mocked. A man reaps what he sows. ⁸The one who sows to please his sinful nature,

Avoiding the Blame Game

Friday

GALATIANS 6:2–5 Have you noticed lately that a large portion of the population claims to be a "victim"? The *New Yorker* magazine recently featured a cover story with the title, "The New Culture of Victimization," and the headline of the inside story was "Don't Blame Me!" On the cover of a recent *Time* magazine these words appeared: "Cry Babies and Eternal Victims!" *Esquire* followed with an article titled "A Confederacy of Complainers." It seems people these days don't want to be held accountable.

We will leave it to the social commentators to explain just how our new culture of victimization will affect society, but we know exactly how it can affect a marriage. Once a husband or wife gets wrapped up in the blame game (blaming parents, genes, a boss or a spouse, for example), a vicious cycle of shirked responsibility can permeate the relationship. Soon each partner is looking for ways to avoid responsibility and shift the blame. Of course, this is nothing new. Ever since Adam blamed Eve, and

Eve blamed the serpent, we have learned the trick of finding excuses. Accused of wrongdoing, we respond, "Who me?—I didn't do it" or "It's only a game" or "Well, you asked for it" or "I didn't mean to."

But let's be honest. We *are* responsible. As human beings with a free will, we have choices, and nobody else makes them for us. While we are not necessarily the cause of all that happens in our lives, we are responsible for what we make of what happens. As Scripture says, "You, my brothers, were called to be free. But do not use your freedom to indulge the sinful nature; rather, serve one another in love" (Galatians 5:13).

Don't let your marriage become a blame game. Don't lay the blame on your church, your parents, your schooling, your income, your siblings, your friends, your government or anything else. Take responsibility for your feelings and your actions and watch your marriage mature.

—Les and Leslie

Go to page 1280 for your next devotional reading.

from that nature*a* will reap destruction; the one who sows to please the Spirit, from the Spirit will reap eternal life. ⁹Let us not become weary in doing good, for at the proper time we will reap a harvest if we do not give up. ¹⁰Therefore, as we have opportunity, let us do good to all people, especially to those who belong to the family of believers.

Not Circumcision but a New Creation

¹¹See what large letters I use as I write to you with my own hand!

¹²Those who want to make a good impression outwardly are trying to compel you to be circumcised. The only reason they do this is to avoid being persecuted for the cross of Christ. ¹³Not even those who are circumcised obey the law, yet they want you to be circumcised that they may boast about your flesh. ¹⁴May I never boast except in the cross of our Lord Jesus Christ, through which*b* the world has been crucified to me, and I to the world. ¹⁵Neither circumcision nor uncircumcision means anything; what counts is a new creation. ¹⁶Peace and mercy to all who follow this rule, even to the Israel of God.

¹⁷Finally, let no one cause me trouble, for I bear on my body the marks of Jesus.

¹⁸The grace of our Lord Jesus Christ be with your spirit, brothers. Amen.

a8 Or *his flesh, from the flesh*   *b14* Or *whom*

Ephesians

Sometimes
what it means to obey Jesus Christ seems abstract, theoretical and difficult to grasp. How do you live out your Christianity at work and at home? How can you maximize your relationship with your spouse? What is the best way to effectively parent your children and motivate them to follow Christ? How can you face and defeat the temptations that constantly swirl around you?

Someone must have asked these very same questions of the apostle Paul, because the book of Ephesians is filled with very practical answers to every one of these questions. The next time someone challenges you with unrealistic and ethereal expectations of your faith, show them this book. By the way, if you're feeling a little overwhelmed by the task of being God's ambassador in the world, you've come to the right place.

1 Paul, an apostle of Christ Jesus by the will of God,

To the saints in Ephesus,*a* the faithful*b* in Christ Jesus:

²Grace and peace to you from God our Father and the Lord Jesus Christ.

Spiritual Blessings in Christ

³Praise be to the God and Father of our Lord Jesus Christ, who has blessed us in the heavenly realms with every spiritual blessing in Christ. ⁴For he chose us in him before the creation of the world to be holy and blameless in his sight. In love

⁵he*c* predestined us to be adopted as his sons through Jesus Christ, in accordance with his pleasure and will— ⁶to the praise of his glorious grace, which he has freely given us in the One he loves. ⁷In him we have redemption through his blood, the forgiveness of sins, in accordance with the riches of God's grace ⁸that he lavished on us with all wisdom and understanding. ⁹And he*d* made known to us the mystery of his will according to his good pleasure, which he purposed in Christ, ¹⁰to be put

a1 Some early manuscripts do not have in Ephesus.
b1 Or believers who are   c4,5 Or sight in love.
5He   d8,9 Or us. With all wisdom and
understanding, 9he

into effect when the times will have reached their fulfillment—to bring all things in heaven and on earth together under one head, even Christ.

[11]In him we were also chosen,[a] having been predestined according to the plan of him who works out everything in conformity with the purpose of his will, [12]in order that we, who were the first to hope in Christ, might be for the praise of his glory. [13]And you also were included in Christ when you heard the word of truth, the gospel of your salvation. Having believed, you were marked in him with a seal, the promised Holy Spirit, [14]who is a deposit guaranteeing our inheritance until the redemption of those who are God's possession—to the praise of his glory.

Thanksgiving and Prayer

[15]For this reason, ever since I heard about your faith in the Lord Jesus and your love for all the saints, [16]I have not stopped giving thanks for you, remembering you in my prayers. [17]I keep asking that the God of our Lord Jesus Christ, the glorious Father, may give you the Spirit[b] of wisdom and revelation, so that you may know him better. [18]I pray also that the eyes of your heart may be enlightened in

order that you may know the hope to which he has called you, the riches of his glorious inheritance in the saints, [19]and his incomparably great power for us who believe. That power is like the working of his mighty strength, [20]which he exerted in Christ when he raised him from the dead and seated him at his right hand in the heavenly realms, [21]far above all rule and authority, power and dominion, and every title that can be given, not only in the present age but also in the one to come. [22]And God placed all things under his feet and appointed him to be head over everything for the church, [23]which is his body, the fullness of him who fills everything in every way.

Made Alive in Christ

2 As for you, you were dead in your transgressions and sins, [2]in which you used to live when you followed the ways of this world and of the ruler of the kingdom of the air, the spirit who is now at work in those who are disobedient. [3]All of us also lived among them at one time, gratifying the cravings of our sinful na-

[a]11 Or *were made heirs*   [b]17 Or *a spirit*

Thank-you Lists

Quiet TIMES with each other

EPHESIANS 1:16 We've been married to each other over half of our lives. We've raised three sons to adulthood. We share the same profession, the same office and even the same car! It's so easy to take each other for granted—especially in a long-term marriage in which you are so comfortable. That's why we often make an "I'm thankful for you" list.

For instance, I might write down how thankful I am for Dave's optimism and his great sense of humor that balances me when I am just too serious. Dave might note how he appreciates my creativity and

the way I focus on my positive points instead of criticizing my weak areas. Then we share our lists and together praise God for each other and for our marriage.

It takes five positive statements to offset one negative statement, so for the next twenty-four hours track your positives against your negatives and see how you're doing. What a difference it makes when we look at our marriage and our lives through a positive filter of thanksgiving and prayer. We encourage you to do the same.

—*Dave and Claudia*

Weekend Warm-up   *If you were to make an "I'm thankful for you" list, what would be on it?*

Go to page 1281 for your next devotional reading.

ture*a* and following its desires and thoughts. Like the rest, we were by nature objects of wrath. ⁴But because of his great love for us, God, who is rich in mercy, ⁵made us alive with Christ even when we were dead in transgressions—it is by grace you have been saved. ⁶And God raised us up with Christ and seated us with him in the heavenly realms in Christ Jesus, ⁷in order that in the coming ages he might show the incomparable riches of his grace, expressed in his kindness to us in Christ Jesus. ⁸For it is by grace you have been saved, through faith—and this not from yourselves, it is the gift of God—⁹not by works, so that no one can boast. ¹⁰For we are God's workmanship, created in Christ Jesus to do good works, which God prepared in advance for us to do.

One in Christ

¹¹Therefore, remember that formerly you who are Gentiles by birth and called "uncircumcised" by those who call themselves "the circumcision" (that done in the body by the hands of men)—¹²remember that at that time you were separate from Christ, excluded from citizenship in Israel and foreigners to the covenants of the promise, without hope and without God in the world. ¹³But now in Christ Jesus you who once were far away have been brought near through the blood of Christ.

¹⁴For he himself is our peace, who has made the two one and has destroyed the barrier, the dividing wall of hostility, ¹⁵by abolishing in his flesh the law with its commandments and regulations. His purpose was to create in himself one new man out of the two, thus making peace, ¹⁶and in this one body to reconcile both of them to God through the cross, by which he put to death their hostility. ¹⁷He came and preached peace to you who were far away and peace to those who were near. ¹⁸For through him we both have access to the Father by one Spirit.

¹⁹Consequently, you are no longer foreigners and aliens, but fellow citizens with God's people and members of God's household, ²⁰built on the foundation of the apostles and prophets, with Christ Jesus himself as the chief cornerstone.

a3 Or our flesh

A Priceless Masterpiece

Monday

EPHESIANS 2:10 Every child could benefit from a grandmother like mine. She was the most affirming person in my life. She spent her time pointing out how special I was. I didn't do anything extraordinary; she just felt that her grandchildren were the greatest people in the world. That was the way she chose to see us. When you were at my grandmother's house, you felt like you could do and be anything.

It is affirming when a grandmother feels that way about her grandchildren, but the fact that the Creator of the universe feels that way about his children should be revolutionary. God's view of us should radically change how we think about ourselves. This passage in Ephesians calls us God's workmanship, but it can also be translated to say that God's children are his "masterpiece." Imagine the significance of know-

ing that you are God's masterpiece. Some dynamics of the marriage relationship can leave us with a low opinion of ourselves. Unresolved conflicts and lack of communication or constant blaming of each other can make a spouse feel as if he or she isn't very special. Unmet needs or dreams we had about the marriage can leave us feeling discouraged or disappointed. Yet the Bible describes us as a treasure in God's eyes. We are God's masterpiece.

Which assessment are you going to trust? When you accept the assessment of the perfect Creator God, you are liberated to love those around you with that same affirming attitude. When you see yourself as God sees you, then you can love others like a proud, encouraging grandparent.

—Bob and Rosemary

Go to page 1283 for your next devotional reading.

²¹In him the whole building is joined together and rises to become a holy temple in the Lord. ²²And in him you too are being built together to become a dwelling in which God lives by his Spirit.

Paul the Preacher to the Gentiles

3 For this reason I, Paul, the prisoner of Christ Jesus for the sake of you Gentiles—

²Surely you have heard about the administration of God's grace that was given to me for you, ³that is, the mystery made known to me by revelation, as I have already written briefly. ⁴In reading this, then, you will be able to understand my insight into the mystery of Christ, ⁵which was not made known to men in other generations as it has now been revealed by the Spirit to God's holy apostles and prophets. ⁶This mystery is that through the gospel the Gentiles are heirs together with Israel, members together of one body, and sharers together in the promise in Christ Jesus.

⁷I became a servant of this gospel by the gift of God's grace given me through the working of his power. ⁸Although I am less than the least of all God's people, this grace was given me: to preach to the Gentiles the unsearchable riches of Christ, ⁹and to make plain to everyone the administration of this mystery, which for ages past was kept hidden in God, who created all things. ¹⁰His intent was that now, through the church, the manifold wisdom of God should be made known to the rulers and authorities in the heavenly realms, ¹¹according to his eternal purpose which he accomplished in Christ Jesus our Lord. ¹²In him and through faith in him we may approach God with freedom and confidence. ¹³I ask you, therefore, not to be discouraged because of my sufferings for you, which are your glory.

A Prayer for the Ephesians

¹⁴For this reason I kneel before the Father, ¹⁵from whom his whole family[a] in heaven and on earth derives its name. ¹⁶I pray that out of his glorious riches he may strengthen you with power through his Spirit in your inner being, ¹⁷so that Christ may dwell in your hearts through faith.

And I pray that you, being rooted and established in love, ¹⁸may have power, together with all the saints, to grasp how wide and long and high and deep is the love of Christ, ¹⁹and to know this love that surpasses knowledge—that you may be filled to the measure of all the fullness of God.

²⁰Now to him who is able to do immeasurably more than all we ask or imagine, according to his power that is at work within us, ²¹to him be glory in the church and in Christ Jesus throughout all generations, for ever and ever! Amen.

Unity in the Body of Christ

4 As a prisoner for the Lord, then, I urge you to live a life worthy of the calling you have received. ²Be completely humble and gentle; be patient, bearing with one another in love. ³Make every effort to keep the unity of the Spirit through the bond of peace. ⁴There is one body and one Spirit—just as you were called to one hope when you were called— ⁵one Lord, one faith, one baptism; ⁶one God and Father of all, who is over all and through all and in all.

⁷But to each one of us grace has been given as Christ apportioned it. ⁸This is why it[b] says:

"When he ascended on high,
   he led captives in his train
   and gave gifts to men."[c]

⁹(What does "he ascended" mean except that he also descended to the lower, earthly regions[d]? ¹⁰He who descended is the very one who ascended higher than all the heavens, in order to fill the whole universe.) ¹¹It was he who gave some to be apostles, some to be prophets, some to be evangelists, and some to be pastors and teachers, ¹²to prepare God's people for works of service, so that the body of Christ may be built up ¹³until we all reach unity in the faith and in the knowledge of the Son of God and become mature, attaining to the whole measure of the fullness of Christ.

¹⁴Then we will no longer be infants, tossed back and forth by the waves, and blown here and there by every wind of

---

a15 Or whom all fatherhood   b8 Or God
c8 Psalm 68:18   d9 Or the depths of the earth

teaching and by the cunning and craftiness of men in their deceitful scheming. ¹⁵Instead, speaking the truth in love, we will in all things grow up into him who is the Head, that is, Christ. ¹⁶From him the whole body, joined and held together by every supporting ligament, grows and builds itself up in love, as each part does its work.

Living as Children of Light

¹⁷So I tell you this, and insist on it in the Lord, that you must no longer live as the Gentiles do, in the futility of their thinking. ¹⁸They are darkened in their understanding and separated from the life of God because of the ignorance that is in them due to the hardening of their hearts. ¹⁹Having lost all sensitivity, they have given themselves over to sensuality so as to indulge in every kind of impurity, with a continual lust for more.

²⁰You, however, did not come to know Christ that way. ²¹Surely you heard of him and were taught in him in accordance with the truth that is in Jesus. ²²You were taught, with regard to your former way of life, to put off your old self, which is being corrupted by its deceitful desires; ²³to be made new in the attitude of your minds; ²⁴and to put on the new self, created to be like God in true righteousness and holiness.

²⁵Therefore each of you must put off falsehood and speak truthfully to his neighbor, for we are all members of one body. ²⁶"In your anger do not sin"ᵃ: Do not let the sun go down while you are still angry, ²⁷and do not give the devil a foothold. ²⁸He who has been stealing must steal no longer, but must work, doing something useful with his own hands, that he may have something to share with those in need.

²⁹Do not let any unwholesome talk come out of your mouths, but only what is helpful for building others up according to their needs, that it may benefit those who listen. ³⁰And do not grieve the Holy Spirit of God, with whom you were sealed for the day of redemption. ³¹Get rid of all bitterness, rage and anger, brawling and slander, along with every form of malice. ³²Be kind and compassionate to one another, forgiving each other, just as in Christ God forgave you.

5 Be imitators of God, therefore, as dearly loved children ²and live a life of love, just as Christ loved us and gave himself up for us as a fragrant offering and sacrifice to God.

³But among you there must not be even a hint of sexual immorality, or of any kind of impurity, or of greed, because

ᵃ26 Psalm 4:4

Listening With the Third Ear

Tuesday

EPHESIANS 4:29 "The road to the heart," wrote Voltaire, "is the ear." So true. Carefully listening to your partner is the quickest path to intimacy. The problem is that most of us confuse hearing with listening. There is a simple skill, however, that can immediately help most couples improve their ability to really listen and build each other up "according to their needs." It is called *reflection*.

Like a mirror reflecting an image, a good listener reflects the emotions of the person he or she is with. Here are some examples:

Husband: I don't care what my boss says, I'm not giving up those vacation days.

Wife: You sound pretty resolved . . .

Wife: I can't believe they canceled the party. I was so excited for this thing.

Husband: You sound really disappointed.

Listening to what your partner is feeling is far more important than hearing what he or she is saying. Theodore Reik calls it listening with "the third ear." It is a way of tapping into the emotional message that underlies nearly every verbal message. When you can do this for each other, you can immediately build each other up and strengthen your bond as soul mates.

—Les and Leslie

Go to page 1284 for your next devotional reading.

these are improper for God's holy people. [4]Nor should there be obscenity, foolish talk or coarse joking, which are out of place, but rather thanksgiving. [5]For of this you can be sure: No immoral, impure or greedy person—such a man is an idolater—has any inheritance in the kingdom of Christ and of God.[a] [6]Let no one deceive you with empty words, for because of such things God's wrath comes on those who are disobedient. [7]Therefore do not be partners with them.

[8]For you were once darkness, but now you are light in the Lord. Live as children of light [9](for the fruit of the light consists in all goodness, righteousness and truth) [10]and find out what pleases the Lord. [11]Have nothing to do with the fruitless deeds of darkness, but rather expose them. [12]For it is shameful even to mention what the disobedient do in secret. [13]But everything exposed by the light becomes visible, [14]for it is light that makes everything visible. This is why it is said:

"Wake up, O sleeper,
    rise from the dead,
and Christ will shine on you."

[15]Be very careful, then, how you live—

not as unwise but as wise, [16]making the most of every opportunity, because the days are evil. [17]Therefore do not be foolish, but understand what the Lord's will is. [18]Do not get drunk on wine, which leads to debauchery. Instead, be filled with the Spirit. [19]Speak to one another with psalms, hymns and spiritual songs. Sing and make music in your heart to the Lord, [20]always giving thanks to God the Father for everything, in the name of our Lord Jesus Christ.

[21]Submit to one another out of reverence for Christ.

Wives and Husbands

[22]Wives, submit to your husbands as to the Lord. [23]For the husband is the head of the wife as Christ is the head of the church, his body, of which he is the Savior. [24]Now as the church submits to Christ, so also wives should submit to their husbands in everything.

[25]Husbands, love your wives, just as Christ loved the church and gave himself up for her [26]to make her holy, cleansing[b]

[a]5 Or kingdom of the Christ and God   [b]26 Or having cleansed

Who's in Charge Here?

Wednesday

EPHESIANS 5:21–33 Tim, a young man recently married, invited me (Les) to lunch one day. He asked, "How can I get my wife to submit to me?" His question threw me. I have counseled many newlyweds, but I had never before heard the question phrased so bluntly.

Tim was a devout Christian who was trying to build his new marriage on Biblical principles, and he wanted to be the "head" of the home. Tim interpreted today's passage to mean literally that it was his job to be the boss of his wife, and it was her job to be submissive to his demands. Tim's wife, however, didn't see things that way. She saw herself, understandably, as an equal partner in the marriage.

Sincere as he was, Tim didn't understand that headship doesn't mean being the first in line. It is not being the boss or

ruler. It is being the first to honor, the first to nurture, the first to meet your partner's needs.

A healthy marriage is built on a mutual desire to submit one's needs to the other. As verse 21 says, "Submit to one another out of reverence for Christ." That's the basic principle. Emptying ourselves of our self-centered desires is the bridge to becoming soul mates. Without mutual submission every marriage, no matter how romantic, will eventually falter.

The key is understanding that submission in marriage is a two-way street. Scripture not only calls husbands and wives to "submit to one another," but we are to also submit to God (see Job 22:21; Hebrews 12:9; James 4:7).

—Les and Leslie

Go to page 1287 for your next devotional reading.

her by the washing with water through the word, ²⁷and to present her to himself as a radiant church, without stain or wrinkle or any other blemish, but holy and blameless. ²⁸In this same way, husbands ought to love their wives as their own bodies. He who loves his wife loves himself. ²⁹After all, no one ever hated his own body, but he feeds and cares for it, just as Christ does the church— ³⁰for we are members of his body. ³¹"For this reason a man will leave his father and mother and be united to his wife, and the two will become one flesh."ᵃ ³²This is a profound mystery—but I am talking about Christ and the church. ³³However, each one of you also must love his wife as he loves himself, and the wife must respect her husband.

Children and Parents

6 Children, obey your parents in the Lord, for this is right. ²"Honor your father and mother"—which is the first commandment with a promise— ³"that it may go well with you and that you may enjoy long life on the earth."ᵇ

⁴Fathers, do not exasperate your children; instead, bring them up in the training and instruction of the Lord.

Slaves and Masters

⁵Slaves, obey your earthly masters with respect and fear, and with sincerity of heart, just as you would obey Christ. ⁶Obey them not only to win their favor when their eye is on you, but like slaves of Christ, doing the will of God from your heart. ⁷Serve wholeheartedly, as if you were serving the Lord, not men, ⁸because you know that the Lord will reward everyone for whatever good he does, whether he is slave or free.

⁹And masters, treat your slaves in the same way. Do not threaten them, since you know that he who is both their Master and yours is in heaven, and there is no favoritism with him.

The Armor of God

¹⁰Finally, be strong in the Lord and in his mighty power. ¹¹Put on the full armor of God so that you can take your stand against the devil's schemes. ¹²For our struggle is not against flesh and blood, but against the rulers, against the authorities, against the powers of this dark world and against the spiritual forces of evil in the heavenly realms. ¹³Therefore put on the full armor of God, so that when the day of evil comes, you may be able to stand your ground, and after you have done everything, to stand. ¹⁴Stand firm then, with the belt of truth buckled around your waist, with the breastplate of righteousness in place, ¹⁵and with your feet fitted with the readiness that comes from the gospel of peace. ¹⁶In addition to all this, take up the shield of faith, with which you can extinguish all the flaming arrows of the evil one. ¹⁷Take the helmet of salvation and the sword of the Spirit, which is the word of God. ¹⁸And pray in the Spirit on all occasions with all kinds of prayers and requests. With this in mind, be alert and always keep on praying for all the saints.

¹⁹Pray also for me, that whenever I open my mouth, words may be given me so that I will fearlessly make known the mystery of the gospel, ²⁰for which I am an ambassador in chains. Pray that I may declare it fearlessly, as I should.

Final Greetings

²¹Tychicus, the dear brother and faithful servant in the Lord, will tell you everything, so that you also may know how I am and what I am doing. ²²I am sending him to you for this very purpose, that you may know how we are, and that he may encourage you.

²³Peace to the brothers, and love with faith from God the Father and the Lord Jesus Christ. ²⁴Grace to all who love our Lord Jesus Christ with an undying love.

ᵃ31 Gen. 2:24   ᵇ3 Deut. 5:16

Philippians

Paul wrote the book of Philippians from a prison cell. This was probably not Paul's preferred ministry base, and it certainly wasn't a pleasant place. But when you read this book, you'll find that it's written from a healthy perspective that reveals Paul's thanksgiving and deep joy. Paul understood that change was inevitable and that times would be tough. So he took the raw materials of his circumstances and built something incredibly encouraging out of them.

If Paul can do this sitting in a jail cell, we can do it no matter what our circumstances. Don't worry if you think your home isn't "good" enough to hold a Bible study in or if you don't feel "gifted" in speaking. If you want to encourage others in your faith, God will clear the way and make it happen.

1 Paul and Timothy, servants of Christ Jesus,

To all the saints in Christ Jesus at Philippi, together with the overseers[a] and deacons:

²Grace and peace to you from God our Father and the Lord Jesus Christ.

Thanksgiving and Prayer

³I thank my God every time I remember you. ⁴In all my prayers for all of you, I always pray with joy ⁵because of your partnership in the gospel from the first day until now, ⁶being confident of this, that he who began a good work in you will carry it on to completion until the day of Christ Jesus.

⁷It is right for me to feel this way about all of you, since I have you in my heart; for whether I am in chains or defending and confirming the gospel, all of you share in God's grace with me. ⁸God can testify how I long for all of you with the affection of Christ Jesus.

⁹And this is my prayer: that your love may abound more and more in knowledge and depth of insight, ¹⁰so that you may be able to discern what is best and may be pure and blameless until the day of Christ, ¹¹filled with the fruit of righ-

a1 Traditionally *bishops*

teousness that comes through Jesus Christ—to the glory and praise of God.

Paul's Chains Advance the Gospel

¹²Now I want you to know, brothers, that what has happened to me has really served to advance the gospel. ¹³As a result, it has become clear throughout the whole palace guard[a] and to everyone else that I am in chains for Christ. ¹⁴Because of my chains, most of the brothers in the Lord have been encouraged to speak the word of God more courageously and fearlessly.

¹⁵It is true that some preach Christ out of envy and rivalry, but others out of goodwill. ¹⁶The latter do so in love, knowing that I am put here for the defense of the gospel. ¹⁷The former preach Christ out of selfish ambition, not sincerely, supposing that they can stir up trouble for me while I am in chains.[b] ¹⁸But what does it matter? The important thing is that in every way, whether from false motives or true, Christ is preached. And because of this I rejoice.

Yes, and I will continue to rejoice, ¹⁹for I know that through your prayers and the help given by the Spirit of Jesus Christ, what has happened to me will turn out for my deliverance.[c] ²⁰I eagerly expect and hope that I will in no way be ashamed, but will have sufficient courage so that now as always Christ will be exalted in my body, whether by life or by death. ²¹For to me, to live is Christ and to die is gain. ²²If I am to go on living in the body, this will mean fruitful labor for me. Yet what shall I choose? I do not know! ²³I am torn between the two: I desire to depart and be with Christ, which is better by far; ²⁴but it is more necessary for you that I remain in the body. ²⁵Convinced of this, I know that I will remain, and I will

a13 Or whole palace   b16,17 Some late manuscripts have verses 16 and 17 in reverse order.   c19 Or salvation

---

Attitude of Gratitude

Thursday

PHILIPPIANS 1:3-6 One of the more negative manifestations of adolescence is ingratitude. No matter how much a parent does, the teenager seems to only see the negative. I remember spending a whole weekend doing only the activities that Torrey, then thirteen, had chosen. We went to see a movie she selected and walked through the mall because she wanted to. Then later that night, when I asked that her phone call be cut to twenty minutes so Rosemary could use the phone, I got blasted with a her blind ingratitude: "Why is it always me that you pick on? I'm not the only one in this house who stays on the phone! I'm the only one you criticize in this house." Ingratitude and adolescents seem to arrive on the same hormone!

That same attitude of ingratitude can creep into our marriages. Husbands and wives can come up with scores of criticisms about their spouses. Some even make these criticisms a matter of prayer, asking that God would change or "fix" their spouse.

It is important to pray for your spouse, and ultimately, God is the only one who is able to effect changes in an individual's life. However, the focus of Paul's prayers in this passage is different from the idea of asking God to change others. Paul approaches God expressing nothing but gratitude for his friends. What a wonderful perspective to develop as you pray on behalf of your spouse! Rather than focusing on what you think needs to be changed, choose to focus on things for which you can be grateful.

Just as every individual needs prayer for areas of weakness, there are many areas of victory and progress to be thankful for. How healthy it would be for marriage partners to change the focus "every time they remember" their spouses and find something about their partners for which to thank God. Being grateful can bring about a change in perspective, attitude and even feelings.

—*Bob and Rosemary*

Go to page 1288 for your next devotional reading.

continue with all of you for your progress and joy in the faith, ²⁶so that through my being with you again your joy in Christ Jesus will overflow on account of me.

²⁷Whatever happens, conduct yourselves in a manner worthy of the gospel of Christ. Then, whether I come and see you or only hear about you in my absence, I will know that you stand firm in one spirit, contending as one man for the faith of the gospel ²⁸without being frightened in any way by those who oppose you. This is a sign to them that they will be destroyed, but that you will be saved—and that by God. ²⁹For it has been granted to you on behalf of Christ not only to believe on him, but also to suffer for him, ³⁰since you are going through the same struggle you saw I had, and now hear that I still have.

Imitating Christ's Humility

2 If you have any encouragement from being united with Christ, if any comfort from his love, if any fellowship with the Spirit, if any tenderness and compassion, ²then make my joy complete by being like-minded, having the same love, being one in spirit and purpose. ³Do nothing out of selfish ambition or vain conceit, but in humility consider others better than yourselves. ⁴Each of you should look not only to your own interests, but also to the interests of others.

⁵Your attitude should be the same as that of Christ Jesus:

⁶Who, being in very nature*ᵃ* God,
did not consider equality with God
something to be grasped,
⁷but made himself nothing,
taking the very nature*ᵇ* of a
servant,
being made in human likeness.
⁸And being found in appearance as a
man,
he humbled himself
and became obedient to death—
even death on a cross!
⁹Therefore God exalted him to the
highest place
and gave him the name that is
above every name,
¹⁰that at the name of Jesus every knee
should bow,
in heaven and on earth and under
the earth,
¹¹and every tongue confess that Jesus
Christ is Lord,
to the glory of God the Father.

Shining as Stars

¹²Therefore, my dear friends, as you have always obeyed—not only in my presence, but now much more in my absence—continue to work out your salvation with fear and trembling, ¹³for it is

ᵃ6 Or *in the form of*   *ᵇ7* Or *the form*

Enjoying Differences

Friday

PHILIPPIANS 2:1–4 It has been suggested that two strangers could be married to each other and have a pretty good marriage if only they were mature enough to work their way through their inevitable differences.

How do you and your spouse handle differences? If you are like most couples, you probably try one of two things: You either sweep your differences under the rug by ignoring them altogether, or you try to make your spouse become like yourself. Unfortunately, both strategies are destined for frustration. For one thing, it is only a matter of time before repressed differences

surface again, and second, we miss out on a tremendous gift of marriage when we do not enjoy each other's uniqueness. That's right, *enjoy* the differences!

God never intended couples to approach life as if they were twins separated at birth. He made us with unique strengths and weaknesses. He gave each of us special gifts and talents.

Sure, some of your spouse's traits make living together tough at times, but appreciating the positive side of your differences will make your marriage more balanced and complete.   **—Les and Leslie**

Go to page 1289 for your next devotional reading.

God who works in you to will and to act according to his good purpose.

¹⁴Do everything without complaining or arguing, ¹⁵so that you may become blameless and pure, children of God without fault in a crooked and depraved generation, in which you shine like stars in the universe ¹⁶as you hold out[a] the word of life—in order that I may boast on the day of Christ that I did not run or labor for nothing. ¹⁷But even if I am being poured out like a drink offering on the sacrifice and service coming from your faith, I am glad and rejoice with all of you. ¹⁸So you too should be glad and rejoice with me.

Timothy and Epaphroditus

¹⁹I hope in the Lord Jesus to send Timothy to you soon, that I also may be cheered when I receive news about you. ²⁰I have no one else like him, who takes a genuine interest in your welfare. ²¹For everyone looks out for his own interests, not those of Jesus Christ. ²²But you know that Timothy has proved himself, because as a son with his father he has served with me in the work of the gospel. ²³I hope, therefore, to send him as soon as I see how things go with me. ²⁴And I am confident in the Lord that I myself will come soon.

²⁵But I think it is necessary to send back to you Epaphroditus, my brother, fellow worker and fellow soldier, who is also your messenger, whom you sent to take care of my needs. ²⁶For he longs for all of you and is distressed because you heard he was ill. ²⁷Indeed he was ill, and almost died. But God had mercy on him, and not on him only but also on me, to spare me sorrow upon sorrow. ²⁸Therefore I am all the more eager to send him, so that when you see him again you may be glad and I may have less anxiety.

a16 Or hold on to

Is Conflict Good or Bad?

Quiet TIMES *with each other*

PHILIPPIANS 2:14 One of the most difficult realizations early in marriage is the number of conflicts that arise. Rosemary and I didn't seem to have many arguments when we were dating. But then we got married! We found ourselves fighting with each other over money, sex, in-laws and just about every other area of importance. We seemed to have such different opinions about so many things.

In the marriage relationship, conflict is going to be a reality. As two people with different perspectives, backgrounds, temperaments and personalities attempt to live together, conflicts, disagreements and differences will surface. The key to having a healthy marriage is found in how we deal with the inevitable conflicts. Conflicts cannot and should not be avoided, but they can be dealt with in a positive way.

First, understand that the conflict itself is no cause for alarm. A conflict simply means you have a relationship and with that comes differences of opinion. In fact, differences of opinion give a couple opportunities to learn new ways of looking at life.

Second, it is important to view each other as members of the same team. When there is an argument, often the focus is on who wins. Instead, we should have the attitude of striving to solve the difference of opinion as a team, rather than win the argument as an individual.

Finally, focus on the opinions of each other, rather than shouting to be heard at all costs. Then we can become, as verse 15 says, "blameless and pure, children of God without fault in a crooked and depraved generation." **—Bob and Rosemary**

Weekend Warm-up *How do you and your spouse handle differences of opinion? Can you agree to disagree?*

Go to page 1290 for your next devotional reading.

²⁹Welcome him in the Lord with great joy, and honor men like him, ³⁰because he almost died for the work of Christ, risking his life to make up for the help you could not give me.

No Confidence in the Flesh

3 Finally, my brothers, rejoice in the Lord! It is no trouble for me to write the same things to you again, and it is a safeguard for you.

²Watch out for those dogs, those men who do evil, those mutilators of the flesh. ³For it is we who are the circumcision, we who worship by the Spirit of God, who glory in Christ Jesus, and who put no confidence in the flesh— ⁴though I myself have reasons for such confidence.

If anyone else thinks he has reasons to put confidence in the flesh, I have more: ⁵circumcised on the eighth day, of the people of Israel, of the tribe of Benjamin, a Hebrew of Hebrews; in regard to the law, a Pharisee; ⁶as for zeal, persecuting the church; as for legalistic righteousness, faultless.

⁷But whatever was to my profit I now consider loss for the sake of Christ. ⁸What is more, I consider everything a loss compared to the surpassing greatness of knowing Christ Jesus my Lord, for whose sake I have lost all things. I consider them rubbish, that I may gain Christ ⁹and be found in him, not having a righteousness of my own that comes from the law, but that which is through faith in Christ—the righteousness that comes from God and is by faith. ¹⁰I want to know Christ and the power of his resurrection and the fellowship of sharing in his sufferings, becoming like him in his death, ¹¹and so, somehow, to attain to the resurrection from the dead.

Pressing on Toward the Goal

¹²Not that I have already obtained all this, or have already been made perfect, but I press on to take hold of that for which Christ Jesus took hold of me. ¹³Brothers, I do not consider myself yet to have taken hold of it. But one thing I do: Forgetting what is behind and straining toward what is ahead, ¹⁴I press on toward the goal to win the prize for which God has called me heavenward in Christ Jesus.

¹⁵All of us who are mature should take such a view of things. And if on some point you think differently, that too God

Pressing On

Monday

COUPLE MINUTES

PHILIPPIANS 3:12–14 We are both list makers. Dave has even been known to make lists after the fact—just so he can mark things off and feel good about his accomplishments. I make lists and then forget where I put them. But seriously, making lists helps us to press on and to focus on the future. Lists can also help us let go of the past.

As we entered the empty nest phase, we realized we were moving into a totally different stage of marriage. An important part of this transition was letting go of unrealistic dreams and expectations. Like Paul, we wanted to press on toward the goal to win the prize. Ironically, we began by making a list of things we knew we would never do.

Our list included things like the reality that Dave will never grow more hair. I will never be competitive in tennis. Our office will probably never be completely organized (or stay that way). What would you put on your "never do" list? Some things will not change. Maybe you keep waiting for the other person to shape up, but it just might not happen. So before pressing on, you must deal with your own disappointments, let go of past hurts and lost dreams.

Then you can make your "pressing on" list as you focus on the future. If you include things like accepting each other as a package deal, being willing to forgive and ask for forgiveness when needed, and committing to growing together in the second half of your marriage, you can win the prize by having a Christian marriage that glorifies Jesus Christ. **—Dave and Claudia**

Go to page 1291 for your next devotional reading.

will make clear to you. [16]Only let us live up to what we have already attained.

[17]Join with others in following my example, brothers, and take note of those who live according to the pattern we gave you. [18]For, as I have often told you before and now say again even with tears, many live as enemies of the cross of Christ. [19]Their destiny is destruction, their god is their stomach, and their glory is in their shame. Their mind is on earthly things. [20]But our citizenship is in heaven. And we eagerly await a Savior from there, the Lord Jesus Christ, [21]who, by the power that enables him to bring everything under his control, will transform our lowly bodies so that they will be like his glorious body.

4 Therefore, my brothers, you whom I love and long for, my joy and crown, that is how you should stand firm in the Lord, dear friends!

Exhortations

[2]I plead with Euodia and I plead with Syntyche to agree with each other in the Lord. [3]Yes, and I ask you, loyal yokefellow,[a] help these women who have contended at my side in the cause of the gospel, along with Clement and the rest of my fellow workers, whose names are in the book of life.

[4]Rejoice in the Lord always. I will say it again: Rejoice! [5]Let your gentleness be evident to all. The Lord is near. [6]Do not be anxious about anything, but in everything, by prayer and petition, with thanksgiving, present your requests to God. [7]And the peace of God, which transcends all understanding, will guard your hearts and your minds in Christ Jesus.

[8]Finally, brothers, whatever is true, whatever is noble, whatever is right, whatever is pure, whatever is lovely, whatever is admirable—if anything is excellent or praiseworthy—think about such things. [9]Whatever you have learned or received or heard from me, or seen in me—put it into practice. And the God of peace will be with you.

Thanks for Their Gifts

[10]I rejoice greatly in the Lord that at last you have renewed your concern for me. Indeed, you have been concerned, but you had no opportunity to show it. [11]I am not saying this because I am in need, for I have learned to be content whatever the circumstances. [12]I know what it is to be in need, and I know what it is to have plenty. I have learned the secret of being content in any and every situation, whether well fed or hungry, whether living in plenty or in want. [13]I can do everything through him who gives me strength.

[14]Yet it was good of you to share in my troubles. [15]Moreover, as you Philippians

[a]3 Or loyal Syzygus

The Marriage Treasure Chest

Tuesday

PHILIPPIANS 4:8-12 Before the wedding day, it's easy to see the positive. But once you're married, did you, like us, discover that the person you thought was just about perfect also had some irritating habits? The reality of living together creates tension, and it's tempting to focus on the negative instead of the positive.

Even when we have pleasant thoughts, their power can only be released when we verbalize them. Positive thoughts are worth developing. However, habits take time and persistence to develop, so be prepared to persevere. You can begin by making your own Philippians "treasure" list. Think about your mate and list one thing that is:

• True, like your spouse's love and commitment
• Noble, or honorable, like his or her integrity in financial affairs
• Right, like making time for your marriage
• Pure, like your mate's faithfulness
• Lovely, like being a creative lover
• Admirable, like helping out at the soup kitchen in the inner city.

When you find yourself thinking negatively about your spouse, pull out your list and dwell on his or her positive qualities.

—Dave and Claudia

Go to page 1292 for your next devotional reading.

know, in the early days of your acquaintance with the gospel, when I set out from Macedonia, not one church shared with me in the matter of giving and receiving, except you only; ¹⁶for even when I was in Thessalonica, you sent me aid again and again when I was in need. ¹⁷Not that I am looking for a gift, but I am looking for what may be credited to your account. ¹⁸I have received full payment and even more; I am amply supplied, now that I have received from Epaphroditus the gifts you sent. They are a fragrant offering, an acceptable sacrifice, pleasing to God. ¹⁹And my God will meet all your needs according to his glorious riches in Christ Jesus.

²⁰To our God and Father be glory for ever and ever. Amen.

final Greetings

²¹Greet all the saints in Christ Jesus. The brothers who are with me send greetings. ²²All the saints send you greetings, especially those who belong to Caesar's household.

²³The grace of the Lord Jesus Christ be with your spirit. Amen.ᵃ

ᵃ23 Some manuscripts do not have *Amen.*

Sharing a Lot or a Little

Wednesday

PHILIPPIANS 4:14 There are times in marriage when we share a lot and yet share little. Although we share the checkbook, the kitchen table, even the same bed, we go through seasons when do not share our lives. We feel alienated from each other and very alone. Our day to day living can become so task-oriented that we lose the intimacy of sharing our lives with one another.

Research reveals that the happiest couples are those who share the mundane details of their days. Most of the time, our lives are filled with the unremarkable. To feel connected with one another, it is mandatory to share small details. We need a listening ear for the small triumphs and frustrations of daily living. Listening and sharing with one another is a choice a couple must make. Make a commitment to one another to carve out time each day to participate in each other's lives. Be available to share in each other's troubles even when they might seem less significant than your own problems. Actively listen.

Sharing each other's life, no matter how insignificant or tedious some of it may seem, helps us feel connected. Listening to each other develops intimacy. Intimacy was what God intended for the marriage relationship— so that we would not feel alone.

—Bob and Rosemary

Go to page 1294 for your next devotional reading.

Colossians

Jesus means different things to different people. Some regard him as a "good man" or a prophet. Some think him a magician or a fraud. The book of Colossians addresses the questions of who Jesus Christ is and how he should affect us. Paul writes to the Colossians to refute teachings that relied on human philosophy and knowledge; he argued that only Jesus Christ is necessary for salvation. To this end, Paul asserts that Jesus is supreme over creation, sin, the church and even our relationships. As you read Colossians, ask yourself what difference it would make in your life if you lived in light of Jesus' supremacy.

1 Paul, an apostle of Christ Jesus by the will of God, and Timothy our brother,

2To the holy and faithful[a] brothers in Christ at Colosse:

Grace and peace to you from God our Father.[b]

Thanksgiving and Prayer

3We always thank God, the Father of our Lord Jesus Christ, when we pray for you, 4because we have heard of your faith in Christ Jesus and of the love you have for all the saints— 5the faith and love that spring from the hope that is stored up for you in heaven and that you have already heard about in the word of truth, the gospel 6that has come to you. All over the world this gospel is bearing fruit and growing, just as it has been doing among you since the day you heard it and understood God's grace in all its truth. 7You learned it from Epaphras, our dear fellow servant, who is a faithful minister of Christ on our[c] behalf, 8and who also told us of your love in the Spirit.

9For this reason, since the day we heard about you, we have not stopped praying for you and asking God to fill you with the knowledge of his will through all spiritual wisdom and understanding. 10And we pray this in order that you may live a life worthy of the Lord and may please him in every way: bearing fruit in every good work, growing in the knowledge of God, 11being strengthened with all power according to his glorious might so that you may have great endurance and patience, and joyfully 12giving thanks to the

a2 Or believing   b2 Some manuscripts Father and the Lord Jesus Christ   c7 Some manuscripts your

Father, who has qualified you[a] to share in the inheritance of the saints in the kingdom of light. [13]For he has rescued us from the dominion of darkness and brought us into the kingdom of the Son he loves, [14]in whom we have redemption,[b] the forgiveness of sins.

The Supremacy of Christ

[15]He is the image of the invisible God, the firstborn over all creation. [16]For by him all things were created: things in heaven and on earth, visible and invisible, whether thrones or powers or rulers or authorities; all things were created by him and for him. [17]He is before all things, and in him all things hold together. [18]And he is the head of the body, the church; he is the beginning and the firstborn from among the dead, so that in everything he might have the supremacy. [19]For God was pleased to have all his fullness dwell in him, [20]and through him to reconcile to himself all things, whether things on earth or things in heaven, by making peace through his blood, shed on the cross.

[21]Once you were alienated from God and were enemies in your minds because of[c] your evil behavior. [22]But now he has reconciled you by Christ's physical body through death to present you holy in his sight, without blemish and free from ac-

cusation— [23]if you continue in your faith, established and firm, not moved from the hope held out in the gospel. This is the gospel that you heard and that has been proclaimed to every creature under heaven, and of which I, Paul, have become a servant.

Paul's Labor for the Church

[24]Now I rejoice in what was suffered for you, and I fill up in my flesh what is still lacking in regard to Christ's afflictions, for the sake of his body, which is the church. [25]I have become its servant by the commission God gave me to present to you the word of God in its fullness— [26]the mystery that has been kept hidden for ages and generations, but is now disclosed to the saints. [27]To them God has chosen to make known among the Gentiles the glorious riches of this mystery, which is Christ in you, the hope of glory.

[28]We proclaim him, admonishing and teaching everyone with all wisdom, so that we may present everyone perfect in Christ. [29]To this end I labor, struggling with all his energy, which so powerfully works in me.

---

[a]12 Some manuscripts *us*   [b]14 A few late manuscripts *redemption through his blood*   [c]21 Or *minds, as shown by*

A Letter of Encouragement

Thursday

COLOSSIANS 1:2-3 We love to get mail, especially when it's personal and uplifting. Paul's letter to the church at Colosse was both. The reason Paul wrote a letter instead of communicating in person was that he was under house arrest, awaiting trial on an appeal to the Roman emperor Nero. Doesn't sound like the best circumstances, does it? Yet Paul's letter begins by wishing the Colossians grace and peace with thanksgiving because of their faithfulness to Christ.

If we had been writing that letter, we might have started by complaining, "Why did this have to happen to me?" Yet Paul underscores the supremacy of Christ and

acknowledges that he is the great Rescuer and Redeemer. Paul truly lives out what it means to trust God in difficult situations.

Paul's positive attitude and advice to the Colossians can help us honor the Lord. Whatever difficult situations we may face, Paul urges us to call on God. He will strengthen us with all power according to his glorious might so that we may have great endurance and patience (see verse 11).

Based on Colossians 1, consider writing your own letter of encouragement to your spouse.

—Dave and Claudia

Go to page 1295 for your next devotional reading.

2 I want you to know how much I am struggling for you and for those at Laodicea, and for all who have not met me personally. ²My purpose is that they may be encouraged in heart and united in love, so that they may have the full riches of complete understanding, in order that they may know the mystery of God, namely, Christ, ³in whom are hidden all the treasures of wisdom and knowledge. ⁴I tell you this so that no one may deceive you by fine-sounding arguments. ⁵For though I am absent from you in body, I am present with you in spirit and delight to see how orderly you are and how firm your faith in Christ is.

Freedom From Human Regulations Through Life With Christ

⁶So then, just as you received Christ Jesus as Lord, continue to live in him, ⁷rooted and built up in him, strengthened in the faith as you were taught, and overflowing with thankfulness.

⁸See to it that no one takes you captive through hollow and deceptive philosophy, which depends on human tradition and the basic principles of this world rather than on Christ.

⁹For in Christ all the fullness of the

Deity lives in bodily form, ¹⁰and you have been given fullness in Christ, who is the head over every power and authority. ¹¹In him you were also circumcised, in the

---

Reconciliation

Friday

COLOSSIANS 1:20 The reconciliation that Jesus Christ provided for each of us was offered before we even asked. The Lord took the first step to reconcile our broken relationship with him. He did that at immeasurable cost as he died for us and rose again. This is a great example for the marriage relationship.

Reconciliation is a necessity. It's more than saying "sorry" or accepting the apology. Reconciliation means a total restoration of the relationship with no conditions. It means loving your spouse as if nothing had ever been done to damage that love. True restoration is a process and a sacrifice. It's a process where one spouse chooses to take the lead and work at expressing love toward the other person—even if it is the

other person who has wronged you. Marriage calls us to a higher plane than fixing blame. It calls us to fix the relationship.

Restoration also calls for sacrifice. When a spouse once again pursues restoration in the marriage relationship, it's a humbling experience. That spouse wonders, "Why is it always me that works on restoring this marriage?" When that sacrifice seems too great, think about how much Almighty God humbled himself. He came down from the throne of heaven and sacrificed himself to restore his love relationship with you. Any sacrifice we could make is insignificant in comparison.

—**Bob and Rosemary**

Go to page 1297 for your next devotional reading.

putting off of the sinful nature,*a* not with a circumcision done by the hands of men but with the circumcision done by Christ, [12]having been buried with him in baptism and raised with him through your faith in the power of God, who raised him from the dead.

[13]When you were dead in your sins and in the uncircumcision of your sinful nature,*b* God made you*c* alive with Christ. He forgave us all our sins, [14]having canceled the written code, with its regulations, that was against us and that stood opposed to us; he took it away, nailing it to the cross. [15]And having disarmed the powers and authorities, he made a public spectacle of them, triumphing over them by the cross.*d*

[16]Therefore do not let anyone judge you by what you eat or drink, or with regard to a religious festival, a New Moon celebration or a Sabbath day. [17]These are a shadow of the things that were to come; the reality, however, is found in Christ. [18]Do not let anyone who delights in false humility and the worship of angels disqualify you for the prize. Such a person goes into great detail about what he has seen, and his unspiritual mind puffs him up with idle notions. [19]He has lost connection with the Head, from whom the whole body, supported and held together by its ligaments and sinews, grows as God causes it to grow.

[20]Since you died with Christ to the basic principles of this world, why, as though you still belonged to it, do you submit to its rules: [21]"Do not handle! Do not taste! Do not touch!"? [22]These are all destined to perish with use, because they are based on human commands and teachings. [23]Such regulations indeed have an appearance of wisdom, with their self-imposed worship, their false humility and their harsh treatment of the body, but they lack any value in restraining sensual indulgence.

Rules for Holy Living

3 Since, then, you have been raised with Christ, set your hearts on things above, where Christ is seated at the right hand of God. [2]Set your minds on things above, not on earthly things. [3]For you died, and your life is now hidden with Christ in God. [4]When Christ, who is your*e* life, appears, then you also will appear with him in glory.

[5]Put to death, therefore, whatever belongs to your earthly nature: sexual immorality, impurity, lust, evil desires and greed, which is idolatry. [6]Because of these, the wrath of God is coming.*f* [7]You used to walk in these ways, in the life you once lived. [8]But now you must rid yourselves of all such things as these: anger, rage, malice, slander, and filthy language from your lips. [9]Do not lie to each other, since you have taken off your old self with its practices [10]and have put on the new self, which is being renewed in knowledge in the image of its Creator. [11]Here there is no Greek or Jew, circumcised or uncircumcised, barbarian, Scythian, slave or free, but Christ is all, and is in all.

[12]Therefore, as God's chosen people, holy and dearly loved, clothe yourselves with compassion, kindness, humility, gentleness and patience. [13]Bear with each other and forgive whatever grievances you may have against one another. Forgive as the Lord forgave you. [14]And over all these virtues put on love, which binds them all together in perfect unity.

[15]Let the peace of Christ rule in your hearts, since as members of one body you were called to peace. And be thankful. [16]Let the word of Christ dwell in you richly as you teach and admonish one another with all wisdom, and as you sing psalms, hymns and spiritual songs with gratitude in your hearts to God. [17]And whatever you do, whether in word or deed, do it all in the name of the Lord Jesus, giving thanks to God the Father through him.

Rules for Christian Households

[18]Wives, submit to your husbands, as is fitting in the Lord.

[19]Husbands, love your wives and do not be harsh with them.

[20]Children, obey your parents in everything, for this pleases the Lord.

---

a 11 Or *the flesh*   *b* 13 Or *your flesh*
c 13 Some manuscripts *us*   *d* 15 Or *them in him*   *e* 4 Some manuscripts *our*   *f* 6 Some early manuscripts *coming on those who are disobedient*

²¹Fathers, do not embitter your children, or they will become discouraged.

²²Slaves, obey your earthly masters in everything; and do it, not only when their eye is on you and to win their favor, but with sincerity of heart and reverence for the Lord. ²³Whatever you do, work at it with all your heart, as working for the Lord, not for men, ²⁴since you know that you will receive an inheritance from the Lord as a reward. It is the Lord Christ you are serving. ²⁵Anyone who does wrong will be repaid for his wrong, and there is no favoritism.

4 Masters, provide your slaves with what is right and fair, because you know that you also have a Master in heaven.

Further Instructions

²Devote yourselves to prayer, being watchful and thankful. ³And pray for us, too, that God may open a door for our message, so that we may proclaim the mystery of Christ, for which I am in chains. ⁴Pray that I may proclaim it clearly, as I should. ⁵Be wise in the way you act toward outsiders; make the most of every opportunity. ⁶Let your conversation be always full of grace, seasoned with salt, so that you may know how to answer everyone.

Final Greetings

⁷Tychicus will tell you all the news about me. He is a dear brother, a faithful minister and fellow servant in the Lord. ⁸I am sending him to you for the express purpose that you may know about our*ᵃ* circumstances and that he may encourage your hearts. ⁹He is coming with Onesimus, our faithful and dear brother, who is one of you. They will tell you everything that is happening here.

¹⁰My fellow prisoner Aristarchus sends you his greetings, as does Mark, the cousin of Barnabas. (You have received instructions about him; if he comes to you, welcome him.) ¹¹Jesus, who is called Justus, also sends greetings. These are the

ᵃ8 Some manuscripts that he may know about your

Seeking Scripture

COLOSSIANS 3:16 We have all sorts of Bibles in our home. They are of all sizes and colors—the *King James,* the *New King James,* the *Good News,* the *New American Standard,* the *Amplified,* the *Living,* the *Message,* the *New International Version,* the *New Revised Standard Bible,* and on and on. And then we have the workbook editions, the pocket editions, the illustrated editions and the devotional editions. Most of these, most of the time, however, sit on a shelf in our study.

But there are two Bibles—our personal Bibles—that are very different. My (Leslie's) Bible is a simple NIV with a brown leather cover that, because of wear, is no longer affixed to the spine (Les gave it to me on December 14, 1979—our first Christmas as a dating couple). Les's Bible is a bigger, black leather reference NIV with thumb indexing. Hardly a day goes by that each of us does not open these familiar books. How about you? Do you make time to study God's Word? Have you discovered the beauty of Bible reading? It's the only way to "Let the word of Christ dwell in you richly . . ." If you and your partner read the Bible together, or on your own throughout each week, your souls will be nourished and your marriage will be blessed (see Luke 11:28, page 1119). For you will have the Word of God written on your hearts (see Deuteronomy 6:6, page 188).

—Les and Leslie

Weekend Warm-up   *What are you learning as you study the Bible together?*

Go to page 1298 for your next devotional reading.

only Jews among my fellow workers for the kingdom of God, and they have proved a comfort to me. [12]Epaphras, who is one of you and a servant of Christ Jesus, sends greetings. He is always wrestling in prayer for you, that you may stand firm in all the will of God, mature and fully assured. [13]I vouch for him that he is working hard for you and for those at Laodicea and Hierapolis. [14]Our dear friend Luke, the doctor, and Demas send greetings. [15]Give my greetings to the brothers at La-odicea, and to Nympha and the church in her house.

[16]After this letter has been read to you, see that it is also read in the church of the Laodiceans and that you in turn read the letter from Laodicea.

[17]Tell Archippus: "See to it that you complete the work you have received in the Lord."

[18]I, Paul, write this greeting in my own hand. Remember my chains. Grace be with you.

The Marriage Salt Shaker

Monday

COLOSSIANS 4:6 We have an ongoing debate about salt. I (Dave) salt everything. Claudia watches her salt intake and continually irritates me by bringing home low-salt snacks from the grocery store. We both agree that food tastes better with salt.

Salt is used as a metaphor several times in the Bible. Christians are to be the "salt of the earth" (Matthew 5:13). And when we are communicating with others, Paul writes that we should let our conversation "be always full of grace, seasoned with salt, so that you may know how to answer everyone" (Colossians 4:6). What a great verse to apply to marriage. Kind, honest, graceful and compassionate words can season our relationship so that we relate in a more positive way.

Besides improving taste, salt also acts as a preservative. And in marriage, wise communication helps spouses build a lasting relationship. Consider what you can do to salt the conversation of your marriage. Not only will you season and preserve your marriage, but you'll also be a model for other couples to follow.

—Dave and Claudia

Go to page 1300 for your next devotional reading.

1 Thessalonians

Though centuries old, 1 Thessalonians was written for times like ours. It speaks to a culture filled with seductive images and sexual pressures. It brings eternal perspective to discussions of material things. It questions the secular values that undermine God's ways. As you read, watch for practical ways that Christian couples can live holy lives in a hostile culture. Overshadowing all this is a perspective on life that is shaped by eternity. And you'll find exciting clues about the end times and Jesus' second coming.

1 Paul, Silas[a] and Timothy,

To the church of the Thessalonians in God the Father and the Lord Jesus Christ:

Grace and peace to you.[b]

Thanksgiving for the Thessalonians' Faith

2We always thank God for all of you, mentioning you in our prayers. 3We continually remember before our God and Father your work produced by faith, your labor prompted by love, and your endurance inspired by hope in our Lord Jesus Christ.

4For we know, brothers loved by God, that he has chosen you, 5because our gospel came to you not simply with words, but also with power, with the Holy Spirit and with deep conviction. You know how we lived among you for your sake. 6You became imitators of us and of the Lord; in spite of severe suffering, you welcomed the message with the joy given by the Holy Spirit. 7And so you became a model to all the believers in Macedonia and Achaia. 8The Lord's message rang out from you not only in Macedonia and Achaia—your faith in God has become known everywhere. Therefore we do not need to say anything about it, 9for they themselves report what kind of reception you gave us. They tell how you turned to God from idols to serve the living and true God, 10and to wait for his Son from heaven, whom he raised from the dead—Jesus, who rescues us from the coming wrath.

Paul's Ministry in Thessalonica

2 You know, brothers, that our visit to you was not a failure. 2We had previously suffered and been insulted in Philippi, as you know, but with the help of our God we dared to tell you his gospel in spite of strong opposition. 3For the ap-

---

a1 Greek *Silvanus*, a variant of *Silas*   *b1* Some early manuscripts *you from God our Father and the Lord Jesus Christ* peal we make does not spring from error or impure motives, nor are we trying to trick you. [4]On the contrary, we speak as men approved by God to be entrusted with the gospel. We are not trying to please men but God, who tests our hearts. [5]You know we never used flattery, nor did we put on a mask to cover up greed—God is our witness. [6]We were not looking for praise from men, not from you or anyone else.

As apostles of Christ we could have been a burden to you, [7]but we were gentle among you, like a mother caring for her little children. [8]We loved you so much that we were delighted to share with you not only the gospel of God but our lives as well, because you had become so dear to us. [9]Surely you remember, brothers, our toil and hardship; we worked night and day in order not to be a burden to anyone while we preached the gospel of God to you.

[10]You are witnesses, and so is God, of how holy, righteous and blameless we were among you who believed. [11]For you know that we dealt with each of you as a father deals with his own children, [12]encouraging, comforting and urging you to live lives worthy of God, who calls you into his kingdom and glory.

[13]And we also thank God continually because, when you received the word of God, which you heard from us, you ac-

cepted it not as the word of men, but as it actually is, the word of God, which is at work in you who believe. [14]For you, brothers, became imitators of God's churches in Judea, which are in Christ Jesus: You suffered from your own countrymen the same things those churches suffered from the Jews, [15]who killed the Lord Jesus and the prophets and also drove us out. They displease God and are hostile to all men [16]in their effort to keep us from speaking to the Gentiles so that they may be saved. In this way they always heap up their sins to the limit. The wrath of God has come upon them at last.[a]

Paul's Longing to See the Thessalonians

[17]But, brothers, when we were torn away from you for a short time (in person, not in thought), out of our intense longing we made every effort to see you. [18]For we wanted to come to you—certainly I, Paul, did, again and again—but Satan stopped us. [19]For what is our hope, our joy, or the crown in which we will glory in the presence of our Lord Jesus when he comes? Is it not you? [20]Indeed, you are our glory and joy.

3 So when we could stand it no longer, we thought it best to be left by ourselves in Athens. [2]We sent Timothy, who

[a]16 Or them fully

Marriage Mentoring

1 THESSALONIANS 2:8 Throughout human history, mentoring has been the primary means of passing on knowledge and skills in every field and in every culture. In the past, mentoring took place in the university where a student learned not only in a classroom but also in the home of a scholar. It took place in the studio where the artist poured himself into the formation of his protégés. The Bible is certainly filled with examples of mentoring (Eli and Samuel, Elijah and Elisha, Moses and Joshua, Naomi and Ruth, Elizabeth and Mary, Paul and Barnabas, Paul and Timothy). Mentoring was a way of life between the generations. But today, mentoring is in short supply.

If you are a seasoned, experienced and happy couple, why not consider sharing your lives with some newlyweds? The single most important factor in effective marriage mentoring is not how much you know or what you've read—it's who you are as a couple. Regardless of your education, training or relational skills, your marriage story, along with your willingness to share it, are all you need to be well on your way to making a difference in another couple's married life. **—Les and Leslie**

Go to page 1301 for your next devotional reading.

is our brother and God's fellow worker[a] in spreading the gospel of Christ, to strengthen and encourage you in your faith, [3]so that no one would be unsettled by these trials. You know quite well that we were destined for them. [4]In fact, when we were with you, we kept telling you that we would be persecuted. And it turned out that way, as you well know. [5]For this reason, when I could stand it no longer, I sent to find out about your faith. I was afraid that in some way the tempter might have tempted you and our efforts might have been useless.

Timothy's Encouraging Report

[6]But Timothy has just now come to us from you and has brought good news about your faith and love. He has told us that you always have pleasant memories of us and that you long to see us, just as we also long to see you. [7]Therefore, brothers, in all our distress and persecution we were encouraged about you because of your faith. [8]For now we really live, since you are standing firm in the Lord. [9]How can we thank God enough for you in return for all the joy we have in the presence of our God because of you? [10]Night and day we pray most earnestly

that we may see you again and supply what is lacking in your faith.

[11]Now may our God and Father himself and our Lord Jesus clear the way for us to come to you. [12]May the Lord make your love increase and overflow for each other and for everyone else, just as ours does for you. [13]May he strengthen your hearts so that you will be blameless and holy in the presence of our God and Father when our Lord Jesus comes with all his holy ones.

Living to Please God

4 Finally, brothers, we instructed you how to live in order to please God, as in fact you are living. Now we ask you and urge you in the Lord Jesus to do this more and more. [2]For you know what instructions we gave you by the authority of the Lord Jesus.

[3]It is God's will that you should be sanctified: that you should avoid sexual immorality; [4]that each of you should learn to control his own body[b] in a way that is holy and honorable, [5]not in passionate lust like the heathen, who do not

---

[a]2 Some manuscripts *brother and fellow worker*; other manuscripts *brother and God's servant*
[b]4 Or *learn to live with his own wife*; or *learn to acquire a wife*

God's Overflowing Love

Wednesday

1 THESSALONIANS 3:12 "I just don't love him anymore," Pam said. "The only reason I'm staying in this marriage is because it's the Christian thing to do!"

As we listened to Pam who had been married to Joe for more than a decade, we were perplexed. Shouldn't loving marriages and Christianity go hand in hand? The apostle Paul writes in this passage that it is the Lord who makes our love increase and overflow for each other. But Pam and Joe who both profess faith in Christ seemed to have settled for a relationship where love was decreasing instead of overflowing.

In our national survey on long-term marriages, we observed an alarming trend. Many who responded that the best aspect

of their marriage was their commitment to Christ often checked "very dissatisfied" for the survey categories that dealt with the marriage relationship—such as communication, conflict resolution, romance and intimacy. Unfortunately, too many couples accept a dysfunctional, loveless relationship just because they have Christianity in common. But it doesn't have to be this way!

Your faith in God can make a radical difference in your relationship with your spouse. God is the one who can enable you to love your mate unconditionally as you love each other with his overflowing love. That's one of the blessings of a truly Christian marriage!   **—Dave and Claudia**

Go to page 1302 for your next devotional reading.

know God; ⁶and that in this matter no one should wrong his brother or take advantage of him. The Lord will punish men for all such sins, as we have already told you and warned you. ⁷For God did not call us to be impure, but to live a holy life. ⁸Therefore, he who rejects this instruction does not reject man but God, who gives you his Holy Spirit.

⁹Now about brotherly love we do not need to write to you, for you yourselves have been taught by God to love each other. ¹⁰And in fact, you do love all the brothers throughout Macedonia. Yet we urge you, brothers, to do so more and more.

¹¹Make it your ambition to lead a quiet life, to mind your own business and to work with your hands, just as we told you, ¹²so that your daily life may win the respect of outsiders and so that you will not be dependent on anybody.

The Coming of the Lord

¹³Brothers, we do not want you to be ignorant about those who fall asleep, or to grieve like the rest of men, who have no hope. ¹⁴We believe that Jesus died and rose again and so we believe that God will bring with Jesus those who have fallen asleep in him. ¹⁵According to the Lord's own word, we tell you that we who are still alive, who are left till the coming of the Lord, will certainly not precede those who have fallen asleep. ¹⁶For the Lord himself will come down from heaven, with a loud command, with the voice of the archangel and with the trumpet call of God, and the dead in Christ will rise first. ¹⁷After that, we who are still alive and are left will be caught up together with them in the clouds to meet the Lord in the air. And so we will be with the Lord forever. ¹⁸Therefore encourage each other with these words.

5 Now, brothers, about times and dates we do not need to write to you, ²for you know very well that the day of the Lord will come like a thief in the night. ³While people are saying, "Peace and safety," destruction will come on them suddenly, as labor pains on a pregnant woman, and they will not escape.

⁴But you, brothers, are not in darkness so that this day should surprise you like a thief. ⁵You are all sons of the light and sons of the day. We do not belong to the night or to the darkness. ⁶So then, let us not be like others, who are asleep, but let us be alert and self-controlled. ⁷For those who sleep, sleep at night, and those who get drunk, get drunk at night. ⁸But since we belong to the day, let us be self-controlled, putting on faith and love as a breastplate, and the hope of salvation as a helmet. ⁹For God did not appoint us to suffer wrath but to receive salvation through our Lord Jesus Christ. ¹⁰He died for us so that, whether we are awake or asleep, we may live together with him.

Gratitude

Thursday

1 THESSALONIANS 5:15–18 "Thanks," said Les. I had just handed him a stack of mail I picked up at his office. "You bet," I replied without giving it a second thought.

"No, I mean it—thank you," Les said with all seriousness. "It was really thoughtful of you to pick up my mail and bring it home. You didn't have to do it, and I appreciate it."

It's always nice to be around somebody who's grateful. Cicero, the Roman philosopher, said, "Gratitude is not only the greatest of virtues, but the parent of all the others." When a person is grateful—when they have an attitude of gratitude— they become a better person.

Saying "thank you" tends to diminish over the years of marriage as we take each other more for granted. One group of social scientists discovered that the words such as "shhh," and "What's on?" are more common in most homes than "thank you."

So keep the attitude of gratitude alive in your marriage. Cultivate it by looking for things to appreciate in your spouse each day. After all, gratitude really is the parent of all virtues. **—Les and Leslie**

Go to page 1305 for your next devotional reading.

[11]Therefore encourage one another and build each other up, just as in fact you are doing.

Final Instructions

[12]Now we ask you, brothers, to respect those who work hard among you, who are over you in the Lord and who admonish you. [13]Hold them in the highest regard in love because of their work. Live in peace with each other. [14]And we urge you, brothers, warn those who are idle, encourage the timid, help the weak, be patient with everyone. [15]Make sure that nobody pays back wrong for wrong, but always try to be kind to each other and to everyone else.

[16]Be joyful always; [17]pray continually; [18]give thanks in all circumstances, for this is God's will for you in Christ Jesus.

[19]Do not put out the Spirit's fire; [20]do not treat prophecies with contempt. [21]Test everything. Hold on to the good. [22]Avoid every kind of evil.

[23]May God himself, the God of peace, sanctify you through and through. May your whole spirit, soul and body be kept blameless at the coming of our Lord Jesus Christ. [24]The one who calls you is faithful and he will do it.

[25]Brothers, pray for us. [26]Greet all the brothers with a holy kiss. [27]I charge you before the Lord to have this letter read to all the brothers.

[28]The grace of our Lord Jesus Christ be with you.

2 Thessalonians

Have you ever been puzzled by what's going on in the world around you? This letter provides something stable—an eternal perspective—with which to evaluate society's shifting views. It reminds us that this world is terminal—careening toward its conclusion. But it also reminds us that Christians have a hope for eternity that enables them to live day-to-day in an anti-Christian environment. This letter, along with 1 Thessalonians, tells us much of what we know about the end times.

1 Paul, Silas*a* and Timothy,

To the church of the Thessalonians in God our Father and the Lord Jesus Christ:

²Grace and peace to you from God the Father and the Lord Jesus Christ.

Thanksgiving and Prayer

³We ought always to thank God for you, brothers, and rightly so, because your faith is growing more and more, and the love every one of you has for each other is increasing. ⁴Therefore, among God's churches we boast about your perseverance and faith in all the persecutions and trials you are enduring.

⁵All this is evidence that God's judgment is right, and as a result you will be counted worthy of the kingdom of God, for which you are suffering. ⁶God is just: He will pay back trouble to those who trouble you ⁷and give relief to you who are troubled, and to us as well. This will happen when the Lord Jesus is revealed from heaven in blazing fire with his powerful angels. ⁸He will punish those who do not know God and do not obey the gospel of our Lord Jesus. ⁹They will be punished with everlasting destruction and shut out from the presence of the Lord and from the majesty of his power ¹⁰on the day he comes to be glorified in his holy people and to be marveled at among all those who have believed. This includes you, because you believed our testimony to you.

¹¹With this in mind, we constantly pray for you, that our God may count you worthy of his calling, and that by his power he may fulfill every good purpose of yours and every act prompted by your faith. ¹²We pray this so that the name of our Lord Jesus may be glorified in you, and you in him, according to the grace of our God and the Lord Jesus Christ.*b*

---

*a*1 Greek *Silvanus*, a variant of *Silas*   *b*12 Or *God and Lord, Jesus Christ*

The Man of Lawlessness

2 Concerning the coming of our Lord Jesus Christ and our being gathered to him, we ask you, brothers, ²not to become easily unsettled or alarmed by some prophecy, report or letter supposed to have come from us, saying that the day of the Lord has already come. ³Don't let anyone deceive you in any way, for ⌊that day will not come⌋ until the rebellion occurs and the man of lawlessness*ᵃ* is revealed, the man doomed to destruction. ⁴He will oppose and will exalt himself over everything that is called God or is worshiped, so that he sets himself up in God's temple, proclaiming himself to be God.

⁵Don't you remember that when I was with you I used to tell you these things? ⁶And now you know what is holding him back, so that he may be revealed at the proper time. ⁷For the secret power of lawlessness is already at work; but the one who now holds it back will continue to do so till he is taken out of the way. ⁸And then the lawless one will be revealed, whom the Lord Jesus will overthrow with the breath of his mouth and destroy by the splendor of his coming. ⁹The coming of the lawless one will be in accordance with the work of Satan displayed in all kinds of counterfeit miracles, signs and wonders, ¹⁰and in every sort of evil that deceives those who are perishing. They perish because they refused to love the truth and so be saved. ¹¹For this reason God sends them a powerful delusion so that they will believe the lie ¹²and so that all will be condemned who have not believed the truth but have delighted in wickedness.

Stand Firm

¹³But we ought always to thank God for you, brothers loved by the Lord, because from the beginning God chose you*ᵇ* to be saved through the sanctifying work of the Spirit and through belief in the truth. ¹⁴He called you to this through our gospel, that you might share in the glory of our Lord Jesus Christ. ¹⁵So then, brothers, stand firm and hold to the

---

ᵃ3 Some manuscripts *sin*   *ᵇ13* Some manuscripts *because God chose you as his firstfruits*

Prayer Reveals the Heart

Friday

2 THESSALONIANS 1:11 Nothing reveals the state of a person's heart better than the focus of that person's prayer life. When you pray, whom do you pray for and what do you pray about? Is the focus on yourself and your own personal needs? During the early and difficult years of our marriage, Rosemary and I were often forced to go to God for answers. The focus of my prayer life was often asking God to help my wife meet my needs. One night while were talking, Rosemary told me about her prayer focus at that time. She was asking God to help her do a better job of understanding my needs. I was shocked to hear how selfless her prayers were.

Our prayers are centered on one of two things: self or others. In this passage Paul once again says that he prays continually for people he loves. He prays that they would reach the great potential that God has for them. Is that the prayer focus you have for your spouse? Rather than desiring to see your spouse reach great spiritual heights, sometimes our prayers focus on our own personal desires.

Perhaps the greatest power lost in marriages today is that marriage partners are not earnestly praying for each other. Far too many spouses begin each day with no one praying for them. Not only should we be making prayer for our spouses a serious focus, but we should also look for what part God would have us play in the answer to those prayers. Is there something God wants you to do that would help your spouse reach the potential God has set out for him or her?

—Bob and Rosemary

Go to page 1306 for your next devotional reading.

teachings[a] we passed on to you, whether by word of mouth or by letter.

[16]May our Lord Jesus Christ himself and God our Father, who loved us and by his grace gave us eternal encouragement and good hope, [17]encourage your hearts and strengthen you in every good deed and word.

Request for Prayer

3 Finally, brothers, pray for us that the message of the Lord may spread rapidly and be honored, just as it was with you. [2]And pray that we may be delivered from wicked and evil men, for not everyone has faith. [3]But the Lord is faithful, and he will strengthen and protect you from the evil one. [4]We have confidence in the Lord that you are doing and will continue to do the things we command. [5]May the Lord direct your hearts into God's love and Christ's perseverance.

Warning Against Idleness

[6]In the name of the Lord Jesus Christ, we command you, brothers, to keep away from every brother who is idle and does not live according to the teaching[b] you received from us. [7]For you yourselves know how you ought to follow our example. We were not idle when we were with you, [8]nor did we eat anyone's food without paying for it. On the contrary, we worked night and day, laboring and toiling so that we would not be a burden to any of you. [9]We did this, not because we do not have the right to such help, but in order to make ourselves a model for you to follow. [10]For even when we were with you, we gave you this rule: "If a man will not work, he shall not eat."

[11]We hear that some among you are idle. They are not busy; they are busybod-

---

[a]15 Or *traditions*   [b]6 Or *tradition*

Marital Super Glue

2 THESSALONIANS 2:15 Chills went down our backs as a participant in a marriage seminar asked us, "Do you really think God intends us to live our whole life with one mate? Maybe we should have 'starter marriages' like 'starter homes.' After all, in Bible times, people didn't live as long as we do today. Sticking together for life may not be practical!"

In a world where the concept of disposable marriages is accepted, we need all the encouragement we can get to stand firm and stick together. We need God's super glue. Many marriages don't make it past the first five years—much less for a lifetime. Yet this passage encourages us to hold on to the teaching of Christ.

While there are no perfect marriages, there are some things you can do that will help you stick together. Consider the following:

- Pray together daily.

- Practice the art of forgiveness. Keep short accounts with each other.
- Talk openly and honestly about issues that create tension. Avoid venting anger on each other. Instead, express your feelings in a way that doesn't attack the other. Stop defending yourself. Remember, you are partners!
- Touch each other in an affectionate way each day. Kiss goodbye and hello. When you give a hug, you get a hug.
- Have some fun. Don't feel guilty when you leave your children (if you have children) to have a date.

Just consider "standing firm" in your marriage as applying God's marital super glue. As you stand firm and hold on to God's teachings, you will model a healthy and thriving marriage that will impact future generations.

—*Dave and Claudia*

Weekend Warm-up Why not try doing one of the items from the list above sometime this week? *Go to page 1307 for your next devotional reading.*

ies. [12]Such people we command and urge in the Lord Jesus Christ to settle down and earn the bread they eat. [13]And as for you, brothers, never tire of doing what is right.

[14]If anyone does not obey our instruction in this letter, take special note of him. Do not associate with him, in order that he may feel ashamed. [15]Yet do not regard him as an enemy, but warn him as a brother.

Final Greetings

[16]Now may the Lord of peace himself give you peace at all times and in every way. The Lord be with all of you.

[17]I, Paul, write this greeting in my own hand, which is the distinguishing mark in all my letters. This is how I write.

[18]The grace of our Lord Jesus Christ be with you all.

Peace . . . and Quiet?

Monday

2 THESSALONIANS 3:16 Peace is something everyone desires but few find it—especially at "all times and in every way." If God is able to give us peace at all times and in every way, why aren't we always experiencing it? Is it because we don't have enough trust?

Or perhaps we are we looking for a different kind of peace. When everything is going well, our kids are not sick, our spouse is being considerate, our boss at work is pleased with our performance, our cash flow is positive—in other words, our circumstances are all pleasant—then will we have peace? Not necessarily. Even if all is well at the moment, peace is still elusive if we fear what may be ahead.

But God offers his peace—a peace that passes all understanding and a peace that this world does not know (see John 14:27 and Philippians 4:4). His peace comforts us not only before or after our difficulties but also in the *middle* of our difficulties. Some of the times we have felt closest to each other and to God have been during really difficult times. I remember when I (Dave) quit my job because I sensed it wasn't where God wanted me to be. At first Claudia didn't understand, but as we looked to God for his plan for our lives, he gave us his peace even before I found a more suitable job.

During stressful times when God's peace seems elusive, seek his will together. We discovered that, whatever the situation, you can handle difficulties better when you know that at least one other person understands—and you can be that person for your spouse. As believers you can pray, support each other and together trust God. Then you can experience his peace that is available to you "at all times and in every way."

—*Dave and Claudia*

Go to page 1309 for your next devotional reading.

1 Timothy

God did not create us to live our lives alone. He gave us marriage, and he also gave us other people to interact with. That, of course, causes both joys and difficulties. What you're about to read is like a handbook on getting along with others. This nitty-gritty wisdom offers practical help to believers in their relationships with each other, with church leaders and with the world around them. Look for the underlying principles. Though specific problems and answers might never be exactly duplicated, the principles of the gospel never change.

1 Paul, an apostle of Christ Jesus by the command of God our Savior and of Christ Jesus our hope,

²To Timothy my true son in the faith:

Grace, mercy and peace from God the Father and Christ Jesus our Lord.

Warning Against False Teachers of the Law

³As I urged you when I went into Macedonia, stay there in Ephesus so that you may command certain men not to teach false doctrines any longer ⁴nor to devote themselves to myths and endless genealogies. These promote controversies rather than God's work—which is by faith. ⁵The goal of this command is love, which comes from a pure heart and a good conscience and a sincere faith. ⁶Some have wandered away from these and turned to meaningless talk. ⁷They want to be teachers of the law, but they do not know what they are talking about or what they so confidently affirm.

⁸We know that the law is good if one uses it properly. ⁹We also know that law*a* is made not for the righteous but for lawbreakers and rebels, the ungodly and sinful, the unholy and irreligious; for those who kill their fathers or mothers, for murderers, ¹⁰for adulterers and perverts, for slave traders and liars and perjurers—and for whatever else is contrary to the sound doctrine ¹¹that conforms to the glorious gospel of the blessed God, which he entrusted to me.

The Lord's Grace to Paul

¹²I thank Christ Jesus our Lord, who has given me strength, that he considered me faithful, appointing me to his service. ¹³Even though I was once a blasphemer and a persecutor and a violent man, I was

a9 Or that the law

shown mercy because I acted in ignorance and unbelief. [14]The grace of our Lord was poured out on me abundantly, along with the faith and love that are in Christ Jesus.

[15]Here is a trustworthy saying that deserves full acceptance: Christ Jesus came into the world to save sinners—of whom I am the worst. [16]But for that very reason I was shown mercy so that in me, the worst of sinners, Christ Jesus might display his unlimited patience as an example for those who would believe on him and receive eternal life. [17]Now to the King eternal, immortal, invisible, the only God, be honor and glory for ever and ever. Amen.

[18]Timothy, my son, I give you this instruction in keeping with the prophecies once made about you, so that by following them you may fight the good fight, [19]holding on to faith and a good conscience. Some have rejected these and so have shipwrecked their faith. [20]Among them are Hymenaeus and Alexander, whom I have handed over to Satan to be taught not to blaspheme.

Instructions on Worship

2 I urge, then, first of all, that requests, prayers, intercession and thanksgiving be made for everyone— [2]for kings and all those in authority, that we may live peaceful and quiet lives in all godliness and holiness. [3]This is good, and pleases God our Savior, [4]who wants all men to be saved and to come to a knowledge of the truth. [5]For there is one God and one mediator between God and men, the man Christ Jesus, [6]who gave himself as a ransom for all men—the testimony given in its proper time. [7]And for this purpose I was appointed a herald and an apostle—I am telling the truth, I am not lying—and a teacher of the true faith to the Gentiles.

[8]I want men everywhere to lift up holy hands in prayer, without anger or disputing.

[9]I also want women to dress modestly, with decency and propriety, not with braided hair or gold or pearls or expensive clothes, [10]but with good deeds, appropriate for women who profess to worship God.

[11]A woman should learn in quietness and full submission. [12]I do not permit a woman to teach or to have authority over a man; she must be silent. [13]For Adam was formed first, then Eve. [14]And Adam was not the one deceived; it was the woman who was deceived and became a sinner. [15]But women[a] will be saved[b]

[a]15 Greek she   [b]15 Or restored

Grab On to God

Tuesday

1 TIMOTHY 2:1 Imagine yourself slowly sliding down a thousand-foot cliff. The cliff is on an angle so that the slide is gradual at first. But as the cliff gets steeper and you slide faster and faster, you know if you don't grab onto something quickly, your destruction is certain. Several options for rescue are within reach. Well-meaning friends are throwing books on climbing at you. Other friends who have experienced cliff sliding before are shouting advice to you. But in the middle of all this ruckus, you are still sliding. Faintly you hear a voice saying, "Turn to me and trust me." You can't see who's talking and the voice seems to get somewhat drowned out by the turmoil all around you. You know

you must choose which voice to listen to, which one to trust.

Many marriages go through frightening times when it seems as if there's no way for the relationship to stop from tumbling to destruction. During times like these, friends want to help but don't know what to do. What can you tell them? Ask them to pray. These are times when you don't know which rope to grab on to, so "grab on to" God in prayer and don't stop praying. He can stop the destruction of a marriage, and he can catch you before you hit bottom. Even when it feels like all is lost and destruction is certain, keep praying.
—**Bob and Rosemary**

Go to page 1310 for your next devotional reading.

through childbearing—if they continue in faith, love and holiness with propriety.

Overseers and Deacons

3 Here is a trustworthy saying: If anyone sets his heart on being an overseer,[a] he desires a noble task. [2]Now the overseer must be above reproach, the husband of but one wife, temperate, self-controlled, respectable, hospitable, able to teach, [3]not given to drunkenness, not violent but gentle, not quarrelsome, not a lover of money. [4]He must manage his own family well and see that his children obey him with proper respect. [5](If anyone does not know how to manage his own family, how can he take care of God's church?) [6]He must not be a recent convert, or he may become conceited and fall under the same judgment as the devil. [7]He must also have a good reputation with outsiders, so that he will not fall into disgrace and into the devil's trap.

[8]Deacons, likewise, are to be men worthy of respect, sincere, not indulging in much wine, and not pursuing dishonest gain. [9]They must keep hold of the deep truths of the faith with a clear conscience. [10]They must first be tested; and then if there is nothing against them, let them serve as deacons.

[11]In the same way, their wives[b] are to be women worthy of respect, not malicious talkers but temperate and trustworthy in everything.

[12]A deacon must be the husband of but one wife and must manage his children and his household well. [13]Those who have served well gain an excellent standing and great assurance in their faith in Christ Jesus.

[14]Although I hope to come to you soon, I am writing you these instructions so that, [15]if I am delayed, you will know how people ought to conduct themselves in God's household, which is the church of the living God, the pillar and foundation of the truth. [16]Beyond all question, the mystery of godliness is great:

> He[c] appeared in a body,[d]
>   was vindicated by the Spirit,
> was seen by angels,
>   was preached among the nations,

---

[a]1 Traditionally *bishop*; also in verse 2   [b]11 Or *way, deaconesses*   [c]16 Some manuscripts *God* [d]16 Or *in the flesh*

The Character of a Marriage

Wednesday

1 TIMOTHY 3:2, 11 Marriage begins when two characters marry each other. Some even say one came from Mars, the other from Venus. We understand that God uniquely created each of us. Certainly gender differences do exist, and wise spouses are aware of them.

Paul, in writing to Timothy, indirectly pointed out some of these differences when he gave instructions for church leaders. Husbands (who are church leaders) should demonstrate temperance, self-control, respectability, hospitality, sobriety and gentleness. Paul warned against being quarrelsome and urged the leaders to have the right perspective about money (see verses 2–3). A husband who demonstrates these qualities—who, for instance, is gentle and not contentious or doesn't have to always be right—will be loved and respected by his wife. What woman would not want to have a husband like that?

And for the wife, Paul's list was shorter but all-inclusive. She is to live her life so as to be worthy of respect. He cautions the wives to avoid malicious gossip and going off on tangents. They should also be temperate and trustworthy in everything (see verse 11). A wife that is calm, collected and well balanced will set a pleasant atmosphere in the home where love can grow and flourish. She will be the kind of wife that a husband can trust. Now *that's* a description of a five-star wife! Just as positive character traits help leadership in the church, they can bring harmony to your marriage.

—Dave and Claudia

Go to page 1311 for your next devotional reading.

was believed on in the world,
was taken up in glory.

Instructions to Timothy

4 The Spirit clearly says that in later times some will abandon the faith and follow deceiving spirits and things taught by demons. [2]Such teachings come through hypocritical liars, whose consciences have been seared as with a hot iron. [3]They forbid people to marry and order them to abstain from certain foods, which God created to be received with thanksgiving by those who believe and who know the truth. [4]For everything God created is good, and nothing is to be rejected if it is received with thanksgiving, [5]because it is consecrated by the word of God and prayer.

[6]If you point these things out to the brothers, you will be a good minister of Christ Jesus, brought up in the truths of the faith and of the good teaching that you have followed. [7]Have nothing to do with godless myths and old wives' tales; rather, train yourself to be godly. [8]For physical training is of some value, but godliness has value for all things, holding promise for both the present life and the life to come.

[9]This is a trustworthy saying that deserves full acceptance [10](and for this we labor and strive), that we have put our hope in the living God, who is the Savior of all men, and especially of those who believe.

[11]Command and teach these things. [12]Don't let anyone look down on you because you are young, but set an example for the believers in speech, in life, in love, in faith and in purity. [13]Until I come, devote yourself to the public reading of Scripture, to preaching and to teaching. [14]Do not neglect your gift, which was given you through a prophetic message when the body of elders laid their hands on you.

[15]Be diligent in these matters; give yourself wholly to them, so that everyone may see your progress. [16]Watch your life and doctrine closely. Persevere in them, because if you do, you will save both yourself and your hearers.

Advice About Widows, Elders and Slaves

5 Do not rebuke an older man harshly, but exhort him as if he were your father. Treat younger men as brothers, [2]older women as mothers, and younger women as sisters, with absolute purity.

[3]Give proper recognition to those widows who are really in need. [4]But if a widow has children or grandchildren, these should learn first of all to put their reli-

In Love for a Lifetime

Thursday

1 TIMOTHY 4:12 Timothy was taking a bold stand for Jesus Christ, and there were those who dismissed his zeal and growth as that of a neophyte. Paul tells Timothy to keep growing and leading others in the proper Christian walk, and to not allow negative talk to discourage him. Apparently there were older people around Timothy who were looking down on his boldness as an error of youth that he would soon outgrow.

Remember hearing that about your marriage? "Oh, they're newly weds; they'll soon outgrow all that romantic stuff!" Like Timothy, there might be older people around you who have given up on the marriage dream they once had. When they hear others talking about how much they love their spouse, these cynical people act like it's a myth of youth, a stage that will soon pass.

Don't let that happen to you! Don't let the mediocrity of some marriages discourage you in yours. Neither age nor years of marriage are the indicator of marital happiness. Effort in the marriage process and commitment to Christ are necessary ingredients in keeping a marriage vibrant throughout the years.

Don't let anyone convince you that you'll get over being in love or that you'll outgrow this time of affection. Choose to be in love for a lifetime, no matter what your age. **—Bob and Rosemary**

Go to page 1312 for your next devotional reading.

gion into practice by caring for their own family and so repaying their parents and grandparents, for this is pleasing to God. [5]The widow who is really in need and left all alone puts her hope in God and continues night and day to pray and to ask God for help. [6]But the widow who lives for pleasure is dead even while she lives. [7]Give the people these instructions, too, so that no one may be open to blame. [8]If anyone does not provide for his relatives, and especially for his immediate family, he has denied the faith and is worse than an unbeliever.

[9]No widow may be put on the list of widows unless she is over sixty, has been faithful to her husband,[a] [10]and is well known for her good deeds, such as bringing up children, showing hospitality, washing the feet of the saints, helping those in trouble and devoting herself to all kinds of good deeds.

[11]As for younger widows, do not put them on such a list. For when their sensual desires overcome their dedication to Christ, they want to marry. [12]Thus they bring judgment on themselves, because they have broken their first pledge. [13]Besides, they get into the habit of being idle and going about from house to house.

And not only do they become idlers, but also gossips and busybodies, saying things they ought not to. [14]So I counsel younger widows to marry, to have children, to manage their homes and to give the enemy no opportunity for slander. [15]Some have in fact already turned away to follow Satan.

[16]If any woman who is a believer has widows in her family, she should help them and not let the church be burdened with them, so that the church can help those widows who are really in need.

[17]The elders who direct the affairs of the church well are worthy of double honor, especially those whose work is preaching and teaching. [18]For the Scripture says, "Do not muzzle the ox while it is treading out the grain,"[b] and "The worker deserves his wages."[c] [19]Do not entertain an accusation against an elder unless it is brought by two or three witnesses. [20]Those who sin are to be rebuked publicly, so that the others may take warning.

[21]I charge you, in the sight of God and Christ Jesus and the elect angels, to keep

[a]9 Or has had but one husband [b]18 Deut. 25:4
[c]18 Luke 10:7

Caring for the Family Tree

Friday

1 TIMOTHY 5:8 Life is lived in seasons, and no season has more potential for family stress than the second half of marriage. Caught in the middle of the family tree, needs of aging parents and adult children confront us from above and below. With so many demands on our time, guilt can be a constant companion. How can you provide for your spouse while keeping the home fires burning for your other family members and relatives? It's not easy, but with God's help, it's possible.

Each generation, from adolescents to the elderly, has similar needs. Besides basic physiological needs, we all need love, affection, tenderness, respect, acceptance, trust and hope. Whatever your family situation, whether the effect on your marriage is positive or negative depends more on

you than on the circumstances. Sometimes a negative situation can even bring you closer together. Help your family and relatives as much as you can, but realize that you can't dictate their responses. Do what you can do while keeping a realistic view of what you cannot do.

Over the years our desire has been to keep our marriage the anchor relationship, while passing on to our own children the legacy of truth that family relationships are precious. If you keep your relationship strong and give each other understanding and support, then you can give your children a legacy of healthy family relationships and a marriage model worth following. —*Dave and Claudia*

Go to page 1314 for your next devotional reading.

these instructions without partiality, and to do nothing out of favoritism.

22Do not be hasty in the laying on of hands, and do not share in the sins of others. Keep yourself pure.

23Stop drinking only water, and use a little wine because of your stomach and your frequent illnesses.

24The sins of some men are obvious, reaching the place of judgment ahead of them; the sins of others trail behind them. 25In the same way, good deeds are obvious, and even those that are not cannot be hidden.

6 All who are under the yoke of slavery should consider their masters worthy of full respect, so that God's name and our teaching may not be slandered. 2Those who have believing masters are not to show less respect for them because they are brothers. Instead, they are to serve them even better, because those who benefit from their service are believers, and dear to them. These are the things you are to teach and urge on them.

Love of Money

3If anyone teaches false doctrines and does not agree to the sound instruction of our Lord Jesus Christ and to godly teaching, 4he is conceited and understands nothing. He has an unhealthy interest in controversies and quarrels about words that result in envy, strife, malicious talk, evil suspicions 5and constant friction between men of corrupt mind, who have been robbed of the truth and who think that godliness is a means to financial gain.

6But godliness with contentment is great gain. 7For we brought nothing into the world, and we can take nothing out of it. 8But if we have food and clothing, we will be content with that. 9People who want to get rich fall into temptation and a trap and into many foolish and harmful desires that plunge men into ruin and destruction. 10For the love of money is a root of all kinds of evil. Some people, eager for money, have wandered from the faith and pierced themselves with many griefs.

Paul's Charge to Timothy

11But you, man of God, flee from all

JUST BETWEEN you & me

Caring for the Family Tree

Check how you are doing at giving basic needs to those in your family tree. Rate yourself (where applicable) on a scale of one to five (one being "needs improvement" and five being "awesome"). Choose one relationship to focus on such as an adult child or one of your parents:

I show love on a daily basis

I am affectionate when appropriate

I try to be sensitive and tender

I am respectful

I demonstrate acceptance

I demonstrate trust and choose to think the best

Choose one area that needs improving, and do something today to care for this person in your family tree.

this, and pursue righteousness, godliness, faith, love, endurance and gentleness. 12Fight the good fight of the faith. Take hold of the eternal life to which you were called when you made your good confession in the presence of many witnesses. 13In the sight of God, who gives life to everything, and of Christ Jesus, who while testifying before Pontius Pilate made the good confession, I charge you 14to keep this command without spot or blame until the appearing of our Lord Jesus Christ, 15which God will bring about in his own time—God, the blessed and only Ruler, the King of kings and Lord of lords, 16who alone is immortal and who lives in unapproachable light, whom no one has seen or can see. To him be honor and might forever. Amen.

17Command those who are rich in this present world not to be arrogant nor to put their hope in wealth, which is so uncertain, but to put their hope in God, who richly provides us with everything for our enjoyment. 18Command them to do good, to be rich in good deeds, and to be generous and willing to share. 19In this way they will lay up treasure for themselves as a firm foundation for the coming age, so that they may take hold of the life that is truly life.

²⁰Timothy, guard what has been entrusted to your care. Turn away from god-less chatter and the opposing ideas of what is falsely called knowledge, ²¹which some have professed and in so doing have wandered from the faith.

Grace be with you.

Love and . . . Money

Quiet TIMES
with each other

1 TIMOTHY 6:10–19 "Why do *you* always make the money decisions?" I asked.

Les and I were standing in the middle of a department store trying to choose a new couch for our apartment. And it seemed to me that he was controlling the purse strings too much.

"I don't make the money decisions," he said. "Our bank account does." That remark was followed by a lengthy, whiny discussion—okay, it was a fight—over how we manage, or should manage, our money. Was he in charge or were *we* in charge?

Money has always provided plenty of fodder for marital discord. It is, after all, the most common source of conflict between couples. And when money problems regularly erupt into shouting matches or hurt feelings, it may be time to seek professional help. But if you are simply trying to avoid the embarrassment of raising your voice in a furniture store, here are some suggestions from experts for trying to work things out on your own. First, educate your spouse about your own upbringing regarding money. Talk over financial matters regularly, at a time when money decisions are not pressing.

And if one person pays the bills, he or she should tell the other where their money is going and when. Finally, agree on and write down your financial goals—short-term and long-term.

When we get too wrapped up in money matters, we need to ask ourselves a tough question: Are we elevating the importance of money? Are we guilty of loving it—yes, *loving* it—over and above God and our spouse? Paul observed that "the love of money is the root of all evils" (verse 10). And it is money's dark side that every marriage must build a fortress against.

—Les and Leslie

Weekend **Warm-up** — What are your short-term and long-term financial goals?

Go to page 1316 for your next devotional reading.

2 Timothy

Languishing in a cold Roman dungeon, chained like a common criminal and realizing he is about to die, Paul attempts to pull together the wisdom of a lifetime of service to God. His words in 2 Timothy, forged in the crucible of life-threatening experiences, point to the hope that belongs to all of us in Jesus Christ.

If you knew your life was about to end and you wanted to pass on your values to your children, or someone close to you, what would you say?

1 Paul, an apostle of Christ Jesus by the will of God, according to the promise of life that is in Christ Jesus,

²To Timothy, my dear son:

Grace, mercy and peace from God the Father and Christ Jesus our Lord.

Encouragement to Be Faithful

³I thank God, whom I serve, as my forefathers did, with a clear conscience, as night and day I constantly remember you in my prayers. ⁴Recalling your tears, I long to see you, so that I may be filled with joy. ⁵I have been reminded of your sincere faith, which first lived in your grandmother Lois and in your mother Eunice and, I am persuaded, now lives in you also. ⁶For this reason I remind you to fan into flame the gift of God, which is in you through the laying on of my hands. ⁷For God did not give us a spirit of timidity, but a spirit of power, of love and of self-discipline.

⁸So do not be ashamed to testify about our Lord, or ashamed of me his prisoner. But join with me in suffering for the gospel, by the power of God, ⁹who has saved us and called us to a holy life—not because of anything we have done but because of his own purpose and grace. This grace was given us in Christ Jesus before the beginning of time, ¹⁰but it has now been revealed through the appearing of our Savior, Christ Jesus, who has destroyed death and has brought life and immortality to light through the gospel. ¹¹And of this gospel I was appointed a herald and an apostle and a teacher. ¹²That is why I am suffering as I am. Yet I am not ashamed, because I know whom I have believed, and am convinced that he is able to guard what I have entrusted to him for that day.

¹³What you heard from me, keep as the pattern of sound teaching, with faith and love in Christ Jesus. ¹⁴Guard the good deposit that was entrusted to you—guard it

with the help of the Holy Spirit who lives in us.

¹⁵You know that everyone in the province of Asia has deserted me, including Phygelus and Hermogenes.

¹⁶May the Lord show mercy to the household of Onesiphorus, because he often refreshed me and was not ashamed of my chains. ¹⁷On the contrary, when he was in Rome, he searched hard for me until he found me. ¹⁸May the Lord grant that he will find mercy from the Lord on that day! You know very well in how many ways he helped me in Ephesus.

2 You then, my son, be strong in the grace that is in Christ Jesus. ²And the things you have heard me say in the presence of many witnesses entrust to reliable men who will also be qualified to teach others. ³Endure hardship with us like a good soldier of Christ Jesus. ⁴No one serving as a soldier gets involved in civilian affairs—he wants to please his commanding officer. ⁵Similarly, if anyone competes as an athlete, he does not receive the victor's crown unless he competes according to the rules. ⁶The hardworking farmer should be the first to receive a share of the crops. ⁷Reflect on what I am saying, for the Lord will give you insight into all this.

⁸Remember Jesus Christ, raised from the dead, descended from David. This is my gospel, ⁹for which I am suffering even to the point of being chained like a criminal. But God's word is not chained. ¹⁰Therefore I endure everything for the sake of the elect, that they too may obtain the salvation that is in Christ Jesus, with eternal glory.

¹¹Here is a trustworthy saying:

If we died with him,
  we will also live with him;
¹²if we endure,
  we will also reign with him.
If we disown him,
  he will also disown us;
¹³if we are faithless,
  he will remain faithful,
  for he cannot disown himself.

A Workman Approved by God

¹⁴Keep reminding them of these things. Warn them before God against

He's Our Rock

Monday

2 TIMOTHY 1:12 The young pastor Timothy was no doubt deeply discouraged as he observed the people around him suffering for the gospel. Likewise today, it is a discouraging and perhaps frightening time as young couples begin their families.

When our children were born, I (Bob) remember how we looked at the culture around us very differently . . . even fearfully. We had thoughts and fears such as, *With the morality of the society around us, in what kind of world are we putting our children? What kind of heart breaks will children cause us? Can we even afford to have children in this day and age? Will we be able to have or maintain the lifestyle that our parents did? What will the future hold as far as education or crime in our communities?* It could have been really discouraging if we had focused on these thoughts alone.

Even as Paul sat in prison, he urged Timothy not to lose heart. Paul reminded Timothy that God is still in control. No matter how grim or uncertain the circumstances, Timothy could be confident that God was at work—even during times when there appeared to be no evidence.

The same message can bring comfort today as couples face uncertain times. No matter what setbacks or problems we face, no matter how insecure we feel about the future, we can trust completely in God. God is fully aware of the condition of our world. Nothing takes him by surprise! We can look to him for guidance and direction when we feel we have no where to turn. As we raised our children in a culture insensitive to the needs of children, we took comfort in the fact that God was still in control . . . and that he loves our children more than we do. **—Bob and Rosemary**

Go to page 1317 for your next devotional reading.

quarreling about words; it is of no value, and only ruins those who listen. ¹⁵Do your best to present yourself to God as one approved, a workman who does not need to be ashamed and who correctly handles the word of truth. ¹⁶Avoid godless chatter, because those who indulge in it will become more and more ungodly. ¹⁷Their teaching will spread like gangrene. Among them are Hymenaeus and Philetus, ¹⁸who have wandered away from the truth. They say that the resurrection has already taken place, and they destroy the faith of some. ¹⁹Nevertheless, God's solid foundation stands firm, sealed with this inscription: "The Lord knows those who are his,"ᵃ and, "Everyone who confesses the name of the Lord must turn away from wickedness."

²⁰In a large house there are articles not only of gold and silver, but also of wood and clay; some are for noble purposes and some for ignoble. ²¹If a man cleanses himself from the latter, he will be an instrument for noble purposes, made holy, useful to the Master and prepared to do any good work.

²²Flee the evil desires of youth, and pursue righteousness, faith, love and peace, along with those who call on the Lord out of a pure heart. ²³Don't have anything to do with foolish and stupid arguments, because you know they produce quarrels. ²⁴And the Lord's servant must not quarrel; instead, he must be kind to everyone, able to teach, not resentful. ²⁵Those who oppose him he must gently instruct, in the hope that God will grant them repentance leading them to a knowledge of the truth, ²⁶and that they will come to their senses and escape from the trap of the devil, who has taken them captive to do his will.

ᵃ19 Num. 16:5 (see Septuagint)

Be a Marriage Mentor

Tuesday

2 TIMOTHY 2:2 One of our greatest joys has been mentoring younger couples. During the years we lived in Europe, we often mentored couples from different cultures than our own. One couple we mentored was Blas and Doris. He was from Spain, and she was from Switzerland. Both cultures are radically different from each other and also different from American culture. Blas and Doris became close friends of ours as we learned to trust each other and to be transparent. We shared our lives with them—they saw the inner workings of our marriage and observed how we dealt with difficult issues. This helped them to work through their unique situations. It wasn't a one-way street. Blas and Doris gave back to us in many ways, such as occasionally staying with our three sons when we taught at a conference for other couples.

During the years we mentored Blas and Doris and other European couples, our greatest challenge was to pass on Biblical principles for a healthy marriage so they could, in turn, mentor other couples.

Nothing can encourage another couple

like a seasoned couple who love each other and enjoy a great relationship. You too can mentor other couples—whether you live in the United States or abroad. You can be part of a mentoring movement that is revolutionizing marriages.

Consider initiating a marriage mentoring program, couples' Bible study or couples' discussion group. Or choose a younger couple to befriend. Invite them into your home, let them get to know you and observe the way you relate to each other. Or start a couples' night out program in your church. By providing married couples with free or low-cost childcare and fun dates based on marriage-enriching themes, you can encourage them while they are experiencing relationship-building times together.

Take some time and brainstorm how you can mentor other couples in such a way that they can mentor others. Then you can begin to live out God's multiplication principle of 2 Timothy 2:2.

—Dave and Claudia

Go to page 1319 for your next devotional reading.

Godlessness in the Last Days

3 But mark this: There will be terrible times in the last days. [2]People will be lovers of themselves, lovers of money, boastful, proud, abusive, disobedient to their parents, ungrateful, unholy, [3]without love, unforgiving, slanderous, without self-control, brutal, not lovers of the good, [4]treacherous, rash, conceited, lovers of pleasure rather than lovers of God— [5]having a form of godliness but denying its power. Have nothing to do with them.

[6]They are the kind who worm their way into homes and gain control over weak-willed women, who are loaded down with sins and are swayed by all kinds of evil desires, [7]always learning but never able to acknowledge the truth. [8]Just as Jannes and Jambres opposed Moses, so also these men oppose the truth—men of depraved minds, who, as far as the faith is concerned, are rejected. [9]But they will not get very far because, as in the case of those men, their folly will be clear to everyone.

Paul's Charge to Timothy

[10]You, however, know all about my teaching, my way of life, my purpose, faith, patience, love, endurance, [11]persecutions, sufferings—what kinds of things happened to me in Antioch, Iconium and Lystra, the persecutions I endured. Yet the Lord rescued me from all of them. [12]In fact, everyone who wants to live a godly life in Christ Jesus will be persecuted, [13]while evil men and impostors will go from bad to worse, deceiving and being deceived. [14]But as for you, continue in what you have learned and have become convinced of, because you know those from whom you learned it, [15]and how from infancy you have known the holy Scriptures, which are able to make you wise for salvation through faith in Christ Jesus. [16]All Scripture is God-breathed and is useful for teaching, rebuking, correcting and training in righteousness, [17]so that the man of God may be thoroughly equipped for every good work.

4 In the presence of God and of Christ Jesus, who will judge the living and the dead, and in view of his appearing and his kingdom, I give you this charge: [2]Preach the Word; be prepared in season and out of season; correct, rebuke and encourage—with great patience and careful instruction. [3]For the time will come when men will not put up with sound doctrine. Instead, to suit their own desires, they will gather around them a great number of teachers to say what their itching ears want to hear. [4]They will turn their ears away from the truth and turn aside to myths. [5]But you, keep your head in all situations, endure hardship, do the work of an evangelist, discharge all the duties of your ministry.

[6]For I am already being poured out like a drink offering, and the time has come for my departure. [7]I have fought the good fight, I have finished the race, I have kept the faith. [8]Now there is in store for me the crown of righteousness, which the Lord, the righteous Judge, will award to me on that day—and not only to me, but also to all who have longed for his appearing.

Personal Remarks

[9]Do your best to come to me quickly, [10]for Demas, because he loved this world, has deserted me and has gone to Thessalonica. Crescens has gone to Galatia, and Titus to Dalmatia. [11]Only Luke is with me. Get Mark and bring him with you, because he is helpful to me in my ministry. [12]I sent Tychicus to Ephesus. [13]When you come, bring the cloak that I left with Carpus at Troas, and my scrolls, especially the parchments.

[14]Alexander the metalworker did me a great deal of harm. The Lord will repay him for what he has done. [15]You too should be on your guard against him, because he strongly opposed our message.

[16]At my first defense, no one came to my support, but everyone deserted me. May it not be held against them. [17]But the Lord stood at my side and gave me strength, so that through me the message might be fully proclaimed and all the Gentiles might hear it. And I was delivered from the lion's mouth. [18]The Lord will rescue me from every evil attack and will bring me safely to his heavenly kingdom. To him be glory for ever and ever. Amen.

Final Greetings

[19]Greet Priscilla[a] and Aquila and the household of Onesiphorus. [20]Erastus stayed in Corinth, and I left Trophimus sick in Miletus. [21]Do your best to get here before winter. Eubulus greets you, and so do Pudens, Linus, Claudia and all the brothers.

[22]The Lord be with your spirit. Grace be with you.

[a]19 Greek *Prisca*, a variant of *Priscilla*

Wanting to Finish Well

Wednesday

2 TIMOTHY 4:7 We will always remember our "empty nest" trip to New England. Over the years we have taken little getaway trips, telling our three sons that it was for their own good. But this trip was different. We were actually initiating the second half of our marriage. As we walked along the rocky coast, the cool, brisk wind and misty spray from the waves energized us as we surveyed the state of our marriage.

We talked about our passion for our marriage and how we could reconnect as a couple, redefine our relationship and let go of some of our unrealistic dreams. As we talked about the future, we thought of older couples we knew who had "finished well." Our deepest desire was (and still is) to finish well.

We asked ourselves a sobering question: "When we finish the race, what do we want our marriage to look like?" We actually made a list of things we hope will describe us when we've been married fifty-plus years. We want to be best friends. We want to have a positive outlook on life. We want to keep growing both spiritually and intellectually. We want to enjoy our family while realizing we can't (and don't want to!) be the center of their lives. And we want our marriage to reflect God's image to other couples who need encouragement.

Now we ask you, "When you reach the finish line, what do you want your marriage to look like?" The answer to that question will make all the difference in how you "run the race."

—Dave and Claudia

Go to page 1321 for your next devotional reading.

Titus

Like Timothy,
Titus was a son in the faith to Paul. Paul expresses confidence in Titus, but he also gives Titus instructions about how to lead the troubled and argumentative church in Crete. Even with God's Spirit at work, church life means hard work and a lot of giving. Putting church difficulties in perspective, Paul offers Titus guidelines for a godly life—including successful relationships between family, friends and society—with an emphasis on faith that overcomes division and disharmony among believers.

1 Paul, a servant of God and an apostle of Jesus Christ for the faith of God's elect and the knowledge of the truth that leads to godliness— ²a faith and knowledge resting on the hope of eternal life, which God, who does not lie, promised before the beginning of time, ³and at his appointed season he brought his word to light through the preaching entrusted to me by the command of God our Savior,

⁴To Titus, my true son in our common faith:

Grace and peace from God the Father and Christ Jesus our Savior.

Titus's Task on Crete

⁵The reason I left you in Crete was that you might straighten out what was left unfinished and appoint*a* elders in every town, as I directed you. ⁶An elder must be blameless, the husband of but one wife, a man whose children believe and are not open to the charge of being wild

and disobedient. ⁷Since an overseer*b* is entrusted with God's work, he must be blameless—not overbearing, not quick-tempered, not given to drunkenness, not violent, not pursuing dishonest gain. ⁸Rather he must be hospitable, one who loves what is good, who is self-controlled, upright, holy and disciplined. ⁹He must hold firmly to the trustworthy message as it has been taught, so that he can encourage others by sound doctrine and refute those who oppose it.

¹⁰For there are many rebellious people, mere talkers and deceivers, especially those of the circumcision group. ¹¹They must be silenced, because they are ruining whole households by teaching things they ought not to teach—and that for the sake of dishonest gain. ¹²Even one of their own prophets has said, "Cretans are always liars, evil brutes, lazy gluttons." ¹³This testimony is true. Therefore, rebuke them sharply, so that they will be

a5 Or *ordain*   *b7* Traditionally *bishop*

sound in the faith ¹⁴and will pay no attention to Jewish myths or to the commands of those who reject the truth. ¹⁵To the pure, all things are pure, but to those who are corrupted and do not believe, nothing is pure. In fact, both their minds and consciences are corrupted. ¹⁶They claim to know God, but by their actions they deny him. They are detestable, disobedient and unfit for doing anything good.

What Must Be Taught to Various Groups

2 You must teach what is in accord with sound doctrine. ²Teach the older men to be temperate, worthy of respect, self-controlled, and sound in faith, in love and in endurance.

³Likewise, teach the older women to be reverent in the way they live, not to be slanderers or addicted to much wine, but to teach what is good. ⁴Then they can train the younger women to love their husbands and children, ⁵to be self-controlled and pure, to be busy at home, to be kind, and to be subject to their husbands, so that no one will malign the word of God.

⁶Similarly, encourage the young men to be self-controlled. ⁷In everything set them an example by doing what is good. In your teaching show integrity, seriousness ⁸and soundness of speech that cannot be condemned, so that those who oppose you may be ashamed because they have nothing bad to say about us.

⁹Teach slaves to be subject to their masters in everything, to try to please them, not to talk back to them, ¹⁰and not to steal from them, but to show that they can be fully trusted, so that in every way they will make the teaching about God our Savior attractive.

¹¹For the grace of God that brings salvation has appeared to all men. ¹²It teaches us to say "No" to ungodliness and worldly passions, and to live self-controlled, upright and godly lives in this present age, ¹³while we wait for the blessed hope—the glorious appearing of our great God and Savior, Jesus Christ, ¹⁴who gave himself for us to redeem us from all wickedness and to purify for himself a people that are his very own, eager to do what is good.

¹⁵These, then, are the things you

Do You Walk Your Talk?

Thursday

COUPLE MINUTES

TITUS 1:16 Inside Dave's grandmother's wedding book (1907), we found this quotation by Elizabeth Barrett Browning which gives a beautiful picture of a marriage when spouses consistently walk their talk:

> "Beloved, let us love so well,
> Our work shall still be better
>   for our love,
> And still our love be sweeter
>   for our work
> And both commended
>   for the sake of each,
> By all true workers and
>   true lovers born."

For Dave and me, walking our talk is a continual struggle. As we seek to encourage other couples to build healthy relationships, we have to make sure we do not neglect ours. We think back to a Valentine's Day when we were doing a media blitz. In the

final interview, the host asked us about our last date—what we did and where we went. Would you believe neither of us could remember . . . and the topic of our interview was why mates should date!

So Paul's warning in this passage is well taken. We must live out our faith and walk our talk. Too often spouses live a compartmentalized life. When they are with other Christians, they look and sound like Christians, but when they are at home behind closed doors, they deny God by their actions. For instance, we hate to admit the times we have yelled at our kids to stop yelling! What is it like at your house when the doors are closed? The answer to this question may reveal how you are doing at living out your faith.

—Dave and Claudia

Go to page 1322 for your next devotional reading.

should teach. Encourage and rebuke with all authority. Do not let anyone despise you.

Doing What Is Good

3 Remind the people to be subject to rulers and authorities, to be obedient, to be ready to do whatever is good, ²to slander no one, to be peaceable and considerate, and to show true humility toward all men.

³At one time we too were foolish, disobedient, deceived and enslaved by all kinds of passions and pleasures. We lived in malice and envy, being hated and hating one another. ⁴But when the kindness and love of God our Savior appeared, ⁵he saved us, not because of righteous things we had done, but because of his mercy. He saved us through the washing of rebirth and renewal by the Holy Spirit, ⁶whom he poured out on us generously through Jesus Christ our Savior, ⁷so that, having been justified by his grace, we

might become heirs having the hope of eternal life. ⁸This is a trustworthy saying. And I want you to stress these things, so that those who have trusted in God may be careful to devote themselves to doing what is good. These things are excellent and profitable for everyone.

⁹But avoid foolish controversies and genealogies and arguments and quarrels about the law, because these are unprofitable and useless. ¹⁰Warn a divisive person once, and then warn him a second time. After that, have nothing to do with him. ¹¹You may be sure that such a man is warped and sinful; he is self-condemned.

Final Remarks

¹²As soon as I send Artemas or Tychicus to you, do your best to come to me at Nicopolis, because I have decided to winter there. ¹³Do everything you can to help Zenas the lawyer and Apollos on their way and see that they have everything they need. ¹⁴Our people must learn to

Mentoring

Friday

TITUS 2   For thousands of years couples were able to turn to older married couples for advice. Society brought people together in a way that made this mentor relationship available to younger couples. Past community interdependence linked young couples and older couples together by doing activities such as barn building, quilting or canning. This kind of community allowed times for younger couples to ask advice of more experienced couples.

As modern society has isolated married couples from these kinds of activities, one would think this mentor relationship is no longer available. Mentoring is not only still available but more needed than ever before. The church can become the new community for both young and older couples. With its church school classes, small groups and cell

groups, the church opens the door of opportunity for the kind of teaching relationship this passage is talking about.

But it's up to each couple to find a comfortable role. Young couples need to get involved and seek mentoring from the church community. Likewise, couples who have worked on building a godly marriage for many years need to accept the challenge. They need to build relationships with young couples and be available to mentor.

The church offers a new community that can help couples both young and old develop their marriages into being more of what God has planned for them: Christ-centered homes that God can use for his kingdom's work.

—*Bob and Rosemary*

Go to page 1323 for your next devotional reading.

devote themselves to doing what is good, in order that they may provide for daily necessities and not live unproductive lives.

[15]Everyone with me sends you greetings. Greet those who love us in the faith.

Grace be with you all.

Avoiding Turbulence

Quiet TIMES *with each other*

TITUS 3:9 Building a marriage is similar to flying a plane. From time to time we all experience some turbulence. Our friend Jake is a pilot who loves to fly. He tells us that, although they are a nuisance, bad weather and air turbulence are just part of flying. We asked Jake what he does when he hits bad weather. His answer? "Slow down." He also says he does everything he can to avoid flying through turbulence altogether.

That's the same basic advice Paul gives in this passage. As Christians, we have common core beliefs about salvation, faith, forgiveness, submitting to God and so on. We agree on these things. But Paul points out that less significant things aren't worth fighting about. It's easy to become embroiled in heated discussions about things that aren't really that important.

In the early years of our marriage, we did this often. And even now when we get stressed, we will let insignificant things irritate us, like why doesn't Claudia do something with the vertical files on her desk or why does Dave have to make hard copies of all of his e-mails?

What are the "foolish controversies" you tend to argue about? Your list is probably different from ours, but we all would benefit from daily applying this passage to our lives.

Not all turbulence is destructive. Thinking differently gives texture to your marriage. Actually a healthy marriage is a safe place to deal with differences and to process feelings. A husband married for thirty years put it this way: "One of the greatest things about our marriage is that we have learned how to disagree, stand our ground and still be friends and lovers."

If you learn the same thing, your marriage will soar above foolish arguments, and you'll be able to fly through turbulent times.

—*Dave and Claudia*

*W*arm-up **Weekend** *What kinds of "foolish controversies" do you tend to argue about?*

Go to page 1325 for your next devotional reading.

Philemon

"I'm sorry, I was wrong. Will you please forgive me?" These words reveal a repentant heart, declare judgment on what has been done or said, and solicit a charitable response from the one who has been offended. These can be difficult words to say to your spouse, your child, your coworker or your friend. But these simple words can have an enormous effect—from soothing a child's hurt feelings to saving a decades-long marriage.

This tiny letter from the apostle Paul to a man named Philemon carries a similarly significant message of repentance and a request for reconciliation. How interesting that we never hear what Philemon did when he received this letter from Paul. Did he, like the father awaiting the lost son, welcome his former slave back home? The fact that this letter found its way into the Bible gives us some indication that he did. It's likely that Philemon found, as many people have, that the only thing more gratifying than *being* pardoned is pardoning.

---

[1]Paul, a prisoner of Christ Jesus, and Timothy our brother,

To Philemon our dear friend and fellow worker, [2]to Apphia our sister, to Archippus our fellow soldier and to the church that meets in your home:

[3]Grace to you and peace from God our Father and the Lord Jesus Christ.

Thanksgiving and Prayer

[4]I always thank my God as I remember you in my prayers, [5]because I hear about your faith in the Lord Jesus and your love for all the saints. [6]I pray that you may be active in sharing your faith, so that you will have a full understanding of every good thing we have in Christ. [7]Your love has given me great joy and encourage-

ment, because you, brother, have refreshed the hearts of the saints.

Paul's Plea for Onesimus

⁸Therefore, although in Christ I could be bold and order you to do what you ought to do, ⁹yet I appeal to you on the basis of love. I then, as Paul—an old man and now also a prisoner of Christ Jesus— ¹⁰I appeal to you for my son Onesimus,ᵃ who became my son while I was in chains. ¹¹Formerly he was useless to you, but now he has become useful both to you and to me.

¹²I am sending him—who is my very heart—back to you. ¹³I would have liked to keep him with me so that he could take your place in helping me while I am in chains for the gospel. ¹⁴But I did not want to do anything without your consent, so that any favor you do will be spontaneous and not forced. ¹⁵Perhaps the reason he was separated from you for a little while was that you might have him back for good— ¹⁶no longer as a slave, but better than a slave, as a dear brother. He is very

dear to me but even dearer to you, both as a man and as a brother in the Lord.

¹⁷So if you consider me a partner, welcome him as you would welcome me. ¹⁸If he has done you any wrong or owes you anything, charge it to me. ¹⁹I, Paul, am writing this with my own hand. I will pay it back—not to mention that you owe me your very self. ²⁰I do wish, brother, that I may have some benefit from you in the Lord; refresh my heart in Christ. ²¹Confident of your obedience, I write to you, knowing that you will do even more than I ask.

²²And one thing more: Prepare a guest room for me, because I hope to be restored to you in answer to your prayers.

²³Epaphras, my fellow prisoner in Christ Jesus, sends you greetings. ²⁴And so do Mark, Aristarchus, Demas and Luke, my fellow workers.

²⁵The grace of the Lord Jesus Christ be with your spirit.

ᵃ10 *Onesimus* means *useful.*

Help Me Be My Best

Monday

PHILEMON The book of Philemon is a wonderful demonstration of one friend helping another friend do the right thing. There's no doubt that Philemon could find justification for his displeasure with Onesimus, but Paul wrote to help his friend do the right thing and restore the broken relationship.

Helping your spouse do the right thing is a very important job for a loving husband or wife. Many times I (Bob) have come home furious because of an injustice one of my associates did at work. After allowing me a time to tell her what had happened, expounding on what the person at work had done to justify my great displeasure, Rosemary always gently helps me to see the situation more clearly. She allows me to tell the story, but she doesn't commiser-

ate or fuel my anger. Slowly and patiently she helps me see that there might be another side to the situation. At first, I sometimes have wondered why she was apparently defending the other person, the "enemy." But my friend and spouse helps me see that it is my attitude or anger that is my real enemy. Next she helps me discover the opportunity that might be found in the difficult situation.

A spouse's role is not always one of agreement. Spouses help one another grow. The next time your spouse encounters a difficult situation or relationship, help him or her get past inappropriate attitudes and anger, in order to go back out into life and do the right thing.

—Bob and Rosemary

Go to page 1327 for your next devotional reading.

Hebrews

How would it feel to lose your job or your home because you follow Jesus Christ? How would it feel to lose the approval of your spouse or your friends? The recipients of this letter were facing these types of losses. They badly needed to be reminded that Jesus was sufficient to meet their needs and to represent them before God. They needed to hear the dangers of drifting from the faith. And they needed to hear about the saints before them who had lived by faith.

As you read, allow the writer of Hebrews to motivate you, as he did the early church, to "fix [your] eyes on Jesus" (12:2). And think about a couple you know who could be your marriage mentor—so you can learn from the saints about what it takes as a married couple to live by faith.

The Son Superior to Angels

1 In the past God spoke to our forefathers through the prophets at many times and in various ways, ²but in these last days he has spoken to us by his Son, whom he appointed heir of all things, and through whom he made the universe. ³The Son is the radiance of God's glory and the exact representation of his being, sustaining all things by his powerful word. After he had provided purification for sins, he sat down at the right hand of the Majesty in heaven. ⁴So he became as much superior to the angels as the name he has inherited is superior to theirs.

⁵For to which of the angels did God ever say,

"You are my Son;
today I have become your
Father*ᵃ*"*ᵇ*?

Or again,

"I will be his Father,
and he will be my Son"*ᶜ*?

⁶And again, when God brings his first-born into the world, he says,

"Let all God's angels worship him."*ᵈ*

⁷In speaking of the angels he says,

"He makes his angels winds,
his servants flames of fire."*ᵉ*

ᵃ5 Or *have begotten you* *ᵇ5* Psalm 2:7
ᶜ5 2 Samuel 7:14; 1 Chron. 17:13
ᵈ6 Deut. 32:43 (see Dead Sea Scrolls and Septuagint) *ᵉ7* Psalm 104:4

8But about the Son he says,

"Your throne, O God, will last for
    ever and ever,
  and righteousness will be the
    scepter of your kingdom.
9You have loved righteousness and
    hated wickedness;
  therefore God, your God, has set
    you above your companions
  by anointing you with the oil of
    joy." [a]

10He also says,

"In the beginning, O Lord, you laid
    the foundations of the earth,
  and the heavens are the work of
    your hands.
11They will perish, but you remain;
  they will all wear out like a
    garment.
12You will roll them up like a robe;
  like a garment they will be
    changed.
But you remain the same,
  and your years will never end." [b]

13To which of the angels did God ever say,

"Sit at my right hand
until I make your enemies
  a footstool for your feet" [c]?

14Are not all angels ministering spirits

sent to serve those who will inherit salvation?

Warning to Pay Attention

2 We must pay more careful attention, therefore, to what we have heard, so that we do not drift away. 2For if the message spoken by angels was binding, and every violation and disobedience received its just punishment, 3how shall we escape if we ignore such a great salvation? This salvation, which was first announced by the Lord, was confirmed to us by those who heard him. 4God also testified to it by signs, wonders and various miracles, and gifts of the Holy Spirit distributed according to his will.

Jesus Made Like His Brothers

5It is not to angels that he has subjected the world to come, about which we are speaking. 6But there is a place where someone has testified:

"What is man that you are mindful
    of him,
  the son of man that you care for
    him?

[a]9 Psalm 45:6,7   [b]12 Psalm 102:25-27
[c]13 Psalm 110:1

God Is Love

Tuesday

HEBREWS 1:10   In the opening scene of *Oliver,* the musical based on the Charles Dickens story of *Oliver Twist,* destitute boys in a London orphanage are hovering over a miserable meal of gruel. Meanwhile, the family and friends of the manager are enjoying heaping platters of succulent fowl and tasty vegetables in an adjoining dining room that the boys can see. Although the paint is peeling on the stark gray wall behind the rough tables where the boys are sitting, there is a huge motto which dares to show itself: GOD IS LOVE.

The audience is left to wonder whether the ragged, coughing urchins ever notice the dusty sign, let alone comprehend its

meaning. But in reality God's love is not part of a theatrical backdrop. It is not meant to have a paradoxical place on stage. God's love is real, and has been since the beginning of time.

How you perceive God's love shapes your love for each other. God's love is self-sacrificing (John 15:13, page 1167), compelling (2 Corinthians 5:14, page 1263) and unchangeable (John 13:1). That's what makes it perfect.

If the GOD IS LOVE sign had the audacity to cling to the scaly wall in Oliver's dreadful orphanage, it can surely abide in the hearts of a husband and wife who care for each other.   **—Les and Leslie**

Go to page 1328 for your next devotional reading.

⁷You made him a little*a* lower than
    the angels;
  you crowned him with glory and
    honor
⁸ and put everything under his feet."*b*

In putting everything under him, God left
nothing that is not subject to him. Yet at
present we do not see everything subject
to him. ⁹But we see Jesus, who was made
a little lower than the angels, now
crowned with glory and honor because he
suffered death, so that by the grace of God
he might taste death for everyone.

¹⁰In bringing many sons to glory, it was
fitting that God, for whom and through
whom everything exists, should make the
author of their salvation perfect through
suffering. ¹¹Both the one who makes men
holy and those who are made holy are of
the same family. So Jesus is not ashamed
to call them brothers. ¹²He says,

"I will declare your name to my
    brothers;
  in the presence of the congregation
    I will sing your praises."*c*

¹³And again,

"I will put my trust in him."*d*

And again he says,

"Here am I, and the children God
    has given me."*e*

¹⁴Since the children have flesh and
blood, he too shared in their humanity so
that by his death he might destroy him
who holds the power of death—that is, the
devil— ¹⁵and free those who all their lives
were held in slavery by their fear of death.

*a*7 Or *him for a little while;* also in verse 9
*b*8 Psalm 8:4-6   *c*12 Psalm 22:22
*d*13 Isaiah 8:17   *e*13 Isaiah 8:18

Overcoming Temptation

Wednesday

HEBREWS 2:18 When you least expect it, you may feel it. We have.
Maybe it was a look, a touch or a
sympathetic listening ear on the
day your spouse was deaf. The
temptation is to momentarily let
down your guard. What starts so innocently can have disastrous results—and
temptation that goes unchecked can devastate your marriage.

    In our culture temptation seems to lurk
behind every corner. Affairs and infidelity
for many are a way of life. Unfortunately,
Christians are not exempt from temptation. The writer of Hebrews reminds us that
even Jesus was tempted. But the really
good news is that Jesus is able to help those
who are being tempted. And in marriage,
we need all the help we can get!

    At sometime you too probably have felt
an attraction to someone other than your
spouse. While you can't control the chemistry, you can control your response. And in
this passage we are reminded that God will
help us when we are tempted.

    Years ago we made a commitment to
each other that in those times if and when
we were tempted, we would take the ini-

tiative to say "no" verbally, non-
verbally or take whatever action
was necessary to remain faithful
to each other. I (Dave) remember
once when we lived in Germany
actually leaving in the middle of a
conference and coming home several
days early. It was better to miss part of the
conference than to remain in a compromis-
ing and tempting situation.

    When we lived in Austria, I (Claudia) re-
member at a party a friend's husband flirting and sending signals that made me feel
uneasy. The next day he stopped by to pick
up a book. I remember leaving the front
door of our apartment wide open and not
inviting him in. I did not want to be alone
with him.

    Temptations are a reminder to look for
ways to energize and ignite the chemistry
with our spouse. They motivate us to plan
romantic getaways or give little silly gifts
to say "I love you." Like us, you can resist
temptation. And you can protect and nurture your own love chemistry.

                   —Dave and Claudia

Go to page 1330 for your next devotional reading.

[16]For surely it is not angels he helps, but Abraham's descendants. [17]For this reason he had to be made like his brothers in every way, in order that he might become a merciful and faithful high priest in service to God, and that he might make atonement for[a] the sins of the people. [18]Because he himself suffered when he was tempted, he is able to help those who are being tempted.

Jesus Greater Than Moses

3 Therefore, holy brothers, who share in the heavenly calling, fix your thoughts on Jesus, the apostle and high priest whom we confess. [2]He was faithful to the one who appointed him, just as Moses was faithful in all God's house. [3]Jesus has been found worthy of greater honor than Moses, just as the builder of a house has greater honor than the house itself. [4]For every house is built by someone, but God is the builder of everything. [5]Moses was faithful as a servant in all God's house, testifying to what would be said in the future. [6]But Christ is faithful as a son over God's house. And we are his house, if we hold on to our courage and the hope of which we boast.

Warning Against Unbelief

[7]So, as the Holy Spirit says:

> "Today, if you hear his voice,
> [8] do not harden your hearts
> as you did in the rebellion,
>   during the time of testing in the
>   desert,
> [9]where your fathers tested and tried
>   me
>   and for forty years saw what I did.
> [10]That is why I was angry with that
>   generation,
>   and I said, 'Their hearts are always
>   going astray,
>   and they have not known my
>   ways.'
> [11]So I declared on oath in my anger,
>   'They shall never enter my rest.' "[b]

[12]See to it, brothers, that none of you has a sinful, unbelieving heart that turns away from the living God. [13]But encourage one another daily, as long as it is called Today, so that none of you may be hardened by sin's deceitfulness. [14]We have come to share in Christ if we hold

firmly till the end the confidence we had at first. [15]As has just been said:

> "Today, if you hear his voice,
>   do not harden your hearts
> as you did in the rebellion."[c]

[16]Who were they who heard and rebelled? Were they not all those Moses led out of Egypt? [17]And with whom was he angry for forty years? Was it not with those who sinned, whose bodies fell in the desert? [18]And to whom did God swear that they would never enter his rest if not to those who disobeyed[d]? [19]So we see that they were not able to enter, because of their unbelief.

A Sabbath-Rest for the People of God

4 Therefore, since the promise of entering his rest still stands, let us be careful that none of you be found to have fallen short of it. [2]For we also have had the gospel preached to us, just as they did; but the message they heard was of no value to them, because those who heard did not combine it with faith.[e] [3]Now we who have believed enter that rest, just as God has said,

> "So I declared on oath in my anger,
>   'They shall never enter my rest.' "[f]

And yet his work has been finished since the creation of the world. [4]For somewhere he has spoken about the seventh day in these words: "And on the seventh day God rested from all his work."[g] [5]And again in the passage above he says, "They shall never enter my rest."

[6]It still remains that some will enter that rest, and those who formerly had the gospel preached to them did not go in, because of their disobedience. [7]Therefore God again set a certain day, calling it Today, when a long time later he spoke through David, as was said before:

> "Today, if you hear his voice,
>   do not harden your hearts."[h]

[a]17 Or *and that he might turn aside God's wrath, taking away*   [b]11 Psalm 95:7-11   [c]15 Psalm 95:7,8   [d]18 Or *disbelieved*   [e]2 Many manuscripts *because they did not share in the faith of those who obeyed*   [f]3 Psalm 95:11; also in verse 5   [g]4 Gen. 2:2   [h]7 Psalm 95:7,8

8For if Joshua had given them rest, God would not have spoken later about another day. 9There remains, then, a Sabbath-rest for the people of God; 10for anyone who enters God's rest also rests from his own work, just as God did from his. 11Let us, therefore, make every effort to enter that rest, so that no one will fall by following their example of disobedience.

12For the word of God is living and active. Sharper than any double-edged sword, it penetrates even to dividing soul and spirit, joints and marrow; it judges the thoughts and attitudes of the heart. 13Nothing in all creation is hidden from God's sight. Everything is uncovered and laid bare before the eyes of him to whom we must give account.

Jesus the Great High Priest

14Therefore, since we have a great high priest who has gone through the heavens,*a* Jesus the Son of God, let us hold firmly to the faith we profess. 15For we do not have a high priest who is unable to sympathize with our weaknesses, but we have one who has been tempted in every way, just as we are—yet was without sin. 16Let us then approach the throne of grace with confidence, so that we may receive mercy and find grace to help us in our time of need.

5 Every high priest is selected from among men and is appointed to rep-resent them in matters related to God, to offer gifts and sacrifices for sins. 2He is able to deal gently with those who are ignorant and are going astray, since he himself is subject to weakness. 3This is why he has to offer sacrifices for his own sins, as well as for the sins of the people.

4No one takes this honor upon himself; he must be called by God, just as Aaron was. 5So Christ also did not take upon himself the glory of becoming a high priest. But God said to him,

"You are my Son;
    today I have become your
        Father.*b" c*

6And he says in another place,

"You are a priest forever,
    in the order of Melchizedek."*d*

7During the days of Jesus' life on earth, he offered up prayers and petitions with loud cries and tears to the one who could save him from death, and he was heard because of his reverent submission. 8Although he was a son, he learned obedience from what he suffered 9and, once made perfect, he became the source of eternal salvation for all who obey him 10and was designated by God to be high priest in the order of Melchizedek.

---

a14 Or *gone into heaven*   *b5* Or *have begotten you*   *c5* Psalm 2:7   *d6* Psalm 110:4

Love Like a Lighthouse

Thursday

HEBREWS 3:13 On a recent trip to the New England coast, we discovered a little lighthouse that has been a source of encouragement to many lonely sailors over the years. Minot's light, near Scituate, Massachusetts, signals the nautical code that spells "I love you." Wives in this sailing town sent out this message to encourage their husbands out at sea and remind them how much they were loved.

Several years ago the Coast Guard decided to upgrade the light by replacing the old equipment. They announced that for technical reasons the new machines would be unable to flash the "I love you" mes-sage. Both the families waiting in town and the sailors protested. The Coast Guard finally weakened. The old equipment, noticeably out of date, was reinstalled and remains in Scituate to faithfully send its encouraging message to the sailing husbands.

Every spouse needs an encouraging word. More than that, we need a marriage that serves as a kind of safe harbor, a place where we can count on being encouraged. Is your marriage such a place? Do you "encourage one another daily"?

—Les and Leslie

Go to page 1331 for your next devotional reading.

Warning Against Falling Away

[11]We have much to say about this, but it is hard to explain because you are slow to learn. [12]In fact, though by this time you ought to be teachers, you need someone to teach you the elementary truths of God's word all over again. You need milk, not solid food! [13]Anyone who lives on milk, being still an infant, is not acquainted with the teaching about righteousness. [14]But solid food is for the mature, who by constant use have trained themselves to distinguish good from evil.

6 Therefore let us leave the elementary teachings about Christ and go on to maturity, not laying again the foundation of repentance from acts that lead to death,[a] and of faith in God, [2]instruction about baptisms, the laying on of hands, the resurrection of the dead, and eternal judgment. [3]And God permitting, we will do so.

[4]It is impossible for those who have once been enlightened, who have tasted the heavenly gift, who have shared in the Holy Spirit, [5]who have tasted the goodness of the word of God and the powers of the coming age, [6]if they fall away, to be brought back to repentance, because[b] to their loss they are crucifying the Son of God all over again and subjecting him to public disgrace.

[7]Land that drinks in the rain often falling on it and that produces a crop useful to those for whom it is farmed receives the blessing of God. [8]But land that produces thorns and thistles is worthless and is in danger of being cursed. In the end it will be burned.

[9]Even though we speak like this, dear friends, we are confident of better things in your case—things that accompany salvation. [10]God is not unjust; he will not forget your work and the love you have shown him as you have helped his people and continue to help them. [11]We want each of you to show this same diligence to the very end, in order to make your hope sure. [12]We do not want you to become lazy, but to imitate those who through faith and patience inherit what has been promised.

The Certainty of God's Promise

[13]When God made his promise to Abraham, since there was no one greater

---

[a]1 Or *from useless rituals*   [b]6 Or *repentance while*

Living in the Word of God

Friday

HEBREWS 4:12 The root system of most trees is as wide and deep as the leaf line is wide and high. That is not true, however, of the redwood, which has a shallow root system that spreads out in all directions. It is just not very deep. That fact of life creates a problem for a redwood standing alone. It can easily be blown over because the lack of deep roots gives it little stability. However, when two redwoods grow together, their root structures intertwine with each other and give one another strength. Though weak as separate trees, they become strong together. The same is true for spouses. "Two are better than one," said King Solomon.

Whether you live in one place for many years or relocate around the country according to job requirements, the most important roots you'll ever establish are in God and his Word. For this spiritual root system will bear much fruit. "I am the vine;" said Jesus, "[and] you are the branches. If a man remains in me and I in him, he will bear much fruit; apart from me you can do nothing . . . If you remain in me and my words remain in you, ask whatever you wish, and it will be given you. This is to my Father's glory, that you bear much fruit, showing yourselves to be my disciples" (John 15:5–8).

As a couple grows together in their understanding of God and his Word, they become all the more "rooted and established in love" (Ephesians 3:17). Never forget that you as a couple, like the redwoods, become stronger together.   —*Les and Leslie*

Go to page 1332 for your next devotional reading.

for him to swear by, he swore by himself, [14]saying, "I will surely bless you and give you many descendants."[a] [15]And so after waiting patiently, Abraham received what was promised.

[16]Men swear by someone greater than themselves, and the oath confirms what is said and puts an end to all argument. [17]Because God wanted to make the unchanging nature of his purpose very clear to the heirs of what was promised, he confirmed it with an oath. [18]God did this so that, by two unchangeable things in which it is impossible for God to lie, we who have fled to take hold of the hope offered to us may be greatly encouraged. [19]We have this hope as an anchor for the soul, firm and secure. It enters the inner

sanctuary behind the curtain, [20]where Jesus, who went before us, has entered on our behalf. He has become a high priest forever, in the order of Melchizedek.

Melchizedek the Priest

7 This Melchizedek was king of Salem and priest of God Most High. He met Abraham returning from the defeat of the kings and blessed him, [2]and Abraham gave him a tenth of everything. First, his name means "king of righteousness"; then also, "king of Salem" means "king of peace." [3]Without father or mother, without genealogy, without beginning of days

[a]14 Gen. 22:17

The Marriage Diet

Quiet TIMES *with each other*

HEBREWS 5:13–14 There is a joke at our house that's not really that funny. It's about our Frosted Mini-Wheats gourmet dinners. When we get overloaded, the first thing to go is our good eating habits. While an occasional crazy dinner is fine, a steady diet of only milk and cereal would be unhealthy. Both in our Christian walk and in our marriages, we need substantial, "solid food." As this passage indicates, solid food helps us mature so we can distinguish good from evil.

Over the years we've struggled to keep our marriage enriched with solid nutrients—and to be honest, we still struggle today. On those Frosted Mini-Wheat days, we're most likely neglecting our own marriage as well as our own health. But the most difficult time we had keeping our marriage healthy was when we had three children ages six and under. During that time we were living in Germany and had no English-speaking neighbors or family around who could give us a hand with the boys. Time alone as a couple was hard to come by. But we remember at least once a

week, putting the boys to bed early—or as early as we could get them settled—and having a stay-at-home date. We would pull out our best dishes and set the table with a real tablecloth. Our meal might have been simple, but it was served with soft music, candlelight and sometimes even fresh flowers. Sure there were those nights Claudia fell asleep in the middle of dessert, but our at-home dates became a ritual that helped us stay connected during those early parenting years.

Now we have our "peel-your-own-shrimp-at-home" dates. When we get back home from a marriage seminar we are usually exhausted and too tired to cook or even go out for a bite to eat. So we stop by the market and buy raw vegetables, dip and a half-pound of fresh shrimp. That's our total menu, but it's relaxing and we enjoy unwinding at home together. It's become a little tradition that we treasure.

Perhaps you will want to take some time and talk about how you can nurture your marriage. —*Dave and Claudia*

*W*eekend Warm-up *Why not plan a quiet dinner date at home sometime soon?*

Go to page 1335 for your next devotional reading.

or end of life, like the Son of God he remains a priest forever.

⁴Just think how great he was: Even the patriarch Abraham gave him a tenth of the plunder! ⁵Now the law requires the descendants of Levi who become priests to collect a tenth from the people—that is, their brothers—even though their brothers are descended from Abraham. ⁶This man, however, did not trace his descent from Levi, yet he collected a tenth from Abraham and blessed him who had the promises. ⁷And without doubt the lesser person is blessed by the greater. ⁸In the one case, the tenth is collected by men who die; but in the other case, by him who is declared to be living. ⁹One might even say that Levi, who collects the tenth, paid the tenth through Abraham, ¹⁰because when Melchizedek met Abraham, Levi was still in the body of his ancestor.

Jesus Like Melchizedek

¹¹If perfection could have been attained through the Levitical priesthood (for on the basis of it the law was given to the people), why was there still need for another priest to come—one in the order of Melchizedek, not in the order of Aaron? ¹²For when there is a change of the priesthood, there must also be a change of the law. ¹³He of whom these things are said belonged to a different tribe, and no one from that tribe has ever served at the altar. ¹⁴For it is clear that our Lord descended from Judah, and in regard to that tribe Moses said nothing about priests. ¹⁵And what we have said is even more clear if another priest like Melchizedek appears, ¹⁶one who has become a priest not on the basis of a regulation as to his ancestry but on the basis of the power of an indestructible life. ¹⁷For it is declared:

"You are a priest forever,
    in the order of Melchizedek." ᵃ

¹⁸The former regulation is set aside because it was weak and useless ¹⁹(for the law made nothing perfect), and a better hope is introduced, by which we draw near to God.

²⁰And it was not without an oath! Others became priests without any oath, ²¹but he became a priest with an oath when God said to him:

"The Lord has sworn
    and will not change his mind:
'You are a priest forever.' " ᵃ

²²Because of this oath, Jesus has become the guarantee of a better covenant.

²³Now there have been many of those priests, since death prevented them from continuing in office; ²⁴but because Jesus lives forever, he has a permanent priesthood. ²⁵Therefore he is able to save completely ᵇ those who come to God through him, because he always lives to intercede for them.

²⁶Such a high priest meets our need—one who is holy, blameless, pure, set apart from sinners, exalted above the heavens. ²⁷Unlike the other high priests, he does not need to offer sacrifices day after day, first for his own sins, and then for the sins of the people. He sacrificed for their sins once for all when he offered himself. ²⁸For the law appoints as high priests men who are weak; but the oath, which came after the law, appointed the Son, who has been made perfect forever.

The High Priest of a New Covenant

8 The point of what we are saying is this: We do have such a high priest, who sat down at the right hand of the throne of the Majesty in heaven, ²and who serves in the sanctuary, the true tabernacle set up by the Lord, not by man.

³Every high priest is appointed to offer both gifts and sacrifices, and so it was necessary for this one also to have something to offer. ⁴If he were on earth, he would not be a priest, for there are already men who offer the gifts prescribed by the law. ⁵They serve at a sanctuary that is a copy and shadow of what is in heaven. This is why Moses was warned when he was about to build the tabernacle: "See to it that you make everything according to the pattern shown you on the mountain." ᶜ ⁶But the ministry Jesus has received is as superior to theirs as the covenant of which he is mediator is superior to the old one, and it is founded on better promises.

⁷For if there had been nothing wrong with that first covenant, no place would

ᵃ17,21 Psalm 110:4   ᵇ25 Or forever
ᶜ5 Exodus 25:40

have been sought for another. ⁸But God found fault with the people and said ᵃ:

"The time is coming, declares the Lord,
    when I will make a new covenant
with the house of Israel
    and with the house of Judah.
⁹It will not be like the covenant
    I made with their forefathers
when I took them by the hand
    to lead them out of Egypt,
because they did not remain faithful
    to my covenant,
and I turned away from them,
                    declares the Lord.
¹⁰This is the covenant I will make with
    the house of Israel
after that time, declares the Lord.
I will put my laws in their minds
    and write them on their hearts.
I will be their God,
    and they will be my people.
¹¹No longer will a man teach his
    neighbor,
or a man his brother, saying,
    'Know the Lord,'
because they will all know me,
    from the least of them to the
    greatest.
¹²For I will forgive their wickedness
    and will remember their sins no
    more." ᵇ

¹³By calling this covenant "new," he has made the first one obsolete; and what is obsolete and aging will soon disappear.

Worship in the Earthly Tabernacle

9 Now the first covenant had regulations for worship and also an earthly sanctuary. ²A tabernacle was set up. In its first room were the lampstand, the table and the consecrated bread; this was called the Holy Place. ³Behind the second curtain was a room called the Most Holy Place, ⁴which had the golden altar of incense and the gold-covered ark of the covenant. This ark contained the gold jar of manna, Aaron's staff that had budded, and the stone tablets of the covenant. ⁵Above the ark were the cherubim of the Glory, overshadowing the atonement cover. ᶜ But we cannot discuss these things in detail now.

⁶When everything had been arranged like this, the priests entered regularly into the outer room to carry on their ministry. ⁷But only the high priest entered the inner room, and that only once a year, and never without blood, which he offered for himself and for the sins the people had committed in ignorance. ⁸The Holy Spirit was showing by this that the way into the Most Holy Place had not yet been disclosed as long as the first tabernacle was still standing. ⁹This is an illustration for the present time, indicating that the gifts and sacrifices being offered were not able to clear the conscience of the worshiper. ¹⁰They are only a matter of food and drink and various ceremonial washings—external regulations applying until the time of the new order.

The Blood of Christ

¹¹When Christ came as high priest of the good things that are already here, ᵈ he went through the greater and more perfect tabernacle that is not man-made, that is to say, not a part of this creation. ¹²He did not enter by means of the blood of goats and calves; but he entered the Most Holy Place once for all by his own blood, having obtained eternal redemption. ¹³The blood of goats and bulls and the ashes of a heifer sprinkled on those who are ceremonially unclean sanctify them so that they are outwardly clean. ¹⁴How much more, then, will the blood of Christ, who through the eternal Spirit offered himself unblemished to God, cleanse our consciences from acts that lead to death, ᵉ so that we may serve the living God!

¹⁵For this reason Christ is the mediator of a new covenant, that those who are called may receive the promised eternal inheritance—now that he has died as a ransom to set them free from the sins committed under the first covenant. ¹⁶In the case of a will, ᶠ it is necessary to prove the death of the one who made it, ¹⁷because a will is in force only when somebody has died; it never takes effect while the one who made it is living.

ᵃ8 Some manuscripts may be translated *fault and said to the people.*   ᵇ12 Jer. 31:31-34
ᶜ5 Traditionally *the mercy seat*   ᵈ11 Some early manuscripts *are to come*   ᵉ14 Or *from useless rituals*   ᶠ16 Same Greek word as *covenant;* also in verse 17

¹⁸This is why even the first covenant was not put into effect without blood. ¹⁹When Moses had proclaimed every commandment of the law to all the people, he took the blood of calves, together with water, scarlet wool and branches of hyssop, and sprinkled the scroll and all the people. ²⁰He said, "This is the blood of the covenant, which God has commanded you to keep."ᵃ ²¹In the same way, he sprinkled with the blood both the tabernacle and everything used in its ceremonies. ²²In fact, the law requires that nearly everything be cleansed with blood, and without the shedding of blood there is no forgiveness.

²³It was necessary, then, for the copies of the heavenly things to be purified with these sacrifices, but the heavenly things themselves with better sacrifices than these. ²⁴For Christ did not enter a manmade sanctuary that was only a copy of the true one; he entered heaven itself, now to appear for us in God's presence. ²⁵Nor did he enter heaven to offer himself again and again, the way the high priest enters the Most Holy Place every year with blood that is not his own. ²⁶Then Christ would have had to suffer many times since the creation of the world. But now he has appeared once for all at the end of the ages to do away with sin by the sacrifice of himself. ²⁷Just as man is destined to die once, and after that to face judg-ment, ²⁸so Christ was sacrificed once to take away the sins of many people; and he will appear a second time, not to bear sin, but to bring salvation to those who are waiting for him.

Christ's Sacrifice Once for All

10 The law is only a shadow of the good things that are coming—not the realities themselves. For this reason it can never, by the same sacrifices repeated endlessly year after year, make perfect those who draw near to worship. ²If it could, would they not have stopped being offered? For the worshipers would have been cleansed once for all, and would no longer have felt guilty for their sins. ³But those sacrifices are an annual reminder of sins, ⁴because it is impossible for the blood of bulls and goats to take away sins.

⁵Therefore, when Christ came into the world, he said:

"Sacrifice and offering you did not
    desire,
  but a body you prepared for me;
⁶with burnt offerings and sin offerings
    you were not pleased.
⁷Then I said, 'Here I am—it is written
    about me in the scroll—

ᵃ20 Exodus 24:8

Pessimists and Optimists

HEBREWS 9:15 Pessimists are people who feel bad when they feel good for fear they'll feel worse when they feel better. In other words, pessimists have simply made negative thinking a habit, a way of life. Optimists, on the other hand, are undaunted by defeat. When they are confronted with the inevitable hard knocks of life, they immediately look for solutions. They see defeat as temporary. Most of all, they look to a bright future.

It is difficult to read about the new covenant of Jesus Christ and not become an optimist. Through his death and resurrection, Jesus is promising an eternal inheri-

tance. He is setting us free from sin. Of course, the Bible has a different word for optimism—*hope*. In the New Testament "hope" appears more than eighty times, and it usually refers to Christ, who is the hope of this world (see Titus 2:13 and 1 Peter 1:3). Colossians 1:5 tells us that love springs from hope. That's an important message for married couples. We can't really love one another without hope, for hope is an "anchor for the soul, firm and secure" (Hebrews 6:19).

—Les and Leslie

Go to page 1337 for your next devotional reading.

I have come to do your will,
O God.'"[a]

[8]First he said, "Sacrifices and offerings, burnt offerings and sin offerings you did not desire, nor were you pleased with them" (although the law required them to be made). [9]Then he said, "Here I am, I have come to do your will." He sets aside the first to establish the second. [10]And by that will, we have been made holy through the sacrifice of the body of Jesus Christ once for all.

[11]Day after day every priest stands and performs his religious duties; again and again he offers the same sacrifices, which can never take away sins. [12]But when this priest had offered for all time one sacrifice for sins, he sat down at the right hand of God. [13]Since that time he waits for his enemies to be made his footstool, [14]because by one sacrifice he has made perfect forever those who are being made holy.

[15]The Holy Spirit also testifies to us about this. First he says:

[16]"This is the covenant I will make
with them
after that time, says the Lord.
I will put my laws in their hearts,
and I will write them on their
minds."[b]

[17]Then he adds:

"Their sins and lawless acts
I will remember no more."[c]

[18]And where these have been forgiven, there is no longer any sacrifice for sin.

A Call to Persevere

[19]Therefore, brothers, since we have confidence to enter the Most Holy Place by the blood of Jesus, [20]by a new and living way opened for us through the curtain, that is, his body, [21]and since we have a great priest over the house of God, [22]let us draw near to God with a sincere heart in full assurance of faith, having our hearts sprinkled to cleanse us from a guilty conscience and having our bodies washed with pure water. [23]Let us hold unswervingly to the hope we profess, for he who promised is faithful. [24]And let us consider how we may spur one another on toward love and good deeds. [25]Let us not give up meeting together, as some are in the habit of doing, but let us encourage one another—and all the more as you see the Day approaching.

[26]If we deliberately keep on sinning after we have received the knowledge of the truth, no sacrifice for sins is left, [27]but only a fearful expectation of judgment and of raging fire that will consume the enemies of God. [28]Anyone who rejected the law of Moses died without mercy on the testimony of two or three witnesses. [29]How much more severely do you think a man deserves to be punished who has trampled the Son of God under foot, who has treated as an unholy thing the blood of the covenant that sanctified him, and who has insulted the Spirit of grace? [30]For we know him who said, "It is mine to avenge; I will repay,"[d] and again, "The Lord will judge his people."[e] [31]It is a dreadful thing to fall into the hands of the living God.

[32]Remember those earlier days after you had received the light, when you stood your ground in a great contest in the face of suffering. [33]Sometimes you were publicly exposed to insult and persecution; at other times you stood side by side with those who were so treated. [34]You sympathized with those in prison and joyfully accepted the confiscation of your property, because you knew that you yourselves had better and lasting possessions.

[35]So do not throw away your confidence; it will be richly rewarded. [36]You need to persevere so that when you have done the will of God, you will receive what he has promised. [37]For in just a very little while,

"He who is coming will come and
will not delay.
[38]   But my righteous one[f] will live by
faith.
And if he shrinks back,
I will not be pleased with him."[g]

[39]But we are not of those who shrink back and are destroyed, but of those who believe and are saved.

[a]7 Psalm 40:6-8 (see Septuagint)
[b]16 Jer. 31:33   [c]17 Jer. 31:34
[d]30 Deut. 32:35   [e]30 Deut. 32:36; Psalm 135:14   [f]38 One early manuscript But the righteous   [g]38 Hab. 2:3,4

By Faith

11 Now faith is being sure of what we hope for and certain of what we do not see. ²This is what the ancients were commended for.

³By faith we understand that the universe was formed at God's command, so that what is seen was not made out of what was visible.

⁴By faith Abel offered God a better sacrifice than Cain did. By faith he was commended as a righteous man, when God spoke well of his offerings. And by faith he still speaks, even though he is dead.

⁵By faith Enoch was taken from this life, so that he did not experience death; he could not be found, because God had taken him away. For before he was taken, he was commended as one who pleased God. ⁶And without faith it is impossible to please God, because anyone who

comes to him must believe that he exists and that he rewards those who earnestly seek him.

⁷By faith Noah, when warned about things not yet seen, in holy fear built an ark to save his family. By his faith he condemned the world and became heir of the righteousness that comes by faith.

⁸By faith Abraham, when called to go to a place he would later receive as his inheritance, obeyed and went, even though he did not know where he was going. ⁹By faith he made his home in the promised land like a stranger in a foreign country; he lived in tents, as did Isaac and Jacob, who were heirs with him of the same promise. ¹⁰For he was looking forward to the city with foundations, whose architect and builder is God.

¹¹By faith Abraham, even though he was past age—and Sarah herself was barren—was enabled to become a father be-

Spurring Each Other On

Tuesday

HEBREWS 10:23-24 Claudia is more time-oriented than I am, so she is continually trying to "spur" me on. That comes naturally. But it's not so natural or easy to "spur one another on toward love and good deeds." Spouses greatly influence one another, and we need to use that influence in a positive way.

One way we spur each other on toward love and good deeds is to pray faithfully for each other and with each other. This passage reminds us that God is faithful and will help us to hold unswervingly to the hope we profess. God fortifies a Christian marriage, and we can fortify our own marriage through prayer.

It hasn't always been easy for me and Claudia to pray together. At first we felt awkward and were hesitant to pray out loud. Someone suggested that we write down our prayer requests before we tried praying together. This really helped us resist sending messages to the other through prayer—like "God, please help her be a little more sensitive to my needs." Also,

keeping a prayer journal over the years has helped us to grow in our faith as we see how God has answered our prayers—and not always in the way we wanted him to answer them—but always in our best interest.

Another way we try to spur each other on is to watch our communication—not just our words but also our tone of voice and non-verbal message. Many times our attitude determines whether we're encouraging or discouraging our spouse. For example if Claudia were to ask me, "Why haven't you finished writing that letter to our prayer partners?" I would probably get angry and resentful. But if she were to say, "Dave, what can I do to help you get that prayer letter underway? Would it be helpful to make a list of things we want to include?" I would probably give her an entirely different response.

Think about your own communication style. Does it spur your spouse on toward love and good deeds? —*Dave and Claudia*

Go to page 1339 for your next devotional reading.

cause he[a] considered him faithful who had made the promise. [12]And so from this one man, and he as good as dead, came descendants as numerous as the stars in the sky and as countless as the sand on the seashore.

[13]All these people were still living by faith when they died. They did not receive the things promised; they only saw them and welcomed them from a distance. And they admitted that they were aliens and strangers on earth. [14]People who say such things show that they are looking for a country of their own. [15]If they had been thinking of the country they had left, they would have had opportunity to return. [16]Instead, they were longing for a better country—a heavenly one. Therefore God is not ashamed to be called their God, for he has prepared a city for them.

[17]By faith Abraham, when God tested him, offered Isaac as a sacrifice. He who had received the promises was about to sacrifice his one and only son, [18]even though God had said to him, "It is through Isaac that your offspring[b] will be reckoned."[c] [19]Abraham reasoned that God could raise the dead, and figuratively speaking, he did receive Isaac back from death.

[20]By faith Isaac blessed Jacob and Esau in regard to their future.

[21]By faith Jacob, when he was dying, blessed each of Joseph's sons, and worshiped as he leaned on the top of his staff.

[22]By faith Joseph, when his end was near, spoke about the exodus of the Israelites from Egypt and gave instructions about his bones.

[23]By faith Moses' parents hid him for three months after he was born, because they saw he was no ordinary child, and they were not afraid of the king's edict.

[24]By faith Moses, when he had grown up, refused to be known as the son of Pharaoh's daughter. [25]He chose to be mistreated along with the people of God rather than to enjoy the pleasures of sin for a short time. [26]He regarded disgrace for the sake of Christ as of greater value than the treasures of Egypt, because he was looking ahead to his reward. [27]By faith he left Egypt, not fearing the king's anger; he persevered because he saw him who is invisible. [28]By faith he kept the Passover and the sprinkling of blood, so

that the destroyer of the firstborn would not touch the firstborn of Israel.

[29]By faith the people passed through the Red Sea[d] as on dry land; but when the Egyptians tried to do so, they were drowned.

[30]By faith the walls of Jericho fell, after the people had marched around them for seven days.

[31]By faith the prostitute Rahab, because she welcomed the spies, was not killed with those who were disobedient.[e]

[32]And what more shall I say? I do not have time to tell about Gideon, Barak, Samson, Jephthah, David, Samuel and the prophets, [33]who through faith conquered kingdoms, administered justice, and gained what was promised; who shut the mouths of lions, [34]quenched the fury of the flames, and escaped the edge of the sword; whose weakness was turned to strength; and who became powerful in battle and routed foreign armies. [35]Women received back their dead, raised to life again. Others were tortured and refused to be released, so that they might gain a better resurrection. [36]Some faced jeers and flogging, while still others were chained and put in prison. [37]They were stoned[f]; they were sawed in two; they were put to death by the sword. They went about in sheepskins and goatskins, destitute, persecuted and mistreated— [38]the world was not worthy of them. They wandered in deserts and mountains, and in caves and holes in the ground.

[39]These were all commended for their faith, yet none of them received what had been promised. [40]God had planned something better for us so that only together with us would they be made perfect.

God Disciplines His Sons

12 Therefore, since we are surrounded by such a great cloud of witnesses, let us throw off everything that hinders and the sin that so easily entangles, and let us run with perseverance the race marked out for us. [2]Let us fix our eyes on

[a]11 Or By faith even Sarah, who was past age, was enabled to bear children because she   [b]18 Greek seed   [c]18 Gen. 21:12   [d]29 That is, Sea of Reeds   [e]31 Or unbelieving   [f]37 Some early manuscripts stoned; they were put to the test;

Jesus, the author and perfecter of our faith, who for the joy set before him endured the cross, scorning its shame, and sat down at the right hand of the throne of God. ³Consider him who endured such opposition from sinful men, so that you will not grow weary and lose heart.

⁴In your struggle against sin, you have not yet resisted to the point of shedding your blood. ⁵And you have forgotten that word of encouragement that addresses you as sons:

> "My son, do not make light of the
>   Lord's discipline,
>   and do not lose heart when he
>   rebukes you,
> ⁶because the Lord disciplines those he
>   loves,
>   and he punishes everyone he
>   accepts as a son."ᵃ

⁷Endure hardship as discipline; God is treating you as sons. For what son is not disciplined by his father? ⁸If you are not disciplined (and everyone undergoes discipline), then you are illegitimate children and not true sons. ⁹Moreover, we

have all had human fathers who disciplined us and we respected them for it. How much more should we submit to the Father of our spirits and live! ¹⁰Our fathers disciplined us for a little while as they thought best; but God disciplines us for our good, that we may share in his holiness. ¹¹No discipline seems pleasant at the time, but painful. Later on, however, it produces a harvest of righteousness and peace for those who have been trained by it.

¹²Therefore, strengthen your feeble arms and weak knees. ¹³"Make level paths for your feet,"ᵇ so that the lame may not be disabled, but rather healed.

Warning Against Refusing God

¹⁴Make every effort to live in peace with all men and to be holy; without holiness no one will see the Lord. ¹⁵See to it that no one misses the grace of God and that no bitter root grows up to cause trouble and defile many. ¹⁶See that no one is sexually immoral, or is godless like Esau,

ᵃ6 Prov. 3:11,12   ᵇ13 Prov. 4:26

Get Rid of the Clutter

Wednesday

HEBREWS 12:1 Nothing makes us feel better than cleaning out a closet. And when we moved into a condo from our family home, we cleared out all of them! But this time, closet cleaning was a real challenge; we were moving into a home with less space—no way could we take everything with us. Actually, this limitation was a positive. We were forced to rid ourselves of "things" we really didn't need.

Closet clutter is easy to deal with—you simply take everything out of your closet and only put back in what you really need. But other kinds of clutter are more difficult to overcome. Over the years we have dealt with corporate clutter—balancing job demands with personal ones—and at times it's been rather difficult. Being a weekend husband and dad was something I didn't handle well, so we chose to de-clutter our lives by finding a different job.

Now in the empty nest, we travel to-

gether and lead marriage and family seminars, so we have to de-clutter our lives in other ways. We choose not to worry about things we cannot control—like delayed flights. And we try to give up unrealistic expectations—like believing we can be gone most weekends and still maintain a social life at home.

We still struggle with the clutter of overcommitment. At times we face writing deadlines and realize that, apart from stressful twenty-hour days, we won't make them.

Consider whether you have too many "things" that require your constant attention, or if the urgent things leave little time for the important things in your life, like building your marriage relationship. Maybe it's time to take Hebrew 12:1 seriously.

—Dave and Claudia

Go to page 1340 for your next devotional reading.

who for a single meal sold his inheritance rights as the oldest son. [17]Afterward, as you know, when he wanted to inherit this blessing, he was rejected. He could bring about no change of mind, though he sought the blessing with tears.

[18]You have not come to a mountain that can be touched and that is burning with fire; to darkness, gloom and storm; [19]to a trumpet blast or to such a voice speaking words that those who heard it begged that no further word be spoken to them, [20]because they could not bear what was commanded: "If even an animal touches the mountain, it must be stoned."[a] [21]The sight was so terrifying that Moses said, "I am trembling with fear."[b]

[22]But you have come to Mount Zion, to the heavenly Jerusalem, the city of the living God. You have come to thousands upon thousands of angels in joyful assembly, [23]to the church of the firstborn, whose names are written in heaven. You have come to God, the judge of all men, to the spirits of righteous men made perfect, [24]to Jesus the mediator of a new covenant, and to the sprinkled blood that speaks a better word than the blood of Abel.

[25]See to it that you do not refuse him who speaks. If they did not escape when they refused him who warned them on earth, how much less will we, if we turn away from him who warns us from heaven? [26]At that time his voice shook the earth, but now he has promised, "Once more I will shake not only the earth but also the heavens."[c] [27]The words "once more" indicate the removing of what can be shaken—that is, created things—so that what cannot be shaken may remain.

[28]Therefore, since we are receiving a kingdom that cannot be shaken, let us be thankful, and so worship God acceptably with reverence and awe, [29]for our "God is a consuming fire."[d]

Concluding Exhortations

13 Keep on loving each other as brothers. [2]Do not forget to entertain strangers, for by so doing some people have entertained angels without knowing

[a]20 Exodus 19:12,13   [b]21 Deut. 9:19
[c]26 Haggai 2:6   [d]29 Deut. 4:24

Your Mate's "Moccasins"

Thursday

COUPLE MINUTES

HEBREWS 13:1–5 There is an old Sioux Indian prayer that says, "Oh Great Spirit, grant me the wisdom to walk in another's moccasins before I criticize or pass judgment." Learning to walk in your mate's moccasins is at the heart of a healthy marriage relationship. Psychologists call it empathy. It is the rare capacity to put ourselves into the shoes of our spouse and accurately see life from his or her perspective.

Empathy combines two important capacities: to analyze and to sympathize—to use our heads and to use our hearts. Our analytical capacities involve collecting facts and observing conditions. We look at a problem and break it down into its causes and then propose solutions. That's analyzing. Sympathizing is feeling for another person. It is feeling the pain of someone who's suffering or the anger of a person in rage. Sympathizing and analyzing together are the twin engines of empathy. One without the other is fine, but their true power is found in combination. We need to love with both our head and our heart to empathize.

The apostle Paul encouraged empathy when he said, "Remember those in prison as if you were their fellow prisoners, and those who are mistreated as if you yourselves were suffering" (verse 3).

When we empathize with our spouse, we put aside our expectation that he or she should be like us. We accept the fact that each of us has brought our unique personality into our marriage, and we ask ourselves questions like, "What is he feeling? What pressures does she have to cope with? What does he fear? What does she need?"

—*Les and Leslie*

Go to page 1343 for your next devotional reading.

it. ³Remember those in prison as if you were their fellow prisoners, and those who are mistreated as if you yourselves were suffering.

⁴Marriage should be honored by all, and the marriage bed kept pure, for God will judge the adulterer and all the sexually immoral. ⁵Keep your lives free from the love of money and be content with what you have, because God has said,

"Never will I leave you;
    never will I forsake you." *a*

⁶So we say with confidence,

"The Lord is my helper; I will not be
    afraid.
What can man do to me?" *b*

⁷Remember your leaders, who spoke the word of God to you. Consider the outcome of their way of life and imitate their faith. ⁸Jesus Christ is the same yesterday and today and forever.

⁹Do not be carried away by all kinds of strange teachings. It is good for our hearts to be strengthened by grace, not by ceremonial foods, which are of no value to those who eat them. ¹⁰We have an altar from which those who minister at the tabernacle have no right to eat.

¹¹The high priest carries the blood of animals into the Most Holy Place as a sin offering, but the bodies are burned outside the camp. ¹²And so Jesus also suffered outside the city gate to make the people holy through his own blood. ¹³Let us, then, go to him outside the camp, bearing the disgrace he bore. ¹⁴For here we do not have an enduring city, but we are looking for the city that is to come.

¹⁵Through Jesus, therefore, let us continually offer to God a sacrifice of praise—the fruit of lips that confess his name. ¹⁶And do not forget to do good and to share with others, for with such sacrifices God is pleased.

¹⁷Obey your leaders and submit to their authority. They keep watch over you as men who must give an account. Obey them so that their work will be a joy, not a burden, for that would be of no advantage to you.

¹⁸Pray for us. We are sure that we have a clear conscience and desire to live honorably in every way. ¹⁹I particularly urge you to pray so that I may be restored to you soon.

²⁰May the God of peace, who through the blood of the eternal covenant brought back from the dead our Lord Jesus, that great Shepherd of the sheep, ²¹equip you with everything good for doing his will, and may he work in us what is pleasing to him, through Jesus Christ, to whom be glory for ever and ever. Amen.

²²Brothers, I urge you to bear with my word of exhortation, for I have written you only a short letter.

²³I want you to know that our brother Timothy has been released. If he arrives soon, I will come with him to see you.

²⁴Greet all your leaders and all God's people. Those from Italy send you their greetings.

²⁵Grace be with you all.

---

*a*5 Deut. 31:6   *b*6 Psalm 118:6,7

James

How should I respond to my spouse when I face hard times? How can I learn to control my temper—and my mouth? How do I find real wisdom?

The book of James is loaded with straightforward advice for everyday life. The refreshing feature about this book is that James takes a no-nonsense approach to hypocrisy. He describes very real situations and offers hard-hitting, practical solutions. James shows that it's possible to believe the right things yet live the wrong way. This book will show you how to turn right doctrine into right living.

1 James, a servant of God and of the Lord Jesus Christ,

To the twelve tribes scattered among the nations:

Greetings.

Trials and Temptations

²Consider it pure joy, my brothers, whenever you face trials of many kinds, ³because you know that the testing of your faith develops perseverance. ⁴Perseverance must finish its work so that you may be mature and complete, not lacking anything. ⁵If any of you lacks wisdom, he should ask God, who gives generously to all without finding fault, and it will be given to him. ⁶But when he asks, he must believe and not doubt, because he who doubts is like a wave of the sea, blown and tossed by the wind. ⁷That man should not think he will receive anything from the Lord; ⁸he is a double-minded man, unstable in all he does.

⁹The brother in humble circumstances ought to take pride in his high position. ¹⁰But the one who is rich should take pride in his low position, because he will pass away like a wild flower. ¹¹For the sun rises with scorching heat and withers the plant; its blossom falls and its beauty is destroyed. In the same way, the rich man will fade away even while he goes about his business.

¹²Blessed is the man who perseveres under trial, because when he has stood the test, he will receive the crown of life that God has promised to those who love him.

¹³When tempted, no one should say, "God is tempting me." For God cannot be tempted by evil, nor does he tempt anyone; ¹⁴but each one is tempted when, by his own evil desire, he is dragged away and enticed. ¹⁵Then, after desire has con-

ceived, it gives birth to sin; and sin, when it is full-grown, gives birth to death.

[16]Don't be deceived, my dear brothers. [17]Every good and perfect gift is from above, coming down from the Father of the heavenly lights, who does not change like shifting shadows. [18]He chose to give us birth through the word of truth, that we might be a kind of firstfruits of all he created.

Listening and Doing

[19]My dear brothers, take note of this: Everyone should be quick to listen, slow to speak and slow to become angry, [20]for man's anger does not bring about the righteous life that God desires. [21]Therefore, get rid of all moral filth and the evil that is so prevalent and humbly accept the word planted in you, which can save you.

[22]Do not merely listen to the word, and so deceive yourselves. Do what it says. [23]Anyone who listens to the word but does not do what it says is like a man who looks at his face in a mirror [24]and, after looking at himself, goes away and immediately forgets what he looks like. [25]But the man who looks intently into the perfect law that gives freedom, and continues to do this, not forgetting what he has heard, but doing it—he will be blessed in what he does.

[26]If anyone considers himself religious and yet does not keep a tight rein on his tongue, he deceives himself and his religion is worthless. [27]Religion that God our Father accepts as pure and faultless is this: to look after orphans and widows in their distress and to keep oneself from being polluted by the world.

Favoritism Forbidden

2 My brothers, as believers in our glorious Lord Jesus Christ, don't show favoritism. [2]Suppose a man comes into your meeting wearing a gold ring and fine clothes, and a poor man in shabby clothes also comes in. [3]If you show special attention to the man wearing fine clothes and say, "Here's a good seat for you," but say to the poor man, "You stand there" or "Sit on the floor by my feet," [4]have you not discriminated among your-

Facing Trials . . . Together

Friday

JAMES 1:2–4 We have some friends who have been married more than thirty years. Now in their mid-fifties, they seem to enjoy all the blessings possible for a healthy married couple—a beautiful home, good friends, bright children and fulfilling careers. But their marriage hasn't been easy. Their second child, a boy, was just four years old when he wandered into a neighbor's yard and drowned in their swimming pool.

Faced with this tragedy and the unbearable grief that followed, this couple could have given up. After all, it is not uncommon for a marriage to dissolve in the face of overwhelming suffering. Strangely, sorrowful couples sometimes retreat to separate corners of misery, and, because misery doesn't always love company, their circumstances tear them apart instead of bring them together. But not this couple. They chose to call upon the power of love to help them weather their tragedy as husband and wife—together.

Are you and your spouse cultivating the power of love? We hope you will never be forced to test its strength, and we pray you will always rest in the courage that can come from a healthy Christian marriage: "Who shall separate us from the love of Christ? Shall trouble or hardship or persecution or famine or nakedness or danger or sword? . . . No, in all these things we are more than conquerors through him who loved us" (Romans 8:35, 37).

What a marvelous resource marriage partners can be to one another. For as we cultivate love, we are strengthening our ability to cope with all that life might bring.

—*Les and Leslie*

Go to page 1344 for your next devotional reading.

selves and become judges with evil thoughts?

⁵Listen, my dear brothers: Has not God chosen those who are poor in the eyes of the world to be rich in faith and to inherit the kingdom he promised those who love him? ⁶But you have insulted the poor. Is it not the rich who are exploiting you? Are they not the ones who are dragging you into court? ⁷Are they not the ones who are slandering the noble name of him to whom you belong?

⁸If you really keep the royal law found in Scripture, "Love your neighbor as yourself,"ᵃ you are doing right. ⁹But if you show favoritism, you sin and are convicted by the law as lawbreakers. ¹⁰For whoever keeps the whole law and yet stumbles at just one point is guilty of breaking all of it. ¹¹For he who said, "Do not commit adultery,"ᵇ also said, "Do not murder."ᶜ If you do not commit adultery but do commit murder, you have become a lawbreaker.

¹²Speak and act as those who are going to be judged by the law that gives freedom, ¹³because judgment without mercy will be shown to anyone who has not been merciful. Mercy triumphs over judgment!

Faith and Deeds

¹⁴What good is it, my brothers, if a man claims to have faith but has no deeds? Can such faith save him? ¹⁵Suppose a brother or sister is without clothes and daily food. ¹⁶If one of you says to him, "Go, I wish you well; keep warm and well fed," but does nothing about his physical needs, what good is it? ¹⁷In the same way, faith by itself, if it is not accompanied by action, is dead.

¹⁸But someone will say, "You have faith; I have deeds."

Show me your faith without deeds, and I will show you my faith by what I do. ¹⁹You believe that there is one God. Good! Even the demons believe that—and shudder.

²⁰You foolish man, do you want evidence that faith without deeds is uselessᵈ? ²¹Was not our ancestor Abraham

ᵃ8 Lev. 19:18   ᵇ11 Exodus 20:14; Deut. 5:18
ᶜ11 Exodus 20:13; Deut. 5:17   ᵈ20 Some early manuscripts *dead*

Wha'd You Say?

Quiet TIMES
with each other

JAMES 1:19 Most people talk at the rate of 120 words per minute. And most spoken material can be comprehended equally well at rates of up to 250 words per minute. What does this mean? It means that plenty of extra time is available for mental activity during a typical conversation. That's what causes us to do just the opposite of what this verse urges—most of us, most of the time, are quick to talk and slow to listen.

Jesus certainly understood the value of taking time to listen. When he encountered the emotionally disturbed, demon-possessed man who lived among the tombs in Gadara, the man was shout-

ing at Jesus: "What do you want...? Have you come here to torture us?" (Matthew 8:29). Jesus could have turned and walked away. He certainly didn't deserve to be talked to like that. Jesus could have left the poor man to his own devices. But instead, Jesus listened. He not only heard the words the man shouted, but he listened for the message of the emotions behind the words. Jesus understood that the man's outburst was really a cry for help.

When we listen to our spouse's words with the same understanding, our conversations will never be the same.

—*Les and Leslie*

Weekend Warm-up *Do you make a conscious effort to listen more than talk?*

Go to page 1345 for your next devotional reading.

considered righteous for what he did when he offered his son Isaac on the altar? ²²You see that his faith and his actions were working together, and his faith was made complete by what he did. ²³And the scripture was fulfilled that says, "Abraham believed God, and it was credited to him as righteousness," ᵃ and he was called God's friend. ²⁴You see that a person is justified by what he does and not by faith alone.

²⁵In the same way, was not even Rahab the prostitute considered righteous for what she did when she gave lodging to the spies and sent them off in a different direction? ²⁶As the body without the spirit is dead, so faith without deeds is dead.

Taming the Tongue

3 Not many of you should presume to be teachers, my brothers, because you know that we who teach will be judged more strictly. ²We all stumble in many ways. If anyone is never at fault in what he says, he is a perfect man, able to keep his whole body in check.

³When we put bits into the mouths of horses to make them obey us, we can turn the whole animal. ⁴Or take ships as an example. Although they are so large and are driven by strong winds, they are steered by a very small rudder wherever the pilot wants to go. ⁵Likewise the tongue is a small part of the body, but it makes great boasts. Consider what a great forest is set on fire by a small spark. ⁶The tongue also is a fire, a world of evil among the parts of the body. It corrupts the whole person, sets the whole course of his life on fire, and is itself set on fire by hell.

⁷All kinds of animals, birds, reptiles and creatures of the sea are being tamed and have been tamed by man, ⁸but no man can tame the tongue. It is a restless evil, full of deadly poison.

⁹With the tongue we praise our Lord and Father, and with it we curse men, who have been made in God's likeness. ¹⁰Out of the same mouth come praise and cursing. My brothers, this should not be. ¹¹Can both fresh water and salt ᵇ water flow from the same spring? ¹²My brothers, can a fig tree bear olives, or a grapevine bear figs? Neither can a salt spring produce fresh water.

Two Kinds of Wisdom

¹³Who is wise and understanding among you? Let him show it by his good life, by deeds done in the humility that comes from wisdom. ¹⁴But if you harbor bitter envy and selfish ambition in your hearts, do not boast about it or deny the truth. ¹⁵Such "wisdom" does not come down from heaven but is earthly, unspiri-

ᵃ23 Gen. 15:6   ᵇ11 Greek *bitter* (see also verse 14)

Playing Favorites

Monday

JAMES 2:1–4 When James writes in the first verse of not showing favoritism, he is saying that we need to have an inclusive attitude toward others. He is talking about letting outsiders in. Do you do that in your marriage?

Most of us become pretty comfortable in our own social circles and don't even think about stepping outside them. The most glaring example, as this passage points out, concerns socio-economic status. But playing favorites can be seen even at a church picnic. How many new people have attempted to plug into the body of Christ only to feel sidelined and forgotten? It's difficult to know. But when we become less discriminating and give a "good seat" to an outsider, something wonderful happens in a marriage. It's called shared service—reaching out to another person as a caring couple. And few things bring spouses closer together.

So the next time you get an opportunity—at a party or simply socializing in the church foyer—try a little experiment and don't play favorites. You might be surprised what it does for your marriage.

—Les and Leslie

Go to page 1346 for your next devotional reading.

tual, of the devil. [16]For where you have envy and selfish ambition, there you find disorder and every evil practice.

[17]But the wisdom that comes from heaven is first of all pure; then peace-loving, considerate, submissive, full of mercy and good fruit, impartial and sincere. [18]Peacemakers who sow in peace raise a harvest of righteousness.

Submit Yourselves to God

4 What causes fights and quarrels among you? Don't they come from your desires that battle within you? [2]You want something but don't get it. You kill and covet, but you cannot have what you want. You quarrel and fight. You do not have, because you do not ask God. [3]When you ask, you do not receive, because you ask with wrong motives, that you may spend what you get on your pleasures.

[4]You adulterous people, don't you know that friendship with the world is hatred toward God? Anyone who chooses to be a friend of the world becomes an enemy of God. [5]Or do you think Scripture says without reason that the spirit he caused to live in us envies intensely?[a] [6]But he gives us more grace. That is why Scripture says:

"God opposes the proud
    but gives grace to the humble."[b]

[7]Submit yourselves, then, to God. Resist the devil, and he will flee from you. [8]Come near to God and he will come near to you. Wash your hands, you sinners, and purify your hearts, you double-minded. [9]Grieve, mourn and wail. Change your laughter to mourning and your joy to gloom. [10]Humble yourselves before the Lord, and he will lift you up.

[11]Brothers, do not slander one another. Anyone who speaks against his brother or judges him speaks against the law and judges it. When you judge the law, you are not keeping it, but sitting in judgment on it. [12]There is only one Lawgiver and Judge, the one who is able to save and

[a]5 Or that God jealously longs for the spirit that he made to live in us; or that the Spirit he caused to live in us longs jealously   [b]6 Prov. 3:34

Living It Out

Tuesday

COUPLE MINUTES

JAMES 2:14 Over the years theologians have debated the relationship between faith and works. Since the early church it's been a hot topic; the book of James, one of the earliest New Testament books to be written, nails the real issue. While it may be possible to believe the right things yet live the wrong way, James challenges us to turn the right doctrine into right living—to let our behavior and actions show our faith. And nowhere is living out our faith more important than in our marriage and family life.

"Kids, stop arguing," one mother said, and her oldest child responded, "It's all right, Mom. Only the family is here." What is it like at your house when only the family or only your spouse is there? We know from experience that children learn what they live. In other words, how you are "when only the family is there" is what you will pass on.

While we made our share of parenting mistakes, we concentrated on building positive and healthy relationships. We tried to be open, honest and kind as we lived out our faith. And on those occasions when we simply blew it, we were quick to ask for forgiveness. Actually we believe our children learned how to ask for forgiveness because we needed to ask them to forgive us so much for harsh words, over-reactions and other transgressions.

Today we are thrilled to see the way our sons and daughters-in-law "live it out" as they relate to our grandchildren with encouragement, kindness, gentleness, love, understanding, patience, compassion and self-control. The cycle of healthy relationships spins on and on. But it can only start when you accept the challenge to live out your faith in your own marriage and family.
—*Dave and Claudia*

Go to page 1347 for your next devotional reading.

destroy. But you—who are you to judge your neighbor?

Boasting About Tomorrow

¹³Now listen, you who say, "Today or tomorrow we will go to this or that city, spend a year there, carry on business and make money." ¹⁴Why, you do not even know what will happen tomorrow. What is your life? You are a mist that appears for a little while and then vanishes. ¹⁵Instead, you ought to say, "If it is the Lord's will, we will live and do this or that." ¹⁶As it is, you boast and brag. All such boasting is evil. ¹⁷Anyone, then, who knows the good he ought to do and doesn't do it, sins.

Warning to Rich Oppressors

5 Now listen, you rich people, weep and wail because of the misery that is coming upon you. ²Your wealth has rotted, and moths have eaten your clothes. ³Your gold and silver are corroded. Their corrosion will testify against you and eat your flesh like fire. You have hoarded wealth in the last days. ⁴Look! The wages you failed to pay the workmen who mowed your fields are crying out against you. The cries of the harvesters have reached the ears of the Lord Almighty. ⁵You have lived on earth in luxury and self-indulgence. You have fattened yourselves in the day of slaughter.ᵃ ⁶You have condemned and murdered innocent men, who were not opposing you.

Patience in Suffering

⁷Be patient, then, brothers, until the Lord's coming. See how the farmer waits for the land to yield its valuable crop and how patient he is for the autumn and spring rains. ⁸You too, be patient and stand firm, because the Lord's coming is near. ⁹Don't grumble against each other, brothers, or you will be judged. The Judge is standing at the door!

¹⁰Brothers, as an example of patience in the face of suffering, take the prophets who spoke in the name of the Lord. ¹¹As you know, we consider blessed those who have persevered. You have heard of Job's perseverance and have seen what the Lord finally brought about. The Lord is full of compassion and mercy.

¹²Above all, my brothers, do not swear—not by heaven or by earth or by anything else. Let your "Yes" be yes, and your "No," no, or you will be condemned.

The Prayer of Faith

¹³Is any one of you in trouble? He should pray. Is anyone happy? Let him sing songs of praise. ¹⁴Is any one of you sick? He should call the elders of the church to pray over him and anoint him with oil in the name of the Lord. ¹⁵And the prayer offered in faith will make the sick person well; the Lord will raise him up. If he has sinned, he will be forgiven.

ᵃ5 Or *yourselves as in a day of feasting*

Easy to Live With

Wednesday

JAMES 3:16 Self-centeredness is a poison to marriage. It is often fueled by envy. And as an old Yiddish proverb states, "Envy breeds hate." We'll say it again, self-centeredness is a poison to couples. It ought to be outlawed. Nothing, or no one, is more difficult to live with than a selfish spouse.

The person who is easy to live with, on the other hand, is cooperative. He or she understands what the psalmist meant in saying, "How good and pleasant it is [to] live together in unity" (Psalm 133:1). Such an individual also has an even and stable emotional tone. Nobody is attracted to an uncontrollable temper. A good spouse communicates his or her needs openly and honestly. What they say is in sync with how they feel and what they want. They do not mask their feelings to protect their pride or even to avoid hurting their spouse's feelings. Instead, they share their innermost thoughts, the good and the bad.

—*Les and Leslie*

Go to page 1348 for your next devotional reading.

¹⁶Therefore confess your sins to each other and pray for each other so that you may be healed. The prayer of a righteous man is powerful and effective.

¹⁷Elijah was a man just like us. He prayed earnestly that it would not rain, and it did not rain on the land for three and a half years. ¹⁸Again he prayed, and the heavens gave rain, and the earth produced its crops.

¹⁹My brothers, if one of you should wander from the truth and someone should bring him back, ²⁰remember this: Whoever turns a sinner from the error of his way will save him from death and cover over a multitude of sins.

Future Plans

Thursday

JAMES 4:14–15 A number of years ago when we were making a shift in our ministry focus, we made two lists. The first was a list of things we had planned and the accompanying results. The second list was things we didn't plan, but that God dropped in our lap and the results. Guess which list was the most significant? The God-initiated plans were the ones with the lasting impact. We now have what we affectionately call our "lap page" where we record God's plans. These are the things he brings into our life. Then we make "our plans" around his.

The Bible never discourages us from planning, preparing and looking expectantly toward the future. But James gives one important qualification: As we make our plans, whether in our personal lives, business or our marriage, we need to plan with the perspective that it is God who ultimately holds the future. James encourages us to say, "If it is the Lord's will, we will live and do this or that."

Actually, knowing God will have the final say is reassuring—especially when things don't go as we planned. Have you recently experienced a change of plans? Perhaps you've just gone through a financial reversal, a career change or health and/or relationship problem. In the middle of broken plans, we can experience his peace. We can know for certain that our infinitely wise and loving heavenly Father is in control of our lives and our circumstances.

—Dave and Claudia

Go to page 1350 for your next devotional reading.

1 Peter

Peter addresses this letter to Christians scattered throughout the Roman world. His readers were suffering because of the culture's fading tolerance of Christianity. Sound familiar? Peter's letter is as relevant today as it was the day he wrote it. The apostle poses some hard challenges. Rugged times require disciplined Christian living. There are no platitudes or easy answers here. But Peter's tough advice is gift-wrapped in the language of hope: "These [sufferings] have come so that your faith—of greater worth than gold, which perishes even though refined by fire—may be proved genuine and may result in praise, glory and honor when Jesus Christ is revealed" (1:7).

1 Peter, an apostle of Jesus Christ,

To God's elect, strangers in the world, scattered throughout Pontus, Galatia, Cappadocia, Asia and Bithynia, ²who have been chosen according to the foreknowledge of God the Father, through the sanctifying work of the Spirit, for obedience to Jesus Christ and sprinkling by his blood:

Grace and peace be yours in abundance.

Praise to God for a Living Hope

³Praise be to the God and Father of our Lord Jesus Christ! In his great mercy he has given us new birth into a living hope through the resurrection of Jesus Christ from the dead, ⁴and into an inheritance that can never perish, spoil or fade—kept in heaven for you, ⁵who through faith are shielded by God's power until the coming of the salvation that is ready to be revealed in the last time. ⁶In this you greatly rejoice, though now for a little while you may have had to suffer grief in all kinds of trials. ⁷These have come so that your faith—of greater worth than gold, which perishes even though refined by fire—may be proved genuine and may result in praise, glory and honor when Jesus Christ is revealed. ⁸Though you have not seen him, you love him; and even though you do not see him now, you believe in him and are filled with an inexpressible and glorious joy, ⁹for you are receiving the goal of your faith, the salvation of your souls.

¹⁰Concerning this salvation, the

prophets, who spoke of the grace that was to come to you, searched intently and with the greatest care, [11]trying to find out the time and circumstances to which the Spirit of Christ in them was pointing when he predicted the sufferings of Christ and the glories that would follow. [12]It was revealed to them that they were not serving themselves but you, when they spoke of the things that have now been told you by those who have preached the gospel to you by the Holy Spirit sent from heaven. Even angels long to look into these things.

Be Holy

[13]Therefore, prepare your minds for action; be self-controlled; set your hope fully on the grace to be given you when Jesus Christ is revealed. [14]As obedient children, do not conform to the evil desires you had when you lived in ignorance. [15]But just as he who called you is holy, so be holy in all you do; [16]for it is written: "Be holy, because I am holy."[a]

[17]Since you call on a Father who judges each man's work impartially, live your lives as strangers here in reverent fear. [18]For you know that it was not with perishable things such as silver or gold that you were redeemed from the empty way of life handed down to you from your forefathers, [19]but with the precious blood of Christ, a lamb without blemish or defect. [20]He was chosen before the creation of the world, but was revealed in these last times for your sake. [21]Through him you believe in God, who raised him from the dead and glorified him, and so your faith and hope are in God.

[22]Now that you have purified yourselves by obeying the truth so that you have sincere love for your brothers, love one another deeply, from the heart.[b] [23]For you have been born again, not of perishable seed, but of imperishable, through the living and enduring word of God. [24]For,

"All men are like grass,

[a]16 Lev. 11:44,45; 19:2; 20:7   [b]22 Some early manuscripts *from a pure heart*

Faith on Trial

Friday

1 PETER 1:6 One way to know if your marriage will go the distance is to expose it to a little "fire." Peter tells us that trials refine our faith and "may result in praise, glory and honor when Jesus Christ is revealed" (verses 6–7).

Frank and Lois, missionaries in a former Eastern-bloc country, experienced more than their share of trials. Having just picked up their daughter at the airport for the Christmas holidays, they were enjoying their reunion. Suddenly, to Frank's horror, he realized a car was stopped in the fast lane of the busy highway. He didn't have any time to warn his family . . . any time to swerve to miss the car. The crash left bruises and Lois with a broken leg, but fortunately there were no fatalities. But there were other trials—their new car was a mess, car insurance had yet to be finalized and the police placed the blame for the accident on Frank.

What a way to start the holidays! We were amazed as we read their letters and e-mails by the wonderful way in which God saw them through each crisis. Never did we read the slightest hint from Lois that she blamed Frank (or God) for the accident or her broken leg. God provided for the repairs of their car. The other family chose not to press charges.

We learned an important lesson from Frank and Lois: Suffering can bring you together when you trust the Lord, or it can push you apart when you focus on your problems. It's your choice. The good news of 1 Peter is that God offers hope and meaning in the midst of our suffering. Let your trials pull you closer to each other and to God as you trust him to refine your own faith and your marriage.

—*Dave and Claudia*

Go to page 1352 for your next devotional reading.

and all their glory is like the
   flowers of the field;
the grass withers and the flowers fall,
25   but the word of the Lord stands
     forever."[a]

And this is the word that was preached to
you.

2 Therefore, rid yourselves of all malice
and all deceit, hypocrisy, envy, and
slander of every kind. [2]Like newborn babies, crave pure spiritual milk, so that by
it you may grow up in your salvation,
[3]now that you have tasted that the Lord is
good.

The Living Stone and a Chosen People

[4]As you come to him, the living Stone—
rejected by men but chosen by God and
precious to him— [5]you also, like living
stones, are being built into a spiritual
house to be a holy priesthood, offering
spiritual sacrifices acceptable to God
through Jesus Christ. [6]For in Scripture it
says:

"See, I lay a stone in Zion,
   a chosen and precious cornerstone,
and the one who trusts in him
   will never be put to shame."[b]

[7]Now to you who believe, this stone is
precious. But to those who do not believe,

"The stone the builders rejected
   has become the capstone,[c]"[d]

[8]and,

"A stone that causes men to stumble
   and a rock that makes them fall."[e]

They stumble because they disobey the
message—which is also what they were
destined for.

[9]But you are a chosen people, a royal
priesthood, a holy nation, a people belonging to God, that you may declare the
praises of him who called you out of
darkness into his wonderful light. [10]Once
you were not a people, but now you are
the people of God; once you had not received mercy, but now you have received
mercy.

[11]Dear friends, I urge you, as aliens and
strangers in the world, to abstain from
sinful desires, which war against your
soul. [12]Live such good lives among the
pagans that, though they accuse you of

doing wrong, they may see your good
deeds and glorify God on the day he visits us.

Submission to Rulers and Masters

[13]Submit yourselves for the Lord's sake
to every authority instituted among men:
whether to the king, as the supreme authority, [14]or to governors, who are sent by
him to punish those who do wrong and
to commend those who do right. [15]For
it is God's will that by doing good you
should silence the ignorant talk of foolish
men. [16]Live as free men, but do not use
your freedom as a cover-up for evil; live
as servants of God. [17]Show proper respect
to everyone: Love the brotherhood of believers, fear God, honor the king.

[18]Slaves, submit yourselves to your
masters with all respect, not only to those
who are good and considerate, but also to
those who are harsh. [19]For it is commendable if a man bears up under the pain of
unjust suffering because he is conscious
of God. [20]But how is it to your credit if
you receive a beating for doing wrong and
endure it? But if you suffer for doing good
and you endure it, this is commendable
before God. [21]To this you were called, because Christ suffered for you, leaving you
an example, that you should follow in his
steps.

[22]"He committed no sin,
   and no deceit was found in his
     mouth."[f]

[23]When they hurled their insults at him,
he did not retaliate; when he suffered, he
made no threats. Instead, he entrusted
himself to him who judges justly. [24]He
himself bore our sins in his body on the
tree, so that we might die to sins and live
for righteousness; by his wounds you
have been healed. [25]For you were like
sheep going astray, but now you have returned to the Shepherd and Overseer of
your souls.

Wives and Husbands

3 Wives, in the same way be submissive
to your husbands so that, if any of
them do not believe the word, they may

---

[a]25 Isaiah 40:6-8   [b]6 Isaiah 28:16   [c]7 Or
cornerstone   [d]7 Psalm 118:22   [e]8 Isaiah 8:14
[f]22 Isaiah 53:9

be won over without words by the behavior of their wives, [2]when they see the purity and reverence of your lives. [3]Your beauty should not come from outward adornment, such as braided hair and the wearing of gold jewelry and fine clothes. [4]Instead, it should be that of your inner self, the unfading beauty of a gentle and quiet spirit, which is of great worth in God's sight. [5]For this is the way the holy women of the past who put their hope in God used to make themselves beautiful. They were submissive to their own husbands, [6]like Sarah, who obeyed Abraham and called him her master. You are her daughters if you do what is right and do not give way to fear.

[7]Husbands, in the same way be considerate as you live with your wives, and treat them with respect as the weaker partner and as heirs with you of the gracious gift of life, so that nothing will hinder your prayers.

Suffering for Doing Good

[8]Finally, all of you, live in harmony with one another; be sympathetic, love as brothers, be compassionate and humble. [9]Do not repay evil with evil or insult with insult, but with blessing, because to this you were called so that you may inherit a blessing. [10]For,

"Whoever would love life
  and see good days
must keep his tongue from evil
  and his lips from deceitful speech.
[11]He must turn from evil and do good;
  he must seek peace and pursue it.
[12]For the eyes of the Lord are on the
    righteous
  and his ears are attentive to their
    prayer,
but the face of the Lord is against
  those who do evil." [a]

[13]Who is going to harm you if you are eager to do good? [14]But even if you should suffer for what is right, you are blessed. "Do not fear what they fear[b]; do not be frightened." [c] [15]But in your hearts set apart Christ as Lord. Always be prepared to give an answer to everyone who asks you to give the reason for the hope that you have. But do this with gentleness and respect, [16]keeping a clear conscience, so that those who speak maliciously

[a]12 Psalm 34:12-16　　[b]14 Or not fear their threats　　[c]14 Isaiah 8:12

The Mosquitos of Marriage

Quiet TIMES with each other

1 PETER 2:23 "You really look tired," I said to Leslie as I climbed into the car with her to run a quick errand.

"What do you mean by that?" Leslie snapped.

"Just what I said," I countered. "I know you haven't gotten much sleep, and it shows."

"Well, I'm not tired," Leslie declared, "and I find your comment very insulting."

Ever had one of these "insulting" conversations? They're a little like trying to swat mosquitos. The insults are not very big, but the more annoyed you get with them, the more irritating they become. These annoying conversations are not un-common in marriage. After all, when a man and a woman live under the same roof and spend time together, insults—intentional or not—are bound to happen.

Happy couples, however, have learned the principle practiced in this passage: When one partner feels that a comment could have been meant as a zinger, he or she makes a decision to overlook it and move one. Think of the excruciating time this saves and the hassles it avoids. To overlook a potentially harmful word is key to avoiding countless annoyances and instead building a happier marriage. —**Les and Leslie**

Weekend Warm-up When was the last time you chose to overlook an "off" comment you made to each other?

Go to page 1353 for your next devotional reading.

against your good behavior in Christ may be ashamed of their slander. [17]It is better, if it is God's will, to suffer for doing good than for doing evil. [18]For Christ died for sins once for all, the righteous for the unrighteous, to bring you to God. He was put to death in the body but made alive by the Spirit, [19]through whom[a] also he went and preached to the spirits in prison [20]who disobeyed long ago when God waited patiently in the days of Noah while the ark was being built. In it only a few people, eight in all, were saved through water, [21]and this water symbolizes baptism that now saves you also—not the removal of dirt from the body but the pledge[b] of a good conscience toward God. It saves you by the resurrection of Jesus Christ, [22]who has gone into heaven and is at God's right hand—with angels, authorities and powers in submission to him.

Living for God

4 Therefore, since Christ suffered in his body, arm yourselves also with the same attitude, because he who has suffered in his body is done with sin. [2]As a result, he does not live the rest of his earthly life for evil human desires, but

rather for the will of God. [3]For you have spent enough time in the past doing what pagans choose to do—living in debauchery, lust, drunkenness, orgies, carousing and detestable idolatry. [4]They think it strange that you do not plunge with them into the same flood of dissipation, and they heap abuse on you. [5]But they will have to give account to him who is ready to judge the living and the dead. [6]For this is the reason the gospel was preached even to those who are now dead, so that they might be judged according to men in regard to the body, but live according to God in regard to the spirit.

[7]The end of all things is near. Therefore be clear minded and self-controlled so that you can pray. [8]Above all, love each other deeply, because love covers over a multitude of sins. [9]Offer hospitality to one another without grumbling. [10]Each one should use whatever gift he has received to serve others, faithfully administering God's grace in its various forms. [11]If anyone speaks, he should do it as one speaking the very words of God. If anyone serves, he should do it with the strength

[a]18,19 Or *alive in the spirit*, [19]*through which*
[b]21 Or *response*

Bring Your Ministry Home

Monday

1 PETER 3:1 It's so much easier to be kind to people outside your own family, especially if your family members do not have the same faith you do. Ministering to strangers or acquaintances removes the element of consistent living. An acquaintance can only see your acts of kindness. They know nothing of your day-to-day lifestyle. Family members, however, know us far too well. Growing up in an unchurched home, I (Bob) was the first to accept Jesus Christ in my family. It was so much easier to live out my newfound faith on the college campus than it was when I went home on vacations. My family knew the old me, and I felt as if they were waiting to see just how long this new "attitude" was going to last. Ministering at home can be the most difficult place of ministry and

requires a very consistent lifestyle. Yet this is what we are called to do. If your spouse is not a believer, this is your great mission field. Your faith in Christ must be seen by your spouse as an asset to the marriage rather than an irritation or intimidation. Your faith must make you such a joyful, consistent servant that your spouse eventually wants to know more about what you believe. This could take more time to accomplish than you might think. But be patient. Let your spouse be won over by your consistent living and servant spirit. Don't ignore your spouse by only going out of the door to minister to others. Bring your ministry home.

—Bob and Rosemary

Go to page 1355 for your next devotional reading.

JUST BETWEEN *you* & *me*

Help for the Romantically Impaired

Take a moment to answer each of these questions on your own. Then compare your answers to your spouse's.

Yes No   In general, if a person holds onto a specific set of expectations about romance in marriage, they are very likely to be disappointed.

Yes No   For the most part, my spouse and I agree on what is romantic.

Yes No   Do I set aside time and work to create special times of romance in our marriage?

Yes No   As unromantic as it may sound, I believe romance sometimes needs to be scheduled.

Yes No   Romance deserves all the time and attention we can afford to give it.

God provides, so that in all things God may be praised through Jesus Christ. To him be the glory and the power for ever and ever. Amen.

Suffering for Being a Christian

¹²Dear friends, do not be surprised at the painful trial you are suffering, as though something strange were happening to you. ¹³But rejoice that you participate in the sufferings of Christ, so that you may be overjoyed when his glory is revealed. ¹⁴If you are insulted because of the name of Christ, you are blessed, for the Spirit of glory and of God rests on you. ¹⁵If you suffer, it should not be as a murderer or thief or any other kind of criminal, or even as a meddler. ¹⁶However, if you suffer as a Christian, do not be ashamed, but praise God that you bear that name. ¹⁷For it is time for judgment to begin with the family of God; and if it begins with us, what will the outcome be for those who do not obey the gospel of God? ¹⁸And,

"If it is hard for the righteous to be saved,

what will become of the ungodly and the sinner?"[a]

¹⁹So then, those who suffer according to God's will should commit themselves to their faithful Creator and continue to do good.

To Elders and Young Men

5 To the elders among you, I appeal as a fellow elder, a witness of Christ's sufferings and one who also will share in the glory to be revealed: ²Be shepherds of God's flock that is under your care, serving as overseers—not because you must, but because you are willing, as God wants you to be; not greedy for money, but eager to serve; ³not lording it over those entrusted to you, but being examples to the flock. ⁴And when the Chief Shepherd appears, you will receive the crown of glory that will never fade away.

⁵Young men, in the same way be submissive to those who are older. All of you, clothe yourselves with humility toward one another, because,

"God opposes the proud
but gives grace to the humble."[b]

⁶Humble yourselves, therefore, under God's mighty hand, that he may lift you up in due time. ⁷Cast all your anxiety on him because he cares for you.

⁸Be self-controlled and alert. Your enemy the devil prowls around like a roaring lion looking for someone to devour. ⁹Resist him, standing firm in the faith, because you know that your brothers throughout the world are undergoing the same kind of sufferings.

¹⁰And the God of all grace, who called you to his eternal glory in Christ, after you have suffered a little while, will himself restore you and make you strong, firm and steadfast. ¹¹To him be the power for ever and ever. Amen.

Final Greetings

¹²With the help of Silas,[c] whom I regard as a faithful brother, I have written to

---

a18 Prov. 11:31   *b5* Prov. 3:34   *c12* Greek *Silvanus,* a variant of Silas you briefly, encouraging you and testifying that this is the true grace of God. Stand fast in it.

¹³She who is in Babylon, chosen together with you, sends you her greetings, and so does my son Mark. ¹⁴Greet one another with a kiss of love.

Peace to all of you who are in Christ.

Help for the Romantically Impaired

Tuesday

1 PETER 4:8 It was our one-year anniversary—June 30, 1985. Whew! A whole year of being married. And now the celebration. Just how would we commemorate this important milestone? A romantic dinner and a walk under the stars? A rosy bouquet or a box of Godiva Chocolates? Nope. We packed a picnic lunch with tunafish sandwiches and diet pop and drove from Pasadena up the coast to Santa Barbara, three or so hours away. It was Les's idea. *Okay,* I thought. *This could be fun.* We'll have time to talk as we drive, and we can eat our lunch on the beach. But Les, now in graduate school, had a different idea. He was one week into a stressful summer school course, taking Greek! So he brought along a taped lecture to listen to on our drive and a pack of flash cards to study for his next exam.

So much for romance, at least on that day. I shouldn't paint an incorrect picture—Les can be very romantic. On my birthday this year, for example, he took me to the swankiest restaurant in town and had prearranged with the maître d' to have a gift delivered to our table with my favorite desert.

Still, in our home, romance can be a hit or miss endeavor. Of course, I do my part. Like the time I planned a weekend getaway as a surprise for Les. That's when I learned he doesn't think surprises are very romantic! Or the time I thought he would enjoy going to a theater production instead of skiing with his friends. He didn't.

Well, in case you haven't already guessed, we haven't discovered *the* secret to romance in marriage. Maybe that makes us romantically impaired. But we have discovered that a big part of cultivating romance is learning to love each other in spite of expectations that aren't met. That's a lesson couples can learn from Peter, when he writes, " . . . love each other deeply, because love covers over a multitude of sins."

—Les and Leslie

Go to page 1357 for your next devotional reading.

2 Peter

Junk mail is a fact of life. Every day your letter carrier delivers one more "once in a lifetime" opportunity or the ever popular "You have already won!" letter. If you were to sit down with the direct marketing experts who write these letters (don't call it "junk mail" to them), they'd reveal that if you want the reader to really pay attention to a bit of information, put it in the postscript—the P.S. at the end of the letter.

Peter knew something about this fact, because he packed this little book—his own P.S.—with information he didn't want his readers to miss. "Make every effort to add to your faith goodness; and to goodness, knowledge; and to knowledge, self-control; and to self-control, perseverance; and to perseverance, godliness; and to godliness, brotherly kindness; and to brotherly kindness, love" (1:5–7). Peter was writing to people who were being challenged by heresy and temptation, much the same as we are today. He said, in effect, "Don't cut corners. Don't miss the basics. Hang in there." Reading 2 Peter gives us the truth in concentrated form. A good dose of marriage "vitamins"!

1 Simon Peter, a servant and apostle of Jesus Christ,

To those who through the righteousness of our God and Savior Jesus Christ have received a faith as precious as ours:

²Grace and peace be yours in abundance through the knowledge of God and of Jesus our Lord.

Making One's Calling and Election Sure

³ His divine power has given us everything we need for life and godliness through our knowledge of him who called us by his own glory and goodness. ⁴Through these he has given us his very great and precious promises, so that through them you may participate in the divine nature and escape the corrup-

tion in the world caused by evil desires.

⁵For this very reason, make every effort to add to your faith goodness; and to goodness, knowledge; ⁶and to knowledge, self-control; and to self-control, perseverance; and to perseverance, godliness; ⁷and to godliness, brotherly kindness; and to brotherly kindness, love. ⁸For if you possess these qualities in increasing measure, they will keep you from being ineffective and unproductive in your knowledge of our Lord Jesus Christ. ⁹But if anyone does not have them, he is nearsighted and blind, and has forgotten that he has been cleansed from his past sins.

¹⁰Therefore, my brothers, be all the more eager to make your calling and election sure. For if you do these things, you will never fall, ¹¹and you will receive a rich welcome into the eternal kingdom of our Lord and Savior Jesus Christ.

Prophecy of Scripture

¹²So I will always remind you of these things, even though you know them and are firmly established in the truth you now have. ¹³I think it is right to refresh your memory as long as I live in the tent of this body, ¹⁴because I know that I will soon put it aside, as our Lord Jesus Christ has made clear to me. ¹⁵And I will make every effort to see that after my departure you will always be able to remember these things.

¹⁶We did not follow cleverly invented stories when we told you about the power and coming of our Lord Jesus Christ, but we were eyewitnesses of his majesty. ¹⁷For he received honor and glory from God the Father when the voice came to him from the Majestic Glory, saying, "This is my Son, whom I love; with him I am well pleased."[a] ¹⁸We ourselves heard this voice that came from heaven when we were with him on the sacred mountain.

¹⁹And we have the word of the prophets made more certain, and you will do well to pay attention to it, as to a light shining in a dark place, until the day dawns and the morning star rises in your hearts. ²⁰Above all, you must understand that no prophecy of Scripture came about by the prophet's own interpretation. ²¹For prophecy never had its origin in the will of man, but men spoke from God as they were carried along by the Holy Spirit.

False Teachers and Their Destruction

2 But there were also false prophets among the people, just as there will be false teachers among you. They will secretly introduce destructive heresies, even denying the sovereign Lord who bought them—bringing swift destruction on themselves. ²Many will follow their shameful ways and will bring the way of truth into disrepute. ³In their greed these teachers will exploit you with stories they have made up. Their condemnation has long been hanging over them, and their destruction has not been sleeping.

⁴For if God did not spare angels when they sinned, but sent them to hell,[b] putting them into gloomy dungeons[c] to be

---

[a]17 Matt. 17:5; Mark 9:7; Luke 9:35   [b]4 Greek *Tartarus*   [c]4 Some manuscripts *into chains of darkness*

Knowing God Together

Wednesday

2 PETER 1:5 One of the saddest questions we ever hear in our counseling office is generally uttered by a couple who has entered the second half of marriage—perhaps with an empty nest—and realizes they have no deep meaning and connection in their marriage. They eventually ask, "Is this all there is?"

This verse points to the reason couples wind up in this place. It has to do with

COUPLE MINUTES

knowing God. Sure, we can work on having faith and being good. But as this passage says, that is not enough. We must learn to know God better and discover what he wants us to do. Take a moment to ponder this issue as a couple. What are you doing alone and together to know God better?

—*Les and Leslie*

Go to page 1358 for your next devotional reading.

held for judgment; [5]if he did not spare the ancient world when he brought the flood on its ungodly people, but protected Noah, a preacher of righteousness, and seven others; [6]if he condemned the cities of Sodom and Gomorrah by burning them to ashes, and made them an example of what is going to happen to the ungodly; [7]and if he rescued Lot, a righteous man, who was distressed by the filthy lives of lawless men [8](for that righteous man, living among them day after day, was tormented in his righteous soul by the lawless deeds he saw and heard)— [9]if this is so, then the Lord knows how to rescue godly men from trials and to hold the unrighteous for the day of judgment, while continuing their punishment.[a] [10]This is especially true of those who follow the corrupt desire of the sinful nature[b] and despise authority.

Bold and arrogant, these men are not afraid to slander celestial beings; [11]yet even angels, although they are stronger and more powerful, do not bring slanderous accusations against such beings in the presence of the Lord. [12]But these men blaspheme in matters they do not understand. They are like brute beasts, creatures of instinct, born only to be caught and destroyed, and like beasts they too will perish.

[13]They will be paid back with harm for the harm they have done. Their idea of pleasure is to carouse in broad daylight. They are blots and blemishes, reveling in their pleasures while they feast with you.[c] [14]With eyes full of adultery, they never stop sinning; they seduce the unstable; they are experts in greed—an accursed brood! [15]They have left the straight way and wandered off to follow the way of Balaam son of Beor, who loved the wages of wickedness. [16]But he was rebuked for his wrongdoing by a donkey—a beast without speech—who spoke with a man's voice and restrained the prophet's madness.

[17]These men are springs without water and mists driven by a storm. Blackest darkness is reserved for them. [18]For they mouth empty, boastful words and, by appealing to the lustful desires of sinful human nature, they entice people who are just escaping from those who live in error. [19]They promise them freedom, while they themselves are slaves of depravity—for a man is a slave to whatever has mastered him. [20]If they have escaped the corruption of the world by knowing our Lord and Savior Jesus Christ and are again en-

[a]9   Or *unrighteous for punishment until the day of judgment*   [b]10   Or *the flesh*   [c]13   Some manuscripts *in their love feasts*

False Teachers

Thursday

2 PETER 2:1–2   A psychology magazine recently exposed the views of a contemporary marriage expert as somewhat suspect. The magazine devoted an entire page to comparing and contrasting him with another, less popular marriage expert. The article described the two men's fundamental messages and their differing approaches. The authors noted the two experts' differing backgrounds and educational levels. They even supplied a chart that made it easy to see how each of them, with best-sellers and sold-out seminar schedules, differed in their credentials. One, it was reported, had a license in marriage and family therapy. The other had a driver's license.

Which one do you want informing your marriage? Not that this "expert" is necessarily giving out only misinformation. His books are selling, and he is apparently helping many people. But this exposé, combined with this Scripture passage, got us thinking. As couples, we need to be careful about the kinds of teaching we look to. We need to beware of false teachers and be sure they are grounded in Biblical wisdom. Just because something or somebody is popular doesn't guarantee credibility and truth.

—*Les and Leslie*

Go to page 1359 for your next devotional reading.

tangled in it and overcome, they are worse off at the end than they were at the beginning. ²¹It would have been better for them not to have known the way of righteousness, than to have known it and then to turn their backs on the sacred command that was passed on to them. ²²Of them the proverbs are true: "A dog returns to its vomit,"ᵃ and, "A sow that is washed goes back to her wallowing in the mud."

The Day of the Lord

3 Dear friends, this is now my second letter to you. I have written both of them as reminders to stimulate you to wholesome thinking. ²I want you to recall the words spoken in the past by the holy prophets and the command given by our Lord and Savior through your apostles.

³First of all, you must understand that in the last days scoffers will come, scoffing and following their own evil desires. ⁴They will say, "Where is this 'coming' he promised? Ever since our fathers died, everything goes on as it has since the beginning of creation." ⁵But they deliberately forget that long ago by God's word the heavens existed and the earth was formed out of water and by water. ⁶By these waters also the world of that time was deluged and destroyed. ⁷By the same word the present heavens and earth are reserved for fire, being kept for the day of judgment and destruction of ungodly men.

⁸But do not forget this one thing, dear friends: With the Lord a day is like a thousand years, and a thousand years are like a day. ⁹The Lord is not slow in keeping his promise, as some understand slowness. He is patient with you, not wanting anyone to perish, but everyone to come to repentance.

¹⁰But the day of the Lord will come like a thief. The heavens will disappear with a roar; the elements will be destroyed by fire, and the earth and everything in it will be laid bare.ᵇ

¹¹Since everything will be destroyed in this way, what kind of people ought you to be? You ought to live holy and godly lives ¹²as you look forward to the day of God and speed its coming.ᶜ That day will bring about the destruction of the heavens by fire, and the elements will melt in the heat. ¹³But in keeping with his promise we are looking forward to a new heaven and a new earth, the home of righteousness.

¹⁴So then, dear friends, since you are looking forward to this, make every effort to be found spotless, blameless and at peace with him. ¹⁵Bear in mind that our Lord's patience means salvation, just as our dear brother Paul also wrote you with the wisdom that God gave him. ¹⁶He writes the same way in all his letters, speaking in them of these matters. His

---

ᵃ22 Prov. 26:11   ᵇ10 Some manuscripts be burned up   ᶜ12 Or as you wait eagerly for the day of God to come

---

You Can't Save Time in a Bottle

Friday

2 PETER 3:8 Imagine there is a bank which credits your account each morning with $86,400, carries over no balance from day to day, allows you to keep no cash balance, and every evening cancels whatever part of the amount you had failed to use during the day. What would you do? Draw out every cent, right?

Well, everyone has such a bank. Its name is "Time." Every morning, it credits you with 86,400 seconds. Every night it writes off, as lost, whatever of this you have failed to invest to good purpose. It al-

lows no overdraft. Each day it opens a new account for you. Each night it burns the record of the day. If you fail to use the day's deposits, the loss is yours. There is no going back. There is no drawing against the "tomorrow."

Time is something we too often take for granted in our marriages. So as you read this passage on God's timing, consider how you "spend" your time together. He wants every day to count.

—Les and Leslie

Go to page 1360 for your next devotional reading.

letters contain some things that are hard to understand, which ignorant and unstable people distort, as they do the other Scriptures, to their own destruction.

[17]Therefore, dear friends, since you already know this, be on your guard so that you may not be carried away by the error of lawless men and fall from your secure position. [18]But grow in the grace and knowledge of our Lord and Savior Jesus Christ. To him be glory both now and forever! Amen.

On Guard

2 PETER 3:17 Because we travel so much, we installed a security system several years ago for our home. Nothing is more jolting than to accidentally set off the alarm, but it will certainly stop anyone who's not supposed to be around! Wouldn't it be great to have a security system like that for your marriage?

Balance and caution are Biblical concepts that are hard to live out—especially in a culture that undervalues marriage. How many couples do you know who have experienced marital breakups because one or the other got out-of-balance or failed to be on their guard? Have you heard statements like, "He was married to his job" or "She spent too much time with her co-worker" or "They never found time to be alone with each other"?

If we heed Peter's warning in this passage to "be on your guard," we can protect our marriage and maintain balance. Consider the following suggestions:

• Never take your partner for granted. Do something each day to intentionally build your relationship.
• Live in the light of eternity. Choose to live out your lasting values such as purity, righteousness and holiness.
• Invest quantity as well as quality time with your partner.
• Study Scripture and pray together often.
• Worship and enjoy fellowship with other Christian couples.

As you safeguard your marriage, you can grow in the grace and knowledge of our Lord and Savior Jesus Christ. And you can glorify him!

—*Dave and Claudia*

Weekend Warm-up *If you had a security system for your marriage, would it be ringing?*

Go to page 1362 for your next devotional reading.

1 John

Many of the worldviews spinning through cyberspace today run counter to Jesus' teachings. That's why 1 John is such a relevant book for us. The apostle John writes to correct a worldview that denied that Jesus was both God and man. Though written to correct dangerous heresy, John's letter is anything but dry. Instead it is a beautiful treatise on the love of God. John stresses that we are to walk in the light of God's love and to love others with the same love we have received from him, to love "with actions and in truth" (3:18). Think about how you can do this for your spouse today.

The Word of Life

1 That which was from the beginning, which we have heard, which we have seen with our eyes, which we have looked at and our hands have touched—this we proclaim concerning the Word of life. ²The life appeared; we have seen it and testify to it, and we proclaim to you the eternal life, which was with the Father and has appeared to us. ³We proclaim to you what we have seen and heard, so that you also may have fellowship with us. And our fellowship is with the Father and with his Son, Jesus Christ. ⁴We write this to make our*ᵃ* joy complete.

Walking in the Light

⁵This is the message we have heard from him and declare to you: God is light; in him there is no darkness at all. ⁶If we claim to have fellowship with him yet walk in the darkness, we lie and do not live by the truth. ⁷But if we walk in the light, as he is in the light, we have fellowship with one another, and the blood of Jesus, his Son, purifies us from all*ᵇ* sin.

⁸If we claim to be without sin, we deceive ourselves and the truth is not in us. ⁹If we confess our sins, he is faithful and just and will forgive us our sins and purify us from all unrighteousness. ¹⁰If we claim we have not sinned, we make him out to be a liar and his word has no place in our lives.

2 My dear children, I write this to you so that you will not sin. But if anybody does sin, we have one who speaks to the Father in our defense—Jesus Christ, the Righteous One. ²He is the atoning sacrifice for our sins, and not only for ours but also for*ᶜ* the sins of the whole world.

³We know that we have come to know

---

a4 Some manuscripts *your*   *b7* Or *every*
c2 Or *He is the one who turns aside God's wrath, taking away our sins, and not only ours but also*

him if we obey his commands. ⁴The man who says, "I know him," but does not do what he commands is a liar, and the truth is not in him. ⁵But if anyone obeys his word, God's love*ᵃ* is truly made complete in him. This is how we know we are in him: ⁶Whoever claims to live in him must walk as Jesus did.

⁷Dear friends, I am not writing you a new command but an old one, which you have had since the beginning. This old command is the message you have heard. ⁸Yet I am writing you a new command; its truth is seen in him and you, because the darkness is passing and the true light is already shining.

⁹Anyone who claims to be in the light but hates his brother is still in the darkness. ¹⁰Whoever loves his brother lives in the light, and there is nothing in him*ᵇ* to make him stumble. ¹¹But whoever hates his brother is in the darkness and walks around in the darkness; he does not know where he is going, because the darkness has blinded him.

¹²I write to you, dear children,
　because your sins have been
　　forgiven on account of his
　　name.
¹³I write to you, fathers,
　because you have known him who
　　is from the beginning.

I write to you, young men,
　because you have overcome the
　　evil one.
I write to you, dear children,
　because you have known the
　　Father.
¹⁴I write to you, fathers,
　because you have known him who
　　is from the beginning.
I write to you, young men,
　because you are strong,
　and the word of God lives in you,
　and you have overcome the evil
　　one.

Do Not Love the World

¹⁵Do not love the world or anything in the world. If anyone loves the world, the love of the Father is not in him. ¹⁶For everything in the world—the cravings of sinful man, the lust of his eyes and the boasting of what he has and does—comes not from the Father but from the world. ¹⁷The world and its desires pass away, but the man who does the will of God lives forever.

Warning Against Antichrists

¹⁸Dear children, this is the last hour; and as you have heard that the antichrist

ᵃ5 Or *word, love for God*　　*ᵇ10* Or *it*

Confession With Discretion

Monday

1 JOHN 1:9 Confession is good for the soul, but false confession causes relational chaos. I know a woman who could win a blue ribbon for the originality and frequency of her confessions. She takes full responsibility for any and every unfortunate situation. She sees herself as responsible for bad weather ("I'm sorry about this rain. I should have known better than to schedule a picnic in late spring"), unexpected road construction ("Why didn't I call AAA before we left home?"), or anyone's disappointment about anything ("I'm so sorry, I would do anything to make you feel better"). Her guilt is boundless. Like Atlas, she tries to carry the whole world on their shoulders.

She has caused such strife in her marriage due to her compulsion for repeated confessions that, in a counseling session, her husband said, "If she says 'I'm sorry' one more time, I'm going to explode!"

Let's make this clear: Confession is a healing process. Sometimes, however, confession can be used as an excuse to wallow in guilt. Therefore, confession must be done with discretion.

If you're confessing just to make yourself feel better—not to change your attitude or behavior—maybe you should rethink it.

—**Les and Leslie**

Go to page 1363 for your next devotional reading.

is coming, even now many antichrists have come. This is how we know it is the last hour. ¹⁹They went out from us, but they did not really belong to us. For if they had belonged to us, they would have remained with us; but their going showed that none of them belonged to us.

²⁰But you have an anointing from the Holy One, and all of you know the truth.ᵃ ²¹I do not write to you because you do not know the truth, but because you do know it and because no lie comes from the truth. ²²Who is the liar? It is the man who denies that Jesus is the Christ. Such a man is the antichrist—he denies the Father and the Son. ²³No one who denies the Son has the Father; whoever acknowledges the Son has the Father also.

²⁴See that what you have heard from the beginning remains in you. If it does, you also will remain in the Son and in the Father. ²⁵And this is what he promised us—even eternal life.

²⁶I am writing these things to you about those who are trying to lead you astray. ²⁷As for you, the anointing you received from him remains in you, and you do not need anyone to teach you. But as his anointing teaches you about all things and as that anointing is real, not counterfeit—just as it has taught you, remain in him.

Children of God

²⁸And now, dear children, continue in him, so that when he appears we may be confident and unashamed before him at his coming.

²⁹If you know that he is righteous, you know that everyone who does what is right has been born of him.

3 How great is the love the Father has lavished on us, that we should be called children of God! And that is what we are! The reason the world does not know us is that it did not know him. ²Dear friends, now we are children of God, and what we will be has not yet

ᵃ20 Some manuscripts *and you know all things*

Material Marriage

1 JOHN 2:15 In our society, it's sometimes easy to lose sight of how things can become more important than relationships. One of the best measures of how you are doing in this area has to do with your giving quotient.

The apostle Paul provides a great example of giving when talking about the Macedonians (2 Corinthians 8). He writes, "For I testify that they gave as much as they were able, and even beyond their ability. Entirely on their own, they urgently pleaded with us for the privilege of sharing in this service to the saints" (verses 3–4). They gave voluntarily, not because somebody twisted their arms behind their backs. They *wanted* to share in the joy of helping. A little later in that same letter, the apostle encourages this spirit of voluntary spontaneity in giving: "Each man should give what he has decided in his heart to give, not reluctantly or under compulsion, for God loves a cheerful giver" (9:7).

Why is our motivation in giving so important? Well, consider the Pharisees and teachers of the law who used tithing to camouflage their selfishness. They were so ritualistic about tithing that they would count the small herbs in their garden to be sure they were tithing on all they had. Of course, they were missing the whole point. Listen to what Jesus said to them: "Woe to you, teachers of the law and Pharisees, you hypocrites! You give a tenth of your spices—mint, dill and cummin. But you have neglected the more important matters of the law—justice, mercy and faithfulness. You should have practiced the latter, without neglecting the former. You blind guides! You strain out a gnat but swallow a camel" (Matthew 23:23–24).

Here's the bottom line. The Bible calls us to give money away. And to do that, we must take Christ's famous exhortation and apply it to our checkbooks: "Where your treasure is," Jesus said, "there your heart will be also" (Matthew 6:21). **—Les and Leslie**

Go to page 1365 for your next devotional reading.

been made known. But we know that when he appears,[a] we shall be like him, for we shall see him as he is. ³Everyone who has this hope in him purifies himself, just as he is pure.

⁴Everyone who sins breaks the law; in fact, sin is lawlessness. ⁵But you know that he appeared so that he might take away our sins. And in him is no sin. ⁶No one who lives in him keeps on sinning. No one who continues to sin has either seen him or known him.

⁷Dear children, do not let anyone lead you astray. He who does what is right is righteous, just as he is righteous. ⁸He who does what is sinful is of the devil, because the devil has been sinning from the beginning. The reason the Son of God appeared was to destroy the devil's work. ⁹No one who is born of God will continue to sin, because God's seed remains in him; he cannot go on sinning, because he has been born of God. ¹⁰This is how we know who the children of God are and who the children of the devil are: Anyone who does not do what is right is not a child of God; nor is anyone who does not love his brother.

Love One Another

¹¹This is the message you heard from the beginning: We should love one another. ¹²Do not be like Cain, who belonged to the evil one and murdered his brother. And why did he murder him? Because his own actions were evil and his brother's were righteous. ¹³Do not be surprised, my brothers, if the world hates you. ¹⁴We know that we have passed from death to life, because we love our brothers. Anyone who does not love remains in death. ¹⁵Anyone who hates his brother is a murderer, and you know that no murderer has eternal life in him.

¹⁶This is how we know what love is: Jesus Christ laid down his life for us. And we ought to lay down our lives for our brothers. ¹⁷If anyone has material possessions and sees his brother in need but has no pity on him, how can the love of God be in him? ¹⁸Dear children, let us not love with words or tongue but with actions and in truth. ¹⁹This then is how we know that we belong to the truth, and how we set our hearts at rest in his presence

²⁰whenever our hearts condemn us. For God is greater than our hearts, and he knows everything.

²¹Dear friends, if our hearts do not condemn us, we have confidence before God ²²and receive from him anything we ask, because we obey his commands and do what pleases him. ²³And this is his command: to believe in the name of his Son, Jesus Christ, and to love one another as he commanded us. ²⁴Those who obey his commands live in him, and he in them. And this is how we know that he lives in us: We know it by the Spirit he gave us.

Test the Spirits

4 Dear friends, do not believe every spirit, but test the spirits to see whether they are from God, because many false prophets have gone out into the world. ²This is how you can recognize the Spirit of God: Every spirit that acknowledges that Jesus Christ has come in the flesh is from God, ³but every spirit that does not acknowledge Jesus is not from God. This is the spirit of the antichrist, which you have heard is coming and even now is already in the world.

⁴You, dear children, are from God and have overcome them, because the one who is in you is greater than the one who is in the world. ⁵They are from the world and therefore speak from the viewpoint of the world, and the world listens to them. ⁶We are from God, and whoever knows God listens to us; but whoever is not from God does not listen to us. This is how we recognize the Spirit[b] of truth and the spirit of falsehood.

God's Love and Ours

⁷Dear friends, let us love one another, for love comes from God. Everyone who loves has been born of God and knows God. ⁸Whoever does not love does not know God, because God is love. ⁹This is how God showed his love among us: He sent his one and only Son[c] into the world that we might live through him. ¹⁰This is love: not that we loved God, but that he loved us and sent his Son as an

a2 Or when it is made known   b6 Or spirit
c9 Or his only begotten Son

atoning sacrifice for[a] our sins. [11]Dear friends, since God so loved us, we also ought to love one another. [12]No one has ever seen God; but if we love one another, God lives in us and his love is made complete in us.

[13]We know that we live in him and he in us, because he has given us of his Spirit. [14]And we have seen and testify that the Father has sent his Son to be the Savior of the world. [15]If anyone acknowledges that Jesus is the Son of God, God lives in him and he in God. [16]And so we know and rely on the love God has for us.

God is love. Whoever lives in love lives in God, and God in him. [17]In this way, love is made complete among us so that we will have confidence on the day of judgment, because in this world we are like him. [18]There is no fear in love. But perfect love drives out fear, because fear has to do with punishment. The one who fears is not made perfect in love.

[19]We love because he first loved us. [20]If anyone says, "I love God," yet hates his brother, he is a liar. For anyone who does not love his brother, whom he has seen, cannot love God, whom he has not seen.

[21]And he has given us this command: Whoever loves God must also love his brother.

Faith in the Son of God

5 Everyone who believes that Jesus is the Christ is born of God, and everyone who loves the father loves his child as well. [2]This is how we know that we love the children of God: by loving God and carrying out his commands. [3]This is love for God: to obey his commands. And his commands are not burdensome, [4]for everyone born of God overcomes the world. This is the victory that has overcome the world, even our faith. [5]Who is it that overcomes the world? Only he who believes that Jesus is the Son of God.

[6]This is the one who came by water and blood—Jesus Christ. He did not come by water only, but by water and blood. And it is the Spirit who testifies, because the Spirit is the truth. [7]For there are three

[a] 10 Or *as the one who would turn aside his wrath, taking away*

Love One Another

Wednesday

1 JOHN 4:7 Remember the Cuban Missile Crisis? While Kennedy and his advisers were making international decisions in the White House, we were making marital decisions in Atlanta, Georgia. The anxiety of whether the world would survive catapulted us into a serious conversation about getting married immediately, before we even finished college. It was about the same time the Beatles were singing "All You Need Is Love." We honestly thought the world was going to get blown up before we would have a chance to live together as husband and wife—so we just did it! We got married. Our love would surely see us through any difficulties. Uh huh . . .

While we quickly discovered that marriage takes more than love, the greatest lesson we learned was that God's love is the very foundation for a successful Chris-

tian marriage. John could have been writing about marriage in verse 7 when he says, "Dear friends, let us love one another, for love comes from God. Everyone who loves has been born of God and knows God."

God's love is central to marriage. And our relationship to him should make a tremendous difference in our relationship with our spouse—especially if we express a Christlike love. God's love is unconditional, sacrificial, accepting, generous, forgiving and lasting.

For a wonderful picture of God's love, flip back to 1 Corinthians 13 and read verses 4–6 (page 1252). Now compare God's love for you with your love for your spouse. Let God's perfect love inspire you to better love your spouse.

—Dave and Claudia

Go to page 1366 for your next devotional reading.

that testify: [8]the[a] Spirit, the water and the blood; and the three are in agreement. [9]We accept man's testimony, but God's testimony is greater because it is the testimony of God, which he has given about his Son. [10]Anyone who believes in the Son of God has this testimony in his heart. Anyone who does not believe God has made him out to be a liar, because he has not believed the testimony God has given about his Son. [11]And this is the testimony: God has given us eternal life, and this life is in his Son. [12]He who has the Son has life; he who does not have the Son of God does not have life.

Concluding Remarks

[13]I write these things to you who believe in the name of the Son of God so that you may know that you have eternal life. [14]This is the confidence we have in approaching God: that if we ask anything according to his will, he hears us. [15]And if we know that he hears us—whatever we ask—we know that we have what we asked of him.

[16]If anyone sees his brother commit a sin that does not lead to death, he should pray and God will give him life. I refer to those whose sin does not lead to death. There is a sin that leads to death. I am not saying that he should pray about that. [17]All wrongdoing is sin, and there is sin that does not lead to death.

[18]We know that anyone born of God does not continue to sin; the one who was born of God keeps him safe, and the evil one cannot harm him. [19]We know that we are children of God, and that the whole world is under the control of the evil one. [20]We know also that the Son of God has come and has given us understanding, so that we may know him who is true. And we are in him who is true—even in his Son Jesus Christ. He is the true God and eternal life.

[21]Dear children, keep yourselves from idols.

[a]7,8 Late manuscripts of the Vulgate *testify in heaven: the Father, the Word and the Holy Spirit, and these three are one. 8And there are three that testify on earth: the* (not found in any Greek manuscript before the sixteenth century)

Are You Listening?

Thursday

1 JOHN 5:14 Nothing is more irritating for me than to start to tell something to Dave and realize he isn't listening! Actually, I often start a sentence and after a few words, I pause to see if Dave is listening. If not, I start over. Frustrating? Extremely! Fortunately when we talk with God, we don't have to work to get his attention. We know before we even say the first word, he is listening. Wouldn't it be wonderful if we knew our spouse always listened?

How well do you listen to your spouse? Listening is more than politely waiting for your turn to talk. To really listen, you need to focus on what the other is saying, and you need to listen with your heart. What are the feelings behind the words you're hearing? The ultimate goal of listening is to understand the other.

According to this passage, not only does God listen to us, but he also understands.

And when we ask for help according to his will, he answers. An even deeper level of listening is when, together, you talk to and listen to God. Praying together has blessed our lives and also our marriage, but it hasn't always been easy. When we first tried to pray together, one of us was more verbal than the other—okay, it was me. I would get "on a roll" and, when I had finished praying, all Dave could say was "Amen." Not a great experience. However, through the years we became more comfortable praying together.

At times we share silence and listen for God to speak to our hearts. Actually, shared silence is the Quaker model of prayer, and it's a great way to listen to God. You can pray silently together. It's an easy first step in praying and worshiping together.

—*Dave and Claudia*

Go to page 1368 for your next devotional reading.

2 John

John carried the name *"elder"* as an endearing nickname among the Christians who knew him. He was an old man when he wrote this tiny letter. Like his other short epistles, the book of 2 John was written to believers who were dealing with frauds and hypocrites: "deceivers, who do not acknowledge Jesus Christ as coming in the flesh" (verse 7). But this letter was especially written for a "chosen lady and her children" (verse 1).

This fact raises certain questions. Was this "chosen lady" a single mother raising children in a fatherless home? Or was John's address a figurative representation of a local church? With both of these possibilities in mind, read this short letter and hear this precious old man's words of encouragement and challenge. It's a very short letter, but it's great.

¹The elder,

To the chosen lady and her children, whom I love in the truth—and not I only, but also all who know the truth— ²because of the truth, which lives in us and will be with us forever:

³Grace, mercy and peace from God the Father and from Jesus Christ, the Father's Son, will be with us in truth and love.

⁴It has given me great joy to find some of your children walking in the truth, just as the Father commanded us. ⁵And now, dear lady, I am not writing you a new command but one we have had from the beginning. I ask that we love one another. ⁶And this is love: that we walk in obedience to his commands. As you have heard from the beginning, his command is that you walk in love.

⁷Many deceivers, who do not acknowledge Jesus Christ as coming in the flesh, have gone out into the world. Any such person is the deceiver and the antichrist. ⁸Watch out that you do not lose what you have worked for, but that you may be rewarded fully. ⁹Anyone who runs ahead and does not continue in the teaching of Christ does not have God; whoever continues in the teaching has both the Father

and the Son. [10]If anyone comes to you and does not bring this teaching, do not take him into your house or welcome him. [11]Anyone who welcomes him shares in his wicked work.

[12]I have much to write to you, but I do not want to use paper and ink. Instead, I hope to visit you and talk with you face to face, so that our joy may be complete.

[13]The children of your chosen sister send their greetings.

Truth or Consequences

Friday

2 JOHN He lied. She lied. Not a little lie, like denying that he ate the last chocolate chip cookie. Or acting like she loved the hot pink scarf she got for Valentine's Day. But it wasn't a huge, marriage-crushing lie, like denying an affair.

He lied about working late when he was out with his buddies from the office. She lied about dropping off some dry-cleaning that was supposed to be ready by the weekend. He lied about the price he paid for his new golf club. She lied about all of the bills being paid, when in reality the checkbook balance didn't even begin to cover the deficits.

If your spouse had been honest, you might have been hurt or angry, you might have had a fight or a long talk, but you almost certainly could have lived with the truth.

What you can't live with is your spouse lying to you. You wonder, *How could he or she pull such a sleazy maneuver? If my partner lied about this, what else might he or she lie about?* How can you ever trust your spouse again? You thought you had an open, honest relationship, and now you feel like it's a sham.

When a partner lies to you, it's natural to feel as if the whole relationship has been called into question—because, in a sense, it has. But before you let suspicion tear the two of you apart, take some time to look for the larger truth behind the lie—the truth about you, about your partner and about what you really expect from each other.

It may be, for instance, that, while you give lip service to the value of honesty, the two of you have actually set up a marriage that encourages lying. This can happen when you try to preserve the perfect, unrealistic world of romance you had as a dating couple, insisting that the marriage remain endlessly loving, fun, tranquil, nonthreatening. Over time, it can seem as if neither one of you will tolerate anything less—won't tolerate, in other words, the truth. Yikes. Thank goodness it doesn't have to remain this way.

—Les and Leslie

Go to page 1370 for your next devotional reading.

3 John

What's the
correct way to handle opposition, especially
when that opposition comes from someone on an ego trip?
Third John provides some insight. It seems that Diotrephes
had rejected the itinerant teachers John sent to his church
and had alienated those who were trying to be hospitable.
John commends his friend Gaius for his faithfulness and love
for those traveling teachers. John doesn't avoid the problem
but deals with it honestly and directly—a great example for
spouses then and now!

¹The elder,

To my dear friend Gaius, whom I love in the truth.

²Dear friend, I pray that you may enjoy good health and that all may go well with you, even as your soul is getting along well. ³It gave me great joy to have some brothers come and tell about your faithfulness to the truth and how you continue to walk in the truth. ⁴I have no greater joy than to hear that my children are walking in the truth.

⁵Dear friend, you are faithful in what you are doing for the brothers, even though they are strangers to you. ⁶They have told the church about your love. You will do well to send them on their way in a manner worthy of God. ⁷It was for the sake of the Name that they went out, receiving no help from the pagans. ⁸We ought therefore to show hospitality to such men so that we may work together for the truth.

⁹I wrote to the church, but Diotrephes, who loves to be first, will have nothing to do with us. ¹⁰So if I come, I will call attention to what he is doing, gossiping maliciously about us. Not satisfied with that, he refuses to welcome the brothers. He also stops those who want to do so and puts them out of the church.

¹¹Dear friend, do not imitate what is evil but what is good. Anyone who does what is good is from God. Anyone who does what is evil has not seen God. ¹²De-

metrius is well spoken of by everyone—and even by the truth itself. We also speak well of him, and you know that our testimony is true. 13I have much to write you, but I do not want to do so with pen and ink. 14I

hope to see you soon, and we will talk face to face.

Peace to you. The friends here send their greetings. Greet the friends there by name.

A Purposeful Home

3 JOHN 4–8 If you came to our house for dinner, you most likely would eat store-bought lasagna, but hopefully it would be served with fun and laughter. And you would probably eat by candlelight—that's the best way to hide dust! Being hospitable has more to do with loving people than it does with gourmet meals and dust-free furniture. Hopefully if you came to our house, you would experience God's love.

God calls us all to hospitality and service—to bring his love and truth to others—and the process can start intentionally in our homes.

You can follow Gaius's example and show hospitality to others. In our fast-paced world, hospitality is a much-needed gift. And it can be a gift to your marriage when together you choose to serve others. But first you need to serve each other. Mar-

Quiet TIMES with each other

riages would be revolutionized if we each had a servant's heart. It's hard to learn to serve each other, especially in the closeness of a marriage relationship, but it is an important part of developing spiritual intimacy.

When we acknowledge that our life together is part of God's divine purpose, we look for ways to live that out in service to others. Why not make a list of ways that you can serve others together? Perhaps God will use your gift of hospitality through hosting a couples' Bible study in your home or by providing a place for visiting missionaries.

Not only will your relationship be enriched, but your children who are watching will also learn the joy of serving others. Think about it. Hospitality and service are wonderful legacies to pass on to future generations.   **—Dave and Claudia**

Weekend Warm-up *How about inviting a couple you know (or would like to know) over to your home for dinner?*

Go to page 1372 for your next devotional reading.

Jude

Sometimes a slight variation of the truth is like a small spark of error that starts an inferno of heresy. Jude understood this, which is why he wrote this letter. Immoral people in the church were trying to convince believers that being saved by God's grace gave them freedom to sin. You can imagine what they said: "Our sins are forgiven by grace and we are no longer under the law; go ahead and sin away because it doesn't matter." Jude's answer sounds an alarm that demands a response of unwavering faith.

When you're tempted to let things slide in your marriage, remember Jude's warning.

¹Jude, a servant of Jesus Christ and a brother of James,

To those who have been called, who are loved by God the Father and kept by*a* Jesus Christ:

²Mercy, peace and love be yours in abundance.

The Sin and Doom of Godless Men

³Dear friends, although I was very eager to write to you about the salvation we share, I felt I had to write and urge you to contend for the faith that was once for all entrusted to the saints. ⁴For certain men whose condemnation was written about*b* long ago have secretly slipped in among you. They are godless men, who change the grace of our God into a license for immorality and deny Jesus Christ our only Sovereign and Lord.

⁵Though you already know all this, I want to remind you that the Lord*c* delivered his people out of Egypt, but later destroyed those who did not believe. ⁶And the angels who did not keep their positions of authority but abandoned their own home—these he has kept in darkness, bound with everlasting chains for judgment on the great Day. ⁷In a similar way, Sodom and Gomorrah and the surrounding towns gave themselves up to sexual immorality and perversion. They serve as an example of those who suffer the punishment of eternal fire.

⁸In the very same way, these dreamers pollute their own bodies, reject authority and slander celestial beings. ⁹But even the archangel Michael, when he was disput-

a1 Or *for; or in*   *b4* Or *men who were marked out for condemnation*   *c5* Some early manuscripts *Jesus* ing with the devil about the body of Moses, did not dare to bring a slanderous accusation against him, but said, "The Lord rebuke you!" [10]Yet these men speak abusively against whatever they do not understand; and what things they do understand by instinct, like unreasoning animals—these are the very things that destroy them.

[11]Woe to them! They have taken the way of Cain; they have rushed for profit into Balaam's error; they have been destroyed in Korah's rebellion.

[12]These men are blemishes at your love feasts, eating with you without the slightest qualm—shepherds who feed only themselves. They are clouds without rain, blown along by the wind; autumn trees, without fruit and uprooted—twice dead. [13]They are wild waves of the sea, foaming up their shame; wandering stars, for whom blackest darkness has been reserved forever.

[14]Enoch, the seventh from Adam, prophesied about these men: "See, the Lord is coming with thousands upon thousands of his holy ones [15]to judge everyone, and to convict all the ungodly of all the ungodly acts they have done in the ungodly way, and of all the harsh words ungodly sinners have spoken against him." [16]These men are grumblers and faultfinders; they follow their own evil desires; they boast about themselves and flatter others for their own advantage.

A Call to Persevere

[17]But, dear friends, remember what the apostles of our Lord Jesus Christ foretold. [18]They said to you, "In the last times there will be scoffers who will follow their own ungodly desires." [19]These are the men who divide you, who follow mere natural instincts and do not have the Spirit.

[20]But you, dear friends, build yourselves up in your most holy faith and pray in the Holy Spirit. [21]Keep yourselves in God's love as you wait for the mercy of our Lord Jesus Christ to bring you to eternal life.

[22]Be merciful to those who doubt; [23]snatch others from the fire and save them; to others show mercy, mixed with fear—hating even the clothing stained by corrupted flesh.

Doxology

[24]To him who is able to keep you from falling and to present you before his glorious presence without fault and with great joy— [25]to the only God our Savior be glory, majesty, power and authority, through Jesus Christ our Lord, before all ages, now and forevermore! Amen.

Honest to Goodness Doubt

Monday

JUDE 22 Are you ever threatened by your partner's doubt? Some people feel uneasy with, or even resent, a spouse who doubts spiritually. They lose sight of the fact that faith matures because of, not in spite of, doubt. They forget that a question that is not seriously asked will not produce the richness and depth of an adequate answer and commitment. The most destructive thing a husband or wife can do to a spouse passing through a period of honest uncertainty is to attempt to silence them. Although the Bible strongly warns against unbelief, there is not a single passage to discourage honest to goodness doubt. In fact, this passage urges us to be merciful to those who doubt.

Doubt and belief are compatible. As odd as this may sound, doubt is not a hazard to faith; it may be the necessary catalyst in bringing a developing faith to maturity.

—**Les and Leslie**

Go to page 1374 for your next devotional reading.

Revelation

We've all experienced the moment when we said, "I do" to our spouse. In some ways, we feel we've reached a culmination, an achievement on our wedding day. But, as with graduation ceremonies that honor young men and women who have successfully completed their course work, our wedding day should be called commencement, which means "initiation" or "beginning." The wedding ceremony signals not so much the end of one era as the beginning of another. The man and woman are starting a new life together as one.

Because it comes at the end of the Bible, some consider the book of Revelation to be the finish line—the end of the story. But we know that our lives on this earth are just the "dating years," just the course work. Revelation is our commencement. We're getting ready to live forever. Live today in the light of that eternal perspective.

Prologue

1 The revelation of Jesus Christ, which God gave him to show his servants what must soon take place. He made it known by sending his angel to his servant John, [2]who testifies to everything he saw— that is, the word of God and the testimony of Jesus Christ. [3]Blessed is the one who reads the words of this prophecy, and blessed are those who hear it and take to heart what is written in it, because the time is near.

Greetings and Doxology

[4]John,

To the seven churches in the province of Asia:

Grace and peace to you from him who is, and who was, and who is to come, and from the seven spirits[a] before his throne, [5]and from Jesus Christ, who is the faithful

---

a 4 Or the sevenfold Spirit

witness, the firstborn from the dead, and the ruler of the kings of the earth.

To him who loves us and has freed us from our sins by his blood, ⁶and has made us to be a kingdom and priests to serve his God and Father—to him be glory and power for ever and ever! Amen.

⁷Look, he is coming with the clouds,
    and every eye will see him,
even those who pierced him;
    and all the peoples of the earth
        will mourn because of him.
            So shall it be! Amen.

⁸"I am the Alpha and the Omega," says the Lord God, "who is, and who was, and who is to come, the Almighty."

One Like a Son of Man

⁹I, John, your brother and companion in the suffering and kingdom and patient endurance that are ours in Jesus, was on the island of Patmos because of the word of God and the testimony of Jesus. ¹⁰On the Lord's Day I was in the Spirit, and I heard behind me a loud voice like a trumpet, ¹¹which said: "Write on a scroll what you see and send it to the seven churches:

to Ephesus, Smyrna, Pergamum, Thyatira, Sardis, Philadelphia and Laodicea."

¹²I turned around to see the voice that was speaking to me. And when I turned I saw seven golden lampstands, ¹³and among the lampstands was someone "like a son of man,"[a] dressed in a robe reaching down to his feet and with a golden sash around his chest. ¹⁴His head and hair were white like wool, as white as snow, and his eyes were like blazing fire. ¹⁵His feet were like bronze glowing in a furnace, and his voice was like the sound of rushing waters. ¹⁶In his right hand he held seven stars, and out of his mouth came a sharp double-edged sword. His face was like the sun shining in all its brilliance.

¹⁷When I saw him, I fell at his feet as though dead. Then he placed his right hand on me and said: "Do not be afraid. I am the First and the Last. ¹⁸I am the Living One; I was dead, and behold I am alive for ever and ever! And I hold the keys of death and Hades.

¹⁹"Write, therefore, what you have seen, what is now and what will take

[a] 13 Daniel 7:13

Fan the Flame

Tuesday

REVELATION 2:4–5   A newfound faith in Christ is exciting. It is also easy to lose. That initial zeal and joy of the Christian walk will not automatically last forever. The newness of the relationship with the Father, free of guilt and full of purpose, is thrilling but must be maintained. If it is not maintained, the pressures of the world around us will douse the fire. Prayer and obedience are essential to keep the original fervor alive.

    This principle also applies to our marriages. We begin our relationships passionately with high expectations. The newness of our love for each other propels us through the initial adjustment period. However, as the complexities and concerns of life begin to place pressure on the relationship, we can lose our excitement. Just as our spiritual lives need continual maintenance, so do our marriages.

    First, it is important to anticipate the reality stage. Knowing that we as a couple will inevitably enter that stage helps us not to become disillusioned. Both spouses are human beings who are going to make mistakes. That is a reality. There will be times of disagreement.

    Second, couples need to maintain communication. They need to talk about how they can keep the joy of their love alive. Relationships take time, effort and thought. Just as the benefits of renewing the enthusiasm for our spiritual lives are immeasurable, so is renewing our marriage. Excitement about the marriage is not a flash of fire that ignites and then quickly burns out. It's an ongoing flame that must be maintained.   **—Bob and Rosemary**

Go to page 1377 for your next devotional reading.

place later. [20]The mystery of the seven stars that you saw in my right hand and of the seven golden lampstands is this: The seven stars are the angels[a] of the seven churches, and the seven lampstands are the seven churches.

To the Church in Ephesus

2 "To the angel[b] of the church in Ephesus write:

These are the words of him who holds the seven stars in his right hand and walks among the seven golden lampstands: [2]I know your deeds, your hard work and your perseverance. I know that you cannot tolerate wicked men, that you have tested those who claim to be apostles but are not, and have found them false. [3]You have persevered and have endured hardships for my name, and have not grown weary.

[4]Yet I hold this against you: You have forsaken your first love. [5]Remember the height from which you have fallen! Repent and do the things you did at first. If you do not repent, I will come to you and remove your lampstand from its place. [6]But you have this in your favor: You hate the practices of the Nicolaitans, which I also hate.

[7]He who has an ear, let him hear what the Spirit says to the churches. To him who overcomes, I will give the right to eat from the tree of life, which is in the paradise of God.

To the Church in Smyrna

[8]"To the angel of the church in Smyrna write:

These are the words of him who is the First and the Last, who died and came to life again. [9]I know your afflictions and your poverty—yet you are rich! I know the slander of those who say they are Jews and are not, but are a synagogue of Satan. [10]Do not be afraid of what you are about to suffer. I tell you, the devil will put some of you in prison to test you, and you will suffer persecution for ten days. Be faithful, even to the

Fan the Flame

Take a moment to answer each of these questions on your own. Then compare your answers to your spouse's.

Yes No I can think of several little things I used to do for my spouse when we were dating that I still do now.

Yes No I get excited when I see something I know my spouse would like and I can get it.

Yes No It makes me happier to do something for my spouse than to have my spouse do something for me.

Yes No When I feel my spouse takes me for granted, I am comfortable talking about it.

point of death, and I will give you the crown of life.

[11]He who has an ear, let him hear what the Spirit says to the churches. He who overcomes will not be hurt at all by the second death.

To the Church in Pergamum

[12]"To the angel of the church in Pergamum write:

These are the words of him who has the sharp, double-edged sword. [13]I know where you live—where Satan has his throne. Yet you remain true to my name. You did not renounce your faith in me, even in the days of Antipas, my faithful witness, who was put to death in your city— where Satan lives.

[14]Nevertheless, I have a few things against you: You have people there who hold to the teaching of Balaam, who taught Balak to entice the Israelites to sin by eating food sacrificed to idols and by committing sexual immorality. [15]Likewise you also have those who hold to the teaching of the Nicolaitans. [16]Re-

[a]20 Or *messengers*   [b]1 Or *messenger*; also in verses 8, 12 and 18

pent therefore! Otherwise, I will soon come to you and will fight against them with the sword of my mouth.

[17]He who has an ear, let him hear what the Spirit says to the churches. To him who overcomes, I will give some of the hidden manna. I will also give him a white stone with a new name written on it, known only to him who receives it.

To the Church in Thyatira

[18]"To the angel of the church in Thyatira write:

These are the words of the Son of God, whose eyes are like blazing fire and whose feet are like burnished bronze. [19]I know your deeds, your love and faith, your service and perseverance, and that you are now doing more than you did at first.

[20]Nevertheless, I have this against you: You tolerate that woman Jezebel, who calls herself a prophetess. By her teaching she misleads my servants into sexual immorality and the eating of food sacrificed to idols. [21]I have given her time to repent of her immorality, but she is unwilling. [22]So I will cast her on a bed of suffering, and I will make those who commit adultery with her suffer intensely, unless they repent of her ways. [23]I will strike her children dead. Then all the churches will know that I am he who searches hearts and minds, and I will repay each of you according to your deeds. [24]Now I say to the rest of you in Thyatira, to you who do not hold to her teaching and have not learned Satan's so-called deep secrets (I will not impose any other burden on you): [25]Only hold on to what you have until I come.

[26]To him who overcomes and does my will to the end, I will give authority over the nations—

[27]'He will rule them with an iron
　　　scepter;
　　　he will dash them to pieces
　　　like pottery'[a]—

just as I have received authority

from my Father. [28]I will also give him the morning star. [29]He who has an ear, let him hear what the Spirit says to the churches.

To the Church in Sardis

3 "To the angel[b] of the church in Sardis write:

These are the words of him who holds the seven spirits[c] of God and the seven stars. I know your deeds; you have a reputation of being alive, but you are dead. [2]Wake up! Strengthen what remains and is about to die, for I have not found your deeds complete in the sight of my God. [3]Remember, therefore, what you have received and heard; obey it, and repent. But if you do not wake up, I will come like a thief, and you will not know at what time I will come to you.

[4]Yet you have a few people in Sardis who have not soiled their clothes. They will walk with me, dressed in white, for they are worthy. [5]He who overcomes will, like them, be dressed in white. I will never blot out his name from the book of life, but will acknowledge his name before my Father and his angels. [6]He who has an ear, let him hear what the Spirit says to the churches.

To the Church in Philadelphia

[7]"To the angel of the church in Philadelphia write:

These are the words of him who is holy and true, who holds the key of David. What he opens no one can shut, and what he shuts no one can open. [8]I know your deeds. See, I have placed before you an open door that no one can shut. I know that you have little strength, yet you have kept my word and have not denied my name. [9]I will make those who are of the synagogue of Satan, who claim to be Jews though they are not, but are liars—I will make them come and fall down at your

[a]27 Psalm 2:9　　[b]1 Or *messenger*; also in verses 7 and 14　　[c]1 Or *the sevenfold Spirit*

feet and acknowledge that I have loved you. [10]Since you have kept my command to endure patiently, I will also keep you from the hour of trial that is going to come upon the whole world to test those who live on the earth.

[11]I am coming soon. Hold on to what you have, so that no one will take your crown. [12]Him who overcomes I will make a pillar in the temple of my God. Never again will he leave it. I will write on him the name of my God and the name of the city of my God, the new Jerusalem, which is coming down out of heaven from my God; and I will also write on him my new name. [13]He who has an ear, let him hear what the Spirit says to the churches.

To the Church in Laodicea

[14]"To the angel of the church in Laodicea write:

These are the words of the Amen, the faithful and true witness, the ruler of God's creation. [15]I know your deeds, that you are neither cold nor hot. I wish you were either one or the other! [16]So, because you are lukewarm—neither hot nor cold—I am about to spit you out of my mouth. [17]You say, 'I am rich; I have acquired wealth and do not need a thing.' But you do not realize that you are wretched, pitiful, poor, blind and naked. [18]I counsel you to buy from me gold refined in the fire, so you can become rich; and white clothes to wear, so you can cover your shameful nakedness; and salve to put on your eyes, so you can see.

[19]Those whom I love I rebuke and discipline. So be earnest, and repent. [20]Here I am! I stand at the door and knock. If anyone hears my voice and opens the door, I will come in and eat with him, and he with me.

[21]To him who overcomes, I will give the right to sit with me on my throne, just as I overcame and sat down with my Father on his throne. [22]He who has an ear, let him hear what the Spirit says to the churches."

The Throne in Heaven

4 After this I looked, and there before me was a door standing open in heaven. And the voice I had first heard speaking to me like a trumpet said, "Come up

---

Open Door Policy

Wednesday

REVELATION 3:20 This verse is often used and even quoted in reference to inviting Jesus Christ into your life as Lord and Savior. It also teaches a wonderful lesson about enjoying his fellowship. The concept of dining with the Lord would certainly imply that. The Lord wants to have fellowship with us and desires for us to open up to him. He is patient and persistent in attempting to get through to us.

Unfortunately, in the fast pace of life, we can forget the most important one in our lives. We can overlook the joy of communicating with the Creator and making him a part of our day. Not only should we individually "dine" with him, but what a blessing in our marriage to fellowship with our divine "guest" together as a couple!

Sharing Scripture or ideas as a couple that we have learned from our own personal study is a wonderful way to fellowship with God together. Making him a part of our decision-making process, through prayer, is another way to fellowship together with Christ. Praying about the needs of the family is a powerful tool available to us. Not only will it deepen our lives as individuals, but it will strengthen the life of the family as well.

Through fellowship with Jesus, we welcome Jesus' life-changing presence and power into our daily walk. Let us always open the door of our lives to him.

—Bob & Rosemary

Go to page 1380 for your next devotional reading.

here, and I will show you what must take place after this." ²At once I was in the Spirit, and there before me was a throne in heaven with someone sitting on it. ³And the one who sat there had the appearance of jasper and carnelian. A rainbow, resembling an emerald, encircled the throne. ⁴Surrounding the throne were twenty-four other thrones, and seated on them were twenty-four elders. They were dressed in white and had crowns of gold on their heads. ⁵From the throne came flashes of lightning, rumblings and peals of thunder. Before the throne, seven lamps were blazing. These are the seven spirits*a* of God. ⁶Also before the throne there was what looked like a sea of glass, clear as crystal.

In the center, around the throne, were four living creatures, and they were covered with eyes, in front and in back. ⁷The first living creature was like a lion, the second was like an ox, the third had a face like a man, the fourth was like a flying eagle. ⁸Each of the four living creatures had six wings and was covered with eyes all around, even under his wings. Day and night they never stop saying:

> "Holy, holy, holy
>   is the Lord God Almighty,
>   who was, and is, and is to come."

⁹Whenever the living creatures give glory, honor and thanks to him who sits on the throne and who lives for ever and ever, ¹⁰the twenty-four elders fall down before him who sits on the throne, and worship him who lives for ever and ever. They lay their crowns before the throne and say:

> ¹¹"You are worthy, our Lord and God,
>   to receive glory and honor and
>   power,
> for you created all things,
>   and by your will they were created
>   and have their being."

The Scroll and the Lamb

5 Then I saw in the right hand of him who sat on the throne a scroll with writing on both sides and sealed with seven seals. ²And I saw a mighty angel proclaiming in a loud voice, "Who is worthy to break the seals and open the scroll?" ³But no one in heaven or on earth or un-

der the earth could open the scroll or even look inside it. ⁴I wept and wept because no one was found who was worthy to open the scroll or look inside. ⁵Then one of the elders said to me, "Do not weep! See, the Lion of the tribe of Judah, the Root of David, has triumphed. He is able to open the scroll and its seven seals."

⁶Then I saw a Lamb, looking as if it had been slain, standing in the center of the throne, encircled by the four living creatures and the elders. He had seven horns and seven eyes, which are the seven spirits*a* of God sent out into all the earth. ⁷He came and took the scroll from the right hand of him who sat on the throne. ⁸And when he had taken it, the four living creatures and the twenty-four elders fell down before the Lamb. Each one had a harp and they were holding golden bowls full of incense, which are the prayers of the saints. ⁹And they sang a new song:

> "You are worthy to take the scroll
>   and to open its seals,
> because you were slain,
>   and with your blood you
>   purchased men for God
>   from every tribe and language and
>   people and nation.
> ¹⁰You have made them to be a
>   kingdom and priests to serve
>   our God,
>   and they will reign on the earth."

¹¹Then I looked and heard the voice of many angels, numbering thousands upon thousands, and ten thousand times ten thousand. They encircled the throne and the living creatures and the elders. ¹²In a loud voice they sang:

> "Worthy is the Lamb, who was slain,
> to receive power and wealth and
>   wisdom and strength
> and honor and glory and praise!"

¹³Then I heard every creature in heaven and on earth and under the earth and on the sea, and all that is in them, singing:

> "To him who sits on the throne and
>   to the Lamb
> be praise and honor and glory and
>   power,
>   for ever and ever!"

a 5,6 Or *the sevenfold Spirit*

14The four living creatures said, "Amen," and the elders fell down and worshiped.

The Seals

6 I watched as the Lamb opened the first of the seven seals. Then I heard one of the four living creatures say in a voice like thunder, "Come!" 2I looked, and there before me was a white horse! Its rider held a bow, and he was given a crown, and he rode out as a conqueror bent on conquest.

3When the Lamb opened the second seal, I heard the second living creature say, "Come!" 4Then another horse came out, a fiery red one. Its rider was given power to take peace from the earth and to make men slay each other. To him was given a large sword.

5When the Lamb opened the third seal, I heard the third living creature say, "Come!" I looked, and there before me was a black horse! Its rider was holding a pair of scales in his hand. 6Then I heard what sounded like a voice among the four living creatures, saying, "A quart*a* of wheat for a day's wages,*b* and three quarts of barley for a day's wages,*b* and do not damage the oil and the wine!"

7When the Lamb opened the fourth seal, I heard the voice of the fourth living creature say, "Come!" 8I looked, and there before me was a pale horse! Its rider was named Death, and Hades was following close behind him. They were given power over a fourth of the earth to kill by sword, famine and plague, and by the wild beasts of the earth.

9When he opened the fifth seal, I saw under the altar the souls of those who had been slain because of the word of God and the testimony they had maintained. 10They called out in a loud voice, "How long, Sovereign Lord, holy and true, until you judge the inhabitants of the earth and avenge our blood?" 11Then each of them was given a white robe, and they were told to wait a little longer, until the number of their fellow servants and brothers who were to be killed as they had been was completed.

12I watched as he opened the sixth seal. There was a great earthquake. The sun turned black like sackcloth made of goat hair, the whole moon turned blood red,

13and the stars in the sky fell to earth, as late figs drop from a fig tree when shaken by a strong wind. 14The sky receded like a scroll, rolling up, and every mountain and island was removed from its place.

15Then the kings of the earth, the princes, the generals, the rich, the mighty, and every slave and every free man hid in caves and among the rocks of the mountains. 16They called to the mountains and the rocks, "Fall on us and hide us from the face of him who sits on the throne and from the wrath of the Lamb! 17For the great day of their wrath has come, and who can stand?"

144,000 Sealed

7 After this I saw four angels standing at the four corners of the earth, holding back the four winds of the earth to prevent any wind from blowing on the land or on the sea or on any tree. 2Then I saw another angel coming up from the east, having the seal of the living God. He called out in a loud voice to the four angels who had been given power to harm the land and the sea: 3"Do not harm the land or the sea or the trees until we put a seal on the foreheads of the servants of our God." 4Then I heard the number of those who were sealed: 144,000 from all the tribes of Israel.

5From the tribe of Judah 12,000
    were sealed,
  from the tribe of Reuben 12,000,
  from the tribe of Gad 12,000,
  6from the tribe of Asher 12,000,
  from the tribe of Naphtali 12,000,
  from the tribe of Manasseh 12,000,
  7from the tribe of Simeon 12,000,
  from the tribe of Levi 12,000,
  from the tribe of Issachar 12,000,
  8from the tribe of Zebulun 12,000,
  from the tribe of Joseph 12,000,
  from the tribe of Benjamin 12,000.

The Great Multitude in White Robes

9After this I looked and there before me was a great multitude that no one could count, from every nation, tribe, people and language, standing before the throne and in front of the Lamb. They

*a*6 Greek *a choinix* (probably about a liter)
*b*6 Greek *a denarius*

were wearing white robes and were holding palm branches in their hands. [10]And they cried out in a loud voice:

"Salvation belongs to our God,
who sits on the throne,
and to the Lamb."

[11]All the angels were standing around the throne and around the elders and the four living creatures. They fell down on their faces before the throne and worshiped God, [12]saying:

"Amen!
Praise and glory
and wisdom and thanks and honor
and power and strength
be to our God for ever and ever.
Amen!"

[13]Then one of the elders asked me, "These in white robes—who are they, and where did they come from?"

[14]I answered, "Sir, you know."

And he said, "These are they who have come out of the great tribulation; they have washed their robes and made them white in the blood of the Lamb. [15]Therefore,

"they are before the throne of God
and serve him day and night in his
temple;

and he who sits on the throne will
spread his tent over them.
[16]Never again will they hunger;
never again will they thirst.
The sun will not beat upon them,
nor any scorching heat.
[17]For the Lamb at the center of the
throne will be their shepherd;
he will lead them to springs of
living water.
And God will wipe away every tear
from their eyes."

The Seventh Seal and the Golden Censer

8 When he opened the seventh seal, there was silence in heaven for about half an hour.

[2]And I saw the seven angels who stand before God, and to them were given seven trumpets.

[3]Another angel, who had a golden censer, came and stood at the altar. He was given much incense to offer, with the prayers of all the saints, on the golden altar before the throne. [4]The smoke of the incense, together with the prayers of the saints, went up before God from the angel's hand. [5]Then the angel took the censer, filled it with fire from the altar, and hurled it on the earth; and there came peals of thunder, rumblings, flashes of lightning and an earthquake.

I'll Cry if I Want to

Thursday

REVELATION 7:15–17 "Don't cry!"

"It's okay to cry," Leslie whimpered.

We were having lunch at a favorite restaurant, talking about I-don't-know-what when out of nowhere, or so it seemed, Leslie's eyes flooded with tears. Only moments before they had been sparkling.

"I know it's okay to cry," I confessed, "but can't you wait until we get in the car?"

My simple request only exacerbated the emotion I was trying to stifle. Leslie dabbed her eyes with a napkin, trying to retain her mascara, but the floodgates soon opened, and the tears flowed like a stream.

I can't tell you how many times we have lived through similar scenes, and neither of us could tell you what the issues were, but we can assure you that tears are a part of every marriage relationship. But here's the good news: Did you know that God keeps a record of your tears? The psalmist says they are listed on a scroll (see Psalm 56:8, page 600). God values our tears. And, as this passage makes clear, God comforts us when we cry.

Part of becoming soul mates is learning that there is no shame in tears. Sure, crying in the middle of a restaurant is nobody's idea of a good time, but if an onlooker doesn't understand the tenderness of tears between a married couple, that's their problem!   —*Les and Leslie*

Go to page 1390 for your next devotional reading.

The Trumpets

⁶Then the seven angels who had the seven trumpets prepared to sound them.

⁷The first angel sounded his trumpet, and there came hail and fire mixed with blood, and it was hurled down upon the earth. A third of the earth was burned up, a third of the trees were burned up, and all the green grass was burned up.

⁸The second angel sounded his trumpet, and something like a huge mountain, all ablaze, was thrown into the sea. A third of the sea turned into blood, ⁹a third of the living creatures in the sea died, and a third of the ships were destroyed.

¹⁰The third angel sounded his trumpet, and a great star, blazing like a torch, fell from the sky on a third of the rivers and on the springs of water— ¹¹the name of the star is Wormwood.ᵃ A third of the waters turned bitter, and many people died from the waters that had become bitter.

¹²The fourth angel sounded his trumpet, and a third of the sun was struck, a third of the moon, and a third of the stars, so that a third of them turned dark. A third of the day was without light, and also a third of the night.

¹³As I watched, I heard an eagle that was flying in midair call out in a loud voice: "Woe! Woe! Woe to the inhabitants of the earth, because of the trumpet blasts about to be sounded by the other three angels!"

9 The fifth angel sounded his trumpet, and I saw a star that had fallen from the sky to the earth. The star was given the key to the shaft of the Abyss. ²When he opened the Abyss, smoke rose from it like the smoke from a gigantic furnace. The sun and sky were darkened by the smoke from the Abyss. ³And out of the smoke locusts came down upon the earth and were given power like that of scorpions of the earth. ⁴They were told not to harm the grass of the earth or any plant or tree, but only those people who did not have the seal of God on their foreheads. ⁵They were not given power to kill them, but only to torture them for five months. And the agony they suffered was like that of the sting of a scorpion when it strikes a man. ⁶During those days men will seek death, but will not find it; they will long to die, but death will elude them.

⁷The locusts looked like horses prepared for battle. On their heads they wore something like crowns of gold, and their faces resembled human faces. ⁸Their hair was like women's hair, and their teeth were like lions' teeth. ⁹They had breastplates like breastplates of iron, and the sound of their wings was like the thundering of many horses and chariots rushing into battle. ¹⁰They had tails and stings like scorpions, and in their tails they had power to torment people for five months. ¹¹They had as king over them the angel of the Abyss, whose name in Hebrew is Abaddon, and in Greek, Apollyon.ᵇ

¹²The first woe is past; two other woes are yet to come.

¹³The sixth angel sounded his trumpet, and I heard a voice coming from the hornsᶜ of the golden altar that is before God. ¹⁴It said to the sixth angel who had the trumpet, "Release the four angels who are bound at the great river Euphrates." ¹⁵And the four angels who had been kept ready for this very hour and day and month and year were released to kill a third of mankind. ¹⁶The number of the mounted troops was two hundred million. I heard their number.

¹⁷The horses and riders I saw in my vision looked like this: Their breastplates were fiery red, dark blue, and yellow as sulfur. The heads of the horses resembled the heads of lions, and out of their mouths came fire, smoke and sulfur. ¹⁸A third of mankind was killed by the three plagues of fire, smoke and sulfur that came out of their mouths. ¹⁹The power of the horses was in their mouths and in their tails; for their tails were like snakes, having heads with which they inflict injury.

²⁰The rest of mankind that were not killed by these plagues still did not repent of the work of their hands; they did not stop worshiping demons, and idols of gold, silver, bronze, stone and wood— idols that cannot see or hear or walk. ²¹Nor did they repent of their murders,

---

ᵃ11 That is, Bitterness   ᵇ11 Abaddon and Apollyon mean Destroyer.   ᶜ13 That is, projections their magic arts, their sexual immorality or their thefts.

The Angel and the Little Scroll

10 Then I saw another mighty angel coming down from heaven. He was robed in a cloud, with a rainbow above his head; his face was like the sun, and his legs were like fiery pillars. ²He was holding a little scroll, which lay open in his hand. He planted his right foot on the sea and his left foot on the land, ³and he gave a loud shout like the roar of a lion. When he shouted, the voices of the seven thunders spoke. ⁴And when the seven thunders spoke, I was about to write; but I heard a voice from heaven say, "Seal up what the seven thunders have said and do not write it down."

⁵Then the angel I had seen standing on the sea and on the land raised his right hand to heaven. ⁶And he swore by him who lives for ever and ever, who created the heavens and all that is in them, the earth and all that is in it, and the sea and all that is in it, and said, "There will be no more delay! ⁷But in the days when the seventh angel is about to sound his trumpet, the mystery of God will be accomplished, just as he announced to his servants the prophets."

⁸Then the voice that I had heard from heaven spoke to me once more: "Go, take the scroll that lies open in the hand of the angel who is standing on the sea and on the land."

⁹So I went to the angel and asked him to give me the little scroll. He said to me, "Take it and eat it. It will turn your stomach sour, but in your mouth it will be as sweet as honey." ¹⁰I took the little scroll from the angel's hand and ate it. It tasted as sweet as honey in my mouth, but when I had eaten it, my stomach turned sour. ¹¹Then I was told, "You must prophesy again about many peoples, nations, languages and kings."

The Two Witnesses

11 I was given a reed like a measuring rod and was told, "Go and measure the temple of God and the altar, and count the worshipers there. ²But exclude the outer court; do not measure it, because it has been given to the Gentiles.

They will trample on the holy city for 42 months. ³And I will give power to my two witnesses, and they will prophesy for 1,260 days, clothed in sackcloth." ⁴These are the two olive trees and the two lampstands that stand before the Lord of the earth. ⁵If anyone tries to harm them, fire comes from their mouths and devours their enemies. This is how anyone who wants to harm them must die. ⁶These men have power to shut up the sky so that it will not rain during the time they are prophesying; and they have power to turn the waters into blood and to strike the earth with every kind of plague as often as they want.

⁷Now when they have finished their testimony, the beast that comes up from the Abyss will attack them, and overpower and kill them. ⁸Their bodies will lie in the street of the great city, which is figuratively called Sodom and Egypt, where also their Lord was crucified. ⁹For three and a half days men from every people, tribe, language and nation will gaze on their bodies and refuse them burial. ¹⁰The inhabitants of the earth will gloat over them and will celebrate by sending each other gifts, because these two prophets had tormented those who live on the earth.

¹¹But after the three and a half days a breath of life from God entered them, and they stood on their feet, and terror struck those who saw them. ¹²Then they heard a loud voice from heaven saying to them, "Come up here." And they went up to heaven in a cloud, while their enemies looked on.

¹³At that very hour there was a severe earthquake and a tenth of the city collapsed. Seven thousand people were killed in the earthquake, and the survivors were terrified and gave glory to the God of heaven.

¹⁴The second woe has passed; the third woe is coming soon.

The Seventh Trumpet

¹⁵The seventh angel sounded his trumpet, and there were loud voices in heaven, which said:

"The kingdom of the world has
    become the kingdom of our
    Lord and of his Christ,
    and he will reign for ever and ever."

16And the twenty-four elders, who were seated on their thrones before God, fell on their faces and worshiped God, 17saying:

"We give thanks to you, Lord God
  Almighty,
  the One who is and who was,
because you have taken your great
    power
  and have begun to reign.
18The nations were angry;
  and your wrath has come.
The time has come for judging the
    dead,
  and for rewarding your servants the
    prophets
and your saints and those who
    reverence your name,
  both small and great—
and for destroying those who destroy
    the earth."

19Then God's temple in heaven was opened, and within his temple was seen the ark of his covenant. And there came flashes of lightning, rumblings, peals of thunder, an earthquake and a great hailstorm.

The Woman and the Dragon

12 A great and wondrous sign appeared in heaven: a woman clothed with the sun, with the moon under her feet and a crown of twelve stars on her head. 2She was pregnant and cried out in pain as she was about to give birth. 3Then another sign appeared in heaven: an enormous red dragon with seven heads and ten horns and seven crowns on his heads. 4His tail swept a third of the stars out of the sky and flung them to the earth. The dragon stood in front of the woman who was about to give birth, so that he might devour her child the moment it was born. 5She gave birth to a son, a male child, who will rule all the nations with an iron scepter. And her child was snatched up to God and to his throne. 6The woman fled into the desert to a place prepared for her by God, where she might be taken care of for 1,260 days.

7And there was war in heaven. Michael and his angels fought against the dragon, and the dragon and his angels fought back. 8But he was not strong enough, and they lost their place in heaven. 9The great dragon was hurled down—that ancient serpent called the devil, or Satan, who leads the whole world astray. He was hurled to the earth, and his angels with him.

10Then I heard a loud voice in heaven say:

"Now have come the salvation and
    the power and the kingdom
    of our God,
  and the authority of his Christ.
For the accuser of our brothers,
  who accuses them before our God
    day and night,
  has been hurled down.
11They overcame him
  by the blood of the Lamb
  and by the word of their
    testimony;
they did not love their lives so much
  as to shrink from death.
12Therefore rejoice, you heavens
  and you who dwell in them!
But woe to the earth and the sea,
  because the devil has gone down
    to you!
He is filled with fury,
  because he knows that his time is
    short."

13When the dragon saw that he had been hurled to the earth, he pursued the woman who had given birth to the male child. 14The woman was given the two wings of a great eagle, so that she might fly to the place prepared for her in the desert, where she would be taken care of for a time, times and half a time, out of the serpent's reach. 15Then from his mouth the serpent spewed water like a river, to overtake the woman and sweep her away with the torrent. 16But the earth helped the woman by opening its mouth and swallowing the river that the dragon had spewed out of his mouth. 17Then the dragon was enraged at the woman and went off to make war against the rest of her offspring—those who obey God's commandments and hold to the testimony of Jesus. **13** 1And the dragon*a* stood on the shore of the sea.

---

*a*1 Some late manuscripts *And I*

The Beast out of the Sea

And I saw a beast coming out of the sea. He had ten horns and seven heads, with ten crowns on his horns, and on each head a blasphemous name. ²The beast I saw resembled a leopard, but had feet like those of a bear and a mouth like that of a lion. The dragon gave the beast his power and his throne and great authority. ³One of the heads of the beast seemed to have had a fatal wound, but the fatal wound had been healed. The whole world was astonished and followed the beast. ⁴Men worshiped the dragon because he had given authority to the beast, and they also worshiped the beast and asked, "Who is like the beast? Who can make war against him?"

⁵The beast was given a mouth to utter proud words and blasphemies and to exercise his authority for forty-two months. ⁶He opened his mouth to blaspheme God, and to slander his name and his dwelling place and those who live in heaven. ⁷He was given power to make war against the saints and to conquer them. And he was given authority over every tribe, people, language and nation. ⁸All inhabitants of the earth will worship the beast—all whose names have not been written in the book of life belonging to the Lamb that was slain from the creation of the world.ª

⁹He who has an ear, let him hear.

¹⁰If anyone is to go into captivity,
    into captivity he will go.
If anyone is to be killedᵇ with the
    sword,
    with the sword he will be killed.

This calls for patient endurance and faithfulness on the part of the saints.

The Beast out of the Earth

¹¹Then I saw another beast, coming out of the earth. He had two horns like a lamb, but he spoke like a dragon. ¹²He exercised all the authority of the first beast on his behalf, and made the earth and its inhabitants worship the first beast, whose fatal wound had been healed. ¹³And he performed great and miraculous signs, even causing fire to come down from heaven to earth in full view of men. ¹⁴Because of the signs he was given power to do on behalf of the first beast, he deceived the inhabitants of the earth. He ordered them to set up an image in honor of the beast who was wounded by the sword and yet lived. ¹⁵He was given power to give breath to the image of the first beast, so that it could speak and cause all who refused to worship the image to be killed. ¹⁶He also forced everyone, small and great, rich and poor, free and slave, to receive a mark on his right hand or on his forehead, ¹⁷so that no one could buy or sell unless he had the mark, which is the name of the beast or the number of his name.

¹⁸This calls for wisdom. If anyone has insight, let him calculate the number of the beast, for it is man's number. His number is 666.

The Lamb and the 144,000

14 Then I looked, and there before me was the Lamb, standing on Mount Zion, and with him 144,000 who had his name and his Father's name written on their foreheads. ²And I heard a sound from heaven like the roar of rushing waters and like a loud peal of thunder. The sound I heard was like that of harpists playing their harps. ³And they sang a new song before the throne and before the four living creatures and the elders. No one could learn the song except the 144,000 who had been redeemed from the earth. ⁴These are those who did not defile themselves with women, for they kept themselves pure. They follow the Lamb wherever he goes. They were purchased from among men and offered as firstfruits to God and the Lamb. ⁵No lie was found in their mouths; they are blameless.

The Three Angels

⁶Then I saw another angel flying in midair, and he had the eternal gospel to proclaim to those who live on the earth—to every nation, tribe, language and people. ⁷He said in a loud voice, "Fear God and give him glory, because the hour of his judgment has come. Worship him

---

ª8 Or *written from the creation of the world in the book of life belonging to the Lamb that was slain*
ᵇ10 Some manuscripts *anyone kills*

who made the heavens, the earth, the sea and the springs of water."

⁸A second angel followed and said, "Fallen! Fallen is Babylon the Great, which made all the nations drink the maddening wine of her adulteries."

⁹A third angel followed them and said in a loud voice: "If anyone worships the beast and his image and receives his mark on the forehead or on the hand, ¹⁰he, too, will drink of the wine of God's fury, which has been poured full strength into the cup of his wrath. He will be tormented with burning sulfur in the presence of the holy angels and of the Lamb. ¹¹And the smoke of their torment rises for ever and ever. There is no rest day or night for those who worship the beast and his image, or for anyone who receives the mark of his name." ¹²This calls for patient endurance on the part of the saints who obey God's commandments and remain faithful to Jesus.

¹³Then I heard a voice from heaven say, "Write: Blessed are the dead who die in the Lord from now on."

"Yes," says the Spirit, "they will rest from their labor, for their deeds will follow them."

The Harvest of the Earth

¹⁴I looked, and there before me was a white cloud, and seated on the cloud was one "like a son of man"ᵃ with a crown of gold on his head and a sharp sickle in his hand. ¹⁵Then another angel came out of the temple and called in a loud voice to him who was sitting on the cloud, "Take your sickle and reap, because the time to reap has come, for the harvest of the earth is ripe." ¹⁶So he who was seated on the cloud swung his sickle over the earth, and the earth was harvested.

¹⁷Another angel came out of the temple in heaven, and he too had a sharp sickle. ¹⁸Still another angel, who had charge of the fire, came from the altar and called in a loud voice to him who had the sharp sickle, "Take your sharp sickle and gather the clusters of grapes from the earth's vine, because its grapes are ripe." ¹⁹The angel swung his sickle on the earth, gathered its grapes and threw them into the great winepress of God's wrath. ²⁰They were trampled in the winepress

outside the city, and blood flowed out of the press, rising as high as the horses' bridles for a distance of 1,600 stadia.ᵇ

Seven Angels With Seven Plagues

15 I saw in heaven another great and marvelous sign: seven angels with the seven last plagues—last, because with them God's wrath is completed. ²And I saw what looked like a sea of glass mixed with fire and, standing beside the sea, those who had been victorious over the beast and his image and over the number of his name. They held harps given them by God ³and sang the song of Moses the servant of God and the song of the Lamb:

"Great and marvelous are your deeds,
    Lord God Almighty.
Just and true are your ways,
    King of the ages.
⁴Who will not fear you, O Lord,
    and bring glory to your name?
For you alone are holy.
All nations will come
    and worship before you,
for your righteous acts have been
    revealed."

⁵After this I looked and in heaven the temple, that is, the tabernacle of the Testimony, was opened. ⁶Out of the temple came the seven angels with the seven plagues. They were dressed in clean, shining linen and wore golden sashes around their chests. ⁷Then one of the four living creatures gave to the seven angels seven golden bowls filled with the wrath of God, who lives for ever and ever. ⁸And the temple was filled with smoke from the glory of God and from his power, and no one could enter the temple until the seven plagues of the seven angels were completed.

The Seven Bowls of God's Wrath

16 Then I heard a loud voice from the temple saying to the seven angels, "Go, pour out the seven bowls of God's wrath on the earth."

²The first angel went and poured out his bowl on the land, and ugly and painful sores broke out on the people who

ᵃ14 Daniel 7:13   ᵇ20 That is, about 180 miles (about 300 kilometers) had the mark of the beast and worshiped his image.

³The second angel poured out his bowl on the sea, and it turned into blood like that of a dead man, and every living thing in the sea died.

⁴The third angel poured out his bowl on the rivers and springs of water, and they became blood. ⁵Then I heard the angel in charge of the waters say:

"You are just in these judgments,
    you who are and who were, the
        Holy One,
    because you have so judged;
⁶for they have shed the blood of your
        saints and prophets,
    and you have given them blood to
        drink as they deserve."

⁷And I heard the altar respond:

"Yes, Lord God Almighty,
    true and just are your judgments."

⁸The fourth angel poured out his bowl on the sun, and the sun was given power to scorch people with fire. ⁹They were seared by the intense heat and they cursed the name of God, who had control over these plagues, but they refused to repent and glorify him.

¹⁰The fifth angel poured out his bowl on the throne of the beast, and his kingdom was plunged into darkness. Men gnawed their tongues in agony ¹¹and cursed the God of heaven because of their pains and their sores, but they refused to repent of what they had done.

¹²The sixth angel poured out his bowl on the great river Euphrates, and its water was dried up to prepare the way for the kings from the East. ¹³Then I saw three evil*a* spirits that looked like frogs; they came out of the mouth of the dragon, out of the mouth of the beast and out of the mouth of the false prophet. ¹⁴They are spirits of demons performing miraculous signs, and they go out to the kings of the whole world, to gather them for the battle on the great day of God Almighty.

¹⁵"Behold, I come like a thief! Blessed is he who stays awake and keeps his clothes with him, so that he may not go naked and be shamefully exposed."

¹⁶Then they gathered the kings together to the place that in Hebrew is called Armageddon.

¹⁷The seventh angel poured out his bowl into the air, and out of the temple came a loud voice from the throne, saying, "It is done!" ¹⁸Then there came flashes of lightning, rumblings, peals of thunder and a severe earthquake. No earthquake like it has ever occurred since man has been on earth, so tremendous was the quake. ¹⁹The great city split into three parts, and the cities of the nations collapsed. God remembered Babylon the Great and gave her the cup filled with the wine of the fury of his wrath. ²⁰Every island fled away and the mountains could not be found. ²¹From the sky huge hailstones of about a hundred pounds each fell upon men. And they cursed God on account of the plague of hail, because the plague was so terrible.

The Woman on the Beast

17 One of the seven angels who had the seven bowls came and said to me, "Come, I will show you the punishment of the great prostitute, who sits on many waters. ²With her the kings of the earth committed adultery and the inhabitants of the earth were intoxicated with the wine of her adulteries."

³Then the angel carried me away in the Spirit into a desert. There I saw a woman sitting on a scarlet beast that was covered with blasphemous names and had seven heads and ten horns. ⁴The woman was dressed in purple and scarlet, and was glittering with gold, precious stones and pearls. She held a golden cup in her hand, filled with abominable things and the filth of her adulteries. ⁵This title was written on her forehead:

MYSTERY
BABYLON THE GREAT
THE MOTHER OF PROSTITUTES
AND OF THE ABOMINATIONS OF THE EARTH.

⁶I saw that the woman was drunk with the blood of the saints, the blood of those who bore testimony to Jesus.

When I saw her, I was greatly astonished. ⁷Then the angel said to me: "Why are you astonished? I will explain to you the mystery of the woman and of the beast she rides, which has the seven heads and ten horns. ⁸The beast, which you saw,

a13 Greek unclean

once was, now is not, and will come up out of the Abyss and go to his destruction. The inhabitants of the earth whose names have not been written in the book of life from the creation of the world will be astonished when they see the beast, because he once was, now is not, and yet will come.

⁹"This calls for a mind with wisdom. The seven heads are seven hills on which the woman sits. ¹⁰They are also seven kings. Five have fallen, one is, the other has not yet come; but when he does come, he must remain for a little while. ¹¹The beast who once was, and now is not, is an eighth king. He belongs to the seven and is going to his destruction.

¹²"The ten horns you saw are ten kings who have not yet received a kingdom, but who for one hour will receive authority as kings along with the beast. ¹³They have one purpose and will give their power and authority to the beast. ¹⁴They will make war against the Lamb, but the Lamb will overcome them because he is Lord of lords and King of kings—and with him will be his called, chosen and faithful followers."

¹⁵Then the angel said to me, "The waters you saw, where the prostitute sits, are peoples, multitudes, nations and languages. ¹⁶The beast and the ten horns you saw will hate the prostitute. They will bring her to ruin and leave her naked; they will eat her flesh and burn her with fire. ¹⁷For God has put it into their hearts to accomplish his purpose by agreeing to give the beast their power to rule, until God's words are fulfilled. ¹⁸The woman you saw is the great city that rules over the kings of the earth."

The Fall of Babylon

18 After this I saw another angel coming down from heaven. He had great authority, and the earth was illuminated by his splendor. ²With a mighty voice he shouted:

> "Fallen! Fallen is Babylon the Great!
>   She has become a home for demons
> and a haunt for every evil*ᵃ* spirit,
>   a haunt for every unclean and
>   detestable bird.
> ³For all the nations have drunk

> the maddening wine of her
>   adulteries.
> The kings of the earth committed
>   adultery with her,
>   and the merchants of the earth
>   grew rich from her excessive
>   luxuries."

⁴Then I heard another voice from heaven say:

> "Come out of her, my people,
>   so that you will not share in her
>   sins,
>   so that you will not receive any of
>   her plagues;
> ⁵for her sins are piled up to heaven,
>   and God has remembered her
>   crimes.
> ⁶Give back to her as she has given;
>   pay her back double for what she
>   has done.
>   Mix her a double portion from her
>   own cup.
> ⁷Give her as much torture and grief
>   as the glory and luxury she gave
>   herself.
> In her heart she boasts,
>   'I sit as queen; I am not a widow,
>   and I will never mourn.'
> ⁸Therefore in one day her plagues will
>   overtake her:
>   death, mourning and famine.
> She will be consumed by fire,
>   for mighty is the Lord God who
>   judges her.

⁹"When the kings of the earth who committed adultery with her and shared her luxury see the smoke of her burning, they will weep and mourn over her. ¹⁰Terrified at her torment, they will stand far off and cry:

> "'Woe! Woe, O great city,
>   O Babylon, city of power!
> In one hour your doom has come!'

¹¹"The merchants of the earth will weep and mourn over her because no one buys their cargoes any more— ¹²cargoes of gold, silver, precious stones and pearls; fine linen, purple, silk and scarlet cloth; every sort of citron wood, and articles of every kind made of ivory, costly wood, bronze, iron and marble; ¹³cargoes of cin-

ᵃ2 Greek unclean

namon and spice, of incense, myrrh and frankincense, of wine and olive oil, of fine flour and wheat; cattle and sheep; horses and carriages; and bodies and souls of men.

14 "They will say, 'The fruit you longed for is gone from you. All your riches and splendor have vanished, never to be recovered.' 15 The merchants who sold these things and gained their wealth from her will stand far off, terrified at her torment. They will weep and mourn 16 and cry out:

" 'Woe! Woe, O great city,
    dressed in fine linen, purple and
        scarlet,
    and glittering with gold, precious
        stones and pearls!
17 In one hour such great wealth has
    been brought to ruin!'

"Every sea captain, and all who travel by ship, the sailors, and all who earn their living from the sea, will stand far off. 18 When they see the smoke of her burning, they will exclaim, 'Was there ever a city like this great city?' 19 They will throw dust on their heads, and with weeping and mourning cry out:

" 'Woe! Woe, O great city,
    where all who had ships on the sea
        became rich through her wealth!
In one hour she has been brought to
        ruin!
20 Rejoice over her, O heaven!
    Rejoice, saints and apostles and
        prophets!
God has judged her for the way she
        treated you.' "

21 Then a mighty angel picked up a boulder the size of a large millstone and threw it into the sea, and said:

"With such violence
    the great city of Babylon will be
        thrown down,
    never to be found again.
22 The music of harpists and musicians,
        flute players and trumpeters,
    will never be heard in you again.
No workman of any trade
    will ever be found in you again.
The sound of a millstone
    will never be heard in you again.
23 The light of a lamp
    will never shine in you again.

The voice of bridegroom and bride
    will never be heard in you again.
Your merchants were the world's great
        men.
    By your magic spell all the nations
        were led astray.
24 In her was found the blood of
        prophets and of the saints,
    and of all who have been killed on
        the earth."

Hallelujah!

19 After this I heard what sounded like the roar of a great multitude in heaven shouting:

"Hallelujah!
Salvation and glory and power belong
        to our God,
2   for true and just are his judgments.
He has condemned the great
        prostitute
    who corrupted the earth by her
        adulteries.
He has avenged on her the blood of
        his servants."

3 And again they shouted:

"Hallelujah!
The smoke from her goes up for ever
        and ever."

4 The twenty-four elders and the four living creatures fell down and worshiped God, who was seated on the throne. And they cried:

"Amen, Hallelujah!"

5 Then a voice came from the throne, saying:

"Praise our God,
    all you his servants,
you who fear him,
    both small and great!"

6 Then I heard what sounded like a great multitude, like the roar of rushing waters and like loud peals of thunder, shouting:

"Hallelujah!
    For our Lord God Almighty reigns.
7 Let us rejoice and be glad
    and give him glory!
For the wedding of the Lamb has
        come,

and his bride has made herself
   ready.
[8]Fine linen, bright and clean,
   was given her to wear."
(Fine linen stands for the righteous acts of
the saints.)

[9]Then the angel said to me, "Write:
'Blessed are those who are invited to the
wedding supper of the Lamb!' " And he
added, "These are the true words of God."
[10]At this I fell at his feet to worship
him. But he said to me, "Do not do it! I
am a fellow servant with you and with
your brothers who hold to the testimony
of Jesus. Worship God! For the testimony
of Jesus is the spirit of prophecy."

The Rider on the White Horse

[11]I saw heaven standing open and
there before me was a white horse, whose
rider is called Faithful and True. With justice he judges and makes war. [12]His eyes
are like blazing fire, and on his head are
many crowns. He has a name written on
him that no one knows but he himself.
[13]He is dressed in a robe dipped in blood,
and his name is the Word of God. [14]The
armies of heaven were following him, riding on white horses and dressed in fine
linen, white and clean. [15]Out of his
mouth comes a sharp sword with which
to strike down the nations. "He will rule
them with an iron scepter."[a] He treads
the winepress of the fury of the wrath of
God Almighty. [16]On his robe and on his
thigh he has this name written:

   KING OF KINGS AND LORD OF LORDS.

[17]And I saw an angel standing in the
sun, who cried in a loud voice to all the
birds flying in midair, "Come, gather together for the great supper of God, [18]so
that you may eat the flesh of kings, generals, and mighty men, of horses and their
riders, and the flesh of all people, free and
slave, small and great."
[19]Then I saw the beast and the kings of
the earth and their armies gathered together to make war against the rider on
the horse and his army. [20]But the beast
was captured, and with him the false
prophet who had performed the miraculous signs on his behalf. With these signs
he had deluded those who had received

the mark of the beast and worshiped his
image. The two of them were thrown alive
into the fiery lake of burning sulfur. [21]The
rest of them were killed with the sword
that came out of the mouth of the rider
on the horse, and all the birds gorged
themselves on their flesh.

The Thousand Years

20 And I saw an angel coming down
out of heaven, having the key to
the Abyss and holding in his hand a great
chain. [2]He seized the dragon, that ancient
serpent, who is the devil, or Satan, and
bound him for a thousand years. [3]He
threw him into the Abyss, and locked and
sealed it over him, to keep him from deceiving the nations anymore until the
thousand years were ended. After that, he
must be set free for a short time.
[4]I saw thrones on which were seated
those who had been given authority to
judge. And I saw the souls of those who
had been beheaded because of their testimony for Jesus and because of the word
of God. They had not worshiped the beast
or his image and had not received his
mark on their foreheads or their hands.
They came to life and reigned with Christ
a thousand years. [5](The rest of the dead
did not come to life until the thousand
years were ended.) This is the first resurrection. [6]Blessed and holy are those who
have part in the first resurrection. The second death has no power over them, but
they will be priests of God and of Christ
and will reign with him for a thousand
years.

Satan's Doom

[7]When the thousand years are over, Satan will be released from his prison [8]and
will go out to deceive the nations in the
four corners of the earth—Gog and Magog—to gather them for battle. In number
they are like the sand on the seashore.
[9]They marched across the breadth of the
earth and surrounded the camp of God's
people, the city he loves. But fire came
down from heaven and devoured them.
[10]And the devil, who deceived them, was
thrown into the lake of burning sulfur,
where the beast and the false prophet had

---

[a]15 Psalm 2:9

been thrown. They will be tormented day and night for ever and ever.

The Dead Are Judged

[11]Then I saw a great white throne and him who was seated on it. Earth and sky fled from his presence, and there was no place for them. [12]And I saw the dead, great and small, standing before the throne, and books were opened. Another book was opened, which is the book of life. The dead were judged according to what they had done as recorded in the books. [13]The sea gave up the dead that were in it, and death and Hades gave up the dead that were in them, and each person was judged according to what he had done. [14]Then death and Hades were thrown into the lake of fire. The lake of fire is the second death. [15]If anyone's name was not found written in the book of life, he was thrown into the lake of fire.

The New Jerusalem

21 Then I saw a new heaven and a new earth, for the first heaven and the first earth had passed away, and there was no longer any sea. [2]I saw the Holy City, the new Jerusalem, coming down out of heaven from God, prepared as a bride beautifully dressed for her husband. [3]And I heard a loud voice from the throne saying, "Now the dwelling of God is with men, and he will live with them. They will be his people, and God himself will be with them and be their God. [4]He will wipe every tear from their eyes. There will be no more death or mourning or crying or pain, for the old order of things has passed away."

[5]He who was seated on the throne said, "I am making everything new!" Then he said, "Write this down, for these words are trustworthy and true."

[6]He said to me: "It is done. I am the Alpha and the Omega, the Beginning and the End. To him who is thirsty I will give to drink without cost from the spring of the water of life. [7]He who overcomes will inherit all this, and I will be his God and he will be my son. [8]But the cowardly, the unbelieving, the vile, the murderers, the sexually immoral, those who practice magic arts, the idolaters and all liars— their place will be in the fiery lake of burning sulfur. This is the second death."

[9]One of the seven angels who had the seven bowls full of the seven last plagues came and said to me, "Come, I will show you the bride, the wife of the Lamb." [10]And he carried me away in the Spirit to a mountain great and high, and showed me the Holy City, Jerusalem, coming down out of heaven from God. [11]It shone with the glory of God, and its brilliance was

---

Anticipation Is Half the Fun

Friday

REVELATION 21:10–27 Each year as a couple, Bob and I have planned a "second" honeymoon trip. Sometimes it's a short trip to a bed and breakfast close to home, and sometimes it has been a spectacular event for which we prepare quite a while. Whether it is a small get-away or an eventful memory maker, it is always a time that helps us get back our perspective as a married couple. For a few days, we shed all our responsibilities and the roles we carry from work, or as parents, and just become lovers.

A wonderful part of this long-awaited trip is the anticipation. Just looking forward to it keeps us going during the daily grind. The planning is half of the fun! That perspective of anticipation should be evident in all of our lives. The Apostle John was overwhelmed with the vision he had of heaven. He used the most beautiful, descriptive words he could think of to help us get a glimpse of the marvelous future that awaits us as Christians.

When we get bogged down in the daily grind or difficulties, let us never lose the perspective that we are headed to that marvelous destination. We are journeying through this life toward the New Jerusalem to share an eternity with Jesus Christ.

—Bob and Rosemary

Go to page 2 for your next devotional reading.

like that of a very precious jewel, like a jasper, clear as crystal. ¹²It had a great, high wall with twelve gates, and with twelve angels at the gates. On the gates were written the names of the twelve tribes of Israel. ¹³There were three gates on the east, three on the north, three on the south and three on the west. ¹⁴The wall of the city had twelve foundations, and on them were the names of the twelve apostles of the Lamb.

¹⁵The angel who talked with me had a measuring rod of gold to measure the city, its gates and its walls. ¹⁶The city was laid out like a square, as long as it was wide. He measured the city with the rod and found it to be 12,000 stadia*a* in length, and as wide and high as it is long. ¹⁷He measured its wall and it was 144 cubits*b* thick,*c* by man's measurement, which the angel was using. ¹⁸The wall was made of jasper, and the city of pure gold, as pure as glass. ¹⁹The foundations of the city walls were decorated with every kind of precious stone. The first foundation was jasper, the second sapphire, the third chalcedony, the fourth emerald, ²⁰the fifth sardonyx, the sixth carnelian, the seventh chrysolite, the eighth beryl, the ninth topaz, the tenth chrysoprase, the eleventh jacinth, and the twelfth amethyst.*d* ²¹The twelve gates were twelve pearls, each gate made of a single pearl. The great street of the city was of pure gold, like transparent glass.

²²I did not see a temple in the city, because the Lord God Almighty and the Lamb are its temple. ²³The city does not need the sun or the moon to shine on it, for the glory of God gives it light, and the Lamb is its lamp. ²⁴The nations will walk by its light, and the kings of the earth will bring their splendor into it. ²⁵On no day will its gates ever be shut, for there will be no night there. ²⁶The glory and honor of the nations will be brought into it. ²⁷Nothing impure will ever enter it, nor will anyone who does what is shameful or deceitful, but only those whose names are written in the Lamb's book of life.

The River of Life

22 Then the angel showed me the river of the water of life, as clear as crystal, flowing from the throne of God and of the Lamb ²down the middle of the great street of the city. On each side of the river stood the tree of life, bearing twelve crops of fruit, yielding its fruit every month. And the leaves of the tree are for the healing of the nations. ³No longer will there be any curse. The throne of God and of the Lamb will be in the city, and his servants will serve him. ⁴They will see his face, and his name will be on their foreheads. ⁵There will be no more night. They will not need the light of a lamp or the light of the sun, for the Lord God will give them light. And they will reign for ever and ever.

⁶The angel said to me, "These words are trustworthy and true. The Lord, the God of the spirits of the prophets, sent his angel to show his servants the things that must soon take place."

Jesus Is Coming

⁷"Behold, I am coming soon! Blessed is he who keeps the words of the prophecy in this book."

⁸I, John, am the one who heard and saw these things. And when I had heard and seen them, I fell down to worship at the feet of the angel who had been showing them to me. ⁹But he said to me, "Do not do it! I am a fellow servant with you and with your brothers the prophets and of all who keep the words of this book. Worship God!"

¹⁰Then he told me, "Do not seal up the words of the prophecy of this book, because the time is near. ¹¹Let him who does wrong continue to do wrong; let him who is vile continue to be vile; let him who does right continue to do right; and let him who is holy continue to be holy."

¹²"Behold, I am coming soon! My reward is with me, and I will give to everyone according to what he has done. ¹³I am the Alpha and the Omega, the First and the Last, the Beginning and the End.

¹⁴"Blessed are those who wash their robes, that they may have the right to the

a16 That is, about 1,400 miles (about 2,200 kilometers)   *b17* That is, about 200 feet (about 65 meters)   *c17* Or *high*   *d20* The precise identification of some of these precious stones is uncertain.

tree of life and may go through the gates into the city. ¹⁵Outside are the dogs, those who practice magic arts, the sexually immoral, the murderers, the idolaters and everyone who loves and practices falsehood.

¹⁶"I, Jesus, have sent my angel to give you*ᵃ* this testimony for the churches. I am the Root and the Offspring of David, and the bright Morning Star."

¹⁷The Spirit and the bride say, "Come!" And let him who hears say, "Come!" Whoever is thirsty, let him come; and whoever wishes, let him take the free gift of the water of life.

¹⁸I warn everyone who hears the words of the prophecy of this book: If anyone adds anything to them, God will add to him the plagues described in this book. ¹⁹And if anyone takes words away from this book of prophecy, God will take away from him his share in the tree of life and in the holy city, which are described in this book.

²⁰He who testifies to these things says, "Yes, I am coming soon."

Amen. Come, Lord Jesus.

²¹The grace of the Lord Jesus be with God's people. Amen.

ᵃ16 The Greek is plural.

Weights & Measures

	Biblical Unit	Approximate American Equivalent	Approximate Metric Equivalent
WEIGHTS	talent (60 minas)	75 pounds	34 kilograms
	mina (50 shekels)	1¼ pounds	0.6 kilogram
	shekel (2 bekas)	⅖ ounce	11.5 grams
	pim (⅔ shekel)	⅓ ounce	7.6 grams
	beka (10 gerahs)	⅕ ounce	5.5 grams
	gerah	1/50 ounce	0.6 gram
LENGTH	cubit	18 inches	0.5 meter
	span	9 inches	23 centimeters
	handbreadth	3 inches	8 centimeters
CAPACITY			
Dry Measure	cor [homer] (10 ephahs)	6 bushels	220 liters
	lethek (5 ephahs)	3 bushels	110 liters
	ephah (10 omers)	⅗ bushel	22 liters
	seah (⅓ ephah)	7 quarts	7.3 liters
	omer (1/10 ephah)	2 quarts	2 liters
	cab (1/18 ephah)	1 quart	1 liter
Liquid Measure	bath (1 ephah)	6 gallons	22 liters
	hin (⅙ bath)	4 quarts	4 liters
	log (1/72 bath)	⅓ quart	0.3 liter

The figures of the table are calculated on the basis of a shekel equaling 11.5 grams, a cubit equaling 18 inches and an ephah equaling 22 liters. The quart referred to is either a dry quart (slightly larger than a liter) or a liquid quart (slightly smaller than a liter), whichever is applicable. The ton referred to in the footnotes is the American ton of 2,000 pounds.

This table is based upon the best available information, but it is not intended to be mathematically precise; like the measurement equivalents in the footnotes, it merely gives approximate amounts and distances. Weights and measures differed somewhat at various times and places in the ancient world. There is uncertainty particularly about the ephah and the bath; further discoveries may shed more light on these units of capacity.

Study HELPS

Subject Index

Couples in the Bible Index

Just Between You and Me Index

Reading Plan

Subject Index

Index
"COUPLES IN THE BIBLE"

Index

"JUST BETWEEN YOU AND ME"

Reading Plan

God's Word is his personal message of love to you today. The best way to grow as a Christian and get to know God in a more personal way is to spend time in his Word. Here are 3 ways for you to read through the Bible.

1 **If you are reading the Bible for the first time:**
   • Begin by reading the Gospel of Mark or the Gospel of John in the New Testament.
   • After reading 1 of these gospels, read the book of Acts or the book of Romans.
   • After reading Acts or Romans, pick an Old Testament book like Genesis or perhaps Psalms.

2 **If you want to read through the entire Bible in 1 year:**
   • Read 3 chapters each day, Monday through Saturday, and 5 chapters on Sunday.

3 **If you want to read through the entire Bible in 2 years:**
   • Read 2 chapters each day, Sunday through Saturday.

The following chart covers every book and chapter of the Bible. To keep track of what you have read, mark off each chapter as you complete it.

GENESIS ☐1 ☐2 ☐3 ☐4 ☐5 ☐6 ☐7 ☐8 ☐9 ☐10 ☐11 ☐12 ☐13 ☐14 ☐15 ☐16 ☐17 ☐18 ☐19 ☐20 ☐21 ☐22 ☐23 ☐24 ☐25 ☐26 ☐27 ☐28 ☐29 ☐30 ☐31 ☐32 ☐33 ☐34 ☐35 ☐36 ☐37 ☐38 ☐39 ☐40 ☐41 ☐42 ☐43 ☐44 ☐45 ☐46 ☐47 ☐48 ☐49 ☐50

EXODUS ☐1 ☐2 ☐3 ☐4 ☐5 ☐6 ☐7 ☐8 ☐9 ☐10 ☐11 ☐12 ☐13 ☐14 ☐15 ☐16 ☐17 ☐18 ☐19 ☐20 ☐21 ☐22 ☐23 ☐24 ☐25 ☐26 ☐27 ☐28 ☐29 ☐30 ☐31 ☐32 ☐33 ☐34 ☐35 ☐36 ☐37 ☐38 ☐39 ☐40

LEVITICUS ☐1 ☐2 ☐3 ☐4 ☐5 ☐6 ☐7 ☐8 ☐9 ☐10 ☐11 ☐12 ☐13 ☐14 ☐15 ☐16 ☐17 ☐18 ☐19 ☐20 ☐21 ☐22 ☐23 ☐24 ☐25 ☐26 ☐27

NUMBERS ☐1 ☐2 ☐3 ☐4 ☐5 ☐6 ☐7 ☐8 ☐9 ☐10 ☐11 ☐12 ☐13 ☐14 ☐15 ☐16 ☐17 ☐18 ☐19 ☐20 ☐21 ☐22 ☐23 ☐24 ☐25 ☐26 ☐27 ☐28 ☐29 ☐30 ☐31 ☐32 ☐33 ☐34 ☐35 ☐36

DEUTERONOMY ☐1 ☐2 ☐3 ☐4 ☐5 ☐6 ☐7 ☐8 ☐9 ☐10 ☐11 ☐12 ☐13 ☐14 ☐15 ☐16 ☐17 ☐18 ☐19 ☐20 ☐21 ☐22 ☐23 ☐24 ☐25 ☐26 ☐27 ☐28 ☐29 ☐30 ☐31 ☐32 ☐33 ☐34

JOSHUA ☐1 ☐2 ☐3 ☐4 ☐5 ☐6 ☐7 ☐8 ☐9 ☐10 ☐11 ☐12 ☐13 ☐14 ☐15 ☐16 ☐17 ☐18 ☐19 ☐20 ☐21 ☐22 ☐23 ☐24

JUDGES ☐1 ☐2 ☐3 ☐4 ☐5 ☐6 ☐7 ☐8 ☐9 ☐10 ☐11 ☐12 ☐13 ☐14 ☐15 ☐16 ☐17 ☐18 ☐19 ☐20 ☐21

RUTH ☐1 ☐2 ☐3 ☐4

1 SAMUEL ☐1 ☐2 ☐3 ☐4 ☐5 ☐6 ☐7 ☐8 ☐9 ☐10 ☐11 ☐12 ☐13 ☐14 ☐15 ☐16 ☐17 ☐18 ☐19 ☐20 ☐21 ☐22 ☐23 ☐24 ☐25 ☐26 ☐27 ☐28 ☐29 ☐30 ☐31

2 SAMUEL ☐1 ☐2 ☐3 ☐4 ☐5 ☐6 ☐7 ☐8 ☐9 ☐10 ☐11 ☐12 ☐13 ☐14 ☐15 ☐16 ☐17 ☐18 ☐19 ☐20 ☐21 ☐22 ☐23 ☐24

1 KINGS ☐1 ☐2 ☐3 ☐4 ☐5 ☐6 ☐7 ☐8 ☐9 ☐10 ☐11 ☐12 ☐13 ☐14 ☐15 ☐16 ☐17 ☐18 ☐19 ☐20 ☐21 ☐22

2 KINGS □1 □2 □3 □4 □5 □6
□7 □8 □9 □10 □11 □12 □13 □14
□15 □16 □17 □18 □19 □20 □21 □22
□23 □24 □25

1 CHRONICLES □1 □2 □3 □4 □5
□6 □7 □8 □9 □10 □11 □12 □13
□14 □15 □16 □17 □18 □19 □20 □21
□22 □23 □24 □25 □26 □27 □28 □29

2 CHRONICLES □1 □2 □3 □4 □5
□6 □7 □8 □9 □10 □11 □12 □13
□14 □15 □16 □17 □18 □19 □20 □21
□22 □23 □24 □25 □26 □27 □28 □29
□30 □31 □32 □33 □34 □35 □36

EZRA □1 □2 □3 □4 □5 □6
□7 □8 □9 □10

NEHEMIAH □1 □2 □3 □4 □5 □6
□7 □8 □9 □10 □11 □12 □13

ESTHER □1 □2 □3 □4 □5 □6
□7 □8 □9 □10

JOB □1 □2 □3 □4 □5 □6 □7
□8 □9 □10 □11 □12 □13 □14 □15
□16 □17 □18 □19 □20 □21 □22 □23
□24 □25 □26 □27 □28 □29 □30 □31
□32 □33 □34 □35 □36 □37 □38 □39
□40 □41 □42

PSALMS □1 □2 □3 □4 □5
□6 □7 □8 □9 □10 □11 □12
□13 □14 □15 □16 □17 □18 □19
□20 □21 □22 □23 □24 □25 □26
□27 □28 □29 □30 □31 □32 □33
□34 □35 □36 □37 □38 □39 □40
□41 □42 □43 □44 □45 □46 □47
□48 □49 □50 □51 □52 □53 □54
□55 □56 □57 □58 □59 □60 □61
□62 □63 □64 □65 □66 □67 □68
□69 □70 □71 □72 □73 □74 □75
□76 □77 □78 □79 □80 □81 □82
□83 □84 □85 □86 □87 □88 □89
□90 □91 □92 □93 □94 □95 □96
□97 □98 □99 □100 □101 □102 □103
□104 □105 □106 □107 □108 □109 □110
□111 □112 □113 □114 □115 □116 □117
□118 □119 □120 □121 □122 □123 □124
□125 □126 □127 □128 □129 □130 □131
□132 □133 □134 □135 □136 □137 □138
□139 □140 □141 □142 □143 □144 □145
□146 □147 □148 □149 □150

PROVERBS □1 □2 □3 □4 □5
□6 □7 □8 □9 □10 □11 □12
□13 □14 □15 □16 □17 □18 □19
□20 □21 □22 □23 □24 □25 □26
□27 □28 □29 □30 □31

ECCLESIASTES □1 □2 □3 □4 □5
□6 □7 □8 □9 □10 □11 □12

SONG OF SONGS □1 □2 □3 □4 □5
□6 □7 □8

ISAIAH □1 □2 □3 □4 □5 □6
□7 □8 □9 □10 □11 □12 □13 □14
□15 □16 □17 □18 □19 □20 □21 □22
□23 □24 □25 □26 □27 □28 □29 □30
□31 □32 □33 □34 □35 □36 □37 □38
□39 □40 □41 □42 □43 □44 □45 □46
□47 □48 □49 □50 □51 □52 □53 □54
□55 □56 □57 □58 □59 □60 □61 □62
□63 □64 □65 □66

JEREMIAH □1 □2 □3 □4 □5 □6
□7 □8 □9 □10 □11 □12 □13 □14
□15 □16 □17 □18 □19 □20 □21 □22
□23 □24 □25 □26 □27 □28 □29 □30
□31 □32 □33 □34 □35 □36 □37 □38
□39 □40 □41 □42 □43 □44 □45 □46
□47 □48 □49 □50 □51 □52

LAMENTATIONS □1 □2 □3 □4 □5

EZEKIEL □1 □2 □3 □4 □5 □6
□7 □8 □9 □10 □11 □12 □13 □14
□15 □16 □17 □18 □19 □20 □21 □22
□23 □24 □25 □26 □27 □28 □29 □30
□31 □32 □33 □34 □35 □36 □37 □38
□39 □40 □41 □42 □43 □44 □45 □46
□47 □48

DANIEL □1 □2 □3 □4 □5 □6
□7 □8 □9 □10 □11 □12

HOSEA □1 □2 □3 □4 □5 □6
□7 □8 □9 □10 □11 □12 □13 □14

JOEL ☐1 ☐2 ☐3

AMOS ☐1 ☐2 ☐3 ☐4 ☐5 ☐6 ☐7 ☐8 ☐9

OBADIAH ☐OBADIAH

JONAH ☐1 ☐2 ☐3 ☐4

MICAH ☐1 ☐2 ☐3 ☐4 ☐5 ☐6 ☐7

NAHUM ☐1 ☐2 ☐3

HABAKKUK ☐1 ☐2 ☐3

ZEPHANIAH ☐1 ☐2 ☐3

HAGGAI ☐1 ☐2

ZECHARIAH ☐1 ☐2 ☐3 ☐4 ☐5 ☐6 ☐7 ☐8 ☐9 ☐10 ☐11 ☐12 ☐13 ☐14

MALACHI ☐1 ☐2 ☐3 ☐4

MATTHEW ☐1 ☐2 ☐3 ☐4 ☐5 ☐6 ☐7 ☐8 ☐9 ☐10 ☐11 ☐12 ☐13 ☐14 ☐15 ☐16 ☐17 ☐18 ☐19 ☐20 ☐21 ☐22 ☐23 ☐24 ☐25 ☐26 ☐27 ☐28

MARK ☐1 ☐2 ☐3 ☐4 ☐5 ☐6 ☐7 ☐8 ☐9 ☐10 ☐11 ☐12 ☐13 ☐14 ☐15 ☐16

LUKE ☐1 ☐2 ☐3 ☐4 ☐5 ☐6 ☐7 ☐8 ☐9 ☐10 ☐11 ☐12 ☐13 ☐14 ☐15 ☐16 ☐17 ☐18 ☐19 ☐20 ☐21 ☐22 ☐23 ☐24

JOHN ☐1 ☐2 ☐3 ☐4 ☐5 ☐6 ☐7 ☐8 ☐9 ☐10 ☐11 ☐12 ☐13 ☐14 ☐15 ☐16 ☐17 ☐18 ☐19 ☐20 ☐21

ACTS ☐1 ☐2 ☐3 ☐4 ☐5 ☐6 ☐7 ☐8 ☐9 ☐10 ☐11 ☐12 ☐13 ☐14 ☐15 ☐16 ☐17 ☐18 ☐19 ☐20 ☐21 ☐22 ☐23 ☐24 ☐25 ☐26 ☐27 ☐28

ROMANS ☐1 ☐2 ☐3 ☐4 ☐5 ☐6 ☐7 ☐8 ☐9 ☐10 ☐11 ☐12 ☐13 ☐14 ☐15 ☐16

1 CORINTHIANS ☐1 ☐2 ☐3 ☐4 ☐5 ☐6 ☐7 ☐8 ☐9 ☐10 ☐11 ☐12 ☐13 ☐14 ☐15 ☐16

2 CORINTHIANS ☐1 ☐2 ☐3 ☐4 ☐5 ☐6 ☐7 ☐8 ☐9 ☐10 ☐11 ☐12 ☐13

GALATIANS ☐1 ☐2 ☐3 ☐4 ☐5 ☐6

EPHESIANS ☐1 ☐2 ☐3 ☐4 ☐5 ☐6

PHILIPPIANS ☐1 ☐2 ☐3 ☐4

COLOSSIANS ☐1 ☐2 ☐3 ☐4

1 THESSALONIANS ☐1 ☐2 ☐3 ☐4 ☐5

2 THESSALONIANS ☐1 ☐2 ☐3

1 TIMOTHY ☐1 ☐2 ☐3 ☐4 ☐5 ☐6

2 TIMOTHY ☐1 ☐2 ☐3 ☐4

TITUS ☐1 ☐2 ☐3

PHILEMON ☐PHILEMON

HEBREWS ☐1 ☐2 ☐3 ☐4 ☐5 ☐6 ☐7 ☐8 ☐9 ☐10 ☐11 ☐12 ☐13

JAMES ☐1 ☐2 ☐3 ☐4 ☐5

1 PETER ☐1 ☐2 ☐3 ☐4 ☐5

2 PETER ☐1 ☐2 ☐3

1 JOHN ☐1 ☐2 ☐3 ☐4 ☐5

2 JOHN ☐2 JOHN

3 JOHN ☐3 JOHN

JUDE ☐JUDE

REVELATION ☐1 ☐2 ☐3 ☐4 ☐5 ☐6 ☐7 ☐8 ☐9 ☐10 ☐11 ☐12 ☐13 ☐14 ☐15 ☐16 ☐17 ☐18 ☐19 ☐20 ☐21 ☐22

Notes between you & me

Notes between you & me

Notes
between
you & *me*

Notes between you & me

Notes between you & me

Notes between you & me

Notes between you & me

Notes
between
you & *me*

NIV Marriage Devotional Bible

Project management and editorial: Catherine DeVries

Editorial Assistance: Shari TeSlaa

Production Management: Jean Entingh

Interior design: Sharon Wright, Belmont, MI

Cover design: Amy Peterman

Typesetting: AutoGraphics, Inc., Pomona, CA

Interior proofreading: Peachtree Editorial
and Proofreading Service, Peachtree City, GA

Printing: Dickinson Press, Grand Rapids, MI

Guarantee

*Zondervan Publishing House guarantees leather
Bibles unconidtionally against manufacturing
defects for six years and hardcover and softcover
Bibles for four years.This guarantee does not apply
to normal wear. Contact Zondervan Customer Service,
800-727-1308, for replacement instructions.*

Care

*We suggest loosening the binding of your new Bible
by gently pressing on a small section of pages at
a time from the center. To ensure against breakage
of the spine, it is best not to bend the cover
backward around the spine or to carry study notes,
church bulletins, pens, etc., inside the cover. Because
a felt-tipped marker will "bleed" through the pages,
we recommend use of a ball-point pen or pencil
to underline favorite passages. Your Bible should not
be exposed to excessive heat, cold, or humidity.*